Congressional Districts in the 2000s

Congressional Districts
in the 2000s

A PORTRAIT OF AMERICA

A Division of Congressional Quarterly Inc.
Washington, D.C.

CQ Press
1255 22nd Street, N.W., Suite 400
Washington, D.C. 20037

202-729-1900; toll-free: 1-866-4CQ-PRESS (1-866-427-7737)

www.cqpress.com

Printed and bound in the United States of America
07   06   05   04   03   5   4   3   2   1

⊗ The paper used in this publication exceeds the requirements of the
American National Standard for Information Sciences—Permanence
of Paper for Printed Library Materials, ANSI Z39.48-1992.

Cover design: Auburn Associates, Inc.

Library of Congress Cataloging-in-Publication Data

Congressional districts in the 2000s : a portrait of America.
        p. cm.
Includes indexes.
    ISBN 1-56802-849-0 (alk. paper)
    1. United States. Congress. House—Election districts. 2. United
States. Congress. House—Election districts—Statistics. I. CQ Press.
II. Title.
JK1341.C65   2003
328.73′07345′090511—dc22   2003065430

Editor's Note

Congressional Districts in the 2000s is the fourth volume produced by Congressional Quarterly and CQ Press over the past 30 years that chronicles the distribution— and redistribution—of political power in the U.S. House of Representatives. This edition again carries the subtitle "A Portrait of America" because—as we noted in 1993— "it is a kind of political hitchhiker's guide to the people, problems, and opportunities before the nation." America's political, social, and economic challenges and opportunities are most often described by reference to states, or cities and towns. This book looks at these issues through the structure of the 435 congressional districts that each send a member to the U.S. House of Representatives. The House is often described as a fair reflection of voter concerns and preferences because representatives—individually and collectively—are close to individual voters and have a good feel for the political pulse of citizens.

The congressional subjects in this picture—the Democrats, Republicans, and occasional independents—are the people who eventually must decide how the federal government will attempt to resolve America's most challenging social and economic issues. Understanding these districts and the people who live in them is essential to understanding how Congress and the other parts of the national government respond or do not respond.

In this volume, the editors have brought together introductory essays for each of the states; text descriptions of each of the districts written by CQ's political reporters; a variety of 2000 census and other data that help explain the needs and political orientation of the population; and maps of all states and many urban areas that show district lines as well as counties and many cities. The reader can learn, for example, the age, race, ancestry, education, employment, and housing patterns of *people* in the district. The district descriptions bring these data into focus by highlighting the economic and political forces that shape the area. Public information sources, such as newspapers and TV and cable stations, are listed along with a compilation of major employers, universities and colleges, and military installations. Editors also have included reconfigured actual voting results for the 2000 presidential race to fit the boundaries of the new districts to show the political orientation of an area had the lines been in place for the historically close contest between Al Gore and George W. Bush.

With each edition of *Congressional Districts,* CQ editors have found the task of collecting, analyzing, and publishing the data both more difficult and more interesting as the ceaseless ingenuity of American politicians, wedded to the power of computers, is brought to bear on the process. The most distinctive feature of redistricting for at least the past 20 years has been the application of computers to the goals of politicians. In the 1990s one objective was meeting the requirements of the Voting Rights Act to enhance the prospects of minorities winning more House seats. An important political goal of the process was to create districts that came to be known as majority-minority, in which certain minority groups in the population had a majority and thus were likely to elect an individual of the same background. Although this was done with some success—primarily in states in the South—it resulted in more than a few bizarrely shaped districts that under legal challenge the Supreme Court said did not stand constitutional muster.

By the time the new redistricting process started, following the 2000 census, less focus was given to majority-minority considerations, so long as districts fit within Voting Rights Act requirements, and more to other considerations, as CQ political reporter Greg Giroux notes in his introduction to the volume, "Redistricting for the 2000s." The result, as before, was many states with unusually shaped districts that generally were drawn to enhance the political power of one entity or another (usually a political party but sometimes a specific community or candidate)—the practice often referred to as gerrymandering.

But the 2000 redistricting process was different in one potentially fundamental way. In two states—Texas and Colorado—the controlling political party, in both cases Republican, sought in effect to re-redistrict to enhance the chances of GOP candidates. The Republicans in these states claimed that the original districts—both drawn by courts rather than the legislature—did not accurately reflect the political orientation of the state as measured in other voting statistics. Texas Republicans spent months before passing into law in late 2003 a hugely redrawn map that, if upheld on legal challenge, was thought likely to end the political careers of at least seven current Democratic members of the House in the 2004 elections. The Colorado changes were less drastic—seeking only to enhance the prospects of Republicans who had won anyway in 2002—but the principal question of whether district lines could be drawn more than once in a decade (other than by court order) remained the same. Democrats and some independent scholars said Republicans were simply refusing to accept the outcome of what had historically been accepted by both parties as a single decennial event. Democrats went to court to challenge both actions on various grounds, including— especially for Texas—that the new lines violated voting rights of minorities. Both challenges were just beginning to work through the courts as this book went to press. But should the courts uphold the Republican actions, scholars said it may mean that other states would do the same, thus making redistricting an ongoing decade-long political event.

How to Use the Book

A reader may find information in this volume in several ways. The book is organized alphabetically by state. Each state profile begins with a general description of the state followed by profiles of each district in numerical sequence. Maps of each state and of a number of urban areas are provided.

National data tables are included in the appendix. These tables bring together the census data for each state that are spread throughout the book, allowing a reader to make quick comparisons between states. In addition, these tables include national figures to allow a reader to compare a state to the same figure for the nation as a whole. These tables begin on page 1012. In addition to the national tables, the appendix includes a compilation of all district demographic data. This information is presented by state and by districts within the states. A particularly useful feature assigns a ranking to each entry to allow a reader to compare a specific district to all others in the country. Also included in the appendix are several tables of highest and lowest numbers for demographic information in approximately 50 to 100 districts. And, completing the appendix are a list of redistricting-related court cases and a profile of the District of Columbia.

Six separate indexes—for major employers, cable companies, cities, counties, military installations, and universities and colleges—help the reader locate specific information. If, for example, a reader needs to know the district in which a certain city or county is located, turning to those indexes will quickly provide the answer. The indexes begin on page 1039.

Contributors

This work is the result of the dedicated effort of many persons at CQ Press, its parent company, Congressional Quarterly Inc., and elsewhere.

Jon Preimesberger, a former senior editor at CQ Press, was the principal manuscript editor for the volume. At CQ Press, production editor Gwenda Larsen organized the thousands of separate tables and pieces of text into a coherent package ready for composition. Assistant editor Grace Hill helped with research and other tasks, including the preparation of the military installations lists.

Ron Elving, senior Washington editor with *National Public Radio News,* wrote the opening essays for all of the states. CQ's political staff, under the direction of David Hawkings and Brian Nutting, wrote the congressional district profiles (all of which first appeared in CQ's *Politics in America 2004*). *CQ Weekly* political reporter Greg Giroux prepared the "Redistricting for the 2000s" essay *(see p. xv),* which analyzes the redistricting that occurred after the 2000 census.

Polidata, under the direction of Clark Bensen with the assistance of Steve Ellis and Bill Steiner, prepared the demographic information in the district profiles—including population, area, counties, cities, race, and ancestry—from Census Bureau data. Clark Bensen also drew the book's maps and reconfigured the census demographic data for the tables that appear in the appendix. Polidata also prepared the presidential and House election returns.

iMapData, under the direction of William Lilley III and Laurence J. DeFranco, prepared the other components in the district profiles—universities and colleges, newspapers, television stations, cable systems, and businesses. Peter W. Fleury and H. Jeffries Macintire handled much of this compilation. iMapData, a private company, provides tailored information to businesses and government agencies using the World Wide Web. Much of the firm's work allows clients to create maps, reports, and aerial images.

David R. Tarr, Volume Editor
November 2003

Sources and Explanations

Congressional Districts in the 2000s presents descriptive and statistical profiles of the 435 congressional districts based on the 2000 census and subsequent reapportionment and redistricting.

State Profiles

The book is organized alphabetically by state. Each state section includes the following information:

- A narrative portrait of political, social, and economic conditions in each state. These essays note important changes that occurred during the 1990s and earlier leading to the new House districts that were created after the 2000 census. The profiles also describe political forces at work during the redistricting process.

- A map of each state that shows the congressional district boundaries. The maps include county names and boundaries and a selection of cities. For some states additional maps are included to show urban districts that are not well defined on the state maps. Many states have unusually shaped districts that generally were drawn to enhance the political power of one entity or another (usually a political party but sometimes a specific community or candidate)—the practice sometimes referred to as gerrymandering. These areas on many of the state maps have shading that shows the area of the state over which the district is spread.

  Congressional Districts in the 2000s has two maps for Maine because it redistricts a year later than other states. The first Maine map shows the district lines in place for 1994–2002; the second map shows the lines for elections starting in 2004. Colorado also has two maps: one used for the 2002 elections and one created in 2003 that may take effect in 2004. The latter was a product of Republican efforts in that state to increase their margins in some districts. The new map was in litigation as of November 2003. Texas Republicans in 2003 also attempted to benefit their party by redrawing districts created in 2002. Their effort proved successful in October, but Democrats and Mexican American groups immediately challenged the new map in court. The original Colorado and Texas maps were drawn by judges when the state legislatures were unable to agree on new district lines.

- Six tables provide census statistics on population, voting strength by race and Hispanic or Latino origin and by age

groups, income and occupation, education, and housing patterns by congressional districts. Data for each district and the state are presented in tabular form to allow easy comparison. All tables were prepared from Census Bureau data on the 2000 census. For easy state-to-state comparisons, the appendix includes a table showing state totals for each data group and national figures where they were available. The appendix also includes a listing of selected data for all districts and a national ranking for each district. *(See pp. 1012–1029.)*

Table 1: Population

This table provides population and age data for each district in the state: total population, population under 18 years of age, voting-age population (all persons 18 and over), and median age as well as percentage of the population that is male and percentage that is female. The voting-age population shows all potential voters, including noncitizens and others not eligible to register, not just persons registered to vote. The median age is the age that divides the population into two equal groups, one half older than the median and one half younger. The median age for the entire United States in the 2000 census was 35.3 years, up from 32.9 years in the 1990 census.

Table 2: Voting-Age Persons by Race and Hispanic or Latino Origin

This table shows the voting-age population of different race and ancestry groups identified in the census. The size of each population group, shown as a percentage of the total voting-age population, provides an estimate of the maximum potential voting strength of each group in the district. The labels in this table correspond to those used by the Census Bureau. The percentages were calculated from the raw census data. Categories of race and ancestry also appear in each district profile but as a percentage of the total district population, rather than only the voting-age population. *(For details of the race and Hispanic/Latino origin categories, see "Racial Classifications" box, p. xii.)*

Table 3: Voting-Age Persons by Age Group

Voters by age group are listed in this table to indicate the potential voting strength of the group in the district. The percentages, which were calculated from census data, are stated as a percentage of the voting-age population.

Table 4: Income and Occupation

This table presents median family income, families that fall below the government's poverty line, white- and blue-collar workers, and service and farm employees.

Median family income is the income level that divides families into two equal groups, with half having incomes above the median and half below the median. The median family income for the entire United States was $50,046 in the 2000 census, up from $35,225 ten years earlier.

The data for families in poverty show the percentage of families with income in 1999 below the poverty level. The Census Bureau prepared these figures based on federal definitions of poverty.

Percentages of white-collar, blue-collar, service, and farm worker occupations are in terms of employed persons age 16 and older and were calculated from census data. The Census Bureau revised the classification of the occupational questions for 2000 to coincide with the standard occupational classification manual. The Census Bureau divides employed persons into 13 major industry groups that *Congressional Districts in the 2000s* combines into four categories in the table that are only generally comparable with previous combinations:

- *White-Collar Workers.* Managerial and professional specialty occupations (including executive, administrative, and managerial occupations, and professional specialty occupations) and technical, sales, and administrative support occupations (including technicians and related support occupations, sales occupations, and administrative support occupations including clerical).

- *Blue-Collar Workers.* Precision production, craft, and repair occupations; and operators, fabricators, and laborers (including machine operators; assemblers and inspectors; transportation and material-moving occupations; and handlers, equipment cleaners, helpers, and laborers).

- *Service Workers.* Service occupations (including private household occupations and protective service occupations, and service occupations except protective and household occupations).

- *Farm Workers.* Farming, forestry, and fishing occupations.

Table 5: Education: School Years Completed

Data on years of school completed refer to the adult population 25 years of age or older. The data that appear in the columns of the table are for discrete groups of individuals. For the nation, 80.4 percent of persons 25 or older reported a high school or higher educational level. Percentages were calculated from census data.

Table 6: Housing and Residential Patterns

Housing units are divided between owner-occupied and renter-occupied units. Housing units include individual houses and individual apartments.

People classified as urban by the Census Bureau were those persons living in urban clusters or urbanized areas, both census definitions. An *urban cluster* was a densely settled territory of at least 2,500 people but fewer then 50,000. An *urbanized area* was a location with at least one central place and ad-joining territory with a population density of at least 1,000 people per square mile and a minimum residential population of at least 50,000 people. People classified as rural were all persons not classified as urban.

In explaining these groupings, the Census Bureau cautioned that the criteria for an urban area were extensively revised for the 2000 census. As a result, some territory that was classified as urbanized for the 1990 census was reclassified as rural, and some areas identified as urban areas in the 1990 count were reclassified as urban clusters in 2000.

District Profiles

Following the summary material and tables for the states, *Congressional Districts in the 2000s* provides information about each congressional district in a state.

- A text overview of the district. This summary describes the political and economic highlights and the impact of redistricting on the politics of the area.

- Election returns for the 2000 presidential race and the 2002 House race in the district. Returns for the presidential race have been recalculated to fit the boundaries of the new districts. The House returns are the actual votes cast for the 2002 contests.

- The 2000 population of the district.

- The total area and land area and the population density of the district.

- Counties or parts of counties in the district and their population.

- Cities and other areas with populations greater than 10,000 or parts of such locations in the district and their population. *Congressional Districts in the 2000s* has retained Census Bureau designations of localities such as "town" or "village" or "Census Designated Place" (CDP). (In Alaska, the designation is "Census Area" or "Borough.") These are included in the book for clarity but usually are not part of a locality's common name. A few states have cities that are independent of counties. These areas will appear in both the Counties and Cities listings with the same or similar name but are independent of one another. The most notable example is Virginia.

   Many counties and cities are split between two or more districts. To quickly determine the districts in which a jurisdiction is located consult the county and city indexes in the back of the volume. These jurisdictions appear alphabetically by name. A jurisdiction in more than one district will be listed two or more times but with different district numbers and page references. Note that only cities and similar areas with populations of 10,000 or more are included in this volume. If a city or similar jurisdiction is split between districts only parts with 10,000 or more population are in the book and index. All counties and their populations are listed.

- The race and ancestry of the district's residents.

- Universities and colleges located in the district and their 2000–2001 enrollment.

- Newspapers that circulate in the district and the district and total circulation of the paper.

- Television stations that serve the district.
- Cable TV companies available in the district.
- Military installations in the district.
- Major employers in the district (those employing 500 or more people), their product or service, and the reported number of employees.

Congressional Districts: The Political Picture

Political reporters for *CQ Weekly* prepared the district profiles in late 2002 and early 2003. The writers' intent was to describe the districts, and in some cases the House members, for the 108th Congress that began in January 2003. The reader should note that specific information in the text may disagree in minor ways with the tabular data that follows. For example, the text may round off numbers. In addition, the text may refer to a figure, such as a city population, that encompasses an entire unit (the full city's population) even though that city straddles a district line. In such cases, the data in tables will show only the portion applicable to the district. The reader also should be alert to the universe for numbers cited in the text and tables. For example, the text may refer to a total population figure while the table uses a comparable number that refers only to the voting-age population. The text material was prepared to show the overall complexion of a district and its place in the politics and economy of the state, which often required including information that applied to more than a single district. The data in the tables apply only to the district.

The reader should note also that census data sets do not generally include percentage calculations; consequently, to attain percentages the reader must first determine the appropriate universe. In addition, for many categories several options are available for demographic research. For example, a reader must determine whether to use the value for "all housing units" or only "specified housing units." The options chosen may result in differences in the data listed in *Congressional Districts in the 2000s* compared to other sources. In general, the differences will not affect the relative differences in the character of one district to another.

Election Returns

Polidata, under the direction of Clark Bensen, with the assistance of Steve Ellis and Bill Steiner, prepared the reconfigured presidential election returns. The returns show how the vote would have been in the district had the district lines for 2002 existed in 2000. In this way, it is possible to see the political history and trends within each current congressional district. The election returns shown for the House races are the actual votes cast in the 2002 election.

The presidential vote is estimated from political databases developed by participants in the reapportionment process following the 2000 census. The databases were developed by different groups or individuals using varying standards. For example, in some states the vote for Ralph Nader was available as a separate figure, in some states the Nader vote was combined with the vote for other minor candidates, and in other states the Nader vote was not available at all. Similarly, the degree to which absentee and early votes were treated varied by state. In general these databases were developed by collecting official returns at the precinct level and assigning these votes to census blocks on the basis of a population factor. These votes were then aggregated, just as census data are, for any redistricting plan for political assessment. Because of the nature of these data and the differing standards used in development, these numbers should be treated as estimates of the generic political strength of the parties. In general, the percentages will be more reliable than the raw numbers, and differences will be noted from other sources in some cases. Readers who have questions about the process or who are interested in updates can visit www.polidata.us.

Population, Area, Density

The population, total area, land area, and population density are shown for all districts. A district's population density is calculated based on the land area, excluding any part of the district covered by water.

Counties

Most states are organized by counties. In Louisiana the equivalent divisions are known as parishes. Alaska has no counties. A few states—including Maryland, Missouri, Nevada, and Virginia—have cities that are independent of any county and therefore are considered equivalent divisions. They usually carry the same name as a city in the state and appear in the county list with the word "city."

Where one county is divided between two or more congressional districts, that is indicated by "(Pt.)"—part—following the county name.

Cities

The Census Bureau recognizes two kinds of cities: those that are incorporated and those that are closely settled but fall outside incorporated areas. *Congressional Districts in the 2000s* lists incorporated places in which total population exceeded 10,000 in the 2000 census.

In addition, widely recognized unincorporated places exceeding 10,000 in population are included for districts and are followed by the abbreviation CDP. In some cases, towns, townships, and villages are also included.

Race and Ancestry

Race. The racial categories that appear in *Congressional Districts in the 2000s* are taken from the Census Bureau's listings and use the Bureau's labeling: white, black or African American, American Indian or Alaska native, Asian, native Hawaiian or other Pacific Islander, some other race, and two or more races. Persons responding to the 2000 census were asked to choose the race or races with which they most closely identify. In reporting the data, the bureau noted that the categories are "socio-political constructs and should not be interpreted as being scientific or anthropological in nature." The bureau also said the race categories included both racial and national-origin groups. People who identify their origin as Hispanic or Latino may be of any race. (*For category components, see box, p. xii.*)

Racial Classifications

The racial classifications used by the Census Bureau in the 2000 census were different from those used in the 1990 census in two ways. First, a new racial category (Native Hawaiian or other Pacific Islander) was separated from the former Asian category. Second, census respondents were allowed to classify themselves as members of more than one racial group. The new classifications were based on standards issued by the U.S. Office of Management and Budget on October 30, 1997. The OMB required five minimum categories (white, black or African American, American Indian or Alaska native, Asian, and native Hawaiian or other Pacific Islander) for race. Those categories are described below with a sixth category, "Some other race," added with OMB approval. In addition to the five race groups, the OMB standards allowed respondents to select one or more races. Note that persons considering themselves Hispanic or Latino may be of any race. The Hispanic origin classification is derived from a separate question on the census form.

- **White.** A person having origins in any of the original peoples of Europe, the Middle East, or North Africa. It includes people who in the 2000 census indicated their race as "White" or reported entries such as Irish, German, Italian, Lebanese, Near Easterner, Arab, or Polish.

- **Black or African American.** A person having origins in any of the black racial groups of Africa. It includes people who indicated their race as "Black, African Am., or Negro," or provided written entries such as African American, Afro American, Kenyan, Nigerian, or Haitian.

- **American Indian or Alaska Native.** A person having origins in any of the original peoples of North and South America (including Central America) and who maintains tribal affiliation or community attachment. It includes people who classified themselves as American Indian, American Indian tribe, or Alaska Native (including Eskimos and Aleuts).

- **Asian.** A person having origins in any of the original peoples of the Far East, Southeast Asia, or the Indian subcontinent including, for example, Cambodia, China, India, Japan, Korea, Malaysia, Pakistan, the Philippine Islands, Thailand, or Vietnam. It includes "Asian Indian," "Chinese," "Filipino," "Korean," "Japanese," "Vietnamese," and "Other Asian."

- **Native Hawaiian or Other Pacific Islander.** A person having origins in any of the original peoples of Hawaii, Guam, Samoa, or other Pacific Islands. It includes people who indicated their race as "Native Hawaiian," "Guamanian or Chamorro," "Samoan," or "Other Pacific Islander."

- **Some Other Race.** This group includes all other responses not included in the five other categories. Respondents who provided write-in entries such as multiracial, mixed, interracial, or a Hispanic/Latino group (for example, Mexican, Puerto Rican, or Cuban) in the "Some other race" write-in space were included in this category.

- **Two or More Races.** Respondents who provided two or more races either by checking two or more race response check boxes, by providing multiple write-in responses, or by some combination of check boxes and write-in responses were placed in this category. There were 57 possible combinations in this category.

Hispanic or Latino Origin

In the 2000 census people who identified with the terms "Hispanic" or "Latino" were those who classified themselves in one of the specific Hispanic or Latino categories listed on census questionnaires—"Mexican," "Puerto Rican," or "Cuban"—as well as those who indicated that they were "other Spanish, Hispanic, or Latino." Origin can be viewed as the heritage, nationality group, lineage, or country of birth of the person or the person's parents or ancestors before their arrival in the United States. People who identify their origin as Spanish, Hispanic, or Latino may be of any race. *(For additional discussion of ancestry information from the 2000 census, see the "Race and Ancestry" section, which begins on p. xi).*

The categories used in the 2000 census incorporated new guidelines that the U.S. Office of Management and Budget (OMB) recently created. The OMB said the revised guidelines reflected "the increasing diversity of our nation's population, stemming from growth in interracial marriages and immigration." One important change allowed respondents to report as many race categories as they wished. As a result of this and other definitional changes, the Census Bureau said the 2000 race data are not directly comparable with data from the 1990 and previous censuses.

Ancestry. Unlike the data in most tables in *Congressional Districts in the 2000s,* ancestry data are subject to different methodological analysis. This is because the ancestry question asked during the census was open-ended and allowed for multiple responses. A person did not have to indicate any ancestry or could have stated one or several. The Census Bureau tabulated the first two responses for purposes of reporting. Analysts can examine these data in different ways using different population universes such as total population, ancestry specified, and total ancestry responses, each of which will give somewhat different pictures of the ancestry of persons living in a congressional district area. Clark Bensen of Polidata prepared the estimates for *Congressional Districts in the 2000s.* For purposes of this book, Polidata used the average number of responses to the ancestry question for any given district to estimate the number of persons who shared this characteristic. This number was then divided by the total population to attain an estimated percentage of the population that is comparable to other percentages. This method disregards any priority to the first response tabulated and does not count persons more than once. It is, however, just an estimate and is subject to error, and it may be affected by differential rates of response to the ancestry question.

Universities and Colleges

Congressional Districts in the 2000s lists schools offering two or more years of study and at least an associate's degree. Certain types of training schools, such as beauty/cosmetology, are not included. Schools are listed if they reported an enrollment of 100 or more students. A few professional or other well-known colleges below that threshold, primarily law schools, are included. Some colleges and universities straddle boundaries, affecting two districts. If a school is listed in more than one district, enrollment figures have not been divided between the two. The schools were located using data from the National Center for Education Statistics in the U.S. Department of Education. Enrollments shown are for fall 2000. The tables include public and private institutions as well as technical, professional, and community schools. In most cases, the city or locality of the institution is not included if it is obvious from the name of the school.

Newspapers

Newspapers that circulate in a congressional district are listed. The purpose of this listing is to show sources of information available to voters in the district. In many cases, the newspaper's home office is located in another district and, in the case of major newspapers, in a district many miles away. A few papers in the lists have national circulations.

Congressional Districts in the 2000s provides two circulation numbers: circulation in a congressional district and total circulation of the paper. The mapping and research firm iMapData calculated both numbers from circulation data reported to the Audit Bureau of Circulations. Most newspapers in the United States report circulation by postal zip code, which allows matching a zip code area to a district's boundaries. However, some papers report circulation only by county. In these cases, iMapData sought to manually assign district circulation using county figures, but the accuracy of these district numbers is less than through the use of zip codes. The papers that report circulation by county are noted by an asterisk.

Some circulation figures are not available through the Audit Bureau of Circulations or other sources and therefore are not included in *Congressional Districts in the 2000s*. Most are smaller local papers but a few are primary papers for a city or region. The most notable example is *The Wall Street Journal,* which is distributed nationally but its local circulation figures are not available. Papers with a circulation under 1,000 are not included.

In some cities, competitive newspapers have combined certain operations—primarily business and printing—under the Failing Newspaper Act, a law enacted by Congress to help struggling papers and maintain journalistic competition. These papers often publish a joint Sunday edition under a combined name. The listings include such editions under their joint name when it was available, as well as the separate daily editions.

Television Stations

Television stations, and their network affiliation if any, are listed for congressional districts. The stations are listed where their signal is likely to be received in some or all of the geographic area in which a district is situated. The impact of political news and advertising in a congressional district can be gauged by knowing the stations and network affiliations that have some or dominant viewership in a district.

iMapData linked stations in *Congressional Districts in the 2000s* to congressional districts through use of Designated Market Areas (DMAs), which is a geographic market design created by the ACNielsen company that defines each TV market exclusive of another based on measurable viewing patterns over time. DMAs are composed of complete or split counties and based on historical viewing patterns. Each county or split county in the country is assigned only to one DMA. iMapData used Federal Communications Commission records to provide information on television stations within DMAs. Any station that was not included in Nielsen's data collection will not appear in the book.

Although DMAs are used primarily for commercial rather than political purposes, they can tell a reader which stations' reports on political news and election advertising may have an influence in a congressional district. For example, station WFUM, a PBS station in Michigan serving the Flint, Saginaw, and Bay City DMA, will be received in all or some of Michigan's 1st, 4th, 5th, 8th, and 10th districts. The geographic names are the DMAs that include the actual cities within the area.

In the listings, the DMA is denoted by a city. In some listings an additional city name follows in parentheses. This indicates that there is a television station located there but the city is outside the metropolitan area that Nielsen defines. The state name abbreviations in some listings are included to make clear when the DMA crosses state borders.

A district may be entirely within one DMA or it may be divided among several DMAs; estimated percentages are given to indicate the portion of the district allocated to each DMA.

Cable Television Systems

Cable television systems serving a district were compiled by iMapData using data from Federal Communications Commission records and matching the information to known cable franchise boundaries provided by Data Mapping Inc. and congressional district boundaries. For most of the nation, this methodology showed the franchises and the number of its subscribers in a district. In a few tightly compacted districts in the New York City and Los Angeles areas, in which the results were unclear, iMapData imputed results by weighing known subscribers of franchises against census data on households. Those districts are marked with asterisks in the tables. Cable systems with fewer than 500 subscribers are not included.

Military Installations

Congressional Districts in the 2000s lists by congressional district military installations and facilities with full-time military and civilian personnel as of September 2001. The information was derived from a Department of Defense report on base structure. The report identifies bases by zip code, which CQ Press editors used to identify a location within a congressional district. Readers should be aware that base closures and staffing requirements—both military and civilian—are under continual review by the Department of Defense and undergo annual changes.

Business and Other Major Employers

This section lists major employers in each congressional district. Included are private profit-making companies, non-profit groups, and government offices. The latter includes federal, state, and local offices including school districts. Employers with 500 or more employees are listed. iMapData assembled the data by using the official address of a company or organization available in standard government and business directories and assigning directory-provided latitude and longitudinal points to a district.

For each employer, *Congressional Districts in the 2000s* lists the name and a division name if applicable, the location, the product or service provided, and the number of employees. The purpose of an employer generally is omitted if it is obvious from the name, such as "state police," "area public schools," or "hospital."

The address used places the employer in a specific district, but in many cases, particularly in cities that straddle district lines, a portion of a workforce may actually be located in an adjoining district. Even in districts where the employing office is entirely within a district, people who work there may live in an adjoining district. As a result, the information presented must be considered a useful but not exact measurement of economic activity in a specific district. The reader should examine the overall picture of the region by looking at listings for each district in an area. The economic impact of a government agency or a private employer in such cases will spread across more than one district and affect several House representatives. The official location of an employer in such cases is less important than the jobs and economic impact the employer has on the region. In some districts, the list will include similar or identical names. Usually this indicates the same employer but different divisions or functions.

With this information, the reader usually can discern the types of industry and business, government employment, and other sources of economic activity prevalent in a con-gressional district. The listed number of employees, however, must be viewed with caution. National companies may report staffing size that reflects employment in the entire company or division even if a portion of the workers are located elsewhere. The databases from which the information was drawn do not always make a clear distinction. However, employment data given for smaller local companies can be expected to more accurately reflect the number of workers actually in the district.

Appendix

An appendix starting on page 1011 includes a number of important features that supplement the data in the state and district profiles.

- *National Census Tables.* These tables provide the state and national figures for each of the data groups used throughout the book. This information allows the reader to make quick comparisons between states and between an individual state and the nation as a whole.

- *Rankings Tables.* A number of the data sets that appear in the book have been combined into a compilation of congressional districts, organized alphabetically by state. The combined table includes a district's ranking compared to other districts. Duplicate numbers are given the same ranking. The total number of rankings appears at the bottom of the table. In addition, a selection of these data sets has been reorganized to show the highest and lowest numbers in some categories, such as districts with the most blacks or Hispanics or the highest and lowest median incomes.

- *Redistricting Court Cases List. Congressional Districts in the 2000s* includes a listing of case names for litigation involving the drawing of lines after a census. The list is organized by state.

- *District of Columbia.* To round out the view of the United States, census and profile data are provided for Washington, D.C.

Indexes

Six subject-specific indexes are included to help the reader quickly locate data: employers of 500 or more persons, cable TV companies, cities, counties, military installations, and universities and colleges. Each index lists the state and the congressional district number of the entry and the page on which the entry will be found.

Redistricting for the 2000s

House incumbents should have dreaded the 2002 midterm elections because those elections were the first to be held under congressional district lines that were redrawn after the 2000 census. Incumbents tend to be more vulnerable when they run in newly drawn districts, which have thousands of new voters with whom they are not familiar, than in districts in which they are well known for years.

But incumbents in both parties fared well in November 2002. Of the 398 House members in 2002 who sought reelection, 382 were successful—a 96 percent success rate. It was the third consecutive election in which fewer than ten House members were defeated in November; that phenomenon had occurred in only three of the 26 previous House elections since World War II.

An important reason for incumbents' high success rate in 2002 was that the district lines were tailored to their overwhelming advantage. Members of Congress in many states forged bipartisan compromises with their legislatures to protect or even strengthen their House districts' partisan leanings, in some cases choosing collective incumbent protection over maps that might have given opportunities to both parties to gain additional seats. Even states that redistricted under the direction of nonpartisan commissions and judicial panels, which might be expected to treat House incumbents less favorably than legislators would, tended to view seniority positively and drew congressional maps that shielded incumbents from political danger.

Redistricting often locks in a party's advantage in a district for an entire decade. Of the 435 House districts, 324 (75 percent) stayed in the same party's hands through the five elections from 1992 through 2000 even though that period included the 1994 election in which Republicans won control of Congress for the first time in four decades. The most recent redistricting process is expected to produce another decade-long partisan lock on most House districts.

Decennial Reapportionment and Redistricting

The redistricting process started in December 2000 with the reapportionment of the 435 House seats, a process based on the population data from the decennial census. Because the membership of the U.S. House is fixed under federal law, reapportionment is a zero-sum game. Fast-growing states gain seats at the expense of slow-growing states.

The reapportionment of U.S. House seats confirmed a continuation of the nation's overriding population trend of the past half-century: continuing growth in large parts of the

South and West outstripping slower growth in the former industrial areas of the East and Midwest. Arizona, Florida, Georgia, and Texas gained two House seats each for the ten-year period that began with the 2002 elections; California, Colorado, Nevada, and North Carolina gained one seat apiece.

Florida, now the nation's fourth-most-populous state, has gained seats in every reapportionment since 1900. Texas, which passed New York in the late 1990s to become the nation's second-most-populous state, after California, has gained seats in all but one reapportionment since 1850, five years after it became a state.

Losing two House seats apiece were New York and Pennsylvania. The Empire State, which had 45 House seats as recently as the 1940s, lost at least two seats for the sixth consecutive reapportionment. Pennsylvania was stripped of at least one House seat for the eighth consecutive reapportionment, and it lost at least two seats for the sixth consecutive reapportionment. At 19 House seats for this decade, Pennsylvania has 17 fewer seats than it had after the 1910 reapportionment. The Keystone State has not had fewer than 20 members in its House delegation since the first decade of the nineteenth century.

Losing one seat apiece were Connecticut, Illinois, Indiana, Michigan, Mississippi, Ohio, Oklahoma, and Wisconsin. The remaining states maintained the number of House seats from the 1990s.

The reapportionment appeared to marginally benefit Republicans, who traditionally have done better in the South and West than in the East and Midwest. Had the 2000 presidential election been held under the postreapportionment electoral college calculus, Republican George W. Bush would have won 278 electoral votes, seven more than he actually received.

Incumbency Protection

With the census and reapportionment complete, state legislatures could begin the task of redrawing congressional district lines to reflect population shifts. In this part of the decennial ballet, the major thrust of redistricting in 2001 and 2002 was to protect incumbents of both parties. Nowhere was proincumbent redistricting more consequential than in California. By far the nation's most populous state, it gained one seat in the 2000 reapportionment, bringing its delegation to an all-time record of 53. One out of every eight seats in the House is held by a Californian.

With Democrat Gray Davis as governor at the time and the Democratic Party solidly in control of the California legislature, some national Democratic strategists argued for drawing a congressional map of the state that would augment the party's already considerable 12-seat advantage in the state's House delegation as the decade began. But this view was not shared by the seven California Democratic House members who were elected or reelected in 2000 with 55 percent of the vote or less, or by their colleagues. They felt their party had reached a high-water mark in the 2000 election, when it gained four House seats in California for a total of 32.

Rather than spreading Democratic voters more widely in hopes of undercutting some Republican incumbents, the Democratic members wanted their political security shored up. Republicans, who had fared terribly in recent California elections, were eager for a deal that they hoped would arrest their precipitous political decline in the state. The outcome was a bargain under which the lines were shifted to add Democratic voters to districts held by Democratic members and Republican voters to districts held by Republicans.

With redistricting ensuring Democrats control of the state's new seat, 33 California Democrats won in 2002 with an average of 68 percent of the vote; just four were elected or reelected with less than 60 percent. The 20 victorious Republicans won with an average of 67 percent, and all of them won at least 60 percent.

The remap brought a radical improvement in political fortune for Democrat Jane Harman, for example. In a politically marginal suburban Los Angeles district, starting in 1992 she won her first three House terms with 48 percent, 48 percent, and 52 percent of the vote. After giving her seat up for a 1998 bid for governor that failed, two years later Harman narrowly won her seat back—again with 48 percent. But for this decade, Harman's district was redrawn with a more solidly Democratic orientation, and she prevailed in 2002 by 26 percentage points.

Also benefiting under redistricting were Democratic representative Lois Capps and Republican representative Elton Gallegly, who represent adjacent districts on the California coast north of Los Angeles. Capps and Gallegly were reelected in 2000 with 53 percent and 54 percent, respectively. In the 2002 election Capps won with 59 percent of the vote, a career high, and Gallegly won with 65 percent.

The proincumbent trend continued apace in Texas, where the 32-member House delegation is second in size only to California. The Democratic-controlled state House and Republican-controlled state Senate could not agree on a plan, so a three-judge federal panel handled the line-drawing duties. The two seats Texas received in reapportionment—a result of burgeoning population growth—were drawn to favor Republican candidates. But it otherwise protected members of both parties, including congressional leaders such as then-House majority whip Tom DeLay and then-Democratic Caucus chairman Martin Frost—a rationale the judges said they took into account when crafting their plan. "It was plain that these members were not harmed in their reelection prospects by this plan and that, indeed, no incumbent was paired with another incumbent or significantly harmed by the plan," the judges wrote. However, in 2003 Republicans—then in full control of the Texas government—set out to undo the judge's work. (*See discussion that follows on p. xviii.*)

In Michigan, Republicans parlayed their control of the legislature and governorship into drawing a map that turned the Democrats' 9–7 advantage in the delegation to a 9–6 Republican edge. One beneficiary of the plan was freshman Republican Mike Rogers, who won by 111 votes in the closest House race of 2000. Under more favorable district lines, Rogers won by 85,605 votes in 2002.

To strengthen Rogers and other GOP candidates, GOP mapmakers pulled Republican voters from Democratic-held districts, thereby packing Democratic voters in districts that Democratic candidates would dominate. Democrat Dale Kildee was vigorously challenged in the 1990s, winning races with 54, 51, 59, and 56 percent of the vote. The GOP map moved Republican voters from Kildee's district to Rogers's district and paired Kildee in one district with Democratic representative James A. Barcia, who chose to retire. The GOP did not even field a nominee against Kildee in his redrawn, staunchly Democratic district.

Some states use a commission to redraw congressional district lines. But even commissions tended to draw district lines that favored incumbents.

New Jersey's commission was far from independent: its 13 members included six Democratic and six Republican appointees and one independent chairperson. The map the commission ultimately enacted made small changes to a map preferred by the state delegation's seven Democrats and six Republicans. Alan Rosenthal, a Rutgers University political scientist who chaired the commission, noted that the new map was "kind to incumbents," particularly Republican Mike Ferguson, who in 2000 won his first term by just 50 percent to 48 percent, and Democratic Rush Holt, who that year won a second term by just 651 votes. In 2002, Ferguson took 58 percent of the vote—the smallest winning percentage in a New Jersey House race that year. Holt zoomed to 61 percent.

To be sure, there were a few exceptions to the proincumbent trend. In Iowa, state law empowers a nonpartisan state legislative agency to draw the lines without regard to political registration data, election results, or even incumbents' home addresses.

The new map was particularly disruptive to Republican representative Jim Leach, who was paired in one district with Republican representative Jim Nussle, and Democratic representative Leonard Boswell, whose residence was drawn into a heavily Republican district in western Iowa. Leach and Boswell moved to different congressional districts to seek reelection. Nussle and Republican Tom Latham, the other two Iowa incumbents who sought reelection, ran in districts that were significantly redrawn. All four incumbents won, but with electoral percentages ranging from 52 percent for Leach to 57 percent for Nussle. For Leach, Boswell, and Latham, their 2002 races were the closest reelection campaigns in their careers.

The Iowa system's backers say it depoliticizes a system that is deeply political. Good-government advocates argue that the Iowa system, if enacted in more states, would produce highly competitive elections and a more responsive Congress. But the Iowa system will require politicians to cede power over a process that may be the most political thing legislatures do.

Smaller Judicial Role

Another reason the redistricting process in 2001 and 2002 was only marginally disruptive to incumbents was the relatively small role courts played in implementing new district plans. The judiciary has long hesitated to get involved in redistricting. Supreme Court Justice Felix Frankfurter wrote in 1946 that redistricting was a "political thicket" that "courts ought not to enter," but in the 1990s the courts thrust themselves deeply into the debate about drawing districts that would maximize the voting power of blacks and Hispanics. North Carolina, where the labyrinthine 12th District was the subject of a decade of litigation, used one map for the 1992, 1994, and 1996 elections; a second map for the 1998 elections; and a third map for the 2000 election. *(See list of redistricting court cases, pp. 1030–1032.)*

In just seven states with 66 House districts—Colorado, Minnesota, Mississippi, New Mexico, Oklahoma, South Carolina, and Texas—did a court issue a binding congressional district plan for the 2002 elections. In the 1990s round, courts played an integral role in the redistricting process in nearly half of the states and actually drew the plans in ten states, including the high-population states of California, Florida, Pennsylvania, Illinois, and Michigan. None of those five states used a court-drawn plan for districts in the 2000s.

Alignment of Members, Constituents

Because most of the 435 districts were drawn to strongly favor one of the two major political parties, the overwhelming majority of House members will be from the same party as most of their constituents.

The consequences on Capitol Hill were already becoming clear by 2003: more lawmakers were feeling less compelled than in the past to appeal to a broad spectrum of views because their constituents were, in considerable measure, ideologically just like them. Political analysts predicted that deepening partisanship in the House was probable, and the divisions were likely to be locked in place until the next congressional maps are drawn after the 2010 census.

This latest political-demographic trend is most readily seen by comparing the party that holds a House seat with the party whose presidential candidate carried the district in the 2000 election. Looking at the districts as they were previously drawn—which were in effect on election day 2000—there were 86 (one out of every five) in which voters elected a House candidate of one party but preferred the presidential nominee of the opposite party. By artfully redrawing congressional district lines for this decade in many states, mapmakers reduced by 28 percent, to 62, the number of ticket-splitting districts in 2002. Thus in only one out of every seven House districts did voters elect a congressional candidate from a party different from what their presidential choice would have been in 2000.

That level of ticket-splitting is the lowest since at least 1952, the earliest election year for which complete presidential-vote-by-district data are available. It is far lower than the 110 split districts (25 percent of the total) after the reelection of both Democratic president Bill Clinton and an all-Republican Congress in 1996, and it pales by comparison with the 192 split districts (44 percent) in the 1972 election that reelected not only Republican president Richard Nixon but also a solidly Democratic Congress.

This might seem at odds with the macrolevel perception of the United States as a nation whose partisan loyalties are divided nearly evenly. This impression was strengthened by the razor's-edge outcome of the 2000 presidential election, in which George W. Bush narrowly won in the electoral college while narrowly losing the popular vote, as well as by the relatively small margins by which Republicans controlled the House and Senate in the Congress that convened in January 2003.

But that near-even national split is the sum total of states and districts that increasingly have hardened into "red" or "blue" strongholds on the political map for either the Republicans or the Democrats. The strength of a district's political leanings is a good indicator of how faithfully its representative will toe the party line. This is particularly true in the House. Far from spurring greater electoral participation and competition, the redistricting that followed the 2000 census and preceded the 2002 elections mainly benefited incumbents and narrowed the field of competitive races.

One part of the country that joined the trend toward partisan fidelity in 2002, with a big assist from redistricting, is essentially on Congress's doorstep. Maryland's reliably Democratic 8th District, which takes in the suburbs just north of Washington, chose Democratic state senator Chris Van Hollen over Constance A. Morella, a moderate Republican who had held the seat for 16 years. Far above average in affluence and education, 8th District residents had long pointed to their support of Morella to deflect suggestions that they were automatic Democratic votes. Morella, in turn, maintained her popularity with a legislative voting record that often was the most liberal among House Republicans.

But Democrats completely controlled Maryland's redistricting process in 2002 and fashioned a map that made the 8th District even more reflexively Democratic and more attractive to prospective challengers. An activist legislator popular among the Democrats' liberal base, Van Hollen won by 4 percentage points.

The partisan impact was immediate. As moderate as Morella was, she still joined with most Democratic members against most of her Republican colleagues on only 41 percent of mostly party-line votes in her final term. Through mid-October 2003, Van Hollen voted the majority Democratic position on 98 percent of the votes that pitted a majority of Democrats against a majority of Republicans.

The redistricting of California ended the political career of Republican Steve Horn, another leading GOP moderate during his decade in the House. His Democratic-leaning district in Los Angeles County was redrawn with an even more strongly liberal slant, and he chose to retire. Much of the territory Horn represented is now held by Democrat Linda T. Sánchez, who through mid-October 2003 had backed her party's leadership more often than any other House Democrat on mostly party-line votes.

Redistricting also ended the political career of Republican Benjamin A. Gilman of New York, who broke with his party's leaders on key votes more often than nearly every other House Republican. Gilman retired rather than run in a district in which he had been paired with Republican representative Sue W. Kelly.

The 2002 elections also thinned the Democratic Party of some of its leading centrists. Ronnie Shows of Mississippi had departed from the national Democratic orthodoxy on issues such as abortion and gun control during his two House terms.

He was nonetheless defeated after a court-imposed redistricting plan compelled him to seek reelection against Republican Charles W. "Chip" Pickering Jr. in Mississippi's heavily Republican district. David Phelps, another socially conservative Democrat first elected in 1998, lost a redistricting-induced matchup with Republican John Shimkus in Illinois.

A handful of members managed to survive against the partisan tides in their districts. They included conservative Democrats such as Kentucky's Ken Lucas, and Texans Charles W. Stenholm and Ralph M. Hall. But during the first decade of the 2000s these members' districts would be so inclined toward the GOP—all favored Bush by lopsided margins in 2000—that their successors were likely, if not certain, to be conservative Republicans.

But Texas Republicans in 2003 were not content waiting for Democratic retirements in districts the GOP long coveted. With the enthusiastic backing of House majority leader Tom DeLay of Texas, GOP legislators spent much of 2003 promoting a new congressional district map they said would better reflect the state's Republican voting patterns than the plan a three-judge federal panel implemented in 2001 for the following year's elections. Under the judges' map, Democrats won 17 of the 32 House seats in Texas even as Republicans were winning every statewide office in 2002.

The legislature finally enacted a new map in October 2003, in a third special session of the state legislature that Republican governor Rick Perry called after Democrats had blocked consideration of redistricting through parliamentary maneuvers, including fleeing the state twice to preclude a quorum from convening.

Opponents of the new Texas map immediately filed federal lawsuits alleging that the plan was unfair to Democrats and unconstitutionally diluted the voting power of blacks and Hispanics. Republicans countered that the new map could elect more Hispanics and blacks to the House.

Opponents also called on the federal courts to delay considering a new Texas map until the Supreme Court in 2004 sheds light on the extent to which political factors can influence congressional redistricting. Oral arguments in *Vieth v. Jubelirer,* which centered around a GOP-drawn congressional redistricting plan in Pennsylvania that Democrats challenged as too partisan, were expected in December 2003.

Should the Justice Department and the federal courts approve the new Texas map, Republicans could win up to 22 Texas seats in the 2004 House elections—seven more than the 15 they held after the 2002 races.

Less disruptive than the Texas plan, but no less controversial, was a new Colorado district map GOP legislators enacted in May 2003 that was expected to boost Republican performance in two districts while not adversely affecting Democratic incumbents. Democrats also challenged that plan in court.

Regardless of how the courts rule, the Texas and Colorado redistricting plans raised the possibility that state legislatures could take up a redrawing of congressional district lines more frequently than once per decade, as has long been the standard.

Greg Giroux
CQ Weekly

Congressional Districts in the 2000s

Reapportionment and Redistricting

Reapportionment, the redistribution of the 435 seats in the House of Representatives among the states to reflect shifts in population, and redistricting, the redrawing of congressional district boundaries for the House within the states, are among the most important and contentious processes in the U.S. political system. They help to determine whether Democrats or Republicans, or liberals or conservatives will dominate the House, and whether districts will be drawn to favor the election of candidates from particular racial or ethnic groups.

Reapportionment and redistricting occur every ten years on the basis of the decennial population census. States where populations grew quickly during the previous ten years typically gain congressional seats, while those that lost population or grew much more slowly than the national average stand to lose seats. The number of House members for the rest of the states remains the same.

The states that gain or lose seats usually must make extensive changes in their congressional maps. Even those states with stable delegations must make modifications to take into account population shifts within their boundaries, in accordance with Supreme Court "one-person, one-vote" rulings.

In most states, the state legislatures are responsible for drafting and enacting the new congressional district map. Thus, the majority party in each state legislature is often in a position to draw a district map that enhances the fortunes of its incumbents and candidates at the expense of the opposing party. "Some members may find their old district no longer recognizable, or their home located in someone else's district. Others will find the music has stopped and they are, quite literally, without a seat. Or they will find themselves thrown together in a single district with another incumbent—often from the same party," wrote one reporter. "The scramble to prevent or minimize such political problems involves some of the most brutal combat in American politics, for the power to draw district lines is the power not only to end one politician's career but often to enfranchise or disenfranchise a neighborhood, a city, a party, a social or economic group or even a race by concentrating or diluting their votes within a given district."[1]

Among the many unique features to emerge in the remarkable nation-creating endeavor of 1787 was a national legislative body whose membership was to be elected by the people and apportioned on the basis of population. In keeping with the nature of the Constitution, however, only fundamental rules and regulations were provided. The interpretation and implementation of the instructions contained in the document were left to future generations.

Within this flexible framework many questions soon arose. How large was the House of Representatives to be? What mathematical formula was to be used in calculating the distribution of seats among the various states? Were the representatives to be elected at large or by districts? If by districts, what standards should be used in fixing their boundaries? Congress and the courts have been wrestling with these questions for more than 200 years.

Until the midtwentieth century such questions generally remained in the hands of the legislators. But with the population increasingly concentrated in urban areas, variations in populations among rural and urban districts in a single state grew more and more pronounced. Efforts to persuade Congress and state legislatures to address the issue of heavily populated but underrepresented areas proved unsuccessful. Legislators from rural areas were so intent on preventing power from slipping from their hands that they managed to block reapportionment of the House for a whole decade after the 1920 census.

Not long afterward, litigants began trying to persuade the Supreme Court to order the states to revise congressional district boundaries to reflect population shifts. For years they found the Court unreceptive, but then there was incremental progress, and a breakthrough finally occurred in 1964 in the case of *Wesberry v. Sanders*. In that case, the Court declared that the Constitution required that "as nearly as practicable, one man's vote in a congressional election is to be worth as much as another's."

In the years that followed, the Court repeatedly reaffirmed its one-person, one-vote requirement. Following the 1980 census, several states adopted new maps with districts of nearly equal population that were designed to benefit one party at the expense of the other. These partisan gerrymanders disregarded other traditional tenets of map-drawing, such as making districts compact and respecting the integrity of county and city lines. But as long as the districts in such maps were drawn to be equal in population, these gerrymanders seemed unassailable in the courts. In 1986, in *Davis v. Bandemer*, a slim majority of the Supreme Court held that partisan gerrymanders were subject to constitutional review by federal courts. But the Court offered no opinion on what might constitute an impermissible partisan gerrymander, and maps drawn with a clear partisan slant continued to appear in the 1990s and 2000s rounds of redistricting.

Starting in the mid-1980s and continuing through the 1990s, the focus of much redistricting controversy and litigation shifted to the practice of racial gerrymandering—designing constituencies to favor the election of candidates from racial or ethnic groups whose numbers in Congress are lower than their proportion in the general population. Although this issue remained contentious, its importance was diminished for redistricting after the 2000 census following a series of Supreme Court rulings that questioned or prohibited the practice. In a landmark 1986 ruling (*Thornburg v. Gingles*), the Supreme Court not only said that gerrymandering that deliberately diluted minority voting strength was illegal, but went even further, imposing a requirement that mapmakers do all they can to maximize minority voting strength. The expansion of minority rights sparked by *Gingles* changed redistricting dramatically. After the 1990 census, redistricting in many states was done with an eye toward creating constituencies designed to elect minority candidates. Those new maps resulted in record numbers of blacks and Hispanics winning House seats in 1992.

As if taken aback by the pace of change wrought by *Gingles*, the Supreme Court issued a series of rulings in the 1990s that discouraged states from going to extremes to draw districts for minorities. As a result, mapmakers in the new century found themselves between legal and political pressures to enhance election opportunities for minority group members and court decisions that posed a rigorous examination of the standards and methods to carry out this obligation.

EARLY HISTORY OF REAPPORTIONMENT

Modern legislative bodies are descended from the councils of feudal lords and gentry that medieval kings summoned for the purpose of raising revenues and armies. The councils represented only certain groups of people, such as the nobility, the clergy, the landed gentry, and town merchants; the notion of equal representation for equal numbers of people or even for all groups of people had not yet begun to develop.

Beginning as little more than administrative and advisory arms of the throne, royal councils in time developed into lawmaking bodies and acquired powers that eventually eclipsed those of the monarchs they served. In England the king's council became Parliament, with the higher nobility and clergy making up the House of Lords and representatives of the gentry and merchants making up the House of Commons. The power struggle between king and council climaxed in the mid-1600s, when the king was executed and a "benevolent" dictatorship was set up under Oliver Cromwell. Although the monarchy was soon restored, by 1800 Parliament was clearly the more powerful branch of government.

The growth of the powers of Parliament, as well as the development of English ideas of representation during the seventeenth and eighteenth centuries, had a profound effect on the colonists in America. Representative assemblies were unifying forces behind the breakaway of the colonies from England and the establishment of the newly independent nation.

Colonists in America generally modeled their legislatures after England's, using both population and land units as bases for apportionment. Patterns of early representation varied. "Nowhere did representation bear any uniform relation to the number of electors. Here and there the factor of size had been crudely recognized," Robert Luce noted in his book *Legislative Principles*.[2]

The Continental Congress, with representation from every colony, proclaimed in the Declaration of Independence in 1776 that governments derive "their just powers from the consent of the governed" and that "the right of representation in the legislature" is an "inestimable right" of the people. The Constitutional Convention of 1787 included representatives from all the states. However, in neither of these bodies were the state delegations or voting powers proportional to population.

In New England the town was usually the basis for representation. In the Middle Atlantic region the county frequently was used. Virginia used the county with additional representation for specified cities. In many areas, towns and counties were fairly equal in population, and territorial representation afforded roughly equal representation for equal numbers of people. Delaware's three counties, for example, were of almost equal population and had the same representation in the legislature. But in Virginia the disparity was enormous (from 951 people in one county to 22,015 in another). Thomas Jefferson criticized the state's constitution on the ground that "among those who share the representation, the shares are unequal."[3]

The Framers' Intentions

What, then, did the Framers of the Constitution have in mind about who would be represented in the House of Representatives and how? The Constitution declares only that each state is to be allotted a certain number of representatives. It does not state specifically that congressional districts must be equal or nearly equal in population. Nor does it explicitly require that a state create districts at all. However, it seems clear that the first clause of Article I, Section 2, providing that House members should be chosen "by the People of the several States," indicates that the House of Representatives, in contrast to the Senate, was to represent people rather than states. *(See box, Constitutional Provisions, p. 3.)*

The third clause of Article I, Section 2, provided that congressional apportionment among the states must be according to population. "There is little point in giving the states congressmen 'according to their respective numbers' if the states do not redistribute the members of their delegations on the same principle," Andrew Hacker argued in his book *Congressional Districting*. "For representatives are not the property of the states, as are the senators, but rather belong to the people who happen to reside within the boundaries of those states. Thus, each citizen has a claim to be regarded as a political unit equal in value to his neighbors."[4]

Hacker also examined the Constitutional Convention, *The Federalist Papers* (essays written by Alexander Hamilton, John Jay, and James Madison in defense of the Constitution), and the state conventions ratifying the Constitution for evidence of the Framers' intentions with regard to representation. He found that the issue of unequal representation arose only once during debate in the Constitutional Convention. The occasion was Madison's defense of Article I, Section 4, of the proposed Constitution, giving Congress the power to override state regulations on "the times . . . and manner" of holding elections for members of Congress. Madison's argument related to the fact that many state legislatures of the time were badly malapportioned: "The inequality of the representation in the legislatures of particular states would produce a like inequality in their representation in the national legislature, as it was presumable that the counties having the power in the former case would secure it to themselves in the latter."[5]

The implication was that states would create congressional districts and that unequal districting was undesirable and should be prevented.

Madison made this interpretation even more clear in his contributions to *The Federalist Papers*. Arguing in favor of the relatively small size of the projected House of Representatives, he wrote in No. 56: "Divide the largest state into ten or twelve districts and it will be found that there will be no peculiar local interests . . . which will not be within the knowledge of the Representative of the district."

In the same paper Madison said, "The Representatives of each state will not only bring with them a considerable knowledge of its laws, and a local knowledge of their respective districts, but will probably in all cases have been members, and may even at the very time be members, of the state legislature, where all the local information and interests of the state are assembled, and from whence they may easily be conveyed by a very few hands into the legislature of the United States." And, finally, in the *Federalist* No. 57 Madison stated that "each Representative of the United States will be elected by five or six thousand citizens." In making these arguments, Madison seems to have assumed that all or most representatives would be elected by districts rather than at large.[6]

In the states' ratifying conventions, the grant to Congress by Article I, Section 4, of ultimate jurisdiction over the "Times, Places and Manner of holding Elections" (except the places of choosing senators) held the attention of many delegates. There were differences over the merits of this section, but no justification of unequal districts was prominently used to attack the grant of power. Further evidence that individual districts were the intention of the Founding Fathers was given in the New York ratifying convention, when Alexander Hamilton said, "The natural and proper mode of holding elections will be to divide the state into districts in proportion to the number to be elected. This state will consequently be divided at first into six."[7]

From his study of the sources relating to the question of congressional districting, Hacker concluded,

> There is, then, a good deal of evidence that those who framed and ratified the Constitution intended that the House of Representatives have as its constituency a public in which the votes of all citizens were of equal weight. . . . The House of Representatives was designed to be a popular chamber, giving the same electoral power to all who had the vote. And the concern of Madison . . . that districts be equal in size was an institutional step in the direction of securing this democratic principle.[8]

REAPPORTIONMENT: THE NUMBER OF SEATS

The Constitution made the first apportionment, which was to remain in effect until the first census was taken. No reliable figures on the population were available at the time. The Constitution's apportionment yielded a 65-member House. The seats were allotted among the 13 states as follows: New Hampshire, three; Massachusetts, eight; Rhode Island and

Constitutional Provisions

Article I, Section 2: The House of Representatives shall be composed of Members chosen every second Year by the People of the several States, and the Electors in each State shall have the Qualifications requisite for Electors of the most numerous Branch of the State Legislature. . . .

Representatives and direct Taxes shall be apportioned among the several States which may be included within this Union, according to their respective Numbers, which shall be determined by adding to the whole Number of free Persons, including those bound to Service for a Term of Years, and excluding Indians not taxed, three fifths of all other Persons. The actual Enumeration shall be made within three Years after the first Meeting of the Congress of the United States, and within every subsequent Term of ten Years, in such Manner as they shall by Law direct. The Number of Representatives shall not exceed one for every thirty thousand, but each State shall have at least one Representative. . . .

Article I, Section 4: The Times, Places and Manner of holding Elections for Senators and Representatives, shall be prescribed in each State by the Legislature thereof; but the Congress may at any time by Law make or alter such Regulations, except as to the Place of Chusing Senators. . . .

Amendment XIV (Ratified July 28, 1868), Section 2: Representatives shall be apportioned among the several States according to their respective numbers, counting the whole number of persons in each State, excluding Indians not taxed. But when the right to vote at any election for the choice of electors for President and Vice President of the United States, Representatives in Congress, the Executive and Judicial officers of a State, or the members of the Legislature thereof, is denied to any of the male inhabitants of such State, being twenty-one years of age, and citizens of the United States, or in any way abridged, except for participation in rebellion, or other crime, the basis of representation therein shall be reduced in the proportion which the number of such male citizens shall bear to the whole number of male citizens twenty-one years of age in such State.

Providence Plantations, one; Connecticut, five; New York, six; New Jersey, four; Pennsylvania, eight; Delaware, one; Maryland, six; Virginia, ten; North Carolina, five; South Carolina, five; and Georgia, three. This apportionment remained in effect during the 1st and 2nd Congresses (1789–1793).

Apparently realizing that apportionment of the House was likely to become a major bone of contention, the First Congress submitted to the states a proposed constitutional amendment containing a formula to be used in future reapportionments. The amendment provided that following the taking of a decennial census one representative would be allotted for every 30,000 people until the House membership reached 100. Once that level was reached, there would be one representative for every 40,000 people until the House membership reached 200, when there would be one representative for every 50,000 people.

First Apportionment by Congress

The states, however, refused to ratify the reapportionment-formula amendment, which forced Congress to enact apportionment legislation after the first census was taken in 1790. The first apportionment bill was sent to the president in March 1792. President George Washington sent the bill back to Congress without his signature—the first presidential veto.

The bill had incorporated the constitutional minimum of 30,000 as the size of each district. But the population of each state was not a simple multiple of 30,000; significant fractions were left over. For example, Vermont was found to be entitled to 2.85 representatives, New Jersey to 5.98, and Virginia to 21.02. A formula had to be found that would deal in the fairest possible manner with unavoidable variations from exact equality.

Accordingly, Congress proposed in the first apportionment bill to distribute the members on a fixed ratio of one representative for each 30,000 inhabitants, and to give an additional member to each state with a fraction exceeding one-half. Washington's veto was based on the belief that eight states would receive more than one representative for each 30,000 people under this formula.

A motion to override the veto was unsuccessful. A new bill meeting the president's objections, approved in April 1792, provided for a ratio of one member for every 33,000 inhabitants and fixed the exact number of representatives to which each state was entitled. The total membership of the House was to be 105. In dividing the population of the various states by 33,000, all remainders were to be disregarded. Thomas Jefferson devised the solution, known as the method of rejected fractions.

Jefferson's Method

Jefferson's method of reapportionment resulted in great inequalities among districts. A Vermont district would contain 42,766 inhabitants, a New Jersey district 35,911, and a Virginia district only 33,187. Jefferson's method emphasized what was considered to be the ideal size of a congressional district rather than what the size of the House ought to be.

The reapportionment act based on the census of 1800 continued the ratio of 33,000, which provided a House of 141 members. The third apportionment bill, enacted in 1811, fixed the ratio at 35,000, yielding a House of 181 members. Following the 1820 census Congress set the ratio at 40,000 inhabitants per district, which produced a House of 213 members. The act of May 22, 1832, fixed the ratio at 47,700, resulting in a House of 240 members.

Dissatisfaction with inequalities produced by the method of rejected fractions grew. Launching a vigorous attack against it, Daniel Webster urged adoption of a method that would assign an additional representative to each state with a large fraction. Webster outlined his reasoning in a report he submitted to Congress in 1832:

The Constitution, therefore, must be understood not as enjoining an absolute relative equality—because that would be demanding an impossibility—but as requiring of Congress to make the apportionment of Representatives among the several states according to their respective numbers, *as near as may be.* That which cannot be done perfectly must be done in a manner as near perfection as can be.... In such a case approximation becomes a rule.[9]

Following the 1840 census Congress adopted a reapportionment method similar to that advocated by Webster. The method fixed a ratio of one representative for every 70,680 people. This figure was reached by deciding on a fixed size of the House in advance (223), dividing that figure into the total national "representative population," and using the result (70,680) as the fixed ratio. The population of each state was then divided by this ratio to find the number of its representatives and the states were assigned an additional representative for each fraction more than one-half. Under this method the actual size of the House dropped. *(See table, p. 5.)*

The modified reapportionment formula adopted by Congress in 1842 was more satisfactory than the previous method, but another change was made following the census of 1850. Proposed by Rep. Samuel F. Vinton of Ohio, the new system became known as the Vinton method.

Vinton Apportionment Formula

Under the Vinton formula Congress first fixed the size of the House and then distributed the seats. The total qualifying population of the country was divided by the desired number of representatives, and the resulting number became the ratio of population to each representative. The population of each state was divided by this ratio, and each state received the number of representatives equal to the whole number in the quotient for that state. Then, to reach the required size of the House, additional representatives were assigned based on the remaining fractions, beginning with the state having the largest fraction. This procedure differed from the 1842 method only in the last step, which assigned one representative to every state having a fraction larger than one-half.

Proponents of the Vinton method pointed out that it had the distinct advantage of fixing the size of the House in advance and taking into account at least the largest fractions. The concern of the House turned from the ideal size of a congressional district to the ideal size of the House itself.

Under the 1842 reapportionment formula, the exact size of the House could not be fixed in advance. If every state with a fraction more than one-half were given an additional representative, the House might wind up with a few more or a few less than the desired number. However, under the Vinton method, only states with the largest fractions were given additional House members and only up to the desired total size of the House.

Vinton Apportionments

Six reapportionments were carried out under the Vinton method. The 1850 census act contained three provisions not included in any previous law. First, it required reapportionment not only after the census of 1850 but also after all the subsequent censuses; second, it purported to fix the size of the House permanently at 233 members; and third, it provided

Congressional Apportionment, 1789–2000

Year of census[1]

	Constitution (1789)[2]	1790	1800	1810	1820	1830	1840	1850	1860	1870	1880	1890	1900	1910	1930[3]	1940	1950	1960	1970	1980	1990	2000
Alabama				1[4]	3	5	7	7	6	8	8	9	9	10	9	9	9	8	7	7	7	7
Alaska																	1[4]	1	1	1	1	1
Arizona														1[4]	1	2	2	3	4	5	6	8
Arkansas						1[4]	1	2	3	4	5	6	7	7	7	7	6	4	4	4	4	4
California					2[4]	2	3	4	6	7	8	11	20	23	30	38	43	45	52	53		
Colorado										1[4]	1	2	3	4	4	4	4	4	5	6	6	7
Connecticut	5	7	7	7	6	6	4	4	4	4	4	4	5	5	6	6	6	6	6	6	6	5
Delaware	1	1	1	2	1	1	1	1	1	1	1	1	1	1	1	1	1	1	1	1	1	1
Florida							1[4]	1	1	2	2	2	3	4	5	6	8	12	15	19	23	25
Georgia	3	2	4	6	7	9	8	8	7	9	10	11	11	12	10	10	10	10	10	10	11	13
Hawaii																	1[4]	2	2	2	2	2
Idaho											1[4]	1	1	2	2	2	2	2	2	2	2	2
Illinois				1[4]	1	3	7	9	14	19	20	22	25	27	27	26	25	24	24	22	20	19
Indiana				1[4]	3	7	10	11	11	13	13	13	13	13	12	11	11	11	11	10	10	9
Iowa							2[4]	2	6	9	11	11	11	11	9	8	8	7	6	6	5	5
Kansas									1	3	7	8	8	8	7	6	6	5	5	5	4	4
Kentucky		2	6	10	12	13	10	10	9	10	11	11	11	11	9	9	8	7	7	7	6	6
Louisiana				1[4]	3	3	4	4	5	6	6	6	7	8	8	8	8	8	8	8	7	7
Maine				7[4]	7	8	7	6	5	5	4	4	4	4	3	3	3	2	2	2	2	2
Maryland	6	8	9	9	9	8	6	6	5	6	6	6	6	6	6	6	7	8	8	8	8	8
Massachusetts	8	14	17	13[5]	13	12	10	11	10	11	12	13	14	16	15	14	14	12	12	11	10	10
Michigan						1[4]	3	4	6	9	11	12	12	13	17	17	18	19	19	18	16	15
Minnesota								2[4]	2	3	5	7	9	10	9	9	9	8	8	8	8	8
Mississippi				1[4]	1	2	4	5	5	6	7	7	8	8	7	7	6	5	5	5	5	4
Missouri					1	2	5	7	9	13	14	15	16	16	13	13	11	10	10	9	9	9
Montana											1[4]	1	1	2	2	2	2	2	2	1	1	1
Nebraska									1[4]	1	3	6	6	6	5	4	4	3	3	3	3	3
Nevada									1[4]	1	1	1	1	1	1	1	1	1	1	2	2	3
New Hampshire	3	4	5	6	6	5	4	3	3	3	2	2	2	2	2	2	2	2	2	2	2	2
New Jersey	4	5	6	6	6	6	5	5	5	7	7	8	10	12	14	14	14	15	15	14	13	13
New Mexico														1[4]	1	2	2	2	2	3	3	3
New York	6	10	17	27	34	40	34	33	31	33	34	34	37	43	45	45	43	41	39	34	31	29
North Carolina	5	10	12	13	13	13	9	8	7	8	9	9	10	10	11	12	12	11	11	11	12	13
North Dakota											1[4]	1	2	3	2	2	2	2	1	1	1	1
Ohio			1[4]	6	14	19	21	21	19	20	21	21	21	22	24	23	23	24	23	21	19	18
Oklahoma													5[4]	8	9	8	6	6	6	6	6	5
Oregon				–				1[4]	1	1	1	2	2	3	3	4	4	4	4	5	5	5
Pennsylvania	8	13	18	23	26	28	24	25	24	27	28	30	32	36	34	33	30	27	25	23	21	19
Rhode Island	1	2	2	2	2	2	2	2	2	2	2	2	2	3	2	2	2	2	2	2	2	2
South Carolina	5	6	8	9	9	9	7	6	4	5	7	7	7	7	6	6	6	6	6	6	6	6
South Dakota											2[4]	2	2	3	2	2	2	2	2	1	1	1
Tennessee		1[4]	3	6	9	13	11	10	8	10	10	10	10	10	9	10	9	9	8	9	9	9
Texas							2[4]	2	4	6	11	13	16	18	21	21	22	23	24	27	30	32
Utah												1[4]	1	2	2	2	2	2	2	3	3	3
Vermont		2	4	6	5	5	4	3	3	3	2	2	2	2	1	1	1	1	1	1	1	1
Virginia	10	19	22	23	22	21	15	13	11	9	10	10	10	10	9	9	10	10	10	10	11	11
Washington											1[4]	2	3	5	6	6	7	7	7	8	9	9
West Virginia									3	4	4	5	6	6	6	6	5	4	4	3	3	
Wisconsin							2[4]	3	6	8	9	10	11	11	10	10	10	10	9	9	9	8
Wyoming											1[4]	1	1	1	1	1	1	1	1	1	1	1
Total	65	106	142	186	213	242	232	237	243	293	332	357	391	435	435	435	437[6]	435	435	435	435	435

1. Apportionment effective with congressional election two years after census.
2. Original apportionment made in Constitution, pending first census.
3. No apportionment was made in 1920.
4. These figures are not based on any census, but indicate the provisional representation accorded newly admitted states by Congress, pending the next census.
5. Twenty members were assigned to Massachusetts, but seven of these were credited to Maine when that area became a state.
6. Normally 435, but temporarily increased two seats by Congress when Alaska and Hawaii became states.

Source: Biographical Directory of the American Congress and Bureau of the Census.

in advance for an automatic apportionment by the secretary of the interior under the method prescribed in the act.

Following the census of 1860 an automatic reapportionment was to be carried out by the Interior Department. However, because the size of the House was to remain at the 1850 level, some states faced loss of representation and others were to gain fewer seats than they expected. To avert that possibility, an act was approved in 1862 increasing the size of the House to 241 and giving an extra representative to eight states—Illinois, Iowa, Kentucky, Minnesota, Ohio, Pennsylvania, Rhode Island, and Vermont.

Apportionment legislation following the 1870 census contained several new provisions. The act fixed the size of the House at 283, with the proviso that the number should be increased if new states were admitted. A supplemental act assigned one additional representative each to Alabama, Florida, Indiana, Louisiana, New Hampshire, New York, Pennsylvania, Tennessee, and Vermont.

With the Reconstruction era at its height in the South, the reapportionment legislation of 1872 reflected the desire of Congress to enforce Section 2 of the new 14th Amendment. That section attempted to protect the right of blacks to vote by providing for reduction of representation in the House of a state that interfered with the exercise of that right. The number of representatives of such a state was to be reduced in proportion to the number of inhabitants of voting age whose right to go to the polls was denied or abridged. The reapportionment bill repeated the language of Section 2, but the provision never was put into effect because of the difficulty of determining the exact number of people whose right to vote was being abridged.

The reapportionment act of 1882 provided for a House of 325 members, with additional members for any new states admitted to the Union. No new apportionment provisions were added. The acts of 1891 and 1901 were routine as far as apportionment was concerned. The 1891 measure provided for a House of 356 members, and the 1901 statute increased the number to 386.

Problems with Vinton Method

Despite the apparent advantages of the Vinton method, certain difficulties revealed themselves as the formula was applied. Zechariah Chafee Jr., of the Harvard Law School summarized these problems in an article in the *Harvard Law Review* in 1929. The method, he pointed out, suffered from what he called the "Alabama paradox." Under that aberration, an increase in the total size of the House might be accompanied by an actual loss of a seat by some states, even though there had been no corresponding change in population. This phenomenon first appeared in tables prepared for Congress in 1881, which gave Alabama eight members in a House of 299 but only seven members in a House of 300. It could even happen that the state that lost a seat was the one state that had expanded in population, while all the others had fewer people.

Chafee concluded from his study of the Vinton method:

> Thus, it is unsatisfactory to fix the ratio of population per Representative before seats are distributed. Either the size of the House comes out haphazard, or, if this be determined in advance, the absurdities of the "Alabama paradox" vitiate the apportion-

ment. Under present conditions, it is essential to determine the size of the House in advance; the problem thereafter is to distribute the required number of seats among the several states as nearly as possible in proportion to their respective populations so that no state is treated unfairly in comparison with any other state.[10]

Maximum Membership of House

In 1911 the membership of the House was fixed at 433. Provision was made for the addition of one representative each from Arizona and New Mexico, which were expected to become states in the near future. Thus, the size of the House reached 435, where it has remained with the exception of a brief period, 1959–1963, when the admission of Alaska and Hawaii raised the total temporarily to 437.

Limiting the size of the House amounted to recognition that the body soon would expand to unmanageable proportions if Congress continued the practice of adding new seats every ten years to match population gains without depriving any state of its existing representation. Agreement on a fixed number made the task of reapportionment even more difficult when the population not only increased but also became much more mobile. Population shifts brought Congress up hard against the politically painful necessity of taking seats away from slow-growing states to give the fast-growing states adequate representation.

A new mathematical calculation was adopted for the reapportionment following the 1910 census. Devised by W. F. Willcox of Cornell University, the new system established a priority list that assigned seats progressively, beginning with the first seat above the constitutional minimum of at least one seat for each state. When there were 48 states, this method was used to assign the 49th member, the 50th member, and so on, until the agreed-upon size of the House was reached. The method was called "major fractions" and was used after the censuses of 1910, 1930, and 1940. There was no reapportionment after the 1920 census.

1920s Struggle

The results of the fourteenth decennial census were announced in December 1920, just after the short session of the 66th Congress convened. The 1920 census showed that for the first time in history most Americans were urban residents. This came as a profound shock to people accustomed to emphasizing the nation's rural traditions and the virtues of life on farms and in small towns as Thomas Jefferson had. Jefferson once wrote:

> Those who labor in the earth are the chosen people of God, if ever He had a chosen people, whose breasts He had made His peculiar deposit for substantial and genuine virtue.... The mobs of great cities add just as much to the support of pure government as sores do to the strength of the human body.... I think our governments will remain virtuous for many centuries as long as they are chiefly agricultural: and this shall be as long as there shall be vacant lands in any part of America. When they get piled up upon one another in large cities as in Europe, they will become corrupt as in Europe.[11]

As their power waned throughout the latter part of the nineteenth century and the early part of the twentieth, farmers clung to the Jeffersonian belief that somehow they were more pure and virtuous than the growing number of urban residents. When faced with the fact that they were in the minority, these country residents put up a strong rearguard action to prevent the inevitable shift of congressional districts to the cities. They succeeded in postponing reapportionment legislation for almost a decade.

Rural representatives insisted that, because the 1920 census was taken as of January 1, the farm population had been undercounted. In support of this contention, they argued that many farm laborers were seasonally employed in the cities at that time of year. Furthermore, midwinter road conditions probably had prevented enumerators from visiting many farms, they said, and other farmers were said to have been uncounted because they were absent on winter vacation trips. The change of the census date to January 1 in 1920 had been made to conform to recommendations of the U.S. Department of Agriculture, which had asserted that the census should be taken early in the year if an accurate statistical picture of farming conditions was to be obtained.

Another point raised by rural legislators was that large numbers of unnaturalized aliens were congregated in northern cities, with the result that these cities gained at the expense of constituencies made up mostly of citizens of the United States. Rep. Homer Hoch, R-Kan., submitted a table showing that in a House of 435 representatives, exclusion from the census count of people not naturalized would have altered the allocation of seats in 16 states. Southern and western farming states would have retained the number of seats allocated to them in 1911 or would have gained, while northern industrial states and California would have lost or at least would have gained fewer seats.

A constitutional amendment to exclude all aliens from the enumeration for purposes of reapportionment was proposed during the 70th Congress (1927–1929) by Hoch, Sen. Arthur Capper, R-Kan., and others. But nothing further came of the proposals.

Reapportionment Bills Opposed

The first bill to reapportion the House according to the 1920 census was drafted by the House Census Committee early in 1921. Proceeding on the principle that no state should have its representation reduced, the committee proposed to increase the total number of representatives from 435 to 483. But the House voted 267–76 to keep its membership at 435. The bill then was blocked by a Senate committee, where it died when the 66th Congress expired March 4, 1921.

Early in the 67th Congress, the House Census Committee again reported a bill, this time fixing the total membership at 460, an increase of 25. Two states—Maine and Massachusetts—would have lost one representative each and sixteen states would have gained. On the House floor an unsuccessful attempt was made to fix the number at the existing 435, and the House sent the bill back to committee.

During the 68th Congress (1923–1925), the House Census Committee failed to report any reapportionment bill. In April 1926, midway through the 69th Congress (1925–1927), it became apparent that the committee would not produce a reapportionment measure. A motion to discharge a reapportionment bill from the committee failed, however, and the matter once again was put aside.

Coolidge Intervention

President Calvin Coolidge, who previously had made no reference to reapportionment in his communications to Congress, announced in January 1927 that he favored passage of a new apportionment bill during the short session of the 69th Congress, which would end in less than two months. The House Census Committee refused to act. Its chairman, Rep. E. Hart Fenn, R-Conn., therefore moved in the House to suspend the rules and pass a bill he had introduced authorizing the secretary of commerce to reapportion the House immediately after the 1930 census. The motion was voted down 183–197.

The Fenn bill was rewritten early in the 70th Congress (1927–1929) to give Congress itself a chance to act before the proposed reapportionment by the secretary of commerce should go into effect. The House passed an amended version of the Fenn bill in January 1929, and it was quickly reported by the Senate Commerce Committee. Repeated efforts to bring it up for floor action ahead of other bills failed. Its supporters gave up the fight when it became evident that senators from states slated to lose representation were ready to carry on a filibuster that would have blocked not only reapportionment but all other measures.

Hoover Intervention

President Herbert Hoover listed provision for the 1930 census and reapportionment as "matters of emergency legislation" that should be acted upon in the special session of the 71st Congress, which was convened on April 15, 1929. In response to this urgent request, the Senate June 13 passed, 48–37, a combined census-reapportionment bill that had been approved by voice vote of the House two days earlier.

The 1929 law established a permanent system of reapportioning the 435 House seats following each census. It provided that immediately after the convening of the 71st Congress for its short session in December 1930, the president was to transmit to Congress a statement showing the population of each state together with an apportionment of representatives to each state based on the existing size of the House. Failing enactment of new apportionment legislation, that apportionment would go into effect without further action and would remain in effect for ensuing elections to the House of Representatives until another census had been taken and another reapportionment made.

Because two decades had passed between reapportionments, a greater shift than usual took place following the 1930 census. California's House delegation was almost doubled, rising from 11 to 20. Michigan gained four seats, Texas three, and New Jersey, New York, and Ohio two each. Twenty-one states lost a total of 27 seats; Missouri lost three, and Georgia, Iowa, Kentucky, and Pennsylvania each lost two.

To test the fairness of two allocation methods—the familiar major fractions and the new equal proportions system—the 1929 act required the president to report the distribution

2000 Reapportionment: Gainers and Losers

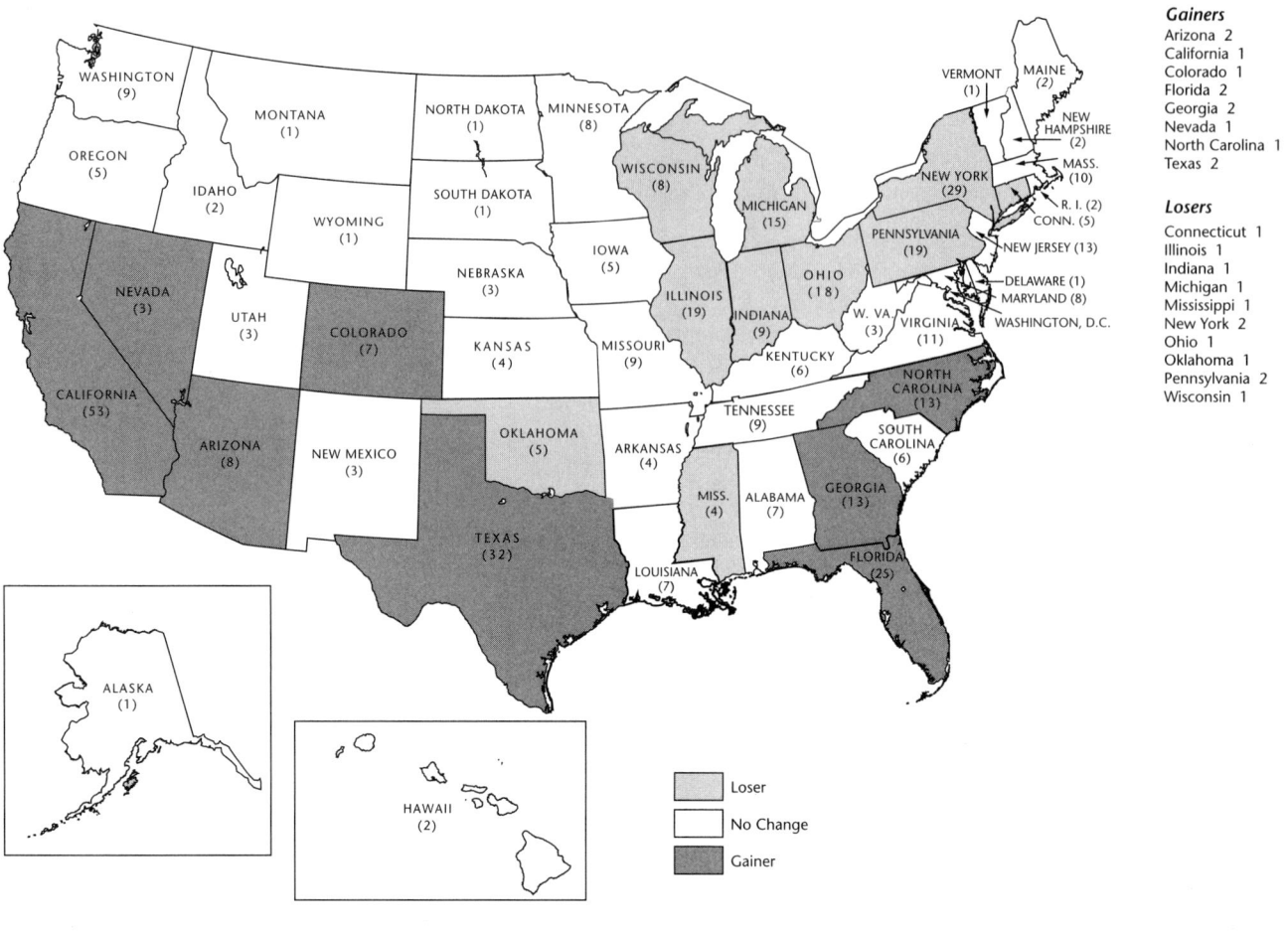

Note: Number in parentheses indicates state's House seats under 2000 reapportionment.

of seats by both methods. But, pending legislation to the contrary, the method of major fractions was to be used.

The two methods gave an identical distribution of seats based on 1930 census figures. However, in 1940 the two methods gave different results: under major fractions, Michigan would gain a seat lost by Arkansas; under equal proportions, no change would occur in either state. The automatic reapportionment provisions of the 1929 act went into effect in January 1941. But the House Census Committee moved to reverse the result, favoring the method of equal proportions and the certain Democratic seat in Arkansas over a possible Republican gain if the seat were shifted to Michigan. The Democratic-controlled Congress went along, adopting equal proportions as the method to be used in reapportionment calculations after the 1950 and subsequent censuses, and making this action retroactive to January 1941 to save Arkansas its seat.

While politics doubtless played a part in the timing of the action taken in 1941, the method of equal proportions had come to be accepted as the best available: It had been worked out by Edward V. Huntington of Harvard

in 1921. At the request of the Speaker of the House, all known methods of apportionment were considered in 1929 by the National Academy of Sciences Committee on Apportionment. The committee expressed its preference for equal proportions.

Method of Equal Proportions

The method of equal proportions involves complicated mathematical calculations. In brief, each of the 50 states is initially assigned the one seat to which it is entitled by the Constitution. Then "priority numbers" for states to receive second seats, third seats, and so on are calculated by dividing the state's population by the square root of $n(n-1)$, where "n" is the number of seats for that state. The priority numbers are then lined up in order and the seats given to the states with priority numbers until 435 are awarded.

The method is designed to make the proportional difference in the average district size in any two states as small as possible. After the 1990 reapportionment, for example,

Montana's single district was the most populous, with 803,655 residents, while Wyoming's single district was the least populous, with 453,588 people. The average population per district nationwide was about 572,500. In 2000 the average population per district increased to 647,000. Montana's single district remained the most populous with 902,195 people; Wyoming's single district remained the least populous with 493,782 residents.

Questioning the Count in the 1980s, 1990s, and 2000s

While the method of equal proportions came to be accepted as the best way to apportion House seats among the states, the 1980s and 1990s brought heated debate over a more fundamental issue: the accuracy of the census itself.

Members of Congress as well as state and local officials have a keen interest in an accurate population count. In addition to being the basis for reapportionment and redistricting, the census also is used to determine the allocation of funding for many federal aid programs.

Concern about the census "undercount" grew after 1980, when the Census Bureau estimated that it counted about 99 percent of the white population but only about 94 percent of the blacks. Democrats, especially those representing inner-city districts where the undercount was comparatively high, argued unsuccessfully for a statistical adjustment to compensate for undercounting.

The controversy over the 1990 count began even before the census was taken, when the Commerce Department, the parent agency to the Census Bureau, announced in 1987 that it would not statistically adjust the 1990 data. New York City, along with other cities, states, and civil rights organizations, pressed a case in court to force the Census Bureau to make a statistical adjustment to account for people who were missed, including sizable numbers of blacks, Hispanics, and Native Americans. In 1996, the Supreme Court rejected adjusting the census.

But by then, the White House had passed from Republican to Democratic hands, and Commerce Department officials were laying plans to have the Census Bureau use statistical sampling techniques that they said would enhance the accuracy of the 2000 census. The Republican majority in Congress gave statistical sampling a cold eye, worrying that it might lead to politically motivated manipulating of the census. (See box, How Should the Census Count the Population?, p. 16.)

The same issue arose after the 2000 census. Advocates for minority groups, fearing that many persons of their race or ethnic background, were missed in the new count, argued vocally for a statistical adjustment to the actual head count in the census. But by the time the issue was to be resolved in early 2001, the White House and both houses of Congress were under Republican control, making a decision to statistically adjust the count unlikely. Unexpectedly, however, on March 1, 2001, professionals in the Census Bureau said the actual count turned out to be more reliable than expected and warned that use of the statistical adjustment methods available could make the count less accurate. Their recom-

mendation against adjustment essentially defused the issue politically.

REDISTRICTING: DRAWING THE LINES

Although the Constitution contained provisions for the apportionment of U.S. House seats among the states, it was silent about how the members should be elected. From the beginning most states divided their territory into geographic districts, permitting only one member of Congress to be elected from each district.

But some states allowed would-be House members to run at large, with voters able to cast as many votes as there were seats to be filled. Still other states created what were known as multimember districts, in which a single geographic unit would elect two or more members of the House. At various times, some states used combinations of these methods. For example, a state might elect ten representatives from ten individual districts and two at large.

In the first few elections to the House, New Hampshire, Pennsylvania, New Jersey, and Georgia elected their representatives at large, as did Rhode Island and Delaware, the two states with only a single representative. Districts were used in Massachusetts, New York, Maryland, Virginia, and South Carolina. In Connecticut a preliminary election was held to nominate three times as many people as the number of representatives to be chosen at large in the subsequent election. In 1840 22 of the 31 states elected their representatives by districts. New Hampshire, New Jersey, Georgia, Alabama, Mississippi, and Missouri, with a combined representation of 33 House seats, elected their representatives at large. Three states, Arkansas, Delaware, and Florida, had only one representative each.

Those states that used congressional districts quickly developed what came to be known as the gerrymander. The term refers to the practice of drawing district lines so as to maximize the advantage of a political party or interest group. The name originated from a salamander-shaped congressional district created by the Massachusetts legislature in 1812 when Elbridge Gerry was governor. (See box, Origins of the Gerrymander, p. 11.)

Constant efforts were made during the early 1800s to lay down national rules, by means of a constitutional amendment, for congressional districting. The first resolution proposing a mandatory division of each state into districts was introduced in Congress in 1800. In 1802 the legislatures of Vermont and North Carolina adopted resolutions in support of such action. From 1816 to 1826 22 states adopted resolutions proposing the election of representatives by districts.

In Congress Sen. Mahlon Dickerson, R-N.J., proposed such an amendment regularly almost every year from 1817 to 1826. It was adopted by the Senate three times, in 1819, 1820, and 1822, but each time it failed to reach a vote in the House. Although the constitutional amendment was unsuccessful, a law passed in 1842 required contiguous single-member congressional districts. That law required representatives to be "elected by districts composed of contiguous territory equal in number to the representatives to which

State Population Totals and House Seat Changes in the 2000s

State	April 1, 1990	April 1, 2000	Population change	% Change	2002 to 2010 seats	Seat change in the 2000s
Alabama	4,040,587	4,447,100	406,513	10.1	7	0
Alaska	550,043	626,932	76,889	14.0	1	0
Arizona	3,665,228	5,130,632	1,465,404	40.0	8	+2
Arkansas	2,350,725	2,673,400	322,675	13.7	4	0
California	29,760,021	33,871,648	4,111,627	13.8	53	+1
Colorado	3,294,394	4,301,261	1,006,867	30.6	7	+1
Connecticut	3,287,116	3,405,565	118,449	3.6	5	−1
Delaware	666,168	783,600	117,432	17.6	1	0
Florida	12,937,926	15,982,378	3,044,452	23.5	25	+2
Georgia	6,478,216	8,186,453	1,708,237	26.4	13	+2
Hawaii	1,108,229	1,211,537	103,308	9.3	2	0
Idaho	1,006,749	1,293,953	287,204	28.5	2	0
Illinois	11,430,602	12,419,293	988,691	8.6	19	−1
Indiana	5,544,159	6,080,485	536,326	9.7	9	−1
Iowa	2,776,755	2,926,324	149,569	5.4	5	0
Kansas	2,477,574	2,688,418	210,844	8.5	4	0
Kentucky	3,685,296	4,041,769	356,473	9.7	6	0
Louisiana	4,219,973	4,468,976	249,003	5.9	7	0
Maine	1,227,928	1,274,923	46,995	3.8	2	0
Maryland	4,781,468	5,296,486	515,018	10.8	8	0
Massachusetts	6,016,425	6,349,097	332,672	5.5	10	0
Michigan	9,295,297	9,938,444	643,147	6.9	15	−1
Minnesota	4,375,099	4,919,479	544,380	12.4	8	0
Mississippi	2,573,216	2,844,658	271,442	10.5	4	−1
Missouri	5,117,073	5,595,211	478,138	9.3	9	0
Montana	799,065	902,195	103,130	12.9	1	0
Nebraska	1,578,385	1,711,263	132,878	8.4	3	0
Nevada	1,201,833	1,998,257	796,424	66.3	3	+1
New Hampshire	1,109,252	1,235,786	126,534	11.4	2	0
New Jersey	7,730,188	8,414,350	684,162	8.9	13	0
New Mexico	1,515,069	1,819,046	303,977	20.1	3	0
New York	17,990,455	18,976,457	986,002	5.5	29	−2
North Carolina	6,628,637	8,049,313	1,420,676	21.4	13	+1
North Dakota	638,800	642,200	3,400	0.5	1	0
Ohio	10,847,115	11,353,140	506,025	4.7	18	−1
Oklahoma	3,145,585	3,450,654	305,069	9.7	5	−1
Oregon	2,842,321	3,421,399	579,078	20.4	5	0
Pennsylvania	11,881,643	12,281,054	399,411	3.4	19	−2
Rhode Island	1,003,464	1,048,319	44,855	4.5	2	0
South Carolina	3,486,703	4,012,012	525,309	15.1	6	0
South Dakota	696,004	754,844	58,840	8.5	1	0
Tennessee	4,877,185	5,689,283	812,098	16.7	9	0
Texas	16,986,510	20,851,820	3,865,310	22.8	32	+2
Utah	1,722,850	2,233,169	510,319	29.6	3	0
Vermont	562,758	608,827	46,069	8.2	1	0
Virginia	6,187,358	7,078,515	891,157	14.4	11	0
Washington	4,866,692	5,894,121	1,027,429	21.1	9	0
West Virginia	1,793,477	1,808,344	14,867	0.8	3	0
Wisconsin	4,891,769	5,363,675	471,906	9.6	8	−1
Wyoming	453,588	493,782	40,194	8.9	1	0
District of Columbia	606,900	572,059	−34,841	−5.7	NA	NA
Total resident population	248,709,873	281,421,906	32,712,033	13.2		

Notes: Consistent with the January 1999 U.S. Supreme Court ruling (*Department of Commerce* v. *House of Representatives,* 525 U.S. 316, 119 S. Ct. 765), these resident population counts do not reflect the use of statistical sampling to correct for overcounting or undercounting. Total resident population includes the population of the 50 states and the District of Columbia. NA = Not applicable.

Sources: U.S. Department of Commerce, U.S. Census Bureau. Internet release date: December 28, 2000.

said state may be entitled, no one district electing more than one Representative."

The districting provisions of the 1842 act were not repeated in the legislation that followed the 1850 census. But in 1862 an act separate from the reapportionment act revived the provisions of the act of 1842 requiring districts to be composed of contiguous territory.

The 1872 reapportionment act again repeated the districting provisions and went even further by adding that districts should contain "as nearly as practicable an equal number of inhabitants." Similar provisions were included in the acts of 1881 and 1891. In the act of 1901, the words "compact territory" were added, and the clause then read "contiguous and compact territory and containing as nearly as practicable an equal number of inhabitants." This requirement appeared also in the legislation of 1911. The "contiguous and compact" provisions of the act subsequently lapsed, and Congress has never replaced them.

Several unsuccessful attempts were made to enforce redistricting provisions. Despite the districting requirements enacted in 1842, New Hampshire, Georgia, Mississippi, and Missouri elected their representatives at large that autumn. When the new House convened for its first session, on December 4, 1843, objection was made to seating the representatives of the four states.

The House debated the matter in February 1844. With the Democratic Party holding a majority of more than 60, and with 18 of the 21 challenged members being Democrats, the House decided to seat the members. However, by 1848 all four states had come around to electing their representatives by districts.

The next challenge a representative encountered over federal districting laws occurred in 1901. A charge was leveled that the existing Kentucky redistricting law did not comply with the reapportionment law of 1901; the charge aimed at preventing the seating of Rep. George G. Gilbert, a Democrat, of Kentucky's 8th District. The committee assigned to investigate the matter turned aside the challenge, asserting that the federal act was not binding on the states. The reasons given were practical and political:

> Your committee are therefore of opinion that a proper construction of the Constitution does not warrant the conclusion that by that instrument Congress is clothed with power to determine the boundaries of Congressional districts, or to revise the acts of a State Legislature in fixing such boundaries; and your committee is further of opinion that even if such power is to be implied from the language of the Constitution, it would be in the last degree unwise and intolerable that it should exercise it. To do so would be to put into the hands of Congress the ability to disfranchise, in effect, a large body of the electors. It would give Congress the power to apply to all the States, in favor of one party, a general system of gerrymandering. It is true that the same method is to a large degree resorted to by the several states, but the division of political power is so general and diverse that notwithstanding the inherent vice of the system of gerrymandering, some kind of equality of distribution results.[12]

In 1908 the Virginia legislature transferred Floyd County from the 5th District to the 6th District. As a result, the population of the 5th was reduced from 175,579 to 160,191 and that of the 6th was increased from 181,571 to 196,959. The average for the state was 185,418. The newly elected Democratic representative from the 5th District, Edward W. Saunders, was challenged by his opponent in the election on

Origins of the Gerrymander

The practice of "gerrymandering"—the excessive manipulation of the shape of a legislative district to benefit certain persons or groups—is probably as old as the Republic, but the name originated in 1812.

In that year the Massachusetts legislature carved out of Essex County a district which historian John Fiske said had a "dragonlike contour." When the painter Gilbert Stuart saw the misshapen district, he penciled in a head, wings, and claws and exclaimed: "That will do for a salamander!"—to which editor Benjamin Russell replied: "Better say a Gerrymander"—after Elbridge Gerry, then governor of Massachusetts.

By the 1990s the term had broadened to include the modern-day practice of drawing maps to benefit racial and ethnic groups. In the past the term was applied largely to districts drawn to benefit incumbents or political parties.

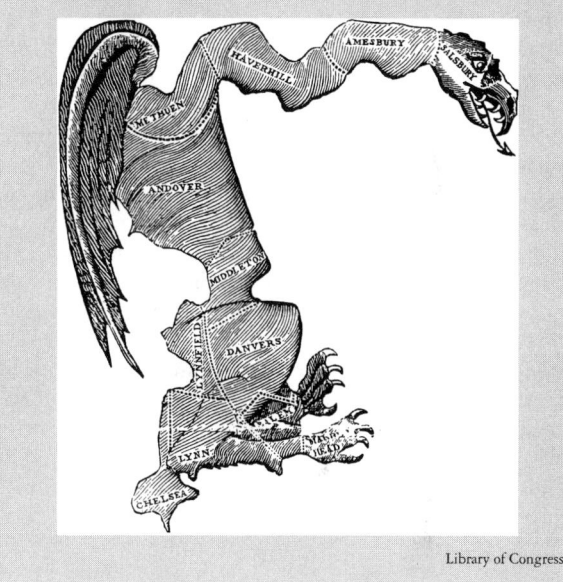

Library of Congress

the ground that the Virginia law of 1908 was null and void because it did not conform with the federal reapportionment law of 1901, or with the constitution of Virginia. Had the district included the counties that were a part of it before enactment of the 1908 state legislation, Saunders's opponent would have had a majority of the votes.

The majority of the congressional investigating committee upheld the challenge and recommended that Saunders's opponent be seated. For the first time, it appeared that the districting legislation would be enforced, but the House did not take action on the committee's report and Saunders was seated.

Court Action on Redistricting

After the long and desultory battle over reapportionment in the 1920s, those who were unhappy over the inaction of

Congress and the state legislatures began taking their cases to court. At first, the protesters had no luck. But as the population disparities grew in both federal and state legislative districts and the Supreme Court began to show a tendency to intervene, the objectors were more successful.

Finally, in a series of decisions beginning in 1962 with *Baker v. Carr* the Court exerted great influence over the redistricting process, ordering that congressional districts as well as state and local legislative districts be drawn so that their populations would be as nearly equal as possible.[13]

Supreme Court's 1932 Decision

Baker v. Carr essentially reversed the direction the Court had taken in 1932. *Wood v. Broom* was a case challenging the constitutionality of a Mississippi redistricting law because it violated the standards of the 1911 federal redistricting act. The question was whether the federal act was still in effect. That law, which required that districts be separate, compact, contiguous, and equally populated, had been neither specifically repealed nor reaffirmed in the 1929 reapportionment act.

Speaking for the Court, Chief Justice Charles Evans Hughes ruled that the 1911 act, in effect, had expired with the approval of the 1929 apportionment act and that the standards of the 1911 act therefore were no longer applicable. The Court reversed the decision of a lower federal court, which had permanently enjoined elections under the new Mississippi redistricting act.

That the Supreme Court upheld a state law that failed to provide for districts of equal population was almost less important than the minority opinion that the Court should not have heard the case. Justices Louis D. Brandeis, Harlan F. Stone, Owen J. Roberts, and Benjamin N. Cardozo, while concurring in the majority opinion, said they would have dismissed the *Wood* case for "want of equity." The "want-of-equity" phrase in this context suggested a policy of judicial self-limitation with respect to the entire question of judicial involvement in essentially "political" questions.

Political Thicket

Not until 1946, in *Colegrove v. Green,* did the Court again rule in a significant case dealing with congressional redistricting. The case was brought by Kenneth Colegrove, a political science professor at Northwestern University, who alleged that congressional districts in Illinois, which varied between 112,116 and 914,053 in population, were so unequal that they violated the 14th Amendment's guarantee of equal protection of the laws. A seven-member Supreme Court divided 4–3 in dismissing the suit.

Justice Felix Frankfurter gave the opinion of the Court, speaking for himself and Justices Stanley F. Reed and Harold H. Burton. Frankfurter's opinion cited *Wood v. Broom* to indicate that Congress had deliberately removed the standard set by the 1911 act. He also said that he, Reed, and Burton agreed with the minority that the Court should have dismissed the case. The issue, Frankfurter said, was of

a peculiarly political nature and therefore not meant for judicial interpretation. . . . The short of it is that the Constitution has conferred upon Congress exclusive authority to secure fair representation by the states in the popular House and has left to that

House determination whether states have fulfilled their responsibility. If Congress failed in exercising its powers, whereby standards of fairness are offended, the remedy lies ultimately with the people. . . . To sustain this action would cut very deep into the very being of Congress. Courts ought not to enter this political thicket. The remedy for unfairness in districting is to secure state legislatures that will apportion properly, or to invoke the ample powers of Congress.

Frankfurter also said that the Court could not affirmatively remap congressional districts and that elections at large would be politically undesirable.

In a dissenting opinion Justice Hugo L. Black, joined by Justices William O. Douglas and Frank Murphy, maintained that the district court did have jurisdiction over congressional redistricting. The three justices cited as evidence a section of the U.S. Code that allowed district courts to redress deprivations of constitutional rights occurring through action of the states. Black's opinion also rested on an earlier case in which the Court had indicated that federal constitutional questions, unless "frivolous," fall under the jurisdiction of the federal courts. Black asserted that the appellants had standing to sue and that the population disparities violated the equal protection clause of the 14th Amendment.

With the Court split 3–3 on whether the judiciary had or should exercise jurisdiction, Justice Wiley B. Rutledge cast the deciding vote in *Colegrove v. Green.* On the question of justiciability, Rutledge agreed with Black, Douglas, and Murphy that the issue could be considered by the federal courts. Thus a majority of the Court participating in the *Colegrove* case felt that congressional redistricting cases were justiciable.

Yet on the question of granting relief in this specific instance, Rutledge agreed with Frankfurter, Reed, and Burton that the case should be dismissed. He pointed out that four of the nine justices in *Wood v. Broom* had felt that dismissal should be for want of equity. Rutledge saw a "want-of-equity" situation in *Colegrove v. Green* as well. "I think the gravity of the constitutional questions raised [are] so great, together with the possibility of collision [with the political departments of the government], that the admonition [against avoidable constitutional decision] is appropriate to be followed here," Rutledge said. Jurisdiction, he thought, should be exercised "only in the most compelling circumstances." He thought that "the shortness of time remaining [before the forthcoming election] makes it doubtful whether action could or would be taken in time to secure for petitioners the effective relief they seek." Rutledge warned that congressional elections at large would deprive citizens of representation by districts, "which the prevailing policy of Congress demands." In the case of at-large elections, he said, "the cure sought may be worse than the disease." For all these reasons he concluded that the case was "one in which the Court may properly, and should, decline to exercise its jurisdiction."

Changing Views

In the ensuing years, law professors, political scientists, and other commentators increasingly criticized the *Colegrove* doctrine and grew impatient with the Supreme Court's reluctance to intervene in redistricting disputes. At the same time, the membership of the Court was changing, and the new members were more inclined toward judicial action on redistricting.

Gerrymandering: The Shape of the House

There are basically three types of gerrymanders. One is the partisan gerrymander, where a single party draws the lines to its advantage. Another is the proincumbent (sometimes called the "bipartisan" or "sweetheart") gerrymander, where the lines are drawn to protect incumbents, with any gains or losses in the number of seats shared between the two parties. In states where control of the state government is divided, proincumbent gerrymanders are common.

A third form of gerrymandering is race-based, where lines are drawn to favor the election of candidates from particular racial or ethnic groups. Initially, racial redistricting referred to the practice of drawing lines to scatter minority voters across several districts, so they would not have a dominant influence in any. But the impact of the 1965 Voting Rights Act and numerous court rulings has resulted in a new version of racial gerrymandering: designing constituencies to concentrate minority voters. These majority-minority districts are more likely to elect a minority candidate.

Sweetheart gerrymandering rarely attracts much attention. But this method of mapping has a powerful effect on the House. "Districts get more Democratic for Democrats and more Republican for Republicans. Competition is minimized," said Bernard Grofman, a political scientist at the University of California at Irvine. Incumbent reelection rates have been high since World War II, in part because a proincumbent spin in much of the line drawing diminishes the prospects for dramatic change in the House's membership.

Still, redistricting at least increases the possibility of turnover, because most states must redraw their districts to accommodate population shifts within the state as well as the gain or loss of any seats. Typically, some House members choose to retire rather than stand for election in redesigned districts.

Partisan gerrymanders do not always achieve their goals. Indiana Republicans redrew their map in 1981 with the hope that it would turn the Democrats' congressional majority into a 7–3 Republican edge. Instead, by the end of the decade Democrats held a 7–3 advantage.

But without question, gerrymandering during redistricting is an important determinant of which party controls the House. Many political analysts predicted that the 1980 reapportionment would alter the political makeup of the House, because most of the states that lost seats tended to favor liberal Democrats, while the states that gained seats were more likely to favor Republicans or conservative Democrats. But in part because of Democrats' gerrymandering successes in the state redistricting battles, their party remained in control of the House throughout the 1980s.

In the 1990 reapportionment, the shift of House seats to more conservative areas in the South and West continued, but successful gerrymandering by Democrats helped the party hold its House majority in 1992. Finally in 1994 a broad surge of support for Republican candidates helped the GOP take control of the House, which they held through the 2002 elections. Population changes recorded in the 2000 census showed a continuing trend toward states that have voted more Republican than Democratic in recent years, some of which received additional House members under the 2000 reapportionment. *(See table, p. 5.)* As a result, the redistricting following the 2000 census—particularly within Republican-leaning states—was expected to be a highly contentious exercise. As it turned out, Democrats and Republicans tacitly agreed in the initial round of redistricting that their primary interests was in protecting incumbents. Much of the drawing of lines focused on creating districts incumbents could hold. There was less emphasis on designing districts for competitive party advantage, although that did occur in many states.

In an unusual development after the 2002 elections, Republicans in Colorado and Texas sought to reopen the redistricting decisions—made in both cases by courts—to create districts that were more likely to elect GOP members. Colorado's new redistricting decisions, which were in litigation in 2003, made changes in a few districts to bring more Republicans into districts already controlled by the GOP. In Texas, however, the Republicans were trying in 2003 to redraw many districts completely in order to elect more GOP members to Congress. The action was being directed by U.S. House Majority Leader Tom DeLay and was being resisted by Democrats in the Texas legislature, some of whom fled the state to Oklahoma and New Mexico in the summer to prevent a quorum that could conduct business.

In the 1950s the Court decided two cases that laid some groundwork for its subsequent reapportionment decisions. The first was *Brown v. Board of Education,* the historic school desegregation case, in which the Court decided that an individual citizen could assert a right to equal protection of the laws under the 14th Amendment, contrary to the "separate but equal" doctrine of public facilities for white and black citizens.

Six years later, in *Gomillion v. Lightfoot,* the Court held that the Alabama legislature could not draw the city limits of Tuskegee so as to exclude nearly every black vote. In his opinion Justice Frankfurter drew a clear line between redistricting challenges based on the 14th Amendment, such as *Colegrove,* and challenges to discriminatory redistricting based on the 15th Amendment's voting rights protections, as in *Gomillion.* But Justice Charles E. Whittaker said that the equal protection clause was the proper constitutional basis for the decision. One commentator later remarked that *Gomillion* amounted to a "dragon" in the "political thicket" of *Colegrove.*

By 1962 only three members of the *Colegrove* Court remained: Justices Black and Douglas, dissenters in that case, and Justice Frankfurter, aging spokesperson for restraint in the exercise of judicial power.

By then it was clear that malapportionment within the states no longer could be ignored. By 1960 not a single state legislative body existed in which there was not at least a two-to-one population disparity between the most and the least heavily populated districts. For example, the disparity was 242–1 in the Connecticut House, 223–1 in the Nevada Senate, 141–1 in the Rhode Island Senate, and 9–1 in the Georgia Senate. Studies of the effective vote of large and small counties in state legislatures between 1910 and 1960 showed that the effective vote of the most populous counties had slipped while their percentage of the national population had more than doubled. The most lightly populated counties, on the other hand, advanced from a position of slight overrepresentation to one of extreme overrepresentation, holding almost twice as many seats as they would be entitled to by population size alone. Predictably, the rural-dominated state legislatures resisted every move toward reapportioning state legislative districts to reflect new population patterns.

Population imbalance among congressional districts was substantially lopsided but by no means so gross. In Texas the 1960 census showed the most heavily populated district had four times as many inhabitants as the most lightly populated. Arizona, Maryland, and Ohio each had at least one district with three times as many inhabitants as the least populated. In most cases rural areas benefited from the population imbalance in congressional districts. As a result of the postwar population movement out of central cities to the surrounding areas, the suburbs were the most underrepresented.

Baker v. Carr

Against this background a group of Tennessee city dwellers successfully broke the long-standing precedent against federal court involvement in legislative apportionment problems. For more than half a century, since 1901, the Tennessee legislature had refused to reapportion itself, even though a decennial reapportionment based on population was specifically required by the state's constitution. In the meantime, Tennessee's population had grown and shifted dramatically to urban areas. By 1960 the House legislative districts ranged from 3,454 to 36,031 in population, while the Senate districts ranged from 39,727 to 108,094. Appeals by urban residents to the rural-controlled Tennessee legislature proved fruitless. A suit brought in the state courts to force reapportionment was rejected on grounds that the courts should stay out of legislative matters.

City dwellers then appealed to the federal courts, stating that they had no redress: the legislature had refused to act for more than half a century, the state courts had refused to intervene, and Tennessee had no referendum or initiative laws. They charged that there was "a debasement of their votes by virtue of the incorrect, obsolete and unconstitutional apportionment" to such an extent that they were being deprived of their right to equal protection of the laws under the 14th Amendment.

The Supreme Court on March 26, 1962, handed down its historic decision in *Baker v. Carr,* ruling 6–2 in favor of the Tennessee city dwellers. In the majority opinion, Justice William J. Brennan Jr., emphasized that the federal judiciary had the power to review the apportionment of state legislatures under the 14th Amendment's equal protection clause. "The mere fact that a suit seeks protec-

tion as a political right," Brennan wrote, "does not mean that it presents a political question" that the courts should avoid.

In a vigorous dissent, Justice Frankfurter said the majority decision constituted "a massive repudiation of the experience of our whole past" and was an assertion of "destructively novel judicial power." He contended that the lack of any clear basis for relief "catapults the lower courts" into a "mathematical quagmire." Frankfurter insisted that "there is not under our Constitution a judicial remedy for every political mischief." Appeal for relief, Frankfurter maintained, should not be made in the courts, but "to an informed civically militant electorate."

The Court had abandoned the view that malapportionment questions were outside its competence. But it stopped there and in *Baker v. Carr* did not address the merits of the challenge to the legislative districts, stating only that federal courts had the power to resolve constitutional challenges to maldistribution of voters among districts.

Gray v. Sanders

The one-person, one-vote rule was set out by the Court almost exactly one year after its decision in *Baker v. Carr.* But the case in which the announcement came did not involve congressional districts.

In *Gray v. Sanders* the Court found that Georgia's county-unit primary system for electing state officials—a system that weighted votes to give advantage to rural districts in statewide primary elections—denied voters equal protection of the laws. All votes in a statewide election must have equal weight, the Court held:

> How then can one person be given twice or 10 times the voting power of another person in a statewide election merely because he lives in a rural area or because he lives in the smallest rural county? Once the geographical unit for which a representative is to be chosen is designated, all who participate in the election are to have an equal vote—whatever their race, whatever their sex, whatever their occupation, whatever their income, and wherever their home may be in that geographical unit. This is required by the Equal Protection Clause of the Fourteenth Amendment. The concept of "we the people" under the Constitution visualizes no preferred class of voters but equality among those who meet the basic qualification. The idea that every voter is equal to every other voter in his State, when he casts his ballot in favor of one of several competing candidates, underlies many of our decisions. . . . The conception of political equality from the Declaration of Independence to Lincoln's Gettysburg Address, to the Fifteenth, Seventeenth, and Nineteenth Amendments can mean only one thing—one person, one vote.

The Rule Applied

The Court's rulings in *Baker* and *Gray* concerned the equal weighting and counting of votes cast in state elections. In 1964, deciding the case of *Wesberry v. Sanders,* the Court applied the one-person, one-vote principle to congressional districts and set equality as the standard for congressional redistricting.

Shortly after the *Baker* decision was handed down, James P. Wesberry Jr., an Atlanta resident and a member of the Georgia Senate, filed suit in federal court in Atlanta claiming that gross disparity in the population of Georgia's congressional districts violated 14th Amendment rights of equal protection of the laws. At the time, Georgia districts ranged in population from 272,154 in the rural 9th District in the northeastern part of the state to 823,860 in the 5th District in Atlanta and its suburbs. District lines had not been changed since 1931. The state's number of House seats remained the same in the interim, but Atlanta's district population—already high in 1931 compared with the others—had more than doubled in 30 years, making a 5th District vote worth about one-third that of a vote in the 9th.

In June 1962 the three-judge federal court divided 2–1 in dismissing Wesberry's suit. The majority reasoned that the precedent of *Colegrove* still controlled in congressional district cases. The judges cautioned against federal judicial interference with Congress and against "depriving others of the right to vote" if the suit should result in at-large elections. They suggested that the Georgia legislature (under court order to reapportion itself) or the U.S. Congress might better provide relief. Wesberry then appealed to the Supreme Court.

On February 17, 1964, the Supreme Court ruled in *Wesberry v. Sanders* that congressional districts must be substantially equal in population. The Court, which upheld Wesberry's challenge by a 6–3 decision, based its ruling on the history and wording of Article I, Section 2, of the Constitution, which states that representatives shall be apportioned among the states according to their respective numbers and be chosen by the people of the several states. This language, the Court stated, meant that "as nearly as is practicable, one man's vote in a congressional election is to be worth as much as another's."

The majority opinion, written by Justice Black and supported by Chief Justice Earl Warren and Justices Brennan, Douglas, Arthur J. Goldberg, and Byron R. White, said: "While it may not be possible to draw congressional districts with mathematical precision, that is no excuse for ignoring our Constitution's plain objective of making equal representation for equal numbers of people the fundamental goal for the House of Representatives."

In a strongly worded dissent, Justice John M. Harlan asserted that the Constitution did not establish population as the only criterion of congressional districting but left the matter to the discretion of the states, subject only to the supervisory power of Congress. "The constitutional right which the Court creates is manufactured out of whole cloth," Harlan concluded.

The *Wesberry* opinion established no precise standards for districting beyond declaring that districts must be as nearly equal in population "as is practicable." In his dissent Harlan suggested that a disparity of more than 100,000 between a state's largest and smallest districts would "presumably" violate the equality standard enunciated by the majority. On that basis, Harlan estimated, the districts of 37 states with 398 representatives would be unconstitutional, "leaving a constitutional House of 37 members now sitting."

Neither did the Court's decision make any reference to gerrymandering, since it discussed only the population, not the shape of districts. In a separate opinion handed down the same day as *Wesberry*, the Court dismissed a challenge to congressional districts in New York City, which had been brought by voters who charged that Manhattan's "silk-stocking" 17th District had been gerrymandered to exclude blacks and Puerto Ricans.

Strict Equality

Five years elapsed between *Wesberry* and the Court's next application of constitutional standards to congressional districting. In 1967 the Court hinted at the strict stance it would adopt two years later. With two unsigned opinions, the Court sent back to Indiana and Missouri for revision those two states' congressional redistricting plans because they allowed variations of as much as 20 percent from the average district population.

Two years later Missouri's revised plan returned to the Court for full review. By a 6–3 vote, the Court rejected the plan. It was unacceptable, the Court held in *Kirkpatrick v. Preisler*, because it allowed a variation of as much as 3.1 percent from perfectly equal population districts. Thus the Court made clear its stringent application of the one-person, one-vote rule to congressional districts.

There was no "fixed numerical or percentage population variance small enough to be considered *de minimis* and to satisfy without question the 'as nearly as practicable' standard," Justice Brennan wrote for the Court. "Equal representation for equal numbers of people is a principle designed to prevent debasement of voting power and diminution of access to elected Representatives. Toleration of even small deviations detracts from these purposes."

The only permissible variances in population, the Court ruled, were those that were unavoidable despite the effort to achieve absolute equality or those that could be legally justified. The variances in Missouri could have been avoided, the Court said.

None of Missouri's arguments for the plan qualified as "legally acceptable" justifications. The Court rejected the argument that population variance was necessary to allow representation of distinct interest groups. It said that acceptance of such variances to produce districts with specific interests was "antithetical" to the basic purpose of equal representation.

Justice White dissented from the majority opinion, which he characterized as "an unduly rigid and unwarranted application of the Equal Protection Clause which will unnecessarily involve the courts in the abrasive task of drawing district lines." White added that some "acceptably small" population variance could be established. He indicated that considerations of existing political boundaries and geographical compactness could justify to him some variation from "absolute equality" of population.

Justice Harlan, joined by Justice Potter Stewart, dissented, saying that "whatever room remained under this Court's prior decisions for the free play of the political process in matters of reapportionment is now all but eliminated by today's Draconian judgments."

Practical Results

As a result of the Court's decisions of the 1960s, nearly every state was forced to redraw its congressional district lines—sometimes more than once. By the end of the decade, 39 of the 45 states with more than one representative had made the necessary adjustments.

However, the effect of the one-person, one-vote standard on congressional districts did not bring about immediate population equality in districts. Most of the new districts were far from equal in population, because the only official

How Should the Census Count the Population?

Counting the number of people in the United States has never been as easy as one, two, three, and that is not just because of logistical problems. When it comes to the decennial census, the political stakes are huge, and so is the interest in how the count is conducted. The constitutionally mandated census not only provides crucial information for reapportioning U.S. House seats among the states, but it also supplies the data for drawing district boundaries for state and local public officials and for determining how billions in federal spending are distributed through dozens of grant programs, including Medicaid, educational assistance to poor children, community development block grants, and job training.

Questions about the accuracy of the census are as old as the Republic. A 1998 report issued by the General Accounting Office (GAO) said, "The census has never counted 100 percent of those it should, in part, because American sensibilities would probably not tolerate more foolproof census-taking methods." For instance, the census could be made more precise if people were required to register with the government. But even proposing such a mandate would stir a huge public fuss.

Disputes over the accuracy of the census have intensified since 1911, when Congress fixed the number of representatives at 435. Since then, a gain of representation in any one state can come only at the loss of representation in another. After the 1920 census showed for the first time that the majority of Americans lived in cities, rural interests objected that the farm population had been undercounted. They pressed their case with such tenacity that legislation reapportioning House seats for the 1920s never passed. In 1941 concerns about the accuracy of the census arose when the number of men turning out for the wartime draft was considerably higher than expectations based on the 1940 census.

In the latter years of the twentieth century, there was intense controversy about the census' undercounting of certain groups, especially minorities. It became more difficult for government census takers to make an accurate population count in crowded inner-city neighborhoods and in some sparsely settled rural areas. The undercount issue became a particular concern for major cities and for the Democrats who tended to represent them. They were in the forefront of an effort to persuade the Census Bureau to use a statistical method to adjust the census for the undercount.

The Census Bureau estimated that it did not count 1.4 percent of the total population in 1980, including roughly 5.9 percent of the nation's blacks. In 1991 Commerce Secretary Robert A. Mosbacher, serving in the administration of Republican president George Bush, said that he would not adjust the 1990 census, even though a postcensus survey found that blacks were undercounted by 4.8 percent, Native Americans by 5 percent, and Hispanics by 5.2 percent. Mosbacher said he was "deeply troubled" by the disproportionate undercount of minorities but decided that sticking with the head count would be "fairest for all Americans."

Several states and cities pursued the matter in court, pressing a suit requesting a statistical adjustment of the census to compensate for the undercount. A 1996 Supreme Court ruling went against them.

By then, though, Democrat Bill Clinton was in the White House, and the Census Bureau was laying the groundwork for a 2000 census that bureau officials said would produce a more accurate count by combining traditional head-tallying methods with large-scale use of statistical sampling techniques. Their plan was to count at least 90 percent of the people in each census tract by tabulating surveys returned in the mail and sending census-takers to interview those who did not respond by mail. Then the remaining population would be estimated by statistically extrapolating the demographics of 750,000 randomly selected homes nationwide.

However, this proposal met with fierce resistance in the Republican-controlled Congress. The GOP majority complained that sampling was unconstitutional and open to political manipulation. "Our Constitution calls for an 'actual enumeration' of citizens, not just an educated guess by Washington bureaucrats," Rep. John A. Boehner, R-Ohio, said. Democrats in Congress retorted that conservatives opposed statistical sampling because they feared

population figures came from the 1960 census. Massive population shifts during the decade rendered most post-*Wesberry* efforts to achieve equality useless.

But redistricting based on the 1970 census resulted in districts that differed only slightly in population from the state average. Among House members elected in 1972, 385 of 435 represented districts that varied by less than 1 percent from the state average district population.

By contrast, only nine of the districts in the 88th Congress (elected in 1962) deviated less than 1 percent from the state average; 81 districts were between 1 and 5 percent; 87 districts from 5 to 10 percent; and in 236 districts the deviation was 10 percent or greater. Additionally, 22 House members were elected at large.

The Supreme Court made only one major ruling concerning congressional districts during the 1970s. In 1973 the Court declared the Texas congressional districts, as redrawn in 1971, unconstitutional because of excessive population variance among districts. The variance between the largest and smallest districts was 4.99 percent. The Court returned the case to a three-judge federal panel, which adopted a new congressional district plan.

Precise Equality

Following the 1980 census, several federal courts accepted or imposed redistricting maps that achieved population equality but were drawn for blatant partisan purposes. In Missouri a federal court accepted the Democrats' remap proposal over the Republican plan because its districts were more nearly equal in population. The Democratic map obtained population equality by dismantling a district in a part of the state

it would cost the GOP seats in the House. "They believe not counting certain minorities and the poor is to their political advantage," said Rep. Carolyn B. Maloney, D-N.Y.

With the Republican House and the Democratic White House at a standoff on allowing statistical sampling in the 2000 census, the dispute headed to the courts. When the Supreme Court heard arguments on the case in late 1998, justices expressed reluctance to get involved in what essentially appeared to be a partisan fight.

In January 1999 in *Department of Commerce v. House of Representatives,* the Court issued an equivocal 5–4 ruling that seemed likely to spur further litigation. Pleasing Republicans, the Court majority said that amendments to the Census Act added in 1976 forbade "the use of sampling in calculating the population for purposes of apportionment." House Speaker Dennis Hastert, R-Ill., declared, "The administration should abandon its illegal and risky polling scheme and start preparing for a true head count."

But Democrats took some solace in the Court majority's position that the Census Act "required" that sampling be used for other purposes (such as establishing the population formulas used to distribute some federal grant monies), if the Census Bureau and the secretary of commerce deemed it "feasible."

The ruling led the Clinton administration to plot a course to produce two sets of numbers in the 2000 census—a count based on traditional methods to be used for reapportionment, and an adjusted count to be used for distributing federal money and other purposes, possibly including redistricting within the states. That decision drew a harsh response from Republicans in Congress. Rep. Dan Miller, R-Fla., chairman of the House Census Committee, said, "It will absolutely be a disaster if we have a two-number census. . . . If we try to divide the census, we'll have two failed censuses." In 2001 Democrats, and racial and ethnic minority groups, pressed hard for the Census Bureau to statistically adjust the numbers of the 2000 count for purposes of redistricting within states, but they were not optimistic that the White House—by then back in the control of Republicans—would do this. Additionally, in early March 2001 Census Bureau profes-

sionals unexpectedly said they could not guarantee that an adjusted number for redistricting would be any better than the actual head count that Republicans favored using. The bureau professionals said unresolved issues in using statistical adjustment could not be solved before the legal deadline of April 1, 2001, to release redistricting data to the states.

Illegal Aliens

Members of Congress and other public officials also have taken a strong interest in the traditional inclusion of illegal aliens in the census. Some complain that the Census Bureau's effort to count all people living in the United States has unfair political ramifications.

The Fourteenth Amendment states that "representatives shall be apportioned among the several states according to their respective numbers, counting the whole number of persons in each state, excluding Indians not taxed." The Census Bureau has never attempted to exclude illegal aliens from the census—a policy troubling to states that fear losing House seats and clout to states with large numbers of illegal aliens.

The Census Bureau does not have a method for excluding illegal aliens, although it has studied some alternatives. Some supporters of the current policy say that any questions used to separate out illegal aliens could discourage others from responding, thus undermining the accuracy of the census.

Overseas Personnel

For the 1990 census the Commerce Department reversed a long-standing policy and counted military personnel and dependents stationed overseas. "Historically we have not included them because the census is based on the concept of usual residence," said Charles Jones, associate director of the Census Bureau. "People overseas have a 'usual residence' overseas." An exception was made once in 1970 during the Vietnam War. This policy was continued in the 2000 census. For the purposes of reapportionment, overseas personnel were assigned to the state each individual considered home.

where population was growing and preserving a district in inner-city St. Louis that had been losing population. The plan cost one Republican incumbent his seat.

Michigan's map for the 1980s offered an extreme example of fealty to precise population equality. In 1982 a court-imposed redistricting plan created sixteen congressional districts with exactly equal populations—514,560. The state's two other districts each had a population of just one person fewer—514,559. To achieve that equality, however, the line for many districts cut through many small cities and towns, dividing their residents among two or three different districts.

Although maps such as these raised the question whether partisan gerrymandering was also a violation of an individual's voting rights, the Supreme Court in 1983 appeared to make it even more difficult to challenge a redistricting map on grounds other than population deviation. In a 5–4

decision, the Court ruled in *Karcher v. Daggett* that states must adhere as closely as possible to the one-person, one-vote standard and bear the burden of proving that deviations from precise population equality were made in pursuit of a legitimate goal. The decision overturned New Jersey's congressional map because the variation between the most populated and the least populated districts was 0.69 percent.

Brennan, who wrote the Court's opinion in *Baker* and *Kirkpatrick,* also wrote the opinion in *Karcher,* contending that population differences between districts "could have been avoided or significantly reduced with a good-faith effort to achieve population equality."

"Adopting any standard other than population equality, using the best census data available, would subtly erode the Constitution's ideal of equal representation," Brennan wrote. "In this case, appellants argue that a maximum deviation of approximately 0.7 percent should be considered *de minimis.* If we accept that argument, how are we to regard deviations of 0.8 percent, 0.95 percent, 1.0 percent or 1.1 percent? . . . To accept the legitimacy of unjustified, though small population deviations in this case would mean to reject the basic premise of *Kirkpatrick* and *Wesberry."*

Brennan said that "any number of consistently applied legislative policies might justify" some population variation. These included "making districts compact, respecting municipal boundaries, preserving the cores of prior districts, and avoiding contests between incumbent Representatives." However, he cautioned, the state must show "with some specificity that a particular objective required the specific deviations in its plan, rather than simply relying on general assertions."

In his dissent Justice White criticized the majority for its "unreasonable insistence on an unattainable perfection in the equalizing of congressional districts." He warned that the decision would invite "further litigation of virtually every congressional redistricting plan in the nation."

Partisan Gerrymandering

In *Karcher* the Court did not address the underlying political issue in the New Jersey case, which was that its map had been drawn to serve Democratic interests. As a partisan gerrymander, the map had few peers, boasting some of the most oddly shaped districts in the country. One constituency, known as the "fishhook" by its detractors, twisted through central New Jersey's industrial landscape, picking up Democratic voters along the way. Another stretched from the suburbs of New York to the fringes of Trenton.

In separate dissents Justices Lewis F. Powell Jr., and John Paul Stevens broadly hinted that they were willing to hear constitutional challenges to instances of partisan gerrymandering. "A legislator cannot represent his constituents properly—nor can voters from a fragmented district exercise the ballot intelligently—when a voting district is nothing more than an artificial unit divorced from, and indeed often in conflict with, the various communities established in the State," wrote Powell.

The Court's opportunity to address that issue came in *Davis v. Bandemer.* On June 30, 1986, the Court ruled that political gerrymanders are subject to constitutional review by federal courts, even if the disputed districts meet the one-person, one-vote test. The case arose from a challenge by Indiana Democrats who argued that the Republican-drawn map so heavily favored the Republican Party that Democrats were denied appropriate representation. But the Court rejected the Democrats' challenge to the alleged gerrymander, saying that one election was insufficient to prove unconstitutional discrimination. Left unclear were what standards the Court would use to find a partisan gerrymander legally unacceptable.

National Republicans expressed delight with the *Bandemer* decision. The GOP had long held that Democratic control over most state legislatures had allowed them to draw congressional and legislative districts to their partisan advantage. In particular, Republicans expressed confidence that the *Bandemer* decision lay the groundwork for overturning California's congressional district map, created by Democratic Rep. Phillip Burton in the early 1980s.

Widely recognized as a classic example of a partisan gerrymander, the map featured a number of oddly shaped districts, drawn neither compactly nor with respect to community boundaries, but all with nearly equal populations. As one commentator described it, "Burton carefully stretched districts from one Democratic enclave to another—sometimes joining them with nothing but a bridge, a stretch of harbor, or a spit of land . . .—avoiding Republicans block for block and household for household."[14] Before the 1982 elections, Democrats held 22 congressional districts, Republicans 21 districts. With the Burton map in place for the 1982 elections, Democrats held 28 seats, Republicans only 17.

Republican Rep. Robert E. Badham filed a lawsuit against the Burton plan in federal district court in 1983. In the wake of the *Bandemer* decision, that court held a hearing on *Badham v. Eu* but dismissed the Republican complaint by a 2–1 vote. The court in essence ruled that a party seeking to overturn a gerrymandered map must show a general pattern of exclusion from the political process, which the California Republican Party, in control of the governorship, a Senate seat, and 40 percent of the House seats, could not do. The Republicans appealed to the Supreme Court, but the Court refused to become involved, voting 6–3 in 1989 to reaffirm the lower court's decision without comment.

Minority Representation

One form of gerrymandering is expressly forbidden by law: redistricting for the purpose of racial discrimination. The Voting Rights Act of 1965, extended in 1970, 1975, and 1982, banned redistricting that diluted the voting strength of black communities. Other minorities, including Hispanics, Asian-Americans, American Indians, and native Alaskans, subsequently were brought under the protection of the law.

In 1980 the Supreme Court for the first time narrowed the reach of the Voting Rights Act in the case of *Mobile v. Bolden,* a challenge to the at-large system of electing city commissioners used in Mobile, Alabama.[15] By a vote of 6–3, the Court ruled that proof of discriminatory intent by the commissioners was necessary before a violation could be found; the fact that no black had ever been elected under the challenged system was not proof enough.

The *Mobile* decision set off an immediate reaction on Capitol Hill. In extending the Voting Rights Act in 1982, Congress amended it to outlaw any practice that has the effect of discriminating against blacks or other minorities—regardless of the lawmakers' intent.

The Justice Department later adopted a similar "results test" for another part of the act (Section 5), which requires certain states and localities with a history of discrimination to have their electoral plans "precleared" by the department. In 1986 the Supreme Court applied this test in *Thornburg v. Gingles,* ruling that six of North Carolina's multimember legislative districts impermissibly diluted black voting strength. Sharply departing from *Mobile,* the Court held that since very few blacks had been elected from these districts, the system must be in violation of the law.

The Court also used the *Thornburg* decision to develop three criteria that, if met, should lead to the creation of a minority legislative district: the minority group must be large and geographically compact enough to constitute a majority in a single-member electoral district; the group must be politically cohesive; and the white majority must vote as a bloc to the degree that it usually can defeat candidates preferred by the minority.

North Carolina's 12th District, 1990s–2000s

1990s

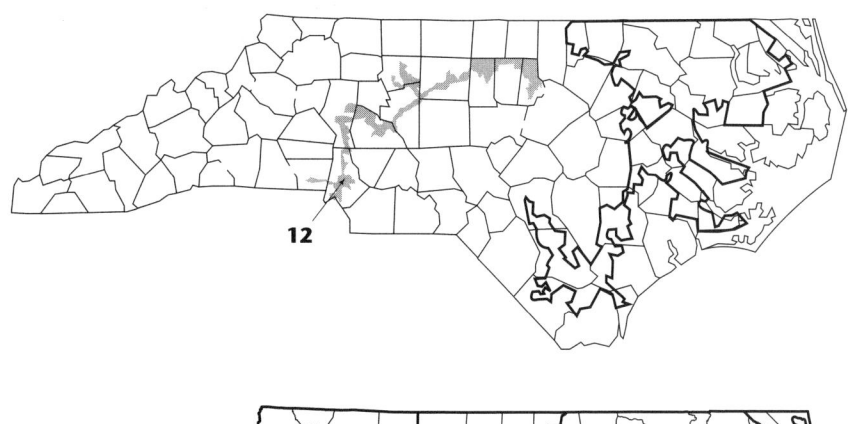

2000s

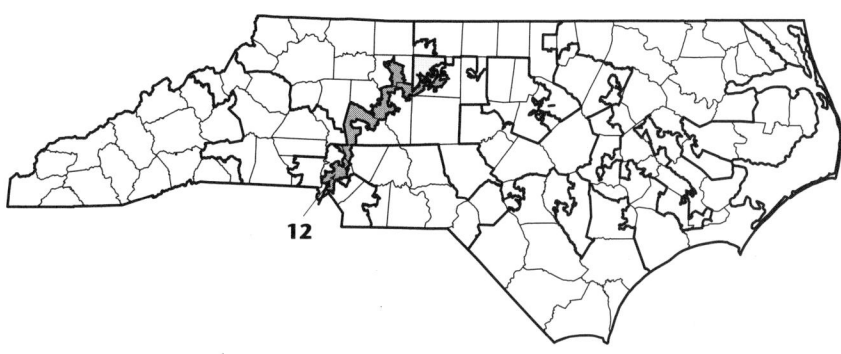

Note: House redistricting in some states after the 1990 census sought to create so-called majority-minority districts that were likely to elect a person from a minority group, usually an African American. The effort resulted in unusually shaped districts such as North Carolina's 12th. The Supreme Court in a series of rulings cast doubt on these configurations, and mapmakers after the 2000 census focused on other concerns, particularly protection of incumbents. Nevertheless, North Carolina's 12th District in 2002 (above, bottom) looked similar to the 1990s version (above, top). States with large minority populations continued efforts after the 2000 count to make sure district configurations provided representation in the House for minority groups.

Thus, within a period of ten years the burden of proof was shifted from minorities, who had been required to show that lines were being drawn to dilute their voting strength, to lawmakers, who had to show that they had done all they could to maximize minority voting strength.

But maps drawn for the 1990s that went to extraordinary lengths to elect minorities came quickly under scrutiny by the Supreme Court. In a 1993 ruling on districts in North Carolina *(Shaw v. Reno),* Justice Sandra Day O'Connor wrote for the Court majority that any map that groups people "who may have little in common with one another but the color of their skin bears an uncomfortable resemblance to political apartheid." The ruling reinstated a suit by five white North Carolinians who contended that the state's congressional district map, which created two oddly shaped majority-minority districts, violated their right to "equal protection under law" by diluting their votes.

And in a 1995 case involving districts in Georgia *(Miller v. Johnson),* the Court ruled that using race as "the predominant factor" in drawing districts is presumed to be unconstitutional, unless it serves a compelling government interest.

The decision struck down a redistricting plan that created three black-majority districts.

Those two rulings represented a speedy swing of the judicial pendulum away from the 1986 *Gingles* doctrine of maximizing minority voting strength in redistricting. As the 1990s unfolded, the constitutionality of majority-minority districts was widely challenged, and eventually, federal courts ordered a number of states—including North Carolina, Georgia, Florida, Louisiana, New York, Texas, and Virginia—to redraw districts that were adjudged to be unconstitutional racial gerrymanders.

But the Supreme Court did not make sweeping determinations affecting all majority-minority districts. In Illinois, a majority-minority district was allowed to stand after the state argued successfully that it had a "compelling state interest" in giving Chicago's large Hispanic population the opportunity to elect one representative of its own. And in a 1999 North Carolina case *(Hunt v. Cromartie),* the Court unanimously ruled that mapmakers could create a district with a "supermajority" of black Democrats as long as the primary reason for doing so was political rather than racial.

Illinois's 17th District, 2000s

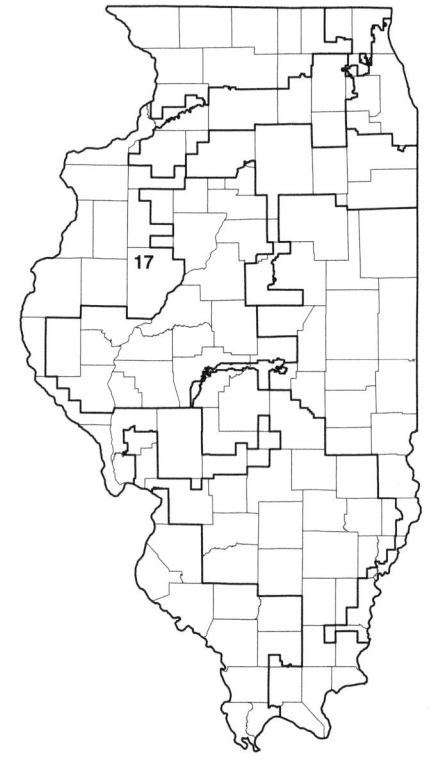

Note: Following the 2000 census, Democrats and Republicans were particularly interested in drawing new House districts that protected incumbents and were less concerned about creating new districts that benefited their party—although a good deal of that went on also. One of the most striking examples of a bizarrely shaped district that was drawn to ensure the reelection of an incumbent was the 17th District in Illinois. The 17th covered nine full counties and parts of 14 others.

Even though numerous majority-minority districts were redrawn in the mid- and late-1990s to reduce minority populations, nearly all those districts retained members of minority groups as their representatives by the end of the twentieth century.

Nevertheless, the mapmakers following the 2000 census devised many bizarrely shaped districts, some for racial reasons, but many for incumbent-protection purposes. Interestingly, the North Carolina 12th District, a serpentine majority-minority creation in the 1990s that was at the focus of the Supreme Court's actions, survived in a roughly similar configuration in 2001. *(See maps, p. 19.)* But in Illinois, mapmakers outdid even North Carolina in creating the 17th District, one of the strangest in the nation, taking in nine full counties and parts of 14 others for the purpose of protecting a Democratic incumbent. *(See map, above.)*

Congress and Redistricting

Congress considered several proposals in the post–World War II period to enact new legislation on redistricting. Only one of these efforts was successful—enactment of a measure barring at-large elections in states with more than one House seat.

In January 1951 President Harry S. Truman asked for a ban on gerrymandering, an end to at-large seats in states having more than one representative, and a sharp reduction in the huge differences in size among congressional districts within most states. On behalf of the administration, Emanuel Celler, D-N.Y., chairman of the House Judiciary Committee, introduced a bill reflecting these requests, but the committee took no action.

Celler regularly introduced his bill throughout the 1950s and early 1960s, but it made no headway until the Supreme Court handed down the *Wesberry* decision in 1964. The House passed a version of the Celler bill in 1965, largely to discourage the Supreme Court from imposing even more rigid criteria. The Senate, however, took no action and the measure died.

In 1967, after defeating a conference report that would have prevented the courts from ordering a state to redistrict or to hold at-large elections until after the 1970 census, Congress approved a measure to ban at-large elections in all states entitled to more than one representative. Exceptions were made for New Mexico and Hawaii, which had a tradition of electing their representatives at large. Both states, however, soon passed districting laws, New Mexico for the 1968 elections and Hawaii for 1970.

Bills to increase the size of the House to prevent states from losing seats as a result of population shifts have been introduced after most recent censuses, but Congress has given little consideration to any of them.

Notes

1. Ronald D. Elving, "Redistricting: Drawing Power with a Map," *Editorial Research Reports,* February 15, 1991, 99.
2. Robert Luce, *Legislative Principles* (New York: Houghton Mifflin, 1930; New York: DaCapo Press, 1971), 342.
3. Thomas Jefferson, *The Portable Thomas Jefferson,* ed. Merrill D. Peterson, part 3, *Notes on the State of Virginia* (New York: Viking, 1965), 163.
4. Andrew Hacker, *Congressional Districting: The Issue of Equal Representation,* rev. ed. (Washington, D.C.: Brookings Institution, 1964), 6–7.
5. Max Farrand, ed., *The Records of the Federal Convention of 1787* (New Haven, Conn.: Yale University Press, 1911, 1966), vol. 2, 241.
6. *The Federalist Papers,* with an introduction by Clinton Rossiter (New York: New American Library, 1961), 347–348, 354.
7. Quoted in Laurence F. Schmeckebier, *Congressional Apportionment* (Washington, D.C.: Brookings Institution, 1941), 131.
8. Hacker, *Congressional Districting,* 14.
9. Quoted in Schmeckebier, *Congressional Apportionment,* 113.
10. Zechariah Chafee Jr., "Congressional Reapportionment," *Harvard Law Review* (1929): 1015–1047.
11. Jefferson, *Notes on the State of Virginia,* 217.
12. Schmeckebier, *Congressional Reapportionment,* 137.
13. The following summary is based on *Congressional Quarterly's Guide to the U.S. Supreme Court,* 2nd ed. (Washington, D.C.: Congressional Quarterly, 1990), 483–493.
14. Elving, "Redistricting," 107.
15. The discussion of minority representation is based on Rhodes Cook, "Map-Drawers Must Toe the Line in Upcoming Redistricting," *Congressional Quarterly Weekly Report,* September 1, 1990, 2786–2793.

Alabama

When the alphabetical roll of the states is read, Alabama's name is called first. But other reasons exist for starting a tour of America's changing political landscape here. Alabama could represent ground zero for many of the forces reshaping power relationships among the political parties, the regions, and the races. The state has seen long-standing presumptions overturned and contributed to momentous changes in the Congress.

From its earliest times Alabama had a small-farm economy in the hilly north and a plantation system based on rich topsoil in the south. The latter was dependent on slavery and was politically dominant. When the Confederacy formed in 1861, its first capital was Alabama's capital of Montgomery in the south.

After the Civil War Alabama awoke to an era of expansion based on the state's iron and coal and the railroad crossing at Birmingham ("the Pittsburgh of the South") in the north. For a time that dynamic seemed to be propelling the state to the forefront of the region in the twentieth century. But in the latter half of that century, while Alabama's cities and suburbs grew and many northerners migrated to the state for jobs or retirement, the New South made its headquarters elsewhere. Neighboring Georgia grew four times as fast and became one of the ten most populous states. Alabama lost ground to other states, as well, and one big reason was its image on matters of race.

Alabama stepped out as a bastion of segregation in 1948 when much of the South first broke away from the Democratic Party over civil rights. A new State's Rights Party formed and nominated for president the governor of South Carolina, J. Strom Thurmond (who would later serve nearly half a century in the U.S. Senate). Thurmond's Dixiecrat campaign fared better in Alabama than almost anywhere else. Of the 30 counties in the South that gave Thurmond his highest percentages (about 95 percent or higher), half were in Alabama.

In the 1950s Montgomery became famous for the Rosa Parks bus boycott that launched the career of Martin Luther King Jr., while in Birmingham the firehoses that were turned on protest marchers and the beatings on the Edmund Pettus Bridge became symbols of the violence sparked by the civil rights movement. Most of all, Alabama Gov. George C. Wallace became famous for standing in the schoolhouse door in opposition to integration. A populist Democrat who was governor for 16 years between 1963 and 1987, Wallace also ran for president three times as the candidate of states' rights and resistance to integration.

Alabama has come a long way since the 1960s. By the time Wallace died in 1998 he had reconciled with many of the same civil rights figures he had vilified in his prime. Mercedes Benz was building new plants in the state, spawning related industrial growth. In 2002 even the song "Sweet Home Alabama," written in defense of Wallace and Dixie defiance 30 years earlier, resurfaced as the soundtrack and title for a Hollywood romantic comedy sentimentalizing the state.

Although race is no longer the issue it once was, it remains a concern. Race was the most important consideration in redrawing the lines between the state's seven congressional districts following the 2000 census, even as it had been ten years earlier. In the early 1990s Alabama received its first congressional district with a black majority. The state legislature was still heavily Democratic but dealing with Gov. Guy Hunt, the state's first Republican governor since Reconstruction. So the remap plan was eventually decided by a federal court in concert with the federal Justice Department, which by terms of the 1964 Civil Rights Act must "preclear" redistricting in states with histories of racial gerrymandering.

The court drew the new 7th District in the state's southwest but projected one long tentacle into the center of the state, deep into the 6th District, folding in black neighborhoods of Tuscaloosa and Birmingham along the way. Roughly two of three voters in the new 7th District were African American, and in 1992 they elected the state's first black member of Congress since Reconstruction, Democrat Earl Hilliard.

After the 2000 census the 7th District was slightly redrawn, moving some black precincts into the east-central 3rd District in an effort to help Democrats capture that swing district when next it came open. In this case the Democrats running the legislature had no interference from the governor, Don Siegelman, who was also a Democrat. Their gambit failed in its aim: the 3rd District stayed Republican despite a vacancy in 2002. But there was an unexpected side effect. With the black majority in the 7th District reduced from about 67 percent to 60 percent, Hilliard was ousted in his primary by another black Democrat, Artur Hill, who held his own among blacks and ran better than Hilliard among whites.

The creation of the black-majority 7th District in 1992 had already had another notable side effect: helping to tip the delegation's partisan balance in favor of Republicans. Before 1992 the state had five Democrats and two Republicans. But in concentrating black Democrats in the new 7th, the remap left adjacent districts distinctly white and Republican. By 1996 the House ratio had reversed itself to favor Republicans five to two, a ratio that held into the new century. The only white Democrat left hailed from the state's northernmost

ALABAMA

Districts established January 31, 2002, for elections first held in 2002.

7 members

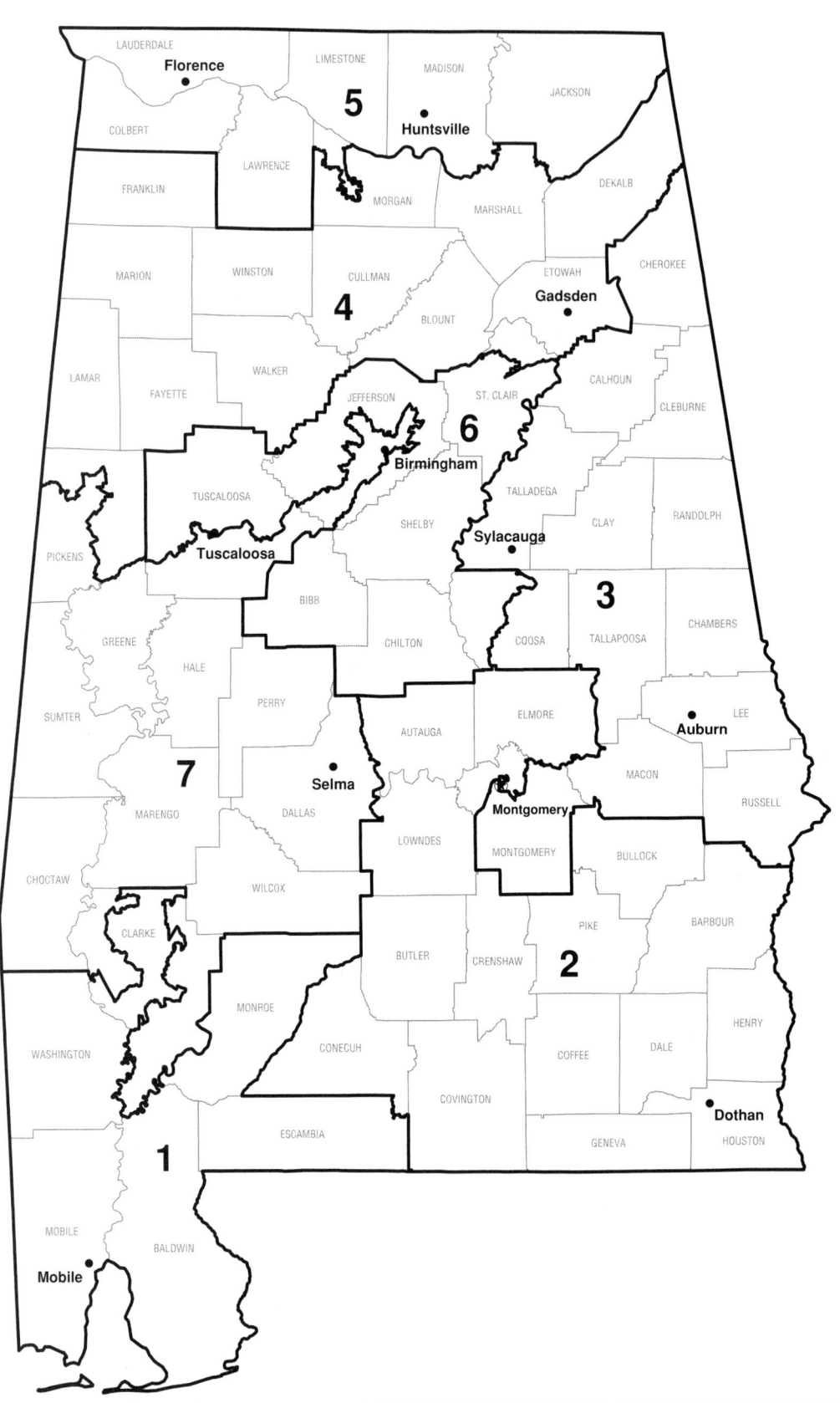

hills, a venue that had resisted secession in the 1860s and thereafter voted Republican for generations when the rest of the state did not.

This pattern of racial redistricting, so well demonstrated in Alabama in the 1990s, was at work elsewhere in the South. It meant a great leap forward for black representation in the House, and it also left a large number of districts that would be difficult for Democrats to win. It was no surprise then that in 1994, for the first time since Reconstruction, Republicans gained a majority of the seats in the South—a majority they would hold into the new century.

Alabama also saw a parallel shift in its Senate delegation. After the GOP gained control of the Senate in 1994, lifelong Democrat Richard C. Shelby switched parties. Two years later he was joined in the Senate by Republican Jeff Sessions (who replaced the state's senior retiring Democrat, Howell Heflin).

The Republican trend has been equally pronounced on other levels. Only one Democratic nominee for president has carried Alabama since the passage of the Civil Rights Act of 1964. That candidate was Jimmy Carter, who had lived just across the Chattahoochie River in Georgia when he carried Alabama in 1976. The incumbent Carter lost Alabama to Ronald Reagan in 1980, and the state voted Republican in the next five presidential years by an average margin of fourteen points.

The governorship, a Democratic preserve since the 1870s, fell to Republican Hunt when Wallace retired for the last time. The GOP then held the office for a dozen years before giving it up for one term in 1998 and winning it back in 2002.

Change has been more glacial in the state legislature, which remained in Democratic hands as of 2003. But the Republicans' share of seats in the state House had risen above 40 percent, signaling a sea change that was likely to result in a GOP majority within the decade.

Table 1 Population

District	Population	Population under 18	Voting-age population	Median age	Male*	Female*
1	635,300	169,329	465,971	35.7	48.3	51.7
2	635,300	162,403	472,897	35.7	48.5	51.5
3	635,300	156,563	478,737	35.0	48.1	51.9
4	635,300	154,022	481,278	37.6	48.8	51.2
5	635,300	158,175	477,125	36.3	48.7	51.3
6	635,300	155,497	479,803	36.5	48.8	51.2
7	635,300	167,433	467,867	33.7	46.5	53.5
State	4,447,100	1,123,422	3,323,678	35.8	48.3	51.7

*As percentage of total population.

Table 2 Voting-Age Persons by Race/Hispanic or Latino Origin

District	White*	Black or African American*	American Indian or Alaska Native*	Asian*	Other or multirace*	Hispanic or Latino*
1	70.7	25.4	0.9	1.0	0.8	1.2
2	69.6	27.1	0.4	0.6	0.8	1.4
3	67.4	29.9	0.3	0.6	0.6	1.1
4	91.4	4.7	0.4	0.2	0.7	2.5
5	79.4	15.8	0.9	1.0	1.1	1.7
6	89.5	7.2	0.3	0.9	0.6	1.5
7	39.5	57.8	0.2	0.6	0.6	1.2
State	72.7	23.8	0.5	0.7	0.7	1.5

*As percentage of voting-age population.

Table 3 Voting-Age Population by Age Groups

District	18 to 24*	25 to 44*	45 to 64*	Over 64*
1	12.7	38.6	31.0	17.7
2	13.0	39.0	30.3	17.8
3	16.1	37.0	29.8	17.1
4	11.3	37.5	32.0	19.2
5	12.2	40.4	31.1	16.4
6	11.2	41.2	31.3	16.3
7	16.2	37.7	28.4	17.7
State	13.2	38.8	30.6	17.4

*As percentage of voting-age population.

Table 4 Income and Occupation

District	Median family income	Families in poverty*	White collar†	Blue collar†	Service†	Farm†
1	$41,406	13.7	54.7	29.7	14.7	0.9
2	$40,062	13.6	55.1	29.5	14.4	1.1
3	$38,959	13.8	51.7	33.1	14.5	0.7
4	$37,916	11.4	46.0	40.8	11.9	1.3
5	$46,350	9.7	57.1	29.6	12.9	0.5
6	$56,307	5.9	67.7	22.1	9.8	0.4
7	$33,398	20.4	53.4	28.6	17.3	0.7
State	$41,657	12.5	55.4	30.3	13.5	0.8

*As percentage of all families.　　†As percentage of employed workers 16 years and over.

Table 5 Education: School Years Completed

District	Less than grade 9*	Grades 9–12 no diploma*	High school diploma no college*	Some college*	College bachelor's degree or higher*
1	6.7	16.4	32.1	26.3	18.5
2	9.0	16.6	30.1	26.2	18.0
3	9.3	18.8	30.8	24.5	16.7
4	11.7	19.4	33.1	24.5	11.3
5	7.4	14.0	28.6	26.5	23.5
6	5.3	11.8	27.0	26.2	29.6
7	8.8	18.1	31.1	26.9	15.1
State	8.3	16.4	30.4	25.9	19.0

*As percentage of persons age 25 and over.

Table 6 Housing and Residential Patterns

District	Median home value	Owner occupied*	Renter occupied*	Urban†	Rural†
1	$78,500	73.1	26.9	64.4	35.6
2	$70,400	71.7	28.3	50.1	49.9
3	$67,700	71.0	29.0	53.3	46.7
4	$67,100	78.1	21.9	26.5	73.5
5	$85,000	72.5	27.5	59.4	40.6
6	$115,000	78.0	22.0	62.1	37.9
7	$62,700	62.8	37.2	72.2	27.8
State	$76,700	72.5	27.5	55.4	44.6

*As percentage of occupied housing units.　　†As percentage of total population.

Alabama 1st District

Southwest — Mobile

Crop fields and pine forests merge with Alabama's shoreline to form the 1st. Although the city of Mobile is the anchor of the state's only Gulf Coast district, a symbiotic relationship between the industrial and rural areas balances the district's economy.

Forestry feeds the district's timber mills and shipping companies, though a deep recession in the Southeast Asian market in the mid- to late-1990s forced cutbacks in the local timber industry. Mobile's State Docks, one of the nation's largest commercial shipping centers, supports a shipbuilding industry that has stagnated in recent years. South Alabama still relies on its rich soil for the staple products—trees, cotton, and soybeans—that have given the region strength for decades.

But the overall contraction of timber, ship-related industries, and a once-thriving textile industry forced the district to diversify. Tourism, based around the Gulf Coast, has been the most immediate remedy. Retail outlets spur employment and chemical and aerospace companies help broaden the district's economy.

The shift to GOP voting seen in much of the South took root early here. Republicans held the House seat from 1965 to 2003, and the district overwhelmingly favored GOP presidential candidates in the 1990s and 2000. Mobile residents lean Republican, though Democrats long have had a foothold in rural parts of the district. Local elections can become battles over issues such as farm subsidies and trade.

Major Industry

Commercial shipping, timber, textiles.

Notable

Gulf Shores' National Shrimp Festival draws more than 200,000 visitors each October; Mobile annually hosts America's Junior Miss competition and college football's Senior Bowl.

Election Returns

	Republican		Democratic		Other	
President 2000	13,938	60.4%	86,142	37.5%	4,798	2.1%
House 2002	108,102	60.5%	67,507	37.8%	3,078	1.7%

District Profile

Population   635,300

Total area (square miles)   7,182
   Land area (square miles)   6,317

Population per square mile   100.6

Counties (2000 population)

Baldwin	140,415	Mobile	399,843
Clarke (pt.)	14,181	Monroe	24,324
Escambia	38,440	Washington	18,097

Cities and other areas over 10,000 (2000 population)

Daphne	16,581	Prichard	28,633
Fairhope	12,480	Saraland	12,288
Mobile	198,915	Tillmans Corner CDP	
		15,685	

Race and Hispanic or Latino origin*

White   67.8%
Black or African American   28.0%
American Indian or Alaska Native   1.0%
Asian   1.0%
Native Hawaiian or other Pacific Islander   0.0%
Some other race   0.1%
Hispanic or Latino origin   1.3%
Two or more races   0.9%

As percentage of total population.

Ancestry*

English	6.6%	Italian	1.3%
French	2.1%	Scotch-Irish	1.9%
German	5.7%	Scottish	1.3%
Irish	6.8%	USA/American	12.4%

As estimated percentage of total population.

Universities and colleges, 2000–2001 enrollment

Alabama Southern Community College, Monroeville   1,261
Bishop State Community College, Mobile   4,058
Faulkner University, Mobile*
James H. Faulkner State Community College, Bay Minette   2,775
Jefferson Davis Community College, Brewton   1,129
Southeast College of Technology, Mobile   578
Spring Hill College, Mobile   1,484
United States Sports Academy, Daphne   354
University of Mobile, Mobile   1,968
University of South Alabama, Mobile   11,673
University of South Alabama-Baldwin, Fairhope   8,342

Enrollment under 100. See Sources and Explanations in the front of the volume.

Newspapers and circulation

	District circulation	Total circulation
Mobile Register	91,634	97,781
Pensacola News Journal	1,900	62,983
*USA Today**	3,347	1,674,376

See Sources and Explanations in the front of the volume.

Television stations and affiliations

Mobile-Pensacola (Ft. Walton Beach)	100%	WALA	FOX
Mobile-Pensacola (Ft. Walton Beach)	100%	WAWD	Independent
Mobile-Pensacola (Ft. Walton Beach)	100%	WEAR	ABC
Mobile-Pensacola (Ft. Walton Beach)	100%	WEIQ	PBS
Mobile-Pensacola (Ft. Walton Beach)	100%	WFGX	Independent
Mobile-Pensacola (Ft. Walton Beach)	100%	WHBR	Independent
Mobile-Pensacola (Ft. Walton Beach)	100%	WJTC	UPN
Mobile-Pensacola (Ft. Walton Beach)	100%	WKRG	CBS
Mobile-Pensacola (Ft. Walton Beach)	100%	WMPV	Independent
Mobile-Pensacola (Ft. Walton Beach)	100%	WPAN	Independent
Mobile-Pensacola (Ft. Walton Beach)	100%	WPMI	NBC
Mobile-Pensacola (Ft. Walton Beach)	100%	WSRE	PBS

Cable systems and subscribers

Cable South Inc.   1,215
Charter   4,334
Comcast   71,894
Galaxy   1,156
Interchange Cable   2,653
Mallard   1,665
Mediacom   35,062
Riviera Utility Cable TV   4,475
Time Warner   623

Businesses and other major employers

University of South Alabama; Mobile   5,403
Infirmary Health System Inc.; Mobile; hospital   2,900
MesaStaff Inc.; Mobile; payroll accounting service   2,500
University of South Alabama; Mobile; physician general and family practice   2,452
Kimberly-Clark Corp.; Mobile; paper mills   2,100
Daniel's Home Improvement; Brewton; home remodeling   1,999
Atlantic Marine-Mobile; Mobile; shipbuilding and repairing   1,600
University of South Alabama Medical Center; Mobile   1,600
Providence Hospital; Mobile   1,537
S. D. Warren Alabama; Mobile; paper products   1,525
International Paper Co.; Mobile; paper mills   1,312
Pilot Catastrophe Services Inc.; Mobile; insurance claim adjusters   1,184
Springhill Medical Complex Inc.; Mobile   1,100
St. Mobile Aerospace Engineering Inc.; Mobile; aircraft maintenance, repair   1,094
Standard Furniture Manufacturing Co.; Bay Minette; wood bedroom furniture   1,000
J-Mar Trucking Inc.; Atmore; contract haulers   950
Springhill Hospitals Inc.; Mobile   900
Teledyne Technologies Inc.; Mobile; electronic and communications products   800
Alabama Mental Health Dept.; Mount Vernon   793
Baldwin County Eastern Shore Health Care Authority; Fairhope; hospital   750
Degussa-Huls Corp.; Theodore; industrial organic chemicals   750
Acordis Cellulosic Fibers Inc.; Axis; rayon fibers, straw, strips, and yarn   730
University of South Alabama Hospital; Mobile   725
Sears Home Services Group; Mobile; computer maintenance services   650
City of Mobile; Mobile; police office   605
Stone Container Corp.; Brewton; corrugated and solid fiber boxes   600
Vanity Fair Intimates Inc.; Atmore; women's and children's underwear   600
Baldwin County; Bay Minette; district attorney's office   600
Vanity Fair Intimates Inc.; Jackson; women's blouses/shirts   600
Alantic Marine Mobil Inc.; Mobile; fishing vessel construction, repair   600
Computer Programs and Systems Inc.; Mobile; computer turnkey vendors   559
Wal-Mart Stores Inc.; Foley; discount department stores   550
Saad's Healthcare Services Inc.; Mobile; home health care services   550
University of South Alabama Medical Center; Mobile   550
West Telemarketing Corp.; Mobile; telemarketing services   532
Boise Cascade Corp.; Jackson; pulp mills   530
Vanity Fair Intimates Inc.; Monroeville; women's and children's undergarments   500
Performance Contractors Inc.; Irvington; industrial buildings construction   500
SkilStaf Inc.; Orange Beach; employment agencies   500
PCH Hotels and Resorts Inc.; Point Clear; resort hotel   500
Hertz Corp.; Saraland; management services   500
ExxonMobil Oil Corp.; Theodore; petroleum refining   500
Mobile County; Mobile; county police   500
Mobile County Sheriff's Dept.; Mobile   500
Sears Roebuck and Co. Inc.; Mobile; department stores   500
U.S. Coast Guard; Mobile   500
Wal-Mart Stores Inc.; Mobile; discount department stores   500
NCO Group Inc.; Mobile; adjustment and collection services   500

Alabama 2nd District

Southeast — part of Montgomery, Dothan

Besides Dothan and part of the state capital, Montgomery, the 2nd consists of scattered small towns. The district is probably best known for its peanut farms, but poultry, cotton, and tree farming are also important. The local economy has suffered in recent years from hurricanes, floods, droughts, and ice storms. Farther south, around Dothan, high-tech and auto parts plants have replaced textile mills that moved overseas.

Defense and state government provide steady employment. Maxwell Air Force Base and its Gunter Annex are responsible for most of the Air Force's computer systems. A Hyundai plant scheduled to open in 2005 in the neighboring 3rd District is expected to employ about 2,000 people.

Tourism also contributes to the economy, particularly in Montgomery, though many historic sites of the civil rights movement are in the 3rd. The Robert Trent Jones Golf Trail, large antebellum homes in Eufaula, and fishing at Lake Eufaula attract visitors to the area.

Redistricting following the 2000 census shuffled the population of Montgomery: the 2nd now shares the city with the 3rd, and the 7th was completely removed from the city. A large military retiree population underscores a conservative constituency that usually votes Republican. On the local level, the 2nd usually sends Democrats to the state legislature.

Major Industry

Agriculture, military, manufacturing.

Notable

Dothan hosts a national peanut festival annually; the Hank Williams Sr. Museum is in Georgiana; the Boll Weevil Monument in Enterprise is a tribute to the insect, whose destruction of the cotton crop persuaded farmers to switch to peanuts.

Election Returns

	Republican		Democratic		Other	
President 2000	137,168	61.1%	84,435	37.6%	3,061	1.4%
House 2002	129,233	68.8%	55,495	29.5%	3,273	1.7%

District Profile

Population 635,300

Total area (square miles) 10,607
    Land area (square miles) 10,501

Population per square mile 60.5

Counties (2000 population)

Autauga 43,671	Dale 49,129
Barbour 29,038	Elmore 65,874
Bullock 11,714	Geneva 25,764
Butler 21,399	Henry 16,310
Coffee 43,615	Houston 88,787
Conecuh 14,089	Lowndes 13,473
Covington 37,631	Montgomery (pt.) 131,536
Crenshaw 13,665	Pike 29,605

Cities and other areas over 10,000 (2000 population)

Dothan 57,737	Montgomery (pt.) 127,986
Enterprise 21,178	Ozark 15,119
Eufaula 13,908	Prattville 24,303
Millbrook 10,386	Troy 13,935

Race and Hispanic or Latino origin*

White 67.0%
Black or African American 29.4%
American Indian or Alaska Native 0.4%
Asian 0.6%
Native Hawaiian or other Pacific Islander 0.0%
Some other race 0.1%
Hispanic or Latino origin 1.5%
Two or more races 0.9%

As percentage of total population.

Ancestry*

English 6.2%	Scotch-Irish 1.7%
French 1.2%	Scottish 1.3%
German 4.5%	USA/American 15.7%
Irish 5.9%	

As estimated percentage of total population.

Universities and colleges, 2000–2001 enrollment

Chauncey Sparks State Technical College, Eufaula 634
Douglas MacArthur State Technical College, Opp 473
Enterprise State Junior College, Enterprise 1,590
Faulkner University, Montgomery 2,704
George C. Wallace State Community College, Dothan 3,612
Huntingdon College, Montgomery 657
J. F. Ingram State Technical College, Deatsville 630
John M. Patterson State Technical College, Montgomery 986
Lurleen B. Wallace Junior College, Andalusia 802
Reid State Technical College, Evergreen 706
South College, Montgomery 207
Trenholm State Technical College, Montgomery 663
Troy State University, Dothan 1,958
Troy State University, Troy 12,541
Troy State University, Montgomery 3,090

Newspapers and circulation

	District circulation	Total circulation
Birmingham News	1,146	149,145
Birmingham News/Post Herald (Sunday)	1,182	160,856
Dothan Eagle	33,707	34,645
Mobile Register	1,226	97,781
Montgomery Advertiser	32,868	50,654
*USA Today**	2,017	1,674,376

See Sources and Explanations in the front of the volume.

Television stations and affiliations

Montgomery (Selma)	55%	WAIQ	PBS
Montgomery (Selma)	55%	WAKA	CBS
Montgomery (Selma)	55%	WCOV	FOX
Montgomery (Selma)	55%	WDIQ	PBS
Montgomery (Selma)	55%	WIIQ	PBS
Montgomery (Selma)	55%	WMCF	Independent
Montgomery (Selma)	55%	WNCF	ABC
Montgomery (Selma)	55%	WSFA	NBC
Dothan	28%	WDFX	FOX
Dothan	28%	WDHN	ABC
Columbus, GA	9%	WACS	PBS
Columbus, GA	9%	WGIQ	PBS
Columbus, GA	9%	WLTZ	NBC
Columbus, GA	9%	WRBL	CBS
Columbus, GA	9%	WSWS	UPN
Columbus, GA	9%	WTVM	ABC
Columbus, GA	9%	WXTX	FOX
Mobile-Pensacola (Ft. Walton Beach)	8%	WALA	FOX
Mobile-Pensacola (Ft. Walton Beach)	8%	WAWD	Independent
Mobile-Pensacola (Ft. Walton Beach)	8%	WEAR	ABC
Mobile-Pensacola (Ft. Walton Beach)	8%	WEIQ	PBS
Mobile-Pensacola (Ft. Walton Beach)	8%	WFGX	Independent
Mobile-Pensacola (Ft. Walton Beach)	8%	WHBR	Independent
Mobile-Pensacola (Ft. Walton Beach)	8%	WJTC	UPN
Mobile-Pensacola (Ft. Walton Beach)	8%	WKRG	CBS
Mobile-Pensacola (Ft. Walton Beach)	8%	WMPV	Independent
Mobile-Pensacola (Ft. Walton Beach)	8%	WPAN	Independent
Mobile-Pensacola (Ft. Walton Beach)	8%	WPMI	NBC
Mobile-Pensacola (Ft. Walton Beach)	8%	WSRE	PBS

Cable systems and subscribers

Adelphia 9,079
Charter 40,191
City Cablevision 2,313
Comcast 22,670
Com-Link 1,233
Community Cable 513
Luverne TV Cable 1,089
Mallard 1,267
Mediacom 1,358
Opp Cablevision 3,471
Time Warner 23,326
TV Cable of Andalusa 4,350

Military installations, September 2001
   Fort Rucker (Army), Daleville   9,079
   Maxwell Air Force Base, Montgomery   7,100
   Dannelly Field Air National Guard, Montgomery   978
   R. W. Shepherd (Army Guard), Hope Hull   385
   Montgomery Air National Guard, Montgomery   234

Businesses and other major employers
   Weyerhaeuser Co.; Montgomery; container board
      7,000
   TMG Staffing Services Inc.; Dothan; employment agency
      6,000
   Alabama Finance Dept. Payroll; Montgomery   3,000
   Baptist Health Hospital; Montgomery   2,000
   Houston County Healthcare Authority; Dothan; hospital
      2,000
   QHG of Alabama Inc.; Dothan; hospital   1,878
   Alabama Dept. of Transportation; Montgomery   1,717
   Charoen Pokphand (USA) Inc.; Eufaula; poultry
      slaughtering/processing   1,500
   Perdue Farms Inc.; Dothan; processed fresh poultry
      1,200
   Sony Magnetic Products Inc. of America; Dothan; audio
      tape   1,200
   ConAgra Foods Inc.; Enterprise; chicken processing
      1,100
   Shaw Industries Inc.; Andalusia; yarn spinning mills
      1,050
   Wiley Sanders Truck Lines Inc.; Troy; trucking   1,000
   U.S. Dept. of Veterans Affairs; Enterprise   1,000
   Piggly Wiggly of Dixieland; Hartford; supermarkets
      1,000
   Johnston Industries Inc.; Opp; child day care services
      1,000
   Colonial Bank; Montgomery; state commercial banks
      925
   Alabama Dept. of Public Health; Montgomery   925
   Alabama Power Co.; Columbia; management services
      900
   Southern Nuclear Operating Co.; Columbia; electric
      power generation   900
   WestPoint Stevens Inc.; Abbeville; fabric sheets   833
   Magnatrax Corp.; Eufaula; prefabricated metal buildings
      800
   Regions Mortgage Inc.; Montgomery; mortgage bankers
      800
   City of Montgomery; Montgomery; county police   734
   United Parcel Service Inc.; Montgomery; parcel delivery
      700
   Alabama Alcoholic Beverage Control Board;
      Montgomery   700
   International Paper Co.; Prattville; paper mills   680
   PYA/Monarch Inc.; Montgomery; food supplier   650
   Pemco Aeroplex Inc.; Dothan; aircraft   650
   ContiGroup Companies Inc.; Union Springs; processed
      poultry   600
   Sylvest Farms Inc.; Montgomery; broiling chickens
      600
   Rheem Manufacturing Co.; Montgomery; water heaters
      600
   Michelin North America Inc.; Dothan; tires and inner
      tubes   600

Phillips-Van Heusen Corp.; Ozark; men's and boys'
   nightwear   600
Hart and Cooley Inc.; Geneva; architectural metalwork
   560
American Buildings Co.; Eufaula; prefabricated metal
   buildings   550
Troy State University; Troy   525
Collins Signs Inc.; Dothan; signs and advertising
   specialties   520
Wal-Mart Stores Inc.; Prattville; supermarkets   500
Neptune Technology Group Inc.; Tallassee; well logging
   500
HB&G Building Products Inc.; Troy; millwork   500
Alabama Dept. of Public Health; Montgomery   500
AAA Cooper Transportation; Dothan; trucking   500
Twitchell Corp.; Dothan; polypropylene broadwoven
   fabrics   500
CMI Industries Inc.; Geneva; cotton broadwoven goods
   500

Alabama 3rd District

East — part of Montgomery, Auburn, Anniston

With agriculture, industry, universities, and part of the capital city of Montgomery, the 3rd can claim to be a microcosm of the state. Revised during 2002 redistricting to decrease its Republican strength, the 3rd now has many socially conservative Democrats who favor GOP presidential candidates, as well as African Americans, who make up one-third of the population, and small pockets of university liberals who support Democrats on all levels.

Anniston relies heavily on the federal government. The Army left Fort McClellan in 1999, but the base has been turned into a training facility for first respondents to chemical, biological, and nuclear terrorist attacks. Honda operates a plant in Lincoln, and Hyundai's first U.S. facility is scheduled to open in 2005 south of Montgomery.

Auburn University is one of the state's largest employers and a leading agricultural research center. Construction of a chemical weapons incinerator at the Anniston Army Depot raised environmental concerns and protests in 2003.

Redistricting removed some western territory, while adding many Montgomery attractions, including the state capitol and the Dexter Avenue Baptist Church, where civil rights leaders launched the 1955 bus boycott.

Major Industry
   Higher education, agriculture, textiles.

Notable
   Tuskegee University, founded in 1881, was one of the nation's first black colleges; Talladega Superspeedway is a big attraction.

Election Returns

	Republican		Democratic		Other	
President 2000	112,320	51.6%	101,431	46.6%	3,769	1.7%
House 2002	91,169	50.3%	87,351	48.2%	2,703	1.5%

District Profile

Population 635,300

Total area (square miles) 7,987
  Land area (square miles) 7,833

Population per square mile 81.1

Counties (2000 population)

Calhoun	112,249	Macon	24,105
Chambers	36,583	Montgomery (pt.)	91,974
Cherokee	23,988	Randolph	22,380
Clay	14,254	Russell	49,756
Cleburne	14,123	Talladega	80,321
Coosa (pt.)	9,000	Tallapoosa	41,475
Lee	115,092		

Cities and other areas over 10,000 (2000 population)

Alexander City	15,008	Phenix City	28,265
Anniston	24,276	Saks CDP	10,698
Auburn	42,987	Smiths CDP	21,756
Montgomery (pt.)	73,582	Sylacauga	12,616
Opelika	23,498	Talladega	15,143
Oxford	14,592	Tuskegee	11,846

Race and Hispanic or Latino origin*

White 64.9%
Black or African American 32.2%
American Indian or Alaska Native 0.3%
Asian 0.6%
Native Hawaiian or other Pacific Islander 0.0%
Some other race 0.1%
Hispanic or Latino origin 1.2%
Two or more races 0.7%

*As percentage of total population.

Ancestry*

English	5.8%	Scotch-Irish	1.4%
German	3.8%	Scottish	1.2%
Irish	6.0%	USA/American	15.9%

*As estimated percentage of total population.

Universities and colleges, 2000–2001 enrollment

Alabama State University, Montgomery 5,269
Auburn University, Auburn University 21,860
Auburn University, Montgomery 4,900
Central Alabama Community College, Alexander City 1,577
Chattahoochee Valley Community College, Phenix City 1,748
Harry M. Ayers State Technical College, Anniston 1,112
Jacksonville State University, Jacksonville 7,844
Southern Christian University, Montgomery 294
Southern Union State Community College, Wadley 4,017
Talladega College, Talladega 475
Tuskegee University, Tuskegee 2,826

Newspapers and Circulation

	District circulation	Total circulation
Anniston Star	25,678	25,680
Atlanta Journal-Constitution	1,875	857,088
Birmingham News	6,734	149,145
Birmingham News/Post Herald (Sunday)	6,743	160,856
Columbus Ledger-Enquirer	9,552	46,345
Gadsden Times	2,889	25,280
Montgomery Advertiser	15,781	50,654
Opelika-Auburn News	13,224	13,229
*USA Today**	2,723	1,674,376

*See Sources and Explanations in the front of the volume.

Television stations and affiliations

Birmingham (Anniston-Tuscaloosa)	32%	WABM	UPN
Birmingham (Anniston-Tuscaloosa)	32%	WBIQ	PBS
Birmingham (Anniston-Tuscaloosa)	32%	WBRC	FOX
Birmingham (Anniston-Tuscaloosa)	32%	WCFT	ABC
Birmingham (Anniston-Tuscaloosa)	32%	WDBB	WB
Birmingham (Anniston-Tuscaloosa)	32%	WIAT	CBS
Birmingham (Anniston-Tuscaloosa)	32%	WJSU	ABC
Birmingham (Anniston-Tuscaloosa)	32%	WPXH	PAX
Birmingham (Anniston-Tuscaloosa)	32%	WTJP	Independent
Birmingham (Anniston-Tuscaloosa)	32%	WTTO	WB
Birmingham (Anniston-Tuscaloosa)	32%	WVTM	NBC
Montgomery (Selma)	30%	WAIQ	PBS
Montgomery (Selma)	30%	WAKA	CBS
Montgomery (Selma)	30%	WCOV	FOX
Montgomery (Selma)	30%	WDIQ	PBS
Montgomery (Selma)	30%	WIIQ	PBS
Montgomery (Selma)	30%	WMCF	Independent
Montgomery (Selma)	30%	WNCF	ABC
Montgomery (Selma)	30%	WSFA	NBC
Columbus, GA	24%	WACS	PBS
Columbus, GA	24%	WGIQ	PBS
Columbus, GA	24%	WLTZ	NBC
Columbus, GA	24%	WRBL	CBS
Columbus, GA	24%	WSWS	UPN
Columbus, GA	24%	WTVM	ABC
Columbus, GA	24%	WXTX	FOX
Atlanta	14%	WAGA	FOX
Atlanta	14%	WATC	Independent
Atlanta	14%	WATL	WB
Atlanta	14%	WCIQ	PBS
Atlanta	14%	WGTV	PBS
Atlanta	14%	WHSG	Independent
Atlanta	14%	WJSP	PBS
Atlanta	14%	WPBA	PBS
Atlanta	14%	WPXA	PAX
Atlanta	14%	WSB	ABC
Atlanta	14%	WTBS	TBN
Atlanta	14%	WUPA	UPN
Atlanta	14%	WXIA	NBC

Cable systems and subscribers

Cable ONE 18,021
Charter 118,891
Comcast 1,003
Com-Link 636
Communicomm 9,053
Lincoln Cable TV 1,538
Phenix City CATV 14,855

Military installations, September 2001

Anniston Army Depot, Anniston 4,439
Fort McClellan (Army), Anniston 470
Nichols Army Reserve, Anniston 309

Businesses and other major employers

Russell Corp.; Alexander City; knit jerseys   7,000

Skilstaf Inc.; Alexander City; employee leasing service   5,000

Auburn University; Auburn   4,100

Alfa Mutual Inc.; Montgomery; accident and health insurance carriers   2,919

Honda Manufacturing of Alabama; Lincoln; automobiles   2,100

Michelin North America Inc.; Opelika; automobile tires   2,000

Auburn University; Auburn   2,000

Baptist Health Hospital; Montgomery   1,700

East Alabama Health Care Authority; Opelika; hospital   1,530

U.S. Veterans Hospital; Tuskegee   1,400

Jackson Hospital and Clinic; Montgomery   1,388

Regional Medical Center Board; Anniston; hospital, medical school   1,232

Wellborn Cabinet Inc.; Ashland; wood kitchen cabinets   1,200

WestPoint Stevens Inc.; Valley; cotton sheets, bedding, table cloths, towels   1,139

AIDB Inc.; Talladega; elementary and secondary schools   1,000

Tyson Foods Inc.; Ashland; processed poultry   1,000

Alabama Dept. of Revenue; Montgomery   800

Jacksonville State University; Jacksonville   800

Quantegy Inc.; Opelika; magnetic and optical recording media   800

Alfa Corp.; Montgomery; personal credit institutions   750

Auburn University; Montgomery   750

MeadWestvaco Corp.; Phenix City; coated paperboard   734

Alabama State University; Montgomery   729

Avondale Mills Inc.; Sylacauga; denims   700

Union Underwear Co.; Leesburg; knit underwear mills   700

Tuskegee University; Tuskegee Institute   700

Werner Co.; Anniston; aluminum sheet, plate, and foil   700

Meadowcraft Inc.; Wadley; metal lawn furniture   650

Johnston Industries Alabama Inc.; Phenix City; polyester broadwoven fabrics   650

WestPoint Stevens Inc.; Lanett; cotton sheets and sheetings   642

Alabama Institute for Deaf and Blind; Talladega   619

Baptist Health System; Sylacauga; hospital, nursing school   600

Coosa Valley Baptist Medical Center Inc.; Sylacauga   600

Leesburg Knitting Mills Inc.; Leesburg; yarn spinning mills   600

Alabama Dept. of Finance; Montgomery   600

North American Bus Industries Inc.; Anniston; bus assembly   594

Bostrom Seating Inc.; Piedmont; vehicle furniture   590

Springs Industries Inc.; Piedmont; household furnishings   508

Hager and Sons Hinge Manufacturing Co.; Montgomery; hardware   500

HCA Inc.; Montgomery; hospital   500

Alabama Dept. of Human Resources; Montgomery   500

Alabama Governor's Office; Montgomery   500

United Defense Industries Inc.; Anniston; steel foundries   500

Russell County Board of Education; Phenix City   500

Alabama 4th District

North central — Gadsden, part of Decatur

Encompassing mountains, foothills, flatlands, and large waterways, the 4th stretches the width of the state, bordering Georgia and Mississippi. A small African American population and the absence of a major city distinguish it from the rest of Alabama.

One of the state's poorest districts, the 4th has suffered through textile companies moving overseas and a decline in coal mining, with some relief from an underlying agricultural economy. Rubber and steel plants in Gadsden, the district's only sizable city, have downsized as a result of strikes and foreign competition.

Efforts by local officials to attract new, moderate-size businesses may be helped by "Corridor X," a road project that locals hope will become an interstate. Many residents work in surrounding metropolitan areas—such as Huntsville in the 5th, and Birmingham, which is split between the 6th and 7th Districts. Mobile home manufacturing plants fuel Marshall County's economy. Cullman County's agricultural industry includes everything from cotton and soybeans to chickens and cattle. DeKalb County, a mountainous region in the northeastern part of the state, includes some of the region's natural sights and tourist destinations.

The rural 4th's population is socially conservative, especially on gun control and religious issues. The district originally adhered to Democratic populism but has voted Republican on recent presidential ballots. In 1996 voters sent a Republican to Congress for just the second time since Reconstruction and have reelected him through 2002.

Major Industry
Agriculture, manufacturing.

Notable
Fort Payne and surrounding DeKalb County, billed as the "sock capital of the world," have more than 100 mills that employ more than 6,000 workers; Winston County briefly became the "free state of Winston" when Alabama seceded from the union; the world's longest yard sale, which starts in Gadsden and ends 450 miles later in Covington, Ky., attracts 400,000 bargain shoppers for one week in August.

Election Returns

	Republican		Democratic		Other	
President 2000	141,285	60.7%	87,062	37.4%	4,240	1.8%
House 2002	139,705	86.7%			21,396	13.3%

District Profile

Population   635,300

Total area (square miles)   8,523
   Land area (square miles)   8,372

Population per square mile   75.9

Counties (2000 population)

Blount	51,024	Marion	31,214
Cullman	77,483	Marshall	82,231
Dekalb	64,452	Morgan (pt.)	49,819
Etowah	103,459	Pickens (pt.)	9,402
Fayette	18,495	St. Clair (pt.)	5,038
Franklin	31,223	Walker	70,713
Lamar	15,904	Winston	24,843

Cities and other areas over 10,000 (2000 population)

Albertville	17,247	Gadsden	38,978
Cullman	13,995	Jasper	14,052
Fort Payne	12,938		

Race and Hispanic or Latino origin*

White 90.4%
Black or African American 5.1%
American Indian or Alaska Native 0.4%
Asian 0.2%
Native Hawaiian or other Pacific Islander 0.0%
Some other race 0.0%
Hispanic or Latino origin 3.0%
Two or more races 0.8%

*As percentage of total population.

Ancestry*

English	6.8%	Scotch-Irish	1.3%
German	4.8%	Scottish	1.1%
Irish	8.2%	USA/American	21.3%

*As estimated percentage of total population.

Universities and colleges, 2000–2001 enrollment

Bevill State Community College, Sumiton 3,558
Bevill State Community College-Walker College, Jasper 1,002
Gadsden State Community College, Gadsden 4,787
George C. Wallace State Community College, Hanceville 4,696
Northeast Alabama State Community College, Rainsville 1,659
Snead State Community College, Boaz 1,579

Newspapers and circulation

	District circulation	Total circulation
Birmingham News	13,124	149,145
Birmingham News/Post Herald (Sunday)	13,134	160,856
Cullman Times	10,859	10,899
Decatur Daily	8,983	24,437
Florence Times Daily	3,629	31,214
Gadsden Times	22,198	25,280
Guntersville Advertiser-Gleam	9,734	10,163
Huntsville Times	4,736	57,734
Jasper Daily Mountain Eagle	11,353	11,580
Tuscaloosa News	3,323	36,423
*USA Today**	1,732	1,674,376

*See Sources and Explanations in the front of the volume.

Television stations and affiliations

Birmingham (Anniston-Tuscaloosa)	63%	WABM	UPN
Birmingham (Anniston-Tuscaloosa)	63%	WBIQ	PBS
Birmingham (Anniston-Tuscaloosa)	63%	WBRC	FOX
Birmingham (Anniston-Tuscaloosa)	63%	WCFT	ABC
Birmingham (Anniston-Tuscaloosa)	63%	WDBB	WB
Birmingham (Anniston-Tuscaloosa)	63%	WIAT	CBS
Birmingham (Anniston-Tuscaloosa)	63%	WJSU	ABC
Birmingham (Anniston-Tuscaloosa)	63%	WPXH	PAX
Birmingham (Anniston-Tuscaloosa)	63%	WTJP	Independent
Birmingham (Anniston-Tuscaloosa)	63%	WTTO	WB
Birmingham (Anniston-Tuscaloosa)	63%	WVTM	NBC
Huntsville-Decatur (Florence)	30%	WAAY	ABC
Huntsville-Decatur (Florence)	30%	WAFF	NBC
Huntsville-Decatur (Florence)	30%	WFIQ	PBS
Huntsville-Decatur (Florence)	30%	WHDF	UPN
Huntsville-Decatur (Florence)	30%	WHIQ	PBS
Huntsville-Decatur (Florence)	30%	WHNT	CBS
Huntsville-Decatur (Florence)	30%	WYLE	Independent
Huntsville-Decatur (Florence)	30%	WZDX	FOX
Columbus-Tupelo-West Point	7%	WCBI	CBS
Columbus-Tupelo-West Point	7%	WLOV	FOX
Columbus-Tupelo-West Point	7%	WMAB	PBS
Columbus-Tupelo-West Point	7%	WTVA	NBC

Cable systems and subscribers

Adelphia 19,658
Charter 50,482
Comcast 23,412
Communicomm 3,405
Galaxy 1,246
Northland 1,600
Otel Co. 2,504
West Alabama TV Cable 6,788

Military installations, September 2001

Martin Air National Guard, Gadsden 136

Businesses and other major employers

Riverview Regional Medical Center; Gadsden 1,910
General Electric Co.; Decatur; household refrigerators 1,600
Goodyear Tire and Rubber Co.; Gadsden; rebuilding and retreading tires 1,400
Tyson Foods Inc.; Gadsden; processed poultry 1,300
Tyson Foods Inc.; Albertville; chicken processing 1,205
Tyson Foods Inc.; Blountsville; processed poultry 1,100
Gold Kist Inc.; Russellville; poultry slaughtering/processing 1,000
QHG of Gadsden; Gadsden; hospital 1,000
Cagle's Inc.; Collinsville; processed poultry 925
Copeland Corp.; Hartselle; refrigeration/air conditioning equipment 900
Gold Kist Inc.; Guntersville; processed poultry 900
Cullman Medical Center; Cullman 834
Southern Energy Homes Inc.; Addison; mobile homes 800
Sara Lee Bakery Group Inc.; Fort Payne; breads and cakes 800
VF Jeanswear; Oneonta; men's and boys' jeans 750
Electrolux Home Products Inc.; Cullman; refrigeration/air conditioning equipment 700
Cavalier Industries Inc.; Addison; mobile homes 700
VF Jeanswear; Russellville; women's and girls' jeans 650
Walker Baptist Medical Center; Jasper 620
Wal-Mart Stores Inc.; Jasper; discount department stores 600

ContiGroup Companies Inc.; Albertville; processed
poultry   600

Marshall Health System; Boaz; hospital, nursing school
600

SCI Systems Inc.; Arab; radio/TV communications
equipment   550

Wallace State Community College; Hanceville   550

Southern Energy Homes Inc.; Double Springs; mobile
homes   550

Chandeleur Homes Inc.; Boaz; mobile homes   550

Mueller Co.; Albertville; cast iron pressure pipe and
fittings   540

Golden Rod Broilers Inc.; Cullman; broiling chickens
500

Rehau Inc.; Cullman; plastics processing   500

Cubigel-USA Division; Cullman; air and gas
compressors   500

ArvinMeritor Inc.; Fayette; motor vehicle exhaust
mufflers   500

NTN-Bower Corp.; Hamilton; roller bearings and parts
500

Sunshine Mills Inc.; Red Bay; dog food   500

Gold Kist Inc.; Boaz; processed poultry   500

Palm Harbor Homes; Boaz; mobile homes   500

TS Tech North America Inc.; Boaz; automobile seats
500

Renfro Corp.; Fort Payne; knit underwear mills   500

Kappler USA Inc.; Guntersville; men's/boys' work
clothing   500

Alabama 5th District

North — Huntsville

A large section of the Tennessee River winds through the 5th, a strip of land across the northern tier of Alabama that borders Georgia, Mississippi, and Tennessee.

Reliant on agriculture before World War II, the district now owes its economic well-being to the federal government. Huntsville is best known for hosting the NASA Marshall Space Flight Center, but the defense industry has contributed more to its economy.

Redstone Arsenal benefited from base closures in the 1990s, incorporating Army aviation duties into its missile command center and increasing its personnel. Redstone has attracted several high-tech plants, and Cummings Research Park in Huntsville, with more than 200 tenants and a workforce of more than 20,000, boasts that it is the second-largest research park in the United States.

Tennessee Valley Authority facilities line the river's shores throughout the 5th. Boeing built a satellite rocket booster plant in Decatur in 1999, which aided the local economy. Toyota began building its first V-8 engine plant outside of Japan in Huntsville in 2001. DaimlerChrysler, the maker of Mercedes cars, has a large operation there also.

Voters in the 5th have never sent a Republican to Congress, but GOP presidential candidates have enjoyed a slight edge recently. The district generally claims a socially conservative constituency.

Major Industry

Defense, government, technology.

Notable

"Muscle Shoals Sound" originated at Fame Recording Studios, where Aretha Franklin, Otis Redding, and Wilson Pickett recorded hit songs; Helen Keller was born in Tuscumbia.

Election Returns

	Republican		Democratic		Other	
President 2000	131,608	54.0%	106,685	43.8%	5,241	2.2%
House 2002	48,226	24.7%	143,029	73.3%	3,916	2.0%

District Profile

Population   635,300

Total area (square miles)   4,688
  Land area (square miles)   4,485

Population per square mile   141.6

Counties (2000 population)

Colbert 54,984	Limestone 65,676
Jackson 53,926	Madison 276,700
Lauderdale 87,966	Morgan (pt.) 61,245
Lawrence 34,803	

Cities and other areas over 10,000 (2000 population)

Athens 18,967	Huntsville 158,216
Decatur (pt.) 44,655	Madison 29,329
Florence 36,264	Muscle Shoals 11,924
Hartselle (pt.) 12,015	Scottsboro 14,762

Race and Hispanic or Latino origin*
  White   77.7%
  Black or African American   16.9%
  American Indian or Alaska Native   0.9%
  Asian   1.0%
  Native Hawaiian or other Pacific Islander   0.0%
  Some other race   0.1%
  Hispanic or Latino origin   2.0%
  Two or more races   1.4%

As percentage of total population.

Ancestry*

English 7.6%	Italian 1.1%
French 1.3%	Scotch-Irish 2.0%
German 6.5%	Scottish 1.4%
Irish 8.0%	USA/American 16.1%

As estimated percentage of total population.

Universities and colleges, 2000–2001 enrollment
  Alabama A&M University, Normal   5,523
  Athens State University, Athens   2,662
  Faulkner University-Florence, Florence*
  J. F. Drake State Technical College, Huntsville   543
  John C. Calhoun State Community College, Decatur
  7,719
  Northwest Shoals Community College, Muscle Shoals
  3,826
  Oakwood College, Huntsville   1,767
  University of Alabama in Huntsville, Huntsville   6,563
  University of North Alabama, Florence   5,601
  Virginia College, Huntsville   446

Enrollment under 100. See Sources and Explanations in the front of the volume.

Newspapers and circulation

	District circulation	Total circulation
Athens News-Courier	7,077	7,075
Birmingham News	2,179	149,145
Birmingham News/Post Herald (Sunday)	2,180	160,856
Decatur Daily	15,131	24,437
Florence Times Daily	26,405	31,214
Huntsville Times	52,166	57,734
USA Today*	4,603	1,674,376

*See Sources and Explanations in the front of the volume.

Television stations and affiliations

Huntsville-Decatur (Florence)	100%	WAAY	ABC
Huntsville-Decatur (Florence)	100%	WAFF	NBC
Huntsville-Decatur (Florence)	100%	WFIQ	PBS
Huntsville-Decatur (Florence)	100%	WHDF	UPN
Huntsville-Decatur (Florence)	100%	WHIQ	PBS
Huntsville-Decatur (Florence)	100%	WHNT	CBS
Huntsville-Decatur (Florence)	100%	WYLE	Independent
Huntsville-Decatur (Florence)	100%	WZDX	FOX

Cable systems and subscribers

Charter   51,065
Comcast   105,146
Mediacom   3,241
New Hope Telephone Co-op   631

Military installations, September 2001

Redstone Arsenal (Army), Huntsville   22,934

Businesses and other major employers

Huntsville Health Care Authority; Huntsville; hospital   4,500

Delphi Corp.; Athens; motor vehicle parts/accessories   3,500

DaimlerChrysler Corp.; Huntsville; motor vehicle electrical equipment   3,000

Florence City Health Care Authority; Florence; hospital   2,700

Intergraph Corp.; Huntsville; computer integrated systems design   2,540

NASA; Huntsville; space research and technology   2,300

University of Alabama; Huntsville   2,139

Jays Tee Industries Inc.; Florence; knit outerwear mills   2,100

International Paper Co.; Courtland; printing and writing paper   2,000

Computer Sciences Corp.; Huntsville; commercial physical research   2,000

Teledyne Brown Engineering Inc.; Huntsville; commercial physical research   1,997

Interstate Fibernet Inc.; Huntsville; telecommunications consultant   1,750

ConAgra Poultry Co.; Athens; poultry services   1,325

U.S. Army Corps of Engineers; Huntsville   1,200

Benchmark Electronics Huntsville Inc.; Huntsville; electrical equipment and supplies   1,100

ContiGroup Companies Inc.; Decatur; poultry and poultry products   1,000

City of Decatur Health Care Authority; Decatur; hospital with residency   1,000

Tennessee Valley Authority; Decatur; electric power generation   1,000

Tennessee Valley Authority; Athens; electric services   1,000

Wise Metals Group; Muscle Shoals; primary aluminum   1,000

Maples Industries Inc.; Scottsboro; tufted rugs   1,000

United Technologies Corp.; Huntsville; space propulsion units and parts   1,000

Adtran Inc.; Huntsville; telephone and telegraph apparatus   969

SCI Systems Inc.; Huntsville; printed circuit boards   900

Alabama A&M University; Huntsville   850

BP Amoco Chemical Co.; Decatur; industrial organic chemicals   820

Sara Lee Corp.; Florence; meat packing plants   800

Computer Systems Technology Inc.; Huntsville; computer integrated systems design   800

SCI Systems Inc.; Huntsville; electronic circuits   800

Madison County; Huntsville; county supervisors' and executives' office   795

Intergraph Public Safety Inc.; Huntsville; communication equipment   773

Solutia Inc.; Decatur; acrylic fibers   750

Boeing Co.; Huntsville; guided missiles and space vehicles   700

Intergraph Process and Building Solutions Inc.; Huntsville; systems software development services   700

Acordis Industrial Fibers Inc.; Scottsboro; manmade and synthetic fiber yarns   673

Shaw Industries Inc.; Stevenson; carpet yarn   665

University of North Alabama; Florence   650

DaimlerChrysler Corp.; Huntsville; automobiles   650

Science Applications International Corp.; Huntsville; commercial research laboratory   640

Steelcase Inc.; Athens; office furniture   625

Northwest Alabama Health Care Authority; Sheffield; hospital   600

CAS Inc.; Huntsville; commercial physical research   600

PPG Industries Inc.; Huntsville; aircraft assemblies, parts   600

Goodyear Tire and Rubber Co.; Decatur; tire cord and fabrics   575

Boeing Aerospace Operations Inc.; Decatur; rocket launchers   550

City of Florence; Florence   550

Tennessee Valley Authority; Stevenson; electric power generation   550

Lozier Corp.; Scottsboro; store fixtures   525

Dynetics Inc.; Huntsville; engineering laboratory   504

Dyneon; Decatur; custom compound purchased resins   500

VF Jeanswear; Florence; men's and boys' jeans   500

Wal-Mart Stores Inc.; Florence; discount department stores   500

Tennessee Valley Authority; Muscle Shoals; agricultural research   500

Calhoun Community College; Tanner   500

Jackson County Health Care Authority; Scottsboro; hospital   500

Mead Corp.; Stevenson; paperboard mills   500
Crestwood Health Care; Huntsville; hospital   500
City of Huntsville; Huntsville; electric services   500
IDT Holdings; Huntsville; electronic/electrical circuits test equipment   500

Alabama 6th District

Central — suburban Birmingham and Tuscaloosa

Alabama's most prosperous district, the 6th is a combination of the whiter and wealthier portions of Birmingham and Tuscaloosa and their suburbs. Rural life still dots the district, but fields and forests are steadily turning into shopping malls.

Birmingham's success beginning in the 1980s started with a shift from steel to white-collar business. Banks and medical facilities have made the city a hub for the deep South. Though most of Birmingham's population is in the neighboring 7th, commuters from suburbs in the 6th enjoy the bulk of the city's wealth. Jefferson County's well-to-do, almost exclusively white bedroom communities such as Homewood, Mountain Brook, and Hoover are home to people who work in Birmingham's business district.

The 6th takes in a small portion of Tuscaloosa, a medium-size city that is starting to feel the effects of Birmingham's expansion. A nearby Mercedes-Benz plant (in the 7th District) joins the city's chemical and rubber manufacturers and adds to the district's employment base. But the area's signature undoubtedly is University of Alabama football, which attracts fanatics statewide to watch the "Crimson Tide." The campus falls just outside of the 6th's borders.

The Republican 6th moved further into the GOP column after redistricting in 2002. GOP-leaning areas in Bibb, Chilton, Coosa, and St. Clair Counties were added from the 3rd District, where Democrats hoped to gain an advantage. More Birmingham- and Tuscaloosa-area voters were shifted from the 6th into the overwhelmingly Democratic, black-majority 7th. The contrast between the 6th and 7th can lead to conflict, particularly when funds for infrastructure are at stake.

Major Industry
Banking, manufacturing, higher education.

Notable
A 55-foot cast-iron statue in Birmingham of Vulcan, the Roman god of fire and metalworking, is one of the world's largest iron figures.

Election Returns

	Republican		Democratic		Other	
President 2000	200,818	73.6%	67,975	24.9%	3,997	1.5%
House 2002	178,171	89.8%			20,175	10.2%

District Profile

Population   635,300

Total area (square miles)   4,648
  Land area (square miles)   4,564

Population per square mile   139.2

Counties (2000 population)
Bibb 20,826	Shelby 143,293
Chilton 39,593	St. Clair (pt.) 59,704
Coosa (pt.) 3,202	Tuscaloosa (pt.) 41,543
Jefferson (pt.) 327,139	

Cities and other areas over 10,000 (2000 population)
Alabaster 22,619	Hueytown (pt.) 12,921
Birmingham (pt.) 26,723	Leeds 10,455
Gardendale 11,626	Mountain Brook 20,604
Helena 10,296	Pelham 14,369
Homewood (pt.) 16,384	Trussville (pt.) 12,924
Hoover 62,742	Vestavia Hills 24,476

Race and Hispanic or Latino origin*
White   88.8%
Black or African American   7.7%
American Indian or Alaska Native   0.3%
Asian   0.9%
Native Hawaiian or other Pacific Islander   0.0%
Some other race   0.0%
Hispanic or Latino origin   1.6%
Two or more races   0.7%

As percentage of total population.

Ancestry*
Dutch 1.1%	Italian 2.0%
English 10.1%	Scotch-Irish 2.5%
French 1.6%	Scottish 2.2%
German 6.6%	USA/American 14.5%
Irish 8.1%	

As estimated percentage of total population.

Universities and colleges, 2000–2001 enrollment
Andrew Jackson University, Birmingham*
ITT Technical Institute, Birmingham   363
Samford University, Birmingham   4,379
University of Montevallo, Montevallo   3,014
Virginia College-Birmingham, Birmingham   1,656

Enrollment under 100. See Sources and Explanations in the front of the volume.

Newspapers and circulation

	District circulation	Total circulation
Birmingham News	76,142	149,145
Birmingham News/Post Herald (Sunday)	82,684	160,856
Birmingham Post Herald	6,533	11,633
Tuscaloosa News	7,645	36,423
*USA Today**	5,046	1,674,376

See Sources and Explanations in the front of the volume.

Television stations and affiliations
Birmingham (Anniston-Tuscaloosa)	94%	WABM	UPN
Birmingham (Anniston-Tuscaloosa)	94%	WBIQ	PBS
Birmingham (Anniston-Tuscaloosa)	94%	WBRC	FOX
Birmingham (Anniston-Tuscaloosa)	94%	WCFT	ABC
Birmingham (Anniston-Tuscaloosa)	94%	WDBB	WB
Birmingham (Anniston-Tuscaloosa)	94%	WIAT	CBS
Birmingham (Anniston-Tuscaloosa)	94%	WJSU	ABC
Birmingham (Anniston-Tuscaloosa)	94%	WPXH	PAX
Birmingham (Anniston-Tuscaloosa)	94%	WTJP	Independent
Birmingham (Anniston-Tuscaloosa)	94%	WTTO	WB

Birmingham (Anniston-Tuscaloosa)	94%	WVTM	NBC
Montgomery (Selma)	6%	WAIQ	PBS
Montgomery (Selma)	6%	WAKA	CBS
Montgomery (Selma)	6%	WCOV	FOX
Montgomery (Selma)	6%	WDIQ	PBS
Montgomery (Selma)	6%	WIIQ	PBS
Montgomery (Selma)	6%	WMCF	Independent
Montgomery (Selma)	6%	WNCF	ABC
Montgomery (Selma)	6%	WSFA	NBC

Cable systems and subscribers
Adelphia   1,715
Charter   86,328
Coosa Cable   8,002
SunTel Communications   602
Time Warner   4,634

Military installations, September 2001
Horace B. Hanson Army Reserve, Birmingham   720

Businesses and other major employers
University of Alabama at Birmingham; Birmingham; hospital, medical school   3,000

Coach Inc.; Birmingham; women's handbags and purses   2,700

Blue Cross and Blue Shield of Alabama; Birmingham; medical service plans   2,273

Protective Life Insurance Co.; Birmingham; life insurance   2,000

St. Vincent's Hospital; Birmingham   1,400

Medical Center East Inc.; Birmingham   1,200

Samford University; Birmingham   1,000

Washington Group International Inc.; Birmingham; engineering services   1,000

HealthSouth Corp.; Birmingham; sports medicine specialist   1,000

Accenture Inc.; Birmingham; computer consulting services   1,000

Rust Constructors Inc.; Birmingham; industrial buildings, warehouses   932

Horizon Health Care; Birmingham; outpatient rehabilitation center   900

A-1 Temporary Services of Birmingham; Birmingham; help supply services   850

EBSCO Industries Inc.; Birmingham; subscription fulfillment services   850

Gold Kist Inc.; Trussville; processed poultry   800

Infinity Insurance Co.; Birmingham; insurance agents   800

Galactic Employer Service Inc.; Birmingham; employment agencies   758

CSC Healthcare Inc.; Birmingham; management consulting   750

BE&K Inc.; Birmingham; construction and civil engineering   700

J. Gordon Gaines Inc.; Birmingham; insurance brokers   650

Baptist Health System; Birmingham; hospital management   603

Drummond Co.; Adger; coal preparation plant   600

Elastic Corp. of America Inc.; Columbiana; narrow fabric mills   600

G&R Plant Maintenance Inc.; Birmingham; building maintenance   600

Pinkerton's Inc.; Birmingham; detective, armored car services   560

Vulcan Construction Materials; Birmingham; crushed and broken limestone   550

U.S. Steel Mining Co.; Adger; coal mining   516

United Chair Co.; Leeds; office chairs   500

Sitel Corp.; Birmingham; telemarketing services   500

Alabama 7th District

West central — parts of Birmingham and Tuscaloosa

The 7th combines large portions of Birmingham and Tuscaloosa with poor, rural communities in west-central Alabama. In contrast to its white, well-to-do neighbor, the Republican 6th District, the 7th's residents tend to be lower- to middle-class blacks who vote overwhelmingly Democratic. The 7th lost its portion of Montgomery to the 3rd during 2002 redistricting, while it gained parts of Jefferson and Tuscaloosa Counties.

The 7th's part of Birmingham, the densely populated downtown area, has lagged behind the rest of the city. Still, there are signs of revitalization: old buildings are being restored into high-rent apartments.

Several steel plants and communications firms have kept district unemployment down. Near Tuscaloosa, a Mercedes-Benz plant in Vance now tops an industrial sector that complements small- to medium-size businesses. One of the district's best-known employers is the University of Alabama in Tuscaloosa.

The Black Belt, named for the traditionally rich soil in rural Alabama, accounts for the rest of the district. This poverty-filled area has not known prosperity since before the Civil War, when cotton plantation owners made fortunes from slave labor.

Power struggles between the region's existing African American political machine and a new generation of black leaders have made for interesting primaries here in recent years.

Major Industry
Agriculture, higher education, manufacturing.

Notable
Edmund Pettus Bridge in Selma was the site of "Bloody Sunday," when Alabama state troopers beat and gassed peaceful civil rights marchers on their way from Selma to Montgomery in 1965.

Election Returns

	Republican		Democratic		Other	
President 2000	78,670	32.9%	158,580	66.3%	1,827	0.8%
House 2002			153,735	92.4%	12,574	7.6%

District Profile

Population   635,300

Total area (square miles)   8,780
   Land area (square miles)   8,668

Population per square mile   73.3

Counties (2000 population)

Choctaw	15,922	Marengo	22,539
Clarke (pt.)	13,686	Perry	11,861
Dallas	46,365	Pickens (pt.)	11,547
Greene	9,974	Sumter	14,798
Hale	17,185	Tuscaloosa (pt.)	123,332
Jefferson (pt.)	334,908	Wilcox	13,183

Cities and other areas over 10,000 (2000 population)

Bessemer (pt.)	27,599	Fairfield	12,381
Birmingham (pt.)	216,097	Selma	20,512
Center Point CDP (pt.)	16,828	Tuscaloosa (pt.)	68,928

Race and Hispanic or Latino origin*

White   35.5%
Black or African American   61.7%
American Indian or Alaska Native   0.2%
Asian   0.6%
Native Hawaiian or other Pacific Islander   0.0%
Some other race   0.1%
Hispanic or Latino origin   1.3%
Two or more races   0.6%

*As percentage of total population.

Ancestry*

English	3.7%	Scotch-Irish	1.2%
German	2.4%	Subsaharan	1.2%
Irish	3.5%	USA/American	7.1%

*As estimated percentage of total population.

Universities and colleges, 2000–2001 enrollment

Bessemer State Technical College, Bessemer   1,314
Birmingham School of Law, Birmingham*
Birmingham Southern College, Birmingham   1,477
Concordia College, Selma   532
George C. Wallace State Community College, Selma 1,445
Herzing College, Birmingham   534
Jefferson State Community College, Birmingham 5,652
Judson College, Marion   321
Lawson State Community College, Birmingham   1,673
Miles College, Fairfield   1,502
Selma University, Selma*
Shelton State Community College, Tuscaloosa   5,330
Stillman College, Tuscaloosa   1,530
University of Alabama, Tuscaloosa   19,277
University of Alabama, Birmingham   14,951
University of West Alabama, Livingston   1,924

*Enrollment under 100. See Sources and Explanations in the front of the volume.

Newspapers and circulation

	District circulation	Total circulation
Birmingham News	49,827	149,145
Birmingham News/Post Herald (Sunday)	55,045	160,856
Birmingham Post Herald	5,208	11,633
Meridian Star	1,080	17,342
Mobile Register	2,651	97,781
Montgomery Advertiser	1,556	50,654
Tuscaloosa News	25,449	36,423
*USA Today**	1,702	1,674,376

*See Sources and Explanations in the front of the volume.

Television stations and affiliations

Montgomery (Selma)	41%	WAIQ	PBS
Montgomery (Selma)	41%	WAKA	CBS
Montgomery (Selma)	41%	WCOV	FOX
Montgomery (Selma)	41%	WDIQ	PBS
Montgomery (Selma)	41%	WIIQ	PBS
Montgomery (Selma)	41%	WMCF	Independent
Montgomery (Selma)	41%	WNCF	ABC
Montgomery (Selma)	41%	WSFA	NBC
Birmingham (Anniston-Tuscaloosa)	29%	WABM	UPN
Birmingham (Anniston-Tuscaloosa)	29%	WBIQ	PBS
Birmingham (Anniston-Tuscaloosa)	29%	WBRC	FOX
Birmingham (Anniston-Tuscaloosa)	29%	WCFT	ABC
Birmingham (Anniston-Tuscaloosa)	29%	WDBB	WB
Birmingham (Anniston-Tuscaloosa)	29%	WIAT	CBS
Birmingham (Anniston-Tuscaloosa)	29%	WJSU	ABC
Birmingham (Anniston-Tuscaloosa)	29%	WPXH	PAX
Birmingham (Anniston-Tuscaloosa)	29%	WTJP	Independent
Birmingham (Anniston-Tuscaloosa)	29%	WTTO	WB
Birmingham (Anniston-Tuscaloosa)	29%	WVTM	NBC
Meridian	21%	WGBC	NBC
Meridian	21%	WMDN	CBS
Meridian	21%	WTOK	ABC
Mobile-Pensacola (Ft. Walton Beach)	9%	WALA	FOX
Mobile-Pensacola (Ft. Walton Beach)	9%	WAWD	Independent
Mobile-Pensacola (Ft. Walton Beach)	9%	WEAR	ABC
Mobile-Pensacola (Ft. Walton Beach)	9%	WEIQ	PBS
Mobile-Pensacola (Ft. Walton Beach)	9%	WFGX	Independent
Mobile-Pensacola (Ft. Walton Beach)	9%	WHBR	Independent
Mobile-Pensacola (Ft. Walton Beach)	9%	WJTC	UPN
Mobile-Pensacola (Ft. Walton Beach)	9%	WKRG	CBS
Mobile-Pensacola (Ft. Walton Beach)	9%	WMPV	Independent
Mobile-Pensacola (Ft. Walton Beach)	9%	WPAN	Independent
Mobile-Pensacola (Ft. Walton Beach)	9%	WPMI	NBC
Mobile-Pensacola (Ft. Walton Beach)	9%	WSRE	PBS

Cable systems and subscribers

Adelphia   1,403
Charter   24,264
Comcast   36,129
Demopolis CATV   2,005
Galaxy   3,259
Mediacom   6,378
Northland   4,949
Sky Cablevision   1,370
Time Warner   89,050

Military installations, September 2001

Birmingham International Airport Air National Guard, Birmingham   967

Businesses and other major employers

University of Alabama at Birmingham; Birmingham 14,000
American Cast Iron Pipe Co.; Birmingham; ductile iron castings   4,400
University of Alabama; Tuscaloosa   3,950
Alabama Power Co.; Birmingham; electric power generation   3,580
DCH Healthcare Authority; Tuscaloosa; hospital   3,000
Carraway Methodist Health Systems; Birmingham; hospital with residency   2,875
U.S. Steel Corp.; Fairfield; blast furnaces and steel mills 2,500

Jefferson County; Birmingham; courts 2,500

Michelin North America Inc.; Tuscaloosa; automobile tires 2,400

U.S. Postal Service; Birmingham 2,200

Alabama Children's Hospital; Birmingham 2,070

NDCHealth Corp.; Bessemer; accounting services 2,000

U.S. Social Security Administration; Birmingham 2,000

Mercedes-Benz U.S. International Inc.; Vance; motor vehicles and car bodies 2,000

Georgia-Pacific Corp.; Pennington; sanitary paper products 2,000

Alabama Mental Health and Mental Retardation Dept.; Tuscaloosa 1,780

Pemco Aeroplex Inc.; Birmingham; aircraft servicing, repairing 1,425

U.S. Veterans Hospital; Birmingham 1,250

Marathon Oil Corp.; Fairfield; structural steel erection 1,200

Jefferson County; Birmingham; county supervisors' and executives' office 1,200

SouthTrust Bank; Birmingham; state commercial banks 1,000

International Paper Co.; Selma; paper mills 972

U.S. Dept. of Veterans Affairs; Tuscaloosa 971

BellSouth Telecommunications Inc.; Birmingham; local/long distance telephone 957

Phifer Wire Products Inc.; Tuscaloosa; screening, woven wire 950

General Welding Co.; Birmingham; welding repair 910

City of Birmingham; Birmingham; police protection 900

Saks Inc.; Birmingham; department stores 900

AmSouth Bank; Birmingham; state commercial banks 900

Buffalo Rock Co.; Birmingham; soft drinks 850

Bruno's Supermarkets Inc.; Birmingham; general warehousing, storage 825

HealthSouth Medical Center Inc.; Birmingham 800

United Parcel Service Inc.; Birmingham; courier services 800

Jefferson County; Birmingham; legislative bodies 800

Weyerhaeuser Co.; Pine Hill; container board 800

University of Alabama Health Services; Birmingham; specialty outpatient clinics 750

SouthTrust Bank; Birmingham; state commercial banks 748

Jefferson County; Birmingham; sheriffs' office 700

Dean Holding Co.; Birmingham; milk processing 700

Meadowcraft Inc.; Birmingham; metal household furniture 700

Jefferson County Hospital; Birmingham 700

Selma Public Schools; Selma 690

UAB Medical West; Bessemer; hospital 656

Deaton Inc.; Birmingham; trucking 650

Linden Lumber Co.; Linden; lumber: rough, sawed, or planed 617

Birmingham News Co.; Birmingham; newspaper 600

Event Service Providers Inc.; Birmingham; stadium event operator services 600

Pliant Corp.; Birmingham; packaging and labeling services 600

Shelton State Community College; Tuscaloosa 600

JVC America Inc.; Tuscaloosa; video recording tape 600

Shelton State Community College; Tuscaloosa 600

Wal-Mart Stores Inc.; Tuscaloosa; discount department stores 600

Jim Walter Resources Inc.; Brookwood; coal mining 576

Burns International Security Services Corp.; Birmingham; security guard service 570

HNB Auto Exchange; Birmingham; commercial banking 565

Regions Financial Corp.; Birmingham; state commercial banks 550

Allstates Technical Services; Birmingham; employment agencies 550

DCH Healthcare Authority; Northport; hospital 545

United States Pipe and Foundry Co.; Bessemer; cast iron soil pipe and fittings 544

Security Engineers Inc.; Birmingham; security guard service 516

Alabama Dept. of Transportation; Birmingham 504

Vaughan Regional Medical Center; Selma 502

Wal-Mart Stores Inc.; Bessemer; discount department stores 500

BellSouth Telecommunications Inc.; Birmingham; local/long distance telephone 500

Norfolk Southern Corp.; Birmingham; railroad freight hauling 500

U.S. Internal Revenue Service; Birmingham 500

SouthTrust Bank; Birmingham; state commercial banks 500

City of Birmingham; Birmingham; waste management agency 500

C&T Holding Inc.; Birmingham; trucking 500

Coca-Cola Bottling Company United Inc.; Birmingham; carbonated soft drinks 500

O'Neal Steel Inc.; Birmingham; iron and steel products 500

Norwood Clinic Inc.; Birmingham; specialty outpatient clinics 500

University of Birmingham; Birmingham; cardiology 500

Delphi Corp.; Tuscaloosa; motor vehicle parts/accessories 500

Gulf States Paper Corp.; Demopolis; paperboard mills 500

Southern Pride Catfish Co.; Greensboro; fresh fish 500

Alaska

laska calls itself America's last frontier, and so it surely is. Vastness of scale and rigors of climate still dominate life here, much as in the American West of the 1800s. Just as the inhabitants of the Old West felt estranged from the cities of the East, so do Alaskans feel removed from the politics and sensibilities of the "Lower 48." Alaska's remoteness belies its dependence on Washington, D.C. The state's proximity to Russia and other Asian nations makes it a military stronghold; the federal government is Alaska's largest employer.

Alaskans also share with older frontier folk a sense of life as an ongoing creation. The state has traveled far from the lawless days of its 1890s gold rush. It now ranks second in percentage of homes with personal computers and Internet access, yet it still exudes a sense of raw possibility. The people are young and adventuresome: the percentage of the population above age 65 in this state is the lowest in the nation.

Population growth has become a near constant in Alaska. Since emerging from a slump in the years after the gold rush a century ago, Alaska has seen seven straight decades of double-digit expansion and fivefold growth since 1950. Big leaps came in the 1970s and 1980s, a 20-year period in which the oil boom pushed the population up by more than 80 percent, from roughly 300,000 to 550,000.

The 1990s, a period of lower oil prices and higher frustration for Alaska's miners and loggers, brought a relatively modest net population gain of about 75,000 but still enough to keep the pressure on housing prices in Anchorage, Fairbanks, and Juneau. As a result, Alaska is no longer the state with the fewest inhabitants, a distinction it ceded to Wyoming after the 1990 census. In fact, the state is now more populous than two other states as well, having surpassed Vermont in the 2000 census and North Dakota (by a few hundred souls) in the census estimates for 2001.

Alaska will probably always be the least densely populated state. It still has only about one person per square mile, while Wyoming has five. Alaska also remains a long way from earning a second seat in Congress. The Census Bureau expects its growth to slow over the first quarter of the twenty-first century, leaving it well shy of 1 million at the 2025 mark (when states will probably need roughly 1.5 million for two districts).

Demographers note that nearly half of the state lies above the Arctic Circle, and the winter night lasts several months. Land is plentiful but most everything else in Alaska must come long distances from its point of manufacture, making this one of the six most expensive states in cost of living.

Another limit on growth is the state's continued dependence on industries of extraction, always subject to cycles of boom and bust. Oil, ore, timber, fish, and other riches from the earth and sea still provide most of the livelihood for residents. Fishing, for example, amounts to roughly half the commercial catch off the shores or in the inland waters of the United States and keeps one fourth of the workforce employed.

Oil has been a special conundrum, a cornucopia that has also been perceived as threatening the state's way of life. Some production was underway even before statehood came in 1959, but it was the historic gusher at the northern Prudhoe Bay in 1968 (the largest in U.S. history) that established the state as the northern answer to Texas. Thanks to the consequent oil royalties, Alaska's state government leads the nation in per capita measures of revenue, nontax revenue, and spending. The state was also able to scrap its sales and income taxes and provide residents with annual oil royalties.

Hopes that Alaskan oil would free the nation from dependence on foreign sources have not been borne out, however, for economic as well as political reasons. The cost and challenge of developing and transporting oil from within the Arctic Circle has been daunting—and especially discouraging in the years when oil prices dropped below $15 per barrel. The notorious 1989 oil spill from the *Exxon Valdez* tanker was an enormous setback, causing even the pro-oil enthusiasts of the state legislature to have second thoughts.

Throughout the 1990s, the memory of that ecological disaster enabled policymakers in Washington to forestall drilling in the 1.5 million acre Arctic National Wildlife Refuge, where some geologists think the next great oil and gas fields lie. Congress in the 1990s approved a first step into exploiting these fields, but it was vetoed by President Bill Clinton. But in the new decade, with oil back above $30 per barrel, pressure to drill in the refuge has intensified. The administration of George W. Bush attached almost iconic importance to the issue. But opposition to the drilling from environmentalists, empowered by the rules of the Senate that can delay action without a three-fifths majority to end filibustering, seemed likely to block the project for years to come.

Politically, Alaska citizens are the most likely of any state's to register to vote and the least inclined to register with one of the two major parties (only two in five do so). Third parties proliferate in this cold, conservative frontier state. Ross Perot received 29 percent of the vote for president here in 1992 and nearly edged out Clinton for second place. In state and local elections, substantial fractions of the vote go to such

alternatives as the Libertarian and Green Parties (which have held several seats in the legislature).

However, since the 1970s, Republicans have dominated Alaska's presidential voting and most of its congressional and legislative elections. Alaska has not elected a Democrat to Congress since 1974. The same three Republicans held the state's Senate seats and House seat from 1980 through 2002. Its congressional delegation vigorously opposed a Clinton-era rule banning road building and most logging in the Tongass National Forest, and the lawmakers have been the most outspoken advocates of opening land to oil and gas exploration.

The Democrats retain strength in some areas of the state. Residents in a few cities, the panhandle, and the sparsely populated tundra tend to vote more Democratic. The governorship in recent years has also been up for grabs—alternating between the Democratic, Republican, and Alaskan Independence Parties.

Major Industry
Oil, defense, tourism, fishing, timber, mining.

Notable
Mt. McKinley is the highest point in North America, at 20,320 feet.

Table 1　Population

District	Population	Population under 18	Voting-age population	Median age	Male*	Female*
At Large	626,932	190,717	436,215	32.4	51.7	48.3

*As percentage of total population.

Table 2　Voting-Age Persons by Race/Hispanic or Latino Origin

District	White*	Black or African American*	American Indian or Alaska Native*	Asian*	Other or multirace*	Hispanic or Latino*
At Large	71.4	3.2	13.7	4.6	3.5	3.6

*As percentage of voting-age population.

Table 3　Voting-Age Population by Age Groups

District	18 to 24*	25 to 44*	45 to 64*	Over 64*
At Large	13.1	46.7	32.0	8.2

*As percentage of voting-age population.

Table 4　Income and Occupation

District	Median family income	Families in poverty*	White collar†	Blue collar†	Service†	Farm†
At Large	$59,036	6.7	60.5	22.4	15.6	1.5

*As percentage of all families.　†As percentage of employed workers 16 years and over.

Table 5　Education: School Years Completed

District	Less than grade 9*	Grades 9–12 no diploma*	High school diploma no college*	Some college*	College bachelor's degree or higher*
At Large	4.1	7.5	27.9	35.7	24.7

*As percentage of persons age 25 and over.

Table 6　Housing and Residential Patterns

District	Median home value	Owner occupied*	Renter occupied*	Urban†	Rural†
At Large	$137,400	62.5	37.5	65.7	34.3

*As percentage of occupied housing units.　†As percentage of total population.

Election Returns

	Republican		Democratic		Other	
President 2000	167,398	58.8%	79,004	27.8%	38,090	13.4%
House 2002	169,685	74.5%	39,357	17.3%	18,683	8.2%

District Profile

Population　626,932

Total area (square miles)　663,267
　Land area (square miles)　571,951

Population per square mile　1.1

Counties (2000 population)
　Aleutians East Borough　2,697
　Aleutians West Census Area　5,465
　Anchorage Municipality　260,283
　Bethel Census Area　16,006
　Bristol Bay Borough　1,258
　Denali Borough　1,893
　Dillingham Census Area　4,922
　Fairbanks North Star Borough　82,840
　Haines Borough　2,392
　Juneau City and Borough　30,711
　Kenai Peninsula Borough　49,691
　Ketchikan Gateway Borough　14,070
　Kodiak Island Borough　13,913
　Lake and Peninsula Borough　1,823
　Matanuska-Susitna Borough　59,322
　Nome Census Area　9,196
　North Slope Borough　7,385
　Northwest Arctic Borough　7,208
　Prince of Wales-Outer Ketchikan Census Area　6,146
　Sitka City and Borough　8,835
　Skagway-Hoonah-Angoon Census Area　3,436
　Southeast Fairbanks Census Area　6,174
　Valdez-Cordova Census Area　10,195
　Wade Hampton Census Area　7,028
　Wrangell-Petersburg Census Area　6,684
　Yakutat City and Borough　808
　Yukon-Koyukuk Census Area　6,551

Cities and other areas over 10,000 (2000 population)
　Anchorage Municipality　260,283
　College CDP　11,402
　Fairbanks　30,224
　Juneau City and Borough　30,711

Race and Hispanic or Latino origin*
　White　67.6%
　Black or African American　3.4%
　American Indian or Alaska Native　15.4%
　Asian　3.9%
　Native Hawaiian or other Pacific Islander　0.5%

Some other race   0.2%
Hispanic or Latino origin   4.1%
Two or more races   4.9%

As percentage of total population.

Ancestry*

Dutch 1.4%	Norwegian 3.2%
English 7.2%	Polish 1.6%
French 2.4%	Scotch-Irish 1.4%
German 12.5%	Scottish 1.9%
Irish 8.1%	Swedish 2.0%
Italian 2.1%	USA/American 4.3%

As estimated percentage of total population.

Universities and colleges, 2000–2001 enrollment
Alaska Pacific University, Anchorage   687
Charter College, Anchorage   486
Ilisagvik College, Barrow   322
Prince William Sound Community College, Valdez   841
University of Alaska Anchorage, Anchorage   14,794
University of Alaska Fairbanks, Fairbanks   7,132
University of Alaska Fairbanks Northwest College, Nome*
University of Alaska Southeast, Juneau   3,470

Enrollment under 100. See Sources and Explanations in the front of the volume.

Newspapers and circulation

	District circulation	Total circulation
*Fairbanks Daily News-Miner**	16,373	16,373
*Homer News**	3,004	3,004

See Sources and Explanations in the front of the volume.

Television stations and affiliations

Non-DMA Area	90%	KTNL	CBS, PAX
Anchorage	8%	KAKM	PBS
Anchorage	8%	KDMD	PAX
Anchorage	8%	KIMO	ABC
Anchorage	8%	KTBY	FOX
Anchorage	8%	KTUU	NBC
Anchorage	8%	KTVA	CBS
Anchorage	8%	KYES	UPN
Fairbanks	1%	KATN	ABC
Fairbanks	1%	KFXF	FOX
Fairbanks	1%	KJNP	Independent
Fairbanks	1%	KTVF	NBC
Fairbanks	1%	KUAC	PBS
Juneau	1%	KJUD	ABC
Juneau	1%	KTOO	PBS

Cable systems and subscribers
Barrow Cable TV   761
Eyecom Inc.   1,586
GCI Cable Inc.   92,417

Military installations, September 2001
Elmendort Air Force Base, Anchorage   7,781
Fort Wainwright (Army), Fairbanks   6,392
Eielson Air Force Base, North Pole   4,088
Fort Richardson (Army), Anchorage   4,061
Kulis Air National Guard Base, Anchorage   1,245
MTA Camp Carroll (Army Guard), Fort Richardson   948
Clear Air Force Base, Anderson   152
Fort Greely (Army), Fairbanks   107

Businesses and other major employers
Providence Health System-Washington; Anchorage; hospital   3,200
University of Alaska; Fairbanks   3,154
Alaska Petroleum Contractors Inc.; Anchorage; oil field services   2,035
U.S. Postal Service; Anchorage;   2,000
Alaska Airlines Inc.; Anchorage; air passenger carrier   1,500
Federal Express Corp.; Anchorage; air cargo carrier   1,500
Banner Health System; Fairbanks; hospital   1,500
Alaska Native Tribal Health Consortium Inc.; Anchorage; social service information exchange   1,200
Indian Health Service; Anchorage   1,200
Cardinal Health; Anchorage; medical equipment and supplies   1,000
Alaska Dept. of Military and Veterans Affairs; Anchorage   1,000
U.S. Bureau of Land Management; Anchorage   1,000
Omega Enterprises; Kodiak; fishing   1,000
Alaska Dept. of Transportation and Public Facilities; Fairbanks   921
University of Alaska; Anchorage; community college   912
Trident Seafoods Corp.; Akutan; fresh or frozen packaged fish   900
Alaskan Professional Employers; Anchorage; employee leasing service   840
BP Exploration (Alaska) Inc.; Anchorage; crude petroleum production   830
GCI Communication Corp.; Anchorage; local telephone communications   788
Wells Fargo Bank Alaska; Kotzebue; commercial bank   754
North Slope Borough; Barrow; town management   743
Doyon Universal Services; Anchorage; recreation outfitters   700
Alaska Dept. of Military and Veterans Affairs; Eielson AFB   680
L. M. Berry and Co.; Anchorage; telemarketing service   650
Alaska Communications Systems Holdings Inc.; Anchorage; telephone communication   620
Galen Hospital Alaska Inc.; Anchorage   600
University of Alaska; Anchorage   600
Phillips Alaska Inc.; Prudhoe Bay; crude petroleum production   574
Phillips Alaska Inc.; Anchorage; crude petroleum pipelines   550
U.S. Army Corps of Engineers; Anchorage   550

Alaska Dept. of Transportation and Public Facilities;
Anchorage   540
Anchorage Daily News Inc.; Anchorage; newspaper
525
Juneau City and Borough; Juneau; city management
510
Alascom Inc.; Anchorage; local telephone
communications   500
Peninsula Airways Inc.; Anchorage; airline passenger
carrier   500

U.S. Dept. of the Interior; Anchorage   500
Veco Alaska Inc.; Anchorage; construction and civil
engineering   500
Alyeska Pipeline Service Co.; Anchorage; crude
petroleum pipelines   500
Yukon-Kuskokwim Health Corp.; Bethel; hospital   500
Alaska Dept. of Labor and Workforce Development;
Dillingham; social and manpower programs   500
Kenai Peninsula Borough School District; Soldotna
500

ARIZONA

Districts established October 12, 2001, for elections first held in 2002.

8 members

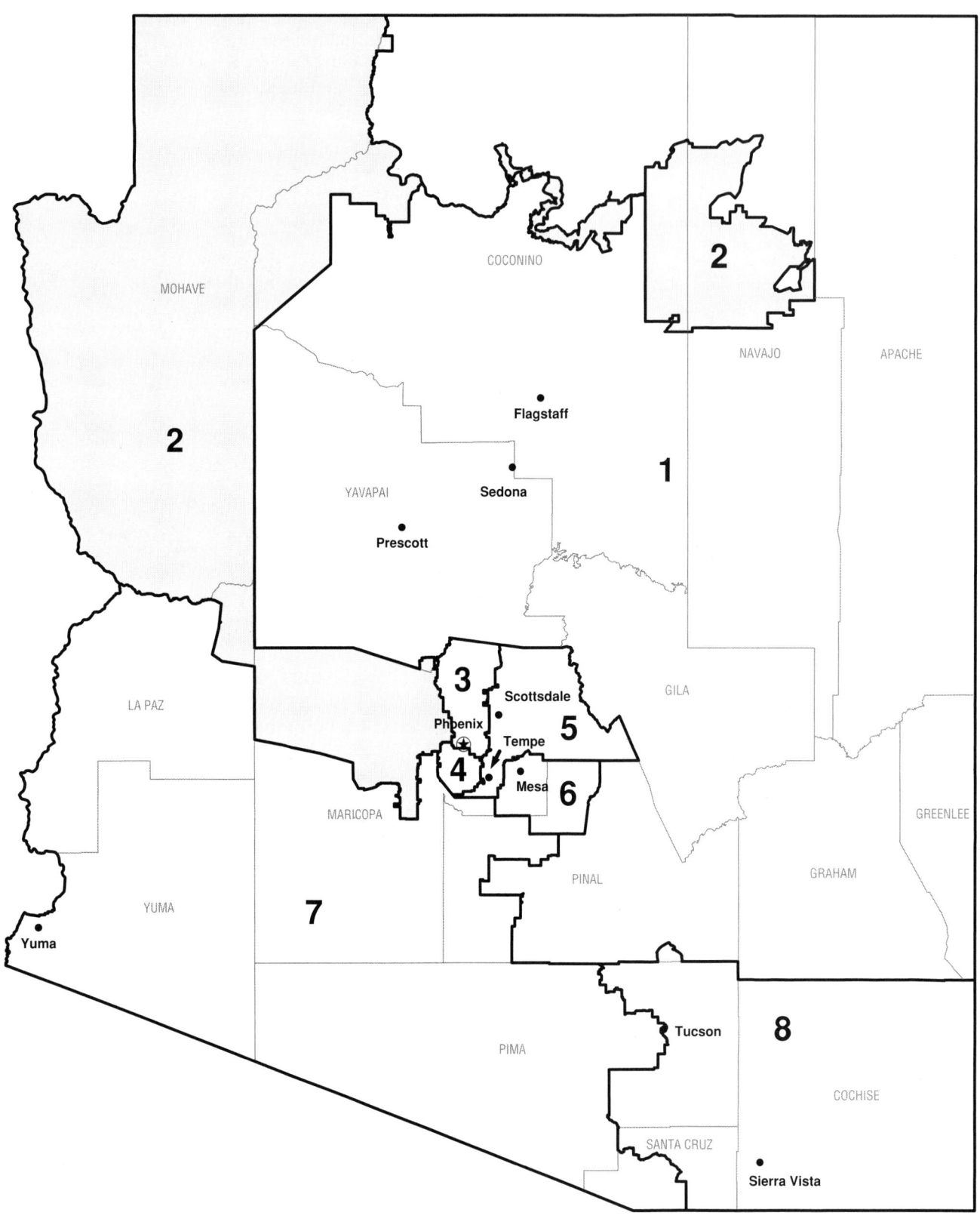

Arizona

Not long ago, one went to Arizona for the Grand Canyon or for the dry, clean air. But the denizens of the East and the Midwest who once thought of Arizona strictly as vacation or retirement territory are now often stunned to learn it is entitled to as much of Congress as their home states. In the 2000 census it drew even with Maryland and Minnesota with eight seats; and if it grew as much by 2010, it would overtake Missouri and Massachusetts with ten.

Many states have been transformed since World War II by the boon of air conditioning, the increasing mobility of auto-borne families, and the renewal of robust immigration. But no state has seen quite so potent a combination of all three as Arizona. California and Florida grabbed the nation's attention by tripling and quintupling their numbers, respectively, in the postwar years, but Arizona over the same period grew even faster. There were 750,000 Arizonans at midcentury, and 5 million in 2000. Only Nevada, rising from a far smaller base, has grown more rapidly over the same time period.

Arizona's growth has been concentrated in the Valley of the Sun, the metroplex of Phoenix-Scottsdale-Tempe-Mesa, which leaped by 45 percent in the single decade of the 1990s to reach 3.3 million people. This area now supports, entirely or in part, five congressional districts, roughly the same as the city of Chicago or the borough of Manhattan. Once described as Los Angeles without the ocean, the Phoenix area is so spread out that it hardly seems to have an urban core. Yet Phoenix proper is now the sixth largest city in America (1.3 million), and a candidate to supplant Philadelphia in fifth place by 2010. To measure how remarkable this would be, consider that Phoenix had a little more than 100,000 inhabitants in 1950, when Philadelphia had more than 2 million.

For decades Phoenix served as the farm team town for San Francisco's baseball Giants, until the city gained its franchise, the Arizona Diamondbacks, in the 1990s. Surely the city's statement of arrival in the national consciousness was made when that expansion team rose up to dethrone the New York Yankees in the World Series of 2001.

But Arizona is less likely to grow at these rates in the new century. Recently, ecologists and other scientists have issued warnings about the state's overreliance on imported water, the increase in air pollution, and the arrival of airborne irritants such as pollen that residents once came here to escape. Still, the pace of growth has seemed to accelerate.

Arizona's population growth has had three sources. Since the 1950s, the state has been a magnet for eastern and midwestern retirees, who came seeking warmer winters and cleaner air. But the state has also seen its general economy boom with electronic manufacturing, attracting younger transplants from other states. They have come from overcrowded southern California, the snowbound Upper Midwest, the boom-and-bust of Texas, and the Deep South. So the median age (34.2) is now among the eight lowest in the country, while the percentage of people sixty-five and older is right in the middle of the pack.

Arizona has also looked like a step up for hundreds of thousands of new residents from the Spanish-speaking countries to the South. The Hispanic influx has mostly come from Mexico but with strong strains of Central and South American nationals as well. The Hispanic population rose from 440,000 in 1980 to 700,000 in 1990 and to more than 1 million in 2000. Arizona is now fourth in the nation in percentage of Hispanic residents (25 percent).

These three streams have given the state some of its mixed political character. Many of the retirees are affluent suburbanites who have transferred here with their Republican affinities intact. Likewise many of the younger arrivals are independent and entrepreneurial in spirit, making them responsive to Republican economics. But the Hispanic immigrants have tended to follow the pattern of their predecessors in preferring the Democratic Party.

These patterns have been evident in the results of the redrawn political maps over the decades of growth. Districts drawn around central Phoenix and Tucson have produced majorities for Democrats and recently for Hispanic Democrats. The more suburban venues have been generally Republican. Democrats had hoped there would also be enough Hispanic, Native American, and rural Democratic voters in the rest of the state to produce another competitive race or two. But these hopes, expressed in the 2000 redistricting plan, were not borne out in the 2002 election.

The remapping process was run by a nonpartisan commission that nonetheless did a solid job of protecting all the incumbents. The commission also created a rural east-northern 1st District the size of the state of Pennsylvania, which provided the state's best competition. In 2002 the 1st elected a Republican and the 2nd District elected a new Republican to succeed its retiring GOP incumbent. The four Republicans seeking reelection all won.

Democrats elected their first Hispanic member in Ed Pastor, who won in 1991, succeeding the Democratic icon Morris Udall in a district drawn to include Spanish-speaking neighborhoods in Phoenix and Tucson. Nowadays the 4th District is entirely within Maricopa (Phoenix) County, and almost 65 percent of its voting age population is composed of Hispanics and other minorities. The state's other majority Hispanic district is the newly drawn 7th District, which includes western portions of the Tucson area and the entire southwestern fifth of the state.

In the near future, Democrats can look ahead to regaining the 1st District and contesting the 8th District. The 8th was nearly a dead heat between the presidential candidates in 2000. A win in these two districts would give the Democrats parity in the House delegation.

Through all its burgeoning decades, Arizona has maintained much of its political character. It has a bipartisan heritage, thanks in part to new residents from the states of Dixie, who settled in rural areas and became known locally as "pinto Democrats." The state's first brace of senators in 1912 were Democrats, and they were followed by the legendary Democrat Carl Hayden, who served seven terms in the Senate from 1927 to 1969.

Democrats have held their own here in recent gubernatorial elections, and the legislature has seesawed between the parties. But the state's image remains distinctly Republican, largely on the basis of presidential politics and the tilt in the congressional delegation since 1994.

Arizona was the only state to have voted Republican in every presidential election from 1952 through 1992. Bill Clinton managed to carry the state narrowly in 1996, largely because of the continuing popularity of maverick Ross Perot, who received 8 percent here even in his second, less successful bid for the presidency. The state returned to its GOP habit in the presidential contest of 2000, when George W. Bush managed a majority of 51 percent.

Along the way, Arizona has been known for the remarkable career of Republican Barry Goldwater, scion of a wealthy Phoenix retailing family, who first came to the Senate in 1952 and was the GOP nominee for president in 1964. He lost every state but Arizona and the Deep South to Lyndon B. Johnson that year but returned to the Senate after Hayden retired and served another 18 years. Unlike others who lost by lopsided margins in presidential elections, Goldwater remained a figure of pride at home and among conservatives generally. He was succeeded by John McCain, a highly decorated Navy pilot and Vietnam POW who would make a bid for the White House of his own in 2000.

McCain shared with Goldwater an image of independence that subordinated their strong conservative principles at times to a kind of Western libertarianism. Goldwater spoke out against his party's strict antiabortion stand in his later years, causing the state party to remove his name from the headquarters building. McCain has had so many rows with party leaders in his home state that he cannot count on winning nomination for a fourth term without an intraparty rival.

It also is noteworthy that three of the state's last four governors have been women. The most recent, Janet Napolitano, is the first to enter office by election, rather than as the successor to an incumbent who resigned.

Table 1 Population

District	Population	Population under 18	Voting-age population	Median age	Male*	Female*
1	641,329	180,555	460,774	35.3	50.8	49.2
2	641,329	153,610	487,719	39.9	48.9	51.1
3	641,329	160,418	480,911	35.0	49.8	50.2
4	641,329	211,241	430,088	27.1	52.0	48.0
5	641,329	145,162	496,167	34.0	49.8	50.2
6	641,329	178,915	462,414	34.1	49.3	50.7
7	641,329	190,263	451,066	30.8	49.7	50.3
8	641,329	146,783	494,546	39.1	49.0	51.0
State	5,130,632	1,366,947	3,763,685	34.2	49.9	50.1

*As percentage of total population.

Table 2 Voting-Age Persons by Race/Hispanic or Latino Origin

District	White*	Black or African American*	American Indian or Alaska Native*	Asian*	Other or multirace*	Hispanic or Latino*
1	64.3	1.3	18.0	0.7	1.0	14.8
2	82.1	1.9	1.8	1.8	1.1	11.4
3	81.4	2.1	1.1	2.2	1.3	11.9
4	35.6	7.3	2.3	1.6	1.4	51.8
5	79.7	2.5	1.6	3.4	1.5	11.3
6	80.1	1.8	0.7	1.9	1.0	14.4
7	45.3	2.7	4.7	1.6	1.2	44.5
8	77.6	2.8	0.8	2.2	1.4	15.3
State	69.0	2.7	3.8	1.9	1.2	21.3

*As percentage of voting-age population.

Table 3 Voting-Age Population by Age Groups

District	18 to 24*	25 to 44*	45 to 64*	Over 64*
1	13.4	36.1	31.4	19.1
2	9.5	34.1	29.5	26.9
3	12.2	43.6	30.4	13.8
4	19.3	47.8	22.8	10.1
5	15.5	42.9	28.3	13.2
6	11.6	41.9	26.3	20.1
7	17.1	39.8	27.0	16.1
8	11.3	35.8	31.1	21.8
State	13.7	40.2	28.4	17.7

*As percentage of voting-age population.

Table 4 Income and Occupation

District	Median family income	Families in poverty*	White collar†	Blue collar†	Service†	Farm†
1	$38,113	15.0	53.5	25.6	19.7	1.2
2	$49,150	5.9	60.3	22.2	16.9	0.6
3	$57,053	5.7	68.2	17.7	13.9	0.2
4	$31,933	21.1	43.8	35.7	20.0	0.5
5	$63,729	4.8	73.1	14.2	12.6	0.1
6	$53,537	5.4	63.3	22.6	13.7	0.4
7	$34,287	17.2	51.4	26.8	19.6	2.2
8	$49,568	7.3	66.7	16.5	16.4	0.4
State	$46,723	9.9	61.2	21.9	16.2	0.6

*As percentage of all families.   †As percentage of employed workers 16 years and over.

Table 5 Education: School Years Completed

District	Less than grade 9*	Grades 9–12 no diploma*	High school diploma no college*	Some college*	College bachelor's degree or higher*
1	9.1	13.6	27.2	32.6	17.5
2	4.6	11.3	29.1	35.7	19.3
3	4.1	8.1	22.3	35.2	30.3
4	21.4	19.5	24.7	24.1	10.2
5	2.8	5.5	17.9	34.3	39.6
6	5.1	9.5	25.1	36.7	23.6
7	15.0	17.0	26.7	28.1	13.3
8	3.9	7.5	21.9	36.0	30.6
State	7.8	11.2	24.3	33.1	23.5

*As percentage of persons age 25 and over.

Table 6 Housing and Residential Patterns

District	Median home value	Owner occupied*	Renter occupied*	Urban†	Rural†
1	$87,600	71.5	28.5	55.5	44.5
2	$109,500	79.3	20.7	89.0	11.0
3	$132,700	66.5	33.5	96.5	3.5
4	$77,500	50.7	49.3	99.5	0.5
5	$152,900	63.0	37.0	97.2	2.8
6	$123,400	77.4	22.6	96.8	3.2
7	$76,300	66.1	33.9	83.6	16.4
8	$115,500	67.1	32.9	87.3	12.7
State	$109,400	68.0	32.0	88.2	11.8

*As percentage of occupied housing units.   †As percentage of total population.

Arizona 1st District

North and east — Flagstaff, Prescott, Navajo reservation

A mix of rural conservatives, artistic liberals, and dependably Democratic Navajo voters makes for unpredictable elections in the immense 1st. However, this mix does not mean the residents have nothing in common.

Tired of being represented by politicians in Phoenix and Mesa, the eight counties of the 1st pushed hard for a district of their own when the state was awarded two new House seats following the 2000 census. Neither party has a distinct voter registration advantage in the 58,608-square-mile swath of Arizona, larger than 30 states, but nearly all locals call themselves environmentalists in a district that includes both sides of the Grand Canyon.

The district, which mostly follows county lines, is missing a chunk of land in its northern section to avoid placing the Hopi Nation in the same district as the Navajo Nation. The two tribes have historical land disputes. To connect the Hopi land with the western Arizona-based 2nd District, mapmakers sliced the Colorado River from the 1st where it cuts through the Grand Canyon. The district has the largest Native American population (22.1 percent) in the nation.

The 1st, home to great natural beauty, tribal lands, and the city of Sedona, felt its tourist economy suffer during the recession that began in the late-1990s. The 1st also faced drought and then forest fires in 2002, wounding the logging industry and straining the resources of local governments in the north.

Major Industry
Tourism, copper mining, logging.

Notable
Arizona's most significant Civil War battle took place at Picacho Peak; Lowell Observatory, in Flagstaff, is where Clyde Tombaugh discovered Pluto in 1930.

Election Returns

	Republican		Democratic		Other	
President 2000	102,068	50.5%	91,920	45.5%	7,931	3.9%
House 2002	85,967	49.2%	79,730	45.6%	8,990	5.1%

District Profile

Population   641,329

Total area (square miles)   58,713
   Land area (square miles)   58,608

Population per square mile   10.9

Counties (2000 population)
Apache   69,423   Greenlee   8,547
Coconino (pt.)   114,795   Navajo (pt.)   91,658
Gila   51,335   Pinal (pt.)   104,566
Graham   33,489   Yavapai (pt.)   167,516

Cities and other areas over 10,000 (2000 population)
Casa Grande   25,224
Cottonwood-Verde Village CDP   10,610
Eloy   10,375
Flagstaff   52,894
Florence town   17,054
Payson town   13,620
Prescott   33,938
Prescott Valley town   23,535
Sedona   10,192

Race and Hispanic or Latino origin*
White   58.4%
Black or African American   1.2%
American Indian or Alaska Native   22.1%
Asian   0.5%
Native Hawaiian or other Pacific Islander   0.1%
Some other race   0.1%
Hispanic or Latino origin   16.4%
Two or more races   1.2%

*As percentage of total population.

Ancestry*
Dutch   1.2%   Norwegian   1.5%
English   8.7%   Polish   1.2%
French   2.0%   Scotch-Irish   1.3%
German   10.3%   Scottish   1.6%
Irish   7.1%   Swedish   1.3%
Italian   2.1%   USA/American   3.9%

*As estimated percentage of total population.

Universities and colleges, 2000–2001 enrollment
Central Arizona College, Coolidge   4,536
Coconino County Community College, Flagstaff   3,167
Din'e College, Tsaile   1,712
Eastern Arizona College, Thatcher   6,223
Northern Arizona University, Flagstaff   19,964

Northland Pioneer College, Holbrook 5,096
Prescott College, Prescott 904
Yavapai College, Prescott 7,915

Newspapers and circulation

	District circulation	Total circulation
Arizona Daily Star	1,984	100,725
Arizona Daily Sun	11,317	11,448
Arizona Republic	36,723	470,415
Casa Grande Dispatch	3,875	9,054
Gallup Independent	5,401	15,519
Mesa East Valley Tribune	2,588	100,990
Tucson Citizen	2,120	138,692
*USA Today**	3,178	1,674,376

See Sources and Explanations in the front of the volume.

Television stations and affiliations

Phoenix (Prescott)	86%	KAET	PBS
Phoenix (Prescott)	86%	KASW	WB
Phoenix (Prescott)	86%	KNAZ	NBC
Phoenix (Prescott)	86%	KNXV	ABC
Phoenix (Prescott)	86%	KPAZ	Independent
Phoenix (Prescott)	86%	KPHO	CBS
Phoenix (Prescott)	86%	KPNX	NBC
Phoenix (Prescott)	86%	KSAZ	FOX
Phoenix (Prescott)	86%	KTVA	Independent
Phoenix (Prescott)	86%	KTVK	Independent
Phoenix (Prescott)	86%	KUTP	UPN
Albuquerque-Santa Fe	14%	KASA	FOX
Albuquerque-Santa Fe	14%	KASY	UPN
Albuquerque-Santa Fe	14%	KAZQ	Independent
Albuquerque-Santa Fe	14%	KBIM	CBS
Albuquerque-Santa Fe	14%	KCHF	Independent
Albuquerque-Santa Fe	14%	KENW	PBS
Albuquerque-Santa Fe	14%	KHFT	UPN
Albuquerque-Santa Fe	14%	KLUZ	Univision
Albuquerque-Santa Fe	14%	KNAT	Independent
Albuquerque-Santa Fe	14%	KNME	PBS
Albuquerque-Santa Fe	14%	KOAT	ABC
Albuquerque-Santa Fe	14%	KOBF	NBC
Albuquerque-Santa Fe	14%	KOBR	NBC
Albuquerque-Santa Fe	14%	KOB	NBC
Albuquerque-Santa Fe	14%	KOCT	ABC
Albuquerque-Santa Fe	14%	KOVT	ABC
Albuquerque-Santa Fe	14%	KREZ	CBS
Albuquerque-Santa Fe	14%	KRPV	Independent
Albuquerque-Santa Fe	14%	KRQE	CBS

Cable systems and subscribers

Cable America 1,292
Cable ONE 105,214
Cablevision 27,008
Citizens Utility 3,850
Cox 4,502
Eagle West 10,036
Indevideo 2,585
San Carlos Cablevision 1,260

Businesses and other major employers

Northern Arizona University; Flagstaff 2,800
Phelps Dodge Morenci Inc.; Morenci; copper ore 2,600
Northern Arizona Healthcare Corp.; Flagstaff; business management 1,500
Navajo Nation Tribal Government; Window Rock 1,500
Asarco Inc.; Hayden; primary copper 1,370
Arizona Dept. of Corrections; Florence 1,100
Abitibi Consolidated Sales Corp.; Snowflake; kraft linerboard and printing paper 1,050
BHP Copper North American; San Manuel; primary copper 1,000
American Youth Soccer Organization; Flagstaff; soccer club 1,000
Amfac Resorts; Grand Canyon; transportation ticket offices 1,000
U.S. National Park Service; Grand Canyon 1,000
Peabody Coal Co.; Kayenta; business management 1,000
Yavapai Community Hospital Assn. Prescott 1,000
Flagstaff Medical Center Inc.; Flagstaff 985
RPM Management Inc.; Sedona; resort hotel 968
Yavapai Community College; Prescott 906
Phelps Dodge Miami Inc.; Claypool; underground copper ore mining 900
Yavapai County; Prescott; government 773
Pinal County Community College District; Coolidge 755
Evergreen Air Center Inc.; Marana; restaurant 702
Arizona Dept. of Corrections; Winslow 700
Salt River Project Agricultural Improvement and Power District; Page; electric power distribution 698
Kellogg Brown and Root Inc.; Morenci; industrial plant construction 687
BHP Copper Inc.; Miami; copper ore 650
Casa Grande Community Hospital; Casa Grande 625
Arizona Dept. of Economic Security; Coolidge 600
Arizona Dept. of Corrections; Safford 600
Indian Health Service; Tuba City 600
Prescott Unified School District; Prescott 600
Northern Arizona VA Health Care System; Prescott; veterans' organization 600
Yavapai Apache Nation; Camp Verde; casino hotel 600
National Bank of Arizona; Sedona; commercial bank 561
Northern Arizona Council of Governments; Flagstaff 550
Metal Industries Inc.; Prescott Valley; metal storm doors or windows 550
Phelps Dodge Bagdad Inc.; Bagdad; copper ore 550
Wal-Mart Stores Inc.; Show Low; discount department stores 535
Hexcel Corp.; Casa Grande; metal stampings 530
Burlington Northern and Santa Fe Railway Co.; Winslow; railroad freight hauling 525
Sonora Quest Laboratories; Pinetop; medical laboratories 521
Navapache Health Care Assn. Inc.; Show Low; hospital 510
Eurofresh Inc.; Willcox; tomato farm 500
Arizona Dept. of Corrections; Willcox 500
Arizona Dept. of Transportation; Flagstaff 500
Sodexho Operations; Flagstaff; eating places 500

Arizona 2nd District

Northwest and central — most of Glendale, Peoria, Lake Havasu City; Hopi reservation

Although the 2nd spans the northwestern corner of Arizona, Republicans living in the fast-growing Phoenix suburbs in the district's southeast dominate its politics. This area, which includes a small portion of the city itself, takes in suburbs such as Peoria, most of Glendale, and the retirement community of Sun City. It is home to the vast majority of the 2nd's voters.

Most of the district's land is in Mohave County, where Lake Havasu City, Bullhead City, and Kingman are located. Democrats maintain isolated areas of influence among Native Americans in the northwest, where younger, lower-income, and larger minority populations live. Overall, the district is almost 80 percent white and gave Republican George W. Bush 56.5 percent of the vote in the 2000 presidential election.

The 2nd also includes the Hopi reservation, an appendage separated from the surrounding Navajo reservation (located in the 1st). To reach the Hopi land, the 2nd follows the Colorado River through the Grand Canyon, though both sides of the canyon are in the 1st.

The district's economy, once grounded in agriculture, has diversified to include manufacturing jobs in the aerospace, electronics, communications, and chemical industries. Diversification helped soften the blow of the early-2000s recession.

Major Industry

Retail, manufacturing, tourism.

Notable

Lake Havasu City has been home to the old London Bridge since 1971; the Phoenix Coyotes hockey team was scheduled to move into a new arena in Glendale in 2003.

Election Returns

	Republican		Democratic		Other	
President 2000	119,386	56.5%	86,251	40.8%	5,760	2.7%
House 2002	100,359	59.9%	61,217	36.5%	5,296	3.5%

District Profile

Population   641,329

Total area (square miles)   20,391
  Land area (square miles)   20,219

Population per square mile   31.7

Counties (2000 population)

Coconino (pt.) 1,525	Mohave 155,032
La Paz (pt.) 23	Navajo (pt.) 5,812
Maricopa (pt.) 478,936	Yavapai (pt.) 1

Cities and other areas over 10,000 (2000 population)
  Bullhead City   33,769
  Glendale (pt.)   146,483
  Goodyear   18,911
  Kingman   20,069
  Lake Havasu City   41,938
  Mohave Valley CDP   13,694
  New Kingman-Butler CDP   14,810
  Peoria   108,364
  Phoenix (pt.)   47,199
  Sun City CDP   38,309
  Sun City West CDP   26,344
  Surprise   30,848

Race and Hispanic or Latino origin*
  White   78.4%
  Black or African American   2.1%
  American Indian or Alaska Native   2.0%
  Asian   1.7%
  Native Hawaiian or other Pacific Islander   0.1%
  Some other race   0.1%
  Hispanic or Latino origin   14.2%
  Two or more races   1.4%

As percentage of total population.

Ancestry*

Dutch 1.5%	Norwegian 1.9%
English 9.4%	Polish 2.4%
French 2.7%	Scotch-Irish 1.4%
German 14.6%	Scottish 1.6%
Irish 9.3%	Swedish 1.7%
Italian 4.0%	USA/American 4.5%

As estimated percentage of total population.

Universities and colleges, 2000–2001 enrollment
  American Graduate School of International Management, Glendale   1,639
  Estrella Mountain Community College, Litchfield Park   4,300
  Glendale Community College, Glendale   20,091
  Midwestern University, Glendale   979
  Mohave Community College, Kingman   5,883

Newspapers and circulation

	District circulation	Total circulation
Arizona Republic	90,369	470,415
Mesa East Valley Tribune	17,022	100,990
Mohave Valley Daily News	6,839	7,439
*USA Today**	8,768	1,674,376

See Sources and Explanations in the front of the volume.

Television stations and affiliations

Phoenix (Prescott)	100%	KAET	PBS
Phoenix (Prescott)	100%	KASW	WB
Phoenix (Prescott)	100%	KNAZ	NBC
Phoenix (Prescott)	100%	KNXV	ABC
Phoenix (Prescott)	100%	KPAZ	Independent
Phoenix (Prescott)	100%	KPHO	CBS
Phoenix (Prescott)	100%	KPNX	NBC
Phoenix (Prescott)	100%	KSAZ	FOX
Phoenix (Prescott)	100%	KTVA	Independent
Phoenix (Prescott)	100%	KTVK	Independent
Phoenix (Prescott)	100%	KUTP	UPN

Cable systems and subscribers
  Cable America   2,044
  Cablevision   30,366
  Cox   37,151

Military installations, September 2001
Luke Air Force Base, Litchfield Park   7,172

Businesses and other major employers
Honeywell International Inc.; Glendale; aircraft flight
instruments   5,000
Banner Health System; Glendale; hospital   1,900
Sun Health Corp.; Sun City; hospital   1,200
Honeywell International Inc.; Glendale; guided missile,
space vehicle parts   800
Arizona Dept. of Corrections; Goodyear   700
Wal-Mart Stores Inc.; Surprise; warehouse club stores
650
Kingman Hospital Inc.; Kingman   626
Del Webb Corp.; Surprise; subdividers and developers
610
American Drug Stores Inc.; Glendale; drug stores   600
City of Peoria; Peoria; city and town management   600
PHC-Lake Havasu Inc.; Lake Havasu City; hospital
550
McLane/Sunwest Inc.; Goodyear; discount department
stores   500
Freedom Plaza Limited Partnership; Peoria; apartment
building operators   500

Arizona 3rd District

Northern Phoenix; Paradise Valley

Encompassing a large northern chunk of Phoenix and the
hills and suburbs north of the city, the 3rd has the state's
least number of minorities—78.5 percent of its residents are
white. Still, the district is changing with the rest of the state
as the number of Hispanics increases.

Nearly half of the district's voters are registered Republicans who consistently support economically and socially
conservative candidates at the local and federal levels. The
district, numbered the 4th until redistricting following the
2000 census, supported GOP candidates in presidential contests in the 1990s and 2000, with George W. Bush capturing
54.5 percent of the vote in 2000.

Democrats are concentrated in the southern part of the
3rd, where the district extends to downtown Phoenix. Seeds
of liberalism also are developing in the more rural sections
north of Phoenix, as young professionals move into planned
communities such as New River.

The entire Phoenix area experienced explosive growth during the 1990s. The city itself (divided among five congressional districts) grew by almost one-third, and even small
Cave Creek north of the city grew by more than one-fourth.
The area is home to many manufacturing companies, including producers of semiconductors, electronics, and aerospace
equipment. Aerospace manufacturer Honeywell has a division headquarters in the 3rd.

Many of the state's most affluent and politically active residents live east of Phoenix in the posh community of Paradise
Valley, where the median household income is more than
$150,000. The town is exclusively zoned for single-family
residential use and collects no property taxes.

Major Industry
Technology, manufacturing, electronics.

Notable
Locally brewed Cave Creek Chili Beer has a pepper in every
bottle; Carefree is home to a giant sundial that locals call the
third-largest working sundial in the Western Hemisphere.

Election Returns

	Republican		Democratic		Other	
President 2000	114,259	54.5%	89,308	42.6%	6,140	2.9%
House 2002	104,847	67.3%	47,173	30.3%	3,731	2.4%

District Profile

Population   641,329

Total area (square miles)   598
Land area (square miles)   598

Population per square mile   1,071.7

Counties (2000 population)
Maricopa (pt.)   641,329

Cities and other areas over 10,000 (2000 population)
New River CDP   10,740
Paradise Valley town   13,664
Phoenix (pt.)   603,604

Race and Hispanic or Latino origin*
White   78.5%
Black or African American   2.3%
American Indian or Alaska Native   1.2%
Asian   2.1%
Native Hawaiian or other Pacific Islander   0.1%
Some other race   0.1%
Hispanic or Latino origin   14.1%
Two or more races   1.6%

*As percentage of total population.

Ancestry*

Dutch 1.4%	Norwegian 1.9%
English 8.6%	Polish 2.7%
French 2.5%	Scotch-Irish 1.3%
German 14.5%	Scottish 1.7%
Irish 10.0%	Swedish 1.6%
Italian 4.8%	USA/American 3.6%

*As estimated percentage of total population.

Universities and colleges, 2000–2001 enrollment
Apollo College, Phoenix   1,013
Arizona State University-West, Phoenix   5,325
Art Institute of Phoenix, Phoenix   1,070
Clinton Technical Institute, Phoenix   1,503
Devry University, Phoenix   3,705
Keller Graduate School of Management, Phoenix   364
Ottawa University, Phoenix   2,171
Paradise Valley Community College, Phoenix   7,000
Western International University, Phoenix   1,520

Newspapers and circulation

	District circulation	Total circulation
Arizona Republic	98,124	470,415
Mesa East Valley Tribune	3,128	100,990
*USA Today**	1,876	1,674,376

*See Sources and Explanations in the front of the volume.

Television stations and affiliations

Phoenix (Prescott)	100%	KAET	PBS
Phoenix (Prescott)	100%	KASW	WB
Phoenix (Prescott)	100%	KNAZ	NBC
Phoenix (Prescott)	100%	KNXV	ABC
Phoenix (Prescott)	100%	KPAZ	Independent
Phoenix (Prescott)	100%	KPHO	CBS
Phoenix (Prescott)	100%	KPNX	NBC
Phoenix (Prescott)	100%	KSAZ	FOX
Phoenix (Prescott)	100%	KTVA	Independent
Phoenix (Prescott)	100%	KTVK	Independent
Phoenix (Prescott)	100%	KUTP	UPN

Cable systems and subscribers

Cox   5,779
Eagle West   619

Businesses and other major employers

Honeywell International Inc.; Phoenix; aircraft engines and parts   5,000

American Express Travel Related Services Co.; Phoenix; credit card service   4,500

Cox Communications Inc.; Phoenix; data processing   2,000

Honeywell Inc.; Phoenix; process control instruments   2,000

Honeywell International Inc.; Phoenix; search and navigation equipment   2,000

John C. Lincoln Health Network; Phoenix; hospital   1,703

Sheraton Phoenician Corp.; Scottsdale; resort hotel   1,700

Hilton Hotels Corp.; Phoenix; hotels   1,672

Cafe and Ice Cream Phoenician; Scottsdale; carry-out restaurant   1,300

Suntron Corp.; Phoenix; computer peripheral equipment   1,248

AZB Partnership; Phoenix; resort hotel   1,200

NDC Health Inc.; Phoenix; health and allied services   1,200

KSI Arizona Biltmore Resort Inc.; Phoenix; resort hotel   1,150

Blue Cross and Blue Shield of Arizona; Phoenix; hospital/medical service plans   1,147

Sears Roebuck and Co. Inc.; Phoenix; credit card services, collection   1,000

Honeywell International Inc.; Phoenix; electronic circuits   1,000

Honeywell International Inc.; Phoenix; rebuilding engines and transmissions   1,000

AG Communication Systems Corp.; Phoenix; telephone switching equipment   946

American Express Travel Related Services Co.; Phoenix; travel agency   900

Cigna Healthcare of Arizona Inc.; Phoenix; health maintenance organization   900

Mayo Clinic; Phoenix   900

Destination Resorts Inc.; Phoenix; personnel management   871

Camelback Inn Assn. LP; Scottsdale; apartment building operators   860

Karsten Manufacturing Corp.; Phoenix; golf equipment   840

Marriott International Inc.; Scottsdale; hotels   800

Western International University; Phoenix   700

Cox Communications Inc.; Phoenix; cable television   700

STMicroelectronics Inc.; Phoenix; semiconductors and related devices   628

Wyndham International Inc.; Carefree; resort hotel   600

Safeway Inc.; Phoenix; supermarkets   575

Weisheimer Companies Inc.; Phoenix; pet food   557

Hypercom Corp.; Phoenix; computer peripheral equipment   544

Charles Schwab and Co. Inc.; Phoenix; security brokers, dealers, flotation companies   500

TP Racing; Phoenix; race track operation   500

Pete King Corp.; Phoenix; painting and paper hanging   500

Arizona State University; Phoenix   500

Honeywell International Inc.; Phoenix; missile guidance systems   500

Hypercom Corp.; Phoenix; electronic computers   500

ING Life Insurance and Annuity Co.; Phoenix; life insurance   500

Arizona 4th District

Downtown and south Phoenix; part of Glendale

Centered around Phoenix in Arizona's rapidly growing "Valley of the Sun," the Hispanic-majority 4th remains a Democratic stronghold in a generally Republican state.

The district is dominated by lower-income neighborhoods in downtown Phoenix that tend to elect Democrats. These areas have been undergoing a slow economic change in the last few years as more white-collar workers buy up housing, but the influx has yet to shake the 4th's solidly liberal base.

The 4th's portion of the city includes the Phoenix airport (one of the nation's busiest), the state capitol, the Heard Museum of Native American art and culture, Mystery Castle, and shopping complexes, including Arizona Center and Desert Sky Mall. Bank One Ballpark and America West Arena, home to most of the Phoenix sports teams, are here, and health care jobs also aid the economy.

Glendale—shared with the 2nd District—is a conservative, prosperous community that nearly doubled its population during the 1990s. A few agricultural or undeveloped areas remain in the southwestern edge of the district, but they probably will be overtaken in the coming years as the city continues to sprawl outward.

Arizona's Hispanic voters tend to break from the Democratic Party on some social issues, opposing abortion rights and favoring some traditionally Republican "family values"-type legislation. The 4th has the state's highest percentage of Hispanic residents (58 percent) and its highest percentage of blacks (7.5 percent).

Major Industry

Retail, government, manufacturing.

Notable

In the late 1800s, residents chose the name "Phoenix" to reflect that the town would rise from the ashes of a once-thriving Native American civilization.

Election Returns

	Republican		Democratic		Other	
President 2000	31,542	34.5%	57,198	62.6%	2,598	2.8%
House 2002	18,381	27.8%	44,517	67.4%	3,167	4.8%

District Profile

Population   641,329

Total area (square miles)   199
  Land area (square miles)   199

Population per square mile   3,216.3

Counties (2000 population)
  Maricopa (pt.)   641,329

Cities and other areas over 10,000 (2000 population)
  Glendale (pt.)   72,329   Phoenix (pt.)   558,408

Race and Hispanic or Latino origin*
  White   29.3%
  Black or African American   7.5%
  American Indian or Alaska Native   2.4%
  Asian   1.3%
  Native Hawaiian or other Pacific Islander   0.1%
  Some other race   0.1%
  Hispanic or Latino origin   58.0%
  Two or more races   1.5%

*As percentage of total population.

Ancestry*

English	3.4%	Irish	4.0%
French	1.1%	Italian	1.6%
German	5.8%	USA/American	2.8%

*As estimated percentage of total population.

Universities and colleges, 2000–2001 enrollment
  Arizona Institute of Business and Technology, Phoenix
    456
  Bryman School, Phoenix   687
  Gateway Community College, Phoenix   7,895
  Grand Canyon University, Phoenix   3,615
  High-Tech Institute, Phoenix   1,487
  ITT Technical Institute, Phoenix   330
  Long Medical Institute, Phoenix   299
  National Education Center, Glendale   277
  Phoenix College, Phoenix   12,386
  South Mountain Community College, Phoenix   3,514
  Universal Technical Institute, Phoenix   2,091
  University of Phoenix, Phoenix   9,152

Newspapers and circulation

	District circulation	Total circulation
Arizona Republic	47,359	470,415

Television stations and affiliations

Phoenix (Prescott)	100%	KAET	PBS
Phoenix (Prescott)	100%	KASW	WB
Phoenix (Prescott)	100%	KNAZ	NBC
Phoenix (Prescott)	100%	KNXV	ABC
Phoenix (Prescott)	100%	KPAZ	Independent
Phoenix (Prescott)	100%	KPHO	CBS
Phoenix (Prescott)	100%	KPNX	NBC
Phoenix (Prescott)	100%	KSAZ	FOX
Phoenix (Prescott)	100%	KTVA	Independent
Phoenix (Prescott)	100%	KTVK	Independent
Phoenix (Prescott)	100%	KUTP	UPN

Cable systems and subscribers
  Cox   249,124

Military installations, September 2001
  Papago Park Military Reservation (Army Guard),
    Phoenix   1,311
  Sky Harbor International Airport Air National Guard,
    Phoenix   887
  Barnes Hall Army Reserve, Phoenix   481

Businesses and other major employers
  University of Arizona; Phoenix   17,000
  City of Phoenix; Phoenix; government   12,111
  Banner Health System; Phoenix; medical laboratories
    10,000
  Motorola Inc.; Phoenix; semiconductors and related
    devices   4,950
  St. Joseph Medical Center; Phoenix   4,000
  Honeywell International Inc. Phoenix; aircraft engines
    and parts   3,900
  Maricopa County Health; Phoenix; hospital   3,600
  Shamrock Foods Co.; Phoenix; packaged frozen goods
    3,600
  City of Phoenix; Phoenix; amusement parks   3,000
  Catholic Healthcare West-Arizona Inc.; Phoenix;
    hospital with residency   3,000
  Simplified Business Solutions Inc.; Phoenix; employee
    leasing service   2,805
  Avnet Inc.; Phoenix; electronic parts   2,800
  City of Phoenix; Phoenix; municipal police   2,680
  Arizona Republic; Phoenix; newspaper   2,500
  Semiconductor Components Industries; Phoenix;
    semiconductors and related devices   2,500
  Swift Transportation Co. Inc.; Phoenix; trucking   2,200
  Arizona Dept. of Corrections; Phoenix   2,120
  RGI Group Inc.; Phoenix; cosmetics   2,014
  Arizona Dept. of Public Safety; Phoenix   2,000
  United Parcel Service Inc.; Phoenix; parcel delivery
    2,000
  Lann Leasing; Phoenix; trucking   1,971
  Belden Wire and Cable Co.; Phoenix; telephone and
    telegraph apparatus   1,800
  Maricopa County; Phoenix; sheriff's office   1,700
  Knipp Brothers Inc.; Glendale; carpentry work   1,625
  Arizona Dept. of Transportaton; Phoenix   1,600
  Leona Group; Phoenix; private junior high school
    1,600
  Maricopa Board of Supervisors; Phoenix   1,500
  Arizona Judiciary Courts; Phoenix   1,500
  ON Semiconductor Corp.; Phoenix; semiconductors and
    related devices   1,500
  U.S. Veterans Hospital; Phoenix   1,500
  Maricopa County; Phoenix; county supervisor's and
    executives' office   1,361
  City of Phoenix; Phoenix; water control and quality
    agency   1,200
  Pediatric Critical Care; Phoenix; pediatrician   1,200
  Kenyon Companies; Phoenix; stucco work   1,200
  U-Haul International Inc.; Phoenix; truck rental   1,100

Donald L. Gaffney; Phoenix; legal services   1,000

United Metro Materials Inc.; Phoenix; ready-mixed concrete   1,000

Qwest Corp.; Phoenix; telecommunication equipment repair   1,000

U.S. Postal Service; Phoenix   1,000

Cartwright School District; Phoenix   1,000

Health Care Cost Containment System; Phoenix; public health programs   1,000

Maricopa County Community College; Phoenix   981

Arizona Dept. of Revenue; Phoenix   930

St. Luke's Health System; Phoenix; hospital   920

Phoenix Elementary School District; Phoenix   900

Aviation Management Systems Inc.; Phoenix; management consulting   900

Woodstuff Manufacturing Inc.; Phoenix; bed frames   900

Destination Resorts Inc.; Phoenix; resort hotel   900

Knight Transportation Inc.; Phoenix; trucking   865

City of Phoenix; Phoenix refuse systems   850

MONY/PSM; Phoenix; resort hotel   850

National Express Corp.; Phoenix; bus line operations   800

Vanguard Health Systems Inc.; Phoenix; hospital   800

Jean E. Harris; Phoenix; general practice law office   800

Sanmina-SCI Corp.; Phoenix; printed circuit boards   758

Corning Gilbert Inc.; Glendale; cord connectors, electric   750

Burns International Security Services Corp.; Phoenix; detective, armored car services   716

CSK Auto Inc.; Phoenix; automotive parts   700

Environmental Quality Dept.; Phoenix; air, water, solid waste management   700

Indian Health Service; Phoenix   700

Vanguard Health Systems Inc.; Phoenix; hospital   700

Hadco Phoenix Inc.; Phoenix; printed circuit boards   700

Maricopa County; Phoenix; courts   600

City of Phoenix; Phoenix; education programs   600

Arizona Public Service Co.; Phoenix; electric power generation   600

Arizona Attorney General; Phoenix   600

Woodstuff Manufacturing Inc.; Phoenix; wood household furniture   600

Avis Rent A Car System Inc.; Phoenix; automobile rental   600

City of Phoenix; Phoenix; airports   600

KFX Building Co. Inc.; Phoenix; framing contractor   600

America West Airlines Inc.; Tempe; air passenger carrier   600

University of Phoenix; Phoenix   584

City of Phoenix; Phoenix; local courts   580

Bonded Cleaning Contractors Inc.; Phoenix; janitorial service   563

Fleming Companies Inc.; Phoenix; food supplier   555

AdobeAir Inc.; Phoenix; air conditioning equipment   550

Southwest Airlines Co.; Phoenix; air passenger carrier   550

Advantage Logistics Southwest Inc.; Phoenix; management consulting   550

Kitchell Corp.; Phoenix; commercial/office building construction   537

Phoenix Childrens Hospital; Phoenix   527

Hyatt Corp.; Phoenix; hotel, franchised   500

Robert C. Bates; Phoenix; general practice law office   500

Triangle Services Inc.; Phoenix; janitorial service   500

Arizona Dept. of Transportaton; Phoenix   500

West Catholic Healthcare; Phoenix; hospital management   500

AT Systems Security Inc.; Phoenix; security guard service   500

Host International Inc.; Phoenix; snack bar services   500

City of Phoenix; Phoenix; transportation department   500

SPI Manufacturing Inc.; Phoenix; commercial mobile buildings   500

Arizona 5th District

Scottsdale; Tempe; part of Phoenix and Mesa

Wealth, beautiful sunsets, and conservative politics abound in the 5th, which takes in a sliver of Phoenix and then spreads east to Tempe, Scottsdale, and the western parts of Chandler and Mesa.

Scottsdale, known for its golf courses and tournaments, and Fountain Hills to the east draw retirees and their bank accounts—the 2000 census showed both communities had higher incomes and median ages than the state and nation.

Farther south, Tempe bucks the trend. The home of Arizona State University, its median age is under 30, compared to 34 years for the 5th as a whole. Its more liberal voters slightly offset but do not heavily endanger the district's GOP bent. Overall, Republicans hold an 18-point voter registration advantage, and George W. Bush carried the district by 10 points in the 2000 presidential election.

Tourism props up much of the area's economy, with resorts, parks, golf courses, rugged scenery, and spring training baseball to convince travelers that the area is the right place for an upscale retreat. The district's small portion of Phoenix includes the city's zoo and the Desert Botanical Garden.

The Salt River and Fort McDowell Native American reservations are attracting guests of their own, and not just for the casinos. The Scottsdale Pavillions shopping mall, just inside the Salt River border, and the Out of Africa Wildlife Park in Fort McDowell are examples of reservations working with private businesses to develop their land.

Major Industry

Tourism, education, health care.

Notable

Fender, the guitar-maker, is based on the Salt River reservation; the fountain at Fountain Hills shoots a stream of water 560 feet into the air; Frank Lloyd Wright's Taliesin West in Scottsdale was the architect's winter home; Taliesin Architects, based in Scottsdale, seeks to continue Wright's practices.

Election Returns

	Republican		Democratic		Other	
President 2000	121,462	53.6%	97,604	43.1%	7,635	3.4%
House 2002	103,870	61.2%	61,559	36.3%	4,383	2.6%

District Profile

Population   641,329

Total area (square miles)   1,422
   Land area (square miles)   1,405

Population per square mile   456.2

Counties (2000 population)
   Maricopa (pt.)   641,329

Cities and other areas over 10,000 (2000 population)
   Chandler (pt.)   66,823   Phoenix (pt.)   85,765
   Fountain Hills town   20,235   Scottsdale   202,705
   Mesa (pt.)   96,622   Tempe   158,625

Race and Hispanic or Latino origin*
   White   76.8%
   Black or African American   2.7%
   American Indian or Alaska Native   1.8%
   Asian   3.3%
   Native Hawaiian or other Pacific Islander   0.2%
   Some other race   0.2%
   Hispanic or Latino origin   13.3%
   Two or more races   1.7%

*As percentage of total population.

Ancestry*
   Dutch   1.4%   Polish   2.7%
   English   9.0%   Russian   1.1%
   French   2.5%   Scotch-Irish   1.4%
   German   14.3%   Scottish   1.9%
   Irish   9.5%   Swedish   1.9%
   Italian   5.1%   USA/American   3.2%
   Norwegian   2.1%

*As estimated percentage of total population.

Universities and colleges, 2000–2001 enrollment
   Al Collins Graphic Design School, Tempe   5,833
   Arizona State University, Tempe   44,126
   Arkansas State University, State University   10,429
   Keller Graduate School-East Valley Center, Mesa*
   Mesa Community College, Mesa   22,821
   Pima Medical Institute, Mesa   422
   Rio Salado Community College, Tempe   11,275
   Scottsdale Community College, Scottsdale   10,391
   Scottsdale Culinary Institute, Scottsdale   602
   Southwest College of Naturopathic Medicine and Health
      Science, Tempe   263
   University of Advancing Computer Technology, Tempe
      931

*Enrollment under 100. See Sources and Explanations in the front of the volume.

Newspapers and circulation

	District circulation	Total circulation
Arizona Republic	94,255	470,415
Mesa East Valley Tribune	25,866	100,990
*USA Today**	4,458	1,674,376

*See Sources and Explanations in the front of the volume.

Television stations and affiliations

Phoenix (Prescott)	100%	KAET	PBS
Phoenix (Prescott)	100%	KASW	WB
Phoenix (Prescott)	100%	KNAZ	NBC
Phoenix (Prescott)	100%	KNXV	ABC
Phoenix (Prescott)	100%	KPAZ	Independent
Phoenix (Prescott)	100%	KPHO	CBS
Phoenix (Prescott)	100%	KPNX	NBC
Phoenix (Prescott)	100%	KSAZ	FOX
Phoenix (Prescott)	100%	KTVA	Independent
Phoenix (Prescott)	100%	KTVK	Independent
Phoenix (Prescott)	100%	KUTP	UPN

Cable systems and subscribers
Cox   96,177

Businesses and other major employers
   Honeywell International Inc.; Tempe; pneumatic tools
      and equipment   9,000
   Motorola Inc.; Mesa; monolithic integrated circuits
      5,000
   Intel Corp.; Chandler; semiconductors and related
      devices   5,000
   Wells Fargo Bank Northwest National Assn.; Tempe;
      commercial bank   3,000
   General Dynamics Decision Systems; Scottsdale; security
      control equipment and systems   2,800
   Arizona Dept. of Emergency and Military Affairs;
      Phoenix   2,700
   Salt River Project Agricultural Improvement and Power
      District; Tempe; electric power distribution   2,500
   Motorola Inc.; Scottsdale; radio/TV communications
      equipment   2,300
   Chase Bankcard Services Inc.; Tempe; state commercial
      banks   2,300
   JP Morgan Chase Bank; Tempe; commercial bank
      2,200
   Koch Industries Inc.; Wichita; petroleum refining
      2,000
   Banner Health System; Mesa; home health care services
      2,000
   Banner Health System; Mesa; office management   2,000
   Motorola Inc.; Tempe; electronic computers   2,000
   Arizona State University; Tempe   1,750
   Mayo Clinic; Scottsdale   1,700
   Bank One National Assn.; Tempe; commercial bank
      1,600
   Banner Health System; Mesa; hospital   1,500
   Scottsdale Healthcare Corp.; Scottsdale; hospital
      management   1,500
   Financial, Administrative, and Credit Services Group
      Inc.; Tempe; credit card service   1,500
   Phillips Petroleum Co.; Tempe; engine fuels and oils
      1,500
   Scottsdale Healthcare Corp.; Scottsdale; hospital
      management   1,499
   Circle K Stores Inc.; Tempe; convenience stores   1,400
   Microchip Technology Inc.; Chandler; semiconductors
      and related devices   1,250
   General Dynamics Decision Systems; Scottsdale; search
      and navigation equipment   1,200
   Wells Fargo Bank Arizona; Tempe; data processing
      1,200

Scottsdale Insurance Co.; Scottsdale; fire, marine, casualty insurance 1,050

West Macy's Inc.; Tempe; department stores 1,050

Town's Ambulance Service Inc.; Scottsdale; ambulance service 1,000

Simply Best Training; Scottsdale; job training services 1,000

Varian Inc.; Tempe; printed circuit boards 1,000

Conseco Finance Corp. Inc.; Tempe; mortgage bankers 1,000

Rhino Staging and Events Productions Inc.; Tempe; promoters of shows and exhibitions 981

Medtronic Inc.; Tempe; electronic circuits 950

BFI Waste Services; Scottsdale; refuse systems 930

City of Scottsdale; Scottsdale; city management 900

Fort McDowell Gaming Center; Scottsdale; gambling 850

Hyatt Corp.; Scottsdale; hotel, franchised 850

Encompass Electrical Technologies Inc.; Tempe; electrical contractor 850

Motorola Inc.; Phoenix; semiconductors and related devices 800

Tosco Marketing Co.; Tempe; convenience stores 790

Dial Corp.; Scottsdale; soap and other detergents 775

Sonora Quest Laboratories; Tempe; medical laboratories 750

Hilti Inc.; Tempe; metal fasteners 725

Professional Event Management; Tempe; signs and advertising specialties 705

Electronic Data Systems Corp.; Phoenix; telemarketing services 700

Arizona Public Service; Chandler 700

Worldwide Security Associates Inc.; Tempe; security guard service 700

Coca-Cola Bottling of Los Angeles; Tempe; soft drinks 700

E-Funds Corp.; Scottsdale; data processing 650

Bashas' Inc.; Chandler; self storage warehousing 600

Sharp Drywall Inc.; Chandler; drywall 600

McKesson Health Solutions Inc.; Scottsdale; business management 600

JDA Software Inc.; Scottsdale; computer programming services 600

MSA Solutions Inc.; Tempe; data processing 600

Park Electrochemical Corp.; Tempe; nonelectric transformers 600

VISA USA Inc.; Tempe; credit card service 600

Vital Processing Services; Tempe; credit card service 575

Laboratory Sciences of Arizona; Tempe; medical laboratories 520

PR Hotel; Scottsdale; hotels 510

Goodrich Corp.; Chandler; model kits 500

Avnet Inc.; Chandler; electronic parts and equipment 500

Salt River Pima Maricopa Indian Community; Scottsdale 500

Kforce Professional Staffing; Scottsdale; medical help service 500

Leisure Co.; Tempe; tour operators 500

Litton Industries Inc.; Tempe; safety equipment and supplies 500

Bank of America Corp.; Tempe; billing, bookkeeping service 500

Performance Hospitality Inn Inc.; Tempe; resort hotel 500

Clopay Corp.; Tempe; wood garage doors 500

Direct Alliance Corp.; Tempe; computer consulting services 500

Arizona 6th District

Southeast Phoenix suburbs — most of Mesa and Chandler, Gilbert, Apache Junction

Rooted in the conservative leanings of an affluent, historically Mormon population, the suburban 6th favors Republican candidates. The district still has a significant population of Mormons, as well as a mix of young couples who commute to Phoenix. The area's warm sunny days have helped draw an established population of retirees from other states.

The district begins east of Phoenix, where it takes in all but the westernmost segments of Mesa and Chandler, both of which have experienced tremendous population growth during the past 20 years. Manufacturing aids the economy in Mesa, the state's third-largest city and now within the nation's top 50 in population.

Chandler, not as dependent on tourism as its neighbors, fuels its economy through retail business while attempting to attract biotechnology firms. Between the two cities is Gilbert, which has several construction-related businesses.

Redistricting following the 2000 census made the 6th—previously numbered the 1st—more conservative by slicing off the Democratic university town of Tempe and the district's portion of Phoenix. The district expanded east to take in part of largely agricultural Pinal County, including Apache Junction on the county's northern border.

Republicans now hold an almost 25-point edge in party registration, and the redrawn district gave George W. Bush 60.9 percent of the vote in the 2000 presidential election. More than 76 percent white, the 6th has more white residents and fewer minorities than the state average.

Major Industry
Manufacturing, high-tech, retail.

Notable
Chandler's Ostrich Festival, held each March, features ostrich races and a parade; Mesa is the spring training home of the Chicago Cubs baseball team, which has led the Arizona Cactus League in attendance for many of the past 20 years; Mesa was founded by Mormons.

Election Returns

	Republican		Democratic		Other	
President 2000	118,278	60.9%	72,093	37.1%	3,942	2.0%
House 2002	103,094	65.9%	49,355	31.6%	3,888	2.5%

District Profile

Population 641,329

Total area (square miles) 723
    Land area (square miles) 723

Population per square mile 886.2

Counties (2000 population)

Maricopa (pt.)	588,659	Pinal (pt.)	52,670

Cities and other areas over 10,000 (2000 population)

Apache Junction	31,814	Mesa (pt.)	299,753
Chandler (pt.)	109,758	Sun Lakes CDP	11,936
Gilbert town	109,697		

Race and Hispanic or Latino origin*

White 76.6%
Black or African American 1.9%
American Indian or Alaska Native 0.8%
Asian 1.8%
Native Hawaiian or other Pacific Islander 0.2%
Some other race 0.1%
Hispanic or Latino origin 17.2%
Two or more races 1.4%

*As percentage of total population.

Ancestry*

Dutch	1.5%	Norwegian	2.2%
English	10.2%	Polish	2.1%
French	2.6%	Scotch-Irish	1.1%
German	14.1%	Scottish	1.8%
Irish	8.6%	Swedish	1.7%
Italian	3.7%	USA/American	4.3%

*As estimated percentage of total population.

Universities and colleges, 2000–2001 enrollment

Arizona Institute of Business and Technology, Mesa
229
Arizona State University East, Mesa 1,939
Chandler/Gilbert Community College, Chandler 6,217

Newspapers and circulation

	District circulation	Total circulation
Arizona Republic	71,022	470,415
Mesa East Valley Tribune	49,982	100,990
*USA Today**	1,019	1,674,376

*See Sources and Explanations in the front of the volume.

Television stations and affiliations

Phoenix (Prescott)	100%	KAET	PBS
Phoenix (Prescott)	100%	KASW	WB
Phoenix (Prescott)	100%	KNAZ	NBC
Phoenix (Prescott)	100%	KNXV	ABC
Phoenix (Prescott)	100%	KPAZ	Independent
Phoenix (Prescott)	100%	KPHO	CBS
Phoenix (Prescott)	100%	KPNX	NBC
Phoenix (Prescott)	100%	KSAZ	FOX
Phoenix (Prescott)	100%	KTVA	Independent
Phoenix (Prescott)	100%	KTVK	Independent
Phoenix (Prescott)	100%	KUTP	UPN

Cable systems and subscribers

Cable America 1,078
Cox 71,891
Mediacom 4,349

Businesses and other major employers

Boeing Co.; Mesa; helicopters 5,000
Arise Inc.; Mesa; social services for the handicapped 3,652
Douglas McDonnell Helicopter Co.; Mesa; helicopters 3,600
Intel Corp.; Chandler; microprocessors 2,600
General Motors Corp.; Mesa; automobile proving, testing 1,500
Innovex Inc.; Chandler; electronic circuits 1,500
Northrop Grumman Corp.; Chandler; engineering services 1,500
Gila River Gaming Enterprises Inc.; Chandler; slot machine 1,500
INTESYS Technologies Inc.; Gilbert; molding primary plastics 1,150
Whiteman Family Corp.; Mesa; construction and mining machinery 1,077
TRW Systems; Mesa; automotive parts, plastic 1,040
Motorola Inc.; Chandler; cellular telephones 1,000
Motorola Inc.; Chandler; mobile communication equipment 1,000
Motorola Inc.; Chandler; semiconductors and related devices 998
Chandler Community Hospital; Chandler 881
Banner Health System; Mesa; hospital 833
TRW Inc.; Mesa; motor vehicle parts/accessories 800
Robson Communities Inc.; Chandler; golf club 800
Special Devices Inc.; Mesa; flares, fireworks 750
Bank of America Corp.; Chandler; telemarketing services 750
Earnhardt's Gilbert Dodge Inc.; Gilbert; automobiles 730
AutoNation Inc.; Mesa; new and used car dealers 600
City of Mesa; Mesa; municipal police 600
NDCHealth Corp.; Mesa; data processing 600
Empire Southwest; Mesa; construction and mining machinery 600
W&A Schafer Enterprises Inc.; Mesa; industrial, commercial cleaning services 575
Orbital Sciences Corp.; Chandler; guided missiles and space vehicles 530
Phase 2 Solutions Inc.; Mesa; telemarketing services 500
Freedom Communications Inc.; Mesa; direct mail advertising 500
Freedom Newspapers of Arizona Inc.; Mesa; newspaper 500
T&H Inc.; Mesa; metal mining services 500
Gorilla Co.; Gilbert; decoration services 500

Arizona 7th District

Southwest — part of Tucson, Yuma, Avondale

Stretching mainly south and west from Phoenix, the Hispanic-majority 7th crosses large reservations and rural areas to take in Yuma, downtown Tucson, and most of Arizona's border with Mexico. The district, most of which was in the 2nd until redistricting following the 2000 census, is a Democratic stronghold.

The 7th includes the University of Arizona in Tucson, southern Arizona's top employer, and the Mexican border town of Nogales. It also climbs to the California border, taking in most of La Paz and all of Yuma counties. The economy is supported by seasonal immigrant workers, who buttress the agriculture and service industries but boost poverty statistics. The 7th has more blue-collar workers and fewer college graduates than any other Arizona district except the 4th.

Some conservative ranching communities exist in Yuma County and elsewhere in the district, but their political impact is largely offset by a Democratic-voting Native American presence. The Tohono O'odham and Gila River reservations are the 7th's largest, and Native Americans make up over 5 percent of the district's population. Overall, Democrats have an almost 2-to-1 advantage over Republicans.

Major Industry

Agriculture, tourism, education.

Notable

Yuma Territorial Prison was turned into a high school, then a shelter for railroad vagrants, and finally a state historic park.

Election Returns

	Republican		Democratic		Other	
President 2000	49,343	38.3%	74,176	57.6%	5,271	4.1%
House 2002	38,474	37.1%	61,256	59.0%	4,088	3.9%

District Profile

Population   641,329

Total area (square miles)   22,891
   Land area (square miles)   22,872

Population per square mile   28

Counties (2000 population)

La Paz (pt.)	19,692	Pinal (pt.)	17,764
Maricopa (pt.)	80,567	Santa Cruz (pt.)	34,231
Pima (pt.)	329,049	Yuma	160,026

Cities and other areas over 10,000 (2000 population)

Avondale	35,883	Phoenix (pt.)	26,069
Drexel Heights CDP	23,849	San Luis	15,322
Fortuna Foothills CDP	20,478	Tucson (pt.)	230,164
Nogales	20,878	Yuma	77,515

Race and Hispanic or Latino origin*
   White   38.6%
   Black or African American   2.8%
   American Indian or Alaska Native   5.3%
   Asian   1.3%
   Native Hawaiian or other Pacific Islander   0.1%
   Some other race   0.1%
   Hispanic or Latino origin   50.6%
   Two or more races   1.3%

*As percentage of total population.

Ancestry*

English	4.8%	Irish	5.4%
French	1.6%	Italian	1.8%
German	7.8%	USA/American	3.2%

*As estimated percentage of total population.

Universities and colleges, 2000–2001 enrollment
   Arizona Western College, Yuma   5,214
   ITT Technical Institute, Tucson   224
   Pima Community College, Tucson   28,078
   University of Arizona, Tucson   34,488

Newspapers and circulation

	District circulation	Total circulation
Arizona Daily Star	23,805	100,725
Arizona Republic	23,904	470,415
Casa Grande Dispatch	5,189	9,054
Tucson Citizen	35,384	138,692
*USA Today**	21,673	1,674,376
Yuma Sun	17,376	17,780

*See Sources and Explanations in the front of the volume.

Television stations and affiliations

Phoenix (Prescott)	43%	KAET	PBS
Phoenix (Prescott)	43%	KASW	WB
Phoenix (Prescott)	43%	KNAZ	NBC
Phoenix (Prescott)	43%	KNXV	ABC
Phoenix (Prescott)	43%	KPAZ	Independent
Phoenix (Prescott)	43%	KPHO	CBS
Phoenix (Prescott)	43%	KPNX	NBC
Phoenix (Prescott)	43%	KSAZ	FOX
Phoenix (Prescott)	43%	KTVA	Independent
Phoenix (Prescott)	43%	KTVK	Independent
Phoenix (Prescott)	43%	KUTP	UPN
Tucson (Sierra Vista)	33%	KGUN	ABC
Tucson (Sierra Vista)	33%	KHRR	Telemundo
Tucson (Sierra Vista)	33%	KMSB	FOX
Tucson (Sierra Vista)	33%	KOLD	CBS
Tucson (Sierra Vista)	33%	KTTU	UPN
Tucson (Sierra Vista)	33%	KUAS	PBS
Tucson (Sierra Vista)	33%	KUAT	PBS
Tucson (Sierra Vista)	33%	KVOA	NBC
Tucson (Sierra Vista)	33%	KWBA	WB
Yuma-El Centro, CA	24%	KECY	FOX
Yuma-El Centro, CA	24%	KSWT	CBS
Yuma-El Centro, CA	24%	KYMA	NBC

Cable systems and subscribers
   Adelphia   24,930
   Cable America   715
   Cablevision   2,896
   Comcast   3,127
   Cox   5,676
   Mediacom   7,448

Military installations, September 2001
   Davis-Monthan Air Force Base Tucson   7,295
   Yuma Marine Corps Air Station, Yuma   4,508
   Yuma Proving Ground (Army), Yuma   1,702
   Tucson International Airport Air National Guard, Tucson   1,647
   Silver Bell AR Helpor (Army Guard), Marana   569

Businesses and other major employers
   University of Arizona; Tucson   13,000
   Raytheon Co.; Tucson; electronic circuits   11,000
   U.S. Marine Corps Personnel Support; Yuma   6,026
   Arizona Public Service Co.; Tonopah; electric services   2,000

Learjet Inc.; Tucson; aircraft 2,000

University Medical Center; Tucson 2,000

Gila River Indian Community; Sacaton; government
1,700

Fiesta Restaurants Inc.; Tucson; Mexican restaurant
1,700

American Airlines Inc.; Tucson; air passenger carrier
1,600

Arizona Dept. of Emergency and Military Affairs; Tucson
1,600

Palo Verde Nuclear Generating Station; Tonopah;
electric power generation 1,500

Union Pacific Corp.; Tucson; switching and terminal
services 1,500

Carondelet Health Network Inc.; Tucson; hospital
1,500

Arizona Public Service Human Resources; Avondale;
electric power distribution 1,400

Intuit Inc.; Tucson; prepackaged software 1,300

Sun Land Beef Co.; Tolleson; meat packing plants
1,200

Yuma Regional Medical Center Inc.; Yuma 1,200

Texas Instruments Tucson Corp.; Tucson; integrated
microcircuits (semiconductor) 1,068

Veterans Health Administration; Tucson 1,033

International Business Machines Corp.; Tucson;
computer hardware 1,000

Weiser Lock Corp.; Tucson; door locks, bolts 1,000

Tucson Electric Power Co.; Tucson; electric power
generation 964

TNI Partners; Tucson; newspaper 946

City of Tucson; Tucson; police protection 900

Bravo Harvesting Inc.; Yuma; citrus fruits 800

Pima County; Tucson; hospital 800

Pascua Yaqui Tribe; Tucson 752

Ak-Chin Indian Community; Maricopa; gambling
machines 750

Tucson Unified School District; Tucson 720

Pimalco Inc.; Chandler; aluminum products 700

Tohono O'odham Nation; Sells; Indian reservation 700

Leoni Wiring Systems Inc.; Tucson; wire cable 675

Sears Home Services Group; Tucson; computer
consulting services 650

CS Integrated; Tolleson; cold storage warehousing 646

Tohono O'odham Nation; Tucson; gambling 630

Flowing Wells School District; Tucson 625

Arizona Mail Order Co.; Tucson; mail order women's
apparel 625

Pima County; Tucson; juvenile correctional facilities
625

Sysco Food Services; Tolleson; packaged frozen goods
610

Pedus Security Services Inc.; Tucson; detective, armored
car services 600

Direct Marketing Inc.; Tucson; telemarketing services
597

Pima County Community College; Tucson 581

Edward Montiel; Yuma; farm labor contractors 562

University of Arizona Hospital; Tucson; cancer hospital
550

Pima County; Tucson; legal counsel 500

City of Tucson; Tucson; air, water, solid waste
management 500

City of Tucson; Tucson; city and town management
500

Tomkins Industries Inc.; Tucson; refrigeration and
heating equipment 500

Systems Implementers Inc.; Tucson; energy conservation
engineering 500

Borderland Construction Co.; Tucson; highway, street
general contractor 500

Professional Transit Management of Tucson Inc.; Tucson;
bus transportation 500

Arizona 8th District

Southeast — part of Tucson and northern suburbs

Located in the state's southeastern corner bordering New
Mexico and Mexico, the 8th contains many swing voters and
independents who often favor moderates in national elections. Most residents live in Pima County, primarily in the
Tucson metropolitan area, although Cochise County makes
up most of the district geographically. Both urban and rural
areas grew by about 20 percent during the 1990s.

Tucson is surrounded by mountain ranges, but the majestic Santa Catalinas just north of the city are the local landmark. Population growth is heavy here as residents literally
"head for the hills" and the wealthy, unincorporated areas of
Casas Adobes and Catalina Foothills. These and other northern suburban communities are home to affluent, retired, and
military residents who moved to the area from other states
in recent years and add to the district's GOP lean. Central
areas of Tucson, including the University of Arizona, are in
the neighboring 7th.

Democrats hold the majority in Santa Cruz and Cochise
Counties, which have large Hispanic populations, but Republicans lead in overall voter registration by about 5 percentage points. George W. Bush won the 2000 presidential
vote here by 3.8 percent.

The various military jets that fly past Tucson on their
way to or from Davis-Monthan Air Force Base reveal two
of the area's economic engines: military and manufacturing.
The city has a number of high-tech defense contractors and
aerospace firms, including Raytheon Missile Systems, but
the district is increasingly dependent on service industries,
including tourism, to support its economic base. Tucson's
growing suburbs have made construction an economic force
as well.

Major Industry

Service, manufacturing, military, aerospace, tourism, agriculture.

Notable

Tombstone, "the town too tough to die," was notorious
for its boomtown lawlessness in the late 1800s.

Election Returns

	Republican		Democratic		Other	
President 2000	123,585	49.7%	114,055	45.9%	10,814	4.4%
House 2002	126,930	63.3%	67,328	33.6%	6,170	3.1%

District Profile

Population 641,329

Total area (square miles) 9,057
  Land area (square miles) 9,006

Population per square mile 71.2

Counties (2000 population)
Cochise 117,755   Pinal (pt.) 4,727
Pima (pt.) 514,697   Santa Cruz (pt.) 4,150

Cities and other areas over 10,000 (2000 population)
Casas Adobes CDP 54,011
Catalina Foothills CDP 53,794
Douglas 14,312
Flowing Wells CDP 15,050
Green Valley CDP 17,283
Màrana town 13,556
Oro Valley town 29,700
Sierra Vista 37,775
Sierra Vista Southeast CDP 14,348
Tanque Verde CDP 16,195
Tucson (pt.) 256,535

Race and Hispanic or Latino origin*
White 73.9%
Black or African American 3.0%
American Indian or Alaska Native 0.8%
Asian 2.1%
Native Hawaiian or other Pacific Islander 0.1%
Some other race 0.1%
Hispanic or Latino origin 18.2%
Two or more races 1.8%

*As percentage of total population.

Ancestry*
Dutch 1.4%   Norwegian 1.8%
English 9.7%   Polish 2.2%
French 2.7%   Scotch-Irish 1.7%
German 14.4%   Scottish 2.1%
Irish 9.1%   Swedish 1.6%
Italian 3.7%   USA/American 3.7%

*As estimated percentage of total population.

Universities and colleges, 2000–2001 enrollment
Art Center, Tucson 350
Chaparral Career College, Tucson 339
Cochise College, Douglas 4,966
Pima Medical Institute, Tucson 364
University of Phoenix, Tucson 2,212

Newspapers and circulation

	District circulation	Total circulation
Arizona Daily Star	74,374	100,725
Arizona Republic	2,089	470,415
Tucson Citizen	100,664	138,692
*USA Today**	2,966	1,674,376

*See Sources and Explanations in the front of the volume.

Television stations and affiliations
Tucson (Sierra Vista)	99%	KGUN	ABC
Tucson (Sierra Vista)	99%	KHRR	Telemundo
Tucson (Sierra Vista)	99%	KMSB	FOX
Tucson (Sierra Vista)	99%	KOLD	CBS
Tucson (Sierra Vista)	99%	KTTU	UPN
Tucson (Sierra Vista)	99%	KUAS	PBS
Tucson (Sierra Vista)	99%	KUAT	PBS
Tucson (Sierra Vista)	99%	KVOA	NBC
Tucson (Sierra Vista)	99%	KWBA	WB

Cable systems and subscribers
Cable ONE 2,675
Comcast 11,453
Cox 108,596

Military installations, September 2001
Fort Huachuca (Army), Sierra Vista 10,078

Businesses and other major employers
Walbro Engine Management; Tucson; carburetors 3,500
U.S. Postal Service; Green Valley 1,745
TMC Healthcare; Tucson; hospital 1,655
Tohono O'odham Gaming Authority; Sahuarita; gambling 1,300
Carondelet Health Network Inc.; Tucson; hospital 1,000
Commission on Accreditation of Rehabilitation Facilities Inc.; Tucson; educational research 1,000
Arizona Dept. of Corrections; Tucson 1,000
Northwest Hospital; Tucson 940
Asarco Inc.; Sahuarita; copper ore 905
Canyon Ranch Management; Tucson; resort hotel 900
Marana Unified School District; Marana 847
Anderson Financial Network; Tucson; business planning, organizing services 800
Honeywell International Inc.; Tucson; turbines and turbine generators 800
Arizona Dept. of Corrections; Douglas; correctional institution 750
Phelps Dodge Sierrita Inc.; Green; Valley; open pit copper ore mining 750
Aegis Communications Group Inc.; Sierra Vista; telemarketing services 724
Convergys Corp.; Tucson; facilities support services 700
Intergroup Prepaid Health Services of Arizona Inc.; Tucson; health maintenance organization 650
Misys Healthcare Systems Inc.; Tucson; computer systems analysis and design 650
Kmart Corp.; Tucson; discount department stores 600
Dependable Nurses Inc.; Tucson; home health care services 600
U.S. Bureau of Citizenship and Immigration Services; Douglas 550
El Dorado Hospital Center; Tucson 522
El Conquistador Hotel Associates; Tucson; resort hotel 515
Sierra Vista Regional Health Center Inc.; Sierra Vista 500
Cross Country Automotive Services Inc.; Tucson; automobile recovery service 500
Health Net of Arizona Inc.; Tucson; health maintenance organization 500
Caesar Park Hotels and Resorts Inc.; Tucson; resort hotel 500
Ventana Canyon Hotel Associates; Tucson; resort hotel 500

Districts established April 20, 2001, for elections first held in 2002.

4 members

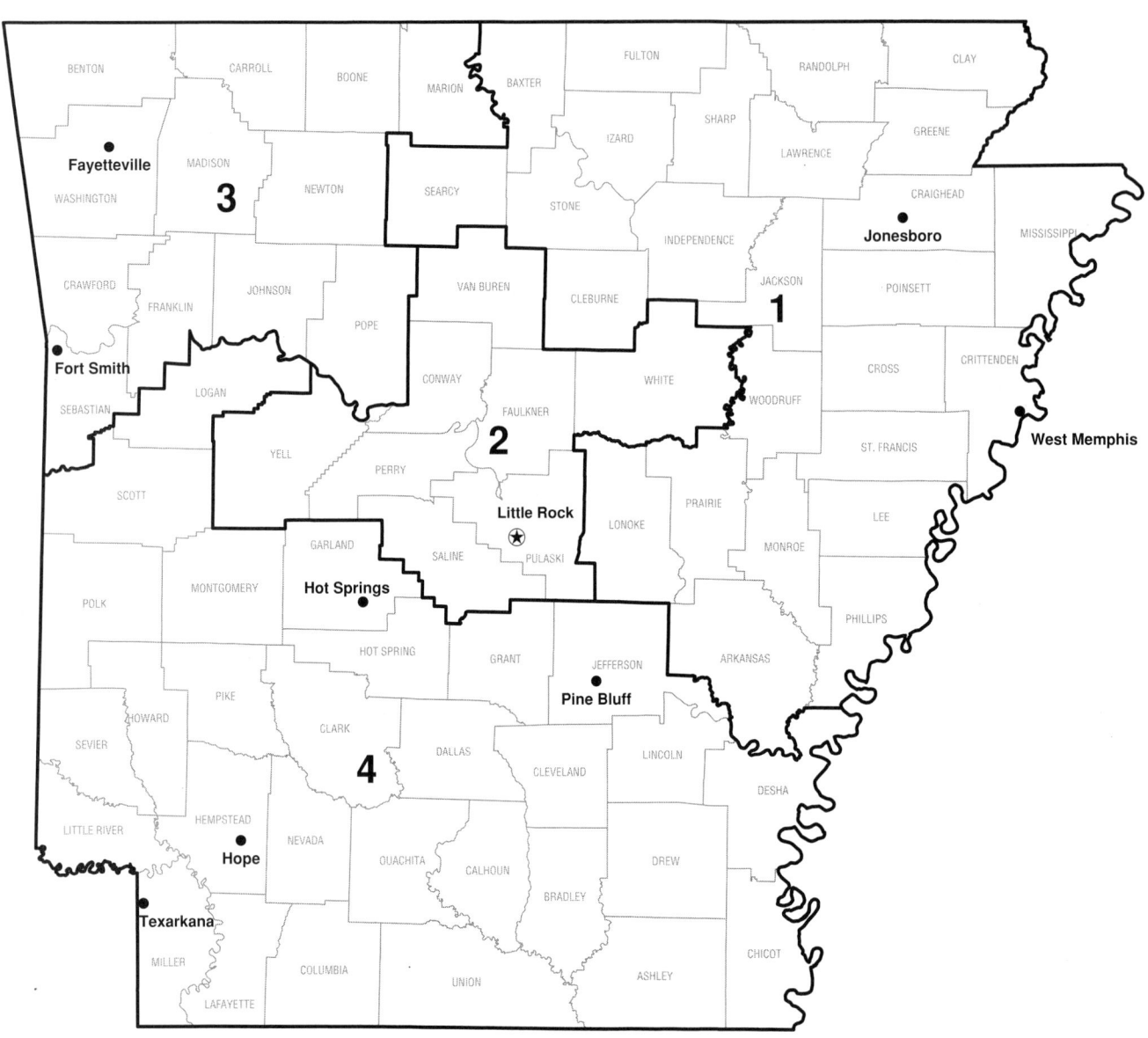

Arkansas

The career of Bill Clinton drove the politics of the 1990s, to one degree or another, in every state in the nation. But in Clinton's home state of Arkansas, his influence spanned a quarter century and left a mark that will last much longer.

From the time Clinton returned from Oxford to attend law school at the University of Arkansas in the early 1970s until he returned to choose a site for his presidential library three decades later, Clinton pursued his personal rendezvous with destiny. He lost a bid for Congress in 1974 but ran for attorney general two years later and won. He was elected governor in 1978, defeated for reelection in 1980, and returned to office in 1982. He held the governor's office for the next decade before leaving for the White House late in 1992.

During most of that time Clinton, and a generation of slightly older but progressive Democrats, held the state against forces eroding their party's historic dominance in the South. The state's nascent suburbs were growing, more managers were arriving from other states to run corporate operations, and more affluent retirees were flocking to the easy living of the Ozarks and other hilly regions of the state. These voters made their presence felt as Republicans carried Arkansas in the presidential election of 1972, and in all three White House contests of the 1980s.

Still, the Democrats managed to keep their grip in Little Rock. Building on the popularity of Democratic governors Dale Bumpers and David Pryor, both of whom moved on to the Senate in the 1970s, Clinton and his supporters survived the years that were dominated by President Ronald Reagan at the head of the GOP. Democrats held three of the four seats in Congress and maintained a smothering advantage in the state legislature.

It was Clinton's ascent to the Oval Office that changed everything. Being the state's first president made him a hero back home at first, but he soon seemed to forget the populist themes on which he had risen. Here as elsewhere in the South there was bitter disappointment with Clinton's early moves—tax increases in the budget, proposed acceptance of gays in the military, and aggressive efforts to appoint women and minorities to high office. Matters did not improve when Clinton and his wife, Hillary Rodham Clinton, moved on to gun control, free trade, and an overhaul of the health care system.

In 1994 a revolt throughout the South gave the Republicans a majority of the region's governorships and Senate and House seats—for the first time since Reconstruction more than a century earlier and all on the same day. Arkansas's

House delegation was suddenly split 2–2. But the Clinton-era earthquakes had only begun.

There soon followed the successful prosecution of a dozen Arkansans who had been associated with a panoply of business schemes collectively known as Whitewater. Prominent among those indicted was Gov. Jim Guy Tucker, Clinton's successor, who was convicted and sentenced to prison. Replacing him in July 1996 was Mike Huckabee, a Baptist preacher who had been regarded as almost a fringe candidate until his election as lieutenant governor in 1992. In 1996 Pryor retired, and when the Republicans captured his Senate seat it was their first in the state since Reconstruction.

Huckabee would win successive four-year terms in his own right thereafter in 1998 and 2002. But Democrats otherwise showed resilience. Clinton carried the state in his reelection year (although with less than 54 percent of the vote). Democrats also held the Bumpers seat in 1998 with Blanche Lambert Lincoln, recaptured the 4th District in 2000, and then recaptured Pryor's old Senate seat in 2002 with Pryor's son, Mark.

Thus the legislature, still solidly Democratic, had little impetus to alter the congressional district lines after the 2000 census except for numerical equity. The black population of Arkansas was less than 16 percent overall and well distributed through three of the state's four districts. The best candidate for a black district has been the southern 4th District, which includes the cities of Hot Springs and Pine Bluff. This district was 26.5 percent black by 2000 and might have been redrawn to include parts of Pulaski County (Little Rock) that would push its black percentage nearer 50 percent. Theoretically, that would have been an opportunity for a black congressional candidate. But the legislature decided instead to move three western, heavily Republican counties—Polk, Scott, and Logan—from the 3rd District to the 4th. The result was to lower slightly the black percentage in the 4th without creating a critical mass for change anywhere else.

That decision was a product of both political and legal factors. The legislature that draws the maps was still dominated by white Democrats with little motivation to draw a black district. Just as important, Arkansas had so far not been part of the federal remapping mandates imposed on other states in the South to correct for previous racial discrimination.

The state was not "put in the penalty box" as were some of its neighbors in the 1964 Civil Rights Act, so it is not required to submit its redistricting plans for "preclearance" by the Justice Department. Nonetheless, a group of black citizens successfully sued to force a new map for state legislative districts after the 1980 census and won. Similar efforts to combat black vote dilution after the 1990 census and again after the 2000 census did not get far before being dismissed by the federal courts.

The loss of those counties did not make the northwestern 3rd District substantially more competitive. The 3rd snuggles against the Missouri line on the north and the Oklahoma line on the west. It is only a short drive from the entertainment complex at Branson, Missouri, and is by far the state's fastest-growing quarter, rich in resorts and retirement communities. It also has been a Republican enclave for several decades and has become one of the most Republican districts in the South. Only about 2 percent of its voters are black.

A handful of Arkansans became very rich in the years Clinton served as governor and president. The Walton family thrived on Sam Walton's Wal-Marts, the Tysons on their poultry empire. But most of their money was made outside of Arkansas and much of it seemed to get spent outside the state as well. The state's growth rate remains slow. Arkansas grew by one-third in the latter half of the 1900s, but that rate was less than half the national average.

The main occupations in the state remain related to agriculture and light manufacture, and the historically low-wage pattern for such work has yet to be broken. Arkansas continues to have a larger percentage of its people living in poverty (about 18 percent) than any other state except Mississippi and a virtual tie with New Mexico. Twelve percent of its families were in the poverty classification, according to the 2000 census. It also ranked third from the bottom in per capita personal income ($22,887) in 2001 and puts up disappointing numbers in terms of welfare dependency.

Table 1   Population

District	Population	Population under 18	Voting-age population	Median age	Male*	Female*
1	668,360	171,601	496,759	36.9	48.5	51.5
2	666,058	167,561	498,497	35.2	48.5	51.5
3	672,756	173,239	499,517	35.0	49.4	50.6
4	666,226	167,968	498,258	37.2	48.8	51.2
State	2,673,400	680,369	1,993,031	36.0	48.8	51.2

*As percentage of total population.

Table 2   Voting-Age Persons by Race/Hispanic or Latino Origin

District	White*	Black or African American*	American Indian or Alaska Native*	Asian*	Other or multirace*	Hispanic or Latino*
1	82.9	14.2	0.4	0.3	0.8	1.4
2	78.3	17.3	0.4	0.9	0.9	2.1
3	89.1	1.8	1.1	1.5	1.3	5.2
4	73.8	22.3	0.5	0.4	0.8	2.3
State	81.0	13.9	0.6	0.8	0.9	2.8

*As percentage of voting-age population.

Table 3   Voting-Age Population by Age Groups

District	18 to 24*	25 to 44*	45 to 64*	Over 64*
1	12.4	36.1	31.2	20.4
2	13.7	40.1	30.0	16.3
3	14.0	38.9	29.6	17.6
4	12.5	35.7	30.9	20.9
State	13.1	37.7	30.4	18.8

*As percentage of voting-age population.

Table 4   Income and Occupation

District	Median family income	Families in poverty*	White collar†	Blue collar†	Service†	Farm†
1	$34,949	14.4	48.8	35.0	14.0	2.2
2	$44,403	9.5	60.5	25.0	13.9	0.5
3	$40,169	9.9	53.0	32.0	13.8	1.1
4	$35,915	14.2	47.8	34.9	14.8	2.4
State	$38,663	12.0	52.8	31.6	14.1	1.5

*As percentage of all families.   †As percentage of employed workers 16 years and over.

Table 5   Education: School Years Completed

District	Less than grade 9*	Grades 9–12 no diploma*	High school diploma no college*	Some college*	College bachelor's degree or higher*
1	12.5	17.2	35.9	22.1	12.3
2	6.0	12.7	31.0	27.1	23.2
3	9.2	14.0	33.1	25.9	17.9
4	9.9	17.4	36.4	23.1	13.3
State	9.4	15.3	34.1	24.5	16.7

*As percentage of persons age 25 and over.

Table 6   Housing and Residential Patterns

District	Median home value	Owner occupied*	Renter occupied*	Urban†	Rural†
1	$59,100	69.6	30.4	44.5	55.5
2	$77,600	67.1	32.9	66.2	33.8
3	$79,400	68.7	31.3	54.4	45.6
4	$54,300	72.2	27.8	44.7	55.3
State	$67,400	69.4	30.6	52.4	47.6

*As percentage of occupied housing units.   †As percentage of total population.

Arkansas 1st District

Northeast — Jonesboro, West Memphis

One of the nation's poorest districts, the 1st stretches across Arkansas's northeastern third, reaching from the Mississippi Delta through fertile plains and into the hilly north, where the Ozark Mountains begin.

Poverty is most notably present within the largely white, older populations in the northwest and the former sharecropping communities in the Democratic Delta. In the mid-1990s the predominantly black Delta communities began working with Arkansas State University in Jonesboro to attract tourism and manufacturing, but they have made little headway. The area receives government support in the form of the Delta Regional Authority, which seeks to increase economic development in the areas along the Mississippi River.

Some of the nation's largest rice and cotton producers farm the Delta and house their corporate headquarters in the 1st. Cattle and poultry businesses are prosperous in the north. Manufacturing is strong in several cities, including Stuttgart, Batesville, and Jonesboro. One of the nation's largest steel production plants bolsters Blytheville, where the population and economy sagged after Eaker Air Force Base closed in 1992.

The 1st elects few Republicans at the state or federal level. A Republican has not represented the district since 1875, and Democratic presidential candidates carried the area in the 1990s and 2000, although Al Gore took the 1st with just under 50 percent in 2000. Western Lonoke County—home to Little Rock suburbanites and some military personnel—leans Republican, as do some of the 1st's northwestern counties. The heavily Christian district is socially conservative in many areas.

Major Industry

Agriculture, steel production, manufacturing.

Notable

Author John Grisham was born in Jonesboro; the world duck calling championship is held annually in Stuttgart.

Election Returns

	Republican		Democratic		Other	
President 2000	105,547	47.9%	109,160	49.6%	5,482	2.5%
House 2002	64,357	33.2%	129,701	66.8%		

District Profile

Population   668,360

Total area (square miles)   17,521
     Land area (square miles)   17,151

Population per square mile   39

Counties (2000 population)

Arkansas	20,749	Lee	12,580
Baxter	38,386	Lonoke	52,828
Clay	17,609	Mississippi	51,979
Cleburne	24,046	Monroe	10,254
Craighead	82,148	Phillips	26,445
Crittenden	50,866	Poinsett	25,614
Cross	19,526	Prairie	9,539
Fulton	11,642	Randolph	18,195
Greene	37,331	Searcy	8,261
Independence	34,233	Sharp	17,119
Izard	13,249	St. Francis	29,329
Jackson	18,418	Stone	11,499
Lawrence	17,774	Woodruff	8,741

Cities and other areas over 10,000 (2000 population)

Blytheville	18,272	Mountain Home	11,012
Cabot	15,261	Paragould	22,017
Forrest City	14,774	West Memphis	27,666
Jonesboro	55,515		

Race and Hispanic or Latino origin*

White   80.2%
Black or African American   16.6%
American Indian or Alaska Native   0.4%
Asian   0.3%
Native Hawaiian or other Pacific Islander   0.0%
Some other race   0.0%
Hispanic or Latino origin   1.6%
Two or more races   0.9%

*As percentage of total population.

Ancestry*

Dutch	1.2%	Irish	7.5%
English	5.6%	Scotch-Irish	1.1%
French	1.3%	USA/American	15.3%
German	6.8%		

*As estimated percentage of total population.

Universities and colleges, 2000–2001 enrollment

Arkansas State University, Mountain Home   916
Black River Technical College, Pocahontas   1,239
Delta Technical Institute, Marked Tree   293
East Arkansas Community College, Forrest City   1,358
Lyon College, Batesville   471
Mississippi County Community College, Blytheville   1,980
Ozarka Technical College, Melbourne   737
University of Arkansas Community College, Batesville   1,024
University of Arkansas Community College-Phillips, Helena   2,364
Williams Baptist College, Walnut Ridge   660

Newspapers and circulation

	District circulation	Total circulation
*Arkansas Democrat Gazette**	23,278	179,875
Baxter Bulletin	9,699	11,063
Jonesboro Sun	26,010	25,992
Memphis Commercial Appeal	4,755	157,808
West Memphis Evening Times	7,347	7,350

*See Sources and Explanations in the front of the volume.

Television stations and affiliations

Little Rock-Pine Bluff	40%	KARK	NBC
Little Rock-Pine Bluff	40%	KASN	UPN
Little Rock-Pine Bluff	40%	KATV	ABC
Little Rock-Pine Bluff	40%	KEMV	PBS
Little Rock-Pine Bluff	40%	KETG	PBS
Little Rock-Pine Bluff	40%	KETS	PBS
Little Rock-Pine Bluff	40%	KLEP	Independent
Little Rock-Pine Bluff	40%	KLRT	FOX
Little Rock-Pine Bluff	40%	KTHV	CBS
Little Rock-Pine Bluff	40%	KVTH	Independent
Little Rock-Pine Bluff	40%	KVTN	Independent
Little Rock-Pine Bluff	40%	KYPX	PAX
Memphis, TN	28%	KVTJ	Independent
Memphis, TN	28%	WBUY	Independent
Memphis, TN	28%	WHBQ	FOX
Memphis, TN	28%	WKNO	PBS
Memphis, TN	28%	WMAE	PBS
Memphis, TN	28%	WMAV	PBS
Memphis, TN	28%	WMC	NBC
Memphis, TN	28%	WPTY	ABC, WB
Memphis, TN	28%	WPXX	PAX
Memphis, TN	28%	WREG	CBS
Jonesboro	25%	KAIT	ABC
Jonesboro	25%	KTEJ	PBS
Springfield, MO	7%	KDEB	FOX
Springfield, MO	7%	KOLR	CBS
Springfield, MO	7%	KOZK	PBS
Springfield, MO	7%	KSPR	ABC
Springfield, MO	7%	KYTV	NBC

Cable systems and subscribers

Augusta Video   878
Blythville TV Cable   6,312
Buford Cable   1,151
Cable ONE   1,578
CableVision Communications   6,584
Charter   2,559
City Cable   8,779
Classic   28,793
Cox   58,546
East Arkansas Video   10,927
Independence County Cable   5,771
Salem Community Cablevision   525
Time Warner   13,152

Businesses and other major employers

American Greetings Corp.; Osceola; greeting cards   2,000
Arkansas State University; Jonesboro   2,000
Loving Garden Gourmet Inc.; Mountain; Home; specialty food items   1,994
St. Bernard's Hospital; Jonesboro   1,500
ConAgra Foods Inc.; Batesville; poultry hatcheries   1,500
L. A. Darling Co.; Paragould; wood store fixtures   1,400
Remington Arms Co.; Lonoke; small arms ammunition   1,000
Tenneco Automotive Operating Co.; Paragould; motor vehicle parts/accessories   1,000
Baxter County Regional Hospital Inc.; Mountain Home   980
Hytrol Conveyor Co.; Jonesboro; belt conveyor systems   910
Baxter Healthcare Corp.; Mountain Home; surgical and medical instruments   825
Nucor-Yamato Steel Co.; Armorel; steel structural shapes and pilings   800
Townsends of Arkansas Inc.; Batesville; broiling chickens   771
Mueller Copper Tube Products Inc.; Wynne; copper tubing   755
Eastman Chemical Co.; Batesville; chemicals and allied products   734
Family Dollar Stores Inc.; West Memphis; general warehousing, storage   700
Quebecor World Inc.; Jonesboro; offset printing   650
White River Medical Center; Batesville   650
Boar's Head Provision Co. Inc.; Forrest City; meats and meat products   600
Delta Consolidated Industries Inc.; Jonesboro; plastic boxes   600
Waterloo Industries Inc.; Pocahontas; metal boxes   600
S-B Power Tool Co.; Heber Springs; power-driven hand tools   600
Sanyo Manufacturing Corp.; Forrest City; television receiving sets   550
Arkansas Methodist Hospital Corp.; Paragould   550
S-B Power Tool Co.; Walnut Ridge; power-driven handtools   550
Trailmobile Parts and Service Corp; Jonesboro; semitrailers for truck tractors   530
Harold Ives Trucking Co.; Stuttgart; trucking   503

Maverick Tube Corp.; Blytheville; welded, lock joint tubes   500
Munro and Co.; Wynne; men's boots   500
Riceland Foods Inc.; Jonesboro; rice milling   500
Wal-Mart Stores Inc.; Jonesboro; discount department stores   500
Wolverine World Wide Inc.; Jonesboro; men's footwear, nonathletic   500
Haworth Inc.; Jonesboro; office furniture   500
L. A. Darling Co.; Corning; nonwood office/store shelving   500
Emerson Electric Co; Paragould; electric motors   500
Capital-Mercury Apparel; Gassville; men's/boys' dress shirts   500

Arkansas 2nd District

Central — Little Rock

Encompassing Little Rock, eight surrounding counties, and part of a ninth, the 2nd is Arkansas's axis of government activity. More than half of the district's population is focused in the Little Rock area, where strong black, union, and university populations offer solid support to Democrats in most elections.

The district includes the state's largest white-collar population and has the highest median income. While the district supported Arkansas' former governor Bill Clinton heavily in the 1992 and 1996 presidential elections, George W. Bush narrowly carried the 2nd in 2000.

Democratic support is concentrated in poor and working-class neighborhoods in east Little Rock, which is heavily black. Rural agriculture and mining communities in outlying areas also tend to support Democrats, although social conservatism is more common.

Affluent neighborhoods in north and west Little Rock are more likely to vote for Republicans. The GOP has gained popularity within rapidly growing suburbs in Faulkner, Saline, and Pulaski Counties, which are fed by affluent whites leaving Little Rock. Republicans also fare well in White County, where Church of Christ-affiliated Harding University is located.

Major Industry

Government, higher education, military.

Notable

The William J. Clinton Presidential Center will be located along the south bank of the Arkansas River in Little Rock; Little Rock Air Force Base has the largest C-130 training and airlift facility in the world; the Arkansas state capitol, completed in 1915, was built on the site of the state penitentiary, partially using prison labor; Gen. Douglas MacArthur was born in Little Rock.

Election Returns

	Republican		Democratic		Other	
President 2000	116,075	49.3%	112,720	47.8%	6,817	2.9%
House 2002	142,752	92.9%	10,874	7.1%		

District Profile

Population   666,058

Total area (square miles)   6,044
  Land area (square miles)   5,922

Population per square mile   112.5

Counties (2000 population)

Conway 20,336	Saline 83,529
Faulkner 86,014	Van Buren 16,192
Perry 10,209	White 67,165
Pulaski 361,474	Yell 21,139

Cities and other areas over 10,000 (2000 population)

Benton 21,906	Maumelle 10,557
Conway 43,167	North Little Rock 60,433
Jacksonville 29,916	Searcy 18,928
Little Rock 183,133	Sherwood 21,511

Race and Hispanic or Latino origin*

White   75.6%
Black or African American   19.4%
American Indian or Alaska Native   0.4%
Asian   0.9%
Native Hawaiian or other Pacific Islander   0.0%
Some other race   0.1%
Hispanic or Latino origin   2.4%
Two or more races   1.1%

*As percentage of total population.

Ancestry*

English 7.2%	Italian 1.2%
French 1.7%	Scotch-Irish 1.7%
German 8.4%	Scottish 1.4%
Irish 7.9%	USA/American 11.7%

*As estimated percentage of total population.

Universities and colleges, 2000–2001 enrollment

Arkansas Baptist College, Little Rock   201
Arkansas State University-Beebe Branch, Beebe   4,899
Baptist Schools of Nursing and Allied Health, Little Rock   567
Central Baptist College, Conway   381
Harding University, Searcy   4,337
Hendrix College, Conway   1,137
ITT Technical Institute, Little Rock   242
Philander Smith College, Little Rock   845
Pulaski Technical College, North Little Rock   893
University of Arkansas, Little Rock   10,968
University of Arkansas Community College, Morrilton   1,142
University of Arkansas for Medical Sciences, Little Rock   1,855
University of Central Arkansas, Conway   8,481

Newspapers and circulation

	District circulation	Total circulation
*Arkansas Democrat Gazette**	89,905	179,875
Benton Courier	7,128	7,166
*USA Today**	2,115	1,674,376

*See Sources and Explanations in the front of the volume.

Television stations and affiliations

Little Rock-Pine Bluff	100%	KARK	NBC
Little Rock-Pine Bluff	100%	KASN	UPN
Little Rock-Pine Bluff	100%	KATV	ABC
Little Rock-Pine Bluff	100%	KEMV	PBS
Little Rock-Pine Bluff	100%	KETG	PBS
Little Rock-Pine Bluff	100%	KETS	PBS
Little Rock-Pine Bluff	100%	KLEP	Independent
Little Rock-Pine Bluff	100%	KLRT	FOX
Little Rock-Pine Bluff	100%	KTHV	CBS
Little Rock-Pine Bluff	100%	KVTH	Independent
Little Rock-Pine Bluff	100%	KVTN	Independent
Little Rock-Pine Bluff	100%	KYPX	PAX

Cable systems and subscribers

Buford Comm.   13,198
Charter   9,310
Classic   2,967
Clinton Cable TV   1,040
Comcast   95,295
Cox   4,385
Independence County Cable   1,028
White County Cable TV   7,713

Military installations, September 2001

Little Rock Air Force Base, Jacksonville   6,015
MTA Camp Robinson, North Little Rock   2,114

Businesses and other major employers

University of Arkansas Hospital; Little Rock; hospital, medical school   8,000
Arkansas Dept. of Human Services; Little Rock   4,954
Washington Group; Jacksonville; special trade contractors   3,900
University of Arkansas; Little Rock   3,600
St. Vincent Hospital; Little Rock   3,200
U.S. Veterans Hospital; Little Rock   3,200
U.S. Veterans Hospital; North Little Rock   3,000
Arkansas Dept. of State Highway and Transportation; Little Rock   3,000
Alltel Information Services Inc.; Little Rock; data processing   3,000
Baptist Health Hospital; Little Rock   2,800
Oklahoma Alltel Corp. Services; Little Rock; local telephone communications   2,500
Arkansas Childrens Hospital; Little Rock   2,490
University of Central Arkansas; Conway   2,176
Arkansas Childrens Hospital; Little Rock   2,100
Union Pacific Railroad Co.; North Little Rock; railroad freight hauling   1,917
Virco Manufacturing Corp.; Conway; wood household tables   1,800
Baptist Health Hospital; North Little Rock   1,800
Arkansas Dept. of Finance and Administration; Little Rock   1,700
Molex Inc.; North Little Rock; electric cord connectors   1,600
Dassault Falcon Jet Corp.; Little Rock; aviation, aeronautical engineering   1,400
Harding University; Searcy   1,320
Wal-Mart Stores Inc.; Searcy; discount department stores; warehousing   1,300

International Union United Automobile Aerospace and
Agricultural Implement Workers of America;
Conway; labor union   1,200
Arkansas Blue Cross and Blue Shield; Little Rock; group
hospitalization   1,200
Tyson Foods Inc.; Dardanelle; processed poultry   1,200
Arkansas National Guard; North Little Rock   1,027
L'Oreal USA Inc.; North Little Rock; hair preparations,
shampoos   1,000
Maybelline Products Co.; North Little Rock; perfumes,
cosmetics, other toilet products   1,000
Alltel Corp.; Little Rock; local/long-distance telephone
1,000
Southwest Grocers Insurance Services Inc.; Little Rock;
insurance agents and brokers   1,000
Arkansas Dept. of Human Services; Little Rock   995
Southwest Airlines Co.; Benton; air passenger carrier
950
Little Rock School District; Little Rock   950
Maverick Transportation Inc.; North Little Rock;
building materials transport   908
Camden News Publishing Co.; Little Rock; newspaper
907
Pulaski County; Little Rock; courts   860
Nuvell Financial Services Corp.; Little Rock; purchaser
accounts receivable/commercial paper   831
American Transportation Corp.; Conway; bus parts   800
Target Corp.; North Little Rock; department stores
800
Heritage Co.; North Little Rock; telemarketing services
800
United Parcel Service Inc.; Little Rock; package delivery
800
Jean Petite Poultry Inc.; Danville; processed poultry
740
Alcoa Inc.; Bauxite; aluminum ore mining   700
Conway Public School District; Conway   700
Regal Ware Inc.; Jacksonville; cooking/kitchen utensils
700
Dimension Carpets; Little Rock; carpets   700
Conway Regional Medical Center; Conway   698
Kimberly-Clark Corp.; Conway; tampons   650
Wal-Mart Stores Inc.; Conway; discount department
stores   650
Land O'Frost Inc.; Searcy; sausages, other prepared meats
650
White County Medical Center; Searcy   650
Stephens Group Inc.; Little Rock; crude petroleum;
natural gas; investment bankers   643
Wal-Mart Stores Inc.; Benton; discount department
stores   600
Eaton Corp.; Searcy; industrial valves   600
Bryan Foods Inc.; Little Rock; meat packing plants   600
Arkansas Health Group; Little Rock; medical doctor
offices, clinics   600
MedCath of Arkansas; Little Rock; hospital   600
Benton Services Center; Benton; convalescent home;
nursing care   550
Quality Foods Inc.; Little Rock; food supplier   550
Spirit Homes Inc.; Conway; mobile homes   525
Affiliated Foods Southwest Inc.; Little Rock; food
supplier   525
Rebsamen Medical Center; Jacksonville   506

Acxiom Rm-Tools Inc.; Conway; data base information
retrieval   500
ICT Group Inc.; Morrilton; personal service agents   500
U.S. Postal Service; North Little Rock   500
Arkansas Dept. of Education; Little Rock   500
Dillard's Inc.; Little Rock; department stores   500
Entergy Arkansas Inc.; Little Rock; electric power
generation   500
Timex Corp.; Little Rock; watches, clocks, watchcases
500
Raytheon Aircraft Co.; Little Rock; aircraft   500
Arkansas State Police; Little Rock   500
Mechanical Refrigeration and Air Conditioning Inc.;
Little Rock; store fixtures   500

Arkansas 3rd District

Northwest — Fort Smith, Fayetteville

Arkansas's hilly northwest subscribes to a rugged conservatism unique in this heavily Democratic state, and its Republican bent remains despite an influx of newcomers. It voted heavily in favor of George W. Bush in 2000 and was the state's only district to withhold hearty support from native-son Bill Clinton in 1996. The 3rd has sent a Republican to Congress since the 1966 election.

Median household income, low in much of Arkansas, ranks in the bottom third of congressional districts nationwide, reflecting the 3rd's population of poor whites who live in the Ozark hills and farming communities. Residents in the Ozark mountains tend to be self-reliant and favor limited government, voting most often for Republicans.

Fayetteville, Springdale, Bentonville, and Rogers in the state's northwest corner represent a wealthier part of the district, where history, religious tradition, and an influx of retirees have created a solid Republican base. The 2000 census rated this northwestern corridor one of the ten fastest-growing metropolitan areas in the country, with 48 percent growth over the 1990s.

Though the northwest sets the political tone, the rest of the 3rd—particularly farming communities and the city of Fort Smith—is more open to electing Democrats at the state level. Fayetteville and Springdale also have some liberal-leaning areas.

Hometown giants Tyson Foods in Springdale and Wal-Mart in Bentonville sustain the 3rd's economy, as does the University of Arkansas in Fayetteville. The significant downsizing of Fort Chaffee Army Base, near Fort Smith, in the late 1990s hit the district hard, but the military has recently made attempts to redevelop the land.

Major Industry

Agriculture, livestock, retail.

Notable

Sen. J. William Fulbright, who established the Fulbright fellowships, lived in Fayetteville; the seven-story Christ of the Ozarks Statue in Eureka Springs was completed in 1966.

Election Returns

	Republican		Democratic		Other	
President 2000	138,977	59.5%	86,739	37.2%	7,691	3.3%
House 2002	141,479	100.0%			1,577	0.01%

District Profile

Population   672,756

Total area (square miles)   8,660
    Land area (square miles)   8,489

Population per square mile   79.2

Counties (2000 population)

Benton	153,406	Madison	14,243
Boone	33,948	Marion	16,140
Carroll	25,357	Newton	8,608
Crawford	53,247	Pope	54,469
Franklin	17,771	Sebastian	115,071
Johnson	22,781	Washington	157,715

Cities and other areas over 10,000 (2000 population)

Bella Vista CDP	16,582	Rogers	38,829
Bentonville	19,730	Russellville	23,682
Fayetteville	58,047	Siloam Springs	10,843
Fort Smith	80,268	Springdale	45,798
Harrison	12,152	Van Buren	18,986

Race and Hispanic or Latino origin*

White   87.3%
Black or African American   2.0%
American Indian or Alaska Native   1.2%
Asian   1.4%
Native Hawaiian or other Pacific Islander   0.2%
Some other race   0.1%
Hispanic or Latino origin   6.3%
Two or more races   1.6%

As percentage of total population.

Ancestry*

Dutch	1.6%	Italian	1.3%
English	7.5%	Scotch-Irish	1.5%
French	1.9%	Scottish	1.2%
German	10.0%	USA/American	11.8%
Irish	8.8%		

As estimated percentage of total population.

Universities and colleges, 2000–2001 enrollment

Arkansas Tech University, Russellville   4,970
John Brown University, Siloam Springs   1,536
North Arkansas College, Harrison   1,817
Northwest Arkansas Community College, Bentonville   4,058
University of Arkansas, Fayetteville   15,346
University of the Ozarks, Clarksville   622
Westark College, Fort Smith   5,286

Newspapers and circulation

	District circulation	Total circulation
*Arkansas Democrat Gazette**	35,880	179,875
Baxter Bulletin	1,204	11,063
*Fort Smith Times Record**	31,749	41,298
Harrison Daily Times	9,112	9,424
Morning News of Northwest Arkansas	35,664	35,393
*USA Today**	2,462	1,674,376

See Sources and Explanations in the front of the volume.

Television stations and affiliations

Fort Smith-Fayetteville-Springdale-Rogers	59%	KAFT	PBS
Fort Smith-Fayetteville-Springdale-Rogers	59%	KFAA	NBC
Fort Smith-Fayetteville-Springdale-Rogers	59%	KFSM	CBS
Fort Smith-Fayetteville-Springdale-Rogers	59%	KHBS	ABC
Fort Smith-Fayetteville-Springdale-Rogers	59%	KHOG	ABC
Fort Smith-Fayetteville-Springdale-Rogers	59%	KPOM	NBC
Fort Smith-Fayetteville-Springdale-Rogers	59%	KSBN	Independent
Springfield, MO	31%	KDEB	FOX
Springfield, MO	31%	KOLR	CBS
Springfield, MO	31%	KOZK	PBS
Springfield, MO	31%	KSPR	ABC
Springfield, MO	31%	KYTV	NBC
Little Rock-Pine Bluff	10%	KARK	NBC
Little Rock-Pine Bluff	10%	KASN	UPN
Little Rock-Pine Bluff	10%	KATV	ABC
Little Rock-Pine Bluff	10%	KEMV	PBS
Little Rock-Pine Bluff	10%	KETG	PBS
Little Rock-Pine Bluff	10%	KETS	PBS
Little Rock-Pine Bluff	10%	KLEP	Independent
Little Rock-Pine Bluff	10%	KLRT	FOX
Little Rock-Pine Bluff	10%	KTHV	CBS
Little Rock-Pine Bluff	10%	KVTH	Independent
Little Rock-Pine Bluff	10%	KVTN	Independent
Little Rock-Pine Bluff	10%	KYPX	PAX

Cable systems and subscribers

Classic   3,204
Cox   121,626
Independence County Cable   1,222
Madison County Cable   1,089

Military installations, September 2001

Fort Smith Municipal Airport Air Force Guard Station, Fort Smith   1,001
Fort Chaffee (Army), Fort Smith   461

Businesses and other major employers

Wal-Mart Stores Inc.; Bentonville; discount department stores   6,650
Whirlpool Corp.; Fort Smith; household refrigerators/freezers   3,300
Sparks Regional Medical Center; Fort Smith   2,800
J. B. Hunt Transport Inc.; Lowell; trucking   2,396
Tyson Breeders Inc.; Springdale; poultry hatcheries   2,000
Wal-Mart Stores Inc.; Bentonville; general warehousing, storage   1,706
Tyson Foods Inc.; Berryville; processed poultry   1,700
Tyson Foods Inc.; Green Forest; processed poultry   1,500
University of Arkansas; Fayetteville   1,500
Tyson Foods Inc.; Clarksville; processed poultry   1,500
Mercy St. Edwards Medical Center; Fort Smith   1,500
Arvest Bank Group Inc.; Lowell; bank holding companies   1,458
Baldor Electric Co.; Fort Smith; electric motor, generator parts   1,458
Northwest Health Systems; Springdale; hospital   1,400
Washington Regional Medical Hospital; Fayetteville   1,300
Superior Industries International Inc.; Fayetteville; aluminum foundries   1,200
ConAgra Foods Inc.; Russellville; frozen dinners   1,200
USA Truck Inc.; Van Buren; trucking   1,197
Peterson Farms Inc.; Decatur; liquefied petroleum gas dealers   1,000
Glad Products Co; Rogers; storage bags   1,000

IMS Health Inc.; London; market analysis or research
1,000

Tyson Foods Inc.; Van Buren; processed poultry   1,000

Danaher Corp.; Springdale; hand and edge tools   900

George's Inc.; Springdale; processed poultry   800

PAM Transport Inc.; Tontitown; trucking   800

Riverside Furniture Corp.; Fort Smith; wood household
furniture   800

Hospice Preferred Choice Inc.; Fort Smith; personal
service agents   800

Wood Manufacturing Co.; Flippin; fiberglass boats   750

Pinnacle Food Corp.; Fayetteville; processed poultry
750

ConAgra Poultry Co.; Huntsville; processed turkey
750

Gates Corp.; Siloam Springs; rubber belting   750

Franklin Electric Co. Inc.; Siloam Springs; motors and
generators   725

American Freightways Inc.; Harrison; freight carrier
717

St. Mary-Rogers Memorial Hospital; Rogers   710

Construction Management and Inspection Co.; Fort
Smith; construction project management consultant
710

Kawneer Co.; Springdale; metal housings, enclosures,
casings, containers   700

Sara Lee Corp.; Clarksville; bras, girdles, and allied
garments   700

Beverly Enterprises-Arizona Inc.; Fort Smith; skilled
nursing care facilities   700

Cargill Inc.; Ozark; turkey processing   680

Rogers Tool Works Inc.; Rogers; cutting tools for
machine tools   652

St. Mary's Regional Medical Center; Russellville   650

Georgia-Pacific Corp.; Fort Smith; paper cups, plates,
dishes, utensils   650

North Arkansas Regional Medical Center; Harrison
600

Pace Industries Inc.; Harrison; aluminum die-castings
600

Wal-Mart Realty Co.; Bentonville; financial
management for business   600

Magee Enterprises Inc.; Springdale; temporary help
service   600

Tyson Foods Inc.; Springdale; processed poultry   600

Wal-Mart Stores Inc.; Clarksville; general warehousing,
storage   600

Trane Co.; Fort Smith; air conditioning equipment   578

Wal-Mart Stores Inc.; Fort Smith; discount department
stores   550

University of Arkansas Fort Smith; Fort Smith   541

Tyson Foods Inc.; Fayetteville; processed poultry and
food   540

Gerber Products Co.; Fort Smith; baby foods   520

U.S. Dept. of Veterans Affairs; Fayetteville   508

Eveready Battery Co.; Fayetteville; industrial storage
batteries   500

Wal-Mart Stores Inc.; Elkins; discount department stores
500

Peterson Farms Inc.; Rogers; chicken processing   500

Tyson Foods Inc.; Rogers; chicken processing   500

Wal-Mart Stores Inc.; Rogers; discount department
stores   500

Tyson Foods Inc.; Springdale; processed poultry   500

Arkansas 4th District

South — Pine Bluff, Hot Springs

Covering much of Arkansas's southern half, from the Mississippi River to the Texas and Oklahoma borders, the 4th is a socially conservative but Democratic district that took a Republican swing in the 1990s.

The district narrowly elected its first GOP representative of the twentieth century in 1992, but overwhelmingly supported Hope-born and Hot Springs-raised Bill Clinton in both his presidential bids. In 2000 the 4th not only supported Al Gore in the presidential race but also elected a Democrat to the House. State legislators in the 4th are almost exclusively Democrats.

Rice, soybeans, cotton, and rural poverty characterize the eastern edge of the 4th, where many Mississippi River communities have black-majority populations. Democrats receive their most faithful support from these areas and from blue-collar and minority populations in Little River and Lafayette counties to the west. Republicans fare better in oil- and chemical-producing southern cities such as El Dorado, as well as in military and white-collar areas near Pine Bluff and Hot Springs. The timber industry here discourages pro-environment candidates.

The Pine Bluff Arsenal, which once produced the nation's supply of biological weapons, is home to an emergency preparedness center and a center for toxicological research. A chemical weapons disposal facility is under construction at the arsenal, and the base hopes to house the nation's first government-owned vaccine production plant to guard against bioterrorism.

Major Industry

Timber, agriculture, livestock.

Notable

Author Maya Angelou was raised in Stamps; country singer Johnny Cash was born in Kingsland; Hot Springs, the state's premier tourist attraction, was a getaway for mobsters such as Charles "Lucky" Luciano and Al Capone in the 1930s.

Election Returns

	Republican		Democratic		Other	
President 2000	112,341	48.3%	114,149	49.1%	6,083	2.6%
House 2002	77,904	39.4%	119,633	60.6%		

District Profile

Population   666,226

Total area (square miles)   20,951
    Land area (square miles)   20,504

Population per square mile   32.5

Counties (2000 population)

Ashley	24,209	Jefferson	84,278
Bradley	12,600	Lafayette	8,559
Calhoun	5,744	Lincoln	14,492
Chicot	14,117	Little River	13,628
Clark	23,546	Logan	22,486
Cleveland	8,571	Miller	40,443
Columbia	25,603	Montgomery	9,245
Dallas	9,210	Nevada	9,955
Desha	15,341	Ouachita	28,790
Drew	18,723	Pike	11,303
Garland	88,068	Polk	20,229
Grant	16,464	Scott	10,996
Hempstead	23,587	Sevier	15,757
Hot Spring	30,353	Union	45,629
Howard	14,300		

Cities and other areas over 10,000 (2000 population)

Arkadelphia	10,912	Hot Springs	35,750
Camden	13,154	Magnolia	10,858
El Dorado	21,530	Pine Bluff	55,085
Hope	10,616	Texarkana	26,448

Race and Hispanic or Latino origin*

White 71.0%
Black or African American 24.4%
American Indian or Alaska Native 0.5%
Asian 0.4%
Native Hawaiian or other Pacific Islander 0.0%
Some other race 0.0%
Hispanic or Latino origin 2.7%
Two or more races 0.9%

*As percentage of total population.

Ancestry*

Dutch	1.1%	Irish	7.3%
English	5.7%	Scotch-Irish	1.3%
French	1.4%	USA/American	14.0%
German	5.5%		

*As estimated percentage of total population.

Universities and colleges, 2000–2001 enrollment

Cossatot Technical College, De Queen 815
Garland County Community College, Hot Springs 2,231
Henderson State University, Arkadelphia 3,549
Ouachita Baptist University, Arkadelphia 1,714
Ouachita Technical College, Malvern 829
Rich Mountain Community College, Mena 943
South Arkansas Community College, El Dorado 905
Southeast Arkansas College, Pine Bluff 1,955
Southern Arkansas University, Magnolia 2,977
Southern Arkansas University Tech, Camden 790
University of Arkansas, Monticello 2,323
University of Arkansas, Pine Bluff 3,042
University of Arkansas Community College, Hope 1,176

Newspapers and circulation

	District circulation	Total circulation
*Arkansas Democrat Gazette**	30,812	179,875
El Dorado News-Times	9,545	9,715
*Fort Smith Times Record**	3,323	41,298
Hot Springs Sentinel-Record	16,781	17,477
Pine Bluff Commercial	18,576	18,576
Texarkana Gazette	11,306	30,429

*See Sources and Explanations in the front of the volume.

Television stations and affiliations

Little Rock-Pine Bluff	58%	KARK	NBC
Little Rock-Pine Bluff	58%	KASN	UPN
Little Rock-Pine Bluff	58%	KATV	ABC
Little Rock-Pine Bluff	58%	KEMV	PBS
Little Rock-Pine Bluff	58%	KETG	PBS
Little Rock-Pine Bluff	58%	KETS	PBS
Little Rock-Pine Bluff	58%	KLEP	Independent
Little Rock-Pine Bluff	58%	KLRT	FOX
Little Rock-Pine Bluff	58%	KTHV	CBS
Little Rock-Pine Bluff	58%	KVTH	Independent
Little Rock-Pine Bluff	58%	KVTN	Independent
Little Rock-Pine Bluff	58%	KYPX	PAX
Shreveport, LA	21%	KLTS	PBS
Shreveport, LA	21%	KMSS	FOX
Shreveport, LA	21%	KPXJ	PAX
Shreveport, LA	21%	KSHV	WB, UPN
Shreveport, LA	21%	KSLA	CBS
Shreveport, LA	21%	KTAL	NBC
Shreveport, LA	21%	KTBS	ABC
Monroe-El Dorado	10%	KAQY	ABC
Monroe-El Dorado	10%	KARD	FOX
Monroe-El Dorado	10%	KLTM	PBS
Monroe-El Dorado	10%	KMCT	Independent
Monroe-El Dorado	10%	KNOE	CBS
Monroe-El Dorado	10%	KTVE	NBC
Monroe-El Dorado	10%	WNTZ	FOX
Fort Smith-Fayetteville-Springdale-Rogers	8%	KAFT	PBS
Fort Smith-Fayetteville-Springdale-Rogers	8%	KFAA	NBC
Fort Smith-Fayetteville-Springdale-Rogers	8%	KFSM	CBS
Fort Smith-Fayetteville-Springdale-Rogers	8%	KHBS	ABC
Fort Smith-Fayetteville-Springdale-Rogers	8%	KHOG	ABC
Fort Smith-Fayetteville-Springdale-Rogers	8%	KPOM	NBC
Fort Smith-Fayetteville-Springdale-Rogers	8%	KSBN	Independent
Greenwood-Greenville	3%	WABG	ABC
Greenwood-Greenville	3%	WLMT	UPN
Greenwood-Greenville	3%	WMAO	PBS
Greenwood-Greenville	3%	WXVT	CBS

Cable systems and subscribers

Bayou Cable 3,215
Cable ONE 7,750
Cam-Tel Co. 5,932
Charter 6,628
Classic 15,035
Community Comm. 8,260
Cox 42,906
Hope Community TV 3,862
Pine Bluff Cable TV 14,405
Prescott Video 1,312
Resort TV Cable 22,629

Military installations, September 2001

Pine Bluff Arsenal (Army), Pine Bluff 3,510

Businesses and other major employers

Georgia-Pacific Corp.; Crossett; millwork; reconstituted wood products 2,600
Tyson Foods Inc.; Pine Bluff; processed poultry 2,100
Tyson Foods Inc.; Nashville; processed poultry 2,000
Murphy Gas Gathering Inc.; El Dorado; petroleum products 1,800
Tyson Foods Inc.; Grannis; processed poultry 1,800
Jefferson Hospital; Pine Bluff 1,695

ConAgra Poultry Co.; El Dorado; processed poultry 1,500

Tyson Foods Inc.; Hope; broiler, fryer, roaster chickens 1,500

Electrolux Home Products Inc.; Nashville; chain saws 1,400

St. Joseph's Regional Hospital; Hot Springs; lumber; rough, sawed, or planed   1,320

Georgia-Pacific Corp.; Ashdown; pulp mills   1,300

Tyson Foods Inc.; Waldron; poultry products   1,200

Albemarle Corp.; Magnolia; brine   1,100

Jean Petite Poultry Inc.; Arkadelphia; processed poultry 800

Area Agency of South East Arkansas Inc.; Pine Bluff; individual and family services   700

Medical Center of South Arkansas; El Dorado   700

Electrolux Home Products Inc.; De Queen; lawn edgers 700

National Park Medical Center; Hot Springs   700

Alcoa Extrusions Inc.; Magnolia; aluminum products 650

Weyerhaeuser Co.; Dierks; lumber: rough, sawed, or planed   600

U.S. Food and Drug Administration; Jefferson   600

Cloyes Gear and Products Inc.; Paris; air conditioner parts, motor vehicle   600

Central Moloney Inc.; Pine Bluff; nonelectric transformers   585

CMC Steel Fabricators Inc.; Hope; expansion joints 569

International Paper Co.; Camden; millwork and lumber 550

Lockheed Martin Corp.; Camden; space and military rockets   530

Aalfs Manufacturing Inc.; Mena; men's/boys' trousers and slacks   530

University of Arkansas; Monticello   500

Atlantic Research Corp.; Camden; guided missile/space vehicle propulsion units   500

Meyer's Bakeries Inc.; Hope; breads and cakes   500

Southern Refrigerated Transport Inc.; Ashdown; contract haulers   500

Munro and Co.; Hot Springs; men's footwear, nonathletic 500

Carrier Corp.; Arkadelphia; electronic equipment hermetic seals   500

Weyerhaeuser Co.; Mountain Pine; sawmills and planing mills   500

Excel Corp.; Booneville; meat packing plants   500

California

California has always had a special relationship to the rest of reality. Most Americans know less about the actual California than they do about the imagined one, with its mythic images of promise: the gold rush, agricultural paradise, Hollywood glamour, Disneyland fantasy, endless beaches, Summer of Love, and, most recently, Silicon Valley.

California is so defined as the state of hope that when riots broke out in Los Angeles, they called into question something profound: a version of the American dream itself. The Watts riots of 1965 were the first repudiation of the Great Society programs that were a central part of President Lyndon B. Johnson's tenure, and a harbinger of things to come in the state (Ronald Reagan would be elected governor in 1966) and nation (Richard Nixon would become president two years later).

Something similar happened in 1992 when rioting followed the acquittal of white police officers accused of beating a black motorist. In this case, as in 1965, the outrage and violence were disquieting portents of larger unrest. In the early 1990s the state's economy, particularly in the Los Angeles Basin, was reeling from cutbacks in the aerospace and defense industries on which it had thrived since World War II. Automaking had also taken a downturn, along with construction and other industries that Angelenos had come to take for granted. For a time the state was also victimized by a series of earthquakes, mudslides, floods, catastrophic fires, and droughts. An aide to Gov. Pete Wilson once remarked that the state was "just two plagues shy of Egypt."

But then there are many economies in California, and when one goes bust there always seems to be another waiting to boom. Hollywood enjoyed one of its biggest decades ever in the 1990s as did the state's agriculture. Despite shortages of water early and energy later in the decade, California's farmers and ranchers produced more product than ever and more than any other state.

Then there was the new gold rush, the digital one. California was not the only source of high-tech innovation or manufacture but an extraordinary matrix for both had grown up around the Bay Area, fed by the research activities at Stanford and the University of California-Berkeley. High-tech industry had long since found a home in former fruit groves in Santa Clara County south of Stanford. Soon the success stories spread down the San Francisco peninsula to San Jose, as the microchip and the Internet and the World Wide Web all spread revolution from this base in so-called Silicon Valley.

By the late 1990s the phenomenal growth of such ventures as Intel and Sun Microsystems had spurred a stock market revolution. The NASDAQ, where many of the dot-coms were traded, topped 5000 and seemed on track to overtake the Dow Jones Industrial Average in fame and capitalization. There were overnight billionaires and many millionaires, but all on paper. When the bubble burst in 2000 most of those paper billions disappeared and the resulting loss of confidence shook the national and world economies.

That falloff also starved the state for revenues at a time when energy shortages were causing brownouts and service interruptions. The fiscal sorrows of the years right after 2000 were such that the state deficit hit $35 billion, an amount larger than the whole budget for most states.

Clearly, California is multidirectional. It is at once ascending and descending, coming in and going out. It is at once the nation's best melting pot and its toughest case of resistance to cultural homogeneity. The home base of the national GOP of the 1970s and 1980s is now national Democrats' best source of both votes and money. It is not only hard to predict, it is hard to describe in its current state, and it is especially hard to describe without the prefix "multi-."

It is often thought of first as multipopulous, the place where all the growth streams of U.S. history flowed together. Here was an historic shift from the eastern states, the more recent exodus from southern and midwestern states, the generations of ship-borne Asians and border-crossing Hispanics. People came for gold, then for land or jobs, then for climate or freedom, and, finally, for excitement. California surpassed New York as the most populous state in 1963. Forty years later, it had 34 million people, more than three times the number it had in 1950.

In the next quarter century, the Census Bureau projects, California will grow by half again, vying with a few smaller states for the fastest growth rate while outstripping them all in absolute numbers. Its expected net gain of 16 million should equal that of the next four big gainers—Texas, Florida, Georgia, and Washington—combined.

With all this expansion it is inevitable California should be the nation's most multicultural state. Even in precolonial times, the state was home to an estimated 100 tribes of Native Americans, and at the millennium diversity has returned to rule.

During the 1990s, an estimated 80 percent of the state's growth was attributable to Hispanics, bringing the Hispanic share of the populace to one-third and the total of non-Anglo residents (including Asian and African Americans) to more than half. Moreover, that only begins to state the case. By the 2000s the Los Angeles suburb of Glendale could count about 60 different languages and dialects being spoken in its public schools.

CALIFORNIA

Districts established September 26, 2001, for elections first held in 2002.

53 members

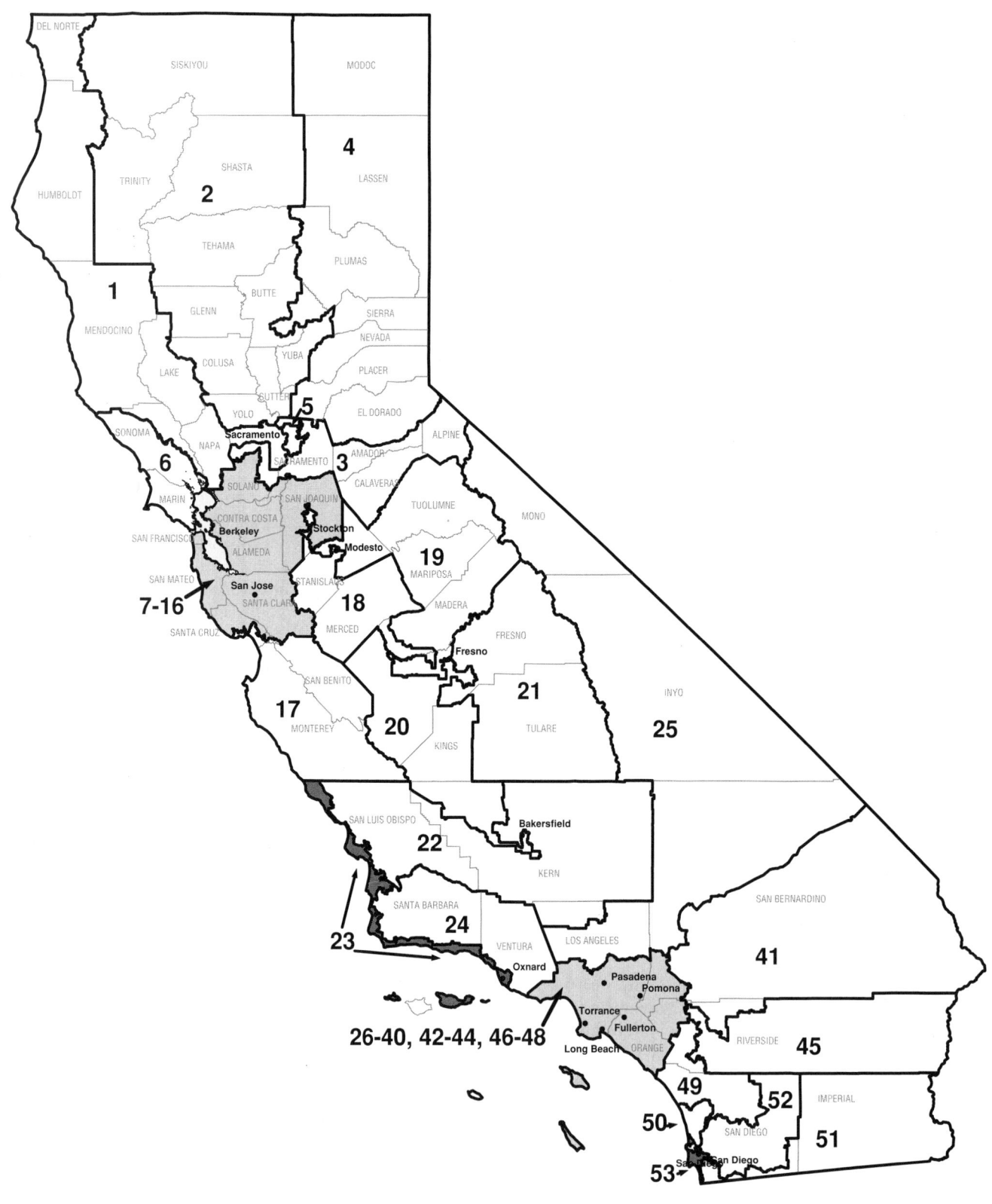

It is this explosion of diversity that has Republicans worried. Before the 1990s, the state had gone Republican for president in nine of ten elections (the exception being Lyndon Johnson's landslide in 1964), often by big margins. Yet in 1992 the state rejected the incumbent Republican George Bush in favor of Democrat Bill Clinton, a shift so strong and so well rooted in the state's new demographics that it gave Democrats a surge of confidence nationally as well as in California. A similar voting pattern emerged in 1996, when Clinton took an outright majority, and in 2000, when Gore did even better.

How did this turnaround happen? One factor was the sudden absence of Californians from the GOP ticket (which had one Californian eight times out of ten from 1948 through 1984.) A second difference came from the shift in state issues. In the elections of the 1990s, economics and social change replaced crime and the cold war as the salient concerns. Clinton was able to focus much of the campaign debate on the future, rather than on the resentments of the past.

But the key element was the degree to which the Republican era of success had relied on Anglo white voters. As this group has declined to plurality status its voting clout has begun to diminish (although Anglo whites still cast most of the votes in the state). In the early 1990s, two million California residents left the state, most of them Anglo whites. They were replaced primarily by Hispanics. Although it takes time for the new arrivals to begin voting, that process has begun.

What made this reliance on Anglo whites especially damaging was the fallout from Proposition 187, a ballot initiative approved in 1994 that sought to deny state services (including school and health care) to illegal immigrants and their families. Many established Hispanics and Asians, including legal immigrants, favored the idea. But the campaign pushing the measure aggravated anti-immigrant feeling in general. The manner in which the incumbent governor, Pete Wilson, used the issue to secure his own reelection left a bruise. Among those who condemned the tactic at the time was the Republican governor of Texas, George W. Bush.

The backlash was swift, as Hispanic votes for Republicans got scarce in the Clinton reelection year in 1996 and stayed down in Democrat Gray Davis's gubernatorial wins in 1998 and 2002. In those elections, Democrats achieved a near sweep of statewide offices and built up formidable margins in the legislature as well. However, in the summer of 2003 a movement to recall Davis because of the state's huge budget deficit qualified for the fall ballot and called into question the future leadership of the state.

Following the 2000 census the Democratic majorities in Sacramento, backed by Davis, were able to do as they wished with the redistricting process. But in an interesting departure from recent state history, the Democrats chose to emphasize the protection of incumbents. Given their distinct edge (32–20) in House seats at the time, the Democrats in Sacramento (some planning congressional campaigns of their own) were more concerned about losing ground than gaining it. Remarkably, Republicans in Sacramento and Washington were generally agreeable to this arrangement. One GOP official called it "a sweetheart gerrymander."

That was what galled critics, including some in both parties, who wanted more competitive districts. It also led to a lawsuit by the Mexican American Legal Defense and Educational Fund (MALDEF), an advocacy group for Hispanics. Their argument was that a wider distribution of Hispanic voters in Los Angeles County might produce more Hispanic members of Congress, albeit at the expense of some incumbent Anglo or African American Democrats. In all, the group challenged four of the districts as racial gerrymandering, but their suit was dismissed. California does not have the burdensome states bear to gain clearance for their redistricting plans from the Justice Department.

Other complainants took their case to the state supreme court, which had drawn the map that emerged from the 1990 census (perhaps the most even-handed map in generations). But the court saw no basis on which to interfere, in part because the new lines were based on the court's own.

A tour of the old-new map begins with the state's mountainous northern third, which has coastal ranges down the west side and portions of the Sierra Nevada on the east. At the center of this is Mount Shasta and, directly below it, the deep cut of the Sacramento Valley (which includes the river and state capital of the same name). This region relies heavily on mining and timber, tourism, and the vast array of farm products pouring each season from the irrigated areas of the Valley. It is lightly populated like the Mountain West but it does support five congressional districts, most of them rural Republican and influenced by the strong Mormon presence in the state's far northeast.

The middle third of the state includes the San Francisco Bay Area, home to ten districts. In the years right before and after 2000 all these districts were represented by Democrats, as were the central-coastal districts extending south to Monterey Bay and Santa Barbara. The dominant political dynamic here is a strong preference for social liberals, a rare breed in the contemporary GOP. It may be said that in 2003 the 12–0 shutout of the GOP in this part of the state is largely responsible for the Democrats' overall advantage in the delegation.

Directly east of the Bay Area, the Sacramento Valley gives way to the San Joaquin (both together are referred to as the Central Valley). Moving south across the Valley there are orchards of all descriptions, grapes on the vine, vast dairy operations, plantations of cotton, and feedlots for finishing steers. Here the votes of landowner farmers and agribusiness people are usually Republican, while those of workers, many of them immigrants, tend to be Democratic.

Further south in the Valley, the energy industry becomes a presence, with its unofficial capital in Bakersfield. Growth here earned another House seat in 2002 for the Republicans who dominate the lower reaches of the Central Valley, and they filled it with a Hispanic farmer named Devin Nunes. Overall, the six Valley House seats from San Joaquin County south split 4–2 Republican in 2003.

The Valley thoroughfares, Interstate 5 and Highway 99, converge in the Tehachapi Mountains. Then below Tejon Pass one descends into the Los Angeles Basin, the second most populous metro area in America after New York City. The area accounts for more than 20 congressional districts (more than Ohio, Illinois, or Pennsylvania). This part of the state is dominated by Los Angeles County, the nation's busiest port and top manufacturing center and by many measures the unofficial capital of the Pacific Rim. If the twenty-first century is to be the Asian century, with trade and immigration redefining relationships across the world's largest ocean, then the city of the future can already be glimpsed in parts of old Los Angeles, teeming with multinational humanity and culture.

Redistricting here was mostly a matter of securing seven suburban venues for Republicans, with six districts held by

Hispanic Democrats, five held by Anglo Democrats, and three held by African American Democrats in 2003. In Long Beach, the mapmakers so altered the old 38th District to prompt the retirement of the Republican incumbent, a moderate who had held on for years in a district Gore won with 58 percent. One beneficiary of this work was a new district, numbered the 39th, that reached from Long Beach south to Orange County. These older suburbs built to accommodate the postwar boom are now filling with immigrants and are rich in Democratic votes. The first winner in 2002 was a Democratic union official, Linda Sanchez, whose sister Loretta won reelection in the neighboring 47th District.

Just east of the Los Angeles Basin, across the San Gabriel and the San Bernardino Mountains, lies what is called the Inland Empire. Riverside and San Bernardino still seem part of the Los Angeles metroplex but beyond them the suburban sprawl seems more free-floating along Interstate 10. Palm Springs has long since been joined by a host of populous resort and retirement towns, all built around old water holes, and the four members of Congress from the area in 2003, split 3–1 Republican.

At the base of the state, still hard by the ocean, lies San Diego County, home port for the largest U.S. Navy base in the world and for many other military installations as well. But if San Diego has long felt this influence, it is also joined by streetcar to Tijuana and Latin America beyond. Broadly defined, the San Diego part of the state also runs east through the Imperial Valley to the Arizona line. These spacious precincts are still subsumed into the 51st and 52nd Districts, which are among the five House seats that are San Diego County based. They split 3–2 Republican in 2003.

Table 1 Population

District	Population	Population under 18	Voting-age population	Median age	Male*	Female*
1	639,087	156,816	482,271	36.1	49.6	50.4
2	639,087	168,711	470,376	36.6	49.3	50.7
3	639,088	167,406	471,682	36.7	49.7	50.3
4	639,088	163,835	475,253	39.1	50.2	49.8
5	639,088	181,090	457,998	31.8	48.6	51.4
6	639,087	145,265	493,822	39.0	49.4	50.6
7	639,088	175,130	463,958	34.5	49.6	50.4
8	639,088	91,089	547,999	36.0	51.4	48.6
9	639,088	147,921	491,167	34.0	48.5	51.5
10	639,088	169,760	469,328	36.4	49.0	51.0
11	639,088	183,598	455,490	35.0	49.5	50.5
12	639,088	132,336	506,752	38.0	48.8	51.2
13	639,088	162,461	476,627	34.7	49.5	50.5
14	639,088	143,765	495,323	36.1	50.6	49.4
15	639,088	154,500	484,588	34.6	50.4	49.6
16	639,088	174,380	464,708	31.8	51.1	48.9
17	639,088	174,560	464,528	32.1	51.0	49.0
18	639,088	214,263	424,825	29.5	50.1	49.9
19	639,088	181,373	457,715	34.1	48.9	51.1
20	639,088	222,964	416,124	26.9	53.8	46.2
21	639,088	206,825	432,263	30.2	49.6	50.4
22	639,088	182,970	456,118	34.2	51.0	49.0
23	639,088	161,300	477,788	31.9	50.2	49.8
24	639,088	176,768	462,320	36.1	49.7	50.3
25	639,087	205,650	433,437	32.2	50.4	49.6
26	639,088	173,104	465,984	35.8	48.6	51.4
27	639,088	163,162	475,926	33.9	49.5	50.5
28	639,087	182,707	456,380	30.8	50.3	49.7
29	639,088	147,093	491,995	36.2	47.9	52.1
30	639,088	108,390	530,698	38.6	48.8	51.2
31	639,088	191,700	447,388	29.0	50.8	49.2
32	639,087	197,856	441,231	29.8	49.4	50.6
33	639,088	155,663	483,425	32.7	48.5	51.5
34	639,088	207,490	431,598	27.9	51.1	48.9
35	639,088	209,968	429,120	28.8	48.3	51.7
36	639,087	148,044	491,043	34.7	49.9	50.1
37	639,088	210,532	428,556	28.7	48.8	51.2
38	639,088	202,914	436,174	29.5	49.6	50.4
39	639,088	207,855	431,233	29.2	49.4	50.6
40	639,088	172,233	466,855	33.5	49.6	50.4
41	639,087	181,923	457,164	34.8	49.4	50.6
42	639,088	180,278	458,810	34.8	49.6	50.4
43	639,087	234,019	405,068	26.7	49.7	50.3
44	639,088	195,859	443,229	31.4	50.0	50.0
45	639,088	185,693	453,395	35.0	50.1	49.9
46	639,088	140,382	498,706	37.0	49.7	50.3
47	639,087	212,267	426,820	27.6	51.4	48.6
48	639,087	149,134	489,953	36.4	48.6	51.4
49	639,087	185,974	453,113	32.1	50.7	49.3
50	639,087	161,450	477,637	36.2	49.7	50.3
51	639,087	196,321	442,766	31.0	50.1	49.9
52	639,087	169,998	469,089	35.5	49.0	51.0
53	639,087	133,084	506,003	30.8	51.9	48.1
State	33,871,648	9,249,829	24,621,819	33.3	49.8	50.2

*As percentage of total population.

Table 2 Voting-Age Persons by Race/Hispanic or Latino Origin

District	White*	Black or African American*	American Indian or Alaska Native*	Asian*	Other or multirace*	Hispanic or Latino*
1	74.6	1.4	2.1	4.3	2.6	15.0
2	80.0	1.1	1.7	3.2	2.5	11.4
3	77.0	4.2	0.8	6.1	2.8	9.1
4	85.7	1.2	1.1	2.3	2.0	7.6
5	49.3	13.0	0.8	14.9	3.9	18.0
6	78.9	2.0	0.6	4.0	2.2	12.4
7	47.3	15.9	0.5	14.2	3.3	18.7
8	46.6	7.8	0.3	28.3	2.9	14.1
9	39.3	24.5	0.4	16.4	3.3	16.2
10	68.7	5.1	0.4	9.9	2.9	12.9
11	67.5	3.3	0.5	8.8	2.6	17.2
12	50.9	2.5	0.2	29.3	3.1	14.0
13	42.1	5.9	0.4	29.1	3.8	18.7
14	62.3	3.0	0.3	17.1	2.2	15.2
15	50.1	2.3	0.3	29.4	2.7	15.2
16	35.5	3.4	0.4	24.4	2.6	33.8
17	51.8	2.8	0.5	5.6	2.3	37.0
18	44.8	5.5	0.7	8.4	3.1	37.5
19	64.8	3.2	1.0	4.3	2.6	24.1
20	26.0	7.9	0.8	5.1	1.7	58.7
21	52.3	2.0	0.9	4.7	2.0	38.1
22	70.5	5.3	0.9	3.1	2.2	18.0
23	54.8	2.0	0.5	5.4	1.8	35.5
24	71.7	1.7	0.5	4.8	1.7	19.6
25	61.4	7.2	0.9	4.3	2.2	24.0
26	56.2	4.3	0.3	15.5	2.3	21.5
27	49.7	4.3	0.3	11.0	2.9	31.8
28	37.2	4.2	0.2	6.7	2.5	49.2
29	42.0	5.6	0.2	24.6	4.5	23.2
30	77.2	2.6	0.2	9.2	3.1	7.7
31	12.1	4.5	0.3	16.0	1.8	65.5
32	17.7	2.5	0.3	20.7	1.3	57.4
33	23.2	29.6	0.2	13.6	3.1	30.2

District	White*	Black or African American*	American Indian or Alaska Native*	Asian*	Other or multirace*	Hispanic or Latino*
34	13.9	5.0	0.3	6.8	1.0	72.9
35	13.0	35.0	0.2	7.2	1.9	42.7
36	53.0	3.8	0.3	14.5	2.5	25.8
37	21.4	24.7	0.3	13.0	2.3	38.2
38	16.5	3.6	0.3	11.9	1.4	66.3
39	25.1	6.0	0.3	10.8	1.4	56.3
40	53.4	2.1	0.4	16.6	2.0	25.6
41	68.4	4.7	1.0	4.1	2.3	19.6
42	56.6	3.0	0.3	16.6	2.1	21.6
43	28.2	11.9	0.5	3.9	1.8	53.7
44	55.8	5.4	0.5	5.6	2.2	30.6
45	56.8	5.7	0.6	3.2	1.5	32.2
46	66.1	1.5	0.3	15.5	2.1	14.4
47	21.2	1.6	0.3	15.9	1.4	59.5
48	70.4	1.3	0.2	13.0	2.3	12.7
49	63.1	4.7	0.9	4.3	1.9	25.1
50	69.4	1.7	0.4	10.7	1.9	15.9
51	25.1	9.5	0.5	13.9	1.9	49.0
52	76.0	3.3	0.6	6.0	2.5	11.7
53	57.3	6.6	0.5	8.8	2.7	24.0
State	51.1	6.2	0.5	11.6	2.4	28.1

As percentage of voting-age population.

Table 3 Voting-Age Population by Age Groups

District	18 to 24*	25 to 44*	45 to 64*	Over 64*
1	15.1	36.3	31.1	17.4
2	13.8	35.1	31.4	19.7
3	10.7	41.2	31.5	16.6
4	9.5	37.3	34.7	18.6
5	14.9	42.9	27.2	15.0
6	10.0	38.9	34.5	16.6
7	12.4	43.3	30.8	13.6
8	10.7	48.8	25.4	15.2
9	14.5	43.1	28.3	14.1
10	10.6	41.6	31.6	16.1
11	11.5	42.8	31.9	13.8
12	10.0	41.9	30.6	17.5
13	11.7	45.8	28.6	14.0
14	11.0	44.4	29.7	14.9
15	11.2	48.3	27.9	12.6
16	14.6	47.2	27.2	11.0
17	15.6	43.2	27.5	13.7
18	15.6	43.3	26.7	14.4
19	13.4	39.8	30.3	16.5
20	18.5	46.8	23.3	11.4
21	15.8	41.0	28.0	15.2
22	13.3	41.5	29.9	15.4
23	19.3	38.9	26.0	15.8
24	10.8	41.7	31.9	15.6
25	12.8	46.5	28.8	11.8
26	12.6	40.1	32.4	15.0
27	13.1	44.6	27.9	14.3
28	14.7	48.4	24.9	12.1
29	11.1	43.0	28.7	17.1
30	10.9	41.9	29.5	17.7
31	17.4	48.8	23.4	10.5
32	16.3	44.7	25.9	13.1
33	14.8	45.9	25.6	13.7
34	17.9	47.9	23.0	11.3
35	16.3	47.1	25.2	11.5
36	11.0	48.0	27.6	13.4
37	16.6	46.4	25.1	11.9
38	16.5	44.2	26.1	13.3
39	16.3	45.3	26.3	12.1
40	13.3	43.8	28.4	14.5
41	13.6	38.0	29.4	18.9
42	11.6	44.9	31.9	11.6
43	17.2	48.6	24.3	9.9
44	14.8	45.1	28.0	12.1
45	12.1	38.4	27.4	22.2
46	10.7	42.3	30.6	16.5
47	17.8	50.7	21.8	9.7
48	11.1	43.5	30.0	15.3
49	16.0	41.2	25.0	17.8
50	11.3	42.3	30.0	16.4
51	15.1	43.8	26.8	14.2
52	11.6	43.0	30.2	15.2
53	20.4	45.6	21.5	12.6
State	13.7	43.5	28.2	14.6

As percentage of voting-age population.

Table 4 Income and Occupation

District	Median family income	Families in poverty*	White collar†	Blue collar†	Service†	Farm†
1	$47,667	9.7	58.3	20.9	17.8	3.1
2	$40,408	12.0	54.9	23.2	18.2	3.6
3	$59,574	5.8	67.8	18.4	13.2	0.6
4	$57,310	6.1	63.1	19.6	16.5	0.8
5	$41,011	15.3	62.9	20.1	16.6	0.4
6	$69,561	4.4	68.0	17.2	14.0	0.8
7	$59,656	7.5	60.1	22.7	16.9	0.2
8	$59,037	8.8	72.9	11.9	15.0	0.1
9	$53,315	12.3	69.0	17.3	13.5	0.2
10	$74,079	4.3	69.0	17.8	12.9	0.3
11	$70,734	6.2	67.6	19.1	11.4	1.9
12	$80,658	3.2	72.8	14.6	12.4	0.1
13	$69,228	5.0	66.8	22.3	10.8	0.2
14	$91,249	3.8	77.1	12.1	10.3	0.5
15	$82,246	4.4	73.6	16.9	9.2	0.4
16	$71,400	6.7	60.9	24.7	13.9	0.5
17	$53,318	9.0	55.4	19.7	16.4	8.4
18	$37,281	18.1	46.0	31.0	16.5	6.5
19	$46,636	11.0	59.3	22.0	15.3	3.5
20	$27,800	27.4	37.8	27.2	19.2	15.8
21	$39,710	15.8	52.8	22.0	15.9	9.3
22	$48,470	10.8	57.8	23.1	17.4	1.7
23	$51,509	9.4	57.3	20.3	16.8	5.6
24	$68,648	5.0	67.8	17.1	13.6	1.5
25	$53,522	9.9	60.3	23.6	15.9	0.3
26	$66,539	6.2	70.7	17.3	11.8	0.2
27	$52,228	10.1	66.2	19.9	13.8	0.1
28	$41,622	16.0	58.0	26.2	15.6	0.2
29	$49,831	11.6	70.2	16.0	13.7	0.1
30	$85,703	4.8	84.4	6.9	8.7	0.0
31	$26,927	27.5	44.1	33.7	22.0	0.3
32	$42,785	14.6	51.3	32.7	15.7	0.3
33	$35,695	19.9	63.9	17.8	18.3	0.1
34	$32,003	22.1	43.7	40.0	16.0	0.4
35	$34,063	23.2	53.0	28.3	18.5	0.2
36	$60,049	9.7	71.1	16.1	12.7	0.1
37	$35,681	22.1	53.5	29.0	17.3	0.2
38	$44,772	13.3	50.7	34.1	14.9	0.3
39	$47,373	12.5	55.0	31.2	13.7	0.2
40	$59,625	7.1	64.5	22.1	13.2	0.2
41	$44,625	11.8	57.3	25.0	17.4	0.4
42	$77,088	4.2	74.1	15.2	10.5	0.2
43	$39,688	17.4	46.4	36.2	16.7	0.7

District	Median family income	Families in poverty*	White collar†	Blue collar†	Service†	Farm†
44	$57,132	8.7	59.3	26.0	14.1	0.5
45	$45,707	11.3	53.2	23.1	20.6	3.1
46	$71,863	5.0	72.7	15.4	11.8	0.1
47	$40,870	15.4	40.9	37.9	20.1	1.1
48	$82,172	3.7	79.8	10.1	10.0	0.1
49	$51,111	8.7	58.1	24.4	16.3	1.2
50	$67,489	5.0	70.8	15.7	13.0	0.5
51	$42,118	13.8	54.7	23.5	19.7	2.1
52	$60,116	5.7	67.7	18.2	14.0	0.2
53	$41,189	15.4	64.6	16.3	18.8	0.4
State	$53,025	10.6	62.7	21.2	14.8	1.3

*As percentage of all families.   †As percentage of employed workers 16 years and over.

District	Less than grade 9*	Grades 9–12 no diploma*	High school diploma no college*	Some college*	College bachelor's degree or higher*
46	5.7	7.6	16.7	33.5	36.4
47	29.8	19.8	19.2	21.2	10.0
48	3.4	4.8	13.3	31.9	46.5
49	9.1	10.8	23.4	36.0	20.7
50	6.0	6.8	15.7	31.4	40.0
51	15.9	15.1	23.1	30.6	15.2
52	3.5	8.0	22.3	37.6	28.6
53	9.6	10.4	17.7	30.2	32.2
State	11.5	11.7	20.1	30.0	26.6

*As percentage of persons age 25 and over.

Table 5 Education: School Years Completed

District	Less than grade 9*	Grades 9–12 no diploma*	High school diploma no college*	Some college*	College bachelor's degree or higher*
1	7.5	11.5	23.2	32.7	25.0
2	7.8	12.8	25.9	36.2	17.4
3	3.5	8.2	23.4	37.9	27.0
4	3.3	8.7	23.6	39.3	25.2
5	9.9	12.4	23.2	33.1	21.4
6	5.3	7.1	17.2	32.6	37.9
7	7.5	11.1	23.8	35.2	22.4
8	11.3	8.8	13.8	22.0	44.0
9	9.9	10.5	16.9	25.3	37.4
10	4.0	6.6	19.7	33.4	36.2
11	6.5	9.6	21.4	33.3	29.1
12	5.9	6.8	17.5	29.1	40.7
13	7.6	9.5	21.3	29.8	31.8
14	5.7	5.7	12.2	24.1	52.2
15	5.9	7.4	16.2	29.0	41.6
16	13.4	12.7	19.1	27.8	26.9
17	16.4	11.2	18.5	28.9	24.9
18	19.8	17.8	25.1	27.6	9.7
19	10.3	12.9	23.8	32.7	20.3
20	30.2	19.6	23.2	20.7	6.3
21	18.4	13.8	23.0	29.8	15.0
22	6.2	13.9	25.7	35.9	18.3
23	14.1	11.0	18.8	29.8	26.2
24	6.2	7.9	20.0	35.9	30.0
25	6.7	12.5	25.1	37.0	18.8
26	5.4	8.9	18.9	34.5	32.4
27	11.5	12.2	20.6	29.8	25.8
28	21.2	15.8	16.6	22.7	23.7
29	11.5	10.1	17.5	27.5	33.4
30	2.8	4.7	13.0	26.0	53.5
31	33.6	18.9	16.5	17.2	13.7
32	23.0	17.9	21.3	24.1	13.6
33	15.1	13.5	18.1	26.4	26.9
34	32.6	21.1	19.1	18.4	8.7
35	20.3	19.1	21.2	26.1	13.3
36	8.9	9.2	16.9	28.1	36.9
37	19.5	17.0	20.6	27.7	15.2
38	22.6	19.0	22.6	23.3	12.5
39	20.4	16.8	22.1	26.0	14.7
40	9.2	10.9	20.9	32.7	26.4
41	6.2	13.6	26.2	35.9	18.1
42	4.8	7.8	18.5	34.2	34.8
43	18.1	20.2	25.5	27.4	8.8
44	9.7	13.1	22.1	34.0	21.1
45	11.3	14.4	24.4	32.5	17.4

Table 6 Housing and Residential Patterns

District	Median home value	Owner occupied*	Renter occupied*	Urban†	Rural†
1	$168,600	60.7	39.3	76.0	24.0
2	$113,600	63.1	36.9	67.7	32.3
3	$160,400	68.6	31.4	86.4	13.6
4	$184,300	73.2	26.8	67.4	32.6
5	$116,700	49.6	50.4	99.7	0.3
6	$339,400	63.3	36.7	89.8	10.2
7	$184,400	64.0	36.0	98.7	1.3
8	$408,800	30.2	69.8	100.0	0.0
9	$276,300	45.6	54.4	99.9	0.1
10	$261,900	69.8	30.2	96.5	3.5
11	$244,600	68.9	31.1	90.1	9.9
12	$429,400	62.3	37.7	99.9	0.1
13	$284,200	60.7	39.3	99.3	0.7
14	$577,000	58.5	41.5	93.6	6.4
15	$418,600	58.0	42.0	99.3	0.7
16	$358,600	64.1	35.9	98.7	1.3
17	$282,900	55.5	44.5	90.0	10.0
18	$106,800	56.9	43.1	91.3	8.7
19	$129,600	64.4	35.6	80.6	19.4
20	$78,700	50.0	50.0	91.2	8.8
21	$103,400	61.7	38.3	79.9	20.1
22	$110,200	65.2	34.8	82.5	17.5
23	$229,000	53.8	46.2	98.0	2.0
24	$245,700	71.0	29.0	94.2	5.8
25	$135,100	70.0	30.0	88.2	11.8
26	$228,400	68.7	31.3	98.8	1.2
27	$202,800	54.1	45.9	99.7	0.3
28	$188,900	43.9	56.1	99.9	0.1
29	$254,800	44.1	55.9	99.4	0.6
30	$440,000	47.7	52.3	97.5	2.5
31	$173,500	23.0	77.0	100.0	0.0
32	$166,300	55.9	44.1	100.0	0.0
33	$218,400	30.5	69.5	100.0	0.0
34	$175,100	30.6	69.4	100.0	0.0
35	$168,000	39.4	60.6	100.0	0.0
36	$305,500	44.8	55.2	100.0	0.0
37	$156,900	44.1	55.9	100.0	0.0
38	$159,700	62.5	37.5	100.0	0.0
39	$182,000	59.5	40.5	100.0	0.0
40	$231,100	60.0	40.0	100.0	0.0
41	$108,300	66.8	33.2	89.4	10.6
42	$254,500	76.5	23.5	98.7	1.3
43	$113,800	59.9	40.1	99.3	0.7
44	$169,600	65.8	34.2	97.7	2.3
45	$123,900	69.2	30.8	89.9	10.1
46	$284,900	61.6	38.4	99.9	0.1
47	$177,200	47.6	52.4	100.0	0.0

District	Median home value	Owner occupied*	Renter occupied*	Urban†	Rural†
48	$306,700	65.1	34.9	99.9	0.1
49	$175,000	66.8	33.2	90.3	9.7
50	$263,600	65.9	34.1	97.8	2.2
51	$149,800	56.7	43.3	95.6	4.4
52	$218,000	63.8	36.2	93.6	6.4
53	$203,800	34.4	65.6	99.9	0.1
State	$198,900	56.9	43.1	94.5	5.5

*As percentage of occupied housing units.   †As percentage of total population.

California 1st District

Northern coast — Eureka, Napa, Davis

It takes about nine hours to travel the length of the 1st, a journey that starts in Yolo County, across the river from Sacramento, and ends at the Oregon border in Del Norte County, one of the district's three coastal counties. In between are wineries and majestic redwoods, for which the northern coast is famous. *(See map p. 85.)*

The 1st is notable for its breadth and diversity. Even the weather patterns vary across the district, with a rainy north and arid farmland in the south. Apart from wine and timber, other dominant industries include commercial fishing in Crescent City, Eureka, and Fort Bragg, and tourism. The University of California, Davis, in Yolo County is another major employer.

To the north, Mendocino, Humboldt, and Del Norte Counties long have been a battleground for environmentalists and the timber industry. Tensions reached a peak in the summer of 1990 with "Redwood Summer" demonstrations over the proposed logging of the Headwaters Forest, one of the last stands of virgin redwood trees. Isolated protests still occur but have not reached the same intensity.

East of Mendocino, Lake County's economy is a mix of ranching, farming, and tourism, centered on Clearlake. Its relatively low cost of living, relative to Bay Area cities, makes it a retirees' haven. South of Mendocino, the 1st takes in part of wine-producing Sonoma County and all of Napa County. Half of the state's wineries are in the district.

Environmental issues, including offshore drilling, continue to make the 1st volatile, despite a Democratic voter registration advantage and the district's backing of Democratic presidential candidates in the 1990s and 2000. Green Party candidate Ralph Nader received 15 percent of the 2000 presidential vote in Mendocino County and 13 percent in Humboldt County. Del Norte was the only county in the 1st to support Republican George W. Bush.

Major Industry

Timber, agriculture, tourism.

Notable

Niebaum-Coppola is the winery owned by film director Francis Ford Coppola; the redwood trees along the northern coast are the tallest in the world.

Election Returns

	Republican		Democratic		Other	
President 2000	98,506	38.8%	131,376	51.7%	24,220	9.5%
House 2002	60,013	32.4%	118,669	64.1%	6,534	3.5%

District Profile

Population 639,087

Total area (square miles) 12,195
Land area (square miles) 11,005

Population per square mile 58.1

Counties (2000 population)
Del Norte 27,507   Napa 124,279
Humboldt 126,518   Sonoma (pt.) 66,816
Lake 58,309   Yolo (pt.) 149,393
Mendocino 86,265

Cities and other areas over 10,000 (2000 population)
Arcata 16,651   McKinleyville CDP 13,599
Clearlake 13,142   Napa 72,585
Davis 60,308   Ukiah 15,497
Eureka 26,128   West Sacramento 31,615
Fortuna 10,497   Windsor town 22,744
Healdsburg 10,722   Woodland (pt.) 39,455

Race and Hispanic or Latino origin*
White 71.2%
Black or African American 1.3%
American Indian or Alaska Native 2.4%
Asian 3.9%
Native Hawaiian or other Pacific Islander 0.2%
Some other race 0.2%
Hispanic or Latino origin 17.9%
Two or more races 2.9%

*As percentage of total population.

Ancestry*
Dutch 1.4%   Polish 1.1%
English 8.9%   Portuguese 1.3%
French 2.7%   Scotch-Irish 1.5%
German 11.3%   Scottish 1.9%
Irish 9.0%   Swedish 1.8%
Italian 4.6%   USA/American 3.6%
Norwegian 1.7%

*As estimated percentage of total population.

Universities and colleges, 2000–2001 enrollment
College of the Redwoods, Eureka 6,986
Humboldt State University, Arcata 7,433
Mendocino College, Ukiah 4,463
Napa Valley College, Napa 7,152
Pacific Union College, Angwin 1,468
University of California, Davis 26,094

Newspapers and circulation

	District circulation	Total circulation
Crescent City Daily Triplicate	4,459	4,512
Davis Enterprise	9,690	9,940
Eureka Times-Standard	18,811	19,090
Lake County Record-Bee	6,625	6,614
Napa Valley Register	17,886	18,373
Sacramento Bee	15,259	293,344
San Francisco Chronicle	19,570	518,725
Santa Rosa Press Democrat	26,011	89,998
Ukiah Daily Journal	7,368	7,385
*USA Today**	2,071	1,674,376
Vallejo Times Herald	2,918	20,751
Woodland Daily Democrat	4,347	9,766

See Sources and Explanations in the front of the volume.

Television stations and affiliations

San Francisco-Oakland-San Jose	53%	KBHK	UPN
San Francisco-Oakland-San Jose	53%	KBWB	WB
San Francisco-Oakland-San Jose	53%	KCNS	Independent
San Francisco-Oakland-San Jose	53%	KCSM	PBS
San Francisco-Oakland-San Jose	53%	KDTV	Univision
San Francisco-Oakland-San Jose	53%	KFTL	Independent
San Francisco-Oakland-San Jose	53%	KFTY	Independent
San Francisco-Oakland-San Jose	53%	KFWU	Independent Spanish
San Francisco-Oakland-San Jose	53%	KGO	ABC
San Francisco-Oakland-San Jose	53%	KICU	Independent
San Francisco-Oakland-San Jose	53%	KKPX	PAX
San Francisco-Oakland-San Jose	53%	KMTP	PBS
San Francisco-Oakland-San Jose	53%	KNTV	NBC
San Francisco-Oakland-San Jose	53%	KPIX	CBS
San Francisco-Oakland-San Jose	53%	KQED	PBS
San Francisco-Oakland-San Jose	53%	KRCB	PBS
San Francisco-Oakland-San Jose	53%	KRON	Independent
San Francisco-Oakland-San Jose	53%	KSTS	Telemundo
San Francisco-Oakland-San Jose	53%	KTEH	PBS
San Francisco-Oakland-San Jose	53%	KTLN	Independent
San Francisco-Oakland-San Jose	53%	KTNC	Independent Spanish
San Francisco-Oakland-San Jose	53%	KTSF	Independent
San Francisco-Oakland-San Jose	53%	KTVU	FOX
Eureka	43%	KAEF	ABC
Eureka	43%	KBVU	FOX, UPN
Eureka	43%	KEET	PBS
Eureka	43%	KIEM	NBC
Eureka	43%	KVIQ	CBS
Sacramento-Stockton-Modesto	4%	KBSV	Independent
Sacramento-Stockton-Modesto	4%	KCRA	NBC
Sacramento-Stockton-Modesto	4%	KMAX	UPN
Sacramento-Stockton-Modesto	4%	KOVR	CBS
Sacramento-Stockton-Modesto	4%	KQCA	WB
Sacramento-Stockton-Modesto	4%	KSPX	PAX
Sacramento-Stockton-Modesto	4%	KTXL	FOX
Sacramento-Stockton-Modesto	4%	KUVS	Univision
Sacramento-Stockton-Modesto	4%	KVIE	PBS
Sacramento-Stockton-Modesto	4%	KXTV	ABC

Cable systems and subscribers

Adelphia 15,796
Boulder Ridge Cable TV 880
Central Valley Cable 523
Charter 20,429
Comcast 67,439
Cox 37,024
Mallard 651
Mediacom 13,997

Businesses and other major employers

California Dept. of Mental Health; Napa 2,500
California Dept. of Corrections; Crescent City 1,200
Queen of Valley Hospital; Napa 1,092
Humboldt County; Eureka; county government 800
Target Corp.; Woodland; general warehousing, storage 765
St. Helena Hospital; Deer Park 750
Cultured Stone Corp.; Napa; cast stone, concrete 739
Dey Inc.; Napa; respiratory system drugs 700
MTS Inc.; West Sacramento; records 700
Valley Media Inc.; Woodland; compact discs 700
Aventis CropScience USA; Woodland; agricultural chemicals 630
Silverado Country Club and Resort Inc.; Napa; country club 600
Simpson Timber Co.; Eureka; sawmills and planing mills 600
St. Joseph Hospital; Eureka 593
Amfac Resorts; Napa; management services 521
Napa Valley Community College District; Napa 500
Walsh Vineyard Management Inc.; Napa; real estate managers 500
Lake County; Lakeport; county government 500
Ukiah Adventist Hospital; Ukiah 500
American Hospital Management Corp.; Arcata; medical and surgical hospital 500
University of California; Davis 500
Fleming Companies Inc.; West Sacramento; food supplier 500

California 2nd District

North central — Redding, Chico

Previously abutting most of the state's border with Nevada north of Lake Tahoe, the mountainous 2nd was reshaped during redistricting following the 2000 census to form a north-south strip down the center of the state, from the Oregon border to just north of Sacramento. It includes the Sutter-Buttes mountain range.

Agriculture dominates the 2nd, which gained five farming counties—Sutter, Colusa, Glenn, Tehama, and part of Yolo—through redistricting. The district is rural, with rice farms and orchards producing walnuts, olives, and peaches. Much of its economic activity is centered in Shasta County, home to mining and forestry interests. Shasta Lake, the state's largest man-made reservoir, attracts tourism. Redding, the 2nd's largest city, is about 160 miles north of Sacramento in Shasta County. Both the city and county experienced strong growth through the 1980s and 1990s.

The 2nd has had to fight to save its agriculture industry from harsh weather—much of it was declared a disaster area after flooding in 1997. Wildfires account for at least one major fire every summer, especially in the northernmost counties of Shasta, Trinity, and Siskiyou. Water also is a perennial issue: two-thirds of the state's supply comes from the upper third of the state. The timber industry has steadily declined since the 1990s, in the process diminishing some of the tension between environmental interests and the industry.

The district retains its overwhelmingly white and Republican character, but there has been a steady influx of Sikhs in the Yuba City area, as well as an infusion of Democratic-leaning Hispanic farmworkers.

Major Industry

Agriculture, timber, tourism, health care.

Notable

The dormant Mt. Shasta volcano in Siskiyou County is near the southern end of the Cascade Mountains; the Sierra Nevada Brewing Co. is in Chico; GOP presidential nominee Bob Dole fell from a stage at a rally in Chico in 1996, saying later that he had "fallen for Chico."

Election Returns

	Republican		Democratic		Other	
President 2000	150,196	61.1%	81,861	33.3%	13,609	5.5%
House 2002	117,747	65.8%	52,455	29.3%	8,783	4.9%

District Profile

Population   639,087

Total area (square miles)   21,977
   Land area (square miles)   21,758

Population per square mile   29.4

Counties (2000 population)

Butte (pt.) 158,796	Sutter 78,930
Colusa 18,804	Tehama 56,039
Glenn 26,453	Trinity 13,022
Shasta 163,256	Yolo (pt.) 19,267
Siskiyou 44,301	Yuba 60,219

Cities and other areas over 10,000 (2000 population)

Chico   59,954
Linda CDP   13,474
Magalia CDP   10,569
Marysville   12,268
Olivehurst CDP   11,061
Paradise town   26,408
Red Bluff   13,147
Redding   80,865
South Yuba City CDP   12,651
Yuba City   36,758

Race and Hispanic or Latino origin*

White   76.2%
Black or African American   1.2%
American Indian or Alaska Native   1.9%
Asian   3.6%
Native Hawaiian or other Pacific Islander   0.1%
Some other race   0.2%
Hispanic or Latino origin   14.0%
Two or more races   2.8%

*As percentage of total population.

Ancestry*

Dutch 1.6%	German 11.8%
English 9.0%	Irish 8.9%
French 2.6%	Italian 3.6%
Norwegian 1.6%	Scottish 1.9%
Portuguese 1.3%	Swedish 1.6%
Scotch-Irish 1.5%	USA/American 5.3%

*As estimated percentage of total population.

Universities and colleges, 2000–2001 enrollment

Butte College, Oroville   11,542
California Northern School of Law, Chico*
California State University, Chico   15,912
College of the Siskiyous, Weed   2,786
Shasta College, Redding   9,112
Simpson College, Redding   1,214%
Yuba College, Marysville   10,295

*Enrollment under 100. See Sources and Explanations in the front of the volume.

Newspapers and circulation

	District circulation	Total circulation
Chico Enterprise-Record	30,250	33,388
Red Bluff Daily News	6,814	6,879
Redding Record Searchlight	34,351	33,888
Sacramento Bee	13,680	293,344
San Francisco Chronicle	5,621	518,725
USA Today*	1,405	1,674,376
Woodland Daily Democrat	5,401	9,766
Yuba-Sutter Appeal Democrat	21,224	21,409

*See Sources and Explanations in the front of the volume.

Television stations and affiliations

Chico-Redding	57%	KCVU	FOX
Chico-Redding	57%	KHSL	CBS
Chico-Redding	57%	KIXE	PBS
Chico-Redding	57%	KNVN	NBC
Chico-Redding	57%	KRCR	ABC
Medford-Klamath Falls, OR	29%	KDKF	ABC
Medford-Klamath Falls, OR	29%	KDRV	ABC
Medford-Klamath Falls, OR	29%	KFTS	PBS
Medford-Klamath Falls, OR	29%	KMVU	FOX
Medford-Klamath Falls, OR	29%	KOBI	NBC
Medford-Klamath Falls, OR	29%	KOTI	NBC
Medford-Klamath Falls, OR	29%	KSYS	PBS
Medford-Klamath Falls, OR	29%	KTVL	CBS
Sacramento-Stockton-Modesto	14%	KBSV	Independent
Sacramento-Stockton-Modesto	14%	KCRA	NBC
Sacramento-Stockton-Modesto	14%	KMAX	UPN
Sacramento-Stockton-Modesto	14%	KOVR	CBS
Sacramento-Stockton-Modesto	14%	KQCA	WB
Sacramento-Stockton-Modesto	14%	KSPX	PAX
Sacramento-Stockton-Modesto	14%	KTXL	FOX
Sacramento-Stockton-Modesto	14%	KUVS	Univision
Sacramento-Stockton-Modesto	14%	KVIE	PBS
Sacramento-Stockton-Modesto	14%	KXTV	ABC

Cable systems and subscribers

Adelphia   1,635
Central Valley Cable   1,000
Charter   72,682
Comcast   83,349
Mallard   2,072
Marks Cablevision   6,050
Northland   9,366
Siskiyou Cablevision   982

Military installations, September 2001
Beale Air Force Base, Marysville   4,576

Businesses and other major employers
California State University Chico; Chico   2,600
Chico CSU Research Foundation; Chico; management services   2,000
Enloe Medical Center Inc.; Chico   1,500
Tenet Healthcare Corp.; Redding; medical and surgical hospital   1,500
United Communities Medical Services Inc.; Yuba City; management services   1,450
Chico Unified School District; Chico   1,425
Rand Corp.; Chico; elementary and secondary schools   1,100
Wal-Mart Stores Inc.; Red Bluff; discount department stores   1,100
City of Redding; Redding; city management   802
Staff Resources Inc.; Chico; personnel management   800
California Dept. of Transportation; Redding   800
Rumsey Indian Tribe; Brooks; Native American reservation   700
Rideout Memorial Hospital; Marysville   700
California Employment Development Dept.; Redding   700
U.S. Forest Service; Redding   700
Mercy Healthcare North Hospital; Redding   700
Shasta-Tehama-Trinity Joint Community College District; Redding   650
Feather River Hospital; Paradise   620
Menlo Logistics Inc.; Woodland; business planning, organizing services   600
Yuba College; Marysville   600
Fremont Hospital; Yuba City   598
California Dept. of Transportation; Marysville   500
Shasta County; Redding; public health programs   500
Siskiyou County; Yreka; county government   500

California 3rd District

Central — Sacramento suburbs

Redistricting following the 2000 census radically changed the 3rd from a north Central Valley district to one that stretches east to west, from Alpine County on the Nevada border to Solano County. The redrawn district is more Republican and more white. *(See map p. 85.)*

The new 3rd used to be Mother Lode country, which drew gold seekers and now attracts those who want to leave the state's crowded cities while still working in a burgeoning high-tech economy. It gets most of its population—about 85 percent—from a chunk of Sacramento County that includes the affluent Sacramento suburbs of Citrus Heights and Rio Linda.

Wineries and agriculture dominate the 3rd's economy, especially grape, almond, and prune production, except in the forestry-heavy eastern county of Alpine, where mountains and skiing are prevalent. The closure of McClellan Air Force Base in 2001 dealt a blow to the area's economy, but it has been mitigated by the base's conversion into a business park (shared with the 5th), which has sought to attract high-tech and defense microelectronics activity.

Sacramento County, whose residents tend to work in state government or the high-tech industries that attract transplants from San Francisco, is the politically competitive heart of the district. Its surrounding areas are largely rural and Republican, and the district as a whole gave GOP presidential nominee George W. Bush 54.9 percent of the vote in 2000.

Water and flood control are important local issues. The Sacramento Valley is prone to flooding from the Sacramento and the American rivers, and while the last major floods occurred in 1995 and 1997, minor flooding happens more often.

Major Industry
Agriculture, timber, technology.

Notable
Angels Camp in Calaveras County hosts the annual jumping frog contest made famous by Mark Twain.

Election Returns

	Republican		Democratic		Other	
President 2000	142,946	54.9%	107,690	41.3%	9,820	3.8%
House 2002	121,732	62.5%	67,136	34.4%	6,050	3.1%

District Profile

Population   639,088

Total area (square miles)   3,422
 Land area (square miles)   3,374

Population per square mile   189.4

Counties (2000 population)
Alpine   1,208   Sacramento (pt.)   550,786
Amador   35,100   Solano (pt.)   11,440
Calaveras   40,554

Cities and other areas over 10,000 (2000 population)
Arden-Arcade CDP (pt.)   53,597
Carmichael CDP   49,742
Citrus Heights   85,071
Elk Grove CDP (pt.)   34,568
Fair Oaks CDP   28,008
Folsom   51,884
Galt   19,472
Laguna CDP   34,309
North Highlands CDP (pt.)   14,777
Rancho Cordova CDP (pt.)   28,869
Rio Linda CDP   10,466
Vineyard CDP   10,109

Race and Hispanic or Latino origin*
White   74.4%
Black or African American   4.3%
American Indian or Alaska Native   0.8%
Asian   5.9%
Native Hawaiian or other Pacific Islander   0.3%
Some other race   0.2%
Hispanic or Latino origin   10.7%
Two or more races   3.5%

As percentage of total population.

Ancestry*

Dutch	1.3%	Polish	1.2%
English	8.9%	Portuguese	1.3%
French	2.7%	Scotch-Irish	1.6%
German	12.4%	Scottish	1.9%
Irish	9.0%	Swedish	1.5%
Italian	4.6%	USA/American	3.8%
Norwegian	1.6%		

*As estimated percentage of total population.

Universities and colleges, 2000–2001 enrollment

American River College, Sacramento   28,420
Heald College School of Business, Rancho Cordova   778
Heald College School of Technology-Sacramento, Sacramento   1,048
ITT Technical Institute, Rancho Cordova   476
MTI College of Business and Technology, Sacramento 1,316

Newspapers and circulation

	District circulation	Total circulation
Lodi News-Sentinel	1,042	16,691
Sacramento Bee	102,296	293,344
San Francisco Chronicle	4,452	518,725
Stockton Record	3,193	58,220
*USA Today**	3,524	1,674,376
Vacaville Reporter	4,894	18,124

*See Sources and Explanations in the front of the volume.

Television stations and affiliations

Sacramento-Stockton-Modesto	78%	KBSV	Independent
Sacramento-Stockton-Modesto	78%	KCRA	NBC
Sacramento-Stockton-Modesto	78%	KMAX	UPN
Sacramento-Stockton-Modesto	78%	KOVR	CBS
Sacramento-Stockton-Modesto	78%	KQCA	WB
Sacramento-Stockton-Modesto	78%	KSPX	PAX
Sacramento-Stockton-Modesto	78%	KTXL	FOX
Sacramento-Stockton-Modesto	78%	KUVS	Univision
Sacramento-Stockton-Modesto	78%	KVIE	PBS
Sacramento-Stockton-Modesto	78%	KXTV	ABC
Reno, NV	22%	KAME	UPN
Reno, NV	22%	KNPB	PBS
Reno, NV	22%	KOLO	ABC
Reno, NV	22%	KREN	PAX
Reno, NV	22%	KRNV	NBC
Reno, NV	22%	KRXI	FOX
Reno, NV	22%	KTVN	CBS
Reno, NV	22%	KWNV	NBC

Cable systems and subscribers

Comcast   21,792
Rancho Murietta Assn.   955
Volcano Vision   2,603

Businesses and other major employers

Intel Corp.; Folsom; semiconductors and related devices 2,600
California Dept. of Corrections; Folsom   2,200
National Staff Specialists Inc.; Rancho Cordova; employee leasing service   2,090
Franklin/Templeton Investor Services Inc.; Rancho Cordova; investment advice   2,000

Mercy Healthcare Sacramento Hospital; Carmichael   1,700
Vision Service Plan; Rancho Cordova; hospital/medical service plans   1,600
Millennium Transportation; Citrus Heights; freight transportation   1,400
Bank of America Corp.; Rancho Cordova; commercial bank 1,400
Aerojet-General Corp.; Rancho Cordova; guided missile/space vehicle propulsion units   1,400
Health Net Federal Services Inc.; Rancho Cordova; group health association   1,400
Cardinal Distribution Corp.; Folsom; pharmaceuticals 1,250
Los Rios Community College District; Sacramento   1,160
Jackson Rancheria Casino; Jackson; bingo hall   1,000
Pacific Bell; Sacramento; telephone communication   1,000
U.S. Internal Revenue Service; North Highlands   900
Electronic Data Systems Corp.; Rancho Cordova; data processing   750
California Dept. of Corrections; Ione   711
Delta Dental Plan of California; Rancho Cordova; dental insurance   700
Premium Retail Services Inc.; Citrus Heights; merchandising consultant   645
JC Penney Corp.; Carmichael; catalog sales   600
Independent Contractor Services Inc.; Volcano; professional organization   600
Franklin/Templeton Investor Services Inc.; Rancho Cordova; security brokers, dealers, flotation companies   574
Governor's Office of Emergency Services; Mather   550
EdFund; Rancho Cordova; student loan marketing association   503
California Youth and Adult Correctional Agency; Ione 500
U.S. Veterans Hospital; Mather   500
LCL Administrators Inc.; Rancho Cordova; employee leasing service   500
JTS Communities Inc.; Sacramento; residential construction 500
Sutter Connect; Sacramento; hospital/health services consultant   500
West Macy's Inc.; Sacramento; department stores   500

California 4th District

Northeast — Roseville, Rocklin

Redistricting following the 2000 census brought major changes to the 4th. Where it previously occupied California's northeast-central belt, moving from Sacramento to Lake Tahoe and then south, the district now heads north after reaching Lake Tahoe, along the Nevada border up to Oregon in the state's northeastern corner.

Laden with rivers, lakes, and the mountain ranges that give their names to Sierra and Nevada Counties, the 4th's new district lines have added timber and agriculture to the economic mainstays of mining and technology.

The mining counties of Placer and El Dorado lend the 4th its gold rush feel, though technology drives one of the fastest growth rates in the state. Placer, El Dorado, and Nevada counties are home to facilities of big technology names such as Hewlett-Packard and Oracle. These three counties, which along with a sliver of Sacramento County make up the southern part of the district, account for more than three-fourths of its population and continue to draw those who want to leave the state's crowded cities but still work in the high-tech economy.

The 4th is a popular vacation destination, with numerous ski resorts dotting the Sierra Nevada mountain range, as well as Lake Tahoe in eastern El Dorado and Placer counties. Placer, with cheap property and abundant natural beauty, is rapidly becoming a draw for retirees. Whites make up 83.8 percent of the population, which gives the district the highest percentage in the state.

This is safe Republican territory. George W. Bush took 58.9 percent of the vote in the 2000 presidential election, and Republicans hold a 13-point edge in party registration.

Major Industry

Computers, agriculture, mining, tourism.

Notable

Squaw Valley, near Lake Tahoe, hosted the 1960 Winter Olympics.

Election Returns

	Republican		Democratic		Other	
President 2000	172,169	58.9%	104,437	35.7%	15,633	5.3%
House 2002	147,997	64.9%	72,860	31.9%	7,247	3.2%

District Profile

Population   639,088

Total area (square miles)   17,158
  Land area (square miles)   16,453

Population per square mile   38.8

Counties (2000 population)

Butte (pt.) 44,375	Placer 248,399
El Dorado 156,299	Plumas 20,824
Lassen 33,828	Sacramento (pt.) 30,326
Modoc 9,449	Sierra 3,555
Nevada 92,033	

Cities and other areas over 10,000 (2000 population)
  Auburn 12,462
  Cameron Park CDP 14,549
  El Dorado Hills CDP 18,016
  Granite Bay CDP 19,388
  Grass Valley 10,922
  Lincoln 11,205
  North Auburn CDP 11,847
  Orangevale CDP 26,705
  Oroville 13,004
  Rocklin 36,330
  Roseville 79,921
  South Lake Tahoe 23,609
  Susanville 13,541
  Truckee town 13,864

Race and Hispanic or Latino origin*
  White 83.8%
  Black or African American 1.2%
  American Indian or Alaska Native 1.1%
  Asian 2.3%
  Native Hawaiian or other Pacific Islander 0.1%
  Some other race 0.2%
  Hispanic or Latino origin 8.9%
  Two or more races 2.4%

*As percentage of total population.

Ancestry*

Dutch 1.5%	Polish 1.3%
English 11.2%	Portuguese 1.2%
French 3.1%	Scotch-Irish 1.6%
German 13.1%	Scottish 2.2%
Irish 10.0%	Swedish 2.0%
Italian 4.7%	USA/American 4.1%
Norwegian 1.9%	

*As estimated percentage of total population.

Universities and colleges, 2000–2001 enrollment
  Feather River Community College District, Quincy 892
  Lake Tahoe Community College, South Lake Tahoe 3,053
  Lassen Community College, Susanville 2,344
  Sierra College, Rocklin 17,517

Newspapers and circulation

	District circulation	Total circulation
Auburn Journal	11,266	11,321
Chico Enterprise-Record	3,128	33,388
Grass Valley Union	16,013	16,111
Placerville Mountain Democrat	12,443	12,481
Reno Gazette/Journal	2,110	66,645
Sacramento Bee	66,775	293,344
San Francisco Chronicle	5,351	518,725
USA Today*	2,402	1,674,376

*See Sources and Explanations in the front of the volume.

Television stations and affiliations

Sacramento-Stockton-Modesto	44%	KBSV	Independent
Sacramento-Stockton-Modesto	44%	KCRA	NBC
Sacramento-Stockton-Modesto	44%	KMAX	UPN
Sacramento-Stockton-Modesto	44%	KOVR	CBS
Sacramento-Stockton-Modesto	44%	KQCA	WB
Sacramento-Stockton-Modesto	44%	KSPX	PAX
Sacramento-Stockton-Modesto	44%	KTXL	FOX
Sacramento-Stockton-Modesto	44%	KUVS	Univision
Sacramento-Stockton-Modesto	44%	KVIE	PBS
Sacramento-Stockton-Modesto	44%	KXTV	ABC
Reno, NV	44%	KAME	UPN
Reno, NV	29%	KNPB	PBS
Reno, NV	29%	KOLO	ABC
Reno, NV	29%	KREN	PAX
Reno, NV	29%	KRNV	NBC
Reno, NV	29%	KRXI	FOX
Reno, NV	29%	KTVN	CBS
Reno, NV	29%	KWNV	NBC
Chico-Redding	27%	KCVU	FOX
Chico-Redding	27%	KHSL	CBS
Chico-Redding	27%	KIXE	PBS
Chico-Redding	27%	KNVN	NBC
Chico-Redding	27%	KRCR	ABC

Cable systems and subscribers
Adelphia   4,587
Boulder Ridge Cable TV   6,899
Charter   22,803
Comcast   43,743
Quincy Community TV   2,342
Suntel Communications   2,198
USA Media Group   34,378

Military installations, September 2001
Sierra Army Depot, Reno   754

Businesses and other major employers
Weber Enterprises; Orangevale; public health programs 5,000
Truckee-Donner Recreation and Park District; Truckee 2,200
HP Americas Integration; Roseville; printers, computers 2,000
Butte County; Oroville; county government   1,290
Sierra Joint Community College District; Rocklin   1,200
NEC Electronics Inc.; Roseville; integrated microcircuits (semiconductor)   1,200
Artesyn Solutions Inc.; Lincoln; electronic equipment repair 1,165
Oroville Hospital; Oroville   1,100
DST Output Inc.; El Dorado Hills; computer maintenance and repair   1,000
Tektronix Inc.; Nevada City; radio/TV communications equipment   773
Marshall Hospital; Placerville   760
Sutter Health; Auburn; insurance agents and brokers   750
Earthlink Inc.; Roseville; online service providers   750
Coherent Inc.; Auburn; laser systems and equipment   700
Roseville Toyota; Roseville; automobiles   700
Sierra Nevada Memorial-Miners Hospitals Inc.; Grass Valley   649
Artesyn Technologies Inc.; Lincoln; computer maintenance services   600
Squaw Creek Associates; Olympic Valley; resort hotel   600
Barton Health Systems Hospital; South Lake Tahoe   535
Placer County; Auburn; county government   500
Calfarm Insurance Co.; Newcastle; insurance agents and brokers   500
Charter School Resource Alliance; Roseville; child day care services   500
Il Fornaio (America) Corp.; Roseville; eating places   500
City of Roseville; Roseville; city management   500

California 5th District

Sacramento

Two things tend to dominate the 5th—state politics and triple-digit temperatures that send air conditioners into overdrive. Located in California's hot Central Valley, the 5th is home to the state capital, Sacramento, and reaches east and south to include a few upper-middle-class suburbs such as Arden-Arcade and Elk Grove (both of which are shared with the 3rd District). *(See map p. 85.)*

Sacramento first attracted fortune seekers as the starting point of the gold rush of 1849. State government now pro-

vides the lion's share of employment, although other sectors are increasing in importance.

The city's economy has improved since a statewide recession in the early 1990s, with real estate value and population numbers growing against turn-of-the-century state and national economic trends. Several big-name technology companies are major employers in the 5th.

Overall, Democrats hold a substantial edge in voter registration. Sacramento used to be a swing district, supporting Ronald Reagan and George Bush in the presidential elections of the 1980s and Republican Pete Wilson in the 1990 gubernatorial race. But Democrats gained strength in the 1992 redistricting, when some of the more affluent, GOP-leaning suburbs were stripped. This trend continued in redistricting following the 2000 census, as mapmakers added suburbs such as Rancho Cordova and North Highlands (both shared with the 3rd). Al Gore captured 60.2 percent of the 5th's vote in the 2000 presidential election.

The city itself is slightly more diverse than neighboring communities, but whites account for about 43 percent of the district's residents, Hispanics about 21 percent, and blacks 14.4 percent.

Major Industry
State government, technology.

Notable
The California State Railroad Museum is one of North America's largest railroad museums; Sacramento is California's oldest incorporated city.

Election Returns

	Republican		Democratic		Other	
President 2000	66,011	34.9%	113,987	60.2%	9,239	4.9%
House 2002	34,749	26.4%	92,726	70.5%	4,103	3.1%

District Profile

Population   639,088

Total area (square miles)   149
     Land area (square miles)   147

Population per square mile   4,347

Counties (2000 population)
Sacramento (pt.)   639,088

Cities and other areas over 10,000 (2000 population)
Arden-Arcade CDP (pt.)   42,428
Elk Grove CDP (pt.)   25,416
Florin CDP   27,653
La Riviera CDP (pt.)   10,056
North Highlands CDP (pt.)   29,410
Parkway-South Sacramento CDP   36,468
Rancho Cordova CDP (pt.)   26,191
Rosemont CDP   22,904
Sacramento   407,018

Race and Hispanic or Latino origin*
White   43.4%
Black or African American   14.4%
American Indian or Alaska Native   0.8%
Asian   14.9%

Native Hawaiian or other Pacific Islander   0.8%
Some other race   0.3%
Hispanic or Latino origin   20.8%
Two or more races   4.7%

As percentage of total population.

Ancestry*

English	5.3%	Italian	3.1%
French	1.8%	Portuguese	1.1%
German	7.5%	Scottish	1.1%
Irish	5.9%	USA/American	2.8%

As estimated percentage of total population.

Universities and colleges, 2000–2001 enrollment

California State University, Sacramento   25,714
Cosumnes River College, Sacramento   16,493
High-Tech Institute, Sacramento   338
Northwestern California University School of Law, Sacramento*
Sacramento City College, Sacramento   20,878
Skills and Business Education Center, Sacramento   4,132
Trinity Life Bible College, Sacramento   300
University of Northern California-Lorenzo Patino School of Law, Sacramento*
University of Phoenix, Sacramento   1,619
University of the Pacific-McGeorge School of Law, Sacramento*
Western Career College, Sacramento   574

Enrollment under 100. See Sources and Explanations in the front of the volume.

Newspapers and circulation

	District circulation	Total circulation
Sacramento Bee	91,033	293,344
San Francisco Chronicle	4,219	518,725

Television stations and affiliations

Sacramento-Stockton-Modesto	100%	KBSV	Independent
Sacramento-Stockton-Modesto	100%	KCRA	NBC
Sacramento-Stockton-Modesto	100%	KMAX	UPN
Sacramento-Stockton-Modesto	100%	KOVR	CBS
Sacramento-Stockton-Modesto	100%	KQCA	WB
Sacramento-Stockton-Modesto	100%	KSPX	PAX
Sacramento-Stockton-Modesto	100%	KTXL	FOX
Sacramento-Stockton-Modesto	100%	KUVS	Univision
Sacramento-Stockton-Modesto	100%	KVIE	PBS
Sacramento-Stockton-Modesto	100%	KXTV	ABC

Cable systems and subscribers

Comcast   221,617

Military installations, September 2001

BT Collins USARC (Army Reserve), Sacramento   1,043

Businesses and other major employers

Sacramento City-County Unified School District; Sacramento   6,383
University of California; Sacramento; x-ray laboratory   5,000
California Board of Equalization; Sacramento   4,000
First Union National Bank; Sacramento; commercial bank   3,500

California Motor Vehicles Dept.; Sacramento   3,100
California Dept. of Transportation; Sacramento   3,000
California Employment Development Dept.; Sacramento   3,000
California State University; Sacramento   3,000
McClatchy Newspapers Inc.; Sacramento; newspaper   2,500
Information Sources Inc.; Sacramento; computer programming services   2,200
California Dept. of Food and Agriculture; Sacramento   2,100
Mercy Healthcare Sacramento; Sacramento; x-ray laboratory   2,000
California Dept. of Justice; Sacramento   2,000
California Federal Bank; Sacramento; federal savings institutions   2,000
California Franchise Tax Board; Sacramento   2,000
Apple Computer Inc.; Elk Grove; electronic computers   1,700
California Dept. of Corrections; Sacramento   1,500
California Water Resources Dept.; Sacramento   1,500
Los Rios Community College District; Sacramento   1,400
United Services Automobile Association; Sacramento; life insurance   1,206
City of Sacramento; Sacramento; police dept.   1,100
Homeq Servicing Corp.; North Highlands; mortgage bankers   1,000
California Controller; Sacramento   1,000
California Dept. of Justice; Sacramento   1,000
California Legislative Office; Sacramento   1,000
City of Sacramento; Sacramento; real estate agents and managers   1,000
Kaiser Foundation Hospitals; Sacramento   1,000
Mercy Healthcare Hospital Sacramento; Sacramento   990
U.S. Army Corps of Engineers; Sacramento   900
Tacoma News Inc.; Sacramento; newspaper   820
California Almond Growers Exchange Sacramento; food preparations   800
California Public Employees' Retirement System; Sacramento   800
Comcast Corp.; Sacramento; architectural services   760
Sacramento Municipal Utility District; Sacramento electric power generation   710
City of Sacramento; Sacramento; public utility association   700
Sacramento County; Sacramento; county government   700
Sacramento Regional Transit District; Sacramento   700
Stat Nursing Services Inc.; Sacramento; employment agencies   700
Sara Lee Bakery Group Inc.; Sacramento; bread baking   700
Los Rios Community College District; Sacramento; child day care services   650
Sacramento County; Sacramento; district attorneys' office   602
California Water Resources Control Board; Sacramento   600
California Lottery Commission; Sacramento   600
City of Sacramento; Sacramento; automotive repair shops   600
Nordstrom Inc.; Sacramento; family clothing stores   585
City of Sacramento; Sacramento; fire dept. engineering   581

California Consumer Affairs Dept.; Sacramento 550

California Dept. of Health Services; Sacramento 550

California State Teachers Retirement System; Sacramento 535

California Dept. of Social Services; Sacramento 531

California Air Resources Board; Sacramento 500

California Dept. of General Services; Sacramento 500

California Office of Legislative Council; Sacramento 500

California State Board of Control; Sacramento 500

California Fish and Game Dept.; Sacramento 500

Interwoven Inc.; Sacramento; business computer software 500

Pick and Pull Auto Dismantler; Sacramento; automotive parts 500

Octel Communications Corp.; Sacramento telephones and telephone apparatus 500

Siemens Transportation Systems Inc.; Sacramento; commercial vehicles 500

United Parcel Service Inc.; Sacramento; parcel delivery 500

Sprint Corp.; Sacramento; local/long distance telephone 500

California 6th District

Northern Bay Area — Sonoma and Marin Counties

Travel north across the Golden Gate Bridge and the scenery changes from the cityscape of San Francisco to the Pacific coastline and inland hills that make up the 6th. This area north of the city is home to upper-middle-class suburbanites who commute to San Francisco and the "Telecom Valley," which extends north from San Rafael to Santa Rosa. *(See map p. 85.)*

The 6th includes all of Marin County and most of Sonoma County. The area has grown significantly since the bridge opened in 1937 and continues to prosper. In recent years, migration from the city has created a tight housing market. As of 2002, the median house price for Marin County was $700,000, while Sonoma County's was $375,000.

Marin is home to San Quentin State Prison, San Rafael (the largest city in the county), and popular getaway spots such as Point Reyes National Seashore, Sausalito, and Muir Woods. To the north, Sonoma County is home to a California State University campus and Santa Rosa, the largest city in the district. Wine and dairy ranching dominate the economy here, although high-tech companies have made inroads. Petaluma, with Victorian architecture left untouched by the 1906 earthquake, is near the Sonoma-Marin county line.

The district's affluent residents think of themselves as progressive and tolerant of diverse views. The 6th is one of the most liberal in the Democrat-dominated Golden State. After flirting with Republicanism in the late 1970s and early 1980s, it turned solidly Democratic, giving Democrat Al Gore 62.2 percent to George W. Bush's 30.3 percent in the 2000 presidential election. Democrats outnumber Republicans two to one in voter registration.

Major Industry

Telecommunications, agriculture, tourism.

Notable

San Rafael is home to film producer and director George Lucas' companies, Industrial Light & Magic, Lucasfilm Ltd., and Skywalker Sound.

Election Returns

	Republican		Democratic		Other	
President 2000	87,082	30.3%	178,746	62.2%	21,514	7.5%
House 2002	62,052	29.6%	139,750	66.7%	7,761	3.7%

District Profile

Population 639,087

Total area (square miles) 2,118
  Land area (square miles) 1,624

Population per square mile 393.4

Counties (2000 population)
  Marin 247,289
  Sonoma (pt.) 391,798

Cities and other areas over 10,000 (2000 population)
  Larkspur 12,014
  Mill Valley 13,600
  Novato 47,630
  Petaluma 54,548
  Rohnert Park 42,236
  San Anselmo town 12,378
  San Rafael 56,063
  Santa Rosa 147,595
  Tamalpais-Homestead Valley CDP 10,691

Race and Hispanic or Latino origin*
  White 76.1%
  Black or African American 2.0%
  American Indian or Alaska Native 0.6%
  Asian 3.7%
  Native Hawaiian or other Pacific Islander 0.2%
  Some other race 0.2%
  Hispanic or Latino origin 14.5%
  Two or more races 2.7%

*As percentage of total population.

Ancestry*

Dutch 1.3%	Polish 1.7%
English 9.8%	Portuguese 1.1%
French 3.0%	Russian 1.7%
German 11.1%	Scotch-Irish 1.6%
Irish 10.6%	Scottish 2.4%
Italian 6.6%	Swedish 1.8%
Norwegian 1.7%	USA/American 2.4%

*As estimated percentage of total population.

Universities and colleges, 2000–2001 enrollment
  College of Marin, Kentfield 8,317
  Dominican College of San Rafael, San Rafael 1,369
  Empire College School of Business, Santa Rosa 363
  Golden Gate Baptist Seminary, Mill Valley 463
  San Francisco Theological Seminary, San Anselmo 637
  Santa Rosa Junior College, Santa Rosa 27,020
  Sonoma State University, Rohnert Park 7,402

Newspapers and circulation

	District circulation	Total circulation
Marin Independent Journal	39,912	40,137
San Francisco Chronicle	51,877	518,725
Santa Rosa Press Democrat	63,746	89,998
*USA Today**	1,755	1,674,376

See Sources and Explanations in the front of the volume.

Television stations and affiliations

San Francisco-Oakland-San Jose	100%	KBHK	UPN
San Francisco-Oakland-San Jose	100%	KBWB	WB
San Francisco-Oakland-San Jose	100%	KCNS	Independent
San Francisco-Oakland-San Jose	100%	KCSM	PBS
San Francisco-Oakland-San Jose	100%	KDTV	Univision
San Francisco-Oakland-San Jose	100%	KFTL	Independent
San Francisco-Oakland-San Jose	100%	KFTY	Independent
San Francisco-Oakland-San Jose	100%	KFWU	Independent Spanish
San Francisco-Oakland-San Jose	100%	KGO	ABC
San Francisco-Oakland-San Jose	100%	KICU	Independent
San Francisco-Oakland-San Jose	100%	KKPX	PAX
San Francisco-Oakland-San Jose	100%	KMTP	PBS
San Francisco-Oakland-San Jose	100%	KNTV	NBC
San Francisco-Oakland-San Jose	100%	KPIX	CBS
San Francisco-Oakland-San Jose	100%	KQED	PBS
San Francisco-Oakland-San Jose	100%	KRCB	PBS
San Francisco-Oakland-San Jose	100%	KRON	Independent
San Francisco-Oakland-San Jose	100%	KSTS	Telemundo
San Francisco-Oakland-San Jose	100%	KTEH	PBS
San Francisco-Oakland-San Jose	100%	KTLN	Independent
San Francisco-Oakland-San Jose	100%	KTNC	Independent Spanish
San Francisco-Oakland-San Jose	100%	KTSF	Independent
San Francisco-Oakland-San Jose	100%	KTVU	FOX

Cable systems and subscribers

Central Valley Cable   705
Comcast   179,905
Horizon Cable TV   1,075

Businesses and other major employers

Associated Indemnity Corp.; Novato; life insurance   2,500
Fireman's Fund Insurance Co.; Novato; fire, marine, casualty insurance   2,242
American Insurance Co.; Novato; fire, marine, casualty insurance   2,000
Guardian Post Acute Services Inc.; Corte Madera; skilled nursing care facilities   1,800
Marin County; San Rafael; county government   1,690
Santa Rosa City Schools; Santa Rosa   1,600
Sonoma County Community College District; Santa Rosa   1,500
Hewlett-Packard Co.; Santa Rosa; electronic computers   1,225
State Farm Mutual Automobile Insurance Co.; Rohnert Park; insurance agents and brokers   1,200
VPA Inc.; Novato; automobile insurance   1,200
Marin General Hospital; Greenbrae   1,100
Kaiser Foundation Hospitals; San Rafael   1,050
Kaiser Foundation Hospitals; Santa Rosa   1,050
Mattel Inc.; Novato; computer software development   1,000
Cisco Systems Inc.; Petaluma; research institute   1,000
P&T Products; Novato; sporting and recreation goods   948
California Dept. of Corrections;   San Rafael   925
Sola International Inc.; Petaluma; lenses, ophthalmic   860

Township Building Services Inc.; Novato; janitorial service   830
North American Mortgage Co.; Santa Rosa; mortgage bankers   750
Community College of Marin; Kentfield   700
Medtronic Ave Inc.; Santa Rosa; surgical instruments and apparatus   700
Sonoma County Office of Education; Santa Rosa   685
Advanced Fibre Communications; Petaluma; fiber optics communications equipment   680
Wine Country Hotel; Sonoma; hotels and motels   627
Santa Rosa Memorial Hospital Inc.; Santa Rosa   614
Isaac Fair and Co.; San Rafael; business computer software   600
Agilent Technologies Inc.; Santa Rosa; electric measuring instruments, meters   600
Sonoma County; Santa Rosa; county government   600
Amy's Kitchen Inc.; Santa Rosa; frozen dinners   600
Golden Gate Bridge Highway and Transportation District; San Rafael   535
Lucas Digital; San Rafael; motion pictures services   500
Managed Health Network; San Rafael; hospital/medical service plans   500
Sheehan Construction Inc.; Novato; single-family housing construction   500
Sunrise Industries; Eldridge; employment agencies   500
Crescent Real Estate Equities Co.; Sonoma; real estate investment trusts   500

California 7th District

Northeastern Bay Area — Vallejo, Richmond

Situated along the San Pablo Bay and home to marshes and wetlands where the Sacramento and San Joaquin deltas feed into the bay, the 7th combines industrial and suburban areas of north Contra Costa County with the western end of more rural Solano County. *(See map p. 85.)*

In Contra Costa County, the district takes in residential Concord (shared with the 10th) and the industrial cities of Richmond and Martinez along San Pablo Bay, home to oil, steel, and biotechnology. Richmond, which has a black plurality, was home to one of the largest World War II shipbuilding operations.

Vallejo, the largest city in the district, was the site of Mare Island Naval Shipyard, which closed in 1996 after more than 140 years of operation. The city converted the island to a private commercial-residential property, which is still in development.

Vallejo and other traditionally Democratic Solano County communities—including Green Valley and Vacaville, which were added to the northern part of the 7th in redistricting following the 2000 census—are home to farm-support services.

Redistricting also shaved off Democratic-voting areas like Suisun City, Fairfield, Cordelia, and Kensington to shore up the neighboring 10th District for Democrats, but the 7th is still a safe Democratic seat.

Major Industry

Petrochemicals, steel, biotechnology, agriculture, health care.

SAN FRANCISCO BAY AREA

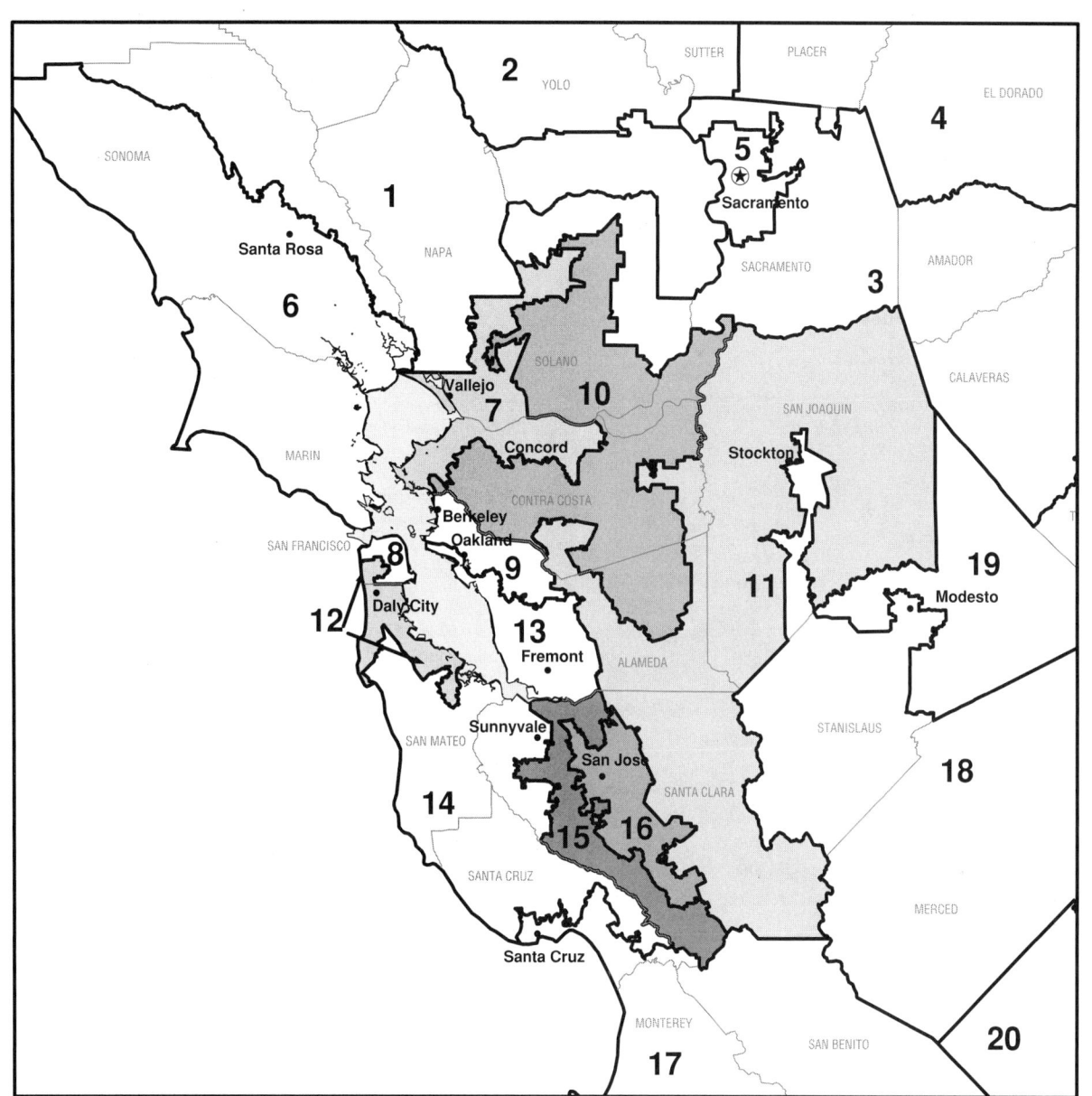

Notable

The forerunner to the martini, the "Martinez Special," became popular in the city of Martinez during the gold rush; Actor Tom Hanks was born in Concord; Vallejo (twice) and Benicia both served as the state capital in the 1850s.

Election Returns

	Republican		Democratic		Other	
President 2000	64,477	30.6%	139,421	66.2%	6,824	3.2%
House 2002	36,584	26.4%	97,849	70.7%	3,943	2.8%

District Profile

Population   639,088

Total area (square miles)   443
   Land area (square miles)   349

Population per square mile   1,831

Counties (2000 population)
   Contra Costa (pt.)   398,978
   Solano (pt.)   240,110

Cities and other areas over 10,000 (2000 population)

Bay Point CDP	21,534	Pinole	19,039
Benicia	26,865	Pittsburg	56,769
Clayton	10,762	Richmond	99,216
Concord (pt.)	49,240	San Pablo	30,215
El Sobrante CDP	12,260	Vacaville	88,625
Hercules	19,488	Vallejo	116,760
Martinez	35,866		

Race and Hispanic or Latino origin*
   White   43.2%
   Black or African American   16.8%
   American Indian or Alaska Native   0.5%
   Asian   13.3%
   Native Hawaiian or other Pacific Islander   0.6%
   Some other race   0.3%
   Hispanic or Latino origin   21.4%
   Two or more races   3.9%

*As percentage of total population.

Ancestry*

English	5.6%	Norwegian	1.1%
French	1.7%	Portuguese	1.3%
German	7.5%	Scottish	1.2%
Irish	6.7%	Swedish	1.1%
Italian	4.1%	USA/American	2.4%

*As estimated percentage of total population.

Universities and colleges, 2000–2001 enrollment
   California Maritime Academy, Vallejo   653
   Contra Costa College, San Pablo   7,133
   Heald College School of Business, Concord   554
   Heald College School of Technology, Martinez   923
   Los Medanos College, Pittsburg   9,212

Newspapers and circulation

	District circulation	Total circulation
Fairfield Daily Republic	5,073	19,756
Oakland Tribune	6,260	68,112
Pleasanton Tri-Valley Herald	1,850	43,384
San Francisco Chronicle	20,759	518,725
Vacaville Reporter	5,138	18,124
Vallejo Times Herald	15,436	20,751
Walnut Creek Contra Costa Times	54,574	182,696

Television stations and affiliations

San Francisco-Oakland-San Jose	74%	KBHK	UPN
San Francisco-Oakland-San Jose	74%	KBWB	WB
San Francisco-Oakland-San Jose	74%	KCNS	Independent
San Francisco-Oakland-San Jose	74%	KCSM	PBS
San Francisco-Oakland-San Jose	74%	KDTV	Univision
San Francisco-Oakland-San Jose	74%	KFTL	Independent
San Francisco-Oakland-San Jose	74%	KFTY	Independent
San Francisco-Oakland-San Jose	74%	KFWU	Independent Spanish
San Francisco-Oakland-San Jose	74%	KGO	ABC
San Francisco-Oakland-San Jose	74%	KICU	Independent
San Francisco-Oakland-San Jose	74%	KKPX	PAX
San Francisco-Oakland-San Jose	74%	KMTP	PBS
San Francisco-Oakland-San Jose	74%	KNTV	NBC
San Francisco-Oakland-San Jose	74%	KPIX	CBS
San Francisco-Oakland-San Jose	74%	KQED	PBS
San Francisco-Oakland-San Jose	74%	KRCB	PBS
San Francisco-Oakland-San Jose	74%	KRON	Independent
San Francisco-Oakland-San Jose	74%	KSTS	Telemundo
San Francisco-Oakland-San Jose	74%	KTEH	PBS
San Francisco-Oakland-San Jose	74%	KTLN	Independent
San Francisco-Oakland-San Jose	74%	KTNC	Independent Spanish
San Francisco-Oakland-San Jose	74%	KTSF	Independent
San Francisco-Oakland-San Jose	74%	KTVU	FOX
Sacramento-Stockton-Modesto	26%	KBSV	Independent
Sacramento-Stockton-Modesto	26%	KCRA	NBC
Sacramento-Stockton-Modesto	26%	KMAX	UPN
Sacramento-Stockton-Modesto	26%	KOVR	CBS
Sacramento-Stockton-Modesto	26%	KQCA	WB
Sacramento-Stockton-Modesto	26%	KSPX	PAX
Sacramento-Stockton-Modesto	26%	KTXL	FOX
Sacramento-Stockton-Modesto	26%	KUVS	Univision
Sacramento-Stockton-Modesto	26%	KVIE	PBS
Sacramento-Stockton-Modesto	26%	KXTV	ABC

Cable systems and subscribers
   Comcast   162,290

Businesses and other major employers
   Shaw Environmental Inc.; Concord; business consulting 6,000
   Ceramic Development Corp.; Richmond; arts and crafts equipment and supplies   1,982
   CCC Hospital Facilities Maintenance; Martinez; hospital, medical school   1,500
   John Muir/Mt. Diablo Hospital; Concord   1,200
   Kaiser Foundation Hospitals; Vallejo   1,050
   Ocular Sciences Inc.; Concord; contact lenses   1,031
   Contra Costa County; Martinez; sheriff's office   1,000
   Kaiser Foundation Hospitals; Martinez   1,000
   Six Flags Inc.; Vallejo; theme park   1,000
   Lucas Film; Vallejo; motion picture production   1,000
   Doctor's Medical Center; San Pablo   1,000
   U.S. Postal Service; Richmond   1,000
   California Dept. of Corrections; Vacaville   1,000
   Bio-Rad Laboratories Inc.; Hercules; analytical instruments 900
   Shell Martinez Refining Co.; Martinez; petroleum refining 900
   Equilon Enterprises; Martinez; petroleum refining   800
   Contra Costa County; Martinez; government   700
   Contra Costa County Dept. of Health Service; Martinez 700

QRS Corp.; Richmond; computer programming services 700

Valero Energy Corp.; Martinez; petroleum refining 670

Ladbrokes Casino San Pablo; San Pablo; casino 670

Alza Corp.; Vacaville; pharmaceuticals 650

Ladbroke San Pablo; San Pablo; gambling and lottery services 547

Sutter Solano Medical Center Inc.; Vallejo 542

C&H Sugar Co.; Crockett; cane sugar refining 520

Wells Fargo Bank; El Monte; management consulting 500

Valero Refining Co.; Benicia; petroleum refining 500

West Macy's Inc.; Concord; discount department stores 500

Tenet Health System Hospitals Inc.; Pinole 500

Tosco Corp.; Rodeo; petroleum refining 500

U.S. Postal Service; Richmond 500

Travis Federal Credit Union; Vacaville; federal credit unions 500

California 8th District

Most of San Francisco

Since the gold rush in the midnineteenth century, San Francisco has attracted visitors, new residents, and fortune seekers from around the globe. "The City," as it is known to natives, is famous for its landmarks, food, and a diverse collection of neighborhoods, from the Italian and Hispanic centers of North Beach and the Mission District to spots such as Chinatown, hippie haven Haight-Ashbury, and the gay mecca of Castro. *(See map p. 85.)*

More than 80 percent of the city's residents live in the 8th, which forms a backward C-shape. The 12th District to the west and south takes in neighborhoods just south of Golden Gate Park and west of Twin Peaks. Whites were 42.9 percent of the 8th's population in the 2000 census, followed by Asians, at 28.7 percent.

A center for protest during the Vietnam War, the city also barred police from arresting illegal immigrants fleeing Central American bloodshed in the 1980s, in opposition to federal immigration officials. More recently, the city has helped fund the largest needle exchange program in the nation and in 2002 approved an initiative to study whether to grow and distribute medical marijuana to seriously ill patients. The city also chose, however, to cut its once-bountiful direct payments to the homeless and shift that money to create more housing and services. The 8th is safe Democratic territory. Democrat Al Gore won the 2000 presidential vote here by 62 percentage points.

Major Industry

Tourism, financial services, health care.

Notable

San Francisco was home to the nation's only declared monarch, Norton I, who named himself Emperor of the United States and Protector of Mexico in 1859; throughout his "reign," Norton issued various proclamations, including orders to bar Congress from meeting in Washington and to construct a bridge between San Francisco and Oakland—more than 60 years before construction of the Bay Bridge;

Alcatraz Island, home to the first West Coast fort and lighthouse and used as a federal maximum-security prison from 1934 to 1963, was occupied in protest by Native Americans from 1969 to 1971.

Election Returns

	Republican		Democratic		Other	
President 2000	37,737	14.8%	196,878	77.1%	20,869	8.2%
House 2002	20,063	12.5%	127,684	79.6%	12,694	7.9%

District Profile

Population 639,088

Total area (square miles) 113
    Land area (square miles) 35

Population per square mile 18,063

Counties (2000 population)
    San Francisco (pt.) 639,088

Cities and other areas over 10,000 (2000 population)
    San Francisco (pt.) 639,088

Race and Hispanic or Latino origin*
    White 42.9%
    Black or African American 8.6%
    American Indian or Alaska Native 0.3%
    Asian 28.7%
    Native Hawaiian or other Pacific Islander 0.5%
    Some other race 0.3%
    Hispanic or Latino origin 15.7%
    Two or more races 2.9%

*As percentage of total population.

Ancestry*

English 5.1%	Polish 1.5%
French 1.9%	Russian 2.2%
German 6.4%	Scottish 1.5%
Irish 6.9%	USA/American 1.3%
Italian 4.1%	

*As estimated percentage of total population.

Universities and colleges, 2000–2001 enrollment
    Academy of Art College, San Francisco 5,995
    American College of Traditional Chinese Medicine, San Francisco 229
    Art Institutes International at San Francisco, San Francisco 329
    California College of Podiatric Medicine, San Francisco 305
    California Culinary Academy, San Francisco 1,486
    California Institute of Integral Studies, San Francisco 951
    Computer Learning Center, San Francisco 532
    Fashion Institute of Design and Merchandising, San Francisco 663
    Golden Gate University, San Francisco 5,322
    Heald College Schools of Business and Technology, San Francisco 1,070
    New College of California, San Francisco 527
    San Francisco Art Institute, San Francisco 625
    San Francisco Law School, San Francisco*
    Saybrook Institute, San Francisco 421

University of California Hastings College of Law, San
Francisco   1,201
University of Phoenix-Online, San Francisco   14,783
University of San Francisco, San Francisco   7,917

Enrollment under 100. See Sources and Explanations in the front of the volume.

Newspapers and circulation

	District circulation	Total circulation
San Francisco Chronicle	108,075	518,725
San Jose Mercury News	4,080	275,971
*USA Today**	6,158	1,674,376

See Sources and Explanations in the front of the volume.

Television stations and affiliations

San Francisco-Oakland-San Jose	100%	KBHK	UPN
San Francisco-Oakland-San Jose	100%	KBWB	WB
San Francisco-Oakland-San Jose	100%	KCNS	Independent
San Francisco-Oakland-San Jose	100%	KCSM	PBS
San Francisco-Oakland-San Jose	100%	KDTV	Univision
San Francisco-Oakland-San Jose	100%	KFTL	Independent
San Francisco-Oakland-San Jose	100%	KFTY	Independent
San Francisco-Oakland-San Jose	100%	KFWU	Independent Spanish
San Francisco-Oakland-San Jose	100%	KGO	ABC
San Francisco-Oakland-San Jose	100%	KICU	Independent
San Francisco-Oakland-San Jose	100%	KKPX	PAX
San Francisco-Oakland-San Jose	100%	KMTP	PBS
San Francisco-Oakland-San Jose	100%	KNTV	NBC
San Francisco-Oakland-San Jose	100%	KPIX	CBS
San Francisco-Oakland-San Jose	100%	KQED	PBS
San Francisco-Oakland-San Jose	100%	KRCB	PBS
San Francisco-Oakland-San Jose	100%	KRON	Independent
San Francisco-Oakland-San Jose	100%	KSTS	Telemundo
San Francisco-Oakland-San Jose	100%	KTEH	PBS
San Francisco-Oakland-San Jose	100%	KTLN	Independent
San Francisco-Oakland-San Jose	100%	KTNC	Independent Spanish
San Francisco-Oakland-San Jose	100%	KTSF	Independent
San Francisco-Oakland-San Jose	100%	KTVU	FOX

Cable systems and subscribers
Comcast   171,054

Businesses and other major employers
United Air Lines Inc.; San Francisco; aircraft maintenance, repair   16,000
International Business Machines Corp.; San Francisco; information technologies   8,500
Wells Fargo Bank; San Francisco; commercial bank   6,000
Pacific Gas and Electric Co.; San Francisco; electric power generation   5,500
San Francisco City and County; San Francisco; local railway passenger operation   3,784
San Francisco City and County; San Francisco; sleeping car and other passenger car services   3,500
Union Pacific Railroad Co.; San Francisco; railroad freight hauling   3,000
San Francisco City and County Hospital; San Francisco   3,000
San Francisco Community College District; San Francisco   2,750
Independent Consulting Network Inc.; San Francisco; professional organization   2,632
California Pacific Medical Center; San Francisco   2,578
Gap Inc.; San Francisco; family clothing stores   2,500
West Macy's Inc.; San Francisco; department stores   2,266
San Francisco City and County; San Francisco; police dept.   2,200

Bechtel Group Inc.; San Francisco; civil engineering   2,100
PricewaterhouseCoopers; San Francisco; accounting services   2,100
San Francisco City and County; San Francisco; utility regulation   2,000
LPMT; San Francisco; charitable organization   2,000
Pacific Bell; San Francisco; local/long distance telephone   2,000
California Pacific Medical Center; San Francisco   2,000
U.S. Veterans Hospital; San Francisco   2,000
University of San Francisco; San Francisco   1,671
California State Automobile Assn. Inter-Insurance Bureau; San Francisco   1,600
Levi Strauss and Co.; San Francisco; men's and boys' jeans   1,600
Lembi Group Inc.; San Francisco; real estate managers   1,510
Broadway Stores Inc.; San Francisco; department stores   1,500
Bank of America Corp.; San Francisco security brokers   1,500
Federal Reserve Bank of San Francisco; San Francisco   1,397
Chronicle Publishing Co.; San Francisco; newspaper   1,350
ChevronTexaco Corp.; San Francisco; petroleum refining   1,329
Genesis Telecom Laboratory; San Francisco; computer software development   1,300
San Francisco Baseball Associates; San Francisco; baseball club   1,240
Coach USA Inc.; San Francisco; tour operators   1,200
San Francisco City and County; San Francisco; public welfare administration   1,200
Charles Schwab Corp.; San Francisco; security brokers   1,200
Hilton Hotels Corp.; San Francisco; hotels   1,117
Madsen Services Inc.; San Francisco; placement agencies   1,100
Barclays California Corp.; San Francisco; investment advisory service   1,100
Stat Nursing Services Inc.; San Francisco; nurses' registry   1,100
Delta Dental Plan of California; San Francisco; dental insurance   1,069
St. Mary's Hospital and Medical Center; San Francisco   1,043
California Compensation Insurance Fund; San Francisco   1,000
Bank of America Corp.; San Francisco; commercial bank   1,000
Kaiser Foundation Hospitals; San Francisco   1,000
Permanente Medical Group Inc.; San Francisco   1,000
Kaiser Foundation Hospitals; San Francisco   1,000
International Total Services Inc.; San Francisco; security guard service   1,000
U.S. Postal Service; San Francisco   1,000
PricewaterhouseCoopers; San Francisco; computer maintenance services   900
Hyatt Corp.; San Francisco; hotel, franchised   900
Unilever Bestfoods Foodservice; San Francisco; retail bakeries   900
Nordstrom Inc.; San Francisco; family clothing stores   856
California Public Utilities Commission; San Francisco   850

Union Bank of California; San Francisco; commercial bank 850

San Francisco Sheriff's Office; San Francisco 820

BRE/St. Francis Hotel; San Francisco; hotels 800

Cap Gemini America Inc.; San Francisco; computer consulting services 800

J. P. Morgan Securities Inc.; San Francisco; security brokers 800

Saint Francis Memorial Hospital; San Francisco 800

PMI Mortgage Insurance Co.; San Francisco; mortgage guarantee insurance 800

McKesson Corp.; San Francisco; pharmaceuticals 755

Volume Services America Inc.; San Francisco; contract food services 750

St. Luke's Hospital; San Francisco 740

Williams-Sonoma Inc.; San Francisco; catalog sales 714

California Physicians Service; San Francisco; hospital/medical service plans 700

Pillsbury Winthrop LLP; San Francisco; general practice law office 700

Marsh USA Inc.; San Francisco; insurance agents and brokers 700

Morrison and Foerster; San Francisco; general practice law office 650

U.S. Postal Service; San Francisco 650

Metreon Inc.; San Francisco; administrative management 600

Barclays Global Investors; San Francisco; investment advisory service 600

Burns International Security Services Corp.; San Francisco; security guard service 600

CNET Networks Inc.; San Francisco; radio/telephone communication 600

Pacific Bell Directory; San Francisco; directories publishing 600

Palace Hotel; San Francisco; hotels and motels 600

Providian Bancorp Service Inc.; San Francisco; financial services 600

CMP Media Inc.; San Francisco; periodicals 600

DHL Holdings Inc.; San Francisco; air courier services 600

Morgan Stanley Dean Witter and Co.; San Francisco; security brokers 600

Thomas Weisel Partners; San Francisco; investment bankers 590

Scient Inc.; New York; computer consulting services 588

Byer California; San Francisco; women's and misses' blouses/shirts 575

AT&T Corp.; San Francisco; long-distance telephone 575

Hebrew Home for Aged Disabled; San Francisco; skilled nursing care facilities 574

Heller Ehrman White & McAuliffe; San Francisco; specialized law offices 560

Brobeck, Phleger & Harrison; San Francisco; general practice law office 550

PricewaterhouseCoopers; San Francisco; acccounting services 550

California Dept. of Rehabilitation; San Francisco 530

Wesley Medical Resources Inc.; San Francisco; temporary help service 504

California Dept. of Industrial Relations; San Francisco 500

U.S. Mint; San Francisco 500

UnionBanCal Corp.; San Francisco; commercial bank 500

ITT Sheraton Corp.; San Francisco; resort hotel 500

Kyo-Ya Co.; San Francisco; hotels 500

Pacific Bell; San Francisco; telephone communication 500

Advent Software Inc.; San Francisco; prepackaged software 500

Delancey Street Foundation; San Francisco; residential rehabilitation center 500

Pacific Bell; San Francisco; telephone communication 500

SBC Communications Inc.; San Francisco; telephone directories 500

California Hyatt Corp.; San Francisco; hotels 500

Neiman Marcus Group Inc.; San Francisco; department stores 500

ABM Security Services Inc.; San Francisco; security guard service 500

First Republic Bank; San Francisco; commercial banking 500

U.S. Bureau of Citizenship and Immigration Services; San Francisco 500

Mattel Inc.; San Francisco; toys and games 500

U.S. National Park Service; San Francisco 500

California 9th District

Northwest Alameda County — Oakland, Berkeley

Across the bay from San Francisco, the 9th is anchored by Oakland and Berkeley, two racially diverse and liberal communities that gained national attention for their political activism in the 1960s. *(See map p. 85.)*

More than 60 percent of district residents live in Oakland, which is 38 percent black. The city's unemployment rate is slightly above the national average, but revitalization efforts have kept the area in good health, despite the closing of several military facilities. In the city's eastern hills, the neighborhoods tend to be wealthy and less diverse. Tension between blacks and police gave birth to the Black Panther Party in 1966.

Just north of Oakland, Berkeley is home to the flagship campus of the University of California system and looks out over the bay from the Berkeley Hills. Home to student protests in the 1960s, Berkeley still looks much the way it did then. The remainder of the district includes smaller communities such as Albany, a suburb at the north end of the district; Piedmont, a residential "suburb in the city" in Oakland's hills; and several additions from redistricting following the 2000 census: Ashland, Castro Valley, Cherryland, and Fairview, which are unincorporated sections of Alameda County southeast of Oakland.

The 9th also includes the fast-growing bayside city of Emeryville, home to biotechnology firms, high-tech companies, and headquarters of animation studio Pixar (*Toy Story, Finding Nemo*).

With a core constituency in the left-leaning cities of Oakland and Berkeley, the 9th is a Democratic stronghold. Republicans account for only 12 percent of registered voters.

Major Industry

Biotechnology, shipping.

Notable

Since 1970, Jack London Square in Oakland has featured the relocated cabin where the author, who ran for Oakland mayor twice, lived during the Yukon gold rush of 1897; West Oakland was a terminus for the transcontinental railroad.

Election Returns

	Republican		Democratic		Other	
President 2000	31,464	13.4%	184,030	78.5%	18,868	8.1%
House 2002	25,333	15.2%	135,893	81.4%	5,691	3.4%

District Profile

Population   639,088

Total area (square miles)   152
   Land area (square miles)   132

Population per square mile   4,831.1

Counties (2000 population)
   Alameda (pt.)   639,088

Cities and other areas over 10,000 (2000 population)
   Albany   16,444
   Ashland CDP   20,793
   Berkeley   102,743
   Castro Valley CDP (pt.)   57,224
   Cherryland CDP (pt.)   11,335
   Oakland (pt.)   399,484
   Piedmont   10,952

Race and Hispanic or Latino origin*
   White   35.2%
   Black or African American   26.0%
   American Indian or Alaska Native   0.4%
   Asian   15.4%
   Native Hawaiian or other Pacific Islander   0.4%
   Some other race   0.4%
   Hispanic or Latino origin   18.7%
   Two or more races   3.6%

*As percentage of total population.

Ancestry*
   English   5.1%   Portuguese   1.1%
   French   1.5%   Russian   1.5%
   German   5.9%   Scottish   1.3%
   Irish   5.0%   Subsaharan   1.8%
   Italian   2.8%   USA/American   1.3%
   Polish   1.2%

*As estimated percentage of total population.

Universities and colleges, 2000–2001 enrollment
   California College of Arts and Crafts, Oakland   1,180
   Graduate Theological Union, Berkeley   263
   Heald College School of Business, Oakland   327
   Holy Names College, Oakland   945
   ITT Technical Institute, Oakland   5,975
   Laney College, Oakland   11,531
   Mills College, Oakland   1,059
   Oakland College of Law, Oakland*
   Pacific School of Religion, Berkeley   231
   Patten College, Oakland   560
   Sierra Academy of Aeronautics Technical Institute, Oakland   477
   University of California, Berkeley   31,277

Vista College, Berkeley   3,984
Wright Institute, Berkeley   281

*Enrollment under 100. See Sources and Explanations in the front of the volume.

Newspapers and circulation

	District circulation	Total circulation
Hayward Daily Review	12,982	38,497
Oakland Tribune	44,085	68,112
San Francisco Chronicle	56,662	518,725
Walnut Creek Contra Costa Times	5,771	182,696

Television stations and affiliations

San Francisco-Oakland-San Jose	100%	KBHK	UPN
San Francisco-Oakland-San Jose	100%	KBWB	WB
San Francisco-Oakland-San Jose	100%	KCNS	Independent
San Francisco-Oakland-San Jose	100%	KCSM	PBS
San Francisco-Oakland-San Jose	100%	KDTV	Univision
San Francisco-Oakland-San Jose	100%	KFTL	Independent
San Francisco-Oakland-San Jose	100%	KFTY	Independent
San Francisco-Oakland-San Jose	100%	KFWU	Independent Spanish
San Francisco-Oakland-San Jose	100%	KGO	ABC
San Francisco-Oakland-San Jose	100%	KICU	Independent
San Francisco-Oakland-San Jose	100%	KKPX	PAX
San Francisco-Oakland-San Jose	100%	KMTP	PBS
San Francisco-Oakland-San Jose	100%	KNTV	NBC
San Francisco-Oakland-San Jose	100%	KPIX	CBS
San Francisco-Oakland-San Jose	100%	KQED	PBS
San Francisco-Oakland-San Jose	100%	KRCB	PBS
San Francisco-Oakland-San Jose	100%	KRON	Independent
San Francisco-Oakland-San Jose	100%	KSTS	Telemundo
San Francisco-Oakland-San Jose	100%	KTEH	PBS
San Francisco-Oakland-San Jose	100%	KTLN	Independent
San Francisco-Oakland-San Jose	100%	KTNC	Independent Spanish
San Francisco-Oakland-San Jose	100%	KTSF	Independent
San Francisco-Oakland-San Jose	100%	KTVU	FOX

Cable systems and subscribers
   Comcast   110,844

Military installations, September 2001
   Oakland USARC/AMSA (Army Reserve), Oakland   214

Businesses and other major employers
   Bigfix Inc.; Berkeley; prepackaged software   10,000
   Praxair Distribution Inc.; Oakland; carbon dioxide   5,000
   Lawrence Berkeley National Laboratory; Berkeley; biological research   5,000
   University of California; Berkeley   3,100
   University of California; Berkeley; research institute   3,000
   U.S. Internal Revenue Service; Oakland   2,500
   Pacific Gas and Electric Co.; Oakland; business consulting   2,500
   Kaiser Foundation Hospitals; Oakland   2,200
   Summit Medical Center; Oakland   2,000
   Northern California Children's Hospital Medical Center; Oakland   1,900
   Berkeley; Albany; public health programs   1,520
   Peralta Community College District; Oakland   1,420
   Alameda County Hospital; Oakland   1,300
   San Francisco Bay Area Rapid Transit District; Oakland   1,300
   Kaiser Foundation Health Plan Inc.; Oakland; hospital/medical service plans   1,300
   City of Berkeley; Berkeley; city government   1,159
   University of California; Oakland   1,100

City of Oakland; Oakland; municipal police   1,000
Eden Township Hospital District Inc.; Castro Valley   968
Alameda County Hospital; San Leandro   900
City of Oakland; Oakland; city government   858
Waste Management of Alameda County Inc.; Oakland;
   rubbish collection and disposal   800
Pinkerton's Inc.; Oakland; detective agency   800
Clorox Co.; Oakland; polishes and sanitation goods   775
KSL Claremont Resort Inc.; Berkeley; resort hotel   725
California Dept. of Transportation; Oakland   700
West Macy's Inc.; Oakland; department stores   700
Harsch Investment Corp.; Berkeley; hotels   700
Alta Bates Medical Center; Berkeley   653
Pixar; Emeryville; movie cartoon production   648
Alameda County; San Leandro; probation office   600
Oakland Unified School District; Oakland   600
APL Information Services; Oakland; management
   consulting   600
Kaiser Foundation Hospitals; Oakland   600
City of Oakland; Oakland; fire dept.   600
Aramark Services Inc.; Oakland; food services   600
Army and Air Force Exchange Service; Oakland;
   warehousing   585
East Bay Municipal Utility District Water System;
   Oakland; water supply   580
University of California; Berkeley; management services
   550
Chiron Diagnostics Corp.; Emeryville; medical diagnostic
   apparatus   525
APL Limited; Oakland; deep sea freight transportation
   523
Kmart Corp.; Oakland; discount department stores   500
Owens-Brockway Glass Container Inc.; Oakland; glass
   containers   500
Chiron Corp.; Emeryville; diagnostic substances   500
Sutter Visiting Nurse Assn. and Hospice; Emeryville;
   visiting nurse service   500
Value Tel; Oakland; long-distance telephone   500
Golden West Financial Corp.; Oakland; federal savings and
   loan associations   500
Permanente Medical Group Inc.; Oakland; business
   management   500
Stealth Security Services Inc.; Oakland; detective, armored
   car services   500
Archway Mothers Cookies; Oakland; cookies and crackers
   500
SOS Professional Service Inc.; Oakland; employment
   agencies   500
Alta Bates Medical Center; Berkeley; medical centers   500
California Dept. of Health Services; Berkeley   500

California 10th District

East Bay suburbs — Fairfield, Antioch, Livermore

Anyone driving through the Caldecott Tunnel across the Alameda-Contra Costa county line or on Interstate 680 during rush hour probably will be surrounded by 10th District residents on their way to and from work in San Francisco or San Jose. Separated from the rest of the Bay Area by the hills east of Oakland, the 10th's residents are mainly well-educated, well-paid professionals who work outside the district. *(See map p. 85.)*

The 10th's residents have managed to fend off overdevelopment from their hills and hidden valleys while keeping pace with the rest of the area economically, giving the district a different feel from its more urban neighbors to the west. Almost two-thirds of residents live in the 10th's portion of Contra Costa County, including Antioch and most of Concord (shared with the 7th District).

Some of the residents here represent white flight from Oakland that is now generations old. But many newer commuters are younger and identify with San Francisco or Berkeley. The district retains a moderate political character—residents tend to be conscious of pocketbook issues but also share their Bay Area neighbors' views on the environment and other quality-of-life issues.

The district's Solano County portion is a growing but still largely agricultural area where commuters may head south to the Bay Area or north to Sacramento. Added along with a sliver of Sacramento County during redistricting following the 2000 census, these areas made the previously competitive district more Democratic. Residents here are more working-class than their "new Democrat" suburban district-mates. Growth will soon make these areas a part of the suburbs.

Major Industry
Research, health care, agriculture, service.

Notable
Lawrence Livermore National Laboratory is one of the country's leading centers of experimental physics research and defense analysis; Fairfield is home to the Jelly Belly jelly bean factory.

Election Returns

	Republican		Democratic		Other	
President 2000	109,149	41.3%	145,996	55.2%	9,273	3.5%
House 2002			126,390	75.6%	40,807	24.4%

District Profile

Population   639,088

Total area (square miles)   1,084
   Land area (square miles)   1,013

Population per square mile   630.7

Counties (2000 population)

Alameda (pt.)	75,162	Sacramento (pt.)	3,299
Contra Costa (pt.)	417,635	Solano (pt.)	142,992

Cities and other areas over 10,000 (2000 population)

Alamo CDP	15,626	Livermore	73,345
Antioch	90,532	Moraga town	16,290
Concord (pt.)	72,540	Oakley	25,619
Dixon	16,103	Orinda	17,599
El Cerrito	23,171	Pleasant Hill	32,837
Fairfield	96,178	Suisun City	26,118
Lafayette	23,908	Walnut Creek	64,296

Race and Hispanic or Latino origin*
   White   65.4%
   Black or African American   5.7%

American Indian or Alaska Native   0.4%
Asian   9.1%
Native Hawaiian or other Pacific Islander   0.4%
Some other race   0.2%
Hispanic or Latino origin   15.0%
Two or more races   3.7%

As percentage of total population.

Ancestry*

Dutch	1.2%	Polish	1.5%
English	8.2%	Portuguese	1.6%
French	2.5%	Scotch-Irish	1.4%
German	10.7%	Scottish	2.0%
Irish	9.1%	Swedish	1.7%
Italian	5.4%	USA/American	2.8%
Norwegian	1.6%		

As estimated percentage of total population.

Universities and colleges, 2000–2001 enrollment
Diablo Valley College, Pleasant Hill   21,581
John F. Kennedy University, Orinda   1,567
Las Positas College, Livermore   6,960
St. Mary's College of California, Moraga   4,150

Newspapers and circulation

	District circulation	Total circulation
Fairfield Daily Republic	13,420	19,756
Oakland Tribune	2,613	68,112
Pleasanton Tri-Valley Herald	8,476	43,384
Sacramento Bee	1,261	293,344
San Francisco Chronicle	37,157	518,725
*USA Today**	3,214	1,674,376
Vacaville Reporter	7,468	18,124
Vallejo Times Herald	1,089	20,751
Walnut Creek Contra Costa Times	88,998	182,696

See Sources and Explanations in the front of the volume.

Television stations and affiliations

San Francisco-Oakland-San Jose	56%	KBHK	UPN
San Francisco-Oakland-San Jose	56%	KBWB	WB
San Francisco-Oakland-San Jose	56%	KCNS	Independent
San Francisco-Oakland-San Jose	56%	KCSM	PBS
San Francisco-Oakland-San Jose	56%	KDTV	Univision
San Francisco-Oakland-San Jose	56%	KFTL	Independent
San Francisco-Oakland-San Jose	56%	KFTY	Independent
San Francisco-Oakland-San Jose	56%	KFWU	Independent Spanish
San Francisco-Oakland-San Jose	56%	KGO	ABC
San Francisco-Oakland-San Jose	56%	KICU	Independent
San Francisco-Oakland-San Jose	56%	KKPX	PAX
San Francisco-Oakland-San Jose	56%	KMTP	PBS
San Francisco-Oakland-San Jose	56%	KNTV	NBC
San Francisco-Oakland-San Jose	56%	KPIX	CBS
San Francisco-Oakland-San Jose	56%	KQED	PBS
San Francisco-Oakland-San Jose	56%	KRCB	PBS
San Francisco-Oakland-San Jose	56%	KRON	Independent
San Francisco-Oakland-San Jose	56%	KSTS	Telemundo
San Francisco-Oakland-San Jose	56%	KTEH	PBS
San Francisco-Oakland-San Jose	56%	KTLN	Independent
San Francisco-Oakland-San Jose	56%	KTNC	Independent Spanish
San Francisco-Oakland-San Jose	56%	KTSF	Independent
San Francisco-Oakland-San Jose	56%	KTVU	FOX
Sacramento-Stockton-Modesto	44%	KBSV	Independent
Sacramento-Stockton-Modesto	44%	KCRA	NBC
Sacramento-Stockton-Modesto	44%	KMAX	UPN
Sacramento-Stockton-Modesto	44%	KOVR	CBS
Sacramento-Stockton-Modesto	44%	KQCA	WB
Sacramento-Stockton-Modesto	44%	KSPX	PAX
Sacramento-Stockton-Modesto	44%	KTXL	FOX
Sacramento-Stockton-Modesto	44%	KUVS	Univision
Sacramento-Stockton-Modesto	44%	KVIE	PBS
Sacramento-Stockton-Modesto	44%	KXTV	ABC

Cable systems and subscribers
Charter   2,306
Comcast   181,027

Military installations, September 2001
Travis Air Force Base, Fairfield   11,691

Businesses and other major employers
University of California; Livermore   9,000
University of California; Livermore; research institute   8,000
Pizza Hut Holdings Inc.; Dixon; fast-food restaurant chain   2,515
Engineered Forest Products; Moraga; venture capital companies   2,000
John Muir/Mt. Diablo Health System; Walnut Creek; management services   1,601
John Muir Medical Center; Walnut Creek   1,600
Valley Care Health System; Livermore   1,100
Providian Bancorp Service Inc.; Suisun City; collection agency   1,000
USS/Posco Industries; Pittsburg; cold or hot-rolled steel sheets or strips   970
Lilja Corp.; Livermore; boiler and furnace contractors   940
St. Mary's College of California; Moraga   900
Davey Tree Surgery Co.; Livermore; ornamental shrub and tree services   873
Livermore Valley Joint Unified School District; Livermore   804
Contra Costa Newspapers Inc.; Walnut Creek   784
Northbay Healthcare Group; Fairfield   760
Frank A. Barcott Security and Investigations; Antioch; detective, armored car services   750
Nordstrom Inc.; Walnut Creek; family clothing stores   643
Pacific Gas and Electric Co.; Concord; electric services   640
Mallard Holding Co.; Lafayette; fast-food restaurant chain   600
City of Alameda; Livermore; fire dept.   600
Kaiser Foundation Hospitals; Livermore   600
Anheuser-Busch Inc.; Suisun City; beer   600
Solano County Community College District; Suisun City   600
Bank of West; Walnut Creek; state commercial banks   600
Safeway Inc.; Walnut Creek; grocery store   600
Sanburn Construction Corp.; Dixon; framing contractor   600
Longs Drug Stores California Inc.; Walnut Creek; variety stores   550
Delta Sutter Medical Hospital; Antioch   535
Army and Air Force Exchange Service; Fairfield; Army-Navy goods stores   530
BEI Sensors and Systems Co.; Concord; electronic circuits   500
Pacific Bell; Concord; local/long-distance telephone   500
Contra Costa County Office of Education; Pleasant Hill   500

Pacific Bell; Pleasant Hill; local/long-distance telephone 500

Pacific Bell; Fairfield; local telephone communications 500

WMA Securities Douglas R. Cain; Fairfield; security brokers, dealers, flotation companies 500

Hospital Committee for Livermore-Pleasanton Areas; Livermore 500

Dow Chemical Co.; Pittsburg; industrial inorganic chemicals 500

Pacific Bell; Walnut Creek; telephone communication 500

Verizon Wireless Inc.; Walnut Creek; communication network services 500

California 11th District

San Joaquin Valley; inland East Bay; part of Stockton

A mix of bedroom communities along commuter corridors east of San Francisco Bay and inland developing agricultural country, the 11th has one common thread: conservative tendencies in the voting booth. The district is wrench-shaped, with the handle running along Interstate 680 and south past San Jose, while the northern end surrounds Stockton on three sides (central Stockton is in the 18th District). *(See map p. 85.)*

The district includes more than 40 percent of Stockton's residents and almost all of surrounding San Joaquin County's area, where farmland is giving way to high-end residential development. Hour-long drives to San Francisco or San Jose can more than double during rush hour. The technology boom has pushed some Bay Area commuters to Stockton, and easing the gridlock is a top concern. The diverse city leans Democratic, but the 11th's portion leans Republican.

Dairy and wine grapes make up the district's biggest agricultural exports. Interstate 205 breaks off from Interstate 5 to head west to San Francisco, making it a key transportation hub. Lodi and Tracy are two main trucking centers through which the district's agricultural products travel. Woodbridge and Lodi produce 40 percent of the state's premium wine grapes—many of which are shipped to the Napa Valley for bottling. Stockton's location as a port city on the San Joaquin River makes it a transportation hub as well.

Residents in the rural, agricultural valley areas are sometimes at odds with their hillier suburban neighbors over water use and the smog that drifts east into the valley.

Major Industry

Agriculture, technology, service.

Notable

Stockton, named for Robert F. Stockton—who proclaimed California as U.S. territory—was the first community in California to have an American name, all others being of Spanish or Native American origin.

Election Returns

	Republican		Democratic		Other	
President 2000	125,876	52.9%	106,354	44.7%	5,882	2.5%
House 2002	104,921	60.3%	69,035	39.7%		

District Profile

Population   639,088

Total area (square miles)   2,315
   Land area (square miles)   2,276

Population per square mile   280.7

Counties (2000 population)
   Alameda (pt.)   90,403
   Contra Costa (pt.)   132,203
   San Joaquin (pt.)   373,933
   Santa Clara (pt.)   42,549

Cities and other areas over 10,000 (2000 population)
   Blackhawk-Camino Tassajara CDP   10,048
   Brentwood   23,302
   Danville town   41,715
   Dublin   29,973
   Lodi   56,999
   Manteca   49,258
   Morgan Hill   33,556
   Pleasanton (pt.)   58,432
   Ripon   10,146
   San Ramon   44,722
   Stockton (pt.)   104,409
   Tracy   56,929

Race and Hispanic or Latino origin*
   White   64.1%
   Black or African American   3.4%
   American Indian or Alaska Native   0.5%
   Asian   8.7%
   Native Hawaiian or other Pacific Islander   0.2%
   Some other race   0.2%
   Hispanic or Latino origin   19.7%
   Two or more races   3.2%

As percentage of total population.

Ancestry*

Dutch 1.5%		Polish 1.1%
English 7.5%		Portuguese 2.7%
French 2.1%		Scotch-Irish 1.1%
German 11.4%		Scottish 1.5%
Irish 8.3%		Swedish 1.5%
Italian 5.7%		USA/American 2.9%
Norwegian 1.5%		

As estimated percentage of total population.

Universities and colleges, 2000–2001 enrollment
   Humphreys College, Stockton   593
   San Joaquin Delta College, Stockton   16,973
   University of the Pacific, Stockton   5,609

Newspapers and circulation

	District circulation	Total circulation
Lodi News-Sentinel	14,901	16,691
Manteca Bulletin	5,765	6,336
Modesto Bee	6,329	85,295
Pleasanton Tri-Valley Herald	26,083	43,384
Sacramento Bee	1,639	293,344
San Francisco Chronicle	15,038	518,725
San Jose Mercury News	15,236	275,971

Stockton Record	42,954	58,220
Tracy Press	8,920	10,504
*USA Today**	7,671	1,674,376
Walnut Creek Contra Costa Times	31,831	182,696

See Sources and Explanations in the front of the volume.

Television stations and affiliations

Sacramento-Stockton-Modesto	57%	KBSV	Independent
Sacramento-Stockton-Modesto	57%	KCRA	NBC
Sacramento-Stockton-Modesto	57%	KMAX	UPN
Sacramento-Stockton-Modesto	57%	KOVR	CBS
Sacramento-Stockton-Modesto	57%	KQCA	WB
Sacramento-Stockton-Modesto	57%	KSPX	PAX
Sacramento-Stockton-Modesto	57%	KTXL	FOX
Sacramento-Stockton-Modesto	57%	KUVS	Univision
Sacramento-Stockton-Modesto	57%	KVIE	PBS
Sacramento-Stockton-Modesto	57%	KXTV	ABC
San Francisco-Oakland-San Jose	43%	KBHK	UPN
San Francisco-Oakland-San Jose	43%	KBWB	WB
San Francisco-Oakland-San Jose	43%	KCNS	Independent
San Francisco-Oakland-San Jose	43%	KCSM	PBS
San Francisco-Oakland-San Jose	43%	KDTV	Univision
San Francisco-Oakland-San Jose	43%	KFTL	Independent
San Francisco-Oakland-San Jose	43%	KFTY	Independent
San Francisco-Oakland-San Jose	43%	KFWU	Independent Spanish
San Francisco-Oakland-San Jose	43%	KGO	ABC
San Francisco-Oakland-San Jose	43%	KICU	Independent
San Francisco-Oakland-San Jose	43%	KKPX	PAX
San Francisco-Oakland-San Jose	43%	KMTP	PBS
San Francisco-Oakland-San Jose	43%	KNTV	NBC
San Francisco-Oakland-San Jose	43%	KPIX	CBS
San Francisco-Oakland-San Jose	43%	KQED	PBS
San Francisco-Oakland-San Jose	43%	KRCB	PBS
San Francisco-Oakland-San Jose	43%	KRON	Independent
San Francisco-Oakland-San Jose	43%	KSTS	Telemundo
San Francisco-Oakland-San Jose	43%	KTEH	PBS
San Francisco-Oakland-San Jose	43%	KTLN	Independent
San Francisco-Oakland-San Jose	43%	KTNC	Independent Spanish
San Francisco-Oakland-San Jose	43%	KTSF	Independent
San Francisco-Oakland-San Jose	43%	KTVU	FOX

Cable systems and subscribers

Charter   12,069

Comcast   64,797

Ponderosa Cable Systems   25,174

Military installations, September 2001

Parks Reserve Forces Training Area (Army Reserve), Dublin 3,311

Defense District West Sharpe Site (Army), Stockton   1,227

Defense District West Tracy (Army), Tracy   1,176

Businesses and other major employers

Safeway New Canada Inc.; Pleasanton; supermarkets 28,000

PeopleSoft Inc.; Pleasanton; business computer software 4,500

PacPizza; San Ramon; pizzeria chain   3,600

Summit Logistics Inc.; Tracy; warehousing   1,426

Software AG Inc.; San Ramon; prepackaged software 1,200

Dillingham Construction Inc.; Pleasanton; waste water/sewage treatment plant construction   1,200

University of Pacific; Stockton   1,200

Farmers Group Inc.; Pleasanton; insurance   1,200

U.S. Defense Logistics Agency; Tracy   1,150

Pacific Bell Wireless; Pleasanton; cellular telephones 1,146

Dillingham Construction Overseas; Pleasanton; dam construction   1,000

Safeway Inc.; Pleasanton; supermarkets   1,000

Anritsu Co.; Morgan Hill; electronic/electric measuring test equipment   850

Providian Financial Corp.; Pleasanton; savings and loan association   800

Abbott Laboratories; Morgan Hill; pharmaceuticals   780

ADP Claims Solutions Group Inc.; San Ramon; research services, insurance   750

Chevron Texaco Overseas Petroleum Inc.; San Ramon; management services   700

San Joaquin Delta Community College District; Stockton 642

Irwin Home Equity Corp.; San Ramon; mortgage bankers 640

Lodi Memorial Hospital; Lodi   607

Alameda County; Dublin; correctional facilities   600

Sybase Inc.; Dublin; business computer software   600

Automatic Data Processing Inc.; San Ramon; data processing   600

H. J. Heinz Co.; Tracy; canned fruits/specialties   600

Dole Food Co.; Stockton; grocery store   555

Micro Dental Laboratories; Dublin; dental laboratories 544

Tenet Healthcare Corp.; Danville; medical doctor offices, clinics   500

Tenet Healthcare Corp. Hospital; San Ramon   500

Clorox Services Co.; Pleasanton; commercial physical research   500

Pacific Coast Producers; Lodi; packaging and labeling services   500

Gardner Trucking; Tracy; trucking   500

Owens-Brockway Glass Container Inc.; Tracy; packers' ware (containers), glass   500

California 12th District

Part of San Mateo County; most of western San Francisco

A mix of scenic coastal mountains and bayside commuter traffic jams, the 12th lies between its two well-known neighbors of San Francisco and the Silicon Valley. *(See map p. 85.)*

The district includes a western section of San Francisco, but most residents live in heavily populated San Mateo County suburbs, either in Daly City or between two main commuter routes—the Junipero Serra Freeway (Interstate 280) and Bayshore Freeway (U.S. Highway 101). The 12th also covers a portion of Pacific coastline from the Great Highway in San Francisco through Pacifica to Moss Beach, and the district stretches southeast to San Carlos and part of Redwood City, about halfway to San Jose.

Despite a downturn in the 12th's high-tech economy and in Silicon Valley to the south, real estate prices have continued to rise in one of the highest-demand retail markets in the country. The district's largest employer remains San Francisco International Airport, though a number of biotechnology firms have set up shop in the South San Francisco area, making biotechnology one of the area's leading industries. Almost 30 percent of the district's residents are Asian, with Daly City home to the district's highest concentration. The

Farallon Islands, a national wildlife refuge about 30 miles west of San Francisco, also belong to the district.

District residents cover a wide range of the political spectrum, but Democrats hold a strong edge in voter registration. At the southern end of the district, residents of the affluent communities of Burlingame and Hillsborough are more conservative, while voters in the San Francisco area are more Democratic.

Major Industry
Biotechnology, airport, software.

Notable
The Museum of Pez Memorabilia is in Burlingame; Daly City has the largest concentration of Filipinos outside of the Philippines; software firm Oracle's corporate headquarters are in Redwood Shores.

Election Returns

	Republican		Democratic		Other	
President 2000	70,468	28.6%	164,490	66.8%	11,103	4.5%
House 2002	38,381	24.8%	105,597	68.1%	11,006	7.1%

District Profile

Population   639,088

Total area (square miles)   362
  Land area (square miles)   116

Population per square mile   5,464.7

Counties (2000 population)
  San Francisco (pt.)   137,645
  San Mateo (pt.)   501,443

Cities and other areas over 10,000 (2000 population)
  Burlingame   28,158
  Daly City   103,621
  Foster City   28,803
  Hillsborough town   10,825
  Millbrae   20,718
  Pacifica   38,390
  Redwood City (pt.)   22,529
  San Bruno   40,165
  San Carlos   27,718
  San Francisco (pt.)   137,645
  San Mateo   92,482
  South San Francisco   60,552

Race and Hispanic or Latino origin*
  White   48.2%
  Black or African American   2.5%
  American Indian or Alaska Native   0.2%
  Asian   28.5%
  Native Hawaiian or other Pacific Islander   0.9%
  Some other race   0.3%
  Hispanic or Latino origin   15.7%
  Two or more races   3.6%

*As percentage of total population.

Ancestry*

Arab-Misc.	1.1%	French	2.0%
English	5.2%	German	7.4%
Irish	8.2%	Scottish	1.3%
Italian	6.4%	Swedish	1.1%
Polish	1.3%	USA/American	1.7%
Russian	1.8%		

*As estimated percentage of total population.

Universities and colleges, 2000–2001 enrollment
Canada College, Redwood City   5,273
City College of San Francisco, San Francisco   39,386
College of San Mateo, San Mateo   10,756
San Francisco Conservatory of Music, San Francisco   263
San Francisco State University, San Francisco   26,826
Skyline College, San Bruno   8,689
University of California, San Francisco   3,517

Newspapers and circulation

	District circulation	Total circulation
Pacifica Tribune	6,979	7,130
San Francisco Chronicle	82,339	518,725
San Jose Mercury News	6,745	275,971
San Mateo County Times	25,561	35,088
*USA Today**	7,919	1,674,376

*See Sources and Explanations in the front of the volume.

Television stations and affiliations

San Francisco-Oakland-San Jose	100%	KBHK	UPN
San Francisco-Oakland-San Jose	100%	KBWB	WB
San Francisco-Oakland-San Jose	100%	KCNS	Independent
San Francisco-Oakland-San Jose	100%	KCSM	PBS
San Francisco-Oakland-San Jose	100%	KDTV	Univision
San Francisco-Oakland-San Jose	100%	KFTL	Independent
San Francisco-Oakland-San Jose	100%	KFTY	Independent
San Francisco-Oakland-San Jose	100%	KFWU	Independent Spanish
San Francisco-Oakland-San Jose	100%	KGO	ABC
San Francisco-Oakland-San Jose	100%	KICU	Independent
San Francisco-Oakland-San Jose	100%	KKPX	PAX
San Francisco-Oakland-San Jose	100%	KMTP	PBS
San Francisco-Oakland-San Jose	100%	KNTV	NBC
San Francisco-Oakland-San Jose	100%	KPIX	CBS
San Francisco-Oakland-San Jose	100%	KQED	PBS
San Francisco-Oakland-San Jose	100%	KRCB	PBS
San Francisco-Oakland-San Jose	100%	KRON	Independent
San Francisco-Oakland-San Jose	100%	KSTS	Telemundo
San Francisco-Oakland-San Jose	100%	KTEH	PBS
San Francisco-Oakland-San Jose	100%	KTLN	Independent
San Francisco-Oakland-San Jose	100%	KTNC	Independent Spanish
San Francisco-Oakland-San Jose	100%	KTSF	Independent
San Francisco-Oakland-San Jose	100%	KTVU	FOX

Cable systems and subscribers
Comcast   109,721
San Bruno Cable TV   11,672

Businesses and other major employers
University of California; San Francisco; medical and surgical hospital   14,500
United Air Lines Inc.; San Francisco; air passenger carrier   12,000
California State University; San Francisco   2,757
Franklin Resources Inc.; San Mateo; mutual funds manager   2,500
Inovant Inc.; Foster City; financial services   2,500
Oracle Corp.; Redwood City; prepackaged software   2,300
Genentech Inc.; South San Francisco; pharmaceuticals   2,000
Applera Corp.; Foster City; analytical instruments   2,000

City College of San Francisco; San Francisco 1,897

San Francisco City and County; San Francisco; medical and surgical hospital 1,800

Franklin Advisers Inc.; San Mateo; investment advice 1,700

Recovery Equity Investors; Redwood City; investors 1,603

American Airlines Inc.; San Francisco; air passenger carrier 1,600

MCN Enterprises Inc.; South San Francisco; air freight handling 1,500

University of California; San Francisco 1,500

Mills-Peninsula Health Services; Burlingame 1,400

Bechtel Group Inc.; Daly City; construction project management consultant 1,200

Franklin/Templeton Investor Services Inc.; San Mateo; security traders 1,200

VISA International Service Assn.; Foster City; financial services 1,200

Siebel Systems Inc.; San Mateo; computer software 1,181

Seton Medical Center; Daly City 1,099

United Air Lines Inc.; San Francisco; air transportation 1,000

San Mateo County; San Mateo; public health programs 1,000

San Mateo County Hospital; San Mateo 1,000

Rudolph and Sletten Inc.; Foster City; industrial buildings, warehouses 1,000

San Francisco City and County; San Francisco; air traffic control 920

E.piphany Inc.; San Mateo; business computer software 856

Northwest Airlines Inc.; San Francisco; air passenger carrier 819

Litton Systems Inc.; San Carlos; infrared sensors 800

Aeroground Inc.; South San Francisco; trucking 800

Pacific Gas and Electric Co.; San Carlos; electrical work 700

Athena Neurosciences Inc.; South San Francisco; pharmaceuticals 700

Lucky Chances; Daly City; gambling 600

Applied Materials Inc.; Sunnyvale; semiconductor manufacturing machinery 600

San Mateo Community College District; San Mateo 600

Sony Computer Entertainment America Inc.; Foster City; video games 600

Judy Madrigal and Associates Inc.; San Mateo; medical doctor offices, clinics 550

OneSource Facility Services Inc.; Foster City; building maintenance 550

Cosine Communications Inc.; Redwood City; telephone, telegraph equipment 506

San Carlos Transfer Facility; San Carlos; refuse collection and disposal services 500

Entenmann's Inc.; South San Francisco; breads and cakes 500

VISA International Service Assn.; San Mateo; financial services 500

U.S. Postal Service; San Mateo 500

California 13th District

East Bay — Fremont, Hayward, Alameda

Bordered by San Francisco Bay to the west, Silicon Valley to the south and Oakland to the north, the 13th is an industrially and culturally diverse suburban area. The district is dotted with many working-class communities and often is described as the less glamorous side of the bay, but its large Hispanic and Asian populations—including immigrants from India, China, Afghanistan, and the Philippines—have flourished culturally. The area's blue-collar industry historically has given Democrats a solid base of support. *(See map p. 85.)*

Fremont and Hayward are the two largest cities in the district. Hayward is home to a campus of the California State University system; Fremont's General Motors-Toyota joint auto plant employs more than 5,000. Both cities have become more oriented toward technology industries as Silicon Valley has extended its influence to the East Bay. The population of the Tri-City area—Newark, Fremont, and Union City—has grown by nearly 120,000 since 1980 and the region's high-tech industry has grown beside it. Computer manufacturers, including Hewlett-Packard and Sun Microsystems, have offices there. San Leandro, just south of Oakland, is home to a Coca-Cola plant, as well as Otis Spunkmeyer's cookie empire and the North Face, which produces outdoor equipment.

Alameda's closed Naval Air Station in the north is being converted into homes and recreational facilities. The island city features 100-year-old Victorian homes and hosts a museum aboard the *USS Hornet,* a World War II aircraft carrier. Oakland International Airport falls within the 13th's boundaries, though Oakland itself is located in the neighboring 9th.

Major Industry

Electronics, industrial machinery, food product processing.

Notable

Ghirardelli Chocolate, the nation's longest continuously operating chocolate manufacturer, has headquarters in San Leandro; Fremont is home to Mission San Jose, which was founded by Father Fermin Lasuen in 1797.

Election Returns

	Republican		Democratic		Other	
President 2000	55,803	29.6%	126,477	67%	6,472	3.4%
House 2002	26,852	22.1%	86,495	71.1%	8,376	6.9%

District Profile

Population 639,088

Total area (square miles) 280
   Land area (square miles) 221

Population per square mile 2,888

Counties (2000 population)
   Alameda (pt.) 639,088

Cities and other areas over 10,000 (2000 population)

Alameda	72,259	San Leandro	79,452
Fremont	203,413	San Lorenzo CDP	21,898
Hayward	140,030	Union City	66,869
Newark	42,471		

Race and Hispanic or Latino origin*

White 38.4%

Black or African American 6.3%

American Indian or Alaska Native 0.4%

Asian 28.2%

Native Hawaiian or other Pacific Islander 0.8%

Some other race 0.3%

Hispanic or Latino origin 21.1%

Two or more races 4.5%

As percentage of total population.

Ancestry*

English	4.8%	Italian	3.4%
French	1.6%	Portuguese	3.0%
German	6.9%	Scottish	1.1%
Irish	5.7%	USA/American	1.8%

As estimated percentage of total population.

Universities and colleges, 2000–2001 enrollment

California School of Professional Psychology Alameda 692

California State University, Hayward 12,705

Chabot College, Hayward 13,615

College of Alameda, Alameda 5,088

Devry University, Fremont 2,149

Heald College Schools of Business and Technology, Hayward 1,241

ITT Technical Institute, Hayward 447

Life Chiropractic College-West, San Lorenzo 688

Ohlone College, Fremont 9,444

Queen of the Holy Rosary College, Fremont*

Santa Barbara Business College, Fremont 309

Sequoia Institute, Fremont 1,249

Silicon Valley College, Fremont 721

Western Career College, San Leandro 345

Enrollment under 100. See Sources and Explanations in the front of the volume.

Newspapers and circulation

	District circulation	Total circulation
Fremont Argus	32,350	32,350
Hayward Daily Review	25,445	38,497
Oakland Tribune	13,163	68,112
San Francisco Chronicle	26,664	518,725
San Jose Mercury News	14,763	275,971
*USA Today**	1,818	1,674,376

See Sources and Explanations in the front of the volume.

Television stations and affiliations

San Francisco-Oakland-San Jose	100%	KBHK	UPN
San Francisco-Oakland-San Jose	100%	KBWB	WB
San Francisco-Oakland-San Jose	100%	KCNS	Independent
San Francisco-Oakland-San Jose	100%	KCSM	PBS
San Francisco-Oakland-San Jose	100%	KDTV	Univision
San Francisco-Oakland-San Jose	100%	KFTL	Independent
San Francisco-Oakland-San Jose	100%	KFTY	Independent
San Francisco-Oakland-San Jose	100%	KFWU	Independent Spanish
San Francisco-Oakland-San Jose	100%	KGO	ABC
San Francisco-Oakland-San Jose	100%	KICU	Independent
San Francisco-Oakland-San Jose	100%	KKPX	PAX
San Francisco-Oakland-San Jose	100%	KMTP	PBS
San Francisco-Oakland-San Jose	100%	KNTV	NBC
San Francisco-Oakland-San Jose	100%	KPIX	CBS
San Francisco-Oakland-San Jose	100%	KQED	PBS
San Francisco-Oakland-San Jose	100%	KRCB	PBS
San Francisco-Oakland-San Jose	100%	KRON	Independent
San Francisco-Oakland-San Jose	100%	KSTS	Telemundo
San Francisco-Oakland-San Jose	100%	KTEH	PBS
San Francisco-Oakland-San Jose	100%	KTLN	Independent
San Francisco-Oakland-San Jose	100%	KTNC	Independent Spanish
San Francisco-Oakland-San Jose	100%	KTSF	Independent
San Francisco-Oakland-San Jose	100%	KTVU	FOX

Cable systems and subscribers

Comcast 94,438

Military installations, September 2001

Alameda Navy Reserve, Alameda 397

Hayward Municipal Airport (Air National Guard), Hayward 297

Businesses and other major employers

Oracle Corp.; Fremont; systems software development services 40,000

New United Motor Manufacturing Inc.; Fremont; automobiles 4,893

Mervyn's; Hayward; department stores 4,200

Chippac Inc.; Fremont; semiconductors and related devices 3,600

Farmers Group Inc.; Alameda; insurance agents and brokers 2,100

Lucent Technologies Inc.; Alameda; computer peripheral equipment 2,000

Ross Stores Inc.; Newark; family clothing stores 1,500

Lam Research Corp.; Fremont; semiconductor manufacturing machinery 1,400

HMT Technology Corp.; Fremont; computer disk drives 1,348

Veritas Software Technology Corp.; Fremont; key-tape equipment 1,300

Washington Township Healthcare District Hospital; Fremont 1,225

Komag Inc.; Fremont; diskette or key-disk equipment 1,200

Chabot-Las Positas Community College District; Hayward 1,200

Sysco Food Services; Fremont; food supplier 1,025

Flextronics International USA Inc.; Fremont; printed circuit boards 1,000

Read-Rite Corp.; Fremont; magnetic recording/playback heads 1,000

Sister Hayward Hospital; Hayward 755

Sanmina-SCI Corp.; Fremont; metal housings, enclosures, casings, containers 750

Southern Wine and Spirits of America Inc.; Union City; bottling wines and liquors 750

Cala Foods Inc.; Compton; supermarkets 737

Avant Corp.; Fremont; computer software development 700

Compaq Computer Corp.; Fremont; computers 700

Kindred Healthcare Hospital; San Leandro 650

Pacific Gas and Electric Co.; Alameda; engineering services 640

Fremont Newark Community College District; Fremont 630

Gillig Corp.; Hayward; motor bus assembly   600
Boston Scientific Corp.; Fremont; surgical and medical
   instruments   550
Southwest Airlines Co.; Oakland; air passenger carrier   529
Alameda Hospital; Alameda   520
U.S. Coast Guard; Alameda   500
Lucent Technologies Inc.; Alameda; general warehousing,
   storage   500
Flash Electronics Inc.; Fremont; printed circuit boards
   500
Sanmina-SCI Corp.; Fremont; electronic computers   500
Diversified Maintenance Services Inc.; Fremont; building
   maintenance   500
Myntahl Corp.; Fremont; communication headgear,
   telephone   500
Manheim Auctions Inc.; Hayward; automobiles   500
Marelich Mechanical Co. Inc.; Hayward; plumbing,
   heating, air-conditioning   500
Pacific Bell; Hayward; telephone communication   500

California 14th District

Southern San Mateo and northwestern Santa Clara
Counties; most of Santa Cruz County

The 14th's economic center is Palo Alto, home to Stanford University and tech giants such as Hewlett-Packard. This Silicon Valley stronghold known for innovation has undergone tremendous economic growth since the 1980s. The orchards surrounding Stanford have given way to some of the nation's most expensive housing, even after the technology bubble burst. *(See map p. 85.)*

The district borders the bay and the Pacific, creeping north toward the San Francisco suburbs and south into Santa Cruz County, almost to the Monterey County line. Most residents live in cities along the bay between San Francisco and San Jose, including Sunnyvale, Mountain View, and Redwood City. Labor from large numbers of Asians and Hispanics aided the tech boom. Soaring housing prices, though stable in the past few years, and traffic snarls were the major results.

The 14th's innovation-minded voters are liberal on many social issues but prefer a laissez-faire government that does not impede change. Environmental consciousness is high, particularly in Santa Cruz County. Conservative pockets do exist in wealthy areas such as Saratoga and Monte Sereno in Santa Clara County, but Democrats hold a 15 percentage point edge in voter registration, and the district gave Democrat Al Gore 61.5 percent of the vote in the 2000 presidential election.

Major Industry
Computers, biotechnology, defense, agriculture.

Notable
A water tower painted as a Libby's fruit cocktail can stands where the cannery operated in Sunnyvale; Hewlett-Packard was founded in 1939 in a Palo Alto garage, which is now a tourist attraction; Half Moon Bay holds an annual pumpkin festival.

Election Returns

	Republican		Democratic		Other	
President 2000	84,637	33.6%	155,165	61.5%	12,451	4.9%
House 2002	48,346	28.2%	117,055	68.2%	6,277	3.7%

District Profile

Population   639,088

Total area (square miles)   1,030
   Land area (square miles)   825

Population per square mile   774.7

Counties (2000 population)
   San Mateo (pt.)   205,718
   Santa Clara (pt.)   361,860
   Santa Cruz (pt.)   71,510

Cities and other areas over 10,000 (2000 population)
   Belmont   25,123
   East Palo Alto   29,506
   Half Moon Bay   11,842
   Los Altos   27,693
   Menlo Park   30,785
   Mountain View   70,708
   North Fair Oaks CDP   15,440
   Palo Alto   58,598
   Redwood City (pt.)   52,873
   Saratoga   29,843
   Scotts Valley   11,385
   Stanford CDP   13,315
   Sunnyvale   131,760

Race and Hispanic or Latino origin*
   White   59.6%
   Black or African American   3.0%
   American Indian or Alaska Native   0.3%
   Asian   16.0%
   Native Hawaiian or other Pacific Islander   0.7%
   Some other race   0.3%
   Hispanic or Latino origin   17.5%
   Two or more races   2.7%

As percentage of total population.

Ancestry*
Dutch 1.1%	Polish 1.6%
English 8.3%	Russian 1.7%
French 2.3%	Scotch-Irish 1.3%
German 9.7%	Scottish 2.0%
Irish 7.2%	Swedish 1.6%
Italian 4.4%	USA/American 2.1%
Norwegian 1.4%	

As estimated percentage of total population.

Universities and colleges, 2000–2001 enrollment
   Bethany College, Scotts Valley   531
   Cogswell College, Sunnyvale   426
   College of Notre Dame, Belmont   1,670
   Foothill College, Los Altos Hills   14,193
   Institute of Transpersonal Psychology, Palo Alto   354

Menlo College, Atherton   649
Pacific Graduate School of Psychology, Palo Alto   279
Stanford University, Stanford   18,549
West Valley College, Saratoga   10,719

Newspapers and circulation

	District circulation	Total circulation
San Francisco Chronicle	38,951	518,725
San Jose Mercury News	73,285	275,971
San Mateo County Times	9,527	35,088
Santa Cruz Sentinel	14,539	26,580
*USA Today**	4,484	1,674,376
Watsonville Register-Pajaronian	2,097	7,331

See Sources and Explanations in the front of the volume.

Television stations and affiliations

San Francisco-Oakland-San Jose	63%	KBHK	UPN
San Francisco-Oakland-San Jose	63%	KBWB	WB
San Francisco-Oakland-San Jose	63%	KCNS	Independent
San Francisco-Oakland-San Jose	63%	KCSM	PBS
San Francisco-Oakland-San Jose	63%	KDTV	Univision
San Francisco-Oakland-San Jose	63%	KFTL	Independent
San Francisco-Oakland-San Jose	63%	KFTY	Independent
San Francisco-Oakland-San Jose	63%	KFWU	Independent Spanish
San Francisco-Oakland-San Jose	63%	KGO	ABC
San Francisco-Oakland-San Jose	63%	KICU	Independent
San Francisco-Oakland-San Jose	63%	KKPX	PAX
San Francisco-Oakland-San Jose	63%	KMTP	PBS
San Francisco-Oakland-San Jose	63%	KNTV	NBC
San Francisco-Oakland-San Jose	63%	KPIX	CBS
San Francisco-Oakland-San Jose	63%	KQED	PBS
San Francisco-Oakland-San Jose	63%	KRCB	PBS
San Francisco-Oakland-San Jose	63%	KRON	Independent
San Francisco-Oakland-San Jose	63%	KSTS	Telemundo
San Francisco-Oakland-San Jose	63%	KTEH	PBS
San Francisco-Oakland-San Jose	63%	KTLN	Independent
San Francisco-Oakland-San Jose	63%	KTNC	Independent Spanish
San Francisco-Oakland-San Jose	63%	KTSF	Independent
San Francisco-Oakland-San Jose	63%	KTVU	FOX
Monterey-Salinas	37%	KCAH	PBS
Monterey-Salinas	37%	KCBA	FOX, UPN
Monterey-Salinas	37%	KION	CBS
Monterey-Salinas	37%	KSBW	NBC
Monterey-Salinas	37%	KSMS	Univision

Cable systems and subscribers
Comcast   132,238
Matrix Cablevision   5,984

Military installations, September 2001
Moffett Field (Air National Guard), Sunnyvale   807
Onizuka Air Force Base, Sunnyvale   319

Businesses and other major employers
Lockheed Martin Corp.; Sunnyvale; guided missiles and space vehicles   8,000
General Dynamics Government Systems Corp.; Mountain View; engineering services   4,000
Sun Microsystems Inc.; Half Moon Bay; minicomputers   3,500
Sun Microsystems Inc.; Palo Alto; minicomputers   3,500
U.S. Veterans Hospital; Palo Alto   3,500
Advanced Micro Devices Inc.; Sunnyvale; integrated circuits, semiconductor networks   3,100
Tyco Electronics/Raychem; Menlo Park; electronic connectors   3,000

Hewlett-Packard Co.; Palo Alto; computer hardware   3,000
Space Systems/Loral Inc.; Palo Alto; radio/TV communications equipment   2,575
America Online Inc.; Mountain View; Internet connectivity services   2,500
Hewlett-Packard Co.; Palo Alto; personal computers   2,500
Veritas Software Technology Corp.; Scotts Valley; computer disk drives   2,500
WebTV; Mountain View; computer-related services   2,000
Philips Semiconductors Inc.; Sunnyvale; integrated circuits, semiconductor networks   2,000
El Camino Hospital; Mountain View   1,975
Acuson International Sales Corp.; Mountain View; medical diagnostic apparatus   1,800
Varian Medical Systems Inc.; Palo Alto; surgical and medical instruments   1,710
Silicon Graphics Inc.; Mountain View; personal computers   1,600
Network Appliance Inc.; Sunnyvale; computer integrated systems design   1,600
Amdahl Information Technology Services Inc.; Sunnyvale; management information systems consultant   1,583
Kaiser Foundation Hospitals; Redwood City   1,500
Tyco Electronics Corp.; Menlo Park; medical and hospital equipment   1,400
U.S. Dept. of Energy; Menlo Park   1,400
Veritas Software Technology Corp.; Scotts Valley; computer disk drives   1,400
Pajaro Valley Unified School District; Watsonville   1,279
SRI International; Menlo Park; scientific research agency   1,200
Margaret S. Kosek MD; Palo Alto; medical doctor offices, clinics   1,200
International Business Machines Corp.; Palo Alto; business research service   1,200
Broadvision Inc.; Redwood City; software programming applications   1,195
Acuson Corp.; Mountain View; hospital equipment repair services   1,000
KPMG; Mountain View; certified public accountant   1,000
PeopleSoft Inc.; Sunnyvale; business computer software   1,000
University of California Children's Hospital; Palo Alto   990
National Aeronautics and Space Administration; Mountain View; noncommercial research organization   958
Maxim Integrated Products Inc.; Sunnyvale; integrated microcircuits (semiconductor)   956
Northrop Grumman Systems Corp.; Sunnyvale; aircraft   950
Wilson Sonsini Goodrich & Rosati Professional Corp.; Palo Alto; corporate partnership and business law   950
San Mateo County; Redwood City; law enforcement statistics   826
Alza Corp.; Mountain View; commercial research laboratory   800
WebTV Networks Inc.; Mountain View; Internet connectivity services   800
Openwave Systems Inc.; Redwood City; custom computer software design   800

San Mateo County; Redwood City; county government 800

Veritas Software Corp.; Sunnyvale; business computer software 800

Communications and Power Industries Holding Corp.; Palo Alto; vacuum tubes 800

McGraw-Hill Companies Inc.; Mountain View; book publishing 750

Trimble Navigation Limited Inc.; Sunnyvale; navigational systems and instruments 750

E Trade Group Inc.; Menlo Park; security brokers 700

Palo Alto Medical Foundation for Health Care Research and Education (inc.); Palo Alto; medical clinic 700

Nordstrom Inc.; Palo Alto; family clothing stores 700

West Macy's Inc.; Palo Alto; department stores 700

West Valley Mission Community College District; Saratoga 684

U.S. Geological Survey; Menlo Park 680

Essex Management Corp.; Palo Alto; real estate investment trusts 654

Varner Illustration; El Granada; commercial art and illustration 625

Lockheed Martin Corp.; Palo Alto; guided missile, space vehicle parts 625

City of Palo Alto; Palo Alto; city management 601

Database Software Inc.; Menlo Park; computer software development 600

Tyco Electronics/Raychem; Menlo Park; unsupported plastic tubes 600

Computer Curriculum Corp.; Sunnyvale; computer turnkey vendors 600

TRW Inc.; Sunnyvale; guided missiles and space vehicles 600

Volex Interconnect Systems Inc.; Sunnyvale; steel cable 600

Alta Vista; Palo Alto; Internet connectivity services 600

Electric Power Research Institute Inc.; Palo Alto; research institute 600

Hewlett-Packard Co.; Palo Alto; electronic computers 600

Williams Communications Group Inc.; Sunnyvale; Internet connectivity services 567

Fujitsu Holdings Inc.; Sunnyvale; computer and data processing 553

Foothill-De Anza Community College District; Los Altos 550

Incyte Genomics Inc.; Palo Alto; database information retrieval 550

Tibco Software Inc.; Palo Alto; systems integration services 550

Camino Medical Group Inc.; Sunnyvale; medical clinic 544

College of Notre Dame; Belmont 500

Guidant Corp.; Menlo Park; medical ultrasonic scanning devices 500

Netscape Communications Corp.; Mountain View; computer software 500

Synopsys Inc.; Mountain View; computer software development 500

Redwood City; Redwood City; city management 500

San Mateo County; Redwood City; sheriff's office 500

Philips Electronics North America Corp.; Sunnyvale; business research service 500

Compaq Computer Corp.; Sunnyvale; computers 500

Interwoven Inc.; Sunnyvale; business computer software 500

Marvell Semiconductor Inc.; Sunnyvale; semiconductors and related devices 500

Inhale Therapeutic Systems; Palo Alto; inhalation therapy equipment 500

Incyte Genomics Inc.; Palo Alto; information retrieval services 500

Xerox Corp.; Palo Alto; commercial physical research 500

Agilent Technologies Inc.; Palo Alto; electricity measuring instruments 500

Cooley Godward LLP; Palo Alto; legal services 500

California 15th District

Santa Clara County — part of San Jose

Home to one-third of San Jose's residents, the 15th touches the southern end of San Francisco Bay in the north, then descends inland through Silicon Valley to still-rural but fast-growing farm towns. *(See map p. 85.)*

The district has a diverse population that includes one of the nation's heaviest concentrations of Asian-Americans outside of Hawaii. Slightly less than 30 percent of residents are Asian, the highest percentage in any California district. Vietnamese, Chinese, and Filipino Americans have flocked to the north to take white- and blue-collar jobs, while Hispanics, 17.2 percent of the 15th's population, make up a big part of the labor force in the south. Immigration is the top issue caseworkers face.

West of San Jose, the district includes Santa Clara, a Spanish mission in the late 1700s, and other more affluent suburbs including Campbell, Cupertino, and Los Gatos. These areas house high-tech companies that boomed in the 1990s but suffered higher unemployment after the tech bubble burst. Housing—stable but still quite expensive—and transit troubles plague the area. The economy remains technology-based, however, and Sun Microsystems is based in Santa Clara.

To the south, Gilroy's famous garlic farms anchor a more traditionally Democratic agricultural community. But open land is quickly being snatched up as the San Jose suburbs continue to bulge southward.

The district gave 60.3 percent to Democrat Al Gore in the 2000 presidential election, though if any political trend is apparent here it is an increase in independent voters who seek moderation. Generally liberal on environmental and social issues, voters also favor less government regulation of business.

Major Industry

Computers, biotechnology, health care, agriculture.

Notable

Santa Clara University, founded in 1851, is California's oldest institution of higher learning; Winchester Mystery House in San Jose is a 160-room Victorian mansion famous for oddities such as staircases that lead nowhere that was built over many years by the heiress to the Winchester rifle fortune because she believed that she would not die so long as construction went on—which it did 24 hours a day; Apple Computer was founded in Cupertino; Gilroy is known as the garlic capital of the world.

Election Returns

	Republican		Democratic		Other	
President 2000	74,974	36.2%	124,880	60.3%	7,108	3.4%
House 2002	41,251	31%	87,482	65.8%	4,289	3.2%

District Profile

Population   639,088

Total area (square miles)   288
   Land area (square miles)   286

Population per square mile   2,232.5

Counties (2000 population)
Santa Clara (pt.)   639,088

Cities and other areas over 10,000 (2000 population)
Campbell 38,138	Milpitas 62,698
Cupertino 50,546	San Jose (pt.) 295,018
Gilroy 41,464	Santa Clara 102,361
Los Gatos town 28,592	

Race and Hispanic or Latino origin*
White   47.1%
Black or African American   2.4%
American Indian or Alaska Native   0.3%
Asian   29.2%
Native Hawaiian or other Pacific Islander   0.3%
Some other race   0.2%
Hispanic or Latino origin   17.2%
Two or more races   3.2%

*As percentage of total population.

Ancestry*
English 6.1%	Polish 1.3%
French 1.9%	Portuguese 1.6%
German 8.0%	Scottish 1.4%
Irish 6.3%	Swedish 1.2%
Italian 4.7%	USA/American 1.9%

*As estimated percentage of total population.

Universities and colleges, 2000–2001 enrollment
De Anza College, Cupertino   22,770
Gavilan College, Gilroy   5,681
Heald College School of Technology, Milpitas   1,329
Mission College, Santa Clara   9,821
San Jose City College, San Jose   11,295
Santa Clara University, Santa Clara   7,356

Newspapers and circulation
	District circulation	Total circulation
San Francisco Chronicle	6,760	518,725
San Jose Mercury News	72,395	275,971
*USA Today**	2,165	1,674,376

*See Sources and Explanations in the front of the volume.

Television stations and affiliations
San Francisco-Oakland-San Jose	100%	KBHK	UPN
San Francisco-Oakland-San Jose	100%	KBWB	WB
San Francisco-Oakland-San Jose	100%	KCNS	Independent
San Francisco-Oakland-San Jose	100%	KCSM	PBS
San Francisco-Oakland-San Jose	100%	KDTV	Univision
San Francisco-Oakland-San Jose	100%	KFTL	Independent
San Francisco-Oakland-San Jose	100%	KFTY	Independent
San Francisco-Oakland-San Jose	100%	KFWU	Independent Spanish
San Francisco-Oakland-San Jose	100%	KGO	ABC
San Francisco-Oakland-San Jose	100%	KICU	Independent
San Francisco-Oakland-San Jose	100%	KKPX	PAX
San Francisco-Oakland-San Jose	100%	KMTP	PBS
San Francisco-Oakland-San Jose	100%	KNTV	NBC
San Francisco-Oakland-San Jose	100%	KPIX	CBS
San Francisco-Oakland-San Jose	100%	KQED	PBS
San Francisco-Oakland-San Jose	100%	KRCB	PBS
San Francisco-Oakland-San Jose	100%	KRON	Independent
San Francisco-Oakland-San Jose	100%	KSTS	Telemundo
San Francisco-Oakland-San Jose	100%	KTEH	PBS
San Francisco-Oakland-San Jose	100%	KTLN	Independent
San Francisco-Oakland-San Jose	100%	KTNC	Independent Spanish
San Francisco-Oakland-San Jose	100%	KTSF	Independent
San Francisco-Oakland-San Jose	100%	KTVU	FOX

Cable systems and subscribers
Charter   6,983
Comcast   73,331

Businesses and other major employers
Solectron Corp.; Milpitas; printed circuit boards   6,700
Intel Corp.; Santa Clara; microprocessors   5,700
National Semiconductor Corp.; Santa Clara; semiconductors and related devices   5,100
Hewlett-Packard Co.; Cupertino; minicomputers   3,000
LSI Logic Corp.; Milpitas; semiconductors and related devices   3,000
Maxtor Corp.; Milpitas; computer storage devices   3,000
Solectron Global Services; Milpitas; industrial machinery/equipment repair   3,000
Sniffer Technologies; Santa Clara; computer tapes and disks   3,000
Flextronics International USA Inc.; San Jose; printed circuit boards   3,000
Maxtor Corp.; Milpitas; computer disk drive components   2,500
Honeywell International Finance Corp.; Santa Clara; management services   2,500
Sun Microsystems Inc.; Santa Clara; computer programming services   2,500
Quantum Corp.; Milpitas; computer storage devices   2,295
Apple Computer Inc.; Cupertino; personal computers   2,000
Hadco Santa Clara Inc.; Santa Clara; printed circuit boards   2,000
Good Samaritan Hospital; San Jose   1,800
Veritas Software Technology Corp.; Milpitas; administrative management   1,700
Read-Rite Corp.; Fremont; magnetic recording/playback heads   1,500
Santa Clara College; Santa Clara   1,380
Atmel Corp.; San Jose; integrated microcircuits (semiconductor)   1,311
Philips Semiconductor VLSI Inc.; San Jose; integrated microcircuits (semiconductor)   1,250
Lucent Technologies Inc.; Milpitas; telephone and telegraph apparatus   1,200
Octel Communications Corp.; Milpitas; telephones and telephone apparatus   1,200
Sanmina-SCI Corp.; Santa Clara; printed circuit boards   1,200
Kaiser Foundation Hospitals; Santa Clara   1,200
Siemens Information and Communication Networks Inc.; Santa Clara; communication network services   1,200

JDS Uniphase Corp.; San Jose; semiconductors and related devices 1,200

Northern Telecom Inc.; Cupertino; engineering services 1,100

Adaptec Inc.; Milpitas; computer input/output equipment 1,100

Sun Microsystems Inc.; Milpitas; computer-related systems engineering 1,100

Coherent Inc.; Santa Clara; laser scientific and engineering instruments 1,082

Align Technology Inc.; Santa Clara; orthodontic appliances 1,065

Pyramid Building Maintenance Corp.; Santa Clara; janitorial service 1,035

Lucent Technologies Inc.; Los Gatos; telephone and telegraph apparatus 1,000

KLA-Tencor Corp.; Milpitas; electricity measuring instruments 1,000

Lifescan Inc.; Milpitas; blood derivative diagnostic agents 1,000

United Defense Industries Inc.; Santa Clara; military motor vehicle assembly 1,000

Advanced Cardiovascular Systems Inc.; Santa Clara; surgical instruments and apparatus 1,000

Novell Inc.; San Jose; computer integrated systems design; computer tapes and disks 1,000

Nortel Networks Inc.; Santa Clara; telephone and telegraph apparatus 1,000

MMC Technology Inc.; San Jose; computer peripheral equipment 1,000

Rosendin Electric Inc.; San Jose; electrical contractor 1,000

Xilinx Inc.; San Jose; integrated microcircuits (semiconductor) 988

Hewlett-Packard Co.; Sunnyvale; computer rental and leasing 900

Burns International Security Services Corp.; Campbell; security guard service 900

Linear Technology Corp.; Milpitas; integrated circuits, semiconductor networks 900

Milpitas Unified School District; Milpitas 900

NEC Electronics Inc.; Santa Clara; semiconductors and related devices 900

Becton Dickinson and Co.; San Jose; surgical and medical instruments 900

Nvidia US Investment Co.; Santa Clara; radio/TV communications equipment 850

West Macy's Inc.; Santa Clara; department stores 800

Analog Devices Inc.; Santa Clara; monolithic integrated circuits 800

Applied Materials Inc.; Santa Clara; semiconductor manufacturing machinery 800

Tenet Healthcare Corp.; Los Gatos; medical and surgical hospital 750

Avantek Inc.; Santa Clara; microwave components 750

Guidant Corp.; Santa Clara; surgical and medical instruments 750

Siliconix Inc.; Santa Clara; semiconductors and related devices 703

San Jose City; Alviso; fire dept. 700

Honeywell-Measurex International Corp.; Cupertino; computer peripherals, software 700

24/7 Customer.com Inc.; Los Gatos; online services technology consultants 700

Network Associates Inc.; Santa Clara; computer software development 700

Vishay Siliconics Inc.; Santa Clara; silicones 700

San Jose City; San Jose; fire dept. 700

Garden City Inc.; San Jose; card rooms 665

Trend Technologies Inc.; San Jose; special dies, tools, jigs, fixtures 650

Palm Inc.; Santa Clara; computer software development 620

Nordstrom Inc.; Santa Clara; family clothing stores 615

Compaq Computer Corp.; Cupertino; electronic computers 600

Granite Rock Co.; Gilroy; excavation work 600

Asia Info Holdings Inc.; Santa Clara; Internet connectivity services 600

Cardiogenesis Corp.; Santa Clara; surgical and medical instruments 600

Hewlett-Packard Co.; Santa Clara; electronic computers 600

Pinkerton's Inc.; Santa Clara; burglar alarms 600

Schlumberger Technology Corp.; San Jose; abrasion, shearing strength test equipment 600

Silicon Valley Bank; Santa Clara; state commercial banks 592

City of Milpitas; Milpitas; city management 557

Joseph J. Albanese Inc.; Santa Clara; concrete work 550

Longs Drug Stores California Inc.; Santa Clara; carpet, upholstery cleaning 550

PA Acquisition Corp.; Santa Clara; gift, novelty, souvenir shop 550

Honeywell Inc.; Cupertino; computer interface equipment 500

Dynamic Details Inc.; Milpitas; printed circuit boards 500

Santa Clara Unified School District; Santa Clara 500

Agilent Technologies Inc.; Santa Clara; electronic/electric measuring test equipment 500

Hewlett-Packard Co.; Santa Clara; mechanical and electromechanical counters/devices 500

Lumenis Inc.; Santa Clara; therapy equipment 500

Team Services Inc.; Santa Clara; janitorial service 500

SCI Systems Inc.; San Jose; electronic computers 500

Hospital Shared Services; San Jose; security guard service 500

California 16th District

Most of San Jose

The high-tech boom of the 1990s propelled San Jose out of San Francisco's shadow and earned it a reputation as "the capital of Silicon Valley." A metropolitan area unto itself, San Jose is now home to the Bay Area's NBC affiliate and a professional hockey franchise. *(See map p. 85.)*

The district includes two-thirds of San Jose and almost 40 percent of Santa Clara County's population, but all but 8 percent of the 16th's residents live in San Jose—the only city in the district and the third largest in the state. Silicon Valley's tremendous growth has rubbed off on the city, creating a white-collar workforce and helping to establish it as a leading exporter of high-tech goods. An economic downturn has sent unemployment, once as low as 2 percent, soaring past 8 percent, but housing prices have remained high. The county has the area's highest median income and highest rate of charitable giving.

The 16th is one of the most ethnically diverse districts in the Bay Area. Its Asian population includes the nation's second-largest Vietnamese community, but Hispanics represent the district's largest group at 37.6 percent. Whites make up 31.9 percent of the population.

Redistricting after the 2000 census concentrated the 16th more around San Jose, removing hilly areas east of the city and southern areas including Morgan Hill (now in the 11th) and Gilroy (now in the 15th).

The 16th has been solidly liberal and Democratic for many years, and an influx of Hispanics has helped continue that trend. However, white-collar workers are becoming more common and could begin to shift the district's politics to the right. Al Gore took 63.9 percent of the district's vote in the 2000 presidential election.

Major Industry
Technology, health care, finance.

Notable
San Jose served as the state capital for a short time after California's annexation by the United States; in 1777 San Jose became the state's first civilian settlement under Spanish rule; Norman Y. Mineta San Jose International Airport is named for the former U.S. representative and secretary of transportation.

Election Returns

	Republican		Democratic		Other	
President 2000	57,160	33.3%	109,632	63.9%	4,832	2.8%
House 2002	32,182	29.8%	72,370	67.0%	3,434	3.2%

District Profile

Population 639,088

Total area (square miles) 232
  Land area (square miles) 229

Population per square mile 2,790.8

Counties (2000 population)
  Santa Clara (pt.) 639,088

Cities and other areas over 10,000 (2000 population)
  Alum Rock CDP 13,479
  San Jose (pt.) 590,306

Race and Hispanic or Latino origin*
  White 31.9%
  Black or African American 3.4%
  American Indian or Alaska Native 0.4%
  Asian 23.4%
  Native Hawaiian or other Pacific Islander 0.4%
  Some other race 0.2%
  Hispanic or Latino origin 37.6%
  Two or more races 2.8%

*As percentage of total population.

Ancestry*

English	4.2%	Italian	3.8%
French	1.3%	Portuguese	1.6%
German	5.7%	USA/American	1.6%
Irish	4.6%		

*As estimated percentage of total population.

Universities and colleges, 2000–2001 enrollment
  Evergreen Valley College, San Jose 12,404
  Heald College School of Business, San Jose 294
  Masters Institute, San Jose 1,131
  National Hispanic University, San Jose 340
  Palmer College of Chiropractic-West, San Jose 582
  San Jose Christian College, San Jose 395
  San Jose State University, San Jose 26,698
  University of Phoenix-Northern California, San Jose 4,317

Newspapers and circulation

	District circulation	Total circulation
San Francisco Chronicle	5,313	518,725
San Jose Mercury News	73,667	275,971
*USA Today**	1,738	1,674,376

*See Sources and Explanations in the front of the volume.

Television stations and affiliations

San Francisco-Oakland-San Jose	100%	KBHK	UPN
San Francisco-Oakland-San Jose	100%	KBWB	WB
San Francisco-Oakland-San Jose	100%	KCNS	Independent
San Francisco-Oakland-San Jose	100%	KCSM	PBS
San Francisco-Oakland-San Jose	100%	KDTV	Univision
San Francisco-Oakland-San Jose	100%	KFTL	Independent
San Francisco-Oakland-San Jose	100%	KFTY	Independent
San Francisco-Oakland-San Jose	100%	KFWU	Independent Spanish
San Francisco-Oakland-San Jose	100%	KGO	ABC
San Francisco-Oakland-San Jose	100%	KICU	Independent
San Francisco-Oakland-San Jose	100%	KKPX	PAX
San Francisco-Oakland-San Jose	100%	KMTP	PBS
San Francisco-Oakland-San Jose	100%	KNTV	NBC
San Francisco-Oakland-San Jose	100%	KPIX	CBS
San Francisco-Oakland-San Jose	100%	KQED	PBS
San Francisco-Oakland-San Jose	100%	KRCB	PBS
San Francisco-Oakland-San Jose	100%	KRON	Independent
San Francisco-Oakland-San Jose	100%	KSTS	Telemundo
San Francisco-Oakland-San Jose	100%	KTEH	PBS
San Francisco-Oakland-San Jose	100%	KTLN	Independent
San Francisco-Oakland-San Jose	100%	KTNC	Independent Spanish
San Francisco-Oakland-San Jose	100%	KTSF	Independent
San Francisco-Oakland-San Jose	100%	KTVU	FOX

Cable systems and subscribers
  Comcast 149,182

Businesses and other major employers
  Lockheed Martin Corp.; San Jose; aircraft 6,000
  San Jose City; San Jose; city management 3,100
  KLA-Tencor Corp.; San Jose; optical test and inspection equipment 3,000
  FMC Corp.; San Jose; military weapons/guns 2,700
  San Jose State University; San Jose 2,581
  Sony Electronics Inc.; San Jose; electronic parts and equipment 2,500
  Lockheed Martin Corp.; San Jose; satellite communications 2,200
  Cadence Design Systems Inc.; San Jose; computer software 2,000

Sony Electronics Inc.; San Jose; electrical appliances   2,000

Coast Personnel Services Inc.; Santa Clara; temporary help service   1,895

Cisco Systems Inc., San Jose; data conversion equipment, media-to-media: computer   1,800

American Airlines Inc.; San Jose; air passenger carrier   1,500

International Business Machines Corp.; San Jose; commercial research laboratory   1,500

International Business Machines Corp.; San Jose; computer software development, applications   1,500

San Jose City; San Jose; police dept.   1,400

United Title Companies Inc.; San Jose; title insurance   1,395

Adobe Systems Inc.; San Jose; computer software   1,300

Cadence Design Systems Inc.; San Jose; computer software   1,102

HCA Inc.; San Jose; medical and surgical hospital   1,100

Santa Clara Valley Transportation Authority; San Jose   1,053

Santa Barbara County; San Jose; county government   1,000

Varian Medical Systems Inc.; San Jose; hangar operation   1,000

Kaiser Foundation Hospitals; San Jose   1,000

Hewlett-Packard Co.; San Jose; printers, computers   1,000

O'Connor Hospital; San Jose   1,000

Hewlett-Packard Co.; San Jose; semiconductors and related devices   1,000

Knight-Ridder Inc.; San Jose; television broadcasting stations   1,000

San Jose Mercury News Inc.; San Jose; newspaper   1,000

Globe Y Manufacturing; San Jose; manufacturing industries   950

Cypress Semiconductor Corp.; San Jose; semiconductors and related devices   930

Novellus Systems Inc.; San Jose; semiconductor manufacturing machinery   900

Veritas Software Technology Corp.; San Jose; computer disk drives   866

Santa Barbara County; San Jose; purchasing agency   828

Brocade Communications Systems Inc.; San Jose; computer peripheral equipment   800

Santa Barbara County; San Jose; probation office   800

Infineon Technologies Corp.; San Jose semiconductors and related devices   800

Nortel Networks Inc.; San Jose; Internet connectivity services   800

San Jose State University Foundation; San Jose; education programs   750

Air Systems Inc.; San Jose; mechanical contractor   750

Altera Corp.; San Jose; metal oxide silicon devices   750

United Technologies Corp.; San Jose; aircraft engines and parts   750

San Jose City; San Jose; fire dept.   720

Service Performance Corp.; San Jose; building cleaning   700

United Parcel Service Inc.; San Jose; parcel delivery   700

MCI Worldcom Network Services Inc.; San Jose; local/long-distance telephone   700

Metropolitan Education District; San Jose; vocational schools   700

Sutter's Place Inc.; San Jose; card rooms   690

Aspect Communications Corp.; San Jose; prepackaged software   670

Kaiser Aerospace and Electronics Corp.; San Jose; aircraft engines and parts   650

Mobile Telesys Inc.; San Jose; cellular telephones   600

Allied Security Inc.; San Jose; security guard service   600

Barton Protective Services Inc.; San Jose; guard services   600

Siemens Information and Communication Mobile; San Jose; minicomputers   600

Spectaguard Acquisition; San Jose; security guard service   600

Oplink Communications Inc.; San Jose; fiber optic cable   570

Integrated Device Technology; San Jose; metal oxide silicon devices   567

Hilton Hotels Corp.; San Jose; hotels and motels   559

Santa Barbara County; San Jose; sheriff's office   550

Bea Systems Inc.; San Jose; computer software development   550

Phoenix Technologies; San Jose; computer software development   515

Santa Clara County Office of Education; San Jose   512

Alteon Websystems Inc.; Nashville; electronic circuits   500

U-Haul Co. of Arizona; San Jose; truck rental and leasing   500

California Drywall Co.; San Jose; drywall   500

Light Tower Associates; San Jose; hotels   500

Mentor Graphics Corp.; San Jose; commercial art and graphic design   500

Pacific Bell; San Jose; telephone communication   500

Sanmina-SCI Corp.; San Jose; electronic circuits   500

Pacific Bell; San Jose; telephone communication   500

Redback Networks Inc.; San Jose; personal service agents   500

Thermo Finnigan; San Jose; analytical instruments   500

California 17th District

Monterey, San Benito, and Santa Cruz Counties — Salinas, Santa Cruz

The 17th includes the most populated part of upscale Santa Cruz County, with its namesake city and several sizable seaside communities. Farther south, in Monterey County, Monterey attracts tourists, and exclusive Pebble Beach is home to celebrities and Silicon Valley executives. While Santa Cruz County is a Democratic stronghold, Republican-leaning farmers and retirees in Monterey and San Benito Counties can pull the Democratic district to the right.

South of Santa Cruz County, agriculture drives the economy. Major wineries and vineyards also dot the landscape. Salinas, the seat of Monterey County and the district's largest city, is known as the nation's "salad bowl" for its fresh vegetables. The district's 43 percent Hispanic population is concentrated in the Salinas Valley, where Hispanics are beginning to win local offices. More than 60 percent of district residents live in Monterey County.

Residents in the 17th expected to suffer economically when they lost Fort Ord in 1994. But California State University Monterey Bay has since opened on a portion of the site, and the influx of students and related jobs is expected to help replace 17,000 military jobs. The region also has developed as a center for marine sciences, with more than a dozen major research institutions located around the Monterey Bay coastline.

Major Industry

Agriculture, tourism, higher education.

Notable

The Monterey Bay National Marine Sanctuary is the nation's largest marine sanctuary.

Election Returns

	Republican		Democratic		Other	
President 2000	68,717	33%	124,580	59.9%	14,819	7.1%
House 2002	40,334	27%	101,632	68.1%	7,330	4.9%

District Profile

Population   639,088

Total area (square miles)   5,386
   Land area (square miles)   4,820

Population per square mile   132.6

Counties (2000 population)
   Monterey   401,762
   San Benito   53,234
   Santa Cruz (pt.)   184,092

Cities and other areas over 10,000 (2000 population)

Capitola 10,033	Pacific Grove 15,522
Greenfield 12,583	Prunedale CDP 16,432
Hollister 34,413	Salinas 151,060
King City 11,094	Santa Cruz 54,593
Live Oak CDP 16,628	Seaside 31,696
Marina 25,101	Soledad 11,263
Monterey 29,674	Watsonville 44,265

Race and Hispanic or Latino origin*
   White   46.3%
   Black or African American   2.6%
   American Indian or Alaska Native   0.4%
   Asian   4.8%
   Native Hawaiian or other Pacific Islander   0.3%
   Some other race   0.3%
   Hispanic or Latino origin   42.9%
   Two or more races   2.5%

*As percentage of total population.

Ancestry*

English 6.3%	Italian 4.1%
French 1.9%	Portuguese 1.3%
German 7.6%	Scottish 1.6%
Irish 6.3%	USA/American 2.4%

*As estimated percentage of total population.

Universities and colleges, 2000–2001 enrollment
   Cabrillo College, Aptos   12,807
   California State University-Monterey Bay, Seaside   2,624
   Hartnell College,   Salinas   7,757
   Heald College School of Business, Salinas   669
   Monterey Institute of International Studies, Monterey   667
   Monterey Peninsula College, Monterey   9,421
   Naval Postgraduate School, Monterey   1,763
   University of California, Santa Cruz   12,144

Newspapers and circulation

	District circulation	Total circulation
Monterey County Herald	34,337	34,506
Salinas Californian	18,124	18,220
San Francisco Chronicle	9,483	518,725
San Jose Mercury News	12,319	275,971
Santa Cruz Sentinel	11,912	26,580
*USA Today**	2,462	1,674,376
Watsonville Register-Pajaronian	5,000	7,331

*See Sources and Explanations in the front of the volume.

Television stations and affiliations

Monterey-Salinas	100%	KCAH	PBS
Monterey-Salinas	100%	KCBA	FOX, UPN
Monterey-Salinas	100%	KION	CBS
Monterey-Salinas	100%	KSBW	NBC
Monterey-Salinas	100%	KSMS	Univision

Cable systems and subscribers
   Charter   46,015
   Comcast   63,182

Military installations, September 2001
   Naval Postgraduate School, Monterey   2,446
   Presidio of Monterey (Army), Monterey   2,013
   Silas B. Hays (Army), Seaside   573
   Camp Roberts Military Training Area, San Miguel   463
   Fort Hunter Liggett (Army Reserve), King City   240

Businesses and other major employers
   Interspanish Bay; Pebble Beach; resort hotel   2,500
   Lone Cypress; Pebble Beach; inns   2,000
   California Dept. of Corrections; Soledad   1,800
   Consolidated Factors Inc.; Monterey; fresh fish   1,695
   University of California; Santa Cruz   1,500
   Salinas Valley Memorial Hospital; Salinas   1,480
   Monterey Peninsula Community Hospital; Monterey   1,450
   West Catholic Healthcare; Santa Cruz; residential rehabilitation center   1,400
   Georgia-Pacific Corp.; Salinas; chemicals and allied products   1,300
   Lone Cypress; Pebble Beach; resort hotel   1,200
   Naval Postgraduate School; Monterey; educational research   1,022
   Monterey County; Salinas; psychiatric hospitals   1,011
   SCO Investment Corp.; Santa Cruz; computer tapes and disks   1,000
   Agrilink Foods Inc.; Watsonville; fruits and fruit products   1,000
   Cabrillo Community College District; Aptos   980
   Santa Cruz County; Santa Cruz; county government   976
   Fresh Express Inc.; Salinas; crop preparation services for market   900

McGraw-Hill Companies Inc.; Monterey; publishing
750

McGraw-Hill Companies Inc.; Monterey; educational
research   700

Century Aluminum Co.; Monterey; primary aluminum
680

Texas Instruments Inc.; Santa Cruz; semiconductors and
related devices   670

Monterey Peninsula Community College District;
Monterey   660

Natividad Hospital Inc.; Salinas   659

Community Health Systems Inc.; Watsonville; medical
and surgical hospital   650

Monterey County; Salinas; county government   600

Sonora Packing Co.; Salinas; vegetable crops market
preparation   600

California Dept. of Parks and Recreation; Monterey
600

Monterey County; Monterey; recreation services   600

Lone Cypress; Pebble Beach; golf goods and equipment
600

Albros Custom Harvesting Inc.; Soledad; crop harvesting
600

Granite Rock Co.; Aromas; gravel mining   600

Newstar Fresh Foods; Salinas; fruits   585

Quality Farm Labor Inc.; Gonzales; farm labor crew
leaders   525

Integrated Device Technology; Salinas; semiconductors
and related devices   514

Monterey Mushrooms Inc.; Watsonville; mushroom
production   501

Boskovich Farms Inc.; Salinas; agriculture extension
service   500

Mann Packing Co.; Salinas; vegetable packing services
500

ConAgra Foods Inc.; King City; dehydrating equipment,
food processing   500

Santa Cruz Seaside Co.; Santa Cruz; amusement pier
500

California 18th District

Central Valley — Merced, parts of Stockton and Modesto

While the location of the Central Valley-based 18th remained largely intact, redistricting after the 2000 census
pushed the district's political lean sharply left. *(See map
p. 85.)*

Fearing that the scandal surrounding then-representative
Gary A. Condit could move the seat into the GOP column,
the Democratic-controlled state legislature redrew it from a
highly competitive seat into one with a 17-point Democratic
registration edge. Though still dominated by agriculture, the
district now includes the central portion of the diverse and
Democratic city of Stockton.

Central California's Merced County, along with half of
Stanislaus County, make up the district's agricultural base.
Modesto, the Stanislaus County seat, has its own canning
and food-processing industry, as well as the Gallo Winery,
which accounts for about one-fourth of domestic wine sales.
The city has grown substantially over the years, spurred by

businesses fleeing California's congested coastal cities and by
the Central Valley's successful agriculture industry.

The port city of Stockton (shared with the 11th), on the
San Joaquin River, is a transportation hub that some Bay
Area commuters call home. Almost 60 percent of the city's
residents—Stockton's most Democratic ground—live in the
18th. Whites and Hispanics each make up about 40 percent
of the district's overall population.

Local issues tend to revolve around water availability and
the preservation of farmland. The seasonal economy has contributed to higher unemployment rates than in other parts
of California.

Major Industry

Agriculture, wine, food processing.

Notable

Stockton has the largest Sikh population in the United
States.

Election Returns

	Republican		Democratic		Other	
President 2000	65,105	44.4%	77,908	53.1%	3,690	2.5%
House 2002	47,528	43.4%	56,181	51.3%	5,884	5.3%

District Profile

Population   639,088

Total area (square miles)   3,100
Land area (square miles)   3,052

Population per square mile   209.4

Counties (2000 population)
Fresno (pt.) 3,194	San Joaquin (pt.) 189,665
Madera (pt.) 2,903	Stanislaus (pt.) 232,772
Merced 210,554	

Cities and other areas over 10,000 (2000 population)
Atwater 23,113	Merced 63,893
Ceres 34,609	Modesto (pt.) 133,975
Lathrop 10,445	Patterson 11,606
Livingston 10,473	Stockton (pt.) 139,362
Los Banos 25,869	

Race and Hispanic or Latino origin*
White   39.1%
Black or African American   5.6%
American Indian or Alaska Native   0.7%
Asian   8.9%
Native Hawaiian or other Pacific Islander   0.3%
Some other race   0.2%
Hispanic or Latino origin   41.9%
Two or more races   3.2%

As percentage of total population.

Ancestry*
Dutch 1.1%	Irish 4.8%
English 4.0%	Italian 2.5%
French 1.3%	Portuguese 3.3%
German 6.2%	USA/American 3.2%

As estimated percentage of total population.

Universities and colleges, 2000–2001 enrollment
Andon College, Modesto   511
Heald College School of Business-Stockton, Stockton 592
Merced College, Merced   10,700
Modesto Junior College, Modesto   15,158

Newspapers and circulation

	District circulation	Total circulation
Fresno Bee	8,254	160,724
Merced Sun Star	15,891	16,511
Modesto Bee	36,472	85,295
Pleasanton Tri-Valley Herald	1,520	43,384
San Francisco Chronicle	5,144	518,725
Stockton Record	11,762	58,220
Tracy Press	1,583	10,504
Turlock Journal	1,239	5,897

Television stations and affiliations
Fresno-Visalia	73%	KAIL	UPN
Fresno-Visalia	73%	KFSN	ABC
Fresno-Visalia	73%	KFTV	Univision
Fresno-Visalia	73%	KGMC	Independent
Fresno-Visalia	73%	KMPH	FOX
Fresno-Visalia	73%	KNSO	Telemundo
Fresno-Visalia	73%	KNXT	Independent
Fresno-Visalia	73%	KSEE	NBC
Fresno-Visalia	73%	KVPT	PBS
Sacramento-Stockton-Modesto	27%	KBSV	Independent
Sacramento-Stockton-Modesto	27%	KCRA	NBC
Sacramento-Stockton-Modesto	27%	KMAX	UPN
Sacramento-Stockton-Modesto	27%	KOVR	CBS
Sacramento-Stockton-Modesto	27%	KQCA	WB
Sacramento-Stockton-Modesto	27%	KSPX	PAX
Sacramento-Stockton-Modesto	27%	KTXL	FOX
Sacramento-Stockton-Modesto	27%	KUVS	Univision
Sacramento-Stockton-Modesto	27%	KVIE	PBS
Sacramento-Stockton-Modesto	27%	KXTV	ABC

Cable systems and subscribers
Charter   6,990
Comcast   127,710

Businesses and other major employers
Ethan Allen Inc.; Modesto; furniture   7,000
Foster Farms Dairy; Livingston; poultry products   6,900
E&J Gallo Winery; Modesto; wines   3,550
Fosters Poultry Farms; Livingston; poultry hatcheries 3,000
San Joaquin County; French Camp; medical and surgical hospital   2,000
Memorial Hospitals Assn.; Modesto   2,000
Tenet Healthcare Corp. Hospital; Modesto   1,800
City of Stockton; Stockton; county police   1,300
California Dept. of Corrections; Tracy   1,000
Gallo Glass Co.; Modesto; glass containers   1,000
Dameron Hospital; Stockton   987
Washington Mutual Bank; Stockton; federal savings banks 950
Yosemite Community College District; Modesto   925

San Joaquin County; Stockton; social and human resources 900
U.S. Postal Service; Stockton   900
Quebecor World Inc.; Merced; offset printing   850
Stanislaus County; Modesto; state education department 800
Stanislaus County; Modesto; public welfare administration 760
Merced Community College District; Merced   730
California Dept. of Transportation; Stockton   700
Swift Transportation Co. Inc.; Lathrop; trucking   700
Merced County; Merced; medical and surgical hospital 700
Procter and Gamble Paper Products Co.; Modesto; paper mills   700
Mater Misericordiae Hospital Inc.; Merced   668
Sutter Health Hospital; Merced   650
San Joaquin County; Stockton; county government   600
Merced County Office of Education; Merced   600
Stanislaus County Hospital; Modesto   600
City of Modesto; Modesto; city management   600
Gould Medical Foundation; Modesto; medical clinic   600
Smart and Final Foodservice Distributors Inc.; Stockton; food supplier   560
California Cedar Products Co.; Stockton; wood pencil slats 533
Fuentes Farms; Merced; ship crew agency   500
Merced County; Merced; public welfare administration 500
Rim Hotel Group; Modesto; hotel or motel management 500

California 19th District

Central Valley — parts of Fresno and Modesto, Turlock, Madera

A fertile farm district, the 19th includes the heart of Central California's San Joaquin Valley. It takes in almost all of Madera County and part of the city of Fresno, home to large numbers of Hispanics, Hmong, and Armenians. All of Mariposa and Tuolumne Counties are in the district, along with about half of Stanislaus County.

The 19th is rural and Republican. The district has had a Republican in Congress since 1995 and supported GOP presidential candidates in 1992, 1996, and 2000—when it gave 57.9 percent of the vote to George W. Bush. Farmers and senior citizens, leery of government regulations and environmental protection laws, tend to be moderate conservatives. Farming and water issues are perpetual hot topics and are becoming more significant as population growth means less water for agricultural use.

The district's portion of Stanislaus County includes less than a third of Modesto's population and the growing city of Turlock. Tuolumne and Mariposa Counties, which along with Madera County to the south are home to Yosemite National Park, are sparsely populated areas that account for only one-tenth of the district's population. They feature Sierra Nevada mountains, skiing, and forests in the east and former gold rush towns such as Jamestown, Columbia, and Mariposa in the west.

Tourism at Yosemite helps keep the 19th's economy afloat, though the district suffers from high unemployment because of the seasonal nature of its driving industries. The district picked up all of Yosemite, which was only partially in the old 19th, in redistricting following the 2000 census. Hispanics make up 28.2 percent of residents.

Major Industry

Agriculture, dairy, tourism.

Notable

The Yosemite Valley was deeded to California in 1864 as a public trust, and Yosemite National Park was created in 1890.

Election Returns

	Republican		Democratic		Other	
President 2000	125,465	57.9%	84,559	39%	6,823	3.1%
House 2002	106,209	67.3%	47,403	30%	4,190	2.7%

District Profile

Population 639,088

Total area (square miles) 6,780
  Land area (square miles) 6,692

Population per square mile 95.5

Counties (2000 population)

Fresno (pt.) 233,026	Stanislaus (pt.) 214,225
Madera (pt.) 120,206	Tuolumne 54,501
Mariposa 17,130	

Cities and other areas over 10,000 (2000 population)

Chowchilla 11,127	Oakdale 15,503
Fresno (pt.) 189,836	Riverbank 15,826
Madera 43,207	Salida CDP 12,560
Modesto (pt.) 54,881	Turlock 55,810

Race and Hispanic or Latino origin*

White 59.9%
Black or African American 3.4%
American Indian or Alaska Native 1.0%
Asian 4.4%
Native Hawaiian or other Pacific Islander 0.1%
Some other race 0.2%
Hispanic or Latino origin 28.2%
Two or more races 2.8%

*As percentage of total population.

Ancestry*

Dutch 1.5%	Norwegian 1.1%
English 7.3%	Portuguese 2.6%
French 2.0%	Scotch-Irish 1.1%
German 10.0%	Scottish 1.3%
Irish 6.9%	Swedish 1.5%
Italian 3.7%	USA/American 3.5%

*As estimated percentage of total population.

Universities and colleges, 2000–2001 enrollment

California State University-Stanislaus, Turlock 7,062
Columbia College, Sonora 3,340
Fresno City College, Fresno 19,351
Heald College School of Business and Technology, Fresno 735
San Joaquin Valley College, Fresno 669

Newspapers and circulation

	District circulation	Total circulation
Fresno Bee	56,228	160,724
Modesto Bee	42,149	85,295
San Francisco Chronicle	5,363	518,725
Sonora Union Democrat	10,464	11,192
Turlock Journal	4,630	5,897
*USA Today**	1,053	1,674,376

*See Sources and Explanations in the front of the volume.

Television stations and affiliations

Fresno-Visalia	55%	KAIL	UPN
Fresno-Visalia	55%	KFSN	ABC
Fresno-Visalia	55%	KFTV	Univision
Fresno-Visalia	55%	KGMC	Independent
Fresno-Visalia	55%	KMPH	FOX
Fresno-Visalia	55%	KNSO	Telemundo
Fresno-Visalia	55%	KNXT	Independent
Fresno-Visalia	55%	KSEE	NBC
Fresno-Visalia	55%	KVPT	PBS
Sacramento-Stockton-Modesto	45%	KBSV	Independent
Sacramento-Stockton-Modesto	45%	KCRA	NBC
Sacramento-Stockton-Modesto	45%	KMAX	UPN
Sacramento-Stockton-Modesto	45%	KOVR	CBS
Sacramento-Stockton-Modesto	45%	KQCA	WB
Sacramento-Stockton-Modesto	45%	KSPX	PAX
Sacramento-Stockton-Modesto	45%	KTXL	FOX
Sacramento-Stockton-Modesto	45%	KUVS	Univision
Sacramento-Stockton-Modesto	45%	KVIE	PBS
Sacramento-Stockton-Modesto	45%	KXTV	ABC

Cable systems and subscribers

Charter 26,993
Comcast 22,024
Meyerhoff Cable 656
Northland 5,301
Ponderosa Cablevision 650
Sun Country Cable 1,765

Military installations, September 2001

Riverbank Army Ammunition Plant, Riverbank 281

Businesses and other major employers

Kaiser Foundation Hospitals; Fresno 2,000
St. Agnes Medical Center; Fresno 1,700
Valley Children's Hospital; Madera 1,500
U.S. National Park Service; Yosemite National Park 1,250
ConAgra Grocery Products Co.; Oakdale; tomato products 1,200
Emanuel Medical Center Inc.; Turlock 1,100
Yosemite Concession Services Corp.; Yosemite National Park; hotels 1,025

California Dept. of Corrections; Chowchilla   1,000
Table Mountain Rancheria Bingo; Friant; gambling   1,000
Vendo Co.; Fresno; vending machines   1,000
Tammie D. Fogle; Turlock; wine   1,000
State Center Community College District; Fresno   900
Valley Fresh Inc.; Turlock; processed canned poultry   900
Fosters Poultry Farms; Turlock; turkey processing   775
Sonora Community Hospital Inc.; Sonora   712
Canandaigua Wine Co.; Madera; wines, brandy, and brandy spirits   700
Kmart Corp.; Fresno; discount department stores   700
California State University; Turlock   600
Madera Community Hospital Inc.; Madera   500
Forest Service; Sonora; land conservation agencies   500
Tuolumne County; Sonora; data processing   500

California 20th District

Central Valley — Kings County, parts of Fresno and Bakersfield

The Hispanic-majority 20th reaches from Fresno to Bakersfield, through rural portions of Fresno, Kern, and Kings Counties. The 20th was a swing district until being redrawn following the 2000 census. Once state lawmakers completed the remap Democrats were left with a 20-point voter registration edge.

The 20th still bears much of the burden of the San Joaquin Valley's urban and rural poor, and is beset by crime and high unemployment. It also is one of California's most rural districts, and has some of the nation's poorest and least-educated residents, many of whom are Hispanic and Hmong immigrants who work in the district's farming community.

The district includes the area known as the Westlands. Here, federal water projects have spawned vast farms with battalions of workers. Motorists on Interstate 5 see nary a town while they pass fields filled with a wide variety of products, including alfalfa, cotton, fruits, sugar beets, wheat, and nuts.

Roughly 40 percent of Fresno—the city is split among the 19th, 20th, and 21st districts—is in the 20th, which takes in much of downtown and Hispanic areas in the southern section of the city. The downtown portion includes a multipurpose stadium, which opened in 2002 and is home to a minor league baseball team, that local leaders hope will give an economic boost to the city once known for its proliferation of car thefts. In recent years, the 20th also has attracted many state and privately run prisons that assist the area's shaky economy.

Major Industry

Agriculture, dairy, prisons.

Notable

Fresno resident Mike Reynolds, whose daughter was murdered, was the catalyst behind California's "three strikes" ballot initiative.

Election Returns

	Republican		Democratic		Other	
President 2000	46,058	43.6%	57,790	54.7%	1,844	1.7%
House 2002	25,628	34.4%	47,403	63.6%	1,515	2%

District Profile

Population   639,088

Total area (square miles)   4,988
    Land area (square miles)   4,982

Population per square mile   128.3

Counties (2000 population)
    Fresno (pt.)   292,120
    Kern (pt.)   217,507
    Kings   129,461

Cities and other areas over 10,000 (2000 population)

Arvin	12,956	Lamont CDP	13,296
Avenal	14,674	Lemoore	19,712
Bakersfield (pt.)	43,284	Parlier	11,145
Coalinga	11,668	Sanger	18,931
Corcoran	14,458	Selma	19,444
Delano	38,824	Shafter	12,736
Fresno (pt.)	154,998	Wasco	21,263
Hanford	41,686		

Race and Hispanic or Latino origin*
    White   21.4%
    Black or African American   7.2%
    American Indian or Alaska Native   0.7%
    Asian   5.6%
    Native Hawaiian or other Pacific Islander   0.1%
    Some other race   0.2%
    Hispanic or Latino origin   63.1%
    Two or more races   1.7%

*As percentage of total population.

Ancestry*

English	2.1%	Portuguese	1.3%
German	3.2%	USA/American	2.3%
Irish	2.6%		

*As estimated percentage of total population.

Universities and colleges, 2000–2001 enrollment
    Fresno Pacific University, Fresno   1,676
    West Hills Community College, Coalinga   4,344

Newspapers and circulation

	District circulation	Total circulation
Bakersfield Californian	11,275	71,386
Fresno Bee	29,332	160,724
Hanford Sentinel	12,601	13,214
Pleasanton Tri-Valley Herald	1,183	43,384

Television stations and affiliations

Fresno-Visalia	75%	KAIL	UPN
Fresno-Visalia	75%	KFSN	ABC
Fresno-Visalia	75%	KFTV	Univision
Fresno-Visalia	75%	KGMC	Independent
Fresno-Visalia	75%	KMPH	FOX
Fresno-Visalia	75%	KNSO	Telemundo
Fresno-Visalia	75%	KNXT	Independent
Fresno-Visalia	75%	KSEE	NBC
Fresno-Visalia	75%	KVPT	PBS
Santa Barbara-Santa Maria-San Luis Obispo	25%	KBAK	CBS
Santa Barbara-Santa Maria-San Luis Obispo	25%	KCOY	CBS

Santa Barbara-Santa Maria-San Luis Obispo	25%	KERO	ABC
Santa Barbara-Santa Maria-San Luis Obispo	25%	KEYT	ABC
Santa Barbara-Santa Maria-San Luis Obispo	25%	KGET	NBC
Santa Barbara-Santa Maria-San Luis Obispo	25%	KSBY	NBC
Santa Barbara-Santa Maria-San Luis Obispo	25%	KTAS	Telemundo
Santa Barbara-Santa Maria-San Luis Obispo	25%	KUVI	UPN

Cable systems and subscribers
Bright House Networks   12,881
Central Valley Cable   2,900
Comcast   126,272
Time Warner   1,454

Military installations, September 2001
Lemoore Naval Air Station, Lemoore   6,450
Fresno Yosemite International, Fresno   982

Businesses and other major employers
Moreles Harvesting and Packing; Lemoore; crop harvesting   4,000
Community Medical Centers; Fresno; hospital management   3,400
Fresno Community Hospital and Medical Center; Fresno   3,000
Kern County Hospital; Bakersfield   2,500
California Dept. of Corrections; Coalinga   2,000
California Dept. of Corrections; Corcoran   2,000
U.S. Internal Revenue Service; Fresno   2,000
Fresno County; Fresno; county government   1,750
Fresno County; Fresno; individual and family services   1,500
Bakersfield City School District; Bakersfield   1,449
California Dept. of Corrections; Avenal   1,100
California Dept. of Transportation; Fresno   1,100
Kings County; Hanford; county government   977
Paramount Farms; Lost Hills; salted and roasted nuts and seeds   940
Kern County; Bakersfield; health and welfare council   900
Up-Right Inc.; Selma; aerial work platforms   900
Fresno County; Fresno; public health programs   900
Fresno County Superintendent of Schools Central Valley; Fresno   900
Diocese of Fresno Education Corp.; Fresno; Catholic schools   800
U.S. Veterans Affairs Dept.; Fresno   800
Fresno County Economic Opportunities Commission; Fresno   800
PCA Farm Management; Delano; farm management services   700
Sunmet Agricultural Inc.; Del Rey; management services   700
Kreger Inc.; Five Points; farm labor contractors   700
Fosters Poultry Farms; Fresno; chicken processing   700
McClatchy Newspapers Inc.; Fresno; newspaper   700
City of Fresno; Fresno; municipal police   675
Pirelli Tire; Hanford; automobile tires   650
Hanford Community Hospital; Hanford   640
Sears Logistics Services Inc.; Delano; trucking terminal facilities   600
Sears Roebuck and Co. Inc.; Delano; self storage warehousing   550
J. G. Boswell Co; Corcoran; cotton   500
ConAgra Grocery Products Co.; Helm; tomato products   500
Pacific Bell; Fresno; shipping agents   500
Fresno County; Fresno; probation office   500
Pepsi Cola Bottling Co.; Fresno; soft drinks   500

California 21st District
Central Valley — Tulare County, part of Fresno

The agriculture-dominated 21st is home to all of Tulare and part of Fresno counties, which vie each year for the title of top farm-goods-producing county in the nation. Tulare was the winner in 2001, with more than $3.5 billion in agricultural commodities. In addition to about 20 percent of Fresno, the district takes in some of the mountains and forests of the Sierra Nevada chain on its eastern edge, including Sequoia National Park.

Tulare County is the world's largest dairy producing area, with more than $1 billion in dairy goods in 2001. But the county produces more than 250 other agricultural goods, including oranges, cattle, grapes, cotton, and nuts. It is no surprise that farming and water issues are perpetual hot topics and are becoming more significant as population growth means less water for agricultural use. Unlike other areas, where supply and transportation are concerns, the big problem here is water storage. The district also faces high unemployment and below-average education rates.

The district includes the eastern, conservative portion of Fresno, including Fresno Yosemite International Airport and the Fresno branch of California State University. It also holds the cities of Visalia and Clovis, agricultural towns that have become cities in their own right. Clovis calls itself the gateway to the Sierra Nevadas.

During redistricting following the 2000 census, the 21st was created as an open seat, merging rural, conservative areas likely to elect a Republican. The district gave George W. Bush 60.5 percent of the vote in the 2000 presidential election, and GOP candidates should dominate for the foreseeable future.

Major Industry
Agriculture, transportation, tourism.

Notable
Mount Whitney, at 14,494 feet, is the tallest point in the lower 48 states; General Sherman, a giant sequoia in Sequoia National Park, is the largest living thing in the world.

Election Returns

	Republican		Democratic		Other	
President 2000	107,645	60.5%	65,268	36.7%	5,120	2.9%
House 2002	87,544	70.5%	32,584	26.2%	4,070	3.3%

District Profile
Population   639,088

Total area (square miles)   8,089
  Land area (square miles)   8,025

Population per square mile   79.6

Counties (2000 population)
Fresno (pt.)   271,067
Tulare   368,021

Cities and other areas over 10,000 (2000 population)

Clovis	68,468	Porterville	39,615
Dinuba	16,844	Reedley	20,756
Fresno (pt.)	82,818	Tulare	43,994
Lindsay	10,297	Visalia	91,565

Race and Hispanic or Latino origin*

White   46.4%
Black or African American   2.1%
American Indian or Alaska Native   0.9%
Asian   4.9%
Native Hawaiian or other Pacific Islander   0.1%
Some other race   0.2%
Hispanic or Latino origin   43.4%
Two or more races   2.2%

*As percentage of total population.

Ancestry*

Dutch	1.4%	Italian	2.2%
English	5.6%	Portuguese	1.8%
French	1.5%	Scottish	1.1%
German	7.7%	Swedish	1.1%
Irish	5.5%	USA/American	4.0%

*As estimated percentage of total population.

Universities and colleges, 2000–2001 enrollment

California School of Professional Psychology, Fresno   409
California State University, Fresno   19,056
College of the Sequoias, Visalia   10,251
Porterville College, Porterville   3,785
Reedley College, Reedley   9,081
San Joaquin College of Law, Clovis   204
San Joaquin Valley College, Visalia   627

Newspapers and circulation

	District circulation	Total circulation
Fresno Bee	65,812	160,724
Porterville Recorder	9,874	9,957
San Francisco Chronicle	1,771	518,725
Tulare Advance-Register	8,111	8,184
Visalia Times-Delta	21,463	21,488

Television stations and affiliations

Fresno-Visalia	100%	KAIL	UPN
Fresno-Visalia	100%	KFSN	ABC
Fresno-Visalia	100%	KFTV	Univision
Fresno-Visalia	100%	KGMC	Independent
Fresno-Visalia	100%	KMPH	FOX
Fresno-Visalia	100%	KNSO	Telemundo
Fresno-Visalia	100%	KNXT	Independent
Fresno-Visalia	100%	KSEE	NBC
Fresno-Visalia	100%	KVPT	PBS

Cable systems and subscribers

Charter   16,227
Comcast   42,757
USA Media Group   943

Businesses and other major employers

U.S. Internal Revenue Service; Fresno   3,000
California Motor Vehicles Dept.; Fresno   2,500
Marko Zaninovich Inc.; McFarland; grapes   2,000

California Dept. of Developmental Services; Porterville   2,000
Kaweah Delta Health Care District; Visalia; hospital with residency   1,600
Tulare County; Visalia   1,500
Cigna Corp.; Visalia; insurance adjusters   1,400
Freedom Aquisitions Inc.; Clovis; television closed circuit equipment   1,100
Wal-Mart Stores Inc.; Porterville; discount department stores   1,000
Tulare County; Visalia; sheriff's office   1,000
Ruiz Food Products Inc.; Dinuba; frozen ethnic foods   1,000
College of Sequoias Community College District; Visalia   995
Dole Food Co.; Earlimart; grapes   800
Fresno Community Hospital and Medical Center; Clovis   800
Sierra View Local Hospital District; Porterville   600
Gap Inc.; Fresno; family clothing stores   600
Sunrise Medical Inc.; Fresno; wheelchairs   590
Monrovia Nursery Co.; Visalia; nursery stock   566
Sun-Maid Growers of California; Kingsburg; raisins   531
Harris Farms Inc.; Selma; meat packing plants   530
Sun Pacific Farming Co.; Exeter; citrus grove management   500
Land O'Lakes Inc.; Tulare; milk processing   500
Tulare Local Health Care District; Tulare; medical and surgical hospital   500
Pacific Bell; Clovis; local/long-distance telephone   500

California 22nd District

Kern and San Luis Obispo Counties — Bakersfield

The 22nd stretches from San Luis Obispo County near the coast inland to Ridgecrest in Kern County, dipping south into northwestern Los Angeles County. The district, previously numbered the 21st, lost its portion of Tulare County in redistricting following the 2000 census, though it remains consistently Republican. More than two-thirds of its residents live in Kern County.

Kern is known for oil production and has a strong agricultural industry. Along with the farm-oriented San Luis Obispo area (the city itself is in the coastal 23rd District), the counties produce billions of dollars each year in crops such as grapes, citrus, cotton, and nuts. San Luis Obispo nurtures vineyards and cattle.

Bakersfield, some of which falls in the 20th District, is Kern County's largest city and sits in the southern end of the San Joaquin Valley. Along with Lancaster in Los Angeles County, it continues to see the most growth. Here, oil and agriculture dominate the economy, although the city is trying to diversify by promoting its growing telecommunications, financial, and light manufacturing sectors.

San Luis Obispo County trends conservative, with many conservative Democrats in the northern part. Agricultural and military aviation issues remain dominant concerns for residents.

Major Industry

Agriculture, oil, military.

Notable

Bakersfield was known as the country music capital of the West; country music star Buck Owens has his Crystal Palace museum and theater in Bakersfield; the nation's first jet- and rocket-powered flights took off from Edwards Air Force Base; the world's largest novelty ice cream plant, for Nestle Ice Cream Co., is in Bakersfield.

Election Returns

	Republican		Democratic		Other	
President 2000	141,156	64.3%	73,338	33.4%	5,043	2.3%
House 2002	120,473	73.3%	38,988	23.7%	4,824	2.9%

District Profile

Population   639,088

Total area (square miles)   10,453
Land area (square miles)   10,416

Population per square mile   61.4

Counties (2000 population)
Kern (pt.)   444,138
Los Angeles (pt.)   73,901
San Luis Obispo (pt.)   121,049

Cities and other areas over 10,000 (2000 population)
Arroyo Grande   15,851
Atascadero   26,411
Bakersfield (pt.)   203,773
El Paso de Robles (Paso Robles)   24,297
Lancaster (pt.)   65,976
Oildale CDP   27,885
Ridgecrest   24,927
Rosamond CDP   14,349
Tehachapi   10,957

Race and Hispanic or Latino origin*
White   66.8%
Black or African American   5.6%
American Indian or Alaska Native   0.9%
Asian   2.9%
Native Hawaiian or other Pacific Islander   0.1%
Some other race   0.2%
Hispanic or Latino origin   21.0%
Two or more races   2.5%

*As percentage of total population.

Ancestry*
Dutch	1.4%	Norwegian	1.2%
English	7.8%	Scotch-Irish	1.3%
French	2.2%	Scottish	1.5%
German	10.7%	Swedish	1.2%
Irish	8.1%	USA/American	5.1%
Italian	3.0%		

*As estimated percentage of total population.

Universities and colleges, 2000–2001 enrollment
Antelope Valley College, Lancaster   10,315
Bakersfield College, Bakersfield   14,466
California State University, Bakersfield   6,397
Cerro Coso Community College, Ridgecrest   5,106
San Joaquin Valley College, Bakersfield   742
Taft College, Taft   7,331

Newspapers and circulation

	District circulation	Total circulation
Bakersfield Californian	58,284	71,386
Daily Variety, Los Angeles*	2,314	27,269
Los Angeles Daily News	6,327	195,376
*Los Angeles Sentinel**	1,406	12,345
Los Angeles Times	10,689	1,044,205
San Luis Obispo Telegram-Tribune	24,457	37,920
Santa Maria Times	2,187	17,797
*USA Today**	6,322	1,674,376

*See Sources and Explanations in the front of the volume.

Television stations and affiliations
Santa Barbara-Santa Maria-San Luis Obispo	73%	KBAK	CBS
Santa Barbara-Santa Maria-San Luis Obispo	73%	KCOY	CBS
Santa Barbara-Santa Maria-San Luis Obispo	73%	KERO	ABC
Santa Barbara-Santa Maria-San Luis Obispo	73%	KEYT	ABC
Santa Barbara-Santa Maria-San Luis Obispo	73%	KGET	NBC
Santa Barbara-Santa Maria-San Luis Obispo	73%	KSBY	NBC
Santa Barbara-Santa Maria-San Luis Obispo	73%	KTAS	Telemundo
Santa Barbara-Santa Maria-San Luis Obispo	73%	KUVI	UPN
Los Angeles	27%	KABC	ABC
Los Angeles	27%	KADY	Independent
Los Angeles	27%	KCAL	Independent
Los Angeles	27%	KCBS	CBS
Los Angeles	27%	KCET	PBS
Los Angeles	27%	KCOP	UPN
Los Angeles	27%	KDOC	Independent
Los Angeles	27%	KHIZ	Independent
Los Angeles	27%	KJLA	Independent
Los Angeles	27%	KLCS	PBS
Los Angeles	27%	KMEX	Univision
Los Angeles	27%	KNBC	NBC
Los Angeles	27%	KOCE	PBS
Los Angeles	27%	KPXN	PAX
Los Angeles	27%	KRCA	PBS
Los Angeles	27%	KSCI	Independent
Los Angeles	27%	KTBN	Independent
Los Angeles	27%	KTLA	WB
Los Angeles	27%	KTTV	FOX
Los Angeles	27%	KVCR	PBS
Los Angeles	27%	KVEA	Telemundo
Los Angeles	27%	KWHY	Independent Spanish

Cable systems and subscribers
Bright House Networks   6,123
Charter   25,358
Cox   79,302
Mediacom   21,337
Mountain Cablevision   2,614

Military installations, September 2001
Edwards Air Force Base, Rosamond   6,485
Naval Air Weapons Station, China Lake   4,078
Vandenberg Air Force Base, Lompoc   4,025
Camp San Luis Obispo Military Training Area, San Luis Obispo   525

Businesses and other major employers
California Polytechnic State University; San Luis Obispo   3,050
Bolthouse Farms Inc.; Bakersfield; carrot farm   2,250
San Luis Obispo County; San Luis Obispo; juvenile correctional facilities   1,900
California Dept. of Corrections; San Luis Obispo   1,700

Antelope Valley Hospital; Lancaster   1,660

California Dept. of Mental Health; Atascadero   1,600

Country Wide Funding; Rosemead; federal home loan mortgage corporation   1,300

Mercy Health Care Bakersfield Hospital; Bakersfield 1,000

Kern County; Bakersfield; sheriff's office   1,000

Boeing Capital Corp.; Edwards; flight instruments, guidance systems   1,000

National Aeronautics and Space Administration; Edwards; space research and development   1,000

Kern County Superintendent of Schools; Bakersfield   975

Kern Community College District; Bakersfield   900

San Joaquin Community Hospital; Bakersfield   850

Aera Energy; Bakersfield; directional oil, gas well drilling 800

Cal Organic Vegetable Co. Inc.; Bakersfield; vegetable crops market preparation   800

Frito-Lay Inc.; Bakersfield; potato chips and snacks   800

U.S. Borax Inc.; Boron; industrial inorganic chemicals   800

Antelope Valley Community College District; Lancaster 773

Bakersfield Memorial Hospital; Bakersfield   735

Bakersfield College; Bakersfield   600

AG Wise Enterprises Inc.; Bakersfield; farm management services   600

Antelope Valley Union High School District; Lancaster 600

La County High Desert Hospital; Lancaster   600

U.S. Dept. of Energy; Tupman   550

Flight Systems; Mojave; aviation, aeronautical engineering 550

Zond Pacific; Tehachapi; electric services   550

Gene Watson Construction; Taft; oil field services   530

Kern Community College District; Ridgecrest   512

Giumarra Vineyards Corp.; Edison; grapes   500

Esparza Enterprises Inc.; Maricopa; employment agency 500

City of Bakersfield; Bakersfield; legislative bodies   500

Kern County; Bakersfield; county government   500

7th Standard Ranch Co.; Bakersfield; grapes   500

Kern County; Bakersfield; fire dept.   500

Pool Company Inc.; Bakersfield; servicing oil and gas wells 500

Kern County; Bakersfield; fire dept.   500

Tenet Healthcare Corp.; Templeton; specialty hospitals 500

Mesa Construction Co.; Tehachapi; power generating equipment installation   500

California 23rd District

Central Coast — Oxnard, Santa Barbara, Santa Maria, San Luis Obispo

The 23rd is a sliver of coastline stretching from north of San Luis Obispo into Ventura County, which lies northwest of Los Angeles. Three main cities—Oxnard, Santa Barbara, and San Luis Obispo—register high numbers of Democrats, especially Oxnard, which has a significant blue-collar Hispanic population. As with much of California's coast, the district is liberal on social issues.

The district's other major city, Santa Maria, is the most Republican, but wealthy members of Hollywood's elite in Santa Barbara County and students at California Polytechnic State University in San Luis Obispo and the University of California, Santa Barbara, tilt the 23rd to the left.

Agriculture is a mainstay in the San Luis Obispo area, as well as in Santa Maria, which also is known for manufacturing. Oxnard is home to large biotech companies and the Port of Hueneme, the only international port on the central coast, which imports and exports the majority of cars in the state. Tourism also helps this beachfront district's economy, and universities contribute to the wealth of the 23rd.

Redistricting following the 2000 census gave the district, previously numbered the 22nd, its coastal shape—at one point it narrows to the width of a strip of shoreline—and its Democratic lean. The new district gave Democrat Al Gore 53.5 percent of the vote in the 2000 presidential election. Hispanics make up two-fifths of the population.

Major Industry
Agriculture, military, tourism.

Notable
The Hearst Castle, a historic state museum at San Simeon, was home to William Randolph Hearst; half of the acreage of Channel Islands National Park is under water.

Election Returns

	Republican		Democratic		Other	
President 2000	90,550	40.4%	119,795	53.5%	13,574	6.1%
House 2002	62,604	38.6%	95,752	59%	3,866	2.4%

District Profile

Population   639,088

Total area (square miles)   2,479
  Land area (square miles)   1,041

Population per square mile   613.9

Counties (2000 population)
  San Luis Obispo (pt.)   125,632
  Santa Barbara (pt.)   286,713
  Ventura (pt.)   226,743

Cities and other areas over 10,000 (2000 population)
  Baywood-Los Osos CDP   14,351
  Carpinteria   14,194
  Goleta CDP   55,204
  Grover Beach   13,067
  Isla Vista CDP   18,344
  Montecito CDP   10,000
  Morro Bay   10,350
  Nipomo CDP   12,626
  Oxnard   170,358
  Port Hueneme   21,845
  San Buenaventura (Ventura) (pt.)   21,500
  San Luis Obispo   44,174
  Santa Barbara   92,325
  Santa Maria   77,423

Race and Hispanic or Latino origin*

White   48.7%
Black or African American   1.9%
American Indian or Alaska Native   0.5%
Asian   4.9%
Native Hawaiian or other Pacific Islander   0.2%
Some other race   0.1%
Hispanic or Latino origin   41.7%
Two or more races   2.0%

*As percentage of total population.

Ancestry*

English	7.2%	Polish	1.1%
French	2.0%	Scotch-Irish	1.1%
German	8.3%	Scottish	1.6%
Irish	6.5%	Swedish	1.2%
Italian	3.2%	USA/American	2.5%
Norwegian	1.2%		

*As estimated percentage of total population.

Universities and colleges, 2000–2001 enrollment

Allan Hancock College, Santa Maria   12,110
Antioch University, Santa Barbara   263
Brooks Institute of Photography, Santa Barbara   670
California Polytechnic State University, San Luis Obispo   16,877
Cuesta College, San Luis Obispo   9,496
Fielding Institute, Santa Barbara   1,237
ITT Technical Institute, Oxnard   503
Oxnard College, Oxnard   7,105
Pacifica Graduate Institute, Carpinteria   837
Santa Barbara City College, Santa Barbara   13,834
University of California, Santa Barbara   19,962
Ventura College of Law, Ventura*
Westmont College, Santa Barbara   1,332

*Enrollment under 100. See Sources and Explanations in the front of the volume.

Newspapers and circulation

	District circulation	Total circulation
Lompoc Record	1,489	7,908
Los Angeles La Opinion	2,060	127,108
Los Angeles Times	17,563	1,044,205
San Luis Obispo Telegram-Tribune	12,792	37,920
Santa Barbara News Press	29,216	44,078
Santa Maria Times	7,585	17,797
Ventura County Star	20,448	96,625

Television stations and affiliations

Santa Barbara-Santa Maria-San Luis Obispo	92%	KBAK	CBS
Santa Barbara-Santa Maria-San Luis Obispo	92%	KCOY	CBS
Santa Barbara-Santa Maria-San Luis Obispo	92%	KERO	ABC
Santa Barbara-Santa Maria-San Luis Obispo	92%	KEYT	ABC
Santa Barbara-Santa Maria-San Luis Obispo	92%	KGET	NBC
Santa Barbara-Santa Maria-San Luis Obispo	92%	KSBY	NBC
Santa Barbara-Santa Maria-San Luis Obispo	92%	KTAS	Telemundo
Santa Barbara-Santa Maria-San Luis Obispo	92%	KUVI	UPN
Los Angeles	8%	KABC	ABC
Los Angeles	8%	KADY	Independent
Los Angeles	8%	KCAL	Independent
Los Angeles	8%	KCBS	CBS
Los Angeles	8%	KCET	PBS
Los Angeles	8%	KCOP	UPN
Los Angeles	8%	KDOC	Independent
Los Angeles	8%	KHIZ	Independent
Los Angeles	8%	KJLA	Independent
Los Angeles	8%	KLCS	PBS
Los Angeles	8%	KMEX	Univision
Los Angeles	8%	KNBC	NBC
Los Angeles	8%	KOCE	PBS
Los Angeles	8%	KPXN	PAX
Los Angeles	8%	KRCA	PBS
Los Angeles	8%	KSCI	Independent
Los Angeles	8%	KTBN	Independent
Los Angeles	8%	KTLA	WB
Los Angeles	8%	KTTV	FOX
Los Angeles	8%	KVCR	PBS
Los Angeles	8%	KVEA	Telemundo
Los Angeles	8%	KWHY	Independent Spanish

Cable systems and subscribers

Adelphia   31,838
Avenue TV Cable   36,040
Charter   45,079
Comcast   16,283
Cox   79,949

Military installations, September 2001

Port Hueneme Naval Construction Battalion Center, Port Hueneme   4,353

Businesses and other major employers

University of California; Santa Barbara   5,000
Santa Barbara County; Santa Barbara; county government   2,620
S Adamo Coffee Co.; Oxnard; coffee shop   2,002
Pacific Gas and Electric Co.; Avila Beach; gas transmission, distribution   2,000
CHW Central Coast Hospital; Santa Barbara   1,850
Raytheon Co.; Goleta; countermeasure simulators   1,800
FHC Hotel Management Co.; Santa Barbara; hotel or motel management   1,700
Goleta Valley Cottage Hospital; Santa Barbara   1,700
Santa Barbara Cottage Hospital; Santa Barbara   1,655
Santa Barbara Elementary School District; Santa Barbara   1,632
Santa Barbara City; Santa Barbara; city government   1,400
CHW Central Coast; Oxnard; medical and surgical hospital   1,200
Sunbelt Enterprises Inc.; Oxnard; nonresidential building operators   1,200
ITT Industries Inc.; Lompoc; missile tracking: telemetry/photography   1,100
Illuminations.com Inc.; Ventura; catalog, mail-order   1,049
Santa Barbara Community College District; Santa Barbara   1,000
Raytheon Infrared Systems; Goleta; defense systems and equipment   1,000
Verizon Inc.; Oxnard; employment agencies   900
Raytheon Co.; Goleta; infrared instruments   900
CHW Central Coast; Santa Maria; medical and surgical hospital   900
Allan Hancock Joint Community College District; Santa Maria; community college   779
Santa Barbara Bank and Trust Inc.; Santa Barbara; state commercial banks   750
QAD Inc.; Carpinteria; computer software development   700
B&S Plastics Inc.; Oxnard; injection molding of plastics   700
McGhan Medical Corp.; Santa Barbara; surgical implants   630
Interim Staffing; Oxnard; temporary help service   600

Procter and Gamble Manufacturing Co.; Oxnard; paper mills   600

San Ramon Regional Medical Center Inc.; San Ramon   600

Sierra Vista Hospital Inc.; San Luis Obispo   575

Employers Depo Inc.; Ventura; help supply services   550

Devereux Foundation; Goleta; psychiatrist   550

Seminis Vegetable Seeds Inc.; Oxnard; garden, flower seeds   500

4 Seasons Biltmore Hotel Resort; Santa Barbara; business management   500

California Dept. of Transportation; San Luis Obispo   500

California 24th District

Ventura and Santa Barbara Counties — Thousand Oaks, Simi Valley

Located north and west of the Los Angeles suburbs, the 24th includes nearly all of Ventura County and inland Santa Barbara County.

Ventura County, where more than four-fifths of district residents live, is a mix of lower-income farming communities and more-upscale residential neighborhoods, such as Moorpark, one of district's fastest-growing cities. The county passed a slow-growth ballot initiative in 1998 in an effort to stave off urban sprawl. After absorbing some destruction from the 1994 Northridge earthquake, Ventura County now has growing electronics, finance, and insurance sectors. Industries ranging from agriculture to biotechnology to construction have contributed to the county's recovery.

Because Ventura borders Los Angeles County to the south and east, it often is identified with its urban neighbor. The central and western portions of the district—mainly in Santa Barbara County—are more agricultural, producing grapes, broccoli, and strawberries, and including most of the Los Padres National Forest. Many residents are employed by hospitals and universities. San Nicolas Island and the Anacapa Islands also fall within the 24th's boundaries.

The district's reliable Republicanism comes from interior Santa Barbara—the neighboring 23rd contains the more Democratic coast. Vandenberg Air Force Base and south Ventura County cities such as Simi Valley and Thousand Oaks also contribute to the GOP base.

Major Industry
Biotechnology, aerospace, service.

Notable
The Ronald Reagan Presidential Library is in Simi Valley; an all-white Simi Valley jury acquitted three police officers accused of beating motorist Rodney King, touching off Los Angeles riots in 1992.

Election Returns

	Republican		Democratic		Other	
President 2000	140,755	53.6%	112,436	42.8%	9,220	3.5%
House 2002	120,585	65.2%	58,755	31.8%	5,666	3.1%

District Profile

Population   639,088

Total area (square miles)   4,156
   Land area (square miles)   3,883

Population per square mile   164.6

Counties (2000 population)
   Santa Barbara (pt.)   112,634
   Ventura (pt.)   526,454

Cities and other areas over 10,000 (2000 population)
   Camarillo   57,077
   Fillmore   13,643
   Lompoc   41,103
   Moorpark   31,415
   Orcutt CDP   28,830
   San Buenaventura (Ventura)   79,416
   Santa Paula   28,598
   Simi Valley   111,351
   Thousand Oaks   117,005

Race and Hispanic or Latino origin*
   White   68.6%
   Black or African American   1.6%
   American Indian or Alaska Native   0.5%
   Asian   4.4%
   Native Hawaiian or other Pacific Islander   0.1%
   Some other race   0.2%
   Hispanic or Latino origin   22.3%
   Two or more races   2.2%

*As percentage of total population.

Ancestry*

Dutch 1.3%	Polish 2.0%
English 9.0%	Russian 1.4%
French 2.5%	Scotch-Irish 1.4%
German 11.7%	Scottish 1.8%
Irish 8.8%	Swedish 1.6%
Italian 4.6%	USA/American 3.6%
Norwegian 1.7%	

*As estimated percentage of total population.

Universities and colleges, 2000–2001 enrollment
   California Lutheran University, Thousand Oaks   2,766
   Moorpark College, Moorpark   13,233
   Thomas Aquinas College, Santa Paula   277
   Ventura College, Ventura   11,837

Newspapers and circulation

	District circulation	Total circulation
Lompoc Record	6,419	7,908
Los Angeles Daily News	19,590	195,376
Los Angeles La Opinion	2,545	127,108
Los Angeles Times	53,617	1,044,205
Santa Barbara News Press	14,547	44,078
Santa Maria Times	7,954	17,797
*USA Today**	2,218	1,674,376
Ventura County Star	74,846	96,625

*See Sources and Explanations in the front of the volume.

Television stations and affiliations

Santa Barbara-Santa Maria-San Luis Obispo	51%	KBAK	CBS
Santa Barbara-Santa Maria-San Luis Obispo	51%	KCOY	CBS
Santa Barbara-Santa Maria-San Luis Obispo	51%	KERO	ABC
Santa Barbara-Santa Maria-San Luis Obispo	51%	KEYT	ABC
Santa Barbara-Santa Maria-San Luis Obispo	51%	KGET	NBC
Santa Barbara-Santa Maria-San Luis Obispo	51%	KSBY	NBC
Santa Barbara-Santa Maria-San Luis Obispo	51%	KTAS	Telemundo
Santa Barbara-Santa Maria-San Luis Obispo	51%	KUVI	UPN
Los Angeles	49%	KABC	ABC
Los Angeles	49%	KADY	Independent
Los Angeles	49%	KCAL	Independent
Los Angeles	49%	KCBS	CBS
Los Angeles	49%	KCET	PBS
Los Angeles	49%	KCOP	UPN
Los Angeles	49%	KDOC	Independent
Los Angeles	49%	KHIZ	Independent
Los Angeles	49%	KJLA	Independent
Los Angeles	49%	KLCS	PBS
Los Angeles	49%	KMEX	Univision
Los Angeles	49%	KNBC	NBC
Los Angeles	49%	KOCE	PBS
Los Angeles	49%	KPXN	PAX
Los Angeles	49%	KRCA	PBS
Los Angeles	49%	KSCI	Independent
Los Angeles	49%	KTBN	Independent
Los Angeles	49%	KTLA	WB
Los Angeles	49%	KTTV	FOX
Los Angeles	49%	KVCR	PBS
Los Angeles	49%	KVEA	Telemundo
Los Angeles	49%	KWHY	Independent Spanish

Cable systems and subscribers

Adelphia   111,312
AmeriCable International   4,204
Comcast   24,191

Military installations, September 2001

Channel Islands Air National Guard Station, Oxnard
1,208

Businesses and other major employers

Amgen Holding Inc.; Thousand Oaks; pharmaceuticals
4,791

Ventura County; Ventura; sheriff's office   4,025

Amy Johnson; Thousand Oaks; education aids   2,300

Advanced Data; Thousand Oaks; Internet host services
2,000

Southern California Edison Co.; Ventura; cooperative
apartment manager   2,000

Technicolor Inc.; Camarillo; household video equipment
2,000

Countrywide Home Loans Inc.; Simi Valley; mortgage
bankers   1,900

Ventura County; Ventura; individual and family services
1,800

Conejo Unified School District; Thousand Oaks   1,600

Ventura County; Ventura; public health programs   1,500

Ventura County; Ventura; county government   1,500

California Dept. of Mental Health; Camarillo   1,500

Technicolor Inc.; Camarillo; video tape or disk reproduction
1,500

Kavlico Corp.; Moorpark; electrical transducers   1,390

San Buenaventura Community Memorial Hospital; Ventura
1,260

Blue Cross of California; Thousand Oaks; health
maintenance organization   1,200

Louis Esparza Services Inc.; New Cuyama; farm labor
contractors   1,100

Los Robles Regional Medical Center; Thousand Oaks
1,000

Central Purchasing Inc.; Camarillo; tools and hardware,
mail order   1,000

ITT Industries Inc.; Lompoc; missile tracking:
telemetry/photography   1,000

Lompoc Unified School District; Lompoc   970

Kinko's Graphics Corp.; Ventura; photocopying and
duplicating services   900

Farmers Group Inc.; Simi Valley; insurance agents and
brokers   900

Truck Underwriters Association; Simi Valley; life insurance
900

Adventist Health System/West; Simi Valley; specialty
hospitals   880

Wellpoint Health Networks Inc.; Newbury Park; health
insurance   806

Cardservice International Inc.; Camarillo; survey service
800

Imation Corp; Camarillo; noncommercial recording studio
800

Verizon California Inc.; Thousand Oaks; telephone
equipment   650

Cardservice International Inc.; Simi Valley; office
equipment   650

City of Simi Valley; Simi Valley; government   650

Wellpoint Health Networks Inc.; Camarillo; health
insurance   620

Amgen Inc.; Newbury Park; pharmaceuticals   600

Ventura County Community College District; Moorpark
600

Crown Golf Properties; Ojai; business management
consultant   600

Ojai Valley Inn-Golf Course; Ojai; public golf courses   600

U.S. Bureau of Prisons; Lompoc   519

Baxter Healthcare Corp.; Thousand Oaks; pharmaceuticals
500

Chronicle Publishing Co.; Newbury Park; cable television
500

Rockwell Scientific Co.; Thousand Oaks; aircraft engine
research and development   500

Pacific Bell; Ventura; local telephone communications   500

CHW Central Coast Hospital; Camarillo   500

Technicolor Videocassette Inc.; Camarillo; video tape or disk
reproduction   500

Unisys Corp.; Camarillo; computer systems analysis and
design   500

Ojai Resort Management Inc.; Ojai; resort hotel   500

Oxnard Harvest; Oxnard; fruit and vegetable markets   500

California 25th District

*Northern Los Angeles and San Bernardino Counties; Inyo
and Mono Counties*

The vast 25th stretches from east-central California on the
Nevada border south along the mountains and through Death
Valley before crossing the Mojave Desert and San Bernardino
County into northern Los Angeles County, where it takes in
the tip of the city.

Nearly three-fourths of residents live in Los Angeles
County, though only 5 percent of the county's overall popu-
lace is in the district. The 25th's suburbs and desert are solidly
Republican, including a mix of upper-middle-class residents

and more-conservative working-class whites. About 27 percent of the district is Hispanic, however.

Most of the land in Mono and Inyo Counties, added during redistricting following the 2000 census, is government-owned, and a few bedroom communities' economies rely on tourism, mining, and agriculture. Santa Clarita Valley is suburban, but attracts manufacturing that cannot afford to locate in Los Angeles proper. The 25th's fastest-growing area is the Antelope Valley desert due north of Los Angeles, home to Lancaster and Palmdale.

Economically, the 25th has suffered more from the dwindling aerospace industry than from the 1994 earthquake that collapsed buildings and a freeway. It now faces the challenges of managing and irrigating vast tracts of desert, much of it federally owned, and spurring its economy by attracting more industry and manufacturing jobs.

Major Industry

Tourism, manufacturing, construction, aerospace, military.

Notable

Badwater in Death Valley is the lowest point in the United States at 282 feet below sea level; Baker has a 134-foot-high thermometer.

Election Returns

	Republican		Democratic		Other	
President 2000	108,627	55.5%	81,893	41.9%	5,055	2.6%
House 2002	80,775	65.0%	38,674	31.1%	4,887	3.9%

District Profile

Population   639,087

Total area (square miles)   21,622
   Land area (square miles)   21,484

Population per square mile   29.7

Counties (2000 population)
   Inyo   17,945
   Los Angeles (pt.)   454,942
   Mono   12,853
   San Bernardino (pt.)   153,347

Cities and other areas over 10,000 (2000 population)
   Adelanto   18,130
   Barstow   21,119
   Lake Los Angeles CDP   11,523
   Lancaster (pt.)   52,742
   Los Angeles (pt.)   22,882
   Palmdale   116,670
   Santa Clarita   151,088
   Victorville   64,029

Race and Hispanic or Latino origin*
   White   57.2%
   Black or African American   7.9%
   American Indian or Alaska Native   0.9%
   Asian   3.7%
   Native Hawaiian or other Pacific Islander   0.2%
   Some other race   0.2%
   Hispanic or Latino origin   27.1%
   Two or more races   2.7%

*As percentage of total population.

Ancestry*

Dutch	1.2%	Norwegian	1.2%
English	7.1%	Polish	1.5%
French	2.3%	Scotch-Irish	1.2%
German	10.3%	Scottish	1.5%
Irish	7.6%	Swedish	1.3%
Italian	4.2%	USA/American	3.7%

*As estimated percentage of total population.

Universities and colleges, 2000–2001 enrollment
   Barstow College, Barstow   2,785
   California Institute of the Arts, Valencia   1,212
   College of the Canyons, Santa Clarita   10,528
   Masters College, Santa Clarita   1,448
   Victor Valley College, Victorville   9,221

Newspapers and circulation

	District circulation	Total circulation
Barstow Desert Dispatch	3,258	5,241
Daily Variety, Los Angeles*	6,779	27,269
Los Angeles Daily News	32,059	195,376
Los Angeles La Opinion	1,848	127,108
*Los Angeles Sentinel**	4,120	12,345
Los Angeles Times	27,840	1,044,205
San Bernardino Sun	3,573	72,213
*USA Today**	12,462	1,674,376
Victorville Daily Press	10,988	29,283

*See Sources and Explanations in the front of the volume.

Television stations and affiliations

Los Angeles	86%	KABC	ABC
Los Angeles	86%	KADY	Independent
Los Angeles	86%	KCAL	Independent
Los Angeles	86%	KCBS	CBS
Los Angeles	86%	KCET	PBS
Los Angeles	86%	KCOP	UPN
Los Angeles	86%	KDOC	Independent
Los Angeles	86%	KHIZ	Independent
Los Angeles	86%	KJLA	Independent
Los Angeles	86%	KLCS	PBS
Los Angeles	86%	KMEX	Univision
Los Angeles	86%	KNBC	NBC
Los Angeles	86%	KOCE	PBS
Los Angeles	86%	KPXN	PAX
Los Angeles	86%	KRCA	PBS
Los Angeles	86%	KSCI	Independent
Los Angeles	86%	KTBN	Independent
Los Angeles	86%	KTLA	WB
Los Angeles	86%	KTTV	FOX
Los Angeles	86%	KVCR	PBS
Los Angeles	86%	KVEA	Telemundo
Los Angeles	86%	KWHY	Independent Spanish
Reno, NV	14%	KAME	UPN
Reno, NV	14%	KNPB	PBS
Reno, NV	14%	KOLO	ABC
Reno, NV	14%	KREN	PAX
Reno, NV	14%	KRNV	NBC
Reno, NV	14%	KRXI	FOX
Reno, NV	14%	KTVN	CBS
Reno, NV	14%	KWNV	NBC

Cable systems and subscribers

Adelphia   60,807
Charter   17,187
Lone Pine TV   3,496
Mediacom   825
NPG Cable   7,583
Time Warner   108,049
Total TV of Fort Irwin   3,575
USA Media Group   2,693

Military installations, September 2001

Fort Irwin/National Training Center (Army), Barstow   8,345
Marine Corps Logistics Base, Barstow   3,005
Production Flight Test Instl. Air Force Plant, Palmdale   111

Businesses and other major employers

Lockheed Martin Corp.; Palmdale; aircraft   4,000
Dyncorp; Fort Irwin; electrical work   1,600
Cal-Aerospace Manufacturers Assn.; Tujunga; aircraft   1,550
Bell Helicopter Textron Inc.; Lancaster; aircraft   1,500
Santa Clarita Community College District; Santa Clarita   1,100
Burlington Northern and Santa Fe Railway Co.; Barstow; interurban railways   1,000
Princess Cruise Line; Santa Clarita; oceanliner transportation   900
HR Textron Inc.; Santa Clarita; electrohydraulic valves   800
Verizon Information Services Inc.; Victorville; telephone directory distribution   800
Classic Wire Cut Co.; Santa Clarita; electrical discharge machining   701
Bertelsmann Services Inc.; Valencia; commercial printing   700
Hydrolic Research Crcd.; Santa Clarita; scientific research agency   700
IMC Global Inc.; Trona; borate compounds (natural) mining   673
Victor Valley Community Hospital; Victorville   617
Victor Valley Community College District; Victorville   600
Lancaster Hospital Corp.; Palmdale   550
Northern Indiana Public Service Co.; Wanatah; digital panel meters   500
Gothic Landscaping Inc.; Valencia; landscape services   500
Roadway Express Inc.; Adelanto; contract haulers   500
Raytheon Technical Services Co.;   Fort Irwin; electrical equipment repair services   500
Constellation Energy Group Inc.; Victorville; electric power distribution   500
Lantz Security Systems Inc.; Lancaster; security guard service   500

California 26th District

Northeastern Los Angeles suburbs

Set in the foothills of the San Gabriel Mountains, the 26th is a mix of Los Angeles bedroom communities and the mountainous Angeles National Forest, which makes up its northern half. The commuter-heavy district takes in middle- to upper-class suburbs, many of which have retained their identities and quaint downtowns. *(See map p. 121.)*

The district includes wealthy, Republican communities surrounding Pasadena, such as La Canada Flintridge and San Marino, and other Los Angeles County cities such as Arcadia, Glendora, Monrovia, and San Dimas. Outside La Canada Flintridge is NASA's Jet Propulsion Laboratory, which contributes to the area's high-tech flavor along with the California Institute of Technology in Pasadena (in the 29th District) and engineering firms in Monrovia. Many of the 26th's residents commute to work in downtown Los Angeles or have high-tech manufacturing jobs just outside the district.

In its chunk of San Bernardino County, where orchard country has given way to rapidly developing suburbs, the district includes the Inland Valley suburbs of Rancho Cucamonga, Upland, and Montclair. Rapid development has brought young, wealthy fiscally minded Republicans to town–not unlike Orange County to the south. The valley is populated by service employers such as corporate call centers and technology groups. Most other industry is confined to small defense subcontractors and service industries, though the area has seen some growth in trade-related import and export businesses.

Like many Los Angeles suburbanites, residents here tend to be socially moderate and economically conservative. The district went for George W. Bush in the 2000 presidential contest by nearly 10 points. While not as diverse as most of its neighbors, the district is one-fourth Hispanic.

Major Industry

Service, manufacturing, health care, biotechnology.

Notable

Santa Anita Park thoroughbred racetrack is in Arcadia; the Huntington Library, a museum and garden in San Marino, has Thomas Gainsborough's painting *The Blue Boy* and a Gutenberg Bible in its collection.

Election Returns

	Republican		Democratic		Other	
President 2000	127,468	53.2%	105,023	43.8%	7,044	2.9%
House 2002	95,360	63.8%	50,081	33.5%	4,089	2.7%

District Profile

Population   639,088

Total area (square miles)   754
   Land area (square miles)   751

Population per square mile   851

Counties (2000 population)
   Los Angeles (pt.)   388,032
   San Bernardino (pt.)   251,056

Cities and other areas over 10,000 (2000 population)
   Arcadia   53,054
   Claremont   33,998
   East San Gabriel CDP (pt.)   13,626
   Glendora   49,415
   La Canada Flintridge   20,318
   La Crescenta-Montrose CDP   18,532

La Verne   31,638
Monrovia   36,929
Montclair   33,049
Rancho Cucamonga   127,743
San Dimas   34,980
San Marino   12,945
Sierra Madre   10,578
Upland   68,393
Walnut   30,004

Race and Hispanic or Latino origin*

White   52.7%
Black or African American   4.4%
American Indian or Alaska Native   0.3%
Asian   15.2%
Native Hawaiian or other Pacific Islander   0.1%
Some other race   0.2%
Hispanic or Latino origin   24.4%
Two or more races   2.6%

*As percentage of total population.

Ancestry*

Dutch 1.2%	Norwegian 1.2%
English 7.5%	Polish 1.4%
French 2.1%	Scotch-Irish 1.2%
German 9.6%	Scottish 1.7%
Irish 6.9%	Swedish 1.3%
Italian 4.3%	USA/American 2.8%

*As estimated percentage of total population.

Universities and colleges, 2000–2001 enrollment

Chaffey Community College, Rancho Cucamonga   15,220
Citrus College, Glendora   11,486
Claremont Graduate University, Claremont   1,969
Claremont McKenna College, Claremont   1,003
Claremont School of Theology, Claremont   490
Harvey Mudd College, Claremont   719
Life Bible College, San Dimas   488
Mt. San Antonio College, Walnut   28,329
Pitzer College, Claremont   924
Pomona College, Claremont   1,574
Scripps College, Claremont   800
University of Laverne, Laverne   6,603

Newspapers and circulation

	District circulation	Total circulation
Daily Variety, Los Angeles*	2,099	27,269
Inland Valley Daily Bulletin	29,785	65,184
Los Angeles Daily News	2,528	195,376
Los Angeles La Opinion	1,366	127,108
Los Angeles Sentinel*	1,276	12,345
Los Angeles Times	46,511	1,044,205
Pasadena Star-News	9,848	34,895
San Bernardino Sun	1,600	72,213
San Gabriel Valley Tribune	12,555	48,476
USA Today*	3,465	1,674,376

*See Sources and Explanations in the front of the volume.

Television stations and affiliations

Los Angeles	100%	KABC	ABC
Los Angeles	100%	KADY	Independent
Los Angeles	100%	KCAL	Independent
Los Angeles	100%	KCBS	CBS
Los Angeles	100%	KCET	PBS
Los Angeles	100%	KCOP	UPN
Los Angeles	100%	KDOC	Independent
Los Angeles	100%	KHIZ	Independent
Los Angeles	100%	KJLA	Independent
Los Angeles	100%	KLCS	PBS
Los Angeles	100%	KMEX	Univision
Los Angeles	100%	KNBC	NBC
Los Angeles	100%	KOCE	PBS
Los Angeles	100%	KPXN	PAX
Los Angeles	100%	KRCA	PBS
Los Angeles	100%	KSCI	Independent
Los Angeles	100%	KTBN	Independent
Los Angeles	100%	KTLA	WB
Los Angeles	100%	KTTV	FOX
Los Angeles	100%	KVCR	PBS
Los Angeles	100%	KVEA	Telemundo
Los Angeles	100%	KWHY	Independent Spanish

Cable systems and subscribers

Adelphia   68,589
Charter   28,359
Time Warner   2,531

Businesses and other major employers

Mt. San Antonio Community College District; Walnut   4,000
4evrnew Inc.; Monrovia; computer maintenance services   3,000
Ashley Furniture Industries Inc.; Glendora; furniture stores   2,500
Los Angeles County; La Canada Flintridge; medical and surgical hospital   2,200
Preferred Framing Inc.; Rancho Cucamonga; framing contractor   1,800
San Antonio Community Hospital; Upland   1,750
Chaffey Community College District; Rancho Cucamonga   1,385
Medquist Inc.; Monrovia; paralegal service   1,200
University of La Verne; La Verne   985
Methodist Hospital of Southern California; Arcadia   933
Vons Companies Inc.; Arcadia; supermarkets   900
Scripto-Tokai Corp.; Rancho Cucamonga; cigarette lighters   870
Automatic Data Processing Inc.; San Dimas; data processing   850
Claremont Graduate University; Claremont   654
Alta Loma School District; Alta Loma   623
Citrus Community College District; Glendora   615
Encompass Services Corp.; Glendora; electrical work   611
Encompass Electrical Technologies Inc.; San Dimas; electrical work   611
Monrovia Nursery Co.; Azusa; nursery stock   567
ATC Distribution Group Inc.; Rancho Cucamonga; rebuilding engines and transmissions   550

Foothill Hospital; Glendora   546

Morrow-Meadows Corp.; Walnut; electrical contractor 520

Kaiser Foundation Hospitals; Pasadena   500

Frito-Lay Inc.; Rancho Cucamonga; potato chips and snacks   500

Southern California Edison Co.; Rancho Cucamonga; electric power distribution   500

U.S. Data Source; Rancho Cucamonga; data processing 500

Ormco Corp.; Glendora; dental equipment   500

Southern California Metropolitan Water District; La Verne   500

California 27th District

Part of the San Fernando Valley; part of Burbank

While most of the 27th is in Los Angeles, few of the district's residents identify themselves as "Angelenos." Instead, they see themselves as part of the region's fast-growing communities: the Van Nuys, Encino, and Sherman Oaks areas of Los Angeles in the San Fernando Valley north of the central city. *(See map p. 121.)*

The Valley—primarily the 27th and 28th districts—was behind a failed ballot measure in 2002 to secede from the rest of the city amid complaints that too much of its taxes went over the mountains to city services in central Los Angeles. Though the measure was initiated by the Valley's traditional white, middle- to upper-class voters, the 27th's suburban havens have been transformed by immigrants and no longer are dominated by that group. The district, with whites making up 45 percent of the residents and Hispanics 36 percent, has seen an explosion of Asian immigrants, particularly from India and Pakistan, who have added to the district's working-class flavor.

The flat, gridlike streets of the 27th hold the Burbank and Van Nuys airports, as well as several colleges, including California State University Northridge. Reservoirs in the northwest corner provide water to more than 10 million Los Angeles residents.

While many San Fernando Valley residents worry about traffic congestion on their commutes to downtown or west Los Angeles, quality-of-life issues including health care and air quality are major concerns as well. Immigration is one among several factors that have made the district solidly Democratic—it gave Democrat Al Gore 60.3 percent of the vote in the 2000 presidential election.

Major Industry

Biotechnology, service.

Notable

The San Fernando Valley is known as the pornography capital of the world.

Election Returns

	Republican		Democratic		Other	
President 2000	70,557	36.3%	117,120	60.3%	6,568	3.4%
House 2002	48,996	38%	79,815	62%		

District Profile

Population   639,088

Total area (square miles)   151
   Land area (square miles)   150

Population per square mile   4,239.5

Counties (2000 population)
   Los Angeles (pt.)   639,088

Cities and other areas over 10,000 (2000 population)
   Burbank (pt.)   45,436
   Los Angeles (pt.)   591,573

Race and Hispanic or Latino origin*
   White   44.9%
   Black or African American   4.5%
   American Indian or Alaska Native   0.3%
   Asian   10.5%
   Native Hawaiian or other Pacific Islander   0.1%
   Some other race   0.2%
   Hispanic or Latino origin   36.5%
   Two or more races   3.1%

As percentage of total population.

Ancestry*

Arab-Misc.	1.1%	Italian	3.4%
English	4.6%	Polish	1.7%
French	1.7%	Russian	2.4%
German	6.3%	USA/American	2.9%
Irish	5.0%		

As estimated percentage of total population.

Universities and colleges, 2000–2001 enrollment
   California State University, Northridge   29,066
   ITT Technical Institute, Sylmar   591
   Los Angeles Pierce College, Woodland Hills   16,111
   Woodbury University, Burbank   1,342

Newspapers and circulation

	District circulation	Total circulation
Los Angeles Daily News	48,280	195,376
Los Angeles La Opinion	4,493	127,108
Los Angeles Times	47,166	1,044,205

Television stations and affiliations

Los Angeles	100%	KABC	ABC
Los Angeles	100%	KADY	Independent
Los Angeles	100%	KCAL	Independent
Los Angeles	100%	KCBS	CBS
Los Angeles	100%	KCET	PBS
Los Angeles	100%	KCOP	UPN
Los Angeles	100%	KDOC	Independent
Los Angeles	100%	KHIZ	Independent
Los Angeles	100%	KJLA	Independent
Los Angeles	100%	KLCS	PBS
Los Angeles	100%	KMEX	Univision
Los Angeles	100%	KNBC	NBC
Los Angeles	100%	KOCE	PBS
Los Angeles	100%	KPXN	PAX
Los Angeles	100%	KRCA	PBS

LOS ANGELES, SAN DIEGO AREAS

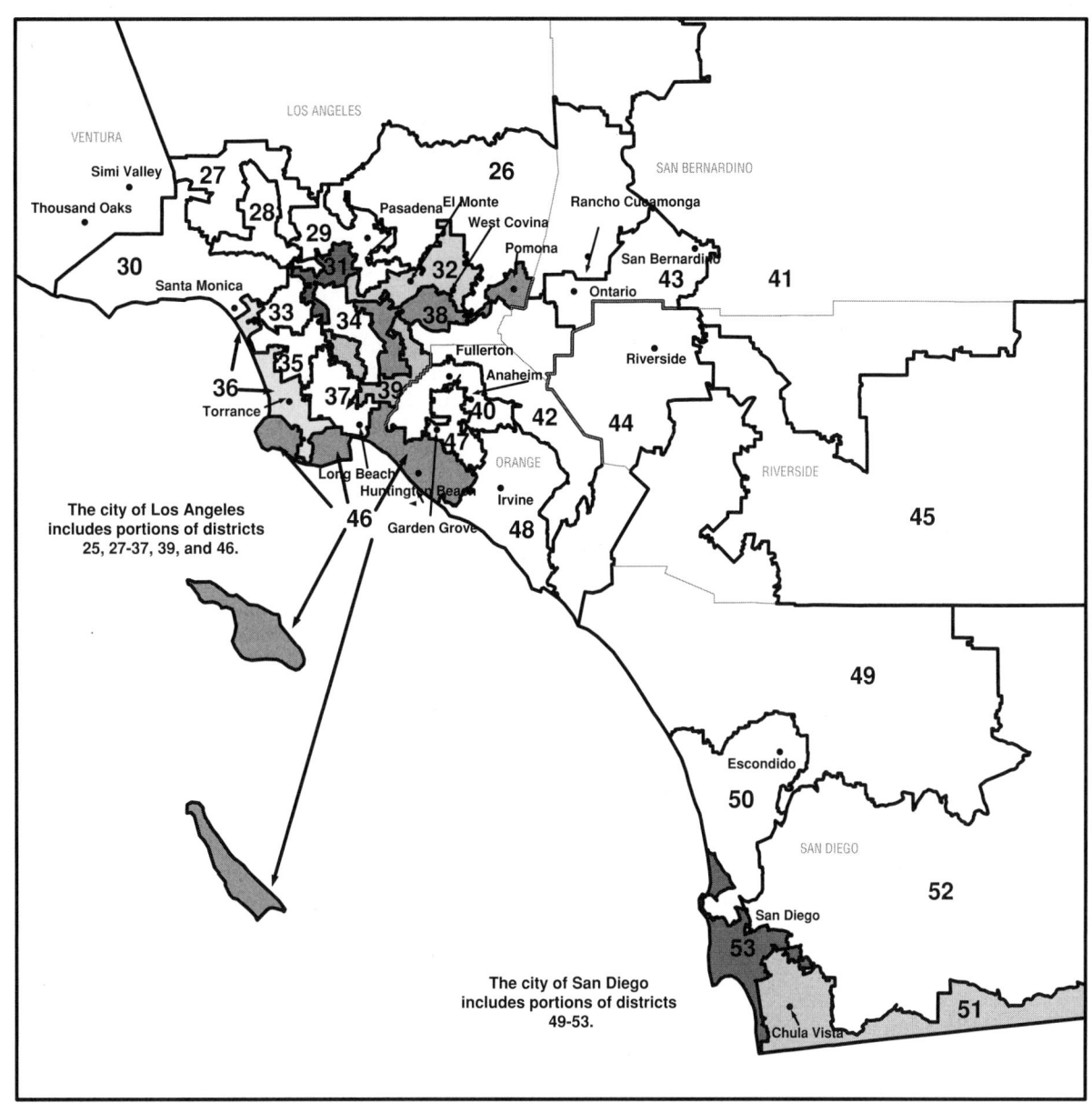

The city of Los Angeles includes portions of districts 25, 27-37, 39, and 46.

The city of San Diego includes portions of districts 49-53.

Los Angeles	100%	KSCI	Independent
Los Angeles	100%	KTBN	Independent
Los Angeles	100%	KTLA	WB
Los Angeles	100%	KTTV	FOX
Los Angeles	100%	KVCR	PBS
Los Angeles	100%	KVEA	Telemundo
Los Angeles	100%	KWHY	Independent Spanish

Cable systems and subscribers
Time Warner*   2,200

See Sources and Explanations in the front of the volume.

Military installations, September 2001
Sepulveda National Guard Station, Van Nuys   132

Businesses and other major employers
Time Warner Entertainment Co.; Burbank; motion picture and video production   4,000
California State University; Northridge   2,713
JBL Inc.; Northridge; household audio equipment   2,000
Valley Care Olive View UCLA Medical Center; Sylmar   2,000
Northridge Hospital Medical Center; Northridge   1,400
Valley Presbyterian Hospital; Van Nuys   1,100
Providence St. Joseph Medical Center; Mission Hills   1,000
Superior Industries International Inc.; Van Nuys; motor vehicle parts/accessories   1,000
U.S. Veterans Hospital; North Hills   900
AMISUB of California Inc.; Tarzana; medical and surgical hospital   900
Washington Mutual Bank; Granada Hills; federal savings and loan associations   800
Superior Astechnology Inc.; Van Nuys; holding companies, nec   800
Mel Bernie and Co.; Burbank; costume jewelry   800
Pacesetter Inc.; Sylmar; electromedical equipment   725
Media News Group; Woodland Hills; newspaper   700
Accessory Plating Inc.; Burbank; plating of metals, formed products   700
Interviewing Service of America Inc.; Van Nuys; market analysis: business/economic research   680
Harman-Becker Automotive Systems Inc.; Northridge; amplifiers   600
Anthony Inc.; Sylmar; glass, metal, plastic containers   600
Disney Enterprises Inc.; Burbank; variety store merchandise   600
United Parcel Service Inc.; Sylmar; parcel delivery   550
Staff Assistance Inc.; Sepulveda; nurses' registry   550
International Philanthropic Hospital Foundation; Granada Hills   520
Medtronic Minimed Inc.; Northridge; medical instruments: blood, bone work   515
American Landscape Inc.; Canoga Park; landscape services   500
Los Angeles Community College District; Sylmar   500
Health Enterprises Life Long Plan Inc.; Tarzana; home health care services   500
Pierce College Foundation; Woodland Hills; civic and social associations   500

Easton Sports Inc.; Van Nuys; sporting and recreation goods   500
U.S. Dept. of Commerce; Van Nuys   500
Hydro-Aire Inc.; Burbank; aircraft parts, equipment   500
American Automobile Assn. Inc.; Burbank; automobile owners' association   500

California 28th District
Part of the San Fernando Valley

The 28th starts in the San Fernando Valley north of Los Angeles, where it takes in the small city of San Fernando and includes the Los Angeles communities of Pacoima, Arleta, Panorama City, North Hollywood, and parts of Van Nuys. The southern border follows in part famed Mulholland Drive, taking in parts of Encino and Sherman Oaks, and Studio City in the Hollywood Hills north of Beverly Hills. *(See map p. 121.)*

Once composed of predominately white, suburban Los Angeles communities, the area has attracted large numbers of Hispanics, who made up 55.6 percent of the district's population in the 2000 census. That majority is a major contributor to the Democratic voting tendency in the district, which gave Democrat Al Gore 72.9 percent of the vote in the 2000 presidential election.

The 28th's thriving commercial district, centered on financial services, is just south of Route 101, along Ventura Boulevard, where bank branch offices in office towers compete with miles of fast-food outlets, trendy restaurants, and strip malls. It passes by the Sherman Oaks Galleria, home of the Valley Girl and recently renovated with businesses and upscale restaurants. A number of movies and TV shows have been filmed at the CBS Studio Center in Studio City, including *Hill Street Blues, Roseanne,* and *Seinfeld.*

Defense industry closures and the 1994 Northridge earthquake hit the district hard. It has stayed afloat, however, fueled by the technology and entertainment industries and the growth of service industries that are increasingly driven by new immigrants. The district has some manufacturing plants, but Van Nuys, which lost a General Motors plant in 1992, got a boost from a new retail center and industrial park that opened on the old GM site in 2000.

Major Industry
Service, entertainment, manufacturing, health care.

Notable
The Academy of Television Arts and Sciences, which presents the annual Emmy Awards, is based in North Hollywood; actors Robert Redford and Marilyn Monroe attended Van Nuys High School; Rock and Roll Hall of Famer Ritchie Valens ("La Bamba") was a native of Pacoima.

Election Returns

	Republican		Democratic		Other	
President 2000	36,762	23.9%	112,332	72.9%	5,021	3.3%
House 2002	23,926	23.2%	73,771	71.4%	5,629	5.4%

District Profile

Population   639,088

Total area (square miles)   77
    Land area (square miles)   77

Population per square mile   8,280.1

Counties (2000 population)
    Los Angeles (pt.)   639,087

Cities and other areas over 10,000 (2000 population)
    Los Angeles (pt.)   615,523
    San Fernando   23,564

Race and Hispanic or Latino origin*
    White   31.4%
    Black or African American   4.1%
    American Indian or Alaska Native   0.2%
    Asian   5.9%
    Native Hawaiian or other Pacific Islander   0.1%
    Some other race   0.2%
    Hispanic or Latino origin   55.6%
    Two or more races   2.4%

*As percentage of total population.

Ancestry*

English	2.9%	Italian	2.4%
French	1.1%	Polish	1.5%
German	3.7%	Russian	2.7%
Irish	3.2%	USA/American	2.4%

*As estimated percentage of total population.

Universities and colleges, 2000–2001 enrollment
    Concorde Career Institute, North Hollywood   444
    Los Angeles Mission College, San Fernando   6,782
    Los Angeles Valley College, Van Nuys   17,393
    Modern Technology College, North Hollywood   355
    Phillips Graduate Institute, Encino   238

Newspapers and circulation

	District circulation	Total circulation
Los Angeles Daily News	30,644	195,376
Los Angeles La Opinion	6,241	127,108
Los Angeles Times	44,153	1,044,205

Television stations and affiliations

Los Angeles	100%	KABC	ABC
Los Angeles	100%	KADY	Independent
Los Angeles	100%	KCAL	Independent
Los Angeles	100%	KCBS	CBS
Los Angeles	100%	KCET	PBS
Los Angeles	100%	KCOP	UPN
Los Angeles	100%	KDOC	Independent
Los Angeles	100%	KHIZ	Independent
Los Angeles	100%	KJLA	Independent
Los Angeles	100%	KLCS	PBS
Los Angeles	100%	KMEX	Univision
Los Angeles	100%	KNBC	NBC
Los Angeles	100%	KOCE	PBS
Los Angeles	100%	KPXN	PAX
Los Angeles	100%	KRCA	PBS
Los Angeles	100%	KSCI	Independent
Los Angeles	100%	KTBN	Independent
Los Angeles	100%	KTLA	WB
Los Angeles	100%	KTTV	FOX
Los Angeles	100%	KVCR	PBS
Los Angeles	100%	KVEA	Telemundo
Los Angeles	100%	KWHY	Independent Spanish

Cable systems and subscribers
    Comcast   6,606
    Time Warner*   1,129

*See Sources and Explanations in the front of the volume.

Businesses and other major employers
    Universal City Studios Inc.; Universal City; motion picture production and distribution   7,000
    W. F. Cinema Holdings; Encino; motion picture theaters   2,000
    Amblin Entertainment Inc.; Universal City; motion picture production   2,000
    Quest Diagnostics Clinical Laboratories Inc.; Van Nuys; medical laboratories   1,200
    Kaiser Foundation Hospitals; Panorama City   1,000
    City of Los Angeles; Sun Valley; utility regulation   900
    Price Pfister Inc.; Pacoima; plumbers' brass goods   800
    Kwikset Corp.; Pacoima; keys, locks, related hardware   700
    Los Angeles Unified School District Inc.; Van Nuys   692
    Equilon Enterprises; North Hollywood; petroleum refining   560
    Sierracin Corp.; Sylmar; windshields   525
    Pacifica of Valley Corp.; Sun Valley; medical and surgical hospital   525
    Vast Resources Inc.; San Fernando; publishing and licensing performance rights   500
    Western Security Inc.; Van Nuys; security protective devices   500

California 29th District

Glendale; Pasadena; Alhambra; part of Burbank

Set in the foothills of the San Gabriel Mountains, the 29th includes the Los Angeles suburbs of Glendale, Pasadena, Alhambra, and part of Burbank. Over the years, immigration and the growing nearby Hollywood economy have transformed once-WASPish neighborhoods, giving the district a Democratic lean. *(See map p. 121.)*

The 29th is home to few movie stars, but many of those whose names appear farther down in movie credits live here. While a high-tech community has sprung up around the California Institute of Technology and a number of colleges, the district is primarily residential.

The area includes a wide mix of ethnicities. Monterey Park (shared with the 32nd) is upper-middle-class and known as "Little Taipei" for its Taiwanese and other Asian immigrants. Glendale is home to about 75,000 Armenians, the largest such community outside of Armenia. Alhambra is heavily Hispanic and Asian, and upscale San Gabriel has a strong Italian community. Overall the district is about one-fourth Asian and one-fourth Hispanic. About 60 different languages are spoken in Glendale's public schools.

Though in the Los Angeles area, Glendale and Pasadena, a lush former resort town, have their separate downtowns.

Television and movie production studios drive the economy in Burbank. Redeveloping landfills is a challenge in Monterey Park, while residents of South Pasadena and Alhambra argue over whether to extend Interstate 710 through their cities.

Major Industry

Entertainment, technology, engineering.

Notable

The Rose Bowl is in Pasadena, which hosts the Tournament of Roses Parade; Burbank is home to the studios of Warner Bros., Disney, and NBC; Griffith Park is one of the nation's largest municipal parks.

Election Returns

	Republican		Democratic		Other	
President 2000	79,210	38.4%	119,396	57.9%	7,671	3.7%
House 2002	40,616	33.4%	76,036	62.6%	4,889	4%

District Profile

Population   639,088

Total area (square miles)   101
   Land area (square miles)   101

Population per square mile   6,302.3

Counties (2000 population)
   Los Angeles (pt.)   639,088

Cities and other areas over 10,000 (2000 population)
   Alhambra   85,804
   Altadena CDP (pt.)   38,306
   Burbank (pt.)   54,880
   Glendale   194,973
   Monterey Park (pt.)   24,922
   Pasadena   133,936
   San Gabriel   39,804
   South Pasadena   24,292
   Temple City   33,377

Race and Hispanic or Latino origin*
   White   39.1%
   Black or African American   5.9%
   American Indian or Alaska Native   0.2%
   Asian   23.7%
   Native Hawaiian or other Pacific Islander   0.1%
   Some other race   0.2%
   Hispanic or Latino origin   26.1%
   Two or more races   4.7%

*As percentage of total population.

Ancestry*
Arab-Misc. 1.2%	Irish 4.4%
English 4.7%	Italian 2.7%
French 1.3%	Scottish 1.1%
German 5.3%	USA/American 1.7%

*As estimated percentage of total population.

Universities and colleges, 2000–2001 enrollment
   American Academy of Dramatic Arts-West, Pasadena   215
   Art Center College of Design, Pasadena   1,459
   California Institute of Technology, Pasadena   1,968
   California School of Professional Psychology, Alhambra   616
   Fuller Theological Seminary, Pasadena   2,475
   Glendale Community College, Glendale   15,596
   Mt. Sierra College, Pasadena   734
   Pacific Oaks College, Pasadena   824
   Pasadena City College, Pasadena   22,948
   Southern California School of Culinary Art, South Pasadena   681

Newspapers and circulation

	District circulation	Total circulation
Los Angeles Daily News	12,343	195,376
Los Angeles La Opinion	3,279	127,108
Los Angeles Times	55,142	1,044,205
Pasadena Star-News	20,296	34,895

Television stations and affiliations
Los Angeles	100%	KABC	ABC
Los Angeles	100%	KADY	Independent
Los Angeles	100%	KCAL	Independent
Los Angeles	100%	KCBS	CBS
Los Angeles	100%	KCET	PBS
Los Angeles	100%	KCOP	UPN
Los Angeles	100%	KDOC	Independent
Los Angeles	100%	KHIZ	Independent
Los Angeles	100%	KJLA	Independent
Los Angeles	100%	KLCS	PBS
Los Angeles	100%	KMEX	Univision
Los Angeles	100%	KNBC	NBC
Los Angeles	100%	KOCE	PBS
Los Angeles	100%	KPXN	PAX
Los Angeles	100%	KRCA	PBS
Los Angeles	100%	KSCI	Independent
Los Angeles	100%	KTBN	Independent
Los Angeles	100%	KTLA	WB
Los Angeles	100%	KTTV	FOX
Los Angeles	100%	KVCR	PBS
Los Angeles	100%	KVEA	Telemundo
Los Angeles	100%	KWHY	Independent Spanish

Cable systems and subscribers
   Charter   120,760
   Time Warner   5,013

Businesses and other major employers
   Disney Enterprises Inc.; Burbank; motion picture production and distribution   6,000
   Walt Disney Co.; Burbank; television broadcasting stations   6,000
   Prolease Pacific Inc. Monterey Park; payroll accounting service   5,500
   Kaiser Foundation Hospitals; Pasadena   5,000
   Inter-Con Security Systems Inc.; Pasadena; guard services   4,500
   MWH Global Inc.; Pasadena; engineering services   3,500
   U.S. Postal Service; Pasadena   3,100
   Los Angeles County; Alhambra; water supply   3,000
   Pasadena Hospital; Pasadena   2,100
   California Institute of Technology; Pasadena   2,000
   Earthlink Inc.; Pasadena; data processing   2,000

California Institute of Technology; Pasadena   2,000

Parsons Corp.; Pasadena; chemical plant and refinery construction   2,000

Parsons International-Cayman Islands; Pasadena; engineering services   2,000

Providence Health System-Southern California Hospital; Burbank   1,700

Pasadena Area Community College District; Pasadena   1,600

Diversified Maintenance Services Inc.; South Pasadena; building maintenance   1,500

UNI-Health Hospital; Glendale   1,500

Garfield Rehabilitation; Monterey Park; management services   1,500

Tenet Healthcare Corp. Hospital; Monterey Park   1,500

Glendale Adventist Medical Center Inc.; Glendale   1,350

Glendale Memorial Hospital and Health Center; Glendale   1,245

IndyMac Bank; Pasadena; federal savings and loan associations   1,217

Parsons Infrastructure and Technology Group Inc.; Pasadena; engineering services   1,200

Nestle USA Inc.; Glendale; evaporated milk   1,200

Glendale Community College District; Glendale   1,180

Sega Gameworks; Glendale; coin-operated amusement devices   1,028

Walt Disney Imagineering; Glendale; design services   1,011

Baxter Healthcare Corp.; Los Angeles; pharmaceuticals   1,000

DreamWorks; Glendale; motion picture production   1,000

Baxter Healthcare Corp.; Glendale; pharmaceuticals   1,000

Warner Bros. (Transatlantic) Inc.; Burbank; motion picture distribution   1,000

Forest Lawn Mortuary; Glendale; funeral home   920

San Gabriel Valley Medical Center; San Gabriel   850

WCO Parent Corp.; Burbank; resort hotel   748

Air Conditioning Co.; Glendale; process piping contractor   700

International Business Machines Corp.; Glendale; minicomputers   700

Columbia Pictures Industries Inc.; Burbank; motion picture production and distribution   700

Fremont Industrial Indemnity Co.; Glendale; workers' compensation insurance   650

Avon Products Inc.; Pasadena; catalog, mail-order   600

Interstate Brands West Corp.; Glendale; breads and cakes   600

Go.com; Burbank; online service providers   600

Alhambra Hospital Medical Center LP; Alhambra   580

Fuller Theological Seminary; Pasadena   500

Pasadena; Pasadena; city management   500

Ritz-Carlton Hotel Co.; Pasadena hotels   500

Lockheed Martin Corp.; Pasadena; search and navigation equipment   500

Ticketmaster Corp.; Pasadena; Internet connectivity services   500

Disney Store Inc.; Glendale; family clothing stores   500

PPG Industries Inc.; Glendale; chemicals and allied products   500

Teleinterpreters Inc.; Glendale; translation services   500

City of Glendale; Glendale; city management   500

Red Horizon Productions Inc.; Burbank; motion picture production   500

Union Pacific Corp.; Monterey Park; administrative management   500

Pacific Bell; Alhambra; local telephone communications   500

California 30th District

West Los Angeles County — Santa Monica, West Hollywood

Boasting such glamorous locales as Beverly Hills, Malibu, Bel Air, and Pacific Palisades, there are few places in the 30th that have not been immortalized by a television show or movie. The district is home to a large Jewish population, the University of California, Los Angeles, and the activist gay community of West Hollywood. *(See map p. 121.)*

Eclectic, wealthy, and Democratic describe many of the district's residents. Members of England's royal family have stayed at the Regent Beverly Wilshire hotel at the southern end of the exclusive Rodeo Drive shopping strip, and thousands annually crowd the streets of West Hollywood to witness the gay and lesbian pride parade. The district votes overwhelmingly Democratic in elections at all levels.

The district stretches north from the Santa Monica and Malibu beaches across the Santa Monica Mountains to Calabasas and Hidden Hills on the north side of the range.

The 30th is about three-fourths white and the economy is overwhelmingly white-collar. Entertainment executives lunch with financial advisers and real estate developers, and tourism brings in large amounts of money. Thousands flock annually to the legendary Grauman's Chinese Theater, where they can compare their handprints and footprints to those of the stars, or see Whoopi Goldberg's braids, preserved in cement. The area's seven medical centers make health care an important economic engine.

Major Industry
Entertainment, higher education, health care.

Notable
Hugh Hefner's Playboy Mansion is where prominent Democrats, including presidential candidates Gary Hart, Jerry Brown, and Jesse Jackson, have held fundraisers; Santa Monica Pier, an amusement park that stretches out into the ocean, was built in 1909 and features an antique carousel.

Election Returns

	Republican		Democratic		Other	
President 2000	81,336	27.8%	199,282	68.2%	11,464	3.9%
House 2002	54,989	29.6%	130,604	70.4%		

District Profile

Population   639,088

Total area (square miles)   387
   Land area (square miles)   285

Population per square mile   2,238.3

Counties (2000 population)
Los Angeles (pt.)   639,088

Cities and other areas over 10,000 (2000 population)
Agoura Hills   20,537
Beverly Hills   33,784
Calabasas   20,033
Los Angeles (pt.)   399,622
Malibu   12,575
Santa Monica   84,084
West Hollywood   35,716

Race and Hispanic or Latino origin*
White   76.4%
Black or African American   2.6%
American Indian or Alaska Native   0.2%
Asian   8.8%
Native Hawaiian or other Pacific Islander   0.1%
Some other race   0.3%
Hispanic or Latino origin   8.3%
Two or more races   3.3%

*As percentage of total population.

Ancestry*
English   6.8%   Polish   3.7%
French   2.3%   Russian   6.7%
German   8.3%   Scottish   1.5%
Hungarian   1.2%   Swedish   1.3%
Irish   6.8%   USA/American   3.7%
Italian   4.4%

*As estimated percentage of total population.

Universities and colleges, 2000–2001 enrollment
American Intercontinental University, Los Angeles   671
Art Institute of Los Angeles, Santa Monica   1,185
Emperors College of Traditional Oriental Medicine, Santa Monica   334
Lee College, West Hills   245
Mount St. Mary's College, Los Angeles   1,973
Pepperdine University, Malibu   7,476
Santa Monica College, Santa Monica   27,868
University of California, Los Angeles   36,890

Newspapers and circulation

	District circulation	Total circulation
Daily Variety, Los Angeles*	1,657	27,269
Los Angeles Daily News	21,580	195,376
Los Angeles La Opinion	2,648	127,108
Los Angeles Times	108,337	1,044,205
USA Today *	2,735	1,674,376
Ventura County Star	1,385	96,625

*See Sources and Explanations in the front of the volume.

Television stations and affiliations
Los Angeles	100%	KABC	ABC
Los Angeles	100%	KADY	Independent
Los Angeles	100%	KCAL	Independent
Los Angeles	100%	KCBS	CBS
Los Angeles	100%	KCET	PBS
Los Angeles	100%	KCOP	UPN
Los Angeles	100%	KDOC	Independent
Los Angeles	100%	KHIZ	Independent
Los Angeles	100%	KJLA	Independent
Los Angeles	100%	KLCS	PBS
Los Angeles	100%	KMEX	Univision
Los Angeles	100%	KNBC	NBC
Los Angeles	100%	KOCE	PBS
Los Angeles	100%	KPXN	PAX
Los Angeles	100%	KRCA	PBS
Los Angeles	100%	KSCI	Independent
Los Angeles	100%	KTBN	Independent
Los Angeles	100%	KTLA	WB
Los Angeles	100%	KTTV	FOX
Los Angeles	100%	KVCR	PBS
Los Angeles	100%	KVEA	Telemundo
Los Angeles	100%	KWHY	Independent Spanish

Cable systems and subscribers
Adelphia*   65,914

*See Sources and Explanations in the front of the volume.

Businesses and other major employers
Cedars-Sinai Medical Center; Los Angeles   6,000
Walt Disney Co.; Pacific Palisades; television broadcasting stations   6,000
Cedars-Sinai Medical Center; Los Angeles   5,500
Edison International; Los Angeles; telephone communication   5,000
Medical Management Consultants Inc.; Los Angeles; hospital/health services consultant   5,000
Boeing Co.; Canoga Park; aircraft   5,000
Magna Entertainment Corp.; Santa Monica; horse race track   4,376
U.S. Veterans Affairs Dept.; Los Angeles   4,000
University of California; Los Angeles   3,200
Premier ASP; Beverly Hills; placement agencies   3,200
Blue Cross of California; Woodland Hills; health maintenance organization   2,543
CBS Broadcasting Inc.; Los Angeles; television broadcasting stations   2,500
Career Group Inc.; Los Angeles; executive placement   2,035
20th Century Fox Home Entertainment Inc.; Beverly Hills; motion picture production and distribution   2,000
21st Century Insurance Group; Woodland Hills; automobile insurance   2,000
Litton Systems Inc.; Woodland Hills; radio/TV transmitting apparatus   2,000
Peninsula Group; Beverly Hills; hotel or motel management   1,979
Sports Club Co.; Los Angeles; health club   1,900
University of California; Los Angeles research institute   1,500
J. Paul Getty Trust Inc.; Los Angeles; museums and art galleries   1,431
Herbalife International of America Inc.; Los Angeles; vitamins and minerals   1,374
Santa Monica Human Services; Santa Monica   1,300
Litton Systems Inc.; Agoura Hills; inertial guidance systems   1,200
Kaiser Foundation Hospitals; Woodland Hills   1,200
University of California Medical Center; Santa Monica   1,111
St. John's Health Center; Santa Monica   1,100

Santa Monica Comunity College District; Santa Monica 1,100

Countrywide Credit Industries Inc.; Calabasas; mortgage bankers 1,100

Prudential Financial; Woodland Hills; insurance agents 1,100

Scripps Networks Inc.; Los Angeles; cable television 1,000

Twentieth Century-Fox TV International Inc.; Los Angeles; television broadcasting stations 1,000

SunAmerica Inc.; Los Angeles; life insurance 1,000

Pepperdine University; Malibu 1,000

Rand Corp.; Santa Monica; research institute 1,000

MGM Studios Inc.; Santa Monica; film developing and printing 1,000

Countrywide Home Loans Inc.; Calabasas; mortgage bankers 1,000

Countrywide Home Loans Inc.; Canoga Park; mortgage bankers 1,000

West Hills Hospital and Medical Center; Canoga Park 1,000

Northrop Grumman Corp.; Woodland Hills; airplanes 1,000

St. Jude Medical Inc.; Woodland Hills; cardiac pacemaker 1,000

Century Plaza Hotel Co.; Los Angeles; hotels 970

Primedia Inc.; Los Angeles; magazine publishing 900

Princess Cruise Line; Los Angeles; cruise line 900

GWI Inc.; Los Angeles; signs and advertising specialties 900

Sanford; Santa Monica; mechanical pencils and pencil parts 900

UCLA Neuropsychiatric Institute; Los Angeles 800

Specialty Laboratories Inc.; Santa Monica; testing laboratories 788

Culinary Services of America Inc.; Los Angeles; temporary help service 750

BAE Systems Aircraft Controls Inc.; Santa Monica; search and navigation equipment 740

U.S. Federal Bureau of Investigation; Los Angeles 700

E! Entertainment Television Inc.; Los Angeles; cable television 700

Beverly Holdings Inc.; Beverly Hills; hotels 700

BW Hotel; Beverly Hills; hotels 700

HCA Inc.; Canoga Park; medical and surgical hospital 700

Prudential Financial; Woodland Hills; group hospitalization 700

SNTL Corp.; Agoura Hills; workers' compensation insurance 665

Tenet Healthcare Corp. Hospital; Los Angeles 650

Sierra Investment Services Corp.; Northridge; security brokers, dealers, flotation companies 650

Los Angeles County Metropolitan Transportation Authority; West Hollywood 640

Sprint Corp.; Santa Monica; cellular telephones 630

Universal City Studios Inc.; Santa Monica; television film production 600

Alphameric Inc.; Calabasas; computer consulting services 600

Wellpoint Pharmacy Management Inc.; Canoga Park hospital/medical service plans 600

Washington Mutual Bank; Northridge; federal savings and loan associations 600

Media Initiative Worldwide Inc.; Los Angeles; media buying service 550

Chef America Inc.; Chatsworth; frozen fruits, fruit juices, vegetables 550

Nordstrom Inc.; Los Angeles; family clothing stores 526

Nordstrom Inc.; Canoga Park; family clothing stores 520

ABC Family Worldwide Inc.; Los Angeles; television cartoon production 500

Lexicon Marketing Corp.; Los Angeles; school supplies 500

Advance Building Maintenance; Beverly Hills; janitorial service 500

Hilton Hawaii Corp; Beverly Hills; hotels 500

Pacific Bell; Beverly Hills; local telephone communications 500

Direct TV Inc.; El Segundo; radio, television, publisher representatives 500

Malibu Conference Center Inc.; Malibu; building operation 500

GC Eye Inc.; Agoura Hills; executive placement 500

NMB (USA) Inc.; Chatsworth; ball bearings and parts 500

Dole Bakersfield Inc.; Westlake Village; grapes 500

Compass Group USA Inc.; Woodland Hills; merchandising machine operators 500

California 31st District

Northeast and south central Los Angeles

The only district completely contained within the city of Los Angeles, the 31st is densely populated, heavily Hispanic and staunchly Democratic. It starts west of downtown Los Angeles and stretches south into south central Los Angeles and northeast toward Pasadena. Hispanics (70.2 percent) and Asians (13.8 percent) outnumber whites (9.8 percent). Voter turnout is usually low. *(See map p. 121.)*

Rapid immigration is changing many of the district's already diverse communities. Asians, Armenians, Russians, and Hispanics have been moving to the 31st, with many settling in the district's western side. This area, which includes part of East Hollywood, the mid-Wilshire area, and Koreatown, was hit hard by the 1992 riots. Pico Union and Westlake are dominated by Central American immigrants. Other heavily Hispanic communities include Highland Park, Cypress Park, and Glassell Park.

Directly west of Elysian Park, where Dodger Stadium is located, is the artsy and gentrifying Echo Park. A nearby area was recognized as Filipinotown in 2002. To the northeast sits Eagle Rock, a hilly, middle-class pocket of relative affluence that votes Democratic but leans more toward the political center than other parts of the 31st. The eastern side leads to Lincoln Heights and El Sereno—heavily Hispanic, blue-collar areas with a significant Mexican immigrant presence. The district also has part of south central Los Angeles east of the University of Southern California.

The 31st has the lowest median family income in the state, at $26,927. It falls mostly outside federal empowerment zone lines drawn after the riots. Entertainment studios and a slew of hospitals contribute to the economy, as do white-collar businesses along Wilshire Boulevard, a central business corridor.

Major Industry

Service, entertainment, tourism, health care.

Notable

Paramount Pictures is the only major motion picture studio still based in Hollywood.

Election Returns

	Republican		Democratic		Other	
President 2000	19,400	18.8%	79,560	77.2%	4,156	4%
House 2002	12,674	18.8%	54,569	81.2%		

District Profile

Population   639,088

Total area (square miles)   39
  Land area (square miles)   39

Population per square mile   16,232.3

Counties (2000 population)
  Los Angeles (pt.)   639,088

Cities and other areas over 10,000 (2000 population)
  Los Angeles (pt.)   639,088

Race and Hispanic or Latino origin*
  White   9.8%
  Black or African American   4.2%
  American Indian or Alaska Native   0.3%
  Asian   13.8%
  Native Hawaiian or other Pacific Islander   0.1%
  Some other race   0.2%
  Hispanic or Latino origin   70.2%
  Two or more races   1.5%

*As percentage of total population.

Ancestry*

English	1.1%	Irish	1.3%
German	1.5%	USA/American	1.6%

*As percentage of total population.

Universities and colleges, 2000–2001 enrollment
  Cleveland Chiropractic College of Los Angeles, Los Angeles   643
  Los Angeles City College, Los Angeles   15,174
  Los Angeles Trade Technical College, Los Angeles   18,164
  Occidental College, Los Angeles   1,729
  Southwestern University School of Law, Los Angeles   837

Newspapers and circulation

	District circulation	Total circulation
Los Angeles Daily News	7,272	195,376
Los Angeles La Opinion	12,828	127,108
Los Angeles Times	32,672	1,044,205
Pasadena Star-News	1,638	34,895

Television stations and affiliations

Los Angeles	100%	KABC	ABC
Los Angeles	100%	KADY	Independent
Los Angeles	100%	KCAL	Independent
Los Angeles	100%	KCBS	CBS
Los Angeles	100%	KCET	PBS
Los Angeles	100%	KCOP	UPN
Los Angeles	100%	KDOC	Independent
Los Angeles	100%	KHIZ	Independent
Los Angeles	100%	KJLA	Independent
Los Angeles	100%	KLCS	PBS
Los Angeles	100%	KMEX	Univision
Los Angeles	100%	KNBC	NBC
Los Angeles	100%	KOCE	PBS
Los Angeles	100%	KPXN	PAX
Los Angeles	100%	KRCA	PBS
Los Angeles	100%	KSCI	Independent
Los Angeles	100%	KTBN	Independent
Los Angeles	100%	KTLA	WB
Los Angeles	100%	KTTV	FOX
Los Angeles	100%	KVCR	PBS
Los Angeles	100%	KVEA	Telemundo
Los Angeles	100%	KWHY	Independent Spanish

Cable systems and subscribers
  Adelphia*   6,000
  Comcast*   50,000

*See Sources and Explanations in the front of the volume.

Military installations, September 2001
  Navy Marine Corps Reserve Center, Los Angeles   418

Businesses and other major employers
  U.S. Veterans Hospital; Los Angeles   4,000
  Los Angeles Childrens Hospital; Los Angeles   3,000
  Cable News Network Inc.; Los Angeles; cable television   2,200
  Bank of America Corp.; Los Angeles; data processing   1,200
  Tenet Health System Hospitals Inc.; Los Angeles   1,195
  St. John's Health Center; Los Angeles   1,100
  Los Angeles Housing Authority; Los Angeles   1,100
  Los Angeles Community College District; Los Angeles   1,057
  Point Denimwear Corp.; Los Angeles; men's and boys' jeans   1,050
  Catholic Healthcare West Southern California; Los Angeles   1,000
  Goodwill Industries of Southern California Inc.; Los Angeles; variety stores   880
  City of Los Angeles; Los Angeles; city government   800
  Los Angeles Community College District; Los Angeles   778
  Hunter Douglas Fashions Inc.; Los Angeles; miniblinds   700
  West Macy's Inc.; Los Angeles; business management   650
  HPM-Stadco Inc.; Los Angeles; machine and other job shop work   603
  Occidental College; Los Angeles   600

Los Angeles Housing Authority; Los Angeles   561
Aramark Services Inc.; Los Angeles; eating places   500
Pacific Bell; Los Angeles; local telephone communications   500
Mrs. Baird's Bakeries Business Trust; Los Angeles; retail bakeries   500
Pacific Bell; Los Angeles; telephone communication   500
Interstate Brands West Corp.; Los Angeles; cakes, bakery products   500

California 32nd District

East Los Angeles; El Monte; West Covina

The 32nd sits just east of the city of Los Angeles. It takes in the southern and central San Gabriel Valley and stretches northeast to Azusa, with several good-size cities in between. *(See map p. 121.)*

Once a largely white community, the 32nd has acquired a Hispanic majority from city residents moving to the suburbs. As a result, once-Republican enclaves have become solid Democratic domains.

The district's shrinking pockets of Republican and older white voters are in Azusa. El Monte, in the heart of the San Gabriel Valley, and Baldwin Park to the east are middle-income, blue-collar cities and the 32nd's Democratic base. El Monte also has some older white voters, mostly Democrats, and the city has a substantial new immigrant population. Monterey Park (shared with the 29th) is upper-middle class—the district's richest area—and is known as "Little Taipei" for its Taiwanese and other Asian immigrants. Another large Asian population lives in wealthy, liberal-leaning West Covina. The district has several daily Chinese-language papers.

The 32nd lacks a dominant industry, and the San Gabriel Valley has suffered from higher unemployment rates than the rest of the nation. Most residents commute outside the district to work. Once a small farming town, El Monte became home to some small aerospace factories. It is now a light manufacturing area with a huge retail auto complex. Irwindale is among the district's industrial centers.

Major Industry
Service, light manufacturing.

Notable
MGM's trademark roaring lion came from Gay's Lion Farm in El Monte, where animal trainer Charles Gay kept African lions until 1942; El Monte's original settlers were drawn by the California gold rush; City of Hope National Medical Center in Duarte is a research hospital specializing in cancer and other life-threatening diseases.

Election Returns

	Republican		Democratic		Other	
President 2000	45,018	31.2%	96,217	66.7%	3,057	2.1%
House 2002	23,366	27.5%	58,530	68.8%	3,183	3.7%

District Profile

Population   639,087

Total area (square miles)   92
  Land area (square miles)   91

Population per square mile   6,958.6

Counties (2000 population)
  Los Angeles (pt.)   639,087

Cities and other areas over 10,000 (2000 population)
  Azusa   44,712
  Baldwin Park   75,837
  Covina   46,837
  Duarte   21,486
  East Los Angeles CDP (pt.)   43,483
  El Monte   115,965
  Los Angeles (pt.)   30,311
  Monterey Park (pt.)   35,129
  Rosemead   53,505
  South El Monte   21,144
  Vincent CDP   15,097
  West Covina   105,080

Race and Hispanic or Latino origin*
  White   14.8%
  Black or African American   2.6%
  American Indian or Alaska Native   0.3%
  Asian   18.4%
  Native Hawaiian or other Pacific Islander   0.1%
  Some other race   0.1%
  Hispanic or Latino origin   62.3%
  Two or more races   1.4%

As percentage of total population.

Ancestry*
  English   2.2%   Italian   1.6%
  German   3.1%   USA/American   1.6%
  Irish   2.5%

As estimated percentage of total population.

Universities and colleges, 2000–2001 enrollment
  Azusa Pacific University, Azusa   6,497
  California State University, Los Angeles   19,593
  Don Bosco Technical Institute, Rosemead   287
  East Los Angeles College, Monterey Park   27,199
  East San Gabriel Valley Regional Occupational Program, West Covina   960
  ITT Technical Institute, West Covina   849

Newspapers and circulation

	District circulation	Total circulation
Los Angeles Daily News	1,255	195,376
Los Angeles La Opinion	7,292	127,108
Los Angeles Times	23,745	1,044,205
Pasadena Star-News	2,024	34,895
San Gabriel Valley Tribune	24,366	48,476

Television stations and affiliations

Los Angeles	100%	KABC	ABC
Los Angeles	100%	KADY	Independent
Los Angeles	100%	KCAL	Independent
Los Angeles	100%	KCBS	CBS
Los Angeles	100%	KCET	PBS
Los Angeles	100%	KCOP	UPN
Los Angeles	100%	KDOC	Independent
Los Angeles	100%	KHIZ	Independent
Los Angeles	100%	KJLA	Independent
Los Angeles	100%	KLCS	PBS
Los Angeles	100%	KMEX	Univision
Los Angeles	100%	KNBC	NBC
Los Angeles	100%	KOCE	PBS
Los Angeles	100%	KPXN	PAX
Los Angeles	100%	KRCA	PBS
Los Angeles	100%	KSCI	Independent
Los Angeles	100%	KTBN	Independent
Los Angeles	100%	KTLA	WB
Los Angeles	100%	KTTV	FOX
Los Angeles	100%	KVCR	PBS
Los Angeles	100%	KVEA	Telemundo
Los Angeles	100%	KWHY	Independent Spanish

Cable systems and subscribers

Adelphia   11,787
Charter   33,332

Businesses and other major employers

Pedus Service Inc.; Monterey Park; industrial help service   4,400

Los Angeles County; Monterey Park; sheriff's office   3,500

Los Angeles County; Los Angeles; fire dept.   2,600

Southern California Edison Co.; Rosemead; electric power generation   2,004

Los Angeles County; Los Angeles; building maintenance   2,000

Hope National Medical Center; Duarte   1,900

C. B. Richard Ellis Inc.; Baldwin Park; real estate brokers and agents   1,800

Azusa Unified School District; Azusa   1,500

Northrop Grumman Information Technology Inc.; Azusa; guided missiles and space vehicles   1,500

Alpha Therapeutic Corp.; Los Angeles; plasmas   1,400

Citrus Valley Medical Center Inc.; West Covina   1,229

Washington Mutual Bank; Irwindale; federal savings and loan associations   1,200

Los Angeles Community College District; Monterey Park   1,058

Miller Brewing Co.; Irwindale; malt beverages   1,036

Verizon Communications Inc.; Covina; telephone and telephone equipment installation   1,000

Azusa Pacific University; Azusa   961

Ready Pac Produce Inc.; Irwindale; fresh or refrigerated salads   900

Community Development Commission; Monterey Park; community and rural development   900

Bank of the West; Monterey Park; state commercial banks   800

Public Health Foundation Enterprises Inc.; Irwindale; public health programs   700

Asian American Assn.; El Monte; telephone services   700

Decore-ative Specialties Inc.; Irwindale; wood doors   650

Los Angeles County; Monterey Park; specialty hospitals   600

Irish Construction; Rosemead; water, sewer, utility lines   600

Medsep Corp.; Covina; medical instruments: blood, bone work   552

West Covina City; West Covina; city council   516

National Service Industries Inc.; Los Angeles; envelopes   500

Eveready Battery Co.; Covina; batteries, dry cell   500

California Air Resources Board; El Monte   500

Pacific Bell; El Monte; local telephone communications   500

Pacific Bell; Rosemead; local/long-distance telephone   500

California 33rd District

West Los Angeles; Culver City

The 33rd is an ethnically diverse, Democratic district that begins about a mile inland from Venice Beach, runs east through Culver City and ends up in south central Los Angeles. From there it runs north through Koreatown, the "Miracle Mile" district, and Hollywood. (*See map p. 121.*)

Blacks, Hispanics, and Asians account for more than three-fourths of the population, but the 33rd has no single racial majority. Nearly 70 percent of the district's registered voters are Democrats. Several major demographic shifts have dramatically changed the makeup. The first was in the 1960s when the district's Jewish population migrated to the area's now more upscale northwest end and the district's center became predominantly black. Since the 1990s, there has been an influx of Hispanic immigrants, who now account for the largest part of the population, at almost 35 percent.

The 33rd has a solid middle class, as well as some sharply contrasting areas such as wealthy Hancock Park—where the mayor's official residence is located—and poor south central Los Angeles, which witnessed intense racial strife during the 1992 riots.

The largest business sector is the service industry, with health care also providing employment for many. Though the 33rd is no longer the film production hub it used to be, it is home to the real Tinseltown—Hollywood—and entertainment continues to be a factor in its overall economy.

For recreation, residents and tourists flock to Exposition Park in downtown Los Angeles. In addition to the Los Angeles County Natural History Museum and the California Science Center, the park boasts the Los Angeles Memorial Coliseum, which has hosted two Olympiads.

Major Industry

Service, entertainment, health care.

The University of Southern California; MGM Studios (now part of Sony Picture Studios); the Academy Awards ceremony moved to the Kodak Theatre in 2002.

Election Returns

	Republican		Democratic		Other	
President 2000	24,214	13.5%	148,978	83.1%	6,067	3.4%
House 2002	16,699	14.1%	97,779	82.5%	3,971	3.4%

District Profile

Population   639,088

Total area (square miles)   48
   Land area (square miles)   48

Population per square mile   13,274.1

Counties (2000 population)
   Los Angeles (pt.)   639,088

Cities and other areas over 10,000 (2000 population)
   Culver City   38,816
   Los Angeles (pt.)   582,746
   View Park-Windsor Hills CDP   10,958

Race and Hispanic or Latino origin*
   White   19.9%
   Black or African American   29.9%
   American Indian or Alaska Native   0.2%
   Asian   12.1%
   Native Hawaiian or other Pacific Islander   0.1%
   Some other race   0.4%
   Hispanic or Latino origin   34.6%
   Two or more races   2.8%

*As percentage of total population.

Ancestry*
English 2.1%	Russian 1.3%
German 2.8%	Subsaharan 1.9%
Irish 2.4%	USA/American 1.8%
Italian 1.5%	West Indian 1.4%

*As estimated percentage of total population.

Universities and colleges, 2000–2001 enrollment
   American Film Institute, Los Angeles   298
   California Design College, Los Angeles   279
   Computer Learning Center, Los Angeles   1,017
   Dongguk Royal University, Los Angeles   381
   Institute of Computer Technology, Los Angeles   329
   Musicians Institute, Hollywood   586
   Nova Institute of Health Technology, Los Angeles   318
   Samra University of Oriental Medicine, Los Angeles   344
   University of Southern California, Los Angeles   29,194
   West Los Angeles College, Culver City   10,404

Newspapers and circulation

	District circulation	Total circulation
Los Angeles Daily News	3,628	195,376
Los Angeles La Opinion	7,222	127,108
Los Angeles Times	49,236	1,044,205
Torrance Daily Breeze	1,597	79,363

Television stations and affiliations

Los Angeles	100%	KABC	ABC
Los Angeles	100%	KADY	Independent
Los Angeles	100%	KCAL	Independent
Los Angeles	100%	KCBS	CBS
Los Angeles	100%	KCET	PBS
Los Angeles	100%	KCOP	UPN
Los Angeles	100%	KDOC	Independent
Los Angeles	100%	KHIZ	Independent
Los Angeles	100%	KJLA	Independent
Los Angeles	100%	KLCS	PBS
Los Angeles	100%	KMEX	Univision
Los Angeles	100%	KNBC	NBC
Los Angeles	100%	KOCE	PBS
Los Angeles	100%	KPXN	PAX
Los Angeles	100%	KRCA	PBS
Los Angeles	100%	KSCI	Independent
Los Angeles	100%	KTBN	Independent
Los Angeles	100%	KTLA	WB
Los Angeles	100%	KTTV	FOX
Los Angeles	100%	KVCR	PBS
Los Angeles	100%	KVEA	Telemundo
Los Angeles	100%	KWHY	Independent Spanish

Cable systems and subscribers
   Comcast   84,389

Businesses and other major employers
   Los Angeles County; Los Angeles; childrens' aid society   6,000
   Kaiser Foundation Hospitals; Los Angeles   4,396
   City of Los Angeles; Los Angeles; municipal police   4,000
   Team-One Employment Specialists; Los Angeles; employment agencies   4,000
   University of Southern California; Los Angeles   4,000
   Sony Pictures Entertainment Inc.; Culver City; motion picture production and distribution   3,000
   Los Angeles Memorial Coliseum Commission; Los Angeles; stadium operator   2,500
   Farmers Insurance Exchange Farmers Group Inc.; Los Angeles; fire, marine, casualty insurance   2,000
   Southern California Permanente Medical Group; Los Angeles   2,000
   Kaiser Foundation Hospitals; Los Angeles   2,000
   Truck Underwriters Assn.; Los Angeles; legal services   1,767
   Paramount Pictures Corp.; Los Angeles; TV motion picture production and distribution   1,700
   Continental Graphics Holdings Inc.; Los Angeles; promotional printing, lithographic   1,650
   All City Management Services; Los Angeles; traffic consultant   1,500
   U.S. Merchants Financial Group Inc.; Los Angeles; packaging and labeling services   1,500
   Merchant of Tennis Inc.; Los Angeles; sporting goods and bicycle shops   1,400
   Ticketmaster Corp.; Los Angeles; sports ticket sales office   1,300
   MGM/United Artist; Culver City; motion picture production   1,300
   Valet Parking Service; Culver City; parking lots   1,268

Los Angeles Community College District; Los Angeles
1,000

Brotman Partners; Culver City; medical and surgical
hospital   1,000

Vision-X Inc.; Los Angeles; marketing consulting
services   900

ABM Security Services Inc.; Los Angeles; protective
services, guard   900

Tenet Healthcare Corp. Hospital; Los Angeles   875

Tracerton Enterprises Inc.; Los Angeles; security guard
service   800

Continental Currency Services Inc.; Los Angeles; check
clearing services   800

Los Angeles County Metropolitan Transportation
Authority; Los Angeles   800

Los Angeles Community College District; Culver City
746

Servicon Systems Inc.; Culver City; janitorial service
720

Burns International Security Services Corp.; Los Angeles;
security guard service   700

Midway Hospital Medical Center; Los Angeles; hospital
with residency   700

Diversified Re-Packaging Corp.; Los Angeles;
management consulting   700

Interstate Brands West Corp.; Los Angeles; bakery
products   700

Deluxe Laboratories Inc.; Los Angeles; motion picture
film processing   617

Capitol Records Inc.; Los Angeles; compact laser discs
600

Totally Secured Inc.; Culver City; security systems
services   600

Los Angeles Doctors Hospital; Los Angeles   550

Pinkerton's Inc.; Los Angeles; security guard service
536

Wackenhut Corp.; Los; Angeles; security guard service
500

Fox Family World Wide; Los Angeles; motion picture
and video production   500

Avnet Inc.; Culver City; computer peripheral equipment
500

Moldex-Metric Inc.; Culver City; personal safety
equipment   500

California 34th District

East central Los Angeles; Downey; Bellflower

The Democratic 34th takes in the heart and southeastern part of Los Angeles and has an overwhelming Hispanic
majority. At 77 percent, the district has the largest concentration of Hispanics in California. *(See map p. 121.)*

The local economy revolves around businesses in the revitalizing downtown area and nearby light manufacturing centers such as Vernon and Commerce. Downtown businesses
include toy, jewelry, and garment manufacturers and retailers. Some spaces downtown are being transformed into lofts.
Many Los Angeles civic buildings, including city hall, court-
houses, and the county prison, are in the 34th.

Vernon's population, according to the 2000 census, is a
mere 91 people, but during the day it jumps to more than
50,000 as workers stream into its food-processing and furniture plants. The district also is attracting new "green" industries, such as recycling companies.

One of California's poorest and least-educated districts,
the 34th had among the lowest voter turnouts of any district
in the nation in 2000. Al Gore won the 2000 presidential
vote with 72.4 percent of the vote—despite the district's inclusion of slightly more suburban and conservative Downey
and Bellflower, located to the south, where there are fewer
Hispanics. Other areas include Little Tokyo and part of Pico
Union and Chinatown. Despite redevelopment and many
small businesses, the area has seen a rise in crime rates.

Brighter spots include the Walt Disney Concert Hall,
which was scheduled to open in 2003 and become the Los Angeles Philharmonic's new home. Transportation hub Union
Station and the end of the 20-mile Alameda Corridor rail
link connecting Los Angeles and the ports of Los Angeles
and Long Beach are in the district, as is the Staples Center, home to basketball's Lakers and Clippers and hockey's
Kings.

Major Industry
Government, manufacturing, service, retail.

Notable
The 2000 Democratic National Convention was held at
the Staples Center; downtown's El Pueblo de Los Angeles
Historic Monument, including Olvera Street, is the oldest
section of Los Angeles.

Election Returns

	Republican		Democratic		Other	
President 2000	27,384	25.8%	76,876	72.4%	1,901	1.8%
House 2002	17,090	26%	48,734	74%		

District Profile

Population   639,088

Total area (square miles)   59
   Land area (square miles)   58

Population per square mile   10,962.9

Counties (2000 population)
   Los Angeles (pt.)   639,088

Cities and other areas over 10,000 (2000 population)
   Bell   36,664
   Bellflower   72,878
   Bell Gardens   44,054
   Commerce   12,568
   Cudahy   24,208
   Downey   107,323
   East Los Angeles CDP (pt.)   27,451
   Florence-Graham CDP (pt.)   20,222
   Huntington Park   61,348
   Los Angeles (pt.)   188,018
   Maywood   28,083
   Walnut Park CDP   16,180

Race and Hispanic or Latino origin*
White   11.4%
Black or African American   4.4%
American Indian or Alaska Native   0.3%
Asian   5.5%
Native Hawaiian or other Pacific Islander   0.1%
Some other race   0.1%
Hispanic or Latino origin   77.2%
Two or more races   0.9%

*As percentage of total population.

Ancestry*
English	1.4%	Irish	1.5%
German	2.0%	USA/American	1.9%

*As estimated percentage of total population.

Universities and colleges, 2000–2001 enrollment
Fashion Institute of Design and Merchandising, Los Angeles   2,648
Loyola Law School, Los Angeles   1,400

Newspapers and circulation
	District circulation	Total circulation
Long Beach Press-Telegram	12,810	94,944
Los Angeles Daily News	4,649	195,376
Los Angeles La Opinion	17,913	127,108
Los Angeles Times	34,177	1,044,205

Television stations and affiliations
Los Angeles	100%	KABC	ABC
Los Angeles	100%	KADY	Independent
Los Angeles	100%	KCAL	Independent
Los Angeles	100%	KCBS	CBS
Los Angeles	100%	KCET	PBS
Los Angeles	100%	KCOP	UPN
Los Angeles	100%	KDOC	Independent
Los Angeles	100%	KHIZ	Independent
Los Angeles	100%	KJLA	Independent
Los Angeles	100%	KLCS	PBS
Los Angeles	100%	KMEX	Univision
Los Angeles	100%	KNBC	NBC
Los Angeles	100%	KOCE	PBS
Los Angeles	100%	KPXN	PAX
Los Angeles	100%	KRCA	PBS
Los Angeles	100%	KSCI	Independent
Los Angeles	100%	KTBN	Independent
Los Angeles	100%	KTLA	WB
Los Angeles	100%	KTTV	FOX
Los Angeles	100%	KVCR	PBS
Los Angeles	100%	KVEA	Telemundo
Los Angeles	100%	KWHY	Independent Spanish

Cable systems and subscribers
Adelphia   2,217
Charter   3,021
Comcast*   426,518

*See Sources and Explanations in the front of the volume.

Military installations, September 2001
Patton Hall U.S. Army Reserve Center, Bell   488

Businesses and other major employers
City of Los Angeles; Los Angeles; city government   11,700
Los Angeles County; Los Angeles; materials management consultant   10,000
Los Angeles County; Los Angeles; county government   6,400
Los Angeles Superior Courthouse; Los Angeles; courts   5,985
U.S. Postal Service; Los Angeles   5,500
Boeing Co.; Downey; aircraft maintenance, repair   5,000
Los Angeles Times Communications; Los Angeles; newspaper   4,325
Los Angeles County Office of Education; Downey   3,959
City of Los Angeles; Los Angeles; fire department   3,650
City of Los Angeles; Los Angeles; electric services   3,500
Southern California Gas Co.; Los Angeles; natural gas distribution   2,500
ABM Janitorial Services; Los Angeles; janitorial service   2,500
California Commerce Club Inc.; Los Angeles; gambling   2,300
Atlantic Richfield Co.; Los Angeles; crude petroleum production   2,200
Transamerica Occidental Life Insurance Co.; Los Angeles; life insurance   2,000
BMK LP; Los Angeles; piece goods and sewing notions   2,000
Kaiser Foundation Hospitals; Bellflower   2,000
Bell Gardens Bicycle Club; Bell; gambling   1,950
Good Samaritan Hospital; Los Angeles   1,800
United Parcel Service Inc.; Los Angeles; shipping agents   1,600
U.S. Bureau of Citizenship and Immigration Services; Los Angeles   1,500
Los Angeles County; Los Angeles; general practice law office   1,500
Coca-Cola Bottling of Los Angeles; Los Angeles; general automotive repair shops   1,500
Sun Pacific Marketing Cooperative Inc.; Los Angeles; fresh fruits and vegetables   1,500
Burlington Northern and Santa Fe Railway Co.; Los Angeles; railroad freight hauling   1,500
Los Angeles County; Los Angeles; psychiatric hospitals   1,500
California Hospital Medical Center; Los Angeles   1,400
Los Angeles County Metropolitan Transportation Authority; Los Angeles   1,200
White Memorial Medical Center Inc.; Los Angeles   1,200
Downey Regional Medical Center-Hospital Inc.; Downey   1,150
Clougherty Packing Co.; Los Angeles; meatpacking plants   1,100
California Dept. of Transportation; Los Angeles   1,000

El Pueblo De Los Angeles Historic Monument; Los Angeles; land, mineral, wildlife conservation   1,000

Los Angeles Unified School District Inc.; Los Angeles   1,000

Los Angeles County; Los Angeles; specialty hospitals   1,000

Bank of America Corp.; Los Angeles; commercial bank   1,000

PricewaterhouseCoopers; Los Angeles; accounting association   1,000

Starwood Hotels and Resorts Worldwide Inc.; Los Angeles; hotels   1,000

U.S. Postal Service; Bell   1,000

City of Los Angeles; Los Angeles; urban and community development   950

Guess Inc.; Los Angeles; men's and boys' sportswear   940

Ernst and Young; Los Angeles; certified public accountant   900

Los Angeles County; Los Angeles; public health programs   863

Union Bank of California; Los Angeles; commercial bank   850

City of Los Angeles; Los Angeles; legal services   800

Los Angeles County; Los Angeles; government finance   800

Pacific Bell; Los Angeles; local/long-distance telephone   800

Servizi Aeroportuali; Los Angeles; base maintenance   800

American Apparel Inc.; Los Angeles; t-shirts and tops   800

Los Angeles Unified School District; Los Angeles   800

United Parcel Service Inc.; Los Angeles; parcel delivery   800

KPMG; Los Angeles; certified public accountant   800

Today's IV; Los Angeles; hotels   750

Los Angeles County; Los Angeles; government finance   720

City of Los Angeles; Los Angeles; online services technology consultants   700

Los Angeles Unified School District Inc.; Los Angeles; data processing   700

Bank of America Corp.; Los Angeles; commercial bank   700

U.S. Army Corps of Engineers; Los Angeles; engineering services   650

Authentic Fitness Corp.; Los Angeles; athletic clothing   650

Federal Reserve Bank of San Francisco; Los Angeles   640

AON Risk Services Inc. of Southern California Insurance Services; Los Angeles; insurance brokers   630

WHB Corp.; Los Angeles; hotels and motels   630

Trust Company of the West; Los Angeles; mutual funds manager   610

Los Angeles County; Los Angeles; specialty hospitals   600

City of Los Angeles; Los Angeles; social and manpower programs   600

Marsh USA Inc.; Los Angeles; insurance brokers   600

Los Angeles Times Communications; Los Angeles; newspaper   600

A Z 3 Inc.; Los Angeles; women's clothing stores   600

Latham & Watkins; Los Angeles; general practice law office   600

O'Melveny & Myers LLP; Los Angeles; general practice law office   600

University of California; Los Angeles; psychologist, psychotherapist offices   600

Central Financial Acceptance Corp.; Los Angeles; security brokers, dealers, flotation companies   592

Hanjin International Corp.; Los Angeles; hotels   560

TCW Funds Management Inc.; Los Angeles; security brokers, dealers, flotation companies   550

Unified Western Grocers Inc.; Los Angeles; food supplier   550

Ancora Capital and Management Group; Los Angeles; mailing service   525

Superba Inc.; Los Angeles; men's/boys' neckwear   520

Southern California Metropolitan Water District; Los Angeles   517

Parsec Inc.; Los Angeles; cargo loading, unloading   514

City of Los Angeles; Los Angeles; treasurers' office   500

United States Attorneys; Los Angeles; legal counsel and prosecution   500

Aramark Services Inc.; Los Angeles; caterers   500

Pinkerton's Inc.; Los Angeles; protective services, guard   500

Gruma Corp.; Los Angeles; tortilla chips   500

Los Angeles County Metropolitan Transportation Authority; Los Angeles   500

Wine Warehouse Imports Inc.; Los Angeles; wine   500

Dekar Industries Inc.; Los Angeles; janitorial service   500

Fortune Fashions Industries; Los Angeles; screen printing of cotton broadwoven fabrics   500

Master Foods USA; Los Angeles; cat food   500

Owens-Brockway Glass Container Inc.; Los Angeles; packers' ware (containers), glass   500

Aames Financial Corp.; Los Angeles; loan brokers   500

Capital Group Companies; Los Angeles; money market mutual funds   500

Gibson, Dunn, & Crutcher LLP; Los Angeles; general practice law office   500

Pacific Bell; Los Angeles; local/long-distance telephone   500

Swett and Crawford; Los Angeles; insurance agents and brokers   500

Stride Rite Corp.; Downey; shoe stores   500

California 35th District

South central Los Angeles; Inglewood

The 35th in south central Los Angeles is one of the most secure Democratic districts in the state. *(See map p. 121.)*

Almost 70 percent of its voters register as Democrats, and Al Gore captured 81.6 percent of the vote here in the 2000 presidential election. Once predominantly black, the district is seeing a huge influx of Hispanics. It still had the state's highest concentration of African Americans at 34.1 percent in the 2000 census, but Hispanics were the district's racial plurality, making up 47.4 percent of the population. Gardena has a large and politically influential Japanese community.

Riots put the 35th in the headlines in 1992 in the wake of a verdict acquitting white police officers accused of beating black motorist Rodney King. Issues of poverty, joblessness, and lack of basic human services remain. Police-community relations, public safety, and economic development are central public policy concerns.

The district is set between downtown Los Angeles to the north, beaches to the west, Torrance to the south, and the industrial Alameda Corridor to the east. Redistricting following the 2000 census added Los Angeles International Airport, the region's largest employer. The 35th is mostly poor, but there are middle-class areas in Inglewood and the South Bay cities of Gardena and Hawthorne. Efforts to lure businesses have met with some success. In 1994 the area became part of a federal empowerment zone set up to help areas affected by the riots.

Gardena receives a strong revenue stream as one of the only cities in Los Angeles County that allows poker parlors, which account for a chunk of the city's budget. In 1999 the Los Angeles Lakers and Kings moved from the Great Western Forum in Inglewood to the new Staples Center in the nearby 34th, a disappointment for the 35th.

Major Industry

Aerospace, service, manufacturing.

Notable

Hollywood Park racetrack is in Inglewood; Hawthorne was the birthplace of the Beach Boys and Northrop Corp., before it became aerospace giant Northrop Grumman Corp.; Central Avenue, on the district's eastern edge, was the West Coast hub of African American entertainment during the jazz age.

Election Returns

	Republican		Democratic		Other	
President 2000	24,495	16.9%	118,450	81.6%	2,262	1.6%
House 2002	18,094	19.4%	72,401	77.5%	2,912	3.1%

District Profile

Population   639,088

Total area (square miles)   55
    Land area (square miles)   55

Population per square mile   11,533.2

Counties (2000 population)
    Los Angeles (pt.)   639,088

Cities and other areas over 10,000 (2000 population)
    Florence-Graham CDP (pt.)   11,403
    Gardena   57,746
    Hawthorne   84,112
    Inglewood   112,580
    Lawndale   31,711
    Los Angeles (pt.)   280,597
    Westmont CDP   31,623

Race and Hispanic or Latino origin*
    White   10.4%
    Black or African American   34.1%
    American Indian or Alaska Native   0.2%
    Asian   5.6%

Native Hawaiian or other Pacific Islander   0.3%
Some other race   0.2%
Hispanic or Latino origin   47.4%
Two or more races   1.8%

*As percentage of total population.

Ancestry*
English	1.5%	Subsaharan	1.6%
German	2.0%	USA/American	1.5%
Irish	1.7%		

*As estimated percentage of total population.

Universities and colleges, 2000–2001 enrollment
    City University-Los Angeles, Inglewood   2,749
    El Camino College, Torrance   24,067
    Los Angeles Southwest College, Los Angeles   5,710
    Loyola Marymount University, Los Angeles   7,500
    Northrop-Rice Aviation, Inglewood   413
    Otis College of Art and Design, Los Angeles   924

Newspapers and circulation

	District circulation	Total circulation
Los Angeles Daily News	1,807	195,376
Los Angeles La Opinion	7,563	127,108
Los Angeles Times	35,424	1,044,205
Torrance Daily Breeze	15,246	79,363

Television stations and affiliations
Los Angeles	100%	KABC	ABC
Los Angeles	100%	KADY	Independent
Los Angeles	100%	KCAL	Independent
Los Angeles	100%	KCBS	CBS
Los Angeles	100%	KCET	PBS
Los Angeles	100%	KCOP	UPN
Los Angeles	100%	KDOC	Independent
Los Angeles	100%	KHIZ	Independent
Los Angeles	100%	KJLA	Independent
Los Angeles	100%	KLCS	PBS
Los Angeles	100%	KMEX	Univision
Los Angeles	100%	KNBC	NBC
Los Angeles	100%	KOCE	PBS
Los Angeles	100%	KPXN	PAX
Los Angeles	100%	KRCA	PBS
Los Angeles	100%	KSCI	Independent
Los Angeles	100%	KTBN	Independent
Los Angeles	100%	KTLA	WB
Los Angeles	100%	KTTV	FOX
Los Angeles	100%	KVCR	PBS
Los Angeles	100%	KVEA	Telemundo
Los Angeles	100%	KWHY	Independent Spanish

Cable systems and subscribers
    Comcast   33,555
    Time Warner   24,892

Businesses and other major employers
    Los Angeles County; Lawndale; community development   14,000
    Los Angeles International Airport; Los Angeles   2,600
    Daniel Freeman Hospitals Inc.; Inglewood   1,940
    Tenet Healthcare Corp. Hospital; Inglewood   1,940

Vivendi Universal Interactive Publishing North America Inc.; Los Angeles; prepackaged software   1,806

U.S. Postal Service; Inglewood   1,700

Northwest Airlines Inc.; Los Angeles; airline tickets   1,681

Century Gaming Management Inc.; Inglewood; casino hotel   1,250

Loyola Marymount University; Los Angeles   1,229

CVHS Hospital Corp.; Inglewood   1,150

El Camino Community College District; Torrance   1,060

Command Security Corp.; Los Angeles; detective, armored car services   1,000

Resource Collection Inc.; Hawthorne; building maintenance   1,000

Marriott International Inc.; Los Angeles; hotels and motels   900

City of Inglewood; Inglewood; city government   900

Hawthorne School District; Hawthorne   836

RPD Hotels 18; Los Angeles; hotels   800

Avnet Marketing Services; Inglewood; advertising   800

Southwest Airlines Co.; Los Angeles; air passenger carrier   700

Robert F. Kennedy Medical Center Inc.; Hawthorne   700

Watts Health Systems Inc.; Inglewood; hospital/health services consultant   700

Los Angeles Community College District; Los Angeles   674

Fortuna Enterprises LP; Los Angeles; hotels   650

Sky Chefs Inc.; Los Angeles; caterers   650

Neutrogena Corp.; Los Angeles; perfumes, cosmetics, other toilet products   600

Normandie Casino; Gardena; casino   600

U.S. Federal Aviation Administration; Lawndale   600

Gategourmet International AG; Los Angeles; contract food services   500

Hallmark Aviation Services; Los Angeles; help supply services   500

ITT Sheraton Corp.; Los Angeles; hotels   500

U.S. Bureau of Customs and Border Protection; Los Angeles   500

United Parcel Service Inc.; Gardena; parcel delivery   500

Uniserve Facilities Services; Torrance; janitorial service   500

California 36th District

Southwest Los Angeles County — Torrance, Redondo Beach, Manhattan Beach

The 36th is home to some of most famous beaches—and biggest aerospace firms—of Los Angeles. It hugs the Pacific Coast south from Venice through El Segundo to Manhattan, Hermosa, and Redondo Beaches. *(See map p. 121.)*

Redistricting following the 2000 census removed the Republican Palos Verdes peninsula to give the district a Democratic lean. Presidential candidate Al Gore took 57.1 percent of the vote here in 2000, and Democrats hold a 13-point voter registration edge.

Venice's eclectic beaches are considered the state's most liberal havens outside of Berkeley. Manhattan Beach, and Marina del Rey, with its huge private marina, are ritzier. Torrance, the district's largest whole city, is split politically. It is wealthier toward the coast, but inland sections include middle- and working-class areas that have conservative and labor-heavy pockets. New immigrants and poorer residents live just west of Interstate 110.

A number of major companies maintain headquarters in the 36th, and aerospace firms in El Segundo and Redondo Beach drive the economy. The district has some of the state's most-educated residents. Some had trouble finding work as defense and aerospace spending shrank, but many employers, such as Hughes Electronics Corp. and Northrop Grumman, have successfully converted to nondefense projects. Such efforts to diversify the economy and encourage dual-use technology resulted in an economic boost.

Major Industry
Aerospace, high-tech, manufacturing.

Notable
The Hyperion sewage treatment plant in Playa del Rey, the subject of a multiple-decade environmental lawsuit, is now one of cleanest plants in the Los Angeles area; Hughes and subsidiary DirecTV are based in El Segundo.

Election Returns

	Republican		Democratic		Other	
President 2000	88,619	38.7%	130,752	57.1%	9,423	4.1%
House 2002	50,328	35%	88,198	61.4%	5,225	3.6%

District Profile

Population   639,087

Total area (square miles)   122
   Land area (square miles)   74

Population per square mile   8,536.3

Counties (2000 population)
   Los Angeles (pt.)   639,087

Cities and other areas over 10,000 (2000 population)
   El Segundo   16,033
   Hermosa Beach   18,566
   Lennox CDP   22,950
   Lomita   20,046
   Los Angeles (pt.)   295,807
   Manhattan Beach   33,852
   Redondo Beach   63,261
   Torrance   137,946
   West Carson CDP (pt.)   20,741

Race and Hispanic or Latino origin*
   White   48.4%
   Black or African American   4.1%
   American Indian or Alaska Native   0.3%
   Asian   13.4%
   Native Hawaiian or other Pacific Islander   0.4%
   Some other race   0.3%
   Hispanic or Latino origin   30.3%
   Two or more races   2.9%

As percentage of total population.

Ancestry*

English	6.2%	Polish	1.6%
French	2.1%	Russian	1.5%
German	8.0%	Scottish	1.4%
Irish	6.6%	Swedish	1.1%
Italian	4.2%	USA/American	2.4%
Norwegian	1.1%		

As estimated percentage of total population.

Universities and colleges, 2000–2001 enrollment

Antioch University, Los Angeles   622
Los Angeles Harbor College, Wilmington   8,741
Southern California Institute of Architecture, Los Angeles   257

Newspapers and circulation

	District circulation	Total circulation
Long Beach Press-Telegram	3,182	94,944
Los Angeles Daily News	1,308	195,376
Los Angeles La Opinion	3,368	127,108
Los Angeles Times	65,303	1,044,205
Torrance Daily Breeze	43,688	79,363

Television stations and affiliations

Los Angeles	100%	KABC	ABC
Los Angeles	100%	KADY	Independent
Los Angeles	100%	KCAL	Independent
Los Angeles	100%	KCBS	CBS
Los Angeles	100%	KCET	PBS
Los Angeles	100%	KCOP	UPN
Los Angeles	100%	KDOC	Independent
Los Angeles	100%	KHIZ	Independent
Los Angeles	100%	KJLA	Independent
Los Angeles	100%	KLCS	PBS
Los Angeles	100%	KMEX	Univision
Los Angeles	100%	KNBC	NBC
Los Angeles	100%	KOCE	PBS
Los Angeles	100%	KPXN	PAX
Los Angeles	100%	KRCA	PBS
Los Angeles	100%	KSCI	Independent
Los Angeles	100%	KTBN	Independent
Los Angeles	100%	KTLA	WB
Los Angeles	100%	KTTV	FOX
Los Angeles	100%	KVCR	PBS
Los Angeles	100%	KVEA	Telemundo
Los Angeles	100%	KWHY	Independent Spanish

Cable systems and subscribers

Adelphia   40,602
Comcast   9,434
Time Warner   37,453

Military installations, September 2001

Los Angeles Air Force Base, El Segundo   2,631

Businesses and other major employers

General Motors Corp.; El Segundo; computer integrated systems design   5,600
Raytheon Co.; El Segundo; radar systems and equipment   5,000
Los Angeles County Hospital; Torrance   5,000
Little Company of Mary Health Services; Torrance; hospital management   4,044
Pinkerton Government Services Inc.; Torrance; detective, armored car services   3,200
Toyota Motor Sales USA Inc.; Torrance; commercial vehicles   3,000
Aerospace Corp.; El Segundo; scientific research agency   2,313
Comcast; El Segundo; cable television   2,300
Canter and Associates Inc.; Los Angeles; continuing education service   2,000
Hughes Electronics Corp.; El Segundo; radio/TV communications equipment   2,000
American Honda Motor Co. Inc.; Torrance; automobiles   2,000
Honeywell International Inc.; Torrance; steel foundries   2,000
Torrance Memorial Medical Center; Torrance   2,000
Ichem; Redondo Beach; chemical cleaning services   1,999
Nippan Rent A Car; Los Angeles; passenger car rental   1,998
Mattel Toy Co.; El Segundo; toys and games   1,900
OrthAlliance Inc.; Torrance; advocacy for orthodontic professionals   1,700
Kaiser Foundation Hospitals; Harbor City   1,700
U.S. Postal Service; Los Angeles   1,500
Little Company of Mary Hospital; Torrance; medical doctor offices, clinics   1,200
Fairchild Corp.; Torrance; fasteners   1,200
Raytheon Co.; Torrance; semiconductors and related devices   1,100
Direct TV Inc.; El Segundo; satellite broadcast services   1,000
Honeywell International Inc.; Torrance; aircraft engines and parts   1,000
Fairchild Corp.; Torrance; aircraft equipment and supplies   1,000
Honeywell International Inc.; Torrance; steam turbines   1,000
Boeing Satellite Systems Inc.; Torrance; traveling wave tubes   904
International Rectifier Corp.; El Segundo; semiconductors and related devices   900
City of Los Angeles; Venice; water control and quality agency   900
Avery Dennison Office Products Co. Inc.; Torrance; albums   900
Motorcar Parts and Accessories Inc.; Torrance; alternators, automotive   825
Accenture Inc.; El Segundo; business consulting   800
CSC Foreign Ventures Inc.; El Segundo; computer systems analysis and design   800
City of Los Angeles; Venice; waste management agency   800
ExxonMobil Oil Corp.; Torrance; petroleum refining   800
Los Angeles Community College District; Wilmington   770
Teledyne Technologies Inc.; Los Angeles; electronic circuits   750
Raytheon Co.; El Segundo; personal document and information services   700

City of Torrance; Torrance; city management   700
City of Torrance; Torrance; police dept.   700
Fairchild Corp.; Torrance; aerospace castings   700
Saatchi and Saatchi North America Inc.; Torrance; advertising   700
Virco Manufacturing Corp.; Torrance; school furniture   650
Boeing Electron Dynamic Devices Inc.; Torrance; traveling wave tubes   620
Citicorp Development Center; Los Angeles; computer systems analysis and design   600
Chipton-Ross Inc.; El Segundo; employment agency   600
Gategourmet International AG; El Segundo; caterers   600
Infonet Services Corp.; El Segundo; data processing   600
Younger Manufacturing Co.; Torrance; lenses, ophthalmic   600
Fairchild Corp.; Torrance; wrenches, hand tools   600
Robinson Helicopter Co.; Torrance; helicopters   600
Port of Los Angeles; San Pedro   600
Tosco Corp.; Wilmington; petroleum refining   575
Infonet Services Corp.; El Segundo; general warehousing, storage   572
Tri-Star Electronics Inc.; El Segundo; contacts, electrical   570
TRG Real Estate Group Inc.; Torrance; real estate brokers and agents   570
San Pedro Peninsula Hospital; San Pedro   556
Parks Mechanical Construction Corp.; Wilmington; plumbing contractors   550
Security First Group Inc.; Los Angeles; life insurance   529
730 Cal Hotel Properties II Inc.; Los Angeles; hotels   500
William Morris Agency Inc.; Los Angeles; theatrical talent agent   500
Plantel Nurseries Inc.; Los Angeles; retail nurseries   500
ABM Janitorial Services; El Segundo; building maintenance   500
ChevronTexaco Corp.; El Segundo; petroleum refining   500
Hughes Aircraft Employees Federal Credit Union Inc.; Manhattan Beach; federal credit unions   500
Skechers USA Inc.; Manhattan Beach; footwear   500
TRW Inc.; Redondo Beach; motor vehicle parts/accessories   500
TBWA Chiat/Day Inc.; Venice; advertising   500
Tenet Healthcare Corp.; Venice; medical and surgical hospital   500
Just Right Help Services Inc.; Torrance; personal care home, with health care   500

California 37th District

Southern Los Angeles County — most of Long Beach, Compton, Carson

The 37th combines some of the state's poorest and most Democratic communities with a large chunk of middle-class Long Beach. Minorities made up about 81 percent of the population in the 2000 census, with Hispanics as the dominant group, totaling 43.2 percent of residents. The district is one-fourth black and more than one-tenth Asian. *(See map p. 121.)*

Many residents are concentrated in the lower- and middle-class cities of Compton and Carson south of Los Angeles; the district also contains a tiny sliver of Los Angeles itself. These communities boost Democratic presidential candidates to high margins of victory in the 37th. Al Gore captured 75.9 percent of the vote here in 2000.

The district's south end contains the noncoastal portion of Long Beach (the port is in the 46th), which holds a more suburban, politically mixed community. It has a sizable Cambodian population, and more than four dozen languages are spoken in the public schools.

The 37th's troubled economy suffered in the 1992 riots when fires ravaged parts of Compton. Despite redevelopment, Compton still has blocks-long stretches of abandoned buildings and vacant lots, and gang problems persist.

There are some bright spots, however. Several national retailers and fast-food chains have moved into communities once considered undevelopable, and home sales have increased. The multibillion-dollar Alameda Corridor project, which links the ports of Long Beach and Los Angeles south of the 27th to distribution areas in Los Angeles north of the district, created construction jobs for the area, and local leaders hope it will continue to provide an economic boost.

Major Industry
Service, manufacturing, oil.

Notable
Toyota, which operates a manufacturing plant in Long Beach, is the title sponsor of the Grand Prix of Long Beach auto race.

Election Returns

	Republican		Democratic		Other	
President 2000	31,832	21.5%	112,235	75.9%	3,712	2.5%
House 2002	20,154	23.2%	63,445	72.9%	3,413	3.9%

District Profile

Population   639,088

Total area (square miles)   75
   Land area (square miles)   74

Population per square mile   8,569.6

Counties (2000 population)
   Los Angeles (pt.)   639,088

Cities and other areas over 10,000 (2000 population)
   Carson   89,730
   Compton   93,493
   Long Beach (pt.)   368,591
   Los Angeles (pt.)   33,808
   Willowbrook CDP (pt.)   21,096

Race and Hispanic or Latino origin*
   White   16.6%
   Black or African American   24.8%
   American Indian or Alaska Native   0.3%
   Asian   11.1%

Native Hawaiian or other Pacific Islander   1.4%
Some other race   0.2%
Hispanic or Latino origin   43.2%
Two or more races   2.4%

As percentage of total population.

Ancestry*

English   2.4%   Italian   1.4%
German   3.2%   USA/American   1.6%
Irish   2.7%

As estimated percentage of total population.

Universities and colleges, 2000–2001 enrollment

Brooks College, Long Beach   1,618
California State University-Dominguez Hills, Carson   12,848
Compton Community College, Compton   6,643
Devry University, Long Beach   2,877
Educorp Career College, Long Beach   487
ITT Technical Institute, Torrance   572
Keller Graduate School of Management, Long Beach   589
Long Beach City College, Long Beach   20,926
Nova Institute of Health Technology, Long Beach   369
Pacific Coast University School of Law, Long Beach*

Enrollment under 100. See Sources and Explanations in the front of the volume.

Newspapers and circulation

	District circulation	Total circulation
Long Beach Press-Telegram	28,110	94,944
Los Angeles La Opinion	4,781	127,108
Los Angeles Times	23,617	1,044,205
Torrance Daily Breeze	6,941	79,363

Television stations and affiliations

Los Angeles	100%	KABC	ABC
Los Angeles	100%	KADY	Independent
Los Angeles	100%	KCAL	Independent
Los Angeles	100%	KCBS	CBS
Los Angeles	100%	KCET	PBS
Los Angeles	100%	KCOP	UPN
Los Angeles	100%	KDOC	Independent
Los Angeles	100%	KHIZ	Independent
Los Angeles	100%	KJLA	Independent
Los Angeles	100%	KLCS	PBS
Los Angeles	100%	KMEX	Univision
Los Angeles	100%	KNBC	NBC
Los Angeles	100%	KOCE	PBS
Los Angeles	100%	KPXN	PAX
Los Angeles	100%	KRCA	PBS
Los Angeles	100%	KSCI	Independent
Los Angeles	100%	KTBN	Independent
Los Angeles	100%	KTLA	WB
Los Angeles	100%	KTTV	FOX
Los Angeles	100%	KVCR	PBS
Los Angeles	100%	KVEA	Telemundo
Los Angeles	100%	KWHY	Independent Spanish

Cable systems and subscribers

Charter   2,023
Comcast   22,664

Businesses and other major employers

Boeing Co.; Long Beach; aircraft   10,000
Memorial Hospital; Long Beach   7,334
Los Angeles County Hospital; Los Angeles   3,800
Coastcast Corp.; Compton; golf equipment   3,500
Inchon Iron and Steel Co.; Gardena; metal scrap and waste materials   3,000
Long Beach Memorial Medical Center; Long Beach   2,705
Maintenance Staff Inc.; Long Beach; janitorial service   2,600
Nissan North America Inc.; Gardena; commercial vehicles   2,500
Leiner Health Products Group Inc.; Carson; vitamin, nutrient, hematinic preparations   1,800
Long Beach Police Officers Assn. Inc.; Long Beach; labor union   1,800
Long Beach Community College District; Long Beach   1,700
United Technologies Corp.; Long Beach; aircraft engines and parts   1,510
California State University System; Carson   1,270
Charles R. Drew University of Medicine and Science; Los Angeles   1,000
Raytheon Technical Services Co.; Long Beach; commercial physical research   950
TRW Inc.; Carson; guided missiles and space vehicles   900
U.S. Postal Service; Long Beach   900
Belkin Components; Compton; computer peripheral equipment   800
Food 4 Less Holdings Inc.; Compton; supermarkets   800
Ralphs Grocery Co.; Compton; supermarkets   800
Jonathan Louis International; Gardena; household furniture   800
TRW Inc.; Carson; satellite communications   800
Lakeshore Learning Materials; Carson; education aids   800
Long Beach Transit; Long Beach   750
Construction Protective Services Inc.; Gardena; protective services, guard   700
Pepsi-Cola Metropolitan Bottling Co.; Carson; soft drinks   700
Irwin Industries Inc.; Long Beach; power plant construction   700
Pacific Hospital of Long Beach; Long Beach   610
Goodhew Ambulance Service Inc.; Torrance; ambulance service   600
R. R. Donnelley and Sons Co.; Torrance; publication printing   600
Langner Security Services Inc.; Long Beach; security guard service   600
AFSA Data Corp.; Long Beach; loan brokers   600
Computer Sciences Corp.; Long Beach; computer integrated systems design   600
Catholic Healthcare West Southern California; Long Beach   600
Long Beach City; Long Beach; public health programs   600
Long Beach Public Transportation Co.; Long Beach   570

TABC Inc.; Long Beach; motor vehicle parts/accessories 543

Epson America Inc.; Long Beach; computer peripherals, software 510

Denso Sales California Inc.; Long Beach; automotive supplies, parts 504

Techmer PM Inc.; Compton; plastics materials and resins 500

DeMenno/Kerdoon; Compton; hazardous waste transport 500

Prime Wheel Corp.; Gardena; motor vehicle wheels 500

Atlantic Richfield Co.; Carson; gasoline stations 500

Los Angeles County Sanitation Districts; Carson 500

Long Beach City; Long Beach; fire dept. 500

Hanger Prosthetics and Orthotics Inc.; Long Beach; orthopedic appliances 500

Ondis Capital Corp.; Long Beach; investment holding company 500

California 38th District

East Los Angeles County — Pomona, Norwalk

The Democratic 38th, once a predominantly white area, has become a middle- and working-class Hispanic-majority district. A sideways "L" shape, it takes in the southeast Los Angeles County city of Norwalk, then stretches north along Interstate 5 to include nearly half of East Los Angeles. It then runs east through Montebello and Pico Rivera, goes north a bit to La Puente, and then extends a thin arm parallel to the 60 Freeway into the Inland Valley to take in Pomona, the district's largest city, at the county's eastern edge. *(See map p. 121.)*

Though mostly blue-collar, the district contains some affluent and conservative areas such as Hacienda Heights, Rowland Heights (shared with the 42nd), and a narrow sliver of Whittier.

Small businesses dominate the 38th, which contains the heart of the East Los Angeles business district. Stores generally are owned or operated by Hispanics. These suburbs are partly populated by what used to be called Muppies— Mexican yuppies who have moved in and fixed up old homes.

Montebello is an upper-middle-class Hispanic area, with a lot of home-grown residents. Pico Rivera has been called a pure Middle American working community, Hispanic-style. The city received a major blow in 2000 with the closure of a Northrop Grumman B-2 plant. Norwalk, the district's second-largest city, is a bedroom community. Santa Fe Springs is an industrial area with light manufacturing and oil wells.

The district's workers and seniors ensure that it is reliably Democratic on all levels as voters focus on health care and small-business support issues. Democratic presidential candidate Al Gore received 70.1 percent of the vote here in 2000. California State Polytechnic University, Pomona College, and Cerritos College add students to the Democratic mix.

Major Industry

Manufacturing, oil.

Notable

The Pomona Swap Meet and Car Show is billed as the largest collection of antique cars, parts, and accessories on the West Coast.

Election Returns

	Republican		Democratic		Other	
President 2000	41,706	27.9%	104,612	70.1%	2,929	2.0%
House 2002	23,126	26.3%	62,600	71.1%	2,301	2.6%

District Profile

Population 639,088

Total area (square miles) 105
   Land area (square miles) 103

Population per square mile 6,151.6

Counties (2000 population)
   Los Angeles (pt.) 639,088

Cities and other areas over 10,000 (2000 population)
   Avocado Heights CDP 15,148
   East Los Angeles CDP (pt.) 53,349
   Hacienda Heights CDP 53,122
   La Puente 41,063
   Montebello 62,150
   Norwalk 103,298
   Pico Rivera 63,428
   Pomona 149,473
   Santa Fe Springs 17,438
   South San Jose Hills CDP 20,218
   Valinda CDP (pt.) 19,001
   West Puente Valley CDP 22,589

Race and Hispanic or Latino origin*
   White 13.6%
   Black or African American 3.6%
   American Indian or Alaska Native 0.3%
   Asian 10.2%
   Native Hawaiian or other Pacific Islander 0.1%
   Some other race 0.1%
   Hispanic or Latino origin 70.6%
   Two or more races 1.4%

*As percentage of total population.

Ancestry*

English 1.8%	Italian 1.3%
German 2.7%	USA/American 1.7%
Irish 1.8%	

*As estimated percentage of total population.

Universities and colleges, 2000–2001 enrollment
   California State Polytechnic University, Pomona 18,424
   Devry University, Pomona 3,674
   Keller Graduate School of Management, Pomona*
   Rio Hondo College, Whittier 19,506
   Western University of Health Sciences, Pomona 1,471

*Enrollment under 100. See Sources and Explanations in the front of the volume.

Newspapers and circulation

	District circulation	Total circulation
Inland Valley Daily Bulletin	6,614	65,184
Long Beach Press-Telegram	4,485	94,944
Los Angeles La Opinion	7,600	127,108
Los Angeles Times	27,564	1,044,205
San Gabriel Valley Tribune	8,087	48,476
Whittier Daily News	5,668	16,991

Television stations and affiliations

Los Angeles	100%	KABC	ABC
Los Angeles	100%	KADY	Independent
Los Angeles	100%	KCAL	Independent
Los Angeles	100%	KCBS	CBS
Los Angeles	100%	KCET	PBS
Los Angeles	100%	KCOP	UPN
Los Angeles	100%	KDOC	Independent
Los Angeles	100%	KHIZ	Independent
Los Angeles	100%	KJLA	Independent
Los Angeles	100%	KLCS	PBS
Los Angeles	100%	KMEX	Univision
Los Angeles	100%	KNBC	NBC
Los Angeles	100%	KOCE	PBS
Los Angeles	100%	KPXN	PAX
Los Angeles	100%	KRCA	PBS
Los Angeles	100%	KSCI	Independent
Los Angeles	100%	KTBN	Independent
Los Angeles	100%	KTLA	WB
Los Angeles	100%	KTTV	FOX
Los Angeles	100%	KVCR	PBS
Los Angeles	100%	KVEA	Telemundo
Los Angeles	100%	KWHY	Independent Spanish

Cable systems and subscribers

Adelphia   50,132
Charter   16,397
Comcast   1,821

Businesses and other major employers

Pomona Valley Hospital Medical Center; Pomona 2,121

Smoke Shop; Norwalk; tobacco stores and stands   2,001

California State University; Pomona   1,814

Rio Hondo Community College District; Whittier 1,500

Norwalk-La Mirada Unified School District; Norwalk 1,300

Rockwell Collins Inc.; Pomona; airborne radio communications equipment   1,200

Lights of America Inc.; Walnut; residential fluorescent lighting fixtures   1,192

Sysco Food Services; Walnut; food supplier   1,175

Sasco Electric; Artesia; electrical contractor   1,100

U.S. Postal Service; City of Industry   1,000

May Department Stores Co.; City of Industry; warehousing   1,000

Beverly Community Hospital Assn.; Montebello   950

Los Angeles County Sanitation Districts; Whittier   850

Rose Hills Mortuary Inc.; Whittier; funeral service and crematories   850

Entenmann's Inc.; Montebello; breads and cakes   850

Vons Companies Inc.; Santa Fe Springs; general warehousing, storage   800

Household International Inc.; Pomona; consumer finance companies   800

Los Angeles County; Norwalk; courts   660

Spectrum International Holdings Inc.; City of Industry; postal lock boxes, mail racks, related products   620

Leegin Creative Leather Products Inc.; City of Industry; apparel belts   600

Laborers International Union of Northamerica Local 806; Pomona; labor union   600

Minson Corp.; Montebello; metal lawn furniture   550

Kim Lighting Inc.; City of Industry; outdoor lighting equipment   550

Bentley Prince Street Inc.; City of Industry; carpets 550

Acorn Engineering Co.; City of Industry; plumbing fixtures: enameled   525

Viking Freight Inc.; Whittier; trucking terminal facilities   500

Industrial Container Services; Montebello; professional instrument repair services   500

Mexican American Opportunity Foundation; Montebello; social service center   500

Initial Security Inc.; Santa Fe Springs; security protective devices   500

McMaster-Carr Supply Co.; Santa Fe Springs; industrial supplies   500

Myers Custom Products; Santa Fe Springs; traffic signals 500

Mike Campbell and Associates; City of Industry; local trucking, without storage   500

Norstar Office Products; City of Industry; office furniture 500

Everett Charles Technologies Inc.; Pomona; electronic/electrical circuits test equipment   500

Lockheed Martin Corp.; Pomona; electronic teaching machines/aids   500

C&C Concessions Inc.; Pomona; concessionaire   500

Owens-Brockway Glass Container Inc.; Walnut; flat glass   500

California 39th District

Southeast Los Angeles County — South Gate, Lakewood

The 39th is a product of the post-2000 census redistricting cycle: state legislators carved the area out as an open seat designed to elect a Hispanic Democrat from Los Angeles County south of downtown. It was 61.2 percent Hispanic in the 2000 census, and registered Democrats outnumber Republicans almost two to one. Despite their external similarities, most of these communities have little interaction with one another. *(See map p. 121.)*

The district has a strong organized-labor movement. Towns like Whittier (shared with the 42nd) and Lakewood have a number of industrial centers, and most residents work in the district or nearby rather than commuting to downtown Los Angeles, Orange County, or Long Beach.

Whittier and South Whittier, on the U-shaped district's northeastern tip, are home to many second- and third-generation Latino families, and pockets of wealth exist there. La Mirada and the Asian-American-heavy Cerritos, on the eastern arm of the U, are slightly more conservative communities that resemble cities in neighboring, richer Orange County—former farm areas now dependent on aerospace and technology jobs. Lakewood, on the southern arc of the U, is more blue-collar, while South Gate, Lynwood, and Paramount, farther west, are heavily working class and include many new immigrants.

Major Industry

Manufacturing, aerospace.

Notable

Whittier, where Richard Nixon lived and attended college, was the epicenter of the area's 1987 earthquake; Paramount is home to Zamboni, maker of the ice resurfacing machines used at skating and hockey rinks; the home of the last Mexican governor of California is in Pio Pico Historical Park.

Election Returns

	Republican		Democratic		Other	
President 2000	56,067	35.5%	98,478	62.4%	3,390	2.1%
House 2002	38,925	40.8%	52,256	54.8%	4,165	4.4%

District Profile

Population   639,088

Total area (square miles)   65
   Land area (square miles)   64

Population per square mile   9,861.2

Counties (2000 population)
   Los Angeles (pt.)   639,088

Cities and other areas over 10,000 (2000 population)
   Artesia   16,380
   Cerritos   51,488
   Florence-Graham CDP (pt.)   28,572
   Hawaiian Gardens   14,779
   Lakewood   79,345
   La Mirada   46,783
   Lynwood   69,845
   Paramount   55,266
   South Gate   96,375
   South Whittier CDP   55,193
   West Whittier-Los Nietos CDP   25,129
   Whittier (pt.)   56,918
   Willowbrook CDP (pt.)   13,042

Race and Hispanic or Latino origin*
   White   21.0%
   Black or African American   6.1%
   American Indian or Alaska Native   0.3%
   Asian   9.5%
   Native Hawaiian or other Pacific Islander   0.3%
   Some other race   0.1%
   Hispanic or Latino origin   61.2%
   Two or more races   1.5%

*As percentage of total population.

Ancestry*

English	3.0%	Italian	1.7%
German	4.3%	USA/American	1.9%
Irish	3.3%		

*As estimated percentage of total population.

Universities and colleges, 2000–2001 enrollment
   Biola University, La Mirada   4,092
   Cerritos College, Norwalk   24,536
   Los Angeles College of Chiropractic, Whittier   638
   Nova Institute of Health Technology, Whittier   352
   Platt College, Cerritos   265

Newspapers and circulation

	District circulation	Total circulation
Long Beach Press-Telegram	22,018	94,944
Los Angeles La Opinion	6,429	127,108
Los Angeles Times	22,005	1,044,205
Orange County Register	2,995	319,326
Whittier Daily News	7,166	16,991

Television stations and affiliations

Los Angeles	100%	KABC	ABC
Los Angeles	100%	KADY	Independent
Los Angeles	100%	KCAL	Independent
Los Angeles	100%	KCBS	CBS
Los Angeles	100%	KCET	PBS
Los Angeles	100%	KCOP	UPN
Los Angeles	100%	KDOC	Independent
Los Angeles	100%	KHIZ	Independent
Los Angeles	100%	KJLA	Independent
Los Angeles	100%	KLCS	PBS
Los Angeles	100%	KMEX	Univision
Los Angeles	100%	KNBC	NBC
Los Angeles	100%	KOCE	PBS
Los Angeles	100%	KPXN	PAX
Los Angeles	100%	KRCA	PBS
Los Angeles	100%	KSCI	Independent
Los Angeles	100%	KTBN	Independent
Los Angeles	100%	KTLA	WB
Los Angeles	100%	KTTV	FOX
Los Angeles	100%	KVCR	PBS
Los Angeles	100%	KVEA	Telemundo
Los Angeles	100%	KWHY	Independent Spanish

Cable systems and subscribers
   Adelphia   7,367
   Charter   10,045
   Comcast   37,432
   Verizon   7,700

Businesses and other major employers
   Roger Mayberry; La Mirada; personal interest organization   2,500
   Southern Wine and Spirits of America Inc.; Cerritos; wine   2,000
   International Business Machines Corp.; La Mirada; computer facilities management   1,500
   United Parcel Service Inc.; Cerritos; parcel delivery   1,500

Lincoln Security Services Inc.; Cerritos; burglary protection   1,130

Interhealth Corp.; Whittier; medical and surgical hospital   1,100

Cerritos Community College District; Norwalk   1,050

Koos Manufacturing Inc.; South Gate; sewing contractor   1,030

Presbyterian Intercommunity Hospital Inc.; Whittier   1,000

Biola University; La Mirada   1,000

Hawaiian Gardens Card Club Inc.; Hawaiian Gardens; gambling   960

U.S. Foodservice Inc.; La Mirada; food supplier   800

Bluepoint Swim Inc.; Mission Viejo; women's and children's sportswear/swimsuits   750

Danka Imaging Distribution Inc. Whittier; management services   700

City of Cerritos; Cerritos; government   675

Southern California Specialty Care Inc.; La Mirada; specialty hospitals   600

AB Cellular Holding Co.; Cerritos; local/long-distance telephone   600

Tenet Healthcare Corp.; Lakewood; medical and surgical hospital   590

Bragg Investment Co.; Long Beach; crane and aerial lift service   580

Crown Bolt Inc.; Cerritos; screws   543

GI Trucking Co.; La Mirada; contract haulers   525

California Youth and Adult Correctional Agency; Whittier   500

Owens-Brockway Plastics Products Inc.; La Mirada; plastic containers   500

Bragg Investment Co.; Paramount; building maintenance   500

Tenet Health Care Systems Inc.; Paramount; occupational therapy   500

California 40th District

North central Orange County — Orange, Fullerton

As with most of Orange County, the 40th is largely affluent and Republican, though these inland areas are less affluent than the coast. The district forms a half circle, extending north from Los Alamitos on the Los Angeles County border to take in most of Fullerton before turning southeast to reach Orange and Villa Park. It wraps around Anaheim and Garden Grove, taking in small chunks of each. *(See map p. 121.)*

Orange, the solidly suburban district's largest city, and Fullerton are both upper middle class, while Stanton and Cypress are the district's more blue-collar communities. The median home value in the district was $231,000 according to the 2000 census, median income is high and, unemployment is low. Whites make up about half of the district's population, which is seeing an influx of wealthier Hispanics. Several cities are nearly half Hispanic, while the district overall was 29.6 percent Hispanic and 15.6 percent Asian in the 2000 census. In the 2000 presidential race, George W. Bush defeated Al Gore here 56.4 percent to 40.8 percent.

Before massive growth in the 1960s and 1970s, Orange County consisted largely of orange and lemon groves, and many cities were dairy farm communities. Now the economy centers on aerospace and defense, and new high-tech firms have sprung up in the district. The 40th also has a sizable senior population.

Fullerton is home to a Raytheon facility and a Kimberly-Clark paper mill, as well as a California State University campus that is the city's major employer. Adams Rite Aerospace in Fullerton makes airplane cockpit security doors, which Congress mandated after the September 11, 2001, terrorist attacks. Orange is a health care center, and the district is home to four major hospitals.

Major Industry

Aerospace, defense, manufacturing, health care.

Notable

Beach Boulevard in Buena Park features attractions such as Knott's Berry Farm—the first theme park in the United States, the Movieland Wax Museum, Ripley's Believe It or Not, Wild Bill's Wild West Dinner Extravaganza, and the Medieval Times dinner and tournament.

Election Returns

	Republican		Democratic		Other	
President 2000	119,443	56.4%	86,460	40.8%	5,886	2.8%
House 2002	92,422	67.6%	40,265	29.5%	3,955	2.9%

District Profile

Population   639,088

Total area (square miles)   101
   Land area (square miles)   100

Population per square mile   6,387.5

Counties (2000 population)
   Orange (pt.)   639,088

Cities and other areas over 10,000 (2000 population)
   Anaheim (pt.)   87,082
   Buena Park   78,282
   Cypress   46,229
   Fullerton (pt.)   108,151
   Garden Grove (pt.)   34,656
   La Palma   15,408
   Los Alamitos   11,536
   Orange   128,821
   Placentia (pt.)   37,356
   Rossmoor CDP   10,298
   Stanton   37,403
   Westminster (pt.)   27,808

Race and Hispanic or Latino origin*
   White   49.3%
   Black or African American   2.2%
   American Indian or Alaska Native   0.3%
   Asian   15.6%
   Native Hawaiian or other Pacific Islander   0.4%
   Some other race   0.2%
   Hispanic or Latino origin   29.6%
   Two or more races   2.4%

As percentage of total population.

Ancestry*

Dutch	1.2%	Norwegian	1.2%
English	6.8%	Polish	1.4%
French	2.1%	Scottish	1.4%
German	9.3%	Swedish	1.2%
Irish	6.8%	USA/American	2.9%
Italian	3.4%		

As estimated percentage of total population.

Universities and colleges, 2000–2001 enrollment

California State University, Fullerton   28,381
Chapman University, Orange   10,498
Cypress College, Cypress   21,361
Fullerton College, Fullerton   19,993
Hope International University, Fullerton   840
Santiago Canyon College, Orange   10,039
Southern California College of Optometry, Fullerton   378
Western State University College of Law, Fullerton   501

Newspapers and circulation

	District circulation	Total circulation
Long Beach Press-Telegram	2,260	94,944
Los Angeles La Opinion	2,795	127,108
Los Angeles Times	34,181	1,044,205
Orange County Register	74,019	319,326
*USA Today**	1,226	1,674,376

See Sources and Explanations in the front of the volume.

Television stations and affiliations

Los Angeles	100%	KABC	ABC
Los Angeles	100%	KADY	Independent
Los Angeles	100%	KCAL	Independent
Los Angeles	100%	KCBS	CBS
Los Angeles	100%	KCET	PBS
Los Angeles	100%	KCOP	UPN
Los Angeles	100%	KDOC	Independent
Los Angeles	100%	KHIZ	Independent
Los Angeles	100%	KJLA	Independent
Los Angeles	100%	KLCS	PBS
Los Angeles	100%	KMEX	Univision
Los Angeles	100%	KNBC	NBC
Los Angeles	100%	KOCE	PBS
Los Angeles	100%	KPXN	PAX
Los Angeles	100%	KRCA	PBS
Los Angeles	100%	KSCI	Independent
Los Angeles	100%	KTBN	Independent
Los Angeles	100%	KTLA	WB
Los Angeles	100%	KTTV	FOX
Los Angeles	100%	KVCR	PBS
Los Angeles	100%	KVEA	Telemundo
Los Angeles	100%	KWHY	Independent Spanish

Cable systems and subscribers

Adelphia   43,367
Comcast   85,299
Cox   26,481
Time Warner   14,648

Military installations, September 2001

Armed Forces Reserve Center, Los Alamitos   2,586

Businesses and other major employers

St. Joseph Health System; Orange; home health care services   7,311
Independent Merchandising Group; Orange; demonstration service   4,000
Sonica Software Corp.; Orange; computer programming services   4,000
Mitsubishi Electric America; Cypress; electrical entertainment equipment   3,900
St. Joseph Heritage Healthcare; Fullerton   3,500
All-Pro Remodeling Inc.; Orange; residential renovation   3,035
University of California; Orange   3,000
St. Jude Hospital Inc.; Fullerton   2,582
Computer Sciences Corp.; Fullerton; computer consulting services   2,000
St. Joseph Hospital of Orange; Orange   2,000
Alliance Imaging Inc.; Anaheim; medical laboratories   1,900
Combat Support Associates; Orange; engineering services   1,500
Beckman Coulter Inc.; Fullerton; analytical instruments   1,200
Chapman University; Orange   1,050
Automatic Data Processing Inc.; La Palma; data processing   1,000
Orange County Children's Hospital; Orange   1,000
Blaine Convention Services Inc.; Buena Park; exhibit construction   959
Valencia Foods Inc.; Fullerton; canned fruits/specialties   850
PacifiCare of California; Cypress; health maintenance organization   800
Pepsi Cola Federal Credit Union; Los Alamitos; merchandising machine operators   800
O'Hart Personnel Group Inc.; Orange; air courier services   800
Wackenhut Corp.; Orange; protective services, guard   800
Frank A. Barcott Security and Investigations; Cypress; security guard service   750
Alticor Inc.; Buena Park; bulk vitamins   700
Atlantic Richfield Co.; La Palma; communication network services   700
Automotive Caliper Exchange Inc.; Anaheim; motor vehicle brake systems/parts   700
Bace Manufacturing Inc.; Anaheim; injection molding of plastics   700
North Orange County Community College District; Fullerton   700
Thales Raytheon Systems Co.; Fullerton; air traffic control systems, equipment   700
AmerisourceBergen Corp.; Orange; drug and proprietary stores   700
JC Penney Corp.; Buena Park; administrative management   690
West Anaheim Community Hospital; Anaheim   650
St. Gobain Abrasives Inc.; Garden Grove; abrasive wheels   650
Taormina Industries Inc.; Anaheim; garbage collection   630

Tenet Healthcare Corp.; Los Alamitos; medical doctor offices, clinics   625

Trend Offset Printing Services Inc.; Los Alamitos; offset printing   609

Bank of America Corp.; Cypress; commercial bank   600

Arrowhead Products Corp.; Los Alamitos; aircraft parts, equipment   600

Verizon Information Services Inc.; Los Alamitos; telephone directories   600

Corewest Banc; Westminster; mortgage bankers   600

Orman Grubb Co.; Anaheim; wood bedroom furniture   600

Harex Holdings Inc.; Fullerton; concrete fireplaces   600

Padilla Construction Co.; Orange; plastering, drywall insulation   600

Bergen Brunswig Corp.; Orange; drugs, proprietaries, and sundries   600

Air Industries Corp.; Garden Grove; metal bolts   550

Knott's Berry Farm; Buena Park; theme park   500

Mitsubishi Motor Sales of America Inc.; Cypress; automobiles   500

Revcare Inc.; Cypress; collection agency   500

Unigraphics Solutions Inc.; Cypress; computer systems analysis and design   500

Yamaha Motor Corp. USA; Cypress; lawn machinery and equipment   500

Horsemen's Quarter Horse Racing Assn.; Los Alamitos; horses, racing   500

Pacific Health Corp.; Anaheim; medical and surgical hospital   500

Dynamic Details Inc.; Anaheim; printed circuit boards   500

Pacific Bell; Anaheim; local telephone communications   500

Kimberly-Clark Corp.; Fullerton; towels, tissues, and napkins   500

ConAgra Grocery Products Co.; Fullerton; tomato products   500

Ameriquest Mortgage Co.; Orange; mortgage bankers   500

California 41st District

Most of San Bernardino County — Redlands

The 41st includes vast desert and mountain stretches and most of the nation's largest county, San Bernardino, but is home to less than one-third of county residents. The district takes in some eastern Inland Valley communities and a northwest sliver of Riverside County before crossing the San Bernardino Mountains and part of the Mojave Desert to reach the mountains along the Nevada and Arizona borders. Republicans enjoy a 10-point edge in voter registration.

Nearly everyone lives in the western quarter of the 41st, where the district's Inland Empire, Victor Valley, and Riverside County areas are located. Redlands, Highland, Yucaipa, and a portion of the city of San Bernardino are nestled south of the San Bernardino Mountains. *(See map p. 121.)*

The Victor Valley high-desert cities of Hesperia and Apple Valley to the north have seen rapid growth. Affordable land and housing have made the area a magnet for Los Angeles and Orange County workers since the 1990s. The Riverside

County portion of the 41st takes in the San Jacinto Valley and the areas of Banning, San Jacinto, Beaumont, and Calimesa.

As the 41st heads northeast, bordered by Interstate 15 on the north and the San Bernardino-Riverside county line on the south, towns become scarce and desert, mountains, and dry lakes dominate. Exits off Interstate 15 lead mostly to dirt roads. Much of the land here is arid or mountainous, making development difficult. Local hospitals and the government remain the largest employers.

Major Industry
Service, manufacturing, military.

Notable
The Mojave National Preserve, designated in 1994, features the Devil's Playground dunes and the Kelso railroad depot, which was built in 1924; Roy Rogers' former ranch was in Apple Valley.

Election Returns

	Republican		Democratic		Other	
President 2000	114,498	56.3%	83,584	41.1%	5,116	2.5%
House 2002	91,326	67.4%	40,155	29.6%	4,052	3.0%

District Profile

Population   639,087

Total area (square miles)   13,350
   Land area (square miles)   13,314

Population per square mile   48

Counties (2000 population)
   Riverside (pt.)   113,246
   San Bernardino (pt.)   525,841

Cities and other areas over 10,000 (2000 population)
   Apple Valley town   54,239
   Banning   23,562
   Beaumont   11,384
   Crestline CDP   10,218
   Desert Hot Springs   16,582
   Grand Terrace   11,626
   Hesperia   62,582
   Highland   44,605
   Loma Linda   18,681
   Redlands   63,591
   San Bernardino (pt.)   54,789
   San Jacinto   23,779
   Twentynine Palms   14,764
   Valle Vista CDP   10,488
   Yucaipa   41,207
   Yucca Valley town   16,865

Race and Hispanic or Latino origin*
   White   63.5%
   Black or African American   5.3%
   American Indian or Alaska Native   1.0%
   Asian   3.7%
   Native Hawaiian or other Pacific Islander   0.2%
   Some other race   0.2%
   Hispanic or Latino origin   23.4%
   Two or more races   2.7%

As percentage of total population.

Ancestry*

Dutch	1.8%	Norwegian	1.3%
English	8.4%	Polish	1.3%
French	2.8%	Scotch-Irish	1.5%
German	11.7%	Scottish	1.6%
Irish	8.3%	Swedish	1.5%
Italian	3.4%	USA/American	4.1%

As estimated percentage of total population.

Universities and colleges, 2000–2001 enrollment

California State University, San Bernardino 14,909
College of the Desert, Joshua Tree 2,172
Crafton Hills College, Yucaipa 5,054
ITT Technical Institute, San Bernardino 817
Loma Linda University, Loma Linda 3,153
Mt. San Jacinto College, San Jacinto 9,045
University of Redlands, Redlands 4,143

Newspapers and circulation

	District circulation	Total circulation
Barstow Desert Dispatch	1,931	5,241
Los Angeles Times	16,735	1,044,205
Palm Springs Desert Sun	3,686	52,122
Redlands Daily Facts	7,015	7,007
Riverside Press-Enterprise	25,624	176,422
San Bernardino Sun	41,947	72,213
*USA Today**	2,562	1,674,376
Victorville Daily Press	17,696	29,283

See Sources and Explanations in the front of the volume.

Television stations and affiliations

Los Angeles	99%	KABC	ABC
Los Angeles	99%	KADY	Independent
Los Angeles	99%	KCAL	Independent
Los Angeles	99%	KCBS	CBS
Los Angeles	99%	KCET	PBS
Los Angeles	99%	KCOP	UPN
Los Angeles	99%	KDOC	Independent
Los Angeles	99%	KHIZ	Independent
Los Angeles	99%	KJLA	Independent
Los Angeles	99%	KLCS	PBS
Los Angeles	99%	KMEX	Univision
Los Angeles	99%	KNBC	NBC
Los Angeles	99%	KOCE	PBS
Los Angeles	99%	KPXN	PAX
Los Angeles	99%	KRCA	PBS
Los Angeles	99%	KSCI	Independent
Los Angeles	99%	KTBN	Independent
Los Angeles	99%	KTLA	WB
Los Angeles	99%	KTTV	FOX
Los Angeles	99%	KVCR	PBS
Los Angeles	99%	KVEA	Telemundo
Los Angeles	99%	KWHY	Independent Spanish
Palm Springs	1%	KESQ	ABC
Palm Springs	1%	KMIR	NBC

Cable systems and subscribers

Adelphia 62,433
Charter 44,549
Citizens Cable 1,348
Time Warner 6,481

Military installations, September 2001

Marine Corps Air Force Combat Center, Twentynine Palms 10,544

Businesses and other major employers

Loma Linda University Medical Center; Loma Linda 4,600
U.S. Veterans Hospital; Loma Linda 2,000
California Dept. of Mental Health; Patton 2,000
Casino Morongo; Cabazon; casino 1,500
San Manuel Indian Bingo and Casino; Highland; bingo hall 1,374
Loma Linda University; Loma Linda 1,339
Environmental Systems Research Institute Inc.; Redlands; computer software 1,300
California State University; San Bernardino 1,283
Epic Management; Redlands; nursing/personal care facility management 1,200
Stater Bros. Markets; Colton; supermarkets 1,000
San Bernardino County; Loma Linda; county government 1,000
Marine Corps Personnel Support; Twentynine Palms; variety stores 968
Redlands Community Hospital Inc.; Redlands 900
University of Redlands; Redlands 900
St. Mary Regional Medical Center; Apple Valley 700
San Bernardino Community College District; Yucaipa 500

California 42nd District

Parts of Orange, Los Angeles, and San Bernardino Counties — Mission Viejo, Chino

Though most of its population lives in Orange County, the Republican 42nd is centered around the area where Orange, Los Angeles, and San Bernardino Counties come together east of Los Angeles proper. *(See map p. 121.)*

From there, the 42nd has a long arm that stretches southeast and then southwest farther into Orange County to Mission Viejo. Its most southeastern city, Rancho Santa Margarita, is also its newest, incorporated in 2000 with a population of 47,214. A chunk of eastern Anaheim also falls within the district's borders.

Chino and Chino Hills in San Bernardino County have an agricultural heritage, but dairy production is giving way to manufacturing and service industries. Diamond Bar, Whittier (shared with the 39th), and Rowland Heights (shared with the 38th) in Los Angeles County have large Asian populations. Hispanics and Asians also are found in the northern Orange County cities of Brea (one of the fastest-growing in the county), La Habra and Placentia (shared with the 40th), though this Orange County segment is predominantly white-collar and white. Conservatism persists even among nonwhites, and Republicans hold a 20 percentage point voter registration edge in the 42nd.

Overall, the district is predominantly middle- and upper-class and is about 24 percent Hispanic and 16 percent Asian. It is home to many married couples and families but has a low percentage of senior citizens. Unemployment is low and housing prices, particularly in Orange County, are above average. Many of the residential communities' commuters travel to work in Los Angeles or nearby Irvine (which is located in the 48th).

Major Industry
Service, manufacturing, dairy.

Notable
Yorba Linda, the birthplace and burial site of President Richard M. Nixon, is the home of the Nixon Library.

Election Returns

	Republican		Democratic		Other	
President 2000	139,655	58.9%	92,169	38.9%	5,157	2.2%
House 2002	98,476	67.8%	42,090	29.0%	4,680	3.2%

District Profile

Population   639,088

Total area (square miles)   317
  Land area (square miles)   313

Population per square mile   2,036.8

Counties (2000 population)
Los Angeles (pt.)   131,473
Orange (pt.)   367,512
San Bernardino (pt.)   140,103

Cities and other areas over 10,000 (2000 population)
Anaheim (pt.)   55,395
Brea   35,410
Chino   67,168
Chino Hills   66,787
Diamond Bar   56,287
La Habra   58,974
Mission Viejo   93,102
Rancho Santa Margarita   47,214
Rowland Heights CDP (pt.)   41,581
Whittier (pt.)   25,151
Yorba Linda   58,918

Race and Hispanic or Latino origin*
White   54.4%
Black or African American   2.9%
American Indian or Alaska Native   0.3%
Asian   15.9%
Native Hawaiian or other Pacific Islander   0.2%
Some other race   0.2%
Hispanic or Latino origin   23.8%
Two or more races   2.4%

*As percentage of total population.

Ancestry*
Dutch 1.3%	Norwegian 1.3%
English 7.4%	Polish 1.7%
French 2.2%	Scottish 1.5%
German 10.2%	Swedish 1.4%
Irish 7.4%	USA/American 2.6%
Italian 4.4%	

*As estimated percentage of total population.

Universities and colleges, 2000–2001 enrollment
Saddleback College, Mission Viejo   18,563
Whittier College, Whittier   2,682

Newspapers and circulation

	District circulation	Total circulation
Inland Valley Daily Bulletin	7,618	65,184
Los Angeles La Opinion	1,378	127,108
Los Angeles Times	40,292	1,044,205
Orange County Register	50,869	319,326
San Gabriel Valley Tribune	2,237	48,476
*USA Today**	2,339	1,674,376
Whittier Daily News	4,007	16,991

*See Sources and Explanations in the front of the volume.

Television stations and affiliations
Los Angeles	100%	KABC	ABC
Los Angeles	100%	KADY	Independent
Los Angeles	100%	KCAL	Independent
Los Angeles	100%	KCBS	CBS
Los Angeles	100%	KCET	PBS
Los Angeles	100%	KCOP	UPN
Los Angeles	100%	KDOC	Independent
Los Angeles	100%	KHIZ	Independent
Los Angeles	100%	KJLA	Independent
Los Angeles	100%	KLCS	PBS
Los Angeles	100%	KMEX	Univision
Los Angeles	100%	KNBC	NBC
Los Angeles	100%	KOCE	PBS
Los Angeles	100%	KPXN	PAX
Los Angeles	100%	KRCA	PBS
Los Angeles	100%	KSCI	Independent
Los Angeles	100%	KTBN	Independent
Los Angeles	100%	KTLA	WB
Los Angeles	100%	KTTV	FOX
Los Angeles	100%	KVCR	PBS
Los Angeles	100%	KVEA	Telemundo
Los Angeles	100%	KWHY	Independent Spanish

Cable systems and subscribers
Adelphia   77,821
Charter   14,757
Cox   28,794

Businesses and other major employers
Boeing Co.; Chino Hills; radio/TV communications equipment   5,000
California Dept. of Corrections; Chino   3,000
Toshiba; Mission Viejo; electric housewares and fans   2,000
Kaiser Foundation Hospitals; Anaheim   1,700
U.S. Postal Service; Yorba Linda   1,600
Hussmann International Inc.; Chino; refrigeration and heating equipment   1,500
Mission Hospital Regional Medical Center; Mission Viejo   1,350
Jasper Electronics; Anaheim; electronic switches   1,200
Walnut Valley Unified School District; Walnut   1,050
South Orange County Community College District; Mission Viejo   1,000
Quest Diagnostics Clinical Laboratories Inc.; Brea; medical laboratories   1,000
Circuit City Stores Inc.; Yorba Linda; radio, television, and electronic stores   1,000
Sundance Spas Inc.; Chino; hot tubs   950
Albertson's Inc.; Brea; general warehousing, storage   950

California Youth and Adult Correctional Agency; Chino 850

San Marino Plastering Inc.; Anaheim; plastering, drywall insulation   820

Parker Hannifin Corp.; Mission Viejo; aircraft parts, equipment   800

South Coast Air Quality Management District Inc.; Diamond Bar   772

Cox Communications Inc.; Rancho Santa Margarita; cable television   750

Keenan Hopkins Suder Stowell Contractors Inc.; Anaheim; plastering, plain or ornamental   700

Mercury General Corp.; Brea; automobile insurance 700

Kirkhill-TA Co.; Brea; reclaimed rubber, specialty rubber compounds   625

First American Real Estate Solutions; Anaheim; real estate agents and managers   600

Whittier Hospital Medical Center Inc.; Whittier   580

Eurodesign Cabinets Inc.; Chino; wood kitchen cabinets 550

Biosense Webster Inc.; Diamond Bar; electromedical apparatus   525

Tenet Healthsystem Medical Inc.; Whittier; medical laboratories   500

Trend Technologies Inc.; Chino; injection molding of plastics   500

Circuit City Stores Inc.; Walnut; radio, television, and electronic stores   500

Coldwell Banker Residential Real Estate; Mission Viejo; real estate brokers and agents   500

Brea Veterans Club; Brea; veterans' organization   500

PBC Concrete Inc.; Brea; concrete work   500

Peterson Brothers Construction Inc.; Brea; concrete work 500

California 43rd District

Southwest San Bernardino County — Ontario, Fontana, most of San Bernardino

The cities of San Bernardino, Fontana, and Ontario form the base of the 43rd, which is located in the heart of the Inland Valley east of Los Angeles in San Bernardino County. (*See map p. 121.*)

The district is part of California's fastest-growing region. Some residents commute into Los Angeles along the Pomona and San Bernardino freeways. The Ontario airport, a recently expanded transportation hub, and the sprawling Ontario Mills mall are here. Fontana and Rialto, farther east, also have seen explosive growth. The high mountains around the city of San Bernardino, however, are partly to blame for some of the worst smog in the Los Angeles basin.

The 43rd was 58.3 percent Hispanic in the 2000 census, and registered Democrats outnumber Republicans almost two to one. Even as some neighboring suburbs trended wealthier and more conservative, ethnically diverse San Bernardino and Colton (both of which are shared with the 41st) consistently vote Democratic. The district favors Democrats on all levels and gave Al Gore a 29.5-point margin of victory in the 2000 presidential contest.

This area was a fruit-packing center in the 1930s. Today, its citrus industry shares space with electronics and aerospace firms. A steel mill bankruptcy in the 1980s and the 1994 closing of nearby Norton Air Force Base hurt the district's employment rolls, but new government jobs and growing high-tech and manufacturing industries prove the economy is recovering.

Though it has prospered like its neighbors in Orange and Los Angeles Counties, the district retains a diverse and working-class feel. Local leaders work on efforts to combine economic growth and smart development.

Major Industry

Manufacturing, electronics, construction.

Notable

Wyatt Earp's brother, Virgil, was the first marshal of Colton; Fontana is the birthplace of the Hell's Angels.

Election Returns

	Republican		Democratic		Other	
President 2000	41,272	34.3%	76,710	63.8%	2,293	1.9%
House 2002	20,821	30.5%	45,374	66.4%	2,145	3.1%

District Profile

Population   639,087

Total area (square miles)   192
Land area (square miles)   190

Population per square mile   3,348.1

Counties (2000 population)
San Bernardino (pt.)   639,087

Cities and other areas over 10,000 (2000 population)
Bloomington CDP   19,318
Colton (pt.)   43,349
Fontana   128,929
Ontario   158,007
Rialto   91,873
San Bernardino (pt.)   130,612

Race and Hispanic or Latino origin*
White   23.4%
Black or African American   12.4%
American Indian or Alaska Native   0.4%
Asian   3.1%
Native Hawaiian or other Pacific Islander   0.3%
Some other race   0.2%
Hispanic or Latino origin   58.3%
Two or more races   1.9%

As percentage of total population.

Ancestry*

English	3.0%	Irish	3.4%
French	1.2%	Italian	1.9%
German	4.6%	USA/American	2.3%

As estimated percentage of total population.

Universities and colleges, 2000–2001 enrollment
Nova Institute of Health Technology, Ontario   294
Platt College-Los Angeles, Ontario   268
San Bernardino Valley College, San Bernardino   12,025

Newspapers and circulation

	District circulation	Total circulation
Inland Valley Daily Bulletin	20,164	65,184
Los Angeles La Opinion	3,657	127,108
Los Angeles Times	13,283	1,044,205
Riverside Press-Enterprise	6,547	176,422
San Bernardino Sun	24,098	72,213

Television stations and affiliations

Los Angeles	100%	KABC	ABC
Los Angeles	100%	KADY	Independent
Los Angeles	100%	KCAL	Independent
Los Angeles	100%	KCBS	CBS
Los Angeles	100%	KCET	PBS
Los Angeles	100%	KCOP	UPN
Los Angeles	100%	KDOC	Independent
Los Angeles	100%	KHIZ	Independent
Los Angeles	100%	KJLA	Independent
Los Angeles	100%	KLCS	PBS
Los Angeles	100%	KMEX	Univision
Los Angeles	100%	KNBC	NBC
Los Angeles	100%	KOCE	PBS
Los Angeles	100%	KPXN	PAX
Los Angeles	100%	KRCA	PBS
Los Angeles	100%	KSCI	Independent
Los Angeles	100%	KTBN	Independent
Los Angeles	100%	KTLA	WB
Los Angeles	100%	KTTV	FOX
Los Angeles	100%	KVCR	PBS
Los Angeles	100%	KVEA	Telemundo
Los Angeles	100%	KWHY	Independent Spanish

Cable systems and subscribers
Adelphia   105,885

Businesses and other major employers
Arrow Head Regional Medical Center; Colton   2,500
Kaiser Foundation Hospitals; Fontana   1,700
St. Bernardine Medical Center Inc.; San Bernardino   1,700
San Bernardino County; San Bernardino; medical and surgical hospital   1,650
San Bernardino Community Hospital; San Bernardino   1,500
Ontario-Montclair School District; Ontario   1,336
U.S. Postal Service; Fontana   1,200
California Dept. of Transportation; San Bernardino   1,200
California Steel Industries Inc.; Fontana; steel slabs   950
Mag Instrument Inc.; Ontario; flashlights   800
Target Corp.; Fontana; discount department stores   800
Manheim Investments Inc.; Fontana; auctioneer   800
San Bernardino County; San Bernardino; mental health agency   800
McLane Co.; San Bernardino; warehousing   650
Marriott International Inc.; Ontario; hotels and motels   624
Fleetwood Travel Trailers of California Inc.; Rialto; travel trailers and campers   571
Yellow Freight System Inc.; San Bernardino; contract haulers   563

Kushwood Manufacturing Inc.; Ontario; wood household furniture   505
Burns International Security Services Corp.; Ontario; security guard service   500
General Electric Co.; Ontario; aircraft, heavy equipment repair   500
U.S. Merchants Financial Group Inc.; Ontario; personal service agents   500
Swift Transportation Co. Inc.; Fontana; building materials transport   500
San Bernardino Community College District; San Bernardino   500
San Bernardino County; San Bernardino; county government   500

California 44th District

Northwestern Riverside County — Riverside, Corona

The 44th is a fast-growing residential district that lies east of Los Angeles and north of San Diego. It contains about one-third of Riverside County's residents and the southeastern portion of Orange County that borders San Diego County. *(See map p. 121.)*

Registered Republicans outnumber Democrats about 50 percent to 35 percent, and George W. Bush won the 2000 presidential vote here with 53.3 percent.

The district includes the city of Riverside and the rest of the burgeoning northwestern edge of Riverside County. Riverside began growing navel oranges—still one of the area's major crops—in the nineteenth century. While the 44th has become increasingly Republican overall, the more blue-collar Riverside communities and the areas around the University of California, Riverside lean Democratic.

The district is undergoing major growth as young, white-collar families move into its cities. The trend is especially true in Norco and Corona, where low real estate prices have produced attractive bedroom communities for commuters into Orange and Los Angeles Counties. Despite the influx, manufacturing and agriculture (including dairy, citrus, grapes, dates, and avocados) contribute to the economy, though they are being driven farther east and out of the district as the Los Angeles area continues to expand. Orange County areas include the coastal city of San Clemente, San Juan Capistrano (shared with the 48th), and Santa Ana Mountain forests.

Local officials are trying to halt illegal drug production in the Inland Empire, dubbed by some as the methamphetamine capital of the world.

Major Industry
Manufacturing, agriculture, health care.

Notable
Riverside's Mission Inn was where Richard and Pat Nixon were married and Ronald and Nancy Reagan stopped on their honeymoon.

Election Returns

	Republican		Democratic		Other	
President 2000	101,897	53.3%	84,048	44%	5,143	2.7%
House 2002	76,686	63.7%	38,021	31.6%	5,756	4.8%

District Profile

Population 639,088

Total area (square miles) 548
    Land area (square miles) 522

Population per square mile 1,223.9

Counties (2000 population)
    Orange (pt.) 85,276
    Riverside (pt.) 553,812

Cities and other areas over 10,000 (2000 population)
    Corona 124,966
    Coto de Caza CDP 13,057
    Glen Avon CDP 14,853
    Mira Loma CDP 17,617
    Norco 24,157
    Pedley CDP 11,207
    Riverside 255,166
    Rubidoux CDP 29,180
    San Clemente 49,936
    San Juan Capistrano (pt.) 17,208

Race and Hispanic or Latino origin*
    White 51.3%
    Black or African American 5.5%
    American Indian or Alaska Native 0.5%
    Asian 4.8%
    Native Hawaiian or other Pacific Islander 0.3%
    Some other race 0.2%
    Hispanic or Latino origin 35.0%
    Two or more races 2.4%

As percentage of total population.

Ancestry*

Dutch 1.3%	Italian 3.5%
English 6.8%	Norwegian 1.2%
French 2.2%	Polish 1.3%
German 9.5%	Scottish 1.3%
Irish 7.0%	USA/American 3.4%

As estimated percentage of total population.

Universities and colleges, 2000–2001 enrollment
    California Baptist University, Riverside 2,043
    California Paramedical and Technical College, Riverside 436
    California Southern Law School, Riverside*
    La Sierra University, Riverside 1,411
    Riverside Community College, Riverside 22,107
    University of California, Riverside 13,015

Enrollment under 100. See Sources and Explanations in the front of the volume.

Newspapers and circulation

	District circulation	Total circulation
Los Angeles La Opinion	1,639	127,108
Los Angeles Times	16,364	1,044,205
Orange County Register	10,686	319,326
Riverside Press-Enterprise	72,723	176,422
*USA Today**	2,466	1,674,376

See Sources and Explanations in the front of the volume.

Television stations and affiliations

Los Angeles	100%	KABC	ABC
Los Angeles	100%	KADY	Independent
Los Angeles	100%	KCAL	Independent
Los Angeles	100%	KCBS	CBS
Los Angeles	100%	KCET	PBS
Los Angeles	100%	KCOP	UPN
Los Angeles	100%	KDOC	Independent
Los Angeles	100%	KHIZ	Independent
Los Angeles	100%	KJLA	Independent
Los Angeles	100%	KLCS	PBS
Los Angeles	100%	KMEX	Univision
Los Angeles	100%	KNBC	NBC
Los Angeles	100%	KOCE	PBS
Los Angeles	100%	KPXN	PAX
Los Angeles	100%	KRCA	PBS
Los Angeles	100%	KSCI	Independent
Los Angeles	100%	KTBN	Independent
Los Angeles	100%	KTLA	WB
Los Angeles	100%	KTTV	FOX
Los Angeles	100%	KVCR	PBS
Los Angeles	100%	KVEA	Telemundo
Los Angeles	100%	KWHY	Independent Spanish

Cable systems and subscribers
    Charter 110,028
    Comcast 16,486
    Cox 16,104

Businesses and other major employers
    Am Personnel Partners Inc.; Riverside; employee leasing service 3,800
    Barney Simmons and Co. Inc.; San Clemente; computer maintenance and repair 2,000
    City of Riverside; Riverside; sheriff's office 1,500
    Quest Diagnostics Clinical Laboratories Inc.; Mission Viejo; medical laboratories 1,300
    Riverside Community Health Systems; Riverside; medical and surgical hospital 1,200
    Parkview Community Hospital Medical Center; Riverside 1,149
    Riverside County Office of Education; Riverside 1,143
    Riverside Community College District; Riverside 1,100
    Press Enterprise Co.; Riverside; newspaper 1,000
    Riverside County; Riverside; school for physically handicapped 1,000
    Riverside County; Riverside; probation office 1,000
    Kaiser Foundation Hospitals; Riverside 1,000
    Quest Diagnostics Clinical Laboratories Inc.; San Juan Capistrano; testing laboratories 1,000
    Quadramed Corp.; Corona; collection agency 900
    Riverside County; Riverside; mental health agency 880
    Vista Hospital; Corona 800
    James Hardie Irrigation Inc.; Riverside; self-propelled irrigation equipment 750
    Watson Laboratories Inc.; Corona; pharmaceuticals 750
    Sunstone Hotel Investors Inc.; San Clemente; hotels 744
    Consolidated Freightways Corp. of Delaware; Mira Loma; trucking terminal facilities 700

Riverside County; Riverside; county government   700
Riverside Medical Clinic Inc.; Riverside   700
Fleetwood Enterprises Inc.; Riverside; prefabricated
   buildings, wood   665
Rohr Inc.; Riverside; aircraft parts, equipment   650
Toro Co.; Riverside; lawn and garden tractors and
   equipment   650
Baier and Baier Inc.; San Juan Capistrano; microwave
   components   650
Jurupa Unified School District; Riverside   612
Fleetwood Enterprises; Riverside; mobile homes   600
Viejo Little League; Mission Viejo; outdoor field clubs
   600
Fender Musical Instruments Corp.; Corona; musical
   instruments   600
City Hall; Corona; business services   600
Blackhawk Furniture Inc.; Riverside; wood bedroom
   furniture   555
City of Riverside; Riverside; police dept.   545
HCI Inc.; Norco; communication tower construction
   529
Addus Healthcare Inc.; Riverside; home health care
   services   528
Nichols Institute Reference Laboratories; San Juan
   Capistrano; testing laboratories   525
RCR Plumbing Inc.; Riverside; plumbing, heating,
   air-conditioning   500
Riverside County; Riverside; county government   500
City of Riverside; Riverside; city management   500

California 45th District

Riverside County — Moreno Valley, Palm Springs

Ritzy desert resorts, a booming service industry, and large, irrigated farms fuel the economy of the 45th, whose residents largely reside in one of two Riverside County areas: rapidly growing Inland Empire communities—such as Moreno Valley, Hemet, and Murrieta in the west—or upscale, resort-filled Coachella Valley cities farther east. *(See map p. 121.)*

The Palm Springs area, including Cathedral City, Indian Wells, La Quinta, and Indio, attracts visitors to its numerous golf courses. Once known as playgrounds for the rich and retired, the resort cities have seen an influx of younger, middle-class families. Still, the 45th has the highest percentage of senior citizens in California.

Although the district leans Republican, pockets in Rancho Mirage and Palm Springs tend to vote Democratic. Overall, the district gave George W. Bush 51.2 percent of its vote in the 2000 presidential election, and Republicans hold an 8-point voter registration advantage.

The 45th has grown into a diverse community that is home to some of the richest and poorest areas in the state, with Palm Springs on one end of the economic spectrum and some of the district's Native American reservations on the other. Many poor residents work as migrant farm laborers, in the growing gaming industry, and at tourist shops. Health care service providers and small educational institutions have begun to settle in the district, spurring an increase in professionals.

The Salton Sea—located mainly in the 51st District—attracted attention in the 1990s as one of the nation's most polluted bodies of water. Congress voted in 1998 to fund a cleanup effort in honor of the late GOP representative Sonny Bono, who represented the Riverside district (at the time numbered the 44th) from 1995 until his death in January 1998.

Major Industry

Services, tourism, agriculture, manufacturing.

Notable

Palm Springs is known as the golf capital of the world; President Gerald R. Ford retired to Rancho Mirage; Joshua Tree National Park (shared with the 41st) boasts an abundance of the namesake yuccas and other desert plants and animals.

Election Returns

	Republican		Democratic		Other	
President 2000	93,802	51.2%	85,427	46.6%	4,029	2.2%
House 2002	87,101	65.2%	43,692	32.7%	2,740	2.1%

District Profile

Population   639,088

Total area (square miles)   6,062
   Land area (square miles)   5,979

Population per square mile   106.9

Counties (2000 population)
   Riverside (pt.)   639,088

Cities and other areas over 10,000 (2000 population)

Blythe 12,155	La Quinta 23,694
Cathedral City 42,647	Moreno Valley 142,381
Coachella 22,724	Murrieta 44,282
East Hemet CDP 14,823	Palm Desert 41,155
Hemet 58,812	Palm Springs 42,807
Indio 49,116	Rancho Mirage 13,249

Race and Hispanic or Latino origin*
   White   50.1%
   Black or African American   6.3%
   American Indian or Alaska Native   0.6%
   Asian   2.8%
   Native Hawaiian or other Pacific Islander   0.2%
   Some other race   0.1%
   Hispanic or Latino origin   38.0%
   Two or more races   1.9%

As percentage of total population.

Ancestry*

Dutch 1.2%	Norwegian 1.1%
English 7.1%	Polish 1.3%
French 2.3%	Scotch-Irish 1.1%
German 8.9%	Scottish 1.4%
Irish 6.6%	Swedish 1.3%
Italian 3.1%	USA/American 3.1%

As estimated percentage of total population.

Universities and colleges, 2000–2001 enrollment
   College of the Desert, Palm Desert   6,972
   Palo Verde College, Blythe   3,312

Newspapers and circulation

	District circulation	Total circulation
Los Angeles La Opinion	1,472	127,108
Los Angeles Times	20,819	1,044,205
North County Times	7,446	93,408
Palm Springs Desert Sun	48,240	52,122
Riverside Press-Enterprise	46,082	176,422
San Diego Union Tribune	1,265	357,315
USA Today*	5,780	1,674,376

*See Sources and Explanations in the front of the volume.

Television stations and affiliations

Los Angeles	87%	KABC	ABC
Los Angeles	87%	KADY	Independent
Los Angeles	87%	KCAL	Independent
Los Angeles	87%	KCBS	CBS
Los Angeles	87%	KCET	PBS
Los Angeles	87%	KCOP	UPN
Los Angeles	87%	KDOC	Independent
Los Angeles	87%	KHIZ	Independent
Los Angeles	87%	KJLA	Independent
Los Angeles	87%	KLCS	PBS
Los Angeles	87%	KMEX	Univision
Los Angeles	87%	KNBC	NBC
Los Angeles	87%	KOCE	PBS
Los Angeles	87%	KPXN	PAX
Los Angeles	87%	KRCA	PBS
Los Angeles	87%	KSCI	Independent
Los Angeles	87%	KTBN	Independent
Los Angeles	87%	KTLA	WB
Los Angeles	87%	KTTV	FOX
Los Angeles	87%	KVCR	PBS
Los Angeles	87%	KVEA	Telemundo
Los Angeles	87%	KWHY	Independent Spanish
Palm Springs	13%	KESQ	ABC
Palm Springs	13%	KMIR	NBC

Cable systems and subscribers

Adelphia   42,640
Comcast   6,487
NPG Cable   3,682
Time Warner   98,700

Businesses and other major employers

KSL Recreation Group Inc.; La Quinta; hotels and motels   5,000
Eisenhower Medical Center; Rancho Mirage   2,000
Samuels Jewelers Inc.; Hemet; jewelry   1,535
Valley Health System Inc. Hospital; Hemet   1,200
National Railroad Passenger Corp.; Moreno Valley; passenger rail transportation   1,000
Tenet Healthsystem Desert Inc.; Palm Springs; medical and surgical hospital   960
Aztec Harvesting; Blythe; farm labor contractors   800
KSL Desert Resorts Inc.; La Quinta; resort hotel   700
Desert Community College District; Palm Desert   700
Renaissance Hotel Group; Indian Wells; resort hotel   650
Mayan King International Inc.; Palm Desert; banana grove   630
Tenet Health System Hospitals Inc.; Indio   627
West Taneem Group; Palm Desert; single-family housing construction   600
Spotlight 29 Enterprises; Coachella; gambling   600
Starwood Hotels and Resorts Worldwide Inc.; Rancho Mirage; resort hotel   550
John F. Kennedy Memorial Hospital; Indio   535
Cabazon Band of Mission Indians; Indio; book printing   500
Fantasy Springs Casino Inc.; Indio; casino   500
Hyatt Corp.; Palm Desert; hotels and motels   500
Western Mission Health; Rancho Mirage; hotels and motels   500
Western Mission Resort; Rancho Mirage; advertising   500
Thor California Inc.; Moreno Valley; recreational vehicles   500
Universal Health Services of Rancho Springs Inc.; Murrieta   500

California 46th District

Coastal Los Angeles and Orange Counties — Huntington Beach, Costa Mesa

The 46th is a comfortably conservative district that runs along the coast south of Los Angeles. *(See map p. 121.)*

An eclectic mix of residents, including senior citizens, surfers, and aerospace workers, live in several communities. In the northwest is an ultra-wealthy, mountainous peninsula containing Rancho Palos Verdes, Palos Verdes Estates, and Rolling Hills Estates. In the center is a more blue-collar area around Long Beach Harbor. The district continues southeast into the wealthier Orange County communities of Huntington Beach and Costa Mesa.

At Seal Beach, just over the line into Orange County, two-thirds of the city's residents are 65 or older and roughly one-third live in Leisure World, a seniors community. Huntington Beach is a hub for both surfers and aerospace workers, many of whom work at the Boeing plant that is a prime design and manufacturing facility for the space station and Delta rocket.

Generally speaking, the coastal areas are more Republican and the inland areas slightly more Democratic. Despite its proximity to Los Angeles, the district was 62 percent white in the 2000 census. The 46th's interior, which includes Costa Mesa, Fountain Valley, and part of Westminster and Santa Ana, tends to be less affluent than the coastal cities. These towns are solidly middle-class residential areas. Many of the area's blue-collar workers are employed by aerospace companies within the district or in Anaheim, Torrance, or Long Beach.

Major Industry

Aerospace, high-tech, manufacturing.

Notable

Huntington Beach hosts major surfing tournaments and is home to the International Surfing Museum; Catalina Island, a tourist destination, and San Clemente Island, which is owned by the Navy, are included in the 46th; Seal Beach is known for its seals and sea lions.

Election Returns

	Republican		Democratic		Other	
President 2000	145,729	54.8%	110,984	41.7%	9,413	3.5%
House 2002	108,807	61.8%	60,890	34.6%	6,568	3.7%

District Profile

Population   639,088

Total area (square miles)   825
   Land area (square miles)   263

Population per square mile   2,424

Counties (2000 population)
   Los Angeles (pt.)   162,849
   Orange (pt.)   476,239

Cities and other areas over 10,000 (2000 population)
   Costa Mesa   108,724
   Fountain Valley   54,978
   Huntington Beach   189,594
   Long Beach (pt.)   83,666
   Palos Verdes Estates   13,340
   Rancho Palos Verdes   41,145
   Santa Ana (pt.)   18,427
   Seal Beach   24,157
   Westminster (pt.)   60,399

Race and Hispanic or Latino origin*
   White   62.8%
   Black or African American   1.4%
   American Indian or Alaska Native   0.3%
   Asian   15.4%
   Native Hawaiian or other Pacific Islander   0.3%
   Some other race   0.2%
   Hispanic or Latino origin   16.9%
   Two or more races   2.6%

*As percentage of total population.

Ancestry*

Dutch 1.4%	
English 8.5%	Polish 1.7%
French 2.4%	Russian 1.1%
German 10.7%	Scotch-Irish 1.3%
Irish 8.4%	Scottish 1.8%
Italian 4.4%	Swedish 1.6%
Norwegian 1.5%	USA/American 3.0%

*As estimated percentage of total population.

Universities and colleges, 2000–2001 enrollment
   California State University, Long Beach   30,918
   Coastline Community College, Fountain Valley   7,873
   College of Oceaneering, Wilmington   245
   Fashion Institute of Design and Merchandising, Costa Mesa   292
   Golden West College, Huntington Beach   13,538
   Marymount College, Rancho Palos Verdes   879
   Orange Coast College, Costa Mesa   23,315
   Southern California College, Costa Mesa   1,654
   University of Phoenix-Southern California, Fountain Valley   18,075

Newspapers and circulation

	District circulation	Total circulation
*Daily Variety, Los Angeles**	3,045	27,269
Long Beach Press-Telegram	19,274	94,944
Los Angeles La Opinion	2,359	127,108
*Los Angeles Sentinel**	1,827	12,345
Los Angeles Times	59,039	1,044,205
Orange County Register	59,127	319,326
Torrance Daily Breeze	10,130	79,363
*USA Today**	6,435	1,674,376

*See Sources and Explanations in the front of the volume.

Television stations and affiliations

Los Angeles	100%	KABC	ABC
Los Angeles	100%	KADY	Independent
Los Angeles	100%	KCAL	Independent
Los Angeles	100%	KCBS	CBS
Los Angeles	100%	KCET	PBS
Los Angeles	100%	KCOP	UPN
Los Angeles	100%	KDOC	Independent
Los Angeles	100%	KHIZ	Independent
Los Angeles	100%	KJLA	Independent
Los Angeles	100%	KLCS	PBS
Los Angeles	100%	KMEX	Univision
Los Angeles	100%	KNBC	NBC
Los Angeles	100%	KOCE	PBS
Los Angeles	100%	KPXN	PAX
Los Angeles	100%	KRCA	PBS
Los Angeles	100%	KSCI	Independent
Los Angeles	100%	KTBN	Independent
Los Angeles	100%	KTLA	WB
Los Angeles	100%	KTTV	FOX
Los Angeles	100%	KVCR	PBS
Los Angeles	100%	KVEA	Telemundo
Los Angeles	100%	KWHY	Independent Spanish

Cable systems and subscribers
   Adelphia   8,068
   Catalina Cable TV   1,205
   Charter   64,614
   Comcast   23,080
   Cox   16,634
   Time Warner   55,148

Military installations, September 2001
   Seal Beach Naval Weapons Center, Seal Beach   947

Businesses and other major employers
   Experian Information Solutions Inc.; Costa Mesa; consumer credit reporting bureau   3,700
   U.S. Veterans Hospital; Long Beach   3,500
   California State University System; Long Beach   2,628
   Boeing Co.; Seal Beach; testing laboratories   2,000
   California Dept. of Transportation; Long Beach   2,000
   Kumlee; Westminster; candy, nut, confectionery stores   1,976
   Coast Community College District; Huntington Beach   1,806
   Reliable Maintenance Inc.; Fountain Valley; building cleaning   1,700

Coast Community College District; Costa Mesa   1,600
Washington Journey; Costa Mesa; periodicals   1,600
Coast Community College District; Fountain Valley
   1,600
California Dept. of Developmental Services; Costa Mesa
   1,500
Inter-Insurance Exchange of Automobile Club of
   Southern California; Costa Mesa; automobile insurance
   1,500
Tarsadia Hotels; Costa Mesa; hotels   1,500
Pacificare Health Systems Inc.; Huntington Beach;
   health insurance   1,500
Fountain Valley Regional Hospital and Medical Center;
   Fountain Valley   1,300
City of Long Beach; Long Beach; city management
   1,200
Kingston Technology Co.; Fountain Valley; computer
   peripheral equipment   1,100
Star-Kist Foods Inc.; San Pedro; packaged tuna fish
   1,020
Boeing Co.; Seal Beach; satellite communications
   1,000
HR Serve Enterprises; Long Beach; payroll accounting
   service   1,000
Bank of America Corp.; Costa Mesa; commercial bank
   1,000
California Dept. of Mental Health; Costa Mesa   1,000
Times Mirror Co.; Costa Mesa; newspaper   1,000
Triad Financial Corp.; Huntington Beach; financial
   services   1,000
City of Huntington Beach; Huntington Beach; economic
   development   1,000
Quiksilver Inc.; Huntington Beach; men's/boys' trousers
   and slacks   1,000
Star-Kist Foods Inc.; San Pedro; dog and cat food   900
Cambro Manufacturing Co.; Huntington Beach; plastic
   trays   850
Express Manufacturing Inc.; Santa Ana; electronic
   circuits   835
TRW Inc.; Palos Verdes Peninsula; acceleration
   indicators and systems components, aerospace   800
Behr Process Corp.; Santa Ana; paints and paint
   additives   800
Ponderosa Builders Inc.; Santa Ana; janitorial service
   800
International Business Machines Corp.; Costa Mesa;
   computers   750
B. Alan Whitson Co.; Santa Ana; corporation organizing
   consultant   750
Cingular Interactive; Huntington Beach; radiotelephone
   communication   725
Deloitte and Touche; Costa Mesa; accounting services
   700
Phillips Petroleum Co.; Costa Mesa; gasoline service
   stations   700
Verizon California Inc.; Huntington Beach; local/
   long-distance telephone   700
RMS Foundation Inc.; Long Beach; hotels   650
Filenet Corp.; Costa Mesa; business computer software
   650
Aluminum Precision Products; Santa Ana; aluminum
   forgings   650
Ditech.com; Costa Mesa; loan brokers   641

West Macy's Inc.; Costa Mesa; department stores   600
Orange Coast Memorial Medical Center; Fountain Valley
   580
Pacificare Health Systems Inc.; Santa Ana; health
   maintenance organization   550
City of Long Beach; Long Beach; fire dept.   538
MGE UPS Systems Inc.; Costa Mesa; power and
   distribution transformers   534
Safeco Insurance Company of America Inc.; Fountain
   Valley; insurance agents and brokers   520
Dynamic Cooking Systems Inc.; Huntington Beach;
   commercial cooking equipment   507
Tri-Union Seafoods; San Pedro; canned, cured
   fish/seafoods   500
Hyatt Corp.; Long Beach; hotels   500
New Port Unified School District; Costa Mesa   500
Midas Auto System Experts; Costa Mesa; automotive
   repair shops   500
City of Huntington Beach; Huntington Beach; city
   management   500
Enviromental Golf Inc.; Santa Ana; golf course
   construction   500
Ceridian Tax Service Inc.; Fountain Valley; payroll
   accounting service   500

California 47th District

*Orange County — most of Santa Ana, Anaheim, and
Garden Grove*

A blue-collar inland strip full of older suburban homes
and younger families, the majority-Hispanic 47th is unlike
its mostly affluent, Republican neighbors in Orange County.
Located about 30 miles southeast of Los Angeles, it takes
in part of four cities: Santa Ana, Anaheim, Garden Grove,
and Fullerton, where a growing number of Hispanics and
other ethnic minorities are changing its demographics and
creating a strong Democratic voter base. *(See map p. 121.)*

Almost half the district's population is in Santa Ana—the
Orange County seat–which has higher unemployment and
more blue-collar jobs than surrounding areas. The city is one
of only three in the county in which registered Democrats
outnumber Republicans.

Three-fourths of residents in diverse and growing Garden
Grove live in the 47th, which includes the center (a mix of
Vietnamese, Koreans, and Hispanics) and the eastern (heavily
Hispanic) sections. An influx of Southeast Asian refugees has
spurred a conservative backlash from some residents who
worry that increased social services will lead to higher taxes.
But the Asian community, some of which is heavily Christian,
has a conservative side of its own.

Anaheim, Orange County's second-largest city after Santa
Ana, has a large tourism industry, and the 47th has some of its
most Democratic areas. The small chunk of Fullerton in the
district's northern end is heavily Hispanic, though that city
leans Republican overall. Apart from Disneyland, no single
employer drives the area's economy. Defense subcontractors
and small businesses are scattered throughout the district.

Major Industry
   Small business, service, defense, tourism.

Notable

The 47th's part of Anaheim is home to Disneyland, the 2002 World Series champion Angels, and the Mighty Ducks hockey team.

Election Returns

	Republican		Democratic		Other	
President 2000	43,752	41.5%	59,515	56.4%	2,257	2.1%
House 2002	24,346	34.7%	42,501	60.6%	3,331	4.7%

District Profile

Population   639,087

Total area (square miles)   55
Land area (square miles)   54

Population per square mile   11,683.9

Counties (2000 population)
Orange (pt.)   639,087

Cities and other areas over 10,000 (2000 population)
Anaheim (pt.)   185,537   Garden Grove (pt.)   125,336
Fullerton (pt.)   17,852   Santa Ana (pt.)   299,552

Race and Hispanic or Latino origin*
White   17.3%
Black or African American   1.5%
American Indian or Alaska Native   0.3%
Asian   13.9%
Native Hawaiian or other Pacific Islander   0.4%
Some other race   0.1%
Hispanic or Latino origin   65.3%
Two or more races   1.3%

*As percentage of total population.

Ancestry*
English   2.3%   Italian   1.3%
German   3.5%   USA/American   2.0%
Irish   2.5%

*As estimated percentage of total population.

Universities and colleges, 2000–2001 enrollment
American College of Law, Anaheim*
Bethesda Christian University, Anaheim   2,749
Computer Learning Center, Anaheim   628
ITT Technical Institute, Anaheim   705
Santa Ana College, Santa Ana   27,571
South Baylo University, Anaheim   711
William Howard Taft University, Santa Ana*

*Enrollment under 100. See Sources and Explanations in the front of the volume.

Newspapers and circulation

	District circulation	Total circulation
Los Angeles La Opinion	5,587	127,108
Los Angeles Times	16,228	1,044,205
Orange County Register	43,480	319,326

Television stations and affiliations

Los Angeles	100%	KABC	ABC
Los Angeles	100%	KADY	Independent
Los Angeles	100%	KCAL	Independent
Los Angeles	100%	KCBS	CBS
Los Angeles	100%	KCET	PBS
Los Angeles	100%	KCOP	UPN
Los Angeles	100%	KDOC	Independent
Los Angeles	100%	KHIZ	Independent
Los Angeles	100%	KJLA	Independent
Los Angeles	100%	KLCS	PBS
Los Angeles	100%	KMEX	Univision
Los Angeles	100%	KNBC	NBC
Los Angeles	100%	KOCE	PBS
Los Angeles	100%	KPXN	PAX
Los Angeles	100%	KRCA	PBS
Los Angeles	100%	KSCI	Independent
Los Angeles	100%	KTBN	Independent
Los Angeles	100%	KTLA	WB
Los Angeles	100%	KTTV	FOX
Los Angeles	100%	KVCR	PBS
Los Angeles	100%	KVEA	Telemundo
Los Angeles	100%	KWHY	Independent Spanish

Cable systems and subscribers
Adelphia   63,686
Time Warner   17,934

Businesses and other major employers
Hitech Metal Fabrication Corp; Anaheim; fabricated structural metal   6,056
Ingram Micro Inc.; Santa Ana; computer software   4,000
City of Anaheim; Anaheim; stadium operator   3,500
Discovery Medical Inc.; Anaheim; fabric dress and work gloves   3,100
Orange County; Santa Ana; county government   2,400
Rancho Santiago Community College District Inc.; Santa Ana   2,300
City of Anaheim; Anaheim; city management   1,990
All Style Apparel and Activewear; Anaheim; shirts   1,800
WCO Hotels Inc.; Anaheim; hotels   1,700
Staffay Inc.; Santa Ana; employee leasing service   1,600
Orange County Dept. of Education; Santa Ana   1,561
IO Interconnect; Santa Ana; electronic connectors   1,500
Penhall International Inc.; Anaheim; concrete breaking   1,500
Anaheim Hotel Partnership; Anaheim; hotels   1,500
Anaheim Memorial Hospital Assn.; Anaheim   1,200
ITT Industries Inc.; Santa Ana; electronic connectors   1,100
Marriott International Inc.; Anaheim; gift, novelty, souvenir shop   1,000
Kwikset Corp.; Anaheim; hand tools   1,000
Freedom Communications Inc.; Santa Ana; newspaper   900
First American Title Insurance Co.; Santa Ana; title insurance   900
Textron Fastening Systems; Santa Ana; fasteners   800
RSI Holding Corp.; Anaheim; kitchen cabinets: metal   700
City of Garden Grove; Garden Grove; city management   700
APW Enclosure Systems; Anaheim; sheet metalwork   644
APW-Wright Line Inc.; Anaheim; plastic foam products   600
Pacific Bell; Anaheim; telephone communication   600

Source Refrigeration and HVAC Inc.; Anaheim; refrigeration service and repair   593

Power Paragon Inc.; Anaheim; nonelectric transformers   585

Tenet Health System Medical Hospital; Garden Grove   580

James Productions Inc.; Anaheim; party planning service   520

Interstate Electronics Corp; Anaheim; search and navigation equipment   520

Lexicon Marketing Corp.; Santa Ana; general warehousing, storage   500

PPS Parking Inc.; Santa Ana; valet parking   500

Deloitte and Touche; Santa Ana; accounting services   500

Ingram Micro Inc.; Santa Ana; warehousing   500

Pacific Bell; Anaheim; telephone communication   500

3 Day Blinds Inc.; Anaheim; miniblinds   500

Hewlett-Packard Co.; Fullerton; electronic parts and equipment   500

California 48th District

Southern Orange County — Irvine, Newport Beach

The 48th covers the Orange County coast from Newport Beach south through Laguna Beach to Dana Point, and it takes in a chunk of the inland county from the coast through Irvine to the foothills of the Santa Ana mountains. Registered Republicans outnumber Democrats nearly two to one here, and the district is distinguished by its large white-collar labor force and its high household income. *(See map p. 121.)*

Newport Beach is a wealthy enclave noted for its beautiful sandy beaches, luxurious housing, and solid Republicanism. Many workers commute from the north or east, where living is cheaper. Laguna Beach attracts more scuba divers than swimmers and is a more liberal enclave known as "the arts colony." Inland is Laguna Woods, home to a significant number of senior citizens, Laguna Niguel, and Laguna Hills. About 68 percent of district residents are white.

Smog, crime, and other problems endemic to Los Angeles do not affect these areas. Transportation troubles are among the toughest problems on the horizon, as traffic backs up and increases the risk of air and water pollution. Toll roads in the area have helped, but residents generally oppose a new commuter train.

While Republicans dominate the 48th, pockets of Democratic strength can be found in the district's inland sections and in the more liberal-leaning community surrounding the University of California, Irvine. The university's engineering and biomedical research programs have attracted a large number of thriving high-tech and biotechnology firms to the area, which is beginning to rival Silicon Valley.

The late-1990s closure of the El Toro and Tustin Marine Corps Air stations did not have a huge impact on the economy, but the El Toro closure did touch off a fierce battle over whether to turn it into a commercial airport. After numerous referenda, the 4,700-acre parcel is set to become a park.

Major Industry

High-tech, biomedical, tourism.

Notable

The El Toro "Y," where Interstates 5 and 405 split, is in Irvine.

Election Returns

	Republican		Democratic		Other	
President 2000	156,340	57.8%	106,809	39.5%	7,421	2.7%
House 2002	122,884	68.4%	51,058	28.4%	5,607	3.1%

District Profile

Population   639,088

Total area (square miles)   301
   Land area (square miles)   212

Population per square mile   3,011

Counties (2000 population)
   Orange (pt.)   639,087

Cities and other areas over 10,000 (2000 population)
   Aliso Viejo CDP   40,166
   Dana Point   35,110
   Foothill Ranch CDP   10,899
   Irvine   143,072
   Laguna Beach   23,727
   Laguna Hills   31,178
   Laguna Niguel   61,891
   Laguna Woods   16,507
   Lake Forest   58,707
   Newport Beach   70,032
   San Juan Capistrano (pt.)   16,618
   Santa Ana (pt.)   19,998
   Tustin   67,504
   Tustin Foothills CDP   24,044

Race and Hispanic or Latino origin*
   White   68.0%
   Black or African American   1.4%
   American Indian or Alaska Native   0.2%
   Asian   12.7%
   Native Hawaiian or other Pacific Islander   0.2%
   Some other race   0.2%
   Hispanic or Latino origin   14.7%
   Two or more races   2.7%

As percentage of total population.

Ancestry*

Dutch 1.3%	Polish 2.0%
English 9.3%	Russian 1.6%
French 2.5%	Scotch-Irish 1.3%
German 11.3%	Scottish 2.0%
Irish 8.3%	Swedish 1.8%
Italian 4.8%	USA/American 2.9%
Norwegian 1.5%	

As estimated percentage of total population.

Universities and colleges, 2000–2001 enrollment
   Art Institute of Southern California, Laguna Beach   268
   Concordia University, Irvine   1,319
   Irvine Valley College, Irvine   10,074
   Keller Graduate School of Management, Irvine*
   Platt College-Newport, Newport Beach   262

Southern California University for Professional Studies, Santa Ana   672

University of California-Irvine, Irvine   20,211

Enrollment under 100. See Sources and Explanations in the front of the volume.

Newspapers and circulation

	District circulation	Total circulation
Los Angeles La Opinion	1,684	127,108
Los Angeles Times	61,887	1,044,205
Orange County Register	73,065	319,326
*USA Today**	3,642	1,674,376

See Sources and Explanations in the front of the volume.

Television stations and affiliations

Los Angeles	100%	KABC	ABC
Los Angeles	100%	KADY	Independent
Los Angeles	100%	KCAL	Independent
Los Angeles	100%	KCBS	CBS
Los Angeles	100%	KCET	PBS
Los Angeles	100%	KCOP	UPN
Los Angeles	100%	KDOC	Independent
Los Angeles	100%	KHIZ	Independent
Los Angeles	100%	KJLA	Independent
Los Angeles	100%	KLCS	PBS
Los Angeles	100%	KMEX	Univision
Los Angeles	100%	KNBC	NBC
Los Angeles	100%	KOCE	PBS
Los Angeles	100%	KPXN	PAX
Los Angeles	100%	KRCA	PBS
Los Angeles	100%	KSCI	Independent
Los Angeles	100%	KTBN	Independent
Los Angeles	100%	KTLA	WB
Los Angeles	100%	KTTV	FOX
Los Angeles	100%	KVCR	PBS
Los Angeles	100%	KVEA	Telemundo
Los Angeles	100%	KWHY	Independent Spanish

Cable systems and subscribers

Adelphia   25,853

Comcast   12,780

Cox   200,235

Businesses and other major employers

University of California; Irvine   12,861

ConAgra Grocery Products Co.; Irvine; food supplier   7,000

Edwards Lifesciences Corp.; Irvine; cardiology   4,700

B. Braun/McGaw Inc.; Irvine; pharmaceuticals   3,000

Pacific Life Insurance Co.; Newport Beach; life insurance   3,000

Fluor Daniel Construction Co.; Aliso Viejo; bridge, tunnel, elevated highway construction   3,000

Fluor Corp.; Aliso Viejo; engineering services   2,600

Conexant Systems Inc.; Newport Beach; semiconductors and related devices   2,500

Advanced Medical Optics Inc.; Santa Ana; pharmaceuticals   2,100

Hoag Memorial Hospital Presbyterian; Newport Beach   2,058

California Dept. of Transportation; Irvine   2,000

New Century Mortgage Corp.; Irvine; mortgage bankers   1,500

Western Assn. for College Admission Counselors; San Juan Capistrano; education programs   1,500

Tenet Healthcare Corp. Hospital; Santa Ana; medical and surgical hospital   1,500

Mindspeed Technologies Inc.; Newport Beach; semiconductors and related devices   1,474

Allergan Inc.; Irvine; pharmaceutical solutions   1,300

Parker Hannifin Corp.; Irvine; aircraft parts, equipment   1,280

Tenet Healthcare Corp. Hospital; Santa Ana; medical and surgical hospital   1,200

Taco Bell Corp.; Irvine; Mexican restaurant   1,025

Saddleback Memorial Medical Center; Laguna Hills   1,020

Sprint Spectrum; Irvine; telephone communication   1,000

Baxter Healthcare Corp.; Irvine; special warehousing and storage   1,000

Freedom Communications Inc.; Irvine; newspaper   1,000

Unisys Corp.; El Toro; systems integration services   1,000

API Motion; Laguna Hills; motor control accessories   1,000

Leisure World Laguna Woods; Laguna Hills; retirement center   1,000

Advantage-Crown Sales and Marketing; Irvine; food brokers   918

Oakley Inc.; El Toro; ophthalmic goods   900

Western Digital Technologies Inc.; Lake Forest; computer disk drives   900

Baxter Healthcare Corp.; Irvine; surgical instruments and apparatus   850

Pacific Building Care Inc.; Irvine; building cleaning   850

Ritz-Carlton Hotel Co.; Dana Point; resort hotel   850

Option One Mortgage Corp.; Irvine; buying and selling mortgages   800

Toshiba America Information Systems Inc.; Irvine; electronic computers   800

CPH Monarch Hotel; Dana Point; resort hotel   800

Glidewell Dental Ceramics Inc.; Newport Beach; dental laboratories   770

Verizon Wireless Inc.; Irvine; mobile telephone equipment   700

South Coast Medical Center; Laguna Beach   690

Life Fitness Inc.; Aliso Viejo; exercise equipment   690

Multek Multilayer Technology Inc.; Irvine; printed circuit boards   650

Downey Savings and Loan Assn.; Newport Beach; federal savings and loan associations   650

Jazz Semiconductor Inc.; Newport Beach; wafers (semiconductor devices)   650

Edison Capital Housing Management; Irvine; real estate managers   639

TDK Electronics Corp.; Irvine; household audio/video equipment   600

Alcon Laboratories Inc.; Irvine; surgical and medical instruments   600

AST Research Inc.; Irvine; personal computers   600

Mitsubishi Digital Electronics America Inc.; Irvine; television receiving sets   600

Pacific Bell; Irvine; telephone communication   600

Sicor Inc.; Irvine; pharmaceuticals   600

Hines Nurseries Inc.; Irvine; ornamental nursery
products   600

United Parcel Service Inc.; Aliso Viejo; parcel delivery
600

Irvine Regional Hospital and Medical Center; Irvine
590

Employer and Occupational Services Group; Irvine; data
processing   590

Multek Multilayer Technology Inc.; Irvine; printed
circuit boards   550

Western Financial Bank; Irvine; federal savings and loan
associations   550

ZC Sterling Insurance Agency Inc.; Irvine; insurance
brokers   550

Next Link Technology; Lake Forest; electrical supplies
550

House2home Inc.; Irvine; home centers   530

Silver Springs Energy Co.; Irvine; electric power
generation   530

Royalty Carpet Mills Inc.; Irvine; carpets   521

Printronix Inc.; Irvine; printers, computers   500

Rosenbluth International Inc.; Irvine; travel agency
500

Edison Housing South Carolina; Irvine; holding
companies   500

Marriott International Inc.; Irvine; hotels   500

PricewaterhouseCoopers; Irvine; accounting services
500

Washington Mutual Bank; Irvine; federal savings banks
500

Quest Software Inc.; Irvine; computer software
development   500

South Orange County Community College District;
Irvine   500

Toshiba America Business Solutions Inc.; Irvine; copying
equipment   500

Toshiba America Information Systems Inc.; Irvine;
computer tapes and disks   500

FutureLink Corp.; Lake Forest; computer consulting
services   500

Del Taco Income Properties IV; Laguna Hills;
nonresidential building operators   500

FSH Newport Beach Inc.; Newport Beach; hotel or
motel management   500

Macarthur Hotels LP; Newport Beach; hotels   500

Federal Deposit Insurance Corp.; Newport Beach; bank
regulation, insurance   500

Kaiser Foundation Hospitals; Tustin; health association
500

California 49th District

North San Diego County; West Riverside County

One of the fastest-growing areas in California, the heavily residential 49th in northwestern San Diego County and western Riverside County is home to many rapidly changing bedroom communities. *(See map p. 121.)*

Commuters travel to jobs in San Diego (a sliver of which falls in the 49th) and, to a lesser extent, Orange County, while tourists visit the wineries in Riverside County. Al-most 60 percent white and solidly conservative, the district gave George W. Bush 58.6 percent of the vote in the 2000 presidential election.

The 1990s saw areas such as Lake Elsinore, Canyon Lake, and Sun City in Riverside County turn from retirement communities into family-oriented commuter towns. Perris, which largely remains a retirement community, is the district's only city in which Democrats hold an edge.

Massive Camp Pendleton Marine Corps Base sits on the district's coast, but the local economy relies less on military contracts than its Orange County and San Diego neighbors. Sony has a plant in Rancho Bernardo (in northeast San Diego) that makes laptop computers, among other electronics. Beach visitors to Oceanside and the Pacific Coast also boost the local economy.

Though most residents live in San Diego County, growth has been prodigious in Temecula, the heart of the district's wine industry, in Riverside County. Ballooning and skydiving are among the tourist attractions in the more-rural northern parts of the district.

Major Industry

Medical devices, services, manufacturing, tourism, defense.

Notable

Fallbrook is a leader in avocado production; Julian sells 10,000 apple pies a week each fall; the San Onofre nuclear power plant is on the Pacific Coast next to Camp Pendleton.

Election Returns

	Republican		Democratic		Other	
President 2000	114,193	58.6%	75,561	38.8%	5,217	2.7%
House 2002	94,594	77.2%			27,903	22.8%

District Profile

Population   639,087

Total area (square miles)   1,777
   Land area (square miles)   1,690

Population per square mile   378.1

Counties (2000 population)
   Riverside (pt.)   239,241
   San Diego (pt.)   399,846

Cities and other areas over 10,000 (2000 population)

Fallbrook CDP	29,100	Sun City CDP	17,773
Lake Elsinore	28,928	Temecula	57,716
Oceanside	161,029	Vista	89,857
Perris	36,189	Wildomar CDP	14,064
San Diego (pt.)	14,520		

Race and Hispanic or Latino origin*
   White   57.9%
   Black or African American   5.0%
   American Indian or Alaska Native   0.9%
   Asian   3.5%
   Native Hawaiian or other Pacific Islander   0.5%
   Some other race   0.2%
   Hispanic or Latino origin   29.5%
   Two or more races   2.5%

*As percentage of total population.

Ancestry*

Dutch	1.2%	Norwegian	1.5%
English	7.8%	Polish	1.6%
French	2.4%	Scotch-Irish	1.3%
German	10.7%	Scottish	1.6%
Irish	7.9%	Swedish	1.3%
Italian	3.8%	USA/American	3.4%

As estimated percentage of total population.

Universities and colleges, 2000–2001 enrollment
Maric College of Medical Careers, Vista   592
Mira Costa College, Oceanside   9,863

Newspapers and circulation

	District circulation	Total circulation
Los Angeles La Opinion	1,142	127,108
Los Angeles Times	8,967	1,044,205
North County Times	55,367	93,408
Orange County Register	4,203	319,326
Riverside Press-Enterprise	24,970	176,422
San Diego Union Tribune	32,959	357,315
USA Today*	4,759	1,674,376

See Sources and Explanations in the front of the volume.

Television stations and affiliations

San Diego	77%	KFMB	CBS
San Diego	77%	KGTV	ABC
San Diego	77%	KNSD	NBC
San Diego	77%	KPBS	PBS
San Diego	77%	KSWB	WB
San Diego	77%	KUSI	Independent
Los Angeles	23%	KABC	ABC
Los Angeles	23%	KADY	Independent
Los Angeles	23%	KCAL	Independent
Los Angeles	23%	KCBS	CBS
Los Angeles	23%	KCET	PBS
Los Angeles	23%	KCOP	UPN
Los Angeles	23%	KDOC	Independent
Los Angeles	23%	KHIZ	Independent
Los Angeles	23%	KJLA	Independent
Los Angeles	23%	KLCS	PBS
Los Angeles	23%	KMEX	Univision
Los Angeles	23%	KNBC	NBC
Los Angeles	23%	KOCE	PBS
Los Angeles	23%	KPXN	PAX
Los Angeles	23%	KRCA	PBS
Los Angeles	23%	KSCI	Independent
Los Angeles	23%	KTBN	Independent
Los Angeles	23%	KTLA	WB
Los Angeles	23%	KTTV	FOX
Los Angeles	23%	KVCR	PBS
Los Angeles	23%	KVEA	Telemundo
Los Angeles	23%	KWHY	Independent Spanish

Cable systems and subscribers
Adelphia   47,280
Cable USA   650
Comcast   5,163
Cox   69,920
Mediacom   11,075
Time Warner   16,085

Military installations, September 2001
Camp Pendleton Marine Corps Base, Camp Pendleton   31,745
Camp Pendleton Marine Corps Air Station, Camp Pendleton   5,082
Camp Pendleton Naval Hospital, Camp Pendleton   1,673

Businesses and other major employers
Guidant Vascular Intervention; Temecula; medical instruments: blood, bone work   4,000
Tri-City Hospital; Oceanside   2,100
Southern California Edison Co.; San Clemente; electric power generation   1,892
Children's Hospital and Health Center; Oceanside   1,700
Starcrest Products of California Inc.; Perris; mail order gifts   1,200
Pechange Development Corp.; Temecula; casino   1,100
RV National Inc.; Perris; motor homes   1,000
Watkins Manufacturing Corp.; Vista; hot tubs, plastics, or fiberglass   800
D. J. Orthopedics Inc.; Vista; orthopedic offices   799
Altman Specialty Plants Inc.; Vista; nursery stock   600
Los Angeles County Metropolitan Transportation Authority; Lake Elsinore   600
International Rectifier Corp.; Temecula; semiconductors and related devices   600
Mira Costa Community College; Oceanside   520
North San Diego County Transit Development Board; Oceanside   500
PSP and D Inc.; Vista; shopping news publishing   500
Inland Valley Regional Medical Center Inc.; Wildomar   500

California 50th District
North San Diego county suburbs; Carlsbad; Escondido

The 50th spans San Diego's "North County" from Interstate 5 along the coast to Interstate 15 in the east. With its beautiful beach communities and upper-middle-class suburbs, the 50th is a steadily growing GOP stronghold. *(See map p. 121.)*

The area's wealth is a testament to a booming technology industry north of San Diego that has been likened to a mini-Silicon Valley. The growth of cellular technology companies, computer software firms, and biotech research has contributed to the area's image. Military firms and defense contractors have diversified the boom. Construction of opulent homes continues apace, especially in Carmel Valley and inland Del Mar and Carlsbad, and locals and tourists compete for time at a plethora of golf courses.

Conservative elements in the district include resident military personnel who work nearby at Camp Pendleton (in the 49th), and the Marine Corps base in Miramar (shared with the 52nd), which until 1996 was home to the Navy's famed "Top Gun" fighter school. As part of downsizing, the Naval Air Station at Miramar moved to Nevada, and Marines from the closing El Toro and Tustin bases, 50 miles to the north in Orange County, moved to Miramar.

Unlike San Diego's south side, the 50th is two-thirds white and heavily Republican. Coastal cities such as Del Mar,

Solana Beach, Encinitas, and Carlsbad, where beach replenishment and the environment are issues, add some liberals to the district, but they are outweighed by inland voters in well-off San Diego communities such as Rancho Santa Fe, Carmel Valley, and upscale parts of Escondido. Republicans have a voter registration advantage of more than 15 points.

Major Industry

Technology, defense, manufacturing.

Notable

Carlsbad grows and distributes most of the West Coast's fresh-cut flowers and is home to several major golf equipment manufacturers, as well as the Legoland theme park; the 2000 census ranked Rancho Santa Fe as the richest community in the country—its median home price was $1.7 million in 2002; the Ecke Ranch produces 80 percent of the world's poinsettias.

Election Returns

	Republican		Democratic		Other	
President 2000	136,311	53.9%	107,436	42.5%	8,996	3.6%
House 2002	111,095	64.3%	55,855	32.3%	5,751	3.3%

District Profile

Population   639,087

Total area (square miles)   364
  Land area (square miles)   300

Population per square mile   2,128.4

Counties (2000 population)
  San Diego (pt.)   639,087

Cities and other areas over 10,000 (2000 population)
Carlsbad 78,247	San Diego (pt.) 262,523
Encinitas 58,014	San Marcos 54,977
Escondido 133,559	Solana Beach 12,979

Race and Hispanic or Latino origin*
  White   65.8%
  Black or African American   1.8%
  American Indian or Alaska Native   0.3%
  Asian   10.3%
  Native Hawaiian or other Pacific Islander   0.2%
  Some other race   0.2%
  Hispanic or Latino origin   18.8%
  Two or more races   2.6%

*As percentage of total population.

Ancestry*
Dutch 1.3%	Polish 2.0%
English 8.8%	Russian 1.3%
French 2.4%	Scotch-Irish 1.4%
German 11.5%	Scottish 1.9%
Irish 8.6%	Swedish 1.6%
Italian 4.3%	USA/American 3.2%
Norwegian 1.5%	

*As estimated percentage of total population.

Universities and colleges, 2000–2001 enrollment
  Advertising Arts College, San Diego   280
  California School of Professional Psychology, San Diego   681
  California State University, San Marcos   6,256
  Design Institute of San Diego, San Diego   358
  Gemological Institute of America, Carlsbad   5,928
  Kelsey-Jenney College, San Diego   679
  National University, San Diego   17,090
  Palomar College, San Marcos   21,062

Newspapers and circulation

	District circulation	Total circulation
Los Angeles Times	6,509	1,044,205
North County Times	27,240	93,408
San Diego Union Tribune	83,489	357,315

Television stations and affiliations
San Diego	100%	KFMB	CBS
San Diego	100%	KGTV	ABC
San Diego	100%	KNSD	NBC
San Diego	100%	KPBS	PBS
San Diego	100%	KSWB	WB
San Diego	100%	KUSI	Independent

Cable systems and subscribers
  Adelphia   38,734
  Cox   42,170
  Time Warner   28,720

Businesses and other major employers
  First Union National Bank; Encinitas; commercial bank   8,849
  Sony Electronics Inc.; San Diego; television receiving sets   5,000
  Safeskin Corp.; San Diego; rubber-coated fabrics and clothing   4,632
  Kaiser Permanente Medical Care; San Diego   4,000
  Palomar Community College District; San Marcos   3,300
  Callaway Golf Co.; Carlsbad; golfing equipment   2,126
  Total Source Manufacturing; San Diego; laboratory equipment   1,800
  BAE Systems Mission Solutions Inc.; San Diego; electronic/electric measuring test equipment   1,800
  Hewlett-Packard Co.; San Diego; electrical equipment and supplies   1,700
  Fidelity National Information Solutions; Santa Barbara; information retrieval services   1,324
  Ericsson Wireless Communications Inc.; San Diego; mobile communication equipment   1,230
  Aviara Four Seasons Resort; Carlsbad; resort hotel   1,200
  Palomar Pomerado Hospital; Escondido   1,200
  Qualcomm Inc.; San Diego; space satellite communications equipment   1,200
  GJL Associates Inc.; San Diego; women's and misses' outerwear   1,200
  REMEC Inc.; Del Mar; search and navigation equipment   1,147

Tyco Healthcare Group; Carlsbad; medical instruments 1,100

Orilio and Associates Inc.; Encinitas; restaurant/food services consultants 1,083

Coastal Audio Visual; Carlsbad; audio-visual program production 1,000

Legoland California Inc.; Carlsbad; theme park 800

Mallinckrodt Inc.; Carlsbad; surgical and medical instruments 800

KSL La Costa Resort Corp.; Carlsbad; resort hotel 800

Wild Animal Park; Escondido; zoo 800

Intuit Inc.; San Diego; prepackaged software 800

City of Escondido; Escondido; city government 775

California Dept. of Food and Agriculture; Del Mar 758

Hunter Industries Inc.; San Marcos; plumbing fixture fittings and trim 750

Alaris Medical Systems Inc.; San Diego; IV transfusion apparatus 675

Unisys Corp.; San Diego; computers 650

Scripps Hospital; Encinitas 625

Gen-Probe Inc.; San Diego; in vitro diagnostics 605

Eldorado Stone; San Marcos; precast concrete products 600

Newgen Results Corp.; San Diego; telephone solicitation service 600

Pyxis Corp.; San Diego; computer integrated systems design 600

Cymer Inc.; San Diego; laser systems and equipment 555

Signet Armorlite Inc.; San Marcos; lenses, ophthalmic 550

Motorola Inc.; San Diego; satellite communications 550

Qualcomm Inc.; San Diego; space satellite communications equipment 527

Hardage Hotels I; San Diego; hotels and motels 520

General Atomics Aeronautical Systems Inc.; San Diego; aircraft 510

Eassist Global Solutions; Carlsbad; computer tapes and disks 500

Viasat Inc.; Carlsbad; space satellite communications equipment 500

Pacific Bell; Escondido; local/long-distance telephone 500

Omnitec International; Rancho Santa Fe; computer system selling services 500

Household Automotive Finance Inc.; San Diego; automobile finance leasing 500

Petco Animal Supplies Inc.; San Diego; pets and pet supplies 500

Berendsen Fluid Power Inc.; San Diego; hydraulic systems equipment 500

U.S. Federal Aviation Administration; San Diego 500

Toppan Electronics Inc.; San Diego; printed circuit boards 500

California 51st District

Central and southern San Diego; Imperial County

The part-urban, part-rural 51st runs the entire length of California's border with Mexico except for the western tip at the Pacific Ocean. It includes part of central San Diego and all of Imperial County, which is sometimes at odds with the city constituency. The Democratic district, previously an urban stronghold numbered the 50th, increased its original area tremendously through post-census 2000 redistricting. *(See map p. 121.)*

The district's San Diego portion, which begins south and east of downtown, is working class and heavily Hispanic, and has some of the worst of the city's problems. Much of the growth that has boosted areas north of San Diego has left the 51st behind. NAFTA and the 2001 terrorist attacks have slowed the border traffic-dependent economy—Mexican shoppers spend more than $3 billion a year at area malls. A sizable military and veteran population has produced a more even party split in the booming residential suburb of Chula Vista.

Imperial County is heavily agricultural, with an annual crop yield of about $1 billion, and about 70 percent Hispanic. Unemployment runs as high as 30 percent in some areas. Voters here are more conservative than their city cousins but still lean Democratic.

Border issues, particularly illegal immigration—which fills agricultural labor jobs—illegal drugs, and wastewater treatment, are important in the Hispanic-majority 51st, which gave 56.9 percent to presidential nominee Al Gore in 2000. Its areas compete for water and are under pressure to reduce dependency on the Colorado River. Environmentalists object to one proposed solution—the Salton Sea (shared with the 45th)—which they say is key to the local ecosystem and to migratory birds.

Major Industry

Service, manufacturing, agriculture, retail.

Notable

San Diego-Tijuana border crossing at San Ysidro is the world's busiest; Otay Mesa is known as the television capital of the world for its consumer electronics manufacturing.

Election Returns

	Republican		Democratic		Other	
President 2000	61,008	40.6%	85,561	56.9%	3,819	2.5%
House 2002	40,430	39.3%	59,541	57.9%	2,816	2.7%

District Profile

Population 639,087

Total area (square miles) 4,896
Land area (square miles) 4,582

Population per square mile 139.5

Counties (2000 population)
Imperial 142,361
San Diego (pt.) 496,726

Cities and other areas over 10,000 (2000 population)
Bonita CDP	12,401	El Centro	37,835
Brawley	22,052	National City	54,260
Calexico	27,109	San Diego (pt.)	239,457
Chula Vista	173,556		

Race and Hispanic or Latino origin*
White   21.3%
Black or African American   9.4%
American Indian or Alaska Native   0.5%
Asian   12.4%
Native Hawaiian or other Pacific Islander   0.6%
Some other race   0.2%
Hispanic or Latino origin   53.3%
Two or more races   2.4%

*As percentage of total population.

Ancestry*
English 2.9%		Irish 3.3%	
French 1.1%		Italian 1.4%	
German 4.2%		USA/American 2.0%	

*As estimated percentage of total population.

Universities and colleges, 2000–2001 enrollment
Imperial Valley College, Imperial   6,775
Southwestern College, Chula Vista   17,994

Newspapers and circulation
	District circulation	Total circulation
Imperial Valley Press	14,612	14,658
Los Angeles Times	1,185	1,044,205
San Diego Union Tribune	52,039	357,315
*USA Today**	1,529	1,674,376

*See Sources and Explanations in the front of the volume.

Television stations and affiliations
Yuma-El Centro	92%	KECY	FOX
Yuma-El Centro	92%	KSWT	CBS
Yuma-El Centro	92%	KYMA	NBC
San Diego	8%	KFMB	CBS
San Diego	8%	KGTV	ABC
San Diego	8%	KNSD	NBC
San Diego	8%	KPBS	PBS
San Diego	8%	KSWB	WB
San Diego	8%	KUSI	Independent

Cable systems and subscribers
Adelphia   19,561
Cable USA   715
Chula Vista Cable   69,091
Cox   26,809

Military installations, September 2001
San Diego Naval Station, San Diego   2,890
El Centro Naval Air Facility, El Centro   401

Businesses and other major employers
Rohr Inc. Credit Corp.; Charlotte; aircraft engines and parts   2,400
Rohr Inc.; Chula Vista; aircraft parts, equipment   2,100
California Dept. of Corrections; San Diego   1,200
Noblesse Oblige Inc.; El Centro; combining services   1,200
Hypermetallics; Bonita; sporting and recreation goods   1,000
Kendall Healthcare; Chula Vista; hypodermic needles and syringes   1,000
Paradise Valley Hospital Inc.; National City   925
Nypro Precision Assemblies Inc.; Chula Vista; surgical and medical instruments   900

California Dept. of Corrections; Calipatria   900
City of Chula Vista; Chula Vista; city management   800
Cox Communications Inc.; San Diego; cable television   750
Imperial Irrigation District Inc.; Imperial; electric, other services   750
Sharp Chula Vista Medical Center; Chula Vista   729
BI Technologies Corp.; Calexico; electronic circuits   700
International Rectifier Corp.; San Diego; security brokers   675
Southwestern Community College District; Chula Vista   646
Imperial County Office of Education; El Centro; educational services   600
Ora Corp.; San Diego; frozen ethnic foods   570
Packer Hughes Interconnect; San Diego; alarm systems   561
Bud Antle Inc.; Holtville; vegetables   555
Imperial Community College District; Imperial   503
Jhane Barnes Collection Inc.; Chula Vista; men's and boys' sportswear   500
Gilbert Martin Woodworking Co.; San Diego; wood household furniture   500
El Centro Community Hospital Inc.; El Centro   500

California 52nd District
Eastern San Diego; inland San Diego County

The 52nd, which wraps around the east side of San Diego from Poway in the north to east of Otay Mesa in the south, is predominantly made up of wealthy, conservative suburbs. It contains about 15 percent of San Diego's residents and is solidly Republican ground, complemented by growing, rich suburbs. (See map p. 121.)

After years of slow economic growth, the late 1990s marked a turn-around, particularly in El Cajon, where property values and home sales rose dramatically. San Diego's large military and defense-related workforce contributes to the district's conservative personality and robust economy. Though most of the area's military bases are in the 53rd, many residents commute to nearby defense and military contracting jobs. Blue- and white-collar employees alike tend to vote Republican in the almost three-fourths white district.

Poway has a more wealthy, rural feel to it than the surrounding suburban sprawl, where growth is becoming a hot issue. Just outside of Poway is an expanse of evenly developed suburbs that includes Rancho Bernardo (shared with the 49th) and Scripps Ranch, areas within San Diego's city limits that have attracted retirees and young families alike.

The district also stretches about 100 miles east and north through mountains and protected desert parks to the San Diego County borders. Until redistricting following the 2000 census, the 52nd also had much of California's border with Mexico and all of rural Imperial County to the east. But those areas were moved into the 51st, making this district more conservative and dominated by suburban interests.

Major Industry
Technology, manufacturing.

Notable

The Unarius society, based in El Cajon, believes UFOs will bring "a new beginning for planet earth."

Election Returns

	Republican		Democratic		Other	
President 2000	143,081	57.3%	98,633	39.5%	7,833	3.1%
House 2002	118,561	70.2%	43,526	25.8%	6,923	4.1%

District Profile

Population   639,087

Total area (square miles)   2,129
   Land area (square miles)   2,113

Population per square mile   302.4

Counties (2000 population)
   San Diego (pt.)   639,087

Cities and other areas over 10,000 (2000 population)
   Alpine CDP   13,143
   Bostonia CDP   15,169
   Casa de Oro-Mount Helix CDP   18,874
   El Cajon   94,869
   Lakeside CDP   19,560
   La Mesa   54,749
   Poway   48,044
   Ramona CDP   15,691
   Rancho San Diego CDP   20,155
   San Diego (pt.)   164,544
   Santee   52,975
   Spring Valley CDP   26,663
   Winter Gardens CDP   19,771

Race and Hispanic or Latino origin*
   White   72.9%
   Black or African American   3.7%
   American Indian or Alaska Native   0.7%
   Asian   5.4%
   Native Hawaiian or other Pacific Islander   0.3%
   Some other race   0.2%
   Hispanic or Latino origin   13.7%
   Two or more races   3.2%

As percentage of total population.

Ancestry*

Dutch	1.2%	Norwegian	1.6%
English	8.5%	Polish	1.9%
French	2.8%	Scotch-Irish	1.5%
German	12.5%	Scottish	1.7%
Irish	9.1%	Swedish	1.5%
Italian	4.4%	USA/American	3.9%

As estimated percentage of total population.

Universities and colleges, 2000–2001 enrollment
   Christian Heritage College, El Cajon   675
   Coleman College, La Mesa   1,256
   Cuyamaca College, El Cajon   6,476
   Grossmont College, El Cajon   16,309
   ITT Technical Institute, San Diego   909
   Maric College, San Diego   1,653
   Pacific College of Oriental Medicine, San Diego   370
   San Diego Miramar College, San Diego   8,439
   U.S. International University, San Diego   1,334
   University of Phoenix, San Diego   2,581

Newspapers and circulation

	District circulation	Total circulation
Los Angeles Times	2,365	1,044,205
North County Times	3,180	93,408
San Diego Union Tribune	99,359	357,315
*USA Today**	6,808	1,674,376

See Sources and Explanations in the front of the volume.

Television stations and affiliations

San Diego	100%	KFMB	CBS
San Diego	100%	KGTV	ABC
San Diego	100%	KNSD	NBC
San Diego	100%	KPBS	PBS
San Diego	100%	KSWB	WB
San Diego	100%	KUSI	Independent

Cable systems and subscribers
   Cable USA   1,658
   Cox   71,490
   Time Warner   28,046

Military installations, September 2001
   Marine Corps Air Station, San Diego   9,183

Businesses and other major employers
   San Diego County; San Diego; sheriff's office   4,000
   GEICO; Poway; insurance agents and brokers   3,000
   Kaiser Foundation Hospitals; San Diego   2,500
   Viejas Casino and Turf Club; Alpine; casino   2,000
   Sycuan Casino; El Cajon; casino   2,000
   U.S. Postal Service; San Diego   2,000
   Grossmont Hospital Corp.; La Mesa   1,740
   ARC of San Diego; San Diego; advocacy   1,664
   Grossmont-Cuyamaca Community College District; El Cajon   1,490
   Cubic Corp.; San Diego; electronic flight simulators   1,243
   Aldila Golf Corp.; Poway; golf club shafts   1,150
   Interinsurance Exchange; La Mesa; insurance agents and brokers   1,000
   San Diego Hospital Assn.; San Diego; health systems agency   1,000
   GKN Aerospace Chem-Tronics Inc.; El Cajon; aircraft engines and parts   873
   Anacomp Inc.; Poway; microfilm recording and developing service   800
   Delta Design Inc.; Poway; electronic/electrical circuits test equipment   800
   Sutherland Group; San Diego; data base information retrieval   800
   TRW Inc.; San Diego; commercial physical research   780
   America Kyocera Inc.; San Diego; integrated circuits, semiconductor networks   775
   San Diego Unified School District; San Diego   700
   San Diego County; San Diego; individual and family services   700
   San Diego County; San Diego; legislative bodies   700

TRW Inc.; San Diego; engineering services   700

San Diego County; Ramona; public elementary school   650

Uniserve Facilities Services; San Diego; building maintenance   650

Addus Healthcare Inc.; San Diego; home health care services   634

Senior Operations Inc.; El Cajon; fabricated structural metal   630

Merck and Co. Inc.; San Diego; medicinals and botanicals   600

REMEC Inc.; San Diego; search and navigation equipment   600

Mitchell International Inc.; San Diego; business newsletters publishing, printing   597

Cubic Defense Systems Inc.; San Diego; electronic flight simulators   590

GEICO; San Diego; insurance agents   575

Cubic Transportation Systems Inc.; San Diego; public transportation fare registers   550

Brookwood Landscape Inc.; San Diego; lawn and garden services   550

Pinkerton's Inc.; San Diego; security guard service   550

CCN Managed Care Inc.; San Diego; medical field-related associations   550

Computer Sciences Corp.; San Diego; computer systems analysis and design   550

Jack In Box Inc.; San Diego; fast-food restaurant chain management   550

Mitchell International Inc.; San Diego; information retrieval services   550

TRW Inc.; San Diego; research institute   525

Guard Management Inc.; San Diego; guard services   510

Campo Band of Missions Indians; Campo; casino   505

Automobile Club of Southern California; La Mesa; automobile owners' association   500

Kiewit Pacific Co.; Lakeside; highway and street construction   500

Ciba Vision Inc.; San Diego; optical instruments and lenses   500

Cox Communications Inc.; San Diego; cable television   500

Pacific Bell; San Diego; local/long-distance telephone   500

Solar Turbines Inc.; San Diego; gas turbine generators   500

Maintenance Warehouse America Corp.; San Diego; hardware   500

Medimpact Healthcare Systems Inc.; San Diego; industry specialist consultants   500

California 53rd District

Downtown San Diego; Imperial Beach

The coastal 53rd is the economic engine that drives surrounding districts. It includes San Diego's downtown, large employers, most of its military bases, and its coastline from the Mexican border to the protected shores of La Jolla. (*See map p. 121.*)

Redistricting following the 2000 census scooped away wealthy and Republican-leaning communities, such as Clairemont and the inland part of La Jolla from the north end, making the district, previously numbered the 49th, much more Democratic.

The 53rd now includes Hispanic Democratic areas east of the city such as Lemon Grove as well as a big chunk of central San Diego. It still contains some Reagan Democrats but also includes blue-collar, central city areas like North Park, City Heights, Barrio Logan, and Hillcrest, one of the area's most liberal and Democratic places and the center of the city's gay community. The result is a 29.4 percent Hispanic district that favored Democrat Al Gore over Republican George W. Bush by 57.5 percent to 37.5 percent in the 2000 presidential election.

Higher education in the district includes the University of California, San Diego, in La Jolla, San Diego State University, and the University of San Diego. Private companies have formed biomedical research partnerships with the schools. The 53rd's economy has benefited from a presence of biotech and telecommunications firms, but the downtown area and military presence have kept it diverse enough to avoid downturns.

Major Industry

Telecommunications, defense, biotechnology.

Notable

Sea World, the San Diego Zoo, and Balboa Park (the city's cultural center) are major tourist attractions; the Coronado Bay Bridge connects downtown with the beach resort of Coronado Island; a new downtown stadium for baseball's Padres opens in 2004; Torrey Pines State Reserve, next to the venerable golf course of the same name, is home to the nation's rarest pine tree.

Election Returns

	Republican		Democratic		Other	
President 2000	74,526	37.5%	114,435	57.5%	9,944	5%
House 2002	43,891	37.8%	72,252	62.2%		

District Profile

Population   639,087

Total area (square miles)   251
    Land area (square miles)   94

Population per square mile   6,731.6

Counties (2000 population)
    San Diego (pt.)   639,087

Cities and other areas over 10,000 (2000 population)
    Coronado   24,100   Lemon Grove   24,918
    Imperial Beach   26,992   San Diego (pt.)   542,356
    La Presa CDP (pt.)   20,721

Race and Hispanic or Latino origin*
    White   51.0%
    Black or African American   7.2%
    American Indian or Alaska Native   0.5%
    Asian   8.3%
    Native Hawaiian or other Pacific Islander   0.4%

Some other race   0.3%
Hispanic or Latino origin   29.4%
Two or more races   3.1%

As percentage of total population.

Ancestry*

English	6.3%	Polish	1.5%
French	2.1%	Scotch-Irish	1.2%
German	8.8%	Scottish	1.6%
Irish	7.4%	Swedish	1.2%
Italian	3.9%	USA/American	2.6%
Norwegian	1.3%		

As estimated percentage of total population.

Universities and colleges, 2000–2001 enrollment
California Western School of Law, San Diego   760
Fashion Institute of Design and Merchandising, San Diego   213
Kelsey-Jenney College, San Diego   311
National University, San Diego   16,848
Platt College-San Diego, San Diego   342
Point Loma Nazarene University, San Diego   2,733
San Diego City College, San Diego   27,165
San Diego Mesa College, San Diego   21,233
San Diego State University, San Diego   31,609
Scripps Research Institute, La Jolla*
Thomas Jefferson School of Law, San Diego   575
University of California-San Diego, La Jolla   20,197
University of San Diego, San Diego   6,943

Enrollment under 100. See Sources and Explanations in the front of the volume.

Newspapers and circulation

	District circulation	Total circulation
Los Angeles Times	6,168	1,044,205
San Diego Union Tribune	87,713	357,315

Television stations and affiliations
San Diego	100%	KFMB	CBS
San Diego	100%	KGTV	ABC
San Diego	100%	KNSD	NBC
San Diego	100%	KPBS	PBS
San Diego	100%	KSWB	WB
San Diego	100%	KUSI	Independent

Cable systems and subscribers
Cox   11,557
Time Warner   296,706

Military installations, September 2001
San Diego Naval Base, San Diego   34,142
North Island Naval Aviation Depot Activity, San Diego   16,604
San Diego Naval Hospital, San Diego   4,646
Space and Naval Warfare Systems Center, San Diego   3,711
San Diego Marine Corps Recruitment Depot, San Diego   3,607
Fleet and Industrial Supply Center (NWCF), San Diego   1,566
Pacific Fleet Combat Training Center, San Diego   1,248
San Diego Naval Submarine Base, San Diego   564
Naval Training Center, San Diego   486
Naval Computer and Telecommunications Station, San Diego   281

Businesses and other major employers
Scripps Foundation for Medicine and Science; San Diego; fund-raising organization   7,800
City of San Diego; San Diego; municipal police   5,000
Science Applications International Corp.; San Diego; commercial physical research   4,300
University of California; San Diego; medical and surgical hospital   4,000
San Diego Gas and Electric Co.; San Diego; electric power distribution   4,000
Science Applications International Corp.; San Diego; commercial physical research   3,500
Scripps Health; La Jolla; skilled nursing care facilities   3,000
U.S. Bureau of Customs and Border Protection   3,000
National Steel and Shipbuilding Co.; San Diego; shipbuilding and repairing   3,000
Sharp Memorial Hospital; San Diego   3,000
Solar Turbines Inc.; San Diego; gas turbine generators   2,700
Scripps Research Institute; La Jolla   2,500
Edix Corp.; San Diego; management services   2,375
Pfizer Corp.; La Jolla; pharmaceuticals   2,000
A Soul Purpose Christian Singles; San Diego; dating service   2,000
International Specialty Products Inc.; San Diego; organic fibers   2,000
San Diego Childrens' Hospital; San Diego   2,000
Sea World/Busch Entertainment Corp.; San Diego; theme park   1,700
Scripps Clinic; La Jolla; management services   1,600
University of San Diego; San Diego   1,516
Zoological Society of San Diego; San Diego; zoo   1,500
Trizec Centers Inc.; San Diego; subdividers and developers   1,500
San Diego County; San Diego; county government   1,350
L-O Coronado Hotel Inc.; Coronado; hotels   1,350
Professional Community Management Inc.; San Diego; real estate managers   1,300
University of California; La Jolla   1,200
Tenet Healthcare Corp. Hospital; San Diego   1,200
Golden Eagle Insurance Corp.; San Diego; fire, marine, casualty insurance   1,100
Sempra Energy; San Diego; electric power generation   1,000
City of San Diego; San Diego; water supply   1,000
Southwest Marine Inc.; San Diego; shipbuilding and repairing   1,000
Agouron Pharmaceuticals Inc.; San Diego; pharmaceuticals   1,000
Kyocera Wireless Corp.; San Diego; communication equipment   1,000
Navy Exchange Service Command; San Diego; general warehousing, storage   1,000
Starwood Hotels and Resorts Worldwide Inc.; San Diego; hotel, franchised   950
San Diego County; San Diego; sheriff's office   950
General Atomics; San Diego; commercial physical research   950
Manchester Resorts; San Diego; hotels   900
San Diego Gas and Electric Co.; San Diego; electric power generation   900

Woodfin Suite Hotels; San Diego; hotels   865
San Diego Sheraton Corp.; San Diego; hotels   850
Equi-Sher San Diego Joint Venture; San Diego; commercial real estate agent   800
San Diego Community College District; San Diego   750
Atlas Hotels Inc.; San Diego; hotels   730
Hyatt Corp.; San Diego; hotels and motels   720
San Diego Unified School District; San Diego   700
Clear Channel Communications Inc.; San Diego; radio broadcasting stations   700
Navy Exchange Service Command; San Diego; Army-Navy goods stores   700
Nielsen Dillingham Builders Inc.; San Diego; specialized public building contractors   669
San Diego Transit Corp.; San Diego; commuter bus operation   650
Sharp Cabrillo Hospital; San Diego   600
Marine Corps Personnel Support; San Diego; variety stores   600
Nordstrom Inc.; San Diego; family clothing stores   596
Anthony's Seafood Group; San Diego; restaurants   585
San Diego County Office of Education; San Diego   577

International Total Services Inc.; San Diego; security systems services   569
Courier Leasing Inc.; San Diego; passenger car leasing   560
American Specialty Health Plan; San Diego; health maintenance organization   550
Business Assn. of Latin American Studies; San Diego; professional organization   550
Allied Global Holdings Inc.; Phoenix; collection agency   500
UCSD Medical Center; La Jolla   500
Pacific Bell; San Diego; telephone communication   500
Pedus Service Inc.; San Diego; security systems services   500
San Diego Paradise Point Resort Inc.; San Diego; resort hotel   500
Westgroup San Diego Associates; San Diego; resort hotel   500
Bazaar Del Mundo Inc.; San Diego; restaurants/shops   500
Sharp Coronado Hospital; Coronado   500
U.S. Veterans Hospital; San Diego   500

Colorado

Colorado stands out even among other western states that bulk large and boxy on the map. It lies at the proximate center of what was once called the Great American Desert—midway between Canada and Mexico, the Pacific and the Mississippi. At the heart of the state is its capital and dominant population center, Denver, a name known to cross-continental travelers in every era since frontier days. Still the biggest town going west from Kansas City to San Francisco, Denver now fills the same role going northwest from the urban centers of Texas to their counterparts in the Pacific Northwest.

The economy here soars and falls rather regularly on the vagaries of commodity markets, including livestock, timber, hard rock minerals, and petroleum. Diversifying into electronics and financial services has helped metro Denver even out the bumps, but even some of the alternative sources of income have had a tendency to feast or famine.

Colorado's growth in the postwar decades has been uneven but impressive. In proportional terms the biggest leap came in the 1950s when the population grew by a third. But because the whole country was growing fast then, the state was still stuck at the four House seats it had earned by the 1910 census. It took until the 1960s, when somewhat slower growth still added another half million people, to fill out that fifth seat.

The 1970s was a pivotal decade, bringing two energy crises nationally, raising energy prices, and renewing interest in Colorado's oil, gas, and hydropower potential. Colorado sits on the world's greatest deposits of oil shale, an expensive source of fuel but one the federal government tried for a time to develop. That push coincided with a surge in skiing in the 1970s and Denver's emergence as a regional financial services center and brought the state a net gain of 680,000 residents, enough for a sixth House seat.

A period of slower growth followed in the 1980s when resistance to sprawl was high and energy prices turned downward (the oil shale experiment was abandoned). But coming out of the recession of 1991 the state found its way into the high-tech boom of the decade, benefiting from Boulder-based growth around the University of Colorado as well as the Colorado Springs growth associated with the Air Force Academy. In the 1990s Colorado grew faster than any state in the union except for Nevada and Arizona, and its biggest numerical gain yet, a full million, would be more than enough for a seventh House seat.

All these changes have affected the state's recent politics. Historically, Colorado has known sharp spasms of populism and socialism. But these have generally given way to steadier epochs of conservative Republicanism in which winning candidates had the backing of the mines, the railroads, and the banks. The last uprising among liberals came in the 1970s and 1980s when an influx of younger people with antiwar backgrounds and environmental causes helped tilt the state to the left. Galvanized by the issue of state funding for the winter Olympics of 1976, this new coalition found its voice and won a referendum that blocked the Olympics.

Soon the new forces were making common cause with traditional farm-and-labor Democrats, which led to some surprising new faces in office: Gov. Richard Lamm, Sen. Gary Hart, and, later, Sen. Timothy Wirth and Rep. Pat Schroeder, all products of elite universities and law schools elected here in the 1970s who would seek to put their stamp on national politics. But their era waned as population growth slowed with falling energy prices in the 1980s, fears of overcrowding eased, and anxiety about economic stagnation took their place. New issues from the right came to the fore, including gun owners' rights, a three-strikes sentencing law, ordinances against homosexuals, and term limits on officeholders. The term limit movement was perhaps less needed here than in many states: leading Democrats such as Lamm, Hart, Wirth, and Schroeder left office voluntarily, as did Republican senators Bill Armstrong and Hank Brown.

The issue shift led to changes in the partisan lineup. After 24 years of Lamm and his successor, Roy Romer, in the governorship, Colorado elected Bill Owen, a Texas-bred conservative Republican, in 1998 and 2002. The moderate Republican Brown gave up his Senate seat to the more conservative Republican Wayne Allard in 1996, who was reelected in 2002. The Senate seat that had been Democratic went to Ben Nighthorse Campbell in 1992, but he switched parties when the Republicans became the majority in 1994. In 2003 he was contemplating his second reelection bid as a Republican.

In presidential races Colorado has generally been a dependable state for Republicans. Only one Democrat won a majority here in the thirteen presidential elections from 1952 to 2000: Lyndon Johnson in his 1964 landslide. Bill Clinton carried the state with just 40 percent of the vote in 1992, when disillusionment with George Bush dropped him to 35 percent of the vote and Ross Perot got 23 percent (one of his best showings anywhere). In 1996 the Perot vote was down to 7 percent and Bob Dole recaptured the state for the GOP. George W. Bush won here with just under 51 percent of the vote in 2000.

The congressional delegation, historically bipartisan, also settled into a Republican configuration in the 1990s. The huge Western Slope district (roughly half the state) reached

Districts established January 25, 2002, for elections first held in 2002.

7 members

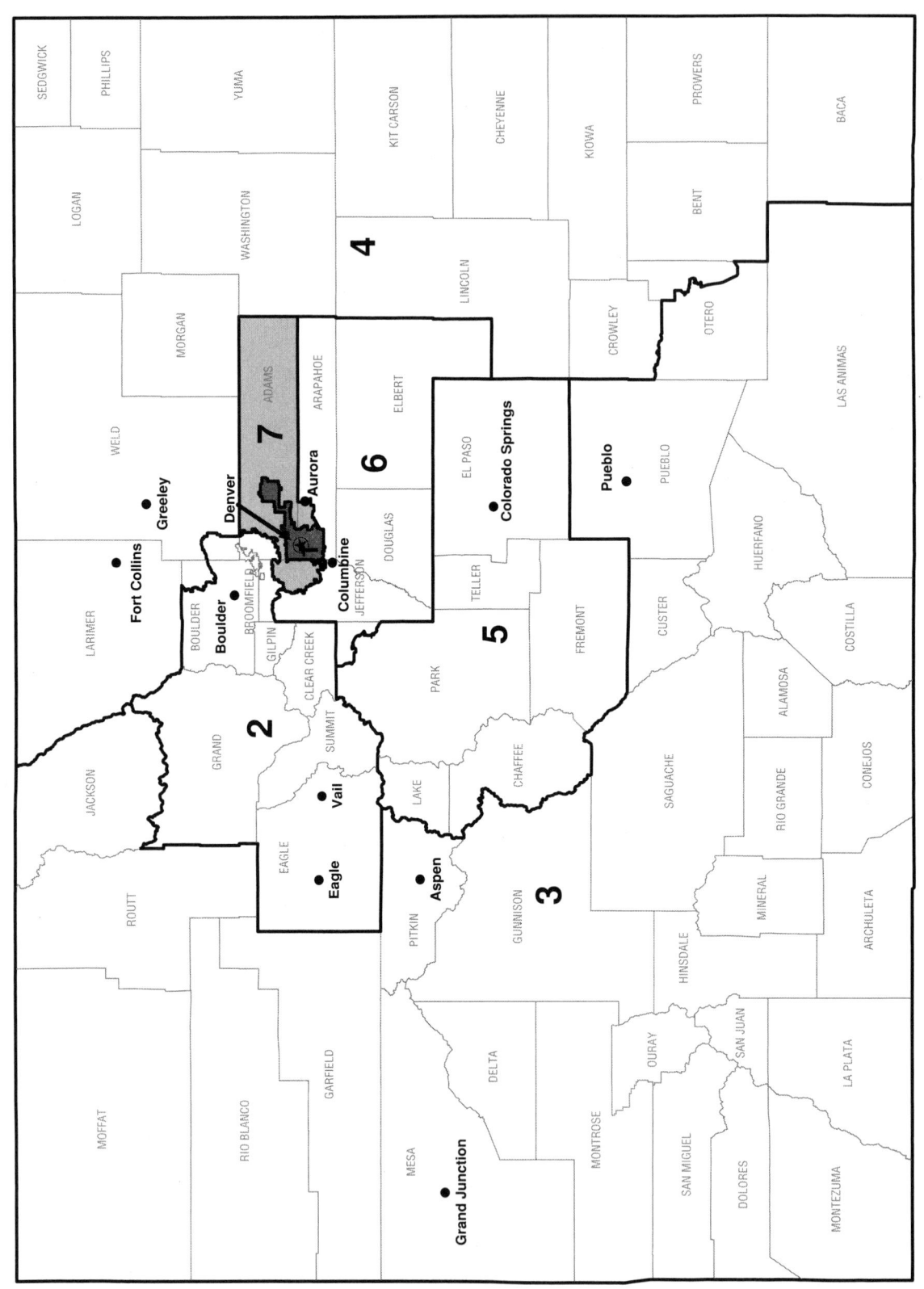

Districts established May 9, 2003, for elections first held in 2004.

7 members

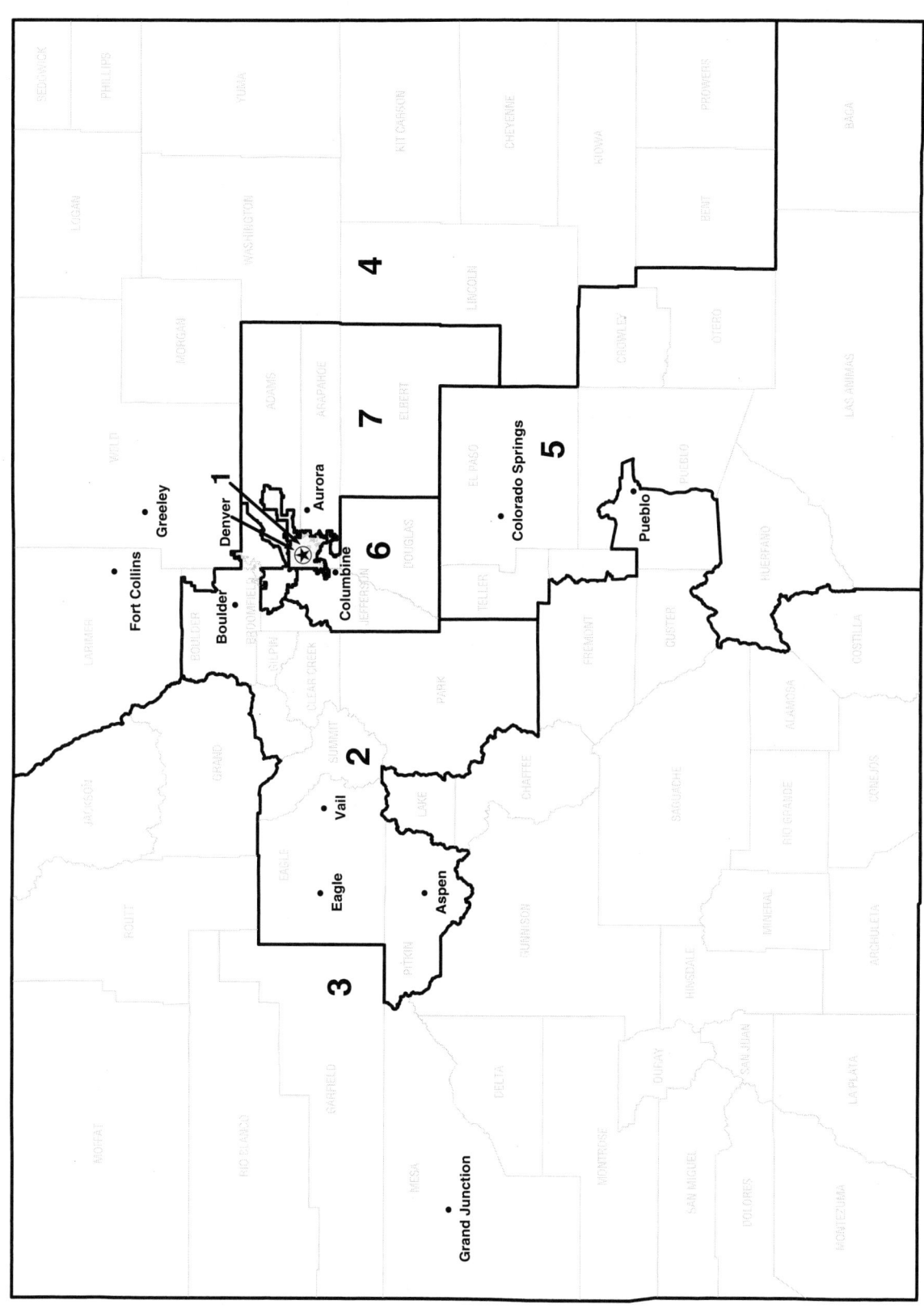

into the southeast to take in Pueblo. The nearly-as-roomy eastern district swung northwest to take in Fort Collins. Both were Republican throughout the 1990s, as were the traditionally Republican districts around Colorado Springs (5th District) and the Denver suburbs (6th District). The Democrats held the districts based in Denver and Boulder.

But after the 2000 census yielded a seventh seat, the state legislature had trouble mapping it. The state house was Republican, and it fashioned a new 7th in Arapahoe and Jefferson Counties, east and south of Denver, that leaned Republican too. But the state senate was Democratic, and its president wanted to draw a new southern district built around his home base in Pueblo. Such a district might also have meant more influence for Hispanics, whose 17 percent share of the population made Colorado the sixth most Hispanic state in 2000.

But with the legislators at loggerheads, the job was done by a state judge in Denver. The judge accepted the general outline of the old map (no new southern district), shrank the eastern rural 4th District (where veteran Bob Schaffer was retiring), and fashioned a highly competitive new 7th District in suburbs east and north of Denver. The new 7th had a partisan split of exactly one third each between Republicans, Democrats, and independents and had actually been carried by Al Gore in 2000, although not by much.

No institution in Colorado is nearly as popular as the Denver Broncos. When the team was winning consecutive Super Bowls in the late 1990s, the local GOP dreamed of nominating legendary quarterback John Elway in the new district (which would coincidentally bear Elway's jersey number). But the legend said no, and both parties suffered through protracted candidate scrambles. In the end, the new 7th proved as competitive as the judge had hoped. It went Republican in 2002 by 121 votes.

The Republican controlled legislature did not want to leave it at that. In early 2003, legislators redrew the court-ordered boundaries to add new Republican voters to the 7th. Democrats protested in vain and took the issue to court. *(See discussion p. 184.)* The controversy remained in litigation as of mid-November 2003.

Table 1　Population

District	Population	Population under 18	Voting-age population	Median age	Male*	Female*
1	614,465	134,420	480,045	33.2	50.5	49.5
2	614,465	152,298	462,167	32.5	51.1	48.9
3	614,467	154,091	460,376	37.2	50.0	50.0
4	614,466	160,160	454,306	33.3	50.4	49.6
5	614,467	164,003	450,464	34.1	50.9	49.1
6	614,466	180,777	433,689	35.8	49.7	50.3
7	614,465	155,046	459,419	34.4	49.9	50.1
State	4,301,261	1,100,795	3,200,466	34.3	50.4	49.6

*As percentage of total population.

Table 2　Voting-Age Persons by Race/Hispanic or Latino Origin

District	White*	Black or African American*	American Indian or Alaska Native*	Asian*	Other or multirace*	Hispanic or Latino*
1	60.3	9.1	0.7	2.9	1.7	25.3
2	81.4	0.9	0.5	3.2	1.3	12.8
3	77.3	0.7	1.3	0.6	1.1	19.0
4	82.2	0.8	0.5	1.3	1.1	14.3
5	79.6	5.5	0.7	2.5	1.8	9.8
6	89.0	1.8	0.4	2.7	1.1	5.1
7	72.7	5.2	0.6	3.0	1.5	16.9
State	77.3	3.5	0.7	2.3	1.4	14.9

*As percentage of voting-age population.

Table 3　Voting-Age Population by Age Groups

District	18 to 24*	25 to 44*	45 to 64*	Over 64*
1	13.7	46.2	25.7	14.5
2	15.7	47.2	28.3	8.8
3	12.6	37.3	32.3	17.8
4	16.5	40.7	28.7	14.1
5	13.7	44.3	29.4	12.6
6	8.3	47.4	35.0	9.3
7	13.3	43.4	29.7	13.6
State	13.4	43.8	29.8	13.0

*As percentage of voting-age population.

Table 4　Income and Occupation

District	Median family income	Families in poverty*	White collar†	Blue collar†	Service†	Farm†
1	$48,541	10.1	64.3	20.4	15.1	0.1
2	$64,006	4.0	66.3	20.2	13.2	0.4
3	$42,668	9.2	56.1	25.0	17.4	1.5
4	$51,590	6.7	59.8	24.0	14.4	1.8
5	$52,482	5.9	63.2	21.3	15.3	0.2
6	$80,910	1.9	77.4	13.2	9.2	0.1
7	$53,624	6.4	62.6	23.8	13.4	0.2
State	$55,883	6.2	64.5	21.0	13.9	0.6

*As percentage of all families.　　†As percentage of employed workers 16 years and over.

Table 5　Education: School Years Completed

District	Less than grade 9*	Grades 9–12 no diploma*	High school diploma no college*	Some college*	College bachelor's degree or higher*
1	8.7	11.7	20.4	24.9	34.3
2	3.4	6.9	21.2	29.2	39.3
3	6.2	10.0	28.6	31.5	23.8
4	6.4	8.3	25.2	31.3	28.7
5	2.6	7.2	24.4	36.0	29.8
6	1.0	3.4	16.5	32.3	46.8
7	5.4	10.0	26.3	32.3	26.0
State	4.8	8.2	23.2	31.0	32.7

*As percentage of persons age 25 and over.

Table 6　Housing and Residential Patterns

District	Median home value	Owner occupied*	Renter occupied*	Urban†	Rural†
1	$159,100	52.1	47.9	100.0	0.0
2	$185,400	69.1	30.9	87.3	12.7
3	$112,500	70.4	29.6	61.0	39.0

District	Median home value	Owner occupied*	Renter occupied*	Urban†	Rural†
4	$146,300	68.0	32.0	75.1	24.9
5	$141,300	66.5	33.5	85.7	14.3
6	$211,800	84.9	15.1	84.7	15.3
7	$154,600	63.2	36.8	97.7	2.3
State	$160,100	67.3	32.7	84.5	15.5

*As percentage of occupied housing units.   †As percentage of total population.

Colorado 1st District

Denver

Mostly within the capital city of Denver, the 1st is a bastion of liberalism in a conservative-leaning state. A Republican last won Denver's House seat in 1970, and Ronald Reagan, in 1980, was the last Republican to carry Denver for president.

Denver's diversity—the fast-growing Hispanic community makes up nearly a third of the city's population while blacks make up more than a tenth—is reflected by residents' electoral decisions. Mayor Wellington Webb, an African American elected in 1991, succeeded Federico Peña, a Hispanic who later served in President Bill Clinton's cabinet. City officials are using the $5 billion Denver International Airport, which opened in 1995 and has become one of the nation's ten busiest, to increase exports and lure European and Asian companies to locate or expand their business here.

Dependent on the region's oil and gas industries, Denver suffered during the oil bust of the 1980s, but the city boomed in the 1990s. The economy became more diversified as technology and telecommunications industries revitalized downtown and surrounding areas. The former Lowry Air Force Base is now an education center; the former Fitzsimons Army Medical Center is home to the University of Colorado medical school and a bioscience research park.

Area sports fans had a lot to cheer about in the 1990s, as football's Broncos won two Super Bowls and hockey's Colorado Avalanche won two Stanley Cups. New baseball (1995) and football (2001) stadiums, as well as a new arena (1999), opened in the city.

Ninety percent of the 1st District's residents live in Denver. The rest live just south of the city, in well-off communities such as Englewood and Cherry Hills Village.

Major Industry

Telecommunications, computers, health care, government.

Notable

The Great American Beer Festival is the nation's largest and oldest annual brewing competition; U.S. Mint coin production facility.

Election Returns

	Republican		Democratic		Other	
President 2000	72,455	32.8%	134,187	60.7%	14,430	6.5%
House 2002	49,884	29.6%	111,718	66.3%	6,962	4.1%

District Profile

Population   614,465

Total area (square miles)   173.0
   Land area (square miles)   171.3

Population per square mile   3,587.1

Counties (2000 population)
   Arapahoe (pt.)   59,825
   Denver   554,636
   Jefferson (pt.)   4

Cities and other areas over 10,000 (2000 population)
   Denver   554,636
   Englewood (pt.)   31,727

Race and Hispanic or Latino origin*
   White   54.3%
   Black or African American   10.1%
   American Indian or Alaska Native   0.7%
   Asian   2.7%
   Native Hawaiian or other Pacific Islander   0.1%
   Some other race   0.2%
   Hispanic or Latino origin   30.0%
   Two or more races   1.9%

*As percentage of total population.

Ancestry*

Dutch 1.3%	Polish 1.6%
English 6.9%	Russian 1.1%
French 2.0%	Scotch-Irish 1.3%
German 11.6%	Scottish 1.6%
Irish 7.8%	Swedish 1.5%
Italian 2.8%	USA/American 2.8%
Norwegian 1.3%	

*As estimated percentage of total population.

Universities and colleges, 2000–2001 enrollment
   College America-Denver, Denver   399
   Colorado Institute of Art, Denver   2,090
   Community College of Denver, Denver   6,635
   Denver Automotive and Diesel College, Denver   390
   Denver Seminary, Englewood   678
   Denver Technical College, Denver   814
   Health One-School of Medical Technology, Denver   1,912
   Iliff School of Theology, Denver   276
   Metropolitan State College of Denver, Denver   17,688
   Platt College, Aurora   217
   Regis University, Denver   9,129
   Rocky Mountain College of Art and Design, Denver   410
   University of Colorado-Denver, Denver   13,737
   University of Colorado Health Sciences Center, Denver   2,399
   University of Denver, Denver   9,444
   Westwood College of Technology, Denver   443

Newspapers and circulation

	District circulation	Total circulation
Denver Post-Rocky Mountain News	89,039	674,801
Denver Rocky Mountain News	103,844	418,717
*USA Today**	8,266	1,674,376

*See Sources and Explanations in the front of the volume.

Television stations and affiliations

Denver	100%	KBDI	PBS
Denver	100%	KCEC	Univision
Denver	100%	KCNC	CBS
Denver	100%	KDUH	ABC
Denver	100%	KDVR	FOX
Denver	100%	KFCT	FOX
Denver	100%	KFNR	ABC
Denver	100%	KMGH	ABC
Denver	100%	KPXC	PAX
Denver	100%	KREG	CBS
Denver	100%	KRMA	CBS
Denver	100%	KRMT	Independent
Denver	100%	KTVD	UPN
Denver	100%	KUSA	NBC
Denver	100%	KWGN	WB
Denver	100%	KWHD	Independent

Cable systems and subscribers

Comcast   106,683

Military installations, September 2001

Joe P. Martinez U.S. Army Reserve Center, Denver   563

Businesses and other major employers

U.S. Geological Survey; Denver   9,000

Tyco International Inc.; Denver; fire detection systems 4,000

Denver Health and Hospital Authority; Denver   3,541

First Data Corp.; Commerce City; data processing 3,000

AT&T Corp.; Denver; cable television   3,000

J. D. Edwards and Co.; Denver; computer software 3,000

Samsonite Corp.; Denver; luggage   2,806

U.S. Veterans Hospital; Denver   2,700

University of Colorado Hospital Authority; Denver 2,595

Children's Health Corp.; Denver; hospital management 2,200

Denver Newspaper Agency; Denver; newspaper   2,100

Hard Rock Cafe International Inc.; Denver; restaurants 2,000

Wells Fargo Bank Minnesota; Denver; commercial bank 2,000

University of Denver Burns School; Denver; business training services   2,000

HCA-HealthONE Hospital; Denver   2,000

St. Joseph Hospital Inc.; Denver; hospital, medical school   2,000

Elitch Gardens Co.; Denver; theme park   1,800

Porter Adventist Health System Inc.; Denver; hospital 1,670

University of Denver; Denver   1,650

U.S. Defense Dept.; Denver   1,600

XCEL Energy Inc.; Denver; electric services   1,500

Colorado Dept. of Revenue; Denver   1,500

Denver City and County; Denver; police dept.   1,500

State Farm Life Insurance Co.; Denver; insurance agents and brokers   1,500

Aramark Services Inc.; Denver; eating places   1,500

Shareholder Services Inc.; Denver; security transfer agents   1,500

Property Asset Management Services; Denver; apartment building operators   1,412

Dillon Companies Inc.; Denver; convenience stores 1,400

HCA Inc.; Englewood; physiotherapist   1,300

Startek USA Inc.; Denver; business computer software 1,255

Qwest Business Resources Inc.; Denver; purchasing service   1,250

U.S. Internal Revenue Service; Denver   1,200

Continental Airlines Inc.; Denver; air passenger carrier 1,200

Rose HealthONE Medical Center; Denver   1,200

Apartment Investment and Management Co.; Denver; real estate investment trusts   1,150

Denver Board of Water Commissioners; Denver   1,100

Gates Corp.; Denver; rubber and plastics hose and beltings   1,100

EPA Employees Assn.; Denver; employees' association 1,036

Qwest Business and Government Services Inc.; Denver; telephone equipment and systems   1,002

Qwest Communications International Inc.; Denver; telephone communication   1,000

University of Colorado; Denver   1,000

ING America Equities Inc.; Denver; security brokers, dealers   1,000

Catholic Health Initiative; Denver; medical doctor offices, clinics   1,000

Janus Investment Fund; Denver; money market mutual funds   1,000

Denver Post Corp.; Denver; newspaper   1,000

U.S. Postal Service; Denver   1,000

Colorado Rockies Baseball Club; Denver; baseball club 990

Bank One Corp.; Denver; state commercial banks   986

National Jewish Medical and Research Center Inc.; Denver   980

Anthem Blue Cross and Blue Shield; Denver; insurance agents and brokers   975

Denver City and County; Denver; airport   950

Regis University; Denver   909

MCI Worldcom Network Services Inc.; Denver; long distance telephone   900

Colorado Federation of Garden Clubs Inc.; Denver; membership sports/recreation clubs   900

U.S. Environmental Protection Agency; Denver   900

HCA-HealthONE Hospital; Denver   850

United Air Lines Inc.; Denver; airline training   850

Colorado Dept. of Transportation; Denver   800

Janus Capital Corp.; Denver; money market mutual funds   800

Compus Logistics Inc.; Denver; food supplier   760

Wynkoop Brewing Co.; Denver; restaurant   750

Nobel/Sysco Food Services Co.; Denver; food supplier 750

Master Klean Janitorial Inc.; Denver; janitorial service 750

Accenture Inc.; Denver; business management consultant   725

Public Service Company of Colorado; Denver; electric services   701

Denver Post Corp.; Denver; newspaper   700

Public Service Company of Colorado; Denver; electric
  power generation   700

Colonial Gardens; Denver; mobile home site operators
  700

Auraria Higher Education Center; Denver; management
  services   700

Pepsi-Cola North America; Denver; soft drinks   700

Denver Regional Transportation District; Denver   700

Keebler Co.; Denver; cookies and crackers   700

Temporary Accounting Personnel Inc.; Denver;
  employment agencies   700

Invesco Funds Group Inc.; Denver; security brokers,
  dealers, flotation companies   700

Denver School District; Denver   650

Aimco Properties LP; Denver; apartment building
  operators   650

Colorado Dept. of Corrections; Denver   650

Security Life of Denver Insurance Co.; Denver; life
  insurance   641

Denver Petroleum Club; Denver; temporary help service
  600

Bonded Maintenance Co.; Denver; janitorial service
  600

Pepsi-Cola Metropolitan Bottling Co.; Denver;
  carbonated beverages   600

Safeway Inc.; Denver; general warehousing, storage
  600

B. G. Service Solutions Inc.; Denver; building
  maintenance   600

Colorado Permanent Medical Group Inc.; Denver   600

Preferred Staffing Inc.; Denver; help supply services
  600

Colorado Dept. of Transportation; Denver   565

Metropolitan Life Insurance Co.; Denver; pension funds
  530

Craig Hospital; Englewood   512

Colorado Dept. of Regulatory Agencies; Denver   504

BGM Industries Inc.; Denver; building maintenance
  500

FlightSafety Services Corp.; Englewood; airline training
  500

American Furniture Warehouse Co. Inc.; Englewood;
  furniture stores   500

Southeast Corridor Constructors; Englewood; highway
  and street construction   500

United Technologies Corp.; Littleton; computer
  peripheral equipment   500

Colorado Labor and Employment Dept.; Denver   500

Dyncorp; Denver; airports   500

Visiting Nurse Support Service Inc.; Denver; visiting
  nurse service   500

Colorado Museum of Natural History; Denver   500

Burlington Northern and Santa Fe Railway Co.; Denver;
  railroad freight hauling   500

Unilever Bestfoods Foodservice; Denver; retail bakeries
  500

U.S. Minerals Management Service; Denver   500

Kinder Morgan Inc.; Lakewood; natural gas distribution
  500

Clay Street Properties; Denver; building operation   500

URS Group Inc.; Denver; engineering services   500

Colorado Compensation Insurance Authority; Denver
  500

Colorado 2nd District

Northwest Denver suburbs; Boulder

The liberal "granola" culture of Boulder—home to
the University of Colorado and a committed corps of
environmentalists—permeates much of the 2nd. But the district is mostly moderate in its political tone, exhibiting a
slight but hardly overwhelming Democratic lean.

After a decade of strong growth, redistricting following
the 2000 census redrew the 2nd to include more of Adams
County, which is adjacent to Denver and has a blue-collar
tone, and less of Boulder County, which had been entirely
within the district. The 2nd also shed most of its share of
fast-growing suburban Jefferson County.

Although they contain only a fraction of the 2nd's voters, Eagle, Grand, and Summit Counties, which were added
during redistricting, form an overwhelming majority of the
district's land area. Skiing is king in these mountain counties on the district's western border; the resort city of Vail is
in Eagle County. The 2nd also includes some communities
north of Denver in southwestern Weld County.

Environmental issues still play heavily here, and because
Boulder has been one of the fastest-growing cities in the
state, urban sprawl has gained some attention. Another concern is the Rocky Flats facility, a former plutonium plant
located near the Boulder-Jefferson county line, which is now
an environmental cleanup site.

Education is a high priority in the 2nd, site of the state's
flagship university and several federal research labs. The liberal strain in the academic community helped Green Party
presidential nominee Ralph Nader garner 12 percent of the
Boulder County vote in 2000, well above his statewide total
of 5 percent. But newcomers—who can overcome Boulder's
slow-growth regulations and afford a home in the resulting high-priced real estate market—tend to be more fiscally
conservative than voters past.

Major Industry

Information technology, government laboratories, higher
education.

Notable

The atomic clock at the National Institute of Standards
and Technology in Boulder is the nation's official timekeeper.

Election Returns

	Republican		Democratic		Other	
President 2000	103,518	42.6%	126,607	52.1%	13,107	5.4%
House 2002	75,564	36.8%	123,504	60.1%	6,454	3.2%

District Profile

Population   614,465

Total area (square miles)   5,664.2
  Land area (square miles)   5,614.8

Population per square mile   109.4

Counties (2000 population)

Adams (pt.)	239,615	Grand	12,442
Boulder (pt.)	216,126	Jefferson (pt.)	53,882
Clear Creek	9,322	Summit	23,548
Eagle	41,659	Weld (pt.)	13,114
Gilpin	4,757		

Cities and other areas over 10,000 (2000 population)

Boulder	94,673	Northglenn	31,575
Broomfield	38,272	Sherrelwood CDP	17,657
Federal Heights	12,065	Thornton (pt.)	82,378
Lafayette	23,197	Welby CDP (pt.)	11,717
Louisville	18,937	Westminster (pt.)	100,850

Race and Hispanic or Latino origin*

White   78.9%
Black or African American   1.0%
American Indian or Alaska Native   0.5%
Asian   3.2%
Native Hawaiian or other Pacific Islander   0.1%
Some other race   0.1%
Hispanic or Latino origin   14.7%
Two or more races   1.5%

*As percentage of total population.

Ancestry*

Dutch	1.4%	Norwegian	2.1%
English	9.1%	Polish	2.2%
French	2.6%	Scotch-Irish	1.6%
German	16.9%	Scottish	2.2%
Irish	9.8%	Swedish	2.2%
Italian	4.0%	USA/American	3.2%

*As estimated percentage of total population.

Universities and colleges, 2000–2001 enrollment

Colorado Aero Tech, Broomfield   1,188
Front Range Community College, Westminster
   12,962
ITT Technical Institute, Thornton   372
Parks College, Denver   330
Naropa Institute, Boulder   1,033
University of Colorado-Boulder, Boulder   29,352
Westwood College of Technology, Denver   904

Newspapers and circulation

	District circulation	Total circulation
Boulder Daily Camera	28,840	34,162
Denver Post-Rocky Mountain News	68,019	674,801
Denver Rocky Mountain News	68,610	418,717
Longmont Daily Times-Call	5,388	21,777
*USA Today**	2,441	1,674,376

*See Sources and Explanations in the front of the volume.

Television stations and affiliations

Denver	100%	KBDI	PBS
Denver	100%	KCEC	Univision
Denver	100%	KCNC	CBS
Denver	100%	KDUH	ABC
Denver	100%	KDVR	FOX
Denver	100%	KFCT	FOX
Denver	100%	KFNR	ABC
Denver	100%	KMGH	ABC
Denver	100%	KPXC	PAX
Denver	100%	KREG	CBS
Denver	100%	KRMA	CBS
Denver	100%	KRMT	Independent
Denver	100%	KTVD	UPN
Denver	100%	KUSA	NBC
Denver	100%	KWGN	WB
Denver	100%	KWHD	Independent

Cable systems and subscribers

Comcast   110,708
Copper Mountain Metro District   878
Galaxy   849
Rocky Mountain Cable   777
Ropir Cablevision   4,450

Businesses and other major employers

University of Colorado; Boulder   20,095
U.S. Dept. of Energy; Golden   8,000
International Business Machines Corp.; Westminster;
   printers, computers   5,000
International Business Machines Corp.; Boulder;
   computer magnetic storage devices   5,000
Avaya Inc.; Denver; online service providers   4,000
Lucent Technologies Inc.; Denver; telecommunication
   equipment repair   4,000
Storage Technology Corp.; Louisville; computer storage
   devices   3,014
AT&T Corp.; Westminster; telephone sets   3,000
Avaya Inc.; Westminster; online service providers
   3,000
Vail Resorts Inc.; Avon; ski lodge   2,000
Ball Aerospace and Technologies Corp.; Boulder; ship,
   boat, machine designing   1,500
Vail Holdings Inc.; Vail; ski instruction   1,500
Community Hospital Assn. Inc.; Boulder   1,316
Lucent Technologies Inc.; Denver; commercial research
   laboratory   1,200
Hyland Hills Park and Recreation; Denver   1,140
U.S. National Oceanic and Atmospheric Administration;
   Boulder   1,100
Hunter Douglas Inc.; Broomfield; mineral wool   1,000
Wells Fargo Bank Colorado; Denver; commercial bank
   1,000
Tyco Healthcare Group; Boulder; medical instruments:
   blood, bone work   893
Micro Motion Inc.; Boulder; liquid meters   800
Emerson Electric Co.; Boulder; industrial
   machinery/equipment   700
Intrado Inc.; Boulder; computer-aided system services
   691
Las Palmas Del Sol Regional Healthcare Systems; Denver
   650
U.S. National Bureau of Standards; Boulder   650
Electronic Data Systems Corp.; Louisville; subscription
   fulfillment services   617
Ball Corp.; Broomfield; food and beverage containers
   600
Buhrmann U.S. Inc.; Broomfield; stationery and office
   supplies   600
HCA-HealthONE Hospital; Thornton   600

Black Hawk Gaming and Development Co.; Black
  Hawk; casino hotel   600

Flextronics USA Inc.; Longmont; machine tool
  accessories   600

Amgen Inc.; Longmont; pharmaceuticals   560

Climax Molybdenum Co.; Empire; molybdenum ores
  mining   515

Colorado Leasing Systems Inc.; Broomfield; employee
  leasing service   500

Corporate Express Inc.; Broomfield; office equipment
  500

Level 3 Communications; Broomfield; telephone
  communication   500

McData Corp.; Broomfield; electronic circuits   500

Avista Hospital Inc.; Louisville   500

Corporate Express Inc.; Louisville; office forms and
  supplies   500

Global Crossing; Denver; telephone/video
  communications   500

Qwest Corp.; Thornton; local/long distance telephone
  500

Teris; Boulder; hazardous waste collection, disposal
  500

American Postal Workers Union; Boulder; labor
  organization   500

MRA Systems Inc.; Boulder; computer software   500

Lodge Casino at Black Hawk; Black Hawk; casino hotel
  500

Summit County School District; Frisco   500

Vail Clinic Inc.; Vail   500

Colorado 3rd District

Western Slope; Pueblo

The expansive 3rd, which captures Colorado's entire western border and all but one county on its southern edge, displays some of the abundant variety found outside the state's urban centers: the rural poor, the resort rich, the old steel mill town and the isolated Hispanic counties. Redistricting following the 2000 census kept the 3rd's character intact while moving the borders farther from Denver.

Residential growth and a substantial agricultural constituency have made water and land two of the 3rd's hottest issues. Most of the state's rivers flow down the Western Slope to Nevada and California. Farmers here would like to see more of that water stored for local use. Meanwhile, residential development has driven up property values.

A century of boom-and-bust mineral speculation—in gold, silver, uranium, and shale oil—has left the Western Slope dotted with small, struggling towns. The San Luis Valley and rural areas west of Interstate 25 have been hardest hit. Profits also have shrunk in the 3rd's other economic mainstays, namely cattle ranching in the west and steel production in Pueblo. But with plenty of national parks and ski resorts, tourism has quickly filled the void.

Residential Colorado has spilled over the Continental Divide onto the Western Slope. The newcomers, many of whom migrated to the area to build rustic retirement homes, tend to vote Republican. But Pueblo County, the district's most populous, is heavily unionized, more than one-third Hispanic,

and voted decisively for Al Gore in 2000. Some heavily Hispanic, sparsely populated counties border New Mexico.

There is a liberal strain in some southwestern Colorado communities. Green Party presidential nominee Ralph Nader's top four counties in Colorado were in the 3rd District, topped by San Miguel County (17.2 percent), which includes Telluride. Farther north, Pitkin County, which takes in the Aspen ski resort, gave Nader 13 percent of the vote.

Major Industry

Tourism, skiing, agriculture.

Notable

The U.S. Government Consumer Information Center is in Pueblo.

Election Returns

	Republican		Democratic		Other	
President 2000	140,191	53.5%	102,100	39.0%	19,585	7.5%
House 2002	143,433	65.8%	68,160	31.3%	6,379	2.9%

District Profile

Population   614,467

Total area (square miles)   54,099.8
  Land area (square miles)   53,963.4

Population per square mile   11.4

Counties (2000 population)

Alamosa 14,966	Mineral 831
Archuleta 9,898	Moffat 13,184
Conejos 8,400	Montezuma 23,830
Costilla 3,663	Montrose 33,432
Custer 3,503	Otero (pt.) 18,459
Delta 27,834	Ouray 3,742
Dolores 1,844	Pitkin 14,872
Garfield 43,791	Pueblo 141,472
Gunnison 13,956	Rio Blanco 5,986
Hinsdale 790	Rio Grande 12,413
Huerfano 7,862	Routt 19,690
Jackson 1,577	Saguache 5,917
La Plata 43,941	San Juan 558
Las Animas 15,207	San Miguel 6,594
Mesa 116,255	

Cities and other areas over 10,000 (2000 population)

Clifton CDP 17,345	Montrose 12,344
Durango 13,922	Pueblo 102,121
Grand Junction 41,986	Pueblo West CDP 16,899

Race and Hispanic or Latino origin*

White   74.6%

Black or African American   0.7%

American Indian or Alaska Native   1.4%

Asian   0.5%

Native Hawaiian or other Pacific Islander   0.1%

Some other race   0.1%

Hispanic or Latino origin   21.5%

Two or more races   1.2%

*As percentage of total population.

Ancestry*

Dutch	1.5%	Norwegian	1.5%
English	9.0%	Polish	1.2%
French	2.4%	Scotch-Irish	1.6%
German	13.6%	Scottish	1.8%
Irish	8.1%	Swedish	1.7%
Italian	3.8%	USA/American	5.3%

As estimated percentage of total population.

Universities and colleges, 2000–2001 enrollment

Adams State College, Alamosa   8,188
Colorado Mountain College, Glenwood Springs   7,407
Colorado Northwestern Community College, Rangely   1,834
Ft. Lewis College, Durango   4,285
Mesa State College, Grand Junction   5,212
Otero Junior College, La Junta   1,361
Pueblo Community College, Pueblo   4,654
San Juan Basin Area Vocational School, Cortez   1,198
Trinidad State Junior College, Trinidad   1,921
University of Southern Colorado, Pueblo   5,531
Western State College Colorado, Gunnison   2,325

Newspapers and circulation

	District circulation	Total circulation
Denver Post-Rocky Mountain News	5,176	674,801
Denver Rocky Mountain News	2,463	418,717
Durango Herald	8,389	8,495
Grand Junction Daily Sentinel	29,716	29,982
Pueblo Chieftain	44,357	51,146
*USA Today**	2,061	1,674,376

See Sources and Explanations in the front of the volume.

Television stations and affiliations

Denver	61%	KBDI	PBS
Denver	61%	KCEC	Univision
Denver	61%	KCNC	CBS
Denver	61%	KDUH	ABC
Denver	61%	KDVR	FOX
Denver	61%	KFCT	FOX
Denver	61%	KFNR	ABC
Denver	61%	KMGH	ABC
Denver	61%	KPXC	PAX
Denver	61%	KREG	CBS
Denver	61%	KRMA	CBS
Denver	61%	KRMT	Independent
Denver	61%	KTVD	UPN
Denver	61%	KUSA	NBC
Denver	61%	KWGN	WB
Denver	61%	KWHD	Independent
Colorado Springs-Pueblo	18%	KKTV	CBS
Colorado Springs-Pueblo	18%	KOAA	NBC
Colorado Springs-Pueblo	18%	KRDO	ABC
Colorado Springs-Pueblo	18%	KTSC	PBS
Colorado Springs-Pueblo	18%	KXRM	FOX
Grand Junction-Montrose	12%	KJCT	ABC
Grand Junction-Montrose	12%	KKCO	NBC
Grand Junction-Montrose	12%	KREX	CBS
Grand Junction-Montrose	12%	KREY	CBS
Grand Junction-Montrose	12%	KRMJ	PBS
Albuquerque-Santa Fe	7%	KASA	FOX
Albuquerque-Santa Fe	7%	KASY	UPN
Albuquerque-Santa Fe	7%	KAZQ	Independent
Albuquerque-Santa Fe	7%	KBIM	CBS
Albuquerque-Santa Fe	7%	KCHF	Independent
Albuquerque-Santa Fe	7%	KENW	PBS
Albuquerque-Santa Fe	7%	KHFT	UPN
Albuquerque-Santa Fe	7%	KLUZ	Univision
Albuquerque-Santa Fe	7%	KNAT	Independent
Albuquerque-Santa Fe	7%	KNME	PBS
Albuquerque-Santa Fe	7%	KOAT	ABC
Albuquerque-Santa Fe	7%	KOBF	NBC
Albuquerque-Santa Fe	7%	KOBR	NBC
Albuquerque-Santa Fe	7%	KOB	NBC
Albuquerque-Santa Fe	7%	KOCT	ABC
Albuquerque-Santa Fe	7%	KOVT	ABC
Albuquerque-Santa Fe	7%	KREZ	CBS
Albuquerque-Santa Fe	7%	KRPV	Independent
Albuquerque-Santa Fe	7%	KRQE	CBS
Salt Lake City	2%	KBYU	PBS
Salt Lake City	2%	KCSG	PAX
Salt Lake City	2%	KENV	NBC
Salt Lake City	2%	KGWR	CBS
Salt Lake City	2%	KJZZ	Independent
Salt Lake City	2%	KSL	NBC
Salt Lake City	2%	KSTU	FOX
Salt Lake City	2%	KTVX	ABC
Salt Lake City	2%	KUED	PBS
Salt Lake City	2%	KULC	PBS
Salt Lake City	2%	KUTV	CBS
Salt Lake City	2%	KUWB	WB

Cable systems and subscribers

Adelphia   8,930
Battlement Mesa Communications   1,230
Bresnan   89,155
Center Municipal Cable   628
Charter   2,020
Comcast   15,381
Galaxy   940
Hermosa Cablevision   838
ICE Cable Holdings   1,399
Rocky Mountain Cable   2,295

Military installations, September 2001

Pueblo Chemical Depot (Army), Pueblo   252

Businesses and other major employers

St. Mary's Hospital and Medical Center; Grand Junction   2,000
Jacobs House; Crested Butte; antiques   1,997
University of Southern Colorado; Pueblo   1,534
Parkview Medical Center Inc.; Pueblo   1,400
St. Mary-Corwin Hospital of Pueblo Colorado; Pueblo   1,168
Convergys Corp.; Pueblo; telemarketing services   1,000
State Board for Community Colleges; Pueblo   1,000
Crested Butte Mountain Resort Inc.; Crested Butte; resort hotel   1,000
Rocky Mountain Steel Mills; Pueblo; blast furnaces and steel mills   850
Target Corp.; Pueblo; general warehousing, storage   750
Mercy Medical Center; Durango   716
Russell Stover Candies Inc.; Montrose; candy   675

Columbia House Co.; Colorado City; mail order music/video record/tape club   550

Colorado Dept. of Human Services; Grand Junction   500

U.S. Postal Service; Grand Junction   500

Wal-Mart Stores Inc.; Grand Junction; discount department stores   500

Colorado 4th District

North and East — Fort Collins

The 4th, which covers Colorado's eastern plains and touches five other states, resembles Kansas more than Colorado. Intensive irrigation has turned these prairies where buffalo roamed into productive wheat and corn fields. Cattle production in the eastern counties ranks among the highest in the nation. But as demand for beef has fallen and wheat prices have declined, ranchers and farmers have faced hard times.

Fort Collins—the district's most populous city and home to Colorado State University—sits more than 50 miles from Boulder and Denver, but it has been able to cash in on the recent economic boom in the Front Range. Some high-tech industry has moved into the city, and the relatively low cost of living has attracted new residents.

The 4th has a long history of supporting GOP House members, and most of the district includes rural Republican territory. Several counties here gave George W. Bush more than two-thirds of their votes in the 2000 presidential election, with Cheyenne County awarding Bush a statewide high of 79 percent and Washington County giving him his second-highest total. Fort Collins is an exception to the district's strong GOP tilt and tends to support Democrats in local elections.

Redistricting following the 2000 census stripped the fast-growing 4th of several counties in the northwestern (Adams, Arapahoe, and Elbert) and southwestern (Las Animas, most of Otero) parts of the district. The Republican-leaning northeastern portion of Boulder County, including the city of Longmont, was added.

Major Industry
Agriculture, meatpacking, higher education.

Notable
The Greeley Independence Stampede is a rodeo and country music festival held annually during the week of July 4th; the Kit Carson County Carousel is in Burlington.

Election Returns

	Republican		Democratic		Other	
President 2000	145,056	57.1%	92,602	36.5%	16,271	6.4%
House 2002	115,359	54.9%	87,499	41.7%	7,097	3.4%

District Profile

Population   614,466

Total area (square miles)   31,047.9
   Land area (square miles)   30,897.8

Population per square mile   19.9

Counties (2000 population)

Baca 4,517	Logan 20,504
Bent 5,998	Morgan 27,171
Boulder (pt.) 75,162	Otero (pt.) 1,852
Cheyenne 2,231	Phillips 4,480
Crowley 5,518	Prowers 14,483
Kiowa 1,622	Sedgwick 2,747
Kit Carson 8,011	Washington 4,926
Larimer 251,494	Weld (pt.) 167,822
Lincoln 6,087	Yuma 9,841

Cities and other areas over 10,000 (2000 population)

Fort Collins 118,652	Longmont 71,093
Fort Morgan 11,034	Loveland 50,608
Greeley 76,930	Sterling 11,360

Race and Hispanic or Latino origin*
White   79.4%
Black or African American   0.7%
American Indian or Alaska Native   0.5%
Asian   1.1%
Native Hawaiian or other Pacific Islander   0.1%
Some other race   0.1%
Hispanic or Latino origin   17.0%
Two or more races   1.2%

As percentage of total population.

Ancestry*

Dutch 1.6%	Norwegian 2.1%
English 8.7%	Polish 1.4%
French 2.3%	Scotch-Irish 1.5%
German 20.3%	Scottish 1.8%
Irish 8.4%	Swedish 2.5%
Italian 2.5%	USA/American 3.9%

As estimated percentage of total population.

Universities and colleges, 2000–2001 enrollment
Aims Community College, Greeley   6,948
Colorado State University, Fort Collins   26,807
Lamar Community College, Lamar   991
Morgan Community College, Fort Morgan   1,757
Northeastern Junior College, Sterling   3,670
University of Northern Colorado, Greeley   12,234

Newspapers and circulation

	District circulation	Total circulation
Boulder Daily Camera	2,478	34,162
Denver Post-Rocky Mountain News	28,380	674,801
Denver Rocky Mountain News	35,254	418,717
Fort Collins Coloradoan	28,637	28,744
Fort Morgan Times	4,246	4,246
Greeley Daily Tribune	23,847	23,992
Lamar Daily News	2,405	2,405
Longmont Daily Times-Call	16,397	21,777
Loveland Daily Reporter-Herald	17,666	17,666
Pueblo Chieftain	3,074	51,146
Sterling Journal-Advocate	5,026	5,026
*USA Today**	1,410	1,674,376

See Sources and Explanations in the front of the volume.

Television stations and affiliations

Denver	78%	KBDI	PBS
Denver	78%	KCEC	Univision
Denver	78%	KCNC	CBS
Denver	78%	KDUH	ABC
Denver	78%	KDVR	FOX
Denver	78%	KFCT	FOX
Denver	78%	KFNR	ABC
Denver	78%	KMGH	ABC
Denver	78%	KPXC	PAX
Denver	78%	KREG	CBS
Denver	78%	KRMA	CBS
Denver	78%	KRMT	Independent
Denver	78%	KTVD	UPN
Denver	78%	KUSA	NBC
Denver	78%	KWGN	WB
Denver	78%	KWHD	Independent
Colorado Springs-Pueblo	22%	KKTV	CBS
Colorado Springs-Pueblo	22%	KOAA	NBC
Colorado Springs-Pueblo	22%	KRDO	ABC
Colorado Springs-Pueblo	22%	KTSC	PBS
Colorado Springs-Pueblo	22%	KXRM	FOX

Cable systems and subscribers

Bresnan   13,417
Cable USA   727
Charter   5,754
Classic   706
Comcast   85,935
Communicomm   1,680
Galaxy   28,164
U.S. Cable   2,417

Businesses and other major employers

General Motors Corp.; Fort Collins   15,000
Colorado State University; Fort Collins   13,658
Poudre School District; Fort Collins   6,585
Hewlett-Packard Co.; Fort Collins; computers   5,000
University of Northern Colorado; Greeley   3,100
North Colorado Medical Center; Greeley   2,000
Excel Corp.; Fort Morgan; meatpacking plants   2,000
Poudre Valley Hospital; Fort Collins   1,850
Agilent Technologies Inc.; Fort Collins; electricity measuring instruments   1,200
Veritas Software Technology Corp.; Longmont; computer disk drives   1,100
Aims Junior College District Inc.; Greeley   1,100
Longmont United Hospital; Longmont   1,085
Forsythe and Dowis Rides Inc.; Merino; carnival machines, equipment   1,000
Maxtor Corp.; Longmont; computer storage   850
Center Partners Inc.; Fort Collins; computer consulting services   850
Advanced Energy Industries Inc.; Fort Collins; power supplies   825
City of Longmont; Longmont; city management   800
Banner Health System Hospital; Loveland   800
Hewlett-Packard Co.; Greeley; computer integrated systems design   800
State Farm Life Insurance Co.; Greeley   750
Anheuser-Busch Inc.; Fort Collins; malt beverages   700
McLane/Western Inc.; Longmont; discount department stores   650

Priority Staffing Health; Longmont; help supply services   621
Celestica Colorado Inc.; Fort Collins; integrated circuits, semiconductor networks   600
Neoplan USA Corp.; Lamar; bus assembly   585
Hach Co.; Loveland; analytical instruments   560
Hewlett-Packard Co.; Loveland; computer tape storage   552
Woodward Governor Co.; Fort Collins; aircraft propeller feathering   550
City of Loveland; Loveland; city management   536
U.S. Federal Aviation Administration; Longmont   500
Wal-Mart Stores Inc.; Fort Collins; retail bakeries   500
Lafarge North America Inc.; Fort Collins; brick, stone, and related material   500
Sykes Enterprises Inc.; Greeley; computer maintenance services   500
ConAgra Beef Co.; Greeley; meatpacking plants   500

Colorado 5th District

South central — Colorado Springs

God and country dominate the 5th, an overwhelmingly conservative district where registered Republicans outnumber Democrats by two-to-one. Military installations employ tens of thousands of people in the Colorado Springs area. The popular resort town is a prime destination for retired military personnel, who come to enjoy the scenery and find like-minded neighbors. James Dobson's Focus on the Family and other evangelical organizations are based in the 5th.

Defense cutbacks threatened the district in the early 1990s when there was an unsuccessful effort to put Fort Carson on the list of base closures. Since then, the district has made itself an indispensable arm of the modern military. Colorado Springs houses the U.S. Space Command, the North American Aerospace Defense Command, and a good portion of the country's satellite defense research.

The city also has broadened its economic base: direct and indirect military expenditures account for about 40 percent of the economy, down from 60 percent a decade ago. But much of the new industry, including superconductor and computer development, depends on the defense industry. Like much of Colorado's Front Range, the city attracts lots of tourists, many of whom come to ascend the 14,110-foot Pikes Peak.

More than 80 percent of district residents live in El Paso County (Colorado Springs), which has topped 500,000 residents. Redistricting in 2002 removed the district's portions of Douglas and Arapahoe Counties near Denver and added three counties farther west.

Major Industry

Military, tourism, semiconductors.

Notable

The U.S. Olympic headquarters is in Colorado Springs.

Election Returns

	Republican		Democratic		Other	
President 2000	151,751	63.3%	74,940	31.3%	13,116	5.5%
House 2002	128,118	69.4%	45,587	24.7%	10,972	5.9%

District Profile

Population   614,467

Total area (square miles)   7,732.4
   Land area (square miles)   7,707.9

Population per square mile   79.7

Counties (2000 population)

Chaffee	16,242	Lake	7,812
El Paso	516,929	Park (pt.)	6,784
Fremont	46,145	Teller	20,555

Cities and other areas over 10,000 (2000 population)

Black Forest CDP   13,247
Canon City   15,431
Cimarron Hills CDP   15,194
Colorado Springs   360,890
Fort Carson CDP   10,566
Fountain   15,197
Security-Widefield CDP   29,845

Race and Hispanic or Latino origin*

White   77.4%
Black or African American   5.7%
American Indian or Alaska Native   0.7%
Asian   2.2%
Native Hawaiian or other Pacific Islander   0.2%
Some other race   0.2%
Hispanic or Latino origin   11.1%
Two or more races   2.5%

*As percentage of total population.

Ancestry*

Dutch	1.5%	Norwegian	1.9%
English	8.9%	Polish	1.8%
French	2.4%	Scotch-Irish	1.6%
German	16.1%	Scottish	2.0%
Irish	9.1%	Swedish	1.6%
Italian	3.4%	USA/American	4.3%

*As estimated percentage of total population.

Universities and colleges, 2000–2001 enrollment

Blair College, Colorado Springs   578
Colorado College, Colorado Springs   1,942
Colorado Technical University, Colorado Springs   1,851
Denver Technical College at Colorado Springs, Colorado Springs   470
Nazarene Bible College, Colorado Springs   473
Pikes Peak Community College, Colorado Springs   9,997
PPI Health Careers School, Colorado Springs   277
Technical Trades Institute, Colorado Springs   252
U.S. Air Force Academy, Colorado Springs   4,330
University of Colorado, Colorado Springs   6,666

Newspapers and circulation

	District circulation	Total circulation
Canon City Daily Record	8,235	8,547
Colorado Springs Gazette	98,459	99,927
Denver Post-Rocky Mountain News	7,345	674,801
Denver Rocky Mountain News	16,908	418,717
Pueblo Chieftain	3,350	51,146
USA Today *	3,203	1,674,376

*See Sources and Explanations in the front of the volume.

Television stations and affiliations

Colorado Springs-Pueblo	55%	KKTV	CBS
Colorado Springs-Pueblo	55%	KOAA	NBC
Colorado Springs-Pueblo	55%	KRDO	ABC
Colorado Springs-Pueblo	55%	KTSC	PBS
Colorado Springs-Pueblo	55%	KXRM	FOX
Denver	45%	KBDI	PBS
Denver	45%	KCEC	Univision
Denver	45%	KCNC	CBS
Denver	45%	KDUH	ABC
Denver	45%	KDVR	FOX
Denver	45%	KFCT	FOX
Denver	45%	KFNR	ABC
Denver	45%	KMGH	ABC
Denver	45%	KPXC	PAX
Denver	45%	KREG	CBS
Denver	45%	KRMA	CBS
Denver	45%	KRMT	Independent
Denver	45%	KTVD	UPN
Denver	45%	KUSA	NBC
Denver	45%	KWGN	WB
Denver	45%	KWHD	Independent

Cable systems and subscribers

Adelphia   99,523
Bresnan   15,883
Charter   20,265
U.S. Cable   2,745

Military installations, September 2001

Fort Carson (Army), Colorado Springs   20,356
Peterson Air Force Base, Colorado Springs   6,559
United States Air Force Academy, Colorado Springs   3,780
Schriever Air Force Base, Ellicott   2,665
Cheyenne Mountain Air Force Base, Colorado Springs   640

Businesses and other major employers

Saturn Corp.; Colorado Springs; automobiles   10,500
Memorial Hospital Corp.; Colorado Springs   2,408
Atmel Corp.; Colorado Springs; semiconductors and related devices   2,000
Hewlett-Packard Co.; Colorado Springs; billing, bookkeeping service   2,000
WCS Inc.; Colorado Springs; fast-food restaurant chain   2,000
United Services Automobile Assn.; Colorado Springs; automobile insurance   2,000
Agilent Technologies Inc.; Colorado Springs; electricity measuring instruments   1,400
Direct Checks Unlimited Inc.; Colorado Springs; checkbooks   1,400
Colorado Springs Shrine Club; Colorado Springs; civic associations   1,300
Futurecall Telemarketing West Inc.; Colorado Springs; telemarketing services   1,300
Focus on Family; Colorado Springs; family service agency   1,300
Les Thompson; Colorado Springs; labor and union relations consultant   1,200

Academy School District; Colorado Springs   1,196

Western Forge Corp.; Colorado Springs; hand and edge tools   1,000

MCI Worldcom Network Services Inc.; Colorado Springs; telemarketing services   1,000

Current USA Inc.; Colorado Springs; mail order cards   1,000

Colorado Dept. of Corrections; Canon City   1,000

Fleet National Bank; Colorado Springs; credit card service   900

Colorado Dept. of Corrections; Buena Vista   900

Ingersoll-Rand Co.; Colorado Springs; locks or lock sets   850

SCI Systems Inc.; Fountain; electronic computers   800

Lockheed Martin Services Inc.; Colorado Springs; engineering services   800

Compassion International Inc.; Colorado Springs; advocacy   764

Quantum Corp.; Colorado Springs; computer disk drives   739

Lanoga Corp.; Fountain; lumber and building materials   700

Oracle Corp.; Peyton; prepackaged software   700

American Postal Workers Union; Colorado Springs; labor organization   670

Oracle Corp.; Colorado Springs; computer integrated systems design   668

Pikes Peak Community College Inc.; Colorado Springs   650

Centura Health Corp. Hospital; Colorado Springs   625

NCR Corp.; Colorado Springs; semiconductors and related devices   625

Colorado Springs School District; Colorado Springs   600

Goodwill Industries of Colorado Springs Inc.; Colorado Springs; used merchandise stores   600

Honeywell Technology Solutions Inc.; Colorado Springs; management services   600

MCI Worldcom Network Services Inc.; Colorado Springs; long distance telephone   600

Wal-Mart Stores Inc.; Colorado Springs; discount department stores   600

Qwest Corp.; Colorado Springs; local telephone communications   586

J. P. McGill's; Cripple Creek; casino hotel   500

Colorado Interstate Production Co.; Colorado Springs; natural gas transmission   500

U.S. Postal Service; Colorado Springs   500

Electronic Data Systems Corp.; Colorado Springs; data processing   500

Schlage Lock Co.; Colorado Springs; locks or lock sets   500

Colorado 6th District

Denver suburbs — part of Aurora; Douglas County

Managing growth is a top priority for the affluent, white-collar suburbs that lie south of Denver and make up the 6th. Highway congestion has become a serious problem as commuters living in suburban bedroom communities head into Denver every morning.

Steep housing prices on the West Coast have resulted in an influx of Californians, especially to Douglas County, which increased its population by 191 percent in the 1990s, the fastest clip in the country.

The 6th was redrawn following the 2000 census to include Douglas, which accounts for 30 percent of the district's population and solidifies it as a Republican stronghold. Douglas supported George W. Bush by a two-to-one ratio in 2000. The county is quickly filling up with young, well-educated professionals with families, and it has the state's highest median income. Technology sector growth in the suburbs has made the 6th one of the most highly educated districts.

Contrasts are evident in Arapahoe County, where a plurality of district residents reside even though the county is overwhelmingly rural. The urban, western portion of Arapahoe, which includes the county seat of Littleton just south of Denver, has many residential and retail areas. Nearly one-third of Aurora, Colorado's third most-populous city, is in the district. Columbine High School, site of a 1999 shooting that left 15 dead, is in Littleton, which makes gun control an emotional issue in the 6th.

The district's total Hispanic population (slightly less than 6 percent) is the lowest percentage in the state. Minorities total 12 percent of residents, making the 6th the only district in Colorado where minorities represent less than 20 percent of the population.

Major Industry

Manufacturing.

Notable

The "Buffalo Bill" Cody grave and museum is near Golden; the Comanche Crossing Railroad Site near Strasburg marks the place where the last spike was driven in 1870 to create the first continuous transcontinental railroad.

Election Returns

	Republican		Democratic		Other	
President 2000	169,205	60.2%	104,126	37.1%	7,580	2.7%
House 2002	158,851	66.9%	71,327	30.0%	7,323	3.1%

District Profile

Population   614,466

Total area (square miles)   4,111.2
   Land area (square miles)   4,103.9

Population per square mile   149.7

Counties (2000 population)

Arapahoe (pt.) 265,663	Jefferson (pt.) 145,426
Douglas 175,766	Park (pt.) 7,739
Elbert 19,872	

Cities and other areas over 10,000 (2000 population)
Aurora (pt.)   78,878
Castle Rock town   20,224
Castlewood CDP   25,567
Columbine CDP   24,095
Greenwood Village   11,035
Highlands Ranch CDP   70,931
Ken Caryl CDP   30,887
Littleton (pt.)   40,340

Parker town   23,558
Southglenn CDP   43,520

Race and Hispanic or Latino origin*
White   87.7%
Black or African American   1.9%
American Indian or Alaska Native   0.4%
Asian   2.6%
Native Hawaiian or other Pacific Islander   0.1%
Some other race   0.1%
Hispanic or Latino origin   5.8%
Two or more races   1.5%

*As percentage of total population.

Ancestry*
Dutch	1.7%	Polish	2.4%
English	10.5%	Russian	1.1%
French	2.9%	Scotch-Irish	1.6%
German	18.9%	Scottish	2.4%
Irish	10.9%	Swedish	2.6%
Italian	4.0%	USA/American	3.6%
Norwegian	2.4%		

*As estimated percentage of total population.

Universities and colleges, 2000–2001 enrollment
Arapahoe Community College, Littleton   7,436
Colorado Technical University, Greenwood Village   383
University of Phoenix-Colorado, Englewood   3,098

Newspapers and circulation
	District circulation	Total circulation
Denver Post-Rocky Mountain News	76,377	674,801
Denver Rocky Mountain News	85,561	418,717
*USA Today**	3,712	1,674,376

*See Sources and Explanations in the front of the volume.

Television stations and affiliations
Denver	100%	KBDI	PBS
Denver	100%	KCEC	Univision
Denver	100%	KCNC	CBS
Denver	100%	KDUH	ABC
Denver	100%	KDVR	FOX
Denver	100%	KFCT	FOX
Denver	100%	KFNR	ABC
Denver	100%	KMGH	ABC
Denver	100%	KPXC	PAX
Denver	100%	KREG	CBS
Denver	100%	KRMA	CBS
Denver	100%	KRMT	Independent
Denver	100%	KTVD	UPN
Denver	100%	KUSA	NBC
Denver	100%	KWGN	WB
Denver	100%	KWHD	Independent

Cable systems and subscribers
Charter   913
Comcast   25,602

Businesses and other major employers
Comcast; Englewood; cable television   9,200
Lockheed Martin Corp.; Littleton; aircraft   8,000
Lockheed Martin Corp.; Larkspur; aircraft   7,000
One Corp.; Englewood; health maintenance organization   4,531
Twentieth Century Manufacturing; Denver; malt beverages   4,000
Centura Health Corp.; Englewood; medical centers   3,096
Acterna Corp.; Englewood; computer software development   3,000
General Electric Co.; Englewood; computer maintenance and repair   2,500
Great-West Life and Annuity Insurance Co.; Englewood; accident and health insurance carriers   1,900
Information Handling Services Group Inc.; Englewood; micropublishing   1,500
EchoStar Communications Corp.; Littleton; satellite broadcast services   1,500
Citigroup Inc.; Englewood; credit card services, collection   1,200
Comcast; Englewood; data telephone communications   1,100
Theramerica Inc.; Englewood; temporary help service   1,000
ICG Communications Inc.; Englewood; telephone communication   1,000
Jeppesen Sanderson Inc.; Englewood; publishing   1,000
Qwest Corp.; Englewood; telephone equipment and systems   1,000
Rhythms NetConnections Inc.; Englewood; data communication services   1,000
Denver Autoliv Operations; Aurora; motor vehicle parts/accessories   900
AT&T Corp.; Englewood; local telephone communications   900
Lucent Technologies Inc.; Englewood; communication equipment   861
Qwest Yellow Pages; Aurora; advertising   800
Pacificare of Colorado; Englewood; health maintenance organization   800
Remco Inc.; Englewood; engineering services   800
Integrated Payment Systems Inc.; Englewood; money order issuance   750
AT&T Corp.; Littleton; radio broadcasting stations   720
Raytheon Co.; Englewood; single-family housing construction   700
United Artists Investments Inc.; Englewood; cable television   700
Nextel Communications Inc.; Littleton; radiotelephone communication   700
Home Lumber Co.; Littleton; lumber, plywood, and millwork   700
Comcast; Denver; cable television   700
U.S. Dept. of Energy; Golden   700
Teletech Holdings Inc.; Englewood; telemarketing services   650
Your Way Enterprises Inc.; Englewood; eating places   605
Time Warner Telecom Inc.; Englewood; telephone communication   600
Washington Group International Inc.; Englewood; engineering services   600

DENVER AREA

Districts established January 25, 2002, for elections first held in 2002.

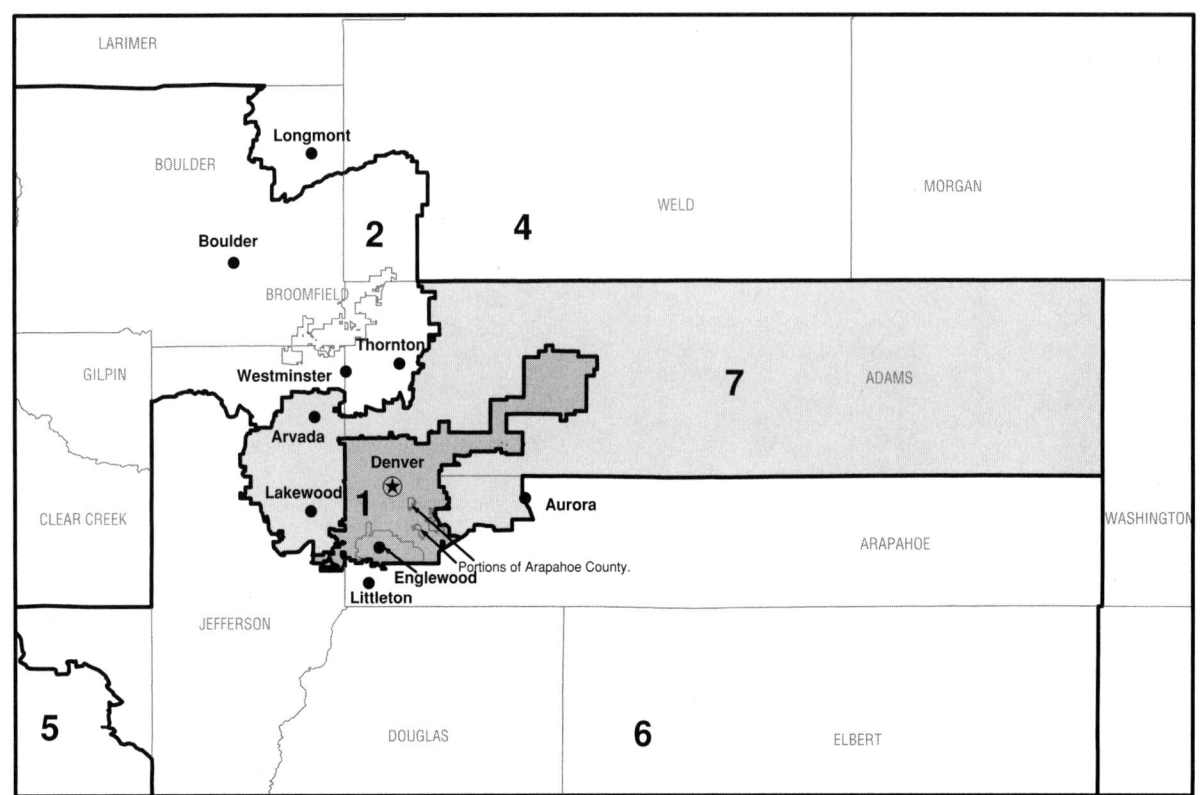

Districts established May 9, 2003, for elections first held in 2004.

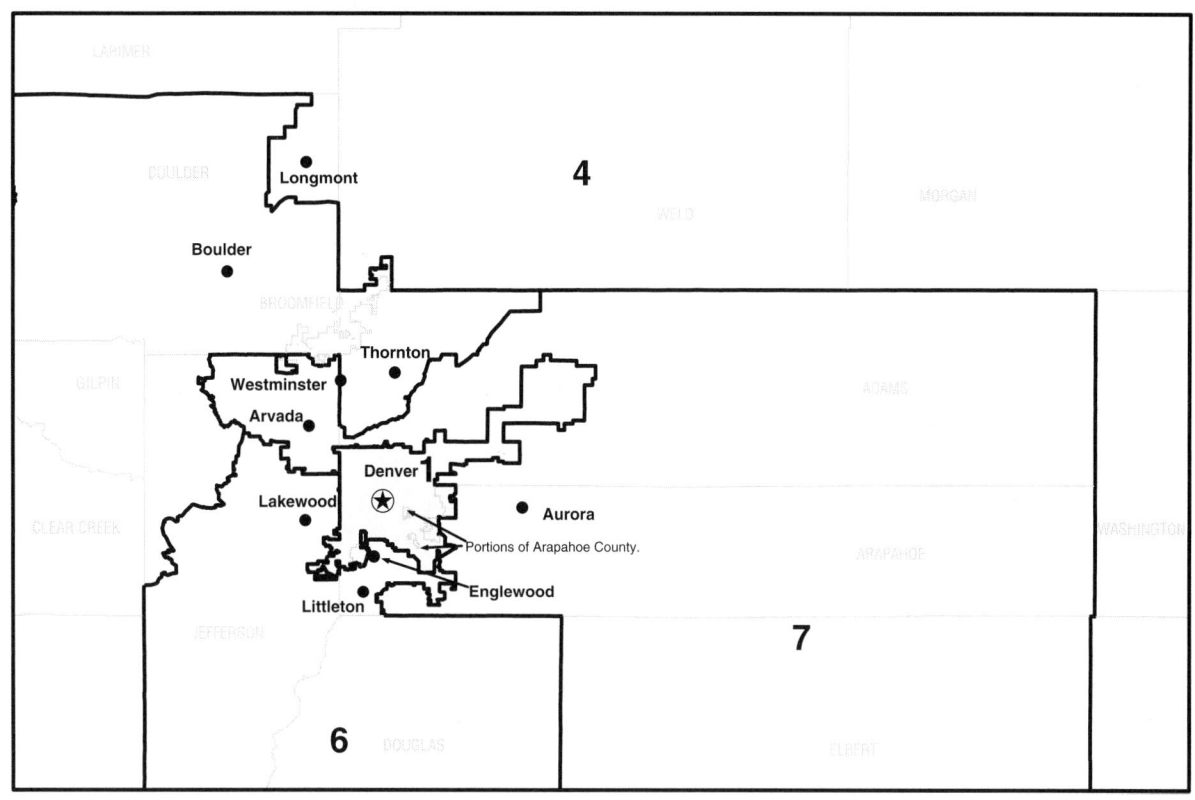

U.S. Food Service; Englewood; commercial cooking, food service equipment   575

Metropolitan Life Insurance Co.; Englewood; hospital/medical service plans   570

Oracle Corp.; Englewood; prepackaged software   550

IMI Norgren Inc.; Littleton; control valves, fluid power   536

Ch2m Hill Companies; Englewood; engineering services   525

MCI Worldcom Network Services Inc.; Englewood; local/long distance telephone   500

Agilent Technologies Inc.; Englewood; electronic/electric measuring test equipment   500

Behavioral Healthcare Inc.; Englewood; counseling services   500

Houston Tracker Systems Inc.; Englewood; cable television   500

Ikon Office Solutions Inc.; Englewood; photocopy machines   500

McGraw-Hill Companies Inc.; Englewood; investment advice   500

OrionAuto Inc.; Englewood; fire, marine, casualty insurance   500

Arapahoe County; Littleton; sheriff's office   500

Syntec Consulting Inc.; Littleton; temporary help service   500

Dillard's Inc.; Littleton; department stores   500

Store 34; Littleton; variety stores   500

Medtronic Inc.; Parker; electromedical equipment   500

Ch2m Hill Corp.; Denver; consulting engineer   500

Colorado 7th District

Denver suburbs — Lakewood, parts of Aurora and Arvada

Awarded to fast-growing Colorado following the 2000 census, the new 7th—as it was configured for the 2002 election—was a middle-class suburban area that surrounded Denver (and the 1st District) from the west, north, and east before extending east to take in the remainder of Adams County.

The bulk of the district's population was in Jefferson County, where more than half of residents lived and which formed its western edge. The 7th included Lakewood, a middle-class area that abuts Denver to the west; Golden, which included the Coors Brewing Co.; and nearly all of Arvada.

Minorities represent a third of the residents, giving the 7th the second-highest total in the state. Commerce City, a Hispanic-majority, lower-middle-class area just north of Denver, and most of the city of Aurora (shared with the 6th) were in the 7th. Aurora had the largest African American percentage (13 percent) in Colorado.

Buckley Air Force Base is a link in the Air Force Space Command satellite tracking system and has attracted aerospace firms to the area. The Rocky Mountain Arsenal, which once produced chemical weapons, is expected to be rid of pollutants by 2011.

The 7th became Colorado's most competitive district. Al Gore narrowly carried the area in 2000, and the two major parties were equal in voter registration. The slight Democratic lean of Adams and Arapahoe Counties was largely offset by the GOP lean in Jefferson.

However, the 2002 district lines for Colorado, including the 7th, were drawn by a Colorado judge. In early 2003, in what appeared to be an unprecedented action, the Republican-controlled legislature redrew the district lines around Denver to put more GOP-leaning voters in the 7th, presumably increasing the chances of the incumbent—a Republican who won in 2002 by 121 votes—winning reelection in 2004. Democrats protested and took the issue to court, where it remained in fall 2003. Redistricting experts said they did not know of any previous time when a state redistricted a second time after the initial redrawing of lines after a census, except in cases of court-ordered changes. *(See maps pp. 182–183.)*

(Note: the tables for all Colorado districts in this volume are based on the district lines that were used in the 2002 election.)

Major Industry

Communications, aerospace, manufacturing.

Notable

Dinosaur Ridge is near Morrison.

Election Returns

	Republican		Democratic		Other	
President 2000	101,632	48.9%	103,592	49.8%	2,783	1.3%
House 2002	81,789	47.3%	81,668	47.3%	9,422	5.4%

District Profile

Population   614,465

Total area (square miles)   1,264.7
Land area (square miles)   1,258.2

Population per square mile   488.4

Counties (2000 population)
Adams (pt.)   124,242
Arapahoe (pt.)   162,479
Jefferson (pt.)   327,744

Cities and other areas over 10,000 (2000 population)

Arvada (pt.) 98,941	Commerce City 20,991
Aurora (pt.) 197,515	Golden 17,159
Berkley CDP 10,743	Lakewood 144,126
Brighton (pt.) 20,751	Wheat Ridge 32,913

Race and Hispanic or Latino origin*
White   68.9%
Black or African American   5.8%
American Indian or Alaska Native   0.6%
Asian   2.9%
Native Hawaiian or other Pacific Islander   0.1%
Some other race   0.1%
Hispanic or Latino origin   19.6%
Two or more races   1.9%

As percentage of total population.

Ancestry*

Dutch	1.3%	Norwegian	1.8%
English	8.4%	Polish	1.6%
French	2.4%	Scotch-Irish	1.5%
German	16.0%	Scottish	1.7%
Irish	8.9%	Swedish	2.1%
Italian	3.7%	USA/American	3.5%

As estimated percentage of total population.

Universities and colleges, 2000–2001 enrollment

Bel-Rea Institute of Animal Technology, Denver 608
Cambridge College, Aurora 426
Colorado Christian University, Lakewood 1,967
Colorado School of Mines, Golden 3,738
Community College of Aurora, Aurora 4,642
Denver Academy of Court Reporting, Denver 213
Heritage College of Health Careers, Denver 271
Parks College-Aurora, Aurora 1,114
Pima Medical Institute, Denver 288
Red Rocks Community College, Lakewood 7,520

Newspapers and circulation

	District circulation	Total circulation
Denver Post-Rocky Mountain News	82,907	674,801
Denver Rocky Mountain News	99,979	418,717
*USA Today**	1,409	1,674,376

See Sources and Explanations in the front of the volume.

Television stations and affiliations

Denver	100%	KBDI	PBS
Denver	100%	KCEC	Univision
Denver	100%	KCNC	CBS
Denver	100%	KDUH	ABC
Denver	100%	KDVR	FOX
Denver	100%	KFCT	FOX
Denver	100%	KFNR	ABC
Denver	100%	KMGH	ABC
Denver	100%	KPXC	PAX
Denver	100%	KREG	CBS
Denver	100%	KRMA	CBS
Denver	100%	KRMT	Independent
Denver	100%	KTVD	UPN
Denver	100%	KUSA	NBC
Denver	100%	KWGN	WB
Denver	100%	KWHD	Independent

Cable systems and subscribers

Comcast 143,751

Military installations, September 2001

Buckley Air National Guard Base (Air Force), Aurora 2,527
Buckley Air National Guard Base (Army), Aurora 984
Fitzsimons Army Medical Center, Aurora 794
Rocky Mountain Arsenal, Commerce City 567
Marine Corps Reserve Center, Denver 358

Businesses and other major employers

Coors Brewing Co.; Golden; malt beverages 4,000
Coorstex; Golden; glass or glass ceramic tableware 2,600
Exempla Lutheran Medical Center; Wheat Ridge; 2,045
Gambro Inc.; Denver; surgical instruments and apparatus 2,000
Jefferson County; Golden; county government 2,000
Raytheon Co.; Aurora; semiconductors and related devices 1,600
Alpine Access Inc.; Lakewood; business consulting 1,600
HealthONE Hospital; Aurora 1,500
U.S. Bureau of Reclamation; Denver 1,500
West La Farge Inc.; Denver; aggregate 1,336
First Tennessee Bank National Assn.; Littleton; personal credit institutions 1,000
Colorado Dept. of Revenue; Denver 1,000
U.S. Geological Survey; Denver 1,000
AON Innovative Solutions Inc.; Golden; management services 1,000
Sun Microsystems Inc.; Arvada; computer programming services 900
Level 3 Communications; Golden; telephone communication 870
Adams County; Brighton; county government 852
Gambro BCT Inc.; Lakewood; surgical instruments and apparatus 835
Cobe Cardiovascular Inc.; Arvada; electrotherapeutic apparatus 825
U.S. National Park Service; Denver 800
Sturgeon Electric Co.; Henderson; electrical contractor 775
Nelnet; Aurora; personal credit institutions 750
Colorado School of Mines; Golden 722
Aurora Regional Transportation District; Aurora 700
Youthtrack Inc.; Denver; residential care 700
Burns International Security Services Corp.; Denver; security guard service 700
State Board for Community Colleges and Occupational Educational System; Lakewood 675
Colorado State Patrol; Lakewood 670
Wagner Equipment Co.; Aurora; construction and mining machinery 650
Colorado Dept. of Natural Resources; Denver 650
TRW Inc.; Aurora; computer software writers 600
City of Lakewood; Denver; city management 600
Jefferson County; Golden; sheriff's office 600
Lockheed Martin Corp.; Aurora; aircraft 575
Dole Food Co.; Aurora; food supplier 555
City of Aurora; Aurora; municipal police 540
Yellow Freight System Inc.; Aurora; automobile transport 510
Navajo Express Inc.; Commerce City; refrigerated products transport 510

Developmental Disabilities Resource Center Inc.; Arvada; sheltered workshop   500

Manheim Auctions Inc.; Aurora; automotive brokers   500

City of Aurora; Aurora; city government   500

McGraw-Hill Companies Inc.; Aurora; technical manual and paper publishing   500

Aurora Loan Services Inc.; Aurora; mortgage bankers   500

Mile High Kennel Club Inc.; Commerce City; dog race track operation   500

Cobe Renal Care Inc.; Lakewood; kidney dialysis centers   500

Sunshine Janitorial Specialists Inc.; Lakewood; janitorial service   500

Gambro Healthcare Inc.; Lakewood; hemodialysis apparatus   500

Clayton Group Services Inc.; Golden; environmental consultant   500

Kmart Corp.; Brighton; general warehousing, storage   500

Fedex Ground Inc.; Henderson; contract haulers   500

Connecticut

Connecticut entered the new century as the nation's wealthiest state, a statistical truth that carries some cachet but also a measure of irony. The characterization of wealth is based mostly on one number: the state's per capita personal income of $41,930 (first in the nation in 2001). Bolstering the impression of affluence was the below-average unemployment rate and the percentage of state residents living in poverty in 2000 (6.3 percent), which was lower than all but two states. Without question, Connecticut features some of the most comfortable communities in the nation, especially in Fairfield County with its bedroom suburbs for commuters or retirees, many of whom spend their days in nearby New York.

But further into Connecticut proper, the main cities of Hartford, Bridgeport, New Haven, and Waterbury have been under economic pressure for decades. Companies have failed, jobs have fled, and expectations are often bleak. In New Haven, for example, the per capita income in 2000 was less than half what it was statewide.

That is why in the 'wealthiest state' economic uncertainties have held down population growth and taken a bite out of the congressional delegation. Connecticut in 2001 had 3.4 million people, a two-thirds increase from 1950. But national population growth was more than 80 percent over the same period, so it was only a matter of time before Connecticut lost the sixth congressional district it had been awarded after the 1930 census. The blow finally fell in 2000 after a decade in which the state population rose just 3.6 percent.

An original colony rich in history dating back to the 1600s, Connecticut developed first as an agricultural economy. Then, in the early 1800s, it helped to lead the industrial revolution, thanks in part to a farmer's son and Yale man named Eli Whitney. A key contributor to the cotton gin and the use of interchangeable parts on assembly lines, Whitney operated from a shop in New Haven and defined the prototype later celebrated in Mark Twain's *A Connecticut Yankee in King Arthur's Court.* Later in the 1800s beneficiaries of his heritage included Samuel Colt, the legendary gun manufacturer. Both Whitney and Colt were progenitors of a defense industry that would later make nuclear submarines at Electric Boat in Groton and manufacture engines and missiles at United Technologies.

The industrial revolution was good to Connecticut. It raised the state capital of Hartford to major status among American cities, as a factory town and as a forerunner of the modern insurance industry. At the turn of the last century Hartford boasted some of the nation's most impressive homes and renowned citizens, including Twain himself. Bridgeport, the coastal city, competed with the major ports of the eastern seaboard and New Haven grew up and thrived around Yale.

This golden age spawned great fortunes, some of which survive as 'old money' in super-exclusive communities such as Old Greenwich. In the 1900s, however, Hartford and much of the state were increasingly in New York's shadow. A third of the state is now included in New York's combined market statistical area and Connecticut's Bridgeport and New Haven are listed as its suburbs.

Part of this slippage was attributable to industrial competition from the Great Lakes region and beyond. But as the century ground on and the mega-metropolis across the state line kept gaining in population and economic power, Hartford was neither dynamic nor nimble enough to keep pace. The city took a fresh round of hits when the insurance industry faltered in the early 1990s. Meanwhile Bridgeport did not modernize when larger ports did, and many parts of New Haven not associated with Yale slowly aged into slums.

Some of these weaknesses were counterbalanced by strong defense spending in the Cold War era but this dependency brought hardship when the cold war ended and Pentagon spending for weapons systems dropped by half. Electric Boat all but closed down, Colt filed for bankruptcy protection in 1992, something like 150,000 manufacturing jobs disappeared statewide, and the political climate of confidence changed into one of fear.

Politically Connecticut had been a Yankee Republican bastion for generations, even voting for Herbert Hoover in 1932 before switching to Franklin D. Roosevelt in 1936. After the war Connecticut voted for the GOP's Thomas E. Dewey in 1948 and twice for Dwight Eisenhower in the 1950s. Since then the state has swung between the parties in intervals measured in decades.

The Democrats in 1960 nominated John F. Kennedy for president largely on the backroom support of John Bailey, the power broker who ran Connecticut's Democratic politics for 30 years and oversaw the power shift from Protestant Republican to Catholic Democrat in the statehouse. Kennedy got 54 percent in Connecticut, which would also vote for Democrats in 1964 and 1968.

In the 1970s and 1980s the state voted for Republicans Richard Nixon, Gerald Ford, Ronald Reagan, and George Bush in five straight elections, largely because blue-collar voters were not enamored of the Democratic alternatives. But beginning in 1992 the state did a pirouette and preferred Bill Clinton and Al Gore in the next three cycles, giving their Republican opponents a paltry 36 percent of the vote on average. This despite the fact that these opponents

CONNECTICUT

Districts established December 21, 2001, for elections first held in 2002.

5 members

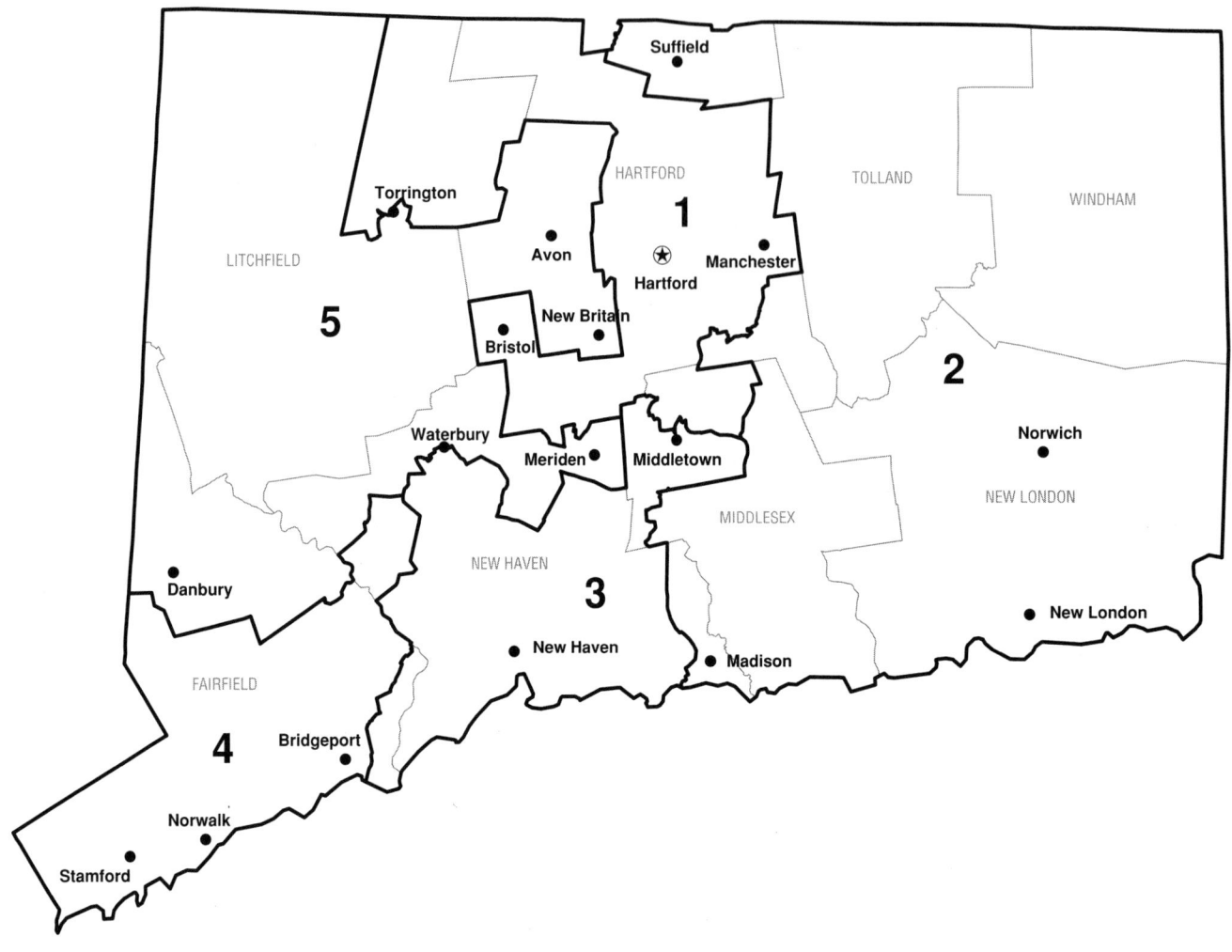

Suffield

HARTFORD

TOLLAND

WINDHAM

Torrington

LITCHFIELD

1

Avon

Hartford

Manchester

5

New Britain

Bristol

Waterbury

Meriden

Middletown

2

Norwich

NEW LONDON

MIDDLESEX

Danbury

NEW HAVEN

3

New Haven

Madison

New London

FAIRFIELD

4

Bridgeport

Norwalk

Stamford

included George Bush (1992) and George W. Bush (2000), the son and grandson of Connecticut's own Prescott Bush, who represented the state in the Senate from 1953 to 1963.

Curiously, the vote for governor in Connecticut has often gone opposite to the presidential vote. While Republicans were dominating presidential voting here in the 1970s and 1980s, the state elected a succession of Democratic governors. But when the White House vote turned around in the 1990s the state elected Republican John Rowland to three terms in the statehouse. A Reagan-inspired conservative, Rowland attracts crossover Catholic votes on abortion.

Democrats dominated Senate elections starting in the 1980s, however, keeping a brace of outspoken labor-friendly Democrats in office with little trouble. One, Christopher Dodd, was the son of a former Democratic senator, and the other, Joseph I. Lieberman, was the first Jew nominated for president or vice president, running with Al Gore in 2000.

But the first real competition of the years after 2000 came with the redrawing of the state's congressional districts to accommodate the loss of the sixth seat. The new map, conceived by a bipartisan commission, left the 1st District (Hartford), 2nd District (Middlesex-New London), 3rd District (New Haven), and 4th District (Fairfield) largely the same but merged the old 6th District and the old 5th District in a new district, bringing roughly equal numbers of the constituents of each. Numerically, however, there were 13,000 more Democrats, and the district had given Gore 52 percent in 2000.

Some of the Democratic advantage in the new 5th District was attributable to the factory town of New Britain. The town received some good news in 2002 when Stanley Works, a local toolmaker with 160 years' history, reversed a plan to move its headquarters to Bermuda for tax reasons. Three Republicans and two Democrats made up the state's House delegation in 2002.

Table 1 Population

District	Population	Population under 18	Voting-age population	Median age	Male*	Female*
1	681,113	166,564	514,549	37.8	47.7	52.3
2	681,113	164,945	516,168	37.2	49.8	50.2
3	681,113	161,307	519,806	37.1	47.9	52.1
4	681,113	177,103	504,010	37.2	48.2	51.8
5	681,113	171,769	509,344	37.7	48.6	51.4
State	3,405,565	841,688	2,563,877	37.4	48.4	51.6

*As percentage of total population.

Table 2 Voting-Age Persons by Race/Hispanic or Latino Origin

District	White*	Black or African American*	American Indian or Alaska Native*	Asian*	Other or multirace*	Hispanic or Latino*
1	75.3	11.4	0.2	2.3	1.5	9.3
2	89.7	3.3	0.4	1.7	1.2	3.7
3	79.1	10.1	0.2	2.6	1.4	6.6
4	73.3	10.0	0.1	3.2	1.7	11.7
5	82.8	4.8	0.2	2.0	1.5	8.7
State	80.1	7.9	0.2	2.4	1.4	8.0

*As percentage of voting-age population.

Table 3 Voting-Age Population by Age Groups

District	18 to 24*	25 to 44*	45 to 64*	Over 64*
1	10.2	39.5	30.8	19.6
2	12.1	40.5	31.1	16.3
3	11.6	39.8	29.3	19.3
4	9.3	41.3	31.3	18.1
5	9.8	40.3	31.5	18.5
State	10.6	40.3	30.8	18.3

*As percentage of voting-age population.

Table 4 Income and Occupation

District	Median family income	Families in poverty*	White collar†	Blue collar†	Service†	Farm†
1	$61,187	7.3	65.8	19.7	14.3	0.2
2	$64,772	3.7	62.9	20.9	15.8	0.4
3	$61,106	6.4	64.7	21.1	14.1	0.1
4	$80,284	5.4	71.8	15.5	12.6	0.1
5	$65,204	5.5	62.9	22.4	14.4	0.2
State	$65,521	5.6	65.6	19.9	14.3	0.2

*As percentage of all families.　　†As percentage of employed workers 16 years and over.

Table 5 Education: School Years Completed

District	Less than grade 9*	Grades 9–12 no diploma*	High school diploma no college*	Some college*	College bachelor's degree or higher*
1	6.6	11.3	29.4	24.6	28.2
2	4.1	9.1	30.8	27.2	28.8
3	5.6	10.8	31.3	24.3	28.0
4	6.2	9.2	22.1	20.3	42.2
5	6.4	10.7	28.7	24.3	29.9
State	5.8	10.2	28.5	24.1	31.4

*As percentage of persons age 25 and over.

Table 6 Housing and Residential Patterns

District	Median home value	Owner occupied*	Renter occupied*	Urban†	Rural†
1	$140,600	63.6	36.4	93.4	6.6
2	$145,400	72.0	28.0	66.7	33.3
3	$148,700	63.5	36.5	96.6	3.4
4	$309,500	67.8	32.2	95.9	4.1
5	$159,400	67.6	32.4	85.9	14.1
State	$160,600	66.8	33.2	87.7	12.3

*As percentage of occupied housing units.　　†As percentage of total population.

Connecticut 1st District

Central — Hartford, Bristol

Situated midway between Boston and New York—roughly 100 miles from each—the 1st is an attractive commercial center for businesses straddling the Northeast Corridor. Insurance companies, banks, and state government are the lifeblood of Hartford and its well-off suburbs.

Hartford saw a renewal in the 1990s, cleaning up its downtown and attracting several high-tech manufacturing firms. But challenges persist: while Hartford remains the most populous city in the 1st District, it experienced a 13 percent population decline in the 1990s. West Hartford, the next most populous city, grew by 6 percent.

Hartford is overwhelmingly minority and staunchly Democratic. The city gave Al Gore 80 percent of the vote in the 2000 presidential election, more than any other city or town in the state. Democrats outnumber Republicans in the 1st by more than a two-to-one ratio. The district gave Gore his largest vote margin in Connecticut, and a Republican has not represented Hartford in the House since 1959.

Hispanics make up 40 percent of Hartford residents; most of them are Puerto Rican. City voters in November 2001 elected Hartford's first Hispanic mayor.

In the 1990s, the 1st was relatively compact in shape. Connecticut lost one seat in the 2000 reapportionment, and the 1st now resembles a backward "C." The new district takes in some sparsely populated towns in northwestern Connecticut and part of Middletown, where Wesleyan University is located. The district also includes Democratic-leaning Bristol, where ESPN has its headquarters.

Major Industry

Insurance, banking, defense, government.

Notable

The *Hartford Courant* (founded in 1764) is the nation's oldest newspaper in continuous circulation; Noah Webster, author of the first American dictionary, was born in West Hartford; Hartford's Wadsworth Atheneum is the nation's oldest public art museum.

Election Returns

	Republican		Democratic		Other	
President 2000	96,411	33.3%	178,977	61.9%	13,731	4.7%
House 2002	66,968	33.2%	134,698	66.8%	22	

District Profile

Population   681,113

Total area (square miles)   672.5
   Land area (square miles)   652.9

Population per square mile   1,043.2

Counties (2000 population)
   Hartford (pt.)   613,955   Middlesex (pt.)   30,441
   Litchfield (pt.)   36,717

Cities and other areas over 10,000 (2000 population)
   Bristol   60,062
   Central Manchester CDP   30,595
   East Hartford CDP   49,575
   Hartford   121,578
   Newington CDP   29,306
   Torrington (pt.)   15,000
   West Hartford CDP   63,589
   Wethersfield CDP   26,271
   Windsor Locks CDP   12,043

Race and Hispanic or Latino origin*
   White   71.6%
   Black or African American   12.6%
   American Indian or Alaska Native   0.2%
   Asian   2.4%
   Native Hawaiian or other Pacific Islander   0.0%
   Some other race   0.2%
   Hispanic or Latino origin   11.4%
   Two or more races   1.7%

*As percentage of total population.

Ancestry*

English	6.9%	Polish	6.7%
Fr. Canadian	3.0%	Russian	1.2%
French	5.8%	Scottish	1.3%
German	6.1%	Swedish	1.6%
Irish	11.1%	USA/American	2.3%
Italian	12.1%	West Indian	2.2%

*As estimated percentage of total population.

Universities and colleges, 2000–2001 enrollment
   Briarwood College, Southington   518
   Capital Community Technical College, Hartford   3,042
   Charter Oak State College, Newington   1,459
   Data Institute, East Hartford   418
   Manchester Community Technical College, Manchester   5,135
   Northwestern Connecticut Community Technical College, Winsted   1,596
   Rensselaer Hartford Graduate Center, Hartford   1,807
   St. Joseph College, West Hartford   1,823
   Trinity College, Hartford   2,246
   University of Hartford, West Hartford   6,895

Newspapers and circulation

	District circulation	Total circulation
Bristol Press	9,988	12,291
Hartford Courant	108,988	201,769
Manchester Journal Inquirer	20,172	43,855
Meriden Record-Journal	3,778	25,795
Middletown Press	2,113	9,544
New Britain Herald Press	5,981	16,280
*New York Daily News**	1,001	723,155
New York Post	2,234	511,412
Torrington Register Citizen	7,302	10,286
*USA Today**	4,862	1,674,376
Waterbury Republican-American	5,199	56,111

*See Sources and Explanations in the front of the volume.

Television stations and affiliations
Hartford-New Haven	100%	WEDH	PBS
Hartford-New Haven	100%	WEDN	PBS
Hartford-New Haven	100%	WEDY	PBS
Hartford-New Haven	100%	WFSB	CBS
Hartford-New Haven	100%	WHPX	PAX
Hartford-New Haven	100%	WSAH	Independent
Hartford-New Haven	100%	WTIC	FOX
Hartford-New Haven	100%	WTNH	ABC
Hartford-New Haven	100%	WTXX	WB
Hartford-New Haven	100%	WVIT	NBC

Cable systems and subscribers
   Charter   2,609
   Comcast   108,121
   Cox   82,880

Military installations, September 2001

Camp Hartell, Windsor Locks   389

John W. Middleton U.S. Army Reserve Center, East
Windsor   207

Businesses and other major employers

Hamilton Sundstrand Corp.; Windsor Locks; aircraft
control systems   8,500

Aetna Inc.; Hartford; life and health insurance   7,800

Travelers Indemnity Co.; Hartford; commodity contracts
brokers, dealers   7,000

Travelers Casualty Co.; Hartford; fire, marine, casualty
insurance   7,000

Connecticut General Corp.; Bloomfield; life insurance
6,476

Hartford Insurance Company of Illinois; Hartford;
insurance agents and brokers   5,000

Hartford Hospital; Hartford   4,870

City of Hartford; Hartford; city management   4,000

Hartford Fire Insurance Co.; Hartford; fire, marine,
casualty insurance   3,500

St. Francis Hospital and Medical Center Foundation Inc.;
Hartford   3,360

Connecticut Dept. of Transportation; Newington
3,100

U.S. Postal Service; Hartford   2,100

Hartford Fire Insurance Co.; Southington; insurance
agents and brokers   2,000

Northeast Utilities System; Berlin; electric power
generation   1,800

United Technologies Corp.; Rocky Hill; aircraft engines
and parts   1,700

Alstom Power Inc.; Windsor; engineering services
1,302

United Technologies Corp.; Southington; engine mount
parts, aircraft   1,300

Eastern Connecticut Health Network Inc.; Manchester;
hospital management   1,200

Hartford Courant Co; Hartford; newspaper publishing
1,200

United Technologies Corp.; East Hartford; aircraft
maintenance, repair   1,200

Bristol Hospital Inc.; Bristol   1,185

Mark Facey and Co.; Bristol; telemarketing services
1,150

Connecticut Institute for the Blind; Hartford;
community-based programs for the visually impaired
1,100

ESPN Inc.; Bristol; cable television   1,000

Northeast Utilities System; Glastonbury; electric power
generation   1,000

Manchester Memorial Hospital Inc.; Manchester   1,000

Ames Department Stores Inc.; Rocky Hill; discount
department stores   1,000

Connecticut Bureau of Financial and Support Services;
Hartford   1,000

United Technologies Corp.; East Hartford; aircraft
engines and parts   1,000

Fleet National Bank; Hartford; commercial bank   1,000

Stanadyne Corp.; Windsor; automotive fuel systems and
parts   950

U.S. Internal Revenue Service; Hartford   950

Connecticut Dept. of Revenue Services; Hartford   950

Connecticut Children's Medical Center; Hartford   850

University of Hartford; West Hartford   846

UTC Fuel Cells; South Windsor; fuel cells, solid state
800

Connecticut Dept. of Social Services; Hartford   800

Connecticut Environmental Protection Dept.; Hartford
800

Mettown Management Construction Inc.; Hartford;
construction project management consultant   800

Kaman Aerospace Corp.; Bloomfield; airframe assemblies
789

Wiremold Co.; West Hartford; noncurrent-carrying
wiring devices   750

Hamilton Sundstrand Corp.; East Windsor; orthopedic,
prosthetic, surgical supplies   700

International Business Machines Corp.; Hartford; data
processing   700

Metropolitan District; Hartford; water supply   700

Connecticut Dept. of Administrative Services; Hartford
700

U.S. Federal Deposit Insurance Corp.; East Hartford
700

U.S. Veterans Hospital; Newington   700

General Cigar Co. Inc.; Windsor; cigars and accessories
675

City of Windsor; Windsor; city management   650

United Technologies Corp.; East Hartford; scientific
research agency   650

Southern Auto Sales Inc.; East Windsor; automobile
auction   600

Konica Business Technologies Inc.; Windsor;
duplicating machines   600

Chelsea Place Care Center; Hartford; skilled nursing
care facilities   600

Capitol Region Education Council; Hartford;
educational services   600

Trinity College; Hartford   600

Boilermakers Northeast Area Apprentice; East Hartford;
labor organization   600

Colt's Manufacturing Co.; West Hartford; small arms
600

Hebrew Home and Hospital Inc.; West Hartford   600

Mercy Community Health Inc.; Hartford; medical
centers   600

United Technologies Corp.; Hartford; administrative
management   550

St. Joseph College; West Hartford   550

Ethicon Inc.; Southington; IV transfusion apparatus
550

Rocky Hill Veterans Home and Hospital; Rocky Hill
525

Johnson and Johnson; Southington; surgical and medical
instruments   525

Ahlstrom Windsor Locks; Windsor Locks; sanitary paper
products   510

Sherwood Industries Inc.; Kensington; paper cups   507

City of Bristol; city management; Bristol   505

HNS Management Co.; Hartford; intercity and rural bus
transportation   501

Vanguard; Glastonbury; business services   500

Dynamic Gunver Technologies; Manchester; sheet metal
specialties   500

City of Manchester; Manchester; city management   500

ING Life Insurance and Annuity Co.; Windsor; life insurance   500

TWA Airlines; Hartford; air transportation   500

Connecticut Adjutant General; Hartford; national security   500

University of Connecticut Inc.; Hartford; child day care services   500

Connecticut Dept. of Public Health; Hartford   500

Belcan Engineering Group Inc.; East Hartford; engineering services   500

BKM Enterprises Inc.; East Hartford; office furniture   500

Connecticut Light and Power Co.; Newington; electric power generation   500

Data Mail Inc.; Newington; addressing service   500

Stop 'n Shop Companies Inc.; East Hartford; drug stores   500

City of Hartford; Hartford; police dept.   500

St. Francis Hospital and Medical Center Foundation Inc.; Portland   500

Connecticut 2nd District

East — Norwich, New London, Storrs

The state's largest and most working-class district, the 2nd runs from the waterfront of Middlesex and New London Counties north to the Massachusetts border through small towns and the main campus of the University of Connecticut in Storrs.

The defense industry continues to be the district's major economic force, but it now shares some of that responsibility with the Native American-owned Foxwoods and Mohegan Sun casinos. The economic shift started in the early 1990s, when some of the submarine contracts in New London and Groton were sent to Newport News, Virginia, just as Foxwoods, and later Mohegan Sun, began attracting visitors.

Defense and casino matters sit atop the district's list of political issues. The stream of gamblers and casino employees traveling through the district has strained the 2nd's highways, making transportation an election-year issue. In addition, the casinos and surrounding towns have quarreled over which regulations should apply to reservation land.

Despite a series of close elections throughout the 1980s and 1990s, Democrats were able to maintain their lock on the 2nd until 2000, when the Republicans took the seat for the first time since 1972. The district became slightly less Democratic in redistricting following the 2000 census, as liberal-leaning Middletown was excised from the 2nd and split up between the 1st and 3rd districts.

Major Industry

Gambling, defense, health care.

Notable

Foxwoods Resort and Casino, owned by the Mashantucket Pequot Tribal Nation, is the largest resort casino in the world, with annual revenue of $1 billion; New London is home to the U.S. Coast Guard Academy; the Mystic Seaport maritime museum is in Mystic.

Election Returns

	Republican		Democratic		Other	
President 2000	119,184	39.5%	162,762	54.0%	19,587	6.5%
House 2002	117,434	54.1%	99,674	45.9%		

District Profile

Population   681,113

Total area (square miles)   2,142.7
Land area (square miles)   2,028.1

Population per square mile   335.8

Counties (2000 population)
Hartford (pt.)   74,625   New London   259,088
Middlesex (pt.)   84,087   Tolland   136,364
New Haven (pt.)   17,858   Windham   109,091

Cities and other areas over 10,000 (2000 population)
Conning Towers-Nautilus Park CDP   10,241
Groton   10,010
New London   25,671
Norwich   36,117
Storrs CDP   10,996
Willimantic CDP   15,823

Race and Hispanic or Latino origin*
White   88.6%
Black or African American   3.3%
American Indian or Alaska Native   0.5%
Asian   1.7%
Native Hawaiian or other Pacific Islander   0.0%
Some other race   0.1%
Hispanic or Latino origin   4.3%
Two or more races   1.5%

As percentage of total population.

Ancestry*
English   10.2%   Polish   6.7%
Fr. Canadian   4.3%   Russian   1.1%
French   7.8%   Scotch-Irish   1.1%
German   8.1%   Scottish   1.9%
Irish   13.3%   Swedish   1.7%
Italian   10.2%   USA/American   2.6%

As estimated percentage of total population.

Universities and colleges, 2000–2001 enrollment
Asnuntuck Community Technical College, Enfield   1,850
Connecticut College, New London   1,856
Eastern Connecticut State University, Willimantic   5,145
Mitchell College, New London   621
Quinebaug Valley Community Technical College, Danielson   1,347
Three Rivers Community Technical College, Norwich   3,574
U.S. Coast Guard Academy, New London   877
University of Connecticut, Storrs   19,393

Newspapers and circulation

	District circulation	Total circulation
Hartford Courant	50,473	201,769
Manchester Journal Inquirer	23,685	43,855
Middletown Press	2,473	9,544
New Haven Register	5,428	98,728
New London Day	39,265	40,270
*New York Daily News**	1,822	723,155
New York Post	1,680	511,412
Norwich Bulletin	27,542	28,043
Springfield Union-News	1,045	89,595
*USA Today**	5,845	1,674,376
Westerly Sun	2,456	10,398
Willimantic Chronicle	10,158	10,158
Worcester Telegram-Gazette	1,600	104,076

See Sources and Explanations in the front of the volume.

Television stations and affiliations

Hartford-New Haven	100%	WEDH	PBS
Hartford-New Haven	100%	WEDN	PBS
Hartford-New Haven	100%	WEDY	PBS
Hartford-New Haven	100%	WFSB	CBS
Hartford-New Haven	100%	WHPX	PAX
Hartford-New Haven	100%	WSAH	Independent
Hartford-New Haven	100%	WTIC	FOX
Hartford-New Haven	100%	WTNH	ABC
Hartford-New Haven	100%	WTXX	WB
Hartford-New Haven	100%	WVIT	NBC

Cable systems and subscribers

Adelphia   21,602
Charter   25,337
Comcast   76,239
Cox   21,914
Eastern Connecticut Cable TV   38,446

Military installations, September 2001

New London Naval Submarine Base, Groton   6,459
Bradley International Airport Air National Guard, Windsor Locks   940
Aviation Classification Repair Activity Depot Groton New London Airport, Groton   351
Camp Rowland Military Training Area, Niantic   235

Businesses and other major employers

Mashantucket Pequot Tribal Nation; Ledyard; casino   11,000
Electric Boat Corp.; Groton; building and repairing submarines   8,000
Pfizer Corp.; Groton; medicinals and botanicals   6,000
Mohegan Tribe of Indians of Connecticut; Uncasville; casino   5,000
Connecticut Light and Power Co.; Waterford; electric power generation   1,700
Dominion Nuclear Connecticut Inc.; Waterford; electric power generation   1,650
Rosenbluth International Inc.; Enfield; travel agency   1,500
Backus Corp.; Norwich; hospital management   1,437
Lawrence and Memorial Hospital; New London   1,400
Wyman-Gordon Investment Castings Inc.; Groton; steel investment foundries   1,359
Lego Systems Inc.; Enfield; toy erector sets   1,350

Connecticut Dept. of Mental Health and Addiction Services; Norwich; psychiatric hospitals   1,100
William Backus Hospital; Norwich   1,045
Retail Brand Alliance Inc.; Enfield; women's ready-to-wear apparel   1,000
Eastern Pequot Development Corp.; North Stonington; Native American reservation   1,000
City of Groton; Groton; city management   957
Day Kimball Medical Office Assn. Inc.; Putnam   900
Healthnet of New England Inc.; Putnam; hospital management   815
Connecticut University System; Willimantic   800
City of Windham; Willimantic; city management   800
Johnson Memorial Corp.; Stafford Springs   770
Connecticut Dept. of Corrections; Enfield   700
Hunter Fan Co.; Enfield   655
Connecticut College; New London   636
Lee Co.; Westbrook; fluidic devices, circuits   635
Windham Community Memorial Hospital; Willimantic   632
Frito-Lay Inc.; Dayville; potato chips and snacks   600
Computer Sciences Corp.; Norwich; computer service bureau   600
Davis-Standard Corp.; Pawcatuck; pumps and pumping equipment   600
Conopco Inc.; Clinton; perfumes, cosmetics, other toilet products   600
Rockville General Hospital Inc.; Vernon-Rockville   580
Franklin Farms Inc.; North Franklin; mushroom production   550
City of Norwich; Norwich; elementary and secondary schools   550
City of Montville; Uncasville; mayor's office   517
Gerber Technology Inc.; Tolland; computer software development   500
Connecticut Dept. of Corrections; Niantic   500
C&M Corp. of Connecticut; Wauregan; communication wire   500
R.R. Donnelley and Sons Co.; Old Saybrook; commercial printing   500

Connecticut 3rd District

South — New Haven, Milford

Working-class, bedrock constituents of the Democratic Party mix with the liberal ivory tower elite in the 3rd. Situated on the state's southern coast, the 3rd encompasses both the working-class elements of New Haven, a busy blue-collar port, and prestigious Yale University. Yale might be the city's largest employer, but labor issues have sometimes caused tension between the university and the city's blue-collar workers. All this stands in contrast to the surrounding towns, where professionals who commute throughout Connecticut and as far as New York City reside. New Haven, as with most Connecticut cities, is far poorer than its surrounding suburbs.

The district is solidly Democratic, with the outlying towns leaning to the right of New Haven. The district picked up most of Democratic stronghold Middletown during redistricting following the 2000 census. The 3rd is home to many minority groups, most living in New Haven, that traditionally support Democrats. New Haven has a high percentage of Hispanics and blacks. The district also is home to many Italian-Americans, who have increasingly moved to the suburbs.

The defense industry plays a large role in the 3rd. Sikorsky Aircraft, a helicopter manufacturer based in Stratford, depends on the military for survival, and Pratt & Whitney has a plant in North Haven. The 3rd was dealt a blow in 1995 when Stratford Army Engine Plant was slated for shut down, and the district has had trouble attracting new industries. New Haven has tried to lure tourists to its waterfront and business groups to its convention centers, with mild success.

Major Industry
Trade, manufacturing, defense.

Notable
The frisbee was invented at Yale University in 1920 when students discovered that empty pie plates from the Frisbee Baking Co. of nearby Bridgeport were fun to toss around on New Haven Green; Milford is home to the headquarters of the Subway sandwich shop chain; polls conducted by Quinnipiac University in Hamden are frequently cited by national news organizations.

Election Returns

	Republican		Democratic		Other	
President 2000	96,446	34.4%	168,196	60.0%	15,455	5.5%
House 2002	54,757	29.5%	121,557	65.6%	9,050	4.9%

District Profile

Population 681,113

Total area (square miles) 484.9
  Land area (square miles) 459.1

Population per square mile 1,483.6

Counties (2000 population)
Fairfield (pt.) 59,885   New Haven (pt.) 580,685
Middlesex (pt.) 40,543

Cities and other areas over 10,000 (2000 population)
Ansonia 18,554
Derby 12,391
East Haven CDP 28,189
Middletown (pt.) 34,329
Milford 50,594
Naugatuck borough 30,989
New Haven 123,626
North Haven CDP 23,035
Orange CDP 13,233
Stratford CDP 49,976
Wallingford Center CDP 17,509
Waterbury (pt.) 18,647
West Haven 52,360

Race and Hispanic or Latino origin*
White 76.1%
Black or African American 11.5%
American Indian or Alaska Native 0.2%
Asian 2.5%
Native Hawaiian or other Pacific Islander 0.0%
Some other race 0.2%
Hispanic or Latino origin 8.0%
Two or more races 1.5%

As percentage of total population.

Ancestry*

English 6.3%	Italian 18.7%
Fr. Canadian 1.5%	Polish 6.2%
French 2.9%	Russian 1.5%
German 6.7%	Scottish 1.1%
Hungarian 1.1%	Swedish 1.2%
Irish 12.5%	USA/American 1.9%

As estimated percentage of total population.

Universities and colleges, 2000–2001 enrollment
Albertus Magnus College, New Haven 2,105
Gateway Community Technical College, New Haven 4,157
Middlesex Community Technical College, Middletown 2,309
Paier College of Art, Hamden 282
Quinnipiac University, Hamden 6,477
Southern Connecticut State University, New Haven 12,127
University of New Haven, West Haven 4,349
Wesleyan University, Middletown 3,158
Yale University, New Haven 11,099

Newspapers and circulation

	District circulation	Total circulation
Connecticut Post	26,452	76,961
Hartford Courant	9,606	201,769
Meriden Record-Journal	8,301	25,795
Middletown Press	4,929	9,544
New Haven Register	87,099	98,728
*New York Daily News**	4,091	723,155
New York Post	4,522	511,412
*New York Times**	9,312	666,228
*USA Today**	4,621	1,674,376
Waterbury Republican-American	11,278	56,111

See Sources and Explanations in the front of the volume.

Television stations and affiliations

Hartford-New Haven	92%	WEDH	PBS
Hartford-New Haven	92%	WEDN	PBS
Hartford-New Haven	92%	WEDY	PBS
Hartford-New Haven	92%	WFSB	CBS
Hartford-New Haven	92%	WHPX	PAX
Hartford-New Haven	92%	WSAH	Independent
Hartford-New Haven	92%	WTIC	FOX
Hartford-New Haven	92%	WTNH	ABC
Hartford-New Haven	92%	WTXX	WB
Hartford-New Haven	92%	WVIT	NBC
New York	8%	WABC	ABC
New York	8%	WCBS	CBS
New York	8%	WEDW	PBS
New York	8%	WFME	Independent
New York	8%	WLIW	PBS
New York	8%	WLNY	Independent
New York	8%	WMBC	Independent

New York	8%	WNBC	NBC
New York	8%	WNET	PBS
New York	8%	WNJB	PBS
New York	8%	WNJN	PBS
New York	8%	WNJU	Telemundo
New York	8%	WNYE	PBS
New York	8%	WNYW	FOX
New York	8%	WPIX	WB
New York	8%	WPXN	PAX
New York	8%	WRNN	Independent
New York	8%	WTBY	Independent
New York	8%	WWOR	UPN
New York	8%	WXTV	Univision

Cable systems and subscribers
Cablevision   36,703
Comcast   138,922
Tele-Media   30,550

Military installations, September 2001
Stratford Army Engine Plant, Stratford   420
Orange Air National Guard Station, New Haven   256

Businesses and other major employers
Sikorsky Aircraft Corp.; Stratford; helicopters   8,300
Yale-New Haven Hospital Inc.; New Haven   5,800
Southern New England Telephone Co.; New Haven; local/long-distance telephone   5,700
U.S. Veterans Hospital; West Haven   3,500
Hospital of St. Raphael; New Haven   3,400
SBC Communications Inc.; New Haven; telephone services   2,500
Bayer Corp.; West Haven; pharmaceuticals   2,000
Anthem Health Plan Inc.; North Haven; group hospitalization   1,800
United Technologies Corp.; North Haven; aircraft engines and parts   1,800
United Technologies Corp.; Middletown; aircraft engines and parts   1,650
United Technologies Corp.; North Haven; aircraft turbines   1,550
City of Middletown; Middletown; city management   1,343
Middlesex Hospital; Middletown   1,174
City of Stratford; Stratford; city management   1,164
U.S. Postal Service; Wallingford   1,100
Honeywell International Inc.; Stratford; aircraft engines and parts   990
Bristol-Myers Squibb Co.; Wallingford; commercial physical research   950
Bic Corp.; Milford; ball point pens and parts   900
Wesleyan University; Middletown   800
Pfizer Corp.; Milford; razor blades and razors   700
CYTEC Industries Inc.; Wallingford; chemical preparations   700
ADC Telecommunications Inc.; Tustin; telephones and telephone apparatus   660
Griffin Hospital Inc.; Derby   651
Sargent Manufacturing Co.; New Haven; locks or lock sets   650
City of East Haven; East Haven; city management   650
Knights of Columbus Supreme Council Inc.; New Haven; insurance agents and brokers   625

New Haven Register Inc.; New Haven; newspaper   620
Stop 'n Shop Companies Inc.; North Haven; industrial buildings, warehouses   600
Telecheck Services Inc.; North Haven; data processing   600
Pritchard Industries Inc.; New Haven; building maintenance   600
City of New Haven; New Haven; police dept.   600
Quinnipiac University; Hamden   581
Northeast Graphics Inc.; North Haven; commercial printing   580
University of New Haven; West Haven   579
Gaylord Farm Assn.; Wallingford; residential rehabilitation center   566
Hewitt Organization Inc.; Shelton; business consulting   550
Hershey Foods Corp.; Naugatuck; confectionery products   517
Milford Hospital Inc.; Milford   500
Sheaffer Pen Corp.; Milford; stationery and office supplies   500
Connecticut Board of Community-Technical Colleges; New Haven   500
City of Hamden; Hamden; city government   500
Dresser Inc.; Stratford; machinists' precision tools   500

Connecticut 4th District

Southwest — Bridgeport, Stamford

The 4th runs along Connecticut's sparkling "Gold Coast," bordering Long Island Sound, from the outskirts of New York City to Bridgeport on the district's southeast border. The contrast between working-class Bridgeport and the district's widespread wealth creates a complex world for politicians to navigate, as polo clubs rub elbows with the decayed city.

Many residents travel to jobs in New York City and Stamford, causing severe traffic problems on Interstate 95, already a congested route. Traffic issues permeate the public debate. Welfare-to-work programs also have become an issue. Having failed to place welfare recipients in good jobs in Bridgeport, the state's largest city, the local government began making moves to find employment for low-income residents in the affluent suburbs.

The 4th's political landscape is driven by the suburban elite, giving the district more registered Republicans than any other in Connecticut. Still, the 4th gave the edge to the Democratic presidential candidate in 1996 and 2000. A majority of the population in the poor, urban areas votes Democratic. Darien and New Canaan were the only two Connecticut jurisdictions to give George W. Bush more than 60 percent of the vote in 2000, while Al Gore's 73 percent showing in Bridgeport was among his highest in the state.

Republican mayors long dominated local politics. But Democrats made big inroads in 2001 when a Democrat won the race for first selectman in Greenwich and Norwalk's incumbent GOP mayor lost a reelection bid.

Major Industry

Manufacturing, banking, medical.

Notable

Republican senator Prescott Bush, the father of the 41st president and a grandfather of the 43rd president, reared his family in Greenwich; General Electric's corporate headquarters are in Fairfield; P. T. Barnum, founder of the Ringling Bros., Barnum & Bailey Circus, made his home in Bridgeport; Bridgeport was the largest producer of ammunition for the Allied forces during both world wars.

Election Returns

	Republican		Democratic		Other	
President 2000	120,140	43.2%	148,022	53.2%	10,219	3.7%
House 2002	113,197	64.4%	62,491	35.6%	7	

District Profile

Population 681,113

Total area (square miles) 538.6
  Land area (square miles) 456.9

Population per square mile 1,490.7

Counties (2000 population)
  Fairfield (pt.) 671,292
  New Haven (pt.) 9,821

Cities and other areas over 10,000 (2000 population)
  Bridgeport 139,529   Stamford 117,083
  Darien CDP 19,607   Trumbull CDP 34,243
  Norwalk 82,951   Westport CDP 25,749
  Shelton (pt.) 28,192

Race and Hispanic or Latino origin*
  White 70.9%
  Black or African American 10.9%
  American Indian or Alaska Native 0.1%
  Asian 3.2%
  Native Hawaiian or other Pacific Islander 0.0%
  Some other race 0.3%
  Hispanic or Latino origin 12.8%
  Two or more races 1.7%

As percentage of total population.

Ancestry*
  English 6.9%   Polish 4.4%
  French 1.8%   Russian 2.1%
  German 7.1%   Scottish 1.5%
  Hungarian 1.7%   Swedish 1.1%
  Irish 11.6%   USA/American 2.7%
  Italian 13.5%   West Indian 2.1%

As estimated percentage of total population.

Universities and colleges, 2000–2001 enrollment
  Fairfield University, Fairfield 5,188
  Gibbs College, Norwalk 554
  Housatonic Community Technical College, Bridgeport 3,902
  Norwalk Community Technical College, Norwalk 5,377
  Sacred Heart University, Fairfield 5,684
  St. Vincent's College, Bridgeport 265
  University of Bridgeport, Bridgeport 2,973

Newspapers and circulation

	District circulation	Total circulation
Connecticut Post	49,319	76,961
Danbury News-Times	3,002	32,710
Fairfield Citizen-News	7,562	7,773
Greenwich Time	11,601	12,177
New Canaan Advertiser	5,676	5,686
New Haven Register	1,973	98,728
*New York Daily News**	8,527	723,155
New York Post	9,118	511,412
*New York Times**	28,447	666,228
Norwalk Hour	15,811	16,196
Stamford Advocate	26,809	27,105
*USA Today**	8,039	1,674,376
*Westport News**	5,782	8,188

See Sources and Explanations in the front of the volume.

Television stations and affiliations

New York	95%	WABC	ABC
New York	95%	WCBS	CBS
New York	95%	WEDW	PBS
New York	95%	WFME	Independent
New York	95%	WLIW	PBS
New York	95%	WLNY	Independent
New York	95%	WMBC	Independent
New York	95%	WNBC	NBC
New York	95%	WNET	PBS
New York	95%	WNJB	PBS
New York	95%	WNJN	PBS
New York	95%	WNJU	Telemundo
New York	95%	WNYE	PBS
New York	95%	WNYW	FOX
New York	95%	WPIX	WB
New York	95%	WPXN	PAX
New York	95%	WRNN	Independent
New York	95%	WTBY	Independent
New York	95%	WWOR	UPN
New York	95%	WXTV	Univision
Hartford-New Haven	5%	WEDH	PBS
Hartford-New Haven	5%	WEDN	PBS
Hartford-New Haven	5%	WEDY	PBS
Hartford-New Haven	5%	WFSB	CBS
Hartford-New Haven	5%	WHPX	PAX
Hartford-New Haven	5%	WSAH	Independent
Hartford-New Haven	5%	WTIC	FOX
Hartford-New Haven	5%	WTNH	ABC
Hartford-New Haven	5%	WTXX	WB
Hartford-New Haven	5%	WVIT	NBC

Cable systems and subscribers
  Cablevision 154,729
  Charter 13,564
  Comcast 6,656
  Tele-Media 14,282

Businesses and other major employers
  Berisford Inc.; Stamford; commercial cooking, food service equipment 6,000
  Pitney Bowes Inc.; Stamford; mailing machines 4,000
  Perkinelmer Instruments; Shelton; analytical instruments 3,300

Coreskills Inc.; Trumbull; checkbooks 3,000

Xl Global Service Inc.; Stamford; insurance agents and brokers 2,700

Reeves Brothers Inc. /Hart Holding Co.; Norwalk; blankets and blanketings 2,490

Employees Assistance Program; Norwalk; employment agencies 2,400

Bridgeport Hospital Inc.; Bridgeport 2,029

Kodak Polychrome Graphics; Norwalk; printing trades machinery equipment/supplies 2,000

Swiss Bank Corp.; Stamford; investment bankers 2,000

Lester Gee Funeral Home Inc.; Bridgeport 1,992

St. Vincent's Medical Center; Bridgeport 1,900

Boehringer Ingelheim Corp.; Ridgefield; medicines 1,900

Arch Chemicals Inc.; Norwalk; industrial inorganic chemicals 1,700

Norwalk Hospital Assn.; Norwalk; hospital, medical school 1,660

United States Surgical Corp.; Norwalk; surgical instruments and apparatus 1,560

Rutledge Capital; Greenwich; investors 1,540

Greenwich Hospital; Greenwich 1,500

Idealife Insurance Co.; Stamford; insurance agents and brokers 1,500

Clairol Inc.; Stamford; hair coloring preparations 1,500

People's Bank; Bridgeport; federal savings and loan associations 1,400

MLGA Fund II; Greenwich; business brokers 1,205

Stamford Hospital; Stamford 1,200

Claricom; Shelton; telephone and communication equipment 1,171

Conopco Inc.; Trumbull; dried fruits, vegetables, soup mixes 1,100

General Atlantic Holding Co. Inc.; Greenwich; discount department stores 1,000

City of Greenwich; Greenwich; city management 1,000

City of Westport; Westport; elementary and secondary schools 1,000

American Television and Communications Corp.; Stamford; cable television 1,000

General Electric Capital Corp.; Stamford; auto purchase financing 1,000

General Re Corp.; Stamford; property damage insurance 950

City of Stamford; Stamford; city management 878

Gartner Inc.; Stamford; market analysis or research 825

Fairfield University Inc.; Fairfield 808

American Skandia Life Assurance Corp.; Shelton; life insurance 800

Emcor Midwest Inc.; Norwalk; electrical contractor 800

ASM Lithography; Wilton; lithographic stones 800

Purdue Pharma LP; Stamford; pharmaceuticals 790

Oxford Health Plans Inc.; Trumbull; health maintenance organization 765

George Weston Bakeries Inc.; Greenwich; trucking 750

GTE Corp.; Stamford; management services 750

Trumbull School District; Trumbull 700

Applera Corp.; Norwalk; analytical instruments 700

Pepperidge Farm Inc.; Norwalk; bread baking 700

Northrop Grumman Norden Systems Inc.; Norwalk; radar systems and equipment 700

Verizon Communications Inc.; Stamford; documentation center 700

Hyperion Solutions Corp.; Stamford; computer software development 700

Stew Leonard's Norwalk Dairy Inc.; Norwalk; supermarkets 642

Stamford Health Center; Stamford 623

Burns International Security Services Corp.; Stamford; security guard service 610

Information Holdings Inc.; Stamford; business computer software 607

Hubbell Inc.; Bridgeport; current-carrying wiring services 600

Bridgeport Health Care Center Inc.; Bridgeport 600

Cendant Corp.; Trumbull; buyers' club 600

Imagistics International Inc.; Trumbull; facsimile equipment 600

National Assn. of Securities Dealers Inc.; Trumbull; data processing 600

News America Marketing In-Store Inc.; Wilton; display advertising service 600

OneSource Facility Services Inc.; Stamford; building cleaning 600

Greenwich Capital Markets Inc.; Greenwich; security dealers 563

General Electric Co.; Fairfield; personal credit institutions 550

Micro Warehouse Inc.; Norwalk; catalog sales 549

United Visiting Nurse Assn. Inc.; Trumbull; visiting nurse service 540

Citizens Utilities Company of California; Stamford; local telephone communications 536

Doncaster Advisory Service; Greenwich; investment advice 500

New Canaan Town; New Canaan; city management 500

Auto Suture Co.; Norwalk; surgical and medical instruments 500

Hewitt Associates; Norwalk; compensation and benefits planning 500

International Business Machines Corp.; Norwalk; industrial machinery/equipment repair 500

Beiersdorf Inc.; Norwalk; face creams or lotions 500

Connoisseur Communications Partners; Westport; radio broadcasting stations 500

TBM Holdings Inc.; Westport; trucks, tractors, loaders, carriers 500

Macy's East Inc.; Stamford; department stores 500

PricewaterhouseCoopers; Stamford; accounting services 500

Omega Engineering Inc.; Stamford; industrial temperature measuring instruments 500

Connecticut 5th District

West — Danbury, New Britain, most of Waterbury

Based in the western part of the state, the 5th is a mix of bucolic farmland and midsize industrial cities that includes nearly equal parts of the old 5th and 6th Districts.

The two were largely combined following the 2000 census when slow-growing Connecticut lost one House seat in reapportionment.

Waterbury is the 5th's most populous city, with about four of five city residents living in the district (the rest live in the 3rd District). The city is middle-class and racially diverse, with blacks and Hispanics together totaling 40 percent of the population. East of Waterbury, in the 5th's eastern edge, is Cheshire, an upper-income, Republican-leaning area, and Meriden, a Democratic-voting area with a large (21 percent) Hispanic population and a sizable Polish-American constituency.

North and east of Waterbury the district branches off to take in New Britain, where in 2002 directors of the toolmaking company Stanley Works voted—before reversing themselves—to reincorporate in Bermuda. New Britain, which lost population in the 1990s, has an ample Hispanic community and votes Democratic.

Danbury, located in the southwestern corner of the district, grew by 14 percent in the 1990s and has attracted immigrants from South America, the Caribbean, and southeast Asia.

The 5th is a politically competitive district. Al Gore and Joseph I. Lieberman won the redrawn area in the 2000 presidential contest by 9 percentage points, their smallest margin in the state. The GOP runs well in the medium-size and small towns in the district's center. George W. Bush carried several towns north and east of Danbury, including burgeoning New Milford and Newtown, in 2000.

Major Industry

Manufacturing, health care, insurance, defense.

Notable

Cheshire was designated the "Bedding Plant Capital of Connecticut" by the state legislature.

Election Returns

	Republican		Democratic		Other	
President 2000	121,424	43.1%	146,599	52.0%	13,887	4.9%
House 2002	113,626	54.2%	90,616	43.3%	5,212	2.5%

District Profile

Population   681,113

Total area (square miles)   1,281.5
Land area (square miles)   1,247.6

Population per square mile   545.9

Counties (2000 population)
Fairfield (pt.)	151,390	Litchfield (pt.)	145,476
Hartford (pt.)	168,603	New Haven (pt.)	215,644

Cities and other areas over 10,000 (2000 population)
Danbury	74,848	Torrington (pt.)	20,202
Meriden	58,244	Waterbury (pt.)	88,624
New Britain	71,538		

Race and Hispanic or Latino origin*
White   80.2%
Black or African American   5.2%
American Indian or Alaska Native   0.2%

Asian   2.1%
Native Hawaiian or other Pacific Islander   0.0%
Some other race   0.3%
Hispanic or Latino origin   10.5%
Two or more races   1.5%

As percentage of total population.

Ancestry*
English	7.3%	Polish	6.7%
Fr. Canadian	2.2%	Russian	1.3%
French	4.6%	Scottish	1.4%
German	8.2%	Swedish	1.4%
Irish	12.7%	USA/American	2.5%
Italian	14.5%		

As estimated percentage of total population.

Universities and colleges, 2000–2001 enrollment
Central Connecticut State University, New Britain   12,252
Naugatuck Valley Community Technical College, Waterbury   5,116
Teikyo Post University, Waterbury   1,356
Tunxis Community Technical College, Farmington   3,412
University of Connecticut School of Medicine and Dentistry, Farmington   486
Western Connecticut State University, Danbury   5,806

Newspapers and circulation

	District circulation	Total circulation
Bristol Press	2,364	12,291
Danbury News-Times	29,177	32,710
Hartford Courant	31,086	201,769
Meriden Record-Journal	13,396	25,795
New Britain Herald Press	10,251	16,280
New Haven Register	2,882	98,728
*New York Daily News**	4,444	723,155
New York Post	4,229	511,412
*New York Times**	10,782	666,228
Torrington Register Citizen	2,874	10,286
*USA Today**	5,671	1,674,376
Waterbury Republican-American	38,829	56,111
*Westport News**	1,849	8,188

See Sources and Explanations in the front of the volume.

Television stations and affiliations
Hartford-New Haven	85%	WEDH	PBS
Hartford-New Haven	85%	WEDN	PBS
Hartford-New Haven	85%	WEDY	PBS
Hartford-New Haven	85%	WFSB	CBS
Hartford-New Haven	85%	WHPX	PAX
Hartford-New Haven	85%	WSAH	Independent
Hartford-New Haven	85%	WTIC	FOX
Hartford-New Haven	85%	WTNH	ABC
Hartford-New Haven	85%	WTXX	WB
Hartford-New Haven	85%	WVIT	NBC
New York	15%	WABC	ABC
New York	15%	WCBS	CBS
New York	15%	WEDW	PBS
New York	15%	WFME	Independent
New York	15%	WLIW	PBS
New York	15%	WLNY	Independent

New York	15%	WMBC	Independent
New York	15%	WNBC	NBC
New York	15%	WNET	PBS
New York	15%	WNJB	PBS
New York	15%	WNJN	PBS
New York	15%	WNJU	Telemundo
New York	15%	WNYE	PBS
New York	15%	WNYW	FOX
New York	15%	WPIX	WB
New York	15%	WPXN	PAX
New York	15%	WRNN	Independent
New York	15%	WTBY	Independent
New York	15%	WWOR	UPN
New York	15%	WXTV	Univision

Cable systems and subscribers
Cablevision 26,156
Charter 37,469
Comcast 80,298
Cox 26,349
Tele-Media 42,288

Military installations, September 2001
Army Aviation Support Facility Bradley International Airport, Windsor Locks 106

Businesses and other major employers
Protocol; Cheshire; telephone services 4,300
International Business Machines Corp.; Southbury; computer peripherals, software 3,500
City of Waterbury; Waterbury; city management 3,200
Hartford Life Inc.; Simsbury; life insurance 3,000
New Britain General Hospital School of Nursing Alumni and Associates Inc.; New Britain 2,450
Hartford Equity Sales Co.; Weatogue; security brokers 2,000
Danbury Hospital; Danbury 1,950
St. Mary's Hospital Corp.; Waterbury 1,500
Union Carbide Corp.; Danbury; industrial organic chemicals 1,500
Waterbury Hospital; Waterbury 1,450
Otis Elevator Co.; Farmington; elevators and equipment 1,200
Pitney Bowes Inc.; Brookfield; office supplies 1,000
Southern New England Telephone Co.; Meriden; telephone communication 961
Connecticut Mental Retardation Office; Farmington 950
University of Connecticut Health Center; Farmington 940
General Electric Co.; Plainville; electric power switches 900

Torrington Co.; Torrington; ball bearings and parts 900
JLT Services; Waterbury; insurance brokers 802
Hospital for Special Care; New Britain 800
Manafort Brothers Inc.; Plainville; excavation work 800
Bozzuto's Inc.; Cheshire; food supplier 800
Grolier Inc.; Danbury; book publishing 790
Meriden; Meriden; city management 760
Stanley Works Inc.; New Britain; builders' hardware 725
Philips Electronics North America Corp.; Cheshire; switchgear and switchboard apparatus 700
United Technologies Corp.; Cheshire; aircraft, heavy equipment repair 700
Northrop Grumman Component Technologies; Watertown; infrared sensors 700
Midstate Medical Center; Meriden 670
Charlotte Hungerford Hospital; Torrington 648
Rescare Premier; Farmington; residential care for handicapped 600
Ensign-Bickford Industries Inc.; Simsbury; high explosives detonators 600
McLean Fund; Simsbury; charitable trust management 600
Gillette Co.; Bethel; storage batteries 600
Cendant Mobility Services Corp.; Danbury; relocation service 600
Goodrich Corp.; Danbury; aircraft research and development 600
MacDermid Graphic Arts; Waterbury; printing plates 599
Pitney Bowes Inc.; Danbury; photographic equipment, supplies 563
New Milford Hospital Holding Corp.; New Milford; hospital management 550
Siemon Co.; Watertown; thermoformed finished plastics products 537
Becton Dickinson and Co.; Canaan; hypodermic needles and syringes 500
Siemens VDO Automotive Corp.; Cheshire; electrical equipment and supplies 500
United Technologies Corp.; Meriden; aircraft engines and parts 500
TI Group Automotive Systems Corp.; Meriden; seamless steel tubes 500
City of Waterbury; Waterbury; police dept. 500
Opticare Eye Health Center; Waterbury 500
City of Torrington; Torrington; public elementary schools 500
General Electric Capital Corp.; Danbury; intermediate investment banks 500

NEW CASTLE

Wilmington

Newark

Dover

KENT

At Large

Rehoboth Beach

SUSSEX

Bethany Beach

Delaware

It is not hard to stump people with a question about Delaware, a small state tucked between parts of larger states in a pocket of the East Coast that is often overlooked. Weighing in at less than 2,500 square miles, Delaware is larger only than Rhode Island (and that only slightly). Its population is likely to be surpassed by Alaska's before 2010.

Swedes established the first permanent European settlement here, building Fort Christina in 1638 where Wilmington is today. They soon gave way to the Dutch, who gave way to the English, who turned it over to William Penn, founder of Pennsylvania. Delaware became the Three Lower Counties of Penn's colony but soon chafed at that status. Shortly after the Revolutionary War began, the three broke away to form their own state. That status was confirmed in the Constitution of 1787, which Delaware was eager to ratify, becoming the first state to do so.

Wilmington is still around, and still Delaware's main city. But it has long been overshadowed by Philadelphia just a few miles up the Delaware River. Nowadays, both Wilmington and its neighbor Newark, Delaware's second-largest city, are considered part of the Philadelphia combined market statistical area—making them suburbs of a city in another state.

Delaware occupies the northeastern third and more of the Delmarva Peninsula, a body of land on the Atlantic seaboard south of New Jersey. It is shaped by Delaware Bay and the ocean on the east and by Chesapeake Bay on the west and south. The rest of the peninsula is occupied by the Eastern Shore of Maryland (which wraps around Delaware on the west and south) and, at the tip, by a vestige of Virginia.

Like other small states Delaware has been largely dependent on a single industry. Before 1800, it was flour milling in the Wilmington area. Just after the turn of that century E. I. du Pont opened a new mill there to make gunpowder. That mill grew into the DuPont Corporation, the most important chemical manufacturer in the country and the most important employer in the state. DuPont (the business is spelled differently) would be important to every American war thereafter and the source of countless products from nylon to Teflon that changed how the world lived.

The du Pont family also sank deep roots in the culture and politics of the state. Descendants of the founder have been a kind of local aristocracy with influence in the private and public spheres. The most recent example was Pierre S. (Pete) du Pont IV, who served as Republican governor for two terms until 1985, then ran for president in 1988.

Since the late 1800s, however, the state has also derived a special identity from its liberal laws of incorporation. The state is still the No. 1 incorporation for Fortune 500 companies and No. 2 for Forbes 500 companies. Many of the nation's largest banks, especially credit card firms, have their legal headquarters here, a point emphasized by the gleaming high-rise office towers that loom over historic Wilmington's otherwise low-rise downtown. Another way to put it: the state ranks first in the nation in financial institution assets, including federally insured commercial banks with $83.5 billion in insured deposits at the close of the 1990s.

All this helped spare Delaware the brunt of the recession in the early 1990s. The state ended the decade with nearly the lowest unemployment rate in the country, ranked in the top 12 states for personal income per capita, and basking in successive rounds of tax cuts by governors from both parties. The population rose over the decade by a respectable 17.6 percent, making this the only state in the Northeast to beat the national growth rate of 13.2 percent. Still, it is hard to imagine Delaware ever recapturing its second seat in Congress, which it lost after the census of 1820.

South of Wilmington and across the Chesapeake-Delaware canal, the landscape stays flat and the population sparse all the way to the coast. The state capital remains in centrally located Dover, where it was moved to escape British troops in Wilmington during the Revolutionary War. The city features the Dover Downs International Speedway, part of the NASCAR circuit and a major tourist attraction in the summer. Outside of town is a major Air Force base of the same name that is home to the main mortuary for the U.S. military.

Agriculture is mostly small scale (soybeans, potatoes, corn) except for the poultry factories that mass-produce for the tables of the Mid-Atlantic region. An agricultural survey in 2002 counted nearly 250 million broilers and 1.3 million chickens other than broilers.

Tourism is a significant contributor, as visitors spent $1.1 billion in 1999. Completion of the towering Chesapeake Bay Bridge helped beach communities such as Rehoboth, Dewey, and Bethany lure license plates from the Baltimore and Washington, D.C., areas as well as from metro Philadelphia and southern New Jersey. The arrival of increasing numbers of Washington people has earned Rehoboth the sobriquet of "the nation's summer capital." The growing number of retirees in these beach communities has made rural Sussex County one of the state's fastest-growing areas and increased its conservative tenor.

Delaware has usually been a bellwether in national elections, voting with the winner consistently from 1952 until

201

2000. In 2000 the state could at least say it went with the winner of the nationwide popular vote, in this case Democrat Al Gore, who got one of his best showings here (55 percent).

Delaware's internal politics tend to be a bipartisan, almost homey affair. Voters pursue ticket-splitting with rare relish at all levels, and the state is generally incumbent-friendly. The state has territory both north and south of the Mason-Dixon line, and it was one of the slave-holding states in the union that did not secede in 1861. Over the years it has had affinity for southern Democrats and for more modern national Democrats, for moderate-to-liberal Republicans and conservatives.

Democrats are strong in Wilmington. Fifty years ago, almost half the state's residents lived here, but the city's 73,000 residents now cast only about 10 percent of Delaware's vote, largely because of migration to the booming suburbs. The pocket-size capital, Dover, set in Kent County, also has a Democratic constituency. Dover is where everyone knows everyone else well, and for their part voters prefer not to be forced to choose between popular politicians. The GOP's strength lies in Wilmington's suburbs and south of the Chesapeake-Delaware canal, in the poultry farms and coastal marshes of the Delmarva Peninsula.

Major Industry

Financial services, manufacturing, tourism.

Notable

Ralph Nader's report, "The Company State" (1971), described the du Pont family's influence on Delaware—the family once owned the newspaper and held the governor's mansion; Delaware in 1787 was the first state to ratify the Constitution.

Table 1 Population

District	Population	Population under 18	Voting-age population	Median age	Male*	Female*
At Large	783,600	194,587	589,013	36.0	48.6	51.4

*As percentage of total population.

Table 2 Voting-Age Persons by Race/Hispanic or Latino Origin

District	White*	Black or African American*	American Indian or Alaska Native*	Asian*	Other or multirace*	Hispanic or Latino*
At Large	75.2	17.4	0.3	2.1	1.0	4.0

*As percentage of voting-age population.

Table 3 Voting-Age Population by Age Groups

District	18 to 24*	25 to 44*	45 to 64*	Over 64*
At Large	12.8	40.1	29.8	17.3

*As percentage of voting-age population.

Table 4 Income and Occupation

District	Median family income	Families in poverty*	White collar†	Blue collar†	Service†	Farm†
At Large	$55,257	6.5	62.9	22.0	14.6	0.5

*As percentage of all families.   †As percentage of employed workers 16 years and over.

Table 5 Education: School Years Completed

District	Less than grade 9*	Grades 9–12 no diploma*	High school diploma no college*	Some college*	College bachelor's degree or higher*
At Large	5.0	12.4	31.4	26.1	25.0

*As percentage of persons age 25 and over.

Table 6 Housing and Residential Patterns

District	Median home value	Owner occupied*	Renter occupied*	Urban†	Rural†
At Large	$122,000	72.3	27.7	80.0	20.0

*As percentage of occupied housing units.   †As percentage of total population.

Election Returns

	Republican		Democratic		Other	
President 2000	137,288	41.9%	180,068	55.0%	10,173	3.1%
House 2002	164,605	72.1%	61,011	26.7%	2,789	1.2%

District Profile

Population 783,600

Total area (square miles) 2,489.2
  Land area (square miles) 1,953.5

Population per square mile 401.1

Counties (2000 population)
  Kent 126,697   Sussex 156,638
  New Castle 500,265

Cities and other areas over 10,000 (2000 population)
  Bear CDP 17,593   Hockessin CDP 12,902
  Brookside CDP 14,806   Newark 28,547
  Dover 32,135   Pike Creek CDP 19,751
  Glasgow CDP 12,840   Wilmington 72,664

Race and Hispanic or Latino origin*
  White 72.5%
  Black or African American 18.9%
  American Indian or Alaska Native 0.3%
  Asian 2.1%
  Native Hawaiian or other Pacific Islander 0.0%
  Some other race 0.1%
  Hispanic or Latino origin 4.8%
  Two or more races 1.3%

*As percentage of total population.

Ancestry*
  Dutch 1.1%   Italian 7.1%
  English 9.2%   Polish 4.0%
  French 1.6%   Scotch-Irish 1.1%
  German 10.9%   Scottish 1.5%
  Irish 12.6%   USA/American 4.6%

*As estimated percentage of total population.

Universities and colleges, 2000–2001 enrollment
Delaware State University, Dover   3,103
Delaware Technical & Community College-Owens, Georgetown   3,439
Delaware Technical & Community College-Stanton-Wilmington, Newark   6,622
Delaware Technical & Community College-Terry, Dover   1,958
Goldey-Beacom College, Wilmington   1,337
University of Delaware, Newark   19,072
Wesley College, Dover   1,595
Widener University-Delaware, Wilmington   1,323
Wilmington College, New Castle   5,298

Newspapers and circulation

	District circulation	Total circulation
Baltimore Sun	2,127	268,280
Philadelphia Daily News	2,813	151,682
Philadelphia Inquirer	3,401	371,901
Salisbury Daily Times	1,902	25,978
*USA Today**	7,001	1,674,376
Washington Post	1,901	779,632
Wilmington News Journal	111,382	121,217

Television stations and affiliations
Philadelphia	52%	KYW	CBS
Philadelphia	52%	WBPH	Independent
Philadelphia	52%	WCAU	NBC
Philadelphia	52%	WFMZ	Independent
Philadelphia	52%	WHYY	PBS
Philadelphia	52%	WLVT	PBS
Philadelphia	52%	WMGM	NBC
Philadelphia	52%	WNJS	PBS
Philadelphia	52%	WNJT	PBS
Philadelphia	52%	WPHL	WB
Philadelphia	52%	WPPX	PAX
Philadelphia	52%	WPSG	UPN
Philadelphia	52%	WPVI	ABC
Philadelphia	52%	WTVE	Independent
Philadelphia	52%	WTXF	FOX
Philadelphia	52%	WWAC	Independent
Philadelphia	52%	WYBE	PBS
Salisbury, MD	48%	WBOC	CBS
Salisbury, MD	48%	WCPB	PBS
Salisbury, MD	48%	WDPB	PBS
Salisbury, MD	48%	WMDT	ABC

Cable systems and subscribers
Charter   1,475
Comcast   170,245
Mediacom   41,572

Military installations, September 2001
Dover Air Force Base, Dover   6,167
New Castle Airport Air Force Guard Station, Newport   1,080

Businesses and other major employers
MBNA Corp.; Wilmington; commercial bank   11,000
E. I. Du Pont De Nemours and Co.; Hockessin; petroleum bulk stations/terminals   6,000
E. I. Du Pont De Nemours and Co.; Wilmington; photographic equipment, supplies   5,000
Phillips Petroleum International Investment Co. Inc.; Wilmington; management consulting   3,500
E. I. Du Pont De Nemours and Co.; Wilmington; explosives   3,500
Dupont Dow Elastomers; Wilmington; synthetic rubber   3,300
University of Delaware; Newark   3,164
Saturn Corp.; Wilmington; automobiles   3,054
DaimlerChrysler Corp.; Newark; motor vehicles and car bodies   3,000
Christiana Care Health System; Newark   3,000
E. I. Du Pont De Nemours and Co.; Wilmington; technical institute   3,000
Appleton Investments; Wilmington; paper mills   2,700
Spring Cave Inc.; Wilmington; women's clothing stores   2,573
AstraZeneca Pharmaceuticals LP; Wilmington; pharmaceuticals   2,500
E. I. Du Pont De Nemours and Co.; Seaford; nylon yarn   2,500
First USA Bank; Wilmington; commercial bank   2,400
General Motors Corp.; Wilmington; motor vehicle parts/accessories   2,100
RBC Insurance Holding (USA) Inc.; Wilmington; life insurance   2,024
E. I. Du Pont De Nemours and Co.; Newark; medical instruments   2,000
Delaware Dept. of Health and Social Services; New Castle   2,000
Du Pont Pharmaceutical Co.; Wilmington; biological research   2,000
Wilmington Trust Co.; Wilmington; mortgage bankers   2,000
Dupont Hospital for Children; Wilmington   1,994
Citicorp International Technology Inc.; New Castle; mortgage bankers   1,600
Chase Manhattan USA Inc.; Wilmington; state commercial banks   1,527
Wilmington Trust Co.; Wilmington; mortgage investment trusts   1,500
PFPC Inc.; Wilmington; accounting services   1,500
J. P. Morgan Chase Bank; Newark; commercial bank   1,400
Sears Roebuck and Co. Inc.; New Castle; department stores   1,400
Bay Health Medical Center Inc.; Dover; hospital   1,355
Prince Telecom Holdings Inc.; New Castle; telecommunication equipment repair   1,250
Delaware Dept. of Transportation; Dover   1,250
Perdue Farms Inc.; Georgetown; processed poultry   1,200
ConAgra Poultry Co.; Milford; processed poultry   1,200
J. P. Morgan Services Inc.; Newark; data processing   1,000
E. I. Du Pont De Nemours and Co.; Newark; biological research   1,000
Christiana Care Health Services; Wilmington   1,000
City of Wilmington; Wilmington; city management   1,000
Delaware Racing Assn. Inc.; Wilmington; horse race track   1,000

St. Francis Hospital Inc.; Wilmington 1,000

TCIM Services; Wilmington; telemarketing services 1,000

E. I. Du Pont De Nemours and Co.; Wilmington; commercial physical research 1,000

Dover Downs Gaming and Entertainment; Dover; casino hotel 1,000

Playtex Manufacturing Inc.; Dover; sanitary paper products 1,000

New Castle County Vocational School District; Wilmington 900

Agilent Technologies Inc.; Wilmington; chromatographic equipment 900

E. I. Du Pont De Nemours and Co.; Newark; industrial organic chemicals 815

E. I. Du Pont De Nemours and Co.; Newark; libraries 800

Ace USA Inc.; Wilmington; fire, marine, casualty insurance 800

Kraft Foods Inc.; Dover; gelatin dessert preparations 800

Allen Family Foods Inc.; Harbeson; processed poultry 800

Beebe Medical Center Inc.; Lewes 782

Delmarva Power and Light Co.; Newark; electric power generation 750

Jones Lang Lasalle Inc.; Wilmington; building operation 750

Delaware Dept. of Health and Social Services; Georgetown 750

Delaware Dept. of Health and Social Services; Smyrna 750

American Postal Workers Union; New Castle; labor union 720

Discover Financial Services Inc.; Newark; credit card service 700

Bank of New York Delaware; Newark; credit card service 700

Rodel Inc.; Newark; polishes and sanitation goods 700

Gannett Co. Inc.; New Castle; newspaper 700

U. S. Postal Service; New Castle 700

U. S. Environmental Protection Agency; Dover; environmental research 700

Capital School District; Dover 700

Nanticoke Memorial Hospital Inc.; Seaford 655

Avon Products Inc.; Newark; drugs, proprietaries, sundries 650

Hercules Inc.; Wilmington; speciality chemicals 650

Zenith Products Corp.; New Castle; organizers for closets, drawers 630

New Castle County; New Castle; county police 616

AstraZeneca Pharmaceuticals LP; Newark; pharmaceuticals 600

Fleet National Bank; Newark; bank holding companies 600

Motiva Enterprises; Delaware City; petroleum refining 600

Christiana Care Health Services; New Castle 600

PNC Bancorp Inc.; Wilmington; commercial trust company 600

Sears Roebuck and Co. Inc.; Wilmington; department stores 600

Delaware Dept. of Corrections; Smyrna 600

Delaware State University; Dover 594

Applied Card Systems Inc.; Wilmington; credit card service 501

Cape May Lewes Ferry; New Castle; ferries 500

Cigna Corp.; New Castle; insurance agents and brokers 500

Atlantic City Electric Co.; Wilmington; electric power generation 500

Computer Aid Inc.; Wilmington; computer programming services 500

Delaware Supreme Court; Wilmington; state courts 500

J. R. Gettier and Associates Inc.; Wilmington; detective services 500

U. S. Veterans Hospital; Wilmington 500

Electronic Payment Services Inc.; Wilmington; investment holding company 500

Bank of America Corp.; Dover; commercial bank 500

Delaware Dept. of Natural Resources; Dover; air, water, solid waste management 500

Polo Retail Corp.; Dover; housewares 500

Catalog Resources Inc.; Dover; catalog, mail-order 500

Wendover Inc.; Dover; fast-food restaurant chain 500

Metal Masters Foodservice Equipment Co.; Clayton; commercial cooking, food service equipment 500

Dentsply International Inc.; Milford; dental equipment 500

Intervet Inc.; Millsboro; veterinary biological products 500

Florida

Until the year 2000, Florida made people think about vacation, sun, beaches, retirement, sports, even swamps—anything but politics. Then came the unforgettable election of 2000. Since then, it has been difficult to think of Florida without recalling butterfly ballots, "hanging chads," and the nightmare struggle to recount one state's vote and determine the nation's leader.

The state did not play much of a role in national politics until late in the twentieth century. It was smaller than Arkansas until World War II and beset with acute growing pains thereafter. But with the 2000 census the state had nearly 16 million residents in the 2000 census, giving it the status of the fourth most populous state and on a trajectory to surpass New York sometime before 2025.

More than any of the other Sun Belt success stories, Florida has been transformed by automobiles and air conditioning, refugees from northern winters, and Caribbean politics. Successive waves of immigrants have created a mélange of culture unique to a place and time that is almost entirely detached from the earlier history of Florida. Yet there was a Florida before the superhighways and luxury high-rises arrived.

Florida was originally annexed as a U.S. territory in 1819, ending three centuries of back-and-forth possession by warring European powers. But it took another quarter century to assemble a critical mass of residents and achieve statehood. The settled parts of the eastern seaboard regarded Florida as not only distant but remote—a pestilential swamp offering little enticement for development.

The parts of the state that settled first were primarily in the northern stretch, near the more populous and established state of Georgia. Here the culture was mostly southern and the economic institutions included slavery. Florida seceded with the Confederacy in 1861 and was not readmitted to the Union until 1868. Thereafter, growth was gradual. The railroads were slow to arrive and proliferate around the state. Florida did not have even a second congressional seat until 1870 and waited another 30 years for its third.

But in the middle decades of the twentieth century, the outward pressure from the great cities of the eastern seaboard began to be felt. A land boom in the 1920s thrived on the first blush of romance between Florida and its distant neighbor, New York, which even today supplies more of Florida's new residents than any other state. This growth was concentrated in South Florida, around Miami, Palm Beach, and the other Gold Coast communities up the coast.

Steady growth from 1900 to 1950 brought the House delegation to eight but then the curve turned sharply upward.

After the 1950s, the decade when air conditioning took hold, Florida claimed 12 House seats—a stunning expansion of 50 percent in a decade. That feat seemed impossible to duplicate, but during the next 30 years the delegation would nearly double again. This third wave of growth greatly benefited Central Florida, particularly the Interstate 4 corridor from Tampa Bay (with its two cities, Tampa and St. Petersburg) across to Orlando and on to the Atlantic Coast section that includes Cape Canaveral. This last was dubbed the "Space Coast" by Al Neuharth, the Gannett newspaper publisher who tested his ideas about TV-style newspapers there before founding *USA Today* in 1982.

The economy of Florida has been a perfect demonstration of how diversity and even tension between ethnicities need not be a bar to growth and prosperity. The state has long since transcended its image as an orange grove surrounded by swamps, becoming a power in manufacturing, trade, financial services, tourism, entertainment, and diversified agriculture—all on a world scale. The complex of attractions that has grown up near Orlando, keyed by the opening of Disney World in 1971, has made that city one of the principal destinations in the Western Hemisphere. Overall, tourism has risen to contribute one-fifth of the overall state economy.

But it took a long time to translate all this growth into commensurate political heft on the national stage. The state has not bred many national figures (former Gov. Reubin Askew ran briefly for president in 1984), and efforts to move its presidential primary to greater prominence have been frustrated. The state's Democratic senators did not leave great marks on Washington, and when Republicans occasionally won the job (1968, 1980, 1988) they were gone after a term or two. In the House, a few of the state's most senior manatees acquired the authority of major committee chairs: Claude Pepper chaired House Rules in the 1980s, C. W. "Bill" Young took over appropriations, and Porter Goss became chairman of Select Intelligence in the 1990s.

That was why Florida took the world by surprise in 2000, becoming the focal point of a presidential contest that wound up in the U.S. Supreme Court. The national election was so close in the Electoral College that without Florida's 25 votes neither Republican George W. Bush nor Democrat Al Gore could claim the White House. On Election Night the news networks called it first for Gore, then for Bush, and then declared it too close to call.

Ballots from contested areas were counted and recounted, impounded, battled over in court, shipped from one end of the state to the other, and finally counted again. After

FLORIDA

Districts established March 27, 2002, for elections first held in 2002.

25 members

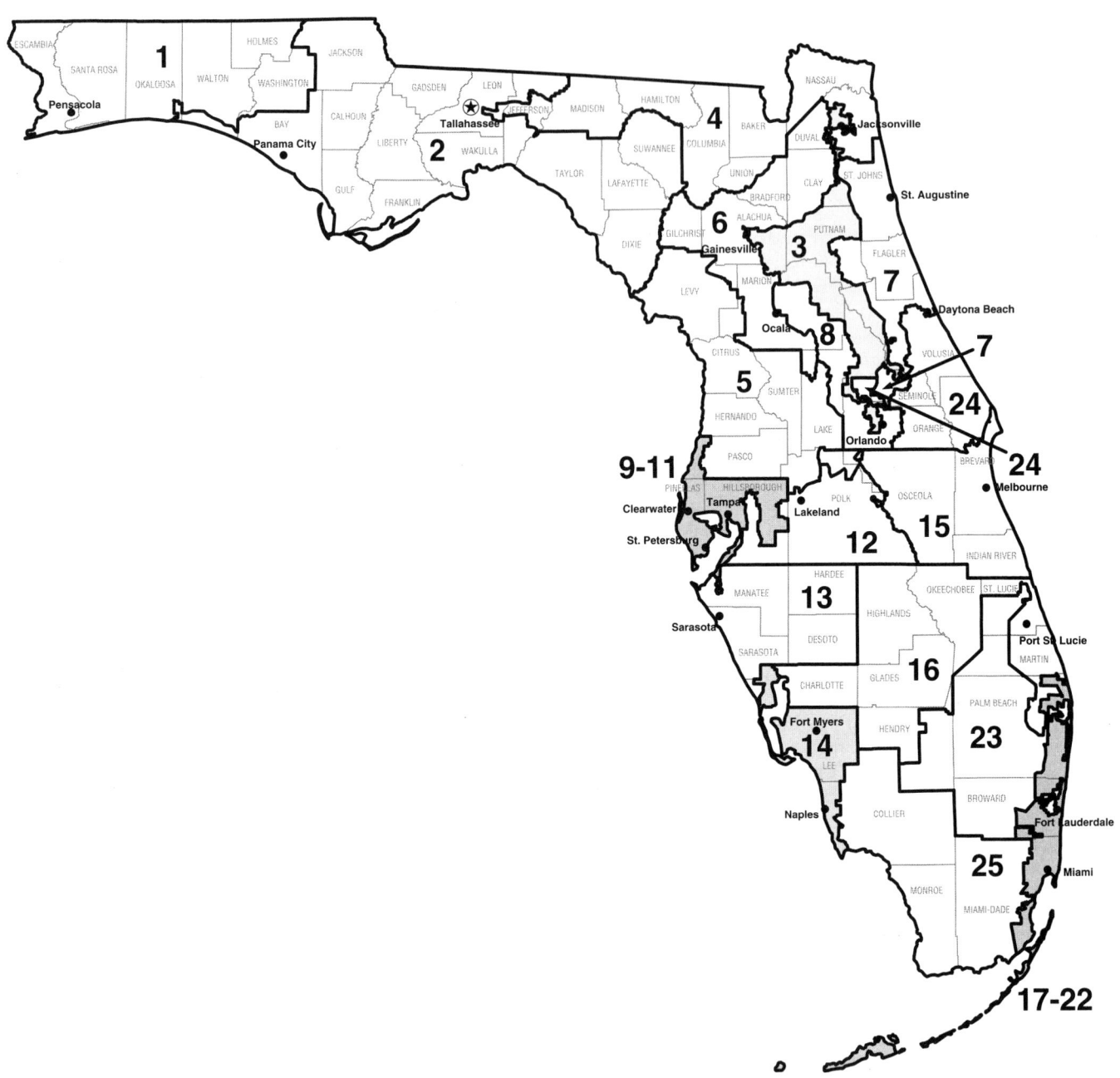

nearly five weeks of uncertainty bordering on chaos, the Supreme Court overruled the Florida supreme court, stopped the counting, and left standing the state of Florida's declared winner: Bush. Democrats were doubly incensed that this happened in a state where the governor was the presidential winner's brother, Jeb Bush, and where the state's election apparatus was in the hands of Republican elected officials closely tied to that governor.

To some degree, the nation moved beyond the Florida fiasco in 2001, especially after the terrorist strikes in September. But in 2002, the wound was reopened. The national Democratic Party leadership decided to concentrate its midterm election resources on gaining revenge for 2000 and experienced instead a stinging rebuke. The Democrats targeted Governor Bush but saw him reelected easily, along with his slate of GOP statewide nominees. Moreover, two of the key Republican figures in the vote-counting controversy—Katherine Harris and Tom Feeney—won seats in Congress. Harris had been the secretary of state who supervised the state's recounts and consistently interpreted state law to favor the Bush campaign. Feeney was the leader in the state House who successfully pressed legislators to meet in special session and declare Bush the winner, even while the controversy over the ballot recount raged.

The Florida ballot controversy brought into high relief a reality that had been developing here for decades. Growth had brought so many new people to the state that the old political paradigm had been broken. The Old South style of Democratic hegemony had been receding for years, leaving behind a mix of Republican domination in legislative races and two-party balance in statewide contests.

Presidential voting had followed a typical southern pattern in the era following the presidency of Democrat Lyndon B. Johnson, with regional Democrats such as Jimmy Carter and Bill Clinton proving competitive (each won once and lost once here), but those from up north (Michael Dukakis, Walter Mondale, George McGovern) getting less than 40 percent of the vote. Democrats did far better in the Senate races, winning eight of the eleven from 1970 to 2000, thanks primarily to three wins each by Lawton Chiles and Bob Graham. The governorship, long a presumptive possession for Democrats, went Republican for a term in 1966 (Claude Kirk) and then again for a term in 1986 (Bob Martinez). Then Jeb Bush got the job in 1998 and became the first Republican ever reelected to the office in 2002.

But in state legislative and congressional elections, Republicans have established a dominance unknown for the GOP elsewhere in the region. With the addition of two more congressional seats after 2000, the state reached a delegation of 25, and split 18 for the GOP and just 7 for Democrats in 2002. This ratio is matched by the partisan tilt of the legislature responsible for creating the districts, a body with nearly twice as many Republicans as Democrats at a time when statewide party registration was essentially even.

The Republicans in Tallahassee were not shy about fashioning district lines to suit their party purposes. The Republican mapmakers had several goals. First, they wanted both the new districts earned by population growth to favor Republican candidates, with one being Cuban American. Second, they wanted to hold on to seats vacated by retirement while shoring up some of their incumbents who had close calls in 2000. Third, they wanted to weaken some

Democratic incumbents enough to be beaten. Fourth and finally, they needed to accomplish all this without too much damage to the three African American districts created in 1992, lest the Justice Department disapprove and spike the whole plan. (Parts of Florida are subject to federal review of all election laws and rules under the Voting Rights Act of 1965.)

Few redistricting schemes achieve all their goals but this one came remarkably close. The first goal was met when Feeney won his newly created 24th District in the Orlando area and Mario Diaz-Balart, brother of an incumbent Republican representative, won the new 25th in Miami (which he had helped shape as chair of the redistricting committee in the state House). The second goal, holding GOP seats, was met perfectly as Harris filled the lone vacancy in the Sarasota-based 13th District even as 14 GOP incumbents were winning reelection with comparative ease. One Republican incumbent in the 22nd District around Fort Lauderdale saw his GOP registration go up 9 percentage points and his share of the November vote go up 11.

The score on the third goal was only a slight disappointment, as the Republicans were able to knock off just one Democratic incumbent in the 5th District north of Tampa Bay. The Democrats in the new 5th suffered the loss of Gainesville, with the University of Florida and many black voters, which left the district slightly more Republican than Democratic. The map was not as successful at destabilizing a more junior Democrat in the Dixie-like 2nd District around Tallahassee, or the black Democratic incumbent in the Jacksonville-based 3rd. Overall, though, the remappers could breathe easily when the Justice Department, and later a federal court, approved the new district designs statewide and specifically the three black districts.

Table 1   Population

District	Population	Population under 18	Voting-age population	Median age	Male*	Female*
1	639,295	155,724	483,571	36.1	50.2	49.8
2	639,295	145,541	493,754	35.1	49.7	50.3
3	639,295	181,062	458,233	32.4	48.5	51.5
4	639,295	155,780	483,515	35.5	49.9	50.1
5	639,295	129,570	509,725	45.5	48.9	51.1
6	639,295	146,508	492,787	36.6	49.0	51.0
7	639,295	141,557	497,738	40.7	48.5	51.5
8	639,295	149,181	490,114	36.3	49.0	51.0
9	639,296	140,136	499,160	41.1	48.0	52.0
10	639,295	115,345	523,950	43.9	47.9	52.1
11	639,295	161,173	478,122	34.2	48.5	51.5
12	639,296	161,119	478,177	37.4	49.1	50.9
13	639,295	115,198	524,097	47.4	48.4	51.6
14	639,295	116,938	522,357	47.4	48.7	51.3
15	639,295	141,291	498,004	41.0	48.8	51.2
16	639,295	134,633	504,662	44.5	49.2	50.8
17	639,296	187,428	451,868	32.6	47.7	52.3
18	639,295	123,522	515,773	39.5	49.4	50.6
19	639,295	120,872	518,423	45.1	46.9	53.1
20	639,295	136,040	503,255	39.2	48.3	51.7
21	639,295	156,004	483,291	36.0	47.9	52.1
22	639,295	120,591	518,704	43.0	48.8	51.2
23	639,295	179,980	459,315	33.1	49.4	50.6
24	639,295	147,987	491,308	37.5	49.5	50.5
25	639,295	183,160	456,135	32.7	49.5	50.5
State	15,982,378	3,646,340	12,336,038	38.7	48.8	51.2

*As percentage of total population.

Table 2 Voting-Age Persons by Race/Hispanic or Latino Origin

District	White*	Black or African American*	American Indian or Alaska Native*	Asian*	Other or multirace*	Hispanic or Latino*
1	80.1	12.5	0.9	2.1	1.6	2.8
2	73.2	20.8	0.5	1.3	1.1	3.1
3	43.2	45.1	0.3	1.9	2.0	7.5
4	79.6	12.4	0.4	2.5	1.3	3.9
5	89.3	4.0	0.3	0.7	0.7	4.8
6	80.9	10.5	0.3	2.4	1.2	4.8
7	83.4	7.9	0.3	1.4	1.0	6.2
8	72.8	6.3	0.3	3.0	1.6	16.0
9	87.2	3.0	0.2	1.7	1.0	6.9
10	89.7	2.9	0.3	2.1	1.1	3.8
11	53.0	23.9	0.3	2.3	1.6	19.0
12	76.1	11.3	0.3	1.1	1.1	10.1
13	88.5	3.6	0.2	0.7	0.7	6.3
14	86.8	4.0	0.2	0.7	0.8	7.5
15	80.6	6.3	0.3	1.6	1.2	9.9
16	84.6	4.9	0.3	0.9	0.8	8.5
17	21.5	51.3	0.1	1.7	3.3	22.0
18	29.6	4.7	0.1	1.0	0.8	63.9
19	80.8	4.9	0.1	1.8	1.3	11.1
20	69.1	7.0	0.2	2.2	1.7	19.8
21	19.1	6.1	0.0	1.8	0.8	72.2
22	84.2	3.2	0.1	1.6	1.2	9.7
23	35.0	46.2	0.2	1.4	4.0	13.2
24	81.8	5.7	0.3	2.0	1.2	8.9
25	23.3	9.2	0.1	1.7	1.4	64.3
State	68.4	12.3	0.3	1.6	1.3	16.1

*As percentage of voting-age population.

Table 3 Voting-Age Population by Age Groups

District	18 to 24*	25 to 44*	45 to 64*	Over 64*
1	13.6	39.6	30.0	16.8
2	17.3	37.6	29.5	15.6
3	14.9	42.0	28.0	15.1
4	12.2	43.4	29.9	14.6
5	7.2	29.3	31.4	32.1
6	15.8	35.4	28.7	20.1
7	10.2	34.4	32.0	23.4
8	11.7	42.2	28.2	18.0
9	8.4	35.3	30.1	26.3
10	7.5	33.5	30.4	28.5
11	13.8	42.3	27.7	16.1
12	11.3	36.7	29.1	22.9
13	7.2	28.0	30.0	34.8
14	6.9	28.2	31.4	33.5
15	9.2	34.7	30.2	25.9
16	7.6	30.1	30.1	32.3
17	14.3	41.8	28.7	15.3
18	10.1	38.4	29.4	22.2
19	7.2	31.1	25.2	36.6
20	8.4	40.7	28.9	22.1
21	11.3	42.2	29.5	17.1
22	7.1	35.4	31.8	25.7
23	13.8	42.8	26.5	16.9
24	12.2	39.0	29.7	19.1
25	13.3	46.4	28.2	12.0
State	10.8	37.0	29.4	22.8

*As percentage of voting-age population.

Table 4 Income and Occupation

District	Median family income	Families in poverty*	White collar†	Blue collar†	Service†	Farm†
1	$42,656	10.3	57.1	24.4	17.9	0.6
2	$43,496	11.1	61.7	19.3	17.7	1.4
3	$34,216	17.4	51.8	26.6	20.7	0.8
4	$51,472	6.6	64.8	20.6	14.1	0.6
5	$40,204	7.6	55.2	26.1	17.4	1.3
6	$44,815	8.3	61.4	21.7	16.0	0.9
7	$48,369	7.0	63.2	20.3	15.8	0.6
8	$48,078	6.9	63.6	19.3	16.8	0.4
9	$49,756	6.0	68.0	17.6	13.9	0.5
10	$47,118	5.8	64.9	19.9	15.0	0.2
11	$39,492	13.4	61.4	21.2	17.0	0.4
12	$43,389	9.0	55.9	26.1	16.0	1.9
13	$47,780	6.1	58.5	21.0	17.9	2.5
14	$49,608	5.9	59.6	21.1	18.5	0.8
15	$45,860	7.1	58.4	21.5	19.4	0.7
16	$45,950	6.7	57.5	21.8	17.3	3.3
17	$33,677	20.0	52.5	24.0	23.2	0.3
18	$38,509	14.5	60.1	20.6	18.5	0.8
19	$51,689	5.2	67.1	17.1	15.4	0.3
20	$54,631	6.8	69.4	16.0	14.4	0.2
21	$44,799	10.6	63.6	22.6	13.7	0.2
22	$64,685	4.6	69.4	16.0	14.4	0.3
23	$35,126	18.3	48.0	25.8	24.5	1.7
24	$50,858	5.5	65.3	19.4	14.9	0.4
25	$46,820	11.0	61.7	20.8	15.3	2.2
State	$45,625	9.0	61.1	21.1	16.9	0.9

*As percentage of all families.   †As percentage of employed workers 16 years and over.

Table 5 Education: School Years Completed

District	Less than grade 9*	Grades 9–12 no diploma*	High school diploma no college*	Some college*	College bachelor's degree or higher*
1	5.2	12.3	29.4	32.9	20.2
2	6.2	13.7	28.8	27.2	24.1
3	8.2	20.4	31.4	27.0	12.9
4	4.1	11.2	28.7	31.6	24.4
5	5.6	15.6	36.6	27.9	14.3
6	4.6	12.6	31.3	30.0	21.4
7	4.3	11.2	28.7	31.3	24.5
8	4.8	11.4	27.6	30.2	25.9
9	4.5	11.9	29.0	30.0	24.6
10	3.8	12.0	30.2	31.5	22.6
11	7.6	15.8	27.5	27.8	21.2
12	7.9	15.8	32.5	27.2	16.6
13	5.2	11.0	31.3	28.8	23.7
14	4.5	11.3	30.6	29.2	24.4
15	4.5	11.7	29.8	31.8	22.3
16	6.0	13.1	31.6	29.3	20.0
17	12.2	21.3	28.6	24.4	13.5
18	16.6	16.2	20.1	21.5	25.6
19	4.1	10.2	30.3	29.6	25.7
20	4.5	10.3	26.3	29.4	29.6
21	14.8	16.4	21.5	24.4	22.9
22	3.2	8.2	23.9	30.7	34.1
23	12.2	21.3	29.8	23.9	12.8
24	3.6	10.1	27.6	33.3	25.5
25	12.5	15.1	24.1	28.0	20.3
State	6.7	13.4	28.7	28.8	22.3

*As percentage of persons age 25 and over.

Table 6 Housing and Residential Patterns

District	Median home value	Owner occupied*	Renter occupied*	Urban†	Rural†
1	$85,000	70.6	29.4	77.5	22.5
2	$81,600	68.4	31.6	62.1	37.9
3	$66,200	55.7	44.3	89.7	10.3
4	$94,500	69.3	30.7	78.2	21.8
5	$78,800	85.2	14.8	64.5	35.5
6	$83,300	72.9	27.1	69.4	30.6
7	$96,700	74.1	25.9	86.7	13.3
8	$97,400	66.3	33.7	91.7	8.3
9	$91,500	76.3	23.7	93.8	6.2
10	$84,700	71.7	28.3	100.0	0.0
11	$78,200	55.5	44.5	99.6	0.4
12	$76,900	72.6	27.4	84.3	15.7
13	$101,700	77.5	22.5	89.4	10.6
14	$112,600	77.3	22.7	90.7	9.3
15	$91,100	73.2	26.8	89.6	10.4
16	$88,900	81.6	18.4	84.5	15.5
17	$84,300	57.4	42.6	100.0	0.0
18	$149,100	47.9	52.1	99.1	0.9
19	$96,600	79.1	20.9	99.6	0.4
20	$110,400	70.0	30.0	99.7	0.3
21	$128,200	61.9	38.1	99.9	0.1
22	$146,900	74.4	25.6	99.2	0.8
23	$77,500	56.5	43.5	97.9	2.1
24	$97,700	74.3	25.7	91.2	8.8
25	$117,100	72.7	27.3	94.4	5.6
State	$93,200	70.1	29.9	89.3	10.7

*As percentage of occupied housing units.   †As percentage of total population.

Florida 1st District

Panhandle — Pensacola, Fort Walton Beach

Some residents of the 1st refer to the area as "Lower Alabama," and in spirit the area is much closer to the Old South than the state's big metropolitan areas. The district, which stretches from north of Panama City to Pensacola, has several large military bases and a mostly white population. Its Gulf Coast beaches and open spaces attract both tourists and residents seeking a small-town feel. Walton and Okaloosa Counties (part of which are in the 2nd) increased their populations by more than 40 percent in the 1990s.

Tourism, health care, and retirement communities helped boost an economy slowed by manufacturing losses in the 1980s and early 1990s. Growth here is slower than in Florida's southern regions, but St. Joe, a paper company turned real estate giant, is planning to develop largely rural northwestern Florida. Interstate 10 slips between the Blackwater River State Forest, which borders Alabama, and Eglin Air Force Base, connecting the western tip and Pensacola to the rest of the state.

The 1st is more staunchly conservative than its slight GOP registration advantage indicates. The district's Democrats are more "Dixiecrats" than liberals, and several local and state officials from the area have switched to the GOP after decades as Democrats. The military presence also plays a significant role in politics; a large segment of the Okaloosa population is military employees. Republican governor Jeb Bush took 77 percent in Okaloosa and 75 percent in Santa Rosa in the 2002 election, his second- and third-best showings in the state.

Major Industry
Defense, health care, tourism.

Notable
The "Blue Angels" flight group is housed at Naval Air Station Pensacola; much of the movie *The Truman Show* was filmed in the town of Seaside.

Election Returns

	Republican		Democratic		Other
President 2000	173,896	68.9%	78,469	31.1%	
House 2002	152,635	74.6%	51,972	25.4%	19

District Profile

Population   639,295

Total area (square miles)   5,241.2
  Land area (square miles)   4,641.7

Population per square mile   137.7

Counties (2000 population)
Escambia 294,410	Santa Rosa 117,743
Holmes 18,564	Walton (pt.) 30,864
Okaloosa (pt.) 156,741	Washington 20,973

Cities and other areas over 10,000 (2000 population)
Bellview CDP   21,201
Brent CDP   22,257
Crestview   14,766
Ensley CDP   18,752
Ferry Pass CDP   27,176
Fort Walton Beach   19,973
Gonzalez CDP   11,365
Myrtle Grove CDP   17,211
Niceville (pt.)   11,552
Pensacola   56,255
Warrington CDP   15,207
West Pensacola CDP   21,939
Wright CDP   21,697

Race and Hispanic or Latino origin*
White   78.0%
Black or African American   14.0%
American Indian or Alaska Native   0.9%
Asian   1.9%
Native Hawaiian or other Pacific Islander   0.1%
Some other race   0.2%
Hispanic or Latino origin   3.0%
Two or more races   2.0%

*As percentage of total population.

Ancestry*
Dutch 1.1%	Italian 2.7%
English 7.7%	Polish 1.3%
French 2.3%	Scotch-Irish 2.0%
German 8.8%	Scottish 1.8%
Irish 8.5%	USA/American 10.7%

*As estimated percentage of total population.

Universities and colleges, 2000–2001 enrollment
George Stone Area Vocational Technical Center, Pensacola   537
Okaloosa Applied Technology Center, Ft. Walton Beach   860

Okaloosa-Walton Community College, Niceville 6,663

Pensacola Junior College, Pensacola   9,985

Radford M. Locklin Technical Center, Milton   322

University of West Florida, Pensacola   8,479

Washington-Holmes Technical Center, Chipley   712

Newspapers and circulation

	District circulation	Total circulation
Northwest Florida Daily News	34,006	38,547
Panama City News Herald	1,639	30,370
Pensacola News Journal	57,903	62,983
*USA Today**	5,721	1,674,376

See Sources and Explanations in the front of the volume.

Television stations and affiliations

Mobile-Pensacola (Ft. Walton Beach)	59%	WALA	FOX
Mobile-Pensacola (Ft. Walton Beach)	59%	WAWD	Independent
Mobile-Pensacola (Ft. Walton Beach)	59%	WEAR	ABC
Mobile-Pensacola (Ft. Walton Beach)	59%	WEIQ	PBS
Mobile-Pensacola (Ft. Walton Beach)	59%	WFGX	Independent
Mobile-Pensacola (Ft. Walton Beach)	59%	WHBR	Independent
Mobile-Pensacola (Ft. Walton Beach)	59%	WJTC	UPN
Mobile-Pensacola (Ft. Walton Beach)	59%	WKRG	CBS
Mobile-Pensacola (Ft. Walton Beach)	59%	WMPV	Independent
Mobile-Pensacola (Ft. Walton Beach)	59%	WPAN	Independent
Mobile-Pensacola (Ft. Walton Beach)	59%	WPMI	NBC
Mobile-Pensacola (Ft. Walton Beach)	59%	WSRE	PBS
Panama City	41%	WFSG	PBS
Panama City	41%	WJHG	NBC, UPN
Panama City	41%	WMBB	ABC
Panama City	41%	WPGX	FOX
Panama City	41%	WTVY	CBS

Cable systems and subscribers

Cable Community Corp.   681

Comcast   1,001

Cox   142,996

Mallard   1,063

Mediacom   24,148

Time Warner   4,283

Military installations, September 2001

Pensacola Naval Air Station, Pensacola   11,176

Eglin Air Force Base, Valparaiso   10,545

Eglin Auxiliary Air Field 9, Mary Esther   7,551

Pensacola Naval Hospital, Pensacola   2,200

Eglin Auxiliary Air Field 3, Crestview   1,528

Whiting Field Naval Air Station, Milton   833

PWC Pensacola (Navy), Pensacola   332

Eglin Auxiliary Air Field 6, Milton   129

Businesses and other major employers

Solutia Inc.; Cantonment; organic fibers   2,500

Paymaster Management Inc.; Fort Walton Beach; employee leasing service   2,500

Florida Dept. of Children and Families; Pensacola   2,000

Sacred Heart Hospital of Pensacola Inc.; Pensacola   1,990

University of West Florida; Pensacola   1,901

Baptist Hospital; Pensacola   1,641

West Florida Regional Medical Center Inc.; Pensacola 1,520

Sikorsky Aircraft Corp.; Pensacola; aircraft   1,505

Santa Rosa Board of Public Instruction; Milton   1,400

Pensacola Christian College Inc.; Pensacola   1,200

Hospital Corporation of America; Pensacola   1,200

Escambia County; Pensacola; sheriff's office   1,100

Pensacola Junior College Inc.; Pensacola   1,000

U.S. Defense Dept.; Pensacola   1,000

SouthTrust Bank; Fort Walton Beach; commercial bank 1,000

City of Pensacola; Pensacola; mayor's office   819

NT Corp.; Pensacola; online service providers   800

Fort Walton Beach Medical Center; Fort Walton Beach 750

Stron International Inc.; Pensacola; management consulting 700

Okaloosa County; Fort Walton Beach; public utility commission   700

Sandestin Resorts Inc.; Destin; resort hotel   700

WestPoint Stevens Inc.; Chipley; broadwoven fabric mills, cotton   691

CBS Corp.; Pensacola; power generators   625

Perdue Farms Inc.; De Funiak Springs; chicken processing 600

Navy Exchange Service Command; Pensacola; Army-Navy goods stores   600

APAC Holdings Inc.; Valparaiso; highway and street construction   600

Army and Air Force Exchange Service; Hurlburt Field; Army-Navy goods stores   550

Wayne-Dalton Corp.; Pensacola; wood garage doors   500

Army and Air Force Exchange Service; Eglin AFB; Army-Navy goods stores   500

Spanish Broadcasting System Inc.; Gulf Breeze; tax return preparation services   500

Florida 2nd District

Panhandle — part of Tallahassee, Panama City

The 2nd stretches around Florida's Big Bend, joining the Panhandle with the state capital of Tallahassee (a small part of which is in the 4th District) and the north-central part of the state. Taking in all or part of 16 counties, the district features tobacco and peanut farms, forests, and uncongested towns. While safely Democratic, the 2nd is not as liberal as districts in southeast Florida.

Democrats outnumber Republicans more than two to one, but many have conservative views on fiscal and social issues. The exception is the Tallahassee area (Leon County), home to Florida State University and Florida A&M University, where a more liberal sentiment exists. Panama City has a stronger conservative element, as do the smaller communities that ring the Gulf Coast. Black residents—the majority of whom live in the Tallahassee area or in neighboring Gadsden County—make up about one-fifth of the district's voting-age population. The 2002 Democratic gubernatorial nominee took at least 60 percent of the vote in Gadsden, Leon, Jefferson, and Liberty Counties.

The 2nd's economy is driven by its land—from the Gulf Coast beaches where oysters are harvested to farms stocked with soybeans and peanuts. Agriculture has struggled occasionally because of bad weather and low prices, but a steady base of government employees buffers any long-term economic effects. Florida's forestry industry has suffered some setbacks but maintains a strong presence. Panama City relies on tourism and the economic benefits of the military community around Tyndall Air Force Base.

Major Industry

Agriculture, government, manufacturing.

Notable

The Suwannee River was made famous by Stephen Foster's song, "Old Folks at Home"; Liberty County has the fewest registered Republicans of any county in the state—206 as of October 2002.

Election Returns

	Republican		Democratic		Other
President 2000	132,275	52.7%	118,758	47.3%	
House 2002	75,275	33.1%	152,164	66.9%	

District Profile

Population 639,295

Total area (square miles) 11,141.1
    Land area (square miles) 9,424.8

Population per square mile 67.8

Counties (2000 population)

Bay 148,217	Lafayette 7,022
Calhoun 13,017	Leon (pt.) 226,973
Dixie 13,827	Liberty 7,021
Franklin 11,057	Okaloosa (pt.) 13,757
Gadsden 45,087	Suwannee 34,844
Gulf 13,332	Taylor 19,256
Jackson 46,755	Wakulla 22,863
Jefferson (pt.) 6,530	Walton (pt.) 9,737

Cities and other areas over 10,000 (2000 population)
    Callaway 14,233
    Lynn Haven 12,451
    Panama City 36,417
    Tallahassee (pt.) 147,167
    Upper Grand Lagoon CDP 10,889

Race and Hispanic or Latino origin*
    White 71.5%
    Black or African American 22.1%
    American Indian or Alaska Native 0.5%
    Asian 1.2%
    Native Hawaiian or other Pacific Islander 0.0%
    Some other race 0.1%
    Hispanic or Latino origin 3.3%
    Two or more races 1.3%

*As percentage of total population.

Ancestry*

English 8.0%	Italian 2.2%
French 2.0%	Scotch-Irish 1.8%
German 7.6%	Scottish 1.7%
Irish 7.9%	USA/American 10.3%

*As estimated percentage of total population.

Universities and colleges, 2000–2001 enrollment
    Chipola Junior College, Marianna 1,845
    Florida Agricultural and Mechanical University, Tallahassee 12,126

Florida Baptist Theological College, Graceville 549
Florida State University, Tallahassee 33,971
Gulf Coast Community College, Panama City 5,341
Lively Technical Center, Tallahassee 1,010
Tallahassee Community College, Tallahassee 10,816
Taylor Technical Institute, Perry 441
Tom P. Haney Technical Center, Panama City 443

Newspapers and circulation

	District circulation	Total circulation
Gainesville Sun	2,834	48,794
Jacksonville Florida Times-Union	2,874	171,667
Northwest Florida Daily News	4,510	38,547
Panama City News Herald	28,750	30,370
Tallahassee Democrat	45,211	48,482
*USA Today**	3,494	1,674,376

*See Sources and Explanations in the front of the volume.

Television stations and affiliations

Panama City	48%	WFSG	PBS
Panama City	48%	WJHG	NBC, UPN
Panama City	48%	WMBB	ABC
Panama City	48%	WPGX	FOX
Panama City	48%	WTVY	CBS
Tallahassee-Thomasville	44%	WCTV	CBS
Tallahassee-Thomasville	44%	WFSU	PBS
Tallahassee-Thomasville	44%	WFXU	UPN
Tallahassee-Thomasville	44%	WTLH	FOX
Tallahassee-Thomasville	44%	WTWC	NBC
Tallahassee-Thomasville	44%	WTXL	ABC
Gainesville	8%	WCJB	ABC
Gainesville	8%	WUFT	PBS

Cable systems and subscribers
    Comcast 114,321
    Communicomm 1,470
    Gulfshores Communications 627
    Knology 6,250
    Mediacom 14,742
    Time Warner 128,462

Military installations, September 2001
    Tyndall Air Force Base, Springfield 4,191
    Naval Surface Warfare Center, Panama City 1,797

Businesses and other major employers
    Florida State University; Tallahassee 7,603
    Florida Dept. of Children and Families; Tallahassee 5,000
    Florida Dept. of Agriculture and Consumer Services; Tallahassee 3,600
    Tallahassee Memorial Hospital; Tallahassee 3,000
    Florida Environmental Protection Dept.; Tallahassee 2,351
    Florida Dept. of Revenue; Tallahassee 2,200
    Florida Dept. of Health; Tallahassee 2,000
    Florida Dept. of Children and Families; Chattahoochee 2,000
    Florida Dept. of Education; Tallahassee 1,900
    Bay Medical Center; Panama City 1,756
    Florida A&M University; Tallahassee 1,700
    Florida Dept. of Highway Safety and Motor Vehicles; Tallahassee 1,581

Florida Legislative Office; Tallahassee   1,457
Florida A&M University; Tallahassee   1,393
Intrawest Sandestin Co.; Destin; resort hotel   1,200
Florida Dept. of Law Enforcement; Tallahassee   1,005
Abbott Resorts Inc.; Destin; resort hotel   1,000
Watkins Engineers and Constructors Inc.; Tallahassee;
   paper/pulp mill construction   969
Florida Dept. of Banking and Finance; Tallahassee   900
Florida Dept. of Business and Professional Regulation;
   Tallahassee   850
Sallie Mae Servicing; Lynn Haven; student loan
   marketing association   847
Resort Hospitality Enterprises; Panama City; hotel or
   motel management   800
Buckeye Florida Corp.; Perry; investment holding
   company   775
Tallahassee Community College; Tallahassee   750
Buckeye Technologies Inc.; Perry; pulp mills   750
Florida Dept. of Corrections; Tallahassee   750
Marianna Sunland Facility; Marianna; facility for
   mentally retarded persons   750
Florida Dept. of Insurance and Treasurer; Tallahassee
   700
Tallahassee Leon County Civic Center; Tallahassee   672
Bay Hospital Inc.; Panama City   650
Leon County; Tallahassee; police dept.   600
Florida Dept. of State; Tallahassee   600
Miracle Strip-Shipwreck Island Corp.; Panama City;
   theme park   580
Quincy Corp.; Quincy; mushroom production   575
Tallahassee Medical Center Inc.; Tallahassee   572
Alliance Laundry Systems; Marianna; commercial
   laundry equipment   570
Stone Container Corp.; Panama City; laundry products,
   wood   568
Florida Dept. of Corrections; Sneads   548
Florida Dept. of Children and Families; Tallahassee   500
Florida Dept. of Transportation; Tallahassee   500
Wal-Mart Stores Inc.; Panama City; discount department
   stores   500

Florida 3rd District

North — parts of Jacksonville, Orlando, and Gainesville

The 3rd, which bounces among three of Florida's northern cities, includes both heavily urban areas and long stretches of swamps and lakes along the St. Johns River. The racial and political demographics of the black-dominated 3rd were hardly changed during redistricting following the 2000 census, though the district no longer includes the Daytona Beach area, and it now extends west from its poles of Jacksonville and Orlando to pick up voters in Gainesville, home to the University of Florida (though the university itself is in the 6th District).

Democrats dominate the 3rd—they make up almost 65 percent of registered voters. Some rural areas are home to Republicans and old-line conservative Democrats, but not enough to counter the district's strong proclivity toward Democratic candidates for federal office. Al Gore won the 2000 presidential vote here by 30 percentage points.

The 3rd includes a large portion of Putnam County. Often referred to as the Bass Fishing Capital of the World, Putnam is a blue-collar region. The 3rd does contain some tinges of conservatism, particularly in Clay County and in the Palatka area (shared with the 7th) on the St. Johns River.

Mostly blue-collar, the district relies on Naval Air Station Jacksonville (in the 4th District) and other area government facilities for jobs. CSX Corp. also is based in Jacksonville. The city's emergence as a financial center has helped the district's economic outlook, while Orlando residents work in tourism jobs at locations such as Walt Disney World (in the 8th District). Most of the areas in between have agricultural land and lack major private employers, contributing to the 3rd's poor overall economic profile.

Major Industry
Defense, government, higher education, transportation.

Notable
Eatonville was the hometown of Harlem Renaissance author Zora Neale Hurston.

Election Returns

	Republican		Democratic		Other
President 2000	59,144	34.9%	110,501	65.1%	
House 2002	60,747	40.7%	88,462	59.3%	4

District Profile

Population   639,295

Total area (square miles)   2,097.2
   Land area (square miles)   1,796.3

Population per square mile   355.9

Counties (2000 population)

Alachua (pt.)	47,668	Orange (pt.)	218,404
Clay (pt.)	14,259	Putnam (pt.)	39,135
Duval (pt.)	251,892	Seminole (pt.)	24,950
Lake (pt.)	19,645	Volusia (pt.)	14,463
Marion (pt.)	8,879		

Cities and other areas over 10,000 (2000 population)

Gainesville (pt.)	35,540	Orlando (pt.)	61,906
Jacksonville (pt.)	251,892	Pine Hills CDP	41,764
Oak Ridge CDP	22,349	Sanford (pt.)	21,786

Race and Hispanic or Latino origin*
White   38.4%
Black or African American   49.3%
American Indian or Alaska Native   0.3%
Asian   1.6%
Native Hawaiian or other Pacific Islander   0.0%
Some other race   0.2%
Hispanic or Latino origin   8.0%
Two or more races   2.1%

*As percentage of total population.

Ancestry*

English	4.4%	Italian	1.8%
French	1.2%	Subsaharan	1.5%
German	5.2%	USA/American	6.4%
Irish	4.9%	West Indian	3.6%

*As estimated percentage of total population.

Universities and colleges, 2000–2001 enrollment
Edward Waters College, Jacksonville   987
Florida Community College, Jacksonville   20,838
Jacksonville University, Jacksonville   2,049
Jones College-Jacksonville, Jacksonville   654
Mid-Florida Tech, Orlando   1,927
Orlando College-South, Orlando   938
St. Johns River Community College, Palatka   4,512
Winter Park Tech, Winter Park   511

Newspapers and circulation

	District circulation	Total circulation
Daytona Beach News-Journal	4,813	99,266
Gainesville Sun	6,547	48,794
Jacksonville Florida Times-Union	32,130	171,667
Leesburg Daily Commercial	1,282	29,286
Ocala Star Banner	1,270	49,279
Orlando Sentinel	23,320	257,293
Palatka Daily News	7,757	11,421
*USA Today**		4,498	1,674,376

See Sources and Explanations in the front of the volume.

Television stations and affiliations
Orlando-Daytona Beach-Melbourne	49%	WACX	Independent
Orlando-Daytona Beach-Melbourne	49%	WBCC	PBS
Orlando-Daytona Beach-Melbourne	49%	WCEU	PBS
Orlando-Daytona Beach-Melbourne	49%	WESH	NBC
Orlando-Daytona Beach-Melbourne	49%	WFTV	ABC
Orlando-Daytona Beach-Melbourne	49%	WKCF	WB
Orlando-Daytona Beach-Melbourne	49%	WKMG	CBS
Orlando-Daytona Beach-Melbourne	49%	WMFE	PBS
Orlando-Daytona Beach-Melbourne	49%	WOFL	FOX
Orlando-Daytona Beach-Melbourne	49%	WOGX	FOX
Orlando-Daytona Beach-Melbourne	49%	WOPX	PAX
Orlando-Daytona Beach-Melbourne	49%	WRBW	UPN
Orlando-Daytona Beach-Melbourne	49%	WTGL	Independent
Jacksonville	40%	WAWS	FOX, UPN
Jacksonville	40%	WJCT	PBS
Jacksonville	40%	WJEB	Independent
Jacksonville	40%	WJWB	WB
Jacksonville	40%	WJXT	Independent
Jacksonville	40%	WJXX	ABC
Jacksonville	40%	WTEV	CBS
Jacksonville	40%	WTLV	NBC
Jacksonville	40%	WXGA	PBS
Gainesville	11%	WCJB	ABC
Gainesville	11%	WUFT	PBS

Cable systems and subscribers
Bright House Networks   7,892
Comcast   188,322
Cox   32,831
Florida Cable   20,411
Time Warner   11,598

Military installations, September 2001
Jacksonville International Airport Air Force Guard Station, Callahan   1,031

Businesses and other major employers
U.S. Internal Revenue Service; Jacksonville   2,000
U.S. Postal Service; Orlando   2,000
Florida Dept. of Children and Families; Gainesville   1,800
Loews Hotels Holding Corp.; Orlando; resort hotel   1,800

U.S. National Aeronautics and Space Administration; Kennedy Space Center   1,800
Florida Dept. of Children and Families; Orlando   1,600
Georgia-Pacific Corp.; Palatka; towels, tissues and napkins   1,500
Precision Response Corp.; Jacksonville; marketing consulting services   1,500
Orange County; Orlando; correctional institutions   1,400
First Coast Service Options Inc.; Jacksonville; management consulting   1,250
Darden Restaurants Inc.; Orlando; seafood restaurants   1,200
Florida Community College; Jacksonville   1,200
Orange County Public Schools; Orlando   1,075
BellSouth Telecommunications Inc.; Jacksonville; local telephone communications   1,000
Embry-Riddle University; Orange Park   1,000
Florida Dept. of Transportation; Deland   1,000
Hyatt Corp.; Orlando; resort hotel   1,000
Morris Communications Corp.; Jacksonville; newspaper   1,000
Walt Disney World Co.; Orlando; resort hotel   1,000
Winn-Dixie Stores Inc.; Jacksonville; supermarkets   1,000
GMRI Inc.; Orlando; restaurants   950
Shands Jacksonville Medical Center Inc.; Jacksonville   914
Florida Dept. of Corrections; Orlando   904
First Union Bank and Trust Co.; Jacksonville; commercial bank   900
Jacksonville Electric Authority; Jacksonville; electric power distribution   900
Anheuser-Busch Inc.; Jacksonville; beer   850
Tyson Foods Inc.; Jacksonville; business management   850
U.S. Postal Service; Jacksonville   802
HCA Inc. Hospital; Jacksonville   800
U.S. Army Corps of Engineers; Jacksonville   800
Winn-Dixie Stores Inc.; Orlando; general warehousing, storage   800
Interline Brands Inc.; Jacksonville; electrical supplies   771
Environmental Care Inc.; Orlando; landscape contractors   750
Swisher International Group Inc.; Jacksonville; cigars   750
Alachua County; Gainesville; police dept.   720
Transpo Electronics Inc.; Orlando; automotive voltage regulators   720
Central Florida Regional Transportation Authority; Orlando   700
Service America; Orlando; contract food services   700
Walgreen Co.; Orlando; general warehousing, storage   700
Cintas Corp.; Orlando; uniform supply   600
CSX Transportation Inc.; Jacksonville; freight transportation   600
Duval County; Jacksonville; public health programs   600
Florida Coca-Cola Bottling Co.; Orlando; carbonated beverages   600
Florida Furniture Industries Inc.; Palatka; bed frames   600
Seven Seventeen HB Corp.; Jacksonville; specialized public building contractors   600
W. W. Gay Mechanical Contractors Inc.; Jacksonville; mechanical contractor   600
City of Jacksonville; Jacksonville; mayor's office   560
Clay County; Green Cove Springs; sheriff's office   550
Winn-Dixie Stores Inc.; Orlando; supermarkets   550

Universal Select Inc.; Jacksonville; employee leasing service   530

Merrill Lynch and Co.; Jacksonville; life insurance   529

ABF Freight System Inc.; Orlando; trucking terminal facilities   500

Allete Corp.; Apopka; water supply   500

City of Jacksonville; Jacksonville; correctional facilities   500

Datamax Corp.; Orlando; computer peripheral encoders   500

Interstate Brands Corp.; Jacksonville; breads and cakes   500

Island One Inc.; Orlando; residential construction   500

Jacksonville Transportation Authority; Jacksonville; transit system   500

MSI Aviation; Maitland; aircraft storage at airports   500

Progressive Driver Services Inc.; Jacksonville; employment agencies   500

Florida 4th District

North — part of Jacksonville, sliver of Tallahassee

The solidly Republican 4th is anchored in Jacksonville and the surrounding beach communities of Duval County. It wraps around the northeast corner of the state and then runs across the northern border counties as far west as Leon County, where it narrows to a finger to take in a small eastern part of Tallahassee, the state capital.

Overall, Democrats outnumber Republicans, who are clustered in Duval County. But many Democrats in the more rural areas of the district are old-line conservatives who now vote Republican. One such example is Baker County, where Democrats hold a six-to-one registration advantage but Republican Jeb Bush won 69 percent of the vote in the 2002 gubernatorial election. Overall, the 4th gave George W. Bush 65.8 percent of the vote in the 2000 presidential election.

The Jacksonville-based 4th was once a thin strip along the East Coast, but redistricting in 2002 gave it an east-west cast that alters the set of issues important to voters. Agriculture and inland water are now vital in a district once dominated by coastal issues. Much of the 4th shadows Interstate 10, a highway that bridges the 150 miles of rural territory between Jacksonville and Tallahassee.

Jacksonville is a major center for the financial services industry, which provides many of the jobs not associated with the Navy's strong presence in the district along the St. Johns River.

Major Industry

Defense, financial services, tourism.

Notable

Fernandina Beach is the only part of the current United States to have existed under eight flags: France, Spain (twice), England, "Patriot," "Green Cross of Florida," Mexico, Confederate, and U.S.

Election Returns

	Republican		Democratic		Other
President 2000	154,615	65.8%	80,227	34.2%	
House 2002	171,152	100.0%			509

District Profile

Population   639,295

Total area (square miles)   4,368.1
   Land area (square miles)   4,117.8

Population per square mile   155.3

Counties (2000 population)

Baker 22,259	Leon (pt.) 12,479
Columbia 56,513	Madison 18,733
Duval (pt.) 438,507	Nassau 57,663
Hamilton 13,327	Union 13,442
Jefferson (pt.) 6,372	

Cities and other areas over 10,000 (2000 population)

Atlantic Beach   13,368
Fernandina Beach   10,549
Jacksonville (pt.)   396,879
Jacksonville Beach   20,990

Race and Hispanic or Latino origin*

White   77.8%
Black or African American   13.5%
American Indian or Alaska Native   0.3%
Asian   2.4%
Native Hawaiian or other Pacific Islander   0.1%
Some other race   0.1%
Hispanic or Latino origin   4.2%
Two or more races   1.5%

*As percentage of total population.

Ancestry*

English 8.7%	Polish 1.4%
French 2.1%	Scotch-Irish 1.8%
German 9.0%	Scottish 1.9%
Irish 8.7%	USA/American 9.7%
Italian 3.3%	

*As estimated percentage of total population.

Universities and colleges, 2000–2001 enrollment

Florida Coastal School of Law, Jacksonville   454
Florida Technical College of Jacksonville, Jacksonville   278
Lake City Community College, Lake City   2,143
North Florida Community College, Madison   1,358
Stenotype Institute of Jacksonville, Jacksonville Beach   209
Ultrasound Diagnostic School, Jacksonville   225
University of North Florida, Jacksonville   12,550

Newspapers and circulation

	District circulation	Total circulation
Gainesville Sun	2,663	48,794
Jacksonville Florida Times-Union	77,508	171,667
Lake City Reporter	8,826	9,761
Tallahassee Democrat	1,888	48,482
*USA Today**	5,651	1,674,376

*See Sources and Explanations in the front of the volume.

Television stations and affiliations

Jacksonville	67%	WAWS	FOX, UPN
Jacksonville	67%	WJCT	PBS

Jacksonville	67%	WJEB	Independent
Jacksonville	67%	WJWB	WB
Jacksonville	67%	WJXT	Independent
Jacksonville	67%	WJXX	ABC
Jacksonville	67%	WTEV	CBS
Jacksonville	67%	WTLV	NBC
Jacksonville	67%	WXGA	PBS
Tallahassee-Thomasville	33%	WCTV	CBS
Tallahassee-Thomasville	33%	WFSU	PBS
Tallahassee-Thomasville	33%	WFXU	UPN
Tallahassee-Thomasville	33%	WTLH	FOX
Tallahassee-Thomasville	33%	WTWC	NBC
Tallahassee-Thomasville	33%	WTXL	ABC

Cable systems and subscribers
Adelphia   1,020
Comcast   44,815
Time Warner   10,241

Military installations, September 2001
Jacksonville Naval Air Station, Jacksonville   13,420
Mayport Naval Station, Mayport   13,216

Businesses and other major employers
AT&T Corp.; Jacksonville; telemarketing services 5,000

Prudential Financial; Jacksonville; life insurance   3,800

Blue Cross and Blue Shield of Florida; Jacksonville; group hospitalization   3,500

St. Vincent's Medical Center Inc.; Jacksonville   2,728

Southern Baptist Hospital of Florida Inc.; Jacksonville 2,300

Kelley-Clarke Inc.; Jacksonville; personal service agents 2,200

Vistakon Vision Products Inc.; Jacksonville; contact lenses   2,200

St. Luke's Hospital Assn.; Jacksonville   2,000

Citicorp Credit Services Inc.; Jacksonville; personal service agents   1,800

Memorial Healthcare Group Inc.; Jacksonville   1,334

Mayo Clinic; Jacksonville   1,250

Florida Dept. of Corrections; Lake Butler   1,200

White Springs Agricultural Chemicals Inc.; White Springs; phosphate rock   1,200

Florida Dept. of Legal Affairs; Tallahassee   1,200

Alltel Mortgage Information Services Inc.; Jacksonville; data processing   1,150

Amelia Island Co.; Fernandina Beach; resort hotel 1,100

Comcast; Jacksonville; cable television   1,100

Florida National Guard; Jacksonville   1,000

Crowley Liner Services Inc.; Jacksonville; coastal freight transportation   900

Metris Companies Inc.; Jacksonville; telemarketing services   900

State Farm Fire and Casualty Co.; Jacksonville; surety insurance   900

University of North Florida; Jacksonville   836

Merrill Lynch Credit Corp.; Jacksonville; mortgage bankers   832

Florida Dept. of Corrections; Raiford   808

Bombardier Capital Inc.; Jacksonville; mercantile financing   800

Dixie Packers Inc.; Madison; meat packing plants   795

Florida Dept. of Transportation; Tallahassee   750

American Heritage Life Insurance Co. Inc.; Jacksonville; accident and health insurance   738

U.S. Federal Aviation Administration; Hilliard   700

Timco; Lake City; aircraft body and parts   700

Honeywell Technology Solutions Inc.; Jacksonville; missile tracking: telemetry/photography   650

Navy Exchange Service Command; Jacksonville; Army-Navy goods stores   640

Dura Operating Corp.; Jacksonville; windshields   620

Smurfit Stone Container Corp.; Fernandina Beach; container board   600

Duval County School Board; Jacksonville   600

Xomed Inc.; Jacksonville; surgical implants   600

Comcast; Jacksonville; cable television   600

Unison Industries Inc.; Jacksonville; ignition apparatus and distributors   600

Baptist Medical Center of Beaches Inc.; Jacksonville 535

Homeside Lending Inc.; Jacksonville; mortgage bankers 501

Florida Dept. of Corrections; Jasper   500

Wal-Mart Stores Inc.; Lake City; discount department stores   500

Johnson and Johnson Vision Care Inc.; Jacksonville; contact lenses   500

Barnett Dealer Financial Services Inc.; Jacksonville; automobile finance leasing   500

EquiCredit Corp. of America; Jacksonville; mortgage bankers   500

Wal-Mart Stores Inc.; Tallahassee; discount department stores   500

Florida 5th District

Northern west coast — Pasco, Hernando Counties

Located north of Tampa on Florida's west coast, the 5th includes Hernando, Citrus, and part of Pasco Counties and portions of five other counties. Its eastern part, in Lake County, extends to the greater Orlando area. *(See map p. 223.)*

During redistricting following the 2000 census, the legislature swapped Democratic strongholds for GOP bailiwicks in an effort to elect a Republican to the House. The resulting electorate is almost evenly divided between Republicans and Democrats, with about 17 percent of voters registered as independents. Two of the most notable changes were the exclusion of Alachua County—which includes the Democratic-leaning Gainesville voters around the University of Florida—and the Pasco County coast. Mapmakers instead added more-conservative areas of Pasco.

Social Security, prescription drugs, and veterans affairs are the dominant political issues in the 5th, where almost a third of the voting age population is 65 or older. Although its populace often has fought development, the district's communities have been filling up more rapidly in recent decades as additional retirees move into the area.

Tougher economic times have hit parts of the 5th, but many communities are thriving anyway. Businesses continue to buy up land in Pasco County, and industrial parks in Pasco and Hernando Counties are havens for small manufacturing companies.

Major Industry
Manufacturing, service, health care.

Notable
Brooksville was named for Rep. Preston Brooks of South Carolina, who in 1856 bludgeoned Sen. Charles Sumner of Massachusetts with a cane after Sumner gave an antislavery speech in which he denounced a senator who was a relative of Brooks.

Election Returns

	Republican		Democratic		Other	
President 2000	147,231	54.1%	124,982	45.9%		
House 2002	121,998	47.9%	117,758	46.2%	14,915	5.8%

District Profile

Population   639,295

Total area (square miles)   4,801.1
Land area (square miles)   4,044.0

Population per square mile   158.1

Counties (2000 population)
Citrus 118,085	Marion (pt.) 14,071
Hernando 130,802	Pasco (pt.) 164,177
Lake (pt.) 78,265	Polk (pt.) 53,920
Levy (pt.) 26,630	Sumter 53,345

Cities and other areas over 10,000 (2000 population)
Homosassa Springs CDP   12,458
Land O' Lakes CDP   20,971
Spring Hill CDP   69,078
Zephyrhills   10,833

Race and Hispanic or Latino origin*
White   87.7%
Black or African American   4.5%
American Indian or Alaska Native   0.3%
Asian   0.8%
Native Hawaiian or other Pacific Islander   0.0%
Some other race   0.1%
Hispanic or Latino origin   5.6%
Two or more races   0.9%

*As percentage of total population.

Ancestry*
Dutch 1.6%	Polish 2.7%
English 10.1%	Scotch-Irish 1.6%
French 2.9%	Scottish 1.7%
German 13.0%	Swedish 1.1%
Irish 10.5%	USA/American 8.0%
Italian 6.0%	

*As estimated percentage of total population.

Universities and colleges, 2000–2001 enrollment
Lake-Sumter Community College, Leesburg   2,751
Pasco-Hernando Community College, New Port Richey   5,165
St. Leo College, St. Leo   8,720
Withlacoochee Technical Institute, Inverness   413

Newspapers and circulation

	District circulation	Total circulation
Citrus County Chronicle	24,959	25,046
Gainesville Sun	2,701	48,794
Lakeland Ledger	8,132	70,629
Leesburg Daily Commercial	13,227	29,286
Ocala Star Banner	4,249	49,279
Orlando Sentinel	17,337	257,293
St. Petersburg Times	53,848	331,636
Tampa Tribune	32,630	218,543
*USA Today**	2,238	1,674,376

*See Sources and Explanations in the front of the volume.

Television stations and affiliations
Tampa-St. Petersburg (Sarasota)	47%	WCLF	Independent
Tampa-St. Petersburg (Sarasota)	47%	WEDU	PBS
Tampa-St. Petersburg (Sarasota)	47%	WFLA	NBC
Tampa-St. Petersburg (Sarasota)	47%	WFTS	ABC
Tampa-St. Petersburg (Sarasota)	47%	WMOR	Independent
Tampa-St. Petersburg (Sarasota)	47%	WTOG	UPN
Tampa-St. Petersburg (Sarasota)	47%	WTSP	CBS
Tampa-St. Petersburg (Sarasota)	47%	WTTA	WB
Tampa-St. Petersburg (Sarasota)	47%	WTVT	FOX
Tampa-St. Petersburg (Sarasota)	47%	WUSF	PBS
Tampa-St. Petersburg (Sarasota)	47%	WWSB	ABC
Tampa-St. Petersburg (Sarasota)	47%	WXPX	PAX
Gainesville	28%	WCJB	ABC
Gainesville	28%	WUFT	PBS
Orlando-Daytona Beach-Melbourne	25%	WACX	Independent
Orlando-Daytona Beach-Melbourne	25%	WBCC	PBS
Orlando-Daytona Beach-Melbourne	25%	WCEU	PBS
Orlando-Daytona Beach-Melbourne	25%	WESH	NBC
Orlando-Daytona Beach-Melbourne	25%	WFTV	ABC
Orlando-Daytona Beach-Melbourne	25%	WKCF	WB
Orlando-Daytona Beach-Melbourne	25%	WKMG	CBS
Orlando-Daytona Beach-Melbourne	25%	WMFE	PBS
Orlando-Daytona Beach-Melbourne	25%	WOFL	FOX
Orlando-Daytona Beach-Melbourne	25%	WOGX	FOX
Orlando-Daytona Beach-Melbourne	25%	WOPX	PAX
Orlando-Daytona Beach-Melbourne	25%	WRBW	UPN
Orlando-Daytona Beach-Melbourne	25%	WTGL	Independent

Cable systems and subscribers
Adelphia   5,932
Bright House Networks   98,428
Comcast   24,282
Communicomm   582
FSN Cable   97,410
Galaxy   589

Businesses and other major employers
Pasco County District School Board; Land O' Lakes   5,800
Time Inc.; Brooksville; magazines   2,000
Delta Management Group Show Services Inc.; Clermont; technical manual preparation   2,000
Citrus County School Board; Inverness   1,640
Wal-Mart Stores Inc.; Brooksville; discount department stores   1,600
Leesburg Regional Medical Center; Leesburg   1,484
Temporary Jobs Inc.; Crystal River; labor resource services   1,000
Oak Hill Hospital; Brooksville   1,000
Villages of Lake-Sumter Inc.; Lady Lake; public golf courses   946
Tenet Health System Hospitals Inc.; Crystal River   925

Citrus Memorial Health Foundation Inc.; Inverness   855
Sumter County School District; Bushnell   840
Saddlebrook Resorts Inc.; Zephyrhills; resort hotel   830
East Pasco Medical Center Inc.; Zephyrhills   708
Florida Bureau of Prisons; Coleman   700
Hernando County; Brooksville; county government   600
Pall Aeropower Corp.; New Port Richey; filters   538
Galen of Florida Inc.; Dade City; hospital   500
Verizon Inc.; Lutz; proprietary online service networks
   500
Florida Dept. of Tourism; Lecanto   500
Florida Dept. of Children and Families; Brooksville   500

Florida 6th District

North central — parts of Jacksonville, Gainesville, and Ocala

The boomerang-shaped 6th takes in large swaths of rural territory, as well as western Duval County, western Gainesville, and part of Ocala. The southern tip is in Leesburg, which is within Orlando's sphere in the center of the state.

Despite a slight Democratic registration advantage, the GOP has a clear edge in most federal races. But voters are willing to support conservative candidates from either major party. In the 2000 presidential election 58.2 percent of voters favored George W. Bush.

The district contains three regions with distinct interests. The northern end is centered in Jacksonville (shared with the 3rd and 4th Districts), which is heavily influenced by the military. Gainesville, shared with the 3rd in the middle of the district, is home to the University of Florida and a major veterans hospital, while the southern area is a haven for retirees.

The district includes all of two small counties—Gilchrist and Bradford—and parts of six others, including Alachua and Marion, each of which contains about one-quarter of the 6th's population. Alachua, which includes Gainesville, is the biggest Democratic outpost in the district, while Republicans have their strongest registration edge in the Clay County Jacksonville suburbs and exurbs west of the St. Johns River. Republican governor Jeb Bush took more than 77 percent of the Clay vote in the 2002 governor's race, his best showing in the state.

Major Industry

Higher education, health care, agriculture, forestry, defense.

Notable

The Florida Museum of Natural History is located on the campus of the University of Florida in Gainesville; Camp Blanding, in Clay County, is a 73,000-acre Florida Army National Guard training center that was used for multiple purposes by the Army during World War II—including serving as a prisoner-of-war camp.

Election Returns

	Republican		Democratic		Other
President 2000	142,489	58.2%	102,179	41.8%	
House 2002	141,570	65.4%	75,046	34.6%	

District Profile

Population   639,295

Total area (square miles)   3,025.6
   Land area (square miles)   2,911.6

Population per square mile   219.6

Counties (2000 population)
Alachua (pt.) 170,287	Gilchrist 14,437
Bradford 26,088	Lake (pt.) 44,611
Clay (pt.) 126,555	Levy (pt.) 7,820
Duval (pt.) 88,480	Marion (pt.) 161,017

Cities and other areas over 10,000 (2000 population)
Bellair-Meadowbrook Terrace CDP (pt.)   16,539
Gainesville (pt.)   59,907
Jacksonville (pt.)   86,846
Lady Lake town   11,828
Lakeside CDP   30,927
Leesburg (pt.)   14,746
Middleburg CDP   10,338
Ocala (pt.)   29,559

Race and Hispanic or Latino origin*
White   78.9%
Black or African American   11.9%
American Indian or Alaska Native   0.3%
Asian   2.2%
Native Hawaiian or other Pacific Islander   0.0%
Some other race   0.1%
Hispanic or Latino origin   5.2%
Two or more races   1.4%

As percentage of total population.

Ancestry*
Dutch 1.3%	Italian 3.8%
English 8.9%	Polish 1.9%
French 2.6%	Scotch-Irish 1.6%
German 10.7%	Scottish 1.7%
Irish 9.1%	USA/American 8.5%

As estimated percentage of total population.

Universities and colleges, 2000–2001 enrollment
Central Florida Community College, Ocala   5,230
City College-Branch, Gainesville   292
ITT Technical Institute, Jacksonville   439
Santa Fe Community College, Gainesville   12,464
Trinity Baptist College, Jacksonville   362
University of Florida, Gainesville   45,114
Webster College, Ocala   328

Newspapers and circulation

	District circulation	Total circulation
Gainesville Sun	34,040	48,794
Jacksonville Florida Times-Union	26,705	171,667
Leesburg Daily Commercial	7,103	29,286
Ocala Star Banner	30,162	49,279
Orlando Sentinel	7,597	257,293
St. Petersburg Times	1,345	331,636
*USA Today**	3,938	1,674,376

See Sources and Explanations in the front of the volume.

Television stations and affiliations

Gainesville	39%	WCJB	ABC
Gainesville	39%	WUFT	PBS
Jacksonville	36%	WAWS	FOX, UPN
Jacksonville	36%	WJCT	PBS
Jacksonville	36%	WJEB	Independent
Jacksonville	36%	WJWB	WB
Jacksonville	36%	WJXT	Independent
Jacksonville	36%	WJXX	ABC
Jacksonville	36%	WTEV	CBS
Jacksonville	36%	WTLV	NBC
Jacksonville	36%	WXGA	PBS
Orlando-Daytona Beach-Melbourne	25%	WACX	Independent
Orlando-Daytona Beach-Melbourne	25%	WBCC	PBS
Orlando-Daytona Beach-Melbourne	25%	WCEU	PBS
Orlando-Daytona Beach-Melbourne	25%	WESH	NBC
Orlando-Daytona Beach-Melbourne	25%	WFTV	ABC
Orlando-Daytona Beach-Melbourne	25%	WKCF	WB
Orlando-Daytona Beach-Melbourne	25%	WKMG	CBS
Orlando-Daytona Beach-Melbourne	25%	WMFE	PBS
Orlando-Daytona Beach-Melbourne	25%	WOFL	FOX
Orlando-Daytona Beach-Melbourne	25%	WOGX	FOX
Orlando-Daytona Beach-Melbourne	25%	WOPX	PAX
Orlando-Daytona Beach-Melbourne	25%	WRBW	UPN
Orlando-Daytona Beach-Melbourne	25%	WTGL	Independent

Cable systems and subscribers

Adelphia   1,506
Bright House Networks   3,127
City of Newberry   705
Comcast   13,553
Communicomm   2,569
Cox   84,238
Galaxy   24,794
Time Warner   603

Military installations, September 2001

Camp Blanding Military Reservation, Starke   225

Businesses and other major employers

University of Florida; Gainesville   18,000
Shands Teaching Hospital and Clinics Inc.; Gainesville   4,000
AMF Alley Katz Inc.; Gainesville; bowling centers   3,534
U.S. Veterans Hospital; Gainesville   1,557
Central Florida Health Care Development Corp.; Leesburg; hospital management   1,500
Leesburg Regional Medical Center Inc.; Leesburg   1,484
North Florida Regional Medical Center Inc.; Gainesville   1,450
Munroe Regional Healthcare Systems Inc.; Ocala   1,300
Shands Teaching Hospital and Clinics Inc.; Gainesville   1,200
Santa Fe Community College; Gainesville   1,100

Marion Community Hospital Inc.; Ocala   1,100
Villages of Lake-Sumter Inc.; Lady Lake; subdividers and developers   946
Lockheed Martin Corp.; Ocala; missile tracking: telemetry/photography   940
Clairson International Corp.; Ocala; fabricated wire products   900
Orange Park Medical Center Inc.; Orange Park   800
Publix Super Markets Inc.; Jacksonville; general warehousing, storage   800
Nationwide Mutual Insurance Co.; Gainesville; insurance agents   800
Mark IV Industries Inc.; Ocala; rubber hose   700
Marion County; Ocala; sheriff's office   700
Marion County; Belleview; city management   650
Kmart Corp.; Ocala; general warehousing, storage   650
U.S. Postal Service; Gainesville   600
Moltech Power Systems Inc.; Alachua; alkaline batteries   595
Florida Dept. of Corrections; Starke   570
Emergency One Inc.; Ocala; fire dept. vehicles   550
Vystar Credit Union; Orange Park; federally sponsored credit agencies   500
Florida National Guard; Starke   500
ACH Financing; Jacksonville; banking and finance consultant   500
Sysco Food Services; Jacksonville; food supplier   500
American Medical Services; Ocala; medical services organization   500

Florida 7th District

East — St. John's County, Daytona Beach

The 7th follows Interstate 95 from southeast of Jacksonville to northern Daytona Beach, where it turns to follow Interstate 4 west into the Orlando area. It includes all of fast-growing Flagler and St. Johns Counties, as well as most of Volusia County, parts of Putnam and Seminole Counties, and a tiny sliver of Orange County. Two-fifths of the district's population lives in Volusia, mostly on the strip of coast stretching from Ormond Beach to Daytona Beach.

Once a major agricultural area, Seminole County now serves as the suburban home to middle- and upper-class Orlando commuters and their families. But inland portions of the district maintain some agrarian heritage, especially in Flagler County. Daytona Beach continues to attract college students, bikers, and race car fans with its beaches and sporting events, including the Daytona 500 stock car race, which is in the nearby 24th District.

The steady influx of people has meant a sustained economic boom but also has pushed growth-management issues to the top of the local agenda. Retirees have flocked to once-small towns closer to the ocean, drawing retail shops but not as many larger employers. The base is broadened by a growing aerospace industry near Daytona Beach, helped by Embry-Riddle Aeronautical University.

Republicans hold a slim party registration edge and won the 1992, 1996, and 2000 presidential elections in the 7th, which was significantly altered in redistricting following the 2000 census to allow for the creation of the new 24th. Republican George W. Bush won 53.9 percent in 2000. But some moderate Democrats also have had success among the 7th's voters.

Major Industry

Tourism, aerospace, service.

Notable

St. Augustine is the oldest continuously inhabited city in the United States; Jackie Robinson Stadium—named for Major League Baseball's first African American player—is in Daytona Beach, where Robinson was the first black player in a spring training game.

Election Returns

	Republican		Democratic		Other
President 2000	143,672	53.9%	122,818	46.1%	
House 2002	142,147	59.6%	96,444	40.4%	

District Profile

Population   639,295

Total area (square miles)   2,221.4
Land area (square miles)   1,797.0

Population per square mile   355.8

Counties (2000 population)

Flagler 49,832	Seminole (pt.) 161,915
Orange (pt.) 9,707	St. Johns 123,135
Putnam (pt.) 31,288	Volusia (pt.) 263,418

Cities and other areas over 10,000 (2000 population)

Altamonte Springs (pt.)   11,070
Casselberry (pt.)   10,339
Daytona Beach (pt.)   53,629
De Bary (pt.)   14,021
De Land (pt.)   15,216
Deltona (pt.)   47,033
Fruit Cove CDP   16,077
Holly Hill   12,119
Lake Mary   11,458
Longwood   13,745
Ormond Beach   36,301
Palm Coast   32,732
Palm Valley CDP   19,860
Sanford (pt.)   16,505
St. Augustine   11,592
Wekiwa Springs CDP   23,169
Winter Springs (pt.)   12,794

Race and Hispanic or Latino origin*

White   81.3%
Black or African American   8.8%
American Indian or Alaska Native   0.3%
Asian   1.4%
Native Hawaiian or other Pacific Islander   0.0%
Some other race   0.1%
Hispanic or Latino origin   6.9%
Two or more races   1.1%

*As percentage of total population.

Ancestry*

Dutch	1.3%	Italian	6.0%
English	9.9%	Polish	2.4%
French	2.8%	Scotch-Irish	1.6%
German	11.7%	Scottish	2.0%
Irish	10.6%	USA/American	6.6%

*As estimated percentage of total population.

Universities and colleges, 2000–2001 enrollment

Bethune Cookman College, Daytona Beach   2,745
Daytona Beach Community College, Daytona Beach   10,420
Embry-Riddle Aeronautical University, Daytona Beach   13,936
Flagler College, St. Augustine   1,830
Florida Technical College, Orange City*
Institute of Specialized Training and Management, Casselberry   204
Seminole Community College, Sanford   9,042
Stetson University, Deland   3,199
University of St. Augustine for Health Sciences, St. Augustine   419

*Enrollment under 100. See Sources and Explanations in the front of the volume.

Newspapers and circulation

	District circulation	Total circulation
Daytona Beach News-Journal	55,806	99,266
Jacksonville Florida Times-Union	14,744	171,667
Orlando Sentinel	41,456	257,293
Palatka Daily News	3,558	11,421
St. Augustine Record	14,617	14,617
*USA Today**	4,303	1,674,376

*See Sources and Explanations in the front of the volume.

Television stations and affiliations

Orlando-Daytona Beach-Melbourne	53%	WACX	Independent
Orlando-Daytona Beach-Melbourne	53%	WBCC	PBS
Orlando-Daytona Beach-Melbourne	53%	WCEU	PBS
Orlando-Daytona Beach-Melbourne	53%	WESH	NBC
Orlando-Daytona Beach-Melbourne	53%	WFTV	ABC
Orlando-Daytona Beach-Melbourne	53%	WKCF	WB
Orlando-Daytona Beach-Melbourne	53%	WKMG	CBS
Orlando-Daytona Beach-Melbourne	53%	WMFE	PBS
Orlando-Daytona Beach-Melbourne	53%	WOFL	FOX
Orlando-Daytona Beach-Melbourne	53%	WOGX	FOX
Orlando-Daytona Beach-Melbourne	53%	WOPX	PAX
Orlando-Daytona Beach-Melbourne	53%	WRBW	UPN
Orlando-Daytona Beach-Melbourne	53%	WTGL	Independent
Jacksonville	47%	WAWS	FOX, UPN
Jacksonville	47%	WJCT	PBS
Jacksonville	47%	WJEB	Independent
Jacksonville	47%	WJWB	WB
Jacksonville	47%	WJXT	Independent
Jacksonville	47%	WJXX	ABC
Jacksonville	47%	WTEV	CBS
Jacksonville	47%	WTLV	NBC
Jacksonville	47%	WXGA	PBS

Cable systems and subscribers

Bright House Networks   84,341
Comcast   4,172
Shaw Communications   7,523
Time Warner   31,239

Businesses and other major employers

Workers Temporary Staffing Inc.; Lake Mary; temporary help service   14,900

Convergys Corp.; Lake Mary; direct mail advertising   2,000

St. Johns County School Board; St. Augustine   1,965

Halifax Hospital Medical Center; Daytona Beach   1,950

Adventist Health System Sunbelt Healthcare Corp. Hospital; Altamonte Springs   1,400

Seminole Community College; Sanford   1,350

Leadership Network Corp.; Altamonte Springs; marketing consulting services   1,200

First USA Bank; Lake Mary; commercial bank   1,200

Northrop Grumman Systems Corp.; St. Augustine; fuselage assembly, aircraft   1,100

Encompass Electrical Technologies Inc.; Altamonte Springs; electrical contractor   1,050

United Parcel Service Inc.; De Land; courier or messenger service   1,000

Central Florida Regional Hospital; Sanford   1,000

Sentinel Communications Co.; Longwood; newspaper   1,000

U.S. Postal Service; Mid Florida   1,000

Palm Coast Data; Palm Coast; subscription fulfillment services   850

Embry-Riddle Aeronautical University Inc.; Daytona Beach   800

Sea Ray Boats Inc.; Palm Coast; fiberglass boats   800

Stetson University; Deland   800

American Automobile Assn. Inc.; Lake Mary; automobile owners' association   800

Flagler County School Board; Bunnell   750

Memorial Health Systems; Ormond Beach   732

Florida School for Deaf and Blind; St. Augustine   700

Cingular Wireless; Lake Mary; radiotelephone communication   700

Orlando Regional Healthcare System Hospital; Longwood   700

Sypris Electronics; Tampa; radio, TV circuit boards   700

St. Johns County; St. Augustine; county government   680

Recoton Corp.; Lake Mary; household audio equipment   650

Gate Petroleum Co.; Ponte Vedra Beach; convenience stores   600

Bethune-Cookman College; Daytona Beach   600

News-Journal Corp.; Daytona Beach; newspaper   600

Tyco Healthcare Group; De Land; orthopedic, prosthetic, surgical supplies   600

Tycal Health Care Kendall; De Land; cleaning equipment   600

AT&T Corp.; Lake Mary; information bureau   600

Memorial Hospital West Volusia Inc.; Deland   563

Putnam Community Medical Center; Palatka; hospital   525

Publix Super Markets Inc.; St. Augustine; supermarkets   500

PGA Tour Inc.; Ponte Vedra Beach; resort hotel   500

Wal-Mart Stores Inc.; St. Augustine; discount department stores   500

Metra Electronics Corp.; Daytona Beach; motor vehicle body components and frame   500

Volusia County; Deland; county government   500

Seminole County; Sanford; sheriff's office   500

Florida 8th District

Central — most of Orlando

The 8th surrounds western Orlando and includes upscale parts of the region, a large chunk of the city, including much of the downtown area, and the Walt Disney World complex. It then pushes north to take in parts of Lake and Marion Counties, giving it a rural element.

One of Florida's few landlocked districts, the 8th is thriving nonetheless, powered by the presence of Walt Disney World and the tourism industry in the Orlando area, the world's top vacation destination. Redistricting in 2002 removed territory in eastern Orange County and near Kissimmee.

Residents of Orlando's suburbs—from middle-class areas near the city to well-heeled Winter Park and Windermere—support conservative Republicans on social and economic issues. The population is younger, wealthier, and more educated than most Florida districts. While conservative Democrats were once competitive here, Republicans now mostly prevail in Orange County elections. But the county's surging Hispanic population, which spurred its 28 percent growth in the 1990s, has put Orange within political reach of Democratic statewide candidates. Unlike Miami-area Hispanics who are of Cuban descent and vote Republican, many Orlando-area Hispanics are of Puerto Rican stock and vote Democratic. Al Gore in 2000 was the first Democratic presidential nominee to carry Orange County since Franklin D. Roosevelt in 1944.

Although tourism leads the economy, the district also relies on a growing technology sector headed by defense and aerospace contractor Lockheed Martin and Oracle Corp. Technology and research have replaced the dwindling military presence—Orlando's Naval Training Center was shut down in 1999, costing about 4,000 full-time jobs. The research park of the University of Central Florida's Institute for Simulation and Training is an economic engine.

Major Industry

Tourism, aerospace, TV production.

Notable

Dozens of well-known professional athletes—including golf's Tiger Woods and baseball's Ken Griffey Jr.—live in the 8th; costumed Disney World employees are members of the Teamsters Union.

Election Returns

	Republican		Democratic		Other
President 2000	119,139	53.7%	102,538	46.3%	
House 2002	123,497	65.1%	66,099	34.9%	

District Profile

Population   639,295

Total area (square miles)   1,157.8
  Land area (square miles)   986.7

Population per square mile   647.9

Counties (2000 population)

Lake (pt.)	68,007	Orange (pt.)	493,093
Marion (pt.)	74,949	Osceola (pt.)	3,246

Cities and other areas over 10,000 (2000 population)

Azalea Park CDP   11,073
Conway CDP   14,394
Eustis   15,106
Fairview Shores CDP (pt.)   12,479
Meadow Woods CDP   11,286
Ocala (pt.)   16,384
Ocoee (pt.)   23,591
Orlando (pt.)   123,842
Winter Garden   14,351
Winter Park (pt.)   11,034

Race and Hispanic or Latino origin*

White   69.9%
Black or African American   7.2%
American Indian or Alaska Native   0.3%
Asian   3.0%
Native Hawaiian or other Pacific Islander   0.1%
Some other race   0.3%
Hispanic or Latino origin   17.6%
Two or more races   1.6%

*As percentage of total population.

Ancestry*

Dutch	1.3%	Polish	2.0%
English	8.6%	Scotch-Irish	1.4%
French	2.5%	Scottish	1.8%
German	10.7%	USA/American	6.6%
Irish	9.0%	West Indian	1.2%
Italian	4.8%		

*As estimated percentage of total population.

Universities and colleges, 2000–2001 enrollment

Career Training Institute, Orlando   215
Florida Hospital College of Health Science, Orlando   581
Florida Technical College, Orlando   571
Lake County Area Vocational Technical Center, Eustis   669
Orange Technical Education Centers Westside Tech, Winter Garden   1,111
Orlando College, Orlando   867
Rollins College, Winter Park   3,553
Southern College, Orlando   318
Valencia Community College, Orlando   27,565

Newspapers and circulation

	District circulation	Total circulation
Leesburg Daily Commercial	7,696	29,286
Ocala Star Banner	13,581	49,279
Orlando Sentinel	85,674	257,293
*USA Today**	9,382	1,674,376

*See Sources and Explanations in the front of the volume.

Television stations and affiliations

Orlando-Daytona Beach-Melbourne	100%	WACX	Independent
Orlando-Daytona Beach-Melbourne	100%	WBCC	PBS
Orlando-Daytona Beach-Melbourne	100%	WCEU	PBS
Orlando-Daytona Beach-Melbourne	100%	WESH	NBC
Orlando-Daytona Beach-Melbourne	100%	WFTV	ABC
Orlando-Daytona Beach-Melbourne	100%	WKCF	WB
Orlando-Daytona Beach-Melbourne	100%	WKMG	CBS
Orlando-Daytona Beach-Melbourne	100%	WMFE	PBS
Orlando-Daytona Beach-Melbourne	100%	WOFL	FOX
Orlando-Daytona Beach-Melbourne	100%	WOGX	FOX
Orlando-Daytona Beach-Melbourne	100%	WOPX	PAX
Orlando-Daytona Beach-Melbourne	100%	WRBW	UPN
Orlando-Daytona Beach-Melbourne	100%	WTGL	Independent

Cable systems and subscribers

Bright House Networks   55,183
Comcast   16,085
Cox   1,180

Businesses and other major employers

Walt Disney World Co.; Lake Buena Vista; theme park and hotels   51,400
Adventist Health System/Sunbelt Healthcare Corp.; Orlando   14,000
Universal City Development Partners; Orlando; theme park   8,500
Orlando Regional Healthcare System Hospital; Orlando   5,250
Co-Advantage Resources Inc.; Orlando; employee leasing service   5,000
Coopeartizea; Orlando; automobile insurance   5,000
Stream International Inc.; Orlando; prepackaged software   5,000
Walt Disney Parks and Resorts; Orlando; entertainment service   2,500
U.S. Defense Dept.; Orlando   2,140
Marriott International Inc.; Orlando; public golf courses   2,000
Sea World of Florida Inc.; Orlando; theme park   2,000
Rosen Hotels and Resorts Inc.; Orlando; hotel, franchised   1,646
Cirent Semiconductor Inc.; Orlando; semiconductors and related devices   1,600
Space Gateway Support; Kennedy Space Center; security systems services   1;500
AirTran Airlines Inc.; Orlando; air passenger carrier   1,500
Continental Group; Orlando; real estate managers   1,372
Sentinel Communications Co.; Orlando; commercial printing, newspaper publishing   1,325
Nurses PRN of Orlando Inc.; Orlando; nurses' registry   1,200
Tempus Resorts International; Orlando; resort hotel   1,200
Precision Response Corp.; Orlando; marketing consulting services   1,100
Hyatt Corp.; Orlando; hotels   1,100
Florida Hospital/Waterman Inc.; Eustis   1,000
Orange County; Winter Park; fire dept.   1,000
UCF Hotel Venture; Orlando; hotels and motels   1,000
RPM Management Inc.; Orlando; time-sharing real estate sales   1,000
Farmland Industries Inc.; Ocoee; farm supplies   1,000
General Motors Corp.; Ocoee; motor vehicles and car bodies   1,000
Harcourt Inc.; Orlando; textbooks   965
Buena Vista Investment Fund; Lake Buena Vista; hotels   949
U.S. Postal Service; Orlando   900
Loews Hotels Holding Corp.; Orlando; hotels   900

Southwind Sales and Marketing; Orlando; marketing consulting services   900

Royal Palace Hotel Associates; Lake Buena Vista; hotels   895

Wyndham Palace Resort and Spa; Lake Buena Vista; hotels   860

Westgate Resorts; Orlando; time-share condominium exchange   803

Navy Exchange Service Command; Orlando; Army-Navy goods stores   800

Adventist Health System Sunbelt Healthcare Corp.; Kissimmee   800

Orlando Regional Lucerne Hospital; Orlando   790

Rosen Plaza Inc.; Orlando; hotels   750

Orange County; Orlando; public service commission   725

Regal Marine Industries Inc.; Orlando; fiberglass boats   725

Walt Disney World Co.; Orlando; golf, tennis, ski shops   700

Portafino Bay Hotel; Orlando; hotels   700

Renaissance Hotel Group; Orlando; resort hotel   700

Starwood Hotels and Resorts Worldwide Inc.; Orlando; resort hotel   700

Mears Destination Services Inc.; Orlando; intra-airport transportation   650

Marion County; Ocala; county government   650

West Orange Health Care District Hospital; Ocoee   646

Hubbard Construction Co.; Winter Park; highway, street general contractor   634

Lake County; Tavares; sheriff's office   604

Greater Orlando Aviation Authority; Orlando; airport   604

Hilton Hotels Corp.; Lake Buena Vista; hotels   602

Church Street Station of Orlando Inc.; Orlando; restaurants   600

CNL Corporate Properties Inc.; Orlando; commercial land development   600

City of Orlando; Orlando; city management   600

Adventist Health System/Sunbelt Healthcare Corp. Hospital; Orlando   600

Avis Rent A Car Systems Inc.; Orlando; automobile rental   600

Grosvenor Properties Inc.; Orlando; resort hotel   600

Tupperware Corp.; Orlando; plastic containers   600

Manheim Investments Inc.; Ocoee; automobile auction   600

Manheim Investments Inc.; Winter Garden; automobile auction   600

Orlando Regional Hospital; Orlando   590

Manheim's Greater Orlando Auto Auction Inc.; Orlando; automobile auction   580

C&L Group Inc.; Orlando; apartment hotel operation   500

Hughes Supply Inc.; Orlando; electrical supplies   500

Orange County; Orlando; legislative bodies   500

Travelers Insurance Group Inc.; Orlando; fire, marine, casualty insurance   500

Interstate Brands Corp.; Orlando; bakery products   500

Data Access; Orlando; computer software and accessories   500

Interstate Hotels; Orlando; restaurants   500

Planet Hollywood Inc.; Orlando; restaurants   500

Marriott International Inc.; Orlando; motels   500

Marriott Ownership Resorts Inc.; Orlando; hotels   500

Marriott Resorts Hospitality Corp.; Orlando; time-sharing real estate sales   500

Walt Disney Co.; Orlando; jobbing and repair machine shop   500

Wildhorse Saloon; Orlando; saloon   500

GNA Corp.; Orlando; insurance agents and brokers   500

Wal-Mart Stores Inc.; Ocala; discount department stores   500

Orlando Hyatt; Kissimmee; resort hotel   500

Sysco Food Services; Ocoee; food supplier   500

Florida 9th District

West — suburbs north of Tampa

Suburban and rural areas north of Tampa and St. Petersburg form the bulk of the 9th, which encompasses coastal areas of Pinellas and Pasco Counties as well as a large chunk of Hillsborough County. *(See map p. 223.)*

The 9th is mostly residential, and more than one-fifth of the population is 65 or older. Clearwater, the largest city, is known as a beach resort and as the "spiritual headquarters" of the Church of Scientology, which has a large community in the city. Palm Harbor and Tarpon Springs have many Greek Orthodox residents, descendants of the area's earliest settlers.

The 9th's economy is driven by tourism, and many residents commute to Tampa and St. Petersburg. Service-oriented industries add to the mix, but the predominance of shopping centers and strip malls has created growth problems in the coastal areas. The 9th's economy has grown along with its population, though its northeast portions have lagged behind the Clearwater area. Hillsborough County is mostly suburban; Pasco County, which is bisected by Interstate 75, lacks major industry, though it has several sources of spring water.

The 9th long has been a home for mostly Republican retirees, and the GOP retains a slight edge in the district because of its dominance in Hillsborough. Many of the county's most heavily Republican precincts are in the 9th, in towns such as Bloomingdale and Valrico east of I-75 and in the upscale Westchase area in western Hillsborough. The parts of Pinellas that are in the 9th also are decidedly Republican. Democrats hold their own in the 9th's share of Pasco County, where Democrats and Republicans are even in voter registration.

Major Industry

Tourism, health care, technology.

Notable

Tarpon Springs' waters were a major source of sea sponges before they were killed off in the 1940s by toxic blooms of algae known as red tides; Jack Eckerd, founder of the Eckerd chain of drug stores that originated in Clearwater, was the Republican gubernatorial nominee in 1978, losing to Democrat Bob Graham.

Election Returns

	Republican		Democratic		Other
President 2000	146,735	54.2%	124,242	45.8%	
House 2002	169,369	71.5%	67,623	28.5%	

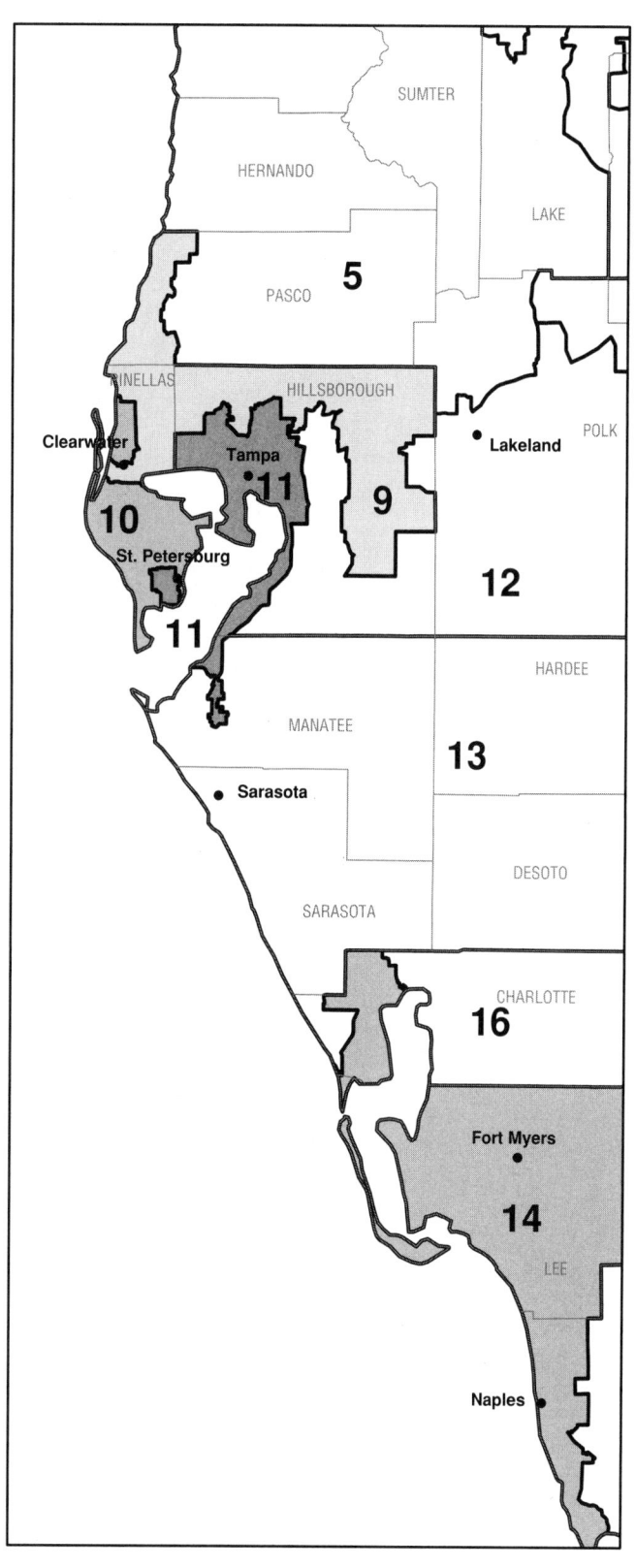

Population   639,296

Total area (square miles)   799.7
   Land area (square miles)   633.9

Population per square mile   1,008.5

Counties (2000 population)
   Hillsborough (pt.)   246,430
   Pasco (pt.)   180,588
   Pinellas (pt.)   212,278

Cities and other areas over 10,000 (2000 population)
   Bayonet Point CDP   23,577
   Bloomingdale CDP (pt.)   13,449
   Clearwater (pt.)   79,189
   East Lake CDP   29,394
   Elfers CDP   13,161
   Greater Carrollwood CDP (pt.)   16,603
   Greater Northdale CDP (pt.)   15,831
   Holiday CDP   21,904
   Hudson CDP   12,765
   Jasmine Estates CDP   18,213
   Keystone CDP   14,627
   Lake Magdalene CDP (pt.)   17,486
   Lutz CDP (pt.)   15,380
   New Port Richey   16,117
   Oldsmar   11,910
   Palm Harbor CDP (pt.)   30,806
   Plant City (pt.)   22,445
   Safety Harbor   17,203
   Tampa (pt.)   19,248
   Tarpon Springs   21,003
   Westchase CDP   11,116

Race and Hispanic or Latino origin*
   White   85.2%
   Black or African American   3.5%
   American Indian or Alaska Native   0.2%
   Asian   1.8%
   Native Hawaiian or other Pacific Islander   0.0%
   Some other race   0.1%
   Hispanic or Latino origin   7.9%
   Two or more races   1.1%

*As percentage of total population.

Ancestry*

Dutch	1.4%	Italian	7.7%
English	9.2%	Polish	3.2%
French	2.8%	Scotch-Irish	1.4%
German	13.3%	Scottish	1.8%
Greek	1.3%	Swedish	1.1%
Irish	11.2%	USA/American	5.8%

*As estimated percentage of total population.

Universities and colleges, 2000–2001 enrollment
   Clearwater Christian College, Clearwater   649
   Florida Metro University-Tampa College-Pinellas,
      Clearwater   1,447

Newspapers and circulation

	District circulation	Total circulation
St. Petersburg Times	87,198	331,636
Tampa Tribune	44,604	218,543
*USA Today**	4,219	1,674,376

*See Sources and Explanations in the front of the volume.

Television stations and affiliations
   Tampa-St. Petersburg (Sarasota)   100%   WCLF   Independent
   Tampa-St. Petersburg (Sarasota)   100%   WEDU   PBS
   Tampa-St. Petersburg (Sarasota)   100%   WFLA   NBC
   Tampa-St. Petersburg (Sarasota)   100%   WFTS   ABC
   Tampa-St. Petersburg (Sarasota)   100%   WMOR   Independent
   Tampa-St. Petersburg (Sarasota)   100%   WTOG   UPN
   Tampa-St. Petersburg (Sarasota)   100%   WTSP   CBS
   Tampa-St. Petersburg (Sarasota)   100%   WTTA   WB
   Tampa-St. Petersburg (Sarasota)   100%   WTVT   FOX
   Tampa-St. Petersburg (Sarasota)   100%   WUSF   PBS
   Tampa-St. Petersburg (Sarasota)   100%   WWSB   ABC
   Tampa-St. Petersburg (Sarasota)   100%   WXPX   PAX

Cable systems and subscribers
   Bright House Networks   19,027
   Verizon   44,752

Businesses and other major employers
   University of South Florida; Odessa   5,000
   U.S. Dept. of Housing and Urban Development; Clearwater
      3,000
   Verizon Data Services Inc.; Tampa; data processing   2,500
   Morton Plant Hospital Assn.; Clearwater   2,100
   Moose International Inc.; Holiday; civic associations
      1,600
   United Services Automobile Assn.; Tampa; fire, marine,
      casualty insurance   1,556
   Times Publishing Co.; Tampa; newspaper   1,500
   Pinellas County; Clearwater; county management   1,400
   HCA Health Services of Florida Inc. Hospital; Port Richey
      1,200
   Church of Scientology Flag Service Organization Inc.;
      Clearwater; religious organization   1,000
   New Port Richey Hospital Inc.; New Port Richey   1,000
   Tarpon Springs Hospital Foundation Inc.; Tarpon Springs
      900
   Golf Host Resorts Inc.; Palm Harbor; resort hotel   850
   Flextronics International Inc.; Palm Harbor; printed circuit
      boards   700
   Bausch and Lomb Pharmaceuticals Inc.; Tampa;
      pharmaceuticals   650
   Time Warner Cable Inc.; Clearwater; cable television   625
   South Florida Baptist Hospital Inc.; Plant City   600
   Reptron Electronics Inc.; Tampa; electronic parts   600
   Salomon Smith Barney Holdings Inc.; Tampa; buying and
      selling mortgages   600
   CGI Group Inc.; Clearwater; computer consulting services
      600
   Wal-Mart Stores Inc.; Port Richey; discount department
      stores   600
   United Healthcare Insurance Co.; Oldsmar; life insurance
      600

CF Industries Inc.; Plant City; phosphatic fertilizers   500
RTG Furniture Corp. of Georgia Inc.; Seffner; furniture stores   500
Regions Bank; Montgomery; commercial banking   500

Florida 10th District

West — most of Pinellas County, St. Petersburg

The 10th takes in about 70 percent of Pinellas County, including most of St. Petersburg and its upscale beachfront communities. From the southern portion of Pinellas, it excludes Clearwater in the central part of the county and captures Dunedin and Palm Harbor. *(See map p. 223.)*

One of Florida's first Republican areas, the district had become increasingly Democratic over the years. But unlike many areas in Florida, the 10th did not see its population boom in the 1990s, a result of the already crowded conditions in most of the district. During redistricting in 2002, it was reshaped to help Republicans stave off a Democratic trend. A significant piece of St. Petersburg—including Pinellas County's southern tip—was ceded to the neighboring, Democratic-held 11th District, and a piece north of Clearwater was added in.

Now Democrats and Republicans appear fairly evenly matched here. Democratic nominee Al Gore won the 2000 presidential race among the voters of the reconfigured 10th by fewer than 5,000 votes. Bill Clinton won here in 1996, and voters favored George Bush in 1992.

Nearly one-fourth of the district's residents are 65 or older, and many retirees reside in Largo and the Gulf Coast towns. Younger residents tend to live in Pinellas Park and St. Petersburg, closer to major employers and Tampa. Tourism has been an economic mainstay for the district, accounting for about $2 billion a year from area hotels and attractions, and the district includes two airports—though the future of the field that serves smaller aircraft is uncertain. High-tech manufacturers and financial services companies have helped to diversify the district's economy.

Major Industry
Tourism, health care, retail.

Notable
Greyhounds have raced at St. Petersburg's Derby Lane, one of several area dog tracks, since the 1920s; St. Petersburg is home to the Salvador Dalí Museum.

Election Returns

	Republican		Democratic		Other
President 2000	133,004	49.2%	137,286	50.8%	
House 2002*					

Uncontested. No vote taken.

District Profile

Population   639,295

Total area (square miles)   448.3
   Land area (square miles)   174.5

Population per square mile   3,663.6

Counties (2000 population)
Pinellas (pt.)   639,295

Cities and other areas over 10,000 (2000 population)
Clearwater (pt.)   29,598
Dunedin   35,691
Gulfport (pt.)   11,763
Largo   69,371
Palm Harbor CDP (pt.)   28,442
Pinellas Park   45,658
Seminole   10,890
St. Petersburg (pt.)   179,087
West and East Lealman CDP   21,753

Race and Hispanic or Latino origin*
White   88.0%
Black or African American   3.6%
American Indian or Alaska Native   0.3%
Asian   2.3%
Native Hawaiian or other Pacific Islander   0.0%
Some other race   0.1%
Hispanic or Latino origin   4.4%
Two or more races   1.3%

As percentage of total population.

Ancestry*
Dutch	1.5%	Polish	3.0%
English	10.2%	Scotch-Irish	1.7%
French	3.3%	Scottish	2.2%
German	14.0%	Swedish	1.2%
Irish	11.6%	USA/American	5.0%
Italian	6.8%		

As estimated percentage of total population.

Universities and colleges, 2000–2001 enrollment
Eckerd College, St. Petersburg   1,572
Pinellas Technical Education Center, Clearwater   1,417
St. Petersburg Junior College, Pinellas Park   19,900
Schiller International University, Dunedin   257

Newspapers and circulation

	District circulation	Total circulation
St. Petersburg Times	152,286	331,636
Tampa Tribune	9,838	218,543
*USA Today**	3,593	1,674,376

See Sources and Explanations in the front of the volume.

Television stations and affiliations
Tampa-St. Petersburg (Sarasota)	100%	WCLF	Independent
Tampa-St. Petersburg (Sarasota)	100%	WEDU	PBS
Tampa-St. Petersburg (Sarasota)	100%	WFLA	NBC
Tampa-St. Petersburg (Sarasota)	100%	WFTS	ABC
Tampa-St. Petersburg (Sarasota)	100%	WMOR	Independent
Tampa-St. Petersburg (Sarasota)	100%	WTOG	UPN
Tampa-St. Petersburg (Sarasota)	100%	WTSP	CBS
Tampa-St. Petersburg (Sarasota)	100%	WTTA	WB
Tampa-St. Petersburg (Sarasota)	100%	WTVT	FOX
Tampa-St. Petersburg (Sarasota)	100%	WUSF	PBS
Tampa-St. Petersburg (Sarasota)	100%	WWSB	ABC
Tampa-St. Petersburg (Sarasota)	100%	WXPX	PAX

Cable systems and subscribers

Bright House Networks   65,808
Verizon   56,188

Businesses and other major employers

Modern Business Associates Inc.; St. Petersburg; employee leasing service   5,000

Tech Data Corp.; Clearwater; computer peripherals, software   3,500

Hospital Housekeeping Systems of Houston Inc.; Largo; janitorial service   3,200

Pinellas County; Largo; sheriff's office   3,000

National Call Center Inc.; St. Petersburg; telemarketing services   2,600

Special Data Processing Corp.; Clearwater; subscription fulfillment services   2,300

U.S. Veterans Hospital; Bay Pines   2,200

Home Shopping Network; St. Petersburg; television, home shopping   2,100

Amfinity Business Solutions Inc.; St. Petersburg; employee leasing service   2,000

ATC Associates Inc.; St. Petersburg; personal service   2,000

Honeywell Inc.; Clearwater; space vehicle guidance systems and equipment   2,000

Raymond James and Associates Inc.; St. Petersburg; security brokers   1,900

Times Publishing Co.; St. Petersburg; newspaper   1,872

Bayfront Medical Center Inc.; St. Petersburg   1,723

Flanders Corp.; St. Petersburg; purification and dust collection equipment   1,546

Honeywell International Inc.; Clearwater; commercial physical research   1,525

U.S. Postal Service; St. Petersburg   1,400

All Children's Hospital Inc.; St. Petersburg   1,358

Jabil Circuit Inc.; St. Petersburg; printed circuit boards   1,344

St. Anthony's Hospital Inc.; St. Petersburg   1,312

Franklin/Templeton Investor Services Inc.; St. Petersburg; security traders   1,200

Raytheon E-Systems Inc.; St. Petersburg; radio broadcasting equipment   1,200

Nielsen Media Research Inc.; Dunedin; market analysis or research   1,116

Certegy Card Services Inc.; St. Petersburg; credit card service   1,100

Eckerd Corp.; Largo; drug stores   1,100

Facs Group Inc.; Clearwater; credit reporting services   1,050

Florida Power Corp.; St. Petersburg; electric services   1,000

Danka Holding Co.; St. Petersburg; photocopy machines   1,000

Baycare Health System Inc.; Clearwater; management services   1,000

Baxter Healthcare Corp.; Largo; pharmaceuticals   1,000

Cox Newspapers Inc.; Largo; newspaper   1,000

Tenet Healthcare Corp.; St. Petersburg; management services   950

Pinellas County School Board; Largo   900

Bankers Insurance Co.; St. Petersburg; fire, marine, casualty insurance   826

Insurance Management Solutions Group Inc.; St. Petersburg; fire, marine, casualty insurance   800

Val-Pak Direct Marketing Systems Inc.; Largo; direct mail advertising   800

Linvatec Corp.; Largo; surgical instruments and apparatus   775

IASIS Healthcare Corp.; St. Petersburg; specialty hospitals   750

Largo Medical Center Inc.; Largo   750

Pinellas County School Board; Largo   750

PSCU Financial Services Inc.; St. Petersburg; credit card service   730

Times Publishing Co.; St. Petersburg; newspaper   700

Resort Inns of America Inc.; St. Petersburg; hotels   700

RP Scherer Corp.; St. Petersburg; gelatin capsules   700

Honeywell International Inc.; Clearwater; aircraft control systems   700

American Retirement Corp.; Seminole; residential care   700

Mease Hospital Inc.; Dunedin   700

Northside Hospital and Heart Institute; St. Petersburg   640

City of St. Petersburg; St. Petersburg; city management   600

St. Petersburg Suncoast Medical Group; St. Petersburg   600

Bic Corp.; St. Petersburg; pens and mechanical pencils   600

Paragon Water Services; Clearwater; telemarketing services   600

U.S. Dept. of Energy; Largo   600

Sun Coast Hospital Inc.; Largo   588

Accenture Inc.; St. Petersburg; management consulting   586

Mortgage Investors Corp.; St. Petersburg; mortgage bankers   580

Vinoy Investments LP; St. Petersburg; hotels   550

U.S. Veterans Affairs; St. Petersburg   550

Verizon Information Services Inc.; St. Petersburg; advertising   550

Galen of Florida Inc.; St. Petersburg; hospital   525

American Retirement Corp.; Seminole; apartment building operators   520

U.S. Coast Guard; Clearwater   500

United Parcel Service Inc.; Clearwater; parcel delivery   500

Instrument Transformers Inc.; Clearwater; instrument transformers   500

Diagnostic Clinic Medical Group; Largo; building operation   500

Transitions Optical Inc.; Pinellas Park; ophthalmic glass   500

Florida 11th District

West — Tampa, south St. Petersburg

The 11th ranges from Tampa to south St. Petersburg and part of Bradenton. One of the younger and more racially diverse districts in the state, the 11th combines what is left of a traditional blue-collar manufacturing base with the newer high-tech and service industries that have transformed Tampa into a major Southern city. The Tampa-St. Petersburg area was a finalist to host the 2004 Republican convention, which was awarded to New York City. *(See map p. 223.)*

The district was reconfigured in 2002 to take in some of the Democrats in the St. Petersburg area who presented a threat to the GOP's security in the neighboring Pinellas County-based 10th. Blacks and Hispanics together make up nearly half of the 11th's population, with heavy concentrations of blacks in south St. Petersburg, east Tampa, and parts of Bradenton, and Hispanics in west Tampa and the Egypt Lake-Leto and Town 'n' Country areas just northwest of the city. It is a heavily Democratic district that gave Al Gore 61 percent of the vote in 2000.

As its economy continues to evolve, the Tampa area has attracted professional sports arenas and a steady military presence at MacDill Air Force Base. Tampa's airport and seaport make it a major shipping and transportation hub, while its traditional cigar industry is attempting a comeback from harder years. The University of South Florida, one of the state's largest schools, is on the city's northern end.

The influence of Cuban and Spanish culture is most pronounced in Ybor City, a downtown Tampa neighborhood named after the man who brought the first cigar factory to Tampa. The neighborhood's success in reinventing itself as a nighttime hot spot has given the area new life.

Major Industry
Retail, health care, finance.

Notable
Pirate Jose Gaspar, better known as Gasparilla, had a hideout in Tampa; Native American tribes named the area Tampa, which means "sticks of fire"; the U.S. Central Command, responsible for U.S. military interests in the Middle East, is based at MacDill Air Force Base.

Election Returns

	Republican		Democratic		Other
President 2000	77,367	39.0%	120,926	61.0%	
House 2002*					

Uncontested. No vote taken.

District Profile

Population 639,295

Total area (square miles) 460.1
  Land area (square miles) 243.8

Population per square mile 2,622.2

Counties (2000 population)
  Hillsborough (pt.) 541,993
  Manatee (pt.) 27,393
  Pinellas (pt.) 69,909

Cities and other areas over 10,000 (2000 population)
  Bradenton (pt.) 10,119
  Citrus Park CDP (pt.) 14,722
  Egypt Lake-Leto CDP 32,782
  Greater Carrollwood CDP (pt.) 16,916
  Lake Magdalene CDP (pt.) 11,269
  Palm River-Clair Mel CDP 17,589
  St. Petersburg (pt.) 69,145
  Tampa (pt.) 284,199

  Town 'n' Country CDP 72,523
  University CDP 30,736

Race and Hispanic or Latino origin*
  White 48.3%
  Black or African American 27.4%
  American Indian or Alaska Native 0.3%
  Asian 2.0%
  Native Hawaiian or other Pacific Islander 0.1%
  Some other race 0.2%
  Hispanic or Latino origin 20.0%
  Two or more races 1.7%

As percentage of total population.

Ancestry*
English	5.8%	Polish	1.4%
French	1.9%	Scotch-Irish	1.1%
German	7.6%	Scottish	1.3%
Irish	6.6%	USA/American	5.0%
Italian	4.4%	West Indian	1.6%

As estimated percentage of total population.

Universities and colleges, 2000–2001 enrollment
  D. G. Erwin Technical Center, Tampa 853
  Education America-Tampa Technical Institute, Tampa 1,244
  Florida Metropolitan University, Tampa 1,038
  International Academy of Merchandising and Design, Tampa 1,325
  ITT Technical Institute, Tampa 742
  Keller Graduate School of Management, Tampa*
  Pinellas Technical Education Center, St. Petersburg 1,232
  University of South Florida, Tampa 35,561
  University of Tampa, Tampa 3,452

Enrollment under 100. See Sources and Explanations in the front of the volume.

Newspapers and circulation

	District circulation	Total circulation
Bradenton Herald	2,681	44,627
St. Petersburg Times	28,286	331,636
Tampa Tribune	74,813	218,543
*USA Today**	2,869	1,674,376

See Sources and Explanations in the front of the volume.

Television stations and affiliations
Tampa-St. Petersburg (Sarasota)	100%	WCLF	Independent
Tampa-St. Petersburg (Sarasota)	100%	WEDU	PBS
Tampa-St. Petersburg (Sarasota)	100%	WFLA	NBC
Tampa-St. Petersburg (Sarasota)	100%	WFTS	ABC
Tampa-St. Petersburg (Sarasota)	100%	WMOR	Independent
Tampa-St. Petersburg (Sarasota)	100%	WTOG	UPN
Tampa-St. Petersburg (Sarasota)	100%	WTSP	CBS
Tampa-St. Petersburg (Sarasota)	100%	WTTA	WB
Tampa-St. Petersburg (Sarasota)	100%	WTVT	FOX
Tampa-St. Petersburg (Sarasota)	100%	WUSF	PBS
Tampa-St. Petersburg (Sarasota)	100%	WWSB	ABC
Tampa-St. Petersburg (Sarasota)	100%	WXPX	PAX

Cable systems and subscribers
  Bright House Networks 333,204

Military installations, September 2001
  MacDill Air Force Base, Tampa 5,926

Businesses and other major employers

LCI Group Inc.; Tampa; employment agencies 8,500

University of South Florida; Tampa 6,767

TECO Energy; Tampa; electric, other services 5,872

Florida Health Sciences Center Inc.; Tampa 3,500

AT&T Global Network Services; Tampa; business consulting 3,500

U.S. Postal Service; Tampa 3,000

J. P. Morgan Chase Bank; Tampa; commercial bank 3,000

St. Joseph's Hospital Inc.; Tampa 2,975

U.S. Veterans Hospital; Tampa 2,500

Hillsborough County; Tampa; county government 2,500

Tropicana Products Inc.; Bradenton; fruit juices 2,500

Sykes Enterprises Inc.; Tampa; computer programming services 2,200

University Community Hospital Inc.; Tampa 2,139

U.S. Postal Service; Tampa 2,000

Pacific Tomato Growers; Palmetto; tomato farm 2,000

City of Tampa; Tampa; police dept. 1,500

International Business Machines Corp.; Tampa; computer programming services 1,500

Verizon New York Inc.; Tampa; telephone equipment 1,500

H. Lee Moffitt Cancer Center and Research Institute Inc.; Tampa; medical research 1,350

Tribune Co.; Tampa; newspaper 1,200

VF Imagewear Inc.; Tampa; athletic clothing 1,200

Hillsborough County; Tampa; correctional facilities 1,190

Manatee Memorial Hospital LP; Bradenton 1,174

Laboratory Corp. America; Tampa; medical laboratories 1,100

Honeywell Inc.; Clearwater; aviation, aeronautical engineering 1,100

Aramark Sports and Entertainment Services Inc.; Tampa; contract food services 1,000

Verizon Information Services Inc.; Tampa; telecommunications consultant 1,000

Continental Airlines Inc.; Tampa; airports 1,000

Metropolitan Life Insurance Co.; Tampa; insurance agents and brokers 1,000

PricewaterhouseCoopers; Tampa; certified public accountant 1,000

Florida Power Corp.; St. Petersburg; electric services 1,000

ABR Benefits Services Inc.; St. Petersburg; software programming applications 1,000

America BPB Inc.; Tampa; gypsum wallboard 900

ConAgra Foods Inc.; Tampa; seafood products 900

Citi Trends Inc.; St. Petersburg; department stores 900

TSI Telecommunications Services Inc.; Tampa; cellular telephones 850

Time Customer Service Inc.; Tampa; customized clothing and apparel 843

Kash N' Karry Food Stores Inc.; Tampa; supermarkets 800

Customer Communications Center Inc.; Tampa; catalog, mail-order 800

U.S. Postal Service; Tampa 800

Tropical Sportswear International Corp.; Tampa; men's/boys' trousers and slacks 712

GTE Telecom Inc.; Tampa; telecommunications consultant 700

Hillsborough County; Tampa 700

Sitel Corp.; Tampa; telemarketing services 700

Software Spectrum Inc.; Tampa; prepackaged software 700

Sypris Electronics; Tampa; printed circuit boards 650

Seminole Tribe of Florida Inc.; Tampa; bingo hall 615

City of Tampa; Tampa; fire dept. 609

Pasco Beverage Co.; Tampa; frozen fruit juice concentrates 600

Quest Diagnostics Clinical Laboratories Inc.; Tampa; medical laboratories 600

Ceridian Benefits Services; St. Petersburg; software programming applications 600

Merck-Medco RX Services of Florida; Tampa; pharmaceuticals, mail order 550

Remington's Steak House Inc.; Tampa; restaurant 545

Hillsborough County School District; Tampa 540

HMS Host Corp.; Tampa; restaurants 530

Cigna Healthcare of Florida Inc.; Tampa; group hospitalization 507

Americana Ships Limited Co.; Tampa; administrative management 500

Hillsborough County; Tampa; county government 500

Hyatt Corp.; Tampa; hotels 500

URS Group Inc.; Tampa; engineering services 500

Electric Machinery Enterprises Inc.; Tampa; electrical contractor 500

Florida Dept. of Transportation; Tampa 500

Continental Airlines Inc.; Tampa; air transportation 500

Time Warner Entertainment Co.; Tampa; cable television 500

BAE Systems Applied Technologies Inc.; Tampa; electronic flight simulators 500

Bank of America Corp.; Tampa; commercial bank 500

Lear Corp.; Tampa; motor vehicle parts/accessories 500

U.S. Postal Service; St. Petersburg 500

Florida 12th District

West central — Polk and Hillsborough Counties

Florida's 12th has plenty of land but much of it is covered by citrus groves and more than 500 natural lakes, not beaches and developments. Centered east of Tampa and southwest of Orlando, it includes almost all of Polk County, suburban and exurban portions of southern and eastern Hillsborough County, and a small slice of western Osceola County. (*See map p. 223.*)

A Democratic registration advantage belies the social and economic conservatism of most residents. The GOP has the edge in the third of the district located in Hillsborough County, and the 12th backed Republican presidential candidates in 1992, 1996, and 2000. Traditional southern Democrats probably could make state and local elections more competitive, but Republicans have had much better success recruiting top-quality candidates for important offices recently.

The 12th's economy is driven by Polk County's agricultural prowess. Polk is the state's top producer of citrus and is Florida's leader in overall farmland. Tomatoes and strawberries are cultivated in the Hillsborough County portion of the district.

The 12th's economy grew steadily during the 1990s, despite some weather-related dips among citrus crops. Florida's phosphate mining industry has its home around Bartow and Mulberry, while Publix Supermarkets is headquartered in Lakeland. These industries provide consistent economic support, while citrus crops are more prone to ups and downs.

Retirees are attracted to the district's significant retirement communities—including Sun City Center—while baseball fans enjoy spring training games at many stadiums in the area.

Major Industry
Agriculture, mining, utilities.

Notable
Spook Hill, in Lake Wales, is a local oddity where cars parked in neutral at the base of the hill will roll up, defying gravity; Cypress Gardens, Florida's first theme park, is in Winter Haven.

Election Returns

	Republican		Democratic		Other
President 2000	121,083	54.8%	99,826	45.2%	
House 2002*					

Uncontested. No vote taken.

District Profile

Population   639,296

Total area (square miles)   2,096.5
Land area (square miles)   1,955.9

Population per square mile   326.9

Counties (2000 population)
Hillsborough (pt.)   210,525
Osceola (pt.)   13,647
Polk (pt.)   415,124

Cities and other areas over 10,000 (2000 population)
Auburndale   11,032
Bartow   15,340
Brandon CDP (pt.)   72,878
Greater Sun Center CDP   16,321
Haines City   13,174
Lakeland (pt.)   71,079
Lakeland Highlands CDP   12,557
Lake Wales   10,194
Poinciana CDP   13,647
Riverview CDP   12,035
Winter Haven   26,487

Race and Hispanic or Latino origin*
White   72.1%
Black or African American   13.0%
American Indian or Alaska Native   0.3%
Asian   1.1%
Native Hawaiian or other Pacific Islander   0.0%
Some other race   0.1%
Hispanic or Latino origin   12.0%
Two or more races   1.3%

As percentage of total population.

Ancestry*

Dutch	1.4%	Italian	3.3%
English	8.2%	Polish	1.5%
French	2.3%	Scotch-Irish	1.4%
German	9.9%	Scottish	1.6%
Irish	8.4%	USA/American	9.8%

As estimated percentage of total population.

Universities and colleges, 2000–2001 enrollment
The Academy, Lakeland   332
Florida College, Temple Terrace   537
Florida Metro University-Tampa College, Lakeland   887
Florida Metropolitan University, Tampa   628
Florida Southern College, Lakeland   2,382
Hillsborough Community College, Tampa   18,497
Polk Community College, Winter Haven   5,611
Southeastern College, Lakeland   1,232
Travis Technical Center, Lakeland   4,380
Ultrasound Diagnostic School, Tampa   285
Warner Southern College, Lake Wales   1,001
Webber College, Babson Park   459

Newspapers and circulation

	District circulation	Total circulation
Lakeland Ledger	60,516	70,629
Orlando Sentinel	1,981	257,293
St. Petersburg Times	3,841	331,636
Tampa Tribune	35,689	218,543
*USA Today**	3,911	1,674,376

See Sources and Explanations in the front of the volume.

Television stations and affiliations

Tampa-St. Petersburg (Sarasota)	98%	WCLF	Independent
Tampa-St. Petersburg (Sarasota)	98%	WEDU	PBS
Tampa-St. Petersburg (Sarasota)	98%	WFLA	NBC
Tampa-St. Petersburg (Sarasota)	98%	WFTS	ABC
Tampa-St. Petersburg (Sarasota)	98%	WMOR	Independent
Tampa-St. Petersburg (Sarasota)	98%	WTOG	UPN
Tampa-St. Petersburg (Sarasota)	98%	WTSP	CBS
Tampa-St. Petersburg (Sarasota)	98%	WTTA	WB
Tampa-St. Petersburg (Sarasota)	98%	WTVT	FOX
Tampa-St. Petersburg (Sarasota)	98%	WUSF	PBS
Tampa-St. Petersburg (Sarasota)	98%	WWSB	ABC
Tampa-St. Petersburg (Sarasota)	98%	WXPX	PAX
Orlando-Daytona Beach-Melbourne	2%	WACX	Independent
Orlando-Daytona Beach-Melbourne	2%	WBCC	PBS
Orlando-Daytona Beach-Melbourne	2%	WCEU	PBS
Orlando-Daytona Beach-Melbourne	2%	WESH	NBC
Orlando-Daytona Beach-Melbourne	2%	WFTV	ABC
Orlando-Daytona Beach-Melbourne	2%	WKCF	WB
Orlando-Daytona Beach-Melbourne	2%	WKMG	CBS
Orlando-Daytona Beach-Melbourne	2%	WMFE	PBS
Orlando-Daytona Beach-Melbourne	2%	WOFL	FOX
Orlando-Daytona Beach-Melbourne	2%	WOGX	FOX
Orlando-Daytona Beach-Melbourne	2%	WOPX	PAX
Orlando-Daytona Beach-Melbourne	2%	WRBW	UPN
Orlando-Daytona Beach-Melbourne	2%	WTGL	Independent

Cable systems and subscribers
Bright House Networks   102,622
Comcast   9,123

Military installations, September 2001
  Craig Field (Army Guard), Jacksonville   379

Businesses and other major employers
  Lakeland Regional Medical Center; Lakeland   3,100
  IMC Global Inc.; Bartow; phosphatic fertilizers   2,800
  Citibank NA; Tampa; commercial bank   2,700
  Meadowbrook Golf Group Inc.; Lakeland; management consulting   2,300
  IMC Phosphates MP Inc.; Mulberry; phosphatic fertilizers   2,112
  Publix Supermarkets Inc.; Lakeland; supermarkets   2,000
  Polk County; Bartow; county government   2,000
  Winter Haven Hospital Inc.; Winter Haven   1,600
  Hillsborough County School District; Thonotosassa   1,500
  Household Finance Corp.; Brandon; consumer finance companies   1,200
  Galencare Inc.; Brandon; hospital   1,200
  Watson Clinic; Lakeland   1,100
  Willis Shaw Express Inc.; Auburndale; trucking   1,046
  IMC Global Inc.; Mulberry; nitrogenous fertilizers   1,037
  Florida Cypress Gardens Inc.; Winter Haven; tourist attraction   1,000
  Florida Power and Light Co.; Homestead; electric power generation   850
  Watkins Motor Lines Inc.; Lakeland; trucking   760
  City of Lakeland; Lakeland; electric, other services   754
  Citrus World Inc.; Lake Wales; fruit juices   740
  Cutrale Citrus Juices USA Inc.; Auburndale; frozen fruits, fruit juices, vegetables   700
  Discount Auto Parts Inc.; Lakeland; auto and home supplies   675
  City of Lakeland; Lakeland; city management   600
  Polk County School Board; Bartow   600
  Pasco Beverage Co.; Lake Hamilton; frozen fruit juice concentrates   600
  W. S. Badcock Corp.; Mulberry; furniture stores   600
  Breed Technologies Inc.; Lakeland; motor vehicle steering systems   550
  Lazy Days RV Center Inc.; Seffner; travel trailers   507
  Albertson's Inc.; Plant City; general warehousing, storage   500
  Florida Southern College; Lakeland   500
  Dundee Citrus Growers Assn.; Dundee; fruit sorting services   500
  Sealy Corp.; Lake Wales; mattresses and foundations   500
  ExxonMobil Oil Corp.; Nichols; crude petroleum production   500

Florida 13th District

Southwest — Sarasota, most of Bradenton

Midwestern retirees flock to the Gulf Coast cities of Sarasota and Bradenton, making the 13th a reliably Republican district. Sarasota and Manatee Counties have nearly 90 percent of the district's population; the more affluent tend to live near Sarasota while middle-class residents are more prevalent around Bradenton. *(See map p. 223.)*

Most residents live near the coast, while farmland and citrus groves are inland. Sarasota County cultivates a refined image with its art museums, theater, and symphony performances. It generally draws a more highly educated and wealthier class of retirees than most other west coast communities in Florida.

The 13th shares Bradenton, the county seat, and retail center of Manatee County, with the 11th District. Bradenton has a more noticeable mix of incomes and ethnic groups. The 13th has the nation's highest median age, and its proportion of people 65 years and older (29 percent of the voting-age population) makes it a popular home for older part-time residents.

Service industries, including investment companies, and trade make up much of the labor force. The district's proximity to Gulf beaches, barrier islands, and a large state park makes the environment a bipartisan concern, with residents attuned to the problems of beach erosion and the effects of rapid population growth.

Republicans outnumber Democrats by nearly 50 percent in registration, and voters overwhelmingly favor GOP candidates in statewide races. Republican nominees won the district in the 1992, 1996, and 2000 presidential elections.

Major Industry
  Health care, financial services.

Notable
  Former circus owner John Ringling brought his circus to the Sarasota area each winter.

Election Returns

	Republican		Democratic		Other
President 2000	152,725	54.5%	127,751	45.5%	
House 2002	139,048	54.8%	114,739	45.2%	22

District Profile

Population   639,295

Total area (square miles)   2,947.7
  Land area (square miles)   2,599.2

Population per square mile   246

Counties (2000 population)
  Charlotte (pt.)   17,582   Manatee (pt.)   236,609
  DeSoto   32,209   Sarasota   325,957
  Hardee   26,938

Cities and other areas over 10,000 (2000 population)
  Bayshore Gardens CDP   17,350
  Bradenton (pt.)   39,385
  Englewood CDP (pt.)   16,088
  Fruitville CDP   12,741
  Gulf Gate Estates CDP   11,647
  North Port   22,797
  Sarasota   52,715
  Sarasota Springs CDP   15,875
  South Bradenton CDP   21,587
  South Venice CDP   13,539
  Venice   17,764

Race and Hispanic or Latino origin*
White   86.0%
Black or African American   4.4%
American Indian or Alaska Native   0.2%
Asian   0.8%
Native Hawaiian or other Pacific Islander   0.0%
Some other race   0.1%
Hispanic or Latino origin   7.7%
Two or more races   0.8%

*As percentage of total population.

Ancestry*
Dutch 1.7%	Polish 2.7%
English 10.8%	Scotch-Irish 1.6%
French 3.1%	Scottish 2.1%
German 14.1%	Swedish 1.3%
Irish 10.2%	USA/American 6.2%
Italian 5.2%	

*As estimated percentage of total population.

Universities and colleges, 2000–2001 enrollment
Manatee Community College, Bradenton   7,834
Manatee Technical Institute, Bradenton   2,721
Ringling School of Art and Design, Sarasota   958
Sarasota County Technical Institute, Sarasota   963
University of Sarasota, Sarasota   766

Newspapers and circulation
	District circulation	Total circulation
Bradenton Herald	41,745	44,627
Charlotte Sun	11,526	34,794
Sarasota Herald Tribune	95,962	106,830
St. Petersburg Times	2,557	331,636
Tampa Tribune	3,524	218,543
*USA Today**	4,087	1,674,376
Venice Gondolier Sun	11,344	11,344

*See Sources and Explanations in the front of the volume.

Television stations and affiliations
Tampa-St. Petersburg (Sarasota)	75%	WCLF	Independent
Tampa-St. Petersburg (Sarasota)	75%	WEDU	PBS
Tampa-St. Petersburg (Sarasota)	75%	WFLA	NBC
Tampa-St. Petersburg (Sarasota)	75%	WFTS	ABC
Tampa-St. Petersburg (Sarasota)	75%	WMOR	Independent
Tampa-St. Petersburg (Sarasota)	75%	WTOG	UPN
Tampa-St. Petersburg (Sarasota)	75%	WTSP	CBS
Tampa-St. Petersburg (Sarasota)	75%	WTTA	WB
Tampa-St. Petersburg (Sarasota)	75%	WTVT	FOX
Tampa-St. Petersburg (Sarasota)	75%	WUSF	PBS
Tampa-St. Petersburg (Sarasota)	75%	WWSB	ABC
Tampa-St. Petersburg (Sarasota)	75%	WXPX	PAX
Ft. Myers-Naples	25%	WBBH	NBC
Ft. Myers-Naples	25%	WFTX	FOX
Ft. Myers-Naples	25%	WGCU	PBS
Ft. Myers-Naples	25%	WINK	CBS
Ft. Myers-Naples	25%	WRXY	Independent
Ft. Myers-Naples	25%	WTVK	WB
Ft. Myers-Naples	25%	WZVN	ABC

Cable systems and subscribers
Bright House Networks   32,414
Comcast   124,012

Businesses and other major employers
Sarasota County Public Hospital Board; Sarasota   2,600
Integrated Health Services at Sarasota Inc.; Sarasota; extended care facility   1,480
National Instore Marketing; Sarasota; advertising, promotion   1,240
HCA Health Services of Florida Inc.; Bradenton; home health care services   1,200
PGT Industries Inc.; Nokomis; window and door frames   1,200
U-Haul International Inc.; Sarasota; truck rental and leasing   1,000
Bon Secours Venice Healthcare Corp.; Venice; hospital   1,000
Wellcraft Marine Corp.; Sarasota; fiberglass boats   936
Sarasota County; Sarasota   825
TWA Airlines; Sarasota; air transportation   800
Beall's Inc.; Bradenton; family clothing stores   784
Staff Leasing Inc.; Bradenton; employee leasing service   700
Circle K Stores Inc.; Sarasota; convenience stores   700
Manatee County; Bradenton   695
Sarasota Doctor's Hospital Inc.; Sarasota   632
Sysco Food Services; Palmetto; canned goods   620
Comdial Corp.; Sarasota; telephones and telephone apparatus   600
GTSI; Sarasota; computers   600
Sarasota County; Sarasota; county government   600
SouthTrust Bank; Sarasota; individual and family services   600
PEO USA Inc.; Sarasota; employment agencies   600
FCCI Services Inc.; Sarasota; insurance agents and brokers   600
Eaton Corp.; Sarasota; electric power relays   600
U.S. Postal Service; Sarasota   600
U.S. Postal Service; Manasota   600
Westport Holdings; Bradenton; nursing home   550
Sarasota Family YMCA Inc.; Sarasota; youth organizations   549
County of Manatee; Bradenton; county government   500
Key Club Associates; Longboat Key; hotels   500
Shannon Hotel Group Inc.; Longboat Key; real estate agents and managers   500
Sarasota County School Board; Sarasota   500
Stoneridge Inc.; Sarasota; engine electrical equipment   500

Florida 14th District

Southwest — Cape Coral, Fort Myers, Naples

A haven for retirees and tourists, the solidly Republican 14th features Gulf Coast beaches and a rapidly expanding population centered in Lee County. It also takes in the coastal edge of Collier County and a small slice of Charlotte County. Most residents live near the coast, between the shore and Interstate 75, which runs through the entire district before turning eastward into the Everglades. (*See map p. 223.*)

The population of Collier County grew by more than 65 percent during the 1990s, while neighboring Lee expanded by almost a third. The increase in Lee County was pushed by Cape Coral, where the population has swelled in recent years. Originally a retirement community, Cape Coral has been attracting young professionals, service industries, and land developers. Wealthier retirees live around Naples, where golf courses and high-rise condominiums are plentiful and new construction helps put the area among the top ten in the state in taxable property value.

Florida Gulf Coast University, which opened in Lee County in 1997, and the nearby Everglades help promote a bustling ecotourism industry and marine biology. The barrier islands act as a magnet for tourists—Sanibel Island is renowned for the seashells that wash up on its beaches from the Gulf of Mexico.

Small Democratic pockets exist within the district's cities, like Fort Myers and Cape Coral, but the 14th has the largest Republican registration edge in the state and regularly gives GOP candidates high vote percentages. In 2002 GOP governor Jeb Bush took 67 percent of the Lee County vote, winning 168 of 175 precincts.

Major Industry
Tourism, health care, agriculture.

Notable
Collier County was created as a favor to land baron and streetcar advertising mogul Baron G. Collier, who helped build the Tamiami Trail, which stretches from Tampa to Miami; the J. N. "Ding" Darling Wildlife Refuge is on Sanibel Island.

Election Returns

	Republican		Democratic		Other
President 2000	163,750	61.4%	103,118	38.6%	
House 2002*					

*Uncontested. No vote taken.

District Profile

Population   639,295

Total area (square miles)   1,717.8
   Land area (square miles)   1,056.5

Population per square mile   605.1

Counties (2000 population)
   Charlotte (pt.)   26,720
   Collier (pt.)   171,687
   Lee   440,888

Cities and other areas over 10,000 (2000 population)
   Bonita Springs   32,797
   Cape Coral   102,286
   Cypress Lake CDP   12,072
   Fort Myers   48,208
   Iona CDP   11,756
   Lehigh Acres CDP   33,430
   Marco Island   14,879
   Naples   20,976
   North Fort Myers CDP   40,214
   San Carlos Park CDP   16,317
   Villas CDP   11,346

Race and Hispanic or Latino origin*
   White   83.8%
   Black or African American   5.1%
   American Indian or Alaska Native   0.2%
   Asian   0.7%
   Native Hawaiian or other Pacific Islander   0.0%
   Some other race   0.1%
   Hispanic or Latino origin   9.0%
   Two or more races   1.0%

*As percentage of total population.

Ancestry*

Dutch	1.5%	Polish	2.9%
English	10.2%	Scotch-Irish	1.4%
French	2.8%	Scottish	2.0%
German	14.4%	Swedish	1.3%
Irish	11.0%	USA/American	5.7%
Italian	6.5%		

*As estimated percentage of total population.

Universities and colleges, 2000–2001 enrollment
   Edison Community College, Fort Myers   8,919
   Florida Gulf Coast University, Fort Myers   3,664
   International College, Fort Myers   575
   International College, Naples   451
   Lee County High Technical Center-Central, Fort Myers   874
   Lorenzo Walker Institute of Technology, Naples   1,607
   Southwest Florida College of Business, Fort Myers   946

Newspapers and circulation

	District circulation	Total circulation
Charlotte Sun	4,127	34,794
Ft. Myers News-Press	86,321	88,633
Marco Island Eagle	6,797	6,912
Naples Daily News	50,213	55,324
Sarasota Herald Tribune	3,947	106,830
*USA Today**	7,307	1,674,376

*See Sources and Explanations in the front of the volume.

Television stations and affiliations
Fort Myers-Naples	100%	WBBH	NBC
Fort Myers-Naples	100%	WFTX	FOX
Fort Myers-Naples	100%	WGCU	PBS
Fort Myers-Naples	100%	WINK	CBS
Fort Myers-Naples	100%	WRXY	Independent
Fort Myers-Naples	100%	WTVK	WB
Fort Myers-Naples	100%	WZVN	ABC

Cable systems and subscribers
   Comcast   106,601
   Marco Island Cable   13,328
   Time Warner   33,663

Businesses and other major employers
   Valley Crest Landscape Inc.; Fort Myers; business services   5,600
   First Union National Bank; Naples; security brokers, dealers   3,000
   Lee County Hospital; Fort Myers   2,275
   Collier County; Naples; sheriff's office   2,000
   Gulf Coast Travel World Inc.; Cape Coral; travel agency   1,982
   Naples Community Hospital Inc.; Naples   1,780
   American Business Solutions Inc.; Naples; data processing   1,700

Southwest Florida Regional Medical Center Inc.; Fort Myers 1,400

General Electric Co.; Fort Myers; electrical work 1,000

Lee County; Fort Myers; sheriff's office 1,000

Collier County; Naples; county government 940

Marriott International Inc.; Marco Island; hotel, franchised 843

Boca Resorts Inc.; Naples; hotels and motels 750

Yoder Brothers Inc.; Alva; flowers 730

Meristar Hospitality Corp.; Captiva; resort hotel 720

City of Cape Coral; Cape Coral; city management 717

Sprint-Florida Inc.; Fort Myers; telephone communication 700

Outreach Programs Inc.; Fort Myers; individual and family services 700

Multimedia Holdings Corp.; Fort Myers; newspaper 650

Associated Therapists Corp.; Naples; physicians' office 607

General Electric Co.; Fort Myers; aircraft engines and parts 600

Beasley Mezzanine Holdings; Naples; radio broadcasting stations 600

Edison Community College; Fort Myers 560

Christian and Missionary Alliance Foundation Inc.; Fort Myers; retirement hotel operation 550

Classic Bentley Village Inc.; Naples; nursing/personal care facility management 550

Doctors Osteopathic Medical Center Inc.; Fort Myers 510

Corral South Inc.; Fort Myers; restaurants 500

Lee County School Board; Fort Myers 500

Wal-Mart Stores Inc.; Fort Myers; discount department stores 500

Liberty Sanibel II LP; Fort Myers; resort hotel 500

Southwest Florida International Airport; Fort Myers 500

Florida 15th District

Central coast — Indian River County; parts of Brevard, Osceola, and Polk Counties

Most people in the GOP-tilting 15th live along the Atlantic Coast in Brevard and Indian River Counties, primarily between the conservative strongholds of Merritt Island and Vero Beach. In addition to all of Indian River County and three-quarters of Brevard County, the 15th contains most of Osceola County and a sliver of Polk County. It is home to the Cape Canaveral Air Force Station, though redistricting in 2002 placed Kennedy Space Center, often associated with Cape Canaveral, in the new, neighboring 24th District. The Air Force Station, Patrick Air Force Base—just a few miles south—and the Kennedy Space Center are the region's economic engine, pushing a thriving technology industry and helping to insulate it from downturns.

Melbourne and Palm Bay in the northeastern portion of the district combine to form a major population center. Most cities in the 15th have seen steady growth, and a Disney complex near Vero Beach is helping to change that sleepy town into a high-profile resort.

Fast-growing Kissimmee, a heavily Hispanic city in the district's portion of Osceola County, depends on the industry built up around Walt Disney World and other nearby tourist destinations. Democrats hold a slight registration edge in Osceola, and conservative Democrats can compete throughout the district. But the GOP holds a significant registration edge in the 15th, and voters here favored the Republican presidential candidate in 1992, 1996, and 2000—including giving George W. Bush a 7 percentage point cushion over Democrat Al Gore.

Major Industry

Technology, defense, tourism.

Notable

Kissimmee used to be known as the cow capital of Florida.

Election Returns

	Republican		Democratic		Other
President 2000	141,242	53.7%	121,611	46.3%	
House 2002	146,414	63.2%	85,433	36.8%	10

District Profile

Population 639,295

Total area (square miles) 3,252.5
  Land area (square miles) 2,544.9

Population per square mile 251.2

Counties (2000 population)
  Brevard (pt.) 355,868   Osceola (pt.) 155,600
  Indian River 112,947   Polk (pt.) 14,880

Cities and other areas over 10,000 (2000 population)
  Cocoa (pt.) 11,088
  Cocoa Beach 12,482
  Florida Ridge CDP 15,217
  Kissimmee 47,814
  Melbourne 71,382
  Merritt Island CDP (pt.) 27,291
  Palm Bay 79,413
  Rockledge 20,170
  Sebastian 16,181
  St. Cloud 20,074
  Vero Beach 17,705
  Vero Beach South CDP 20,362
  Yeehaw Junction CDP 21,778

Race and Hispanic or Latino origin*
  White 77.8%
  Black or African American 7.3%
  American Indian or Alaska Native 0.3%
  Asian 1.6%
  Native Hawaiian or other Pacific Islander 0.0%
  Some other race 0.2%
  Hispanic or Latino origin 11.3%
  Two or more races 1.4%

As percentage of total population.

Ancestry*

Dutch	1.4%	Italian	6.0%
English	9.7%	Polish	2.5%
French	3.0%	Scotch-Irish	1.6%
German	12.2%	Scottish	1.9%
Irish	10.6%	USA/American	5.8%

As estimated percentage of total population.

Universities and colleges, 2000–2001 enrollment

Florida Christian College, Kissimmee   222
Florida Institute of Technology, Melbourne   4,248

Newspapers and circulation

	District circulation	Total circulation
Florida Today, Melbourne	67,419	86,199
Lakeland Ledger	1,253	70,629
Orlando Sentinel	23,933	257,293
Treasure Coast News/Press-Tribune	31,288	33,204
*USA Today**	6,786	1,674,376

See Sources and Explanations in the front of the volume.

Television stations and affiliations

Orlando-Daytona Beach-Melbourne	77%	WACX	Independent
Orlando-Daytona Beach-Melbourne	77%	WBCC	PBS
Orlando-Daytona Beach-Melbourne	77%	WCEU	PBS
Orlando-Daytona Beach-Melbourne	77%	WESH	NBC
Orlando-Daytona Beach-Melbourne	77%	WFTV	ABC
Orlando-Daytona Beach-Melbourne	77%	WKCF	WB
Orlando-Daytona Beach-Melbourne	77%	WKMG	CBS
Orlando-Daytona Beach-Melbourne	77%	WMFE	PBS
Orlando-Daytona Beach-Melbourne	77%	WOFL	FOX
Orlando-Daytona Beach-Melbourne	77%	WOGX	FOX
Orlando-Daytona Beach-Melbourne	77%	WOPX	PAX
Orlando-Daytona Beach-Melbourne	77%	WRBW	UPN
Orlando-Daytona Beach-Melbourne	77%	WTGL	Independent
West Palm Beach-Ft. Pierce	19%	WFLX	FOX
West Palm Beach-Ft. Pierce	19%	WPBF	ABC
West Palm Beach-Ft. Pierce	19%	WPEC	CBS
West Palm Beach-Ft. Pierce	19%	WPTV	NBC
West Palm Beach-Ft. Pierce	19%	WPXP	PAX
West Palm Beach-Ft. Pierce	19%	WTCE	Independent
West Palm Beach-Ft. Pierce	19%	WTVX	UPN, WB
West Palm Beach-Ft. Pierce	19%	WXEL	PBS
Tampa-St. Petersburg (Sarasota)	4%	WCLF	Independent
Tampa-St. Petersburg (Sarasota)	4%	WEDU	PBS
Tampa-St. Petersburg (Sarasota)	4%	WFLA	NBC
Tampa-St. Petersburg (Sarasota)	4%	WFTS	ABC
Tampa-St. Petersburg (Sarasota)	4%	WMOR	Independent
Tampa-St. Petersburg (Sarasota)	4%	WTOG	UPN
Tampa-St. Petersburg (Sarasota)	4%	WTSP	CBS
Tampa-St. Petersburg (Sarasota)	4%	WTTA	WB
Tampa-St. Petersburg (Sarasota)	4%	WTVT	FOX
Tampa-St. Petersburg (Sarasota)	4%	WUSF	PBS
Tampa-St. Petersburg (Sarasota)	4%	WWSB	ABC
Tampa-St. Petersburg (Sarasota)	4%	WXPX	PAX

Cable systems and subscribers

Adelphia   8,945
Bright House Networks   123,821
Comcast   41,426

Military installations, September 2001

Patrick Air Force Base, Cocoa Beach   3,407
Cape Canaveral Air Force Station, Port Canaveral   565

Businesses and other major employers

Harris Corp.; Palm Bay; electronic circuits   5,300
Harris Inc.; Melbourne; computer integrated systems design   5,000
FlightSafety International Inc.; Vero Beach; courier services   3,200
U.S. Dept. of Housing and Urban Development; Kissimmee   3,000
Northrop Grumman Corp.; Melbourne; radar systems and equipment   1,800
Fairways Golf Corp.; Davenport; public golf courses   1,500
Wuesthoff Health Systems Inc.; Rockledge   1,346
Sterling Hospitality Inc.; Kissimmee; hotel or motel management   1,300
Indian River Memorial Hospital Inc.; Vero Beach   1,290
New Piper Aircraft Inc.; Vero Beach; airplanes   1,200
Brevard County; Melbourne; county government   1,000
Oracle Corp.; Kissimmee; management information systems consultant   1,000
S &A Restaurant Corp.; Kissimmee; restaurants   1,000
Central Florida Investments Inc.; Kissimmee; condominium manager   1,000
Florida Institute of Technology; Melbourne   967
Boeing Co.; Cape Canaveral; government space flight operations   900
McLane/Suneast Inc.; Kissimmee; discount department stores   900
Cape Canaveral Hospital Inc.; Cocoa Beach   800
Cocoa Beach Area Health Service Inc.; Cocoa Beach   800
Force Computers Inc.; Melbourne; electronic computers   788
Rockwell Collins Inc.; Melbourne; radio/TV communications equipment   750
Brevard Community College; Melbourne   750
Cape Publications Inc.; Melbourne; newspaper   709
Wal-Mart Stores Inc.; Melbourne; discount department stores   700
Orlando Regional South Seminole Hospital; Longwood   600
Profile Services Inc.; Melbourne; janitorial service   600
Coastal Refining and Marketing; Cape Canaveral; petroleum/chemical bulk stations/terminals   600
Dictaphone Corp.; Melbourne; word processing equipment   600
Wal-Mart Stores Inc.; Melbourne; discount department stores   600
Sunag; Fellsmere; citrus fruits   600
Harris Corp.; Malabar; semiconductors and related devices   600
Haines City Health Management Assn. Inc.; Davenport; hospital   597
Tyco Electronics; Melbourne; printed circuit boards   585
Lockheed Martin Corp.; Cocoa Beach; radio/TV communications equipment   580
Creative Management Technology; Cocoa Beach; management consulting   550
Reed and Barton Corp.; Vero Beach; jewelry   550
Osceola Regional Hospital Inc.; Kissimmee   522
MC Test Service Inc.; Melbourne; printed circuit boards   520
Sterling Casino Lines; Cape Canaveral; deep sea freight transportation   500

Devereux Foundation Children's Hospital; Melbourne   500
Florida Dept. of Corrections; Vero Beach   500
Tempus Resorts International; Kissimmee; time-sharing
real estate sales   500

Florida 16th District

South central — Port St. Lucie, parts of Port Charlotte and Wellington

The 16th sprawls across south-central Florida, connecting wealthy east coast communities with Charlotte Harbor on the west coast. In between, rural Floridians raise cattle and grow sugar cane, particularly around Lake Okeechobee. The district surrounds the western side of the lake and includes most of St. Lucie County's white population near the Atlantic Ocean, from the southern part of the Fort Pierce area to Port St. Lucie. With the lake and beaches, environmental issues play a significant role in local politics.

St. Lucie County is the most populous jurisdiction in the 16th, accounting for about one-fourth of the district population. It has a slight Republican lean: in 2002 GOP governor Jeb Bush took 55 percent of the vote in the 16th's share of St. Lucie, which includes all of Port St. Lucie and most of Fort Pierce and Lakewood Park. Martin County, which is older and even more solidly Republican, includes wealthy Jupiter Island.

Robust population growth required the 16th to shed 120,000 people in 2002 redistricting to meet the population equality requirement. Mapmakers accomplished this by excising 240,000 Palm Beach County residents and adding others in Republican-leaning Charlotte County on the state's west coast. The 16th's remaining share of Palm Beach County includes parts of Jupiter and Palm Beach Gardens, as well as most of Wellington, a growing, wealthy subdivision southwest of West Palm Beach.

The 16th had a slight Democratic tilt in the 1990s, but changes in redistricting gave it a slight Republican edge. George W. Bush won 53.1 percent of the vote here in the 2000 presidential race.

Major Industry
Agriculture, government, health care.

Notable
LaBelle, on the shores of the Caloosahatchee River, hosts the annual Swamp Cabbage Festival, held at the end of February.

Election Returns

	Republican		Democratic		Other	
President 2000	141,029	53.1%	124,752	46.9%		
House 2002	176,171	78.9%			47,169	21.1%

District Profile

Population   639,295

Total area (square miles)   5,249.0
Land area (square miles)   4,538.4

Population per square mile   140.9

Counties (2000 population)

Charlotte (pt.)	97,325	Martin (pt.)	122,220
Glades	10,576	Okeechobee	35,910
Hendry (pt.)	28,980	Palm Beach (pt.)	102,230
Highlands	87,366	St. Lucie (pt.)	154,688

Cities and other areas over 10,000 (2000 population)
Fort Pierce (pt.)   13,717
Hobe Sound CDP   11,376
Jensen Beach CDP   11,100
Jupiter town (pt.)   10,566
Palm City CDP   20,097
Port Charlotte CDP (pt.)   39,610
Port Salerno CDP   10,141
Port St. Lucie   88,769
Punta Gorda   14,344
Royal Palm Beach village (pt.)   13,769
Stuart   14,633
Wellington village (pt.)   35,797

Race and Hispanic or Latino origin*
White   81.8%
Black or African American   5.8%
American Indian or Alaska Native   0.3%
Asian   1.0%
Native Hawaiian or other Pacific Islander   0.0%
Some other race   0.1%
Hispanic or Latino origin   10.1%
Two or more races   1.0%

*As percentage of total population.

Ancestry*

Dutch	1.3%	Polish	2.6%
English	9.7%	Scotch-Irish	1.4%
French	2.8%	Scottish	1.7%
German	12.3%	USA/American	6.5%
Irish	11.3%	West Indian	1.3%
Italian	7.3%		

*As estimated percentage of total population.

Universities and colleges, 2000–2001 enrollment
Charlotte Vocational Technical Center, Port Charlotte   1,276
South Florida Community College, Avon Park   2,199

Newspapers and circulation

	District circulation	Total circulation
Charlotte Sun	19,132	34,794
Ft. Myers News-Press	3,405	88,633
Palm Beach Post	32,647	171,457
Sarasota Herald Tribune	6,315	106,830
Tampa Tribune	11,543	218,543
Treasure Coast News/Press-Tribune	1,860	33,204
*USA Today**	2,385	1,674,376

*See Sources and Explanations in the front of the volume.

Television stations and affiliations

Fort Myers-Naples	42%	WBBH	NBC
Fort Myers-Naples	42%	WFTX	FOX
Fort Myers-Naples	42%	WGCU	PBS
Fort Myers-Naples	42%	WINK	CBS
Fort Myers-Naples	42%	WRXY	Independent

Fort Myers-Naples	42%	WTVK	WB
Fort Myers-Naples	42%	WZVN	ABC
West Palm Beach-Fort Pierce	37%	WFLX	FOX
West Palm Beach-Fort Pierce	37%	WPBF	ABC
West Palm Beach-Fort Pierce	37%	WPEC	CBS
West Palm Beach-Fort Pierce	37%	WPTV	NBC
West Palm Beach-Fort Pierce	37%	WPXP	PAX
West Palm Beach-Fort Pierce	37%	WTCE	Independent
West Palm Beach-Fort Pierce	37%	WTVX	UPN, WB
West Palm Beach-Fort Pierce	37%	WXEL	PBS
Tampa-St. Petersburg (Sarasota)	21%	WCLF	Independent
Tampa-St. Petersburg (Sarasota)	21%	WEDU	PBS
Tampa-St. Petersburg (Sarasota)	21%	WFLA	NBC
Tampa-St. Petersburg (Sarasota)	21%	WFTS	ABC
Tampa-St. Petersburg (Sarasota)	21%	WMOR	Independent
Tampa-St. Petersburg (Sarasota)	21%	WTOG	UPN
Tampa-St. Petersburg (Sarasota)	21%	WTSP	CBS
Tampa-St. Petersburg (Sarasota)	21%	WTTA	WB
Tampa-St. Petersburg (Sarasota)	21%	WTVT	FOX
Tampa-St. Petersburg (Sarasota)	21%	WUSF	PBS
Tampa-St. Petersburg (Sarasota)	21%	WWSB	ABC
Tampa-St. Petersburg (Sarasota)	21%	WXPX	PAX

Cable systems and subscribers
Adelphia   30,120
Comcast   73,397
Time Warner   2,227

Businesses and other major employers
U.S. Sugar Corp.; Clewiston; sugarcane farm   2,500
Commercial Communications; Okeechobee; cellular telephones   1,998
Martin Memorial Medical Center Inc.; Stuart   1,776
Charlotte County; Port Charlotte; county government   1,027
Sprint Corp.; Okeechobee; local/long distance telephone   1,000
Florida Hospital Heartland; Sebring; hospital   900
Fawcett Memorial Hospital Inc.; Port Charlotte   900
QVC Inc.; Fort Pierce; television, home shopping   900
Highlands County School Board; Sebring   800
Liberty Medical Supply Inc.; Port St. Lucie; mail order   745
Asplundh Tree Expert Co.; Jupiter; ornamental shrub and tree services   700
Florida Power and Light Co.; Jensen Beach; electric services   700
Punta Gorda HMA Inc. Hospital; Punta Gorda   680
St. Lucie Medical Center; Port St. Lucie   600
Armellini Industries Inc.; Palm City; trucking   600
Aegis Communications Group Inc.; Port St. Lucie; telemarketing services   549
Martin County School District; Stuart   520
Reithoffer Shows; West Palm Beach; carnival operation   500
A. Duda and Sons Inc.; Felda; vegetables and melons   500
Plantation Botanicals Inc.; Felda; botanical products   500
Wal-Mart Stores Inc.; Port Charlotte; department stores   500
Charlotte County; Punta Gorda; school board   500
St. Lucie County; Fort Pierce; county government   500

Florida 17th District
Southeast — parts of Miami and Hollywood

The black-majority 17th, once a long strip running from the Broward County border through Miami to points south, became more compact during redistricting following the 2000 census. The new district takes in some well-to-do areas and some of the region's most destitute but is confined to northeast Miami-Dade County and southeast Broward County. *(See map p. 237.)*

Overtown, once the hub of African American wealth in the region, spent decades in decline. But that area, along with others in the district, is part of Miami-Dade's federal empowerment zone, and revitalization efforts are under way. Officials are encouraging public-private partnerships as a means to rebuild communities.

Infrastructure is a big part of the picture in the 17th: Miami International Airport is located just outside the district, and another airport in Opa-Locka serves as a base for civilian pilots. Interstate 95 and Route 1 wind through the district. Health concerns are a major topic for residents, many of whom are uninsured. In addition, the HIV/AIDS epidemic has hit the 17th hard, particularly in the black community.

Democrats are a lock at all levels in the 17th, where Republican candidates in statewide races often get less than 25 percent of the vote. Al Gore won 84.8 percent here in the 2000 presidential race—his best showing in the state.

Major Industry
Transportation, service, entertainment.

Notable
Overtown's Lyric Theater, which for decades hosted eminent black entertainers, has been restored.

Election Returns
	Republican		Democratic		Other
President 2000	26,081	15.2%	145,341	84.8%	
House 2002			113,749	100.0%	73

District Profile
Population   639,296

Total area (square miles)   98.8
  Land area (square miles)   96.5

Population per square mile   6,624.8

Counties (2000 population)
  Broward (pt.)   165,847
  Miami-Dade (pt.)   473,449

Cities and other areas over 10,000 (2000 population)
  Brownsville CDP (pt.)   13,792
  Carol City CDP (pt.)   35,858
  Gladeview CDP (pt.)   13,048
  Golden Glades CDP   32,623
  Hallandale (pt.)   13,942
  Hollywood (pt.)   57,267

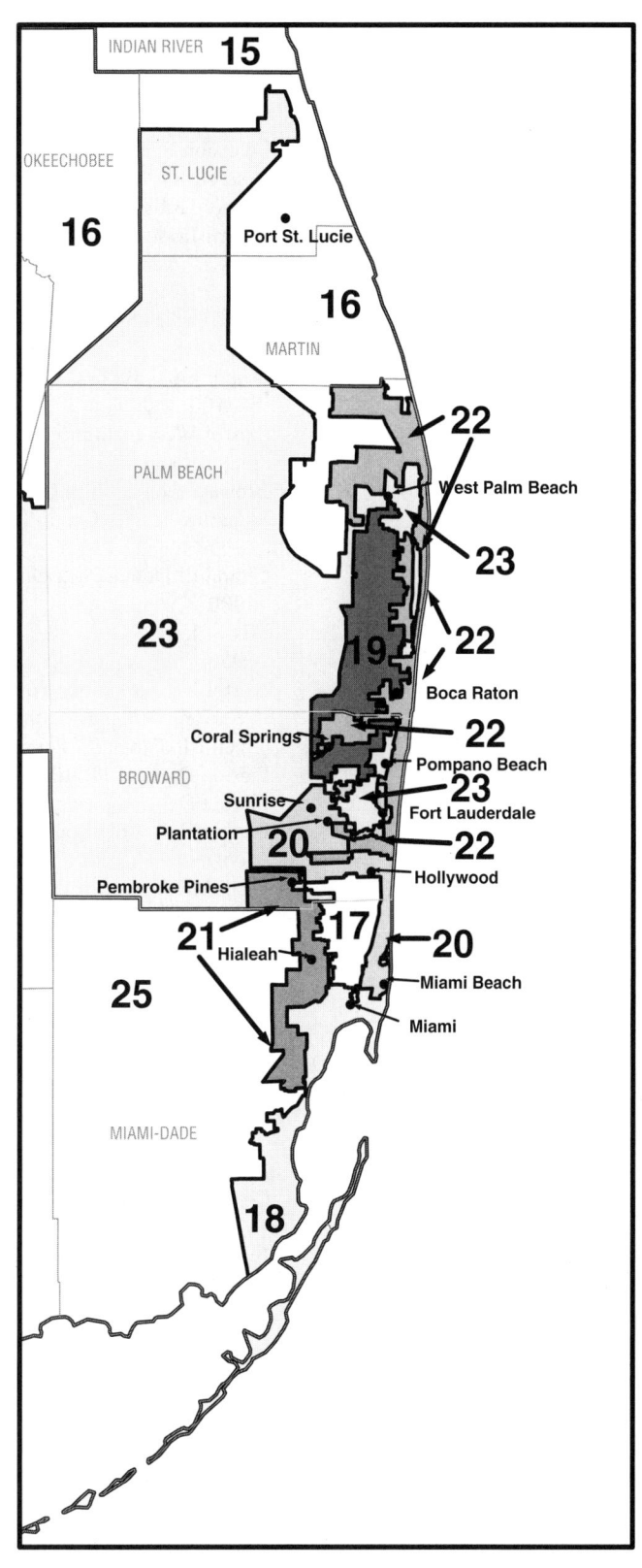

Ives Estates CDP   17,586
Miami (pt.)   81,688
Miramar (pt.)   41,272
Norland CDP   22,995
North Miami (pt.)   50,514
North Miami Beach (pt.)   34,859
Ojus CDP   16,642
Opa-Locka (pt.)   14,603
Pembroke Pines (pt.)   34,354
Pinewood CDP   16,523
Scott Lake CDP   14,401
West Little River CDP (pt.)   26,573

Race and Hispanic or Latino origin*

White   18.4%
Black or African American   55.2%
American Indian or Alaska Native   0.2%
Asian   1.5%
Native Hawaiian or other Pacific Islander   0.0%
Some other race   0.3%
Hispanic or Latino origin   21.2%
Two or more races   3.1%

*As percentage of total population.

Ancestry*

English   1.5%   Subsaharan   1.3%
German   2.3%   USA/American   4.7%
Irish   2.3%   West Indian   20.3%
Italian   2.4%

*As estimated percentage of total population.

Universities and colleges, 2000–2001 enrollment

ATI Health Education Center, Miami   269
Barry University, Miami   8,650
Florida Memorial College, Miami   1,985
Johnson & Wales University, North Miami   1,620
National School of Technology, North Miami Beach   393
St. Thomas University, Miami   2,295

Newspapers and circulation

	District circulation	Total circulation
El Nuevo Herald, Miami	8,977	88,384
Miami Herald	53,933	312,757
South Florida Sun-Sentinel	8,134	251,736

Television stations and affiliations

Miami-Fort Lauderdale	100%	WAMI	Telefutura
Miami-Fort Lauderdale	100%	WBFS	UPN
Miami-Fort Lauderdale	100%	WBZL	WB
Miami-Fort Lauderdale	100%	WEYS	Independent Spanish
Miami-Fort Lauderdale	100%	WFOR	CBS
Miami-Fort Lauderdale	100%	WHFT	Independent
Miami-Fort Lauderdale	100%	WLRN	PBS
Miami-Fort Lauderdale	100%	WLTV	Univision
Miami-Fort Lauderdale	100%	WPBT	PBS
Miami-Fort Lauderdale	100%	WPLG	ABC
Miami-Fort Lauderdale	100%	WPXM	PAX
Miami-Fort Lauderdale	100%	WSCV	Telemundo
Miami-Fort Lauderdale	100%	WSVN	FOX
Miami-Fort Lauderdale	100%	WTVJ	NBC

Cable systems and subscribers

Comcast   102,021

Businesses and other major employers

American Airlines Inc.; Miami; air passenger carrier   10,000
Ecclesiastical Province; Miami; religious organization   5,500
Koning Restaurants International; Miami; restaurants   3,000
Precision Response Corp.; Miami; marketing consulting services   3,000
City of Hollywood; Hollywood; city management   1,500
Miami-Dade County School Board; Miami   1,200
Barry University Inc.; Miami   1,171
City of Miami; Miami; police dept.   1,111
Tenet Health System North Shore Inc. Hospital; Miami   1,100
Mount Sinai Medical Center of Florida; Miami; hospital   1,100
Bristol West Insurance Service Inc.; Hollywood; insurance agents and brokers   1,000
Broward Community College Inc.; Hollywood   1,000
Signature Service Group Inc.; Miami; help supply services   925
Churchill Downs Inc.; Opa-Locka; race track operation   900
Miami Jewish Home and Hospital for Aged Inc.; Miami   900
Nortel Networks Inc.; Fort Lauderdale; telecommunication equipment repair   900
Green Isle Partners; Fort Lauderdale; hotels   900
Florida Dept. of Health; Pembroke Pines   743
Florida Dept. of Revenue; Hollywood   700
Florida Coca-Cola Bottling Co.; Hollywood; soft drinks   650
Tenet Health System Hospitals Inc.; Hollywood   600
U.S. Bureau of Customs and Border Protection; Miami   600
Southern Wine and Spirits of America Inc.; Miami; bottling wines and liquors   600
Sysco Food Services; Miami; dried or canned foods   600
City of Pembroke Pines; Hollywood; city government   565
U.S. Postal Service; Hollywood   560
Fifty State Security Service Inc.; Miami; security guard service   550
Perko Inc.; Miami; marine hardware   525
City of Hollywood; Hollywood; police dept.   500
University of Miami Hospital; Miami   500
Ivax Bioscience Inc.; Miami; pharmaceuticals   500
American Skyhawk Insurance Co.; Miami; property damage insurance   500
U.S. Federal Bureau of Investigation; Miami   500

Florida 18th District

Southeast — most of Miami; Florida Keys

The 18th features the glitz of downtown Miami and the southern part of Miami Beach, but its political base comes from the Latin-dominated areas west of downtown—though it gave up some Hispanic suburbs when a third GOP-leaning, Hispanic-majority South Florida district was drawn during redistricting in 2002. From Miami, the 18th winds its way south along the coast and then follows U.S. 1 through the Florida Keys. More than three-fifths of the district's residents are of Hispanic origin and many are stridently anti-Castro. *(See map p. 237.)*

The district has a wide mix of areas, from the downtrodden sections of Little Havana to wealthy Coral Gables (home to the University of Miami), Key Biscayne, and Fisher Island. Residents tend to be conservative on foreign policy issues but more in line with Democrats on welfare and other social issues. A strong economy that does not rely solely on tourism has translated into little opposition for Republican incumbents.

The Keys, particularly Key West, have a significant gay and lesbian population in addition to older natives who adhere to the independence and environmentalism of the "Conch Republic." The Port of Miami and Miami International Airport, which is in the 21st District, are major transportation centers that feed thriving trade and tourism industries.

In 2000 the district was the center of national attention when federal agents seized Cuban refugee Elían Gonzalez, then six years old, from the Little Havana home of his relatives.

Major Industry
Trade, transportation, tourism.

Notable
Little Havana dominoes players gather at "Domino Park"—actually named Maximo Gomez Park, after a Cuban revolutionary; a giant sculpted hand stretches out toward the sky at the Holocaust Memorial in Miami Beach; Richard M. Nixon vacationed regularly on Key Biscayne.

Election Returns

	Republican		Democratic		Other	
President 2000	109,596	56.8%	83,524	43.2%		
House 2002	103,512	69.1%	42,852	28.6%	3,423	2.3%

District Profile

Population   639,295

Total area (square miles)   3,195.8
   Land area (square miles)   354.9

Population per square mile   1,801.3

Counties (2000 population)
   Miami-Dade (pt.)   559,766
   Monroe (pt.)   79,529

Cities and other areas over 10,000 (2000 population)
   Coral Gables   42,249
   Coral Terrace CDP   24,380
   Key Biscayne village   10,507
   Key Largo CDP   11,886
   Key West   25,478
   Marathon   10,255
   Miami (pt.)   270,214
   Miami Beach (pt.)   75,172
   Pinecrest village (pt.)   12,437
   South Miami   10,741
   Westchester CDP   30,271

Race and Hispanic or Latino origin*
   White   29.7%
   Black or African American   5.7%
   American Indian or Alaska Native   0.1%
   Asian   0.9%
   Native Hawaiian or other Pacific Islander   0.0%
   Some other race   0.1%
   Hispanic or Latino origin   62.7%
   Two or more races   0.7%

As percentage of total population.

Ancestry*

English	3.5%	Polish	1.3%
French	1.5%	Russian	1.2%
German	4.0%	USA/American	3.3%
Irish	3.3%	West Indian	1.3%
Italian	2.9%		

As estimated percentage of total population.

Universities and colleges, 2000–2001 enrollment
   City College, South Miami   232
   Florida Keys Community College, Key West   1,625
   Florida National College, Miami   274
   International Fine Arts College, Miami   997
   Lindsey Hopkins Technical Education Center, Miami   275
   Miami-Dade Community College, Miami   46,834
   Trinity International University, Miami   334
   University of Miami, Coral Gables   13,963

Newspapers and circulation

	District circulation	Total circulation
El Nuevo Herald, Miami	25,295	88,384
*Key West Citizen**	5,784	8,460
Miami Herald	70,678	312,757
*USA Today**	4,633	1,674,376

See Sources and Explanations in the front of the volume.

Television stations and affiliations
Miami-Fort Lauderdale	100%	WAMI	Telefutura
Miami-Fort Lauderdale	100%	WBFS	UPN
Miami-Fort Lauderdale	100%	WBZL	WB
Miami-Fort Lauderdale	100%	WEYS	Independent Spanish
Miami-Fort Lauderdale	100%	WFOR	CBS
Miami-Fort Lauderdale	100%	WHFT	Independent
Miami-Fort Lauderdale	100%	WLRN	PBS
Miami-Fort Lauderdale	100%	WLTV	Univision
Miami-Fort Lauderdale	100%	WPBT	PBS
Miami-Fort Lauderdale	100%	WPLG	ABC
Miami-Fort Lauderdale	100%	WPXM	PAX
Miami-Fort Lauderdale	100%	WSCV	Telemundo
Miami-Fort Lauderdale	100%	WSVN	FOX
Miami-Fort Lauderdale	100%	WTVJ	NBC

Cable systems and subscribers
   Charter   177,589
   Comcast   90,434

Military installations, September 2001
   Homestead Air Force Base, Homestead   1,569
   Key West Naval Air Station, Key West   1,114
   Key West Naval Medical Clinic, Key West   100

Businesses and other major employers

Baptist Health System Hospital; Coral Gables   7,169
Miami-Dade County Hospital; Miami   7,000
University of Miami; Miami   4,000
Royal Caribbean Cruises; Miami; deep sea passenger transportation   3,300
U.S. Veterans Hospital; Miami   3,000
Style View Products Inc.; Miami; awnings   2,800
Knight-Ridder Inc.; Miami; newspaper   2,535
Miami-Dade County; Coral Gables; air, water, solid waste management   2,500
South Miami Hospital Inc.; Miami   2,200
Variety Children's Hospital; Miami   2,200
Florida Dept. of Children and Families; Miami   2,000
Miami-Dade County; Miami; county government   2,000
Miami-Dade County School Board; Miami   2,000
Arthur J. England Jr.; Miami; general practice law office   1,991
Miami-Dade County; Miami; recreation services   1,900
Cedars Medical Center; Miami   1,800
Mercy Hospital Inc.; Miami   1,700
Miami-Dade County School Board; Miami   1,700
U.S. Postal Service; Miami   1,500
Miami-Dade Community College; Miami   1,382
City of Miami; Miami; police dept.   1,322
Pan American Hospital Corp.; Miami   1,152
Federal Aviation Administration; Miami; aircraft inspection   1,103
U.S. Coast Guard; Miami   1,000
Norwegian Cruise Line Ltd.; Miami   1,000
HCA Inc.; Coral Gables; hospital   1,000
United Healthcare of Florida Inc.; Coral Gables; hospital/medical service plans   1,000
American Airlines Aircraft Maintenance; Miami; aircraft maintenance, repair   1,000
Interval Holdings Inc.; Miami; travel agency   1,000
Sunglass Hut International Inc.; Cincinnati; sunglasses   1,000
Goodwill Industries of South Florida Inc.; Miami; work experience center   945
Flordia Dept. of Health; Miami   900
American Sales and Management Organization Corp.; Miami; aircraft cleaning and janitorial service   900
City of Miami; Miami; city government   900
Loews Miami Beach Hotel Operating Co.; Miami Beach; hotels and motels   900
Burdines Inc.; Miami; general warehousing, storage   900
H. I. G. P-Xi Holdings Inc.; Miami; collection agency   702
Ocean Reef Club Inc.; Key Largo; resort hotel   700
Baxter Healthcare Corp.; Miami; analytical instruments   700
Miami-Dade County; Miami; detention center   700
Certified Security Services; Miami; guard services   700
Ladstock Holding Corp.; Coral Gables; horse race track   670
HealthSouth Doctors' Hospital Inc.; Coral Gables   644
Geriatrics Service Complex Foundation Inc.; Miami   640
CB Richard Ellis Memphis; Coral Gables; real estate agents and managers   603
Central Parking System Inc.; Miami; parking lots   600

Union Planters Bank NA; Coral Gables; commercial bank   600
Sheraton Bal Harbour Beach Resort; Miami; hotel, franchised   600
Ocean Bank; Miami; state commercial banks   570
Sky Chefs Inc.; Miami; cafeteria   562
Tenet Health System Hospitals Inc.; Miami   552
Delta Airlines Inc.; Miami; air cargo carrier   521
Entenmann's Inc.; Miami; cakes, pies, and pastries   520
Avborne Heavy Maintenance Inc.; Miami; aircraft servicing, repairing   501
Florida Power and Light Co.; Homestead; electric power generation   500
Nature Conservancy; Summerland Key; environmental protection   500
Miami-Dade County; Miami; environmental protection   500
Inter-Continental Hotels Corp.; Miami; hotels   500
Renaissance Miami Biscayne Bay; Miami; hotel, franchised   500
Tri-State Employment Service Inc.; Miami; employment agencies   500
Seaway Hospitality Corp.; Miami; hotel or motel management   500
Miami-Dade County; Miami; attorney general's office   500
City of Miami Beach; Miami Beach; police dept.   500
Global Baggage Protection Systems Inc.; Miami; airport terminal   500

Florida 19th District

Southeast — parts of Coral Springs, Margate, and Boca Raton

Two-thirds of the heavily Democratic 19th's residents live in Palm Beach County and one-third live in Broward County, mostly west of Interstate 95, where subdivisions dot the landscape. The 19th stretches from West Palm Beach as far south as Margate and includes parts of Boca Raton and Deerfield Beach. Older, upper-middle-class residents make it one of the most educated and white-collar districts in the state. *(See map p. 237.)*

Almost exclusively white, the 19th supports Democrats by overwhelming margins at the state and national levels. Democratic senator Bill Nelson and presidential candidate Al Gore both won this district with more than 70 percent in the 2000 election. Retirees, including many Jewish condominium residents, provide a consistent base of support throughout much of the district.

The 19th has one of the highest percentage of voting-age residents age 65 or older (36.6 percent) of any district in the nation, and elderly voters make up more than 80 percent of the electorate in the 19th's portion of Palm Beach County. Accordingly, the "condo commandos" who run condominium associations serve as local power brokers. Redistricting in 2002 removed some wealthy residents of gated communities in Boca Raton, adding to the 19th's Democratic tilt.

The portion of Boca Raton included in the 19th long has been home to corporate headquarters. Sensormatic Electronics Corp. (acquired by Tyco International in 2001) and Rexall Sundown, a vitamin producer, have major facilities there.

Major Industry

Health care, electronics, financial services.

Notable

A photo editor for *The Sun,* a supermarket tabloid, contracted the first fatal case of anthrax in 2001 while working at the newspaper's Boca Raton office; Boca Raton is known for its pink municipal buildings and the Spanish revival architecture of Addison Mizner.

Election Returns

	Republican		Democratic		Other
President 2000	71,544	27.2%	191,382	72.8%	
House 2002	60,477	27.8%	156,747	72.2%	

District Profile

Population   639,295

Total area (square miles)   234.0
  Land area (square miles)   231.0

Population per square mile   2,767.5

Counties (2000 population)
  Broward (pt.)   210,320
  Palm Beach (pt.)   428,975

Cities and other areas over 10,000 (2000 population)
  Boca Del Mar CDP (pt.)   14,641
  Boca Raton (pt.)   18,818
  Boynton Beach (pt.)   15,211
  Coconut Creek (pt.)   24,901
  Coral Springs (pt.)   74,195
  Deerfield Beach (pt.)   24,728
  Delray Beach (pt.)   17,064
  Greenacres   27,569
  Hamptons at Boca Raton CDP   11,306
  Kings Point CDP   12,207
  Lake Worth Corridor CDP (pt.)   11,459
  Margate (pt.)   42,284
  Pompano Beach (pt.)   13,049
  Sandalfoot Cove CDP   16,582
  Tamarac (pt.)   25,756

Race and Hispanic or Latino origin*
  White   77.5%
  Black or African American   6.1%
  American Indian or Alaska Native   0.1%
  Asian   2.0%
  Native Hawaiian or other Pacific Islander   0.0%
  Some other race   0.3%
  Hispanic or Latino origin   12.7%
  Two or more races   1.4%

*As percentage of total population.

Ancestry*
Austrian	1.1%	Italian	9.0%
English	4.8%	Polish	5.0%
French	1.8%	Russian	5.7%
German	8.4%	USA/American	5.8%
Hungarian	1.1%	West Indian	2.7%
Irish	7.6%		

*As estimated percentage of total population.

Universities and colleges, 2000–2001 enrollment

Atlantic Vocational Technical Center, Coconut Creek   1,570
Florida Atlantic University, Boca Raton   21,046
Lynn University, Boca Raton   2,034
Northwood University-Florida Education Center, West Palm Beach   969

Newspapers and circulation

	District circulation	Total circulation
Miami Herald	5,713	312,757
New York Post	1,677	511,412
Palm Beach Post	37,129	171,457
South Florida Sun-Sentinel	74,671	251,736
*USA Today**	1,065	1,674,376

*See Sources and Explanations in the front of the volume.

Television stations and affiliations

West Palm Beach-Fort Pierce	79%	WFLX	FOX
West Palm Beach-Fort Pierce	79%	WPBF	ABC
West Palm Beach-Fort Pierce	79%	WPEC	CBS
West Palm Beach-Fort Pierce	79%	WPTV	NBC
West Palm Beach-Fort Pierce	79%	WPXP	PAX
West Palm Beach-Fort Pierce	79%	WTCE	Independent
West Palm Beach-Fort Pierce	79%	WTVX	UPN, WB
West Palm Beach-Fort Pierce	79%	WXEL	PBS
Miami-Fort Lauderdale	21%	WAMI	Telefutura
Miami-Fort Lauderdale	21%	WBFS	UPN
Miami-Fort Lauderdale	21%	WBZL	WB
Miami-Fort Lauderdale	21%	WEYS	Independent Spanish
Miami-Fort Lauderdale	21%	WFOR	CBS
Miami-Fort Lauderdale	21%	WHFT	Independent
Miami-Fort Lauderdale	21%	WLRN	PBS
Miami-Fort Lauderdale	21%	WLTV	Univision
Miami-Fort Lauderdale	21%	WPBT	PBS
Miami-Fort Lauderdale	21%	WPLG	ABC
Miami-Fort Lauderdale	21%	WPXM	PAX
Miami-Fort Lauderdale	21%	WSCV	Telemundo
Miami-Fort Lauderdale	21%	WSVN	FOX
Miami-Fort Lauderdale	21%	WTVJ	NBC

Cable systems and subscribers

Adelphia   48,170
Comcast   28,138

Businesses and other major employers

Florida Atlantic University; Boca Raton   2,420
Tenet Health System Hospitals Inc.; Delray Beach   2,000
Siemens Information and Communication Networks Inc.; Boca Raton; telephone and telegraph apparatus   1,800
Applied Card Systems Inc.; Boca Raton; credit card service   1,626
Sensormatic Electronics Corp.; Boca Raton; detection apparatus   1,050
South Palm Beach County Jewish Federation Inc.; Boca Raton; religious organization   1,000
National Car Rental System Inc.; Boca Raton; passenger car rental   1,000
Medical Staffing Network Holdings Inc.; Boca Raton; medical help service   876
U.S. Postal Service; West Palm Beach   800
Cingular Wireless; Boca Raton; cellular telephones   800
North Broward Hospital District; Coral Springs   750
Tenet Health System Hospitals Inc.; Boca Raton   700

Broward County; Pompano Beach; transportation regulation   648

International Business Machines Corp.; Boca Raton; market analysis: business/economic research   600

Sun-Sentinel Co.; Deerfield Beach; newspaper   600

Fifty Second Avenue Associates Inc.; Boca Raton; real estate agents and managers   600

Nortel Networks Inc.; Boca Raton; telecommunications consultant   600

Prime Management Group Inc.; Boca Raton; condominium manager   529

Publix Super Markets Inc.; Deerfield Beach; warehousing   520

First Data Corp.; Coral Springs; credit reporting services   500

OneSource Facility Services Inc.; Pompano Beach; janitorial service   500

Life Care Home Health Services Corp.; Delray Beach   500

Silly Boy Records Inc.; Lake Worth; noncommercial recording studio   500

NABI International Inc.; Boca Raton; plasmapherous center   500

Sensormatic Electronics Corp.; Boca Raton; radio and television repair   500

Florida 20th District

Southeast — parts of Hollywood, Sunrise, Davie, and Fort Lauderdale

Middle-class suburbs mix with beach communities as the 20th snakes through heavily Democratic territory in Broward and Miami-Dade Counties from as far north as Village Park to as far south as Miami Beach. The district takes in a slice of Fort Lauderdale and accounts for about one-third of Broward's population, much of it in suburbs such as Sunrise, Plantation, and Davie. Western Broward teems with shopping centers and suburban development as many former Miami residents have moved north in search of suburban life. *(See map p. 237.)*

Though it takes in those western Broward suburbs, the district wraps around the eastern side of the Miami area. It twists through portions of Hollywood and Hallandale in Broward and moves south into Aventura, with its growing community of young professionals, and North Miami before jumping the Intracoastal Waterway to take in Bal Harbor and a chunk of Miami Beach.

About two-thirds of residents are white and about one-fifth are Hispanic. Some liberal-leaning areas, such as most of Wilton Manors, were added to the 20th in 2002 redistricting. Wilton Manors has a significant gay and lesbian community, and Dania Beach is becoming a more prominent gay resort area. Jewish retirees also contribute to the district's overall Democratic bent.

Davie, with its cattle ranches, has retained some of its rural feel. Plantation has more-expensive homes and light industry. Democrats tend to win elections in Broward County, where they rack up especially large margins in the 20th's parts of Sunrise and Lauderhill. Al Gore took 69 percent of the district's vote in the 2000 presidential election.

Major Industry

Tourism, business services, retail.

Notable

Wilton Manors has a gay mayor and a gay-majority city council; the architecture in downtown Davie is designed to resemble the Old West, and the local McDonald's has a hitching post for horses.

Election Returns

	Republican		Democratic		Other
President 2000	72,553	31.0%	161,154	69.0%	
House 2002*					

Uncontested. No vote taken.

District Profile

Population   639,295

Total area (square miles)   217.9
   Land area (square miles)   160.4

Population per square mile   3,985.6

Counties (2000 population)
   Broward (pt.)   543,879
   Miami-Dade (pt.)   95,416

Cities and other areas over 10,000 (2000 population)
   Aventura (pt.)   22,645
   Cooper City (pt.)   17,148
   Dania Beach (pt.)   19,982
   Davie town (pt.)   70,142
   Fort Lauderdale (pt.)   31,504
   Hallandale (pt.)   20,340
   Hollywood (pt.)   81,921
   Lauderhill (pt.)   10,214
   Miami (pt.)   10,568
   Miami Beach (pt.)   12,761
   Oakland Park (pt.)   11,288
   Pembroke Pines (pt.)   37,466
   Plantation (pt.)   66,264
   Sunny Isles Beach   15,315
   Sunrise (pt.)   71,670
   Tamarac (pt.)   10,374
   Weston (pt.)   49,286

Race and Hispanic or Latino origin*
   White   66.9%
   Black or African American   7.9%
   American Indian or Alaska Native   0.2%
   Asian   2.3%
   Native Hawaiian or other Pacific Islander   0.0%
   Some other race   0.3%
   Hispanic or Latino origin   20.6%
   Two or more races   1.6%

As percentage of total population.

Ancestry*

English 4.7%	Polish 3.7%
French 2.0%	Russian 3.8%
German 7.7%	USA/American 5.9%
Irish 7.5%	West Indian 3.7%
Italian 7.9%	

As estimated percentage of total population.

Universities and colleges, 2000–2001 enrollment

Broward Community College, Fort Lauderdale   27,389
ITT Technical Institute, Fort Lauderdale   543
Nova Southeastern University, Fort Lauderdale   18,587
Sheridan Vocational Center, Hollywood   1,487
William T. McFatter Vocational Technical Center, Davie   986

Newspapers and circulation

	District circulation	Total circulation
El Nuevo Herald, Miami	6,876	88,384
Miami Herald	56,831	312,757
South Florida Sun-Sentinel	54,785	251,736
*USA Today**	1,441	1,674,376

See Sources and Explanations in the front of the volume.

Television stations and affiliations

Miami-Fort Lauderdale	100%	WAMI	Telefutura
Miami-Fort Lauderdale	100%	WBFS	UPN
Miami-Fort Lauderdale	100%	WBZL	WB
Miami-Fort Lauderdale	100%	WEYS	Independent Spanish
Miami-Fort Lauderdale	100%	WFOR	CBS
Miami-Fort Lauderdale	100%	WHFT	Independent
Miami-Fort Lauderdale	100%	WLRN	PBS
Miami-Fort Lauderdale	100%	WLTV	Univision
Miami-Fort Lauderdale	100%	WPBT	PBS
Miami-Fort Lauderdale	100%	WPLG	ABC
Miami-Fort Lauderdale	100%	WPXM	PAX
Miami-Fort Lauderdale	100%	WSCV	Telemundo
Miami-Fort Lauderdale	100%	WSVN	FOX
Miami-Fort Lauderdale	100%	WTVJ	NBC

Cable systems and subscribers

Advanced Cable Communications   3,221
Charter   5,738
Comcast   89,354

Businesses and other major employers

Broward County School Board Inc.; Fort Lauderdale   25,600
Broward County; Fort Lauderdale; county government   7,000
Charlies Happy Cleaners; Fort Lauderdale; cleaning and dyeing   6,000
South Broward Hospital District; Hollywood   5,664
Miami-Dade County; Miami; police dept.   5,000
GEICO; Fort Lauderdale; insurance agents and brokers   5,000
North Broward Hospital District; Fort Lauderdale   4,000
American Express Travel Related Services Co.; Fort Lauderdale; credit card services, collection   4,000
Mount Sinai Medical Center of Florida; Miami   3,125
Broward General Medical Center; Fort Lauderdale   3,000
Motorola Inc.; Fort Lauderdale; radio/TV communications equipment   3,000
City of Fort Lauderdale; Fort Lauderdale; city management   2,019
Maxim Integrated Products Inc.; Hallandale; semiconductors and related devices   2,000
Nova Southeastern University; Fort Lauderdale   1,500
Fort Lauderdale Transportation Inc.; Fort Lauderdale; valet parking   1,180
Florida Medical Center Inc.; Fort Lauderdale   1,024

HCA Corp. Hospital; Miami   1,000
Kemper National Services Inc.; Fort Lauderdale; medical services organization   1,000
Nursing Administration; Fort Lauderdale; skilled nursing care facilities   900
City of Sunrise; Fort Lauderdale; city management   892
Columbia Hospital Corp. of South Broward Inc.; Fort Lauderdale   875
Turnberry Country Club; Miami; hotels and motels   800
Certified Tours Inc.; Fort Lauderdale; travel packages   800
Williams Island Associates; Miami; residential land development   600
Nortel Network Cala Inc.; Fort Lauderdale; communication equipment   600
HCA Inc.; Fort Lauderdale; temporary employment service   600
U.S. Internal Revenue Service; Fort Lauderdale   600
Macy's East Inc.; Fort Lauderdale; department stores   600
Precision Response Corp.; Fort Lauderdale; marketing consulting services   600
Gulfstream International Airlines Inc.; Dania; air passenger carrier   579
Macy's East Inc.; Miami; department stores   550
Templeton International Inc.; Fort Lauderdale; security dealers   550
Elite Health Care Management; Miami; skilled nursing care facilities   525
Renaissance Cruises Inc.; Fort Lauderdale; deep sea passenger transportation   520
DCA Grantor Trust; Miami; investment bankers   500
Alamo Rent-A-Car; Fort Lauderdale; automobile rental   500
Navarro Group Inc.; Fort Lauderdale; detective, armored car services   500
Wyndham International Inc.; Fort Lauderdale; resort hotel   500
Ruby Tuesday South Florida Franchise; Fort Lauderdale; restaurants   500
Harwood Companies Inc.; Fort Lauderdale; men's/boys' underwear and nightwear   500
BellSouth Telecommunications Inc.; Fort Lauderdale; local telephone communications   500
Tenet Health System Hospitals Inc.; Fort Lauderdale   500

Florida 21st District

Southeast — most of Hialeah and Kendall

The Hispanic-dominated 21st is a dependable Republican district that includes middle-class suburbs in central-west Miami-Dade County, from part of Miami Lakes in the north through most of Hialeah in its center and much of Kendall to the south. It includes one-fourth of Miami-Dade's population and a slice of southwestern Broward County. Traditionally, the district's politics center around opposition to Fidel Castro. But economic and foreign policy conservatism are balanced somewhat by residents' more moderate views on labor and social policy matters. *(See map p. 237.)*

Many residents commute from Hialeah, a vibrant, blue-collar residential area filled with Cuban-Americans, to other parts of the 21st. Transportation-related businesses, including Carnival Cruise Lines, have set up facilities close to Miami

International Airport, which was moved into the 21st during 2002 redistricting. Officials say the area is well-positioned to capitalize on trade pacts with Latin American countries.

South Florida's healthy economic scene during the 1990s meant more jobs and homes for the 21st and neighboring districts. The 21st also picks up parts of Miramar and Pembroke Pines, which boast many young professionals from Latin America.

The district's large, suburban Cuban-American community accounts for its Republican bent in statewide and federal elections. Few areas in Florida are as heavily Republican as Hialeah, which has a large contingent of elderly Cuban-American voters and which gave Republican governor Jeb Bush more than 80 percent of the vote in the 2002 election. Bob Dole only narrowly won the district in 1996, but George W. Bush carried the 21st by 16 percentage points in 2000.

Major Industry

Trade, technology, small business.

Notable

Hialeah boasts 15,000 multilingual businesses; Amelia Earhart's final flight began in 1937 in Hialeah.

Election Returns

	Republican		Democratic		Other
President 2000	104,888	57.9%	76,322	42.1%	
House 2002*					

*Uncontested. No vote taken.

District Profile

Population   639,295

Total area (square miles)   139.7
    Land area (square miles)   134.9

Population per square mile   4,739.0

Counties (2000 population)
    Broward (pt.)   74,109
    Miami-Dade (pt.)   565,186

Cities and other areas over 10,000 (2000 population)
    Carol City CDP (pt.)   23,585
    Country Club CDP   36,310
    Cutler CDP (pt.)   12,304
    Fountainbleau CDP (pt.)   52,244
    Glenvar Heights CDP (pt.)   10,600
    Hialeah (pt.)   208,552
    Kendall CDP (pt.)   59,676
    Miami Lakes CDP (pt.)   12,898
    Miami Springs (pt.)   13,712
    Miramar (pt.)   19,863
    Olympia Heights CDP (pt.)   13,452
    Pembroke Pines (pt.)   54,246
    Sunset CDP   17,150
    Sweetwater   14,226
    University Park CDP   26,538
    Westwood Lakes CDP   12,005

Race and Hispanic or Latino origin*
    White   21.0%
    Black or African American   6.5%
    American Indian or Alaska Native   0.1%
    Asian   1.8%
    Native Hawaiian or other Pacific Islander   0.0%
    Some other race   0.2%
    Hispanic or Latino origin   69.7%
    Two or more races   0.8%

*As percentage of total population.

Ancestry*
English	2.0%	Italian	2.5%
German	2.6%	USA/American	3.2%
Irish	2.4%	West Indian	2.6%

*As estimated percentage of total population.

Universities and colleges, 2000–2001 enrollment
    Caribbean Center for Advanced Studies, Miami   606
    Florida College of Natural Health, Miami   314
    Florida Computer and Business School, Miami   971
    Florida International University, Miami   31,945
    Florida National College, Hialeah   1,352
    Florida National College-Flagler, Miami   370
    ITT Technical Institute, Miami   363
    Miami Lakes Technical Education Center, Miami   1,098
    National School of Technology, Hialeah   502

Newspapers and circulation

	District circulation	Total circulation
El Nuevo Herald, Miami	20,699	88,384
Miami Herald	54,519	312,757
New York Post	1,012	511,412
South Florida Sun-Sentinel	5,271	251,736

Television stations and affiliations
Miami-Fort Lauderdale	100%	WAMI	Telefutura
Miami-Fort Lauderdale	100%	WBFS	UPN
Miami-Fort Lauderdale	100%	WBZL	WB
Miami-Fort Lauderdale	100%	WEYS	Independent Spanish
Miami-Fort Lauderdale	100%	WFOR	CBS
Miami-Fort Lauderdale	100%	WHFT	Independent
Miami-Fort Lauderdale	100%	WLRN	PBS
Miami-Fort Lauderdale	100%	WLTV	Univision
Miami-Fort Lauderdale	100%	WPBT	PBS
Miami-Fort Lauderdale	100%	WPLG	ABC
Miami-Fort Lauderdale	100%	WPXM	PAX
Miami-Fort Lauderdale	100%	WSCV	Telemundo
Miami-Fort Lauderdale	100%	WSVN	FOX
Miami-Fort Lauderdale	100%	WTVJ	NBC

Cable systems and subscribers
    Comcast   92,978

Businesses and other major employers
    University of Miami; Miami   7,618
    Baptist Hospital Inc.; Miami   3,050
    International Parts; Miami; automotive parts   3,000
    Florida International University; Miami   2,800
    BellSouth Telecommunications Inc.; Miami; telephone communication   2,500
    Unity International Trading Corp.; Miami; electrical equipment   2,000
    DMC Retail Resource; Miami; cosmetics   2,000
    Ryder Truck Rental Inc.; Miami; truck leasing   2,000
    Phineas Corp.; Miami; home for mentally retarded persons   2,000

Carnival Corp.; Miami; deep sea passenger transportation 1,800

Cordis Corp.; Hialeah; surgical and medical instruments 1,600

Palmetto General Hospital; Hialeah   1,400

Alterman Corp.; Opa-Locka; trucking   1,305

Hialeah Hospital Inc.; Hialeah   1,200

Parkway Regional Medical Center; Miami   1,200

Florida KSL Holdings Inc.; Miami; resort hotel   1,200

Miami-Dade County; Miami; waste management program 1,100

Althin Healthcare Inc.; Hialeah; surgical and medical instruments   1,000

Kitty Hawk Cargo Inc.; Miami; freight forwarding   1,000

Knight-Ridder Inc.; Coral Gables; advertising   1,000

Symbiosis Corp.; Miami; surgical and medical instruments 1,000

U.S. Postal Service; Pembroke Pines   875

Norwegian Cruise Line Ltd.; Miami; deep sea passenger transportation   850

Ocean Bank; Hollywood; commercial bank   800

Univision Network LP; Miami; investment holding company   798

Interval Travel Inc.; Miami; travel agency   710

Professional Aviation Management; Miami; employment agencies   700

Host International Inc.; Miami; snack bar   700

Vanguard Security Inc.; Miami; security guard service   640

Palm Springs General Hospital Inc.; Hialeah   600

Amadeus Global Travel Distribution; Miami; computer rental and leasing   600

Edna W. Lopez; Miami; general practice law office   600

Miami-Dade County School Board; Miami   550

Dole Fresh Flowers Inc.; Miami; flowers   550

Bloomingdale's Inc.; Miami; department stores   550

QCS Inet Aquisition Corp.; Miami; photograph transmission services   533

Fine Air Services Corp.; Miami; air cargo carrier   523

Alubia; Pembroke Pines; export/import bank   521

STS Apparel Corp.; Hialeah; embroidered emblems   500

Electronic Data Systems Corp.; Hollywood; computer programming services   500

Danzas AEI Inc.; Miami; domestic freight forwarding   500

Miami-Dade County Hospital; Miami   500

Cingular Wireless; Miami; cellular telephones   500

Daniel Electrical of Treasure Coast Inc.; Miami; electrical contractor   500

Miami-Dade County; Miami; passenger train services   500

Multi-Builder Acceptance Corp.; Miami; mortgage bankers 500

Miami-Dade County; Miami; county government   500

Electronic Data Systems Corp.; Miami; management services   500

Miami-Dade County; Miami; waste management program 500

Florida 22nd District

Southeast — coastal Broward and Palm Beach Counties, parts of Fort Lauderdale and Boca Raton

The 22nd follows picturesque Route A1A down the Southeast coast from northern Palm Beach County to Fort Lauderdale in Broward County. Though its projections reach inland in places to pick up middle-class suburbs and gated communities, the district is mostly identifiable by its upscale beachfront cities and towns, including parts of Boca Raton. The 22nd no longer has the highest percentage of elderly residents in the state after 2002 redistricting, but one-quarter of its voting-age population is 65 or older. *(See map p. 237.)*

The district's residents are mostly well-off and overwhelmingly white. Republicans count Palm Beach, Pompano Beach, and Fort Lauderdale as their base. Many of the old 22nd's Democratic strongholds—including all of the district's territory in Miami-Dade County—were excised during redistricting to help bolster GOP candidates here.

Both Palm Beach, where a majority of residents live, and Broward Counties lean Democratic, but redistricting lassoed in enough Republican precincts to transform the 22nd from a Democratic-leaning district into a politically competitive battleground that backed Al Gore by just 5 percentage points in the 2000 elections. The Republican incumbent captured 61 percent of the vote in the new district in 2002.

Exclusive hotels and shopping centers lie within the district, while the ports of Palm Beach and Fort Lauderdale attract shipping and cruise line business. The area's elderly population supports several large hospitals. The wealth of many district residents helps insulate them from economic pressures, but the area depends heavily on tourism.

Major Industry
Health care, tourism, shipping.

Notable
The International Swimming Hall of Fame Museum is in Fort Lauderdale.

Election Returns

	Republican		Democratic		Other
President 2000	123,302	47.6%	135,868	52.4%	
House 2002	131,930	60.8%	83,265	38.4%	1,902

District Profile

Population   639,295

Total area (square miles)   500.2
  Land area (square miles)   267.7

Population per square mile   2,388.1

Counties (2000 population)
Broward (pt.)   277,367
Palm Beach (pt.)   361,928

Cities and other areas over 10,000 (2000 population)
Boca Raton (pt.)   55,946
Boynton Beach (pt.)   25,208
Coconut Creek (pt.)   18,665
Cooper City (pt.)   10,791
Coral Springs (pt.)   43,354
Deerfield Beach (pt.)   28,259
Delray Beach (pt.)   24,274
Fort Lauderdale (pt.)   61,509
Jupiter town (pt.)   28,762
Lighthouse Point   10,767
North Palm Beach village   12,064
Palm Beach Gardens (pt.)   30,649
Palm Beach town   10,468
Parkland (pt.)   13,765
Pompano Beach (pt.)   34,925
West Palm Beach (pt.)   26,467

Race and Hispanic or Latino origin*
White   82.3%
Black or African American   3.8%
American Indian or Alaska Native   0.1%
Asian   1.7%
Native Hawaiian or other Pacific Islander   0.0%
Some other race   0.2%
Hispanic or Latino origin   10.7%
Two or more races   1.2%

*As percentage of total population.

Ancestry*
Dutch 1.2%	Russian 2.3%
English 8.7%	Scotch-Irish 1.3%
French 2.8%	Scottish 1.8%
German 11.7%	Swedish 1.1%
Irish 11.0%	USA/American 4.8%
Italian 9.5%	West Indian 1.6%
Polish 3.4%	

*As estimated percentage of total population.

Universities and colleges, 2000–2001 enrollment
Art Institute of Fort Lauderdale, Fort Lauderdale   3,145
Florida Metropolitan University, Fort Lauderdale   1,483
North Technical Education Center, Riviera Beach   1,661
Palm Beach Atlantic College, West Palm Beach   2,295
Palm Beach Community College, Lake Worth   17,326
Ultrasound Diagnostic School, Pompano Beach   668

Newspapers and circulation
	District circulation	Total circulation
El Nuevo Herald, Miami	2,694	88,384
Miami Herald	15,932	312,757
New York Post	2,125	511,412
Palm Beach Post	54,607	171,457
South Florida Sun-Sentinel	62,282	251,736
*USA Today**	2,459	1,674,376

*See Sources and Explanations in the front of the volume.

Television stations and affiliations
West Palm Beach-Fort Pierce	70%	WFLX	FOX
West Palm Beach-Fort Pierce	70%	WPBF	ABC
West Palm Beach-Fort Pierce	70%	WPEC	CBS
West Palm Beach-Fort Pierce	70%	WPTV	NBC
West Palm Beach-Fort Pierce	70%	WPXP	PAX
West Palm Beach-Fort Pierce	70%	WTCE	Independent
West Palm Beach-Fort Pierce	70%	WTVX	UPN, WB
West Palm Beach-Fort Pierce	70%	WXEL	PBS
Miami-Fort Lauderdale	30%	WAMI	Telefutura
Miami-Fort Lauderdale	30%	WBFS	UPN
Miami-Fort Lauderdale	30%	WBZL	WB
Miami-Fort Lauderdale	30%	WEYS	Independent Spanish
Miami-Fort Lauderdale	30%	WFOR	CBS
Miami-Fort Lauderdale	30%	WHFT	Independent
Miami-Fort Lauderdale	30%	WLRN	PBS
Miami-Fort Lauderdale	30%	WLTV	Univision
Miami-Fort Lauderdale	30%	WPBT	PBS
Miami-Fort Lauderdale	30%	WPLG	ABC
Miami-Fort Lauderdale	30%	WPXM	PAX
Miami-Fort Lauderdale	30%	WSCV	Telemundo
Miami-Fort Lauderdale	30%	WSVN	FOX
Miami-Fort Lauderdale	30%	WTVJ	NBC

Cable systems and subscribers
Adelphia   82,566
Advanced Cable Communications   27,179
Comcast   51,504
Shaw Communications   115,348

Businesses and other major employers
Club Corp. Inc.; West Palm Beach; membership sports/recreation clubs   23,000
Equitable Life Assurance Society of United States; Boca Raton; real estate investment trusts   5,859
Good Samaritan Medical Center; West Palm Beach   3,100
Palm Beach County School Board; West Palm Beach   3,000
Office Depot Inc.; Delray Beach; office supplies   2,400
Palm Beach Community College; Lake Worth   2,362
Holy Cross Hospital Inc.; Deerfield Beach   2,300
Holy Cross Hospital Inc.; Fort Lauderdale   2,085
Florida Power and Light Co.; West Palm Beach; electric power generation   2,000
Private Care Inc.; Palm Beach Gardens; home health care services   2,000
American Media Operations Inc.; Delray Beach; newspaper   1,955
Panthers BRHC; Boca Raton; resort hotel   1,800
Boca Raton Community Hospital Inc.; Boca Raton   1,800
Fleming Gannett Inc.; North Palm Beach; engineering services   1,500
U.S. Veterans Hospital; West Palm Beach   1,300
Boca Raton; Boca Raton; town government   1,300
U.S. Postal Service; Boynton Beach   1,130
Birdsall Inc.; West Palm Beach; shipping and steamship company association   1,058
GEE SDA Inc.; Fort Lauderdale; loan brokers   1,000
Westport Senior Living Investment Fund; Palm Beach Gardens; community and rural development   1,000
Executive Incentives and Travel Inc.; Deerfield Beach; travel agency   1,000
AJG Investment Inc.; Palm Beach; investment offices   1,000

Palm Beach Gardens Community Hospital Inc.; Palm Beach Gardens   994

North Amisub Ridge Hospital Inc.; Fort Lauderdale   990

Divosta Building Corp.; Palm Beach Gardens; new single-family houses   925

Palm Beach County; Palm Beach Gardens; fire dept.   900

Jupiter Medical Center Inc.; Jupiter   819

NCCI Holdings Inc.; Boca Raton; workers' compensation insurance   800

Breakers Palm Beach Inc.; Palm Beach; hotels   750

Excel Administrative Solutions; Boca Raton; employee leasing service   700

North Broward Hospital District; Fort Lauderdale   600

Vacation Break USA Inc.; Fort Lauderdale; time-sharing real estate sales   600

HRS Broward County Health Hospital; Fort Lauderdale   600

Palm Beach County; West Palm Beach; county government   600

Allied Interstate Inc.; West Palm Beach; collection agency   600

Wackenhut Corp.; Palm Beach Gardens; security guard service   550

Broward County; Pompano Beach; police dept.   500

City of Coral Springs; Pompano Beach; city government   500

HR Network; Fort Lauderdale; employment agency   500

Form Works Inc.; Fort Lauderdale; concrete work   500

GE Medical Systems Information Technologies; Jupiter; medical equipment rental   500

Churchill Benefit Corp.; Delray Beach; prepackaged software   500

Florida 23rd District

Southeast — parts of Fort Lauderdale, West Palm Beach, and Lauderhill

One of two black-majority districts in the state, the heavily Democratic 23rd stretches westward from working-class Fort Pierce to the eastern shores of Lake Okeechobee and back east toward some of the coastal hubs, such as West Palm Beach and Fort Lauderdale. Most residents live in Broward County, and much of the area west of Interstate 95 is rural and unpopulated. A significant portion of the Everglades was added to the 23rd in 2002 redistricting. The eastern borders of the 23rd tend to be several blocks off the coast, with the neighboring 22nd taking in much of the prime beachfront property. *(See map p. 237.)*

Most urban areas in the 23rd—such as Lauderhill, Lauderdale Lakes, Riviera Beach, and portions of West Palm Beach—contain largely black neighborhoods and attract local government employees, educators and other middle-class professionals. The 23rd is growing more diverse, drawing in people from around the world. Hispanics make up 13.7 percent of the population. Citrus, sugar cane, and rice growers work the large but sparsely populated rural portions of the district. The 23rd lacks a major employment sector, and the vulnerability of citrus crops to bad weather contributes to making it one of the poorest districts in the state.

Democrats outnumber Republicans by a ratio of more than three to one, and voters routinely give Democratic candidates more than 75 percent of the vote in competitive statewide elections. Indeed, many heavily black precincts—including some in western Fort Lauderdale and Lauderdale Lakes—gave the Democratic gubernatorial nominee more than 90 percent of the vote in 2002.

Major Industry

Agriculture, local government, small business.

Notable

Lake Okeechobee, part of which is in the 23rd, is the second-largest freshwater lake contained wholly within the United States; Lauderdale Lakes has 22 churches within its four square miles.

Election Returns

	Republican		Democratic		Other
President 2000	33,034	20.2%	130,518	79.8%	
House 2002	27,986	22.5%	96,347	77.5%	5

District Profile

Population   639,295

Total area (square miles)   3,703.2
Land area (square miles)   3,362.2

Population per square mile   190.1

Counties (2000 population)
Broward (pt.)   351,496   Palm Beach (pt.)   238,051
Hendry (pt.)   7,230   St. Lucie (pt.)   38,007
Martin (pt.)   4,511

Cities and other areas over 10,000 (2000 population)
Belle Glade   14,906
Boynton Beach (pt.)   19,970
Deerfield Beach (pt.)   11,596
Delray Beach (pt.)   18,682
Fort Lauderdale (pt.)   57,387
Fort Pierce (pt.)   23,799
Lake Worth (pt.)   26,775
Lauderdale Lakes (pt.)   30,895
Lauderhill (pt.)   47,371
Margate (pt.)   11,625
Miramar (pt.)   11,604
North Lauderdale   32,264
Oakland Park (pt.)   13,265
Pembroke Pines (pt.)   11,361
Pompano Beach (pt.)   30,217
Riviera Beach (pt.)   22,615
Sunrise (pt.)   14,109
Tamarac (pt.)   19,458
West Palm Beach (pt.)   52,330

Race and Hispanic or Latino origin*
White   29.4%
Black or African American   51.2%
American Indian or Alaska Native   0.2%
Asian   1.2%
Native Hawaiian or other Pacific Islander   0.1%
Some other race   0.4%
Hispanic or Latino origin   13.7%
Two or more races   3.9%

As percentage of total population.

Ancestry*

English	2.9%	Polish	1.3%
French	1.1%	Subsaharan	1.2%
German	4.1%	USA/American	5.0%
Irish	4.0%	West Indian	16.2%
Italian	3.3%		

As estimated percentage of total population.

Universities and colleges, 2000–2001 enrollment

ATI Career Training Center, Fort Lauderdale 534
City College, Fort Lauderdale 322
Cooper Career Institute, West Palm Beach 207
Indian River Community College, Fort Pierce 13,186
Institute of Career Education, West Palm Beach 206
Keiser College, Fort Lauderdale 3,086
New England Institute of Technology, West Palm Beach 836
South College, West Palm Beach 381

Newspapers and circulation

	District circulation	Total circulation
Miami Herald	9,581	·312,757
New York Post	2,680	511,412
Palm Beach Post	36,646	171,457
South Florida Sun-Sentinel	30,337	251,736
*USA Today**	13,397	1,674,376

See Sources and Explanations in the front of the volume.

Television stations and affiliations

West Palm Beach-Fort Pierce	60%	WFLX	FOX
West Palm Beach-Fort Pierce	60%	WPBF	ABC
West Palm Beach-Fort Pierce	60%	WPEC	CBS
West Palm Beach-Fort Pierce	60%	WPTV	NBC
West Palm Beach-Fort Pierce	60%	WPXP	PAX
West Palm Beach-Fort Pierce	60%	WTCE	Independent
West Palm Beach-Fort Pierce	60%	WTVX	UPN, WB
West Palm Beach-Fort Pierce	60%	WXEL	PBS
Miami-Fort Lauderdale	24%	WAMI	Telefutura
Miami-Fort Lauderdale	24%	WBFS	UPN
Miami-Fort Lauderdale	24%	WBZL	WB
Miami-Fort Lauderdale	24%	WEYS	Independent Spanish
Miami-Fort Lauderdale	24%	WFOR	CBS
Miami-Fort Lauderdale	24%	WHFT	Independent
Miami-Fort Lauderdale	24%	WLRN	PBS
Miami-Fort Lauderdale	24%	WLTV	Univision
Miami-Fort Lauderdale	24%	WPBT	PBS
Miami-Fort Lauderdale	24%	WPLG	ABC
Miami-Fort Lauderdale	24%	WPXM	PAX
Miami-Fort Lauderdale	24%	WSCV	Telemundo
Miami-Fort Lauderdale	24%	WSVN	FOX
Miami-Fort Lauderdale	24%	WTVJ	NBC
Fort Myers-Naples	16%	WBBH	NBC
Fort Myers-Naples	16%	WFTX	FOX
Fort Myers-Naples	16%	WGCU	PBS
Fort Myers-Naples	16%	WINK	CBS
Fort Myers-Naples	16%	WRXY	Independent
Fort Myers-Naples	16%	WTVK	WB
Fort Myers-Naples	16%	WZVN	ABC

Cable systems and subscribers

Adelphia 72,505
Comcast 118,995
Shaw Communications 19,876

Businesses and other major employers

CSR Business Service Center; West Palm Beach; lumber and building materials 9,200
Broward County; Fort Lauderdale; fire dept. 7,500
Answer Group Inc.; Pompano Beach; computer programming services 3,200
Palm Beach County; West Palm Beach; correctional institutions 3,000
St. Mary's Hospital; West Palm Beach 3,000
ADP Total Source; West Palm Beach; labor resource services 2,900
Range Systems Engineering Suppport; West Palm Beach; engineering services 2,096
Maria C. Munoz; West Palm Beach; certified public accountant 2,002
American Multiline Corp.; Pompano Beach; temporary help service 2,000
U.S. Postal Service; Fort Lauderdale 2,000
Indian River Community College Inc.; Fort Pierce 1,800
Disabled American Veteran Inc.; West Palm Beach; veterans' organization 1,600
Sun Energy Products USA Corp.; Fort Lauderdale; industrial supplies 1,580
South Broward Hospital District; Hollywood 1,500
Ohio Savings Financial Corp.; Fort Lauderdale; federal savings institutions 1,400
Bethesda Memorial Hospital Inc.; Boynton Beach 1,283
University Hospital; Fort Lauderdale 1,100
Lawnwood Medical Center Inc.; Fort Pierce 1,050
Florida Agent Investigations; West Palm Beach; private investigator 1,000
North Broward Hospital District; Pompano Beach 983
Broward County; Fort Lauderdale; correctional facilities 900
Plantation General Hospital; Fort Lauderdale 900
Ocwen Federal Bank; West Palm Beach; federal savings banks 850
Cleveland Clinic Florida; Fort Lauderdale 800
Palm Beach County; West Palm Beach; public health programs 800
Broward County School Board; Fort Lauderdale 760
American Medical Response Inc.; Fort Lauderdale; ambulance service 700
St. Lucie County; Fort Pierce; county government 700
South Florida Water Management District; West Palm Beach; water control and quality agency 680
Columbia Hospital; West Palm Beach 625
Citrix Systems Inc.; Fort Lauderdale; computer software development 600
Florida Dept. of Transportation; Fort Lauderdale 600
Sports Authority Inc.; Fort Lauderdale; sporting goods and bicycle shops 600
Paddock Restaurant; West Palm Beach; restaurants 600
Wellington Regional Medical Center Inc.; West Palm Beach 525
Comcast; Pompano Beach; cable television 500
Sugar Cane Growers Cooperative of Florida; Belle Glade; raw cane sugar 500

Florida 24th District

East central — Orlando suburbs, part of Space Coast

Created following the 2000 census, the 24th takes in much of the area between the GOP-leaning Orlando suburbs and the so-called Space Coast, drawing nearly equally from Orange, Seminole, and Volusia Counties, with just a bit less than one-fifth of its population coming from its portion of Brevard County.

Fashioned out of slices of the old Republican-held 7th, 8th, and 15th districts, the 24th is a potentially competitive district with a small but distinct Republican lean. The GOP nominee won the 1992, 1996, and 2000 presidential contests among voters in what would have been the 24th, with George W. Bush capturing 53.4 percent of the vote in 2000.

The Space Coast, home of the Kennedy Space Center, is an economic driver in the region, providing a tourist attraction and a base for technology companies.

North of the Space Coast are popular beach communities and the city of Daytona Beach, most of which is in the neighboring 7th District. College students and bikers flock to Daytona's famous coastline during spring and summer.

The 24th takes in one of Daytona Beach's jewels—Daytona International Speedway, which is home to NASCAR's Daytona 500 stock car race.

The district, which has a relatively young population for Florida, sweeps west to pick up suburban communities outside Orlando, including most of Altamonte Springs and all of Oviedo.

Major Industry

Aerospace, technology, tourism.

Notable

Star Systems, an electronic payments network using ATMs and retailers, is based in Maitland (shared with the 7th).

Election Returns

	Republican		Democratic		Other
President 2000	133,531	53.4%	116,502	46.6%	
House 2002	135,576	61.8%	83,667	38.2%	

District Profile

Population   639,295

Total area (square miles)   1,914.5
   Land area (square miles)   1,583.2

Population per square mile   403.8

Counties (2000 population)

Brevard (pt.)	120,362	Seminole (pt.)	178,331
Orange (pt.)	175,140	Volusia (pt.)	165,462

Cities and other areas over 10,000 (2000 population)

Altamonte Springs (pt.)   30,130
Apopka (pt.)   18,505
Casselberry (pt.)   12,290
Daytona Beach (pt.)   10,483
Deltona (pt.)   22,510
Edgewater   18,668
Forest City CDP   12,612
Goldenrod CDP   12,871
Lockhart CDP (pt.)   11,005
New Smyrna Beach   20,048
Oviedo   26,316
Port Orange   45,823
Port St. John CDP   12,112
Titusville   40,670
Winter Springs (pt.)   18,872

Race and Hispanic or Latino origin*

White   80.0%
Black or African American   6.3%
American Indian or Alaska Native   0.3%
Asian   2.0%
Native Hawaiian or other Pacific Islander   0.0%
Some other race   0.2%
Hispanic or Latino origin   9.8%
Two or more races   1.4%

As percentage of total population.

Ancestry*

Dutch	1.4%	Italian	6.1%
English	9.3%	Polish	2.3%
French	2.8%	Scotch-Irish	1.6%
German	12.4%	Scottish	1.9%
Irish	10.5%	USA/American	6.2%

As estimated percentage of total population.

Universities and colleges, 2000–2001 enrollment

Brevard Community College, Cocoa   13,265
Full Sail Real World Education, Winter Park   1,910
ITT Technical Institute, Maitland   342
University of Central Florida, Orlando   33,713
University of Phoenix-Orlando, Maitland   3,992

Newspapers and circulation

	District circulation	Total circulation
Daytona Beach News-Journal	38,391	99,266
Florida Today, Melbourne	18,474	86,199
Orlando Sentinel	54,734	257,293
*USA Today**	14,752	1,674,376

See Sources and Explanations in the front of the volume.

Television stations and affiliations

Orlando-Daytona Beach-Melbourne	100%	WACX	Independent
Orlando-Daytona Beach-Melbourne	100%	WBCC	PBS
Orlando-Daytona Beach-Melbourne	100%	WCEU	PBS
Orlando-Daytona Beach-Melbourne	100%	WESH	NBC
Orlando-Daytona Beach-Melbourne	100%	WFTV	ABC
Orlando-Daytona Beach-Melbourne	100%	WKCF	WB
Orlando-Daytona Beach-Melbourne	100%	WKMG	CBS
Orlando-Daytona Beach-Melbourne	100%	WMFE	PBS
Orlando-Daytona Beach-Melbourne	100%	WOFL	FOX
Orlando-Daytona Beach-Melbourne	100%	WOGX	FOX
Orlando-Daytona Beach-Melbourne	100%	WOPX	PAX
Orlando-Daytona Beach-Melbourne	100%	WRBW	UPN
Orlando-Daytona Beach-Melbourne	100%	WTGL	Independent

Cable systems and subscribers

Bright House Networks   78,790

Military installations, September 2001

Naval Air War Center, Orlando   1,161

Businesses and other major employers

Washington Mutual Inc.; Altamonte Springs; federal
savings institutions   26,450

Fuel-Tech Inc.; Mims; tank repair   3,832

University of Central Florida; Orlando   3,401

Adventist Health System/Sunbelt Healthcare Corp.;
Orlando; medical laboratories   3,000

Siemens Westinghouse Power Corp.; Orlando; turbines and
turbine generators   3,000

RadioShack Corp.; Oviedo; consumer electronic equipment
2,300

Lockheed Martin Corp.; Orlando; missile tracking:
telemetry/photography   2,000

Winter Park Health Care Group; Winter Park; hospital
with residency   1,600

Boeing Co.; Kennedy Space Center; security guard service
1,500

Time Warner Entertainment Co.; Maitland; cable television
1,100

Valley Forge Life Insurance Co.; Maitland; data processing
1,000

North Brevard County Hospital District; Titusville   910

Campus Crusade for Christ Inc.; Orlando; religious
organization   900

Florida Dept. of Corrections; Orlando   800

Brevard County; Titusville; police dept.   750

Sprint-Florida Inc.; Apopka; local telephone
communications   700

Wal-Mart Stores Inc.; Orlando; discount department stores
700

Computer Science Raytheon; Cocoa; missile tracking:
telemetry/photography   700

Boston Whaler; Edgewater; boatbuilding and repairing
600

Massey Services Inc.; Maitland; pest control services   550

Brevard Community College; Cocoa   550

Bert Fish Medical Center Inc.; New Smyrna Beach   520

Wal-Mart Stores Inc.; Daytona Beach; department stores
500

Ocwen Federal Bank; Orlando; federal savings institutions
500

Florida 25th District

South — western Miami-Dade County, the Everglades

One of two seats Florida gained following the 2000 census, the 25th takes in a broad swath of land covering the western portion of Miami-Dade County, most of Collier County, and almost all of Monroe County. Geographically, it is centered in Everglades National Park and Big Cypress National Preserve. *(See map p. 237.)*

The district was constructed to elect a Republican of Cuban descent. A majority of residents are Hispanic—many of them Cuban-American—and Republicans have a 43 percent to 35 percent registration edge over Democrats. Though Bill Clinton won the area with a plurality in his 1996 reelection bid, Republicans have won the area in most statewide elections, especially those involving members of the Bush family.

Nearly 90 percent of the district's population lives in Miami-Dade County, much of it on the western edge of the Miami region and in communities south of the city.

National parks give the 25th an ecosystem and an array of wildlife—everything from manatees to panthers—not commonly found in North America. Restoration of the Everglades, oil drilling, and the pace of development promise to remain contentious issues here for some time.

Republican support for a hard line against Fidel Castro-led Cuba has helped the GOP forge a long-standing alliance with South Florida's large Cuban-American community.

Major Industry

Tourism.

Notable

Everglades National Park covers 1.5 million acres—which is just a small portion of the Everglades.

Election Returns

	Republican		Democratic		Other
President 2000	88,308	55.1%	72,050	44.9%	
House 2002	81,845	64.6%	44,757	35.4%	

District Profile

Population   639,295

Total area (square miles)   4,724.2
Land area (square miles)   4,267.9

Population per square mile   149.8

Counties (2000 population)
Collier (pt.)   79,690
Miami-Dade (pt.)   559,545
Monroe (pt.)   60

Cities and other areas over 10,000 (2000 population)
Country Walk CDP   10,653
The Crossings CDP   23,557
Cutler Ridge CDP (pt.)   24,482
Doral CDP (pt.)   11,416
Golden Gate CDP (pt.)   20,951
The Hammocks CDP   47,379
Hialeah (pt.)   17,834
Hialeah Gardens   19,297
Homestead   31,909
Immokalee CDP   19,763
Kendale Lakes CDP (pt.)   56,901
Kendall CDP (pt.)   15,550
Kendall West CDP   38,034
Leisure City CDP (pt.)   22,137
Richmond West CDP   28,082
South Miami Heights CDP   33,522
Tamiami CDP (pt.)   54,788

Race and Hispanic or Latino origin*
White   24.3%
Black or African American   10.0%
American Indian or Alaska Native   0.1%
Asian   1.6%

Native Hawaiian or other Pacific Islander   0.0%
Some other race   0.2%
Hispanic or Latino origin   62.4%
Two or more races   1.4%

As percentage of total population.

Ancestry*
English   2.3%   Italian   2.4%
German   3.2%   USA/American   3.8%
Irish   3.0%   West Indian   3.7%

As estimated percentage of total population.

Universities and colleges, 2000–2001 enrollment
National School of Technology, Miami   544
Robert Morgan Vocational Technical Institute, Miami   1,075

Newspapers and circulation

	District circulation	Total circulation
El Nuevo Herald, Miami	22,162	88,384
*Key West Citizen**	2,675	8,460
Miami Herald	44,422	312,757
Naples Daily News	4,855	55,324
*USA Today**	13,083	1,674,376

See Sources and Explanations in the front of the volume.

Television stations and affiliations
Miami-Fort Lauderdale	59%	WAMI	Telefutura
Miami-Fort Lauderdale	59%	WBFS	UPN
Miami-Fort Lauderdale	59%	WBZL	WB
Miami-Fort Lauderdale	59%	WEYS	Independent Spanish
Miami-Fort Lauderdale	59%	WFOR	CBS
Miami-Fort Lauderdale	59%	WHFT	Independent
Miami-Fort Lauderdale	59%	WLRN	PBS
Miami-Fort Lauderdale	59%	WLTV	Univision
Miami-Fort Lauderdale	59%	WPBT	PBS
Miami-Fort Lauderdale	59%	WPLG	ABC
Miami-Fort Lauderdale	59%	WPXM	PAX
Miami-Fort Lauderdale	59%	WSCV	Telemundo
Miami-Fort Lauderdale	59%	WSVN	FOX
Miami-Fort Lauderdale	59%	WTVJ	NBC
Fort Myers-Naples	41%	WBBH	NBC
Fort Myers-Naples	41%	WFTX	FOX
Fort Myers-Naples	41%	WGCU	PBS
Fort Myers-Naples	41%	WINK	CBS
Fort Myers-Naples	41%	WRXY	Independent
Fort Myers-Naples	41%	WTVK	WB
Fort Myers-Naples	41%	WZVN	ABC

Cable systems and subscribers
Adelphia   6,529
Comcast   3,438
Time Warner   62,877

Military installations, September 2001
Luis E. Martinez U.S. Army Reserve, Miami   1,090

Businesses and other major employers
Miami-Dade Community College; Miami   2,106
American Bankers Acceptance Corp.; Miami; insurance agents and brokers   2,000
Miami-Dade County; Miami; airport transportation   1,700
United Technologies Corp.; Hialeah; aircraft engines and parts   1,503
Kendall Health Care Group Hospital; Miami   1,300
Miccosukee Tribe of Indians of Florida; Miami; bingo hall   1,215
Transportation Office of Miami-Dade Schools; Miami   1,001
Coulter Corp.; Miami; fluid meters and counting devices   1,000
Sara Lee Corp.; Miami; novelties, leather   950
Paragon Produce Corp.; Immokalee; tomato farm   860
Wal-Mart Stores Inc.; Hialeah; discount department stores   800
Interstate Brands Corp.; Miami; bakery products   715
Wal-Mart Stores Inc.; Hialeah; automotive tires   700
Costa Nursery Farms Inc.; Goulds; nursery stock   700
Aneco Inc.; Miami; electrical contractor   700
Florida Dept. of Corrections; Homestead   650
Homestead Hospital Inc.; Homestead   500
Sears Roebuck and Co. Inc.; Miami; department stores   500

GEORGIA

Districts established October 1, 2001, for elections first held in 2002.

13 members

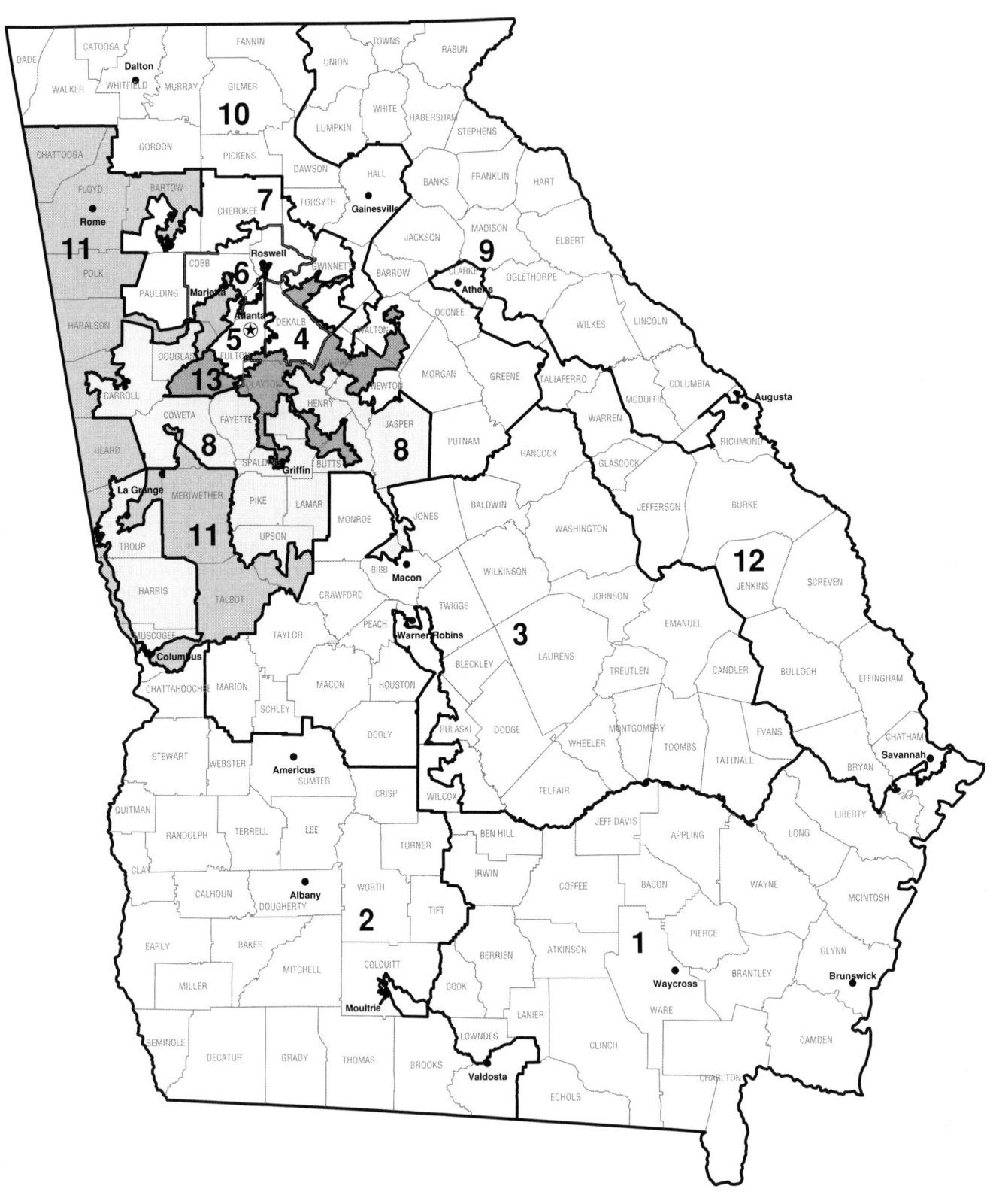

Georgia

At the turn of the new century, Georgia has assumed unprecedented importance not only in the South but in the nation. The state had grown by one-fourth in the 1990s, and the historic relationship between its races, subregions, and major parties had undergone unprecedented changes.

All these influences were on display in November 2002 when the stunning results of midterm elections for Congress and statewide office both secured and epitomized Republican successes nationally. By ousting an incumbent Democratic senator, Georgia broke the 50–50 partisan tie in the Senate and restored the Republican majority there. By ousting an incumbent Democratic governor (in an even larger upset), Georgia elected its first Republican governor in more than a century and kept the majority of all governorships Republican (26 to 24). Moreover, by winning two more seats in Congress than anyone had expected, Georgia Republicans held their control of the delegation and completely frustrated the redistricting aims of state and national Democrats. It is not too much to say that if Florida's prolonged presidential recount was the featured national election story of 2000, Georgia's upsets and partisan shift were the most important results in the midterms of 2002.

As with Florida, its alphabetical and geographical next-door neighbor, Georgia has risen suddenly to the first rank of national politics through explosive population growth and new economic muscle. If these two states were one, they would now be the second most populous state behind California (and well ahead of Texas). Taken together or separately, they are now pivotal in the partisan battle for the South in the decade after 2000 and probably for decades thereafter.

While Texas and Florida have leaped into the second and fourth places nationally in terms of population, neither grew as fast as Georgia in the 1990s. This latest spurt made Georgia the tenth most populous state and marked it for further moves up the rankings soon. In the first 25 years of the new millennium, only California, Texas, and Florida are expected to add more to their populations than Georgia.

Georgia's growth has had all the elements of the general national expansion—people moving to new states, people arriving from other countries, and people seeking life in the suburbs. Most of this confluence in Georgia centers around the megalopolis of Atlanta, the inland city and airport hub that has become the capital of the New South. Despite the rise of half a dozen rival urban centers in the region, Atlanta continues to drain talent from around the South, attract new residents from other parts of the country, provide opportunity for Hispanics (already 5 percent of the state in 2000) and

other immigrants, and demonstrate America's continuing eagerness to live in newly constructed suburbs.

Part of Atlanta's expansion has been homegrown, as symbolized by the worldwide success of Coca-Cola, a local product for more than a century. But more fuel has come from the arrival of companies from other states and overseas, as international companies have chosen to make this hot and humid inland metropolis their base for southern, and sometimes national, operations. Hartsfield Airport, named for Bill Hartsfield, Atlanta's far-sighted mayor for a quarter century ending in 1961, has become one of the two or three busiest hubs in the world. Atlanta also has the unusual distinction of being the home of the cable giant CNN, in part because the cable news operation's founder, sports and media mogul Ted Turner, was based here. Like Turner's perennially powerful baseball team, the Atlanta Braves, CNN helped elevate the city's profile worldwide.

All the growth and the new business began increasing the state's Republican population substantially in the postwar decades, as the GOP attracted arrivals from the North and the Midwest along with native conservative Democrats embittered by the policies of their national party on civil rights and other issues. Republicans started winning here in White House voting. In fact, no Democratic nominee has won a majority in Georgia since John F. Kennedy in 1960, with the exception of native son and former governor Jimmy Carter. (Bill Clinton carried the state with a 43 percent plurality in 1992 but lost it in 1996.)

For years, however, the GOP could not extend its appeal beyond the presidential line. There was briefly a Republican senator in the 1980s and another in the 1990s, but the congressional delegation was nine to one Democratic as late as 1992. Georgia was the last southern state to break the "since Reconstruction" skein and elect a Republican governor, doing so after a dozen decades. During that time, the legislature had also remained Democratic in both chambers (by four-to-one ratios as late as 1991).

One reason for this hard-core Democratic survival was that the party here kept producing candidates who could hold white rural populists' votes even after the civil rights movement and the widespread registration of African Americans changed the fundamentals of Southern elections. Georgia's black population (28 percent in 2000) was largely concentrated in metropolitan Atlanta but mapmakers made sure they parceled it out in a pinwheel of districts that would all elect Democrats without ever getting a black Democratic nominee. Still, the critical mass of the blacks in Atlanta raised up many powerful black activists, including

Martin Luther King Jr. They elected black Democrats Andrew Young, Julian Bond, Maynard Jackson, and John Lewis and sent them all on to national notice. But they also provided the winning margins for white Democrats in statewide votes: Carter and Sam Nunn, Max Cleland, and Roy Barnes.

In their several ways, these white men were able to persuade Georgia voters they were not beholden to the national Democratic Party, no matter how prominent they were in it. But renewing that feat of persuasion became more difficult every time a national Democratic initiative was perceived to be directed against Georgia—as in the civil rights acts or the various Democratic proposals to curtail gun ownership and public acts of worship while promoting the rights of women and gays to serve in the military.

Republicans have long argued that the state's bedrock attitudes favored their philosophy, and that only old habits and structural advantages kept the Democrats running the state. Evidence for that came in the elections of 2002, when a strong midterm turnout among conservatives in both parties (and among rural white voters in particular) toppled the incumbent Democratic governor and senator and delivered eight of the states' 13 new congressional districts to Republicans.

The great irony of these shifts was that before the 2002 elections the governor and party leaders in the legislature had taken great pains to ensure Democratic gains in the congressional delegation. They had drawn the two new districts, and revised the preexisting 11, to make it highly likely the Democrats would hold the three districts they had (all represented by African Americans) and capture four of the other ten. The idea was to get to seven seats altogether for a bare majority in the new delegation.

The new districts were drawn in metro Atlanta (the 13th) and in a central-eastern corridor anchored by Athens and Augusta (the 12th), each with combined black-Hispanic populations right around 50 percent. Assuming both these districts would be won by black Democrats, the mapmakers went on to scramble the south-central counties around Macon to create an open-seat district (renumbered the 3rd) and to appropriate most of the old 7th to form a new 11th District. In both cases, districts were created that a Democrat could reasonably expect to win. Along the way, the Democratic mapmakers also put two Republican incumbents together in the southeastern 1st District and two others in the Atlanta suburban 7th District.

This aggressive approach to redistricting was neither unprecedented nor without parallel in states where Republicans had the whip hand. But it generated great controversy in Georgia, where interested voters could easily see what was afoot and, in many cases, take offense. The gerrymander became an issue in the elections of 2002, along with intraparty struggles in the Democratic primaries and removal of the Confederate battle flag from the current state flag.

In the end, the Democratic remapping offensive flopped. While the new 13th and the redrawn 3rd fell to the Democrats as planned, the new 12th and the redrawn 11th went Republican, keeping the delegation's Republican contingent at eight. Adding an ironic note, one of the two Republicans driven out of their home district by the map ran for the Senate and won.

It should be noted that the Democrats whose map strategy overreached in 2001 had ample warning of what might happen. In 1991 Democrats in charge of redistricting had also used their power to the fullest, creating two new districts where a black candidate could win, weakening the white Democrats in surrounding districts and dismantling the district of Newt Gingrich, who was the only Republican in the delegation and the number two GOP leader in the House.

The 1991 plan backfired badly. Gingrich simply moved to another district with no incumbent and won a new term easily in 1992. As he was winning, so were three other Republicans, all beneficiaries to some degree of the map that made districts either more black or more white than they were before. In 1994 three more Republicans arrived, making the delegation seven to four GOP just in time to cheer Gingrich becoming the first Republican Speaker in 42 years in 1995. Later that year, the last white Democrat in the delegation switched parties, making the delegation eight to three.

In his four years as Speaker, Gingrich pushed the limits of that powerful position and became a national figure. In so doing, he helped highlight the growing importance of his home state. His high-handed style also attracted attention, however, and prompted rebellions in the House. In the election of 1998, the national GOP suffered small but unexpected losses in the House for which Gingrich took the blame. He resigned, but it was a sign of the new Georgia reality that the district immediately elected another Republican.

In the years after 2000 the memory of Gingrich faded both in Washington and in Georgia. But the House maintained the Republican majority he had helped establish, and Georgia maintained the Republican course he had charted. As of 2003, election results and party switches had made the state senate Republican for the first time since Reconstruction. Perhaps even more than the governorship and the other offices, this shift signaled that the Republican wave had not yet crested.

Table 1 Population

District	Population	Population under 18	Voting-age population	Median age	Male*	Female*
1	629,761	173,461	456,300	33.3	50.1	49.9
2	629,735	174,571	455,164	32.6	48.4	51.6
3	629,748	165,116	464,632	34.9	49.1	50.9
4	629,690	156,905	472,785	32.1	48.6	51.4
5	629,727	137,289	492,438	31.4	49.3	50.7
6	629,725	173,920	455,805	35.4	49.4	50.6
7	629,706	185,213	444,493	33.6	50.0	50.0
8	629,700	171,729	457,971	35.3	49.2	50.8
9	629,762	162,530	467,232	36.1	49.1	50.9
10	629,702	165,744	463,958	34.6	50.0	50.0
11	629,730	164,246	465,484	33.3	49.1	50.9
12	629,735	159,534	470,201	30.8	48.3	51.7
13	629,732	178,976	450,756	30.9	49.1	50.9
State	8,186,453	2,169,234	6,017,219	33.4	49.2	50.8

As percentage of total population.

Table 2 Voting-Age Persons by Race/Hispanic or Latino Origin

District	White*	Black or African American*	American Indian or Alaska Native*	Asian*	Other or multirace*	Hispanic or Latino*
1	73.6	20.6	0.3	1.1	0.8	3.7
2	54.2	40.9	0.3	0.6	0.6	3.2
3	59.2	37.2	0.2	0.6	0.5	2.3
4	36.5	48.8	0.2	4.4	1.6	8.5
5	39.2	51.0	0.2	2.4	1.3	5.9
6	83.9	6.5	0.2	3.9	1.1	4.4

District	White*	Black or African American*	American Indian or Alaska Native*	Asian*	Other or multirace*	Hispanic or Latino*
7	83.4	6.5	0.2	3.8	1.0	5.1
8	83.9	11.8	0.2	1.3	0.7	2.0
9	82.8	12.8	0.3	1.1	0.7	2.3
10	87.0	3.2	0.3	0.7	0.6	8.2
11	65.0	25.8	0.2	1.3	1.0	6.7
12	56.1	38.4	0.2	1.7	1.0	2.7
13	46.1	37.3	0.2	5.2	1.3	9.8
State	65.2	26.4	0.2	2.1	1.0	5.0

*As percentage of voting-age population.

Table 3 Voting-Age Population by Age Groups

District	18 to 24*	25 to 44*	45 to 64*	Over 64*
1	14.4	41.8	29.2	14.6
2	16.1	39.1	28.3	16.5
3	13.8	39.7	29.9	16.5
4	14.6	48.9	26.2	10.3
5	16.8	47.8	24.2	11.2
6	9.4	47.7	33.5	9.5
7	10.2	51.0	30.3	8.5
8	11.4	42.9	32.7	13.0
9	11.9	39.7	32.0	16.5
10	12.2	43.0	30.6	14.2
11	13.9	44.0	27.4	14.8
12	21.2	38.4	26.2	14.3
13	14.7	49.4	26.3	9.7
State	13.9	44.1	28.9	13.1

*As percentage of voting-age population.

Table 4 Income and Occupation

District	Median family income	Families in poverty*	White collar†	Blue collar†	Service†	Farm†
1	$42,042	11.7	53.3	30.2	14.9	1.6
2	$34,793	18.3	50.2	31.1	16.6	2.1
3	$38,410	15.9	48.9	32.5	17.0	1.7
4	$54,221	7.6	67.4	19.6	12.9	0.1
5	$43,324	16.5	68.1	16.7	15.0	0.2
6	$86,640	2.4	79.7	11.2	9.0	0.1
7	$68,828	3.2	69.1	20.6	10.1	0.2
8	$59,258	4.6	60.7	27.5	11.6	0.3
9	$46,212	8.6	53.5	32.8	12.7	1.0
10	$47,474	7.5	51.4	36.9	11.1	0.7
11	$42,834	10.7	52.3	33.4	13.9	0.4
12	$38,566	15.9	53.6	28.0	17.8	0.6
13	$47,840	8.8	55.9	29.6	14.3	0.1
State	$49,280	9.9	59.5	26.5	13.4	0.6

*As percentage of all families.   †As percentage of employed workers 16 years and over.

Table 5 Education: School Years Completed

District	Less than grade 9*	Grades 9–12 no diploma*	High school diploma no college*	Some college*	College bachelor's degree or higher*
1	7.8	14.9	32.7	26.6	17.9
2	10.6	19.1	33.0	23.4	13.9
3	10.3	19.1	36.6	21.2	12.8
4	5.5	9.1	20.4	29.1	35.9
5	6.2	13.0	21.0	22.5	37.3
6	2.0	4.1	15.8	27.4	50.7
7	4.3	8.9	25.3	29.7	31.9
8	5.2	11.8	31.5	28.1	23.4
9	8.6	16.0	33.2	23.7	18.5
10	11.9	16.7	31.8	23.7	15.9
11	10.3	17.1	32.0	23.7	16.9
12	8.5	16.5	30.8	24.9	19.3
13	7.8	14.4	29.5	28.9	19.4
State	7.6	13.8	28.7	25.6	24.3

*As percentage of persons age 25 and over.

Table 6 Housing and Residential Patterns

District	Median home value	Owner occupied*	Renter occupied*	Urban†	Rural†
1	$74,100	71.4	28.6	57.9	42.1
2	$62,500	62.5	37.5	58.6	41.4
3	$62,900	69.0	31.0	48.8	51.2
4	$133,000	57.7	42.3	99.6	0.4
5	$136,900	42.1	57.9	99.5	0.5
6	$183,400	79.1	20.9	97.8	2.2
7	$141,000	84.9	15.1	85.9	14.1
8	$116,500	80.7	19.3	58.5	41.5
9	$93,400	76.9	23.1	34.1	65.9
10	$98,200	76.4	23.6	52.0	48.0
11	$85,900	64.1	35.9	72.3	27.7
12	$74,600	58.4	41.6	74.5	25.5
13	$98,000	59.2	40.8	92.1	7.9
State	$100,600	67.5	32.5	71.7	28.3

*As percentage of occupied housing units. †As percentage of total population.

Georgia 1st District

Southeast — Savannah suburbs, part of Valdosta

The 1st takes in a swath of southeast Georgia and its entire coastline, stretching from South Carolina to Florida. In the redistricting plan enacted in 2001, the 1st was altered to become a Republican-leaning district with a substantial military population. Like much of the rest of Georgia, the district is ancestrally Democratic but has shown Republican trends in federal races. George W. Bush received 63.9 percent of the vote here in 2000.

The 1st has no population center; redistricting removed the urban, Democratic areas of Savannah that were the nucleus of the old 1st. The district now has large, mostly rural chunks, reaching into the Republican suburbs of Savannah and parts of Valdosta. It also travels up Interstate 75, taking in parts of Warner Robins, the Republican areas outside of Macon and Robins Air Force Base. The district includes five of the state's 12 major military bases.

Despite a drought, storms, and hurricanes that severely hurt the area's farmers in 1998, peanuts, onions, cotton, tobacco, and other crops help sustain the economy, as do timber, defense, shrimping, and tourism. The district's ports and coastline make trade and coastal conservation dominant issues.

Georgia's coast is becoming a popular destination for retirees and is seeing an influx of new residents settling between Hilton Head, South Carolina, and Florida. This growing part of the population adds to the Republican lean of the district, outnumbering older, agricultural Democrats.

Major Industry
Agriculture, military, manufacturing.

Notable
The Okefenokee Swamp, which covers 436,000 acres, is home to an estimated 35,000 alligators and 234 species of birds.

Election Returns

	Republican		Democratic		Other	
President 2000	119,133	63.9%	65,744	35.3%	1,524	0.8%
House 2002	103,661	72.1%	40,026	27.9%	13	

District Profile

Population   629,761

Total area (square miles)   12,070.6
   Land area (square miles)   11,232.3

Population per square mile   56.1

Counties (2000 population)

Appling	17,419	Glynn	67,568
Atkinson	7,609	Houston (pt.)	45,937
Bacon	10,103	Irwin	9,931
Ben Hill	17,484	Jeff Davis	12,684
Berrien	16,235	Lanier	7,241
Brantley	14,629	Liberty	61,610
Bryan (pt.)	7,197	Long	10,304
Camden	43,664	Lowndes (pt.)	40,315
Charlton	10,282	McIntosh	10,847
Chatham (pt.)	52,575	Pierce	15,636
Clinch	6,878	Pulaski (pt.)	6,313
Coffee	37,413	Ware	35,483
Colquitt (pt.)	14,745	Wayne	26,565
Cook	15,771	Wilcox (pt.)	3,569
Echols	3,754		

Cities and other areas over 10,000 (2000 population)

Brunswick   15,600
Douglas   10,639
Fort Stewart CDP   11,205
Hinesville   30,392
Kingsland   10,506
Moultrie (pt.)   10,083
St. Marys   13,761
St. Simons CDP   13,381
Valdosta (pt.)   15,442
Waycross   15,333
Wilmington Island CDP   14,213

Race and Hispanic or Latino origin*

White   71.0%
Black or African American   22.5%
American Indian or Alaska Native   0.3%
Asian   0.9%
Native Hawaiian or other Pacific Islander   0.1%
Some other race   0.1%
Hispanic or Latino origin   4.1%
Two or more races   1.0%

As percentage of total population.

Ancestry*

English	7.2%	Italian	1.6%
French	1.4%	Scotch-Irish	1.5%
German	5.9%	Scottish	1.5%
Irish	7.0%	USA/American	15.3%

As estimated percentage of total population.

Universities and colleges, 2000–2001 enrollment

Altamaha Technical Institute, Jesup   1,110
Armstrong Atlantic State University, Savannah   5,444
Coastal Georgia Community College, Brunswick   1,912
East Central Technical Institute, Fitzgerald   1,434
Georgia Military College, Moody AFB   454
Georgia Military College, Robins AFB   340
Middle Georgia Technical Institute, Warner Robins   2,124
Moultrie Area Technical Institute, Moultrie   1,376
Okefenokee Technical Institute, Waycross   1,263
South Georgia College, Douglas   1,267
Valdosta Technical Institute, Valdosta   2,049
Waycross College, Waycross   861

Newspapers and circulation

	District circulation	Total circulation
Atlanta Journal-Constitution	10,271	857,088
Jacksonville Times-Union	11,594	171,667
Macon Telegraph	6,672	63,666
Savannah Morning News	21,322	58,145
*USA Today**	3,772	1,674,376
Valdosta Daily Times	7,683	18,691

See Sources and Explanations in the front of the volume.

Television stations and affiliations

Jacksonville, FL	32%	WAWS	FOX, UPN
Jacksonville, FL	32%	WJCT	PBS
Jacksonville, FL	32%	WJEB	Independent
Jacksonville, FL	32%	WJWB	WB
Jacksonville, FL	32%	WJXT	Independent
Jacksonville, FL	32%	WJXX	ABC
Jacksonville, FL	32%	WTEV	CBS
Jacksonville, FL	32%	WTLV	NBC
Jacksonville, FL	32%	WXGA	PBS
Savannah	32%	WGSA	UPN
Savannah	32%	WJCL	ABC
Savannah	32%	WSAV	NBC
Savannah	32%	WTGS	FOX
Savannah	32%	WTOC	CBS
Savannah	32%	WVAN	PBS
Albany	19%	WABW	PBS
Albany	19%	WALB	NBC
Albany	19%	WFXL	FOX
Albany	19%	WSST	Independent
Tallahassee-Thomasville	13%	WCTV	CBS
Tallahassee-Thomasville	13%	WFSU	PBS

Tallahassee-Thomasville	13%	WFXU	UPN
Tallahassee-Thomasville	13%	WTLH	FOX
Tallahassee-Thomasville	13%	WTWC	NBC
Tallahassee-Thomasville	13%	WTXL	ABC
Macon	4%	WDCO	PBS
Macon	4%	WGNM	UPN
Macon	4%	WGXA	FOX
Macon	4%	WMAZ	CBS
Macon	4%	WMGT	NBC
Macon	4%	WPGA	ABC

Cable systems and subscribers
Adelphia 7,800
Blackshear TV Cable 1,626
Cable Vu TV 1,985
Charter 19,896
Comcast 31,288
Communicomm 1,721
Cox 15,800
Dixie Cable Television 4,838
Kings Bay Communications 2,261
Mallard 771
Mediacom 14,061
U.S. Cable 8,369
Waycross Cable Co. 10,383

Military installations, September 2001
Robins Air Force Base, Warner Robins 19,895
Fort Stewart (Army), Hinesville 19,063
Kings Bay Naval Submarine Base, Kings Bay 5,669
Hunter Army Airfield, Savannah 4,830
Moody Air Force Base, Valdosta 3,827

Businesses and other major employers
U.S. Navy Public Affairs; Kings Bay 6,000
Valdosta/Lowndes Counties Hospital Authority; Valdosta 1,800
Gold Kist Inc.; Douglas; processed poultry 1,400
Amoco Fabrics and Fibers Co.; Hazlehurst; polyethylene resins 1,280
Glynn-Brunswick Memorial Hospital Authority; Brunswick 1,272
Camden County School District; Kingsland 1,200
Frito-Lay Inc.; Kathleen; corn chips and snacks 1,100
Georgia Power Co.; Baxley; electric services 1,003
Sea Island Co.; Sea Island; resort hotel 1,000
Amoco Fabrics and Fibers Co.; Nashville; rug backing compounds 1,000
Valdosta State University; Valdosta 1,000
General Manufactured Housing Inc.; Waycross; mobile homes 900
Southern Nuclear Operating Co.; Baxley; electric power distribution 900
PCC Airfoils Inc.; Douglas; airfoils, aircraft engines 900
Gateway Community Service Board; Darien 875
Durango-Georgia Paper Co.; St. Marys; paper mills 854
Rayonier Inc.; Jesup; pulp mills 800
Georgia-Pacific Corp.; Brunswick; millwork 775
Hospital Authority of Colquitt County; Moultrie 725
Georgia Forestry Commission; Homerville 702
Satilla Health Services Inc. Hospital; Waycross 700
Tecumseh Products Co.; Douglas; heating, cooling equipment 700

Chaparral Boats Inc.; Nashville; fiberglass boats 700
First Union National Bank; Hinesville; mortgage bankers 679
Cady Industries Inc.; Pearson; bags and containers 593
Armstrong Atlantic State University; Savannah 592
Destiny Industries Inc.; Moultrie; mobile homes 550
Coffee Regional Medical Center Inc.; Douglas 530
Lockheed Martin Corp.; St. Marys; missile guidance systems 525
Financial Management Service; Brunswick; treasurers' office 521
Shaw Industries Inc.; Fitzgerald; wool yarn 520
Rich-Seapak Corp.; Brunswick; fresh or frozen packaged fish 511
Wal-Mart Stores Inc.; Waycross; discount department stores 500
Wal-Mart Stores Inc.; Brunswick; discount department stores 500
Corrections Corp. of America; Nicholls; correctional facilities 500
Brockway Standard Inc.; Homerville; metal cans 500

Georgia 2nd District

Southwest — Albany, part of Columbus and Valdosta

Georgia's 2nd takes in the state's entire southwest corner and extends south from Columbus to the Florida border. It contains parts of Columbus and Valdosta and all of Albany, Bainbridge, and Thomasville.

Although it was once a black-majority district, redistricting in 1995 reduced its black population, changing it from a strongly Democratic area to one in which Republicans were competitive. Redistricting changes enacted in 2001 made the 2nd significantly more Democratic again, adding predominantly black areas of Columbus to the district. Nearly forty-one percent of the voting-age population is black.

Democrats hold most local offices and are strong in the northwestern counties that have higher black populations. Pockets of GOP strength exist in Lee County, in the central part of the 2nd, as well as in Thomasville and other southern parts of the district. Dougherty County, with Albany as the county seat, is the district's most populous and is reliably Democratic. Nonetheless, George W. Bush narrowly won the district in 2000, with 50.6 percent of the vote.

The 2nd's largely rural and heavily agricultural regions have struggled economically for decades and are heavily dependent on farm loan assistance. Farming and livestock are key to the economy, and the district grows more peanuts than any other place in the United States.

Major Industry
Agriculture, military, manufacturing, health care.

Notable
Jackie Robinson, who broke baseball's color barrier in 1947, was born in Cairo; Plains is the hometown of former president Jimmy Carter.

Election Returns

	Republican		Democratic		Other	
President 2000	84,854	50.6%	81,684	48.7%	1,160	0.7%
House 2002			102,925	100.0%		

District Profile

Population 629,735

Total area (square miles) 9,886.8
   Land area (square miles) 9,723.9

Population per square mile 64.8

Counties (2000 population)

Baker	4,074	Mitchell	23,932
Brooks	16,450	Muscogee (pt.)	83,973
Calhoun	6,320	Quitman	2,598
Chattahoochee	14,882	Randolph	7,791
Clay	3,357	Seminole	9,369
Colquitt (pt.)	27,308	Stewart	5,252
Crisp	21,996	Sumter	33,200
Decatur	28,240	Terrell	10,970
Dougherty	96,065	Thomas	42,737
Early	12,354	Tift	38,407
Grady	23,659	Turner	9,504
Lee	24,757	Webster	2,390
Lowndes (pt.)	51,800	Worth	21,967
Miller	6,383		

Cities and other areas over 10,000 (2000 population)

Albany 76,939
Americus 17,013
Bainbridge 11,722
Columbus (pt.) 83,973
Cordele 11,608
Fort Benning South CDP 11,737
Thomasville 18,162
Tifton 15,060
Valdosta (pt.) 28,282

Race and Hispanic or Latino origin*

White 50.3%
Black or African American 44.5%
American Indian or Alaska Native 0.3%
Asian 0.6%
Native Hawaiian or other Pacific Islander 0.1%
Some other race 0.1%
Hispanic or Latino origin 3.5%
Two or more races 0.8%

*As percentage of total population.

Ancestry*

English	5.0%	Scotch-Irish	1.2%
German	3.6%	Subsaharan	1.1%
Irish	4.7%	USA/American	12.2%

*As estimated percentage of total population.

Universities and colleges, 2000–2001 enrollment

Abraham Baldwin Agricultural College, Tifton 2,630
Albany State University, Albany 3,525
Albany Technical Institute, Albany 2,444
Andrew College, Cuthbert 329
Bainbridge College, Bainbridge 1,311
Darton College, Albany 2,805
Georgia Military College, Fort Benning 239
Georgia Southwestern State University, Americus 2,622
Meadows Junior College, Columbus*
South Georgia Technical Institute, Americus 1,319

Thomas Technical Institute, Thomasville 1,465
Thomas University, Thomasville 594
Valdosta State University, Valdosta 8,792

*Enrollment under 100. See Sources and Explanations in the front of the volume.

Newspapers and circulation

	District circulation	Total circulation
Albany Herald	27,265	27,310
Atlanta Journal-Constitution	13,742	857,088
Columbus Ledger-Enquirer	10,611	46,345
Jacksonville Times-Union	1,385	171,667
Tallahassee Democrat	1,236	48,482
*USA Today**	1,384	1,674,376
Valdosta Daily Times	10,472	18,691

*See Sources and Explanations in the front of the volume.

Television stations and affiliations

Albany	41%	WABW	PBS
Albany	41%	WALB	NBC
Albany	41%	WFXL	FOX
Albany	41%	WSST	Independent
Tallahassee-Thomasville	28%	WCTV	CBS
Tallahassee-Thomasville	28%	WFSU	PBS
Tallahassee-Thomasville	28%	WFXU	UPN
Tallahassee-Thomasville	28%	WTLH	FOX
Tallahassee-Thomasville	28%	WTWC	NBC
Tallahassee-Thomasville	28%	WTXL	ABC
Columbus	23%	WACS	PBS
Columbus	23%	WGIQ	PBS
Columbus	23%	WLTZ	NBC
Columbus	23%	WRBL	CBS
Columbus	23%	WSWS	UPN
Columbus	23%	WTVM	ABC
Columbus	23%	WXTX	FOX
Dothan	8%	WDFX	FOX
Dothan	8%	WDHN	ABC

Cable systems and subscribers

Baconton Cable TV 6,372
Blakely Cable TV 1,772
Charter 48,217
Citizens Cable TV 109,692
Comcast 1,103
Mallard 4,354
Mediacom 110,157
Southeast Cable TV 1,041
Time Warner 4,450

Military installations, September 2001

Marine Corps Logistics Base, Albany 4,589
Fort Benning,* Columbus 17,964

*Fort Benning is shared with the 11th District.

Businesses and other major employers

Salomon Smith Barney Holdings Inc.; Albany; security brokers, dealers, flotation companies 28,000
U.S. Social Security Administration; Albany 15,000
American Family Life Assurance Co. of Columbus; Columbus; health insurance 2,920
Cagle's Inc.; Camilla; chicken processing 2,900
Phoebe Putney Memorial Hospital Inc.; Albany 2,618

Total System Services Inc.; Columbus; data processing
2,500

Osborne Construction Co. Inc.; Valdosta;
commercial/office building construction   2,013

Procter and Gamble Paper Products Co.; Albany;
sanitary paper products   1,525

Columbus Regional Healthcare System Inc. Medical
Center; Columbus   1,500

John D. Archbold Memorial Hospital Inc.; Thomasville
1,300

Cooper Tire and Rubber Co.; Albany; pneumatic tires
1,200

Riverside Manufacturing Co.; Moultrie; men's/boys'
work clothing   1,200

City of Columbus; Columbus; city government   1,200

St. Francis Hospital Inc.; Columbus   1,148

Burns International Security Services Corp.; Columbus;
protective services, guard   1,000

Amoco Fabrics and Fibers Co.; Bainbridge; polyethylene
resins   950

Target Corp.; Tifton; department stores   950

Levi Strauss and Co.; Valdosta; men's and boys' jeans
900

Tom's Foods Inc.; Columbus; potato chips and snacks
900

Georgia-Pacific Corp.; Cedar Springs; kraft linerboard
830

Tift Regional Medical Center; Tifton   800

Interstate Brands Corp.; Columbus; breads and cakes
800

Mental Retardation and Development Service;
Columbus; speech defect clinic   750

Keebler Co.; Columbus; bakery products   675

Columbus Police Dept.; Columbus   650

Shaw Industries Inc.; Tifton; yarn spinning mills   630

Miller Brewing Co.; Albany; beer   600

Crisp Regional Hospital; Cordele   553

Georgia Southwestern State University; Americus   540

Wight Nurseries Inc.; Cairo; shrubbery plants   525

Manor Corp. Inc.; Columbus; rehabilitation services
525

Columbus Doctors Hospital Inc.; Columbus   520

Atlanta Winn-Dixie Inc.; Valdosta; cookies   500

Bayliner Marine Corp.; Valdosta; fiberglass boats   500

Dillard's Inc.; Valdosta; general warehousing, storage
500

Roadway Express Inc.; Lake Park; trucking terminal
facilities   500

Merck and Co. Inc.; Albany; industrial inorganic
chemicals   500

Mars Inc.; Albany; candy bars   500

Sumter Regional Hospital Foundation Inc.; Americus
500

Tyson Foods Inc.; Dawson   500

Prestolite Wire Corp.; Tifton; automotive ignition coils
500

Georgia 3rd District

Middle Georgia — Macon

Created to encompass the rural heart of Georgia, the 3rd takes in mostly agricultural counties in the center of the state. Farm issues are paramount here, increasingly so since drought has put the area's economy in peril.

The district stretches from Marion County in the west to Hancock County in the north, while Telfair and Tattnall Counties flank its southern border. Peaches, pecans, and cotton are primary crops in the center of the district. Peanuts dominate the southern area, and onions and tobacco are prevalent in the southeast. Forestry also is a major industry. Aerospace jobs and textile manufacturing have helped sustain the economy, though some textile plants have closed in recent years.

The 3rd was drawn in redistricting after the 2000 census to elect a Democrat. But like much of the South, voters will support Republicans, and the 3rd can be politically competitive—George W. Bush received 51.8 percent of the vote here in the 2000 presidential election. Blacks make up 37.2 percent of the voting-age population.

The 3rd is almost split in two by a gash up its center, in which the 1st District takes in Warner Robins Air Force Base and Republican suburbs south of Macon. The 8th also descends into the area, taking in Republican suburbs north of Macon. The 3rd includes the rest of Macon, including the heavily Democratic city center.

Major Industry

Agriculture, distribution, aerospace.

Notable

Milledgeville served as the state capital from 1803 until 1868, when the capital was moved to Atlanta during Reconstruction; Vidalia is known for its sweet onions; Claxton is known for its fruitcake.

Election Returns

	Republican		Democratic		Other	
President 2000	98,100	51.8%	89,374	47.2%	1,766	0.9%
House 2002	73,866	49.5%	75,394	50.5%		

District Profile

Population   629,748

Total area (square miles)   11,002.6
   Land area (square miles)   10,914.7

Population per square mile   57.7

Counties (2000 population)
| Baldwin | 44,700 | Bleckley | 11,666 |
| Bibb (pt.) | 127,664 | Candler | 9,577 |

Crawford 12,495
Dodge 19,171
Dooly 11,525
Emanuel 21,837
Evans 10,495
Hancock 10,076
Houston (pt.) 64,828
Johnson 8,560
Jones (pt.) 21,318
Laurens 44,874
Macon 14,074
Marion 7,144
Monroe 21,757
Montgomery 8,270

Peach 23,668
Pulaski (pt.) 3,275
Schley 3,766
Tattnall 22,305
Taylor 8,815
Telfair 11,794
Toombs 26,067
Treutlen 6,854
Twiggs 10,590
Washington 21,176
Wheeler 6,179
Wilcox (pt.) 5,008
Wilkinson 10,220

Cities and other areas over 10,000 (2000 population)
Dublin 15,857
Macon (pt.) 89,507
Milledgeville 18,757
Vidalia 10,491
Warner Robins (pt.) 38,969

Race and Hispanic or Latino origin*
White 56.2%
Black or African American 39.8%
American Indian or Alaska Native 0.2%
Asian 0.5%
Native Hawaiian or other Pacific Islander 0.0%
Some other race 0.1%
Hispanic or Latino origin 2.6%
Two or more races 0.7%

*As percentage of total population.

Ancestry*
English 5.4%   Scotch-Irish 1.1%
German 3.1%   USA/American 15.3%
Irish 4.8%

*As estimated percentage of total population.

Universities and colleges, 2000–2001 enrollment
Brewton-Parker College, Mt. Vernon 1,062
East Georgia College, Swainsboro 1,313
Fort Valley State University, Fort Valley 2,561
Georgia College and State University, Milledgeville 5,090
Georgia Military College, Milledgeville 963
Heart of Georgia Technical Institute, Dublin 1,068
Macon State College, Macon 4,116
Macon Technical Institute, Macon 3,787
Mercer University, Macon 6,908
Middle Georgia College, Cochran 1,938
Sandersville Regional Technical Institute, Sandersville 601
Southeastern Technical Institute, Vidalia 1,139
Swainsboro Technical Institute, Swainsboro 775

Newspapers and circulation

	District circulation	Total circulation
Atlanta Journal-Constitution	13,640	857,088
Augusta Chronicle	1,143	68,807
Dublin Courier Herald	10,701	10,701
Macon Telegraph	50,297	63,666
Savannah Morning News	4,409	58,145
*USA Today**	1,196	1,674,376

*See Sources and Explanations in the front of the volume.

Television stations and affiliations
Macon	71%	WDCO	PBS
Macon	71%	WGNM	UPN
Macon	71%	WGXA	FOX
Macon	71%	WMAZ	CBS
Macon	71%	WMGT	NBC
Macon	71%	WPGA	ABC
Savannah	14%	WGSA	UPN
Savannah	14%	WJCL	ABC
Savannah	14%	WSAV	NBC
Savannah	14%	WTGS	FOX
Savannah	14%	WTOC	CBS
Savannah	14%	WVAN	PBS
Columbus	8%	WACS	PBS
Columbus	8%	WGIQ	PBS
Columbus	8%	WLTZ	NBC
Columbus	8%	WRBL	CBS
Columbus	8%	WSWS	UPN
Columbus	8%	WTVM	ABC
Columbus	8%	WXTX	FOX
Augusta	7%	WAGT	NBC
Augusta	7%	WCES	PBS
Augusta	7%	WEBA	PBS
Augusta	7%	WFXG	FOX
Augusta	7%	WJBF	ABC
Augusta	7%	WRDW	CBS

Cable systems and subscribers
Charter 13,672
Comcast 15,369
Communicomm 3,516
Cox 45,401
Flint Cable TV 3,735
Forsyth Municipal 14,955
Kennedy Cablevision 966
Mallard 10,648
Mediacom 6,489
Northland 11,614
SunTel Communications 3,349
Valley Cable TV 4,408

Businesses and other major employers
Central Georgia Health System Inc.; Macon; management services 3,600
Medical Center of Central Georgia Inc.; Macon 3,300
GEICO Corp.; Macon; fire, marine, casualty insurance 2,500
Teresa Boston; Alamo; business services 2,000
Georgia Dept. of Human Resources; Milledgeville 2,000
Lithonia Lighting Inc.; Cochran; fluorescent lighting fixtures 1,400
Cargill Inc.; Buena Vista; processed poultry 1,380
Bird Blue Body Co.; Fort Valley; motor vehicles and car bodies 1,300
Fries Farms; Claxton; broiling chickens 1,200
Georgia Dept. of Corrections; Hardwick 1,200
Engelhard Corp.; McIntyre; inorganic pigments 1,161

Rheem Manufacturing Co.; Milledgeville; air conditioning equipment   1,100

Mercer University; Macon   900

Houston County Hospital Authority; Warner Robins   850

Coliseum Park Hospital Inc.; Macon   850

Imerys USA Inc.; Sandersville; whiting mining   800

U.S. Veterans Affairs; Dublin   772

Bibb County; Macon; county government   750

Lucas Aerospace Cargo Systems; Macon; aircraft assemblies, parts   735

Victor Forstmann Inc.; Dublin; broadwoven fabric mills, wool   730

Georgia Forestry Commission; Dry Branch   702

Mohawk Industries Inc.; Dublin; carpet manufacturing   700

Boeing Co.; Macon; aircraft   700

Dublin Community Hospital Inc.; Dublin   675

Vought Aircraft Industries Inc.; Milledgeville; aircraft   600

Engelhard Corp.; Sandersville; chalk   600

Georgia Dept. of Transportation; Tennille   600

W. L. Sparkay O'Caine; Macon; fund-raising organization   600

Keebler Co.; Macon; cookies and crackers   600

Dan River Inc.; Fort Valley; bedspreads and comforters   559

U.S. Postal Service; Macon   550

Oconee Regional Health Systems Inc.; Milledgeville   543

Warner Robins City; Warner Robins; city government   530

HBE Corp.; Vidalia; hotels and motels   500

Imerys Kaolin Inc.; Dry Branch; kaolin and ball clay   500

Early Childhood Education; Dublin; child day care services   500

Dodge County Board of Education; Eastman   500

Georgia College and State University; Milledgeville   500

Cagle's Inc.; Perry; chicken processing   500

Armstrong World Industries Inc.; Macon; wall and ceiling squares   500

Norfolk Southern Corp.; Macon; switching and terminal services   500

Riverwood International Corp.; Macon; kraft linerboard   500

Georgia 4th District

Atlanta suburbs — DeKalb County

Already decidedly Democratic, the DeKalb County-based 4th became more so in redistricting after the 2000 census. The voting-age population in the district at the 2000 census was just under 49 percent African American. *(See map p. 262.)*

DeKalb County, which sits just east of Atlanta, accounts for almost 97 percent of the district's population and is the most Democratic county in the state. Democratic candidates receive a warm reception in the county's racially diverse central and western portions, while Republicans run well in northern DeKalb's more white, affluent areas.

Like the rest of Atlanta, south DeKalb—which has one of the nation's most affluent concentrations of African Americans—has seen rapid growth. This growth has changed the tenor of the 4th, bringing more moderate, business-oriented African Americans into the district and lessening the influence of more-liberal voices, such as that of five-term representative Cynthia A. McKinney, who was defeated in the 2002 primary.

Jobs in the 4th center around health care and higher education. Emory University, home to a university hospital, is a major employer. The Centers for Disease Control and Prevention also employs a sizable number of the area's health care workers. Decatur was a nineteenth century commercial hub until it lost out as a railroad center to Atlanta, but it still has many government-related jobs.

Major Industry

Retail, health care, government.

Notable

Stone Mountain Park features a huge granite outcropping into which a sculpture of Robert E. Lee and other Confederate heroes is carved.

Election Returns

	Republican		Democratic		Other	
President 2000	58,338	28.7%	140,767	69.3%	4,107	2.0%
House 2002	35,202	23.0%	118,045	77.0%		

District Profile

Population   629,690

Total area (square miles)   253.6
Land area (square miles)   250.9

Population per square mile   2,509.7

Counties (2000 population)
DeKalb (pt.)   607,648   Gwinnett (pt.)   22,042

Cities and other areas over 10,000 (2000 population)
Belvedere Park CDP   18,945
Candler-McAfee CDP   28,294
Decatur (pt.)   18,137
Druid Hills CDP   12,741
Dunwoody CDP   32,808
North Atlanta CDP   38,579
North Decatur CDP   15,270
Panthersville CDP   11,791
Redan CDP   33,841
Tucker CDP   26,532

Race and Hispanic or Latino origin*
White   32.0%
Black or African American   53.1%
American Indian or Alaska Native   0.2%
Asian   4.2%
Native Hawaiian or other Pacific Islander   0.0%
Some other race   0.2%
Hispanic or Latino origin   8.5%
Two or more races   1.7%

As percentage of total population.

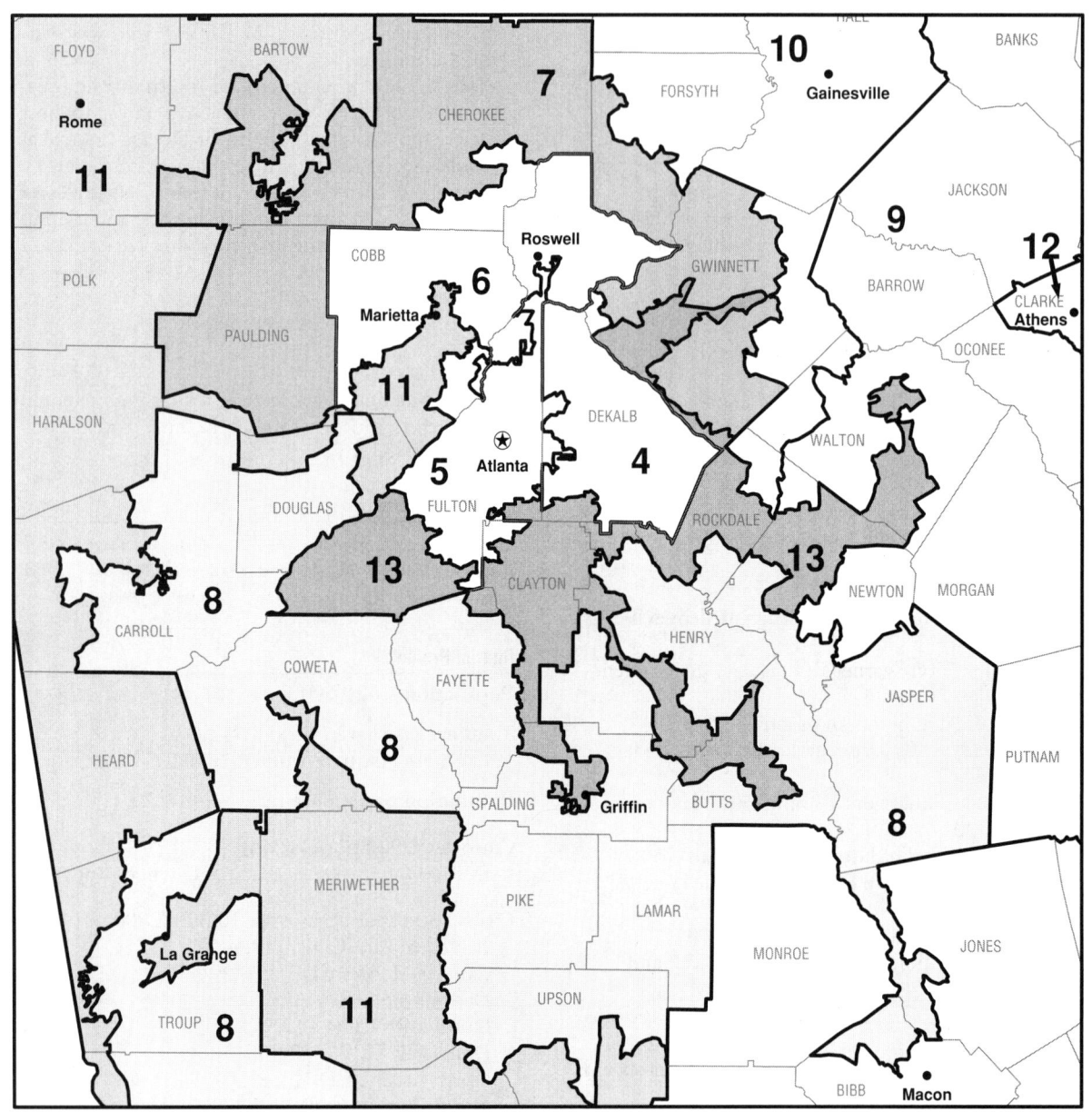

Ancestry*

English	5.4%	Scotch-Irish	1.4%
French	1.2%	Scottish	1.3%
German	4.6%	Subsaharan	3.2%
Irish	4.2%	USA/American	3.5%
Italian	1.3%	West Indian	2.1%

As estimated percentage of total population.

Universities and colleges, 2000–2001 enrollment

Agnes Scott College, Atlanta   901
Columbia Theological Seminary, Decatur   303
DeKalb Technical Institute, Clarkston   3,315
Devry University, Decatur   2,916
Emory University, Atlanta   11,398
Georgia Perimeter College, Decatur   13,708
Interactive College of Technology, Chamblee   280
Keller Graduate School of Management, Decatur   820
Luther Rice Seminary, Lithonia   1,692
Oglethorpe University, Atlanta   1,267

Newspapers and circulation

	District circulation	Total circulation
Atlanta Journal-Constitution	156,347	857,088
*USA Today**	5,343	1,674,376

See Sources and Explanations in the front of the volume.

Television stations and affiliations

Atlanta	100%	WAGA	FOX
Atlanta	100%	WATC	Independent
Atlanta	100%	WATL	WB
Atlanta	100%	WCIQ	PBS
Atlanta	100%	WGTV	PBS
Atlanta	100%	WHSG	Independent
Atlanta	100%	WJSP	PBS
Atlanta	100%	WPBA	PBS
Atlanta	100%	WPXA	PAX
Atlanta	100%	WSB	ABC
Atlanta	100%	WTBS	TBN
Atlanta	100%	WUPA	UPN
Atlanta	100%	WXIA	NBC

Cable systems and subscribers

Comcast   91,361

Military installations, September 2001

Decatur U.S. Army Reserve, Decatur   1,111

Businesses and other major employers

CVS Pharmacy Inc.; Decatur; drug and proprietary stores   30,000
Georgia-Pacific Corp.; Atlanta; timber tracts   8,500
Emory University; Atlanta   8,017
Bristol Hotel Tenant Co.; Atlanta; hotels and motels   8,000
Transplant Outpatient SVC; Atlanta; home health care services   6,000
Holiday Pacific Partners LP; Atlanta; hotel, franchised   3,000
Emory Clinic; Atlanta   2,500
DeKalb Medical Center Inc.; Decatur   2,212
Sears Roebuck and Co. Inc.; Atlanta; catalog, mail-order   2,000
McKesson Corp.; Atlanta; prepackaged software   2,000

DeKalb County; Decatur; police dept.   1,800
Centers for Disease Control and Prevention; Atlanta; public health programs   1,648
Georgia Public Health Service; Atlanta   1,600
DeKalb County; Decatur; county government   1,500
U.S. Veterans Hospital; Decatur   1,500
Cox Texas Publications Inc.; Atlanta; newspaper   1,500
University of Georgia; Atlanta   1,500
NDC Health Corp.; Atlanta; data processing   1,450
Mercer University; Norcross   1,360
Gulf Capital Services; Atlanta; investment offices   1,302
NWS Holdings; Norcross; furniture stores   1,200
Lanier Worldwide Inc.; Atlanta; office equipment   1,100
Aramark Services Inc.; Decatur; contract food services   1,000
DeKalb County; Decatur; county police   1,000
Federated Retail Holdings Inc.; Decatur; department stores   1,000
Georgia Dept. of Human Resources; Decatur   1,000
American Premier Insurance Co.; Norcross; property and casualty insurance agent   1,000
Quest Diagnostics Clinical Laboratories Inc.; Tucker; medical laboratories   1,000
Cox Communications Inc.; Atlanta; cable television   1,000
U.S. Internal Revenue Service; Atlanta   1,000
Six Continents Hotels Inc.; Atlanta; resort hotel   1,000
MCI Worldcom Network Services Inc.; Atlanta; data telephone communications   975
Georgia Dept. of Human Resources; Atlanta   950
Metropolitan Atlanta Rapid Transit Authority; Decatur; bus line operations   922
Florida Auto Auction of Orlando Inc.; Atlanta; automobiles   800
Federated Department Stores Inc.; Atlanta; department stores   800
Georgia Bureau of Investigations; Decatur   776
Rich's Department Stores Inc.; Stone Mountain; department stores   750
General Motors Corp.; Atlanta; warehousing   750
American Building Maintenance Co. of Georgia; Atlanta; janitorial service   710
Georgia Dept. of Human Resources; Decatur   700
DeKalb County; Decatur; correctional institution   700
Matrix Resources Inc.; Atlanta; labor resource services   700
Macy's East Inc.; Decatur; general warehousing, storage   650
Georgia Dept. of Transportation; Atlanta   650
Camden Fire Insurance Assn.; Atlanta; fire, marine, casualty insurance   650
DBC Holding Corp.; Atlanta; computer software development   650
Federated Department Stores Inc.; Norcross; data processing   600
Innovative Hospitality Management Inc.; Tucker; industry specialist consultants   600
Pinkerton's Inc.; Atlanta; security guard service   600
U.S. Centers for Disease Control and Prevention; Atlanta   600
Macy's East Inc.; Atlanta; department stores   600

General Electric Capital Corp.; Atlanta; equipment, vehicle finance leasing   600

Rich's Department Stores Inc.; Atlanta; department stores   600

Federated Department Stores Inc.; Stone Mountain; general warehousing, storage   550

BellSouth Telecommunications Inc.; Tucker; local/long distance telephone   550

McKenney's Inc.; Atlanta; plumbing contractors   550

Per-Se Technologies Inc.; Atlanta; management services 550

BellSouth Business Systems Inc.; Atlanta; marketing consulting services   532

John H. Harland Co.; Decatur; checkbooks   500

Atlanta Casualty Co.; Norcross; insurance agents and brokers   500

General Electric Co.; Norcross; electrical repair shops 500

Scandura Inc.; Scottdale; rubber belting   500

Aegis Communications Group Inc.; Tucker; telemarketing services   500

Sears Roebuck and Co. Inc.; Tucker; men's/boys' clothing stores   500

Macy's East Inc.; Atlanta; department stores   500

Crawford and Co.; Atlanta; insurance adjusters   500

Georgia 5th District

Atlanta

The heart of the 5th lies in downtown Atlanta, the symbolic capital of the New South and the commercial center of the Southeast. The district takes in almost all of the city of Atlanta and much of surrounding Fulton County. The most populous county in Georgia, Fulton is reliably Democratic. A few pockets of GOP strength exist in the district's wealthier northern suburbs, such as Buckhead. *(See map p. 262.)*

The 5th is the only black-majority district in the state. Its 51 percent black population—concentrated mostly in the southern part of the district—keeps it a Democratic bastion, though whites have flooded into the recently revitalized Midtown area. A large gay population in Midtown also has a significant influence on local politics.

During the 1990s Atlanta saw a 13 percent increase in white residents, while the black population declined by 3 percent. Overall, the city's population grew by about 6 percent. New apartment buildings and condominiums are going up almost daily as the city attempts to keep up with the increase.

Along with Atlanta's downtown business district, Hartsfield Atlanta International Airport in Clayton County is the 5th's major economic generator. The airport, a small part of which is located in the 13th District, is one of the nation's busiest and employs more than 44,000 people. The 5th's strategic location also has made it the headquarters for transportation-related industries, distribution companies, and other major firms. At the same time, air pollution, gridlock, and urban sprawl from the expanding economy are a concern.

Major Industry

Transportation, distribution.

Notable

Martin Luther King Jr. was born in Atlanta and served as a pastor of Ebenezer Baptist Church; Atlanta hosted the 1996 Summer Olympics; Coca-Cola and CNN headquarters are in Atlanta.

Election Returns

	Republican		Democratic		Other	
President 2000	55,605	28.5%	136,606	69.9%	3,232	1.7%
House 2002			116,230	100.0%		

District Profile

Population   629,727

Total area (square miles)   253.9
  Land area (square miles)   251.8

Population per square mile   2,500.9

Counties (2000 population)
  Clayton (pt.)   9,019
  Cobb (pt.)   57,356
  DeKalb (pt.)   45,971
  Fulton (pt.)   517,381

Cities and other areas over 10,000 (2000 population)
  Atlanta (pt.)   403,925
  College Park (pt.)   18,348
  East Point (pt.)   39,595
  North Druid Hills CDP (pt.)   16,132
  Sandy Springs CDP (pt.)   44,738
  Smyrna (pt.)   26,781

Race and Hispanic or Latino origin*
  White   34.4%
  Black or African American   55.7%
  American Indian or Alaska Native   0.2%
  Asian   2.2%
  Native Hawaiian or other Pacific Islander   0.0%
  Some other race   0.2%
  Hispanic or Latino origin   6.1%
  Two or more races   1.2%

As percentage of total population.

Ancestry*

English 5.4%	Scotch-Irish 1.3%
French 1.2%	Scottish 1.4%
German 4.5%	Subsaharan 1.8%
Irish 4.4%	USA/American 3.2%
Italian 1.6%	

As estimated percentage of total population.

Universities and colleges, 2000–2001 enrollment
  American Intercontinental University, Atlanta   860
  Art Institute of Atlanta, Atlanta   934
  Atlanta Christian College, East Point   385
  Atlanta College of Art, Atlanta   375
  Atlanta Metropolitan College, Atlanta   1,907
  Atlanta Technical Institute, Atlanta   2,884
  Bauder College, Atlanta   598
  Beulah Heights Bible College, Atlanta   579
  Clark Atlanta University, Atlanta   5,060
  Georgia Baptist College of Nursing, Atlanta   311
  Georgia Military College, Fort McPherson   310

National Service Industries Inc.; Smyrna; envelopes 500

City of Atlanta; Atlanta; correctional institutions   500

Tomahawk Land Co.; Atlanta; paper mills   500

Kaiser Permanente Medical Center; Atlanta   500

Marsh and McLennan Companies Inc.; Atlanta; insurance agents and brokers   500

Atlanta Board of Education; Atlanta   500

U.S. Small Business Administration; Atlanta   500

H. C. Beck; Atlanta; special trade contractors   500

Emory University Hospital; Atlanta   500

Spelman College; Atlanta   500

CS Integrated; Atlanta; warehousing   500

Barton Protective Services Inc.; Atlanta; management consulting   500

Ernst and Young; Atlanta; management consulting 500

BellSouth Telecommunications Inc.; Atlanta; telephone communication   500

NDC Health Information SE; Atlanta; medical insurance claim processing   500

Georgia Dept. of Administrative Services; Atlanta   500

Atlanta Winn-Dixie Inc.; Atlanta; supermarkets   500

Printpack Inc.; Atlanta; bags   500

Moore Group Inc.; Atlanta; investment holding company   500

Per-Se Technologies Inc.; Atlanta; business management 500

CSX Transportation Inc.; Atlanta; railroad terminals 500

BSC Ventures; Atlanta; envelopes   500

Georgia 6th District

Atlanta suburbs — Roswell, part of Marietta

Anchored in Atlanta's burgeoning northern suburbs, the 6th covers parts of three counties that are home to Republican voters who work in technology and other white-collar occupations. The 2000 census showed the old 6th as the most highly populated district in the state, a reflection of the massive growth taking place here. *(See map p. 262.)*

The mostly white 6th is one of Georgia's most affluent, educated, and Republican districts. Office parks, malls, and housing subdivisions dominate the landscape. This area is referred to as the Golden Crescent: it is sandwiched between three of the state's major highways—Interstate 75, Interstate 85, and the Interstate 285 perimeter highway. Cobb County, northwest of Atlanta, accounts for more than 50 percent of the district's vote, and many of its residents work at Lockheed Martin, across the district line in the 11th.

Along with its defense industry, Marietta (shared with the 11th) provides Cobb County with its own thriving commercial center. Numerous corporations have office space in the "Platinum Triangle," shared with the 5th, a huge employment center that has begun to rival Atlanta's business district. But the growth and prospering economy also have brought gridlock and air pollution, causing some businesses to reconsider locating here.

In the central part of the 6th are solidly GOP suburbs in northern Fulton County. Alpharetta was once home to large farms that since have been converted into suburban developments. Roswell, formerly a cotton-milling center, is now a booming bedroom community in Fulton County.

Major Industry
Communications, aerospace, finance, technology.

Notable
Former Republican representative Newt Gingrich represented the 6th from 1979 to 1999 and served as House Speaker from 1995 to 1999; Confederate troops defeated Northern general William Sherman's army on June 27, 1864, at what is now Kennesaw Mountain National Battlefield Park.

Election Returns

	Republican		Democratic		Other	
President 2000	174,414	67.5%	77,646	30.1%	6,303	2.4%
House 2002	163,203	79.9%	41,043	20.1%		

District Profile

Population   629,725

Total area (square miles)   440.9
  Land area (square miles)   434.9

Population per square mile   1,448.0

Counties (2000 population)
  Cherokee (pt.)   43,212
  Cobb (pt.)   346,988
  Fulton (pt.)   239,525

Cities and other areas over 10,000 (2000 population)
  Acworth   13,422
  Alpharetta   34,854
  Kennesaw   21,675
  Marietta (pt.)   18,614
  Roswell (pt.)   71,848
  Sandy Springs CDP (pt.)   41,043

Race and Hispanic or Latino origin*
  White   83.0%
  Black or African American   6.9%
  American Indian or Alaska Native   0.2%
  Asian   4.0%
  Native Hawaiian or other Pacific Islander   0.0%
  Some other race   0.2%
  Hispanic or Latino origin   4.5%
  Two or more races   1.2%

*As percentage of total population.

Ancestry*

Dutch 1.2%	Polish 2.2%
English 11.0%	Russian 1.1%
French 2.4%	Scotch-Irish 2.2%
German 11.1%	Scottish 2.5%
Irish 10.1%	USA/American 7.8%
Italian 4.2%	

*As estimated percentage of total population.

Universities and colleges, 2000–2001 enrollment
  Keller Graduate School of Management, Alpharetta*
  Kennesaw State University, Kennesaw   13,360

*Enrollment under 100. See Sources and Explanations in the front of the volume.

Newspapers and circulation

	District circulation	Total circulation
Atlanta Journal-Constitution	207,384	857,088
Marietta Daily Journal	10,753	18,321
*USA Today**	11,910	1,674,376

*See Sources and Explanations in the front of the volume.

Television stations and affiliations

Atlanta	100%	WAGA	FOX
Atlanta	100%	WATC	Independent
Atlanta	100%	WATL	WB
Atlanta	100%	WCIQ	PBS
Atlanta	100%	WGTV	PBS
Atlanta	100%	WHSG	Independent
Atlanta	100%	WJSP	PBS
Atlanta	100%	WPBA	PBS
Atlanta	100%	WPXA	PAX
Atlanta	100%	WSB	ABC
Atlanta	100%	WTBS	TBN
Atlanta	100%	WUPA	UPN
Atlanta	100%	WXIA	NBC

Cable systems and subscribers

Charter   15,545
Comcast   13,434

Military installations, September 2001

Atlanta Naval Air Station, Marietta   1,097

Businesses and other major employers

Kennestone Hospital Inc.; Marietta   2,900
ADC Telecommunications Inc.; Kennesaw; fiber optics communications equipment   2,300
Pep Snack Foods Inc.; Kennesaw   2,050
Nortel; Alpharetta; telephone communication   2,000
Road Link USA Inc.; Marietta; passenger car rental   2,000
Kimberly-Clark Corp.; Roswell; paper mills   2,000
General Electric Co.; Atlanta; electronic parts and equipment   2,000
Ciba Vision Corp.; Duluth; optical goods   1,900
Utiliquest; Kennesaw; underground utilities contractor   1,800
Alliance Data Systems Corp.; Kennesaw; credit card service   1,675
Law International Inc.; Alpharetta; construction and civil engineering   1,600
Kennesaw State University; Kennesaw   1,561
Arris Group Inc.; Duluth; radio/TV communications equipment   1,366
Vopak USA Inc.; Atlanta; chemicals   1,348
AT&T Corp.; Alpharetta; data processing   1,200
Worldcom Inc.; Alpharetta; telephone communication   1,200
Brentwood Healthcare; Roswell; nursing home   1,200
ING America Insurance Holdings Inc.; Atlanta; life insurance   1,200
Hyco Holdings; Atlanta; fluid power cylinders   1,100
SRI Integrated Facilities; Marietta; real estate listing services   1,032
Equifax Inc.; Alpharetta; credit reporting bureau   1,000
Oracle Corp.; Roswell; computer consulting services   1,000
Heidelberg USA Inc.; Kennesaw; printing trades machinery equipment/supplies   1,000
North Fulton Medical Center Inc.; Roswell   820
Compdent Corp.; Roswell; dental insurance   800
Fulton County Board of Education; Duluth   800
First North American National Bank; Kennesaw; commercial bank   800
Hewlett-Packard Co.; Kennesaw; electronic computers   800
International Business Machines Corp.; Atlanta; electronic computers   800
Sprint Communications Co.; Atlanta; long distance telephone   780
Worldspan; Atlanta; reservation services   750
ChoicePoint Inc.; Alpharetta; insurance information, consulting services   700
Lucent Technologies Inc.; Alpharetta; electric intercommunication systems   700
Federated Systems Group Inc.; Duluth; data processing   700
Cobb County Fire Dept.; Acworth   700
Hewitt Associates; Atlanta; business management consultant   700
Sita Information Networking Computing USA Inc.; Atlanta; communication network services   700
Thomson U.S. Inc.; Alpharetta; prepackaged software   670
Atlanta Casualty Group Inc.; Alpharetta; insurance agents   613
PricewaterhouseCoopers; Alpharetta; business consulting   600
United Parcel Service Inc.; Roswell; air courier services   600
Equant Network Services International Corp.; Atlanta; management consulting   600
Georgia Power Co.; Alpharetta; electric services   550
Manhattan Associates Inc.; Atlanta; prepackaged software   550
Compaq Computer Corp.; Alpharetta; computers   500
United Parcel Service Inc.; Alpharetta; online services technology consultants   500
E Trade Group Inc.; Alpharetta; security brokers   500
Lin R. Rogers Electrical Contractors Inc.; Alpharetta; electrical contractor   500
Ryder Truck Rental Inc.; Alpharetta; truck leasing   500
Delta Airlines Inc.; Marietta; air transportation   500
Oracle Corp.; Marietta; computer and data processing   500
Equifax Inc.; Marietta; consumer credit reporting bureau   500
American Medical Response Inc.; Kennesaw; local passenger transportation   500
Renaissance Hotel Group; Atlanta; hotels   500
ACS State Healthcare; Atlanta; computer integrated systems design   500

Georgia 7th District

North of Atlanta — outer Atlanta suburbs

The 7th takes in overflow from many of the Atlanta suburbs contained in the 6th District. Forming a horseshoe shape around the top of Atlanta, the district is characterized by rapid suburban growth, including many newcomers to the state. As the suburbs close to the city become increasingly populated, the areas represented by the 7th are becoming outer suburbs. Many of the towns are transitioning from rural to suburban. *(See map p. 262.)*

(See map p. 262.)

In addition to those who commute to Atlanta, many who live in the district work at Lockheed Martin in the nearby 11th or at one of a host of technology companies in Norcross. The home-building industry is burgeoning as the explosion of housing developments and wealthy subdivisions extends farther north from the city.

Voters in the 7th range from social conservatives living in rural areas to fiscal conservatives living in suburban areas. Redistricting following the 2000 census shifted the district's politics further right, as many Democratic and swing voters were removed, leaving a solid GOP base. In 2000 George W. Bush received 69.8 percent of the vote in the new 7th, more than in any other district in the state. The bulk of voters live in Gwinnett County, considered the most-moderate and fastest-growing county in the district.

Water use is a major issue. The state has been affected by droughts, and the increasing population is depleting the area's water supply. Lake Lanier (shared with the 10th) and Allatoona Lake are major bodies of water in the district.

Major Industry

Technology, retail, homebuilding, manufacturing.

Notable

Mall of Georgia, in Buford, covers 2 million square feet and features themed courtyards that represent areas of the state; Duluth elected the first woman mayor in Georgia, Alice H. Strickland, in 1921; she promised to "clean up Duluth and rid it of demon rum."

Election Returns

	Republican		Democratic		Other	
President 2000	154,575	69.8%	60,082	27.1%	6,694	3.0%
House 2002	138,997	78.9%	37,124	21.1%	24	

District Profile

Population   629,706

Total area (square miles)   1,219.8
 Land area (square miles)   1,195.0

Population per square mile   527.0

Counties (2000 population)
Bartow (pt.)	37,638	Gwinnett (pt.)	366,460
Cherokee (pt.)	98,691	Paulding (pt.)	79,045
Forsyth (pt.)	47,872		

Cities and other areas over 10,000 (2000 population)
Buford (pt.)	10,100	Snellville (pt.)	15,346
Duluth	22,122	Sugar Hill	11,399
Lawrenceville (pt.)	18,269		

Race and Hispanic or Latino origin*
 White   82.4%
 Black or African American   6.9%
 American Indian or Alaska Native   0.2%
 Asian   3.8%
 Native Hawaiian or other Pacific Islander   0.0%
 Some other race   0.1%
 Hispanic or Latino origin   5.4%
 Two or more races   1.1%

As percentage of total population.

Ancestry*
Dutch	1.1%	Italian	3.0%
English	9.5%	Polish	1.5%
French	1.9%	Scotch-Irish	1.9%
German	9.4%	Scottish	2.0%
Irish	9.2%	USA/American	11.9%

As estimated percentage of total population.

Universities and colleges, 2000–2001 enrollment

Gwinnett Technical Institute, Lawrenceville   4,814
North Metro Technical Institute, Acworth   1,567
Reinhardt College, Waleska   1,108

Newspapers and circulation

	District circulation	Total circulation
Atlanta Journal-Constitution	149,780	857,088
Cartersville Daily Tribune News	4,888	7,902
Marietta Daily Journal	1,122	18,321
*USA Today**	3,013	1,674,376

See Sources and Explanations in the front of the volume.

Television stations and affiliations

Atlanta	100%	WAGA	FOX
Atlanta	100%	WATC	Independent
Atlanta	100%	WATL	WB
Atlanta	100%	WCIQ	PBS
Atlanta	100%	WGTV	PBS
Atlanta	100%	WHSG	Independent
Atlanta	100%	WJSP	PBS
Atlanta	100%	WPBA	PBS
Atlanta	100%	WPXA	PAX
Atlanta	100%	WSB	ABC
Atlanta	100%	WTBS	TBN
Atlanta	100%	WUPA	UPN
Atlanta	100%	WXIA	NBC

Cable systems and subscribers

Adelphia   15,066
Charter   101,291
Comcast   37,014

Businesses and other major employers

Staffing Concepts Inc.; Duluth; employee leasing service   15,960
Siemens Corp.; Alpharetta; nonelectric transformers   3,500
Kawneer-Alcoa; Norcross; architectural services   3,000
Delta Apparel Inc.; Duluth; men's and boys' sports shirts   2,600
Childtime Childcare Inc.; Snellville; child day care services   1,518
Qwest Corp.; Norcross; telephone communication   1,500
NCR Corp.; Buford; personal service agents   1,500

Nextel Communications Inc.; Norcross; radiotelephone communication 1,444

World Technology Group Inc.; Lawrenceville; voice telephone communications 1,300

Alcoa Inc.; Norcross; aluminum sheet, plate, and foil 1,300

Gulf Power Co.; Norcross; electric services 1,300

Mississippi Power Co.; Norcross; electric services 1,300

Business Alliance Group Inc.; Alpharetta; help supply services 1,200

Solectron Corp.; Suwanee; electronic computers 1,200

Reed Elsevier Inc.; Norcross; pamphlet publishing, printing 1,100

Scientific Games Finance Corp.; Alpharetta; commercial printing 1,000

Gwinnett County; Lawrenceville; county government 1,000

EHCA Eastside Medical Center; Snellville 900

Gwinnett County; Lawrenceville; county police 800

Herman Miller Inc.; Canton; office furniture 800

ConAgra Poultry Co.; Canton; poultry slaughtering/processing 800

Avon Products Inc.; Suwanee; cosmetics 725

OKI Telecom Inc.; Suwanee; transportation signaling devices 700

Network Communications Inc.; Lawrenceville; periodicals 700

Radiant Systems Inc.; Alpharetta; computer integrated systems design 650

Checkfree Corp.; Norcross; custom computer software design 650

Galey and Lord Industries Inc.; Shannon; broadwoven fabric mills, man-made 650

Hoover Universal Inc.; Suwanee; automobile seats 600

Micro Motion Inc.; Lawrenceville; fluid meters and counting devices 600

EMS Technologies Inc.; Norcross; microwave communication equipment 600

Ikon Office Solutions Inc.; Norcross; photocopy machines 600

Glad Products Co.; Cartersville; plastic bags 600

Metso Automation USA Inc.; Norcross; control valves, fluid power 557

General Electric Capital Corp.; Alpharetta; data processing 550

Mitel Networks Inc.; Lawrenceville; telephone and communication equipment 521

MCI Worldcom Network Services Inc.; Alpharetta; long-distance telephone 500

Intervoice-Brite Inc.; Lawrenceville; telephone and telegraph apparatus 500

KMC Telecom Inc.; Lawrenceville; local/long-distance telephone 500

Unisys Corp.; Norcross; computer software development 500

Shaw Industries Inc.; Cartersville; fabrics: linen, jute, hemp, ramie 500

Makita Corp. of America; Buford; power-driven handtools 500

Georgia 8th District

West — suburbs of Atlanta, Columbus, and Macon

Created in redistricting after the 2000 census, the 8th was drawn to elect a Republican. Mostly within the rough triangle of Macon, Columbus, and the south-central suburbs of Atlanta, the 8th jumps all around western Georgia, taking in Republican suburbs of those cities. The 11th and 13th districts wind in and around the 8th, encompassing Democratic areas. *(See map p. 262.)*

Much of the 8th used to be agricultural but is now suburban, though many rural areas remain. Textile and poultry processing plants dot the landscape, and the timber industry flourishes here. The home-building industry also is becoming a larger force in the suburbs, as additional housing developments and malls are constructed.

South of Atlanta, the district includes suburbs that were cut out of the heavily Democratic 13th. Peachtree City, in Fayette County, is a planned community 15 miles south of Atlanta that attracts commuters and home builders. Fayette County is home to many workers at nearby Hartsfield Atlanta International Airport. Henry County, east of Fayette, is the second-fastest-growing county in the state.

Farther east, the district encompasses all of rural Jasper County and snakes into Bibb County, covering the Republican suburbs north of Macon. Some workers from Robins Air Force Base, in the 1st District, live in the 8th, along with commuters to Macon.

The district's western edge includes rural Carroll and Coweta Counties and extends south into Harris County, a wealthy bedroom community outside Columbus. The 8th also includes the northern part of Muscogee County and its immediate suburbs of Columbus.

Major Industry

Textiles, agriculture, timber, poultry processing, home building.

Notable

Callaway Gardens, a 14,000-acre resort and gardens in Pine Mountain, holds the Sky High Hot Air Balloon Festival every Labor Day.

Election Returns

	Republican		Democratic		Other	
President 2000	157,703	68.9%	67,192	29.3%	4,098	1.8%
House 2002	142,505	78.3%	39,422	21.7%		

District Profile

Population 629,700

Total area (square miles) 3,553.3
    Land area (square miles) 3,512.2

Population per square mile 179.3

Counties (2000 population)

Bibb (pt.)	26,223	Jones (pt.)	2,321
Butts (pt.)	10,925	Lamar	15,912
Carroll (pt.)	58,201	Muscogee (pt.)	53,778
Coweta (pt.)	74,266	Newton (pt.)	19,213
Douglas (pt.)	58,766	Pike	13,688
Fayette (pt.)	86,826	Rockdale (pt.)	18,764
Harris (pt.)	21,296	Spalding (pt.)	30,871
Henry (pt.)	77,898	Troup (pt.)	27,944
Jasper	11,426	Upson (pt.)	21,382

Cities and other areas over 10,000 (2000 population)
Columbus (pt.) 53,778
Douglasville (pt.) 13,553
Fayetteville 11,148
Peachtree City 31,580

Race and Hispanic or Latino origin*
White 82.8%
Black or African American 12.5%
American Indian or Alaska Native 0.2%
Asian 1.3%
Native Hawaiian or other Pacific Islander 0.0%
Some other race 0.1%
Hispanic or Latino origin 2.1%
Two or more races 0.9%

As percentage of total population.

Ancestry*

English	8.8%	Italian	1.9%
French	1.6%	Scotch-Irish	1.8%
German	7.4%	Scottish	1.8%
Irish	8.7%	USA/American	15.6%

As estimated percentage of total population.

Universities and colleges, 2000–2001 enrollment
Columbus State University, Columbus 5,187
Gordon College, Barnesville 2,890
LaGrange College, LaGrange 917
State University of West Georgia, Carrollton 8,959
Wesleyan College, Macon 577

Newspapers and circulation

	District circulation	Total circulation
Atlanta Journal-Constitution	98,492	857,088
Carrollton Times-Georgian	5,247	9,543
Columbus Ledger-Enquirer	14,119	46,345
Douglas County Sentinel	3,606	6,255
Griffin Daily News	9,299	11,029
Macon Telegraph	5,367	63,666
*USA Today**	2,642	1,674,376

See Sources and Explanations in the front of the volume.

Television stations and affiliations

Atlanta	83%	WAGA	FOX
Atlanta	83%	WATC	Independent
Atlanta	83%	WATL	WB
Atlanta	83%	WCIQ	PBS
Atlanta	83%	WGTV	PBS
Atlanta	83%	WHSG	Independent
Atlanta	83%	WJSP	PBS
Atlanta	83%	WPBA	PBS
Atlanta	83%	WPXA	PAX
Atlanta	83%	WSB	ABC
Atlanta	83%	WTBS	TBN
Atlanta	83%	WUPA	UPN
Atlanta	83%	WXIA	NBC
Columbus	14%	WACS	PBS
Columbus	14%	WGIQ	PBS
Columbus	14%	WLTZ	NBC
Columbus	14%	WRBL	CBS
Columbus	14%	WSWS	UPN
Columbus	14%	WTVM	ABC
Columbus	14%	WXTX	FOX
Macon	3%	WDCO	PBS
Macon	3%	WGNM	UPN
Macon	3%	WGXA	FOX
Macon	3%	WMAZ	CBS
Macon	3%	WMGT	NBC
Macon	3%	WPGA	ABC

Cable systems and subscribers
Charter 46,099
Comcast 29,167
Mediacom 751

Businesses and other major employers
Pilot SVCS Inc.; Winston; telephone communication 6,000
Cagle's Inc.; Pine Mountain Valley; poultry slaughtering/processing 1,800
Washington Inventory Service Inc.; Fayetteville; inventory computing service 1,300
West Georgia Health System Inc. Hospital; LaGrange; 1,270
United Technologies Corp.; Columbus; aircraft engines and parts 1,200
Callaway Gardens Resort Inc.; Pine Mountain; golf goods and equipment 1,000
Kmart Corp.; Newnan; general warehousing, storage 950
Photocircuits Corp.; Peachtree City; printed circuit boards 950
Matsushita Communication Industrial Corp.; Peachtree City; pagers 920
West Georgia State University; Carrollton 850
Wal-Mart Stores Inc.; Fayetteville; discount department stores 800
Quad Graphics Inc.; The Rock; commercial printing 800
Callaway Gardens Resort Inc.; Pine Mountain; hotels and motels 800
Fayette Community Hospital Inc.; Fayetteville 750
Georgia Forestry Commission; Macon 702
Cooper-Standard Automotive Inc.; Griffin; automotive rubber goods 650
Yamaha Motor Manufacturing Corp. of America; Newnan; golf carts 650
Yokogawa Trading USA Inc.; Newnan; electric measuring instruments, meters 650
NCR Corp.; Peachtree City; office equipment 650
Ace USA; Macon; insurance agents and brokers 600
Bradley Marketing Services; Midland; catalog sales 600
William Carter Co.; Griffin; women's and children's undergarments 558

Wal-Mart Stores Inc.; Newnan; department stores   550
Newnan Hospital; Newnan   549
Total System Services Inc.; Columbus; commercial printing   545
Eckerd Corp.; Newnan; drug and proprietary stores 510
Quad Graphics Inc.; Thomaston; magazine publishing 500
Georgia Farm Bureau Casualty Insurance Co.; Macon 500
Harris County School District; Hamilton   500
Columbus State University; Columbus   500

Georgia 9th District

Northeast — part of Augusta

The 9th starts in northeastern Georgia, encompassing agricultural and mountain areas, and travels down the South Carolina border to take in parts of Augusta. It also extends west to take in some suburbs east of Atlanta.

Created following the 2000 census, the 9th is solidly Republican. An arm from the neighboring 12th cuts north into the center of the district to strip out liberal Athens and the University of Georgia. A growing suburban population contributes to the GOP bent, and George W. Bush received 66.4 percent of the district's vote in the 2000 presidential election.

Suburban areas around Augusta and Athens are less developed than those bordering Atlanta. The district takes in part of the city of Augusta as well, including much of the Augusta National Golf Club (shared with the 12th). Many of the 9th's suburbs are rural in character, dotted with dairy farms and ranches. The mountainous northern region is the most rural, with dairy, timber, and mining industries sustaining the economy. The area also depends on tourism dollars from visitors to a chain of lakes on the South Carolina border: Lake Russell, Lake Thurmond, and Lake Hartwell.

The Savannah River valley makes water a major issue. Legislators representing this part of the state often have fought against exporting water to Atlanta, hoping to keep the resources on their own turf.

Major Industry

Agriculture, tourism, retail.

Notable

Augusta National Golf Club (shared with the 12th) hosts the annual Masters golf tournament; the movies *Deliverance* and *Smokey and the Bandit* were set in Rabun County; Helen, a hamlet in White County, is a replica of a Swiss village; Elberton is known as the granite capital of the world.

Election Returns

	Republican		Democratic		Other	
President 2000	141,065	66.4%	67,451	31.7%	4,025	1.9%
House 2002	123,313	72.8%	45,974	27.2%		

District Profile

Population   629,762

Total area (square miles)   7,123.7
  Land area (square miles)   6,946.8

Population per square mile   90.7

Counties (2000 population)

Banks	14,422	Morgan	15,457
Barrow	46,144	Newton (pt.)	11,560
Columbia	89,288	Oconee	26,225
Elbert	20,511	Oglethorpe (pt.)	10,410
Franklin	20,285	Putnam	18,812
Greene	14,406	Rabun	15,050
Habersham	35,902	Richmond (pt.)	37,392
Hart	22,997	Stephens	25,435
Jackson	41,589	Towns	9,319
Lincoln	8,348	Union	17,289
Lumpkin	21,016	Walton (pt.)	30,313
Madison	25,730	White	19,944
McDuffie	21,231	Wilkes	10,687

Cities and other areas over 10,000 (2000 population)

Augusta (pt.)   36,679
Evans CDP   17,727
Martinez CDP   27,749
Winder   10,201

Race and Hispanic or Latino origin*

White   81.2%
Black or African American   13.6%
American Indian or Alaska Native   0.3%
Asian   1.2%
Native Hawaiian or other Pacific Islander   0.0%
Some other race   0.1%
Hispanic or Latino origin   2.6%
Two or more races   0.9%

*As percentage of total population.

Ancestry*

English	8.1%	Italian	1.5%
French	1.3%	Scotch-Irish	1.8%
German	6.4%	Scottish	1.5%
Irish	7.8%	USA/American	16.8%

*As estimated percentage of total population.

Universities and colleges, 2000–2001 enrollment

Emmanuel College, Franklin Springs   786
Georgia Military College, Fort Gordon   993
North Georgia College and State University, Dahlonega 3,622
North Georgia Technical Institute, Clarkesville   1,482
Piedmont College, Demorest   1,728
Toccoa Falls College, Toccoa Falls   941
Truett-McConnell College, Cleveland   2,033
Young Harris College, Young Harris   620

Newspapers and circulation

	District circulation	Total circulation
Anderson Independent-Mail	7,797	38,854
Athens Banner-Herald	13,962	25,775
Atlanta Journal-Constitution	46,386	857,088
Augusta Chronicle	22,065	68,807
Gainesville Times	4,126	21,011
*USA Today**	1,949	1,674,376

*See Sources and Explanations in the front of the volume.

Television stations and affiliations

Atlanta	65%	WAGA	FOX
Atlanta	65%	WATC	Independent
Atlanta	65%	WATL	WB
Atlanta	65%	WCIQ	PBS
Atlanta	65%	WGTV	PBS
Atlanta	65%	WHSG	Independent
Atlanta	65%	WJSP	PBS
Atlanta	65%	WPBA	PBS
Atlanta	65%	WPXA	PAX
Atlanta	65%	WSB	ABC
Atlanta	65%	WTBS	TBN
Atlanta	65%	WUPA	UPN
Atlanta	65%	WXIA	NBC
Augusta	20%	WAGT	NBC
Augusta	20%	WCES	PBS
Augusta	20%	WEBA	PBS
Augusta	20%	WFXG	FOX
Augusta	20%	WJBF	ABC
Augusta	20%	WRDW	CBS
Greenville-Spartanburg-Asheville-Anderson	15%	WASV	UPN
Greenville-Spartanburg-Asheville-Anderson	15%	WBSC	WB
Greenville-Spartanburg-Asheville-Anderson	15%	WGGS	Independent
Greenville-Spartanburg-Asheville-Anderson	15%	WHNS	FOX
Greenville-Spartanburg-Asheville-Anderson	15%	WLOS	ABC
Greenville-Spartanburg-Asheville-Anderson	15%	WNEG	CBS
Greenville-Spartanburg-Asheville-Anderson	15%	WNEH	PBS
Greenville-Spartanburg-Asheville-Anderson	15%	WNTV	PBS
Greenville-Spartanburg-Asheville-Anderson	15%	WRET	PBS
Greenville-Spartanburg-Asheville-Anderson	15%	WSPA	CBS
Greenville-Spartanburg-Asheville-Anderson	15%	WUNF	PBS
Greenville-Spartanburg-Asheville-Anderson	15%	WYFF	NBC

Cable systems and subscribers

Adelphia   2,340
Alltel Communications   16,389
Charter   11,812
Comcast   33,899
Communicomm   5,323
Galaxy   1,056
Knology   2,731
Northland   42,503
Plantation Cablevision   1,005
Water, Light, and Gas Commission   9,152

Military installations, September 2001

Fort Gordon, Augusta   11,686

Businesses and other major employers

Horton Homes Inc.; Eatonton; mobile homes   1,450
Fieldale Farms Corp.; Cornelia; processed poultry   1,400
ContiGroup Companies Inc.; Pendergrass; poultry slaughtering/processing   1,200
Coats American Inc.; Toccoa; thread: bleaching, dyeing, finishing   1,200
Club Car Inc.; Evans; off-highway cars   1,100
New FOL Inc.; Rabun Gap; men's and boys' underwear   1,000
Quebecor World Inc.; Evans; commercial printing   800
Futurecall Telemarketing West Inc.; Augusta; telemarketing services   800
Mount Vernon Mills Inc.; Alto; upholstery fabrics   750
Georgia Dept. of Corrections; Grovetown   750
Springs Industries Inc.; Hartwell; textile goods   720
Columbia County School District; Appling   700
Thermal Ceramics Inc.; Augusta; electrical insulators, insulation materials   700
Chateau Elan Resorts Inc.; Braselton; resort hotel   600
ConAgra Poultry Co.; Elberton; poultry slaughtering/processing   600
Tenneco Automotive Operating Co.; Hartwell; automotive shock absorbers   600
Scovill Fasteners Inc.; Clarkesville; fasteners, buttons, needles, and pins   550
Harrison Poultry Inc.; Bethlehem; chicken hatchery   550
Ethicon Inc.; Cornelia; sutures   500
Wellington Leisure Products Inc.; Madison; water skis   500
Duck Head Apparel Co.; Winder; men's/boys' sportswear and athletic clothing   500
Carole Fabrics Corp.; Augusta; draperies   500

Georgia 10th District

North — Dalton, Gainesville

Anchored by North Georgia's mountains, the 10th runs across the western half of the state's northern border. It includes the Cloudland Canyon, the man-made Lake Lanier, and several growing Atlanta suburbs, as well as bedroom communities outside of Chattanooga, Tennessee.

Residents are overwhelmingly white and strongly Republican; only 3.2 percent of the district's voting-age population is black. While Democrats have long dominated local politics, the GOP allegiance in some north-central counties is unwavering and dates to the Civil War. George W. Bush received 69.4 percent of the district's vote in 2000.

Economically, the 10th has benefited from a population boom. A surge of new residents in the south has brought white-collar and service-sector jobs to the district but is straining local water resources. Many of the new residents are Hispanic immigrants who work in the district's poultry processing and carpet-making industries in Hall and Whitfield counties. Tourist dollars also play a role in the economy, as visitors flock to Lake Lanier (shared with the 7th).

The district also dips down into the Atlanta area, where it takes in Republican suburbs north and east of the city, most of them dominated by housing subdivisions and shopping malls.

Major Industry

Poultry processing, carpet manufacturing, textiles.

Notable

Dalton is known as the carpet capital of the world; Gainesville, dubbed the poultry capital of the world, displays the Georgia Poultry Federation's monument to the industry in the center of town—an obelisk with a chicken statue on top; Springer Mountain is the southern terminus of the Appalachian National Scenic Trail, which is 2,167 miles long and extends to Maine.

Election Returns

	Republican		Democratic		Other	
President 2000	134,619	69.4%	54,633	28.2%	4,614	2.4%
House 2002	129,242	100.0%				

District Profile

Population   629,702

Total area (square miles)   3,819.6
  Land area (square miles)   3,741.1

Population per square mile   168.3

Counties (2000 population)

Catoosa	53,282	Hall	139,277
Dade	15,154	Murray	36,506
Dawson	15,999	Pickens	22,983
Fannin	19,798	Rockdale (pt.)	4,497
Forsyth (pt.)	50,535	Walker	61,053
Gilmer	23,456	Walton (pt.)	16,187
Gordon	44,104	Whitfield	83,525
Gwinnett (pt.)	43,346		

Cities and other areas over 10,000 (2000 population)

Calhoun   10,667
Dalton   27,912
Gainesville   25,578

Race and Hispanic or Latino origin*

White   85.4%
Black or African American   3.3%
American Indian or Alaska Native   0.3%
Asian   0.7%
Native Hawaiian or other Pacific Islander   0.0%
Some other race   0.1%
Hispanic or Latino origin   9.4%
Two or more races   0.8%

*As percentage of total population.

Ancestry*

Dutch	1.1%	Italian	1.4%
English	7.8%	Scotch-Irish	1.5%
French	1.3%	Scottish	1.5%
German	6.2%	USA/American	17.9%
Irish	8.3%		

*As estimated percentage of total population.

Universities and colleges, 2000–2001 enrollment

Brenau University, Gainesville   2,266
Covenant College, Lookout Mountain   1,149
Dalton College, Dalton   3,137
Gainesville College, Oakwood   3,248
Lanier Technical Institute, Oakwood   1,987
Northwestern Technical Institute, Rock Spring   1,500
Pickens Technical Institute, Jasper   950

Newspapers and circulation

	District circulation	Total circulation
Atlanta Journal-Constitution	63,472	857,088
Chattanooga Times Free Press	13,071	72,730
Dalton Daily Citizen News	12,881	12,881
Gainesville Times	16,194	21,011
USA Today *	3,129	1,674,376

*See Sources and Explanations in the front of the volume.

Television stations and affiliations

Atlanta	52%	WAGA	FOX
Atlanta	52%	WATC	Independent
Atlanta	52%	WATL	WB
Atlanta	52%	WCIQ	PBS
Atlanta	52%	WGTV	PBS
Atlanta	52%	WHSG	Independent
Atlanta	52%	WJSP	PBS
Atlanta	52%	WPBA	PBS
Atlanta	52%	WPXA	PAX
Atlanta	52%	WSB	ABC
Atlanta	52%	WTBS	TBN
Atlanta	52%	WUPA	UPN
Atlanta	52%	WXIA	NBC
Chattanooga, TN	48%	WCLP	PBS
Chattanooga, TN	48%	WDEF	CBS
Chattanooga, TN	48%	WDSI	FOX
Chattanooga, TN	48%	WELF	Independent
Chattanooga, TN	48%	WFLI	WB
Chattanooga, TN	48%	WRCB	NBC
Chattanooga, TN	48%	WTCI	PBS
Chattanooga, TN	48%	WTVC	ABC

Cable systems and subscribers

Adelphia   1,196
Charter   35,551
Comcast   18,663

Businesses and other major employers

Beaulieu of America Inc.; Dalton; carpets   5,017
Shaw Industries Inc.; Dalton; carpets, rugs   3,300
Northeast Georgia Medical Center Inc.; Gainesville   2,600
SI Corp.; Chickamauga; polypropylene broadwoven fabrics   1,800
Roper Corp.; La Fayette; indoor cooking equipment   1,700
Shaw Industries Inc.; Ringgold; carpet finishing   1,600
ConAgra Poultry Co.; Gainesville; poultry processing   1,500
Aladdin Manufacturing Corp.; Sugar Valley; carpet finishing   1,500
Hamilton Medical Center Inc.; Dalton   1,380
Tyson Foods Inc.; Cumming; processed poultry   1,200
Hutcheson Medical Center; Fort Oglethorpe   1,100
Mar-Jac Holdings Inc.; Gainesville; chicken processing   1,005
Carriage Investments Ltd.; Calhoun; investors   1,000
Fieldale Farms Corp.; Murrayville; processed poultry   900
Mannington Carpets Inc.; Calhoun; carpets   850
Fieldale Farms Corp.; Gainesville; processed fresh poultry   800
Calfee Company of Dalton Inc.; Dalton; convenience stores   800
Cottrell Inc.; Gainesville; car carrier bodies   750
J&J Industries Inc.; Dalton; carpets   730
Gold Kist Inc.; Ellijay; processed poultry   700
ConAgra Poultry Co.; Dalton; processed poultry   700
Beaulieu Group; Dalton; carpets, rugs   700
Aladdin Manufacturing Corp.; Chatsworth; carpet finishing   700
Gress Foods; Gainesville; processed fresh poultry   670
Mohawk Industries Inc.; Calhoun; bedspreads   616
McLeodUSA Inc.; Cumming; telephone communication   600
Peachtree Doors and Windows Inc.; Gainesville; millwork   550
GM Nameplate Inc.; Flowery Branch; paper labels   513
Georgia Tufters; Calhoun; tufted rugs   503
Wal-Mart Stores Inc.; Dalton; discount department stores   500

Wal-Mart Stores Inc.; Fort Oglethorpe; discount
  department stores 500
Shaw Industries Inc.; Calhoun; carpet yarn 500
Regions Financial Corp.; Gainesville; data processing
  500
Liberty Mutual Insurance Co.; Gainesville; fire, marine,
  casualty insurance 500
Georgia Phillips State Prison; Buford 500
Aladdin Manufacturing Corp.; Dalton; carpet yarn 500

Georgia 11th District

Northwest — Rome, parts of Columbus and Marietta

Running south along the Alabama border from northwest
Georgia to Columbus, the oddly shaped 11th stretches east
to take in Atlanta's northwestern suburbs and connect several
Democratic areas. While the district includes all or part of
17 counties, the majority of its voters live in three—Cobb
(suburbs of Atlanta and part of Marietta), Floyd (Rome), and
Muscogee (Columbus).

The 11th was drawn following the 2000 census to lean
Democratic. Although 25.8 percent of the voting-age population is African American, the district's white population
tends to be socially conservative and supportive of GOP candidates. George W. Bush captured 51.4 percent of the district's vote in the 2000 presidential election.

Cobb County is a collection of largely white-collar,
middle-income suburbs with a rapidly growing minority
population. The 11th takes in southern parts of the county
and much of Marietta (shared with the 6th). Small businesses and corporate headquarters, as well as military- and
aerospace-related jobs in Marietta, spark the economy. Lockheed Martin employs many. Other major industries include
electrical wire in Carroll County and carpet manufacturing
in the north.

Areas outside the district's three cities are largely agricultural, and some small towns are reliant on textile trades. The
beef and timber industries and a few manufacturers provide
jobs for workers along the border.

Major Industry
Defense, carpet manufacturing, electronics.

Notable
Like its Italian namesake, Rome is built on seven hills.

Election Returns

	Republican		Democratic		Other	
President 2000	93,359	51.4%	85,542	47.1%	2,632	1.4%
House 2002	69,260	51.6%	64,922	48.4%		

District Profile

Population 629,730

Total area (square miles) 3,750.3
  Land area (square miles) 3,700.6

Population per square mile 170.2

Counties (2000 population)

Bartow (pt.)	38,381	Chattooga	25,470
Carroll (pt.)	29,067	Cobb (pt.)	203,407
Coweta (pt.)	14,949	Muscogee (pt.)	48,540
Douglas (pt.)	33,408	Paulding (pt.)	2,633
Floyd	90,565	Polk	38,127
Haralson	25,690	Talbot	6,498
Harris (pt.)	2,399	Troup (pt.)	30,835
Heard	11,012	Upson (pt.)	6,215
Meriwether	22,534		

Cities and other areas over 10,000 (2000 population)
  Carrollton (pt.) 12,953
  Cartersville (pt.) 15,925
  Columbus (pt.) 48,030
  LaGrange (pt.) 18,380
  Mableton CDP (pt.) 28,140
  Marietta (pt.) 40,133
  Rome 34,980
  Smyrna (pt.) 14,218

Race and Hispanic or Latino origin*
  White 61.7%
  Black or African American 28.2%
  American Indian or Alaska Native 0.2%
  Asian 1.2%
  Native Hawaiian or other Pacific Islander 0.0%
  Some other race 0.2%
  Hispanic or Latino origin 7.2%
  Two or more races 1.1%

As percentage of total population.

Ancestry*

English	5.7%	Scottish	1.1%
German	4.5%	Subsaharan	1.3%
Irish	6.3%	USA/American	13.7%
Scotch-Irish	1.2%		

As estimated percentage of total population.

Universities and colleges, 2000–2001 enrollment
  Berry College, Mt. Berry 2,033
  Carroll Technical Institute, Carrollton 2,032
  Chattahoochee Technical Institute, Marietta 3,287
  Columbus Technical Institute, Columbus 1,754
  Coosa Valley Technical Institute, Rome 2,313
  Flint River Technical Institute, Thomaston 605
  Floyd College, Rome 2,090
  Life University, Marietta 3,161
  Shorter College, Rome 1,925
  Southern Polytechnic State University, Marietta 3,546
  West Georgia Technical Institute, LaGrange 1,201

Newspapers and circulation

	District circulation	Total circulation
Atlanta Journal-Constitution	63,276	857,088
Carrollton Times-Georgian	4,282	9,543
Cartersville Daily Tribune News	2,717	7,902
Columbus Ledger-Enquirer	11,018	46,345
Douglas County Sentinel	2,163	6,255
Marietta Daily Journal	5,578	18,321
Rome News-Tribune	16,059	16,702
*USA Today**	3,045	1,674,376

See Sources and Explanations in the front of the volume.

Television stations and affiliations

Atlanta	77%	WAGA	FOX
Atlanta	77%	WATC	Independent
Atlanta	77%	WATL	WB
Atlanta	77%	WCIQ	PBS
Atlanta	77%	WGTV	PBS
Atlanta	77%	WHSG	Independent
Atlanta	77%	WJSP	PBS
Atlanta	77%	WPBA	PBS
Atlanta	77%	WPXA	PAX
Atlanta	77%	WSB	ABC
Atlanta	77%	WTBS	TBN
Atlanta	77%	WUPA	UPN
Atlanta	77%	WXIA	NBC
Columbus	14%	WACS	PBS
Columbus	14%	WGIQ	PBS
Columbus	14%	WLTZ	NBC
Columbus	14%	WRBL	CBS
Columbus	14%	WSWS	UPN
Columbus	14%	WTVM	ABC
Columbus	14%	WXTX	FOX
Chattanooga, TN	9%	WCLP	PBS
Chattanooga, TN	9%	WDEF	CBS
Chattanooga, TN	9%	WDSI	FOX
Chattanooga, TN	9%	WELF	Independent
Chattanooga, TN	9%	WFLI	WB
Chattanooga, TN	9%	WRCB	NBC
Chattanooga, TN	9%	WTCI	PBS
Chattanooga, TN	9%	WTVC	ABC

Cable systems and subscribers

Adelphia   6,666
Charter   64,639
Comcast   26,074
Community Television   7,075
SunTel Communications   8,501

Military installations, September 2001

Fort Benning,* Columbus   17,964
Dobbins Air Force Reserve Base, Marietta   2,162
Naval Marine Corps Reserve Center, Atlanta   515

Fort Benning is shared with the 2nd District.

Businesses and other major employers

Lockheed Martin Corp.; Marietta; aircraft   7,500
Southwire Co.; Carrollton; wire, aluminum   2,800
Mount Vernon Mills Inc.; Trion; upholstery fabrics   2,500
Tanner Medical Center Inc.; Carrollton   1,600
Wellstar Cobb Hospital; Austell   1,525
Floyd Healthcare Management Inc. Hospital; Rome   1,525
Cobb County School District; Marietta   1,500
Blue Cross and Blue Shield of Georgia; Columbus; health maintenance organization   1,400
Southern Polytechnic State University; Marietta   1,100
AT&T Corp.; Marietta; cellular telephones   1,000
Power Industry Consultants Inc.; Marietta; consulting engineer   1,000
Redmond Park Hospital Inc.; Rome   1,000
General Electric Co.; Franklin; electric power systems contractors   1,000
C&M Holdings Inc.; Rome; carpets   950

Greenwood Mills Inc.; Lindale; broadwoven fabric mills, cotton   900
Gold Kist Inc.; Carrollton; processed poultry   878
Goody Products Inc.; Manchester; hair and hair-based products   851
Auto Nation; Lithia Springs; automobile sales   827
Wal-Mart Stores Inc.; LaGrange; general warehousing, storage   800
Interface Flooring Systems Inc.; LaGrange; carpet finishing   750
Wellstar Windy Hill Hospital; Marietta; management services   700
Tillotson Corp.; Menlo; fabric dress and work gloves   700
Yellow Freight System Inc.; Marietta; local trucking, without storage   681
Kellogg Co.; Rome; cookies   650
Swift Spinning Mills Inc.; Columbus; cotton yarn   640
Goodyear Tire and Rubber Co.; Cartersville; tire cord and fabrics   600
Crews Chemicals Inc.; Rome; chemicals and allied products   600
Inland Paperboard and Packaging Inc.; Rome; linerboard   600
ITC Holding Co.; West Point; telephone communications broker   600
Columbus Internet Foundry; Columbus; ductile iron castings   600
William L. Bonnell Co.; Newnan; aluminum products   587
Tip Top Poultry Inc.; Marietta; processed fresh poultry   550
Cluett American Corp.; Cedartown; men's/boys' clothing   550
Aladdin Manufacturing Corp.; Lyerly; tufted rugs   520
Life University Inc.; Marietta   510
Solvay Pharmaceuticals Inc.; Marietta; antihistamine preparations   500
Tyco Healthcare Group; Marietta; sanitary paper products   500
Public Storage Inc.; Adairsville; general warehousing, storage   500
Hon Industries Inc.; Cedartown; office furniture   500
Northwest Georgia Hospital; Rome   500
Zartic Inc.; Rome; processed frozen poultry   500
United Forming Inc.; Austell; concrete work   500
Gillette Co.; LaGrange; storage batteries   500
Berry College Inc.; Summerville   500

Georgia 12th District

East — Athens, most of Augusta and Savannah

The 12th resembles the Statue of Liberty, with Athens at the torch, Augusta at the head, and Savannah at the feet. It covers the southern half of Georgia's border with South Carolina, extending down from Augusta into Chatham County to cover most of the city of Savannah. The district's arm travels through agricultural communities to take in Athens and the University of Georgia's main campus.

Drawn during redistricting following the 2000 census to elect a Democrat, the 12th encompasses Savannah's city center, including the inner city and historic areas. While all of Savannah was included in the old 1st District, the new map split the city to separate predominantly Democratic and Republican areas. Over thirty-eight percent of the 12th's voting-age population is black.

Effingham, a rapidly growing Savannah suburb, is the most Republican part of the district. Farther north, the 12th takes in the urban areas of Augusta. Most of Augusta National Golf Club is in the 9th, but the 13th hole, part of "Amen Corner," is in the 12th.

The agricultural areas south of Athens are heavily African American, specializing in row farming and timber production. Textile factories had a presence here, but many have shut down in recent years. The Medical College of Georgia is in the district.

Major Industry
Agriculture, manufacturing, timber.

Notable
Part of the movie *Forrest Gump* was filmed at Chippewa Square in Savannah.

Election Returns

	Republican		Democratic		Other	
President 2000	80,665	45.0%	95,845	53.5%	2,636	1.5%
House 2002	77,479	55.2%	62,904	44.8%	74	

District Profile

Population 629,735

Total area (square miles) 5,264.9
Land area (square miles) 5,224.0

Population per square mile 120.5

Counties (2000 population)
Bryan (pt.) 16,220	Jefferson 17,266
Bulloch 55,983	Jenkins 8,575
Burke 22,243	Oglethorpe (pt.) 2,225
Chatham (pt.) 179,473	Richmond (pt.) 162,383
Clarke 101,489	Screven 15,374
Effingham 37,535	Taliaferro 2,077
Glascock 2,556	Warren 6,336

Cities and other areas over 10,000 (2000 population)
Athens-Clarke County 100,266
Augusta (pt.) 158,503
Garden City 11,289
Savannah (pt.) 126,598
Statesboro 22,698

Race and Hispanic or Latino origin*
White 51.9%
Black or African American 42.3%
American Indian or Alaska Native 0.2%
Asian 1.4%
Native Hawaiian or other Pacific Islander 0.1%
Some other race 0.1%
Hispanic or Latino origin 2.9%
Two or more races 1.1%

*As percentage of total population.

Ancestry*
English 5.8%	Scotch-Irish 1.3%
French 1.3%	Scottish 1.4%
German 5.5%	Subsaharan 1.2%
Irish 5.8%	USA/American 8.8%
Italian 1.4%	

*As estimated percentage of total population.

Universities and colleges, 2000–2001 enrollment
Athens Area Technical Institute, Athens 2,747
Augusta State University, Augusta 5,070
Augusta Technical Institute, Augusta 3,265
Georgia Southern University, Statesboro 14,184
Medical College of Georgia, Augusta 1,932
Ogeechee Technical Institute, Statesboro 1,764
Savannah College of Art and Design, Savannah 4,923
Savannah State University, Savannah 2,166
Savannah Technical Institute, Savannah 2,048
South College, Savannah 491
University of Georgia, Athens 31,288

Newspapers and circulation

	District circulation	Total circulation
Athens Banner-Herald	11,677	25,775
Atlanta Journal-Constitution	19,367	857,088
Augusta Chronicle	29,103	68,807
Savannah Morning News	28,597	58,145
*USA Today**	2,931	1,674,376

*See Sources and Explanations in the front of the volume.

Television stations and affiliations
Augusta	49%	WAGT	NBC
Augusta	49%	WCES	PBS
Augusta	49%	WEBA	PBS
Augusta	49%	WFXG	FOX
Augusta	49%	WJBF	ABC
Augusta	49%	WRDW	CBS
Savannah	46%	WGSA	UPN
Savannah	46%	WJCL	ABC
Savannah	46%	WSAV	NBC
Savannah	46%	WTGS	FOX
Savannah	46%	WTOC	CBS
Savannah	46%	WVAN	PBS
Atlanta	5%	WAGA	FOX
Atlanta	5%	WATC	Independent
Atlanta	5%	WATL	WB
Atlanta	5%	WCIQ	PBS
Atlanta	5%	WGTV	PBS
Atlanta	5%	WHSG	Independent
Atlanta	5%	WJSP	PBS
Atlanta	5%	WPBA	PBS
Atlanta	5%	WPXA	PAX
Atlanta	5%	WSB	ABC
Atlanta	5%	WTBS	TBN
Atlanta	5%	WUPA	UPN
Atlanta	5%	WXIA	NBC

Cable systems and subscribers
Charter 35,344
Comcast 112,574
Mallard 3,407
Northland 9,115

Military installations, September 2001

Savannah International Airport (Air National Guard), Savannah 947

Navy Supply Corps School, Athens 166

Businesses and other major employers

Medical College of Georgia; Augusta 10,000

Gulfstream Aerospace Corp.; Savannah; aircraft 4,157

Memorial Health University Medical Center Inc.; Savannah 3,500

University Health Services Inc. Hospital; Augusta 2,600

United Technologies Corp.; East Syracuse; aircraft engines and parts 2,500

Athens Regional Medical Center; Athens 2,100

U.S. Veterans Hospital; Augusta 1,988

ConAgra Poultry Co.; Athens; poultry slaughtering/processing 1,700

St. Joseph's Candler Health System; Savannah 1,674

Georgia Southern University; Statesboro 1,600

City of Savannah; Savannah; city management 1,555

Georgia Dept. of Human Resources; Gracewood 1,500

Doctors Hospital of Augusta Inc.; Augusta 1,400

Georgia-Pacific Corp.; Rincon; towels, tissues and napkins 1,400

St. Mary's Health Care System Inc.; Athens 1,247

Textron Inc.; Augusta; golf carts 1,176

St. Joseph's Candler Health System; Savannah 1,100

Gold Kist Inc.; Athens; processed poultry 1,000

Southeastern Newspapers Corp.; Augusta; newspaper 1,000

Memorial Health University Medical Center Inc.; Richmond Hill 1,000

Great Dane LP; Savannah; truck trailers 1,000

Reliance Electric Industrial Co.; Athens; electric motors 950

University of Georgia; Athens 950

International Paper Co.; Augusta; paper mills 937

Thermal Ceramics Inc.; Augusta; ceramic fiber 925

Viracon Inc.; Statesboro; laminated glass 850

Georgia Power Co.; Waynesboro; electric services 850

Unified Athens-Clarke County; Athens; county government 821

Austin Industrial Inc.; Augusta; industrial buildings construction 800

Briggs and Stratton Corp.; Statesboro; internal combustion engines 790

Savannah Foods Industrial Inc.; Savannah; refined cane sugar 762

St. Joseph Hospital; Augusta 760

Savannah College of Art and Design; Savannah 750

Sizemore Inc.; Augusta; security guard service 749

Kerr McGee Pigments; Savannah; titanium dioxide (pigments) 714

General Time Corp.; Athens; clock assembly 689

Tyco Healthcare Group; Augusta; medical device manufacturer 685

Murray Biscuits; Augusta; biscuits 655

Georgia Power Co.; Athens; electric services 653

Health Management Associates Inc.; Statesboro; hospital 650

Wal-Mart Stores Inc.; Statesboro; department stores 650

Wal-Mart Stores Inc.; Athens; department stores 600

Georgia Ports Authority; Savannah 600

McLane Co.; Athens; discount department store 580

Augusta State University; Augusta 520

Stone Container Corp.; Port Wentworth; linerboard 520

Georgia Dept. of Human Resources; Augusta 508

Thermo King Corp.; Louisville; refrigeration equipment 500

Jockey International Inc.; Millen; men's and women's underwear 500

Torrington Co.; Sylvania; ball bearings and parts 500

ABB Inc.; Athens; nonelectric transformers 500

McLane Co.; Athens; discount department store 500

Avondale Mills Inc.; Augusta; broadwoven fabric mills, cotton 500

Memorial Health University Medical Center Inc.; Springfield 500

Georgia Dept. of Human Resources; Savannah 500

Morris Communications Corp.; Savannah; radio broadcasting stations 500

Sun Healthcare Group Inc.; Savannah; home health care services 500

Georgia 13th District

Southern Atlanta suburbs

One of two new districts created in Georgia following the 2000 census, the 13th covers a spidery area south of Atlanta with tentacles extending outward from the city. The district was created by Democratic state legislators to represent the growing black population on the outskirts of Atlanta.

The district has a slim white plurality: 46 percent of the 13th's voting-age population is white, while 37 percent is African American. Roughly 10 percent of residents are Hispanic, though voter turnout is much lower among that population. Solidly Democratic, 56.8 percent of residents voted for Al Gore in the 2000 presidential election.

The 13th takes in an array of middle-income urban, suburban, and rural areas. Many residents in the urban areas—the two fingers that run along Interstate 85, north of Atlanta in Gwinnett County and south of the city in Fulton County—live in apartment communities and commute to Atlanta. The heart of the district is suburban Clayton County, which formerly was populated by blue-collar white residents and is now a haven for African American families moving south from Atlanta. The 13th's fingers run through some Republican areas to reach rural, Democratic-leaning towns at the district's fingertips.

The 13th includes a small section of Atlanta and a small part of Hartsfield Atlanta International Airport. The airport, one of the nation's busiest, helps bolster the economy.

Major Industry

Agriculture, distribution, aerospace.

Notable

Jonesboro was the setting for Tara, the plantation in Margaret Mitchell's novel *Gone With the Wind*; TV show *Dukes of Hazzard* was filmed in Covington.

Election Returns

	Republican		Democratic		Other	
President 2000	66,576	41.1%	91,895	56.8%	3,392	2.1%
House 2002	47,405	40.4%	70,011	59.6%		

District Profile

Population 629,732

Total area (square miles) 784.2
  Land area (square miles) 777.4

Population per square mile 810.0

Counties (2000 population)

Butts (pt.)	8,597	Henry (pt.)	41,443
Clayton (pt.)	227,498	Newton (pt.)	31,228
DeKalb (pt.)	12,246	Rockdale (pt.)	46,850
Fayette (pt.)	4,437	Spalding (pt.)	27,546
Fulton (pt.)	59,100	Walton (pt.)	14,187
Gwinnett (pt.)	156,600		

Cities and other areas over 10,000 (2000 population)

Atlanta (pt.)	12,515	Griffin (pt.)	17,783
Conyers (pt.)	10,135	Riverdale (pt.)	12,478
Covington	11,547	Union City	11,621
Forest Park (pt.)	21,447		

Race and Hispanic or Latino origin*
White 42.1%
Black or African American 40.7%
American Indian or Alaska Native 0.2%
Asian 5.1%
Native Hawaiian or other Pacific Islander 0.0%
Some other race 0.2%
Hispanic or Latino origin 10.2%
Two or more races 1.5%

As percentage of total population.

Ancestry*

English	4.6%	Scotch-Irish	1.1%
German	4.4%	Subsaharan	1.7%
Irish	5.1%	USA/American	8.2%
Italian	1.3%		

As estimated percentage of total population.

Universities and colleges, 2000–2001 enrollment
Clayton College and State University, Morrow 4,455
Georgia Institute of Technology, Atlanta 14,805
Griffin Technical Institute, Griffin 2,689

Newspapers and circulation

	District circulation	Total circulation
Atlanta Journal-Constitution	93,856	857,088
Griffin Daily News	1,755	11,029
*USA Today**	10,855	1,674,376

See Sources and Explanations in the front of the volume.

Television stations and affiliations

Atlanta	100%	WAGA	FOX
Atlanta	100%	WATC	Independent
Atlanta	100%	WATL	WB
Atlanta	100%	WCIQ	PBS
Atlanta	100%	WGTV	PBS
Atlanta	100%	WHSG	Independent
Atlanta	100%	WJSP	PBS
Atlanta	100%	WPBA	PBS
Atlanta	100%	WPXA	PAX
Atlanta	100%	WSB	ABC
Atlanta	100%	WTBS	TBN
Atlanta	100%	WUPA	UPN
Atlanta	100%	WXIA	NBC

Cable systems and subscribers
Charter 3,348
Comcast 16,510
Covington Cable TV 3,570
Mediacom 2,340

Military installations, September 2001
Fort Gillem (Army), Forest Park 3,530

Businesses and other major employers
Lalji Investors; Conyers; hotels and motels 5,852
Clayton County Board of Education; Jonesboro 4,000
Dundee Mills Inc.; Griffin; broadwoven fabric mills, cotton 3,650
U.S. Postal Service; Atlanta 2,500
Ford Motor Co.; Atlanta; automobiles 2,366
Southern Regional Medical Center Inc.; Riverdale 2,315
JC Penney Corp.; Forest Park; mail order 2,100
Fitel USA; Norcross; fiber optic cable 2,000
Ciba Vision; Duluth; contact lenses 2,000
U.S. Postal Service; Duluth 1,700
Delta Technology Inc.; Atlanta; computer integrated systems design 1,700
Primerica Life Insurance Co.; Duluth; life insurance 1,576
Allstaff Management Inc.; Lawrenceville; employee leasing service 1,500
Lithonia Lighting Inc.; Conyers; commercial lighting fixtures 1,425
Gwinnett Hospital System Inc.; Lawrenceville 1,300
AT&T Corp.; Conyers; long-distance telephone 1,200
American Express Travel Related Services Co.; Norcross; travel agency 1,200
Nexpak Corp.; Duluth; plastics containers 1,036
PFS Investments Inc.; Duluth; insurance agents and brokers 1,000
Nacom Corp.; Griffin; printed circuit boards 1,000
Henry Medical Center; Stockbridge 1,000
National Service Industries Inc.; Conyers; commercial lighting fixtures 900
Victory Packaging Inc.; Norcross; paper products 900
Army and Air Force Exchange Service; Forest Park; Army-Navy goods stores 900
U.S. Federal Aviation Administration; Atlanta 900
Clayton County; Jonesboro; county government 860
Rockdale Hospital and Health System Inc.; Conyers 800
Encompass Group; McDonough; men's medical and hospital uniforms 800
Snapper Inc.; McDonough; lawn and garden mowers 800
Gat Security Services Inc.; Atlanta; security systems services 785

Kindred Healthcare Inc. Hospital; Griffin 750

Tenet Health System Spalding Inc. Hospital; Griffin 740

Pactiv Corp.; Covington; bags 703

Applejam Inc.; Duluth; restaurant 700

Kysor Industrial Corp.; Conyers; refrigeration/air conditioning equipment 650

JB Hunt Transport Inc.; Forest Park; trucking 630

Rockdale County; Conyers; county government 600

Wal-Mart Stores Inc.; Conyers; discount department stores 600

Stonebridge Industries Inc.; Conyers; electric motor, generator parts 600

Owens Corning; Fairburn; fiberglass insulation 600

Georgia Dept. of Corrections; Jackson 600

Kmart Corp.; Forest Park; general warehousing, storage 600

Sweetheart Cup Co.; Conyers; plastic pallets 550

Heartland Industries Inc.; Norcross; prefabricated wood buildings 550

Springs Industries Inc.; Griffin; cotton towels and toweling 540

Sara Lee Bakery Group Inc.; Decatur; bread baking 525

Auto Ventshade Co.; Lawrenceville; motor vehicle parts/accessories 512

American Freightways Inc.; Conley; trucking 500

AAA Cooper Transportation; Ellenwood; trucking 500

Hawaii

The thought of Hawaii fills the minds of mainlanders with sweet, colorful images of paradise. This remains true for most who have actually visited the islands, as well as for those who have done so only in their dreams. But for permanent residents of this premier vacation destination, reality means good times and bad times like anywhere else. The 1990s were not a good time.

In fact, despite its image of robust happiness, Hawaii ended the century lagging the nation in most measures of economic health and growth. Having more than doubled in population from 1950 to 1990, the state slowed to a comparatively glacial 9.3 percent growth rate in the 1990s—tied for the slowest among western states and 31st among all states. In another indicator of decline, Hawaii was the only state experiencing big increases in welfare caseloads in the late 1990s.

Over the long haul, prognosticators expect Hawaii to rebound. The Census Bureau has projected the islands' population to grow by better than 50 percent by the year 2025, a rate that could be tops in the nation. There were also signs of economic turnaround before the September 11, 2001, terrorist attacks. But the prevailing mood immediately after the year 2000 was still glum. Economic doldrums had struck simultaneously in several of Hawaii's core industries, including agriculture, defense, and, of course, tourism. Agriculture here has traditionally focused on sugar and pineapples, with lesser attention paid to coffee, floriculture, and various kinds of animal husbandry. Most of these things can be produced more cheaply elsewhere, putting Hawaii at a distinct disadvantage given its remote location. The great plantations that established the islands' economy and grand family fortunes over two centuries have waned and now employ only a fraction of the workers they did a generation ago.

Another blow came from the ending of the cold war and concomitant cuts in the nation's military spending, a mainstay for the islands since well before World War II. The Navy's grand dame, Pearl Harbor, has never ceased to contribute to Honolulu's hub of economic activity, but its functions have been shared with other, more modern bases around the world. The state's many other Air Force, Army, and Marine facilities also remain important but not to the degree of the postwar and Vietnam periods.

Finally, and most telling, the tourism industry that provides one third or more of the islands' economy was suffering from weaker bookings long before the shock of the 2001 terrorist attacks. Recession on the West Coast in the early 1990s was one factor, but the long slump in the Japanese economy was far more serious and sustained. Japanese tourists have been as important to the resort and hotel business in Hawaii as Japanese-Americans have been to the islands' permanent resident community.

As might be expected, softening economic conditions have made life harder for incumbent officeholders. Democrats had held sway in all the major offices on the islands for 40 years, beginning just a few years after statehood was granted in 1959. But 2002 finally brought a breakthrough Republican governor in Linda Lingle, a transplant from New York who had been mayor of Maui, the islands' second largest city. Lingle had lost narrowly to the last incumbent Democratic governor in 1998, and she had plenty to run against. Besides the sour economy, the ruling Democrats had endured internal divisions and a scandal over the management of the Bishop Estate. The Bishop fortune, two centuries old in origin, had been willed to the benefit of native Hawaiians but its board was packed with political appointees who were taking care of themselves. Lingle argued the fault lay with one-party government, and many voters agreed.

There may be more Lingles in the future for Hawaii, but they will need to fight their way through demographics and voting habits long in place. Only about one-quarter of the population is white, and the faster growing groups tend to be Filipinos, Hispanics, and Native Hawaiians. The state has had a strong postwar labor movement and been staunchly Democratic since shortly after statehood. Democratic presidential nominees have carried Hawaii with just two exceptions: the 49-state GOP landslides of 1972 and 1984. As of 2003, both senators, Daniel Inouye and Daniel Akaka, were veterans of the World War II generation who helped to build the modern Democratic Party here and who flourished with it for half a century. When they are gone, these seats are likely to be more competitive. The same should be true for the two House seats, which have usually, but not always, been held by Democrats.

The 1st District congressional seat is Honolulu city and close-in suburbs and has a two-thirds majority of Asian and Islander descent. The 2nd District consists of the rest of the island of Oahu and all of the other seven major "neighbor islands"—including Hawaii ("the big island"), Kauai, and Maui. But most of the 2nd District population still lives on Oahu, in the outer suburbs of Honolulu and the sizable towns of Kailua and Kaneohe. Redistricting is handled by a nine-member citizen commission, named by the leaders of the two parties and the two chambers in the state legislature. Redistricting Hawaii entails the movement of one line on one island to make sure the populations of the two districts match numerically.

HAWAII

Districts established November 30, 2001, for elections first held in 2002.

2 members

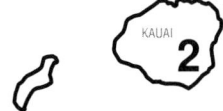

Table 1   Population

District	Population	Population under 18	Voting-age population	Median age	Male*	Female*
1	606,718	131,993	474,725	37.4	49.9	50.1
2	604,819	163,774	441,045	34.9	50.6	49.4
State	1,211,537	295,767	915,770	36.2	50.2	49.8

*As percentage of total population.

Table 2   Voting-Age Persons by Race/Hispanic or Latino Origin

District	White*	Black or African American*	American Indian or Alaska Native*	Asian*	Other or multirace*	Hispanic or Latino*
1	19.3	1.9	0.2	62.7	11.5	4.4
2	31.9	1.5	0.3	41.7	17.4	7.2
State	25.4	1.7	0.2	52.6	14.3	5.7

*As percentage of voting-age population.

Table 3   Voting-Age Population by Age Groups

District	18 to 24*	25 to 44*	45 to 64*	Over 64*
1	11.8	39.5	29.4	19.3
2	13.4	39.7	31.3	15.6
State	12.6	39.6	30.4	17.5

*As percentage of voting-age population.

Table 4   Income and Occupation

District	Median family income	Families in poverty*	White collar†	Blue collar†	Service†	Farm†
1	$60,609	6.6	63.8	15.7	20.0	0.5
2	$53,852	8.7	56.7	19.3	21.9	2.1
State	$56,961	7.6	60.3	17.5	20.9	1.3

*As percentage of all families.   †As percentage of employed workers 16 years and over.

Table 5   Education: School Years Completed

District	Less than grade 9*	Grades 9–12 no diploma*	High school diploma no college*	Some college*	College bachelor's degree or higher*
1	8.1	7.8	26.6	28.6	28.9
2	6.2	8.7	30.6	31.3	23.1
State	7.2	8.2	28.5	29.9	26.2

*As percentage of persons age 25 and over.

Table 6   Housing and Residential Patterns

District	Median home value	Owner occupied*	Renter occupied*	Urban†	Rural†
1	$280,200	53.1	46.9	99.3	0.7
2	$220,600	60.2	39.8	83.8	16.2
State	$249,300	56.5	43.5	91.6	8.4

*As percentage of occupied housing units.   †As percentage of total population.

Hawaii 1st District

Oahu — Honolulu, Waipahu, Pearl City

Located on the southern coast of Oahu Island, the compact 1st takes in the narrow plain south of the Koolau mountain range, encompassing the city of Honolulu—the engine that drives all of Hawaii. Redistricting following the 2000 census added only one town, Waipahu, which lies west of Honolulu. Pearl Harbor is the district's unforgettable landmark.

Honolulu is Hawaii's capital, home to most of its business and about a third of its people. To the east lies Waikiki and the heart of Hawaii's leading industry: tourism. The state experienced a downturn in the mid-1990s as Asia's economic problems meant fewer Japanese visitors and less Japanese investment in the state. The September 11, 2001, terrorist attacks also hurt tourism, but it has largely rebounded. The district's other major economic plank—the military— managed to escape major cuts and is holding steady.

The 1st is a Democratic stronghold and has elected only one Republican to Congress in its history. Japanese-Americans—particularly of the older generation—dominate the Democratic Party and are joined by many other nonwhite constituents who form the majority of the 1st's residents. Locally, Democrats do very well in elections, although some moderate Republican enclaves exist in the suburbs of East Honolulu and Waikiki.

Major Industry

Tourism, military, construction.

Notable

Iolani Palace in Honolulu is believed to be the only palace in the United States; Ala Wai Golf Course in Waikiki, now with roughly 165,000 rounds a year, has been rated "busiest course" by the *Guinness Book of Records*.

Election Returns

	Republican		Democratic		Other	
President 2000	70,674	39.0%	100,403	55.4%	10,211	5.6%
House 2002	45,032	24.9%	131,673	72.9%	4,028	2.2%

District Profile

Population   606,718

Total area (square miles)   325.7
   Land area (square miles)   190.8

Population per square mile   3,179.9

Counties (2000 population)
   Honolulu (pt.)   606,718

Cities and other areas over 10,000 (2000 population)
   Ewa Beach CDP   14,650
   Halawa CDP   13,891
   Honolulu CDP   371,657
   Mililani Town CDP   28,608
   Pearl City CDP   30,976
   Waimalu CDP   29,371
   Waipahu CDP   33,108
   Waipio CDP   11,672

Race and Hispanic or Latino origin*

White   17.7%
Black or African American   1.9%
American Indian or Alaska Native   0.1%
Asian   53.6%
Native Hawaiian or other Pacific Islander   6.6%
Some other race   0.2%
Hispanic or Latino origin   5.4%
Two or more races   14.4%

As percentage of total population.

Ancestry*

English   2.9%   Italian   1.2%
German   3.8%   Portuguese   2.0%
Irish   2.8%

As estimated percentage of total population.

Universities and colleges, 2000–2001 enrollment

American School of Professional Psychology, Honolulu   231
Chaminade University of Honolulu, Honolulu   2,620
Education America, Honolulu   409
Hawaii Pacific University, Honolulu   7,553
Heald College School of Business and Technology, Honolulu   1,134
Honolulu Community College, Honolulu   4,487
Kapiolani Community College, Honolulu   6,760
Leeward Community College, Pearl City   5,259
University of Hawaii-Manoa, Honolulu   17,263
University of Hawaii-West Oahu, Pearl City   665
University of Phoenix-Hawaii, Honolulu   1,063

Television stations and affiliations

Honolulu	100%	KAAH	Independent
Honolulu	100%	KAII	FOX, UPN
Honolulu	100%	KBFD	Independent
Honolulu	100%	KFVE	WB
Honolulu	100%	KGMB	CBS, UPN
Honolulu	100%	KGMD	CBS, UPN
Honolulu	100%	KGMV	CBS, UPN
Honolulu	100%	KHAW	FOX, UPN
Honolulu	100%	KHBC	NBC
Honolulu	100%	KHET	PBS
Honolulu	100%	KHNL	NBC
Honolulu	100%	KHON	FOX, UPN
Honolulu	100%	KHVO	ABC
Honolulu	100%	KIKU	Independent
Honolulu	100%	KITV	ABC
Honolulu	100%	KLEI	PAX
Honolulu	100%	KMAU	ABC
Honolulu	100%	KMEB	PBS
Honolulu	100%	KOGG	NBC
Honolulu	100%	KPXO	PAX
Honolulu	100%	KWHE	UPN
Honolulu	100%	KWHH	UPN
Honolulu	100%	KWHM	UPN

Cable systems and subscribers

Cable TV Services   5,860
Time Warner   142,342

Military installations, September 2001

Kaneohe Bay Marine Corps Base, Kaneohe Bay   12,134
Schofield Barracks Military Reserve (Army), Wahiawa   12,055
Pearl Harbor Naval Submarine Base, Pearl Harbor   8,589
Pearl Harbor Naval Shipyard, Pearl Harbor   7,587
Hickam Air Force Base, Honolulu   6,893
Fort Shafter, Honolulu   5,835
Pearl Harbor Naval Station, Pearl Harbor   3,988
Tripler Army Medical Center, Honolulu   3,371
Wheeler Army Airfield, Wahiawa   2,307
Kalaeloa (Barbers Point), Kapolei   1,032
PWC Pearl Harbor, Pearl Harbor   948
Fort De Russy (Army), Honolulu   858
Fort Ruger (Army Guard), Honolulu   332
Fleet and Industrial Supply Center, Pearl Harbor   329
TS Waiawa Gulch, Pearl City   284

Businesses and other major employers

University of Hawaii; Honolulu   8,000
Kyo-Ya Co.; Honolulu; resort hotel   3,800
Queen's Medical Center; Honolulu   2,982
Bank of Hawaii Corp.; Honolulu; state commercial banks   2,100
Hilton Hawaiian Village; Honolulu; resort hotel   2,000
Outrigger Hotels Hawaii; Honolulu; hotels   2,000
Aloha Airlines Inc.; Honolulu; air passenger carrier   1,893
First Hawaiian Bank; Honolulu; state commercial banks   1,850
Straub Clinic and Hospital Inc.; Honolulu   1,800
Buyco Inc.; Honolulu; sugarcane farm   1,760
United Air Lines Corp.; Honolulu; air transportation   1,500
St. Francis Medical Center; Honolulu   1,350
Kuakini Health System Hospital; Honolulu   1,331
Hawaiian Electric Co.; Honolulu; electric power generation   1,321
Hawaii Medical Service Assn.; Honolulu; hospital/medical service plans   1,300
ITT Sheraton Corp.; Honolulu; hotels   1,300
Kamehameha Schools Bernice Pauahi Bishop Estate; Honolulu   1,300
Northwest Airlines Inc.; Honolulu; air passenger carrier   1,192
Hawaii Pacific University; Honolulu   1,000
Polynesian Voyaging Society; Honolulu; charitable organization   1,000
Hyatt Corp.; Honolulu; hotel, franchised   1,000
Kaiser Foundation Hospitals; Honolulu   1,000
Navy Exchange Service Command; Honolulu; Army-Navy goods stores   1,000
Hawaii Dept. of Transportation; Honolulu   900
Oahu Transit Services Inc.; Honolulu; bus line operations   900
Sports Shinko Co.; Mililani; resort hotel   802
Dick Pacific Construction Co.; Honolulu; single-family housing construction   800
Gannett Co. Inc.; Honolulu; newspaper   800

Unicco Service Co.; Honolulu; building maintenance 800

Pacific Beach Corp.; Honolulu; resort hotel 800

Great Hawaiian Cruise Line Inc.; Honolulu; deep sea passenger transportation 765

Halekulani Hotel; Honolulu; hotels 750

Punahou School; Honolulu 750

Honolulu Board of Water Supply; Honolulu 720

Hawaii Dept. of Labor and Industrial Relations; Honolulu 700

Kapiolani Medical Center for Women and Children; Honolulu 682

HTH Corp.; Honolulu; resort hotel 670

Otaka LP; Honolulu; hotels and motels 650

Kapiolani Medical Center at Pali Momi; Aiea 618

HND/Hawaiian Dredging; Honolulu; residential construction 600

St. Francis Medical Center; Ewa Beach 581

Azabu USA Corp.; Honolulu; resort hotel 550

Burns International Security Services Corp.; Honolulu; security guard service 543

American Savings Bank; Honolulu; federal savings banks 500

Sora Management Inc.; Honolulu; management services 500

Neiman Marcus Group Inc.; Honolulu; department stores 500

Robert's Tours and Transportation Inc.; Honolulu; general automotive repair shops 500

Filipino Chamber of Commerce of Hawaii; Honolulu 500

UH Financial Aid Services; Honolulu; financial services 500

Hawaii 2nd District

Suburban and Outer Oahu; 'Neighbor Islands'

Some visitors call these Pacific islands paradise. With beaches, volcanoes, rain forests, and deserts, the 2nd is amazing in its geographic diversity. It includes part of Oahu and all of the other seven major islands that make up the state.

The 2nd's economy struggled through rough times in the 1990s with both of its major industries, tourism and agriculture, in crisis. The more luxury-oriented tourism offered in the 2nd was not as hard-hit as in Honolulu. But the Japanese yen's depreciation and Asia's economic woes resulted in Asian visitors spending less in the latter part of the decade—a worrisome development in a state that welcomes more than one-fourth of its tourists from Japan. A wave of sugar plantation closures also shook the economy, but growers are diversifying by adding more coffee, macadamia nuts, and bananas. Tax incentives have helped attract biotech and information technology companies.

The 2nd has large Asian sections and is heavily Democratic. While there are some predominately white, conservative-leaning communities on Oahu and Maui, these areas barely make a dent. Economic problems can give the GOP grounds to make inroads at the local level, but the liberal 2nd has kept Democrats in office.

Major Industry

Tourism, agriculture, military.

Notable

Kauai's Waialeale, the wettest spot on earth, averages 300 inches of rain annually.

Election Returns

	Republican		Democratic		Other	
President 2000	67,118	36.0%	104,830	56.2%	14,577	7.8%
House 2002	71,661	40.0%	100,671	56.2%	6,919	3.9%

District Profile

Population 604,819

Total area (square miles) 10,605.2
Land area (square miles) 6,231.7

Population per square mile 97.1

Counties (2000 population)
Hawaii 148,677   Kauai 58,463
Honolulu (pt.) 269,438   Maui 128,094
Kalawao 147

Cities and other areas over 10,000 (2000 population)
Hilo CDP 40,759
Kahului CDP 20,146
Kailua CDP 36,513
Kaneohe CDP 34,970
Kaneohe Station CDP 11,827
Kihei CDP 16,749
Makakilo City CDP 13,156
Nanakuli CDP 10,814
Schofield Barracks CDP 14,428
Wahiawa CDP 16,151
Waianae CDP 10,506
Wailuku CDP 12,296

Race and Hispanic or Latino origin*
White 28.0%
Black or African American 1.5%
American Indian or Alaska Native 0.3%
Asian 28.0%
Native Hawaiian or other Pacific Islander 11.3%
Some other race 0.2%
Hispanic or Latino origin 9.0%
Two or more races 21.7%

As percentage of total population.

Ancestry*
English 3.9%   Italian 1.6%
French 1.3%   Portuguese 4.2%
German 5.4%   USA/American 1.2%
Irish 4.0%

As estimated percentage of total population.

Universities and colleges, 2000–2001 enrollment
Brigham Young University-Hawaii, Laie 2,353
Hawaii Community College, Hilo 2,090
Kauai Community College, Lihue 1,052
Maui Community College, Kahului 2,678
University of Hawaii-Hilo, Hilo 2,874
Windward Community College, Kaneohe 1,451

Newspapers and circulation

	District circulation	Total circulation
*USA Today**	1,952	1,674,376

See Sources and Explanations in the front of the volume.

Television stations and affiliations

Honolulu	100%	KAAH
Honolulu	100%	KAII
Honolulu	100%	KBFD
Honolulu	100%	KFVE
Honolulu	100%	KGMB
Honolulu	100%	KGMD
Honolulu	100%	KGMV
Honolulu	100%	KHAW
Honolulu	100%	KHBC
Honolulu	100%	KHET
Honolulu	100%	KHNL
Honolulu	100%	KHON
Honolulu	100%	KHVO
Honolulu	100%	KIKU
Honolulu	100%	KITV
Honolulu	100%	KLEI
Honolulu	100%	KMAU
Honolulu	100%	KMEB
Honolulu	100%	KOGG
Honolulu	100%	KPXO
Honolulu	100%	KWHE
Honolulu	100%	KWHH
Honolulu	100%	KWHM

Cable systems and subscribers

Time Warner   87,280

Military installations, September 2001

Naval Computer and Telecommunications Area Master Station, Wahiawa   698

Helemano Radio Station, Wahiawa   551

TS Keaukaha Military Reserve, Hilo   228

Businesses and other major employers

Pan Global Partners; Kamuela; resort hotel   1,396

Brigham Young University-Hawaii; Laie   1,330

Four Seasons Resort Kaupulehu Makai Venture; Kailua Kona; vacation lodges   1,200

Hyatt Regency Maui Resort; Lahaina; hotels   1,200

Polynesian Cultural Center Inc.; Laie; tourist attraction   1,100

Marriott International Inc.; Lihue; resort hotel   1,100

KSL Grand Wailea Resort and Spa Inc.; Kihei; hotels and motels   1,000

Wilcox Memorial Hospital; Lihue   950

Maui County; Wailuku; county government   950

Alexander and Baldwin Inc.; Paia; cane sugar   933

Kawailoa Development Co.; Koloa; hotels and motels   900

Alexander and Baldwin Inc.; Puunene; cane sugar   900

Kauai County; Lihue; county government   875

Westin Maui Hotel; Lahaina; resort hotel   850

Hawaii Dept. of Health; Hilo   800

Castle Medical Center; Kailua   800

ITT Sheraton Corp.; Kamuela; hotels   700

Hawaii County; Hilo; police dept.   668

Hawaii County; Hilo; county government   666

Hawaii County; Hilo; courts   666

Del Monte Fresh Produce Inc.; Kunia; pineapple farm   650

Mauna Kea Beach Hotel Corp.; Kamuela; resort hotel   630

Four Seasons Resort Maui; Kihei; resort hotel   630

Mauna Lani Resort Operation; Kamuela; hotels   600

Ritz Carlton Maui; Lahaina; resort hotel   600

Brewer Co.; Pepeekeo; sugarcane and sugar beets   600

Dole Food Co.; Wahiawa; fruits   555

Hapuna Beach Hotel Corp.; Kamuela; resort hotel   550

Oahu Transit Services Inc.; Haleiwa; bus line operations   500

Robert's Tours and Transportation Inc.; Hilo; travel agency   500

Princeville Hotel Associates; Princeville; resort hotel   500

Maui Pineapple Co.; Kahului; fruits   500

ITT Industries Inc.; Kekaha; electrical work   500

Prince Maui Hotel; Kihei; resort hotel   500

Wahiawa Hospital Assoc.; Wahiawa   500

Idaho

It is hardly a surprise to learn that Nevada, Arizona, or Colorado were the fastest growing states in the 1990s. Each has a booming metropolitan area with a high profile in the national media. Idaho has none of these things, yet it attracted permanent residents almost as fast in the decade before the year 2000. Its growth rate of 28.5 percent was the fifth best in the country.

Indeed, moving to Idaho became something of a fad, like the SUVs and snowmobiles new residents often brought with them. While fads tend to fade, Idaho is projected by the Census Bureau to grow another 30 percent through the first quarter of the new century. To be sure, the state was building on a low base. Idaho has historically been among the half dozen least densely populated states, which accounts for much of its appeal in the age of antisprawl. But there are other factors at work here as well, economic and cultural, that lure new residents in a variety of income categories.

In past years, Idaho's best-known employers were timber giants such as Boise-Cascade or food processors such as Ore-Ida. Now employers are as likely to be high-tech outfits, such as Micron Technology or Hewlett-Packard, which together employed 11,000 people in the Boise area in 2001. Although Idaho for generations depended on the volatile markets for commodities—minerals, timber, agriculture—it now thrives as well on smokeless industries such as recreation and tourism.

As elsewhere in the West, Idaho has a deep tradition of populism, based in the self-reliant and defiant spirit of its original settlers, many of whom were fleeing economic, social, or political oppression in the East or overseas. In 1892 the first presidential election after Idaho became a state, the state's electoral votes were cast for James B. Weaver, the candidate of the People's Party. At this early date, the sentiments of pioneer farmers and ranchers, miners, and timber cutters predominated, and they held sway for a time after the state began choosing between the major party candidates. The state favored William Jennings Bryan twice and progressives Theodore Roosevelt and Woodrow Wilson a total of three times. After an interlude of Republican presidential preferences in the 1920s, Idaho went four times for Franklin Roosevelt and once for Harry Truman from 1932 to 1948.

But in the years since the New Deal, Idaho has grown restive with the federal presence (only four states have more federally owned land) and the burden of government. Populist resentment of capital shifted to focus on bureaucratic power and distant decision-makers. A tilt to the GOP returned and settled in: Idaho has since voted Demo-cratic for president only once (1964). In 1992 Bill Clinton almost finished third here behind Ross Perot; and in 2000 Al Gore received less than 27 percent of the popular vote.

Contests for other offices have been competitive, with notable figures emerging from the rugged populist tradition in both parties. Republican William Borah was an exemplar of the isolationist strain in populism in the era after World War I, making himself influential as chairman of the Senate Foreign Relations Committee. Half a century later, Frank Church would occupy the same position as a Democrat and use it to support the United Nations and President Jimmy Carter's efforts to find peace for the Middle East. But Church lost in 1980 to a hard-edged conservative who represented the "sagebrush rebellion," an antigovernment and especially anti-Washington movement strong in the rural stretches of the Mountain West in that era. Conservative Republicans would win every Senate race in the state from 1978 into the years after 2000.

The governor's races remained competitive longer but mostly because of two men, Cecil Andrus and John V. Evans. One or the other was the state's Democratic nominee for governor from 1966 through 1990, and they won six out of seven. Both managed to call forth the populist tradition in their party without disconcerting the state's swing voters. Andrus had worked as, among other things, a lumberjack and Interior Secretary under President Jimmy Carter. But after his second tour in office ended in 1994, Republicans easily added the governorship to the lengthening list of state offices for which the GOP primary is the most important contest.

Idaho has had two House seats since 1910 and now seems in no danger of losing one. Since 1994 the residents of the state have settled into the double-Republican pattern that had prevailed from 1966 to 1986. Before that, the postwar years had usually seen one seat held by each party. All this makes it uncommonly easy for the heavily Republican legislature to handle its redistricting chores. The one decision is where to draw the line through metropolitan Boise that divides the two congressional districts. The 1st District starts in Boise and climbs straight north up the Panhandle to Canada, taking in spectacular mountain ranges and towns with romantic names such as Moscow and Coeur d'Alene. The 2nd District also begins in Boise and runs east to Wyoming, taking in Pocatello, Idaho Falls, and a clutch of southeastern Mormon towns closer to Salt Lake City than Boise. This district has become one of the more reliable bases for Mormon candidates in recent decades.

IDAHO

Districts established August 22, 2001, for elections first held in 2002.

2 members

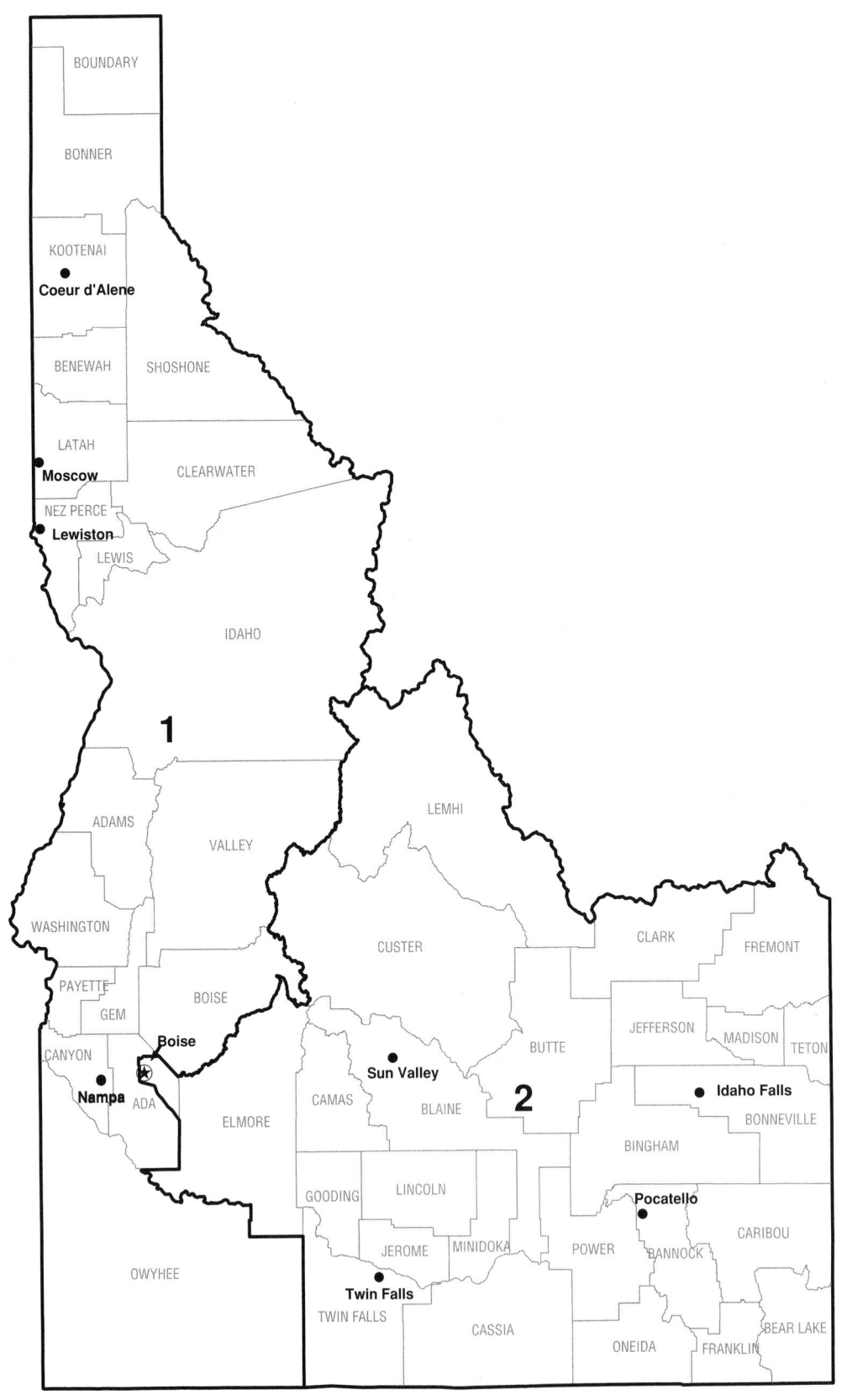

Table 1   Population

District	Population	Population under 18	Voting-age population	Median age	Male*	Female*
1	648,774	182,608	466,166	34.7	50.1	49.9
2	645,179	186,422	458,757	31.6	50.2	49.8
State	1,293,953	369,030	924,923	33.2	50.1	49.9

*As percentage of total population.

Table 2   Voting-Age Persons by Race/Hispanic or Latino Origin

District	White*	Black or African American*	American Indian or Alaska Native*	Asian*	Other or multirace*	Hispanic or Latino*
1	90.8	0.2	1.2	1.1	1.3	5.5
2	89.0	0.5	1.1	1.1	1.1	7.2
State	89.9	0.4	1.1	1.1	1.2	6.4

*As percentage of voting-age population.

Table 3   Voting-Age Population by Age Groups

District	18 to 24*	25 to 44*	45 to 64*	Over 64*
1	13.0	39.4	31.5	16.1
2	17.1	39.0	28.5	15.4
State	15.0	39.2	30.0	15.8

*As percentage of voting-age population.

Table 4   Income and Occupation

District	Median family income	Families in poverty*	White collar†	Blue collar†	Service†	Farm†
1	$44,109	7.9	56.1	26.2	15.5	2.2
2	$42,800	8.7	57.3	23.8	15.7	3.2
State	$43,490	8.3	56.7	25.0	15.6	2.7

*As percentage of all families.   †As percentage of employed workers 16 years and over.

Table 5   Education: School Years Completed

District	Less than grade 9*	Grades 9–12 no diploma*	High school diploma no college*	Some college*	College bachelor's degree or higher*
1	5.2	10.5	30.0	33.9	20.3
2	5.2	9.6	26.8	35.2	23.1
State	5.2	10.1	28.5	34.6	21.7

*As percentage of persons age 25 and over.

Table 6   Housing and Residential Patterns

District	Median home value	Owner occupied*	Renter occupied*	Urban†	Rural†
1	$109,500	75.7	24.3	65.8	34.2
2	$94,900	69.0	31.0	67.0	33.0
State	$102,100	72.4	27.6	66.4	33.6

*As percentage of occupied housing units.   †As percent of total population.

Idaho 1st District

West — Nampa, Panhandle, part of Boise

Stretching the 500-mile height of western Idaho, from British Columbia in the north to Nevada in the south, the 1st is mostly rural, punctuated by urban pockets. White-collar workers in Idaho's capital, Boise (shared with the 2nd), combine with agricultural voters to give it a GOP base. Redistricting after the 2000 census had little effect on the district, with the 1st losing a small part of Boise.

Boise and its surroundings contain about one-fourth of the district's population and house the headquarters of many lumber, paper, food processing, electronics, and construction companies. The strongest Democratic voting bloc is found among the timber and metal miners in the Panhandle and around Coeur d'Alene, but Democrats are outnumbered in nearly every other part of the district.

The 1st's midsize cities have attracted new high-tech businesses, such as Hewlett-Packard in Boise, and created new white-collar jobs. Some technology companies also reside along the Interstate 90 corridor in the northern part of the district. Nampa, west of Boise, has experienced high growth due to cheaper housing and a solid job market. Some small towns have not fared as well, as the 1st has become increasingly urbanized. Small timber mills have suffered, and the mining industry has struggled with low prices. Many rural communities are attempting to attract tourists to the state's forests, lakes, and mountains.

Republicans dominate the district. Since 1967, Democrats have held the congressional seat for only four years, from 1991 to 1995. Only three counties—Latah, Shoshone, and Nez Perce—supported Bill Clinton in his two presidential elections. Al Gore fared even worse in 2000, as George W. Bush swept all of the counties in the 1st.

Major Industry

Manufacturing, agriculture, timber.

Notable

The Sunshine Mine Memorial near Kellogg in Shoshone County memorializes the 1972 Sunshine Mine fire, which killed 91 miners; at nearly 20 carats, one of the largest diamonds found in the United States was discovered near McCall.

Election Returns

	Republican		Democratic		Other	
President 2000	171,364	67.5%	70,523	27.8%	11,983	4.7%
House 2002	120,743	58.6%	80,269	38.9%	5,129	2.5%

District Profile

Population   648,774

Total area (square miles)   39,971.7
    Land area (square miles)   39,524.7

Population per square mile   16.4

Counties (2000 population)

Ada (pt.) 164,290	Kootenai 108,685
Adams 3,476	Latah 34,935
Benewah 9,171	Lewis 3,747
Boise 6,670	Nez Perce 37,410
Bonner 36,835	Owyhee 10,644
Boundary 9,871	Payette 20,578
Canyon 131,441	Shoshone 13,771
Clearwater 8,930	Valley 7,651
Gem 15,181	Washington 9,977
Idaho 15,511	

Cities and other areas over 10,000 (2000 population)

Boise (pt.) 59,680	Meridian 34,919
Caldwell 25,967	Moscow 21,291
Coeur d'Alene 34,514	Nampa 51,867
Eagle 11,085	Post Falls 17,247
Lewiston 30,904	

Race and Hispanic or Latino origin*

White   89.0%
Black or African American   0.3%
American Indian or Alaska Native   1.2%
Asian   0.9%
Native Hawaiian or other Pacific Islander   0.1%
Some other race   0.1%
Hispanic or Latino origin   6.8%
Two or more races   1.5%

*As percentage of total population.

Ancestry*

Danish 1.2%	Italian 2.1%
Dutch 2.0%	Norwegian 3.1%
English 10.6%	Scotch-Irish 1.5%
French 2.4%	Scottish 2.1%
German 15.4%	Swedish 2.5%
Irish 8.2%	USA/American 6.0%

*As estimated percentage of total population.

Universities and colleges, 2000–2001 enrollment

Albertson College of Idaho, Caldwell   774
ITT Technical Institute, Boise   420
Lewis-Clark State College, Lewiston   2,693
North Idaho College, Coeur d'Alene   4,049
Northwest Nazarene College, Nampa   1,316
University of Idaho, Moscow   11,635

Newspapers and circulation

	District circulation	Total circulation
Idaho Press-Tribune	19,520	19,599
Idaho Statesman	41,552	63,960
Spokane Spokesman-Review	17,073	104,394
*USA Today**	1,847	1,674,376

*See Sources and Explanations in the front of the volume.

Television stations and affiliations

Spokane	53%	KAYU	FOX
Spokane	53%	KCDT	PBS
Spokane	53%	KHQ	NBC
Spokane	53%	KLEW	CBS, UPN
Spokane	53%	KREM	CBS
Spokane	53%	KSKN	WB
Spokane	53%	KSPS	PBS
Spokane	53%	KUID	PBS
Spokane	53%	KWSU	PBS
Spokane	53%	KXLY	ABC
Boise	47%	KAID	PBS
Boise	47%	KBCI	CBS
Boise	47%	KIVI	ABC
Boise	47%	KNIN	UPN
Boise	47%	KTRV	FOX
Boise	47%	KTVB	NBC

Cable systems and subscribers

Adelphia   25,307
Cable ONE   30,057
Charter   5,274
Northland   7,434
USA Media Group   9,642

Businesses and other major employers

Hewlett-Packard Co.; Meridian; computers   4,500
University of Idaho; Moscow   3,360
St. Alphonsus Regional Medical Center Inc.; Boise   2,234
Potlatch Corp.; Lewiston; sawmills and planing mills   2,200
Church of Jesus Christ of Latter-Day Saints Corp.; Caldwell; religious organization   2,000
Kootenai Medical District Hospital; Coeur d'Alene   1,360
Micron PC; Nampa; computer peripherals, software   1,000
SCP Global Technologies Inc.; Boise; electronic component manufacturing machinery   1,000
Sears Roebuck and Co. Inc.; Boise; credit card service   1,000
Potlatch Corp.; Lewiston; pulp mills   900
Direct TV Inc.; Boise; cable television   900
St. Joseph's Regional Medical Center Inc.; Lewiston   830
Woodgrain Millwork Inc.; Fruitland; millwork   800
Electronic Assembly Corp.; Nampa; printed circuit boards   791
Alliant Techsystems Inc.; Lewiston; small arms ammunition   700
Zilog Inc.; Nampa; wafers (semiconductor devices)   617
Kit Manufacturing Co.; Caldwell; travel trailers and campers   600
Trace Inc.; Eagle; employment agencies   600
Hagadone Hospitality; Coeur d'Alene; resort hotel   600
Kootenai County; Coeur d'Alene; county government   600
Hansen-Rice Inc.; Nampa; commercial/office building contractors   567
Kimball International Inc.; Post Falls; office panel systems and partitions   550
Mercy Medical Center; Nampa   542
Idaho Dept. of Health and Welfare; Nampa   520
Lewis-Clark State College; Lewiston   500
Coldwater Creek Inc.; Coeur d'Alene; mail order women's apparel   500
Coldwater Creek Inc.; Sandpoint; mail order   500

Idaho 2nd District

East — Pocatello, Idaho Falls, part of Boise

Covering eastern and central Idaho, the 2nd includes part of Boise, a few midsize towns, and a vast swath of agricultural land irrigated by the Snake River. To the west, in Elmore County, is the Mountain Home Air Force Base. But most of the district subsists on agriculture, primarily potatoes, sugar beets, and grain. Blackfoot, in Bingham County, is known as the potato-producing capital of the world.

The 2nd's manufacturing economy revolves around food processing, including Ore-Ida's frozen french fries. The district also is home to technology firms, including Micron, which provide thousands of jobs. The 2nd's fortunes have risen and fallen on agriculture, with farms faring poorly but expected to benefit from the 2002 farm law that reinstated federal subsidies for staple crops. Farmers have expanded into dairy, beef, and cheese processing, especially in Twin Falls and Jerome counties.

Tourism is the district's third-leading industry. With natural wonders such as Shoshone Falls and ski resorts such as Sun Valley, and its gateway location to Yellowstone National Park just across the border in Wyoming, the 2nd attracts a steady stream of vacationers.

The district consistently votes Republican at the state and national level. Members of the Church of Jesus Christ of Latter-day Saints make up the largest religious group; like most Mormon areas, the district is strongly conservative. Since 1992, only Blaine County, with its resorts, has voted Democratic in presidential elections. The district gained only a small part of Boise in redistricting, which did little to alter its political makeup.

Major Industry
Agriculture, food processing, tourism.

Notable
Nearly 85 percent of all commercial trout sold in the United States is produced in the Hagerman Valley near Twin Falls; Sun Valley was America's first ski resort; in 1955, Arco became the first town powered solely by atomic energy—for one hour.

Election Returns

	Republican		Democratic		Other	
President 2000	165,559	67.3%	68,055	27.7%	12,319	5.0%
House 2002	135,605	68.2%	57,769	29.0%	5,508	2.8%

District Profile

Population   645,179

Total area (square miles)   43,598.2
  Land area (square miles)   43,222.4

Population per square mile   14.9

Counties (2000 population)

Ada (pt.)	136,614	Blaine	18,991
Bannock	75,565	Bonneville	82,522
Bear Lake	6,411	Butte	2,899
Bingham	41,735	Camas	991
Caribou	7,304	Jerome	18,342
Cassia	21,416	Lemhi	7,806
Clark	1,022	Lincoln	4,044
Custer	4,342	Madison	27,467
Elmore	29,130	Minidoka	20,174
Franklin	11,329	Oneida	4,125
Fremont	11,819	Power	7,538
Gooding	14,155	Teton	5,999
Jefferson	19,155	Twin Falls	64,284

Cities and other areas over 10,000 (2000 population)

Blackfoot	10,419	Pocatello	51,466
Boise (pt.)	126,107	Rexburg	17,257
Idaho Falls	50,730	Twin Falls	34,469
Mountain Home	11,143		

Race and Hispanic or Latino origin*
White   87.1%
Black or African American   0.5%
American Indian or Alaska Native   1.2%
Asian   0.9%
Native Hawaiian or other Pacific Islander   0.1%
Some other race   0.1%
Hispanic or Latino origin   8.9%
Two or more races   1.3%

As percentage of total population.

Ancestry*

Danish	2.9%	Norwegian	2.2%
Dutch	1.6%	Scotch-Irish	1.2%
English	15.9%	Scottish	2.5%
French	1.9%	Swedish	2.7%
German	12.2%	USA/American	6.2%
Irish	6.4%	Welsh	1.5%
Italian	1.8%		

As estimated percentage of total population.

Universities and colleges, 2000–2001 enrollment
American Institute of Health Technology, Boise   235
Boise State University, Boise   16,287
College of Southern Idaho, Twin Falls   5,452
Eastern Idaho Technical College, Idaho Falls   595
Idaho State University, Pocatello   13,040
Ricks College, Rexburg   8,949

Newspapers and circulation

	District circulation	Total circulation
Idaho Falls Post Register	23,293	23,675
Idaho State Journal	16,898	16,977
Idaho Statesman	21,737	63,960
Logan Herald Journal	1,079	14,458
Twin Falls Times-News	22,783	22,846
*USA Today**	1,837	1,674,376

See Sources and Explanations in the front of the volume.

Television stations and affiliations

Idaho Falls-Pocatello	59%	KIDK	CBS, UPN
Idaho Falls-Pocatello	59%	KIFI	ABC
Idaho Falls-Pocatello	59%	KISU	PBS
Idaho Falls-Pocatello	59%	KJWY	NBC
Idaho Falls-Pocatello	59%	KPVI	NBC
Twin Falls	24%	KIPT	PBS
Twin Falls	24%	KMVT	CBS

Twin Falls	24%	KXTF	FOX
Boise	10%	KAID	PBS
Boise	10%	KBCI	CBS
Boise	10%	KIVI	ABC
Boise	10%	KNIN	UPN
Boise	10%	KTRV	FOX
Boise	10%	KTVB	NBC
Salt Lake City	7%	KBYU	PBS
Salt Lake City	7%	KCSG	PAX
Salt Lake City	7%	KENV	NBC
Salt Lake City	7%	KGWR	CBS
Salt Lake City	7%	KJZZ	Independent
Salt Lake City	7%	KSL	NBC
Salt Lake City	7%	KSTU	FOX
Salt Lake City	7%	KTVX	ABC
Salt Lake City	7%	KUED	PBS
Salt Lake City	7%	KULC	PBS
Salt Lake City	7%	KUTV	CBS
Salt Lake City	7%	KUWB	WB

Cable systems and subscribers

Adelphia 4,658
Cable ONE 108,608
Comcast 914
Cox 4,159
Mallard 4,951
Millennium Digital Media 1,519

Military installations, September 2001

Mountain Home Air Force Base, Mountain Home 4,922
Gowen Field Military Training Area, Boise 1,655
Boise Air Terminal Air Guard Station, Boise 1,309

Businesses and other major employers

Micron Technology Inc.; Boise; random access memory 9,000
Lockheed Martin Corp.; Idaho Falls; engineering laboratory 7,000
Ada County; Boise; county government 5,000
Idaho Dept. of Health and Welfare; Boise 4,000
Bechtel BWXT Idaho; Idaho Falls; environmental research 2,300
St. Luke's Regional Medical Center; Boise 2,200
St. Alphonsus Regional Medical Center Inc.; Boise 2,100
Boise State University; Boise 1,784
J. R. Simplot Co.; Heyburn; frozen/cold pack vegetables 1,500
Jewel-Osco Inc.; Boise; supermarkets 1,500
Idaho State University; Pocatello 1,400
Washington Group International Inc.; Boise; highway, street general contractor 1,400

Eastern Idaho Regional Medical Center Inc.; Idaho Falls 1,300
Brigham Young University-Idaho; Rexburg 1,289
J. R. Simplot Co.; Boise; agricultural equipment repair 1,200
J. R. Simplot Co.; Pocatello; phosphatic fertilizers 1,130
CBS Corp.; Idaho Falls; nuclear reactors 1,000
MK-Ferguson of Oak Ridge Co.; Boise; heavy construction 1,000
Albertson's Inc.; Boise; supermarkets 950
AMI Semiconductor Inc.; Pocatello; semiconductors and related devices 900
Boise Cascade Corp.; Boise; trucking terminal facilities 900
Boise Cascade Corp.; Boise; stationery and office supplies 900
Melaleuca Inc.; Idaho Falls; bulk vitamins 816
Bannock Regional Medical Center; Pocatello 810
Lamb-Weston Inc.; Twin Falls; frozen/cold pack potato products 800
McCain Foods Inc.; Burley; frozen/cold pack vegetables 800
Magic Valley Regional Medical Center; Twin Falls 775
Basic American Inc.; Blackfoot; potato curing services 700
College of Southern Idaho; Twin Falls 700
University of Chicago; Idaho Falls; noncommercial research organization 700
U.S. Land Management Bureau; Boise 700
FMC Corp.; Pocatello; industrial inorganic chemicals 600
Convergys Corp.; Pocatello; telemarketing services 600
Sinclair Oil Corp.; Sun Valley; resort hotel 600
Blaine Larsen Processing Inc.; Hamer; potato curing services 600
Morrison-Knudsen Engineers Inc.; Boise; bridge construction 600
Lamb-Weston Inc.; American Falls; frozen/cold pack vegetables 570
White Cloud Consulting Inc.; Rexburg; business consulting 550
U.S. Veterans Hospital; Boise 530
Idaho Dept. of Transportation; Boise 529
Madison County Memorial Hospital; Rexburg 522
Intermountain Health Care Inc.; Pocatello 510
Fort Hall Agency Inc.; Fort Hall; city government 500
Nonpareil Corp.; Blackfoot; dried/dehydrated potato products 500
Idaho Power Co.; Boise; electric power generation 500
Qwest Corp.; Boise; paging services 500
Wabtec Corp.; Boise; locomotives and parts 500

Illinois

Illinois still calls itself the Land of Lincoln, after the man who will always be its most famous political son. But within a generation after Lincoln's death, Illinois came to be known chiefly as the state of Chicago, the city that has dominated its image, for better or worse, ever since. Chicago was where the Great Lakes met the prairies, where water transport met the rail lines as they crossed the country. Its skyline rises from the landscape much as a feudal castle loomed over obeisant fields and dwellings below, drawing its life from them and ordering their existence.

Chicago's factories, stockyards, and other engines of commerce have now been the center of the regional economy for more than a century and a factor in the world economy for nearly as long. Everyone brought everything to the city with the full-throttle attitude, and that applied to culture as well. The city Sinclair Lewis fictionalized as "Zenith" has had an impact on art and architecture, theater, classical music, fiction, jazz, blues, and other folk arts second only to that of New York. That is one reason the ambivalent sobriquet "Second City" has lingered in usage long after Los Angeles became second in population.

Roughly two-thirds of the state's population lives in the greater Chicago area, which stretches from Kenosha (Wisconsin) on the north to Gary (Indiana) on the southeast. This megalopolis grew by more than 10 percent in the 1990s (providing all the state's growth overall), holding its ground as the third most populous metropolitan area in the country. Yet, as with New York, Chicago stands at one end of its state and in uneasy relation to its state capital and power structures.

The city tends to regard its politics as a world unto itself. The mayor is, for many people in the city, a more important elected official than any other (save perhaps the president). The city's Democratic machine is as much a part of the national mythos as its bootlegging gangster (an icon and an era still being exploited in the media, as witness the 2003 best picture Oscar for the musical *Chicago*). That machine has managed to rule City Hall and most of the 50 city wards for generations; many observers still believe that Mayor Richard J. Daley found just enough votes to carry the state (and thus the presidential election) for John F. Kennedy in 1960.

In reality, Chicago party bosses have not been so successful at winning elections for the Democrats statewide and national nominees in the rest of the postwar era. After the Kennedy squeaker and Lyndon B. Johnson's landslide in 1964, the state voted Republican for president eight times in a row. These years also brought Republican dominance in Springfield, the state capital. The GOP won ten of the 14 elections for governor after 1950, including seven in a row

ending in 2002. The Senate seats have usually been split, although Democrats held both seats from 1984 to 1998.

Traditionally, the Democrats in Chicago could count on working people, many of them first- or second-generation immigrants from Europe, often organized politically by labor unions. They also got votes from African Americans and, later, Hispanics, drawn by the same lure of living wages for unskilled as well as skilled work. The great migration of blacks up the Mississippi had no destination more common than Chicago; the South Side neighborhoods where these workers lived elected the first black member of Congress to serve after Reconstruction (Oscar De Priest) in 1928. The city now easily elects three black members, and in 1993 it produced the only black woman ever elected to the U.S. Senate, Carol Moseley-Braun.

The renewed potency of this coalition was evident in 2002 when the state elected a Democratic governor for the first time in 30 years. Just as remarkable was the political profile of the winner, Rod Blagojevich, a Chicago-based representative who came to politics as the son-in-law of a longtime Daley lieutenant. Blagojevich's win was perhaps as much a testament to Republican disarray as to Democratic resurgence. The GOP suffered a scandal that engulfed its incumbent governor, then the party nominated a successor with the same last name.

Historically, Republican strength was downstate in the farm counties and the small cities (Rockford, Peoria, Kankakee) and towns that served them. This is the Illinois celebrated in the state song and motto (the Prairie State), and it generally resembles the rich breadbasket of the states to its east and west (Indiana and Iowa). The Mississippi River, which forms the irregular western boundary, flows past rough old river towns such as Rock Island and Moline (commemorated in another movie from 2002, *The Road to Perdition*). Further south are Alton, site of a major lock and dam, and East St. Louis, a downtrodden industrial suburb just across the bridge from St. Louis, Missouri. The rest of southern Illinois is a somewhat separate element, historically dependent on coal mining and culturally akin to the neighboring states of Missouri and Kentucky. It has been observed that this part of the state is closer to Memphis than Chicago, and not just geographically.

But since the 1950s, the old dichotomy of city and downstate has slowly given way to the growing importance of Chicago's suburbs, which spread beyond Cook (Chicago) County to the counties of DuPage to the west, Lake to the north, and Will to the south. Home at first to affluent whites who commuted to downtown Chicago, the suburban

ILLINOIS

Districts established May 31, 2001, for elections first held in 2002.

19 members

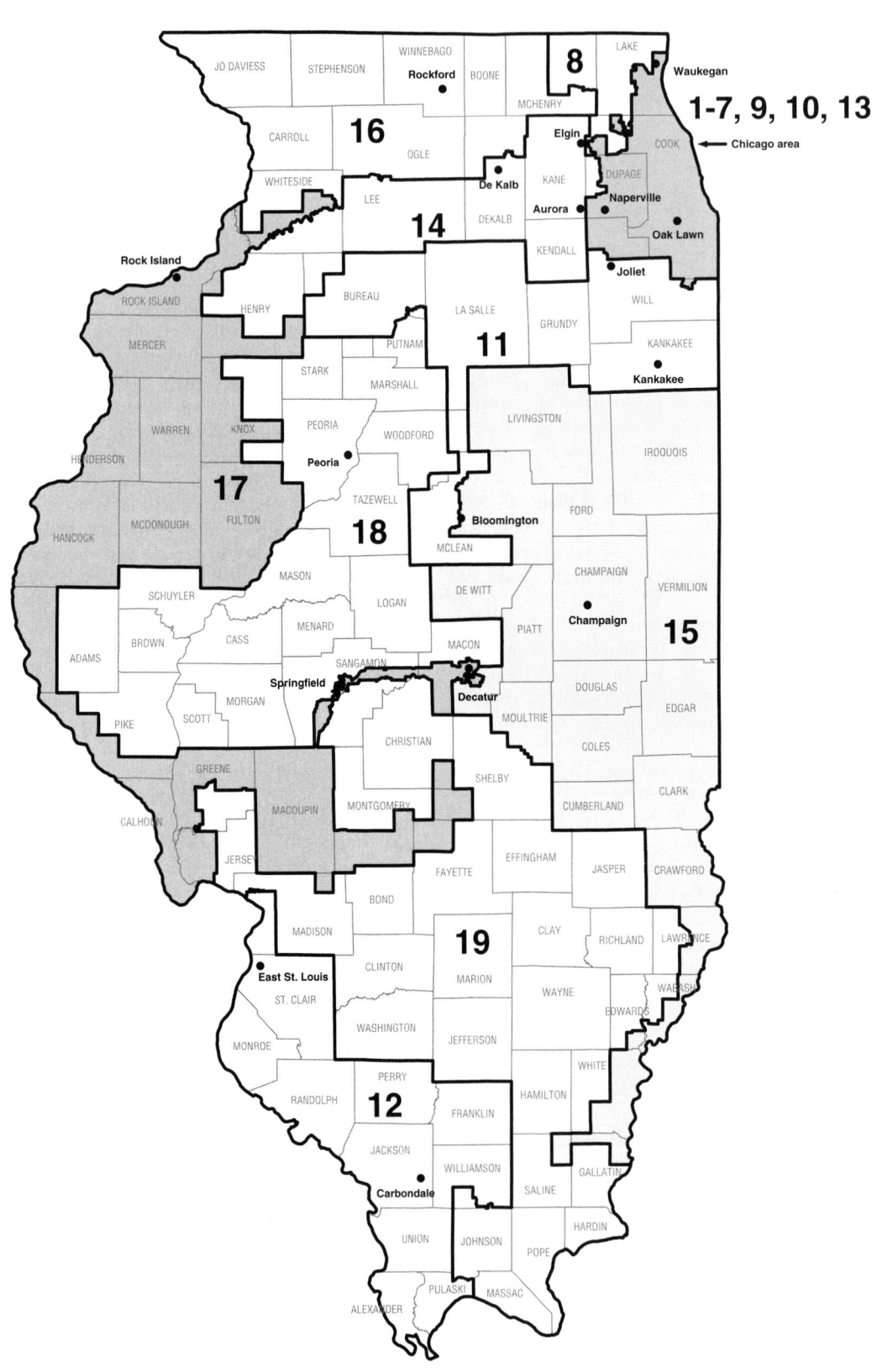

1-7, 9, 10, 13

← Chicago area

developments welcomed successive waves of middle-class and working families, some fleeing the city's decay and changing racial makeup. As they arrived in the suburbs, some of these new residents took up golf and an interest in the GOP. Eventually the changes led to an Illinois member becoming Speaker of the House in 1998. But it was not the chamber's longtime Republican leader Bob Michel from Peoria (who retired in 1992). It was J. Dennis Hastert, a former high school wrestling coach from the suburban town of Yorkville, on the outskirts of metro Chicago.

In the 1990s a new dynamic developed. The suburbs had grown so much that they were no longer bedrooms but job centers in their own right, with increasing economic, racial, and ethnic diversity. The Democrats who had suffered from the flight from the city—and from the racial divisions of the 1960s and 1970s—found themselves luring back younger suburban voters on issues such as sprawl, environmental safety, abortion rights, and health care. Even though the suburban venues continued to lean Republican, the margins shrank enough to allow Democrats to win statewide elections again. DuPage County, with more than 900,000 residents in 2000, had long been the mother lode for Republican candidates, who once could count on two-thirds of its vote. But in the presidential elections of 1992, 1996, and 2000, the Republican nominees averaged less than 52 percent in DuPage; as a consequence each one failed to carry the state. Lake and Will Counties have had even weaker Republican performance in these cycles.

Another factor helping the Democrats do better statewide has been the refurbishing of the old Daley machine in Chicago. After the senior Daley's death in 1976, his organization was divided in the election of 1979. Four years later, Richard M. Daley, the mayor's son, opposed the incumbent Democrat and divided the white vote in the primary. The result was the election of Harold Washington, the city's first black mayor. In the 1990s, however, Daley the younger reemerged, restored the party apparatus, and reclaimed his father's place. He made accommodations with most of the city's African American and Hispanic politicians and brought their voters back into the fold.

Events that followed felt like a return to normality for many Chicagoans. The period has coincided with an era of prosperity in the city's economy and a return of investment in its physical capital. In 1996 the city hosted the Democratic National Convention, its first for either party since the riot-torn anti-Vietnam debacle of 1968. The success of the event captured a sense of return for Chicago, the longtime leader in hosting the national nominating conventions.

This renewed spirit of pride in Chicago has also helped pull its population up after three decades of net decline. That helped fuel the metro growth of 11 percent and pull the whole state forward by 8.5 percent, which reversed the statewide slow-growth or no-growth trend. But none of this was enough when it came to reapportionment following the 2000 census: Illinois lost another seat in the House. That brought the state below 20 seats for the first time since 1880 (its peak had been 27 in the decades after 1910). Despite the legislature's Republican leanings, and the presence of a Republican governor in 2001, it was clear the burden of redistricting pain would fall downstate, where population had not grown.

The map that became law was essentially the work of Speaker Hastert and William Lipinski, the senior Democrat

in the congressional delegation. It was mostly focused on incumbent protection for both parties.

The one competitive district was the downstate, Decatur-based 19th, held by a conservative Democrat. The old district had been divided between several of its neighbors, and the incumbent found himself battling another incumbent, Republican John Shimkus, who had already been representing three-fifths of the new, shared district. Shimkus prevailed, predictably, as did all the other Illinois incumbents who chose to run for reelection. Most all were running in districts designed to be almost impossible to lose. That left the GOP with a one-seat edge in the overall House delegation after the 2002 elections.

Table 1 Population

District	Population	Population under 18	Voting-age population	Median age	Male*	Female*
1	653,647	185,643	468,004	33.8	46.2	53.8
2	653,647	192,586	461,061	33.8	46.5	53.5
3	653,647	168,184	485,463	35.8	48.5	51.5
4	653,647	208,188	445,459	27.2	51.7	48.3
5	653,647	129,274	524,373	33.7	49.3	50.7
6	653,647	170,327	483,320	34.8	49.6	50.4
7	653,647	174,672	478,975	31.9	47.3	52.7
8	653,647	184,387	469,260	34.2	49.8	50.2
9	653,647	134,645	519,002	37.3	48.6	51.4
10	653,647	177,123	476,524	36.8	49.5	50.5
11	653,647	174,967	478,680	34.5	49.3	50.7
12	653,647	164,373	489,274	36.0	48.7	51.3
13	653,647	184,687	468,960	35.0	49.3	50.7
14	653,647	187,620	466,027	32.5	50.2	49.8
15	653,647	153,381	500,266	35.1	49.2	50.8
16	653,647	180,155	473,492	35.9	49.4	50.6
17	653,647	156,878	496,769	37.6	48.6	51.4
18	653,647	159,238	494,409	37.8	48.8	51.2
19	653,647	159,123	494,524	37.9	49.6	50.4
State	12,419,293	3,245,451	9,173,842	34.7	49.0	51.0

*As percentage of total population.

Table 2 Voting-Age Persons by Race/Hispanic or Latino Origin

District	White*	Black or African American*	American Indian or Alaska Native*	Asian*	Other or multirace*	Hispanic or Latino*
1	29.8	63.2	0.1	1.7	1.0	4.2
2	29.4	59.4	0.1	0.7	1.1	9.3
3	72.4	5.1	0.1	2.9	1.5	18.0
4	23.6	3.6	0.2	2.0	1.6	69.0
5	70.0	2.1	0.2	6.5	2.0	19.2
6	77.4	2.4	0.1	8.1	1.1	11.0
7	32.8	55.9	0.1	4.5	1.2	5.4
8	81.0	2.8	0.1	5.7	1.0	9.4
9	65.7	9.7	0.2	12.1	2.4	9.9
10	77.3	4.9	0.1	5.9	0.9	10.9
11	85.9	6.9	0.1	0.8	0.6	5.6
12	82.1	14.4	0.2	0.9	0.7	1.6
13	82.8	4.7	0.1	6.6	0.9	4.9
14	77.0	4.2	0.1	1.8	0.8	16.1
15	89.3	5.2	0.2	2.6	0.8	2.0
16	87.9	4.6	0.2	1.3	0.6	5.4
17	89.3	6.2	0.2	0.6	0.6	3.0
18	91.4	5.6	0.2	0.9	0.5	1.3
19	94.3	3.6	0.2	0.5	0.5	0.9
State	70.9	13.7	0.1	3.5	1.1	10.7

*As percentage of voting-age population.

Table 3 Voting-Age Population by Age Groups

District	18 to 24*	25 to 44*	45 to 64*	Over 64*
1	13.8	39.4	29.1	17.7
2	12.8	39.9	30.9	16.4
3	12.0	39.9	28.7	19.5
4	19.4	50.3	21.3	8.9
5	13.2	47.2	24.9	14.7
6	12.0	44.3	29.8	14.0
7	14.7	44.9	27.3	13.1
8	10.7	47.4	30.5	11.4
9	12.3	40.0	28.1	19.6
10	11.4	39.0	32.8	16.8
11	14.6	40.3	28.8	16.3
12	13.8	38.0	28.9	19.3
13	10.3	45.7	31.6	12.3
14	14.9	43.7	28.8	12.7
15	17.7	36.1	28.0	18.2
16	10.5	41.8	31.1	16.7
17	13.7	35.0	30.0	21.3
18	11.8	36.9	31.3	19.9
19	11.6	37.5	30.7	20.3
State	13.2	41.4	29.1	16.4

*As percentage of voting-age population.

Table 4 Income and Occupation

District	Median family income	Families in poverty*	White collar†	Blue collar†	Service†	Farm†
1	$44,422	15.9	61.3	21.6	17.0	0.1
2	$47,809	12.3	60.1	23.8	16.0	0.1
3	$57,104	6.4	58.1	27.6	14.2	0.1
4	$37,143	17.8	43.5	39.2	17.1	0.3
5	$56,881	6.2	64.9	21.5	13.5	0.1
6	$71,991	3.0	69.5	20.2	10.2	0.1
7	$43,748	20.5	70.6	15.5	13.8	0.0
8	$71,398	3.2	67.3	21.8	10.7	0.2
9	$60,033	7.7	69.8	16.1	14.0	0.0
10	$85,990	3.1	75.9	14.4	9.6	0.1
11	$56,971	5.7	55.3	29.4	14.9	0.4
12	$43,580	11.4	55.1	26.2	18.2	0.4
13	$82,413	1.9	74.9	15.8	9.3	0.0
14	$64,330	4.6	59.9	26.8	12.9	0.4
15	$48,961	6.6	57.7	26.3	15.2	0.7
16	$57,434	5.2	57.2	29.7	12.5	0.5
17	$43,200	9.0	51.7	29.9	17.6	0.7
18	$51,009	6.2	59.1	24.7	15.5	0.7
19	$47,058	6.6	55.4	28.2	15.5	0.9
State	$55,545	7.8	61.8	24.0	13.9	0.3

*As percentage of all families.   †As percentage of employed workers 16 years and over.

Table 5 Education: School Years Completed

District	Less than grade 9*	Grades 9–12 no diploma*	High school diploma no college*	Some college*	College bachelor's degree or higher*
1	6.0	16.5	28.0	30.7	18.7
2	6.6	14.0	27.7	33.5	18.1
3	9.8	12.9	30.5	26.3	20.5
4	29.5	18.9	21.9	16.1	13.6
5	9.6	11.1	23.5	22.0	33.9
6	5.8	7.6	23.8	28.3	34.6
7	7.2	16.7	20.5	23.5	32.1
8	4.6	7.3	25.7	30.3	32.1
9	7.4	8.6	20.4	24.0	39.6
10	5.3	6.0	17.3	23.9	47.5
11	5.5	10.4	34.8	30.7	18.5
12	7.5	13.0	32.0	30.8	16.8
13	2.6	5.5	20.7	28.7	42.4
14	8.1	9.8	27.0	28.8	26.3
15	5.6	9.6	33.5	28.1	23.2
16	5.2	10.5	32.9	30.2	21.1
17	6.1	12.6	37.8	28.7	14.7
18	5.2	10.3	34.3	29.6	20.7
19	7.6	10.9	34.3	30.1	17.1
State	7.5	11.1	27.7	27.6	26.1

*As percentage of persons age 25 and over.

Table 6 Housing and Residential Patterns

District	Median home value	Owner occupied*	Renter occupied*	Urban†	Rural†
1	$115,700	54.5	45.5	100.0	0.0
2	$95,400	66.2	33.8	99.9	0.1
3	$143,000	72.6	27.4	100.0	0.0
4	$142,900	39.2	60.8	100.0	0.0
5	$184,000	49.7	50.3	100.0	0.0
6	$174,100	75.8	24.2	100.0	0.0
7	$157,200	41.8	58.2	100.0	0.0
8	$165,100	77.6	22.4	96.1	3.9
9	$198,800	54.7	45.3	100.0	0.0
10	$245,900	78.7	21.3	99.6	0.4
11	$113,800	74.7	25.3	78.2	21.8
12	$64,700	69.4	30.6	76.7	23.3
13	$195,300	80.6	19.4	98.8	1.2
14	$148,000	74.8	25.2	86.2	13.8
15	$77,100	68.8	31.2	64.2	35.8
16	$111,200	75.5	24.5	78.4	21.6
17	$65,400	71.0	29.0	71.1	28.9
18	$83,500	73.5	26.5	68.0	32.0
19	$73,300	78.1	21.9	52.2	47.8
State	$127,800	67.3	32.7	87.8	12.2

*As percentage of occupied housing units.   †As percentage of total population.

Illinois 1st District

Chicago — South Side and southwest

The nation's first black-majority district, the 1st covers much of Chicago's South Side. It begins at 26th Street in the historic black hub and spreads out to the south and west through mainly residential neighborhoods. The district narrows considerably through the southwestern Chicago neighborhoods of Washington Heights, Beverly, and Morgan Park, then expands outside the city to scoop up nearby suburbs. About 70 percent of the 1st's residents live in Chicago (down from 90 percent under the district's 1990s configuration). *(See map p. 297.)*

Long a relatively compact district, the 1st's boundaries have expanded gradually in the past few decades to adjust for declining populations in some of the area's most economically distressed neighborhoods. Redistricting following the 2000 census stretched the 1st as far south as Cook County's border with Will County.

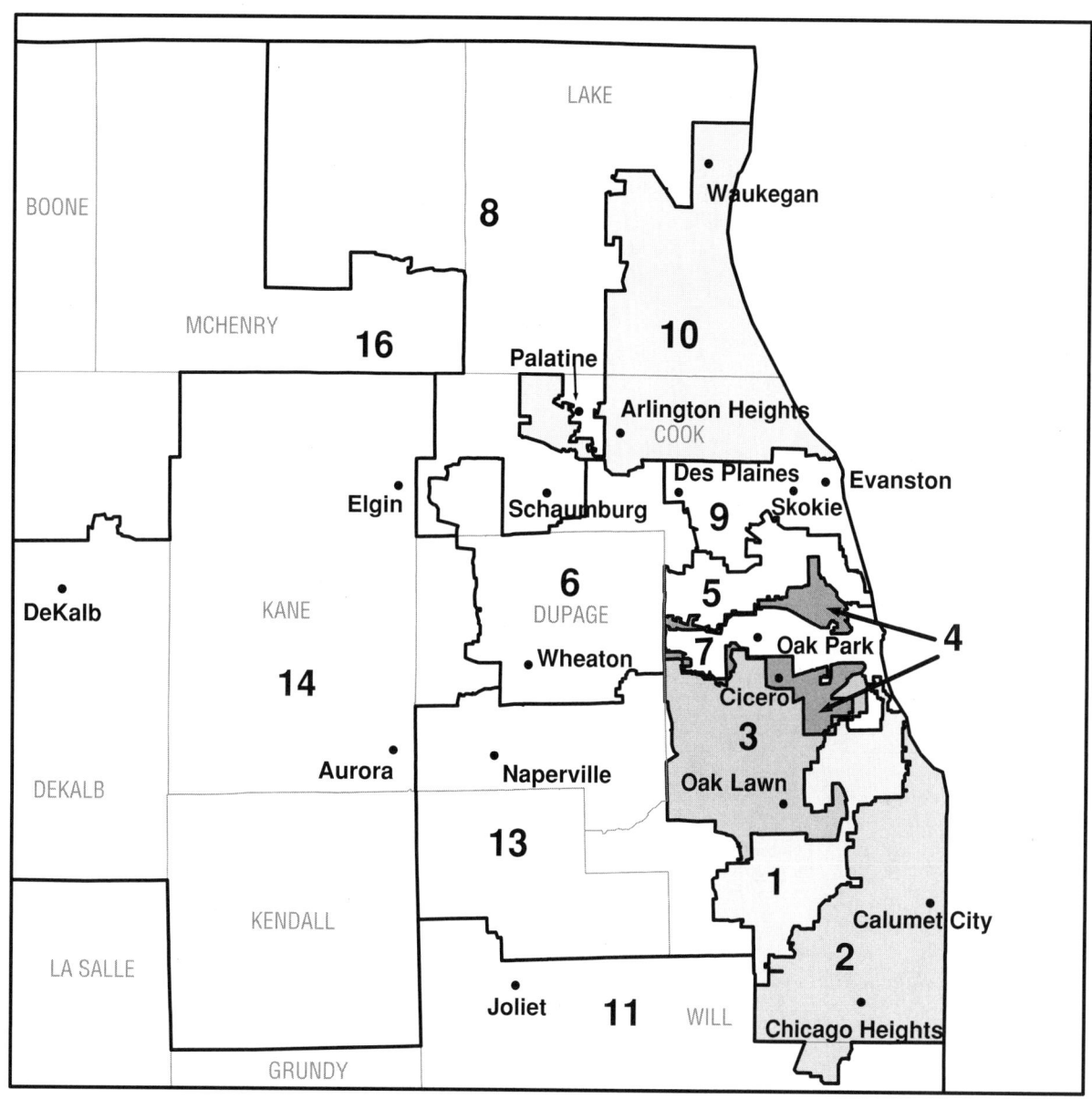

When the steel industry left the South Side in the 1970s, it decimated the district's middle class and many black-owned businesses. Now the 1st is home to some of the city's largest subsidized housing projects, and almost 16 percent of the families are classified as living under the poverty line. The district still has several solidly middle-class black neighborhoods, including Chatham and Avalon Park. The north end takes in part of Bronzeville, which has seen young black professionals move in and rehabilitate old houses instead of leaving for the suburbs. Blue Island, one southwest suburb, is 40 percent Hispanic and 25 percent black.

The 1st, represented by black representatives since 1929, has the nation's largest percentage of African Americans (65.2 percent). White voters are concentrated outside the city or in some southwestern neighborhoods. The 1st is perhaps the state's most Democratic district: it gave 2000 presidential nominee Al Gore his best showing in Illinois (83.7 percent).

Major Industry

Hospitals, higher education, manufacturing.

Notable

The 1st is home to the national headquarters of Jesse Jackson's Rainbow/PUSH Coalition; the University of Chicago is in the Hyde Park neighborhood.

Election Returns

	Republican		Democratic		Other	
President 2000	39,400	15.5%	213,244	83.7%	2,097	0.8%
House 2002	29,776	16.2%	149,068	81.2%	4,812	2.6%

District Profile

Population   653,647

Total area (square miles)   98.5
  Land area (square miles)   97.8

Population per square mile   6,683.5

Counties (2000 population)
  Cook (pt.)   653,647

Cities and other areas over 10,000 (2000 population)
  Alsip village (pt.)   18,631
  Blue Island (pt.)   23,436
  Chicago (pt.)   451,488
  Crestwood village   11,251
  Evergreen Park village   20,821
  Midlothian village   14,315
  Oak Forest (pt.)   28,041
  Orland Park village (pt.)   27,342
  Tinley Park village (pt.)   23,863

Race and Hispanic or Latino origin*
  White   27.3%
  Black or African American   65.2%
  American Indian or Alaska Native   0.1%
  Asian   1.4%
  Native Hawaiian or other Pacific Islander   0.0%
  Some other race   0.1%
  Hispanic or Latino origin   4.8%
  Two or more races   1.0%

*As percentage of total population.

Ancestry*

Dutch	1.1%	Italian	3.2%
English	1.4%	Polish	4.5%
German	6.2%	Subsaharan	1.4%
Irish	7.1%		

*As estimated percentage of total population.

Universities and colleges, 2000–2001 enrollment
  Catholic Theological Union, Chicago   746
  Chicago State University, Chicago   6,914
  Chicago Theological Seminary, Chicago   231
  City Colleges of Chicago-Kennedy-King College, Chicago   6,029
  Illinois College of Optometry, Chicago   650
  Illinois Institute of Technology, Chicago   6,003
  Lutheran School of Theology, Chicago   517
  McCormick Theological Seminary, Chicago   421
  Trinity Christian College, Palos Heights   854
  University of Chicago, Chicago   12,531
  Vandercook College of Music, Chicago   216

Newspapers and circulation

	District circulation	Total circulation
Chicago Sun-Times	47,370	474,127
Chicago Tribune	28,224	664,927
Daily Southtown, Chicago	12,899	47,715
*USA Today**	2,304	1,674,376

*See Sources and Explanations in the front of the volume.

Television stations and affiliations

Chicago	100%	WBBM	CBS
Chicago	100%	WCIU	Independent
Chicago	100%	WCPX	PAX
Chicago	100%	WFLD	FOX
Chicago	100%	WGBO	Univision
Chicago	100%	WGN	WB
Chicago	100%	WJYS	Independent
Chicago	100%	WLS	ABC
Chicago	100%	WMAQ	NBC
Chicago	100%	WPWR	UPN
Chicago	100%	WSNS	Telemundo
Chicago	100%	WTTW	PBS
Chicago	100%	WWTO	Independent
Chicago	100%	WYCC	PBS
Chicago	100%	WYIN	PBS

Cable systems and subscribers
  Comcast   41,653

Businesses and other major employers
  University of Chicago Hospitals; Chicago   4,150
  Cook County Hospital; Oak Forest   2,225
  Palos Community Hospital; Palos Heights   2,185
  Little Company of Mary Hospital and Health Care Centers; Chicago   1,700
  Staff Leasing Corp.; Palos Heights; employee leasing service   1,500
  Holy Cross Hospital; Chicago   1,380
  SSM Health Care Hospital; Blue Island   1,175
  Chicago State University; Chicago   1,100
  Panduit Corp.; Tinley Park; electric conduits and fittings   900

Cook County Hospital; Chicago   850
Ashley's Cleaning Service; Chicago; building
  maintenance   850
Jackson Park Hospital Foundation; Chicago   750
Chicago Transit Authority; Chicago   700
Kraft Foods Inc.; Chicago salad dressings   700
St. Bernard Hospital and Healthcare Center; Chicago
  684
A&R Security Services Inc.; Blue Island; security guard
  service   650
Illinois Institute of Technology; Chicago   650
Parco Foods; Blue Island; cookies   594
Hilton Hotels Corp.; Chicago; hotels   573
Sonnenschein Nath and Rosenthal; Chicago; general
  practice law office   540
Midwest Suburban Publishing Inc.; Tinley Park;
  commercial printing, newspaper publishing   520
City of Chicago; Chicago; police dept.   510
Board of Trustees of Community College District;
  Chicago   500
William Thurman; Chicago; glass bottles   500

Illinois 2nd District

Chicago — far South Side; Chicago Heights

The 2nd begins in Chicago's South Side along Lake Michigan and extends south along the Indiana border and southwest to take in Chicago Heights and Cook County suburbs. Redistricting following the 2000 census extended the southern border into University Park in Will County. (*See map p. 297.*)

About 40 percent of district residents live in Chicago. The 2nd runs from the Hyde Park area near the University of Chicago, south through such neighborhoods as South Shore, South Chicago, East Side, Roseland, and Pullman. East Side is heavily Hispanic.

U.S. Steel was once a dominant employer in the 2nd. When the steel industry collapsed in the late 1970s, it devastated the district's industrial-based economy. Ford Motor Co. is one of the few large manufacturing businesses remaining in the district.

A proposed new airport in nearby Peotone (in the 11th District) could rejuvenate the 2nd's economy. Advocates hope the airport would attract corporate headquarters, hotels, distributors, and other new businesses. Unemployment remains high, and many residents have fled the South Side to find jobs. Before redistricting in 2001, the 2nd had the smallest population of any Illinois district.

In Chicago's south suburbs it is not unusual to find heavily black areas like Harvey, Dolton, and Ford Heights, or largely white areas like Homewood, Flossmoor, and Thornton. Other areas are more racially mixed—in Chicago Heights, whites and blacks are about equal in population, and one-fourth of residents are Hispanic.

Overall, the 2nd's 62-percent black population and working-class base shape a staunchly Democratic district.

Major Industry

Automotive and wire manufacturing, steel production, health care.

Notable

Pullman, now part of Chicago near Lake Calumet, originally was a factory town built by the Pullman Palace Car Co., maker of railroad sleeping cars.

Election Returns

	Republican		Democratic		Other	
President 2000	41,005	16.5%	204,372	82.5%	2,455	1.0%
House 2002	32,567	17.7%	151,443	82.3%		

District Profile

Population   653,647

Total area (square miles)   192.1
  Land area (square miles)   184.6

Population per square mile   3,540.9

Counties (2000 population)
  Cook (pt.)   643,178
  Will (pt.)   10,469

Cities and other areas over 10,000 (2000 population)
  Calumet City   39,071
  Chicago (pt.)   265,814
  Chicago Heights   32,776
  Country Club Hills (pt.)   16,159
  Dolton village   25,614
  Harvey (pt.)   29,926
  Hazel Crest village   14,816
  Homewood village   19,543
  Lansing village   28,332
  Matteson village (pt.)   12,928
  Park Forest village   23,462
  Richton Park village   12,533
  Riverdale village (pt.)   15,055
  Sauk Village village (pt.)   10,411
  South Holland village   22,147

Race and Hispanic or Latino origin*
  White   25.6%
  Black or African American   62.0%
  American Indian or Alaska Native   0.1%
  Asian   0.6%
  Native Hawaiian or other Pacific Islander   0.0%
  Some other race   0.1%
  Hispanic or Latino origin   10.4%
  Two or more races   1.2%

As percentage of total population.

Ancestry*
  Dutch   1.5%   Italian   3.1%
  English   1.8%   Polish   4.4%
  German   5.8%   Subsaharan   1.7%
  Irish   4.4%   USA/American   1.2%

As estimated percentage of total population.

Universities and colleges, 2000–2001 enrollment
  City Colleges of Chicago-Olive-Harvey College, Chicago   6,569
  Governors State University, University Park   6,105
  ITT Technical Institute, Matteson   246

Prairie State College, Chicago Heights   4,795
South Suburban College, South Holland   6,751

Newspapers and circulation

	District circulation	Total circulation
Chicago Sun-Times	45,660	474,127
Chicago Tribune	26,438	664,927
Daily Southtown, Chicago	7,755	47,715
Munster Times	8,256	88,021
*USA Today**	6,958	1,674,376

See Sources and Explanations in the front of the volume.

Television stations and affiliations

Chicago	100%	WBBM	CBS
Chicago	100%	WCIU	Independent
Chicago	100%	WCPX	PAX
Chicago	100%	WFLD	FOX
Chicago	100%	WGBO	Univision
Chicago	100%	WGN	WB
Chicago	100%	WJYS	Independent
Chicago	100%	WLS	ABC
Chicago	100%	WMAQ	NBC
Chicago	100%	WPWR	UPN
Chicago	100%	WSNS	Telemundo
Chicago	100%	WTTW	PBS
Chicago	100%	WWTO	Independent
Chicago	100%	WYCC	PBS
Chicago	100%	WYIN	PBS

Cable systems and subscribers
Comcast   75,393

Military installations, September 2001
P. Schulstad U.S. Army Reserve Center, Arlington Heights   535
Vietnam Veterans Memorial U.S. Army Reserve Center, Homewood   204

Businesses and other major employers
Ford Motor Co.; Chicago; automobiles   2,479
Ingalls Memorial Hospital; Harvey   2,293
Ford Motor Co.; Chicago Heights; automotive stampings 1,920
Advocate South Suburban Hospital; Hazel Crest   1,300
Roadway Express Inc.; Chicago Heights; local trucking, without storage   1,200
St. James Hospital and Health Centers Inc.; Chicago Heights   1,200
Acme Steel Co.; Chicago; blast furnaces and steel mills 1,200
Illinois Community College District; Chicago Heights 1,000
Allied Tube and Conduit Corp.; Harvey; storage   1,000
Anheuser-Busch Inc.; Country Club Hills; business consulting   1,000
First Data Financial Services; Matteson; data processing 850
Allied Tube and Conduit Corp.; Harvey; electric conduits and fittings   826
Consolidated Medical Transport; Dolton; local passenger transportation   800
South Suburban College; South Holland   799

Sears Roebuck and Co. Inc.; Calumet City; discount department stores   700
Illinois Dept. of Human Services; Park Forest; residential care   700
St. James Hospital and Health Centers Inc.; Olympia Fields   650
GNU Inc.; Chicago Heights; motor vehicle parts/accessories   550
Morgan Marshall Industries Inc.; Chicago Heights; nonwood office/store shelving   550
Norfolk Southern Corp.; Chicago; railroad terminals 519
ABF Freight System Inc.; Chicago Heights; trucking 500
Silver Line Building Products Corp.; Lansing; window screening, plastics   500
Jays Foods; Chicago; potato chips   500
Joseph T. Ryerson & Son Inc.; Chicago; rails and accessories   500
Museum of Science and Industry; Chicago   500

Illinois 3rd District

Chicago — southwest side; south and west suburbs

The 3rd covers the southwest corner of Chicago and adjacent suburbs, part of a working-class region known as the "Bungalow Belt" that is stocked with voters of Eastern European, Italian, and Irish descent. *(See map p. 297.)*

This once urban, Chicago-machine district shifted west into suburban territory when a new Hispanic-majority district was created to its north in 1991 redistricting. The change inserted an ample GOP vote from the district's more affluent suburbs, especially in western Cook County. The townships of Lyons, Palos, and Riverside voted for Republican George W. Bush in the 2000 presidential election.

Further redistricting following the 2000 census added more of Chicago; city residents now make up about 40 percent of the district population. The 3rd includes the historically Irish neighborhood of Bridgeport, which is the former home and political base of the powerful Daley family, and southwest Chicago neighborhoods such as Beverly, West Lawn, Clearing, and Garfield Ridge (where Midway Airport is located). The West Lawn and West Eldson neighborhoods have experienced rapid Hispanic growth. The 3rd has more Hispanics than all but two districts in Illinois.

Crisscrossed by highways, railroads, and the Chicago Sanitary and Ship Canal, the 3rd is a center of manufacturing and distribution. Expansion at Midway has broadened the district's retail and service base and created new jobs for district residents.

In national elections, the 3rd typically votes Democratic, but not by the same wide margins as in other Chicago-based districts. Many working- and middle-class voters lean to the right on social issues.

Major Industry
Metals and other heavy manufacturing, trucking, warehouses.

Notable

The Berwyn Houby Festival, celebrating Czech heritage, is named after the Czech word for mushroom.

Election Returns

	Republican		Democratic		Other	
President 2000	91,471	40.1%	131,650	57.7%	4,913	2.2%
House 2002			156,042	100.0%		

District Profile

Population   653,647

Total area (square miles)   125.7
   Land area (square miles)   124.4

Population per square mile   5,254.4

Counties (2000 population)
   Cook (pt.)   653,647

Cities and other areas over 10,000 (2000 population)
   Berwyn (pt.)   51,179
   Bridgeview village   15,335
   Brookfield village (pt.)   18,980
   Burbank   27,902
   Chicago (pt.)   266,264
   Chicago Ridge village   14,127
   Cicero town (pt.)   12,407
   Hickory Hills   13,926
   Justice village   12,193
   LaGrange Park village   13,295
   LaGrange village   15,608
   Lyons village   10,255
   Oak Lawn village   55,245
   Palos Hills   17,665
   Summit village   10,637
   Western Springs village   12,493

Race and Hispanic or Latino origin*
   White   68.2%
   Black or African American   5.8%
   American Indian or Alaska Native   0.1%
   Asian   2.8%
   Native Hawaiian or other Pacific Islander   0.0%
   Some other race   0.1%
   Hispanic or Latino origin   21.3%
   Two or more races   1.7%

As percentage of total population.

Ancestry*

Arab-Misc. 1.3%	Italian 6.9%
English 2.7%	Lithuanian 1.8%
French 1.2%	Polish 13.5%
German 11.0%	Swedish 1.4%
Irish 14.2%	USA/American 1.4%

As estimated percentage of total population.

Universities and colleges, 2000–2001 enrollment
   City Colleges of Chicago-Richard J. Daley College,
      Chicago   9,800
   Moraine Valley Community College, Palos Hills
      12,972
   Morton College, Cicero   4,465

Northwestern Business College-Southwestern, Hickory
   Hills   744
St. Xavier University, Chicago   4,602

Newspapers and circulation

	District circulation	Total circulation
Chicago Sun-Times	52,185	474,127
Chicago Tribune	44,896	664,927
Daily Southtown, Chicago	15,090	47,715
*USA Today**	2,939	1,674,376

See Sources and Explanations in the front of the volume.

Television stations and affiliations

Chicago	100%	WBBM	CBS
Chicago	100%	WCIU	Independent
Chicago	100%	WCPX	PAX
Chicago	100%	WFLD	FOX
Chicago	100%	WGBO	Univision
Chicago	100%	WGN	WB
Chicago	100%	WJYS	Independent
Chicago	100%	WLS	ABC
Chicago	100%	WMAQ	NBC
Chicago	100%	WPWR	UPN
Chicago	100%	WSNS	Telemundo
Chicago	100%	WTTW	PBS
Chicago	100%	WWTO	Independent
Chicago	100%	WYCC	PBS
Chicago	100%	WYIN	PBS

Cable systems and subscribers
   Comcast   209,323

Businesses and other major employers
   United Parcel Service Inc.; LaGrange; parcel delivery
      6,000
   Advocate Health Care Network Hospital; Oak Lawn
      4,000
   TCF Bank; Hinsdale; commercial bank   2,500
   LaGrange Memorial Hospital Inc.; LaGrange   1,719
   West Suburban Hospital Medical Center; Berwyn
      1,568
   Yellow Transportation; Chicago Ridge; trucking   1,432
   Moraine Valley Community College; Palos Hills   1,200
   MacNeal Memorial Hospital Assn.; Berwyn   1,000
   Tootsie Roll Co.; Chicago; confectionery products
      1,000
   Suntory International Corp.; Chicago; bottled water
      1,000
   Greater Chicago Metropolitan Water Reclamation
      District; Cicero   1,000
   Wrigley Manufacturing Co.; Chicago; chewing gum
      992
   Aargus Security Systems Inc.; Chicago; security guard
      service   900
   Corn Products International Inc.; Bedford Park; wet corn
      milling   800
   St. Xavier University; Chicago   758
   M&R Tile and Remodeling Inc.; Western Springs; home
      remodeling   750
   Commonwealth Edison Co.; Chicago; electric services
      750

3M Co.; Bedford Park; papeteries   700

Morse Automotive Corp.; Chicago; motor vehicle brake systems/parts   700

Harper Leather Goods Manufacturing Co.; Bedford Park; dog products   700

Landis Plastics Inc.; Chicago Ridge; plastic containers   600

Consolidated Freightways; Bedford Park; trucking   600

PepsiAmericas Inc.; Chicago; carbonated beverages   600

Morand Bros. Beverage Co.; Chicago; wine   600

Certified Grocers Midwest Inc.; LaGrange; general warehousing, storage   550

Ondeo Nalco Co.; Chicago; medicinals and botanicals   550

Rose Packing Co.; Chicago; pork products   530

Ferrara Pan Candy Co.; Forest Park; confectionery products   500

Executive Mailing Service Inc.; Palos Hills; mailing service   500

American Heritage Protective Services; Worth; security guard service   500

Chicago Zoological Society Inc.; Brookfield; noncommercial zoo   500

Grayhill Inc.; LaGrange; electronic switches   500

Don Edward and Co.; Riverside; restaurant equipment and supplies   500

AT&T Corp.; Chicago; cable television   500

Aramark Sports and Entertainment Services Inc.; Chicago; concessionaire   500

Illinois 4th District

Chicago — parts of North Side, southwest side

Surrounding the black-majority 7th District in the center of Chicago, the horseshoe-shaped 4th was drawn to unite the city's Hispanic neighborhoods into one voting bloc. Slightly less than 90 percent of district residents live in Chicago. *(See map p. 297.)*

The district, created after the 1990 census revealed that the city's Hispanic population had passed 500,000, is three-fourths Hispanic, and after slight boundary revisions in 2001 includes 45 percent of Cook County's 1.1 million Hispanics. Solidly Democratic, the 4th is plagued by low voter turnout.

A narrow strip of land—about ten miles in length and running along railroad tracks, highways, and cemeteries—attaches the Puerto Rican neighborhood of Logan Square in the northern part of the 4th to Mexican American communities in Little Village and Pilsen in the southern part. In 1998 the Supreme Court declined to hear a suit alleging that the district had been unconstitutionally drawn with race as the major factor.

More than 90 percent of residents are Hispanic in parts of the Lower West Side and South Lawndale neighborhoods around Cermak Road. Hispanic growth also has been impressive in some close-in suburbs: Cicero, a once heavily Slavic town infamous for being the center of operations for Al Capone's mob and the site of a 1966 race riot, is now three-fourths Hispanic. Stone Park, located in the district's

northwestern corner (near the DuPage County line), was once largely Italian but is now four-fifths Hispanic.

The 4th has the state's largest percentage of blue-collar workers, and includes significant immigrant populations in both its Hispanic communities and adjacent Ukrainian and Polish neighborhoods. It also takes in part of Back of the Yards, an area in Chicago that declined when the city's famed stockyards closed in the early 1970s.

Major Industry
Light manufacturing, county administration, electronics.

Notable
The Mexican Fine Arts Center Museum is located in the Lower West Side neighborhood.

Election Returns

	Republican		Democratic		Other	
President 2000	23,809	20.3%	93,266	79.4%	317	0.3%
House 2002	12,778	15.1%	67,339	79.7%	4,396	5.2%

District Profile

Population   653,647

Total area (square miles)   39.4
   Land area (square miles)   39.1

Population per square mile   16,717.3

Counties (2000 population)
   Cook (pt.)   653,647

Cities and other areas over 10,000 (2000 population)
   Chicago (pt.)   560,373
   Cicero town (pt.)   73,209

Race and Hispanic or Latino origin*
   White   18.4%
   Black or African American   3.7%
   American Indian or Alaska Native   0.1%
   Asian   1.7%
   Native Hawaiian or other Pacific Islander   0.0%
   Some other race   0.1%
   Hispanic or Latino origin   74.5%
   Two or more races   1.4%

As percentage of total population.

Ancestry*
   German   3.4%   Polish   5.0%
   Irish   3.1%   USA/American   1.2%
   Italian   1.9%

As estimated percentage of total population.

Universities and colleges, 2000–2001 enrollment
   College of Office Technology, Chicago   443

Newspapers and circulation

	District circulation	Total circulation
Chicago Sun-Times	28,753	474,127
Chicago Tribune	17,217	664,927

See Sources and Explanations in the front of the volume.

Television stations and affiliations

Chicago	100%	WBBM	CBS
Chicago	100%	WCIU	Independent
Chicago	100%	WCPX	PAX
Chicago	100%	WFLD	FOX
Chicago	100%	WGBO	Univision
Chicago	100%	WGN	WB
Chicago	100%	WJYS	Independent
Chicago	100%	WLS	ABC
Chicago	100%	WMAQ	NBC
Chicago	100%	WPWR	UPN
Chicago	100%	WSNS	Telemundo
Chicago	100%	WTTW	PBS
Chicago	100%	WWTO	Independent
Chicago	100%	WYCC	PBS
Chicago	100%	WYIN	PBS

Cable systems and subscribers

Comcast   223,995

Businesses and other major employers

In Elite Staffing; Chicago; temporary help service
  14,000

U.S. Veterans Hospital; Hines   3,000

City of Chicago; Chicago; city management   1,600

International Truck and Engine Corp.; Melrose Park;
  truck and tractor truck assembly   1,500

Edsal Manufacturing Co.; Chicago; nonwood office/store
  shelving   1,500

Target Corp.; Chicago; warehousing   1,500

Central Steel and Wire Co.; Chicago; metals service
  centers and offices   1,250

U.S. Veterans Affairs; Hines   1,000

Chicago Sun-Times Inc.; Chicago; newspaper   1,000

Exelon Corp.; Chicago; telephone answering service
  1,000

St. Elizabeth's Hospital of Chicago Inc.; Chicago   923

Culinary Foods Inc.; Chicago; frozen specialties   900

Union Pacific Railroad Co.; Melrose Park; railroad
  freight hauling   800

ABN Amro Inc.; Chicago; security brokers, dealers   800

Chicago Transit Authority; Chicago   800

Banco Popular North America; Chicago; state
  commercial banks   750

Norwegian American Hospital Inc.; Chicago   700

Mars Inc.; Chicago; chocolate and cocoa products   700

Packaging Dynamics Corp.; Chicago; coated and
  laminated packaging paper   613

Olmarc Packaging Co. Inc.; Melrose Park; packaging
  and labeling services   550

NWS Inc.; Chicago; wine and distilled beverages   550

Westlake Hospital; Melrose Park   500

Kraft Foods Inc.; Chicago; confectionery products   500

RC Cola Bottling Co.; Chicago; carbonated beverages
  500

Illinois 5th District

Chicago — North Side

The 5th spans the North Side of Chicago, from Lake Michigan to near O'Hare International Airport (located in the 6th District). One of the city's few remaining active in- dustrial sectors runs through the middle of the district, along the north branch of the Chicago River. The district's 2 per- cent black population is the lowest in the state. (*See map p. 297.*)

On the east side, the 5th includes most of Lincoln Park, a wealthy community of "lakefront liberals" known for their expensive homes and opposition to Democratic machine pol- itics. Voters here rarely support establishment candidates in the primary but then vote Democratic in general elections.

The west side of the district covers part of the "Bun- galow Belt," a strip of 1930s brick homes built by Cen- tral and Eastern European families. This section of town is still dominated by middle- and working-class German and Polish neighborhoods, but has seen an increasing num- ber of Hispanic newcomers. Voters here also lean Demo- cratic but sometimes vote for Republicans in the general election.

The west's working-class base routinely supports candi- dates trumpeting populist-style economic causes. But west- ern side neighborhoods also have been known to elect a few Republicans to local offices. On the federal level, the dis- trict supported Democratic presidential candidates in 1992, 1996, and 2000.

Major Industry

Warehousing and storage, electronics, manufacturing, health care.

Notable

Wrigley Field is home to baseball's Chicago Cubs; fa- mous gangster death sites: the S. M. C. Cartage Co. garage, where Al Capone ordered "Bugs" Moran's gangsters shot in the 1929 St. Valentine's Day Massacre; and the Biograph Theatre, where federal agents gunned down outlaw John Dillinger in 1934.

Election Returns

	Republican		Democratic		Other	
President 2000	73,793	33.9%	143,106	65.7%	885	0.4%
House 2002	46,008	28.9%	106,514	66.8%	6,913	4.3%

District Profile

Population   653,647

Total area (square miles)   57.8
  Land area (square miles)   56.9

Population per square mile   11,487.6

Counties (2000 population)
  Cook (pt.)   653,647

Cities and other areas over 10,000 (2000 population)
  Chicago (pt.)   549,762
  Elmwood Park village (pt.)   23,741
  Franklin Park village   19,434
  Melrose Park village (pt.)   17,415
  Northlake (pt.)   10,852
  River Grove village   10,668
  Schiller Park village   11,850

Race and Hispanic or Latino origin*
  White   65.9%
  Black or African American   2.2%

American Indian or Alaska Native   0.2%
Asian   6.5%
Native Hawaiian or other Pacific Islander   0.0%
Some other race   0.2%
Hispanic or Latino origin   23.0%
Two or more races   2.2%

As percentage of total population.

Ancestry*

English	2.9%	Italian	7.5%
French	1.2%	Polish	13.5%
German	11.5%	Russian	1.1%
Greek	1.3%	Swedish	1.5%
Irish	9.9%	USA/American	1.6%

As estimated percentage of total population.

Universities and colleges, 2000–2001 enrollment

City Colleges of Chicago-Wilbur Wright College, Chicago   12,015
Devry University, Chicago   4,095
North Park University, Chicago   2,387
Northeastern Illinois University, Chicago   10,941
Northwestern Business College, Chicago   719
Triton College, River Grove   16,927

Newspapers and circulation

	District circulation	Total circulation
Chicago Sun-Times	47,529	474,127
Chicago Tribune	47,609	664,927
*USA Today**	2,582	1,674,376

See Sources and Explanations in the front of the volume.

Television stations and affiliations

Chicago	100%	WBBM	CBS
Chicago	100%	WCIU	Independent
Chicago	100%	WCPX	PAX
Chicago	100%	WFLD	FOX
Chicago	100%	WGBO	Univision
Chicago	100%	WGN	WB
Chicago	100%	WJYS	Independent
Chicago	100%	WLS	ABC
Chicago	100%	WMAQ	NBC
Chicago	100%	WPWR	UPN
Chicago	100%	WSNS	Telemundo
Chicago	100%	WTTW	PBS
Chicago	100%	WWTO	Independent
Chicago	100%	WYCC	PBS
Chicago	100%	WYIN	PBS

Cable systems and subscribers

Comcast   17,449

Businesses and other major employers

Illinois Masonic Medical Center; Chicago   3,100
Sinai Health System Inc.; Chicago; hospital management   3,000
Zenith Electronics Corp.; Melrose Park; household audio/video equipment   2,500
Children's Memorial Hospital Inc.; Chicago   2,000
Dr. Pepper/Seven Up Bottling Group Inc.; Melrose Park; carbonated soft drinks   1,900
Swedish Covenant Hospital; Chicago   1,550
Northeastern Illinois University; Chicago   1,400

Alberto-Culver USA Inc.; Melrose Park; perfumes, cosmetics, other toilet products   1,350
Advocate North Side Health Network Hospital; Chicago   1,300
Gottlieb Memorial Hospital; Melrose Park   1,200
Advocate Health Care Network Hospital; Chicago   1,100
Our Lady of Resurrection Medical Center; Chicago   1,012
Werner Co.; Franklin Park; aluminum sheet, plate, and foil   800
Triton Community College; River Grove   795
Illinois Dept. of Human Services; Chicago   780
Chicago Contract Cleaning and Supply Co.; Chicago; janitorial service   735
Entenmann's Inc.; Melrose Park; breads and cakes   700
Capital Cleaning Inc.; Chicago; building maintenance   700
Beltone Electronics Corp.; Chicago; hearing aids   700
Life Fitness Inc.; Franklin Park; exercising cycles   690
Tempel Steel Co.; Chicago; laminating steel   650
Safety Service Systems Inc.; Chicago; protective services, guards   620
Burns International Security Services Corp.; Chicago; insurance inspection and investigation   600
Sloan Valve Co.; Franklin Park; valves and pipe fittings   595
Grant Hospital Inc.; Chicago   595
Bethany Home and Hospital of Methodist Church Inc.; Chicago   550
Redi-Cut Foods Inc.; Franklin Park; pickles, sauces, salad dressings   500
Unilever Bestfoods Foodservice; Franklin Park; pickles, sauces, salad dressings   500
Dominick's Finer Foods Inc.; Melrose Park; general warehousing, storage   500
Follett Corp.; River Grove; book stores   500
Gategourmet International AG; Schiller Park; caterers   500
Aramark Services Inc.; Chicago; concession operator   500
John O. Butler Co.; Chicago; nonelectric toothbrushes   500
D-A Lubricant Co.; Chicago; electronic parts and equipment   500
S-B Power Tool Co.; Chicago; power-driven handtools   500
SOO Line Railroad Co.; Franklin; railroad freight hauling   500

Illinois 6th District

Northwest and west Chicago suburbs

Just west of Chicago, the 6th includes northern DuPage County and part of northwest Cook County. It is full of older, mostly built-out bedroom communities along commuter rail lines running into the city. Many of these suburbs have been revitalizing their downtown districts. *(See map p. 297.)*

Most residents of the 6th traditionally have commuted to Chicago, but some now travel to booming northwest satellite cities. The district's eastern boundary is O'Hare International

Airport (an extension of the city of Chicago), which is one of the nation's busiest airports and the focus of the 6th's commercial district. Hotels and other travel-related businesses, and companies seeking close airport access, are located in the area.

The district has a reputation as a Republican bastion, historically working in opposition to Chicago's Democrats. It includes more than half of DuPage County, which accounts for three-fourths of the population. DuPage is decidedly Republican (it backed George W. Bush by 13 percentage points in the 2000 presidential election), but not as heavily so as in the 1980s, when it backed Ronald Reagan and George Bush by better than two-to-one ratios. Overall, George W. Bush won the 6th with 53.3 percent of the vote in 2000.

The 6th is one-eighth Hispanic, and DuPage is becoming more racially diverse. Addison and Bensenville have many Hispanic residents, and Asians and Hispanics each tally 20 percent in Glendale Heights. Many Hispanics came to the district when agriculture was a dominant industry and stayed as Chicago's suburbs crept westward in the 1970s and 1980s and took over farmland.

The Cook County portions of the district also have a conservative lean. Under redistricting following the 2000 census, the 6th ceded nearly all of Maine township (Des Plaines, Park Ridge) to the 9th District and gained most of Hanover township (the westernmost township in Cook) from the 8th District.

Major Industry
Airport, light manufacturing, health care.

Notable
United Airlines headquarters is in Elk Grove Village.

Election Returns

	Republican		Democratic		Other	
President 2000	126,254	53.3%	103,616	43.8%	6,945	2.9%
House 2002	113,174	65.1%	60,698	34.9%		

District Profile

Population   653,647

Total area (square miles)   214.8
   Land area (square miles)   213.4

Population per square mile   3,063.0

Counties (2000 population)
   Cook (pt.)   164,512
   DuPage (pt.)   489,135

Cities and other areas over 10,000 (2000 population)
   Addison village   35,914
   Bartlett village (pt.)   24,122
   Bensenville village (pt.)   20,703
   Bloomingdale village   21,675
   Carol Stream village   40,438
   Des Plaines (pt.)   17,691
   Elk Grove Village village (pt.)   30,241
   Elmhurst (pt.)   42,762
   Glendale Heights village   31,765
   Glen Ellyn village   26,999
   Hanover Park village (pt.)   28,012
   Lombard village   42,322
   Mount Prospect village (pt.)   29,898
   Roselle village (pt.)   22,479
   Streamwood village (pt.)   34,885
   Villa Park village   22,075
   Wheaton (pt.)   55,416
   Wood Dale   13,535

Race and Hispanic or Latino origin*
   White   75.3%
   Black or African American   2.7%
   American Indian or Alaska Native   0.1%
   Asian   8.1%
   Native Hawaiian or other Pacific Islander   0.0%
   Some other race   0.1%
   Hispanic or Latino origin   12.5%
   Two or more races   1.3%

*As percentage of total population.

Ancestry*

Dutch	1.1%	Italian	9.3%
English	5.0%	Norwegian	1.6%
French	1.6%	Polish	9.4%
German	16.7%	Swedish	2.5%
Irish	11.0%	USA/American	1.7%

*As estimated percentage of total population.

Universities and colleges, 2000–2001 enrollment
   College of DuPage, Glen Ellyn   28,862
   Devry University, Addison   4,006
   Elmhurst College, Elmhurst   2,611
   Illinois School of Professional Psychology, Rolling Meadows   205
   Keller Graduate School of Management, Oakbrook Terrace   2,591
   Midwestern University, Downers Grove   1,499
   National College of Chiropractic, Lombard   710
   Northern Baptist Theological Seminary, Lombard   275
   Universal Technical Institute, Glendale Heights   1,407
   Wheaton College, Wheaton   2,827

Newspapers and circulation

	District circulation	Total circulation
Arlington Heights Daily Herald	41,345	148,825
Chicago Suburban Newspapers	2,236	116,127
Chicago Sun-Times	31,374	474,127
Chicago Tribune	59,675	664,927
Elgin Courier News	1,938	16,812
*USA Today**	5,316	1,674,376

*See Sources and Explanations in the front of the volume.

Television stations and affiliations

Chicago	100%	WBBM	CBS
Chicago	100%	WCIU	Independent
Chicago	100%	WCPX	PAX
Chicago	100%	WFLD	FOX
Chicago	100%	WGBO	Univision
Chicago	100%	WGN	WB
Chicago	100%	WJYS	Independent
Chicago	100%	WLS	ABC
Chicago	100%	WMAQ	NBC
Chicago	100%	WPWR	UPN

Chicago	100%	WSNS	Telemundo
Chicago	100%	WTTW	PBS
Chicago	100%	WWTO	Independent
Chicago	100%	WYCC	PBS
Chicago	100%	WYIN	PBS
Chicago	100%	WBBM	CBS

Cable systems and subscribers
Comcast   135,354

Businesses and other major employers
United Air Lines Corp.; Elk Grove Village; air passenger carrier   4,500

Advocate Health and Hospitals Corp.; Oak Brook   4,000

Wes Shore Pipeline Co.; Arlington Heights; gas production, distribution   3,400

Elmhurst Memorial Hospital Inc.; Elmhurst   2,429

U.S. Postal Service; Chicago   2,075

PMI-Eisenhart Inc.; Lombard; food supplier   2,000

Advocate Health Care Network Hospital; Downers Grove   2,000

Alexian Brothers Medical Center Inc.; Elk Grove Village   1,800

Household Credit Services Inc.; Wood Dale; financial services   1,700

Central DuPage Hospital Assn.; Winfield   1,627

Illinois National Guard; Chicago   1,400

Illinois Community College District; Glen Ellyn   1,369

McMaster-Carr Supply Co.; Elmhurst; industrial supplies   1,250

CTS Wireless Components Inc.; Bloomingdale; household audio/video equipment   1,200

Compass Group USA Inc.; Elmhurst; food vending machines   1,200

McDonald's Restaurants of Michigan Inc.; Oak Brook; fast-food restaurant chain   1,200

Sky Chefs Inc.; Chicago; caterers   1,200

Fellowes Inc.; Itasca; corrugated boxes   1,150

Automatic Data Processing Inc.; Elk Grove Village; data processing   1,100

Field Container Co.; Elk Grove Village; folding paperboard boxes   1,062

Acxiom-May and Speh Inc.; Downers Grove; data processing   1,050

Flextronics Enclosures Inc.; Villa Park; electrical equipment and supplies   1,025

3 Com Corp.; Rolling Meadows; computer integrated systems design   1,000

Ciba Vision Inc.; Des Plaines; contact lenses   1,000

Wesley-Jessen Corp.; Des Plaines; contact lenses   1,000

First Hospitality Group Inc.; Des Plaines; hotel or motel management   953

Glen Ellyn Clinic; Glen Ellyn   940

Paddock Publications Inc.; Arlington Heights; newspaper   900

Comark Inc.; Bloomingdale; computers   900

AFC Enterprises Inc.; Bartlett; chicken restaurant   900

Boise Cascade Office Products Corp.; Itasca; general warehousing, storage   900

HMS Host Corp.; Chicago; restaurants   900

Chamberlain Manufacturing Corp.; Elmhurst; door opening/closing devices   865

Nordstrom Inc.; Oak Brook; family clothing stores   855

Senior Operations Inc.; Bartlett; flexible metallic hose   850

Spiegel Inc.; Downers Grove; catalog sales   850

Enesco Group Inc.; Itasca; gifts and novelties   800

First Health Group Corp.; Downers Grove; medical insurance claim processing   800

Dominick's Finer Foods Inc.; Oak Brook; supermarkets   800

Wheaton College; Wheaton   736

Arthur J. Gallagher and Co.; Itasca; insurance brokers   700

Imperial Service Systems Inc.; Villa Park; janitorial service   700

Spraying Systems Co.; Carol Stream; spray nozzles: aerosol, paint, insecticide   700

Wackenhut Corp.; Downers Grove; protective services, guard   700

America FIC Corp.; Carol Stream; metal stampings   685

Natural Gas Pipeline Company of America; Lombard; natural gas pipelines   650

Prism Partners; Wood Dale; management consulting   650

Videojet Technologies Inc.; Wood Dale; addressing machines, plates and plate embossers   650

Glenoaks Medical Center; Glendale Heights   613

Elmhurst College; Elmhurst   604

Pampered Chef; Addison; party-plan merchandising   600

County of DuPage; Wheaton; county government   600

Berlin Industries Inc.; Carol Stream; commercial printing   600

Rockwell Firstpoint Contact Corp.; Wood Dale; telephones and telephone apparatus   600

International Business Machines Corp.; Hinsdale; sales consultant   600

Guardsmark Inc.; Oak Brook; security guard service   570

Joint Commission on Accreditation of Healthcare Organizations; Villa Park; medical field-related associations   550

R. R. Donnelley and Sons Co.; Downers Grove; commercial printing   550

Advance Dial Co.; Elmhurst; injection molding of plastics   546

PDV America Inc.; Rolling Meadows; engine fuels and oils   540

Focal Communications Corp.; Elk Grove Village; local telephone communications   500

John B. San Filippo and Son Inc.; Elk Grove Village; nuts: dried, dehydrated, salted or roasted   500

Kmart Corp.; Elk Grove Village; discount department stores   500

STS Operating Inc.; Addison; hydraulic systems equipment   500

Bartlett Park District; Bartlett; city government   500

Sara Lee Corp.; Bensenville; roasted coffee   500

Keebler Co.; Elmhurst; cookies   500

Scholle Corp.; Elmhurst; packing materials, plastics sheet   500

Central DuPage Hospital Assn.; Glen Ellyn   500

Eveready Battery Co.; Glen Ellyn; electrical equipment 500

Saks Inc.; Lombard; department stores   500

Devry University Inc.; Villa Park   500

AAR International Inc.; Wood Dale; aircraft engines and parts   500

Market Day Corp.; Wood Dale; food brokers   500

ConAgra Poultry Co.; Downers Grove; turkey processing 500

Intelistaf Holdings Inc.; Oak Brook; medical help service 500

Sears Roebuck and Co. Inc.; Hinsdale; department stores 500

Worldcom Inc.; Oak Brook; electronic research   500

Illinois 7th District

Chicago — downtown, West Side; west suburbs

East to west, the 7th stretches from the Loop, Chicago's downtown business district, almost to the DuPage County line, taking in the well-to-do western suburbs of Oak Park and River Forest. North to south, the district runs from the upscale Lincoln Park neighborhood to 57th Street on the South Side. *(See map p. 297.)*

The eastern end of the 7th houses some of Chicago's gems, including the Sears Tower, the plush high-rises of River North, several museums, and about a dozen colleges and universities. Chicago's "Magnificent Mile" on Michigan Avenue includes some prestigious shops and first-rate hotels and museums. Business giants such as Boeing, Sara Lee, and Quaker Foods and Beverages have their corporate headquarters in the 7th.

But most of the district lives in the poverty-stricken neighborhoods that stretch from the western Loop to the edge of the county. Except for a few communities of middle-class blacks, the West Side has had problems with gang violence, unemployment, and crumbling infrastructure. The situation is beginning to change in the West Loop, once dominated by the Cabrini-Green housing project, where young couples and development companies have rehabilitated old apartment buildings and warehouses, turning them into condos and lofts.

The district fills with white commuters during the day, but more than 61 percent of the district's permanent residents are black. A reliably Democratic district across the ballot, the only genuine political contests in the 7th are the Democratic primaries.

Major Industry
Insurance, banking, accounting.

Notable
The United Center, arena for the Chicago Bulls and Blackhawks, Soldier Field, stadium for the Chicago Bears and Fire, and Comiskey Park (U.S. Cellular Field), stadium for the Chicago White Sox, are in the district; the Ernest Hemingway birthplace and museum are in Oak Park; Oprah Winfrey's Harpo Productions is in Chicago; Architect Frank Lloyd Wright's home and studio are in Oak Park.

Election Returns

	Republican		Democratic		Other	
President 2000	38,196	16.0%	199,064	83.2%	1,985	0.8%
House 2002	25,280	15.3%	137,933	83.2%	2,543	1.5%

District Profile

Population   653,647

Total area (square miles)   58.9
  Land area (square miles)   56.3

Population per square mile   11,610.1

Counties (2000 population)
  Cook (pt.)   653,647

Cities and other areas over 10,000 (2000 population)
  Bellwood village   20,535
  Chicago (pt.)   502,445
  Maywood village (pt.)   24,895
  Oak Park village   52,524
  River Forest village   11,635

Race and Hispanic or Latino origin*
  White   27.3%
  Black or African American   61.6%
  American Indian or Alaska Native   0.1%
  Asian   3.8%
  Native Hawaiian or other Pacific Islander   0.0%
  Some other race   0.1%
  Hispanic or Latino origin   5.8%
  Two or more races   1.2%

As percentage of total population.

Ancestry*

English	2.5%	Polish	2.7%
German	5.6%	Russian	1.1%
Irish	5.2%	Subsaharan	1.4%
Italian	2.9%	USA/American	1.1%

As estimated percentage of total population.

Universities and colleges, 2000–2001 enrollment
  Adler School of Professional Psychology, Chicago   332
  American Academy of Art, Chicago   398
  Argosy University-Chicago, Chicago   590
  Chicago School of Professional Psychology, Chicago 201
  City Colleges of Chicago-Harold Washington College, Chicago   8,147
  City Colleges of Chicago-Malcolm X. College, Chicago 8,638
  Cooking and Hospitality Institute of Chicago, Chicago 761
  Columbia College Chicago, Chicago   9,056
  Concordia University, River Forest   1,900
  DePaul University, Chicago   20,548
  Dominican University, River Forest   2,317
  Dr. William Scholl College of Podiatric Medicine, Chicago   271
  East-West University, Chicago   744
  Harrington Institute of Interior Design, Chicago   646
  Illinois Institute of Art, Chicago   1,395

International Academy of Merchandising and Design, Chicago   1,739
John Marshall Law School, Chicago   1,392
Lake Forest Graduate School of Management, Chicago*
Loyola University of Chicago, Chicago   12,605
MacCormac College, Chicago   511
Moody Bible Institute, Chicago   1,470
Robert Morris College, Chicago   4,938
Roosevelt University, Chicago   7,359
Rush University, Chicago   1,282
School of the Art Institute of Chicago, Chicago   2,578
Spertus College, Chicago   259
University of Illinois-Chicago, Chicago   24,942

*Enrollment under 100. See Sources and Explanations in the front of the volume.

Newspapers and circulation

	District circulation	Total circulation
Chicago Sun-Times	78,527	474,127
Chicago Tribune	66,831	664,927
Daily Southtown, Chicago	2,382	47,715
*USA Today**	3,311	1,674,376

*See Sources and Explanations in the front of the volume.

Television stations and affiliations

Chicago	100%	WCIU	Independent
Chicago	100%	WCPX	PAX
Chicago	100%	WFLD	FOX
Chicago	100%	WGBO	Univision
Chicago	100%	WGN	WB
Chicago	100%	WJYS	Independent
Chicago	100%	WLS	ABC
Chicago	100%	WMAQ	NBC
Chicago	100%	WPWR	UPN
Chicago	100%	WSNS	Telemundo
Chicago	100%	WTTW	PBS
Chicago	100%	WWTO	Independent
Chicago	100%	WYCC	PBS
Chicago	100%	WYIN	PBS

Cable systems and subscribers
Comcast   30,885

Businesses and other major employers
Boeing Co.; Chicago; airplanes   26,000
City of Chicago; Chicago; city management   21,148
University of Illinois; Chicago   12,000
ERP Operating LP; Chicago; apartment building operators   7,000
Rush-Presbyterian St. Lukes Medical Center; Chicago   7,000
CNA Healthcare Systems Inc.; Chicago; insurance agents and brokers   7,000
Cook County; Chicago; sheriff's office   6,000
Continental Casualty Co.; Chicago; fire, marine, casualty insurance   6,000
Leo Burnett Worldwide Inc.; Chicago; advertising   5,612
Northern Trust Corp.; Chicago; commercial banking   5,400
Northwestern Memorial Hospital; Chicago   5,000
Cook County Hospital; Chicago   5,000

Commonwealth Edison Co.; Chicago; electric power generation   4,900
Harris Bankcorp Inc.; Chicago; state commercial banks   4,200
AT&T; Chicago; telephone services   4,000
Chicago Board of Education; Chicago   3,854
BP America Inc.; Chicago; petroleum products   3,600
General Growth Properties LP; Chicago; commercial real estate agent   3,500
KPMG; Chicago; accounting services   3,400
ABN Amro North America Inc.; Chicago; commercial banking   3,100
Health Care Professionals Inc.; Chicago; hospital/medical service plans   3,000
LPI Service Corp.; Chicago; employment agencies   3,000
Illinois Bell Telephone Co.; Chicago; local/long-distance telephone   3,000
Chicago Tribune Co.; Chicago; newspaper   2,800
Target Corp.; Chicago; department stores   2,500
Illinois National Insurance Co. Inc.; Chicago; fire, marine, casualty insurance   2,400
SBC Global Services Inc.; Chicago; custom computer software design   2,390
West Suburban Hospital Medical Center; Oak Park   2,300
Cook County; Chicago; legislative bodies   2,300
Excess Underwriters Agency Inc.; Chicago; insurance brokers   2,200
Illinois Judiciary Courts; Chicago; courts   2,000
Bank of America Corp.; Chicago; state commercial banks   2,000
Real Property Management; Chicago; real estate managers   2,000
PricewaterhouseCoopers; Chicago; accounting services   2,000
ComPsych Corp.; Chicago; personnel management consultant   2,000
International Business Machines Corp.; Chicago; computer peripherals, software   2,000
Urban Retail Properties Co.; Chicago; shopping center   2,000
U.S. Veterans Hospital; Chicago   2,000
Mercy Hospital and Medical Center; Chicago   1,900
City of Chicago; Chicago; sewerage systems   1,800
ABN Amro Services Co.; Chicago; data processing   1,748
Mount Sinai Hospital Medical Center of Chicago; Chicago   1,696
Lakeside Building Maintenance Inc.; Chicago; janitorial service   1,674
Park Hyatt Beaver Creek Resort and Spa; Chicago; hotels and motels   1,600
Mario Tricoci Hair Salon Chicago Inc.; Chicago; hairdressers   1,600
U.S. Social Security Administration; Chicago   1,600
Bankers Life and Casualty Co; Chicago; health insurance   1,590
Oak Park Hospital; Oak Park   1,500
Allied Security Inc.; Chicago; protective services, guards   1,500
Heller Interstate Inc.; Chicago; investment holding company   1,500

Information Resources Inc.; Chicago; market analysis or research   1,500

Suburban Job-Link Corp.; Chicago; temporary help service   1,500

Federal Reserve Bank of Chicago; Chicago   1,475

Chicago Symphony Orchestra; Chicago; symphony orchestra   1,410

City of Chicago; Chicago; transportation regulation   1,400

Citibank F. S. B. Inc.; Chicago; federal savings and loan associations   1,400

St. Mary of Nazareth Hospital Center; Chicago   1,390

Focal Financial Services Inc.; Chicago; telephone communication   1,300

Chicago Sun-Times Inc.; Chicago; newspaper   1,300

DiamondCluster International Inc.; Chicago; management consulting   1,300

Heidrick and Struggles International Inc.; Chicago; employment agencies   1,280

Hilton Hotels Corp.; Chicago; hotels   1,217

Sargent and Lundy; Chicago; consulting engineer   1,200

Gatorade Co.; Chicago; soft drinks   1,200

Hollinger International Publishing Inc.; Chicago; newspaper   1,200

U.S. Veterans Hospital; Chicago   1,200

Chicago Transit Authority; Chicago   1,200

Rezko Enterprises Inc.; Chicago; pizzeria chain   1,168

Hilton Hotels Corp.; Chicago; hotels   1,153

DePaul University; Chicago   1,126

Peoples Gas Light and Coke Inc.; Chicago; gas   1,115

Kirkland and Ellis; Chicago; general practice law office   1,100

Adam Oyebanji; Chicago; general practice law office   1,100

Loyola University of Chicago Inc.; Chicago   1,100

Michael Reese Medical Center Corp.; Chicago   1,100

Chicago Mercantile Exchange Holdings Inc.; Chicago; commodity contract exchanges   1,060

System Parking Inc.; Chicago; parking garage   1,000

American National Bank and Trust Co. of Chicago; Chicago; commercial bank   1,000

Mayer Brown Rowe and Maw; Chicago; general practice law office   1,000

Thomson Professional and Regulatory Inc.; Chicago; tax return preparation services   1,000

U.S. Internal Revenue Service; Chicago   1,000

ADT Security Services Inc.; Chicago; home security services   1,000

Continental Assurance Co.; Chicago; insurance agents and brokers   1,000

MHC Operating LP; Chicago; mobile home site operators   1,000

Northern Trust Co.; Chicago; nondeposit trust facilities   1,000

United Parcel Service Inc.; Chicago; parcel delivery   1,000

Quaker Oats Co.; Chicago; soft drinks   1,000

Foote Cone and Belding Inc.; Chicago; advertising   1,000

Marriott International Inc.; Chicago; hotels   1,000

Hyatt Corp.; Chicago; hotel, franchised   1,000

Transunion; Chicago; consumer credit reporting bureau   1,000

Sidley Austin Brown and Wood; Chicago; general practice law office   1,000

Illinois Dept. of Transportation; Chicago   1,000

Bank One Corp.; Chicago; commercial bank   1,000

Chicago Board of Trade; Chicago; contract futures exchange   916

City of Chicago; Chicago; public library   916

William Blair and Co.; Chicago; stock brokers and dealers   900

Kemper Growth Fund; Chicago; open-ended management investment   900

Union Pacific Railroad Co.; Chicago; railroad terminals   900

Zurich Scudder Investments Inc.; Chicago; security brokers, dealers, flotation companies   900

Pepper Construction Co.; Chicago; commercial/office building contractors   900

True North Communications Inc.; Chicago; advertising   900

U.S. Railroad Retirement Board; Chicago   900

Addus Healthcare Inc.; Chicago; home health care services   891

La Salle National Bancorp Inc.; Chicago; bank holding companies   879

Stokely-Van Camp Inc.; Chicago; soft drinks   854

Amli Residential Properties; Chicago; apartment building operators   850

Levy Security Corp.; Chicago; security guard service   850

Great Hawaiian Properties Corp.; Chicago; deep sea passenger transportation   825

Winston and Strawn; Chicago; general practice law office   820

ABN Amro Inc.; Chicago; security brokers, dealers   820

RREEF America; Chicago; real estate consultant   806

American Medical Assn.; Chicago; medical field-related associations   800

Roosevelt University; Chicago   800

Janssen Pharmaceutical Inc.; Chicago; pharmaceuticals   800

Virginia Surety Co.; Chicago; automobile warranty insurance   800

Bloomingdale's Inc.; Chicago; department stores   800

ITT Sheraton Corp.; Chicago; hotels   800

Fuji America Holdings Inc.; Chicago; short-term business credit   800

Rush Presbyterian St. Luke's Hospital; Chicago   800

Katten Muchin Zavis Rosenman; Chicago; general practice law office   799

Chicago Board Options Exchange Inc.; Chicago; security exchanges   795

India Tourism; Chicago; travel agency   780

Rehabilitation Institute of Chicago; Chicago   777

Accenture Inc.; Chicago; management information systems consultant   750

Piper Marbury Rudnick and Wolfe; Chicago; general practice law office   750

Perot Systems Corp.; Chicago; computer facilities management   750

Combined Insurance Company of America; Chicago; accident insurance carriers   750

Chicago Baking Co.; Chicago; baked goods 750

U.S. Federal Bureau of Investigation; Chicago 740

Greater Chicago Metropolitan Water Reclamation District; Chicago 720

Bcom3 Group Inc.; Chicago; advertising 700

Buckingham Fountain; Chicago; hotels 700

Jones Lang La Salle Americas Inc.; Chicago; real estate agents and managers 700

Bruce R. Duffield; Chicago; general practice law office 700

Marsh and McLennan Companies Inc.; Chicago; insurance brokers 700

McDermott, Will & Emery; Chicago; corporate partnership and business law 700

American Bar Association; Chicago; lawyer association 700

City of Chicago; Chicago; legislative bodies 700

CCC Information Services Inc.; Chicago; insurance information, consulting services 700

Marsh USA Inc.; Chicago; insurance brokers 700

Jenner and Block; Chicago; general practice law office 670

R. R. Donnelley and Sons Co.; Chicago; commercial printing 665

Fairmont Hotel Management; Chicago; hotels 650

United Healthcare of Illinois Inc.; Chicago; health maintenance organization 650

Vandenburg Organization; Chicago; subdividers and developers 650

Morningstar Inc.; Chicago; statistical reports 650

USG Corp.; Chicago; gypsum products 650

Boulevard Bancorp Inc.; Chicago; commercial bank 650

Illinois Institute of Technology; Chicago 650

Moody Bible Institute of Chicago; Chicago; religious organization 640

Chapman and Cutler; Chicago; general practice law office 621

Board of Trustees of Community College District; Chicago 619

Frontenac Co.; Chicago; management services 612

Sanford; Bellwood; pens and mechanical pencils 600

Independence Plus Inc.; Oak Park; home health care services 600

Consoer Townsend Envirodyne Engineers Inc.; Chicago; civil engineering 600

Edelman Public Relations; Chicago; public relations services 600

Renaissance Hotel Group; Chicago; hotels 600

Interpark Holdings Inc.; Chicago; automobile parking 600

Stafford Trading Inc.; Chicago; business computer software 600

Giordanos Enterprises Inc.; Chicago; restaurant/food services consultants 600

Archibald Candy Corp.; Chicago; confectionery products 600

East Bank Club Venture; Chicago; health club 600

Federated Industries Inc.; Chicago; nonresidential building operators 600

Playboy Gaming Greece; Chicago; gambling 600

Titan Corp.; Chicago; satellite communications 600

Vista International Inc.; Chicago; hotels 600

Wrigley Manufacturing Co.; Chicago; chewing gum 600

Northeast Illinois Regional Commuter Railroad Corp.; Chicago 600

Cancer Treatment Centers of America Inc.; Arlington Heights 600

McDermott, Will & Emery; Chicago; general practice law office 597

Alpha Baking Co. Inc.; Chicago; bread baking 570

City of Chicago; Chicago; commerical regulation 562

Schiff Hardin and Waite; Chicago; general practice law office 560

Blue Cross and Blue Shield Assn.; Chicago; health association 550

Valet Parking Service Inc.; Chicago; automobile parking 550

Lord, Bissell and Brook; Chicago; general practice law office 550

Field Museum of Natural History; Chicago 550

Royal Imperial Group Inc.; Chicago; commercial land development 550

Illinois Dept. of Children and Family Services; Chicago 550

Loretto Hospital; Chicago 550

Metropolitan Pier and Exposition Authority Inc.; Chicago 548

City of Chicago; Chicago; police dept. 541

Smith Bucklin and Associates Inc.; Chicago; management consulting 530

Elkay Manufacturing Co.; Broadview; enameled iron, metal sinks 500

Robert Bosch Corp.; Broadview; household audio equipment 500

Dry Storage Corp.; Berkeley; general warehousing, storage 500

Baker and McKenzie; Chicago; general practice law office 500

Chicago Title Insurance Co.; Chicago; title abstract offices 500

Frankel; Chicago; promotion service 500

U.S. National Institutes of Health; Chicago 500

Parking Service Inc.; Chicago; parking garage 500

Excell Personnel Services Inc.; Chicago; employment agencies 500

Michael P. Morrison; Chicago; general practice law office 500

ED&F Man International Inc.; Chicago; security brokers, dealers, flotation companies 500

United Service Companies; Chicago; janitorial service 500

American Building Maintenance Co. of Illinois; Chicago; janitorial service 500

Hartmarx Corp.; Chicago; men's and boys' suits 500

MEPC American Holdings Inc.; Chicago; subdividers and developers 500

Nuveen Municipal Advantage Fund Inc.; Chicago; mutual fund sales 500

OneSource Building Services Inc.; Chicago; janitorial service 500

VNU Business Media Inc.; Chicago; grocery stores 500

Flying Food Group Inc.; Chicago; caterers 500

Helene Curtis Industries Inc.; Chicago; hair shampoos, rinses, conditioners 500

Mesirow Financial Holdings Inc.; Chicago; stock brokers and dealers   500

CBS Broadcasting Inc.; Chicago; radio broadcasting stations   500

City of Chicago; Chicago; air, water, solid waste management   500

Four Seasons Hotels Inc.; Chicago; hotel, franchised   500

Hilton International Co.; Chicago; direct selling   500

Intercontinental Chicago Operating Corp.; Chicago; hotel, franchised   500

JMB Income Properties; Chicago; building operation   500

National Broadcasting Co.; Chicago; television broadcasting stations   500

Near North National Group Inc.; Chicago; insurance agents   500

Lakewood Engineering and Manufacturing Co.; Chicago; electric housewares and fans   500

White Cap Inc.; Chicago; jar tops and crowns   500

Grant Thornton; Chicago; certified public accountant   500

Ametek Dixson; Chicago; automotive water, oil gauges   500

Illinois 8th District

Northwest Cook County — Schaumburg; part of Lake and McHenry Counties

Most of the 8th's population lies in the affluent, well-established suburbs northwest of Chicago, although population growth has spurred new developments farther north through western Lake County and into the Chain-O-Lakes vacation communities near the Wisconsin border. *(See map p. 297.)*

The district became a huge employment center in the late 1980s, drawing commuters away from Chicago and causing serious traffic problems. The 8th is still struggling with these negatives that come with rapid development and suburban sprawl.

As in other northwestern Chicago suburban districts, some of the 8th's cities, such as Palatine (which is shared with the 10th) and Schaumburg, have lured corporate headquarters. Motorola is based in Schaumburg. The biggest development boom in Cook County has been abetted by access to Interstates 90 and 290 and proximity to O'Hare International Airport (in the 6th District).

Redistricting in 2001 gave the 8th more of Lake County, where a slight majority of district residents live. The district now takes in all of Lake County's border with Wisconsin. This area is mostly upscale and well-educated; in the southwest Lake townships of Cuba and Ela, the median family income is more than $100,000. Redistricting also added the northeastern part of fast-growing McHenry County, located west of Lake.

The 8th's strong Republican tradition—it gave George W. Bush 55.5 percent of the vote in 2000—has been moderated only slightly by newcomers and a small but growing minority population. Hispanics make up one-tenth of district residents.

Major Industry
Health care, insurance, retail.

Notable
Six Flags Great America amusement park is in Gurnee; the Volo Illinois Auto Museum features classic and celebrity cars.

Election Returns

	Republican		Democratic		Other	
President 2000	131,967	55.5%	98,664	41.5%	6,954	2.9%
House 2002	95,275	57.4%	70,626	42.6%		

District Profile

Population   653,647

Total area (square miles)   645.8
   Land area (square miles)   617.8

Population per square mile   1,058.0

Counties (2000 population)
   Cook (pt.)   222,765
   Lake (pt.)   329,314
   McHenry (pt.)   101,568

Cities and other areas over 10,000 (2000 population)
   Elgin (pt.)   15,552
   Grayslake village (pt.)   17,804
   Gurnee village (pt.)   24,403
   Hanover Park village (pt.)   10,266
   Hoffman Estates village (pt.)   39,568
   Lake Zurich village   18,104
   Lindenhurst village   12,539
   McHenry   21,501
   Mundelein village (pt.)   28,416
   Palatine village (pt.)   47,077
   Round Lake Beach village   25,859
   Schaumburg village (pt.)   71,577
   Woodstock (pt.)   19,668
   Zion   22,866

Race and Hispanic or Latino origin*
   White   78.8%
   Black or African American   3.2%
   American Indian or Alaska Native   0.1%
   Asian   5.6%
   Native Hawaiian or other Pacific Islander   0.0%
   Some other race   0.1%
   Hispanic or Latino origin   10.8%
   Two or more races   1.2%

As percentage of total population.

Ancestry*

Dutch 1.1%	Norwegian 2.0%
English 5.3%	Polish 8.3%
French 1.9%	Scottish 1.1%
German 19.5%	Swedish 2.6%
Irish 11.0%	USA/American 2.5%
Italian 6.3%	

As estimated percentage of total population.

Universities and colleges, 2000–2001 enrollment

College of Lake County, Grayslake   14,441
ITT Technical Institute, Hoffman Estates   418
McHenry County College, Crystal Lake   5,086
Illinois Institute of Art, Schaumburg   870
University of St. Mary of the Lake, Mundelein   262

Newspapers and circulation

	District circulation	Total circulation
Arlington Heights Daily Herald	34,921	148,825
Chicago Suburban Newspapers	17,996	116,127
Chicago Sun-Times	13,814	474,127
Chicago Tribune	43,916	664,927
Crystal Lake Northwest Herald	14,093	34,938
Elgin Courier News	1,639	16,812
*USA Today**	3,833	1,674,376
Waukegan News Sun	12,716	21,251

*See Sources and Explanations in the front of the volume.

Television stations and affiliations

Chicago	100%	WBBM	CBS
Chicago	100%	WCIU	Independent
Chicago	100%	WCPX	PAX
Chicago	100%	WFLD	FOX
Chicago	100%	WGBO	Univision
Chicago	100%	WGN	WB
Chicago	100%	WJYS	Independent
Chicago	100%	WLS	ABC
Chicago	100%	WMAQ	NBC
Chicago	100%	WPWR	UPN
Chicago	100%	WSNS	Telemundo
Chicago	100%	WTTW	PBS
Chicago	100%	WWTO	Independent
Chicago	100%	WYCC	PBS
Chicago	100%	WYIN	PBS

Cable systems and subscribers

Comcast   101,614
Mediacom   591

Businesses and other major employers

Sears Roebuck and Co. Inc.; Schaumburg; department stores   6,800
Illinois Dept. of Transportation; Schaumburg   5,000
American Guarantee and Liability Insurance Co.; Schaumburg; property damage insurance   3,393
Ameritech Services Inc.; Hoffman Estates; purchasing service   2,500
Centegra Health System Hospital; McHenry   2,300
Kemper Insurance Companies; Long Grove; fire, marine, casualty insurance   2,000
Motorola Communications and Electronics Inc.; Schaumburg; electronic parts   1,800
Allstate Insurance Co.; Barrington; real estate insurance agents   1,500
Experian Information Solutions Inc.; Schaumburg; credit reporting services   1,500
GE Capital Auto Financial Services Inc.; Barrington; licensed loan companies   1,300
Takeda America Holdings Inc.; Vernon Hills; drugs, proprietaries, sundries   1,100
St. Alexius Medical Center; Hoffman Estates   1,070
Advocate Health Care Network Hospital; Barrington   1,000
Allegiance Healthcare Corp.; Waukegan; medical and hospital equipment   1,000
Target Corp.; Schaumburg; department stores   1,000
Northern Illinois Medical Center; McHenry   925
Cherry Corp.; Waukegan; electric switches   900
Siemens Medical Systems Inc.; Schaumburg; medical diagnostic apparatus   850
Intermatic Inc.; Spring Grove; residential lighting fixtures   818
Life Fitness Inc.; Lake Zurich; exercise facilities   800
Lacosta Inc.; Wauconda; building office cleaning   800
Illinois Judiciary Courts; Woodstock   800
Mascon Information Technologies; Schaumburg; computer software writing services   800
Market Facts Inc.; Arlington Heights; market analysis or research   700
Medcor Inc.; McHenry; first aid service   700
Bel-Rae Inc.; Wauconda; janitors' supplies   700
A. C. Nielsen Co.; Schaumburg; business research service   700
Echo Inc.; Lake Zurich; lawn and garden equipment   690
Follett Corp.; McHenry; books   684
Woodland Consolidated School District; Grayslake   660
Northrop Grumman Systems Corp.; Rolling Meadows; radio broadcasting equipment   637
WMS Gaming Inc.; Waukegan; coin-operated amusement machines   621
Baxter Healthcare Corp.; Waukegan; medical equipment and supplies   600
American General Assurance Co.; Schaumburg; life insurance   600
Ameritech Mobile Communications Inc.; Schaumburg; cellular telephones   600
Comcast; Schaumburg; telephone services   600
McHenry County College; Crystal Lake   579
Transamerica Commercial Finance Corp.; Hoffman Estates; mercantile financing   575
U.S. Can Corp.; Elgin; metal cans   560
Gruner and Jahr Printing and Publishing Co.; Woodstock; magazine publishing   550
JC Penney Corp.; Schaumburg; department stores   550
Evangelical Retirement Homes of Greater Chicago Inc.; Schaumburg   550
McHenry County; Woodstock; county government   548
Automotive Brake Co.; McHenry; motor vehicle brake systems/parts   540
Elgin Sweeper Co.; Elgin; street sprinklers and sweepers   520
Tempel Steel Co.; Libertyville; stamping metal   500
McHenry School District; McHenry   500
Medline Industries Inc.; Mundelein; surgical and medical instruments   500
Baxter Healthcare Corp.; Round Lake; noncommercial research organization   500
Automatic Liquid Packaging Inc.; Woodstock; packaging and labeling services   500
Memorial Medical Center; Woodstock   500
Midwestern Regional Medical Center Inc.; Zion   500

Sharp Electronics Corp.; Schaumburg; electronic
connectors   500
Ameritech Mobile Communications Inc.; Hoffman
Estates; cellular telephones   500

Illinois 9th District

Chicago — North Side lakefront; Evanston

The 9th starts in upscale Wilmette (shared with the 10th), runs south through the liberal suburbs of Evanston and Skokie and Chicago's multi-ethnic North Side, and then drops into one of the city's most prosperous lakefront neighborhoods. It also extends west to industrial and blue-collar Des Plaines and Rosemont (both shared with the 6th). *(See map p. 297.)*

About 62 percent of the district's population is white, with the remainder almost evenly divided among Asians, blacks, and Hispanics. More than one in five who live in Skokie, Morton Grove, and Lincolnwood are Asian.

Slightly less than half of the district's population lives in Chicago. The neighborhoods of Rogers Park, Edgewater, and Uptown once housed Eastern European and Irish immigrants; they are now an eclectic mix of Asian, European, and African immigrants. Rogers Park, tucked in the city's northeast corner, takes in the campus of Loyola University. Uptown is mainly working-class, with some low-income areas. Southeast Asians, the area's newest arrivals, have opened shops and restaurants, revitalizing the area's economy.

Lakeview, the district's southernmost point, includes a large gay population. The area near Wrigley Field (which lies in the adjacent 5th District) is a mecca for affluent young professionals and is home to a hot real estate market.

Most of the other Chicagoans in the 9th live in the far northwestern part of the city, near O'Hare Airport (which is located in the neighboring 6th).

The mix of immigrants, affluent urbanites, and Northwestern University students makes the 9th solidly Democratic. Although the "lakefront liberals" tend not to vote for machine candidates, they are reliably Democratic. The district's suburbs contain a sizable Jewish population.

Major Industry

Health care, insurance, light manufacturing.

Notable

The North Shore Center for the Performing Arts is in Skokie.

Election Returns

	Republican		Democratic		Other	
President 2000	71,064	30.8%	155,529	67.4%	4,331	1.9%
House 2002	45,307	26.8%	118,642	70.3%	4,887	2.9%

District Profile

Population   653,647

Total area (square miles)   77.5
   Land area (square miles)   75.3

Population per square mile   8,680.6

Counties (2000 population)
Cook (pt.)   653,647

Cities and other areas over 10,000 (2000 population)
Chicago (pt.)   299,868
Des Plaines (pt.)   39,632
Evanston   74,239
Lincolnwood village   12,359
Morton Grove village   22,451
Niles village   30,068
Norridge village   14,582
Park Ridge   37,775
Skokie village   63,348
Wilmette village (pt.)   11,344

Race and Hispanic or Latino origin*
White   62.5%
Black or African American   10.7%
American Indian or Alaska Native   0.2%
Asian   12.3%
Native Hawaiian or other Pacific Islander   0.1%
Some other race   0.3%
Hispanic or Latino origin   11.5%
Two or more races   2.6%

As percentage of total population.

Ancestry*

English	3.5%	Polish	8.4%
French	1.1%	Russian	3.0%
German	10.6%	Subsaharan	1.3%
Greek	1.5%	Swedish	1.7%
Irish	8.2%	USA/American	2.2%
Italian	5.1%		

As estimated percentage of total population.

Universities and colleges, 2000–2001 enrollment
City Colleges of Chicago-Harry S. Truman College, Chicago   15,466
Garrett Evangelical Theological Seminary, Evanston   302
Hebrew Theological College, Skokie   224
Kendall College, Evanston   629
Lincoln Technical Institute, Norridge   1,325
National Louis University, Evanston   7,222
Northwestern University, Evanston   16,952
Oakton Community College, Des Plaines   11,551
St. Augustine College, Chicago   1,543

Newspapers and circulation

	District circulation	Total circulation
Arlington Heights Daily Herald	4,219	148,825
Chicago Sun-Times	35,492	474,127
Chicago Tribune	58,870	664,927
*USA Today**	7,607	1,674,376

See Sources and Explanations in the front of the volume.

Television stations and affiliations

Chicago	100%	WBBM	CBS
Chicago	100%	WCIU	Independent
Chicago	100%	WCPX	PAX
Chicago	100%	WFLD	FOX

Chicago	100%	WGBO	Univision
Chicago	100%	WGN	WB
Chicago	100%	WJYS	Independent
Chicago	100%	WLS	ABC
Chicago	100%	WMAQ	NBC
Chicago	100%	WPWR	UPN
Chicago	100%	WSNS	Telemundo
Chicago	100%	WTTW	PBS
Chicago	100%	WWTO	Independent
Chicago	100%	WYCC	PBS
Chicago	100%	WYIN	PBS

Cable systems and subscribers

Comcast   60,342

Businesses and other major employers

Northwestern University; Evanston   5,928

Advocate Lutheran General Hospital; Park Ridge   4,800

Advocate Health Care Network; Park Ridge   4,200

Pechiney Plastic Packaging Inc.; Chicago; packaging and shipping materials   2,900

CR/Pl Management Co. Inc.; Evanston; management consulting   2,800

Beco Inc.; Park Ridge; temporary help service   2,662

Rexam Beverage Can Co.; Chicago   2,400

UOP; Des Plaines; catalysts, chemical   2,000

Kimco Corp.; Chicago; janitorial service   2,000

Our Lady of Resurrection Medical Center; Chicago   1,907

St. Francis Hospital of Evanston; Evanston   1,850

John Crane Inc.; Morton Grove; gaskets and sealing devices   1,800

S&C Electric Co.; Chicago; electric fuses   1,700

Evanston School District; Evanston   1,640

Federal-Mogul Corp.; Skokie; gaskets; packing and sealing devices   1,600

Oakton Community College; Des Plaines   1,500

Rosemont Exposition Services Inc.; Des Plaines; industrial buildings renovation   1,500

Resurrection Health Care Corp. Hospital; Chicago   1,400

Illinois National Guard; Chicago   1,400

Wells Lamont Industrial Products Inc.; Niles; gloves   1,400

Millard Group; Lincolnwood; janitorial service   1,300

Arlington Hospitality Staffing Inc.; Des Plaines; employee leasing service   1,250

Honeywell International Inc.; Des Plaines; automotive supplies, parts   1,200

Littelfuse Inc.; Des Plaines; fuses and fuse equipment   1,200

Peapod Inc.; Skokie; delivery service   1,190

Louis A. Weiss Memorial Hospital Inc.; Chicago   1,100

Rush North Shore Medical Center; Skokie   1,098

Target Corp.; Skokie; department stores   1,000

RDIS Corp.; Lincolnwood; automobile insurance   1,000

Professional Nursing Inc.; Chicago; nurses' registry   950

Comdisco Inc.; Des Plaines; computer rental and leasing   900

Hart Schaffner and Marx; Des Plaines; men's and boys' apparel   882

Sears Roebuck and Co. Inc.; Skokie; catalog sales   830

Hyatt Corp.; Des Plaines; hotel, franchised   800

Burns International Security Services Corp.; Chicago; detective, armored car services   800

Argenbright Security Inc.; Chicago; security guard service   800

ITT Industries Inc.; Morton Grove; industrial pumps and parts   780

Sysco Food Services; Des Plaines; canned goods   750

Misericordia Home; Chicago; facility for mentally retarded persons   725

Central States Southeast and Southwest Areas Health and Welfare Fund; Des Plaines; union welfare, benefit, health funds   719

Holy Family Medical Center; Des Plaines   716

Market Facts Inc.; Des Plaines; market analysis or research   700

U.S. Federal Aviation Administration; Des Plaines; air traffic control   700

Sprint Corp.; Des Plaines; long-distance telephone   700

Cap Enterprises Inc.; Chicago; nonbank personal holding companies   687

United Stationers Supply Co. Inc.; Des Plaines; stationery and office supplies   650

Juno Lighting Inc.; Des Plaines; commercial lighting fixtures   650

Anixter Inc.; Skokie; electrical equipment   650

U.S. Cellular Inc.; Chicago; radiotelephone communication   650

Stratos Lightwave Inc.; Chicago; light-sensitive devices   633

Shure Inc.; Evanston; microphones   600

VoiceStream Wireless Corp.; Chicago; mobile telephones and equipment   600

AB Dick Co.; Niles; duplicating machines   600

Edwin Knowles China Co. Inc.; Niles; pottery cooking and kitchen articles   600

Kraft Foods Inc.; Niles; cookies and crackers   600

Norman Rockwell Gallery Ltd.; Niles; mail-order collectibles and antiques   600

Sierra Systems Inc.; Park Ridge; drafting service   556

Grace Brothers; Evanston; security brokers   550

Eastman Kodak Co.; Lincolnwood; microfilm equipment   550

Interim Healthcare Inc.; Chicago; temporary help service   543

Klein Tools Inc.; Skokie; hand and edge tools   530

Starwood Hotels and Resorts Worldwide Inc.; Des Plaines; hotels   525

Illinois State Police; Des Plaines   500

Wheels Inc.; Des Plaines; truck leasing   500

Nurse Staffers Inc.; Des Plaines; employment agencies   500

Cheesecake Factory Restaurants Inc.; Skokie; restaurants   500

Oakton Community College; Skokie   500

Pharmacia Corp.; Skokie; commercial physical research   500

Truserv Corp.; Chicago; lumber: rough, dressed, and finished   500

Illinois Community College District; Chicago   500

Oce-USA Inc.; Chicago; copying equipment   500

Illinois 10th District

North and northwest Chicago suburbs — Waukegan

The mostly upscale 10th hugs Lake Michigan, taking in southeast Lake County and northeast Cook County. Along the lakefront, Chicagoland's old-money elite live in exclusive towns like Wilmette (shared with the 9th), Kenilworth, and Winnetka, where homes routinely sell for $500,000 or more. *(See map p. 297.)*

To the north, the district's industrial sector, in Waukegan and North Chicago, found new life in 1994 when nearby Great Lakes Naval Training Center became the nation's only naval recruit training facility. Most of the district's minorities live in Waukegan, which is about 45 percent Hispanic and 20 percent black. Minorities also make up a majority in North Chicago, located just south of Waukegan. There also is a large Jewish constituency in the district.

Suburban and working-class residents combine to make the 10th a moderate "swing" district—fiscally conservative but socially liberal, especially on abortion rights and gun control. With the 10th's proximity to Lake Michigan, environmental protection is a major issue.

Within the 10th, Cook County is slightly more populous than Lake County. In 2001 redistricting, the 10th shed part of Wilmette to the south and some communities on the Wisconsin border (which had been the district's northern boundary). The western border was extended to pick up part of Palatine and Inverness. The revised 10th is slightly more Republican than its 1990s configuration, though residents within the new lines narrowly backed Bill Clinton in 1996 and Al Gore in 2000.

Major Industry
Pharmaceutical research, insurance, military.

Notable
Berto Center, the Chicago Bulls basketball training facility, is in Deerfield; the Chicago Botanic Garden is in Glencoe.

Election Returns

	Republican		Democratic		Other	
President 2000	123,982	46.9%	134,149	50.8%	6,097	2.3%
House 2002	128,611	68.8%	58,300	31.2%		

District Profile

Population 653,647

Total area (square miles) 252.4
  Land area (square miles) 249.5

Population per square mile 2,619.8

Counties (2000 population)
  Cook (pt.) 338,605
  Lake (pt.) 315,042

Cities and other areas over 10,000 (2000 population)
  Arlington Heights village (pt.) 69,414
  Buffalo Grove village 42,909
  Deerfield village 18,420
  Glenview village (pt.) 33,328
  Highland Park 31,365

Lake Forest 20,059
Libertyville village (pt.) 20,740
Mount Prospect village (pt.) 26,367
Northbrook village 33,435
North Chicago 35,918
Palatine village (pt.) 18,402
Prospect Heights 17,081
Vernon Hills village (pt.) 20,120
Waukegan (pt.) 79,726
Wheeling village 34,496
Wilmette village (pt.) 16,307
Winnetka village 12,419

Race and Hispanic or Latino origin*
White 75.2%
Black or African American 5.3%
American Indian or Alaska Native 0.1%
Asian 5.9%
Native Hawaiian or other Pacific Islander 0.0%
Some other race 0.2%
Hispanic or Latino origin 12.3%
Two or more races 1.1%

As percentage of total population.

Ancestry*

English 5.6%	Norwegian 1.4%
French 1.5%	Polish 7.3%
German 14.4%	Russian 3.9%
Greek 1.2%	Scottish 1.2%
Irish 9.9%	Swedish 2.4%
Italian 5.6%	USA/American 3.0%

As estimated percentage of total population.

Universities and colleges, 2000–2001 enrollment
Barat College, Lake Forest 799
Finch University of Health Science-Chicago Medical School, North Chicago 1,360
Lake Forest College, Lake Forest 1,270
Lake Forest Graduate School of Management, Lake Forest 652
Trinity International University, Deerfield 2,663
William Rainey Harper College, Palatine 15,021

Newspapers and circulation

	District circulation	Total circulation
Arlington Heights Daily Herald	31,098	148,825
Chicago Suburban Newspapers	10,500	116,127
Chicago Sun-Times	21,664	474,127
Chicago Tribune	73,479	664,927
*USA Today**	8,325	1,674,376
Waukegan News Sun	8,489	21,251

See Sources and Explanations in the front of the volume.

Television stations and affiliations

Chicago	100%	WBBM	CBS
Chicago	100%	WCIU	Independent
Chicago	100%	WCPX	PAX
Chicago	100%	WFLD	FOX
Chicago	100%	WGBO	Univision
Chicago	100%	WGN	WB
Chicago	100%	WJYS	Independent
Chicago	100%	WLS	ABC

Chicago	100%	WMAQ	NBC
Chicago	100%	WPWR	UPN
Chicago	100%	WSNS	Telemundo
Chicago	100%	WTTW	PBS
Chicago	100%	WWTO	Independent
Chicago	100%	WYCC	PBS
Chicago	100%	WYIN	PBS

Cable systems and subscribers
Comcast   132,003

Military installations, September 2001
Great Lakes National Training Center, Great Lakes
  5,492
Sheridan Reserve Complex, Highland Park   1,910
Great Lakes Naval Hospital, Great Lakes   1,772
PWC Great Lakes, Great Lakes   481

Businesses and other major employers
Hewitt Associates Inc.; Lincolnshire; human resource
  consulting   13,018
Abbott Laboratories; North Chicago; pharmaceuticals
  12,284
Motorola Inc.; Libertyville; communication equipment
  repair   5,000
Allstate Insurance Corp.; Northbrook; fire, marine,
  casualty insurance   5,000
CDW Technologies Inc.; Vernon Hills; computers
  3,300
BTI Americas Inc.; Northbrook; travel agency   3,300
HFC Funding Corp.; Prospect Heights; personal credit
  institutions   3,300
Northwest Community Healthcare Corp. Hospital;
  Arlington Heights   3,000
Aurora Casket Co.; Libertyville burial caskets   3,000
Patriot Parent Assn.; Buffalo Grove; business services
  3,000
Dayton Electric Manufacturing Co.; Lake Forest; electric
  motors   2,337
Discover Financial Services Inc.; Deerfield; credit card
  services, collection   2,000
Novus Credit Services Inc.; Deerfield; consumer finance
  companies   2,000
Evanston Northwestern Healthcare Corp. Hospital;
  Glenview   2,000
U.S. Veterans Hospital; North Chicago   2,000
Kraft Foods Inc.; Winnetka; cheese products   2,000
Underwriters Laboratories Inc.; Northbrook; product
  testing laboratory   1,841
Trailmobile Trailer; Northbrook; truck trailers   1,700
CDW Computer Centers Inc.; Vernon Hills; direct
  selling   1,563
Empower HR Inc.; Arlington Heights; single-family
  housing construction   1,500
Baxter International Inc.; Deerfield; pharmaceuticals
  1,500
Commodities Inc.; Deerfield; mail order   1,500
Trustmark Insurance Co.; Lake Forest; health insurance
  1,500
Condell Medical Center; Libertyville   1,500
Motorola Communications and Electronics Inc.;
  Northbrook; motor vehicle parts/accessories   1,500

Evanston Northwestern Healthcare Corp. Hospital;
  Highland Park   1,400
International Society for the Study of Dissociation;
  Northbrook; mental health professionals   1,400
William Rainey Harper Community College; Palatine
  1,307
Household Financial Group; Prospect Heights; business
  and consumer lending, credit   1,300
Courtesy Corp.; Buffalo Grove; injection molding of
  plastics   1,300
Forest Lake Hospital; Lake Forest   1,286
Walgreen Co.; Deerfield; drug stores   1,200
W. W. Grainger Inc.; Lake Forest; electric motors
  1,200
Siemens Building Technologies Inc.; Buffalo Grove; air
  conditioning, refrigeration controls   1,200
Federal Cleaning Contractors Inc.; Northbrook;
  janitorial service   1,153
Bond Drug Co. of Illinois; Deerfield; drug stores   1,100
Takeda Pharmaceuticals North America Inc.;
  Lincolnshire; pharmaceuticals   1,100
Victory Memorial Hospital Assn.; Waukegan   1,088
Motorola Inc.; Arlington Heights; cellular telephones
  1,000
Walgreens Health Initiatives Inc.; Deerfield;
  pharmaceuticals, mail order   1,000
Zenith Electronics Corp.; Glenview; household
  audio/video equipment   1,000
Medline Industries Inc.; Mundelein; orthopedic,
  prosthetic, surgical supplies   1,000
Hasbro Inc.; Vernon Hills; dolls and stuffed toys   1,000
Tiger Electronics; Vernon Hills; toys   1,000
Quill Corp.; Lincolnshire; mail order   1,000
Caremark Inc.; Northbrook; medical and hospital
  equipment   900
Fill-Mor Holding Inc.; Winnetka; jewelry   900
American Seating Co.; Highwood; public building and
  related furniture   895
Lake County; Waukegan; county government   850
Motorola Automotive Energy and Controls Products Inc.;
  Northbrook; automotive electrical equipment   800
Tap Holdings Inc.; Lake Forest; pharmaceuticals   740
Paslode Corp. Inc.; Vernon Hills; hand and edge tools
  740
Illinois Dept. of Human Services; Waukegan   731
Addison Wesley Educational Publisher Inc.; Glenview;
  textbooks   730
Montclair Hotel Investors Inc.; Deerfield; management
  services   700
William M. Mercer Inc.; Deerfield; compensation and
  benefits planning   700
Zenith Electronics Corp.; Lincolnshire; household
  audio/video equipment   700
Navy Exchange Service Command; Waukegan;
  Army-Navy goods stores   700
Bombardier Motor Corp. of America; Waukegan;
  outboard motors   700
Pactiv Corp.; Wheeling; box-making machines   700
Hewitt Associates; Deerfield; human resource consulting
  675
American Hotel Register Co.; Vernon Hills; hotel
  equipment and supplies   650

Marriott International Inc.; Lincolnshire; resort hotel 610

American Colloid Co.; Arlington Heights; bentonite mining 604

Lutheran Home and Services for the Aged Inc.; Arlington Heights 600

CCH Inc.; Riverwoods; statistical reports 600

Lifesource Blood Services; Glenview; blood-related health services 600

Allstate Life Insurance Co.; Vernon Hills; life insurance 600

Zebra Technologies Corp.; Vernon Hills; bar code (magnetic ink) printers 600

Deluxe Video Services Inc.; Northbrook; video tape or disk reproduction 600

Handi-Foil Corp.; Wheeling; bakery goods, frozen foods foil containers 600

Solo Cup Co.; Highland Park; plastic cups 575

New Trier Township High School District; Winnetka 573

Lieberman Management Services Inc.; Buffalo Grove; nonresidential building operators 565

Kraft Foods Inc.; Glenview; food research 560

Illinois Student Assistance Commission; Deerfield 550

Pactiv Corp.; Lake Forest; pressed/molded pulp and fiber products 550

Logs Financial Services Inc.; Northbrook; financial management for business 550

Northshore School District; Highland Park 528

Fujisawa Healthcare Inc.; Deerfield; pharmaceuticals 515

Woodhead Industries Inc.; Deerfield; power and distribution transformers 500

Illinois Tool Works Inc.; Glenview; metal strapping 500

Scott Foresman Inc.; Glenview; book publishing 500

Mitsubishi Electronics America Inc.; Vernon Hills; electronic parts and equipment 500

Sears Roebuck and Co. Inc.; Vernon Hills; department stores 500

Borden Inc.; Northbrook; dried fruits, vegetables, soup mixes 500

Herman M. Finch University of Health Sciences/Chicago Medical School; North Chicago 500

Pactiv Corp.; Lincolnshire; honeycomb core and board 500

First Data Resources Inc.; Buffalo Grove; data processing 500

Orval Kent Food Co. Inc.; Wheeling; ready-to-eat food 500

Illinois 11th District

South Chicago exurbs — Joliet; part of Bloomington-Normal

Beginning south of Chicago in suburban Will County, the 11th heads west through the old industrial city of Joliet and into farming country, with a sliver making a left turn in La Salle County to run south parallel to Interstate 39 as it heads to Bloomington-Normal. *(See map p. 297.)*

Will County (shared mostly with the 13th District) is the district's most populous jurisdiction and has seen an influx of young suburban families. Will had a 41 percent growth rate in the 1990s and voted narrowly for GOP presidential nominee George W. Bush in 2000. The county is at the nexus of a plan to build a third Chicago metro-area airport in Peotone. Residents in the 11th's northern reaches say a new airport would boost the suburbs, though rural residents worry it may disrupt their way of life.

South of Will, the 11th includes Kankakee County before assuming a more rural posture west of those two counties as it takes in a small portion of Livingston County, all of Grundy and La Salle Counties, and most of Bureau County before its jaunt south to Bloomington.

In the 1990s the 11th was the most eclectic district in Illinois, running from southeastern Chicago through some racially diverse Cook County suburbs and ending in La Salle's farming communities. But 2001 redistricting made the district less urban and suburban by moving the Cook County portions to the 2nd and adding the southern leg to McLean County's Bloomington-Normal region, which is home to Illinois State University and is shared with the 15th District.

The 11th remains politically competitive on the numbers, but the removal of Democratic-leaning southern Cook County lessened the district's Democratic influence. The old 11th voted for Al Gore in 2000 by 8 percentage points; the new district backed Bush by 2 points.

Major Industry

Farm equipment manufacturing, agriculture.

Notable

The Midewin National Tallgrass Prairie is in Will County.

Election Returns

	Republican		Democratic		Other	
President 2000	128,280	49.6%	122,979	47.6%	7,269	2.8%
House 2002	124,192	64.3%	68,893	35.7%		

District Profile

Population 653,647

Total area (square miles) 4,284.2
Land area (square miles) 4,240.9

Population per square mile 154.1

Counties (2000 population)

Bureau (pt.) 28,021	Livingston (pt.) 411
Grundy 37,535	McLean (pt.) 81,582
Kankakee 103,833	Will (pt.) 287,644
La Salle 111,509	Woodford (pt.) 3,112

Cities and other areas over 10,000 (2000 population)
Bloomington (pt.) 30,298
Bourbonnais village 15,256
Bradley village 12,784
Frankfort village (pt.) 10,391
Joliet (pt.) 105,052
Kankakee 27,491
Mokena village 14,583
Morris 11,928
New Lenox village (pt.) 17,742
Normal town (pt.) 30,662
Ottawa 18,307
Streator (pt.) 13,948

Race and Hispanic or Latino origin*
White 83.7%
Black or African American 7.8%
American Indian or Alaska Native 0.1%
Asian 0.8%
Native Hawaiian or other Pacific Islander 0.0%
Some other race 0.1%
Hispanic or Latino origin 6.7%
Two or more races 0.9%

*As percentage of total population.

Ancestry*
Dutch 1.7%   Italian 6.0%
English 5.8%   Norwegian 1.8%
French 2.8%   Polish 5.6%
German 18.4%   Swedish 2.2%
Irish 11.8%   USA/American 3.4%

*As estimated percentage of total population.

Universities and colleges, 2000–2001 enrollment
Illinois State University, Normal 20,755
Illinois Valley Community College, Oglesby 3,794
Illinois Wesleyan University, Bloomington 2,027
Joliet Junior College, Joliet 11,334
Kankakee Community College, Kankakee 3,120
Mennonite College of Nursing, Bloomington 207
Olivet Nazarene University, Bourbonnais 2,859
University of St. Francis, Joliet 4,332

Newspapers and circulation

	District circulation	Total circulation
Bloomington Pantagraph	19,474	47,270
Chicago Suburban Newspapers	28,120	116,127
Chicago Sun-Times	9,329	474,127
Chicago Tribune	14,493	664,927
Daily Southtown, Chicago	3,001	47,715
Juliet Herald News	27,353	37,243
Kankakee Daily Journal	22,389	27,278
La Salle News Tribune	14,485	18,234
Ottawa Times	10,935	11,348
Peoria Journal Star	1,248	67,115
Streator Times Press	5,027	7,350
*USA Today**	2,801	1,674,376

*See Sources and Explanations in the front of the volume.

Television stations and affiliations
Chicago	69%	WBBM	CBS
Chicago	69%	WCIU	Independent
Chicago	69%	WCPX	PAX
Chicago	69%	WFLD	FOX
Chicago	69%	WGBO	Univision
Chicago	69%	WGN	WB
Chicago	69%	WJYS	Independent
Chicago	69%	WLS	ABC
Chicago	69%	WMAQ	NBC
Chicago	69%	WPWR	UPN
Chicago	69%	WSNS	Telemundo
Chicago	69%	WTTW	PBS
Chicago	69%	WWTO	Independent
Chicago	69%	WYCC	PBS
Chicago	69%	WYIN	PBS
Davenport-Rock Island-Moline	16%	KLJB	FOX
Davenport-Rock Island-Moline	16%	KLJB	FOX
Davenport-Rock Island-Moline	16%	KQCT	PBS
Davenport-Rock Island-Moline	16%	KWQC	NBC
Davenport-Rock Island-Moline	16%	WHBF	CBS
Davenport-Rock Island-Moline	16%	WQAD	ABC
Davenport-Rock Island-Moline	16%	WQPT	PBS
Peoria-Bloomington	15%	WEEK	NBC
Peoria-Bloomington	15%	WHOI	ABC
Peoria-Bloomington	15%	WMBD	CBS
Peoria-Bloomington	15%	WTVP	PBS
Peoria-Bloomington	15%	WYZZ	FOX

Cable systems and subscribers
Comcast 67,528
Galaxy 1,073
Insight 53,402
Manhattan Cable TV 1,203
Mediacom 23,082
Seneca Cable TV 893

Military installations, September 2001
Marseilles Military Training Area, Marseilles 122

Businesses and other major employers
Royce Group Inc.; Frankfort; temporary help service 4,764
Mitsubishi Motor Manufacturing of America Inc.; Normal; automobiles 3,300
Provena Hospital; Joliet 2,300
Caterpillar Inc.; Joliet; construction machinery 2,000
Empress Casino Joliet Corp.; Joliet; gambling 2,000
Riverside Hospital; Kankakee 1,500
Silver Cross Hospital; Joliet 1,400
Illinois Dept. of Human Services; Kankakee 1,350
Illinois Dept. of Corrections; Joliet 1,200
Provena Health St. Mary's Hospital; Kankakee 1,100
Harrah's Entertainment Inc.; Joliet; hotels 1,050
Panduit Corp.; New Lenox; electric conduits and fittings 1,000
Aventis Behring; Bradley; blood derivatives 1,000
Exelon Corp.; Marseilles; electric services 850
Joliet Junior College District; Joliet 814
Exelon Corp.; Morris; electric power generation 812
Commonwealth Edison Co.; Braceville; power plant construction 750
Olivet Nazarene University Inc.; Bourbonnais 750
Will County; Joliet; county government 700
Equistar Chemicals; Morris; industrial organic chemicals 700
Illinois State Board of Education; Normal 700
Joliet Public School District; Joliet 655
ExxonMobil Oil Corp.; Channahon; oil/gas exploration services 650
Bloomington School District; Bloomington 650
Applied Systems Inc.; University Park; computer software development 600
Illinois Valley Community College; Oglesby 600
Anderson Financial Network Inc.; Bloomington; business planning, organizing services 587
Illinois Valley Community Hospital Inc.; Peru 570
Federal Signal Corp.; University Park; vehicle, marine, industrial sirens 568
Georgia-Pacific Corp.; University Park; lumber, plywood, and millwork 550

Illinois Dept. of Transportation; Ottawa   550
Harper-Wyman Co.; Princeton; valves and pipe fittings
  550
Illinois Wesleyan University; Bloomington   550
Ottawa Community Hospital; Ottawa   540
Illinois Dept. of Corrections; Joliet   500
T. J. Lambrecht Construction Inc.; Joliet; excavation
  work   500
Morris Hospital; Morris   500
Johnson and Johnson; Wilmington; sanitary paper
  products   500
Kraft Foods Inc.; Kankakee; coupon redemption service
  500
Kmart Corp.; Manteno; department stores   500
Sears Logistics Services Inc.; Manteno; packaging and
  labeling services   500
Baker and Taylor Inc.; Momence; books   500
Monterey Mushrooms Inc.; Princeton; mushroom
  production   500
Myers Peabody Corp.; Streator; off-highway trucks   500
Heartland Community College District; Normal   500

Illinois 12th District

Southwest — Belleville, East St. Louis, Carbondale

The 12th begins in the St. Louis suburbs along the Mississippi River and extends south along the river to the end of the state, where the Mississippi and Ohio Rivers converge near Cairo.

Illinois' worst urban blight is not in Chicago—it is 300 miles southwest in East St. Louis, where severe white flight and industrial decay nearly bankrupted the city. In the late 1980s the city cut off most municipal services, including trash collection. Federal and state intervention, coupled with new revenue from casino gambling, restored most city services by the mid-1990s, but residents still face high unemployment and poverty.

Other cities in the 12th also stand on precarious ground. Alton had to bolster its industrial base with riverboat gambling. Residents of Belleville, where nearby Scott Air Force Base is the largest employer, worry about defense cutbacks. Coal mining has almost disappeared from the hilly, southern end of the district with the mechanization of the industry and enactment of the 1990 Clean Air Act. Higher education remains one of the few steadfast employers: Jackson County's economy is bolstered by Southern Illinois University in Carbondale, which has 22,000 students.

The district's economic anxiety and relatively large minority population (blacks make up 16 percent of the population) make it solid Democratic turf. Democrat Rod R. Blagojevich carried nine of the 11 counties wholly or partly within the 12th in his successful 2002 race for governor. St. Clair County, which includes East St. Louis, is the only Illinois county other than Chicago-based Cook to vote Democratic in the past seven presidential elections. Some corn and hog farmers in western counties lean Republican, but they are too few to sway the district.

Major Industry
Manufacturing, higher education, riverboat gambling, agriculture.

Notable
Cahokia Mounds, a prehistoric civilization, was designated by the United Nations as a World Heritage Site in 1982.

Election Returns

	Republican		Democratic		Other	
President 2000	116,724	43.4%	144,548	53.8%	7,634	2.8%
House 2002	58,440	30.8%	131,580	69.2%		

District Profile

Population   653,647

Total area (square miles)   4,556.3
  Land area (square miles)   4,424.8

Population per square mile   147.7

Counties (2000 population)

Alexander	9,590	Pulaski	7,348
Franklin	39,018	Randolph	33,893
Jackson	59,612	St. Clair	256,082
Madison (pt.)	121,186	Union	18,293
Monroe	27,619	Williamson (pt.)	57,912
Perry	23,094		

Cities and other areas over 10,000 (2000 population)
  Alton   30,496
  Belleville   41,410
  Cahokia village   16,391
  Carbondale   20,681
  East St. Louis   31,542
  Fairview Heights   15,034
  Granite City   31,301
  Herrin   11,298
  Marion (pt.)   16,032
  Murphysboro   13,295
  O'Fallon   21,910
  Swansea village   10,579
  Wood River (pt.)   11,296

Race and Hispanic or Latino origin*
  White   79.7%
  Black or African American   16.3%
  American Indian or Alaska Native   0.2%
  Asian   0.8%
  Native Hawaiian or other Pacific Islander   0.0%
  Some other race   0.1%
  Hispanic or Latino origin   1.8%
  Two or more races   1.0%

As percentage of total population.

Ancestry*

Dutch	1.3%	Italian	2.4%
English	6.6%	Polish	1.8%
French	2.9%	Scotch-Irish	1.1%
German	18.6%	USA/American	6.4%
Irish	8.7%		

As estimated percentage of total population.

Universities and colleges, 2000–2001 enrollment
  Belleville Area College, Belleville   13,351
  John A. Logan College, Carterville   7,675

McKendree College, Lebanon 1,993
Metropolitan Community College, East St. Louis 1,095
Shawnee Community College, Ullin 1,880
Southern Illinois University-Carbondale, Carbondale 22,552

Newspapers and circulation

	District circulation	Total circulation
Alton Telegraph	8,684	27,005
Belleville News-Democrat	41,772	53,540
Carbondale Southern Illinoisan	23,135	26,254
St. Louis Post-Dispatch	21,856	295,281
USA Today*	1,839	1,674,376

*See Sources and Explanations in the front of the volume.

Television stations and affiliations

Paducah-Cape Girardeau-Harrisburg-Mt. Vernon	61%	KBSI	FOX
Paducah-Cape Girardeau-Harrisburg-Mt. Vernon	61%	KFVS	CBS
Paducah-Cape Girardeau-Harrisburg-Mt. Vernon	61%	KPOB	ABC
Paducah-Cape Girardeau-Harrisburg-Mt. Vernon	61%	WDKA	WB
Paducah-Cape Girardeau-Harrisburg-Mt. Vernon	61%	WKMU	PBS
Paducah-Cape Girardeau-Harrisburg-Mt. Vernon	61%	WKPD	PBS
Paducah-Cape Girardeau-Harrisburg-Mt. Vernon	61%	WPSD	NBC
Paducah-Cape Girardeau-Harrisburg-Mt. Vernon	61%	WSIL	ABC
Paducah-Cape Girardeau-Harrisburg-Mt. Vernon	61%	WSIU	PBS
Paducah-Cape Girardeau-Harrisburg-Mt. Vernon	61%	WTCT	Independent
St. Louis	39%	KDNL	ABC
St. Louis	39%	KETC	PBS
St. Louis	39%	KMOV	CBS
St. Louis	39%	KNLC	Independent
St. Louis	39%	KPLR	WB
St. Louis	39%	KSDK	NBC
St. Louis	39%	KTVI	FOX
St. Louis	39%	WHSL	Independent
St. Louis	39%	WPXS	PAX

Cable systems and subscribers

Charter 92,675
Galaxy 2,158
Mediacom 30,034
Suscom 7,289

Military installations, September 2001

Scott Air Force Base, Shiloh 10,213
Charles Melvin Price Support Center, Granite City 576

Businesses and other major employers

National Steel Corp.; Granite City; hot-rolled steel sheet or strip 3,450
Protestant Memorial Medical Center Inc.; Belleville 1,975
Belleville Community College; Belleville 1,839
St. Elizabeth's Hospital; Belleville 1,600
Olin Corp.; East Alton; small arms ammunition 1,500
Casino Queen Inc.; East St. Louis; gambling 1,250
Sky Chefs Inc.; Chicago; caterers 1,100
Illinois Dept. of Corrections; Menard 1,071
Alton Memorial Hospital; Alton 1,000
Argosy Gaming Co.; Alton; gambling and lottery services 1,000
Alton Gaming Co.; Alton; nonresidential building operators 950
Community Health Systems Inc.; Granite City; skilled nursing care facilities 900
Cerro Copper Products Company Inc.; East St. Louis; copper tubing 900
Southern Illinois Hospital Services; Carbondale 900
St. Anthony's Hospital; Alton 836

Amsted Industries Inc.; Granite City; iron and steel forgings 800
Maytag Corp.; Herrin; laundry dryers, household or coin-operated 800
Toscopetro Corp.; Roxana; petroleum refining 750
John A. Logan College; Carterville 744
Gateway Regional Medical Center Inc.; Granite City 731
ASF-Keystone Inc.; Granite City; railroad equipment 700
Lanter Co.; Madison; trucking 700
Tosco Corp.; Wood River; gasoline service stations 700
Phillips Petroleum Co.; Roxana; petroleum refining 680
Illinois Dept. of Human Services; Anna 660
Southern Illinois University; Carbondale 650
Spartan Light Metal Products Inc.; Sparta; aluminum die-castings 634
Cintas Corp.; Chicago; uniforms and work clothing 600
Wal-Mart Stores Inc.; Carbondale; discount department stores 600
Tower Automotive Inc.; Granite City; automotive frames 566
Solutia Inc.; East St. Louis; industrial organic chemicals 560
Crownline Boats Inc.; West Frankfort; fiberglass boats 550
Challenge Unlimited Inc.; Granite City; sheltered workshop 500
Midcoast Aviation Inc.; East St. Louis; aircraft servicing, repairing 500
Belleville Public School District; Belleville 500
St. Clair County; Belleville; county government 500
U.S. Defense Dept.; Scott Air Force Base 500
Illinois Dept. of Human Services; Chester 500
Old Ben Coal Co.; Coulterville; bituminous strip mining 500
PCA International Inc.; Sparta; photographic studios, portrait 500
Gilster-Mary Lee Corp.; Steeleville; packaging and labeling services 500

Illinois 13th District

Southwest Chicago suburbs — Naperville

More than half of the suburban Chicago-based 13th's population lives in the southern part of booming DuPage County. The district's most populous city is Naperville, which has tripled its population since 1980. Sprawling subdivisions and a newly refurbished downtown characterize this fairly young suburb. *(See map p. 297.)*

Argonne National Laboratory, in southeast DuPage, and Fermi National Accelerator Laboratory, just over the border in the 14th District, have made the area a scientific research hub and provide a prime source of jobs for district residents.

Naperville and Oak Brook have become leading business centers outside Chicago and are home to a growing number of corporate headquarters. Oak Brook, home to headquarters for McDonald's, is about ten miles south of O'Hare Airport and sits near the nexus of Interstates 88, 294, and 290, which has abetted its development. These cities increasingly draw in commuters, creating serious traffic problems in suburban communities.

Nearly one-third of the population lives in northern Will County communities such as Bolingbrook and Romeoville. The rest live in the southwestern corner of Cook. Redistricting in 2001 required the 13th, Illinois's fastest-growing district in the 1990s, to shed more than 100,000 people (mostly to the 1st and 11th districts).

Voters in the 13th tend to be white-collar executive types, loyal to free enterprise. It is a reliably Republican district that comfortably backed George W. Bush in the 2000 presidential election. Many residents, however, hold moderate views on family and women's issues (such as equal pay and child care) and environmental protection.

Major Industry
Scientific research, health care, insurance.

Notable
Hamburger University, McDonald's management training center, is located in Oak Brook.

Election Returns

	Republican		Democratic		Other	
President 2000	148,621	55.2%	113,450	42.1%	7,166	2.7%
House 2002	139,546	70.3%	59,069	29.7%		

District Profile

Population   653,647

Total area (square miles)   361.5
Land area (square miles)   354.5

Population per square mile   1,843.9

Counties (2000 population)
Cook (pt.)   85,799
DuPage (pt.)   363,695
Will (pt.)   204,153

Cities and other areas over 10,000 (2000 population)
Aurora (pt.)   40,846
Bolingbrook village   56,321
Crest Hill (pt.)   10,782
Darien   22,860
Downers Grove village (pt.)   45,139
Goodings Grove CDP   17,084
Hinsdale village (pt.)   17,349
Lemont village   13,098
Lisle village (pt.)   20,993
Lockport   15,191
Naperville (pt.)   128,358
Orland Park village (pt.)   23,729
Plainfield village (pt.)   10,815
Romeoville village   21,153
Tinley Park village (pt.)   22,020
Westmont village (pt.)   23,310
Woodridge village   30,934

Race and Hispanic or Latino origin*
White   81.6%
Black or African American   4.9%
American Indian or Alaska Native   0.1%
Asian   6.6%
Native Hawaiian or other Pacific Islander   0.0%
Some other race   0.1%
Hispanic or Latino origin   5.5%
Two or more races   1.2%

*As percentage of total population.

Ancestry*
Dutch   1.5%
English   5.3%
French   1.7%
German   16.5%
Irish   13.1%
Italian   7.7%
Lithuanian   1.4%
Norwegian   1.2%
Polish   10.0%
Swedish   2.2%
USA/American   1.9%

*As estimated percentage of total population.

Universities and colleges, 2000–2001 enrollment
Benedictine University, Lisle   2,842
ITT Technical Institute, Burr Ridge   204
Lewis University, Romeoville   4,304
North Central College, Naperville   2,532

Newspapers and circulation

	District circulation	Total circulation
Arlington Heights Daily Herald	9,439	148,825
Chicago Suburban Newspapers	10,562	116,127
Chicago Sun-Times	24,980	474,127
Chicago Tribune	67,797	664,927
Daily Southtown, Chicago	5,225	47,715
Juliet Herald News	8,963	37,243
Naperville Sun	20,534	21,230
*USA Today**	5,080	1,674,376

*See Sources and Explanations in the front of the volume.

Television stations and affiliations
Chicago	100%	WBBM	CBS
Chicago	100%	WCIU	Independent
Chicago	100%	WCPX	PAX
Chicago	100%	WFLD	FOX
Chicago	100%	WGBO	Univision
Chicago	100%	WGN	WB
Chicago	100%	WJYS	Independent
Chicago	100%	WLS	ABC
Chicago	100%	WMAQ	NBC
Chicago	100%	WPWR	UPN
Chicago	100%	WSNS	Telemundo
Chicago	100%	WTTW	PBS
Chicago	100%	WWTO	Independent
Chicago	100%	WYCC	PBS
Chicago	100%	WYIN	PBS

Cable systems and subscribers
Comcast   95,716
Optel Cable   843

Military installations, September 2001
Parkhurst U.S. Army Reserve Center, Darien   428

Businesses and other major employers

Employco Inc.; Westmont; human resource consulting 15,000

Aramark SM Management Services Inc.; Downers Grove; management services 11,805

Chicago Bridge and Iron Co.; Plainfield structural steel erection 5,950

University of Chicago; Lemont; energy research 4,000

ServiceMaster Aviation Management Co.; Downers Grove; building maintenance 3,000

BP America Inc.; Warrenville; petroleum products 2,500

Edward Hospital; Naperville 2,442

BP America Inc.; Naperville; petroleum products 2,000

Illinois Toll Highway Authority; Downers Grove 1,900

Glen Ellyn Clinic; Downers Grove 1,500

McDonald's Corp.; Oak Brook; fast-food restaurant chain 1,500

Andrew International Services Corp.; Orland Park; microwave communication equipment 1,400

Tellabs Operations Inc.; Bolingbrook; telephone and telegraph apparatus 1,300

International Truck and Engine Corp.; Warrenville; truck and tractor truck assembly 1,200

Ondeo Nalco Co.; Naperville; corrosion preventive lubricant 1,155

Meijers; Aurora; grocery stores 1,000

Worldcom Inc.; Downers Grove; local/long-distance telephone 1,000

Ace Hardware Corp.; Oak Brook; paints, varnishes, and supplies 1,000

Metropolitan Life Insurance Co.; Aurora; insurance agents and brokers 950

Copley Memorial Hospital Inc.; Aurora 930

Mid America Bank; Clarendon Hills; federal savings banks 900

Tyco Electronics Corp.; Downers Grove; primary batteries 800

Material Management; Hinsdale; materials management consultant 800

Molex Inc.; Lisle; electronic connectors 800

Allied Van Lines Inc.; Naperville; household goods transport 800

Northern Illinois Gas Co.; Naperville; natural gas distribution 800

U.S. Postal Service; Fox Valley 800

Citgo Petroleum Corp.; Lemont; petroleum refining 700

Quantum Foods Inc.; Bolingbrook; prepared beef products 700

Kehe Food Distributors Inc.; Romeoville; food supplier 700

Westell Inc.; Aurora; telephone and telegraph apparatus 700

Initial Security Inc.; Naperville; automobile recovery service 650

Valley View Public Schools; Lockport 618

Dynagear Inc.; Downers Grove; motor vehicle parts/accessories 600

Tellabs Operations Inc.; Lisle; telephone and telegraph apparatus 600

PDV Midwest Refining; Bolingbrook; petroleum refining 540

First Student Inc.; Joliet; bus charters 500

Sears Roebuck and Co. Inc.; Orland Park; department stores 500

Pepperidge Farm Inc.; Downers Grove; bread baking 500

Tricon Industries Inc.; Downers Grove; molding primary plastics 500

Wilton Industries Inc.; Downers Grove; kitchen tools and utensils 500

ADT Security Services Inc.; Oak Brook; electrical equipment 500

Illinois 14th District

North Central — Aurora, Elgin, DeKalb

Most people in the 14th live on the district's eastern side, in established towns along the Fox River valley. West of the river, prairies and farms stretch to the district's end in Henry County, nearly to the Mississippi River. Rich in hay, soybeans, and corn, the flat landscape is interrupted only by Northern Illinois University in DeKalb. *(See map p. 297.)*

The district's population center is Kane County, a fast-growing area on the outskirts of metropolitan Chicago. The district's largest cities, Aurora and Elgin, suffered a period of heavy manufacturing decline in the 1980s but have recovered by promoting industrial parks and opening riverboat casinos. One of Aurora's major employers is the heavy-equipment manufacturer Caterpillar. The cities also have benefited from job growth in nearby Naperville and Schaumburg, suburban cities that have emerged as business centers outside Chicago.

Both Elgin and Aurora are about one-third Hispanic, a vestige of the days when DuPage County farms were cultivated by migrant labor. Those farms have now been paved over and built upon, but many of the migrant workers remained in the area. Only three other Illinois districts—the Chicago-area 3rd, 4th, and 5th—have a larger Hispanic population than the 14th, which is almost one-fifth Hispanic.

While the minority influence tends to help Democrats, the 14th overall has a strong Republican tilt, mostly because of the GOP leanings of Kane County, Kendall County (which includes U.S. House Speaker J. Dennis Hastert's hometown of Yorkville), and northwestern DuPage County. GOP-friendly suburban and rural voters far outnumber the cities' blue-collar and minority Democrats. George W. Bush carried the district by 12 percentage points in the 2000 presidential election.

Major Industry

Farm machinery and other manufacturing, riverboat gambling, agriculture.

Notable

Former President Ronald Reagan's birthplace in Tampico and boyhood home in Dixon are operated as local museums.

Election Returns

	Republican		Democratic		Other	
President 2000	129,745	54.4%	101,369	42.5%	7,428	3.1%
House 2002	135,198	74.1%	47,165	25.9%		

District Profile

Population 653,647

Total area (square miles) 2,866.2
  Land area (square miles) 2,851.6

Population per square mile 229.2

Counties (2000 population)

Bureau (pt.)	976	Kane	404,119
DeKalb (pt.)	72,925	Kendall	54,544
DuPage (pt.)	51,331	Lee	36,062
Henry (pt.)	22,612	Whiteside (pt.)	11,078

Cities and other areas over 10,000 (2000 population)

Aurora (pt.) 102,144
Batavia 23,866
Carpentersville village 30,586
DeKalb 39,018
Dixon 15,941
Elgin (pt.) 74,013
Geneva 19,515
North Aurora village 10,585
Oswego village 13,326
South Elgin village 16,100
St. Charles 27,896
Sycamore (pt.) 12,007
West Chicago (pt.) 23,449

Race and Hispanic or Latino origin*

White 74.0%
Black or African American 4.6%
American Indian or Alaska Native 0.1%
Asian 1.8%
Native Hawaiian or other Pacific Islander 0.0%
Some other race 0.1%
Hispanic or Latino origin 18.5%
Two or more races 1.0%

*As percentage of total population.

Ancestry*

Dutch	1.4%	Norwegian	2.3%
English	6.0%	Polish	4.7%
French	1.9%	Scottish	1.1%
German	18.9%	Swedish	3.3%
Irish	9.9%	USA/American	2.9%
Italian	4.3%		

*As estimated percentage of total population.

Universities and colleges, 2000–2001 enrollment

Aurora University, Aurora 2,391
Elgin Community College, Elgin 10,174
Judson College, Elgin 1,111
Northern Illinois University, DeKalb 23,248
Sauk Valley Community College, Dixon 2,386
Waubonsee Community College, Sugar Grove 7,602

Newspapers and circulation

	District circulation	Total circulation
Arlington Heights Daily Herald	22,075	148,825
*Aurora Beacon News**	26,635	28,061
Chicago Suburban Newspapers	45,592	116,127
Chicago Sun-Times	9,645	474,127
Chicago Tribune	29,917	664,927
DeKalb Daily Chronicle	5,929	9,035
Dixon Telegraph	6,930	9,165
Elgin Courier News	12,043	16,812
Kane County Chronicle	13,287	13,332
Moline Dispatch	4,520	27,065
Quad-City Times, Davenport	1,122	51,390
Sterling Daily Gazette	4,767	12,472
*USA Today**	2,663	1,674,376

*See Sources and Explanations in the front of the volume.

Television stations and affiliations

Chicago	45%	WBBM	CBS
Chicago	45%	WCIU	Independent
Chicago	45%	WCPX	PAX
Chicago	45%	WFLD	FOX
Chicago	45%	WGBO	Univision
Chicago	45%	WGN	WB
Chicago	45%	WJYS	Independent
Chicago	45%	WLS	ABC
Chicago	45%	WMAQ	NBC
Chicago	45%	WPWR	UPN
Chicago	45%	WSNS	Telemundo
Chicago	45%	WTTW	PBS
Chicago	45%	WWTO	Independent
Chicago	45%	WYCC	PBS
Chicago	45%	WYIN	PBS
Davenport-Rock Island-Moline	30%	KLJB	FOX
Davenport-Rock Island-Moline	30%	KLJB	FOX
Davenport-Rock Island-Moline	30%	KQCT	PBS
Davenport-Rock Island-Moline	30%	KWQC	NBC
Davenport-Rock Island-Moline	30%	WHBF	CBS
Davenport-Rock Island-Moline	30%	WQAD	ABC
Davenport-Rock Island-Moline	30%	WQPT	PBS
Rockford	25%	WIFR	CBS
Rockford	25%	WQRF	FOX
Rockford	25%	WREX	NBC
Rockford	25%	WTVO	ABC

Cable systems and subscribers

Comcast 80,788
Insight 6,238
Mediacom 6,599

Businesses and other major employers

Northern Illinois University Inc.; DeKalb 3,970
Dial Corp.; Montgomery; soap and other detergents 3,716
Caterpillar Inc.; Aurora; construction machinery 3,300
Universities Research Assn. Inc.; Batavia; noncommercial research organization 2,293
Specialty Equipment Manufacturing Corp.; Aurora; commercial cooking equipment 2,290
Fermi National Accelerator Laboratory; Batavia; noncommercial research organization 2,150
Hollywood Casino-Aurora Inc.; Aurora; gambling 1,700
Grand Victoria Casino; Elgin; gambling 1,500
Sherman Hospital; Elgin 1,300
Illinois Dept. of Human Services; Elgin 1,250
Delnor-Community Hospital; Geneva 1,200
Illinois Office of Emergency Management; Geneva 1,200

Eastman Chemical Co.; Carpentersville; plastic materials and resins 1,100

Dreyer Clinic Inc.; Aurora 1,100

East Aurora Council; Aurora; labor organization 1,000

Elgin Community College; Elgin 950

Ameritech Mobile Communications Inc.; Elgin; cellular telephones 900

Provena Hospitals; Elgin 900

Kane County; Geneva; county government 900

A. C. Nielsen Co.; Oswego; market analysis or research 900

Provena Health Hospital; Aurora 880

Waubonsee Community College; Sugar Grove 850

U.S. Federal Aviation Administration; Aurora 800

Suncast Corp.; Batavia; lawn furniture 800

Carmax Auto SuperStores Inc.; Naperville; new and used car dealers 800

Raynor Manufacturing Co.; Dixon; metal garage doors 800

Kishwaukee Community Hospital; DeKalb 650

International Teams; Elgin; religious organization 600

Matsushita Electric Corp. of America; Elgin; electric power distribution 600

Montgomery Production Inc.; Montgomery; food preparations 600

Katherine Shaw Bethea Hospital Inc.; Dixon 600

SKF USA Inc.; Elgin; ball and roller bearings 550

Lyon Workspace Products; Montgomery; nonwood office/store shelving 550

Dukane Corp.; St. Charles; radio/TV communications equipment 535

AGCO Corp.; DeKalb; farm machinery and equipment 500

Goodyear Tire and Rubber Co.; DeKalb 500

Wal-Mart Stores Inc.; DeKalb; discount department stores 500

Ventana Medical Systems; St. Charles; computer and software stores 500

Farmers Group Inc.; Aurora; insurance agents and brokers 500

Illinois Dept. of Corrections; Dixon 500

Illinois Dept. of Transportation; Dixon 500

Illinois 15th District

East central — Champaign, Bloomington, Danville

Agriculture is the dominant industry in the 15th, which takes in all or part of 22 counties. Corn and soybean fields cover much of this area, and the crop yields are the state's highest in the counties south of Champaign, the district's main population center. Farmers produce feed and raw material for food products manufactured just over the border at Decatur-based Archer Daniels Midland Co. in the 17th District.

Scattered amid the farms are several midsize towns, including Danville, that are centered around agribusiness and manufacturing. Higher education is big business in this district, with 38,000 students at the University of Illinois flagship campus in Urbana, adjacent to Champaign. Bloomington-Normal has Illinois State and Illinois Wesleyan Universities, which are just outside the district in

the 11th. Bloomington, home to State Farm Insurance, leads downstate Illinois in insurance and finance.

Redistricting in 2001 altered the 15th's boundaries after slow growth in downstate Illinois cost the state one seat in reapportionment. Mapmakers dismantled the southeastern 19th District, and the remnants that were attached to the 15th form a long, narrow appendage that hugs the Indiana border. North to south, the 15th runs for more than 250 miles.

The district has a strong GOP lean. Republicans typically run strongest in counties north of Champaign, including Iroquois, Livingston, and Ford counties, which gave presidential candidate George W. Bush in 2000 and the GOP gubernatorial nominee in 2002 comfortable majorities, though both lost Illinois. Champaign County's academic community helps keep Democrats competitive: Champaign was the only county east of Decatur and south of Chicago that Bush lost in Illinois in 2000, though only narrowly.

Major Industry

Agriculture, higher education, food processing.

Notable

The Lincoln Log Cabin State Historic Site in Coles County preserves the last home of Abraham Lincoln's father and stepmother.

Election Returns

	Republican		Democratic		Other	
President 2000	148,176	54.0%	116,436	42.5%	9,616	3.5%
House 2002	134,650	65.2%	64,131	31.0%	7,836	3.8%

District Profile

Population 653,647

Total area (square miles) 10,122.4
Land area (square miles) 10,072.4

Population per square mile 64.9

Counties (2000 population)

Champaign 179,669	Iroquois 31,334
Clark 17,008	Lawrence (pt.) 8,624
Coles 53,196	Livingston (pt.) 39,267
Crawford 20,452	Macon (pt.) 15,221
Cumberland 11,253	McLean (pt.) 68,851
DeWitt 16,798	Moultrie 14,287
Douglas 19,922	Piatt 16,365
Edgar 19,704	Saline (pt.) 6,430
Edwards (pt.) 1,105	Vermilion 83,919
Ford 14,241	Wabash (pt.) 10,783
Gallatin (pt.) 1,171	White (pt.) 4,047

Cities and other areas over 10,000 (2000 population)
Bloomington (pt.) 34,510
Champaign 67,518
Charleston 21,039
Danville 33,904
Mattoon 18,291
Normal town (pt.) 14,724
Pontiac 11,864
Rantoul village 12,857
Urbana 36,395

Race and Hispanic or Latino origin*
White 88.5%
Black or African American 5.7%
American Indian or Alaska Native 0.2%
Asian 2.3%
Native Hawaiian or other Pacific Islander 0.0%
Some other race 0.1%
Hispanic or Latino origin 2.2%
Two or more races 1.0%

*As percentage of total population.

Ancestry*
Dutch 1.6%   Polish 1.6%
English 8.4%   Scotch-Irish 1.2%
French 2.2%   Scottish 1.3%
German 18.8%   Swedish 1.4%
Irish 9.2%   USA/American 7.9%
Italian 1.9%

*As estimated percentage of total population.

Universities and colleges, 2000–2001 enrollment
Danville Area Community College, Danville 2,505
Eastern Illinois University, Charleston 10,637
Heartland Community College, Bloomington 4,205
Illinois Eastern Community Colleges-Lincoln Trail
    College, Robinson 1,279
Illinois Eastern Community Colleges-Wabash Valley
    College, Mt. Carmel 3,421
Lake Land College, Mattoon 5,925
Parkland College, Champaign 8,026
University of Illinois-Urbana, Champaign 38,465

Newspapers and circulation

	District circulation	Total circulation
Bloomington Pantagraph	22,794	47,270
Champaign News Gazette	41,748	42,108
Charleston Times-Courier	6,668	6,769
Danville Commercial-News	13,924	16,253
Decatur Herald &Review	9,723	33,425
Evansville Courier &Press	1,579	69,254
Kankakee Daily Journal	4,881	27,278
Mattoon Journal Gazette	9,885	10,951
Streator Times Press	2,053	7,350
Terre Haute Tribune Star	2,331	29,738
*USA Today**	4,229	1,674,376
Vincennes Sun-Commercial	1,419	11,883

*See Sources and Explanations in the front of the volume.

Television stations and affiliations
Champaign-Springfield-Decatur	67%	WAND
Champaign-Springfield-Decatur	67%	WBUI
Champaign-Springfield-Decatur	67%	WCCU
Champaign-Springfield-Decatur	67%	WCFN
Champaign-Springfield-Decatur	67%	WCIA
Champaign-Springfield-Decatur	67%	WEIU
Champaign-Springfield-Decatur	67%	WICD
Champaign-Springfield-Decatur	67%	WICS
Champaign-Springfield-Decatur	67%	WILL
Champaign-Springfield-Decatur	67%	WRSP
Champaign-Springfield-Decatur	67%	WSEC
Peoria-Bloomington	17%	WEEK
Peoria-Bloomington	17%	WHOI
Peoria-Bloomington	17%	WMBD
Peoria-Bloomington	17%	WTVP
Peoria-Bloomington	17%	WYZZ
Terre Haute, IN	11%	WBAK
Terre Haute, IN	11%	WTHI
Terre Haute, IN	11%	WTWO
Terre Haute, IN	11%	WUSI
Terre Haute, IN	11%	WVUT
Evansville, IN	4%	WEHT
Evansville, IN	4%	WEVV
Evansville, IN	4%	WFIE
Evansville, IN	4%	WKMA
Evansville, IN	4%	WKOH
Evansville, IN	4%	WNIN
Evansville, IN	4%	WTVW
Paducah-Cape Girardeau-Harrisburg-Mt. Vernon	1%	KBSI
Paducah-Cape Girardeau-Harrisburg-Mt. Vernon	1%	KFVS
Paducah-Cape Girardeau-Harrisburg-Mt. Vernon	1%	KPOB
Paducah-Cape Girardeau-Harrisburg-Mt. Vernon	1%	WDKA
Paducah-Cape Girardeau-Harrisburg-Mt. Vernon	1%	WKMU
Paducah-Cape Girardeau-Harrisburg-Mt. Vernon	1%	WKPD
Paducah-Cape Girardeau-Harrisburg-Mt. Vernon	1%	WPSD
Paducah-Cape Girardeau-Harrisburg-Mt. Vernon	1%	WSIL
Paducah-Cape Girardeau-Harrisburg-Mt. Vernon	1%	WSIU
Paducah-Cape Girardeau-Harrisburg-Mt. Vernon	1%	WTCT

Cable systems and subscribers
CableVision Communications 3,643
Charter 16,713
Comcast 2,405
Galaxy 2,738
Heartland Cable 581
Illinet Communications 2,756
Illini Cablevision 4,515
Insight 60,491
Mediacom 53,803

Businesses and other major employers
State Farm Mutual Automobile Insurance Co.;
    Bloomington; automobile insurance 11,000
State Farm Life and Accident Assurance Co. Inc.;
    Bloomington; life insurance 4,226
Carle Clinic Inc.; Urbana 2,600
Country Mutual Insurance Co. Inc.; Bloomington;
    automobile insurance 2,000
Eastern Illinois University; Charleston 1,988
Bromenn Healthcare; Normal; hospital, nursing school
    1,700
Illinois State University; Champaign 1,500
R.R. Donnelley and Sons Co.; Mattoon; commercial
    printing 1,500
Christie Clinic Assn.; Champaign 1,500
Provena Covenant Medical Center; Urbana 1,450
U.S. Veterans Hospital; Danville 1,400
Sarah Bush Lincoln Health Center; Mattoon 1,216
United Air Lines Inc.; Rankin; air passenger carrier
    1,200
Verizon North Inc.; Bloomington; telephone
    communication 1,200
Textron Automotive Co.; Rantoul; molded plastics
    products 1,100
Provena Hospital; Danville 1,080
University of Illinois; Urbana 1,077

R. R. Donnelley and Sons Co.; Dwight; commercial printing 1,000

Caterpillar Inc.; Pontiac; automotive radiators 1,000

Illinois Dept. of Corrections; Champaign 1,000

Lake Land College; Mattoon 1,000

Illinois Power Co.; Clinton; electric power generation 957

Amergen Energy Co.; Clinton; electric services 925

Illinois Dept. of Corrections; Pontiac 902

OSF Healthcare System; Bloomington; hospital 900

Nacco Materials Handling Group Inc.; Danville; forklift trucks 900

State Farm Mutual Automobile Insurance Co.; Bloomington; insurance adjusters 800

Parkland College; Champaign 800

Independent Lift Truck Union; Danville; labor organization 800

McLane Co.; Danville; food supplier 787

Hershey Foods Corp.; Robinson; confectionery products 750

Masterbrand Cabinets Inc.; Arthur; wood kitchen cabinets 730

Snap-On Inc.; Mount Carmel; hand and edge tools 714

Supervalu Inc.; Urbana; warehousing 700

Hobbico Inc.; Champaign; model kits 700

U.S. Army Corps of Engineers; Champaign 700

Aid Assoc. for Lutherans/Lutheran Brotherhood; Mahomet; fraternal life insurance organization 700

Wal-Mart Stores Inc.; Normal; discount department stores 650

Jeld-Wen Inc.; Rantoul; millwork 640

R. R. Donnelley and Sons Co.; Pontiac; commercial printing 600

University of Illinois; Champaign 600

CCL Custom Manufacturing Inc.; Danville; filling pressure containers 600

Heatcraft Inc.; Danville; parts for heating, cooling, and refrigerating equipment 600

Genesis Health Ventures Inc.; Monticello; billing, bookkeeping service 600

Simonton Building Products Inc.; Paris; window frames and sash 600

Marathon Ashland Petroleum; Robinson; partly refined oils 600

General Electric Co.; Bloomington; electrical work 550

Quaker Oats Co.; Danville; food preparations 550

Herff Jones Inc.; Champaign; academic vestments (caps and gowns) 500

Meijer Inc.; Champaign; discount department stores 500

Bell Sports Inc.; Rantoul; athletic helmets 500

Wal-Mart Stores Inc.; Savoy 500

General Electric Co.; Mattoon; photoflash and photoflood lamps 500

Illinois Consolidated Telephone Co.; Mattoon; local telephone communications 500

Casey Tool and Machine Co. Inc.; Casey; spinning metal for the trade 500

TRW Inc.; Marshall; electron tubes 500

Illinois 16th District

North — Rockford, part of McHenry County

The 16th spans most of the Illinois-Wisconsin border, taking in Rockford and covering the rolling northern prairie where family farmers grow corn and raise dairy cows. (*See map p. 297.*)

At its eastern end, the district includes most of McHenry County, the fastest-growing county in Illinois during the 1990s at 42 percent. Located at the edge of Chicago's flourishing northwest counties, McHenry is quickly filling up with new suburban bedroom communities. Solidly GOP, it voted for George W. Bush by 20 percentage points in the 2000 presidential election. To the west is Boone County, which also is fast-growing and Republican-leaning.

About one-fourth of the district's voters live in Rockford (Winnebago County), an industrial hub and the state's second-largest city. Once the self-styled tool and die capital of the world, in the 1980s it became a poster child of Rust Belt decline, with unemployment often exceeding 20 percent. The city recovered by upgrading to high-tech manufacturing and expanding its exports to China, Mexico, and Canada.

Other counties in the 16th are among Illinois' leading dairy producers. Jo Daviess County, in the northwest corner, is a state leader in raising beef cattle and producing hay. Galena, in rolling hills near the Mississippi River, has a tourist-based economy.

Redistricting following the 2000 census made the 16th somewhat more rural by shedding part of McHenry to the 8th District and adding parts of the counties to the southwest.

More than 90 percent of the district's black residents live in Rockford, giving the city a base of loyal Democrats. But the 16th covers mostly conservative, Republican territory. Only once in the twentieth century did district voters elect a Democrat to the House.

Major Industry

Manufacturing, aircraft and machine parts, agriculture, trade.

Notable

The Ulysses S. Grant Home is in Galena; Rockford is known as the world's largest producer of fasteners.

Election Returns

	Republican		Democratic		Other	
President 2000	141,878	53.9%	113,020	43.0%	8,163	3.1%
House 2002	133,339	70.6%	55,488	29.4%		

District Profile

Population 653,647

Total area (square miles) 4,157.6
  Land area (square miles) 4,098.2

Population per square mile 159.5

Counties (2000 population)

Boone	41,786	Ogle	51,032
Carroll	16,674	Stephenson	48,979
DeKalb (pt.)	16,044	Whiteside (pt.)	19,916
Jo Daviess	22,289	Winnebago	278,418
McHenry (pt.)	158,509		

Cities and other areas over 10,000 (2000 population)

Algonquin village (pt.)   18,254
Belvidere   20,820
Cary village   15,531
Crystal Lake (pt.)   37,740
Freeport   26,443
Lake in the Hills village   23,152
Loves Park   20,044
Machesney Park village   20,759
Rockford   150,115

Race and Hispanic or Latino origin*

White   85.7%
Black or African American   5.3%
American Indian or Alaska Native   0.2%
Asian   1.3%
Native Hawaiian or other Pacific Islander   0.0%
Some other race   0.1%
Hispanic or Latino origin   6.5%
Two or more races   1.0%

*As percentage of total population.

Ancestry*

Dutch	2.0%	Italian	4.8%
English	6.7%	Norwegian	2.8%
French	1.9%	Polish	4.2%
German	21.8%	Swedish	4.9%
Irish	10.0%	USA/American	3.6%

*As estimated percentage of total population.

Universities and colleges, 2000–2001 enrollment

Highland Community College, Freeport   2,595
Kishwaukee College, Malta   3,663
Rock Valley College, Rockford   7,699
Rockford Business College, Rockford   318
Rockford College, Rockford   1,395

Newspapers and circulation

	District circulation	Total circulation
Arlington Heights Daily Herald	3,434	148,825
Chicago Sun-Times	2,227	474,127
Chicago Tribune	8,823	664,927
Clinton Herald	2,182	12,763
Crystal Lake Northwest Herald	18,180	34,938
DeKalb Daily Chronicle	3,007	9,035
Dixon Telegraph	2,208	9,165
Dubuque Telegraph Herald	2,495	28,283
Freeport Journal-Standard	13,323	13,493
Quad-City Times, Davenport	1,396	51,390
Rockford Register Star	58,508	69,985
Sterling Daily Gazette	4,984	12,472
USA Today*	2,655	1,674,376

*See Sources and Explanations in the front of the volume.

Television stations and affiliations

Rockford	51%	WIFR	CBS
Rockford	51%	WQRF	FOX
Rockford	51%	WREX	NBC
Rockford	51%	WTVO	ABC
Davenport-Rock Island-Moline	34%	KLJB	FOX
Davenport-Rock Island-Moline	34%	KLJB	FOX
Davenport-Rock Island-Moline	34%	KQCT	PBS
Davenport-Rock Island-Moline	34%	KWQC	NBC
Davenport-Rock Island-Moline	34%	WHBF	CBS
Davenport-Rock Island-Moline	34%	WQAD	ABC
Davenport-Rock Island-Moline	34%	WQPT	PBS
Chicago	15%	WBBM	CBS
Chicago	15%	WCIU	Independent
Chicago	15%	WCPX	PAX
Chicago	15%	WFLD	FOX
Chicago	15%	WGBO	Univision
Chicago	15%	WGN	WB
Chicago	15%	WJYS	Independent
Chicago	15%	WLS	ABC
Chicago	15%	WMAQ	NBC
Chicago	15%	WPWR	UPN
Chicago	15%	WSNS	Telemundo
Chicago	15%	WTTW	PBS
Chicago	15%	WWTO	Independent
Chicago	15%	WYCC	PBS
Chicago	15%	WYIN	PBS

Cable systems and subscribers

Charter   12,379
Comcast   24,768
Insight   88,807
Mediacom   14,892

Businesses and other major employers

Motorola Inc.; Harvard; telephone and communication equipment   4,000
DaimlerChrysler Corp.; Belvidere; automobiles   3,500
Rockford Memorial Hospital Inc.; Rockford   2,500
Honeywell International Inc.; Freeport; switchgear and switchboard apparatus   2,000
Quebecor Printing Mt. Morris Inc.; Mt. Morris; commercial printing   1,677
Ingersoll Milling Machine Co.; Rockford; metal-cutting machine tools   1,500
OSF Healthcare System Hospital; Rockford   1,500
Invensys Building Systems Inc.; Loves Park; building services monitoring controls   1,400
Winnebago County; Rockford; county government   1,350
Rock Valley Community College; Rockford   1,130
Newell Operating Co.; Rockford; market analysis or research   1,000
MCI Worldcom Communications Inc.; Rockford; local/long-distance telephone   1,000
Freeport Regional Health Care Foundation; Freeport; hospital management   950
American Bowling Congress; Poplar Grove; bowling center   920
Warner-Lambert Co.; Loves Park; chewing gum   902
AG Communication Systems Corp.; Genoa; telephone or telegraph switchboards   900

Woodward Governor Co.; Rockford; aircraft engines and parts   900

U.S. Postal Service; Cherry Valley   850

Precision Twist Drill Co.; Crystal Lake; drills (machine tool accessories)   800

Carpenter Contractors of America Inc.; Belvidere; carpentry work   800

Goodyear Tire and Rubber Co.; Freeport; truck or bus tires   800

Textron Fastening Systems; Rockford; nuts, rivets, and washers   800

Swedish American Hospital Assn. Inc.; Rockford   773

Conseco Annuity Assurance Co.; Rockford; medical insurance claim processing   750

Exelon Corp.; Byron; electric power generation   739

Economy Fire and Casualty Co. Inc.; Freeport; automobile insurance   700

Textron Fastening Systems; Rockford; metal heat treating   700

DOT Black Graphics Inc.; Crystal Lake; printing trade photocomposition   639

Rockford Products Corp.; Rockford; metal screws   630

Carrier Commerical Refrigeration Inc.; Rockton; ice cream manufacturing machinery   627

Rock YMCA River Valley; Rockford; youth organizations   620

Kable News Co.; Mt. Morris; magazines   600

U.S. Postal Service; Rockford   600

Eagle Ridge Lease Co.; Galena; inns   550

United Parcel Service Inc.; Rockford; courier services   550

General Electric Co.; Morrison; electric control equipment   550

Wal-Mart Stores Inc.; Sterling; discount department stores   510

Kishwaukee College; Malta   500

Amcore Financial Inc.; Rockford; commercial bank   500

Ron Weber and Associates Inc.; Machesney Park; telemarketing services   500

Illinois 17th District

West — Moline, Rock Island; part of Decatur and Springfield

The 17th is a vivid demonstration of the extremes Illinois mapmakers went to in 2001 to draw safe districts for incumbent House members. In the 1990s the 17th was a relatively compact district that split just two counties. The redrawn 17th is a geographic monstrosity, taking in nine full counties and parts of 14 others, hugging much of Illinois' border with the Mississippi River but reaching with tentacle-like appendages as far inland as Springfield and Decatur.

In 1837 John Deere developed the first self-cleaning steel plow in the present-day 17th, which includes rich farmland along the Mississippi and the cities of Rock Island and Moline, two of the four industrial Quad Cities that straddle the river into Iowa. Defense cutbacks have drained jobs from one of the district's industrial mainstays, the Rock Island Arsenal.

Corn, soybeans, and hogs fuel most of the rest of the district's economy. Even the industrial sector depends on agriculture: it is dominated by the nation's two largest farm equipment manufacturers. Sliding farm profits have forced the Quad Cities to recruit new types of manufacturing.

Redistricting gave the 17th—a politically competitive district in the 1990s—a decided Democratic tilt. Six of the nine counties wholly within the 17th voted for Al Gore in the 2000 presidential election. The Democratic vote in Rock Island, coupled with the Democratic lean of the parts of Springfield and Decatur that were drawn into the district, are enough to overcome the Republican tendencies of some rural areas.

Major Industry

Farm equipment manufacturing, agriculture, defense.

Notable

The Carl Sandburg Home in Galesburg is where the late poet was born; Wyatt Earp was born in Monmouth; Bishop Hill was established in 1846 by Swedish religious dissidents searching for a "utopia on the prairie."

Election Returns

	Republican		Democratic		Other	
President 2000	119,563	43.6%	146,548	53.5%	7,807	2.9%
House 2002	76,519	37.6%	127,093	62.4%		

District Profile

Population   653,647

Total area (square miles)   8,289.1
Land area (square miles)   8,120.1

Population per square mile   80.5

Counties (2000 population)

Adams (pt.) 55,850	Macoupin 49,019
Calhoun 5,084	Madison (pt.) 1,746
Christian (pt.) 6,860	McDonough 32,913
Fayette (pt.) 2,467	Mercer 16,957
Fulton 38,250	Montgomery (pt.) 15,278
Greene (pt.) 8,476	Pike (pt.) 4,809
Hancock 20,121	Rock Island 149,374
Henderson 8,213	Sangamon (pt.) 36,348
Henry (pt.) 28,408	Shelby (pt.) 1,960
Jersey (pt.) 3,646	Warren 18,735
Knox (pt.) 49,281	Whiteside (pt.) 29,659
Macon (pt.) 70,193	

Cities and other areas over 10,000 (2000 population)

Canton 15,288	Moline 43,768
Decatur (pt.) 58,701	Quincy 40,366
East Moline 20,333	Rock Island 39,684
Galesburg 33,706	Springfield (pt.) 28,952
Kewanee 12,944	Sterling (pt.) 13,775
Macomb 18,558	

Race and Hispanic or Latino origin*
White   87.3%
Black or African American   7.2%
American Indian or Alaska Native   0.2%
Asian   0.6%

Native Hawaiian or other Pacific Islander   0.0%
Some other race   0.1%
Hispanic or Latino origin   3.7%
Two or more races   1.0%

As percentage of total population.

Ancestry*

Belgian	1.3%	Italian	2.0%
Dutch	1.7%	Polish	1.1%
English	7.7%	Scotch-Irish	1.2%
French	1.7%	Scottish	1.2%
German	18.2%	Swedish	3.2%
Irish	9.0%	USA/American	7.2%

As estimated percentage of total population.

Universities and colleges, 2000–2001 enrollment
Augustana College, Rock Island   2,230
Black Hawk College, Moline   6,118
Blackburn College, Carlinville   540
Carl Sandburg College, Galesburg   3,220
John Wood Community College, Quincy   2,167
Knox College, Galesburg   1,199
Millikin University, Decatur   2,334
Monmouth College, Monmouth   1,069
Quincy University, Quincy   1,188
Spoon River College, Canton   1,894
Western Illinois University, Macomb   13,089

Newspapers and circulation

	District circulation	Total circulation
Alton Telegraph	4,191	27,005
Burlington Hawk-Eye	1,807	19,485
Decatur Herald &Review	9,647	33,425
Galesburg Register-Mail	14,278	15,332
Jacksonville Journal-Courier	1,226	14,451
Moline Dispatch	21,930	27,065
Peoria Journal Star	7,388	67,115
Quad-City Times, Davenport	9,565	51,390
Quincy Herald Whig	10,802	22,635
Rock Island Argus	12,264	12,699
Springfield State Journal Register	11,806	58,065
St. Louis Post-Dispatch	2,796	295,281
Sterling Daily Gazette	2,548	12,472
*USA Today**	1,859	1,674,376

See Sources and Explanations in the front of the volume.

Television stations and affiliations

Davenport-Rock Island-Moline	34%	KLJB	FOX
Davenport-Rock Island-Moline	34%	KLJB	FOX
Davenport-Rock Island-Moline	34%	KQCT	PBS
Davenport-Rock Island-Moline	34%	KWQC	NBC
Davenport-Rock Island-Moline	34%	WHBF	CBS
Davenport-Rock Island-Moline	34%	WQAD	ABC
Davenport-Rock Island-Moline	34%	WQPT	PBS
Quincy-Hannibal-Keokuk	25%	KHQA	CBS
Quincy-Hannibal-Keokuk	25%	WGEM	NBC
Quincy-Hannibal-Keokuk	25%	WMEC	PBS
Quincy-Hannibal-Keokuk	25%	WQEC	PBS
Quincy-Hannibal-Keokuk	25%	WTJR	Independent
St. Louis	25%	KDNL	ABC
St. Louis	25%	KETC	PBS
St. Louis	25%	KMOV	CBS
St. Louis	25%	KNLC	Independent
St. Louis	25%	KPLR	WB
St. Louis	25%	KSDK	NBC
St. Louis	25%	KTVI	FOX
St. Louis	25%	WHSL	Independent
St. Louis	25%	WPXS	PAX
Peoria-Bloomington	11%	WEEK	NBC
Peoria-Bloomington	11%	WHOI	ABC
Peoria-Bloomington	11%	WMBD	CBS
Peoria-Bloomington	11%	WTVP	PBS
Peoria-Bloomington	11%	WYZZ	FOX
Champaign-Springfield-Decatur	5%	WAND	ABC
Champaign-Springfield-Decatur	5%	WBUI	WB
Champaign-Springfield-Decatur	5%	WCCU	FOX
Champaign-Springfield-Decatur	5%	WCFN	UPN
Champaign-Springfield-Decatur	5%	WCIA	CBS
Champaign-Springfield-Decatur	5%	WEIU	PBS
Champaign-Springfield-Decatur	5%	WICD	NBC
Champaign-Springfield-Decatur	5%	WICS	NBC
Champaign-Springfield-Decatur	5%	WILL	PBS
Champaign-Springfield-Decatur	5%	WRSP	FOX
Champaign-Springfield-Decatur	5%	WSEC	PBS

Cable systems and subscribers
Adams Telcom   750
CableVision Communications   1,948
Charter   10,433
Diverse Communications   627
Galaxy   1,818
Green County Cable   1,169
Insight   86,621
Madison Communications   2,819
Mediacom   52,545

Military installations, September 2001
Rock Island Arsenal (Army), Rock Island   5,440

Businesses and other major employers
Archer Daniels Midland Co.; Decatur; wet corn milling   10,000
Caterpillar Inc.; Decatur; construction tractors   3,300
Deere and Co.; Moline; farm machinery and equipment   2,955
Memorial Medical Center; Springfield   2,535
Burlington Northern and Santa Fe Railway Co.; Galesburg; switching and terminal services   2,500
Illinois University; Macomb   2,500
Deere and Co.; East Moline; combines (harvester-threshers)   2,400
Maytag Corp.; Galesburg; household refrigerators/freezers   2,200
Methodist Medical Center of Illinois; Galesburg   2,100
Decatur Memorial Hospital; Decatur   2,100
Deere and Co.; Rock Island   1,918
Bridgestone/Firestone North American Tire; Decatur; tires and inner tubes   1,800
Western Illinois University Inc.; Macomb   1,700
United Parcel Service Inc.; Decatur; courier services   1,600
Trinity Medical Center; Rock Island   1,572
Northwestern Steel and Wire Co.; Sterling; steel structural shapes and pilings   1,500
Methode Electronics Inc.; Carthage; electronic connectors   1,500

A. E. Staley Manufacturing Co.; Decatur; high fructose corn syrup   1,500

Illinois Power Co.; Decatur; electric power generation   1,356

Illinois Dept. of Natural Resources; Springfield   1,300

Southern Illinois University; Springfield   1,300

St. Mary's Hospital; Decatur   1,200

Blessing Hospital; Quincy   1,100

Titan International Inc.; Quincy; motor vehicle wheels   1,100

Army and Air Force Exchange Service; Rock Island   1,000

U.S. Defense Dept.; Rock Island   1,000

U.S. Army Corps of Engineers; Rock Island; engineering services   950

National Manufacturing Co.; Sterling; builders' hardware   845

Butler Manufacturing Co.; Galesburg; prefabricated metal buildings   836

Galesburg Cottage Hospital; Galesburg   800

U.S. Postal Service; Springfield   740

Mueller Co.; Decatur; industrial process flow instruments   728

Community Unit School District; Galesburg   726

Wahl Clipper Corp.; Sterling; hair clippers   720

Commonwealth Edison Co.; Cordova; electric power generation   710

Black Hawk College District; Moline   700

Norfolk Southern Corp.; Decatur; railroad freight hauling   700

Franklin Life Insurance Co.; Springfield; life insurance   700

Illini Hospital; Silvis   680

Brake Parts Inc.; Litchfield; automotive brakes   650

John Deere Insurance Group Inc.; Moline; fire, marine, casualty insurance   640

Moline Public School District; Moline   631

Pro Emp Inc.; Decatur; employee leasing service   630

CGH Medical Center; Sterling   600

McDonough County Hospital District; Macomb   600

Farmland Foods Inc.; Monmouth; meatpacking plants   600

Quincy Physicians Clinic; Quincy   600

Gardner Denver Inc.; Quincy; industrial pumps and parts   600

U.S. Veterans Hospital; Quincy   581

Kone Inc.; Moline; elevator inspection, service, repair   580

NTN-Bower Corp.; Macomb; roller bearings and parts   550

Glenayre Electronics Inc.; Quincy; radio/TV communications equipment   550

Promotion Support Services Inc.; Rock Island; promotion service   500

Deere and Co.; Milan; general warehousing, storage   500

Export Packaging Co. Inc.; Milan; packing and crating   500

Wal-Mart Stores Inc.; Moline; discount department stores   500

Decatur Intermet Foundry; Decatur; iron foundry   500

Illinois Environmental Protection Agency; Springfield   500

Illinois 18th District

Central — Peoria, part of Springfield and Decatur

When Richard M. Nixon spoke to the silent majority, his message hit home in Peoria, an American Everytown filled with hard-working, conservative, middle-class folks.

Thirty years later, Peoria is a politically competitive region in a sea of mostly rural Republicanism. A large black population on the south side and a substantial union constituency allow Democratic candidates to prevail in Peoria, as Al Gore did in the city and its namesake county in the 2000 presidential election. Republicans run stronger to the north: the GOP gubernatorial nominee's strong showing there helped him carry the city and county in 2002.

The 18th takes in all or part of 20 counties in central and western Illinois, with Peoria County accounting for nearly 30 percent of the population. In the south, the 18th takes in the northern part of Springfield, the state capital, some Republican-leaning suburbs north and west of the city, and rural turf that stretches west of the capital almost to the Mississippi River. In its southeastern reaches, the 18th runs to north Decatur.

In much of this predominantly agricultural district, voters worry about crop prices, ethanol, free trade, and estate taxes. But the district's economic health still depends largely on Peoria-based Caterpillar Inc., which manufactures earth-moving equipment and other heavy machinery.

The Republican lean of the rural areas, primarily those north and east of Peoria and north of Springfield, tips the 18th to the GOP. Woodford County, which abuts Peoria to the east, was George W. Bush's fourth-best Illinois county in the 2000 presidential election.

Major Industry

Construction machinery, ethanol and grain products, agriculture.

Notable

Pekin (Tazewell County) was the hometown of former Senate minority leader Everett McKinley Dirksen; Abraham Lincoln's tomb in Springfield is a state historic site.

Election Returns

	Republican		Democratic		Other	
President 2000	159,475	54.0%	128,411	43.5%	7,464	2.5%
House 2002	192,567	100.0%				

District Profile

Population   653,647

Total area (square miles)   8,301.5
  Land area (square miles)   8,186.3

Population per square mile   79.8

Counties (2000 population)

Adams (pt.) 12,427	Logan 31,183
Brown 6,950	Macon (pt.) 29,292
Bureau (pt.) 6,506	Marshall 13,180
Cass 13,695	Mason 16,038
Knox (pt.) 6,555	Menard 12,486

Morgan   36,616
Peoria   183,433
Pike (pt.)   12,575
Putnam   6,086
Sangamon (pt.)   86,725

Schuyler   7,189
Scott   5,537
Stark   6,332
Tazewell   128,485
Woodford (pt.)   32,357

Cities and other areas over 10,000 (2000 population)
Decatur (pt.)   15,571
East Peoria   22,638
Jacksonville   18,940
Lincoln   15,369
Morton village   15,198

Pekin   33,857
Peoria   112,936
Springfield (pt.)   57,209
Washington   10,841

Race and Hispanic or Latino origin*
White   90.0%
Black or African American   6.4%
American Indian or Alaska Native   0.2%
Asian   0.9%
Native Hawaiian or other Pacific Islander   0.0%
Some other race   0.1%
Hispanic or Latino origin   1.5%
Two or more races   0.9%

*As percentage of total population.

Ancestry*
Dutch   1.5%
English   8.8%
French   2.1%
German   21.2%
Irish   9.7%
Italian   2.6%

Polish   1.3%
Scotch-Irish   1.2%
Scottish   1.4%
Swedish   1.5%
USA/American   6.6%

*As estimated percentage of total population.

Universities and colleges, 2000–2001 enrollment
Bradley University, Peoria   5,951
Eureka College, Eureka   498
Illinois Central College, East Peoria   11,053
Illinois College, Jacksonville   909
Lincoln Christian College and Seminary, Lincoln   851
Lincoln College, Lincoln   1,010
MacMurray College, Jacksonville   739
Midstate College, Peoria   324
Richland Community College, Decatur   3,243
Springfield College in Illinois, Springfield   323

Newspapers and circulation

	District circulation	Total circulation
Bloomington Pantagraph	4,872	47,270
Decatur Herald &Review	8,809	33,425
Jacksonville Journal-Courier	12,659	14,451
Kewanee Star Courier	6,302	6,341
La Salle News Tribune	3,297	18,234
Peoria Journal Star	57,119	67,115
Quincy Herald Whig	8,014	22,635
Springfield State Journal Register	28,991	58,065
*USA Today**	3,933	1,674,376

*See Sources and Explanations in the front of the volume.

Television stations and affiliations
Peoria-Bloomington	38%	WEEK	NBC
Peoria-Bloomington	38%	WHOI	ABC
Peoria-Bloomington	38%	WMBD	CBS
Peoria-Bloomington	38%	WTVP	PBS
Peoria-Bloomington	38%	WYZZ	FOX
Quincy-Hannibal-Keokuk	30%	KHQA	CBS
Quincy-Hannibal-Keokuk	30%	WGEM	NBC
Quincy-Hannibal-Keokuk	30%	WMEC	PBS
Quincy-Hannibal-Keokuk	30%	WQEC	PBS
Quincy-Hannibal-Keokuk	30%	WTJR	Independent
Champaign-Springfield-Decatur	27%	WAND	ABC
Champaign-Springfield-Decatur	27%	WBUI	WB
Champaign-Springfield-Decatur	27%	WCCU	FOX
Champaign-Springfield-Decatur	27%	WCFN	UPN
Champaign-Springfield-Decatur	27%	WCIA	CBS
Champaign-Springfield-Decatur	27%	WEIU	PBS
Champaign-Springfield-Decatur	27%	WICD	NBC
Champaign-Springfield-Decatur	27%	WICS	NBC
Champaign-Springfield-Decatur	27%	WILL	PBS
Champaign-Springfield-Decatur	27%	WRSP	FOX
Champaign-Springfield-Decatur	27%	WSEC	PBS
Davenport-Rock Island-Moline	5%	KLJB	FOX
Davenport-Rock Island-Moline	5%	KLJB	FOX
Davenport-Rock Island-Moline	5%	KQCT	PBS
Davenport-Rock Island-Moline	5%	KWQC	NBC
Davenport-Rock Island-Moline	5%	WHBF	CBS
Davenport-Rock Island-Moline	5%	WQAD	ABC
Davenport-Rock Island-Moline	5%	WQPT	PBS

Cable systems and subscribers
CableVision Communications   4,531
Cass Cable TV   10,598
Green County Cable   3,910
Insight   125,862
Mediacom   33,939

Military installations, September 2001
Greater Peoria Regional Airport Air National Guard, Bartonville   1,268
Peoria Army Aviation Support Facility, Peoria   342

Businesses and other major employers
Illinois Dept. of Children and Family Services; Springfield   4,500
OSF Healthcare System Hospital; Peoria   4,300
Caterpillar Inc.; Mossville; construction machinery   4,200
St. John's Hospital of Hospital; Springfield   2,900
Sleep Disorders Center; Peoria   2,500
Caterpillar Inc.; Morton; road construction equipment   2,400
Excel Corp.; Beardstown; meat packing plants   1,900
Cargill Inc.; Beardstown; grain and field beans   1,800
City of Springfield; Springfield; social and human resources   1,800
Illinois Central College; Peoria   1,600
Keystone Consolidated Industries Inc.; Peoria; steel billets   1,470
Teachers Insurance Co.; Springfield; automobile insurance   1,300
Illinois Dept. of Public Health; Springfield; public health programs   1,300
Horace Mann Educators Corp.; Springfield; property damage insurance   1,285
Christian Homes Inc.; Lincoln; skilled nursing care facilities   1,228
Caterpillar Logistics Services Inc.; Peoria; computer peripherals, software   1,200

Caterpillar Inc.; Peoria; construction machinery   1,176

Par-a-Dice Gaming Corp.; East Peoria; gambling and
   lottery services   1,100

Proctor Hospital; Peoria   1,040

Kennametal Inc.; Mossville; industrial supplies   1,000

Boyd Gaming Corp.; East Peoria; casino hotel   1,000

Foster and Gallagher Inc.; Peoria; mail order   1,000

Mobil Chemical Co.; Jacksonville; chemical preparations
   1,000

Bradley University; Peoria   990

Affina Corp.; Peoria; management consulting   900

Capitol-EMI Music Inc.; Jacksonville; record and
   prerecorded tape stores   900

Eaton Corp.; Lincoln; switchgear and switchboard
   apparatus   900

DOT Foods Inc.; Mount Sterling; food supplier   853

Caterpillar Inc.; Mapleton; iron foundry   800

Affina Corp.; Peoria; telephone communication   800

Pactiv Corp.; Jacksonville; plastic and pliofilm bags
   800

Morton Custom Plastics; Morton; injection molding of
   plastics   700

Caterpillar Inc.; Mossville; construction machinery   700

Farmers Automobile Management Corp.; Pekin;
   management services   700

Illinois Judiciary Courts; Springfield   700

Illinois State Board of Education; Springfield   700

Passavant Memorial Area Hospital Assn. Inc.;
   Jacksonville   670

U.S. Postal Service; Peoria   650

Illinois Dept. of Public Health; Springfield   650

Dept. of Agriculture; Springfield; agricultural marketing
   regulation   622

Pampered Chef; Peoria; restaurants   600

Hertzberg-New Method Inc.; Jacksonville; books   600

Illinois Dept. of Human Services; Jacksonville   600

Illinois Secretary of State; Springfield   600

University of Illinois; Springfield   600

Farmers Automobile Insurance Assn.; Pekin; life
   insurance   560

Citizen's Equity First Credit Union; Peoria; state credit
   unions   541

Pekin Memorial Hospital; Pekin   525

Case Corp.; Goodfield; farm machinery and equipment
   520

City of Peoria; Peoria; city management   500

Fleming Companies Inc.; East Peoria; food supplier
   500

Lincoln University; Lincoln   500

Central Illinois Public Service Co.; Springfield; electric
   power generation   500

Illinois Dept. of Natural Resources; Springfield   500

Illinois State Police; Springfield   500

Illinois State Board of Education; Springfield; education
   programs   500

Illinois 19th District

South — southern rural counties; part of Springfield

Following a decade of slow population growth, Illinois
lost one of its 20 House districts in 2001 reapportionment.

In general, the new map merged the 19th and 20th districts,
creating a sprawling district in southern Illinois that touches
three states (Missouri, Indiana, and Kentucky) and takes in
all or part of 30 counties.

The northern counties cover typical midwestern
country—acres of corn and soybean fields dotted by small
towns. This area leans Republican, as do more-populous areas
such as the 19th's share of Madison County and the Sangamon
County suburbs of Springfield, the state capital.

The southern half looks more like Appalachia than Midwestern prairie. Its hilly, forested counties depend on timber
and coal mining. Unemployment is an endemic problem in
much of the region. Mechanization of mining has caused job
losses and reduced demand for the region's high-sulfur coal.
Pope County, the state's least populous, is almost entirely
within the Shawnee National Forest.

The district has an ancestrally conservative Democratic
tradition but leaned Republican in the 2000 presidential
election, backing George W. Bush with 56.1 percent of the
vote. While the economic populism of the region can help
conservative Democrats win, voters will cast a GOP ballot if they perceive Democrats as too liberal on cultural
issues. In the 2000 election, Wayne and Effingham Counties gave Bush his top vote percentages in the state. Edwards County, which is shared with the 15th District, gave
2002 the GOP gubernatorial nominee a statewide high of
70 percent.

Major Industry

Agriculture, coal mining, manufacturing, food products.

Notable

Metropolis (Massac County) was declared the official
hometown of Superman by the Illinois House in 1972—the
town is closer to Birmingham, Alabama, than to Chicago.

Election Returns

	Republican		Democratic		Other	
President 2000	164,541	56.1%	121,210	41.3%	7,621	2.6%
House 2002	133,956	54.8%	110,517	45.2%		

District Profile

Population   653,647

Total area (square miles)   11,646.0
   Land area (square miles)   11,518.7

Population per square mile   56.7

Counties (2000 population)

Bond 17,633	Jersey (pt.) 18,022
Christian (pt.) 28,512	Johnson 12,878
Clay 14,560	Lawrence (pt.) 6,828
Clinton 35,535	Madison (pt.) 136,009
Edwards (pt.) 5,866	Marion 41,691
Effingham 34,264	Massac 15,161
Fayette (pt.) 19,335	Montgomery (pt.) 15,374
Gallatin (pt.) 5,274	Pope 4,413
Greene (pt.) 6,285	Richland 16,149
Hamilton 8,621	Saline (pt.) 20,303
Hardin 4,800	Sangamon (pt.) 65,878
Jasper 10,117	Shelby (pt.) 20,933
Jefferson 40,045	Wabash (pt.) 2,154

Washington 15,148   White (pt.) 11,324
Wayne 17,151   Williamson (pt.) 3,384

Cities and other areas over 10,000 (2000 population)
Centralia 14,136   Godfrey village 16,286
Collinsville (pt.) 21,803 Mount Vernon 16,269
Edwardsville (pt.) 21,478 Springfield (pt.) 25,293
Effingham 12,384   Taylorville 11,427
Glen Carbon village 10,425

Race and Hispanic or Latino origin*
White 94.0%
Black or African American 3.5%
American Indian or Alaska Native 0.2%
Asian 0.5%
Native Hawaiian or other Pacific Islander 0.0%
Some other race 0.1%
Hispanic or Latino origin 1.1%
Two or more races 0.7%

*As percentage of total population.

Ancestry*
Dutch 1.5%   Italian 2.3%
English 8.0%   Polish 1.5%
French 2.2%   Scotch-Irish 1.1%
German 21.5%   Scottish 1.1%
Irish 8.6%   USA/American 8.8%

*As estimated percentage of total population.

Universities and colleges, 2000–2001 enrollment
Greenville College, Greenville 1,169
Illinois Eastern Community Colleges-Frontier
  Community College, Fairfield 1,519
Illinois Eastern Community Colleges, Olney 1,648
Kaskaskia College, Centralia 2,676
Lewis and Clark Community College, Godfrey 6,629
Lincoln Land Community College, Springfield 6,789
Principia College, Elsah 558
Rend Lake College, Ina 2,739
Southeastern Illinois College, Harrisburg 2,508
Southern Illinois University-Edwardsville, Edwardsville
  12,193
University of Illinois-Springfield, Springfield 3,942

Newspapers and circulation

	District circulation	Total circulation
Alton Telegraph	13,906	27,005
Belleville News-Democrat	10,264	53,540
Carbondale Southern Illinoisan	3,019	26,254
Decatur Herald &Review	4,956	33,425
Edwardsville Intelligencer	5,460	5,930
Effingham Daily News	12,279	12,673
Evansville Courier &Press	2,416	69,254
Paducah Sun	1,840	26,236
Springfield State Journal Register	16,932	58,065
St. Louis Post-Dispatch	16,647	295,281
Taylorville Breeze-Courier	5,550	5,934
*USA Today**	2,757	1,674,376

*See Sources and Explanations in the front of the volume.

Television stations and affiliations
St. Louis	34%	KDNL	ABC
St. Louis	34%	KETC	PBS
St. Louis	34%	KMOV	CBS
St. Louis	34%	KNLC	Independent
St. Louis	34%	KPLR	WB
St. Louis	34%	KSDK	NBC
St. Louis	34%	KTVI	FOX
St. Louis	34%	WHSL	Independent
St. Louis	34%	WPXS	PAX
Paducah-Cape Girardeau-Harrisburg-Mt. Vernon	24%	KBSI	FOX
Paducah-Cape Girardeau-Harrisburg-Mt. Vernon	24%	KFVS	CBS
Paducah-Cape Girardeau-Harrisburg-Mt. Vernon	24%	KPOB	ABC
Paducah-Cape Girardeau-Harrisburg-Mt. Vernon	24%	WDKA	WB
Paducah-Cape Girardeau-Harrisburg-Mt. Vernon	24%	WKMU	PBS
Paducah-Cape Girardeau-Harrisburg-Mt. Vernon	24%	WKPD	PBS
Paducah-Cape Girardeau-Harrisburg-Mt. Vernon	24%	WPSD	NBC
Paducah-Cape Girardeau-Harrisburg-Mt. Vernon	24%	WSIL	ABC
Paducah-Cape Girardeau-Harrisburg-Mt. Vernon	24%	WSIU	PBS
Paducah-Cape Girardeau-Harrisburg-Mt. Vernon	24%	WTCT	Independent
Champaign-Springfield-Decatur	18%	WAND	ABC
Champaign-Springfield-Decatur	18%	WBUI	WB
Champaign-Springfield-Decatur	18%	WCCU	FOX
Champaign-Springfield-Decatur	18%	WCFN	UPN
Champaign-Springfield-Decatur	18%	WCIA	CBS
Champaign-Springfield-Decatur	18%	WEIU	PBS
Champaign-Springfield-Decatur	18%	WICD	NBC
Champaign-Springfield-Decatur	18%	WICS	NBC
Champaign-Springfield-Decatur	18%	WILL	PBS
Champaign-Springfield-Decatur	18%	WRSP	FOX
Champaign-Springfield-Decatur	18%	WSEC	PBS
Terre Haute, IN	13%	WBAK	FOX
Terre Haute, IN	13%	WTHI	CBS, UPN
Terre Haute, IN	13%	WTWO	NBC
Terre Haute, IN	13%	WUSI	PBS
Terre Haute, IN	13%	WVUT	PBS
Evansville, IN	11%	WEHT	ABC
Evansville, IN	11%	WEVV	CBS
Evansville, IN	11%	WFIE	NBC
Evansville, IN	11%	WKMA	PBS
Evansville, IN	11%	WKOH	PBS
Evansville, IN	11%	WNIN	PBS
Evansville, IN	11%	WTVW	FOX

Cable systems and subscribers
Adelphia 1,121
CableVision Communications 1,076
Cass Cable TV 1,960
Charter 73,937
Comcast 2,681
Galaxy 6,349
Green County Cable 1,661
Insight 5,780
Madison Communications 575
Mediacom 14,469
Mid-America Cablevision 2,186
Suscom 4,013

Military installations, September 2001
Springfield (TS Cp Lincoln), Springfield 1,240

Businesses and other major employers
Argenbright Inc.; Taylorville; security guard service
  6,224
Royster-Clark Group Inc.; Collinsville; farm supplies
  2,245
Illinois State Government; Springfield 2,000
Continental Tire North America Inc.; Mount Vernon;
  automotive tires 2,000
Sangamon Co.; Taylorville; management consulting
  1,860

Champion Laboratories Inc.; West Salem; automotive air, fuel, oil filters   1,856

Southern Illinois University; Edwardsville   1,800

Illinois Dept. of Transportation; Springfield   1,500

Laidlaw Inc.; Edwardsville; school buses   1,200

Illinois Dept. of Public Aid; Springfield   1,200

Walgreen Co.; Mount Vernon   1,100

Decoma International Inc.; Nashville; automotive bumpers   1,000

Quebecor World Inc.; Effingham; periodicals   1,000

International Paper Co.; Shelbyville; food containers   1,000

International Union, United Automobile, Aerospace, and Agricultural Implement Workers of America; Centralia; labor organization   1,000

North American Lighting Inc.; Flora; automotive lighting   1,000

Computer Network Technology Corp.; Edwardsville; computer integrated systems design   950

St. Mary's Good Samaritan Inc. Hospital; Centralia   900

UIS Inc.; Fairfield; motor vehicle engines/parts   855

Madison County; Edwardsville; courts   850

SSM Health Care Hospital; Mount Vernon   845

North American Lighting Inc.; Salem; automotive lighting   802

Fedders Corp.; Effingham; air conditioning equipment   800

GSI Group Inc.; Assumption; crop storage bins   800

Southern Illinois/Riverboat Casino Cruises Inc.; Metropolis; gambling   800

Petty Co. Inc.; Effingham; offset printing   720

Illinois Dept. of Transportation; Collinsville; highway and street maintenance   700

St. Anthony Memorial Hospital; Effingham   700

McLane/Midwest Inc.; Carmi; discount department stores   680

Southwestern Illinois Health Facilities Inc.; Maryville   670

Meridian Automotive Systems Inc.; Shelbyville; motor vehicle parts/accessories   650

Basler Electric Co.; Highland; electric power transformers   609

Lewis and Clark Community College; Godfrey   600

Illinois Dept. of Human Services; Centralia   600

Earl L. Henderson Trucking Co.; Salem; contract haulers   600

American Coal Co.; Galatia; coal, other minerals and ores   575

Illinois Dept. of Corrections; Vandalia   560

Stevens Industries Inc.; Teutopolis; wood cabinets   550

OI Plastic Products FTS Inc.; Vandalia; plastic pallets   550

Hella Electronics Corp.; Flora; relays and industrial controls   540

Wal-Mart Stores Inc.; Olney; discount department stores   530

Rend Lake College; Ina   510

Owens-Brockway Glass Container Inc.; Godfrey; glass containers   500

ExxonMobil Oil Corp.; Albers; coal mining   500

Cooper B-Line Inc.; Highland; fabricated structural metal   500

Wal-Mart Stores Inc.; Effingham; discount department stores   500

Ryder Truck Rental Inc.; Taylorville; truck rental and leasing   500

CC Services Inc.; Centralia; insurance claim processing   500

Illinois Dept. of Corrections; Centralia   500

Champion Laboratories Inc.; Albion; automotive air, fuel, oil filters   500

Indiana

Indiana is the smallest of the eight states that ring the Great Lakes, sixth among them in population, and dead last in personal income per capita. Compared to its immediate, more populous neighbors—Illinois, Michigan, and Ohio—it has sometimes seemed a country cousin, more akin in culture and voting patterns to the midwestern states at the edge of the Great Plains than to those on the shores of the Great Lakes.

This is partly because, with Chicago right across the state line, Indiana did not develop a major city of its own on Lake Michigan. Instead, its population center lies inland at Indianapolis, smack in the middle of the state. Indianapolis grew up as a farm market and the state capital, later becoming a center for the insurance and pharmaceutical industries. The metro area is now more than 1.5 million people, one fourth of the statewide total, and host to big league football and basketball. But having skipped over the machine age and rise of organized labor, Indianapolis has retained more of its Republican flavor from the nineteenth century (in 2003 the GOP had held the mayor's office for 32 years running). Its suburbs and surrounding counties have been so many Republican locks; some gave George W. Bush two-thirds of their vote in 2000.

But at its northern and southern ends, the state's economy and political culture are quite different. Near the lake, the Chicago metro area has its eastern terminus in the Indiana cities of Gary and Hammond. Taken with other factory towns such as South Bend and Fort Wayne, this was the heart of the industrial Midwest in the middle decades of the 1900s. Then it became a buckle on what was called the Rust Belt in the downturn of the 1970s and 1980s (Gary lost 23 percent of its people in the 1980s, the worst decline of any American city, and was still losing population in the 1990s). As with the rest of the region, northern Indiana has since found ways to reinvent its steel-based manufacturing and rebound. Politically, autoworkers and other metal-bender unions have long been strong here, and Gary is 80 percent African American (the state as a whole is 8.5 percent). So this part of the state supports one Democratic district easily and makes a second competitive.

At the state's southern end, many residents have long had an affinity with Dixie and thus with the old Democratic Party. Some are still descendants of the original settlers, who came from below the Mason-Dixon line and were Southern sympathizers in the Civil War era. The state's southern border is the Ohio River, and on the other side lies Kentucky. In these hills, small-scale farming and big-scale mining remain the mainstays of the economy, and the culture is more traditional. Downstate counties vote Democratic for state offices,

and Bill Clinton ran well in many of them in the 1990s. But Republicans have leverage as the party of social conservatism, and their candidates have also benefited from the growth of bedroom suburbs for Cincinnati, Ohio, at Indiana's southeastern extreme.

In presidential elections, Indiana has been as loyal to the GOP as any state in the union. Only once since World War II have the Hoosiers gone Democratic for the White House, and that was in Lyndon B. Johnson's 1964 landslide. Richard Nixon and Ronald Reagan both topped 60 percent of the Indiana vote in their reelection years. In fact, exit polling data from early-closing Indiana precincts have come to be regarded as a harbinger for national GOP landslides in the making.

Democrats have had more luck in races for statewide office, most notably the governorship, which Democrats have won seven times in the postwar era, including four in a row beginning in 1996 (the Republicans had won five in a row before that). The outcomes of races for the U.S. Senate have been even more inclined to streaks. Republicans dominated the 1940s and 1950s, then Democrats reeled off a string of six straight wins. Then the GOP answered with eight in a row of its own, ending with the election of Democrat Evan Bayh in 1998. Bayh had previously served two terms as governor, and his father, Birch Bayh, won three terms in the Senate. Without the Bayhs' winning ways, and the more recent skein of two-term governor Frank O'Bannon, the GOP would have been utterly in command.

The congressional district lines in Indiana generally favored Republicans after the 1980 and 1990 censuses, but the state GOP has actually done somewhat better since the 2001 remap, which was dominated by Democrats on a special commission. The map fashioned after the 1980 census was a heavy-handed gerrymander intended to whittle the Democrats down to two or three of the state's ten seats. Instead, it produced a classic backfire by spreading the Republican vote too thin across too many districts. Democrats held even in the delegation, then became the majority in 1986, pushed it to 7–3 in a 1989 special election and peaked at a stunning 8–2 advantage after the election of 1990. Adjustments were made in the next remapping but it took until 1994, and the historic Republican takeover of the House, for the Hoosier GOP to climb back into the majority.

Drawing post-2000 lines was complicated by the state's loss of a seat in reapportionment. The decrease came because the statewide population growth, while respectable at 9.7 percent, did not increase enough to keep pace with other states. The Indianapolis area grew by 60,000 net residents but Gary, the old steel town that abuts Chicago at the

INDIANA

Districts established May 16, 2001, for elections first held in 2002.

9 members

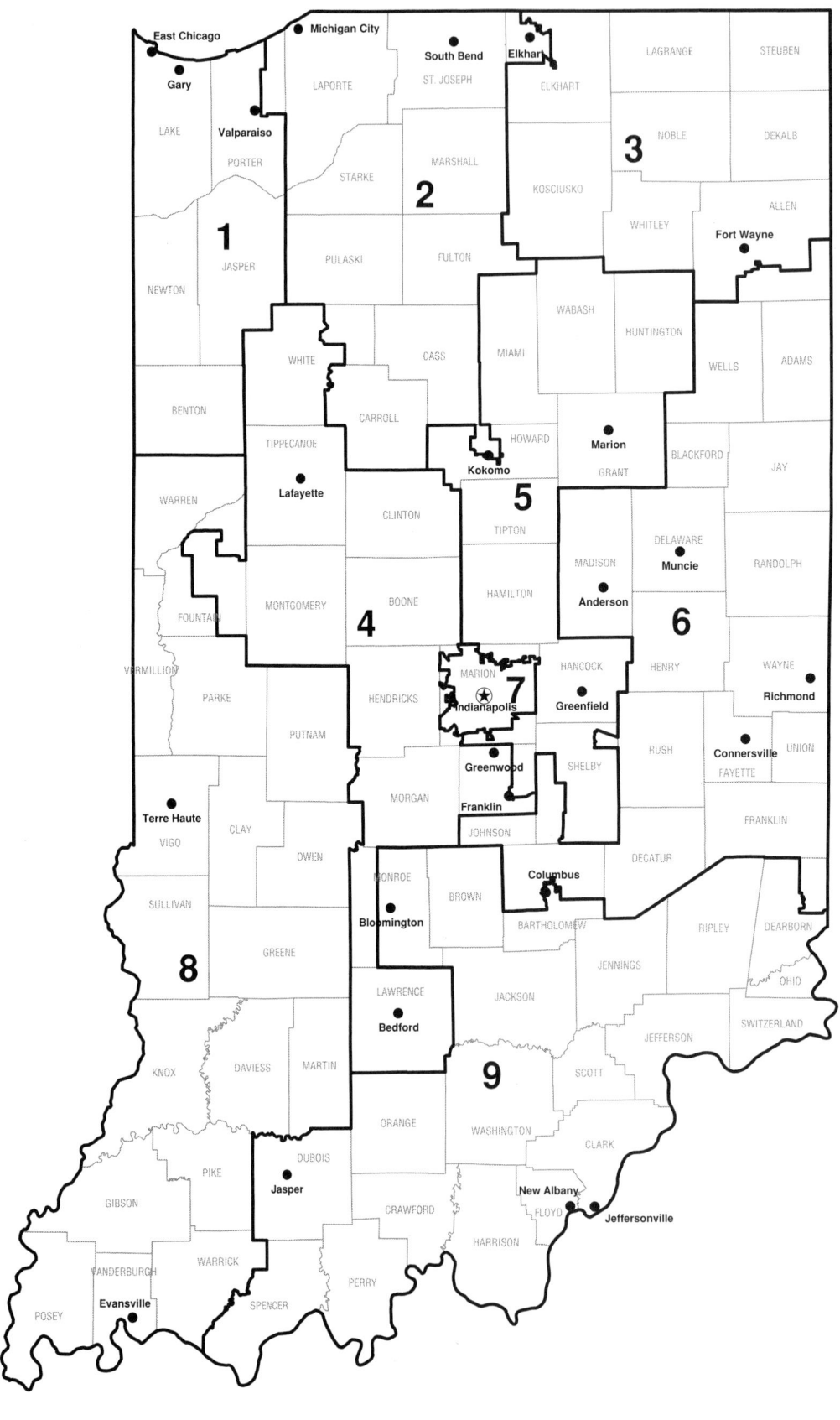

northwest corner of the state, lost another 14,000. The new map was drawn by a five-member commission in 2001 after the two chambers of the legislature (Democrats in the state House, Republicans in the Senate) failed to agree on a plan. The Democratic governor's appointee on the panel tipped the balance toward his party and the commission adopted lines close to those passed by the state House.

The new lines lumped together two midstate members in GOP districts who had to face off in a 2002 primary. The more senior of them (Steve Buyer) won this primary and was reelected. The most closely watched district was the newly designed 2nd, in South Bend and adjacent parts of the northern end of the state. The new map had added Kokomo, a blue-collar town from just below the old 2nd District line. This was to help Democrats hold the seat, which was being vacated by a five-term Democrat. But here, as elsewhere in a frustrating election year for Democrats nationwide, tweaking the lines was not enough. A Republican newcomer who was brave enough to talk about partially privatizing Social Security won the new 2nd.

In the rest of the state, four other Republicans were reelected easily in 2002, securing a 6–3 advantage in the delegation that could well be a pattern for the decade. The winners included one in the southern end of the state (Evansville) whom the Democrats had tried hard to dislodge. The three Democratic survivors included the state's only woman and only black representative, who carried the Indianapolis-based 7th District despite the introduction of roughly 100,000 new constituents from the mostly Republican suburbs. Veteran Democrats also held on to seats based in the 1st District (Gary) and the 9th District at the state's southeastern corner. The latter had to be bolstered by the addition to that district of Bloomington, home to Indiana University.

The Democrats' loss of ground in Indiana in 2002 was particularly discouraging because the national party had hoped the state would contribute one or two seats to the net gain it needed to regain the House majority. The failure to do so was a major reason observers were asking whether the Democrats would regain that majority anytime soon.

Table 1 Population

District	Population	Population under 18	Voting-age population	Median age	Male*	Female*
1	675,562	179,764	495,798	35.9	48.4	51.6
2	675,766	176,438	499,328	35.4	49.3	50.7
3	675,457	190,447	485,010	34.0	49.6	50.4
4	675,617	173,930	501,687	34.2	49.7	50.3
5	675,577	181,365	494,212	35.9	49.0	51.0
6	675,669	169,732	505,937	36.5	48.9	51.1
7	675,674	174,411	501,263	32.9	48.3	51.7
8	675,564	164,491	511,073	36.8	49.1	50.9
9	675,599	163,818	511,781	35.1	49.3	50.7
State	6,080,485	1,574,396	4,506,089	35.2	49.0	51.0

*As percentage of total population.

Table 2 Voting-Age Persons by Race/Hispanic or Latino Origin

District	White*	Black or African American*	American Indian or Alaska Native*	Asian*	Other or multirace*	Hispanic or Latino*
1	72.5	17.0	0.2	0.8	0.9	8.7
2	86.6	7.2	0.3	0.8	1.0	4.2
3	89.2	5.0	0.2	0.9	0.8	3.9
4	94.0	1.3	0.2	1.6	0.6	2.3
5	93.9	2.5	0.3	1.3	0.6	1.4
6	94.1	3.5	0.2	0.5	0.6	1.1
7	66.5	26.7	0.2	1.4	1.1	4.1
8	94.2	3.5	0.2	0.6	0.5	0.8
9	94.5	2.2	0.2	1.0	0.8	1.4
State	87.3	7.6	0.2	1.0	0.7	3.1

*As percentage of voting-age population.

Table 3 Voting-Age Population by Age Groups

District	18 to 24*	25 to 44*	45 to 64*	Over 64*
1	12.8	38.7	31.3	17.2
2	13.5	38.8	29.7	18.0
3	13.0	41.0	30.1	15.9
4	15.6	40.1	29.4	14.9
5	10.8	42.2	31.5	15.5
6	13.2	37.0	31.0	18.8
7	14.3	44.6	26.2	15.0
8	13.8	37.0	30.2	19.0
9	15.8	38.5	29.6	16.0
State	13.6	39.8	29.9	16.7

*As percentage of voting-age population.

Table 4 Income and Occupation

District	Median family income	Families in poverty*	White collar†	Blue collar†	Service†	Farm†
1	$52,076	8.1	53.1	31.2	15.5	0.2
2	$48,153	6.9	50.7	34.7	14.2	0.4
3	$51,664	5.5	51.7	35.9	12.0	0.5
4	$54,668	4.9	56.5	29.6	13.4	0.5
5	$62,335	3.5	63.2	24.4	12.0	0.4
6	$46,778	6.7	49.7	35.0	14.8	0.5
7	$43,721	10.6	57.7	26.2	16.0	0.1
8	$45,199	7.7	51.9	31.9	15.7	0.5
9	$47,129	6.7	50.6	34.4	14.4	0.6
State	$50,261	6.7	54.0	31.4	14.2	0.4

*As percentage of all families.   †As percentage of employed workers 16 years and over.

Table 5 Education: School Years Completed

District	Less than grade 9*	Grades 9–12 no diploma*	High school diploma no college*	Some college*	College bachelor's degree or higher*
1	5.5	12.1	38.3	26.9	17.1
2	5.5	14.2	38.1	25.0	17.2
3	6.2	11.7	36.4	27.2	18.4
4	3.9	10.5	38.4	25.2	22.1
5	3.1	8.5	31.9	25.9	30.6
6	5.7	13.6	42.0	23.9	14.7
7	5.4	16.1	31.4	25.9	21.2
8	5.5	13.2	39.3	26.1	15.9
9	6.8	13.1	38.9	23.9	17.3
State	5.3	12.6	37.2	25.5	19.4

*As percentage of persons age 25 and over.

Table 6   Housing and Residential Patterns

District	Median home value	Owner occupied*	Renter occupied*	Urban†	Rural†
1	$100,500	71.0	29.0	87.0	13.0
2	$84,800	72.8	27.2	72.8	27.2
3	$92,400	75.0	25.0	65.1	34.9
4	$109,900	73.5	26.5	68.2	31.8
5	$119,600	76.0	24.0	74.5	25.5
6	$83,300	74.3	25.7	59.3	40.7
7	$85,400	55.8	44.2	99.7	0.3
8	$76,500	74.0	26.0	58.1	41.9
9	$90,500	71.7	28.3	52.3	47.7
State	$92,500	71.4	28.6	70.8	29.2

*As percentage of occupied housing units.   †As percentage of total population.

Indiana 1st District

Northwest — Gary, Hammond

Bordered to the north by Lake Michigan and to the west by Illinois, the 1st is home to steelworkers and large union and minority populations that offer Democrats solid support. More steel is produced here than in any other district in the nation—more than 30,000 steelworkers reside in Gary, Hammond, and East Chicago. Most of the 1st's population lives in the far northwest corner, where more than 80 percent of Gary residents are black and more than half of East Chicago residents are Hispanic. The 1st also is home to many Eastern European ethnic neighborhoods.

Residents around Gary still struggle with the effects of unemployment, suburban flight, and urban decay that began when the steel industry took a dive in the early 1980s. As recently as 1970, Gary and Fort Wayne (located in the 3rd) were equal in population. Thirty years later, Gary had only half the population of Fort Wayne.

Another crisis hit in 1998 when cheap, imported steel flooded the U.S. market in record amounts. At least one steel company went out of business and there were thousands of layoffs. The district has attracted some lake boat gambling, but so far it is not a replacement for steel's place in the economy.

Democrats carry congressional and presidential elections by strong margins. Republicans have a meager base in growing Porter County and in Lake County suburbs such as Crown Point and Merrillville, where an influx of white Chicago commuters has raised incomes.

Redistricting following the 2000 census added southern Lake County and three rural counties, and altered the district's portion of Porter County.

Major Industry
Steel, manufacturing, gaming.

Notable
Indiana Dunes National Lakeshore; Singer Michael Jackson was raised in Gary; John Dillinger's infamous jailbreak occurred in Crown Point.

Election Returns

	Republican		Democratic		Other	
President 2000	104,917	41.8%	141,163	56.3%	4,759	1.9%
House 2002	41,909	31.0%	90,443	66.9%	2,759	2.0%

District Profile

Population   675,562

Total area (square miles)   2,443.0
    Land area (square miles)   2,209.3

Population per square mile   305.8

Counties (2000 population)
Benton   9,421   Newton   14,566
Jasper   30,043   Porter (pt.)   136,968
Lake   484,564

Cities and other areas over 10,000 (2000 population)
Chesterton town (pt.)   10,472
Crown Point   19,806
Dyer town   13,895
East Chicago   32,414
Gary   102,746
Griffith town   17,334
Hammond   83,048
Highland town   23,546
Hobart   25,363
Lake Station   13,948
Merrillville town   30,560
Munster town   21,511
Portage   33,496
Schererville town   24,851
Valparaiso (pt.)   27,362

Race and Hispanic or Latino origin*
White   69.8%
Black or African American   18.2%
American Indian or Alaska Native   0.2%
Asian   0.8%
Native Hawaiian or other Pacific Islander   0.0%
Some other race   0.1%
Hispanic or Latino origin   10.0%
Two or more races   1.0%

*As percentage of total population.

Ancestry*
Dutch   2.5%   Italian   3.2%
English   4.9%   Polish   7.3%
French   1.6%   Slovak   1.7%
German   13.8%   Swedish   1.5%
Hungarian   1.1%   USA/American   3.6%
Irish   8.9%

*As estimated percentage of total population.

Universities and colleges, 2000–2001 enrollment
Calumet College of St. Joseph, Whiting   975
Davenport College-Merrillville, Merrillville   587
Indiana University-Northwest, Gary   4,649
Ivy Tech State College-Northwest, Gary   4,675
Purdue University-Calumet, Hammond   9,045
St. Joseph's College, Rensselaer   935
Valparaiso University, Valparaiso   3,614

Newspapers and circulation

	District circulation	Total circulation
USA Today*	1,890	1,674,376

See Sources and Explanations in the front of the volume.

Television stations and affiliations

Chicago	83%	WBBM	CBS
Chicago	83%	WCIU	Independent
Chicago	83%	WCPX	PAX
Chicago	83%	WFLD	FOX
Chicago	83%	WGBO	Univision
Chicago	83%	WGN	WB
Chicago	83%	WJYS	Independent
Chicago	83%	WLS	ABC
Chicago	83%	WMAQ	NBC
Chicago	83%	WPWR	UPN
Chicago	83%	WSNS	Telemundo
Chicago	83%	WTTW	PBS
Chicago	83%	WWTO	Independent
Chicago	83%	WYCC	PBS
Chicago	83%	WYIN	PBS

Cable systems and subscribers

Comcast   109,279
Galaxy   584
Insight   2,185
Mediacom   5,011
TV Cable of Rensselaer   2,376

Businesses and other major employers

Ispat Inland Inc.; East Chicago; blast furnaces and steel mills   7,000

Bethlehem Steel Corp.; Chesterton; blast furnaces and steel mills   5,900

Bethlehem Steel Corp.; Valparaiso; steel foundries   5,000

St. Margaret Mercy Health Care Center; Dyer   3,000

Lake County; Crown Point; county government   2,000

Munster Medical Research Foundation Inc.; Munster   2,000

Harrahs East Chicago Casino; East Chicago; casino hotel   1,700

Empress Casino Hammond Corp.; Hammond; gambling   1,700

Methodist Hospitals Inc.; Gary   1,671

St. Margaret Mercy Healthcare Centers Inc.; Hammond   1,633

Marina Showboat Casino Partnership; East Chicago; casino hotel   1,500

Franciscan Sisters of Chicago Hospital; Crown Point   1,400

St. Anthony Medical Center; Crown Point   1,400

Gary Community School Corp.; Gary   1,300

Porter Memorial Hospital; Valparaiso   1,270

U.S. Steel Corp.; Gary; steel foundries   1,200

Indiana Trump Inc.; Gary; gambling   1,200

Barden Companies Inc.; Gary; computer software development   1,100

National Steel Corp.; Portage; hot-rolled steel sheet or strip   1,000

Whiteco Industries Inc.; Merrillville; billboard advertising   1,000

Lutheran University Assn. Inc.; Valparaiso   935

St. Catherine's Hospital Inc.; East Chicago   900

Con-Way Transportation Services Inc.; Hammond; combination utilities   800

Green Leaf Acquisitions; Hammond; automotive supplies, used   800

Northern Indiana Public Service Co.; Gary; gas and other services   800

Elgin Joliet and Eastern Railway Co.; Gary; railroad switching   750

State Farm Mutual Automobile Insurance Co.; West Lafayette; insurance agents and brokers   750

St. Mary Medical Center; Hobart   700

Conopco Inc.; Hammond; soap   650

City of Hammond; Hammond; city management   640

Indiana Harbor Belt Railroad Co.; Hammond; switching and terminal services   600

Indiana Family and Social Services Admin.; Gary   586

Cerestar USA Inc.; Hammond; wet corn milling   569

Hammond Clinic; Munster   557

Purdue University; Hammond   540

Whiteco Industries Inc.; Merrillville; resort hotel   530

Marathon Oil Corp.; East Chicago; tin   510

City of East Chicago; East Chicago; government   502

Franciscan Communities Inc.; Crown Point; rest home, with health care   500

Lear Corp.; Hammond; motor vehicle parts/accessories   500

Kenny Industrial Service; Hammond; building maintenance   500

Indiana University; Gary   500

Meijer Inc.; Merrillville; discount department stores   500

Indiana 2nd District

North central — South Bend, parts of Elkhart and Kokomo

The 2nd touches a southeastern corner of Lake Michigan and stretches across Indiana's northern border, but also drops south to Kokomo. Traditionally a politically competitive area, it has been considered a barometer of national political trends.

The district takes in St. Joseph County (South Bend), which is home to an ideologically diverse and economically disparate population. Here, the wealthy, Catholic Notre Dame community is joined by low-income, minority populations downtown, as well as blue-collar communities east of the city. Farther west, Michigan City's steel-producing areas and blue-collar La Porte provide solid Democratic support.

Farming and business in Elkhart County (shared with the 3rd)—a national center for the manufactured housing industry—create a faithful conservative constituency. Elkhart's large Amish population helps make it the state's leading milk producer.

The 2nd takes in some rural, Republican-leaning counties in north-central Indiana. Redistricting following the 2000 census extended the district (numbered the 3rd in the 1990s) south to Kokomo in Howard County. Kokomo (shared with the 5th) is dependent on the automobile industry, with Delphi and DaimlerChrysler as the area's dominant employers, and has a working-class, Democratic orientation. The 2nd is less GOP-leaning than the old 3rd, but George W. Bush won it by 9 points in the 2000 presidential election.

Major Industry
Manufacturing, higher education, agriculture.

Notable
The College Football Hall of Fame and Studebaker National Museum are located in South Bend.

Election Returns

	Republican		Democratic		Other	
President 2000	128,803	53.4%	107,344	44.5%	5,276	2.2%
House 2002	95,081	50.5%	86,253	45.8%	7,124	3.8%

District Profile

Population   675,766

Total area (square miles)   3,719.3
  Land area (square miles)   3,679.0

Population per square mile   183.7

Counties (2000 population)

Carroll 20,165	Marshall 45,128
Cass 40,930	Porter (pt.) 9,830
Elkhart (pt.) 86,033	Pulaski 13,755
Fulton 20,511	Starke 23,556
Howard (pt.) 36,062	St. Joseph 265,559
La Porte 110,106	White (pt.) 4,131

Cities and other areas over 10,000 (2000 population)

Elkhart (pt.) 48,783	Logansport 19,684
Granger CDP 28,284	Michigan City 32,900
Kokomo (pt.) 32,007	Mishawaka 46,557
La Porte 21,621	South Bend 107,789

Race and Hispanic or Latino origin*
  White   84.4%
  Black or African American   8.1%
  American Indian or Alaska Native   0.3%
  Asian   0.8%
  Native Hawaiian or other Pacific Islander   0.0%
  Some other race   0.1%
  Hispanic or Latino origin   5.0%
  Two or more races   1.3%

*As percentage of total population.

Ancestry*

Dutch 2.0%	Italian 2.3%
English 5.6%	Polish 5.8%
French 1.8%	Scottish 1.1%
German 18.3%	Swedish 1.2%
Hungarian 1.4%	USA/American 6.4%
Irish 8.8%	

*As estimated percentage of total population.

Universities and colleges, 2000–2001 enrollment
  Ancilla College, Donaldson   473
  Bethel College, Mishawaka   1,647
  Commonwealth Business College, Michigan City   200
  Davenport College-South Bend-Mishawaka, Granger   505
  Holy Cross College, Notre Dame   485
  Indiana University-South Bend, South Bend   7,252
  Ivy Tech State College, Kokomo   1,812
  Ivy Tech State College-North Central, South Bend   3,475
  Purdue University-North Central, Westville   3,459
  St. Mary's College, Notre Dame   1,449
  University of Notre Dame, Notre Dame   10,800

Newspapers and circulation

	District circulation	Total circulation
Gary Post-Tribune	3,381	59,665
Kokomo Tribune	2,976	21,336
La Porte Herald-Argus	11,785	11,785
Lafayette Journal and Courier	2,974	36,884
Logansport Pharos-Tribune	10,620	10,987
Michigan City News-Dispatch	11,911	11,911
Munster Times	3,227	88,021
South Bend Tribune	58,989	72,305
*USA Today**	4,529	1,674,376

*See Sources and Explanations in the front of the volume.

Television stations and affiliations

South Bend-Elkhart	57%	WHME	Independent
South Bend-Elkhart	57%	WNDU	NBC
South Bend-Elkhart	57%	WNIT	PBS
South Bend-Elkhart	57%	WSBT	CBS
South Bend-Elkhart	57%	WSJV	FOX
Indianapolis	25%	WCLJ	Independent
Indianapolis	25%	WFYI	PBS
Indianapolis	25%	WHMB	Independent
Indianapolis	25%	WIPB	PBS
Indianapolis	25%	WIPX	PAX
Indianapolis	25%	WISH	CBS
Indianapolis	25%	WLFI	CBS
Indianapolis	25%	WNDY	UPN
Indianapolis	25%	WRTV	ABC
Indianapolis	25%	WTBU	Independent
Indianapolis	25%	WTHR	NBC
Indianapolis	25%	WTIU	PBS
Indianapolis	25%	WTTK	WB
Indianapolis	25%	WTTV	WB
Indianapolis	25%	WXIN	FOX
Chicago	18%	WBBM	CBS
Chicago	18%	WCIU	Independent
Chicago	18%	WCPX	PAX
Chicago	18%	WFLD	FOX
Chicago	18%	WGBO	Univision
Chicago	18%	WGN	WB
Chicago	18%	WJYS	Independent
Chicago	18%	WLS	ABC
Chicago	18%	WMAQ	NBC
Chicago	18%	WPWR	UPN
Chicago	18%	WSNS	Telemundo
Chicago	18%	WTTW	PBS
Chicago	18%	WWTO	Independent
Chicago	18%	WYCC	PBS
Chicago	18%	WYIN	PBS

Cable systems and subscribers
  Comcast   105,115
  Galaxy   1,377

Insight   28,819
Mediacom   20,436
TV Cable of Winamac   1,259

Businesses and other major employers

University of Notre Dame; Notre Dame   3,584

Memorial Hospital of South Bend Inc.; South Bend
2,000

IBP Inc.; Logansport; meatpacking plants   2,000

St. Joseph's Regional Medical Center Inc.; South Bend
1,505

Indiana Packers Corp.; Delphi; pork products   1,350

Elkhart General Hospital; Elkhart   1,300

Boyd Gaming Corp.; Michigan City; excursion boat
operators   1,090

La Porte Hospital; La Porte   1,000

Indiana Correction Dept.; Westville   1,000

Sodexho Inc.; Elkhart; restaurants   1,000

Norfolk Southern Railway Co.; Elkhart; railroad freight
hauling   1,000

Honeywell International Inc.; South Bend; aircraft parts,
equipment   1,000

AM General Corp.; Mishawaka; military motor vehicle
assembly   900

St. Joseph Hospital and Health Center Inc.; Kokomo
887

Crowe Chizek and Co.; South Bend; certified public
accountant   814

Indiana Correction Dept.; Logansport   807

Sisters of St. Francis Health Services Inc.; Michigan City
800

Meijer Inc.; South Bend; discount department stores
800

Exterior Systems Inc.; Elkhart; sheet metal siding   760

Haynes International Inc.; Kokomo; nickel   748

United Steel Workers of America; Osceola; labor
organization   700

Associates Corp. of North America; South Bend;
administrative management   700

St. Joseph's Regional Medical Center Inc.; Mishawaka
693

Nishikawa Standard Co.; Bremen; sponge rubber
weather stripping   652

Indiana Dept. of Transportation; La Porte   650

Indiana Correction Dept.; Michigan City   650

Elkhart Products Corp.; Elkhart; pipe fittings   650

Consolidated Rail Corp.; Elkhart; railroad and subway
construction   650

Madison Center Inc.; South Bend; outpatient mental
health clinic   650

Howmet Corp.; La Porte; steel investment foundries
645

Henkels and McCoy Inc.; Elkhart; water, sewer, utility
lines   632

Whirlpool Corp.; La Porte; appliance parts   625

Jaymar-Ruby Inc.; Michigan City; men's, youths', boys'
dress slacks   600

Sullair Corp.; Michigan City; air and gas compressors
600

City of South Bend; South Bend; recreational program
600

T. M. Morris Manufacturing Co.; Logansport; harness
assemblies, electronic use   600

Godfrey Conveyor Co. Inc.; Elkhart; pontoons   550

Bayer Corp.; Mishawaka; medical instruments: blood,
bone work   550

Federal-Mogul Corp.; Logansport; ignition systems
550

CTS Corp.; Elkhart; electronic switches   541

Honeywell International Inc.; South Bend; search and
navigation equipment   530

Meijer Inc.; Michigan City; discount department stores
500

Wal-Mart Stores Inc.; Valparaiso; discount department
stores   500

Culver Educational Foundation; Culver; military
academy   500

Tomkins Industries Inc.; Elkhart; metal doors   500

Crown Audio Inc.; Elkhart; amplifiers   500

Meijer Inc.; Goshen; discount department stores   500

Meijer Inc.; Mishawaka; discount department stores
500

South Bend Tribune Corp.; South Bend; newspaper
500

Meijer Inc.; Kokomo; discount department stores   500

Wal-Mart Stores Inc.; Kokomo; discount department
stores   500

Memorial Hospital; Logansport   500

Braun Corp.; Winamac; wheelchair lifts   500

Indiana 3rd District

Northeast — Fort Wayne

Agricultural communities with deep-rooted religious be-
liefs shape the character of the 3rd, a solidly Republican
district in Indiana's northeast corner. The district's long tradition of social conservatism begins in the large Amish communities to the northwest, which are not overtly politically
active but form and reflect the area's traditional values. Rural
voters bolster the state's Republican leanings.

The 3rd's population center is Allen County, which includes Fort Wayne and accounts for nearly half of the district
population. Fort Wayne, the state's most populous city after
Indianapolis, has white-collar suburban neighborhoods and
German-Americans that cement the 3rd's conservative loyalties. Like many midsize midwestern cities, Fort Wayne has
a substantial manufacturing sector. While the surrounding
area has lost thousands of manufacturing jobs since the late
1990s, the region has been cushioned somewhat by a strong
white-collar service sector. Technology and financial-service
jobs have attracted professionals into Allen County, which
had a slightly higher growth rate in the 1990s than Indiana at large. Noble County, northwest of Allen, grew by 22
percent in the 1990s.

After Allen, the district's next most populous counties are
Elkhart (shared with the 2nd) and Kosciusko, which were
added to the 3rd in redistricting following the 2000 census. Both counties are solidly conservative: Kosciusko gave
George W. Bush a statewide high of 76 percent of the vote in
the 2000 election. East of Elkhart is LaGrange County, where
nearly one-third of residents speak a language at home other
than English; the county's Amish population speaks a German dialect.

Democrats find support in minority and blue-collar neighborhoods in Fort Wayne, but little backing elsewhere. In 2000, George W. Bush won every county in the 3rd with at least 60 percent of the vote.

Major Industry
Manufacturing, agriculture, health care.

Notable
Author and naturalist Gene Stratton-Porter's former home is a state historical site on Sylvan Lake in Noble County.

Election Returns

	Republican		Democratic		Other	
President 2000	147,106	65.5%	73,775	32.9%	3,682	1.6%
House 2002	92,566	63.1%	50,509	34.5%	3,531	2.4%

District Profile

Population   675,457

Total area (square miles)   3,292.4
Land area (square miles)   3,239.7

Population per square mile   208.5

Counties (2000 population)
Allen (pt.)	319,252	LaGrange	34,909
DeKalb	40,285	Noble	46,275
Elkhart (pt.)	96,758	Steuben	33,214
Kosciusko	74,057	Whitley	30,707

Cities and other areas over 10,000 (2000 population)
Auburn	12,074	New Haven	12,406
Fort Wayne (pt.)	202,769	Warsaw	12,415
Goshen (pt.)	26,611		

Race and Hispanic or Latino origin*
White   87.6%
Black or African American   5.6%
American Indian or Alaska Native   0.2%
Asian   0.9%
Native Hawaiian or other Pacific Islander   0.0%
Some other race   0.1%
Hispanic or Latino origin   4.5%
Two or more races   1.1%

*As percentage of total population.

Ancestry*
Dutch	1.9%	Italian	1.6%
English	6.2%	Polish	1.5%
French	2.6%	Scottish	1.2%
German	22.8%	Swiss	1.4%
Irish	7.1%	USA/American	8.4%

*As estimated percentage of total population.

Universities and colleges, 2000–2001 enrollment
Concordia Theological Seminary, Fort Wayne   416
Goshen College, Goshen   1,041
Grace College and Theological Seminary, Winona Lake   1,331
Indiana Institute of Technology, Fort Wayne   2,293
Indiana University-Purdue University, Fort Wayne   10,531
International Business College, Fort Wayne   642
ITT Technical Institute, Fort Wayne   510
Ivy Tech State College-Northeast, Fort Wayne   3,392
Taylor University-Fort Wayne, Fort Wayne   477
Tri-State University, Angola   1,267
University of St. Francis, Fort Wayne   1,570

Newspapers and circulation

	District circulation	Total circulation
Angola Herald-Republican	3,727	3,727
Auburn Evening Star	6,317	6,317
Fort Wayne Journal Gazette	46,053	58,705
Fort Wayne News-Sentinel	38,867	44,999
Goshen News	15,675	16,431
Kendallville News-Sun	6,789	7,075
South Bend Tribune	2,564	72,305
*USA Today**	4,958	1,674,376
Warsaw Times-Union	11,710	12,460

*See Sources and Explanations in the front of the volume.

Television stations and affiliations
Fort Wayne	60%	WANE	CBS
Fort Wayne	60%	WFFT	FOX
Fort Wayne	60%	WFWA	PBS
Fort Wayne	60%	WKJG	NBC
Fort Wayne	60%	WPTA	ABC
South Bend-Elkhart	40%	WHME	Independent
South Bend-Elkhart	40%	WNDU	NBC
South Bend-Elkhart	40%	WNIT	PBS
South Bend-Elkhart	40%	WSBT	CBS
South Bend-Elkhart	40%	WSJV	FOX

Cable systems and subscribers
Comcasts   63,228
Galaxy   1,086
Insight   12,745
Mediacom   30,833

Military installations, September 2001
Fort Wayne International Airport (Air National Guard), Fort Wayne   978

Businesses and other major employers
Lincoln National Risk Management Inc.; Fort Wayne; fire, marine, casualty insurance   3,650
Parkview Hospital Inc.; Fort Wayne   3,400
HBOS Manufacturing; Middlebury; mobile homes   3,200
General Motors Corp.; Roanoke; motor vehicles and car bodies   3,000
General Electric Co.; Fort Wayne; tube transformer assemblies   3,000
Verizon Communications Inc.; Fort Wayne; telephone communication   2,500
Zimmer Inc.; Warsaw; orthopedic appliances   2,200
General Electric Co.; Fort Wayne; motors and generators   2,000
Lincoln National Mezzanine Corp.; Fort Wayne; investors   2,000
Lincoln National Special Opportunity Fund; Fort Wayne; insurance agents and brokers   2,000
IOM Health System Hospital; Fort Wayne   2,000
ITT Industries Inc.; Fort Wayne; aircraft flight instruments   1,800

North American Van Lines Inc.; Fort Wayne; trucking 1,800

Forest River Inc.; Goshen; tent-type camping trailers 1,648

Monaco Coach Corp.; Wakarusa; truck bodies and parts 1,500

International Truck and Engine Corp.; Fort Wayne; truck and tractor truck assembly 1,400

St. Joseph Health System; Fort Wayne; investment holding company 1,200

SuperValu Inc.; Fort Wayne; food supplier 1,100

Allied Worldwide Inc.; Fort Wayne; household goods transport 1,100

Coachmen Industries Inc.; Middlebury; motor homes 1,015

Supreme Corp.; Goshen; truck bodies 1,000

Syndicate Systems Inc.; Middlebury; office, store display fixtures 1,000

Utilimaster Corp.; Wakarusa; motor vehicles and car bodies 1,000

R. R. Donnelley and Sons Co.; Warsaw; offset printing 1,000

Raytheon Co.; Columbia City; electronic circuits 1,000

Purdue University; Fort Wayne 1,000

Biomet Inc.; Warsaw; surgical implants 950

Cooper Tire and Rubber Co.; Auburn 900

Karl Schmidt Unisia Inc.; Fort Wayne; pistons and piston rings 900

Shambaugh and Son; Fort Wayne; plumbing, heating, air-conditioning 900

Waterfield Mortgage Co.; Fort Wayne; mortgage bankers 893

Fairmont Homes Inc.; Nappanee; mobile homes 860

H-C Liquidating Corp.; Goshen; wood kitchen cabinets 850

Dalton Corp.; Warsaw; gray iron castings 829

CTB Inc.; Milford; bins 800

Newmar Corp.; Nappanee; motor homes 800

Depuy Orthopaedics Inc.; Warsaw; orthopedic, prosthetic, surgical supplies 800

Auburn Foundry Inc.; Auburn; gray iron castings 750

Dutch Housing Inc.; LaGrange; mobile homes 750

Bank One Corp.; Fort Wayne; commercial bank 750

AON Innovative Solutions Inc.; Fort Wayne; management services 750

Mennonite Board of Education Inc.; Goshen; Catholic schools 749

Goshen Hospital Assn. Inc.; Goshen 736

Wells Fargo Bank Indiana; Fort Wayne; commercial trust company 719

Jayco Inc.; Middlebury; house trailers 700

Dana Corp.; Columbia City; hose and tube fittings, assemblies 700

Mattel Inc.; Fort Wayne; automobiles 700

Raytheon Co.; Fort Wayne; ship, boat, machine designing 700

Tokheim Corp.; Fort Wayne; measuring and dispensing pumps 687

Dana Corp.; Syracuse; motor vehicle axles 650

BAE Systems North America Inc.; Fort Wayne; aircraft 650

Norfolk Southern Corp.; Fort Wayne; railroad freight hauling 650

Sears Roebuck and Co. Inc.; Fort Wayne; teleconferencing services 650

Poly-Hi Solidur Inc.; Fort Wayne; plastics processing 642

Nishikawa Standard Co.; Topeka; sponge rubber weather stripping 622

Tech Computers Inc.; Fort Wayne; computer software development 622

Johnson Controls Inc.; Goshen; limit and fan controls 600

Tomkins Industries Inc.; Albion; motor vehicle axles 600

Parker Hannifin Corp.; New Haven; hose and tube fittings, assemblies 600

Fort Wayne Newspapers Inc.; Fort Wayne; newspaper 600

International Business Machines Corp.; Fort Wayne; welcoming services 600

North American Van Lines Inc.; Fort Wayne; household moving/storage 600

Slater Steels Corp.; Fort Wayne; steel ingots 561

Kosciusko Community Hospital Inc.; Warsaw 560

Hayes Lemmerz International Inc.; Bristol; industrial molds 550

Greencroft Inc.; Goshen; nursing/personal care facility management 550

TI Group Automotive Systems Corp.; Ashley; nonferrous rolling and drawing 550

Therma-Tru Corp.; Butler; window and door frames 550

Reese Products Inc.; Elkhart; trailer hitches 529

Steel Dynamics Inc.; Butler; primary finished or semifinished shapes 527

Parker Hannifin Corp.; Goshen; mechanical rubber goods 500

Aero Manufacturing; Goshen; travel trailers and campers 500

Gulf Stream Coach Inc.; Nappanee; motor homes 500

Redman Industries Inc.; Topeka; mobile homes 500

Wal-Mart Stores Inc.; Warsaw; discount department stores 500

International Union United Automobile Aerospace and Agricultural Implement Workers of America; Auburn; denomination church 500

Dalton Corp. Kendallville Manufacturing Facility; Kendallville; gray iron castings 500

Silgan Plastics Corp.; Ligonier; plastics bottles 500

Allen County; Fort Wayne; county government 500

Data Bank Inc.; Fort Wayne; marketing consulting services 500

Essex Group Inc.; Fort Wayne; building wire and cable 500

Verizon Communications Inc.; Fort Wayne; telephone communication 500

Meijer Inc.; Fort Wayne; discount department stores 500

Swiss RE; Fort Wayne; insurance agents and brokers 500

Meijer Inc.; Fort Wayne; discount department stores 500

Avo International Inc.; Dallas; electrical work 500

Indiana 4th District

West central — Indianapolis suburbs, Lafayette

Traversing the 4th by car requires a 175-mile trip through a slender district that takes in a mixture of farmland, small towns, and suburbs. It spans from White County, which is roughly halfway between Chicago and Indianapolis, south to Lawrence County, which is about halfway between Indianapolis and Louisville.

The 4th, as redrawn following the 2000 census, includes remnants of the 7th District that existed under the 1990s map. White County, the district's northernmost (and which is shared with the 2nd District), tops the state in corn and soybean production. Farther south, Montgomery and Clinton Counties also produce corn and soybeans. In between is Tippecanoe County, the district's most populous, which takes in Lafayette and West Lafayette. The latter is home to the main campus of Purdue University, which has an enrollment of more than 38,000. The school's engineering bent helps give Tippecanoe a conservative hue.

South and east of fast-growing, GOP-friendly Boone and Hendricks Counties, the 4th takes in a western sliver of Marion County (Indianapolis) and curves south of Indianapolis to take in most of Johnson County, which is filling up with young, well-educated families.

Moving west and south, the district encompasses all of mostly rural Morgan County before narrowing considerably to take in western Monroe County (but not Bloomington, which is in the 9th District). South of Monroe is Lawrence County.

The 4th includes some of the most overwhelmingly Republican territory in Indiana. In the 2000 election, Boone and Hendricks gave George W. Bush 72 percent of the vote, a performance he surpassed in just two other Indiana counties. Bush did not lose a single county in the 4th.

Major Industry
Higher education, agriculture, manufacturing.

Notable
Ben-Hur Museum is in Crawfordsville; Tippecanoe Battlefield was where troops led by then-governor (and later president) William Henry Harrison fought off a Native American attack in 1811.

Election Returns

	Republican		Democratic		Other	
President 2000	156,747	66.1%	74,660	31.5%	5,739	2.4%
House 2002	112,760	71.4%	41,314	26.1%	3,934	2.5%

District Profile

Population 675,617

Total area (square miles) 4,032.8
  Land area (square miles) 4,016.4

Population per square mile 168.2

Counties (2000 population)

Boone	46,107	Marion (pt.)	40,207
Clinton	33,866	Monroe (pt.)	28,062
Fountain (pt.)	6,103	Montgomery	37,629
Hendricks	104,093	Morgan	66,689
Johnson (pt.)	96,848	Tippecanoe	148,955
Lawrence	45,922	White (pt.)	21,136

Cities and other areas over 10,000 (2000 population)
Bedford 13,768
Brownsburg town 14,520
Crawfordsville 15,243
Frankfort 16,662
Franklin (pt.) 16,122
Greenwood 36,037
Indianapolis (pt.) 39,244
Lafayette 56,397
Lebanon 14,222
Martinsville 11,698
Plainfield town 18,396
West Lafayette 28,778

Race and Hispanic or Latino origin*
White 93.6%
Black or African American 1.3%
American Indian or Alaska Native 0.2%
Asian 1.5%
Native Hawaiian or other Pacific Islander 0.0%
Some other race 0.1%
Hispanic or Latino origin 2.6%
Two or more races 0.8%

As percentage of total population.

Ancestry*

Dutch	2.0%	Italian	1.6%
English	8.3%	Polish	1.4%
French	1.9%	Scotch-Irish	1.2%
German	17.0%	Scottish	1.6%
Irish	8.9%	USA/American	11.7%

As estimated percentage of total population.

Universities and colleges, 2000–2001 enrollment
Ivy Tech State College, Lafayette 3,013
Purdue University, West Lafayette 39,667
Wabash College, Crawfordsville 858

Newspapers and circulation

	District circulation	Total circulation
Bedford Times-Mail	10,170	12,971
Bloomington Herald-Times	7,374	26,750
*Crawfordsville Journal &Review**	8,845	9,446
Indianapolis Star	45,880	252,714
Lafayette Journal and Courier	28,988	36,884
Martinsville Reporter-Times	6,307	6,608
*USA Today**	3,769	1,674,376

See Sources and Explanations in the front of the volume.

Television stations and affiliations

Indianapolis	88%	WCLJ	Independent
Indianapolis	88%	WFYI	PBS
Indianapolis	88%	WHMB	Independent
Indianapolis	88%	WIPB	PBS

Indianapolis	88%	WIPX	PAX
Indianapolis	88%	WISH	CBS
Indianapolis	88%	WLFI	CBS
Indianapolis	88%	WNDY	UPN
Indianapolis	88%	WRTV	ABC
Indianapolis	88%	WTBU	Independent
Indianapolis	88%	WTHR	NBC
Indianapolis	88%	WTIU	PBS
Indianapolis	88%	WTTK	WB
Indianapolis	88%	WTTV	WB
Indianapolis	88%	WXIN	FOX

Cable systems and subscribers

Bright House Networks   6,939
Charter   2,572
Comcast   19,187
Frontier Communications   11,797
Galaxy   2,912
Insight   89,496
Tri-County Communications   764

Businesses and other major employers

Purdue University; West Lafayette   16,650
Subaru-Isuzu Automotive Inc.; Lafayette; automobile bodies   3,100
Wabash National Corp.; Lafayette; truck trailers   3,000
Lafayette Home Hospital Inc.; Lafayette   2,600
American Trans Air Inc.; Indianapolis; nonscheduled charter services   2,200
General Electric Co.; Bloomington; household cooking equipment   2,200
Cinergy Corp.; Plainfield; electric services   2,000
Caterpillar Inc.; Lafayette; internal combustion engines   1,800
North Central Health Services Inc.; Lafayette; management services   1,700
Target Corp.; Indianapolis; variety stores   1,500
United Parcel Service Inc.; Indianapolis; package delivery   1,500
General Motors Corp.; Bedford; automotive body parts   1,500
Alcoa Inc.; Lafayette; aluminum tubes   1,400
Eli Lilly and Co.; Lafayette; pharmaceuticals   1,165
Fairfield Manufacturing Co.; Lafayette; motor vehicle differentials, parts   1,130
Siemens Metering Inc.; Lafayette; meters: electric, pocket, portable, panelboard   1,100
Sisters of St. Francis Health Services Inc.; Lafayette   1,100
Hendricks Community Hospital; Danville   1,000
PSI Energy Inc.; Plainfield; commercial printing   1,000
Hendrix Community Hospital; Cartersburg   970
Heritage Environmental Services; Indianapolis; refuse systems   900
Visteon Corp.; Bedford; motor vehicle parts/accessories   850
Lafayette Venetian Blind Inc.; West Lafayette; drapery hardware, window blinds/shades   850
Federal-Mogul Corp.; Frankfort; gaskets; packing and sealing devices   800
Weston Mills Inc.; Brownsburg; frozen bakery products   800

Carrier Corp.; Coatesville; plumbing, heating, air-conditioning   800
Carrier Corp.; Indianapolis; refrigeration and heating equipment   800
Preferred Technical Group Inc.; Mitchell; assembly line robots   800
Raybestos Products Co.; Crawfordsville; automotive power transmission equipment   800
Phycor-Lafayette; Lafayette; management services   750
Meijer Inc.; Greenwood; drug and proprietary stores   740
Dow Agrosciences; Indianapolis; agricultural chemicals   700
Covance Central Laboratory Services LP; Indianapolis; testing laboratories   690
Harman-Becker Automotive Systems Inc.; Martinsville; amplifiers   660
TRW Inc.; Lafayette; automotive power steering equipment   655
Flex-N-Gate Corp.; Veedersburg; motor vehicle parts/accessories   650
Indiana Dept. of Health; Lafayette   620
Johnson Memorial Hospital; Franklin   600
Nice-Pak Products Inc.; Mooresville; towels, tissues, and napkins   550
Miller Pipeline Corp.; Indianapolis; pipeline construction   550
Lithonia Lighting Inc.; Crawfordsville; commercial lighting fixtures   542
Emerson Electric Co.; Frankfort; automotive electrical equipment   500
Frito-Lay Inc.; Frankfort; potato chips and snacks   500
Indiana Correction Dept.; Plainfield   500
Meijer Inc.; Plainfield; discount department stores   500
Cook Inc.; Bloomington; catheters   500
Lafayette School Corp.; Lafayette   500

Indiana 5th District

East central — part of Indianapolis and suburbs

Dominated by Indianapolis suburbanites and rural farmers, the 5th is Indiana's wealthiest district and is staunchly Republican turf. The trend might well continue; the suburbanites, who are rapidly taking the region's countryside, have been a largely GOP constituency.

The district's most affluent residents and its few minorities live in northern Indianapolis (Marion County) and in the Hamilton County suburbs of Carmel, Fishers, and Noblesville. Here, growing populations of white-collar workers in electronics and financial services bring median incomes well above state and national averages. Hamilton's median family income, $80,000 in 1999, was the state's highest and was nearly $20,000 above the next-highest county, Hancock (which is east of Indianapolis and also in the 5th District).

Hamilton, Marion, and Hancock Counties make up more than half of the 5th's population. Southeast of Indianapolis, the district also takes in most of Shelby County and northeastern Johnson County.

The suburban affluence does not extend to the northern part of the district, which is more middle-class. Miami County lost population in the 1990s, in part because of the

1994 realignment of what is now Grissom Air Reserve Base. Wabash and Grant Counties, adjacent to Miami, also lost population in the 1990s. The district also takes in most of Howard County, including parts of working-class Kokomo (shared with the 2nd).

While the rural communities are not as affluent as their suburban counterparts, they too are solidly Republican. George W. Bush won all of the counties at least partly within the 5th in the 2000 presidential election. Four of the counties were among his ten best statewide.

Major Industry

Financial services, electronics, agriculture.

Notable

The Dan Quayle Center and U.S. Vice Presidential Museum is in Quayle's hometown of Huntington; Peru is the birthplace of Cole Porter and the site of the International Circus Hall of Fame; the Elwood Haynes Museum, in Kokomo, honors the inventor who was among the first to build a gasoline-powered automobile.

Election Returns

	Republican		Democratic		Other	
President 2000	187,489	68.5%	80,945	29.6%	5,110	1.9%
House 2002	129,442	72.0%	45,283	25.2%	5,130	2.9%

District Profile

Population   675,577

Total area (square miles)   3,290.8
  Land area (square miles)   3,266.1

Population per square mile   206.8

Counties (2000 population)
Grant 73,403	Marion (pt.) 144,573
Hamilton 182,740	Miami 36,082
Hancock 55,391	Shelby (pt.) 38,679
Howard (pt.) 48,902	Tipton 16,577
Huntington 38,075	Wabash 34,960
Johnson (pt.) 6,195	

Cities and other areas over 10,000 (2000 population)
Carmel 37,733	Lawrence (pt.) 10,829
Fishers town 37,835	Marion 31,320
Greenfield 14,600	Noblesville 28,590
Huntington 17,450	Peru 12,994
Indianapolis (pt.) 130,195	Shelbyville 17,951
Kokomo (pt.) 14,106	Wabash 11,743

Race and Hispanic or Latino origin*

White   93.2%
Black or African American   2.6%
American Indian or Alaska Native   0.3%
Asian   1.3%
Native Hawaiian or other Pacific Islander   0.0%
Some other race   0.1%
Hispanic or Latino origin   1.6%
Two or more races   0.9%

*As percentage of total population.

Ancestry*

Dutch	1.7%	Italian	2.0%
English	8.7%	Polish	1.4%
French	2.0%	Scotch-Irish	1.2%
German	18.7%	Scottish	1.7%
Irish	9.1%	USA/American	9.6%

*As estimated percentage of total population.

Universities and colleges, 2000–2001 enrollment

Franklin College of Indiana, Franklin   1,020
Huntington College, Huntington   938
Indiana University-Kokomo, Kokomo   2,682
Indiana Wesleyan University, Marion   7,088
International Business College, Indianapolis   274
Manchester College, North Manchester   1,067
Taylor University-Upland, Upland   1,843

Newspapers and circulation

	District circulation	Total circulation
Chronicle-Tribune	18,762	19,831
Fort Wayne Journal Gazette	2,592	58,705
Indianapolis Star	70,047	252,714
Kokomo Tribune	18,098	21,336
Shelbyville News	6,853	9,915
USA Today*	7,632	1,674,376

*See Sources and Explanations in the front of the volume.

Television stations and affiliations

Indianapolis	75%	WCLJ	Independent
Indianapolis	75%	WFYI	PBS
Indianapolis	75%	WHMB	Independent
Indianapolis	75%	WIPB	PBS
Indianapolis	75%	WIPX	PAX
Indianapolis	75%	WISH	CBS
Indianapolis	75%	WLFI	CBS
Indianapolis	75%	WNDY	UPN
Indianapolis	75%	WRTV	ABC
Indianapolis	75%	WTBU	Independent
Indianapolis	75%	WTHR	NBC
Indianapolis	75%	WTIU	PBS
Indianapolis	75%	WTTK	WB
Indianapolis	75%	WTTV	WB
Indianapolis	75%	WXIN	FOX
Fort Wayne	25%	WANE	CBS
Fort Wayne	25%	WFFT	FOX
Fort Wayne	25%	WFWA	PBS
Fort Wayne	25%	WKJG	NBC
Fort Wayne	25%	WPTA	ABC

Cable systems and subscribers

Bright House Networks   24,188
Comcast   11,548
Galaxy   1,542
Insight   33,647
Mediacom   1,447
Oak Hill Cablevision   1,080
Suscom   5,384
Warren Cable TV   12,374

Military installations, September 2001

Camp Atterbury Military Training Area, Edinburgh   958

Businesses and other major employers

General Motors Corp.; Marion; automotive stampings 15,000

Delphi Corp.; Kokomo; automotive instrument boards 10,000

Pioneer Life Insurance Co.; Carmel; life insurance 3,600

Conseco Variable Insurance Co.; Carmel; life insurance 3,500

Vulcan Life Insurance Co.; Carmel; life insurance 3,000

Apple American LP of Indiana; Indianapolis; restaurant chain 2,000

Roche Diagnostics Corp.; Indianapolis; blood testing apparatus 2,000

Thomson Multimedia Inc.; Indianapolis; household audio/video equipment 2,000

DaimlerChrysler Corp.; Kokomo; electric power transmission 1,800

Knauf Fiber Glass GMBH Inc.; Shelbyville; mineral wool 1,800

Resort Condominiums International; Carmel; time-share condominium exchange 1,400

Marion General Hospital Inc.; Marion 1,204

Keihin Indiana Precision Technology Inc.; Greenfield; automotive fuel systems and parts 1,200

DaimlerChrysler Corp.; Kokomo; motor vehicle parts/accessories 1,075

Charles Schwab and Co. Inc.; Fishers; security brokers 1,000

Riverview Hospital; Noblesville 941

Cendant Corp.; Carmel; real estate agents and managers 900

Voluntary Enterprises Inc.; Indianapolis; management consulting 853

Carrier Corp.; Huntington; printed circuit boards 850

Ryobi Die Castings USA Inc.; Shelbyville; automotive transmission housings, parts 850

ArvinMeritor Inc.; Franklin; motor vehicle parts/accessories 800

Community Hospitals of Indiana Inc.; Indianapolis 800

Indiana Wesleyan University; Marion 800

Sunshine Promotions Inc.; Noblesville; entertainment promotion 800

Verizon Inc.; Westfield; radiotelephone communication 800

American Health Network of Indiana Inc.; Indianapolis; hospital/medical service plans 787

AdminaStar Federal Inc.; Indianapolis; medical insurance claim processing 780

Howard Community Hospital; Kokomo 775

Haynes International Inc.; Kokomo; gold and gold alloy 700

Meijer Inc.; Carmel; drug and proprietary stores 700

Indiana Mills and Manufacturing Inc.; Westfield; belting and belt products 665

Ford Meter Box Co.; Wabash; plumbers' brass goods 650

Best Lock Corp.; Indianapolis; locks or lock sets 630

Meridian Automotive Systems-Composites Operations Inc.; Shelbyville; motor vehicles and car bodies 600

Rich's Department Stores Inc.; Indianapolis; department stores 600

Square D Co.; Peru; electrical equipment 600

Worksmart Systems Inc.; Indianapolis; business consulting 600

Pilkington North America Inc.; Shelbyville; flat glass 550

Hancock Memorial Hospital and Health Services Inc.; Greenfield 522

Wabash Technologies; Huntington; electronic coils and transformers 520

JD Restaurants Inc.; Tipton; restaurant chain 500

Liberty Mutual Insurance Co.; Indianapolis; fire, marine, casualty insurance 500

Meijer Inc.; Indianapolis; department stores 500

Peerless Insurance Co. Inc.; Indianapolis; property damage insurance 500

Spicer Driveshaft Manufacturing Inc.; Marion; universal joints, motor vehicle 500

St. Vincent Hospital and Health Care Center Inc.; Carmel 500

Talent Tree Inc.; Indianapolis; temporary help service 500

Universal Studios Inc.; Fishers; chamber music groups or artists 500

Indiana 6th District

East — Muncie, Anderson, Richmond

Covering most of Indiana's eastern border with Ohio, the 6th is a mix of farm, midsize-city, and suburban populations. The district's major population centers are Muncie and Anderson, in the center of the district.

In the 1920s Muncie was the model for the "Middletown Studies," a research study on small-town American life. Today, it is home to Ball State University, as well as two large automotive plants. The city's economy was unsteady for much of the 1990s, with unemployment rates well above the state average. Delaware and adjacent Blackford were among the 11 Indiana counties that lost population in the 1990s. Anderson, another former auto manufacturing hub, also has seen industrial decline.

South and east of Muncie and Anderson, the 6th takes in Wayne and Henry Counties, where the percentage of residents over age 65 is among the highest in Indiana. Richmond, in Wayne County, is the main city on the 6th's eastern edge. Rush County is a top state producer of corn and soybeans.

Redistricting following the 2000 census elongated the district (previously numbered the 2nd). The new 6th extends as far south as Dearborn County, just a few miles from the Ohio River, and stretches as far north as Allen County, just south of Fort Wayne.

The 6th has a Democratic past but now leans conservative, in part because the decline of manufacturing weakened the district's Democratic labor base. Bill Clinton carried Delaware and Madison Counties, where Muncie and Anderson are located, respectively, in the 1996 presidential election, but George W. Bush carried all 19 counties that lie wholly or partly in the 6th in 2000.

Major Industry

Auto manufacturing, agriculture, light industry.

Notable

The Indiana Basketball Hall of Fame is in New Castle; Elwood was the hometown of 1940 GOP presidential nominee Wendell Willkie.

Election Returns

	Republican		Democratic		Other	
President 2000	148,415	58.5%	100,231	39.5%	5,090	2.0%
House 2002	118,436	63.8%	63,871	34.4%	3,346	1.8%

District Profile

Population   675,669

Total area (square miles)   5,572.0
Land area (square miles)   5,550.4

Population per square mile   121.7

Counties (2000 population)

Adams	33,625	Jay	21,806
Allen (pt.)	12,597	Johnson (pt.)	12,166
Bartholomew (pt.)	37,514	Madison	133,358
Blackford	14,048	Randolph	27,401
Dearborn (pt.)	14,510	Rush	18,261
Decatur	24,555	Shelby (pt.)	4,766
Delaware	118,769	Union	7,349
Fayette	25,588	Wayne	71,097
Franklin	22,151	Wells	27,600
Henry	48,508		

Cities and other areas over 10,000 (2000 population)

Anderson	59,734	Muncie	67,430
Columbus (pt.)	15,427	New Castle	17,780
Connersville	15,411	Richmond	39,124
Greensburg	10,260		

Race and Hispanic or Latino origin*

White   93.4%
Black or African American   3.8%
American Indian or Alaska Native   0.2%
Asian   0.5%
Native Hawaiian or other Pacific Islander   0.0%
Some other race   0.1%
Hispanic or Latino origin   1.3%
Two or more races   0.8%

As percentage of total population.

Ancestry*

Dutch	1.4%	Irish	7.5%
English	7.7%	Italian	1.2%
French	1.6%	Scottish	1.2%
German	16.8%	USA/American	12.7%

As estimated percentage of total population.

Universities and colleges, 2000–2001 enrollment

Anderson University, Anderson   2,381
Ball State University, Muncie   19,004
Earlham College, Richmond   1,156
Indiana Business College, Anderson   207
Indiana Business College, Muncie   237
Indiana Business College, Columbus   217
Indiana University-East, Richmond   2,335
Ivy Tech State College-Columbus, Columbus   3,288
Ivy Tech State College-East Central, Muncie   3,351
Ivy Tech State College-Whitewater, Richmond   1,261

Newspapers and circulation

	District circulation	Total circulation
Anderson Herald Bulletin	25,274	26,120
Cincinnati Enquirer	2,123	189,326
Fort Wayne Journal Gazette	6,896	58,705
Fort Wayne News-Sentinel	4,770	44,999
Indianapolis Star	2,050	252,714
Muncie Star Press	32,256	32,514
Richmond Palladium-Item	16,728	18,474
Shelbyville News	3,063	9,915
*USA Today**	4,246	1,674,376

See Sources and Explanations in the front of the volume.

Television stations and affiliations

Indianapolis	60%	WCLJ	Independent
Indianapolis	60%	WFYI	PBS
Indianapolis	60%	WHMB	Independent
Indianapolis	60%	WIPB	PBS
Indianapolis	60%	WIPX	PAX
Indianapolis	60%	WISH	CBS
Indianapolis	60%	WLFI	CBS
Indianapolis	60%	WNDY	UPN
Indianapolis	60%	WRTV	ABC
Indianapolis	60%	WTBU	Independent
Indianapolis	60%	WTHR	NBC
Indianapolis	60%	WTIU	PBS
Indianapolis	60%	WTTK	WB
Indianapolis	60%	WTTV	WB
Indianapolis	60%	WXIN	FOX
Fort Wayne	22%	WANE	CBS
Fort Wayne	22%	WFFT	FOX
Fort Wayne	22%	WFWA	PBS
Fort Wayne	22%	WKJG	NBC
Fort Wayne	22%	WPTA	ABC
Cincinnati	11%	WCET	PBS
Cincinnati	11%	WCPO	ABC
Cincinnati	11%	WCVN	PBS
Cincinnati	11%	WKOI	Independent
Cincinnati	11%	WKON	PBS
Cincinnati	11%	WKRC	CBS
Cincinnati	11%	WLWT	NBC
Cincinnati	11%	WPTO	PBS
Cincinnati	11%	WSTR	WB
Cincinnati	11%	WXIX	FOX
Dayton, OH	7%	WBDT	WB, PAX
Dayton, OH	7%	WDTN	ABC
Dayton, OH	7%	WHIO	CBS
Dayton, OH	7%	WKEF	NBC
Dayton, OH	7%	WPTD	PBS
Dayton, OH	7%	WRGT	FOX

Cable systems and subscribers

CableVision Communications   2,734
Charter   1,960
Comcast   27,799
Galaxy   1,554
Insight   95,900
Mediacom   6,602
Suscom   13,704
Time Warner   1,416

Businesses and other major employers

Ball State University; Muncie 6,096

Visteon Corp.; Connersville; motor vehicle heaters 3,300

Ball Memorial Hospital Inc.; Muncie 2,100

Reid Hospital and Health Care Services Inc.; Richmond 1,525

Delphi Corp.; Anderson; motor vehicle electrical equipment 1,475

St. John's Health System Corp.; Anderson 1,387

Belden Wire and Cable Co.; Richmond; nonferrous wiredrawing and insulating 1,300

DaimlerChrysler Corp.; New Castle; motor vehicle parts/accessories 1,300

GECOM Corp.; Greensburg; motor vehicle body components and frame 1,235

Baxter Healthcare Corp.; Muncie; blood bank 1,200

Delphi Corp.; Anderson; commercial physical research 1,200

Kroger Co.; Bluffton; general warehousing, storage 1,200

New Venture Gear Inc.; Muncie; motor vehicle transmissions, drive assemblies 1,184

Fleetwood Motor Homes of Indiana Inc.; Decatur; mobile homes 1,119

Community Hospital of Anderson and Madison County Inc.; Anderson 900

Franklin Electric Co. Inc.; Bluffton; electric motors 878

Caylor-Nickel Research Institute Inc.; Bluffton 700

Delphi Corp.; Anderson; generators for gas-electric or oil-electric vehicles 700

Indiana Family and Social Services Admin.; Richmond 690

Indiana Correction Dept.; Pendleton 625

Henry County Memorial Hospital; New Castle 623

ELSA Corp.; Elwood; automotive exhaust systems 600

Fayette Memorial Hospital; Connersville 564

CTS Corp.; Berne; resistor networks 520

Hoosier Park; Anderson; race track operation 517

All American Homes; Decatur; wood modular homes 500

Bluffton Regional Medical Center; Bluffton 500

Cummins Inc.; Columbus; automotive fuel systems and parts 500

Delco Remy America Inc.; Anderson; engine electrical equipment 500

Intat Precision Inc.; Rushville; ductile iron castings 500

J&J Packaging Inc.; Brookville; packing goods for shipping 500

Lear Corp.; Edinburgh; injection molding of plastics 500

Meijer Inc.; Muncie; discount department stores 500

Owens-Brockway Glass Container Inc.; Lapel; glass containers 500

Premium Marcor Group Inc.; Richmond; help supply services 500

Primex Plastics Corp.; Richmond; plastics hardware and building products 500

Indiana 7th District

Most of Indianapolis

Indiana's largest concentration of minorities lives in the urban 7th, which boasts one of the state's biggest white-collar workforces but also has one of its lowest median incomes. Almost four times bigger than Fort Wayne, the state's next most-populous city Indianapolis is the state's capital as well as its banking and commercial center. Heavy industry also plays a role in the city's economy, with a few automotive plants hanging on despite industry downturns.

Redistricting in 2001 changed the district's number (from 10th to 7th) and slightly reduced the district's black population and Democratic lean. But even with those changes, the 7th gave Al Gore a solid 55.5 percent of the vote in the 2000 presidential election, and its substantial minority influence makes it hard for a Republican to win.

Large minority populations, particularly African Americans, in central Indianapolis form the 7th's Democratic core. The joint Indiana University-Purdue University campus is here, and some neighborhoods are up to 65 percent black. In the city's northern tier, white-collar residents are some of the wealthiest in the state and are more receptive to Republican candidates. In the southern part of the district, blue-collar, mostly white populations built around the city's manufacturing industry are more socially conservative and generally supported Republicans on the local level in the 1990s.

Indianapolis has a reputation for being one of the nation's more conservative metropolitan areas: Richard G. Lugar (before he became senator), William Hudnut, and Stephen Goldsmith kept the mayor's office in Republican hands for 32 years, until Democrat Bart Peterson took office in 2000. On the federal level, George W. Bush carried Marion County (which is shared with the 4th and 5th districts) by slightly more than 1 percentage point in 2000, a smaller margin than Bob Dole took in 1996.

Major Industry
Manufacturing, health care, higher education.

Notable
Indianapolis Motor Speedway; President Benjamin Harrison, John Dillinger, poet James Whitcomb Riley, three vice presidents, and ten Indiana governors are buried in the Crown Hill Cemetery.

Election Returns

	Republican		Democratic		Other	
President 2000	84,362	42.6%	109,800	55.5%	3,795	1.9%
House 2002	64,379	44.2%	77,478	53.1%	3,919	2.7%

District Profile

Population 675,674

Total area (square miles) 264.5
  Land area (square miles) 261.5

Population per square mile 2,583.8

Counties (2000 population)
  Marion (pt.) 675,674

Cities and other areas over 10,000 (2000 population)

Beech Grove	14,880	Lawrence (pt.)	28,086
Indianapolis (pt.)	612,431	Speedway town	12,881

Race and Hispanic or Latino origin*

White 63.0%
Black or African American 29.4%
American Indian or Alaska Native 0.2%
Asian 1.3%
Native Hawaiian or other Pacific Islander 0.0%
Some other race 0.2%
Hispanic or Latino origin 4.4%
Two or more races 1.5%

*As percentage of total population.

Ancestry*

Dutch	1.2%	Irish	7.8%
English	5.5%	Italian	1.6%
French	1.4%	Scottish	1.2%
German	12.3%	USA/American	7.7%

*As estimated percentage of total population.

Universities and colleges, 2000–2001 enrollment

Butler University, Indianapolis 4,168
Christian Theological Seminary, Indianapolis 292
Indiana Business College, Indianapolis 920
Indiana University-Purdue University, Indianapolis 27,525
ITT Technical Institute, Indianapolis 821
Ivy Tech State College-Central Indiana, Indianapolis 6,748
Lincoln Technical Institute, Indianapolis 703
Marian College, Indianapolis 1,271
Martin University, Indianapolis 577
Professional Careers Institute, Indianapolis 462
University of Indianapolis, Indianapolis 3,599

Newspapers and circulation

	District circulation	Total circulation
Indianapolis Star	93,405	252,714
*USA Today**	8,391	1,674,376

*See Sources and Explanations in the front of the volume.

Television stations and affiliations

Indianapolis	100%	WCLJ	Independent
Indianapolis	100%	WFYI	PBS
Indianapolis	100%	WHMB	Independent
Indianapolis	100%	WIPB	PBS
Indianapolis	100%	WIPX	PAX
Indianapolis	100%	WISH	CBS
Indianapolis	100%	WLFI	CBS
Indianapolis	100%	WNDY	UPN
Indianapolis	100%	WRTV	ABC
Indianapolis	100%	WTBU	Independent
Indianapolis	100%	WTHR	NBC
Indianapolis	100%	WTIU	PBS
Indianapolis	100%	WTTK	WB
Indianapolis	100%	WTTV	WB
Indianapolis	100%	WXIN	FOX

Cable systems and subscribers

Bright House Networks 80,486
Comcast 24,269

Military installations, September 2001

Fort Benjamin Harrison (Army Reserve), Lawrence 1,434

Businesses and other major employers

General Motors Corp.; Indianapolis; motor vehicle parts/accessories 9,600
Clarian Health Partners Inc. Hospital; Indianapolis 9,013
St. Vincent Hospital and Health Care Center Inc.; Indianapolis 6,228
Eli Lilly International Corp.; Indianapolis; business management consultant 5,500
Rolls-Royce Corp.; Indianapolis; aircraft engines and parts 4,700
Indiana University Hospital; Indianapolis 4,640
Suncare Respiratory Services Inc.; Indianapolis; health clinic 3,550
Community Hospitals of Indiana Inc.; Indianapolis 3,000
Federal Express Corp.; Indianapolis; air cargo carrier 3,000
Marion County Health and Hospital Corp.; Indianapolis 3,000
General Motors Corp.; Indianapolis; truck bodies and parts 2,800
City of Indianapolis; Indianapolis; fire dept. 2,500
Indiana Dept. of Transportation; Indianapolis 2,500
International Truck and Engine Corp.; Indianapolis; diesel, dual-fuel engines 2,500
John Sexton and Co.; Indianapolis; management consulting 2,450
Bank One Corp.; Indianapolis; commercial bank 2,335
U.S. Postal Service; Indianapolis 2,300
Indiana University; Indianapolis 2,284
U.S. Defense Dept.; Indianapolis 2,200
AmeriTech; Indianapolis; local/long-distance telephone 2,000
Brylane Inc.; Indianapolis; mail-order women's apparel 2,000
Eli Lilly and Co.; Indianapolis; pharmaceuticals 2,000
Sisters of St. Francis Health Services Inc.; Beech Grove 2,000
Celadon Trucking Services Inc.; Indianapolis; trucking 1,900
Indiana Dept. of Environmental Management; Indianapolis 1,800
Indiana Dept. of Health; Indianapolis 1,600
American United Life Insurance Co.; Indianapolis; pension funds 1,580
Indiana Newspapers Inc.; Indianapolis; newspaper 1,500
Raytheon Technical Services Co.; Indianapolis; electrical equipment repair services 1,500
LDI Ltd.; Indianapolis; video cassettes, accessories 1,300
Marion County; Indianapolis; county government 1,250
Be Music Services; Indianapolis; mail-order music/video record/tape club 1,200
DaimlerChrysler Corp.; Indianapolis; aluminum foundries 1,150

Republic Airways Holdings Inc.; Indianapolis; air passenger carrier   1,118

Autozone Inc.; Indianapolis; automotive accessories   1,015

American Economy Insurance Co. Inc.; Indianapolis; fire, marine, casualty insurance   1,000

BMG Music; Indianapolis; prerecorded records and tapes   1,000

Simon Property Group; Indianapolis; nonresidential building operators   1,000

Meijer Inc.; Indianapolis; discount department stores   1,000

National Railroad Passenger Corp.; Beech Grove; railroad terminals   950

American States Life Insurance Co. Inc.; Indianapolis; life insurance   850

Melvin Simon and Associates Inc.; Indianapolis; shopping center property operation   825

Indiana Dept. of Revenue; Indianapolis   800

LogoAthletic Inc.; Indianapolis; men's and boys' sportswear   800

Simon Property Group; Indianapolis; community development   800

Butler University Inc.; Indianapolis   797

GSF Safeway; Indianapolis; janitorial service   750

Marsh Supermarkets Inc.; Indianapolis; caterers   749

Indiana Dept. of Natural Resources; Indianapolis   730

Golden Rule Insurance Co.; Indianapolis; insurance agents and brokers   700

Ingersoll-Rand Co.; Indianapolis; door opening/closing devices   700

Superior Insurance Group Management Inc.; Indianapolis; automobile insurance   700

United Farm Family Mutual Insurance Co.; Indianapolis; fire, marine, and casualty insurance   700

Kindred Healthcare Inc. Hospital; Indianapolis   650

Metropolitan School District Wayne Township; Indianapolis   629

Indianapolis Casting Corp.; Indianapolis; iron foundry   625

Indiana Dept. of Workforce Development; Indianapolis   600

Indiana University Childrens Hospital; Indianapolis   600

Indopco Inc.; Indianapolis; plastic materials and resins   600

Meridian Citizens Mutual Insurance Co.; Indianapolis; fire, marine, and casualty insurance   600

Roadway Express Inc.; Indianapolis; trucking terminal facilities   600

U.S. Federal Aviation Administration; Indianapolis   600

Yellow Freight System Inc.; Indianapolis; local trucking, without storage   587

University of Indianapolis; Indianapolis   579

Banc One Mortgage Corp.; Indianapolis; mortgage bankers   567

Amsted Industries Inc.; Indianapolis; automotive power transmission equipment   550

Tenet Healthcare Corp. Hospital; Indianapolis   550

Reilly Industries Inc. Indianapolis; testing laboratories   540

Emmis Communications Corp.; Indianapolis; radio, television, publisher representatives   506

Citizens Gas and Coke Utility; Indianapolis; liquified petroleum gas, distribution through mains   500

City of Indianapolis; Indianapolis; city government   500

CNF Inc.; Indianapolis; trucking   500

First Data Corp.; Indianapolis; telemarketing services   500

Indiana Family and Social Services Administration; Indianapolis   500

Swift-Eckrich Inc.; Indianapolis; sausages, other prepared meats   500

Union Acceptance Corp.; Indianapolis; installment sales finance   500

Von Duprin Inc.; Indianapolis; builders' hardware   500

Indiana 8th District

West — Evansville, Terre Haute

Indiana's southwest corner, formed by the converging Wabash and Ohio rivers, houses the 8th District, characterized by laborers and social conservatives. It is known in political circles as the "Bloody Eighth" for its aggressive and close elections, including a 1984 barnburner in which four votes separated the candidates.

Evansville, an Ohio River port and the state's third-largest city, is southern Indiana's industrial center. It is located in Vanderburgh County, the district's most populous, and is home to the 8th's only substantial minority and liberal populations.

North of Evansville the district takes on a more rural and culturally conservative flavor. Gibson and Knox Counties are among Indiana's top corn producing areas. Nearly one in six people in Daviess County, east of Knox, speak a language other than English at home. The county also has a large Amish population. Martin County, east of Daviess, includes the Naval Surface Warfare Center in Crane.

Owen County, northwest of Bloomington and about 50 miles southwest of Indianapolis, has just 22,000 residents but had a higher population growth rate in the 1990s than all but three other Indiana counties. West of Owen is Vigo County, the district's other major population center and home of Indiana State University in Terre Haute. Redistricting following the 2000 census extended the district's northern boundary to Warren County, which is closer to Chicago than to Evansville.

The 8th's manufacturing base and history as a mining center long gave Democrats an edge. But cultural issues, including gun control, strongly thrust the 8th in George W. Bush's direction in 2000; he carried every county in the district except for sparsely populated Vermillion.

Major Industry
Manufacturing, agriculture, higher education.

Notable
Labor leader Jimmy Hoffa was born in Brazil.

Election Returns

	Republican		Democratic		Other	
President 2000	144,848	56.5%	106,850	41.7%	4,808	1.9%
House 2002	98,952	51.3%	88,763	46.0%	5,150	2.7%

District Profile

Population 675,564

Total area (square miles) 7,132.4
Land area (square miles) 7,041.6

Population per square mile 95.9

Counties (2000 population)

Clay 26,556	Pike 12,837
Daviess 29,820	Posey 27,061
Fountain (pt.) 11,851	Putnam 36,019
Gibson 32,500	Sullivan 21,751
Greene 33,157	Vanderburgh 171,922
Knox 39,256	Vermillion 16,788
Martin 10,369	Vigo 105,848
Owen 21,786	Warren 8,419
Parke 17,241	Warrick 52,383

Cities and other areas over 10,000 (2000 population)

Evansville 121,582	Vincennes 18,701
Terre Haute 59,614	Washington 11,380

Race and Hispanic or Latino origin*

White 93.7%
Black or African American 3.7%
American Indian or Alaska Native 0.2%
Asian 0.6%
Native Hawaiian or other Pacific Islander 0.0%
Some other race 0.1%
Hispanic or Latino origin 0.9%
Two or more races 0.8%

As percentage of total population.

Ancestry*

Dutch 1.5%	Italian 1.3%
English 7.7%	Scotch-Irish 1.1%
French 2.1%	Scottish 1.3%
German 18.1%	USA/American 11.9%
Irish 8.1%	

As estimated percentage of total population.

Universities and colleges, 2000–2001 enrollment

DePauw University, Greencastle 2,223
Indiana Business College, Terre Haute 276
Indiana Business College, Evansville 241
Indiana State University, Terre Haute 11,051
ITT Technical Institute, Newburgh 323
Ivy Tech State College-Southwest, Evansville 3,448
Ivy Tech State College-Wabash Valley, Terre Haute 3,325
Oakland City University, Oakland City 1,418
Rose-Hulman Institute of Technology, Terre Haute 1,725
St. Mary-of the-Woods College, St. Mary-of-the-Woods 1,439
Trinity Theological Seminary-Trinity College, Newburgh 6,954
University of Evansville, Evansville 2,636
University of Southern Indiana, Evansville 9,012
Vincennes University, Vincennes 9,169

Newspapers and circulation

	District circulation	Total circulation
Bloomington Herald-Times	3,706	26,750
Danville Commercial-News	1,932	16,253
Evansville Courier &Press	55,738	69,254
Lafayette Journal and Courier	1,722	36,884
Terre Haute Tribune Star	27,214	29,738
*USA Today**	2,737	1,674,376
Vincennes Sun-Commercial	9,848	11,883
Washington Times-Herald	8,725	8,921

See Sources and Explanations in the front of the volume.

Television stations and affiliations

Terre Haute	53%	WBAK	FOX
Terre Haute	53%	WTHI	CBS, UPN
Terre Haute	53%	WTWO	NBC
Terre Haute	53%	WUSI	PBS
Terre Haute	53%	WVUT	PBS
Evansville	27%	WEHT	ABC
Evansville	27%	WEVV	CBS
Evansville	27%	WFIE	NBC
Evansville	27%	WKMA	PBS
Evansville	27%	WKOH	PBS
Evansville	27%	WNIN	PBS
Evansville	27%	WTVW	FOX
Indianapolis	15%	WCLJ	Independent
Indianapolis	15%	WFYI	PBS
Indianapolis	15%	WHMB	Independent
Indianapolis	15%	WIPB	PBS
Indianapolis	15%	WIPX	PAX
Indianapolis	15%	WISH	CBS
Indianapolis	15%	WLFI	CBS
Indianapolis	15%	WNDY	UPN
Indianapolis	15%	WRTV	ABC
Indianapolis	15%	WTBU	Independent
Indianapolis	15%	WTHR	NBC
Indianapolis	15%	WTIU	PBS
Indianapolis	15%	WTTK	WB
Indianapolis	15%	WTTV	WB
Indianapolis	15%	WXIN	FOX
Champaign-Springfield-Decatur	5%	WAND	ABC
Champaign-Springfield-Decatur	5%	WBUI	WB
Champaign-Springfield-Decatur	5%	WCCU	FOX
Champaign-Springfield-Decatur	5%	WCFN	UPN
Champaign-Springfield-Decatur	5%	WCIA	CBS
Champaign-Springfield-Decatur	5%	WEIU	PBS
Champaign-Springfield-Decatur	5%	WICD	NBC
Champaign-Springfield-Decatur	5%	WICS	NBC
Champaign-Springfield-Decatur	5%	WILL	PBS
Champaign-Springfield-Decatur	5%	WRSP	FOX
Champaign-Springfield-Decatur	5%	WSEC	PBS

Cable systems and subscribers

CableVision Communications 11,029
Capital Cable 927
Charter 45,411
Clinton Cable TV 2,273
Galaxy 15,569
Insight 85,724
Time Warner 19,867

Military installations, September 2001
Naval Surface Warfare Center Division, Crane 3,410
Hulman Regional Airport, Terre Haute 1,006
Newport Chemical Depot, Terre Haute 393
Evansville Armed Forces Reserve Center, Evansville
188

Businesses and other major employers
Alcoa Inc.; Newburgh; primary aluminum 2,800
Whirlpool Corp.; Evansville; household refrigerator
cabinets 2,700
Bristol-Myers Squibb Co.; Evansville; pharmaceuticals
2,400
Mead Johnson and Co.; Evansville; food preparations
2,400
St. Mary's Medical Center; Evansville 2,400
Bristol-Myers Squibb Co.; Mount Vernon;
pharmaceuticals 2,300
Deaconess Hospital; Evansville 2,150
Rural/Metro Corp.; Terre Haute; ambulance service
2,000
University of Southern Indiana; Evansville 1,868
Union Hospital; Terre Haute 1,818
General Electric Co.; Mount Vernon; plastic materials
and resins 1,700
Good Samaritan Hospital; Vincennes 1,600
St. Mary's Health Care Services/Welborn Campus;
Evansville 1,600
Indiana State University; Terre Haute 1,500
Operative Plasterers and Cement Masons; Terre Haute;
labor organization 1,500
Aztar Indiana Gaming Corp.; Evansville; gambling
1,400
Columbia House Co.; Terre Haute; records/tapes
preparation 1,200
Digital Audio Disc Corp.; Terre Haute; optical disks and
tape 1,200
Vincennes University; Vincennes 1,150
Bemis Co.; Terre Haute; polyethylene film 1,000
Great Dane LP; Brazil; truck trailers 900
Industrial Contractors Inc.; Evansville; industrial
buildings construction 900
Lear Corp.; Greencastle; automotive trimmings, fabric
852
Terre Haute Regional Hospital Inc.; Terre Haute 800
Boston Scientific Corp.; Spencer; surgical and medical
instruments 780
Harrison Steel Castings Co.; Attica; steel foundries 700
Yosemite Insurance Co.; Evansville; property damage
insurance 700
American General Finance Management Corp.;
Evansville; personnel management 698
Applied Extrusion Technologies Inc.; Terre Haute;
polypropylene film and sheet 603
Berry Plastics Corp.; Evansville; injection molding of
plastics 600
Indiana Dept. of Transportation; Vincennes 600
Pfizer Corp.; Terre Haute; medicinals and botanicals
600
U.S. Postal Service; Evansville 600
Welborn Clinic Inc.; Evansville 600
Indiana Correction Dept.; Greencastle 590

PSI Energy Inc.; Owensville; electric services 568
Indian Industries Inc.; Evansville; ping-pong tables
540
DePauw University; Greencastle 528
Indiana Correction Dept.; Carlisle 512
Ivy Hill Corp.; Terre Haute; commercial printing 510
U.S. Bureau of Prisons; Terre Haute 509
City of Evansville; Evansville; city government 500
Gemtron Corp.; Vincennes; tempered glass 500
Indiana Family and Social Services Admin.; Evansville
500
PPG Industries Inc.; Evansville; flat glass 500
U.S. Dept. of Justice; Terre Haute 500
Wal-Mart Stores Inc.; Evansville; discount department
stores 500

Indiana 9th District

Southeast — Bloomington, New Albany

Bordering the Ohio River to the south, the 9th shares socially conservative roots and, more recently, competitive politics with other river valley districts. Manufacturing forms the district's economic foundation, although agriculture and retail trade also are prevalent in Indiana's southeastern quadrant.

The 9th's northeastern counties are seeing an influx of Cincinnati migrants, who have started to change the district from rural to slightly suburban. To the south, Clark and Floyd counties are adding residents due to Louisville metropolitan area growth. Clark is the 9th's most populous county.

Much of Monroe, the next most-populous county, was drawn into the 9th following the 2000 census, including Bloomington. Indiana University's presence gives the city a Democratic lean, and in some city precincts the write-in tally for Green Party presidential candidate Ralph Nader was higher than that of George W. Bush in 2000.

While the university makes Monroe one of Indiana's best-educated counties, the 9th as a whole is blue-collar with a low percentage of college graduates. Unemployment in some counties, including Orange and Crawford, can run substantially above Indiana's otherwise low average, and areas of rural poverty exist in the district. Crawford has the state's second-highest poverty rate and the longest commute time: many residents work in Louisville, due east on Interstate 64.

While the 9th has a Democratic heritage, the area's deep conservatism on cultural issues propelled Bush to a double-digit victory in 2000. Although Bush's statewide showing was only 10 percentage points higher than that of Republican Bob Dole four years earlier, in the 9th Bush exceeded Dole's 1996 numbers by more than 16 percentage points in Dubois, Crawford, Jennings, Orange, Switzerland, and Ohio Counties.

Major Industry
Manufacturing, agriculture, retail.

Notable
Basketball star Larry Bird is from French Lick; Corydon, hometown of Gov. Frank L. O'Bannon, was Indiana's first state capital from 1816 to 1825.

Election Returns

	Republican		Democratic		Other	
President 2000	142,694	56.3%	106,417	42.0%	4,288	1.7%
House 2002	87,169	46.1%	96,654	51.2%	5,134	2.7%

District Profile

Population 675,599

Total area (square miles) 6,670.1
Land area (square miles) 6,602.6

Population per square mile 102.3

Counties (2000 population)

Bartholomew (pt.)	33,921	Jennings	27,554
Brown	14,957	Monroe (pt.)	92,501
Clark	96,472	Ohio	5,623
Crawford	10,743	Orange	19,306
Dearborn (pt.)	31,599	Perry	18,899
Dubois	39,674	Ripley	26,523
Floyd	70,823	Scott	22,960
Harrison	34,325	Spencer	20,391
Jackson	41,335	Switzerland	9,065
Jefferson	31,705	Washington	27,223

Cities and other areas over 10,000 (2000 population)

Bloomington (pt.) 66,459
Clarksville town 21,400
Columbus (pt.) 23,632
Jasper 12,100
Jeffersonville 27,362
Madison 12,004
New Albany 37,603
Seymour 18,101

Race and Hispanic or Latino origin*

White 94.0%
Black or African American 2.3%
American Indian or Alaska Native 0.2%
Asian 0.9%
Native Hawaiian or other Pacific Islander 0.0%
Some other race 0.1%
Hispanic or Latino origin 1.5%
Two or more races 0.9%

*As percentage of total population.

Ancestry*

Dutch	1.2%	Italian	1.4%
English	7.2%	Scotch-Irish	1.1%
French	2.0%	Scottish	1.3%
German	20.0%	USA/American	12.2%
Irish	8.7%		

*As estimated percentage of total population.

Universities and colleges, 2000–2001 enrollment

Hanover College, Hanover 1,142
Indiana University-Bloomington, Bloomington 37,076
Indiana University-Southeast, New Albany 6,427
Ivy Tech State College-South Central, Sellersburg 1,933
Ivy Tech State College-Southeast, Madison 1,418

Newspapers and circulation

	District circulation	Total circulation
Bedford Times-Mail	2,483	12,971
Bloomington Herald-Times	15,646	26,750
Cincinnati Enquirer	3,188	189,326
Evansville Courier &Press	5,913	69,254
Louisville Courier Journal	32,404	220,676
*USA Today**	2,673	1,674,376

*See Sources and Explanations in the front of the volume.

Television stations and affiliations

Louisville, KY	56%	WAVE	NBC
Louisville, KY	56%	WBNA	PAX
Louisville, KY	56%	WDRB	FOX
Louisville, KY	56%	WFTE	UPN
Louisville, KY	56%	WHAS	ABC
Louisville, KY	56%	WKMJ	PBS
Louisville, KY	56%	WKPC	PBS
Louisville, KY	56%	WKZT	PBS
Louisville, KY	56%	WLKY	CBS
Louisville, KY	56%	WWWB	WB
Evansville	18%	WEHT	ABC
Evansville	18%	WEVV	CBS
Evansville	18%	WFIE	NBC
Evansville	18%	WKMA	PBS
Evansville	18%	WKOH	PBS
Evansville	18%	WNIN	PBS
Evansville	18%	WTVW	FOX
Cincinnati	15%	WCET	PBS
Cincinnati	15%	WCPO	ABC
Cincinnati	15%	WCVN	PBS
Cincinnati	15%	WKOI	Independent
Cincinnati	15%	WKON	PBS
Cincinnati	15%	WKRC	CBS
Cincinnati	15%	WLWT	NBC
Cincinnati	15%	WPTO	PBS
Cincinnati	15%	WSTR	WB
Cincinnati	15%	WXIX	FOX
Indianapolis	11%	WCLJ	Independent
Indianapolis	11%	WFYI	PBS
Indianapolis	11%	WHMB	Independent
Indianapolis	11%	WIPB	PBS
Indianapolis	11%	WIPX	PAX
Indianapolis	11%	WISH	CBS
Indianapolis	11%	WLFI	CBS
Indianapolis	11%	WNDY	UPN
Indianapolis	11%	WRTV	ABC
Indianapolis	11%	WTBU	Independent
Indianapolis	11%	WTHR	NBC
Indianapolis	11%	WTIU	PBS
Indianapolis	11%	WTTK	WB
Indianapolis	11%	WTTV	WB
Indianapolis	11%	WXIN	FOX

Cable systems and subscribers

Adelphia 12,820
Charter 4,196
Comcast 8,652
Galaxy 1,821
Insight 84,805
Suscom 8,415

Businesses and other major employers

American Commercial Lines; Jeffersonville; canal barge operations   3,000

Bloomington Hospital Inc.; Bloomington   2,800

Indiana Gaming Co. LP; Lawrenceburg; casino hotel   2,400

RDI/Caesars Riverboat Casino; Elizabeth; casino hotel   2,000

Pinnacle Entertainment Inc.; Florence; casino hotel   1,500

Clark Memorial Hospital; Jeffersonville   1,498

Columbus Regional Hospital; Columbus   1,400

Batesville Casket Co.; Batesville; burial caskets   1,300

Hill-Rom Co.; Batesville; hospital beds   1,200

U.S. Census Bureau; Jeffersonville; economic programs   1,200

Valeo-Sylvania; Seymour; electric lamps   1,200

Grand Victoria Casino and Resort; Rising Sun; gambling   1,100

Aisin USA Manufacturing Inc.; Seymour; motor vehicle parts/accessories   1,000

Grote Industries Inc.; Madison; vehicular lighting equipment   1,000

Floyd Memorial Hospital; New Albany   990

Indiana University; Bloomington   900

Jasper Engine Exchange Inc.; Jasper; rebuilding engines and transmissions   900

Jasper Rubber Products Inc.; Jasper; mechanical rubber goods   869

Little Company of Mary Hospital of Indiana Inc.; Jasper   820

Kimball Electronics Inc.; Jasper; printed circuit boards   750

ArvinMeritor Inc.; Columbus; motor vehicle parts/accessories   739

NTN Driveshaft Inc.; Columbus; joints and couplings   735

Discount Labels Inc.; New Albany; paper labels   720

Beach Mold and Tool Inc.; New Albany; finishing services   705

Indiana University; New Albany   703

Enkei America Inc.; Columbus; motor vehicle wheels   670

Paoli Inc.; Orleans; wood office furniture   650

Best Chairs Inc.; Ferdinand; chairs   600

Cummins Inc.; Seymour; diesel, dual-fuel engines   600

Lawrenceburg Distillers and Importers; Lawrenceburg; distilled and blended liquors   600

Lowe's Home Centers Inc.; North Vernon; lumber, plywood, and millwork   600

Tyson Foods Inc.; Corydon; chicken processing   600

Indiana Family and Social Services Admin.; Madison   550

Interstate Brands Corp.; Columbus; bakery products   550

PTS Corp.; Bloomington; electronic circuits   543

Jackson County Schneck Memorial Hospital; Seymour   526

Arvin Sango Inc.; Madison; automotive exhaust systems   500

Dearborn County Hospital; Lawrenceburg   500

GKN Sinter Metals; Salem; friction material   500

Kimball International Inc.; Santa Claus; office furniture   500

Kimball International Manufacturing Inc.; Borden; wood office furniture   500

Kimball International Manufacturing Inc.; Jasper; office chairs   500

Morgan Foods Inc.; Austin; packaged soups   500

Reliance Electric Industrial Co.; Madison; electric motors   500

Samtec; New Albany; electronic circuits   500

Tecumseh Products Co.; Salem; refrigeration/air conditioning equipment   500

Wal-Mart Stores Inc.; Scottsburg; discount department stores   500

Districts established June 22, 2001, for elections first held in 2002.

5 members

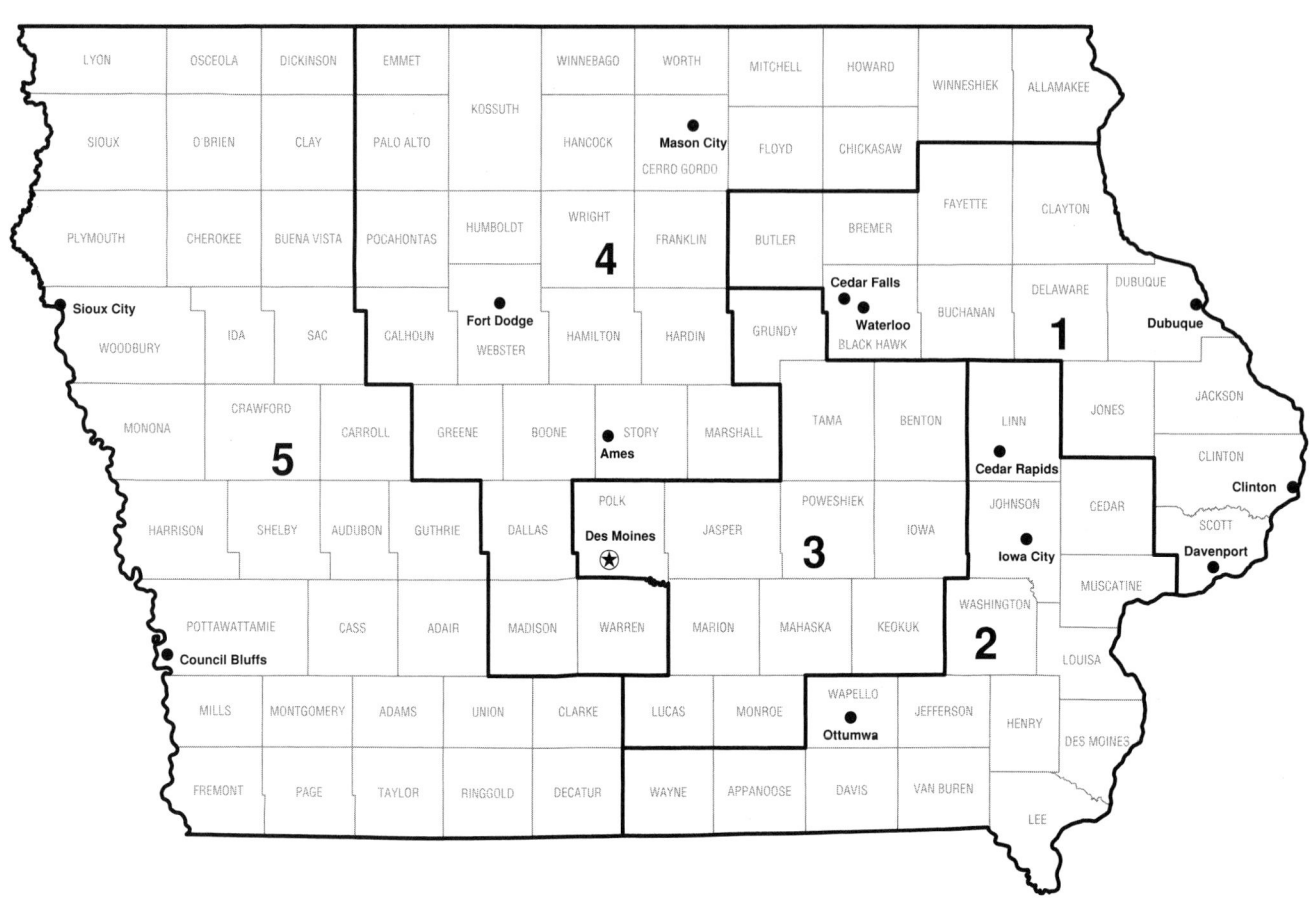

Iowa

Sturdy, squarish, set near the center of the national map, Iowa has long been a symbol for the agricultural Midwest, if not for all of rural America and its values. *The Music Man* is set here, in one of the Mississippi River towns on the state's eastern border (although the musical's author actually hailed from further west in Mason City), and its idealization of small town, old-fashioned America is still being revived every few years on Broadway.

There is science underpinning such sentiment. Iowa soil is among the deepest and richest black earth in the world, left by the retreating glaciers and irresistible to waves of eager tillers from back East and across the Atlantic. They made a fabulous success of farming here in the 1800s, and the state had a million residents shortly after the Civil War.

More recently, the state's longtime devotion to education, research, and innovation has helped lead the global Green Revolution that has made agriculture so productive it is difficult to make it profitable. As more and more can be produced with astonishing efficiency, the number of people engaged in agriculture has plummeted. In bad market cycles, commodity and land prices drop and crop loans and equipment loans come due. The factories, shops, packing houses, and other commerce that sprang up to service the farms have found it hard to survive. The state has striven to find new uses for its high-skill workers and farm families. But Iowa has been competing against many other farm states desperately seeking high-tech firms and venture capitalists. In 2002, to its chagrin, Iowa was dead last among the states in the number of new companies setting up shop within the state.

These long-term trends, coupled with the lack of a major metro area, gradually slowed the state's growth, then brought stagnation and, in the 1980s, actual decline. The population aged as many of the young left, skewing the population's average age. Only three states, all retirement destinations, now have a higher percentage of their residents over age 65. These trends have been deadly for the state's clout in Congress. Having increased its seats in the House from two to six in the 1850s, Iowa by 1880 topped out at 11 seats. But that would prove to be the plateau from which it fell. When the 1930 reapportionment finally accounted for the nation's urban shift, Iowa dropped to nine seats. It has dropped a seat each decade or so since; projections suggest it may drop another in 2010.

Still, in recent decades, Iowa has found some new ways to make itself matter, both economically and politically. Its unemployment rate has remained among the lowest in the country, as has its number of bankruptcy filings. Home ownership and net farm income still rank in the top ten, and the state remains among the national leaders in spending on schools and in the educational attainments of its people.

One reason the state has weathered uncertain economic times well is that it has striven to keep its government close and well examined, and it has usually gotten the maximum from its federal officials by keeping them in office. By 2003 Republican Chuck Grassley and Democrat Tom Harkin each had served about 20 years in the U.S. Senate. The governorship has been through a long Republican period courtesy of Terry Branstad, who held the job for 16 years ending in 1998, but Democrat Tom Vilsack was given a second term in 2002. The legislature, however, remained Republican in 2003.

On the presidential level, Iowa is best known not for its vote in November but for the winter night chats called caucuses that its party activists hold in January. These caucuses began in the early 1970s as fairly informal and often private events. But they were soon discovered by the national news media as a new way to steal a march on the nomination story. As the caucuses became the first stop on the long presidential march, they proved a tremendous marketing campaign and political contact festival for Iowa.

Since the caucuses began, Iowa has also been trending Democratic in the general election vote for president. In part this reflected the appeal of personalities. The state had launched George Bush as a national politician in its caucuses in 1980. But in 1988 Iowans turned on him, landing him fourth in the GOP caucuses. That presaged a vote for Michael Dukakis in November, and three more cycles of voting Democratic thereafter. The state has also concocted a notable cocktail of antiwar feelings (some left over from Vietnam), interest in global trade, and old-fashioned isolationism in becoming a leading opponent of U.S. intervention in foreign wars.

A perfect example of Iowa's vaunted sense of good government is its approach to redistricting. It begins with a nonpartisan advisory commission that proposes maps based on equal district size, geographical logic, and community of interest. The legislature can then pass or reject the maps (after two rejections, legislators are allowed to offer amendments), and the governor has a veto. After the 2000 census, the commission proposed one map and the Republican legislature failed to approve it. The commission then offered a second map, and Vilsack called a special session to vote it up or down. They voted for it, and Vilsack signed the plan in June 2001.

The result was a quick scramble for some incumbents who found their homes left out of their new districts. Republican Jim Leach, finding himself sharing a district with party colleague Jim Nussle, moved his home to be in the new 2nd district, which had most of his old constituents from the old 1st. Republican Tom Latham and Democrat Leonard Boswell also found they had to move to newly drawn districts with different numbers to stay with the main body of their constituents.

In the end though, the map did not cause much carnage in the 2002 elections. Latham quickly laid claim to the north-central district from Ames to the Minnesota line (and west to Fort Dodge) and won there. Boswell went from Decatur to Des Moines to claim the largely Democratic seat based there. The new district, in the western half of the state including Council Bluffs and Sioux City, went to a Republican state legislator named Steve King.

Table 1　Population

District	Population	Population under 18	Voting-age population	Median age	Male*	Female*
1	585,302	148,277	437,025	36.6	48.8	51.2
2	585,241	141,405	443,836	35.5	49.2	50.8
3	585,305	149,945	435,360	35.8	48.8	51.2
4	585,305	143,093	442,212	37.4	49.4	50.6
5	585,171	150,918	434,253	38.1	49.0	51.0
State	2,926,324	733,638	2,192,686	36.6	49.1	50.9

*As percentage of total population.

Table 2　Voting-Age Persons by Race/Hispanic or Latino Origin

District	White*	Black or African American*	American Indian or Alaska Native*	Asian*	Other or multirace*	Hispanic or Latino*
1	93.7	3.1	0.2	0.8	0.6	1.6
2	93.6	1.8	0.2	1.5	0.6	2.2
3	91.7	2.8	0.3	1.8	0.8	2.6
4	95.5	0.7	0.1	1.1	0.4	2.0
5	95.0	0.5	0.3	0.8	0.4	2.9
State	93.9	1.8	0.2	1.2	0.5	2.3

*As percentage of voting-age population.

Table 3　Voting-Age Population by Age Groups

District	18 to 24*	25 to 44*	45 to 64*	Over 64*
1	14.0	36.3	30.4	19.4
2	15.4	37.8	29.3	17.5
3	12.1	40.6	29.4	17.9
4	14.7	34.4	29.2	21.7
5	11.7	35.2	30.0	23.1
State	13.6	36.9	29.7	19.9

*As percentage of voting-age population.

Table 4　Income and Occupation

District	Median family income	Families in poverty*	White collar†	Blue collar†	Service†	Farm†
1	$47,321	6.9	55.7	28.3	15.2	0.8
2	$50,101	6.0	58.6	26.5	14.2	0.7
3	$52,260	5.4	62.0	23.5	14.0	0.6
4	$46,867	5.5	56.2	27.2	15.0	1.6
5	$44,322	6.3	53.3	29.5	15.5	1.6
State	$48,005	6.0	57.2	27.0	14.8	1.1

*As percentage of all families.　　†As percentage of employed workers 16 years and over.

Table 5　Education: School Years Completed

District	Less than grade 9*	Grades 9–12 no diploma*	High school diploma no college*	Some college*	College bachelor's degree or higher*
1	5.9	8.6	37.5	28.1	20.0
2	4.7	7.8	33.2	29.3	25.0
3	4.6	8.2	34.2	28.4	24.6
4	5.6	7.7	36.1	30.2	20.4
5	7.1	9.3	39.3	28.2	16.1
State	5.6	8.3	36.1	28.8	21.2

*As percentage of persons age 25 and over.

Table 6　Housing and Residential Patterns

District	Median home value	Owner occupied*	Renter occupied*	Urban†	Rural†
1	$82,400	72.6	27.4	66.3	33.7
2	$86,900	70.8	29.2	66.0	34.0
3	$91,300	71.5	28.5	73.1	26.9
4	$76,400	73.3	26.7	50.5	49.5
5	$73,100	73.6	26.4	49.4	50.6
State	$82,100	72.3	27.7	61.1	38.9

*As percentage of occupied housing units.　　†As percentage of total population.

Iowa 1st District

East — Davenport, Waterloo, Dubuque

The 1st takes in half of Iowa's Mississippi River counties and is dominated by three midsize industrial cities: Davenport, Waterloo, and Dubuque.

Davenport and Bettendorf in Scott County (Iowa's half of the Quad Cities that straddle the river into Illinois) are old, industrial river cities whose economies suffered badly during the 1980s but are recovering by capitalizing on tourists drawn to riverboat gambling. Waterloo, slightly more than 100 miles northwest of Davenport, grew up around the farm-implement and meatpacking industries. While hogs still are slaughtered here, the economy diversified in the 1990s to include finance and insurance. Neighboring Cedar Falls relies on the influence of the University of Northern Iowa.

Dubuque, built against the bluffs facing the Mississippi River, is Iowa's oldest city. Its economic base shifted in the 1990s from manufacturing and meatpacking to service, including insurance, finance, and telecommunications.

Democrats outnumber Republicans in the 1st, but voters have tended to demonstrate their independence at the polls in recent years. Black Hawk County, with Cedar Falls and Waterloo, has a strong Democratic base from its labor and academic communities. Scott County narrowly voted for Al Gore in 2000 but has a centrist Republican tradition. Democrats have the advantage in Clinton County, located north of Scott. Overall, Gore carried the district with 52.2 percent of the vote.

Dubuque County, which is heavily Catholic, gave Gore a greater percentage of the vote than any other county in the 1st. Dubuque has a culturally conservative lean, though, and Rep. Nussle has consistently outperformed Republican presidential candidates there. The rest of the 1st's residents live in rural areas that by and large are Republican-leaning but politically competitive.

Major Industry

Farm machinery, meatpacking, health care, agriculture.

Notable

Dyersville is home to the baseball field in the movie *Field of Dreams*.

Election Returns

	Republican		Democratic		Other	
President 2000	116,588	44.8%	135,856	52.2%	7,737	3.0%
House 2002	112,280	57.3%	83,779	42.7%	369	

District Profile

Population   585,302

Total area (square miles)   7,291.1
  Land area (square miles)   7,216.7

Population per square mile   81.1

Counties (2000 population)

Black Hawk	128,012	Delaware	18,404
Bremer	23,325	Dubuque	89,143
Buchanan	21,093	Fayette	22,008
Butler	15,305	Jackson	20,296
Clayton	18,678	Jones	20,221
Clinton	50,149	Scott	158,668

Cities and other areas over 10,000 (2000 population)

Bettendorf	31,275	Davenport	98,359
Cedar Falls	36,145	Dubuque	57,686
Clinton	27,772	Waterloo	68,747

Race and Hispanic or Latino origin*

White   92.1%
Black or African American   3.8%
American Indian or Alaska Native   0.2%
Asian   0.8%
Native Hawaiian or other Pacific Islander   0.0%
Some other race   0.1%
Hispanic or Latino origin   2.0%
Two or more races   1.0%

*As percentage of total population.

Ancestry*

Danish	1.2%	Irish	11.1%
Dutch	1.8%	Norwegian	2.9%
English	6.0%	Swedish	1.6%
French	1.8%	USA/American	4.8%
German	31.5%		

*As estimated percentage of total population.

Universities and colleges, 2000–2001 enrollment

Allen College, Waterloo   251
American Institute of Commerce, Cedar Falls   272
American Institute of Commerce, Davenport   376
Clarke College, Dubuque   1,249
Eastern Iowa Community College, Davenport   6,179
Emmaus Bible College, Dubuque   294
Hamilton Technical College, Davenport   344
Hawkeye Community College, Waterloo   4,263
Loras College, Dubuque   1,725
Marycrest International University, Davenport   721
Mount St. Clare College, Clinton   616
Northeast Iowa Community College, Peosta*
Palmer College of Chiropractic, Davenport   1,729
St. Ambrose University, Davenport   3,011
University of Dubuque, Dubuque   953
University of Northern Iowa, Cedar Falls   14,106
Upper Iowa University, Fayette   4,859
Wartburg College, Waverly   1,600

*Enrollment under 100. See Sources and Explanations in the front of the volume.

Newspapers and circulation

	District circulation	Total circulation
*Cedar Rapids Gazette**	8,894	64,798
Clinton Herald	10,202	12,763
Des Moines Register	6,624	152,945
Dubuque Telegraph Herald	21,183	28,283
Quad-City Times, Davenport	35,627	51,390
*USA Today**	2,901	1,674,376
Waterloo-Cedar Falls Courier	34,267	43,765

*See Sources and Explanations in the front of the volume.

Television stations and affiliations

Cedar Rapids-Waterloo-Iowa City-Dubuque	75%	KCRG	ABC
Cedar Rapids-Waterloo-Iowa City-Dubuque	75%	KFXA	FOX
Cedar Rapids-Waterloo-Iowa City-Dubuque	75%	KGAN	CBS
Cedar Rapids-Waterloo-Iowa City-Dubuque	75%	KIIN	PBS
Cedar Rapids-Waterloo-Iowa City-Dubuque	75%	KPXR	PAX
Cedar Rapids-Waterloo-Iowa City-Dubuque	75%	KRIN	PBS
Cedar Rapids-Waterloo-Iowa City-Dubuque	75%	KWKB	WB
Cedar Rapids-Waterloo-Iowa City-Dubuque	75%	KWWL	NBC
Cedar Rapids-Waterloo-Iowa City-Dubuque	75%	KYOU	FOX, UPN
Davenport-Rock Island-Moline	25%	KLJB	FOX
Davenport-Rock Island-Moline	25%	KLJB	FOX
Davenport-Rock Island-Moline	25%	KQCT	PBS
Davenport-Rock Island-Moline	25%	KWQC	NBC
Davenport-Rock Island-Moline	25%	WHBF	CBS
Davenport-Rock Island-Moline	25%	WQAD	ABC
Davenport-Rock Island-Moline	25%	WQPT	PBS

Cable systems and subscribers

Alpine Communications   1,076
Bellevue Municipal Cable   1,977
Butler Bremer Cablevision   654
Dixon Telephone   978
Jessup Cablevision   712
Mediacom   127,158
Northeast Iowa Telephone   780
Shellsburg Cablevision   884
Telnet   566

Businesses and other major employers

Canadian National Railway Co.; Waterloo; railroad freight hauling   3,200
Deere and Co.; Dubuque; farm tractors   2,500
Deere and Co.; Jesup; plant, dock, terminal tractors   2,000
Covenant Health System Inc. Hospital; Waterloo   1,789
Mercy Health Network Hospital; Dubuque   1,750
Memorial Foundation of Allen Hospital; Waterloo; fund-raising organization   1,500
Kraft Foods Inc.; Davenport; meatpacking plants   1,500

University of Northern Iowa; Cedar Falls   1,415
Hawkeye Community College; Waterloo   1,390
Genesis Medical Center; Davenport   1,307
Deere and Co.; Waterloo; farm tractors   1,225
Viking Pump Inc.; Cedar Falls; iron foundry   1,210
IBP Foodservice; Waterloo; meatpacking plants   1,200
MidAmerican Energy Co.; Davenport; electric services   1,200
Allen Memorial Hospital Corp.; Waterloo   1,175
APAC Customer Services Inc.; Davenport; telemarketing services   1,000
Interstate Power and Light Co.; Dubuque; electric services   960
Isle of Capri Bettendorf; Bettendorf; casino hotel   950
Deere and Co.; Davenport; excavation work   950
Omega Cabinets; Waterloo; wood kitchen cabinets   900
Finley Hospital; Dubuque   900
GMAC Mortgage Corp.; Waterloo; general and industrial loan institutions   800
Flexsteel Industries Inc.; Dubuque; upholstered household furniture   750
Deere and Co.; Cedar Falls; engineering services   730
Isle of Capri Davenport; Davenport; gambling   700
CUNA Mutual Life Insurance Co.; Waverly; life insurance   650
Eagle Window and Door Inc.; Dubuque; millwork   650
M&S Foods of Iowa Inc.; Davenport; fast-food restaurant   629
Alliant Energy Corp.; Dubuque; electric, other services   600
International Paper Co.; Clinton; food containers   600
Deere and Co.; Waterloo; engineering services   575
Custom Pak Inc.; Clinton; plastics products   550
APAC Customer Services Inc.; Waterloo; telemarketing services   500
Advanced Data-Comm Inc.; Dubuque; telemarketing services   500
Wal-Mart Stores Inc.; Dubuque; discount department stores   500
Family Dollar Stores Inc.; Maquoketa; general warehousing, storage   500
Isle of Capri Casino and Hotel; Marquette; gambling   500
Archer Daniels Midland Co.; Clinton; wet corn milling   500
Nestle Purina Petcare Co.; Davenport; dog and cat food   500
Sears Manufacturing Co.; Davenport; vehicle furniture   500
United Parcel Service Inc.; Davenport; parcel delivery   500
Target Corp.; Davenport; department stores   500

Iowa 2nd District

Southeast — Cedar Rapids, Iowa City

The 2nd, a Democratic-leaning region of 15 southeastern Iowa counties, takes in part of the state's eastern border with the Mississippi River and about half of the state's southern border with Missouri.

In the district's north is Cedar Rapids (in Linn County), the most populous city in the district and, after the state capital of Des Moines, the most populous in the state. Long a center for grain processing, Cedar Rapids has weathered hard economic times of late with help from telecommunication equipment firms.

Iowa City (Johnson County), located south of Cedar Rapids, is home to the University of Iowa and a growing number of high-tech companies. The academic community gives Iowa City a strong liberal tilt; one of the city's precincts gave more votes to Ralph Nader than George W. Bush in the 2000 presidential election. Johnson County has not backed a Republican presidential nominee since Richard Nixon in 1960.

The 2nd's other population center runs along the Mississippi River in the district's southeast, in Des Moines and Lee Counties. Unions retain some influence in the area, but an economy once centered on manufacturing is headed toward tourism and riverboat gambling.

The counties that form the district's southwestern arm are predominantly rural; the economy here relies on exporting agricultural products, including corn, tomatoes, soybeans, and pork. With the exception of Wapello County (Ottumwa), this area leans Republican.

Linn, Johnson, and the river counties together give the 2nd a decidedly Democratic tilt even though a Republican held the area for more than two decades even before the 2000 redistricting by mixing fiscal conservatism with moderate-to-liberal social views.

Major Industry

Electronics, telecommunications, health care, grain processing.

Notable

University of Iowa Hospitals and Clinics is one of the largest teaching hospitals in the world; Cedar Rapids' government buildings are located on an island in the center of the city.

Election Returns

	Republican		Democratic		Other	
President 2000	113,255	42.5%	141,487	53.1%	11,581	4.3%
House 2002	108,130	52.2%	94,767	45.8%	4,274	2.0%

District Profile

Population   585,241

Total area (square miles)   7,684.1
  Land area (square miles)   7,565.7

Population per square mile   77.4

Counties (2000 population)

Appanoose 13,721	Linn 191,701
Cedar 18,187	Louisa 12,183
Davis 8,541	Muscatine 41,722
Des Moines 42,351	Van Buren 7,809
Henry 20,336	Wapello 36,051
Jefferson 16,181	Washington 20,670
Johnson 111,006	Wayne 6,730
Lee 38,052	

Cities and other areas over 10,000 (2000 population)

Burlington   26,839
Cedar Rapids   120,758
Coralville   15,123
Fort Madison   10,715
Iowa City   62,220
Keokuk   11,427
Marion   26,294
Muscatine   22,697
Ottumwa   24,998

Race and Hispanic or Latino origin*

White   92.4%
Black or African American   2.0%
American Indian or Alaska Native   0.2%
Asian   1.5%
Native Hawaiian or other Pacific Islander   0.0%
Some other race   0.1%
Hispanic or Latino origin   2.7%
Two or more races   1.0%

*As percentage of total population.

Ancestry*

Dutch   2.2%
English   7.3%
French   2.0%
German   24.0%
Irish   10.4%
Italian   1.3%
Norwegian   2.4%
Scotch-Irish   1.2%
Scottish   1.2%
Swedish   2.1%
USA/American   5.5%

*As estimated percentage of total population.

Universities and colleges, 2000–2001 enrollment

Coe College, Cedar Rapids   1,301
Cornell College, Mount Vernon   987
Hamilton College, Cedar Rapids   345
Indian Hills Community College, Ottumwa   3,615
Iowa Wesleyan College, Mount Pleasant   777
Kirkwood Community College, Cedar Rapids   11,645
Maharishi University of Management, Fairfield   734
Mount Mercy College, Cedar Rapids   1,363
Southeastern Community College, West Burlington   2,537
University of Iowa, Iowa City   28,311

Newspapers and circulation

	District circulation	Total circulation
Burlington Hawk-Eye	17,556	19,485
*Cedar Rapids Gazette**	47,147	64,798
Des Moines Register	8,509	152,945
Iowa City Press Citizen	14,741	14,995
Muscatine Journal	7,650	7,731
Ottumwa Courier	12,952	16,215
Quad-City Times, Davenport	3,491	51,390
*USA Today**	2,620	1,674,376

*See Sources and Explanations in the front of the volume.

Television stations and affiliations

Cedar Rapids-Waterloo-Iowa City-Dubuque	32%	KCRG	ABC
Cedar Rapids-Waterloo-Iowa City-Dubuque	32%	KFXA	FOX
Cedar Rapids-Waterloo-Iowa City-Dubuque	32%	KGAN	CBS
Cedar Rapids-Waterloo-Iowa City-Dubuque	32%	KIIN	PBS
Cedar Rapids-Waterloo-Iowa City-Dubuque	32%	KPXR	PAX
Cedar Rapids-Waterloo-Iowa City-Dubuque	32%	KRIN	PBS
Cedar Rapids-Waterloo-Iowa City-Dubuque	32%	KWKB	WB
Cedar Rapids-Waterloo-Iowa City-Dubuque	32%	KWWL	NBC
Cedar Rapids-Waterloo-Iowa City-Dubuque	32%	KYOU	FOX, UPN
Ottumwa-Kirksville	24%	KTVO	ABC
Davenport-Rock Island-Moline	23%	KLJB	FOX
Davenport-Rock Island-Moline	23%	KLJB	FOX
Davenport-Rock Island-Moline	23%	KQCT	PBS
Davenport-Rock Island-Moline	23%	KWQC	NBC
Davenport-Rock Island-Moline	23%	WHBF	CBS
Davenport-Rock Island-Moline	23%	WQAD	ABC
Davenport-Rock Island-Moline	23%	WQPT	PBS
Des Moines-Ames	14%	KCCI	CBS
Des Moines-Ames	14%	KDIN	PBS
Des Moines-Ames	14%	KDSM	FOX
Des Moines-Ames	14%	KTIN	PBS
Des Moines-Ames	14%	WHO	NBC
Quincy-Hannibal-Keokuk	7%	KHQA	CBS
Quincy-Hannibal-Keokuk	7%	WGEM	NBC
Quincy-Hannibal-Keokuk	7%	WMEC	PBS
Quincy-Hannibal-Keokuk	7%	WQEC	PBS
Quincy-Hannibal-Keokuk	7%	WTJR	Independent

Cable systems and subscribers

Galaxy   2,150
Mediacom   129,564
Mediapolis Cablevision   593
Shellsburg Cablevision   599
Springville Cable   543
Starwest Cable   825

Military installations, September 2001

Iowa Army Ammunition Plant, Burlington   923

Businesses and other major employers

Iowa State University; Iowa City   14,777
Rockwell Collins Inc.; Cedar Rapids; search and navigation equipment   9,000
University of Iowa Hospitals and Clinics; Iowa City   6,894
Michael Paar; Muscatine; office furniture   4,000
University of Iowa; Iowa City   3,000
Metzeler Automotive Systems Iowa Inc.; Keokuk; rubber automotive products   3,000
Aegon USA Inc.; Cedar Rapids; health insurance   2,600
Heartland Express of Iowa; Iowa City; contract haulers   1,906
Mercy Medical Center; Cedar Rapids   1,800
McLeodUSA Telecommunications Services Inc.; Cedar Rapids; local telephone communications   1,800
Wal-Mart Stores Inc.; Cedar Rapids; discount department stores   1,750
Alliant Energy Corp.; Cedar Rapids; electric power generation   1,555
Iowa State University Hospital; Iowa City   1,500
MCI Worldcom Network Services Inc.; Cedar Rapids; local telephone communications   1,400
Excel Corp.; Ottumwa; meatpacking plants   1,400
U.S. Veterans Hospital; Iowa City   1,306
St. Luke's Methodist Hospital Inc.; Cedar Rapids   1,300
RuffaloCODY; Cedar Rapids; political fundraising   1,200
Farmland Foods Inc.; Bennett; auctioning livestock   1,200
Wal-Mart Stores Inc.; Mount Pleasant; general warehousing, storage   1,100
Great River Health Systems Inc. Hospital; Burlington   1,050
Mercy Hospital Iowa City Iowa Inc.; Iowa City   1,000
Iowa Turkey Growers Cooperative; West Liberty; turkey processing   1,000
Great River Medical Center; West Burlington   980
Lear Corp.; Iowa City; automobile seats   972

ACT Inc.; Iowa City; educational/personnel test service
950

NCS Pearson Inc.; Iowa City; testing services   850

Ottumwa Regional Health Center Inc.; Ottumwa   850

Rockwell Collins Inc.; Coralville; printed circuit boards
800

Transamerica Holding Co. Inc.; Cedar Rapids; mutual
funds manager   800

General Electric Co.; West Burlington; electric power
switches   800

Grain Processing Corp.; Muscatine; industrial grain
alcohol   780

American Ordnance; Middletown; ammunition plant
750

Procter and Gamble Manufacturing Co.; Iowa City;
toilet cleaners   663

Motorola Inc.; Mount Pleasant; radio/TV
communications equipment   650

Stanley Consultant International Inc.; Muscatine;
management consulting   650

Premium Retail Services Inc.; Marion; merchandising
consultant   645

City of Iowa City; Iowa City; city government   640

Square D Co.; Cedar Rapids; power circuit breakers
609

MCI Worldcom Network Services Inc.; Iowa City;
telemarketing services   600

Linn-Mar Community School; Marion   600

Sabine Transportation Co.; Cedar Rapids; deep-sea
freight transportation   600

Case Corp.; Burlington; construction machinery   600

Federal-Mogul Corp.; Burlington; engine spark plugs
600

Experian Information Solutions Inc.; Mount Pleasant;
direct mail advertising   600

Johnson County; Iowa City; county government   562

Interstate Power and Light Co.; Palo; electric power
generation   560

Vista Bakery Inc.; Burlington; bakery products   550

Dexter Co.; Fairfield; commercial washing machines
540

International Paper Co.; Cedar Rapids; paper mills   512

U.S. Postal Service; Cedar Rapids   500

Dial Corp.; Fort Madison; soap and other detergents
500

Keokuk Area Hospital; Keokuk   500

Meridian Rail Corp.; Keokuk; steel foundries   500

Celestica Corp.; Mount Pleasant; radio, TV circuit
boards   500

Hearth Technologies Inc.; Mount Pleasant; heating
equipment, non-electric   500

R. J. Personnel Inc.; Muscatine; temporary help service
500

Iowa 3rd District

Central and east central — Des Moines

The 12-county 3rd is somewhat microcosmic of the Hawkeye state. It includes relatively well-off urban and suburban areas, as well as rural counties, industrial cities, and scattered towns with hopes for economic development. It is roughly one-third urban, suburban, and rural.

The district is anchored in Des Moines, the state's largest city and the region's commercial, financial, and governmental center. Almost two-thirds of the district's residents live in Des Moines and the surrounding towns in Polk County. The capital has flourished since the 1980s, partly because of its diverse, white-collar employment base and its partial independence from agriculture. There is a sizable African American and Hispanic population north of downtown, between Interstate 235 and Drake University.

Outside of Polk the 3rd takes on a more rural and conservative flavor. No other county has more than 40,000 residents, and George W. Bush won nine of the district's 11 other counties in the 2000 presidential election. Mahaska and Grundy counties are among the most heavily Republican territories in Iowa.

But the 3rd is competitive in its voting: it gave Al Gore a 49 percent plurality of its votes, as did Iowa as a whole. The influence of Des Moines and surrounding Polk County gives the 3rd its slight Democratic lean. Polk has been more reliably Democratic than many parts of the nation, even supporting Democratic presidential nominees in the GOP presidential landslides of 1984 and 1988. Polk has not given a Republican presidential candidate a majority of its votes since Richard Nixon in 1972.

Major Industry

Insurance, health care, manufacturing.

Notable

F. L. Maytag built the first mechanized washer in Newton; legendary western lawman and gunfighter Wyatt Earp grew up in Pella; Pella is home to window and door manufacturer Pella Corp.

Election Returns

	Republican		Democratic		Other	
President 2000	131,319	48.4%	132,890	49.0%	7,226	2.7%
House 2002	97,285	45.1%	115,367	53.4%	3,333	1.5%

District Profile

Population   585,305

Total area (square miles)   7,033.8
   Land area (square miles)   6,979.2

Population per square mile   83.9

Counties (2000 population)

Benton	25,308	Mahaska	22,335
Grundy	12,369	Marion	32,052
Iowa	15,671	Monroe	8,016
Jasper	37,213	Polk	374,601
Keokuk	11,400	Poweshiek	18,815
Lucas	9,422	Tama	18,103

Cities and other areas over 10,000 (2000 population)

Altoona   10,345
Ankeny   27,117
Clive (pt.)   10,486
Des Moines   198,682

Newton 15,579
Oskaloosa 10,938
Urbandale (pt.) 28,745
West Des Moines (pt.) 42,525

Race and Hispanic or Latino origin*
White 90.1%
Black or African American 3.2%
American Indian or Alaska Native 0.4%
Asian 1.9%
Native Hawaiian or other Pacific Islander 0.0%
Some other race 0.1%
Hispanic or Latino origin 3.2%
Two or more races 1.1%

*As percentage of total population.

Ancestry*
Danish 1.2%	Italian 1.9%
Dutch 4.8%	Norwegian 3.0%
English 7.7%	Scotch-Irish 1.2%
French 1.8%	Scottish 1.3%
German 20.7%	Swedish 2.3%
Irish 9.6%	USA/American 5.3%

*As estimated percentage of total population.

Universities and colleges, 2000–2001 enrollment
American Institute of Business, Des Moines 875
Central College, Pella 1,336
Des Moines Community College, Ankeny 10,998
Drake University, Des Moines 5,126
Faith Baptist Bible College and Theological Seminary, Ankeny 494
Grand View College, Des Moines 1,378
Grinnell College, Grinnell 1,344
Hamilton College, Des Moines 472
Mercy College of Health Sciences, Des Moines 409
Mercy Hospital Medical Center-School of Cytotech, Des Moines 238
University of Osteopathic Medicine and Health Sciences, Des Moines 1,149
Vatterott College, Des Moines 281
William Penn College, Oskaloosa 1,384

Newspapers and circulation
	District circulation	Total circulation
*Cedar Rapids Gazette**	6,682	64,798
Des Moines Register	82,677	152,945
Marshalltown Times-Republican	1,224	9,595
Oskaloosa Herald	4,060	4,114
Ottumwa Courier	3,248	16,215
*USA Today**	3,647	1,674,376
Waterloo-Cedar Falls Courier	4,744	43,765

*See Sources and Explanations in the front of the volume.

Television stations and affiliations
Des Moines-Ames	56%	KCCI	CBS
Des Moines-Ames	56%	KDIN	PBS
Des Moines-Ames	56%	KDSM	FOX
Des Moines-Ames	56%	KTIN	PBS
Des Moines-Ames	56%	WHO	NBC
Cedar Rapids-Waterloo-Iowa City-Dubuque	44%	KCRG	ABC
Cedar Rapids-Waterloo-Iowa City-Dubuque	44%	KFXA	FOX
Cedar Rapids-Waterloo-Iowa City-Dubuque	44%	KGAN	CBS
Cedar Rapids-Waterloo-Iowa City-Dubuque	44%	KIIN	PBS
Cedar Rapids-Waterloo-Iowa City-Dubuque	44%	KPXR	PAX
Cedar Rapids-Waterloo-Iowa City-Dubuque	44%	KRIN	PBS
Cedar Rapids-Waterloo-Iowa City-Dubuque	44%	KWKB	WB
Cedar Rapids-Waterloo-Iowa City-Dubuque	44%	KWWL	NBC
Cedar Rapids-Waterloo-Iowa City-Dubuque	44%	KYOU	FOX, UPN

Cable systems and subscribers
Inter-County Cable 958
Mediacom 115,427
Montezuma Telephone 976
Telnet South 1,161

Military installations, September 2001
Camp Dodge Military Training Area, Johnston 2,246
Des Moines Army Reserve Complex, Des Moines 1,128
Des Moines International Airport (Air National Guard), Des Moines 976

Businesses and other major employers
Principal Life Insurance Co.; Des Moines; life insurance 5,109
Mercy Hospital Medical Center-Des Moines; Des Moines 4,500
Iowa Health System; Des Moines; hospital management 4,110
Pella Corp.; Pella; windows, wood 4,000
Central Iowa Hospital Corp.; Des Moines 3,300
Maytag Corp.; Amana; freezers 3,100
Blue Cross and Blue Shield of Iowa; Des Moines; health insurance 3,000
Well Mark Insurance Co.; Des Moines; insurance brokers 2,500
Seabury and Smith Inc.; Ankeny; insurance agents and brokers 2,000
Iowa Assn. of Community College Trustees; Des Moines; educational trust management 1,971
Marsh USA Inc.; Des Moines; insurance agents and brokers 1,900
Vermeer Manufacturing Co.; Pella; construction machinery 1,800
Iowa Governor's Office; Johnston 1,700
Deere and Co.; Ankeny; farm machinery and equipment 1,500
Pioneer Hybrid International; Johnston; manufacturing industries 1,500
AARP; West Des Moines; elder citizen organization 1,500
Communications Data Services Inc.; Des Moines; data processing 1,500
U.S. Postal Service; Des Moines 1,500
Allied Group Inc.; Des Moines; property damage insurance 1,388
Wells Fargo Home Mortgage Inc.; Des Moines; mortgage bankers 1,300
West Des Moines Community Schools District; West Des Moines 1,200
Annett Holdings Inc.; Des Moines; building materials transport 1,200
SAC and Fox Tribe of Mississippi and Iowa Inc.; Tama; bingo hall 1,200
Hy-Vee Inc.; Chariton; general warehousing, storage 1,100
Sears Roebuck and Co. Inc.; West Des Moines; credit card service 1,100

Polk County; Des Moines; county government 1,100

Employers Mutual Casualty Co.; Des Moines; fire, marine, casualty insurance 1,033

Equitrust Life Insurance Co.; West Des Moines; insurance agents and brokers 1,000

Iowa Health Physicians; Des Moines; medical centers 1,000

R. R. Donnelley and Sons Co.; Des Moines; rotogravure printing 1,000

Racing Assn. of Central Iowa; Altoona; horse race track 900

U.S. Veterans Hospital; Knoxville 900

Broadlawns Medical Center; Des Moines 900

Midland Homes Inc.; Des Moines; federal savings banks 842

John Deere Credit Co.; Johnston; installment note buying 825

Citigroup Inc.; West Des Moines; consumer finance companies 800

Qwest Corp.; Des Moines; local telephone communications 800

Wells Fargo Financial Inc.; Des Moines; consumer finance companies 800

Drake University; Des Moines 748

Vernon Co.; Newton; advertising 744

Tone Brothers Inc.; Ankeny; spices, including grinding 715

Des Moines Register and Tribune Co.; Des Moines; newspaper 700

U.S. Veterans Hospital; Des Moines 700

Iowa National Guard; Des Moines 700

Guideone Life Insuance Co.; West Des Moines; insurance agents and brokers 690

Continental Western Insurance Co.; Des Moines; fire, marine, casualty insurance 688

Titan Tire Corp.; Des Moines; automobile tires 650

Associates Corp. of North America; West Des Moines; credit card service 600

Wells Fargo Iowa; Des Moines; commercial bank 600

SuperValu Inc.; Des Moines; food supplier 600

Southeast Polk Community School District 6101; Runnells 599

F. C. Stone; West Des Moines; commodity futures brokers, dealers 570

Grinnell Mutual Reinsurance Co.; Grinnell; fire, marine, casualty insurance 560

Pella Regional Health Center; Pella 550

Grinnell College; Grinnell 530

American Republic Insurance Co.; Des Moines; accident insurance carriers 525

Emco Enterprises Inc.; Des Moines; metal storm doors or windows 508

City of Des Moines; Des Moines; police dept. 501

3M Co.; Knoxville; pressure-sensitive tape 500

Electronic Data Systems Corp.; Des Moines; direct-mail advertising 500

Sears Roebuck and Co. Inc.; Des Moines; department stores 500

Iowa Dept. of Human Services; Des Moines 500

Iowa Workforce Development Dept.; Des Moines 500

Ship Drop Express; Des Moines; mailing service 500

Gannett Co. Inc.; Des Moines; newspaper 500

Inland Finance Co.; Clive; vending machines 500

Dieomatic Inc.; Williamsburg; motor vehicle parts/accessories 500

Kinze Manufacturing Inc.; Williamsburg; farm machinery and equipment 500

Iowa 4th District

North and central — Ames, Mason City

The vast 4th takes up most of the state's northern border and dips deeply south, past the state capital of Des Moines (in the 3rd District), dividing Republican-leaning western Iowa and Democratic-leaning eastern Iowa.

Ames is the district's most populous city and is home to Iowa State University, about 30 miles north of Des Moines. Ames leans Democratic but does not have a strong liberal strain. The city, which accounts for almost two-thirds of Story County residents, backed Al Gore by just 7 percentage points in the 2000 presidential election.

Democrats fare well in Cerro Gordo County, which includes Mason City, the 4th's next most-populous city. Two-thirds of Mason City's employers are involved in manufacturing. A third urban center is Fort Dodge in Webster County, an industrial center that has relied on gypsum factories to support the area's economy. The city also emerged as a leader in veterinary pharmaceuticals. There are many Irish Catholic Democrats in this area.

But the 4th may have a slight GOP lean. George W. Bush won the district with 49 percent in 2000, capturing 13 of the 20 counties that have fewer than 20,000 residents.

The southern reaches of the district buttonhook counterclockwise around Des Moines to take in the Republican-leaning counties of Dallas, Madison, and Warren. Dallas is a big exception to Iowa's sluggish population growth; suburban growth west of Des Moines fueled Dallas' 37 percent growth rate in the 1990s, by far the fastest clip in the state. Warren (13 percent) and Madison (12 percent) also registered impressive growth.

Major Industry

Meatpacking, health care, veterinary pharmaceuticals.

Notable

Film star John Wayne was born in Winterset; Madison County's covered bridges were popularized in Robert James Waller's book; Mason City inspired native son Meredith Willson to compose the musical *The Music Man.*

Election Returns

	Republican		Democratic		Other	
President 2000	131,391	48.8%	129,280	48.0%	8,506	3.2%
House 2002	115,430	54.8%	90,784	43.1%	4,560	2.1%

District Profile

Population 585,305

Total area (square miles) 15,832.9
   Land area (square miles) 15,760.0

Population per square mile 37.1

Counties (2000 population)

Allamakee	14,675	Humboldt	10,381
Boone	26,224	Kossuth	17,163
Calhoun	11,115	Madison	14,019
Cerro Gordo	46,447	Marshall	39,311
Chickasaw	13,095	Mitchell	10,874
Dallas	40,750	Palo Alto	10,147
Emmet	11,027	Pocahontas	8,662
Floyd	16,900	Story	79,981
Franklin	10,704	Warren	40,671
Greene	10,366	Webster	40,235
Hamilton	16,438	Winnebago	11,723
Hancock	12,100	Winneshiek	21,310
Hardin	18,812	Worth	7,909
Howard	9,932	Wright	14,334

Cities and other areas over 10,000 (2000 population)

Ames	50,731	Indianola	12,998
Boone	12,803	Marshalltown	26,009
Fort Dodge	25,136	Mason City	29,172

Race and Hispanic or Latino origin*

White 94.7%
Black or African American 0.8%
American Indian or Alaska Native 0.2%
Asian 1.1%
Native Hawaiian or other Pacific Islander 0.0%
Some other race 0.1%
Hispanic or Latino origin 2.5%
Two or more races 0.6%

As percentage of total population.

Ancestry*

Danish	1.9%	Irish	8.9%
Dutch	2.2%	Norwegian	9.1%
English	6.8%	Scottish	1.1%
French	1.7%	Swedish	2.8%
German	27.1%	USA/American	4.2%

As estimated percentage of total population.

Universities and colleges, 2000–2001 enrollment

Hamilton College, Mason City 251
Iowa Central Community College, Fort Dodge 4,294
Iowa Lakes Community College, Estherville 2,743
Iowa State University, Ames 26,845
Iowa Valley Community College, Marshalltown 2,198
Luther College, Decorah 2,621
North Iowa Area Community College, Mason City 2,803
Northeast Iowa Community College, Calmar 3,480
Simpson College, Indianola 1,912
Waldorf College, Forest City 600

Newspapers and circulation

	District circulation	Total circulation
*Cedar Rapids Gazette**	2,075	64,798
Des Moines Register	39,300	152,945
Fort Dodge Messenger	17,267	17,848
Marshalltown Times-Republican	8,367	9,595
Mason City Globe Gazette	18,934	19,097
*USA Today**	1,162	1,674,376
Waterloo-Cedar Falls Courier	4,604	43,765
Webster City Freeman-Journal	2,889	2,889

See Sources and Explanations in the front of the volume.

Television stations and affiliations

Des Moines-Ames	61%	KCCI	CBS
Des Moines-Ames	61%	KDIN	PBS
Des Moines-Ames	61%	KDSM	FOX
Des Moines-Ames	61%	KTIN	PBS
Des Moines-Ames	61%	WHO	NBC
Rochester-Mason City-Austin	21%	KAAL	ABC
Rochester-Mason City-Austin	21%	KIMT	CBS
Rochester-Mason City-Austin	21%	KSMQ	PBS
Rochester-Mason City-Austin	21%	KTTC	NBC
Rochester-Mason City-Austin	21%	KXLT	FOX
Rochester-Mason City-Austin	21%	KYIN	PBS
Rochester-Mason City-Austin	21%	WCCO	CBS
Cedar Rapids-Waterloo-Iowa City-Dubuque	12%	KCRG	ABC
Cedar Rapids-Waterloo-Iowa City-Dubuque	12%	KFXA	FOX
Cedar Rapids-Waterloo-Iowa City-Dubuque	12%	KGAN	CBS
Cedar Rapids-Waterloo-Iowa City-Dubuque	12%	KIIN	PBS
Cedar Rapids-Waterloo-Iowa City-Dubuque	12%	KPXR	PAX
Cedar Rapids-Waterloo-Iowa City-Dubuque	12%	KRIN	PBS
Cedar Rapids-Waterloo-Iowa City-Dubuque	12%	KWKB	WB
Cedar Rapids-Waterloo-Iowa City-Dubuque	12%	KWWL	NBC
Cedar Rapids-Waterloo-Iowa City-Dubuque	12%	KYOU	FOX, UPN
Sioux City, NE	6%	KCAU	ABC
Sioux City, NE	6%	KMEG	CBS, UPN
Sioux City, NE	6%	KSIN	PBS
Sioux City, NE	6%	KTIV	NBC
Sioux City, NE	6%	KUSD	PBS
Sioux City, NE	6%	KXNE	PBS

Cable systems and subscribers

Complete Communications 1,739
Huxley Communications 883
Mediacom 97,221
Northwest Communications 857
Ogden Telephone 948
Telepartners 1,255
Telnet Communications 2,932
Video Services Limited 676
Winnebago Co-op Cablevision 1,055

Businesses and other major employers

Iowa State University of Science and Technology; Ames 6,000
Fisher Controls International Inc.; Marshalltown; valves and pipe fittings 2,734
Winnebago Industries Inc.; Forest City; motor homes 2,600
Mercy Medical Center; Mason City 2,100
Aerus; Webster City; household vacuum cleaners 2,000
Compass Facility Management Inc.; Ames; auditoriums and theaters operations 1,800
Iowa Dept. of Transportation; Ames 1,300
Mary Greeley Medical Center; Ames 1,240
Assa Abloy Door Group; Mason City; metal doors 1,200
Lennox Industries Inc.; Marshalltown; furnaces 1,100
Northeast Iowa Community College; Calmar 1,100
IBP Inc.; Perry; meatpacking plants 1,000
ISU Research Park Corp.; Ames; research institute 900
Trinity Regional Hospital; Fort Dodge 825
Barr-Nunn Transportation Inc.; Granger; trucking 701
Advanta USA Inc.; Slater; vegetable seeds 700
Iowa Dept. of Human Services; Woodward 700

Sara Lee Corp.; New Hampton; frozen bakery products
700

Featherlite Inc.; Cresco; farm machinery and equipment
700

Marshalltown Medical and Surgical Center;
Marshalltown   670

Sauer-Danfoss Co.; Ames; hydraulic power transfer
pumps   650

U.S. Dept. of Energy; Ames   600

Principal Life Insurance Co.; Mason City; insurance
agents   583

Fleetguard Inc.; Lake Mills; motor vehicle
parts/accessories   550

Luther College; Decorah   550

McFarland Clinic; Ames   502

Snap-On Inc.; Algona; sheet metal specialties   500

Comprehensive Systems Inc.; Charles City; outpatient
mental health clinic   500

Mercy Health Network Hospital; New Hampton   500

Iowa 5th District

West — Sioux City, Council Bluffs

The 32-county 5th takes in miles of fertile soil and gently undulating hills in the western part of the state. The bountiful land has allowed the region to remain more like the Iowa of old than any other part of the state.

Sioux City, the district's largest metropolitan center, has developed into a service center for a region that includes part of Nebraska and South Dakota. Some Sioux City businesses have moved across the river to take advantage of more-favorable tax laws in other states, but Woodbury County has sprouted numerous bedroom communities where many workers live. Sioux City long has leaned Republican, and surrounding rural towns are home to many independent farmers who tend to vote Republican.

The district's second-largest city, Council Bluffs, also is located on the state's western border, though farther south. Built against bluffs, the city was a bustling crossroads for three westward trails in the early 1800s, and five railroads later met there. Today, many workers cross the Missouri River to work for Omaha businesses that have been lured to Nebraska by lower tax rates.

Southwest Iowa is less wedded to social conservatism than the northwest region and is more likely to back GOP-establishment candidates. This area gave big percentages to George W. Bush in the 2000 caucuses, and it backed state House Speaker Brent Siegrist in the 2002 5th District primary over more-conservative challengers.

Overall, the solidly Republican district backed Bush by 17 percentage points in the 2000 general election. Bush's six top-performing counties in Iowa, and 11 of his best 13, are in the 5th District (topped by Sioux County with 83 percent of the vote).

Major Industry
Meatpacking, agriculture.

Notable
The annual Donna Reed Festival is held in the actress's hometown of Denison; the largest rural Danish settlement in the United States is in Elk Horn.

Election Returns

	Republican		Democratic		Other	
President 2000	141,820	57.1%	99,004	39.8%	7,623	3.1%
House 2002	113,257	62.2%	68,853	37.8%	127	

District Profile

Population   585,171

Total area (square miles)   18,429.4
   Land area (square miles)   18,347.5

Population per square mile   31.9

Counties (2000 population)

Adair 8,243	Lyon 11,763
Adams 4,482	Mills 14,547
Audubon 6,830	Monona 10,020
Buena Vista 20,411	Montgomery 11,771
Carroll 21,421	O'Brien 15,102
Cass 14,684	Osceola 7,003
Cherokee 13,035	Page 16,976
Clarke 9,133	Plymouth 24,849
Clay 17,372	Pottawattamie 87,704
Crawford 16,942	Ringgold 5,469
Decatur 8,689	Sac 11,529
Dickinson 16,424	Shelby 13,173
Fremont 8,010	Sioux 31,589
Guthrie 11,353	Taylor 6,958
Harrison 15,666	Union 12,309
Ida 7,837	Woodbury 103,877

Cities and other areas over 10,000 (2000 population)

Carroll 10,106	Spencer 11,317
Council Bluffs 58,268	Storm Lake 10,076
Sioux City 85,013	

Race and Hispanic or Latino origin*
White   93.7%
Black or African American   0.6%
American Indian or Alaska Native   0.4%
Asian   0.9%
Native Hawaiian or other Pacific Islander   0.0%
Some other race   0.0%
Hispanic or Latino origin   3.6%
Two or more races   0.7%

As percentage of total population.

Ancestry*

Danish 3.2%	Irish 9.2%
Dutch 5.7%	Norwegian 3.2%
English 6.6%	Swedish 3.0%
French 2.0%	USA/American 4.7%
German 26.8%	

As estimated percentage of total population.

Universities and colleges, 2000–2001 enrollment

Briar Cliff College, Sioux City 917
Buena Vista University, Storm Lake 2,732
Dordt College, Sioux Center 1,426
Graceland College, Lamoni 3,211
Iowa Western Community College, Council Bluff 4,503
Morningside College, Sioux City 1,049
Northwest Iowa Community College, Sheldon 912
Northwestern College, Orange City 1,243
Southwestern Community College, Creston 1,211
Western Iowa Tech Community College, Sioux City 4,365

Newspapers and circulation

	District circulation	Total circulation
Council Bluffs Nonpareil	16,481	16,506
Des Moines Register	13,152	152,945
Omaha World Herald	20,234	194,150
Sioux City Journal	38,855	46,030
Sioux Falls Argus Leader	1,919	51,753

See Sources and Explanations in the front of the volume.

Television stations and affiliations

Sioux City, NE	38%	KCAU	ABC
Sioux City, NE	38%	KMEG	CBS, UPN
Sioux City, NE	38%	KSIN	PBS
Sioux City, NE	38%	KTIV	NBC
Sioux City, NE	38%	KUSD	PBS
Sioux City, NE	38%	KXNE	PBS
Omaha, NE	30%	KBIN	PBS
Omaha, NE	30%	KETV	ABC
Omaha, NE	30%	KHIN	PBS
Omaha, NE	30%	KMTV	CBS
Omaha, NE	30%	KPTM	FOX
Omaha, NE	30%	KUON	PBS
Omaha, NE	30%	KXVO	WB
Omaha, NE	30%	KYNE	PBS
Omaha, NE	30%	WOWT	NBC
Des Moines-Ames	27%	KCCI	CBS
Des Moines-Ames	27%	KDIN	PBS
Des Moines-Ames	27%	KDSM	FOX
Des Moines-Ames	27%	KTIN	PBS
Des Moines-Ames	27%	WHO	NBC
Sioux Falls (Mitchell), SD	5%	KABY	ABC
Sioux Falls (Mitchell), SD	5%	KCSD	PBS
Sioux Falls (Mitchell), SD	5%	KDLO	CBS
Sioux Falls (Mitchell), SD	5%	KDLV	NBC
Sioux Falls (Mitchell), SD	5%	KDSD	PBS
Sioux Falls (Mitchell), SD	5%	KELO	CBS
Sioux Falls (Mitchell), SD	5%	KESD	PBS
Sioux Falls (Mitchell), SD	5%	KPLO	CBS
Sioux Falls (Mitchell), SD	5%	KPRY	ABC
Sioux Falls (Mitchell), SD	5%	KQSD	PBS
Sioux Falls (Mitchell), SD	5%	KRNE	PBS
Sioux Falls (Mitchell), SD	5%	KSFY	ABC
Sioux Falls (Mitchell), SD	5%	KSMN	PBS
Sioux Falls (Mitchell), SD	5%	KTSD	PBS
Sioux Falls (Mitchell), SD	5%	KTTM	FOX
Sioux Falls (Mitchell), SD	5%	KTTW	FOX

Cable systems and subscribers

Cable ONE 22,770
Community Cable TV 899
Comserv 3,686
Cox 17,459
Galaxy 1,551
Hartley Municipal Cable 696
HTC Cablecom 2,578
Interstate Cablevision 620
Lenox Municipal Cable 540
Manning Municipal 600
Marine & Elk Horn Telephone & Cable 1,063
Mediacom 45,375
Milford Cable TV 1,596
Modern Communications 960
New Century Communications 1,461
Northwest Iowa Telephone 540
Premier Center 1,448
Premier Communications 1,167
Telepartners 3,925
Telnet South 775
Tip Top Communications 1,150
Vernon Communications 1,842
Wetherell Satelite Cable TV 563

Military installations, September 2001

Sioux Gateway Airport (Air National Guard), Sergeant Bluff 984

Businesses and other major employers

Mutual of Omaha; Council Bluffs; insurance brokers 6,000
Trinity Health Corp.; Sioux City 2,000
Wells Dairy Inc.; Le Mars; packaged and molded ice cream 1,600
IBP Inc.; Storm Lake; meatpacking plants 1,500
Union Pacific Railroad Co.; Council Bluffs; railroad freight hauling 1,500
St. Luke's Regional Medical Center of Sioux City; Sioux City 1,450
Harveys Iowa Management Co.; Council Bluffs; casino hotel 1,306
Ameristar Casino Council Bluffs Inc.; Council Bluffs; casino hotel 1,250
John Morrell and Co. Inc.; Sioux City; meatpacking plants 1,200
Farmland Foods Inc.; Denison; meatpacking plants 1,200
IBP Inc.; Council Bluffs; meatpacking plants 1,057
Klaussner Corporate Services Inc.; Milford; upholstered household furniture 950
Iowa Dept. of Human Services; Glenwood 900
Southern Iowa Gaming Co.; Osceola; casino hotel 800
Alegent Health Inc. Medical Center; Council Bluffs 800
ConAgra Foods Inc.; Council Bluffs; frozen specialties 800
Jennie Edmundson Memorial Hospital; Council Bluffs 750
Eaton Corp.; Shenandoah; electric power transmission 750

Continental Deli Foods Inc.; Cherokee; prepared pork products   700

Pure Fishing Inc.; Spirit Lake; fishing equipment   650

American Marketing Industries Inc.; Orange City; uniform hats and caps   630

Communications Data Services Inc.; Red Oak; data processing   625

Pella Corp.; Carroll; metal doors, sash, and trim   600

Wal-Mart Stores Inc.; Council Bluffs; discount department stores   600

Pella Corp.; Shenandoah; windows, wood   600

Excel Corp.; Orange City; meatpacking plants   575

Western Iowa Tech Community College; Sioux City   525

Iowa Western Community College Inc.; Council Bluffs   510

Sara Lee Corp.; Storm Lake; turkey farm   500

Bunn-O-Matic Corp.; Creston; household cooking utensils   500

Polaris Industries Inc.; Spirit Lake; jet skis   500

Farner-Bocken Co.; Carroll; cigarettes   500

Oakland Foods; Oakland; sausages, other prepared meats   500

Intier Automotive Seating of America Inc.; Red Oak; farm machinery and equipment   500

Kansas

Kansas, the second largest state in the Midwest by area, calls forth images of wheat fields and wide horizons befitting its state song ("Home on the Range"). Yet in the new century, Kansas's economic and political destiny is increasingly influenced by Kansas City, the growing metropolis that straddles its eastern state line, at the confluence of the Kansas and Missouri Rivers. There are, in fact, two municipalities named Kansas City, founded on opposite river banks. The one that matters most to the metro area is the one on the Missouri side, because it is three times more populous than its rival Kansas City, Kansas. The big Kansas City is also the main economic engine for a metro area that's rising toward 2 million and locating more and more of its new residents in suburbs on the Kansas side of the rivers and of State Line Road.

The new residents are expanding the established suburbs of Johnson County, the largest of which (Overland Park) now has more people than Kansas City, Kansas, and onetime exurbs such as Olathe, Lenexa, and Ottawa. With 465,000 people in 2001, Johnson is now the most populous county in Kansas, having just surpassed Sedgwick (Wichita). Still the moving vans keep arriving, rolling into new developments further west on Interstate 70 and south on Interstate 35.

Historically, Kansas is that rare case of a state that reached its peak of political importance even before it entered the Union. In the 1850s "bleeding Kansas" was the site of incendiary cross-border raids by abolitionist and proslavery paramilitaries that preceded the Civil War. More recently, like so many of its neighbors, Kansas has been striving to replace the jobs disappearing from its agriculture (wheat, beef cattle, corn, hay, soybeans, sorghum, and hogs) and related manufacturing sectors. The loss of farm-related employment has driven a long-running population decline, shrinking the state's House delegation from a high of eight (first achieved in 1890) to the current four, with the fourth seat under pressure in the decades ahead.

Politically, Kansas alternates eras of Republican near-domination with eras of Republican total domination. When the White House is on the ballot, Kansas sets the GOP loyalty standard. The GOP nominee has carried the state in every presidential election since 1940, with the one exception of Lyndon B. Johnson's landslide in 1964. The Senate seats have been even more uniformly Republican. No Democrat has won either since George McGill sneaked in with a plurality in 1932. The GOP senators in 2003, Pat Robert and Sam Brownback, brought together two conservatives from different eras and schools. Brownback has been an outspoken advocate for social causes; Roberts chairs the Senate Intelli-gence Committee and also focuses on agricultural trade and international commerce. Their predecessors, Bob Dole and Nancy Landon Kassebaum, were remarkably popular at home and in Washington and were elected a total of eight times. The last close Senate race the state saw was in 1974, when first-termer Bob Dole was reelected with less than 51 percent in a race that turned on how many abortions had been done by the Democratic physician who was challenging Dole.

The abortion issue has fueled a strong social conservatives' movement here, and in 1999 that movement got control of the state's school board and promptly changed the rules for teaching evolution and big bang theory. A torrent of negative publicity descended on the state, and the board was pilloried as a latter day version of the 1920s Scopes "monkey trial" in Tennessee. At their next opportunity, state voters changed the mix on that board and the curriculum decision was reversed.

The one place where Democrats have held their own is in the gubernatorial contests of the postwar era. Democrats have come close to parity here, and moderate Republicans have tended to win over more orthodox conservatives—as if the voters wanted a chief executive to leaven the consistently conservative legislature. In 2002 the state elected its second woman Democrat as governor in a decade, Kathleen Sebelius.

In redistricting, the Kansas that lies beyond the Kansas City metro area is loath to be the dog wagged by its upstart suburban tail. Still, there is little way around the fact that without Johnson and the adjacent counties that drove overall growth in the 1990s (8.7 percent statewide), the state would be static. That is why these suburbs may soon rate a district all their own. Right now they are the bulk of the 3rd District, which also includes Wyandotte County, a trove of minority and blue-collar voters who make it competitive for a Democrat. In 2002 the 3rd was won by a Democrat only by a slim margin.

The 1st District includes Russell, the ancestral home of Bob Dole, the 1996 Republican nominee for president. One of the largest districts in the country, the 1st covers two-thirds of the state's counties, from Colorado eastward to within a short drive of Missouri at its easternmost points. In each decade's redistricting, the 1st needs to enfold a few more eastern counties to reach parity with the other districts. This district includes most all of the state's energy industry, and stripper wells still dot the landscape as it rises gradually into the high plains of eastern Colorado.

The 2nd combines the capital of Topeka and an array of historic towns from Atchison (at the northeast corner near Nebraska) to Leavenworth to Coffeyville (nearly at the Oklahoma line). If Wyandotte County were returned to the

Districts established May 31, 2002, for elections first held in 2002.

4 members

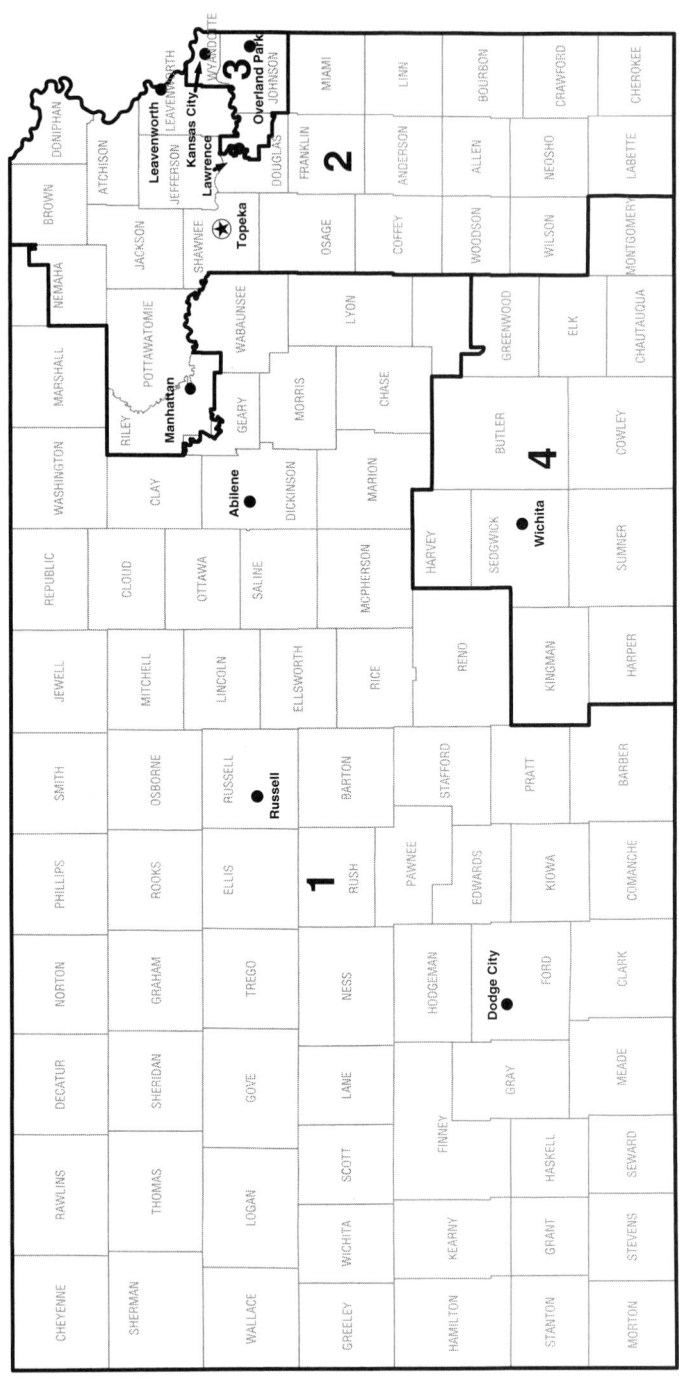

2nd District at some point in time, this could become the new swing district. But in 2001 the remappers, a special committee from both chambers of the state legislature, went the other way, to the relief of the 3rd District's Democratic incumbent. The new map made few changes, other than adjusting the lines to keep the population of the districts equal, and shrinking the 3rd to include somewhat less of Douglas County (Lawrence), the home of the University of Kansas.

The 4th District is the city of Wichita (344,000), plus the rest of Sedgwick County and the surrounding counties, none far from the Oklahoma state line. Wichita got a boost from the oil and gas industry that began here in the 1890s and has known some boom decades since. But the larger success story for Wichita has been the aircraft industry, which centered small plane production here in World War II. Cessna and its chief rivals are still here, and Wichita folks are glad to remind you they still manufacture more small aircraft than any other city in the world.

Table 1   Population

District	Population	Population under 18	Voting-age population	Median age	Male*	Female*
1	672,091	177,815	494,276	36.9	49.6	50.4
2	672,102	170,318	501,784	35.3	49.8	50.2
3	672,124	178,776	493,348	33.6	48.9	51.1
4	672,101	186,084	486,017	35.0	49.3	50.7
State	2,688,418	712,993	1,975,425	35.2	49.4	50.6

*As percentage of total population.

Table 2   Voting-Age Persons by Race/Hispanic or Latino Origin

District	White*	Black or African American*	American Indian or Alaska Native*	Asian*	Other or multirace*	Hispanic or Latino*
1	87.3	2.0	0.4	0.9	0.8	8.6
2	88.7	4.7	1.1	1.1	1.3	3.2
3	81.5	8.0	0.6	2.6	1.2	6.0
4	83.5	6.2	1.1	2.4	1.5	5.4
State	85.3	5.2	0.8	1.7	1.2	5.8

*As percentage of voting-age population.

Table 3   Voting-Age Population by Age Groups

District	18 to 24*	25 to 44*	45 to 64*	Over 64*
1	12.9	35.7	29.1	22.3
2	15.9	36.9	29.1	18.1
3	14.3	43.1	28.8	13.8
4	12.6	40.1	29.3	18.0
State	14.0	38.9	29.1	18.0

*As percentage of voting-age population.

Table 4   Income and Occupation

District	Median family income	Families in poverty*	White collar†	Blue collar†	Service†	Farm†
1	$42,292	7.8	52.8	28.5	16.1	2.7
2	$47,095	7.1	57.6	26.1	15.5	0.8
3	$62,695	4.9	70.4	17.3	12.2	0.2
4	$49,650	7.0	57.0	28.3	14.2	0.5
State	$49,624	6.7	59.7	24.9	14.4	1.0

*As percentage of all families.   †As percentage of employed workers 16 years and over.

Table 5   Education: School Years Completed

District	Less than grade 9*	Grades 9–12 no diploma*	High school diploma no college*	Some college*	College bachelor's degree or higher*
1	8.1	9.6	32.9	31.4	18.0
2	4.5	8.6	34.2	29.5	23.2
3	3.4	6.7	21.7	29.1	39.1
4	4.8	10.2	30.5	31.5	23.0
State	5.2	8.8	29.8	30.4	25.8

*As percentage of persons age 25 and over.

Table 6   Housing and Residential Patterns

District	Median home value	Owner occupied*	Renter occupied*	Urban†	Rural†
1	$61,900	71.4	28.6	52.4	47.6
2	$75,400	69.0	31.0	59.8	40.2
3	$129,900	67.7	32.3	94.7	5.3
4	$74,400	68.8	31.2	78.8	21.2
State	$81,000	69.2	30.8	71.4	28.6

*As percentage of occupied housing units.   †As percentage of total population.

Kansas 1st District

West — Salina, Hutchinson, Dodge City

The fiscally conservative 1st takes in all of western Kansas and stretches east across farmland to reach Nemaha County in the north and Emporia in the center, covering most of rural Kansas in the process. The district covers 70 percent of the state and in land area is bigger than most U.S. states (including 25 of the 26 states east of the Mississippi River).

The 1st's economy is wedded to agriculture, an industry that suffered from weather disasters in the 1980s and falling commodity prices in the 1990s. More and more rural residents have packed their bags for the city to escape the tough farming life.

The largest population center is in the district's eastern portion. Salina (Saline County) is a traditional farm-market town but has an industrial element—Raytheon has a factory here. Hutchinson, site of the Kansas State Fair, is dominated by farm- and food-related businesses. Junction City is home to many civilian workers who commute to Fort Riley in the 2nd District. In the west, towns such as Garden City and Dodge City rely on meatpacking and tourism. Thriving beef processing plants continue to draw Mexican and Asian immigrants.

The 1st is comfortably Republican, although it did exhibit an independent streak in the 1992 presidential election, giving Ross Perot 29 percent of the vote. The district overwhelmingly voted for George W. Bush in the 2000 presidential contest, giving him two-thirds of the vote. The GOP also dominates local offices, except in Hays, where Fort Hays State University is located, and in Hutchinson.

Major Industry

Agriculture, manufacturing, oil, and gas.

President Dwight D. Eisenhower's burial place and presidential library are in Abilene; former Senate majority leader and 1996 Republican presidential nominee Bob Dole is from Russell.

Election Returns

	Republican		Democratic		Other	
President 2000	177,857	66.7%	76,448	28.7%	12,514	4.7%
House 2002	189,976	91.1%			18,585	8.9%

District Profile

Population   672,091

Total area (square miles)   57,575.5
  Land area (square miles)   57,373.2

Population per square mile   11.7

Counties (2000 population)

Barber	5,307	Meade	4,631
Barton	28,205	Mitchell	6,932
Chase	3,030	Morris	6,104
Cheyenne	3,165	Morton	3,496
Clark	2,390	Nemaha (pt.)	7,085
Clay	8,822	Ness	3,454
Cloud	10,268	Norton	5,953
Comanche	1,967	Osborne	4,452
Decatur	3,472	Ottawa	6,163
Dickinson	19,344	Pawnee	7,233
Edwards	3,449	Phillips	6,001
Ellis	27,507	Pratt	9,647
Ellsworth	6,525	Rawlins	2,966
Finney	40,523	Reno	64,790
Ford	32,458	Republic	5,835
Geary (pt.)	23,682	Rice	10,761
Gove	3,068	Rooks	5,685
Graham	2,946	Rush	3,551
Grant	7,909	Russell	7,370
Gray	5,904	Saline	53,597
Greeley	1,534	Scott	5,120
Greenwood (pt.)	2,110	Seward	22,510
Hamilton	2,670	Sheridan	2,813
Haskell	4,307	Sherman	6,760
Hodgeman	2,085	Smith	4,536
Jewell	3,791	Stafford	4,789
Kearny	4,531	Stanton	2,406
Kiowa	3,278	Stevens	5,463
Lane	2,155	Thomas	8,180
Lincoln	3,578	Trego	3,319
Logan	3,046	Wabaunsee	6,885
Lyon	35,935	Wallace	1,749
Marion	13,361	Washington	6,483
Marshall	10,965	Wichita	2,531
McPherson	29,554		

Cities and other areas over 10,000 (2000 population)

Dodge City	25,176	Hutchinson	40,787
Emporia	26,760	Junction City	18,886
Garden City	28,451	Liberal	19,666
Great Bend	15,345	McPherson	13,770
Hays	20,013	Salina	45,679

Race and Hispanic or Latino origin*

White   84.5%
Black or African American   2.1%
American Indian or Alaska Native   0.4%
Asian   0.9%
Native Hawaiian or other Pacific Islander   0.0%
Some other race   0.1%
Hispanic or Latino origin   10.9%
Two or more races   1.1%

*As percentage of total population.

Ancestry*

Dutch	1.9%	Scotch-Irish	1.2%
English	7.3%	Scottish	1.1%
French	2.3%	Swedish	2.4%
German	23.2%	USA/American	7.2%
Irish	7.2%		

*As estimated percentage of total population.

Universities and colleges, 2000–2001 enrollment

Barton County Community College, Great Bend   4,612
Bethany College, Lindsborg   608
Cloud County Community College, Concordia   2,668
Colby Community College, Colby   2,160
Dodge City Community College, Dodge City   1,999
Emporia State University, Emporia   5,616
Flint Hills Technical College, Emporia   391
Fort Hays State University, Hays   5,498
Garden City Community College, Garden City   2,107
Hutchinson Community College, Hutchinson   3,466
Kansas Wesleyan University, Salina   747
McPherson College, McPherson   463
North Central Kansas Technical College, Beloit   411
Northwest Kansas Area Vocational Technical School, Goodland   593
Pratt Community College, Pratt   1,331
Salina Area Vocational Technical School, Salina   310
Seward County Community College, Liberal   1,750
Sterling College, Sterling   440
Tabor College, Hillsboro   586

Newspapers and circulation

	District circulation	Total circulation
Emporia Gazette	7,622	7,999
Garden City Telegram	9,851	9,897
Great Bend Tribune	6,719	6,719
Hutchinson News	30,986	34,007
Junction City Daily Union	5,350	5,514
Kansas City Star	1,242	261,945
Salina Journal	29,242	29,562
Topeka Capital Journal	5,686	56,641
*USA Today**	1,795	1,674,376
Wichita Eagle	5,394	87,687

*See Sources and Explanations in the front of the volume.

Television stations and affiliations

Wichita-Hutchinson	83%	KAAS	FOX
Wichita-Hutchinson	83%	KAKE	ABC
Wichita-Hutchinson	83%	KBSD	CBS
Wichita-Hutchinson	83%	KBSH	CBS
Wichita-Hutchinson	83%	KBSL	CBS

Wichita-Hutchinson	83%	KDCK	PBS
Wichita-Hutchinson	83%	KLBY	ABC
Wichita-Hutchinson	83%	KOOD	PBS
Wichita-Hutchinson	83%	KPTS	PBS
Wichita-Hutchinson	83%	KSAS	FOX
Wichita-Hutchinson	83%	KSNC	NBC
Wichita-Hutchinson	83%	KSNG	NBC
Wichita-Hutchinson	83%	KSNK	NBC
Wichita-Hutchinson	83%	KSNW	NBC
Wichita-Hutchinson	83%	KSWK	PBS
Wichita-Hutchinson	83%	KUPK	ABC
Wichita-Hutchinson	83%	KWCH	CBS
Topeka	11%	KSNT	NBC
Topeka	11%	KTKA	ABC
Topeka	11%	KTWU	PBS
Topeka	11%	WIBW	CBS
Lincoln-Hastings-Kearney	6%	KGIN	CBS
Lincoln-Hastings-Kearney	6%	KHAS	NBC
Lincoln-Hastings-Kearney	6%	KHGI	ABC
Lincoln-Hastings-Kearney	6%	KHNE	PBS
Lincoln-Hastings-Kearney	6%	KLKE	ABC
Lincoln-Hastings-Kearney	6%	KLKN	ABC
Lincoln-Hastings-Kearney	6%	KLNE	PBS
Lincoln-Hastings-Kearney	6%	KMNE	PBS
Lincoln-Hastings-Kearney	6%	KOLN	CBS
Lincoln-Hastings-Kearney	6%	KSNB	FOX
Lincoln-Hastings-Kearney	6%	KTVG	FOX
Lincoln-Hastings-Kearney	6%	KWNB	ABC

Cable systems and subscribers
Adelphia   5,400
Atwood Cable System   572
Cable ONE   9,445
Carson Communications   563
Charter   5,589
Classic   26,667
Community Antenna Systems   1,048
Cox   72,718
Cunningham Cable   2,760
Eagle Communications   13,711
Epic Touch   1,045
Five Star Cable   784
Galaxy   10,791
GBT Communications   1,358
H&B Cable Services   886
Nex-Tech   2,989
Pioneer Communications   9,174
Time Warner   2,834
Twin Valley Communications   574
United Communications Assn.   1,349
Washington Cable TV   559

Businesses and other major employers
IBP Inc.; Holcomb; meatpacking plants   3,000
Raytheon Aircraft Co.; Salina; airplanes   2,000
Farmland National Beef Packing Co.; Dodge City; meatpacking plants   1,600
U.S. Postal Service; Salina   1,555
Emporia State University; Emporia   1,500
Fort Hays State University; Hays   1,500
Blue Beacon U.S.A. LP; Salina; truck wash   900
Hutchinson Hospital Corp.; Hutchinson   900
Salina Regional Health Center; Salina   800

Exide Technologies; Salina; storage batteries   781
Eaton Corp.; Hutchinson; fluid power cylinders   750
Russell Stover Candies Inc.; Abilene; candy   740
Interstate Brands Corp.; Emporia; breads and cakes   700
Salina Unified School District; Salina   680
Eastbay Inc.; Junction City; general warehousing, storage   630
Kansas Dept. of Corrections; Hutchinson   621
Philips Electronics North America Corp.; Salina; fluorescent lamps   600
Knight-Ridder Inc.; Canton; newspaper   600
Mossberg Sanitation Inc.; Great Bend; livestock services   600
Sykes Enterprises Inc.; Hays; computer peripherals, software   600
Fouard Tax Service; Hutchinson; tax return preparation services   596
Barton County Community College Inc.; Great Bend   596
Hays Medical Center Inc.; Hays   575
Swift-Eckrich Inc.; Junction City; sausages, other prepared meats   500
Great Plains Health Alliance Inc.; Beloit; skilled nursing care facilities   500
Hutchinson Community College; Hutchinson   500
Centex Construction Products Inc.; Hutchinson; paperboard mills   500
Hutchinson Clinic; Hutchinson   500
Central Kansas Medical Center Inc.; Great Bend   500
ConAgra Beef Co.; Garden City; meatpacking plants   500

Kansas 2nd District

East — Topeka, Manhattan, Leavenworth

The 2nd runs the length of the state in east Kansas from Nebraska to Oklahoma, passing west of the Kansas City area. This moderately conservative district is a combination of rural farm communities and urbanized areas, including the state capital of Topeka. One-fourth of district residents live in Topeka or surrounding Shawnee County.

Republicans do well in the district's rural regions, while Democrats are more successful in Topeka and the state's blue-collar southeast corner. Although the 2nd is conservative, it is not overwhelmingly Republican; it was the only congressional district in Kansas where native son Bob Dole failed to win 50 percent or more of the vote in the 1996 presidential election. The district also favored Democrat Kathleen Sebelius in the 2002 governor's election. George W. Bush won the district with 54.1 percent of the vote in the 2000 presidential election.

The 2nd's economy has experienced slow but steady growth, and unemployment is low. Most of the jobs revolve around agriculture, particularly wheat. State government is Topeka's largest employer. Fort Riley and Fort Leavenworth also aid the 2nd's economy, though Fort Riley suffered a round of cutbacks in the mid-1990s.

Redistricting following the 2000 census added part of Lawrence—the Democratic-leaning home of the University of Kansas (the university itself is in the 3rd District)—but the political impact was offset by the 2nd's acquisition of conservative Miami County. The district also includes Manhattan, home to Kansas State University.

Major Industry

Agriculture, defense, higher education.

Notable

Robert Stroud, the "Birdman of Alcatraz," served 30 years in the federal penitentiary in Leavenworth before being transferred to Alcatraz; the Kansas Museum of History is in Topeka; Mine Creek Battlefield near Pleasanton was the site of Kansas' only major Civil War battle.

Election Returns

	Republican		Democratic		Other	
President 2000	144,721	54.1%	109,133	40.8%	13,723	5.1%
House 2002	127,477	60.4%	79,160	37.5%	4,340	2.1%

District Profile

Population 672,102

Total area (square miles) 14,317.8
Land area (square miles) 14,133.5

Population per square mile 47.6

Counties (2000 population)

Allen	14,385	Jefferson	18,426
Anderson	8,110	Labette	22,835
Atchison	16,774	Leavenworth	68,691
Bourbon	15,379	Linn	9,570
Brown	10,724	Miami	28,351
Cherokee	22,605	Nemaha (pt.)	3,632
Coffey	8,865	Neosho	16,997
Crawford	38,242	Osage	16,712
Doniphan	8,249	Pottawatomie	18,209
Douglas (pt.)	36,806	Riley	62,843
Franklin	24,784	Shawnee	169,871
Geary (pt.)	4,265	Wilson	10,332
Jackson	12,657	Woodson	3,788

Cities and other areas over 10,000 (2000 population)

Atchison	10,232	Ottawa	11,921
Lawrence (pt.)	25,768	Parsons	11,514
Leavenworth	35,420	Pittsburg	19,243
Manhattan	44,831	Topeka	122,377

Race and Hispanic or Latino origin*

White 87.3%
Black or African American 4.9%
American Indian or Alaska Native 1.2%
Asian 1.0%
Native Hawaiian or other Pacific Islander 0.1%
Some other race 0.1%
Hispanic or Latino origin 3.8%
Two or more races 1.7%

As percentage of total population.

Ancestry*

Dutch	1.7%	German	19.3%
English	8.2%	Irish	9.1%
French	2.3%	Italian	1.6%
Scotch-Irish	1.5%	Swedish	1.8%
Scottish	1.4%	USA/American	7.1%

As estimated percentage of total population.

Universities and colleges, 2000–2001 enrollment

Allen County Community College, Iola   1,968
Baker University College of Arts and Sciences, Baldwin City   828
Benedictine College, Atchison   1,369
Fort Scott Community College, Fort Scott   1,677
Highland Community College, Highland   2,693
Kansas State University, Manhattan   21,929
Labette Community College, Parsons   1,338
Manhattan Area Technical College, Manhattan   320
Manhattan Christian College, Manhattan   406
Neosho County Community College, Chanute   1,479
Ottawa University, Ottawa   429
Pittsburg State University, Pittsburg   6,418
Saint Mary College, Leavenworth   766
Topeka Technical College, Topeka   260
U.S. Army Command and General Staff College, Fort Leavenworth   1,108
University of Kansas,* Lawrence   25,920
Washburn University of Topeka, Topeka   5,917

Principally located in the 3rd District, some portions in the 2nd District.

Newspapers and circulation

	District circulation	Total circulation
Joplin Globe	3,058	30,638
Kansas City Star	15,909	261,945
Lawrence Journal-World	9,976	18,512
Manhattan Mercury	9,452	10,243
St. Joseph News-Press	2,966	39,144
Topeka Capital Journal	50,182	56,641
*USA Today**	2,452	1,674,376

See Sources and Explanations in the front of the volume.

Television stations and affiliations

Topeka	40%	KSNT	NBC
Topeka	40%	KTKA	ABC
Topeka	40%	KTWU	PBS
Topeka	40%	WIBW	CBS
Joplin-Pittsburg	32%	KOAM	CBS
Joplin-Pittsburg	32%	KODE	ABC
Joplin-Pittsburg	32%	KOZJ	PBS
Joplin-Pittsburg	32%	KSNF	NBC
Kansas City	25%	KCPT	PBS
Kansas City	25%	KCTV	CBS
Kansas City	25%	KCWE	UPN
Kansas City	25%	KMBC	ABC
Kansas City	25%	KMCI	Independent
Kansas City	25%	KPXE	PAX
Kansas City	25%	KSHB	NBC
Kansas City	25%	KSMO	WB
Kansas City	25%	WDAF	FOX
St. Joseph, MO	3%	KQTV	ABC
St. Joseph, MO	3%	KTAJ	Independent

Cable systems and subscribers

Baxter Springs Cablevision   1,492
Cable ONE   9,418

Carson Communications   3,646
Charter   7,277
Classic   10,164
CLR Video   3,637
Columbus Municipal Cable TV   952
Cox   79,416
Galaxy   2,749
Mediacom   8,635
National Cable   538
Sunflower Cablevision   1,185
Time Warner   10,206
Wamengo Community Cable   2,110

Military installations, September 2001
Fort Riley (Army), Junction City   13,905
Fort Leavenworth (Army), Leavenworth   5,552
Forbes Field (Air National Guard), Pauline   950
Topeka Future (Army Reserve), Topeka   428
Topeka Forbes Field (Army Guard), Topeka   258
Kansas Army Ammunition Plant, Parsons   153

Businesses and other major employers
Goodyear Tire and Rubber Co.; Topeka; pneumatic tires   7,000
Kansas Dept. of Social and Rehabilitation Services; Topeka   2,755
Stormont-Vail Regional Health Center; Topeka   2,393
Burlington Northern and Santa Fe Railway Co.; Topeka; railroad freight hauling   2,000
St. Francis Health Center; Topeka   1,500
Pittsburg State University; Pittsburg   1,500
U.S. Veterans Hospital; Topeka   1,260
Kansas State University; Manhattan   1,200
Menninger Clinic Inc.; Topeka   1,185
Wolf Creek Nuclear Operating Corp.; Burlington; electric power generation   1,006
U.S. Veterans Hospital; Leavenworth   1,000
Prairie Band of Potawatomi; Mayetta; casino hotel   1,000
Jostens Inc.; Topeka; commercial printing   980
Blue Cross and Blue Shield of Kansas; Topeka; hospital/medical service plans   950
Kansas Dept. of Administration; Topeka   930
Mount Carmel Regional Medical Center Inc.; Pittsburg   900
Kansas Dept. of Human Resources; Topeka   850
Kansas Dept. of Health and Environment; Topeka   845
Southwestern Bell Telephone Co.; Topeka; telephone equipment and systems   800
Hallmark Cards Inc.; Topeka; greeting cards   800
Payless Shoesource Financial Inc.; Topeka; shoe stores   750
TeleTech Services Corp.; Topeka; telemarketing services   750
Payless Shoesource Inc.; Topeka; general warehousing, storage   750
Washburn University; Topeka   716
Farm Bureau Insurance Agency Inc.; Manhattan; insurance brokers   700
Hill's Pet Nutrition Inc.; Topeka; pet food   700
City of Topeka; Topeka; city management   700
Superior Industries International Inc.; Pittsburg; aluminum foundries   700

Kansas Dept. of Social and Rehabilitation Services; Topeka   650
Atchison Casting Corp.; Atchison; steel foundries   620
Snorkel International Inc.; Elwood; backhoes, tractors, cranes, plows   600
Northrop Grumman Information Technology Inc.; Fort Leavenworth; engineering services   600
Church of Jesus Christ of Latter-Day Saints Corp.; Leavenworth; religious organization   600
Kansas State University Veterinary College; Manhattan   600
Westar Energy Inc.; Topeka; electric power generation   600
Security Benefit Life Insurance Co.; Topeka; life insurance   600
Frito-Lay Inc.; Topeka; cheese curls and puffs   580
Kansas Dept. of Social and Rehabilitation Services; Osawatomie   575
Kansas Dept. of Social and Rehabilitation Services; Parsons   563
U.S. Bureau of Prisons; Leavenworth   561
Gates Corp.; Iola; rubber and plastic hose and beltings   540
Fiberglass Engineering Inc.; Neodesha; fiberglass boats   510
Highland Community College; Highland   500
Checkrite; Manhattan; check-clearing services   500
Mercy Health Center of Manhattan Inc.; Manhattan   500
Sykes Enterprises Inc.; Manhattan; computer programming services   500
Wal-Mart Stores Inc.; Topeka; discount department stores   500
Reser's Fine Foods Inc.; Topeka; packaged tortillas   500
Burlington Northern and Santa Fe Railway Co.; Topeka; railroad terminals   500
Monarch Cement Co.; Humboldt; portland cement   500

Kansas 3rd District

Kansas City region — Overland Park, eastern Lawrence

Eastern Kansas's 3rd District differs markedly from the state's other districts. Geographically compact, it is almost entirely within the metropolitan sphere of Kansas City, Missouri, and most of its population lives either in Kansas City, Kansas, or in Johnson County suburbs. It boasts three of the state's five most-populous cities.

The district is hardly uniform in its economic character. Poverty and unemployment are prevalent in Wyandotte County and Kansas City itself. Overshadowed by its namesake across the Missouri River, Kansas City, Kansas, is an industrial town that has had its share of Rust Belt blues because of factory closures and the long-term decline of urban stockyards. But Kansas City maintains a large industrial base and has attracted some growth in its biotechnology sector.

Johnson County is one of the state's richest, with company headquarters, suburban developments, and a strong service sector. While Kansas City lost population in the 1990s, many Johnson County areas are booming. Overland Park grew by one-third, passing Topeka and Kansas City to become the state's second-largest city, and Olathe grew by nearly 50 percent during the decade.

Heading west, the 3rd takes in the eastern part of Douglas County and two-thirds of Lawrence (shared with the 2nd). Lawrence is home to the University of Kansas, which falls principally within the 3rd's boundaries (some of the campus is in the 2nd), and is considered the most liberal area in the state.

Large, wealthy Johnson County is a Republican stronghold, and it gives the 3rd a GOP lean. But Democratic strength in Wyandotte County and parts of Douglas County keep the district competitive.

Major Industry

Long-distance phone service, auto manufacturing, service.

Notable

James Naismith, inventor of basketball, was the University of Kansas' first coach and the only one with a losing record.

Election Returns

	Republican		Democratic		Other	
President 2000	152,832	52.9%	122,463	42.4%	13,452	4.7%
House 2002	102,882	46.9%	110,095	50.2%	6,412	2.9%

District Profile

Population   672,124

Total area (square miles)   787.1
  Land area (square miles)   777.5

Population per square mile   864.5

Counties (2000 population)
| Douglas (pt.) | 63,156 | Wyandotte | 157,882 |
| Johnson | 451,086 | | |

Cities and other areas over 10,000 (2000 population)
Kansas City	146,866	Olathe	92,962
Lawrence (pt.)	54,330	Overland Park	149,080
Leawood	27,656	Prairie Village	22,072
Lenexa	40,238	Shawnee	47,996
Merriam	11,008		

Race and Hispanic or Latino origin*
White   79.6%
Black or African American   8.8%
American Indian or Alaska Native   0.6%
Asian   2.6%
Native Hawaiian or other Pacific Islander   0.0%
Some other race   0.1%
Hispanic or Latino origin   6.8%
Two or more races   1.5%

*As percentage of total population.

Ancestry*
Dutch	1.4%	Norwegian	1.1%
English	9.0%	Polish	1.6%
French	2.3%	Scotch-Irish	1.6%
German	18.0%	Scottish	1.7%
Irish	10.5%	Swedish	1.8%
Italian	2.2%	USA/American	4.8%

*As estimated percentage of total population.

Universities and colleges, 2000–2001 enrollment

Baker University School of Professional and Graduate Studies, Overland Park   1,894
Donnelly College, Kansas City   318
Haskell Indian Nations University, Lawrence   918
Johnson County Community College, Overland Park   16,383
Kansas City Kansas Community College, Kansas City   5,238
Midamerica Nazarene University, Olathe   1,717
Ottawa University-Kansas City, Overland Park   1,144
University of Kansas,* Lawrence   25,920
University of Kansas Medical Center, Kansas City   2,409

*Principally located in the 3rd District, some portions in the 2nd District.

Newspapers and circulation

	District circulation	Total circulation
Kansas City Star	92,057	261,945
Lawrence Journal-World	8,508	18,512
Olathe Daily News	5,795	6,130
*USA Today**	5,766	1,674,376

*See Sources and Explanations in the front of the volume.

Television stations and affiliations

Kansas City	100%	KCPT	PBS
Kansas City	100%	KCTV	CBS
Kansas City	100%	KCWE	UPN
Kansas City	100%	KMBC	ABC
Kansas City	100%	KMCI	Independent
Kansas City	100%	KPXE	PAX
Kansas City	100%	KSHB	NBC
Kansas City	100%	KSMO	WB
Kansas City	100%	WDAF	FOX

Cable systems and subscribers

Classic   595
Comcast   17,895
Sunflower Cablevision   20,622
Time Warner   127,521

Businesses and other major employers

University of Kansas; Lawrence   9,229
Ford Motor Co.; Kansas City; cars   6,000
University of Kansas Hospital Authority; Kansas City   6,000
Sprint Communications Co.; Shawnee Mission; telephone communication   5,000
Leopoldstadt Inc.; Shawnee Mission; temporary help service   4,300
United Parcel Service Inc.; Shawnee Mission; parcel delivery   4,000
Kansas City/Wyandotte County Unified Government; Kansas City; city government   3,200
Burlington Northern and Santa Fe Railway Co.; Kansas City; trucking terminal facilities   2,000
Johnson County Community College; Shawnee Mission   2,000
Shawnee Mission Medical Center Inc.; Shawnee Mission   1,783
Honeywell International Inc.; Olathe; aircraft engines and parts   1,400

Health Midwest Hospital; Shawnee Mission   1,200

Deffenbaugh Industries Inc.; Shawnee Mission; sanitary landfill operation   1,200

JC Penney Corp.; Shawnee Mission; warehousing   1,200

Olathe Medical Center Inc.; Olathe   1,000

Kansas City/Wyandotte County Unified Government; Kansas City; county government   1,000

First Excess and Reinsurance Corp.; Shawnee Mission; fire, marine, casualty insurance   1,000

First Specialty Insurance Corp.; Shawnee Mission; fire, marine, casualty insurance   1,000

Grafton Inc.; Shawnee Mission; help supply services   1,000

Yellow Transportation; Shawnee Mission; freight carrier   1,000

Lawrence Memorial Hospital; Lawrence   900

United Telephone Company of Kansas; Shawnee Mission; telephone communication   896

John Deere-NAAMC Inc.; Shawnee Mission; farm and garden machinery   850

Bethany Medical Center; Kansas City   831

LabOne Inc.; Shawnee Mission; testing laboratories   826

Johnson County; Olathe; county government   800

Encore Receivable Management; Olathe; personal service agents   800

Occupational Health Services; Kansas City   800

TeleTech Services Corp.; Kansas City; telemarketing services   800

Keebler Co.; Kansas City; biscuits   720

City of Lawrence; Lawrence; city management   700

U.S. Postal Service; Kansas City   700

Waddell and Reed Financial Services Inc.; Shawnee Mission; security brokers, dealers   700

Sprint Corp.; Shawnee Mission; local/long-distance telephone   700

American Valet Parking Inc.; Shawnee Mission; automobile parking   700

Clorox Products Manufacturing Co.; Shawnee Mission; degreasing solvent   700

Transam Trucking Inc.; Olathe; trucking   699

Kansas Board of Public Utilities; Kansas City   680

Menorah Medical Center Inc.; Shawnee Mission   650

Garmin International Inc.; Olathe; search and navigation equipment   625

United Telephone Company of Kansas; New Century; telephone communication   600

Elite Logistics Inc.; Kansas City; cold storage warehousing   600

Owens Corning; Kansas City; fiberglass insulation   600

RETEC Group Inc.; Shawnee Mission; engineering services   600

W & R Insurance Agency; Shawnee Mission; life insurance   600

Farmers Insurance Exchange Farmers Group Inc.; Shawnee Mission; insurance agents and brokers   600

GFSI Holdings Inc.; Shawnee Mission; men's/boys' sportswear and athletic clothing   600

Kansas Dept. of Social and Rehabilitation Services; Kansas City   570

Sysco Food Services; Olathe; food supplier   563

Lock Line; Shawnee Mission; insurance claim processing   550

PTEK Holdings Inc.; Shawnee Mission; teleconferencing services   520

Remel Inc.; Shawnee Mission; culture media   505

Johnson County; New Century; correctional institutions   500

Garage Door Group Inc.; Lawrence; metal garage doors   500

Honeywell International Inc.; Lawrence; business consulting   500

Kmart Corp.; Lawrence; warehousing   500

U.S. Federal Aviation Admin.; Olathe   500

Wal-Mart Stores Inc.; Olathe; discount department stores   500

Colgate-Palmolive Co.; Kansas City; soap   500

Swift-Eckrich Inc.; Kansas City; sausages, other prepared meats   500

Certainteed Corp.; Kansas City; asbestos products   500

Sprint Corp.; Shawnee Mission; long-distance telephone   500

Dillard's Inc.; Shawnee Mission; department stores   500

Sprint Spectrum; Shawnee Mission; communication services   500

Sprint Corp.; Shawnee Mission; telephone communication   500

Sprint Spectrum; Shawnee Mission; telephone communication   500

Kansas 4th District

South central — Wichita

Seeing an airplane is about as commonplace as seeing a bird to residents of the 4th. The moderately conservative district is centered around the state's largest city, Wichita, with its large aviation industry. Much of the rest of the 4th is farmland.

Boeing, one of the state's largest employers, has a plant here. Cessna, Raytheon Aircraft, and Learjet are among the other airplane manufacturers that have operations in the Wichita area. Although the industry has helped keep the economy healthy, aviation business downturns have led the city to look for ways to diversify. Wichita also benefits from a regional medical center and universities.

Sumner County, on the Oklahoma border, is one of Kansas's leading wheat-growing counties. Wheat also is important in Harper and Kingman Counties to the west. Cattle graze in sparsely populated Greenwood, Elk, and Chautauqua Counties to the east.

Redistricting in the 1990s made the politically marginal 4th more favorable to Republicans by taking out Democratic-leaning Reno County and bringing in Republican-oriented Montgomery County (in the district's far southeast corner). This change helped Republicans win the district in 1994 and keep it since then. Redistricting following the 2000 census made minor changes and did not alter the 4th's political outlook. Locally, Republicans usually win here, but Democrats capture some offices. Cowley County, in the south-central part of the district, tilts more Democratic.

Major Industry

Aviation, defense, agriculture.

Notable

Omar Knedlik of Coffeyville invented the first frozen carbonated drink machine in 1961; Old Cowtown Museum in Wichita recreates life in Sedgwick County and Wichita from 1865 to 1880.

Election Returns

	Republican		Democratic		Other	
President 2000	146,921	59.0%	91,232	36.6%	10,918	4.4%
House 2002	115,691	60.6%	70,656	37.0%	4,616	2.4%

District Profile

Population   672,101

Total area (square miles)   9,596.2
  Land area (square miles)   9,530.5

Population per square mile   70.5

Counties (2000 population)

Butler 59,482	Harvey 32,869
Chautauqua 4,359	Kingman 8,673
Cowley 36,291	Montgomery 36,252
Elk 3,261	Sedgwick 452,869
Greenwood (pt.) 5,563	Sumner 25,946
Harper 6,536	

Cities and other areas over 10,000 (2000 population)

Arkansas City 11,963	Newton 17,190
Coffeyville 11,021	Wichita 344,284
Derby 17,807	Winfield 12,206
El Dorado 12,057	

Race and Hispanic or Latino origin*

White   81.0%
Black or African American   6.8%
American Indian or Alaska Native   1.1%
Asian   2.4%
Native Hawaiian or other Pacific Islander   0.0%
Some other race   0.1%
Hispanic or Latino origin   6.6%
Two or more races   2.0%

*As percentage of total population.

Ancestry*

Dutch 1.9%	Italian 1.2%
English 8.0%	Scotch-Irish 1.5%
French 2.3%	Scottish 1.4%
German 17.7%	Swedish 1.3%
Irish 7.9%	USA/American 7.7%

*As estimated percentage of total population.

Universities and colleges, 2000–2001 enrollment

Bethel College, North Newton   506
Butler County Community College, El Dorado   7,911
Coffeyville Community College, Coffeyville   1,680
Cowley County Community College, Arkansas City   3,986
Friends University, Wichita   3,247
Hesston College, Hesston   436
Independence Community College, Independence   1,144
Newman University, Wichita   1,967
Southwestern College, Winfield   1,143
Wichita Area Technical College, Wichita   3,829
Wichita State University, Wichita   14,810

Newspapers and circulation

	District circulation	Total circulation
Hutchinson News	2,018	34,007
*USA Today**	3,772	1,674,376
Wichita Eagle	81,808	87,687
Winfield Daily Courier	4,764	5,054

Television stations and affiliations

Wichita-Hutchinson	86%	KAAS	FOX
Wichita-Hutchinson	86%	KAKE	ABC
Wichita-Hutchinson	86%	KBSD	CBS
Wichita-Hutchinson	86%	KBSH	CBS
Wichita-Hutchinson	86%	KBSL	CBS
Wichita-Hutchinson	86%	KDCK	PBS
Wichita-Hutchinson	86%	KLBY	ABC
Wichita-Hutchinson	86%	KOOD	PBS
Wichita-Hutchinson	86%	KPTS	PBS
Wichita-Hutchinson	86%	KSAS	FOX
Wichita-Hutchinson	86%	KSNC	NBC
Wichita-Hutchinson	86%	KSNG	NBC
Wichita-Hutchinson	86%	KSNK	NBC
Wichita-Hutchinson	86%	KSNW	NBC
Wichita-Hutchinson	86%	KSWK	PBS
Wichita-Hutchinson	86%	KUPK	ABC
Wichita-Hutchinson	86%	KWCH	CBS
Tulsa, OK	14%	KDOR	Independent
Tulsa, OK	14%	KJRH	NBC
Tulsa, OK	14%	KOED	PBS
Tulsa, OK	14%	KOET	PBS
Tulsa, OK	14%	KOKI	FOX
Tulsa, OK	14%	KOTV	CBS
Tulsa, OK	14%	KRSC	PBS
Tulsa, OK	14%	KTFO	UPN
Tulsa, OK.	14%	KTPX	PAX
Tulsa, OK	14%	KTUL	ABC
Tulsa, OK	14%	KWBT	WB
Tulsa, OK	14%	KWHB	Independent

Cable systems and subscribers

Cable ONE   4,284
Charter   1,553
Classic   3,164
Clearwater Cablevision   1,626
Cox   135,954
Galaxy   6,323
Mediacom   1,333
Southern Kansas Telephone   1,915
Sumner Cable TV   3,200

Military installations, September 2001

McConnell Air Force Base, Wichita   4,768

Businesses and other major employers

Boeing Co.; Wichita; aircraft   16,000
Raytheon Aircraft Co.; Wichita; airplanes   9,000
Cessna Aircraft Co.; Wichita; airplanes   4,840
Learjet Inc.; Wichita; aircraft   4,000
Via Christi Regional Medical Center; Wichita   4,000
Wichita State University; Wichita   3,380

Wesley Medical Center; Wichita   3,080
City of Wichita; Wichita; city management   2,221
Kansas National Guard; Wichita   1,600
Koch Industries Inc.; Wichita; oil/gas exploration
   services   1,500
American Pizza Partners LP; Wichita; pizzeria chain
   1,422
Sedgwick County; Wichita; legislative bodies   1,350
Evcon Industries Inc.; Wichita; heating equipment
   1,350
Case Corp.; Hesston; farm machinery and equipment
   1,300
AGCO Corp.; Hesston; haying machines   1,100
Coleman International Holdings; Wichita; barbecues,
   grills, and braziers   1,100
Aramark Service Master Facility Services; Wichita; house
   and babysitting services   1,000
Cessna Aircraft Co.; Independence; airplanes   1,000
Dana Corp.; Independence; automotive maintenance
   equipment   961
American Coin Merchandising Inc.; Wichita;
   merchandising machine operators   900
Intrust Bank NA; Wichita; commercial trust company
   820
U.S. Postal Service; Wichita   800
Amazon.com Inc.; Coffeyville; book and record clubs
   800
Emerson Electric Co.; Independence; electric motors
   750
General Electric Co.; Arkansas City; aircraft, heavy
   equipment repair   700

Vulcan Materials Co.; Wichita; chlorine   700
U.S. Veterans Hospital; Wichita   694
Lodging Enterprises Inc.; Wichita; hotels and motels
   678
Cox Communications Inc.; Wichita; cable television
   670
Wichita Eagle and Beacon Publishing Co.; Wichita;
   newspaper   650
IFR Systems Inc.; Wichita; electricity measuring
   instruments   610
Wal-Mart Stores Inc.; Derby; discount department stores
   600
Haysville Unified School District; Haysville   600
Apple Corps.; Wichita; restaurants   600
Case Corp.; Wichita; entrenching machines   600
Wal-Mart Stores Inc.; Wichita; discount department
   stores   600
Excel Corp.; Wichita; meatpacking plants   575
Southwestern Bell Telephone Co.; Wichita; telephone
   communication   566
Air Midwest Inc.; Wichita; air passenger carrier   545
Norcraft Companies; Newton; wood kitchen cabinets
   500
Sedgwick County; Wichita; sheriff's office   500
Scholfield Auto Inc.; Wichita; general automotive repair
   shops   500
Edward A. Hall Dental Offices; Wichita   500
Wichita Clinic; Wichita   500
Latour Management Inc.; Wichita; restaurant
   management   500
Love Transport Co.; Wichita; trucking   500

Districts established January 31, 2002, for elections first held in 2002.

6 members

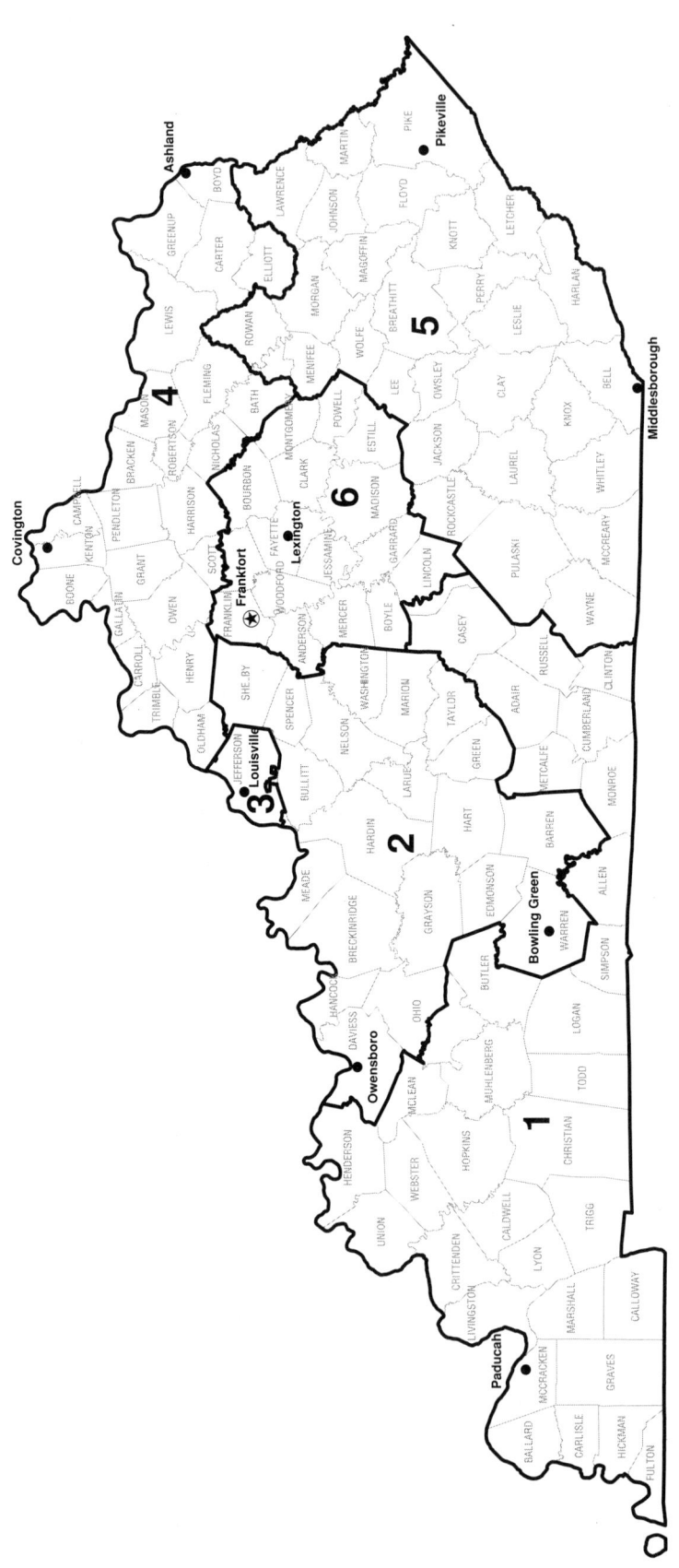

Kentucky

The name Kentucky conjures a rich blend of American sensations. One sees wide grassy valleys and white-fenced corrals filled with well-bred horses. In the state's central region the grass produces blue blossoms, inspiring the state nickname: the Blue Grass State. Bill Monroe adopted the name bluegrass for his music when he went south to Nashville with his mandolin and "high lonesome" tenor. Here too are the Kentucky Derby, the county where bourbon whiskey was first made and the Hillerich, and Bradsby factory that makes baseball's "Louisville Sluggers." King Coal long ruled in the hills, but basketball reigns in towns of all sizes, enabling both the University of Kentucky and the University of Louisville to field perennial national powers even as lots of local stars are exported out of state.

Kentucky is a state of many well-used roads and residents on wheels. It ranks eighth nationally in street and highway miles, and ninth in vehicle miles per capita. A lot of this travel has to do with farming, and Kentucky still gets more of its gross product from agriculture than most states. Long known for tobacco, Kentucky still has more farms growing that controversial crop than any other state, but important mainstays for the future are more likely to be beef cattle, horse breeding, dairy, corn, and soybeans.

Changing markets have cast shadows on tobacco, soft coal, and hard liquor, so Kentucky officials have looked to new frontiers in recent years. They worked hard to attract a General Motors Saturn plant and a Toyota factory, and the state's low-wage scale has helped it climb into the top dozen states for manufacturing employment and value added in manufacturing. Nonetheless, in 2000 Kentucky still ranked among the poorest dozen states in gross state product and personal income per capita. Its population increased by only about one-third in the latter half of the twentieth century, and its growth rate again lagged the national rate for the 1990s. Census experts foresee even slower growth over the next generation.

Many of Kentucky's glories are of the past. Once the western portion of the immense Virginia colony, its heritage dates to such illustrious residents as Daniel Boone, the quintessential frontiersman, and Henry Clay, the brilliant politician who came to the House in 1811 and was promptly elected Speaker. The state's largest delegation in the House (thirteen seats) occurred in the 1830s, but the westward movement soon moved on to Indiana, Illinois, and Missouri, all of which leaped forward in the census of 1840. Kentucky's delegation settled at 11 seats in the Reconstruction period, remaining there for 40 years before taking another long slide in the

twentieth century: down to nine in 1930, eight in 1950, and seven in 1960. After the census of 1990, the state had just half a dozen seats, less than half its peak, with no realistic prospect of reversing the trend.

Kentucky will always be considered a border state, meaning its politics, culture, and economics are a mix of the North and the South. Both Abraham Lincoln and Jefferson Davis were born here, less than 100 miles apart. The state's eastern, high-elevation counties were ill-suited to slave-based plantations and their residents opposed the practice, as did the immigrants in the fledgling city of Louisville to the west on the Ohio River. But much of antebellum Kentucky was growing tobacco with slave labor, and as a matter of heart and spirit, the state has always been closer to Dixie than to the Great Lakes states to the north or the Atlantic states to the east. Most of the Kentucky men who took up arms did so on behalf of the Confederacy.

Generally speaking, that affinity made good ground for old-school Democrats. At certain high-water marks, the GOP could elect a governor or senator or a majority in the congressional delegation. After the election of 1928, for example, the state sent nine Republicans to the House. But that interlude was quickly canceled in the first Depression election of 1930, and Democrats usually held sway for several decades thereafter.

In presidential voting, a new pattern emerged after World War II as the state caught some of the early migration of northerners seeking new opportunities. The suburbs across the river from Cincinnati boomed, as did the Louisville metro. In part as a consequence, resurgent Republicans captured the state's electoral college votes in 1956 and 1960, then again in 1968 and 1972. Jimmy Carter carried the state in 1976 but lost it in 1980. Bill Clinton won it in 1992 by a small margin and in 1996 by an even smaller one. But in 2000, Al Gore (a well-known nemesis of tobacco and coal) abandoned the state early. George W. Bush prevailed by more than 233,000 votes, dominating the rural counties as well as the suburbs and suggesting the state had finally decided on a permanent home in the GOP.

That suggestion has been bolstered by the trend in congressional voting. Both Senate seats were held by Republicans after the elections of 1998 and the retirement of longtime statewide officeholder Wendell Ford. The new powerbroker in the 1990s became Republican senator Mitch McConnell, who by 2003 had risen to Ford's old job of Senate majority whip. Along the way he helped engineer the turnover of the state's House delegation by recruiting and bankrolling candidates.

As recently as 1992, the state elected four Democrats to the House and just two Republicans, with the latter coming from eastern districts that had been contrarian since Civil War times. But that template was shattered in the big GOP breakthough of 1994 when Republicans won five seats.

They carried that lopsided advantage into the years after 2000 when court-supervised redistricting broke the partisan gridlock in Lexington, where the legislature was under split control. The results left the GOP in solid control. Three seats still considered competitive are the Louisville-based 3rd District with a black population of 19 percent, the largest in the state; the northern 4th, which includes Covington and other communities across the river from Cincinnati; and the Lexington-based 6th, which had a Democratic representative until 1999. The other three districts were, in varying degrees, drawn safe for their Republican incumbents, and perhaps for Republican successors for years to come. As of 2003, all but the 4th District were in Republican hands, and the 4th looked likely to join them when next left vacant.

One other shared characteristic with the states to the south: despite increasingly Republican voting patterns, Democrats still enjoy a numerical advantage in voter registration. Moreover, by 2002 the important office of governor was won by Democrats in 13 of the previous 14 elections. The state legislature in Frankfort, while far less Democratic than usual, was still under split control at mid-decade. Kentucky still offers an opportunity for Democrats at various levels who combine the personality and issue profile it takes to win in what remains a primarily rural and Southern environment.

Table 1   Population

District	Population	Population under 18	Voting-age population	Median age	Male*	Female*
1	673,629	162,240	511,389	36.9	48.9	51.1
2	673,224	173,414	499,810	35.3	49.3	50.7
3	674,032	162,732	511,300	36.8	47.7	52.3
4	673,588	174,720	498,868	35.7	49.3	50.7
5	673,670	165,673	507,997	36.2	49.1	50.9
6	673,626	156,039	517,587	34.3	48.8	51.2
State	4,041,769	994,818	3,046,951	35.9	48.9	51.1

*As percentage of total population.

Table 2   Voting-Age Persons by Race/Hispanic or Latino Origin

District	White*	Black or African American*	American Indian or Alaska Native*	Asian*	Other or multirace*	Hispanic or Latino*
1	90.9	6.6	0.2	0.4	0.6	1.3
2	91.5	5.3	0.2	0.8	0.7	1.5
3	78.5	17.2	0.2	1.4	1.0	1.7
4	95.5	2.2	0.2	0.5	0.5	1.0
5	97.2	1.2	0.2	0.3	0.5	0.6
6	88.0	7.8	0.2	1.2	0.8	2.0
State	90.2	6.7	0.2	0.7	0.7	1.3

*As percentage of voting-age population.

Table 3   Voting-Age Population by Age Groups

District	18 to 24*	25 to 44*	45 to 64*	Over 64*
1	12.9	36.9	30.9	19.3
2	13.6	40.4	30.5	15.6
3	11.7	40.0	30.2	18.1
4	11.8	41.6	30.9	15.7
5	12.9	38.8	31.9	16.4
6	16.1	40.8	28.8	14.3
State	13.2	39.7	30.5	16.6

*As percentage of voting-age population.

Table 4   Income and Occupation

District	Median family income	Families in poverty*	White collar†	Blue collar†	Service†	Farm†
1	$37,022	12.7	46.6	37.3	14.6	1.5
2	$42,124	10.3	49.6	35.2	14.1	1.0
3	$49,426	9.5	62.0	23.7	14.1	0.2
4	$47,648	9.1	56.0	29.6	13.7	0.7
5	$26,627	24.0	48.4	35.3	15.2	1.1
6	$46,939	9.6	58.8	25.8	14.3	1.1
State	$40,939	12.7	54.1	30.7	14.3	0.9

*As percentage of all families. †As percentage of employed workers 16 years and over.

Table 5   Education: School Years Completed

District	Less than grade 9*	Grades 9–12 no diploma*	High school diploma no college*	Some college*	College bachelor's degree or higher*
1	13.4	15.3	37.2	22.3	11.8
2	10.8	13.7	37.6	23.9	13.9
3	5.3	12.6	28.8	28.0	25.3
4	9.2	13.4	35.3	24.7	17.5
5	22.6	18.2	32.8	16.9	9.6
6	8.9	11.9	29.9	24.6	24.6
State	11.7	14.2	33.6	23.4	17.1

*As percentage of persons age 25 and over.

Table 6   Housing and Residential Patterns

District	Median home value	Owner occupied*	Renter occupied*	Urban†	Rural†
1	$62,300	74.0	26.0	36.5	63.5
2	$82,100	73.5	26.5	47.2	52.8
3	$102,300	64.7	35.3	98.3	1.7
4	$89,100	73.5	26.5	59.7	40.3
5	$45,900	76.3	23.7	21.3	78.7
6	$94,300	63.2	36.8	71.3	28.7
State	$79,600	70.8	29.2	55.7	44.3

*As percentage of occupied housing units. †As percentage of total population.

Kentucky 1st District

West — Hopkinsville, Henderson, Paducah

Located in the western part of the Bluegrass State, Kentucky's rural, 34-county 1st is a hub of agricultural activity. Here, slaves once helped cultivate cotton and tobacco crops, and tobacco still dominates the economy (particularly in the counties south of the Ohio River city of Henderson), though its future is uncertain. The 1st also has seen a steady decline in its coal industry to the north.

The Ohio River port of Paducah (McCracken County) traditionally has been the political and population center of western Kentucky, but its population has been surpassed by Hopkinsville (Christian County), an agricultural market center dependent on nearby Fort Campbell, and by Henderson.

While the 1st has seen its coal and mining industries decline precipitously, Hopkins County has weathered the loss by evolving into a regional industrial and medical center. Tourism and recreation also play a role in the economy, especially near the Land Between the Lakes recreation area, where management functions in 1999 were transferred from the Tennessee Valley Authority to the Forest Service.

The 1st's Confederate legacy traditionally translated into Democratic votes, but the 1994 GOP wave sent the district's first Republican to Congress. While conservative Democrats continue to dominate local offices in western Kentucky, the region votes for Republican presidential candidates. George W. Bush carried 30 of the district's 34 counties in the 2000 election. Redistricting following the 2000 census changed the district little, but marginally increased the 1st's conservative lean by giving it some GOP-voting rural counties in south-central Kentucky.

Major Industry
Agriculture, manufacturing.

Notable
The Jefferson Davis Monument, located at his birthplace in Fairview, is a 351-foot obelisk; the nation's only plant that turns uranium into nuclear fuel is operated by USEC Inc. in Paducah.

Election Returns

	Republican		Democratic		Other	
President 2000	147,486	58.3%	101,551	40.1%	3,961	1.6%
House 2002	117,600	65.3%	62,617	34.7%		

District Profile

Population   673,629

Total area (square miles)   12,057.5
   Land area (square miles)   11,683.1

Population per square mile   57.7

Counties (2000 population)

Adair	17,244	Lincoln (pt.)	5,892
Allen	17,800	Livingston	9,804
Ballard	8,286	Logan	26,573
Butler	13,010	Lyon	8,080
Caldwell	13,060	Marshall	30,125
Calloway	34,177	McCracken	65,514
Carlisle	5,351	McLean	9,938
Casey	15,447	Metcalfe	10,037
Christian	72,265	Monroe	11,756
Clinton	9,634	Muhlenberg	31,839
Crittenden	9,384	Ohio (pt.)	12,831
Cumberland	7,147	Russell	16,315
Fulton	7,752	Simpson	16,405
Graves	37,028	Todd	11,971
Henderson	44,829	Trigg	12,597
Hickman	5,262	Union	15,637
Hopkins	46,519	Webster	14,120

Cities and other areas over 10,000 (2000 population)
Fort Campbell North CDP   14,338
Henderson   27,373
Hopkinsville   30,089
Madisonville   19,307
Mayfield   10,349
Murray   14,950
Paducah   26,307

Race and Hispanic or Latino origin*
White   89.7%
Black or African American   7.2%
American Indian or Alaska Native   0.2%
Asian   0.3%
Native Hawaiian or other Pacific Islander   0.0%
Some other race   0.1%
Hispanic or Latino origin   1.5%
Two or more races   0.9%

*As percentage of total population.

Ancestry*
English	7.8%	Scotch-Irish	1.3%
French	1.2%	Scottish	1.1%
German	7.1%	USA/American	19.5%
Irish	7.7%		

*As estimated percentage of total population.

Universities and colleges, 2000–2001 enrollment
Henderson Community College, Henderson   1,170
Hopkinsville Community College, Hopkinsville   2,554
Lindsey Wilson College, Columbia   1,364
Madisonville Community College, Madisonville   1,915
Madisonville Technical College, Madisonville   556
Mid-Continent College, Mayfield   455
Murray State University, Murray   9,136
Paducah Community College, Paducah   2,881
Rets Medical and Business Institute, Hopkinsville   275
West Kentucky Technical College, Paducah   1,518

Newspapers and circulation

	District circulation	Total circulation
Bowling Green Daily News	4,215	20,612
Danville Advocate-Messenger	1,318	10,619
Evansville Courier &Press	3,411	69,254
Glasgow Daily Times	1,207	8,877
Hopkinsville Kentucky New Era	11,550	11,550
Louisville Courier Journal	4,441	220,676
Owensboro Messenger Inquirer	5,023	30,216
Paducah Sun	24,456	26,236
*USA Today**	2,249	1,674,376

*See Sources and Explanations in the front of the volume.

Television stations and affiliations

Paducah-Cape Girardeau-Harrisburg-Mt. Vernon	32%	KBSI	FOX
Paducah-Cape Girardeau-Harrisburg-Mt. Vernon	32%	KFVS	CBS
Paducah-Cape Girardeau-Harrisburg-Mt. Vernon	32%	KPOB	ABC
Paducah-Cape Girardeau-Harrisburg-Mt. Vernon	32%	WDKA	WB
Paducah-Cape Girardeau-Harrisburg-Mt. Vernon	32%	WKMU	PBS
Paducah-Cape Girardeau-Harrisburg-Mt. Vernon	32%	WKPD	PBS
Paducah-Cape Girardeau-Harrisburg-Mt. Vernon	32%	WPSD	NBC
Paducah-Cape Girardeau-Harrisburg-Mt. Vernon	32%	WSIL	ABC
Paducah-Cape Girardeau-Harrisburg-Mt. Vernon	32%	WSIU	PBS
Paducah-Cape Girardeau-Harrisburg-Mt. Vernon	32%	WTCT	Independent
Nashville	27%	WCTE	PBS
Nashville	27%	WHTN	Independent
Nashville	27%	WJFB	Independent

Nashville	27%	WKRN	ABC
Nashville	27%	WNAB	WB
Nashville	27%	WNPX	PAX
Nashville	27%	WPGD	Independent
Nashville	27%	WSMV	NBC
Nashville	27%	WTVF	CBS
Nashville	27%	WUXP	UPN
Nashville	27%	WZTV	FOX
Evansville, IN	22%	WEHT	ABC
Evansville, IN	22%	WEVV	CBS
Evansville, IN	22%	WFIE	NBC
Evansville, IN	22%	WKMA	PBS
Evansville, IN	22%	WKOH	PBS
Evansville, IN	22%	WNIN	PBS
Evansville, IN	22%	WTVW	FOX
Bowling Green	12%	WBKO	ABC
Bowling Green	12%	WKGB	PBS
Bowling Green	12%	WKYU	PBS
Lexington	7%	WDKY	FOX
Lexington	7%	WKHA	PBS
Lexington	7%	WKLE	PBS
Lexington	7%	WKMR	PBS
Lexington	7%	WKSO	PBS
Lexington	7%	WKYT	CBS
Lexington	7%	WLEX	NBC
Lexington	7%	WLJC	Independent
Lexington	7%	WTVQ	ABC
Lexington	7%	WYMT	CBS

Cable systems and subscribers
Access Cable TV   5,160
Adelphia   6,197
Charter   47,422
Comcast   32,831
Galaxy   9,202
Insight   10,492
Mediacom   28,264
Tele-Media   7,547

Military installations, September 2001
Fort Campbell (Army), Clarksville   30,544

Businesses and other major employers
Continental Tire North America Inc.; Mayfield; tires and inner tubes   2,000

Knights of Columbus Supreme Council Inc.; Murray; fraternal association   1,800

U.S. Enrichment Corp.; Paducah; public utilities consultant   1,510

Cagle's Inc.; Albany; poultry slaughtering/processing   1,500

Baptist Health System Hospital; Paducah   1,409

Mattel Inc.; Murray; games, toys, children's vehicles   1,400

Gibbs Die Casting Corp.; Henderson; aluminum die-castings   1,400

Tyson Foods Inc.; Robards; poultry slaughtering/processing   1,400

Trover Clinic Foundation Inc.; Madisonville   1,250

Sisters of Lourdes Hospital; Paducah   1,200

Murray State University; Murray   1,056

ConAgra Poultry Co. of Kentucky Inc.; Hickory; chicken processing   1,000

Briggs and Stratton Corp.; Murray; internal combustion engines   1,000

Logan Aluminum Inc.; Russellville; aluminum rolling and drawing   980

Sumitomo Electric Wiring Systems Inc.; Edmonton; electrical work   920

A. O. Smith Corp.; Scottsville; electric motors   875

Murray-Calloway County Public Hospital Corp.; Murray   874

Perdue Farms Inc.; Beaver Dam; chicken processing   850

General Electric Co.; Madisonville; airfoils, aircraft engine   800

Genuine Parts Co.; Morganfield; rebuilding engines and transmissions   780

Dolgencorp Inc.; Scottsville; variety stores   760

Alcan Aluminum Corp.; Henderson; aluminum smelting and refining   750

Community United Methodist Hospital Inc.; Henderson   744

Tyco International Inc.; Franklin; orthopedic, prosthetic, surgical supplies   715

JSE Inc.; Paducah; employee leasing service   700

Army and Air Force Exchange Service; Fort Campbell; Army-Navy goods stores   700

Sykes Enterprises Inc.; Morganfield; computer programming services   700

Lodestar Energy Inc.; Clay; coal mining   665

Kentucky Health Services; Hopkinsville   620

International Specialty Products Inc.; Calvert City; chemicals   600

Westvaco Corp.; Wickliffe; paper mills   600

Emhart Teknologies Inc.; Hopkinsville; nuts, rivets, and washers   600

Flynn Enterprises Inc.; Hopkinsville; dungarees: men's, youths', and boys'   600

Res-Care Inc.; Morganfield; vocational apprentice training   600

Alcan Aluminum Corp.; Robards; primary aluminum   600

Tarter Gate and Wood Products Inc.; Dunnville; wood pallets   600

Jennie Stuart Medical Center Inc.; Hopkinsville   575

Union Planters Bank NA; Paducah; commercial bank   560

Carhartt Inc.; Madisonville; overalls and coveralls   560

Carpenter Co.; Russellville; foamed plastic insulation or cushioning   550

Muhlenberg Community Hospital Inc.; Greenville   550

Quebecor World Inc.; Franklin; rotogravure printing   500

Flynn Enterprises Inc.; Elkton; dungarees: men's, youths', and boys'   500

Dana Corp.; Hopkinsville; motor vehicles and car bodies   500

Accuride Corp.; Henderson; motor vehicle parts/accessories   500

Bremner Inc.; Princeton; crackers   500

Lodestar Energy Inc.; Sturgis; coal mining   500

Kentucky 2nd District

West central — Owensboro, Bowling Green

The mostly rural 2nd, anchored in Kentucky's west-central heartland, takes in some suburban areas near Louisville and runs through rolling tobacco country, ending in the river country to the west.

While tobacco remains the district's dominant crop, the 2nd's economy relies on more than agriculture. Oil and coal help make Owensboro western Kentucky's leading trade center, while the General Motors Corvette plant in Bowling Green also provides jobs. Although substantially smaller than either Louisville or Lexington, the two cities are the state's third and fourth most populous. Away from the main population areas, the economic picture has been somewhat grim. In Taylor County, the closing of a textile plant in the late 1990s helped ratchet its unemployment rate above 20 percent at one point. An Amazon.com facility has helped steady the area.

The eastern portion of the district includes several of the distilleries that constitute Kentucky's "Bourbon Trail." Bardstown, in Nelson County, bills itself as the bourbon capital of the world (there is a whiskey museum in the city). Redistricting following the 2000 census brought the 2nd's northern boundary to Shelby County, which is sandwiched between Louisville and the state capital of Frankfort.

The 2nd includes the birthplace of Abraham Lincoln (in Larue County), the first Republican president, and district voters now side with the GOP in federal elections after a long period of Democratic dominance following the Reconstruction era. In the 2000 election George W. Bush did not lose any of the 19 counties that lie wholly within the 2nd District, and just five gave him less than 60 percent of the vote.

Major Industry

Tobacco, tourism, manufacturing.

Notable

The U.S. bullion depository at Fort Knox, or "Gold Vault," houses the largest portion of the U.S. gold reserve; Bardstown includes Federal Hill Mansion, which inspired Stephen Foster to compose the ballad "My Old Kentucky Home."

Election Returns

	Republican		Democratic		Other	
President 2000	152,236	61.7%	90,086	36.5%	4,288	1.7%
House 2002	122,773	69.6%	51,431	29.2%	2,084	1.2%

District Profile

Population 673,224

Total area (square miles) 7,668.7
  Land area (square miles) 7,567.0

Population per square mile 89.0

Counties (2000 population)

Barren 38,033	Larue 13,373
Breckinridge 18,648	Marion 18,212
Bullitt 61,236	Meade 26,349
Daviess 91,545	Nelson 37,477
Edmonson 11,644	Ohio (pt.) 10,085
Grayson 24,053	Shelby 33,337
Green 11,518	Spencer 11,766
Hancock 8,392	Taylor 22,927
Hardin 94,174	Warren 92,522
Hart 17,445	Washington 10,916
Jefferson (pt.) 19,572	

Cities and other areas over 10,000 (2000 population)
  Bardstown 10,374
  Bowling Green 49,296
  Campbellsville 10,498
  Elizabethtown 22,542
  Fort Knox CDP 12,377
  Glasgow 13,019
  Owensboro 54,067
  Radcliff 21,961
  Shelbyville 10,085

Race and Hispanic or Latino origin*
  White 90.6%
  Black or African American 5.7%
  American Indian or Alaska Native 0.2%
  Asian 0.7%
  Native Hawaiian or other Pacific Islander 0.1%
  Some other race 0.1%
  Hispanic or Latino origin 1.7%
  Two or more races 1.0%

*As percentage of total population.

Ancestry*

English 7.7%	Italian 1.1%
French 1.4%	Scotch-Irish 1.3%
German 9.2%	Scottish 1.2%
Irish 8.5%	USA/American 18.7%

*As estimated percentage of total population.

Universities and colleges, 2000–2001 enrollment
  Bowling Green Technical College, Bowling Green 854
  Brescia University, Owensboro 729
  Campbellsville University, Campbellsville 1,601
  Draughons Junior College, Bowling Green 304
  Elizabethtown Community College, Elizabethtown 3,484
  Elizabethtown Technical College, Elizabethtown 637
  Kentucky Advanced Technology Institute, Bowling Green 325
  Kentucky Wesleyan College, Owensboro 680
  Owensboro Community College, Owensboro 2,248
  Owensboro Junior College of Business, Owensboro 211
  Owensboro Technical College, Owensboro 802
  Owensboro Technical College-Davies County, Owensboro 343
  St. Catharine College, St. Catharine 525
  Western Kentucky University, Bowling Green 15,481

Newspapers and circulation

	District circulation	Total circulation
Bowling Green Daily News	17,194	20,612
Elizabethtown News-Enterprise	15,886	15,886
Glasgow Daily Times	7,618	8,877
Louisville Courier Journal	36,902	220,676
Owensboro Messenger Inquirer	24,784	30,216
*USA Today**	2,475	1,674,376

*See Sources and Explanations in the front of the volume.

Television stations and affiliations

Louisville	63%
Louisville	63%
Louisville	63%

Louisville	63%
Louisville	63%
Louisville	63%
Louisville	63%
Louisville	63%
Louisville	63%
Louisville	63%
Bowling Green	23%
Bowling Green	23%
Bowling Green	23%
Evansville, IN	14%
Evansville, IN	14%
Evansville, IN	14%
Evansville, IN	14%
Evansville, IN	14%
Evansville, IN	14%
Evansville, IN	14%

Cable systems and subscribers
Access Cable TV   925
Adelphia   28,111
Bardstown Cable TV   2,641
Comcast   24,318
Insight   46,607
Mediacom   6,050

Military installations, September 2001
Fort Knox (Army), Radcliff   12,631

Businesses and other major employers
Mercy Owensboro Health Systems Hospital; Owensboro 2,134

Western Kentucky University; Bowling Green   1,723

Hardin Memorial Hospital; Elizabethtown   1,470

National Institute for Animal Agriculture; Bowling Green   1,200

R. R. Donnelley and Sons Co.; Glasgow; magazine publishing   1,200

TechnoTrim Inc.; Glasgow; automobile seat covers 1,195

Publishers Printing Co.; Shepherdsville; periodicals 1,100

Catholic Health Initiative Hospital; Nazareth   1,000

Ambrake Corp.; Elizabethtown; motor vehicle brake systems/parts   950

Samson Community Hospital; Glasgow   948

General Motors Corp.; Bowling Green; automobiles 874

Century Aluminum Co.; Hawesville; aluminum smelting and refining   800

Commonwealth Aluminum Corp.; Lewisport; flat rolled shapes   800

American Greetings Corp.; Bardstown; greeting cards 763

Holley Performance Products; Bowling Green; carburetors, pistons, piston rings, valves   750

Cox Interior Inc.; Campbellsville; wood moldings   725

Dana Corp.; Glasgow; motor vehicle axles   700

Eagle Industries; Bowling Green; home entertainment wood cabinets   697

U.S. Defense Dept.; Fort Knox   600

Huish Detergents Inc.; Bowling Green; soap and other detergents   600

AFG Industries Inc.; Elizabethtown; safety glass   590

Leggett and Platt Inc.; Simpsonville; bed frames   550

SKF USA Inc.; Glasgow; ball and roller bearings   542

Miller and Hartman South; Leitchfield; smoking tobacco 540

Gates Corp.; Elizabethtown; automobile hose   535

Wal-Mart Stores Inc.; Elizabethtown; department stores 535

Nielsen Media Research Inc.; Radcliff; market analysis or research   500

Meijer Inc.; Louisville; discount department stores   500

Union Underwear Co.; Bowling Green; shorts, briefs, drawers   500

HCA Inc. Hospital; Bowling Green   500

J. L. French Corp.; Glasgow; aluminum die-castings 500

Kroger Co; Owensboro; supermarkets   500

Texas Gas Transmission Corp.; Owensboro; natural gas pipelines   500

Kentucky 3rd District
Louisville and suburbs

With the Ohio River forming its western border, the 3rd sprawls across ethnically and economically diverse neighborhoods in Jefferson County, taking in Louisville. Compared with the rest of the state, Louisville has a sizable black population (nearly one-third of the state's blacks live in the city), as well as a large Catholic community, a legacy of a massive German immigration in the mid-19th century. The city of Louisville was scheduled to merge with the county government in 2003.

Despite some job losses from industrial decline, labor strength runs deep among the blue-collar, white residents of the South End. Blacks, who live near downtown in the West End, also make up a strong Democratic voting bloc. Republicans live in the affluent East End by the Ohio River. The bulk of the 3rd's recent population growth came in northeastern and southeastern Jefferson County.

Although tobacco is a part of the 3rd's hearty economy, other sectors, such as the service industry, have rivaled it. Louisville claims a booming health care industry, and the United Parcel Service operates an air-freight hub out of Louisville International Airport. A Ford assembly plant provides thousands of jobs. Tourism, already big, was boosted by the 1998 opening of a massive floating casino on the Indiana bank of the Ohio River.

The 3rd is Kentucky's most Democratic district in electoral performance, but it is politically competitive. Democrats run well at the local level, especially in downtown Louisville. But more-upscale areas favor Republicans, and the increasing muscle of white-collar suburbanites appears to be swinging the 3rd closer to the GOP. Redistricting following the 2000 census added more Republicans to the district.

Major Industry
Service, manufacturing, trade, tobacco.

Notable
The Kentucky Derby, called "the greatest two minutes in sports," is held at Churchill Downs in south Louisville;

Louisville is the birthplace of Muhammad Ali (1942) and is home to the Louisville Slugger Museum; the cheeseburger was invented in Louisville in 1934.

Election Returns

	Republican		Democratic		Other	
President 2000	134,234	47.7%	141,337	50.3%	5,628	2.0%
House 2002	118,228	51.6%	110,846	48.4%		

District Profile

Population   674,032

Total area (square miles)   378.6
  Land area (square miles)   366.6

Population per square mile   1,838.6

Counties (2000 population)
  Jefferson (pt.)   674,032

Cities and other areas over 10,000 (2000 population)
  Fern Creek CDP   17,870
  Highview CDP   15,161
  Jeffersontown   26,633
  Louisville   256,231
  Newburg CDP   20,636
  Okolona CDP (pt.)   15,640
  Pleasure Ridge Park CDP   25,776
  Shively   15,157
  St. Matthews   15,852
  Valley Station CDP   22,946

Race and Hispanic or Latino origin*
  White   76.0%
  Black or African American   19.1%
  American Indian or Alaska Native   0.2%
  Asian   1.4%
  Native Hawaiian or other Pacific Islander   0.0%
  Some other race   0.2%
  Hispanic or Latino origin   1.8%
  Two or more races   1.3%

*As percentage of total population.

Ancestry*

Dutch 1.2%	Italian 1.8%
English 8.0%	Scotch-Irish 1.4%
French 1.7%	Scottish 1.4%
German 14.8%	USA/American 8.8%
Irish 10.4%	

*As estimated percentage of total population.

Universities and colleges, 2000–2001 enrollment
  Bellarmine College, Louisville   2,848
  ITT Technical Institute, Louisville   354
  Jefferson Community College, Louisville   9,520
  Jefferson Technical College, Louisville   1,512
  Louisville Presbyterian Theological Seminary, Louisville   250
  Louisville Technical Institute, Louisville   612
  Rets Electronic Institute, Louisville   365
  Southern Baptist Theological Seminary, Louisville   2,320
  Spalding University, Louisville   1,632
  Spencerian College, Louisville   201
  Sullivan College-Louisville, Louisville   3,212
  University of Louisville, Louisville   19,771

Newspapers and circulation

	District circulation	Total circulation
Louisville Courier Journal	133,335	220,676
*USA Today**	4,943	1,674,376

*See Sources and Explanations in the front of the volume.

Television stations and affiliations

Louisville	100%	WAVE	NBC
Louisville	100%	WBNA	PAX
Louisville	100%	WDRB	FOX
Louisville	100%	WFTE	UPN
Louisville	100%	WHAS	ABC
Louisville	100%	WKMJ	PBS
Louisville	100%	WKPC	PBS
Louisville	100%	WKZT	PBS
Louisville	100%	WLKY	CBS
Louisville	100%	WWWB	WB

Cable systems and subscribers
Insight   180,938

Military installations, September 2001
  Standiford Field (Air National Guard), Louisville   1,143
  Louisville (Army), Louisville   1,009

Businesses and other major employers
  U.S. Postal Service; Louisville   10,000
  Senior Kapson Quarters Corp.; Louisville; real estate managers   7,500
  Ford Motor Co.; Louisville; motor trucks assembly   6,183
  WKT Restaurant Corp.; Louisville; restaurant management   4,088
  University of Louisville; Louisville   4,039
  Ford Motor Co.; Louisville; automobiles   3,824
  Norton Hospitals Inc.; Louisville   3,800
  Jewish Hospital Healthcare Services Inc.; Louisville   3,450
  St. Gobain Advanced Materials Corp.; Louisville; industrial inorganic chemicals   3,300
  United Parcel Service Inc.; Louisville; courier services   2,800
  Baptist Health System Hospital; Louisville   2,000
  Norton Healthcare Inc. Hospital; Louisville   2,000
  Anthem Blue Cross and Blue Shield; Louisville; medical insurance plan   2,000
  MG & A Inc.; Louisville; videotape rental   1,973
  University Medical Center Inc.; Louisville   1,955
  Sud-Chemie Inc.; Louisville; catalysts, chemical   1,750
  BellSouth Telecommunications Inc.; Louisville; local/long-distance telephone   1,700
  Caritas Health Services Inc.; Louisville   1,630
  International Business Machines Corp.; Louisville; electronic computers   1,500
  Swift-Eckrich Inc.; Louisville; meatpacking plants   1,500
  General Electric Co.; Louisville; household cooking equipment   1,500

UPS Aviation Services Inc.; Louisville; aircraft fueling services   1,400

National Processing Inc.; Louisville; data processing   1,387

Norton Healthcare Inc. Hospital; Louisville   1,350

Sears Roebuck and Co. Inc.; Louisville; credit card service   1,300

Courier-Journal and Louisville Times Co.; Louisville; newspaper   1,200

National City Bank; Louisville; commercial bank   1,159

Bank One Corp.; Louisville; commercial bank   1,140

Humana Inc.; Louisville; health maintenance organization   1,100

U.S. Veterans Hospital; Louisville   1,100

Brown-Forman Corp.; Louisville; bourbon whiskey   1,100

LG & E Energy Services Inc.; Louisville; personal services   1,000

Catholic Health Initiative; Louisville; hospital management   1,000

Churchill Downs Inc.; Louisville; thoroughbred horse racing   1,000

City of Louisville; Louisville; advertising, promotional   1,000

Kentucky Fried Chicken; Louisville; fast-food restaurant chain   1,000

BellSouth Corp.; Louisville; telephone communication   982

Murray Biscuits; Louisville; cookies   900

Brown and Williamson Tobacco Co.; Louisville; cigarettes   879

Bank of America Mortgage; Louisville; urban mortgage   800

Kindred Healthcare Inc.; Louisville; investment holding company   800

UPS Full Service Brokerage; Louisville; security brokers   735

Rohm and Haas Co.; Louisville; acrylic resins   700

Sykes Healthplan Service Bureau Inc.; Louisville; administrative management   700

Jefferson County Board of Education; Louisville   680

Trover Solutions Inc.; Louisville; adjustment and collection services   675

River City Transit Authority; Louisville   670

Sam Swope Auto Group Inc.; Louisville; automobiles   650

Southern Baptist Theological Seminary; Louisville   641

Jefferson County; Louisville; police dept.   631

Jefferson County; Louisville; county government   628

City of Louisville; Louisville; fire dept.   610

Hilliard Lyons Inc.; Louisville; security brokers, dealers, flotation companies   600

Presbyterian Church USA; Louisville; religious organization   600

Brown and Williamson Tobacco Co.; Louisville; management services   600

United Parcel Service Inc.; Louisville; courier services   600

Dillard's Inc.; Louisville; department stores   600

Sears Roebuck and Co. Inc.; Louisville; industrial equipment services   600

Louisville Gas and Electric Co.; Louisville; gas production, distribution   594

Sysco Food Services; Louisville; food supplier   575

D-J Inc.; Louisville; injection molding of plastics   550

West Virginia Residential Care Inc.; Louisville   502

Home Supply Co.; Louisville; hotels   500

City of Louisville; Louisville; courts   500

City of Louisville; Louisville; mayor's office   500

William M. Mercer Inc.; Louisville; actuarial consultant   500

Kentucky Packaging Service; Louisville; textile converters   500

Dillard's Inc.; Louisville; department stores   500

Louisville Ladder Group; Louisville; wood ladders   500

R. C. Tway Co.; Louisville; truck trailers   500

Kentucky Dept. of Highways; Louisville   500

Norfolk Southern Railway Co.; Louisville; railroad freight hauling   500

CSX Transportation Inc.; Louisville; railroad freight hauling   500

All Trades Direct Inc.; Louisville; labor resource services   500

Meijer Inc.; Louisville; discount department stores   500

Sam Swope Auto Group Inc.; Louisville; automobiles   500

Kentucky 4th District

North — Covington, Florence, Ashland

About half of the 4th's residents live in Cincinnati's suburbs, which helps explain the district's dual economic personality and its consistently conservative politics. Starting near the industrial city of Ashland along the Ohio River, the 4th picks up tobacco farms and small towns and passes through the Ohio commuters' region in northern Kentucky, eventually reaching the suburbs northeast of Louisville.

Covington (Kenton County) and the northern part of the district have enjoyed steady economic growth, partly because of Cincinnati-Northern Kentucky International Airport located in Boone County. Covington also serves as a regional center for the IRS, a major employer. Boone County increased its population by about 50 percent in the 1990s. Suburban Boone, Campbell, and Kenton counties account for just less than half of the 4th's population.

At the district's western end is Oldham County, which abuts Jefferson County (Louisville) and has the highest median income in the state. Oldham joins the Cincinnati-area counties in voting reliably Republican.

The economic picture is gloomier in the eastern counties. Ashland struggled to cope with the relocation of Ashland Inc. to Covington and the downsizing of other businesses, and the city has become a declining industrial hub. Boyd County, which includes Ashland, was the only county in the 4th to lose population in the 1990s.

The district is rivaled only by the west-central 2nd District in its steadfast backing of Republican presidential candidates. George W. Bush topped 60 percent of the vote in the 4th, and Al Gore carried just two counties, both in the far east: Elliott, which has voted Democratic for president since before 1920 and where 97 percent of registered voters are Democrats, and Boyd, which Bush only narrowly lost. The

Covington-area district had sent a Republican to Congress since 1967 until a conservative Democrat won in 1998.

Major Industry

Service, manufacturing, health care.

Notable

The Kentucky Speedway racetrack is near Sparta in Gallatin County.

Election Returns

	Republican		Democratic		Other	
President 2000	152,856	60.7%	92,768	36.9%	6,060	2.4%
House 2002	81,651	47.5%	87,776	51.1%	2,308	1.3%

District Profile

Population   673,588

Total area (square miles)   5,770.0
Land area (square miles)   5,678.5

Population per square mile   118.6

Counties (2000 population)

Bath (pt.) 8,260	Harrison 17,983
Boone 85,991	Henry 15,060
Boyd 49,752	Kenton 151,464
Bracken 8,279	Lewis 14,092
Campbell 88,616	Mason 16,800
Carroll 10,155	Nicholas 6,813
Carter 26,889	Oldham 46,178
Elliott 6,748	Owen 10,547
Fleming 13,792	Pendleton 14,390
Gallatin 7,870	Robertson 2,266
Grant 22,384	Scott (pt.) 4,243
Greenup 36,891	Trimble 8,125

Cities and other areas over 10,000 (2000 population)

Ashland 21,981	Florence 23,551
Burlington CDP 10,779	Fort Thomas 16,495
Covington 43,370	Independence 14,982
Erlanger 16,676	Newport 17,048

Race and Hispanic or Latino origin*

White   95.1%
Black or African American   2.2%
American Indian or Alaska Native   0.2%
Asian   0.5%
Native Hawaiian or other Pacific Islander   0.0%
Some other race   0.1%
Hispanic or Latino origin   1.1%
Two or more races   0.8%

*As percentage of total population.

Ancestry*

Dutch 1.3%	Italian 1.7%
English 8.2%	Scotch-Irish 1.2%
French 1.6%	Scottish 1.2%
German 17.6%	USA/American 13.6%
Irish 10.4%	

*As estimated percentage of total population.

Universities and colleges, 2000–2001 enrollment

Ashland Community College, Ashland   2,232
Ashland Technical College, Ashland   503
KCTCS-Maysville Community College, Maysville   1,219
Kentucky Career Institute, Florence   231
Kentucky Christian College, Grayson   569
Northern Kentucky Technical College, Covington   1,024
Northern Kentucky University, Highland Heights   12,080
Southern Ohio College-Fort Mitchell, Fort Mitchell   338
Thomas More College, Crestview Hills   1,416

Newspapers and circulation

	District circulation	Total circulation
Ashland Daily Independent	18,458	20,149
Cincinnati Enquirer	23,282	189,326
Cincinnati Post	28,356	52,163
Huntington Herald Dispatch	2,220	35,241
Louisville Courier Journal	9,689	220,676
*USA Today**	4,131	1,674,376

*See Sources and Explanations in the front of the volume.

Television stations and affiliations

Cincinnati	37%	WCET	PBS
Cincinnati	37%	WCPO	ABC
Cincinnati	37%	WCVN	PBS
Cincinnati	37%	WKOI	Independent
Cincinnati	37%	WKON	PBS
Cincinnati	37%	WKRC	CBS
Cincinnati	37%	WLWT	NBC
Cincinnati	37%	WPTO	PBS
Cincinnati	37%	WSTR	WB
Cincinnati	37%	WXIX	FOX
Charleston-Huntington, WV	29%	WCHS	ABC
Charleston-Huntington, WV	29%	WHCP	WB, UPN
Charleston-Huntington, WV	29%	WKAS	PBS
Charleston-Huntington, WV	29%	WKPI	PBS
Charleston-Huntington, WV	29%	WOUB	PBS
Charleston-Huntington, WV	29%	WOWK	CBS
Charleston-Huntington, WV	29%	WPBO	PBS
Charleston-Huntington, WV	29%	WPBY	PBS
Charleston-Huntington, WV	29%	WSAZ	NBC
Charleston-Huntington, WV	29%	WTSF	Independent
Charleston-Huntington, WV	29%	WVAH	FOX
Lexington	21%	WDKY	FOX
Lexington	21%	WKHA	PBS
Lexington	21%	WKLE	PBS
Lexington	21%	WKMR	PBS
Lexington	21%	WKSO	PBS
Lexington	21%	WKYT	CBS
Lexington	21%	WLEX	NBC
Lexington	21%	WLJC	Independent
Lexington	21%	WTVQ	ABC
Lexington	21%	WYMT	CBS
Louisville	13%	WAVE	NBC
Louisville	13%	WBNA	PAX
Louisville	13%	WDRB	FOX
Louisville	13%	WFTE	UPN
Louisville	13%	WHAS	ABC
Louisville	13%	WKMJ	PBS
Louisville	13%	WKPC	PBS

Louisville	13%	WKZT	PBS
Louisville	13%	WLKY	CBS
Louisville	13%	WWWB	WB

Cable systems and subscribers
Adelphia   35,614
Armstrong   5,639
Bracken Cable Vision   1,067
Insight   66,710
Limestone Cablevision   3,779
Thompson Cablevision   1,121
Williamstown Cable TV   847

Military installations, September 2001
Brooks-Lawler U.S. Army Reserve Center, Newport
376

Businesses and other major employers
St. Elizabeth Medical Center Inc.; Covington; medical
centers   3,500
Catlettsburg Refining; Catlettsburg; petroleum refining
1,941
Ashland Hospital Corp.; Ashland   1,850
Northern Kentucky University; Highland Heights
1,400
Corporate Cleaning Systems Inc.; Erlanger; janitorial
service   1,200
TechnoTrim Inc.; Maysville; automobile seat covers
1,195
Onyx Industrial Services Inc.; Ashland; industrial,
commercial cleaning services   1,100
Our Lady of Bellefonte Hospital Inc.; Ashland   1,069
Good Samaritan Hospital; Erlanger   1,000
AK Steel Corp.; Ashland; steel slabs   1,000
Marathon Ashland Petroleum; Catlettsburg; petroleum
refining   1,000
Grandview Hotel LP; Fort Mitchell; hotels and motels
861
St. Luke Hospital Inc.; Fort Thomas   831
Gap Inc.; Erlanger; warehousing   800
Applied Card Systems Inc.; Russell; credit card service
785
Toyota Motor Manufacturing North America; Erlanger;
motor vehicles and car bodies   755
Worldspan; Prospect; reservation services   750
Cinergy Inc.; Independence; public utility association
700
St. Luke Hospital Inc.; Florence   650
Cingular Wireless; Grayson; wire telephone   625
SSE Manufacturing Inc.; Florence; frozen pizza   600
Addington Mining Inc.; Ashland; surface mining,
bituminous   600
Cook Family Foods; Grayson; food products machinery
600
Speedway SuperAmerica; Russell; grocery store   600
Marrowbone Development Co.; Ashland; coal mining
services   579
North American Stainless; Ghent; steel finishing   575
Newport Steel Corp.; Newport; steel and iron tubes
565
TFE Group Inc.; Hebron; help supply services   550
Sara Lee Corp.; Alexandria; meats and meat products
540

3M Co.; Cynthiana; writing paper   520
Kentucky Dept. of Corrections; La Grange   500
Mazak Corp.; Florence; industrial machinery/equipment
500
Nielsen Co.; Florence; commercial printing   500
Levi Strauss and Co.; Hebron; men's/boys' sportswear
and athletic clothing   500
Thomson Learning Inc.; Independence; textbooks   500
Emerson Power Transmission Corp.; Maysville; steel
chains   500
CSX Transportation Inc.; Raceland; freight cars and
equipment   500

Kentucky 5th District

East and southeast — Somerset, Middlesboro

No area of Kentucky has lower levels of income and education than the rural 5th, which takes in eastern Kentucky's hardscrabble coal country and whose largest city, Somerset, has a population of just over 11,000.

Coal mining once was a thriving industry in this sparsely populated, Appalachian region, but its decline has brought even harder times to the region's mountain people. Mining still provides thousands of jobs in the area—particularly in high-producing coal areas such as Pike, Perry, Harlan, and Knott counties—but the eastern counties are trying to diversify their economies. Some community leaders are trying to attract tourists by highlighting the area's country music heritage, building new arts centers, and showcasing the area's coal history.

Population in the western section is concentrated in Pulaski and Laurel Counties. Like the rest of the west, Somerset relies heavily on tourism and recreation. Lake Cumberland is nearby, as is the Big South Fork National River and Recreation Area. The Daniel Boone National Forest extends from Rowan County in the north to the Tennessee border.

The 5th is secure GOP territory—Democrats have not represented the southeast Kentucky district since 1889. Republicans run particularly well in the more populous central and western parts. Jackson and Owsley Counties, in the west, gave George W. Bush more than 80 percent of the vote in 2000, and five other counties in the southern part gave Bush more than 70 percent. Bush carried the district overall with 57 percent.

Democrats maintain a strong presence in the far eastern coal counties where the United Mine Workers of America union is strong. Seven of the 15 Kentucky counties Al Gore won in 2000 are in the 5th; Democratic voter registration tops 90 percent in some of the counties. But Bush cracked the Democratic dominance by winning Menifee, Morgan, and Wolfe Counties in 2000.

Major Industry
Health care, service, tourism, coal.

Notable
The 5th has the nation's highest percentage of white residents (97 percent); Colonel Harland Sanders began making what would later be known as Kentucky Fried Chicken at his service station in Corbin.

Election Returns

	Republican		Democratic		Other	
President 2000	131,494	56.7%	97,104	41.9%	3,423	1.5%
House 2002	137,986	78.3%	38,254	21.7%		

District Profile

Population   673,670

Total area (square miles)   10,758.7
   Land area (square miles)   10,676.3

Population per square mile   63.1

Counties (2000 population)

Bath (pt.) 2,825	Magoffin 13,332
Bell 30,060	Martin 12,578
Breathitt 16,100	McCreary 17,080
Clay 24,556	Menifee 6,556
Floyd 42,441	Morgan 13,948
Harlan 33,202	Owsley 4,858
Jackson 13,495	Perry 29,390
Johnson 23,445	Pike 68,736
Knott 17,649	Pulaski 56,217
Knox 31,795	Rockcastle 16,582
Laurel 52,715	Rowan 22,094
Lawrence 15,569	Wayne 19,923
Lee 7,916	Whitley 35,865
Leslie 12,401	Wolfe 7,065
Letcher 25,277	

Cities and other areas over 10,000 (2000 population)

Middlesborough   10,384
Somerset   11,352

Race and Hispanic or Latino origin*

White   97.1%
Black or African American   1.1%
American Indian or Alaska Native   0.2%
Asian   0.3%
Native Hawaiian or other Pacific Islander   0.0%
Some other race   0.0%
Hispanic or Latino origin   0.7%
Two or more races   0.6%

*As percentage of total population.

Ancestry*

English 6.8%	Irish 5.7%
German 4.1%	USA/American 29.5%

*As estimated percentage of total population.

Universities and colleges, 2000–2001 enrollment

Alice Lloyd College, Pippa Passes   557
Cumberland College, Williamsburg   1,702
Frontier School of Midwifery and Family Nursing,
   Hyden   205
Hazard Community College, Hazard   2,241
Hazard Technical College, Hazard   405
Laurel Technical College, London   404
Laurel Technical College-Cumberland Valley, Pineville
   516
Mayo Technical College, Paintsville   1,052
Morehead State University, Morehead   8,316
Pikeville College, Pikeville   1,156
Prestonsburg Community College, Prestonsburg   2,207
Somerset Community College, Somerset   2,383
Somerset Technical College, Somerset   546
Southeast Community College, Cumberland   2,411
Union College, Barbourville   893

Newspapers and circulation

	District circulation	Total circulation
Ashland Daily Independent	1,302	20,149
Louisville Courier Journal	1,109	220,676

Television stations and affiliations

Lexington	59%	WDKY	FOX
Lexington	59%	WKHA	PBS
Lexington	59%	WKLE	PBS
Lexington	59%	WKMR	PBS
Lexington	59%	WKSO	PBS
Lexington	59%	WKYT	CBS
Lexington	59%	WLEX	NBC
Lexington	59%	WLJC	Independent
Lexington	59%	WTVQ	ABC
Lexington	59%	WYMT	CBS
Charleston-Huntington, WV	22%	WCHS	ABC
Charleston-Huntington, WV	22%	WHCP	WB, UPN
Charleston-Huntington, WV	22%	WKAS	PBS
Charleston-Huntington, WV	22%	WKPI	PBS
Charleston-Huntington, WV	22%	WOUB	PBS
Charleston-Huntington, WV	22%	WOWK	CBS
Charleston-Huntington, WV	22%	WPBO	PBS
Charleston-Huntington, WV	22%	WPBY	PBS
Charleston-Huntington, WV	22%	WSAZ	NBC
Charleston-Huntington, WV	22%	WTSF	Independent
Charleston-Huntington, WV	22%	WVAH	FOX
Knoxville, TN	12%	WATE	ABC
Knoxville, TN	12%	WBIR	NBC
Knoxville, TN	12%	WBXX	WB
Knoxville, TN	12%	WKOP	PBS
Knoxville, TN	12%	WPXK	PAX
Knoxville, TN	12%	WTNZ	FOX
Knoxville, TN	12%	WVLT	CBS
Bristol-Johnson City-Kingsport	7%	WCYB	NBC
Bristol-Johnson City-Kingsport	7%	WEMT	FOX
Bristol-Johnson City-Kingsport	7%	WJHL	CBS
Bristol-Johnson City-Kingsport	7%	WKPT	ABC
Bristol-Johnson City-Kingsport	7%	WLFG	Independent
Bristol-Johnson City-Kingsport	7%	WMSY	PBS
Bristol-Johnson City-Kingsport	7%	WSBN	PBS
Bristol-Johnson City-Kingsport	7%	WSJK	PBS

Cable systems and subscribers

Access Cable TV   6,133
Adelphia   41,832
Barbourville Cable TV   3,306
Big Sandy TV Cable   1,914
C & W Cable   912
Charter   47,576
Community TV Inc.   5,566
Eastern Cable Corp.   1,988
Howards Cable TV   3,175
Inter Mountain Cable   22,506
Kentucky West Virginia Cable Inc.   1,090
Louisa Cable TV   1,797
McKee Television   1,175
Tele-Media   19,335
TV Service Inc.   8,296

Businesses and other major employers

Kentucky Health Services; Somerset; public health programs 1,350

Morehead State University; Morehead 1,180

Baptist Health System Hospital; Corbin 1,024

Pikeville United Methodist Hospital of Kentucky Inc.; Pikeville 1,000

Affiliated Computer Services Inc.; London; computer service bureau 900

Lifepoint Hospitals Inc.; Somerset 850

Mid-South Electronics Inc.; Annville; printed circuit boards 800

Sykes Enterprises Inc.; Pikeville; technical institute 700

St. Claire Medical Center Inc.; Morehead 650

Wal-Mart Stores Inc.; London; department stores 600

Super Service Inc.; Somerset; trucking 600

CTA Acoustics Acquistion Corp.; Corbin; motor vehicle body components and frame 550

Wal-Mart Stores Inc.; Corbin; department stores 500

Hassel Finance; London; financial services 500

Image Entry Inc.; London; data processing 500

Mountaintop Baking Co.; Kimper; breads, rolls, and buns 500

Consolidated Health Systems Hospital; Endicott 500

Appalachian Regional Healthcare Inc. Hospital; Whitesburg 500

Wal-Mart Stores Inc.; Somerset; discount department stores 500

Toyotetsu America Inc.; Somerset; automotive stampings 500

Kentucky 6th District

East central — Lexington, Frankfort

The 6th embodies the culture and economic pursuits that most outsiders associate with the state of Kentucky. This is the heart of the Bluegrass region, which spawns Kentucky Derby champions and is host to considerable tobacco and liquor interests.

A patchwork of urban, suburban, and rural areas, the 6th experienced steady economic growth in the 1990s. Lexington, the district's largest city, continues to have a strong equine industry and is known as the thoroughbred capital of the world. The city is home to the University of Kentucky, where the basketball team plays at Rupp Arena. A Toyota manufacturing facility in Georgetown, just north of Lexington, is one of the largest employers in the state.

Tobacco, always a highly charged subject in this region, held strong in the 1990s despite mounting concerns about its future. Kentucky's top three producers of burley tobacco in 2000—Bourbon, Fayette, and Madison Counties—are in the 6th District.

The 6th swung sharply to George W. Bush in the 2000 election after narrowly backing Bill Clinton in 1996. As in other Kentucky districts, the cultural themes of the 2000 election helped the GOP. District voters tend to be socially conservative, especially on gun control. The House seat switched from Republican to Democrat and back again in the 1990s.

Government workers in Frankfort contribute to Franklin County's Democratic lean; it was the only county in the 6th to back Al Gore for president in 2000. Democratic support dips in Woodford and Scott Counties, which border Franklin and have among the highest incomes in Kentucky. Republicans run up big margins in the farmland south of Lexington—Bush took district-wide highs of 69 percent in Garrard County and 67 percent in Jessamine County.

Major Industry

Manufacturing, service, tobacco, retail.

Notable

The whiskey bourbon was named after Bourbon County.

Election Returns

	Republican		Democratic		Other	
President 2000	145,606	55.5%	109,602	41.8%	7,282	2.8%
House 2002	115,622	72.0%			45,066	28.0%

District Profile

Population 673,626

Total area (square miles) 3,775.3
   Land area (square miles) 3,756.5

Population per square mile 179.3

Counties (2000 population)

Anderson 19,111	Jessamine 39,041
Bourbon 19,360	Lincoln (pt.) 17,469
Boyle 27,697	Madison 70,872
Clark 33,144	Mercer 20,817
Estill 15,307	Montgomery 22,554
Fayette 260,512	Powell 13,237
Franklin 47,687	Scott (pt.) 28,818
Garrard 14,792	Woodford 23,208

Cities and other areas over 10,000 (2000 population)

Danville 15,477	Nicholasville 19,680
Frankfort 27,741	Richmond 27,152
Georgetown 18,080	Winchester 16,724
Lexington-Fayette 260,512	

Race and Hispanic or Latino origin*

White 87.1%
Black or African American 8.2%
American Indian or Alaska Native 0.2%
Asian 1.2%
Native Hawaiian or other Pacific Islander 0.0%
Some other race 0.1%
Hispanic or Latino origin 2.1%
Two or more races 1.1%

*As percentage of total population.

Ancestry*

English 9.5%	Italian 1.5%
French 1.4%	Scotch-Irish 1.9%
German 9.2%	Scottish 1.6%
Irish 8.9%	USA/American 15.3%

*As estimated percentage of total population.

Universities and colleges, 2000–2001 enrollment

Asbury College, Wilmore   1,359
Asbury Theological Seminary, Wilmore   1,288
Berea College, Berea   1,590
Central Kentucky Technical College, Lexington   1,501
Central Kentucky Technical College-Anderson, Lawrenceburg   2,199
Centre College, Danville   1,055
Eastern Kentucky University, Richmond   13,285
Fugazzi College, Lexington   309
Georgetown College, Georgetown   1,736
Kentucky College of Business, Lexington   1,723
Kentucky State University, Frankfort   2,254
Lexington Community College, Lexington   7,214
Midway College, Midway   834
Spencerian College-Lexington, Lexington   254
Transylvania University, Lexington   1,083
University of Kentucky, Lexington   23,114

Newspapers and circulation

	District circulation	Total circulation
Danville Advocate-Messenger	9,061	10,619
*Harrodsburg Herald**	4,628	4,628
Louisville Courier Journal	3,291	220,676
Richmond Register	6,784	6,983
*USA Today**	2,897	1,674,376

See Sources and Explanations in the front of the volume.

Television stations and affiliations

Lexington	100%	WDKY
Lexington	100%	WKHA
Lexington	100%	WKLE
Lexington	100%	WKMR
Lexington	100%	WKSO
Lexington	100%	WKYT
Lexington	100%	WLEX
Lexington	100%	WLJC
Lexington	100%	WTVQ
Lexington	100%	WYMT

Cable systems and subscribers

Adelphia   69,431
Frankfort Community Cable Service   18,550
Insight   80,330
Irvine Community TV   3,782

Military installations, September 2001

Blue Grass Army Depot, Richmond   837

Businesses and other major employers

Kentucky General Government; Frankfort   40,000
Executive Office of Kentucky; Frankfort   10,000
University of Kentucky; Lexington   8,000
Toyota Motor Manufacturing Kentucky Inc.; Georgetown; automobiles   7,773
Lexmark International Inc.; Lexington; typing and word processing machines   6,500
Lexmark International Inc.; Lexington; printers, computers   5,000
University of Kentucky Medical Center; Lexington; medical centers   5,000
Baptist Health System Hospital; Lexington   2,496
University of Kentucky Hospital; Lexington   2,350

Kentucky Utilities Co.; Lexington; electric power distribution   2,300
Eastern Kentucky University; Richmond   1,800
Kentucky Natural Resources and Environmental Protection Cabinet; Frankfort   1,700
Matsushita Electric Corp. of America; Danville; household vacuum cleaners   1,555
Ephraim McDowell Regional Medical Center Inc.; Danville   1,500
Ashland Inc.; Lexington; petroleum refining   1,500
Kentucky Health Services; Frankfort   1,500
Kentucky Labor Cabinet; Frankfort   1,200
Square D Co.; Lexington; electric power switches   1,150
R. R. Donnelley and Sons Co.; Danville; magazine printing   1,100
L-3 Communications Corp.; Lexington; aircraft cleaning and janitorial service   1,000
Kentucky Workforce Development; Frankfort; equal employment opportunity office   1,000
Hitachi Automotive Products USA Inc.; Harrodsburg; alternators, automotive   940
Quebecor World Inc.; Versailles; publishing   900
Ashland Inc.; Lexington; lubricating oils and greases   900
Bank One Corp.; Lexington; banking, insurance   850
Johnson Controls Inc.; Georgetown; automobile seats   800
American Greetings Corp.; Danville; greeting cards   800
Lexington-Fayette Urban County; Lexington; county government   800
Osram Sylvania Inc.; Versailles; electric lamps   750
Tokico Inc.; Berea; automotive shock absorbers   723
Chef America East Inc.; Mount Sterling; frozen specialties   700
Texas Instruments Inc.; Versailles; appliance regulators   700
U.S. Defense Dept.; Lexington   700
Kentucky Education Arts and Humanities; Frankfort   700
Kentucky Finance and Admin.; Frankfort   700
Kentucky State University; Frankfort   700
Trim Masters Inc.; Harrodsburg; public building and related furniture   671
Link-Belt Construction Equipment Co.; Lexington; cranes   665
ATR Wire and Cable Co. Inc.; Danville; steel tire cords and tire cord fabrics   640
Good Samaritan Hospital of Lexington; Lexington   630
Johnson Controls Inc.; Georgetown; plastic bottles   600
Dillard's Inc.; Lexington; department stores   600
Verizon Communications Inc.; Lexington; telephone communication   600
United Parcel Service Inc.; Lexington; parcel delivery   600
Frankfort Regional Medical Center; Frankfort   600
Lexington Herald-Leader Co.; Lexington; newspaper   569
U.S. Bureau of Prisons; Lexington   560
Pattie A. Clay Infirmary; Richmond   550
Meijer Inc.; Lexington; discount department stores   550

CHCK Inc.; Lexington; hospital management   540

Jewish Hospital Healthcare Services Inc.; Lexington   520

Nacco Materials Handling Group Inc.; Berea; industrial trucks and tractors   505

McLane Co.; Nicholasville; discount department stores   500

Kentucky Easter Seal Society Inc.; Lexington; specialty hospitals   500

Kentucky Health Services; Lexington   500

Speedway SuperAmerica; Lexington; convenience stores   500

U.S. Postal Service; Lexington   500

Topy Corp.; Frankfort; motor vehicle wheels   500

Louisiana

Louisiana and its main city of New Orleans have a special fascination for visitors, artists, historians, and social scientists. From the Vieux Carre and its Bourbon Street to Mardi Gras, the jazz clubs, and the riverfront, New Orleans exudes an air of adventure tinged with indulgence. Its rich food and history draw conventioneers and vacationers by the millions. It is the home of exuberant and knowing music, touted as the cradle of jazz and, at a minimum, the birthplace and home of Dixieland. Louisianans have been proud of being more worldly than their country cousins in neighboring Arkansas, Mississippi, and East Texas.

The politics of the state have reflected some of this exaggerated sophistication, sometimes stretching the colorful to the point of corruption and beyond. The dynasty founded by Huey Long as governor, senator, and presidential aspirant between the two world wars, dominated Baton Rouge and federal elections for several generations. Some of what the Longs did was undeniably beneficial to the state, even as it was undeniably good for the Longs. Several Hollywood movies have assayed this subject material, including one based on Robert Penn Warren's classic *All the Kings Men*. That film won the Best Picture Oscar but barely began to convey the mélange of legend, language, and attitude that makes this state unique.

More recently, Louisiana has endured several terms under Democratic governor Edwin Edwards, whose connection to gambling and other criminal activities landed him in jail. Edwards, though, was still considered preferable in his last reelection campaign to the 1991 Republican nominee, former Ku Klux Klan leader David Duke. "Vote for the crook," one local bumper sticker read that year, "it's important."

Behind this wry sense of resignation, however, the state has suffered from years of official neglect. The Pelican State is now 49th in high-tech jobs and percentage of homes with computers. It is dead last in objective measures of public health. Its death rate is the nation's third highest, its child poverty rate the fourth highest, and its unemployment rate in the top ten. The state has the nation's highest murder rate and highest incarceration rate, and the highest percentage of families with just one parent. "I'm tired of Louisiana being last in everything good and first in everything bad," said Cleo Fields, the Democratic nominee for governor in 1995.

Named for the great King Louis XIV in the 1600s, Louisiana is the most distinctly French in its cultural influences of all 50 states. The French held sway here off and on for generations from the late Renaissance to the post-Revolution 1800s, and their mark is on the names and notions affixed in the state's consciousness (counties, for example, are called parishes). In 1803, Napoleon gave up his toehold in the new world to finance more wars of conquest in the old. But there remains a defiant remembrance here, as there does in Quebec (from which many of the early French settlers once migrated to escape the British: "Acadians" known today as Cajuns).

The port city of New Orleans was most important in the economic life of the country from the 1850s to the 1960s. The port is still the point where barge traffic from down the Mississippi River meets the ocean-going vessels from the Gulf of Mexico. But contemporary Louisiana products are often from the oil and gas sector, leaving the state by pipeline, truck, and rail tanker. These resources have also made the chemical industry as important to the state as any other.

When the port was at its height as a bearer of the great river's abundance, Louisiana grew faster than the country as a whole and reached eight House seats in 1910. For nearly the rest of the century, Louisiana's growth rate was just close enough to the national norm to keep these eight. But in the past generation, growth has stalled and the number of seats has begun to dwindle again, even as new seats have sprouted across much of the South.

The loss of one seat after the 1990 census forced a long look at the map and a difficult redistricting process that dragged on for years. Republicans in Washington and some black Democrats in Baton Rouge wanted to draw two black majority seats, one in New Orleans and one outside it. One motivation for this was racial balance in the delegation: 29.5 percent of the voting-age population is African American, the second highest percentage in the country behind Mississippi. Another motivation was to pack the Democrats' most reliable votes into as few districts as possible, strengthening Republicans in the other five districts.

Lawsuits were filed by a variety of parties who felt aggrieved by the plan, and the long and irregular swaths it cut across the upstate parishes in search of more black voters. This artwork also displeased the U.S. Supreme Court, which ordered new lines drawn. One of the two black members elected under the 1992 lines was defeated under the new plan. By the late 1990s the state had settled down to one black Democrat in the 2nd District (New Orleans), a white conservative Democrat in the southwestern bayou country of the 7th District, and five white conservative Republicans representing the rest of the state.

The post-2000 redistricting process was, by contrast, an expeditious process, with the Democratic state legislature passing a plan that was signed into law by Republican governor Mike Foster. The new scheme made few major changes, as if neither party and neither race was ready for another

LOUISIANA

Districts established October 19, 2001, for elections first held in 2002.

7 members

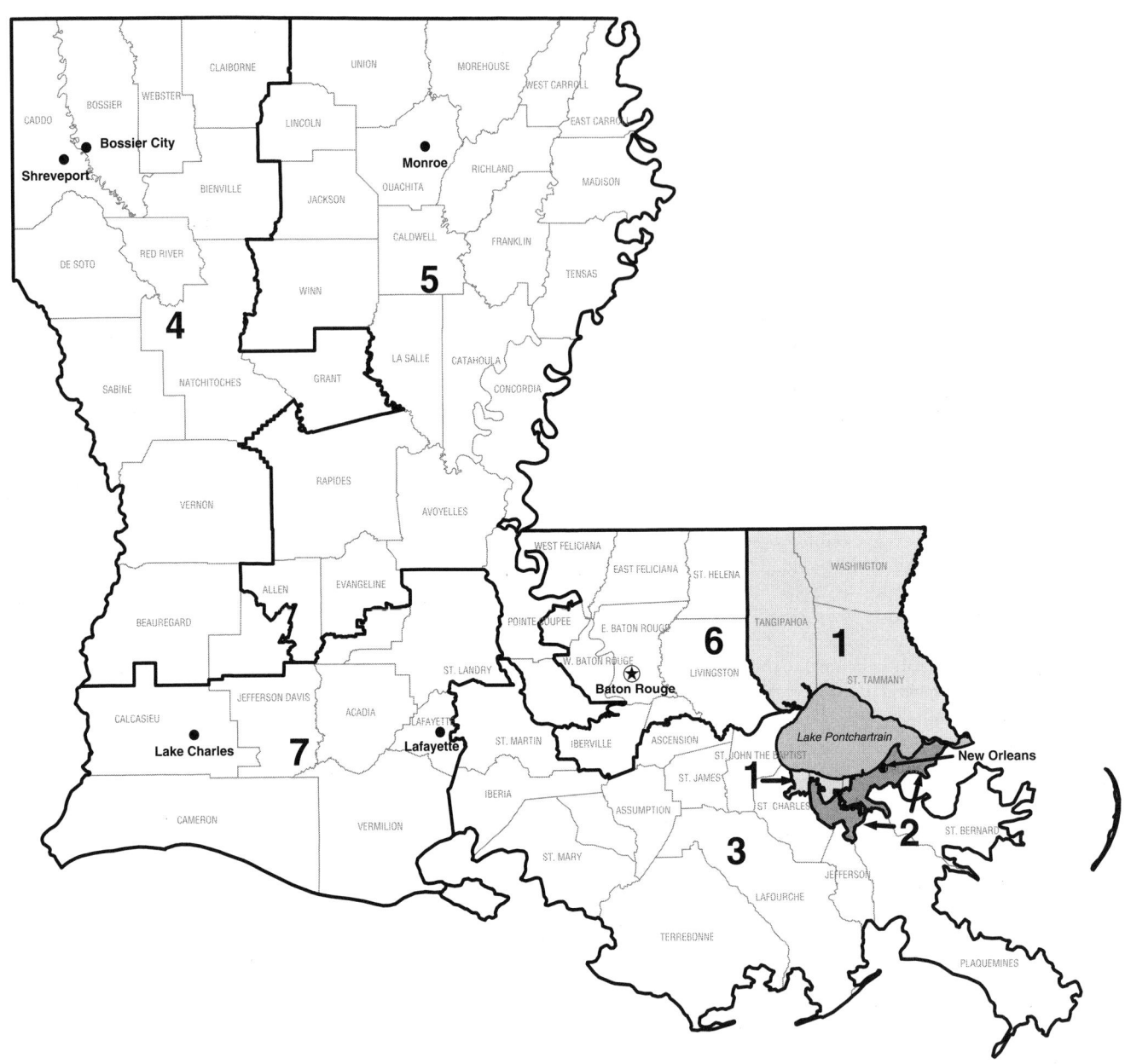

pitched battle so soon. There are three districts in the metro New Orleans area, one upriver in Baton Rouge, one in the Cajun southwest from Lake Charles to Lafayette, one in the northwestern "oil patch" quadrant around Shreveport, and one in the northeast bordered by the Mississippi Delta.

Three of these were in Democratic hands in 2003: the 2nd District, which represents the city of New Orleans and its primarily African American constituents; the northeastern 5th; and the southwestern 7th.

In statewide voting, Louisiana has become unpredictable and is likely to remain so. Roughly three-fifths of the state's registered voters continued to call themselves official Democrats after 2000, but polls found increasing numbers of Louisianans describing themselves as independents who leaned Republican. Surely they were willing to vote that way. Louisiana has been part of the great southern shift to the GOP, going along at its own pace and in its own style.

The state first rebelled against the Democrats by voting for Strom Thurmond and the States Rights Party in 1948, then by backing Dwight D. Eisenhower in 1956, and joining the Deep South swing to Barry Goldwater in 1964. Jimmy Carter claimed the state for the Democrats in 1976 but lost it in 1980. Bill Clinton won by a slim margin in 1992 and a slimmer one in 1996, but in 2000 the state went heavily for George W. Bush.

The trend has penetrated to the governor's mansion, as well. The GOP's David Treen broke the party bar in 1979 but lasted just one term. Mike Foster, a state senator from St. Mary Parish near the Gulf ran and won as a populist conservative Republican in 1995 and 1999.

But for all this movement, Louisiana remains the only state not to have had a Republican in the Senate since Reconstruction. There have been close calls, notably in 1986, 1996, and 2002, when GOP nominees for the Senate seemed on the verge of winning. Each time, a surge in participation by black voters helped the Democratic nominee survive. But given the larger trends in the state's politics, it is still possible the state will have one or even two Republican senators by 2010.

Table 1 Population

District	Population	Population under 18	Voting-age population	Median age	Male*	Female*
1	638,355	158,956	479,399	36.9	48.4	51.6
2	638,562	180,741	457,821	32.3	47.1	52.9
3	638,322	183,698	454,624	33.8	48.7	51.3
4	638,466	173,339	465,127	34.5	48.5	51.5
5	638,517	172,615	465,902	34.3	48.5	51.5
6	638,324	170,817	467,507	32.4	49.0	51.0
7	638,430	179,633	458,797	33.8	48.5	51.5
State	4,468,976	1,219,799	3,249,177	34.0	48.4	51.6

*As percentage of total population.

Table 2 Voting-Age Persons by Race/Hispanic or Latino Origin

District	White*	Black or African American*	American Indian or Alaska Native*	Asian*	Other or multirace*	Hispanic or Latino*
1	81.3	11.4	0.3	1.5	0.9	4.6
2	32.7	59.3	0.3	2.7	1.2	3.9
3	72.7	22.2	1.4	0.9	0.9	2.0
4	65.1	30.5	0.7	0.8	1.0	1.9
5	66.3	30.8	0.4	0.5	0.5	1.3
6	65.3	30.7	0.2	1.5	0.7	1.6
7	74.5	22.6	0.2	0.7	0.7	1.3
State	65.5	29.5	0.5	1.2	0.8	2.4

*As percentage of voting-age population.

Table 3 Voting-Age Population by Age Groups

District	18 to 24*	25 to 44*	45 to 64*	Over 64*
1	11.7	39.6	31.8	16.9
2	15.6	40.9	29.1	14.3
3	13.6	41.4	30.0	15.0
4	14.3	38.2	29.7	17.8
5	15.3	37.4	29.2	18.0
6	17.2	40.9	28.9	13.1
7	14.4	40.2	29.2	16.2
State	14.6	39.8	29.7	15.9

*As percentage of voting-age population.

Table 4 Income and Occupation

District	Median family income	Families in poverty*	White collar†	Blue collar†	Service†	Farm†
1	$50,317	9.1	65.3	20.2	14.1	0.4
2	$32,306	22.8	56.2	21.4	22.1	0.2
3	$39,990	15.6	50.3	33.6	14.7	1.5
4	$37,414	16.0	52.7	28.5	18.0	0.9
5	$34,260	18.7	53.5	26.9	17.8	1.8
6	$46,699	12.5	61.5	23.6	14.7	0.3
7	$38,189	16.2	54.9	27.9	16.5	0.7
State	$39,774	15.8	56.6	25.8	16.7	0.8

*As percentage of all families. †As percentage of employed workers 16 years and over.

Table 5 Education: School Years Completed

District	Less than grade 9*	Grades 9–12 no diploma*	High school diploma no college*	Some college*	College bachelor's degree or higher*
1	5.7	11.9	28.0	27.0	27.4
2	9.0	18.8	27.1	25.6	19.4
3	13.9	17.2	38.2	19.9	10.8
4	7.4	16.0	34.7	25.2	16.7
5	10.9	18.5	34.1	21.0	15.5
6	5.8	13.8	31.3	24.9	24.1
7	12.4	15.3	33.6	22.1	16.6
State	9.3	15.9	32.4	23.7	18.7

*As percentage of persons age 25 and over.

Table 6 Housing and Residential Patterns

District	Median home value	Owner occupied*	Renter occupied*	Urban†	Rural†
1	$115,600	70.2	29.8	79.6	20.4
2	$80,000	50.5	49.5	99.4	0.6
3	$72,700	77.4	22.6	73.0	27.0
4	$63,100	68.5	31.5	59.3	40.7

District	Median home value	Owner occupied*	Renter occupied*	Urban†	Rural†
5	$58,600	70.3	29.7	52.9	47.1
6	$91,200	68.7	31.3	75.5	24.5
7	$68,700	70.3	29.7	68.9	31.1
State	$77,500	67.9	32.1	72.7	27.3

*As percentage of occupied housing units. †As percentage of total population.

Louisiana 1st District

East — Metairie, part of Florida Parishes

A short distance from festive downtown New Orleans, the conservative 1st skims the edges of the city and reaches north across Lake Pontchartrain to the Mississippi border. The mostly white-collar population is among the wealthiest and most educated in the state.

The 1st's population center is on the south side of the lake and includes the upscale Metairie suburbs. The area is packed with white-collar conservatives who generally vote Republican.

North of the lake, the 1st includes three of the "Florida Parishes," so named because they were part of Spanish Florida until 1810. Once a community of seasonal homes for residents escaping the heat and humidity of New Orleans, the north shore is now a booming suburban haven, replete with suburbanites who commute across Lake Pontchartrain Causeway to their jobs in New Orleans. St. Tammany Parish was the fastest-growing area in the 1st during the 1990s. Local developments include petrochemical and oil industries, and leaders hope to attract high-tech firms related to the expansion of the Avondale Shipyard in the 2nd. The northern parishes are still heavily agricultural, producing mainly cotton, corn, and soybeans.

Democrats held the 1st for a little more than a century before it became a GOP possession in 1977. Now, residents warmly welcome Republicans on the local and federal level. George W. Bush took 66.5 percent of the district's vote in 2000, making the 1st the only Louisiana district to give him more than 57 percent. Reliably Democratic African Americans make up 13 percent of the 1st's population—the only district in the state with less than 24 percent. Democrats do manage to win a few local offices in the northern, rural Washington and Tangipahoa Parishes.

Major Industry
Petrochemicals, oil, agriculture, tourism.

Notable
Lake Pontchartrain Causeway, the world's longest highway bridge over water, spans about 23.9 miles; former Ku Klux Klansman David Duke held the Metairie state House seat from 1989 to 1993; pop singer Britney Spears is from Kentwood in Tangipahoa Parish.

Election Returns

	Republican		Democratic		Other	
President 2000	179,196	66.5%	83,779	31.1%	6,650	2.5%
House 2002	147,117	81.5%			33,453	18.5%

District Profile

Population 638,355

Total area (square miles) 2,840.2
 Land area (square miles) 2,402.0

Population per square mile 265.8

Counties (2000 population)
 Jefferson Parish (pt.) 253,565
 Orleans Parish (pt.) 37,451
 St. Charles Parish (pt.) 11,557
 St. Tammany Parish 191,268
 Tangipahoa Parish 100,588
 Washington Parish 43,926

Cities and other areas over 10,000 (2000 population)
 Bogalusa 13,365
 Hammond 17,639
 Kenner (pt.) 46,007
 Mandeville 10,489
 Metairie CDP (pt.) 140,916
 New Orleans (pt.) 37,451
 River Ridge CDP (pt.) 13,324
 Slidell 25,695
 Terrytown CDP (pt.) 15,232

Race and Hispanic or Latino origin*
 White 79.6%
 Black or African American 12.8%
 American Indian or Alaska Native 0.3%
 Asian 1.5%
 Native Hawaiian or other Pacific Islander 0.0%
 Some other race 0.1%
 Hispanic or Latino origin 4.7%
 Two or more races 1.0%

*As percentage of total population.

Ancestry*

English 5.8%		Irish 9.4%	
Fr. Canadian 1.2%		Italian 8.7%	
French 13.3%		Scotch-Irish 1.2%	
German 10.9%		USA/American 6.0%	

*As estimated percentage of total population.

Universities and colleges, 2000–2001 enrollment
 Delgado Community College, New Orleans 12,784
 Education America-Southeast College of Technology, Metairie 652
 Louisiana Technical College-Hammond, Hammond 218
 Louisiana Technical College-Jefferson, Metairie 257
 Louisiana Technical College-Slidell, Slidell 531
 Louisiana Technical College-Sullivian, Bogalusa 849
 Louisiana Technical College-West Jefferson, Harvey 422
 Southeastern Louisiana University, Hammond 14,525
 University of Phoenix-Louisiana, Kenner 1,394

Newspapers and circulation

	District circulation	Total circulation
Hammond Daily Star	9,905	12,096
New Orleans Times-Picayune	106,371	256,823
*USA Today**	2,453	1,674,376

*See Sources and Explanations in the front of the volume.

Television stations and affiliations

New Orleans	100%	WDSU	NBC
New Orleans	100%	WGNO	ABC
New Orleans	100%	WHNO	Independent
New Orleans	100%	WLAE	PBS
New Orleans	100%	WNOL	WB
New Orleans	100%	WPXL	PAX
New Orleans	100%	WUPL	UPN
New Orleans	100%	WVUE	FOX
New Orleans	100%	WWL	CBS
New Orleans	100%	WYES	PBS

Cable systems and subscribers

Charter   57,524
Cox   102,786
Galaxy   616

Military installations, September 2001

Camp Villere Military Training Area (Army Guard), Slidell   161

Businesses and other major employers

United Parcel Service Inc.; New Orleans; parcel delivery 4,500

Alton Ochsner Medical Foundation Inc.; Jefferson 3,000

Keenan Staffing Inc.; Metairie; employment agencies 2,305

Congoleum Corp.; Metairie; floor or wall covering 1,200

Treasure Chest Casino; Kenner; gambling   1,200

Tangipahoa Parish Hospital; Hammond   1,200

Children's Hospital; New Orleans   1,192

Universal Sodexho; Harahan; caterers   1,000

DynMcDermott Petroleum Operations Co.; New Orleans; administrative management   950

St. Tammany Parish Hospital; Covington   920

Louisiana Dept. of Health and Hospitals; Hammond 900

Southeastern Louisiana University; Hammond   900

St. Tammany Parish Hospital; Slidell   880

Community Behavioral Health System Inc.; Metairie 850

Advantage Nursing Services Inc.; Metairie; nurses' registry   800

Lakeview Regional Medical Center Corp.; Covington 800

Louisiana Dept. of Health and Hospitals; Mandeville 749

Coca-Cola Enterprises Inc.; New Orleans; soft drinks 700

Sanderson Farms Inc.; Hammond; chicken processing 700

Wal-Mart Stores Inc.; Hammond; discount department stores   697

Orion Refining Corp.; New Sarpy; petroleum refining 638

Gaylord Container Corp.; Bogalusa; kraft paper   635

Intralox Inc.; Harahan; conveyors and conveying equipment   607

Tenet Healthcare Corp. Hospital; Gretna   602

Louisiana Coca-Cola Bottling Co.; Harahan; soft drinks 600

Wal-Mart Stores Inc.; Covington; discount department stores   600

Louisiana Dept. of Health and Hospitals; Independence 600

Pampered Chef; Slidell; restaurants   600

Tenet Healthcare Corp.; Slidell; hospital   600

Jefferson Parish School Board; Metairie   590

U.S. Minerals Management Service; New Orleans   560

Advance Polybag Inc.; Metairie; plastic bags   550

American Nursing Services Inc.; Metairie; nurses' registry   550

Krewe of Cleopatra; Gretna; carnival operation   550

Delgado Community College; New Orleans   514

Dillard's Inc.; Metairie; department stores   500

Tenet Healthcare Corp. Hospital; Kenner   500

Bank One National Assn.; Harahan; commercial bank 500

St. Tammany Parish; Covington; sheriff's office   500

Louisiana 2nd District

New Orleans

French street names, strands of Spanish moss, and snake-bearing, fortune-telling voodoo queens add to New Orleans's unique cultural mix. But beyond its reputation as the "Big Easy," the comfortably Democratic 2nd, which takes in much of the city and some middle-class suburbs, has dealt with serious issues. While the crime rate has fallen, widespread poverty continues to cause some flight from the city. Since its peak in 1960, New Orleans's population has declined by almost one-fourth.

Famed for its food and jazz traditions, New Orleans is one of the most popular tourist destinations in the country. Mardi Gras and the annual Jazz and Heritage Festival alone attract millions of visitors and billions of dollars each year.

Other staples of the 2nd's economic diet—the New Orleans port, shipbuilding, and petroleum industries—have held strong in recent years. The Avondale shipyard, recently purchased by defense contractor Northrop Grumman, built a new high-tech center that has created jobs and drawn businesses to the area. Meanwhile, after a decade of decline, the oil and gas industry experienced a resurgence in the 1990s that has leveled off in recent years.

Three rounds of redistricting in the 1990s left the 2nd as Louisiana's only black-majority district. Revisions following the 2000 census did not alter that status and left the district 64 percent black. Democratic presidential candidates routinely garner more than 60 percent of the vote here. In 2000 Al Gore received 75.7 percent.

Major Industry

Tourism, shipbuilding, oil, and gas.

Notable

The St. Charles Streetcar Line, created in 1835, is the oldest continuously operating line in the world; Lindy Boggs, mother of newscaster Cokie Roberts and widow of Rep. Hale Boggs, was elected to the U.S. House in 1973 and held the 2nd until 1991.

Election Returns

	Republican		Democratic		Other	
President 2000	48,726	22.3%	165,587	75.7%	4,457	2.0%
House 2002	15,440	10.9%	90,310	63.5%	36,405	25.6%

District Profile

Population   638,562

Total area (square miles)   444.2
  Land area (square miles)   265.9

Population per square mile   2,401.5

Counties (2000 population)
Jefferson Parish (pt.)   191,339
Orleans Parish (pt.)   447,223

Cities and other areas over 10,000 (2000 population)
Estelle CDP (pt.)   15,228
Harvey CDP (pt.)   20,058
Kenner (pt.)   24,510
Marrero CDP (pt.)   35,796
New Orleans (pt.)   447,223
Terrytown CDP (pt.)   10,198
Westwego   10,763
Woodmere CDP   13,058

Race and Hispanic or Latino origin*
White   28.3%
Black or African American   63.7%
American Indian or Alaska Native   0.3%
Asian   2.7%
Native Hawaiian or other Pacific Islander   0.0%
Some other race   0.2%
Hispanic or Latino origin   3.8%
Two or more races   1.0%

*As percentage of total population.

Ancestry*
English	2.3%	Italian	3.2%
French	6.3%	Subsaharan	1.2%
German	4.3%	USA/American	2.5%
Irish	3.6%		

*As estimated percentage of total population.

Universities and colleges, 2000–2001 enrollment
Dillard University, New Orleans   1,953
Louisiana State University-Medical Center, New Orleans   2,720
Louisiana Technical College-Sidney N. Collier, New Orleans   890
Loyola University-New Orleans, New Orleans   5,279
New Orleans Baptist Theological Seminary, New Orleans   2,468
Our Lady of Holy Cross College, New Orleans   1,233
Southern University-New Orleans, New Orleans   3,999
Tulane University of Louisiana, New Orleans   11,652
University of New Orleans, New Orleans   16,218
Xavier University of Louisiana, New Orleans   3,797

Newspapers and circulation

	District circulation	Total circulation
New Orleans Times-Picayune	102,080	256,823
*USA Today**	9,033	1,674,376

*See Sources and Explanations in the front of the volume.

Television stations and affiliations
New Orleans	100%	WDSU	NBC
New Orleans	100%	WGNO	ABC
New Orleans	100%	WHNO	Independent
New Orleans	100%	WLAE	PBS
New Orleans	100%	WNOL	WB
New Orleans	100%	WPXL	PAX
New Orleans	100%	WUPL	UPN
New Orleans	100%	WVUE	FOX
New Orleans	100%	WWL	CBS
New Orleans	100%	WYES	PBS

Cable systems and subscribers
Cox   120,836

Military installations, September 2001
New Orleans Naval Air Station (Navy Reserve), Belle Chase   1,583
New Orleans Naval Air Station (Air National Guard), Belle Chase   1,011

Businesses and other major employers
Avondale Industries of New York Inc.; Westwego; barges   6,000
Northrop Grumman Ship Systems; Westwego; shipbuilding and repairing   6,000
Hibernia Corp.; New Orleans; commercial bank   5,366
Litton Avondale Industries Inc.; Westwego; military ships: building and repairing   5,300
Louisiana State University; New Orleans   5,000
J. Ray McDermott Holdings Inc.; New Orleans; marine construction   4,330
Louisiana Dept. of Health and Hospitals; New Orleans   4,000
U.S. Postal Service; New Orleans   2,887
Tulane Medical Center; New Orleans   2,752
Tenet Healthcare Corp. Hospital; New Orleans   2,600
Lockheed Martin Corp.; New Orleans; metal plate tanks   2,500
Jazz Casino Co.; New Orleans; casino hotel   2,500
Jefferson Parish Inc.; Harahan; law enforcement   1,900
Continental Airlines Inc.; New Orleans; airline tickets   1,800
U.S. Dept. of Agriculture; New Orleans   1,750
U.S. Veterans Hospital; New Orleans   1,700
City of New Orleans; New Orleans; refuse systems   1,562
Hospital Service District; Marrero   1,548
Regional Transit Authority; New Orleans   1,400
Touro Infirmary and Hebrew Benevolent Assn.; New Orleans   1,323
Hilton Hotels Corp.; New Orleans; hotels   1,302
City of New Orleans; New Orleans city government   1,300
U.S. Army Corps. of Engineers; New Orleans   1,300
City of New Orleans; New Orleans; police dept.   1,300

Jazzland Inc.; New Orleans; theme park 1,300

Pendleton Memorial Methodist Hospital; New Orleans 1,210

Louisiana-I Gaming; Harvey; gambling 1,200

U.S. Coast Guard; New Orleans 1,200

University of New Orleans; New Orleans 1,150

Tenet Healthcare Corp. Hospital; New Orleans 1,100

Xavier University of Louisiana; New Orleans 1,000

Texaco Exploration and Production Inc.; New Orleans; administrative management 1,000

Bank One Corp.; New Orleans; commercial bank 1,000

Entergy Louisiana; New Orleans; electric, other services 932

Pellerin Milnor Corp.; Kenner; commercial laundry equipment 900

City of New Orleans; New Orleans; fire dept. 860

Loyola University New Orleans Inc.; New Orleans 850

Park Place Entertainment Corp.; New Orleans; casino hotel 850

Emeril's Homebase; New Orleans; cajun restaurant 850

Bollinger Shipyards Lockport; Lockport; shipbuilding and repairing 845

Hyatt Corp.; New Orleans; hotels 830

CS&M Associates; New Orleans; hotel, franchised 800

Hospitality Enterprises Inc.; New Orleans; travel packages 800

Pan American Life Insurance Inc.; New Orleans; life insurance 800

Facility Management of Louisiana Inc.; New Orleans; nonresidential building operators 725

Nabors Offshore Corp.; Harvey; drilling oil and gas wells 700

Starwood Hotels and Resorts Worldwide Inc.; New Orleans; resort hotel 700

City of Kenner; Kenner; city government 678

CYTEC Industries Inc.; Westwego; chemical preparations 650

Hibernia National Bank; New Orleans; commercial bank 650

Associated Catholic Charities of New Orleans Inc.; New Orleans; charitable trust management 650

Southern Holdings Inc.; New Orleans; scrap and waste materials 650

Louisiana National Guard; New Orleans 650

New Orleans Roosevelt Venture; New Orleans; hotels 600

Orleans Parish School Board; New Orleans 600

U.S. Internal Revenue Service; New Orleans 600

Tenet Healthcare Corp. Hospital; New Orleans 550

ExxonMobil Oil Corp.; New Orleans; crude petroleum production 500

Fairmont Hotel Management; New Orleans; hotels 500

OneSource Facility Services Inc.; New Orleans; janitorial service 500

National Building Services and Maintenance Inc.; New Orleans; janitorial service 500

Aramark Sports and Entertainment Services Inc.; New Orleans; concessionaire 500

Orient-Express Hotels Louisiana Inc.; New Orleans; hotels 500

Royal Sonesta Inc.; New Orleans; hotel, franchised 500

Tidewater Marine; New Orleans; chartering of commercial boats 500

Louisiana 3rd District

South central — New Iberia, Houma

A maze of interconnected bayous, swamps, and marshes, the southern 3rd District runs along the coast of the Gulf of Mexico and takes in the Mississippi River delta and the eastern half of Cajun country. Folks here know the intricate details of catching and cleaning fish, a major industry in the 3rd, and are adept at stockpiling canned goods and plywood during hurricane season. River Road, a highway running the length of the Mississippi River, originates in the 3rd and is lined by symbols of the Old South—antebellum sugar plantations.

After a decade of decline, the 3rd rebounded somewhat in the 1990s, in large part because of the oil and gas industry, which is especially big in parishes along the Gulf. The district helps the state lead the nation in crawfish, catfish, blue crab, and shrimp production. Further inland, petrochemical plants along the Mississippi have recovered since the 1980s but still struggle with declining overseas demand. Sugar cane, which dominated the regional economy into the twentieth century, continues to be profitable. Employment remains seasonal, and the unemployment rate soars in the off-season.

Democrats dominated the region for nearly a century, with a Progressive Party interlude, but the Catholic 3rd now favors Republicans. The historical tendency of the district, however, remains: conservative Democrats fare well in local elections.

Major Industry

Oil and gas, petrochemicals, fishing, shipbuilding, sugar cane.

Notable

Morgan City hosts the Louisiana Shrimp and Petroleum Festival each Labor Day; New Iberia is home to the Conrad Rice Mill, the oldest working rice mill in the United States; the main Battle of New Orleans, fought on Chalmette battlefield January 8, 1815, was waged after a peace treaty had been signed by the United States and Great Britain.

Election Returns

	Republican		Democratic		Other	
President 2000	133,749	52.0%	115,734	45.0%	7,967	3.1%
House 2002	130,323	86.7%			20,019	13.3%

District Profile

Population 638,322

Total area (square miles) 12,675.2
Land area (square miles) 7,010.3

Population per square mile 91.1

Counties (2000 population)
Ascension Parish (pt.) 39,785
Assumption Parish 23,388
Iberia Parish 73,266

Jefferson Parish (pt.)   10,562
Lafourche Parish   89,974
Plaquemines Parish   26,757
St. Bernard Parish   67,229
St. Charles Parish (pt.)   36,515
St. James Parish   21,216
St. John the Baptist Parish   43,044
St. Martin Parish   48,583
St. Mary Parish   53,500
Terrebonne Parish   104,503

Cities and other areas over 10,000 (2000 population)

Bayou Cane CDP   17,046
Chalmette CDP   32,069
Houma   32,393
Laplace CDP   27,684
Luling CDP   11,512
Meraux CDP   10,192
Morgan City   12,703
New Iberia   32,623
Raceland CDP   10,224
Thibodaux   14,431

Race and Hispanic or Latino origin*

White   69.7%
Black or African American   24.6%
American Indian or Alaska Native   1.6%
Asian   1.0%
Native Hawaiian or other Pacific Islander   0.0%
Some other race   0.1%
Hispanic or Latino origin   2.1%
Two or more races   1.0%

*As percentage of total population.

Ancestry*

English   2.6%
Fr. Canadian   5.4%
French   17.4%
German   5.9%
Irish   4.0%
Italian   4.6%
USA/American   8.7%

*As estimated percentage of total population.

Universities and colleges, 2000–2001 enrollment

Elaine P. Nunez Community College, Chalmette   1,884
Louisiana Technical College-Ascension, Sorrento   238
Louisiana Technical College-Lafourche, Thibodaux   482
Louisiana Technical College-River Parishes, Reserve   315
Louisiana Technical College-South Louisiana, Houma   950
Louisiana Technical College-Teche Area, New Iberia   460
Louisiana Technical College-Young Memorial, Morgan City   1,014
Nicholls State University, Thibodaux   7,326
South Louisiana Community College, New Iberia*

*Enrollment under 100. See Sources and Explanations in the front of the volume.

Newspapers and circulation

	District circulation	Total circulation
Baton Rouge Advocate	4,566	91,744
Houma Courier	17,662	17,662
Lafayette Daily Advertiser	5,966	44,373
New Orleans Times-Picayune	43,145	256,823
Thibodaux Daily Comet	11,408	11,408
*USA Today**	3,113	1,674,376

*See Sources and Explanations in the front of the volume.

Television stations and affiliations

New Orleans	72%	WDSU	NBC
New Orleans	72%	WGNO	ABC
New Orleans	72%	WHNO	Independent
New Orleans	72%	WLAE	PBS
New Orleans	72%	WNOL	WB
New Orleans	72%	WPXL	PAX
New Orleans	72%	WUPL	UPN
New Orleans	72%	WVUE	FOX
New Orleans	72%	WWL	CBS
New Orleans	72%	WYES	PBS
Lafayette	15%	KADN	FOX
Lafayette	15%	KATC	ABC
Lafayette	15%	KLFY	CBS
Lafayette	15%	KLPB	PBS
Lafayette	15%	KLTL	PBS
Lafayette	15%	KPLC	NBC
Baton Rouge	13%	WAFB	CBS
Baton Rouge	13%	WBRZ	ABC
Baton Rouge	13%	WGMB	FOX
Baton Rouge	13%	WLPB	PBS
Baton Rouge	13%	WVLA	NBC

Cable systems and subscribers

Allen's TV Cable   10,445
Cable South Inc.   5,429
Callais Cablevision   9,820
Charter   37,107
Classic   6,094
Cox   63,228
Plaquemines Cablevision   4,404
Time Warner   19,826

Businesses and other major employers

Martin Mills Inc.; St. Martinville; men's and boys' underwear   2,700
Builders Central; Laplace; lumber and building materials   2,001
McDermott Inc.; Amelia; marine construction   2,000
Terrebonne Parish Hospital; Houma   1,397
R&B Falcon Drilling USA Inc.; Houma; drilling oil and gas wells   1,300
Pride Offshore Inc.; Houma; drilling oil and gas wells   1,250
U.S. Dept. of Defense; Belle Chasse   1,000
McDermott Inc.; Amelia; oil and gas drilling bits   1,000
Cypress Bayou Casino; Charenton; gambling   1,000
BASF Corp.; Geismar; industrial inorganic chemicals   1,000
Honeywell Inc.; Geismar; electrical equipment and supplies   1,000
Edison Chouest Offshore; Galliano; marine cargo handling   975
Bruce Foods Corp.; St. Martinville; Mexican foods   890
North American Shipbuilding; Larose; building/repairing offshore supply boats   850
A. M. E. Services Inc.; Norco; building maintenance   825
Corporate Personnel Services and Temps Inc.; Larose; help supply services   800
Oceaneering International Inc.; Morgan City; drilling oil and gas wells   800

Louisiana Dept. of Health and Hospitals; Houma   742
Nicholls State University; Thibodaux   728
Entergy Operations Inc.; Killona; electric power
    generation   700
UNIFAB International Inc.; New Iberia; fabricated
    structural metal for ships   700
Trico Marine Operators Inc.; Houma; boat and ship
    rental, leasing   695
Cameco Industries Inc.; Thibodaux; planting, haying,
    harvesting, processing machinery   685
Lafourche Parish Hospital; Thibodaux   681
Kaiser Aluminum and Chemical Corp.; Gramercy;
    alumina fused refractories   600
Transamerican Natural Gas Corp.; New Sarpy;
    petroleum refining   600
Terrebonne Parish Consolidated Govt.; Houma   600
Global Divers and Contractors Inc.; New Iberia; oil/gas
    wells building/repairing/dismantling   600
Parker Drilling Co.; New Iberia; service well drilling
    600
Wal-Mart Stores Inc.; Gonzales; discount department
    stores   600
E. I. Du Pont De Nemours and Co.; Laplace; industrial
    inorganic chemicals   590
Shell Oil Co.; Geismar; catalysts, chemical   542
St. Bernard Parish; Chalmette; parish government   528
Marathon Ashland Petroleum; Garyville; petroleum
    refining   500
Transtar Metals Inc.; St. Martinville; metals service
    centers and offices   500
Rubicon Inc.; Geismar; aniline, nitrobenzene   500

Louisiana 4th District

Northwest and west — Shreveport, Bossier City

Removed from the Cajun influence that much of Louisiana is known for, the mostly white-collar 4th identifies more with Dallas than New Orleans. Covering most of western Louisiana, the conservative district takes in Shreveport at its north end and wanders into timber country in Beauregard and Allen Parishes in the south.

The oil industry that fueled the economy in the 4th fizzled in the 1980s. But Shreveport and Bossier City responded to a 1995 gambling proposal that allowed for 15 casinos in the state; five riverboat casinos now are docked on the Red River that separates the two cities. A wave of riverfront renewal, accompanied by a large influx of retail and service industries, has helped drive the economy in recent years. Other industries remain intact: General Motors has invested millions in a new Shreveport facility, and the city has remained a health care hub for northern Louisiana as well as for eastern Texas and southern Arkansas. The Barksdale Air Force Base near Bossier City also is a major employer for both cities. Forestry and poultry production scattered throughout the 4th add to the economy.

Redistricted three times in the 1990s, the old 4th briefly had a black majority, but African Americans now make up a third of the population. The area sent conservative Democrats to Congress from 1874 until a 1988 special election. The GOP incumbent has won comfortably since (briefly in the old 5th), even though registered Democrats outnumber Re-

publicans. Locally, the 4th still favors Democrats, although the suburbs around Shreveport and Bossier City have elected some Republicans in recent elections.

Major Industry
Military, riverboat gambling, health care, timber.

Notable
Bank robbers Bonnie and Clyde were gunned down south of Gibsland in 1934—the town reenacts the shooting every year.

Election Returns

	Republican		Democratic		Other	
President 2000	129,908	54.7%	102,228	43.0%	5,466	2.3%
House 2002	114,649	71.6%	42,340	26.4%	3,104	1.9%

District Profile

Population   638,466

Total area (square miles)   11,150.6
    Land area (square miles)   10,764.7

Population per square mile   59.3

Counties (2000 population)
    Allen Parish (pt.)   11,691
    Beauregard Parish   32,986
    Bienville Parish   15,752
    Bossier Parish   98,310
    Caddo Parish   252,161
    Claiborne Parish   16,851
    De Soto Parish   25,494
    Grant Parish   18,698
    Natchitoches Parish   39,080
    Red River Parish   9,622
    Sabine Parish   23,459
    Vernon Parish   52,531
    Webster Parish   41,831

Cities and other areas over 10,000 (2000 population)
    Bossier City   56,461
    Fort Polk South CDP   11,000
    Minden   13,027
    Natchitoches   17,865
    Shreveport   200,145

Race and Hispanic or Latino origin*
    White   62.0%
    Black or African American   33.3%
    American Indian or Alaska Native   0.8%
    Asian   0.7%
    Native Hawaiian or other Pacific Islander   0.1%
    Some other race   0.1%
    Hispanic or Latino origin   2.0%
    Two or more races   1.1%

As percentage of total population.

Ancestry*

English	5.6%	Italian	1.4%
French	4.1%	Scotch-Irish	1.5%
German	5.2%	USA/American	10.2%
Irish	6.9%		

As estimated percentage of total population.

Universities and colleges, 2000–2001 enrollment

Bossier Parish Community College, Bossier City 4,332
Centenary College of Louisiana, Shreveport 1,035
Louisiana State University, Shreveport 4,108
Louisiana Technical College-Lamar Salter, Leesville 259
Louisiana Technical College-Natchitoches, Natchitoches 345
Louisiana Technical College-Northwest Louisiana, Minden 755
Louisiana Technical College-Shreveport-Bossier, Shreveport 1,067
Northwestern State University of Louisiana, Natchitoches 9,292
Southern University-Shreveport-Bossier City, Shreveport 1,176

Newspapers and circulation

	District circulation	Total circulation
Alexandria Town Talk	5,701	34,774
Dallas Morning News	1,628	495,624
Lake Charles American Press	3,416	36,621
Shreveport Times	63,563	66,644
*USA Today**	1,848	1,674,376

See Sources and Explanations in the front of the volume.

Television stations and affiliations

Shreveport	68%	KLTS	PBS
Shreveport	68%	KMSS	FOX
Shreveport	68%	KPXJ	PAX
Shreveport	68%	KSHV	WB, UPN
Shreveport	68%	KSLA	CBS
Shreveport	68%	KTAL	NBC
Shreveport	68%	KTBS	ABC
Alexandria	18%	KALB	NBC
Alexandria	18%	KLAX	ABC
Alexandria	18%	KLPA	PBS
Lake Charles	14%	KVHP	FOX

Cable systems and subscribers

Charter 2,442
Clairborne Cablevision 2,058
Classic 12,594
Communicomm 1,014
Cox 35,398
Macco Cable 8,420
Mansfield Cable TV 2,932
Northeast Louisiana Cablevision 2,113
Pleasant Vision 694
Time Warner 57,268

Military installations, September 2001

Fort Polk (Army), Leesville 13,626
Barksdale Air Force Base, Bossier City 7,764

Businesses and other major employers

Louisiana State University; Shreveport 4,000
General Motors Corp.; Shreveport; automobiles 3,000
Willis-Knighton Medical Center; Shreveport 2,600
Horseshoe Entertainment; Bossier City; gambling 2,500
Life Care Holdings Inc.; Shreveport; business consulting 2,500
Lucent Technologies Inc.; Shreveport; telephone and telegraph apparatus 1,850
Ditto Apparel of California Inc.; Colfax; men's/boys' trousers and slacks 1,650
Grand Casino's of Louisiana Inc.; Kinder; game parlor 1,600
Boom Town Bossier Casino and Hotel; Bossier City; amusement and recreation 1,500
Harrah's Shreveport Investment Co.; Shreveport; gambling 1,500
Louisiana Riverboat Gaming Partnership; Bossier City; gambling 1,308
Libbey Glass Inc.; Shreveport; tableware 1,000
City of Shreveport; Shreveport; water supply 900
U.S. Veterans Hospital; Shreveport 900
Red River Sanitors Inc.; Shreveport; janitorial service 670
Fibrebond Corp.; Minden; concrete products 650
Frymaster; Shreveport; cooking equipment 650
Christus Health Hospital; Shreveport 638
Calcasieu Parish; Hayes; police dept. 600
Cellxion; Shreveport; cellular telephones 600
City of Shreveport; Shreveport; fire dept. 600
General Electric Co.; Shreveport; electronic transformers 600
Reliant Energy Resources Corp.; Shreveport; electric power generation 600
International Paper Co.; Mansfield; paper mills 560
International Paper Co.; Springhill; lumber: rough, sawed, or planed 550
Wal-Mart Stores Inc.; Shreveport; discount department stores 550
Northwestern State University of Louisiana; Natchitoches 532
City of Shreveport; Shreveport; sheriff's office 500
ConAgra Poultry Co.; Natchitoches; poultry hatcheries 500
Louisiana Dept. of Transportation and Development; Bossier City 500
Martco LP; Chopin; sawmills and planing mills 500
Wal-Mart Stores Inc.; Bossier City; supermarkets 500

Louisiana 5th District

Northeast and central — Monroe, Alexandria

Taking in most of northeastern and central Louisiana, the conservative 5th District stretches from the delta parishes along the Mississippi River to central Louisiana—a region known as the Crossroads for its mix of Native Americans, Cajuns, and European settlers.

Although the rich, black soil along the Mississippi produces much of the state's cotton and soybeans, poor education and transportation systems slow economic growth—poverty and unemployment in the delta parishes can affect as many as one-fourth of residents. A move toward larger farms has altered the economy of Monroe, the 5th's largest city. Located between the delta farms in the east and the small lumber and paper mills that dot the western parishes, Monroe now depends increasingly on health care, service, and retail industries.

The central part of the state is focused around Alexandria in Rapides Parish. Although military base closings in the 1990s hurt the regional economy, the 1992 conversion of England Air Force Base into an industrial park has helped the area.

This historically Democratic district leans Republican, but voters will support conservatives of either party. Democrats hold some local offices. George W. Bush took 57.1 percent of the 5th's vote in the 2000 presidential election. Most residents classify themselves as conservative Democrats, but the Baptists and Pentecostals in the north are more likely to vote for Republicans than the Catholics in the south. About one-third of residents are African American.

Major Industry
Agriculture, health care.

Notable
Former governor and senator Huey Long was born in Winn Parish in 1893; Delta Air Lines started in Monroe and was based there until moving to Atlanta in 1941.

Election Returns

	Republican		Democratic		Other	
President 2000	143,628	57.1%	100,287	39.9%	7,706	3.1%
House 2002*	85,744	49.7%	86,718	50.3%	974	

Runoff election December 2002.

District Profile

Population   638,517

Total area (square miles)   14,225.1
   Land area (square miles)   13,775.0

Population per square mile   46.4

Counties (2000 population)
   Allen Parish (pt.)   13,749
   Avoyelles Parish   41,481
   Caldwell Parish   10,560
   Catahoula Parish   10,920
   Concordia Parish   20,247
   East Carroll Parish   9,421
   Evangeline Parish (pt.)   12,878
   Franklin Parish   21,263
   Iberville Parish (pt.)   14,932
   Jackson Parish   15,397
   La Salle Parish   14,282
   Lincoln Parish   42,509
   Madison Parish   13,728
   Morehouse Parish   31,021
   Ouachita Parish   147,250
   Pointe Coupee Parish (pt.)   12,932
   Rapides Parish   126,337
   Richland Parish   20,981
   Tensas Parish   6,618
   Union Parish   22,803
   West Carroll Parish   12,314
   Winn Parish   16,894

Cities and other areas over 10,000 (2000 population)
   Alexandria   46,342
   Bastrop   12,988
   Monroe   53,107
   Pineville   13,829
   Ruston   20,546
   West Monroe   13,250

Race and Hispanic or Latino origin*
   White   63.4%
   Black or African American   33.7%
   American Indian or Alaska Native   0.4%
   Asian   0.5%
   Native Hawaiian or other Pacific Islander   0.0%
   Some other race   0.0%
   Hispanic or Latino origin   1.3%
   Two or more races   0.6%

As percentage of total population.

Ancestry*
English	4.8%	Irish	6.4%
Fr. Canadian	1.1%	Italian	1.4%
French	5.6%	Scotch-Irish	1.1%
German	3.5%	USA/American	13.2%

As estimated percentage of total population.

Universities and colleges, 2000–2001 enrollment
   Charles B. Coreil Technical Institute, Ville Platte   256
   Delta-Ouachita Regional Technical Institute, West Monroe   652
   Grambling State University, Grambling   4,716
   Louisiana College, Pineville   1,125
   Louisiana State University, Alexandria   2,386
   Louisiana Tech University, Ruston   10,363
   Louisiana Technical College, Winnsboro   230
   Louisiana Technical College-Alexandria, Alexandria   300
   Louisiana Technical College-Avoyelles, Cottonport   219
   Louisiana Technical College-Bastrop, Bastrop   280
   Louisiana Technical College-Oakdale, Oakdale   278
   Louisiana Technical College-Ruston, Ruston   213
   Louisiana Technical College-Tallulah, Tallulah   580
   Louisiana Technical College-Westside, Plaquemine   265
   Northeast Louisiana University, Monroe   9,405

Newspapers and circulation

	District circulation	Total circulation
Alexandria Town Talk	28,864	34,774
Monroe News-Star	35,668	36,015
Shreveport Times	1,517	66,644
*USA Today**	1,575	1,674,376

See Sources and Explanations in the front of the volume.

Television stations and affiliations
Monroe-El Dorado, AR	73%	KAQY	ABC
Monroe-El Dorado, AR	73%	KARD	FOX
Monroe-El Dorado, AR	73%	KLTM	PBS
Monroe-El Dorado, AR	73%	KMCT	Independent
Monroe-El Dorado, AR	73%	KNOE	CBS
Monroe-El Dorado, AR	73%	KTVE	NBC
Monroe-El Dorado, AR	73%	WNTZ	FOX
Alexandria	16%	KALB	NBC
Alexandria	16%	KLAX	ABC
Alexandria	16%	KLPA	PBS
Baton Rouge	5%	WAFB	CBS
Baton Rouge	5%	WBRZ	ABC
Baton Rouge	5%	WGMB	FOX
Baton Rouge	5%	WLPB	PBS
Baton Rouge	5%	WVLA	NBC

Lafayette	3%	KADN	FOX
Lafayette	3%	KATC	ABC
Lafayette	3%	KLFY	CBS
Lafayette	3%	KLPB	PBS
Lafayette	3%	KLTL	PBS
Lafayette	3%	KPLC	NBC
Lake Charles	3%	KVHP	FOX

Cable systems and subscribers
Bayou Cable TV 1,120
Broadband Cablevision 1,320
Cable ONE 2,969
Charter 16,614
Classic 10,804
Communicomm 7,523
Cox 49,416
Delta Cablevision 4,607
Southwest Cablevision 1,556
Spillway Communications 965
Tallulah Cable TV 2,406
Time Warner 31,616

Military installations, September 2001
Camp Beauregard Military Training Area, Pineville
1,208

Businesses and other major employers
Dupont Dow Elastomers; Plaquemine; synthetic rubber
2,000
ConAgra; Farmerville; poultry processing 1,800
Louisiana Dept. of Public Education; Pineville 1,800
Riverwood International Corp.; Monroe; industrial
machinery/equipment 1,700
Rapid Healthcare System Hospital; Alexandria 1,642
Columbia Healthcare of Central Virginia Inc.;
Alexandria 1,600
Riverwood International Corp.; West Monroe; paper
mills 1,600
St. Francis Medical Center; Monroe 1,584
University of Louisiana at Monroe; Monroe 1,250
Christus Health Central Louisiana Hospital; Alexandria
1,247
Century Supply Group Inc.; Monroe;
telecommunications consultant 1,200
Glenwood Regional Medical Center; West Monroe
1,200
Rapides Regional Medical Center Hospital; Alexandria
1,200
Grambling State University; Grambling 996
Cleco Power; Pineville; electric power distribution 981
International Paper Co.; Bastrop; stationery 900
Louisiana Dept. of Health and Hospitals; Monroe 870
Red Simpson Inc.; Alexandria; electric power line
construction 860
Louisiana Tech University; Ruston 851
Stone Container Corp.; Hodge; grocers' bags 706
City of Monroe; Monroe; city government 700
General Motors Corp.; Monroe; automotive lighting
700
Iberville Parish School Board Inc.; Plaquemine 667
Georgia Gulf Corp.; Plaquemine; plastics materials and
resins 613
Allen Canning Co.; Hessmer; packaged vegetables 600
Avoyelles Parish; Marksville; sheriff's office 583

Lincoln Health System Hospital; Ruston 510
Louisiana Dept. of Health and Hospitals; Pineville 500
Tedco Inc.; West Monroe; soap 500
Wal-Mart Stores Inc.; Alexandria; discount department
stores 500
Wal-Mart Stores Inc.; Pineville; department stores 500

Louisiana 6th District

East central — Baton Rouge

Centered around the state capital of Baton Rouge, the socially conservative 6th takes in a slew of petrochemical plants along the Mississippi River as well as rural parishes along the Mississippi border. Baton Rouge's economic and population growth has spilled over into neighboring parishes, which attract commuters with superior schools and lower crime rates.

The decline of the domestic oil industry in the 1980s made Baton Rouge's government and university employees even more vital to the district's economy—Southern and Louisiana State universities are both located in the city. While oil and petrochemicals rebounded in the 1990s, local officials were concerned with the exodus of white-collar workers. A 1996 "Plan Baton Rouge" to redevelop downtown brought more tourism to the area—aided by the addition of two docked riverboat casinos. Although the port is no longer the centerpiece of the 6th's economy, it remains important.

Agriculture fuels the rural parishes on the outskirts of the district—sugar cane is produced in the west, while the northeastern part is lined with paper mills and potato farms.

As in most of the South, socially conservative suburban and rural voters have shifted toward the GOP. But the minority and blue-collar residents of Baton Rouge still vote Democratic. Rounds of redistricting in the 1990s gave the 6th more and more of Baton Rouge, transforming it into a politically competitive district. Democrats fare well locally in the northern and western parts of the 6th, while East Baton Rouge, Livingston, and Ascension Parishes consistently vote Republican. George W. Bush received 54.8 percent of the district's vote in 2000.

Major Industry
Government, higher education, petrochemicals.

Notable
The state capitol, completed in 1932, is the tallest in the United States; Gov. Huey Long, who led the fight for the new capitol, was assassinated there in 1935 and is buried on the capitol grounds; the five-campus Southern University System is the only historically black university system in the country.

Election Returns

	Republican		Democratic		Other	
President 2000	142,239	54.8%	111,602	43.0%	5,716	2.2%
House 2002	146,932	84.0%			27,898	16.0%

District Profile

Population 638,324

Total area (square miles) 3,209.7
Land area (square miles) 3,075.8

Population per square mile 207.5

Counties (2000 population)
Ascension Parish (pt.)   36,842
East Baton Rouge Parish   412,852
East Feliciana Parish   21,360
Iberville Parish (pt.)   18,388
Livingston Parish   91,814
Pointe Coupee Parish (pt.)   9,831
St. Helena Parish   10,525
West Baton Rouge Parish   21,601
West Feliciana Parish   15,111

Cities and other areas over 10,000 (2000 population)
Baker   13,793   Shenandoah CDP   17,070
Baton Rouge   227,818   Zachary   11,275
Merrydale CDP   10,427

Race and Hispanic or Latino origin*
White   62.7%
Black or African American   33.2%
American Indian or Alaska Native   0.2%
Asian   1.4%
Native Hawaiian or other Pacific Islander   0.0%
Some other race   0.1%
Hispanic or Latino origin   1.6%
Two or more races   0.7%

*As percentage of total population.

Ancestry*
English   5.4%   Irish   6.3%
Fr. Canadian   2.1%   Italian   3.7%
French   10.3%   Scotch-Irish   1.4%
German   5.7%   USA/American   7.4%

*As estimated percentage of total population.

Universities and colleges, 2000–2001 enrollment
Camelot College, Baton Rouge   226
Delta College of Arts and Technology, Baton Rouge   249
ITI Technical College, Baton Rouge   320
Louisiana State University, Baton Rouge   31,527
Louisiana Technical College-Baton Rouge, Baton Rouge   1,015
Louisiana Technical College-Folkes, Jackson   230
Louisiana Technical College-Jumonville Memorial, New Roads   607
Our Lady of the Lake College, Baton Rouge   1,053
Southern University and A&M College, Baton Rouge   9,449

Newspapers and circulation

	District circulation	Total circulation
Baton Rouge Advocate	64,430	91,744
Hammond Daily Star	2,345	12,096
New Orleans Times-Picayune	1,211	256,823
*USA Today**	2,242	1,674,376

*See Sources and Explanations in the front of the volume.

Television stations and affiliations
Baton Rouge	100%	WAFB	CBS
Baton Rouge	100%	WBRZ	ABC
Baton Rouge	100%	WGMB	FOX
Baton Rouge	100%	WLPB	PBS
Baton Rouge	100%	WVLA	NBC

Cable systems and subscribers
Audubon Cablevision   820
Cable South Inc.   2,622
Charter   14,097
Cox   141,863

Businesses and other major employers
Shaw Environmental and Infrastructure Inc.; Baton Rouge; pollution control engineering   6,000
Harmony Corp.; Baton Rouge; industrial buildings, warehouses   3,780
Our Lady of Lake Hospital Inc.; Baton Rouge   3,500
ExxonMobil Oil Corp.; Baton Rouge; petroleum refining   3,200
Stone and Webster Construction Inc.; Baton Rouge; building construction   3,200
Louisiana State University; Baton Rouge   3,000
Southern University System; Baton Rouge; elementary and secondary schools   2,300
General Health System; Baton Rouge; medical laboratories   2,000
Ochsner Clinic Health Services Corp.; Baton Rouge   2,000
Louisiana Dept. of Corrections; Angola   1,800
Southern University Agricultural and Mechanical College; Baton Rouge   1,750
Anco Industries Inc.; Baton Rouge; insulation   1,445
Newtron Group Inc.; Baton Rouge; electrical work   1,342
Louisiana Dept. of Health and Hospitals; Baton Rouge   1,250
Louisiana Dept. of Health and Hospitals; Jackson   1,200
Woman's Hospital Foundation Inc.; Baton Rouge   1,200
Louisiana Health Service and Indemnity Co.; Baton Rouge; group hospitalization   1,137
Ecolab Inc.; Zachary; soap and other detergents   1,050
City of Baton Rouge; Baton Rouge; public utility commission   1,000
City of Baton Rouge; Baton Rouge; city management   1,000
Jennifer Johnson; Baton Rouge; legal services   1,000
Louisiana Dept. of Public Education; Baton Rouge   1,000
Syngenta Inc.; Saint Gabriel; chemicals   1,000
Louisiana Casino Cruises Inc.; Baton Rouge; gambling   960
Argosy of Louisiana; Baton Rouge; gambling   900
Georgia-Pacific Corp.; Zachary; printing paper   900
Industrial Specialty Contractors; Baton Rouge; electrical work   900
Louisiana Dept. of Transportation and Development; Baton Rouge   900
Louisiana Dept. of Health and Hospitals; Baton Rouge   845
Gilbert Southern Corp.; Saint Gabriel; highway and street construction   800
Associated Grocers Inc.; Baton Rouge; food supplier   724
City of Baton Rouge; Baton Rouge; police dept.   700
Entergy Operations Inc.; St. Francisville; electric services   700

U.S. Dept. of Labor; Baton Rouge; labor regulatory agency   700

Louisiana Dept. of Corrections; Saint Gabriel   674

City of Baton Rouge; Baton Rouge; sheriff's office   670

Petrin Corp.; Port Allen; insulation of pipes and boilers   670

JE Merit Constructors Inc.; Baton Rouge; industrial plant construction   651

Louisiana Environmental Quality Dept.; Baton Rouge; government finance   650

Nichols Construction Corp.; Baton Rouge; equipment rental and leasing   635

Louisiana Dept. of Revenue and Taxation; Baton Rouge   617

American Building Maintenance of Louisiana Inc.; Baton Rouge; janitorial service   600

Harmony Corp.; Baton Rouge; construction machinery and equipment   600

Jacobs Engineering Group Inc.; Baton Rouge; engineering services   600

Lamar Corp.; Baton Rouge; billboard advertising   600

East Baton Rouge Parish Hospital; Zachary   568

International Maintenance Corp.; Baton Rouge; industrial buildings renovation   530

Wal-Mart Stores Inc.; Baton Rouge; discount department stores   525

Bank One National Assn.; Baton Rouge; commercial bank   500

City of Baton Rouge; Baton Rouge; city council   500

Compass Group USA Inc.; Baton Rouge; contract food services   500

Ferrara Fire Apparatus Inc.; Holden; fire dept. vehicles   500

Louisiana Dept. of Revenue and Taxation; Baton Rouge   500

National Building Service and Maintenance Inc.; Baton Rouge; janitorial service   500

Shaw Sunland Fabricators Inc.; Walker; pipe sections   500

Southern University Agricultural and Mechanical College; Baton Rouge   500

Target Corp.; Baton Rouge; department stores   500

U.S. Attorneys; Baton Rouge; legal counsel and prosecution   500

Louisiana 7th District

Southwest — Lafayette, Lake Charles

Anchored by blue-collar Lake Charles in the west, white-collar Lafayette in the east and the Gulf of Mexico in the south, the 7th takes in both coastal and city life. A sizable Catholic citizenry bolsters the district's socially conservative leanings.

The 7th's economy is firmly centered around agriculture, as well as oil and gas production. After the statewide petroleum depression in the 1980s, local officials worked to diversify the economy. But with recovery in the 1990s, attention has refocused on the offshore and inland oil wells. The rural parishes between Lafayette and Lake Charles produce rice and soybeans. Rice farmers also have had success raising crawfish in fallow rice fields.

Dotted with waterfowl and wildlife refuges, the 7th's Gulf edge serves sports and commercial fishermen. Lake Charles, a refining and chemical-producing hub in Calcasieu Parish, offers a sharp industrial contrast to the district's coastal and rural areas.

Despite the 7th's conservative tenor, the area tends to vote for moderate Democrats and has sent a Democrat to Congress in every election since 1884. Lafayette Parish, in the eastern part of the district, is the most Republican-leaning area.

Three stabs at redistricting in the 1990s did little to change the 7th, and the redraw following the 2000 census also left the district largely intact. The only changes in 2001 were the removal of the old 7th's portions of Allen and St. Martin Parishes. George W. Bush captured 55.2 percent of the 7th's vote in 2000. In 1996, the district regained some black neighborhoods in Lafayette Parish that it had lost in 1992. African Americans now make up one-fourth of the population.

Major Industry
Oil and gas, petrochemicals, agriculture, fishing.

Notable
Dr. Michael E. DeBakey, born in Lake Charles, was the first person to successfully use an artificial heart in a patient; Rayne, the self-proclaimed frog capital of the world, hosts an annual frog festival.

Election Returns

	Republican		Democratic		Other	
President 2000	141,378	55.2%	107,190	41.9%	7,357	2.9%
House 2002			138,659	86.8%	21,051	13.2%

District Profile

Population   638,430

Total area (square miles)   7,294.4
Land area (square miles)   6,267.8

Population per square mile   101.9

Counties (2000 population)
Acadia Parish   58,861
Calcasieu Parish   183,577
Cameron Parish   9,991
Evangeline Parish (pt.)   22,556
Jefferson Davis Parish   31,435
Lafayette Parish   190,503
St. Landry Parish   87,700
Vermilion Parish   53,807

Cities and other areas over 10,000 (2000 population)

Abbeville 11,887	Lake Charles 71,757
Crowley 14,225	Moss Bluff CDP 10,535
Eunice 11,499	Opelousas 22,860
Jennings 10,986	Sulphur 20,512
Lafayette 110,257	

Race and Hispanic or Latino origin*
White   72.0%
Black or African American   24.8%
American Indian or Alaska Native   0.2%
Asian   0.7%

Native Hawaiian or other Pacific Islander   0.0%
Some other race   0.1%
Hispanic or Latino origin   1.4%
Two or more races   0.7%

As percentage of total population.

Ancestry*

English	3.8%	Irish	4.1%
Fr. Canadian	6.6%	Italian	1.8%
French	14.1%	USA/American	11.6%
German	5.1%		

As estimated percentage of total population.

Universities and colleges, 2000–2001 enrollment

Delta School of Business and Technology, Lake Charles   308
Louisiana State University-Eunice, Eunice   2,704
Louisiana Technical College-Acadian, Crowley   254
Louisiana Technical College-Gulf Area, Abbeville   241
Louisiana Technical College-Lafayette, Lafayette   519
Louisiana Technical College-Sowela, Lake Charles   1,243
Louisiana Technical College-T. H. Harris, Opelousas   699
McNeese State University, Lake Charles   7,603
Remington College, Lafayette   472
University of Southwestern Louisiana, Lafayette   15,742

Newspapers and circulation

	District circulation	Total circulation
Lafayette Daily Advertiser	38,243	44,373
Lake Charles American Press	33,037	36,621
Opelousas Daily World	9,983	10,965
*USA Today**	1,619	1,674,376

See Sources and Explanations in the front of the volume.

Television stations and affiliations

Lafayette	58%	KADN	FOX
Lafayette	58%	KATC	ABC
Lafayette	58%	KLFY	CBS
Lafayette	58%	KLPB	PBS
Lafayette	58%	KLTL	PBS
Lafayette	58%	KPLC	NBC
Lake Charles	42%	KVHP	FOX

Cable systems and subscribers

Allen's TV Cable   5,599
Cable South Inc.   1,098
Charter   15,537
Classic   5,615
Communicomm   8,120
Cox   94,999

Businesses and other major employers

Isle of Capri-Lake Charles; Westlake; casino hotel   2,021
PPG Industries Inc.; Lake Charles; alkalies and chlorine   2,000
St. Charles Gaming Co.; Lake Charles; casino hotel   2,000
Harrah's Entertainment Inc.; Lake Charles; casino hotel   1,800
Citgo Petroleum Corp.; Lake Charles; self-storage warehousing   1,500
Southwest Louisiana Hospital Assn.; Lake Charles   1,500
Lafayette General Medical Center Inc.; Lafayette   1,494
University of Louisiana at Lafayette; Lafayette   1,475
St. Patrick Hospital Inc.; Lake Charles   1,450
Our Lady of Lourdes Regional Medical Center Inc.; Lafayette   1,375
Citgo Petroleum Corp.; Westlake; petroleum refining   1,345
Delta Downs Inc.; Vinton; horse race track   1,100
McNeese State University; Lake Charles   888
Louisiana Dept. of Health and Hospitals; Lafayette   850
SHRM Catering Services Inc.; Lafayette; caterers   800
Wal-Mart Stores Inc.; Opelousas; department stores   800
Conoco Inc.; Westlake; petroleum refining   750
Opelousas General Hospital; Opelousas   730
TMC Foods; Lafayette; fast-food restaurant chain   726
Calcasieu Parish; Lake Charles; parish government   700
Lyondell Chemical Co.; Lake Charles; industrial organic chemicals   700
Rapides Health Care System; Mamou   700
City of Lake Charles; Lake Charles   600
Petroleum Helicopters Inc.; Lafayette; air transportation   600
West Calcasieu Cameron Hospital; Sulphur   580
West Telemarketing Corp.; Lafayette; telemarketing services   550
US Unwired Inc.; Lake Charles; cellular telephones   520
Cajundome Commission; Lafayette; auditorium operation   519
Lafayette City Parish Consolidated Govt.; Lafayette; sheriffs' office   518
Basell USA Inc.; Lake Charles; plastics materials and resins   500
Boh Bros. Construction Co.; Westlake; single-family housing construction   500
Lafayette City Parish Consolidated Govt.; Lafayette; parish government   500
Louisiana Dept. of Transportation and Development; Lake Charles   500
Louisiana Pigment Co.; Westlake; titanium dioxide (pigments)   500
Old Republic National Title Insurance Co.; York; insurance agents and brokers   500
Operators and Consulting Services Inc.; Lafayette; oil consultants   500
Stuller Inc.; Lafayette; jewel settings and mountings   500
Triad Electric and Controls Inc.; Lake Charles; electrical work   500
West Calcasieu Cameron Hospital; Westlake   500

Maine

The people of Maine were touting their independent streak long before that characteristic came into vogue nationally in the 1990s, and they are still at it. A Gallup poll in 2002 found 44 percent of the state's voters liked to think of themselves as independents. No surprise then that this was the best state in the nation for freelance presidential candidate Ross Perot in both 1992 and 1996. Perot actually finished ahead of the incumbent president George Bush, who had long spent his summers at his family's place in Kennebunkport. Maine also had one independent governor in the 1970s and another, Angus King, through most of the 1990s. The Green and Libertarian parties have found converts here, too, and the state seems pleased with a two-party congressional delegation for which partisan loyalty is often a secondary concern.

Republicans did win their fifth straight Senate election here in 2002, but the candidates who have been winning these races are moderate Republicans often out of step with their party's leaders in Washington. One was William Cohen, who left the Senate to be secretary of defense for President Bill Clinton, passing the torch to two former staff members, Olympia Snowe and Susan Collins. These have since made Maine the first state with two Republican women in the Senate at once—a fitting tribute to Maine's trailblazing Margaret Chase Smith, a moderate Republican force in the Senate from the 1940s into the 1970s.

At the same time, however, Democrats in 2002 were extending their winning streak in Maine's House elections, and carrying the state for the third presidential race in a row. The surprise in these Democratic victories was their defiance of state history. Maine was once as rock-ribbed a Republican redoubt as any, one of just two states to vote against Franklin D. Roosevelt's 1936 landslide (the occasion for FDR's famous crack, "as Maine goes, so goes Vermont"). But in recent decades, the "Down Easters" got picky about their Republicans, rejecting Richard Nixon in 1960 and Barry Goldwater four years later. More recently still, the state's GOP has been discomfited by the Sun Belt bent of their party's national leaders (even adoptive son George Bush senior had decided he was from Texas).

At the same time, the state's old Democratic base, composed of Catholics, unionists, and ethnic groups has lately been augmented by lifestyle liberals and environmentalists who chose the state for its off-trail charms. The rise of tourism in the state has also enlarged the service industries, bringing in new voters with Democratic voting habits acquired elsewhere.

When Gallup in 2002 pressed Maine's self-described independents to lean toward one party or the other, the tilt was Democratic. In fact, Maine registered the sharpest increase in Democratic identification (counting leaners) in the 50 states in a comparison of polls done by Gallup in 1993 and 2002. In the earlier year, 45 percent of Maine residents were Democrats or independents who leaned Democratic (as compared with 42 percent Republicans or independents who leaned to the right). But in 2002, the gap had grown from three percentage points to 11, with Democrats and their leaners near 50 percent while the GOP's combined total had slipped below 40.

It is highly unusual to see such a shift in Democrats' favor in a state with virtually no minority population at all (less than 1 percent each for African Americans, Asian Americans, and Hispanics). Maine is still composed overwhelmingly of descendants from Yankees, Irish, French Canadians, and various Europeans. Such relatively static demographics have given Maine the third oldest median age in the country at nearly 39. Population grew by only 38 percent between 1950 and 2000, less than half the national average, and in the 1990s it was one of the five slowest growing states. Projections show the state's population rising only by about 14 percent by 2025.

Economic opportunities, including jobs in shipyards with military contracts, have not been quite enough to overcome the remoteness of the topography and the harsh winters. The rugged northern reaches of the Appalachians run up the western spine of the state, yet there are white sand beaches along part of its southeastern seacoast and the moderating effects of the Atlantic keep the coastal towns relatively temperate in winter. Inland, there may be 100 inches of snow or more.

As remote and forbidding as Maine can seem today, it was far less hospitable for its early settlers. The first forays by the French and English failed after 1600, and nearly a century later the British simply attached the territory to the colony of Massachusetts. This state of affairs survived until 1820, when Maine entered the union as a separate state—the next to last Atlantic Coast state admitted (Florida would come 25 years later). Maine would peak at eight seats in the House in 1830 before beginning a long decline to the two seats it has had since 1960.

Fishing on the Grand Banks was a mainstay of Maine's economy from the beginning, as were timbering and the few forms of agriculture that could survive the short growing season. Logically, the state developed an early shipbuilding industry around Portland and other natural harbors. Today, the timber and lumber industry is much attenuated but there remains enough connection to the mills that a candidate campaigned for one of Maine's House seats by showing himself driving a fork lift at a paper mill.

Since 1960, the state's two districts have been divided to give one to Portland and vicinity (counting the capital of Augusta) and the other to Bangor, Lewiston, and the rest of the state. Maine's huge and largely wild 2nd District (most of it further north than Montreal) is the answer to this trivia question: which is the largest congressional district in the area east of the Mississippi River? The 2nd is also the more politically competitive of Maine's pair, having preferred Al Gore in 2000 by just under two percentage points over George W. Bush. While many environmentalists live here and tend to vote Democratic, the state also has 254,000 residents who own firearms for hunting—one fifth of the total population, heavily concentrated in the 2nd.

Table 1   Population

District	Population	Population under 18	Voting-age population	Median age	Male*	Female*
1	666,936	158,755	508,181	38.5	48.5	51.5
2	607,987	142,483	465,504	38.8	48.8	51.2
State	1,274,923	301,238	973,685	38.6	48.7	51.3

*As percentage of total population.

Table 2   Voting-Age Persons by Race/Hispanic or Latino Origin

District	White*	Black or African American*	American Indian or Alaska Native*	Asian*	Other or multirace*	Hispanic or Latino*
1	97.0	0.5	0.3	0.8	0.8	0.7
2	97.2	0.3	0.7	0.5	0.7	0.5
State	97.1	0.4	0.5	0.7	0.7	0.6

*As percentage of voting-age population.

Table 3   Voting-Age Population by Age Groups

District	18 to 24*	25 to 44*	45 to 64*	Over 64*
1	10.1	39.3	32.3	18.4
2	11.4	36.7	32.6	19.3
State	10.7	38.1	32.4	18.8

*As percentage of voting-age population.

Table 4   Income and Occupation

District	Median family income	Families in poverty*	White collar†	Blue collar†	Service†	Farm†
1	$50,419	6.2	61.3	23.0	14.6	1.1
2	$40,113	9.5	52.8	28.7	16.2	2.3
State	$45,179	7.8	57.4	25.6	15.3	1.7

*As percentage of all families.   †As percentage of employed workers 16 years and over.

Table 5   Education: School Years Completed

District	Less than grade 9*	Grades 9–12 no diploma*	High school diploma no college*	Some college*	College bachelor's degree or higher*
1	4.2	7.9	32.8	27.6	27.5
2	6.8	10.7	39.8	25.0	17.7
State	5.4	9.2	36.2	26.3	22.9

*As percentage of persons age 25 and over.

Table 6   Housing and Residential Patterns

District	Median home value	Owner occupied*	Renter occupied*	Urban†	Rural†
1	$115,600	70.4	29.6	50.4	49.6
2	$77,400	72.8	27.2	29.0	71.0
State	$94,300	71.6	28.4	40.2	59.8

*As percentage of occupied housing units.   †As percentage of total population.

Maine 1st District

South — Portland, Augusta

Rural oceanfront property draws residents to the 1st, a district incorporating the southern reaches of Maine that are also bustling with new technology jobs. Residents of Maine's largest city, Portland, are moving into outlying areas, replacing farmland and uninterrupted forests with single-family homes.

Although textile- and shoe-manufacturing plants have been downsized or closed, a high-tech boom has kept unemployment low. Companies seeking a strong infrastructure and a high quality of life have moved to southern Maine, where Interstate 95 offers a straight shot to Boston. Well-to-do and largely seasonal residents live on the coast, where former president George Bush travels for retreats at his Kennebunkport estate.

Tourism is important in the lower part of the state, as residents from across New England and Canada head to popular beaches and shopping areas along the York County coast. The military's influence also is strong in the 1st.

In a state with one of the weakest party systems in the nation, personalities play the largest role in elections; little difference exists between Democrats and Republicans in many local elections. A plurality of the state's voters register as "unenrolled" or independent. Grounded in Maine's strong communities, the state's voting participation is second only to Minnesota—67 percent in 2000.

Major Industry

Military shipbuilding, fishing, high-tech.

MAINE

Districts established April 4, 1994, for elections held from 1994 through 2002.

2 members

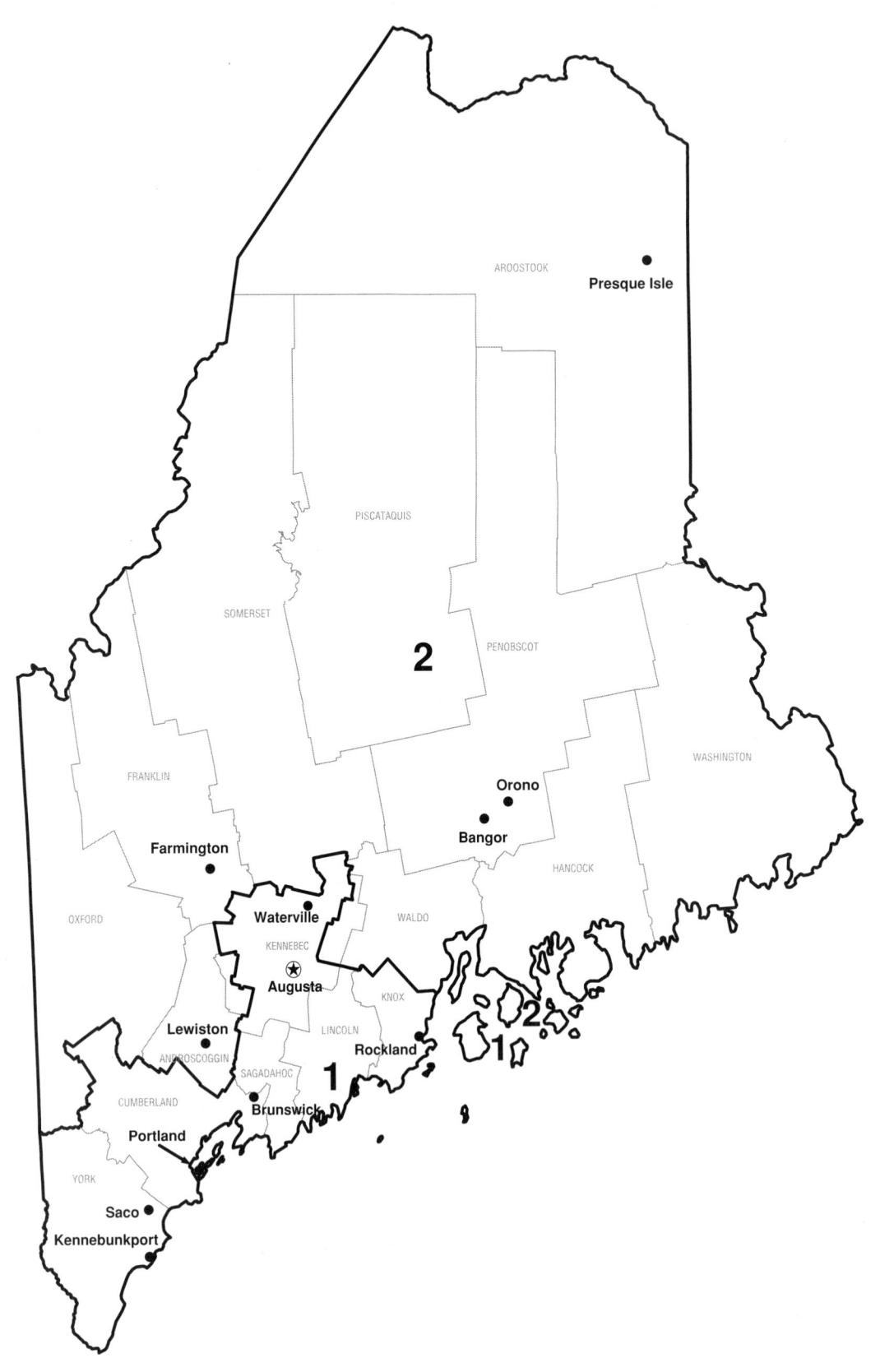

MAINE

Districts established July 2, 2003, for elections first held in 2004.

2 members

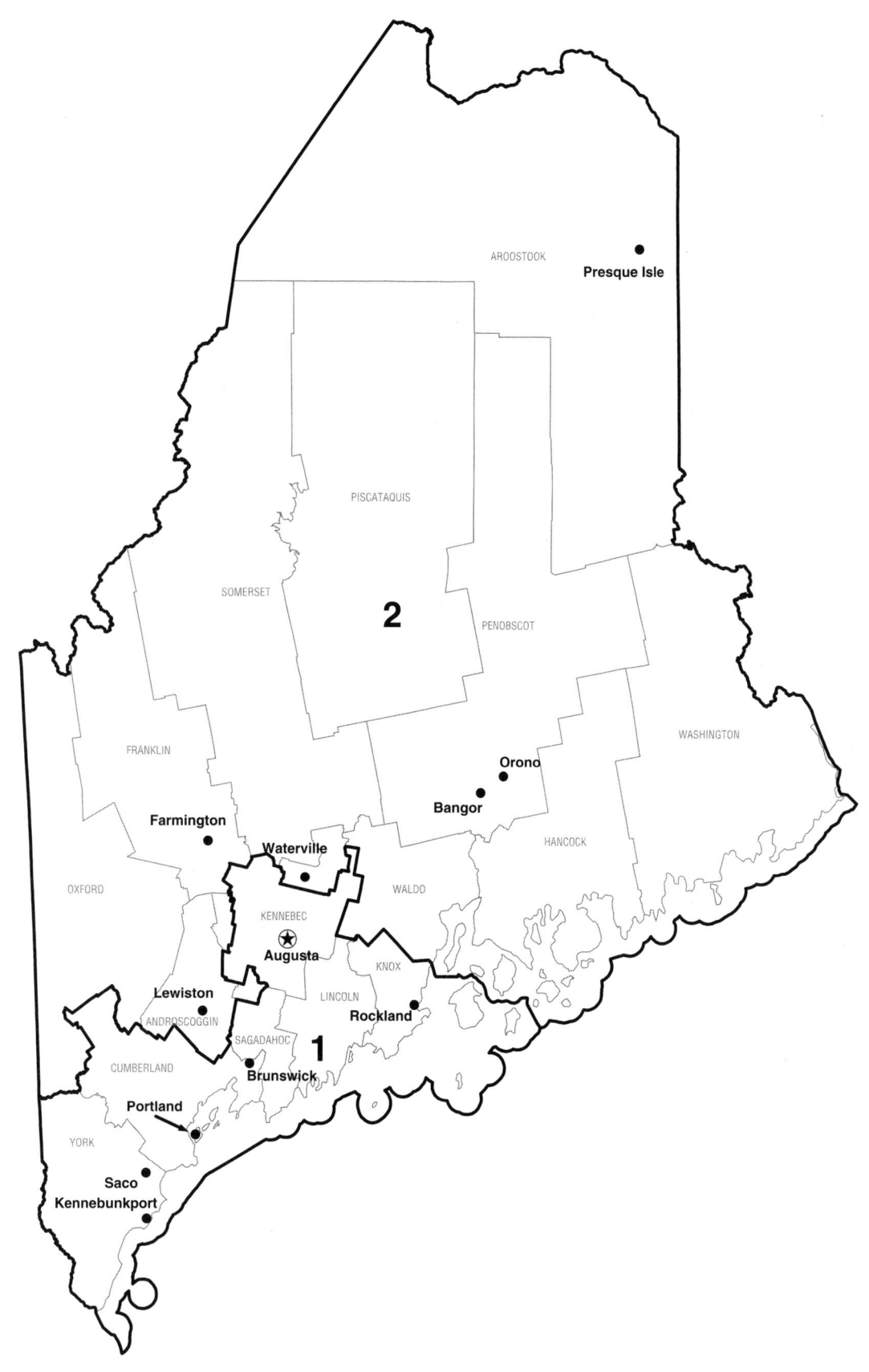

The 1st helped lead the Prohibition crusade when Neal Dow discontinued the traditional "rum break" for his Portland tannery workers because it interfered with productivity; Dow was the Prohibition Party's presidential candidate in 1880.

Election Returns[1]

	Republican		Democratic		Other	
President 2000	148,618	42.6%	176,293	50.6%	23,741	6.8%
House 2002	97,931	36.2%	172,646	63.8%		

District Profile[1]

Population 666,936

Total area (square miles) 5,480.1
    Land area (square miles) 3,617.1

Population per square mile 184.4

Counties (2000 population)

Cumberland 265,612	Lincoln 33,616
Kennebec (pt.) 106,134	Sagadahoc 35,214
Knox 39,618	York 186,742

Cities and other areas over 10,000 (2000 population)

Augusta 18,560	Sanford CDP 10,133
Biddeford 20,942	South Portland 23,324
Brunswick CDP 14,816	Waterville 15,605
Portland 64,249	Westbrook 16,142
Saco 16,822	

Race and Hispanic or Latino origin*

White 96.3%
Black or African American 0.6%
American Indian or Alaska Native 0.3%
Asian 0.9%
Native Hawaiian or other Pacific Islander 0.0%
Some other race 0.1%
Hispanic or Latino origin 0.8%
Two or more races 0.9%

*As percentage of total population.

Ancestry*

English 16.1%	Polish 1.7%
Fr. Canadian 6.1%	Scotch-Irish 2.0%
French 9.7%	Scottish 3.7%
German 5.6%	Swedish 1.4%
Irish 11.9%	USA/American 5.6%
Italian 4.3%	

*As estimated percentage of total population.

Universities and colleges, 2000–2001 enrollment

Andover College, Portland 566
Bowdoin College, Brunswick 1,609
Colby College, Waterville 1,814
Maine College of Art, Portland 440
Southern Maine Technical College, South Portland 2,334
St. Joseph's College, Standish 4,837
Thomas College, Waterville 737

University of Maine-Augusta, Augusta 5,617
University of New England, Biddeford 2,684
University of Southern Maine, Portland 10,820
York County Technical College, Wells 706

Newspapers and circulation

	District circulation	Total circulation
Bangor Daily News	3,469	63,711
Biddeford Journal Tribune	8,856	8,914
Boston Globe	4,836	465,248
Boston Herald	3,039	257,071
Brunswick Times Record	10,430	10,814
Foster's Daily Democrat	3,201	23,144
Kennebec Journal	12,888	13,948
Lewiston Sun-Journal	1,836	34,373
Portland Press Herald Telegram	70,094	73,672
Portsmouth Herald	3,839	14,788
*USA Today**	4,663	1,674,376
Waterford Morning Sentinel	9,431	19,672

*See Sources and Explanations in the front of the volume.

Television stations and affiliations

Portland-Auburn	100%	WCBB	PBS
Portland-Auburn	100%	WCSH	NBC
Portland-Auburn	100%	WGME	CBS
Portland-Auburn	100%	WMEA	PBS
Portland-Auburn	100%	WMTW	ABC
Portland-Auburn	100%	WPXT	WB

Cable systems and subscribers

Adelphia 62,408
Casco Cable Television Inc. 530
Comcast 8,127
Metrocast 8,393
Suscom 16,068
Time Warner 80,177

Military installations, September 2001

Portsmouth Naval Shipyard, Portsmouth 4,453
Brunswick Naval Air Station (Multi-Sites), Brunswick 4,009

Businesses and other major employers

Bath Iron Works Corp.; Bath; combat vessels 6,000
Maine Medical Center; Portland 5,000
Wilson Boney and Sons Inc.; Scarborough; supermarkets 5,000
Midcoast Seamless Gutters; Warren; gutter and downspout contractor 1,986
Fairchild Semiconductor Corp.; South Portland; semiconductors and related devices 1,800
L. L. Bean Inc.; Freeport; clothing, outdoor equipment 1,574
Maine Dept. of Transportation; Augusta 1,500
City of Portland; Portland; city government 1,200
U.S. Postal Service; Portland 1,200
UNUM Life Insurance Company of America; Portland; disability health insurance 1,200
University of Maine System; Portland 1,128
Mercy Hospital; Portland 1,032
U.S. Veterans Hospital; Augusta 1,000
University of Maine System; Gorham 1,000

[1]This information is for districts in effect between 1994 and 2002. Maine redistricts a year later than other states.

Warnaco Inc.; Waterville; men's/boys' dress shirts 1,000

Webber Hospital Assn.; Biddeford 1,000

Anthem Blue Cross and Blue Shield of Maine; South Portland; group hospitalization 990

Sprague Sanford Inc.; Sanford; capacitors and condensers 930

Roman Catholic Bishop of Portland; Portland; religious organization 927

MidCoast Hospital; Brunswick 925

Maine General Medical Center; Augusta 900

Verizon Communications Inc.; Portland; local telephone communications 900

Central Office of Maine Veterans Homes; Augusta 815

Hannaford Bros. Co.; South Portland; food supplier 800

Maine Dept. of Human Services; Augusta 800

Bar Mills School District; Bar Mills 784

Barber Foods Inc.; Portland; processed poultry 750

City of Biddeford; Biddeford; education programs 741

Idexx Laboratories Inc.; Westbrook; surgical/medical instruments 710

Penobscot Bay Medical Center Inc.; Rockport 700

Sanmina-SCI Corp.; Westbrook; electronic computers 700

School Administrative District; Buxton; elementary and secondary schools 700

SCI Systems Inc.; Augusta; electronic circuits 700

Spencer Press Inc.; Wells; offset printing 700

Unemployment Compensation Bureau; Augusta; labor regulatory agency 700

Interstate Brands Corp.; Biddeford; breads and cakes 600

Sodexho Inc.; Rockland; lunchrooms and cafeterias 600

Bowdoin College; Brunswick 580

President and Trustees of Colby College; Waterville 569

Huhtamkaki Co. Mfg.; Waterville; pressed/molded pulp and fiber products 550

S. D. Warren Co.; Westbrook; commercial physical research 509

Seattle Times Co.; Portland; newspaper 502

City of Westbrook; Westbrook; city government 500

Envisionet Computer Services Inc.; Brunswick; computer consulting services 500

General Electric Co.; Westbrook; electric services 500

Maine Dept. of Conservation; Augusta 500

Parker Hannifin Corp.; Portland; motor vehicle parts/accessories 500

Shape Inc.; Kennebunk; audiotape 500

Maine 2nd District

North — Lewiston, Bangor

Millions of acres of trees surround the small towns of northern Maine's 2nd, one of the most politically independent districts in the nation. The largest district in a state east of the Mississippi, the 2nd attracts millions of visitors to Acadia National Park, Baxter State Park, and Maine's many lakes and ski resorts.

A billion-dollar lobster industry dominates the East Coast, and the timber industry reigns in the rest of the 2nd. Sparsely populated in parts, the region is less wealthy than the 1st, which has benefited from an influx of high-tech jobs. Aroostook County, on the Canadian border, lost more than 10,000 people after Loring Air Force Base closed in the 1990s, though recent revitalization efforts have brought 1,000 new jobs to the 8,700-acre base. As the national economy has become more service-based, the 2nd has felt the pinch. Manufacturing jobs, especially in shoes and textiles, have gone overseas, and residents are heading south for jobs. Farming is in decline as well, though the district remains one of the largest producers of potatoes and blueberries in the nation. When redistricting takes place before the 2004 elections, the 2nd will expand southward to pick up more people. *(See maps pp. 412–413.)*

Democrats and Yankee Republicans often vote across party lines in a state with weak party loyalties. In 1992 Ross Perot finished second in the presidential election, behind Bill Clinton but ahead of George Bush. Active participation in town activities helps encourage one of the highest voter turnouts in the nation.

Major Industry

Logging, fishing, textile manufacturing, tourism, higher education.

Notable

Author Stephen King lives in Bangor; Abraham Lincoln's first vice president, Hannibal Hamlin, was born in Paris Hill; essayist E. B. White, author of *Charlotte's Web,* lived on a farm in North Brooklin.

Election Returns[1]

	Republican		Democratic		Other	
President 2000	137,998	45.6%	143,658	47.4%	21,179	7.0%
House 2002	107,849	48.0%	116,868	52.0%		

District Profile[1]

Population 607,987

Total area (square miles) 29,904.4
Land area (square miles) 27,244.4

Population per square mile 22.3

Counties (2000 population)

Androscoggin 103,793	Penobscot 144,919
Aroostook 73,938	Piscataquis 17,235
Franklin 29,467	Somerset 50,888
Hancock 51,791	Waldo 36,280
Kennebec (pt.) 10,980	Washington 33,941
Oxford 54,755	

Cities and other areas over 10,000 (2000 population)

Auburn 23,203	Lewiston 35,690
Bangor 31,473	

Race and Hispanic or Latino origin*
White 96.7%
Black or African American 0.4%

[1]This information is for districts in effect between 1994 and 2002. Maine redistricts a year later than other states.

American Indian or Alaska Native   0.8%
Asian   0.5%
Native Hawaiian or other Pacific Islander   0.0%
Some other race   0.1%
Hispanic or Latino origin   0.7%
Two or more races   0.9%

*As percentage of total population.

Ancestry*

English 15.9%	Polish 1.1%	
Fr. Canadian 6.7%	Scotch-Irish 2.0%	
French 11.6%	Scottish 3.4%	
German 4.2%	Swedish 1.1%	
Irish 10.4%	USA/American 8.6%	
Italian 2.5%		

*As estimated percentage of total population.

Universities and colleges, 2000–2001 enrollment

Bates College, Lewiston   1,694
Beal College, Bangor   338
Central Maine Technical College, Auburn   1,318
College of the Atlantic, Bar Harbor   262
Eastern Maine Technical College, Bangor   1,354
Husson College, Bangor   1,944
Kennebec Valley Technical College, Fairfield   834
Maine Maritime Academy, Castine   721
Northern Maine Technical College, Presque Isle   784
Unity College, Unity   507
University of Maine, Farmington   2,413
University of Maine, Fort Kent   886
University of Maine, Machias   927
University of Maine, Presque Isle   1,427
University of Maine, Orono   10,282
Washington County Technical College, Calais   239

Newspapers and circulation

	District circulation	Total circulation
Bangor Daily News	58,706	63,711
Boston Globe	1,083	465,248
Lewiston Sun-Journal	31,661	34,373
Portland Press Herald Telegram	1,848	73,672
*USA Today**	1,747	1,674,376
Waterford Morning Sentinel	9,885	19,672

*See Sources and Explanations in the front of the volume.

Television stations and affiliations

Bangor	62%	WABI	CBS
Bangor	62%	WLBZ	NBC
Bangor	62%	WMEB	PBS
Bangor	62%	WMED	PBS
Bangor	62%	WVII	ABC
Presque Isle	23%	WAGM	CBS, NBC, UPN
Presque Isle	23%	WMEM	PBS
Portland-Auburn	15%	WCBB	PBS
Portland-Auburn	15%	WCSH	NBC
Portland-Auburn	15%	WGME	CBS
Portland-Auburn	15%	WMEA	PBS
Portland-Auburn	15%	WMTW	ABC
Portland-Auburn	15%	WPXT	WB

Cable systems and subscribers

Adelphia   95,086
Bee Line Cable   9,731
Houlton Cable TV   3,907
Lincolnville Communications   587
Moosehead Enterprises   2,452
Pine Tree Cablevision   4,579
Suscom   645
Time Warner   9,539

Military installations, September 2001

Bangor International Airport (Air National Guard), Bangor   926
Winter Harbor Naval Security Group Activity, Winter Harbor   118

Businesses and other major employers

University of Maine System; Orono   3,000
Eastern Maine Medical Center Inc.; Bangor   2,400
Great Northern Paper Inc.; Millinocket; paper mills   1,329
International Paper Co.; Jay; paper mills   1,200
Mead Corp.; Rumford; paper products   1,200
Central Maine Medical Center Inc.; Lewiston   1,190
International Paper Co.; Bucksport; paper mills   1,100
McCain Foods Inc.; Easton; frozen fruits/vegetables   1,100
Nexfor (USA) Inc.; Madawaska; paper mills   1,100
Jackson Laboratory; Bar Harbor; noncommercial research organization   1,070
SD Warren Co.; Skowhegan; paper mills   912
Dexter Shoe Co.; Dexter; shoes   900
Fraser Papers Inc.; Madawaska; paper mills   900
Yankee Candle Co.; Bangor; candle shops   900
St. Mary's Regional Medical Center; Lewiston   850
St. Joseph Hospital; Bangor   840
Faithworks Inc.; Lewiston; packaging/labeling services   800
Panolam Industries International Inc.; Auburn; plastic laminated table/counter tops   800
MBNA America Bank; Belfast; commercial bank   798
Interface Fabrics Group Inc.; Guilford; manmade and synthetic broadwoven fabrics   700
Aroostook Medical Center Inc.; Presque Isle   624
Fort James Corp.; Old Town; pulp mills   613
Great Northern Paper Inc.; East Millinocket; paper mills   607
Burrelle's Information Services; Presque Isle; press clipping service   606
City of Bangor; Bangor; education programs   600
Combined Management Inc.; Auburn; employment agencies   600
Georgia-Pacific Corp.; Baileyville; printing paper   600
Maine Dept. of Behavioral and Developmental Services; Bangor   600
Irving Tanning Co.; Hartland; leather tanning/finishing   540
Eastern Maine Medical Center; Bangor; hydrostatic testing laboratory   500
General Electric Co.; Bangor; turbines/turbine generators   500
Maine Dept. of Transportation; Bangor   500
Maine Dept. of Transportation; Presque Isle   500
SPX Corp.; Pittsfield; electrical equipment and supplies   500
Wal-Mart Stores Inc.; Auburn; discount department stores   500

Maryland

Maryland is another state that can be viewed as a microcosm of America as a whole. The state has an eastern seashore, a major industrial seaport (Baltimore), a quaintly historic capital (Annapolis), a slice of ocean beach, a Piedmont midsection full of traditional farms, and a far western portion dominated by scenic mountains on the forested Blue Ridge, Appalachian Ridge, and Appalachian Plateau. There are suburbs in Maryland largely interchangeable with those of New York or Chicago, yet there are also lowland counties along the Chesapeake where accents and customs connect to the Old South (and even to colonial times). Maryland has long attracted new residents from all over the country, in part because the nation's capital, Washington, D.C., occupies land Maryland ceded in 1791 on the north bank of the Potomac River. The U.S. Naval Academy at Annapolis enrolls its midshipmen from every state, and many return to retire here.

Maryland is also a case study of national trends in urban and suburban development after World War II. Baltimore benefited from the seaport wartime boom and attracted workers from the upland counties of surrounding states and from throughout the Mid-Atlantic region and beyond. In the 1950s the city took a big league baseball team away from St. Louis (the Browns becoming the Orioles) and developed its professional football team, the Colts, into one of the legends of the sport.

Meanwhile, down the highway, the enormous influx of workers to Washington, D.C., during and after the war brought waves of growth first to the city and then to the suburban counties of Montgomery and Prince Georges. Statewide, the growth rate of 120 percent in the half century beginning in 1950 was among the 15 fastest in the country. Growth along the Interstate 95 corridor between Baltimore and Washington narrowed the gap between them until the Census Bureau began considering them one consolidated market statistical area (CMSA). In the 2000 census this was the fourth largest CMSA after New York, Los Angeles, and Chicago.

During the later decades of the twentieth century, Baltimore became a majority black city, while the ethnic Europeans who had peopled the city's neighborhoods for generations moved into suburban Baltimore County. This led to a steady erosion of population in the city itself, which dropped another 11.5 percent in the 1990s (a rate of decline exceeded only by that of St. Louis). In the Washington end of the metroplex, Montgomery County on the west remained primarily white-collar and Caucasian, with an influx of Asian and Hispanic minorities. The county's dependence on professional jobs in government, science, and technology helped the state as a whole to register a high incidence of college degrees: nearly one-third of Maryland residents over 25 have at least a bachelor's degree.

Prince Georges, on the east side of Washington, adjacent to predominantly black wards of the city, went from being primarily white and blue collar to being a majority black county, the most affluent majority black county in the country, in the 1990s. Along the way, its transformation was marked by this shift: the 1968 Democratic presidential primary here was won by George Wallace, the segregationist; but in 1988 it was won by Jesse Jackson, the civil rights activist.

But if Maryland fits into patterns seen elsewhere, it also differs in both kind and degree. It is even more suburban (72 percent) than most, having the Baltimore suburbs and much of the Washington suburbs as well. It has a low rate of poverty (only two states were lower). As its name implies, Maryland has a distinctly Catholic history, having been granted in 1632 to the Catholic Calvert family, specifically Lord Baltimore, by one of the last Catholic kings of England. It was the only Catholic colony among the original 13, and many of its voters still assign some premium to adherents of the Church of Rome. Just as significant, Maryland has the fifth largest percentage of African Americans (28 percent) among the states, double the national average and the largest of any state that did not secede. Baltimore became a black majority city in the 1980 census, and the black population of Prince Georges County doubled in that same decade.

Combined with union households, Catholics and blacks have made a potent combination for Democrats in recent generations, and Maryland has lately become something of a Democratic lake. Al Gore got 56 percent here in 2000, one of his best showings anywhere, and it was the eighth Democratic win here in the past eleven presidential races. This largely defies the larger trend toward the GOP over the same period, especially in other states below the Mason-Dixon line (an actual historic product of a famous surveying collaboration which defined the border between Maryland and Pennsylvania and came to be regarded as the dividing line between free and slave states).

Senate races have been just as one-sided, as no Republican has won here since Charles Mathias last did so in 1980. Mathias was one of just three Republicans to win a Senate seat here since World War II. The governors' mansion has

MARYLAND

Districts established May 6, 2002, for elections first held in 2002.

8 members

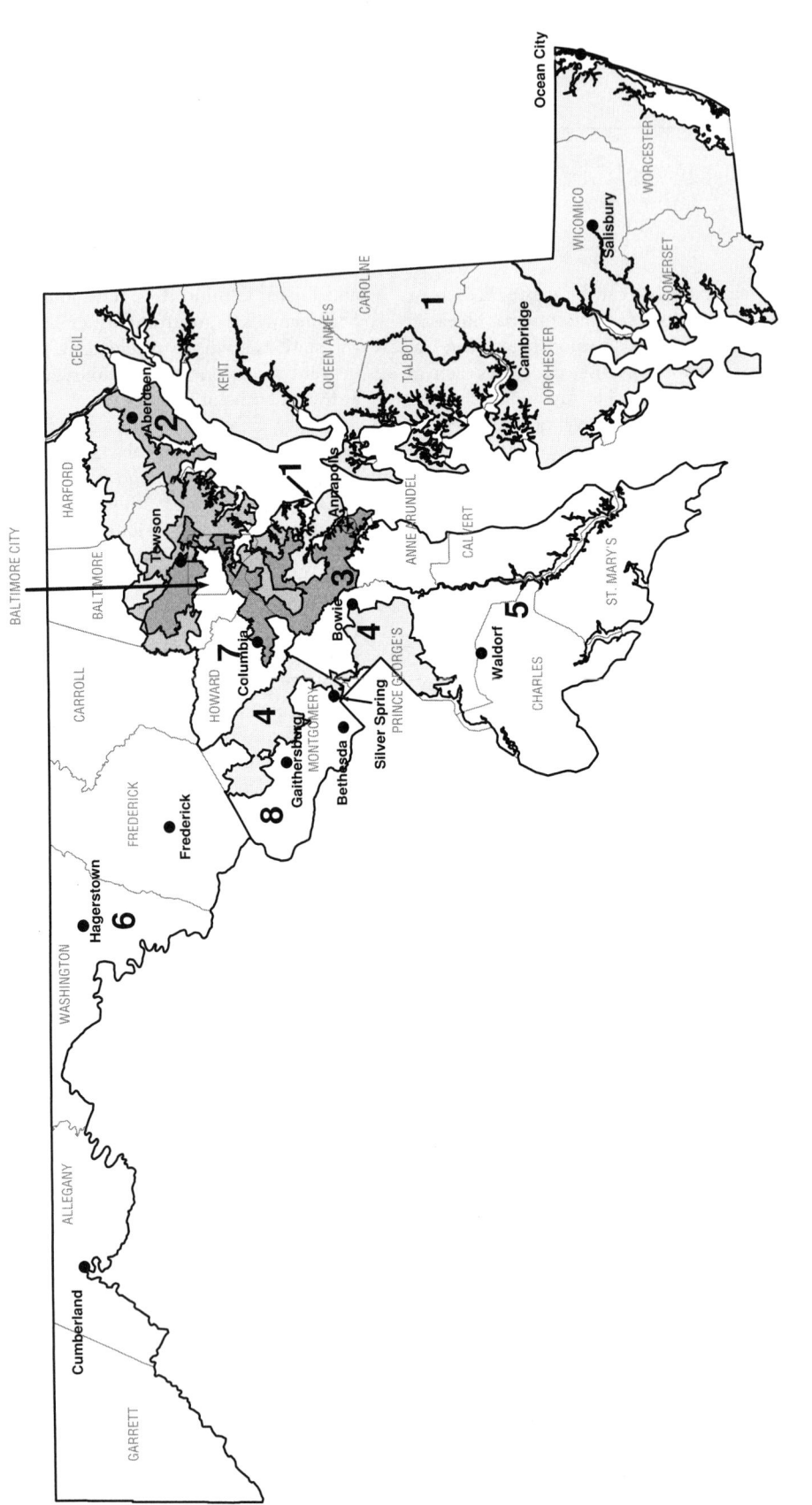

had just three Republican occupants over the same time span. The second was Spiro T. Agnew, elected in 1966, and no GOP wins followed until 2002, when popular representative Bob Ehrlich defeated Lt. Gov. Kathleen Kennedy Townsend, a daughter of Robert F. Kennedy who proved maladroit as a campaigner.

The steady if unspectacular growth and prosperity of Maryland have kept the size of its delegation in Congress almost exactly the same for 200 years. The state began the first Congress with six of the original 65 seats in the House. That meant it was tied with New York for the fourth largest delegation (behind Virginia, Pennsylvania, and Massachusetts). As the nation grew and the House expanded, Maryland rose quickly to nine House seats but saw its share of the total decline. After the 1840 census the state was back to six seats, where it remained (with a brief dip to five) for more than a century. After 1950, growth in the Washington, D.C., suburbs gave the state a seventh and then an eighth seat, which is where it stood after the year 2000.

Drawing the map for those eight districts was the job of a partisan Democratic majority in the legislature and a lame-duck Democratic governor. They fashioned districts that left two Republican incumbents secure at either end of the state—in the western highlands of the Appalachians (Frederick, Hagerstown) and on the marshy Atlantic coastal plain on either side of Chesapeake Bay and down the Eastern Shore to the ocean (Easton, Salisbury). In between these extremes, the mapmakers drew six districts they presumed Democrats could win. Three districts (two white and one black) were for Baltimore, its suburbs and satellites, and Annapolis. The mapmakers then divided the populous precincts of the D.C. suburbs into three districts (two white and one black), with surrounding rural areas ringing their respective fringes.

The result was that all six of these districts elected Democrats in 2002. The 60,000 voters that had been shifted from the Democratic Prince Georges County district into the Montgomery County district provided just enough reliable Democratic votes to oust a longtime moderate Republican there. The new map also allowed the Democrats to win what had been a Republican seat in the suburbs of Baltimore. This arrangement looks likely to hold through 2010. In fact, the Democrats might even find themselves targeting one or both of these two remaining Republican districts in 2004, or when next they fall vacant.

Table 1 Population

District	Population	Population under 18	Voting-age population	Median age	Male*	Female*
1	662,062	166,222	495,840	38.6	48.9	51.1
2	662,060	169,980	492,080	35.4	47.5	52.5
3	662,062	152,069	509,993	36.1	48.6	51.4
4	662,062	187,881	474,181	33.6	47.4	52.6
5	662,060	173,993	488,067	35.0	49.0	51.0
6	662,060	171,782	490,278	37.0	49.7	50.3
7	662,060	172,817	489,243	35.4	47.3	52.7
8	662,060	161,428	500,632	37.1	48.0	52.0
State	5,296,486	1,356,172	3,940,314	36.0	48.3	51.7

*As percentage of total population.

Table 2 Voting-Age Persons by Race/Hispanic or Latino Origin

District	White*	Black or African American*	American Indian or Alaska Native*	Asian*	Other or multirace*	Hispanic or Latino*
1	85.6	10.8	0.2	1.3	0.7	1.4
2	69.8	24.3	0.3	2.5	1.1	1.9
3	77.7	14.9	0.3	3.2	1.2	2.7
4	29.6	55.3	0.2	5.9	1.9	7.1
5	62.5	28.5	0.4	3.9	1.5	3.1
6	92.1	4.9	0.2	1.0	0.7	1.3
7	36.2	57.0	0.2	3.7	1.2	1.6
8	58.2	15.7	0.2	11.0	2.3	12.6
State	64.2	26.2	0.3	4.1	1.3	4.0

*As percentage of voting-age population.

Table 3 Voting-Age Population by Age Groups

District	18 to 24*	25 to 44*	45 to 64*	Over 64*
1	10.0	38.0	34.0	18.0
2	11.9	42.6	28.9	16.6
3	11.8	42.5	29.3	16.4
4	11.8	46.4	31.6	10.2
5	12.9	44.1	31.2	11.8
6	10.4	41.4	32.0	16.3
7	13.3	40.8	30.1	15.9
8	9.6	42.3	31.7	16.4
State	11.4	42.3	31.1	15.2

*As percentage of voting-age population.

Table 4 Income and Occupation

District	Median family income	Families in poverty*	White collar†	Blue collar†	Service†	Farm†
1	$60,620	5.2	63.3	21.9	13.9	0.9
2	$51,916	7.5	61.5	23.0	15.4	0.1
3	$63,408	5.2	71.7	15.7	12.4	0.1
4	$65,107	5.5	70.7	15.0	14.2	0.1
5	$70,571	3.4	68.0	18.8	12.9	0.2
6	$59,362	4.6	61.5	23.9	14.1	0.5
7	$48,649	13.6	66.7	16.2	17.0	0.1
8	$81,922	4.2	77.1	10.6	12.2	0.1
State	$61,876	6.1	67.7	18.1	13.9	0.3

*As percentage of all families.   †As percentage of employed workers 16 years and over.

Table 5 Education: School Years Completed

District	Less than grade 9*	Grades 9–12 no diploma*	High school diploma no college*	Some college*	College bachelor's degree or higher*
1	4.6	11.2	30.7	26.2	27.3
2	5.9	14.3	32.0	27.5	20.3
3	5.2	10.8	23.6	24.0	36.5
4	4.3	9.4	24.8	28.8	32.7
5	3.5	8.9	28.8	30.2	28.7
6	5.1	11.1	34.2	25.9	23.7
7	6.8	17.0	25.4	23.3	27.5
8	5.4	6.2	14.6	20.1	53.7
State	5.1	11.1	26.7	25.7	31.4

*As percentage of persons age 25 and over.

Table 6   Housing and Residential Patterns

District	Median home value	Owner occupied*	Renter occupied*	Urban†	Rural†
1	$144,800	78.6	21.4	64.2	35.8
2	$108,000	62.3	37.7	98.3	1.7
3	$131,200	67.6	32.4	98.6	1.4
4	$151,400	62.9	37.1	97.9	2.1
5	$156,700	74.8	25.2	75.2	24.8
6	$144,300	75.7	24.3	60.5	39.5
7	$102,300	55.5	44.5	94.9	5.1
8	$211,500	65.3	34.7	98.8	1.2
State	$143,300	67.7	32.3	86.1	13.9

*As percentage of occupied housing units.   †As percentage of total population.

Maryland 1st District

East — Eastern Shore, part of Anne Arundel County

The 1st includes the rural counties of the Eastern Shore and, across the Chesapeake Bay, some of the fast-growing suburbs of Anne Arundel County. It also moves across the Susquehanna River in the northeastern part of the state and claims large chunks of Harford County, including Bel Air, and Baltimore County. *(See map p. 422.)*

Although the district's regions are different in many ways, they share a conservative lean that benefits Republicans. The 1st supported the Republican presidential candidate in 1992, 1996, and 2000. During redistricting following the 2000 census, some GOP-leaning voters were pushed into the 1st from the 2nd and 3rd Districts.

The Eastern Shore, which holds about three-fifths of the district's population, has a steady economic grounding in agriculture. The central, more rural, part of the Eastern Shore is GOP heartland. The northern counties, closer to Baltimore and Philadelphia, and southern counties, with larger black and working-class populations, are more Democratic. Ocean City is a popular beach town that swells with visitors during the summer months.

Across the bay, some conservative parts of Anne Arundel County remain in the district. Annapolis, the Democratic-leaning state capital, was removed during redistricting. Part of Baltimore's fast-growing, GOP-leaning northern suburbs also are included in the district.

Major Industry
Agriculture, manufacturing, tourism.

Notable
Wild ponies can be seen roaming Assateague Island, a barrier island on the Atlantic Ocean; residents of Smith Island, which calls itself Maryland's only inhabited offshore island in the Chesapeake Bay, speak an Elizabethan-English-based dialect.

Election Returns

	Republican		Democratic		Other	
President 2000	160,402	57.2%	111,807	39.8%	8,424	3.0%
House 2002	192,004	76.8%	57,986	23.2%	423	

District Profile

Population   662,062

Total area (square miles)   3,701.7
   Land area (square miles)   3,653.1

Population per square mile   181.2

Counties (2000 population)
Anne Arundel (pt.) 101,514	Kent 19,197
Baltimore (pt.) 58,678	Queen Anne's 40,563
Caroline 29,772	Somerset 24,747
Cecil 85,951	Talbot 33,812
Dorchester 30,674	Wicomico 84,644
Harford (pt.) 105,967	Worcester 46,543

Cities and other areas over 10,000 (2000 population)
Arnold CDP (pt.)   23,422
Bel Air North CDP (pt.)   25,372
Bel Air South CDP (pt.)   35,353
Bel Air town   10,080
Cambridge (pt.)   10,911
Easton town (pt.)   11,708
Elkton town (pt.)   11,893
Lake Shore CDP (pt.)   12,962
Ocean Pines CDP (pt.)   10,496
Perry Hall CDP (pt.)   17,145
Salisbury (pt.)   23,743
Severna Park CDP (pt.)   26,646

Race and Hispanic or Latino origin*
White   84.7%
Black or African American   11.2%
American Indian or Alaska Native   0.2%
Asian   1.4%
Native Hawaiian or other Pacific Islander   0.0%
Some other race   0.1%
Hispanic or Latino origin   1.6%
Two or more races   0.9%

*As percentage of total population.

Ancestry*
English 10.7%	Polish 3.3%
French 1.7%	Scotch-Irish 1.4%
German 15.5%	Scottish 1.8%
Irish 12.1%	USA/American 6.4%
Italian 5.1%	

*As estimated percentage of total population.

Universities and colleges, 2000–2001 enrollment
Anne Arundel Community College, Arnold   11,761
Cecil Community College, North East   1,293
Chesapeake College, Wye Mills   2,186
Harford Community College, Bel Air   4,821
Salisbury State University, Salisbury   6,421
University of Maryland-Eastern Shore, Princess Anne   3,297
Washington College, Chestertown   1,225
Wor-Wic Community College, Salisbury   2,329

Newspapers and circulation

	District circulation	Total circulation
Annapolis Capital	17,005	45,981
Baltimore Sun	46,136	268,280
Hartford County Aegis	35,049	59,155
Havre de Grace Record	2,272	3,874
Maryland Gazette	8,549	32,911
Salisbury Daily Times	23,044	25,978
*USA Today**	4,567	1,674,376
Washington Post	9,843	779,632
Washington Times	2,228	101,367
Wilmington News Journal	4,831	121,217

See Sources and Explanations in the front of the volume.

Television stations and affiliations

Salisbury	51%	WBOC	CBS
Salisbury	51%	WCPB	PBS
Salisbury	51%	WDPB	PBS
Salisbury	51%	WMDT	ABC
Baltimore	49%	WBAL	NBC
Baltimore	49%	WBFF	FOX
Baltimore	49%	WJZ	CBS
Baltimore	49%	WMAR	ABC
Baltimore	49%	WMPB	PBS
Baltimore	49%	WMPT	PBS
Baltimore	49%	WNUV	WB
Baltimore	49%	WUTB	UPN

Cable systems and subscribers

Armstrong 554
Charter 9,967
Clearview CATV Inc. 41,875
Comcast 93,901
Easton Utilities 6,281
Gans 12,634
Mediacom 4,839

Military installations, September 2001

U.S. Naval Academy, Annapolis 6,406
Gunpowder Military Reservation, Glen Arm 183
Annapolis Naval Medical Clinic, Annapolis 123

Businesses and other major employers

Airpax Corp.; Cambridge; switchgear and accessories 3,000
Peninsula Regional Medical Center; Salisbury 2,000
U.S. Postal Service; Greensboro 1,976
AT&T Corp.; Hunt Valley; engineering services 1,700
Perdue Farms Inc.; Salisbury; chicken processing 1,600
Upper Chesapeake Medical Center Inc.; Bel Air 1,524
Tyson Foods Inc.; Berlin; chicken processing 1,445
Anne Arundel Community College; Arnold 1,200
North DaimlerChyrsler American Holding Corp.; Elkton; automobiles 1,200
Memorial Hospital of Easton Inc.; Easton 1,175
McCormick and Co.; Hunt Valley; spices 1,000
Procter and Gamble Co.; Hunt Valley; towels, napkins, tissue paper products 1,000
Becton Dickinson and Co.; Cockeysville; bacteriological media 900
Union Hospital of Cecil County Health Services Inc.; Elkton 900

Verizon Maryland Inc.; Cockeysville; local/long-distance telephone 900
Maryland Dept. of Public Safety and Corrections; Westover 876
Black and Decker Corp.; Easton; power-driven handtools 850
University System of Maryland; Princess Anne 850
Dresser Inc.; Salisbury; measuring and dispensing pumps 800
Lankford-Sysco Food Services Inc.; Pocomoke City; food supplier 800
Northrop Grumman Systems Corp.; Annapolis; acoustical engineering 800
Anne Arundel County; Millersville; county police 776
Harford Community College; Bel Air 772
United Call Center Services Inc.; Salisbury; telephone services 650
Seton Center; Princess Anne; individual and family services 619
Allen Family Foods Inc.; Hurlock; poultry slaughtering/processing 600
Piedmont Airlines Inc. (US Airways Express); Salisbury; air passenger carrier 541
Allen Family Foods Inc.; Cordova; poultry slaughtering/processing 500
Exponent Failure Analysis; Severna Park; engineering services 500
Northrop Grumman Systems Corp.; Hunt Valley; engineering services 500
U.S. Veterans Hospital; Perry Point 500

Maryland 2nd District

Part of Baltimore and suburbs — Dundalk, Essex

The 2nd includes northern and eastern parts of Baltimore, suburbs in most directions around the city, and most of the territory east of Interstate 95 between Baltimore and the Susquehanna River. *(See map p. 422.)*

Redrawn during redistricting following the 2000 census to increase Democratic strength, the 2nd ranges northeast from Baltimore along the Chesapeake Bay and south into Anne Arundel County, where it picks up Baltimore-Washington International Airport and Fort George G. Meade (including the National Security Agency). The district's northwest branch moves through the GOP-heavy northern suburbs and then hooks into largely African American suburbs west of Baltimore, such as Randallstown. Blacks make up 27 percent of the 2nd's population.

In eastern Baltimore County, the blue-collar industrial sector—including Dundalk—has struggled with unemployment. But Bethlehem Steel, one of the county's major employers, opened a new mill in 2000 at its Sparrows Point complex, which is seen as a valuable asset for the area's economy. A General Motors plant in the district is an important source of employment.

The 2nd gave Al Gore 57 percent of its vote in the 2000 presidential election. But many Democrats in the Baltimore suburbs have favored GOP candidates in past House races.

Major Industry

Manufacturing, defense, product distribution.

BALTIMORE, WASHINGTON, DC, AREA

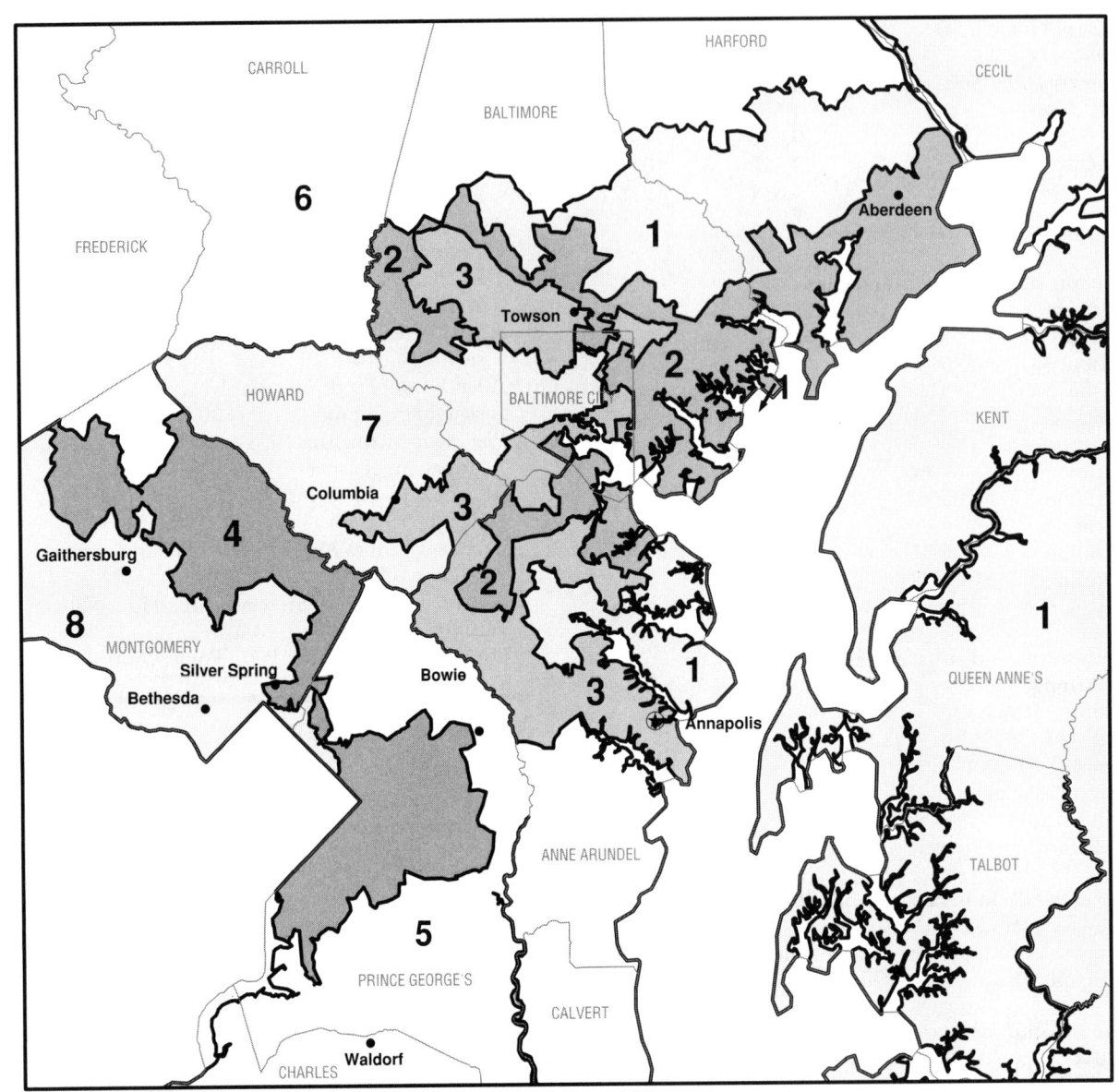

Notable

The stadium complex in Aberdeen is home to Cal Ripken Baseball, a youth division of the amateur Babe Ruth League, and minor league baseball's Aberdeen IronBirds, a team owned by Ripken.

Election Returns

	Republican		Democratic		Other	
President 2000	91,677	40.8%	127,510	56.8%	5,285	2.4%
House 2002	88,954	45.7%	105,718	54.3%	530	

District Profile

Population 662,060

Total area (square miles) 359.1
　Land area (square miles) 354.9

Population per square mile 1,865.5

Counties (2000 population)
Anne Arundel (pt.) 107,337
Baltimore (pt.) 359,711
Baltimore City (pt.) 111,715
Harford (pt.) 83,297

Cities and other areas over 10,000 (2000 population)
Aberdeen 13,842
Baltimore (pt.) 111,715
Brooklyn Park CDP 10,938
Carney CDP (pt.) 28,264
Cockeysville CDP (pt.) 16,422
Dundalk CDP (pt.) 62,306
Edgewood CDP (pt.) 23,378
Essex CDP (pt.) 39,078
Ferndale CDP (pt.) 13,779
Glen Burnie CDP (pt.) 10,293
Green Haven CDP (pt.) 17,415
Havre de Grace (pt.) 11,331
Joppatowne CDP (pt.) 10,606
Lutherville-Timonium CDP 15,814
Middle River CDP (pt.) 23,958
Parkville CDP (pt.) 13,308
Perry Hall CDP (pt.) 11,560
Randallstown CDP (pt.) 29,097
Riviera Beach CDP (pt.) 12,695
Rosedale CDP (pt.) 19,199
Rossville CDP (pt.) 10,672
Severn CDP (pt.) 25,095
Towson CDP (pt.) 23,736

Race and Hispanic or Latino origin*
White 66.3%
Black or African American 27.1%
American Indian or Alaska Native 0.3%
Asian 2.4%
Native Hawaiian or other Pacific Islander 0.0%
Some other race 0.2%
Hispanic or Latino origin 2.2%
Two or more races 1.5%

*As percentage of total population.

Ancestry*

English	5.9%	Italian	5.1%
French	1.4%	Polish	4.6%
German	15.6%	Subsaharan	1.2%
Irish	10.4%	USA/American	4.1%

*As estimated percentage of total population.

Universities and colleges, 2000–2001 enrollment
Dundalk Community College, Dundalk 2,800
Essex Community College, Baltimore 8,233
Goucher College, Baltimore 1,971
Towson University, Towson 16,729

Newspapers and circulation

	District circulation	Total circulation
Baltimore Sun	59,748	268,280
Hartford County Aegis	14,177	59,155
Havre de Grace Record	1,444	3,874
Maryland Gazette	10,906	32,911
*USA Today**	4,069	1,674,376
Washington Post	2,710	779,632
Washington Times	1,019	101,367

*See Sources and Explanations in the front of the volume.

Television stations and affiliations

Baltimore	100%	WBAL	NBC
Baltimore	100%	WBFF	FOX
Baltimore	100%	WJZ	CBS
Baltimore	100%	WMAR	ABC
Baltimore	100%	WMPB	PBS
Baltimore	100%	WMPT	PBS
Baltimore	100%	WNUV	WB
Baltimore	100%	WUTB	UPN

Cable systems and subscribers
Comcast 68,700

Military installations, September 2001
Fort George G. Meade (Army), Baltimore 29,441
Aberdeen Proving Ground (Army), Aberdeen 10,898
Martin State Airport (Air National Guard), Baltimore 1,701
Adam S. Brandt U.S. Army Reserve Center, Baltimore 590
Havre de Grace Military Reserve, Havre de Grace 106

Businesses and other major employers
Bethlehem Steel Corp.; Baltimore; blast furnaces and steel mills 5,061
U.S. Postal Service; Baltimore 5,000
General Motors Corp.; Baltimore; motor vehicle parts/accessories 3,500
Jaeger Inc.; Aberdeen; commercial/office building construction 3,020
Franklin Square Hospital Center Inc.; Baltimore 2,100
Good Samaritan Hospital of Maryland; Baltimore 1,861
Computer Sciences Corp.; Hanover; computer-related systems engineering 1,750
Black and Decker Corp.; Baltimore; power-driven handtools 1,500

MRA Systems Inc.; Baltimore; aircraft engines/parts 1,500

Maryland Dept. of Transportation; Baltimore 1,400

Rite Aid Corp.; Perryman; general merchandise, nondurable 1,400

Oak Crest Village Inc.; Baltimore; nursing home 1,200

Harbor Hospital Center Inc.; Baltimore 1,110

AAI Corp.; Hunt Valley; electronic training devices 1,000

R. C. Theatres Management; Reisterstown; circuit management for theaters 1,000

T. Rowe Price Group Inc.; Owings Mills; investment advisory service 1,000

University of Baltimore; Baltimore 1,000

Northwest Hospital Center Inc.; Randallstown 981

Harford County Board of Education; Aberdeen 909

Baltimore Gas and Electric Co.; Baltimore; electric services 900

Lockheed Martin Corp.; Hanover; commercial physical research 800

Metris Companies Inc.; Baltimore; collection agency 800

Stella Maris Inc.; Lutherville Timonium; real property lessors 780

Northrop Grumman Systems Corp.; Linthicum Heights; infrared sensors 750

Master-Halco Inc.; Edgewood; wire fence, gates, accessories 720

Conopco Inc.; Baltimore; soap 650

Whiting-Turner Contracting Co.; Baltimore; nonresidential construction 629

Harford Memorial Hospital Inc.; Havre de Grace 625

HelixCare; Baltimore; management services 600

Host International Inc.; Baltimore; snack bar 600

Poly-Seal Corp.; Baltimore; plastic products 525

Cintas Corp.; Baltimore; industrial uniform supply 500

Frito-Lay Inc.; Aberdeen; warehousing 500

Goucher College; Baltimore 500

Lockheed Martin Corp.; Baltimore; aircraft assemblies, parts 500

Maryland Dept. of Transportation; Glen Burnie 500

Millennium Inorganic Chemicals Inc.; Baltimore; titanium dioxide (pigments) 500

Operations Management Inc.; Aberdeen; restaurants 500

Science Applications International Corp.; Edgewood; engineering services 500

U.S. Filter Corp.; Lutherville Timonium; sewage and water treatment equipment 500

Maryland 3rd District

Part of Baltimore; eastern Columbia; Annapolis

Like a Z-shaped lightning bolt, the 3rd District flashes through three of Maryland's largest urban centers—Baltimore, Columbia, and Annapolis. *(See map p. 422.)*

Starting in the traditionally Jewish suburbs northwest of Baltimore, the district snakes east, then south, to pick up parts of northeastern Baltimore's suburbs and parts of downtown Baltimore, including Fells Point and the stadiums that house Baltimore's major-league sports teams: baseball's

Orioles and football's Ravens. Many of eastern Baltimore's ethnic neighborhoods are included in the district, but it lost much of downtown to the neighboring 7th in redistricting following the 2000 census. The 3rd then twists south and west through suburban Arbutus and Elkridge on its way to the eastern part of Columbia. Finally, the district moves southeast toward Annapolis.

State and local governments provide employment in Annapolis, which is both the state capital and the Anne Arundel County seat, while technology, financial services and health care businesses push the economy of the Columbia area. Fort George G. Meade—including the National Security Agency—and Baltimore-Washington International Airport, which are both located in the neighboring 2nd District, attract defense-related companies to the region.

The district includes some GOP-leaning areas in Anne Arundel and Baltimore counties, including recently added Towson, but was designed to favor Democratic candidates for federal office.

Major Industry
Government, technology, defense-related business.

Notable
The Preakness Stakes, the second event in horse racing's Triple Crown, is held at Pimlico in northwestern Baltimore; both of Maryland's senators in 2003, Democrats Paul S. Sarbanes and Barbara A. Mikulski, represented the 3rd before their election to the Senate.

Election Returns

	Republican		Democratic		Other	
President 2000	107,481	41.4%	143,685	55.3%	8,456	3.3%
House 2002	75,721	34.2%	145,589	65.8%		

District Profile

Population 662,062

Total area (square miles) 293.4
Land area (square miles) 292.7

Population per square mile 2,261.9

Counties (2000 population)
Anne Arundel (pt.) 231,799
Baltimore (pt.) 185,400
Baltimore City (pt.) 168,687
Howard (pt.) 76,176

Cities and other areas over 10,000 (2000 population)
Annapolis (pt.) 35,838
Arbutus CDP 20,116
Baltimore (pt.) 168,687
Columbia CDP (pt.) 40,311
Crofton CDP 20,091
Elkridge CDP 22,042
Glen Burnie CDP (pt.) 28,629
Lansdowne-Baltimore Highlands CDP 15,724
Odenton CDP (pt.) 19,805
Overlea CDP (pt.) 12,148
Owings Mills CDP (pt.) 15,214
Parkville CDP (pt.) 17,810
Parole CDP (pt.) 14,031
Pikesville CDP (pt.) 29,123

Reisterstown CDP (pt.) 18,052
South Gate CDP (pt.) 28,672
Towson CDP (pt.) 28,057

Race and Hispanic or Latino origin*
White 75.7%
Black or African American 16.2%
American Indian or Alaska Native 0.3%
Asian 3.2%
Native Hawaiian or other Pacific Islander 0.0%
Some other race 0.2%
Hispanic or Latino origin 2.9%
Two or more races 1.5%

*As percentage of total population.

Ancestry*

English 7.7%	Polish 4.2%
French 1.6%	Russian 2.2%
German 14.3%	Scotch-Irish 1.1%
Irish 11.1%	Scottish 1.5%
Italian 4.8%	USA/American 4.2%

*As estimated percentage of total population.

Universities and colleges, 2000–2001 enrollment
College of Notre Dame-Maryland, Baltimore 3,178
Loyola College, Baltimore 6,111
Ner Israel Rabbinical College, Baltimore 565
St. John's College, Annapolis 537
St. Mary's Seminary and University, Baltimore 278
U.S. Naval Academy, Annapolis 4,172
University of Phoenix-Maryland, Columbia 499
Villa Julie College, Stevenson 2,259

Newspapers and circulation

	District circulation	Total circulation
Annapolis Capital	19,276	45,981
Baltimore Sun	67,082	268,280
Maryland Gazette	13,331	32,911
*USA Today**	5,462	1,674,376
Washington Post	16,399	779,632
Washington Times	3,360	101,367

*See Sources and Explanations in the front of the volume.

Television stations and affiliations

Baltimore	100%	WBAL	NBC
Baltimore	100%	WBFF	FOX
Baltimore	100%	WJZ	CBS
Baltimore	100%	WMAR	ABC
Baltimore	100%	WMPB	PBS
Baltimore	100%	WMPT	PBS
Baltimore	100%	WNUV	WB
Baltimore	100%	WUTB	UPN

Cable systems and subscribers
Comcast 170,158

Military installations, September 2001
Camp Fretterd Military Training Area, Reisterstown 811

Businesses and other major employers
Magellan Behavorial Health Services; Columbia; health maintenance organization 6,309

Northrop Grumman Systems Corp.; Linthicum Heights; infrared sensors 6,300

John Hopkins Hospital; Baltimore; charitable trust management 4,000

CBS Corp.; Linthicum Heights; commercial physical research 3,300

Fidelty and Guaranty Insurance; Baltimore; property damage insurance 3,000

Johns Hopkins Bayview Medical Center; Baltimore 3,000

Maryland Dept. of Transportation; Hanover 3,000

Abacus Corp.; Baltimore; employee leasing service 2,950

Greater Baltimore Medical Center Inc.; Baltimore 2,900

Johns Hopkins Hospital Inc.; Laurel 2,800

CareFirst of Maryland Inc.; Owings Mills; health maintenance organization 2,500

St. Agnes Healthcare Inc. Hospital; Baltimore 2,469

GlaxoSmithKline; Glen Burnie; medical laboratories 2,400

St. Joseph Medical Center; Baltimore 2,185

Arundel North Hospital Assn. Inc.; Glen Burnie 2,079

Loyola College in Maryland Inc.; Baltimore 2,050

Maryland Dept. of Transportation; Glen Burnie 2,000

Anne Arundel Medical Center Inc.; Annapolis 1,800

Sweetheart Cup Co.; Owings Mills; plastics kitchenware, tableware, houseware 1,800

ARINC Inc.; Annapolis; aviation, aeronautical engineering 1,500

Corvis Operations Inc.; Columbia; telephone and telegraph apparatus 1,400

Monumental Investment Corp.; Baltimore; mechanical contractor 1,400

Sheppard Pratt Health System; Baltimore; psychiatric hospitals 1,399

Zurich American Insurance Co.; Baltimore; fire, marine, casualty insurance 1,300

Wise Alloys; Linthicum Heights; aluminum sheet, plate, and foil 1,250

Broadway Services Inc.; Baltimore; hospital housekeeping 1,200

Eagle Alliance; Annapolis Junction; custom computer software design 1,200

Baltimore County; Baltimore; county government 1,114

District of Columbia Government; Laurel; juvenile correctional home 1,100

Humana Source Inc.; Glen Burnie; employee leasing service 1,000

Maryland Dept. of Natural Resources; Annapolis 1,000

Poole and Kent Corp.; Baltimore; mechanical contractor 1,000

Sage Dining Services Inc.; Baltimore; cafeteria 1,000

University System of Maryland; Baltimore 1,000

Verizon Communications Inc.; Davidsonville; telephone services 1,000

Ciena Corp.; Linthicum Heights; fiber optics communications equipment 964

International Paper Co.; Odenton; packing materials, plastics sheet 950

Northrop Grumman Corp.; Annapolis; airplanes 800

Quest Diagnostics Clinical Laboratories Inc.; Baltimore; medical laboratories   800

Rentokil Inc.; Baltimore; janitorial service   751

Initial Contract Services Inc.; Baltimore; janitorial service   750

U.S. Airways Inc.; Baltimore; aircraft servicing, repairing   733

Allegis Group Inc.; Hanover; temporary help service   700

Amerix Corp.; Columbia; process serving service   700

Arbitron Inc.; Columbia; market analysis: business/economic research   700

U.S. Foodservice Inc.; Severn; food supplier   700

Maryland Dept. of Public Safety and Corrections; Jessup   649

Illinois Fruit and Produce Corp.; Columbia; packaged frozen goods   640

American Pool Management Inc.; Owings Mills; swimming pool/hot tub service   600

Black and Decker Corp.; Glen Burnie; hardware   600

Honeywell Technology Solutions Inc.; Columbia; satellite earth stations   600

Laurel Racing Assn. LP; Laurel; thoroughbred horse racing   600

Micros Systems Inc.; Columbia; point-of-sale devices   600

Morgan State University; Crownsville   550

American Sugar Refining Co.; Baltimore; cane sugar refining   500

Arundel North Hospital Assn. Inc.; Baltimore   500

Brentwood BWI; Linthicum Heights; hotels and motels   500

Global Payments Inc.; Owings Mills; credit card service   500

Johns Hopkins Health System Corp.; Baltimore; management services   500

Host International Inc.; Glen Burnie; snack bar   500

Maryland Automobile Insurance Fund; Annapolis   500

Maryland Environmental Service; Annapolis   500

Nationwide Mutual Insurance Co.; Annapolis; insurance agents and brokers   500

Science Applications International Corp.; Columbia; computer integrated systems design   500

Maryland 4th District

Inner Prince George's County; part of Montgomery County

The only suburban district in the nation with a black majority, the 4th includes the eastern suburbs of Washington, D.C., in Prince George's County and a sizable swath of northern Montgomery County. Democrats have a strong hold on the district's largely middle-class, black population. (*See map p. 422.*)

The 4th's thriving economy is built on small business and the spillover of high-tech firms from Montgomery County and northern Virginia. The district includes major parts of the Prince George's County High Technology Triangle, home to companies such as Raytheon and anchored by the University of Maryland and NASA (both nearby in the 5th). Prince George's is a national leader for black business formation, home ownership, and education. Many of its residents are federal employees who have made the exodus from Washington. The 4th has the nation's highest percentage of government employees (29 percent).

But some of Prince George's County's low-income areas inside the Capital Beltway, which surrounds Washington, share the capital's problems of drug trafficking and violent crime.

Mapmakers altered the 4th in redistricting following the 2000 census to make the neighboring 8th District more Democratic. They exchanged some of the 4th's heavily minority neighborhoods in western Prince George's County and eastern Montgomery County for farther-out Montgomery County suburbs and exurbs, like Burtonsville, Olney, and Sandy Spring. Nearly 40 percent of the new 4th's population resides in Montgomery County, and 57 percent of residents are black.

Major Industry

Retail grocery, computers, recreation, technology.

Notable

Air Force One is kept at Andrews Air Force Base; FedEx Field is the home of the NFL's Washington Redskins.

Election Returns

	Republican		Democratic		Other	
President 2000	49,202	21.4%	176,780	76.8%	4,098	1.8%
House 2002	34,890	21.0%	131,644	79.0%	233	

District Profile

Population   662,062

Total area (square miles)   317.6
Land area (square miles)   315.2

Population per square mile   2,100.5

Counties (2000 population)
Montgomery (pt.)   251,258
Prince George's (pt.)   410,804

Cities and other areas over 10,000 (2000 population)
Aspen Hill CDP (pt.)   13,342
Camp Springs CDP (pt.)   14,915
Chillum CDP (pt.)   12,599
Coral Hills CDP   10,720
Fairland CDP   21,738
Forestville CDP   12,707
Fort Washington CDP (pt.)   11,717
Germantown CDP (pt.)   30,112
Greater Landover CDP   22,900
Greater Upper Marlboro CDP (pt.)   12,861
Hillcrest Heights CDP   16,359
Kettering CDP   11,008
Montgomery Village CDP (pt.)   17,649
Olney CDP   31,438
Oxon Hill-Glassmanor CDP   35,355
Silver Spring CDP (pt.)   46,910
Suitland-Silver Hill CDP   33,515
Walker Mill CDP   11,104
White Oak CDP (pt.)   17,618

Race and Hispanic or Latino origin*
White   27.6%
Black or African American   56.8%
American Indian or Alaska Native   0.2%
Asian   5.6%
Native Hawaiian or other Pacific Islander   0.0%
Some other race   0.2%
Hispanic or Latino origin   7.5%
Two or more races   2.0%

*As percentage of total population.

Ancestry*
English   4.0%   Polish   1.2%
German   5.3%   Subsaharan   3.5%
Irish   5.0%   USA/American   2.6%
Italian   2.3%   West Indian   2.0%

*As estimated percentage of total population.

Universities and colleges, 2000–2001 enrollment
National Labor College, Silver Spring   826
Prince George's Community College, Largo   11,563
Strayer University-Prince George's County, Suitland   1,022

Newspapers and circulation

	District circulation	Total circulation
USA Today*	4,092	1,674,376
Washington Post	79,191	779,632
Washington Times	9,013	101,367

*See Sources and Explanations in the front of the volume.

Television stations and affiliations
Washington, DC (Hagerstown)	100%	WBDC	WB
Washington, DC (Hagerstown)	100%	WDCA	UPN
Washington, DC (Hagerstown)	100%	WETA	PBS
Washington, DC (Hagerstown)	100%	WFPT	PBS
Washington, DC (Hagerstown)	100%	WHAG	NBC
Washington, DC (Hagerstown)	100%	WHSV	ABC
Washington, DC (Hagerstown)	100%	WHUT	PBS
Washington, DC (Hagerstown)	100%	WJAL	ABC
Washington, DC (Hagerstown)	100%	WJLA	ABC
Washington, DC (Hagerstown)	100%	WNVC	Independent
Washington, DC (Hagerstown)	100%	WNVT	PBS
Washington, DC (Hagerstown)	100%	WPXW	PAX
Washington, DC (Hagerstown)	100%	WRC	NBC
Washington, DC (Hagerstown)	100%	WTTG	FOX
Washington, DC (Hagerstown)	100%	WUSA	CBS
Washington, DC (Hagerstown)	100%	WVPY	PBS
Washington, DC (Hagerstown)	100%	WWPB	PBS
Washington, DC (Hagerstown)	100%	WWPX	PAX

Cable systems and subscribers
Comcast   73,970

Military installations, September 2001
Andrews Air Force Base, Camp Springs   10,205

Businesses and other major employers
U.S. National Oceanic and Atmospheric Admin.; Silver Spring   5,000
U.S. Postal Service; Capitol Heights   3,100
Dimensions Health Corp. Hospital; Hyattsville   2,500
U.S. Veterans Medical Center; Washington   1,700
Prince George's Community College Inc.; Upper Marlboro   1,700
Acterna Corp.; Germantown; electrical energy equipment   1,500
Prince George's County; Hyattsville; police dept.   1,400
Potomac Electric Power Co.; Upper Marlboro; electric services   1,200
Montgomery General Hospital Inc.; Olney   1,190
U.S. Coast Guard; Upper Marlboro   1,172
U.S. Internal Revenue Service; Lanham   1,000
U.S. National Oceanic and Atmospheric Admin.; Suitland   900
Winkler Pool Management; Hyattsville; swimming pool, nonmembership   700
Tru Green LP; Ashton; lawn and garden services   700
U.S. Centers for Disease Control and Prevention; Hyattsville   650
Knight Protective Services Inc.; Capitol Heights; private investigator   600
Giant Food Inc.; Landover; supermarkets   600
Seventh-Day Adventists Church; Silver Spring; religious organization   600
Orbital Sciences Corp.; Sterling; space vehicles   500
Wackenhut Corp.; Suitland; detective, armored car services   500
IIT Research Institute; Hyattsville; scientific research agency   500
Verizon Communications Inc.; Silver Spring; local telephone communications   500

Maryland 5th District

Outer Prince George's County; southern Maryland

The 5th includes part of Prince George's County, southern Anne Arundel County, and all of the three rapidly growing southern counties of Charles, Calvert, and St. Mary's. The mix of liberals in Prince George's County and conservative Democrats and Republicans throughout much of the rest of the district gives the 5th a broad array of political interests. *(See map. p. 422.)*

Prince George's County, which accounts for half the district's population—and nearly 60 percent of its registered Democrats—includes many liberal black communities and College Park, home of the University of Maryland's main campus. "P. G." County, as locals call it, was the only county in the 5th to back Bill Clinton in 1996, allowing Democrats to carry the district. In 2000 a growing black population helped Al Gore take largely exurban Charles County while winning the 5th handily. The GOP holds a slight registration edge among the Anne Arundel residents in the district, but Democrats have the advantage in every other county.

The district is enjoying a moderate amount of economic success due to the technology boom, both in Prince George's County and in Southern Maryland. Many residents and companies have left the Washington, D.C., metropolitan area for the southern counties, attracted by the abundance of land and the military presence. Its proximity to Washington gives the 5th the nation's second-highest percentage of government workers, behind the neighboring 4th District. The Tri-County area retains its southern rural character, however, with tobacco as its major crop and a conservative, but strongly Democratic tradition.

Major Industry
Defense, agriculture, technology.

Notable
NASA Goddard Space Flight Center; cliffs along the Chesapeake Bay in Calvert County contain more than 600 species of fossils; St. Mary's was the first capital of Maryland.

Election Returns

	Republican		Democratic		Other	
President 2000	101,056	41.1%	139,068	56.5%	5,871	2.4%
House 2002	60,758	30.6%	137,903	69.4%		

District Profile

Population 662,060

Total area (square miles) 1,509.1
Land area (square miles) 1,504.2

Population per square mile 440.1

Counties (2000 population)
Anne Arundel (pt.) 49,006
Calvert 74,563
Charles 120,546
Prince George's (pt.) 331,734
St. Mary's 86,211

Cities and other areas over 10,000 (2000 population)
Beltsville CDP 15,690
Bowie (pt.) 47,714
Chesapeake Ranch Estates-Drum Point CDP
(pt.) 11,503
Clinton CDP 26,064
College Park 24,657
Fort Washington CDP (pt.) 12,128
Glenn Dale CDP (pt.) 10,377
Greenbelt 21,456
Lanham-Seabrook CDP (pt.) 10,065
Laurel 19,960
Lexington Park CDP (pt.) 11,021
Rosaryville CDP 12,322
South Laurel CDP 20,479
St. Charles CDP 33,379
Waldorf CDP 22,312

Race and Hispanic or Latino origin*
White 60.4%
Black or African American 30.0%
American Indian or Alaska Native 0.4%
Asian 3.7%
Native Hawaiian or other Pacific Islander 0.0%
Some other race 0.2%
Hispanic or Latino origin 3.5%
Two or more races 1.9%

As percentage of total population.

Ancestry*

English 8.1%	Polish 1.9%
French 1.7%	Scotch-Irish 1.3%
German 10.5%	Scottish 1.3%
Irish 9.9%	Subsaharan 1.9%
Italian 3.9%	USA/American 5.2%

As estimated percentage of total population.

Universities and colleges, 2000–2001 enrollment
Bowie State University, Bowie 4,700
Capitol College, Laurel 787
Charles County Community College, La Plata 6,358
St. Mary's College of Maryland, St. Mary's City 1,547
University of Maryland-College Park, College Park 33,189
University of Maryland-University College, College Park 18,276
Washington Bible College-Capital Bible Seminary, Lanham 567

Newspapers and circulation

	District circulation	Total circulation
Annapolis Capital	9,435	45,981
Baltimore Sun	3,371	268,280
*USA Today**	6,653	1,674,376
Washington Post	65,036	779,632
Washington Times	12,146	101,367

See Sources and Explanations in the front of the volume.

Television stations and affiliations

Washington, DC (Hagerstown)	91%	WBDC	WB
Washington, DC (Hagerstown)	91%	WDCA	UPN
Washington, DC (Hagerstown)	91%	WETA	PBS
Washington, DC (Hagerstown)	91%	WFPT	PBS
Washington, DC (Hagerstown)	91%	WHAG	NBC
Washington, DC (Hagerstown)	91%	WHSV	ABC
Washington, DC (Hagerstown)	91%	WHUT	PBS
Washington, DC (Hagerstown)	91%	WJAL	ABC
Washington, DC (Hagerstown)	91%	WJLA	ABC
Washington, DC (Hagerstown)	91%	WNVC	Independent
Washington, DC (Hagerstown)	91%	WNVT	PBS
Washington, DC (Hagerstown)	91%	WPXW	PAX
Washington, DC (Hagerstown)	91%	WRC	NBC
Washington, DC (Hagerstown)	91%	WTTG	FOX
Washington, DC (Hagerstown)	91%	WUSA	CBS
Washington, DC (Hagerstown)	91%	WVPY	PBS
Washington, DC (Hagerstown)	91%	WWPB	PBS
Washington, DC (Hagerstown)	91%	WWPX	PAX
Baltimore	9%	WBAL	NBC
Baltimore	9%	WBFF	FOX
Baltimore	9%	WJZ	CBS
Baltimore	9%	WMAR	ABC
Baltimore	9%	WMPB	PBS
Baltimore	9%	WMPT	PBS
Baltimore	9%	WNUV	WB
Baltimore	9%	WUTB	UPN

Cable systems and subscribers
Comcast 53,312
Gans 20,672

Military installations, September 2001
Patuxent River Naval Air Test Center, Patuxent River 9,568
Indian Head Naval Ordnance Station, Indian Head 2,790
U.S. Adelphi Laboratory Center, Adelphi 1,122

Businesses and other major employers
National Aeronautics and Space Admin.; Greenbelt; space research and development 12,000
United Parcel Service Inc.; Laurel; parcel delivery 5,000

University System of Maryland; College Park   4,580

Simmons Investigative and Security Agency; Bowie; private investigator   3,500

John Sexton and Co.; Indian Head; plumbing, heating, air-conditioning   2,500

U.S. Treasury; Hyattsville   2,000

CBMC Capital Building Maintenance Corp.; College Park; janitorial service   1,800

Baltimore Gas and Electric Co.; Lusby; electric services   1,500

Maryland Hospitality Inc.; Greenbelt; welcoming services   1,500

Maryland Southern Hospital Inc.; Clinton   1,270

Calvert Cliffs Nuclear Power Plant Inc.; Lusby; electric power generation   1,200

District Photo Inc.; Beltsville; photofinishing laboratory   1,200

U.S. Agricultural Research Service; Beltsville   1,200

Swales and Associates Inc.; Beltsville; commercial physical research   1,100

Cadmus Communications Corp.; Greenbelt; color lithography   950

BAE Systems Applied Techonolgies Inc.; California; engineering services   900

Digex Inc.; Laurel; online service providers   900

Washington Suburban Sanitary Commission; Laurel water and sewer systems   900

Doctors' Hospital Inc.; Lanham   850

Beautify Professional Service Corp.; Greenbelt; janitorial service   800

Calvert County; Prince Frederick; county government   800

Compaq Federal; Greenbelt; minicomputers   800

Maryland Dept. of Natural Resources; Greenbelt   800

Matu Newsprint Inc.; Glenn Dale; waste materials recycling   800

Medstar Visiting Nurse Assn.; Beltsville; skilled nursing care facilities   800

Micros Systems Inc.; Beltsville; accounting equipment   800

Veridian Engineering; Lexington Park; commercial physical research   800

St. Mary's Hospital; Leonardtown   759

Calvert County Memorial Hospital; Prince Frederick   700

Dimensions Health Corp. Hospital; Laurel   700

Leonardtown School District; Leonardtown   700

Civista Medical Center; La Plata   643

Dyncorp; Lexington Park; aircraft servicing   610

Melwood Horticultural Training Center Inc.; Upper Marlboro; vocational training agency   600

NYLCare Health Plans; Greenbelt; health maintenance organization   600

Martex E-Technology; Laurel; computer software development   599

Eagan McAllister Associates Inc.; Lexington Park; engineering services   570

University System of Maryland; Bowie   570

St. Mary's County; Leonardtown; sheriff's office   550

Washington/Baltimore Cellular; Greenbelt; telephone communication   550

Calvert Memorial Hospital; Prince Frederick   500

Charles County; La Plata; sheriff's office   500

Dianne Nichols; Hollywood; medical doctor offices, clinics   500

Duron Inc.; Beltsville; paint   500

Honeywell Technology Solutions Inc.; Lanham; engineering services   500

Northrop Grumman Computer Systems Inc.; Greenbelt; aircraft   500

Maryland 6th District

North and west — Frederick, Hagerstown

The 6th reaches across the northern tier of the state from western Maryland to the Susquehanna River. It takes in all of Garrett, Allegany, Washington, Frederick, and Carroll Counties, as well as significant portions of Baltimore and Harford Counties and a small, exurban slice of Montgomery County. The 6th has a rural tradition and a conservative bent that often benefit the GOP. Though Frederick and Carroll Counties are thriving economically, the demise of old-line industry has left the Appalachian Mountain area struggling. Some local leaders have tried to promote the region as a destination for vacationers.

Frederick and Carroll are experiencing rapid growth from new residents escaping the city and inner suburbs and commuting to Baltimore and Washington, D.C. Carroll County, however, still has an agricultural economy and remains a Republican stronghold.

During redistricting following the 2000 census, northern portions of Baltimore and Harford Counties, where Republicans and old-line conservative Democrats reign, were taken out of the 2nd and folded into the district, bolstering the GOP's hold on the 6th.

The three western counties are less populous and remain solidly conservative. Washington County, with its strong manufacturing base, is the only one experiencing economic prosperity. With companies such as Kelly-Springfield closing their operations, Allegany and Garrett Counties both are struggling and have become dependent on tourism.

Major Industry

Manufacturing, technology, agriculture, tourism.

Notable

Camp David, the president's retreat; Whittaker Chambers's pumpkin patch in Westminster produced evidence for Richard M. Nixon during the Alger Hiss trial; Fort Detrick specializes in biomedical research and development.

Election Returns

	Republican		Democratic		Other	
President 2000	160,263	60.8%	95,282	36.2%	8,029	3.0%
House 2002	147,825	66.2%	75,575	33.8%	426	

District Profile

Population   662,060

Total area (square miles)   3,094.3
  Land area (square miles)   3,062.2

Population per square mile   216.2

Counties (2000 population)

Allegany	74,930	Garrett	29,846
Baltimore (pt.)	30,861	Harford (pt.)	29,326
Carroll	150,897	Montgomery (pt.)	19,000
Frederick	195,277	Washington	131,923

Cities and other areas over 10,000 (2000 population)

Ballenger Creek CDP   13,518
Cumberland   21,518
Damascus CDP   11,430
Eldersburg CDP   27,741
Frederick   52,767
Green Valley CDP   12,262
Hagerstown   36,687
Halfway CDP   10,065
Linganore-Bartonsville CDP   12,529
Westminster   16,731

Race and Hispanic or Latino origin*

White   91.5%
Black or African American   4.8%
American Indian or Alaska Native   0.2%
Asian   1.0%
Native Hawaiian or other Pacific Islander   0.0%
Some other race   0.1%
Hispanic or Latino origin   1.4%
Two or more races   0.9%

*As percentage of total population.

Ancestry*

Dutch	1.2%	Italian	4.0%
English	8.4%	Polish	2.2%
French	1.6%	Scotch-Irish	1.2%
German	20.1%	Scottish	1.7%
Irish	10.6%	USA/American	7.7%

*As estimated percentage of total population.

Universities and colleges, 2000–2001 enrollment

Allegany College of Maryland, Cumberland   2,592
Carroll Community College, Westminster   2,488
Frederick Community College, Frederick   4,343
Frostburg State University, Frostburg   5,348
Garrett Community College, McHenry   685
Hagerstown Business College, Hagerstown   776
Hagerstown Junior College, Hagerstown   2,516
Hood College, Frederick   1,702
Mount St. Mary's College, Emmitsburg   1,859
Western Maryland College, Westminster   3,146

Newspapers and circulation

	District circulation	Total circulation
Baltimore Sun	20,315	268,280
Carroll County Times	20,636	22,464
Cumberland Times-News	21,984	30,232
Frederick News-Post	38,311	41,146
Hagerstown Daily Mail	14,305	14,651
Hagerstown Morning Herald	12,917	21,015
Hagerstown Morning Herald /Daily Mail	27,222	35,668
Hartford County Aegis	8,860	59,155
*Oakland Republican**	8,022	8,818
*USA Today**	4,463	1,674,376
Washington Post	13,003	779,632
Washington Times	1,619	101,367

*See Sources and Explanations in the front of the volume.

Television stations and affiliations

Washington, DC (Hagerstown)	52%	WBDC
Washington, DC (Hagerstown)	52%	WDCA
Washington, DC (Hagerstown)	52%	WETA
Washington, DC (Hagerstown)	52%	WFPT
Washington, DC (Hagerstown)	52%	WHAG
Washington, DC (Hagerstown)	52%	WHSV
Washington, DC (Hagerstown)	52%	WHUT
Washington, DC (Hagerstown)	52%	WJAL
Washington, DC (Hagerstown)	52%	WJLA
Washington, DC (Hagerstown)	52%	WNVC
Washington, DC (Hagerstown)	52%	WNVT
Washington, DC (Hagerstown)	52%	WPXW
Washington, DC (Hagerstown)	52%	WRC
Washington, DC (Hagerstown)	52%	WTTG
Washington, DC (Hagerstown)	52%	WUSA
Washington, DC (Hagerstown)	52%	WVPY
Washington, DC (Hagerstown)	52%	WWPB
Washington, DC (Hagerstown)	52%	WWPX
Baltimore	27%	WBAL
Baltimore	27%	WBFF
Baltimore	27%	WJZ
Baltimore	27%	WMAR
Baltimore	27%	WMPB
Baltimore	27%	WMPT
Baltimore	27%	WNUV
Baltimore	27%	WUTB
Pittsburgh, PA	21%	KDKA
Pittsburgh, PA	21%	WCWB
Pittsburgh, PA	21%	WGPT
Pittsburgh, PA	21%	WNPA
Pittsburgh, PA	21%	WNPB
Pittsburgh, PA	21%	WPCB
Pittsburgh, PA	21%	WPGH
Pittsburgh, PA	21%	WPXI
Pittsburgh, PA	21%	WQED
Pittsburgh, PA	21%	WQEX
Pittsburgh, PA	21%	WTAE
Pittsburgh, PA	21%	WTOV
Pittsburgh, PA	21%	WWCP

Cable systems and subscribers

Adelphia   59,614
Antietam Cable TV   22,068
CableVision Communications   6,004
Charter   26,162
Tele-Media   6,587

Military installations, September 2001

Fort Detrick (Army), Frederick   6,118

Businesses and other major employers

Bechtel Corp.; Frederick; civil engineering   2,500
Sacred Heart Hospital of Sisters of Charity Inc.; Cumberland   2,500
Frederick Memorial Hospital Inc.; Frederick   2,000
National Institutes of Health; Frederick; public health programs   2,000
Wells Fargo Home Mortgage Inc.; Frederick; mortgage bankers   2,000
Integrated Health Services Inc.; Sparks; skilled nursing care facilities   1,900
Washington County Hospital Assn.; Hagerstown   1,737

Westvaco Corp.; Luke; paper mills   1,550

Becton Dickinson and Co.; Sparks; hypodermic needles and syringes   1,500

Frederick County; Frederick; county government   1,500

GEICO; Mount Airy; automobile insurance   1,500

JLG Industries Inc.; Hagerstown; construction machinery   1,500

Noxell Corp.; Cockeysville; cosmetics   1,500

First Nationwide Mortgage Corp.; Frederick; mortgage bankers   1,366

University System of Maryland; Frostburg   1,350

Science Applications International Corp.; Frederick; commercial physical research   1,300

Carroll County General Hospital Inc.; Westminster   1,100

Carroll County Med-Services Inc.; Westminster; nonresidential building operators   1,100

Maryland Dept. of Health and Mental Hygiene; Sykesville   1,000

Memorial Hospital and Medical Center of Cumberland Inc.; Cumberland   1,000

Monongahela Power Co.; Fairmont; electric power generation   1,000

PHH Vehicle Management Services; Hunt Valley; management services   1,000

Western Enterprise Fire Company; Hagerstown; fire dept.   1,000

Allegany College of Maryland; Cumberland   854

Asplundh Tree Expert Co.; Frostburg; shrub and tree services   800

Northrop Grumman Systems Corp.; Sykesville; inertial guidance systems   750

KCI Technologies; Cockeysville; engineering services   740

Alcoa Eastalco Works; Frederick; primary aluminum   730

CSX Transportation Inc.; Cumberland; freight cars and equipment   700

Carroll County; Westminster; county government   677

Black and Decker Corp.; Hampstead; power tools/accessories   600

C. M. Offray and Son Inc.; Hagerstown; narrow fabric mills   600

First USA Bank; Frederick; commercial bank   600

Maryland Dept. of Public Safety and Corrections; Hagerstown   600

Waterside Community Assn.; Frederick; homeowners' association   551

Allegheny County; Cumberland; county government   550

CyberRep Inc.; Frostburg; telemarketing services   540

LM Service Co.; Cumberland; pajamas and bedjackets   540

Washington County; Hagerstown; county government   506

Hunter Douglas Inc.; Cumberland; vertical blinds   500

First Data Corp.; Hagerstown; data processing   500

Maryland 7th District

Downtown Baltimore; part of Columbia

The 7th takes in both the low-income neighborhoods of West Baltimore and much of downtown, including the bustling retail center of the Inner Harbor. The 7th follows the black migration west to include Baltimore County's middle-class southwestern suburbs, and it also includes the bulk of Howard County, including the western portion of Columbia, a liberal-leaning planned community between Baltimore and Washington. *(See map p. 422.)*

The 7th's black majority (almost 60 percent) gives Democrats a distinct advantage in national and local contests through much of the district. But Republicans regularly win on the local level in the more rural parts of Howard County.

Efforts to improve Baltimore's poor neighborhoods have been slow, and urban problems, such as crime, drug abuse, teen pregnancy, and unemployment, have prompted many of the city's middle-class residents to head to the suburbs.

But the picture within the city is not all bleak. Many of Baltimore's most identifiable landmarks and businesses are in the 7th. The gentrified Mount Vernon area, home of the Walters Art Museum and the Peabody Institute, are within its boundaries. Farther north are Johns Hopkins University and the Baltimore Museum of Art.

In addition to the revitalized Inner Harbor waterfront, the old retail section west of the downtown hub still survives; Lexington Market and the Baltimore Arena are here. There are middle-class black communities along Liberty Heights Road in West Baltimore.

The University of Maryland, Baltimore County, in Catonsville and its adjacent research area are attracting technology firms.

Major Industry

Health care, manufacturing, technology.

Notable

The 7th's portion of Baltimore is home to NAACP national headquarters, author Edgar Allan Poe's grave site, and the National Aquarium.

Election Returns

	Republican		Democratic		Other	
President 2000	57,262	25.0%	166,410	72.5%	5,766	2.5%
House 2002	49,172	26.4%	137,047	73.6%	175	

District Profile

Population   662,060

Total area (square miles)   295.9
  Land area (square miles)   294.2

Population per square mile   2,250.4

Counties (2000 population)
  Baltimore (pt.)   119,642
  Baltimore City (pt.)   370,752
  Howard (pt.)   171,666

Cities and other areas over 10,000 (2000 population)
Baltimore (pt.)   370,752
Catonsville CDP   39,820
Columbia CDP (pt.)   47,943
Ellicott City CDP (pt.)   56,231
Lochearn CDP (pt.)   22,026
Milford Mill CDP (pt.)   18,120
North Laurel CDP   20,468
Savage-Guilford CDP (pt.)   10,395
Woodlawn CDP   36,079

Race and Hispanic or Latino origin*
White   34.2%
Black or African American   58.8%
American Indian or Alaska Native   0.2%
Asian   3.5%
Native Hawaiian or other Pacific Islander   0.0%
Some other race   0.2%
Hispanic or Latino origin   1.7%
Two or more races   1.3%

As percentage of total population.

Ancestry*
English 4.6%	Polish 1.7%
German 7.9%	Subsaharan 1.5%
Irish 6.0%	USA/American 2.2%
Italian 2.8%	

As estimated percentage of total population.

Universities and colleges, 2000–2001 enrollment
Baltimore City Community College, Baltimore   5,883
Baltimore International College, Baltimore   456
Catonsville Community College, Catonsville   8,850
Community College of Baltimore County, Catonsville   18,168
Coppin State College, Baltimore   3,890
Howard Community College, Columbia   5,452
Johns Hopkins University, Baltimore   17,774
Maryland Institute College of Art, Baltimore   1,747
Morgan State University, Baltimore   6,269
Sojourner-Douglas College, Baltimore   845
Traditional Acupuncture Institute, Columbia   206
University of Baltimore, Baltimore   4,674
University of Maryland-Baltimore, Baltimore   5,337
University of Maryland-Baltimore County, Baltimore   10,759

Newspapers and circulation
	District circulation	Total circulation
Baltimore Sun	63,302	268,280
Carroll County Times	1,060	22,464
*USA Today**	5,120	1,674,376
Washington Post	12,465	779,632
Washington Times	1,129	101,367

See Sources and Explanations in the front of the volume.

Television stations and affiliations
Baltimore	100%	WBAL	NBC
Baltimore	100%	WBFF	FOX
Baltimore	100%	WJZ	CBS
Baltimore	100%	WMAR	ABC
Baltimore	100%	WMPB	PBS
Baltimore	100%	WMPT	PBS
Baltimore	100%	WNUV	WB
Baltimore	100%	WUTB	UPN

Cable systems and subscribers
Comcast   247,126

Businesses and other major employers
U.S. Social Security Admin.; Baltimore   15,000
CBS Corp.; Baltimore; radar systems and equipment   10,000
Maryland Dept. of Human Resources; Baltimore   7,000
University System of Maryland; Baltimore   6,985
Johns Hopkins Hospital; Baltimore; hospital, medical school   6,900
City of Baltimore; Baltimore; air, water, solid waste management   6,000
University of Maryland Medical System Corp.; Baltimore   4,800
Johns Hopkins University; Baltimore   3,000
Maryland Dept. of Transportation; Baltimore   2,977
Maryland Dept. of Transportation; Baltimore   2,800
U.S. Centers for Medicare and Medicaid Services; Baltimore   2,700
Sinai Hospital of Baltimore Inc.; Baltimore   2,690
Union Memorial Hospital; Baltimore   2,025
Northrop Grumman Information Technology Inc.; Baltimore; radar systems and equipment   2,000
Maryland Dept. of Health and Mental Hygiene; Baltimore   1,874
U.S. Army Corps. of Engineers Baltimore   1,700
Baltimore Sun Co.; Baltimore; newspaper   1,650
Bon Secours Hospital Baltimore Inc.; Baltimore   1,500
Morgan State University; Baltimore   1,437
LifeBridge Health Inc.; Baltimore; management services   1,403
Mercy Medical Center; Baltimore   1,324
Charlestown Community Inc.; Baltimore; retirement hotel operation   1,300
Baltimore Gas and Electric Co.; Baltimore; electric generation and services   1,250
Kennedy Krieger Children's Hospital Inc.; Baltimore   1,200
U.S. Veterans Hospital; Baltimore   1,200
Verizon Maryland Inc.; Baltimore; telephone communication   1,200
Maryland General Hospital; Baltimore   1,100
Howard County General Hospital Inc.; Columbia   1,090
Aegon USA Inc.; Baltimore; life insurance   1,000
Lake Grove School; Baltimore   1,000
Legg Mason Inc.; Baltimore; security brokers, dealers, flotation companies   1,000
Maryland Dept. of Environment; Ellicott City   1,000
Deutsche Bank; Baltimore; security brokers, dealers   900
Stewart Information Services Corp.; Jessup; title insurance   900
T. Rowe Price Group Inc.; Baltimore; investment advisory service   850
Commercial Credit Plan Inc.; Baltimore; personal credit institutions   800
Giant Food Inc.; Jessup; warehousing   800

Shelter Group; Baltimore; apartment building operators 800

University Physicians Inc.; Baltimore; medical clinic 800

Sysco Food Services; Jessup; packaged frozen goods 787

Alpharma USPD Inc.; Baltimore; pharmaceuticals 700

Coleman and Associates Enterprises Inc.; Columbia; computer integrated systems design 695

Baltimore County Community College; Baltimore 657

Wackenhut Corp.; Baltimore; security guard service 650

Advanced Imaging Partners Inc.; Baltimore; radiologist 600

Pimlico Racing Assn. Inc.; Baltimore; horse race track 600

Renaissance Hotel Group; Baltimore; hotels 600

Johns Hopkins Medical Services Corp.; Baltimore; health maintenance organization 570

City of Baltimore; Baltimore; government finance 555

Ainet Corp.; Columbia; online service providers 550

Goodell DeVries Leech and Dann; Baltimore; law office 550

Maryland Dept. of Juvenile Service; Baltimore 530

Peabody Institute of Johns Hopkins University; Baltimore 520

Burns International Security Services Corp.; Baltimore; security guard service 518

Maryland Dept. of Public Safety and Corrections; Jessup 506

Assn. of Universities for Research in Astronomy Inc.; Baltimore; space research and technology 500

City of Baltimore; Baltimore; city management 500

Greenebaum Cancer Center; Baltimore 500

Outlet Square of Atlanta Inc.; Columbia; management services 500

RWD Technologies; Columbia; computer consulting services 500

VNA Management Services; Baltimore; visiting nurse service 500

Zurich American Insurance Co.; Baltimore; surety insurance bonding 500

Maryland 8th District

Parts of Montgomery County — Bethesda, Gaithersburg

The 8th contains wealthy Montgomery County suburbs northwest of Washington, D.C., such as Bethesda, Chevy Chase, and Potomac, as well as less-affluent suburbs in eastern Montgomery and western Prince George's County. It also includes rural areas northwest of Potomac and the Interstate 270 technology corridor, a hotbed for high-tech and biotechnology companies that runs through Rockville and Gaithersburg. *(See map p. 422.)*

The district was redrawn to elect a Democrat in redistricting following the 2000 census. Mapmakers removed some GOP-leaning areas in northern Montgomery County and added liberal Takoma Park, as well as heavily black and Hispanic neighborhoods in western Prince George's County.

Government is the dominant employer in the 8th, where federal agencies abound and Rockville is the Montgomery County seat. The large contingent of educated professionals supports a thriving economy that is bolstered by a wide array of big-name business interests, including Lockheed Martin, Marriott, and IBM.

Potomac, in the western part of the district, is known for its horse farms and expensive estates. In the far west, officials struggle to preserve an agricultural heritage.

Major Industry

Government, technology, services, retail.

Notable

Author F. Scott Fitzgerald is buried in Rockville.

Election Returns

	Republican		Democratic		Other	
President 2000	84,088	31.0%	177,475	65.5%	9,382	3.5%
House 2002	103,587	47.5%	112,788	51.7%	1,738	0.8%

District Profile

Population 662,060

Total area (square miles) 306.7
Land area (square miles) 297.0

Population per square mile 2,229.2

Counties (2000 population)
Montgomery (pt.) 603,083
Prince George's (pt.) 58,977

Cities and other areas over 10,000 (2000 population)
Aspen Hill CDP (pt.) 36,886
Bethesda CDP 55,277
Chillum CDP (pt.) 21,653
Colesville CDP 19,810
Gaithersburg (pt.) 52,613
Germantown CDP (pt.) 25,307
Langley Park CDP (pt.) 13,969
Montgomery Village CDP (pt.) 20,402
North Bethesda CDP 38,610
North Potomac CDP 23,044
Potomac CDP 44,822
Rockville (pt.) 47,388
Silver Spring CDP (pt.) 29,630
Takoma Park 17,299
Wheaton-Glenmont CDP 57,694

Race and Hispanic or Latino origin*
White 56.1%
Black or African American 16.4%
American Indian or Alaska Native 0.2%
Asian 10.9%
Native Hawaiian or other Pacific Islander 0.0%
Some other race 0.3%
Hispanic or Latino origin 13.7%
Two or more races 2.4%

As percentage of total population.

Ancestry*

English 6.6%	Italian 3.5%
French 1.6%	Polish 2.5%
German 8.2%	Russian 3.1%
Irish 8.0%	Scotch-Irish 1.1%

| Scottish | 1.6% | USA/American | 3.4% |
| Subsaharan | 2.9% | West Indian | 1.6% |

As estimated percentage of total population.

Universities and colleges, 2000–2001 enrollment
Columbia Union College, Takoma Park   1,030

Montgomery College-Germantown, Germantown 3,558

Montgomery College-Rockville, Rockville   20,923

Montgomery College-Takoma Park, Takoma Park 4,306

Ultrasound Diagnostic School, Silver Spring   225

Uniformed Services University of the Health Sciences, Bethesda   843

Newspapers and circulation

	District circulation	Total circulation
*USA Today**	4,573	1,674,376
Washington Post	113,650	779,632
Washington Times	9,097	101,367

See Sources and Explanations in the front of the volume.

Television stations and affiliations
Washington, DC (Hagerstown)	100%	WBDC	WB
Washington, DC (Hagerstown)	100%	WDCA	UPN
Washington, DC (Hagerstown)	100%	WETA	PBS
Washington, DC (Hagerstown)	100%	WFPT	PBS
Washington, DC (Hagerstown)	100%	WHAG	NBC
Washington, DC (Hagerstown)	100%	WHSV	ABC
Washington, DC (Hagerstown)	100%	WHUT	PBS
Washington, DC (Hagerstown)	100%	WJAL	ABC
Washington, DC (Hagerstown)	100%	WJLA	ABC
Washington, DC (Hagerstown)	100%	WNVC	Independent
Washington, DC (Hagerstown)	100%	WNVT	PBS
Washington, DC (Hagerstown)	100%	WPXW	PAX
Washington, DC (Hagerstown)	100%	WRC	NBC
Washington, DC (Hagerstown)	100%	WTTG	FOX
Washington, DC (Hagerstown)	100%	WUSA	CBS
Washington, DC (Hagerstown)	100%	WVPY	PBS
Washington, DC (Hagerstown)	100%	WWPB	PBS
Washington, DC (Hagerstown)	100%	WWPX	PAX

Cable systems and subscribers
Comcast   62,322

Military installations, September 2001
National Naval Medical Center, Bethesda   5,768

Naval Surface Warfare Center, Bethesda   1,880

Businesses and other major employers
U.S. National Institutes of Health; Bethesda   13,000

U.S. Dept. of Health and Human Services; Rockville 7,200

Adventist Healthcare Inc. Hospital; Rockville   4,119

National Institute of Standards and Technology; Gaithersburg   3,500

Council for Scientific and Industrial Research; Bethesda; research services   3,000

Marriott International Inc.; Washington; hotels and motels   3,000

Marriott Worldwide Corp.; Bethesda; hotel or motel management   3,000

U.S. Dept. of Energy; Silver Spring   3,000

Red Coats Inc.; Bethesda; building cleaning   2,700

GE Global Exchange Services Inc.; Gaithersburg; online service providers   2,500

Westat Inc.; Rockville; market analysis   2,300

Holy Cross Hospital of Silver Spring Inc.; Silver Spring 2,200

U.S. Nuclear Regulatory Commission; Rockville   2,200

Naval Medical Research Center; Silver Spring; research institute   1,800

U.S. National Ocean Service; Rockville   1,800

U.S. Secretary of Defense; Bethesda; service academy 1,750

BAE Systems Applied Technologies Inc.; Rockville; computer systems analysis/design   1,700

Montgomery Community College; Rockville; community college   1,700

Suburban Hospital Inc.; Bethesda   1,550

GEICO; Chevy Chase; insurance agents   1,500

U.S. Postal Service; Gaithersburg   1,200

Montgomery County; Rockville; police dept.   1,154

Aspen Systems Corp.; Rockville; data processing 1,000

Manugistics Inc.; Washington Grove; management services   1,000

U.S. National Institutes of Health; Rockville   1,000

Hughes Network Systems Inc.; Germantown; communication network services   959

U.S. Food and Drug Admin.; Rockville   950

Montgomery County; Rockville; county government 900

U.S. National Weather Service; Silver Spring   825

Hebrew Home of Greater Washington; Rockville; skilled nursing care facilities   800

John J. Kirlin Inc.; Rockville; mechanical contractors 800

Mid-Atlantic Medical Services Inc.; Rockville; insurance agents and brokers   800

Montgomery County Board of Education; Rockville 750

University System of Maryland; Hyattsville   750

Thomson Financial Inc.; Rockville; investment advice; 677

Alpha Scientific Inc.; Rockville; scientific and engineering equipment   600

International Business Machines Corp.; Bethesda; office equipment   600

Kaiser Foundation Health Plan of Mid-Atlantic States Inc.; Rockville; health maintenance organization 600

Wackenhut Corp.; Takoma Park; protective services, guard   600

Celera Genomics Corp.; Rockville; scientific research agency   590

Asbury Methodist Village Inc.; Gaithersburg; nursing home   575

Human Genome Sciences Inc.; Rockville; diagnostic substances   575

Worldwide Parking Inc.; Rockville; automobile parking 570

ACS Government Services Inc.; Rockville; computer consulting services   550

National Assn. of Securities Dealers Inc.; Rockville; data processing   550

Nordstrom Inc.; Bethesda; family clothing stores   540

Gali Service Industries Inc.; Bethesda; industrial, commercial cleaning services   500

Hughes Electronics Corp.; Gaithersburg; radio/TV communications equipment   500

Manugistics Group Inc.; Rockville; computer software development, applications   500

Navy Exchange Service Command; Bethesda; Army-Navy goods stores   500

Oracle Corp.; Bethesda; prepackaged software   500

Raytheon E-Systems Inc.; Hyattsville; airborne radio communications equipment   500

Sears Roebuck and Co. Inc.; Gaithersburg; department stores   500

Thomson Financial Inc.; Bethesda; information retrieval services   500

U.S. Food and Drug Admin.; Bethesda   500

U.S. National Imagery and Mapping Agency; Bethesda 500

U.S. Postal Service; Rockville   500

MASSACHUSETTS

Districts established February 11, 2002, for elections first held in 2002.

10 members

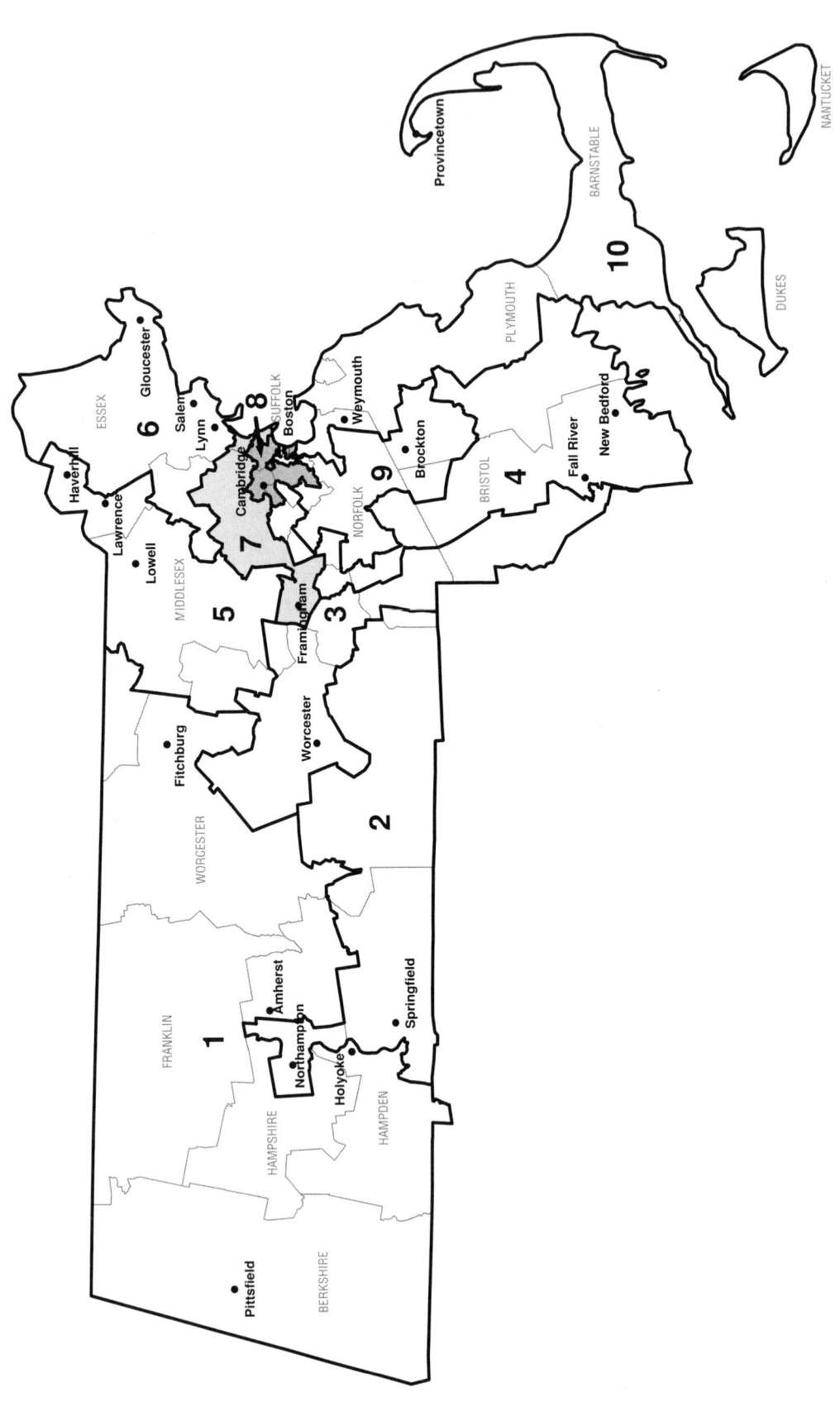

Massachusetts

When the Democratic Party announced it would hold its 2004 National Convention in Boston, many were surprised to learn that neither major party had ever held its presidential nominating event in the city before. Boston has been one of the nation's leading commercial and political centers as far back as the Revolution and anchors its seventh largest metropolitan area today. Residents and tabloid headlines still call it "The Hub," a reference to Oliver Wendell Holmes' paean to Boston as "The Hub of the Universe."

On the other hand, some were surprised that Boston was chosen at all by this party at this particular moment. Why would the Democrats come to Massachusetts at a time when they needed desperately to reach out to states in between their bicoastal bases of support? The Bay State is as much a symbol of eastern establishment liberalism as can be imagined.

Surely, the choice was made partly in gratitude. No state has been friendlier to Democratic nominees in recent decades. The Massachusetts congressional delegation consists of two Democratic senators (who have been elected and reelected eleven times) and a ten-seat House contingent that was all Democratic as of 2003 with no change in sight (half the ten incumbents went without GOP challengers in 2002). No Republican had served the state in the House since 1996, making this by far the largest one-party state delegation in Congress.

Surely having the convention here is not an attempt to capture this state's 12 electoral votes, which are as close to automatic for a Democratic nominee as any in the nation. The state even went for George McGovern in 1972, when 49 other states preferred Richard Nixon.

Of course, the GOP has not been as invisible as these examples suggest. While GOP registration is down below 15 percent, roughly half of Massachusetts' voters now register with neither major party. Among these voters the GOP has found support in recent years for its gubernatorial candidates, perhaps as brakes on an otherwise single-party system. When Mitt Romney, a Mormon businessperson, won the governorship in 2002, it was the fourth straight win for the GOP, which has held the office since the 1990 retirement of Michael Dukakis. Two of those wins belonged to William Weld, the embodiment of the Ivy ideal. Weld's liberal views on social issues helped him win reelection in 1994 with 70 percent of the vote but were not enough when he challenged the incumbent Democratic senator John Kerry in 1996.

The GOP has also been able to benefit at times from a Democratic schism over social issues such as abortion. Seven of the ten House members as of 2003 were Catholics. The most interesting contests here are often primaries, where social conservatives from traditional Irish and Italian parishes clash with social liberals, often based in the state's teeming campus culture.

About 35 percent of the state's residents (25 and older) have a bachelor's degree or better, which is tops in the country. The state also has the highest number of physicians per 100,000 residents. But then this is the home of Harvard and the Massachusetts Institute of Technology, of Tufts and Boston University, and of dozens of liberal arts colleges from Amherst to Williams to Wellesley.

This more-than-critical mass of higher learning has helped the state survive downturns in its basic industries and industrial towns and thrive in the age of high-tech and financial services. That is why the state is now better known for Route 128, the high-tech corridor, than the classic factory towns of Quincy, Waltham, Lawrence, and Lowell. It is why businesspeople now think of Worcester for computers and biotech, not machine shops and spools of thread. That was a big part of the "Massachusetts Miracle" that helped raise Dukakis to national leadership in the Democratic Party in the 1980s (and to drag him down later on).

But now that the high-tech industry has survived a pair of boom-and-bust cycles, it is proving itself a boon for the long haul. This keeps the state's unemployment numbers down below the national average and its real estate values far higher. As of 2000, the state had the third highest personal income per capita and the fourth largest gross state product. While most of the wealth is in the Boston metro area, the Census Bureau now considers the Boston-Worcester-Lawrence metroplex to extend through half the state (and over the state line into New Hampshire), with less than a tenth of its total population in the city of Boston proper. It is easy to forget the portion of the state west of the Connecticut River, where Springfield and Pittsfield largely support a congressional district along with farmers producing beef cattle, dairy, vegetables, and, at one time, a little tobacco.

The high-tech era has also helped Massachusetts renew its reputation for welcoming new residents from around the country and the world, people selected by the competitive academic institutions and people needed to do the work longer-time residents no longer want. The state was long dominated by its old-line WASPs, epitomized by the Henry Cabot Lodge dynasty, and this oligarchy is still able to elect governors now and then. But the center of political gravity shifted to the immigrants in the Depression years and has remained there since.

Massachusetts has never had large numbers of African Americans (just 4.6 percent of the voting-age population in 2000). But lately the state has begun to register substantial populations with Hispanic roots (5.6 percent of the voting-age population) and Asian descent (3.7 percent). Higher rates of immigration will be necessary for the state to catch up to national growth rates, because the existing population is aging. In 2000 Massachusetts was twelfth in residents 65 and older, forty-eighth in residents aged 17 and under.

Without some change in these demographics, Massachusetts will see further shrinkage in its congressional delegation. It was among the Big Three (with Virginia and Pennsylvania) when the first Congress met in 1789, in part because its state lines then included the territory that would later break off as the state of Maine. In the middle 1800s, the Massachusetts numbers were surpassed by those of burgeoning midwestern states. In the watershed reapportionment of 1930, Massachusetts had 15 seats. In 1960, the year John F. Kennedy won the presidency, the census downgraded the state to just 12 seats, and after the 1990 count Massachusetts was down to ten seats and no longer among the top ten. Now the challenge is to stay in double digits after the census of 2010.

Redistricting was not a problem of the 2000 census. All the incumbents were from one party, all were seeking reelection and all had been reelected most recently with at least 68 percent of the vote. The main conflicts in such situations arise among rivals in the legislature who want to shape a district friendly to their future ambitions.

Table 1   Population

District	Population	Population under 18	Voting-age population	Median age	Male*	Female*
1	634,479	153,625	480,854	37.1	48.5	51.5
2	634,444	162,196	472,248	36.6	47.8	52.2
3	634,585	161,815	472,770	36.2	48.5	51.5
4	634,624	152,082	482,542	37.1	47.6	52.4
5	635,326	173,586	461,740	35.7	49.0	51.0
6	636,554	154,112	482,442	38.6	48.1	51.9
7	634,287	130,150	504,137	37.8	47.6	52.4
8	634,835	117,175	517,660	30.0	48.6	51.4
9	634,062	150,719	483,343	37.0	48.1	51.9
10	635,901	144,604	491,297	40.1	48.0	52.0
State	6,349,097	1,500,064	4,849,033	36.5	48.2	51.8

*As percentage of total population.

Table 2   Voting-Age Persons by Race/Hispanic or Latino Origin

District	White*	Black or African American*	American Indian or Alaska Native*	Asian*	Other or multirace*	Hispanic or Latino*
1	90.8	1.5	0.2	1.6	1.0	4.8
2	85.4	4.9	0.2	1.3	1.0	7.2
3	88.1	2.3	0.2	3.0	1.5	4.9
4	88.8	1.9	0.2	3.2	3.2	2.7
5	82.3	1.7	0.1	4.8	1.2	9.9
6	91.4	1.7	0.1	2.3	1.0	3.6
7	85.2	3.0	0.1	5.4	2.1	4.2
8	54.6	18.7	0.2	8.6	4.5	13.4
9	81.8	7.1	0.2	3.6	3.5	3.9
10	92.8	1.5	0.3	2.7	1.5	1.1
State	83.9	4.6	0.2	3.7	2.0	5.6

*As percentage of voting-age population.

Table 3   Voting-Age Population by Age Groups

District	18 to 24*	25 to 44*	45 to 64*	Over 64*
1	13.8	37.4	30.4	18.4
2	11.6	40.1	30.0	18.4
3	11.1	42.3	29.2	17.4
4	11.5	39.9	30.5	18.1
5	10.4	43.7	30.7	15.2
6	9.0	40.0	32.0	19.0
7	10.3	41.8	28.3	19.5
8	22.9	45.2	20.5	11.4
9	10.3	41.6	29.5	18.5
10	7.8	38.1	32.4	21.7
State	12.0	41.0	29.3	17.7

*As percentage of voting-age population.

Table 4   Income and Occupation

District	Median family income	Families in poverty*	White collar†	Blue collar†	Service†	Farm†
1	$52,561	7.3	59.8	23.9	16.0	0.4
2	$54,851	8.2	60.6	24.1	15.1	0.2
3	$61,768	6.6	65.5	20.6	13.7	0.1
4	$65,100	6.2	67.6	19.2	12.8	0.3
5	$67,846	6.7	66.9	20.9	12.0	0.1
6	$70,858	4.3	69.7	17.2	12.8	0.3
7	$69,501	4.6	72.9	14.3	12.7	0.1
8	$42,246	15.6	70.6	12.4	16.9	0.1
9	$67,060	5.4	68.9	17.3	13.7	0.1
10	$63,464	4.1	66.7	18.1	14.9	0.4
State	$61,664	6.7	67.0	18.7	14.1	0.2

*As percentage of all families.   †As percentage of employed workers 16 years and over.

Table 5   Education: School Years Completed

District	Less than grade 9*	Grades 9–12 no diploma*	High school diploma no college*	Some college*	College bachelor's degree or higher*
1	5.2	10.4	32.2	26.8	25.4
2	6.4	11.8	32.1	26.6	23.1
3	6.9	10.6	26.7	24.9	30.8
4	8.5	9.4	23.8	21.4	36.9
5	6.5	9.9	26.5	23.5	33.6
6	4.0	7.6	27.4	25.8	35.1
7	4.4	8.0	26.1	22.0	39.5
8	9.9	11.6	21.5	17.1	39.8
9	4.3	8.8	28.2	24.9	33.8
10	2.4	6.8	28.0	29.4	33.5
State	5.8	9.4	27.3	24.3	33.2

*As percentage of persons age 25 and over.

Table 6   Housing and Residential Patterns

District	Median home value	Owner occupied*	Renter occupied*	Urban†	Rural†
1	$125,500	65.5	34.5	69.3	30.7
2	$129,600	65.8	34.2	84.8	15.2
3	$162,400	62.9	37.1	93.4	6.6
4	$183,500	65.1	34.9	88.2	11.8
5	$194,600	67.2	32.8	93.5	6.5
6	$231,100	68.9	31.1	94.9	5.1

District	Median home value	Owner occupied*	Renter occupied*	Urban†	Rural†
7	$243,800	57.1	42.9	99.5	0.5
8	$232,900	28.3	71.7	100.0	0.0
9	$199,200	64.4	35.6	98.4	1.6
10	$191,400	73.6	26.4	92.2	7.8
State	$182,800	61.7	38.3	91.4	8.6

*As percentage of occupied housing units.   †As percentage of total population.

Massachusetts 1st District

West — Pittsfield, Leominster, Westfield

The oranges of autumn, the whites of winter, and the greens of spring and summer attract vacationers to the 1st. The Berkshire Mountains of western Massachusetts once protected Native Americans from encroaching whites. But 300 years later, the area serves as home to a shrinking blue-collar and stable rural population.

Tourist areas include the kind of serene New England towns depicted in films, books, and Norman Rockwell paintings. Tanglewood, the summer home of the Boston Symphony Orchestra, also attracts jazz and chamber music fans to its outdoor theater in Lenox. The Yankee Candle Company, one of the largest manufacturers of scented candles, is based in South Deerfield.

After decades as a dominant textile mill area and the world's top plastics producer, factory closures and downsizing decimated the region during the recession of the late 1980s and early 1990s. Pittsfield and Fitchburg suffered the most. While the economy of Pittsfield is diversifying, General Electric reduced its defense-related workforce there from 11,000 in the 1980s to 2,000 a decade later. A strong retail and plastics industry has spurred growth in Leominster, a western outgrowth of the Boston suburbs that sits on the crossing of two major highways at the eastern edge of the district.

Once a Republican stronghold, the 1st was held by liberal GOP representative Silvio Conte for more than three decades until his death in 1991. Some rural areas east of Interstate 91 support Republicans, but the sparse population is overwhelmed by Democratic union voters in the northeast and university liberals around Amherst, where the state's flagship university is located. Seven of the 13 cities and towns in which 2002 Democratic gubernatorial nominee Shannon O'Brien received at least two-thirds of the vote are in the 1st.

Major Industry
Plastics, paper, tourism, higher education.

Notable
John Chapman, known as Johnny Appleseed, was born in Leominster; NAACP founder W. E. B. DuBois was born in Great Barrington in 1868.

Election Returns

	Republican		Democratic		Other	
President 2000	88,690	33.2%	150,418	56.4%	27,700	10.4%
House 2002	66,061	32.4%	137,841	67.6%	117	

District Profile

Population   634,479

Total area (square miles)   3,191.6
Land area (square miles)   3,101.1

Population per square mile   204.6

Counties (2000 population)
Berkshire   134,953   Hampshire (pt.)   101,284
Franklin   71,535   Middlesex (pt.)   23,185
Hampden (pt.)   123,424   Worcester (pt.)   180,098

Cities and other areas over 10,000 (2000 population)
Amherst Center CDP   17,050
Easthampton   15,994
Fitchburg   39,102
Gardner   20,770
Greenfield CDP   13,716
Holyoke   39,838
Leominster   41,303
North Adams   14,681
Pittsfield   45,793
Westfield   40,072
West Springfield CDP   27,899

Race and Hispanic or Latino origin*
White   88.8%
Black or African American   1.6%
American Indian or Alaska Native   0.2%
Asian   1.7%
Native Hawaiian or other Pacific Islander   0.0%
Some other race   0.1%
Hispanic or Latino origin   6.3%
Two or more races   1.2%

*As percentage of total population.

Ancestry*
English   9.0%   Polish   6.8%
Fr. Canadian   6.0%   Scotch-Irish   1.1%
French   10.7%   Scottish   2.0%
German   5.7%   Swedish   1.3%
Irish   13.5%   USA/American   3.0%
Italian   8.5%

*As estimated percentage of total population.

Universities and colleges, 2000–2001 enrollment
Amherst College, Amherst   1,695
Berkshire Community College, Pittsfield   2,494
Fitchburg State College, Fitchburg   5,715
Greenfield Community College, Greenfield   2,277
Hampshire College, Amherst   1,175
Holyoke Community College, Holyoke   5,754
Massachusetts College of Liberal Arts, North Adams   1,590
Mount Wachusett Community College, Gardner   3,367
Simons Rock College of Bard, Great Barrington   387
University of Massachusetts-Amherst, Amherst   24,416
Westfield State College, Westfield   5,005
Williams College, Williamstown   2,066

Newspapers and circulation

	District circulation	Total circulation
Berkshire Eagle	30,088	31,162
Boston Globe	6,654	465,248
Boston Herald	5,242	257,071
Daily Hampshire Gazette	11,088	19,522
Fitchburg Sentinel & Enterprise	16,206	16,718
Gardner News	6,671	6,704
Greenfield Recorder	13,877	14,452
Lowell Sun	1,471	51,598
North Adams Transcript	6,545	6,982
Springfield Union-News	29,334	89,595
*USA Today**	6,095	1,674,376
Worcester Telegram-Gazette	15,038	104,076

See Sources and Explanations in the front of the volume.

Television stations and affiliations

Springfield-Holyoke	47%	WGBY	PBS
Springfield-Holyoke	47%	WGGB	ABC
Springfield-Holyoke	47%	WWLP	NBC
Albany-Schenectady-Troy, NY	30%	WCDC	ABC
Albany-Schenectady-Troy, NY	30%	WEWB	WB
Albany-Schenectady-Troy, NY	30%	WMHT	PBS
Albany-Schenectady-Troy, NY	30%	WRGB	CBS
Albany-Schenectady-Troy, NY	30%	WTEN	ABC
Albany-Schenectady-Troy, NY	30%	WXXA	FOX
Albany-Schenectady-Troy, NY	30%	WYPX	PAX
Boston (Manchester)	23%	WBPX	PAX
Boston (Manchester)	23%	WBZ	CBS
Boston (Manchester)	23%	WCVB	ABC
Boston (Manchester)	23%	WDPX	PAX
Boston (Manchester)	23%	WEKW	PBS
Boston (Manchester)	23%	WFXT	FOX
Boston (Manchester)	23%	WGBH	PBS
Boston (Manchester)	23%	WGBX	PBS
Boston (Manchester)	23%	WHDH	NBC
Boston (Manchester)	23%	WLVI	WB
Boston (Manchester)	23%	WMFP	Independent
Boston (Manchester)	23%	WMUR	ABC
Boston (Manchester)	23%	WNDS	Independent
Boston (Manchester)	23%	WPXB	Independent
Boston (Manchester)	23%	WPXG	PAX
Boston (Manchester)	23%	WSBK	UPN
Boston (Manchester)	23%	WUNI	Univision
Boston (Manchester)	23%	WWDP	Independent
Boston (Manchester)	23%	WYDN	Independent

Cable systems and subscribers
Adelphia   21,912
Charter   14,986
Comcast   103,890
Time Warner   26,183

Military installations, September 2001
Barnes Municipal Airport (Air National Guard), Westfield   958

Businesses and other major employers
HealthAlliance Hospital Inc.; Leominster   3,000
University of Massachusetts; Amherst   2,500
City of Holyoke; Holyoke; city government   2,000
Frito-Lay Inc.; Lunenburg; snack foods   2,000
General Dynamics Defense Systems Inc.; Pittsfield; search and detection systems   1,800
Resource Management Inc.; Fitchburg; employee leasing service   1,800
Simplex Time Recorder Co.; Westminster; clocks and time recording devices   1,500
Berkshire Medical Center Inc.; Pittsfield   1,375
Valley Health System Inc. Hospital; Holyoke   1,209
City of Westfield; Westfield; city government   1,200
L. S. Starrett Co.; Athol; precision measuring tools   1,200
Franklin Medical Center; Greenfield   1,163
Crane and Co.; Dalton; business form paper   1,000
General Electric Co.; Fitchburg; turbines and turbine generators   1,000
Massachusetts National Guard; Westfield   1,000
Hillcrest Foundation Inc. Hospital; Pittsfield   980
Williams College; Williamstown   950
AAA South Central New England; Leominster; insurance agents and brokers   900
Yankee Candle Co.; South Deerfield; candles   900
HealthAlliance Hospitals Inc.; Fitchburg   800
McCormick and Co.; Easthampton; unsupported plastic tubes   800
Tubed Products Inc.; Easthampton; plastic containers   800
Holyoke Hospital Inc.; Holyoke   772
Canyon Ranch in the Berkshires; Lenox; resort hotel   700
Henry Heywood Memorial Hospital; Gardner   680
Fitchburg State College; Fitchburg   600
Noble Health Systems Inc.; Westfield; hospital management   600
Amherst College; Amherst   577
Northfield Mount Hermon School Inc.; Northfield   525
Ames Department Stores Inc.; Westfield   500
Greenfield Community College; Greenfield   500

Massachusetts 2nd District

South central — Springfield, Chicopee, Northampton

The rolling hills and thick forests of the 2nd extend along the state's southern border from Springfield and Northampton in the west to Bellingham in the east. Springfield dwarfs all other communities in the 2nd; small, rural towns and intermittent farms fill out the rest of south-central Massachusetts.

Much of Springfield's economic success in the 1990s was tied to its history as a hub for inventions, although the region's future rests with the insurance and health care industries—most notably Mass Mutual and Baystate Health System—which have replaced some of the city's shrinking manufacturing base. Service and government jobs, some of which are generated by Chicopee's Westover Air Reserve Base, are important to the region's economy. The construction of a new home for the Basketball Hall of Fame and restoration of the civic center should bring more visitors to Springfield.

Hispanics—many of whom moved to the 2nd in the 1950s to work in the tobacco fields—once gravitated to Springfield's North End but are now more dispersed through the city. Most African Americans live near the city's center.

Residents in and around Springfield, many of whom are blue-collar and Irish Catholic, vote Democratic and dominate the district's elections. Smith College produces a strongly liberal vote in Northampton, which gave 2000 Green Party presidential nominee Ralph Nader a greater share of the vote than Republican George W. Bush. Despite the district's strong Democratic lean, some Republicans can be competitive, particularly among small-town and rural voters. Mitt Romney, the 2002 GOP gubernatorial nominee, narrowly won the 2nd.

Major Industry
Insurance, health care, higher education, tourism.

Notable
Important local inventions or "firsts" include the U.S. Armory (1794), Pullman rail car (1850), monkey wrench (1854), and the gasoline-powered car (1893).

Election Returns

	Republican		Democratic		Other	
President 2000	89,775	34.6%	150,148	57.9%	19,588	7.5%
House 2002			153,387	99.1%	1,341	0.9%

District Profile

Population   634,444

Total area (square miles)   951.6
Land area (square miles)   921.6

Population per square mile   688.4

Counties (2000 population)
Hampden (pt.)   332,804   Norfolk (pt.)   15,314
Hampshire (pt.)   50,967   Worcester (pt.)   235,359

Cities and other areas over 10,000 (2000 population)
Agawam   28,144
Chicopee   54,653
Longmeadow CDP   15,633
Milford CDP   24,230
Northampton   28,978
Southbridge CDP   12,878
Springfield   152,082
Webster CDP   11,600

Race and Hispanic or Latino origin*
White   82.5%
Black or African American   5.5%
American Indian or Alaska Native   0.2%
Asian   1.3%
Native Hawaiian or other Pacific Islander   0.0%
Some other race   0.1%
Hispanic or Latino origin   9.2%
Two or more races   1.2%

*As percentage of total population.

Ancestry*
English   7.3%   Polish   8.1%
Fr. Canadian   6.1%   Portuguese   1.6%
French   10.8%   Scottish   1.7%
German   4.3%   Swedish   1.5%
Irish   13.4%   USA/American   2.5%
Italian   8.9%

*As estimated percentage of total population.

Universities and colleges, 2000–2001 enrollment
American International College, Springfield   1,548
Bay Path College, Longmeadow   800
Becker College, Leicester   400
Elms College, Chicopee   782
Mount Holyoke College, South Hadley   2,069
Nichols College, Dudley   1,380
Smith College, Northampton   3,113
Springfield College, Springfield   4,722
Springfield Technical Community College, Springfield   6,705
Ultrasound Diagnostic School, Springfield   269
Western New England College, Springfield   4,826

Newspapers and circulation

	District circulation	Total circulation
Boston Globe	7,158	465,248
Boston Herald	4,661	257,071
Daily Hampshire Gazette	8,409	19,522
Framington Metrowest Daily News	10,102	53,458
Springfield Union-News	58,844	89,595
*USA Today**	3,064	1,674,376
Woonsocket Call	2,296	15,580
Worcester Telegram-Gazette	29,213	104,076

*See Sources and Explanations in the front of the volume.

Television stations and affiliations
Boston (Manchester)	59%	WBPX	PAX
Boston (Manchester)	59%	WBZ	CBS
Boston (Manchester)	59%	WCVB	ABC
Boston (Manchester)	59%	WDPX	PAX
Boston (Manchester)	59%	WEKW	PBS
Boston (Manchester)	59%	WFXT	FOX
Boston (Manchester)	59%	WGBH	PBS
Boston (Manchester)	59%	WGBX	PBS
Boston (Manchester)	59%	WHDH	NBC
Boston (Manchester)	59%	WLVI	WB
Boston (Manchester)	59%	WMFP	Independent
Boston (Manchester)	59%	WMUR	ABC
Boston (Manchester)	59%	WNDS	Independent
Boston (Manchester)	59%	WPXB	Independent
Boston (Manchester)	59%	WPXG	PAX
Boston (Manchester)	59%	WSBK	UPN
Boston (Manchester)	59%	WUNI	Univision
Boston (Manchester)	59%	WWDP	Independent
Boston (Manchester)	59%	WYDN	Independent
Springfield-Holyoke	41%	WGBY	PBS
Springfield-Holyoke	41%	WGGB	ABC
Springfield-Holyoke	41%	WWLP	NBC

Cable systems and subscribers
Charter   93,030
Comcast   91,724
Cox   683

Military installations, September 2001
Westover Air Reserve Base, Chicopee   2,795
Westover Armed Forces Reserve Center, Chicopee   187

Businesses and other major employers
Massachusetts Mutual Life Insurance Co.; Springfield; life insurance   5,000
Baystate Medical Center Inc.; Springfield   4,400

U.S. Postal Service; Springfield   4,000

United Healthcare Services Inc.; East Longmeadow; hospital/medical service plans   2,000

Ladd Accounting and Tax Service; Chicopee; accounting services   1,981

Hasbro Inc.; East Longmeadow; games, toys, children's vehicles   1,800

Commerce Group Inc.; Webster; fire, marine, casualty insurance   1,574

EMC Corp.; Milford; computer storage devices   1,500

Mercy Hospital; Springfield   1,300

Millipore Corp.; Milford; water quality monitoring and control systems   1,200

Smith College; Northampton   1,100

Cooley Dickinson Health Care Corp.; Northampton; management services   1,079

Flexcon; Spencer; plastics film and sheet   1,000

Massachusetts Turnpike Authority; Millbury   1,000

Mount Holyoke College; South Hadley   1,000

Solutia Inc.; Springfield; plastics materials/resins   1,000

Milford-Whitinsville Regional Hospital Inc.; Milford 952

WellPoint Health Networks Inc.; Springfield; health insurance   900

Wyman-Gordon Co.; North Grafton; nonferrous forgings   897

Tyco Healthcare Group; Chicopee; orthopedic, prosthetic, surgical supplies   850

Springfield Wire Inc.; Springfield; electric appliance heating units   773

Harrington Memorial Hospital Inc.; Southbridge 700

U.S. Veterans Hospital; Northampton   700

Western New England College; Springfield   625

Republican Co.; Springfield; newspaper   623

American Saw and Manufacturing Co.; East Longmeadow; hand/power saw blades   600

Rexam Image Products Inc.; South Hadley; packaging paper   600

Westvaco Corp.; Springfield; paper products   600

Smith and Wesson Corp.; Springfield; revolvers, revolver parts   552

City of Southbridge; Southbridge; city management 543

Aearo Corp.; Southbridge; ophthalmic goods   500

City of South Hadley; South Hadley; town government 500

Fibermark Inc.; South Hadley; warehousing   500

Jewish Geriatric Services Inc.; Longmeadow; nursing/personal care facility management   500

Ludlow Co.; Chicopee; coated and laminated paper 500

Massachusetts Dept. of Corrections; Milford   500

OFS Fitel; Sturbridge; fiber optics strands   500

Phoenix Home Life; Wilbraham; insurance agents and brokers   500

Sears Roebuck and Co. Inc.; Springfield; department stores   500

Springfield; Springfield; police dept.   500

Springfield College; Springfield   500

Massachusetts 3rd District

Central and south — Worcester, Attleboro, part of Fall River

The 3rd District cuts a diagonal sliver from the mountains of Princeton to the fishing community of Fall River, winding its way from areas north and west of Boston almost to the Atlantic Ocean south of the city.

Worcester, a working-class city with a strong biotechnology presence, is the 3rd's population hub and has been revitalizing its downtown. A late-1990s project centralizing its respected hospitals, research institutes, and drug manufacturing plants into a medical center has sparked economic development. Still, Worcester registered slow population growth in the 1990s. Hispanics and blacks have been displacing whites. Communities to the north and south have been filling up with suburbanites who commute to jobs in Boston or Providence, Rhode Island.

At the district's southern end, Fall River (shared with the 4th District) has long been a bastion of blue-collar white ethnic Democrats. The city has long had one of the highest unemployment rates in the state.

The Democratic dominance in Worcester and Fall River allows Democrats to overcome the ring of Republican support that binds the towns surrounding Worcester, including Paxton, Holden, the Boylstons, and Shrewsbury. George W. Bush came close to winning those areas, as well as Princeton and the well-off towns of Southborough and Hopkinton in the north-central part of the district, but he failed to carry a single city or town in the 3rd in the 2000 presidential election.

Despite the dominance of Democratic presidential candidates, the 3rd can support moderate-to-liberal Republicans, as shown by its backing of Mitt Romney in the 2002 gubernatorial election. Romney won every city and town in the 3rd except Fall River, Worcester, and two others.

Major Industry

Biotechnology, health care, heavy manufacturing, retail.

Notable

Worcester boasts two important "firsts," more than two centuries apart: the publication of the first American novel, William Hill Brown's *The Power of Sympathy,* in 1789, and the successful cloning of human embryos by a Worcester-based biotech company in 2001.

Election Returns

	Republican		Democratic		Other	
President 2000	90,375	34.6%	153,044	58.6%	17,711	6.8%
House 2002			155,697	98.8%	1,848	1.2%

District Profile

Population   634,585

Total area (square miles)   612.3
   Land area (square miles)   581.0

Population per square mile   1,092.2

Counties (2000 population)

Bristol (pt.) 180,647   Norfolk (pt.) 60,245
Middlesex (pt.) 78,076   Worcester (pt.) 315,617

Cities and other areas over 10,000 (2000 population)

Attleboro   42,068
Fall River (pt.)   53,704
Franklin   29,560
Marlborough   36,255
North Attleborough Center CDP   16,796
Somerset CDP   18,234
Worcester   172,648

Race and Hispanic or Latino origin*

White   86.2%
Black or African American   2.6%
American Indian or Alaska Native   0.2%
Asian   3.2%
Native Hawaiian or other Pacific Islander   0.0%
Some other race   0.3%
Hispanic or Latino origin   6.0%
Two or more races   1.5%

As percentage of total population.

Ancestry*

English   8.5%   Polish   3.8%
Fr. Canadian   4.2%   Portuguese   6.3%
French   7.9%   Scottish   1.6%
German   4.1%   Swedish   2.1%
Irish   16.1%   USA/American   3.0%
Italian   9.5%

As estimated percentage of total population.

Universities and colleges, 2000–2001 enrollment

Anna Maria College, Paxton   1,255
Assumption College, Worcester   2,754
Atlantic Union College, South Lancaster   755
Becker College-Worcester, Worcester   1,166
Clark University, Worcester   2,910
College of the Holy Cross, Worcester   2,826
Dean College, Franklin   1,379
Quinsigamond Community College, Worcester   5,617
University of Massachusetts Medical School, Worcester   664
Worcester Polytechnic Institute, Worcester   3,874
Worcester State College, Worcester   5,303
Worcester Technical Institute, Worcester   265

Newspapers and circulation

	District circulation	Total circulation
Attleboro Sun Chronicle	14,936	20,530
Boston Globe	23,356	465,248
Boston Herald	9,728	257,071
Fall River Herald News	12,745	22,943
Framington Metrowest Daily News	14,596	53,458
Providence Journal	9,534	161,108
Shrewsburg Chronicle	2,542	2,544
*USA Today**	2,971	1,674,376
Westborough News	2,793	2,798
Worcester Telegram-Gazette	55,221	104,076

See Sources and Explanations in the front of the volume.

Television stations and affiliations

Boston (Manchester)	74%	WBPX	PAX
Boston (Manchester)	74%	WBZ	CBS
Boston (Manchester)	74%	WCVB	ABC
Boston (Manchester)	74%	WDPX	PAX
Boston (Manchester)	74%	WEKW	PBS
Boston (Manchester)	74%	WFXT	FOX
Boston (Manchester)	74%	WGBH	PBS
Boston (Manchester)	74%	WGBX	PBS
Boston (Manchester)	74%	WHDH	NBC
Boston (Manchester)	74%	WLVI	WB
Boston (Manchester)	74%	WMFP	Independent
Boston (Manchester)	74%	WMUR	ABC
Boston (Manchester)	74%	WNDS	Independent
Boston (Manchester)	74%	WPXB	Independent
Boston (Manchester)	74%	WPXG	PAX
Boston (Manchester)	74%	WSBK	UPN
Boston (Manchester)	74%	WUNI	Univision
Boston (Manchester)	74%	WWDP	Independent
Boston (Manchester)	74%	WYDN	Independent
Providence-New Bedford	26%	WJAR	NBC
Providence-New Bedford	26%	WLNE	ABC
Providence-New Bedford	26%	WLWC	UPN, WB
Providence-New Bedford	26%	WNAC	FOX
Providence-New Bedford	26%	WPRI	CBS
Providence-New Bedford	26%	WPXQ	PAX
Providence-New Bedford	26%	WSBE	PBS

Cable systems and subscribers

Charter   79,898
Comcast   65,510
Shrewsbury Community Television   9,582

Businesses and other major employers

Allmerica Securities Trust; Worcester; closed-end management investment   25,000
University of Massachusetts Memorial Hospitals Inc.; Worcester   8,683
Raytheon Co.; Marlborough; air traffic control systems, equipment   5,000
Texas Instruments Inc.; Attleboro; electronic circuits   3,800
St. Gobain Abrasives Inc.; Worcester; abrasive wheels   2,500
St. Vincent Hospital; Worcester   2,200
Quaker Fabric Corp.; Fall River; upholstery fabrics   2,100
Putnam Investments; Franklin; open-ended management investment   1,800
Maxtor Corp.; Shrewsbury; computer hardware   1,465
EMC Corp.; Hopkinton; computer hardware   1,300
Massachusetts Dept. of Mental Retardation; Wrentham   1,200
Thermo Optek Corp.; Franklin; process control instruments   1,150
St. Anne's Hospital Corp.; Fall River   1,110
Sturdy Memorial Hospital Inc.; Attleboro   1,100
PFPC Inc.; Westborough; accounting services   1,020
Marshalls Inc.; Worcester; discount department stores   1,000
Nypro Inc.; Clinton; injection molding of plastics   1,000

TJX Companies Inc.; Worcester; general warehousing, storage 1,000

Shipley Co.; Marlborough; industrial organic chemicals 900

Verizon Communications Inc.; Marlborough; telephone communication 900

College of Holy Cross; Worcester 842

City of Somerset; Somerset; city management 830

Astra USA Inc.; Westborough; pharmaceuticals 801

Allegro Microsystems Inc.; Worcester; semiconductors and related devices 800

Massachusetts Dept. of Mental Health; Westborough 760

Worcester Polytechnic Institute; Worcester 730

City of Marlborough; Marlborough; city management 722

City of Attleboro; Attleboro; elementary and secondary schools 720

Garelick Farms Inc.; Franklin; milk processing 700

Metso Automation Inc.; Shrewsbury; process control instruments 700

North Attleborough Town; North Attleboro; town management 674

Massachusetts Dept. of Mental Health; Worcester 600

Pinkerton's Inc.; Westborough; protective services, guard 600

Worcester State College; Worcester 600

New England Center for Children; Southborough; school for retarded 550

City of Boston; West Boylston; correctional institutions 525

Marlborough Hospital; Marlborough 515

Kidde-Fenwal Inc.; Ashland; fire detection systems 512

Act Manufacturing Inc.; Marlborough; printed circuit boards 500

City of Worcester; Worcester; city government 500

Hilti Inc.; Ashland; electrical construction materials 500

Quinsigamond Community College; Worcester 500

Paul Revere Life Insurance Co.; Worcester; life insurance 500

Swank Inc.; Attleboro; apparel belts 500

Toys R Us Inc.; Northborough; general warehousing, storage 500

U.S. Postal Service; Worcester 500

Worcester Telegram and Gazette Corp.; Worcester; periodicals 500

Massachusetts 4th District

New Bedford; Boston suburbs — Newton; Taunton

Downtowns replete with eighteenth- and nineteenth-century town hall buildings dot the Yankee communities in the 4th, several of which have celebrated their 300th or 350th anniversaries. The district encompasses thickly settled Boston suburbs, rural cranberry bogs, and urban New Bedford and Fall River (shared with the 3rd District). *(See map p. 445)*

The economic health of the 4th reflects a split between the northern and southern tiers of the district. The northern well-to-do towns and Boston suburbs benefited from a strong economy in the 1990s, due in large part to the Route 128 high-tech corridor, though moderate unemployment started to affect the area at the end of the 1990s. The southern fishing and former textile mill communities, including Fall River and New Bedford, struggled to stave off double-digit unemployment as the textile industry declined to almost nothing and commercial fishermen faced sparse catches. In the 4th's center, the cranberry bogs in Middleboro and biotechnology firms farther north provide a strong economic base.

The blue-collar, immigrant-laden southern section of the district gives the 4th a strong Democratic lean. New Bedford, which has the lowest median household income in the state, and Fall River are heavily Portuguese and vote solidly Democratic. So does the district's wealthiest community, Westport, located south of Fall River and west of New Bedford. The wealthy northwestern towns of Wellesley, Dover, and Sherborn tend to lean Republican, but the well-to-do and densely populated Newton and Brookline opt for liberal Democrats.

Major Industry

Fishing, cranberries, health care, textile manufacturing.

Notable

Fig Newtons originated in Newton; former governor Michael S. Dukakis commuted downtown by trolley from his home in Brookline; Ocean Spray is headquartered in Lakeville-Middleboro.

Election Returns

	Republican		Democratic		Other	
President 2000	79,201	28.7%	178,354	64.7%	18,067	6.6%
House 2002			166,125	99.0%	1,691	1.0%

District Profile

Population 634,624

Total area (square miles) 843.8
    Land area (square miles) 731.8

Population per square mile 867.2

Counties (2000 population)
    Bristol (pt.) 331,732   Norfolk (pt.) 141,294
    Middlesex (pt.) 88,029   Plymouth (pt.) 73,569

Cities and other areas over 10,000 (2000 population)
    Brookline CDP 57,107   Newton 83,829
    Fall River (pt.) 38,234   Taunton 55,976
    New Bedford 93,768   Wellesley CDP 26,613

Race and Hispanic or Latino origin*
    White 87.9%
    Black or African American 2.0%
    American Indian or Alaska Native 0.2%
    Asian 3.2%
    Native Hawaiian or other Pacific Islander 0.0%
    Some other race 1.6%
    Hispanic or Latino origin 3.3%
    Two or more races 1.9%

As percentage of total population.

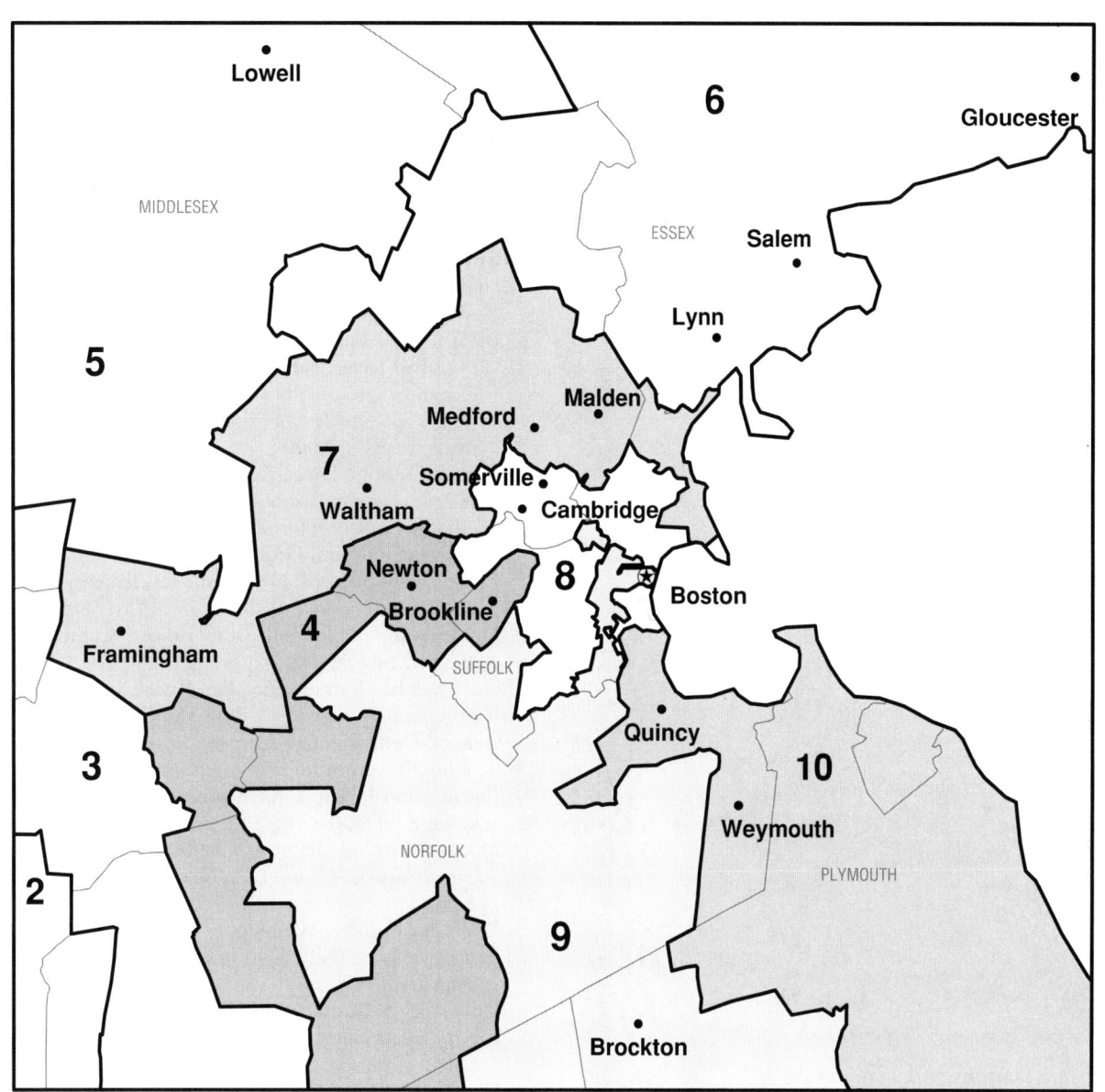

Lowell

6

Gloucester

MIDDLESEX

ESSEX

Salem

5

Lynn

Medford

Malden

Somerville

7

Cambridge

Waltham

Newton

Brookline

8

Boston

4

SUFFOLK

Framingham

Quincy

3

NORFOLK

10

Weymouth

2

PLYMOUTH

9

Brockton

Ancestry*

English	9.0%	Portuguese	13.4%
Fr. Canadian	3.4%	Russian	2.4%
French	6.1%	Scottish	1.5%
German	4.0%	Subsaharan	1.7%
Irish	13.5%	Swedish	1.1%
Italian	6.7%	USA/American	3.0%
Polish	3.3%		

As estimated percentage of total population.

Universities and colleges, 2000–2001 enrollment

Andover Newton Theological School, Newton Centre 396

Babson College, Wellesley 3,397

Boston College, Chestnut Hill 15,240

Bristol Community College, Fall River 6,054

Lasell College, Newton 841

Massachusetts Bay Community College, Wellesley Hills 4,458

Mount Ida College, Newton Centre 1,196

Newbury College-Brookline, Brookline 2,152

Pine Manor College, Chestnut Hill 372

University of Massachusetts, North Dartmouth 7,122

Wellesley College, Wellesley 2,287

Wheaton College, Norton 1,474

Newspapers and circulation

	District circulation	Total circulation
Attleboro Sun Chronicle	5,450	20,530
Boston Globe	47,963	465,248
Boston Herald	15,476	257,071
Brockton Enterprise	7,504	40,861
Dover/Sherborn Press	1,673	1,716
Fall River Herald News	8,347	22,943
Mansfield News	3,322	3,328
Norton Mirror	1,676	1,679
Providence Journal	2,303	161,108
Sharon Advocate	3,772	4,172
Standard-Times	35,502	35,723
Taunton Daily Gazette	12,066	12,303
*USA Today**	3,444	1,674,376
Wellesley Townsman	6,033	6,392

See Sources and Explanations in the front of the volume.

Television stations and affiliations

Providence-New Bedford	53%	WJAR	NBC
Providence-New Bedford	53%	WLNE	ABC
Providence-New Bedford	53%	WLWC	UPN, WB
Providence-New Bedford	53%	WNAC	FOX
Providence-New Bedford	53%	WPRI	CBS
Providence-New Bedford	53%	WPXQ	PAX
Providence-New Bedford	53%	WSBE	PBS
Boston (Manchester)	47%	WBPX	PAX
Boston (Manchester)	47%	WBZ	CBS
Boston (Manchester)	47%	WCVB	ABC
Boston (Manchester)	47%	WDPX	PAX
Boston (Manchester)	47%	WEKW	PBS
Boston (Manchester)	47%	WFXT	FOX
Boston (Manchester)	47%	WGBH	PBS
Boston (Manchester)	47%	WGBX	PBS
Boston (Manchester)	47%	WHDH	NBC
Boston (Manchester)	47%	WLVI	WB
Boston (Manchester)	47%	WMFP	Independent
Boston (Manchester)	47%	WMUR	ABC
Boston (Manchester)	47%	WNDS	Independent
Boston (Manchester)	47%	WPXB	Independent
Boston (Manchester)	47%	WPXG	PAX
Boston (Manchester)	47%	WSBK	UPN
Boston (Manchester)	47%	WUNI	Univision
Boston (Manchester)	47%	WWDP	Independent
Boston (Manchester)	47%	WYDN	Independent

Cable systems and subscribers

Adelphia 1,845

Charter 4,031

Comcast 151,096

Businesses and other major employers

Southcoast Hospital Group Inc.; New Bedford 4,000

Boston College; Chestnut Hill 3,000

Brylane Inc.; Taunton; women's clothing stores 3,000

City of Fall River; Fall River; public elementary/secondary school 2,000

Invensys Systems Inc.; Foxboro; process control instruments 2,000

Roman Catholic Diocese of Fall River; Fall River; religious organization 2,000

Wellesley Newton Hospital Corp.; Newton 1,800

Southcoast Hospital Group Inc.; Fall River 1,794

City of New Bedford; New Bedford; elementary and secondary schools 1,200

Motorola Inc.; Mansfield; radio/TV communications equipment 1,200

Genzyme Bio-Surgery Inc.; Fall River; biological products 1,144

General Dynamics Government Systems Corp.; Taunton; radio/TV communications equipment 1,000

Johnson and Johnson; Raynham; general warehousing, storage 1,000

Morton Hospital; Taunton 1,000

Summit Services Group Inc.; Newton; linen supply 1,000

Wellesley College; Wellesley 1,000

Accenture Inc.; Wellesley; business management consultant 953

University of Massachusetts; Dartmouth 900

City of Dartmouth; North Dartmouth; treasurer's office 850

City of Brookline; Brookline; city management 848

City of Taunton; Taunton; education programs 800

Massasoit Greyhound Assn. Inc.; Raynham; dog racing 800

Reed Elsevier Inc.; Newton; trade journals 800

Talbots Inc.; Lakeville; women's apparel 800

Northeast Security Inc.; Brookline; security guard service 775

Acushnet Co.; Acushnet; golf equipment 700

Aerovox Inc.; New Bedford; capacitors and condensers 700

Tyco Healthcare Group; Mansfield; orthopedic, prosthetic, surgical supplies 700

Verizon Communications Inc.; Taunton; telephone communication 700

Babson College; Babson Park 650

Bristol County; Taunton; county government 650

Joan Fabrics Corp.; Fall River; textiles   650
Main Street Textiles; Fall River; upholstery fabrics   640
Globe Manufacturing Corp.; Fall River; rubber treat 625
Massachusetts Dept. of Mental Health; Taunton   600
Ocean Spray Employees Federal Credit Union; Lakeville 600
Ocean Spray Cranberries Inc.; Middleboro; fruits and fruit products   550
Riverside Manufacturing Corp.; New Bedford; men's and boys' suits   530
Robert Allen Group Inc.; Mansfield; home furnishings 530
Helix Technology Corp.; Mansfield; vacuum pumps 520
Acushnet Co.; New Bedford; athletic balls   500
Bloomingdale's Inc.; Chestnut Hill; department stores 500
City of Dartmouth; North Dartmouth; police dept. 500
City of New Bedford; New Bedford; water supply   500
Genlyte Group Inc.; Fall River; residential lighting fixtures   500
Neponset Valley Health System Inc. Hospital; Norfolk 500
Polaroid Corp.; New Bedford; films: cameras, motion picture, x-ray   500

Massachusetts 5th District

North central — Lowell, Lawrence, Haverhill

More than a generation ago, billowing smokestacks put Lawrence and Lowell among the nation's leading industrial centers. Today, the cities continue to be the population hubs for the 5th, but the wealthy suburbs and rural communities—home to technology workers and some of the nation's most prestigious prep schools—give the district a more upscale flavor.

Textiles are still vital to struggling Lawrence, where immigration has put its sizable Hispanic population—made up mostly of Dominicans and Puerto Ricans—in the majority. Lowell and surrounding suburbs, meanwhile, continue to reinvent themselves. The early 1990s recession hobbled Digital Equipment Corporation and toppled computer giant Wang, both major employers in the area, but the subsequent Internet boom attracted software firms and other high-tech companies. The upswing spurred growth in small towns, as aging buildings that once housed textile mills, and then defense contractors, became home to startups and financial services firms.

While political rivalries among European immigrants are giving way to contests featuring Puerto Ricans, Dominicans, and Cambodians, the blue-collar and low-income minority residents of Lowell and Lawrence vote strongly Democratic, as do many well-educated suburban liberals.

The southern part of the 5th is generally wealthy, with Carlisle, Sudbury, Harvard, and Bolton all registering six-figure median household incomes. These areas demonstrated their political independence in backing Al Gore in the 2000 presidential election and Republican Mitt Romney in the 2002 gubernatorial election.

Major Industry
Computer software, defense, textiles.

Notable
Concord was the site of the first day of fighting in the Revolutionary War on April 19, 1775 (now celebrated each year as Patriots' Day); Paul Revere's ride and the first Revolutionary battles in towns in the 5th and 7th Districts are reenacted every year; Walden Pond served as temporary home to Henry David Thoreau.

Election Returns

	Republican		Democratic		Other	
President 2000	93,406	36.3%	145,277	56.5%	18,433	7.2%
House 2002	69,337	34.1%	122,562	60.2%	11,878	5.8%

District Profile

Population   635,326

Total area (square miles)   581.9
  Land area (square miles)   565.7

Population per square mile   1,123.1

Counties (2000 population)
Essex (pt.)   206,048
Middlesex (pt.)   409,389
Worcester (pt.)   19,889

Cities and other areas over 10,000 (2000 population)
Haverhill   58,969   Lowell   105,167
Hudson CDP   14,388   Maynard CDP   10,433
Lawrence   72,043   Methuen   43,789

Race and Hispanic or Latino origin*
White   79.7%
Black or African American   1.7%
American Indian or Alaska Native   0.1%
Asian   5.2%
Native Hawaiian or other Pacific Islander   0.0%
Some other race   0.2%
Hispanic or Latino origin   11.6%
Two or more races   1.4%

As percentage of total population.

Ancestry*

English 8.9%	Polish 3.0%
Fr. Canadian 4.9%	Portuguese 2.1%
French 6.7%	Scotch-Irish 1.2%
German 4.4%	Scottish 2.0%
Greek 1.3%	Swedish 1.1%
Irish 16.6%	USA/American 2.8%
Italian 9.8%	

As estimated percentage of total population.

Universities and colleges, 2000–2001 enrollment
Bradford College, Haverhill   586
Massachusetts School of Law, Andover   441
Northern Essex Community College, Haverhill 6,580
University of Massachusetts-Lowell, Lowell   12,189

Newspapers and circulation

	District circulation	Total circulation
Beacon-Villager	3,373	3,373
Billerica Minuteman	5,240	5,306
Boston Globe	40,891	465,248
Boston Herald	16,548	257,071
Chelmsford Independent	4,764	4,859
Concord Journal	5,371	5,539
Framington Metrowest Daily News	3,226	53,458
Lawrence Eagle-Tribune	32,849	54,109
Littleton Independent	1,843	1,920
Lowell Sun	46,828	51,598
Tewskbury Advertiser	2,643	2,659
*USA Today**	5,789	1,674,376
Westford Eagle	4,534	4,617
Worcester Telegram-Gazette	2,010	104,076

As estimated percentage of total population.

Television stations and affiliations

Boston (Manchester)	100%	WBPX	PAX
Boston (Manchester)	100%	WBZ	CBS
Boston (Manchester)	100%	WCVB	ABC
Boston (Manchester)	100%	WDPX	PAX
Boston (Manchester)	100%	WEKW	PBS
Boston (Manchester)	100%	WFXT	FOX
Boston (Manchester)	100%	WGBH	PBS
Boston (Manchester)	100%	WGBX	PBS
Boston (Manchester)	100%	WHDH	NBC
Boston (Manchester)	100%	WLVI	WB
Boston (Manchester)	100%	WMFP	Independent
Boston (Manchester)	100%	WMUR	ABC
Boston (Manchester)	100%	WNDS	Independent
Boston (Manchester)	100%	WPXB	Independent
Boston (Manchester)	100%	WPXG	PAX
Boston (Manchester)	100%	WSBK	UPN
Boston (Manchester)	100%	WUNI	Univision
Boston (Manchester)	100%	WWDP	Independent
Boston (Manchester)	100%	WYDN	Independent

Cable systems and subscribers
Charter 4,622
Comcast 151,031

Military installations, September 2001
Hanscom Air Force Base, Bedford 3,434
Devens Reserve Forces Training Area, Devens 1,998

Businesses and other major employers
Raytheon Co.; Tewksbury; search and navigation equipment 3,500
U.S. Internal Revenue Service; Andover 3,500
Intel Corp.; Hudson; computers 3,000
Raytheon Co.; Sudbury; research institute 3,000
Hewlett-Packard Co.; Andover; surgical and medical instruments 2,000
M/A-Com Inc.; Lowell; solid state diodes 2,000
City of Lowell; Lowell; city management 1,993
Emerson Hospital Inc.; Concord 1,300
City of Haverhill; Haverhill; elementary and secondary schools 1,200
Lawrence General Hospital; Lawrence 1,200
Lowell General Hospital; Lowell 1,200

QualxServ; Tewksbury; systems integration services 1,200
Holy Family Hospital Inc.; Methuen 1,180
Massachusetts Dept. of Mental Health; Tewksbury 1,030
Main Central Railroad Inc.; North Billerica; railroad ferries 1,000
Nortel Networks Inc.; Billerica; computer integrated systems design 1,000
Northern Essex Community College; Haverhill 1,000
St. Memorial Medical Center Inc.; Lowell 1,000
Avid Technology Inc.; Tewksbury; motion picture editing equipment 950
Compaq Computer Corp.; Littleton; electronic computers 900
C. R. Bard Inc.; Billerica; electromedical equipment 800
Compaq Computer Corp.; Andover; general warehousing, storage 800
Future Electronics Corp.; Bolton; electronic parts 800
Home Health Foundation Inc.; Lawrence; home health care services 800
Regency Hotel Management Ltd.; Westford; hotel or motel management 750
Stratus Technologies Inc.; Maynard; minicomputers 750
Picturetel Corp.; Andover; visual communication systems 740
New England Business Service Inc.; Groton; commercial printing 738
Brooks Automation Inc.; Chelmsford; computer programming services 700
H. N. Bull Information Systems Inc.; Lowell; mainframe computers 700
Cisco Systems Inc.; Chelmsford; computer peripherals, software 680
City of Concord; Concord; city management 659
Gillette Co.; Andover; toilet preparations 650
City of Billerica; Billerica; elementary and secondary schools 600
Phillips Academy; Andover 600
Teradyne Inc.; Westford; electronic/electric measuring test equipment 600
Verizon New England Inc.; Andover; telephone communication 600
Vicor Corp.; Andover; electronic generation equipment 600
Globalware Solutions of Massachusettes Inc.; Haverhill; technical manuals: publishing and printing 550
City of Haverhill; Haverhill; city government 528
U.S. Army Corps of Engineers; Concord 525
City of Chelmsford; North Chelmsford; elementary and secondary schools 500
City of Sudbury; Sudbury; city management 500
Comverse Network Systems Inc.; Andover; telephone and telegraph apparatus 500
Lucent Technologies Inc.; Westford; computer peripheral equipment 500
Massachusetts Dept. of Corrections; Shirley 500
New Balance Inc.; Lawrence; athletic shoes 500
Nortel Networks Inc.; Acton; computer peripheral equipment 500
SuperValu Inc.; Andover; food supplier 500

Massachusetts 6th District

North Shore — Lynn, Peabody

Pristine beaches line the cool ocean of Boston's North Shore, home to some of the state's largest homes. Country clubs, fox hunting, and polo matches are popular diversions for residents of the northern inland, where the population is sparse but wealthy.

The population is denser along the Route 128 high-tech corridor, which cuts through the southern part of the district. Like much of Massachusetts in the 1990s, communities along Route 128 turned from manufacturing to an information-based economy. Fueled in part by Boston's universities, technology firms have flourished from Burlington (where Sun Microsystems has offices) to Gloucester, which also supports a major fishing industry. Burlington has a major new industrial park, reflecting the continued growth of the district's economy.

Lynn, the 6th's largest community, is home to aerospace and defense contractors and includes a General Electric jet engine plant. Urban dwellers are concentrated mostly in Lynn and Peabody and provide blue-collar and minority votes for Democrats. Other population centers in the district include the adjacent coastal cities of Beverly, which residents describe as the birthplace of the Navy because its first commissioned ship sailed from the city's harbor, and Salem, which has a rich history as the hometown of Nathaniel Hawthorne and the locale of the 1692 witch trials. Salem is middle-class and has a Democratic slant, while Beverly is more politically independent.

Republicans can do well in upscale towns such as Boxford, Lynnfield, Topsfield, and Wenham, which gave 2002 GOP gubernatorial nominee Mitt Romney more than two-thirds of the vote. While the district has a Democratic tilt, it is not overwhelming, and the GOP can win by attracting independent-minded "unenrolled" voters.

Major Industry

Computer software, defense, fishing.

Notable

The 6th includes territory that spawned the original "gerrymander," a state legislative district named for Gov. Elbridge Gerry in 1812.

Election Returns

	Republican		Democratic		Other	
President 2000	107,415	35.7%	172,840	57.4%	20,760	6.9%
House 2002	75,462	31.7%	162,900	68.3%	253	

District Profile

Population 636,554

Total area (square miles) 804.5
Land area (square miles) 480.3

Population per square mile 1,325.3

Counties (2000 population)
Essex (pt.) 517,371
Middlesex (pt.) 119,183

Cities and other areas over 10,000 (2000 population)

Amesbury CDP	12,327	Newburyport	17,189
Beverly	39,862	Peabody	48,129
Burlington CDP	22,876	Reading CDP	23,708
Danvers CDP	25,212	Salem	40,407
Gloucester	30,273	Saugus CDP	26,078
Lynn	89,050	Swampscott CDP	14,412
Lynnfield CDP	11,542	Wakefield CDP	24,804
Marblehead CDP	20,377	Wilmington CDP	21,363

Race and Hispanic or Latino origin*

White 89.8%
Black or African American 1.9%
American Indian or Alaska Native 0.1%
Asian 2.5%
Native Hawaiian or other Pacific Islander 0.0%
Some other race 0.2%
Hispanic or Latino origin 4.4%
Two or more races 1.1%

*As percentage of total population.

Ancestry*

English	10.6%	Polish	3.2%
Fr. Canadian	3.6%	Portuguese	1.8%
French	5.3%	Russian	1.4%
German	4.0%	Scotch-Irish	1.4%
Greek	1.7%	Scottish	2.5%
Irish	18.6%	Swedish	1.4%
Italian	13.1%	USA/American	3.1%

*As estimated percentage of total population.

Universities and colleges, 2000–2001 enrollment

Endicott College, Beverly 1,697
Essex Agricultural Technical Institute, Hathorne 414
Gordon College, Wenham 1,620
Gordon-Conwell Theological Seminary, South Hamilton 1,578
Marian Court College, Swampscott 281
Merrimack College, North Andover 2,660
Middlesex Community College, Bedford 7,451
Montserrat College of Art, Beverly 392
North Shore Community College, Danvers 6,285
Salem State College, Salem 8,587

Newspapers and circulation

	District circulation	Total circulation
Amesbury News	1,893	1,936
Bedford Minuteman	2,984	3,052
Beverly Citizen	3,982	4,061
Boston Globe	56,713	465,248
Boston Herald	30,729	257,071
Burlington Union	3,414	3,414
Danvers Herald	3,971	4,065
Georgetown Record	1,654	1,745
Gloucester Daily Times	11,385	11,405
Hamilton-Wenham Chronicle	2,465	2,564
Ipswich Chronicle	3,797	3,930
Lawrence Eagle-Tribune	7,586	54,109
Lowell Sun	1,070	51,598
Lynn Daily Item	17,819	18,551
Marblehead Reporter	6,042	6,121
Newburyport Daily News	13,193	13,853

North Andover Citizen	2,884	2,991
Salem Evening News	33,744	33,825
Saugus Advertiser	4,329	4,380
Swampscott Reporter	3,281	3,308
*USA Today**	4,007	1,674,376
Wakefield Observer	1,994	2,019

As estimated percentage of total population.

Television stations and affiliations

Boston (Manchester)	100%	WBPX	PAX
Boston (Manchester)	100%	WBZ	CBS
Boston (Manchester)	100%	WCVB	ABC
Boston (Manchester)	100%	WDPX	PAX
Boston (Manchester)	100%	WEKW	PBS
Boston (Manchester)	100%	WFXT	FOX
Boston (Manchester)	100%	WGBH	PBS
Boston (Manchester)	100%	WGBX	PBS
Boston (Manchester)	100%	WHDH	NBC
Boston (Manchester)	100%	WLVI	WB
Boston (Manchester)	100%	WMFP	Independent
Boston (Manchester)	100%	WMUR	ABC
Boston (Manchester)	100%	WNDS	Independent
Boston (Manchester)	100%	WPXB	Independent
Boston (Manchester)	100%	WPXG	PAX
Boston (Manchester)	100%	WSBK	UPN
Boston (Manchester)	100%	WUNI	Univision
Boston (Manchester)	100%	WWDP	Independent
Boston (Manchester)	100%	WYDN	Independent

Cable systems and subscribers

Adelphia   23,464
Comcast   148,717

Military installations, September 2001

Camp Curtis Guild Military Training Area,
   Reading   325

Businesses and other major employers

General Electric Co.; Lynn; aircraft engines and parts
   7,700
Guthrie North America Inc.; Wakefield; aircraft cleaning
   service   5,996
North Shore Medical Center; Lynn; hospital   3,524
Lahey Clinic; Burlington; hospital   3,500
North Shore Medical Center; Salem   3,500
MITRE Corp.; Bedford; noncommercial research
   organization   2,000
Sun Microsystems Inc.; Burlington; computer
   peripherals, software   2,000
Northeast Hospital Corp.; Beverly   1,900
Axcelis Technologies Inc.; Beverly; ion chambers   1,882
Massachusetts Dept. of Mental Retardation; Hathorne
   1,450
U.S. Veterans Hospital; Bedford   1,400
City of Beverly; Beverly; city government   1,200
Textron Inc.; Wilmington; energy research   1,200
AtlantiCare Medical Center Inc.; Lynn; hospital   1,100
Analogic Corp.; Peabody; analog-digital converters
   1,000
Comverse Network Systems Inc.; Wakefield; telephone
   and telegraph apparatus   1,000
Millipore Corp.; Bedford; analytical instruments   1,000
Teradyne Inc.; North Reading; semiconductor test
   equipment   1,000

Anna Jaques Hospital Inc.; Newburyport   950
Altron Inc.; Wilmington; printed circuit boards   864
Osram Sylvania Inc.; Danvers; fluorescent lamps   825
City of Wakefield; Wakefield; town government   805
Aggregate Industries Inc.; Saugus; concrete   800
Cleaning Service Group Inc.; Danvers; building
   maintenance   800
Abbott Laboratories; Bedford; blood testing apparatus
   750
Medtronic Interventional Vascular Inc.; Danvers;
   catheters   750
Verizon Yellow Pages Co.; Middleton; telephone
   directories   729
AGFA Corp.; Wilmington; printing trade
   photocomposition   700
Lotus Development Corp.; Cambridge; prepackaged
   software   700
City of Saugus; Saugus; city management   695
Schneider Automation Inc.; North Andover;
   environmental controls   660
All Care Visiting Nurse Assn.; Lynn; home health care
   services   600
International Protective Services Inc.; Danvers; guard
   services   600
Macy's East Inc.; Burlington; department stores   600
MRO Software Inc.; Bedford; computer software   600
Munters Corp.; Amesbury; housing construction   600
AMETEK Inc.; Wilmington; flight instruments,
   guidance systems   550
City of Burlington; Burlington; elementary and
   secondary schools   500
Eastern Bank; Lynn; savings institutions   500
Hewlett-Packard Co.; Burlington; computer
   maintenance and repair   500
NFI Massachusetts Inc.; Middleton; family counseling
   services   500
Northrop Grumman Corp.; Reading; systems
   integration services   500
Sears Roebuck and Co. Inc.; Burlington; department
   stores   500
Sears Roebuck and Co. Inc.; Salem; credit card service
   500
Simon Worldwide Inc.; Wakefield; screen printing of
   fabrics   500
State Street Corp.; North Reading; state trust company
   500

Massachusetts 7th District

Northwest Boston suburbs — Framingham

The affluent strip along Route 128 and Interstate 95, a
Silicon Valley of the East, shapes the 7th's character. Stretching east from an urban retail center on Route 9 in Framingham, north along Route 128 as it rings Boston and then
north of the city to reach the middle-class coastal town of Revere, the district includes some of the state's most well-to-do
communities. *(See map p. 445.)*

The area takes pride in its history; each year, Lexington
reenacts Paul Revere's ride and the first Revolutionary War
battles (which took place in towns in the 7th and 5th Districts) on Patriots' Day.

The economy is driven by a strong software and Internet industry. Many Medford and Malden residents commute to blue-collar jobs in Boston. Malden has a rapidly growing Asian community. For decades, Revere has attracted middle-class vacationers to its beaches.

The 7th's political roots are a mix of Protestant Yankee Republican and Irish Democrat. But as with all Massachusetts districts, the 7th votes Democratic in federal races. Redistricting following the 2000 census only increased the 7th's already strong Democratic leanings. Al Gore won the 2000 presidential vote here; George W. Bush's best showing was in Weston, the only locale in the 7th that gave him even 40 percent of the vote.

The wealthy sections of the 7th vary from the more conservative Weston to liberal Lincoln. Democrats also draw votes from a blue-collar, middle-class base in Framingham and in the district's east, including Revere, Everett, and Malden.

Major Industry
Computer software, telecommunications, defense.

Notable
James Pierpont is said to have written "Jingle Bells" in 1850 while visiting Medford Square; Richard B. Fitzgibbon Jr. and Richard B. Fitzgibbon III of Stoneham were the only known American father and son to die in the Vietnam War.

Election Returns

	Republican		Democratic		Other	
President 2000	82,250	28.9%	181,417	63.8%	20,891	7.3%
House 2002			170,968	98.2%	3,069	1.8%

District Profile

Population   634,287

Total area (square miles)   187.6
Land area (square miles)   170.2

Population per square mile   3,726.7

Counties (2000 population)
Middlesex (pt.)   568,701
Suffolk (pt.)   65,586

Cities and other areas over 10,000 (2000 population)

Arlington CDP 42,389	Revere 47,283
Belmont CDP 24,194	Stoneham CDP 22,219
Everett 38,037	Waltham 59,226
Framingham CDP 66,910	Watertown 32,986
Lexington CDP 30,355	Winchester CDP 20,810
Malden 56,340	Winthrop CDP 18,303
Medford 55,765	Woburn 37,258
Melrose 27,134	

Race and Hispanic or Latino origin*
White   83.5%
Black or African American   3.3%
American Indian or Alaska Native   0.1%
Asian   5.7%
Native Hawaiian or other Pacific Islander   0.0%
Some other race   0.5%
Hispanic or Latino origin   4.8%
Two or more races   1.9%

*As percentage of total population.

Ancestry*

English 7.5%	Polish 2.3%
Fr. Canadian 2.4%	Portuguese 1.4%
French 2.9%	Russian 1.8%
German 4.2%	Scotch-Irish 1.3%
Greek 1.2%	Scottish 1.8%
Irish 18.5%	Swedish 1.2%
Italian 16.9%	USA/American 2.7%

*As estimated percentage of total population.

Universities and colleges, 2000–2001 enrollment
Bentley College, Waltham   5,728
Brandeis University, Waltham   4,774
Framingham State College, Framingham   5,763
New England School of Acupuncture, Watertown 271
Regis College, Weston   1,138
Tufts University, Medford   9,106

Newspapers and circulation

	District circulation	Total circulation
Arlington Advocate	8,018	8,219
Belmont Citizen Herald	4,485	4,610
Boston Globe	72,485	465,248
Boston Herald	34,674	257,071
Framington Metrowest Daily News	12,688	53,458
Lexington Minuteman	7,275	7,555
Lincoln Journal	1,316	1,437
Malden Observer	3,716	3,784
Medford Transcript	6,127	6,244
Melrose Free Press	5,535	5,626
*USA Today**	4,180	1,674,376
Weston Town Crier & Tab	2,309	2,341
Winchester Star	4,360	4,440

*As estimated percentage of total population.

Television stations and affiliations

Boston (Manchester)	100%	WBPX	PAX
Boston (Manchester)	100%	WBZ	CBS
Boston (Manchester)	100%	WCVB	ABC
Boston (Manchester)	100%	WDPX	PAX
Boston (Manchester)	100%	WEKW	PBS
Boston (Manchester)	100%	WFXT	FOX
Boston (Manchester)	100%	WGBH	PBS
Boston (Manchester)	100%	WGBX	PBS
Boston (Manchester)	100%	WHDH	NBC
Boston (Manchester)	100%	WLVI	WB
Boston (Manchester)	100%	WMFP	Independent
Boston (Manchester)	100%	WMUR	ABC
Boston (Manchester)	100%	WNDS	Independent
Boston (Manchester)	100%	WPXB	Independent
Boston (Manchester)	100%	WPXG	PAX
Boston (Manchester)	100%	WSBK	UPN
Boston (Manchester)	100%	WUNI	Univision
Boston (Manchester)	100%	WWDP	Independent
Boston (Manchester)	100%	WYDN	Independent

Cable systems and subscribers
Comcast   167,445

Military installations, September 2001
Soldier Systems Center, Natick   2,570

Businesses and other major employers

Raytheon Constructors International Inc.; Lexington; management consultant: construction   6,000

Dennison Manufacturing Co.; Framingham; tablets and pads   3,000

Staples Inc.; Framingham; stationery and office supplies   2,500

Massachusetts State Police; Framingham   2,300

Accenture Inc.; Belmont; management consulting   2,000

Bose Corp.; Framingham; loudspeakers   2,000

Polaroid Corp.; Waltham; photographic equipment, supplies   2,000

City of Framingham; Framingham; city management   1,900

Massachusetts Dept. of Mental Retardation; Waltham   1,900

TJX Companies Inc.; Framingham; family clothing stores   1,800

Winchester Hospital; Winchester   1,800

Tufts Associated Health Maintenance Organization Inc.; Watertown; hospital/medical service plans   1,780

American Medical Response of Massachusetts Inc.; Natick; ambulance service   1,600

Mellon Bank; Everett; investment bankers   1,500

American Chamber of Commerce Inc.; Everett; industrial development planning   1,400

City of Woburn; Woburn; city management   1,300

Hallmark Health System Hospital; Melrose   1,300

Cross Country Motor Club; Medford; automobile owners' association   1,241

Senior Epoch Living Inc.; Waltham; nursing home   1,225

Brandeis University; Waltham   1,200

McLean Hospital Corp.; Belmont   1,200

Marshalls Inc.; Woburn; general warehousing, storage   1,150

Metrowest Medical Healthcare System Ltd.; Natick   1,100

Genuity Solutions Inc.; Woburn; online service providers   1,029

Hallmark Health System Hospital; Malden   1,000

Tufts Associated Health Plans Inc.; Waltham; hospital/medical service plans   1,000

Bentley College; Waltham   911

Mathworks Inc.; Natick; computer software   900

New England Rehabilitation Hospital Inc.; Woburn   805

Hallmark Health System Hospital; Medford   800

City of Arlington; Arlington; elementary/secondary schools   778

Boston Scientific Corp.; Natick; surgical and medical instruments   750

City of Everett; Everett; elementary/secondary schools   750

Skyworks Solutions Inc.; Haverhill; microwave components   750

Verizon Communications Inc.; Waltham; commercial research laboratory   750

Deaconess Waltham Hospital; Waltham   740

Bio-Medical Applications of Rhode Island Inc.; Lexington; kidney dialysis centers   700

BJ's Wholesale Club Inc.; Natick; warehouse club stores   700

Medical Information Technology Inc.; Framingham; computer software development   700

Perkins School for the Blind; Watertown   700

International Business Machines Corp.; Waltham; computer peripherals, software   688

Boston Coach Corp.; Everett; limousine rental   665

Private Healthcare Systems; Waltham; management services   653

AM-PM Cleaning Corp.; Waltham; janitorial service   650

Dimock Community Foundation; Brockton; medical doctor offices, clinics   650

U.S. Army Corps of Engineers; Waltham   640

Automatic Data Processing Inc.; Waltham; data processing   600

Cambridge Health Alliance Hospital; Everett   600

City of Belmont; Belmont; elementary/secondary schools   600

City of Medford; Medford; elementary/secondary schools   600

City of Weston;   Weston; city management   600

Commonwealth Maintenance Systems Inc.; Woburn; janitorial service   600

Hurley of America; Stoneham; industrial, commercial cleaning services   600

Instrumentation Laboratory Inc.; Lexington; medical diagnostic apparatus   600

Panametrics Inc.; Waltham; industrial moisture meters   600

City of Revere; Revere; city management   577

Nova Biomedical Corp.; Waltham; blood testing apparatus   560

Lifeline Systems Inc.; Framingham; emergency alarms   544

EDS Personal Communications Corp.; Waltham; cellular telephones   500

Framingham State College; Framingham   500

Germany Cognex Inc.; Natick; eye examining instruments   500

Global Insight Inc.; Waltham; commercial physical research   500

Lycos Inc.; Waltham; information retrieval services   500

Oracle Corp.; Waltham; prepackaged software   500

Parker Hannifin Corp.; Woburn; adhesives and sealants   500

Massachusetts 8th District

Parts of Boston and suburbs — Cambridge, Somerville

The 8th combines Boston's historic Revolutionary War sites with neighborhoods that reflect its evolving future. *(See map p. 445.)*

From the North End and South End—the neighboring 9th takes in places in between like Beacon Hill and the financial district—the 8th grabs much of the city west of Interstate 93. In doing so, it picks up the Back Bay area, Chinatown, and many largely black and Hispanic neighborhoods in areas like Roxbury, Dorchester, and Jamaica Plain, making it the state's only district where a majority of residents are minorities.

Among the many Beantown sights found in the 8th are the Old North Church, Bunker Hill, the *USS Constitution*, and Logan International Airport (shared with the 7th). Most of the land involved in the "Big Dig," a long-running transportation project that will route the city's central highway underground, is in the 8th.

Two of the world's most respected universities—Harvard and the Massachusetts Institute of Technology—lie across the Charles River in Cambridge. Typifying the district's monolithically liberal politics, Cambridge gave George W. Bush just 13 percent of the vote in the 2000 presidential election—a showing topped by Green Party nominee Ralph Nader.

The district also takes in dozens of other colleges and universities, which drive much of the economy, whether through blue-collar service employees who work at the schools and teaching hospitals or through biotechnology software firms that employ local talent. Somerville, just north of Cambridge, has a thriving arts community, while Chelsea, with more-affordable housing and blue-collar jobs, has seen its Hispanic population expand to comprise one-half of the city's residents.

Major Industry
Biotechnology, higher education, health care, tourism.

Notable
The 8th is the descendant of the district once represented by President John F. Kennedy and Speaker of the House Thomas P. "Tip" O'Neill Jr.

Election Returns

	Republican		Democratic		Other	
President 2000	28,903	14.8%	142,500	73.2%	23,374	12.0%
House 2002			111,861	100.0%	495	

District Profile

Population   634,835

Total area (square miles)   92.3
   Land area (square miles)   40.7

Population per square mile   15,597.9

Counties (2000 population)
   Middlesex (pt.)   178,833
   Suffolk (pt.)   456,002

Cities and other areas over 10,000 (2000 population)
   Boston (pt.)   420,922   Chelsea   35,080
   Cambridge   101,355   Somerville   77,478

Race and Hispanic or Latino origin*
   White   48.9%
   Black or African American   21.9%
   American Indian or Alaska Native   0.2%
   Asian   8.1%
   Native Hawaiian or other Pacific Islander   0.1%
   Some other race   1.5%
   Hispanic or Latino origin   15.9%
   Two or more races   3.5%

As percentage of total population.

Ancestry*

English	4.3%	Portuguese	1.7%
Fr. Canadian	1.1%	Russian	1.8%
French	1.8%	Scottish	1.2%
German	3.9%	Subsaharan	2.9%
Irish	9.9%	USA/American	2.5%
Italian	7.3%	West Indian	5.2%
Polish	2.0%		

As estimated percentage of total population.

Universities and colleges, 2000–2001 enrollment
   Art Institute of Boston, Boston   514
   Bay State College, Boston   608
   Berklee College of Music, Boston   3,361
   Boston Architectural Center, Boston   531
   Boston Conservatory, Boston   488
   Boston University, Boston   28,318
   Bunker Hill Community College, Boston   6,385
   Burdett College, Boston   235
   Cambridge College, Cambridge   2,733
   Emmanuel College, Boston   1,765
   Fisher College, Boston   1,513
   Franklin Institute of Boston, Boston   327
   Harvard University, Cambridge   24,279
   Katharine Gibbs School, Boston   1,069
   Lesley College, Cambridge   6,840
   Massachusetts College of Art, Boston   2,328
   Massachusetts College of Pharmacy, Boston   1,877
   Massachusetts Communication College, Boston   581
   Massachusetts Institute of Technology, Cambridge   10,090
   New England College of Finance, Boston   889
   New England College of Optometry, Boston   425
   New England Conservatory of Music, Boston   812
   New England School of Law, Boston   981
   Northeastern University, Boston   23,897
   Radcliffe College, Cambridge*
   Roxbury Community College, Roxbury Crossing   2,699
   School of the Museum of Fine Arts, Boston   1,300
   Simmons College, Boston   3,488
   Urban College of Boston, Boston   244
   Wentworth Institute of Technology, Boston   3,187
   Wheelock College, Boston   1,012

Enrollment under 100. See Sources and Explanations in the front of the volume.

Newspapers and circulation

	District circulation	Total circulation
Allston/Brighton Tab	1,917	1,919
Boston Globe	55,395	465,248
Boston Herald	42,399	257,071
Cambridge Chronicle	5,888	6,039
Somerville Journal	5,959	6,347
*USA Today**	8,689	1,674,376

See Sources and Explanations in the front of the volume.

Television stations and affiliations

Boston (Manchester)	100%	WBPX	PAX
Boston (Manchester)	100%	WBZ	CBS
Boston (Manchester)	100%	WCVB	ABC
Boston (Manchester)	100%	WDPX	PAX
Boston (Manchester)	100%	WEKW	PBS

Boston (Manchester)	100%	WFXT	FOX
Boston (Manchester)	100%	WGBH	PBS
Boston (Manchester)	100%	WGBX	PBS
Boston (Manchester)	100%	WHDH	NBC
Boston (Manchester)	100%	WLVI	WB
Boston (Manchester)	100%	WMFP	Independent
Boston (Manchester)	100%	WMUR	ABC
Boston (Manchester)	100%	WNDS	Independent
Boston (Manchester)	100%	WPXB	Independent
Boston (Manchester)	100%	WPXG	PAX
Boston (Manchester)	100%	WSBK	UPN
Boston (Manchester)	100%	WUNI	Univision
Boston (Manchester)	100%	WWDP	Independent
Boston (Manchester)	100%	WYDN	Independent

Cable systems and subscribers

Comcast   46,643

Military installations, September 2001

South Boston Support Activity, Boston   1,278

Businesses and other major employers

Harvard College Hospital; Boston   15,000

Gillette Safety Razor Co.; Boston; electric razors 12,000

Boston University; Boston   10,000

Harvard University; Cambridge   9,679

Brigham and Women's Hospital Inc.; Boston   7,500

Massachusetts Institute of Technology; Cambridge 5,500

Beth Israel Deaconess Medical Center Inc.; Boston 5,000

John Hancock Life Insurance Co.; Boston; life insurance 4,650

Arista Technologies Inc.; Boston; computer software 4,000

Boston Medical Center; Boston   4,000

New England Medical Center Inc.; Boston   4,000

Children's Hospital Corp.; Boston   3,832

Liberty International Holdings Inc.; Boston; investment holding company   3,400

NSTAR; Boston; electric power distribution   3,300

Boston University School of Medicine; Boston   3,000

Massachusetts Investors Trust; Boston; open-ended management investment   3,000

Modern Continental Construction Co. Inc.; Cambridge; bridge, tunnel, elevated highway construction   3,000

Blue Cross and Blue Shield of Massachusetts; Boston; hospital/medical service plans   2,600

Massachusetts Dept. of Transitional Assistance; Boston 2,600

Boston City Hospital; Boston   2,400

St. Elizabeth's Medical Center of Boston Inc.; Boston 2,327

New England Life Insurance Co.; Boston; real estate agents and managers   2,000

Polaroid Corp.; Cambridge; photographic equipment, supplies   2,000

U.S. Postal Service; Boston   2,000

Dana-Farber Cancer Institute Inc.; Boston   1,995

Browning-Ferris Industries Inc.; Chelsea; refuse collection/disposal   1,920

Mount Auburn Hospital; Cambridge   1,874

Northeastern University; Boston   1,800

Tappet Brothers Associates; Cambridge; radio producers 1,800

Investors Financial Services Corp.; Boston; bank holding companies   1,679

City of Cambridge; Cambridge; elementary and secondary schools   1,560

Sun Life Assurance Corp. of Canada (US) Inc.; Boston; life insurance   1,500

Teradyne Inc.; Boston; semiconductor test equipment 1,400

American Cleaning Co. Inc.; Brighton; janitorial service 1,300

Arthur D. Little Inc.; Cambridge; environmental consultant   1,200

Smithsonian Institution; Cambridge; scientific research agency   1,200

U.S. Coast Guard; Boston   1,200

WGBH Educational Foundation Inc.; Boston; television film production   1,200

Arnold Worldwide; Boston; advertising   1,100

Marriott International Inc.; Boston; hotel, franchised 1,100

New England Baptist Hospital Inc.; Boston   1,100

Charles Stark Draper Laboratory Inc.; Cambridge; research institute   1,050

Bain Capitol Information Partners; Boston; venture capital companies   1,010

BEC Energy; Boston; electric power generation   1,000

Cambridge Health Alliance; Cambridge; hospital management   1,000

Harvard College; Boston   1,000

Massachusetts Electric Construction Co.; Boston; electrical contractor   1,000

Quest Diagnostics Clinical Laboratories Inc.; Cambridge; testing laboratories   1,000

Somerville School Department; Somerville   1,000

U.S. Dept. of Transportation; Cambridge   1,000

Assn. of Literary Scholars and Critics; Boston; literary, film, or cultural club   999

Houghton Mifflin Co.; Boston; books publishing   970

John Hancock Signature Services Inc.; Charlestown; security transfer agents   941

Lotus Development Corp.; Cambridge; computer software   875

Boston Housing Authority; Boston   856

Massachusetts Port Authority; Boston   850

Boston Herald Inc.; Boston; commercial printing, newspaper publishing   830

Biogen Inc.; Cambridge; commercial research laboratory 800

Children's Medical Center Corp.; Jamaica Plain   800

City of Boston; Boston; libraries   800

Continental Airlines Inc.; Boston; air passenger carrier 800

Deloitte and Touche; Boston; certified public accountant 800

Genetics Institute Inc.; Cambridge; pharmaceuticals 800

Liberty Funds Group; Boston; security brokers, dealers 800

U.S. Dept. of Transportation; Cambridge   800

Northwest Airlines Inc.; Boston; air passenger carrier 784

First Church of Christ Scientist Boston; Boston; religious organization   780

Mintz Levin Cohn Ferris Glovsky and Popeo; Boston; law office   775

Baymed Collection Inc.; Brighton; collection agency   766

Museum of Fine Arts; Boston   757

Camp Dresser and McKee Inc.; Cambridge; engineering services   750

Ernst and Young; Boston; certified public accountant   750

Sheraton Boston Corp.; Boston; hotels   750

Digitas Inc.; Boston; computer consulting services   700

Franciscan Children's Hospital and Rehabilitation Center Inc.; Boston   700

JMB/Urban Development Co.; Boston; hotels   700

Simmons College; Boston   687

New England Confectionery Co.; Cambridge; confectionery products   680

Cambridge Health Alliance Hospital; Somerville   663

Dimock Community Foundation; Boston; outpatient rehabilitation center   650

Genuity Inc.; Cambridge; systems integration services   650

Starwood Hotels and Resorts Worldwide Inc.; Boston; hotels   650

Suffolk County; Boston; county police   650

Lesley University; Cambridge   623

Berklee College of Music Inc.; Boston   600

Genzyme Corp.; Cambridge; enzyme, isoenzyme diagnostic agents   600

HMSHost Corp.; Boston; restaurants   600

Massachusetts Dept. of Highway; Boston   600

Massachusetts Financial Services Co.; Boston; investment advisory service   600

Suburban Homemaking and Maternity Agency Inc.; Boston; homemakers' service   600

Bechtel/Parsons Brinkerhoff; Boston; tunnel construction   575

Manufacturers' Life Insurance Company of North America; Boston; insurance information, consulting services   550

Burns International Security Services Corp.; Boston; security guard service   515

ABT Associates Inc.; Cambridge; commercial nonphysical research   500

Akamai Technologies Inc.; Cambridge; data communication services   500

Ames Safety Envelope Co.; Somerville; filing folders   500

Boston School District; Boston   500

CHI International Inc.; Boston; cutlery   500

City of Cambridge; Cambridge; secondary school   500

Federal Transit Admin.; Cambridge   500

Hill Holliday Connors Cosmopulos Inc.; Boston; advertising   500

Massachusetts Dept. of Public Health; Boston   500

Sapient Corp.; Cambridge; computer software development   500

State Street Investment Trust; Boston; open-ended management investment   500

Whitehead Institute for Bio-Medical Research; Cambridge; noncommercial biological research   500

Massachusetts 9th District

Part of Boston; southern suburbs — Brockton, Braintree

The 9th begins with a central swath of downtown Boston, covering Beacon Hill, the West End, and the financial district. *(See map p. 445.)*

The statehouse and brokerage houses—the 9th is home to one of the world's largest centers for mutual fund investing—are dominant in this part of Boston. They share the area with sprawling Boston Common park and several of New England's major tourist attractions. Faneuil Hall Marketplace anchors the retail industry. Some of the wealthiest neighborhoods in the state are along the Charles River.

From central Boston the district hops the Fort Point Channel into South Boston—long referred to as "Southie"—and closely hugs Interstate 93 on its way into Milton. It connects through Dedham to West Roxbury, a mostly white suburban enclave in the southwestern part of Boston.

The "Brahmin" homes of Beacon Hill are counterbalanced by the poor and working-class neighborhoods of traditionally Irish Southie and middle-class suburban communities south and west of the city. Though solidly Democratic, Southie's political tradition is one of supporting prolabor Democrats who are more conservative on social issues.

The 9th's areas outside of Boston are relatively conservative for Massachusetts. While the district's suburbs have helped elect Republicans to the governor's mansion in recent years, the district's mostly blue-collar base in Boston and Brockton keeps it solidly Democratic in federal elections.

Major Industry
Financial services, government, tourism.

Notable
Patriots tossed boxes of tea into Boston Harbor during the Boston Tea Party in 1773, a catalyst for the Revolutionary War; the John F. Kennedy Library and Museum is in Boston; a new federal courthouse in South Boston was named for the late representative Joe Moakley, who represented the district from 1973 until his death in 2001.

Election Returns

	Republican		Democratic		Other	
President 2000	93,529	33.4%	167,059	59.7%	19,051	6.8%
House 2002			168,055	100.0%	921	

District Profile

Population   634,062

Total area (square miles)   319.3
   Land area (square miles)   313.0

Population per square mile   2,025.8

Counties (2000 population)
Bristol (pt.)	22,299	Plymouth (pt.)	159,363
Norfolk (pt.)	284,181	Suffolk (pt.)	168,219

Cities and other areas over 10,000 (2000 population)
Boston (pt.)	168,219	Brockton	94,304
Braintree CDP	33,698	Dedham CDP	23,464

Holbrook CDP   10,785   Norwood CDP   28,587
Milton CDP   26,062   Randolph CDP   30,963
Needham CDP   28,911

Race and Hispanic or Latino origin*
White   79.3%
Black or African American   8.1%
American Indian or Alaska Native   0.2%
Asian   3.7%
Native Hawaiian or other Pacific Islander   0.0%
Some other race   1.8%
Hispanic or Latino origin   4.6%
Two or more races   2.4%

*As percentage of total population.

Ancestry*
English   7.0%   Portuguese   1.6%
Fr. Canadian   1.9%   Russian   1.3%
French   2.6%   Scotch-Irish   1.3%
German   4.1%   Scottish   1.8%
Greek   1.1%   Subsaharan   2.1%
Irish   23.2%   Swedish   1.5%
Italian   10.4%   USA/American   3.3%
Polish   2.5%   West Indian   2.2%

*As estimated percentage of total population.

Universities and colleges, 2000–2001 enrollment
Bridgewater State College, Bridgewater   8,839
Brockton Hospital School of Nursing, Brockton   265
Curry College, Milton   2,330
Emerson College, Boston   4,074
Laboure College, Boston   284
Massasoit Community College, Brockton   6,706
MGH Institute of Health Professions, Boston   524
Stonehill College, North Easton   2,650
Suffolk University, Boston   6,908
University of Massachusetts, Boston   13,346

Newspapers and circulation

	District circulation	Total circulation
Boston Globe	67,017	465,248
Boston Herald	46,660	257,071
Braintree Forum	4,021	4,089
Brockton Enterprise	28,029	40,861
Canton Journal	1,399	1,413
Easton Journal	3,593	3,599
Framington Metrowest Daily News	5,050	53,458
Holbrook Sun	1,713	1,734
Medfield Press	2,765	2,762
Parkway Transcript	1,478	2,089
Quincy Patriot Ledger	16,648	67,219
Stoughton Journal	1,679	1,687
*USA Today**	3,845	1,674,376
West Roxbury Transcript	3,703	3,818
Westwood Press	2,104	2,106

*See Sources and Explanations in the front of the volume.

Television stations and affiliations
Boston (Manchester)	91%	WBPX	PAX
Boston (Manchester)	91%	WBZ	CBS
Boston (Manchester)	91%	WCVB	ABC
Boston (Manchester)	91%	WDPX	PAX
Boston (Manchester)	91%	WEKW	PBS
Boston (Manchester)	91%	WFXT	FOX
Boston (Manchester)	91%	WGBH	PBS
Boston (Manchester)	91%	WGBX	PBS
Boston (Manchester)	91%	WHDH	NBC
Boston (Manchester)	91%	WLVI	WB
Boston (Manchester)	91%	WMFP	Independent
Boston (Manchester)	91%	WMUR	ABC
Boston (Manchester)	91%	WNDS	Independent
Boston (Manchester)	91%	WPXB	Independent
Boston (Manchester)	91%	WPXG	PAX
Boston (Manchester)	91%	WSBK	UPN
Boston (Manchester)	91%	WUNI	Univision
Boston (Manchester)	91%	WWDP	Independent
Boston (Manchester)	91%	WYDN	Independent
Providence-New Bedford	9%	WJAR	NBC
Providence-New Bedford	9%	WLNE	ABC
Providence-New Bedford	9%	WLWC	UPN, WB
Providence-New Bedford	9%	WNAC	FOX
Providence-New Bedford	9%	WPRI	CBS
Providence-New Bedford	9%	WPXQ	PAX
Providence-New Bedford	9%	WSBE	PBS

Cable systems and subscribers
Comcast   233,527

Military installations, September 2001
G. M. Craig U.S. Army Reserve Center, Brockton   254

Businesses and other major employers
State Street Bank and Trust Co.; Boston; state trust company   15,000
MGH Health Services Corp.; Boston; home health care services   14,000
Putnam Investment Inc.; Boston; open-ended management investment   6,000
General Dynamics Network Systems; Needham; telephone and telegraph apparatus   4,000
U.S. Coast Guard; Boston   4,000
Massachusetts General Hospital; Boston   3,647
American Employers' Insurance Co.; Boston; fire, marine, casualty insurance   2,933
All Seasons Services; Canton; advertising, promotional, trade shows   2,600
FleetBoston Financial; Boston; commercial bank   2,500
Stone and Webster Engineering Corp.; Boston; professional engineer   2,200
Boston Group Holdings Inc.; Boston; investment holding company   2,000
City of Brockton; Brockton; elementary/secondary schools   2,000
Fidelity Brokerage Services; Boston; general brokerage investment   2,000
Verizon Communications Inc.; Boston; telephone communication   2,000
Analog Devices Inc.; Norwood; semiconductors and related devices   1,500
Stone and Webster Engineering Corp.; Stoughton; engineering services   1,500
Symantec Corp.; Westwood; computer tapes and disks   1,500
Brockton Hospital Inc.; Brockton   1,300
Parametric Technology Corp.; Needham; computer software   1,300

Quest Software Inc.; Needham; computer software development 1,300

Stream International Inc.; Canton; computer software 1,300

Commonwealth of Massachusetts; Boston; air, water, solid waste management 1,200

Media CP Inc.; Needham; newspaper 1,200

Polaroid Corp.; Norwood; photographic equipment, supplies 1,200

University of Massachusetts; Boston 1,200

Massachusetts Eye and Ear Infirmary Inc.; Boston 1,174

Carney Hospital Inc.; Boston 1,099

U.S. Veterans Hospital; West Roxbury 1,050

Faulkner Hospital Inc.; Boston 1,040

3 Executive Campus Corp.; Boston; engineering services 1,000

Andersen Consulting; Boston; administrative services consultant 1,000

City of Boston; Boston; city government 1,000

Equiserve Partnership; Canton; stock transfer agents 1,000

KPMG; Boston; certified public accountant 1,000

Thomson Financial Inc.; New York; book publishing and printing 1,000

Brown Bros. Harriman and Co.; Boston; commercial banking 971

Federal Reserve Bank of Boston; Boston 950

Spaulding Rehabilitation Hospital Corp.; Boston 950

Good Samaritan Medical Center; Brockton 930

Goodwin Procter; Boston; general practice law office 925

Pioneer Investments; Boston; metals service centers and offices 900

PricewaterhouseCoopers; Boston; certified public accountant 900

Ropes and Gray; Boston; general practice law office 900

National Mentor Healthcare Inc.; Boston; home for mentally handicapped persons 851

Hebrew Rehabilitation Center for Aged; Boston 830

Beacon Companies; Boston; hotel/motel new construction 800

Boston Financial; Braintree; computer programming services 800

Jordan's Furniture Inc.; Avon; furniture stores 800

Point Group Health Care Group and Senior Living Center Inc.; Brockton 800

U.S. Postal Service; Brockton 800

Sheraton Operating Corp.; Boston; hotels and motels 781

City of Randolph; Randolph; town government 750

Fidelity Brokerage Services; Boston; security brokers 750

BEC Energy; Boston; electric services 725

Ground Round of Minn. Inc.; Braintree; restaurant chain 722

Casual Male Corp.; Canton; men's/boys' clothing stores 715

Caritas Norwood Hospital Inc.; Norwood 710

Emcor Facilities Services of North America Inc.; Boston; heating and air conditioning contractors 710

American Building Maintenance Co.; Boston; janitorial service 700

American Red Cross; Dedham; individual and family services 700

AOL Time Warner Inc.; Boston; books publishing 700

Baltimore Technologies Inc.; Needham; computer programming services 700

Cingular Wireless; Westwood; cellular telephones 700

City of Walpole; Walpole; city government 700

Haemonetics Corp.; Braintree; medical instruments 700

Hale and Dorr; Boston; law offices 700

Massachusetts Dept. of Employment and Training; Boston 700

South Shore Hospital Inc.; Braintree; physical therapist 700

Suffolk University; Boston 700

Bridgewater State College; Bridgewater 695

State Street Corp.; Westwood; state trust company 663

Macy's East Inc.; Braintree; department stores 650

New England Sinai Hospital Inc.; Stoughton 650

United Group; West Bridgewater; liquor 650

Apollo Security Inc.; Walpole; security guard service 625

Stoneridge Inc.; Canton; motor vehicle electrical equipment 625

Divine Inc.; Westwood; specialized libraries 617

De Matteo Construction Co.; Braintree; bridge construction 600

May Department stores Co.; Boston; department stores 600

Medical Information Technology Inc.; Canton; computer programming services 600

Nextel Communications Inc.; Boston; business consulting 600

PFPC Inc.; Boston; acccounting services 600

Shaw's Supermarkets Inc.; West Bridgewater; supermarkets 600

Testa Hurwitz and Thibeault; Boston; general practice law office 600

Whitman-Hanson Regional School District; Whitman 600

Chase Global Funds Services Co.; Boston; mutual funds manager 599

CorpSoft Inc.; Norwood; systems software development services 580

Boston Consulting Group Inc.; Boston; management consulting 566

Simon and Schuster Inc.; Needham Heights; textbooks 560

City of Westwood; Westwood; city management 530

Bingham Dana; Boston; general practice law office 522

VT Administrative Inc.; Needham; restaurants 520

Clean Harbors Inc.; Braintree; hazardous waste collection, disposal 508

Stonehill College Inc.; North Easton 502

Allied Domecq Spirits and Wine USA Inc.; Westport restaurants 500

Alvin Hollis and Co. Inc.; South Weymouth; fuel oil dealers 500

Bayer Corp.; East Walpole; medicinals and botanicals 500

Bechtel Corp.; Boston; engineering services   500
City of Brockton; Brockton; educational services   500
Contemporary Services Co.; Foxboro; security guard
   service   500
Dunkin' Donuts Inc.; Randolph; franchise   500
Fallon Service Inc.; Milton; ambulance service   500
Fidelity Investments Institutional Services Co.; Boston;
   security brokers, dealers   500
General Dynamics Government Systems Corp.;
   Needham; data communication services   500
Globe Newspaper Co.; Boston; newspaper   500
Lawrence Instron Corp.; Canton; manufacturing
   industries   500
Massachusetts Dept. of Corrections; South Walpole
   500
Massachusetts Dept. of Corrections; Bridgewater   500
Omni Hotels Management Corp.; Boston; hotels   500
Parsons Energy and Chemicals Group Inc.; Canton;
   engineering services   500
Putnam Investments; Boston; open-ended management
   investment   500
Stop 'n Shop Companies Inc.; Boston; grocery store   500
Suffolk County; Boston; correctional facilities   500
Tab Community Newspapers Inc.; Needham; newspaper
   500
U.S. Federal Bureau of Investigation; Boston   500
U.S. Postal Service; Brockton   500
W. B. Johnson Properties; Boston; hotels   500

Massachusetts 10th District

South Shore — Quincy, Cape Cod, islands

Cool coastal breezes in the summer and warm ocean air in the winter attract retirees and tourists to the 10th, where most towns border the ocean. The area that spawned the nation's puritanical streak and the Thanksgiving holiday still retains a Yankee flavor, but the northern part of the 10th has attracted residents from Boston's ethnic neighborhoods. A rail line from Boston to several South Shore communities is contributing to the area's population boom. The old 10th was the fastest-growing Massachusetts district in the 1990s.

Other than tourism, maritime technology and research are burgeoning industries along the Cape, especially in Woods Hole. To the north, a booming software industry helped the area recover from a recession in the early 1990s.

The mainland coastal towns of the 10th are commonly referred to as the South Shore. With the exception of a handful of thriving cranberry bogs, most of the South Shore towns consist of bedroom developments for Boston's professionals or Quincy's blue-collar workers. The state's most liberal population lives on the far end of Cape Cod, where Provincetown, a predominantly gay artists' colony, thrives. Provincetown gave 75 percent of the vote to Democrat Shannon O'Brien in the 2002 gubernatorial race, her statewide high, and 80 percent to Al Gore in 2000, his second-highest state total.

But those totals belie the 10th's overall political character, which is more politically independent than Democratic. The state's least heavily Democratic district in the 2000 presidential race, the 10th opted for Republican Mitt Romney by 17 points in the 2002 gubernatorial race, thanks to GOP

strength in coastal communities southeast of Quincy and northwest of Plymouth.

Major Industry
Marine technology, biotechnology, health care, tourism.

Notable
Presidents John Adams and John Quincy Adams were from Quincy; Plymouth Rock; the John Alden House in Duxbury is named for the Pilgrim who sailed on the *Mayflower*.

Election Returns

	Republican		Democratic		Other	
President 2000	124,956	38.7%	175,426	54.3%	22,722	7.0%
House 2002	79,624	30.8%	179,238	69.2%	140	

District Profile

Population   635,901

Total area (square miles)   2,969.2
   Land area (square miles)   934.2

Population per square mile   680.7

Counties (2000 population)
Barnstable	222,230	Norfolk (pt.)	149,274
Dukes	14,987	Plymouth (pt.)	239,890
Nantucket	9,520		

Cities and other areas over 10,000 (2000 population)
   Abington CDP   14,605
   Barnstable Town   47,821
   Hull CDP   11,050
   Quincy   88,025
   South Yarmouth CDP   11,603
   Weymouth CDP   53,988

Race and Hispanic or Latino origin*
   White   92.2%
   Black or African American   1.5%
   American Indian or Alaska Native   0.3%
   Asian   2.7%
   Native Hawaiian or other Pacific Islander   0.0%
   Some other race   0.6%
   Hispanic or Latino origin   1.3%
   Two or more races   1.3%

*As percentage of total population.

Ancestry*
English 11.9%	Polish 2.4%
Fr. Canadian 2.3%	Portuguese 2.5%
French 4.0%	Scotch-Irish 1.8%
German 5.4%	Scottish 2.9%
Irish 23.9%	Swedish 2.1%
Italian 9.9%	USA/American 3.0%

*As estimated percentage of total population.

Universities and colleges, 2000–2001 enrollment
   Cape Cod Community College, West Barnstable   3,884
   Eastern Nazarene College, Quincy   1,381
   Massachusetts Maritime Academy, Buzzards Bay   830
   Quincy College, Quincy   4,508

Newspapers and circulation

	District circulation	Total circulation
Abington/Rockland Mariner	2,746	2,765
Boston Globe	44,209	465,248
Boston Herald	26,964	257,071
Brockton Enterprise	5,246	40,861
Cape Cod Times	49,494	49,957
Cohasset Mariner	1,834	1,919
Hanover Mariner	2,334	2,380
Harwich Oracle	2,567	2,651
Hingham Journal	4,482	4,597
Marshfield Mariner	4,149	4,224
Norwell Mariner	2,048	2,089
Pembroke Mariner	1,542	1,574
Quincy Patriot Ledger	48,981	67,219
Scituate Mariner	3,787	3,843
*USA Today**	3,920	1,674,376
Weymouth News	4,589	4,627

See Sources and Explanations in the front of the volume.

Television stations and affiliations

Boston (Manchester)	98%	WBPX	PAX
Boston (Manchester)	98%	WBZ	CBS
Boston (Manchester)	98%	WCVB	ABC
Boston (Manchester)	98%	WDPX	PAX
Boston (Manchester)	98%	WEKW	PBS
Boston (Manchester)	98%	WFXT	FOX
Boston (Manchester)	98%	WGBH	PBS
Boston (Manchester)	98%	WGBX	PBS
Boston (Manchester)	98%	WHDH	NBC
Boston (Manchester)	98%	WLVI	WB
Boston (Manchester)	98%	WMFP	Independent
Boston (Manchester)	98%	WMUR	ABC
Boston (Manchester)	98%	WNDS	Independent
Boston (Manchester)	98%	WPXB	Independent
Boston (Manchester)	98%	WPXG	PAX
Boston (Manchester)	98%	WSBK	UPN
Boston (Manchester)	98%	WUNI	Univision
Boston (Manchester)	98%	WWDP	Independent
Boston (Manchester)	98%	WYDN	Independent
Providence-New Bedford	2%	WJAR	NBC
Providence-New Bedford	2%	WLNE	ABC
Providence-New Bedford	2%	WLWC	UPN, WB
Providence-New Bedford	2%	WNAC	FOX
Providence-New Bedford	2%	WPRI	CBS
Providence-New Bedford	2%	WPXQ	PAX
Providence-New Bedford	2%	WSBE	PBS

Cable systems and subscribers
Adelphia   71,577
Comcast   125,406

Military installations, September 2001
Otis Air National Guard Base, Falmouth   1,353

Businesses and other major employers
Boston Financial Data Services Inc.; Quincy; mutual fund sales   3,000
Bartlett Nuclear Inc.; Plymouth; economic consultant   2,500
South Shore Hospital Inc.; South Weymouth   2,200
Putnam Investments; Quincy; mutual fund sales   1,300
American Federation of State County; Boston; employees' association   1,200
Cape Cod Hospital; Hyannis   1,200
Linchris Hotel Corp.; Hanover; management services   1,200
Stop 'n Shop Companies Inc.; Quincy; supermarkets   1,100
CitiStreet; Quincy; compensation and benefits planning   1,000
Jordan Hospital; Plymouth   1,000
Woods Hole Oceanographic Graphics Institution Inc.; Woods Hole   1,000
Delta Airlines Inc.; Quincy; air passenger carrier   960
Stone and Webster Co.; Weymouth; consulting engineer   900
Wear-Guard Corp.; Norwell; uniforms and work clothing   876
VNA of Cape Cod Inc.; South Dennis; visiting nurse service   830
Talbots Inc.; Hingham; catalog sales   825
Plymouth Public Schools; Plymouth   800
Quincy Medical Center Inc.; Quincy; hospital   800
Silverstream Software Inc.; Centerville; computer software development   800
Massachusetts National Guard; Buzzards Bay   743
City of Weymouth; Weymouth; elementary/secondary schools   741
Falmouth Hospital; Falmouth   700
Harvard Pilgrim Health Care Inc.; Quincy; health maintenance organization   680
Arbella Mutual Insurance Co.; Quincy; property damage insurance   600
Dennis Yarmouth Regional School District; South Yarmouth   560
Anodyne Medical Services Corp.; Quincy; medical help service   500
City of Carver; Carver; city management   500
City of Plymouth; Plymouth; city government   500
George W. Prescott Publishing Co.; Quincy; newspaper   500
Raytheon Co.; Quincy; hybrid integrated circuits   500
Vetcor Professional Practices Inc.; Hingham; business consulting   500

MICHIGAN

Districts established September 11, 2001, for elections first held in 2002.

15 members

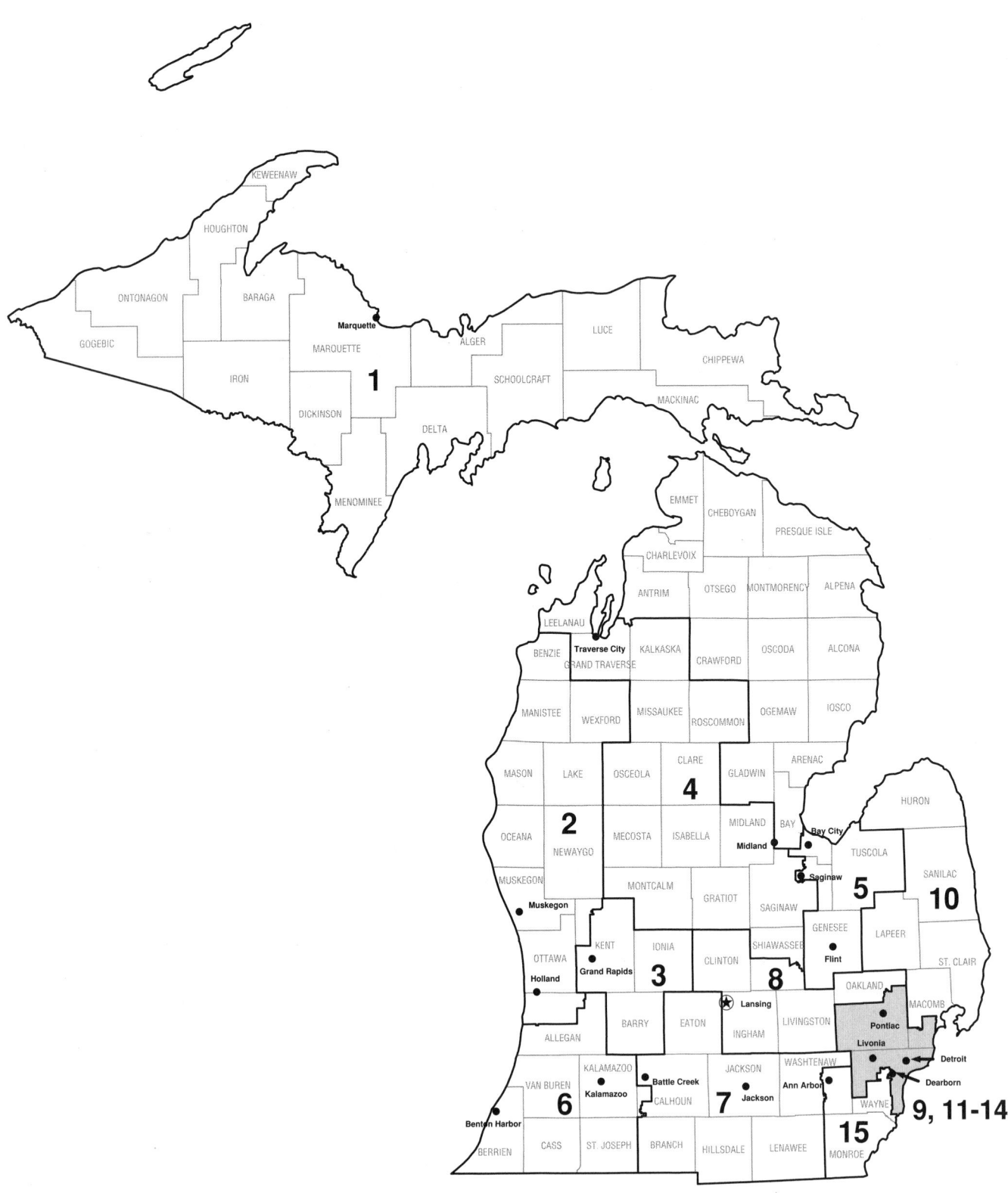

Michigan

When the industrial revolution brought its blessings and strains to the Great Lakes region, no state felt both more than Michigan. When that revolution passed its peak and faltered, no state felt the downturn more acutely than Michigan. At the end of the twentieth century, both the surge of the mechanical age and its wrenching aftermath had begun to give way to a new era. Michigan was once again at the forefront of the experience. The future may never be as robust as the glory days of the mid-twentieth century. In terms of population, Detroit may never again be among the top five cities (it is now tenth in rank), and Michigan may slip from the roster of the top ten states (it is now eighth). But the state has begun its transition to an economy beyond its golden age, and it can count on one of the best support systems of human and natural resources in the nation.

This was just one more agricultural state in the Upper Midwest when Henry Ford was born on a farm near Dearborn during the Civil War. But in 1903, at the age of 40, he established his auto company, and during the next two decades he changed personal transportation and mass market manufacturing forever. Detroit became the nation's unofficial industrial capital, drawing its workforce from every direction—from dozens of states and other countries and former walks of life. Having conquered the world, Ford, the man and the company, found the 1920s and 1930s tougher, given growing competition and a protracted struggle with workers and their unions. Ford finally signed a contract with the United Auto Workers (UAW) in 1941, on the eve of World War II, unleashing the production that would soon help win that war and then drive the postwar economic boom.

As autos changed the way Americans lived, they changed how Michigan worked. The forests, farms, and mines that had been the livelihood of the 1800s were forsaken by generations of young workers. The smaller cities that had spread out to the remote reaches of the state to serve these enterprises lost much of their vigor. Many converted to servicing aspects of the auto industry. Others turned to tourism, which grew in importance as hundreds of thousands of autoworkers gained the means and time off to hunt and fish and take families on vacation.

But by the end of the 1960s, with UAW members increasingly comfortable, middle-aged, and middle-class, there arose a new era of market competition, this time coming from overseas and most especially from Japan. This challenge gained strength with the Arab oil embargo of 1973 and the spike in gasoline prices that followed. The car-making industry stalled and then slid into reverse, losing 150,000 jobs between 1978 and 1982. Michigan's population, which had surged by hundreds of thousands in each decade of the century (peaking at a 1.4 million gain in the 1950s), grew by just 33,000 in the 1980s. And the automakers collectively known as "Detroit" would need the rest of the century to adjust, automate, downsize, and come back.

Along the way, it must be said, Michigan has owed not only its prosperity but also many of its persistent troubles to the auto industry's gargantuan appetite for workers. The huge plants attracted millions over the generations, first from farms and forests in the surrounding states and Canada, then from rural poverty or lesser jobs in cities far away. Along the way each wave of new arrivals had to endure crowded conditions, hardships, and friction among ethnic, religious, and racial groups. The most visible of the outsiders were the African Americans, who came in great numbers from the Depression South, established themselves in Detroit, and grew rapidly as a percentage of the city's population.

Eventually they made Detroit the nation's largest black-majority city (more than 80 percent black in the 2000 census), electing its mayors as far back as the 1970s, and redefining its cultural identity to the nation and the world. For most Americans, the title "Motown" ceased to be the city and became the record label by that name and the enormously popular music it marketed (The Temptations, the Supremes, and many more). But race relations in the city were traumatic even in the 1940s, when violent riots broke out over blacks in public housing. Years of white flight followed World War II and tore the fabric of the city. Then came the week of rioting in the summer of 1967 that left 43 dead and the city's pride shattered. Over the next 20 years, the city shed another third of its population (1990 census). Having once dreamed of surpassing Chicago and challenging New York, Detroit found itself compared instead to shrinking St. Louis or even violence-ridden Beirut.

The 1990s were a better decade for Detroit. Although population declined another 7.5 percent for the decade, falling below the million mark for the first time since Henry Ford's day, the rate of loss slowed and the larger metro area gained by about 5 percent. As of the 2000 census, only about one metro resident in six lived within the city limits. And many of the new residents in the area were immigrants intent on bettering themselves and their new home.

The new immigrant presence extends to many of the smaller cities and towns of the Detroit-Flint-Ann Arbor area. That includes Ford's old hometown of Dearborn (which had long since become a working-class suburb of Detroit) where a third of the residents are now of Arab descent. Throughout southeastern Michigan one can see reinvestment dollars at work, and a new dynamic is evident in both the public and private leadership. In the recession of 2001, Michigan's unemployment rate was only slightly above the national average, while its percentage of population in living poverty was well below.

All the turmoil of recent decades has taken a toll on the state's political status. Michigan had 19 seats in the House as recently as the 1970s, but only 15 were left after the 2000 census. The remapping of those remaining districts for 2002 was handled by the Republicans in charge of the state Senate and overseen by Republican governor John Engler, wrapping up his third term as governor. After decades as the minority party in the state's House delegation (still 9–7 Democratic as of 1992), Michigan Republicans made no bones about their eagerness to break through and their efforts were among the most aggressive and successful in the country.

The Republican remappers' first priority was to ensure the reelection of their seven incumbent Republicans, who represented the GOP strongholds (the Lake Michigan counties, Grand Rapids, Midland, Battle Creek, Kalamazoo) as well as the most affluent of Detroit's suburbs. But the plan also eliminated one Democratic district entirely (to accommodate the loss of a seat in reapportionment) and drew two other Democratic districts in the Detroit suburbs of Wayne and Macomb Counties to make them more vulnerable to takeover. The GOP succeeded on all counts, winding up with a new delegation that was 9–6 Republican when Congress convened in January 2003.

The district erased entirely was the Ann Arbor home base of Lynn Rivers, a four-termer popular among labor families and academics from the University of Michigan as well. Rivers chose to move to an adjacent district (the new 15th), in hopes that its incumbent Democrat, John Dingell, dean of the delegation and eldest member of the House, might retire. Instead, Dingell ran again and beat Rivers in the primary. Also departing were Democrats David Bonior, long the Democratic whip in the House, who sought the party nomination for governor, and Saginaw Bay's James Barcia, who retired rather than face a primary against Democratic colleague Dale Kildee, the longtime incumbent from Flint.

That left the Democrats with Dingell's Dearborn-based district plus two black districts based in Detroit, two white working-class districts in Flint and Warren (with some Detroit suburbs), and just one Democratic district outside the great populated metroplex: the far northern 1st that includes the Upper Peninsula between Lake Michigan and Lake Superior. And that district's loyalty may have been primarily a function of the personal popularity of the Democratic incumbent, a conservative on social issues.

The partisan shift in the House delegation reflected a good year for Republicans, however, that ran counter to the respective parties' fortunes in other recent elections. In 2002 Engler was term-limited, and his departure allowed the election of a Democrat, Jennifer Granholm, who was the first woman to hold the job. The venerable senator Carl Levin also won a fifth term easily, surpassing his previous high in vote share. In 2000 Al Gore won the state, which had been hotly contested by both campaigns. He even managed to eke out a true majority of 51.3 percent despite a relatively strong showing by Green Party nominee Ralph Nader (2 percent). It was the third consecutive win for Democratic presidential nominees in the state, a skein that had been preceded by five straight

wins for the GOP. Also in 2000, Democrats captured the state's junior Senate seat with Debbie Stabenow.

Table 1   Population

District	Population	Population under 18	Voting-age population	Median age	Male*	Female*
1	662,563	153,006	509,557	40.2	50.4	49.6
2	662,563	183,103	479,460	35.1	49.6	50.4
3	662,563	185,956	476,607	33.0	49.6	50.4
4	662,563	162,772	499,791	36.7	49.4	50.6
5	662,563	181,146	481,417	35.4	48.1	51.9
6	662,563	171,892	490,671	35.5	48.9	51.1
7	662,563	172,460	490,103	36.7	49.7	50.3
8	662,563	174,499	488,064	33.9	49.4	50.6
9	662,563	161,943	500,620	37.5	48.9	51.1
10	662,562	176,379	486,183	36.2	49.8	50.2
11	662,563	168,410	494,153	36.3	49.0	51.0
12	662,563	150,222	512,341	37.5	48.1	51.9
13	662,563	199,308	463,255	31.9	48.1	51.9
14	662,563	191,881	470,682	33.2	47.1	52.9
15	662,563	162,790	499,773	33.1	49.2	50.8
State	9,938,444	2,595,767	7,342,677	35.5	49.0	51.0

*As percentage of total population.

Table 2   Voting-Age Persons by Race/Hispanic or Latino Origin

District	White*	Black or African American*	American Indian or Alaska Native*	Asian*	Other or multirace*	Hispanic or Latino*
1	94.5	1.2	2.0	0.4	1.1	0.7
2	89.4	4.1	0.6	0.9	0.8	4.1
3	84.5	7.2	0.4	1.5	1.1	5.3
4	93.6	2.1	0.7	0.7	0.8	2.0
5	78.3	16.4	0.5	0.7	1.3	2.9
6	86.7	7.7	0.5	1.1	1.2	2.9
7	89.8	5.4	0.4	0.8	1.0	2.6
8	89.1	4.5	0.4	1.9	1.2	2.9
9	83.3	7.3	0.2	5.3	1.3	2.6
10	94.4	1.4	0.3	1.2	0.9	1.7
11	90.4	3.6	0.3	2.9	1.1	1.7
12	83.3	11.2	0.3	2.3	1.7	1.2
13	32.5	57.9	0.3	1.1	1.6	6.6
14	35.1	58.9	0.3	1.2	2.9	1.7
15	80.9	10.6	0.3	4.0	1.6	2.5
State	80.7	13.0	0.5	1.7	1.3	2.7

*As percentage of voting-age population.

Table 3   Voting-Age Population by Age Groups

District	18 to 24*	25 to 44*	45 to 64*	Over 64*
1	11.0	34.0	33.0	22.1
2	13.3	39.5	30.2	17.1
3	14.2	43.1	28.1	14.6
4	14.7	36.2	31.2	18.0
5	12.1	40.1	30.9	16.9
6	14.4	38.0	30.7	16.9
7	11.5	39.4	32.2	16.9
8	16.1	41.3	30.6	12.0
9	9.3	41.8	32.5	16.4
10	10.7	42.0	32.2	15.1
11	10.0	44.2	30.4	15.5
12	10.3	40.7	28.8	20.3
13	13.5	42.7	27.5	16.4

District	18 to 24*	25 to 44*	45 to 64*	Over 64*
14	12.6	40.9	29.2	17.3
15	17.1	41.4	28.3	13.2
State	12.7	40.3	30.4	16.6

*As percentage of voting-age population.

Table 4 Income and Occupation

District	Median family income	Families in poverty*	White collar†	Blue collar†	Service†	Farm†
1	$41,241	7.8	50.7	28.8	19.5	1.0
2	$50,227	6.3	51.3	33.1	14.5	1.1
3	$54,123	6.2	56.7	29.5	13.3	0.5
4	$46,500	6.6	53.5	28.7	17.0	0.8
5	$47,051	10.6	51.0	31.4	17.3	0.3
6	$49,402	7.5	53.0	31.3	14.7	1.1
7	$53,227	5.4	53.6	31.3	14.6	0.6
8	$64,336	4.9	62.6	23.0	14.1	0.3
9	$80,897	3.5	75.2	14.7	10.0	0.1
10	$61,930	4.3	55.2	31.5	12.9	0.5
11	$70,224	3.0	64.8	23.4	11.7	0.1
12	$56,748	5.4	59.7	26.7	13.5	0.1
13	$37,220	19.8	50.7	29.3	19.9	0.2
14	$41,967	15.9	53.0	28.4	18.5	0.1
15	$59,541	6.3	59.0	26.2	14.5	0.3
State	$53,457	7.4	57.1	27.6	14.8	0.5

*As percentage of all families. †As percentage of employed workers 16 years and over.

Table 5 Education: School Years Completed

District	Less than grade 9*	Grades 9–12 no diploma*	High school diploma no college*	Some college*	College bachelor's degree or higher*
1	5.3	11.7	38.6	28.9	15.6
2	5.2	11.1	35.1	30.2	18.3
3	4.5	10.9	29.9	30.9	23.9
4	4.4	11.1	35.9	30.0	18.6
5	4.7	13.3	34.8	32.1	15.1
6	5.0	11.5	32.3	30.1	21.1
7	3.9	10.7	33.8	32.4	19.1
8	2.7	7.8	26.8	33.7	29.0
9	2.9	7.0	20.0	26.6	43.5
10	4.6	10.8	34.6	33.1	16.9
11	2.9	9.2	28.0	31.5	28.5
12	5.0	13.5	31.4	30.5	19.5
13	8.4	22.1	29.3	26.0	14.1
14	6.5	17.9	31.1	30.3	14.2
15	4.1	11.2	28.7	28.5	27.5
State	4.7	11.9	31.3	30.3	21.8

*As percentage of persons age 25 and over.

Table 6 Housing and Residential Patterns

District	Median home value	Owner occupied*	Renter occupied*	Urban†	Rural†
1	$79,200	80.1	19.9	33.4	66.6
2	$101,800	80.0	20.0	56.2	43.8
3	$110,000	72.5	27.5	77.1	22.9
4	$92,500	77.7	22.3	41.4	58.6
5	$84,700	73.8	26.2	79.4	20.6
6	$96,000	72.9	27.1	58.3	41.7
7	$102,600	76.8	23.2	54.0	46.0
8	$141,300	75.2	24.8	70.0	30.0
9	$191,900	74.3	25.7	99.3	0.7
10	$144,800	82.1	17.9	66.0	34.0
11	$146,900	78.5	21.5	97.0	3.0
12	$119,100	73.0	27.0	100.0	0.0
13	$69,500	55.7	44.3	100.0	0.0
14	$83,900	64.9	35.1	100.0	0.0
15	$124,800	68.3	31.7	87.7	12.3
State	$110,300	73.8	26.2	74.7	25.3

*As percentage of occupied housing units. †As percentage of total population.

Michigan 1st District

Upper Peninsula; northern Lower Michigan

Rolling, forested hills, and some Upper Peninsula (UP) mountains that get hundreds of inches of snow make the 1st one of the few places suited to skiing in the Midwest. Beaches and resorts around Petoskey also lure summer vacationers from Detroit, Chicago, and Cleveland, feeding the area's tourist industry. But most of the district saw its economic foundations erode in the 1990s.

The UP, surrounded by three of the Great Lakes and connected to the rest of the state by the Mackinac Bridge, is still recovering from the closure of K. I. Sawyer Air Force Base in the 1990s. Mining, which once drew immigrants to remote parts of the state, has not been a growth industry since the early twentieth century. NAFTA has effectively killed most remaining copper, paper, and iron production.

Tourism and timber products companies are the only growth industries. Snowmobiling makes up at least 40 percent of winter revenues for restaurants and hotels. Slow population growth in northern Michigan and the UP gradually has led to the expansion of the district's territory to encompass more than 40 percent of the state's land mass. After the 2000 census, the 1st needed to add about 23,000 people to meet the population equality requirement; a new map drawn in 2001 did this by shedding some northwestern Michigan counties (including Grand Traverse) and adding some northeastern counties along the Saginaw Bay. The 1st reaches nearly as far south as Bay City (which is in the 5th).

As a whole, the 1st backs Democrats, but there is a strong strain of social conservatism, particularly on gun rights. A long tradition of union organization among miners and mill workers has left the western and central UP strongly Democratic, a preference shared by the eastern counties in the northern part of the state. But George W. Bush made major inroads in the area in the 2000 presidential election, decisively winning counties that Bob Dole had lost in 1996. The northern counties at the top of the "mitten" also tend to support Republicans.

Major Industry
Mining, logging, tourism, auto parts.

Notable
Isle Royale National Park; the National Ski Hall of Fame is in Ishpeming.

Election Returns

	Republican		Democratic		Other	
President 2000	154,772	51.7%	135,503	45.2%	9,371	3.1%
House 2002	69,254	31.1%	150,701	67.7%	2,732	1.2%

District Profile

Population   662,563

Total area (square miles)   27,808.7
   Land area (square miles)   24,887.2

Population per square mile   26.6

Counties (2000 population)

Alcona	11,719	Houghton	36,016
Alger	9,862	Iosco	27,339
Alpena	31,314	Iron	13,138
Antrim	23,110	Keweenaw	2,301
Arenac	17,269	Luce	7,024
Baraga	8,746	Mackinac	11,943
Bay (pt.)	30,835	Marquette	64,634
Charlevoix	26,090	Menominee	25,326
Cheboygan	26,448	Montmorency	10,315
Chippewa	38,543	Ogemaw	21,645
Crawford	14,273	Ontonagon	7,818
Delta	38,520	Oscoda	9,418
Dickinson	27,472	Otsego	23,301
Emmet	31,437	Presque Isle	14,411
Gladwin	26,023	Schoolcraft	8,903
Gogebic	17,370		

Cities and other areas over 10,000 (2000 population)

Alpena	11,304	Marquette	19,661
Escanaba	13,140	Sault Ste. Marie	16,542

Race and Hispanic or Latino origin*

White   93.8%
Black or African American   1.0%
American Indian or Alaska Native   2.4%
Asian   0.4%
Native Hawaiian or other Pacific Islander   0.0%
Some other race   0.0%
Hispanic or Latino origin   0.9%
Two or more races   1.4%

*As percentage of total population.

Ancestry*

Dutch	1.8%	Italian	3.1%
English	7.7%	Norwegian	1.3%
Finnish	5.0%	Polish	6.5%
Fr. Canadian	2.9%	Scottish	1.6%
French	7.1%	Swedish	3.4%
German	15.8%	USA/American	3.5%
Irish	7.2%		

*As estimated percentage of total population.

Universities and colleges, 2000–2001 enrollment

Alpena Community College, Alpena   1,853
Bay De Noc Community College, Escanaba   2,073
Bay Mills Community College, Brimley   360
Finlandia University, Hancock   383
Gogebic Community College, Ironwood   1,106
Kirtland Community College, Roscommon   1,307
Lake Superior State University, Sault Ste. Marie   3,118
Michigan Technological University, Houghton   6,336
North Central Michigan College, Petoskey   2,196
Northern Michigan University, Marquette   8,427

Newspapers and circulation

	District circulation	Total circulation
Alpena News	10,800	10,953
Bay City Times	15,525	36,101
Detroit Free Press	11,818	363,536
Detroit News	5,858	238,950
Detroit News/Free Press (Sunday)	17,678	603,915
Escanaba Daily Press	9,893	9,966
Houghton Daily Mining Gazette	9,690	9,770
Iron Mountain Daily News	8,052	9,616
Marquette Mining Journal	16,275	16,292
Midland Daily News	1,965	16,372
Petoskey News-Review	10,502	10,530
Saginaw News	1,114	47,648
Traverse City Record-Eagle	4,033	28,373
*USA Today**	2,065	1,674,376

*See Sources and Explanations in the front of the volume.

Television stations and affiliations

Marquette	50%	WBKP	ABC
Marquette	50%	WJMN	CBS
Marquette	50%	WLUC	NBC
Marquette	50%	WNMU	PBS
Traverse City-Cadillac	29%	WCML	PBS
Traverse City-Cadillac	29%	WCMV	PBS
Traverse City-Cadillac	29%	WCMW	PBS
Traverse City-Cadillac	29%	WGTQ	ABC
Traverse City-Cadillac	29%	WGTU	ABC
Traverse City-Cadillac	29%	WPBN	NBC
Traverse City-Cadillac	29%	WTOM	NBC
Traverse City-Cadillac	29%	WWTV	CBS
Traverse City-Cadillac	29%	WWUP	CBS
Flint-Saginaw-Bay City	8%	WAQP	Independent
Flint-Saginaw-Bay City	8%	WCMU	PBS
Flint-Saginaw-Bay City	8%	WDCP	PBS
Flint-Saginaw-Bay City	8%	WDCQ	PBS
Flint-Saginaw-Bay City	8%	WEYI	NBC
Flint-Saginaw-Bay City	8%	WFUM	PBS
Flint-Saginaw-Bay City	8%	WJRT	ABC
Flint-Saginaw-Bay City	8%	WNEM	CBS
Flint-Saginaw-Bay City	8%	WSMH	FOX
Alpena	7%	WBKB	CBS
Duluth-Superior, MN	3%	KBJR	NBC, UPN
Duluth-Superior, MN	3%	KDLH	CBS
Duluth-Superior, MN	3%	KQDS	FOX
Duluth-Superior, MN	3%	WDIO	ABC
Duluth-Superior, MN	3%	WDSE	PBS
Duluth-Superior, MN	3%	WIRT	ABC
Green Bay-Appleton, WI	3%	WACY	UPN
Green Bay-Appleton, WI	3%	WBAY	ABC
Green Bay-Appleton, WI	3%	WFRV	CBS
Green Bay-Appleton, WI	3%	WGBA	NBC
Green Bay-Appleton, WI	3%	WIWB	WB, PAX
Green Bay-Appleton, WI	3%	WJFW	NBC
Green Bay-Appleton, WI	3%	WLUK	FOX
Green Bay-Appleton, WI	3%	WPNE	PBS

Cable systems and subscribers
Caspian Community TV   557
Charter   125,374
Negaunee Cable TV   2,248
Northwoods Cable TV   838
Norway CATV   1,022
Stambaugh Cable   645
Time Warner   4,093
Upper Peninsula Communications   2,133

Military installations, September 2001
Grayling Airfield (Army Guard), Grayling   568
Alpena County Regional Airport, Alpena   117

Businesses and other major employers
Marquette General Hospital Inc.; Marquette   1,857
Sault Ste. Marie Tribe of Chippewa Indians; Sault Ste. Marie; gambling   1,800
Mead Corp.; Trout Lake; paper broadwoven fabrics   1,500
Michigan Technological University; Houghton   1,235
Escanaba Paper Co.; Escanaba; magazine paper   1,200
Empire Iron Mining Partnership; Palmer; iron ores   1,000
Northern Michigan University; Marquette   1,000
Northern Michigan Hospital Inc.; Petoskey   950
Alpena General Hospital; Alpena   900
Tilden Mining Co.; Ishpeming; iron ores   820
Michigan Dept. of Corrections; Standish   734
Bay Mills Indian Community; Brimley; Native American reservation   710
East Jordan Iron Works Inc.; East Jordan; iron foundry   700
Michigan Dept. of Corrections; Kincheloe   666
Alpena Public Schools; Alpena   600
Dickinson County Health Care System Hospital; Iron Mountain   600
Lec Viewx Desert Band of Lake Superior Chippewa Indians; Watersmeet; Native American reservation   600
International Paper Co.; Quinnesec; paper/pulp mill construction   580
Iron Mountain Kingsford Community School; Iron Mountain   550
Cable Constructors Inc.; Iron Mountain; electronic parts and equipment   500
Grede Foundries Inc.; Iron Mountain; gray iron castings   500
Huron Concrete Co.; Alpena; investment holding company   500
ITT Industries Inc.; Oscoda; plastics products   500
Kimberly-Clark Corp.; Munising; printing paper   500
Northern Michigan Staffing; Standish; employee leasing service   500
OSF Healthcare System Hospital; Escanaba   500

Michigan 2nd District

West — Muskegon, Holland

The 2nd stretches 140 miles along Lake Michigan, covering counties full of cherry trees and asparagus farms. Pioneers, most of them Dutch, were drawn to the region by rich logging opportunities. Now, heavy industrial manufacturing dominates the most populated counties, including Ottawa, Muskegon, and Allegan, but the early settlers' pioneering spirit persists. Dutch independence has made the 2nd one of the most staunchly Republican districts in Michigan.

That Republicanism is led by Ottawa County, which gave George W. Bush a statewide high of 71 percent of the vote in the 2000 presidential election. Ottawa added more than 50,000 residents in the 1990s, more than all but three other Michigan counties, and grew by 27 percent. More than 35 percent of district residents live in Ottawa County.

Support for Democratic candidates can be found among minority voters in the district's largest city, Muskegon, which has struggled to keep manufacturing jobs. But local tax incentives have drawn in new automotive parts suppliers, helping the economy rebound. Western Michigan also hosts several of the nation's top office furniture makers, including Herman Miller in Zeeland and Holland and Haworth in Holland.

Holland, south of Muskegon, is a conservative, Dutch-settled port town that draws tourists from all over the Midwest. It is the westernmost point of the "Dutch Triangle," formed by Holland, Grand Rapids, and Kalamazoo. The Dutch lifestyle of the early twentieth century is recreated in Dutch Village theme park, complete with wooden shoes and Klompen dancers. Holland's annual tulip festival draws hundreds of thousands of visitors every May.

Redistricting following the 2000 census did not significantly alter the 2nd's borders. The new map added Benzie County, a fast-growing area in northwest Michigan, and reconfigured the boundaries in the south.

Major Industry
Metal, furniture, tourism, agriculture.

Notable
The world's largest weather vane is in Montague; Oceana County hosts the National Asparagus Festival.

Election Returns

	Republican		Democratic		Other	
President 2000	172,428	59.3%	111,739	38.4%	6,550	2.3%
House 2002	156,937	70.4%	61,749	27.7%	4,221	1.9%

District Profile

Population   662,563

Total area (square miles)   5,508.3
Land area (square miles)   5,364.9

Population per square mile   123.5

Counties (2000 population)

Allegan (pt.) 38,641	Muskegon 170,200
Benzie 15,998	Newaygo 47,874
Kent (pt.) 30,045	Oceana 26,873
Lake 11,333	Ottawa 238,314
Manistee 24,527	Wexford 30,484
Mason 28,274	

Cities and other areas over 10,000 (2000 population)
Allendale CDP   11,555
Cadillac   10,000

Grand Haven   11,168
Holland   35,048
Jenison CDP   17,211
Muskegon   40,105
Muskegon Heights   12,049
Norton Shores   22,527

Race and Hispanic or Latino origin*

White   87.5%
Black or African American   4.5%
American Indian or Alaska Native   0.6%
Asian   1.0%
Native Hawaiian or other Pacific Islander   0.0%
Some other race   0.1%
Hispanic or Latino origin   5.2%
Two or more races   1.2%

*As percentage of total population.

Ancestry*

Dutch 14.8%		Italian 1.6%	
English 7.0%		Norwegian 1.1%	
Fr. Canadian 1.2%		Polish 4.4%	
French 3.2%		Scottish 1.2%	
German 15.3%		Swedish 2.5%	
Irish 7.0%		USA/American 4.1%	

*As estimated percentage of total population.

Universities and colleges, 2000–2001 enrollment

Baker College-Cadillac, Cadillac   864
Baker College-Muskegon, Muskegon   2,727
Davenport College of Business, Holland   820
Grand Valley State University, Allendale   18,569
Hope College, Holland   3,015
Muskegon Community College, Muskegon   4,311
West Shore Community College, Scottville   1,273

Newspapers and circulation

	District circulation	Total circulation
Detroit Free Press	4,460	363,536
Detroit News	2,116	238,950
Detroit News/Free Press (Sunday)	6,581	603,915
Grand Haven Tribune	10,030	10,030
Grand Rapids Press	38,077	139,414
Holland Sentinel	17,629	18,282
Ludington Daily News	8,078	8,174
Muskegon Chronicle	46,327	46,327
Traverse City Record-Eagle	4,031	28,373
*USA Today**	3,067	1,674,376

*See Sources and Explanations in the front of the volume.

Television stations and affiliations

Grand Rapids-Kalamazoo-Battle Creek	57%	WGVK	PBS
Grand Rapids-Kalamazoo-Battle Creek	57%	WGVU	PBS
Grand Rapids-Kalamazoo-Battle Creek	57%	WLLA	Independent
Grand Rapids-Kalamazoo-Battle Creek	57%	WOOD	NBC
Grand Rapids-Kalamazoo-Battle Creek	57%	WOTV	ABC
Grand Rapids-Kalamazoo-Battle Creek	57%	WTLJ	Independent
Grand Rapids-Kalamazoo-Battle Creek	57%	WWMT	CBS
Grand Rapids-Kalamazoo-Battle Creek	57%	WXMI	FOX
Grand Rapids-Kalamazoo-Battle Creek	57%	WZZM	ABC
Traverse City-Cadillac	43%	WCML	PBS
Traverse City-Cadillac	43%	WCMV	PBS
Traverse City-Cadillac	43%	WCMW	PBS
Traverse City-Cadillac	43%	WGTQ	ABC
Traverse City-Cadillac	43%	WGTU	ABC
Traverse City-Cadillac	43%	WPBN	NBC
Traverse City-Cadillac	43%	WTOM	NBC
Traverse City-Cadillac	43%	WWTV	CBS
Traverse City-Cadillac	43%	WWUP	CBS

Cable systems and subscribers

Charter   55,037
Comcast   53,443

Businesses and other major employers

Haworth Inc.; Holland; office furniture   4,000
Herman Miller Inc.; Zeeland; office furniture   2,800
Herman Miller Inc.; Holland; office furniture   1,630
Mercy General Health Partners Hospital; Muskegon   1,543
E. C. Aviation Services Inc.; Zeeland; air passenger carrier   1,400
Meijer Inc.; Muskegon; discount department stores   1,300
Hackley Hospital; Muskegon   1,268
Johnson Controls Interiors; Holland; automotive trimmings, fabric   1,250
CP Industries Inc.; Grand Haven; aluminum die-castings   1,200
Marriott International Inc.; Muskegon; restaurants   1,200
Sara Lee Corp.; Zeeland; prepared meats   1,100
Holland Community Hospital Inc.; Holland   993
A&E Products Group Inc.; Zeeland; plastics film and sheet   900
Grand Valley State University; Allendale   898
Delphi Corp.; Coopersville; motor vehicle choker rods   850
Meridian Inc.; Spring Lake; office furniture   850
Hart and Cooley Inc.; Holland; metal air registers   800
Meijer Inc.; Holland; discount department stores   700
US Xchange; Grand Rapids; local/long-distance telephone   650
Behr Industries Corp.; Comstock Park; motor vehicle parts/accessories   625
S. D. Warren Co.; Muskegon; paper mills   617
Cadillac Rubber and Plastics Inc.; Cadillac; mechanical rubber goods   614
Gerber Products Co.; Fremont; baby foods   600
Hope College; Holland   600
Little River Casino Resort; Manistee; casino hotel   600
S2 Yachts Inc.; Holland; fiberglass boats   600
Integrated Metal Technology Inc.; Spring Lake; sheet metalwork   575
GNA and Associates Inc.; Grand Haven; physical therapist   530
Brunswick Bowling and Billiards Corp.; Muskegon; sporting goods   500
Four Winns Boats; Cadillac; motorboats building and repairing   500
Howard Miller Clock Co.; Zeeland; clocks   500
Recreational Boat Group; Cadillac; motorboats building and repairing   500
Venturedyne; Holland; environmental testing equipment   500

Michigan 3rd District

West central — Grand Rapids

Grand Rapids, Michigan's second-most-populous city, teems with auto plants and metals manufacturing, but it is a world away from Detroit. Conservative Dutch Republicans—not auto union Democrats—control the district, making the 3rd one of Michigan's heaviest GOP regions. Its staunch conservatism is rivaled only by the neighboring 2nd; both districts gave 61 percent of the two-party vote to George W. Bush in the 2000 presidential election.

Also unlike Detroit, Grand Rapids has escaped complete dependence on the auto industry. The city is a leading producer of metal office furniture, in addition to making avionics systems, tools, and home appliances. The city's economy prospered in the 1970s when modular furniture became popular, but it suffered in the early 1990s when companies began to downsize their managerial staffs and cut back on office space. In a major effort to revitalize downtown Grand Rapids, the city built a new arena and recruited three minor league sports teams.

Gerald R. Ford made his way to the House and then the presidency from Grand Rapids (the area airport is named for the him), and his brand of small-government Republicanism and fiscal restraint still holds sway in the 3rd. One of the district's largest employers, Amway, based in Ada, consistently contributes to Republicans around the nation. This direct sales company, which markets personal- and home-care products, promotes its philosophy of private philanthropy by donating generously to area universities, hospitals, and churches.

More than 80 percent of residents live in Kent County, which grew by 15 percent in the 1990s largely because of rapid growth outside of Grand Rapids (which grew by just 5 percent). The rest live in Ionia and Barry Counties, located east and southeast of Kent, respectively. Redistricting following the 2000 census made minimal changes to the 3rd.

Major Industry
Office furniture, auto parts, metals manufacturing.

Notable
The Norton Mound Group, one of the best-preserved burial centers of the Hopewell culture, is in Grand Rapids.

Election Returns

	Republican		Democratic		Other	
President 2000	170,622	59.5%	110,121	38.4%	5,942	2.1%
House 2002	153,131	70.0%	61,987	28.3%	3,737	1.7%

District Profile

Population   662,563

Total area (square miles)   1,897.4
   Land area (square miles)   1,854.3

Population per square mile   357.3

Counties (2000 population)
Barry   56,755
Ionia   61,518
Kent (pt.)   544,290

Cities and other areas over 10,000 (2000 population)
Cutlerville CDP   15,114
East Grand Rapids   10,764
Forest Hills CDP   20,942
Grand Rapids   197,800
Grandville   16,263
Ionia   10,569
Kentwood   45,255
Northview CDP   14,730
Walker   21,842
Wyoming   69,368

Race and Hispanic or Latino origin*
White   82.2%
Black or African American   7.9%
American Indian or Alaska Native   0.4%
Asian   1.6%
Native Hawaiian or other Pacific Islander   0.0%
Some other race   0.1%
Hispanic or Latino origin   6.2%
Two or more races   1.5%

*As percentage of total population.

Ancestry*
Dutch	13.1%	Italian	1.9%
English	7.8%	Polish	5.2%
French	2.7%	Scottish	1.2%
German	14.6%	Swedish	1.5%
Irish	7.9%	USA/American	3.9%

*As estimated percentage of total population.

Universities and colleges, 2000–2001 enrollment
Aquinas College, Grand Rapids   2,605
Calvin College, Grand Rapids   4,309
Calvin Theological Seminary, Grand Rapids   264
Cornerstone College, Grand Rapids   1,877
Davenport College, Grand Rapids   2,322
Grand Rapids Baptist Seminary, Grand Rapids   216
Grand Rapids Community College, Grand Rapids   13,400
ITT Technical Institute, Grand Rapids   404
Kendall College of Art and Design, Grand Rapids   744

Newspapers and circulation

	District circulation	Total circulation
Battle Creek Enquirer	2,921	24,908
Detroit Free Press	3,203	363,536
Detroit News	1,935	238,950
Detroit News/Free Press (Sunday)	5,145	603,915
Grand Rapids Press	92,340	139,414
Greenville Daily News	2,271	8,576
Kalamazoo Gazette	1,514	56,200
Lansing State Journal	1,851	69,782
*USA Today**	4,364	1,674,376

*See Sources and Explanations in the front of the volume.

Television stations and affiliations
Grand Rapids-Kalamazoo-Battle Creek	100%	WGVK	PBS
Grand Rapids-Kalamazoo-Battle Creek	100%	WGVU	PBS
Grand Rapids-Kalamazoo-Battle Creek	100%	WLLA	Independent
Grand Rapids-Kalamazoo-Battle Creek	100%	WOOD	NBC
Grand Rapids-Kalamazoo-Battle Creek	100%	WOTV	ABC
Grand Rapids-Kalamazoo-Battle Creek	100%	WTLJ	Independent

Grand Rapids-Kalamazoo-Battle Creek	100%	WWMT	CBS
Grand Rapids-Kalamazoo-Battle Creek	100%	WXMI	FOX
Grand Rapids-Kalamazoo-Battle Creek	100%	WZZM	ABC

Cable systems and subscribers
Charter 12,308
Comcast 47,603
Lowell Cable TV 1,891
Millennium Digital Media 5,254

Military installations, September 2001
ITA Fort Custer Training Center, Battle Creek 437

Businesses and other major employers
Steelcase Inc.; Grand Rapids; office furniture 9,500
Amway Corp.; Ada; detergents 6,000
Navigant International Inc.; Grand Rapids; travel management services 6,000
Alticor Inc.; Ada; chemicals and allied products 4,800
General Motors Corp.; Grand Rapids; motor vehicle parts/accessories 2,700
West Michigan Volleyball Centers Ltd. Liability Co.; Grand Rapids; physical fitness facilities 2,700
Meijer Inc.; Grand Rapids; discount department stores 2,200
Mastercuts Inc.; Grandville; hairdressers 2,000
Olender/Bessire Inc.; Grand Rapids; baking supplies 1,920
Spectrum Health-Blodgett Campus Hospital; Grand Rapids 1,900
Hope Network; Grand Rapids; vocational rehabilitation agency 1,569
Foremost Corp. of America; Caledonia; fire, marine, casualty insurance 1,500
Meridian Automotive Systems Inc.; Ionia; automotive stampings 1,500
Meridian Automotive Systems Inc.; Grand Rapids; molded plastics products 1,500
Siemens Dematic Corp.; Grand Rapids; accounting services 1,500
City of Grand Rapids; Grand Rapids; public roads 1,400
CBS Corp.; Grand Rapids; electrical equipment 1,217
Spartan Stores; Grand Rapids; food supplier 1,200
Metropolitan Hospital; Grand Rapids 1,050
Batts Group; Grand Rapids; clothes hangers 1,000
Diesel Technology Co.; Grand Rapids; automotive camshafts 1,000
Lacks Exterior Systems; Grand Rapids; plastics hardware and building products 1,000
Smiths Industries Aerospace and Defense Systems Inc.; Grand Rapids; search and navigation equipment 1,000
Bradford White Corp.; Middleville; household hot water heaters 900
Cascade Engineering; Grand Rapids; injection molding of plastics 900
Delphi Corp.; Grand Rapids; combustion engines 900
Grand Valley State University; Grand Rapids 900
Pine Rest Southwood; Grand Rapids; group foster home 900
Loeks-Star Partners; Grand Rapids; movie theaters 895
Bissell Homecare Inc.; Grand Rapids; vacuum cleaners 800

Gordon Food Service Inc.; Grand Rapids; food supplier 800
Holland Nursing Home; Grand Rapids 800
Keebler Co.; Grand Rapids; cookies 800
Pridgeon and Clay Inc.; Grand Rapids; automotive stampings 750
Knape and Vogt Manufacturing Co.; Grand Rapids; partitions and fixtures 748
Irwin Seating Co.; Grand Rapids; public building furniture 745
American Seating Co.; Grand Rapids; office furniture 700
Sears Roebuck and Co. Inc.; Grand Rapids; department stores 700
Steelcase Inc.; Caledonia; household furniture 700
U.S. Postal Service; Grand Rapids 700
Grand Rapids Community College; Grand Rapids 680
Bank One Corp.; Grand Rapids; commercial trust company 650
Magna Mirror Systems Inc.; Alto; automobile mirrors 650
Mary Free Bed Hospital and Rehabilitation Center; Grand Rapids 622
Autodie International Inc.; Grand Rapids; dies, tools, jigs, fixtures 600
Knoll Inc.; Grand Rapids; office furniture 600
Sysco Food Services; Grand Rapids; food supplier 600
Calvin College; Grand Rapids 595
Canteen Services Inc.; Belmont; vending machines 562
Guardian Protective Services Inc.; Grand Rapids; protective services, guard 530
Benteler Automotive Corp.; Grand Rapids; automotive exhaust systems 510
Flexfab Horizons International Inc.; Hastings; rubber and plastics hose and beltings 508
Amway Hotel Corp.; Grand Rapids; restaurants 500
Coca-Cola Enterprises Inc.; Grand Rapids; soft drinks 500
CSX Transportation Inc.; Grand Rapids; switching and terminal services 500
Display Pack Inc.; Grand Rapids; plastics processing 500
Herald Co.; Grand Rapids; newspaper 500
Magna Mirror Systems Inc.; Grand Rapids; automobile mirrors 500
Michigan Dept. of Corrections; Ionia 500
Pennock Hospital; Hastings 500
Target Corp.; Grand Rapids; department stores 500

Michigan 4th District
North central — Midland, Traverse City

Forests and farms cover much of the 14 central Michigan counties that lie wholly or partly in the 4th, which is the state's second-largest district in land area. The white pine forests north of Midland, the district's largest city, were once some of the most bountiful logging lands in the state. Now, retirees and vacationers build second homes in the sparsely populated woods, and tourists come to ski, camp, and hunt in these remote counties.

Midland, on the district's eastern border, is home to Dow Chemical and Dow Corning, makers of chemicals, plastics, and silicone products. Dow Chemical headquarters sits on a 2,150-acre campus in Midland, giving the city more engineers, chemists, and metallurgists per capita than any other city in the nation. The area is vulnerable to Dow's corporate restructuring, but also has benefited from Dow's generous philanthropy, with churches, schools, and libraries built by the Dow fortune.

West and south of Midland, the district turns agricultural. Farmers—who till fields of sugar beets, dry beans, corn, wheat, and oats—worry about free trade, price supports, and crop insurance. The number of farms and small towns throughout the 4th give it a Republican lean.

Redistricting following the 2000 census gave the 4th some solidly Republican, sparsely populated but fast-growing counties in northwest Michigan. The proximity to Lake Michigan and distance from noisy population centers make the area especially attractive to retirees. Leelanau County, in the northwest corner, grew by 28 percent in the 1990s, and Grand Traverse County (Traverse City), grew by 21 percent. Almost every county in the 4th that is west and north of Midland saw its population grow by at least 15 percent.

Major Industry

Agriculture, chemical and plastics manufacturing, tourism.

Notable

Interlochen Center for the Arts, south of Traverse City, includes a camp and an academy for students of the arts.

Election Returns

	Republican		Democratic		Other	
President 2000	154,539	53.6%	126,282	43.8%	7,468	2.6%
House 2002	149,090	68.2%	65,950	30.2%	3,533	1.6%

District Profile

Population   662,563

Total area (square miles)   8,052.5
   Land area (square miles)   7,451.4

Population per square mile   88.9

Counties (2000 population)

Clare 31,252	Midland 82,874
Grand Traverse 77,654	Missaukee 14,478
Gratiot 42,285	Montcalm 61,266
Isabella 63,351	Osceola 23,197
Kalkaska 16,571	Roscommon 25,469
Leelanau 21,119	Saginaw (pt.) 121,205
Mecosta 40,553	Shiawassee (pt.) 41,289

Cities and other areas over 10,000 (2000 population)
Big Rapids   10,849
Midland (pt.)   41,463
Mount Pleasant   25,946
Owosso   15,713
Saginaw Township North CDP   24,994
Saginaw Township South CDP   13,801
Traverse City (pt.)   14,532

Race and Hispanic or Latino origin*
White   92.8%
Black or African American   2.1%
American Indian or Alaska Native   0.8%
Asian   0.7%
Native Hawaiian or other Pacific Islander   0.0%
Some other race   0.1%
Hispanic or Latino origin   2.4%
Two or more races   1.1%

*As percentage of total population.

Ancestry*

Dutch 3.0%	Italian 1.8%
English 8.9%	Polish 4.7%
Fr. Canadian 1.6%	Scottish 1.9%
French 4.1%	Swedish 1.2%
German 19.5%	USA/American 5.1%
Irish 8.2%	

*As estimated percentage of total population.

Universities and colleges, 2000–2001 enrollment
Alma College, Alma   1,409
Baker College of Owosso, Owosso   1,905
Central Michigan University, Mount Pleasant   26,845
Ferris State University, Big Rapids   9,847
Great Lakes College, Midland   1,694
Mid-Michigan Community College, Harrison   2,316
Montcalm Community College, Sidney   1,545
Northwestern Michigan College, Traverse City   3,965
Northwood University, Midland   3,835

Newspapers and circulation

	District circulation	Total circulation
Bay City Times	1,617	36,101
Detroit Free Press	8,264	363,536
Detroit News	4,887	238,950
Detroit News/Free Press (Sunday)	13,165	603,915
Flint Journal	2,407	88,130
Grand Rapids Press	5,110	139,414
Greenville Daily News	6,144	8,576
Lansing State Journal	1,503	69,782
Midland Daily News	14,504	16,372
Mount Pleasant Morning Sun	11,600	11,600
Saginaw News	28,624	47,648
Traverse City Record-Eagle	20,281	28,373
*USA Today**	4,411	1,674,376

*See Sources and Explanations in the front of the volume.

Television stations and affiliations

Traverse City-Cadillac	67%	WCML	PBS
Traverse City-Cadillac	67%	WCMV	PBS
Traverse City-Cadillac	67%	WCMW	PBS
Traverse City-Cadillac	67%	WGTQ	ABC
Traverse City-Cadillac	67%	WGTU	ABC
Traverse City-Cadillac	67%	WPBN	NBC
Traverse City-Cadillac	67%	WTOM	NBC
Traverse City-Cadillac	67%	WWTV	CBS
Traverse City-Cadillac	67%	WWUP	CBS
Flint-Saginaw-Bay City	26%	WAQP	Independent
Flint-Saginaw-Bay City	26%	WCMU	PBS
Flint-Saginaw-Bay City	26%	WDCP	PBS
Flint-Saginaw-Bay City	26%	WDCQ	PBS
Flint-Saginaw-Bay City	26%	WEYI	NBC
Flint-Saginaw-Bay City	26%	WFUM	PBS
Flint-Saginaw-Bay City	26%	WJRT	ABC

Flint-Saginaw-Bay City	26%	WNEM	CBS
Flint-Saginaw-Bay City	26%	WSMH	FOX
Grand Rapids-Kalamazoo-Battle Creek	7%	WGVK	PBS
Grand Rapids-Kalamazoo-Battle Creek	7%	WGVU	PBS
Grand Rapids-Kalamazoo-Battle Creek	7%	WLLA	Independent
Grand Rapids-Kalamazoo-Battle Creek	7%	WOOD	NBC
Grand Rapids-Kalamazoo-Battle Creek	7%	WOTV	ABC
Grand Rapids-Kalamazoo-Battle Creek	7%	WTLJ	Independent
Grand Rapids-Kalamazoo-Battle Creek	7%	WWMT	CBS
Grand Rapids-Kalamazoo-Battle Creek	7%	WXMI	FOX
Grand Rapids-Kalamazoo-Battle Creek	7%	WZZM	ABC

Cable systems and subscribers
Charter   99,622
Comcast   593
Crystal Cable TV   535

Businesses and other major employers
Michigan State Police; Lakeview   3,500
Dow Chemical Co.; Midland; thermoplastic materials 3,000
Munson Medical Center; Traverse City   2,723
Electrolux Home Products Inc.; Greenville; refrigerators 1,800
Central Michigan University; Mount Pleasant   1,500
Dow Corning Corp.; Midland; silicone-based technology 1,500
Mid-Michigan Regional Medical Center Inc.; Midland 1,375
Traverse City Area Public Schools; Traverse City 1,104
Michigan Dept. of Corrections; Saint Louis; detention center   1,000
Dow Corning Corp.; Midland; silicones   900
Gratiot Health System Hospital; Alma   900
KSL Recreation Group Inc.; Acme; health club   900
Memorial Healthcare Center; Owosso   820
Ferris State University; Big Rapids   800
Grand Traverse Band of Ottawa and Chippewa Indians; Suttons Bay; gambling   800
Meijer Inc.; Mount Pleasant; discount department stores 800
Lear Corp.; Traverse City; automotive electrical equipment   750
Meijer Inc.; Midland; discount department stores   700
Meijer Inc.; Traverse City; discount department stores 700
Sara Lee Corp.; Traverse City; frozen bakery products 700
Nabco Inc.; Reed City; electric motor controls   697
Delfield Co.; Mount Pleasant; commercial cooking, food service equipment   650
Federal-Mogul Corp.; Greenville; bearings, motor vehicle   600
Meijer Inc.; Saginaw; discount department stores   600
Michigan Community Health Dept.; Mount Pleasant 585
Northwestern Michigan College; Traverse City   575
Michigan Dept. of Corrections; Carson City; correctional institutions   550
Quebecor World Pendell Inc.; Midland; publication printing, lithographic   535
Central Michigan Community Hospital Inc.; Mount Pleasant   512

Blue Care Network of Michigan; Saginaw; hospital/medical service plans   500
Consumers Energy; Saginaw; electric power distribution 500
KSL Grand Traverse Resort Inc.; Acme; resort hotel 500
Meijer Inc.; Corunna; discount department stores   500
Saginaw Township Community Schools; Saginaw   500
Total Petroleum Inc.; Alma; petroleum refining   500

Michigan 5th District
East — Flint, Saginaw, Bay City

Flint, the birthplace of General Motors in 1908, gave rise to the modern labor movement 30 years later when sit-down strikes at two Flint plants forced the auto giant to recognize the power of the United Auto Workers (UAW) union. Farther north, the 5th takes in Saginaw and Bay City.

From the turn of the century until the late 1960s, Flint, the largest city in the 5th, grew along with the U.S. auto industry. Then the 1970s oil shock and an increase in inexpensive imports undercut demand for GM cars and drove the economy into a downward spiral. The industry recovered from that slump, but automation and overseas production have reduced the number of jobs. Although GM jobs are not as plentiful, a number of small, spin-off companies employ a significant number of people.

The district's blue-collar voters are populist on economics and more conservative on cultural issues, but they identify strongly with the Democratic Party. Genesee County, which accounts for two-thirds of the district's population, is strongly influenced by the UAW and gave 63 percent of its vote to Al Gore in the 2000 presidential election, his second-best showing in Michigan. Gore received 84 percent in Flint, which is majority-black. The Green Party's Ralph Nader, despite his anticorporate stance, took just 2 percent of the vote in Genesee.

Autoworkers and Democratic voters also are plentiful in Saginaw, which backed Gore by a better than three-to-one ratio. The district also includes parts of Bay County and all of Tuscola County, part of Michigan's "Thumb."

Redistricting following the 2000 census cut counties from the old 5th's north and east. Mapmakers expanded the district's southern border to include the remainder of Genesee County, including Flint. The county had been split between the 5th, 8th, and 9th Districts in the 1990s.

Major Industry
Auto parts manufacturing, agriculture, sugar processing.

Notable
Famous natives include Stevie Wonder (Saginaw); Bay City was once known as the lumber capital of the world; Flint native Michael Moore's documentary film, *Roger & Me*, chronicled the effect of GM's layoffs in the 1980s.

Election Returns

	Republican		Democratic		Other	
President 2000	106,445	37.1%	174,788	60.9%	5,811	2.0%
House 2002			158,709	91.6%	14,630	8.4%

District Profile

Population   662,563

Total area (square miles)   1,779.9
   Land area (square miles)   1,753.9

Population per square mile   377.8

Counties (2000 population)
Bay (pt.) 79,322	Saginaw (pt.) 88,834
Genesee 436,141	Tuscola 58,266

Cities and other areas over 10,000 (2000 population)
Bay City 36,817	Fenton 10,582
Beecher CDP 12,793	Flint 124,943
Burton 30,308	Saginaw (pt.) 61,799

Race and Hispanic or Latino origin*
White   75.0%
Black or African American   18.5%
American Indian or Alaska Native   0.5%
Asian   0.7%
Native Hawaiian or other Pacific Islander   0.0%
Some other race   0.1%
Hispanic or Latino origin   3.6%
Two or more races   1.7%

As percentage of total population.

Ancestry*
Dutch 1.5%	Irish 7.6%
English 7.3%	Italian 1.7%
Fr. Canadian 1.9%	Polish 5.6%
French 4.6%	Scottish 1.5%
German 15.3%	USA/American 4.5%

As estimated percentage of total population.

Universities and colleges, 2000–2001 enrollment
Baker College Center for Graduate Studies, Flint   1,592
Baker College Corporate Services, Flint   1,048
Baker College-Flint, Flint   3,896
Delta College, University Center   9,358
Detroit College of Business-Flint, Flint   1,015
Kettering University, Flint   3,331
Mott Community College, Flint   8,659
Saginaw Valley State University, University Center   8,622
University of Michigan-Flint, Flint   6,316

Newspapers and circulation

	District circulation	Total circulation
Bay City Times	17,738	36,101
Detroit Free Press	6,714	363,536
Detroit News	4,173	238,950
Detroit News/Free Press (Sunday)	10,896	603,915
Flint Journal	75,351	88,130
Oakland Press	1,123	74,996
Saginaw News	17,646	47,648
*USA Today**	3,429	1,674,376

See Sources and Explanations in the front of the volume.

Television stations and affiliations
Flint-Saginaw-Bay City	100%	WAQP	Independent
Flint-Saginaw-Bay City	100%	WCMU	PBS
Flint-Saginaw-Bay City	100%	WDCP	PBS
Flint-Saginaw-Bay City	100%	WDCQ	PBS
Flint-Saginaw-Bay City	100%	WEYI	NBC
Flint-Saginaw-Bay City	100%	WFUM	PBS
Flint-Saginaw-Bay City	100%	WJRT	ABC
Flint-Saginaw-Bay City	100%	WNEM	CBS
Flint-Saginaw-Bay City	100%	WSMH	FOX

Cable systems and subscribers
Charter   74,484
Comcast   73,851

Businesses and other major employers
General Motors Corp.; Flint; automobiles   20,000
Delphi Corp.; Saginaw; motor vehicle parts/accessories   10,000
Delphi Corp.; Flint; motor vehicle parts/accessories   7,000
United Auto Workers Local Union; Flint; labor union   5,500
Genesys Regional Medical Center; Grand Blanc   3,178
General Motors Corp.; Flint; business management   3,000
Hurley Medical Center Inc.; Flint   2,650
General Motors Corp.; Grand Blanc; motor vehicles and car bodies   2,600
Delta College; Bay City   2,000
McLaren Regional Medical Center; Flint   2,000
Covenant Medical Center Inc.; Saginaw   1,950
St. Mary's Medical Center; Saginaw   1,794
Bay Medical Center; Bay City   1,700
Delphi Corp.; Burton; automotive instrument boards   1,700
General Motors Corp.; Bay City; automotive body parts   1,500
General Motors Corp.; Saginaw; castings   1,350
Patrick Ruff; Flint; instruction schools, camps, services   1,300
International Union UAW of America; Bay City; labor union   1,200
Saginaw Valley State University; Bay City   860
Charles Stewart Mott Community College; Flint   850
General Motors Corp.; Saginaw; iron foundry   850
Citizens Bank-Michigan; Flint; state commercial banks   650
Meijer Inc.; Bay City; discount department stores   650
United Retired Government Employees Local 1; Flint; labor organization   600
ADT Security Services Inc.; Saginaw; telephone communication   525
City of Flint; Flint; city government   500
Electronic Data Systems Corp.; Burton; computer programming   500
Frankenmuth Bavarian Inn Inc.; Frankenmuth; restaurant   500
Manufacturing Personnel Inc.; Flint; employment agency   500
Michigan Community Health Dept.; Caro   500
Michigan Dept. of Transportation; Saginaw   500
Vemco Inc.; Grand Blanc; molded plastics   500
Zehnder's of Frankenmuth Inc.; Frankenmuth; restaurant chain   500

Michigan 6th District

Southwest — Kalamazoo, Portage, Benton Harbor

Lush forests in Michigan's southwest corner make the 6th a prime spot for tourists and orchards. Cherries and peaches grow in the fruit belt that extends north from St. Joseph and Benton Harbor—once a stop on the Underground Railroad—through Van Buren County. Many affluent Chicagoans keep second homes in the wooded area along the Lake Michigan shoreline, which has become known as "Harbor County."

Kalamazoo, the 6th's most-populous city, has a strong and diverse manufacturing economy. Cities throughout the district have escaped dependence on Detroit's automaker economy.

Home appliance manufacturer Whirlpool is based in Benton Harbor, and pharmaceutical maker Pharmacia has facilities in Kalamazoo. Education is another economic pillar, led by Western Michigan University's 29,000 students.

Kalamazoo's blue-collar workforce makes it one of the few Democratic parts of the 6th; Al Gore carried the city by a 25 percentage point margin in the 2000 presidential election, helping him narrowly win Kalamazoo County.

But the city's voters are no match for the Republican influences in the district—namely, its conservative Dutch heritage, white-collar corporate managers, and rural conservatives. Berrien County, the district's second-most-populous county, went decisively for George W. Bush (though heavily black Benton Harbor overwhelmingly went for Gore).

The 6th also includes all of Republican-leaning Van Buren, St. Joseph, and Cass Counties (the latter abuts the Indiana state line near South Bend and Elkhart). Redistricting gave the district more of Allegan County, a solidly Republican lake county between Kalamazoo and Grand Rapids.

Major Industry

Manufacturing, higher education, agriculture.

Notable

The first outdoor pedestrian shopping mall in the United States was built in Kalamazoo in 1959.

Election Returns

	Republican		Democratic		Other	
President 2000	138,658	52.2%	119,740	45.0%	7,413	2.8%
House 2002	126,936	69.2%	53,793	29.3%	2,788	1.5%

District Profile

Population   662,563

Total area (square miles)   3,420.1
Land area (square miles)   3,331.3

Population per square mile   198.9

Counties (2000 population)

Allegan (pt.)	67,024	Kalamazoo	238,603
Berrien	162,453	St. Joseph	62,422
Calhoun (pt.)	4,694	Van Buren	76,263
Cass	51,104		

Cities and other areas over 10,000 (2000 population)

Benton Harbor	11,182	Portage	44,897
Kalamazoo	77,145	Sturgis	11,285
Niles	12,204		

Race and Hispanic or Latino origin*

White   84.3%
Black or African American   8.8%
American Indian or Alaska Native   0.5%
Asian   1.1%
Native Hawaiian or other Pacific Islander   0.0%
Some other race   0.1%
Hispanic or Latino origin   3.6%
Two or more races   1.6%

*As percentage of total population.

Ancestry*

Dutch	6.4%	Italian	2.2%
English	8.3%	Polish	3.6%
French	2.5%	Scottish	1.4%
German	17.2%	Swedish	1.3%
Irish	8.3%	USA/American	5.3%

*As estimated percentage of total population.

Universities and colleges, 2000–2001 enrollment

Andrews University, Berrien Springs   2,749
Davenport College-Kalamazoo, Kalamazoo   1,207
Glen Oaks Community College, Centreville   1,601
Kalamazoo College, Kalamazoo   1,322
Kalamazoo Valley Community College, Kalamazoo   9,319
Lake Michigan College, Benton Harbor   3,411
Southwestern Michigan College, Dowagiac   3,047
Western Michigan University, Kalamazoo   28,657

Newspapers and circulation

	District circulation	Total circulation
Detroit Free Press	2,432	363,536
Detroit News	1,622	238,950
Detroit News/Free Press (Sunday)	4,056	603,915
Grand Rapids Press	3,145	139,414
Kalamazoo Gazette	50,044	56,200
South Bend Tribune	10,565	72,305
St. Joseph Herald Palladium	25,730	25,774
*USA Today**	4,609	1,674,376

*See Sources and Explanations in the front of the volume.

Television stations and affiliations

Grand Rapids-Kalamazoo-Battle Creek	61%	WGVK	PBS
Grand Rapids-Kalamazoo-Battle Creek	61%	WGVU	PBS
Grand Rapids-Kalamazoo-Battle Creek	61%	WLLA	Independent
Grand Rapids-Kalamazoo-Battle Creek	61%	WOOD	NBC
Grand Rapids-Kalamazoo-Battle Creek	61%	WOTV	ABC
Grand Rapids-Kalamazoo-Battle Creek	61%	WTLJ	Independent
Grand Rapids-Kalamazoo-Battle Creek	61%	WWMT	CBS
Grand Rapids-Kalamazoo-Battle Creek	61%	WXMI	FOX
Grand Rapids-Kalamazoo-Battle Creek	61%	WZZM	ABC
South Bend-Elkhart, IN	39%	WHME	Independent
South Bend-Elkhart, IN	39%	WNDU	NBC
South Bend-Elkhart, IN	39%	WNIT	PBS
South Bend-Elkhart, IN	39%	WSBT	CBS
South Bend-Elkhart, IN	39%	WSJV	FOX

Cable systems and subscribers
- Charter   64,280
- Comcast   51,251
- Mediacom   811
- Parish Communications   2,078

Military installations, September 2001
- W. K. Kellogg Airport (Air National Guard), Battle Creek   1,012

Businesses and other major employers
- Williamson Employment Services Inc.; St. Joseph; temporary help service   3,000
- Borgess Medical Center Inc.; Kalamazoo   2,414
- Lakeland Hospitals at Niles and St. Joseph Inc.; St. Joseph   2,250
- Whirlpool Corp.; Benton Harbor; washing machines   2,200
- Andrews University Inc.; Berrien Springs   2,100
- Bronson Methodist Hospital Inc.; Kalamazoo   2,045
- Perrigo Co.; Allegan; pharmaceuticals   1,800
- Meijer Inc.; Kalamazoo; discount department stores   1,550
- U.S. Veterans Hospital; Battle Creek   1,500
- Robert Bosch Corp.; St. Joseph; motor vehicle brake systems/parts   1,200
- Murco Foods Inc.; Plainwell; boxed beef   1,100
- American Electric Power Co.; Bridgman; electric services   900
- City of Kalamazoo; Kalamazoo; city management   900
- Meijer Inc.; Portage; discount department stores   900
- Parker Hannifin Corp.; Kalamazoo; aircraft parts, equipment   900
- American Axle and Manufacturing Inc.; Three Rivers; automotive forgings   800
- Benteler Automotive Corp.; Galesburg; motor vehicle axles   800
- Engineered Plastic Components Inc.; Mattawan; injection molding of plastics   800
- Transamerica Commercial Finance Corp.; St. Joseph; equipment, vehicle finance leasing   767
- Kalamazoo County; Kalamazoo; government   764
- Eaton Corp.; Galesburg; motor vehicle parts/accessories   750
- Southwestern Michigan College; Dowagiac   711
- Leco Corp.; St. Joseph; laboratory apparatus   700
- Duncan Aviation Inc.; Portage; aircraft rental   680
- Carrier Commerical Refrigeration Inc.; Niles; refrigerated display cabinets   600
- General Motors Corp.; Three Rivers; motor vehicle parts/accessories   600
- Georgie Boy Manufaturing; Edwardsburg; motor homes   600
- Michigan State University Medical Studies; Kalamazoo   600
- IPC Communication Services Inc.; St. Joseph; periodicals   525
- Allegan County; Allegan; government   500
- Atlantic Automotive Components; Benton Harbor; injection molding of plastics   500
- Lakeland Regional Health System Hospital; Berrien Center   500
- Lear Corp.; Mendon; motor vehicle body components and frame   500
- Meijer Inc.; Benton Harbor; discount department stores   500
- Parker Hannifin Corp.; Otsego; bushings and bearings   500
- Whirlpool Corp.; St. Joseph; electrical or electronic engineering   500

Michigan 7th District

South central — Battle Creek, Jackson

The southern Michigan counties that make up the 7th take in small towns, farming communities, and a few midsize cities. Kellogg's Tony the Tiger makes his home in Battle Creek, the district's largest city. The cereal giant is not only one of the city's largest employers, but it also maintains one of the nation's top philanthropic organizations, donating some gifts to the Battle Creek area.

Outside Battle Creek, auto parts manufacturing drives small-town economies, especially in Jackson. Agriculture dominates most of the rest of the 7th, with soybeans and corn as the staple crops. The farming counties of Branch, Eaton, Hillsdale, Jackson, and Lenawee have been fertile ground for the GOP: George W. Bush and former senator Spencer Abraham carried all five in 2000 even as they were losing statewide.

Rural and small-town voters tend to overwhelm the influence of the cities' blue-collar population, but even Democrats tend to be socially conservative. Unlike Detroit's autoworkers, many of those living here have roots in the surrounding Republican countryside. Hillsdale County is home to Hillsdale College, which does not accept federal funding and has a free-market orientation.

The district's political and social culture has been shaped by Quaker settlements that made the area a station on the Underground Railroad and left many residents sensitive to issues such as racial segregation and the Vietnam War.

Redistricting following the 2000 census did not make major changes to the 7th, though the district needed to gain population due to the state's one-seat loss in reapportionment. The 7th took on a larger slice of Washtenaw County (though county seat Ann Arbor is in the 15th District) and abuts the Detroit-area Wayne County.

Major Industry

Agriculture, food processing, auto parts manufacturing, health care.

Notable

Sojourner Truth lived in Battle Creek; Battle Creek's annual Cereal Festival culminates in the world's longest breakfast table; Grand Ledge, a late-1800s resort town, featured a merry-go-round on one of its islands.

Election Returns

	Republican		Democratic		Other	
President 2000	141,647	51.4%	127,344	46.2%	6,682	2.4%
House 2002	121,142	59.7%	78,412	38.6%	3,515	1.7%

District Profile

Population   662,563

Total area (square miles)   4,365.4
   Land area (square miles)   4,295.3

Population per square mile   154.3

Counties (2000 population)
Branch	45,787	Jackson	158,422
Calhoun (pt.)	133,291	Lenawee	98,890
Eaton	103,655	Washtenaw (pt.)	75,991
Hillsdale	46,527		

Cities and other areas over 10,000 (2000 population)
Adrian	21,574	Jackson	36,316
Battle Creek	53,364	Waverly CDP	16,194
Coldwater	12,697		

Race and Hispanic or Latino origin*
White   88.5%
Black or African American   5.6%
American Indian or Alaska Native   0.4%
Asian   0.8%
Native Hawaiian or other Pacific Islander   0.0%
Some other race   0.1%
Hispanic or Latino origin   3.2%
Two or more races   1.4%

As percentage of total population.

Ancestry*
Dutch	2.7%	Italian	1.9%
English	9.7%	Polish	3.7%
French	3.0%	Scottish	1.7%
German	17.4%	USA/American	5.9%
Irish	8.3%		

As estimated percentage of total population.

Universities and colleges, 2000–2001 enrollment
Adrian College, Adrian   1,081
Albion College, Albion   1,525
Baker College of Jackson, Jackson   1,027
Great Lakes Christian College, Lansing   213
Hillsdale College, Hillsdale   1,196
Jackson Community College, Jackson   5,069
Kellogg Community College, Battle Creek   5,300
Olivet College, Olivet   1,022
Siena Heights College, Adrian   1,972
Spring Arbor University, Spring Arbor   2,558

Newspapers and circulation
	District circulation	Total circulation
Adrian Telegram	15,296	15,353
Ann Arbor News	21,740	55,446
Battle Creek Enquirer	21,473	24,908
Detroit Free Press	12,423	363,536
Detroit News	6,736	238,950
Detroit News/Free Press (Sunday)	19,171	603,915
Jackson Citizen Patriot	34,287	35,240
Lansing State Journal	13,298	69,782
Toledo Blade	3,147	138,304
*USA Today**	5,358	1,674,376

See Sources and Explanations in the front of the volume.

Television stations and affiliations
Lansing	43%	WILX	NBC
Lansing	43%	WKAR	PBS
Lansing	43%	WLAJ	ABC
Lansing	43%	WLNS	CBS
Lansing	43%	WSYM	FOX
Lansing	43%	WZPX	PAX
Grand Rapids-Kalamazoo-Battle Creek	28%	WGVK	PBS
Grand Rapids-Kalamazoo-Battle Creek	28%	WGVU	PBS
Grand Rapids-Kalamazoo-Battle Creek	28%	WLLA	Independent
Grand Rapids-Kalamazoo-Battle Creek	28%	WOOD	NBC
Grand Rapids-Kalamazoo-Battle Creek	28%	WOTV	ABC
Grand Rapids-Kalamazoo-Battle Creek	28%	WTLJ	Independent
Grand Rapids-Kalamazoo-Battle Creek	28%	WWMT	CBS
Grand Rapids-Kalamazoo-Battle Creek	28%	WXMI	FOX
Grand Rapids-Kalamazoo-Battle Creek	28%	WZZM	ABC
Toledo, OH	17%	WBGU	PBS
Toledo, OH	17%	WGTE	PBS
Toledo, OH	17%	WINM	Independent
Toledo, OH	17%	WLMB	PAX
Toledo, OH	17%	WNWO	NBC
Toledo, OH	17%	WTOL	CBS
Toledo, OH	17%	WTVG	ABC
Toledo, OH	17%	WUPW	FOX
Detroit	12%	WADL	Independent
Detroit	12%	WDIV	NBC
Detroit	12%	WDWB	WB
Detroit	12%	WJBK	FOX
Detroit	12%	WKBD	UPN
Detroit	12%	WPXD	PAX
Detroit	12%	WTVS	PBS
Detroit	12%	WWJ	CBS
Detroit	12%	WXYZ	ABC

Cable systems and subscribers
Charter   11,568
Comcast   105,049
Millennium Digital Media   20,422

Businesses and other major employers
Kellogg USA Inc.; Battle Creek; breakfast cereals
   5,000
Bill Knapp's Midland Inc.; Battle Creek; restaurants
   3,000
DENSO Manufacturing Michigan Inc.; Battle Creek;
   motor vehicle parts/accessories   2,501
W. A. Foote Memorial Hospital; Jackson   2,200
Consumers Energy; Jackson; electric services   2,000
Battle Creek Health System Hospital; Battle Creek
   1,600
Kraft Foods Inc.; Battle Creek; breakfast cereals   1,500
Delphi Corp.; Adrian; injection molding of plastics
   1,455
McDonald's of Calhoun Inc.; Battle Creek; restaurant
   chain   1,448
Hayes Lemmerz International-Laredo Inc.; Northville;
   dies and tools   1,400
Michigan Dept. of Corrections; Jackson   1,400
Dawn Investment Co.; Jackson; flour mixes and doughs
   1,200
Tecumseh Products Co.; Tecumseh; parts for heating,
   cooling, and refrigerating equipment   1,100
Washtenaw Community College; Ann Arbor   1,100
United Parcel Service Inc.; Ann Arbor; package delivery
   1,000
Viking Pump Inc.; Saline; pumping equipment   913
Eaton Corp.; Marshall; motor vehice differentials, parts
   850
Chelsea Community Hospital Inc.; Chelsea   805

Grand Trunk Western Railroad Inc.; Battle Creek; freight hauling   800

Meijer Inc.; Lansing; discount department stores   800

JAC Products Inc.; Saline; plastics products   722

Emma L. Bixby Medical Center; Adrian   710

ASMO Manufacturing Inc.; Battle Creek; electric motors   700

Automatic Data Processing Inc.; Ann Arbor; computer time-sharing   700

Auto-Owners Insurance Co.; Lansing; accident insurance carriers   700

General Motors Corp.; Lansing; warehousing   700

Meijer Inc.; Jackson; discount department stores   700

I. I. Stanley Co. Inc.; Battle Creek; motor vehicle lighting equipment   672

Jackson Community College; Jackson   669

Walters-Dimmick Petroleum Inc.; Litchfield; gasoline service stations   620

Eaton Corp.; Jackson; valves for aircraft   600

Harvard Industries Inc.; Albion; iron castings   600

Meijer Inc.; Battle Creek; discount department stores   600

Michigan Automotive Compressor; Parma; air conditioning, motor vehicle   600

Michigan Dept. of Corrections; Adrian   600

TRMI Inc.; Battle Creek; motor vehicle electrical equipment   600

Duncan Aviation Inc.; Battle Creek; aircraft servicing, repairing   590

Collins and Aikman Plastics Inc.; Manchester; injection molding of plastics   575

Spartan Motors Inc.; Charlotte; motor vehicle chassis   570

Branch County Community Health Center; Coldwater   550

DaimlerChrysler Corp.; Chelsea; automobile proving, testing   550

Teleflex Inc.; Hillsdale; process control instruments   550

Jacobson Stores Inc.; Jackson; department stores   530

TRW Inc.; Jackson; motor vehicle parts/accessories   520

Blue Cross and Blue Shield of Michigan; Lansing; group hospitalization   500

International Union UAW of America; Albion; labor union   500

Tenneco Automotive Operating Co.; Litchfield; motor vehicle exhaust mufflers   500

Wacker Chemical Holding Corp.; Adrian; chemical preparations   500

Michigan 8th District

Central — Lansing

Michigan's capital district, where Ransom Eli Olds founded Olds Motor Vehicle Co. in 1897, covers Lansing, East Lansing, and some agricultural communities to the east. The local dominance of General Motors, which makes Chevrolets, Cadillacs, and Pontiacs, is matched only by state government. Together, they employ thousands of people in the 8th.

Michigan State, the nation's first land-grant university, gave birth to the district's second-largest city, East Lansing. State government workers, university students, faculty, and autoworkers make Ingham County strongly Democratic. In 2000 elections, Al Gore took 57 percent in Ingham (his fourth-best showing in Michigan) and then-representative Debbie Stabenow took 58 percent in her Senate race.

Ingham's liberal leanings are nearly counterbalanced by the strong GOP tendencies of Livingston County, a fast-growing area just to the east. Livingston increased its population by 36 percent in the 1990s and has been absorbing whites leaving Detroit, Flint, Lansing, and Pontiac. In contrast to Livingston, Ingham lost population in the 1990s. Combined, the two counties account for two-thirds of residents in the 8th District.

Most of the rest of the 8th's voters live in northern Oakland County, an upscale region that is closer to Flint and Detroit than to Lansing. The 8th also includes Clinton County, just north of Lansing, and parts of Shiawassee County, located between Lansing and Flint.

In redistricting following the 2000 census, Republican mapmakers drew more of Oakland into the 8th to give a GOP lean to a district that was highly competitive in the 1990s. The old 8th's share of Genesee County, including many Democratic voters, was shifted to the 5th District.

Major Industry

State government, auto manufacturing, higher education.

Notable

Basketball star Earvin "Magic" Johnson hails from Lansing and played college ball at Michigan State University; Howell celebrates the honeydew harvest with its annual Melon Festival.

Election Returns

	Republican		Democratic		Other	
President 2000	153,798	50.6%	141,770	46.6%	8,426	2.8%
House 2002	156,525	67.9%	70,920	30.8%	3,152	1.4%

District Profile

Population   662,563

Total area (square miles)   2,288.3
   Land area (square miles)   2,253.6

Population per square mile   294.0

Counties (2000 population)
Clinton 64,753	Oakland (pt.) 131,141
Ingham 279,320	Shiawassee (pt.) 30,398
Livingston 156,951	

Cities and other areas over 10,000 (2000 population)
East Lansing 46,525	Lansing (pt.) 114,321
Haslett CDP 11,283	Okemos CDP 22,805
Holt CDP 11,315	

Race and Hispanic or Latino origin*
White   87.7%
Black or African American   4.8%
American Indian or Alaska Native   0.4%
Asian   1.9%

Native Hawaiian or other Pacific Islander   0.0%
Some other race   0.1%
Hispanic or Latino origin   3.5%
Two or more races   1.6%

As percentage of total population.

Ancestry*

Dutch 2.1%	Italian 3.2%
English 9.6%	Polish 5.3%
Fr. Canadian 1.4%	Scotch-Irish 1.2%
French 3.4%	Scottish 2.2%
German 17.3%	Swedish 1.2%
Irish 9.2%	USA/American 4.2%

As estimated percentage of total population.

Universities and colleges, 2000–2001 enrollment

Cleary College, Howell   393
Davenport College-Lansing, Lansing   1,168
Detroit College of Law at Michigan State University, East Lansing   703
Lansing Community College, Lansing   16,011
Michigan State University, East Lansing   43,366
Thomas M. Cooley Law School, Lansing   1,688

Newspapers and circulation

	District circulation	Total circulation
Ann Arbor News	4,196	55,446
Detroit Free Press	13,023	363,536
Detroit News	9,982	238,950
Detroit News/Free Press (Sunday)	23,016	603,915
Flint Journal	5,533	88,130
Lansing State Journal	53,067	69,782
Oakland Press	31,665	74,996
*USA Today**	7,172	1,674,376

See Sources and Explanations in the front of the volume.

Television stations and affiliations

Lansing	50%	WILX	NBC
Lansing	50%	WKAR	PBS
Lansing	50%	WLAJ	ABC
Lansing	50%	WLNS	CBS
Lansing	50%	WSYM	FOX
Lansing	50%	WZPX	PAX
Detroit	39%	WADL	Independent
Detroit	39%	WDIV	NBC
Detroit	39%	WDWB	WB
Detroit	39%	WJBK	FOX
Detroit	39%	WKBD	UPN
Detroit	39%	WPXD	PAX
Detroit	39%	WTVS	PBS
Detroit	39%	WWJ	CBS
Detroit	39%	WXYZ	ABC
Flint-Saginaw-Bay City	11%	WAQP	Independent
Flint-Saginaw-Bay City	11%	WCMU	PBS
Flint-Saginaw-Bay City	11%	WDCP	PBS
Flint-Saginaw-Bay City	11%	WDCQ	PBS
Flint-Saginaw-Bay City	11%	WEYI	NBC
Flint-Saginaw-Bay City	11%	WFUM	PBS
Flint-Saginaw-Bay City	11%	WJRT	ABC
Flint-Saginaw-Bay City	11%	WNEM	CBS
Flint-Saginaw-Bay City	11%	WSMH	FOX

Cable systems and subscribers

Charter   26,076
Comcast   84,651
Millennium Digital Media   11,716

Businesses and other major employers

General Motors Corp.; Lansing; automotive stampings   5,000
Michigan State University; East Lansing   5,000
Michigan Dept. of Community Health; Lansing   3,000
Sparrow Hospital Assn.; Lansing   3,000
Michigan Dept. of State; Lansing   2,600
Lansing Community College; Lansing   2,300
Michigan Family Independence Agency; Lansing   2,279
Ingham Regional Medical Center; Lansing   1,700
Michigan Community Health Dept.; Lansing   1,400
U.S. Dept. of Treasury; Lansing   1,400
Leona Group; East Lansing; management consulting   1,200
Valeo Inc.; Holly; electric power switches   1,200
Michigan Community Health Dept.; Lansing   1,100
City of Lansing; Lansing; utility regulation   1,000
Electronic Data Systems Corp.; Lansing; data communication services   1,000
Memorial Healthcare Center; Elsie   1,000
Michigan Dept. of Management and Budget; Lansing   1,000
Michigan Dept. of Transporation; Lansing   1,000
U.S. Postal Service; Lansing   1,000
Ingham County; Mason; county government   999
Jackson National Life Insurance Co. Inc.; Lansing; life insurance   850
Meijer Inc.; Okemos; discount department stores   800
Spherion Corp.; Brighton; temporary help service   800
Lear Corp.; Elsie; motor vehicle parts/accessories   785
Meijer Inc.; Lansing; discount department stores   750
Trinity Health Corp. Hospital; Howell   750
Delphi Corp.; Lansing; automobile seats   700
Meijer Inc.; East Lansing; discount department stores   615
Ogihara America Corp.; Howell; automotive body parts   614
ADT Security Services Inc.; Lansing; telephone communication   600
L&L Food Centers; Lansing; supermarkets   600
Federal-Mogul Corp.; St. Johns; motor vehicle parts/accessories   550
Consumers Energy; Lansing; electric, other services   540
Michigan Dept. of Corrections; Lansing   518
Intier Automotive Interiors of America Inc.; Brighton; motor vehicle parts/accessories   500
Michigan National Guard; Lansing   500
Michigan State Police; East Lansing   500

Michigan 9th District

Suburban Detroit — eastern Oakland County

Michigan's 9th—the wealthiest and most-educated district in the state—is wholly contained within Oakland County, one of the most affluent counties in the nation and home to the American headquarters for DaimlerChrysler (in

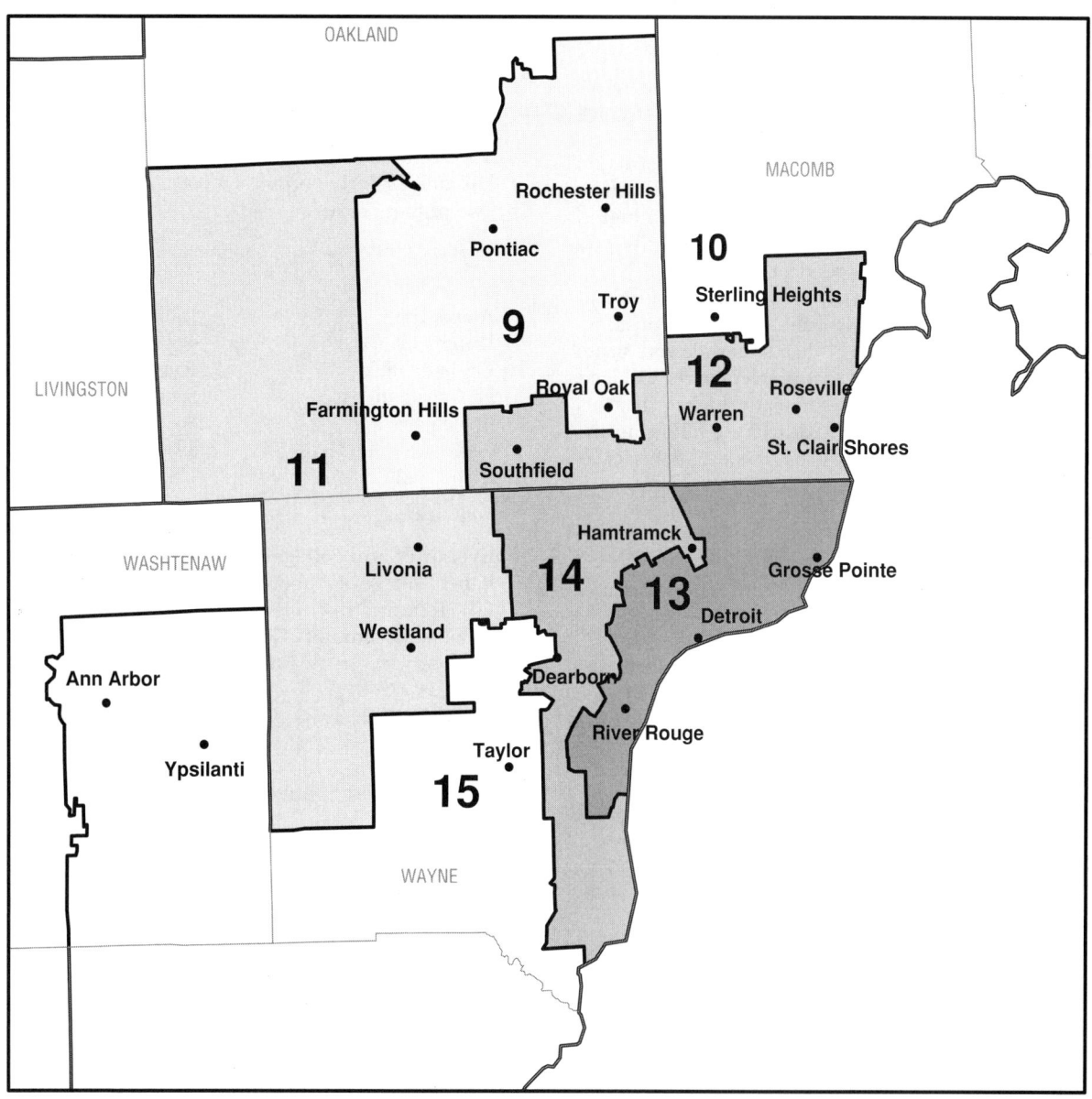

Auburn Hills) and Kmart (in Troy). The district includes more than half of the 1.2 million people who lived in Oakland County at the time of the 2000 census. *(See map p. 477.)*

Communities such as Farmington Hills, north of the northern Detroit boundary cut by 8 Mile Road, form a corridor between Grand River Avenue and the Northwestern Highway that has served as one of the major routes for white exodus from Detroit. Troy, in the southeast corner of the district, has benefited from growth in high-tech automotive research and design, and is also a major office center. The area has a large Asian population.

Troy, Bloomfield, and Rochester Hills give the district its Republican lean, but Democrats fare well in Pontiac, where blacks are a plurality. Al Gore narrowly carried Farmington Hills, the most-populous city in the district, and easily won West Bloomfield in the 2000 presidential election.

Republican candidates have slipped somewhat in Oakland County. In the 1980s Ronald Reagan and George Bush ran 6 to 8 percentage points ahead of their statewide vote share. In 2000 George W. Bush received 48 percent of the Oakland County vote, which was only marginally higher than his 46 percent showing statewide. Redistricting following the 2000 census shuffled the county's congressional districts, as Michigan lost one seat in reapportionment. The redrawn 9th contains part of the old 9th, 11th, and 12th districts.

Major Industry

Auto manufacturing, engineering, health care, insurance.

Notable

The first Holocaust museum built in the United States is in West Bloomfield; the Rev. Charles Coughlin broadcast his controversial weekly radio programs from the Shrine of the Little Flower Church in Royal Oak in the 1930s.

Election Returns

	Republican		Democratic		Other	
President 2000	164,149	51.0%	151,996	47.2%	5,987	1.9%
House 2002	141,102	58.1%	96,856	39.9%	4,922	2.0%

District Profile

Population   662,563

Total area (square miles)   323.2
   Land area (square miles)   311.3

Population per square mile   2,128.4

Counties (2000 population)
   Oakland (pt.)   662,563

Cities and other areas over 10,000 (2000 population)
   Auburn Hills   19,837
   Berkley   15,531
   Beverly Hills village   10,437
   Birmingham   19,291
   Bloomfield Township CDP   43,021
   Clawson   12,732
   Farmington   10,423
   Farmington Hills   82,111
   Pontiac   66,337
   Rochester   10,467
   Rochester Hills   68,825

Royal Oak (pt.)   54,536
Troy   80,959
Waterford CDP (pt.)   66,316
West Bloomfield Township CDP   64,862

Race and Hispanic or Latino origin*
   White   81.4%
   Black or African American   8.0%
   American Indian or Alaska Native   0.2%
   Asian   5.6%
   Native Hawaiian or other Pacific Islander   0.0%
   Some other race   0.1%
   Hispanic or Latino origin   3.0%
   Two or more races   1.6%

As percentage of total population.

Ancestry*

Arab-Misc. 1.3%	Italian 4.4%
Dutch 1.3%	Polish 7.1%
English 8.5%	Russian 1.9%
Fr. Canadian 1.3%	Scotch-Irish 1.1%
French 3.1%	Scottish 2.3%
German 13.6%	Swedish 1.1%
Irish 9.2%	USA/American 3.2%

As estimated percentage of total population.

Universities and colleges, 2000–2001 enrollment
   Baker College of Auburn Hills, Auburn Hills   1,910
   ITT Technical Institute, Troy   607
   Oakland Community College, Bloomfield Hills   23,188
   Oakland University, Rochester Hills   15,235
   Rochester College, Rochester Hills   794
   Walsh College, Troy   2,978
   William Tyndale College, Farmington Hills   625

Newspapers and circulation

	District circulation	Total circulation
Detroit Free Press	54,648	363,536
Detroit News	28,328	238,950
Detroit News/Free Press (Sunday)	82,978	603,915
Oakland Press	85,420	74,996
Royal Oak Daily Tribune	16,462	15,840
*USA Today**	3,691	1,674,376

See Sources and Explanations in the front of the volume.

Television stations and affiliations

Detroit	100%	WADL	Independent
Detroit	100%	WDIV	NBC
Detroit	100%	WDWB	WB
Detroit	100%	WJBK	FOX
Detroit	100%	WKBD	UPN
Detroit	100%	WPXD	PAX
Detroit	100%	WTVS	PBS
Detroit	100%	WWJ	CBS
Detroit	100%	WXYZ	ABC

Cable systems and subscribers
   Bright House Networks   26,401
   Comcast   117,025

Businesses and other major employers
   DaimlerChrysler Corp.; Auburn Hills; automobiles
      14,000

General Motors Corp.; Pontiac; motor vehicles and car bodies   14,000

William Beaumont Hospital Inc.; Royal Oak   7,500

Guardian Automotive Products Inc.; Auburn Hills; flat glass   6,600

General Motors Corp.; Orion; motor vehicles and car bodies   5,500

General Motors Corp.; Pontiac; truck and bus bodies   4,500

Takata Seat Belts Inc.; San Antonio; automobile and aircraft seat belts   4,300

GMC Cadillac; Troy; automobiles   4,000

Delphi Mechatronic Systems Inc.; Troy; motor vehicle parts/accessories   3,850

Compuware Corp.; Farmington Hills; software development   3,500

Kmart Corp.; Troy   3,500

NCR Corp.; Farmington Hills; accounting equipment   3,000

Oakland County; Pontiac; county government   2,744

VDO North America; Troy; automotive water, oil gauges   2,525

Ameritech Publishing International Inc.; Troy; business management consultant   2,500

Comerica Bank; Auburn Hills; state commercial banks   2,000

Continental Teves Inc.; Auburn Hills; automotive supplies, parts   2,000

Creative Staffing Concepts Inc.; Troy; employee leasing service   2,000

General Motors Corp.; Troy; motor vehicles and car bodies   2,000

Michigan Real Estate and Const.; West Bloomfield; real estate agents and managers   1,999

Emerald Interiors; Oakland; interior design services   1,991

Oakland University; Rochester   1,831

Carolina Builders Corp.; Troy; lumber and building materials   1,700

Crittenton Hospital; Rochester   1,685

ADP Total Source; Auburn Hills; employee leasing service   1,600

Haden MacLellan Inc.; Auburn Hills; metal finishing equipment for plating   1,500

Richard Miller Associates Inc.; Birmingham; market analysis/research   1,500

Standard Federal Bank; Troy; commercial bank   1,500

Botsford General Hospital; Farmington Hills   1,475

Kelly Services Inc.; Troy; temporary help service   1,400

Pontiac General Hospital and Medical Center; Pontiac   1,400

Robert Bosch Corp.; Farmington Hills; automotive supplies, parts   1,200

William Beaumont Hospital; Troy   1,200

Consumers Energy; Royal Oak; electric, other services   1,102

ArvinMeritor Inc.; Troy; motor vehicle parts/accessories   1,000

Electronic Data Systems Corp.; Troy; data processing   1,000

Emery Lobdell Corp.; Troy; motor vehicle body components and frame   1,000

Ford Motor Co.; Farmington Hills; software development   1,000

NBD Service Corp.; Troy; credit card service   1,000

Thyssen Intermediate Corp.; Troy; automotive body parts   1,000

Amerisure Insurance Co.; Farmington Hills; workers' compensation insurance   980

POH Medical Center; Pontiac   940

Pentamark Worldwide Inc.; Troy; advertising   900

Textron Automotive Co.; Troy; motor vehicle parts/accessories   900

FANUC Robotics North America; Rochester Hills; metal finishing equipment   864

Flagstar Bank; Troy; federal savings banks   841

Flagstar Bank; Bloomfield Hills; federal savings banks   841

Delphi Corp.; Troy; engineering services   800

JMC Motorhomes; West Bloomfield; motor homes   800

Meritor Light Vehicles Inc.; Troy; motor vehicle parts/accessories   800

Saturn Corp.; Troy; automobiles   800

Solvay Automotive Plastics and Systems Inc.; Troy; plastics products   780

Birmingham School District; Birmingham   743

Interone Marketing Group; Troy; advertising   730

E. I. Du Pont De Nemours and Co.; Troy; commercial physical research   700

Eagle Ottawa Rochester Hills; Rochester Hills; leather processing   700

Jervis B. Webb Co.; Farmington Hills; conveyors and conveying equipment   700

Meijer Inc.; Waterford; discount department stores   700

Valeo Inc.; Auburn Hills; motor vehicle parts/accessories   700

Eaton Corp.; Rochester Hills; motor vehicle parts/accessories   650

Sign of Beefcarver Inc.; Birmingham; restaurant chain   640

Bower Enterprises Inc.; Troy; business consulting   600

Detroit Medical Center; Troy; accounting services   600

General Motors Corp.; Pontiac; commercial trucks   600

Nordstrom Inc.; Troy; clothing stores   600

Quest Diagnostics Clinical Laboratories Inc.; Auburn Hills; testing laboratories   600

Rosenbluth International Inc.; Troy; travel agency   600

OH Inc.; Troy; advertising, promotional, trade shows   550

U.S. Postal Service; Pontiac   550

Webasto Roof Systems Inc.; Rochester Hills; metal stampings   550

ABB Inc.; Auburn Hills; auto body repair, paint supplies   500

Cranbrook Educational Community Schools; Bloomfield Hills   500

Jabil Circuit Inc.; Auburn Hills; circuit boards   500

Oakland County Road Commission; Waterford   500

PPG Industries Inc.; Troy; paints, varnishes, and supplies   500

Rochester Community Schools District; Rochester   500

Sears Roebuck and Co. Inc.; Troy; department stores   500

Visual Services Inc.; Bloomfield Hills; sales promotion   500

Michigan 10th District

Southeast — northern Macomb County, Port Huron, most of the "Thumb"

Stretching from Sterling Heights in the Macomb County suburbs north of Detroit to the Michigan "Thumb," the 10th combines suburban, lakefront, and rural communities. Statewide candidates who carry Macomb, an electoral bellwether where half of the 10th's residents live, usually win the state.

Macomb, while still home to some auto plants, largely has shed its blue-collar past and "Reagan Democrat" reputation and is becoming more white-collar and upscale. Democrats have made major inroads in northern-state suburban counties such as Macomb. But Republican lawmakers who controlled Michigan's redistricting process following the 2000 census were careful to draw Macomb's most solidly Republican territories, including Shelby, Macomb, and Washington townships, into the 10th. Mapmakers put Democratic-leaning southern Macomb in the 12th District.

North of Macomb is St. Clair County, a politically competitive region where one-fourth of residents live. Port Huron, a source of blue-collar Democratic votes, has grown with the expansion of Detroit's metropolitan area. Water quality issues are important to residents along Lake Huron and Lake St. Clair. The 10th also has thriving small businesses based on the boating industry.

The rest of the district has a rural feel, with communities that are dependent on fruit, soybeans, corn, and dairy products. The 10th has some of the most productive navy bean and sugar beet fields in the state. Sanilac County leads Michigan in dairy production.

Major Industry

Auto manufacturing, agriculture, recreation.

Notable

The 10th has the highest number of registered recreational boats per capita in the nation.

Election Returns

	Republican		Democratic		Other	
President 2000	152,780	53.3%	127,640	44.5%	6,242	2.2%
House 2002	137,339	63.3%	77,053	35.5%	2,536	1.2%

District Profile

Population 662,562

Total area (square miles) 3,663.3
    Land area (square miles) 3,549.4

Population per square mile 186.7

Counties (2000 population)
    Huron   36,079   Sanilac   44,547
    Lapeer   87,904   St. Clair 164,235
    Macomb (pt.) 329,797

Cities and other areas over 10,000 (2000 population)
    Harrison CDP (pt.)   24,461
    Port Huron   32,338
    Shelby CDP   65,159
    Sterling Heights (pt.) 86,536

Race and Hispanic or Latino origin*
    White 93.6%
    Black or African American 1.5%
    American Indian or Alaska Native 0.3%
    Asian 1.2%
    Native Hawaiian or other Pacific Islander 0.0%
    Some other race 0.1%
    Hispanic or Latino origin 2.1%
    Two or more races 1.2%

As percentage of total population.

Ancestry*
Belgian 1.3%	Irish 8.2%
Dutch 1.2%	Italian 6.3%
English 7.2%	Polish 10.5%
Fr. Canadian 1.9%	Scotch-Irish 1.1%
French 4.4%	Scottish 2.1%
German 19.1%	USA/American 3.7%

As estimated percentage of total population.

Universities and colleges, 2000–2001 enrollment
    Baker College of Port Huron, Port Huron   1,230
    St. Clair County Community College, Port Huron
    3,972

Newspapers and circulation

	District circulation	Total circulation
Detroit Free Press	26,197	363,536
Detroit News	20,978	238,950
Detroit News/Free Press (Sunday)	47,181	603,915
Flint Journal	4,502	88,130
Huron Daily Tribune	7,234	7,528
Macomb Daily	19,079	53,194
Oakland Press	3,415	74,996
Port Huron Times Herald	29,825	29,931
Romeo Observer	5,286	5,890
*USA Today**	4,537	1,674,376

See Sources and Explanations in the front of the volume.

Television stations and affiliations
Detroit	62%	WADL	Independent
Detroit	62%	WDIV	NBC
Detroit	62%	WDWB	WB
Detroit	62%	WJBK	FOX
Detroit	62%	WKBD	UPN
Detroit	62%	WPXD	PAX
Detroit	62%	WTVS	PBS
Detroit	62%	WWJ	CBS
Detroit	62%	WXYZ	ABC
Flint-Saginaw-Bay City	38%	WAQP	Independent
Flint-Saginaw-Bay City	38%	WCMU	PBS
Flint-Saginaw-Bay City	38%	WDCP	PBS
Flint-Saginaw-Bay City	38%	WDCQ	PBS
Flint-Saginaw-Bay City	38%	WEYI	NBC
Flint-Saginaw-Bay City	38%	WFUM	PBS
Flint-Saginaw-Bay City	38%	WJRT	ABC
Flint-Saginaw-Bay City	38%	WNEM	CBS
Flint-Saginaw-Bay City	38%	WSMH	FOX

Cable systems and subscribers
Charter   10,500
Comcast   91,634

Businesses and other major employers
Michigan National Guard; Harrison Township   8,542

Visteon Corp.; Utica; motor vehicle body components and frame   3,000

Ford Motor Co.; Chesterfield; automotive supplies, parts   2,200

Ford Motor Co.; Sterling Heights; electric power transmission   2,157

Ford Motor Co.; Romeo; motor vehicles and car bodies   1,584

Army and Air Force Exchange Service; Harrison Township; Army-Navy goods stores   1,500

General Dynamics Land Systems Inc.; Sterling Heights; amphibian tanks, military   1,300

Port Huron Hospital; Port Huron   1,142

Craft Industries Inc.; Shelby Township; electric resistance welders   1,000

Lapeer Regional Hospital; Lapeer   950

Schefenacker Vision Systems USA Inc.; Marysville; products of purchased glass   850

Trinity Health Corp.; Port Huron   800

Utica Enterprises Inc.; Shelby Township; welding apparatus   800

Tower Automotive Inc.; Elkton; automotive stampings   750

TRW Vehicle Safety Systems Inc.; Washington; motor vehicle parts/accessories   700

Breed Safety Restraint Systems Inc.; Sterling Heights; motor vehicle steering systems   600

MNP Corp.; Utica; metal bolts   600

Mueller Brass Co.; Port Huron; copper rolling and drawing   500

General Dynamics Land Systems Inc.; Sterling Heights; small arms ammunition   500

Target Corp.; Sterling Heights; department stores   500

Meijer Inc.; Utica; discount department stores   500

Lear Corp.; Marlette; motor vehicle parts/accessories   500

Michigan 11th District

Southeast — Livonia, Westland, Novi

The 11th, which takes in suburbs west and north of Detroit, stands out as a Republican-leaning area in a region renowned for its support of prolabor Democrats. *(See map p. 477.)*

Although Detroit's presence makes Wayne County, where 70 percent of the district's residents live, a Democratic stronghold, the 11th's portion of Wayne is politically competitive. Residents here split their presidential votes almost evenly in 2000 between George W. Bush and Al Gore.

Republicans run well in upper-middle-class communities such as Livonia, the most populous city in the district, and Canton, a rapidly developing residential area in western Wayne County, east of Ann Arbor (located in the 15th). While Wayne County lost population in the 1990s, Canton's population increased by more than one-third.

Also rapidly growing are Northville and Plymouth townships, which are upscale areas just west of Livonia. Bush took about 60 percent of the vote in these areas.

Democrats run better in more middle-class areas such as Redford Township, just west of Detroit, and Westland, an area south of Livonia that gave 58 percent to Gore.

The 11th also covers southwestern Oakland County. The area is more Republican-leaning: Bush captured almost all of this territory in 2000. Novi, the most populous Oakland County jurisdiction in the 11th, grew by 47 percent in the 1990s.

Auto manufacturing is important here, with several Ford facilities among the area plants.

Major Industry
Auto manufacturing, engineering, health care, insurance.

Notable
Novi, first settled around 1825, is said to have been named for being the sixth stop—VI in Roman numerals—on a stagecoach route.

Election Returns

	Republican		Democratic		Other	
President 2000	150,692	51.0%	138,735	47.0%	6,022	2.0%
House 2002	126,050	57.2%	87,402	39.7%	6,953	3.2%

District Profile

Population   662,563

Total area (square miles)   413.0
  Land area (square miles)   398.5

Population per square mile   1,662.6

Counties (2000 population)
  Oakland (pt.)   196,241
  Wayne (pt.)   466,322

Cities and other areas over 10,000 (2000 population)
  Canton CDP   76,366
  Dearborn Heights (pt.)   13,570
  Garden City   30,047
  Livonia   100,545
  Novi   47,386
  Plymouth Township CDP   27,798
  Redford CDP   51,622
  South Lyon   10,036
  Wayne   19,051
  Westland   86,602
  Wixom   13,263

Race and Hispanic or Latino origin*
  White   89.5%
  Black or African American   3.7%
  American Indian or Alaska Native   0.3%
  Asian   3.0%
  Native Hawaiian or other Pacific Islander   0.0%
  Some other race   0.1%
  Hispanic or Latino origin   2.0%
  Two or more races   1.4%

As percentage of total population.

Ancestry*

Dutch	1.3%	Irish	10.8%
English	8.2%	Italian	5.1%
Fr. Canadian	1.7%	Polish	9.8%
French	3.8%	Scotch-Irish	1.4%
German	15.5%	Scottish	2.5%
Hungarian	1.1%	USA/American	3.2%

As estimated percentage of total population.

Universities and colleges, 2000–2001 enrollment

Madonna University, Livonia   3,968
Michigan Institute of Aeronautics, Belleville   315
Schoolcraft College, Livonia   9,016

Newspapers and circulation

	District circulation	Total circulation
Ann Arbor News	2,155	55,446
Detroit Free Press	49,973	363,536
Detroit News	32,748	238,950
Detroit News/Free Press (Sunday)	82,726	603,915
*Michigan Chronicle**	8,529	32,251
Oakland Press	25,546	74,996
*USA Today**	6,540	1,674,376

See Sources and Explanations in the front of the volume.

Television stations and affiliations

Detroit	100%	WADL	Independent
Detroit	100%	WDIV	NBC
Detroit	100%	WDWB	WB
Detroit	100%	WJBK	FOX
Detroit	100%	WKBD	UPN
Detroit	100%	WPXD	PAX
Detroit	100%	WTVS	PBS
Detroit	100%	WWJ	CBS
Detroit	100%	WXYZ	ABC

Cable systems and subscribers

Bright House Networks   51,503
Charter   2,313
Comcast   111,214

Businesses and other major employers

General Motors Corp.; Ypsilanti; motor vehicle parts/accessories   6,132
General Motors Corp.; Milford; engineering services   5,000
Ford Motor Co.; Wayne; motor vehicles and car bodies   3,500
Ford Motor Co.; Wixom; motor vehicle parts/accessories   3,492
Visteon Climate Control Systems; Plymouth; motor vehicle parts/accessories   2,625
Hoover Universal Inc.; Plymouth; automobile seats   1,700
United Auto Workers Local Union; Livonia; labor organization   1,700
St. Mary Mercy Hospital; Livonia   1,500
Unisys Corp.; Plymouth; computer systems integration   1,400
Yazaki North America Inc.; Canton; automotive supplies, parts   1,400
Bank One Corp.; Belleville; commercial bank   1,300
Ford Motor Co.; Livonia; automotive supplies, parts   1,300
Michigan Community Health Dept.; Northville   1,300
Comerica Bank; Livonia   1,200
Garden City Hospital Osteopathic; Garden City   1,200
Huron Valley School District; Milford   1,100
United Parcel Service Inc.; Livonia; parcel delivery   1,000
Trinity Health Corp. Hospital; Novi   925
General Motors Corp.; Waterford; motor vehicle parts/accessories   900
TRW Inc.; Livonia; motor vehicle brake systems/parts   900
Wayne County Assn. for Retarded Children; Livonia   850
Key Plastics; Plymouth; molded plastics products   800
Meijer Inc.; Northville; discount department stores   800
Madonna University; Livonia   768
MAC Valves Inc.; Wixom; control valves, fluid power   740
Ford Motor Co.; Livonia; motor vehicle supplies/parts   700
Meijer Inc.; Canton; discount department stores 700
Quicken Loans Inc.; Livonia; mortgage bankers   700
Sky Chefs Inc.; Plymouth; restaurants   700
Morbark Inc.; Winn; jobbing and repair machine shop   675
Sysco Food Services; Canton; food supplier   650
Huron Valley Hospital Inc.; Commerce Township   607
American Blind and Wallpaper Factory Inc.; Plymouth; mail order   600
Hometown Communications Network Inc.; Livonia; commercial printing, newspaper publishing   600
Meijer Inc.; Belleville; discount department stores   600
Meijer Inc.; Westland; discount department stores   600
Technicolor Videocassette of Michigan Inc.; Livonia; video or disk reproduction   600
Ford Motor Co.; Redford; warehousing   575
Advantage Logistics-Michigan Inc.; Livonia; food supplier   550
Johnson Electric Automotive Inc.; Plymouth; automotive supplies   550
Hayes Lemmerz International-Bristol Inc.; Northville; dies and tools   507
Allied Staffing Inc.; Livonia; temporary help service   500
American Community Mutual Insurance Co.; Livonia; accident and health insurance   500
Aramark Industrial Services; Livonia; management services   500
Corporate Personnel Services Inc.; Livonia; temporary help service   500
Distinctive Maintenance Inc.; Livonia; building maintenance   500
Howard Delivery Service Inc.; Livonia; trucking terminal facilities   500
L&W Inc.; Belleville; automotive stampings   500
Meijer Inc.; Wixom; discount department stores   500
Target Corp.; Westland; department stores   500
USA Jet Airlines Inc.; Belleville; air cargo carrier   500
Williams International Co.; Walled Lake; aircraft turbines   500

Michigan 12th District

Suburban Detroit — Warren, Clinton, Southfield

Well-settled suburbs north of 8 Mile Road, Detroit's northern boundary, form Michigan's 12th. The district is fertile ground for Democratic candidates and depends heavily on automobile manufacturing, making the United Auto Workers union a potent political force. *(See map p. 477.)*

Roughly 70 percent of district residents live in Macomb County, once a largely blue-collar area that typified the "Reagan Democrats," those socially conservative, ancestrally Democratic blue-collar voters who had strong union loyalties but overwhelmingly backed Republican presidential candidates in the 1980s. But Macomb is becoming more white-collar, and Democrats have made progress here: Bill Clinton won Macomb in 1996, and Al Gore and now-senator Debbie Stabenow narrowly carried the county in 2000.

The district is lined with auto manufacturing facilities. Warren, the district's most populous city and a traditional Democratic stronghold (it voted for Gore by 56 percent to 41 percent in 2000), is home to the General Motors Technical Center, a 330-acre design and engineering campus. The Army's Tank Automotive Command also is in Warren.

The western part of the district takes in several areas in southern Oakland County, near the Detroit boundary, that are heavily Democratic and African American: Southfield, which has become a haven for black urban professionals escaping Detroit's crime, Lathrup Village, Oak Park, and Royal Oak. Other Oakland County communities in the 12th include Ferndale, Hazel Park, and Madison Heights, which also are solidly Democratic but mostly white.

Redistricting following the 2000 census pushed the largely Democratic district firmly into the Democrats' column. Republican mapmakers removed some GOP-leaning areas from the 12th to improve their party's chances in adjacent districts.

Major Industry

Auto and tank manufacturing, auto research and design.

Notable

The Detroit Zoo is in Royal Oak.

Election Returns

	Republican		Democratic		Other	
President 2000	106,628	37.0%	175,524	60.9%	5,940	2.1%
House 2002	61,502	29.8%	140,970	68.3%	4,056	2.0%

District Profile

Population   662,563

Total area (square miles)   160.3
   Land area (square miles)   160.3

Population per square mile   4,133.3

Counties (2000 population)
   Macomb (pt.)   458,352
   Oakland (pt.)   204,211

Cities and other areas over 10,000 (2000 population)
   Clinton CDP   95,648
   Eastpointe   34,077
   Ferndale   22,105
   Fraser   15,297
   Hazel Park   18,963
   Madison Heights   31,101
   Mount Clemens   17,312
   Oak Park   29,793
   Roseville   48,129
   Southfield   78,296
   St. Clair Shores (pt.)   63,096
   Sterling Heights (pt.)   37,935
   Warren   138,247

Race and Hispanic or Latino origin*

White   81.7%
Black or African American   12.0%
American Indian or Alaska Native   0.3%
Asian   2.3%
Native Hawaiian or other Pacific Islander   0.0%
Some other race   0.2%
Hispanic or Latino origin   1.5%
Two or more races   2.1%

As percentage of total population.

Ancestry*

Arab-Misc. 1.7%	Irish 8.0%
Belgian 1.1%	Italian 7.6%
English 5.4%	Polish 11.4%
Fr. Canadian 1.7%	Russian 1.1%
French 3.6%	Scottish 1.5%
German 14.1%	USA/American 2.7%

As estimated percentage of total population.

Universities and colleges, 2000–2001 enrollment

Baker College of Mount Clemens, Clinton Township   2,559
Detroit College of Business, Warren   2,561
Lawrence Technological University, Southfield   4,087
Macomb Community College, Warren   22,001
University of Phoenix-Michigan, Southfield   2,090

Newspapers and circulation

	District circulation	Total circulation
Detroit Free Press	57,484	363,536
Detroit News	37,732	238,950
Detroit News/Free Press (Sunday)	95,219	603,915
Macomb Daily	33,619	53,194
Oakland Press	7,254	74,996
Royal Oak Daily Tribune	14,509	15,840
*USA Today**	1,527	1,674,376

See Sources and Explanations in the front of the volume.

Television stations and affiliations

Detroit	100%	WADL	Independent
Detroit	100%	WDIV	NBC
Detroit	100%	WDWB	WB
Detroit	100%	WJBK	FOX
Detroit	100%	WKBD	UPN
Detroit	100%	WPXD	PAX
Detroit	100%	WTVS	PBS

| Detroit | 100% | WWJ | CBS |
| Detroit | 100% | WXYZ | ABC |

Cable systems and subscribers
Comcast 144,371

Military installations, September 2001
Detroit Arsenal (Army), Detroit 4,047
Selfridge Air National Guard Base, Mount Clemens 3,088
Selfridge U.S. Army Garrison, Mount Clemens 859
Southfield U.S. Army Reserve Center, Southfield 629

Businesses and other major employers
General Motors Corp.; Warren; engineering services 15,000
General Motors Corp.; Warren; motor vehicle parts/accessories 10,500
DaimlerChrysler Corp.; Warren; truck and tractor truck assembly 7,000
CMI Management Services Inc.; Southfield; aluminum castings 3,873
DaimlerChrysler Corp.; Sterling Heights; automotive stampings 3,500
General Motors Corp.; Warren; motor vehicle parts/accessories 3,000
Human Capital; Southfield; help supply services 3,000
Providence Hospital; Southfield 2,900
Valenite-Modco International Inc.; Madison Heights; metal cutting machine tools 2,100
DaimlerChrysler Corp.; Warren; automotive stampings 2,000
General Motors Corp.; Warren; motor vehicles and car bodies 2,000
International Business Machines Corp.; Southfield; administrative management 2,000
Mount Clemens General Hospital Inc.; Mount Clemens 2,000
Detroit-Macomb Hospital Corp.; Warren 1,800
Mercy Mount Clemens Corp. Hospital; Clinton Township 1,700
Peregrine U.S. Inc.; Southfield; automotive body parts 1,570
Trianon Industries Corp.; Center Line; automotive stampings 1,500
Macomb Community College; Warren 1,200
Titan Holdings; Southfield; fast-food restaurant chain 1,200
Unique Restaurant Corp.; Franklin; employee leasing service 1,200
DaimlerChrysler Corp.; Center Line; warehousing and storage 1,000
Detroit Osteopathic Hospital Corp.; Warren 1,000
E. I. Du Pont De Nemours and Co.; Mount Clemens; paints and allied products 1,000
Federal-Mogul Venture Corp.; Southfield; warehousing and storage 1,000
Salomon Smith Barney Holdings Inc.; Southfield; brokers' services 1,000
City of Warren; Warren; city management 977
Aetna Industries Inc.; Warren; automotive body parts 900
Blue Cross and Blue Shield of Michigan; Southfield; group hospitalization 900

Meijer Inc.; Roseville; discount department stores 900
D-M-E Co.; Madison Heights; dies, tools, jigs, fixtures 874
Chippewa Valley Schools; Clinton Township 840
Oakland Hospital; Madison Heights 800
City of Southfield; Southfield; city management 800
UNOVA Industrial Automation Systems Inc.; Warren; conveyors and conveying equipment 800
C. A. Muer Corp.; Southfield; restaurants 746
Burns International Security Services Corp.; Oak Park; security guard service 700
Delphi Corp.; Warren; automotive stampings 700
General Electric Co.; Southfield; plastics 650
Inductoheat Inc.; Madison Heights; induction heating equipment 650
TRW Inc.; Sterling Heights; automotive steering mechanisms 627
RCO Engineering Inc.; Roseville; motor vehicle parts/accessories 620
Cameron and Barkley Co.; Mount Clemens; automotive paint shop 600
DaimlerChrysler Services; Southfield; automotive dealer financing 600
Henkel Corp.; Madison Heights; anticorrosion lubricant 600
Meijer Inc.; Mount Clemens; discount department stores 600
Meijer Inc.; Sterling Heights; discount department stores 600
National Coney Island Inc.; Roseville; fast-food restaurants and stands 600
Blue Care Network of Michigan; Southfield; group hospitalization 550
Credit Acceptance Corp.; Southfield; auto financing 550
Lawrence Technological University; Southfield 550
Nation Wide Services Inc.; Southfield; security guard service 550
Detroit Edison Co.; Southfield; electric services 531
St. John's Hospital; Warren 505
Ciber Inc.; Southfield; computer software design 500
FCB Worldwide Inc.; Southfield; advertising 500
Fisher and Co.; St. Clair Shores; motor vehicle parts/accessories 500
Hygrade Food Products Corp.; Southfield; investment holding company 500
Plante and Moran Investment Partnership; Southfield; realty investment trusts 500
TechTeam Global Inc.; Southfield; housing construction 500
Van Dyke Public School District; Warren 500
Vemco Inc.; Fraser; molding primary plastics 500

Michigan 13th District

Part of Detroit; Lincoln Park; Wyandotte

General Motors helped build Detroit through a thriving American auto industry over the first half of the twentieth century. Then riots in 1967 and the oil crisis of the 1970s decimated the city's economy and turned it into a virtual war zone. The 13th suffered the worst of the 1967 riots in terms of property damage and deaths. For a time, Detroit was even known as the "Beirut of America." The city still has a reputation for crime and relatively high taxes, and many of the affluent suburbs that surround Detroit have become regional office centers and have lured companies away from the city. *(See map p. 477.)*

Detroit is divided between the 13th and 14th Districts, with a slightly larger share of the city's population living in the 13th. The 13th is a black-majority district, and about three-fourths of its residents live in Detroit. The city steadily declined in population in the 1990s, and fell below 1 million in the 2000 census.

Detroit remains overwhelmingly Democratic (Al Gore won the city with 94 percent in 2000) and black (80 percent of Detroit's population). Pockets of poverty exist, and the 13th has the state's highest percentage of households with incomes under $10,000. Wealthy communities to the northeast, such as Grosse Pointe, also are losing population.

Downtown Detroit and the waterfront, covered by the 13th, have been a target for intensive redevelopment. There are two new sporting venues downtown that are part of a massive entertainment complex—Comerica Park opened in 2000 for baseball's Detroit Tigers, and Ford Field opened in 2002 for the National Football League's Detroit Lions. There also are several new casinos.

Redistricting following the 2000 census renumbered the district from the 15th to the 13th and added the cities of Wyandotte and Lincoln Park, but the changes did not shift the district's overwhelmingly Democratic tilt.

Major Industry
Auto and auto parts manufacturing, government.

Notable
The Belle Isle Zoo and the Charles H. Wright Museum of African American History are in the 13th.

Election Returns

	Republican		Democratic		Other	
President 2000	39,024	18.7%	167,830	80.4%	1,975	0.9%
House 2002			120,869	91.6%	11,072	8.4%

District Profile

Population 662,563

Total area (square miles) 108.4
  Land area (square miles) 108.0

Population per square mile 6,134.8

Counties (2000 population)
  Wayne (pt.) 662,563

Cities and other areas over 10,000 (2000 population)
  Detroit (pt.) 511,449
  Ecorse (pt.) 11,229
  Grosse Pointe Park (pt.) 12,443
  Grosse Pointe Woods 17,080
  Harper Woods 14,254
  Lincoln Park 40,008
  Wyandotte (pt.) 28,006

Race and Hispanic or Latino origin*
White 28.9%
Black or African American 60.5%
American Indian or Alaska Native 0.3%
Asian 1.2%
Native Hawaiian or other Pacific Islander 0.0%
Some other race 0.2%
Hispanic or Latino origin 7.2%
Two or more races 1.8%

As percentage of total population.

Ancestry*
English	2.4%	Italian	2.4%
French	1.6%	Polish	4.2%
German	5.4%	Subsaharan	1.2%
Irish	4.2%	USA/American	1.7%

As estimated percentage of total population.

Universities and colleges, 2000–2001 enrollment
Center for Creative Studies College of Art and Design, Detroit 1,086
Sacred Heart Major Seminary, Detroit 377
Wayne County Community College, Detroit 9,008
Wayne State University, Detroit 30,408

Newspapers and circulation

	District circulation	Total circulation
Detroit Free Press	40,462	363,536
Detroit News	31,357	238,950
Detroit News/Free Press (Sunday)	71,821	603,915
*Michigan Chronicle**	6,153	32,251
*USA Today**	3,000	1,674,376

See Sources and Explanations in the front of the volume.

Television stations and affiliations
Detroit	100%	WADL	Independent
Detroit	100%	WDIV	NBC
Detroit	100%	WDWB	WB
Detroit	100%	WJBK	FOX
Detroit	100%	WKBD	UPN
Detroit	100%	WPXD	PAX
Detroit	100%	WTVS	PBS
Detroit	100%	WWJ	CBS
Detroit	100%	WXYZ	ABC

Cable systems and subscribers
Comcast 154,547
Wyandotte TV Cable 10,007

Businesses and other major employers
General Motors Corp.; Detroit; automobiles 13,600
City of Detroit; Detroit; police dept. 7,000
DaimlerChrysler Corp.; Detroit; motor vehicles and car bodies 5,000
National Steel Corp.; Detroit; hot-rolled steel shees or strips 4,400
Michigan Family Independence Agency; Detroit 3,700
American Axle and Manufacturing Inc.; Detroit; aircraft forgings 3,300
Blue Cross and Blue Shield of Michigan; Detroit; group hospitalization 3,000
MGM Grand Detroit; Detroit; gambling 3,000
Motor City Casino; Detroit; casino hotel 2,900

Greektown Casino; Detroit; casino hotel   2,700
Detroit Newspapers; Detroit; newspaper   2,600
Ford Motor Co.; Detroit; automotive services   2,500
Harper Hospital; Detroit   2,400
MichCon Gathering Co.; Detroit; natural gas pipelines   2,300
Michigan Children's Hospital; Detroit   2,210
DaimlerChrysler Corp.; Detroit; motor vehicle axles   2,200
Michigan Bell Telephone Co.; Detroit; local/long-distance telephone   2,200
City of Detroit; Detroit; city government   2,000
Delphi Corp.; Detroit; interior design services   2,000
Detroit Edison Co.; Detroit; electric power generation   2,000
Detroit Medical Center; Detroit   2,000
General Motors Corp.; Detroit; accounting services   2,000
Detroit Board of Education; Detroit   1,800
Detroit Receiving Hospital and University Health Center; Detroit   1,740
Budd Co.; Detroit; automotive body parts   1,500
J. Walter Thompson Co.; Detroit; advertising   1,500
Wayne County; Detroit; transportation regulation   1,500
Wyandotte Hospital and Medical Center; Wyandotte   1,500
City of Detroit; Detroit; trucking terminal facilities   1,497
Mexican Industries in Michigan Inc.; Detroit; automotive trimmings, fabric   1,370
U.S. Veterans Hospital; Detroit   1,300
Wayne State University; Detroit   1,259
Michigan Consolidated Gas Co.; Detroit; natural gas distribution   1,200
U.S. Internal Revenue Service; Detroit   1,100
PricewaterhouseCoopers; Detroit; certified public accountant   1,080
American Natural Offshore Co.; Detroit; natural gas transmission   1,000
BASF Corp.; Wyandotte; chemicals and allied products   1,000
Bon Secours-Cottage Health Services Hospital; Detroit   1,000
City of Detroit; Detroit; recreation services   1,000
DaimlerChrysler Corp.; Detroit; diesel engines   1,000
Barden Companies Inc.; Detroit; computer software   985
City of Detroit; Detroit; sewerage systems   950
DaimlerChrysler Corp.; Detroit; products of purchased glass   950
Michigan Judiciary Courts; Detroit   900
St. John Northeast Community Hospital; Detroit   900
DTE Energy Co.; Detroit; electric power generation   800
H&R Block Financial Advisors; Detroit; stock brokers and dealers   800
Henry Ford Health System Hospital; Grosse Pointe   800
International Union UAW of America; Detroit; labor union   800
Olympia Entertainment Inc.; Detroit; subscription services   800

OneSource Facility Services Inc.; Detroit; building maintenance   800
Ace-Tex Corp.; Detroit; industrial launderers   750
Deloitte and Touche; Detroit; certified public accountant   700
General Motors Acceptance Corp.; Detroit; automotive dealer financing   700
Meijer Inc.; Southgate; discount department stores   700
St. John Hospital and Medical Center; Detroit   700
Lear Corp.; Detroit; public building furniture   663
Lavan Hawkins and Associates of Chicago Inc.; Detroit; restaurants   600
Sears Roebuck and Co. Inc.; Lincoln Park; department stores   600
Accenture Inc.; Detroit; management consulting   578
Wellness Plan; Detroit; health maintenance organization   550
CoEnergy MidContinent Inc.; Detroit; natural gas production   500
Health Alliance Plan of Michigan; Detroit; health maintenance organization   500
Ilitch Holdings; Detroit; investment holding company   500
Mark IV Automotive; Detroit; welded, lock joint tubes   500
Marriott International Inc.; Detroit; hotels and motels   500
Newton Security Systems Inc.; Detroit; security guard service   500
Rehabilitation Institute of Michigan; Detroit   500
SBC Communications Inc.; Detroit; data telephone communications   500
Target Corp.; Harper Woods; department stores   500
Wayne County; Detroit; courts   500
Wayne County Community College District; Detroit   500

Michigan 14th District

Parts of Detroit and Dearborn

The auto industry kept Detroit humming for most of this century. The early factories drew people from rural Michigan, Appalachia, the South, and Eastern Europe. Then race riots during the summer of 1967 and the oil crisis of the early 1970s sparked an evacuation of the Motor City. Many residents fled to the suburbs, and automakers moved to Mexico and nonunion U.S. towns, leaving Detroit with some of the poorest and most crime-ridden neighborhoods in the nation. In 1960, 1.7 million people lived in Detroit; in 2000 its population was 951,000. *(See map p. 477.)*

The 14th covers the residential neighborhoods that sprang up north of Detroit's auto plants. It includes slightly less than half of Detroit, which accounts for two-thirds of the district's total population. Long an economically distressed area, the district has seen a few signs of renewal. Property values are beginning to pick up, and crime rates are starting to fall—additional signs that Detroit's worst days may be past.

As redrawn following the 2000 census, the 14th includes two-thirds of Dearborn, which is home to Ford Motor Co. and its River Rouge factory—once the largest in the world. Dearborn has a large Arab American population, with 30 percent of city residents claiming Arab ancestry. The district also includes two areas enveloped by Detroit: Hamtramck, an ethnically diverse enclave where more than 10 percent of residents consider themselves biracial, and Highland Park, an overwhelmingly African American area that in 2000 had the highest poverty rate (38 percent) in metropolitan Detroit.

The 14th has the nation's seventh-largest percentage of black residents (61 percent), and is safely Democratic. Detroit's unyielding Democratic bent keeps Republicans from carrying the seat or Wayne County.

Major Industry
Auto and auto parts manufacturing, health care.

Notable
Woodward Avenue, between 6 Mile and 7 Mile roads, was the nation's first paved road (1909); the Henry Ford Museum houses the rocking chair that President Abraham Lincoln sat in when he was assassinated at Ford's Theatre in Washington, D.C., on April 14, 1865.

Election Returns

	Republican		Democratic		Other	
President 2000	44,345	18.1%	198,687	80.9%	2,449	1.0%
House 2002	26,544	15.2%	145,285	83.2%	2,779	1.6%

District Profile

Population   662,563

Total area (square miles)   122.8
 Land area (square miles)   122.6

Population per square mile   5,404.3

Counties (2000 population)
 Wayne (pt.)   662,563

Cities and other areas over 10,000 (2000 population)
 Allen Park   29,376
 Dearborn (pt.)   64,759
 Detroit (pt.)   439,821
 Grosse Ile CDP (pt.)   10,894
 Hamtramck   22,976
 Highland Park   16,746
 Melvindale   10,735
 Riverview (pt.)   13,272
 Southgate   30,136
 Trenton (pt.)   19,584

Race and Hispanic or Latino origin*
 White   32.1%
 Black or African American   61.1%
 American Indian or Alaska Native   0.3%
 Asian   1.2%
 Native Hawaiian or other Pacific Islander   0.0%
 Some other race   0.2%
 Hispanic or Latino origin   1.8%
 Two or more races   3.3%

*As percentage of total population.

Ancestry*

Arab-Misc.	4.7%	Irish	3.7%
English	2.4%	Italian	2.3%
French	1.7%	Polish	4.8%
German	5.0%	Subsaharan	1.2%
Hungarian	1.1%	USA/American	1.7%

*As estimated percentage of total population.

Universities and colleges, 2000–2001 enrollment
 Detroit College of Business, Dearborn   3,158
 Lewis College of Business, Detroit   323
 Marygrove College, Detroit   5,744
 University of Detroit Mercy, Detroit   6,023

Newspapers and circulation

	District circulation	Total circulation
Detroit Free Press	37,473	363,536
Detroit News	27,396	238,950
Detroit News/Free Press (Sunday)	64,875	603,915
*Michigan Chronicle**	5,593	32,251
*USA Today**	2,727	1,674,376

*See Sources and Explanations in the front of the volume.

Television stations and affiliations
Detroit	100%	WADL	Independent
Detroit	100%	WDIV	NBC
Detroit	100%	WDWB	WB
Detroit	100%	WJBK	FOX
Detroit	100%	WKBD	UPN
Detroit	100%	WPXD	PAX
Detroit	100%	WTVS	PBS
Detroit	100%	WWJ	CBS
Detroit	100%	WXYZ	ABC

Cable systems and subscribers
 Charter   2,140
 Comcast   62,599

Businesses and other major employers
 Ford Motor Co.; Dearborn; motor vehicle parts/accessories   13,000
 Detroit Diesel Corp.; Detroit; diesel, dual-fuel engines   3,500
 Oakwood Hospital Corp.; Dearborn   3,500
 Utility Workers Union of America AFL/CIO; Dearborn; trade union   3,310
 DaimlerChrysler Corp.; Trenton; diesel engines   3,000
 Rouge Steel Co.; Dearborn; steel sheets or strips   2,684
 Visteon Corp.; Allen Park; motor vehicles and car bodies   2,500
 Visteon Corp.; Dearborn; automotive electrical equipment   2,500
 Ford Motor Credit Co.; Dearborn; automotive dealer financing   2,126
 Commonwealth Service Sales Corp.; Dearborn; electric motor repair   1,985
 Carhartt Inc.; Dearborn; men's/boys' work clothing   1,755
 Sinai-Grace Hospital; Detroit   1,622
 City of Detroit; Detroit; public service commission   1,400
 City of Dearborn; Dearborn; city government   1,220

U.S. Postal Service; Allen Park   1,200
American Axle and Manufacturing Inc.; Detroit;
   nonferrous forgings   850
Detroit Osteopathic Hospital Corp.; Trenton   700
Edison Institute; Dearborn; museum   700
University of Detroit Mercy Hospital; Detroit   695
Bartech Inc.; Dearborn; temporary help service   507
ASC Inc.; Southgate; top and body repair and paint
   shops   500
Borman's Inc.; Detroit; grocery store   500
Henry Ford Health System; Detroit; health maintenance
   organization   500
Initial Security Inc.; Southgate; guard services   500
Lear Corp.; Allen Park; motor vehicle parts/accessories
   500
Oakwood Health Promotions Inc.; Dearborn; personal
   care home, with health care   500
Solutia Inc.; Trenton; detergents   500
U.S. Dept. of Veterans Affairs; Allen Park   500

Michigan 15th District

Southeast — Ann Arbor, Taylor, parts of Dearborn and Dearborn Heights

Situated on the flat land west and south of Detroit, the 15th contains a mix of autoworkers, engineers, and academics. As redrawn following the 2000 census, the 15th is a Democratic bastion that takes in parts of the old 13th, based in Ann Arbor, and the old 16th, based in Wayne County outside Detroit. *(See map p. 477.)*

Interstate 94, which joins the eastern and western ends of the 15th in the north, has emerged as an engineering and research corridor where robotics companies, developing ways to automate auto manufacturing, have helped turn Detroit assembly line jobs into highly skilled, computerized work.

At the district's northwestern corner is Ann Arbor, the district's most populous city and home to the University of Michigan's academic community. Ann Arbor votes reliably Democratic: Al Gore took 69 percent of the vote here in the 2000 presidential election. Ypsilanti, a working-class town southeast of Ann Arbor, is home to Eastern Michigan University and also reliably backs Democratic candidates.

A little more than 40 percent of the district's residents live in the blue-collar, reliably Democratic suburbs of Wayne County. The 15th's most populous city here is Taylor, which is just east of Detroit Metropolitan Wayne County Airport in Romulus. Dearborn, the western third of which is in the 15th, Dearborn Heights (shared with the 11th), and Inkster form the district's northeast corner.

Monroe County, south of Wayne and Washtenaw Counties, borders Lake Erie to the east and the Toledo, Ohio, area to the south.

Major Industry

Auto and auto parts manufacturing, higher education, medical research, steel.

Notable

NOAA's Great Lakes Environmental Research Laboratory is in Ann Arbor.

Election Returns

	Republican		Democratic		Other	
President 2000	101,607	37.5%	161,913	59.8%	7,086	2.6%
House 2002	48,626	25.7%	136,518	72.2%	3,919	2.1%

District Profile

Population   662,563

Total area (square miles)   981.0
   Land area (square miles)   961.2

Population per square mile   689.3

Counties (2000 population)
Monroe 145,945		Wayne (pt.) 269,714
Washtenaw (pt.) 246,904		

Cities and other areas over 10,000 (2000 population)
Ann Arbor   114,024
Dearborn (pt.)   33,016
Dearborn Heights (pt.)   44,694
Inkster   30,115
Monroe   22,076
Romulus   22,979
Taylor   65,868
Woodhaven   12,530
Ypsilanti   22,362

Race and Hispanic or Latino origin*
White   79.2%
Black or African American   11.7%
American Indian or Alaska Native   0.4%
Asian   3.7%
Native Hawaiian or other Pacific Islander   0.0%
Some other race   0.2%
Hispanic or Latino origin   2.8%
Two or more races   2.0%

As percentage of total population.

Ancestry*
Arab-Misc. 1.1%	Hungarian 1.5%
Dutch 1.4%	Irish 8.4%
English 6.7%	Italian 3.8%
Fr. Canadian 1.4%	Polish 6.7%
French 4.2%	Scottish 1.7%
German 15.0%	USA/American 3.6%

As estimated percentage of total population.

Universities and colleges, 2000–2001 enrollment
Cleary College, Ypsilanti   705
Concordia College, Ann Arbor   604
Eastern Michigan University, Ypsilanti   23,561
Henry Ford Community College, Dearborn   12,742
Monroe County Community College, Monroe   3,555
University of Michigan, Ann Arbor   38,103
University of Michigan, Dearborn   8,400
Washtenaw Community College, Ann Arbor   11,089

Newspapers and circulation
	District circulation	Total circulation
Ann Arbor News	27,350	55,446
Detroit Free Press	28,874	363,536

Detroit News	19,353	238,950
Detroit News/Free Press (Sunday)	48,235	603,915
Michigan Chronicle *	9,002	32,251
Monroe Evening News	21,610	21,794
Toledo Blade	7,028	138,304
USA Today *	5,731	1,674,376

See Sources and Explanations in the front of the volume.

Television stations and affiliations

Detroit	100%	WADL	Independent
Detroit	100%	WDIV	NBC
Detroit	100%	WDWB	WB
Detroit	100%	WJBK	FOX
Detroit	100%	WKBD	UPN
Detroit	100%	WPXD	PAX
Detroit	100%	WTVS	PBS
Detroit	100%	WWJ	CBS
Detroit	100%	WXYZ	ABC

Cable systems and subscribers
Charter   3,740
Comcast   130,664

Businesses and other major employers
University of Michigan; Ann Arbor   4,900
University of Michigan Medical Center; Ann Arbor   3,300
General Motors Corp.; Romulus; gasoline engines   2,500
SGC Holding Co.; Dearborn; motor vehicle parts/accessories   2,500
Ford Motor Co.; Ypsilanti; medical laboratories   2,300
Visteon Corp.; Monroe; motor vehicle parts/accessories   2,000
Auto Club Group Insurance Co.; Dearborn; fire, marine, casualty insurance   1,943
Auto Club Insurance Assn. and Affiliates; Dearborn; automobile insurance   1,900
City of Ann Arbor; Ann Arbor; city government   1,900
AutoAlliance International Inc.; Flat Rock; motor vehicles and car bodies   1,847
Eastern Michigan University; Ypsilanti   1,800
Ford Motor Co.; Dearborn; automobiles   1,800
U.S. Veterans Hospital; Ann Arbor   1,750
Lear Corp.; Dearborn; automobile seats   1,500

Pfizer Corp.; Ann Arbor; commercial physical research   1,500
Visteon Corp.; Ypsilanti; automotive horns   1,300
Washtenaw County; Ann Arbor; county government   1,150
Meridian Automotive Systems Inc.; Dearborn; automotive stampings   1,100
Visteon Corp.; Milan; motor vehicle parts/accessories   1,100
Dearborn School District; Dearborn   1,000
Ford Motor Co.; Dearborn; automotive supplies, parts   1,000
Oakwood Healthcare Inc. Hospital; Taylor   900
Mercy-Memorial Hospital Corp.; Monroe   896
Detroit Edison Co.; Newport; electric services   877
McNaughton-McKay Electric Co.; Ypsilanti; electrical equipment   850
Borders Inc.; Ann Arbor; bookstores   750
Michigan Community Health Dept.; Ypsilanti   750
Hyatt Corp.; Dearborn; franchised hotel   700
LSG Lufthansa Service Inc.; Detroit; caterers   700
ProQuest Co.; Ann Arbor; book publishing   667
Meijer Inc.; Trenton; discount department stores   650
Johnson Controls Inc.; Taylor; public building furniture   600
Meijer Inc.; Ann Arbor; discount department stores   600
Meijer Inc.; Monroe; discount department stores   600
La-Z-Boy Inc.; Monroe; chairs   568
Masco Corp.; Taylor; faucets and spigots   559
NES Equipment Rental; Taylor; heavy construction equipment rental   550
North Star Steel Co. Inc.; Monroe; blast furnaces and steel mills   543
Eaton Corp.; Ann Arbor; relays and industrial controls   530
Arrow Uniform Rental LP; Taylor; uniform supply   500
Conway Now; Ann Arbor; trucking   500
Ford Motor Co.; Ann Arbor; car dealers   500
Guardian Industries Corp.; Carleton; flat glass   500
Michigan Consolidated Gas Co.; Ypsilanti; natural gas distribution   500
Romulus Board of Education; Romulus   500
Target Corp.; Dearborn; grocery store   500
Van Kampen Funds Inc.; Ann Arbor; mutual fund sales   500

MINNESOTA

Districts established March 19, 2002, for elections first held in 2002.

8 members

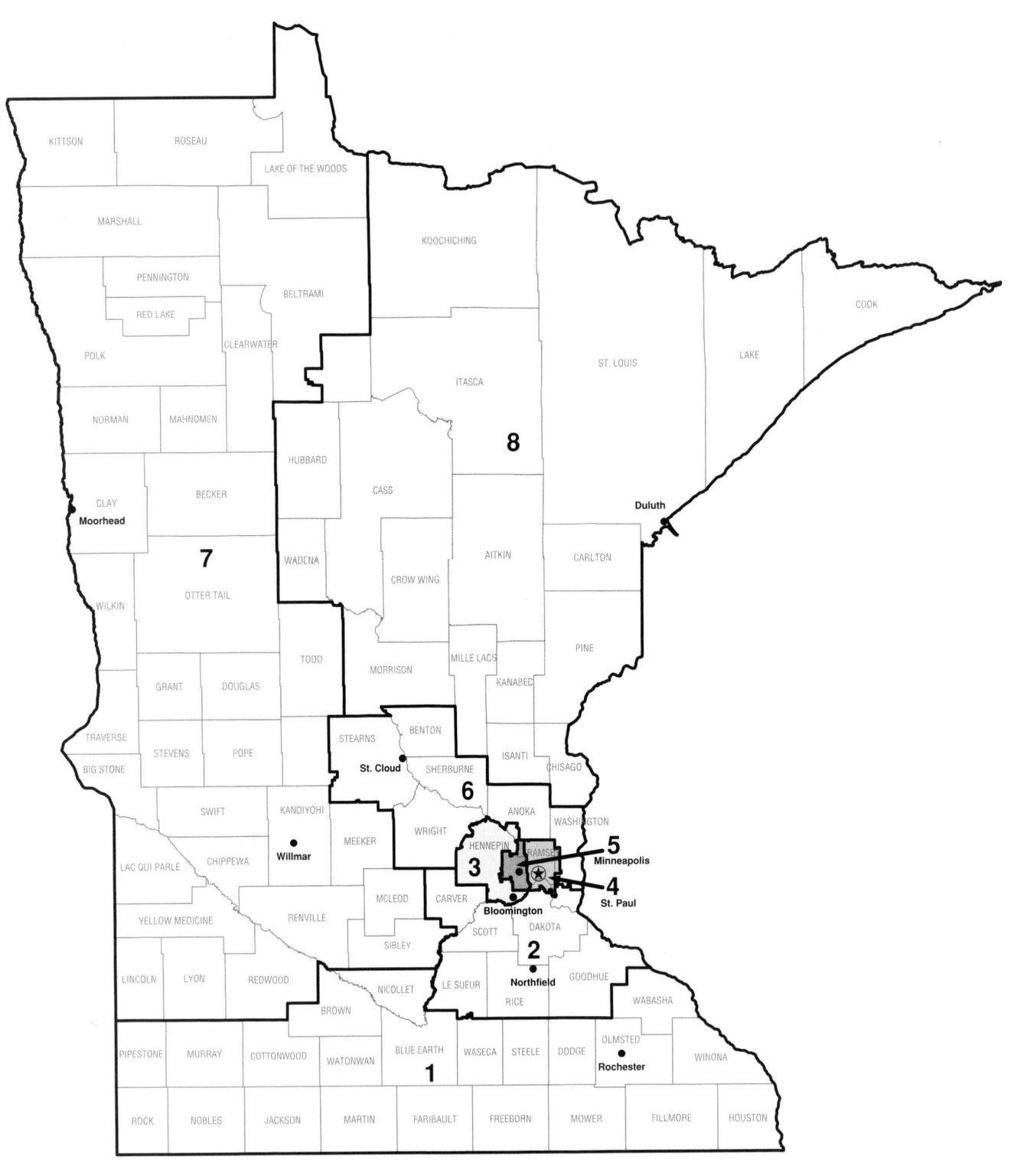

Minnesota

Every state has a political reputation rooted in its past, and these characterizations can be difficult to outgrow. Minnesota has for decades been known as a bastion of liberalism, even though its political climate and voting record are much closer to those of the Midwest region as a whole. The persistent image rests largely on the careers of two men, Hubert H. Humphrey and Walter F. Mondale. Both were senators from the state's left-populist Democratic-Farm-Labor Party (DFL), each served one term as vice president and won the Democratic nomination for president. Together they were on the party's national ticket five times from 1964 through 1984. Humphrey lost by a whisker to Richard Nixon in 1968; Mondale lost 49 states to Ronald Reagan in 1984. But the one state Mondale (barely) won was his own.

There have also been other high-profile Minnesotans on the left whose careers did not go as far. Sen. Eugene McCarthy was a peace candidate for president in 1968 and later a third-party Don Quixote. Subsequent senators Paul Wellstone, the professorial liberal killed in a plane crash while campaigning for a third term in 2002, and the self-financing department store heir Mark Dayton, kept the flame lit in the Senate.

But quite apart from the drama of these careers there exists another political identity in Minnesota, one that has prevailed through most of the state's history and reasserted itself in the years since Humphrey and Mondale's heyday. It is a tradition of independence and unpredictability. Sometimes it has favored populists, other times it has chosen millionaire retailers famous for their commercials. In 1998 the state elected Jesse "The Body" Ventura, a native son who had been a Navy SEAL, a professional wrestler, an action movie actor, a radio talk show host, and finally a plainspoken Perot-style candidate for governor. In a tight three-way race with two conventional politicians, Ventura won with 37 percent of the vote. There followed four tumultuous years in which Ventura fought with the legislature and the media, flirted with a presidential candidacy, and frittered away his early popularity. In 2002 he chose to retire rather than seek a second term.

Ventura was succeeded in 2003 by Republican legislative leader Tim Pawlenty, who prevailed in a three-way contest complicated by the Wellstone tragedy. But Pawlenty himself was no surprise, at least not to Minnesotans. This state has always been friendlier to the GOP than its image would suggest. George W. Bush may have lost it in 2000, but only by two percentage points. Statewide officeholders have as often as not been from the GOP, usually from that centrist subset known as "Main Street" Republicans and long labeled on the ballot here as Independent Republicans.

Minnesota has elected four different Republicans to the Senate a total of seven times since 1978. These included moderates such as three-termer David Durenberger and hard-line conservatives such as former TV news personality Rod Grams. The latest is a former Democrat and former mayor of St. Paul, Norm Coleman, who ran against Wellstone in 2002. After Wellstone's death, Coleman found himself facing no less an obstacle than Mondale himself, who had been recalled from retirement in fine fettle and was presumed unbeatable until Coleman beat him.

Setting politics aside, though, many Americans know Minnesota chiefly as a summer vacation spot. Known as the "Land of 10,000 Lakes," the state actually has more than twice that many, and each seems to be home to at least a few fishing resorts. But the principal livelihood of the state has not been fishing, farming, or tourism; it has long been mining and manufacturing, as signified in the original name of 3M (Minnesota Manufacturing and Mining), the highly diversified, worldwide company known for its Scotch tape line.

The processing of farm goods, primarily grains and meats, laid a base for the factories that made the Twin Cities in the late 1800s. In more recent times the likes of Honeywell in high-tech and IDS in financial services have shown the way to a new economic tomorrow. In 2000 Minnesota ranked among the nation's top ten in high-tech jobs.

That job growth, plus a progressive atmosphere and community spirit have boosted the Minneapolis and St. Paul metroplex even as other midwestern cities have faded. The two, which Minnesotans call simply "The Cities," now coanchor the nation's sixteenth largest metropolitan area, spreading well up the Mississippi River, which is at this point a swift river springing from its source further to the northwest. Nowadays, the metro area actually enfolds the river town of Anoka, the boyhood home of writer Garrison Keillor and the inspiration for his fictional Lake Wobegon. While still in the second tier of metro areas (and constantly threatened with the loss of its Major League Baseball team), the Twin Cities posted a growth rate of 11.5 percent for the 1990s, and that was the best any metro area did outside the Sun Belt and the Pacific Northwest.

In the growth rate lies a potential secret to understanding Minnesota's seemingly mercurial political behavior. The traditionally Democratic cities of Minneapolis and St. Paul now account for just one-fifth of the votes cast in their metro area. The lion's share is in the suburbs, which have always been white, more affluent, more independent, and less friendly to organized labor. Here (and in parts of rural Minnesota) the families still have lots of children, helping the state rank among the top 15 for children under 17. Minnesota looks good in quality of life rankings of all kinds: forty-ninth in poverty percentage, first in health rating and in percentage of voting-age population turning out to vote.

It took the first 60 years of Minnesota's statehood to get to ten House seats after the census of 1910. Then in the next reapportionment (done in 1930 because Congress could not agree on reapportionment in 1920), the state dropped back down to nine seats. In 1960 it slid to eight, because the farms and small towns were thinning out and the Twin Cities could not keep pace with boomtowns elsewhere. Since then, however, Minnesota has not only stabilized but grown steadily, hanging on to all eight of those seats while all its midwestern neighbors to the south and east have seen their numbers erode.

Redistricting for the 2002 cycle was probably doomed from the start as a project for politicians. The Democrats controlled one chamber of the legislature, Republicans the other. And Ventura, despite his independent status, had ideas of his own about drawing new districts. Although Minnesota was not gaining (or losing) any new seats, the governor wanted a new district drawn in the suburbs north of Minneapolis and St. Paul, an area where he had served as a suburban mayor and maintained a base of support. He thought that seat could be freed by throwing two Democratic incumbents located south of Minneapolis and St. Paul into one district. Not surprisingly, Republicans in the legislature liked this idea too.

In the end, however, the three-way tug-of-war wound up catapulting the decision into the courts, where a panel of five judges appointed by the chief justice of the state supreme court got the job done. The incumbents all kept their districts to run in, with four districts dividing the Minneapolis and St. Paul metro area and four others dividing the rest of the state into four enormous quadrants. The four metro districts included one each for Minneapolis and St. Paul (each with its most immediately adjacent suburbs), a third on the west with the populous Hennepin County suburbs, and a fourth wrapping around St. Paul on the north, east, and south.

In the end, with all eight incumbents running, all managed to win in 2002 except one Democratic incumbent, Bill Luther, who had less than half his previous district intact but once again faced his two-time challenger John Kline. This time, Kline won easily and evened the state's House delegation at four seats for each party. With the same split now obtaining in the Senate, Minnesota continues to confound its old reputation.

Table 1 Population

District	Population	Population under 18	Voting-age population	Median age	Male*	Female*
1	614,935	156,560	458,375	36.6	49.4	50.6
2	614,934	183,238	431,696	33.5	49.9	50.1
3	614,935	163,836	451,099	36.5	48.9	51.1
4	614,935	158,447	456,488	34.1	48.2	51.8
5	614,935	132,223	482,712	33.3	49.5	50.5
6	614,935	179,817	435,118	33.1	50.6	49.4
7	614,935	160,294	454,641	38.0	49.7	50.3
8	614,935	152,479	462,456	38.9	49.9	50.1
State	4,919,479	1,286,894	3,632,585	35.4	49.5	50.5

*As percentage of total population.

Table 2 Voting-Age Persons by Race/Hispanic or Latino Origin

District	White*	Black or African American*	American Indian or Alaska Native*	Asian*	Other or multirace*	Hispanic or Latino*
1	94.5	0.8	0.2	1.5	0.5	2.4
2	93.1	1.4	0.4	2.2	0.8	2.2
3	90.5	3.2	0.3	3.6	0.9	1.5
4	82.8	5.4	0.6	5.5	1.4	4.3
5	76.9	10.2	1.3	4.4	2.2	5.2
6	95.6	0.9	0.4	1.3	0.6	1.0
7	94.7	0.3	1.9	0.6	0.6	1.9
8	95.7	0.5	2.1	0.4	0.7	0.6
State	90.3	2.9	0.9	2.4	1.0	2.4

*As percentage of voting-age population.

Table 3 Voting-Age Population by Age Groups

District	18 to 24*	25 to 44*	45 to 64*	Over 64*
1	14.0	36.6	29.1	20.3
2	11.6	48.2	29.5	10.7
3	9.9	43.4	32.8	13.9
4	14.5	41.5	28.2	15.8
5	15.5	44.8	24.8	14.9
6	13.8	46.2	29.3	10.8
7	12.6	34.5	30.1	22.8
8	11.5	35.1	32.4	21.0
State	13.0	41.2	29.5	16.4

*As percentage of voting-age population.

Table 4 Income and Occupation

District	Median family income	Families in poverty*	White collar†	Blue collar†	Service†	Farm†
1	$50,143	5.3	56.7	26.8	15.0	1.5
2	$68,944	2.5	65.0	22.3	12.2	0.4
3	$75,042	2.3	73.1	16.7	10.0	0.1
4	$58,913	6.6	67.0	19.2	13.6	0.1
5	$53,149	8.2	67.2	17.9	14.8	0.1
6	$64,348	2.8	60.3	26.9	12.3	0.4
7	$44,925	6.8	53.3	29.2	15.5	1.9
8	$46,275	6.9	52.9	28.9	17.1	1.0
State	$56,874	5.1	62.3	23.3	13.7	0.7

*As percentage of all families.   †As percentage of employed workers 16 years and over.

Table 5 Education: School Years Completed

District	Less than grade 9*	Grades 9–12 no diploma*	High school diploma no college*	Some college*	College bachelor's degree or higher*
1	7.4	7.5	32.7	30.9	21.6
2	3.3	5.1	26.8	33.6	31.2
3	1.8	4.1	21.3	32.7	40.1
4	4.8	7.1	26.1	29.0	33.0
5	4.8	8.1	23.3	28.8	34.9
6	3.4	6.1	31.1	35.0	24.5
7	9.4	8.4	34.5	31.3	16.4
8	5.2	9.7	35.1	32.4	17.7
State	5.0	7.0	28.8	31.7	27.4

*As percentage of persons age 25 and over.

Table 6   Housing and Residential Patterns

District	Median home value	Owner occupied*	Renter occupied*	Urban†	Rural†
1	$89,900	76.8	23.2	56.5	43.5
2	$148,400	82.2	17.8	80.1	19.9
3	$155,800	77.4	22.6	95.8	4.2
4	$124,400	65.3	34.7	99.9	0.1
5	$119,700	57.2	42.8	100.0	0.0
6	$136,100	82.8	17.2	63.8	36.2
7	$77,900	77.8	22.2	34.0	66.0
8	$86,700	80.2	19.8	37.4	62.6
State	$118,100	74.6	25.4	70.9	29.1

*As percentage of occupied housing units.   †As percentage of total population.

Minnesota 1st District

South — Rochester, Mankato

One of Minnesota's three rural districts, the 1st runs across the state's entire southern border from South Dakota to the Mississippi River, cut horizontally by Interstate 90 and vertically by Interstate 35. While the rural areas continue to lose population, cities such as Rochester, home to the Mayo Clinic and an IBM facility, and Mankato thrive. But the district's economy is dominated by agriculture and food processing.

Corn, soybeans, sugar beets, hogs, and dairy are staples of the agricultural economy. Food processing—from fresh turkey to canned soups—is more prevalent in the western half of the district, where there is no town with more than 20,000 people. Though still more than 90 percent white, Hispanic, Hmong, Lao, and Somali immigrants have come to take agricultural jobs in towns such as Worthington, which has the state's second-highest enrollment of non-English speakers in its schools, following St. Paul.

While many towns and small farmers support the Democratic-Farmer-Labor Party, Republicans have made gains by preaching fiscal conservatism and stressing rural and farm issues. George W. Bush took just over half of the district's vote in the 2000 presidential election.

Larger farms—particularly dairy—in the east support Republicans. Redistricting following the 2000 census added western farmlands that support Democrats and may make the 1st more competitive in the future. Rochester, once solidly Republican, also has begun to support some Democrats. Blue-collar workers from the Austin-based Hormel meatpacking company, as well as the city of Albert Lea, form a Democratic stronghold. College communities in Mankato (Minnesota State University) and Winona (Winona State University) also support Democrats.

Major Industry

Agriculture, food processing, health care.

Notable

Austin, the birthplace of Spam, is home to the Spam Museum.

Election Returns

	Republican		Democratic		Other	
President 2000	146,212	49.3%	133,078	44.8%	17,501	5.9%
House 2002	163,570	61.5%	92,165	34.7%	10,247	3.8%

District Profile

Population   614,935

Total area (square miles)   13,521.3
  Land area (square miles)   13,321.7

Population per square mile   46.2

Counties (2000 population)

Blue Earth 55,941	Murray 9,165
Brown 26,911	Nicollet 29,771
Cottonwood 12,167	Nobles 20,832
Dodge 17,731	Olmsted 124,277
Faribault 16,181	Pipestone 9,895
Fillmore 21,122	Rock 9,721
Freeborn 32,584	Steele 33,680
Houston 19,718	Wabasha 21,610
Jackson 11,268	Waseca 19,526
Le Sueur (pt.) 569	Watonwan 11,876
Martin 21,802	Winona 49,985
Mower 38,603	

Cities and other areas over 10,000 (2000 population)

Albert Lea 18,356	North Mankato 11,798
Austin 23,314	Owatonna 22,434
Fairmont 10,889	Rochester 85,806
Mankato (pt.) 32,427	Winona 27,069
New Ulm 13,594	Worthington 11,283

Race and Hispanic or Latino origin*

White   93.2%
Black or African American   1.0%
American Indian or Alaska Native   0.2%
Asian   1.7%
Native Hawaiian or other Pacific Islander   0.0%
Some other race   0.1%
Hispanic or Latino origin   3.0%
Two or more races   0.8%

*As percentage of total population.

Ancestry*

Danish 1.8%	Irish 7.1%
Dutch 2.5%	Norwegian 14.3%
English 4.3%	Polish 2.4%
French 1.9%	Swedish 3.4%
German 31.7%	USA/American 2.4%

*As estimated percentage of total population.

Universities and colleges, 2000–2001 enrollment

Bethany Lutheran College, Mankato   440
Gustavus Adolphus College, St. Peter   2,388
Martin Luther College, New Ulm   1,026
Mayo Graduate School, Rochester   246
Mayo School of Health Related Sciences, Rochester   248
Minnesota State University, Mankato   12,842
Minnesota West Community and Technical College, Worthington   582
Riverland Community College, Austin   3,182
Rochester Community and Technical College, Rochester   4,778
South Central Technical College, North Mankato   3,220
St. Mary's University of Minnesota, Winona   5,010

University of Minnesota, Waseca*
Winona State University, Winona 7,386

Enrollment under 100. See Sources and Explanations in the front of the volume.

Newspapers and circulation

	District circulation	Total circulation
Fairmont Sentinel	6,884	7,635
La Crosse Tribune	2,824	31,589
Mankato Free Press	20,032	23,283
New Ulm Journal	7,076	8,767
Rochester Post-Bulletin	40,241	42,167
Sioux Falls Argus Leader	1,892	51,753
St. Paul Pioneer Press	3,659	200,578
*USA Today**	2,799	1,674,376
Winona Daily News	9,440	11,538

See Sources and Explanations in the front of the volume.

Television stations and affiliations

Minneapolis-St. Paul	29%	KARE	NBC
Minneapolis-St. Paul	29%	KAWB	PBS
Minneapolis-St. Paul	29%	KAWE	PBS
Minneapolis-St. Paul	29%	KCCO	CBS
Minneapolis-St. Paul	29%	KCCW	CBS
Minneapolis-St. Paul	29%	KMSP	FOX
Minneapolis-St. Paul	29%	KMWB	WB
Minneapolis-St. Paul	29%	KPXM	PAX
Minneapolis-St. Paul	29%	KRWF	ABC
Minneapolis-St. Paul	29%	KSAX	ABC
Minneapolis-St. Paul	29%	KSTP	ABC
Minneapolis-St. Paul	29%	KTCA	PBS
Minneapolis-St. Paul	29%	KTCI	PBS
Minneapolis-St. Paul	29%	KWCM	PBS
Minneapolis-St. Paul	29%	WFTC	UPN
Rochester-Mason City-Austin	25%	KAAL	ABC
Rochester-Mason City-Austin	25%	KIMT	CBS
Rochester-Mason City-Austin	25%	KSMQ	PBS
Rochester-Mason City-Austin	25%	KTTC	NBC
Rochester-Mason City-Austin	25%	KXLT	FOX
Rochester-Mason City-Austin	25%	KYIN	PBS
Rochester-Mason City-Austin	25%	WCCO	CBS
Mankato	19%	KEYC	CBS, UPN
Sioux Falls (Mitchell), SD	18%	KABY	ABC
Sioux Falls (Mitchell), SD	18%	KCSD	PBS
Sioux Falls (Mitchell), SD	18%	KDLO	CBS
Sioux Falls (Mitchell), SD	18%	KDLV	NBC
Sioux Falls (Mitchell), SD	18%	KDSD	PBS
Sioux Falls (Mitchell), SD	18%	KELO	CBS
Sioux Falls (Mitchell), SD	18%	KESD	PBS
Sioux Falls (Mitchell), SD	18%	KPLO	CBS
Sioux Falls (Mitchell), SD	18%	KPRY	ABC
Sioux Falls (Mitchell), SD	18%	KQSD	PBS
Sioux Falls (Mitchell), SD	18%	KRNE	PBS
Sioux Falls (Mitchell), SD	18%	KSFY	ABC
Sioux Falls (Mitchell), SD	18%	KSMN	PBS
Sioux Falls (Mitchell), SD	18%	KTSD	PBS
Sioux Falls (Mitchell), SD	18%	KTTM	FOX
Sioux Falls (Mitchell), SD	18%	KTTW	FOX
La Crosse-Eau Claire, WI	9%	WEAU	NBC
La Crosse-Eau Claire, WI	9%	WEUX	FOX
La Crosse-Eau Claire, WI	9%	WEUX	FOX
La Crosse-Eau Claire, WI	9%	WHLA	PBS
La Crosse-Eau Claire, WI	9%	WHWC	PBS
La Crosse-Eau Claire, WI	9%	WKBT	CBS
La Crosse-Eau Claire, WI	9%	WLAX	FOX
La Crosse-Eau Claire, WI	9%	WQOW	ABC
La Crosse-Eau Claire, WI	9%	WXOW	ABC

Cable systems and subscribers
Charter 89,764
Jackson Municipal TV 1,586
Lakefield Cable TV 674
Mediacom 27,578
North American Communications Corp. 811
Prairiewave 1,487
Terril Cable System 646
Time Warner 5,959
U.S. Cable 6,352
Windom Cable 1,480

Businesses and other major employers
Mayo Clinic; Rochester 24,500
Mayo Medical Center Inc.; Rochester 21,856
Rochester Methodist Hospital; Rochester 20,000
International Business Machines Corp.; Rochester 5,100
Auto Owners Insurance Co.; Essig; automobile insurance 3,000
Hormel Foods Corp.; Austin; meatpacking plants 1,900
Swift and Co.; Worthington; meatpacking plants 1,700
Mankato Rehabilitation Center Inc.; Mankato 1,300
Minnesota State University; Mankato 1,300
Viracon Inc.; Owatonna; laminated glass 1,250
Federated Mutual Insurance Co.; Owatonna; fire, marine, casualty insurance 1,200
Immanuel-St. Joseph Hospital of Mankato Inc.; Mankato 1,100
Albert Lea Medical Center-Mayo Health System Hospital; Albert Lea 1,000
Quality Pork Processors Inc.; Austin; pork products 1,000
Truth Hardware Corp.; Owatonna; windows, window parts, and trim 950
AGCO Corp.; Jackson; farm machinery and equipment 900
Benchmark Electronics Inc.; Winona; harness assemblies, electronic use 900
3M Co.; New Ulm; photographic equipment, supplies 800
Minnesota Dept. of Human Services; St. Peter 800
Olmsted County Hospital; Rochester 800
Winona State University; Winona 800
National Toothpick Holder; Mankato; membership organization 750
Alliance Health Care Inc.; Mankato; home health care services 700
Fastenal Co.; Winona; metalworking machinery 700
SPX Corp.; Owatonna; hand tools 700
Winona Community Memorial Hospital; Winona 675
Austin Medical Center-Mayo Health System; Austin; health systems agency 650
Streater Inc.; Albert Lea; store fixtures 635
Kraft Foods Inc.; New Ulm; processed cheese 600
McNeilus Companies Inc.; Dodge Center; cement mixer bodies 600
Gustavus Adolphus College; St. Peter 595

Cabela's Retail Inc.; Owatonna; sporting goods and bicycle shops   590

Hearth Technologies Inc.; Lake City; heating equipment, nonelectric   560

Emerson Electric Co.; Mankato; electric generators   515

Campbell Soup Co.; Worthington; processed poultry   500

Farmland Foods Inc.; Albert Lea; pork products   500

Federal-Mogul Corp.; Lake City; iron foundry   500

Independent School District; St. Peter   500

Norwood Promotional Products Inc.; Sleepy Eye; publishing   500

Olmsted County; Rochester; county government   500

Pemstar Inc.; Rochester; computers   500

RTP International Holdings Inc.; Winona; textile mill waste   500

Swift-Eckrich Inc.; St. James; sausages, other meats   500

Toro Co.; Windom; lawn mowers   500

Union Pacific Corp.; Winona; switching and terminal services   500

Minnesota 2nd District

Southern Twin Cities suburbs

Located south of the Twin Cities, the 2nd includes all or part of seven rapidly growing counties. Transformed from largely rural to suburb-dominated during redistricting following the 2000 census, the district now reflects the 1990s population influx to the Minneapolis-St. Paul metro area. *(See map. p. 497.)*

Residents can hop on Interstate 35 and shoot into the Twin Cities from Dakota and Scott Counties (Scott is the fastest-growing county in the state). New, expensive housing developments underscore the area's higher incomes, and population increases in Carver, Scott, and particularly Dakota (shared with the 4th District) have made these counties younger and wealthier.

Goodhue, Le Sueur, and Rice Counties retain an agricultural feel, though people are beginning to move here as well. The cost of living has not yet skyrocketed, however.

Scott and Carver Counties propel conservative Republicans to office, while Dakota County has some working-class areas that are faithful Democratic-Farmer-Labor Party supporters. But their political voice is competing with growing numbers of young families, who tend to vote socially progressive but fiscally conservative.

The Rice County towns of Northfield—home to St. Olaf and Carleton colleges—and Faribault also provide Democratic votes, while Goodhue County remains a conservative farming area.

Despite a downturn in the airline industry, Northwest Airlines remains an economic linchpin for the area. Casinos are big business for the Shakopee Mdewakanton Sioux tribe in Prior Lake.

Major Industry

Manufacturing, casinos, aviation.

Notable

The late senator Paul Wellstone was a professor at Carleton College; Green Giant was founded in Le Sueur.

Election Returns

	Republican		Democratic		Other	
President 2000	150,366	50.7%	131,414	44.4%	14,526	4.9%
House 2002	152,970	53.4%	121,121	42.3%	12,769	4.3%

District Profile

Population   614,934

Total area (square miles)   3,153.8
   Land area (square miles)   3,035.2

Population per square mile   202.6

Counties (2000 population)
   Carver   70,205   Rice   56,665
   Dakota (pt.)   295,646   Scott   89,498
   Goodhue   44,127   Washington (pt.)   33,936
   Le Sueur (pt.)   24,857

Cities and other areas over 10,000 (2000 population)
   Apple Valley   45,527
   Burnsville   60,220
   Chanhassen   20,321
   Chaska   17,449
   Cottage Grove   30,582
   Eagan   63,557
   Faribault   20,818
   Farmington   12,365
   Hastings   18,204
   Inver Grove Heights (pt.)   21,248
   Lakeville   43,128
   Northfield   17,147
   Prior Lake   15,917
   Red Wing   16,116
   Rosemount   14,619
   Savage   21,115
   Shakopee   20,568

Race and Hispanic or Latino origin*
   White   91.8%
   Black or African American   1.6%
   American Indian or Alaska Native   0.4%
   Asian   2.3%
   Native Hawaiian or other Pacific Islander   0.0%
   Some other race   0.1%
   Hispanic or Latino origin   2.6%
   Two or more races   1.1%

As percentage of total population.

Ancestry*
   Danish   1.2%   Italian   1.6%
   Dutch   1.4%   Norwegian   11.3%
   English   4.5%   Polish   2.7%
   French   2.7%   Swedish   6.1%
   German   28.4%   USA/American   2.0%
   Irish   9.2%

As estimated percentage of total population.

Universities and colleges, 2000–2001 enrollment
   Carleton College, Northfield   1,936
   Dakota County Technical College, Rosemount   3,086
   Inver Hills Community College, Inver Grove Heights   4,304

Minnesota State College, Red Wing 1,242
Rasmussen College, Eagan 308
St. Olaf College, Northfield 3,014

Newspapers and circulation

	District circulation	Total circulation
Mankato Free Press	2,623	23,283
Minneapolis Star Tribune	45,212	341,251
Red Wing Republican Eagle	6,299	7,410
Rochester Post-Bulletin	1,933	42,167
St. Paul Pioneer Press	29,554	200,578
USA Today*	1,985	1,674,376

*See Sources and Explanations in the front of the volume.

Television stations and affiliations

Minneapolis-St. Paul	100%	KARE	NBC
Minneapolis-St. Paul	100%	KAWB	PBS
Minneapolis-St. Paul	100%	KAWE	PBS
Minneapolis-St. Paul	100%	KCCO	CBS
Minneapolis-St. Paul	100%	KCCW	CBS
Minneapolis-St. Paul	100%	KMSP	FOX
Minneapolis-St. Paul	100%	KMWB	WB
Minneapolis-St. Paul	100%	KPXM	PAX
Minneapolis-St. Paul	100%	KRWF	ABC
Minneapolis-St. Paul	100%	KSAX	ABC
Minneapolis-St. Paul	100%	KSTP	ABC
Minneapolis-St. Paul	100%	KTCA	PBS
Minneapolis-St. Paul	100%	KTCI	PBS
Minneapolis-St. Paul	100%	KWCM	PBS
Minneapolis St. Paul	100%	WFTC	UPN

Cable systems and subscribers

Charter 30,852
Comcast 35,639
Mediacom 11,883
North American Communications Corp. 649
Pine Island Telephone 726
Time Warner 10,214
U.S. Cable 1,016

Businesses and other major employers

3M Co.; St. Paul; pressure sensitive tape 20,000
Thomson Corp.; St. Paul; book publishing and printing 7,000
Independent School District; Rosemount 4,000
Little Six Inc.; Prior Lake; gambling 3,600
BCBSM Inc.; St. Paul; hospital/medical service plans 3,560
Entegris Inc.; Chaska; management services 2,750
Treasure Island Resort and Casino; Welch; bingo hall 1,700
Lockheed Martin Corp.; St. Paul; computers 1,600
Field Container Co.; Chanhassen; packing and crating 1,500
Ecolab Inc.; Savage; soap and other detergents 1,050
3M Co.; Cottage Grove; chemical preparations 980
Coca-Cola Enterprises Inc.; St. Paul; soft drinks 900
Flint Hills Resources; Inver Grove Heights; petroleum refining 900
North America Uponor Inc.; St. Paul; pipes and tubes 900
Red Wing Shoe Co.; Red Wing; men's footwear 900
Ridgeview Medical Center; Waconia 900

Rosemount Aerospace Inc.; Burnsville; thermostats 900
Smead Manufacturing Co.; Hastings; cards, folders, mats 891
St. Olaf College; Northfield 870
Malt-O-Meal Co.; Northfield; breakfast cereals 824
Fairview Health Services Hospital; Burnsville 800
U.S. Postal Service; St. Paul 800
Alliance Health Care Inc.; Burnsville; home health care services 700
Dakota County; Hastings; county government 700
Lake Region Manufacturing Inc.; Chaska; surgical instruments 700
Noridian Mutual Insurance Co.; St. Paul; hospital/medical service plans 700
Northwest Airlines Inc.; St. Paul; administrative management 700
Unisys Corp.; St. Paul; marketing consulting services 700
Carleton College; Northfield 650
Afton Alps Inc.; Hastings; ski lodge 600
Sheldahl Inc.; Northfield; printed circuit boards 600
Society of Manufacturing Engineers; Hastings; engineering services 600
Flexfab Horizons International Inc.; Hastings; flexible metal hose, tubing 550
Target Corp.; Burnsville; department stores 550
Medallion Cabinetry Inc.; Waconia; kitchen cabinets 525
Yellow Freight System Inc.; Burnsville; trucking terminal facilities 525
Regina Medical Center; Hastings 520
Carlisle Power Transmission Products Inc.; Red Wing; motor vehicle parts/accessories 500
FSI International Inc.; Chaska; semiconductor manufacturing machinery 500
Northern Tool and Equipment Co.; Burnsville; pumping equipment 500
Pepsi-Cola Metropolitan Bottling Co.; Burnsville; soft drinks 500
U.S. Federal Aviation Admin.; Farmington 500
XCEL Energy Inc.; Welch; electric services 500
Young America Corp.; Chanhassen; advertising, promotional 500

Minnesota 3rd District

Hennepin County suburbs — Bloomington, Brooklyn Park, Plymouth

Minnesota's most affluent district, the 3rd encompasses Minneapolis' western suburbs, where large white-collar populations are grounded in fiscal conservatism but adhere to moderate views on social issues, particularly abortion. (See map p. 497.)

With abundant technology industries, white-collar workers, golf courses, and middle-class homes, the 3rd is a classic picture of suburban living. Several Fortune 500 corporations, such as State Farm Insurance, have their headquarters in the district, and many residents commute to large companies just outside the 3rd, such as Northwest Airlines and General Mills. Traffic snarls for commuters driving east from the Lake

MINNEAPOLIS-ST. PAUL AREA

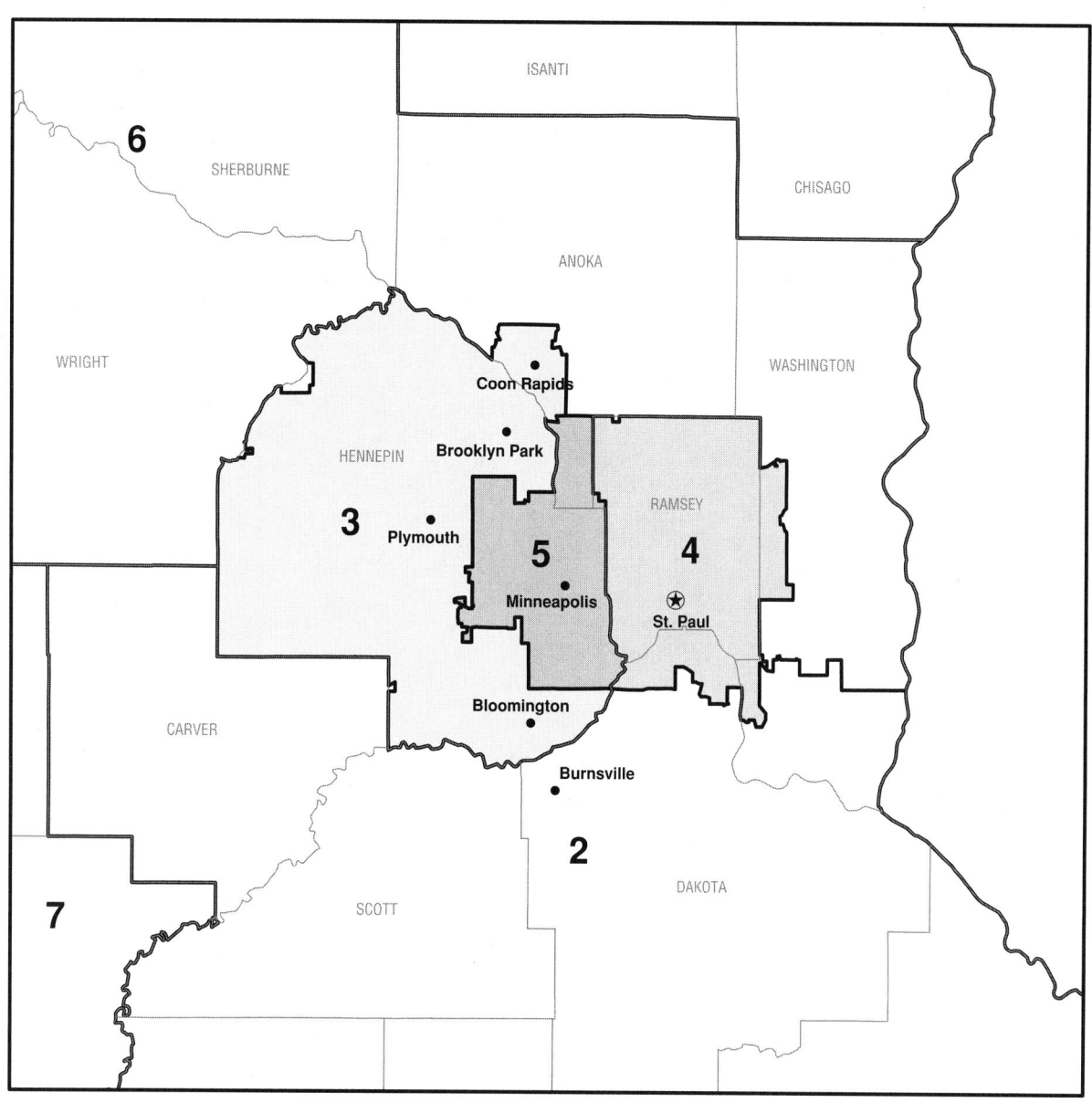

Minnetonka area have worsened considerably from sustained regional growth.

Brooklyn Park was governed in the early 1990s by Mayor Jesse Ventura, who later became governor with the 3rd's electoral blessing, though the white-collar areas did not favor him. Unlike the faster-growing, more conservative outlying suburbs in the 2nd and 6th Districts, the 3rd has sent moderate Republicans to Congress since 1970. The district also elects Republicans to the state legislature, but supported Bill Clinton for president in 1992 and 1996. George W. Bush defeated Al Gore, 49.9 percent to 46 percent, here in the 2000 presidential election.

Brooklyn Park, Coon Rapids (shared with the 6th), and Brooklyn Center's blue-collar residents are older, conservative Democratic-Farmer-Labor Party voters, but the affluent, Republican south and west portions of the 3rd cast most of the votes, giving the 3rd a tilt to the right.

Major Industry

Electronics, manufacturing, food processing.

Notable

Southdale, in Edina, was the nation's first fully enclosed shopping mall (1956); the Mall of America in Bloomington, the nation's largest shopping mall at 4.2 million square feet, attracts more than 40 million visitors a year and employs more than 11,000.

Election Returns

	Republican		Democratic		Other	
President 2000	161,999	49.9%	149,277	46.0%	13,483	4.2%
House 2002	213,334	72.1%	82,575	27.9%	309	

District Profile

Population 614,935

Total area (square miles) 513.1
Land area (square miles) 467.6

Population per square mile 1,315.1

Counties (2000 population)
Anoka (pt.) 58,396
Hennepin (pt.) 556,539

Cities and other areas over 10,000 (2000 population)
Bloomington 85,172
Brooklyn Center 29,172
Brooklyn Park 67,388
Champlin 22,193
Coon Rapids (pt.) 58,396
Eden Prairie 54,901
Edina 47,425
Maple Grove 50,365
Minnetonka 51,301
Plymouth 65,894

Race and Hispanic or Latino origin*
White 88.6%
Black or African American 3.8%
American Indian or Alaska Native 0.3%
Asian 4.0%
Native Hawaiian or other Pacific Islander 0.0%
Some other race 0.1%
Hispanic or Latino origin 1.8%
Two or more races 1.4%

*As percentage of total population.

Ancestry*

Danish	1.3%	Italian	1.8%
Dutch	1.3%	Norwegian	11.3%
English	5.8%	Polish	3.2%
Finnish	1.2%	Scottish	1.1%
French	2.9%	Swedish	7.8%
German	22.8%	USA/American	2.0%
Irish	8.6%		

*As estimated percentage of total population.

Universities and colleges, 2000–2001 enrollment
Academy Education Center, Minneapolis 301
Anoka-Ramsey Community College, Coon Rapids 5,844
Crown College, St. Bonifacius 897
Hennepin Technical College, Brooklyn Park 5,843
High Tech Institute, Brooklyn Center 574
Medical Institute of Minnesota, Bloomington 505
Minnesota School of Business, Brooklyn Center 306
Minnesota School of Professional Psychology, Minneapolis 337
Normandale Community College, Bloomington 7,347
North Hennepin Community College, Brooklyn Park 5,261
Northwestern College of Chiropractic, Bloomington 866

Newspapers and circulation

	District circulation	Total circulation
Minneapolis Star Tribune	88,499	341,251
St. Paul Pioneer Press	5,830	200,578
*USA Today**	11,752	1,674,376

*See Sources and Explanations in the front of the volume.

Television stations and affiliations

Minneapolis-St. Paul	100%	KARE	NBC
Minneapolis-St. Paul	100%	KAWB	PBS
Minneapolis-St. Paul	100%	KAWE	PBS
Minneapolis-St. Paul	100%	KCCO	CBS
Minneapolis-St. Paul	100%	KCCW	CBS
Minneapolis-St. Paul	100%	KMSP	FOX
Minneapolis-St. Paul	100%	KMWB	WB
Minneapolis-St. Paul	100%	KPXM	PAX
Minneapolis-St. Paul	100%	KRWF	ABC
Minneapolis-St. Paul	100%	KSAX	ABC
Minneapolis-St. Paul	100%	KSTP	ABC
Minneapolis-St. Paul	100%	KTCA	PBS
Minneapolis-St. Paul	100%	KTCI	PBS
Minneapolis-St. Paul	100%	KWCM	PBS
Minneapolis-St. Paul	100%	WFTC	UPN

Cable systems and subscribers
Comcast 53,650
Mediacom 27,081
Time Warner 45,245

Military installations, September 2001

Minneapolis/St. Paul International Airport Air Force
Reserve Station, Minneapolis   2,593

Naval Air Research Center, Minneapolis   1,135

Businesses and other major employers

Uniprise Inc.; Hopkins; health maintenance organization
12,000

American Express Asset Management Group;
Minneapolis; open-ended management investment
7,000

Fairview Health Services Hospital; Minneapolis   5,000

Nath Companies Inc.; Minneapolis; restaurant   4,200

Riscomp Industries Inc.; Minneapolis; employee leasing
service   3,800

Holiday Companies Inc.; Minneapolis; gasoline service
stations   3,700

Vertical Systems Inc.; Eden Prairie; computer software
design   3,528

Park Nicollet Health Services Hospital; Excelsior
2,500

ADC Telecommunications Inc.; Eden Prairie; telephone
apparatus   2,300

Best Buy Co. Inc.; Eden Prairie; appliance stores   2,200

Carlson Marketing Group Inc.; Minneapolis; training
and development consultant   2,126

Manor Care Inc.; Hopkins; home health care services
2,055

Accenture Inc.; Eden Prairie; business management
consultant   2,000

Cargill Inc.; Wayzata; grain and field beans   2,000

Rosemount Inc.; Eden Prairie; process control
instruments   1,659

SuperValu Inc.; Eden Prairie; warehousing, storage
1,600

REM Health Inc.; Minneapolis; home health care
services   1,560

Citigroup Inc.; Minneapolis; automobile finance leasing
1,450

MTS Systems Corp.; Eden Prairie; measuring and
controlling devices   1,340

Ovations Inc.; Hopkins; hospital/medical service plans
1,305

Express Scripts Inc.; Minneapolis; mail-order
pharmaceuticals   1,300

Allina Health Systems Inc.; Hopkins; hospital/medical
service plans   1,200

Allina Health Systems Inc. Hospital; Minneapolis
1,200

Datacard Corp.; Hopkins; embossing machines   1,200

Prudential Financial; Minneapolis; insurance brokers
1,200

Target Corp.; Minneapolis; lawn and garden supplies
1,200

Medtronic Inc.; Minneapolis; medical help service
1,150

Schoenecker's Inc.; Minneapolis; incentive/award
program consultant   1,100

Group Health Plan Inc.; Minneapolis; health
maintenance organization   1,090

Starkey Laboratories Inc.; Eden Prairie; hearing aids
1,050

Radisson Hotels International Inc.; Hopkins; hotel or
motel management   1,000

SuperValu Inc.; Eden Prairie; food supplier   1,000

Target Corp.; Minneapolis; facilities support services
1,000

Wayzata Independent School District; Minneapolis
1,000

TCF Financial Corp.; Wayzata; commercial bank   914

Fingerhut Corp.; Hopkins; mail-order catalog   900

Metris Companies Inc.; Hopkins; personal credit
institutions   900

DAIG Corp.; Hopkins; catheters   880

Veritas Software Technology Corp.; Minneapolis;
computer disk drive components   852

General Electric Capital Corp.; Eden Prairie; vehicle
finance leasing   820

C. W. Government Travel Inc.; Minneapolis;
transportation ticket offices   800

Donaldson Co.; Minneapolis; air intake filters   800

Eaton Hydraulics Inc.; Eden Prairie; motor controls and
accessories   800

General Dynamics Information Systems Inc.;
Minneapolis; electronic computers   800

Hartford Life Inc.; Minneapolis; life insurance   800

Honeywell International Inc.; Minneapolis; aircraft
parts, equipment   800

Kurt Manufacturing Co.; Minneapolis; metal machine
bases   800

Suncoast Motion Picture Co.; Hopkins; prerecorded
video discs   800

Valu Ventures 2 Inc.; Eden Prairie; grocery store   800

Ziegler Inc.; Minneapolis; construction and mining
machinery   790

Eaton Corp.; Eden Prairie; auto steering power pumps
750

Taher Inc.; Hopkins; contract food services   743

MLT Inc.; Minneapolis; travel packages   740

Boston Scientific Corp.; Osseo; surgical and medical
instruments   700

Deloitte and Touche; Minneapolis; accounting services
700

Glendale Foods Inc.; Eden Prairie; food services   700

Media Valuevision Inc.; Eden Prairie; catalog sales   700

ShopNBC; Eden Prairie; mail-order catalog   700

West Macy's Inc.; Minneapolis; department stores   700

Nordstrom Inc.; Minneapolis; clothing stores   655

Ceridian Corp.; Minneapolis; payroll accounting service
635

Advantek Inc.; Hopkins; packaging paper   630

Toro Co.; Minneapolis; lawn tractors and equipment
625

Leeann Chin Inc.; Minneapolis; restaurant   605

American Family Mutual Insurance Co. Inc.; Eden
Prairie; insurance adjusters   600

ConAgra Foods Inc.; Minneapolis; packaged popcorn
600

Unisys Corp.; Minneapolis; telemarketing services   600

Douglas Corp.; Eden Prairie; injection molding of
plastics   588

Alternative Staffing Inc.; Minneapolis; temporary help
service   581

Minnertainment Co.; Minneapolis; theme park   561

Carlson Travel Group Inc.; Minneapolis; travel agency 550

Honeywell International Inc.; Minneapolis; semiconductors and related devices   550

Thermo King Corp.; Minneapolis; refrigeration equipment   550

Nilfisk-Advance Inc.; Minneapolis; commercial floor washing, polishing machines   547

Cypress Semiconductor Inc.; Minneapolis; integrated circuits, semiconductor networks   525

City of Bloomington; Minneapolis; city management 515

Merrill/May Inc.; Minneapolis; commercial printing 505

Computer Network Technology Corp.; Minneapolis; systems integration services   500

Compuware Corp.; Minneapolis; software   500

Deltak; Minneapolis; industrial boilers   500

Honeywell Advanced Circuits Inc.; Hopkins; circuit boards   500

Innovex Precision Components Inc.; Maple Plain; electronic circuits   500

Lifetouch National School Studios Inc.; Minneapolis; school photographer   500

Loram Maintenance of Way Inc.; Hamel; railroad maintenance and repair   500

Minnesota Vikings Food Services; Minneapolis; merchandising machine operators   500

Musicland Group Inc.; Hopkins; record and prerecorded tape stores   500

Nash-Finch Co.; Minneapolis; business management 500

PolarFab; Minneapolis; integrated circuits, semiconductor networks   500

Radisson Hotels International Inc.; Minneapolis; hotels 500

United Parcel Service Inc.; Eden Prairie; packaging and labeling services   500

WinCom Systems Inc.; Eden Prairie; music and broadcasting services   500

Minnesota 4th District

Ramsey County — St. Paul and suburbs

St. Paul's liberal university communities, bedroom neighborhoods, state government, and labor populations provide a consistent stronghold for the Democratic-Farmer-Labor Party. *(See map p. 497.)*

Represented in Congress by a Democrat since 1949, voters in the 4th—slightly less than half of whom live in St. Paul—have elected DFL candidates at all levels of government. But as with much of central Minnesota, the district has an independent streak, as demonstrated by support for Ross Perot in the 1992 presidential election and Jesse Ventura in the 1998 gubernatorial race.

St. Paul gained population in the 1990s, though it grew much slower than surrounding areas. The district includes independent and moderate voters in parts of fast-growing Washington County and affluent northern suburbs such as North Oaks and White Bear Lake.

St. Paul is a traditionally Democratic city with a large German and Irish Catholic population. The city developed as a major port and railroading center and still has a strong labor tradition. Today, blue-collar, black, and Hispanic communities contribute to the city's Democratic flavor. It also is a center of Hmong culture in the United States. Forty percent of students in St. Paul's schools are non-English speakers.

Home to the state capital and the headquarters of 3M, the 4th has a large percentage of white-collar workers who live in middle- and high-income neighborhoods. Several colleges, including the University of Minnesota's agriculture school, are located in affluent communities around St. Paul. The limited Republican base is in the growing suburbs to the north of the city that have drawn city residents and newcomers.

Major Industry
State government, higher education, manufacturing.

Notable
Supreme Court Justices Warren E. Burger and Harry A. Blackmun grew up in St. Paul; St. Paul was originally called Pig's Eye Landing, after bootlegger Pierre "Pig's Eye" Parrant; in 2002 the area elected Mee Moua to the state Senate, making her the first Hmong state legislator in the United States.

Election Returns

	Republican		Democratic		Other	
President 2000	109,670	37.2%	166,919	56.6%	18,146	6.2%
House 2002	89,705	33.9%	164,597	62.2%	10,238	3.9%

District Profile

Population   614,935

Total area (square miles)   219.7
Land area (square miles)   201.8

Population per square mile   3,047.2

Counties (2000 population)
Dakota (pt.)   60,258
Ramsey (pt.)   508,687
Washington (pt.)   45,990

Cities and other areas over 10,000 (2000 population)
Maplewood 34,947	Shoreview 25,924
Mendota Heights 11,434	South St. Paul 20,167
Mounds View 12,738	St. Paul 287,151
New Brighton 22,206	Vadnais Heights 13,069
North St. Paul 11,929	West St. Paul 19,405
Oakdale 26,653	White Bear Lake 24,325
Roseville 33,690	

Race and Hispanic or Latino origin*
White   77.7%
Black or African American   6.5%
American Indian or Alaska Native   0.7%
Asian   7.5%
Native Hawaiian or other Pacific Islander   0.0%
Some other race   0.1%
Hispanic or Latino origin   5.2%
Two or more races   2.2%

As percentage of total population.

Ancestry*

English	4.2%	Norwegian	7.7%
French	3.2%	Polish	3.4%
German	22.0%	Swedish	6.1%
Irish	9.5%	USA/American	1.5%
Italian	2.5%		

As estimated percentage of total population.

Universities and colleges, 2000–2001 enrollment

Bethel College, St. Paul   2,953
Bethel Theological Seminary, St. Paul   924
Brown Institute, Mendota Heights   2,179
Century Community and Technical College, White Bear Lake   6,937
College of St. Catherine, St. Paul   4,487
College of Visual Arts, St. Paul   285
Concordia University, St. Paul   1,647
Globe College, Oakdale   642
Hamline University, St. Paul   3,408
Luther Seminary, St. Paul   743
Macalester College, St. Paul   1,794
Metropolitan State University, St. Paul   5,622
Minneapolis Business College, Roseville   322
National American University, St. Paul   586
Northwestern College, St. Paul   2,081
St. Paul Technical College, St. Paul   5,247
United Theological Seminary, New Brighton   215
University of St. Thomas, St. Paul   11,288
William Mitchell College of Law, St. Paul   999

Newspapers and circulation

	District circulation	Total circulation
Minneapolis Star Tribune	29,646	341,251
St. Paul Pioneer Press	95,626	200,578
*USA Today**	1,824	1,674,376

See Sources and Explanations in the front of the volume.

Television stations and affiliations

Minneapolis-St. Paul	100%	KARE	NBC
Minneapolis-St. Paul	100%	KAWB	PBS
Minneapolis-St. Paul	100%	KAWE	PBS
Minneapolis-St. Paul	100%	KCCO	CBS
Minneapolis-St. Paul	100%	KCCW	CBS
Minneapolis-St. Paul	100%	KMSP	FOX
Minneapolis-St. Paul	100%	KMWB	WB
Minneapolis-St. Paul	100%	KPXM	PAX
Minneapolis-St. Paul	100%	KRWF	ABC
Minneapolis-St. Paul	100%	KSAX	ABC
Minneapolis-St. Paul	100%	KSTP	ABC
Minneapolis-St. Paul	100%	KTCA	PBS
Minneapolis-St. Paul	100%	KTCI	PBS
Minneapolis-St. Paul	100%	KWCM	PBS
Minneapolis-St. Paul	100%	WFTC	UPN

Cable systems and subscribers

Comcast   91,729

Military installations, September 2001

Arden Hills U.S. Army Reserve Center, New Brighton   532
Twin Cities Army Ammunition Plant, New Brighton   293

Businesses and other major employers

3M Co.; St. Paul; paper/mineral products, medical instruments   24,700
Minnesota Dept. of Transportation; St. Paul   9,727
St. Paul Fire and Marine Insurance Co.; St. Paul; fire, marine, casualty insurance   6,347
Minnesota Information and Education Bureau; St. Paul   3,000
Regions Hospital; St. Paul   2,900
U.S. Postal Service; St. Paul   2,673
Children's Health Care Services Inc.; St. Paul; medical doctor offices, clinics   2,500
Marsden Building Maintenance Co. Inc.; St. Paul; janitorial service   2,200
Ford Motor Co.; St. Paul; motor vehicles and car bodies   2,034
Burlington Northern and Santa Fe Railway Co.; South St. Paul; safety and security specialization   2,000
Cardiac Pacemakers Inc.; St. Paul; cardiac pacemaker   2,000
Minnesota Life Insurance Co.; St. Paul; mutual association life insurance   2,000
Best Inc.; St. Paul; management services   1,986
Minnesota Dept. of Human Services; St. Paul   1,700
Account Inc.; St. Paul; computer software applications   1,500
Conseco Finance Corp. Inc.; St. Paul; finance companies   1,500
Eastman Kodak Co.; St. Paul; digital test equipment   1,500
Minnesota Dept. of Revenue; St. Paul   1,500
Merrill Corp.; St. Paul; commercial printing   1,200
Unisys Corp.; St. Paul; computer hardware   1,200
Minnesota Dept. of Public Safety; St. Paul   1,200
HealthEast St. Joseph's Hospital; St. Paul   1,164
University of St. Thomas; St. Paul   1,100
Bethesda Lutheran Medical Center; St. Paul   1,000
Ecolab Inc.; St. Paul; soap and detergents   1,000
Lawson Software Inc.; St. Paul; computer software   1,000
Agriliance; Inver Grove Heights; petroleum bulk stations/terminals   900
Minnesota Dept. of Administration; St. Paul   900
Northwest Publications Inc.; St. Paul; newspaper   900
US Bancorp Information Services Corp.; St. Paul; data processing   848
Allina Home Health Servcies Inc.; St. Paul; home health care services   800
American Security Corp.; St. Paul; protective services, guard   800
Cenex Harvest States Cooperatives; Inver Grove Heights; grain and field beans   800
E-Funds Corp.; St. Paul; data processing   800
Land O'Lakes Inc.; St. Paul; cheese   800
McGough Construction Co. Inc.; St. Paul; nonresidential construction   800
REM-Ramsey Inc.; St. Paul; social services for the handicapped   800
U.S. Bank Trust National Assn.; St. Paul; nondeposit trust facilities   765
Century College; St. Paul   750
Independent School District; St. Paul   750

U.S. Army Corps of Engineers; St. Paul   750

Unisys Corp.; St. Paul; telephone equipment   750

City of St. Paul; St. Paul; police dept.   725

HealthEast St. John's Hospital; St. Paul   713

Honeywell Advanced Circuits Inc.; St. Paul; printed circuit boards   700

Hubbard Broadcasting Inc.; St. Paul; television broadcasting stations   700

Minnesota Dept. of Economic Security; St. Paul   700

Mutual Service Co-operative; St. Paul; administrative management   700

Minnesota State Colleges and Universities; St. Paul   670

IC System; St. Paul; adjustment and collection services   650

Presbyterian Homes Housing and Assisted Living Inc.; St. Paul; retirement hotel operation   650

St. Jude Medical Inc.; St. Paul; cardiac pacemaker   650

Sysco Food Services; St. Paul; food brokers   640

Bethel College and Seminary; St. Paul   638

Sportsman's Guide Inc.; South St. Paul; catalog sales   630

American Red Cross; St. Paul; blood bank   600

Green Tree Financial Corp.; St. Paul; finance companies   600

Pinnacle Airlines Corp.; St. Paul; air passenger carrier   600

Pins and Needles Inc.; St. Paul; garment making, alteration, repair   600

U.S. Internal Revenue Service; St. Paul   600

University of Minnesota; St. Paul   600

College of St. Catherine; St. Paul   579

Macalester College; St. Paul   550

SOO Line Railroad Co.; St. Paul; freight hauling   550

Land O'Lakes Inc.; South St. Paul; farm supplies   531

Banta Corp.; St. Paul; commercial printing   500

Dept. of Health; St. Paul; public health programs   500

First Student Inc.; St. Paul; bus charters   500

GCS Service Inc.; St. Paul; commercial cooking, food service equipment   500

Fair, Isaac Corp.; St. Paul; business computer software   500

Manufacturers' Services Central U.S. Operations Inc.; St. Paul; computer peripheral equipment   500

Mendakota Insurance Co.; St. Paul; property damage insurance   500

Metropolitan Council; St. Paul; urban planning and development   500

Minnesota Dept. of State Colleges and Universities; St. Paul   500

Minnesota Natural Resources Department; St. Paul   500

Ramsey County; St. Paul; county government   500

Sara Lee Bakery Group Inc.; St. Paul; breads and cakes   500

St. Paul Technical College; St. Paul   500

Target Corp.; St. Paul; department stores   500

Minnesota 5th District

Minneapolis and suburbs

Established at the northernmost navigable point on the Mississippi River, Minneapolis accounts for most of the 5th's liberal vote. The 2000 round of redistricting may have made the district even more Democratic, moving the affluent suburb of Edina into the 3rd District and adding first-ring northern suburbs. For the first time in a half-century, Minneapolis gained population in the 1990s, though it grew much slower than surrounding areas. *(See map p. 497.)*

Minneapolis is home to many large corporations, such as General Mills, Target Corp., and U.S. Bancorp. The 5th attracted well-educated white-collar workers in the economic boom of the 1990s, but the shift has not changed the area's liberal-mindedness. Minneapolis has the highest number of theater seats per capita in the United States outside of New York City. This strong arts community's liberal lean is bolstered by the University of Minnesota in eastern Minneapolis. Residents who flock to the area's many lakes also support environmental protections. Green Party presidential candidate Ralph Nader received 8 percent of the 5th's vote in 2000—one of his best showings in the nation.

Traffic and the lack of affordable housing have become large problems here. Though Minneapolis was dubbed "murderapolis" by the *New York Times* in 1996, the city has managed to cut crime and redevelop downtown riverfront areas.

Although Minneapolis is known for its Scandinavian heritage, the 5th is the state's most racially diverse district. Asian and black communities—including a sizable Somali population—contribute to the district's Democratic-Farmer-Labor voter rolls. The district's poorer communities lie north of downtown.

Major Industry
Corporate administration, banking, higher education.

Notable
The Minneapolis Sculpture Garden at Walker Art Center features an enormous metal spoon holding a cherry; Democrat Hubert H. Humphrey was elected mayor of Minneapolis in 1945.

Election Returns

	Republican		Democratic		Other	
President 2000	85,447	28.9%	185,874	62.8%	24,577	8.3%
House 2002	66,271	25.9%	171,572	67.0%	18,139	7.1%

District Profile

Population   614,935

Total area (square miles)   129.7
   Land area (square miles)   123.9

Population per square mile   4,963.2

Counties (2000 population)
   Anoka (pt.)   53,402
   Hennepin (pt.)   559,185
   Ramsey (pt.)   2,348

Cities and other areas over 10,000 (2000 population)

Columbia Heights   18,520
Crystal   22,698
Fridley   27,449
Golden Valley   20,281
Hopkins (pt.)   13,921
Minneapolis   382,618
New Hope   20,873
Richfield   34,439
Robbinsdale   14,123
St. Louis Park   44,126

Race and Hispanic or Latino origin*

White   71.2%
Black or African American   12.8%
American Indian or Alaska Native   1.5%
Asian   5.1%
Native Hawaiian or other Pacific Islander   0.1%
Some other race   0.2%
Hispanic or Latino origin   6.0%
Two or more races   3.0%

As percentage of total population.

Ancestry*

English   4.6%   Polish   3.4%
French   2.6%   Scottish   1.1%
German   17.6%   Subsaharan   2.3%
Irish   7.6%   Swedish   6.7%
Italian   1.6%   USA/American   1.4%
Norwegian   9.3%

As estimated percentage of total population.

Universities and colleges, 2000–2001 enrollment

Art Institutes International at Minnesota, Minneapolis   760
Augsburg College, Minneapolis   3,040
College of St. Catherine, Minneapolis   1,015
Dunwoody Industrial Institute, Minneapolis   1,059
KRS Computer and Business School, St. Louis Park   1,012
Lakeland Medical and Dental Academy, Minneapolis   286
Minneapolis College of Art and Design, Minneapolis   615
Minneapolis Community and Technical College, Minneapolis   6,363
Minnesota School of Business, Richfield   701
Musicians Technical Training Center, Minneapolis   265
NEI College of Technology, Columbia Heights   413
North Central University, Minneapolis   1,168
University of Minnesota, Minneapolis   45,481
Walden University, Minneapolis   1,544

Newspapers and circulation

	District circulation	Total circulation
Minneapolis Star Tribune	87,393	341,251
St. Paul Pioneer Press	11,322	200,578
*USA Today**	2,703	1,674,376

See Sources and Explanations in the front of the volume.

Television stations and affiliations

Minneapolis-St. Paul	100%	KARE	NBC
Minneapolis-St. Paul	100%	KAWB	PBS
Minneapolis-St. Paul	100%	KAWE	PBS
Minneapolis-St. Paul	100%	KCCO	CBS
Minneapolis-St. Paul	100%	KCCW	CBS
Minneapolis-St. Paul	100%	KMSP	FOX
Minneapolis-St. Paul	100%	KMWB	WB
Minneapolis-St. Paul	100%	KPXM	PAX
Minneapolis-St. Paul	100%	KRWF	ABC
Minneapolis-St. Paul	100%	KSAX	ABC
Minneapolis-St. Paul	100%	KSTP	ABC
Minneapolis-St. Paul	100%	KTCA	PBS
Minneapolis-St. Paul	100%	KTCI	PBS
Minneapolis-St. Paul	100%	KWCM	PBS
Minneapolis-St. Paul	100%	WFTC	UPN

Cable systems and subscribers

Comcast   16,351
Time Warner   92,080

Military installations, September 2001

Fort Snelling U.S. Army Reserve Center, Minneapolis   1,432

Businesses and other major employers

Wells Fargo Bank; Minneapolis; mortgage bankers   8,700
American Express Financial Corp.; Minneapolis; investment advisory service   8,500
Fairview Health Services Hospital; Minneapolis   6,200
University of Minnesota; Minneapolis   6,000
Allina Hospitals and Clinics; Minneapolis   5,167
City of Minneapolis; Minneapolis; city management   5,000
Rainbow Foods Inc.; Hopkins; supermarkets   4,800
Medtronic Inc.; Minneapolis; electromedical equipment   4,300
RBC Capital Market; Minneapolis; data processing   4,100
Rooftop Inc.; Minneapolis; purchasing service   4,000
Target Corp.; Minneapolis; department stores   3,700
United Parcel Service Inc.; Minneapolis; package delivery   3,500
American Express Financial Corp.; Minneapolis; mutual fund sales   3,300
North Memorial Health Care Hospital; Minneapolis   3,300
Carlson Holdings Inc. Minneapolis; hotels and motels   3,100
Hennepin County Hospital; Minneapolis   3,075
ABM Janitorial Services; Minneapolis; janitorial service   3,000
Hennepin County Schools; Minneapolis   3,000
Methodist Hospital; Minneapolis   2,800
Honeywell Inc.; Minneapolis; air conditioning, refrigeration controls   2,500
U.S. Veterans Hospital; Minneapolis   2,500
Children's Health Care Services Inc.; Minneapolis   2,340
American Express Financial Advisors Inc.; Minneapolis; investment advice   2,295

Honeywell International Inc.; Minneapolis; radio broadcasting equipment 2,200

General Mills Inc.; Minneapolis; breakfast cereals 2,000

Northwest Airlines Corp.; St. Paul; air passenger carrier 2,000

Pillsbury Co.; Minneapolis; doughs and batters 1,800

XCEL Energy Inc.; Minneapolis; electric power generation 1,800

U.S. Bancorp Piper Jaffray Inc.; Minneapolis; security brokers, dealers 1,650

Mesaba Aviation Inc.; Minneapolis; helicopter carrier 1,500

United Defense Industries Inc.; Minneapolis; air intake filters 1,500

Excel Energy Services Inc.; Minneapolis; management services 1,464

Onan Corp.; Minneapolis; electric generators 1,300

Accenture Inc.; Minneapolis; management consulting 1,200

Hennepin County; Minneapolis; county government 1,200

Star Tribune Co.; Minneapolis; newspaper 1,200

Federal Reserve Bank of Minneapolis; Minneapolis 1,074

Minnesota Dept. of Corrections; Minneapolis 1,030

Children's Health Care Services Inc.; Minneapolis 1,000

Graco Inc.; Minneapolis; lubrication systems and parts 1,000

Minnesota Masonic Home North Ridge; Minneapolis; skilled nursing care facilities 1,000

Richard Solum; Minneapolis; law office 1,000

ING Reliastar; Minneapolis; life insurance 900

Walker Methodist Health Center Inc.; Minneapolis 900

Volume Services America Inc.; Minneapolis; contract food services 856

Minnesota Orchestral Assn.; Minneapolis; symphony orchestra 850

Park Nicollet Medical Center Inc.; Minneapolis 800

U.S. Bank National Assn.; Minneapolis; commercial bank 768

Wells Fargo Services Inc.; Minneapolis; data processing 760

Minco Products Inc.; Minneapolis; printed circuit boards 750

Prudential Financial; Minneapolis; life insurance 750

Deloitte and Touche; Minneapolis; accounting services 700

Dorsey and Whitney; Minneapolis; legal services 700

Firstar Bank NA; Minneapolis; credit card service 700

Retek Inc.; Minneapolis; prepackaged software 700

Hennepin Faculty Associates Inc.; Minneapolis; medical research 670

Allied Interstate Inc.; Minneapolis; collection agency 650

ING Life Insurance and Annuity Co.; Minneapolis; life insurance 650

Augsburg College; Minneapolis 622

Japs-Olson Co.; Minneapolis; circular or form letters 619

Campbell-Mithun; Minneapolis; advertising 605

Hilton Hotels Corp. Minneapolis; restaurants 600

Mano Services Inc.; Minneapolis; employment agencies 600

Minneapolis Community and Technical College; Minneapolis 600

New Horizon Child Care Inc.; Minneapolis; preschool center 600

Personnel Decisions International Corp.; Minneapolis; personnel management consultant 600

St. Therese Convalescent Home Inc.; Minneapolis 600

Pohlad Companies; Minneapolis; nightwear 579

Fallon; Minneapolis; advertising 575

Fairview Home Care and Hospice Inc.; Minneapolis 560

Faegre and Benson Minneapolis; law office 557

Travelers Express Co.; Minneapolis; money order issuance 550

U.S. Veterans Affairs Dept.; St. Paul 550

Minnesota Judiciary Courts; Minneapolis 535

Tennant Co.; Minneapolis; industrial dirt sweeping units 530

Minnesota State; Minneapolis; local and suburban transit 525

Minnesota Twins; Minneapolis; baseball club 525

Alliant Integrated Defense Co.; Hopkins; ordnance and accessories 500

Allianz Life Insurance Co. of North America; Minneapolis; life insurance 500

AT&T Corp.; Minneapolis; telephone equipment 500

City of Minneapolis; Minneapolis; recreational program 500

Elizabeth M. Reiskytl; Minneapolis; law office 500

Ernst and Young; Minneapolis; certified public accountant 500

Honeywell International Inc.; Minneapolis; commercial physical research 500

Hyatt Corp.; Minneapolis; hotel, franchised 500

International Total Services Inc.; Minneapolis; airport terminal 500

Leonard Street and Deinard; Minneapolis; legal services 500

Medtronic Inc.; Minneapolis; x-ray apparatus and tubes 500

Minnesota Vikings Food Services; Minneapolis; vending machines 500

NRG Energy Inc.; Minneapolis; electric, other services 500

NRG Operating Services Inc.; Minneapolis; electric, other services 500

PricewaterhouseCoopers; Minneapolis; accounting services 500

SOO Line Railroad Co.; Minneapolis; freight hauling 500

Minnesota 6th District

North and east Twin Cities suburbs; St. Cloud

One of Minnesota's three suburban-oriented districts, the 6th stretches from east and north of the Twin Cities through conservative, developing areas northwest to St. Cloud. The district is tied together by Interstate 94, which runs from St.

Cloud through the Twin Cities to Wisconsin, and the burgeoning Northstar Corridor that runs along the Mississippi River. Officials hope a planned 82-mile commuter train line to link Rice in Benton County with the Twin Cities will help alleviate traffic congestion along the corridor and create jobs. *(See map. p. 497.)*

Development has not yet made St. Cloud a Twin Cities suburb, though the former granite quarrying city is one of the fastest-growing in the state. Home to a mix of blue-collar Democrats and white-collar Republicans, it lies within heavily Catholic Stearns County.

Anoka and Wright Counties, to the north and west of Minneapolis and its first-ring suburbs, include new, wealthy suburban developments and also exurban hobby farms. Washington County, to the east and north of St. Paul, includes Woodbury (a small part of which is in the 2nd), which doubled in population in the 1990s, and the cosmopolitan small town of Stillwater on the St. Croix River, which marks the Wisconsin border. Sherburne County grew by more than 50 percent in the 1990s.

The 6th is a competitive district with a slight GOP lean. Young, high-income families that fuel the region's growth tend to favor fiscal conservatism except on social issues such as public safety and education. Transplants from the north are more liberal on government spending but are likely to be socially conservative. Blue-collar communities in the suburbs of Anoka and Washington Counties are faithful Democratic-Farmer-Labor Party supporters. Anoka as a whole is a swing county that also includes conservative Democrats and young Republicans. Independent Jesse Ventura won every county in the 6th during his 1998 gubernatorial bid.

Major Industry

Corporate administration, manufacturing.

Notable

Writer and radio show host Garrison Keillor was born in Anoka.

Election Returns

	Republican		Democratic		Other	
President 2000	152,977	52.4%	123,247	42.2%	15,954	5.5%
House 2002	164,747	57.3%	100,738	35.1%	21,827	7.6%

District Profile

Population   614,935

Total area (square miles)   3,236.7
   Land area (square miles)   3,080.5

Population per square mile   199.6

Counties (2000 population)

Anoka (pt.) 186,286	Stearns (pt.) 118,340
Benton 34,226	Washington (pt.) 121,204
Hennepin (pt.) 476	Wright 89,986
Sherburne 64,417	

Cities and other areas over 10,000 (2000 population)

Andover 26,588	East Bethel 10,941
Anoka 18,076	Elk River 16,447
Blaine 44,942	Ham Lake 12,710
Buffalo 10,097	Lino Lakes 16,791
Ramsey 18,510	Stillwater 15,143
Sauk Rapids 10,213	Woodbury (pt.) 44,767
St. Cloud 59,107	

Race and Hispanic or Latino origin*
White   94.9%
Black or African American   0.9%
American Indian or Alaska Native   0.4%
Asian   1.4%
Native Hawaiian or other Pacific Islander   0.0%
Some other race   0.1%
Hispanic or Latino origin   1.3%
Two or more races   1.0%

*As percentage of total population.

Ancestry*

Dutch 1.1%	Irish 8.0%
English 3.7%	Italian 1.6%
Finnish 1.4%	Norwegian 10.0%
Fr. Canadian 1.1%	Polish 4.9%
French 3.4%	Swedish 7.2%
German 29.9%	USA/American 2.3%

*As estimated percentage of total population.

Universities and colleges, 2000–2001 enrollment
Anoka-Hennepin Technical College, Anoka   2,046
College of St. Benedict, St. Joseph   2,024
St. Cloud State University, St. Cloud   15,181
St. Cloud Technical College, St. Cloud   2,949
St. John's University, Collegeville   2,020

Newspapers and circulation

	District circulation	Total circulation
Minneapolis Star Tribune	30,421	341,251
St. Cloud Times	24,068	27,872
St. Paul Pioneer Press	26,110	200,578
USA Today*	2,129	1,674,376

*See Sources and Explanations in the front of the volume.

Television stations and affiliations

Minneapolis-St. Paul	100%	KARE	NBC
Minneapolis-St. Paul	100%	KAWB	PBS
Minneapolis-St. Paul	100%	KAWE	PBS
Minneapolis-St. Paul	100%	KCCO	CBS
Minneapolis-St. Paul	100%	KCCW	CBS
Minneapolis-St. Paul	100%	KMSP	FOX
Minneapolis-St. Paul	100%	KMWB	WB
Minneapolis-St. Paul	100%	KPXM	PAX
Minneapolis-St. Paul	100%	KRWF	ABC
Minneapolis-St. Paul	100%	KSAX	ABC
Minneapolis-St. Paul	100%	KSTP	ABC
Minneapolis-St. Paul	100%	KTCA	PBS
Minneapolis-St. Paul	100%	KTCI	PBS
Minneapolis-St. Paul	100%	KWCM	PBS
Minneapolis-St. Paul	100%	WFTC	UPN

Cable systems and subscribers
Benton Telephone   848
Charter   12,727
Comcast   33,250
Heart of the Lakes Cable Co.   533
Mediacom   1,195
U.S. Cable   8,655

Businesses and other major employers

Andersen Corp.; Bayport; windows, wood   4,300
Fingerhut Corp.; St. Cloud; mail order   2,400
Electrolux Home Products Inc.; St. Cloud; refrigerators/freezers   1,800
St. Cloud Hospital Inc.; St. Cloud   1,750
Hoffman Enclosures Inc.; Anoka; housings for business machines   1,500
Lens Vision-Ease Inc.; Anoka; ophthalmic goods   1,500
St. Cloud State University; St. Cloud   1,300
Anoka County; Anoka; county government   1,025
U.S. Veterans Hospital; St. Cloud   875
Bankers Systems Inc.; St. Cloud; business forms printing   850
Cold Spring Granite Co.; Rockville; cut stone and stone products   850
Federal Cartridge Co.; Anoka; shot, steel (ammunition)   850
Washington County; Stillwater; county government   811
BSI Graphics; St. Cloud; shopping news publishing   800
Cold Spring Granite Co.; Cold Spring; stone for buildings   800
Fingerhut Corp.; St. Cloud; collection agency   750
Gold'n Plump Poultry Inc.; Cold Spring; processed poultry   750
Bermo Inc.; Circle Pines; stamping metal   700
International Paper Co.; Sartell; book, bond, and printing papers   670
Wilson Tool International Inc.; St. Paul; forming and stamping punches   650
Crystal Cabinet Works Inc.; Princeton; kitchen cabinets   604
Anoka County; Anoka; mental hospital   600
Cornelius IMI Inc.; Anoka; beverage dispensing equipment   600
General Signal Corp.; Sartell; industrial valves   600
Merrill Corp.; St. Cloud; commercial printing   600
Quebecor World Inc.; St. Cloud; offset printing   600
St. Benedict's Center; St. Cloud; skilled nursing care facilities   530
Centennial Independent School District; Circle Pines   525
Lakeview Memorial Hospital Assn. Inc.; Stillwater   500

Minnesota 7th District

West — Moorhead, Willmar

Stretching 330 miles from north to south, the vast 7th spans almost all of the state's western third. It shifts from flat prairie in the west to hills, lakes, and heavy forests in the middle of the state. Besides Willmar in the southern part of the district, the 7th's population centers, Moorhead and East Grand Forks, are on the Red River, which forms the border between Minnesota and North Dakota, and have much larger companion cities across the border.

While the river irrigates some of the nation's blackest soil, floods in 1997 and 2001 capped a decade of agricultural struggle in the area. Though it lost some population,

East Grand Forks largely has been rebuilt since 1997. Sugar beets and sunflowers are the dominant crops in the fertile west, while soybeans, wheat, corn, and other staples are more prevalent in the east and south. The district also is a top producer of turkeys. Concern over the sugar market, the floods, drought, and crop disease has left farmers looking to diversify and has sent younger residents fleeing. The Prairie Correctional Facility, a private prison taking inmates from as far away as Hawaii, is located in Appleton.

The district's manufacturing firms lend some stability to the area. The 7th produces hockey sticks, windows, skis, and snowmobiles. Lakes in the north and east drive many resorts catering to retirees.

The 7th was George W. Bush's strongest Minnesota district in 2000, but residents will support either party. The 7th is also the state's most competitive district in statewide races. Traditional small-farm and labor support for Democrats still exists, particularly in the south, but these voters tend to oppose gun control and abortion. The district's most conservative voters live along the state's western border.

Major Industry

Agriculture, light manufacturing, recreation.

Notable

Writer Sinclair Lewis, the first American to win the Nobel Prize in Literature, grew up in Sauk Center; Walnut Grove was the childhood home of Laura Ingalls Wilder, author of the *Little House on the Prairie* book series.

Election Returns

	Republican		Democratic		Other	
President 2000	155,794	53.6%	116,099	40.0%	18,706	6.4%
House 2002	90,342	34.7%	170,234	65.3%	237	

District Profile

Population   614,935

Total area (square miles)   33,745.3
  Land area (square miles)   31,796.4

Population per square mile   19.3

Counties (2000 population)

Becker	30,000	Norman	7,442
Beltrami (pt.)	29,082	Otter Tail	57,159
Big Stone	5,820	Pennington	13,584
Chippewa	13,088	Polk	31,369
Clay	51,229	Pope	11,236
Clearwater	8,423	Red Lake	4,299
Douglas	32,821	Redwood	16,815
Grant	6,289	Renville	17,154
Kandiyohi	41,203	Roseau	16,338
Kittson	5,285	Sibley	15,356
Lac qui Parle	8,067	Stearns (pt.)	14,826
Lake of the Woods	4,522	Stevens	10,053
Lincoln	6,429	Swift	11,956
Lyon	25,425	Todd	24,426
Mahnomen	5,190	Traverse	4,134
Marshall	10,155	Wilkin	7,138
McLeod	34,898	Yellow Medicine	11,080
Meeker	22,644		

Cities and other areas over 10,000 (2000 population)

Bemidji	11,917	Marshall	12,735
Fergus Falls	13,471	Moorhead	32,177
Hutchinson	13,080	Willmar	18,351

Race and Hispanic or Latino origin*

White   93.1%
Black or African American   0.3%
American Indian or Alaska Native   2.4%
Asian   0.5%
Native Hawaiian or other Pacific Islander   0.0%
Some other race   0.0%
Hispanic or Latino origin   2.6%
Two or more races   0.9%

*As percentage of total population.

Ancestry*

Danish	1.5%	Irish	5.0%
Dutch	1.7%	Norwegian	20.3%
English	3.1%	Polish	2.5%
French	2.6%	Swedish	7.0%
German	28.5%	USA/American	1.9%

*As estimated percentage of total population.

Universities and colleges, 2000–2001 enrollment

Alexandria Technical College, Alexandria   2,192
Bemidji State University, Bemidji   4,118
Concordia College at Moorhead, Moorhead   2,826
Fergus Falls Community College, Fergus Falls   2,082
Minnesota West Community and Technical College, Granite Falls   3,296
Moorhead State University, Moorhead   7,418
Northland Community and Technical College, Thief River Falls   1,991
Northwest Technical College-Bemidji, Bemidji 4,638
Ridgewater College, Willmar   3,762
Southwest State University, Marshall   4,746
University of Minnesota, Crookston   2,775
University of Minnesota, Morris   1,842
White Earth Tribal and Community College, Mahnomen*

*Enrollment under 100. See Sources and Explanations in the front of the volume.

Newspapers and circulation

	District circulation	Total circulation
Fargo Forum	16,198	49,865
Grand Forks Herald	10,981	33,151
Marshall Independent	7,145	7,423
Minneapolis Star Tribune	2,770	341,251
New Ulm Journal	1,752	8,767
St. Cloud Times	1,881	27,872
*USA Today**	1,444	1,674,376

*See Sources and Explanations in the front of the volume.

Television stations and affiliations

Fargo-Valley City, ND	51%	KBRR	FOX
Fargo-Valley City, ND	51%	KFME	PBS
Fargo-Valley City, ND	51%	KGFE	PBS
Fargo-Valley City, ND	51%	KJRE	PBS
Fargo-Valley City, ND	51%	KJRR	FOX
Fargo-Valley City, ND	51%	KNRR	FOX
Fargo-Valley City, ND	51%	KVLY	NBC
Fargo-Valley City, ND	51%	KVRR	FOX
Fargo-Valley City, ND	51%	KXJB	CBS
Fargo-Valley City, ND	51%	WDAY	ABC
Fargo-Valley City, ND	51%	WDAZ	ABC
Minneapolis-St. Paul	47%	KARE	NBC
Minneapolis-St. Paul	47%	KAWB	PBS
Minneapolis-St. Paul	47%	KAWE	PBS
Minneapolis-St. Paul	47%	KCCO	CBS
Minneapolis-St. Paul	47%	KCCW	CBS
Minneapolis-St. Paul	47%	KMSP	FOX
Minneapolis-St. Paul	47%	KMWB	WB
Minneapolis-St. Paul	47%	KPXM	PAX
Minneapolis-St. Paul	47%	KRWF	ABC
Minneapolis-St. Paul	47%	KSAX	ABC
Minneapolis-St. Paul	47%	KSTP	ABC
Minneapolis-St. Paul	47%	KTCA	PBS
Minneapolis-St. Paul	47%	KTCI	PBS
Minneapolis-St. Paul	47%	KWCM	PBS
Minneapolis-St. Paul	47%	WFTC	UPN
Sioux Falls (Mitchell), SD	2%	KABY	ABC
Sioux Falls (Mitchell), SD	2%	KCSD	PBS
Sioux Falls (Mitchell), SD	2%	KDLO	CBS
Sioux Falls (Mitchell), SD	2%	KDLV	NBC
Sioux Falls (Mitchell), SD	2%	KDSD	PBS
Sioux Falls (Mitchell), SD	2%	KELO	CBS
Sioux Falls (Mitchell), SD	2%	KESD	PBS
Sioux Falls (Mitchell), SD	2%	KPLO	CBS
Sioux Falls (Mitchell), SD	2%	KPRY	ABC
Sioux Falls (Mitchell), SD	2%	KQSD	PBS
Sioux Falls (Mitchell), SD	2%	KRNE	PBS
Sioux Falls (Mitchell), SD	2%	KSFY	ABC
Sioux Falls (Mitchell), SD	2%	KSMN	PBS
Sioux Falls (Mitchell), SD	2%	KTSD	PBS
Sioux Falls (Mitchell), SD	2%	KTTM	FOX
Sioux Falls (Mitchell), SD	2%	KTTW	FOX

Cable systems and subscribers

Barnesville Cablevision   538
Cable ONE   7,787
Charter   38,311
Data Video Systems   1,027
Garden Valley Telephone   1,298
Loretel Cablevision   4,514
Mediacom   20,921
Midcontinent Cable   8,370
Runestone Communications   1,289
Sjoberg's Cable TV   7,646
Stephen Cable TV   991
Tekstar   6,890
U.S. Cable   2,126

Businesses and other major employers

Marvin Lumber and Cedar Co.; Warroad; windows, wood 3,000
Schwan's Sales Enterprises Inc.; Marshall; frozen pizza 2,500
Polaris Industries Inc.; Roseau; snowmobiles   1,800
Hutchinson Technology Inc.; Hutchinson; electronic circuits   1,774
3M Co.; Hutchinson; magnetic tape   1,700
Jennie-O Turkey Store Inc.; Willmar; turkey processing 1,600

White Earth Reservation Tribal Council; Mahnomen; gambling   1,100

Arctic Cat Inc.; Thief River Falls; snowmobiles   1,000

Jennie-O Foods Inc.; Melrose; processed turkey   815

Land O'Lakes Inc.; Mentor; sunflower farm   800

Jackpot Junction Casino Hotel; Morton; casino hotel   768

Minnesota State University Moorhead; Moorhead   750

Jennie-O Foods Inc.; Pelican Rapids; turkey processing   740

St. Francis Health Services of Morris Inc.; Morris   688

American Business Forms Inc.; Glenwood; business forms   650

Rice Memorial Hospital; Willmar   650

Concordia College Corp.; Moorhead   630

Lake Region Healthcare Corp. Hospital; Fergus Falls   610

Douglas County Hospital; Alexandria   600

G&S Staffing Services Inc.; Willmar; telemarketing services   600

Bemidji State University; Bemidji   596

Banta Corp.; Long Prairie; magazine printing   585

Otter Tail County; Fergus Falls; county government   528

Minnesota Dept. of Human Services; Willmar   520

Affiliated Community Medical Centers PA; Willmar; medical clinic   500

Innovex Inc.; Litchfield; integrated circuits   500

Otter Tail County; Fergus Falls; waste materials recycling   500

Minnesota 8th District

Northeast — Duluth, Iron Range

The expansive 8th covers Minnesota's northeast quadrant, including Duluth and the Iron Range—taconite mining communities that stretch across the middle of the state through Cass, Crow Wing, and St. Louis Counties. It is the only one of Minnesota's three rural districts to include any of the Minneapolis-St. Paul metro area, though that area makes up only 12 percent of its population.

Logging and mining still provide a solid base for the region, though the work force is less than half what it was in the 1980s. These blue-collar workers with strong ties to labor cement the 8th's long affiliation with the Democratic-Farmer-Labor Party. The 8th has not sent a Republican to Congress since the 1944 election.

Duluth, the largest city, is the shipping point for much of the grain from the Plains states, and the westernmost deep sea port to the Atlantic. It remains a Democratic stronghold. The rural areas also are Democratic, but voters favor a hands-off approach to federal land management and tend to oppose gun control and abortion.

The southern end of the district grew in the 1990s by attracting Twin Cities commuters. The GOP is making inroads in this rapidly expanding area, where voters are willing to stray from the 8th's solid Democratic stance.

The district has the most varied terrain in the state, from farms in the south and west through the Iron Range and a watery northern border to rugged terrain in the northeastern arrowhead region. Huge tracts of land are designated as state and national forests, and the Boundary Waters Canoe Area along the Canadian border is noted for its motor-free beauty.

Major Industry

Mining, timber, recreation.

Notable

Actress Judy Garland hailed from Grand Rapids; the nation's only gas station designed by Frank Lloyd Wright is in Cloquet; Eveleth is home to the U.S. Hockey Hall of Fame; Little Falls was the boyhood home of aviator Charles Lindbergh; International Falls calls itself "the icebox of the nation" and claims to be the coldest spot in the lower 48 states.

Election Returns

	Republican		Democratic		Other	
President 2000	136,884	43.7%	153,962	49.2%	22,302	7.1%
House 2002	88,673	31.3%	194,909	68.7%	349	

District Profile

Population   614,935

Total area (square miles)   32,418.9
  Land area (square miles)   27,582.6

Population per square mile   22.3

Counties (2000 population)

Aitkin 15,301	Itasca 43,992
Beltrami (pt.) 10,568	Kanabec 14,996
Carlton 31,671	Koochiching 14,355
Cass 27,150	Lake 11,058
Chisago 41,101	Mille Lacs 22,330
Cook 5,168	Morrison 31,712
Crow Wing 55,099	Pine 26,530
Hubbard 18,376	St. Louis 200,528
Isanti 31,287	Wadena 13,713

Cities and other areas over 10,000 (2000 population)

Brainerd 13,178	Duluth 86,918
Cloquet 11,201	Hibbing 17,071

Race and Hispanic or Latino origin*
  White   94.6%
  Black or African American   0.5%
  American Indian or Alaska Native   2.5%
  Asian   0.4%
  Native Hawaiian or other Pacific Islander   0.0%
  Some other race   0.0%
  Hispanic or Latino origin   0.8%
  Two or more races   1.0%

As percentage of total population.

Ancestry*

Danish 1.1%	Irish 6.4%
Dutch 1.2%	Italian 2.1%
English 4.3%	Norwegian 10.8%
Finnish 4.8%	Polish 4.0%
Fr. Canadian 1.2%	Swedish 9.6%
French 3.2%	USA/American 2.4%
German 20.2%	

As estimated percentage of total population.

Universities and colleges, 2000–2001 enrollment
Cambridge Community College, Cambridge*
Central Lakes College, Brainerd   3,138
College of St. Scholastica, Duluth   2,054
Duluth Business University, Duluth   267
Fond Du Lac Tribal and Community College, Cloquet   999
Hibbing Community College, Hibbing   3,143
Itasca Community College, Grand Rapids   1,033
Lake Superior College, Duluth   3,972
Leech Lake Tribal College, Cass Lake   240
Mesabi Range Community and Technical College, Eveleth   1,440
Mesabi Range Community and Technical College, Virginia   1,486
Pine Technical College, Pine City   996
Rainy River Community College, International Falls   617
University of Minnesota, Duluth   9,087
Vermilion Community College, Ely   885

*Enrollment under 100. See Sources and Explanations in the front of the volume.

Newspapers and circulation

	District circulation	Total circulation
Brainerd Daily Dispatch	12,965	13,293
Duluth News-Tribune	39,826	45,647
Minneapolis Star Tribune	4,030	341,251
St. Cloud Times	1,739	27,872
St. Paul Pioneer Press	4,442	200,578
*USA Today**	1,376	1,674,376

*See Sources and Explanations in the front of the volume.

Television stations and affiliations
Duluth-Superior	62%	KBJR	NBC, UPN
Duluth-Superior	62%	KDLH	CBS
Duluth-Superior	62%	KQDS	FOX
Duluth-Superior	62%	WDIO	ABC
Duluth-Superior	62%	WDSE	PBS
Duluth-Superior	62%	WIRT	ABC
Minneapolis-St. Paul	38%	KARE	NBC
Minneapolis-St. Paul	38%	KAWB	PBS
Minneapolis-St. Paul	38%	KAWE	PBS
Minneapolis-St. Paul	38%	KCCO	CBS
Minneapolis-St. Paul	38%	KCCW	CBS
Minneapolis-St. Paul	38%	KMSP	FOX
Minneapolis-St. Paul	38%	KMWB	WB
Minneapolis-St. Paul	38%	KPXM	PAX
Minneapolis-St. Paul	38%	KRWF	ABC
Minneapolis-St. Paul	38%	KSAX	ABC
Minneapolis-St. Paul	38%	KSTP	ABC
Minneapolis-St. Paul	38%	KTCA	PBS
Minneapolis-St. Paul	38%	KTCI	PBS
Minneapolis-St. Paul	38%	KWCM	PBS
Minneapolis-St. Paul	38%	WFTC	UPN

Cable systems and subscribers
Charter   42,939
Crosslake Cablevision   2,053
Mediacom   22,935
Range TV Cable   5,693
Savage Communications   2,864
Tekstar Cablevision   911
U.S. Cable   9,361

Military installations, September 2001
Camp Ripley Military Training Area, Little Falls   1,056
Duluth International Airport (Air National Guard), Duluth   1,022

Businesses and other major employers
Allete Inc.; Duluth; automobiles 2,000
U.S. Steel Corp.; Mountain Iron; taconite mining   1,700
St. Mary's Medical Center; Duluth   1,544
Marathon Oil Corp.; Mountain Iron; tantalite mining   1,500
University of Minnesota; Duluth   1,500
St. Luke's Hospital of Duluth; Duluth   1,240
Corporate Commission of Mille Lacs Band of Chippewa Indians; Hinckley; gambling   1,200
Corporate Commission of Mille Lacs Band of Chippewa Indians; Onamia; gambling   1,200
Boise Cascade Corp.; International Falls; paper mills   1,130
National Steel Pellet Co.; Keewatin; iron ore mining   1,100
Potlatch Corp.; Cloquet; pressed pulp products   1,000
United Healthcare Services Inc.; Duluth; health maintenance organization   950
Leech Lake Palace and Casino Corp.; Cass Lake; bingo hall   900
St. Joseph's Medical Center; Brainerd   900
Larson/Glastron Boats Inc.; Little Falls; fiberglass boats   876
Hibbing Taconite Co.; Hibbing; taconite mining   871
Blandin Paper Co.; Grand Rapids; printing paper   860
Miller-Dwan Medical Center Inc.; Duluth   830
Cleveland-Cliffs Inc.; Hibbing; iron ore mining   800
S. D. Warren Co.; Cloquet; pulp produced from wood base   800
Allina Health Systems Inc. Cambridge Hospital; Cambridge   770
LTV Steel Co.; Hoyt Lakes; steel sheets or strips   750
Duluth Missabe and Iron Range Railway Co.; Duluth; freight hauling   700
Independent Union Papermill Workers; Grand Rapids; labor organization   700
Potlatch Corp.; Brainerd; pulp mills   700
St. Louis County; Duluth; county government   700
Fairview Health Services Hospital; Wyoming   680
Minnesota Dept. of Human Services; Brainerd   650
North Country Health Services Inc. Hospital; Bemidji   650
Premium Retail Services Inc.; Cambridge; merchandising consultant   645
Hazelden Foundation; Center City; residential rehabilitation center   605
Hibbings Electronics Corp.; Hibbing; printed circuit boards   600
Duluth Entertainment Convention Center; Duluth; convention and show services   586

Mississippi

No state is more steeped in Dixie tradition than Mississippi, in many ways the deepest of the Deep South. Few states also have made a greater contribution to American literature than this birthplace of William Faulkner, Eudora Welty, Willie Morris, Tennessee Williams, Richard Wright, and other twentieth-century writers of note. It was also the cradle of the Delta blues and the home of Elvis Presley, who helped make those blues into rock 'n' roll. The stories and songs these artists embedded in the national consciousness were often rooted in the life and history of their state: rich in feeling, hardships, and sorrows.

Before the Civil War, the economy was divided between the large landowners with their slaves and the small farmers and woodsmen working their small plots. The big plantations were located primarily in the alluvial plain just east of the mythic geographical feature that gives the state its name. Towns included the capital Jackson, the old territorial capital and picturesque riverport of Natchez, and the river fortress of Vicksburg that was called the "Gibraltar of the South."

The Civil War and Reconstruction were cruel to the Magnolia State. Mississippi had little economy beyond cotton, and freed slaves had few places to go. Most stayed on or near the land they knew and fell into the penury of sharecropping. As a result, the rural poverty that enveloped much of the region after the war was particularly acute and persistent in the Mississippi Delta, throughout the nineteenth and twentieth centuries.

When Reconstruction ended, the reempowered white majority passed laws that would keep African Americans in reduced status for generations, rarely able to vote and barred from white schools. During and after the world wars and the Depression, the prospect of a job and a measure of freedom in the cities in the North lured hundreds of thousands of African Americans up the Mississippi to the North, particularly to the industrial cities of the Midwest. The state lost 900,000 black residents in the period from 1940–1970 alone.

Much of the lore of that great regional migration attaches to the specific journey up a single two-lane road from the Delta to Chicago, from the land of legendary country blues performer Robert Johnson to the urban turf of Chicago blues performer Muddy Waters. Both men were born in Mississippi, as were B. B. King and Mississippi John Hurt and a host of blues figures. But all these decades of out-migration did not defuse the tension in Mississippi, which remained the highest concentration of African Americans in the nation and still the Gibraltar of the South in its resistance to integration.

As the civil rights movement gained momentum in the early 1960s it had some of its historic turning points here.

A black student named James Meredith enrolled at the University of Mississippi in 1962, touching off days of rioting that changed the tone of the movement and its resistance. In the years since there have been considerable strides made in integrating schools and workplaces and elected offices. But progress has been slow, in part because the state remains mired at the bottom in key measures of economic and social rank: dead last in per capita personal income, near last in college degrees. Even the new economy here has depended on cyclical industries such as shipbuilding and oil refining along the Gulf, petrochemicals in the southern counties, and agriculture further north. In the 1990s, the state got a boost from legalized gambling on the Mississippi, which has become a major source of growth and tax revenue, but which is subject to intense competition.

Along the way, the state has always had substantial help from the federal government. It maximized its weight in Washington by electing members of Congress young and keeping them in office for life. They would never be numerous, but seniority would give them gavels to wield as committee chairs. Few states have worked that system better. At one point in the 1980s, the state had the Appropriations chair in both the House (Jamie Whitten, who served more than 50 years) and in the Senate (John Stennis, who served more than 40) at the same time. Both men were Democrats, as nearly all Mississippi members had been for generations. But in 1972, two former cheerleaders from Ole Miss, Trent Lott and Thad Cochran, won House seats as Republicans. Both later moved to the Senate, where in 2003 Cochran chaired Agriculture and Lott chaired Rules.

Presidential voting here has been dominated not by a party but by an issue: states' rights. When Strom Thurmond ran for president as the nominee of the States' Rights Party in 1948, he got more than 80 percent of the vote here. When Barry Goldwater was the Republican nominee and opposed the Civil Rights Act in 1964, he got 87 percent (at a time when only 7 percent of the states' blacks could vote). After passage of the Voting Rights Act in 1965 integrated voting booths, George Wallace still carried the state in 1968 with better than 60 percent. Since then, the black vote has been heavily Democratic and the white vote heavily Republican (with the single exception of Jimmy Carter's first run in 1976). Setting aside 1976, Mississippi has been in the GOP column for president.

For a time in the 1990s, the romance between the GOP and Mississippi was quite passionate. Yazoo City native Haley Barbour was the chairman of the Republican National Committee and two other state products were right behind

MISSISSIPPI

Districts established February 4, 2002, for elections first held in 2002.

4 members

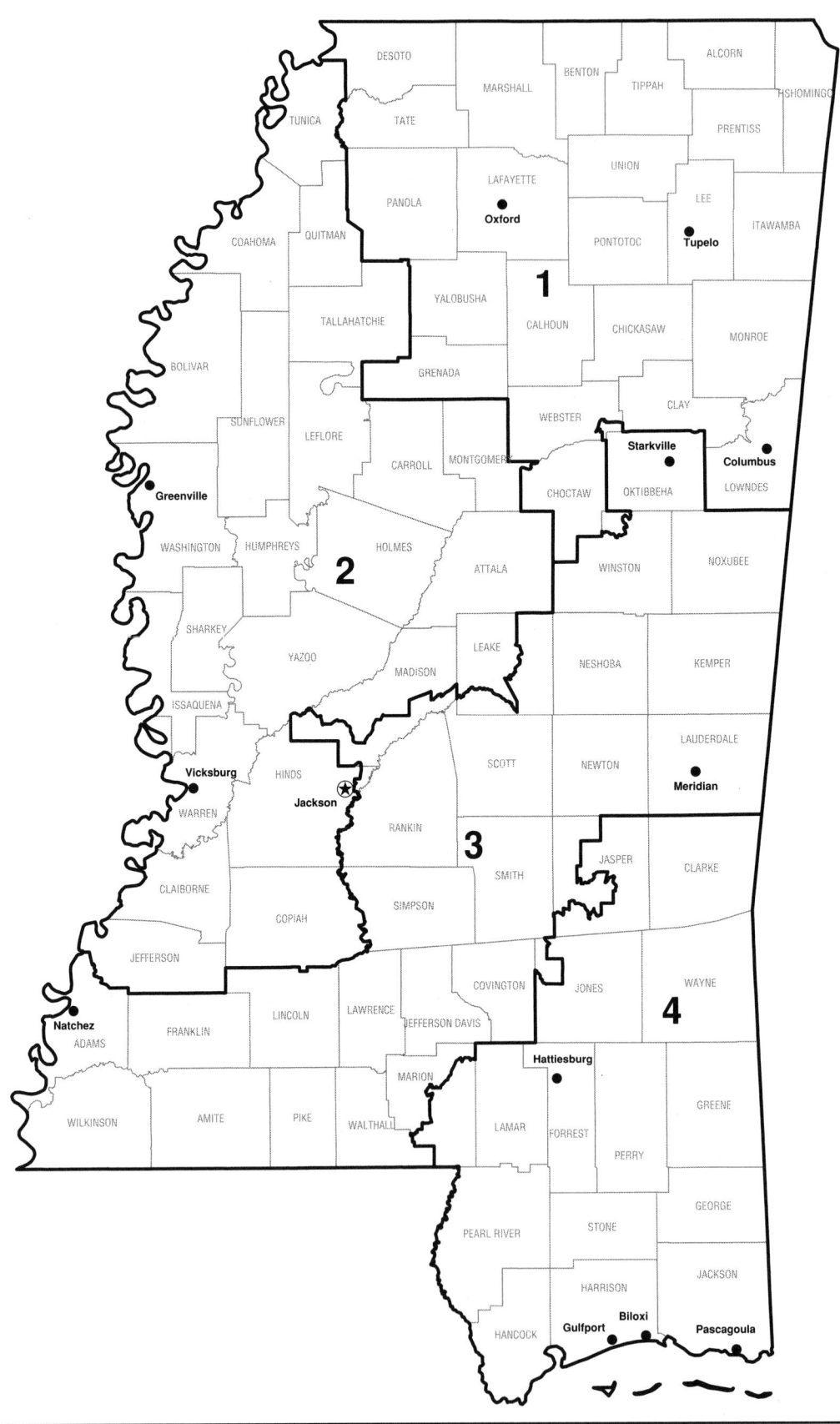

him in the RNC hierarchy. Mississippi elected its first post-Reconstruction Republican governor in 1991. Three of the five House seats switched to the GOP in 1994. That same month, Trent Lott was elected to the number two spot in the Senate Republican hierarchy, becoming the majority leader in 1996.

But Mississippi had yet to cut all ties to its historic party. The state legislature remained Democratic, which helped Ronnie Musgrove win the governorship back for his party in 1999. Democrats then controlled all aspects of the redistricting here, but disagreed over how to deal with the loss of one seat in the post-2000 reapportionment (the state has fallen to four seats from a peak of eight). In the end, the state courts got involved and the white suburbs of Jackson in two counties wound up in the new 3rd District, which became a battleground between two incumbents.

This new map also had one district (the 2nd) drawn to include virtually all the counties of the Delta plus the black precincts of Jackson. Concentrating the black vote this way since the 1980s has reversed the previous practice of distributing it as widely as possible to dilute its effect. It ensures the election of black voters' choice in the 2nd, but it tends to make the other three districts more Republican. The other districts divide the state among a northeastern corner 1st District (some Memphis suburbs plus Tupelo and Columbus), the new central 3rd that slashes across from the Louisiana corner in the southwest upstate to the Alabama line (taking in those Jackson suburbs plus Meridian), and a southeastern 4th that includes Hattiesburg but is dominated by Gulf Coast towns of Gulfport, Biloxi, and Pascagoula.

There was also a postscript written shortly after the election of 2002 that underscored the enduring dilemma of state history. Lott was preparing to return as Senate majority leader after an 18-month period of Democratic control. He attended a 100th birthday party for Thurmond, who was finally retiring from the Senate. In his remarks, Lott said his state was proud to have voted for Thurmond in 1948 and that if the rest of country had done so "maybe we wouldn't have had some of these problems." The comment was taken as nostalgia for the segregated past, fairly or not, and Lott was soon forced to step down as leader to spare his party embarrassment.

Table 1   Population

District	Population	Population under 18	Voting-age population	Median age	Male*	Female*
1	711,160	189,415	521,745	34.5	48.3	51.7
2	711,164	209,277	501,887	31.6	47.6	52.4
3	711,115	187,544	523,571	34.7	48.1	51.9
4	711,219	188,951	522,268	34.2	49.1	50.9
State	2,844,658	775,187	2,069,471	33.8	48.3	51.7

*As percentage of total population.

Table 2   Voting-Age Persons by Race/Hispanic or Latino Origin

District	White*	Black or African American*	American Indian or Alaska Native*	Asian*	Other or multirace*	Hispanic or Latino*
1	74.0	23.7	0.2	0.4	0.5	1.3
2	38.8	58.9	0.2	0.4	0.4	1.2
3	66.8	30.2	0.7	0.6	0.4	1.1
4	76.0	20.0	0.3	1.1	0.7	1.7
State	64.2	33.0	0.4	0.6	0.5	1.3

*As percentage of voting-age population.

Table 3   Voting-Age Population by Age Groups

District	18 to 24*	25 to 44*	45 to 64*	Over 64*
1	14.2	39.2	29.7	16.9
2	16.7	38.8	28.3	16.2
3	14.4	38.6	29.7	17.4
4	14.9	39.4	29.8	15.9
State	15.0	39.0	29.4	16.6

*As percentage of voting-age population.

Table 4   Income and Occupation

District	Median family income	Families in poverty*	White collar†	Blue collar†	Service†	Farm†
1	$39,449	12.9	48.5	38.6	12.1	0.8
2	$32,114	22.7	52.2	28.8	17.2	1.7
3	$38,626	15.4	56.7	28.9	13.0	1.5
4	$39,063	13.4	51.9	29.7	17.4	1.0
State	$37,406	16.0	52.3	31.6	14.9	1.2

*As percentage of all families.   †As percentage of employed workers 16 years and over.

Table 5   Education: School Years Completed

District	Less than grade 9*	Grades 9–12 no diploma*	High school diploma no college*	Some college*	College bachelor's degree or higher*
1	10.7	18.9	31.7	24.7	13.9
2	12.1	19.3	26.2	25.6	16.8
3	8.6	16.6	28.6	26.0	20.2
4	7.2	15.4	30.8	29.9	16.7
State	9.6	17.5	29.4	26.6	16.9

*As percentage of persons age 25 and over.

Table 6   Housing and Residential Patterns

District	Median home value	Owner occupied*	Renter occupied*	Urban†	Rural†
1	$67,200	75.1	24.9	38.5	61.5
2	$55,100	65.7	34.3	62.8	37.2
3	$64,900	75.7	24.3	40.3	59.7
4	$70,600	72.4	27.6	53.7	46.3
State	$64,700	72.3	27.7	48.8	51.2

*As percentage of occupied housing units.   †As percentage of total population.

Mississippi 1st District

North — Tupelo, Southaven, Columbus

The northeastern Hill Country and rich farmland on the edge of the Delta region in northwestern Mississippi support an agricultural economy in the 1st, while manufacturing dominates in Lee County (Tupelo) and surrounding areas.

Tupelo, the region's largest city, is a major producer of upholstered furniture; it hosts a biannual national furniture market that draws enough visitors to temporarily double the local population. Fortune 500 companies abound, drawing job-seekers from poorer parts of the state. The Tennessee-Tombigbee Waterway, which cuts through the 1st's eastern edge, has spawned a boom of forestry-related business.

In the district's northwest corner, DeSoto County is becoming a haven for residents who commute to Memphis over the Tennessee border. DeSoto is the district's most populous county and its fastest growing: its population expanded by nearly 50 percent in the 1990s. Just to the east, Marshall and Benton Counties are home to many of the district's African Americans, a group that makes up more than one-fourth of the population.

Redistricting following the 2000 census did little to change the district's boundaries, politics, or economy, but the 1st did pick up Lowndes County, which includes Columbus and Columbus Air Force Base.

Democrats held the congressional seat for more than a century until a Republican captured it in 1994. Voters have gradually turned away from Democrats in federal elections, favoring GOP presidential candidates in 1992, 1996, and 2000. Democrats, however, dominate state and local elections, stemming from the party's provincial political monopoly since Reconstruction.

Major Industry
Furniture, agriculture, manufacturing.

Notable
Jamie L. Whitten, who represented the district from 1941 to 1995, was the House's longest-serving member—53 years and two months.

Election Returns

	Republican		Democratic		Other	
President 2000	146,197	58.9%	98,350	39.6%	3,690	1.5%
House 2002	95,404	71.4%	32,318	24.2%	5,845	4.4%

District Profile

Population   711,160

Total area (square miles)   11,647.2
Land area (square miles)   11,412.8

Population per square mile   62.3

Counties (2000 population)

Alcorn	34,558	Marshall	34,993
Benton	8,026	Monroe	38,014
Calhoun	15,069	Panola	34,274
Chickasaw	19,440	Pontotoc	26,726
Choctaw	9,758	Prentiss	25,556
Clay	21,979	Tate	25,370
DeSoto	107,199	Tippah	20,826
Grenada	23,263	Tishomingo	19,163
Itawamba	22,770	Union	25,362
Lafayette	38,744	Webster (pt.)	9,544
Lee	75,755	Winston (pt.)	134
Lowndes	61,586	Yalobusha	13,051

Cities and other areas over 10,000 (2000 population)

Columbus	25,944	Oxford	11,756
Corinth	14,054	Southaven	28,977
Grenada	14,879	Tupelo	34,211
Horn Lake	14,099	West Point	12,145
Olive Branch	21,054		

Race and Hispanic or Latino origin*
White   71.3%
Black or African American   26.2%
American Indian or Alaska Native   0.2%
Asian   0.4%
Native Hawaiian or other Pacific Islander   0.0%
Some other race   0.0%
Hispanic or Latino origin   1.4%
Two or more races   0.5%

*As percentage of total population.

Ancestry*

English	6.1%	Scotch-Irish	1.5%
German	3.9%	Scottish	1.1%
Irish	7.1%	USA/American	16.6%

*As estimated percentage of total population.

Universities and colleges, 2000–2001 enrollment
Blue Mountain College, Blue Mountain   371
East Mississippi Community College-Golden Triangle, Mayhew*
Itawamba Community College, Fulton   3,467
Mary Holmes College, West Point   292
Mississippi University for Women, Columbus   2,814
Northeast Mississippi Community College, Booneville 2,796
Northwest Mississippi Community College, Senatobia 4,776
Rust College, Holly Springs   853
University of Mississippi, University   12,118

*Enrollment under 100. See Sources and Explanations in the front of the volume.

Newspapers and circulation

	District circulation	Total circulation
Jackson Clarion-Ledger	4,902	100,657
Memphis Commercial Appeal	18,660	157,808
Tupelo Northeast Mississippi Daily Journal	33,907	34,036
USA Today*	1,367	1,674,376

*See Sources and Explanations in the front of the volume.

Television stations and affiliations

Columbus-Tupelo-West Point	59%	WCBI	CBS
Columbus-Tupelo-West Point	59%	WLOV	FOX
Columbus-Tupelo-West Point	59%	WMAB	PBS
Columbus-Tupelo-West Point	59%	WTVA	NBC
Memphis, TN	37%	KVTJ	Independent
Memphis, TN	37%	WBUY	Independent
Memphis, TN	37%	WHBQ	FOX
Memphis, TN	37%	WKNO	PBS
Memphis, TN	37%	WMAE	PBS
Memphis, TN	37%	WMAV	PBS
Memphis, TN	37%	WMC	NBC
Memphis, TN	37%	WPTY	ABC, WB
Memphis, TN	37%	WPXX	PAX
Memphis, TN	37%	WREG	CBS

Greenwood-Greenville	4%	WABG	ABC
Greenwood-Greenville	4%	WLMT	UPN
Greenwood-Greenville	4%	WMAO	PBS
Greenwood-Greenville	4%	WXVT	CBS

Cable systems and subscribers
Branch Cable   740
Cable ONE   25,959
Cable South Inc.   2,138
Charter   1,383
Comcast   27,895
Galaxy   8,793
Mediacom   6,498
Ripley Video Cable   3,486
Southtel Communications   1,127
Time Warner   19,188
Vista III Media   27,411

Military installations, September 2001
Columbus Air Force Base, Columbus   1,456

Businesses and other major employers
North Mississippi Medical Center Inc.; Tupelo   5,000
Heatcraft Inc.; Grenada; electric motors/generator coils   2,800
University of Mississippi; University   2,500
Bryan Foods Inc.; West Point; meatpacking plants   2,000
Lennox Industries Inc.; Grenada; heating and air conditioning   2,000
Universal Furniture; Blue Mountain; commercial printing   1,600
Genlyte Thomas Group; Tupelo; lighting equipment   1,400
Cooper Tire and Rubber Co.; Tupelo; automobile tires   1,200
Thyssen Elevator Capital Corp.; Horn Lake; elevators   1,150
Cavalier Enterprises Inc.; Belmont; mobile homes   1,013
Baptist Memorial Hospital; Columbus   1,000
U.S. Rural Development Agency; Batesville   1,000
Baptist Memorial Hospital; Oxford   900
Lane Furniture Industries Inc.; Tupelo; recliners   900
Wal-Mart Stores Inc.; Southaven   900
Sanderson Plumbing Products Inc.; Columbus; toilet seats   810
Act Manufacturing Inc.; Corinth; management consulting   800
Leggett and Platt Inc.; Tupelo; metal furniture parts   800
Magnolia Regional Health Center; Corinth   800
Mississippi Dept. of Public Safety; Booneville   800
Quanex Corp.; New Albany; steel bars   800
Caterpillar Inc.; Corinth; motor vehicle engines/parts   750
Lane Furniture Industries Inc.; Pontotoc; recliners   700
Lane Furniture Industries Inc.; Saltillo; upholstered furniture   700
Tupelo Furniture Market Inc.; Tupelo; shows/exhibitions promoters   700
Landau Uniforms Inc.; Olive Branch; work uniforms   678
Corinthian Inc.; Corinth; furniture   650

Omnova Solutions Inc.; Columbus; organic fibers   650
Weyerhaeuser Co.; Columbus; sawmills and planing mills   650
Grenada Lake Medical Center; Grenada   630
Krueger International Inc.; Tupelo; metal furniture   621
Baptist Memorial Hospital; Southaven   600
Borg-Warner Air/Fluid Systems Inc.; Water Valley; carburetors   600
Chromcraft Corp.; Senatobia; furniture   600
Danskin Inc.; Grenada; hosiery   600
Wal-Mart Stores Inc.; Tupelo   600
Advanced Distributor Products; Grenada; heating and air conditioning units   585
Caye Upholstery; New Albany; furniture   550
Lane Furniture Industries Inc.; Belden; recliners   550
Whirlpool Corp.; Oxford; refrigerators/freezers   530
Babcock and Wilcox Co.; West Point; heating equipment, nonelectric   500
Biltrite Corp.; Ripley; shoe/boot heels   500
Carpenter Co.; Verona; foamed insulation   500
Emerson Electric Co.; Oxford; electric motors   500
Fleming Companies Inc.; Southaven; food supplier   500
Lowndes Co. School District; Columbus   500
Mueller Copper Tube Products Inc.; Fulton; multiservice center   500
PeopLoungers Inc.; Nettleton; furniture   500

Mississippi 2nd District

West central — Jackson, Mississippi Delta

The 2nd combines most of Jackson, the state's capital and largest city, with the nutrient-rich flatlands of the Mississippi Delta. The agricultural economy stemming from the Delta has promoted landowner/tenant relationships that have made the 2nd one of the poorest districts in the nation. Parts of the Delta still lack centralized running water.

Most of the district lies west of Interstate 55 and north of Interstate 20. Traveling west from Jackson, the 2nd moves into Vicksburg on the Louisiana border. Just north of Vicksburg, the road drops 15 feet in Issaquena County, marking the beginning of the flat Delta, where some of the nation's most fertile soil supports cotton and soybeans. Although some low-income white residents call the 2nd home, it is the only black-majority district in a state with the highest percentage of black residents in the nation.

While casinos in Tunica County—a popular gaming destination—have helped erase its standing as the nation's poorest county, many casino workers do not live in the district and instead commute from the Memphis region. Since the end of the 1990s, the 2nd has lost many manufacturing jobs to Mexico, which has contributed to high unemployment in some areas. But government, service, and small-scale manufacturing jobs have kept unemployment in check in Jackson, and a new Nissan assembly plant outside Canton (north of Jackson) is providing jobs. Vicksburg is another economic bright spot, where a mixture of tourism, casinos, and a Mississippi River port have fostered local prosperity.

Democratic since 1987, the 2nd's politics are dominated by the African American vote, though Republicans hold small areas around Jackson and the district's northeast.

Major Industry

Agriculture, government, casinos.

Notable

The Delta was the real birthplace of blues music: blues pioneer Muddy Waters was born in Rolling Fork in 1915, and blues legend B. B. King was born in Indianola in 1925.

Election Returns

	Republican		Democratic		Other	
President 2000	97,979	41.3%	134,513	56.8%	4,464	1.9%
House 2002	69,711	42.8%	89,913	55.1%	3,426	2.1%

District Profile

Population 711,164

Total area (square miles) 13,936.6
 Land area (square miles) 13,624.9

Population per square mile 52.2

Counties (2000 population)

Attala	19,661	Leflore	37,947
Bolivar	40,633	Madison (pt.)	27,631
Carroll	10,769	Montgomery	12,189
Claiborne	11,831	Quitman	10,117
Coahoma	30,622	Sharkey	6,580
Copiah	28,757	Sunflower	34,369
Hinds (pt.)	218,968	Tallahatchie	14,903
Holmes	21,609	Tunica	9,227
Humphreys	11,206	Warren	49,644
Issaquena	2,274	Washington	62,977
Jefferson	9,740	Yazoo	28,149
Leake (pt.)	11,361		

Cities and other areas over 10,000 (2000 population)

Canton (pt.)	12,867	Greenwood	18,425
Clarksdale	20,645	Indianola	12,066
Cleveland	13,841	Jackson (pt.)	152,424
Clinton	23,347	Vicksburg	26,407
Greenville	41,633	Yazoo City	14,550

Race and Hispanic or Latino origin*

White 34.5%
Black or African American 63.2%
American Indian or Alaska Native 0.2%
Asian 0.4%
Native Hawaiian or other Pacific Islander 0.0%
Some other race 0.0%
Hispanic or Latino origin 1.2%
Two or more races 0.5%

*As percentage of total population.

Ancestry*

English	3.3%	Scotch-Irish	1.4%
German	2.2%	USA/American	6.8%
Irish	3.7%		

*As estimated percentage of total population.

Universities and colleges, 2000–2001 enrollment

Alcorn State University, Alcorn State 2,936
Antonelli College, Jackson 215
Coahoma Community College, Clarksdale 277
Copiah-Lincoln Community College, Wesson 1,885
Delta State University, Cleveland 3,875
Hinds Community College, Jackson*
Hinds Community College, Raymond 16,032
Hinds Community College, Utica*
Hinds Community College, Vicksburg*
Holmes Community College, Goodman 3,022
Jackson State University, Jackson 6,820
Mississippi College, Clinton 3,423
Mississippi Delta Community College, Moorhead 2,673
Mississippi Valley State University, Itta Bena 2,687
Tougaloo College, Tougaloo 1,000
University of Mississippi Medical Center, Jackson 1,674

*Enrollment under 100. See Sources and Explanations in the front of the volume.

Newspapers and circulation

	District circulation	Total circulation
Bolivar Commercial	6,993	6,993
Clarksdale Press Register	5,850	5,850
Greenville Delta Democrat Times	11,032	11,335
Greenwood Commonwealth	7,460	7,550
Jackson Clarion-Ledger	43,045	100,657
Memphis Commercial Appeal	4,539	157,808
*USA Today**	2,428	1,674,376
Vicksburg Post	13,505	13,927

*See Sources and Explanations in the front of the volume.

Television stations and affiliations

Jackson	56%	WAPT	ABC
Jackson	56%	WDBD	WB
Jackson	56%	WJTV	CBS
Jackson	56%	WLBT	NBC
Jackson	56%	WMAU	PBS
Jackson	56%	WMPN	PBS
Greenwood-Greenville	31%	WABG	ABC
Greenwood-Greenville	31%	WLMT	UPN
Greenwood-Greenville	31%	WMAO	PBS
Greenwood-Greenville	31%	WXVT	CBS
Memphis, TN	10%	KVTJ	Independent
Memphis, TN	10%	WBUY	Independent
Memphis, TN	10%	WHBQ	FOX
Memphis, TN	10%	WKNO	PBS
Memphis, TN	10%	WMAE	PBS
Memphis, TN	10%	WMAV	PBS
Memphis, TN	10%	WMC	NBC
Memphis, TN	10%	WPTY	ABC, WB
Memphis, TN	10%	WPXX	PAX
Memphis, TN	10%	WREG	CBS
Columbus-Tupelo-West Point	3%	WCBI	CBS
Columbus-Tupelo-West Point	3%	WLOV	FOX
Columbus-Tupelo-West Point	3%	WMAB	PBS
Columbus-Tupelo-West Point	3%	WTVA	NBC

Cable systems and subscribers

Adelphia 10,097
Bailey Cable TV 1,320
Branch Cable 873
Broadband Cablevision 2,840
Cable Entertainment 860
Cable ONE 17,807
Cable TV of Belzoni 625

Cablevision   543
Charter   647
Cox   13,458
Galaxy   9,297
Mid-South Cablevision   4,758
Northland   4,103
Suscom   2,789
Time Warner   62,377
Vicksburg Video   12,179
Yazoo Answer Call   627

Military installations, September 2001
George Morris U.S. Army Reserve Center, Vicksburg   238

Businesses and other major employers
U.S. Army Corps of Engineers; Vicksburg   5,000
BellSouth Communications Inc.; Jackson; communication services   3,000
BL Development Corp.; Robinsonville; casino hotel   3,000
Grand Casinos Inc.; Robinsonville; casino hotel   3,000
Horseshoe Gaming Holding Corp.; Tunica; casino hotel   3,000
Mississippi Baptist Medical Center; Jackson   2,800
Mississippi Dept. of Transportation; Jackson   2,000
Boyd Gaming Corp.; Robinsonville; casino hotel   1,700
Delphi Corp.; Clinton; automotive wiring harness sets   1,700
Barden Mississippi Gaming; Robinsonville; casino hotel   1,500
Mississippi Dept. of Corrections; Drew   1,500
Triad Hospitals Inc.; Vicksburg   1,500
Vicksburg Healthcare Hospital; Vicksburg   1,500
Hollywood Casino-Tunica Inc.; Robinsonville; casino   1,300
Jackson State University; Jackson   1,300
Trustmark National Bank; Jackson; commercial bank   1,259
Ameristar Casino Vicksburg Inc.; Vicksburg; hotels   1,200
Cisco Systems Inc.; Jackson; telephone equipment and systems   1,200
Harrah's Tunica Corp.; Robinsonville; gambling and lottery services   1,200
Central Mississippi Medical Center; Jackson   1,150
Fitzgeralds Mississippi Inc.; Robinsonville; casino   1,100
MCI Worldcom Communications Inc.; Clinton; telephone communication   1,100
Olympia Bally's LP; Robinsonville; casino   1,077
PCS Tritel Inc.; Jackson; cellular telephones   1,000
Great Dane LP; Greenville; truck trailers   900
Tyson Foods Inc.; Jackson; feed milling, custom services   876
Circus Circus Mississippi Inc.; Robinsonville; casino   850
LeTourneau Inc.; Vicksburg; construction machinery   850
Alcorn State University; Lorman   812
Eaton Aerospace; Jackson; aircraft engines and parts   800
Saks Inc.; Jackson; department stores   800

City of Jackson; Jackson; police dept.   700
Entergy Operations Inc.; Port Gibson; electric services   700
Harrah's Entertainment Inc.; Vicksburg; hotels   700
MCI Worldcom Communications Inc.; Jackson; paging services   700
Mississippi Dept. of Health; Jackson   700
Riverboat Corp. of Mississippi; Vicksburg; riverboat casino   700
Skytel Communications Inc.; Jackson; radiotelephone communication   700
Greenwood Leflore Hospital; Greenwood   684
Delta Regional Medical Center; Greenville   633
Entergy Nuclear Generation Co.; Jackson; electric power generation   625
Northwest Mississippi Regional Medical Center; Clarksdale   616
Confish Inc.; Isola; fresh fish   600
Irvin Automotive Products Inc.; Greenwood; automobile and aircraft seat belts   600
MTD Products Inc.; Indianola; lawn mowers   600
National Energy Production Corp.; Sallis; power plant construction   600
Southern Farm Bureau Universal Life Insurance Co.; Jackson; life insurance   600
Tyson Foods Inc.; Cleveland; poultry processing   550
Mississippi Dept. of Human Services; Jackson   525
Delta State University; Cleveland   520
Alliance Gaming Corp.; Vicksburg; casino hotel   500
Anderson-Tully Co.; Vicksburg; sawmills and planing mills   500
Bally's Saloon Gambling Hall Hotel; Robinsonville; casino hotel   500
Brintons U.S. Axminster Inc.; Greenville; carpets   500
Kuhlman Electric Corp.; Crystal Springs; power switching equipment   500
U.S. Postal Service; Jackson   500
Wal-Mart Stores Inc.; Jackson   500

Mississippi 3rd District

East central to southwest — Jackson suburbs

The 3rd sprawls across 28 counties, moving from Oktibbeha and Noxubee Counties in the east central part of the state to the Mississippi River in the southwest corner. The GOP stronghold picks up Jackson's northeast corner and some of its mostly white northern and eastern suburbs.

Timber is dominant in the 3rd, but health care and defense also are important industries, especially in Meridian. A new Nissan plant—just outside the district in the neighboring 2nd—is expected to boost Jackson's economy. Small rural communities, filled with poultry and dairy farms, are prevalent. Rankin County is one of the fastest-growing regions of the state, spurred by nearby Jackson residents moving to the suburbs. Kemper and Noxubee Counties on the eastern border include areas as poor as the Delta.

The recession of the late 1980s and early 1990s decimated Natchez's oil and gas industry, but tourism helped the southwestern outpost's economy stay afloat; the small river city, with its antebellum homes and dockside casinos, attracts nearly 150,000 visitors per year.

Republicans now dominate the federal politics of the 3rd, as Democrats did for most of the twentieth century. George W. Bush took 64.3 percent of the vote in 2000. The new 3rd, created in redistricting following the 2000 census, combines the old 3rd and 4th districts to create a GOP district.

Major Industry

Timber, poultry, agriculture.

Notable

Some call Natchez, the oldest settled city on the Mississippi River (1716), the "City of Five Flags"—it has been controlled by the French, British, Spanish, the Confederacy, and the United States; Neshoba County is known as the site of an annual fair in Philadelphia, and as the place where three civil rights workers were murdered by members of the Ku Klux Klan in 1964, an event partly fictionalized for the movie *Mississippi Burning*.

Election Returns

	Republican		Democratic		Other	
President 2000	173,434	64.3%	93,454	34.7%	2,752	1.0%
House 2002	139,329	63.6%	76,184	34.8%	3,638	1.7%

District Profile

Population   711,115

Total area (square miles)   13,310.3
   Land area (square miles)   13,168.3

Population per square mile   54.0

Counties (2000 population)

Adams 34,340	Marion (pt.) 9,742
Amite 13,599	Neshoba 28,684
Covington 19,407	Newton 21,838
Franklin 8,448	Noxubee 12,548
Hinds (pt.) 31,832	Oktibbeha 42,902
Jasper (pt.) 7,163	Pike 38,940
Jefferson Davis 13,962	Rankin 115,327
Jones (pt.) 2,235	Scott 28,423
Kemper 10,453	Simpson 27,639
Lauderdale 78,161	Smith 16,182
Lawrence 13,258	Walthall 15,156
Leake (pt.) 9,579	Webster (pt.) 750
Lincoln 33,166	Wilkinson 10,312
Madison (pt.) 47,043	Winston (pt.) 20,026

Cities and other areas over 10,000 (2000 population)

Brandon 16,436	Natchez 18,464
Jackson (pt.) 31,832	Pearl 21,961
Madison (pt.) 14,603	Ridgeland 20,173
McComb 13,337	Starkville 21,869
Meridian 39,968	

Race and Hispanic or Latino origin*

White   63.7%
Black or African American   33.1%
American Indian or Alaska Native   0.9%
Asian   0.6%
Native Hawaiian or other Pacific Islander   0.0%
Some other race   0.0%
Hispanic or Latino origin   1.2%
Two or more races   0.5%

As percentage of total population.

Ancestry*

English 6.0%	Scotch-Irish 2.3%
French 1.5%	Scottish 1.3%
German 3.8%	USA/American 13.5%
Irish 6.1%	

As estimated percentage of total population.

Universities and colleges, 2000–2001 enrollment

Belhaven College, Jackson   1,594
Copiah-Lincoln Community College, Natchez   779
East Central Community College, Decatur   2,291
East Mississippi Community College, Scooba   2,534
Hinds Community College-Rankin Campus, Pearl*
Meridian Community College, Meridian   3,096
Millsaps College, Jackson   1,280
Mississippi State University, Mississippi State   16,561
Southwest Mississippi Community College, Summit   1,651

Enrollment under 100. See Sources and Explanations in the front of the volume.

Newspapers and circulation

	District circulation	Total circulation
Hattiesburg American	2,069	22,649
Jackson Clarion-Ledger	47,582	100,657
McComb Enterprise-Journal	11,634	11,634
Meridian Star	13,043	17,342
*USA Today**	2,080	1,674,376
West Point Daily Times Leader	6,521	6,919

See Sources and Explanations in the front of the volume.

Television stations and affiliations

Jackson	49%	WAPT	ABC
Jackson	49%	WDBD	WB
Jackson	49%	WJTV	CBS
Jackson	49%	WLBT	NBC
Jackson	49%	WMAU	PBS
Jackson	49%	WMPN	PBS
Meridian, AL	20%	WGBC	NBC
Meridian, AL	20%	WMDN	CBS
Meridian, AL	20%	WTOK	ABC
Columbus-Tupelo-West Point	13%	WCBI	CBS
Columbus-Tupelo-West Point	13%	WLOV	FOX
Columbus-Tupelo-West Point	13%	WMAB	PBS
Columbus-Tupelo-West Point	13%	WTVA	NBC
Baton Rouge, LA	11%	WAFB	CBS
Baton Rouge, LA	11%	WBRZ	ABC
Baton Rouge, LA	11%	WGMB	FOX
Baton Rouge, LA	11%	WLPB	PBS
Baton Rouge, LA	11%	WVLA	NBC
Hattiesburg-Laurel	7%	WDAM	NBC
Hattiesburg-Laurel	7%	WHLT	CBS
Hattiesburg-Laurel	7%	WMAW	PBS

Cable systems and subscribers

Branch Cable   1,290
Cable ONE   19,925
Cable South Inc.   1,274
Cable TV Inc.   1,387

Collins Communications 730
Comcast 20,187
Galaxy 4,097
Mediacom 5,363
Northland 15,975
Suscom 15,592
Time Warner 11,446
Video Inc. 1,178

Military installations, September 2001
Jackson International Airport, Flowood 1,170
Key Field Air National Guard, Meridian 1,035
Meridian Naval Air Station, Meridian 869

Businesses and other major employers
Mississippi State University; Mississippi State 6,213
Mississippi Band of Choctaw Indians; Philadelphia; Native American reservation 3,000
Mississippi Mental Health Dept.; Whitfield 2,200
Sanderson Farms Inc.; Summit; poultry processing 2,029
Rush Foundation Hospital; Meridian 1,900
St. Dominic Jackson Memorial Hospital; Jackson 1,880
Koch Foods; Morton; poultry processing 1,500
Peavey Electronics Corp.; Meridian; audio electronic systems 1,500
Koch Foods; Forest; poultry and poultry products 1,450
La-Z-Boy Inc.; Newton; furniture 1,325
Mississippi Mental Health Dept.; Meridian 1,200
Peco Foods Inc.; Bay Springs; poultry processing 1,200
Mississippi National Guard; Meridian 1,150
W. G. Yates and Sons Construction Co.; Philadelphia; building construction 1,110
Tyson Foods Inc.; Forest; poultry processing 1,026
Helmerich and Payne International Drilling Co.; Pearl; directional oil, gas well drilling 900
Southwest Mississippi Regional Medical Center; McComb 900
International Paper Co.; Natchez; pulp mills 897
Anderson Infirmary Benevolent Assn.; Meridian 881
Ellis Holding Co.; Brandon; fast-food restaurant chain 880
Emerson Electric Co.; Philadelphia; electric motors 800
Health Management Associates Inc.; Meridian; psychiatric hospitals 800
Koch Foods; McComb; fruit and vegetable markets 800
Blue Cross and Blue Shield of Mississippi; Jackson; hospital/medical service plans 777
Air Cruisers Co.; Liberty; air-supported rubber structures 750
River Oaks Hospital Inc.; Jackson 750
University of Mississippi Clinic; Jackson 736
Georgia-Pacific Corp.; Monticello; pulp produced from wood base 610
Cingular Wireless; Ridgeland; cellular telephones 600
Mississippi Methodist Hospital and Rehabilitation Center Inc.; Jackson 550
Multicraft International Ltd.; Madison; automotive electrical equipment 542

City of Meridian; Meridian; city government 530
Delphi Corp.; Meridian; automotive electrical equipment 500
Mississippi Dept. of Transportation; Newton 500
Peco Farms Inc.; Sebastopol; poultry processing 500
Rankin Medical Center; Brandon 500
Sara Lee Corp.; Forest; frozen bakery products 500
U.S. Veterans Hospital; Jackson 500
Wal-Mart Stores Inc.; McComb; discount department stores 500
Warner Inc.; Jackson; industrial, commercial cleaning services 500

Mississippi 4th District
Southeast — Gulf Coast, Hattiesburg

The pristine white Gulf Coast beaches of the 4th are surrounded by casino resorts that have popped up since Hancock and Harrison Counties changed their gaming laws in 1992. Despite slow statewide population growth during the 1990s, many parts of the 4th, including Hancock, experienced population booms. Small forested rural communities dominate where strip malls and suburban sprawl do not. The district's healthy economy and general lack of poverty differentiate it from the rest of the state.

The military, defense-related businesses—most notably Northrop Grumman's Ingalls shipbuilding yard in Pascagoula—and casinos are the dominant industries. Large medical facilities at Keesler Air Force Base and the University of Southern Mississippi, as well as new golf courses, have attracted retirees to the region.

The 4th, which includes the core of the old 5th District, picked up Clarke County, the rest of Wayne County, and parts of Marion, Jones, and Jasper Counties in redistricting following the 2000 census, but the additions are unlikely to change the political outlook of the district.

A conservative Democrat holds the 4th's congressional seat, but the district tends to swing between the parties locally. Republican presidential candidates won the district in 1992, 1996, and 2000.

Major Industry
Military, shipbuilding, casinos.

Notable
Sen. Trent Lott was the only Republican since 1877 to hold the area's congressional seat for more than one year—he held it from 1973 until 1989; Harrison County claims to have the largest man-made beach in the nation at 26 miles; Barq's Root Beer was created in 1898 by Edward Barq Sr. of Biloxi.

Election Returns

	Republican		Democratic		Other	
President 2000	154,997	65.3%	78,224	33.0%	4,152	1.7%
House 2002	34,373	21.2%	121,742	75.2%	5,753	3.6%

District Profile

Population 711,219

Total area (square miles) 9,535.9
   Land area (square miles) 8,700.8

Population per square mile 81.7

Counties (2000 population)

Clarke	17,955	Jones (pt.)	62,723
Forrest	72,604	Lamar	39,070
George	19,144	Marion (pt.)	15,853
Greene	13,299	Pearl River	48,621
Hancock	42,967	Perry	12,138
Harrison	189,601	Stone	13,622
Jackson	131,420	Wayne	21,216
Jasper (pt.)	10,986		

Cities and other areas over 10,000 (2000 population)

Biloxi	50,644	Long Beach	17,320
Gautier	11,681	Moss Point	15,851
Gulfport	71,127	Ocean Springs	17,225
Hattiesburg	44,779	Pascagoula	26,200
Laurel	18,393	Picayune	10,535

Race and Hispanic or Latino origin*

White 73.5%
Black or African American 22.1%
American Indian or Alaska Native 0.3%
Asian 1.2%
Native Hawaiian or other Pacific Islander 0.0%
Some other race 0.1%
Hispanic or Latino origin 1.8%
Two or more races 0.9%

*As percentage of total population.

Ancestry*

English	6.3%	Italian	2.2%
French	4.7%	Scotch-Irish	1.8%
German	6.0%	Scottish	1.3%
Irish	7.3%	USA/American	13.4%

*As estimated percentage of total population.

Universities and colleges, 2000–2001 enrollment

Jones County Junior College, Ellisville 4,514
Mississippi Gulf Coast Community College, Perkinston 8,768
Pearl River Community College, Poplarville 2,800
University of Southern Mississippi, Hattiesburg 14,509
William Carey College, Hattiesburg 2,402

Newspapers and circulation

	District circulation	Total circulation
Biloxi Sun Herald	46,255	47,650
Hattiesburg American	20,153	22,649
Jackson Clarion-Ledger	4,698	100,657
Laurel Leader-Call	6,777	7,354
Meridian Star	2,748	17,342
Mississippi Press	19,487	19,709
Mobile Register	1,457	97,781
New Orleans Times-Picayune	3,444	256,823
Picayune Item	6,060	6,060
*USA Today**	3,915	1,674,376

*See Sources and Explanations in the front of the volume.

Television stations and affiliations

Hattiesburg-Laurel	40%	WDAM	NBC
Hattiesburg-Laurel	40%	WHLT	CBS
Hattiesburg-Laurel	40%	WMAW	PBS
Biloxi-Gulfport	31%	WLOX	ABC
Biloxi-Gulfport	31%	WMAH	PBS
Biloxi-Gulfport	31%	WXXV	FOX
New Orleans	14%	WDSU	NBC
New Orleans	14%	WGNO	ABC
New Orleans	14%	WHNO	Independent
New Orleans	14%	WLAE	PBS
New Orleans	14%	WNOL	WB
New Orleans	14%	WPXL	PAX
New Orleans	14%	WUPL	UPN
New Orleans	14%	WVUE	FOX
New Orleans	14%	WWL	CBS
New Orleans	14%	WYES	PBS
Mobile-Pensacola (Ft. Walton Beach)	8%	WALA	FOX
Mobile-Pensacola (Ft. Walton Beach)	8%	WAWD	Independent
Mobile-Pensacola (Ft. Walton Beach)	8%	WEAR	ABC
Mobile-Pensacola (Ft. Walton Beach)	8%	WEIQ	PBS
Mobile-Pensacola (Ft. Walton Beach)	8%	WFGX	Independent
Mobile-Pensacola (Ft. Walton Beach)	8%	WHBR	Independent
Mobile-Pensacola (Ft. Walton Beach)	8%	WJTC	UPN
Mobile-Pensacola (Ft. Walton Beach)	8%	WKRG	CBS
Mobile-Pensacola (Ft. Walton Beach)	8%	WMPV	Independent
Mobile-Pensacola (Ft. Walton Beach)	8%	WPAN	Independent
Mobile-Pensacola (Ft. Walton Beach)	8%	WPMI	NBC
Mobile-Pensacola (Ft. Walton Beach)	8%	WSRE	PBS
Meridian, AL	7%	WGBC	NBC
Meridian, AL	7%	WMDN	CBS
Meridian, AL	7%	WTOK	ABC

Cable systems and subscribers

Cable ONE 85,456
Charter 5,185
Comcast 31,266
Galaxy 2,400
Mediacom 5,323
Twin County Cablevision 2,466

Military installations, September 2001

Keesler Air Force Base, Biloxi 7,060
CBC Gulfport (Navy), Gulfport 4,947
Camp Shelby Military Training Area, Hattiesburg 2,113
NS Pascagoula, Pascagoula 1,928
Gulfport-Biloxi Regional Airport, Gulfport 452

Businesses and other major employers

Northrop Grumman Ship Systems; Pascagoula; combat vessels 4,000
Grand Casinos of Mississippi Inc.; Biloxi; casino hotel 3,500
Beau Rivage Resorts Inc.; Biloxi; casino hotel 3,145
University of Southern Mississippi; Hattiesburg 2,900
Howard Industries Inc.; Laurel; electric power transformers 2,742
Dictaphone Corp.; Bay St. Louis; video cameras, recorders 2,500
Forrest County General Hospital; Hattiesburg 2,500
Bank of Wiggins; Wiggins; banking and finance consultant 1,940
Memorial Hospital at Gulfport; Gulfport; hospital 1,850
Sunbeam Products Inc.; Hattiesburg; electronic parts and equipment 1,800
Singing River Hospital System; Pascagoula 1,700
U.S. Veterans Hospital; Biloxi 1,700
Mississippi Mental Health Dept.; Ellisville 1,500
BSL Inc.; Bay St. Louis; casino hotel 1,240
Imperial Palace of Mississippi Inc.; Biloxi; casino hotel 1,200

Treasure Bay Corp.; Biloxi; casino hotel   1,200
Mississippi Gulf Coast Community College; Perkinston   1,100
South Central Regional Medical Center; Laurel   1,082
BTN Inc.; Biloxi; casino   1,000
Masonite Corp.; Laurel; fiberboard, wood   1,000
Biloxi Casino Corp.; Biloxi; casino   900
New Palace Casino; Biloxi; gambling and lottery services   900
ContiGroup Companies Inc.; Laurel; poultry processing   850
Friede Goldman Halter Inc.; Pascagoula; shipbuilding and repairing   800
President Riverboat Casino-Mississippi Inc.; Biloxi; gambling   800
Sunbeam Products Inc.; Waynesboro; electric blankets   800
Hattiesburg Medical Clinic Professional Assn.; Hattiesburg   777
Kellogg Brown and Root Inc.; Pascagoula; highway and street construction   762
Marshall Durbin Food Corp.; Hattiesburg; processed poultry   758
Gulf Coast Community Hospital Inc.; Biloxi   750
Gulfport Building Inc.; Gulfport; building maintenance   750
Wesley Health Systems Hospital; Hattiesburg   716
Burlington Industries Inc.; Stonewall; denims   700

Lamar County School District; Purvis   700
Medical Systems Inc.; Hattiesburg; medical help service   700
Sanderson Farms Inc.; Laurel; poultry processing   675
E. I. Du Pont De Nemours and Co.; Pass Christian; industrial inorganic chemicals   643
Mississippi Mental Health Dept.; Long Beach   615
Mississippi Space Services; Bay St. Louis; space research and technology   604
Lockheed Martin Space Operations Co.; Bay St. Louis; aircraft   600
Mississippi Dept. of Transportation; Hattiesburg   600
Wal-Mart Stores Inc.; Gulfport; discount department stores   600
Gulfside Casinos Inc.; Gulfport; casino   550
Johnson Controls World Services Inc.; Bay St. Louis; building maintenance   523
American Medical Response Inc.; Gulfport; local passenger transportation   500
Chevron Phillips Chemical Co.; Pascagoula; plastics materials and resins   500
Friede Goldman Offshore Inc.; Pascagoula; dies, tools, jigs, fixtures   500
Howard Industries Inc.; Laurel; contract haulers   500
Mississippi Dept. of Corrections; Leakesville   500
University of Southern Mississippi; Long Beach   500
Wal-Mart Stores Inc.; Hattiesburg   500

Districts established June 1, 2001, for elections first held in 2002.

9 members

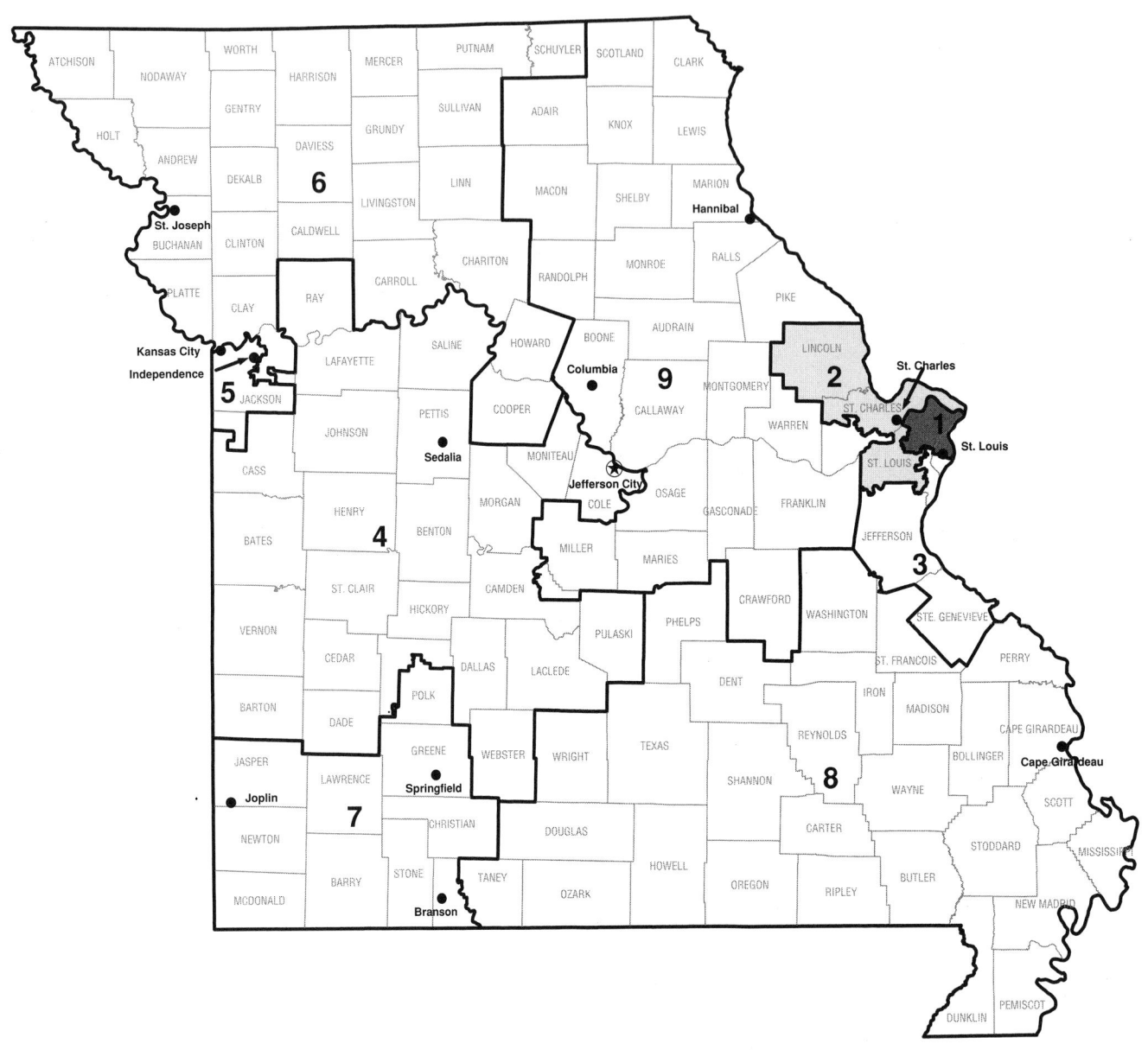

Missouri

Missouri comes in at number 25 in the alphabetical list of the 50 states and appears smack in the middle of the map of the contiguous 48. It is also the home of the national population midpoint as of the 2000 census. As with the country as a whole, it has seen its population move from the farms to small towns to big cities and back out to the suburbs. The mix of education and income levels here closely resembles the national numbers for each, as do the numbers for white and black people. Remarkably, it has voted with the winner in every presidential election since 1900 save one. (The curious exception: it went for Adlai Stevenson in the midst of Dwight Eisenhower's landslide in 1956.)

That is why some Missourians have long advertised their state as a good core sample of the nation as a whole. But others prefer a less generic image for the state, something like the gimlet-eyed skepticism expressed in the state's motto: the Show Me State. This is not a state for frills. Aside from the grandeur of the passing rivers and the rolling loveliness of the Ozarks in the south, the landscape is undramatic. It was good for farming, and Missourians were farmers for a long time. Nostalgia for the past is almost palpable in parts of this state.

Historically, Missouri lent its name to the famous congressional compromise of 1820 that determined which territories would have legal slavery and which would not. Missouri itself entered the Union the following year on the slave-holding side, but being in the middle of things, Missouri had plenty of people on both sides of the question—before, during, and after the Civil War.

The most exciting thing about the state's first century was the city of St. Louis, which became the first gateway to the developing West. Even today the landmark of the city is its Gateway Arch, erected in the late twentieth century. Situated near the confluence of the Mississippi and Missouri Rivers, this city attracted migrants from every state and many of the countries of Europe, particularly Germans seeking asylum after the political upheavals of 1848. St. Louis proper reached its zenith half a century later when it was the nation's fourth largest city and its burghers were busy erecting museums and other public buildings as monuments to their wealth and civic pride. The World's Fair came here in 1904, as if to affix the final imprimatur of global importance.

But all this eminence turned out to be a peak. To the north, Chicago won the battle for the railroads and Detroit became the leading automaker, both developments that increased the importance of other cities on the Great Lakes. To the West, the movement St. Louis helped happen soon created competing centers of growth on the Pacific and then in the interior as well. And as the century wore on, St. Louis lost ground even within its own state to Kansas City, which St. Louis residents had long regarded as a simple cow town.

Besides competition, St. Louis was done in by a case of white flight matched by few other central cities. Although African Americans had been part of the city's mix from the early 1800s, their arrival in greater numbers from the Depression South eventually made the north side of the city majority black. This dynamic dovetailed with postwar governmental policies of the 1940s and 1950s that built freeways and otherwise encouraged suburban growth. Soon there were more people in St. Louis County than in St. Louis the city (the two are legally separate). As this trend intensified and fed upon itself, much of St. Louis took on the look of an abandoned city. Soon blacks too were joining the move across the city line, seeking better schools, neighborhoods, and services.

Between 1950 and 1980, the population of St. Louis was cut in half, and its political influence was downgraded even further. In 1948 the city itself had cast 22 percent of the state's vote for president; just 8 percent in 1980; and only 5.3 percent in 2000. St. Louis County, by contrast, cast more than four times as many votes. As of the 2000 census, St. Louis is the second largest city in the state behind Kansas City, even though the St. Louis metro remains about twice the size of its cross-state rival.

All this has contributed to Missouri's shift from traditional Democratic ties to two-party politics, with Republicans enjoying a slight edge as of the early years after 2000. Like the other border states, Missouri tended to elect Democrats but tolerated Republicans through most of the century after the Civil War. In good times it might elect a Republican governor or senator, and it always had a Republican enclave in its deep southwestern corner, where the neighbors were Kansans and a hill-dwelling breed of Arkansans who had always been pro-Union.

Some of this dynamic remains in the district today. The largest city, Springfield, is the home of the Assembly of God branch of Pentecostalism, and not coincidentally the hometown of George W. Bush's attorney general, John Ashcroft, a former governor and senator from Missouri. The other southwestern city, Joplin, first went Republican after Woodrow Wilson allowed tin imports from South America and devastated the local tin mine.

But Republicans did not have an era of their own statewide until John Danforth emerged on the scene in the late 1960s. Danforth was an heir to the Ralston-Purina fortune in

St. Louis, a Princeton graduate with additional degrees in law and divinity from Yale. Although an ordained Episcopal priest, he chose politics for his ministry and was elected the state's attorney general in 1968, as Richard Nixon was carrying the state. Danforth served in this job until he was elected to the Senate in 1976, and along the way he fostered the careers of other ambitious young Republicans, including Christopher "Kit" Bond and Ashcroft, both of whom would be elected governor and then senator.

Missourians have always been on the conservative side on social issues—including race, abortion, and school prayer—and that fact gave Republicans an opening. Ashcroft, in particular, embodied this spirit when he was attorney general, filing a famous case that led the U.S. Supreme Court to allow state-imposed limits on abortions. Ashcroft's appeal to religious voters and other conservatives on such issues was combined with an antitax program that has also benefited the GOP in Missouri, a traditionally low-tax state, in recent decades. Outside the St. Louis and Kansas City metro areas, roughly 100 rural counties were historically Democratic. But these issues have made them reliably Republican in recent elections.

Democrats, however, still carry the metro areas on the strength of their vote in the cities and near suburbs. They also made something of a comeback in the state with the governorship of Mel Carnahan (1993–2000), who hailed from the small, central city of Rolla. But Carnahan was killed in a plane crash just weeks before his showdown with Ashcroft in the Senate race of 2000. Carnahan won the vote posthumously, and his replacement as governor, Bob Holden, appointed the widow, Jean Carnahan, to fill the seat for two years. In 2002 Mrs. Carnahan was defeated by Republican Jim Talent in a tight race that indicated once again how closely matched the two parties are in the state.

Redistricting in Missouri was completed before the election year of 2002 even began. Holden, still governor, was lucky to have nearly all the state's nine House members, Republican and Democrat, approve the compromise (drawn to protect them all) and avoid a confrontation in the split-control Legislature. The job was also simplified by the manageable and well-distributed population change during the 1990s. Missouri was glad to see its numbers going up again (9 percent), even though its rate was thirtieth in the nation. A freshman Republican from the St. Louis County 2nd District protested the split of some suburbs northwest of the city between his and another district. But he wound up with a constituency that gave 58.6 percent of its vote to George W. Bush in 2000 (his old district had given 55 percent).

Other changes in the St. Louis area pushed the line between the two Democratic districts (the 1st and the 3rd further south) that balances the population numbers after a decade of slow growth in the north side 1st but keeping it just under 50 percent African American. The 3rd District, represented by Richard Gephardt since 1977, the House Democratic leader until he stepped down after the 2002 election, was shored up by the Democrats on the expectation he would run for president in 2004 (and a potential successor Democrat would need more help).

On the western side of the state, even fewer changes were necessary to achieve the population balance and political satisfaction required for approval. The traditionally Democratic 5th District entails Kansas City proper and much of the surrounding Jackson County, plus a tailhook section of

Cass County to the south. The northern suburbs are in the 6th District, which runs north to the Iowa line and east half way across the state. The far southern and southeastern regions of metro Kansas City, traditional Democratic territory, are in the 4th.

Down in the southwestern corner of the state is the 7th District, which in addition to burgeoning Springfield has the vacationland to its south around Branson. This has become Nashville's home away from home, drawing 7 million visitors a year to its theaters and country music halls. More recently it has sent Republican Roy Blunt to the Congress, watching him ascend to the number three GOP leadership job in the House in just a few elected terms.

The 7th shares the Ozarks with the much larger 8th District on its east. This "Bootheel" section of Missouri closely resembles its Arkansas neighbors to the south. Its most famous son may be Cape Girardeau native Rush Limbaugh. Democratic for generations, it has now been in Republican hands long enough to seem comfortably so. And the same can be said of the "Little Dixie" northeastern 9th District, which takes in part of the state capital area around Jefferson City, all of the University of Missouri home campus at Columbia, and nearly all the state's northeast quadrant (including the Mark Twain boyhood home at Hannibal).

Table 1 Population

District	Population	Population under 18	Voting-age population	Median age	Male*	Female*
1	621,690	164,665	457,025	35.4	46.5	53.5
2	621,690	169,886	451,804	36.6	48.8	51.2
3	621,690	153,832	467,858	35.7	48.3	51.7
4	621,690	158,471	463,219	36.7	49.9	50.1
5	621,691	159,010	462,681	35.3	48.1	51.9
6	621,690	157,612	464,078	36.4	49.2	50.8
7	621,690	152,303	469,387	35.8	48.7	51.3
8	621,690	155,944	465,746	37.7	48.8	51.2
9	621,690	155,969	465,721	35.4	49.2	50.8
State	5,595,211	1,427,692	4,167,519	36.1	48.6	51.4

*As percentage of total population.

Table 2 Voting-Age Persons by Race/Hispanic or Latino Origin

District	White*	Black or African American*	American Indian or Alaska Native*	Asian*	Other or multirace*	Hispanic or Latino*
1	50.0	45.8	0.2	1.7	1.1	1.2
2	93.9	2.1	0.2	2.0	0.7	1.2
3	87.7	7.6	0.2	1.7	1.2	1.6
4	93.0	3.2	0.5	0.7	1.0	1.6
5	69.9	21.8	0.4	1.4	1.5	4.9
6	93.1	2.8	0.4	0.9	0.8	2.0
7	93.8	1.2	0.9	0.8	1.4	2.1
8	93.6	3.6	0.6	0.5	1.0	0.8
9	93.2	3.8	0.3	0.9	0.8	0.9
State	85.4	10.1	0.4	1.1	1.1	1.8

*As percentage of voting-age population.

Table 3 Voting-Age Population by Age Groups

District	18 to 24*	25 to 44*	45 to 64*	Over 64*
1	13.0	39.1	29.1	18.8
2	10.2	41.5	32.7	15.6

District	18 to 24*	25 to 44*	45 to 64*	Over 64*
3	12.4	42.0	28.4	17.3
4	12.8	37.2	30.6	19.3
5	12.3	41.6	28.6	17.5
6	12.5	39.5	30.3	17.7
7	14.8	37.1	29.8	18.4
8	12.3	35.4	31.3	21.1
9	15.5	37.9	29.2	17.4
State	12.9	39.0	30.0	18.1

*As percentage of voting-age population.

Table 4   Income and Occupation

District	Median family income	Families in poverty*	White collar†	Blue collar†	Service†	Farm†
1	$44,444	12.4	61.9	20.7	17.3	0.1
2	$70,863	2.5	71.3	17.5	11.1	0.1
3	$50,835	7.4	60.4	24.2	15.3	0.1
4	$40,995	8.9	51.4	31.9	15.5	1.2
5	$47,363	9.4	61.8	22.7	15.3	0.1
6	$49,428	6.2	58.6	25.9	14.6	0.9
7	$39,859	9.0	55.0	28.5	15.7	0.8
8	$33,951	13.7	47.7	34.5	16.0	1.8
9	$45,159	7.7	54.4	29.7	15.0	0.9
State	$46,044	8.6	58.3	26.0	15.0	0.6

*As percentage of all families.   †As percentage of employed workers 16 years and over.

Table 5   Education: School Years Completed

District	Less than grade 9*	Grades 9–12 no diploma*	High school diploma no college*	Some college*	College bachelor's degree or higher*
1	6.3	13.7	28.5	29.1	22.4
2	3.1	6.1	23.5	29.0	38.3
3	6.8	12.7	29.8	27.5	23.2
4	7.5	12.9	38.7	25.3	15.6
5	4.6	12.6	30.1	29.8	22.9
6	4.6	9.7	36.4	28.1	21.2
7	5.6	12.7	34.6	28.3	18.8
8	12.8	16.8	37.3	21.2	11.9
9	7.5	12.0	35.7	24.8	19.9
State	6.5	12.1	32.7	27.0	21.6

*As percentage of persons age 25 and over.

Table 6   Housing and Residential Patterns

District	Median home value	Owner occupied*	Renter occupied*	Urban†	Rural†
1	$72,200	62.1	37.9	99.2	0.8
2	$144,200	81.5	18.5	91.7	8.4
3	$94,000	69.0	31.0	86.7	13.3
4	$79,700	73.5	26.5	39.9	60.1
5	$82,600	62.4	37.6	96.1	3.9
6	$90,600	72.0	28.0	66.3	33.7
7	$81,400	68.8	31.2	59.1	40.9
8	$62,000	72.0	28.0	39.6	60.4
9	$84,600	72.6	27.4	45.8	54.2
State	$86,900	70.3	29.7	69.4	30.6

*As percentage of occupied housing units.   †As percentage of total population.

Missouri 1st District

North St. Louis; northeast St. Louis County

Flanked by the Mississippi and Missouri Rivers, the St. Louis-based 1st is a mixture of poor center-city communities and middle-class suburbs. Redistricting following the 2000 census extended the district further west in St. Louis County to offset a population decline fueled by crime and deteriorating housing conditions.

The 1st takes in the northern half of St. Louis, including most of the city's popular attractions, such as the Gateway Arch and Forest Park, which attracts more than 12 million visitors a year. Many of the area's largest employers are scattered throughout the 1st, including BJC HealthCare, one of the largest nonprofit health care organizations in the United States.

Suburbs in St. Louis County include the region's main airport (one of the nation's ten busiest) and a Boeing jet plant added in redistricting. Residents here are concerned about Ford's plan to close its Hazelwood assembly plant by about 2005.

By far the state's most heavily Democratic district, the 1st handed Al Gore a 46-point victory in 2000. Local and state contests almost always favor Democrats. The black population, which stood at just under 60 percent after the 1990 census, has decreased considerably, though African Americans still make up almost 50 percent of district voters.

Deep state budget cuts have led to cutbacks in city spending, making education, health care, and housing key issues for voters at the polls. Allegations of voting fraud in the 2000 Senate and gubernatorial elections thrust St. Louis into the national debate over an election standards bill and made officials eager to replace the district's aging voting equipment.

Major Industry

Manufacturing, aircraft, higher education.

Notable

The Missouri History Museum, St. Louis Art Museum, St. Louis Zoo, and St. Louis Science Center are located in 1,400-acre Forest Park, which calls itself the nation's seventh-largest urban park.

Election Returns

	Republican		Democratic		Other	
President 2000	65,686	26.0%	182,323	72.1%	5,022	2.0%
House 2002	51,755	27.1%	133,946	70.1%	5,354	2.8%

District Profile

Population   621,690

Total area (square miles)   226.9
   Land area (square miles)   217.1

Population per square mile   2,863.6

Counties (2000 population)
   St. Louis (pt.)   458,670
   St. Louis city (pt.)   163,020

Cities and other areas over 10,000 (2000 population)

Bellefontaine Neighbors   11,271
Berkeley   10,063
Bridgeton   15,550
Creve Coeur (pt.)   16,157
Ferguson   22,406
Florissant   50,497
Hazelwood   26,206
Jennings   15,469
Maryland Heights (pt.)   12,220
Overland   16,838
Spanish Lake CDP   21,337
St. Ann   13,607
St. Louis (pt.)   163,020
University City (pt.)   24,075

Race and Hispanic or Latino origin*

White   45.8%
Black or African American   49.7%
American Indian or Alaska Native   0.2%
Asian   1.5%
Native Hawaiian or other Pacific Islander   0.0%
Some other race   0.1%
Hispanic or Latino origin   1.3%
Two or more races   1.3%

*As percentage of total population.

Ancestry*

English 4.3%	Italian 2.6%
French 2.2%	Polish 1.7%
German 13.6%	Subsaharan 1.2%
Irish 7.8%	USA/American 2.9%

*As estimated percentage of total population.

Universities and colleges, 2000–2001 enrollment

Aquinas Institute of Theology, St. Louis   250
Covenant Theological Seminary, St. Louis   789
Harris-Stowe State College, St. Louis   1,835
Hickey School, St. Louis   380
ITT Technical Institute, Earth City   533
Jewish Hospital-College of Nursing and Allied Health, St. Louis   413
Keller Graduate School of Management, St. Louis*
Missouri Baptist College, St. Louis   2,806
Missouri Technical School, St. Louis   204
Ranken Technical College, St. Louis   1,329
Sanford-Brown College, Hazelwood   323
St. Louis College of Pharmacy, St. Louis   915
St. Louis Community College-Florissant Valley, St. Louis   6,690
St. Louis University, St. Louis   13,847
University of Missouri-St. Louis, St. Louis   15,397
Vatterott College, St. Ann   337
Washington University, St. Louis   12,118

*Enrollment under 100. See Sources and Explanations in the front of the volume.

Newspapers and circulation

	District circulation	Total circulation
St. Louis Post-Dispatch	67,883	295,281
*USA Today**	9,561	1,674,376

*See Sources and Explanations in the front of the volume.

Television stations and affiliations

St. Louis	100%	KDNL	ABC
St. Louis	100%	KETC	PBS
St. Louis	100%	KMOV	CBS
St. Louis	100%	KNLC	Independent
St. Louis	100%	KPLR	WB
St. Louis	100%	KSDK	NBC
St. Louis	100%	KTVI	FOX
St. Louis	100%	WHSL	Independent
St. Louis	100%	WPXS	PAX

Cable systems and subscribers

Charter   191,449

Military installations, September 2001

Lambert/St. Louis International Airport (Air National Guard), St. Ann   1,245
St. Louis #3/Sverdrup U.S. Army Reserve, St. Louis   167

Businesses and other major employers

Southwestern Bell Telephone Co.; St. Louis; local/long-distance telephone   10,000
St. Louis University School of Social Service; St. Louis   5,752
Daughters of Charity of St. Vincent De Paul; St. Louis; religious organization   5,388
St. John's Mercy Medical Center Inc.; St. Louis   4,541
Tyco Healthcare Group; Hazelwood; medical instruments   4,100
A. G. Edwards and Sons Inc.; St. Louis; security brokers, dealers   4,000
BJC HealthCare System; St. Louis; hospital management   4,000
St. Louis University; St. Louis   3,688
Union Electric Development Corp.; St. Louis; electric power generation   3,200
Barnes-Jewish Hospital; St. Louis   3,000
University of Missouri System; St. Louis   2,524
Ford Motor Co.; Hazelwood; automobile assembly plant   2,500
Washington University; St. Louis   2,461
City of St. Louis; St. Louis; police dept.   2,290
St. Louis Children's Hospital; St. Louis   2,078
AT&T Corp.; St. Louis; telephone communication   2,000
Boeing Co.; Hazelwood; systems integration services   2,000
McDonnell Douglas Corp.; St. Louis; search and navigation equipment   2,000
Tenet Healthcare Corp.; St. Louis; job training and related services   2,000
Union Pacific Railroad Co.; St. Louis; freight hauling   2,000
Alberici Constructors Inc.; St. Louis; industrial buildings, warehouses   1,800
Hussmann International Inc.; Bridgeton; refrigeration and heating equipment   1,800
U.S. Veterans Hospital; St. Louis   1,800
WellPoint Health Networks Inc.; St. Louis; hospital/medical service plans   1,800
Missouri National Guard; Bridgeton   1,650
St. Louis University Hospital; St. Louis   1,600
AmerenUE; St. Louis; electric power generation   1,500

Cardinal Glennon Childrens Hospital; St. Louis   1,500
May Department Stores Co.; St. Louis   1,417
GKN Aerospace North America Inc.; St. Louis; aircraft parts, equipment   1,300
Varsity Group Inc.; St. Louis; employee leasing service 1,300
Christian Hospital Northeast-Northwest Inc.; St. Louis 1,226
De Paul Health Center Inc.; Bridgeton   1,200
Kiel Center Partners; St. Louis; auditorium operation 1,200
MCI Worldcom Network Services Inc.; St. Louis; telephone communications   1,200
Mercantile Bank; St. Louis; commercial bank   1,200
Nestle Purina Petcare Co.; St. Louis; dog and cat food 1,200
Spectrum Healthcare Resources Inc.; St. Louis; personnel management   1,100
Mitch Murch's Maintenance Management; St. Louis; janitorial service   1,006
City of St. Louis; St. Louis; city government   1,000
Intensive Maintenance Care Inc.; St. Louis; janitorial service   1,000
Mallinckrodt Inc.; Hazelwood; medical instruments 1,000
U.S. Veterans Medical Center; St. Louis   1,000
State Street Bank and Trust Co.; St. Louis; state trust company   940
Clean Tech Co; St. Louis; janitorial service   900
Interstate Brands Corp.; St. Louis; bread baking   900
Missouri Sportservice Inc.; St. Louis; concessionaire 900
President Riverboat Casinos-Missouri Inc.; St. Louis; gambling   900
McDonnell Douglas Corp.; Hazelwood; computers   860
CPI Corp.; St. Louis; photographer   837
Federal Reserve Bank of St Louis; St. Louis   814
Forest Pharmaceuticals Inc.; Earth City; pharmaceuticals 800
Interstate Cleaning Corp.; St. Louis; janitorial service 800
Jacobs Engineering Group Inc.; St. Louis; architectural services   800
Jewish Community Centers; St. Louis; social associations 800
Lear Corp.; St. Louis; automobile seats   800
MCI Worldcom Network Services Inc.; Earth City; long-distance telephone   800
Physician Groups; St. Louis; health services consultant 800
TWA Airlines; St. Ann; air transportation   800
Witt-Fiala-Flannery and Associates Inc.; St. Louis; janitorial service   800
Quest Diagnostics Clinical Laboratories Inc.; St. Louis; medical laboratories   750
Alvey Systems Inc.; St. Louis; industrial machinery/ equipment   700
BioMerieux Inc.; Hazelwood; medical help service   700
Cervantes Convention Center at Americas Center; St. Louis; trade show arrangement   700
Consumer Programs Inc.; St. Louis; photographer   700
TWA Airlines; St. Louis; aircraft maintenance, repair 700

U.S. Postal Service; Hazelwood   700
Watlow Electric Manufacturing Co.; St. Louis; industrial electric heating units   700
National General Assurance Co.; St. Louis; automobile insurance   650
Missouri-Illinois Bi-State Development Agency; St. Louis; commuter bus operation   644
Deloro Stellite Co.; St. Louis; coating of metals and formed products   633
U.S. Agriculture Dept. Rural Housing Service; St. Louis 633
HealthLink Inc.; St. Louis; health maintenance organization   630
SuperValu Inc.; Hazelwood; food supplier   620
National General Insurance Co.; Earth City; property damage insurance   611
Laclede Gas Co.; St. Louis; natural gas distribution   605
Crane Co.; Hazelwood; vending machines   600
Marriott International Inc.; St. Louis; hotels   600
PS Services Inc.; St. Louis; security guard service   600
Systems and Electronics Inc.; St. Louis; semitrailers 600
Western Union Financial Services Inc.; Bridgeton; telegraph communications   600
American Red Cross; St. Louis; blood bank   550
HBE Corp.; St. Louis; hotels   550
MGI Services Corp.; St. Louis; janitorial service   550
Coburn Thompson; St. Louis; general practice law office 530
St. Louis City; St. Louis; airport   530
Missouri Dept. of Social Services; St. Louis   520
Ceres Investment Co.; St. Louis; security brokers, dealers 506
Emerson Electric Co.; Maryland Heights; relays and industrial controls   505
Allied Security Inc.; St. Louis; protective services, guard 500
Bridge Information Systems America Inc.; St. Louis; information retrieval services   500
Business Response Inc.; St. Louis; mailing service   500
Compass Group USA Inc.; Hazelwood; administrative management   500
Conopco Inc.; St. Louis; detergents   500
Corrigan Brothers Inc.; St. Louis; heating/air conditioning contractor   500
Creative Management Service; St. Louis; planning consultant   500
Detroit Technologies Inc.; St. Louis; motor vehicle parts/accessories   500
Dial Corp.; St. Louis; polishes and sanitation goods   500
Integon Specialty Insurance Co.; Earth City; insurance agents and brokers   500
May Department Stores Co.; St. Ann; department stores 500
McDonnell Douglas Corp.; St. Louis; airplanes   500
Mosby Inc.; St. Louis; book publishing   500
Sigma Chemical Co.; St. Louis; biological products   500
Saint Louis ConnectCare; St. Louis; home health care services   500
Stella ABG Acquisition Inc.; Hazelwood; blood, body fluid analyzers   500
TWA Airlines; St. Louis; air passenger carrier   500

U.S. Army Corps of Engineers; St. Louis   500
United Parcel Service Inc.; St. Louis; courier services
  500
Washington University in St. Louis; St. Louis   500

Missouri 2nd District

Western St. Louis County; north and eastern St. Charles County — St. Charles

Composed mostly of upper-middle-class white suburbanites, the 2nd is one of the state's richest and fastest-growing districts. Western St. Louis and St. Charles Counties continue to prosper from a westward migration started by mass population departures from St. Louis in the 1980s.

Commuter traffic into the St. Louis business district remains heavy, but local residents are increasingly finding lucrative jobs away from the city. Boeing employs many 2nd District residents, though redistricting following the 2000 census moved the company's main manufacturing facility into the neighboring 1st District. DaimlerChrysler and a General Motors plant in Wentzville are major employers, along with biotechnology and financial services companies. A dwindling but diverse agriculture industry supports the northern fringes around the Mississippi-Missouri River junction.

Although Democrats held the 2nd during most of the latter part of the twentieth century, Republicans have dominated in recent years. GOP presidential candidates won the district in 1992, 1996, and 2000, and Republicans have an edge in state and local races.

Wealthy communities such as Ladue and Frontenac are unshakably Republican, and the removal of union-laden Florissant, St. Ann, and Bridgeton during redistricting moved the district further into the GOP column. Lincoln County, added in redistricting, threw a Democratic-leaning constituency into the mix, but the 2nd supported George W. Bush by a 58.6 percent to 39.1 percent tally in the 2000 presidential race, a 7 percentage point gain over Bush's victory margin under the old boundaries.

Major Industry

Auto manufacturing, biotechnology, agriculture.

Notable

Route 66 State Park near Eureka is located on what was Times Beach, the site of an environmental disaster where soil became tainted with dioxin.

Election Returns

	Republican		Democratic		Other	
President 2000	179,633	58.6%	119,907	39.1%	6,744	2.2%
House 2002	167,057	67.1%	77,223	31.0%	4,548	1.8%

District Profile

Population   621,690

Total area (square miles)   1,287.9
  Land area (square miles)   1,247.8

Population per square mile   498.2

Counties (2000 population)

Lincoln	38,944	St. Louis (pt.)	337,065
St. Charles (pt.)	245,681		

Cities and other areas over 10,000 (2000 population)

Ballwin   31,283
Chesterfield   46,802
Concord CDP (pt.)   14,358
Kirkwood (pt.)   24,325
Manchester   19,161
Maryland Heights (pt.)   13,536
O'Fallon (pt.)   44,949
St. Charles   60,321
St. Peters (pt.)   50,001
Town and Country (pt.)   10,894
Wildwood   32,884

Race and Hispanic or Latino origin*

White   93.2%
Black or African American   2.2%
American Indian or Alaska Native   0.2%
Asian   2.0%
Native Hawaiian or other Pacific Islander   0.0%
Some other race   0.1%
Hispanic or Latino origin   1.4%
Two or more races   0.9%

As percentage of total population.

Ancestry*

Dutch	1.3%	Italian	4.2%
English	8.2%	Polish	2.3%
French	3.6%	Scotch-Irish	1.2%
German	26.7%	Scottish	1.3%
Irish	12.7%	USA/American	4.8%

As estimated percentage of total population.

Universities and colleges, 2000–2001 enrollment

Lindenwood University, St. Charles   6,056
Logan College of Chiropractic, Chesterfield   854
Maryville University of St. Louis, St. Louis   3,055
Missouri College, St. Louis   544
Sanford-Brown College, Des Peres   316
St. Charles County Community College, St. Peters   5,565
St. Louis Community College-Meramec, Kirkwood   12,518

Newspapers and circulation

	District circulation	Total circulation
St. Louis Post-Dispatch	83,535	295,281

Television stations and affiliations

St. Louis	100%	KDNL	ABC
St. Louis	100%	KETC	PBS
St. Louis	100%	KMOV	CBS
St. Louis	100%	KNLC	Independent
St. Louis	100%	KPLR	WB
St. Louis	100%	KSDK	NBC
St. Louis	100%	KTVI	FOX
St. Louis	100%	WHSL	Independent
St. Louis	100%	WPXS	PAX

Cable systems and subscribers
Charter   66,277

Businesses and other major employers

Express Scripts Inc.; Maryland Heights; pharmaceuticals
6,000

Southwestern Bell Telephone Co.; St. Louis; telephone
communications   4,500

University of Phoenix Inc.; Hazelwood   4,000

Edward D. Jones and Co.; St. Louis; security brokers
3,732

Jones Financial Cos.; St. Louis; stock brokers and dealers
3,700

DaimlerChrysler Corp.; Fenton; motor vehicles and car
bodies   3,650

School District of St. Louis County; St. Louis   3,600

General American Life Insurance Co.; St. Louis   3,000

General Motors Corp.; Wentzville; truck assembly
3,000

Tri-County Journal; Pacific; newspaper   3,000

McCarthy Interface; St. Louis; housing construction
2,500

St. Luke's Hospital; Chesterfield   2,400

Maritz Inc.; Fenton; travel packages   2,344

DaimlerChrysler Corp.; Fenton; truck and bus bodies
2,300

CitiMortgage Inc.; St. Louis; mortgage bankers   2,000

Harrah's Maryland Heights Operating Co. Inc.;
Maryland Heights; casino hotel   2,000

McDonnell Douglas Corp.; St. Charles; defense systems
and equipment   2,000

St. Luke's Episcopal-Presbyterian Hospitals; Chesterfield
1,803

MEMC Electronic Materials Inc.; St. Peters; silicon
wafers   1,770

Union Corp.; Chesterfield; collection agency   1,700

Missouri Baptist Medical Center; St. Louis; hospital
1,520

Monsanto Co.; Chesterfield; agricultural chemicals
1,250

SSM Health Care; St. Charles; hospital   1,250

St. Joseph Hospital of Kirkwood; St. Louis   1,178

GTE Corp.; Wentzville; telephone communication
1,000

Lucent Technologies Inc.; Chesterfield;
intercommunication systems   1,000

Verizon Wireless Messaging Services; Wentzville;
telephone communication   1,000

Stifel Nicolaus; Chesterfield; security brokers, dealers
935

Missouri Dept. of Transportation; Chesterfield   820

American Healthcare Management Inc.; Chesterfield;
nursing facility management   800

Solutia Inc.; St. Louis; organic fibers   800

St. Charles County Community College; St. Peters   750

Magellan Behavioral Health Services; Maryland Heights;
individual and family services   740

UniGroup Inc.; Fenton; household goods transport   727

America Reuters Inc.; St. Louis; general brokerage
investment firm   700

Bodine Aluminum Inc.; Troy; aluminum die-castings
700

Barnes St. Peters Hospital; St. Peters   690

Des Peres Hospital; St. Louis   650

Maritz Inc.; Fenton; business consulting   620

United Healthcare of Midwest Inc.; Maryland Heights;
health maintenance organization   590

St. Louis County Library District; St. Louis   552

Coca-Cola Enterprises Inc.; St. Charles; soft drinks   550

Cooper Bussmann Inc.; Ballwin; electric fuses   525

Bausch and Lomb Inc.; St. Louis; intraocular lenses
500

Bresnan Capital Corp.; St. Louis; cable television   500

Lutheran Church-Missouri Synod; St. Louis; religious
organization   500

May Department Stores Co.; St. Louis; department stores
500

St. Charles County; St. Charles; county government
500

Transportation Services Group Inc.; Fenton; trucking
500

Missouri 3rd District

*South St. Louis; southeast St. Louis County; Jefferson
and Ste. Genevieve Counties*

Bordered on the east by the Mississippi River, the 3rd
includes the southern half of St. Louis, as well as older, established
suburbs and newer, sprawling ones. Most of the suburban
middle-class residents commute to St. Louis County's
business district, although there are traces of small-scale
farming, manufacturing, and river trading.

Whereas St. Louis as a whole (shared with the 1st District)
has declined in population in the past few decades, south
St. Louis' residential areas have remained stable. Large Italian
and German neighborhoods continue to present a strong
voice. To the south, Jefferson County has been one of the
state's fastest-growing areas since 1980. Bedroom communities
such as Arnold and Imperial continue to prosper.

Many suburban residents work outside the district.
Anheuser-Busch, headquartered in the 3rd's portion of
St. Louis, is a major provider of jobs to the region. The National
Imagery and Mapping Agency also has facilities in
the district. Farther south, on the fringes of Ste. Genevieve
County, small farming complements a sizable trading industry
along the docks of the Mississippi River, where chemical
facilities also are located.

The district's blue-collar base favors Democrats, although
the GOP finds significant support in middle-class communities
such as Arnold and a large Catholic contingent gives
the district an antiabortion tilt. The 3rd's communities often
fight over education and economic development funding.
Redistricting following the 2000 census removed some
traditionally conservative areas, such as Sunset Hills. The revised
3rd gave Al Gore 53.9 percent of the vote in the 2000
presidential election.

Major Industry
Beer manufacturing, defense, health care.

Notable
The Missouri Botanical Garden is in St. Louis.

Election Returns

	Republican		Democratic		Other	
President 2000	112,460	43.0%	140,954	53.9%	7,972	3.0%
House 2002	80,551	38.9%	122,181	59.1%	4,146	2.0%

District Profile

Population 621,690

Total area (square miles) 1,265.5
  Land area (square miles) 1,247.0

Population per square mile 498.5

Counties (2000 population)
Jefferson	198,099	St. Louis (pt.)	220,580
Ste. Genevieve	17,842	St. Louis city (pt.)	185,169

Cities and other areas over 10,000 (2000 population)
Affton CDP (pt.) 20,328
Arnold 19,965
Clayton (pt.) 12,788
Lemay CDP 17,215
Mehlville CDP (pt.) 27,055
Oakville CDP 35,309
St. Louis (pt.) 185,169
University City (pt.) 13,353
Webster Groves 23,230

Race and Hispanic or Latino origin*
White 85.7%
Black or African American 9.1%
American Indian or Alaska Native 0.2%
Asian 1.6%
Native Hawaiian or other Pacific Islander 0.0%
Some other race 0.1%
Hispanic or Latino origin 1.8%
Two or more races 1.4%

*As percentage of total population.

Ancestry*
Dutch	1.1%	Irish	11.6%
English	5.9%	Italian	4.2%
French	4.4%	Polish	1.8%
German	23.1%	USA/American	5.1%

*As estimated percentage of total population.

Universities and colleges, 2000–2001 enrollment
Concordia Seminary, St. Louis 548
Deaconess College of Nursing, St. Louis 229
Fontbonne College, St. Louis 2,060
ITT Technical Institute, Arnold 367
Jefferson College, Hillsboro 3,876
St. Louis Community College-Forest Park, St. Louis 6,749
Webster University, St. Louis 13,783

Newspapers and circulation
	District circulation	Total circulation
Park Hills Daily Journal	1,254	8,509
St. Louis Post-Dispatch	69,939	295,281
*USA Today**	7,238	1,674,376

*See Sources and Explanations in the front of the volume.

Television stations and affiliations
St. Louis	100%	KDNL	ABC
St. Louis	100%	KETC	PBS
St. Louis	100%	KMOV	CBS
St. Louis	100%	KNLC	Independent
St. Louis	100%	KPLR	WB
St. Louis	100%	KSDK	NBC
St. Louis	100%	KTVI	FOX
St. Louis	100%	WHSL	Independent
St. Louis	100%	WPXS	PAX

Cable systems and subscribers
Cable Direct 1,318
Charter 78,837

Military installations, September 2001
Jefferson Barracks Air National Guard Station, St. Louis 334

Businesses and other major employers
Brown Shoe Co.; St. Louis; shoe stores 6,700
Tenet Healthcare Corp. Hospital; St. Louis 5,475
SBC Communications Inc.; St. Louis; telephone communication 3,000
St. Louis County; St. Louis; city council 2,500
Anheuser-Busch Inc.; St. Louis; beer 2,310
U.S. Veterans Hospital; St. Louis 2,000
St. Louis Charter School; St. Louis 1,965
Jefferson Memorial Hospital Assn.; Festus; hospital 1,600
Jefferson Memorial Hospital Assn.; Crystal City 1,400
St. Louis Linux Users' Group Inc.; St. Louis; software training 1,400
Reliable Life Corp.; St. Louis; insurance agents 1,250
Building One Commercial Inc.; St. Louis; janitorial service 1,200
Mississippi Lime Co.; Ste. Genevieve; limestone 900
Von Hoffmann Corp.; St. Louis; book publishing 900
Yellow Freight System Inc.; St. Louis; trucking 800
Graybar Electric Co.; St. Louis; electrical equipment 731
Centaur Building Services Inc.; St. Louis; cleaning services 650
International Business Machines Corp.; St. Louis; computer programming services 650
Semco Plastic Co.; St. Louis; injection molding of plastics 650
Webster University; St. Louis 650
KV Pharmaceutical Co.; St. Louis; pharmaceuticals 637
Fox School District; Arnold 600
Guarantee Electrical Construction Co.; St. Louis; electrical work 600
J. H. Berra Construction Co. Inc.; St. Louis; highway and street construction 600
Missouri Mental Health Dept.; St. Louis 600
Union Pacific Technologies Inc.; St. Louis; computer programming services 594
School Sisters of Notre Dame of St. Louis; St. Louis; religious organization 564
Lutheran Senior Services; St. Louis; geriatric residential care 560

Jefferson County; Hillsboro; county government   550

Enterprise Rent-A-Car Co.; St. Louis; automobile rental   541

Jacobs Engineering Group Inc.; St. Louis; personal service agents   500

Millennium Digital Media Holdings; St. Louis; investment holding company   500

Missouri-Illinois Bi-State Development Agency; St. Louis; bus maintenance facilities   500

Nooter Fabricators Inc.; St. Louis; metal plate tanks   500

St. Louis County; St. Louis; public health agency   500

Missouri 4th District

West central — Kansas City suburbs, Jefferson City

Laden with lakes, rivers, and farmland, the 4th follows the Missouri River on much of its northern border. Besides portions of southeast Kansas City suburbs, state capital Jefferson City, and medium-size Sedalia, the district typifies rural and small-town Missouri.

Most residents work at small-scale farming—row crops, soybeans, and livestock—or moderate-size manufacturing of household goods. The farming communities generally have recovered from "hundred-year" Missouri River floods in 1993 and 1995. Tourism helps the rural areas. In Camden County, the Lake of the Ozarks region (shared with the 9th), with modern hotels and retail outlets, attracts 300,000 boaters a weekend during peak times. The lake areas also draw many retirees.

The 4th's piece of the Kansas City suburbs has not grown as fast as the area north of the city (in the 6th), and the suburbs are not as affluent, but they provide some blue-collar manufacturing jobs. Across the district, in Jefferson City, state government employs more than 15,000 people.

Congressional elections heavily favor Democrats in the western counties while Republican votes can be tilled farther east, especially in Webster and Camden Counties, and in counties in the southwest, such as Cedar and Barton, which were added from the old 7th during 2001 redistricting. The district may be trending Republican—GOP state legislators outnumber their Democratic counterparts two-to-one in the state districts covering the 4th, and George W. Bush took 58.2 percent of the vote in the 2000 presidential election.

Major Industry
Government, defense, agriculture, manufacturing.

Notable
President Harry S. Truman was born in Lamar; Sedalia hosts the Scott Joplin Ragtime Festival each June; the restored home of George Caleb Bingham in Arrow Rock honors the late American artist.

Election Returns

	Republican		Democratic		Other	
President 2000	147,694	58.2%	100,171	39.5%	6,024	2.4%
House 2002	64,451	30.7%	142,204	67.6%	3,583	1.7%

District Profile

Population   621,690

Total area (square miles)   14,824.7
Land area (square miles)   14,544.1

Population per square mile   42.7

Counties (2000 population)

Barton	12,541	Laclede	32,513
Bates	16,653	Lafayette	32,960
Benton	17,180	Moniteau	14,827
Camden (pt.)	34,811	Morgan	19,309
Cass (pt.)	39,026	Pettis	39,403
Cedar	13,733	Polk (pt.)	6,225
Cole	71,397	Pulaski	41,165
Dade	7,923	Ray	23,354
Dallas	15,661	Saline	23,756
Henry	21,997	St. Clair	9,652
Hickory	8,940	Vernon	20,454
Jackson (pt.)	18,907	Webster	31,045
Johnson	48,258		

Cities and other areas over 10,000 (2000 population)
Fort Leonard Wood CDP   13,666
Jefferson City (pt.)   39,611
Lebanon   12,155
Marshall   12,433
Sedalia   20,339
Warrensburg   16,340

Race and Hispanic or Latino origin*
White   92.4%
Black or African American   3.2%
American Indian or Alaska Native   0.5%
Asian   0.6%
Native Hawaiian or other Pacific Islander   0.1%
Some other race   0.1%
Hispanic or Latino origin   1.9%
Two or more races   1.3%

As percentage of total population.

Ancestry*

Dutch	1.6%	Italian	1.4%
English	7.7%	Scotch-Irish	1.4%
French	2.2%	Scottish	1.2%
German	17.4%	USA/American	11.0%
Irish	8.6%		

As estimated percentage of total population.

Universities and colleges, 2000–2001 enrollment
Central Missouri State University, Warrensburg   10,936
Cottey College, Nevada   311
Lincoln University, Jefferson City   3,347
Missouri Valley College, Marshall   1,549
State Fair Community College, Sedalia   3,207
Wentworth Military Academy, Lexington   309

Newspapers and circulation

	District circulation	Total circulation
Jefferson City Post Tribune	14,080	17,069
Joplin Globe	1,598	30,638

Kansas City Star	17,556	261,945
Springfield News-Leader	6,430	63,177
St. Louis Post-Dispatch	2,711	295,281
*USA Today**	2,556	1,674,376
Warrensburg Daily Star Journal	4,013	4,013

See Sources and Explanations in the front of the volume.

Television stations and affiliations

Springfield	42%	KDEB	FOX
Springfield	42%	KOLR	CBS
Springfield	42%	KOZK	PBS
Springfield	42%	KSPR	ABC
Springfield	42%	KYTV	NBC
Kansas City	38%	KCPT	PBS
Kansas City	38%	KCTV	CBS
Kansas City	38%	KCWE	UPN
Kansas City	38%	KMBC	ABC
Kansas City	38%	KMCI	Independent
Kansas City	38%	KPXE	PAX
Kansas City	38%	KSHB	NBC
Kansas City	38%	KSMO	WB
Kansas City	38%	WDAF	FOX
Columbia-Jefferson City	10%	KMIZ	ABC
Columbia-Jefferson City	10%	KMOS	PBS
Columbia-Jefferson City	10%	KNLJ	Independent
Columbia-Jefferson City	10%	KOMU	NBC
Columbia-Jefferson City	10%	KRCG	CBS
Joplin-Pittsburg	10%	KOAM	CBS
Joplin-Pittsburg	10%	KODE	ABC
Joplin-Pittsburg	10%	KOZJ	PBS
Joplin-Pittsburg	10%	KSNF	NBC

Cable systems and subscribers

Alltel Communications 780
Cable America 4,585
Cable Direct 7,617
Charter 31,480
Classic 5,279
Comcast 4,313
Cox 1,431
Galaxy 4,204
Mediacom 25,001
Time Warner 4,565

Military installations, September 2001

Fort Leonard Wood (Army), Waynesville 9,049
Whiteman Air Force Base, Knob Noster 4,826
TS Ike Skelton (Army Guard), Jefferson City 779

Businesses and other major employers

U.S. Army Corps of Engineers; Fort Leonard Wood 3,000
Scholastic Inc.; Jefferson City; books, periodicals 2,000
Tyson Foods Inc.; Sedalia; poultry processing 1,800
O'Sullivan Industries Inc.; Lamar; office furniture 1,600
Missouri Legislature; Jefferson City 1,500
Missouri Dept. of Revenue; Jefferson City 1,443
Capital Region Medical Center; Jefferson City 1,172
Missouri Dept. of Transportation; Jefferson City 1,154
Central Missouri State University; Warrensburg 1,146
Missouri Executive Office; Jefferson City 1,100
Missouri Mental Health Dept.; Marshall 1,000
St. Mary's Health Center; Jefferson City 1,000

VF Jeanswear; Lebanon; men's/boys' trousers 850
Copeland Corp.; Lebanon; refrigeration/air conditioning equipment 800
Excel Corp.; Marshall; meatpacking plants 800
Stahl Specialty Co.; Kingsville; aluminum foundries 800
Scholastic Inc.; Jefferson City; bookstores 700
Missouri Dept. of Corrections; Jefferson City 688
Bothwell Regional Health Center; Sedalia 650
Missouri Dept. of Labor and Industrial Relations; Jefferson City 635
ConAgra Foods Inc.; Marshall; frozen fruits, fruit juices, vegetables 600
Conopco Inc.; Jefferson City; cosmetics 600
John Fitzgibbon Health Care Center; Marshall 600
Kohl's Department Stores Inc.; Grain Valley; warehousing, storage 600
Missouri National Guard; Jefferson City 600
Von Hoffmann Corp.; Jefferson City; book printing and binding 600
Missouri Dept. of Health; Jefferson City 555
Marriott International Inc.; Osage Beach; hotels 550
St. Mary's Hospital of Blue Springs Inc.; Blue Springs 550
Lake Regional Health System Hospital; Osage Beach 547
Pathways Community Behavioral Healthcare Inc.; Camdenton 535
Camdenton School District; Camdenton 530
Missouri Mental Health Dept.; Higginsville 515
3M Co.; Nevada; laminated building paper 500
ABB Inc.; Jefferson City; nonelectric transformers 500
Columbia Properties Ozark; Osage Beach; resort hotel 500
Detroit Tool and Engineering Co.; Lebanon; tool and die steel 500
Golden Valley Memorial Hospital; Clinton 500
Holmes Group Inc.; Clinton; housewares and fans 500
Missouri Mental Health Dept.; Jefferson City; mental health agency 500
Tracker Marine; Lebanon; boatbuilding and repairing 500
Wal-Mart Stores Inc.; Jefferson City 500

Missouri 5th District

Kansas City and suburbs

Mostly middle-class Democratic residents live in Kansas City and the Jackson and Cass County suburbs that make up the 5th. Although the city's suburban growth is greatest in its Kansas portion, Missouri communities have prospered.

A diverse economic base has enabled Kansas City to grow from a cow town to a transportation and telecommunications hub. Steel and automobile production facilities highlight a solid industrial base. Many district residents travel to Kansas or neighboring districts to work at companies such as Sprint Communications and General Motors. The federal government also is a large employer. The city remains a viable market for feeder cattle and winter wheat, although on a smaller scale than in years past.

Hallmark Cards, one of Kansas City's largest employers, built a popular entertainment complex in the downtown area. Resurgence in high-end loft communities has lured younger, well-to-do residents to the city. Still, the contrasting neighborhoods on opposite sides of Troost Avenue remind residents of the economic disparity in the city, which largely runs along racial lines. Taking in nearly all of Kansas City's black neighborhoods, the district has a 24.2 percent black population. About half its voters are in Kansas City, half in the suburbs. Offshoot cities such as Lee's Summit and the 5th's portion of Cass County experienced rapid population growth during the first half of the 1990s. The city of Independence (a small part of which is in the 6th) still accounts for about one-fifth of the district's vote.

The 5th is reliably Democratic and socially moderate. Democrats have held the Kansas City seat since 1931, and Al Gore captured 60.4 percent of the district's vote in the 2000 presidential election.

Major Industry
Auto manufacturing, agriculture.

Notable
President Harry S. Truman hailed from Independence.

Election Returns

	Republican		Democratic		Other	
President 2000	91,626	37.0%	149,621	60.4%	6,625	2.7%
House 2002	60,245	32.4%	122,645	65.9%	3,277	1.8%

District Profile

Population   621,691

Total area (square miles)   519.3
   Land area (square miles)   511.5

Population per square mile   1,215.4

Counties (2000 population)
   Cass (pt.)   43,066
   Jackson (pt.)   578,625

Cities and other areas over 10,000 (2000 population)
   Belton   21,730
   Grandview   24,881
   Independence (pt.)   110,822
   Kansas City (pt.)   322,910
   Lee's Summit (pt.)   65,498
   Raymore   11,146
   Raytown   30,388

Race and Hispanic or Latino origin*
   White   66.3%
   Black or African American   24.2%
   American Indian or Alaska Native   0.4%
   Asian   1.3%
   Native Hawaiian or other Pacific Islander   0.2%
   Some other race   0.1%
   Hispanic or Latino origin   5.6%
   Two or more races   1.9%

*As percentage of total population.

Ancestry*
Dutch	1.3%	Italian	2.4%
English	7.6%	Scotch-Irish	1.5%
French	1.9%	Scottish	1.3%
German	13.5%	Swedish	1.1%
Irish	8.8%	USA/American	5.5%

*As estimated percentage of total population.

Universities and colleges, 2000–2001 enrollment
   Avila College, Kansas City   1,412
   Calvary Bible College, Kansas City   291
   Cleveland Chiropractic College, Kansas City   579
   Devry University, Kansas City   2,708
   Kansas City Art Institute, Kansas City   527
   Keller Graduate School of Management, Kansas City   314
   Longview Community College, Lee's Summit   8,117
   Midwestern Baptist Theological Seminary, Kansas City   515
   National American University, Kansas City   286
   Nazarene Theological Seminary, Kansas City   383
   Penn Valley Community College, Kansas City   4,366
   Rockhurst College, Kansas City   2,727
   St. Paul School of Theology, Kansas City   310
   University of Health Sciences-College of Osteopathy, Kansas City   871
   University of Missouri, Kansas City   12,762
   Vatterott College, Independence   414

Newspapers and circulation

	District circulation	Total circulation
Call	11,608	14,229
Kansas City Star	82,818	261,945
*USA Today**	4,062	1,674,376

*See Sources and Explanations in the front of the volume.

Television stations and affiliations
Kansas City	100%	KCPT	PBS
Kansas City	100%	KCTV	CBS
Kansas City	100%	KCWE	UPN
Kansas City	100%	KMBC	ABC
Kansas City	100%	KMCI	Independent
Kansas City	100%	KPXE	PAX
Kansas City	100%	KSHB	NBC
Kansas City	100%	KSMO	WB
Kansas City	100%	WDAF	FOX

Cable systems and subscribers
   Comcast   52,977
   Galaxy   3,957
   Time Warner   95,964

Military installations, September 2001
   Lake City Army Ammunition Plant, Independence   941
   Marine Corps Support Activity, Kansas City   388

Businesses and other major employers
   St. Luke's-Shawnee Mission Health System Inc.; Kansas City   7,000
   Comfort Inn of Lee's Summit Inc.; Lee's Summit; bed and breakfast inn   6,000

Midwest Heritage Inn of Lee's Summit Inc.; Lee's Summit; bed and breakfast inn 6,000

Hallmark Cards Inc.; Kansas City; greeting cards 5,900

Honeywell International Inc.; Kansas City; search and navigation equipment 4,500

AT&T Corp.; Kansas City; local/long distance telephone 3,450

University of Missouri System; Kansas City 3,368

Kansas City Power and Light Co.; Kansas City; electric services 3,300

Dunn Industries Inc.; Independence; building construction 3,000

U.S. Internal Revenue Service; Kansas City 3,000

U.S. Social Security Admin.; Kansas City 3,000

First Horizon Home Loans Corp.; Kansas City; mortgage bankers 2,870

Honeywell Inc.; Kansas City; radar systems and equipment 2,800

St. Luke's Hospital of Kansas City; Kansas City 2,800

Hallmark Marketing Corp.; Kansas City; greeting cards 2,542

Research Medical Center; Kansas City 2,300

Black and Veatch Corp.; Kansas City; engineering services 2,265

Commerce Bank NA; Kansas City; commercial bank 2,200

DST Systems Inc.; Kansas City; data processing 2,200

Sprint Communications Co.; Kansas City; long distance telephone 2,100

Cosentino Group II Inc.; Kansas City; supermarkets 2,000

Jackson County; Kansas City; county government 2,000

City of Kansas City; Kansas City; police dept. 1,934

BGM Industries Inc.; Kansas City; building maintenance 1,850

Mercy Children's Hospital; Kansas City 1,850

AT&T Corp.; Lee's Summit; telephone apparatus 1,800

Truman Medical Center Inc.; Kansas City 1,800

U.S. Postal Service; Kansas City 1,800

UMB Bank; Kansas City; commercial bank 1,700

American Century Services Corp.; Kansas City; data processing 1,573

Baptist-Lutheran Medical Center; Kansas City 1,500

Kansas City Star Co.; Kansas City; newspaper 1,500

St. Joseph Health Center Inc.; Kansas City 1,500

J. E. Dunn Construction Co.; Kansas City; building construction 1,450

Health Midwest Hospital; Independence 1,440

City of Kansas City; Kansas City; city management 1,400

Sprint Spectrum; Kansas City; telephone communication 1,400

U.S. Defense Dept.; Kansas City 1,400

U.S. Census Bureau; Kansas City 1,200

Farm Service Agency; Kansas City; agricultural marketing regulation 1,100

Kansas City Area Transportation Authority; Kansas City 1,100

State Street Corp.; Kansas City; money market mutual funds 1,080

Quintiles Transnational Corp.; Kansas City; research services 1,060

Burns and McDonnell Engineering Co.; Kansas City; consulting engineer 1,050

Bayer Corp.; Kansas City; agricultural chemicals 1,000

Burlington Northern and Santa Fe Railway Co.; Kansas City; freight hauling 1,000

Defense Finance and Accounting Service; Kansas City; accounting services 1,000

John Knox Village; Lee's Summit; skilled nursing care facilities 1,000

Volume Services America Inc.; Kansas City; cafe 1,000

Yellow Transportation; Kansas City; trucking terminal facilities 1,000

U.S. Veterans Hospital; Kansas City 985

Federal Reserve Bank of Kansas City; Kansas City; banking regulation 960

Blue Cross and Blue Shield of Kansas City; Kansas City; hospital/medical service plans 900

Shook Hardy and Bacon; Kansas City; law office 900

Trinity Lutheran Hospital; Kansas City 893

Mid America Care Foundation Inc.; Kansas City; skilled nursing care facilities 873

Alliant Techsystems Inc.; Independence; small arms ammunition 850

Isle of Capri; Kansas City; gambling and lottery services 832

Government Employees Hospital Assn. Inc.; Independence; health insurance 825

Aventis Pharmaceuticals Inc.; Kansas City; pharmaceuticals 800

Butler Manufacturing Co.; Kansas City; administrative management 800

Fortis Inc.; Kansas City; life insurance 800

AGCO Corp.; Independence; combines (harvester-threshers) 770

City of Kansas City; Kansas City; fire dept. 750

Bank of America Corp.; Kansas City; commercial bank 730

DST Output Illinois Inc.; Kansas City; telemarketing services 700

International Business Machines Corp.; Kansas City; computer and software stores 700

Marriott International Inc.; Kansas City; hotels 700

Missouri Mental Health Dept.; Kansas City 700

Transamerica Occidental Life Insurance Co.; Kansas City; life insurance 700

Burns International Security Services Corp.; Kansas City; security guard service 684

Peterson Manufacturing Co.; Grandview; motor vehicle lighting equipment 674

Hospital Hill Health Services Corp.; Kansas City 648

Kansas City Life Insurance Co.; Kansas City; life insurance 638

Hyatt Corp.; Kansas City; hotels 620

Aquila Merchant Services Inc.; Kansas City; natural gas distribution 600

Kansas City Cable Partners; Kansas City; cable television 600

Missouri Dept. of Social Services; Kansas City 600

Wal-Mart Stores Inc.; Raymore 600

Wal-Mart Stores Inc.; Kansas City 600

Guardsmark Inc.; Kansas City; security guard service 550

Western Missouri Mental Health Center; Kansas City 550

U.S. Army Corps of Engineers; Kansas City 540

General Board of Church of Nazarene; Kansas City; religious organization 530

Integrated HealthSystems Inc.; Kansas City; hospital/medical service plans 525

Southwestern Bell Telephone Co.; Kansas City; local/long-distance telephone 522

Butler Manufacturing Co.; Kansas City; sheet metalwork 500

Butler Manufacturing Co.; Kansas City; noncommercial research organization 500

ConAgra Foods Inc.; Kansas City; meatpacking plants 500

St. Gobain Calmar Inc.; Lee's Summit; plastic containers 500

Unity School of Christianity; Lee's Summit 500

UtiliCorp UK Inc.; Kansas City; natural gas distribution 500

Missouri 6th District

Northwest — St. Joseph, part of Kansas City

A mixture of suburbanites and farmers, the 6th is bordered by Iowa to the north, Nebraska and Kansas to the west, and the Missouri River to the west and most of the south.

Kansas City's suburban boom in the 1980s provided steady growth for the middle-class residents of Platte, Clay, and eastern Jackson Counties, who work mainly for the city's steel, transportation, and communications companies. Kansas City International Airport in Platte County and American Airlines also are large employers, and the Kansas City area is home to Farmland, a large farm cooperative, and the Dairy Farmers of America, a large cooperative milk supplier. The suburbs have attracted some insurance, financial services, and agribusiness companies.

Outside of the metropolitan area, the river town of St. Joseph serves as the economic hub. In the 1990s the economy began to speed up, but agrarian life still prevails in most of the district's counties, where corn and livestock are pervasive. New processing plants have created a growing market for soybeans as well.

Although historically Democratic, the district was competitive during the last quarter of the twentieth century. The 6th now seems in strong GOP hands. Democrat Bill Clinton won the 1992 and 1996 presidential elections, but GOP Senate candidates did well during the same period, and George W. Bush carried the district with 53.1 percent of the vote in 2000. Republicans seeking state office also have fared better recently, especially in the northern, rural areas.

Major Industry

Agriculture, international shipping, manufacturing.

Notable

Jesse James was raised near Kearney and is buried there; the Jesse James Home in St. Joseph was where the outlaw was shot and killed in 1882; the Pony Express carried mail between St. Joseph and California from April 1860 through October 1861.

Election Returns

	Republican		Democratic		Other	
President 2000	143,954	53.1%	119,861	44.2%	7,380	2.7%
House 2002	131,151	63.0%	73,202	35.2%	3,735	1.8%

District Profile

Population   621,690

Total area (square miles)   13,123.8
  Land area (square miles)   13,031.9

Population per square mile   47.7

Counties (2000 population)

Andrew	16,492	Harrison	8,850
Atchison	6,430	Holt	5,351
Buchanan	85,998	Howard	10,212
Caldwell	8,969	Jackson (pt.)	57,348
Carroll	10,285	Linn	13,754
Chariton	8,438	Livingston	14,558
Clay	184,006	Mercer	3,757
Clinton	18,979	Nodaway	21,912
Cooper	16,670	Platte	73,781
Daviess	8,016	Putnam	5,223
DeKalb	11,597	Schuyler	4,170
Gentry	6,861	Sullivan	7,219
Grundy	10,432	Worth	2,382

Cities and other areas over 10,000 (2000 population)
  Blue Springs (pt.)   39,698
  Excelsior Springs (pt.)   10,670
  Gladstone   26,365
  Kansas City (pt.)   118,635
  Liberty   26,232
  Maryville   10,581
  St. Joseph   73,990

Race and Hispanic or Latino origin*
  White   92.4%
  Black or African American   2.8%
  American Indian or Alaska Native   0.4%
  Asian   0.8%
  Native Hawaiian or other Pacific Islander   0.1%
  Some other race   0.1%
  Hispanic or Latino origin   2.4%
  Two or more races   1.1%

*As percentage of total population.

Ancestry*

Dutch	1.6%	Polish	1.1%
English	8.5%	Scotch-Irish	1.6%
French	2.0%	Scottish	1.4%
German	17.1%	Swedish	1.1%
Irish	9.8%	USA/American	8.9%
Italian	2.2%		

*As estimated percentage of total population.

Universities and colleges, 2000–2001 enrollment
  Central Methodist College, Fayette   1,231
  Kemper Military School and College, Boonville   317
  Maple Woods Community College, Kansas City   5,294
  Missouri Western State College, St. Joseph   5,089
  North Central Missouri College, Trenton   1,402

Northwest Missouri State University, Maryville   6,442
Park College, Parkville   9,223
William Jewell College, Liberty   1,442

Newspapers and circulation

	District circulation	Total circulation
Kansas City Star	49,861	261,945
St. Joseph News-Press	35,825	39,144
*USA Today**	5,400	1,674,376

See Sources and Explanations in the front of the volume.

Television stations and affiliations

Kansas City	49%	KCPT	PBS
Kansas City	49%	KCTV	CBS
Kansas City	49%	KCWE	UPN
Kansas City	49%	KMBC	ABC
Kansas City	49%	KMCI	Independent
Kansas City	49%	KPXE	PAX
Kansas City	49%	KSHB	NBC
Kansas City	49%	KSMO	WB
Kansas City	49%	WDAF	FOX
St. Joseph	22%	KQTV	ABC
St. Joseph	22%	KTAJ	Independent
Columbia-Jefferson City	14%	KMIZ	ABC
Columbia-Jefferson City	14%	KMOS	PBS
Columbia-Jefferson City	14%	KNLJ	Independent
Columbia-Jefferson City	14%	KOMU	NBC
Columbia-Jefferson City	14%	KRCG	CBS
Ottumwa-Kirksville	11%	KTVO	ABC
Omaha	4%	KBIN	PBS
Omaha	4%	KETV	ABC
Omaha	4%	KHIN	PBS
Omaha	4%	KMTV	CBS
Omaha	4%	KPTM	FOX
Omaha	4%	KUON	PBS
Omaha	4%	KXVO	WB
Omaha	4%	KYNE	PBS
Omaha	4%	WOWT	NBC

Cable systems and subscribers

Cable Direct   6,998
Charter   5,193
City of Unionville Cable   980
Classic   11,993
Comcast   11,815
Galaxy   1,031
Green Hills Communications   561
Mediacom   9,876
Northwest Communications   775
Rock Port Cablevision   1,667
St. Joseph Cablevision   26,682
Time Warner   27,693

Military installations, September 2001

Rosecrans Memorial Airport (Air National Guard), Elwood   1,045

Businesses and other major employers

TWA Airlines; Kansas City; air passenger carrier 7,000

Harrah's Entertainment Inc.; Kansas City; gambling 2,500

Heartland Regional Medical Center; St. Joseph   2,400

Ameristar Casino Hotel Kansas City Inc.; Kansas City; casino hotel   2,200

Cerner Healthwise Inc.; Kansas City; business computer software   2,100

Farmland Industries Inc.; Kansas City; meatpacking plants   1,500

Missouri Western State College; St. Joseph   1,300

Premium Standard Farms Inc.; Princeton; hog feedlot 1,300

New Liberty Hospital District of Clay County; Liberty 1,200

Premium Standard Farms Inc.; Milan; pork products 900

Missouri Gaming Co.; Kansas City; gambling and lottery services   875

Level 3 Communications; Lee's Summit; telephone communication   869

Isle of Capri of Boonville; Boonville; casino hotel   800

Systems and Services Technologies Inc.; St. Joseph; data processing   800

Tyco International Inc.; St. Joseph; medical instruments 800

ConAgra Foods Inc.; Milan; processed frozen poultry 750

Mead Corp.; St. Joseph; stationery products   750

Walsworth Publishing Co.; Brookfield; yearbook publishing   750

American Family Mutual Insurance Co. Inc.; St. Joseph; insurance brokers   700

Quaker Oats Co.; St. Joseph; extracts, flavoring   700

Wire Rope Corp. of America Inc.; St. Joseph; woven wire products   700

Missouri Dept. of Corrections; Cameron   650

Northwest Missouri State University; Maryville   629

Missouri Dept. of Corrections; St. Joseph   620

GE Transportation Systems Global Signaling; Grain Valley; transportation signaling devices   600

Guy's Foods Inc.; Liberty; potato snacks   600

Hallmark Cards Inc.; Liberty; general warehousing, storage   600

J. B. Hunt Transport Inc.; Kansas City; trucking   600

St. Joseph Foods; St. Joseph; prepared meats   600

Wagner Industries Inc.; Kansas City; local trucking with storage   600

Golden Rule Farms Inc.; Queen City; corn   595

Eveready Battery Co.; Maryville; dry cell batteries   579

General Electric Co.; Grain Valley; railroad signaling devices   563

Horizon Pharmacies Inc.; Mendon; drug and proprietary stores   555

Altec Industries Inc.; St. Joseph; derricks   550

Kawasaki Motors Manufacturing Corp.; Maryville; motors and generators   548

Johnson Controls Inc.; St. Joseph; plastics working machinery   525

Cox Enterprises Inc.; Kansas City; commercial printing, newspaper publishing   500

Missouri 7th District

Southwest — Springfield, Joplin

Two decades of rapid growth helped lift southwest Missouri from a rural hideaway to a burgeoning resort and industrial region. Since the 1970s, this part of Missouri has outpaced the rest of the state in population growth, increasing by 24 percent in the 1990s.

Springfield, in Greene County, is the 7th's industrial and commercial center and has become a manufacturing hub. More than 40 percent of district residents live in Greene or neighboring Christian County on the 7th's eastern edge. Large hospital facilities in Springfield draw patients from as far as Arkansas. The district's other population center, Joplin, is across the district in Jasper County. Once a lead and zinc mining town, it is now a manufacturing and trucking center.

Branson, in the southeast corner, leads the 7th's thriving tourism industry as a magnet for country music fans. A town of 6,000, it draws more than six million visitors a year and boasts more than 40 theaters, including the Andy Williams and Mel Tillis theaters. The area also relies on the resort industry surrounding Table Rock and Taneycomo lakes.

The southwest corner of the district supports beef and dairy cattle, along with poultry. Many of the small, rural communities in the Ozarks have not quite yielded to development. Expansion along U.S. Highway 71, which runs from Kansas City into Arkansas, is expected to improve the area's accessibility and economic prospects.

The 7th has been long considered a Republican bastion. The Assemblies of God, headquartered in Springfield, is among the active religious organizations that reflect the area's devout, conservative population. Springfield has become slightly more Democratic since the 1980s, partly because of the influx of new residents, but the city still leans Republican.

Major Industry

Manufacturing, agriculture, tourism.

Notable

Springfield is home to Fantastic Caverns, which calls itself the nation's only ride-through cave; George Washington Carver's boyhood home is now a national monument in Diamond; Wilson's Creek National Battlefield Park is in Republic.

Election Returns

	Republican		Democratic		Other	
President 2000	153,453	62.1%	87,663	35.5%	6,124	2.5%
House 2002	149,519	74.8%	45,964	23.0%	4,380	2.2%

District Profile

Population   621,690

Total area (square miles)   5,555.2
   Land area (square miles)   5,479.7

Population per square mile   113.5

Counties (2000 population)

Barry 34,010	McDonald 21,681
Christian 54,285	Newton 52,636
Greene 240,391	Polk (pt.) 20,767
Jasper 104,686	Stone 28,658
Lawrence 35,204	Taney (pt.) 29,372

Cities and other areas over 10,000 (2000 population)

Carthage 12,668	Nixa 12,124
Joplin 45,504	Springfield 151,580
Neosho 10,505	

Race and Hispanic or Latino origin*

White   92.9%
Black or African American   1.2%
American Indian or Alaska Native   1.0%
Asian   0.7%
Native Hawaiian or other Pacific Islander   0.1%
Some other race   0.1%
Hispanic or Latino origin   2.6%
Two or more races   1.5%

As percentage of total population.

Ancestry*

Dutch 1.8%	Italian 1.5%
English 8.2%	Scotch-Irish 1.6%
French 2.2%	Scottish 1.3%
German 13.4%	USA/American 10.8%
Irish 9.2%	

As estimated percentage of total population.

Universities and colleges, 2000–2001 enrollment

Assemblies of God Theological Seminary, Springfield   404
Baptist Bible College, Springfield   852
Central Bible College, Springfield   849
College of the Ozarks, Point Lookout   1,414
Crowder College, Neosho   1,719
Drury College, Springfield   4,348
Evangel University, Springfield   1,538
Forest Institute of Professional Psychology, Springfield   261
Lester E. Cox College of Nursing and Health Science, Springfield   294
Missouri Southern State College, Joplin   5,785
Ozark Christian College, Joplin   739
Ozarks Technical Community College, Springfield   6,343
Southwest Baptist University, Bolivar   3,593
Southwest Missouri State University, Springfield   17,703
Springfield College, Springfield   861
Vatterott College, Springfield   214

Newspapers and circulation

	District circulation	Total circulation
Joplin Globe	23,866	30,638
Springfield News-Leader	52,486	63,177
*USA Today**	4,110	1,674,376

See Sources and Explanations in the front of the volume.

Television stations and affiliations

Springfield	68%	KDEB	FOX
Springfield	68%	KOLR	CBS
Springfield	68%	KOZK	PBS
Springfield	68%	KSPR	ABC
Springfield	68%	KYTV	NBC
Joplin-Pittsburg	32%	KOAM	CBS
Joplin-Pittsburg	32%	KODE	ABC
Joplin-Pittsburg	32%	KOZJ	PBS
Joplin-Pittsburg	32%	KSNF	NBC

Cable systems and subscribers

Alltel Communications   2,379
Cable America   1,855
Cable ONE   16,399
Classic   9,399
Cox   15,859
Mediacom   67,122

Military installations, September 2001

Springfield Armed Forces Reserve Center, Springfield
   426

Businesses and other major employers

New Prime Inc.; Springfield; refrigerated products
   transport   4,100
St. John's Regional Health Center; Springfield   4,000
Southwest Missouri State University; Springfield
   2,500
Lester E. Cox Medical Center; Springfield   2,400
Contract Freighters Inc.; Joplin; trucking   2,241
Dillon Companies Inc.; Springfield; administrative
   management   1,700
Bass Pro Inc.; Springfield; administrative management
   1,600
EFCO Corp.; Monett; window and door frames   1,500
Freeman Health System Hospital; Joplin   1,500
St. John's Regional Medical Center; Joplin   1,310
Kraft Foods Inc.; Springfield; cheese products   1,300
La-Z-Boy Inc.; Neosho; chairs/couches   1,300
Lester E. Cox Medical Center; Springfield   1,300
MCI Worldcom Network Services Inc.; Springfield;
   telephone communication   1,200
Tyson Foods Inc.; Monett; processed poultry   1,200
General Council of Assemblies of God; Springfield;
   religious organization   1,100
Litton Systems Inc.; Springfield; radio broadcasting
   equipment   1,000
Fasco Industries Inc.; Cassville; electrical equipment
   980
Willow Brook Foods Inc.; Springfield; processed turkey
   964
ConAgra Poultry Co.; Carthage; turkey farm   900
Eagle-Picher Technologies; Joplin; primary batteries
   900
Loren Cook Co.; Springfield; exhaust fans   900
U.S. Postal Service; Springfield   900
O'Reilly Automotive Inc.; Springfield; automotive parts
   861
City Utilities of Springfield Inc.; Springfield; utility
   regulation   816
City of Springfield; Springfield; city government   800
General Electric Co.; Springfield; electric motors   800

George's Inc.; Butterfield; poultry processing   800
Sweetheart Cup Co.; Springfield; plastic cups and plates
   800
Indiana Western Express Inc.; Springfield; trucking
   780
Cox Alternative Care of Ozarks; Joplin; home health care
   services   750
Paul Mueller Co.; Springfield; metal plate tanks   730
George's Inc.; Cassville; cafeterias   700
Greene County; Springfield; county government   700
New Creative Enterprises Inc.; Bolivar; artificial flowers
   700
U.S. Bureau of Prisons; Springfield   676
Simmons Foods Inc.; South West City; processed poultry
   650
American National Property and Casualty Companies;
   Springfield; insurance agents   600
Citizens Memorial Hospital District of Polk County;
   Bolivar   600
Elite Logistics Inc.; Springfield; cold storage
   warehousing   600
Healthcare Services of Ozarks; Springfield; temporary
   help service   600
Junior College District of Central Southwest Missouri;
   Springfield   600
Leggett and Platt Inc.; Carthage; box springs   600
Missouri Dept. of Transportation; Springfield   600
Schreiber Foods Inc.; Carthage; cheese products   600
Smith Glynn Callaway Clinic Inc.; Springfield   600
Jack Henry and Associates Inc.; Monett; software
   development   572
Sunbeam Products Inc.; Neosho; barbecues, grills, and
   braziers   550
Wal-Mart Stores Inc.; Springfield   550
Positronic Industries Inc.; Springfield; electronic
   connectors   546
Carlisle Power Transmission Products Inc.; Springfield;
   motor vehicle parts   500
Missouri Dept. of Health; Springfield   500
Reckitt Benckiser Inc.; Springfield; mustard   500
Skaggs Community Hospital Assn.; Branson   500
Sportsman's Distribution Co.; Springfield; warehousing
   500
Wal-Mart Stores Inc.; Neosho   500

Missouri 8th District

Southeast — Cape Girardeau, Ozark Plateau

Some of the state's most bountiful farmland can be found in the 8th, which takes in the mountains, forests, and Mississippi Valley towns of Missouri's southeastern corner.

The district spans the political spectrum from solidly Republican counties in the west and northeast along the Mississippi River to "Yellow Dog" Democratic territory in the southeast area, dubbed the boot heel because of its shape. Voters tend to be socially conservative on issues such as abortion and gun control and leery of environmental regulations, and the GOP has made inroads in the boot heel in elections for offices higher than the county level.

The 8th is slowly recovering from a decline in the textile industry since the 1980s. Agriculture and lead mining fuel the central counties, while the boot heel is a former wheat-growing region that now produces soybean, corn, cotton, and rice.

Major growth centers in the district include the northern counties of Phelps and St. Francois, which have been boosted by light manufacturing and defense subcontracts. Lumber also features heavily in the 8th's industry, and four-fifths of Mark Twain National Forest's 1.5 million acres lies in the 8th.

Frequent flooding and earthquakes from the New Madrid fault line that runs through southeast Missouri make the 8th a disaster-prone region, though reinforced levees and highways have reduced the risk. The last major flooding of the Mississippi River was in 1995, but preparation for smaller floods is still an annual spring ritual in the border towns.

Major Industry

Agriculture, lead mining, lumber.

Notable

The Census Bureau estimates that the population center of the United States is near Edgar Springs; Astronaut Linda M. Godwin, who has logged more than 38 days in space, was born in Cape Girardeau; the New Madrid region has more earthquakes than any other part of the United States east of the Rocky Mountains.

Election Returns

	Republican		Democratic		Other	
President 2000	143,511	59.2%	93,244	38.5%	5,635	2.3%
House 2002	135,144	71.8%	50,686	26.9%	2,491	1.3%

District Profile

Population   621,690

Total area (square miles)   18,818.3
　　Land area (square miles)   18,681.0

Population per square mile   33.3

Counties (2000 population)

Bollinger 12,029	Pemiscot 20,047
Butler 40,867	Perry 18,132
Cape Girardeau 68,693	Phelps 39,825
Carter 5,941	Reynolds 6,689
Dent 14,927	Ripley 13,509
Douglas 13,084	Scott 40,422
Dunklin 33,155	Shannon 8,324
Howell 37,238	St. Francois 55,641
Iron 10,697	Stoddard 29,705
Madison 11,800	Taney (pt.) 10,331
Mississippi 13,427	Texas 23,003
New Madrid 19,760	Washington 23,344
Oregon 10,344	Wayne 13,259
Ozark 9,542	Wright 17,955

Cities and other areas over 10,000 (2000 population)

Cape Girardeau 35,349	Poplar Bluff 16,651
Farmington 13,924	Rolla 16,367
Jackson 11,947	Sikeston 16,992
Kennett 11,260	West Plains 10,866

Race and Hispanic or Latino origin*

White   92.5%
Black or African American   4.3%
American Indian or Alaska Native   0.6%
Asian   0.4%
Native Hawaiian or other Pacific Islander   0.0%
Some other race   0.0%
Hispanic or Latino origin   1.0%
Two or more races   1.1%

*As percentage of total population.

Ancestry*

Dutch	1.5%	German	12.7%
English	6.2%	Irish	8.5%
French	2.9%	USA/American	13.7%

*As estimated percentage of total population.

Universities and colleges, 2000–2001 enrollment

Mineral Area College, Park Hills   2,702
Rolla Technical Institute, Rolla   280
Southeast Missouri State University, Cape Girardeau   8,948
Southwest Missouri State University, West Plains   1,525
Three Rivers Community College, Poplar Bluff   2,641
University of Missouri-Rolla, Rolla   4,626

Newspapers and circulation

	District circulation	Total circulation
Park Hills Daily Journal	7,274	8,509
Springfield News-Leader	3,860	63,177
St. Louis Post-Dispatch	8,331	295,281
*USA Today**	2,035	1,674,376

*See Sources and Explanations in the front of the volume.

Television stations and affiliations

Paducah-Cape Girardeau-Harrisburg-Mt. Vernon	48%	KBSI	FOX
Paducah-Cape Girardeau-Harrisburg-Mt. Vernon	48%	KFVS	CBS
Paducah-Cape Girardeau-Harrisburg-Mt. Vernon	48%	KPOB	ABC
Paducah-Cape Girardeau-Harrisburg-Mt. Vernon	48%	WDKA	WB
Paducah-Cape Girardeau-Harrisburg-Mt. Vernon	48%	WKMU	PBS
Paducah-Cape Girardeau-Harrisburg-Mt. Vernon	48%	WKPD	PBS
Paducah-Cape Girardeau-Harrisburg-Mt. Vernon	48%	WPSD	NBC
Paducah-Cape Girardeau-Harrisburg-Mt. Vernon	48%	WSIL	ABC
Paducah-Cape Girardeau-Harrisburg-Mt. Vernon	48%	WSIU	PBS
Paducah-Cape Girardeau-Harrisburg-Mt. Vernon	48%	WTCT	Independent
Springfield	43%	KDEB	FOX
Springfield	43%	KOLR	CBS
Springfield	43%	KOZK	PBS
Springfield	43%	KSPR	ABC
Springfield	43%	KYTV	NBC
St. Louis	9%	KDNL	ABC
St. Louis	9%	KETC	PBS
St. Louis	9%	KMOV	CBS
St. Louis	9%	KNLC	Independent
St. Louis	9%	KPLR	WB
St. Louis	9%	KSDK	NBC
St. Louis	9%	KTVI	FOX
St. Louis	9%	WHSL	Independent
St. Louis	9%	WPXS	PAX

Cable systems and subscribers

CableVision Communications   17,458
Charter   67,270
Classic   1,434
Fidelity Cablevision   6,825
Houston Cable   1,093
Licking Cable   630

Mediacom   6,328
Semo Communications   1,781
Time Warner   5,733

Businesses and other major employers

University of Missouri System; Rolla   2,000

Procter and Gamble Paper Products Co.; Jackson;
disposable diapers   1,300

Southeast Missouri Hospital Assn.; Cape Girardeau
1,300

Three Rivers Health Care Hospital; Poplar Bluff   1,300

Briggs and Stratton Corp.; Poplar Bluff; internal
combustion engines   1,200

St. Francis Medical Center; Cape Girardeau   1,105

Siegel-Robert Inc.; Portageville; plastics processing
1,000

TG Missouri Corp.; Perryville; injection molding of
plastics   1,000

Ozarks Medical Center; West Plains   974

Tenet Health System Medical Center; Poplar Bluff   954

Rowe Furniture Inc.; Poplar Bluff; household furniture
900

Southeast Missouri State University; Cape Girardeau
887

Briggs and Stratton Corp.; Rolla; internal combustion
engines   800

Doe Run Resources Corp.; Viburnum; lead ores mining
800

Newell Rubbermaid Inc.; Jackson; garment hangers
800

Phelps County Regional Medical Center; Rolla   800

Marathon Electric Manufacturing Corp.; West Plains;
electric motors   726

Tyson Foods Inc.; Dexter; poultry processing   725

Pemiscot County Memorial Hospital; Hayti   700

Missouri Delta Medical Center Inc.; Sikeston   696

Huffy Corp.; Farmington; bicycles and parts   600

Missouri Dept. of Transportation; Sikeston   600

Systems and Electronics Inc.; West Plains; truck bodies
550

Wal-Mart Stores Inc.; Poplar Bluff; department stores
550

Hart Schaffner and Marx; Cape Girardeau; men's/boys'
suits and coats   540

Malden School District; Malden   539

Missouri Dept. of Corrections; Farmington   520

Galaxy Cable Inc.; Sikeston; cable television   500

Mary Lee Packaging Corp.; Perryville; breakfast cereals
500

Trinity Industries Inc.; Caruthersville; barges   500

Wal-Mart Stores Inc.; Cape Girardeau; discount
department stores   500

Wheaton USA Inc.; Flat River; glass bottles   500

Missouri 9th District

Northeast — Columbia, St. Louis exurbs

Besides Columbia and some western St. Louis suburbs,
the 9th consists of small towns spread among farmlands.
Residents include many middle-class, socially conservative
Democrats, but the arrival of new wealth has led to rapid
suburban growth and a rise in Republican-leaning areas.

The 9th splits St. Charles County with the neighboring 2nd District and encompasses all of nearby Warren and
Franklin counties. A General Motors plant and a Boeing hub
in nearby districts provide jobs, but much of the area's growth
has come from small businesses. A wine industry that dates
back to the 19th century provides income for Gasconade and
surrounding counties.

Columbia, a steadily growing and mostly middle-class
city across the district from St. Charles County, is home to
the University of Missouri's flagship campus and a handful of
medical facilities, including the Harry S. Truman Memorial
Veterans Hospital. Despite a significant exodus of young people from farming families, the district's economy still thrives
on cattle, soybean, corn, and winter wheat.

Traditionally Democratic, the 9th is becoming increasingly Republican with the growth of suburban St. Louis and
the decline of "Yellow Dog" Democrats in rural communities. Before 1996, voters elected a Republican member of
Congress only once in the twentieth century, in 1920. Still
predominantly Democratic at the local level, the district expanded southwest in 2001 redistricting to gain new counties
that have contributed to a GOP base for state offices. George
W. Bush carried the redrawn district by 12.6 percentage
points in the 2000 presidential election.

Major Industry

Higher education, electronics, agriculture.

Notable

Samuel Clemens (Mark Twain) was born in Florida in
Monroe County and grew up in Hannibal, which attracts
visitors to Twain's boyhood home; Westminster College in
Fulton was the site of Winston Churchill's "Iron Curtain"
speech after World War II; the August A. Busch wildlife
area in St. Charles County was purchased by the state in 1947
after Busch's widow made a donation toward the purchase.

Election Returns

	Republican		Democratic		Other	
President 2000	145,604	55.0%	112,239	42.4%	7,093	2.7%
House 2002	146,032	68.2%	61,126	28.5%	6,967	3.3%

District Profile

Population   621,690

Total area (square miles)   14,082.3
Land area (square miles)   13,925.4

Population per square mile   44.6

Counties (2000 population)

Adair	24,977	Macon	15,762
Audrain	25,853	Maries	8,903
Boone	135,454	Marion	28,289
Callaway	40,766	Miller	23,564
Camden (pt.)	2,240	Monroe	9,311
Clark	7,416	Montgomery	12,136
Crawford	22,804	Osage	13,062
Franklin	93,807	Pike	18,351
Gasconade	15,342	Ralls	9,626
Knox	4,361	Randolph	24,663
Lewis	10,494	Scotland	4,983

Shelby 6,799   Warren 24,525
St. Charles (pt.) 38,202

Cities and other areas over 10,000 (2000 population)
Columbia 84,531
Fulton 12,128
Hannibal 17,757
Kirksville 16,988
Lake St. Louis (pt.) 10,017
Mexico 11,320
Moberly 11,945
Washington 13,243

Race and Hispanic or Latino origin*
White 92.6%
Black or African American 3.9%
American Indian or Alaska Native 0.3%
Asian 0.9%
Native Hawaiian or other Pacific Islander 0.0%
Some other race 0.1%
Hispanic or Latino origin 1.1%
Two or more races 1.1%

*As percentage of total population.

Ancestry*
Dutch 1.3%   Italian 1.9%
English 7.8%   Scotch-Irish 1.3%
French 2.5%   Scottish 1.2%
German 21.7%   USA/American 9.2%
Irish 9.3%

*As estimated percentage of total population.

Universities and colleges, 2000–2001 enrollment
Columbia College, Columbia 7,948
Culver-Stockton College, Canton 821
East Central College, Union 3,190
Hannibal-LaGrange College, Hannibal 1,150
Kirksville College of Osteopathic Medicine, Kirksville
  1,028
Linn State Technical College, Linn 377
Moberly Area Community College, Moberly 2,938
Stephens College, Columbia 771
Truman State University, Kirksville 6,111
University of Missouri, Columbia 23,309
Westminster College, Fulton 686
William Woods University, Fulton 1,479

Newspapers and circulation

	District circulation	Total circulation
Columbia Daily Tribune	17,641	18,902
Hannibal Courier-Post	7,989	8,017
Jefferson City Capital News	1,202	2,150
Jefferson City Post Tribune	3,008	17,069
Kansas City Star	1,462	261,945
Quincy Herald Whig	3,671	22,635
St. Louis Post-Dispatch	20,354	295,281
*USA Today**	3,122	1,674,376

*See Sources and Explanations in the front of the volume.

Television stations and affiliations
Columbia-Jefferson City	35%	KMIZ	ABC
Columbia-Jefferson City	35%	KMOS	PBS
Columbia-Jefferson City	35%	KNLJ	Independent
Columbia-Jefferson City	35%	KOMU	NBC
Columbia-Jefferson City	35%	KRCG	CBS
Quincy-Hannibal-Keokuk	26%	KHQA	CBS
Quincy-Hannibal-Keokuk	26%	WGEM	NBC
Quincy-Hannibal-Keokuk	26%	WMEC	PBS
Quincy-Hannibal-Keokuk	26%	WQEC	PBS
Quincy-Hannibal-Keokuk	26%	WTJR	Independent
St. Louis	25%	KDNL	ABC
St. Louis	25%	KETC	PBS
St. Louis	25%	KMOV	CBS
St. Louis	25%	KNLC	Independent
St. Louis	25%	KPLR	WB
St. Louis	25%	KSDK	NBC
St. Louis	25%	KTVI	FOX
St. Louis	25%	WHSL	Independent
St. Louis	25%	WPXS	PAX
Ottumwa-Kirksville	13%	KTVO	ABC
Springfield	1%	KDEB	FOX
Springfield	1%	KOLR	CBS
Springfield	1%	KOZK	PBS
Springfield	1%	KSPR	ABC
Springfield	1%	KYTV	NBC

Cable systems and subscribers
Cable Direct 1,830
Cable ONE 6,475
Cass County Cable 1,011
Charter 26,907
Galaxy 2,678
Kahoka Communications 642
Mediacom 33,311
St. Joseph Cablevision 2,220
U.S. Cable 24,748

Businesses and other major employers
Memorial Union University; Columbia 25,000
Boone Hospital Center; Columbia 2,000
University of Missouri; Columbia 2,000
University of Missouri Hospital; Columbia 2,000
Phillips Co.; Centralia; wood partitions and fixtures
  1,997
International Management Services Co.; Columbia;
  employee leasing service 1,940
Shelter Insurance; Columbia; insurance brokers 1,100
3M Co.; Columbia; electronic connectors 1,000
AmerenUE; Fulton; electric services 1,000
Missouri Mental Health Dept.; Fulton 1,000
U.S. Veterans Hospital; Columbia 1,000
AB Chance Co.; Centralia; electric distribution
  transformers 950
Ameriwood Industries; Wright City; wood console tables
  850
State Farm Mutual Automobile Insurance Co.;
  Columbia; insurance claim adjusters 800
St. John's Mercy Hospital; Washington 785

Fasco Industries Inc.; Eldon; electric motors   750
MBS Textbook Exchange Inc.; Columbia; books   750
Northeast Regional Medical Center; Kirksville   750
Truman State University; Kirksville   750
K/W Builders; Lancaster; new single-family houses
   720
Hannibal Regional Hospital Inc.; Hannibal   605
Audrain Health Care Inc. Hospital; Mexico   600
Kraft Foods Inc.; Columbia; frankfurters   600
Missouri Dept. of Corrections; Bowling Green   600
Wal-Mart Stores Inc.; Columbia; discount department
   stores   600
Hannibal School District; Hannibal   550

BASF Corp.; Palmyra; pharmaceuticals   500
ConAgra Foods Inc.; Macon; frozen specialties   500
Dura Automotive Systems Inc.; Hannibal; brake
   systems/parts   500
Dura Automotive Systems Inc.; Moberly; motor vehicle
   brake systems/parts   500
Missouri Dept. of Corrections; Moberly   500
Osage County Historical Society; Linn; historical society
   500
Quaker Window Products Co.; Freeburg; window and
   door frames   500
Regional Alternative Health Services Inc.; Columbia;
   home health care services   500

Montana

Montana is called the Big Sky Country, a salute to its sense of limitless horizon. Once explored by Lewis and Clark and later by fur trappers and gold seekers, Montana is now a prime destination for high-tech tycoons, celebrities, and telecommuters who want to buy their own small piece of the frontier.

Other western states offer much the same topography, yet on the map or on the landscape it is Montana's breadth that remains truly breathtaking. However, the challenge for Montana and the other states of scenic grandeur has been to develop an economy diversified and adaptable enough to support a large population. With an economy based on natural resources, Montana finds itself exploiting its terrain while also striving to protect it. In ballot initiatives, voters have rejected some environmental regulations. Yet Butte, the site of years of mining, is the center of a massive Superfund cleanup effort.

With all its vast territory, Montana has never reached the million mark in residents. As a result, in 1990 and again in 2000, it fell just shy of the cutoff point for earning a second congressional district. This reality was a shock after the 1990 census. A decade of almost no growth at all in the 1980s cost the state the second seat it had earned in the census of 1910 and kept ever since. While growth resumed in the 1990s (the state added more than 100,000 residents for the first time since the decade of World War I) and initial indications in the late 1990s held out hope for a restored second seat, the actual census of 2000 found the state just above 900,000 and well shy of the cutoff for a second seat. Montana had to content itself once more with being the most populous of the single-district states.

The 2000 shortfall came as a surprise to many Montanans, who had regarded the slow growth of the previous decades as an aberration and believed the 11 percent jump in the 1990s was, if anything, excessive growth in the state. Some residents regard the latest newcomers with suspicion, even contempt, but the state is increasingly reliant on the outsiders known as tourists, who have become a mainstay of an economy otherwise long dependent on commodity prices and the volatile markets that set them.

Montana grew up as a Wild West paradigm, a land of cattle drives, ore strikes, and boomtowns. Over the generations, the two-thirds of the state east of the Continental Divide settled into ranching and wheat farming, much like the Dakotas. This eastern flat plain follows a tradition of rural Republicanism.

The western third of the state, which features the northern ranges of the Rocky Mountains, leans Democratic, with its environmental base, union tradition in mining and lumber mills, and home to the state's university community in Missoula. This part of the state got its early economic vitality from mining operations around Anaconda and other rich deposits of copper, lead, and zinc. Digging these riches required armies of workers, and there soon followed a labor movement of considerable force. Montana was at one time a major focus of the Western Federation of Miners, a precursor of the International Workers of the World or Wobblies. These socialist burgeonings were suppressed during World War I and lost momentum thereafter. But miners and the more conventional unions that arose later became and remained a force in the state's politics.

One of them, Mike Mansfield, came out of the mine to become the state's best known politician of the century, and his 16 years as Senate majority leader still stands as the record in that job. Through much of the twentieth century, Mansfield-style Democrats held sway in the state's politics by dominating the western mountain counties and holding their own in the rolling hills of the eastern counties. This farm-labor coalition, not unlike its counterparts in the Dakotas and Minnesota, was strong enough to win 13 consecutive Senate races in the state from 1948 through 1984. Mansfield and his fellow Democrat Lee Metcalf served a total of seven terms. Thereafter, Democrats John "Doc" Melcher, a rough-edged veterinarian, and Max Baucus, a Stanford-trained lawyer, carried on the tradition. Baucus won his fifth term in 2002 and was senior Democrat on the Senate Committee on Finance. But Melcher lost in 1988 to a folksy radio personality, Conrad Burns, who held the seat into the years after 2000.

Democrats have also done well in governorships here. Since Montana became a state in 1889, 13 of the 22 governors have been Democrats, although Republicans have more than held their own since World War II. In 2000 the GOP won its fifth straight term in the office, a streak preceded by five straight Democratic wins and before that four by the GOP.

In the late 1990s, the struggle for the state's single House seat seemed to have resolved itself for the Republicans. When the two districts were merged in 1992, the contest between liberal Democrat Pat Williams and conservative Republican Ron Marlenee could not have been a more stark illustration of the state's competing political forces and traditions. Williams narrowly won that round, but when he retired in 1996 the seat went Republican and has so remained.

The GOP has also been the usual favorite here in presidential balloting, as Montanans have shown little interest in the easterners and southerners the Democrats tend to nominate. The voters here have felt affinity with other

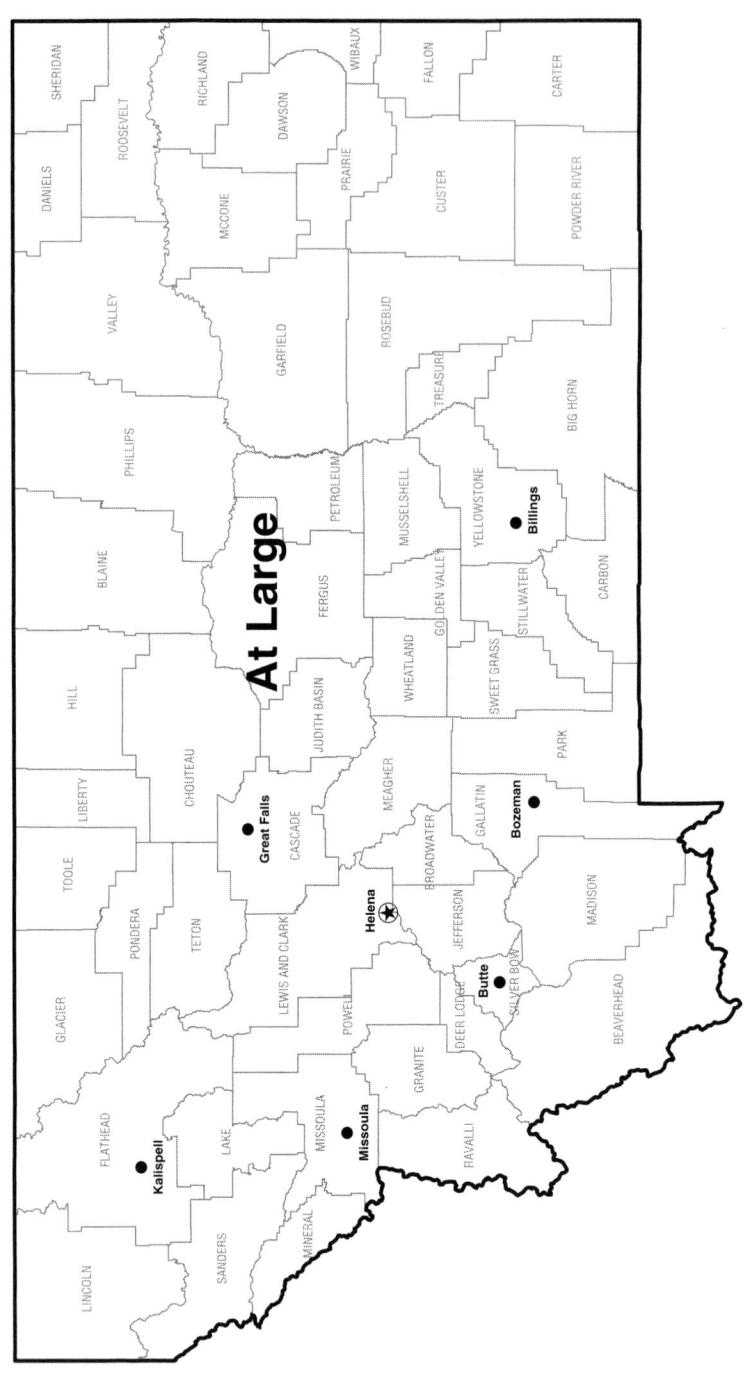

westerners, however, and since 1952, the GOP nominees have been from Texas, Kansas, California, and Arizona (with one, Gerald Ford, from western Michigan).

The only Democrats to capture Montana's electoral votes in that period were Texan Lyndon B. Johnson and, in 1992, Arkansan Bill Clinton. The latter, however, won with a plurality of just 37.6 percent of the vote, thanks to the strong presence of Texan Ross Perot, who got 26 percent. Clinton managed just 41.2 percent here in 1996, not enough to beat Bob Dole of Kansas. In 2000 Texan George W. Bush cruised to victory with more than 58 percent, winning 51 of the 56 counties. Democrat Al Gore managed to reach one-third of the vote, having to share the non-Bush vote with Ralph Nader (6 percent) and a variety of other third-party candidates.

Major Industry
Agriculture, tourism, forestry.

Notable
Montana elected the first woman, Jeannette Rankin, to Congress in 1916; Glacier National Park is located in the northwest part of the state; Jordan was the site of a 1996 standoff between federal authorities and an antitax group called the Freemen.

Table 1 Population

District	Population	Population under 18	Voting-age population	Median age	Male*	Female*
At Large	902,195	230,062	672,133	37.5	49.8	50.2

*As percentage of total population.

Table 2 Voting-Age Persons by Race/Hispanic or Latino Origin

District	White*	Black or African American*	American Indian or Alaska Native*	Asian*	Other or multirace*	Hispanic or Latino*
At Large	91.5	0.3	4.9	0.5	1.3	1.6

*As percentage of voting-age population.

Table 3 Voting-Age Population by Age Groups

District	18 to 24*	25 to 44*	45 to 64*	Over 64*
At Large	12.8	36.5	32.8	18.0

*As percentage of voting-age population.

Table 4 Income and Occupation

District	Median family income	Families in poverty*	White collar†	Blue collar†	Service†	Farm†
At Large	$40,487	10.5	58.6	22.0	17.2	2.2

*As percentage of all families.   †As percentage of employed workers 16 years and over.

Table 5 Education: School Years Completed

District	Less than grade 9*	Grades 9–12 no diploma*	High school diploma no college*	Some college*	College bachelor's degree or higher*
At Large	4.3	8.6	31.3	31.5	24.4

*As percentage of persons age 25 and over.

Table 6 Housing and Residential Patterns

District	Median home value	Owner occupied*	Renter occupied*	Urban†	Rural†
At Large	$95,800	69.1	30.9	54.0	46.0

*As percentage of occupied housing units.   †As percentage of total population.

Election Returns

	Republican		Democratic		Other	
President 2000	240,178	58.4%	137,126	33.4%	33,682	8.2%
House 2002	214,100	64.6%	108,233	32.7%	8,988	2.7%

District Profile

Population   902,195

Total area (square miles)   147,042.4
Land area (square miles)   145,552.4

Population per square mile   6.2

Counties (2000 population)

Beaverhead	9,202	McCone	1,977
Big Horn	12,671	Meagher	1,932
Blaine	7,009	Mineral	3,884
Broadwater	4,385	Missoula	95,802
Carbon	9,552	Musselshell	4,497
Carter	1,360	Park	15,694
Cascade	80,357	Petroleum	493
Chouteau	5,970	Phillips	4,601
Custer	11,696	Pondera	6,424
Daniels	2,017	Powder River	1,858
Dawson	9,059	Powell	7,180
Deer Lodge	9,417	Prairie	1,199
Fallon	2,837	Ravalli	36,070
Fergus	11,893	Richland	9,667
Flathead	74,471	Roosevelt	10,620
Gallatin	67,831	Rosebud	9,383
Garfield	1,279	Sanders	10,227
Glacier	13,247	Sheridan	4,105
Golden Valley	1,042	Silver Bow	34,606
Granite	2,830	Stillwater	8,195
Hill	16,673	Sweet Grass	3,609
Jefferson	10,049	Teton	6,445
Judith Basin	2,329	Toole	5,267
Lake	26,507	Treasure	861
Lewis and Clark	55,716	Valley	7,675
Liberty	2,158	Wheatland	2,259
Lincoln	18,837	Wibaux	1,068
Madison	6,851	Yellowstone	129,352

Cities and other areas over 10,000 (2000 population)

Billings	89,847	Helena	25,780
Bozeman	27,509	Kalispell	14,223
Butte-Silver Bow	33,892	Missoula	57,053
Great Falls	56,690		

Race and Hispanic or Latino origin*
White   89.5%
Black or African American   0.3%
American Indian or Alaska Native   6.0%
Asian   0.5%
Native Hawaiian or other Pacific Islander   0.0%

Some other race   0.1%
Hispanic or Latino origin   2.0%
Two or more races   1.5%

As percentage of total population.

Ancestry*
Danish   1.2%   Norwegian   7.4%
Dutch   1.8%   Polish   1.4%
English   8.8%   Scotch-Irish   1.8%
French   2.9%   Scottish   2.1%
German   18.8%   Swedish   2.4%
Irish   10.3%   USA/American   3.6%
Italian   2.2%

As estimated percentage of total population.

Universities and colleges, 2000–2001 enrollment
Blackfeet Community College, Browning   299
Carroll College, Helena   1,251
Dawson Community College, Glendive   449
Dull Knife Memorial College, Lame Deer   461
Flathead Valley Community College, Kalispell   1,822
Fort Belknap College, Harlem   295
Fort Peck Community College, Poplar   400
Helena College of Technology, Helena   763
Little Big Horn College, Crow Agency   320
Montana State University, Billings   3,799
Montana State University, Bozeman   11,666
Montana State University-College of Technology, Billings   497
Montana State University-Northern, Havre   1,512
Montana Tech-College of Technology, Butte   401
Montana Tech of the University of Montana, Butte   1,509
Rocky Mountain College, Billings   784
Salish Kootenai College, Pablo   1,042
University of Montana, Missoula   12,413
University of Great Falls, Great Falls   1,005
Western Montana College-University of Montana, Dillon   1,160

Newspapers and circulation

	District circulation	Total circulation
Billings Gazette	40,062	46,010
Bozeman Daily Chronicle	14,721	14,960
Butte Montana Standard	13,837	13,906
Great Falls Tribune	32,848	33,055
Helena Independent Record	12,870	13,008
Missoula Missoulian	28,949	29,296
*USA Today**	1,402	1,674,376

See Sources and Explanations in the front of the volume.

Television stations and affiliations
Billings	29%	KHMT	FOX
Billings	29%	KSVI	ABC
Billings	29%	KTVQ	CBS
Billings	29%	KULR	NBC
Billings	29%	KYUS	NBC
Great Falls	28%	KFBB	ABC
Great Falls	28%	KRTV	CBS
Great Falls	28%	KTGF	NBC
Butte-Bozeman	12%	KTVM	NBC
Butte-Bozeman	12%	KUSM	PBS
Butte-Bozeman	12%	KWYB	ABC
Butte-Bozeman	12%	KXLF	CBS
Missoula	12%	KCFW	NBC
Missoula	12%	KECI	NBC
Missoula	12%	KPAX	CBS
Missoula	12%	KTMF	ABC
Missoula	12%	KUFM	PBS
Minot-Bismarck-Dickinson	8%	KBME	PBS
Minot-Bismarck-Dickinson	8%	KBMY	ABC
Minot-Bismarck-Dickinson	8%	KDSE	PBS
Minot-Bismarck-Dickinson	8%	KFYR	NBC
Minot-Bismarck-Dickinson	8%	KMOT	NBC
Minot-Bismarck-Dickinson	8%	KQCD	NBC
Minot-Bismarck-Dickinson	8%	KSRE	PBS
Minot-Bismarck-Dickinson	8%	KUMV	NBC
Minot-Bismarck-Dickinson	8%	KWSE	PBS
Minot-Bismarck-Dickinson	8%	KXMA	CBS
Minot-Bismarck-Dickinson	8%	KXMB	CBS
Minot-Bismarck-Dickinson	8%	KXMC	CBS
Minot-Bismarck-Dickinson	8%	KXMD	CBS
Glendive	4%	KXGN	CBS, NBC
Helena	3%	KTVH	NBC
Rapid City, SD	2%	KBHE	PBS
Rapid City, SD	2%	KCLO	CBS
Rapid City, SD	2%	KEVN	FOX
Rapid City, SD	2%	KHSD	ABC
Rapid City, SD	2%	KIVV	FOX
Rapid City, SD	2%	KOTA	ABC
Rapid City, SD	2%	KPSD	PBS
Rapid City, SD	2%	KSGW	ABC
Rapid City, SD	2%	KTNE	PBS
Rapid City, SD	2%	KZSD	PBS
Spokane, WA	2%	KAYU	FOX
Spokane, WA	2%	KCDT	PBS
Spokane, WA	2%	KHQ	NBC
Spokane, WA	2%	KLEW	CBS, UPN
Spokane, WA	2%	KREM	CBS
Spokane, WA	2%	KSKN	WB
Spokane, WA	2%	KSPS	PBS
Spokane, WA	2%	KUID	PBS
Spokane, WA	2%	KWSU	PBS
Spokane, WA	2%	KXLY	ABC

Cable systems and subscribers
Adelphia   1,184
Bresnan   156,560
Cable Montana   2,973
Fibervision   4,062
Lincoln Cable TV   2,274
Mallard   5,666
Mid-Rivers Cable TV   1,204
Tobacco Valley Communications   620

Military installations, September 2001
Malmstrom Air Force Base, Great Falls   3,953
Great Falls International Airport (Air National Guard), Great Falls   939
Helena Armory (Army Guard), Helena   369
Fort William Henry Harrison Military Training Area, Helena   258
Ernest Veuve Hall (Army Reserve), Missoula   171
Fort Missoula (Army Guard), Missoula   143

Businesses and other major employers

St. Patrick Hospital Corp.; Missoula   2,341
Benefis Health Care Hospital; Great Falls   2,000
Billings School District; Billings   2,000
University of Montana; Missoula   1,900
Deaconess-Billings Clinic; Billings   1,800
St. Vincent Healthcare Hospital; Billings   1,407
Stillwater Mining Co.; Nye; palladium group ores mining   1,200
DJC Inc.; Billings; collection agency   1,000
Kalispell Regional Medical Center Inc.; Kalispell   934
Omniflight Helicopters Inc.; Billings; health practitioner   900
Community Medical Center Inc.; Missoula   850
Blackfeet Nation; Browning; Native American reservation   800
Burlington Northern and Santa Fe Railway Co.; Havre; freight hauling   800
Northwestern Corp.; Butte; engineering services   800
Sampler's Plus; Billings; demonstration service   800
Semitool Inc.; Kalispell; semiconductor manufacturing machinery   730
St. Peter's Hospital; Helena   686
Boyne USA Inc.; Big Sky; resort hotel   675
Smurfit-Stone Container Corp.; Missoula; kraft linerboard   675
Watkins and Shepard Trucking Inc.; Missoula; trucking   666

Bozeman Deaconess Hospital; Bozeman   661
Great Falls Public School District; Great Falls   654
Montana Tech of University of Montana; Butte   652
Montana Taxation Dept.; Helena   650
Flathead Valley Community College Inc.; Kalispell   612
Michael N. Murphy MD; Great Falls; health practitioner   600
Montana State University; Billings   600
Northern Montana Hospital; Havre   600
Crow Tribe of Indians; Crow Agency; Native American reservation   593
Entech Inc.; Butte; surface mining   584
Columbia Falls Aluminum Co.; Columbia Falls; primary aluminum   579
Confederated Salish and Kootenai Tribes Inc.; Pablo; Native American reservation   550
Aware Inc.; Great Falls; social services   500
Blue Cross and Blue Shield of Montana; Helena; group hospitalization   500
Glacier Gas Co.; Butte; crude petroleum and natural gas   500
Missoula County; Missoula; group health association   500
Montana Dept. of Transportation; Helena   500
Montana State University; Bozeman   500
Stimson Lumber Co.; Bonner; plywood, hardwood   500
U.S. Postal Service; Billings   500

NEBRASKA

Districts established May 30, 2001, for elections first held in 2002.

3 members

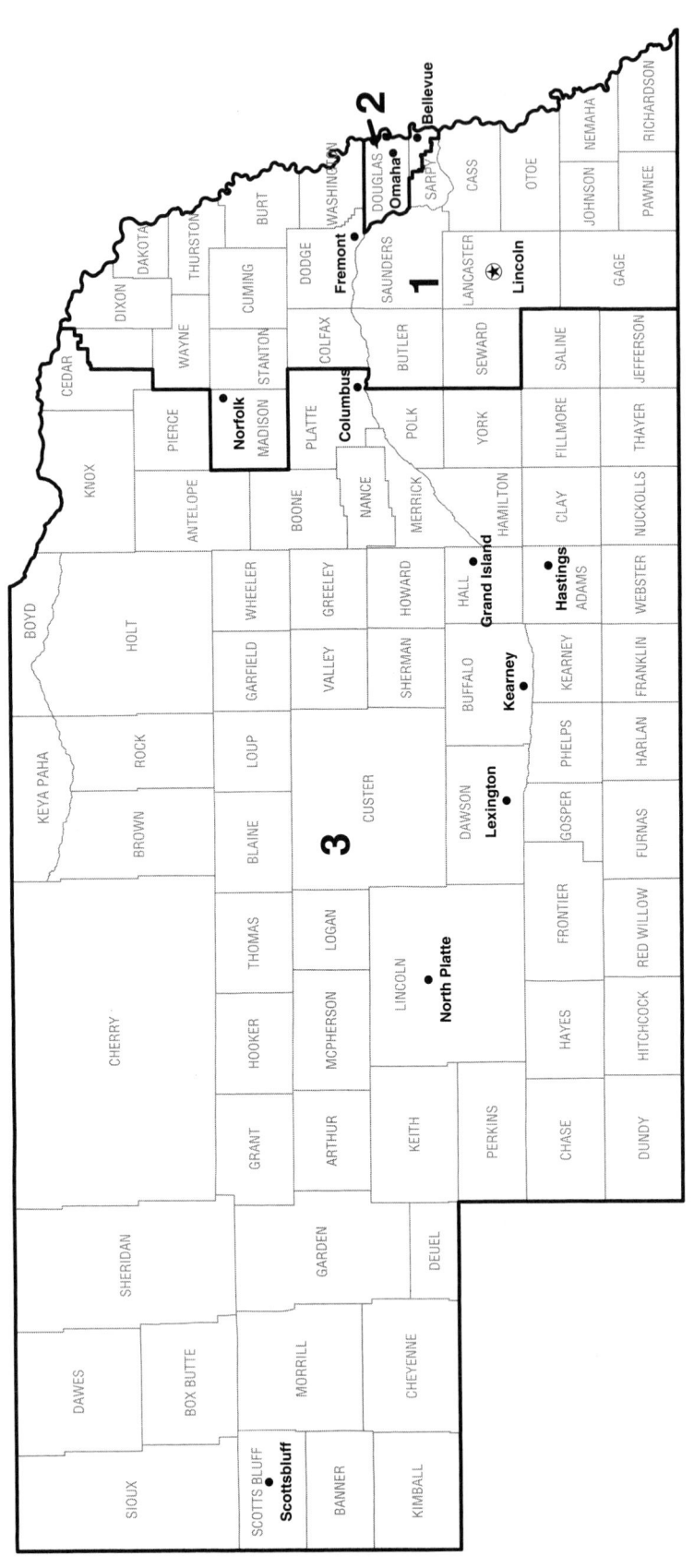

Nebraska

The name means "flat water," the Oto Indians' name for the placid river, now known as the Platte, traversing what is now known as Nebraska. But the image might also be applied to the landscape as a whole, one of the most topographically consistent in the union and one of the most homogenous. Driving across Nebraska, particularly on the well-traveled ribbon of Interstate 80 that largely tracks the Platte, the impression is of crossing one enormous, fenceless farm with only an occasional outcropping of rock or cluster of buildings. Nebraska is in fact the one state with the highest proportion of its land devoted to farming and ranching (95 percent). In population density it ranks forty-second, in average annual pay it ranks forty-first—but in cost of living it was thirty-third. Only South Dakota, the neighbor to the north, had a lower unemployment rate in 2002 than Nebraska's 3.6 percent.

Here, in the eastern counties that border on Iowa, the farming is about corn and soybeans, sorghum, and hogs, much as in the neighboring state. But as the traveler goes west, the emphasis shifts to wheat—and more wheat—in vast stretches of grain that stretch without discernible end. In the north, the soil and water table are less generous, and cattle grazing takes over. But corn remains the single most important crop, justifying the nickname Cornhusker State given long ago that lives on in the mascot of the University of Nebraska football team. In a state with no major league professional sports, the Huskers receive supreme loyalty. Yet it also conveys something of the Nebraska ethos that wherever their team travels it tends to win—often by big scores—yet the accompanying fans are known for their sportsmanship and manners. It is also significant that when the Huskers' highly successful coach, Tom Osborne, retired from the game and won a seat in Congress, it was widely regarded as a step down.

Omaha, on the Iowa line, is the population center, a long-time terminus for cattle drives where stock was fattened for slaughter and marketing. For nearly as long, Omaha has been a regional center for financial services as well. Lincoln is principally known as the home of the University of Nebraska but as such is the lodestar for much of the state's fledgling high-tech economy as well. These two communities are also home to virtually all the state's African Americans (3.5 percent of voting-age population statewide), although the Hispanics (4.5 percent) and other racial groups (2.7 percent) are more widely dispersed throughout the state.

Nebraska has some unusual political traditions, many of them rooted in the hard-eyed practicality of the original

Nebraskans or added in the difficult years of the Great Depression of the 1930s. For example, the state has maintained the only unicameral—single chamber—legislature in the land, and the only one in which the members state no party affiliation. The 49 members are known as senators, and they view themselves as a cross between a corporate board and a gaggle of citizen tribunes.

Despite this nonpartisan gesture, Nebraska's statewide politicians have usually been Republicans, dating back to the first years of statehood in the 1850s, the birth decade of the GOP. But there is within this one-party dominance a long-standing competition between conservatives and progressives that had its beginnings more than a century ago. In more recent years, the role of the progressives in this relationship has been danced by the contemporary Democratic Party, which might well pass for a Republican Party in many states on either coast. Democrats here tend to be semi-detached from the national party, as may be said of Ben Nelson, first elected in 2000, who was one of the three Democrats in the Senate most likely to side with President George W. Bush. The same could be said of Nelson's three recent predecessors as Democrats in the Senate: Bob Kerrey, Jim Exon, and Edward Zorinksy.

Nelson had been a highly popular governor of the state from 1991 through 1999 but his first bid for Senate, in 1996, was frustrated by Republican candidate Chuck Hagel, who in 2002 was reelected practically by acclamation. A decorated Vietnam vet who had worked as a broadcaster, bartender, Washington lobbyist, and telecommunications entrepreneur before running for office, Hagel has established himself as a free thinker within his party, as well. The state has alternated its governorship between the parties fairly regularly, but as with most of the interior West, it has become reliably Republican in presidential elections. Since World War I, Nebraska has voted Democratic only in the huge landslides of Franklin D. Roosevelt (1932, 1936) and Lyndon B. Johnson (1964).

Nebraska hit its peak at six congressional seats in the 1890 census and held them for 40 years before the slide began: down a seat each time in the 1930, 1940, and 1960 censuses. Since then the state has held at three, although every ten years the 3rd District gets bigger and creeps closer to Lincoln, while the 2nd constricts more tightly around Omaha and the 1st is defined as the space between them. The 2nd reaches its one-third share of the state population (around 570,000) by encompassing all of Douglas County and the suburban turf in far northeastern Sarpy County.

Given that all seats have been held by Republicans since the mid-1990s, and all three returned big majorities to George W. Bush in 2000, there was little need for rancor and the redistricting was completed in May 2001. The 3rd District gained about 40,000 voters from the 1st District by taking over York and Saline Counties, the 2nd District passed about 30,000 to the 1st, and that left all three equal.

Table 1 Population

District	Population	Population under 18	Voting-age population	Median age	Male*	Female*
1	570,325	144,447	425,878	34.9	49.6	50.4
2	570,421	156,070	414,351	33.0	49.1	50.9
3	570,517	149,725	420,792	38.3	49.2	50.8
State	1,711,263	450,242	1,261,021	35.3	49.3	50.7

*As percentage of total population.

Table 2 Voting-Age Persons by Race/Hispanic or Latino Origin

District	White*	Black or African American*	American Indian or Alaska Native*	Asian*	Other or multirace*	Hispanic or Latino*
1	92.1	1.3	0.9	1.5	0.7	3.4
2	82.2	9.0	0.5	2.0	1.0	5.4
3	93.5	0.2	0.6	0.5	0.4	4.8
State	89.3	3.5	0.7	1.3	0.7	4.5

*As percentage of voting-age population.

Table 3 Voting-Age Population by Age Groups

District	18 to 24*	25 to 44*	45 to 64*	Over 64*
1	15.9	37.8	28.4	17.9
2	14.0	43.7	28.4	13.9
3	11.6	34.5	30.6	23.4
State	13.8	38.6	29.1	18.4

*As percentage of voting-age population.

Table 4 Income and Occupation

District	Median family income	Families in poverty*	White collar†	Blue collar†	Service†	Farm†
1	$49,295	5.9	57.7	26.2	15.0	1.1
2	$55,674	6.0	66.8	19.5	13.5	0.2
3	$41,316	8.1	53.5	27.6	15.2	3.6
State	$48,032	6.7	59.4	24.4	14.6	1.6

*As percentage of all families.   †As percentage of employed workers 16 years and over.

Table 5 Education: School Years Completed

District	Less than grade 9*	Grades 9–12 no diploma*	High school diploma no college*	Some college*	College bachelor's degree or higher*
1	5.4	7.8	32.0	30.9	23.9
2	3.8	7.8	25.9	32.0	30.5
3	6.8	8.5	35.7	31.8	17.1
State	5.4	8.0	31.3	31.6	23.7

*As percentage of persons age 25 and over.

Table 6 Housing and Residential Patterns

District	Median home value	Owner occupied*	Renter occupied*	Urban†	Rural†
1	$92,000	67.4	32.6	65.1	34.9
2	$102,000	63.8	36.2	97.8	2.2
3	$66,700	71.0	29.0	46.1	53.9
State	$86,900	67.4	32.6	69.7	30.3

*As percentage of occupied housing units.   †As percentage of total population.

Nebraska 1st District

East — Lincoln, Fremont, Norfolk

The 1st takes in eastern Nebraska, excluding Omaha and its suburbs. The region includes the state's capital, Lincoln, and the University of Nebraska's Memorial Stadium, which could qualify as the district's second-largest city and the state's third-largest when filled to its 74,000-seat capacity during a home football game. Despite the area's small-town reputation, growing industry in Omaha exurbs, including Lincoln, Norfolk, and South Sioux City, is helping to make the eastern portion of the state more urban.

Lincoln, in particular, is thriving and has seen a major population increase led by the expanding state and city governments and the university. Hospitals and a banking and insurance industry also help sustain the city's economy.

Although the district was home to populist William Jennings Bryan and many supporters of his politics at the turn of the twentieth century, the 1st now votes consistently Republican at all levels. The University of Nebraska's main campus in Lincoln makes the city more liberal, but voter registration favors the GOP in both the city and surrounding Lancaster County. The strongest Democratic areas are in the northeast, in Dakota County, with a sizable blue-collar contingent, and in Thurston County, made up of the Winnebago and Omaha Native American reservations. Democratic-leaning Saline County was moved from the 1st District to the western 3rd in redistricting following the 2000 census.

The region depends on agriculture but with a modern twist. Traditional crop and hog farming are supplemented by other agribusiness, such as meat processing, food packaging, and fertilizer production. Telemarketing and polling companies, such as the Gallup Organization, also add to white-collar job opportunities. Flood control is a problem in the area.

Major Industry

Agriculture, meat processing, health care, government.

Notable

Johnny Carson, former host of *The Tonight Show,* grew up in Norfolk; Arbor Day was first celebrated in Nebraska City in 1872; a phone booth in Wahoo has been the fictional home office for *The Late Show with David Letterman* since 1996.

Election Returns

	Republican		Democratic		Other	
President 2000	138,799	58.6%	85,634	36.2%	12,242	5.2%
House 2002	133,013	85.4%			22,831	14.6%

District Profile

Population   570,325

Total area (square miles)   12,034.0
  Land area (square miles)   11,950.8

Population per square mile   47.7

Counties (2000 population)

Burt	7,791	Madison	35,226
Butler	8,767	Nemaha	7,576
Cass	24,334	Otoe	15,396
Cedar (pt.)	3,107	Pawnee	3,087
Colfax	10,441	Richardson	9,531
Cuming	10,203	Sarpy (pt.)	15,759
Dakota	20,253	Saunders	19,830
Dixon	6,339	Seward	16,496
Dodge	36,160	Stanton	6,455
Gage	22,993	Thurston	7,171
Johnson	4,488	Washington	18,780
Lancaster	250,291	Wayne	9,851

Cities and other areas over 10,000 (2000 population)

Beatrice	12,496	Norfolk	23,516
Fremont	25,174	South Sioux City	11,925
Lincoln	225,581		

Race and Hispanic or Latino origin*

White   90.5%
Black or African American   1.4%
American Indian or Alaska Native   1.2%
Asian   1.5%
Native Hawaiian or other Pacific Islander   0.0%
Some other race   0.1%
Hispanic or Latino origin   4.2%
Two or more races   1.1%

*As percentage of total population.

Ancestry*

Danish	2.2%	Italian	1.2%
Dutch	1.8%	Norwegian	1.7%
English	6.8%	Polish	1.7%
French	1.9%	Swedish	3.7%
German	30.8%	USA/American	3.2%
Irish	8.7%		

*As estimated percentage of total population.

Universities and colleges, 2000–2001 enrollment

Concordia University, Seward   1,270
Dana College, Blair   583
Lincoln School of Commerce, Lincoln   445
Midland Lutheran College, Fremont   1,025
Nebraska Wesleyan University, Lincoln   1,699
Northeast Community College, Norfolk   4,520
Peru State College, Peru   1,698
Southeast Community College Area, Lincoln   7,396
Union College, Lincoln   788
University of Nebraska at Lincoln, Lincoln   22,268
Wayne State College, Wayne   3,518

Newspapers and circulation

	District circulation	Total circulation
Beatrice Daily Sun	6,330	7,915
Columbus Telegram	2,624	9,104
Fremont Tribune	7,525	7,646
Lincoln Journal Star	67,105	75,540
Norfolk News	10,229	17,361
Omaha World Herald	37,110	194,150
Sioux City Journal	4,665	46,030
*USA Today**	2,281	1,674,376

*See Sources and Explanations in the front of the volume.

Television stations and affiliations

Omaha	54%	KBIN	PBS
Omaha	54%	KETV	ABC
Omaha	54%	KHIN	PBS
Omaha	54%	KMTV	CBS
Omaha	54%	KPTM	FOX
Omaha	54%	KUON	PBS
Omaha	54%	KXVO	WB
Omaha	54%	KYNE	PBS
Omaha	54%	WOWT	NBC
Sioux City	24%	KCAU	ABC
Sioux City	24%	KMEG	CBS, UPN
Sioux City	24%	KSIN	PBS
Sioux City	24%	KTIV	NBC
Sioux City	24%	KUSD	PBS
Sioux City	24%	KXNE	PBS
Lincoln-Hastings-Kearney	22%	KGIN	CBS
Lincoln-Hastings-Kearney	22%	KHAS	NBC
Lincoln-Hastings-Kearney	22%	KHGI	ABC
Lincoln-Hastings-Kearney	22%	KHNE	PBS
Lincoln-Hastings-Kearney	22%	KLKE	ABC
Lincoln-Hastings-Kearney	22%	KLKN	ABC
Lincoln-Hastings-Kearney	22%	KLNE	PBS
Lincoln-Hastings-Kearney	22%	KMNE	PBS
Lincoln-Hastings-Kearney	22%	KOLN	CBS
Lincoln-Hastings-Kearney	22%	KSNB	FOX
Lincoln-Hastings-Kearney	22%	KTVG	FOX
Lincoln-Hastings-Kearney	22%	KWNB	ABC

Cable systems and subscribers

Cable ONE   14,202
Cable TV of Stanton   1,080
Charter   9,741
Galaxy   28,569
Great Plains Cable TV   1,078
HunTel Cablevision   9,571
Telepartners   764
Time Warner   86,190

Military installations, September 2001

Lincoln Municipal Airport (Air National Guard), Lincoln   908
Camp Ashland (National Guard), Ashland   209

Businesses and other major employers

Drivers Management; Omaha; employee leasing service   8,000
BryanLGH Medical Center; Lincoln   3,000
MDS Pharma Services Inc.; Lincoln; testing laboratories   2,871
Excel Corp.; Schuyler; meatpacking plants   2,000
Goodyear Tire and Rubber Co.; Lincoln; automobile hose   1,800
Gallup Inc.; Lincoln; management consulting   1,400
St. Elizabeth Regional Medical Center; Lincoln   1,300

Duncan Aviation Inc.; Lincoln; aircraft, heavy equipment repair 1,200

Nebraska Public Power District; Hadar; electric power systems contractors 1,200

Omaha Public Power District; Fort Calhoun; electric power distribution 1,200

Werner Enterprises Inc.; Omaha; trucking 1,170

State Farm Mutual Automobile Insurance Co.; Lincoln; insurance agents and brokers 1,100

IBP Inc.; Madison; meats and meat products 1,000

Nebraska Health System Hospital; Omaha 1,000

Ameritas Life Insurance Corp.; Lincoln; life insurance 950

Kawasaki Motors Manufacturing Corp.; Lincoln; all-terrain vehicles 900

Tabitha Inc.; Lincoln; aged home 900

Fremont Area Medical Center; Fremont 850

Lincoln Benefit Life Co.; Lincoln; life insurance 820

Madonna Rehabilitation Hospital; Lincoln 820

Nebraska National Guard; Lincoln 800

Ransomes America Corp.; Lincoln; turf and grounds equipment 800

Experian Information Solutions Inc.; Lincoln; direct mail advertising 750

Nebraska Dept. of Roads; Lincoln 750

Square D Co.; Lincoln; switchgear and switchboard apparatus 750

Pfizer Corp.; Lincoln; medicinals and botanicals 700

Affiliated Independent Development Corp.; Norfolk; store equipment 600

American Meter Co.; Nebraska City; meters 600

Kmart Corp.; Lincoln; discount department stores 600

Nebraska Book Co.; Lincoln; bookstores 600

Southeast Community College; Lincoln 600

Tyco Healthcare Group; Norfolk; hypodermic needles and syringes 550

Textron Inc.; Lincoln; turf and grounds equipment 525

Vishay-Dale Electronics Inc.; Norfolk; electronic resistors 520

Affiliated Foods Midwest Cooperative Inc.; Norfolk; food supplier 500

B&R Stores Inc.; Lincoln; grocery store 500

ConAgra Foods Inc.; Lincoln; meatpacking plants 500

Experian Information Solutions Inc.; Seward; direct-mail advertising 500

Nebraska Dept. of Health and Human Services; Lincoln 500

Pegler Sysco Corp.; Lincoln; domestic freight forwarding 500

Nebraska 2nd District

East — Omaha and suburbs

Formerly the eastern terminus of the Union Pacific Railroad, Omaha is the heart of the 2nd. Omaha grew up as a blue-collar city: a railroad center, a Missouri River port, and a place where cattle became steaks. To outsiders, this broad-shouldered, gritty image remains. But the city has become mainly a place of downtown office buildings and white-collar jobs in agriculture and insurance businesses. It also is known as the nation's 1-800 capital, thanks to a glut of telecommunications and credit processing companies.

As its core has filled with people through the years, the 2nd has become more compact. The district lost its slice of Cass County and much of Sarpy County in redistricting following the 2000 census, and now contains just Douglas County and eastern Sarpy County.

Although the district votes consistently Republican, Omaha's dwindling blue-collar base still supports some Democrats, and victory in the city's south side is essential for Democrats to win statewide. The 2nd has always been antiabortion, but social conservatives are gaining ground once held by more-moderate European immigrants.

Douglas County is reliably Republican, having voted for the GOP presidential candidate every time but once since Harry S. Truman. Omaha is home to three-fourths of Nebraska's growing black population, but the state's first black candidate for Congress lost the district by more than 30 percent in 1998. George W. Bush took 56.7 percent of the 2nd's vote in the 2000 presidential election, his lowest tally in the state.

Major Industry

Toll-free service centers, food processing.

Notable

President Gerald R. Ford and political activist Malcolm X were born in Omaha; Father Flanagan's Boys Town, incorporated in 1936, was the only village in the nation run by children; billionaire investor Warren Buffett lives in Omaha—his father, Republican Howard Buffett, represented Omaha in the House in the 1940s and early 1950s.

Election Returns

	Republican		Democratic		Other	
President 2000	125,973	56.7%	85,853	38.7%	10,183	4.6%
House 2002	89,917	63.3%	46,843	33.0%	5,254	3.7%

District Profile

Population 570,421

Total area (square miles) 420.9
  Land area (square miles) 410.5

Population per square mile 1,389.6

Counties (2000 population)
  Douglas 463,585   Sarpy (pt.) 106,836

Cities and other areas over 10,000 (2000 population)
  Bellevue 44,382   Omaha 390,007
  La Vista 11,699   Papillion 16,363

Race and Hispanic or Latino origin*
  White 79.6%
  Black or African American 10.2%
  American Indian or Alaska Native 0.5%
  Asian 1.8%
  Native Hawaiian or other Pacific Islander 0.1%
  Some other race 0.1%
  Hispanic or Latino origin 6.3%
  Two or more races 1.5%

As percentage of total population.

Ancestry*

Danish	2.1%	Italian	3.5%
Dutch	1.4%	Norwegian	1.9%
English	6.6%	Polish	3.6%
French	2.0%	Swedish	2.9%
German	22.1%	USA/American	2.7%
Irish	11.6%		

*As estimated percentage of total population.

Universities and colleges, 2000–2001 enrollment

Bellevue University, Bellevue 3,445
Clarkson College, Omaha 401
College of St. Mary, Omaha 947
Creighton University, Omaha 6,237
Grace University, Omaha 578
ITT Technical Institute, Omaha 353
Metropolitan Community College Area, Omaha 11,534
Nebraska College of Business, Omaha 487
Nebraska Methodist College of Nursing, Omaha 400
Omaha College of Health Careers, Omaha 269
University of Nebraska, Omaha 13,479
University of Nebraska Medical Center, Omaha 2,695

Newspapers and circulation

	District circulation	Total circulation
Omaha World Herald	107,926	194,150
*USA Today**	5,290	1,674,376

*See Sources and Explanations in the front of the volume.

Television stations and affiliations

Omaha	100%	KBIN	PBS
Omaha	100%	KETV	ABC
Omaha	100%	KHIN	PBS
Omaha	100%	KMTV	CBS
Omaha	100%	KPTM	FOX
Omaha	100%	KUON	PBS
Omaha	100%	KXVO	WB
Omaha	100%	KYNE	PBS
Omaha	100%	WOWT	NBC

Cable systems and subscribers

Cox 121,573
Galaxy 610

Military installations, September 2001

Offutt Air Force Base, Bellevue 9,645

Businesses and other major employers

Legion Health; Omaha; medical doctor offices, clinics 7,000
Mutual of Omaha Insurance Co.; Omaha; life insurance 6,000
First Data Resources Inc.; Omaha; data processing 4,000
University of Nebraska Medical Center; Omaha 4,000
Excel Cabinets and Interiors; Papillion; wood kitchen cabinets 3,545
Avaya Inc.; Omaha; current-carrying wiring services 3,500
Baker's Supermarkets Inc.; Omaha; supermarkets 3,000

ConAgra Foods Inc.; Omaha; meatpacking plants 3,000
Creighton University; Omaha 2,500
West Telemarketing Corp.; Omaha; telemarketing services 2,362
First National Bank of Omaha Inc.; Omaha; commercial bank 2,200
Alegent Health-Immanuel Medical Center; Omaha; hospital with residency 2,000
Lucent Technologies; Omaha; telephone station equipment and parts 2,000
United of Omaha Life Insurance Co.; Omaha; life insurance 2,000
Kiewit Construction Co.; Omaha; industrial buildings, warehouses 1,850
Omaha Public Power District; Omaha; electric power distribution 1,800
United Parcel Service Inc.; Omaha; parcel delivery 1,700
Convergys Corp.; Omaha; telephone solicitation service 1,600
Oriental Trading Co.; Omaha; toy novelties and amusements 1,500
Valmont Industries Inc.; Valley; farm machinery and equipment 1,500
Metropolitan Community College; Omaha 1,451
Millard Refrigerated Services; Omaha; frozen or refrigerated goods storage 1,400
Nebraska Furniture Mart Inc.; Omaha; furniture stores 1,400
Pinnacle Foods Corp.; Omaha; frozen dinners 1,300
Creighton University St. Joseph Hospital; Omaha 1,290
Children's Hospital; Omaha 1,250
Nebraska Methodist Hospital; Omaha 1,250
Physicians Life Insurance Co.; Omaha; life reinsurance carriers 1,250
Coxcom Inc.; Omaha; cable television 1,200
Lozier Corp.; Omaha; store fixtures 1,200
Valmont Industries Inc.; Omaha; fabricated structural metal 1,200
Sitel Corp.; Omaha; telemarketing services 1,150
Vickers Inc.; Omaha; pumps and pumping equipment 1,100
Father Flanagan's Boys' Home Inc.; Boys Town; boys' home 1,000
Nebraska Beef; Omaha; meatpacking plants 1,000
Omaha Steaks Inc.; Omaha; mail-order food 1,000
West Corp.; Omaha; telemarketing services 1,000
Children's Health Care Services Inc.; Omaha; medical equipment rental 965
Blue Cross and Blue Shield of Nebraska; Omaha; group hospitalization 954
CSG Systems Inc.; Omaha; data processing 925
Omaha World Herald Co.; Omaha; newspaper 920
Eastern Nebraska Human Services Agency; Omaha 850
Kellogg Co.; Omaha; cereal breakfast foods 850
Cunningham Field and Research Service Inc.; Omaha; commercial nonphysical research 800
Kwik Kafe Co. Inc.; Omaha; concessionaire 800
Metropolitan Utilities District; Omaha; gas and other services 800

Pamida Holdings Corp.; Omaha; variety stores 800

Ameritrade Inc.; Bellevue; mineral leasing dealers 795

Gilbert Network Services; Omaha; highway and street construction 760

City of Omaha; Omaha; city government 750

Commercial Federal Bank; Omaha; federal savings and loan associations 700

InfoUSA Inc.; Omaha; mailing list compilers 700

Jefferson Pilot Financial Insurance Co.; Omaha; insurance agents and brokers 700

Qwest Corp.; Omaha; data processing 700

Wells Fargo Bank Nebraska; Omaha; commercial bank 682

Greater Omaha Packing Co.; Omaha; meat by-products 675

Data Transmission Network Corp.; Omaha; remote database information retrieval 650

First Data Resources Inc.; Omaha; credit card service 620

Transaction Systems Architects Inc.; Omaha; business computer software 611

Douglas County; Omaha; county government 600

Omaha Public Power District; Omaha; electric services 600

Precision Industries Inc.; Omaha; industrial machine parts 600

Papillion-La Vista Public Schools; Papillion 552

Greyhound Lines Inc.; Omaha; freight rate information service 550

Omaha Public Schools; Omaha 550

HDR Inc.; Omaha; architectural services 548

ADT Security Services Inc.; Papillion; security systems services 500

Alegent Health Inc.; Papillion; hospital 500

American Direct Publishing; Omaha; publishing 500

American Security Service Inc.; Omaha; security protective devices 500

Carlson Hospitality Group Inc.; Omaha; subdividers and developers 500

Compaq Computer Corp.; Omaha; electronic computers 500

Crown Cork and Seal Co.; Omaha; plastic bottles 500

Douglas County; Omaha; psychiatric hospitals 500

FBG Service Corp.; Omaha; janitorial service 500

Fleming Companies Inc.; Omaha; supermarkets 500

Hyatt Corp.; Omaha; hotel, motel reservations 500

Hy-Vee Inc.; Omaha; grocery store 500

Nebraska Methodist Hospital; Omaha 500

Tyson Foods Inc.; Omaha; bacon 500

U.S. Veterans Hospital; Omaha 500

Union Pacific Railroad Co.; Omaha; railroad freight hauling 500

Nebraska 3rd District

West — Grand Island, North Platte, Scottsbluff

Scouting what would later become the Oregon Trail, early nineteenth century explorers described this section of the country as the "Great American Desert." Most of the 3rd's land is arid, and most of the district's population lives along the meager Platte River.

Grand Island, North Platte, and Scottsbluff each serve as regional centers, providing for the retail and health care needs of the surrounding counties. Industry and manufacturing also locate around these areas, as well as in Columbus, Hastings, and Kearney. The rest of the land in the district's 69 counties is left to cattle ranchers and sugar beet and wheat farmers. The economy is susceptible to changes in the region's climate. Droughts in the early part of the 1990s battered western Nebraska. The district has a number of the nation's poorest counties.

The 3rd is fiercely independent politically—it gave more votes to Ross Perot than to Bill Clinton in 1992—but the majority is conservative and strongly Republican. In the 2000 presidential contest, George W. Bush carried the district with 70.9 percent of the vote. Reflecting the area's isolation, most voters are against government intervention. The 1st and 2nd Districts dominate state politics, leaving the 3rd resentful that despite its massive land size, its interests, such as farm subsidies and property taxes, are not top priorities.

Saline County, a Democratic-leaning pocket, was added to the 3rd in redistricting following the 2000 census, but the change is not expected to alter the district's outlook.

Major Industry

Agriculture, food processing, tourism.

Notable

Pulitzer Prize-winning author Willa Cather grew up in Red Cloud and based several of her novels in the central-southern region of the state; Carhenge, a full-size replica of Britain's Stonehenge made of cars, stands in Alliance; Fort Robinson near Crawford, now a state park, served as a German prisoner-of-war camp during World War II; the Great Platte River Road Archway Monument, across Interstate 80 near Kearney, was built to memorialize westward expansion.

Election Returns

	Republican		Democratic		Other	
President 2000	169,090	70.9%	60,293	25.3%	8,952	3.8%
House 2002	163,939	93.2%			12,017	6.8%

District Profile

Population 570,517

Total area (square miles) 64,898.7
 Land area (square miles) 64,511.0

Population per square mile 8.8

Counties (2000 population)

Adams	31,151	Cheyenne	9,830
Antelope	7,452	Clay	7,039
Arthur	444	Custer	11,793
Banner	819	Dawes	9,060
Blaine	583	Dawson	24,365
Boone	6,259	Deuel	2,098
Box Butte	12,158	Dundy	2,292
Boyd	2,438	Fillmore	6,634
Brown	3,525	Franklin	3,574
Buffalo	42,259	Frontier	3,099
Cedar (pt.)	6,508	Furnas	5,324
Chase	4,068	Garden	2,292
Cherry	6,148	Garfield	1,902

Gosper	2,143	
Grant	747	
Greeley	2,714	
Hall	53,534	
Hamilton	9,403	
Harlan	3,786	
Hayes	1,068	
Hitchcock	3,111	
Holt	11,551	
Hooker	783	
Howard	6,567	
Jefferson	8,333	
Kearney	6,882	
Keith	8,875	
Keya Paha	983	
Kimball	4,089	
Knox	9,374	
Lincoln	34,632	
Logan	774	
Loup	712	
McPherson	533	
Merrick	8,204	
Morrill	5,440	
Nance	4,038	
Nuckolls	5,057	
Perkins	3,200	
Phelps	9,747	
Pierce	7,857	
Platte	31,662	
Polk	5,639	
Red Willow	11,448	
Rock	1,756	
Saline	13,843	
Scottsbluff	36,951	
Sheridan	6,198	
Sherman	3,318	
Sioux	1,475	
Thayer	6,055	
Thomas	729	
Valley	4,647	
Webster	4,061	
Wheeler	886	
York	14,598	

Cities and other areas over 10,000 (2000 population)

Columbus	20,971	Lexington	10,011
Grand Island	42,940	North Platte	23,878
Hastings	24,064	Scottsbluff	14,732
Kearney	27,431		

Race and Hispanic or Latino origin*

White 91.9%
Black or African American 0.3%
American Indian or Alaska Native 0.7%
Asian 0.5%
Native Hawaiian or other Pacific Islander 0.0%
Some other race 0.0%
Hispanic or Latino origin 6.0%
Two or more races 0.6%

*As percentage of total population.

Ancestry*

Danish	2.3%	Irish	8.5%
Dutch	1.7%	Norwegian	1.4%
English	7.2%	Polish	2.6%
French	1.8%	Swedish	4.1%
German	30.3%	USA/American	3.8%

*As estimated percentage of total population.

Universities and colleges, 2000–2001 enrollment

Central Community College Area, Grand Island 7,126
Chadron State College, Chadron 2,686
Doane College, Crete 2,135
Hastings College, Hastings 1,130
McCook Community College, McCook 760
Mid Plains Community College, North Platte 1,934
Nebraska College of Technical Agriculture, Curtis 234
University of Nebraska-Kearney, Kearney 6,506
Western Nebraska Community College, Scottsbluff 2,264
York College, York 497

Newspapers and circulation

	District circulation	Total circulation
Beatrice Daily Sun	1,039	7,915
Columbus Telegram	6,530	9,104
Grand Island Independent	22,722	22,722
*Holdrege Daily Citizen**	2,690	2,690
Kearney Hub	12,053	12,053
Lincoln Journal Star	7,769	75,540
Norfolk News	7,252	17,361
Omaha World Herald	27,049	194,150
Scottsbluff Star-Herald	13,899	15,180

*See Sources and Explanations in the front of the volume.

Television stations and affiliations

Lincoln-Hastings-Kearney	50%	KGIN	CBS
Lincoln-Hastings-Kearney	50%	KHAS	NBC
Lincoln-Hastings-Kearney	50%	KHGI	ABC
Lincoln-Hastings-Kearney	50%	KHNE	PBS
Lincoln-Hastings-Kearney	50%	KLKE	ABC
Lincoln-Hastings-Kearney	50%	KLKN	ABC
Lincoln-Hastings-Kearney	50%	KLNE	PBS
Lincoln-Hastings-Kearney	50%	KMNE	PBS
Lincoln-Hastings-Kearney	50%	KOLN	CBS
Lincoln-Hastings-Kearney	50%	KSNB	FOX
Lincoln-Hastings-Kearney	50%	KTVG	FOX
Lincoln-Hastings-Kearney	50%	KWNB	ABC
Denver	12%	KBDI	PBS
Denver	12%	KCEC	Univision
Denver	12%	KCNC	CBS
Denver	12%	KDUH	ABC
Denver	12%	KDVR	FOX
Denver	12%	KFCT	FOX
Denver	12%	KFNR	ABC
Denver	12%	KMGH	ABC
Denver	12%	KPXC	PAX
Denver	12%	KREG	CBS
Denver	12%	KRMA	CBS
Denver	12%	KRMT	Independent
Denver	12%	KTVD	UPN
Denver	12%	KUSA	NBC
Denver	12%	KWGN	WB
Denver	12%	KWHD	Independent
Rapid City, SD	12%	KBHE	PBS
Rapid City, SD	12%	KCLO	CBS
Rapid City, SD	12%	KEVN	FOX
Rapid City, SD	12%	KHSD	ABC
Rapid City, SD	12%	KIVV	FOX
Rapid City, SD	12%	KOTA	ABC
Rapid City, SD	12%	KPSD	PBS
Rapid City, SD	12%	KSGW	ABC
Rapid City, SD	12%	KTNE	PBS
Rapid City, SD	12%	KZSD	PBS
North Platte	11%	KNOP	NBC
North Platte	11%	KPNE	PBS
Sioux Falls (Mitchell), SD	9%	KABY	ABC
Sioux Falls (Mitchell), SD	9%	KCSD	PBS
Sioux Falls (Mitchell), SD	9%	KDLO	CBS
Sioux Falls (Mitchell), SD	9%	KDLV	NBC
Sioux Falls (Mitchell), SD	9%	KDSD	PBS
Sioux Falls (Mitchell), SD	9%	KELO	CBS

Sioux Falls (Mitchell), SD	9%	KESD	PBS
Sioux Falls (Mitchell), SD	9%	KPLO	CBS
Sioux Falls (Mitchell), SD	9%	KPRY	ABC
Sioux Falls (Mitchell), SD	9%	KQSD	PBS
Sioux Falls (Mitchell), SD	9%	KRNE	PBS
Sioux Falls (Mitchell), SD	9%	KSFY	ABC
Sioux Falls (Mitchell), SD	9%	KSMN	PBS
Sioux Falls (Mitchell), SD	9%	KTSD	PBS
Sioux Falls (Mitchell), SD	9%	KTTM	FOX
Sioux Falls (Mitchell), SD	9%	KTTW	FOX
Sioux City	3%	KCAU	ABC
Sioux City	3%	KMEG	CBS, UPN
Sioux City	3%	KSIN	PBS
Sioux City	3%	KTIV	NBC
Sioux City	3%	KUSD	PBS
Sioux City	3%	KXNE	PBS
Cheyenne-Scottsbluff	1%	KGWN	CBS
Cheyenne-Scottsbluff	1%	KKTU	NBC
Cheyenne-Scottsbluff	1%	KLWY	FOX
Cheyenne-Scottsbluff	1%	KSTF	CBS
Omaha	1%	KBIN	PBS
Omaha	1%	KETV	ABC
Omaha	1%	KHIN	PBS
Omaha	1%	KMTV	CBS
Omaha	1%	KPTM	FOX
Omaha	1%	KUON	PBS
Omaha	1%	KXVO	WB
Omaha	1%	KYNE	PBS
Omaha	1%	WOWT	NBC
Wichita-Hutchinson, KS	1%	KAAS	FOX
Wichita-Hutchinson, KS	1%	KAKE	ABC
Wichita-Hutchinson, KS	1%	KBSD	CBS
Wichita-Hutchinson, KS	1%	KBSH	CBS
Wichita-Hutchinson, KS	1%	KBSL	CBS
Wichita-Hutchinson, KS	1%	KDCK	PBS
Wichita-Hutchinson, KS	1%	KLBY	ABC
Wichita-Hutchinson, KS	1%	KOOD	PBS
Wichita-Hutchinson, KS	1%	KPTS	PBS
Wichita-Hutchinson, KS	1%	KSAS	FOX
Wichita-Hutchinson, KS	1%	KSNC	NBC
Wichita-Hutchinson, KS	1%	KSNG	NBC
Wichita-Hutchinson, KS	1%	KSNK	NBC
Wichita-Hutchinson, KS	1%	KSNW	NBC
Wichita-Hutchinson, KS	1%	KSWK	PBS
Wichita-Hutchinson, KS	1%	KUPK	ABC
Wichita-Hutchinson, KS	1%	KWCH	CBS

Cable systems and subscribers

Benkelman Telephone Co.   867
Cable ONE   880
Cedar Vision   665
Charter   84,595
Classic   2,484
Consolidated Cable   1,285
Galaxy   10,954
Glenwood Telecommunications   1,018
Great Plains Cable TV   5,772
Hebron Cable TV   579
HunTel Cablevision   694
Midcontinent Cable   2,321

Mid-State Community TV   2,035
Pinpoint Communications   705
Sky Scan Cable   610
Time Warner   15,386

Military installations, September 2001

Cornhusker Army Ammunition Plant, Grand Island   304

Businesses and other major employers

Nebraska Alltel Inc.; Scottsbluff; telephone equipment and systems   8,000
ConAgra Beef Co.; Grand Island; meatpacking plants   2,400
Cabela's Inc.; Sidney; fishing, hunting, camping equipment   2,000
Union Pacific Railroad Co.; North Platte; railroad freight hauling   2,000
Farmland Foods Inc.; Crete; pork products   1,500
Becton Dickinson and Co.; Columbus; surgical and medical instruments   1,200
Regional West Medical Center; Scottsbluff   1,000
St. Francis Medical Center Inc.; Grand Island   1,000
Grand Island Liederkranz; Grand Island; bars and restaurants   850
Burlington Northern and Santa Fe Railway Co.; Alliance; hydrostatic testing laboratory   800
University of Nebraska; Kearney   800
Mary Lanning Memorial Hospital Inc.; Hastings   770
Behlen Manufacturing Co.; Columbus; farm machinery and equipment   750
Dale Test Laboratories Inc.; Columbus; electronic resistors   750
New Holland North America Inc.; Grand Island; farm machinery and equipment   735
Eaton Corp.; Kearney; engine valves   720
Tenneco Automotive Operating Co.; Cozad; automotive shock absorbers   700
Baldwin Filters Inc.; Kearney; automotive air, fuel, oil filters   650
Principal Life Insurance Co.; Grand Island; insurance agents and brokers   650
American Tool Companies Inc.; De Witt; hand and edge tools   600
Camaco; Columbus; public building and related furniture   600
Petersen Manufacturing Co. Inc.; De Witt; screwdrivers, pliers, chisels   600
Becton Dickinson and Co.; Holdrege; hypodermic needles and syringes   594
North Platte Nebraska Hospital Corp.; North Platte   586
Emerson Electric Co.; Columbus; electric motors   550
Nebraska Public Power District; Columbus; electric power generation   510
Crete Carrier Corp.; York; trucking   500
Lindsay Manufacturing Co.; Omaha; self-propelled irrigation equipment   500
Swift-Eckrich Inc.; Hastings; meatpacking plants   500

Nevada

In the decade of the 1990s, no state in the union grew faster than Nevada. But that does not begin to cover the scope or sustained strength of this phenomenon. At first glance, the state's 2000 census total looked like a misprint: could there really be 2 million people in Nevada? In 1990 there had barely been 1.2 million, and a decade earlier only 800,000. Can a state in our time gain 50 percent in population one decade and then 66 percent the next? Yet that is what happened in Nevada. The state's growth rates have averaged 70 percent in each of the previous three decades. Perhaps the best way to sum the population growth in this arid, remote, intermountain state is to say that from 1950 to 2000 it grew by more than 1,000 percent. The second greatest growth rate over that half century was in Arizona, which only grew roughly half as fast.

This growth has been concentrated in Las Vegas, the nation's fastest-growing city (up 85 percent in the decade), its metro area (now more than 1.3 million, the nation's fastest-growing and already larger than the Buffalo or New Orleans metro areas), and surrounding Clark County, which by 2000 was home to seven Nevadans out of ten. How popular is Las Vegas? Its McCarren International Airport in 2000 was the sixth busiest in the United States with 35 million passenger arrivals and departures. New York's JFK, by comparison, had fewer than 30 million. With this ferocious rate of growth has also come a sudden flowering of diversity. The percentage of African Americans in the state hit 10 percent in 2000, not far behind the national average. And the Hispanic share of Nevada's people is now 20 percent, making this the fifth most Hispanic state in the union.

It is no secret that the vast majority of the new people and new dollars coming to this city were lured, directly or indirectly, by gambling. It was the legalization of gambling in the Great Depression of the 1930s that reversed the fortunes of a state that had declined to a population of less than 100,000 in that decade's census. Today, the industry locally referred to as gaming drives the tourism industry statewide: the hotels, resorts, restaurants, and spas, and nowhere is it flashier or more overwhelming than on the Strip in Vegas. The genesis of this playground, which attracts the proverbial high rollers from every continent, has been chronicled in books, novels, and popular films, including Francis Ford Coppola's *The Godfather* series, Warren Beatty's *Bugsy,* and Martin Scorcese's *Casino,* all of which dwelt on the role of organized crime. But to many contemporary Las Vegans, this lurid history seems as quaint as the tales about billionaire recluse Howard Hughes renting whole floors of local hotels

for years at a time (and buying up the casinos once owned by the crime syndicates back East).

The new Vegas is characterized by immense, contemporary, world-class nine-figure hotel-resorts such as Bellagio, Mandalay Bay, Mirage, and New York New York, which have transformed the skyline and taken the notion of marquee lighting into another dimension. The original landmarks on the Strip have not only been eclipsed, some have even been dynamited to make room for their successors. The entertainment is still gaudy and heavy on big name entertainers but with a growing admixture of country western and family fare. The new Las Vegas is a global competitor for convention business and sporting events. The "gaming industry" is also portrayed as just a part of the package, although surely the quintessential part.

The gaming industry was for many years the most important component of Nevada politics, too, eclipsing the old pols who represented the interests of cattle, sheep, mining, and timber. But the entire state economy has become more sophisticated in recent years, with high-tech industry becoming a factor in Clark County, where Las Vegas is located, and elsewhere. Even the people who staff the casinos themselves are a sometimes surprising mix. Mormons, for example, are among the fastest-growing segments of the Clark County population, something of an irony given that Mormons were among the first occupants of the area in the 1850s.

Few expect the recent explosive growth to continue here. The Census Bureau foresees a rate of less than 30 percent in the years from 2000 to 2025, far less growth than took place in the 1990s alone. This is in part because the water supply, always problematic in the West, seems unlikely to support growth indefinitely. But the main reason may be that the success of the gaming industry is fostering greater competition all over the country, from Native American reservations, which are prominently next door in California, to riverboat casinos to outright legalization of gambling.

But for now the state has more than enough new people, investment, and energy to absorb into its economy, community, and power structure. Politics to some degree remains the province of the long-term owner class and the sophisticated organizations. In part because so many residents were new, Nevada had one of the lowest rates of participation in the 2000 election, ranking forty-sixth among the states in votes cast as a percentage of voting-age population. The newness of so much of the constituency makes past voting less indicative of current and future sympathies, but Nevada has been a two-party state throughout nearly all its statehood, rarely

NEVADA

Districts established June 15, 2001, for elections first held in 2002.

3 members

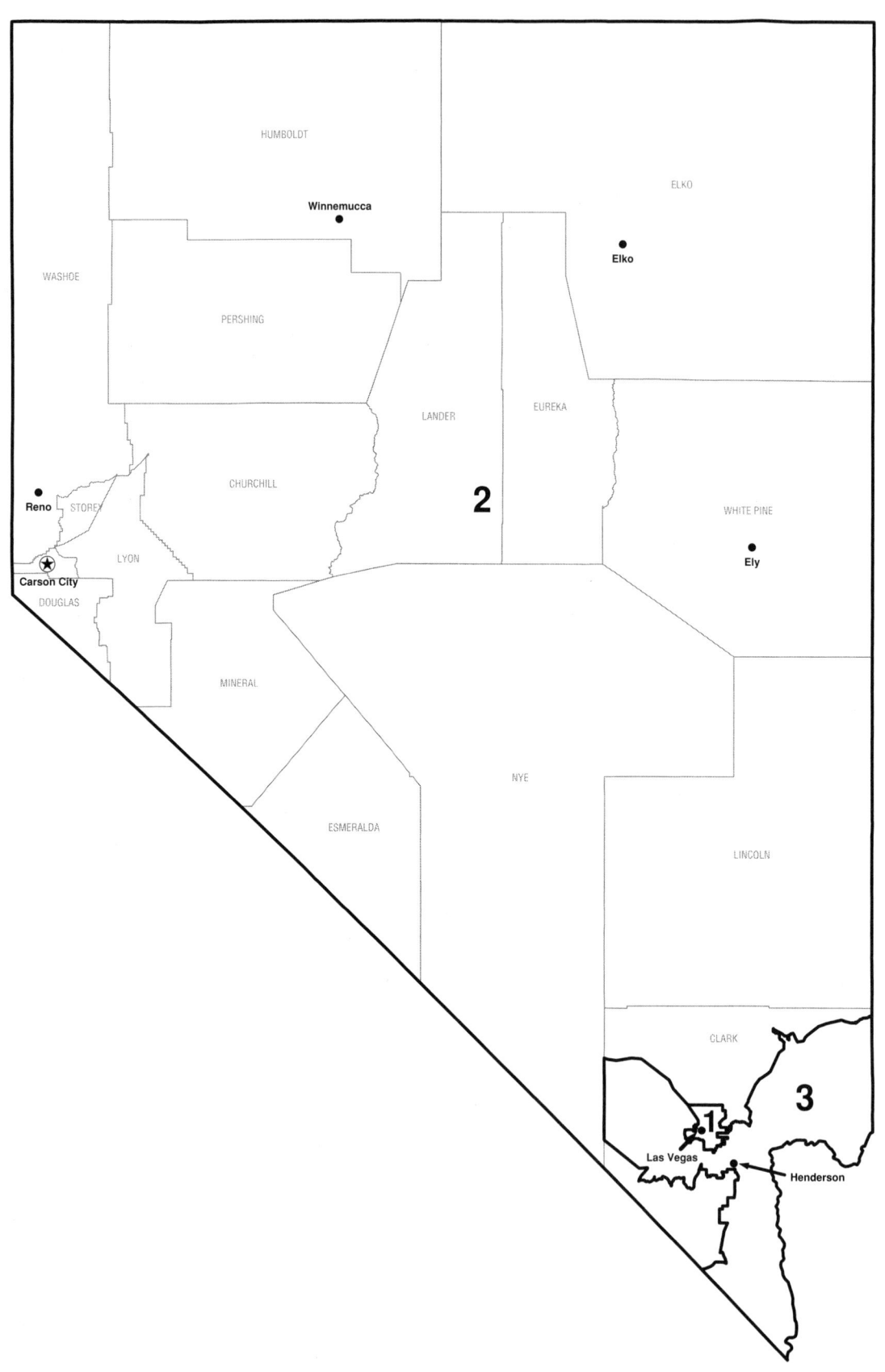

leaving its governorship in the hands of one party for more than a term or two. Democrats won 14 of the 20 Senate elections after World War II (Alan Bible and Howard Cannon won four each), but Republicans were showing greater strength toward the end of the 1990s and stood in good position to hold one or both in the years after 2000.

In presidential voting, the state has generally followed the Western trend in postwar voting but has also shown a tendency to back the winner. Gerald Ford in 1976 was the state's only miscue. It preferred Truman and Eisenhower, then Kennedy and Johnson, then went twice for Nixon and Reagan and once each for the first and second George Bush in 1988 and 2000. Democrats got a break in 1992 and 1996 when Bill Clinton carried the state with pluralities of 37.4 percent and 43.9 percent, respectively (both times owing to a strong showing by Ross Perot).

Nevada had but one House seat from its entry into the union during Lincoln's presidency until 1982, during Reagan's. But it now has three, and that might have posed a problem for the divided legislature and Republican governor Kenny Guinn in 2001. As it turned out, the surplus of new residents made it easy to strike a deal in a special one-day session. The deal protected each of the previous incumbents, Democrat Shelley Berkley and Republican Jim Gibbons, and created a new 3rd District in the Clark County suburbs that was evenly balanced between the parties. George W. Bush and Al Gore had each received 48 percent in the new 3rd (although in November 2002 the Republicans' nominee for the House won here handily).

Berkley's new 1st District remains focused on the city itself (which was approaching half a million residents) and its immediate environs. That gave her several additional percentage points of Democratic vote and helped her win more easily in 2002. The new arrivals in the city proper include many service workers needed in the hotels, and they are among the most unionized workers in the state.

The new 3rd District took in Henderson (Clark County's second city, which had grown from 65,000 to 175,000 in the decade) and other booming areas to the south, west, and east. Even then, the remappers still had more than 40,000 county residents to contribute to the 2nd District, which otherwise consists of the 16 counties in the rest of the state. This district is more Republican as a result of the remap, as Democratic precincts were channeled toward the two districts Democrats thought they were likeliest to win.

Outstate Nevada includes Reno, the one-time rival that competes for attention largely because it is closer to the populous San Francisco Bay Area, a substantial source of regular gamblers. Reno grew by a third in the 1990s to 180,000, barely staying ahead of Henderson for the distinction of being the state's second largest. Reno is in Washoe County, which also takes in Lake Tahoe on the Nevada side and gave the county a total of nearly 340,000 residents in 2000.

Table 1   Population

District	Population	Population under 18	Voting-age population	Median age	Male*	Female*
1	666,088	177,436	488,652	32.9	51.5	48.5
2	666,087	172,771	493,316	36.1	51.3	48.7
3	666,082	161,592	504,490	36.2	50.0	50.0
State	1,998,257	511,799	1,486,458	35.0	50.9	49.1

*As percentage of total population.

Table 2   Voting-Age Persons by Race/Hispanic or Latino Origin

District	White*	Black or African American*	American Indian or Alaska Native*	Asian*	Other or multirace*	Hispanic or Latino*
1	56.4	11.0	0.6	5.5	2.2	24.3
2	78.0	2.3	2.0	3.3	1.7	12.7
3	72.6	5.1	0.5	6.5	2.1	13.2
State	69.1	6.1	1.0	5.1	2.0	16.7

*As percentage of voting-age population.

Table 3   Voting-Age Population by Age Groups

District	18 to 24*	25 to 44*	45 to 64*	Over 64*
1	13.3	45.0	28.1	13.6
2	11.9	40.4	32.5	15.2
3	11.2	41.5	32.0	15.3
State	12.1	42.3	30.9	14.7

*As percentage of voting-age population.

Table 4   Income and Occupation

District	Median family income	Families in poverty*	White collar†	Blue collar†	Service†	Farm†
1	$45,242	10.3	47.8	23.0	29.1	0.1
2	$50,813	7.1	54.9	24.3	20.3	0.6
3	$55,902	5.4	56.8	18.4	24.7	0.1
State	$50,849	7.5	53.3	21.8	24.6	0.3

*As percentage of all families.   †As percentage of employed workers 16 years and over.

Table 5   Education: School Years Completed

District	Less than grade 9*	Grades 9–12 no diploma*	High school diploma no college*	Some college*	College bachelor's degree or higher*
1	9.7	16.1	30.2	29.5	14.6
2	5.5	11.7	28.4	35.1	19.3
3	4.3	11.1	29.4	34.8	20.4
State	6.4	12.9	29.3	33.2	18.2

*As percentage of persons age 25 and over.

Table 6   Housing and Residential Patterns

District	Median home value	Owner occupied*	Renter occupied*	Urban†	Rural†
1	$119,700	51.8	48.2	99.9	0.1
2	$131,400	63.6	36.4	78.5	21.5
3	$143,400	66.9	33.1	96.3	3.7
State	$132,500	60.9	39.1	91.6	8.4

*As percentage of occupied housing units.   †As percentage of total population.

Nevada 1st District

Las Vegas

Neon lights and the chance of easy money continue to reel pleasure seekers into the 1st, which includes Las Vegas and its immediate areas. The city, the state's largest, experienced phenomenal growth in the 1990s; the metropolitan area has been the fastest growing in the nation. One of the downsides is that traffic congestion is now a major concern.

Gambling and tourism drive the 1st's economy. With a healthy economy in the late 1990s, large and small gaming companies continued to thrive. Several new luxury resorts were built on Las Vegas Boulevard, the newest part of the famed "Strip." About 36 million people visited Las Vegas in 2000, with an economic impact of $31 billion.

The 2001 terrorist attacks sharply affected tourism in 2001, forcing many workers out of jobs. One year later most service workers were cautiously optimistic that business was starting to pick back up. Discussion in California about adding more Native American casinos increases the industry's worries, but local leaders are excited over the Las Vegas Monorail project, a four-mile line slated to open in early 2004 that will run along the east side of the Strip.

Besides the gambling industry, the 1st also attracts tourists to its surrounding national parks and desert topography. The area's record growth has made home building a major industry as well, and the city relies on distribution and trade because of its central Western location.

The 1st was a competitive swing district that attracted quite a bit of national attention and money in recent elections, but it became significantly more Democratic in redistricting after the 2000 census when many of the rapidly growing suburbs of the city were placed in the new 3rd District. Though some pockets of Republicans live in the district, the 1st has a strong Democratic base in unionized service workers.

Major Industry

Tourism, casinos, conventions.

Notable

The Little White Wedding Chapel on Las Vegas Boulevard has a drive-through window for weddings.

Election Returns

	Republican		Democratic		Other	
President 2000	63,163	40.7%	87,345	56.2%	4,801	3.1%
House 2002	51,148	42.7%	64,312	53.7%	4,254	3.6%

District Profile

Population   666,088

Total area (square miles)   177.3
  Land area (square miles)   177.2

Population per square mile   3,759.0

Counties (2000 population)
  Clark (pt.)   666,088

Cities and other areas over 10,000 (2000 population)
  Las Vegas (pt.)   362,908
  North Las Vegas (pt.)   115,488
  Paradise CDP (pt.)   77,893
  Sunrise Manor CDP (pt.)   68,288
  Winchester CDP   26,958

Race and Hispanic or Latino origin*
  White   51.5%
  Black or African American   11.9%

American Indian or Alaska Native   0.6%
Asian   4.6%
Native Hawaiian or other Pacific Islander   0.4%
Some other race   0.1%
Hispanic or Latino origin   28.2%
Two or more races   2.6%

*As percentage of total population.

Ancestry*

English	5.9%	Norwegian	1.1%
French	2.1%	Polish	1.8%
German	8.8%	Scottish	1.2%
Irish	7.1%	USA/American	3.4%
Italian	4.7%		

*As estimated percentage of total population.

Universities and colleges, 2000–2001 enrollment
  Academy of Medical Careers, Las Vegas   749
  Community College of Southern Nevada, Las Vegas   29,905
  Heritage College, Las Vegas   253
  University of Nevada, Las Vegas   22,041
  University of Phoenix, Las Vegas   1,840

Newspapers and circulation

	District circulation	Total circulation
Las Vegas Review Journal	68,009	167,168
Las Vegas Review-Journal/Sun (Sunday)	82,848	200,303
Las Vegas Sun	14,835	33,135
Los Angeles Times	1,768	1,044,205

Television stations and affiliations

Las Vegas	100%	KBLR	Telemundo
Las Vegas	100%	KFBT	Independent
Las Vegas	100%	KINC	Univision
Las Vegas	100%	KLAS	CBS
Las Vegas	100%	KLVX	PBS
Las Vegas	100%	KTNV	ABC
Las Vegas	100%	KVBC	NBC
Las Vegas	100%	KVVU	FOX
Las Vegas	100%	KVWB	WB

Cable systems and subscribers
  Cox   94,236

Businesses and other major employers
  Bellagio Resort and Casino; Las Vegas; casino hotel   9,500
  Mirage Casino-Hotel; Las Vegas; casino hotel   7,500
  MGM Grand Hotel Inc.; Las Vegas; casino hotel   5,996
  Desert Palace Inc.; Las Vegas; casino hotel   4,800
  Rio Hotel and Casino Inc.; Las Vegas; casino hotel   4,800
  Venetian Casino Resort; Las Vegas; resort hotel   4,740
  Treasure Island Corp.; Las Vegas; casino hotel   4,500
  New Castle Corp.; Las Vegas; casino hotel   4,200
  Las Vegas Hilton Corp.; Las Vegas; casino hotel   4,011
  Aladdin Gaming; Las Vegas; casino hotel   4,000
  Paris Hotel Casino Resort; Las Vegas; casino hotel   4,000
  Park Place Entertainment Corp.; Las Vegas; hotels and motels   4,000

Park Place Entertainment Corp.; Las Vegas; casino hotel 3,829

Harrah's Las Vegas Inc.; Las Vegas; casino hotel 3,700

GNLV Corp.; Las Vegas; casino hotel 3,145

Victoria Partners; Las Vegas; casino hotel 3,100

Coast Resorts Inc.; Las Vegas; casino hotel 3,000

Las Vegas Police Dept.; Las Vegas 3,000

Sunrise Hospital and Medical Center; Las Vegas 2,750

Hotel Ramada of Nevada; Las Vegas; casino hotel 2,700

Imperial Palace Inc.; Las Vegas; casino hotel 2,500

Sam-Will Inc.; Las Vegas; casino hotel 2,500

Valley Health System Inc. Hospital; Las Vegas 2,386

New York New York Hotel and Casino; Las Vegas; casino hotel 2,300

Stratosphere Gaming Corp.; Las Vegas; hotels and motels 2,300

Horseshoe Club Operating Co.; Las Vegas; casino hotel 2,200

University Medical Center of Southern Nevada; Las Vegas 2,200

Riviera Operating Corp.; Las Vegas; casino hotel 2,175

Palace Station Hotel and Casino Inc.; Las Vegas; casino hotel 2,100

Station Casinos Inc.; Las Vegas; casino hotel 2,100

City of Las Vegas; Las Vegas; city government 2,010

Coast Hotels and Casinos Inc.; Las Vegas; casino hotel 2,000

HCA Inc. Hospital; Las Vegas; hospital 2,000

Mare-Bear Inc.; Las Vegas; casino hotel 2,000

Fiesta Palm; Las Vegas; hotels and motels 1,700

Texas Station Gambling Hall and Hotel Inc.; North Las Vegas; casino hotel 1,700

Boulder Station Inc.; Las Vegas; casino hotel 1,600

Household International Inc.; Las Vegas; credit card service 1,600

GPX Corp.; Las Vegas; personal service agents 1,500

Bechtel Nevada Corp.; North Las Vegas; civil engineering 1,400

Gordon Gaming Corp.; Las Vegas; casino hotel 1,400

Resort at Summerlin Inc.; Las Vegas; resort hotel 1,400

Arizona Charlie's Inc.; Las Vegas; casino hotel 1,200

California Hotel and Casino; Las Vegas; casino hotel 1,200

Central Telephone Co.; Las Vegas; telephone communication 1,200

Ruffin Gaming; Las Vegas; casino hotel 1,200

Exber Inc.; Las Vegas; casino hotel 1,150

Union Plaza Operating Co.; Las Vegas; casino hotel 1,150

Fiesta Station Inc.; Las Vegas; casino hotel 1,100

City of North Las Vegas; North Las Vegas; city management 1,098

Hard Rock Hotel Inc.; Las Vegas; casino hotel 1,040

Citadel Broadcasting Corp.; Las Vegas; radio broadcasting stations 1,034

Ark Las Vegas Restaurant Corp.; Las Vegas; restaurant 1,000

Bechtel SAIC Co.; Las Vegas; construction and civil engineering 1,000

Santa Fe Station Inc.; Las Vegas; casino hotel 1,000

Security Unlimited Inc.; Las Vegas; security guard service 1,000

U.S. Dept. of Energy; Las Vegas 1,000

VSS Enterprises; Las Vegas; casino hotel 1,000

Fitzgeralds Las Vegas Inc.; Las Vegas; casino hotel 995

Republic Silver State Disposal Inc.; Las Vegas; refuse collection and disposal services 995

Barden Nevada Gaming; Las Vegas; casino hotel 924

Las Vegas Convention and Visitors Authority; Las Vegas; advertising, promotional 915

Leisure Homes Corp.; Las Vegas; real estate selling agent 842

Westward Ho Properties; Las Vegas; casino hotel 825

APL Healthcare Group Inc.; Las Vegas; medical laboratories 800

Whittlesea Bell Inc.; Las Vegas; taxicabs 800

Coast Hotels and Casinos Inc.; Las Vegas; hotels and motels 800

Four Queens Inc.; Las Vegas; casino hotel 800

Isle of Capri Inc.; Las Vegas; casino hotel 800

Boyd Gaming Corp.; Las Vegas; hotels and motels 775

Cox Communication Las Vegas Inc.; Las Vegas; cable television 750

Las Vegas Valley Water District; Las Vegas 725

Boardwalk Casino Inc.; Las Vegas; casino hotel 700

Diamond Resorts; Las Vegas; time-share condominium exchange 700

NLVH Inc. Hospital; North Las Vegas 625

Grand Lux Cafe; Las Vegas; restaurants 600

Rainforest Cafe Inc.; Las Vegas; restaurants 600

Summerlin Hospital Medical Center; Las Vegas 600

Williams-Sonoma Inc.; Las Vegas; cookware 600

Sierra Health Services Inc.; Las Vegas; hospital/medical service plans 584

Mountainview Hospital Inc.; Las Vegas 569

American Medical Response Inc.; Las Vegas; ambulance service 530

Burns International Security Services Corp.; Las Vegas; security guard service 500

Jerry's Nugget; North Las Vegas; gambling 500

Lockheed Martin Corp.; Las Vegas; radio/TV communications equipment 500

Mission of Nevada Inc.; North Las Vegas; linen supply 500

Mrs. Fields Original Cookies Inc.; Las Vegas; retail bakeries 500

Official Security Inc.; Las Vegas; security systems services 500

Pete King Corp.; North Las Vegas; painting and paper hanging 500

Wal-Mart Stores Inc.; Las Vegas; discount department stores 500

Nevada 2nd District

Reno, Carson City, and the "Cow Counties"

The conservative-leaning 2nd takes in everything outside of Las Vegas and its suburbs—almost all of the state's vast rural areas. Reno and the capital, Carson City, anchor the 2nd in the west, and in the district's "Cow Counties," agriculture, mining, and ranching dominate. Nearly 90 percent of the district's land is federally owned.

In the 1800s the gold rush attracted fortune seekers to Reno. Fortune seekers now are more inclined to try their luck in the city's casinos or head to Lake Tahoe. Gambling has not fared as well in Reno in recent years, and the industry is concerned that customers will flock to new Native American casinos in California. Yucca Mountain, the proposed national nuclear waste storage site located northwest of Las Vegas in Nye County, also has been a contentious issue in the 2nd.

The 2nd has sent Republicans to Congress since its creation in 1982. It votes mostly Republican in local elections and is becoming increasingly conservative. Redistricting in 2001 further increased the district's Republican voting base by removing some urban territory in Clark County to create the new 3rd District.

Though the 3rd was drawn to take in most of the Las Vegas suburbs, the 2nd dips into Clark County in the southern part of the state. It takes in Nellis Air Force Base and much of the northern part of Clark, as well as a few suburban communities in the southwestern area of the county.

Major Industry
Gambling, mining, manufacturing, warehousing.

Notable
White King, a ten-foot, four-inch tall polar bear on display in Elko, is said to be the world's largest polar bear; Battle Mountain was selected by the *Washington Post Magazine* in 2001 as "the armpit of America."

Election Returns

	Republican		Democratic		Other	
President 2000	134,540	57.3%	87,705	37.4%	12,493	5.3%
House 2002	149,574	74.3%	40,189	20.0%	11,437	5.7%

District Profile

Population   666,087

Total area (square miles)   105,634.6
Land area (square miles)   105,078.9

Population per square mile   6.3

Counties (2000 population)

Carson City 52,457	Lincoln 4,165
Churchill 23,982	Lyon 34,501
Clark (pt.) 43,595	Mineral 5,071
Douglas 41,259	Nye 32,485
Elko 45,291	Pershing 6,693
Esmeralda 971	Storey 3,399
Eureka 1,651	Washoe 339,486
Humboldt 16,106	White Pine 9,181
Lander 5,794	

Cities and other areas over 10,000 (2000 population)
Carson City   52,457
Elko   16,708
Gardnerville Ranchos CDP   11,054
Pahrump CDP   24,631
Reno   180,480
Sparks   66,346
Spring Creek CDP   10,548
Sunrise Manor CDP (pt.)   20,153
Sun Valley CDP   19,461

Race and Hispanic or Latino origin*
White   74.8%
Black or African American   2.4%
American Indian or Alaska Native   2.1%
Asian   2.8%
Native Hawaiian or other Pacific Islander   0.3%
Some other race   0.1%
Hispanic or Latino origin   15.3%
Two or more races   2.1%

*As percentage of total population.

Ancestry*

Dutch 1.5%	Norwegian 2.0%
English 9.6%	Polish 1.3%
French 2.8%	Scotch-Irish 1.5%
German 12.7%	Scottish 1.8%
Irish 9.7%	Swedish 1.7%
Italian 4.6%	USA/American 3.9%

*As estimated percentage of total population.

Universities and colleges, 2000–2001 enrollment
Career College of Northern Nevada, Reno   241
Deep Springs College, Dyer   287
Great Basin College, Elko   2,978
Sierra Nevada College, Incline Village   586
Truckee Meadows Community College, Reno   9,930
University of Nevada, Reno   13,149
Western Nevada Community College, Carson City   5,117

Newspapers and circulation

	District circulation	Total circulation
Carson City Nevada Appeal	14,381	14,401
Las Vegas Review Journal	6,016	167,168
Las Vegas Sun	6,910	200,303
Reno Gazette/Journal	63,952	66,645
San Francisco Chronicle	2,739	518,725
*USA Today**	10,114	1,674,376

*See Sources and Explanations in the front of the volume.

Television stations and affiliations

Reno	41%	KAME	UPN
Reno	41%	KNPB	PBS
Reno	41%	KOLO	ABC
Reno	41%	KREN	PAX
Reno	41%	KRNV	NBC
Reno	41%	KRXI	FOX
Reno	41%	KTVN	CBS
Reno	41%	KWNV	NBC
Las Vegas	30%	KBLR	Telemundo
Las Vegas	30%	KFBT	Independent
Las Vegas	30%	KINC	Univision
Las Vegas	30%	KLAS	CBS
Las Vegas	30%	KLVX	PBS
Las Vegas	30%	KTNV	ABC
Las Vegas	30%	KVBC	NBC
Las Vegas	30%	KVVU	FOX
Las Vegas	30%	KVWB	WB
Salt Lake City	29%	KBYU	PBS
Salt Lake City	29%	KCSG	PAX
Salt Lake City	29%	KENV	NBC
Salt Lake City	29%	KGWR	CBS

Salt Lake City	29%	KJZZ	Independent
Salt Lake City	29%	KSL	NBC
Salt Lake City	29%	KSTU	FOX
Salt Lake City	29%	KTVX	ABC
Salt Lake City	29%	KUED	PBS
Salt Lake City	29%	KULC	PBS
Salt Lake City	29%	KUTV	CBS
Salt Lake City	29%	KUWB	WB

Cable systems and subscribers
Charter 117,040
Clark Cablevision 90,941
Cox 2,209
Eagle West 3,351
HFU TV 4,171
Lovelock Cable TV 850
Mallard/SunTel 2,771
Precis Communications 3,407
Rainbow Cable 842

Military installations, September 2001
Nellis Air Force Base, Las Vegas 7,382
Fallon Naval Air Station, Fallon 1,552
Reno/Tahoe International Airport, Reno 1,004
Indian Springs AF Auxiliary Field, Indian Springs 705
Hawthorne Army Depot, Reno 463

Businesses and other major employers
Circus and El Dorado Joint Venture; Reno; casino hotel 3,000
Harrah's Entertainment Inc.; Reno; casino hotel 3,000
Primadonna Resort and Casino; Jean; casino hotel 3,000
Sparks Nugget Inc.; Sparks; casino hotel 2,800
Reno Hilton Resort Corp.; Reno; hotels 2,500
Washoe Medical Center Inc.; Reno 2,274
El Dorado Resorts; Reno; casino hotel 2,200
Golden Road Motor Inn Inc.; Reno; casino hotel 1,900
St. Mary's Regional Medical Center Inc.; Reno 1,800
Peppermill Casinos Inc.; Reno; hotels and motels 1,700
Pacer International Inc.; Reno; Internet host services 1,655
Barrick Goldstrike Mines Inc.; Carlin; gold ores 1,650
Harveys Casino Resorts; Stateline; casino hotel 1,600
Desert Palace Inc.; Stateline; casino hotel 1,500
Jim's Enterprises Inc.; Wendover; gambling 1,500
Newmont Mining Corp.; Carlin; gold ores 1,500
Odyssey Business Services Inc.; Carson City; employment agencies 1,500
Sierra Development Co.; Reno; bar 1,300
Boomtown Hotel and Casino Inc.; Verdi; gambling 1,200
Jean Development Co; Jean; casino hotel 1,100
JC Penney Corp.; Reno; department stores 1,000
Nevada Dechtel Corp.; Mercury; business services 1,000
Washoe County; Reno; county government 1,000
WSR Inc.; Mesquite; golf club 1,000
City of Reno; Reno; city management 970
Newmont Mining Corp.; Winnemucca; gold ores 950

Bently Nevada Corp.; Minden; measuring and controlling devices 900
Fitzgeralds Gaming Corp.; Reno; casino hotel 900
IGT; Reno; slot machines 900
Sierra Pacific Power Co.; Reno; electric power generation 900
Wild Game NG; Reno; hotels and motels 900
Wimar Tahoe Corp.; Stateline; casino hotel 850
State Line Hotel Inc.; Wendover; casino hotel 828
Casa Blanca Resorts; Mesquite; casino hotel 800
Virgin River Hotel and Casino; Mesquite; casino hotel 800
Carson-Tahoe Hospital; Carson City 750
Hyatt Corp.; Incline Village; casino hotel 750
Cactus Petes Inc.; Jackpot; casino hotel 720
Washoe County; Reno; correctional facilities 715
Mikohn Gaming Corp.; Sparks; personal service agents 711
Nevada Office of Military; Reno; national guard 710
Day and Zimmermann Group; Hawthorne; bombs and parts 700
Zante Inc.; Reno; casino hotel 700
Kids Behavioral Health; Reno; specialty outpatient clinics 650
U.S. Veterans Hospital; Reno 633
Peppermill Casino Wendover Inc.; Wendover; casino hotel 620
AngloGold Corp.; Elko; gold ores 600
Hyatt Tahoe Casino Management Inc.; Incline Village; casino hotel 600
John Deere Capital Corp.; Reno; installment note buying 600
Peppermill Casinos Inc.; Sparks; casino hotel 600
U.S. Postal Service; Reno 600
West Telemarketing Corp.; Reno; telemarketing services 600
Carson Nugget Inc.; Carson City; gambling 550
Getchell Gold Corp.; Golconda; gold ores 550
Carson Valley Inn Inc.; Minden; casino hotel 530
Sundowner Hotel-Casino; Reno; casino hotel 525
Silver Club; Sparks; gambling 520
Round Mountain Gold Corp.; Round Mountain; placer gold mining 509
Washoe County; Reno; sheriff's office 503
Amazon.com Inc.; Fernley; book and record clubs 500
American Skiing Co.; Zephyr Cove; resort hotel 500
Baldini's Casino; Sparks; casino hotel 500
Capital City Entertainment Inc.; Carson City; casino hotel 500
CMS International; Sparks; gambling machines 500
Community College System of Nevada; Reno 500
Gannett Co. Inc.; Reno; newspaper advertising representative 500
Nevada Dept. of Motor Vehicles and Public Safety; Carson City; transportation regulation 500
Northern Nevada Medical Center; Sparks 500
R. R. Donnelley and Sons Co.; Reno; publication printing 500

Nevada 3rd District

Las Vegas suburbs

Roughly pinwheel-shaped, the new 3rd District is located in Clark County, which has absorbed much of the 66 percent population gain that made Nevada the nation's fastest-growing state in the 1990s. The district includes a chunk of Las Vegas, but it is mainly composed of suburbs such as Henderson and Boulder City.

Though most of the city's casinos are located in the urban 1st District, the 3rd is home to many who work in the gambling industry and are part of the area's strong union structure. The district has a 16 percent Hispanic population. It also contains the busy Las Vegas airport.

The 3rd was drawn to be a partisan swing district. When it was created in 2001, its voting makeup was 42 percent Democratic and 42 percent Republican, with the rest of the voters unaffiliated. Al Gore narrowly beat George W. Bush in the 2000 presidential contest here by 48.8 percent to 48.3 percent.

Republicans may have an advantage in the future, however, as the GOP suburban areas are expanding rapidly. The district takes in most of the suburbs, including Summerlin to the west, a massive planned community along the western rim of Las Vegas Valley. These areas are populated with many white-collar new arrivals to the state, as well as one of the fastest-growing elderly populations in the country. To the east, along the Arizona border near Utah, the population is largely Mormon—an influence that has spread into suburbs such as Henderson. In the south, the district contains lightly populated mining communities around Laughlin on the Arizona border.

Major Industry

Mining, gambling, ranching.

Notable

Hoover Dam, about 30 miles southeast of Las Vegas, often is called one of the greatest engineering works in history.

Election Returns

	Republican		Democratic		Other	
President 2000	103,720	48.3%	104,772	48.8%	6,119	2.9%
House 2002	100,378	56.1%	66,659	37.2%	11,957	6.7%

District Profile

Population   666,082

Total area (square miles)   4,748.8
  Land area (square miles)   4,569.7

Population per square mile   145.8

Counties (2000 population)
  Clark (pt.)   666,082

Cities and other areas over 10,000 (2000 population)
  Boulder City   14,966
  Enterprise CDP (pt.)   14,438
  Henderson   175,381
  Las Vegas (pt.)   115,526
  Paradise CDP (pt.)   108,177
  Spring Valley CDP   117,390
  Sunrise Manor CDP (pt.)   67,679
  Whitney CDP   18,273

Race and Hispanic or Latino origin*
  White   69.3%
  Black or African American   5.5%
  American Indian or Alaska Native   0.5%
  Asian   5.9%
  Native Hawaiian or other Pacific Islander   0.4%
  Some other race   0.1%
  Hispanic or Latino origin   15.6%
  Two or more races   2.7%

As percentage of total population.

Ancestry*

Dutch	1.2%	Norwegian	1.4%
English	7.7%	Polish	2.4%
French	2.4%	Scottish	1.4%
German	11.1%	Swedish	1.4%
Irish	8.7%	USA/American	3.8%
Italian	6.2%		

As estimated percentage of total population.

Universities and colleges, 2000–2001 enrollment
  ITT Technical Institute, Henderson   417
  Las Vegas College, Las Vegas   429

Newspapers and circulation

	District circulation	Total circulation
Las Vegas Review Journal	85,376	167,168
Las Vegas Review-Journal/Sun (Sunday)	101,734	200,303
Las Vegas Sun	16,349	33,135
Los Angeles Times	1,274	1,044,205
*USA Today**	9,964	1,674,376

See Sources and Explanations in the front of the volume.

Television stations and affiliations

Las Vegas	100%	KBLR	Telemundo
Las Vegas	100%	KFBT	Independent
Las Vegas	100%	KINC	Univision
Las Vegas	100%	KLAS	CBS
Las Vegas	100%	KLVX	PBS
Las Vegas	100%	KTNV	ABC
Las Vegas	100%	KVBC	NBC
Las Vegas	100%	KVVU	FOX
Las Vegas	100%	KVWB	WB

Cable systems and subscribers
  Clark Cablevision   1,115
  Cox   32,638

Businesses and other major employers
  Mandalay Corp.; Las Vegas; casino hotel   8,000
  Circus Circus Casinos Inc.; Las Vegas; casino hotel   3,600
  Citibank; Las Vegas; credit card service   2,300
  Coast Hotels and Casinos Inc.; Las Vegas; casino hotel   2,100
  Donald J. Laughlin; Laughlin; gambling machines   2,010

Ivantage Network Solutions; Las Vegas; telecommunications consultant 2,000

JT3; Las Vegas; engineering services 2,000

Park Place Entertainment Corp.; Laughlin; casino hotel 2,000

U.S. Postal Service; Las Vegas 2,000

Bechtel National Inc.; Las Vegas; industrial plant construction 1,800

Sunset Station Hotel and Casino Inc.; Henderson; casino hotel 1,800

Harrah's Laughlin Inc.; Laughlin; casino hotel 1,500

Colorado Belle Corp.; Laughlin; casino hotel 1,476

Ramada Express Inc.; Laughlin; casino hotel 1,400

Edgewater Hotel Corp.; Laughlin; gambling machines 1,350

Gold River Operating Corp.; Laughlin; casino hotel 1,200

Ameristar Casino Las Vegas Inc.; Henderson; casino hotel 1,000

Clark County; Las Vegas; airport 1,000

NOSVA LP; Las Vegas; long-distance telephone 1,000

America West Airlines Inc.; Las Vegas; air transportation 900

First National Bank of Marin Inc.; Las Vegas; commercial bank 844

Pioneer Hotel Inc.; Laughlin; casino hotel 840

GNL Corp.; Laughlin; casino hotel 805

Interstate Plumbing and Air Conditioning Inc.; Las Vegas; plumbing, heating, air-conditioning 700

Nevada Power Co.; Las Vegas; electric power generation 700

Silverton Casino; Las Vegas; casino hotel 700

Sun City Anthem; Henderson; single-family housing construction 700

Fresca; Las Vegas; casino hotel 650

AVI Casino Enterprise Inc.; Laughlin; casino hotel 623

Greater Nevada Auto Auction Inc.; Las Vegas; auctioneer 600

Westcor Construction; Las Vegas; framing contractor 600

Titanium Metals Corp.; Henderson; titanium and titanium alloy bars, sheets, strips 560

ETT Inc.; Las Vegas; slot machines 550

Cardivan Co.; Las Vegas; slot machines 500

Full Throttle Apparel Co.; Las Vegas; inflatable life jackets 500

RCR Plumbing Inc.; Las Vegas; plumbing contractors 500

Southwest Gas Corp.; Las Vegas; natural gas distribution 500

United Parcel Service Inc.; Las Vegas; courier services 500

Wal-Mart Stores Inc.; Las Vegas; discount department stores 500

NEW HAMPSHIRE

Districts established April 8, 2002, for elections first held in 2002.

2 members

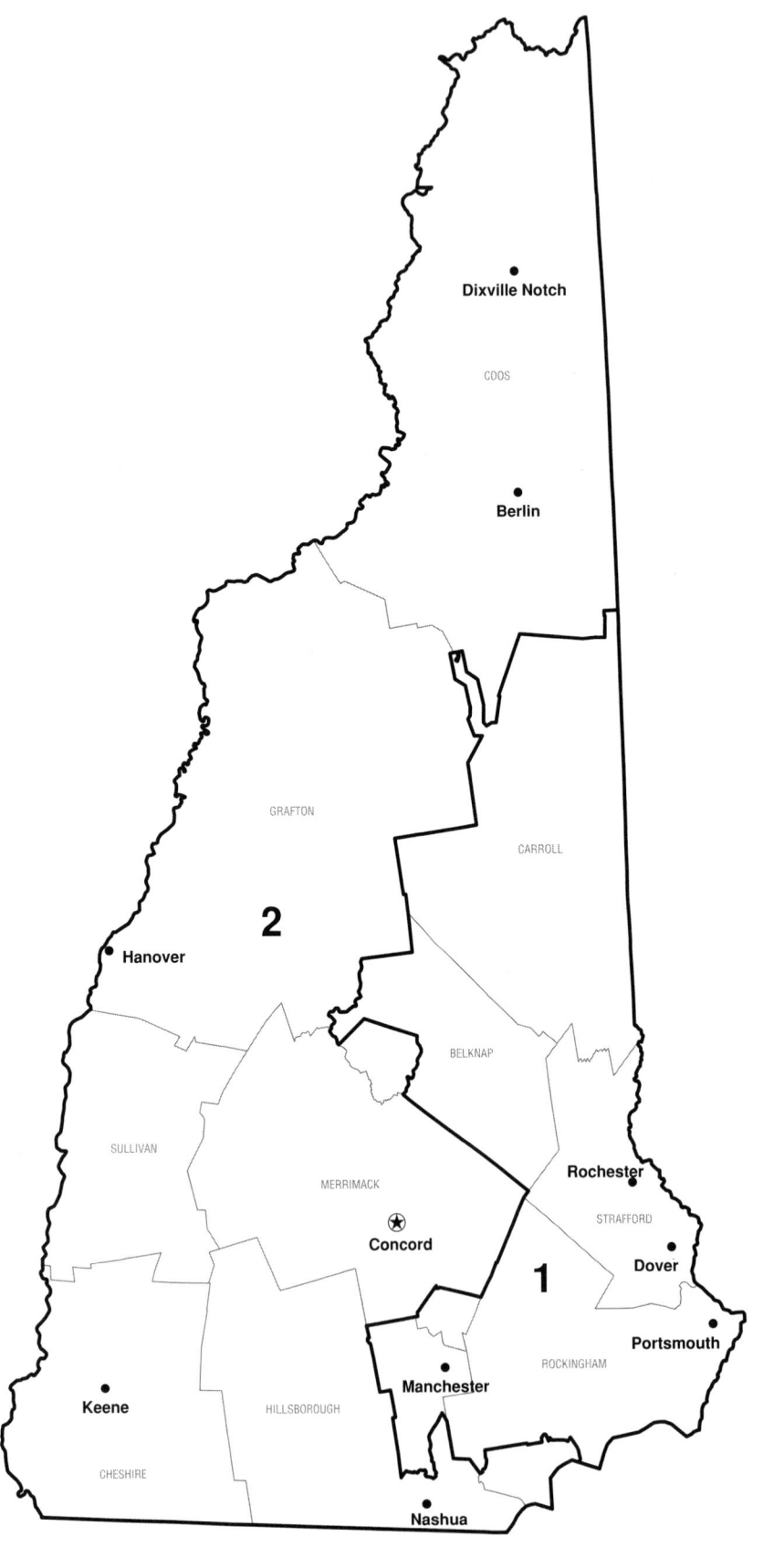

New Hampshire

In spring 2003 New Hampshire sustained a serious indignity when its "Old Man of the Mountain" fell down because of natural causes. The famed profile, a cluster of natural rock ledges on a bluff in Franconia Notch State Park, had been a visitor attraction and symbol since colonial times. It was celebrated by Daniel Webster and Nathaniel Hawthorne, seen on state road signs and even featured on the new quarter saluting the state. To many locals, it was a loss of heritage and a challenge to the "Granite State" image. Some even saw in this event a portent for another local phenomenon steeped in lore: the first-in-the-nation presidential primary.

Although preference primaries got their start elsewhere, New Hampshire's came to prominence at mid-century when it began to attract attention from candidates and reporters. Dwight D. Eisenhower used the 1952 primary here to advance his claim to the Republican nomination, and John F. Kennedy did the same on the Democratic side in 1960. Thereafter, the legend grew. Now the quadrennial event has become a source of local pride, political clout, and economic benefit. Other states have looked jealously upon all these benefits, and by 2004 their encroachment on the calendar had driven New Hampshire's primary into January. It does not seem to matter that in recent years New Hampshire has lost its knack for predicting the winner of the nomination, let alone of the election itself (both George W. Bush and Bill Clinton finished second here the year they first won the White House).

New Hampshire has also been known for its fierce sense of independence ("Live Free or Die" read the license plates) and opposition to taxes. The state has neither an income tax nor a sales tax and the prevailing political imperatives have required winning candidates for statewide office to "take the pledge" to oppose both (until incumbent Democratic governor Jeanne Shaheen won without doing so in 2000). New Hampshire is one of those states that put the rock in "rock-ribbed Republican." Shaheen was one of just three Democrats elected governor after World War II, while the state elected 11 Republicans to that office. During the same period, the state's seats in the U.S. Senate went to Republicans seventeen times in 20 elections. The state legislature was usually predominantly GOP, particularly in the 400-seat House where members earn $100 a year. In presidential voting, Franklin D. Roosevelt and Lyndon B. Johnson were the only Democrats to carry the state between 1920 and 1990.

During the last two decades of the century, however, the Democrats began to advance in state politics. New Hampshire's population grew steadily, faster than any northeastern state except Delaware and nearly as fast as the national average. Some of the arrivals were fleeing the high taxes of Massachusetts and New York, others the crowding, pace, and prices of the Boston and New York metro areas. The state remained overwhelmingly white (forty-third among the states in percentage of both African Americans and Hispanics), but issues shifted. Protecting the environment gained in importance, especially on the Democratic side.

By the early 1990s, the new residents in concert with teachers and the traditionally Democratic union families constituted a new plurality. The recession hit old and new industries hard in New Hampshire, and in that year's three-way November vote for president, Bill Clinton's 38.9 percent eclipsed incumbent President George Bush's 37.6 percent (with independent Ross Perot taking 22.5 percent). Four years later, cruising to reelection, Clinton got close to half the vote here (49.3 percent) with Perot down below 10 percent. But in 2000, with Ralph Nader the choice of nearly 4 percent, Democrat Al Gore fell just shy of Clinton's 1996 share and lost. The Democrats were also dealt a setback in 2002, as Shaheen lost her bid for the Senate, Republicans recaptured the governorship and held on to both House seats.

New Hampshire is unique among the original 13 colonies in that it has fewer seats in Congress today than it had in the first Congress that met in 1789. The state's delegation in the House began at three seats, growing to six in 1810 but falling back after just 20 years. As the rest of the country grew rapidly, New Hampshire saw its House seats dwindle to five after 1830 and down another notch after each of the next two censuses. After 1880 it was reduced to two seats, where it still stands today. To form the districts, the state map was split standing up, like a piece of firewood, with the large but least populous northern Coos County making the western district look top heavy. The center-south of the state is Republican, as the big cities of Manchester and Nashua combine Yankee tradition with the entrepreneurial leanings of new arrivals lured by high-tech opportunity (the state is now ninth in percentage of residents with a college degree). The towns on the western (Vermont) and eastern (Maine) sides have more Catholics and more Democratic tradition.

Although the cost of living is surprisingly high here (one of the ten highest in the nation) New Hampshire remains a state with very little poverty: less than 5 percent of its population meets the statistical definition, the smallest percentage of poor among the 50 states. In the years after 2000 that state had escaped the high unemployment that cost George Bush in 1992; in 2002 the state jobless rate was below 5 percent and more than a full percentage point below the national average.

Table 1 Population

District	Population	Population under 18	Voting-age population	Median age	Male*	Female*
1	617,575	154,454	463,121	36.8	49.1	50.9
2	618,211	155,108	463,103	37.5	49.3	50.7
State	1,235,786	309,562	926,224	37.1	49.2	50.8

*As percentage of total population.

Table 2 Voting-Age Persons by Race/Hispanic or Latino Origin

District	White*	Black or African American*	American Indian or Alaska Native*	Asian*	Other or multirace*	Hispanic or Latino*
1	95.7	0.7	0.2	1.2	0.8	1.3
2	95.6	0.6	0.2	1.3	0.8	1.4
State	95.7	0.6	0.2	1.3	0.8	1.4

*As percentage of voting-age population.

Table 3 Voting-Age Population by Age Groups

District	18 to 24*	25 to 44*	45 to 64*	Over 64*
1	11.2	42.2	31.1	15.6
2	11.1	40.2	32.4	16.4
State	11.2	41.2	31.7	16.0

*As percentage of voting-age population.

Table 4 Income and Occupation

District	Median family income	Families in poverty*	White collar†	Blue collar†	Service†	Farm†
1	$58,351	4.4	62.7	23.6	13.3	0.4
2	$56,966	4.2	62.1	24.7	12.6	0.5
State	$57,575	4.3	62.4	24.1	13.0	0.4

*As percentage of all families.   †As percentage of employed workers 16 years and over.

Table 5 Education: School Years Completed

District	Less than grade 9*	Grades 9–12 no diploma*	High school diploma no college*	Some college*	College bachelor's degree or higher*
1	4.0	8.5	29.3	29.7	28.5
2	3.9	8.8	30.8	27.7	28.9
State	3.9	8.7	30.1	28.7	28.7

*As percentage of persons age 25 and over.

Table 6 Housing and Residential Patterns

District	Median home value	Owner occupied*	Renter occupied*	Urban†	Rural†
1	$133,200	68.5	31.5	66.6	33.4
2	$121,600	70.8	29.2	51.7	48.3
State	$127,500	69.7	30.3	59.2	40.8

*As percentage of occupied housing units.   †As percentage of total population.

New Hampshire 1st District

East — Manchester, Rochester

Nestled in the southeast corner of the state, the 1st covers about one-fourth of New Hampshire's land yet contains 12 of the 17 most populous communities, including the largest, Manchester.

Most people live in and around Manchester or in Rockingham County along the coast. Some residents of southeastern towns, such as Dover, Portsmouth, Hampton, and Exeter, commute to Boston.

Manchester, which boasts many technology and manufacturing companies, grew slowly in the 1990s. But the city is surrounded by rapidly growing areas such as upper-income Bedford to the southwest and Hooksett to the north.

In the eastern part of the district, the Portsmouth Naval Shipyard, across the state line in Kittery, Maine, has served as an economic anchor. Portsmouth experienced a big population drop in the 1990s, in part because of the closing of Pease Air Force Base.

Democratic-leaning Strafford County, where Durham (home to the University of New Hampshire) and Dover are located, gives Democrats healthy margins at the polls. Carroll County, in the north end of the district, is a rural, GOP-friendly area that thrives primarily on tourism and farming.

The 1st exhibits a Republican lean, albeit a small one. Republicans do well in medium-size and small towns, but no longer roll up big margins in population centers such as Manchester, which elected a Democratic mayor in 1999 and backed Al Gore in the 2000 presidential election.

Major Industry

Health care, insurance, computer manufacturing.

Notable

President Franklin Pierce was born in Hillsborough; Robert Frost operated a farm in Derry that is now a state historic site.

Election Returns

	Republican		Democratic		Other	
President 2000	136,474	49.4%	128,278	46.4%	11,545	4.2%
House 2002	128,993	58.1%	85,426	38.5%	7,568	3.4%

District Profile

Population   617,575

Total area (square miles)   2,688.0
   Land area (square miles)   2,448.6

Population per square mile   252.2

Counties (2000 population)
   Belknap (pt.)   50,267
   Carroll   43,666
   Hillsborough (pt.)   167,328
   Merrimack (pt.)   11,721
   Rockingham (pt.)   232,360
   Strafford   112,233

Cities and other areas over 10,000 (2000 population)

Derry CDP	22,661	Manchester	107,006
Dover	26,884	Portsmouth	20,784
Laconia	16,411	Rochester	28,461
Londonderry CDP	11,417	Somersworth	11,477

Race and Hispanic or Latino origin*

White 95.1%
Black or African American 0.7%
American Indian or Alaska Native 0.2%
Asian 1.2%
Native Hawaiian or other Pacific Islander 0.0%
Some other race 0.1%
Hispanic or Latino origin 1.6%
Two or more races 0.9%

*As percentage of total population.

Ancestry*

English	12.7%	Italian	6.4%
Fr. Canadian	7.6%	Polish	3.1%
French	10.5%	Scotch-Irish	1.6%
German	6.0%	Scottish	3.0%
Greek	1.1%	Swedish	1.4%
Irish	14.6%	USA/American	4.0%

*As estimated percentage of total population.

Universities and colleges, 2000–2001 enrollment

Hesser College, Manchester 2,766
McIntosh College, Dover 1,143
New Hampshire Community Technical College, Manchester 4,024
Notre Dame College, Manchester 1,121
Southern New Hampshire University, Manchester 4,584
St. Anselm College, Manchester 1,985
University of New Hampshire, Durham 14,689

Newspapers and circulation

	District circulation	Total circulation
Boston Globe	14,815	465,248
Boston Herald	7,068	257,071
Concord Monitor	2,120	20,234
Exeter News-Letter	5,704	5,704
Foster's Daily Democrat	19,859	23,144
Hampton Union	4,836	4,860
Laconia Citizen	6,915	9,051
Lawrence Eagle-Tribune	5,959	54,109
*Manchester Union Leader-News**	20,344	62,791
Nashua Telegraph	3,213	26,239
Portsmouth Herald	10,830	14,788
*USA Today**	4,576	1,674,376

*See Sources and Explanations in the front of the volume.

Television stations and affiliations

Boston (Manchester)	63%	WBPX	PAX
Boston (Manchester)	63%	WBZ	CBS
Boston (Manchester)	63%	WCVB	ABC
Boston (Manchester)	63%	WDPX	PAX
Boston (Manchester)	63%	WEKW	PBS
Boston (Manchester)	63%	WFXT	FOX
Boston (Manchester)	63%	WGBH	PBS
Boston (Manchester)	63%	WGBX	PBS
Boston (Manchester)	63%	WHDH	NBC
Boston (Manchester)	63%	WLVI	WB
Boston (Manchester)	63%	WMFP	Independent
Boston (Manchester)	63%	WMUR	ABC
Boston (Manchester)	63%	WNDS	Independent
Boston (Manchester)	63%	WPXB	Independent
Boston (Manchester)	63%	WPXG	PAX
Boston (Manchester)	63%	WSBK	UPN
Boston (Manchester)	63%	WUNI	Univision
Boston (Manchester)	63%	WWDP	Independent
Boston (Manchester)	63%	WYDN	Independent
Portland-Auburn	37%	WCBB	PBS
Portland-Auburn	37%	WCSH	NBC
Portland-Auburn	37%	WGME	CBS
Portland-Auburn	37%	WMEA	PBS
Portland-Auburn	37%	WMTW	ABC
Portland-Auburn	37%	WPXT	WB

Cable systems and subscribers

Adelphia 29,472
Comcast 110,675
Metrocast 51,451

Military installations, September 2001

Pease Air Force Base, Portsmouth 993
Armed Forces Reserve Center, Londonderry, Manchester 622

Businesses and other major employers

FMR Corp.; Merrimack; help supply services 3,000
University System of New Hampshire; Durham; elementary and secondary schools 2,793
Enterasys Networks Inc.; Portsmouth; computer peripheral equipment 2,100
Gentek Inc.; Hampton; automotive parts, used 2,000
Manchester Elliot Hospital; Manchester 1,937
Sanmina-SCI Corp.; Derry; printed circuit boards 1,700
Catholic Medical Center; Manchester 1,200
BAE Systems North America Inc.; Merrimack; business consulting 1,100
North Atlantic Energy Corp.; Seabrook; electric services 1,000
Timberland Netherlands Inc.; Stratham; foreign trade consultant 1,000
Tyco International Inc.; Exeter; surgical and medical instruments 1,000
U.S. Postal Service; Manchester 1,000
Anthem Blue Cross and Blue Shield of NH Inc.; Manchester; health insurance 970
General Electric Co.; Somersworth; instrument transformers 962
Tycom Integrated Cable Systems Inc.; Portsmouth; fiber optic cable 950
Wentworth-Douglass Hospital; Dover 936
RESCO Holdings Inc.; Hampton; waste disposal plant construction 900
Textron Automotive Co.; Dover; automotive moldings or trim 900
Heidelberg Web System Inc.; Dover; printing presses 802
Nike Bauer Hockey Inc.; Greenland; athletic goods 800
South Hampton School District; Hampton 800

Roman Catholic Bishop of Manchester; Manchester; religious organization   791

Osram Sylvania Inc.; Manchester; infrared, ultraviolet health lamps   785

HCA Health Services Hospital; Portsmouth   769

Collins and Aikman Products Co.; Farmington; motor vehicle body components and frame   750

Exeter Hospital Inc.; Exeter   740

St. Gobain Performance Plastics Corp.; Merrimack; chemically coated and treated fabrics   738

Lakes Region Hospital Assn.; Laconia   730

Fluor Enterprises Inc.; Portsmouth; industrial plant construction   700

Liberty Mutual Insurance Co.; Portsmouth; liability insurance   700

Ocean Hospitalities Inc.; Portsmouth; hotel, franchised   700

Prime Tanning Co.; Rochester; leather tannery   700

General Electric Co.; Hooksett; aircraft engines and parts   695

Velcro USA Inc.; Manchester; fabric tapes   650

U.S. Veterans Hospital; Manchester   610

Foss Manufacturing Co.; Hampton; nonwoven fabrics   600

Oxford Health Insurance Inc.; Hooksett; health maintenance organization   600

Pan American Airways Corp.; Portsmouth; air transportation   600

Anheuser-Busch Inc.; Merrimack; beer   592

Jac Pac Foods; Manchester; frozen meats   550

Aavid Thermalloy; Laconia; electronic circuits   535

Car Component Technologies Inc.; Bedford; motor vehicle axles   520

Phillips Exeter Academy; Exeter   503

Frisbie Memorial Hospital; Rochester   500

HCA Health Services Hospital; Derry   500

Liberty Life Assurance Company of Boston; Dover; life insurance   500

New Hampshire Ball Bearings Inc.; Laconia; ball bearings and parts   500

Rockingham County; Exeter; county government   500

Roman Catholic Bishop of Manchester; Bedford; religious organization   500

Unitrode Corp.; Manchester; integrated microcircuits (semiconductor)   500

University System of New Hampshire; Durham   500

Verizon New England Inc.; Manchester; telephone communication   500

New Hampshire 2nd District

West — Nashua, Concord

The 2nd encompasses the entire western half of New Hampshire and most of the state's southern border with Massachusetts, spanning from white-collar territory in the southern tier to the mountains and forests of the sparsely populated "North Country."

The district has an economy as varied as its population. Many of the upwardly mobile refugees who fled Massachusetts' higher tax rates reside along the populous southern tier of the district in towns such as Salem, Windham,

and Atkinson, but still work across the state line. Nashua, the 2nd's most populous city, has experienced ups and downs with industries deeply involved in computers and electronics.

The economy of the heavily forested North Country is closely tied to paper manufacturing and wood products. In the far northern reaches of the state, about 20 miles from the border with Quebec, is tiny Dixville Notch, where residents cast the nation's first votes at the stroke of midnight election day. In between lie smaller blue-collar towns, many of which depend on tourist dollars from lake visitors and skiers.

Once rock-ribbed Republican, the 2nd has become more competitive in recent years. Al Gore carried the district in 2000, thanks to the Democratic lean of Nashua and the liberalism of Concord, the state capital, and the college towns of Hanover and Keene. Other population centers are politically competitive: George W. Bush carried Salem by 2 votes and lost Hudson by 46 votes in 2000. The northern counties tend to lean Republican.

Redistricting in 2002 made minimal changes to the 2nd, which retained all of its territory from the 1990s map but added the Merrimack County towns of Epsom and Pittsfield, just east of Concord.

Major Industry

Electronics, computer technology, health care.

Notable

The "Old Man of the Mountain" stone profile in the White Mountains—the source for the state emblem—crumbled down in 2003; the statehouse in Concord is the oldest legislative building in America in which both houses continue to sit in their original chambers; Daniel Webster's birthplace is in Franklin.

Election Returns

	Republican		Democratic		Other	
President 2000	132,336	47.4%	134,343	48.1%	12,801	4.6%
House 2002	125,804	56.8%	90,479	40.9%	5,173	2.3%

District Profile

Population   618,211

Total area (square miles)   6,661.9
Land area (square miles)   6,519.4

Population per square mile   94.8

Counties (2000 population)

Belknap (pt.)	6,058	Hillsborough (pt.)	213,513
Cheshire	73,825	Merrimack (pt.)	124,504
Coos	33,111	Rockingham (pt.)	44,999
Grafton	81,743	Sullivan	40,458

Cities and other areas over 10,000 (2000 population)

Berlin	10,331	Keene	22,563
Claremont	13,151	Lebanon	12,568
Concord	40,687	Nashua	86,605

Race and Hispanic or Latino origin*

White   95.1%

Black or African American   0.6%

American Indian or Alaska Native   0.2%

Asian   1.3%

Native Hawaiian or other Pacific Islander   0.0%
Some other race   0.1%
Hispanic or Latino origin   1.7%
Two or more races   0.9%

*As percentage of total population.

Ancestry*

English 12.9%	Polish 2.7%
Fr. Canadian 7.0%	Scotch-Irish 1.6%
French 10.3%	Scottish 3.2%
German 6.2%	Swedish 1.4%
Irish 13.0%	USA/American 4.5%
Italian 5.7%	

*As estimated percentage of total population.

Universities and colleges, 2000–2001 enrollment

Antioch New England Graduate School, Keene   960
Colby-Sawyer College, New London   845
College for Lifelong Learning, Concord   2,087
Daniel Webster College, Nashua   1,099
Dartmouth College, Hanover   5,386
Franklin Pierce College, Rindge   704
Franklin Pierce Law Center, Concord   466
Keene State College, Keene   4,573
New England College, Henniker   835
New Hampshire Community Technical College, Berlin   1,471
New Hampshire Community Technical College, Nashua   2,176
New Hampshire Technical Institute, Concord   2,809
Plymouth State College, Plymouth   4,041
Rivier College, Nashua   2,320

Newspapers and circulation

	District circulation	Total circulation
Boston Globe	11,323	465,248
Boston Herald	4,944	257,071
Brattleboro Reformer	1,049	10,178
Claremont Eagle Times	5,179	7,049
Concord Monitor	17,868	20,234
Keene Sentinel	13,892	14,186
Laconia Citizen	2,013	9,051
Lawrence Eagle-Tribune	7,519	54,109
Lebanon Valley News	9,234	17,284
Lowell Sun	2,122	51,598
*Manchester Union Leader-News**	42,271	62,791
Nashua Telegraph	22,837	26,239
St. Johnsbury Caledonian-Record	2,613	10,315
*USA Today**	5,411	1,674,376

*See Sources and Explanations in the front of the volume.

Television stations and affiliations

Boston (Manchester)	38%	WBPX	PAX
Boston (Manchester)	38%	WBZ	CBS
Boston (Manchester)	38%	WCVB	ABC
Boston (Manchester)	38%	WDPX	PAX
Boston (Manchester)	38%	WEKW	PBS
Boston (Manchester)	38%	WFXT	FOX
Boston (Manchester)	38%	WGBH	PBS
Boston (Manchester)	38%	WGBX	PBS
Boston (Manchester)	38%	WHDH	NBC
Boston (Manchester)	38%	WLVI	WB
Boston (Manchester)	38%	WMFP	Independent
Boston (Manchester)	38%	WMUR	ABC
Boston (Manchester)	38%	WNDS	Independent
Boston (Manchester)	38%	WPXB	Independent
Boston (Manchester)	38%	WPXG	PAX
Boston (Manchester)	38%	WSBK	UPN
Boston (Manchester)	38%	WUNI	Univision
Boston (Manchester)	38%	WWDP	Independent
Boston (Manchester)	38%	WYDN	Independent
Burlington-Plattsburgh	35%	WCAX	CBS
Burlington-Plattsburgh	35%	WCFE	PBS
Burlington-Plattsburgh	35%	WETK	PBS
Burlington-Plattsburgh	35%	WLED	PBS
Burlington-Plattsburgh	35%	WNNE	NBC
Burlington-Plattsburgh	35%	WPTZ	NBC
Burlington-Plattsburgh	35%	WVER	PBS
Burlington-Plattsburgh	35%	WVNY	ABC
Burlington-Plattsburgh	35%	WVTB	PBS
Portland-Auburn	27%	WCBB	PBS
Portland-Auburn	27%	WCSH	NBC
Portland-Auburn	27%	WGME	CBS
Portland-Auburn	27%	WMEA	PBS
Portland-Auburn	27%	WMTW	ABC
Portland-Auburn	27%	WPXT	WB

Cable systems and subscribers

Adelphia   59,318
Beryl Mountain Cable   1,299
Charter   3,462
Comcast   57,563
MCT Cable   2,243
Metrocast   8,586
Pine Tree Cablevision   2,549
Time Warner   21,438
White Mountain Cablevision   1,504

Businesses and other major employers

BAE Systems Information and Electronic Systems Integration; Nashua; computer integrated systems design   5,000
Mary Hitchcock Memorial Hospital; Lebanon   5,000
New Hampshire Dept. of Health and Human Services; Concord   3,000
Hitchiner Manufacturing Co.; Milford; steel investment foundries   1,687
Compaq Computer Corp.; Nashua; software development   1,500
Concord Hospital Inc.; Concord   1,400
Lockheed Martin Corp.; Nashua; countermeasure simulators   1,200
Teradyne Inc.; Nashua; printed circuit boards   1,200
Southern New Hampshire Medical Center; Nashua   1,000
St. Joseph Hospital of Nashua; Nashua   1,000
Osram Sylvania Inc.; Hillsborough; electric lamps   900
Cheshire Medical Center; Keene   850
MPB Corp.; Keene; ball bearings and parts   850
Sturm Ruger and Co.; Newport; carbines   823
United Natural Foods Inc.; Chesterfield; food brokers   800
MPB Corp.; Lebanon; ball bearings and parts   750
J. Jill Group Inc.; Tilton; telemarketing   727

Peerless Insurance Co. Inc.; Keene; property damage insurance 720

Hitchiner Manufacturing Co.; Littleton; metal finishing equipment 700

New Hampshire Corrections Dept.; Concord 700

Timken Co.; Keene; ball and roller bearings 700

Lockheed Martin Corp.; Hudson; security control equipment and systems 680

Dartmouth College; Hanover 661

Polyclad Laminates Inc.; Franklin; laminated plastics plate and sheet 650

Oxford Health Insurance Inc.; Nashua; health maintenance organization 640

Chubbhealth Holdings Inc.; Concord; health maintenance organization 600

Dartmouth College Hospital; Hanover 600

Geographic Data Technology Inc.; Lebanon; data processing 600

Keene School District; Keene 600

Main Street America Assurance Co.; Keene; fire, marine, casualty insurance 600

Markem Corp.; Keene; printing trades machinery 600

Technical Needs North Inc.; Salem; temporary help service 600

University System of New Hampshire; Keene 600

Watts Regulator Co.; Franklin; industrial valves 600

Portex Inc.; Keene; plastics processing 576

Merrimack County; Concord; county government 550

National Grange Mutual Insurance Co.; Keene; fire, marine, casualty insurance 550

Fitz Vogt and Associates; Walpole; contract food services 540

Granite State Credit Union; Franklin; state credit unions 500

ING America Insurance Holdings Inc.; Keene; life insurance 500

Liberty Regional Agency Market; Keene; insurance agents 500

New Hampshire Ball Bearings Inc.; Peterborough; ball bearings and parts 500

New Hampshire Dept. of Transportation; Concord 500

Stow Mills Inc.; Chesterfield; specialty food items 500

U.S. Federal Aviation Admin.; Nashua 500

University System of New Hampshire; Plymouth 500

New Jersey

In spring 2003 New Jersey's professional teams in basketball and hockey, the Nets and the Devils, were closing in on championships. The question arose: where to stage the victory parade? Where is downtown in New Jersey? The leading suggestion: in the parking lot at the Meadowlands Sports Complex, the facility these teams share with the New York Giants, who have also rusticated to East Rutherford, New Jersey. New Jersey has long been the state with open arms, welcoming millions of former New Yorkers, and former Pennsylvanians too. The latter half of the twentieth century was the golden era of the American suburb, when the percentage of Americans living in suburbs more than doubled (from 23 percent to 50 percent, leaving 30 percent in central cities and 20 percent in nonmetro areas). As America moved to the 'burbs it found that New Jersey was already there.

You could say New Jersey was suburban before suburban was cool—before, in fact, the word itself was in widespread use. People were following basically suburban impulses to New Jersey as far back as colonial times and in waves that have continued to the present. The affluent were seeking space, privacy, and escape from the contemporary social ills of New York and Philadelphia. Others came out of the city looking for cheaper land and affordable rents. But rich or poor, suburbanites in those times and afterward were still connected to the economics and culture of the city they left behind. In New Jersey's case, that meant the great city across the river: the Hudson in the northeast (New York) or the Delaware in the southwest (Philadelphia).

In fact, as suburbs proliferated in rings around the nation's cities, they often seemed modeled on the bedroom communities of this state, each less a town than a "development," with look-alike tract homes for nearly every budget. There was something for middle-class and even working-class families eager to escape to what one Broadway song title called "Somewhere That's Green." Even the first drive-in theater was opened in Camden in 1933 (a carload could be admitted for a dollar). As the century and the outward trend aged, of course, the suburbs in New Jersey aged too. The state suffered from concentrated development, countless cars and trucks, and the roadways built to hold them. Some of this crush and decay can be seen in the mesmerizing title sequence of *The Sopranos,* the cable TV show that has spent years exploring the psychology of a Jersey mob boss.

As the suburbs have grown, here as elsewhere, they have enfolded many older communities that once stood on their own. Prominent in the case of New Jersey's sprawl are cities that got their names from their original Puritan and Dutch settlers—Newark, Hackensack, Paterson, Elizabeth, and Jersey City. Even the town of Princeton, midway across the state between the metro areas, is now a commuter community for some. At the same time, as the suburbs became the typical America, they also lost much of their early character as havens for the white and well-off. With each new census, the bigger suburbs are becoming more diverse—racially, economically, and politically. Just as suburban school administrators now find their student bodies speaking more languages, they also find themselves with more gangs and other social pathogens once regarded as inner-core phenomena.

New Jersey has been reasonably populous and prosperous from colonial times onward, owing in large measure to its natural role in trade and its long-standing history of innovative industry. The state's most prominent son was no less an inventive force than Thomas Edison, and Albert Einstein lived in Princeton for much of his life. The many literary products of the state included James Fenimore Cooper, Walt Whitman, William Carlos Williams, and Norman Mailer. Countless popular entertainers have come from the state but the headliners would have to be Paul Robeson, Frank Sinatra, Jack Nicholson, and Bruce Springsteen.

In the later twentieth century, much of the old industry in the state stagnated. Riding the Metroliner south from New York, passengers gaze out at empty factories and decaying housing left over from the industrial age. But the state has also known recent growth, in high-tech centers far removed from the old rail routes and in such contemporary activities as tourism, entertainment, and gambling. Atlantic City, a faded flower in the 1970s, has bloomed again with the coming of giant casinos.

Revival has been slower in the central cities: Camden, Trenton, Newark, and Jersey City. As with other older cities, these saw their older neighborhoods largely deserted by the white middle class and working class in the decades after World War II. The families moving in were usually African American, often arriving directly from rural poverty in the Deep South or from urban ghettoes in other cities. Their concentration in these urban cores accelerated the white exodus to the suburbs, integrated schools and other public facilities, and upended long-standing political and cultural arrangements. Sometimes this led to violence; some of the worst urban rioting of the period took place in 1967 in Newark, by then a black-majority city, and its central ward has never fully recovered. Although it is still the state's most populous community (263,000 in 2000), it continued to lose population in the 1990s.

573

NEW JERSEY

Districts established October 26, 2001, for elections first held in 2002.

13 members

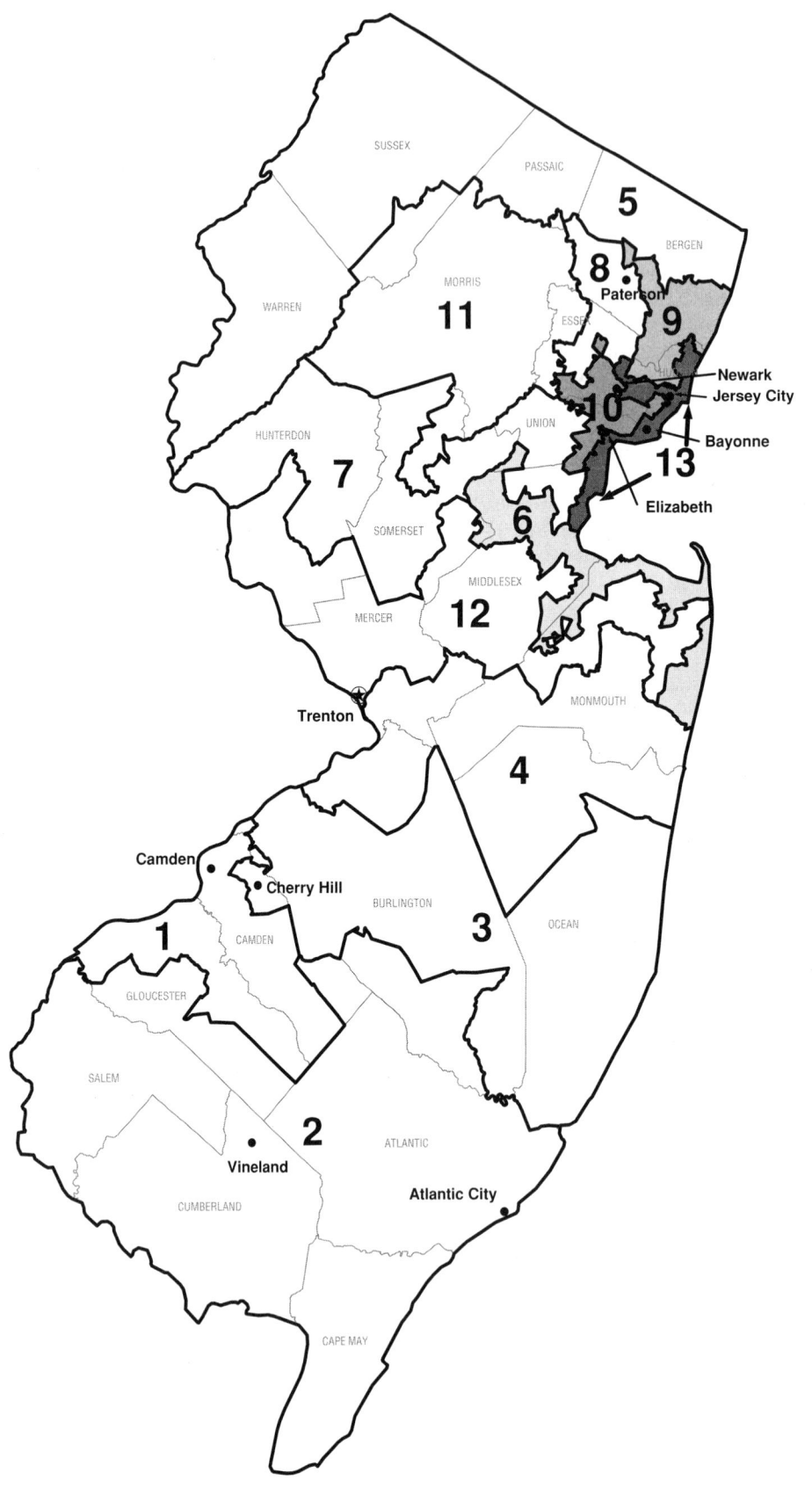

Most of Newark is in the 10th District, which kept an Italian representative until black Democrat Donald Payne was elected in 1988. The more Hispanic parts of the city are in the 13th District, a creation of redistricting in 1991 that aggregated the fast-growing Hispanic communities of Newark and Jersey City. That new district promptly elected the state's first Hispanic member of Congress, Robert Menendez, who in 2003 was third highest in the House Democratic leadership. The district now includes Ellis Island in New York Harbor and an appropriately broad mix of immigrants from Russia, India, Korea, and the Philippines. But its heart is still Spanish-speaking, and as these South and Central Americans become citizens they tend to vote Democratic (the Cubans among them excepted). The state as a whole was nearly 14 percent Hispanic in the 2000 census—just above the national figure. New Jersey became more Hispanic than African American slightly before the nation at large did the same.

For generations, New Jersey's suburbs generally outvoted its cities and gave the state a Republican cast in Congress and national elections. The southwestern 1st District in Camden County, just over the Delaware border from Philadelphia, elected Republicans from 1900 to 1974. But in that year, the changing nature of the suburban population (in this case, more Philadelphians with Democratic habits) tilted the balance of power between the city of Camden and surrounding suburbs. The district has been Democratic ever since.

A similar dynamic has been manifest in statewide voting as well, as the black and Hispanic populations have asserted themselves alongside the newer suburban arrivals. While the state's rural venues and more affluent suburbs remain Republican, there has been evidence that the new GOP of the 1990s, dominated by southern conservatives, is less appealing here than the more traditional GOP. Taken together, these forces have transformed the state into something of a Democratic bastion in statewide voting. In the stated party preference of residents as measured by the Gallup Poll, New Jersey moved farther toward the Democrats than any other state but Maine in the decade ending in 2002.

Election results tell the same story. Before the 1990s, New Jersey had voted Republican for president six times in a row and nine times since World War II, yet in 2000 it was one of George W. Bush's worst states at 40 percent (down a striking 16 percentage points from his father's showing here in 1988). The change began in 1992, when Bill Clinton carried the state with a plurality of 43 percent (matching his national vote share). Four years later Clinton was back 11 percentage points stronger, carrying the state with an outright majority. Al Gore did even better yet in 2000, carrying the state with 56 percent despite Ralph Nader's showing of 3 percent.

Similarly, the governor's office returned to Democratic hands in 2001 when James McGreevey won easily over a conservative Republican mayor. That ended eight years of Republican rule in Trenton under Christine Todd Whitman, who had moved on early to join the cabinet of George W. Bush (from which she resigned in spring 2003). Before Whitman, Democrats had won eight times to the GOP's five in gubernatorial elections since World War II.

Senate elections have been the greatest area of success for Democrats. Although one Republican served briefly as an appointee in 1982, the last GOP win in a Senate race was Clifford P. Case's last election in 1972, after which Democrats won the next ten in a row (three by Bill Bradley, four by

Frank Lautenberg). Lautenberg's win in 2002 was a sign of how much the state has changed. Lautenberg had retired in 2000 but was called back in 2002 as a last-minute replacement for incumbent Robert Torricelli, who had given up the nomination following a rebuke from the Senate Ethics Committee. Lautenberg's relatively easy win that November was a testament to the relative strength of the two parties in the new decade.

Still, Democrats have struggled to translate their gains at the congressional level. They had held a small majority in the House delegation in the 1980s and into the 1990s, but reapportionment after the 1990 census cost the state a seat and scrambled the districts. A new map drawn by a state arbitrator (after the state's bipartisan redistricting commission had deadlocked) helped the GOP win eight of the 13 seats in 1994. But that proved a high tide. In 1996 the Paterson-based 8th District ousted its incumbent Republican and in 1998 the north-central 12th did the same.

Democrats held that 7–6 edge into the decade after 2000, having improved their district lines slightly in the remapping of 2001. This time around, the bipartisan commission was badly split over state legislators' districts but adopted a bipartisan revision of the congressional map months ahead of schedule. One reason was the unusual degree of agreement among the incumbents, who mostly endorsed a map of their own protecting all 13 members at the time (the one member with reason to complain decided instead to retire). The overall redistricting challenge was also eased by the state's healthy growth rate of nearly 9 percent in the 1990s (nearly 700,000 higher than 1990). It was close enough to the national average (13.2 percent) that, for the first time since 1970, the state did not have to give up a seat. That trend suggests robust times for New Jersey in the new century.

Table 1   Population

District	Population	Population under 18	Voting-age population	Median age	Male*	Female*
1	647,258	171,537	475,721	35.4	48.3	51.7
2	647,258	163,388	483,870	37.4	49.0	51.0
3	647,257	155,472	491,785	39.6	48.5	51.5
4	647,258	162,213	485,045	37.9	48.3	51.7
5	647,258	169,146	478,112	38.8	48.6	51.4
6	647,257	154,012	493,245	35.2	48.7	51.3
7	647,257	160,812	486,445	38.2	48.8	51.2
8	647,258	162,152	485,106	35.8	48.0	52.0
9	647,257	137,560	509,697	37.7	48.2	51.8
10	647,258	175,371	471,887	33.3	47.0	53.0
11	647,258	162,692	484,566	38.0	48.9	51.1
12	647,258	161,367	485,891	37.4	48.7	51.3
13	647,258	151,836	495,422	32.8	49.8	50.2
State	8,414,350	2,087,558	6,326,792	36.7	48.5	51.5

*As percentage of total population.

Table 2   Voting-Age Persons by Race/Hispanic or Latino Origin

District	White*	Black or African American*	American Indian or Alaska Native*	Asian*	Other or multirace*	Hispanic or Latino*
1	74.1	15.2	0.2	2.6	1.1	6.9
2	74.4	12.8	0.3	2.4	1.2	8.9
3	84.9	7.9	0.1	2.6	1.0	3.4
4	82.8	7.0	0.1	2.2	1.0	6.9
5	87.3	1.4	0.1	6.2	0.8	4.1

District	White*	Black or African American*	American Indian or Alaska Native*	Asian*	Other or multirace*	Hispanic or Latino*
6	64.4	14.8	0.1	8.4	1.6	10.7
7	80.2	4.3	0.1	7.9	1.0	6.5
8	57.4	11.7	0.1	5.2	2.1	23.5
9	63.9	6.3	0.1	10.4	2.1	17.2
10	24.2	54.3	0.2	3.8	3.1	14.5
11	83.6	2.7	0.1	6.2	0.9	6.5
12	74.1	10.8	0.1	8.7	1.2	5.0
13	35.7	10.5	0.1	5.8	2.9	44.9
State	68.2	12.2	0.1	5.6	1.5	12.3

*As percentage of voting-age population.

Table 3 Voting-Age Population by Age Groups

District	18 to 24*	25 to 44*	45 to 64*	Over 64*
1	11.9	42.2	29.6	16.4
2	10.4	39.8	30.9	18.9
3	8.7	37.4	31.6	22.4
4	9.7	39.4	29.2	21.8
5	7.9	40.0	34.2	18.0
6	13.7	42.4	28.5	15.3
7	7.9	42.4	32.3	17.4
8	11.7	41.4	29.1	17.9
9	10.0	41.7	29.4	18.9
10	14.0	42.8	28.4	14.9
11	8.2	42.3	33.6	15.9
12	10.5	41.2	31.5	16.9
13	14.6	46.3	25.1	14.1
State	10.7	41.5	30.2	17.6

*As percentage of voting-age population.

Table 4 Income and Occupation

District	Median family income	Families in poverty*	White collar†	Blue collar†	Service†	Farm†
1	$56,329	7.6	62.4	22.8	14.7	0.1
2	$52,213	7.6	53.6	23.0	22.5	0.8
3	$64,418	3.5	67.6	18.6	13.6	0.1
4	$64,505	4.5	65.3	20.1	14.2	0.3
5	$83,194	2.3	72.9	16.3	10.7	0.1
6	$65,888	6.2	66.1	20.1	13.6	0.1
7	$86,430	2.2	74.5	15.7	9.7	0.2
8	$61,172	8.1	64.1	22.4	13.4	0.1
9	$62,187	5.6	66.8	20.3	12.8	0.1
10	$45,403	14.9	58.0	23.6	18.4	0.1
11	$91,571	2.2	76.2	14.0	9.7	0.1
12	$82,529	3.4	75.7	13.8	10.3	0.1
13	$40,326	15.6	55.7	28.4	15.9	0.1
State	$65,370	6.3	66.5	19.7	13.6	0.2

*As percentage of all families.   †As percentage of employed workers 16 years and over.

Table 5 Education: School Years Completed

District	Less than grade 9*	Grades 9–12 no diploma*	High school diploma no college*	Some college*	College bachelor's degree or higher*
1	5.6	14.2	34.8	24.7	20.7
2	7.0	15.4	36.0	23.7	17.9
3	3.4	10.3	32.7	26.4	27.2
4	5.1	11.1	32.4	26.1	25.4
5	3.2	6.6	27.3	24.2	38.6
6	5.9	10.7	29.5	24.2	29.7
7	4.1	6.8	25.8	21.8	41.5
8	10.1	13.1	28.8	20.0	28.0
9	8.4	11.1	29.4	21.6	29.5
10	9.2	18.1	31.4	23.0	18.3
11	3.3	5.8	23.4	22.3	45.2
12	3.7	7.5	23.8	22.7	42.3
13	17.7	17.7	27.1	17.0	20.5
State	6.6	11.3	29.4	22.9	29.8

*As percentage of persons age 25 and over.

Table 6 Housing and Residential Patterns

District	Median home value	Owner occupied*	Renter occupied*	Urban†	Rural†
1	$107,200	70.0	30.0	98.6	1.4
2	$113,800	71.1	28.9	79.0	21.0
3	$135,000	82.5	17.5	96.2	3.8
4	$141,700	77.7	22.3	93.2	6.8
5	$234,700	81.6	18.4	82.7	17.3
6	$160,800	61.3	38.7	99.7	0.3
7	$218,700	78.6	21.4	90.4	9.6
8	$192,100	56.7	43.3	100.0	0.0
9	$195,800	52.8	47.2	100.0	0.0
10	$144,700	38.6	61.4	100.0	0.0
11	$249,900	77.9	22.1	93.5	6.5
12	$197,200	75.1	24.9	93.2	6.8
13	$157,400	28.8	71.2	100.0	0.0
State	$167,900	65.6	34.4	94.3	5.7

*As percentage of occupied housing units.   †As percentage of total population.

New Jersey 1st District

Southwest — Camden, Pennsauken

Across the Delaware River from Philadelphia, in southwestern New Jersey, the 1st is a Democratic stronghold. The largest concentration of its population lives in the troubled city of Camden, one of the poorest in the nation. Almost two-thirds of the district's residents live in Camden County, with most of the rest in Gloucester County and a handful in the southwestern edge of Burlington County.

For decades, Camden has been plagued by the departure of residents and businesses, a shrinking tax base, surging unemployment, and crime—particularly drug trafficking. The state government assumed control of the city's finances and in 2002 approved a $175 million plan to redevelop and revitalize the area.

There are some good signs for the city. An aquarium and a 25,000-seat outdoor amphitheater have attracted more tourists to Camden's waterfront. In 2000 the waterfront was the site of a welcoming ceremony for the Republican National Convention. The city also joined its port facilities with Philadelphia's to create one of the largest on the eastern seaboard, and the Environmental Protection Agency launched a redevelopment initiative to clean up industrial waste. Camden also is home to the Campbell Soup Company.

As distressed as the city is, the southern suburbs that fill out the 1st—such as Gloucester and Collingswood—are developing. Voorhees Township also grew at a steady clip in the 1990s.

African and Hispanic Americans form a majority of the population in Camden, while many whites live in the surrounding suburbs. Overall, blacks make up 16.3 percent of district residents and Hispanics total 8.2 percent. The 1st has a large working-class contingent, and Al Gore took nearly two-thirds of the vote here in the 2000 presidential election.

Major Industry
Shipping, manufacturing, education, health care.

Notable
Poet Walt Whitman lived in Camden at the time of his death.

Election Returns

	Republican		Democratic		Other	
President 2000	77,367	33.8%	144,226	63.0%	7,261	3.2%
House 2002			121,846	92.7%	9,543	7.3%

District Profile

Population   647,258

Total area (square miles)   351.7
   Land area (square miles)   334.7

Population per square mile   1,933.8

Counties (2000 population)
   Burlington (pt.)   28,929
   Camden (pt.)   428,473
   Gloucester (pt.)   189,856

Cities and other areas over 10,000 (2000 population)
   Bellmawr borough   11,262
   Camden   79,904
   Collingswood borough   14,326
   Echelon CDP   10,440
   Glassboro borough   19,068
   Gloucester City   11,484
   Haddonfield borough   11,659
   Lindenwold borough   17,414
   Pennsauken CDP   35,737
   Pine Hill borough   10,880
   Williamstown CDP   11,812
   Woodbury   10,307

Race and Hispanic or Latino origin*
   White   71.2%
   Black or African American   16.3%
   American Indian or Alaska Native   0.2%
   Asian   2.6%
   Native Hawaiian or other Pacific Islander   0.0%
   Some other race   0.1%
   Hispanic or Latino origin   8.2%
   Two or more races   1.3%

*As percentage of total population.

Ancestry*

English	6.6%	Italian	14.8%
French	1.3%	Polish	4.5%
German	13.0%	USA/American	2.0%
Irish	16.8%		

*As estimated percentage of total population.

Universities and colleges, 2000–2001 enrollment
   Camden County College, Blackwood   12,131
   Gloucester County College, Sewell   4,669
   Pennco Tech, Blackwood   289
   Rowan University, Glassboro   9,364
   Rutgers University-Camden, Camden   5,136

Newspapers and circulation

	District circulation	Total circulation
Burlington County Times	1,520	38,633
Camden Courier Post	53,629	81,850
Gloucester County Times	15,875	22,872
Greater Philadelphia Newspapers	1,457	152,790
Philadelphia Daily News	7,448	151,682
Philadelphia Inquirer	29,632	371,901
*USA Today**	2,040	1,674,376

*See Sources and Explanations in the front of the volume.

Television stations and affiliations

Philadelphia	100%	KYW	CBS
Philadelphia	100%	WBPH	Independent
Philadelphia	100%	WCAU	NBC
Philadelphia	100%	WFMZ	Independent
Philadelphia	100%	WHYY	PBS
Philadelphia	100%	WLVT	PBS
Philadelphia	100%	WMGM	NBC
Philadelphia	100%	WNJS	PBS
Philadelphia	100%	WNJT	PBS
Philadelphia	100%	WPHL	WB
Philadelphia	100%	WPPX	PAX
Philadelphia	100%	WPSG	UPN
Philadelphia	100%	WPVI	ABC
Philadelphia	100%	WTVE	Independent
Philadelphia	100%	WTXF	FOX
Philadelphia	100%	WWAC	Independent
Philadelphia	100%	WYBE	PBS

Cable systems and subscribers
   Comcast   142,221

Businesses and other major employers
   Virtual Health Inc.; Gibbsboro; hospital management   8,800
   Lockheed Martin Corp.; Voorhees; aerospace and defense contractor   4,000
   Our Lady of Lourdes Medical Center; Camden   3,500
   Campbell Soup Co.; Camden; canned soup   2,800
   Kennedy Health Care Foundation Hospital; Stratford   2,800
   Cooper Health System; Camden   2,250
   Rowan University; Glassboro   1,913
   U.S. Federal Aviation Admin.; Lawnside   1,500
   United Assn. of Plumbers and Steamfitters Local 322; Winslow; labor organization   1,500
   Underwood Memorial Hospital Inc.; Woodbury   1,401

Virtua-West Jersey Health System Inc. Hospital; Camden   1,394

Virtua-West Jersey Health System Inc. Hospital; Voorhees   1,311

General Electric Co.; Camden; aerospace castings   1,200

New Jersey Dept. of Human Services; Hammonton   1,200

Camden County; Camden; county courts   1,000

Camden County; Camden; county government   1,000

Pepsico Inc.; Pennsauken; soft drinks   1,000

Visiting Nurse Custom Care Inc.; Runnemede; medical and hospital equipment   1,000

Camden County College; Blackwood   960

Aluminum Shapes LLC; Delair; aluminum products   800

ExxonMobil Oil Corp.; Paulsboro; gas refinery   750

Bancroft NeuroHealth Inc.; Haddonfield; residential care   700

Cigna Corp.; Voorhees; computer programming services   700

Mobil Research and Development Corp.; Paulsboro; commercial research laboratory   700

Holt Cargo Systems Inc.; Gloucester City; local trucking with storage   686

Camden County; Camden; social and manpower programs   680

Camden County; Blackwood; health systems agency   600

Rutgers State University; Camden   600

Rapidforms Inc.; Thorofare; business forms   598

Camden County; Blackwood; skilled nursing care facilities   550

MacAndrews and Forbes Group Inc.; Camden; flavoring extracts and syrups   500

U.S. Postal Service; Swedesboro   500

New Jersey 2nd District

South — Atlantic City, Vineland

One of the state's most politically and economically diverse districts, the 2nd stretches from the Philadelphia suburbs in Gloucester County to the beach communities of Ocean City and Cape May, taking in much of the southern tier of the state. This is a Republican-leaning district, and locals generally support smaller government and oppose gun control. However, Democrats fare well in statewide elections and have a stronghold in south Cumberland County and in some of the district's more industrial towns.

The western corner of the 2nd is largely rural Salem County, home to a nuclear energy plant. The district's center includes Cumberland and Atlantic Counties, where farmers' markets and small agrarian communities grow peaches, blueberries, cranberries, tomatoes, and soybeans. South Cumberland County is the 2nd's most industrial area, although the economy is shifting from glass and plastics manufacturing to service. The area has been plagued with an unemployment rate higher than the state average.

Tourism is the cash crop in shore communities, where environmental and economic issues are one and the same; the local economy was hit hard when medical waste washed ashore in the late 1980s.

The 2nd includes one of the nation's most well-known gambling resort destinations, Atlantic City, where hotels and casinos create huge numbers of jobs, but where the poorer parts of the city are ravaged by crime and urban blight.

The Delaware River's busy port and one of the nation's largest petroleum centers also contribute to the economy.

Major Industry

Gambling, tourism, agriculture, petroleum, manufacturing.

Notable

The main federal air marshal training facility is in Pomona at Atlantic City International Airport; Delaware Memorial Bridge, the world's longest twin suspension bridge, crosses the Delaware River from Salem County; Cape May Lighthouse, at the southern tip of New Jersey, was built in 1859 and is still in operation.

Election Returns

	Republican		Democratic		Other	
President 2000	105,630	42.6%	134,345	54.2%	7,906	3.2%
House 2002	116,834	69.2%	47,735	28.3%	4,230	2.5%

District Profile

Population   647,258

Total area (square miles)   2,683.2
  Land area (square miles)   1,981.7

Population per square mile   326.6

Counties (2000 population)

Atlantic 252,552	Cumberland 146,438
Burlington (pt.) 6,346	Gloucester (pt.) 64,817
Camden (pt.) 10,494	Salem 64,285
Cape May 102,326	

Cities and other areas over 10,000 (2000 population)

Atlantic City 40,517	Pennsville CDP 11,657
Bridgeton 22,771	Pleasantville 19,012
Brigantine 12,594	Somers Point 11,614
Hammonton town 12,604	Ventnor City 12,910
Millville 26,847	Vineland 56,271
Ocean City 15,378	

Race and Hispanic or Latino origin*

White   71.7%
Black or African American   13.8%
American Indian or Alaska Native   0.3%
Asian   2.4%
Native Hawaiian or other Pacific Islander   0.0%
Some other race   0.1%
Hispanic or Latino origin   10.3%
Two or more races   1.4%

As percentage of total population.

Ancestry*

English 7.5%	Italian 13.0%
French 1.5%	Polish 3.2%
German 12.5%	USA/American 2.9%
Irish 13.9%	

As estimated percentage of total population.

Universities and colleges, 2000–2001 enrollment

Atlantic Cape Community College, Mays Landing
5,162

Cumberland County College, Vineland   2,735

Richard Stockton College of New Jersey, Pomona
6,312

Salem Community College, Carneys Point   1,166

Newspapers and circulation

	District circulation	Total circulation
Atlantic City Press	68,123	73,979
Bridgeton News	7,156	7,212
Camden Courier Post	7,149	81,850
Gloucester County Times	6,885	22,872
Newark Star Ledger	1,476	407,706
*New York Daily News**	1,396	723,155
New York Post	1,123	511,412
Philadelphia Daily News	5,154	151,682
Philadelphia Inquirer	14,003	371,901
*USA Today**	4,896	1,674,376
Vineland Daily Journal	17,237	17,366

See Sources and Explanations in the front of the volume.

Television stations and affiliations

Philadelphia	100%	KYW	CBS
Philadelphia	100%	WBPH	Independent
Philadelphia	100%	WCAU	NBC
Philadelphia	100%	WFMZ	Independent
Philadelphia	100%	WHYY	PBS
Philadelphia	100%	WLVT	PBS
Philadelphia	100%	WMGM	NBC
Philadelphia	100%	WNJS	PBS
Philadelphia	100%	WNJT	PBS
Philadelphia	100%	WPHL	WB
Philadelphia	100%	WPPX	PAX
Philadelphia	100%	WPSG	UPN
Philadelphia	100%	WPVI	ABC
Philadelphia	100%	WTVE	Independent
Philadelphia	100%	WTXF	FOX
Philadelphia	100%	WWAC	Independent
Philadelphia	100%	WYBE	PBS

Cable systems and subscribers

Comcast   168,655

Military installations, September 2001

Atlantic City International Airport, Pleasantville   989

Businesses and other major employers

Trump Taj Mahal Associates; Atlantic City; casino hotel
6,000

Aztar Corp.; Atlantic City; resort hotel   5,500

B. W. Realty Corp.; Atlantic City; automobile parking
5,000

Trump Hotels and Casino Resorts Inc.; Atlantic City;
casino hotel   5,000

Trump Plaza Hotel and Casino; Atlantic City; casino
hotel   5,000

Adamar of New Jersey Inc.; Atlantic City; casino hotel
4,000

New Jersey Dept. of Law and Public Safety; Atlantic
City   4,000

Boardwalk Regency Corp.; Atlantic City; casino hotel
3,999

Harrah's Entertainment Inc.; Atlantic City; casino hotel
3,600

Harrah's Atlantic City Inc.; Atlantic City; casino hotel
3,570

Trump Marina Hotel and Casino Inc.; Atlantic City;
casino hotel   3,500

Bally's Park Place Inc.; Atlantic City; casino hotel
3,400

Resorts International Hotel; Atlantic City; casino hotel
3,300

BFAA Tech Center; Atlantic City; aircraft maintenance
3,000

General Motors Corp.; Salem; automobiles   3,000

Temple University Hospital; Vineland   3,000

GNOC Corp.; Atlantic City; casino hotel   2,800

Trump Castle Associates; Atlantic City; casino hotel
2,700

Greate Bay Hotel and Casino Inc.; Atlantic City; casino
hotel   2,500

New Jersey Dept. of Human Services; Woodbine   2,400

Clairidge Casino; Atlantic City; casino hotel   2,000

Du Pont Pharmaceutical Co.; Deepwater; industrial
organic chemicals   2,000

New Jersey Dept. of Human Services; Vineland   2,000

Wheaton USA Inc.; Millville; glass containers   2,000

Shore Memorial Hospital; Somers Point   1,450

Atlantic City Medical Center Inc.; Atlantic City   1,341

Richard Stockton College of New Jersey; Pomona
1,250

Atlantic City Medical Center; Pomona   1,119

Viking Yacht Co.; New Gretna; yacht building and
repairing   1,100

Cape May County; Cape May Court House; county
government   1,000

Kimble Holdings Inc.; Vineland; medical and laboratory
glassware   1,000

New Jersey National Guard; Egg Harbor Township
1,000

Sony Music Entertainment Inc.; Pitman; compact laser
discs   1,000

Burdette Tomlin Memorial Hospital; Cape May Court
House   950

South Jersey Hospital System; Bridgeton   873

Durand Glass Manufacturing Co. Inc.; Millville; glass or
glass ceramics   800

Mannington Mills Inc.; Salem; floor coverings   800

HR Solutions Inc.; Northfield; employee programs
administration   750

Memorial Hospital of Salem County; Salem   735

South Jersey Hospital System; Vineland   730

New Jersey Dept. of Corrections; Leesburg   685

Atlantic County; Atlantic City; county government
664

William B. Kessler Memorial Hospital Inc.;
Hammonton   650

Archway Programs Inc.; Atco; specialty education   600

Patriot Manufacturing Inc.; Hammonton; window
frames and sash   600

Lenox Inc.; Pomona; china tableware   530

Calvi Electric Co.; Atlantic City; electrical contractor
500

New Jersey Dept. of the Treasury; Atlantic City   500

Wheaton USA Inc.; Mays Landing; plastic bottles   500

New Jersey 3rd District

South central — Cherry Hill, Toms River

Covering one of New Jersey's oldest and wealthiest areas, the 3rd crosses the south-central section of the state from the southern shores of Ocean County to the Philadelphia suburbs along the Delaware River. It includes most of Burlington County and Cherry Hill in Camden County.

Industrial growth dominates the short strip of land that abuts the Delaware River and encompasses the affluent, Republican-leaning suburbs of Cinnaminson, Delran, and Moorestown. Across the district near the Atlantic Ocean, communities around Toms River are concerned that offshore waste disposal and other environmental issues may affect their beach tourist industry. Local officials, most of whom are Republicans, emphasize their "green" credentials.

McGuire Air Force Base and Fort Dix (shared with the 4th District) make defense another salient issue in the 3rd. During the 1990s, the federal government funneled more than $500 million into modernization projects at McGuire, once slated to be closed, including $20 million for a new air terminal.

This politically competitive district has lots of wealthy elderly voters, many of whom live in retirement communities along Route 70, and the lowest percentage of Hispanic residents of any district in the state. Municipal and school budgets, as well as tax rates, are among the lowest in the state—in part because of the high turnout by elderly voters.

Major Industry

Retail sales, health care, agriculture.

Notable

Burlington County, three-fourths of which is in the 3rd District, is the second-largest cranberry-producing county in the nation; Toms River was one of two American teams to win the Little League World Series in the 1990s.

Election Returns

	Republican		Democratic		Other	
President 2000	114,621	43.3%	141,964	53.6%	8,208	3.1%
House 2002	123,375	65.0%	64,364	33.9%	2,000	1.1%

District Profile

Population   647,257

Total area (square miles)   1,179.5
   Land area (square miles)   925.6

Population per square mile   699.3

Counties (2000 population)
   Burlington (pt.)   320,669
   Camden (pt.)   69,965
   Ocean (pt.)   256,623

Cities and other areas over 10,000 (2000 population)
   Barclay-Kingston CDP   10,728
   Beachwood borough   10,375
   Browns Mills CDP   11,257
   Cherry Hill CDP   13,238
   Greentree CDP   11,536
   Holiday City-Berkeley CDP   13,884
   Marlton CDP   10,260
   Moorestown-Lenola CDP   13,860
   Ocean Acres CDP   13,155
   Springdale CDP   14,409
   Toms River CDP   86,327

Race and Hispanic or Latino origin*
   White   83.4%
   Black or African American   8.5%
   American Indian or Alaska Native   0.1%
   Asian   2.7%
   Native Hawaiian or other Pacific Islander   0.0%
   Some other race   0.1%
   Hispanic or Latino origin   3.8%
   Two or more races   1.3%

As percentage of total population.

Ancestry*

Dutch 1.1%	Italian 14.9%
English 7.0%	Polish 5.4%
French 1.5%	Russian 1.6%
German 13.5%	Scottish 1.3%
Irish 15.8%	USA/American 2.6%

As estimated percentage of total population.

Universities and colleges, 2000–2001 enrollment
   Burlington County College, Pemberton   6,122
   Ocean County College, Toms River   7,143

Newspapers and circulation

	District circulation	Total circulation
Asbury Park Press	39,889	167,085
Atlantic City Press	4,649	73,979
Burlington County Times	28,767	38,633
Camden Courier Post	20,499	81,850
Greater Philadelphia Newspapers	29,944	152,790
Newark Star Ledger	6,889	407,706
*New York Daily News**	3,495	723,155
New York Post	2,859	511,412
*New York Times**	2,591	666,228
Philadelphia Daily News	2,990	151,682
Philadelphia Inquirer	27,925	371,901
Trenton Times	2,312	76,719
Trenton Trentonian	3,844	48,680
*USA Today**	3,037	1,674,376

See Sources and Explanations in the front of the volume.

Television stations and affiliations

New York	51%	WABC	ABC
New York	51%	WCBS	CBS
New York	51%	WEDW	PBS
New York	51%	WFME	Independent
New York	51%	WLIW	PBS
New York	51%	WLNY	Independent
New York	51%	WMBC	Independent
New York	51%	WNBC	NBC
New York	51%	WNET	PBS
New York	51%	WNJB	PBS
New York	51%	WNJN	PBS
New York	51%	WNJU	Telemundo

New York	51%	WNYE	PBS
New York	51%	WNYW	FOX
New York	51%	WPIX	WB
New York	51%	WPXN	PAX
New York	51%	WRNN	Independent
New York	51%	WTBY	Independent
New York	51%	WWOR	UPN
New York	51%	WXTV	Univision
Philadelphia	49%	KYW	CBS
Philadelphia	49%	WBPH	Independent
Philadelphia	49%	WCAU	NBC
Philadelphia	49%	WFMZ	Independent
Philadelphia	49%	WHYY	PBS
Philadelphia	49%	WLVT	PBS
Philadelphia	49%	WMGM	NBC
Philadelphia	49%	WNJS	PBS
Philadelphia	49%	WNJT	PBS
Philadelphia	49%	WPHL	WB
Philadelphia	49%	WPPX	PAX
Philadelphia	49%	WPSG	UPN
Philadelphia	49%	WPVI	ABC
Philadelphia	49%	WTVE	Independent
Philadelphia	49%	WTXF	FOX
Philadelphia	49%	WWAC	Independent
Philadelphia	49%	WYBE	PBS

Cable systems and subscribers
Cablevision   6,338
Comcast   136,921

Military installations, September 2001
Fort Dix (Army Reserve), Trenton   10,717
McGuire Air Force Base, Wrightstown   9,243

Businesses and other major employers
Lockheed Martin Space Operations Co.;
Cherry Hill; nongovernment space flight operations
5,950
Cherry Hill Photo Enterprises Inc.; Cherry Hill;
photographic studios   5,500
America's PEO Inc.; Cherry Hill; payroll accounting
service   5,200
Cendant Mortgage Corp.; Mount Laurel; mortgage
bankers   4,500
Memorial Hospital of Burlington County; Mount Holly
2,485
Community Medical Center Inc.; Toms River   2,450
Burlington County; Mount Holly; county government
2,000
Protocall New Jersey Inc.; Cherry Hill; temporary help
1,850
Kennedy Health Systems Hospital; Cherry Hill   1,600
New Jersey National Guard; Trenton   1,600
New Jersey Dept. of Human Services; New Lisbon
1,400
Deborah Heart and Lung Center; Browns Mills   1,225
Computer Sciences Corp.; Moorestown; computer
programming services   1,200
Jevic Transportation Inc.; Riverside; contract haulers
1,100
CVS Pharmacy Inc.; Lumberton; drug and proprietary
stores   1,000
Inrange Technologies; Lumberton; digital test
equipment   1,000

Our Lady of Lourdes Medical Center; Willingboro   825
Electronic Health Information Inc.; Marlton; duplicating
services   800
Duckrey Enterprises II Inc.; Marlton; restaurant chain
750
Nu Horizons Electronics Corp.; Moorestown; circuit
boards   736
Merck-Medco Rx Services Inc.; Willingboro; mail-order
pharmaceuticals   705
Ocean County College Inc.; Toms River   616
Gannett Satellite Information Network Inc.; Cherry
Hill; newspaper   600
Oki Data Americas Inc.; Mount Laurel; management
services   600
Ocean County; Toms River; county government   584
Burlington County; Mount Holly; public education
575
Automotive Rentals Inc.; Mount Laurel; truck rental and
leasing   550
Inductotherm Industries Inc.; Rancocas; industrial
furnaces   550
OPEX Corp.; Moorestown; mailing, addressing
machines   550
Automatic Data Processing Inc.; Mount Laurel; data
processing   500
Prudential Investment Corp.; Toms River; investment
advice   500
Southern Ocean County Hospital; Manahawkin   720
Sports Arena Employees; Cherry Hill; employee
association   900
Strober-Haddonfield Group Inc.; Cherry Hill; building
materials   500
Toms River Regional Schools; Toms River   1,933
U.S. Bureau of Prisons; Fort Dix   597
Virtua-West Jersey Health System Inc. Hospital;
Marlton   800
Visiting Homemaker Service of Ocean County Inc.;
Toms River; home health care   500
Wyeth Laboratories Inc.; Cherry Hill; pharmaceuticals
800

New Jersey 4th District

Central — part of Trenton, Lakewood

The 4th spreads across the center of the state, where the Garden State begins its transition from South to North Jersey, extending from Trenton and the Delaware River to the Jersey Shore and coastal communities such as Point Pleasant and Spring Lake.

The district includes much of the southern and eastern portions of the state capital, Trenton. Democratic-leaning parts of the city, including largely black neighborhoods, were shifted into the 12th District in redistricting following the 2000 census, making the 4th more Republican and the 12th more Democratic.

Most of Trenton's white residents live in the reconfigured 4th, which includes the historically Italian neighborhood of Chambersburg. But the area is not without diversity. More than 25 percent of the 4th's Trenton population is black, while 30 percent is Hispanic.

The Republican lean of the 4th is strengthened by more-conservative areas in the eastern half of the district. But voters here can exhibit an independent streak in local elections, although they tend to prefer Republicans for federal office.

Military bases are important to the economy, but the district does not rely solely on defense. Trenton and its suburbs have a diverse range of businesses, and the towns along the Jersey Shore in Ocean and Monmouth Counties depend heavily on tourism.

Major Industry

State government, tourism, manufacturing.

Notable

Trenton, a Revolutionary War battleground, was temporarily the U.S. capital; John A. Roebling and his sons, of Trenton, made the cable for the Brooklyn, Manhattan, George Washington, and Golden Gate bridges, among others; an illuminated sign on a bridge over the Delaware River proclaims, "Trenton Makes, The World Takes."

Election Returns

	Republican		Democratic		Other	
President 2000	114,309	46.4%	123,764	50.2%	8,301	3.4%
House 2002	115,293	66.1%	55,967	32.1%	3,041	1.7%

District Profile

Population   647,258

Total area (square miles)   761.6
  Land area (square miles)   718.7

Population per square mile   900.6

Counties (2000 population)

Burlington (pt.)	67,450	Monmouth (pt.)	160,251
Mercer (pt.)	165,264	Ocean (pt.)	254,293

Cities and other areas over 10,000 (2000 population)
Freehold borough   10,976
Lakewood CDP   36,065
Leisure Village West-Pine Lake Park CDP   11,085
Mercerville-Hamilton Square CDP   26,419
Point Pleasant borough   19,306
Trenton (pt.)   37,745
West Freehold CDP   12,498

Race and Hispanic or Latino origin*
White   81.3%
Black or African American   7.5%
American Indian or Alaska Native   0.1%
Asian   2.3%
Native Hawaiian or other Pacific Islander   0.0%
Some other race   0.1%
Hispanic or Latino origin   7.6%
Two or more races   1.1%

*As percentage of total population.

Ancestry*

Dutch	1.1%	Hungarian	1.7%
English	5.9%	Irish	15.2%
French	1.4%	Italian	15.9%
German	11.8%	Polish	6.6%

Russian	1.5%	USA/American	2.4%
Scottish	1.2%		

*As estimated percentage of total population.

Universities and colleges, 2000–2001 enrollment
Beth Medrash Govoha, Lakewood   2,993
Georgian Court College, Lakewood   2,483

Newspapers and circulation

	District circulation	Total circulation
Asbury Park Press	64,992	167,085
Burlington County Times	7,355	38,633
Greater Philadelphia Newspapers	7,044	152,790
Jersey City Journal	1,859	42,116
Newark Star Ledger	10,922	407,706
New York Daily News*	5,553	723,155
New York Post	5,334	511,412
New York Times*	9,639	666,228
Philadelphia Inquirer	2,164	371,901
Trenton Times	34,795	76,719
Trenton Trentonian	22,829	48,680
USA Today*	2,664	1,674,376

*See Sources and Explanations in the front of the volume.

Television stations and affiliations

New York	75%	WABC	ABC
New York	75%	WCBS	CBS
New York	75%	WEDW	PBS
New York	75%	WFME	Independent
New York	75%	WLIW	PBS
New York	75%	WLNY	Independent
New York	75%	WMBC	Independent
New York	75%	WNBC	NBC
New York	75%	WNET	PBS
New York	75%	WNJB	PBS
New York	75%	WNJN	PBS
New York	75%	WNJU	Telemundo
New York	75%	WNYE	PBS
New York	75%	WNYW	FOX
New York	75%	WPIX	WB
New York	75%	WPXN	PAX
New York	75%	WRNN	Independent
New York	75%	WTBY	Independent
New York	75%	WWOR	UPN
New York	75%	WXTV	Univision
Philadelphia	25%	KYW	CBS
Philadelphia	25%	WBPH	Independent
Philadelphia	25%	WCAU	NBC
Philadelphia	25%	WFMZ	Independent
Philadelphia	25%	WHYY	PBS
Philadelphia	25%	WLVT	PBS
Philadelphia	25%	WMGM	NBC
Philadelphia	25%	WNJS	PBS
Philadelphia	25%	WNJT	PBS
Philadelphia	25%	WPHL	WB
Philadelphia	25%	WPPX	PAX
Philadelphia	25%	WPSG	UPN
Philadelphia	25%	WPVI	ABC
Philadelphia	25%	WTVE	Independent
Philadelphia	25%	WTXF	FOX
Philadelphia	25%	WWAC	Independent
Philadelphia	25%	WYBE	PBS

Cable systems and subscribers
Cablevision   45,053
Comcast   57,758

Military installations, September 2001
Naval Air Engineering Station, Lakehurst   2,793
Weapons Support Facility, Earle   2,123
Sea Girt Military Training Area, Sea Girt   376

Businesses and other major employers
Lucent Technologies Inc.; Neptune; semiconductors and related   2,500
CentraState Healthcare System Inc.; Freehold; hospital management   1,825
Kimball Medical Center Inc.; Lakewood   1,500
Presbyterian Homes and Services Inc.; Hightstown; residential care   1,300
Robert Wood Johnson University Hospital; Trenton   1,300
Burlington Coat Factory Warehouse of Montville Inc.; Burlington; clothing stores   1,200
International Brotherhood of Electrical Workers Local; Belmar; union   1,200
Jackson Board of Education; Jackson   1,200
McGraw-Hill Companies Inc.; Hightstown; credit card services, collection   1,200
St. Francis Medical Center; Trenton   1,050
Trane Co.; Trenton; heating equipment   900
Bay Head Yacht Club; Point Pleasant Beach; yacht club   800
Building Maintenance Systems Inc.; Trenton; janitorial service   800
Micro Warehouse Inc.; Lakewood; office supplies   800
All Clean Building Services Inc.; Trenton; building cleaning   700
Hamilton Township; Trenton; town government   700
New Jersey Dept. of Corrections; Trenton   674
Masonic Charity Foundation of New Jersey; Burlington; nursing care facilities   644
New Jersey Dept. of Human Services; Trenton   640
KSI Contracting; Freehold; heating/air conditioning contractors   605
Meridian Hospitals Corp.; Brick   600
Aberdeen Sportswear Inc.; Trenton; warehousing   580
New Jersey Dept. of Corrections; Bordentown   572
Mercer County Board of Social Services; Trenton   550
Lucent Technologies Inc.; Hackettstown; fiber optics   530
American Standard Inc.; Trenton; plumbing fixtures   500
New Jersey Legislative Office; Freehold   500
Washington Group International Inc.; Hightstown; engineering services   500

New Jersey 5th District

North and west — Bergenfield, Paramus

Taking in the northernmost portion of New Jersey, the 5th is largely suburban and includes some of the most scenic and affluent areas of the state. It stretches from northern Bergen County through parts of Passaic and the hill-enclosed regions of Sussex County, crossing the Appalachian Mountains and running southwest into Warren County. It has the smallest minority population of New Jersey's 13 districts.

Property values and income levels are among the highest in the state, and no municipality here has more than 30,000 residents. About three-fifths of the district's population is in wealthy Bergen County, which includes Saddle River and its multimillion-dollar homes. The scenic back country of Sussex and Warren Counties traditionally has been rural but grew about 10 percent in the 1990s as young professionals from New York City moved to the area. Warren County continues to experience significant housing development.

Many businesses make northern New Jersey their home, including Sony Electronics America and the Hertz rental car company in Park Ridge, Toys "R" Us in Paramus, and candy giant Mars in Hackettstown.

The 5th tends to vote Republican, though most voters register as independent. GOP strength lies more in the growing western areas than in older Bergen County areas. At the local level, pockets of Democratic strength include Phillipsburg in south Warren County and sections of Bergen County, where races are often close. George W. Bush captured 52 percent of the district's vote in the 2000 presidential election, his second-highest percentage in the state.

Major Industry
Pharmaceuticals, electronics, shipping.

Notable
President Richard Nixon retired to Park Ridge.

Election Returns

	Republican		Democratic		Other	
President 2000	140,132	52.0%	120,142	44.5%	9,431	3.5%
House 2002	118,881	59.5%	76,504	38.3%	4,466	2.2%

District Profile

Population   647,258

Total area (square miles)   1,130.3
Land area (square miles)   1,099.0

Population per square mile   589.0

Counties (2000 population)
Bergen (pt.)   390,879
Passaic (pt.)   52,783
Sussex (pt.)   101,159
Warren   102,437

Cities and other areas over 10,000 (2000 population)
Bergenfield borough   26,247
Dumont borough   17,503
Franklin Lakes borough   10,422
Glen Rock borough   11,546
Hackettstown town   10,403
Hillsdale borough   10,087
New Milford borough (pt.)   14,976
Oakland borough   12,466
Paramus borough   25,737
Phillipsburg town   15,166
Ramsey borough   14,351
Ridgewood village   24,936
Ringwood borough   12,396

River Edge borough 10,946
Tenafly borough 13,806
Wanaque borough 10,266
West Milford CDP 26,410
Westwood borough 10,999
Wyckoff CDP 16,508

Race and Hispanic or Latino origin*
White 86.3%
Black or African American 1.5%
American Indian or Alaska Native 0.1%
Asian 6.6%
Native Hawaiian or other Pacific Islander 0.0%
Some other race 0.1%
Hispanic or Latino origin 4.5%
Two or more races 1.0%

*As percentage of total population.

Ancestry*

Dutch	2.6%	Italian	16.2%
English	5.7%	Polish	5.0%
French	1.5%	Russian	2.2%
German	13.2%	Scottish	1.2%
Hungarian	1.2%	USA/American	2.9%
Irish	15.3%		

*As estimated percentage of total population.

Universities and colleges, 2000–2001 enrollment
Bergen Community College, Paramus 11,993
Centenary College, Hackettstown 1,335
Ramapo College of New Jersey, Mahwah 5,195
Sussex County Community College, Newton 2,286
Warren County Community College, Washington 797

Newspapers and circulation

	District circulation	Total circulation
Easton Express-Times	14,082	48,585
Hackensack Record	56,928	182,466
Hunterdon County Democrat	1,051	22,216
Newark Star Ledger	19,107	407,706
New Jersey Herald	13,375	16,282
*New York Daily News**	18,775	723,155
New York Post	6,102	511,412
*New York Times**	25,747	666,228
Parsippany Daily Record	2,346	42,659
Ridgewood News	6,034	6,049
*USA Today**	5,149	1,674,376

*See Sources and Explanations in the front of the volume.

Television stations and affiliations

New York	100%	WABC	ABC
New York	100%	WCBS	CBS
New York	100%	WEDW	PBS
New York	100%	WFME	Independent
New York	100%	WLIW	PBS
New York	100%	WLNY	Independent
New York	100%	WMBC	Independent
New York	100%	WNBC	NBC
New York	100%	WNET	PBS
New York	100%	WNJB	PBS
New York	100%	WNJN	PBS
New York	100%	WNJU	Telemundo
New York	100%	WNYE	PBS
New York	100%	WNYW	FOX
New York	100%	WPIX	WB
New York	100%	WPXN	PAX
New York	100%	WRNN	Independent
New York	100%	WTBY	Independent
New York	100%	WWOR	UPN
New York	100%	WXTV	Univision

Cable systems and subscribers
Cablevision 107,075
Comcast 30,793
Service Electric Co. 60,550
U.S. Cable 8,594

Businesses and other major employers
United Parcel Service Inc.; Mahwah 3,000
Valley Hospital; Ridgewood 3,000
PSEG Energy Holdings Inc.; Newfoundland; natural gas distribution 1,865
Bergen Regional Medical Center; Paramus 1,700
Howmedica Osteonics Corp.; Allendale; medical supplies 1,600
Becton Dickinson and Co.; Franklin Lakes; hypodermic needles and syringes 1,500
Macy's East Inc.; Paramus; department stores 1,500
Pascack Valley Hospital; Westwood 1,206
United Water Services Inc.; Harrington Park; water supply 1,154
Loving Hands; Paramus; medical help service 1,100
Toys "R" Us Inc.; Paramus; toys and games 1,100
Bergen Community College; Paramus 1,053
KPMG; Montvale; certified public accountants 1,000
Saft America Inc.; Bergenfield; primary batteries 1,000
Selective Insurance Group Inc.; Branchville; automobile insurance 1,000
Sony Electronics Inc.; Park Ridge; audio/video equipment 1,000
Cantor Fitzgerald and Co.; Rochelle Park; security brokers 979
Flowserve Corp.; Phillipsburg; pumping equipment 920
Ferolie Group; Montvale; food supplier 900
North Jersey Health Care Corp.; Newton; management services 850
Sharp Electronics Corp.; Mahwah; office equipment 850
Hertz Corp.; Park Ridge; automobile rental 800
Roche Vitamins Inc.; Belvidere; pharmaceuticals 800
Great Atlantic and Pacific Tea Co. Inc.; Montvale; supermarkets 750
Nordstrom Inc.; Paramus; clothing stores 750
Christian Health Care Center; Wyckoff 725
Warren Hospital; Phillipsburg 724
TNS Nursing Homes Inc.; Norwood; nursing facility management 720
GoGo Tours Inc.; Ramsey; travel agency 700
Mars Inc.; Hackettstown; confectionery products 700
Sony Electronics Inc.; Woodcliff Lake; prerecorded records/tapes 700
Hanjin Shipping Co.; Paramus; steamship leasing 691
Mercedes-Benz; Montvale; automobiles 650

Thomas R. Bryant Corp.; Emerson; temporary help
635

Addison Wesley Longman Inc.; Upper Saddle River;
textbooks   600

BMW of North America; Westwood; automobiles   600

Burns and Roe Enterprises Inc.; Oradell; engineering
services   600

DialAmerica Marketing Inc.; Mahwah; telemarketing
600

St. Francis Hospital Inc.; Ridgewood   600

Hackettstown Community Hospital; Hackettstown
570

Medical Economics Co.; Montvale; medical research
550

Andover Intermediate Care Center; Andover; nursing
care   500

Friends of Long Pond Ironworks Inc.; Hewitt; museum
500

Hudson United Bancorp; Mahwah; state commercial
banks   500

International Licensees; Paramus; data communication
services   500

Minolta Corp.; Ramsey; photographic equipment,
supplies   500

Pechiney Plastic Packaging Inc.; Washington; packaging
materials   500

Ramapo College of New Jersey; Mahwah   500

Sony Electronics Inc.; Montvale; photographic
equipment, supplies   500

Troll Communications; Mahwah; book publishing   500

Vernon School District; Vernon   500

New Jersey 6th District

East central — New Brunswick, Plainfield, part of Edison

Wedged in the heart of the suburbs south of New York and Newark, the 6th combines industrial communities in Middlesex County with a long, thin stretch that incorporates beach towns in Monmouth County. *(See map p. 586.)*

Like much of the state, the district was previously politically competitive but has leaned toward Democrats in recent years. Redistricting following the 2000 census added Democratic areas. The 6th now hops the Union County line to take in Plainfield and crosses the Somerset County line to grab most of Somerset. Al Gore captured 61.4 percent of the revised district's vote in the 2000 presidential election.

In the southwest corner, New Brunswick consolidates two Democratic-voting blocs: students from Rutgers University and African Americans. Nearby Piscataway and the wealthier suburb of Highland Park also favor Democrats. Major area employers include Johnson & Johnson, headquartered in New Brunswick, and Telcordia Technologies, a communications technology firm that has multiple facilities around Piscataway.

Middle-class and independent-voting residents cluster around Edison (shared with the 7th), the district's largest city and home to corporate offices and some manufacturing. Two-thirds of Edison's population lives in the 6th. Exceptionally fast growth in this area after World War II established Middlesex County as the state's leader in industrial growth.

In Monmouth County, the problems of Asbury Park are an exception to the area's generally sunny outlook. Once a vacation site made famous by rocker Bruce Springsteen, the town saw crime grow as the local economy declined.

Major Industry

Higher education, technology, pharmaceuticals, manufacturing.

Notable

Edison was named after inventor Thomas Edison; the Sandy Hook Light, opened in 1764, is the nation's oldest standing lighthouse.

Election Returns

	Republican		Democratic		Other	
President 2000	74,828	34.6%	132,583	61.4%	8,638	4.0%
House 2002	42,479	30.9%	91,379	66.5%	3,637	2.6%

District Profile

Population   647,257

Total area (square miles)   388.4
Land area (square miles)   196.3

Population per square mile   3,297.3

Counties (2000 population)
| Middlesex (pt.) | 286,093 | Somerset (pt.) | 18,268 |
| Monmouth (pt.) | 295,067 | Union (pt.) | 47,829 |

Cities and other areas over 10,000 (2000 population)
Asbury Park   16,930
Edison CDP (pt.)   65,782
Highland Park borough   13,999
Keansburg borough   10,732
Long Branch   31,340
Metuchen borough   12,840
Middlesex borough   13,717
New Brunswick   48,573
Plainfield   47,829
Red Bank borough   11,844
Sayreville borough   40,377
Somerset CDP (pt.)   18,201

Race and Hispanic or Latino origin*
White   61.7%
Black or African American   16.1%
American Indian or Alaska Native   0.1%
Asian   8.3%
Native Hawaiian or other Pacific Islander   0.0%
Some other race   0.3%
Hispanic or Latino origin   11.7%
Two or more races   1.7%

*As percentage of total population.

Ancestry*
English 3.7%	Polish 5.8%
German 8.1%	Russian 2.0%
Hungarian 1.5%	USA/American 2.2%
Irish 12.6%	West Indian 1.4%
Italian 12.7%	

*As estimated percentage of total population.

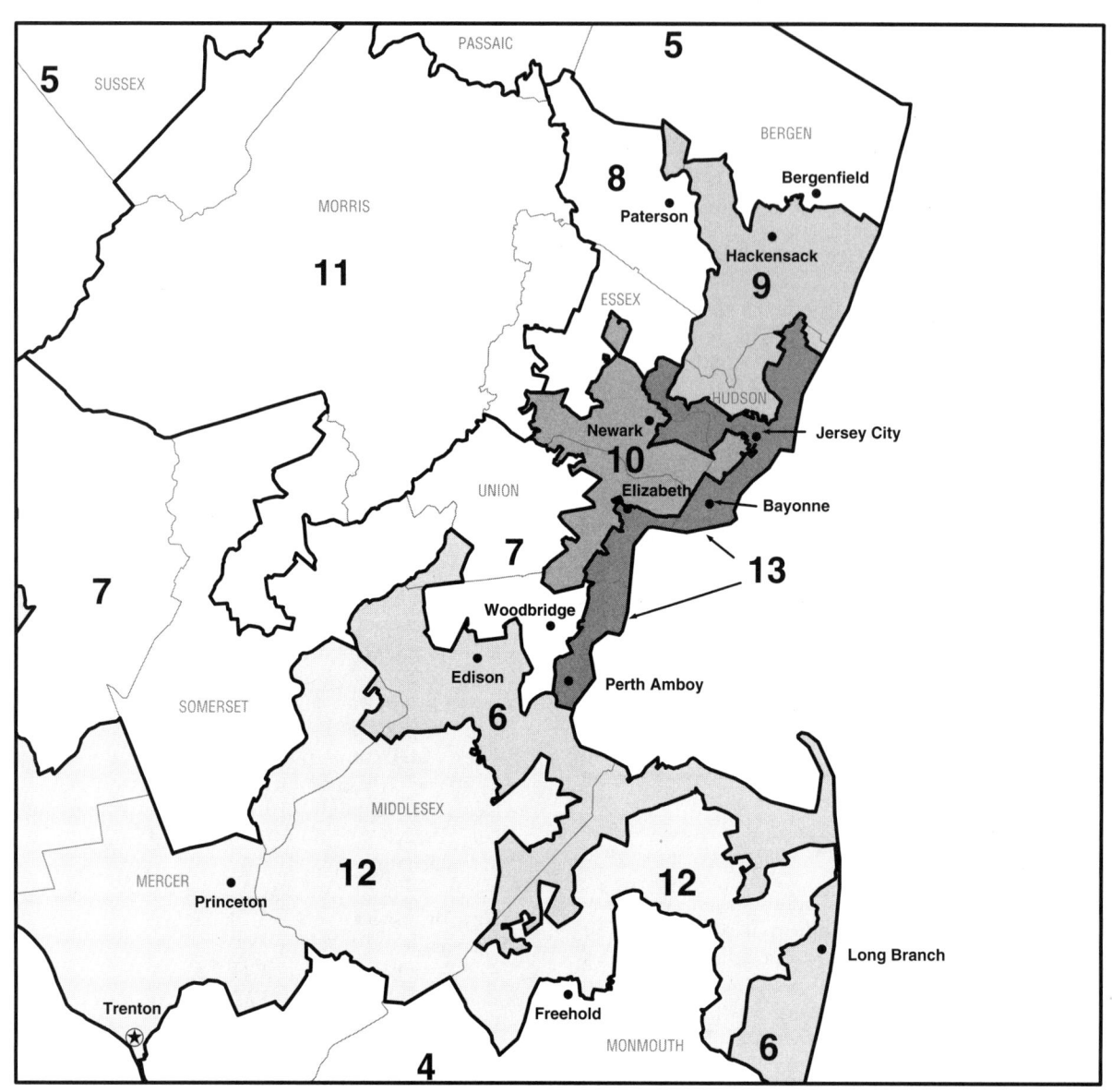

Universities and colleges, 2000–2001 enrollment

Devry University, North Brunswick   3,779
Katharine Gibbs School, Piscataway   440
Middlesex County College, Edison   10,398
Monmouth University, West Long Branch   5,636
Muhlenberg Regional Medical Center-School of
Nursing, Plainfield   273
New Brunswick Theological Seminary, New Brunswick
240
Rutgers University-New Brunswick, New Brunswick
35,236

Newspapers and circulation

	District circulation	Total circulation
Asbury Park Press	35,167	167,085
Bridgewater Courier News	7,318	41,079
Newark Star Ledger	30,319	407,706
New Brunswick Home News Tribune	21,392	65,592
New York Daily News*	6,197	723,155
New York Post	5,909	511,412
New York Times*	9,596	666,228
USA Today*	2,646	1,674,376

*See Sources and Explanations in the front of the volume.

Television stations and affiliations

New York	100%	WABC	ABC
New York	100%	WCBS	CBS
New York	100%	WEDW	PBS
New York	100%	WFME	Independent
New York	100%	WLIW	PBS
New York	100%	WLNY	Independent
New York	100%	WMBC	Independent
New York	100%	WNBC	NBC
New York	100%	WNET	PBS
New York	100%	WNJB	PBS
New York	100%	WNJN	PBS
New York	100%	WNJU	Telemundo
New York	100%	WNYE	PBS
New York	100%	WNYW	FOX
New York	100%	WPIX	WB
New York	100%	WPXN	PAX
New York	100%	WRNN	Independent
New York	100%	WTBY	Independent
New York	100%	WWOR	UPN
New York	100%	WXTV	Univision

Cable systems and subscribers

Cablevision   115,917
Comcast   35,742
Patriot Media   7,882

Military installations, September 2001

J. W. Joyce Kilmer U.S. Army Reserve Center, New
Brunswick   586

Businesses and other major employers

Rutgers University; New Brunswick   6,400
University of Medicine and Dentistry of New Jersey;
Piscataway   3,500
AT&T Corp.; Piscataway; telephone communication
2,900
Robert Wood Johnson University Hospital; New
Brunswick   2,814
United Parcel Service Inc.; Edison   2,800
St. Peter's University Hospital; New Brunswick   2,572
Telcordia Technologies Inc.; Piscataway; commercial
physical research   2,500
Monmouth Medical Center; Long Branch   2,200
Johnson and Johnson; North Brunswick; medical
instruments   1,900
Electrolux Home Products Inc.; Edison; air conditioning
equipment   1,700
Ford Motor Co.; Edison; truck bodies and parts   1,665
Muhlenberg Regional Medical Center Inc.; Plainfield
1,619
Bristol-Myers Squibb Co.; New Brunswick;
pharmaceuticals   1,500
Meridian Health System Inc.; Neptune; billing,
bookkeeping service   1,500
Johnson and Johnson; New Brunswick; noncommercial
research organization   1,200
Continental Service Systems Inc.; North Brunswick;
janitorial service   1,146
CitiStreet; East Brunswick; security brokers, dealers
1,100
Chanel Inc.; Piscataway; perfumes   1,000
E. I. Du Pont De Nemours and Co.; Parlin; medical
equipment   1,000
Macy's East Inc.; Edison; department stores   1,000
Monmouth University; West Long Branch   1,000
Visiting Nurse Assn. of Central Jersey Inc.; Red Bank
1,000
Middlesex County College; Edison   976
Nomura Securities International Inc.; Piscataway;
security dealers   950
New Jersey Press Inc.; Neptune; newspaper   900
Precision Partners Inc.; Hazlet; medical instruments
900
Colgate-Palmolive Co.; Piscataway; dentifrices   800
Roosevelt Care Center; Edison; nursing care facilities
740
Continental Insurance Co.; Neptune; data processing
700
Fujitsu Consulting; Edison; computer programming
700
New Brunswick Public School District; New Brunswick
700
Amserv Healthcare of New Jersey Inc.; Edison; visiting
nurse service   650
Aqualon Co.; Parlin; industrial organic chemicals   650
Tekmark Global Solutions; Edison; computer consulting
650
Amersham Biosciences; Piscataway; scientific recording
equipment   600
Dr. Leonard's Health Care Corp.; Edison; catalog sales
600
Edison Township; Edison; town government   600
L'Oreal USA Inc.; Piscataway; hair preparations   600
Copeland Associates Inc.; East Brunswick; security
brokers, dealers   535
Marlboro Township Board of Education; Marlboro   530
Prudential Mutual Fund Services Inc.; Edison; mutual
funds   525
Ocean Township Board of Education; Oakhurst   520
American Standard Inc.; Piscataway;
refrigeration/heating equipment   500

Bagel Pantry; Metuchen; bagels   500

Career Network Affiliates Inc.; Englishtown; employment agencies   500

Chase Manhattan Mortgage Corp.; Edison; mortgage bankers   500

Great-West Life and Annuity Insurance Co.; Piscataway; life insurance   500

Meridian Hospitals Corp.; Red Bank; management services   500

Middlesex County; New Brunswick; social services   500

PricewaterhouseCoopers; Edison; data processing   500

Revlon International Corp.; Edison; cosmetics   500

Robert Plan of New Jersey Corp.; Edison; insurance agents and brokers   500

Rutgers State University; Piscataway   500

Sears Roebuck and Co. Inc.; New Brunswick; department stores   500

New Jersey 7th District

North central — Woodbridge Township

Beginning in Woodbridge Township near the border with New York City, the 7th meanders west through north central New Jersey, taking in parts of Union, Somerset, and Hunterdon Counties before reaching the Delaware River on the Pennsylvania border. Many of its residents live in bedroom communities and commute to Newark or New York. *(See map p. 586.)*

Redistricting following the 2000 census removed Democratic areas such as Plainfield and added wealthy, heavily Republican areas in Somerset and Hunterdon Counties. The district now leans Republican, and George W. Bush won the vote here by a percentage point in the 2000 presidential election.

Although the new, western areas of the district are less densely populated, the entire 7th has experienced some corporate and industrial growth. Parts of Somerset and Hunterdon Counties, once dotted by horse farms, have been developed into office parks and shopping malls. Drug manufacturers fuel the economy, led by Merck and Co. in Whitehouse Station. Telecommunications giant Lucent Technologies is based in Union County.

All four of the district's counties boast long histories, with charters dating back centuries. During the Revolutionary War, New Providence residents dumped the town's supply of salt into a brook to prevent the British from taking it.

The district has several of New Jersey's Superfund toxic waste sites, and residents tend to be environmentally conscious. Other important local issues include aircraft noise from nearby Newark Liberty International Airport (in the 10th and 13th Districts) and money for infrastructure.

Major Industry

Pharmaceuticals, manufacturing, telecommunications.

Notable

Gov. James E. McGreevey, elected in 2001, was the longtime mayor of Woodbridge Township.

Election Returns

	Republican		Democratic		Other	
President 2000	127,702	48.8%	124,699	47.7%	9,099	3.5%
House 2002	106,055	58.0%	74,879	40.9%	2,068	1.1%

District Profile

Population   647,257

Total area (square miles)   602.5
    Land area (square miles)   595.0

Population per square mile   1,087.8

Counties (2000 population)
    Hunterdon (pt.)   97,985
    Middlesex (pt.)   144,185
    Somerset (pt.)   182,882
    Union (pt.)   222,205

Cities and other areas over 10,000 (2000 population)
    Avenel CDP   17,552
    Berkeley Heights CDP   13,407
    Bound Brook borough   10,155
    Clark CDP   14,597
    Colonia CDP   17,811
    Cranford CDP   22,578
    Edison CDP (pt.)   31,905
    Fords CDP   15,032
    Iselin CDP   16,698
    Manville borough   10,343
    New Providence borough   11,907
    North Plainfield borough   21,103
    Roselle Park borough   13,281
    Scotch Plains CDP   22,732
    South Plainfield borough   21,810
    Springfield CDP   14,429
    Summit   21,131
    Union CDP (pt.)   27,066
    Westfield town   29,644
    Woodbridge CDP (pt.)   18,147

Race and Hispanic or Latino origin*
    White   79.0%
    Black or African American   4.4%
    American Indian or Alaska Native   0.1%
    Asian   8.2%
    Native Hawaiian or other Pacific Islander   0.0%
    Some other race   0.2%
    Hispanic or Latino origin   6.9%
    Two or more races   1.2%

As percentage of total population.

Ancestry*
Dutch 1.1%	
English 5.3%	Polish 7.5%
French 1.2%	Russian 2.3%
German 11.7%	Scottish 1.3%
Hungarian 1.8%	Ukrainian 1.2%
Irish 13.0%	USA/American 2.3%
Italian 15.3%	

As estimated percentage of total population.

Universities and colleges, 2000–2001 enrollment

Raritan Valley Community College, Somerville   5,751
Ultrasound Diagnostic School, Iselin   404
Union County College, Cranford   8,655

Newspapers and circulation

	District circulation	Total circulation
Bridgewater Courier News	24,401	41,079
Delaware Valley News	1,471	2,976
Easton Express-Times	3,209	48,585
Hunterdon County Democrat	15,111	22,216
Newark Star Ledger	75,773	407,706
New Brunswick Home News Tribune	10,855	65,592
*New York Daily News**	5,694	723,155
New York Post	5,304	511,412
*New York Times**	13,585	666,228
Trenton Times	1,206	76,719
*USA Today**	5,009	1,674,376

*See Sources and Explanations in the front of the volume.

Television stations and affiliations

New York	100%	WABC	ABC
New York	100%	WCBS	CBS
New York	100%	WEDW	PBS
New York	100%	WFME	Independent
New York	100%	WLIW	PBS
New York	100%	WLNY	Independent
New York	100%	WMBC	Independent
New York	100%	WNBC	NBC
New York	100%	WNET	PBS
New York	100%	WNJB	PBS
New York	100%	WNJN	PBS
New York	100%	WNJU	Telemundo
New York	100%	WNYE	PBS
New York	100%	WNYW	FOX
New York	100%	WPIX	WB
New York	100%	WPXN	PAX
New York	100%	WRNN	Independent
New York	100%	WTBY	Independent
New York	100%	WWOR	UPN
New York	100%	WXTV	Univision

Cable systems and subscribers

Cablevision   24,518
Comcast   83,763
Patriot Media   59,474
Service Electric Co.   2,158

Businesses and other major employers

Pharmacia and Upjohn Co.; Peapack; pharmaceuticals 6,700
Solaris Health System Hospital; Edison   5,000
Omni Facility Resources Inc.; South Plainfield; landscape services   4,400
Zeman Medical System; Iselin; medical equipment 3,000
AT&T Corp.; Bedminster; long-distance telephone 2,700
Chubb Insurance Co. of New Jersey; Warren; property damage insurance   2,000
BOC Group Inc.; New Providence; industrial gases 2,000

Foster Wheeler; Clinton; industrial engineers   2,000
Puretec Corp.; Somerville; garden hoses   1,750
Hunterdon Medical Center; Flemington   1,680
Schering Corp.; Kenilworth; pharmaceuticals   1,600
Aetna Inc.; Iselin; health insurance   1,600
Merck and Co. Inc.; Whitehouse Station; pharmaceuticals   1,600
NetJets Inc.; Woodbridge; flying charter service   1,475
ExxonMobil Research and Engineering Co.; Annandale; industrial laboratory   1,400
Lucent Technologies Inc.; New Providence; telephone apparatus   1,300
Celanese Americas Corp.; Summit; cigarette tow, cellulosic fiber   1,200
New Jersey Dept. of Human Services; Clinton   1,200
Union Hospital; Union   1,163
New Jersey Dept. of Human Services; Woodbridge 1,100
Laboratory Corp. of America; Cranford; medical laboratories   1,000
Federal Insurance Co.; Warren; fire, marine, casualty insurance   1,000
Lucent Technologies Inc.; Warren; telephone apparatus 1,000
New Jersey Dept. of Human Services; Skillman   1,000
Indopco Inc.; Bridgewater; adhesives   1,000
Standard Automotive Corp.; New York; truck trailer chassis   1,000
Engelhard Corp.; Iselin; catalysts, chemical   925
Hess Oil Virgin Island Corp.; Woodbridge; petroleum refining   900
Reed Elsevier Inc.; New Providence; book publishing 800
Perfect Window Cleaning Corp.; Fanwood; janitorial service   797
Woodbridge Township; Woodbridge; city management 750
Prudential Financial; South Plainfield; business financial management   700
Sheridan Transportation Co.; Woodbridge; coastal freight transportation   700
Conopco Inc.; Flemington; dried foods   660
Phillips-Van Heusen Corp.; Bridgewater; shirts   635
Pinkerton's Inc.; Springfield; security guard service   600
Johnson and Johnson Inc.; Skillman; medical supplies 600
Westfield Board of Education; Westfield   573
New Jersey Dept. of Corrections; Annandale   566
Inn America Hospitality; Iselin; restaurant chain   550
Raritan Valley Community College Inc.; Somerville 550
Pegasus Consulting Group Inc.; Woodbridge; computer software development   525
New Jersey Dept. of Corrections; Clinton   524
Carrier Foundation Inc.; Belle Mead; psychiatric hospitals   510
Vantage Custom Classics Inc.; Avenel; men's/boys' sportswear   500
AT&T Corp.; Warren; telephone communication   500
L'Oreal USA Inc.; Clark; hair preparations   500
Amerada Hess Corp.; Woodbridge; petroleum/chemical bulk stations/terminals   500

Art Rose Industries Inc.; Woodbridge; stationery products   500

Novell Inc.; Summit; computer software design   500

Union County; Berkeley Heights; hospitals   500

Cooper Interests LLC; Princeton; general brokerage investment firm   500

Adesa Corp.; Manville; automobile auction   500

A. M. Best Co.; Oldwick; book publishing   500

New Jersey 8th District

Northeast — Paterson, Clifton, Passaic

The 8th begins in Pompton Lakes and moves south through the southern part of Passaic County into northern Essex County, extending into parts of Livingston, West Orange, and South Orange, just to the west of Newark. The district is a diverse combination of urban centers and suburban towns, and includes Paterson, the state's third-largest city, as well as Clifton and Passaic. *(See map p. 586.)*

Paterson was once known for silk mills that made it a leading textile producer in the late nineteenth century. But after labor strife and the introduction of rayon and other materials, the city experienced a serious economic downfall from which it never fully recovered. Today, Paterson suffers from chronic unemployment and poverty.

The district's Essex County portion, by contrast, is mostly suburban, from wealthy Montclair to the blue-collar and middle-class towns of Nutley and Belleville. Italian Catholics make up a large segment of this area, and there also are pockets of Jewish voters in Essex and Passaic Counties. Many residents commute into Newark or New York.

The district is politically competitive, but recently its voters have favored Democrats in federal elections. Al Gore won 60.4 percent of the vote in the 2000 presidential election.

Overall the district is more than one-fourth Hispanic and almost 13 percent African American, but Paterson, home to dozens of ethnic groups, is half Hispanic and nearly one-third black. The city has a deep-seated labor tradition, making it voter-rich territory for Democratic candidates.

Major Industry

Pharmaceuticals, manufacturing, communications.

Notable

George Washington made his headquarters at Dey Mansion in Wayne during the Revolutionary War for much of the summer and fall of 1780; Samuel Colt patented his first Colt revolver in Paterson and opened his first factory there in 1836.

Election Returns

	Republican		Democratic		Other	
President 2000	78,446	36.5%	129,906	60.4%	6,784	3.2%
House 2002	40,318	30.6%	88,101	66.8%	3,400	2.6%

District Profile

Population   647,258

Total area (square miles)   109.5
Land area (square miles)   106.7

Population per square mile   6,066.1

Counties (2000 population)
Essex (pt.)   233,109
Passaic (pt.)   414,149

Cities and other areas over 10,000 (2000 population)
Belleville CDP   35,928
Bloomfield CDP   47,683
Cedar Grove CDP   12,300
Clifton   78,672
Little Falls CDP   10,855
Livingston CDP (pt.)   11,167
Montclair CDP (pt.)   20,955
Nutley CDP   27,362
Passaic   67,861
Paterson   149,222
Pompton Lakes borough   10,640
South Orange CDP (pt.)   13,075
Verona CDP   13,533
Wayne CDP   54,069
West Orange CDP (pt.)   43,835
West Paterson borough   10,987

Race and Hispanic or Latino origin*
White   53.7%
Black or African American   12.7%
American Indian or Alaska Native   0.1%
Asian   5.3%
Native Hawaiian or other Pacific Islander   0.0%
Some other race   0.3%
Hispanic or Latino origin   25.8%
Two or more races   2.1%

As percentage of total population.

Ancestry*

Arab-Misc. 1.5%	Italian 15.3%
Dutch 1.4%	Polish 4.9%
English 2.7%	Russian 2.0%
German 6.0%	USA/American 2.4%
Irish 8.0%	West Indian 1.7%

As estimated percentage of total population.

Universities and colleges, 2000–2001 enrollment
Berkeley College, West Paterson   1,994
Bloomfield College, Bloomfield   1,785
Montclair State University, Upper Montclair   13,502
Passaic County Community College, Paterson   4,633
William Paterson University of New Jersey, Wayne   9,945

Newspapers and circulation

	District circulation	Total circulation
Hackensack Record	58,358	182,466
Hoy, New York City	1,400	59,949
Newark Star Ledger	43,257	407,706
*New York Daily News**	3,744	723,155
New York Post	4,580	511,412
*New York Times**	7,946	666,228
*USA Today**	2,016	1,674,376
West Essex Tribune	1,752	6,596

See Sources and Explanations in the front of the volume.

Television stations and affiliations

New York	100%	WABC	ABC
New York	100%	WCBS	CBS
New York	100%	WEDW	PBS
New York	100%	WFME	Independent
New York	100%	WLIW	PBS
New York	100%	WLNY	Independent
New York	100%	WMBC	Independent
New York	100%	WNBC	NBC
New York	100%	WNET	PBS
New York	100%	WNJB	PBS
New York	100%	WNJN	PBS
New York	100%	WNJU	Telemundo
New York	100%	WNYE	PBS
New York	100%	WNYW	FOX
New York	100%	WPIX	WB
New York	100%	WPXN	PAX
New York	100%	WRNN	Independent
New York	100%	WTBY	Independent
New York	100%	WWOR	UPN
New York	100%	WXTV	Univision

Cable systems and subscribers

Cablevision   85,748
Comcast   61,308

Businesses and other major employers

St. Joseph's Regional Medical Center; Paterson   3,155
Hoffmann-La Roche Inc.; Nutley; pharmaceuticals   3,000
ITT Industries Inc.; Clifton; electric intercommunication systems   3,000
Passaic County; Paterson; county government   3,000
Lincoln Middle School; Passaic   2,000
AHS Hospital Corp.; Montclair; hospital   1,800
Montclair State University; Montclair   1,760
City of Paterson; Paterson; city management   1,701
Clara Maass Medical Center; Belleville   1,649
Cathedral Healthcare System Inc. Hospital; Newark   1,500
U.S. Dept. of Justice; Newark   1,500
Valley National Bank; Wayne; commercial bank   1,410
ITT Industries Inc.; Nutley; industrial controls   1,400
Datascope Corp.; Bloomfield; medical instruments   1,350
William Paterson University; Wayne   1,300
Kearfott Guidance and Navigation Corp.; Wayne; search/navigation equipment   1,100
Essex County; Cedar Grove; mental hospital   1,016
AHS Hospital Corp.; Passaic   1,000
Organon Inc.; West Orange; pharmaceuticals   1,000
Kessler Rehabilitation Corp.; West Orange; hospital management   970
New Jersey Dept. of Human Services; Totowa   953
Professional Security Bureau; Nutley; detective, armored car services   950
Wayne General Hospital Corp.; Wayne   922
Building Material Corp. of America; Wayne; insulation and roofing material   900
St. Mary's Hospital; Passaic   900
BAE Systems Aerospace Inc.; Wayne; search/navigation equipment   800

Passaic County; Paterson; correctional facilities   800
Roche Laboratories Inc.; Nutley; medical laboratories   800
International Specialty Products Inc.; Wayne; amines, acids, salts, esters   725
Macy's East Inc.; Wayne; department stores   725
JVC Americas Corp.; Wayne; computer peripherals, software   704
Interstate Brands Corp.; Wayne; breads and cakes   700
Reckitt Benckiser Inc.; Wayne; deodorants   700
Beth Israel Hospital Assn. Inc.; Passaic   650
Passaic County Community College; Paterson   650
Vitamin World Inc.; Wayne; vitamin stores   650
Passaic County Board of Social Services; Paterson   645
Barnert Hospital; Paterson   610
Citigroup Inc.; Wayne; mortgage bankers   600
Fortunoff Fine Jewelry and Silverware Inc.; Wayne; silverware   600
Passaic County; Wayne; convalescent home   600
Belleville Board of Education; Belleville   540
City of Passaic; Passaic; city government   512
Automatic Data Processing Inc.; Clifton; data processing   500
Belleville Township; Belleville; town government   500
Boston Scientific Corp.; Wayne; medical instruments   500
Linens 'n Things Inc.; Clifton; beddings and linens   500
Sears Roebuck and Co. Inc.; Wayne; department stores   500

New Jersey 9th District

Northeast — Hackensack, part of Jersey City

Across the Hudson River from northern Manhattan, the 9th is a predominantly wealthy district, but it falls in the middle of New Jersey's generally affluent suburbs. The most prestigious neighborhoods lie to the north, including Englewood and Fort Lee. High rises have sprung up along the river for New York City commuters. The district becomes more middle-class and blue-collar as it runs south into Lyndhurst and Jersey City. *(See map p. 586.)*

Redevelopment has strengthened this district's already solid economy. Anchored by the Meadowlands Sports Complex in East Rutherford, the southern part of the district has seen increased commercial and residential development. But concerns about wetlands preservation have kept growth at a moderate pace. Lipton is based in Englewood Cliffs in the district's northeast corner.

With a strong Hispanic population around Jersey City (shared with the 10th and 13th) and a sizable proportion of black and Asian voters, Democrats far outnumber Republicans. In the district's southern areas, the working-class towns of North Arlington, Lyndhurst, and Kearny (shared with the 13th) provide a strong Democratic vote. The large population of Jewish voters in the northern towns of Teaneck and Fair Lawn also supports Democrats. Bergen County as a whole tends to lean Republican, though several of the older, affluent towns in the county have a history of Democratic voting. Al Gore took nearly two-thirds of the 9th's vote in the 2000 presidential election.

Major Industry

Manufacturing, health care, shipping, stadium events.

Notable

The Meadowlands Sports Complex includes Continental Airlines Arena, Giants Stadium, and Meadowlands Racetrack; Teterboro Airport is home to the Aviation Hall of Fame and Museum of New Jersey; the George Washington Bridge crosses the Hudson River into Manhattan from Fort Lee.

Election Returns

	Republican		Democratic		Other	
President 2000	72,695	33.9%	135,406	63.2%	6,110	2.9%
House 2002	42,088	30.2%	97,108	69.8%		

District Profile

Population   647,257

Total area (square miles)   100.4
   Land area (square miles)   93.1

Population per square mile   6,952.3

Counties (2000 population)
   Bergen (pt.)   493,239   Passaic (pt.)   18,218
   Hudson (pt.)   135,800

Cities and other areas over 10,000 (2000 population)
   Cliffside Park borough   23,007
   Elmwood Park borough   18,925
   Englewood   26,203
   Fair Lawn borough   31,637
   Fairview borough   13,255
   Fort Lee borough   35,461
   Garfield   29,786
   Hackensack   42,677
   Hasbrouck Heights borough   11,662
   Hawthorne borough   18,218
   Jersey City (pt.)   58,129
   Kearny town (pt.)   38,250
   Little Ferry borough   10,800
   Lodi borough   23,971
   Lyndhurst CDP   19,383
   North Arlington borough   15,181
   Palisades Park borough   17,073
   Ridgefield borough   10,830
   Ridgefield Park village   12,873
   Rutherford borough   18,110
   Saddle Brook CDP   13,155
   Secaucus town   15,931
   Teaneck CDP   39,260
   Wallington borough   11,583

Race and Hispanic or Latino origin*
   White   61.3%
   Black or African American   6.6%
   American Indian or Alaska Native   0.1%
   Asian   10.7%
   Native Hawaiian or other Pacific Islander   0.0%
   Some other race   0.3%
   Hispanic or Latino origin   18.8%
   Two or more races   2.1%

*As percentage of total population.

Ancestry*

Arab-Misc.	1.6%	Polish	6.4%
English	2.1%	Russian	2.2%
German	6.6%	USA/American	2.3%
Irish	9.0%	West Indian	1.1%
Italian	16.2%		

*As estimated percentage of total population.

Universities and colleges, 2000–2001 enrollment
   American Business Academy, Hackensack   266
   Fairleigh Dickinson University, Teaneck   9,382
   Felician College, Lodi   1,544

Newspapers and circulation

	District circulation	Total circulation
Hackensack Record	55,309	182,466
Jersey City Journal	9,175	42,116
Newark Star Ledger	13,927	407,706
*New York Daily News**	13,168	723,155
New York Post	8,083	511,412
*New York Times**	13,025	666,228
*USA Today**	2,568	1,674,376

*See Sources and Explanations in the front of the volume.

Television stations and affiliations
New York	100%	WABC	ABC
New York	100%	WCBS	CBS
New York	100%	WEDW	PBS
New York	100%	WFME	Independent
New York	100%	WLIW	PBS
New York	100%	WLNY	Independent
New York	100%	WMBC	Independent
New York	100%	WNBC	NBC
New York	100%	WNET	PBS
New York	100%	WNJB	PBS
New York	100%	WNJN	PBS
New York	100%	WNJU	Telemundo
New York	100%	WNYE	PBS
New York	100%	WNYW	FOX
New York	100%	WPIX	WB
New York	100%	WPXN	PAX
New York	100%	WRNN	Independent
New York	100%	WTBY	Independent
New York	100%	WWOR	UPN
New York	100%	WXTV	Univision

Cable systems and subscribers
   Cablevision   56,661
   Comcast   34,459
   Time Warner   48,379

Businesses and other major employers
   United Parcel Service Inc.; Secaucus; courier services
      5,000
   Hackensack University Medical Center; Hackensack
      4,300
   U.S. Postal Service; Jersey City   3,500
   Quest Diagnostics Clinical Laboratories Inc.; Teterboro;
      medical laboratories   2,800
   Meadowlands Racetrack; East Rutherford; horse racing
      2,700
   Donaldson Lufkin and Jenrette Securities Corp.; Jersey
      City; security brokers, dealers   2,000

Englewood Hospital Assn.; Englewood 2,000

Honeywell International Inc.; Teterboro; aircraft 2,000

Matsushita Electric Corp. of America; Secaucus; televisions and radios 2,000

Fashion Outlets of America Inc.; Lyndhurst 1,945

Quest Diagnostics Clinical Laboratories Inc.; Rutherford; medical laboratories 1,900

Holy Name Hospital; Teaneck 1,780

Howmedica Osteonics Corp.; Rutherford; medical supplies 1,600

North Jersey Media Group Inc.; Hackensack; newspaper 1,275

ASCI Holdings Mexico Inc.; Fort Lee; motor vehicle parts/accessories 1,235

Christ Hospital; Jersey City 1,200

Unilever Bestfoods Foodservice; Englewood Cliffs; management services 1,200

ACS State and Local Solutions Inc.; Teaneck; data processing 1,000

Kraft Foods Inc.; Fair Lawn; food products 1,000

Marcal Paper Mills Inc.; Elmwood Park; paper products 1,000

Nextel Communications Inc.; Rutherford; radiotelephone communication 1,000

Port Authority Police Benevolent Assn.; Englewood Cliffs; labor organization 1,000

Fairleigh Dickinson University; Teaneck 982

Bergen County; Hackensack; county government 970

Control Construction Group; Secaucus; janitorial service 900

U.S. Postal Service; South Hackensack 900

Bloomingdale's Inc.; Hackensack; department stores 800

Kearny School District; Kearny 800

City of Jersey City; Jersey City; pension, health, welfare funds 727

Arrow Fastener Co.; Saddle Brook; stapling machines 700

Emery Air Freight Corp.; Kearny 700

Myron Corp.; Maywood; novelties, plastics 695

Malt Products Corp.; Saddle Brook; malt 650

Palisades General Hospital; North Bergen 631

Bibong Apparel Corp.; Englewood Cliffs; men's/boys' outerwear 600

Care Finders Inc.; Hackensack; nurses' registry 600

CS Integrated; Secaucus; refrigerated warehousing and storage 600

Delta Building Services Inc.; Rutherford; janitorial service 600

PricewaterhouseCoopers; Fort Lee; management consulting 600

West Hudson Hospital Assn.; Kearny 572

Meadowlands Hospital Medical Center; Secaucus 570

American Consolidation Services North America; Secaucus; warehousing 550

New Jersey Transit Corp.; Kearny 550

Retailers and Manufacturers Distribution Marking Service Inc.; Secaucus; packaging/labeling services 550

U.S.A. Security Services Inc.; Hackensack; security specialization 550

Unilever Bestfoods Foodservice; Moonachie; breads and cakes 550

Bowne Business Communications Inc.; Secaucus; offset printing 525

Unilever U.S. Inc.; Edgewater; commercial physical research 520

Teaneck Board of Education; Teaneck 516

Eastern Nursing Services Inc.; Hackensack; home health care 505

AGFA Corp.; Ridgefield Park; photographic equipment, supplies 500

Allied Beverage Group; Carlstadt; wine 500

Cluett Peabody and Co.; Secaucus; men's/boys' clothing 500

Equitable Life Assurance Society of U.S.; Secaucus; pension funds 500

Lantis Eyewear Corp.; Moonachie; optical goods stores 500

Lantis Eyewear Corp.; Secaucus; sunglasses 500

Popular Club Plan Inc.; Garfield; mail-order clothing 500

Reed Elsevier Inc.; Los Angeles; magazine publishing 500

Riviera Trading Inc.; Secaucus; sunglasses 500

U.S. Postal Service; Paterson 500

New Jersey 10th District

Northeast — parts of Newark and Jersey City

Covering a multiracial, urban region centered in Newark, the black-majority 10th provides a solid base for Democrats. Outside Newark (which is shared with the 13th), the district extends into Essex County's working-class suburbs of Irvington, East Orange, and Orange. Largely blue-collar and packed with minorities, the district's cities contribute to its Democratic leanings. It takes in portions of Jersey City (shared with the 9th and 13th Districts) and Elizabeth (shared with the 13th). *(See map p. 586.)*

The 10th's portion of Newark is made up of the largely central, south, and west of the city. The central ward was decimated in the 1967 riots and never fully recovered. The decade after the riots saw a steep decline in the number of jobs and an increase in the number of departing whites. As the Irish and Italians headed to the suburbs, blacks became a majority and grabbed the reins of power at city hall; African Americans have held the mayoralty since 1970.

Although deep poverty continues to be a problem in some spots, efforts to revitalize the area have had some success. An infusion of new housing is helping some of Newark's worst neighborhoods. The population exodus largely has ceased, and the city has several major employers, including Prudential Financial. A large performing arts center that opened in 1997 is helping, as are new retail outlets in Essex County. Newark Liberty International Airport (a small part of which is in the 13th) is a transportation hub for travelers to New York City and is home to large Continental Airlines facilities that employ thousands of residents. Port Newark-Elizabeth (in the 13th) also provides jobs for the region.

The district votes consistently Democratic at all levels, although Rahway and Roselle include some Republicans. Bill Clinton won by comfortable margins in the 1992 and 1996 presidential contests, and Al Gore got 82.7 percent here in 2000, his statewide high.

Major Industry

Aviation, shipping, insurance, higher education, pharmaceuticals.

Notable

Thomas Edison's first shop opened in Newark in 1871.

Election Returns

	Republican		Democratic		Other	
President 2000	27,718	15.6%	147,112	82.7%	3,004	1.7%
House 2002	15,913	15.5%	86,433	84.5%		

District Profile

Population   647,258

Total area (square miles)   69.4
  Land area (square miles)   66.0

Population per square mile   9,806.9

Counties (2000 population)
  Essex (pt.)   375,956
  Hudson (pt.)   69,102
  Union (pt.)   202,200

Cities and other areas over 10,000 (2000 population)
  East Orange   69,824
  Elizabeth (pt.)   74,984
  Hillside CDP   21,747
  Irvington CDP   60,695
  Jersey City (pt.)   63,725
  Linden (pt.)   30,356
  Maplewood CDP   23,868
  Millburn CDP (pt.)   10,269
  Montclair CDP (pt.)   18,022
  Newark (pt.)   155,413
  Orange CDP   32,868
  Rahway   26,500
  Roselle borough   21,274
  Union CDP (pt.)   27,339

Race and Hispanic or Latino origin*
  White   21.4%
  Black or African American   56.6%
  American Indian or Alaska Native   0.2%
  Asian   3.6%
  Native Hawaiian or other Pacific Islander   0.0%
  Some other race   0.5%
  Hispanic or Latino origin   15.0%
  Two or more races   2.8%

*As percentage of total population.

Ancestry*

English 1.1%	Portuguese 1.6%
German 2.5%	Subsaharan 2.8%
Irish 3.6%	USA/American 2.0%
Italian 4.2%	West Indian 6.4%
Polish 3.0%	

*As estimated percentage of total population.

Universities and colleges, 2000–2001 enrollment
  Essex County College, Newark   8,868
  Katharine Gibbs School, Montclair   1,202
  Kean University, Union   11,468
  New Jersey City College, Jersey City   8,342
  New Jersey Institute of Technology, Newark   8,820
  Rutgers University-Newark, Newark   9,352
  Seton Hall University, South Orange   9,920
  University of Medicine and Dentistry of New Jersey, Newark   4,666

Newspapers and circulation

	District circulation	Total circulation
Jersey City Journal	3,810	42,116
Newark Star Ledger	70,177	407,706
New Brunswick Home News Tribune	1,924	65,592
New York Daily News*	4,569	723,155
New York Post	4,180	511,412
New York Times*	9,215	666,228
USA Today*	2,379	1,674,376

*See Sources and Explanations in the front of the volume.

Television stations and affiliations

New York	100%	WABC	ABC
New York	100%	WCBS	CBS
New York	100%	WEDW	PBS
New York	100%	WFME	Independent
New York	100%	WLIW	PBS
New York	100%	WLNY	Independent
New York	100%	WMBC	Independent
New York	100%	WNBC	NBC
New York	100%	WNET	PBS
New York	100%	WNJB	PBS
New York	100%	WNJN	PBS
New York	100%	WNJU	Telemundo
New York	100%	WNYE	PBS
New York	100%	WNYW	FOX
New York	100%	WPIX	WB
New York	100%	WPXN	PAX
New York	100%	WRNN	Independent
New York	100%	WTBY	Independent
New York	100%	WWOR	UPN
New York	100%	WXTV	Univision

Cable systems and subscribers
  Cablevision   44,145
  Comcast   65,336

Military installations, September 2001
  Caven Point U.S. Army Reserve Center, Jersey City   346

Businesses and other major employers
  Prudential Financial Inc.; Newark; life insurance   13,100
  University of Medicine and Dentistry of New Jersey; Newark   6,000
  Schering-Plough Corp.; Union; pharmaceuticals   5,000
  Continental Airlines Inc.; Newark   4,000
  International Union United Auto Workers of America; Linden; labor union   3,000
  Newark Beth Israel Medical Center; Newark   2,700
  Essex County; Newark; county government   2,500
  Gateway Security Inc.; Newark; detective, armored car services   2,400
  Oxford Applied Research USA; Newark; marketing consulting services   2,001

U.S. Veterans Hospital; East Orange   2,000
U.S. Veterans Medical Center; Orange   1,900
Kean University; Union   1,800
Maersk Inc.; Elizabeth; deep-sea freight transportation
   1,700
Public Service Electric and Gas Co.; Newark; electric
   power generation   1,500
Rutgers University; Newark   1,500
Newark Housing Authority; Newark   1,300
New Community Corp.; Newark; commercial printing
   1,150
ExxonMobil Oil Corp.; Linden; crude petroleum and
   natural gas   1,100
New Jersey Institute of Technology; Newark   1,037
TMC Services Inc.; Irvington; warehousing and storage
   1,000
Rahway Hospital; Rahway   935
Seton Hall University; South Orange   900
General Motors Corp.; Linden; automobiles   800
New Jersey City University; Jersey City   800
New Jersey Dept. of Corrections; Newark   800
New Jersey Dept. of Corrections; Rahway   782
Interbake Foods Inc.; Elizabeth; cookies and crackers
   770
East Orange General Hospital Inc.; East Orange   700
Orange Hospital Center; Orange   700
Tuscan/Lehigh Dairies; Union; fluid milk   700
Irvington County; Irvington; county government   600
Newark Housing Authority; Newark   600
Orange Board of Education; Orange   600
U.S. Bureau of Customs and Border Protection; Newark
   600
United Air Lines Inc.; Newark   600
Visiting Nurse Assn. of Essex Valley Inc.; East Orange;
   nurses, medical assistants   600
International Total Services Inc.; Newark; airport
   terminal   525
Irvington General Hospital; Irvington   525
American Airlines Inc.; Newark   500
Arrow International Inc.; Elizabeth; catheters   500
New Jersey Transit Bus Operations Inc.; Orange   500
Newark Extended Care Facility Inc.; Newark   500
Newark Morning Ledger Co.; Newark; newspaper   500
Port Newark Container Terminal; Newark; stevedoring
   500
Revlon Holdings Inc.; Irvington; manicure preparations
   500
USF Red Star Inc.; Newark; trucking   500

New Jersey 11th District

North central — Morris County

Exclusive, pastoral estates and Fortune 500 firms make the 11th one of the most privileged districts in the nation. Located in northern New Jersey and centered in Morris County, the district has the nation's second-highest median income. (*See map p. 586.*)

Its voters tend to be socially moderate, family-centered, and ardently fiscally conservative. The 11th is one of the most solidly Republican districts in the northeast. George

W. Bush captured 53.7 percent of the vote here in the 2000 presidential election, his highest total in the state.

Downsizing in the telecommunications industry increased the amount of empty office space in Morris County. But overall the district's office market is still strong. Corporate giants AT&T (in Basking Ridge), Kraft Foods (in East Hanover), Honeywell (in Morristown), and BASF (in Budd Lake) have facilities here. Pharmaceutical companies have found the 11th particularly attractive, with Warner-Lambert Co. (Morris Plains) and Novartis (East Hanover) basing major operations in the district and Wyeth headquartered in Madison.

In addition to all of Morris County, the district takes in chunks of Essex County in the east, Somerset County in the south, Sussex County in the northwest, and a sliver of Passaic County in the northeast.

Some district residents commute to Manhattan, but the region's attractiveness to large employers and high-paying white-collar jobs means fewer residents are leaving the area for work. Dover's Picatinny Arsenal experienced some cutbacks in the 1990s but appears to be safe from further cuts.

Major Industry

Pharmaceuticals, finance, telecommunications, manufacturing.

Notable

Morristown National Historical Park, the first national historic park established by the federal government, includes George Washington's 1779–1780 Revolutionary War headquarters.

Election Returns

	Republican		Democratic		Other	
President 2000	151,617	53.7%	121,036	42.9%	9,763	3.5%
House 2002	132,938	72.4%	48,477	26.4%	2,263	1.2%

District Profile

Population   647,258

Total area (square miles)   627.6
   Land area (square miles)   610.0

Population per square mile   1,061.1

Counties (2000 population)
Essex (pt.)   66,435   Somerset (pt.)   63,705
Morris   470,212   Sussex (pt.)   43,007
Passaic (pt.)   3,899

Cities and other areas over 10,000 (2000 population)
Dover town   18,188
Hopatcong borough   15,888
Lincoln Park borough   10,930
Livingston CDP (pt.)   16,224
Madison borough   16,530
Morristown town   18,544
Somerville borough   12,423
Succasunna-Kenvil CDP   12,569
West Caldwell CDP   11,233

Race and Hispanic or Latino origin*
White   82.9%
Black or African American   2.6%

American Indian or Alaska Native   0.1%
Asian   6.3%
Native Hawaiian or other Pacific Islander   0.0%
Some other race   0.1%
Hispanic or Latino origin   6.8%
Two or more races   1.0%

*As percentage of total population.

Ancestry*

Dutch	1.6%	Italian	16.8%
English	6.1%	Polish	5.5%
French	1.4%	Russian	2.3%
German	11.8%	Scottish	1.5%
Hungarian	1.1%	USA/American	2.7%
Irish	14.4%		

*As estimated percentage of total population.

Universities and colleges, 2000–2001 enrollment
Caldwell College, Caldwell   2,094
College of St. Elizabeth, Morristown   1,771
County College of Morris, Randolph   7,919
Drew University, Madison   2,412
Metropolitan Technical Institute, Fairfield   240
Rabbinical College of America, Morristown   259
Somerset County Technical Institute, Bridgewater   532

Newspapers and circulation

	District circulation	Total circulation
Bridgewater Courier News	4,535	41,079
Hackensack Record	4,586	182,466
Newark Star Ledger	70,951	407,706
New Jersey Herald	2,585	16,282
*New Jersey Law Journal**	1,350	7,466
*New York Daily News**	5,375	723,155
New York Post	3,996	511,412
*New York Times**	18,463	666,228
Parsippany Daily Record	36,318	42,659
*USA Today**	6,408	1,674,376
West Essex Tribune	4,771	6,596

*See Sources and Explanations in the front of the volume.

Television stations and affiliations
New York	100%	WABC	ABC
New York	100%	WCBS	CBS
New York	100%	WEDW	PBS
New York	100%	WFME	Independent
New York	100%	WLIW	PBS
New York	100%	WLNY	Independent
New York	100%	WMBC	Independent
New York	100%	WNBC	NBC
New York	100%	WNET	PBS
New York	100%	WNJB	PBS
New York	100%	WNJN	PBS
New York	100%	WNJU	Telemundo
New York	100%	WNYE	PBS
New York	100%	WNYW	FOX
New York	100%	WPIX	WB
New York	100%	WPXN	PAX
New York	100%	WRNN	Independent
New York	100%	WTBY	Independent
New York	100%	WWOR	UPN
New York	100%	WXTV	Univision

Cable systems and subscribers
Cablevision   132,939
Comcast   12,501
Patriot Media   6,629
Service Electric Co.   6,276

Military installations, September 2001
Picatinny Arsenal (Army), Dover   3,831

Businesses and other major employers
Novartis Pharmaceuticals Corp.; East Hanover; pharmaceuticals   5,600
AT&T Corp.; Basking Ridge; long-distance telephone   5,300
CSA International; Randolph; electric lab standards   5,000
AT&T Corp.; Morristown; telephone communication   3,900
NRT Inc.; Parsippany; real estate brokers and agents   3,700
RCM Technologies Co.; Succasunna; engineering services   3,000
Sodexho Inc.; Whippany; cafeteria   3,000
St. Clare's Hospital Inc.; Denville   2,800
Warner-Lambert Co.; Morris Plains; pharmaceuticals   2,800
Cendant Corp.; Parsippany; mortgage bankers   2,500
Ethicon Inc.; Somerville; sutures   2,500
St. Barnabas Medical Center Inc.; Livingston   2,500
AT&T Corp.; Parsippany; online information retrieval   2,000
Automatic Data Processing Inc.; Roseland   2,000
Somerset County; Somerville; county government   1,977
North River Insurance Co.; Morristown; property damage insurance   1,700
Somerset Medical Center; Somerville   1,700
Schering-Plough Corp.; Bridgewater; pharmaceuticals   1,600
BASF Corp.; Budd Lake; industrial organic chemicals   1,500
ExxonMobil Oil Corp.; Florham Park; commercial physical research   1,500
Honeywell International Inc.; Morristown; aircraft engines and parts   1,500
Metropolitan Life Insurance Co.; Bridgewater; insurance agents and brokers   1,500
VTech Innovation; Pine Brook; telephones and telephone apparatus   1,500
Fireman's Fund Insurance Co.; Denville; insurance agents and brokers   1,400
Lucent Technologies Inc.; Parsippany; data processing   1,400
St. Clare's Hospital Inc.; Dover   1,400
Monarch Building Maintenance Inc.; Rockaway   1,300
U.S. Veterans Hospital; Lyons   1,300
United Parcel Service Inc.; Morristown; courier services   1,300
Allan Industries Inc.; Rockaway; building cleaning   1,200
Automatic Switch Co.; Florham Park; solenoid valves   1,200
County College of Morris; Dover   1,200

Roche Vitamins Inc.; Parsippany; pharmaceuticals 1,200

Forrest S. Chilton III Memorial Hospital Inc.; Pompton Plains; hospital 1,160

Automatic Data Processing Inc.; Parsippany 1,000

Avis Rent a Car Systems Inc.; Parsippany 1,000

HFS Car Rental Inc.; Parsippany; franchise 1,000

Johnson and Johnson Inc.; Raritan; pharmaceuticals 1,000

Kraft Foods Inc.; East Hanover; cookies 1,000

Medco Health Solutions Inc.; Parsippany; mail-order catalog 1,000

Morris County; Morristown; county government 1,000

Museum Company Acquisition Corp.; Fairfield; gifts and novelties 1,000

Ortho Clinical Diagnostic Inc.; Raritan; diagnostic agents 1,000

Quest International Fragrances Co.; Budd Lake; perfumes, cosmetics 1,000

TechSoft Information Technology Inc.; Succasunna; computer operator training 1,000

TMC Services Inc.; Livingston; janitorial service 1,000

United Jewish Federation of Metro West; Whippany; recreation association 1,000

Villager Franchise Systems Inc.; Parsippany; franchise 1,000

Weichert Co.; Morris Plains; real estate brokers and agents 1,000

Accenture Inc.; Florham Park; business management consultant 985

Reliant Pharmaceuticals; Liberty Corner 950

CRS Facility Services; Elmwood Park; janitorial service 900

Howmet Corp.; Dover; commercial castings 900

River Corridor Closure; Morris Plains; environmental consultant 900

Wyeth Laboratories Inc.; Madison; pharmaceuticals 850

TyCom Inc.; Morristown; current-carrying wiring services 815

Laboratory Corp. of America; Raritan; testing laboratories 800

Macy's East Inc.; Livingston; department stores 800

North America Fedders Inc.; Liberty Corner; air conditioning equipment 800

National Prescription Administrators Inc.; East Hanover; medical services organization 780

Kvaerner U.S. Inc.; Bridgewater; engineering services 775

Aventis Pharmaceuticals Inc.; Bridgewater 750

Corporate Express Office Products Inc.; Whippany; office supplies 750

Dendrite International; Morristown; computer software development 725

AT&T Corp.; Short Hills 700

Global Consultants Inc.; Parsippany; software 700

KPMG; Short Hills; certified public accountant 700

Transistor Devices Inc.; Hackettstown; electronic devices 700

Verizon Wireless Inc.; Morristown; cellular telephones 700

Prudential Insurance Company of America; Florham Park; retirement plan consultants 670

American Safety Razor Co.; Cedar Knolls; cotton swabs 650

Kushner Companies Inc.; Florham Park; single-family houses 650

Telcordia Technologies Inc.; Morristown; software development 610

ASCO Power Technologies; Florham Park; electrical equipment and supplies 600

Beneficial Louisiana Inc.; Bridgewater; licensed loan companies 600

Deloitte and Touche; Parsippany; certified public accountant 600

Greystone Psychiatric Hospital; Morris Plains 600

Macy's East Inc.; Rockaway; department stores 600

Ricoh Corp.; Caldwell; photocopy machines 600

Sears Roebuck and Co. Inc.; Rockaway; department stores 600

MCI WorldCom Network Services Inc.; Parsippany; telephone communication 600

Morris County; Morris Plains; nursing care facilities 570

Drew University; Madison 550

Vita Quest International Inc.; Caldwell; vitamin preparations 549

Dialogic Corp.; Parsippany; telephone and telegraph apparatus 535

Lincoln Park Subacute and Rehab Center; Lincoln Park; nursing care 529

AIGDC; Livingston; insurance agents and brokers 500

CIT Group/Sales Financing Inc.; Livingston; working capital financing 500

Fireman's Fund Insurance Co.; Parsippany; insurance agents 500

Maple Leaf Foods USA Inc.; Livingston; breads and cakes 500

Morristown Memorial Hospital; Morristown 500

New York Life Investment Management; Parsippany; security brokers, dealers 500

Odyssey Pharmaceuticals Inc.; East Hanover; drugs/herbs 500

Planned Building Services Inc.; Fairfield; building maintenance 500

Prudential Financial; Roseland; insurance agents and brokers 500

Prudential New Jersey Properties; Basking Ridge; real estate agents and managers 500

U.S. Postal Service; Whippany 500

Verizon New Jersey Inc.; Cedar Knolls; telephone communication 500

New Jersey 12th District

Central — part of Trenton, East Brunswick, Princeton

Set in the middle of the state, the 12th begins in Hunterdon County, hitting ethnically diverse Trenton (shared with the 4th) and East Brunswick as it winds east to Monmouth County. It ends in shore communities such as Rumson just short of the Atlantic Ocean. *(See map p. 586.)*

Despite its jagged shape, many of the district's towns are similar. Office parks dominate the landscape in these affluent and white communities. But there are pockets of blue-collar diversity. Redistricting following the 2000 census made the 12th more Democratic by exchanging part of predominantly white Hunterdon County for a sizable portion of the state capital, Trenton, where more than 70 percent of the residents are black. Plainsboro in Middlesex County has a large Asian population.

The 12th has benefited from economic growth, though midsize towns such as Ewing must contend with the side effects of suburban sprawl. Delaware River towns, such as Frenchtown and Lambertville, offer quaint antique shops and bed and breakfasts. In addition to the Capitol, the district also boasts the governor's official residence, the stately and imposing Drumthwacket in Princeton.

Old money and suburban affluence made the area historically Republican, except for a small Democratic constituency anchored by Princeton's academic community. But due to an influx of independents, the 12th became politically competitive even before mapmakers pushed it to the left in redistricting. Al Gore took 56.2 percent of the new district's vote in the 2000 presidential election, about 5 percentage points higher than under the old lines.

Major Industry
Higher education, military, pharmaceuticals.

Notable
The Lenox Inc. china company, founded in Trenton, is based in Lawrenceville.

Election Returns

	Republican		Democratic		Other	
President 2000	101,145	40.2%	141,568	56.2%	9,188	3.6%
House 2002	62,938	36.7%	104,806	61.0%	3,969	2.3%

District Profile

Population   647,258

Total area (square miles)   642.4
  Land area (square miles)   633.2

Population per square mile   1,022.2

Counties (2000 population)
  Hunterdon (pt.)   24,004
  Mercer (pt.)   185,497
  Middlesex (pt.)   245,139
  Monmouth (pt.)   159,983
  Somerset (pt.)   32,635

Cities and other areas over 10,000 (2000 population)
  East Brunswick CDP   46,756
  Eatontown borough   14,008
  Ewing CDP   35,707
  North Brunswick Township CDP   36,287
  Old Bridge CDP (pt.)   20,293
  Princeton borough   14,203
  Princeton Meadows CDP   13,436
  South River borough   15,322
  Tinton Falls borough   15,053
  Trenton (pt.)   47,658

Race and Hispanic or Latino origin*
White   72.4%
Black or African American   11.4%
American Indian or Alaska Native   0.1%
Asian   9.1%
Native Hawaiian or other Pacific Islander   0.0%
Some other race   0.2%
Hispanic or Latino origin   5.5%
Two or more races   1.4%

*As percentage of total population.

Ancestry*

English	5.2%	Italian	13.7%
French	1.2%	Polish	6.4%
German	9.3%	Russian	3.0%
Hungarian	1.7%	Scottish	1.1%
Irish	12.1%	USA/American	2.4%

*As estimated percentage of total population.

Universities and colleges, 2000–2001 enrollment
  Brookdale Community College, Lincroft   11,552
  College of New Jersey, Trenton   6,861
  Mercer County Community College, Trenton   7,751
  Princeton Theological Seminary, Princeton   743
  Princeton University, Princeton   6,547
  Rider University, Lawrenceville   5,274
  Thomas A. Edison State College, Trenton   8,137

Newspapers and circulation

	District circulation	Total circulation
Asbury Park Press	26,019	167,085
Bridgewater Courier News	1,783	41,079
Hunterdon County Democrat	5,288	22,216
Newark Star Ledger	28,597	407,706
New Brunswick Home News Tribune	24,006	65,592
*New York Daily News**	7,248	723,155
New York Post	5,554	511,412
*New York Times**	16,536	666,228
Trenton Times	35,623	76,719
Trenton Trentonian	16,558	48,680
*USA Today**	5,279	1,674,376

*See Sources and Explanations in the front of the volume.

Television stations and affiliations

New York	77%	WABC	ABC
New York	77%	WCBS	CBS
New York	77%	WEDW	PBS
New York	77%	WFME	Independent
New York	77%	WLIW	PBS
New York	77%	WLNY	Independent
New York	77%	WMBC	Independent
New York	77%	WNBC	NBC
New York	77%	WNET	PBS
New York	77%	WNJB	PBS
New York	77%	WNJN	PBS
New York	77%	WNJU	Telemundo
New York	77%	WNYE	PBS
New York	77%	WNYW	FOX
New York	77%	WPIX	WB
New York	77%	WPXN	PAX
New York	77%	WRNN	Independent

New York	77%	WTBY	Independent
New York	77%	WWOR	UPN
New York	77%	WXTV	Univision
Philadelphia	23%	KYW	CBS
Philadelphia	23%	WBPH	Independent
Philadelphia	23%	WCAU	NBC
Philadelphia	23%	WFMZ	Independent
Philadelphia	23%	WHYY	PBS
Philadelphia	23%	WLVT	PBS
Philadelphia	23%	WMGM	NBC
Philadelphia	23%	WNJS	PBS
Philadelphia	23%	WNJT	PBS
Philadelphia	23%	WPHL	WB
Philadelphia	23%	WPPX	PAX
Philadelphia	23%	WPSG	UPN
Philadelphia	23%	WPVI	ABC
Philadelphia	23%	WTVE	Independent
Philadelphia	23%	WTXF	FOX
Philadelphia	23%	WWAC	Independent
Philadelphia	23%	WYBE	PBS

Cable systems and subscribers
Cablevision   28,206
Comcast   97,255
Patriot Media   6,273
Service Electric Co.   2,992

Military installations, September 2001
Fort Monmouth Main Post, Red Bank   8,038
Lawrenceville DMAVA Complex, Lawrenceville   516
Trenton Aviation Armory/Mercer, Trenton   338

Businesses and other major employers
New Jersey Executive Office; Trenton   20,000
AT&T Corp.; Holmdel; telephone communication   6,000
Lucent Technologies Inc.; Holmdel; commercial physical research   4,100
New Jersey Dept. of Labor; Trenton   4,000
U.S. Environmental Protection Agency; Trenton   3,600
New Jersey Dept. of Law and Public Safety; Trenton   3,500
Princeton University; Princeton   3,400
CSI International Inc.; Red Bank; facilities support services   3,085
Trenton School District; Trenton   3,000
Capital Health Systems Inc. Hospital; Trenton   2,712
General Electric Co.; Princeton; satellite communications   2,700
New Jersey Dept. of Transportation; Trenton   2,700
Silver Line Building Products Corp.; North Brunswick; windows, plastics   2,600
Educational Testing Service Inc.; Princeton; educational/personnel test service   2,199
Armkel LLC; Princeton; barber/beauty shop equipment   2,100
AT&T Corp.; Somerset; telephone communication   2,000
Bristol-Myers Squibb Co.; Princeton; commercial physical research   2,000
Dow Jones and Co.; Cranbury; newspaper   2,000
New Jersey Dept. of Transportation; Trenton; transportation regulation   2,000

Seagull Project; South River; investment holding company   1,820
City of Trenton; Trenton; city management   1,800
New Jersey Dept. of Corrections; Trenton   1,800
New Jersey Dept. of Education; Trenton   1,700
New Jersey Judiciary Courts; Trenton   1,537
Medical Center at Princeton; Princeton   1,500
Telcordia Technologies Inc.; Red Bank; commercial physical research   1,500
Mercer County Community College; Trenton   1,400
New Jersey Manufacturers Insurance Co.; Trenton; workers' compensation insurance   1,345
Bayshore Community Health Services Inc.; Holmdel; hospital management   1,300
Capital Health System at Mercer; Trenton   1,280
American Reinsurance Co.; Princeton; fire, marine, casualty insurance   1,200
Covance Inc.; Princeton; commercial physical research   1,100
Janssen Pharmaceutical Inc.; Titusville; anesthetics   1,100
Air Safety Equipment Inc.; Holmdel; aircraft servicing   1,000
Berlitz GlobalNet Inc.; Princeton; language school   1,000
First Union National Bank; New Brunswick; commercial bank   1,000
Johnson and Johnson; North Brunswick; pharmaceuticals   1,000
Merrill Lynch Asset Management Inc.; Plainsboro; mutual fund sales   1,000
New Jersey Dept. of Community Affairs; Trenton   1,000
New Jersey Dept. of the Treasury; Trenton   1,000
Professional Detailing Network Inc.; Lawrenceville; marketing consulting services   1,000
Bristol-Myers Squibb Co.; Plainsboro; pharmaceuticals   920
Reiss Manufacturing Inc.; Englishtown; plastics molding   900
AT&T Corp.; Lincroft; computer hardware   850
New Jersey Dept. of the Treasury; Trenton   850
Rhodia Inc.; Cranbury; boric acid   825
College of New Jersey; Trenton   800
Dow Jones and Co.; Monmouth Junction; newspaper   800
New Jersey Dept. of Education; Trenton   800
New Jersey Dept. of Human Services; Trenton   800
Journal News Inc.; Trenton; newspaper   793
Sarnoff Corp.; Princeton; commercial nonphysical research   757
Macy's East Inc.; Eatontown; department stores   750
Times of Trenton Publishing Corp.; Trenton; newspaper   735
Lawrenceville School District; Trenton   725
FMC Corp.; Princeton; chemical laboratory   700
New Jersey Dept. of Health and Senior Services; Trenton   700
Brookdale Community College Inc.; Lincroft; community college   695
Cosmetic Essence Inc.; Holmdel; perfumes, cosmetics   675

Wackenhut Corp.; Somerset; protective services, guard
650

Geneva Pharmaceuticals Inc.; Plainsboro   620

New Jersey Dept. of Personnel; Trenton   608

Barnes and Noble Distribution; Jamesburg; books
600

L'Oreal USA Inc.; Somerset; hair preparations   600

Lucent Technologies Inc.; Eatontown; fiber optics
equipment   600

Merck and Co. Inc.; Somerset; pharmaceuticals   600

Software House International Inc.; Somerset; computer
software   600

Teleport Communications Group Inc.; Dayton;
telephone communication   600

U.S. Postal Service; Eatontown   600

Vertis Direct Marketing Inc.; North Brunswick;
advertising   600

Webcraft; North Brunswick; accounting services
600

Maxim Health Care Services; North Brunswick; home
health care   590

New Jersey Dept. of Banking and Insurance; Trenton
580

Wyeth Laboratories Inc.; Monmouth Junction; medical
laboratories   573

Rider University; Trenton   560

Firmenich Inc.; Plainsboro; perfumes   550

Verizon Information Services Inc.; Somerset; telephone
directory distribution   550

Millennium Chemicals Inc.; Red Bank; titanium dioxide
(pigments)   540

Public Service Electric and Gas Co.; Somerset; electric
power generation   505

ABB Susa Inc.; North Brunswick; sewage treatment
plant construction   500

All Health Care Services Inc.; Middletown; visiting
nurse service   500

AT&T Communications of New Jersey Inc.; Hopewell;
engineering laboratory   500

Citibank; Plainsboro; commercial bank   500

City of Trenton; Trenton; police dept.   500

Cosmetic Essence Inc.; Cranbury; cosmetics   500

Hibbert Co.; Trenton; direct mail advertising   500

L'Oreal USA Inc.; Franklin; hair preparations   500

MedPointe Inc.; Somerset; pharmaceuticals   500

Merrill Lynch, Pierce, Fenner and Smith Inc.; Holmdel;
stock brokers and dealers   500

Philips Electronics North America Corp.; Somerset;
electric light bulbs   500

Princeton University; Princeton; commercial research
laboratory   500

RCN Corp.; Princeton; cable television   500

Schweitzer-Mauduit International Inc.; Spotswood; paper
mills   500

Tellium Inc.; Oceanport; multiplex equipment   500

TyCom Ltd.; Eatontown; engineering services   500

Wakefern Food Corp.; Jamesburg; grocery store
500

Washington Group International Inc.; Princeton;
management services   500

New Jersey 13th District

Northeast — parts of Jersey City and Newark

Covering a long, thin swath from North Bergen to Perth Amboy along the Hudson River, Newark Bay, and Arthur Kill, the diverse 13th takes in parts of Jersey City and Newark. *(See map p. 586.)*

Hispanics, many of whom came in a wave of immigration from Central and South America that followed a loosening of restrictions in 1965, constitute a plurality, though just short of a majority. The 13th was drawn in 1992 to combine scattered Hispanic neighborhoods, and the district elected the state's first Hispanic representative, Robert Menendez, that year.

Within sight of some of the nation's best-known landmarks, including the Statue of Liberty and Manhattan's gleaming skyscrapers, the 13th now has a major landmark on its own turf—Ellis Island. After a protracted legal battle, the U.S. Supreme Court decided in 1998 that New Jersey can lay claim to 80 percent of the immigration gateway, whose lure has helped form the 13th's colorful character.

Russian, Indian, Korean, and Filipino communities add to the district's diversity and its overwhelming Democratic vote. A few Republican presidential ballots are cast by members of Cuban communities in West New York, Union City, North Bergen, and Guttenberg, though much of the Cuban population has moved to Bergen County.

The district is a transportation hub, with Port Newark-Elizabeth and a small part of Newark Liberty International Airport (shared with the 10th). Several lines, including Hudson-Bergen Light Rail, carry commuters across the district, and PATH trains, ferries, and tunnels bring passengers to and from New York. Hoboken has seen gentrification, as young professionals and financial services companies have moved across the river from Manhattan. Officials are hoping to turn long-suffering Jersey City into "Wall Street West."

Major Industry
Transportation, health care, retail, financial services.

Notable
Bayonne Bridge, the world's longest steel arch bridge from 1931 until 1977, connects Bayonne and Staten Island over the Kill Van Kull; Frank Sinatra was born and raised in Hoboken.

Election Returns

	Republican		Democratic		Other	
President 2000	39,554	25.0%	114,586	72.3%	4,338	2.7%
House 2002	16,852	18.2%	72,605	78.3%	3,274	3.5%

District Profile

Population   647,258

Total area (square miles)   74.1
   Land area (square miles)   56.7

Population per square mile   11,415.5

Counties (2000 population)

Essex (pt.)   118,133   Middlesex (pt.)   74,745
Hudson (pt.)   404,073   Union (pt.)   50,307

Cities and other areas over 10,000 (2000 population)

Bayonne (pt.)   56,465
Carteret borough   20,709
Elizabeth (pt.)   45,584
Guttenberg town   10,807
Harrison town   14,424
Hoboken   38,577
Jersey City (pt.)   118,201
Newark (pt.)   118,133
Perth Amboy   47,303
Union City   67,088
West New York town   45,768

Race and Hispanic or Latino origin*

White   32.3%
Black or African American   11.3%
American Indian or Alaska Native   0.1%
Asian   5.5%
Native Hawaiian or other Pacific Islander   0.0%
Some other race   0.6%
Hispanic or Latino origin   47.6%
Two or more races   2.4%

*As percentage of total population.

Ancestry*

Arab-Misc.   1.1%   Italian   7.3%
English   1.1%   Polish   3.8%
German   2.8%   Portuguese   3.0%
Irish   5.3%   USA/American   2.1%

*As estimated percentage of total population.

Universities and colleges, 2000–2001 enrollment

Hudson County Community College, Jersey City
   4,854
Stevens Institute of Technology, Hoboken   4,121
St. Peter's College, Jersey City   3,282

Newspapers and circulation

	District circulation	Total circulation
El Diario-La Prensa, New York City	1,679	54,695
Hackensack Record	1,620	182,466
Hoy, New York City	2,503	59,949
Jersey City Journal	28,371	42,116
Newark Star Ledger	27,012	407,706
New Brunswick Home News Tribune	6,248	65,592
New York Daily News*	16,190	723,155
New York Post	8,310	511,412
New York Times*	9,863	666,228
USA Today*	2,447	1,674,376

*See Sources and Explanations in the front of the volume.

Television stations and affiliations

New York	100%	WABC	ABC
New York	100%	WCBS	CBS
New York	100%	WEDW	PBS
New York	100%	WFME	Independent
New York	100%	WLIW	PBS
New York	100%	WLNY	Independent
New York	100%	WMBC	Independent
New York	100%	WNBC	NBC
New York	100%	WNET	PBS
New York	100%	WNJB	PBS
New York	100%	WNJN	PBS
New York	100%	WNJU	Telemundo
New York	100%	WNYE	PBS
New York	100%	WNYW	FOX
New York	100%	WPIX	WB
New York	100%	WPXN	PAX
New York	100%	WRNN	Independent
New York	100%	WTBY	Independent
New York	100%	WWOR	UPN
New York	100%	WXTV	Univision

Cable systems and subscribers

Cablevision   74,633
Comcast   58,050

Businesses and other major employers

New Jersey Transit Corp.; Newark   3,287
Horizon Healthcare Services Inc.; Newark;
   hospital/medical service plans   2,700
Automatic Data Processing Inc.; Jersey City   2,000
Lucky Brand Dungarees Stores Inc.; North Bergen;
   men's/boys' jeans   2,000
Cathedral Healthcare System Hospital; Newark   1,800
Jersey City Medical Center Inc.; Jersey City   1,770
Raritan Bay Medical Center Corp.; Perth Amboy   1,625
Fraternal Order of Police; Newark; fraternal association
   1,600
Haynes Security Inc.; Newark; security guard service
   1,500
Verizon New Jersey Inc.; Newark; telephone
   communication   1,400
Liz Claiborne Sales Inc.; North Bergen; men's/boys'
   clothing   1,300
Community Corrections Corp.; Caldwell; facilities
   support services   1,300
Union County; Elizabeth; county government   1,300
Trinitas Hospital Inc.; Elizabeth   1,265
Insurance Services Office Inc.; Jersey City; insurance
   agents and brokers 1,217
City of Newark; Newark; city management   1,200
Oil, Chemical and Atomic Workers; Bayonne; labor
   union   1,200
Bayonne Hospital; Bayonne   1,164
St. Mary Hospital Inc.; Hoboken   1,138
Anheuser-Busch Inc.; Newark; beer   1,000
Fleet NJ Community Development Corp.; Jersey City;
   equipment finance leasing   1,000
LCI Holdings Inc.; North Bergen; family clothing stores
   1,000
Marine Personnel and Provisioning Inc.; Weehawken;
   ship crew agency   1,000
Phillips Petroleum Co.; Linden; petroleum refining
   1,000
Plainbridge Inc.; Carteret; supermarkets   1,000
Air Dock Systems Inc.; North Bergen; local trucking
   900
Bayonne Board of Education; Bayonne   857
Block Drug Co.; Jersey City; denture cleaners   850

First Chicago Trust Company of New York Inc.; Jersey City; commercial bank   850

Jersey City; Jersey City; police dept.   830

City of Bayonne; Bayonne; city government   812

Columbus Hospital Inc.; Newark   800

New York and New Jersey Port Authority; Jersey City   800

Sleepmaster; Linden; mattresses and foundations   770

St. Peter's College; Jersey City   734

Bravo Cleaning Services Inc.; Piscataway; janitorial service   710

Brown Bros. Harriman and Co.; Jersey City; nondeposit trust facilities   700

Citicorp North America Inc.; Harrison; commercial bank   700

New Jersey Transit Corp.; Hoboken; railroad terminals   700

Safer Holding Corp.; Newark; investment holding company   700

Sysco Food Services; Jersey City; food supplier   700

U.S. Coast Guard; Bayonne   700

New Jersey Judiciary Courts; Jersey City   650

Hudson Group; North Bergen; magazines   648

Boilermakers Local Union; Bayonne; labor union   600

Hudson County; Jersey City; nursing care facilities   600

JP Morgan Chase Bank; Jersey City; state commercial banks   600

National Retail Systems Inc.; North Bergen; trucking   600

St. Francis Hospital Inc.; Jersey City   600

U.S. Postal Service; Kearny   600

Passaic Valley Sewerage Commission; Newark   595

Citicorp Data Systems Inc.; Weehawken; mortgage bankers   594

City of Union City; Union City; city management   593

Bon Secours New Jersey Health System Inc.; Jersey City   579

Jersey City; Jersey City; fire dept.   571

Hudson County Schools of Technology; North Bergen   550

Kmart Corp.; North Bergen; warehousing   550

Papetti's Hygrade Egg Products Inc.; Elizabeth; egg processing   550

Port Authority Trans-Hudson Corp.; Jersey City   550

Di Giorgio Corp.; Carteret; food supplier   545

U.S. Postal Service; Jersey City   532

American Institute of Certified Public Accountants (Inc.); Jersey City; accounting association   525

Lehman Commercial Paper Inc.; Jersey City; mutual funds   525

North Bergen Township; North Bergen; city management   515

City of Hoboken; Hoboken; city management   505

Coupon Service Corp.; Jersey City; direct-mail advertising   500

Essex County Welfare Board Inc.; Newark   500

Hellas Fashions Inc.; Newark; sewing contractor   500

Port Imperial Ferry Corp.; Weehawken; ferries   500

St. Gobain-Container Inc.; Carteret; glass containers   500

Top Job Personnel Inc.; Jersey City; employee leasing service   500

U.S. News and World Report; Jersey City; periodicals   500

New Mexico

New Mexico was the first part of the country to become comfortable with the idea of having two languages. It happened more than 150 years ago, and the new language was English. Because Spanish-speaking New Mexico has been present, prosperous, and numerous for so long, longtime residents of this state relate to the notion of Hispanic power differently.

New Mexico is the most Hispanic state in the nation at 42 percent, fully 10 percentage points ahead of California and Texas. Topics that generate tension in Texas and Arizona (the neighbor states to the east and west) are old news here, in part because bilingual life has long been the norm and because the Hispanic population is settled in its sense of place and relationships. There is surprisingly little demand for illegal immigrants as labor here; only seven-tenths of one percent of the undocumented workers estimated to be in the country are thought to be in New Mexico. Four times as many are thought to be in New Jersey.

What is new in many parts of New Mexico is the sensation of acceleration—faster population growth, economic development, and social reordering. A major factor prompting all these changes is the North American Free Trade Agreement and the growing trade across the Mexican border. New Mexico grew by about 150 percent in the latter half of the twentieth century and 20 percent in the 1990s alone. While that rate remains well below that of Nevada and Arizona, New Mexico is just hitting its stride. The Census Bureau now projects the Land of Enchantment will grow faster than either Nevada or Arizona in the first 25 years of the new century. In fact, New Mexico is expected to grow faster than any of the 48 contiguous states during that time and increase its numbers by half.

Unfortunately, New Mexico has not derived nearly as much prosperity from its growth as its neighbor states to date. The state ranked fortieth in average annual pay in 2001 and forty-eighth in per capita income in 2000. Nearly 19 percent of the population here lived in what the Census Bureau considered poverty in 2001—the highest percentage in the country.

Recent years have also brought growing pains of other kinds. Forest fires have been among the worst in the state's history, and the jewel in the state's high-tech crown, the legendary nuclear laboratories at Los Alamos, was beset with problems over security. Still, the underlying prospects for New Mexico are excellent, given the coming generation's likely focus on trade, energy, and the empowerment of a new Hispanic power structure.

New Mexico had a pitched partisan battle over redistricting in 2001. The Democratic legislature passed a congressional map that would have made the 2nd District friendlier to their party by making it majority Hispanic. That would have given a Democrat a chance to win there, especially given the retirement of 11-term GOP veteran Joe Skeen. The plan needed the signature of Republican governor Gary Johnson, so the Democrats added an incentive for him. They made the marginal 1st District more Republican, conferring long-term security on incumbent Heather Wilson.

The basic design of the proposed map was a three-slice pie with each slice pointing into Albuquerque, the population center that is fast approaching half a million residents (there are already more than 700,000 in its metro area). But Johnson did not take the bait, preferring to risk the loss of both Republican districts rather than hand one over without a fight. Following his veto, a state court took over and produced a map with few changes in the lines from the 1990s. The court preferred keeping the 1st focused on Albuquerque to the creation of a majority Hispanic district in the 2nd. So the new 1st District retained the bulk of Bernalillo County (Albuquerque), all of Torrance County to the east, and small-but-populous sections of surrounding Sandoval, Santa Fe, and Valencia Counties.

The new 2nd, incorporating most of the state, remains one of the largest districts in the country and actually grew a bit larger in the remapping. It now reaches farther up the Arizona line to take in all of Cibola County and a portion of McKinley County to the north. Its biggest population centers are Las Cruces and Carlsbad, whose counties (Dona Ana County with about 175,000 people and Eddy County with about 52,000) sit on the Mexican border. Nonetheless, the new 2nd is somewhat less Hispanic than before (43 percent versus 48 percent).

The new 3rd was much like the old, retaining most of the counties of Sandoval and Santa Fe, along with the western and northern communities of Gallup and Farmington. It also ran across the entire top third of the state to entail Las Vegas (New Mexico version) and Tucumcari and tracked south along the Texas state line, taking in the city of Clovis and four of the five border counties.

In fall 2002 the 1st and 3rd reelected incumbents Wilson and Tom Udall, a Democrat. respectively. The new 2nd, considered competitive for both parties, was won by a Republican, Ed Pearce, who flew for the Air Force in Vietnam and ran an oilfield services company. But if Johnson's veto kept the state's delegation Republican for a time, dispersing

NEW MEXICO

Districts established January 2, 2002, for elections first held in 2002.

3 members

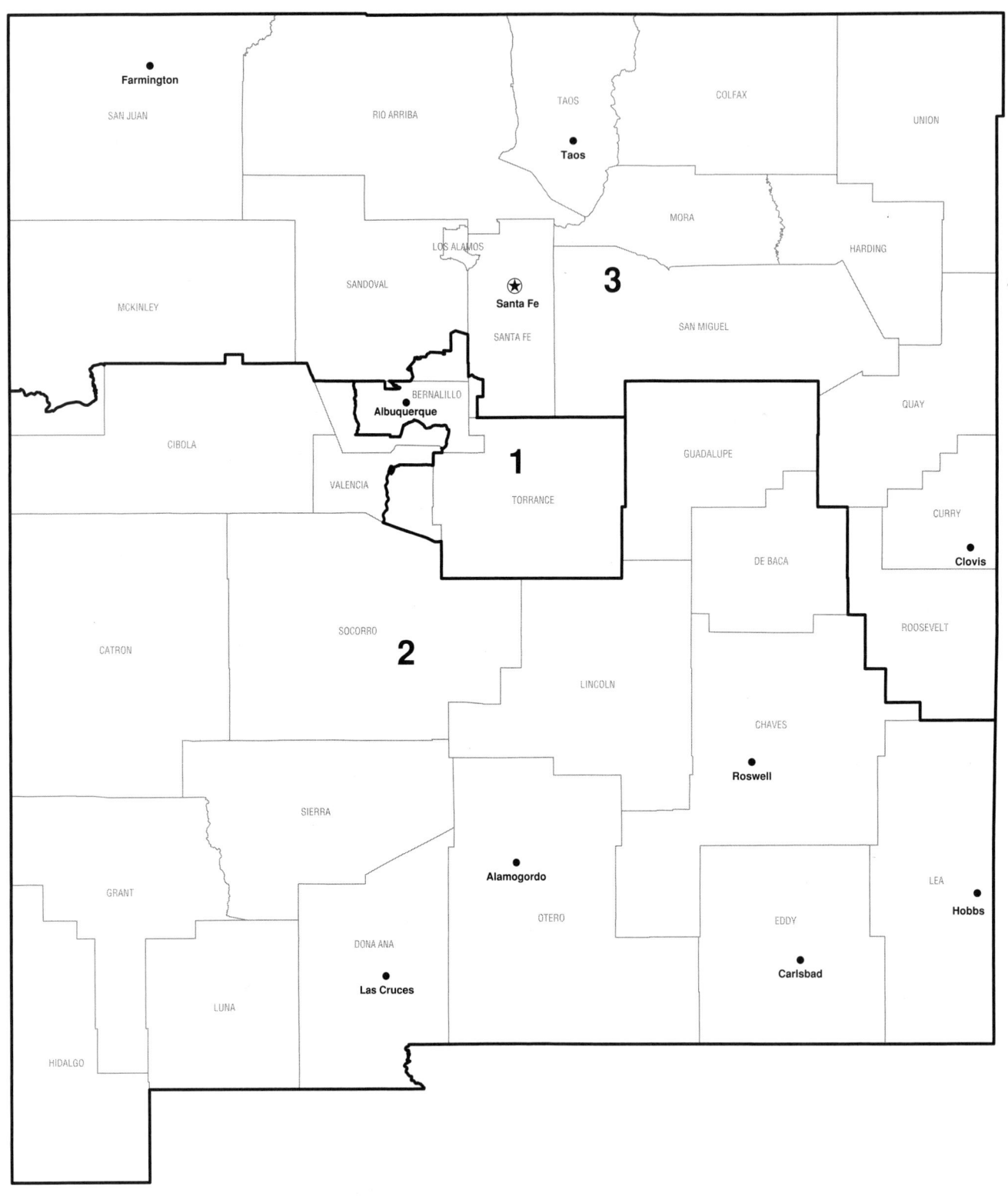

the Hispanic vote may mean that whites fall into minority status in two or even three districts before long.

New Mexico has been one of the Democrats' better territories in the West. They held both Senate seats from the New Deal years until 1972, when Republican Pete Domenici began his multi-decade run. Both Senate seats were Republican from 1976 until 1982, when Democrat Jeff Bingaman upset the incumbent. He and Domenici thereafter formed one of the longest running and successful bipartisan tandems in Senate history. As of 2003 they held the chair and ranking member's seats on the Energy and Natural Resources Committee.

From 1946 to 2002, Democrats won the governorship a dozen times to Republicans' nine. These races have tended to be close: only twice since World War II did the winner's share exceed 55 percent of the vote. In 2003 the governor was Democrat Bill Richardson, a former representative who served as Bill Clinton's U.N. ambassador and secretary of energy. Richardson, whose mother was Mexican, has been mentioned as a prospect for the national ticket.

In presidential voting, this state's unique mix of Hispanic voters with largely rural Anglo populists has managed somehow to march in almost perfect step with the national will. From the 1930s to 2000, New Mexico voted for the winner of the national popular vote every time except in 1976, when it went for Republican Gerald R. Ford by a narrow margin. In 2000 the much-inspected tally here was even closer than Florida's (although it received far less attention): a whopping 366 votes in favor of Al Gore.

New Mexico also has developed one of the strongest state-level third-party movements of recent years, challenging Democrats for environment-minded voters in several elections. Green Party nominee Ralph Nader received 3.5 percent of the presidential vote in 2000 while the Greens' nominee in the 1st District received 6.4 percent.

Table 1   Population

District	Population	Population under 18	Voting-age population	Median age	Male*	Female*
1	606,400	156,200	450,200	35.1	49.0	51.0
2	606,406	175,295	431,111	34.2	49.4	50.6
3	606,240	177,079	429,161	34.3	49.1	50.9
State	1,819,046	508,574	1,310,472	34.6	49.2	50.8

*As percentage of total population.

Table 2   Voting-Age Persons by Race/Hispanic or Latino Origin

District	White*	Black or African American*	American Indian or Alaska Native*	Asian*	Other or multirace*	Hispanic or Latino*
1	52.8	2.3	2.8	1.9	1.5	38.8
2	49.5	1.6	4.4	0.6	1.2	42.5
3	45.9	1.1	16.3	0.9	1.2	34.6
State	49.5	1.7	7.8	1.2	1.4	38.7

*As percentage of voting-age population.

Table 3   Voting-Age Population by Age Groups

District	18 to 24*	25 to 44*	45 to 64*	Over 64*
1	13.6	40.7	30.4	15.3
2	14.3	37.2	30.2	18.2
3	12.8	40.2	32.0	15.1
State	13.6	39.4	30.9	16.2

*As percentage of voting-age population.

Table 4   Income and Occupation

District	Median family income	Families in poverty*	White collar†	Blue collar†	Service†	Farm†
1	$45,837	10.4	65.2	18.9	15.8	0.2
2	$33,637	17.9	52.9	26.7	18.4	2.0
3	$39,673	15.2	60.3	21.7	16.9	1.0
State	$39,425	14.5	59.9	22.2	17.0	1.0

*As percentage of all families.   †As percentage of employed workers 16 years and over.

Table 5   Education: School Years Completed

District	Less than grade 9*	Grades 9–12 no diploma*	High school diploma no college*	Some college*	College bachelor's degree or higher*
1	6.3	9.8	25.2	29.2	29.5
2	13.1	13.7	28.2	28.0	16.9
3	8.5	12.3	26.4	29.2	23.7
State	9.3	11.9	26.6	28.8	23.5

*As percentage of persons age 25 and over.

Table 6   Housing and Residential Patterns

District	Median home value	Owner occupied*	Renter occupied*	Urban†	Rural†
1	$120,100	65.4	34.6	91.3	8.7
2	$67,300	72.0	28.0	71.0	29.0
3	$96,500	72.9	27.1	62.8	37.2
State	$94,600	70.0	30.0	75.0	25.0

*As percentage of occupied housing units.   †As percentage of total population.

New Mexico 1st District

Central — Albuquerque

Built around Albuquerque, New Mexico's largest city, the 1st is the only urban district in a sparsely populated, desert state. Since the Manhattan Project set the region on a technology-driven course in the 1940s, Albuquerque has grown from 35,000 people before World War II to more than 440,000 in 2000.

Sandia National Laboratories—born out of the Manhattan Project—is the basis for a steady defense industry. Sandia, which employs 7,200 workers, coordinates with the two other major employers in the district—the University of New Mexico and Kirtland Air Force Base—to conduct nuclear and national security research. Sandia's success has contributed to a surge in computer, laser, and other high-tech companies in the area. The city's concentration of technology firms draws a disproportionate number of PhD's to the area.

Although the 1st became slightly more conservative as a result of redistricting following the 2000 census, the large government workforce and predominantly Hispanic South Valley provide registered Democrats with a slight edge. Democrats hold most local offices and the district's Hispanics, who make up 42.6 percent of the population, overwhelmingly favor Democrats. The Green Party also makes a strong showing, sometimes winning double-digit percentages in congressional races. But the GOP has held the congressional seat since its creation in 1968; the area traditionally sends fiscally conservative, defense-oriented moderate Republicans to Congress. Much of the GOP vote comes from the mainly white, upper-middle-class Northeast Heights section of Albuquerque.

Major Industry

Higher education, scientific research, government.

Notable

Albuquerque's annual International Balloon Fiesta is the world's largest hot air balloon event; the National Atomic Museum in Albuquerque is owned by the Department of Energy and operated by Sandia Labs.

Election Returns

	Republican		Democratic		Other	
President 2000	103,770	47.0%	106,572	48.3%	10,385	4.7%
House 2002	95,711	55.3%	77,234	44.7%		

District Profile

Population   606,400

Total area (square miles)   4,720.0
Land area (square miles)   4,716.5

Population per square mile   128.6

Counties (2000 population)
Bernalillo (pt.)   543,212   Torrance   16,911
Sandoval (pt.)   16,916   Valencia (pt.)   24,717
Santa Fe (pt.)   4,644

Cities and other areas over 10,000 (2000 population)
Albuquerque (pt.)   442,365
North Valley CDP   11,923
South Valley CDP (pt.)   39,060

Race and Hispanic or Latino origin*
White   48.5%
Black or African American   2.3%
American Indian or Alaska Native   2.9%
Asian   1.7%
Native Hawaiian or other Pacific Islander   0.1%
Some other race   0.2%
Hispanic or Latino origin   42.6%
Two or more races   1.6%

*As percentage of total population.

Ancestry*
English   7.0%   Norwegian   1.1%
French   1.9%   Polish   1.2%
German   9.6%   Scotch-Irish   1.4%
Irish   6.9%   Scottish   1.6%
Italian   2.8%   USA/American   3.6%

*As estimated percentage of total population.

Universities and colleges, 2000–2001 enrollment
Albuquerque Technical Vocational Institute, Albuquerque   17,265
Art Center, Albuquerque   297
Century University, Albuquerque   921
ITT Technical Institute, Albuquerque   379
Metropolitan College of Court Reporting, Albuquerque 265
National American University, Albuquerque   579
Parks College, Albuquerque   722
Pima Medical Institute, Albuquerque   385
Southwestern Indian Polytechnic Institute, Albuquerque 304
University of New Mexico, Albuquerque   23,670
University of New Mexico-Valencia County, Los Lunas 1,514
University of Phoenix, Albuquerque   3,261

Newspapers and circulation

	District circulation	Total circulation
Albuquerque Journal	73,728	109,672
Albuquerque Journal/Tribune (Sunday)	89,151	126,856
Albuquerque Tribune	15,416	17,006
*USA Today**	2,948	1,674,376

*See Sources and Explanations in the front of the volume.

Television stations and affiliations
Albuquerque-Santa Fe	100%	KASA	FOX
Albuquerque-Santa Fe	100%	KASY	UPN
Albuquerque-Santa Fe	100%	KAZQ	Independent
Albuquerque-Santa Fe	100%	KBIM	CBS
Albuquerque-Santa Fe	100%	KCHF	Independent
Albuquerque-Santa Fe	100%	KENW	PBS
Albuquerque-Santa Fe	100%	KHFT	UPN
Albuquerque-Santa Fe	100%	KLUZ	Univision
Albuquerque-Santa Fe	100%	KNAT	Independent
Albuquerque-Santa Fe	100%	KNME	PBS
Albuquerque-Santa Fe	100%	KOAT	ABC
Albuquerque-Santa Fe	100%	KOBF	NBC
Albuquerque-Santa Fe	100%	KOBR	NBC
Albuquerque-Santa Fe	100%	KOB	NBC
Albuquerque-Santa Fe	100%	KOCT	ABC
Albuquerque-Santa Fe	100%	KOVT	ABC
Albuquerque-Santa Fe	100%	KREZ	CBS
Albuquerque-Santa Fe	100%	KRPV	Independent
Albuquerque-Santa Fe	100%	KRQE	CBS

Cable systems and subscribers
Comcast   106,244

Military installations, September 2001
Kirtland Air Force Base, Albuquerque   6,662
Albuquerque Armed Forces Reserve Center (Jenkins), Albuquerque   734

Businesses and other major employers
Sandia Corp.; Albuquerque; nuclear research   7,200
Presbyterian Healthcare Services Hospital; Albuquerque 7,000
City of Albuquerque; Albuquerque; city management 3,500
University of New Mexico; Albuquerque   2,500

University of New Mexico Hospital; Albuquerque
2,375

Lovelace Health Systems Inc.; Albuquerque; health
maintenance organization   1,967

Philips Semiconductors Inc.; Albuquerque; industrial
process control instruments   1,500

Albuquerque Technical-Vocational Institutes;
Albuquerque   1,400

U.S. Veterans Hospital; Albuquerque   1,400

Wal-Mart Stores Inc.; Albuquerque; department stores
1,350

America Online Inc.; Albuquerque; Internet services
1,300

Honeywell International Inc.; Albuquerque; aircraft
1,240

City of Albuquerque; Albuquerque; police dept.   1,066

St. Joseph Health Care System; Albuquerque   1,000

U.S. Dept. of Energy; Albuquerque   1,000

Voicestream Wireless Corp.; Albuquerque;
radiotelephone communication   1,000

Qwest Corp.; Albuquerque; local telephone
communications   900

U.S. Postal Service; Albuquerque   900

Albuquerque Publishing Co.; Albuquerque; newspaper
805

Ethicon Inc.; Albuquerque; medical supplies   800

University of California; Los Alamos; health association
800

Pueblo of Sandia; Albuquerque; casino   750

Regency Rehabilitation Management and Consulting
Inc.; Albuquerque; nursing care facilities   750

Flagstone Hospitality Management; Albuquerque;
motels   703

Bernalillo County; Albuquerque; county government
700

ClientLogic Corp.; Albuquerque; personal service agents
700

Levi Strauss and Co.; Albuquerque; jeans   700

Victoria's Secret Stores Inc.; Albuquerque; lingerie   700

Presbyterian Health Plan Inc.; Albuquerque; medical
service plans   670

ARCA Community Programs; Albuquerque; individual
and family services   600

PNM Resources Inc.; Albuquerque; electrical services
600

Thomas and Betts Corp.; Albuquerque; pyrometers,
industrial process type   600

Express Scripts Inc.; Albuquerque; medical service plans
556

Public Service Company of New Mexico; Albuquerque;
electric services   550

AT&T Network Systems Inc.; Albuquerque;
local/long-distance telephone   500

Green Party of New Mexico; Placitas; environmental
research   500

New Mexico 2nd District

South — Las Cruces, Roswell

Before hosting the first atomic bomb explosion in 1945,
the mostly rural 2nd, covering the southern half of the
state, looked like the old American West. Since then, the
area has attracted nuclear research and waste facilities to the
Chihuahua Desert's deep salt beds and remote location. The
first permanent underground low-level nuclear waste reposi-
tory opened in abandoned salt mines near Carlsbad in 1999.

Towns in the 2nd have built a stable economy on traditional Western industries: copper and lead mining in the
Mexican Highlands along the Arizona border, and oil and
gas, as well as cattle and sheep ranching, in the southeastern
corner of the state, dubbed Little Texas after the Texans who
settled the region in the early twentieth century. The northern New Mexico technology industry has spilled over into
the 2nd, supported by New Mexico State and other universities. Severe water shortages have prevented large-scale industrial development and larger corporate farming, although the
northern part of the district is a major producer of pistachios.

Beginning in the 1970s, ranchers and conservative
Democrats steered away from a long liberal tradition.
Democrats hold the vast majority of local offices, but the
district is now competitive at the national level.

Major Industry
Agriculture, mining, oil and gas production.

Notable
White Sands National Monument is the world's largest
gypsum dune field; Roswell hosts an annual UFO festival
near the site where a UFO allegedly crashed in 1947; Ted
Turner, one of the nation's largest private landowners, owns
more than 1.1 million acres in New Mexico, much of it in
the 2nd.

Election Returns

	Republican		Democratic		Other	
President 2000	96,161	53.8%	76,868	43.0%	5,667	3.2%
House 2002	79,631	56.3%	61,916	43.7%	82	

District Profile

Population   606,406

Total area (square miles)   69,598.4
   Land area (square miles)   69,492.9

Population per square mile   8.7

Counties (2000 population)

Bernalillo (pt.)	3,752	Hidalgo	5,932
Catron	3,543	Lea	55,511
Chaves	61,382	Lincoln	19,411
Cibola	25,595	Luna	25,016
De Baca	2,240	McKinley (pt.)	6,921
Dona Ana	174,682	Otero	62,298
Eddy	51,658	Sierra	13,270
Grant	31,002	Socorro	18,078
Guadalupe	4,680	Valencia (pt.)	41,435

Cities and other areas over 10,000 (2000 population)
Alamogordo   35,582
Artesia   10,692
Carlsbad   25,625
Deming   14,116
Hobbs   28,657
Las Cruces   74,267

Los Lunas village (pt.)   10,034
Roswell   45,293
Silver City town   10,545
Sunland Park   13,309

Race and Hispanic or Latino origin*
White   44.3%
Black or African American   1.6%
American Indian or Alaska Native   4.8%
Asian   0.5%
Native Hawaiian or other Pacific Islander   0.0%
Some other race   0.2%
Hispanic or Latino origin   47.3%
Two or more races   1.2%

*As percentage of total population.

Ancestry*
English 5.9%		Italian 1.3%	
French 1.4%		Scotch-Irish 1.2%	
German 7.4%		Scottish 1.1%	
Irish 5.7%		USA/American 5.4%	

*As estimated percentage of total population.

Universities and colleges, 2000–2001 enrollment
College of the Southwest, Hobbs   508
Eastern New Mexico University, Roswell   2,980
Eastern New Mexico University, Ruidoso   592
New Mexico Institute of Mining and Technology,
  Socorro   1,549
New Mexico Junior College, Hobbs   3,200
New Mexico Military Institute, Roswell   451
New Mexico State University, Alamogordo   1,738
New Mexico State University, Carlsbad   1,051
New Mexico State University, Grants   575
New Mexico State University, Las Cruces   14,958
New Mexico State University-Dona Ana, Las Cruces
  4,640
Western New Mexico University, Silver City   2,669

Newspapers and circulation
	District circulation	Total circulation
Alamogordo Daily News	7,235	7,259
Albuquerque Journal	11,562	109,672
Albuquerque Journal/Tribune (Sunday)	12,341	126,856
Carlsbad Current-Argus	8,266	8,266
El Paso Times	6,949	74,595
Gallup Independent	1,541	15,519
Hobbs News-Sun	9,261	9,261
Las Cruces Sun-News	21,995	22,121
Lubbock Avalanche Journal	1,502	54,669
*USA Today**	2,899	1,674,376

*See Sources and Explanations in the front of the volume.

Television stations and affiliations
Albuquerque-Santa Fe	93%	KASA	FOX
Albuquerque-Santa Fe	93%	KASY	UPN
Albuquerque-Santa Fe	93%	KAZQ	Independent
Albuquerque-Santa Fe	93%	KBIM	CBS
Albuquerque-Santa Fe	93%	KCHF	Independent
Albuquerque-Santa Fe	93%	KENW	PBS
Albuquerque-Santa Fe	93%	KHFT	UPN
Albuquerque-Santa Fe	93%	KLUZ	Univision
Albuquerque-Santa Fe	93%	KNAT	Independent
Albuquerque-Santa Fe	93%	KNME	PBS
Albuquerque-Santa Fe	93%	KOAT	ABC
Albuquerque-Santa Fe	93%	KOBF	NBC
Albuquerque-Santa Fe	93%	KOBR	NBC
Albuquerque-Santa Fe	93%	KOB	NBC
Albuquerque-Santa Fe	93%	KOCT	ABC
Albuquerque-Santa Fe	93%	KOVT	ABC
Albuquerque-Santa Fe	93%	KREZ	CBS
Albuquerque-Santa Fe	93%	KRPV	Independent
Albuquerque-Santa Fe	93%	KRQE	CBS
El Paso, TX	5%	KCOS	PBS
El Paso, TX	5%	KDBC	CBS
El Paso, TX	5%	KFOX	FOX
El Paso, TX	5%	KINT	Univision
El Paso, TX	5%	KRWG	PBS
El Paso, TX	5%	KSCE	Independent
El Paso, TX	5%	KTSM	NBC
El Paso, TX	5%	KVIA	ABC
Odessa-Midland, TX	5%	KMID	ABC
Odessa-Midland, TX	5%	KMLM	Independent
Odessa-Midland, TX	5%	KOCV	PBS
Odessa-Midland, TX	5%	KOSA	CBS
Odessa-Midland, TX	5%	KPEJ	FOX, UPN
Odessa-Midland, TX	5%	KWAB	NBC
Odessa-Midland, TX	5%	KWES	NBC

Cable systems and subscribers
Cable ONE   14,533
Chaparral Cable Co.   795
Charter   19,232
City TV Cable   1,172
Classic   3,216
Comcast   50,809
Time Warner   912
U.S. Cable   22,591

Military installations, September 2001
White Sands Missile Range, Las Cruces   5,916
Holloman Air Force Base, Alamogordo   4,775

Businesses and other major employers
New Mexico State University; Las Cruces   4,500
Memorial Medical Center; Las Cruces   1,350
Mescalero Apache Tribe; Mescalero Native American
  reservation   1,239
Border Foods Inc.; Deming; chili pepper/powder
  1,100
City of Las Cruces; Las Cruces; city management   964
Chino Mines Co.; Hurley; copper ore mining   800
Stream International Inc.; Silver City; personal service
  agents   750
Hobbs Municipal Schools; Hobbs   695
Westinghouse TRU Solutions; Carlsbad; education
  consultant   680
Eastern New Mexico Medical Center; Roswell   670
IMC Global Operations Inc.; Carlsbad; minerals   660
Honeywell Technology Solutions Inc.; Las Cruces;
  satellite earth stations   650
Washington Group International Inc.; Carlsbad;
  radioactive waste disposal   640
National Aeronautics and Space Admin.; Las Cruces;
  space research and technology   621

Wal-Mart Stores Inc.; Las Cruces; department stores
600
Honeywell International Inc.; Las Cruces; space
propulsion units and parts   600
TCIM Services; Las Cruces; telemarketing   567
New Mexico Institute of Mining and Technology;
Socorro   550
Phelps Dodge Corp.; Playas; primary copper   550
New Mexico Technology Group; Las Cruces; facilities
support services   500
Phelps Dodge Tyrone Inc.; Tyrone; copper ore   500
Mississippi Potash Inc.; Carlsbad; minerals   500
New Mexcio Dept. of Health; Carlsbad   500
Wal-Mart Stores Inc.; Alamogordo; department stores
500

New Mexico 3rd District

North — Santa Fe, Rio Rancho, Farmington

Since artist Georgia O'Keeffe began painting northern
New Mexico in 1929, the 3rd District's breathtaking scenery
and unique Spanish and Native American heritage have attracted thousands of artists and beauty seekers. Today, art
galleries and ski resorts still attract tourists, while an influx
of retirees made the district the most rapidly growing part
of the state in the 1990s.

But the 3rd is a district of extremes. Alongside the bountiful art trade is extraordinary poverty. Gallup, in McKinley
County, boasts the most millionaires per capita in the world,
while the county itself remains one of the poorest in the nation. Large Native American populations in the northwest
struggle with modest farming and ranching ventures in the
same area that provides lofty incomes for oil and gas producers. Many western reservations are plagued with alcoholism,
while Rio Arriba County in the north has the highest drug
mortality rate in the nation.

Hispanics and Native Americans—alongside a wealthy,
liberal base in the state capital of Santa Fe—give Democrats
a two-to-one edge in voter registration. Conservative pockets
exist in areas such as Rio Rancho, where Intel employs about
6,500 workers; Los Alamos, where the A-bomb was developed during World War II; and among energy producers in
San Juan County in the district's northwest.

Major Industry
State government, ranching, farming, tourism.

Notable
Santa Fe, the nation's second-oldest city, was founded in
1607, 13 years before the Pilgrims landed at Plymouth Rock;
roughly 100 tribes show their work at the Santa Fe Indian
Market each August; the Aztec Ruins National Monument
in Aztec features structures and artifacts from the 1100s and
1200s; Camel Rock, near Tesuque, is a natural sandstone
formation that the elements have eroded into the shape of a
camel.

Election Returns

	Republican		Democratic		Other	
President 2000	86,004	43.3%	102,809	51.8%	9,676	4.9%
House 2002			122,921	100.0%		

District Profile

Population   606,240

Total area (square miles)   47,270.9
Land area (square miles)   47,146.1

Population per square mile   12.9

Counties (2000 population)

Bernalillo (pt.) 9,714	Rio Arriba 41,190
Colfax 14,189	Roosevelt 18,018
Curry 45,044	Sandoval (pt.) 72,992
Harding 810	San Juan 113,801
Los Alamos 18,343	San Miguel 30,126
McKinley (pt.) 67,877	Santa Fe (pt.) 124,648
Mora 5,180	Taos 29,979
Quay 10,155	Union 4,174

Cities and other areas over 10,000 (2000 population)

Clovis 32,667	Los Alamos CDP 11,909
Farmington 37,844	Portales 11,131
Gallup 20,209	Rio Rancho (pt.) 46,701
Las Vegas 14,565	Santa Fe 62,203

Race and Hispanic or Latino origin*
White   41.4%
Black or African American   1.1%
American Indian or Alaska Native   18.9%
Asian   0.7%
Native Hawaiian or other Pacific Islander   0.1%
Some other race   0.1%
Hispanic or Latino origin   36.3%
Two or more races   1.4%

*As percentage of total population.

Ancestry*

English 6.0%	Italian 1.8%
French 1.6%	Scotch-Irish 1.2%
German 7.4%	Scottish 1.3%
Irish 5.6%	USA/American 3.9%

*As estimated percentage of total population.

Universities and colleges, 2000–2001 enrollment
Clovis Community College, Clovis   2,895
College of Santa Fe, Santa Fe   1,629
Crownpoint Institute of Technology, Crownpoint   841
Eastern New Mexico University, Portales   3,564
Luna Vocational Technical Institute, Las Vegas   973
Mesa Technical College, Tucumcari   465
New Mexico Highlands University, Las Vegas   3,275
Northern New Mexico Community College, Espanola
681
San Juan College, Farmington   4,282
Santa Fe Community College, Santa Fe   3,606
St. John's College, Santa Fe   491
University of New Mexico, Gallup   2,594
University of New Mexico, Los Alamos   792
University of New Mexico, Taos   1,028

Newspapers and circulation

	District circulation	Total circulation
Albuquerque Journal	24,562	109,672
Albuquerque Journal/Tribune (Sunday)	25,462	126,856

Clovis News Journal	7,516	8,027
Farmington Daily Times	16,561	17,139
Gallup Independent	8,346	15,519
Santa Fe New Mexican	22,156	24,956
Taos News	8,901	9,146
USA Today*	1,801	1,674,376

*See Sources and Explanations in the front of the volume.

Television stations and affiliations

Albuquerque-Santa Fe	78%	KASA	FOX
Albuquerque-Santa Fe	78%	KASY	UPN
Albuquerque-Santa Fe	78%	KAZQ	Independent
Albuquerque-Santa Fe	78%	KBIM	CBS
Albuquerque-Santa Fe	78%	KCHF	Independent
Albuquerque-Santa Fe	78%	KENW	PBS
Albuquerque-Santa Fe	78%	KHFT	UPN
Albuquerque-Santa Fe	78%	KLUZ	Univision
Albuquerque-Santa Fe	78%	KNAT	Independent
Albuquerque-Santa Fe	78%	KNME	PBS
Albuquerque-Santa Fe	78%	KOAT	ABC
Albuquerque-Santa Fe	78%	KOBF	NBC
Albuquerque-Santa Fe	78%	KOBR	NBC
Albuquerque-Santa Fe	78%	KOB	NBC
Albuquerque-Santa Fe	78%	KOCT	ABC
Albuquerque-Santa Fe	78%	KOVT	ABC
Albuquerque-Santa Fe	78%	KREZ	CBS
Albuquerque-Santa Fe	78%	KRPV	Independent
Albuquerque-Santa Fe	78%	KRQE	CBS
Amarillo, TX	22%	KACV	PBS
Amarillo, TX	22%	KAMR	NBC
Amarillo, TX	22%	KCIT	FOX
Amarillo, TX	22%	KFDA	CBS
Amarillo, TX	22%	KVIH	ABC
Amarillo, TX	22%	KVII	ABC

Cable systems and subscribers

Cable ONE 8,282
Charter 1,853
Citizens Utility 5,618
Comcast 79,398
Cox 10,050
U.S. Cable 4,832

Military installations, September 2001

Cannon Air Force Base, Clovis 3,718
Onate Complex Training Site, Sante Fe 796

Businesses and other major employers

PPG Industries Inc.; Santa Fe; paints and allied products 35,600

Intel Corp.; Rio Rancho; semiconductors 6,500

Johnson Controls World Services Inc.; Los Alamos; automobile seats 1,500

Central Consolidated School District; Kirtland 1,230

Wal-Mart Stores Inc.; Gallup; department stores 1,200

St. Vincent Hospital Inc.; Santa Fe 1,023

New Mexico Dept. of Health; Las Vegas 1,000

New Mexico Dept. of Highway and Transportation; Santa Fe 800

San Juan Regional Medical Center Inc.; Farmington 787

New Jersey Dept. of Corrections; Santa Fe 750

Santa Fe Community College; Santa Fe 750

Bank of America Corp.; Rio Rancho; credit union administration 700

U.S. Postal Service; Taos Ski Valley 700

Presbyterian Healthcare Services Hospital; Clovis 645

New Mexico Dept. of Children, Youth, and Families; Santa Fe 635

San Felipe Hollywood Casino; Algodones; casino 600

JC Penney Corp.; Albuquerque; catalog sales 600

Indian Health Service Clinic; Gallup 589

Arizona Public Service Co.; Fruitland; electric services 566

PNM Resources Inc.; Waterflow; gas transmission, distribution 550

Indian Health Service Hospital; Shiprock 525

New Mexico Office of Cultural Affairs; Santa Fe 520

Taos Municipal Schools; Taos 500

Wal-Mart Stores Inc.; Clovis; department stores 500

New York

The events of September 11, 2001, had many repercussions in American life, not the least of which was the return of New York to the forefront of the national consciousness. The name of New York has been a powerful invocation before, but now it calls up the images of Ground Zero that were seared upon the world's imagination that autumn, along with all the emotions, fears, and resolve attached to the numbers 9-11.

It seems self-evident that the terrorists chose New York for the symbolic value of the World Trade Center, the twin towers standing for a national pride and a global economics they despised. New York has long been an international symbol for business, for Western culture in its American permutation, for Americanism in general. Some of this is a media creation, of course, built around the tall buildings and the Statue of Liberty. Some is based in the city's image as the epitome of worldliness and urbane sophistication, free minds, and free will. For those who despise such values, nothing could be more galling than New York. All this matters again in a special way since September 11, the day the nation forgot its resentments about the city of Wall Street. After decades of watching the national energy flow from other cities, including far-flung rivals once ignored, the Big Apple was once again the center of all. That is why the city remained on a high alert for fresh acts of terror for years afterward, whatever the alert level was for the country as a whole.

New York first asserted its primacy among the United States in the early 1800s. In the decade of the Louisiana Purchase and the expedition of Lewis and Clark, the big growth story in people terms was New York. Led by the bustling commercial communities of Manhattan and Brooklyn with their piers and wharves on New York Harbor, the Empire State showed just how fast the settled parts of the fledgling nation could grow. When the first Congress met in 1789 in what is now called Federal Hall, a customs house for the Port of New York, there were only a third of a million New Yorkers. By 1800 there would be nearly 600,000, and no one could fail to notice. At the time, both Virginia and Pennsylvania were still bigger. But the census of 1810 found nearly a million New Yorkers, and the rivals were left in the dust. By 1830 the state would have almost two million, and almost a sixth of the burgeoning nation would be living here in just one state.

Grand waves of population growth were to follow: nearly 800,000 in the decade before the Civil War; more than 1.25 million in the 1890s; close to 2 million in the decade after 1900 and as many again in the 1920s. Most of this was driven by the extraordinary engine of New York City, a magnet to Americans born elsewhere and an almost mystical attraction for foreigners. The city has known boom times and bust, but it has always weathered the latter far better than most thanks to its enormous economic diversity, its position atop the economic food chain, and its nearly always open window on the world.

Nonetheless, the latter half of the twentieth century was a period of adjustment. Rivals had arisen. The wars and the New Deal made Washington, D.C., begin to shed its historic southern shell and grow (by 2000 it would be, with Baltimore and environs, the nation's fourth most populous metropolitan area). Farther away, but more bothersome, was Los Angeles, which supplanted Chicago as the second largest city and metropolitan area after World War II. More consequential, Los Angeles rose from being the movie capital to being the center of the entertainment industry generally—appropriating one of Gotham's most glamorous roles. Los Angeles also stole the Brooklyn Dodgers baseball franchise, which seemed somehow a greater enormity than the loss of the New York Giants to San Francisco.

But Los Angeles was only a subset of the larger California problem. California first surpassed New York in population in the mid-1960s, when both had about 17 million people. But while California was climbing to 20 million and beyond in the 1970s, New York state was actually losing population for the first time ever, closing the decade with roughly 700,000 fewer people than it had at the beginning. The upstate cities of Schenectady and Albany, Rochester, and Buffalo were hemorrhaging population, as were the still smaller cities and towns of the old Empire State. Growth did not resume until well into the 1980s, and the state did not return to its previous peak (18.2 million in the census of 1970) until late in the 1990s. In the meantime, yet another rival arose. Texas, growing fast, caught New York right around the 18 million mark in the early 1990s—and kept right on going. In 2000 Texas had the larger population, 20.8 million to 19 million. If present trends and growth rates continue, New York could fall to fourth place, behind Florida, sometime in the second decade after 2000.

For a time in the 1970s the city and its region seemed to be suffering from vertigo. The fiscal crisis of mid-decade, and the cold shoulder from President Gerald R. Ford that prompted the tabloid headline "Ford to City: Drop Dead," seemed to leave Gotham in free fall. It took the more generous impulses of Jimmy Carter's administration (Carter was nominated at the first national nominating convention to be held in New York since the 1950s) to put the city back on track. But it took the boom times on Wall Street in the

NEW YORK

Districts established June 5, 2002, for elections first held in 2002.

29 members

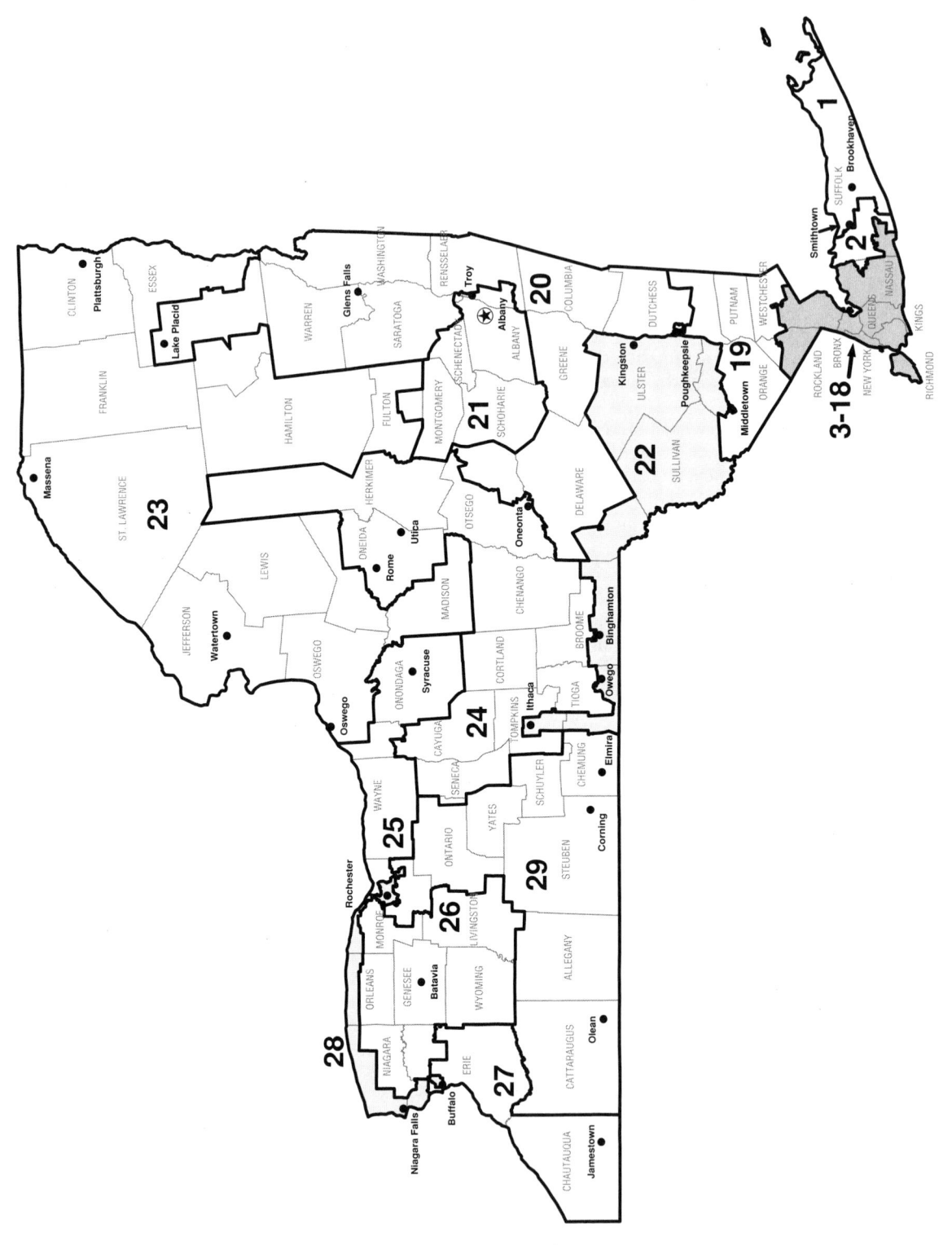

1980s to put the city back on top. Since that conspicuous recovery the city has again known slippage—particularly after the Dow Jones took a spill in 1987, when the tech boom went bust in 2000, and again with the terror attacks of 2001. But these dips have been regarded more as rough spots than reversals. The city's many neighborhoods are broadly, if not universally, in an improved condition today. The statewide incidence of poverty (13.4 percent statistically, tenth nationally) owes as much to downturns in outstate areas as it does to the five boroughs. And real New Yorkers never lost their presumptive faith. When he was mayor in the 1990s, Rudy Giuliani liked to acknowledge visitors from Albany (the "capital of New York") and Washington, D.C. (the "capital of the United States") before welcoming all to New York City, the "capital of the world."

Of course the other source of greatness in New York has been its historic ethnic diversity. From the earliest days as a New Amsterdam, the city has been the great intake valve of the nation, the most common first landfall for immigrants. While some groups tended to step only lightly here and move on, others stayed and started dynasties that have lasted many generations. That is why the notion of an emblematic New Yorker has changed many times from a Dutchman to a Yankee to an Irishman, an Italian, a Jew, a Puerto Rican, a rapper from Harlem. To this day, the expression "New York Ticket" refers to a political slate that is balanced among many, if not all, ethnic constituencies. To some, this suggests a politics short on principle and preoccupied with distributing power. But such can also be called the essence of democracy in the present of varied demography. Today's New York state is 17 percent African American, the tenth blackest state in the union and blacker than any other state north of the Mason-Dixon. It is also 15 percent Hispanic, the eighth highest percentage in the country. And the allure for immigrants continues. In 2000 the United States legally admitted about 850,000 immigrants, and New York was the metro area most often cited as their intended residence. More than 10 percent wanted to stay where the Statue of Liberty stays.

Throughout the twentieth century, New York had either the largest or second largest basket of electoral votes to bestow. That simple math, combined with the strong talent Albany has produced, meant New Yorkers could often vote for one of their own for the White House. It began in the 1800s, when Democrats nominated three New York governors, including Grover Cleveland, who won twice in 1884 and 1892. In the twentieth century the parade of New York governors nominated was bipartisan: Theodore and Franklin D. Roosevelt and three losers: Charles Evans Hughes, Alfred E. Smith, and Thomas E. Dewey. From 1904 to 1948, the state's current or former governor was nominated for president ten times. (In addition, the 1940 GOP nominee, Wendell Wilkie, was a Hoosier transplanted to Manhattan). Counting vice-presidential nominees, there was a New Yorker on at least one major party's national ticket in every cycle save two from 1884 to 1948.

But this changed after 1950, with the switch from Northeast to Sun Belt hegemony. Thereafter, while several New Yorkers yearned for the White House, the only ones nominated for president were legal residents of Manhattan—Dwight Eisenhower in 1952 and Richard Nixon in 1968—whose real roots were in the West. Once freed from its favorite-son obligations, New York tended to vote for the eventual winner (with the exceptions being Nixon in 1968

and the two Presidents Bush (in 1988 and 2000). The only time it has been egregiously out of step was in 2000, when it gave the younger Bush just 35 percent of its vote—quite nearly his worst showing anywhere.

A similar pattern has obtained in voting for top statewide offices. New Yorkers generally sent Republicans to the Senate when that was the fashion for northeastern states a century ago, but switched to the Democrats in the FDR years and then alternated between the parties after World War II. But the kind of Republicans and Democrats who have won these offices has changed. The mainstream and even liberal Republicans of another day—Nelson Rockefeller and Jacob Javits principal among them—are no more. Beginning with Long Island-based neoconservative Alphonse D'Amato in 1980, the statewide nominees of the GOP have been harder edged and more inclined to support the new Republican national consensus, which emerges more from the South and West than from the party's historic roots in the Northeast and Midwest. The same could be said of the state's three-term Republican governor George Pataki, who first won the office in 1994 by denying Democratic icon Mario Cuomo a fourth term. In the wake of September 11, Pataki enjoyed some of the popular affection lavished on Giuliani, helping him win a third term in 2002 with less than 50 percent of the vote.

The Democrats, too, have traveled far from the era of Tammany Hall. Sen. Charles Schumer is a high school valedictorian from Brooklyn who went to Harvard at age sixteen and won a seat in the state assembly the same year he graduated from Harvard Law. Hillary Rodham Clinton, of course, was the first first lady to enter politics. A daughter of Illinois, Wellesley, and Yale, she was more acquainted with the state's resorts (where she had gone first as a child) than with its grittier precincts. But upon becoming a candidate in her own right, Clinton surprised and impressed the state's old political hands. She spent her early campaign weeks upstate, winning over swing voters and minimizing the margin by which she would lose these historically Republican regions in November 2000. When Giuliani's health would not let him make the race, a late GOP stand-in stood little chance.

The final sign of strength for Democrats in New York has been their continued domination of the House delegation as it has dwindled away. New York's seat total has fallen by more than a third from its peak of forty-five during the 1940s. But although the state slipped from thirty-one seats to twenty-nine after the 2000 census, Democrats managed to keep their share constant at nineteen seats while the GOP fell from twelve to ten. This was accomplished without any redistricting legerdemain. In Albany, where a divided legislature was to draw the map while the governor looked on wielding veto power, a relatively easy truce was struck. It was clear early on that the population losses were upstate, not metro New York City. So both parties managed to persuade senior upstate members to retire and facilitate the merger of their districts with those of other incumbents of the same party. Thus the GOP's thirty-year representative Ben Gilman saw his Hudson River suburban district combined with that of up-and-comer Sue Kelly. The Democrats' twenty-eight-year veteran John LaFalce let his Buffalo-Niagara district disappear into those of Louise Slaughter and Jack Quinn. That cost each party one seat, but the Democrats managed to compensate for their loss. Tim Bishop, a college administrator, upset freshman Republican Felix Grucci in the 1st District, the eastern Suffolk County portion of suburban Long Island.

Table 1 Population

District	Population	Population under 18	Voting-age population	Median age	Male*	Female*
1	654,360	167,566	486,794	36.7	49.1	50.9
2	654,360	174,637	479,723	36.5	48.9	51.1
3	654,361	159,786	494,575	38.7	48.5	51.5
4	654,360	164,515	489,845	37.3	47.9	52.1
5	654,361	142,375	511,986	37.5	48.6	51.4
6	654,361	176,441	477,920	33.9	46.7	53.3
7	654,360	154,625	499,735	35.1	47.7	52.3
8	654,360	117,107	537,253	36.2	49.3	50.7
9	654,360	138,169	516,191	38.8	47.6	52.4
10	654,361	197,964	456,397	31.1	45.6	54.4
11	654,361	177,627	476,734	32.5	45.5	54.5
12	654,360	168,001	486,359	31.7	49.1	50.9
13	654,361	154,855	499,506	36.7	48.2	51.8
14	654,361	86,734	567,627	36.5	47.1	52.9
15	654,361	157,169	497,192	33.1	47.8	52.2
16	654,360	226,075	428,285	27.5	46.5	53.5
17	654,360	174,227	480,133	34.9	46.7	53.3
18	654,360	161,945	492,415	37.9	48.1	51.9
19	654,360	176,400	477,961	36.7	49.9	50.1
20	654,360	159,881	494,479	38.3	49.9	50.1
21	654,361	152,671	501,690	37.3	48.1	51.9
22	654,361	155,726	498,635	36.1	49.0	51.0
23	654,361	163,964	490,397	35.5	50.8	49.2
24	654,361	159,382	494,979	37.7	49.3	50.7
25	654,361	169,768	484,593	37.0	48.2	51.8
26	654,361	161,232	493,129	37.6	49.0	51.0
27	654,361	156,781	497,580	38.0	48.4	51.6
28	654,360	170,445	483,915	35.3	47.3	52.7
29	654,361	164,039	490,322	37.7	49.2	50.8
State	18,976,457	4,690,107	14,286,350	35.9	48.2	51.8

As percentage of total population.

Table 2 Voting-Age Persons by Race/Hispanic or Latino Origin

District	White*	Black or African American*	American Indian or Alaska Native*	Asian*	Other or multirace*	Hispanic or Latino*
1	85.7	3.7	0.3	2.5	1.0	6.8
2	73.9	8.9	0.2	3.0	1.3	12.7
3	87.9	2.0	0.1	2.9	0.9	6.3
4	64.9	16.4	0.1	4.3	1.7	12.7
5	46.3	5.1	0.1	24.2	2.2	22.0
6	14.5	51.1	0.5	9.1	8.6	16.2
7	30.8	15.8	0.2	13.1	3.2	37.0
8	70.5	5.0	0.1	10.8	2.8	10.7
9	66.4	3.7	0.1	14.1	3.3	12.3
10	16.8	60.0	0.2	3.0	3.4	16.5
11	23.6	56.8	0.2	4.3	3.5	11.6
12	26.9	8.1	0.2	16.9	3.2	44.7
13	73.8	5.4	0.1	9.0	2.2	9.6
14	68.6	4.2	0.1	11.1	3.4	12.5
15	19.0	30.5	0.2	3.3	2.2	44.8
16	3.6	30.6	0.2	1.8	2.2	61.5
17	44.1	29.3	0.2	4.6	3.0	18.7
18	69.2	9.1	0.1	5.1	1.6	15.0
19	84.3	5.1	0.2	2.2	1.0	7.2
20	93.8	2.5	0.2	0.8	0.8	2.0
21	87.6	6.5	0.2	2.1	1.0	2.6
22	82.1	6.9	0.2	2.8	1.4	6.7
23	92.9	2.9	0.8	0.6	0.7	2.1
24	92.9	3.2	0.2	0.8	0.8	2.0
25	88.8	6.0	0.6	1.7	1.0	1.8
26	92.6	3.2	0.3	1.5	0.6	1.7
27	90.6	3.7	0.7	0.7	0.8	3.6
28	67.4	24.9	0.5	1.5	1.3	4.4
29	93.3	2.6	0.5	1.7	0.7	1.2
State	64.4	13.8	0.2	5.6	2.0	13.8

As percentage of voting-age population.

Table 3 Voting-Age Population by Age Groups

District	18 to 24*	25 to 44*	45 to 64*	Over 64*
1	10.8	41.2	31.7	16.3
2	9.9	42.4	32.0	15.8
3	8.5	40.5	31.7	19.3
4	11.1	38.9	30.8	19.2
5	11.3	40.1	29.8	18.8
6	13.8	42.4	29.3	14.6
7	12.4	42.8	28.0	16.8
8	11.7	44.2	27.2	16.8
9	10.3	38.4	30.0	21.3
10	15.2	42.6	28.5	13.7
11	14.3	44.4	28.6	12.7
12	15.5	45.9	26.0	12.7
13	11.1	41.1	30.4	17.5
14	10.9	47.2	26.7	15.3
15	15.5	43.9	26.6	14.0
16	17.9	46.1	25.7	10.3
17	12.1	41.0	29.5	17.4
18	9.6	39.7	31.6	19.0
19	10.6	41.9	32.6	15.0
20	10.3	38.5	33.0	18.2
21	13.2	37.0	29.6	20.2
22	15.8	37.0	29.4	17.8
23	14.8	39.1	29.5	16.6
24	12.6	36.6	30.7	20.0
25	11.5	39.1	30.8	18.7
26	12.2	38.3	30.9	18.7
27	11.3	37.7	30.2	20.8
28	13.2	39.3	28.2	19.3
29	12.5	36.5	32.1	18.8
State	12.4	40.8	29.7	17.1

As percentage of voting-age population.

Table 4 Income and Occupation

District	Median family income	Families in poverty*	White collar†	Blue collar†	Service†	Farm†
1	$69,971	4.0	64.4	20.3	14.8	0.4
2	$77,224	3.9	66.3	20.1	13.5	0.1
3	$78,874	2.8	69.3	17.0	13.5	0.1
4	$75,653	4.4	67.9	16.6	15.4	0.1
5	$58,694	9.4	65.2	18.2	16.6	0.0
6	$49,563	12.1	57.4	20.5	22.0	0.0
7	$42,003	14.9	57.4	21.1	21.5	0.1
8	$50,615	15.5	79.2	10.1	10.7	0.0
9	$53,950	9.9	68.4	17.6	13.9	0.0
10	$33,698	25.8	60.4	17.5	22.1	0.0
11	$36,637	21.1	61.2	15.7	23.1	0.0
12	$30,215	25.5	50.9	27.5	21.5	0.1
13	$59,749	9.6	65.0	18.3	16.6	0.0
14	$72,594	9.4	82.1	7.8	10.2	0.0
15	$29,416	27.6	63.8	14.8	21.3	0.0
16	$20,924	39.9	46.4	23.6	29.8	0.1
17	$53,201	13.4	64.9	16.0	19.0	0.1

District	Median family income	Families in poverty*	White collar†	Blue collar†	Service†	Farm†
18	$85,771	5.5	73.2	12.8	13.9	0.1
19	$74,699	4.2	67.2	18.5	14.1	0.2
20	$52,099	5.5	61.1	22.7	15.3	0.9
21	$51,647	7.8	66.0	18.9	14.8	0.3
22	$48,489	9.3	60.8	21.4	17.3	0.5
23	$41,845	9.5	52.4	27.4	18.8	1.4
24	$44,280	8.8	57.3	24.4	17.3	1.0
25	$53,779	7.2	65.0	20.8	13.8	0.4
26	$55,616	4.7	61.7	23.4	14.2	0.7
27	$46,520	8.8	57.9	25.3	16.3	0.5
28	$40,361	15.3	58.3	23.2	18.3	0.2
29	$50,475	6.8	61.3	23.0	14.9	0.8
State	$51,691	11.5	63.8	19.3	16.6	0.3

*As percentage of all families.   †As percentage of employed workers 16 years and over.

Table 5   Education: School Years Completed

District	Less than grade 9*	Grades 9–12 no diploma*	High school diploma no college*	Some college*	College bachelor's degree or higher*
1	3.8	8.9	31.5	28.5	27.2
2	5.0	9.5	29.2	25.7	30.6
3	3.8	7.8	30.4	26.8	31.3
4	6.9	9.8	27.9	24.4	31.0
5	11.4	10.8	23.9	20.4	33.6
6	9.6	17.5	29.6	25.4	18.0
7	12.2	16.1	29.0	22.9	19.8
8	8.5	9.7	17.7	16.3	47.8
9	7.7	11.6	27.6	22.1	31.0
10	11.4	20.9	27.8	22.3	17.5
11	9.9	17.9	25.6	21.6	25.0
12	22.8	20.8	23.2	16.1	17.1
13	8.1	12.5	31.9	23.5	24.0
14	6.4	7.0	13.9	15.7	56.9
15	16.9	20.0	19.8	18.3	25.0
16	22.4	27.1	23.2	19.4	7.8
17	8.4	13.9	25.0	24.3	28.5
18	7.0	8.7	20.8	19.7	43.8
19	4.3	9.2	27.2	26.9	32.3
20	4.4	11.2	32.3	27.4	24.7
21	4.7	11.2	30.6	26.6	27.0
22	5.8	12.8	30.9	26.5	23.9
23	6.1	14.3	37.5	26.1	16.0
24	5.7	13.4	33.8	27.8	19.3
25	4.1	10.1	29.7	28.4	27.8
26	4.0	10.3	31.5	28.7	25.5
27	5.8	12.9	33.1	28.2	19.9
28	5.7	15.1	30.6	27.4	21.2
29	4.2	10.2	32.0	27.5	26.1
State	8.0	12.9	27.8	23.9	27.4

*As percentage of persons age 25 and over.

Table 6   Housing and Residential Patterns

District	Median home value	Owner occupied*	Renter occupied*	Urban†	Rural†
1	$174,700	79.4	20.6	94.0	6.0
2	$201,900	81.7	18.3	99.7	0.3
3	$223,300	81.7	18.3	99.6	0.4
4	$222,800	77.3	22.7	100.0	0.0
5	$287,000	53.2	46.8	100.0	0.0
6	$184,100	52.6	47.4	100.0	0.0
7	$196,900	32.3	67.7	100.0	0.0
8	$321,900	26.2	73.8	100.0	0.0
9	$226,300	46.2	53.8	100.0	0.0
10	$202,900	28.6	71.4	100.0	0.0
11	$228,900	21.6	78.4	100.0	0.0
12	$207,100	18.7	81.3	100.0	0.0
13	$230,600	54.0	46.0	100.0	0.0
14	$331,200	25.8	74.2	100.0	0.0
15	$240,200	10.1	89.9	100.0	0.0
16	$152,400	7.2	92.8	100.0	0.0
17	$214,200	41.1	58.9	99.9	0.1
18	$302,000	63.7	36.3	99.3	0.7
19	$183,700	75.2	24.8	78.7	21.3
20	$105,500	73.8	26.2	44.9	55.1
21	$97,100	60.8	39.2	84.3	15.7
22	$96,100	61.2	38.8	67.8	32.2
23	$68,200	71.0	29.0	34.7	65.3
24	$72,000	69.7	30.3	50.5	49.5
25	$88,200	69.1	30.9	79.0	21.0
26	$95,600	75.0	25.0	71.2	28.8
27	$82,500	66.1	33.9	81.5	18.5
28	$74,800	55.4	44.6	93.5	6.5
29	$83,700	74.0	26.0	58.4	41.6
State	$147,600	53.0	47.0	87.5	12.5

*As percentage of occupied housing units.   †As percentage of total population.

New York 1st District

Eastern Suffolk County — Hamptons, Smithtown

Covering the eastern two-thirds of Long Island's Suffolk County, the 1st reaches out into the Atlantic Ocean. At its far eastern end, the district takes in the elite estates of some of New York's wealthiest in the Hamptons and Shelter Island. The rural end of the island has retained its pastoral character, with fishing villages, farms, and wineries scattered throughout. Many duck farms have disappeared, but Long Island's wine industry has expanded rapidly.

Moving west, the 1st takes in some blue-collar towns, populated by conservative Irish Catholics and Italian Americans. Farther west, Smithtown and Brookhaven have boomed with suburban growth. Defense once dominated the economy, but many of those jobs have been replaced by scientific research, attracted by the State University of New York at Stony Brook and Brookhaven National Laboratory.

The 1st's lingering rural temperament and small-town feel make it one of the most conservative districts near New York City. Registration favors Republicans, but many residents have more liberal views on abortion and gun laws. Environmental issues rank high, as many towns depend on the ocean for fish and tourism.

Although Republicans dominate at the local level, Democrats make the 1st competitive in federal elections. Voters have sent a Democrat to the House in 14 of the previous 22 elections. Al Gore outpolled George W. Bush by a 52.3 percent to 43.6 percent tally in the 2000 presidential election, and Bill Clinton carried the district in 1996.

Major Industry

Higher education, medicine, research.

Notable

The Montauk Point Lighthouse, built in 1796, was the first lighthouse in New York state.

Election Returns

	Republican		Democratic		Other	
President 2000	116,308	43.6%	139,490	52.3%	10,705	4.0%
House 2002	81,524	48.6%	84,276	50.2%	1,991	1.2%

District Profile

Population   654,360

Total area (square miles)   1,944.4
    Land area (square miles)   646.4

Population per square mile   1,012.3

Counties (2000 population)
    Suffolk (pt.)   654,360

Cities and other areas over 10,000 (2000 population)
    Centereach CDP   27,285
    Coram CDP   34,923
    East Patchogue CDP   20,824
    Farmingville CDP   16,458
    Hampton Bays CDP   12,236
    Holtsville CDP (pt.)   14,317
    Kings Park CDP (pt.)   14,167
    Lake Grove village   10,250
    Lake Ronkonkoma CDP   19,701
    Manorville CDP   11,131
    Mastic Beach CDP   11,543
    Mastic CDP   15,436
    Medford CDP   21,985
    Miller Place CDP   10,580
    Nesconset CDP   11,992
    Patchogue village   11,919
    Ridge CDP   13,380
    Riverhead CDP   10,513
    Rocky Point CDP   10,185
    Selden CDP   21,861
    Setauket-East Setauket CDP   15,931
    Shirley CDP   25,395
    Smithtown CDP (pt.)   20,875
    St. James CDP   13,268
    Stony Brook CDP   13,727
    Terryville CDP   10,589

Race and Hispanic or Latino origin*
    White   84.5%
    Black or African American   4.0%
    American Indian or Alaska Native   0.3%
    Asian   2.4%
    Native Hawaiian or other Pacific Islander   0.0%
    Some other race   0.1%
    Hispanic or Latino origin   7.5%
    Two or more races   1.2%

*As percentage of total population.

Ancestry*

English	4.9%	German	13.7%
French	1.5%	Irish	17.5%
Italian	21.1%	Russian	1.7%
Polish	4.9%	USA/American	2.1%

*As estimated percentage of total population.

Universities and colleges, 2000–2001 enrollment
    Long Island University-Southampton College,
        Southampton   2,595
    State University of New York-Stony Brook, Stony Brook
        19,924
    St. Joseph's College-Suffolk, Patchogue   3,234
    Suffolk County Community College-Ammerman, Selden
        10,300
    Suffolk County Community College-Eastern, Riverhead
        2,170

Newspapers and circulation

	District circulation	Total circulation
East Hampton Star	9,529	10,854
Long Island Newsday	100,475	575,889
New York Daily News*	24,058	723,155
New York Post	7,155	511,412
New York Times*	20,838	666,228
USA Today*	2,631	1,674,376

*See Sources and Explanations in the front of the volume.

Television stations and affiliations

New York	100%	WABC	ABC
New York	100%	WCBS	CBS
New York	100%	WEDW	PBS
New York	100%	WFME	Independent
New York	100%	WLIW	PBS
New York	100%	WLNY	Independent
New York	100%	WMBC	Independent
New York	100%	WNBC	NBC
New York	100%	WNET	PBS
New York	100%	WNJB	PBS
New York	100%	WNJN	PBS
New York	100%	WNJU	Telemundo
New York	100%	WNYE	PBS
New York	100%	WNYW	FOX
New York	100%	WPIX	WB
New York	100%	WPXN	PAX
New York	100%	WRNN	Independent
New York	100%	WTBY	Independent
New York	100%	WWOR	UPN
New York	100%	WXTV	Univision

Cable systems and subscribers
    Cablevision   223,492

Military installations, September 2001
    Francis S. Gabreski Airport (Air National Guard),
        Westhampton Beach   821

Businesses and other major employers
    Mid East Suffolk Teacher Center; Middle Island; business
        associations   10,000
    Brookhaven Science Associates; Upton; nuclear energy
        regulation   2,950
    Research Foundation of State University of New York;
        Stony Brook; noncommercial research organization
        2,400

State University of New York Health Science Center; Stony Brook   2,000

Symbol Technologies Inc.; Holtsville; magnetic ink and optical scanning devices   1,800

Brookhaven Memorial Hospital; East Patchogue   1,700

Mather Memorial Hospital of Port Jefferson Inc.; Port Jefferson   1,590

Peconic Health Corp.; Aquebogue; hospital   1,400

Catholic Health Systems of Long Island Inc. Hospital; Smithtown   1,200

State University of New York; Stony Brook   1,000

St. Charles Hospital; Port Jefferson   985

Clinical Practice Management Plan; Stony Brook; management services   970

Suffolk County; Yaphank; county government   940

U.S. Internal Revenue Service; Riverhead   897

Three Village Central School District; Stony Brook   800

Southampton Hospital Assn.; Southampton   746

Splish Splash at Adventureland Inc.; Riverhead; amusement parks   700

Independent Group Home Living Inc.; East Moriches; mentally handicapped home   685

Suffolk County Community College; Selden   658

Central Suffolk Hospital; Riverhead   560

Compass Group USA Inc.; Stony Brook; contract food services   500

Kurt Weiss Greenhouses Inc.; Center Moriches; plants   500

Maryhaven Center of Hope; Port Jefferson Station; community center   500

New York 2nd District

Long Island— Brentwood, Commack

Taking in the central part of Long Island and covering almost all of western Suffolk County, the 2nd is full of suburban communities that popped up all over the county's potato fields during the post–World War II suburban boom. Now the 2nd, which also takes in a small piece of east-central Nassau County, has a burgeoning computer sector and the state's highest median income.

Much of the district's white-collar workforce commutes to New York City, and the indigenous industry has long been blue-collar. Defense plants hummed during the height of the cold war, but cutbacks brought job losses. Computer and electronics firms have helped fill the void. The 2nd houses a relatively diverse population, mixing well-to-do communities such as Dix Hills with solidly middle- and working-class neighborhoods. During the summer many New Yorkers flock to Fire Island, a beach community that lies partly in the 2nd.

Redistricting in 2002 gave the 2nd all of Huntington— which it previously shared with the 5th—and stripped it of more-conservative coastal communities in Islip and Babylon to the south. The 2nd also acquired most of Plainview and part of Jericho in Nassau County, both of which have large Jewish populations.

With a nearly 30 percent minority population, a significant Jewish community, and a blue-collar base, the 2nd has a substantial, but not overwhelming, Democratic vote. A Republican held the seat for most of the 1990s before it reverted to Democratic control in 2000. The district remains compet-

itive, but redistricting did push it leftward. Al Gore captured almost 58 percent of the vote here in the 2000 presidential election.

Major Industry

Computers, electronics, service.

Notable

Fire Island National Seashore separates the Atlantic Ocean from the Great South Bay; Islip Long Island MacArthur Airport is near Ronkonkoma; the Walt Whitman Birthplace State Historic Site and Interpretive Center is in West Hills (South Huntington).

Election Returns

	Republican		Democratic		Other	
President 2000	100,708	39.4%	146,723	57.4%	8,165	3.2%
House 2002	59,117	40.5%	85,451	58.5%	1,558	1.1%

District Profile

Population   654,360

Total area (square miles)   329.7
   Land area (square miles)   239.3

Population per square mile   2,734.5

Counties (2000 population)
   Nassau (pt.)   48,613   Suffolk (pt.)   605,747

Cities and other areas over 10,000 (2000 population)
   Bay Shore CDP (pt.)   17,246
   Brentwood CDP   53,917
   Central Islip CDP   31,950
   Commack CDP (pt.)   36,363
   Deer Park CDP   28,316
   Dix Hills CDP   26,024
   East Northport CDP   20,845
   Elwood CDP   10,916
   Greenlawn CDP   13,286
   Hauppauge CDP (pt.)   13,261
   Holbrook CDP (pt.)   22,476
   Huntington CDP   18,403
   Huntington Station CDP   29,910
   Islip CDP (pt.)   13,980
   Melville CDP   14,533
   North Amityville CDP   16,572
   North Bay Shore CDP   14,992
   Plainview CDP (pt.)   23,199
   Ronkonkoma CDP   20,029
   Sayville CDP   16,735
   West Babylon CDP (pt.)   18,975
   Wyandanch CDP   10,546

Race and Hispanic or Latino origin*
   White   71.5%
   Black or African American   9.8%
   American Indian or Alaska Native   0.2%
   Asian   3.0%
   Native Hawaiian or other Pacific Islander   0.0%
   Some other race   0.2%
   Hispanic or Latino origin   13.9%
   Two or more races   1.4%

*As percentage of total population.

Ancestry*

English	3.3%	Polish	3.9%
French	1.1%	Russian	2.5%
German	10.2%	USA/American	2.6%
Irish	14.1%	West Indian	1.7%
Italian	18.8%		

*As estimated percentage of total population.

Universities and colleges, 2000–2001 enrollment

Dowling College, Oakdale   5,680
Five Towns College, Dix Hills   932
Long Island University, Brentwood   910
New York Institute of Technology, Central Islip   908
State University of New York College of Technology, Farmingdale   5,045
Stenotopia Business School, Plainview   290
Suffolk County Community College-Western, Brentwood   5,574

Newspapers and circulation

	District circulation	Total circulation
Hoy, New York City	3,408	59,949
Long Island Newsday	123,863	575,889
*New York Daily News**	5,355	723,155
New York Post	7,814	511,412
*New York Times**	5,002	666,228

*See Sources and Explanations in the front of the volume.

Television stations and affiliations

New York	100%	WABC	ABC
New York	100%	WCBS	CBS
New York	100%	WEDW	PBS
New York	100%	WFME	Independent
New York	100%	WLIW	PBS
New York	100%	WLNY	Independent
New York	100%	WMBC	Independent
New York	100%	WNBC	NBC
New York	100%	WNET	PBS
New York	100%	WNJB	PBS
New York	100%	WNJN	PBS
New York	100%	WNJU	Telemundo
New York	100%	WNYE	PBS
New York	100%	WNYW	FOX
New York	100%	WPIX	WB
New York	100%	WPXN	PAX
New York	100%	WRNN	Independent
New York	100%	WTBY	Independent
New York	100%	WWOR	UPN
New York	100%	WXTV	Univision

Cable systems and subscribers

Cablevision   66,282

Military installations, September 2001

Amityville U.S. Army Reserve Center, New York   127

Businesses and other major employers

Alcott Staff Leasing Inc.; Farmingdale; employee leasing service   3,400
Empire HealthChoice Inc.; New York; medical service plans   3,135
New York Mental Health Office; Brentwood   3,000
Levitz Home Furnishings Inc.; Woodbury   2,770
Brunswick Hospital Center Inc.; Amityville   2,700
Computer Associates International Inc.; Islandia; business software   2,700
Whelan's International Co.; Ronkonkoma; floor waxing   2,120
Entenmann's Inc.; Bay Shore; bakery products   2,000
GEICO; Woodbury; benevolent insurance associations   2,000
U.S. Postal Service; Melville   2,000
U.S. Veterans Hospital; Northport   1,800
Brentwood Union Free School District; Brentwood   1,755
Computer Associates International Inc.; Central Islip; software   1,500
Sigma Temps Inc.; Melville; employment agencies   1,500
CSC Holdings Inc.; Jericho; cable television   1,200
Huntington Hospital Assn.; Huntington   1,200
Fleet National Bank; Melville   1,100
JBL Inc.; Woodbury; speaker systems   1,090
Dowling College; Oakdale   1,020
City of Huntington; Huntington; social services   1,000
New York Office of General Services; Hauppauge   1,000
WSNCHS East Inc.; Amityville; psychiatric hospitals   1,000
AIL Technologies Inc.; Deer Park; electricity measuring instruments   893
NBTY Inc.; Bohemia; bulk vitamins   870
Bay Shore Union Free School District; Bay Shore   800
Middle American Tissue Inc.; Hauppauge; facial tissues   800
North Shore University Hospital; Plainview   800
Acme Bus Corp.; Ronkonkoma; school buses   750
Parker Hannifin Corp.; Smithtown; measuring and controlling devices   750
Statewide Catering Inc.; Ronkonkoma; contract food services   748
UPR Care Corp.; Woodbury; nursing care facilities   730
Hilti Inc.; Hauppauge; metal fasteners   725
Adecco Staffing Inc.; Melville; temporary help service   700
Creative Bath Products Inc.; Central Islip; bathroom accessories   700
Henry Schein Inc.; Melville; dental equipment   700
JP Morgan Chase Bank; Melville; commercial bank   680
BAE Systems; Greenlawn; digital displays of process variables   670
Comforce Corp.; Woodbury; labor resource services   650
Twin Laboratories Inc.; Hauppauge; medicinals and botanicals   646
Automatic Data Processing Inc.; Brentwood   600
J. D'Addario and Co.; Farmingdale; string instruments and parts   600
Marchon Eyewear Inc.; Melville; frames, ophthalmic   600
Olympus America Inc.; Melville; medical equipment and supplies   600
Quality Technical Services Inc.; Farmingdale; employee leasing service   600

Telephonics Corp.; Farmingdale; electric
intercommunication systems   600

United Cerebral Palsy Assn. of Greater Suffolk Inc.;
Hauppauge; family service agency   600

Underwriters Laboratories Inc.; Melville; testing
laboratories   586

City of Huntington; Huntington; city government   550

Lockheed Martin Corp.; Syosset; search and detection
systems/instruments   550

Watchdog Patrols Inc.; Huntington Station; security
guard service   550

Central Islip Union Free School District 13; Central Islip
540

Altana Inc.; Melville; pharmaceuticals   500

American Institute of Physics Inc.; Melville; trade
journals   500

Arrow Electronics Inc.; Melville; electronic parts   500

Citicorp Retail Service Inc.; Melville; credit card services
500

Commercial Building Maintenance Corp.; Syosset;
janitorial service   500

Copiague Union Free School District; Copiague   500

Lason Inc.; Melville; data processing   500

Macy's East Inc.; Huntington Station; department stores
500

Nikon Inc.; Melville; photographic equipment, supplies
500

North Hills Office Services Inc.; Woodbury; industrial,
commercial cleaning services   500

North Shore University Hospital; Syosset   500

Polytechnic University; Farmingdale   500

Quality King Distributors Inc.; Ronkonkoma; drugs,
proprietaries, sundries   500

Rubie's Costume Co.; Bay Shore; costumes   500

Suffolk Transportation Service Inc.; Bay Shore; school
buses   500

Summit Security Services Inc.; Melville; protective
services, guard   500

New York 3rd District

Long Island — Levittown, Hicksville, Long Beach

Most of Long Island's eastern Nassau County and the
south shore of western Suffolk County make up the 3rd,
where extravagant estates mingle with some of the nation's
oldest middle-class suburbs. The district boasts New York
state's second-highest median income. *(See map p. 620.)*

The Republican Party has long been a potent force in
the 3rd, and redistricting in 2002 strengthened the party's
hand even further by adding southwestern Suffolk. The addition was headlined by the acquisition of coastal portions of
Islip and Babylon. Even with the district's significant labor
presence from construction and professional unions, most of
the 3rd's elected officials are Republicans, though Democrats
have made some gains in Nassau County overall. Pockets of
Democratic support in Plainview and Jericho, where many
of the residents are Jewish, were moved into the neighboring
2nd District in redistricting.

While Democratic presidential candidates have held a
modest edge district-wide in recent years (Al Gore captured

52.1 percent of the vote here in 2000), they have not done as
well as in other Long Island districts. The 3rd easily favors
Republicans in state and congressional races.

The economy faltered in the 1980s when aircraft and electronics manufacturing giant Northrup Grumman downsized
following defense cutbacks after the end of the cold war. But
the 3rd has rebounded, expanding its information technology
base and enjoying a low unemployment rate.

The district is overwhelmingly white, with the lowest
percentage of black residents (2.1 percent) in the state and
the lowest percentage of Hispanics (6.9 percent) in the New
York City area.

Major Industry

Information technology, higher education.

Notable

Bethpage State Park hosted the 2002 U.S. Open golf tournament; President Theodore Roosevelt's Sagamore Hill estate is in Oyster Bay; Roosevelt's grave is at nearby Youngs
Memorial Cemetery.

Election Returns

	Republican		Democratic		Other	
President 2000	127,869	44.4%	150,165	52.1%	10,251	3.6%
House 2002	121,537	71.9%	46,022	27.2%	1,513	0.9%

District Profile

Population   654,361

Total area (square miles)   393.3
Land area (square miles)   183.3

Population per square mile   3,569.9

Counties (2000 population)
Nassau (pt.)   495,099
Suffolk (pt.)   159,262

Cities and other areas over 10,000 (2000 population)
Babylon village   12,615
Bellmore CDP   16,441
Bethpage CDP   16,543
Copiague CDP (pt.)   16,577
East Massapequa CDP   19,565
Glen Cove   26,622
Hicksville CDP (pt.)   39,670
Levittown CDP   53,067
Lindenhurst village (pt.)   27,162
Long Beach   35,462
Massapequa CDP   22,652
Massapequa Park village   17,499
Merrick CDP (pt.)   21,330
North Babylon CDP (pt.)   10,163
North Bellmore CDP (pt.)   11,300
North Massapequa CDP   19,152
North Wantagh CDP   12,156
Seaford CDP   15,791
South Farmingdale CDP   15,061
Wantagh CDP   18,971
West Babylon CDP (pt.)   24,477
West Islip CDP (pt.)   27,171

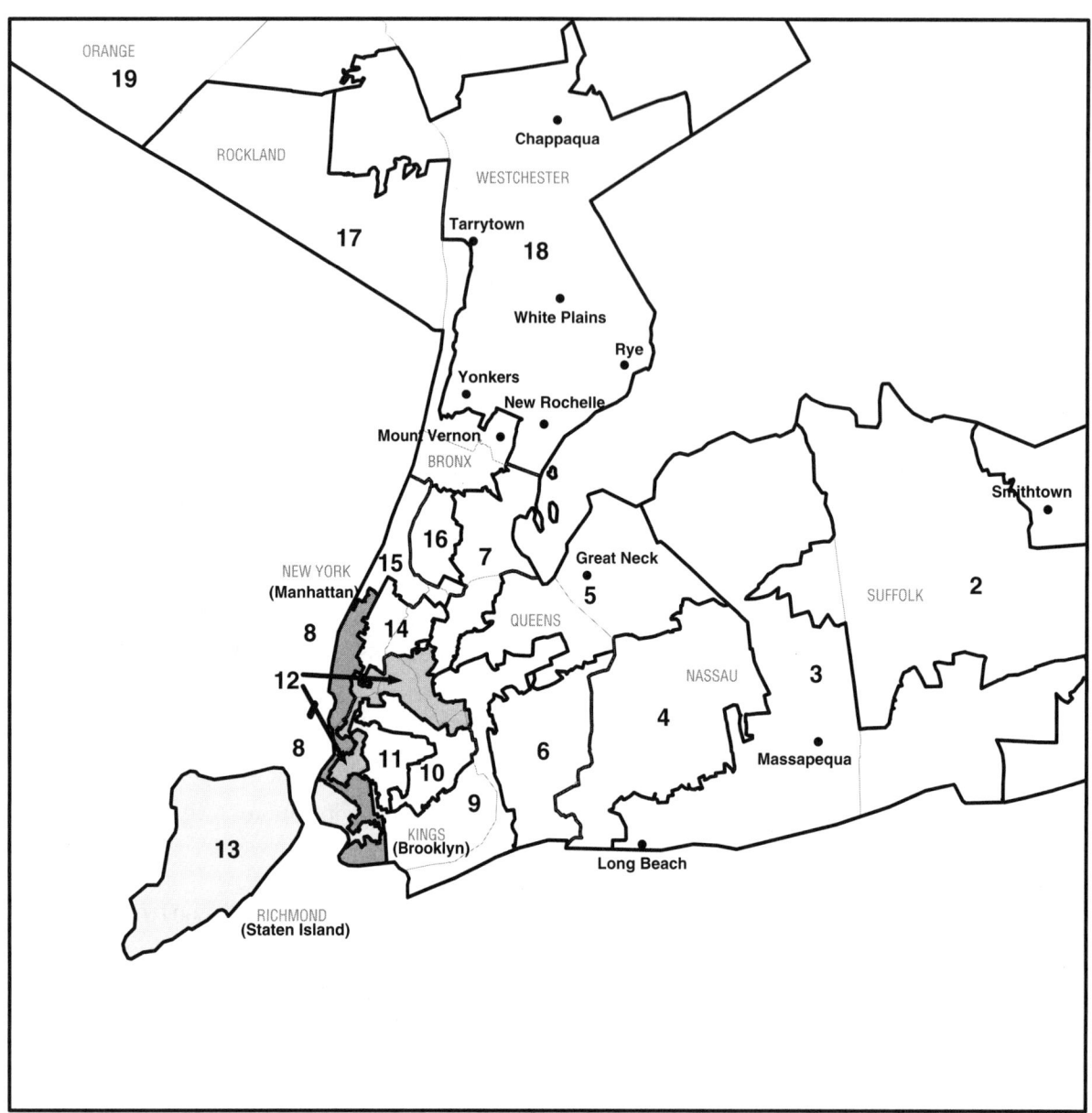

Race and Hispanic or Latino origin*
White   86.9%
Black or African American   2.1%
American Indian or Alaska Native   0.1%
Asian   3.0%
Native Hawaiian or other Pacific Islander   0.0%
Some other race   0.1%
Hispanic or Latino origin   6.9%
Two or more races   1.0%

*As percentage of total population.

Ancestry*
English	3.5%	Italian	23.1%
French	1.1%	Polish	4.6%
German	12.0%	Russian	2.8%
Greek	1.3%	USA/American	2.8%
Irish	17.7%		

*As estimated percentage of total population.

Universities and colleges, 2000–2001 enrollment
Briarcliffe College, Bethpage   1,790
Island Drafting and Technical Institute, Amityville   229
New Center for Holistic Health Education, Syosset   885
New York Institute of Technology, Old Westbury   5,898

Newspapers and circulation
	District circulation	Total circulation
Bellmore Life*	1,856	2,999
Hoy, New York City	1,444	59,949
Long Island Newsday	113,350	575,889
Merrick Life*	2,892	4,671
New York Daily News*	30,512	723,155
New York Post	10,622	511,412
New York Times*	33,744	666,228
USA Today*	2,066	1,674,376
Wantagh-Seaford Citizen*	1,822	2,943

*See Sources and Explanations in the front of the volume.

Television stations and affiliations
New York	100%	WABC	ABC
New York	100%	WCBS	CBS
New York	100%	WEDW	PBS
New York	100%	WFME	Independent
New York	100%	WLIW	PBS
New York	100%	WLNY	Independent
New York	100%	WMBC	Independent
New York	100%	WNBC	NBC
New York	100%	WNET	PBS
New York	100%	WNJB	PBS
New York	100%	WNJN	PBS
New York	100%	WNJU	Telemundo
New York	100%	WNYE	PBS
New York	100%	WNYW	FOX
New York	100%	WPIX	WB
New York	100%	WPXN	PAX
New York	100%	WRNN	Independent
New York	100%	WTBY	Independent
New York	100%	WWOR	UPN
New York	100%	WXTV	Univision

Cable systems and subscribers
Cablevision   221,228

Businesses and other major employers
North Shore University Hospital; Glen Cove   3,500
Interpool Temporary Personnel Inc.; Hicksville   3,000
Good Samaritan Hospital Medical Center; West Islip   2,400
Photocircuits Corp.; Glen Cove; circuit boards   2,078
Southside Hospital Inc.; Bay Shore   1,900
BestCare Inc.; Levittown; home health care   1,806
Ajax Wire Specialty Co. Inc.; Hicksville; wire springs   1,513
Sanofi Winthrop Pharmaceuticals; Massapequa   1,000
Cablevision Systems New York City Corp.; Bethpage; cable TV   950
Recco Home Care Service Inc.; Massapequa; home health care   850
Long Beach Medical Center; Long Beach   776
Compass Group USA Inc.; Wantagh; merchandising machine operators   700
Sears Roebuck and Co. Inc.; Hicksville; department stores   700
Robert Plan of New York Corp.; Bethpage; insurance agents   622
City of Hempstead; Merrick; garbage collection   600
Macy's East Inc.; Massapequa; department stores   600
Massapequa American Legion Post; Massapequa; veterans' organization   600
Board of Cooperative Educational Services of Nassau County; Seaford   600
Family Aides Inc.; Hicksville; home health care services   600
Cold Spring Harbor Laboratory Inc.; Cold Spring Harbor; noncommercial biological research organization   575
Quest Diagnostics Clinical Laboratories Inc.; Syosset; medical laboratories   550
Ladenburg Capital Management Inc.; Bethpage; investors   500
Star Industries Inc.; Syosset; beer and ale   500
Our Lady of Consolation Geriatric Care Center; West Islip   500

New York 4th District
Southwest Nassau County — Hempstead

The 4th's diverse array of residents includes wealthy New York City suburbanites and Wall Street commuters, as well as low- and middle-income residents. The district consumes the southwest corner of Long Island's Nassau County and borders eastern Queens. (See map p. 620.)

With the largest minority population of Long Island's four congressional districts, the 4th has a Democratic base, particularly in Hempstead and Uniondale, which include large black and Hispanic communities. The affluent and largely Jewish "Five Towns" (Inwood, Lawrence, Cedarhurst, Woodmere, and Hewlett), in the 4th's southwestern corner, also lean Democratic. But overall voter registration favors the GOP.

District politics were competitive in the 1990s, with independent and socially moderate voters electing four different representatives during the decade. In 1996 the 4th elected a Democrat who strongly supported gun control. The district voted for Bill Clinton in both of his presidential bids, overwhelmingly so in 1996. In the 2000 presidential contest Al Gore secured the district with almost 60 percent of the vote.

Some of the political upheaval may be tied to economic turmoil that began in the 1980s with the decline of the defense industry, on which Long Island was heavily dependent. The 4th continues to rebuild and diversify, focusing on technology and small businesses. A number of working-class residents are employed by John F. Kennedy International Airport (across the district line in Queens' 6th District), Belmont Park race track, and large shopping centers such as Roosevelt Field Mall in Garden City.

Pocketbook issues and unique regional concerns—such as airplane noise—dominate political discussion in the 4th and help keep it competitive.

Major Industry
Health care, technology, higher education.

Notable
Nassau Coliseum is home to the New York Islanders hockey team.

Election Returns

	Republican		Democratic		Other	
President 2000	99,263	37.6%	156,276	59.2%	8,612	3.3%
House 2002	72,882	43.2%	94,806	56.3%	852	0.5%

District Profile

Population 654,360

Total area (square miles) 103.1
  Land area (square miles) 89.8

Population per square mile 7,286.9

Counties (2000 population)
  Nassau (pt.) 654,360

Cities and other areas over 10,000 (2000 population)
  Baldwin CDP 23,455
  East Meadow CDP 37,461
  East Rockaway village 10,414
  Elmont CDP 32,657
  Floral Park village 15,967
  Franklin Square CDP 29,342
  Freeport village (pt.) 34,958
  Garden City village 21,672
  Hempstead village 56,554
  Lynbrook village 19,911
  Mineola village 19,234
  New Cassel CDP 13,298
  North New Hyde Park CDP (pt.) 14,500
  North Valley Stream CDP 15,789
  Oceanside CDP (pt.) 28,747
  Rockville Centre village 24,568
  Roosevelt CDP 15,854
  Salisbury CDP 12,341
  Uniondale CDP 23,011
  Valley Stream village 36,368
  Westbury village 14,263

West Hempstead CDP 18,713
Woodmere CDP 16,447

Race and Hispanic or Latino origin*
  White 62.3%
  Black or African American 17.6%
  American Indian or Alaska Native 0.1%
  Asian 4.5%
  Native Hawaiian or other Pacific Islander 0.0%
  Some other race 0.3%
  Hispanic or Latino origin 13.6%
  Two or more races 1.6%

*As percentage of total population.

Ancestry*

English	2.3%	Polish	3.7%
German	8.0%	Russian	2.7%
Irish	12.4%	USA/American	3.2%
Italian	17.5%	West Indian	4.8%

*As estimated percentage of total population.

Universities and colleges, 2000–2001 enrollment
  Adelphi University, Garden City 5,908
  Hofstra University, Hempstead 13,144
  Molloy College, Rockville Center 2,478
  Nassau Community College, Garden City 19,621
  Ultrasound Diagnostic School, Carle Place 354

Newspapers and circulation

	District circulation	Total circulation
Hoy, New York City	4,770	59,949
Long Island Newsday	91,239	575,889
*New York Daily News**	10,709	723,155
New York Post	11,428	511,412
*New York Times**	11,966	666,228

*See Sources and Explanations in the front of the volume.

Television stations and affiliations

New York	100%	WABC	ABC
New York	100%	WCBS	CBS
New York	100%	WEDW	PBS
New York	100%	WFME	Independent
New York	100%	WLIW	PBS
New York	100%	WLNY	Independent
New York	100%	WMBC	Independent
New York	100%	WNBC	NBC
New York	100%	WNET	PBS
New York	100%	WNJB	PBS
New York	100%	WNJN	PBS
New York	100%	WNJU	Telemundo
New York	100%	WNYE	PBS
New York	100%	WNYW	FOX
New York	100%	WPIX	WB
New York	100%	WPXN	PAX
New York	100%	WRNN	Independent
New York	100%	WTBY	Independent
New York	100%	WWOR	UPN
New York	100%	WXTV	Univision

Cable systems and subscribers
  Cablevision* 94,443

*See Sources and Explanations in the front of the volume.

Businesses and other major employers

Nassau County; Mineola; police dept.   3,500

Nassau Health Care Corp.; East Meadow; health systems agency   3,100

Plaza Employment Agency Inc.; Lynbrook; home health care   3,000

Nassau Community College; Garden City   2,965

Avis Rent a Car Systems Inc.; Garden City   2,500

Winthrop-University Hospital Inc.; Mineola   2,500

FJC Security Service Inc.; Floral Park; security guard service   2,200

Hofstra University; Hempstead   2,000

Citibank NA; Uniondale; state commercial banks 1,700

Mercy Medical Center; Rockville Centre   1,420

Adelphi University; Garden City   1,388

Nassau County; Mineola; environmental management 1,300

Franklin Hospital Medical Center; Valley Stream   1,058

South Nassau Communities Hospital Inc.; Oceanside 1,035

First National Maintenance Service Inc.; Inwood; window cleaning   1,000

Fortunoff Fine Jewelry and Silverware Inc.; Westbury; warehousing   1,000

Primerica Financial Services Inc.; Hempstead; financial services   1,000

Verizon Communications Inc.; Lynbrook; planning consultant   1,000

Propoco Inc.; Lynbrook; facilities support services   950

United Parcel Service Inc.; Uniondale   900

Laboratory Corp. of America; Uniondale; testing laboratories   800

Depository Trust and Clearing Corp.; Garden City; clearance, settlement, and information services for equities, bonds, securities   700

North Shore Long Island Jewish Health System Hospital; Westbury   700

U.S. Postal Service; Garden City   700

United Brotherhood of Carpenters; Uniondale; labor organization   700

Baldwin Union Free School District; Baldwin   697

Arbor National Holdings Inc.; Uniondale; mortgage bankers   650

Queens-Long Island Medical Group; Uniondale; medical offices   630

Deutsche Lufthansa; East Meadow; air passenger carrier 600

NPD Group Inc.; Uniondale; personal service agents 600

Metropolitan Suburban Bus Authority; Garden City; bus line operations   570

1-800-Flowers.com Inc.; Westbury; florists   500

Better Home Health Care Agency Inc.; Rockville Centre; home health care   500

Bloomingdale's Inc.; Garden City; department stores 500

Dreyfus Service Corp.; Uniondale; personal service agents 500

Hempstead; Hempstead; city management   500

Marriott International Inc.; Uniondale; hotel, franchised 500

Mineola Union Free School District; Mineola   500

Molloy College; Rockville Centre   500

New York Racing Assn. Inc.; Elmont; horse racing   500

Ultimate Parking Services; Valley Stream; personal item care and storage services   500

United Cerebral Palsy Assn. of Nassau County Inc.; Roosevelt; home for physically handicapped   500

New York 5th District

Northeast Queens; northwest Nassau County

The 5th stretches east from south of LaGuardia Airport in Queens into northwestern Nassau County, reaching Roslyn and East Hills. *(See map p. 620.)*

Redistricting in 2002 made significant alterations to the district, which previously had skirted Long Island Sound's North Shore into Suffolk County to take in part of Huntington. By removing Suffolk and adding more of Queens, the new district is more Democratic. Almost 80 percent of the 5th's residents live in Queens and 20 percent live in Nassau.

The minority population grew substantially with redistricting, particularly in Hispanic and Asian communities. Half of New York City's Asians live in Queens, and Elmhurst, downtown Flushing, Murray Hill, and Queensboro Hill have a heavy Asian presence. The neighborhoods of North Corona and South Corona have a strong Hispanic influence.

Although pockets of low-income neighborhoods exist in the 5th, northeastern Queens has affluent areas such as the Douglaston and Little Neck neighborhoods near the Nassau County line. Before fanning eastward into Nassau, the district buttonhooks to the south and west along the Grand Central Parkway to take in some communities around St. John's University (which itself is in the 6th District).

Many of the district's residents commute to white-collar jobs outside the 5th, but the local economy is boosted by the U.S. Merchant Marine Academy at Kings Point, Shea Stadium (home to the Mets baseball team), and the USTA National Tennis Center in Flushing Meadows-Corona Park, where the U.S. Open tennis tournament is held each year.

Nassau tends to be politically competitive, but the strong Democratic tilt of Queens contributes to the district's more than two-to-one Democratic registration advantage.

Major Industry

Higher education, health care, small business.

Notable

In 1662 religious freedom advocate John Bowne was arrested for allowing Quakers to worship in his Flushing home, which is now one of the oldest remaining structures in New York state.

Election Returns

	Republican		Democratic		Other	
President 2000	56,027	29.6%	127,288	67.1%	6,256	3.3%
House 2002			68,773	92.3%	5,718	7.7%

District Profile

Population   654,361

Total area (square miles)   85.3
  Land area (square miles)   66.2

Population per square mile   9,884.6

Counties (2000 population)
Nassau (pt.)   136,472
Queens (pt.)   517,889

Cities and other areas over 10,000 (2000 population)
New York (pt.)   517,889
Port Washington CDP   15,215

Race and Hispanic or Latino origin*
White   44.2%
Black or African American   5.1%
American Indian or Alaska Native   0.1%
Asian   24.5%
Native Hawaiian or other Pacific Islander   0.0%
Some other race   0.4%
Hispanic or Latino origin   23.5%
Two or more races   2.1%

*As percentage of total population.

Ancestry*
English 1.3%	Polish 3.1%
German 3.7%	Russian 3.3%
Greek 2.4%	USA/American 2.9%
Irish 5.8%	West Indian 1.5%
Italian 9.7%	

*As estimated percentage of total population.

Universities and colleges, 2000–2001 enrollment
City University of New York College at Old Westbury, Old Westbury   2,995
City University of New York Queensborough Community College, New York   10,598
City University of New York School of Law, Flushing   383
Long Island University-C. W. Post, Greenvale   9,627
Plaza Business Institute, Jackson Heights   603
U.S. Merchant Marine Academy, Kings Point   885

Newspapers and circulation
	District circulation	Total circulation
El Diario-La Prensa, New York City	3,481	54,695
Hoy, New York City	5,152	59,949
Long Island Newsday	45,214	575,889
*New York Daily News**	24,157	723,155
New York Post	15,021	511,412
*New York Times**	14,874	666,228

*See Sources and Explanations in the front of the volume.

Television stations and affiliations
New York	100%	WABC	ABC
New York	100%	WCBS	CBS
New York	100%	WEDW	PBS
New York	100%	WFME	Independent
New York	100%	WLIW	PBS
New York	100%	WLNY	Independent
New York	100%	WMBC	Independent
New York	100%	WNBC	NBC
New York	100%	WNET	PBS
New York	100%	WNJB	PBS
New York	100%	WNJN	PBS
New York	100%	WNJU	Telemundo
New York	100%	WNYE	PBS
New York	100%	WNYW	FOX
New York	100%	WPIX	WB
New York	100%	WPXN	PAX
New York	100%	WRNN	Independent
New York	100%	WTBY	Independent
New York	100%	WWOR	UPN
New York	100%	WXTV	Univision

Cable systems and subscribers
Cablevision*   50,745
Time Warner*   50,745

*See Sources and Explanations in the front of the volume.

Military installations, September 2001
Ernie Pyle U.S. Army Reserve Center, New York   1,585

Businesses and other major employers
New York City; Flushing; environmental management   7,000
Long Island Jewish Medical Center; New Hyde Park   6,000
North Shore University Hospital; Manhasset   3,500
New York Hospital Medical Center of Queens; Flushing   2,200
St. Francis Hospital; Roslyn   2,084
New York Mental Health Office; Queens Village   2,000
State University of New York; Flushing   2,000
MFW Acquisition Holdings Corp.; Manhasset; periodicals   1,822
JP Morgan Chase Bank; New Hyde Park; commercial bank   1,700
Flushing Hospital Medical Center; Flushing   1,568
Long Island University; Greenvale   1,550
Health Acquisition Corp.; Jamaica; home health care   1,500
St. Vincent's Hospital and Medical Center; Elmhurst   1,414
Pall Corp.; Greenvale; medical supplies   1,200
Parker Jewish Institute for Health Care and Rehabilitation; New Hyde Park   1,070
Canon USA Inc.; New Hyde Park; software development   1,000
NPD Group Inc.; Port Washington; market research/analysis   780
Leviton Manufacturing Co.; Little Neck; wiredrawing and insulating   700
Long Island Platform Tennis Assn.; Flushing; tennis club   700
Verizon Communications Inc.; Flushing; telecommunications consultant   700
Thomson Industries Inc.; Port Washington; ball bearings and parts   650
New York City; Corona; city government   600
Ozanam Hall of Queens Nursing Home Inc.; Bayside   600
State University of New York; Old Westbury   600
Art Leather Manufacturing Co. Inc.; Elmhurst; albums   569
Aramark Services Inc.; Flushing; sports field or stadium operator   550
City-Wide Building Services Corp.; Port Washington; building cleaning   500
Macy's East Inc.; Elmhurst; department stores   500
United Cerebral Palsy of Queens Inc.; Bellerose; individual and family services   500

New York 6th District

Southeast Queens — Jamaica, St. Albans

A black-majority, mostly middle-class area, the 6th is economically focused around John F. Kennedy International Airport on Jamaica Bay in southeastern Queens. It is the only district wholly within the 2.2 million-resident borough of Queens. *(See map p. 620.)*

Redistricting in 2002 only marginally changed the lines of the 6th, which is bound roughly by Cross Bay Boulevard to the west, Grand Central Parkway to the north, and the Nassau County line to the east. South of the airport, across Jamaica Bay, the 6th takes in part of Rockaway, including Edgemere and Far Rockaway. Included in the 6th's boundaries are St. John's University, located at the far north, and Aqueduct Racetrack, at the far west.

More than a generation ago, communities such as Springfield Gardens and St. Albans were settled by a burgeoning Irish and Italian Roman Catholic middle class. Today, while the economic profile of these areas is not much different, the demographics are completely changed—most of the residents are African American. Overall the district is 52.1 percent African American.

The 6th is one of the nation's most economically sound black-majority districts, though some areas such as South Jamaica have been troubled by unemployment and other urban ills. JFK Airport, its largest employer, provides a steady job base and, combined with health care, municipal government, and construction jobs, helps create a strong union constituency.

With a sizable Hispanic constituency to go along with its black majority, the district has an overwhelmingly Democratic lean: Al Gore won 86.6 percent of the vote here in the 2000 presidential election, and Democrats outnumber Republicans 14-to-1 in voter registration.

Major Industry
Airport, health care, education.

Notable
Roy Wilkins Park in Jamaica is named for the civil rights leader; Floyd H. Flake, who represented the 6th from 1987 until he resigned in 1997, is the senior pastor at the 15,000-member Greater Allen Cathedral of New York in Jamaica; residents of the 6th have the nation's longest average travel time to work—more than 47 minutes, according to the 2000 census.

Election Returns

	Republican		Democratic		Other	
President 2000	17,632	10.5%	145,684	86.6%	4,874	2.9%
House 2002			72,799	96.5%	2,632	3.5%

District Profile

Population   654,361

Total area (square miles)   46.2
   Land area (square miles)   39.5

Population per square mile   16,566.1

Counties (2000 population)
Queens (pt.)   654,361

Cities and other areas over 10,000 (2000 population)
New York (pt.)   654,361

Race and Hispanic or Latino origin*
White   12.8%
Black or African American   52.1%
American Indian or Alaska Native   0.5%
Asian   8.9%
Native Hawaiian or other Pacific Islander   0.1%
Some other race   2.6%
Hispanic or Latino origin   16.9%
Two or more races   6.1%

As percentage of total population.

Ancestry*
German	1.5%	Subsaharan	2.1%
Irish	2.2%	USA/American	3.0%
Italian	3.4%	West Indian	15.9%

As estimated percentage of total population.

Universities and colleges, 2000–2001 enrollment
City University of New York, York College, Jamaica   5,357

Newspapers and circulation

	District circulation	Total circulation
El Diario-La Prensa, New York City	1,659	54,695
Hoy, New York City	5,181	59,949
Long Island Newsday	25,190	575,889
*New York Daily News**	28,395	723,155
New York Post	8,983	511,412
*New York Times**	13,033	666,228

See Sources and Explanations in the front of the volume.

Television stations and affiliations

New York	100%	WABC	ABC
New York	100%	WCBS	CBS
New York	100%	WEDW	PBS
New York	100%	WFME	Independent
New York	100%	WLIW	PBS
New York	100%	WLNY	Independent
New York	100%	WMBC	Independent
New York	100%	WNBC	NBC
New York	100%	WNET	PBS
New York	100%	WNJB	PBS
New York	100%	WNJN	PBS
New York	100%	WNJU	Telemundo
New York	100%	WNYE	PBS
New York	100%	WNYW	FOX
New York	100%	WPIX	WB
New York	100%	WPXN	PAX
New York	100%	WRNN	Independent
New York	100%	WTBY	Independent
New York	100%	WWOR	UPN
New York	100%	WXTV	Univision

Cable systems and subscribers
Time Warner*   90,819

See Sources and Explanations in the front of the volume.

Businesses and other major employers

TWA Airlines; Jamaica   5,000
American Airlines Inc.; Jamaica   4,000
Jamaica Hospital Medical Center; Jamaica   3,050
St. John's University New York; Jamaica   2,900
St. Vincent Catholic Medical Centers of New York; Jamaica   1,490
Rockaway Home Attendant Services Inc.; Far Rockaway; home health care   1,200
Federal Express Corp.; Jamaica; package delivery   960
U.S. Bureau of Customs and Border Protection; Jamaica   960
Kwik Care; Richmond Hill; home health care   950
New York State Unified Court System; Kew Gardens   950
Peninsula Hospital Center; Far Rockaway   940
New York and New Jersey Port Authority; Jamaica; airport   900
Episcopal Health Services Inc.; Far Rockaway; nursing care facilities   750
Social Concern Community Development Corp. Inc.; Jamaica; individual and family services   750
United Air Lines Inc.; Jamaica   750
Verizon Communications Inc.; Springfield Gardens; telephone communication   700
Worldwide Security Associates Inc.; Jamaica; security guard service   700
Worldwide Flight Services Inc.; Jamaica; airports   612
City University of New York; Jamaica   600
Green Bus Lines Inc.; Jamaica   600
New York State Unified Court System; Jamaica   600
Swissport CFE Inc.; Jamaica; air freight handling   600
Argenbright Security Inc.; Jamaica; detective, armored car services   550
U.S. Veterans Hospital; Jamaica   550
Command Security Corp.; Jamaica; security systems services   520
Long Island Rail Road Co.; Jamaica; rail passenger operation   500
New York City; Jamaica; county police   500
New York Racing Assn. Inc.; Ozone Park; race track operation   500
Rubie's Costume Co.; Richmond Hill; costumes   500
Verizon New York Inc.; Jamaica; telephone communication   500
Westminster Hospitality Inc.; Jamaica; hotels   500

New York 7th District

Part of Queens and the Bronx

Few districts in the nation are as ethnically and racially diverse as the 7th, which takes in part of northern Queens and the eastern part of the Bronx. Blacks, Hispanics, and Asians each compose more than 10 percent of the population, with Hispanics a clear plurality of residents at 39.5 percent. *(See map p. 620.)*

The rapid-growth 7th was one of the few New York districts to see substantial change in 2002 redistricting. Under the district's 1990s configuration, nearly three-fourths of the registered voters came out of Queens. Now, two-thirds of registered voters come from the Bronx.

The district climbs north from near the intersection of the Brooklyn-Queens and Long Island expressways (in the neighboring 12th) to take in Woodside, Jackson Heights, East Elmhurst, and LaGuardia Airport. This fast-growing area is heavily Hispanic and spurred much of Queens' 14 percent population growth rate in the 1990s.

The district continues northeast to the College Point neighborhood, then jumps across the Whitestone Bridge to envelop parts of the Bronx, reaching as far west as the Bronx Zoo and the New York Botanical Garden and as far north as Co-op City and the Westchester County line. The Bronx portion of the district includes Morris Park and Pelham Bay, which have an Italian influence. While the Bronx overall has economic struggles, the areas around Eastchester Bay have some of the borough's highest incomes.

Like most New York City districts, the 7th has a strong Democratic lean, though a bit less monolithically so. It is mostly middle class and residential, though steady growth tied to the city has spurred new businesses. LaGuardia makes the Queens area a transportation hub, and the health care industry is a major employer in the Bronx.

Major Industry

Airport, health care, service.

Notable

The Maritime Industry Museum and State University of New York-Maritime College are at Fort Schuyler in Throgs Neck, where the East River meets Long Island Sound.

Election Returns

	Republican		Democratic		Other	
President 2000	31,682	20.8%	114,365	75.1%	6,236	4.1%
House 2002	18,572	26.7%	50,967	73.3%		

District Profile

Population   654,360

Total area (square miles)   42.3
   Land area (square miles)   26.3

Population per square mile   24,880.6

Counties (2000 population)
   Bronx (pt.)   373,087
   Queens (pt.)   281,273

Cities and other areas over 10,000 (2000 population)
   New York (pt.)   654,360

Race and Hispanic or Latino origin*
   White   27.6%
   Black or African American   16.5%
   American Indian or Alaska Native   0.2%
   Asian   12.8%
   Native Hawaiian or other Pacific Islander   0.0%
   Some other race   0.6%
   Hispanic or Latino origin   39.5%
   Two or more races   2.7%

As percentage of total population.

Ancestry*

German	2.6%	Subsaharan	1.1%
Irish	5.0%	USA/American	1.8%
Italian	9.6%	West Indian	3.6%
Polish	1.7%		

*As estimated percentage of total population.

Universities and colleges, 2000–2001 enrollment

College of Aeronautics, Flushing   1,297
State University of New York-Maritime College,
Bronx   776

Newspapers and circulation

	District circulation	Total circulation
El Diario-La Prensa, New York City	5,595	54,695
Hoy, New York City	3,189	59,949
Long Island Newsday	7,280	575,889
New York Daily News*	49,014	723,155
New York Post	15,812	511,412
New York Times*	14,367	666,228

*See Sources and Explanations in the front of the volume.

Television stations and affiliations

New York	100%	WABC	ABC
New York	100%	WCBS	CBS
New York	100%	WEDW	PBS
New York	100%	WFME	Independent
New York	100%	WLIW	PBS
New York	100%	WLNY	Independent
New York	100%	WMBC	Independent
New York	100%	WNBC	NBC
New York	100%	WNET	PBS
New York	100%	WNJB	PBS
New York	100%	WNJN	PBS
New York	100%	WNJU	Telemundo
New York	100%	WNYE	PBS
New York	100%	WNYW	FOX
New York	100%	WPIX	WB
New York	100%	WPXN	PAX
New York	100%	WRNN	Independent
New York	100%	WTBY	Independent
New York	100%	WWOR	UPN
New York	100%	WXTV	Univision

Cable systems and subscribers

Cablevision*   63,776
Time Warner*   42,517

*See Sources and Explanations in the front of the volume.

Businesses and other major employers

New York City Health and Hospitals Corp.; Elmhurst   3,500
American Airlines Inc.; Flushing   2,120
Consolidated Edison Company of New York Inc.; Bronx; automotive machine shop   1,000
River Bay Corp.; Bronx; apartment building operators   900
Beth Abraham Health Services; Bronx; nursing home   820
New York City; Bronx; recreational program   800
Bronx Harbor Health Care Complex Inc.; Bronx; nursing care facilities   800

Queens Surface Corp.; Flushing; intercity bus line   800
T&V Rental Co. Inc.; Woodside; television rental   750
New York Westchester Square Medical Center Inc.; Bronx   700
Our Lady of Mercy Medical Center; Bronx   700
Calvary Hospital Inc.; Bronx   685
Copstat Security Inc.; Bronx; safety/security specialization   600
South East Bronx Neighborhood Center Quality Vending Services Inc.; Bronx; home health care   600
New York Mental Health Office; Bronx   500
Welsbach Electric Corp.; College Point; electrical work   500
Hudson General Corp.; Flushing; aircraft storage facilities   500
U.S. Airways Inc.; Flushing   500

New York 8th District

West Side Manhattan; Borough Park; Coney Island

Starting just west of Central Park, the 8th moves south through Manhattan's West Side, taking in part of the Theater District and Times Square, then Chelsea, Greenwich Village, SoHo, and Wall Street. It continues across the East River to skim Brooklyn's western waterfront, followed by some working-class areas, much of Brighton Beach, and some of Brooklyn's south coastline in Coney Island. *(See map p. 620.)*

It was in the 8th that terrorists crashed commercial airliners into the twin towers of the World Trade Center on September 11, 2001, killing thousands of people and leveling the buildings. Despite the generally varied interests of the winding district, the logistics of rebuilding Lower Manhattan promise to dominate political and economic discussion in the 8th for some time to come.

The manufacturing industry that once sustained Brooklyn has been neglected in a surge of white-collar financial growth, though most of Brooklyn's well-to-do neighborhoods are in other districts.

Manhattan's heavily Democratic West Side has sent liberal representatives to Congress for decades. The Brooklyn portion, added in 1992 redistricting, increased the district's diversity, and Green Party presidential candidate Ralph Nader received 6 percent of the 8th's vote in 2000, his highest percentage in the state.

The 8th's politically active communities—gay, Jewish, minority, artistic, and student—have supported Democratic presidential candidates overwhelmingly in recent years. Some GOP voters live in Brooklyn's middle-class neighborhoods, such as Borough Park and Bensonhurst, backing candidates with more-conservative views.

Major Industry

Finance, tourism, manufacturing, small business.

Notable

The Statue of Liberty, Empire State Building, Governors Island, South Street Seaport, American Museum of Natural History, Lincoln Center, Penn Station, Madison Square Garden, New York City Hall, and New York University are in the 8th.

Election Returns

	Republican		Democratic		Other	
President 2000	39,280	17.9%	162,240	73.8%	18,448	8.4%
House 2002	19,674	18.5%	81,002	76.1%	5,805	5.5%

District Profile

Population   654,360

Total area (square miles)   28.1
Land area (square miles)   14.8

Population per square mile   44,213.5

Counties (2000 population)
Kings (pt.)   318,816
New York (pt.)   335,544

Cities and other areas over 10,000 (2000 population)
New York (pt.)   654,360

Race and Hispanic or Latino origin*
White   68.7%
Black or African American   5.4%
American Indian or Alaska Native   0.1%
Asian   11.0%
Native Hawaiian or other Pacific Islander   0.0%
Some other race   0.5%
Hispanic or Latino origin   11.7%
Two or more races   2.5%

*As percentage of total population.

Ancestry*

Arab-Misc. 1.5%	Italian 8.7%
English 3.5%	Polish 4.3%
French 1.3%	Russian 7.2%
German 4.8%	Ukrainian 2.1%
Hungarian 1.5%	USA/American 2.8%
Irish 5.7%	

*As estimated percentage of total population.

Universities and colleges, 2000–2001 enrollment
American Musical and Dramatic Academy, New York   586
Audrey Cohen College, New York 1,282
Blanton Peale Graduate Institute, New York   263
City University of New York John Jay College, New York   10,612
City University of New York Manhattan Community College, New York   15,875
College of Insurance, New York   330
Cooper Union for the Advancement of Science and Art, New York   906
Cope Institute, New York   211
Fashion Institute of Technology, New York   10,813
Globe Institute of Technology, New York   669
Interboro Institute, New York   570
Juilliard School, New York   987
New School University, New York   7,867
New York Career Institute, New York   473
New York Institute of Technology-Manhattan, New York   2,501
New York Law School, New York   1,374
New York Restaurant School, New York   1,281

New York University, New York   37,150
Pace University, New York   7,911
Rabbinical College Bobover Yeshiva Bnei Zion, Brooklyn   282
Swedish Institute, New York   388
Syrit College, Brooklyn   472
Taylor Business Institute, New York   600
Technical Career Institute, New York   4,010
Touro College, New York   8,092

Newspapers and circulation

	District circulation	Total circulation
Daily Variety, Los Angeles*	1,366	27,269
El Diario-La Prensa, New York City	4,844	54,695
El Vocero de Puerto Rico, New York City*	4,512	22,299
Hoy, New York City	2,695	59,949
Long Island Newsday	7,852	575,889
New York Amsterdam News	2,109	16,414
*New York Daily News**	60,484	723,155
*New York Law Journal**	2,081	11,519
New York Post	62,942	511,412
*New York Times**	64,984	666,228
*USA Today**	7,977	1,674,376
Washington Post	1,407	779,632

*See Sources and Explanations in the front of the volume.

Television stations and affiliations

New York	100%	WABC	ABC
New York	100%	WCBS	CBS
New York	100%	WEDW	PBS
New York	100%	WFME	Independent
New York	100%	WLIW	PBS
New York	100%	WLNY	Independent
New York	100%	WMBC	Independent
New York	100%	WNBC	NBC
New York	100%	WNET	PBS
New York	100%	WNJB	PBS
New York	100%	WNJN	PBS
New York	100%	WNJU	Telemundo
New York	100%	WNYE	PBS
New York	100%	WNYW	FOX
New York	100%	WPIX	WB
New York	100%	WPXN	PAX
New York	100%	WRNN	Independent
New York	100%	WTBY	Independent
New York	100%	WWOR	UPN
New York	100%	WXTV	Univision

Cable systems and subscribers
Cablevision*   80,861
Time Warner*   53,907

*See Sources and Explanations in the front of the volume.

Businesses and other major employers
City University of New York; New York   16,700
Merrill Lynch and Co.; New York; security brokers, dealers   10,000
New York University; New York   9,500
Morgan Stanley Dean Witter and Co.; New York; security brokers, dealers   9,238

American Express Co.; New York; credit card service 7,000

American International Group Inc.; New York; mortgage guarantee insurance 5,700

Prudential Securities Inc.; New York; security brokers 5,700

Deloitte Consulting; New York; certified public accountant 5,100

National Union Insurance Co.; New York; accident and health insurance 5,000

New York City Housing Authority; New York; housing agency 5,000

Salomon Smith Barney Inc.; New York; security brokers, dealers 5,000

U.S. Postal Service; New York 5,000

Alliance Capital Management Holding Inc.; New York; investment holding company 4,400

New Partners Inc.; New York; home health care 4,400

New York Times Co.; New York; newspaper 4,200

St. Vincent's Catholic Medical Centers of New York; New York 4,200

Maimonides Medical Center; Brooklyn 3,950

New York City; New York; housing agency 3,600

J. Crew Operating Corp.; New York; mail-order apparel 3,500

New York City Board of Education; Brooklyn 3,200

Metropolitan Opera Assn. Inc.; New York; opera company 3,002

Ogden Confection Corp.; New York; concessionaire 3,000

Smokefree Educational Services; New York; substance abuse counseling 3,000

Federal Reserve Bank of New York; New York 2,827

JP Morgan Securities Inc.; New York; security dealers 2,800

New York City; New York; city government 2,800

St. Luke's-Roosevelt Hospital Center; New York 2,504

New York City; New York; social and human resources 2,500

Tri-State Employment Service Inc.; New York; employment agencies 2,500

American Express Travel Related Services Co.; New York; credit card service 2,250

Brylane Inc.; New York; mail-order apparel 2,250

Advance Magazine Publishers Inc.; New York; magazine publishing 2,200

TD Waterhouse Investor Services Inc.; New York; security brokers 2,200

State Insurance Fund; New York; social and manpower programs 2,050

Auxilliary Police Bene Assn. Inc.; New York; professional organization 2,000

Goldman Sachs and Co; New York; security brokers, dealers 2,000

Instinet Corp.; New York; security brokers 2,000

New York Attorney General; New York 2,000

New York City; New York; legal counsel and prosecution 2,000

New York City; New York; youth organizations 2,000

Ogilvy and Mather Worldwide Inc.; New York; telemarketing 2,000

People Care Inc.; New York; temporary help service 2,000

Progressive Home Health Services Inc.; New York; home health care 1,950

U.S. Federal Bureau of Investigation; New York 1,817

Skadden Arps Slate Meagher and Flom; New York; law office 1,800

Depository Trust and Clearing Corp.; New York; security custodians 1,760

Centennial Insurance Co.; New York; property damage insurance 1,700

Namdor Inc.; New York; supermarkets 1,700

Legal Aid Society; New York; public defender's office 1,600

New York State Court Officers Assn. Security Benefit Fund; New York 1,600

New York State Unified Court System; New York 1,600

Cement and Concrete Works Training; Brooklyn; labor organization 1,500

New York Stock Exchange Inc.; New York; security and commodity exchange 1,500

Pace University; New York 1,500

American Museum of Natural History; New York 1,400

Building Maintenance Service Corp.; New York; office cleaning 1,400

Group Health Inc.; New York; medical service plans 1,400

JP Morgan Chase Bank; New York; stock transfer agents 1,400

Metropolitan Jewish Health Systems; Brooklyn; home health care 1,400

State University of New York; New York 1,400

Sullivan and Cromwell; New York; law office 1,392

Forest Electric Corp.; New York; electrical contractor 1,300

Saatchi and Saatchi North America Inc.; New York; advertising 1,300

Cravath Swaine and Moore; New York; law office 1,250

Barnesandnoble.com Inc.; New York; bookstores 1,237

Barclays Group Inc.; New York; investment bankers 1,200

Fashion Institute of Technology; New York; community college 1,200

Guardian Life Insurance Company of America; New York 1,200

Madison Square Garden; New York; basketball club 1,200

HSBC Asset Management Americas Inc.; New York; investment advice 1,150

Moody's Investors Service Inc.; New York; technical manual and paper publishing 1,150

Reliance Insurance Inc.; New York; insurance agents and brokers 1,144

Village Care of New York Inc.; New York; nursing/personal care facility management 1,050

New York University Downtown Hospital; New York 1,020

AIG Funding Inc.; New York; purchaser accounts receivable/commercial paper 1,000

American Broadcasting Companies Inc.; New York; TV broadcasting stations 1,000

Cede and Co.; New York; security transfer agents 1,000

Cleary Gottlieb Steen and Hamilton; New York; law office   1,000

Global Crossing North America Inc.; New York; local/long-distance telephone   1,000

Health Insurance Plan of Greater NY; New York; medical service plans   1,000

Merrill Lynch Pierce Fenner and Smith Inc.; New York; security brokers   1,000

National Assn. of Holy Name Society; New York; religious organization   1,000

National Benefit Fund for Health and Human Service Employees; New York; union trust funds   1,000

New York City; New York; legal services   1,000

New York City; New York; city government   1,000

New York City; New York; police dept.   1,000

Proskauer Rose; New York; law office   1,000

Reliance National Insurance Co.; New York; insurance agents and brokers   1,000

Standard and Poor's Corp.; New York; statistical reports   1,000

VGP Corp.; New York; security brokers, dealers   1,000

VNU Business Media Inc.; New York; trade journals   1,000

New York City; New York; commercial regulation   996

Spear Leeds and Kellogg; New York; security brokers   955

Brown Bros. Harriman and Co; New York; security dealers   950

International Business Machines Corp.; New York; computer peripherals, software   950

Prestige Care Inc.; New York; home health care   950

Denihan Benjamin and Patrick; New York; hotels and motels   900

First Chinese Presbyterian Community Affairs Home Attendent Corp.; New York; home health care services   900

Information Builders Inc.; New York; computer systems analysis and design   900

Riese New York Inc.; New York; restaurant chain   900

Universal Studios Inc.; New York; entertainment service   900

State Insurance Fund; New York; insurance agents   850

Cadwalader Wickersham and Taft; New York; law office   845

Burns International Security Services Corp.; New York; security guard service   816

Community School District; New York   814

New York Dept. of Transportation; New York   811

Century 21 Department Stores; New York; department stores   805

Hachette Filipacchi Magazines Inc.; New York; magazine publishing   800

Initial Security Inc.; New York; guard services   800

Polygram Holding Inc.; New York; prerecorded audio magnetic tapes   800

Thomson Professional and Regulatory Inc.; New York; software development   800

U.S. Drug Enforcement Admin.; New York   800

West Telemarketing Corp.; New York; sales consultant   760

Bernstein and Co.; New York; investment research   750

New York City; New York; correctional institutions   750

Scholastic Inc.; New York; book publishing   750

Venator Group Retail Inc.; New York; shoe stores   750

Fried Frank Harris Shriver and Jacobson; New York; law office   740

MJG Nursing Home Co. Inc.; Brooklyn; nursing care facilities   725

D'Arcy Masius Benton and Bowles Inc.; New York; advertising   712

St. Clare Hospital and Health Center; New York   710

HealthFirst Inc.; New York; health maintenance organization   700

Messner Vetere Berger McNamee Schmetterer; New York; advertising   700

New York Assistant Secretary for Admin. and Management; New York   700

New York Dept. of State; New York   700

U.S. Coast Guard; Brooklyn   700

Milbank Tweed Hadley and McCloy; New York; law office   677

Macy's East Inc.; New York; department stores   650

Royal Care Inc.; Brooklyn; employment agencies   650

Pillsbury Winthrop LLP; New York; law office   646

New York Mercantile Exchange Inc.; New York; commodity traders, contracts   625

Kateri Residence; New York; nursing care facilities   612

AIG Global Investment Corp.; New York; open-ended management investment   605

Alternate Staffing Inc.; Brooklyn; medical help service   600

Cahill Gordon and Reindel; New York; law office   600

Electra Cleaning Contractors Corp.; New York; building maintenance   600

Fairchild Publications Inc.; New York; periodicals   600

Geneva Staffing Services Inc.; New York; employment agencies   600

Georgeson Shareholder Inc.; New York; management consulting   600

HSBC Markets Inc.; New York; security dealers   600

Lifetime Entertainment Services; New York; cable TV   600

Madison Square Garden; New York; business planning, organizing services   600

McGraw-Hill Companies Inc.; New York; public relations services   600

New School University; New York   600

New York City; New York; city management   600

New York City; New York; police dept.   600

New York City Board of Education; New York   600

New York City Health and Hospitals Corp.; New York   600

New York Daily News; New York; newspaper publishing   600

New York Foundling Hospital; New York   600

New York Pressmen's Union; New York; labor organization   600

Penguin Putnam Inc.; New York; book publishing   600

Remco Maintenance Corp.; New York; exterior cleaning   600

U.S. Army Corps of Engineers; New York   600

U.S. Dept. of Housing and Urban Development; New York   600

Winfield Security Corp.; New York; protective services, guard 600

Daiwa Securities of America Inc.; New York; security brokers, dealers 579

America Daiwa Corp.; New York; security dealers 575

Boston Concessions Group of New York; New York; facilities support services 550

Elite Investigations; New York; protective services, guard 550

FCB Worldwide Inc.; New York; advertising 550

Juilliard School; New York 550

New York Penta Hotel; New York; hotels and motels 550

New Yorker Hotel Management Co.; New York; hotel, franchised 550

Zurich American Insurance Co.; New York; life insurance 550

Parsons Brinckerhoff Inc.; New York; management consulting 546

Foot Locker Inc.; New York; shoe stores 527

Lincoln Center for Performing Arts Inc.; New York; theatrical producers 511

SG Cowen Securities Corp.; New York; security brokers 510

Order of Friars Minor of Province of Most Holy Name; New York; religious organization 504

Amalgamated Life Insurance; New York; life insurance 500

American Express Travel Related Services Co.; New York; reservation services 500

B&H Foto and Electronics Corp.; New York; photographic supplies 500

Bank of America Corp.; New York; security brokers 500

City Center of Music and Drama Inc.; New York; theatrical producers 500

Coach Inc.; New York; handbags 500

Cooper Union for Advancement of Science and Art Inc.; New York; real property lessors 500

Deutsch Inc.; New York; advertising 500

Fedcap Rehabilitation Services Inc.; New York; home health care 500

Federation Employment and Guidance Service Inc.; New York; vocational rehabilitation agency 500

Gap Inc.; New York; clothing 500

J&R Sound; New York; high-fidelity equipment 500

JGB Health Facilities; New York; nursing care facilities 500

Lansdell Protective Agency Inc.; New York; guard services 500

Man International Inc.; New York; commodity traders, contracts 500

Metropolitan Jewish Geriatric Center Inc.; Brooklyn; nursing care facilities 500

Mitchell International Inc.; New York; periodicals 500

Mulligan Security Corp.; New York; detective, armored car services 500

National Railroad Passenger Corp.; New York; passenger rail transportation 500

New York City; New York; transportation department 500

New York City; New York; personal service agents 500

New York City; Brooklyn; police dept. 500

New York Dept. of Insurance; New York 500

New York Health Care Inc.; Brooklyn; home health care 500

New York State Liquidation Bureau; New York 500

Prism Communication Services Inc.; New York; alarm, safety equipment 500

Reed Elsevier Inc.; New York; periodicals 500

Stanley Morgan Mortgage Capital Inc.; New York; mortgage bankers 500

T&M Protection Resources Inc.; New York; protective services, guard 500

Thomas Publishing Co.; New York; data processing 500

U.S. District Court Southern District of New York; New York 500

U.S. Veterans Affairs Dept.; New York 500

UMG Recordings Inc.; New York; prerecorded records and tapes 500

Video Monitoring Services of America Inc.; New York; information retrieval services 500

Visiting Nurse Service of New York; New York 500

New York 9th District

Part of Brooklyn and Queens — Forest Hills, Rockaway, Sheepshead Bay

The Democratic-leaning 9th takes in north-central and western Queens and segues into southeastern Brooklyn. The district was divided almost equally between Brooklyn and Queens in the late 1990s, but 2002 redistricting left the 9th with 70 percent of its registered voters living in Queens. *(See map p. 620.)*

The new map extended the 9th farther east in Queens, past the Grand Central Parkway and through the Hillcrest and Fresh Meadows neighborhoods to the edge of Oakland Gardens, which is only a few exits from Nassau County on the Long Island Expressway. Many of Queens' wealthiest communities are in the northern part of the 9th.

The 9th narrows and runs south from Forest Park, taking in part of the Woodhaven, Ozone Park, and Lindenwood neighborhoods. A decade ago, these areas were mostly white. Hispanics now outnumber whites, and the Asian population is rapidly expanding.

The 9th also takes in much of the Rockaway area in far southwestern Queens along the Atlantic Ocean. In Brooklyn, the district includes Floyd Bennett Field and most of Gateway National Recreation Area on Jamaica Bay. Farther west, the Sheepshead Bay area has seen an influx of Russian immigrants.

A sizable Jewish population contributes to the district's Democratic heft. Registered Democrats outnumber Republicans by a three-to-one ratio, and Al Gore topped two-thirds of the vote here in 2000.

Major Industry

Service, finance, insurance, manufacturing.

Notable

Kings Plaza Shopping Center and Marina, billed as the first indoor mall in New York City, opened in 1970 near Mill Basin.

Election Returns

	Republican		Democratic		Other	
President 2000	54,699	29.5%	123,763	66.9%	6,649	3.6%
House 2002	31,698	34.3%	60,737	65.7%		

District Profile

Population   654,360

Total area (square miles)   103.2
Land area (square miles)   37.0

Population per square mile   17,685.4

Counties (2000 population)
Kings (pt.)   203,888
Queens (pt.)   450,472

Cities and other areas over 10,000 (2000 population)
New York (pt.)   654,360

Race and Hispanic or Latino origin*
White   64.0%
Black or African American   4.0%
American Indian or Alaska Native   0.1%
Asian   14.5%
Native Hawaiian or other Pacific Islander   0.0%
Some other race   0.7%
Hispanic or Latino origin   13.6%
Two or more races   3.0%

*As percentage of total population.

Ancestry*

Arab-Misc. 1.2%		Polish 4.3%	
German 4.7%		Russian 7.2%	
Greek 1.1%		Ukrainian 2.0%	
Irish 7.5%		USA/American 3.4%	
Italian 12.3%		West Indian 1.2%	

*As estimated percentage of total population.

Universities and colleges, 2000–2001 enrollment
Bramson ORT Technical Institute, Forest Hills   621
Central Yeshiva Tomchei Tmimim Lubavitz, Brooklyn
465
City University of New York Kingsborough College,
Brooklyn   14,801
City University of New York Queens College, Flushing
15,061
St. John's University-New York, Jamaica   18,621

Newspapers and circulation

	District circulation	Total circulation
El Diario-La Prensa, New York City	1,853	54,695
Hoy, New York City	4,062	59,949
Long Island Newsday	22,601	575,889
*New York Daily News**	80,837	723,155
New York Post	24,452	511,412
*New York Times**	34,461	666,228
*USA Today**	2,044	1,674,376

*See Sources and Explanations in the front of the volume.

Television stations and affiliations

New York	100%	WABC	ABC
New York	100%	WCBS	CBS
New York	100%	WEDW	PBS
New York	100%	WFME	Independent
New York	100%	WLIW	PBS
New York	100%	WLNY	Independent
New York	100%	WMBC	Independent
New York	100%	WNBC	NBC
New York	100%	WNET	PBS
New York	100%	WNJB	PBS
New York	100%	WNJN	PBS
New York	100%	WNJU	Telemundo
New York	100%	WNYE	PBS
New York	100%	WNYW	FOX
New York	100%	WPIX	WB
New York	100%	WPXN	PAX
New York	100%	WRNN	Independent
New York	100%	WTBY	Independent
New York	100%	WWOR	UPN
New York	100%	WXTV	Univision

Cable systems and subscribers
Cablevision*   45,551
Time Warner*   68,327

*See Sources and Explanations in the front of the volume.

Military installations, September 2001
Navy Marine Corps Reserve Center, Brooklyn   447

Businesses and other major employers
Mount Sinai Hospital; Jamaica   3,900
Home Attendant Vendor Agency Inc.; Brooklyn; home
health care   1,500
B&G Registry Inc.; Brooklyn; nurses' registry   1,200
Parkway Hospital Inc.; Forest Hills   940
North Shore University Hospital; Forest Hills   845
Consolidated Edison Company of New York Inc.; Forest
Hills; electric services   800
Defender Security Services Inc.; Rego Park; security
guard service   675
Pomonok Home Services Inc.; Fresh Meadows; home
health care   650
Silver Crest Extended Care Facility; Flushing   600
St. Vincent's Hospital and Medical Center; Flushing
600
City University of New York; Brooklyn   500

New York 10th District

Part of Brooklyn — Bedford-Stuyvesant, Canarsie, Downtown Brooklyn, East New York

The 10th begins just inland of Brooklyn's industrial waterfront and heads east before bounding back southwest after reaching the Queens border. The district encompasses one of New York's most economically and ethnically diverse constituencies but is homogeneously Democratic, with a 13-to-1 Democratic registration advantage. Al Gore took almost 88 percent of the area's vote in the 2000 presidential contest. (See map p. 620.)

Redistricting in 2002 brought the black-majority 10th west of Flatbush Avenue to include part of Midwood in south-central Brooklyn. East of this area, the district takes in growing Georgetown and Canarsie. Canarsie's racial composition has changed dramatically, as many blacks of Caribbean descent are moving to an area that was once predominantly white. Many of these families have solid middle-class incomes, which is the exception rather than the rule for most of the district. At its northwest corner, the 10th cups the Brooklyn Navy Yard (located in the 12th) to take in Fort Greene and part of Williamsburg—diverse areas with large black and Hispanic populations.

Joblessness has aggravated poverty, violent crime, and racial tensions in some working-class and low-income communities like East New York and Bedford-Stuyvesant. Erosion in the 10th's manufacturing base has caused unemployment, though government jobs in Downtown Brooklyn, which includes Borough Hall and several court facilities, and education jobs at the district's colleges, which include Brooklyn College and Long Island University-Brooklyn, aid the economy.

Aging infrastructure is a problem, as water and sewer lines are prone to collapse and heavy truck traffic is eroding the Brooklyn-Queens Expressway and residential streets leading to the Brooklyn and Manhattan bridges (both in the 12th District).

Major Industry

Government, higher education, small business, pharmaceuticals.

Notable

Spike Lee's film, *Do the Right Thing,* is set in Bedford-Stuyvesant.

Election Returns

	Republican		Democratic		Other	
President 2000	13,058	7.7%	149,018	87.6%	8,029	4.7%
House 2002			73,859	97.8%	1,639	2.2%

District Profile

Population   654,361

Total area (square miles)   18.0
   Land area (square miles)   17.8

Population per square mile   36,761.9

Counties (2000 population)
   Kings (pt.)   654,361

Cities and other areas over 10,000 (2000 population)
   New York (pt.)   654,361

Race and Hispanic or Latino origin*
   White   16.2%
   Black or African American   60.2%
   American Indian or Alaska Native   0.2%
   Asian   2.7%
   Native Hawaiian or other Pacific Islander   0.0%
   Some other race   0.9%

Hispanic or Latino origin   17.2%
Two or more races   2.6%

*As percentage of total population.

Ancestry*

Irish 1.2%	Subsaharan 2.5%
Italian 2.3%	USA/American 3.9%
Russian 1.1%	West Indian 14.8%

*As estimated percentage of total population.

Universities and colleges, 2000–2001 enrollment
   ASA Institute of Business and Computer Technology, Brooklyn   1,432
   Brooklyn Law School, Brooklyn   1,499
   City University of New York Technical College, Brooklyn   11,028
   Institute of Design and Construction, Brooklyn   215
   Long Island University-Brooklyn, Brooklyn   7,780
   Polytechnic University, Brooklyn   3,059
   Pratt Institute, Brooklyn   4,272
   St. Joseph's College, Brooklyn   1,351
   United Talmudical Seminary, Brooklyn   1,640
   Yeshiva of Nitra Rabbinical College, Brooklyn   224

Newspapers and circulation

	District circulation	Total circulation
El Diario-La Prensa, New York City	2,202	54,695
Hoy, New York City	1,321	59,949
Long Island Newsday	3,700	575,889
New York Amsterdam News	1,710	16,414
*New York Daily News**	23,599	723,155
New York Post	12,555	511,412
*New York Times**	8,934	666,228

*See Sources and Explanations in the front of the volume.

Television stations and affiliations

New York	100%	WABC	ABC
New York	100%	WCBS	CBS
New York	100%	WEDW	PBS
New York	100%	WFME	Independent
New York	100%	WLIW	PBS
New York	100%	WLNY	Independent
New York	100%	WMBC	Independent
New York	100%	WNBC	NBC
New York	100%	WNET	PBS
New York	100%	WNJB	PBS
New York	100%	WNJN	PBS
New York	100%	WNJU	Telemundo
New York	100%	WNYE	PBS
New York	100%	WNYW	FOX
New York	100%	WPIX	WB
New York	100%	WPXN	PAX
New York	100%	WRNN	Independent
New York	100%	WTBY	Independent
New York	100%	WWOR	UPN
New York	100%	WXTV	Univision

Cable systems and subscribers
   Cablevision*   90,207
   Time Warner*   10,023

*See Sources and Explanations in the front of the volume.

Businesses and other major employers

Brookdale University Hospital Medical Center Inc.; Brooklyn 3,700

Brookdale Hospital Center Housing Co. Inc.; Brooklyn; rooming and boarding houses 3,508

Verizon Communications Inc.; Brooklyn; telephone services 3,000

Brooklyn Hospital Center; Brooklyn 2,700

U.S. Postal Service; Brooklyn 2,500

New York City Transit Authority; Brooklyn 2,200

City University of New York; Brooklyn 2,000

Linroc Community Services Corp.; Brooklyn; nursing/personal care facility management 2,000

New York Mental Health Office; Brooklyn 1,800

Cabs Home Attendants Service Inc.; Brooklyn; home health care 1,750

Bear Stearns Securities Corp.; Brooklyn; security exchange clearinghouse 1,500

Consolidated Edison Company of New York Inc.; Brooklyn; electric, other services 1,500

Keyspan Gas East Corp.; Brooklyn; natural gas distribution 1,500

Transcare Corp.; Brooklyn; ambulance service 1,500

Human Development Assn. Inc.; Brooklyn; home health care 1,450

St. Mary's Hospital of Brooklyn Inc.; Brooklyn 1,400

New York City; Brooklyn; district attorney's office 1,100

Securities Industry Automation Corp.; Brooklyn; security exchange clearinghouse 1,070

New York City; Brooklyn; fire dept. 1,000

New York City; Brooklyn; public welfare administration 1,000

New York City Health and Hospitals Corp.; Brooklyn 1,000

Pratt Institute; Brooklyn 840

Long Island University; Brooklyn 800

New York City; Brooklyn; taxation department 800

Empire Insurance Co.; Brooklyn; property insurance 730

Pfizer Corp.; Brooklyn; medicinals/botanicals 620

Medical Associates of Woodhull; Brooklyn; medical help service 550

Dorothy and David Schachne Institute for Nursing and Rehab Inc.; Brooklyn; nursing home 500

New York Dept. of Taxation and Finance; Brooklyn 500

Starrett City Inc.; Brooklyn; apartment building operators 500

New York 11th District

Part of Brooklyn — Flatbush, Crown Heights, Brownsville, Park Slope

A black-majority residential district in central Brooklyn, the 11th is predominantly working-class but also contains some of the borough's wealthiest neighborhoods. *(See map p. 620.)*

Redistricting in 2002 did not significantly alter the district's boundaries, other than to extend it westward through Carroll Gardens into parts of Cobble Hill and Brooklyn Heights to compensate for slow population growth in the 1990s. The changes did not affect the district's reliably Democratic vote: Democrats outnumber Republicans 12 to one. George W. Bush finished with less than 9 percent of the vote here in the 2000 presidential election.

At the heart of the district is Flatbush, a working-class black and Hispanic neighborhood that has become home to numerous Caribbean immigrants from Jamaica, Haiti, the Dominican Republic, and Trinidad and Tobago. The 11th's West Indian Carnival Parade attracts hundreds of thousands of visitors each year, a feature that economic development officials hope to exploit to draw tourists into Brooklyn.

In the district's north is Crown Heights, made infamous in 1991 when a car driven by an orthodox rabbi's assistant struck and killed a black child, setting off four days of riots between African Americans and Hasidic Jews.

While New York City gained population in the 1990s, the Crown Heights region lost population during that period. Brownsville, east of Crown Heights, also is heavily black. Pockets of affluence in the 11th include Park Slope, just northwest of Prospect Park, and part of Brooklyn Heights near the Brooklyn Bridge.

Major Industry

Health care, retail.

Notable

Ebbets Field, where the Brooklyn Dodgers played from 1913 to 1957, was demolished in 1960 and is now a housing complex; the Brooklyn Museum of Art and Brooklyn Botanic Garden are in the 11th.

Election Returns

	Republican		Democratic		Other	
President 2000	15,652	8.6%	149,740	82.6%	15,828	8.7%
House 2002	11,149	12.5%	76,917	86.6%	798	0.9%

District Profile

Population 654,361

Total area (square miles) 12.1
   Land area (square miles) 12.0

Population per square mile 54,530.1

Counties (2000 population)
   Kings (pt.) 654,361

Cities and other areas over 10,000 (2000 population)
   New York (pt.) 654,361

Race and Hispanic or Latino origin*
   White 21.4%
   Black or African American 58.5%
   American Indian or Alaska Native 0.2%
   Asian 4.1%
   Native Hawaiian or other Pacific Islander 0.0%
   Some other race 0.6%
   Hispanic or Latino origin 12.1%
   Two or more races 3.0%

As percentage of total population.

Ancestry*

English	1.2%	Russian	2.4%
German	1.6%	Subsaharan	2.3%
Irish	2.6%	USA/American	4.1%
Italian	2.8%	West Indian	23.2%
Polish	1.5%		

As estimated percentage of total population.

Universities and colleges, 2000–2001 enrollment

City University of New York Brooklyn College, Brooklyn   15,039

City University of New York Medgar Evers College, Brooklyn   4,614

Gamla College, Brooklyn   249

Grace Institute of Business Technology, Brooklyn   301

Mesivta Torah Vodaath Rabbinical Seminary, Brooklyn   338

Mirrer Yeshiva Cent Institute, Brooklyn   252

Rabbinical Academy Mesivta Rabbi Chaim Berlin, Brooklyn   388

State University of New York Downstate Medical Center, Brooklyn   1,470

St. Francis College, Brooklyn   2,304

Talmudical Seminary of Oholei Torah, Brooklyn   292

Torah Temimah Talmudical Seminary, Brooklyn   207

Newspapers and circulation

	District circulation	Total circulation
El Diario-La Prensa, New York City	1,658	54,695
Long Island Newsday	2,520	575,889
New York Amsterdam News	1,608	16,414
*New York Daily News**	15,868	723,155
New York Post	13,374	511,412
*New York Times**	6,008	666,228

See Sources and Explanations in the front of the volume.

Television stations and affiliations

New York	100%	WABC	ABC
New York	100%	WCBS	CBS
New York	100%	WEDW	PBS
New York	100%	WFME	Independent
New York	100%	WLIW	PBS
New York	100%	WLNY	Independent
New York	100%	WMBC	Independent
New York	100%	WNBC	NBC
New York	100%	WNET	PBS
New York	100%	WNJB	PBS
New York	100%	WNJN	PBS
New York	100%	WNJU	Telemundo
New York	100%	WNYE	PBS
New York	100%	WNYW	FOX
New York	100%	WPIX	WB
New York	100%	WPXN	PAX
New York	100%	WRNN	Independent
New York	100%	WTBY	Independent
New York	100%	WWOR	UPN
New York	100%	WXTV	Univision

Cable systems and subscribers

Cablevision*   84,670

Time Warner*   21,167

See Sources and Explanations in the front of the volume.

Businesses and other major employers

New York City Health and Hospitals Corp.; Brooklyn   6,000

State University of New York; Brooklyn   3,000

New York Methodist Hospital; Brooklyn   2,881

Kingsbrook Jewish Medical Center Inc.; Brooklyn   2,100

Interfaith Medical Center; Brooklyn   2,000

New York City Board of Education; Brooklyn   1,986

Project OHR Inc.; Brooklyn; homemakers' service   1,550

Assn. for Services for Aged Inc.; Brooklyn; convalescent home   1,300

BHRAGS Inc.; Brooklyn; home health care   1,000

UHS Home Attendants Inc.; Brooklyn; home health care   850

Independence Community Bank; Brooklyn; state commercial banks   800

Rutland Nursing Home Inc.; Brooklyn; nursing care facilities   725

Brooklyn Hospital Center; Brooklyn   600

City University of New York; Brooklyn   500

New York 12th District

Lower East Side of Manhattan; parts of Brooklyn and Queens

The 12th, which touches parts of Manhattan, Brooklyn, and Queens, was created in 1992 to form a Hispanic-majority district under the Voting Rights Act. Once known as the Bullwinkle District because of its resemblance to the cartoon moose, the 12th was redrawn by court decree in 1998 to have a more compact shape and a decreased Hispanic population. Marginal changes in 2002 retained the district's basic contours and pegged its Hispanic population at 48.5 percent. *(See map p. 620.)*

Even with a significant immigrant population that is not eligible to vote and low turnout among Hispanic voters, the 12th elected and continues to send a Puerto Rican representative to Congress. The district's numerous working-class and minority residents make it a Democratic bastion.

Two-thirds of the 12th's registered voters live in Brooklyn. In its southwest corner, the district begins in Sunset Park, which has a large Hispanic population, then segues north along the East River and jumps across the Brooklyn and Manhattan bridges into Manhattan to take in Chinatown, part of Little Italy, and the Lower East Side. Nearly one in five registered voters lives in Manhattan.

Back in northern Brooklyn (the 12th also includes the Williamsburg Bridge), it takes in Greenpoint, which has a large Polish population, and moves east along the Brooklyn-Queens border to the heavily Hispanic neighborhoods of East Williamsburg, Bushwick, and Cypress Hills. In Queens the 12th takes in parts of the Sunnyside and Woodside neighborhoods, which are experiencing rapid Hispanic growth.

Major Industry

Health care, manufacturing, service.

Notable

Brooklyn's Green-Wood Cemetery, where the more than 560,000 interred include Leonard Bernstein, Horace Greeley, and notorious nineteenth century New York politician William M. "Boss" Tweed; Brooklyn Navy Yard; the Brooklyn Heights Promenade, built over the Brooklyn-Queens Expressway, looks out at the lower Manhattan skyline.

Election Returns

	Republican		Democratic		Other	
President 2000	19,604	14.7%	102,465	76.8%	11,268	8.5%
House 2002			48,408	95.8%	2,119	4.2%

District Profile

Population   654,360

Total area (square miles)   19.9
Land area (square miles)   18.7

Population per square mile   34,992.5

Counties (2000 population)
Kings (pt.)   423,267
New York (pt.)   110,623
Queens (pt.)   120,470

Cities and other areas over 10,000 (2000 population)
New York (pt.)   654,360

Race and Hispanic or Latino origin*
White   23.3%
Black or African American   8.8%
American Indian or Alaska Native   0.2%
Asian   15.9%
Native Hawaiian or other Pacific Islander   0.0%
Some other race   0.7%
Hispanic or Latino origin   48.5%
Two or more races   2.5%

*As percentage of total population.

Ancestry*
German 2.3%	Polish 4.4%
Irish 3.4%	USA/American 1.8%
Italian 4.7%	West Indian 1.7%

*As estimated percentage of total population.

Newspapers and circulation

	District circulation	Total circulation
El Diario-La Prensa, New York City	5,584	54,695
Hoy, New York City	2,914	59,949
Long Island Newsday	9,727	575,889
*New York Daily News**	27,290	723,155
New York Post	20,042	511,412
*New York Times**	19,475	666,228
*USA Today**	1,926	1,674,376

*See Sources and Explanations in the front of the volume.

Television stations and affiliations
New York	100%	WABC	ABC
New York	100%	WCBS	CBS
New York	100%	WEDW	PBS
New York	100%	WFME	Independent
New York	100%	WLIW	PBS
New York	100%	WLNY	Independent
New York	100%	WMBC	Independent
New York	100%	WNBC	NBC
New York	100%	WNET	PBS
New York	100%	WNJB	PBS
New York	100%	WNJN	PBS
New York	100%	WNJU	Telemundo
New York	100%	WNYE	PBS
New York	100%	WNYW	FOX
New York	100%	WPIX	WB
New York	100%	WPXN	PAX
New York	100%	WRNN	Independent
New York	100%	WTBY	Independent
New York	100%	WWOR	UPN
New York	100%	WXTV	Univision

Cable systems and subscribers
Cablevision*   50,021
Time Warner*   50,021

*See Sources and Explanations in the front of the volume.

Businesses and other major employers
Lutheran Medical Center; Brooklyn   2,918
Long Island College Hospital Inc.; Brooklyn   2,679
Western Beef Inc.; Ridgewood; fresh meats   2,000
Wyckoff Heights Medical Center; Brooklyn   1,615
New York City; Woodside; rubbish collection and disposal   1,500
New York City Health and Hospitals Corp.; New York   1,100
New York Dept. of Labor; Brooklyn   1,000
St. Nicholas Youth and Family Center; Brooklyn; helping-hand service   999
United Jewish Council of East Side Home Attendance Service Corp.; New York; home health care   850
New York State Unified Court System; Brooklyn   700
School Settlement-Home Attendant Service Corp.; Brooklyn; home health care   700
Peerless Importers Inc.; Brooklyn; wine   677
Morgan Stanley and Co.; Brooklyn; security brokers, dealers   600
Cobble Hill Nursing Home Inc.; Brooklyn; nursing care facilities   550
TASR Co.; Brooklyn; cane sugar refining   550
Educational Alliance Inc.; New York; community development   500
Blue Ridge Farms Inc.; Brooklyn; fresh or refrigerated salads   500
B&H Staffing Inc.; Brooklyn; medical help service   500
White Glove Placement Inc.; Brooklyn; nurses' registry   500
Metaldyne Corp.; Brooklyn; floor attachment partitions   500
Avon Products Inc.; Brooklyn; cosmetics   500
Creative Solutions Group Inc.; Woodside; window/lobby displays   500

New York 13th District

Staten Island; part of southwest Brooklyn

Staten Island's large retired population and white, upper-middle-class suburban residents make the 13th more amenable to Republicans than any of New York City's other districts. *(See map p. 620.)*

The 13th's predominantly Italian American and Catholic conservatives that live on both sides of the Verrazano Narrows Bridge, which connects Staten Island and Brooklyn, have elected a Republican representative since 1982. While Democrat Al Gore carried Staten Island with 52 percent in the 2000 presidential election, Republican Michael R. Bloomberg took 77 percent en route to his mayoral victory in 2001. Gore won the 13th overall with 52.4 percent.

Staten Island was so disenchanted with New York City's Democratic leadership that in 1993 residents overwhelmingly approved a referendum to secede from the city, though the state legislature blocked its enactment. Chief among Staten Island's complaints had been the presence of the Fresh Kills landfill, which the city sanitation department closed in March 2001 but which some have argued should be reopened at least temporarily.

The least diverse of the five boroughs, Staten Island is the only one in which non-Hispanic whites make up a majority of the residents (70.9 percent). The Hispanic and black populations are concentrated mostly in the borough's northeastern neighborhoods. There is an Asian presence in some of the borough's north-central neighborhoods.

Almost three-fourths of registered voters live in Staten Island. The Brooklyn portions of the district include Bay Ridge, Dyker Heights, and part of Bensonhurst near the Verrazano Narrows Bridge. South of Bensonhurst, the 13th buttonhooks south of Cropsey Avenue and moves east to Ocean Parkway, taking in the Gravesend neighborhood.

Major Industry
Health care, retail, communications.

Notable
Bay Ridge was the setting for the 1977 disco movie *Saturday Night Fever*; Todt Hill is touted as the highest point on the eastern seaboard south of Maine.

Election Returns

	Republican		Democratic		Other	
President 2000	85,119	44.2%	101,079	52.4%	6,538	3.4%
House 2002	72,204	69.6%	29,366	28.3%	2,123	2.0%

District Profile

Population   654,361

Total area (square miles)   113.4
   Land area (square miles)   64.7

Population per square mile   10,113.8

Counties (2000 population)
   Kings (pt.)   210,633
   Richmond   443,728

Cities and other areas over 10,000 (2000 population)
   New York (pt.)   654,361

Race and Hispanic or Latino origin*
White   70.9%
Black or African American   6.3%
American Indian or Alaska Native   0.1%
Asian   9.1%
Native Hawaiian or other Pacific Islander   0.0%
Some other race   0.2%
Hispanic or Latino origin   11.0%
Two or more races   2.3%

As percentage of total population.

Ancestry*
Arab-Misc.	2.2%	Italian	29.5%
English	1.6%	Norwegian	1.2%
German	4.3%	Polish	3.1%
Greek	1.4%	Russian	3.0%
Irish	11.5%	USA/American	1.9%

As estimated percentage of total population.

Universities and colleges, 2000–2001 enrollment
City University of New York College of Staten Island, Staten Island   11,115
Wagner College, Staten Island   2,049

Newspapers and circulation

	District circulation	Total circulation
Long Island Newsday	1,571	575,889
*New York Daily News**	37,525	723,155
New York Post	23,669	511,412
*New York Times**	13,543	666,228
Staten Island Advance	67,066	67,637

See Sources and Explanations in the front of the volume.

Television stations and affiliations
New York	100%	WABC	ABC
New York	100%	WCBS	CBS
New York	100%	WEDW	PBS
New York	100%	WFME	Independent
New York	100%	WLIW	PBS
New York	100%	WLNY	Independent
New York	100%	WMBC	Independent
New York	100%	WNBC	NBC
New York	100%	WNET	PBS
New York	100%	WNJB	PBS
New York	100%	WNJN	PBS
New York	100%	WNJU	Telemundo
New York	100%	WNYE	PBS
New York	100%	WNYW	FOX
New York	100%	WPIX	WB
New York	100%	WPXN	PAX
New York	100%	WRNN	Independent
New York	100%	WTBY	Independent
New York	100%	WWOR	UPN
New York	100%	WXTV	Univision

Cable systems and subscribers
Cablevision*   10,708
Time Warner*   96,368

See Sources and Explanations in the front of the volume.

Military installations, September 2001
Fort Hamilton (Army), New York   1,335
Staten Island U.S. Army Reserve Center, Brooklyn   481

Businesses and other major employers
Staten Island University Hospital; Staten Island   4,075
Sanitation Officers Associates Local; Brooklyn; union
3,700
American Express; New York; credit card services
2,250
U.S. Veterans Hospital; Brooklyn   2,000
Stella Orton Home Care Agency Inc.; Staten Island;
home health care   1,200
Victory Memorial Hospital; Brooklyn   1,085
New York Mental Health Office; Staten Island   1,000
Staten Island University Hospital; Staten Island   990
Metropolitan Escort Services Inc.; Staten Island;
employment agencies   800
New York Mental Retardation and Developmental
Disabilities Office; Staten Island   800
City University of New York; Staten Island   750
Cardiac Management Systems; Brooklyn; administrative
management   700
Nicholas Demisay; Staten Island; nursing care facilities
650
Patient Care Inc.; Brooklyn; home health care   630
Eger Health Care Center; Staten Island   620
New York City Health and Hospitals Corp.; Staten
Island   620
New York City; Staten Island; ferries   600
Carmel Richmond Nursing Home Inc.; Staten Island;
nursing care facilities   575
Sisters of Charity Health Care System Nursing Home
Inc.; Staten Island; nursing care facilities   500
Macy's East Inc.; Staten Island; department stores   500
New York Dept. of Environmental Conservation; Staten
Island   500
New York Dept. of Health; Staten Island   500
Sears Roebuck and Co. Inc.; Staten Island; department
stores   500
Amboy Bus Co. Inc.; Brooklyn; school buses   500

New York 14th District

East Side Manhattan; western Queens

Wealthy Republicans engineered politics on Manhattan's East Side when this "Silk Stocking District" was created. But starting in the 1960s, the old-money elite was gradually supplanted by "limousine liberals," highly educated young professionals devoted to the arts. The 14th has the nation's highest percentage of residents with at least a bachelor's degree (56.9 percent) and the highest percentage who walk to work. *(See map p. 620.)*

Republicans can still compete locally, and the 14th supported GOP Mayor Rudolph Giuliani in 1997. But the district sent a Democrat to Congress in 1992, and its residents have given overwhelming support to Democratic presidential candidates in recent years.

Taking in all of Central Park in the district's northwest corner, the 14th's western edge then roughly follows Broadway south toward Union Square before narrowing to reach the Lower East Side. Landmarks include Carnegie Hall, Rocke-feller Center, Grand Central Terminal, the United Nations, Trump Tower, and Fifth Avenue's Museum Mile.

But the chic neighborhoods of Manhattan's East Side do not tell the whole story of a district that crosses Roosevelt Island to pick up ethnic working-class sections of Queens, such as Astoria, and some poorer sections. Long Island City, once an industrial powerhouse, experienced decline but is seeing some resurgence as a haven for artists. It is also home to Queens West—a massive new commercial and residential development along the riverfront.

Though redistricting in 2002 changed some of the eastern contours of the 14th, it still includes most of the northwestern edge of Queens, which has a mix of ethnic communities. In the 1980s and 1990s, the region attracted immigrants from abroad, particularly Greeks, Asians, and Hispanics. Now it draws Manhattanites in search of more-affordable housing.

Major Industry
Finance, publishing, communications, advertising, health care, tourism.

Notable
The American Museum of the Moving Image is in Astoria; Republican John V. Lindsay and Democrat Edward I. Koch held the East Side congressional seat at the time each was elected mayor of New York.

Election Returns

	Republican		Democratic		Other	
President 2000	56,055	23.2%	168,842	69.8%	16,908	7.0%
House 2002	31,548	24.7%	95,931	75.3%		

District Profile

Population   654,361

Total area (square miles)   14.6
Land area (square miles)   12.5

Population per square mile   52,348.9

Counties (2000 population)
New York (pt.)   449,447
Queens (pt.)   204,914

Cities and other areas over 10,000 (2000 population)
New York (pt.)   654,361

Race and Hispanic or Latino origin*
White   65.9%
Black or African American   4.8%
American Indian or Alaska Native   0.1%
Asian   11.4%
Native Hawaiian or other Pacific Islander   0.0%
Some other race   0.6%
Hispanic or Latino origin   14.0%
Two or more races   3.1%

**As percentage of total population.*

Ancestry*
Arab-Misc.   1.2%   Greek   3.0%
English   4.1%   Hungarian   1.2%
French   1.7%   Irish   8.1%
German   6.1%   Italian   7.7%

Polish   3.8%   USA/American   2.8%
Russian   5.0%

*As estimated percentage of total population.

Universities and colleges, 2000–2001 enrollment

Berkeley College of New York City, New York   1,640
Cornell University Medical College, New York   717
City University of New York Bernard M. Baruch College, New York   15,698
City University of New York Graduate School, New York   3,567
City University of New York Hunter College, New York   20,011
City University of New York La Guardia Community College, Long Island City   11,778
Devry University, Long Island City   1,652
Katharine Gibbs School, New York   2,394
Laboratory Institute of Merchandising, New York   285
Marymount Manhattan College, New York   2,497
Mount Sinai School of Medicine, New York   609
New York Institute of Business Technology, New York   945
New York School of Interior Design, New York   700
Pacific College of Oriental Medicine, New York   439
Rabbinical Seminary of America, New York   384
School of Visual Arts, New York   5,286
State University of New York College of Optometry, New York   289
Wood Tobe-Coburn School, New York   455

Newspapers and circulation

	District circulation	Total circulation
Daily Variety, Los Angeles*	1,135	27,269
El Diario-La Prensa, New York City	6,044	54,695
El Vocero de Puerto Rico, New York City*	3,821	22,299
Hoy, New York City	4,115	59,949
Long Island Newsday	13,991	575,889
New York Amsterdam News	1,437	16,414
*New York Daily News**	34,778	723,155
*New York Law Journal**	1,658	11,519
New York Post	49,671	511,412
*New York Times**	49,112	666,228
*USA Today**	6,658	1,674,376
Washington Post	1,380	779,632

*See Sources and Explanations in the front of the volume.

Television stations and affiliations

New York	100%	WABC	ABC
New York	100%	WCBS	CBS
New York	100%	WEDW	PBS
New York	100%	WFME	Independent
New York	100%	WLIW	PBS
New York	100%	WLNY	Independent
New York	100%	WMBC	Independent
New York	100%	WNBC	NBC
New York	100%	WNET	PBS
New York	100%	WNJB	PBS
New York	100%	WNJN	PBS
New York	100%	WNJU	Telemundo
New York	100%	WNYE	PBS
New York	100%	WNYW	FOX
New York	100%	WPIX	WB
New York	100%	WPXN	PAX
New York	100%	WRNN	Independent
New York	100%	WTBY	Independent
New York	100%	WWOR	UPN
New York	100%	WXTV	Univision

Cable systems and subscribers
Time Warner*   151,141

*See Sources and Explanations in the front of the volume.

Businesses and other major employers

New York City; New York; police dept.   40,000
Hearst Communications Inc.; New York; publishing   20,000
News Publishing Australia; New York   14,890
Forstmann Little and Co.; New York; investment bankers   14,351
New York Presbyterian Hospital; New York   13,899
Mount Sinai School of Medicine City University of New York; New York   12,000
New York University Medical Center; New York   10,000
Paramount Communications Acquisition Corp.; New York; investment holding company   8,000
Mount Sinai Hospital; New York   7,869
New York University Hospital; New York   7,500
RAC Holdings Corp.; New York; restaurant chain   7,500
Verizon Communications Inc.; New York; telephone communication   7,000
Memorial Sloan-Kettering Cancer Center Inc.; New York   6,600
Bear Stearns and Co. Inc.; New York; investment bankers   6,000
Citicorp Credit Services Inc.; Long Island City; credit card service   6,000
Beth Israel Medical Center Inc.; New York   5,500
Metro North Commuter Railroad Co.; New York   5,200
Cornell University; New York   5,000
Lowe Group Inc.; New York; advertising   5,000
Time Inc.; New York; magazine publishing   5,000
United Nations; New York; international organization of nations   5,000
UBS Warburg Inc.; New York; stock brokers and dealers   4,781
Bloomberg; New York; news reporting services   4,500
Columbia University; New York   4,500
New York Life Insurance Co.; New York   4,400
CIBC of Delaware Holdings Inc.; New York; commercial bank   4,200
Credit Suisse Financial Products Inc.; New York; security brokers, dealers   4,190
Teachers Insurance and Annuity Assn. of America; New York; life insurance   4,131
Big Flower Press Holdings Inc.; New York; offset printing   4,100
Consolidated Edison Company of New York Inc.; New York; electric power generation   4,100
Bear Stearns Companies Inc.; New York; security brokers, dealers   4,000

Citibank NA; Long Island City; commercial bank 4,000

Equitable Life Assurance Society of U.S.; New York; life insurance 4,000

New York City Health and Hospitals Corp.; New York 3,825

Waldorf Astoria Hotel Corp.; New York; hotels 3,700

Ernst and Young; New York; certified public accountant 3,300

ARKaid; New York; executive placement 3,025

Toyota Motor North America Inc.; New York; motor vehicles and car bodies 3,005

Colgate-Palmolive Co.; New York; dentifrices 3,000

Home Shopping Network Inc.; New York; TV broadcasting stations 3,000

Lehman Brothers Inc.; New York; security brokers, dealers 3,000

Metropolitan Insurance and Annuity Co; New York; life insurance 3,000

Lenox Hill Hospital; New York 2,850

Deutsche Bank Americas Holding Corp.; New York; personal credit institutions 2,847

PricewaterhouseCoopers; New York; certified public accountant 2,800

Insight Communications Co.; New York; cable TV 2,720

Council of European Union; New York; international organization of nations 2,700

National Broadcasting Co.; New York; TV broadcasting stations 2,600

KPMG; New York; certified public accountant 2,561

Pfizer Corp.; New York; pharmaceuticals 2,500

UBS Painewebber Inc.; New York; security brokers, dealers 2,500

Young and Rubicam Inc.; New York; public relations services, advertising 2,450

City University of New York; New York 2,400

TotalFina USA; New York; petroleum refining 2,371

Donaldson Lufkin and Jenrette Securities Corp.; New York; security brokers 2,200

Chartwell Investments Inc.; New York; investment firm 2,100

Bee Cee Inc.; New York; TV broadcasting stations 2,000

Bloomingdale's Inc.; New York; engineering services 2,000

Citibank NA; New York; commercial bank 2,000

Citigroup Inc.; New York; commercial bank 2,000

HBO Direct Inc.; New York; motion picture distribution 2,000

Maxwell Group Holdings Inc.; New York; newspaper 2,000

Metropolitan Museum of Art; New York 2,000

Sony Music Entertainment Inc.; New York; prerecorded records and tapes 2,000

The Related Companies LP; New York; real estate developers 2,000

Cabrini Medical Center; New York 1,900

New York City Board of Education; Long Island City 1,900

Random House Inc.; New York; book publishing 1,900

U.S. Veterans Hospital; New York 1,900

CBS Broadcasting Inc.; New York; TV broadcasting 1,800

Home Services Systems Inc.; Long Island City; health systems agency 1,800

JP Morgan Chase Bank; New York; state commercial banks 1,800

Sunnyside Home Care Project Inc.; Sunnyside; geriatric residential care 1,700

Viacom Inc.; New York; subscription TV services 1,700

HSS Fund Inc.; New York; hospital 1,600

Rockefeller University; New York 1,600

Taunus Corp.; New York; personal credit institutions 1,600

Meridian Sports Holdings Inc.; New York; boatbuilding and repairing 1,537

Donna Karan International Inc.; New York; women's apparel 1,525

Fleet Bank; New York; commercial banking 1,500

Instinet Corp.; New York; security brokers 1,500

AON Risk Services Inc. of New York; New York; insurance brokers 1,400

Hyatt Corp.; New York; hotels 1,400

Philip Morris Inc.; New York; cigarettes 1,400

Forstmann and Co.; New York; wool fabrics 1,375

Accessory Corp.; New York; apparel 1,350

ABN Amro Inc.; New York; security brokers 1,300

Grey Global Group Inc.; New York; advertising 1,300

Luggage Holding Corp.; New York; luggage 1,300

Courtaulds Textiles U.S. Inc.; New York; fabric mills 1,273

J. Walter Thompson Co.; New York; advertising 1,250

Wellspring Capital Managment; New York; investment holding company 1,250

Bristol-Myers Squibb Co.; New York; pharmaceuticals 1,200

Calvin Klein Co.; New York; jeans 1,200

Desai Capital Management Inc.; New York; investment advisory service 1,200

Lazard Freres and Co.; New York; security dealers 1,200

Liz Claiborne Inc.; New York; women's apparel 1,200

Marsh USA Inc.; New York; insurance brokers 1,200

Plaza Operating Partners; New York; resort hotel 1,200

Terence Cardinal Cooke Health Care Center Inc.; New York 1,200

Simpson Thacher and Bartlett; New York; law office 1,200

Tiffany and Co.; New York; jewelry 1,200

Joseph Littlejohn and Levy; New York; investment bankers 1,171

Shearman and Sterling; New York; law office 1,123

Media WRC Inc.; New York; book publishing 1,100

Park Hyatt Beaver Creek Resort and Spa; New York; hotels and motels 1,100

Weil, Gotshal & Manges; New York; law office 1,100

Cantor Fitzgerald Securities Corp.; New York; security brokers 1,097

Hospital for Joint Diseases and Medical Center/Orthopaedic Institute; New York 1,088

Spartan Security Services Inc.; New York; security guard service   1,070

Neuberger Berman Management Inc.; New York; investment advisory service   1,023

Simplicity Pattern; New York; catalogs   1,005

Bates Advertising USA Inc.; New York   1,000

Bell Security Inc.; New York; guard services   1,000

Bertelsmann Publishing Group Inc.; New York; book publishing   1,000

BNP-Paribas Bank; New York; commercial banking   1,000

Catholic Archdiocese of New York; New York; religious organization   1,000

Choice Courier Systems Inc.; New York; courier/messenger service   1,000

Clifford Chance Rogers and Wells; New York; law office   1,000

Credit Lyonnais; New York; banking   1,000

Debevoise and Plimpton; New York; law office   1,000

Estee Lauder Companies Inc.; New York; perfumes and toiletries   1,000

Global Airlines Corp.; New York; investment holding company   1,000

Holiday Statistics Inc.; New York; temporary help service   1,000

Home Health Management Services Inc.; New York; home health care services   1,000

Mana Products Inc.; Long Island City; cosmetics   1,000

McCann-Erickson Inc.; New York; advertising   1,000

New York City School Construction Authority; Long Island City   1,000

Renco Holdings Inc.; New York; steel   1,000

TeleRep Inc.; New York; telephone services   1,000

U.S. Postal Service; New York   1,000

Bookspan; New York; mail-order book club   950

Davis Polk and Wardwell; New York; law office   950

Deutsche Bank Trust Co.; New York; state trust company   950

Palace Co.; New York; hotels   950

CS Security Inc.; New York; security guard service   945

Character Foundations Inc.; New York; undergarments   920

Jewish Home and Hospital for Aged; New York   900

Paul Weiss Rifkind Wharton and Garrison; New York; law office   900

Pepsi-Cola of New York Inc.; Long Island City; soft drinks   900

Willkie Farr and Gallagher; New York; law office   894

Young Men and Young Women's Hebrew Assn.; New York; youth organizations   880

Ketchum Inc.; New York; public relations   877

Charmer Industries Inc.; Long Island City; liquor   850

Nazareth/Century Corp.; New York; men's/boys' sportswear   833

Amedeo Hotels LP; New York; hotels and motels   800

Associated Press; New York; news reporting services   800

BMG Music; New York; prerecorded records and tapes   800

Board of Cooperative Educational Services; New York; medical research   800

Bovis Lend Lease LMB Inc.; New York; construction project management consultant   800

Dreyfus Corp.; New York; financial services   800

Initial Contract Services Inc.; New York; building maintenance   800

International Delights; Long Island City; breads and cakes   800

Kaye Scholer LLP; New York; law office   800

Simon and Schuster Inc.; New York; book publishing   800

UNICEF United Nations Childrens Fund; New York; search and rescue service   800

BBDO Worldwide Inc.; New York; advertising   790

Collins Building Services Corp.; New York; janitorial service   775

NEC Holding Corp.; Long Island City; envelopes   764

FCB International Inc.; New York; advertising   750

Lintas Campbell-Ewald Co.; New York; advertising   750

McGraw-Hill Companies Inc.; New York; book publishing   750

Mutual of America Life Insurance Co.; New York; mutual association life insurance   750

Revlon Consumer Products Corp.; New York; perfumes and toiletries   750

NYP Holdings Inc.; New York; commercial printing, newspaper publishing   725

Two East 61st Street Corp.; New York; hotels   725

ACCO Brands Inc.; Long Island City; stapling machines   700

Bergdorf Goodman Inc.; New York; women's apparel   700

Fieldston Investors LP; New York; investors   700

Fink Baking Co.; Long Island City; breads, rolls, and buns   700

Media Edge Inc.; New York; media buying service   700

New York City; New York; detention center   700

Pritchard Industries Inc.; New York; janitorial service   700

Seligman Income Fund Inc.; New York; management investment   700

Steinway and Sons Inc.; Long Island City; pianos   700

UST Financial Services Corp.; New York; security brokers, dealers   700

Visiting Nurse Service of New York; New York   700

White and Case; New York; law office   700

ZDNet Inc.; New York; book publishing   700

Chadbourne and Parke; New York; law office   685

Land 'n Sea Inc.; New York; blouses   671

American Jewish Joint Distribution Committee Inc.; New York; charitable organization   650

Bantam Doubleday Dell Publishing Group Inc.; New York; book publishing   650

City University of New York; Long Island City   650

Four Seasons Hotels Inc.; New York; hotels   650

LaBoeuf, Lamb, Greene, & McRae; New York; law office   650

Metrocare Home Services Inc.; New York; visiting nurses   650

SLC Operating; New York; hotels   650

Unilever U.S. Inc.; New York; soap   650

Granite Broadcasting Corp.; New York; TV broadcasting stations   646

Hotel Nikko of New York Inc.; New York; hotels   645

Marilyn Lichtman; New York; nursing care facilities 621

KPMG; New York; accounting services 601

Assessment Solutions Inc.; New York; human resource consulting 600

Brazil Fund Inc.; New York; open-ended management investment 600

CDL West 45th St; New York; hotels and motels 600

Cushman and Wakefield Inc.; New York; real estate brokers and agents 600

Dewey Ballantine; New York; law office 600

Dexia Holding Inc.; New York; surety insurance 600

Gruntal Financial; New York; security dealers 600

HarperCollins Publishers Inc.; New York; book publishing 600

Katz Media Group Inc.; New York; radio, TV, publisher representatives 600

Morgan Lewis and Bockius; New York; law office 600

New York and New Jersey Port Authority; New York 600

New York Dept. of Transportation; Long Island City 600

New York Eye and Ear Infirmary; New York 600

New York Public Library; New York 600

Roosevelt Hotel Corp.; New York; hotels 600

Starwood Hotels and Resorts Worldwide Inc.; New York; hotels 600

Temporary Time Capital Corp.; New York; employment agencies 600

Time Warner Inc.; New York; compact laser discs 600

Ford Foundation; New York; charitable trust management 584

Sidley Austin Brown and Wood; New York; legal services 578

57-57th LLC; New York; hotels and motels 575

Blackrock Inc.; New York; security brokers, dealers 573

ING Financial Holdings Corp.; New York; security brokers 562

FJJ Bank Ltd.; New York; commercial banking 560

61st Street Service Corp.; New York; personnel management 550

CIT Group Inc.; New York; working capital financing 550

Command Security Corp.; New York; security guard service 550

Durst Organization Inc.; New York; investment holding company 550

Earlybird Delivery Systems; New York; courier/messenger service 550

New Rio; New York; clothing stores 550

Omni Hotels Management Corp.; New York; hotels 550

Yves Saint Laurent Parfums Corp.; New York; perfumes 550

DDB Worldwide Communications Group Inc.; New York; advertising 547

Gruner and Jahr Publishing Co.; New York; periodicals 542

Time Publishing Ventures Inc.; New York; magazine publishing 530

KCI Protective Service Inc.; New York; security guard service 525

New York Document Exchange Corp.; New York; courier services 525

York Service Industries Inc.; New York; building maintenance 523

Essex Associates Inc.; New York; nonresidential building operators 520

Fiserv Solutions Inc.; New York; data processing 520

Paul Hastings Janofsky and Walker; New York; law office 511

British Airways Enterprises PLC; Flushing; air transportation 510

Mount Sinai Queens Community Hospital; Long Island City 510

CIC International; Astoria; security brokers 503

Katten Muchin Zavis Rosenman; New York; law office 502

Alexander and Alexander Services Inc.; New York; insurance agents and brokers 500

AOL Time Warner Inc.; New York; online service providers 500

B. Dalton Bookseller Inc.; New York; bookstores 500

Bank of America Business Credit; New York; commercial banking 500

Canadian Imperial Bank of Commerce Inc.; New York; foreign currency exchange 500

Emmigrant Agency Inc.; New York; state savings bank 500

Gruner and Jahr Printing and Publishing Co.; New York; magazine publishing 500

Holtzbrinck Publishers; New York; book publishing 500

Hydro-Electric Associates Inc.; New York; electrical work 500

Inter-Continental Hotels Corp.; New York; resort hotel 500

Josephthal and Co. Inc.; New York; security brokers, dealers 500

Marriott International Inc.; New York; hotels 500

Mary Manning Walsh Nursing Home Co.; New York; nursing care facilities 500

New York City Off-Track Betting Corp.; New York; off-track betting 500

Paribas North America Inc.; New York; security brokers 500

Polo Ralph Lauren Corp.; New York; men's/boys' clothing 500

Reservoir Capital Group; New York; financial services 500

School of Visual Arts; New York 500

St. Luke's-Roosevelt Hospital Center; New York 500

St. Vincent's Catholic Medical Centers of New York; New York 500

Standard Motor Products Inc.; Long Island City; motor vehicle parts/accessories 500

United Federation of Teachers Local; New York; labor union 500

Vivendi Universal; New York; liquors 500

Warner-Elektra-Atlantic Corp.; New York; audio and video recording tapes 500

Westdeutsche Landesbank; New York; agencies of foreign banks 500

Western International Media Inc.; New York; media-buying service 500

Wilson Elser Moskowitz Edelman and Dicker; New York; law office 500

Zurich Scudder Investments Inc.; New York; investment advisory service 500

New York 15th District

Northern Manhattan — Harlem, Washington Heights

Harlem was a nexus of black political and cultural power during its heyday in the 1920s and 1930s. But by the time the district was created in 1944, the Great Depression, an influx of poor migrants, and race riots had contributed to severe decline. Two highly popular black Democrats—Adam Clayton Powell Jr. and Charles Rangel—have controlled the 15th since its creation; Powell served 12 terms and part of a 13th; Rangel had been elected 17 times as of 2003. A solidly Democratic district, Bill Clinton won overwhelming majorities here in 1992 and 1996, and Al Gore got 86.5 percent of the vote in 2000. *(See map p. 620.)*

The past 20 years have brought substantial change to the 15th, with Puerto Rican and Dominican immigration supplanting the district's African American majority. Hispanics now far outnumber non-Hispanic blacks, but low voter participation among Hispanics means the smaller black population (31 percent of residents) continues to dominate the district's politics.

Harlem's 1996 designation as a federal empowerment zone has brought the beginning of an economic resurgence. Refurbished brownstones, new restaurants, national retail chains, and prominent corporations are moving into the area. In early 2001 Harlem also received a public relations boon when Clinton decided to lease office space in a building on 125th Street, the area's main thoroughfare.

The district's hospitals and colleges, along with many small businesses, provide much of the employment. But for less-educated residents, many of the jobs are out of reach. The district's doctors, lawyers, and other professionals reside in Harlem's affluent black neighborhoods like Strivers Row, the white, affluent Upper West Side or around Columbia University in Morningside Heights.

Major Industry

Health care, higher education, retail.

Notable

Legendary venues such as the Cotton Club and the Apollo Theater drew jazz greats and comedians; the district includes Randalls, Wards, and Rikers islands.

Election Returns

	Republican		Democratic		Other	
President 2000	12,430	6.5%	165,002	86.5%	13,292	7.0%
House 2002	11,008	11.5%	84,367	88.5%		

District Profile

Population   654,361

Total area (square miles)   15.7
    Land area (square miles)   10.2

Population per square mile   64,153.0

Counties (2000 population)
    Bronx (pt.)   12,780
    New York (pt.)   641,581

Cities and other areas over 10,000 (2000 population)
    New York (pt.)   654,361

Race and Hispanic or Latino origin*
    White   16.4%
    Black or African American   30.5%
    American Indian or Alaska Native   0.2%
    Asian   2.8%
    Native Hawaiian or other Pacific Islander   0.0%
    Some other race   0.4%
    Hispanic or Latino origin   47.9%
    Two or more races   1.8%

As percentage of total population.

Ancestry*

English	1.4%	Russian	1.5%
German	2.0%	Subsaharan	1.9%
Irish	2.0%	USA/American	1.9%
Italian	1.6%	West Indian	2.8%
Polish	1.1%		

As estimated percentage of total population.

Universities and colleges, 2000–2001 enrollment
    Bank Street College of Education, New York   1,022
    Barnard College, New York   2,285
    Boricua College, New York   1,271
    City University of New York City College, New York   11,055
    Columbia University, New York   19,639
    Helene Fuld College of Nursing, New York   202
    Jewish Theological Seminary of America, New York   589
    Manhattan School of Music, New York   837
    New York College of Podiatric Medicine, New York   353
    Rabbi Isaac Elchanan Seminary, New York   338
    Teachers College at Columbia University, New York   4,949
    Union Theological Seminary, New York   276
    Yeshiva University, New York   5,814

Newspapers and circulation

	District circulation	Total circulation
Daily Variety, Los Angeles*	1,829	27,269
El Diario-La Prensa, New York City	4,591	54,695
El Vocero de Puerto Rico, New York City*	6,186	22,299
Hoy, New York City	2,378	59,949
Long Island Newsday	1,751	575,889
New York Amsterdam News	2,760	16,414
*New York Daily News**	50,071	723,155
*New York Law Journal**	2,653	11,519
New York Post	17,582	511,412
*New York Times**	76,650	666,228
*USA Today**	10,563	1,674,376

See Sources and Explanations in the front of the volume.

Television stations and affiliations

New York	100%	WABC	ABC
New York	100%	WCBS	CBS
New York	100%	WEDW	PBS
New York	100%	WFME	Independent
New York	100%	WLIW	PBS
New York	100%	WLNY	Independent
New York	100%	WMBC	Independent
New York	100%	WNBC	NBC
New York	100%	WNET	PBS
New York	100%	WNJB	PBS
New York	100%	WNJN	PBS
New York	100%	WNJU	Telemundo
New York	100%	WNYE	PBS
New York	100%	WNYW	FOX
New York	100%	WPIX	WB
New York	100%	WPXN	PAX
New York	100%	WRNN	Independent
New York	100%	WTBY	Independent
New York	100%	WWOR	UPN
New York	100%	WXTV	Univision

Cable systems and subscribers

Time Warner*   109,913

See Sources and Explanations in the front of the volume.

Businesses and other major employers

Columbia University; New York   4,500

New York City Health and Hospitals Corp.; New York   3,500

St. Luke's-Roosevelt Hospital Center; New York   3,000

New York Presbyterian Hospital; New York   2,000

Manhattan Psychiatric Center; New York   1,370

Columbia University; New York; environmental research   1,000

New York Mental Retardation and Developmental Disabilities Office; New York   1,000

Isabella Geriatric Center Inc.; New York; nursing care facilities   1,000

North General Hospital; New York   925

Jewish Home and Hospital for Aged; New York   900

Columbia University Teachers College; New York   800

Research Foundation for Mental Hygiene Inc.; New York; medical research   800

Vivendi Universal; New York; motion picture production   650

Barnard College; New York   635

FEGS Home Attendant Services Inc.; New York; home health care   624

Booz Allen and Hamilton Inc.; New York; management consulting   510

Carnegie Partners Inc.; New York; nursing care facilities   500

Yeshiva University; New York   500

Institute Home Care Services Inc.; New York; individual and family services   500

New York 16th District

South Bronx

The 16th, which covers the distressed neighborhoods of the South Bronx, is the nation's poorest district in terms of median income. One-third of families live on a household income of less than $10,000, and the area is plagued by urban ills and low rates of home ownership. But some South Bronx neighborhoods have started to turn around, thanks to grass-roots community work and federal empowerment zone money. *(See map p. 620.)*

The South Bronx, overtaken by a post–World War II influx of Hispanics to New York City, has since 1970 elected men of Puerto Rican origin to the House. The Puerto Rican influence has long been strong in the 16th, though the district also is home to many African and South and Central American immigrants. The district's 3 percent non-Hispanic white population is the lowest in the nation.

Democratic presidential candidates regularly top 90 percent of the vote in the 16th, which might be the most strongly Democratic district in the nation. But as with many districts with large minority and immigrant populations, voter turnout is low. Redistricting in 2002 made the 16th a bit longer and narrower in shape; the district now reaches almost as far north as the convergence of the Harlem and Hudson Rivers.

Like frontier settlements, several downtown developments of single-family homes and low-rise housing have been built on vacated lots by subsidized economic development organizations, and they are occupied by people who grew up in the district, worked their way out and are now returning to help rebuild the neighborhoods.

Light manufacturing firms also have set up shop, replacing some of the heavy industry that moved out decades ago. Local baseball fans hope New York Yankees owner George Steinbrenner does not make good on threats to move the team out of the Bronx. Fordham University is in the 16th as well.

Major Industry

Health care, light manufacturing.

Notable

The Edgar Allan Poe Cottage in the Bronx (the writer's last home) is owned by New York City.

Election Returns

	Republican		Democratic		Other	
President 2000	6,634	5.4%	112,786	92.4%	2,630	2.2%
House 2002	4,366	7.9%	50,716	92.1%		

District Profile

Population   654,360

Total area (square miles)   12.7
 Land area (square miles)   11.8

Population per square mile   55,454.2

Counties (2000 population)
 Bronx (pt.)   654,360

Cities and other areas over 10,000 (2000 population)
 New York (pt.)   654,360

Race and Hispanic or Latino origin*
 White   2.9%
 Black or African American   30.3%

American Indian or Alaska Native   0.3%
Asian   1.6%
Native Hawaiian or other Pacific Islander   0.0%
Some other race   0.5%
Hispanic or Latino origin   62.8%
Two or more races   1.6%

As percentage of total population.

Ancestry*
Subsaharan   3.1%   West Indian   3.9%
USA/American   2.3%

As estimated percentage of total population.

Universities and colleges, 2000–2001 enrollment
City University of New York Bronx Community
   College, Bronx   6,928
City University of New York Hostos Community
   College, Bronx   3,115
Fordham University, Bronx   13,650
Monroe College, Bronx   3,387

Newspapers and circulation

	District circulation	Total circulation
El Diario-La Prensa, New York City	4,778	54,695
Hoy, New York City	3,944	59,949
Long Island Newsday	1,418	575,889
New York Amsterdam News	1,396	16,414
*New York Daily News**	17,228	723,155
New York Post	10,926	511,412
*New York Times**	4,591	666,228

See Sources and Explanations in the front of the volume.

Television stations and affiliations
New York	100%	WABC	ABC
New York	100%	WCBS	CBS
New York	100%	WEDW	PBS
New York	100%	WFME	Independent
New York	100%	WLIW	PBS
New York	100%	WLNY	Independent
New York	100%	WMBC	Independent
New York	100%	WNBC	NBC
New York	100%	WNET	PBS
New York	100%	WNJB	PBS
New York	100%	WNJN	PBS
New York	100%	WNJU	Telemundo
New York	100%	WNYE	PBS
New York	100%	WNYW	FOX
New York	100%	WPIX	WB
New York	100%	WPXN	PAX
New York	100%	WRNN	Independent
New York	100%	WTBY	Independent
New York	100%	WWOR	UPN
New York	100%	WXTV	Univision

Cable systems and subscribers
Cablevision*   93,922

See Sources and Explanations in the front of the volume.

Businesses and other major employers
New York City Health and Hospitals Corp.; Bronx
   4,000
New York City; Bronx; police dept.   2,200
U.S. Postal Service; Bronx   2,000

Bronx Lebanon Hospital Center; Bronx   2,000
New York City; Bronx; education programs   2,000
U.S. Veterans Hospital; Bronx   2,000
St. Barnabas Hospital; Bronx   1,950
Fordham University; Bronx   1,820
Jewish Home and Hospital; Bronx   1,300
Wildlife Conservation Society; Bronx; noncommercial
   zoological garden   1,100
DAOR Security Inc.; Bronx; security guard service
   1,000
City University of New York; Bronx   900
Volume Services America Inc.; Bronx; caterers   900
New York City; Bronx; child-related social services   800
Cooperative Home Care Associates Inc.; Bronx; home
   health care   620
New York State Unified Court System; Bronx; legal
   services   550
Ferdinand Arrigoni Inc.; Bronx; bus line operations
   550
New York Botanical Garden; Bronx   539
Daughters of Jacob Nursing Home Co.; Bronx   525
Allied Waste North America Inc.; Bronx; refuse systems
   500
Manhattan Beer Distributors; Bronx; beer and ale   500
Clay-Park Labs Inc.; Bronx; pharmaceuticals   500
Port Morris Tile and Marble Corp.; Bronx; terrazzo, tile,
   marble and mosaic work   500
Viele Manufacturing Corp.; Bronx; plastics   500
Morrisania Bus Service Inc.; Bronx; bus charters
   500

New York 17th District

*North Bronx; part of Westchester and Rockland
Counties — Mount Vernon, part of Yonkers*

The 17th is an economically, racially, and ethnically diverse territory that takes in the northwestern part of the Bronx and parts of Westchester and Rockland Counties northwest of New York City. Blacks and Hispanics together constitute a majority of residents in the district.

Riverdale, a heavily Jewish neighborhood, sits at the western edge of the Bronx and is one of New York's most affluent areas. East of Riverdale, on the other side of Van Cortlandt Park and Woodlawn Cemetery, there is a large black population. The 17th reaches almost as far east as the mammoth Co-op City apartment complex (in the 7th District). About 45 percent of district residents live in the Bronx. *(See map p. 620.)*

In Westchester County, home to one-fourth of the 17th's residents, the district takes in all of Mount Vernon, which is heavily black, some black and Hispanic communities in western Yonkers, and predominantly white communities, many of Italian and Irish descent, in southeastern Yonkers.

The 17th narrows significantly in northern Yonkers, meandering north along Route 9 and the Hudson River to cross the Tappan Zee Bridge into Rockland County, parts of which were appended to the 17th in 2002 redistricting. Rockland leans Democratic, but not overwhelmingly so.

The new district lines excised some of the Bronx's Democratic faithful, but Al Gore nonetheless took 69.3 percent of the vote here in the 2000 presidential election, and Democrats hold a substantial registration edge over the GOP.

Major Industry

Health care, higher education, city government.

Notable

Duke Ellington, Elizabeth Cady Stanton, F. W. Woolworth, Nellie Bly, and "Bat" Masterson are among those buried in Woodlawn Cemetery in the Bronx.

Election Returns

	Republican		Democratic		Other	
President 2000	54,362	26.6%	141,525	69.3%	8,438	4.1%
House 2002	42,634	34.4%	77,535	62.6%	3,674	3.0%

District Profile

Population   654,360

Total area (square miles)   145.6
  Land area (square miles)   126.6

Population per square mile   5,168.7

Counties (2000 population)
  Bronx (pt.)   292,423
  Rockland (pt.)   197,839
  Westchester (pt.)   164,098

Cities and other areas over 10,000 (2000 population)
  Monsey CDP   14,504
  Mount Vernon   68,381
  Nanuet CDP   16,707
  New York (pt.)   292,423
  Pearl River CDP   15,553
  Spring Valley village   25,464
  Suffern village   11,006
  Yonkers (pt.)   87,617

Race and Hispanic or Latino origin*
  White   41.3%
  Black or African American   30.4%
  American Indian or Alaska Native   0.2%
  Asian   4.5%
  Native Hawaiian or other Pacific Islander   0.0%
  Some other race   0.5%
  Hispanic or Latino origin   20.4%
  Two or more races   2.6%

*As percentage of total population.

Ancestry*

English 1.7%	Russian 2.1%
German 3.6%	Subsaharan 1.6%
Irish 8.7%	USA/American 3.4%
Italian 8.4%	West Indian 10.1%
Polish 2.3%	

*As estimated percentage of total population.

Universities and colleges, 2000–2001 enrollment
  City University of New York Lehman College, Bronx   8,768
  College of Mount St. Vincent, Bronx   1,512
  Dominican College of Blauvelt, Orangeburg   1,636
  Long Island University-Rockland, Orangeburg   382
  Manhattan College, Bronx   3,070
  Nyack College, Nyack   2,226
  Rockland Community College, Suffern   6,262
  St. Thomas Aquinas College, Sparkill   2,120
  Yeshivath Viznitz, Monsey   234

Newspapers and circulation

	District circulation	Total circulation
El Diario-La Prensa, New York City	1,987	54,695
Hoy, New York City	1,143	59,949
Long Island Newsday	1,707	575,889
Middletown Times Herald Record	1,045	82,615
*New York Daily News**	21,508	723,155
New York Post	13,130	511,412
*New York Times**	12,052	666,228
White Plains Journal News	37,282	144,547

*See Sources and Explanations in the front of the volume.

Television stations and affiliations

New York	100%	WABC	ABC
New York	100%	WCBS	CBS
New York	100%	WEDW	PBS
New York	100%	WFME	Independent
New York	100%	WLIW	PBS
New York	100%	WLNY	Independent
New York	100%	WMBC	Independent
New York	100%	WNBC	NBC
New York	100%	WNET	PBS
New York	100%	WNJB	PBS
New York	100%	WNJN	PBS
New York	100%	WNJU	Telemundo
New York	100%	WNYE	PBS
New York	100%	WNYW	FOX
New York	100%	WPIX	WB
New York	100%	WPXN	PAX
New York	100%	WRNN	Independent
New York	100%	WTBY	Independent
New York	100%	WWOR	UPN
New York	100%	WXTV	Univision

Cable systems and subscribers
  Cablevision   84,962
  Time Warner   14,942

Military installations, September 2001
  Orangeburg U.S. Army Reserve Center, Nyack   360

Businesses and other major employers
  Montefiore Medical Center; Bronx   3,500
  New York City Transit Authority; Mount Vernon   3,200
  City University of New York; Bronx   2,000
  Good Samaritan Hospital; Suffern   1,600
  Our Lady of Mercy Medical Center; Bronx   1,500
  Verizon Wireless Inc.; Orangeburg; radiotelephone communication   1,500
  Nyack Hospital Inc.; Nyack   1,160
  Hebrew Home for Aged at Riverdale Inc.; Bronx   915
  New York Mental Health Office; Orangeburg   900
  Mount Vernon Hospital Inc.; Mount Vernon   700

Wartburg Home of Evangelical Lutheran Church; Mount Vernon; nursing care facilities   700

Workmen's Circle Home and Geriatrics Center; Bronx; nursing care facilities   650

Michael Anthony Jewelers Inc.; Mount Vernon; jewelry   639

Novartis Corp.; Suffern; pharmaceuticals   625

City of Mount Vernon; Mount Vernon   612

Alliance Home Service Inc.; Bronx; individual and family services   600

Chromalloy Gas Turbine Corp.; Orangeburg; metals coating and formed products   600

Manhattan College Corp.; Bronx   600

New York Foundling Hospital; Nanuet   600

Parochial Bus System Inc.; Bronx; bus charter service   600

Leake and Watts Services Inc.; Yonkers; child-related social services   578

Avon Products Inc.; Suffern; toiletries   500

Columbia University; Palisades   500

Cosner Construction Corp.; Yonkers; concrete work   500

Dominican College of Blauvelt; Orangeburg   500

Palisades Nursing Home Co.; Bronx   500

Rockland County; Pomona; social and manpower programs   500

Sears Roebuck and Co. Inc.; Nanuet; department stores   500

Verizon Services Group Inc.; Pearl River; management consulting   500

Yonkers Racing Corp.; Yonkers; harness horse racing   500

New York 18th District

Most of Westchester County — New Rochelle, most of Yonkers

The 18th encompasses most of southern and central Westchester County, excluding parts of Yonkers bordering the Hudson River and the Bronx, and all of Mount Vernon. The district hops the Hudson to pick up most of New City and Congers and all of Haverstraw in Rockland County. Redistricting in 2002 pushed the district completely out of New York City, where it had taken in a swath of the Bronx and Queens. *(See map p. 620.)*

The 18th is a well-to-do residential district that leans Democratic, but not overwhelmingly. Westchester County has a Republican base but enough affluent Democrats to make it competitive. Wealthy New York suburbs such as Scarsdale and Mamaroneck are the district's hallmark. Many of the district's residents enjoy an easy commute to white-collar jobs in Manhattan.

But the district also takes in working-class communities, including Port Chester and urban sections of White Plains and New Rochelle. Al Gore carried the reconfigured district with 58.1 percent of the vote in the 2000 presidential election. The 18th has the largest portion of Yonkers, Westchester's most populous city. It also includes Ossining, site of Sing Sing prison; its location north of the city on the Hudson River led New Yorkers to refer to prison-bound criminals being "sent up the river."

Hospitals and colleges provide employment opportunities in the district, and officials are trying to attract more technology firms to the region, particularly to Yonkers. Purchase is home to PepsiCo., IBM's corporate headquarters are in Armonk, and Reader's Digest is based in Pleasantville.

Major Industry
Health care, higher education.

Notable
North Tarrytown was renamed Sleepy Hollow in honor of the Washington Irving story set there; Thomas Paine Cottage and Museum is in New Rochelle; former president Bill Clinton and Sen. Hillary Rodham Clinton have a home in Chappaqua.

Election Returns

	Republican		Democratic		Other	
President 2000	103,248	38.5%	155,700	58.1%	9,268	3.5%
House 2002			98,957	92.0%	8,558	8.0%

District Profile

Population   654,360

Total area (square miles)   270.3
  Land area (square miles)   222.1

Population per square mile   2,946.2

Counties (2000 population)
  Rockland (pt.)   60,910
  Westchester (pt.)   593,450

Cities and other areas over 10,000 (2000 population)
  Eastchester CDP   18,564
  Harrison village   24,154
  Haverstraw village   10,117
  Mamaroneck village   18,752
  New City CDP (pt.)   30,260
  New Rochelle   72,182
  Ossining village   24,010
  Port Chester village   27,867
  Rye   14,955
  Scarsdale village   17,823
  Tarrytown village (pt.)   10,874
  White Plains   53,077
  Yonkers (pt.)   108,469

Race and Hispanic or Latino origin*
  White   67.1%
  Black or African American   9.5%
  American Indian or Alaska Native   0.1%
  Asian   5.2%
  Native Hawaiian or other Pacific Islander   0.0%
  Some other race   0.3%
  Hispanic or Latino origin   16.2%
  Two or more races   1.6%

As percentage of total population.

Ancestry*

English	3.4%	Irish	11.0%
French	1.2%	Italian	17.2%
German	6.2%	Polish	3.4%

Russian   3.6%   West Indian   1.8%
USA/American   3.0%

As estimated percentage of total population.

Universities and colleges, 2000–2001 enrollment

Berkeley College, White Plains   615
College of New Rochelle, New Rochelle   6,817
Concordia College, Bronxville   578
Iona College, New Rochelle   4,469
Manhattanville College, Purchase   2,443
Marymount College, Tarrytown   938
Mercy College, Dobbs Ferry   9,244
Monroe College-New Rochelle, New Rochelle   933
New York Medical College, Valhalla   1,502
Pace University-Pleasantville Briarcliff, Pleasantville
   3,471
Pace University-White Plains, White Plains   1,940
Sarah Lawrence College, Bronxville   1,449
State University of New York, Purchase   4,077
State University of New York Westchester Community
   College, Valhalla   10,819
Ultrasound Diagnostic School, Elmsford   208
Westchester Business Institute, White Plains   1,072

Newspapers and circulation

	District circulation	Total circulation
El Diario-La Prensa, New York City	1,508	54,695
Hoy, New York City	1,918	59,949
*New York Daily News**	15,962	723,155
New York Post	15,516	511,412
*New York Times**	30,227	666,228
*USA Today**	2,771	1,674,376
White Plains Journal News	72,978	144,547

See Sources and Explanations in the front of the volume.

Television stations and affiliations

New York	100%	WABC	ABC
New York	100%	WCBS	CBS
New York	100%	WEDW	PBS
New York	100%	WFME	Independent
New York	100%	WLIW	PBS
New York	100%	WLNY	Independent
New York	100%	WMBC	Independent
New York	100%	WNBC	NBC
New York	100%	WNET	PBS
New York	100%	WNJB	PBS
New York	100%	WNJN	PBS
New York	100%	WNJU	Telemundo
New York	100%	WNYE	PBS
New York	100%	WNYW	FOX
New York	100%	WPIX	WB
New York	100%	WPXN	PAX
New York	100%	WRNN	Independent
New York	100%	WTBY	Independent
New York	100%	WWOR	UPN
New York	100%	WXTV	Univision

Cable systems and subscribers

Cablevision   109,325

Businesses and other major employers

Westchester Medical Center; Valhalla   3,900
Highcrest Investors Corp.; Mount Kisco; investment
   holding company   2,600
Yonkers Contracting Co.; Yonkers; highway, street
   general contractor   2,000
Texaco Inc.; White Plains; crude petroleum production
   1,700
International Business Machines Corp.; Armonk;
   computers   1,550
International Business Machines Corp.; White Plains;
   market analysis: business/economic research   1,500
Pepsico Inc.; Purchase; snacks   1,500
Sound Shore Medical Center Inc.; New Rochelle   1,400
Gannett Satellite Information Network Inc.; White
   Plains; newspaper   1,300
White Plains Hospital Center; White Plains   1,300
Bayer Corp.; Tarrytown; medical diagnostic apparatus
   1,200
Fujifilm America Inc.; Elmsford; photographic
   equipment, supplies   1,200
Reader's Digest Assn. Inc.; Pleasantville; magazine
   publishing   1,100
St. John's Riverside Hospital Inc.; Yonkers   1,100
Phelps Memorial Hospital Assn.; Tarrytown   1,055
St. Joseph's Hospital; Yonkers   935
International Business Machines Corp.; Hawthorne;
   commercial physical research   850
New York United Hospital Medical Center Inc.; Port
   Chester   813
Mastercard International Inc.; Purchase; credit card
   service   800
Lawrence Hospital Center Inc.; Bronxville   760
Accent Maintenance Corp.; Ossining; janitorial service
   750
City of White Plains; White Plains; city management
   749
Avon Products Inc.; Rye; cosmetics and perfumes   700
Precision Valve Corp.; Yonkers; aerosol valves   700
Westchester County; White Plains; county government
   700
Macy's East Inc.; White Plains; department stores   673
Iona College; New Rochelle   650
Swiss RE America Holding Corp.; Armonk; fire, marine,
   casualty insurance   650
Kraft Foods Inc.; Tarrytown   610
New York Dept. of Health; West Haverstraw; public
   health agency   610
AT&T Corp.; Harrison; data processing   600
Bloomingdale's Inc.; White Plains; department stores
   600
Burke Rehabilitation Hospital Inc.; White Plains   600
Children's Village Inc.; Dobbs Ferry; children's home
   600
City of Yonkers; Yonkers; city government   600
Entergy Nuclear Generation Co.; White Plains; electric
   power generation   600
Liberty Lines Transit Inc.; Yonkers; bus line operations
   600
Richard L. Aronson Inc.; White Plains; temporary help
   service   600

State University of New York; Purchase   600

Yonkers General Hospital Inc.; Yonkers   585

Ciba Specialty Chemicals Corp.; Tarrytown; industrial
inorganic chemicals   554

A&T Health Care; New City; home health care   550

Carol Management Corp.; Port Chester; hotels   500

Citigroup Inc.; Harrison; commercial bank   500

FRMO Corp.; New Rochelle; financial risk management
500

International Business Machines Corp.; Purchase;
administrative management   500

Jawonio Inc.; New City; outpatient clinics   500

Louis Hornick and Co. Inc.; Haverstraw; curtains and
fabrics   500

New York Medical College; Valhalla   500

Pinkerton's Inc.; White Plains; security guard service
500

Rockland County; New City; county government
500

U.S. Internal Revenue Service; White Plains   500

Verizon Communications Inc.; White Plains; telephone
communication   500

New York 19th District

Hudson Valley — Peekskill, West Point

Wedged between Connecticut and New Jersey, the 19th follows a sizable portion of the Hudson River. On the east side of the river, the 19th spans the southern tier of Dutchess County, all of Putnam County, and the northern section of Westchester County. It also takes in some land west of the Hudson in Orange County and the northern edge of Rockland County.

The southeastern, Westchester County, portion of the district is known for its elegant exurban homes and horse country that attract wealthy professionals and celebrities from Manhattan, where some residents work. The median family income approaches $200,000 in some locations in the district. Nearly 84 percent of the district's residents are white. Racially, ethnically, and economically diverse Peekskill, with a working- and middle-class base, sits on the eastern shore of the Hudson River in northwestern Westchester.

The wealth in the southern part of the district and the rural character of its northern and western reaches—which extend to the foothills of the Catskill Mountains—help give the 19th a solidly Republican tilt. Although Republican George W. Bush did not receive a majority of the district's vote in the 2000 presidential election, his plurality here made the 19th one of only six New York districts he carried.

Drawn by the groundwork built by IBM—a longtime presence in Yorktown—technical and research firms have moved into the lower Hudson Valley. Dutchess County, Putnam County, and Orange County, where farmers grow onions, lettuce, and celery, are more rural. The U.S. Military Academy at West Point, which celebrated its bicentennial in 2002, also aids the district's economy.

Major Industry

Computers, telecommunications, agriculture.

Notable

The home of John Jay, Continental Congress president and first chief justice of the United States.

Election Returns

	Republican		Democratic		Other	
President 2000	133,157	49.0%	126,785	46.7%	11,698	4.3%
House 2002	121,129	70.0%	44,967	26.0%	7,016	4.1%

District Profile

Population   654,361

Total area (square miles)   1,470.2
Land area (square miles)   1,401.1

Population per square mile   467.0

Counties (2000 population)
Dutchess (pt.)   151,923
Orange (pt.)   212,778
Putnam   95,745
Rockland (pt.)   28,004
Westchester (pt.)   165,911

Cities and other areas over 10,000 (2000 population)
Arlington CDP (pt.)   12,329
Beacon   13,808
Jefferson Valley-Yorktown CDP   14,891
Kiryas Joel village   13,138
Peekskill   22,441
Stony Point CDP   11,744

Race and Hispanic or Latino origin*
White   83.5%
Black or African American   5.0%
American Indian or Alaska Native   0.2%
Asian   2.2%
Native Hawaiian or other Pacific Islander   0.0%
Some other race   0.2%
Hispanic or Latino origin   7.7%
Two or more races   1.2%

As percentage of total population.

Ancestry*

Dutch 1.4%	Italian 17.6%
English 5.4%	Polish 4.0%
French 1.6%	Russian 1.9%
German 10.6%	Scottish 1.2%
Hungarian 1.1%	USA/American 2.8%
Irish 16.5%	

As estimated percentage of total population.

Universities and colleges, 2000–2001 enrollment
U.S. Military Academy, West Point   4,088
Vassar College, Poughkeepsie   2,400

Newspapers and circulation

	District circulation	Total circulation
Middletown Times Herald Record	36,605	82,615
*New York Daily News**	25,365	723,155
New York Post	10,995	511,412
*New York Times**	38,784	666,228

Poughkeepsie Journal	18,762	39,831
*USA Today**	4,599	1,674,376
White Plains Journal News	32,842	144,547

See Sources and Explanations in the front of the volume.

Television stations and affiliations

New York	100%	WABC	ABC
New York	100%	WCBS	CBS
New York	100%	WEDW	PBS
New York	100%	WFME	Independent
New York	100%	WLIW	PBS
New York	100%	WLNY	Independent
New York	100%	WMBC	Independent
New York	100%	WNBC	NBC
New York	100%	WNET	PBS
New York	100%	WNJB	PBS
New York	100%	WNJN	PBS
New York	100%	WNJU	Telemundo
New York	100%	WNYE	PBS
New York	100%	WNYW	FOX
New York	100%	WPIX	WB
New York	100%	WPXN	PAX
New York	100%	WRNN	Independent
New York	100%	WTBY	Independent
New York	100%	WWOR	UPN
New York	100%	WXTV	Univision

Cable systems and subscribers
Cablevision   91,007
RCN of Southeast New York   16,327
Time Warner   20,398

Military installations, September 2001
West Point Military Reservation, New York   5,599
Stewart Newburgh U.S. Army Reserve Center, New Windsor   199

Businesses and other major employers
International Business Machines Corp.; Hopewell Junction; computers   8,000
International Business Machines Corp.; Poughkeepsie; computers   4,500
Mediacom Communications Corp.; Middletown; cable television   3,200
U.S. Military Academy; West Point   3,200
International Business Machines Corp.; Somers; software development   3,000
International Business Machines Corp.; Yorktown Heights; commercial physical research   3,000
New York Mental Retardation and Developmental Disabilities Office; Thiells   3,000
New York Mental Health Office; Thiells   2,800
Hastings Health Systems Inc.; Poughkeepsie; hospital management   1,950
New York Power Authority; Buchanan; electric power generation   1,500
New York Dept. of Transportation; Poughkeepsie   1,484
St. Francis Hospital; Poughkeepsie   1,220
General Cinema Beverages of West Virginia Inc.; Somers; soft drinks   1,200
International Business Machines Corp.; Sterling Forest; data processing   1,200

Orange County; Goshen; county government   1,104
Northern Westchester Hospital Assn.; Mount Kisco; hospital   1,100
Vassar College Inc.; Poughkeepsie   950
Putnam Hospital Center; Carmel   900
Wakefern Food Corp.; Middletown; grocery store   850
Arden Hill Hospital; Goshen   840
Kolmar Laboratories Inc.; Port Jervis; toiletries   800
U.S. Veterans Hospital; Castle Point   760
Putnam/Northern Westchester BOCES; Yorktown Heights; education programs   750
Empire Blue Cross and Blue Shield; Middletown; medical service plans   727
Kohlberg and Co.; Mount Kisco; banker's organization, advisory services   675
Orange County; Goshen; convalescent home   675
Mercy Community Hospital; Port Jervis   650
Cornwall Hospital Inc.; Cornwall   600
Orange-Ulster BOCES Inc.; Goshen; vocational training   590
Hudson Central School District Board of Education; Montrose   550
Four Winds Inc.; Katonah; psychiatric hospitals   500
Mount Kisco Medical Group; Mount Kisco; administrative management   500
New York Mental Health Office; Middletown; mental hospital   500
New York Office of Parks, Recreation, and Historic Preservation; Bear Mountain   500
Pepsi Bottling Group Inc.; Somers; soft drinks   500
Putnam County; Carmel; county government   500

New York 20th District

North Hudson Valley — Saratoga Springs

New York's 20th runs along the state's eastern border, starting just outside Poughkeepsie and stretching into the Adirondack Mountains. It covers much of the primarily residential Hudson River Valley, including the site of the Battle of Saratoga, America's first significant victory against the British in the Revolutionary War. A western branch of the 20th picks up rural territory as far west as Delaware and Otsego Counties.

The 20th's population hub is in its center, in the Albany-Schenectady-Troy metropolitan area. The district includes none of those cities (they are all in the 21st), but does claim much of their GOP suburbia. The three cities helped fuel a suburban boom in southern Saratoga County in the 1980s. Saratoga Springs, synonymous with world-class horse racing, attracts tourists during the summer months.

The district follows Interstate 87 north into mountainous, scenic Adirondack Park and the resort areas of Lake George and Essex County. Lake Placid, site of the 1932 and 1980 Winter Olympics, is in Essex County at the northern tip of the district.

The southern end is made up of mainly rural and mountainous territory in Otsego, Delaware, Greene, Columbia, and northern Dutchess Counties. It includes mansions built along the Hudson River by the nation's elite, including the Vanderbilts, Martin Van Buren, and Franklin Delano Roosevelt.

A heavy presence of unionized state workers outside Albany makes labor an important constituency, but dairy farmers and small-town voters give the GOP a solid edge. The 20th (previously the 22nd) has the lowest minority percentage in the state and was one of only three districts to give George W. Bush a majority in the 2000 presidential election.

Major Industry

Agriculture, tourism, paper manufacturing.

Notable

Franklin Roosevelt lost Dutchess County, site of his Hyde Park home, in seven of nine general elections in which he competed.

Election Returns

	Republican		Democratic		Other	
President 2000	146,792	50.7%	127,419	44.0%	15,232	5.3%
House 2002	140,238	73.3%	45,878	24.0%	5,162	2.7%

District Profile

Population   654,360

Total area (square miles)   7,199.6
   Land area (square miles)   7,017.8

Population per square mile   93.2

Counties (2000 population)

Columbia 63,094	Otsego (pt.) 12,054
Delaware (pt.) 41,814	Rensselaer (pt.) 60,192
Dutchess (pt.) 98,356	Saratoga (pt.) 192,120
Essex (pt.) 14,190	Warren 63,303
Greene 48,195	Washington 61,042

Cities and other areas over 10,000 (2000 population)
   Glens Falls   14,354
   Saratoga Springs   26,186

Race and Hispanic or Latino origin*
   White   93.4%
   Black or African American   2.4%
   American Indian or Alaska Native   0.2%
   Asian   0.8%
   Native Hawaiian or other Pacific Islander   0.0%
   Some other race   0.1%
   Hispanic or Latino origin   2.2%
   Two or more races   0.9%

*As percentage of total population.

Ancestry*

Dutch 2.9%	Italian 9.8%
English 9.0%	Polish 3.7%
Fr. Canadian 1.9%	Scotch-Irish 1.2%
French 5.8%	Scottish 1.8%
German 11.8%	USA/American 3.8%
Irish 15.1%	

*As estimated percentage of total population.

Universities and colleges, 2000–2001 enrollment
   Adirondack Community College, Queensbury   3,151
   Bard College, Annandale-on-Hudson   1,512
   Columbia-Greene Community College, Hudson   1,598

Culinary Institute of America, Hyde Park   2,028
Dutchess Community College, Poughkeepsie   6,582
Marist College, Poughkeepsie   5,498
North Country Community College, Saranac Lake   1,086
Skidmore College, Saratoga Springs   2,503
State University of New York College of Technology, Delhi   2,151
State University of New York Empire State College, Saratoga Springs   8,009
Word of Life Bible Institute, Pottersville   693

Newspapers and circulation

	District circulation	Total circulation
Albany Times Union	28,570	99,549
Bennington Banner	1,022	7,356
Binghamton Press & Sun-Bulletin	1,290	58,790
Catskill Daily Mail	3,483	3,542
Glens Falls Post-Star	31,286	32,423
Hudson Register Star	6,314	6,454
Kingston Daily Freeman	3,261	21,179
*New York Daily News**	6,111	723,155
New York Post	7,373	511,412
*New York Times**	3,255	666,228
Oneonta Daily Star	9,770	17,652
Poughkeepsie Journal	16,918	39,831
Saratoga Saratogian	10,539	10,681
Schenectady Gazette	11,629	53,596
Troy Record	12,706	21,180
*USA Today**	3,246	1,674,376

*See Sources and Explanations in the front of the volume.

Television stations and affiliations

Albany-Schenectady-Troy	62%	WCDC	ABC
Albany-Schenectady-Troy	62%	WEWB	WB
Albany-Schenectady-Troy	62%	WMHT	PBS
Albany-Schenectady-Troy	62%	WRGB	CBS
Albany-Schenectady-Troy	62%	WTEN	ABC
Albany-Schenectady-Troy	62%	WXXA	FOX
Albany-Schenectady-Troy	62%	WYPX	PAX
Binghamton	16%	WBNG	CBS
Binghamton	16%	WICZ	FOX
Binghamton	16%	WIVT	ABC
Binghamton	16%	WSKG	PBS
Burlington-Plattsburgh	10%	WCAX	CBS
Burlington-Plattsburgh	10%	WCFE	PBS
Burlington-Plattsburgh	10%	WETK	PBS
Burlington-Plattsburgh	10%	WLED	PBS
Burlington-Plattsburgh	10%	WNNE	NBC
Burlington-Plattsburgh	10%	WPTZ	NBC
Burlington-Plattsburgh	10%	WVER	PBS
Burlington-Plattsburgh	10%	WVNY	ABC
Burlington-Plattsburgh	10%	WVTB	PBS
New York	8%	WABC	ABC
New York	8%	WCBS	CBS
New York	8%	WEDW	PBS
New York	8%	WFME	Independent
New York	8%	WLIW	PBS
New York	8%	WLNY	Independent
New York	8%	WMBC	Independent
New York	8%	WNBC	NBC
New York	8%	WNET	PBS

New York	8%	WNJB	PBS
New York	8%	WNJN	PBS
New York	8%	WNJU	Telemundo
New York	8%	WNYE	PBS
New York	8%	WNYW	FOX
New York	8%	WPIX	WB
New York	8%	WPXN	PAX
New York	8%	WRNN	Independent
New York	8%	WTBY	Independent
New York	8%	WWOR	UPN
New York	8%	WXTV	Univision
Utica	4%	WFXV	FOX
Utica	4%	WKTV	NBC
Utica	4%	WUTR	ABC

Cable systems and subscribers

Adelphia   23,934
Cablevision   11,172
Charter   4,574
Hamilton County Cable TV   543
Hilltop Communications   915
Mid-Hudson Cablevision   14,849
MTC Cable   1,432
Star Video   595
Time Warner   307,126

Businesses and other major employers

New York Mental Retardation and Developmental
   Disabilities Office; Wassaic   2,500
Glens Falls Hospital; Glens Falls   1,925
Johnsonville United Methodist Church; Johnsonville;
   religious organization   1,900
Dutchess Community College; Poughkeepsie   1,700
State Farm Mutual Automobile Insurance Co.; Ballston
   Spa; insurance agents and brokers   1,200
Boston Scientific Corp.; Glens Falls; medical instruments
   1,137
Amphenol Corp.; Sidney; electronic connectors   1,000
Mead Corp.; Sidney; commercial printing   1,000
Saratoga Care Inc.; Saratoga Springs; hospital
   management   1,000
Finch Pruyn and Co.; Glens Falls; paper mills   988
Green Island Associates; Bolton Landing; resort hotel
   800
Skidmore College; Saratoga Springs   764
Columbia Memorial Hospital; Hudson   750
Marist College; Poughkeepsie   740
Sonoco-Crellin International Inc.; Chatham; plastics
   molding   700
Culinary Institute of America; Hyde Park   675
Shanty Hollow Corp.; Hunter; ski lodge   650
Premium Retail Services Inc.; Saratoga Springs;
   merchandising consultant   645
Olympic Regional Development Authority; Lake Placid;
   sporting and recreational camps   600
C. R. Bard Inc.; Glens Falls; medical instruments   550
New York Correctional Services Dept.; Coxsackie   550
New York State Unified Court System; Catskill   550
New York Correctional Services Dept.; Comstock   534
Great Atlantic and Pacific Tea Co. Inc.; Lagrangeville;
   supermarkets   525
Wesley Health Care Center Inc.; Saratoga Springs;
   nursing care facilities   515

Adirondack Community College; Queensbury   500
Berkshire Farm Center and Services for Youth Inc.;
   Canaan; residential care   500
New York Racing Assn. Inc.; Saratoga Springs; sports
   field or stadium operator   500
Tyco Healthcare Group; Argyle; medical instruments
   500

New York 21st District

Capital District — Albany, Schenectady

As the terminus of the Erie Canal, which connects the Great Lakes to the Hudson River, New York's Capital District was one of the state's earliest industrial centers. Blue-collar workers and state employees give the Albany-Schenectady-Troy area a substantial union population and a solidly Democratic vote—unusual for an upstate district.

Albany is home to one of the nation's last big-city political machines, formed in 1921. During the heyday of Daniel O'Connell and Mayor Erastus Corning II, the Albany machine used to ensure Democratic victories throughout the area, but it now holds less sway over the area's ever-expanding suburbs. Few of the district's Democrats can be described as liberal. Most are quite conservative when it comes to social issues. The winning Democratic candidate in 2002 ran the Conservative and Independence Party lines, in addition to the Democratic Party line.

The 21st was expanded during 2002 redistricting and now includes all of Albany, Schenectady, Schoharie, and Montgomery Counties, as well as parts of Fulton, Saratoga, and Rensselaer Counties.

Despite large-scale industrial losses in the 1980s and 1990s, manufacturing remains a force. Job losses have been mitigated by an intensive effort to recruit small manufacturing and technology firms. Retail and wholesale jobs saw a real boom during the 1990s, and service jobs now account for about one-third of non-farm employment.

Major Industry

State government, services, manufacturing, retail.

Notable

The Mohawk and Hudson Rail Road, chartered in 1826 and opened in 1831, ran between Albany and Schenectady and was the state's first railroad; Samuel Wilson, a meatpacker who provided the Army with much of its rations during the War of 1812, is believed to be the inspiration for "Uncle Sam" and is buried in Troy; the original Shaker settlement was established in Watervliet in 1776.

Election Returns

	Republican		Democratic		Other	
President 2000	114,979	39.0%	165,003	55.9%	15,101	5.1%
House 2002	53,525	24.9%	161,329	75.1%		

District Profile

Population   654,361

Total area (square miles)   1,962.4
   Land area (square miles)   1,934.9

Population per square mile   338.2

Counties (2000 population)

Albany 294,565	Saratoga (pt.) 8,515
Fulton (pt.) 31,090	Schenectady 146,555
Montgomery 49,708	Schoharie 31,582
Rensselaer (pt.) 92,346	

Cities and other areas over 10,000 (2000 population)

Albany 95,658	Rotterdam CDP 20,536
Amsterdam 18,355	Schenectady 61,821
Cohoes 15,521	Troy 49,170
Gloversville 15,413	Watervliet 10,207

Race and Hispanic or Latino origin*

White 85.5%
Black or African American 7.5%
American Indian or Alaska Native 0.2%
Asian 2.1%
Native Hawaiian or other Pacific Islander 0.0%
Some other race 0.2%
Hispanic or Latino origin 3.2%
Two or more races 1.3%

*As percentage of total population.

Ancestry*

Dutch 3.0%	Irish 15.1%
English 6.8%	Italian 12.4%
Fr. Canadian 1.6%	Polish 5.3%
French 4.7%	Scottish 1.3%
German 11.8%	USA/American 2.8%

*As estimated percentage of total population.

Universities and colleges, 2000–2001 enrollment

Albany College of Pharmacy, Albany 691
Albany Law School, Albany 740
Albany Medical College, Albany 641
Bryant and Stratton Business Institute, Albany 265
College of St. Rose, Albany 4,231
Fulton-Montgomery Community College, Johnstown 1,885
Hudson Valley Community College, Troy 9,304
Maria College of Albany, Albany 721
Mildred Elley School, Latham 1,013
Regents College-University of the State of New York, Albany 18,067
Rensselaer Polytechnic Institute, Troy 8,022
Sage College, Albany 2,407
Sage College, Troy 819
Schenectady County Community College, Schenectady 3,473
Siena College, Loudonville 3,286
State University of New York, Albany 16,751
State University of New York College of Agriculture and Technology, Cobleskill 2,303
Union College, Schenectady 2,439

Newspapers and circulation

	District circulation	Total circulation
Albany Times Union	68,853	99,549
Amsterdam Recorder	6,906	9,374
Gloversville Leader-Herald	4,545	11,058
*New York Daily News**	2,619	723,155
New York Post	7,146	511,412
Schenectady Gazette	39,098	53,596
Troy Record	8,021	21,180
*USA Today**	3,883	1,674,376

*See Sources and Explanations in the front of the volume.

Television stations and affiliations

Albany-Schenectady-Troy	100%	WCDC	ABC
Albany-Schenectady-Troy	100%	WEWB	WB
Albany-Schenectady-Troy	100%	WMHT	PBS
Albany-Schenectady-Troy	100%	WRGB	CBS
Albany-Schenectady-Troy	100%	WTEN	ABC
Albany-Schenectady-Troy	100%	WXXA	FOX
Albany-Schenectady-Troy	100%	WYPX	PAX

Cable systems and subscribers

Adelphia 2,271
Mid-Hudson Cablevision 1,979
MidTel Cable TV 865
Time Warner 161,510

Military installations, September 2001

Schenectady Airport (Air National Guard), Schenectady 1,328
Watervliet Arsenal, Watervliet 772
Horace D. Bradt U.S. Army Reserve Center, Schenectady 605

Businesses and other major employers

Albany Medical Center; Albany 6,500
Albany Medical Center Hospital; Albany 6,000
General Electric Co.; Schenectady; gas turbine generators 5,000
New York Dept. of Taxation and Finance; Albany 5,000
New York Correctional Services Dept.; Albany 3,250
St. Peter's Health Care Services Hospital; Albany 3,188
University of the State of New York; Albany; state education department 3,000
New York Dept. of Health; Albany 2,608
New York Dept. of Education; Albany 2,565
New York Office of General Services; Albany 2,455
KAPL Inc.; Schenectady; energy research 2,200
New York Dept. of Transportation; Albany 2,079
Center Residence Corp.; Albany; individual and family services 2,000
General Electric Co.; Niskayuna; aircraft engine research and development 2,000
New York Office of State Controller; Albany 2,000
Empire Blue Cross and Blue Shield; Albany; insurance agents 1,800
New York Dept. of Labor; Albany 1,800
New York Motor Vehicles Dept.; Albany 1,752
New York Mental Health Office; Albany 1,731
New York Dept. of Environmental Conservation; Albany 1,700
Albany International Corp.; Albany; paper 1,600
Ellis Hospital; Schenectady 1,535
CSX Transportation Inc.; Selkirk; railroad freight hauling 1,500
U.S. Veterans Hospital; Albany 1,500
Samaritan Hospital; Troy 1,353
Eden Park Health Services Inc.; Albany; nursing care facilities 1,300

U.S. Postal Service; Albany   1,300
St. Clare Hospital; Schenectady   1,150
Memorial Hospital of Albany; Albany   1,105
New York Legislative Office; Albany   1,004
Rensselaer Polytechnic Institute; Troy   1,002
Albany County; Albany; convalescent home; nursing care   1,000
Albany-Schoharie-Schenectady-Saratoga BOCES; Albany; educational services   1,000
Hudson Valley Community College; Troy   1,000
Keybank National Assn.; Albany; state commercial banks   1,000
New York State Assembly; Albany   1,000
New York Temporary and Disability Assistance Office; Albany   1,000
Niagara Mohawk Power Corp.; Albany; electric power transmission   1,000
State Health Wadsworth Center; Albany   1,000
Health Research Inc.; Rensselaer; health services consultant   900
Keymark Inc.; Fonda; windows, plastics   900
New York State Division of Budget; Albany   900
Seton Health System Hospital; Troy   867
Golub Corp.; Schenectady; supermarkets   850
Albany County; Albany; county government   800
Loyal Order of Moose; Cohoes; civic and social associations   800
MVP Health Plan Inc.; Schenectady; health maintenance organization   800
New York Attorney General; Albany   800
New York Civil Service Department; Albany   800
New York Executive Office; Albany   800
U.S. Postal Service; Cohoes   800
St. Mary's Hospital at Amsterdam Inc.; Amsterdam   775
LIA Group; Schenectady; automobiles   758
Nathan Littauer Hospital Assn.; Gloversville   750
New York Dept. of Health; Troy   750
Schenectady/Saratoga Counties Cooperative Educational Services; Albany; elementary and secondary schools   750
Union College; Schenectady   735
Albany County; Albany; home health care   700
Capital District Physicians Health Plan Inc.; Albany; health maintenance organization   700
Hearst Corp.; Albany; periodicals   700
Marriott International Inc.; Albany; hotels, restaurants   700
New York Correctional Services Dept.; Sonyea   700
New York Dept. of State; Albany   700
New York Office of Alcoholism and Substance Abuse Services; Albany   700
New York Office of Children and Family Services; Rensselaer   700
New York State Thruway Authority; Albany   700
Combined Life Insurance Co. of New York Inc.; Latham; accident insurance carriers   690
New York Dept. of State; Albany; government   650
Siena College; Albany   650
General Electric Co.; Selkirk; plastics   600
Guilford Mills Inc.; Cobleskill; knit goods   600
New York National Guard; Scotia   600
New York State Police; Albany   600

Record Town Inc.; Albany; audio tapes   600
Bali Leathers Inc.; Johnstown; gloves, sport, athletic gear   599
National Railroad Passenger Corp.; Rensselaer   583
Burns International Security Services Corp.; Albany; security guard service   556
Capital Region Ford Nursing Home Co.; Cohoes; nursing care facilities   550
New York State and Local Retirement System; Albany   550
New York State Banking Dept.; Albany   550
Rensselaer County; Troy   550
Schenectady County; Schenectady; nursing care facilities   550
St. Gobain Abrasives Inc.; Watervliet; abrasive products   545
City of Albany; Albany; urban planning and development   526
Trans World Entertainment Corp.; Albany; compact discs   520
New York State Dept. of Public Safety; Albany   515
Amsterdam Memorial Health Care System; Amsterdam; hospital management   500
Bard College; Troy   500
Beech-Nut Nutrition Corp.; Canajoharie; baby foods   500
Fulton Montgomery Community College; Johnstown   500
Knights of Columbus Supreme Council Inc.; Albany; fraternal association   500
Macy's East Inc.; Albany; department stores   500
New York Office of Children and Family Services; Johnstown   500
SMG; Albany; real estate managers   500
Sysco Food Services; Clifton Park; canned goods   500
TDY Industries Inc.; Albany; stainless steel   500
United Cerebral Palsy Assn. of Capital District Inc.; Albany; school for physically handicapped   500
Wal-Mart Stores Inc.; Johnstown; department stores   500

New York 22nd District

South central — Binghamton, Poughkeepsie, Ithaca

The elongated 22nd reaches from the hills above Cayuga Lake to the east bank of the Hudson River. Most residents are found at those extremes: the Ithaca and Binghamton areas in the west and the Hudson Valley region, including Poughkeepsie, Newburgh, and Kingston, on the eastern edge.

In general, the district is rural, with a large portion of the Catskill Mountains in the center and apple and dairy farms throughout. Taking in all of Sullivan and Ulster Counties and parts of six others, the mixture of cities and farmland creates a politically competitive environment, though Democrats enjoy a slight advantage.

Ithaca, in the 22nd's far northwest, is home to Cornell University, Ithaca College, and a corps of liberal activists. Residents elected a socialist mayor three times in the 1990s, and Republican George W. Bush took just 28 percent of the vote in this area in the 2000 presidential election.

The district extends along the Pennsylvania border from Tioga County to Sullivan County, taking in Broome County's Triple Cities—Binghamton, Johnson City, and Endicott. Once an industrial hub, Binghamton saw a decline in manufacturing jobs during the 1980s and 1990s, and the economy has been hit hard by recessions. Defense companies are still a major force, though IBM, which at one time was headquartered in Endicott, has significantly reduced operations in the area. Officials now hope to use the state university in Binghamton as an anchor for economic development.

The Catskills' Borscht Belt, a prominent Jewish resort area, declined as tourists began vacationing in more exotic locales. Officials hope to lure tourists back with casinos that have been approved by the state.

Major Industry

Higher education, agriculture, electronics.

Notable

Gen. George Washington had his headquarters and residence in Newburgh from 1782 to 1783; Bethel was the site of the marathon Woodstock rock concert in 1969; Mohonk Mountain House, near New Paltz, has hosted four presidents since its opening in 1869.

Election Returns

	Republican		Democratic		Other	
President 2000	108,460	42.1%	131,421	51.0%	17,578	6.8%
House 2002	58,008	32.9%	113,280	64.2%	5,196	2.9%

District Profile

Population   654,361

Total area (square miles)   3,333.5
   Land area (square miles)   3,246.1

Population per square mile   201.6

Counties (2000 population)
Broome (pt.) 155,671	Sullivan 73,966
Delaware (pt.) 6,241	Tioga (pt.) 31,782
Dutchess (pt.) 29,871	Tompkins (pt.) 50,492
Orange (pt.) 128,589	Ulster 177,749

Cities and other areas over 10,000 (2000 population)
Binghamton   47,380
Endicott village   13,038
Endwell CDP   11,706
Ithaca   29,287
Johnson City village   15,535
Kingston   23,456
Middletown   25,388
Newburgh   28,259
Poughkeepsie   29,871

Race and Hispanic or Latino origin*
White   79.9%
Black or African American   7.7%
American Indian or Alaska Native   0.2%
Asian   2.5%
Native Hawaiian or other Pacific Islander   0.0%
Some other race   0.2%
Hispanic or Latino origin   7.8%
Two or more races   1.7%

*As percentage of total population.

Ancestry*
Dutch 2.6%		Italian 11.1%	
English 7.3%		Polish 4.1%	
French 1.9%		Russian 1.6%	
German 11.8%		Scottish 1.2%	
Irish 13.2%		USA/American 3.1%	

*As estimated percentage of total population.

Universities and colleges, 2000–2001 enrollment
Broome Community College, Binghamton   5,663
Cornell University, Ithaca   20,126
Ithaca College, Ithaca   6,170
Mount St. Mary College, Newburgh   2,107
Orange County Community College, Middletown   5,374
Practical Bible College, Bible School Park   252
State University of New York, Binghamton   12,473
State University of New York, New Paltz   7,723
State University of New York-Ulster County Community College, Stone Ridge   2,671
Sullivan County Community College, Loch Sheldrake   1,552

Newspapers and circulation

	District circulation	Total circulation
Binghamton Press & Sun-Bulletin	28,731	58,790
Ithaca Journal	5,426	18,422
Kingston Daily Freeman	17,899	21,179
Middletown Times Herald Record	41,943	82,615
*New York Daily News**	4,923	723,155
New York Post	4,523	511,412
*New York Times**	3,480	666,228
Poughkeepsie Journal	4,084	39,831
*USA Today**	1,639	1,674,376

*See Sources and Explanations in the front of the volume.

Television stations and affiliations
New York	70%	WABC	ABC
New York	70%	WCBS	CBS
New York	70%	WEDW	PBS
New York	70%	WFME	Independent
New York	70%	WLIW	PBS
New York	70%	WLNY	Independent
New York	70%	WMBC	Independent
New York	70%	WNBC	NBC
New York	70%	WNET	PBS
New York	70%	WNJB	PBS
New York	70%	WNJN	PBS
New York	70%	WNJU	Telemundo
New York	70%	WNYE	PBS
New York	70%	WNYW	FOX
New York	70%	WPIX	WB
New York	70%	WPXN	PAX
New York	70%	WRNN	Independent
New York	70%	WTBY	Independent
New York	70%	WWOR	UPN
New York	70%	WXTV	Univision
Binghamton	27%	WBNG	CBS

Binghamton	27%	WICZ	FOX
Binghamton	27%	WIVT	ABC
Binghamton	27%	WSKG	PBS
Syracuse	3%	WCNY	PBS
Syracuse	3%	WIXT	ABC
Syracuse	3%	WNYS	WB
Syracuse	3%	WNYT	NBC
Syracuse	3%	WSPX	PAX
Syracuse	3%	WSTM	NBC
Syracuse	3%	WSYT	FOX
Syracuse	3%	WTVH	CBS

Cable systems and subscribers
Cablevision 11,450
Haefele TV Inc. 2,982
Hancock Video Inc. 993
Time Warner 182,505

Military installations, September 2001
Stewart International Airport, New Windsor 2,391

Businesses and other major employers
International Business Machines Corp.; Poughkeepsie; computers 6,100
International Business Machines Corp.; Endicott; computers 6,000
State University of New York; Binghamton 5,000
New York State Electric and Gas Corp.; Ithaca; electric power distribution 4,000
Newburgh City School District; Newburgh 2,312
Cornell University; Ithaca 2,000
Youth Advocate Programs Inc.; Middletown; advocacy 2,000
United Health Services Hospitals Inc.; Johnson City 1,600
Our Lady of Lourdes Memorial Hospital Inc.; Binghamton 1,420
Vassar Bros. Hospital; Poughkeepsie 1,300
Horton Memorial Hospital; Middletown 1,295
Hadco Corp.; Owego; circuit boards 1,289
BAE Systems Controls Inc.; Johnson City; flight instruments, guidance systems 1,250
Ithaca College Inc.; Ithaca 1,200
Yellow Freight System Inc.; Maybrook; trucking terminal facilities 1,051
Central Hudson Gas and Electric Corp.; Poughkeepsie; electric services 900
Energy East Corp.; Binghamton; electric power distribution 900
New York Dept. of Transportation; Binghamton; transportation regulation 900
United Health Services Hospitals Inc.; Binghamton 900
Frito-Lay Inc.; Binghamton; snacks 850
American Postal Workers Union; Newburgh; labor organization 800
Benedictine Hospital; Kingston 800
Metropolitan Life Insurance Co.; Kingston; insurance agents and brokers 800
Sullivan County; Monticello; county government 767
Sullivan County Community General Hospital; Harris 750
St. Luke's Hospital of Newburgh; Newburgh 716

Poughkeepsie City School District; Poughkeepsie 700
Flextronics USA Inc.; Conklin; electronic circuits 700
Frito-Lay Inc.; Kirkwood; food products plant construction 700
Imperial Schrade Corp.; Ellenville; cutlery 700
Kingston Hospital; Kingston 700
Maines Paper and Food Service Inc.; Conklin; packaged frozen goods 700
Nevele Hotel; Ellenville; resort hotel 700
U.S. Postal Service; Newburgh 700
Cayuga Medical Center at Ithaca; Ithaca 674
Orange County Community College; Middletown 670
Wegmans Food Markets Inc.; Johnson City 613
City of Binghamton; Binghamton; city government 600
Cox Enterprises Inc.; Newburgh; automobile auction 600
Energy East Corp.; Ithaca; electric, other services 600
Wal-Mart Stores Inc.; Vestal; department stores 600
Wegmans Food Markets Inc.; Ithaca 600
Amphenol Corp.; Endicott; industry specialist consultants 550
State University of New York Health Science Center; Binghamton 550
Emerson Power Transmission Corp.; Ithaca; motor vehicle transmissions, drive assemblies 525
New York Correctional Services Dept.; Wallkill 525
Ottaway Newspapers Inc.; Middletown 521
Broome County; Vestal; nursing care facilities 520
Broome County; Binghamton; county government 500
Marriott International Inc.; Binghamton; caterers 500
Shipley Co.; Ithaca; industrial organic chemicals 500
Telespectrum Worldwide Inc.; Endicott; telemarketing 500

New York 23rd District

North — Watertown, Plattsburgh, Oswego

The vast 23rd covers roughly one-fourth of the state, bordering Lake Champlain, the St. Lawrence Seaway, and Lake Ontario. The waterways provide an inexpensive source of electricity, which has lured some heavy industry to the district and given it a number of blue-collar voters. But most of the district is rural, full of small towns, dairy farms, maple syrup producers, and colleges. It reaches south to Oneida Lake and Madison County.

Fort Drum (near Watertown, the district's largest city) is one of the largest and most modern Army facilities on the East Coast. It thus far has been safe from post–Cold War base closures, but district residents did experience some economic hardship when Plattsburgh Air Force Base shut down in 1995. A business park has sprung from its ashes, attracting roughly 60 tenants.

Still, unemployment remains a problem throughout the district; harsh winters and high transportation costs make attracting jobs difficult. Bright spots include seasonal tourism—the 23rd covers much of the Adirondack Mountains. The proximity to waterways and forests made paper production a major industry for a long while, but many mills have been forced to close their doors, though Georgia Pacific retains its presence in Plattsburgh. Officials see the expansion of broadband Internet access as a means of stoking economic development.

The northeast corner of the state has sent Republicans to the House since the 1872 election. But George W. Bush barely won here in the 2000 presidential election, and Democrats have had increasing success at the local level in recent years.

Major Industry
Agriculture, manufacturing, tourism, defense.

Notable
In 1775 Ethan Allen led the Green Mountain Boys—and Benedict Arnold—in seizing Fort Ticonderoga from the British; Whiteface Mountain is a top East Coast skiing destination.

Election Returns

	Republican		Democratic		Other	
President 2000	119,472	48.6%	115,611	47.1%	10,520	4.3%
House 2002	124,682	100.0%				

District Profile

Population 654,361

Total area (square miles) 14,739.3
Land area (square miles) 13,234.7

Population per square mile 49.4

Counties (2000 population)
Clinton	79,894	Lewis	26,944
Essex (pt.)	24,661	Madison	69,441
Franklin	51,134	Oneida (pt.)	26,879
Fulton (pt.)	23,983	Oswego	122,377
Hamilton	5,379	St. Lawrence	111,931
Jefferson	111,738		

Cities and other areas over 10,000 (2000 population)
Fort Drum CDP	12,123	Oneida	10,987
Fulton	11,855	Oswego	17,954
Massena village	11,209	Plattsburgh	18,816
Ogdensburg	12,364	Watertown	26,705

Race and Hispanic or Latino origin*
White 92.9%
Black or African American 2.6%
American Indian or Alaska Native 0.9%
Asian 0.6%
Native Hawaiian or other Pacific Islander 0.0%
Some other race 0.1%
Hispanic or Latino origin 2.1%
Two or more races 0.8%

*As percentage of total population.

Ancestry*
Dutch	2.1%	Irish	12.0%
English	9.4%	Italian	5.4%
Fr. Canadian	3.7%	Polish	2.8%
French	9.9%	Scottish	1.8%
German	9.9%	USA/American	5.6%

*As estimated percentage of total population.

Universities and colleges, 2000–2001 enrollment
Cazenovia College, Cazenovia 964
Clarkson University, Potsdam 2,877
Clinton Community College, Plattsburgh 1,697
Colgate University, Hamilton 2,820
Jefferson Community College, Watertown 3,652
Mater Dei College, Ogdensburg 268
North Country Community College, Malone 3,421
North Country Community College, Ticonderoga 3,421
Paul Smiths College of Arts and Science, Paul Smiths 760
State University of New York, Oswego 8,149
State University of New York, Plattsburgh 6,153
State University of New York, Potsdam 4,231
State University of New York College of Agriculture and Technology, Morrisville 3,033
State University of New York College of Technology, Canton 2,126
St. Lawrence University, Canton 2,092

Newspapers and circulation

	District circulation	Total circulation
Amsterdam Recorder	1,835	9,374
Gloversville Leader-Herald	6,169	11,058
New York Post	1,150	511,412
Oneida Daily Dispatch	4,613	6,776
Plattsburgh Press-Republican	19,787	21,015
Rome Daily Sentinel	4,009	14,523
Schenectady Gazette	2,650	53,596
Syracuse Post-Standard	23,344	122,222
*USA Today**	2,984	1,674,376
Utica Observer-Dispatch	2,279	45,856
Watertown Daily Times	31,897	32,226

*See Sources and Explanations in the front of the volume.

Television stations and affiliations

Watertown	41%	WNPI	PBS
Watertown	41%	WPBS	PBS
Watertown	41%	WWNY	CBS
Watertown	41%	WWTI	ABC
Burlington-Plattsburgh	27%	WCAX	CBS
Burlington-Plattsburgh	27%	WCFE	PBS
Burlington-Plattsburgh	27%	WETK	PBS
Burlington-Plattsburgh	27%	WLED	PBS
Burlington-Plattsburgh	27%	WNNE	NBC
Burlington-Plattsburgh	27%	WPTZ	NBC
Burlington-Plattsburgh	27%	WVER	PBS
Burlington-Plattsburgh	27%	WVNY	ABC
Burlington-Plattsburgh	27%	WVTB	PBS
Syracuse	16%	WCNY	PBS
Syracuse	16%	WIXT	ABC
Syracuse	16%	WNYS	WB
Syracuse	16%	WNYT	NBC
Syracuse	16%	WSPX	PAX
Syracuse	16%	WSTM	NBC
Syracuse	16%	WSYT	FOX
Syracuse	16%	WTVH	CBS
Albany-Schenectady-Troy	15%	WCDC	ABC
Albany-Schenectady-Troy	15%	WEWB	WB
Albany-Schenectady-Troy	15%	WMHT	PBS
Albany-Schenectady-Troy	15%	WRGB	CBS

Albany-Schenectady-Troy	15%	WTEN	ABC
Albany-Schenectady-Troy	15%	WXXA	FOX
Albany-Schenectady-Troy	15%	WYPX	PAX
Utica	1%	WFXV	FOX
Utica	1%	WKTV	NBC
Utica	1%	WUTR	ABC

Cable systems and subscribers
Adelphia   5,658
Castle Cable TV   715
Charter   15,033
Hamilton County Cable TV   1,003
Selectavision of Cazadonia   10,517
Time Warner   113,869

Military installations, September 2001
Fort Drum (Army), Watertown   13,815

Businesses and other major employers
International Business Machines Corp.; Oswego; computer peripherals, software   3,500

Champlain Valley Physicians Hospital; Plattsburgh   2,000

State University of New York; Plattsburgh   1,600

Alcoa Inc.; Massena; primary aluminum   1,500

New York Dept. of Education; Oswego   1,500

Alcan Aluminum Corp.; Oswego; aluminum sheet, plate, and foil   1,410

New York Mental Retardation and Developmental Disabilities Office; Oneida   1,400

Wyeth Laboratories Inc.; Rouses Point; pharmaceuticals   1,313

Constellation Nuclear Services; Lycoming; electric services   1,300

New York Correctional Services Dept.; Dannemora   1,300

Samaritan Medical Center; Watertown   1,250

Bombardier Mass Transit Corp.; Plattsburgh; railroad equipment   1,200

Niagara Mohawk Power Corp.; Lycoming; conducted tours   1,200

Oswego County; Fulton; county government   1,200

Chemipulp Process Inc.; Watertown; petroleum storage tank installation   1,000

State University of New York; Potsdam   1,000

International Paper Co.; Ticonderoga; paper mills   950

Oswego County Board of Cooperative Education Services; Mexico   903

Colgate University; Hamilton   857

Oneida Health Systems Inc.; Oneida; hospital   850

Wolverine World Wide Inc.; Malone; men's footwear   800

Reynolds Metals Co.; Massena; aluminum   765

New York Dept. of Transportation; Watertown   750

Entergy Nuclear Generation Co.; Oswego; electric power generation   700

New York Correctional Services Dept.; Cape Vincent   700

New York Power Authority; Lycoming; electric power generation   700

State University of New York; Morrisville   625

Fulton City School District; Fulton   600

General Motors Corp.; Massena   600

Huhtamaki Consumer Packaging-West Inc.; Fulton; pressed pulp products   600

St. Lawrence County; Canton; county government   600

St. Lawrence University; Canton   586

New York Correctional Services Dept.; Malone   580

Lewis County; Lowville; county government   570

HCA Genesis Inc.; Watertown; rest home, with health care   563

Claxton-Hepburn Medical Center; Ogdensburg   550

Jefferson Rehabilitation Center Inc.; Watertown   550

Jefferson Rehabilitation Center Inc.; Sackets Harbor   550

Oswego Hospital Inc.; Oswego   550

St. Lawrence County; Canton; vocational schools   544

Georgia-Pacific Corp.; Plattsburgh; paper mills   540

Harden Furniture Inc.; McConnellsville; home furniture   540

Clarkson University; Potsdam   525

Akwesasne Mohawk Casino; Hogansburg; casino hotel   500

Computer Curriculum Corp.; Phoenix; educators' association   500

Madison County Preventive Health; Oneida   500

NYSARC Inc.; Watertown; job training and related services   500

St. Lawrence County; Potsdam; public vocational/technical school   500

New York 24th District

Central — Utica, Rome, Auburn

The J-shaped 24th starts at the western edge of the Adirondack Mountains, sweeps through the central part of the state—south of Syracuse and north of Binghamton—and extends into the Finger Lakes region. Pristine countryside is dotted by the small towns and rural hamlets of central New York. James Fenimore Cooper's tales of the frontier days gave central New York its nickname, the "Leatherstocking Region." Along with dairy farms, the 24th contains halls of fame and other historical gems, including the Women's Rights Convention and the National Women's Hall of Fame in Seneca Falls and the National Baseball Hall of Fame in Cooperstown.

Utica and Rome, aging industrial cities on the Mohawk River, suffered as manufacturing jobs left the state, but blue-collar jobs remain critical to these cities and give the 24th many of its Democratic voters.

The region took a major hit when Griffiss Air Force Base closed in 1995. An effort to turn the Mohawk River Valley into a high-tech information center—aided by the Air Force's Rome research laboratory, which works with many of the state's universities—has replaced some of those jobs.

The 24th also is home to the Oneida Indian Nation, which runs a profitable casino in Verona and has a long-running lawsuit against the state to reclaim its native lands. In the western part of the district, the Cayuga Indian Nation won $250 million in damages from New York in a similar claim, but the state is appealing the award.

The district's natural beauty gives voters a proclivity for earth-friendly policies, but they are traditional Yankee Republicans. The 24th gives solid support to Republican congressional candidates, and voters favored George W. Bush by a slim margin in the 2000 presidential election.

Major Industry

Higher education, agriculture, tourism, manufacturing.

Notable

The National Soccer Hall of Fame is in Oneonta, and the National Distance Running Hall of Fame is in Utica.

Election Returns

	Republican		Democratic		Other	
President 2000	129,050	48.2%	126,021	47.1%	12,639	4.7%
House 2002	108,017	70.7%			44,760	29.3%

District Profile

Population 654,361

Total area (square miles) 6,356.0
Land area (square miles) 6,163.7

Population per square mile 106.2

Counties (2000 population)

Broome (pt.)	44,865	Ontario (pt.)	16,906
Cayuga (pt.)	70,598	Otsego (pt.)	49,622
Chenango	51,401	Seneca	33,342
Cortland	48,599	Tioga (pt.)	20,002
Herkimer	64,427	Tompkins (pt.)	46,009
Oneida (pt.)	208,590		

Cities and other areas over 10,000 (2000 population)

Auburn	28,574	Oneonta	13,292
Cortland	18,740	Rome	34,950
Geneva	13,617	Utica	60,651

Race and Hispanic or Latino origin*

White 92.2%
Black or African American 3.3%
American Indian or Alaska Native 0.2%
Asian 0.9%
Native Hawaiian or other Pacific Islander 0.0%
Some other race 0.1%
Hispanic or Latino origin 2.3%
Two or more races 1.1%

*As percentage of total population.

Ancestry*

Dutch	2.7%	Italian	10.9%
English	10.6%	Polish	4.9%
Fr. Canadian	1.1%	Scottish	1.4%
French	3.2%	USA/American	4.2%
German	11.9%	Welsh	1.6%
Irish	12.3%		

*As estimated percentage of total population.

Universities and colleges, 2000–2001 enrollment

Cayuga County Community College, Auburn 2,498
Hamilton College, Clinton 1,765
Hartwick College, Oneonta 1,431
Herkimer County Community College, Herkimer 2,591
Hobart and William Smith Colleges, Geneva 1,844
Mohawk Valley Community College, Utica 5,092
New York Chiropractic College, Seneca Falls 794
State University of New York, Cortland 7,178
State University of New York, Oneonta 5,584
State University of New York Institute of Technology, Utica 2,660
Tompkins-Cortland Community College, Dryden 2,674
Utica College of Syracuse University, Utica 2,188
Utica School of Commerce, Utica 507
Wells College, Aurora 458

Newspapers and circulation

	District circulation	Total circulation
Auburn Citizen	11,311	12,948
Binghamton Press & Sun-Bulletin	26,072	58,790
Geneva Finger Lakes Times	7,519	17,192
Ithaca Journal	12,106	18,422
*New York Daily News**	1,104	723,155
New York Post	3,335	511,412
Oneida Daily Dispatch	2,086	6,776
Oneonta Daily Star	6,704	17,652
Rochester Democrat and Chronicle	1,458	177,300
Rome Daily Sentinel	10,606	14,523
Syracuse Post-Standard	11,574	122,222
*USA Today**	3,202	1,674,376
Utica Observer-Dispatch	43,400	45,856

*See Sources and Explanations in the front of the volume.

Television stations and affiliations

Utica	39%	WFXV	FOX
Utica	39%	WKTV	NBC
Utica	39%	WUTR	ABC
Syracuse	36%	WCNY	PBS
Syracuse	36%	WIXT	ABC
Syracuse	36%	WNYS	WB
Syracuse	36%	WNYT	NBC
Syracuse	36%	WSPX	PAX
Syracuse	36%	WSTM	NBC
Syracuse	36%	WSYT	FOX
Syracuse	36%	WTVH	CBS
Binghamton	24%	WBNG	CBS
Binghamton	24%	WICZ	FOX
Binghamton	24%	WIVT	ABC
Binghamton	24%	WSKG	PBS
Rochester	1%	WHEC	NBC
Rochester	1%	WROC	CBS
Rochester	1%	WUHF	FOX
Rochester	1%	WXXI	PBS

Cable systems and subscribers

Adelphia 81,692
Haefele TV Inc. 897
NU-View TV 1,702
Time Warner 89,964

Businesses and other major employers

Mary Imogene Bassett Hospital Inc.; Cooperstown 2,000
Borg-Warner Morse TEC Inc.; Ithaca; motor vehicle parts/accessories 1,600
Graphic Arts Mutual Insurance Co.; New Hartford; property insurance 1,325

Broome Community College Foundation Inc.;
Binghamton; community affairs/services 1,231

New York Mental Health Office; Utica 1,200

Fleet Services Corp.; Utica; data processing 1,139

Goulds Pumps Inc.; Seneca Falls; pumping equipment
1,100

New York Dept. of Education; Oneonta 1,075

ConMed Corp.; Utica; electromedical apparatus 1,000

New York State Electric and Gas Corp.; Binghamton;
electric power distribution 1,000

Oneida County; Utica; county government 1,000

Orange and Rockland Utilities Inc.; Cooperstown;
electric services 1,000

Remington Arms Co.; Ilion; small arms 1,000

St. Elizabeth Medical Center; Utica 1,000

Rome Memorial Hospital; Rome 998

State University of New York; Cortland 950

Mohawk Valley Community College; Utica 890

International Paper Co.; Binghamton 831

Orion Bus Industries Parts Inc.; Oriskany; automotive
supplies, parts 800

Raymond Corp.; Greene; industrial trucks and tractors
800

Auburn Memorial Hospital; Auburn 767

Pall Corp.; Cortland; medical supplies 750

Cortland Memorial Hospital Inc.; Cortland 742

Procter and Gamble Pharmaceuticals Inc.; Norwich
703

AAF-McQuay Inc.; Auburn; heating and air
conditioning units 700

Cortland County; Cortland; county government 700

Utica Mutual Insurance Co.; New Hartford; fire, marine,
casualty insurance 700

Wal-Mart Stores Inc.; Marcy; warehousing 700

New York Central Mutual Fire Insurance Co; Edmeston;
fire, marine, casualty insurance 691

Aurelia Osborn Fox Memorial Hospital Society; Oneonta
683

Geneva General Hospital Inc.; Geneva 635

Binghamton Board of Cooperative Education Services;
Binghamton 615

Metropolitan Property and Casualty Insurance Co.;
Utica; property damage insurance 600

New York Correctional Services Dept.; Marcy 600

New York Correctional Services Dept.; Rome 600

Special Metals International Corp.; New Hartford;
metals service centers and offices 550

New York Correctional Services Dept.; Moravia 545

Vail-Ballou Press Inc.; Binghamton; book printing and
binding 525

APAC Customer Services Inc.; Utica; telemarketing
services 500

BMC Industries Inc.; Cortland; ophthalmic goods
500

Geneva City School District; Geneva 500

Hamilton College; Clinton 500

Hofmann Laces; Herkimer; draperies 500

Madison-Oneida County Board of Cooperative Education
Services; Verona 500

New York Correctional Services Dept.; Romulus 500

White Management Corp.; Clinton; home remodeling
500

New York 25th District

North central — Syracuse, most of Irondequoit

Located in the center of the state, Syracuse is the only major city and economic hub of the 25th, which stretches from Onondaga County west along Lake Ontario to Irondequoit, a suburb of Rochester. Small towns and farms fill out the rest of the area in this moderately conservative district.

Syracuse is still suffering from a steep decline in manufacturing jobs that began in the 1980s and continued through the 1990s, though the city has held on to some blue-collar jobs by encouraging light manufacturing. Other growth comes from service-related work in hospitals and universities. State officials are working to turn upstate New York cities into university-based technology centers, and they hope Syracuse (home to Syracuse University) will become such a hub for environmental systems. Outside of Syracuse, small towns rely on dairy farming.

In this previously strong Republican territory, the area's GOP organization once held the loyalties of Irish Italian, Polish, and Jewish constituencies in and around Syracuse. The electorate's Republican leanings were reinforced by the typical upstate antipathy toward Democratic New York City. But the Republican machine has faded; economic stagnation in the 1990s and the decline of the city's industrial sector have helped the Democratic Party gain ground. Minorities and blue-collar workers contribute to the Democratic vote in Syracuse, as does an upscale Jewish population in DeWitt.

Redistricting in 2002 added parts of Monroe County and all of Wayne County, padding the sizable Republican base in Syracuse's suburbs and outlying areas. The revised 25th gave a slight majority to Al Gore in the 2000 presidential election, but by a smaller margin than under the old lines.

Major Industry
Agriculture, service, manufacturing, higher education.

Notable
The Brannock Device—used to measure feet for shoe size—was invented by Syracuse native Charles F. Brannock, and the company is based in Liverpool, a Syracuse suburb; Joseph Smith, founder of the Mormon Church, grew up and had his first visions in Palmyra.

Election Returns

	Republican		Democratic		Other	
President 2000	132,126	45.0%	148,623	50.7%	12,619	4.3%
House 2002	144,610	72.3%	53,290	26.6%	2,131	1.1%

District Profile

Population 654,361

Total area (square miles) 2,560.5
Land area (square miles) 1,619.7

Population per square mile 404.0

Counties (2000 population)

Cayuga (pt.)	11,365	Onondaga	458,336
Monroe (pt.)	90,895	Wayne	93,765

Cities and other areas over 10,000 (2000 population)
Fairmount CDP   10,795
Irondequoit CDP (pt.)   32,661
Syracuse   147,306

Race and Hispanic or Latino origin*
White   86.6%
Black or African American   7.1%
American Indian or Alaska Native   0.6%
Asian   1.8%
Native Hawaiian or other Pacific Islander   0.0%
Some other race   0.1%
Hispanic or Latino origin   2.3%
Two or more races   1.5%

As percentage of total population.

Ancestry*
Dutch 3.0%		Irish 13.9%
English 9.7%		Italian 12.4%
Fr. Canadian 1.4%		Polish 4.8%
French 3.6%		Scottish 1.4%
German 13.9%		USA/American 2.9%

As estimated percentage of total population.

Universities and colleges, 2000–2001 enrollment
Bryant and Stratton Business Institute, Syracuse   233
Le Moyne College, Syracuse   3,130
Onondaga Community College, Syracuse   7,848
State University of New York College of Environmental Science and Forestry, Syracuse   1,749
State University of New York Upstate Medical University, Syracuse   1,096
Syracuse University, Syracuse   18,186

Newspapers and circulation
	District circulation	Total circulation
Auburn Citizen	1,628	12,948
Geneva Finger Lakes Times	3,365	17,192
New York Post	1,377	511,412
Rochester Democrat and Chronicle	32,384	177,300
Syracuse Post-Standard	86,041	122,222
*USA Today**	4,558	1,674,376

See Sources and Explanations in the front of the volume.

Television stations and affiliations
Rochester	57%	WHEC	NBC
Rochester	57%	WROC	CBS
Rochester	57%	WUHF	FOX
Rochester	57%	WXXI	PBS
Syracuse	43%	WCNY	PBS
Syracuse	43%	WIXT	ABC
Syracuse	43%	WNYS	WB
Syracuse	43%	WNYT	NBC
Syracuse	43%	WSPX	PAX
Syracuse	43%	WSTM	NBC
Syracuse	43%	WSYT	FOX
Syracuse	43%	WTVH	CBS

Cable systems and subscribers
Adelphia   1,941
Time Warner   169,160

Military installations, September 2001
Hancock Field (Air National Guard), North Syracuse   1,156
D. W. Holleder U.S. Army Reserve Center, Webster   407

Businesses and other major employers
St. Joseph's Hospital Health Center; Syracuse   5,000
Carrier Corp.; Syracuse; air-conditioning equipment   4,300
State University of New York Health Science Center; Syracuse   4,200
Carrier Corp.; Syracuse; billing, bookkeeping service   4,000
Carrier Corp.; Syracuse; refrigeration/air-conditioning defrost controls   4,000
Syracuse University; Syracuse   4,000
New Venture Gear Inc.; East Syracuse; automotive gears   3,500
Penfield School District; Rochester   3,500
Central New York Developmental Disabilities Services Office; Syracuse   3,000
Staff Leasing of Central New York Inc.; Liverpool; employee leasing service   2,500
Crouse Health Hospital Inc.; Syracuse   2,300
Onondaga County; Syracuse; county government   2,000
Penn Traffic Co.; Syracuse; supermarkets   2,000
Empire Blue Cross and Blue Shield; Syracuse; medical service plans   1,530
New York Mental Retardation and Developmental Disabilities Office; Newark   1,500
Agway Inc.; DeWitt; prepared feeds   1,300
U.S. Veterans Hospital; Syracuse   1,300
Community-General Hospital of Greater Syracuse Inc.; Syracuse   1,240
New York National Guard; Syracuse   1,200
Niagara Mohawk Power Corp.; Syracuse; electric power generation   1,200
Pyramid Management Group Inc.; Syracuse; real estate managers   1,200
Welch Allyn Inc.; Skaneateles Falls; medical diagnostic apparatus   1,200
Excellus Health Plan Inc.; Baldwinsville; health maintenance organization   1,100
Anheuser-Busch Inc.; Baldwinsville; beer   1,000
Bristol-Myers Squibb Co.; East Syracuse; pharmaceuticals   1,000
Excellus Health Plan Inc.; Syracuse   1,000
Onondaga County; Syracuse; child-related social services   1,000
Ontario and Seneca and Yates and Cay; East Palmyra; education programs   1,000
United Parcel Service Inc.; East Syracuse; parcel delivery   1,000
Onondaga Community College; Syracuse   988
Garlock Inc.; Palmyra; gaskets, packing/sealing devices   950
Crucible Materials Corp.; Solvay; blast furnaces and steel mills   900
MONY Group Inc.; Syracuse; life insurance   900
Philips Broadband Networks Inc.; Manlius; cable TV equipment   900

Visiting Nurse Service of Rochester and Monroe County Inc.; Webster; home health care   875

Loretto Rest Nursing Home Co. Inc.; Syracuse   850

Huen New York Inc.; Syracuse; electrical work   800

John Mezzalingua Associates Inc.; East Syracuse; cable TV equipment   800

New York Civil Service Dept.; Syracuse   800

New York Dept. of Transportation; Syracuse   800

New York Mental Health Office; Syracuse   800

Research Foundation of State University of New York; Syracuse; educational research   756

Fayetteville-Manlius School District; Manlius   750

Stickley-Audi Inc.; Manlius; furniture and cabinets   720

City of Syracuse; Syracuse; sanitary district   700

Fiskars Consumer Products Inc.; Baldwinsville; furniture hardware   700

Via Health Newark-Wayne Community Hospital; Newark   700

Onondaga County; Syracuse; sheriff's office   650

St. Camillus Residential Health Care Facility; Syracuse   630

Onondaga County; Syracuse; rest home, with health care   605

HSBC Inc.; Syracuse; commercial banking   600

Parker Hannifin Corp.; Lyons; refrigeration equipment   600

Rochester Gas and Electric Corp.; Ontario; electric power generation   600

Onondaga County Convention Center; Syracuse   575

Eagle Comtronics Inc.; Liverpool; cable TV equipment   550

Wegmans Food Markets Inc.; Rochester; grocery store   542

State University of New York; Syracuse   540

Beebee Island Corp.; Syracuse; electric services   500

Central New York Regional Transportation Authority; Syracuse   500

City of Syracuse; Syracuse; fire dept.   500

Herald Co.; Syracuse; newspaper   500

James Square Nursing Home Inc.; Syracuse; nursing care facilities   500

Morris Protective Service Inc.; Syracuse; security guard service   500

Pennysavers Scotsman Press; Syracuse; newspaper   500

Pinkerton's Inc.; Liverpool; security guard service   500

Verizon Communications Inc.; Phoenix; voice telephone communications   500

Wayne County; Lyons; county government   500

West Irondequoit Central School District; Rochester; public schools   500

New York 26th District

Suburban Buffalo and Rochester; rural west

The Republican-leaning 26th spreads from the Buffalo to the Rochester suburbs, scooping up mainly rural areas in between and to the south. It takes in all or part of seven counties, but slightly less than half of residents live in Niagara and Erie Counties in the westernmost part of the district.

The population is anchored in Amherst, a white-collar suburb northeast of Buffalo. The State University of New York at Buffalo and corporate office parks are mainstays. Amherst and Lancaster, a town to the southeast, voted narrowly for Al Gore in the 2000 presidential election. Less-populous areas in northeastern Erie, including Clarence and Newstead, lean Republican.

The 26th's share of Niagara County, including Lockport and North Tonawanda, was added during 2002 redistricting, which renumbered the district from the 27th. As in Erie, the Niagara portion is politically competitive, with registered Republicans only slightly outnumbering Democrats.

The New York State Thruway links Erie County to the Rochester suburbs of western Monroe County, which include Greece and have a Republican lean.

Between Buffalo and Rochester are the dairy, vegetable, and grain farms of rural western New York. Wyoming County is solidly Republican and heavily agricultural, with an abundance of dairy farms. Wyoming also has a facility that is distinctly unbucolic: the state penitentiary at Attica, which in 1971 had one of the worst prison riots in U.S. history. Livingston County, east of Wyoming, includes Conesus Lake, which is at the western edge of New York's Finger Lakes region, and part of the Genesee River, which flows north into Rochester.

Major Industry

Manufacturing, agriculture, service.

Notable

The Herschell Carrousel Factory Museum in North Tonawanda hosts about 20,000 visitors a year; the Jell-O museum in LeRoy celebrates the beginnings of the famous gelatin dessert.

Election Returns

	Republican		Democratic		Other	
President 2000	144,516	50.6%	126,693	44.4%	14,188	5.0%
House 2002	135,089	73.6%	41,140	22.4%	7,230	3.9%

District Profile

Population   654,361

Total area (square miles)   2,748.5
  Land area (square miles)   2,731.0

Population per square mile   239.6

Counties (2000 population)
  Erie (pt.)   193,273   Niagara (pt.)   112,598
  Genesee   60,370   Orleans (pt.)   35,863
  Livingston   64,328   Wyoming   43,424
  Monroe (pt.)   144,505

Cities and other areas over 10,000 (2000 population)
  Batavia   16,256
  Greece CDP   14,614
  Lancaster village   11,188
  Lockport   22,279
  North Tonawanda   33,262

Race and Hispanic or Latino origin*
  White   92.3%
  Black or African American   3.0%

American Indian or Alaska Native   0.3%
Asian   1.5%
Native Hawaiian or other Pacific Islander   0.0%
Some other race   0.1%
Hispanic or Latino origin   1.9%
Two or more races   0.8%

As percentage of total population.

Ancestry*

Dutch	1.7%	Italian	11.9%
English	9.6%	Polish	8.2%
French	2.6%	Scottish	1.5%
German	20.6%	USA/American	2.8%
Irish	12.3%		

As estimated percentage of total population.

Universities and colleges, 2000–2001 enrollment

Bryant and Stratton Business Institute-Rochester, Rochester   200
Daemen College, Amherst   1,824
Erie Community College, Williamsville   4,665
Genesee Community College, Batavia   4,521
ITT Technical Institute, Getzville   480
Niagara County Community College, Sanborn   4,641
State University of New York, Brockport   8,524
State University of New York, Buffalo   24,830
State University of New York, Geneseo   5,477

Newspapers and circulation

	District circulation	Total circulation
Batavia Daily News	14,906	15,019
Buffalo News	59,094	222,695
Niagara Gazette	5,020	24,260
Rochester Democrat and Chronicle	42,389	177,300
Tonawanda News	7,076	10,743
*USA Today**	5,466	1,674,376

See Sources and Explanations in the front of the volume.

Television stations and affiliations

Buffalo	68%	WGRZ	NBC
Buffalo	68%	WIVB	CBS
Buffalo	68%	WKBW	ABC
Buffalo	68%	WNED	PBS
Buffalo	68%	WNYB	Independent
Buffalo	68%	WNYO	WB
Buffalo	68%	WUTV	FOX
Rochester	32%	WHEC	NBC
Rochester	32%	WROC	CBS
Rochester	32%	WUHF	FOX
Rochester	32%	WXXI	PBS

Cable systems and subscribers

Adelphia   83,288
Cooney Cable Associates   1,607
Time Warner   61,064

Military installations, September 2001

Niagara Falls International Airport Air Reserve Station, Niagara Falls   2,214
Niagara Falls Armed Forces Reserve Center, Niagara Falls   359

Businesses and other major employers

Gap Inc.; Rochester; clothing stores   2,500
Delphi Corp.; Lockport; air conditioner parts, motor vehicle   1,800
Employer Service Corp.; Amherst; employee leasing service   1,800
Ingram Micro Inc.; Williamsville; computer peripherals, software   1,500
Research Foundation of State University of New York; Buffalo; noncommercial research organization   1,200
New York Correctional Services Dept.; Attica   1,100
Dialogic; Amherst; software development   994
Brockport Central School District; Brockport   983
Unity Health System Hospital; Rochester   955
State University of New York; Brockport   900
Monroe Board of Cooperative Education Services; Spencerport   800
State University of New York; Geneseo   800
Genesee County; Batavia; county government   790
Independent Health Assn. Inc.; Williamsville; management consulting   750
Sweet Home Central School District of Amherst and Tonawanda; Amherst   750
Independent Health Assn. Inc.; Buffalo; medical service plans   701
Bank of Amercia Mortgage; Getzville; mortgage bankers   700
Buffalo Medical Group; Williamsville; medical offices   670
Erie County; Alden; convalescent home   652
Bank of America Corp.; Amherst; banking   650
International Imaging Materials Inc.; Amherst; inked ribbons   650
Excellus Health Plan Inc.; Buffalo; health maintenance organization   600
New York Correctional Services Dept.; Albion   600
North American Health Care Inc.; Amherst; insurance agents and brokers   600
Tops Markets Inc.; Williamsville; supermarkets   600
Wyoming County Community Hospital; Warsaw; hospital, nursing school   596
Brothers of Mercy Nursing Home Co. Inc.; Clarence   550
United Memorial Medical Center; Batavia   550
Wegmans Food Markets Inc.; Amherst; supermarkets   524
Citibank NA; Amherst; check clearing services   500
Genesee Board of Cooperative Education Services; Geneseo   500
Wilson Greatbatch Ltd.; Clarence; defibrillator   500

New York 27th District

West — most of Buffalo, south and east suburbs

Tucked along the shores of Lake Erie in western New York, the 27th contains all of Erie County south of Buffalo and all but the northeastern portion of the city itself. Most of Buffalo's minority residents are in the neighboring 28th.

The region has battled to shed its high unemployment rate and Rust Belt image. Auto manufacturing remains important in the area, and the city has a large concentration of blue-collar workers. Buffalo has seen an increase in finance, insurance, and real estate industry jobs—driven mostly by two thriving banks, HSBC and M&T. As part of a larger plan to help the beleaguered economy of upstate New York, officials hope university-based research will turn the Buffalo region into a bioinformatics center, promoting the use of computer technology to study genomes, proteins, and biomolecules.

Adelphia, a major cable telecommunications company, planned to move its headquarters—and high-paying executive jobs—to the waterfront from Pennsylvania, but the plan was scrapped when the company filed for bankruptcy in 2002. Still, local leaders see the waterfront as the locus for Buffalo's renaissance. Sports teams, particularly the NFL's Buffalo Bills, who play in Orchard Park, are the pride of the city. The rest of Erie County and Chautauqua County, a grape-growing region, are mostly rural.

The 27th has a Democratic tradition but was made more Republican in 2002 redistricting: An incumbent-protection plan added the GOP stronghold of Chautauqua County to the old 30th, which was renumbered the 27th. Residents have shown a willingness to vote for moderate Republicans with union sympathies.

Major Industry

Auto manufacturing, government, agriculture, tourism.

Notable

All major cities in the northeastern part of North America are within a 500-mile radius of Buffalo; President Franklin D. Roosevelt gave his 1936 "I Hate War" speech at the Chautauqua Institution.

Election Returns

	Republican		Democratic		Other	
President 2000	114,859	40.9%	149,840	53.4%	16,090	5.7%
House 2002	120,117	69.1%	47,811	27.5%	5,991	3.4%

District Profile

Population   654,361

Total area (square miles)   2,443.6
  Land area (square miles)   1,830.2

Population per square mile   357.5

Counties (2000 population)
  Chautauqua   139,750
  Erie (pt.)   514,611

Cities and other areas over 10,000 (2000 population)
  Buffalo (pt.)   163,179
  Cheektowaga CDP   79,988
  Depew village (pt.)   10,228
  Dunkirk   13,131
  Fredonia village   10,706
  Hamburg village   10,116
  Jamestown   31,730
  Lackawanna   19,064
  West Seneca CDP   45,943

Race and Hispanic or Latino origin*
  White   88.8%
  Black or African American   4.0%
  American Indian or Alaska Native   0.8%
  Asian   0.7%
  Native Hawaiian or other Pacific Islander   0.0%
  Some other race   0.1%
  Hispanic or Latino origin   4.6%
  Two or more races   1.0%

*As percentage of total population.

Ancestry*
Dutch	1.1%	Italian	11.2%
English	6.4%	Polish	14.7%
French	2.1%	Scottish	1.1%
German	19.2%	Swedish	2.4%
Irish	12.5%	USA/American	2.0%

*As estimated percentage of total population.

Universities and colleges, 2000–2001 enrollment
  Bryant and Stratton Business Institute, Buffalo   313
  Bryant and Stratton Business Institute, Lackawanna   215
  Canisius College, Buffalo   4,814
  D'Youville College, Buffalo   2,397
  Erie Community College, Buffalo   2,220
  Erie Community College, Orchard Park   3,122
  Hilbert College, Hamburg   888
  Jamestown Business College, Jamestown   271
  Jamestown Community College, Jamestown   4,041
  Medaille College, Buffalo   1,670
  State University of New York, Buffalo   11,399
  State University of New York, Fredonia   5,086
  Trocaire College, Buffalo   681
  Villa Maria College, Buffalo   405

Newspapers and circulation

	District circulation	Total circulation
Buffalo News	105,766	222,695
Dunkirk Observer Daily	11,019	11,945
Jamestown Post-Journal	18,438	20,591
*USA Today**	10,152	1,674,376

*See Sources and Explanations in the front of the volume.

Television stations and affiliations
Buffalo	100%	WGRZ	NBC
Buffalo	100%	WIVB	CBS
Buffalo	100%	WKBW	ABC
Buffalo	100%	WNED	PBS
Buffalo	100%	WNYB	Independent
Buffalo	100%	WNYO	WB
Buffalo	100%	WUTV	FOX

Cable systems and subscribers
  Adelphia   171,569
  Chautauqua Cable Inc.   573
  Time Warner   23,879

Businesses and other major employers
  U.S. Postal Service; Buffalo   3,228
  Mercy Hospital of Buffalo; Buffalo   2,869
  Erie County; Buffalo; county government   2,500
  New York Dept. of Transportation; Buffalo   2,500
  HSBC Inc.; Buffalo; mortgage bankers   2,322
  Moog Inc.; East Aurora; aircraft control systems   2,100
  Ford Motor Co.; Buffalo; automotive body parts   1,944

Western New York Developmental Disabilities Services Office; West Seneca 1,800

Bush Industries Inc.; Jamestown; home furniture 1,700

New York Dept. of Education; Buffalo 1,600

Clientlogic Operating Corp.; Buffalo; software 1,500

Cummins Inc.; Buffalo; internal combustion engines 1,500

HSBC Arena; Buffalo; convention and show services 1,403

Cummins Inc.; Lakewood; internal combustion engines 1,300

Erie County; Buffalo; sheriff's office 1,200

Woman's Christian Assn. Hospital; Jamestown 1,200

Rich Products Corp.; Buffalo; condensed/evaporated dairy products 1,059

Quebecor World Buffalo Inc.; Depew; book printing 1,050

Contract Staffing Inc.; Buffalo; employee programs administration 1,000

Motorola Inc.; Elma; engine electrical equipment 1,000

Berkshire Hathaway Inc.; Buffalo; newspaper 925

Carriage House Companies Inc.; Fredonia; canned fruits 900

St. Joseph Hospital; Buffalo 849

Baker Victory Services; Lackawanna; self-help group home 800

Bethlehem Steel Corp.; Lackawanna; pipes, plates, sheets 800

City of Buffalo; Buffalo; city management 800

New York Mental Health Office; Buffalo 800

Verizon Communications Inc.; Buffalo; data telephone communications 800

Fisher-Price Inc.; East Aurora; toys and games 765

Outokumpu American Brass Inc.; Buffalo; copper rolling and drawing 760

New ERA Cap Co.; Derby; uniform hats/caps 750

State University of New York; Fredonia 750

United Parcel Service Inc.; Buffalo; parcel delivery 750

Westwood-Squibb Pharmaceuticals Inc.; Buffalo; pharmaceuticals 730

HSBC Mortgage Corp.; Depew; mortgage bankers 676

Buffalo China Inc.; Buffalo; china tableware 650

Graphic Controls Corp.; Buffalo; data processing 650

Hodgson Russ Law Firm; Buffalo; law office 600

TLC Health Network Hospital; Irving 600

Hamburg Central School System Inc.; Hamburg 592

Chautauqua County; Mayville; county government 550

MRC Bearings Inc.; Falconer; ball bearings and parts 550

Niagara Frontier Transportation Authority; Buffalo 536

Wegmans Food Markets Inc.; Buffalo; grocery store 532

Zemco Industries Inc. Del.; Buffalo; prepared meats 530

Child and Family Services; Buffalo; counseling services 500

Cooper Turbocompressor Inc.; Buffalo; air and gas compressors 500

E. I. Du Pont De Nemours and Co.; Buffalo; cellulosic fibers 500

Evans Brant Central School District; Angola 500

Fleet Services Corp.; Buffalo; data processing 500

M. Wile and Co.; Buffalo; men's and boys' suits 500

New York 28th District

Northwest — Rochester, part of Buffalo

A small strip of land along the shore of Lake Ontario serves as a connector for the ends—Buffalo and Rochester—of the telephone receiver-shaped 28th. The old Rochester-based 28th and Buffalo-based 29th were merged during 2002 redistricting to create one district that encompasses the northeastern portion of Buffalo, all of Niagara Falls, and almost all of Rochester, giving the new 28th most of the Democratic-rich voting areas in western New York.

Blacks make up more than one-fourth of the population, and minorities combined total more than one-third, giving the district a far higher proportion of minority residents than any of the surrounding districts.

While manufacturing powered by the Niagara River long has been the base of Buffalo's economy, Rochester has been a technology center. Both cities are trying to recover from economic decline in the 1990s.

Optic and imaging manufacturing firms drive Rochester's economy, joined by high-tech startup companies that benefit from proximity to the area's major corporations, Eastman Kodak and Xerox Corp., and academic institutions.

Rochester suffered from high unemployment during the 1990s, but the situation has been improving. While much of the slack in the manufacturing sector has been picked up by the service industries, the lower salaries have exacerbated the problems of Rochester's low-income residents.

Unlike many northeastern cities with blue-collar bases, the Rochester area long held to a moderate Republican tradition typical of upstate New York. But it has begun to lean the other way. Both the old 28th and old 29th supported Democratic presidential candidates in 1992, 1996, and 2000. Al Gore won the new district by 25 percentage points in 2000.

Major Industry

Service, manufacturing, tourism.

Notable

About 50,000 honeymooners visit Niagara Falls each year; the Rochester home of women's rights activist Susan B. Anthony is now a museum.

Election Returns

	Republican		Democratic		Other	
President 2000	88,461	34.8%	151,402	59.6%	14,160	5.6%
House 2002	59,547	37.5%	99,057	62.5%		

District Profile

Population 654,360

Total area (square miles) 2,282.0

Land area (square miles) 534.0

Population per square mile 1,225.4

Counties (2000 population)

Erie (pt.)	242,381	Niagara (pt.)	107,248
Monroe (pt.)	296,423	Orleans (pt.)	8,308

Cities and other areas over 10,000 (2000 population)

Buffalo (pt.)   129,469
Irondequoit CDP (pt.)   19,693
Kenmore village   16,426
Niagara Falls   55,593
Rochester (pt.)   219,729
Tonawanda   16,136
Tonawanda CDP   61,729

Race and Hispanic or Latino origin*

White   62.0%
Black or African American   28.7%
American Indian or Alaska Native   0.5%
Asian   1.4%
Native Hawaiian or other Pacific Islander   0.0%
Some other race   0.1%
Hispanic or Latino origin   5.5%
Two or more races   1.7%

*As percentage of total population.

Ancestry*

Dutch	1.2%	Italian	11.0%
English	6.3%	Polish	5.5%
French	2.0%	Scottish	1.3%
German	13.4%	USA/American	1.9%
Irish	9.7%		

*As estimated percentage of total population.

Universities and colleges, 2000–2001 enrollment

Monroe Community College, Rochester   3,421
Niagara University, Lewiston   3,146
Rochester Business Institute, Irondequoit   803
University of Rochester, Rochester   8,071

Newspapers and circulation

	District circulation	Total circulation
Buffalo News	51,698	222,695
Niagara Gazette	19,234	24,260
Rochester Democrat and Chronicle	46,097	177,300
Tonawanda News	3,649	10,743
*USA Today**	7,503	1,674,376

*See Sources and Explanations in the front of the volume.

Television stations and affiliations

Buffalo	64%	WGRZ	NBC
Buffalo	64%	WIVB	CBS
Buffalo	64%	WKBW	ABC
Buffalo	64%	WNED	PBS
Buffalo	64%	WNYB	Independent
Buffalo	64%	WNYO	WB
Buffalo	64%	WUTV	FOX
Rochester	36%	WHEC	NBC
Rochester	36%	WROC	CBS
Rochester	36%	WUHF	FOX
Rochester	36%	WXXI	PBS

Cable systems and subscribers

Adelphia   62,962
Time Warner   75,635

Businesses and other major employers

Eastman Kodak Co.; Rochester; films: cameras, motion picture, x-ray   8,200
Xerox Corp.; Rochester; administrative management   5,000
Delphi Corp.; Rochester; motor vehicle parts/accessories   4,000
General Motors Corp.; Tonawanda; automobiles   4,000
General Motors Corp.; Buffalo; automotive engine forgings   4,000
Bausch and Lomb Inc.; Rochester; ophthalmic goods   3,500
Rochester General Hospital; Rochester   3,100
Excellus Health Plan Inc.; Rochester; group hospitalization   3,000
Erie County Medical Center; Buffalo   2,500
Xerox Corp.; Rochester; management services   2,500
National Fuel Gas Co.; Buffalo; gas transmission, distribution   2,200
American Axle and Manufacturing Inc.; Buffalo; automotive forgings   2,000
New York Dept. of Health; Buffalo   1,800
U.S. Veterans Hospital; Buffalo   1,800
Praxair Inc.; Tonawanda; cryogenic tanks   1,500
Radiologists of University of Rochester; Rochester   1,500
Niagara Frontier Transportation Authority; Buffalo; bus terminals   1,300
V&J National and United Enterprises; Rochester; restaurants   1,300
Highland Hospital of Rochester Inc.; Rochester   1,275
HealthNow New York Inc.; Buffalo; group hospitalization   1,150
New York Mental Health Office; Rochester   1,059
Gannett Co. Inc.; Rochester; newspaper   1,000
Gleason Corp.; Rochester; metal-cutting machine tools   1,000
Monroe Community Hospital; Rochester   1,000
Osmose Inc.; Buffalo; lacquers, other coatings   1,000
Pinkerton's Inc.; Rochester; detective, armored car services   1,000
Sisters of Charity Hospital; Buffalo   1,000
Nalge Nunc International Corp.; Rochester; plastics   903
Monroe County; Rochester; social/human resources   900
Paychex Inc.; Rochester; data processing   900
City of Niagara Falls; Niagara Falls; city government   870
Rochester Gas and Electric Corp.; Rochester; electric power generation   850
St. Ann's Home for Aged; Rochester   850
Kenmore Mercy Hospital; Kenmore   827
American Axle and Manufacturing Inc.; Tonawanda; iron and steel forgings   825
Hickey-Freeman Co. Inc.; Rochester; men's/boys' suits   750

Mt. Saint Mary's Hospital of Niagara Falls Inc.; Lewiston 722

E. I. Du Pont De Nemours and Co.; Niagara Falls; industrial inorganic chemicals 710

Niagara Falls Memorial Medical Center Inc.; Niagara Falls 700

City of Rochester; Rochester; police dept. 650

Regional Transit Service Inc.; Rochester; bus line operations 614

NexPress Solutions; Rochester; photographic toners 610

City of Rochester; Rochester; city management 600

City of Rodchester; Rochester; recreation center 600

E. I. Du Pont De Nemours and Co.; Rochester; photographic supplies 600

Monroe County; Rochester; county government 600

Plumbers Benefit Office Local; Rochester; union 600

Woodman of World Life Insurance Society; Tonawanda; life insurance 600

First Synder Corp.; Buffalo; commercial land development 550

Bell Justice Facilities Corp.; Rochester; commercial/ office building contractors 500

Frontier Telephone of Rochester Inc.; Rochester; local/long-distance telephone 500

Interstate Brands Corp.; Buffalo; bread baking 500

Nortel Networks Inc.; Rochester; telephone switching equipment 500

OneSource Facility Services Inc.; Tonawanda; janitorial service 500

New York 29th District

Southern Tier — Elmira, Corning; Rochester suburbs

The 29th blankets much of the southwestern portion of New York known as the Southern Tier, encompassing a mix of forests, lakes, and farms. Small towns and villages dot the countryside. It also reaches north to take in Rochester suburbs.

The district has a large presence of blue-collar workers and is home to diverse manufacturing interests including glassware, furniture, and diesel engines. Agriculture also helps drive the economy, mostly through dairy farms and wineries. The Finger Lakes and surrounding parks draw thousands of visitors annually. Like much of the upstate region, the district's population was stagnant in the 1990s, with four counties losing population and the other four registering single-digit growth.

The 29th curls north and west to take in southern parts of Monroe County outside Rochester, where a plurality of the district's residents live. It wraps around the west, south, and east sides of the city, taking in mostly GOP-leaning towns such as Chili, Pittsford, and Perinton.

With Chautauqua County (Jamestown) moved to the Buffalo-area 27th in 2002 redistricting, the 29th's westernmost point is Cattaraugus County, a rural area that includes Allegany State Park and St. Bonaventure University. To the east, the GOP holds a better than two-to-one registration advantage over Democrats in Allegany, Steuben, and Yates Counties. Steuben County contains Corning, one of America's better-known company towns because of its glass products and costly crystal pieces.

Republicans hold an edge over Democrats in voter registration, and George W. Bush received 53.4 percent of the area's vote in the 2000 presidential election—his best showing in the state. The 29th also has the lowest percentage of Hispanic residents in any New York district.

Major Industry

Agriculture, manufacturing, tourism.

Notable

The Corning Museum of Glass is a major tourist attraction.

Election Returns

	Republican		Democratic		Other	
President 2000	152,004	53.4%	121,596	42.7%	11,318	4.0%
House 2002	127,657	73.1%	37,128	21.3%	9,846	5.6%

District Profile

Population 654,361

Total area (square miles) 5,761.1
Land area (square miles) 5,660.1

Population per square mile 115.6

Counties (2000 population)

Allegany 49,927	Ontario (pt.) 83,318
Cattaraugus 83,955	Schuyler 19,224
Chemung 91,070	Steuben 98,726
Monroe (pt.) 203,520	Yates 24,621

Cities and other areas over 10,000 (2000 population)
Brighton CDP (pt.) 25,869
Canandaigua 11,264
Corning 10,842
Elmira 30,940
Gates-North Gates CDP 15,138
Olean 15,347

Race and Hispanic or Latino origin*
White 92.5%
Black or African American 2.7%
American Indian or Alaska Native 0.5%
Asian 1.8%
Native Hawaiian or other Pacific Islander 0.0%
Some other race 0.1%
Hispanic or Latino origin 1.4%
Two or more races 1.0%

*As percentage of total population.

Ancestry*

Dutch 2.7%	Italian 8.3%
English 11.1%	Polish 4.0%
French 2.5%	Scottish 1.7%
German 16.3%	USA/American 4.6%
Irish 12.1%	

*As estimated percentage of total population.

Universities and colleges, 2000–2001 enrollment

Alfred University, Alfred   1,607
Bryant and Stratton Business Institute, Rochester   288
Corning Community College, Corning   4,306
Elmira Business Institute, Elmira   202
Elmira College, Elmira   1,933
Finger Lakes Community College, Canandaigua   4,667
Houghton College, Houghton   1,409
Jamestown Community College-Cattaraugus County, Olean   3,421
Keuka College, Keuka Park   952
Monroe Community College, Rochester   15,315
Nazareth College of Rochester, Rochester   3,075
New York State College of Ceramics-Alfred University, Alfred   803
Roberts Wesleyan College, Rochester   1,596
Rochester Institute of Technology, Rochester   14,106
State University of New York College of Technology, Alfred   2,735
St. Bonaventure University, St. Bonaventure   2,800
St. John Fisher College, Rochester   2,739

Newspapers and circulation

	District circulation	Total circulation
Buffalo News	5,421	222,695
Canandaigua Daily Messenger	12,330	12,672
Corning Leader	13,276	13,750
Elmira Star Gazette	22,804	28,670
Geneva Finger Lakes Times	6,139	17,192
Jamestown Post-Journal	1,667	20,591
Olean Times Herald	13,890	16,751
Rochester Democrat and Chronicle	54,339	177,300
*USA Today**	4,923	1,674,376

See Sources and Explanations in the front of the volume.

Television stations and affiliations

Buffalo	41%	WGRZ	NBC
Buffalo	41%	WIVB	CBS
Buffalo	41%	WKBW	ABC
Buffalo	41%	WNED	PBS
Buffalo	41%	WNYB	Independent
Buffalo	41%	WNYO	WB
Buffalo	41%	WUTV	FOX
Elmira	37%	WENY	ABC
Elmira	37%	WETM	NBC
Elmira	37%	WYDC	FOX
Rochester	22%	WHEC	NBC
Rochester	22%	WROC	CBS
Rochester	22%	WUHF	FOX
Rochester	22%	WXXI	PBS

Cable systems and subscribers

Adelphia   27,628
Alfred Cable System   665
Bath TV & Service   3,944
Charter   3,144
Haefele TV Inc.   1,065
Time Warner   83,777

Businesses and other major employers

Corning Inc.; Corning; glass   6,300
Finger Lake Development Mental Disability Service Office; Rochester   5,000
Rochester Institute of Technology; Rochester   2,000
Monroe Community College Inc.; Rochester   1,640
Canandaigua Wine Co.; Canandaigua   1,515
Corning Inc.; Painted Post; glass   1,400
Arnot Ogden Medical Center; Elmira   1,400
Wegmans Food Markets Inc.; Rochester; supermarkets   1,375
U.S. Veterans Hospital; Canandaigua   1,200
Toshiba Display Devices Inc.; Horseheads; cathode ray tubes   1,150
New York Mental Retardation and Developmental Disabilities Office; Perrysburg   1,100
Frederick Ferris Thompson Hospital; Canandaigua   1,000
Allstate Insurance Co.; Fairport; insurance agents and brokers   1,000
U.S. Postal Service; Rochester   1,000
Washington Group International Inc.; Hornell; railroad car rebuilding   1,000
St. Joseph's Hospital; Elmira   1,000
St. James Mercy Hospital; Hornell   983
Dresser-Rand Co.; Painted Post; air and gas compressors   975
Hardinge Inc.; Elmira; metal-cutting machine tools   956
F. F. Thompson Health System Inc.; Canandaigua; hospital management   931
New York Correctional Services Dept.; Gowanda   900
Alcas Corp.; Olean; cutlery   870
Allstrom Transportation; Hornell; freight/passenger train cars, equipment   860
Gates Chili Central School District; Rochester   825
West Valley Nuclear Services Co.; West Valley; hazardous waste collection, disposal   750
Steuben County; Bath; county government   750
Mercury Aircraft Inc.; Hammondsport; sheet metalwork   750
Dresser-Rand Co.; Wellsville; turbines and turbine generators   745
Heidelberg Digital; Rochester; photocopiers   700
New York Dept. of Transportation; Hornell   700
Gunlocke Co.; Wayland; office furniture   650
Philips Electronics North America Corp.; Bath; residential lighting   650
Ontario County; Canandaigua; county government   642
Clifton Springs Sanitarium Co. Inc.; Clifton Springs   600
Citibank NA; Pittsford; state commercial banks   600
Time Warner Entertainment Co.; Pittsford; cable TV   600
Delphi Corp.; West Henrietta; automotive engines and parts   600
Jewish Home of Rochester Inc.; Rochester; nursing care facilities   600
Roberts Wesleyan College; Rochester   600
U.S. Veterans Hospital; Bath   600

Alstom Power Inc.; Wellsville; engineering services 600

Corning Hospital; Corning   570

Genesee Region Home Care Assn. Inc.; Rochester; home health care   550

Wegmans Food Markets Inc.; Canandaigua; supermarkets   531

Monroe Adult and Community Education Department; Fairport   500

Xerox Corp.; Victor; printers, computers   500

Element K Corp.; Rochester; computer integrated systems design   500

ENI Technology Inc.; Rochester; electronic loads and power supplies   500

Schlegel Systems Inc.; Rochester; sponge rubber pillows 500

State University of New York; Alfred   500

Schweizer Aircraft Corp.; Big Flats; airplanes   500

Thomas and Betts Corp.; Horseheads; cable TV equipment   500

NORTH CAROLINA

Districts established December 5, 2001, for elections first held in 2002.

13 members

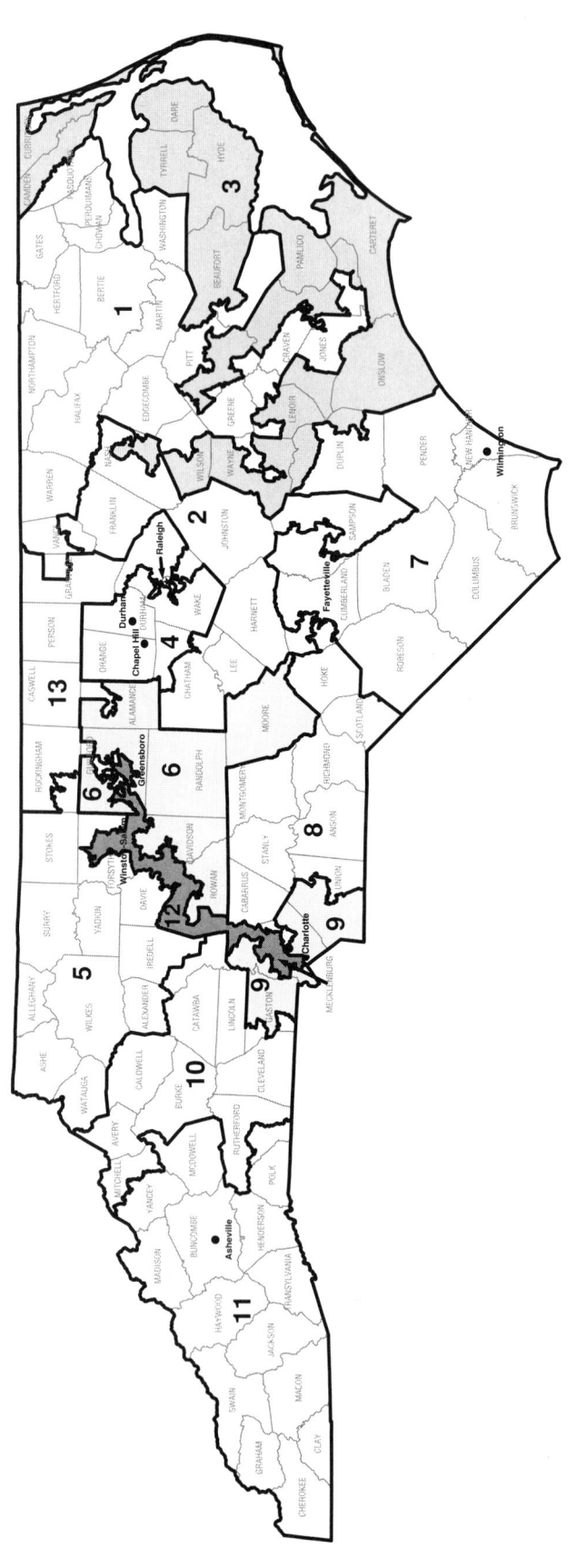

North Carolina

North Carolina has been associated with the rise of the New South since that phrase was first used (probably not long after the Civil War). That reflects North Carolina's long-standing image as a moderate state: temperate in climate, reluctant to secede, relatively balanced in its economic elements, and less bitter in its racial history. The state had a fabulous cash crop in tobacco and kept it within the state for processing, building one of the great profit centers of the twentieth century. It also developed the nation's leading textile and furniture-making industries, again making use of local resources but adding value and reaping wealth within the state.

In the civil rights era, North Carolina had its struggles but was rarely the focus of national attention. Sen. Sam Ervin, a onetime segregationist, became a favorite of the media after the Senate Watergate committee he chaired in 1973 helped drive Richard Nixon from the White House. At about the same time, a succession of progressive governors (Luther Hodges, Terry Sanford, James Hunt) got good press for preaching education and diversity (Sanford was named one of the best governors in U.S. history by a Harvard University study). Their administrations helped build up the Research Triangle—based on the relationship between the University of North Carolina in Chapel Hill, Duke University in Durham, and North Carolina State in Raleigh. Think tanks and high-tech industries sprang up in the piney woods between these campuses, helping replace the jobs and cash flow of tobacco (an industry under siege both socially and legally), textiles, and furniture (industries under pressure from imports). North Carolina emerged as a rival to Georgia as the leader of the new southern dynamic.

North Carolina's population grew another 21 percent in the 1990s, qualifying the state for a thirteenth seat in the House (for the first time since 1830) and bringing the state once again to the brink of the national top ten (just behind Georgia). What surprises some is that this relatively northern outpost in the Sun Belt had been among the nation's more populous states before. In the first Congress, the two Carolinas had as many seats as New York and New Jersey combined. In the 1830s, when North Carolina last had 13 seats, only New York, Pennsylvania, Ohio, and Virginia had more. In the Civil War, North Carolina provide more troops to the Confederate armies than any other state and sustained a quarter of the South's fatalities. Growth relative to the nation as a whole resumed after that conflagration. The size of the House delegation actually grew through the later decades of that century and the first half of the next. By 1930, North Carolina had surpassed its proud neighbor Virginia, and in the census of 1950 it crept into the top ten (only to fall out again a decade later).

One reason North Carolina's numbers raise eyebrows is that until recently, it had no big city. It had Charlotte and Raleigh, then Greensboro and Durham a notch smaller, Winston-Salem and Wilmington a notch smaller yet. But unlike the megastates of the North and Far West, the population here was distributed across the state, in hundreds of towns and hamlets and farming counties. When growth came back to the state in the 1980s and 1990, it did so almost across the board. Five of the state's cities of 100,000 or more grew by 30 percent or more.

The most impressive of these was Charlotte, which added 36 percent to its population and passed the half million mark in 2000. A mining boomtown in the early days of the Republic, Charlotte had long since settled into a quiet, largely white-collar service existence and was one of the state's first Republican enclaves. But in the past two decades it has boomed again, becoming a financial services center of the first order (it bills itself as the second most important banking town after New York) and the alternative to overgrown Atlanta for companies seeking locations on the southeastern seaboard. There are major league franchises here in football and basketball. The metro area, which takes in Gastonia (and Rock Hill on the South Carolina side of the state line), grew by more than a fifth in the same time and is approaching 1.5 million people. That is not enough to crack the top 30 metro areas list, but it is a start.

Just as important to the state overall, the next 12 metro areas in size include two more in North Carolina. Greensboro, taken together with Winston-Salem and High Point (the center of the furniture industry), has also passed 1.2 million and the Research Triangle cities have passed 1.1 million after growing 26 percent in the 1990s (nearly matching the growth rate of Atlanta). For the decade, North Carolina was the ninth fastest growing state, and the fourth fastest in the South behind Georgia, Florida, and Texas.

Today's North Carolina represents a kind of midpoint between the demographics of the South and those of the nation as a whole. The median age (35.3) matches the national median. The percentage of African Americans (22 percent) is nine points higher than the national average but close to the southern norm (six other states below the Mason-Dixon have higher percentages). The Hispanic population (380,000 or 4.7 percent) is twenty-fifth among the states, right in the middle of the pack. The discouraging deviations from this pattern are the unemployment rate—nearly 7 percent in 2002, fifth highest in the country—and the poverty rate (13 percent), one of the 15 worst in 2002.

Like most of the South, North Carolina voted Democratic for president for nearly a century after Reconstruction (except when the Democrats nominated a Catholic in 1928). But in the 1960s, the civil rights era and the alienation of southerners from the party took their toll and Nixon's "southern strategy" worked here in 1968 and 1972. Southerner Jimmy Carter carried the state in 1976, but in 1980 Ronald Reagan won it back. No Democrat has won here since (although Bill Clinton came close in 1992), and George W. Bush got to 56 percent here in 2000.

In other statewide voting, however, the state has been a mixed bag. The first Republican senator to win in the 1900s was former Democrat Jesse Helms, a newspaper editor and broadcast commentator whose homilies and broadsides were well known before he made his first bid for office in 1972. Helms soon established himself as an outspoken advocate of tradition in matters foreign and domestic and a key Reagan acolyte. When Reagan's political star was fading in the spring of 1976—he had yet to win a primary against incumbent Republican Gerald R. Ford—it was Helms and North Carolina who brought the win that kept his presidential ambitions alive. In 1980 Helms was joined by a second conservative Republican, John P. East. Former governor Sanford took that seat back for the Democrats in 1986 but lost it in 1992 to former Democrat Lauch Faircloth, who lost in turn to rising Democratic star John Edwards in 1998. Through all this, Helms held on, rising to chair the Foreign Relations Committee and retiring in 2002. He was succeeded by Republican Elizabeth Hanford Dole, a native of Salisbury, North Carolina, a two-time cabinet member, and the wife of the Republican senator and presidential nominee Bob Dole. The ease with which Dole won suggested the underlying currents of the state's vote continue to move toward the GOP.

The governorship and control of the legislature were Democratic for generations after Reconstruction but began experiencing Republican interludes in the Nixon era. One Republican won the governorship in 1972, serving one term. A second, James G. Martin, won two terms in the mansion during the 1980s. But the main figure in the statehouse in the last quarter century was James B. Hunt, who served eight years in the 1970s and 1980s and another eight in the 1990s, shepherding the state through two periods of substantial growth, and passing the office on to another Democrat in 2000.

A greater source of vexation for both parties has been the House, which has seen its district map redrawn multiple times over the course of the last dozen years. After the 1990 census, the Justice Department required the state to create not just one black-majority district but two, applying what the department saw as the mandate of the 1965 Voting Rights Act. Drawing one fairly natural black district was easy in the largely rural, tobacco counties of the state's northeast-central section—home to a substantial fraction of the state's African Americans. But to do a second black district in a state without a central city required a creativity bound to create controversy. The mappers had to separate black communities from larger white communities, then aggregate them via long stretches of Interstate 85. The new 12th District connected the Charlotte area to sections of Winston-Salem, Greensboro, and Durham, with the visual effect of a bug splattered across a windshield.

The sheer ungainliness of the district became a symbol of "racial gerrymandering" throughout the country and was the main reason the North Carolina map made four trips to the U.S. Supreme Court over the course of the decade. Changes were made along the way, with the Court basically ruling that race could be a factor in drawing district lines but should not be the predominant factor, especially not if it required such severe cartographic contortions. The most recent version of the 12th, drawn in 2001, still starts the snake southwest of Charlotte but now stops it in Greensboro.

Both the 1st and the 13th elected black representatives in 1992 and throughout the decade, helping to raise the number of African American members in the House to a record level. But this map had another side effect. By concentrating black voters in these two districts, the map made all adjoining districts whiter and so less Democratic. Soon after the map took effect, the state delegation flipped. Before the new map, there had been eight Democrats and three Republicans. After the 1994 election, there were eight Republicans and just three Democrats. It took another decade, and another remapping, for the Democrats to return to near parity.

After 2000, North Carolina found itself with yet another new district (won by a margin of less than a thousand people over Utah). The Democrats in control of the legislature promptly fashioned a new 13th that begins in populous Wake County (Raleigh) but has about half its population in four counties to the north and west, all touching the Virginia line. The new district was about one-fourth black, enough to fortify its 25-point Democratic bulge in party registration but not enough to make a black Democratic nominee inevitable. The first winner in the new district was Brad Miller, who had been chair of the state senate committee that drew the map.

Miller's win brought Democrats back to six seats in the House, but they had hoped for a seventh. By shifting the 8th and 9th District boundary in Charlotte, the Democrats put 100,000 more residents of that city in the 8th and made it more Democratic. But that party's favored challenger there lost his primary, and in November the incumbent Republican Robin Hayes, an heir to the Cannon textile fortune, won by nine points.

Creating the 13th prompted the shift of several counties of the old 5th to the west and southwest and into the Brushy Mountains west of Winston-Salem. Likewise the new 10th was obliged to move south and become centered on the South Mountains northwest of Charlotte. These elevated hills signal the arrival of the southern reaches of the Appalachians. Most of the truly mountainous country is in the Great Smoky and the Blue Ridge Mountains, which reach their highest elevations in the western 11th District (Asheville). The 11th has several peaks greater than 6,000 feet including Mount Mitchell, at 6,684 feet the highest point east of the Mississippi, and Clingman's Dome, at 6,643 the second highest, on the Tennessee line.

Table 1 Population

District	Population	Population under 18	Voting-age population	Median age	Male*	Female*
1	619,178	161,242	457,936	36.1	47.6	52.4
2	619,178	157,893	461,285	32.0	50.3	49.7
3	619,178	147,496	471,682	34.3	50.6	49.4
4	619,178	152,240	466,938	33.1	48.7	51.3
5	619,178	143,281	475,897	37.7	48.9	51.1
6	619,178	147,777	471,401	37.6	49.0	51.0

District	Population	Population under 18	Voting-age population	Median age	Male*	Female*
7	619,178	151,703	467,475	36.3	48.8	51.2
8	619,178	161,687	457,491	32.9	49.1	50.9
9	619,178	156,954	462,224	35.5	48.8	51.2
10	619,178	150,223	468,955	36.9	49.3	50.7
11	619,177	131,956	487,221	40.6	48.3	51.7
12	619,178	158,499	460,679	32.8	48.4	51.6
13	619,178	143,096	476,082	33.9	49.1	50.9
State	8,049,313	1,964,047	6,085,266	35.3	49.0	51.0

*As percentage of total population.

Table 2   Voting-Age Persons by Race/Hispanic or Latino Origin

District	White*	Black or African American*	American Indian or Alaska Native*	Asian*	Other or multirace*	Hispanic or Latino*
1	47.9	47.6	0.7	0.5	0.6	2.8
2	61.9	28.5	0.6	1.1	0.9	7.0
3	78.3	15.5	0.4	1.1	0.9	3.9
4	70.3	19.6	0.3	3.9	1.1	4.8
5	89.3	6.2	0.2	0.7	0.5	3.1
6	86.8	8.1	0.4	0.9	0.5	3.3
7	66.3	21.2	7.7	0.5	0.7	3.5
8	65.1	24.5	1.6	1.7	1.0	6.0
9	84.3	9.4	0.3	2.0	0.7	3.3
10	86.6	8.4	0.2	1.1	0.5	3.2
11	91.0	4.2	1.3	0.5	0.7	2.2
12	48.1	41.9	0.4	2.0	1.0	6.7
13	66.0	25.1	0.3	2.0	1.0	5.6
State	72.6	19.9	1.1	1.3	0.8	4.3

*As percentage of voting-age population.

Table 3   Voting-Age Population by Age Groups

District	18 to 24*	25 to 44*	45 to 64*	Over 64*
1	13.0	37.7	30.3	19.0
2	17.2	42.9	26.7	13.2
3	17.5	38.2	29.1	15.2
4	15.2	46.3	27.7	10.8
5	11.3	39.0	32.2	17.5
6	10.4	39.9	31.7	18.0
7	12.8	38.7	31.7	16.8
8	14.3	44.1	27.3	14.3
9	9.5	46.6	30.6	13.4
10	11.0	40.0	31.8	17.2
11	10.4	34.4	32.7	22.6
12	15.5	42.9	27.0	14.5
13	14.6	44.0	27.3	14.1
State	13.3	41.1	29.7	15.9

*As percentage of voting-age population.

Table 4   Income and Occupation

District	Median family income	Families in poverty*	White collar†	Blue collar†	Service†	Farm†
1	$34,523	17.1	45.5	34.8	18.0	1.8
2	$42,230	10.9	52.1	32.6	14.0	1.2
3	$44,273	8.8	55.9	27.3	14.9	1.9
4	$67,201	5.7	74.8	14.3	10.7	0.2
5	$47,339	6.5	54.1	33.2	11.9	0.8
6	$51,119	5.8	55.8	32.3	11.5	0.4

District	Median family income	Families in poverty*	White collar†	Blue collar†	Service†	Farm†
7	$40,612	12.7	50.5	32.4	15.7	1.5
8	$44,245	9.7	53.3	31.8	14.2	0.7
9	$64,759	4.3	69.5	20.4	10.0	0.1
10	$44,138	7.8	45.4	41.9	12.2	0.5
11	$41,579	8.4	51.9	31.5	15.8	0.8
12	$42,127	12.4	51.9	32.1	15.8	0.2
13	$49,168	8.1	60.5	25.7	13.4	0.4
State	$46,335	9.0	56.0	29.7	13.5	0.8

*As percentage of all families.   †As percentage of employed workers 16 years and over.

Table 5   Education: School Years Completed

District	Less than grade 9*	Grades 9–12 no diploma*	High school diploma no college*	Some college*	College bachelor's degree or higher*
1	11.5	19.3	33.0	24.2	12.0
2	8.7	15.0	31.1	29.3	15.9
3	6.3	12.3	30.4	30.9	20.1
4	4.2	7.3	16.3	24.1	48.0
5	9.3	14.3	30.5	25.7	20.1
6	7.1	13.8	29.4	27.0	22.7
7	8.4	16.0	30.5	27.3	17.8
8	8.0	14.5	29.7	29.6	18.2
9	4.4	9.3	21.4	29.0	35.9
10	10.0	18.2	31.9	25.9	14.1
11	8.1	13.4	30.4	27.7	20.5
12	8.5	16.9	29.2	26.3	19.2
13	7.3	12.3	25.9	27.2	27.3
State	7.8	14.0	28.4	27.2	22.5

*As percentage of persons age 25 and over.

Table 6   Housing and Residential Patterns

District	Median home value	Owner occupied*	Renter occupied*	Urban†	Rural†
1	$65,300	63.4	36.6	47.7	52.3
2	$87,200	66.5	33.5	49.5	50.5
3	$87,600	70.9	29.1	53.2	46.8
4	$161,200	64.1	35.9	83.2	16.8
5	$97,400	76.8	23.2	42.9	57.1
6	$104,400	76.7	23.3	51.6	48.4
7	$83,100	73.1	26.9	45.1	54.9
8	$86,700	66.2	33.8	69.4	30.6
9	$141,500	72.9	27.1	84.2	15.8
10	$85,700	75.2	24.8	49.9	50.1
11	$93,600	75.4	24.6	43.9	56.1
12	$90,400	56.8	43.2	88.5	11.5
13	$107,800	62.4	37.6	73.7	26.3
State	$95,800	69.4	30.6	60.2	39.8

*As percentage of occupied housing units.   †As percentage of total population.

North Carolina 1st District

Northeast — part of Goldsboro, Rocky Mount, and Greenville

Situated among the tobacco fields and Baptist churches of eastern North Carolina, the 1st is a poor, rural Democratic stronghold. It has the lowest education and income levels of any North Carolina congressional district.

The main body of the district rests along the Virginia border, with appendages winding south to take in parts of several of the region's commercial centers—Goldsboro, Greenville, and Kinston. Redistricting following the 2000 census kept the 1st's basic shape intact, and it remains the most heavily black district in North Carolina (50.5 percent).

The area's economy is based overwhelmingly on manufacturing and agriculture. Cotton and peanut fields prevail in the northern counties, while tobacco, hogs, and poultry dominate farther south. Manufacturing, primarily of textiles and lumber products, is scattered throughout.

Registered Democrats outnumber Republicans by more than four-to-one in the 1st, which backed Democrat Michael F. Easley with 70 percent in the 2000 governor's race. Many white voters claim the Democratic roots of their forefathers but often support GOP candidates at the state and national level. Republicans also find support in the increasingly affluent coastal areas of Beaufort and Craven Counties.

Major Industry
Agriculture, manufacturing, health care.

Notable
Caleb Bradham started selling "Brad's Drink" in 1898 at his New Bern drug store—the beverage is now known as Pepsi Cola.

Election Returns

	Republican		Democratic		Other	
President 2000	82,204	42.2%	111,558	57.3%	928	0.5%
House 2002	50,907	34.8%	93,157	63.7%	2,093	1.4%

District Profile

Population 619,178

Total area (square miles) 7,664.2
  Land area (square miles) 7,198.8

Population per square mile 86.0

Counties (2000 population)

Beaufort (pt.) 16,287	Martin 25,593
Bertie 19,773	Nash (pt.) 14,765
Chowan 14,526	Northampton 22,086
Craven (pt.) 39,000	Pasquotank 34,897
Edgecombe 55,606	Perquimans 11,368
Gates 10,516	Pitt (pt.) 54,674
Granville (pt.) 11,992	Vance (pt.) 28,240
Greene 18,974	Warren 19,972
Halifax 57,370	Washington 13,723
Hertford 22,601	Wayne (pt.) 52,962
Jones (pt.) 6,756	Wilson (pt.) 36,795
Lenoir (pt.) 30,702	

Cities and other areas over 10,000 (2000 population)
  Elizabeth City (pt.) 17,188
  Goldsboro (pt.) 36,187
  Greenville (pt.) 22,028
  Havelock (pt.) 13,839
  Henderson (pt.) 16,047
  Kinston (pt.) 16,502

New Bern (pt.) 15,186
Roanoke Rapids 16,957
Rocky Mount (pt.) 32,062
Tarboro town 11,138
Wilson (pt.) 25,068

Race and Hispanic or Latino origin*
White 44.4%
Black or African American 50.5%
American Indian or Alaska Native 0.7%
Asian 0.5%
Native Hawaiian or other Pacific Islander 0.0%
Some other race 0.1%
Hispanic or Latino origin 3.1%
Two or more races 0.8%

*As percentage of total population.

Ancestry*

English 6.1%		Scotch-Irish 1.1%	
German 3.3%		USA/American 10.7%	
Irish 3.6%			

*As estimated percentage of total population.

Universities and colleges, 2000–2001 enrollment
  Barton College, Wilson 1,202
  Chowan College, Murfreesboro 739
  College of the Albemarle, Elizabeth City 2,311
  Edgecombe Community College, Tarboro 1,877
  Elizabeth City State University, Elizabeth City 2,035
  Halifax Community College, Weldon 1,308
  Lenoir Community College, Kinston 2,057
  Martin Community College, Williamston 666
  North Carolina Wesleyan College, Rocky Mount 1,996
  Pitt Community College, Greenville 4,973
  Roanoke-Chowan Community College, Ahoskie 1,014
  Vance-Granville Community College, Henderson 3,480
  Wayne Community College, Goldsboro 2,958
  Wilson Technical Community College, Wilson 1,596

Newspapers and circulation

	District circulation	Total circulation
Durham Herald-Sun	1,389	51,061
Elizabeth City Daily Advance	9,004	11,217
Goldsboro-News Argus	5,063	21,216
Greenville Daily Reflector	7,606	20,586
Henderson Daily Dispatch	5,073	8,347
Kinston Free Press	6,691	12,226
Norfolk Virginian-Pilot	7,681	192,929
Raleigh News & Observer	9,221	164,952
Roanoke Rapids Daily Herald	12,195	12,212
Rocky Mount Telegram	5,496	14,430
*USA Today**	2,018	1,674,376
Washington Daily News	2,649	9,479
Wilson Daily Times	4,657	16,229

*See Sources and Explanations in the front of the volume.

Television stations and affiliations

Greenville-New Bern-Washington	44%	WCTI	ABC
Greenville-New Bern-Washington	44%	WEPX	PAX
Greenville-New Bern-Washington	44%	WFXI	FOX
Greenville-New Bern-Washington	44%	WITN	NBC
Greenville-New Bern-Washington	44%	WNCT	CBS

Greenville-New Bern-Washington	44%	WUND	PBS
Greenville-New Bern-Washington	44%	WUNK	PBS
Greenville-New Bern-Washington	44%	WUNM	PBS
Greenville-New Bern-Washington	44%	WYDO	FOX
Norfolk-Portsmouth-Newport News	28%	WAVY	NBC
Norfolk-Portsmouth-Newport News	28%	WGNT	UPN
Norfolk-Portsmouth-Newport News	28%	WHRO	PBS
Norfolk-Portsmouth-Newport News	28%	WPXV	PAX
Norfolk-Portsmouth-Newport News	28%	WTKR	CBS
Norfolk-Portsmouth-Newport News	28%	WTVZ	WB
Norfolk-Portsmouth-Newport News	28%	WVBT	FOX
Norfolk-Portsmouth-Newport News	28%	WVEC	ABC
Raleigh-Durham (Fayetteville)	28%	WGPX	PAX
Raleigh-Durham (Fayetteville)	28%	WKFT	Independent
Raleigh-Durham (Fayetteville)	28%	WLFL	WB
Raleigh-Durham (Fayetteville)	28%	WNCN	NBC
Raleigh-Durham (Fayetteville)	28%	WRAL	CBS
Raleigh-Durham (Fayetteville)	28%	WRAY	Independent
Raleigh-Durham (Fayetteville)	28%	WRAZ	FOX
Raleigh-Durham (Fayetteville)	28%	WRDC	UPN
Raleigh-Durham (Fayetteville)	28%	WRPX	PAX
Raleigh-Durham (Fayetteville)	28%	WTVD	ABC
Raleigh-Durham (Fayetteville)	28%	WUNC	PBS
Raleigh-Durham (Fayetteville)	28%	WUNP	PBS

Cable systems and subscribers
Adelphia   22,359
Charter   26,489
Cox   48,658
Mediacom   16,393
Time Warner   74,097

Military installations, September 2001
Marine Corps Air Station (Multi-Sites), Cherry Point 14,109
Seymour Johnson Air Force Base, Goldsboro   5,587

Businesses and other major employers
Warehouser; Plymouth; grocery store   3,000
U.S. Coast Guard; Elizabeth City   2,500
Standard Commercial Tobacco Co.; Wilson   1,700
Carolina Telephone and Telegraph Co.; Tarboro; local telephone communications   1,500
E. I. Du Pont De Nemours and Co.; Kinston; outerwear 1,500
Moore North America Inc.; Goldsboro; business forms 1,500
DSM Pharmaceuticals Inc.; Greenville; commercial physical research   1,250
Weyerhaeuser Co.; Plymouth; paperboard mills   1,200
Wayne Memorial Hospital Inc.; Goldsboro   1,184
Sara Lee Corp.; Tarboro; frozen bakery products   1,100
VF Jeanswear; Wilson; knit outerwear mills   1,000
Albemarle Hospital Inc.; Elizabeth City   976
Maxwell Foods Inc.; Goldsboro; hogs   975
Pitt County; Greenville; county government   956
Lenoir Memorial Hospital Inc.; Kinston   814
Glenoit Corp.; Tarboro; fabric mills   800
Collins and Aikman Products Co.; Farmville; automotive fabrics   768
Case Foods Inc.; Dudley; broiling chickens   750
Rose's Stores Inc.; Henderson; department stores   707
Halifax Regional Medical Center Inc.; Roanoke Rapids 706
Perdue Farms Inc.; Robersonville; processed poultry 700
Americal Corp.; Henderson; hosiery   650

Virginia Electric and Power Co.; Roanoke Rapids; electric power generation   650
Maria Parham Hospital Assn. Inc.; Henderson   602
Centura Bank; Rocky Mount; state commercial banks 600
City of Greenville; Greenville; city government   600
International Paper Co.; Roanoke Rapids; pulp mills 600
John Smith Inc.; Wilson; meatpacking plants   520
Smithfield Packing Co.; Kinston; meatpacking plants 515
Wilson County; Wilson; county government   505
ASMO Greenville of North Carolina Inc.; Greenville; fluid power motors   500
Cooper-Standard Automotive Inc.; Goldsboro; automotive rubber goods   500
CSX Transportation Inc.; Rocky Mount; railroad freight hauling   500
Ex-Cell Home Fashions Inc.; Goldsboro; bed pillows 500
Georgia-Pacific Corp.; Dudley; particleboard   500
Honeywell International Inc.; Rocky Mount; search and navigation equipment   500
Meadowbrook Meat Co.; Rocky Mount   500
Paper-Pak Products Inc.; Greenville; sanitary paper products   500
Royal Home Fashions Inc.; Henderson; bedding, table cloths   500
WestPoint Stevens Inc.; Roanoke Rapids; dishcloths/washcloths   500

North Carolina 2nd District
Central — parts of Raleigh and Fayetteville

From the thriving state capital of Raleigh, the 2nd pinwheels east, north, and south to take in several surrounding rural counties and part of Fayetteville. While the high-tech Research Triangle Park, the area's economic hub, lies in the neighboring 4th, its influence radiates through the low hills of this eastern Piedmont district. *(See map p. 679.)*

Research Triangle techies, university academics, and government employees live in Raleigh and form the basis of the district's Democratic tilt. Much of the region consists of booming and increasingly urban bedroom communities such as Garner. Sprawl has begun to infiltrate surrounding counties as well, but they still rely primarily on tobacco farming (especially in Johnston and Harnett Counties) and blue-collar manufacturing jobs. Redistricting after the 2000 census added a strong military presence, as the 2nd now contains Pope Air Force Base and part of Fort Bragg, located at the southwestern edge of the district.

Redistricting also lessened the 2nd's conservative lean by excising parts of Wake and Nash Counties and adding a black-majority section of Fayetteville. The 2nd contains the mostly black and strongly Democratic southeastern section of Raleigh, and it has a higher percentage of Hispanic residents (7.9 percent) than any other district in the state. While the Democrats' 30-point registration advantage exaggerates the party's edge—Republicans run well in areas such as Johnston County even though Democrats have more registrants—the GOP has a tough time here.

Major Industry

State government, higher education, agriculture.

Notable

A highway sign outside Sanford claims that it is the brick capital of the United States; the Harnett County town of Erwin grew up around a denim plant, formerly called itself the denim capital of the world, and still holds a fall festival called "Denim Days."

Election Returns

	Republican		Democratic		Other	
President 2000	98,607	53.1%	85,552	46.1%	1,378	0.7%
House 2002	50,965	33.3%	100,121	65.4%	2,098	1.4%

District Profile

Population   619,178

Total area (square miles)   3,979.1
   Land area (square miles)   3,955.9

Population per square mile   156.5

Counties (2000 population)

Chatham (pt.) 33,037	Lee 49,040
Cumberland (pt.) 108,056	Nash (pt.) 45,749
Franklin 47,260	Sampson (pt.) 32,896
Harnett 91,025	Vance (pt.) 14,714
Johnston 121,965	Wake (pt.) 75,436

Cities and other areas over 10,000 (2000 population)

Fayetteville (pt.)   49,899
Fort Bragg CDP   29,183
Garner town (pt.)   17,731
Raleigh (pt.)   45,368
Rocky Mount (pt.)   11,541
Sanford   23,220
Smithfield town   11,510

Race and Hispanic or Latino origin*

White   59.1%
Black or African American   30.1%
American Indian or Alaska Native   0.6%
Asian   0.9%
Native Hawaiian or other Pacific Islander   0.1%
Some other race   0.1%
Hispanic or Latino origin   7.9%
Two or more races   1.2%

*As percentage of total population.

Ancestry*

English 6.7%	Italian 1.6%
French 1.2%	Scotch-Irish 2.0%
German 5.7%	Scottish 1.6%
Irish 5.3%	USA/American 12.3%

*As estimated percentage of total population.

Universities and colleges, 2000–2001 enrollment

Campbell University, Buies Creek   5,880
Central Carolina Community College, Sanford   4,113
Fayetteville State University, Fayetteville   4,487
Johnston Community College, Smithfield   3,061
Louisburg College, Louisburg   544
North Carolina State University, Raleigh   28,619
Sampson Community College, Clinton   1,275

Newspapers and circulation

	District circulation	Total circulation
Dunn Daily Record	6,544	9,760
Fayetteville Observer	12,782	64,750
Greensboro News & Record	1,474	88,143
Henderson Daily Dispatch	2,598	8,347
Raleigh News & Observer	31,566	164,952
Rocky Mount Telegram	3,707	14,430
Sampson Independent	5,514	8,379
Sanford Herald	7,082	10,723
Smithfield Herald	13,486	14,350
*USA Today**	2,519	1,674,376
Wilson Daily Times	2,031	16,229

*See Sources and Explanations in the front of the volume.

Television stations and affiliations

Raleigh-Durham (Fayetteville)	100%	WGPX	PAX
Raleigh-Durham (Fayetteville)	100%	WKFT	Independent
Raleigh-Durham (Fayetteville)	100%	WLFL	WB
Raleigh-Durham (Fayetteville)	100%	WNCN	NBC
Raleigh-Durham (Fayetteville)	100%	WRAL	CBS
Raleigh-Durham (Fayetteville)	100%	WRAY	Independent
Raleigh-Durham (Fayetteville)	100%	WRAZ	FOX
Raleigh-Durham (Fayetteville)	100%	WRDC	UPN
Raleigh-Durham (Fayetteville)	100%	WRPX	PAX
Raleigh-Durham (Fayetteville)	100%	WTVD	ABC
Raleigh-Durham (Fayetteville)	100%	WUNC	PBS
Raleigh-Durham (Fayetteville)	100%	WUNP	PBS

Cable systems and subscribers

Adelphia   2,643
Charter   17,991
Cox   1,478
Starvision   2,103
Time Warner   37,469

Military installations, September 2001

Fort Bragg (Army), Fayetteville   50,519
Pope Air Force Base, Spring Lake   5,323

Businesses and other major employers

North Carolina State University; Raleigh   10,500
Carolina Power and Light Co.; Raleigh; electric power generation   2,000
Progress Energy Inc.; Raleigh; electric services   2,000
Wildwynn Stables; Youngsville; amusement and recreation   1,998
Consolidated Diesel Co.; Whitakers; diesel, dual-fuel engines   1,800
CDC Product Engineering; Whitakers; wire products   1,400
North Carolina State Highway Patrol; Raleigh   1,400
Swift Textiles Inc.; Erwin; fabric mills   1,300
Bayer Corp.; Clayton; pharmaceuticals   1,200
Wake County; Raleigh; county government   1,200
Lundy Packing Co.; Clinton; meatpacking plants   1,080
North Carolina Executive Office; Raleigh   1,048
Army and Air Force Exchange Service; Fort Bragg; Army-Navy goods stores   1,000

Static Control Components Inc.; Sanford; static
elimination equipment   980

North Carolina Division of Prisons; Raleigh   900

Morganite Inc.; Dunn; carbon and graphite products
850

Channel Master; Smithfield; antennas   845

City of Rocky Mount; Rocky Mount; city government
810

Campbell University Inc.; Buies Creek   800

Gold Kist Inc.; Siler City; poultry processing   800

National Welders Supply Co.; Garner; welding supplies
800

Coty U.S. Inc.; Sanford; perfumes   750

U.S. Veterans Hospital; Fayetteville   750

Prestage Farms Inc.; Clinton; hogs   750

Goodmark Foods Inc.; Garner; prepared meats   721

AMISUB of North Carolina Inc. Hospital; Sanford   700

Caterpillar Inc.; Clayton; farm machinery and equipment
700

City of Raleigh; Raleigh; police dept.   700

Townsends Inc.; Siler City; poultry processing   700

First Union Mortgage Corp.; Raleigh; mortgage bankers
700

Magneti Marelli Powertrain U.S.A. Inc.; Sanford;
automotive fuel systems and parts   675

McLane Co.; Battleboro; food supplier   635

GKN Automotive Inc.; Sanford; automotive electrical
equipment   615

Johnston Memorial Hospital; Smithfield   613

Mastercraft Fabrics; Siler City; upholstery fabrics   610

Gold Kist Inc.; Sanford; processed poultry   600

Moen Inc.; Sanford; plumbing fixtures   600

Chicopee Inc.; Benson; personal service agents   565

Food Lion; Dunn; warehousing   550

Pentair Pool Products Inc.; Sanford; pool filter/water
conditioning systems   550

Winn-Dixie Stores Inc.; Clayton; warehousing   550

Phantom USA Inc.; Siler City; hosiery   525

Fayetteville State University; Fayetteville   500

Flanders/Precisionaire Corp.; Smithfield; filters   500

J. A. Jones Inc.; Moncure; nonresidential construction
500

Taylor Co.; Henderson; tobacco redrying   500

North Carolina 3rd District

East — Jacksonville, part of Greenville, Outer Banks

The 3rd runs along the eastern shore from the Virginia
border to north of Wilmington, sweeping from the fragile
barrier islands of the Outer Banks to the tobacco and peanut
fields of the coastal plain. It is a large swath of rural land
inlaid with waterways, affluent vacation towns, and military
facilities; the closest thing to skyscrapers here are historic
lighthouses that dot the shoreline.

Many residents earn their living through fishing, farming, and tourism. The district's military bases have a large
impact on the economy, notably Camp Lejeune, which de-
ployed a high percentage of its Marines abroad in 2003. At
the southern end, two fingers of land stretch west, taking in
turkey, hog, and wheat farms.

Redistricting following the 2000 census did not significantly overhaul the district's jagged shape. One leg of the
3rd stretches from Onslow County in the south, where Jacksonville and Camp Lejeune are located, all the way north to
Nash County, including part of Rocky Mount.

The remap enhanced the 3rd's conservative lean by ced-
ing to the 1st some northeastern counties with large black
populations. In the 2002 Senate race, Republican Elizabeth
Dole topped 60 percent of the vote in Onslow, Wayne, and
Cartaret Counties, three of the four most-populous jurisdictions in the 3rd.

Major Industry
Military, agriculture, tourism.

Notable
Kitty Hawk is where Wilbur and Orville Wright made
their first flight; Dare County is named for Virginia Dare,
the first child born of English parents in America (1587).

Election Returns

	Republican		Democratic		Other	
President 2000	134,471	64.3%	73,035	34.9%	1,589	0.8%
House 2002	131,448	90.7%			13,486	9.3%

District Profile

Population   619,178

Total area (square miles)   10,047.9
  Land area (square miles)   6,192.0

Population per square mile   100.0

Counties (2000 population)

Beaufort (pt.)	28,671	Lenoir (pt.)	28,946
Camden	6,885	Nash (pt.)	26,906
Carteret	59,383	Onslow	150,355
Craven (pt.)	52,436	Pamlico	12,934
Currituck	18,190	Pitt (pt.)	79,124
Dare	29,967	Tyrrell	4,149
Duplin (pt.)	14,395	Wayne (pt.)	60,367
Hyde	5,826	Wilson (pt.)	37,019
Jones (pt.)	3,625		

Cities and other areas over 10,000 (2000 population)
  Greenville (pt.)   38,448
  Jacksonville   66,715
  Piney Green CDP   11,658
  Rocky Mount (pt.)   12,290
  Wilson (pt.)   19,337

Race and Hispanic or Latino origin*
  White   76.3%
  Black or African American   16.6%
  American Indian or Alaska Native   0.4%
  Asian   0.9%
  Native Hawaiian or other Pacific Islander   0.1%
  Some other race   0.1%
  Hispanic or Latino origin   4.4%
  Two or more races   1.2%

As percentage of total population.

Ancestry*

English	9.9%	Polish	1.2%
French	1.7%	Scotch-Irish	1.9%
German	7.6%	Scottish	1.8%
Irish	7.4%	USA/American	12.9%
Italian	2.5%		

*As estimated percentage of total population.

Universities and colleges, 2000–2001 enrollment

Beaufort County Community College, Washington 1,366

Carteret Community College, Morehead City 1,470

Coastal Carolina Community College, Jacksonville 3,780

Craven Community College, New Bern 2,513

East Carolina University, Greenville 18,750

Mount Olive College, Mount Olive 1,713

Nash Community College, Rocky Mount 2,150

Pamlico Community College, Grantsboro 299

Newspapers and circulation

	District circulation	Total circulation
Carteret County News Times	9,670	9,934
Elizabeth City Daily Advance	2,049	11,217
Goldsboro-News Argus	15,175	21,216
Greenville Daily Reflector	12,996	20,586
Jacksonville Daily News	20,277	21,266
Kinston Free Press	5,371	12,226
Norfolk Virginian-Pilot	7,410	192,929
Raleigh News & Observer	12,234	164,952
Rocky Mount Telegram	5,129	14,430
*USA Today**	4,540	1,674,376
Washington Daily News	6,902	9,479
Wilmington Star-News	1,027	53,945
Wilson Daily Times	9,539	16,229

*See Sources and Explanations in the front of the volume.

Television stations and affiliations

Greenville-New Bern-Washington	68%	WCTI	ABC
Greenville-New Bern-Washington	68%	WEPX	PAX
Greenville-New Bern-Washington	68%	WFXI	FOX
Greenville-New Bern-Washington	68%	WITN	NBC
Greenville-New Bern-Washington	68%	WNCT	CBS
Greenville-New Bern-Washington	68%	WUND	PBS
Greenville-New Bern-Washington	68%	WUNK	PBS
Greenville-New Bern-Washington	68%	WUNM	PBS
Greenville-New Bern-Washington	68%	WYDO	FOX
Norfolk-Portsmouth-Newport News	24%	WAVY	NBC
Norfolk-Portsmouth-Newport News	24%	WGNT	UPN
Norfolk-Portsmouth-Newport News	24%	WHRO	PBS
Norfolk-Portsmouth-Newport News	24%	WPXV	PAX
Norfolk-Portsmouth-Newport News	24%	WTKR	CBS
Norfolk-Portsmouth-Newport News	24%	WTVZ	WB
Norfolk-Portsmouth-Newport News	24%	WVBT	FOX
Norfolk-Portsmouth-Newport News	24%	WVEC	ABC
Raleigh-Durham (Fayetteville)	8%	WGPX	PAX
Raleigh-Durham (Fayetteville)	8%	WKFT	Independent
Raleigh-Durham (Fayetteville)	8%	WLFL	WB
Raleigh-Durham (Fayetteville)	8%	WNCN	NBC
Raleigh-Durham (Fayetteville)	8%	WRAL	CBS
Raleigh-Durham (Fayetteville)	8%	WRAY	Independent
Raleigh-Durham (Fayetteville)	8%	WRAZ	FOX
Raleigh-Durham (Fayetteville)	8%	WRDC	UPN
Raleigh-Durham (Fayetteville)	8%	WRPX	PAX
Raleigh-Durham (Fayetteville)	8%	WTVD	ABC
Raleigh-Durham (Fayetteville)	8%	WUNC	PBS
Raleigh-Durham (Fayetteville)	8%	WUNP	PBS

Cable systems and subscribers

Adelphia 1,483

Belhaven Cable TV 935

Charter 39,507

Cox 17,971

Mediacom 5,538

Time Warner 56,552

Military installations, September 2001

Camp Lejeune Marine Corps Base, Camp Lejeune 38,334

Camp Lejeune Naval Hospital, Camp Lejeune 2,902

Businesses and other major employers

Pitt County Memorial Hospital Inc.; Greenville 3,520

East Carolina University; Greenville 3,094

East Carolina University; Greenville; medical and dental assistant school 2,000

North Carolina Dept. of Health and Human Services; Kinston 1,800

Craven Regional Medical Center; New Bern 1,310

Nash Hospitals Inc.; Rocky Mount 1,300

Coastal Carolina Community College; Jacksonville 1,100

Hatteras Yachts Inc.; New Bern; sailboat building and repairing 1,100

Convergys Corp.; Jacksonville; direct-mail advertising 1,000

Onslow County Hospital Authority; Jacksonville 1,000

Pitt Community College; Winterville 1,000

Wilson Medical Center Inc.; Wilson 890

E-Commerce Support Centers Inc.; Jacksonville; computer consulting services 780

Lenoir Community College; Kinston 771

Ellison Co. Inc.; Welcome; storm doors, windows 710

Onslow County Hospital Authority; Jacksonville 700

Carteret General Hospital; Morehead City 635

Cooper-Standard Automotive Inc.; Rocky Mount; automotive rubber goods 615

Weyerhaeuser Co.; Vanceboro; paper mills 610

Interim HealthCare-Morris Group Inc.; Wilson; home health care 600

Electrolux Home Products Inc.; Kinston; dishwashers 600

First Carolina Management Inc.; Rocky Mount; hotel management 550

Beaufort County Hospital Assn. Inc.; Washington 500

Mount Olive Pickle Co. Inc.; Mount Olive; pickles, vinegar 500

Ashland Inc.; Kinston; highway/street paving contractor 500

Gibraltar Publishing Inc.; Jacksonville; statistical reports 500

North Carolina 4th District

Central — Durham, Chapel Hill, part of Raleigh

With more than three-fourths of the district's population living in Durham and Wake Counties, to understand Research Triangle Park is to understand the 4th. *(See map p. 679.)*

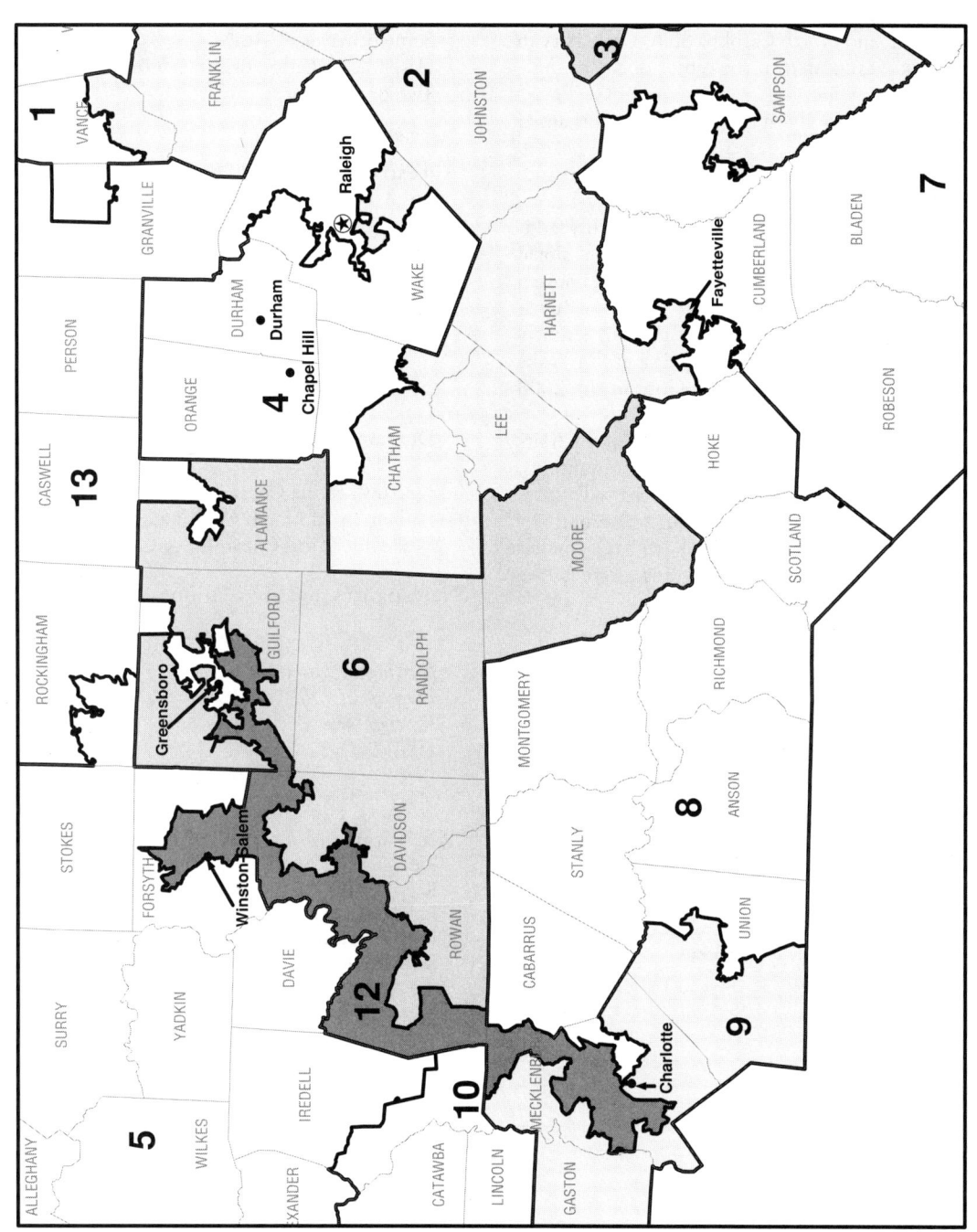

The medical and technological research park was created in the 1950s by a group of academics, politicians, and businesspeople who saw the need to diversify the state's economy beyond the traditional tobacco and textile industries. To tap the brainpower of the three surrounding universities—Duke University in Durham, the University of North Carolina in Chapel Hill, and North Carolina State University in Raleigh—the park was located in the center of the triangle the schools create.

As the park grew, especially in the 1980s, the Durham of James B. Duke's Lucky Strike cigarettes largely disappeared. And as developers began converting tobacco warehouses into apartment buildings, concerns arose over quality-of-life issues. While the district leans to the left, its highly educated voters—one in five holds a postgraduate or professional degree—can be independent-minded. Democrats are boosted by the large black population in the city of Durham. Redistricting following the 2000 census made the 4th slightly more Democratic by cutting out some GOP areas in Wake County. Residents of the 4th favored Al Gore in the 2000 presidential election with 53.1 percent of the vote.

The new map also slimmed the shape of the 4th, which sits halfway between the ocean and the Blue Ridge Mountains. While based primarily in the Triangle, the district still passes through rolling hills of evergreen forests. But some rural territory was excised in redistricting, and the 4th has a smaller rural element than all but two North Carolina districts (the 9th and the 12th).

Major Industry

Technology research, higher education.

Notable

Home to the Durham Bulls baseball team; the 1988 movie, *Bull Durham*, starring Kevin Costner, was filmed here; the nation's first state university, the University of North Carolina at Chapel Hill, was chartered in 1789 and opened to students in 1795.

Election Returns

	Republican		Democratic		Other	
President 2000	112,885	45.6%	131,532	53.1%	3,180	1.3%
House 2002	78,095	36.1%	132,185	61.2%	5,766	2.7%

District Profile

Population 619,178

Total area (square miles) 1,298.0
  Land area (square miles) 1,253.2

Population per square mile 494.1

Counties (2000 population)

Chatham (pt.) 16,292	Orange 118,227
Durham 223,314	Wake (pt.) 261,345

Cities and other areas over 10,000 (2000 population)

Apex town 20,212
Carrboro town 16,782
Cary town (pt.) 83,478
Chapel Hill town 48,715
Durham 187,035
Raleigh (pt.) 38,149

Race and Hispanic or Latino origin*

White 68.8%
Black or African American 20.6%
American Indian or Alaska Native 0.3%
Asian 3.9%
Native Hawaiian or other Pacific Islander 0.0%
Some other race 0.2%
Hispanic or Latino origin 5.0%
Two or more races 1.3%

*As percentage of total population.

Ancestry*

English 10.2%	Polish 1.8%
French 1.8%	Scotch-Irish 2.6%
German 9.8%	Scottish 2.4%
Irish 7.8%	USA/American 6.4%
Italian 3.4%	

*As estimated percentage of total population.

Universities and colleges, 2000–2001 enrollment

Duke University, Durham 12,192
Durham Technical Community College, Durham 4,915
North Carolina Central University, Durham 5,476
University of North Carolina, Chapel Hill 24,892
Wake Technical Community College, Raleigh 9,654

Newspapers and circulation

	District circulation	Total circulation
Burlington Times-News	1,565	27,412
Durham Herald-Sun	42,652	51,061
Raleigh News & Observer	65,052	164,952
*USA Today**	7,945	1,674,376

*See Sources and Explanations in the front of the volume.

Television stations and affiliations

Raleigh-Durham (Fayetteville)	100%	WGPX	PAX
Raleigh-Durham (Fayetteville)	100%	WKFT	Independent
Raleigh-Durham (Fayetteville)	100%	WLFL	WB
Raleigh-Durham (Fayetteville)	100%	WNCN	NBC
Raleigh-Durham (Fayetteville)	100%	WRAL	CBS
Raleigh-Durham (Fayetteville)	100%	WRAY	Independent
Raleigh-Durham (Fayetteville)	100%	WRAZ	FOX
Raleigh-Durham (Fayetteville)	100%	WRDC	UPN
Raleigh-Durham (Fayetteville)	100%	WRPX	PAX
Raleigh-Durham (Fayetteville)	100%	WTVD	ABC
Raleigh-Durham (Fayetteville)	100%	WUNC	PBS
Raleigh-Durham (Fayetteville)	100%	WUNP	PBS

Cable systems and subscribers

Time Warner 90,495

Businesses and other major employers

Duke University; Durham 20,000
Duke University Medical Center; Durham 18,000
GlaxoSmithKline; Durham; pharmaceuticals 7,500
University of North Carolina; Chapel Hill 6,500
University of North Carolina Hospitals; Chapel Hill 4,200
International Business Machines Corp.; Research Triangle Park; computer equipment and electronics 4,000
SAS Institute Inc.; Cary; software 2,915

Nortel Networks Inc.; Apex; cellular telephones 2,100

MCI WorldCom Network Services Inc.; Cary; telephone communication 2,000

Laboratory Corp. of America; Durham; testing laboratories 1,500

U.S. Environmental Protection Agency; Durham 1,500

Research Triangle Institute Inc.; Research Triangle Park; commercial physical research 1,430

U.S. Veterans Hospital; Durham 1,400

City of Durham; Durham; city government 1,378

Austin Quality Foods Inc.; Cary; crackers 1,250

General Electric Co.; Mebane; control circuit relays 1,200

Powerware Group Inc.; Raleigh; AC/DC power conversion units 1,200

Wake Technical Community College; Raleigh 1,188

Aventis CropScience USA; Research Triangle Park; fungicides, herbicides 1,150

Duke University Hospital; Durham; medical doctor offices, clinics 1,000

Ericsson Inc.; Research Triangle Park; radio/TV communications equipment 1,000

PricewaterhouseCoopers; Cary; accounting services 1,000

Nortel Networks Inc.; Raleigh; job training services 900

North Carolina Central University; Durham 825

Acterna Corp.; Durham; electronic test equipment 800

American Eagle Airlines Inc.; Raleigh 800

BASF Corp.; Research Triangle Park; farm management services 800

Biogen Inc.; Research Triangle Park; commercial research lab 800

First Union Mortgage Corp.; Raleigh; mortgage bankers 800

Nationwide Mutual Insurance Co.; Raleigh; insurance agents and brokers 800

U.S. Postal Service; Raleigh 800

Blue Cross and Blue Shield of North Carolina; Durham; group hospitalization 750

Honeywell International Inc.; Moncure; textile mills 726

Duke Clinical Research Institute; Durham; medical labs 700

Educare Community Living Corp.; Apex; mentally handicapped home 680

Peopletree Staffing Solutions; Durham; help supply services 650

PharmaNet; Cary; research services 650

Tyco/Electronics Raychem; Fuquay-Varina; thermoplastics 650

Capital Area Young Men's Christian Assn. Inc.; Cary; civic and social associations 600

Durham Technical Community College Inc.; Durham 600

Misys Healthcare Systems; Raleigh; computer systems integration 600

National Bank of Commerce; Durham; state commercial banks 600

Reichhold Inc.; Durham; plastics 600

U.S. National Institutes of Health; Research Triangle Park 600

Orange County; Hillsborough; county government 580

Underwriters Laboratories Inc.; Research Triangle Park; testing labs 575

North Carolina Division of Prisons; Butner 560

Quintiles Inc.; Durham; commercial medical research 550

Midway Airlines Corp.; Morrisville 525

Sumitomo Electric Lightwave Corp.; Research Triangle Park; wiredrawing and insulating 510

ADP Marshall Inc.; Durham; office building construction 500

American Airlines Inc.; Raleigh 500

BioMerieux Inc.; Durham; blood, body fluid analyzers 500

Diosynth RTP Inc.; Research Triangle Park; pharmaceuticals 500

Ericsson Inc.; Durham; radio/TV communications equipment 500

Forbo Adhesives; Durham; adhesives, chemical 500

International Business Machines Corp.; Durham; computers 500

PhyAmerica Government Services Inc.; Durham; medical help service 500

SpectraSite Communications Inc.; Cary; cellular telephones 500

Ticketmaster Corp.; Durham; events ticketing service 500

Verizon Communications Inc.; Durham; telephone communication 500

Wackenhut Corp.; Raleigh; detective, armored car services 500

North Carolina 5th District

Northwest — part of Winston-Salem

In this northern Piedmont district, Mayberry meets R. J. Reynolds. The district's northern counties, which run along the Virginia border, are filled with small rural towns such as Mount Airy, the childhood home of Andy Griffith and the inspiration for the fictional setting of his 1960s television series. The district's major population center is Winston-Salem and surrounding Forsyth County, home to R. J. Reynolds Tobacco Co. The company's corporate headquarters is in the 12th District (which has most of Winston-Salem), but the company has a plant in the 5th, in the appropriately named town of Tobaccoville.

The economy of Forsyth County has changed over the past few years, veering away from its one-time mainstays, textiles and tobacco. While tobacco production still employs several thousand, it now ranks second to health care, partly because of Wake Forest University's medical center. Banking also is on the rise. Textile and blue-collar manufacturing still prevail throughout the other counties, and grazing cattle wander over Surry County's low, rolling hills.

Redistricting following the 2000 census moved the 5th's lines to the west and south to make room for the state's new 13th District, which includes some territory that had been in the northeastern part of the old 5th. But the new map kept the 5th's strong Republican leanings intact: The district backed Republican Richard Vinroot by a 12-point margin in the 2000 governor's race, and the GOP has a voter-registration advantage. Republicans dominate in Davie and Yadkin Counties, located west of Winston-Salem, which were two of the three counties to give Republican Elizabeth Dole more than 70 percent of the vote in the 2002 Senate race. Even the 5th's share of Forsyth leans Republican, as most of Winston-Salem's sizable black population was drawn into the 12th.

Major Industry
Health care, tobacco, textiles, agriculture.

Notable
Ashe County's "New River," in existence for roughly 300 million years, is regarded as one of the oldest rivers in the United States.

Election Returns

	Republican		Democratic		Other	
President 2000	163,705	66.1%	81,704	33.0%	2,147	0.9%
House 2002	137,879	70.2%	58,558	29.8%		

District Profile

Population 619,178

Total area (square miles) 4,423.5
Land area (square miles) 4,401.8

Population per square mile 140.7

Counties (2000 population)

Alexander 33,603	Rockingham (pt.) 11,112
Alleghany 10,677	Stokes 44,711
Ashe 24,384	Surry 71,219
Davie 34,835	Watauga 42,695
Forsyth (pt.) 175,378	Wilkes 65,632
Iredell (pt.) 68,584	Yadkin 36,348

Cities and other areas over 10,000 (2000 population)
Boone town 13,472
Clemmons village 13,827
Kernersville town (pt.) 17,126
Statesville (pt.) 23,280
Winston-Salem (pt.) 69,790

Race and Hispanic or Latino origin*
White 87.9%
Black or African American 6.7%
American Indian or Alaska Native 0.2%
Asian 0.8%
Native Hawaiian or other Pacific Islander 0.0%
Some other race 0.1%
Hispanic or Latino origin 3.6%
Two or more races 0.7%

*As percentage of total population.

Ancestry*

Dutch 1.3%	Italian 1.6%
English 9.9%	Scotch-Irish 2.8%
French 1.2%	Scottish 1.8%
German 9.5%	USA/American 15.7%
Irish 6.3%	

*As estimated percentage of total population.

Universities and colleges, 2000–2001 enrollment
Appalachian State University, Boone 13,227
Forsyth Technical Community College, Winston-Salem 5,860
Lees-McRae College, Banner Elk 712
Mitchell Community College, Statesville 1,830
Surry Community College, Dobson 2,946
Wilkes Community College, Wilkesboro 2,127

Newspapers and circulation

	District circulation	Total circulation
Charlotte Observer	3,207	237,693
Greensboro News & Record	3,279	88,143
Hickory Daily Record	1,835	19,888
Statesville Record & Landmark	9,727	14,338
*USA Today**	4,281	1,674,376
Winston-Salem Journal	59,417	85,775

*See Sources and Explanations in the front of the volume.

Television stations and affiliations

Greensboro-High Point-Winston-Salem	68%	WDRL	UPN
Greensboro-High Point-Winston-Salem	68%	WFMY	CBS
Greensboro-High Point-Winston-Salem	68%	WGHP	FOX
Greensboro-High Point-Winston-Salem	68%	WLXI	Independent
Greensboro-High Point-Winston-Salem	68%	WUNL	PBS
Greensboro-High Point-Winston-Salem	68%	WUPN	UPN
Greensboro-High Point-Winston-Salem	68%	WXII	NBC
Greensboro-High Point-Winston-Salem	68%	WXLV	ABC
Charlotte	32%	WAXN	Independent
Charlotte	32%	WBTV	CBS
Charlotte	32%	WCCB	FOX
Charlotte	32%	WCNC	NBC
Charlotte	32%	WHKY	Independent
Charlotte	32%	WJZY	UPN
Charlotte	32%	WNSC	PBS
Charlotte	32%	WSOC	ABC
Charlotte	32%	WTVI	PBS
Charlotte	32%	WUNE	PBS
Charlotte	32%	WUNG	PBS

Cable systems and subscribers
Adelphia 18,605
Charter 27,551
Mediacom 4,342
Time Warner 26,100

Businesses and other major employers
Carolina North Baptist Hospitals Inc.; Winston-Salem 5,435
Appalachian State University Inc.; Boone 3,455
Forsyth Medical Center Inc.; Winston-Salem 3,220
Tyson Foods Inc.; Wilkesboro; chicken 3,000
Wake Forest University; Winston-Salem 2,600
Lowe's Companies Inc.; Wilkesboro; home centers 2,330
Remington Arms Co.; Madison; hunting, trapping, game propagation 2,229
UNIFI Inc.; Yadkinville; yarns 2,000
Sara Lee Corp.; Winston-Salem; hosiery, underwear 1,700
Iredell Memorial Hospital; Statesville 1,197
Roadway Express Inc.; Kernersville; contract haulers 1,000
Ansell-Edmont Industrial Inc.; Wilkesboro; work gloves 900

Budd Group Inc.; Winston-Salem; building cleaning
900

ContiGroup Companies Inc.; Dobson; poultry processing
850

U.S. Airways Inc.; Winston-Salem   850

Wilkes Regional Medical Center; North Wilkesboro
845

North Carolina ASMO Inc.; Statesville; gasoline engines
825

Chatham Inc.; Elkin; upholstery fabrics   820

Wherehouse Entertainment Inc.; Boone; records   810

Renfro Corp.; Mount Airy; socks   800

Lucent Technologies Inc.; Winston-Salem; telephone
apparatus   777

Clayton Marcus Co.; Hickory; furniture   700

Lowe's Companies Inc.; Olin; home centers   700

Davis Community Hospital; Statesville   650

Johnson Controls Inc.; Kernersville; automobile seats
650

Siemens Westinghouse Power Corp.; Rural Hall; motors
and generators   650

Kobe Copper Products Inc.; Pine Hall; copper tubing
610

Northern Hospital District of Surry County; Mount Airy
610

Dana Corp.; Statesville; motor vehicle axles   600

Ingersoll-Rand Co.; Mocksville; electrical equipment
and supplies   600

Kmart Corp.; Wilkesboro; department stores   600

Lowe's Companies Inc.; North Wilkesboro; home centers
600

Watauga Medical Center Inc.; Boone   600

Kraft Foods Inc.; Kernersville; breads and cakes   550

Cross Creek Apparel Inc.; Mount Airy; textile mills
542

Kewaunee Scientific Corp.; Statesville; lab furniture
525

Mitchell Gold Co.; Taylorsville; home furniture   512

Forsyth Technical Community College; Winston-Salem
500

Iredell-Statesville Schools; Statesville   500

Lowe's Companies Inc.; Statesville; home centers   500

Sara Lee Corp.; Yadkinville; hosiery   500

Vaughan-Bassett Furniture Co.; Elkin; furniture   500

Western State University; Kernersville   500

North Carolina 6th District

Central — parts of Greensboro and High Point

Located in the heart of the state, the 6th takes in part of
the city of Greensboro and surrounding Guilford County and
then spreads south to include the famed golf course towns
of Southern Pines and Pinehurst, near Fort Bragg. Already
solid GOP turf, the 6th became even more Republican after
redistricting following the 2000 census. *(See map p. 679.)*

The new map shed about 100,000 people in Guilford,
mainly to facilitate the creation of the state's new 13th District, and added territory in Alamance County to the east. As
redrawn, the 6th takes in two large chunks of Guilford that
are connected at a single point, on the Reedy Fork Creek in
the northeastern part of the county.

Greensboro, the third-most-populous city in the state, is
home to a blend of manufacturing and service companies.
Textiles, furniture, and tobacco processing long have been
the economic backbone of both the city and the district,
including Lorillard Tobacco Company, the manufacturer of
Kent and Newport cigarettes. However, the influence of tobacco on the economy has somewhat decreased. Insurance
companies, an American Express regional credit card service
center, and six colleges and universities have helped to diversify Greensboro's economy. Nearby High Point is a furniture
manufacturing hub.

As in much of North Carolina, trade issues loom large in
the 6th District, particularly in textiles and furniture manufacturing. An increase in furniture imports nationwide at
the expense of Greensboro's industry has become a major
concern.

The 6th includes all of Randolph County, a heavily Republican area located south of Greensboro, and most of Alamance,
which votes Republican in part because of the union-resistant
textile industry. Moore County includes the upscale golf and
retirement centers in Pinehurst. The rest of the district is
mostly rural, tobacco country.

Major Industry

Tobacco, textiles, furniture manufacturing.

Notable

The Richard Petty Museum in Level Cross honors the
NASCAR legend, who was the Republican nominee for secretary of state in 1996.

Election Returns

	Republican		Democratic		Other	
President 2000	160,141	67.2%	76,315	32.0%	1,727	0.7%
House 2002	151,430	90.4%			16,067	9.6%

District Profile

Population   619,178

Total area (square miles)   2,988.5
Land area (square miles)   2,943.8

Population per square mile   210.3

Counties (2000 population)

Alamance (pt.)	91,085	Moore	74,769
Davidson (pt.)	74,170	Randolph	130,454
Guilford (pt.)	177,949	Rowan (pt.)	70,751

Cities and other areas over 10,000 (2000 population)
Asheboro   21,672
Burlington (pt.)   21,081
Greensboro (pt.)   59,010
High Point (pt.)   33,404
Southern Pines town   10,918
Thomasville (pt.)   13,331

Race and Hispanic or Latino origin*
White   85.3%
Black or African American   8.6%
American Indian or Alaska Native   0.4%
Asian   1.0%
Native Hawaiian or other Pacific Islander   0.0%

Some other race 0.1%
Hispanic or Latino origin 3.9%
Two or more races 0.7%

As percentage of total population.

Ancestry*

Dutch	1.2%	Italian	1.8%
English	8.9%	Scotch-Irish	3.0%
French	1.3%	Scottish	2.2%
German	10.1%	USA/American	15.3%
Irish	6.7%		

As estimated percentage of total population.

Universities and colleges, 2000–2001 enrollment

Davidson County Community College, Lexington
2,356

Elon University, Elon 4,138

Guilford Technical Community College, Jamestown
8,008

Randolph Community College, Asheboro 1,951

Sandhills Community College, Pinehurst 2,933

Newspapers and circulation

	District circulation	Total circulation
Alamance News	4,227	5,645
Asheboro Courier Tribune	9,499	15,727
Burlington Times-News	19,619	27,412
Fayetteville Observer	4,932	64,750
Greensboro News & Record	44,410	88,143
High Point Enterprise	16,477	29,095
Kannapolis Independent Tribune	2,007	20,324
Lexington Dispatch	10,578	12,469
Raleigh News & Observer	2,311	164,952
Salisbury Post	11,251	23,473
*USA Today**	8,863	1,674,376
Winston-Salem Journal	3,997	85,775

See Sources and Explanations in the front of the volume.

Television stations and affiliations

Greensboro-High Point-Winston-Salem	67%	WDRL	UPN
Greensboro-High Point-Winston-Salem	67%	WFMY	CBS
Greensboro-High Point-Winston-Salem	67%	WGHP	FOX
Greensboro-High Point-Winston-Salem	67%	WLXI	Independent
Greensboro-High Point-Winston-Salem	67%	WUNL	PBS
Greensboro-High Point-Winston-Salem	67%	WUPN	UPN
Greensboro-High Point-Winston-Salem	67%	WXII	NBC
Greensboro-High Point-Winston-Salem	67%	WXLV	ABC
Raleigh-Durham (Fayetteville)	23%	WGPX	PAX
Raleigh-Durham (Fayetteville)	23%	WKFT	Independent
Raleigh-Durham (Fayetteville)	23%	WLFL	WB
Raleigh-Durham (Fayetteville)	23%	WNCN	NBC
Raleigh-Durham (Fayetteville)	23%	WRAL	CBS
Raleigh-Durham (Fayetteville)	23%	WRAY	Independent
Raleigh-Durham (Fayetteville)	23%	WRAZ	FOX
Raleigh-Durham (Fayetteville)	23%	WRDC	UPN
Raleigh-Durham (Fayetteville)	23%	WRPX	PAX
Raleigh-Durham (Fayetteville)	23%	WTVD	ABC
Raleigh-Durham (Fayetteville)	23%	WUNC	PBS
Raleigh-Durham (Fayetteville)	23%	WUNP	PBS
Charlotte	10%	WAXN	Independent
Charlotte	10%	WBTV	CBS
Charlotte	10%	WCCB	FOX
Charlotte	10%	WCNC	NBC
Charlotte	10%	WHKY	Independent
Charlotte	10%	WJZY	UPN
Charlotte	10%	WNSC	PBS
Charlotte	10%	WSOC	ABC
Charlotte	10%	WTVI	PBS
Charlotte	10%	WUNE	PBS
Charlotte	10%	WUNG	PBS

Cable systems and subscribers

Adelphia 811
Carolina Cable Partners 571
Charter 752
Time Warner 116,407

Businesses and other major employers

Klaussner Furniture Industries Inc.; Asheboro; home furniture 3,500

American Express Travel Related Services Co.; Greensboro; credit card services, collection 3,000

Moses H. Cone Memorial Hospital Operating Corp.; Greensboro 3,000

Duke and St. Joseph's Home Care; Pinehurst; home health care 2,000

Lucent Technologies Inc.; McLeansville; telephone apparatus 2,000

FirstHealth of Carolinas Inc.; Pinehurst; hospital 1,800

Timco Aviation Services Inc.; Greensboro; aircraft servicing 1,800

Freightliner; High Point; motor vehicles and car bodies 1,500

Gilbarco; Greensboro; gasoline pumps 1,500

Times Mirror Co.; Oak Ridge; business consulting 1,500

Alamance Regional Medical Center Inc.; Burlington 1,050

Applica Inc.; Asheboro; electric housewares 1,000

Caddie Master Enterprises Inc.; West End; management services 1,000

PPG Industries Inc.; Lexington; fiberglass fabrics 1,000

Eveready Battery Co.; Asheboro 996

Alamance Community College Inc.; Graham 911

Oakwood Mobile Homes Inc.; Greensboro; mobile home dealers 900

Furnitureland South Inc.; Jamestown; furniture stores 870

Tyco Electronics Corp.; Greensboro; programmers, process type 848

GDX Automotive; Salisbury; gaskets and sealing devices 797

Guilford Technical Community College Inc.; Jamestown 785

Ramtex Inc.; Ramseur; fabric mills 744

WestPoint Stevens Inc.; Burlington; bedding 732

GKN Automotive Inc.; Mebane; automotive electrical equipment 725

Elon University; Elon 700

Preferred Building Maintenance Inc.; Greensboro; janitorial service 650

General Electric Co.; Mebane; control circuit relays 600

Randolph Hospital Inc.; Asheboro 596

Burlington Industries Inc.; Burlington; fabrics 535

Gold Toe Brands Inc.; Burlington; socks 517

Arrow International Inc.; Asheboro; surgical instruments 500

Carolina Biological Supply Co.; Burlington; biological products 500

Center for Creative Leadership; Trinity; arts and crafts schools   500

General Dynamics Advanced Technology Systems Inc.; McLeansville; engineering services   500

Lexington Furniture Industries Inc.; Lexington   500

Pinehurst Inc.; Pinehurst; resort hotel   500

Volkert and Associates Inc.; Summerfield; consulting engineer   500

North Carolina 7th District

Southeast — Wilmington, part of Fayetteville

The 7th stretches from the well-off historic port city of Wilmington in the southeast to the military-based commercial hub of Fayetteville in the north. In between lie tobacco fields, hog farms, and manufacturing plants.

Fort Bragg is just outside the 7th (it is shared by the 2nd and 8th Districts), but the huge military base is integral to the Fayetteville area. Tobacco, agriculture, and textiles also drive the district's economy, though textile declines have given some counties high unemployment. Free-trade agreements are viewed with suspicion here.

Like Fayetteville (shared with the 2nd and 8th), Wilmington grew significantly in the 1990s, reflected in its expanding medical center and emerging biotechnology industry.

Wealthy condo-dwellers in Wilmington and surrounding New Hanover County exert a rightward influence. But the region's poor farmers, Lumbee Native Americans (mainly in Robeson County), and cohesive black community in Fayetteville and rural Bladen and Columbus Counties give the district a small Democratic lean. The 7th voted narrowly for George W. Bush in the 2000 presidential election but went decisively for Democrat Michael F. Easley in the 2000 governor's race.

Redistricting following the 2000 census made minimal changes to the 7th, but did give the district all of Robeson County. As a result, the new 7th has the fifth-largest percentage of Native Americans of any district in the nation, and the largest percentage of any district east of the Mississippi River. The Hispanic population is rising. Duplin County (shared with the 3rd), in the northeast, was profiled in a 2002 *New York Times* story about how rural school districts have few qualified people to teach English to immigrants.

Major Industry

Agriculture, military, manufacturing, tourism.

Notable

Wilmington has a strong film and television production industry, with such movies as *Sleeping with the Enemy, Blue Velvet,* and *Domestic Disturbance* and the TV series *Dawson's Creek* filmed there; basketball star Michael Jordan grew up in Wilmington.

Election Returns

	Republican		Democratic		Other	
President 2000	108,091	51.6%	100,025	47.7%	1,420	0.7%
House 2002	45,537	27.3%	118,543	71.1%	2,574	1.5%

District Profile

Population   619,178

Total area (square miles)   6,510.3
 Land area (square miles)   6,087.3

Population per square mile   101.7

Counties (2000 population)

Bladen 32,278	New Hanover 160,307
Brunswick 73,143	Pender 41,082
Columbus 54,749	Robeson 123,339
Cumberland (pt.) 72,152	Sampson (pt.) 27,265
Duplin (pt.) 34,668	Scotland (pt.) 195

Cities and other areas over 10,000 (2000 population)
 Fayetteville (pt.)   19,418
 Lumberton   20,795
 Masonboro CDP   11,812
 Wilmington   75,838

Race and Hispanic or Latino origin*
 White   63.0%
 Black or African American   23.1%
 American Indian or Alaska Native   8.5%
 Asian   0.5%
 Native Hawaiian or other Pacific Islander   0.0%
 Some other race   0.1%
 Hispanic or Latino origin   3.9%
 Two or more races   0.9%

As percentage of total population.

Ancestry*

English 7.7%	Italian 1.9%
French 1.4%	Scotch-Irish 2.9%
German 6.1%	Scottish 2.0%
Irish 5.8%	USA/American 11.1%

As estimated percentage of total population.

Universities and colleges, 2000–2001 enrollment
 Bladen Community College, Dublin   990
 Brunswick Community College, Supply   924
 Cape Fear Community College, Wilmington   5,470
 James Sprunt Community College, Kenansville   1,276
 Methodist College, Fayetteville   2,134
 Miller-Motte Business College, Wilmington   466
 Robeson Community College, Lumberton   1,843
 Southeastern Community College, Whiteville   1,883
 University of North Carolina, Pembroke   3,445
 University of North Carolina, Wilmington   10,100

Newspapers and circulation

	District circulation	Total circulation
Dunn Daily Record	3,137	9,760
Fayetteville Observer	28,465	64,750
Lumberton Robesonian	12,895	12,960
Myrtle Beach Sun News	2,509	48,171
Raleigh News & Observer	1,278	164,952
Sampson Independent	2,915	8,379
*USA Today**	4,172	1,674,376
Wilmington Star-News	52,714	53,945

See Sources and Explanations in the front of the volume.

Television stations and affiliations

Wilmington	64%	WECT	NBC
Wilmington	64%	WSFX	FOX
Wilmington	64%	WUNJ	PBS
Wilmington	64%	WWAY	ABC
Florence-Myrtle Beach, SC	15%	WBTW	CBS
Florence-Myrtle Beach, SC	15%	WFPX	PAX
Florence-Myrtle Beach, SC	15%	WFXB	FOX
Florence-Myrtle Beach, SC	15%	WHMC	PBS
Florence-Myrtle Beach, SC	15%	WJPM	PBS
Florence-Myrtle Beach, SC	15%	WPDE	ABC
Florence-Myrtle Beach, SC	15%	WUNU	PBS
Florence-Myrtle Beach, SC	15%	WWMB	UPN
Raleigh-Durham (Fayetteville)	12%	WGPX	PAX
Raleigh-Durham (Fayetteville)	12%	WKFT	Independent
Raleigh-Durham (Fayetteville)	12%	WLFL	WB
Raleigh-Durham (Fayetteville)	12%	WNCN	NBC
Raleigh-Durham (Fayetteville)	12%	WRAL	CBS
Raleigh-Durham (Fayetteville)	12%	WRAY	Independent
Raleigh-Durham (Fayetteville)	12%	WRAZ	FOX
Raleigh-Durham (Fayetteville)	12%	WRDC	UPN
Raleigh-Durham (Fayetteville)	12%	WRPX	PAX
Raleigh-Durham (Fayetteville)	12%	WTVD	ABC
Raleigh-Durham (Fayetteville)	12%	WUNC	PBS
Raleigh-Durham (Fayetteville)	12%	WUNP	PBS
Greenville-New Bern-Washington	9%	WCTI	ABC
Greenville-New Bern-Washington	9%	WEPX	PAX
Greenville-New Bern-Washington	9%	WFXI	FOX
Greenville-New Bern-Washington	9%	WITN	NBC
Greenville-New Bern-Washington	9%	WNCT	CBS
Greenville-New Bern-Washington	9%	WUND	PBS
Greenville-New Bern-Washington	9%	WUNK	PBS
Greenville-New Bern-Washington	9%	WUNM	PBS
Greenville-New Bern-Washington	9%	WYDO	FOX

Cable systems and subscribers

Adelphia   16,853
Atlantic Telephone   12,851
Carolina Cable   544
Charter   9,452
Southern Cable   5,943
Starvision   2,044
Time Warner   101,676

Military installations, September 2001

Military Ocean Terminal Sunny Point, Wilmington
   337

Businesses and other major employers

Smithfield Packing Co.; Tar Heel; pork products   5,200
General Electric Co.; Wilmington; nuclear fuels   3,500
New Hanover Regional Medical Center; Wilmington
   3,485
International Paper Co.; Riegelwood; paper mills
   1,600
University of North Carolina; Wilmington   1,296
Cumberland County; Fayetteville; county government
   1,210
Campbell Soup Co.; Maxton; canned foods   1,200
Carolina Power and Light Co.; Southport; electric power
   generation   1,100
Southeastern Regional Medical Center; Lumberton
   1,100
CVEO Corp.; Lumberton; footwear   1,000
M. J. Soffe Co; Fayetteville; athletic clothing   1,000
Guilford Mills Inc.; Kenansville; finishing plants   900
Kayser-Roth Corp.; Lumberton; hosiery   900
Alamac Knit Fabrics Inc.; Lumberton; outerwear mills
   700

House of Raeford Farms Inc.; Rose Hill; processed
   poultry   700
Murphy Farms; Rose Hill; hogs   700
Wal-Mart Stores Inc.; Wilmington; department stores
   700
Cutler-Hammer Inc.; Fayetteville; relays and industrial
   controls   680
Extreme Networks; Leland; local area network systems
   680
Brunswick County; Bolivia; legislative bodies   650
Croft Metals Inc.; Lumber Bridge; metal doors   600
PPD Development Inc.; Wilmington; commercial
   physical research   600
Sampson Regional Medical Center; Clinton   580
Columbus County Hospital; Whiteville   555
ConAgra Poultry Co.; Wallace; processed poultry
   550
Fayetteville City Public Works Commission;
   Fayetteville; utilities   535
City of Fayetteville; Fayetteville; city government
   533
Alamac Knit Fabrics Inc.; Elizabethtown   530
City of Fayetteville; Fayetteville; sheriff's office   522
E. I. Du Pont De Nemours and Co.; Fayetteville; plastics
   520
Clayson Knitting Co.; Red Springs; outerwear mills
   500
Cumberland County Schools; Fayetteville   500
Georgia-Pacific Corp.; Whiteville; plywood, hardwood
   500
U.S. Postal Service; Fayetteville   500
Wilmington Health Associates Inc.; Wilmington; family
   health care   500

North Carolina 8th District

South central — parts of Charlotte, Fayetteville, Concord, and Kannapolis

The 8th connects the worlds of eastern and western North Carolina, spanning from Charlotte in the west to military-dominated Fayetteville in the east. *(See map p. 679.)*

This is a district split along geographic, economic, and political lines. Redistricting following the 2000 census extended the 8th west to take in a large portion of Charlotte, giving the previously suburban and rural district an urban component.

Cabarrus, a fast-growing county north of Charlotte, and Cumberland, which includes the 8th's share of Fayetteville, are the district's most-populous counties. Cabarrus is largely white and heavily Republican. Cumberland is more politically competitive.

In Mecklenburg County, which includes Charlotte and is the 8th's third major population center, the district reaches as far west as Memorial Stadium and Independence Park, nearly reaching downtown Charlotte. The 8th's share of Charlotte is almost 40 percent black, giving the district's portion of Mecklenburg a decidedly Democratic lean.

Textile-based economies in the cities along Interstate 85, notably Concord and Kannapolis, have suffered major losses over the last few years as manufacturing jobs have headed overseas. In the east, the district becomes poorer and more rural as it reaches into the Sandhills region. This part of the 8th also has a strong military flavor—Fort Bragg (shared with the 2nd) takes up land in Hoke and Cumberland Counties.

The 8th is politically competitive. In 2000 George W. Bush took 53.6 percent of the vote in the presidential election, while Democrat Michael F. Easley captured 53 percent in the gubernatorial contest.

Major Industry

Military, manufacturing, agriculture, livestock.

Notable

North Carolina Speedway and Rockingham Dragway, known collectively as "The Rock," can draw 250,000 NASCAR fans to races.

Election Returns

	Republican		Democratic		Other	
President 2000	105,484	53.6%	89,672	45.6%	1,568	0.8%
House 2002	80,298	53.6%	66,819	44.6%	2,619	1.7%

District Profile

Population   619,178

Total area (square miles)   3,317.8
    Land area (square miles)   3,282.7

Population per square mile   188.6

Counties (2000 population)
    Anson   25,275
    Cabarrus (pt.)   125,527
    Cumberland (pt.)   122,755
    Hoke   33,646
    Mecklenburg (pt.)   107,392
    Montgomery   26,822
    Richmond   46,564
    Scotland (pt.)   35,803
    Stanly   58,100
    Union (pt.)   37,294

Cities and other areas over 10,000 (2000 population)
    Albemarle   15,680
    Charlotte (pt.)   100,756
    Concord (pt.)   55,938
    Fayetteville (pt.)   51,698
    Hope Mills town (pt.)   11,229
    Kannapolis (pt.)   27,786
    Laurinburg   15,874
    Monroe (pt.)   17,928

Race and Hispanic or Latino origin*
    White   61.8%
    Black or African American   26.6%
    American Indian or Alaska Native   1.7%
    Asian   1.7%
    Native Hawaiian or other Pacific Islander   0.1%
    Some other race   0.2%
    Hispanic or Latino origin   6.6%
    Two or more races   1.4%

*As percentage of total population.

Ancestry*

English	5.9%	Italian	1.7%
French	1.1%	Scotch-Irish	2.9%
German	7.6%	Scottish	1.9%
Irish	5.3%	USA/American	10.8%

*As estimated percentage of total population.

Universities and colleges, 2000–2001 enrollment
Barber-Scotia College, Concord   543
Cabarrus College of Health Sciences, Concord   259
Central Piedmont Community College, Charlotte   14,908
Fayetteville Technical Community College, Fayetteville   8,310
Montgomery Community College, Troy   674
Pfeiffer University, Misenheimer   1,496
Richmond Community College, Hamlet   1,335
South Piedmont Community College, Polkton   323
St. Andrews Presbyterian College, Laurinburg   644
Stanly Community College, Albemarle   1,532
University of North Carolina, Charlotte   17,241
Wingate University, Wingate   1,283

Newspapers and circulation

	District circulation	Total circulation
Charlotte Observer	33,829	237,693
Fayetteville Observer	18,287	64,750
Kannapolis Independent Tribune	14,219	20,324
Monroe Enquirer Journal	2,954	10,296
Richmond County Daily Journal	8,036	8,189
Salisbury Post	1,109	23,473
Stanly News and Press	8,832	9,037
*USA Today**	1,852	1,674,376

*See Sources and Explanations in the front of the volume.

Television stations and affiliations

Charlotte	61%	WAXN	Independent
Charlotte	61%	WBTV	CBS
Charlotte	61%	WCCB	FOX
Charlotte	61%	WCNC	NBC
Charlotte	61%	WHKY	Independent
Charlotte	61%	WJZY	UPN
Charlotte	61%	WNSC	PBS
Charlotte	61%	WSOC	ABC
Charlotte	61%	WTVI	PBS
Charlotte	61%	WUNE	PBS
Charlotte	61%	WUNG	PBS
Greensboro-High Point-Winston-Salem	15%	WDRL	UPN
Greensboro-High Point-Winston-Salem	15%	WFMY	CBS
Greensboro-High Point-Winston-Salem	15%	WGHP	FOX
Greensboro-High Point-Winston-Salem	15%	WLXI	Independent
Greensboro-High Point-Winston-Salem	15%	WUNL	PBS
Greensboro-High Point-Winston-Salem	15%	WUPN	UPN
Greensboro-High Point-Winston-Salem	15%	WXII	NBC
Greensboro-High Point-Winston-Salem	15%	WXLV	ABC
Raleigh-Durham (Fayetteville)	14%	WGPX	PAX
Raleigh-Durham (Fayetteville)	14%	WKFT	Independent
Raleigh-Durham (Fayetteville)	14%	WLFL	WB
Raleigh-Durham (Fayetteville)	14%	WNCN	NBC
Raleigh-Durham (Fayetteville)	14%	WRAL	CBS
Raleigh-Durham (Fayetteville)	14%	WRAY	Independent
Raleigh-Durham (Fayetteville)	14%	WRAZ	FOX
Raleigh-Durham (Fayetteville)	14%	WRDC	UPN
Raleigh-Durham (Fayetteville)	14%	WRPX	PAX
Raleigh-Durham (Fayetteville)	14%	WTVD	ABC
Raleigh-Durham (Fayetteville)	14%	WUNC	PBS
Raleigh-Durham (Fayetteville)	14%	WUNP	PBS
Florence-Myrtle Beach, SC	10%	WBTW	CBS

Florence-Myrtle Beach, SC	10%	WFPX	PAX
Florence-Myrtle Beach, SC	10%	WFXB	FOX
Florence-Myrtle Beach, SC	10%	WHMC	PBS
Florence-Myrtle Beach, SC	10%	WJPM	PBS
Florence-Myrtle Beach, SC	10%	WPDE	ABC
Florence-Myrtle Beach, SC	10%	WUNU	PBS
Florence-Myrtle Beach, SC	10%	WWMB	UPN

Cable systems and subscribers
Adelphia   6,580
Charter   807
Time Warner   113,415

Businesses and other major employers
Presbyterian Hospital; Charlotte   3,075
Cabarrus Memorial Hospital; Concord   3,000
Cumberland County Hospital System Inc.; Fayetteville   2,711
Philip Morris Inc.; Concord; cigarettes   2,600
Black and Decker Corp.; Fayetteville; power-driven handtools   1,500
House of Raeford Farms Inc.; Raeford; turkey processing   1,300
Tyson Foods Inc.; Monroe; processed poultry   1,300
Charlotte Mecklenburg Hospital Authority; Charlotte   1,250
Abbott Laboratories; Laurinburg; pharmaceuticals   1,100
ArvinMeritor Inc.; Fayetteville; auto exhaust systems   1,100
Fayetteville Technical Community College Inc.; Fayetteville   1,100
Central Piedmont Community College; Charlotte   1,000
Cabarrus County School District; Concord   941
Faison Associates; Fayetteville; shopping center operation   895
Perdue Farms Inc.; Rockingham; dressed poultry   850
Pillowtex Corp.; Concord; bedding   850
Perdue Farms Inc.; Concord; poultry processing   825
Allied Security Inc.; Charlotte; security guard service   800
Clayson Knitting Co.; Star; socks   800
Concord Telephone Long Distance Co.; Concord; long-distance telephone   800
Purolator Co.; Fayetteville; motor vehicle parts/accessories   800
FirstHealth of Carolinas Inc.; Rockingham; hospital   750
Union Regional Medical Center; Monroe   750
Burlington Industries Inc.; Cordova; fabrics   725
Scottish Food Systems Inc.; Laurinburg; restaurant management   725
City of Concord; Concord; city government   700
Renfro Corp.; Star; socks   700
Pilkington North America Inc.; Laurinburg; flat glass   675
Cumberland County; Fayetteville; social service center   640
Morton Custom Plastics; Harrisburg   610
Conopco Inc.; Raeford; cosmetics   600
Fieldcrest Cannon Inc.; Laurel Hill; toweling   600
Hartford Casualty Insurance Co.; Charlotte; fire, marine, casualty insurance   600
Sara Lee Corp.; Rockingham; warehousing   600
Scotland Health Care System Hospital; Laurinburg   600
Collins and Aikman Products Co; Albemarle; automobile floor coverings   557
Pass and Seymour Inc.; Concord; current-carrying wiring services   550
Dan River Inc.; Morven; home furnishings   536
WestPoint Stevens Inc.; Wagram; bedding, table cloths   529
CSX Transportation Inc.; Hamlet; railroad freight hauling   502
Allegheny Technologies Inc.; Monroe; nickel   500
Michelin Aircraft Tire Corp.; Norwood   500
Oakwood Homes Corp.; Richfield; mobile homes   500
Toastmaster Inc.; Laurinburg; clock assembly   500
Wal-Mart Stores Inc.; Concord; department stores   500

North Carolina 9th District
South central — parts of Charlotte and Gastonia

Redistricting following the 2000 census strengthened the 9th's ties to Charlotte, the largest metropolitan area in the state. Nearly 40 percent of district residents live within its city limits and nearly 60 percent live in Mecklenburg County, which includes Charlotte. *(See map p. 679.)*

The primarily white suburbs on the southern side of Charlotte feed the city many of its bankers, brokers, accountants, health care professionals, and other white-collar workers. Most of Charlotte's African American residents are in the 8th and 12th Districts. The 9th has the second-highest median family income in North Carolina, thanks to upper-middle-class areas such as Huntersville, in northern Mecklenburg. It also has the lowest percentage of families in poverty.

The region's tremendous growth, much of it sparked by 1990s consolidation in the banking industry, has brought the traffic congestion, shopping malls, and higher home values that usually accompany suburban sprawl. Charlotte is now known as the nation's biggest banking center after New York.

To the west, Gastonia and its surrounding towns have been hurt by the continuing decline of the textile industry. But the 9th has decreased its dependence on manufacturing and textiles, and Gastonia's population still grew by 20 percent in the 1990s.

Redistricting kept the 9th's Republican lean intact. The district's GOP registration advantage increased with the addition of most of Union County, a suburban bedroom community located southeast of Charlotte, and the excision of Democratic-leaning Cleveland County in the west. Republican Richard Vinroot, a former Charlotte mayor, received his best vote percentages in the state from the 9th in the 2000 gubernatorial election.

Major Industry
Finance, service, retail, manufacturing.

Notable
After six years of planning, a Gaston County veterans group in December 1998 succeeded in hoisting the largest flying American flag in the nation—114 by 65 feet.

Election Returns

	Republican		Democratic		Other	
President 2000	157,734	62.8%	91,353	36.4%	2,066	0.8%
House 2002	140,095	72.4%	49,974	25.8%	3,374	1.7%

District Profile

Population   619,178

Total area (square miles)   1,018.1
   Land area (square miles)   990.6

Population per square mile   625.1

Counties (2000 population)
Gaston (pt.)   163,874
Mecklenburg (pt.)   368,921
Union (pt.)   86,383

Cities and other areas over 10,000 (2000 population)
Charlotte (pt.)   243,947
Cornelius town   11,969
Gastonia (pt.)   60,498
Huntersville town   24,960
Indian Trail town   11,905
Matthews town   22,127
Mint Hill town   14,922

Race and Hispanic or Latino origin*
White   82.9%
Black or African American   10.3%
American Indian or Alaska Native   0.3%
Asian   2.0%
Native Hawaiian or other Pacific Islander   0.0%
Some other race   0.1%
Hispanic or Latino origin   3.5%
Two or more races   0.8%

*As percentage of total population.

Ancestry*
Dutch	1.2%	Italian	3.1%
English	9.0%	Polish	1.5%
French	1.8%	Scotch-Irish	4.2%
German	11.2%	Scottish	2.3%
Irish	8.2%	USA/American	9.6%

*As estimated percentage of total population.

Universities and colleges, 2000–2001 enrollment
Belmont Abbey College, Belmont   886
Carolinas College of Health Sciences, Charlotte   226
Gaston College, Dallas   3,954
Queens College, Charlotte   1,596

Newspapers and circulation

	District circulation	Total circulation
Charlotte Observer	99,868	237,693
Gastonia Gazette	22,289	31,214
Monroe Enquirer Journal	6,983	10,296
*USA Today**	7,650	1,674,376

*See Sources and Explanations in the front of the volume.

Television stations and affiliations
Charlotte	100%	WAXN	Independent
Charlotte	100%	WBTV	CBS
Charlotte	100%	WCCB	FOX
Charlotte	100%	WCNC	NBC
Charlotte	100%	WHKY	Independent
Charlotte	100%	WJZY	UPN
Charlotte	100%	WNSC	PBS
Charlotte	100%	WSOC	ABC
Charlotte	100%	WTVI	PBS
Charlotte	100%	WUNE	PBS
Charlotte	100%	WUNG	PBS

Cable systems and subscribers
Adelphia   1,350
Charter   723
Time Warner   48,092

Businesses and other major employers
J. A. Jones Inc.; Charlotte; office building construction   7,500
Charlotte Mecklenburg Hospital Authority; Charlotte   4,900
Medcath Corp. Hospital; Charlotte   2,600
Dana Corp.; Gastonia; industrial filters   2,300
Duke Energy Corp.; Huntersville; electric services   2,200
Parkdale America; Gastonia; spun polyester yarn   2,000
Gaston Memorial Hospital Inc.; Gastonia   1,900
Lance Inc.; Charlotte; bakery products   1,500
Family Dollar Stores Inc.; Matthews; variety stores   1,200
Watermill Ventures; Gastonia; investors   1,097
City of Charlotte; Charlotte; private elementary school   1,000
Stowe-Pharr Mills Inc.; McAdenville   1,000
Mecklenburg County; Charlotte; social and manpower programs   950
McGee Brothers Co. Inc.; Monroe; masonry/stonework   937
City of Charlotte; Charlotte; fire dept.   900
Merkert American Co.; Charlotte; food brokers   900
Deere and Co.; Gastonia; construction machinery   850
CBS Corp.; Charlotte; turbines/turbine generators   800
Danaher Corp.; Gastonia; machine tool accessories   750
Equitable; Charlotte; insurance agents   700
Siemens Medical Systems Inc.; Gastonia   700
TJX Companies Inc.; Charlotte; general warehousing   700
Black and Decker Corp.; Charlotte; packaging/labeling services   600
Emerson Electric Holding Corp.; Indian Trail; fluid meters and counting devices   600
Jaars Inc.; Waxhaw; job training and related services   596
Charlotte Pipe and Foundry Co.; Monroe; plastics pipe   550
Prairie Pizza Inc.; Charlotte; pizzeria chain   550
Wilton Connor Packaging; Charlotte; corrugated display items   550
Ruan Leasing Co.; Indian Trail; truck leasing   520

Maersk Inc.; Charlotte; deep-sea freight transportation 515

Gaston College; Dallas 504

American Studios Inc.; Matthews; photographic studios 500

Distribution and Marking Services Inc.; Charlotte; warehousing 500

Frito-Lay Inc.; Charlotte; snacks 500

Parsons Communications Group Inc.; Charlotte; communication line construction 500

PCA International Inc.; Matthews; photographer 500

Wal-Mart Stores Inc.; Gastonia; department stores 500

North Carolina 10th District

West — Hickory

Set among the small towns of the western part of the state, the 10th has a rustic, small-business, and conservative flavor.

While the 10th includes some suburban communities near Charlotte, it is mostly rural—only one town, Hickory, has a population of more than 20,000. The economy of the southern counties is based largely on textile and furniture manufacturing. Redistricting following the 2000 census added some cotton-growing areas. High-tech manufacturing is on the upswing, especially involving fiber-optic cable. Tourists visit the mountains near the Tennessee state line and ski in areas like Banner Elk (Avery County).

Some suburban sprawl has reached into the eastern and southern edges of the 10th, especially in Hickory, where the furniture industry employs a large part of the workforce. Iredell County is mostly rural and agricultural, with some manufacturing.

Redistricting removed a swath of rock-ribbed Republican counties to the north and east and added cotton-producing, politically competitive Cleveland County. The changes reduced the GOP registration advantage, but many Democratic voters are conservatives who will support Republicans in federal races.

The 10th's GOP lean is set by Catawba County (Hickory), the district's most populous, which backed Republican Elizabeth Dole by a 30-point margin in the 2002 Senate race. Democrats run better in Cleveland and Burke Counties, but Caldwell and Lincoln Counties lean heavily Republican. Mitchell and Avery Counties, on the Tennessee border, are strongly Republican as well. Avery was Dole's best county in the state (73 percent) in 2002.

Major Industry
Manufacturing, agriculture, livestock.

Notable
In 1917 the Elliott-Carnegie Public Library in Hickory was the last public library in the country to receive a grant from the Carnegie Foundation.

Election Returns

	Republican		Democratic		Other	
President 2000	143,124	64.9%	75,592	34.3%	1,693	0.8%
House 2002	102,768	59.3%	65,587	37.8%	4,937	2.8%

District Profile

Population   619,178

Total area (square miles)   3,362.1
    Land area (square miles)   3,302.0

Population per square mile   187.5

Counties (2000 population)
Avery 17,167	Gaston (pt.) 26,491
Burke 89,148	Iredell (pt.) 54,076
Caldwell 77,415	Lincoln 63,780
Catawba 141,685	Mitchell 15,687
Cleveland 96,287	Rutherford (pt.) 37,442

Cities and other areas over 10,000 (2000 population)
Hickory   37,222
Lenoir   16,793
Mooresville town (pt.)   18,782
Morganton   17,310
Newton   12,560
Shelby   19,477

Race and Hispanic or Latino origin*
White   84.9%
Black or African American   9.2%
American Indian or Alaska Native   0.2%
Asian   1.5%
Native Hawaiian or other Pacific Islander   0.0%
Some other race   0.1%
Hispanic or Latino origin   3.5%
Two or more races   0.7%

As percentage of total population.

Ancestry*
Dutch 1.5%	Italian 1.3%
English 6.9%	Scotch-Irish 2.7%
French 1.1%	Scottish 1.7%
German 10.4%	USA/American 16.5%
Irish 5.9%	

As estimated percentage of total population.

Universities and colleges, 2000–2001 enrollment
Caldwell Community College and Technical Institute, Lenoir   3,191
Catawba Valley Community College, Hickory   3,731
Cleveland Community College, Shelby   2,225
Gardner-Webb University, Boiling Springs   3,194
Lenoir-Rhyne College, Hickory   1,515
Mayland Community College, Spruce Pine   989
Western Piedmont Community College, Morganton   2,248

Newspapers and circulation

	District circulation	Total circulation
Asheville Citizen-Times	1,485	55,057
Charlotte Observer	28,855	237,693
Gastonia Gazette	8,166	31,214
Hickory Daily Record	18,072	19,888
Lenoir News-Topic	9,683	9,738
Morganton News Herald	11,455	11,455

Shelby Star	14,598	14,670
Statesville Record & Landmark	4,231	14,338
*USA Today**	2,903	1,674,376

See Sources and Explanations in the front of the volume.

Television stations and affiliations

Charlotte	80%	WAXN	Independent
Charlotte	80%	WBTV	CBS
Charlotte	80%	WCCB	FOX
Charlotte	80%	WCNC	NBC
Charlotte	80%	WHKY	Independent
Charlotte	80%	WJZY	UPN
Charlotte	80%	WNSC	PBS
Charlotte	80%	WSOC	ABC
Charlotte	80%	WTVI	PBS
Charlotte	80%	WUNE	PBS
Charlotte	80%	WUNG	PBS
Greenville-Spartanburg-Asheville-Anderson	20%	WASV	UPN
Greenville-Spartanburg-Asheville-Anderson	20%	WBSC	WB
Greenville-Spartanburg-Asheville-Anderson	20%	WGGS	Independent
Greenville-Spartanburg-Asheville-Anderson	20%	WHNS	FOX
Greenville-Spartanburg-Asheville-Anderson	20%	WLOS	ABC
Greenville-Spartanburg-Asheville-Anderson	20%	WNEG	CBS
Greenville-Spartanburg-Asheville-Anderson	20%	WNEH	PBS
Greenville-Spartanburg-Asheville-Anderson	20%	WNTV	PBS
Greenville-Spartanburg-Asheville-Anderson	20%	WRET	PBS
Greenville-Spartanburg-Asheville-Anderson	20%	WSPA	CBS
Greenville-Spartanburg-Asheville-Anderson	20%	WUNF	PBS
Greenville-Spartanburg-Asheville-Anderson	20%	WYFF	NBC

Cable systems and subscribers

Adelphia   3,252
Charter   74,687
City of Morganton   10,029
Country Cablevision   660
Northland   5,876
Time Warner   11,126

Businesses and other major employers

Siecor Operations; Hickory; fiber-optic cable
  4,500
CommScope Inc.; Catawba; coaxial cable   1,500
PPG Industries Fiber Glass Products Inc.; Shelby;
  pressed and blown glass   1,500
Grace Hospital; Morganton   1,400
North Carolina Dept. of Health and Human Services;
  Morganton   1,380
Case Farms of North Carolina Inc.; Morganton; poultry
  processing   1,375
Century Furniture Industries Inc.; Hickory   1,330
Frye Regional Medical Center Inc.; Hickory   1,290
Alcatel NA Cable Systems Inc.; Claremont;
  communication wire   1,100
Catawba Memorial Hospital; Hickory   1,055
Alcatel USA Inc.; Hickory; fiber-optic cable   1,000
General Electric Co.; Hickory; nonelectric transformers
  1,000
Henredon Furniture; Morganton   1,000
Leviton Manufacturing Co. Inc.; Morganton;
  current-carrying wiring services   1,000
Shurtape Technologies Inc.; Hickory; pressure-sensitive
  tape   900
Cleveland Memorial Hospital Inc.; Shelby   830
Bassett Furniture Industries Inc.; Newton   800
Cone Mills Corp.; Cliffside; denims   800
Mohican Mills Inc.; Lincolnton; cloth   760
CommScope Inc.; Claremont; coaxial cable   750
Thomasville Furniture Industries Inc.; Lenoir
  750

Continental Teves Inc.; Morganton; brake systems/parts
  700
Sherrill Furniture Co.; Hickory   675
Ellis Hosiery Mills Inc.; Hickory   650
City of Hickory; Hickory; social and manpower
  programs   645
Case Foods Inc.; Morganton; processed poultry   630
Eaton Corp.; Kings Mountain; electric power
  transmission   600
Lane Furniture Industries Inc.; Hickory; chairs   600
La-Z-Boy Inc.; Lenoir; furniture stores   600
Transport Drivers Inc.; Morganton; truck rental   570
Neuville Industries Inc.; Hildebran; socks   550
Timken Co.; Iron Station; blast furnaces and steel mills
  550
Universal Manufacturing and Logistics Inc.; Grover;
  optical disks and tape   550
Burlington Industries Inc.; Forest City; fabrics   540
Caldwell Memorial Hospital Inc.; Lenoir   525
Charles A. Cannon Jr. Memorial Hospital Inc.; Linville
  520
Sears Roebuck and Co. Inc.; Shelby; heating/air
  conditioning contractor   513
Avery Health Care Systems Inc.; Newland; health
  services consultant   500
Bali Co.; Kings Mountain; brassieres   500
Broyhill Furniture Industries Inc.; Lenoir   500
Cleveland County; Shelby; county government   500
Cochrane Furniture Co.; Lincolnton   500
Corning Cable Systems; Hickory; fiber-optic cable
  500
Ethan Allen Inc.; Maiden; furniture   500
Fairfield Chair Co.; Lenoir   500
Lincoln Health System; Lincolnton; management
  services   500
Wal-Mart Stores Inc.; Mooresville; department stores
  500

North Carolina 11th District

West — Asheville

Based in the Great Smoky Mountain region, the 11th is a largely rural district dotted with tree farms, wood mills, and campgrounds. While agriculture and forestry long have played a key role in the region's economy, retail trade, health care, and education are becoming major employers. Tourism also has a large role, with people flocking to the area's ski slopes, as well as to the hiking trails in national parks and on Mount Mitchell (the highest peak east of the Mississippi River). Tourists also enjoy the palatial Biltmore House, once home of Cornelius Vanderbilt's grandson.

Asheville—which along with surrounding Buncombe County takes in one-third of the district's residents—is the 11th's economic focal point. Residents recently spruced up the city's downtown, and efforts are underway to attract high-tech businesses. The decline of the textile industry has led to a loss of jobs in the district.

Attractive to retirees, the 11th has the highest median age (40.6) of any North Carolina district. It also has the smallest black population, as the only sizable African American constituency is in Asheville. The Cherokee Reservation in Swain and Jackson Counties gives the district a larger-than-average Native American population.

The 11th leans Republican. Buncombe voted for George W. Bush in the 2000 presidential election, as did every other county in the district. But Buncombe was a classic swing county in the 2002 Senate race, in the end backing Republican Elizabeth Dole by exactly one vote out of more than 63,000 cast. Henderson County, the district's second-most-populous, votes solidly Republican.

Major Industry

Retail trade, forest products, tourism, health care.

Notable

Many of the state's Cherokees are descendants of the estimated 1,000 Cherokees who hid in the mountains of western North Carolina to avoid the forced migration to Oklahoma along the path now known as the Trail of Tears; the Billy Graham Evangelistic Association operates a 1,500-acre training center called "The Cove" in Asheville; the movie *Forrest Gump* was filmed partly at Asheville's Biltmore House.

Election Returns

	Republican		Democratic		Other	
President 2000	150,004	58.4%	102,321	39.8%	4,514	1.8%
House 2002	112,335	55.5%	86,664	42.8%	3,261	1.6%

District Profile

Population 619,177

Total area (square miles) 6,087.8
  Land area (square miles) 6,025.0

Population per square mile 102.8

Counties (2000 population)

Buncombe 206,330	Madison 19,635
Cherokee 24,298	McDowell 42,151
Clay 8,775	Polk 18,324
Graham 7,993	Rutherford (pt.) 25,457
Haywood 54,033	Swain 12,968
Henderson 89,173	Transylvania 29,334
Jackson 33,121	Yancey 17,774
Macon 29,811	

Cities and other areas over 10,000 (2000 population)

Asheville 68,889	Hendersonville 10,420

Race and Hispanic or Latino origin*

White   89.8%
Black or African American   4.6%
American Indian or Alaska Native   1.5%
Asian   0.5%
Native Hawaiian or other Pacific Islander   0.0%
Some other race   0.1%
Hispanic or Latino origin   2.6%
Two or more races   0.9%

As percentage of total population.

Ancestry*

Dutch 1.6%	French 1.6%
English 9.8%	German 8.7%
Irish 8.2%	Scottish 2.6%
Italian 1.6%	USA/American 13.2%
Scotch-Irish 4.4%	

As estimated percentage of total population.

Universities and colleges, 2000–2001 enrollment

Asheville Buncombe Technical Community College, Asheville   4,940
Blue Ridge Community College, Flat Rock   1,826
Brevard College, Brevard   710
Haywood Community College, Clyde   1,653
Isothermal Community College, Spindale   1,863
Mars Hill College, Mars Hill   1,219
McDowell Technical Community College, Marion   1,074
Montreat College, Montreat   1,203
Southwestern Community College, Sylva   1,665
Tri-County Community College, Murphy   984
University of North Carolina, Asheville   3,292
Warren Wilson College, Swannanoa   799
Western Carolina University, Cullowhee   6,699

Newspapers and circulation

	District circulation	Total circulation
Asheville Citizen-Times	53,478	55,057
Atlanta Journal-Constitution	3,303	857,088
Charlotte Observer	1,224	237,693
Enterprise-Mountaineer	9,654	9,654
Hendersonville Times-News	19,864	19,892
Spartanburg Herald-Journal	1,142	52,383
*USA Today**	6,031	1,674,376

See Sources and Explanations in the front of the volume.

Television stations and affiliations

Greenville-Spartanburg-Asheville-Anderson	89%	WASV	UPN
Greenville-Spartanburg-Asheville-Anderson	89%	WBSC	WB
Greenville-Spartanburg-Asheville-Anderson	89%	WGGS	Independent
Greenville-Spartanburg-Asheville-Anderson	89%	WHNS	FOX
Greenville-Spartanburg-Asheville-Anderson	89%	WLOS	ABC
Greenville-Spartanburg-Asheville-Anderson	89%	WNEG	CBS
Greenville-Spartanburg-Asheville-Anderson	89%	WNEH	PBS
Greenville-Spartanburg-Asheville-Anderson	89%	WNTV	PBS
Greenville-Spartanburg-Asheville-Anderson	89%	WRET	PBS
Greenville-Spartanburg-Asheville-Anderson	89%	WSPA	CBS
Greenville-Spartanburg-Asheville-Anderson	89%	WUNF	PBS
Greenville-Spartanburg-Asheville-Anderson	89%	WYFF	NBC
Chattanooga, TN	8%	WCLP	PBS
Chattanooga, TN	8%	WDEF	CBS
Chattanooga, TN	8%	WDSI	FOX
Chattanooga, TN	8%	WELF	Independent
Chattanooga, TN	8%	WFLI	WB
Chattanooga, TN	8%	WRCB	NBC
Chattanooga, TN	8%	WTCI	PBS
Chattanooga, TN	8%	WTVC	ABC
Atlanta	3%	WAGA	FOX
Atlanta	3%	WATC	Independent
Atlanta	3%	WATL	WB
Atlanta	3%	WCIQ	PBS
Atlanta	3%	WGTV	PBS
Atlanta	3%	WHSG	Independent
Atlanta	3%	WJSP	PBS
Atlanta	3%	WPBA	PBS
Atlanta	3%	WPXA	PAX
Atlanta	3%	WSB	ABC
Atlanta	3%	WTBS	TBN
Atlanta	3%	WUPA	UPN
Atlanta	3%	WXIA	NBC

Cable systems and subscribers

Andrews Cable Board   1,409
Cable TV   1,117
Carolina Country Cable   4,038
Charter   71,359
Cherokee Cablevision   1,364
Mediacom   8,326
Northland   4,607
Sylvan Valley CATV   8,621
Tele-Media   1,941

Businesses and other major employers

Memorial Mission Hospital Inc.; Asheville   4,300
RHA of North Carolina Operations; Asheville; mentally handicapped home   2,000
North Carolina Dept. of Health and Human Services; Black Mountain   1,700
Blue Ridge Paper Products Inc.; Canton; papeteries   1,400
Baxter Healthcare Corp.; Marion; pharmaceuticals   1,350
BASF Corp.; Enka; agricultural chemicals   1,200
Eastern Band of Cherokee Indians Inc.; Cherokee; gambling   1,200
General Electric Co.; Hendersonville; lighting fixtures   1,200
Western Carolina University Inc.; Cullowhee   1,200
Mastercraft Fabrics; Spindale; upholstery fabrics   1,100
Sonopress; Weaverville; prerecorded tapes   1,085
U.S. Veterans Hospital; Asheville   1,068
Henderson County Hospital Corp.; Hendersonville   1,006
Ahold U.S.A. Inc.; Hendersonville; grocery store   1,000
Community CarePartners Inc.; Asheville; rehabilitation services   1,000
RFS Ecusta Inc.; Pisgah Forest; paper mills   960
Wilsonart International Inc.; Fletcher; plastics laminating   900
City of Asheville; Asheville; city government   850
National Textiles; Forest City; knit jerseys   830
Moose International Inc.; Black Mountain; civic associations   810
Arteva Specialties SARL Ltd.; Shelby; cellulosic fibers   800
Coats American Inc.; Marion; thread mills   800
National Welders Supply Co.; Canton; welding machinery   800
ClientLogic Corp.; Asheville; telecommunications consultant   750
Steelcase Inc.; Fletcher; office furniture   750
Collins and Aikman Products Co.; Old Fort; automobile floor coverings   749
Grove Park Inn Resort Spa; Asheville; resort hotel   738
Watts Regulator Co.; Spindale; industrial pressure valves and regulators   700
Harris Regional Hospital; Sylva   688
Haywood Regional Medical Center; Clyde   675
Rutherford Hospital Inc.; Rutherfordton   672
Square D Co.; Asheville; electric control panels   651
Charles D. Owen Manufacturing Co.; Swannanoa; fabric mills   650
Continental Teves Inc.; Asheville; brake systems/parts   650
Watts Regulator Co.; Forest City; pressure valves and regulators   650
Asheville-Buncombe Technical Community College; Asheville   646
Fletcher Hospital Inc.; Fletcher   622
Cutler-Hammer Inc.; Arden; electric motor controls   600
Visiting Health Professionals Inc.; Asheville; home health care   600
Stanley Furniture Co.; Robbinsville   563
Borg-Warner Cooling Systems Corp.; Fletcher; electric control equipment   550
Galey and Lord Industries Inc.; Marion; woven goods   550
University of North Carolina; Asheville   530
M. B. Haynes Corp.; Asheville; electrical contractor   525
Cherokee Boys Club Inc.; Cherokee; community development   520
Drexel Heritage Furnishings Inc.; Marion; furniture   520
Borg Warner Turbo Systems; Arden; motor vehicle parts/accessories   500
Honeywell International Inc.; Mars Hill; electric power switches   500
J. Crew Inc.; Asheville; mail-order catalog   500
Kimberly-Clark Corp.; Hendersonville; fabrics   500
Regent Food Systems Inc.; Asheville; restaurant chain   500
Transylvania Community Hospital Inc.; Brevard   500
Wal-Mart Stores Inc.; Sylva; department stores   500

North Carolina 12th District

Central — parts of Charlotte, Winston-Salem, and Greensboro

The 12th became known as the mother of all racial gerrymanders when it was originally drawn for the 1992 elections. Struck down by the courts and widely ridiculed for a serpentine shape that aimed to maximize the black population, the 12th was redrawn twice in the 1990s. Redistricting following the 2000 census made only minimal changes to the district that finally survived challenge. The new 12th includes parts of six counties, is 44.6 percent African American and, among North Carolina districts, is rivaled only by the black-majority 1st in its overwhelming Democratic lean. *(See map p. 679.)*

While not as wildly contorted as its 1990s predecessors, the current 12th forms a zigzag shape that begins in Charlotte, parallels Interstate 85 north and east to take in part of Salisbury, then branches out to scoop up large black populations in Winston-Salem, High Point, and Greensboro. The 12th includes about one-third of Charlotte's population but two-thirds of its black population, and 60 percent of Winston-Salem's population but nearly 90 percent of its black residents. Most black constituents in the 12th are lower- to middle-class.

Charlotte, where nearly one-third of district residents live, has a booming economy. After a decade of consolidation among banks, the city surprised many by becoming the nation's biggest banking center outside of New York—the massive Bank of America is headquartered here. But the city's downtown—known as "uptown"—also has its share of poverty and crime. The Biddleville neighborhood, west of the business district, is a hub of the black community and home to the predominantly black Johnson C. Smith University. Outside of the city, transplants accustomed to New York City real estate prices have built upscale suburban neighborhoods with matching decorative street signs.

Major Industry

Finance, transportation, health care.

Notable

A Woolworth's lunch counter in Greensboro was the site of the first major civil rights sit-in in 1960.

Election Returns

	Republican		Democratic		Other	
President 2000	85,950	42.4%	115,445	56.9%	1,495	0.7%
House 2002	49,588	32.8%	98,821	65.3%	2,830	1.9%

District Profile

Population   619,178

Total area (square miles)   827.1
  Land area (square miles)   821.4

Population per square mile   753.8

Counties (2000 population)
  Cabarrus (pt.)   5,536
  Davidson (pt.)   73,076
  Forsyth (pt.)   130,689
  Guilford (pt.)   131,147
  Mecklenburg (pt.)   219,141
  Rowan (pt.)   59,589

Cities and other areas over 10,000 (2000 population)
  Charlotte (pt.)   196,125
  Greensboro (pt.)   62,075
  High Point (pt.)   52,429
  Lexington (pt.)   19,941
  Salisbury (pt.)   26,399
  Winston-Salem (pt.)   115,986

Race and Hispanic or Latino origin*
  White   44.6%
  Black or African American   44.6%
  American Indian or Alaska Native   0.4%
  Asian   2.1%
  Native Hawaiian or other Pacific Islander   0.0%
  Some other race   0.1%
  Hispanic or Latino origin   7.1%
  Two or more races   1.1%

*As percentage of total population.

Ancestry*

English	4.6%	Scotch-Irish	1.8%
German	6.5%	Scottish	1.1%
Irish	4.1%	Subsaharan	1.2%
Italian	1.2%	USA/American	8.0%

*As estimated percentage of total population.

Universities and colleges, 2000–2001 enrollment
  Bennett College, Greensboro   619
  Catawba College, Salisbury   1,342
  Davidson College, Davidson   1,679
  High Point University, High Point   2,788
  Johnson C. Smith University, Charlotte   1,576
  Livingstone College, Salisbury   1,018
  North Carolina Agricultural and Technical State
    University, Greensboro   7,748
  North Carolina School of the Arts, Winston-Salem   768
  Piedmont Baptist College, Winston-Salem   299
  Rowan-Cabarrus Community College, Salisbury   4,469
  Salem College, Winston-Salem   1,027
  Wake Forest University, Winston-Salem   6,173
  Winston-Salem State University, Winston-Salem
    2,857

Newspapers and circulation

	District circulation	Total circulation
Charlotte Observer	34,628	237,693
Greensboro News & Record	14,614	88,143
High Point Enterprise	12,100	29,095
Kannapolis Independent Tribune	3,850	20,324
Lexington Dispatch	1,815	12,469
Salisbury Post	10,238	23,473
*USA Today**	5,209	1,674,376
Winston-Salem Journal	20,428	85,775

*See Sources and Explanations in the front of the volume.

Television stations and affiliations

Charlotte	52%	WAXN	Independent
Charlotte	52%	WBTV	CBS
Charlotte	52%	WCCB	FOX
Charlotte	52%	WCNC	NBC
Charlotte	52%	WHKY	Independent
Charlotte	52%	WJZY	UPN
Charlotte	52%	WNSC	PBS
Charlotte	52%	WSOC	ABC
Charlotte	52%	WTVI	PBS
Charlotte	52%	WUNE	PBS
Charlotte	52%	WUNG	PBS
Greensboro-High Point-Winston-Salem	48%	WDRL	UPN
Greensboro-High Point-Winston-Salem	48%	WFMY	CBS
Greensboro-High Point-Winston-Salem	48%	WGHP	FOX
Greensboro-High Point-Winston-Salem	48%	WLXI	Independent
Greensboro-High Point-Winston-Salem	48%	WUNL	PBS
Greensboro-High Point-Winston-Salem	48%	WUPN	UPN
Greensboro-High Point-Winston-Salem	48%	WXII	NBC
Greensboro-High Point-Winston-Salem	48%	WXLV	ABC

Cable systems and subscribers
  Adelphia   7,361
  Time Warner   292,676

Military installations, September 2001
  Charlotte/Douglas International Airport (Air National
    Guard), Charlotte   1,233

Businesses and other major employers
  Jeffrey Brent Furniture; High Point; furniture stores
    41,995
  Wachovia Corp.; Charlotte; bank holding companies
    8,849
  Bank of America Corp.; Charlotte; commercial bank
    8,000

First Union National Bank; Charlotte; commercial bank
8,000

R. J. Reynolds Tobacco Co.; Winston-Salem; cigarettes
6,110

City of Charlotte; Charlotte; city council   5,000

International Business Machines Corp.; Charlotte; office
equipment   4,000

Kmart Corp.; High Point; warehousing   3,500

University of North Carolina; Charlotte   3,030

BellSouth Telecommunications Inc.; Charlotte;
telephone communication   3,000

Freightliner; Cleveland; truck and bus bodies   3,000

Sara Lee Corp.; Winston-Salem; hosiery, underwear
2,900

Schneider National Carriers Inc.; Charlotte; trucking
2,500

U.S. Airways Inc.; Charlotte   2,500

Duke Energy Corp.; Charlotte; electric services   2,000

Royal and SunAlliance USA Inc.; Charlotte; fire, marine,
casualty insurance   2,000

WilcoHess; Winston-Salem; convenience stores   2,000

Thomas Built Buses Inc.; High Point; bus bodies
1,999

Belk Inc.; Charlotte; department stores   1,978

Continental Tire North America Inc.; Charlotte; tires
and inner tubes   1,800

Lorillard Inc.; Greensboro; cigarettes   1,800

Wachovia Bank; Winston-Salem; commercial bank
1,800

High Point Regional Hospital; High Point   1,790

Solectron Technology Inc.; Charlotte; printed circuit
boards   1,700

Sprint Corp.; Charlotte; telephone communications
1,700

Show Pros Entertainment Services Inc.; Charlotte; labor
resource services   1,509

Forsyth Technical Community College; Winston-Salem
1,300

Integon Indemnity Corp.; Winston-Salem; fire, marine,
casualty insurance   1,300

U.S. Veterans Hospital; Salisbury   1,300

Wachovia Bank; Charlotte; financial services   1,200

Rowan Regional Medical Center Inc.; Salisbury   1,160

Forsyth County; Winston-Salem; county government
1,157

Knight Publishing Co.; Charlotte; newspaper   1,050

Arteva Specialities SARL Ltd.; Salisbury; sewing thread
1,000

City of Charlotte; Charlotte; city government   1,000

Mecklenburg County; Charlotte; correctional facilities
1,000

Microsoft Corp.; Charlotte; software design   1,000

Vanguard Group Inc.; Charlotte; mutual funds
investment   1,000

Branch Banking and Trust Co.; Winston-Salem; state
commercial banks   932

Diversco; Greensboro; office cleaning   900

City of Charlotte; Charlotte; police dept.   873

City of Charlotte; Charlotte; fire dept.   851

U.S. Postal Service; Greensboro   850

Cone Mills Corp.; Salisbury; fabrics   800

Davidson County; Lexington; county government   800

U.S. Postal Service; Charlotte   800

Sears Roebuck and Co. Inc.; Greensboro; automobile
loans   750

Ballard Medical Products Inc.; Winston-Salem;
gastroscopes   747

City of High Point; High Point; city government   733

AT&T Corp.; Charlotte; telephone communication   722

BE Aerospace Inc.; Winston-Salem; aircraft seats   700

Compass Group USA Inc.; Charlotte; restaurants   700

Pepsi-Cola Metropolitan Bottling Co.; Winston-Salem;
beverage services   700

Polo Ralph Lauren Corp.; Greensboro; men's/boys'
clothing   700

Syngenta Crop Protection Inc.; Greensboro;
agrochemicals   700

Tyco International Inc.; Winston-Salem; electrical
equipment   700

Winston-Salem State University; Winston-Salem   700

Cato Corp.; Charlotte; women's apparel   650

Douglas Battery Manufacturing Co. Inc.; Winston-
Salem; storage batteries   650

J. M. Huber Corp.; Charlotte; forest products   650

PricewaterhouseCoopers; Charlotte; accounting services
650

Davidson College; Davidson   644

AC Corp.; Greensboro; heating/air conditioning
contractor   600

APAC Customer Services Inc.; Greensboro;
telemarketing   600

City of Winston-Salem; Winston-Salem; police dept.
600

Consolidated Coin Caterers Corp.; Charlotte; vending
machines   600

Framatome Inc.; Charlotte; engineering services   600

Highland Mills Inc.; Charlotte; hosiery   600

Marriott International Inc.; Charlotte; administrative
management   600

Marsh Furniture Co.; High Point; kitchen cabinets
600

Sauder Woodworking Co.; High Point; furniture stores
600

Volvo Trucks North America Inc.; Greensboro; highway
truck tractor assembly   600

Womble Carlyle Sandridge and Rice; Winston-Salem;
law office   600

North Carolina Agricultural and Technical State
University; Greensboro   594

Duke Capital Corp.; Charlotte; public utility holding
companies   590

Burns International Security Services Corp.; Charlotte;
security guard service   574

Lexington Furniture Industries Inc.; Lexington   570

Stanley Furniture Co.; Lexington; bed frames   556

North Carolina Dept. of Health and Human Services;
Winston-Salem   550

RF Micro Devices Inc.; Greensboro; integrated
microcircuits   550

U.S. Postal Service; Winston-Salem   540

Accenture Inc.; Charlotte; business management
consultant   536

Banner Pharmacaps Inc.; High Point; pharmaceuticals
515

Republic Mortgage Insurance Co.; Winston-Salem;
mortgage guarantee insurance   505

Blythe Construction Inc.; Charlotte; highway/street construction   500

CCAir Inc.; Charlotte; air passenger carrier   500

Charlotte Mecklenburg Hospital Authority; Charlotte   500

Davidson Health Care Inc.; Lexington; drug and proprietary stores   500

Eastern Omni Constructors Inc.; High Point; antenna installation   500

Exult Inc.; Charlotte; business consulting   500

First Union Securities Inc.; Charlotte; stock brokers and dealers   500

Gillette Co.; Lexington; primary batteries   500

Metrolina Restaurant Group; Charlotte; fast food restaurants and stands   500

Microsoft Corp.; Charlotte; software   500

Old Dominion Freight Line Inc.; Greensboro; trucking   500

U.S. Airways Inc.; Winston-Salem   500

VF Jeanswear; Winston-Salem; women's clothing   500

North Carolina 13th District

North central — parts of Raleigh and Greensboro

The newly drawn 13th, awarded to growing North Carolina in the 2000 reapportionment, is defined by its urban anchors of Greensboro and Raleigh, which sandwich several rural counties along the Virginia border. Almost half the population lives in Wake County (Raleigh), including a large number of government employees and recent out-of-state transplants. *(See map p. 679.)*

The district encompasses northern and central Raleigh, an area that falls into the Research Triangle and is built around an economy of high technology, biotechnology, and financial services. The 13th takes in about 70 percent of Raleigh, which it shares with the 2nd and 4th Districts. The 13th's slice of the city includes most of downtown and the state Capitol.

While Raleigh and Greensboro have grown rapidly and feature diverse economies, the northern, rural areas of Caswell and Alamance Counties still rely heavily on manufacturing and farming, particularly textiles and tobacco.

The 13th has an overall Democratic lean, in part because of a sizable black population and a number of white moderates and liberals in the urban areas. Registered Democrats outnumber Republicans by nearly two-to-one, but the actual Democratic advantage at the polls is smaller. The potential for swing voting exists in both the cities and suburbs. District voters almost tied in the 2000 presidential election, giving George W. Bush a margin 647 votes, but voted more decisively for Democrat Michael F. Easley in the 2000 gubernatorial race.

Major Industry

Biotechnology, financial services, textiles, agriculture.

Notable

Caswell County features one of the largest Amish communities in the South.

Election Returns

	Republican		Democratic		Other	
President 2000	113,600	49.6%	112,953	49.3%	2,429	1.1%
House 2002	77,688	42.4%	100,287	54.7%	5,295	2.9%

District Profile

Population   619,178

Total area (square miles)   2,293.5
  Land area (square miles)   2,255.7

Population per square mile   274.5

Counties (2000 population)
  Alamance (pt.)   39,715
  Caswell   23,501
  Granville (pt.)   36,506
  Guilford (pt.)   111,952
  Person   35,623
  Rockingham (pt.)   80,816
  Wake (pt.)   291,065

Cities and other areas over 10,000 (2000 population)
  Burlington (pt.)   23,836
  Cary town (pt.)   11,058
  Eden   15,908
  Greensboro (pt.)   102,806
  Raleigh (pt.)   192,576
  Reidsville   14,485
  Wake Forest town   12,588

Race and Hispanic or Latino origin*
  White   63.3%
  Black or African American   26.9%
  American Indian or Alaska Native   0.3%
  Asian   2.0%
  Native Hawaiian or other Pacific Islander   0.0%
  Some other race   0.2%
  Hispanic or Latino origin   6.0%
  Two or more races   1.2%

As percentage of total population.

Ancestry*

English 8.7%	Polish 1.1%
French 1.4%	Scotch-Irish 2.4%
German 6.8%	Scottish 1.9%
Irish 6.0%	Subsaharan 1.4%
Italian 2.1%	USA/American 10.0%

As estimated percentage of total population.

Universities and colleges, 2000–2001 enrollment
  Alamance Community College, Graham   3,414
  Greensboro College, Greensboro   973
  Guilford College, Greensboro   1,246
  Meredith College, Raleigh   2,595
  Peace College, Raleigh   603
  Piedmont Community College, Roxboro   1,930
  Rockingham Community College, Wentworth   1,964
  Shaw University, Raleigh   2,527
  Southeastern Baptist Theological Seminary, Wake Forest   1,660
  St. Augustine's College, Raleigh   1,465
  University of North Carolina, Greensboro   13,125

Newspapers and circulation

	District circulation	Total circulation
Alamance News	1,172	5,645
Burlington Times-News	6,088	27,412
Danville Register & Bee	1,537	21,896
Durham Herald-Sun	6,378	51,061
Greensboro News & Record	23,697	88,143
Raleigh News & Observer	41,305	164,952
USA Today*	4,297	1,674,376

*See Sources and Explanations in the front of the volume.

Television stations and affiliations

Raleigh-Durham (Fayetteville)	54%	WGPX	PAX
Raleigh-Durham (Fayetteville)	54%	WKFT	Independent
Raleigh-Durham (Fayetteville)	54%	WLFL	WB
Raleigh-Durham (Fayetteville)	54%	WNCN	NBC
Raleigh-Durham (Fayetteville)	54%	WRAL	CBS
Raleigh-Durham (Fayetteville)	54%	WRAY	Independent
Raleigh-Durham (Fayetteville)	54%	WRAZ	FOX
Raleigh-Durham (Fayetteville)	54%	WRDC	UPN
Raleigh-Durham (Fayetteville)	54%	WRPX	PAX
Raleigh-Durham (Fayetteville)	54%	WTVD	ABC
Raleigh-Durham (Fayetteville)	54%	WUNC	PBS
Raleigh-Durham (Fayetteville)	54%	WUNP	PBS
Greensboro-High Point-Winston-Salem	46%	WDRL	UPN
Greensboro-High Point-Winston-Salem	46%	WFMY	CBS
Greensboro-High Point-Winston-Salem	46%	WGHP	FOX
Greensboro-High Point-Winston-Salem	46%	WLXI	Independent
Greensboro-High Point-Winston-Salem	46%	WUNL	PBS
Greensboro-High Point-Winston-Salem	46%	WUPN	UPN
Greensboro-High Point-Winston-Salem	46%	WXII	NBC
Greensboro-High Point-Winston-Salem	46%	WXLV	ABC

Cable systems and subscribers

Charter 7,353
Time Warner 174,100

Businesses and other major employers

WakeMed Hospital; Raleigh 5,000
University of North Carolina at Greensboro; Greensboro 4,000
Rex Hospital Inc.; Raleigh 3,800
North Carolina Executive Office; Raleigh 3,200
North Carolina Dept. of Transportation; Raleigh 2,200
Guilford County; Greensboro; government 2,116
Guilford Technical Community College; Greensboro 2,000
Murdoch Center; Butner; child health care 1,700
Guilford Mills Inc.; Greensboro; cloth 1,600
Jefferson-Pilot Life Insurance Co.; Greensboro; life insurance 1,500
North Carolina Dept. of Health and Human Services; Butner 1,500
Cone Mills Corp.; Greensboro; denims 1,455
Alcatel NA Network Systems Inc.; Raleigh; telephones and telephone apparatus 1,400
North Carolina Division of Highways; Raleigh 1,400
North Carolina Dept. of Health and Human Services; Raleigh 1,329
American Airlines Inc.; Cary 1,200
Square D Co.; Knightdale; switchgear and switchboard apparatus 1,200
Burlington Industries Inc.; Greensboro; fabrics 1,100
SRI/Surgical Express Inc.; Burlington; linen supply 1,089

Collins and Aikman Products Co.; Roxboro; weaving mill 1,066
U.S. Bureau of Prisons; Butner 1,000
VF Jeanswear; Greensboro; men's/boys' apparel 1,000
North Carolina Dept. of Environment and Natural Resources; Raleigh 968
Bank of America Corp.; Greensboro; commercial bank 900
Crown Crafts Inc.; Timberlake; comforters and quilts 900
Health Works; Eden; health services consultant 850
Raleigh HCA Community Hospital Inc.; Raleigh 845
Newton Instrument Co.; Butner; telephone apparatus 800
North Carolina Employment Security Commission; Raleigh 800
U.S. Internal Revenue Service; Greensboro 800
United Guaranty Insurance Co.; Greensboro; surety insurance 800
Greensboro News and Record Inc.; Greensboro; newspaper 754
Miller Brewing Co.; Eden; beer 750
Moses H. Cone Health System Inc.; Greensboro 750
North Carolina Dept. of Admin.; Raleigh 740
General Electric Capital Corp.; Raleigh; mortgage guarantee insurance 700
GlaxoSmithKline; Zebulon; pharmaceuticals 700
Gregory Poole Equipment Co.; Raleigh; motor vehicle parts/accessories 700
News and Observer Publishing Co.; Raleigh; newspaper 700
North Carolina Dept. of Revenue; Raleigh 700
Owens Corning Metal Systems Inc.; Raleigh; metal siding 700
Precision Walls Inc.; Raleigh; drywall 700
Rockingham County; Wentworth; county government 700
Siemens Energy and Automation Inc.; Wendell; circuit breakers 700
Morehead Memorial Hospital Inc.; Eden 660
Fieldcrest Cannon Inc.; Eden; home furnishings 650
Central Telephone Company of Virginia; Wake Forest; local telephone communications 625
U.S. Postal Service; Greensboro 625
Asplundh Tree Expert Co.; Raleigh; planting, pruning, trimming services 600
Belk Inc.; Raleigh; department stores 600
Business Telecom Inc.; Raleigh; long-distance telephone 600
Crown Automotive Co.; Greensboro; car dealers 600
Emergency Services; Reidsville; government 600
Liberty Embroidery Inc.; Madison; embroidery products 600
North Carolina Correction Dept.; Raleigh 600
Powerware Corp.; Raleigh; AC/DC power conversion units 600
United Telephone-Southeast Inc.; Wake Forest; long-distance telephone 600
Culp Inc.; Graham; fabrics 550
International Business Machines Corp.; Raleigh; office equipment 550

North Carolina Dept. of Justice; Raleigh   550
UNIFI Inc.; Reidsville; fabric finishing   550
Burns International Security Services Corp.; Raleigh;
   security guard service   508
Aladdin Manufacturing Corp.; Eden; carpets   500
Burlington Industries Inc.; Reidsville; draperies
   500
City of Greensboro; Greensboro; city government
   500
GKN Automotive Inc.; Timberlake; engine electrical
   equipment   500
Guardsmark Inc.; Raleigh; security guard service   500
Guilford Mills Inc.; Greensboro; fabric mills   500
Laboratory Corp. of America; Burlington; testing labs
   500

Moses H. Cone Memorial Hospital Operating Corp.;
   Reidsville   500
North Carolina Dept. of Cultural Resources; Raleigh
   500
North Carolina Dept. of Labor; Raleigh   500
North Carolina Farm Bureau Mutual Insurance Co.;
   Raleigh   500
Procter and Gamble Co.; Browns Summit; hair
   preparations   500
Sears Roebuck and Co. Inc.; Greensboro; department
   stores   500
Siemens Power Transmission and Distribution Inc.;
   Raleigh; electric power switches   500
Textilease; Providence; clothing rental services   500
Wake County Public Health Center; Raleigh   500

North Dakota

North Dakota includes fertile eastern Red River farm-lands, wheat-covered plains, arid grasslands farther west, and Teddy Roosevelt's beloved ranches near the western border. The state's agriculture-based economy was shaken in the 1990s by floods, blizzards, foreign competition, and the reduction of federal support systems. Agricultural income dropped drastically in the wake of devastating Red River floods and steep declines in the price of wheat. Economic trends intensified a migration of the state's young people away from rural farming communities and into the cities, where a diversified economy and several universities provide greater job choice.

It has recently been suggested, perhaps only half in jest, that North Dakota would fare better in the twenty-first century if it changed its name—or at least dropped the first half. The idea was that prospective residents and investors were put off by the chill and remote connotations of the word "north." Wags observed that anyone discouraged by such a connotation might well be discouraged by North Dakota itself—a High Plains plateau on the Canadian border, precisely at the center of the North American continent and a day's drive from an American city of any size. The name change idea was taken no more seriously than periodic proposals to merge the two Dakotas and pool their resources. But keeping the state from depopulating remains a challenge. In the 1990s North Dakota increased by just 3,400 souls—roughly one half of one percent—the closest to zero growth in the fifty states.

The great exception to the growth doldrums was Fargo, the state's largest community, in the Red River Valley on the Minnesota line. Fargo had a hot decade and saw its population rise by more than 20 percent to 90,000. One big reason was the opening of telecommunications centers, pushed by Gov. Ed Schaefer, where operators process telephone transactions from all over the world. Also growing, if not so quickly, were Bismarck, the state capital, Minot, and Mandan. The refreshing trend in these communities has led the Census Bureau to project that North Dakota will grow, if slowly, over the first quarter of the twenty-first century. But many other towns got smaller in the 1990s, including Grand Forks (devastated by flooding during the decade) and Minot Air Force Base (always in danger of closure).

The people drain is most serious outside the towns, in the vast spaces between where the wheat fields rush away to the horizons in all directions and the roads stretch unbending for miles. Only Alaska, Montana, and Wyoming have less density of population. The state's most notable geographic demarcation is the Missouri River, which wanders into the

state's northwest corner near Williston and meanders to the east and south before exiting near the midpoint of the South Dakota line. This parabola defines the southwestern quarter of the state, with 14 counties (some with population less than 1,000) and one town (Dickinson, population 16,000 in 1990 and again in 2000). Here the old prairie has less often been plowed for wheat or beans and more often given to grazing land, much similar to the counties west of the same river in South Dakota.

Demographically, North Dakotans still show the stamp of the northern European immigrants who came here in the decades after statehood in 1889. Only 1 percent of the current residents are Hispanic, even fewer are African American or Asian. Easily the largest minority are the Native Americans (3.8 percent), including many descended from the local Plains tribes such as the Sioux and Ojibwa. Three-fourths of the current residents were born in the state. North Dakota has little unemployment (4 percent in 2001, lower than all but three states). But the average annual pay was low too, forty-eighth among the states at $25,707 in 2001. The 12.4 percent poverty rate was among the 20 highest. To some degree, these figures reflected the low pay in phone service and data processing jobs and the poverty on Native American reservations in the state.

Republicans are more numerous and unwavering in the western part of the state, while eastern communities and Native American reservations are more supportive of Democrats. Overall, the state has historically been among the staunchest supporters of Republican presidential candidates. North Dakotans split their electoral votes three ways in their first presidential vote (1892) and have since voted consistently for GOP nominees, often giving them more than 60 percent of the vote. The only exceptions: Woodrow Wilson twice, Franklin D. Roosevelt twice, and Lyndon B. Johnson once. North Dakota's Republicans consistently outregister (as well as outvote) the Democrats. George W. Bush handily carried the state in 2000.

But if the residents here are conservatives on most issues, they do believe in the role of government to regulate the economy, particularly as it affects farm products and trade. They are also political pragmatists who care more about results than ideology. So state elections tend to be dominated by Republicans who will go to Bismarck, do their business, and go home. The state legislators are two-to-one Republican and are paid $3,000 a year plus $111 for each day the legislature is in session. The governor has also been a Republican since 1992. But before that, Democrats had a stunning run in the office, thanks to George Sinner, Arthur Link, and

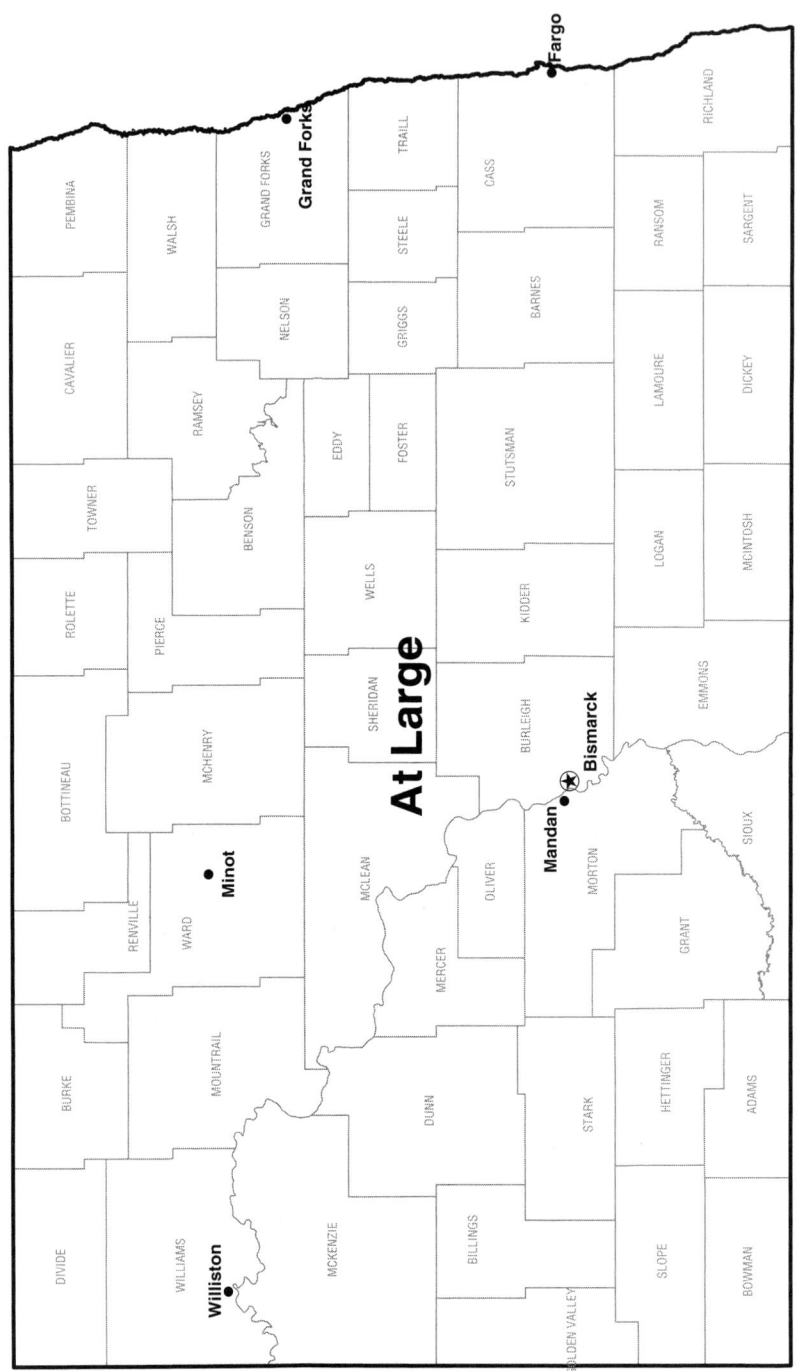

William L. Guy. These three Democrats had the gubernatorial nomination every time from 1960 through 1988 and won every election but one (1980).

But when it comes to sending North Dakotans to Washington, the electorate prefers dogged negotiators who will go to great lengths on their behalf, regardless of party. This applies to both chambers of Congress. The House delegation has dwindled from three seats to one (since 1970), and Democrats have represented North Dakota in the House since 1981. The state's congressional delegation has been entirely Democratic since 1987. As of 2003, its two Democratic senators were Kent Conrad (first elected in 1986) and Byron Dorgan (first elected in 1992). Before their rise, the only Democrat to win a Senate race here after World War II was Quentin Burdick, who was elected six times beginning in 1960 and died in office in 1992.

Major Industry

Agriculture, health care, higher education.

Notable

Lewis and Clark met Sacagawea, the Shoshone Native American woman who guided them to the Pacific Ocean, near the Mandan Indian village; Sitting Bull surrendered at Fort Buford in 1881; Gen. George Custer was stationed at Fort Lincoln, near Bismarck, in 1876 when his unit headed west to ultimate defeat at Little Big Horn; the National Buffalo Museum is in Jamestown; the downbeat movie *Fargo* was mostly filmed in Minnesota.

Table 1 Population

District	Population	Population under 18	Voting-age population	Median age	Male*	Female*
At Large	642,200	160,849	481,351	36.2	49.9	50.1

*As percentage of total population.

Table 2 Voting-Age Persons by Race/Hispanic or Latino Origin

District	White*	Black or African American*	American Indian or Alaska Native*	Asian*	Other or multirace*	Hispanic or Latino*
At Large	93.5	0.5	3.8	0.6	0.7	1.0

*As percentage of voting-age population.

Table 3 Voting-Age Population by Age Groups

District	18 to 24*	25 to 44*	45 to 64*	Over 64*
At Large	15.2	36.3	28.9	19.6

*As percentage of voting-age population.

Table 4 Income and Occupation

District	Median family income	Families in poverty*	White collar†	Blue collar†	Service†	Farm†
At Large	$43,654	8.3	59.4	22.2	16.7	1.7

*As percentage of all families. †As percentage of employed workers 16 years and over.

Table 5 Education: School Years Completed

District	Less than grade 9*	Grades 9–12 no diploma*	High school diploma no college*	Some college*	College bachelor's degree or higher*
At Large	8.7	7.4	27.9	34.0	22.0

*As percentage of persons age 25 and over.

Table 6 Housing and Residential Patterns

District	Median home value	Owner occupied*	Renter occupied*	Urban†	Rural†
At Large	$68,300	66.6	33.4	55.8	44.2

*As percentage of occupied housing units. †As percentage of total population.

Election Returns

	Republican		Democratic		Other	
President 2000	174,852	60.7%	95,284	33.1%	18,120	6.3%
House 2002	109,957	47.6%	121,073	52.4%		

District Profile

Population 642,200

Total area (square miles) 70,699.7
Land area (square miles) 68,975.9

Population per square mile 9.3

Counties (2000 population)

Adams	2,593	McLean	9,311
Barnes	11,775	Mercer	8,644
Benson	6,964	Morton	25,303
Billings	888	Mountrail	6,631
Bottineau	7,149	Nelson	3,715
Bowman	3,242	Oliver	2,065
Burke	2,242	Pembina	8,585
Burleigh	69,416	Pierce	4,675
Cass	123,138	Ramsey	12,066
Cavalier	4,831	Ransom	5,890
Dickey	5,757	Renville	2,610
Divide	2,283	Richland	17,998
Dunn	3,600	Rolette	13,674
Eddy	2,757	Sargent	4,366
Emmons	4,331	Sheridan	1,710
Foster	3,759	Sioux	4,044
Golden Valley	1,924	Slope	767
Grand Forks	66,109	Stark	22,636
Grant	2,841	Steele	2,258
Griggs	2,754	Stutsman	21,908
Hettinger	2,715	Towner	2,876
Kidder	2,753	Traill	8,477
LaMoure	4,701	Walsh	12,389
Logan	2,308	Ward	58,795
McHenry	5,987	Wells	5,102
McIntosh	3,390	Williams	19,761
McKenzie	5,737		

Cities and other areas over 10,000 (2000 population)

Bismarck	55,532	Mandan	16,718
Dickinson	16,010	Minot	36,567
Fargo	90,599	West Fargo	14,940
Grand Forks	49,321	Williston	12,512
Jamestown	15,527		

Race and Hispanic or Latino origin*

White 91.7%
Black or African American 0.6%
American Indian or Alaska Native 4.8%
Asian 0.6%
Native Hawaiian or other Pacific Islander 0.0%
Some other race 0.0%
Hispanic or Latino origin 1.2%
Two or more races 1.0%

*As percentage of total population.

Ancestry*

English	3.4%	Polish	1.9%
French	2.7%	Russian	2.4%
German	30.6%	Swedish	3.5%
Irish	5.4%	USA/American	1.7%
Norwegian	20.9%		

*As estimated percentage of total population.

Universities and colleges, 2000–2001 enrollment

Bismarck State College, Bismarck 2,744
Dickinson State University, Dickinson 2,012
Jamestown College, Jamestown 1,161
Mayville State University, Mayville 776
Minot State University, Bottineau 450
Minot State University, Minot 3,081
North Dakota State College of Science, Wahpeton 2,425
North Dakota State University, Fargo 9,902
Trinity Bible College, Ellendale 332
Turtle Mountain Community College, Belcourt 686
United Tribes Technical College, Bismarck 204
University of Mary, Bismarck 2,343
University of North Dakota, Grand Forks 11,031
University of North Dakota, Williston 517
University of North Dakota-Lake Region, Devils Lake 1,219
Valley City State University, Valley City 1,090

Newspapers and circulation

	District circulation	Total circulation
Bismarck Tribune	22,156	26,157
Fargo Forum	32,750	49,865
Grand Forks Herald	20,254	33,151
Minot Daily News	21,651	21,844
*USA Today**	1,591	1,674,376

*See Sources and Explanations in the front of the volume.

Television stations and affiliations

Minot-Bismarck-Dickinson	65%	KBME	PBS
Minot-Bismarck-Dickinson	65%	KBMY	ABC
Minot-Bismarck-Dickinson	65%	KDSE	PBS
Minot-Bismarck-Dickinson	65%	KFYR	NBC
Minot-Bismarck-Dickinson	65%	KMOT	NBC
Minot-Bismarck-Dickinson	65%	KQCD	NBC
Minot-Bismarck-Dickinson	65%	KSRE	PBS
Minot-Bismarck-Dickinson	65%	KUMV	NBC
Minot-Bismarck-Dickinson	65%	KWSE	PBS
Minot-Bismarck-Dickinson	65%	KXMA	CBS
Minot-Bismarck-Dickinson	65%	KXMB	CBS
Minot-Bismarck-Dickinson	65%	KXMC	CBS
Minot-Bismarck-Dickinson	65%	KXMD	CBS
Fargo-Valley City	35%	KBRR	FOX
Fargo-Valley City	35%	KFME	PBS
Fargo-Valley City	35%	KGFE	PBS
Fargo-Valley City	35%	KJRE	PBS
Fargo-Valley City	35%	KJRR	FOX
Fargo-Valley City	35%	KNRR	FOX
Fargo-Valley City	35%	KVLY	NBC
Fargo-Valley City	35%	KVRR	FOX
Fargo-Valley City	35%	KXJB	CBS
Fargo-Valley City	35%	WDAY	ABC
Fargo-Valley City	35%	WDAZ	ABC

Cable systems and subscribers

Cable ONE 25,469
Cable Services Inc. 9,989
Consolidated Cable 4,909
Dickey Rural Cable 905
Midcontinent Cable 94,240
Polar Cablevision 2,412
Reservation Telephone Co-op 863
Souris River Telephone Co-op 991

Military installations, September 2001

Minot Air Force Base, Minot 5,251
Grand Forks Air Force Base, Emerado 3,050
Hector International Airport, Fargo 1,026
Bismarck (RJB Complex), Bismarck 791
Camp Grafton Military Training Area, Devils Lake 259
Minot Armed Forces Reserve Center, Minot 244
Bismarck AASF Armory (Army Guard), Bismarck 176

Businesses and other major employers

University of North Dakota; Grand Forks 5,153
Meritcare Hospital; Fargo 3,500
Altru Health System; Grand; hospital 3,057
North Dakota State University; Fargo 3,000
North Dakota Executive Office; Bismarck 1,900
St. Alexius Medical Center; Bismarck 1,800
Clark Equipment Co.; Gwinner; compaction equipment 1,200
MedCenter One; Bismarck 1,145
Ecolab Inc.; Grand Forks; exterminating/fumigating 1,000
North Dakota Dept. of Human Services; Grafton 874
Ingersoll-Rand Co.; Bismarck; machinery 850
Ingersoll-Rand Co.; Gwinner; machinery 800
Microsoft Corp.; Fargo; software 800
Sykes Enterprises Inc.; Bismarck; computer programming 800
Z Tel Teleservices; Minot; telemarketing 800
Noridian Mutual Insurance Co.; Fargo; group hospitalization 755
Minot State University; Minot 750
U.S. Veterans Hospital; Fargo 700
City of Fargo; Fargo; city government 700
Dakota Clinic; Fargo 700

OHIO

Districts established January 24, 2002, for elections first held in 2002.

18 members

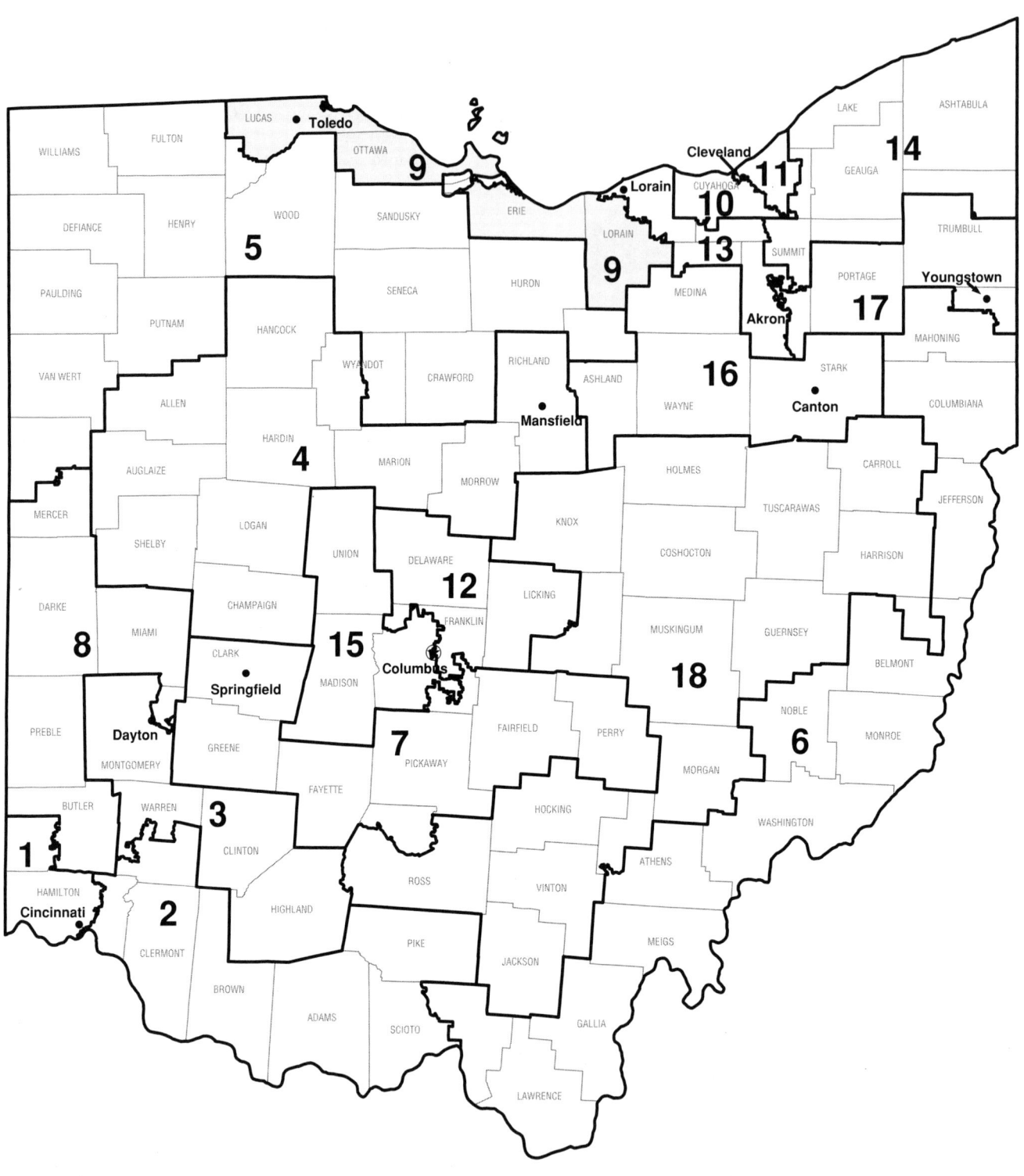

Ohio

In May 2003 the Cleveland Cavaliers learned they would have the first pick in the next National Basketball Association draft, ensuring them of the chance to add LeBron James to their roster. Although still in high school, James was already so celebrated that he had signed a $91-million endorsement contract with Nike sportswear. The fact that he hailed from Akron, just a few miles down the freeway, was almost incidental. James was the hottest thing to hit the sport in years, and Cleveland had him.

Why this story matters beyond the sports page is because the city of Cleveland, as with many of its urban cohorts around the Great Lakes, has long been striving to add more glamour and excitement to its image. This campaign has inspired a new lakefront baseball park (Jacobs Field, known as "The Jake") and football stadium, along with an internationally famous Museum of Rock and Roll and other more classical cultural offerings.

All these are bids not only for tourists' attention but for recognition and respect. Cleveland was once the fifth largest city in the country and second only to New York as a headquarters for major corporations (including that of John D. Rockefeller's Standard Oil). Ohio was the fourth most populous state through most of the nation's history. So it is painful to see this proud city fall below 500,000 in population, down to thirty-third in the nation and a distant second even within Ohio (white-collar Columbus is booming with high-tech industry and has grown half again as big as Cleveland). With another decade like the 1990s, Cleveland proper will be smaller than Albuquerque. While the rest of the state has not suffered the drop that Cleveland has, one cannot miss the degree of its continuing eclipse. The Census Bureau projects that Ohio will add about the same number to its population between 2000 and 2025 as the state of Idaho. That would be good growth, for Idaho. But for Ohio, it would be less than 5 percent for the quarter century. Some 47 other states are projected to grow faster.

Dressing up the state's media appeal is not a new challenge, of course. Even in the years of plenty, when the Great Lakes region led the nation's surge to the forefront of the industrial world, the states that were churning out all that smoke and product seemed as gray and sooty as their factories. Then came a change, and not for the better. The smoking factories of one era became the idled factories of another— victims of age, pollution, and a lack of reinvestment in the Rust Belt. The notion gained currency, both here and abroad, that other countries did manufacturing better.

In strictly economic terms, Ohio has been a righted ship for some years. It remains seventh nationally in personal income and tenth in the presence of Fortune 500 and Forbes 500 corporations. It was third in value-added by manufacturing in 2000, and second in payroll from manufacturing. While Cleveland proper has shrunk, its metro area (which includes Akron and other shoreline communities) is approaching 3 million and is still the nation's fifteenth largest. As a state, Ohio's unemployment and poverty figures are below the national average. Long-term improvements in the environment and transportation system have long since erased the old 1970s insult "the Mistake by the Lake." Much of the credit for the turnaround at both the city and state level has gone to former mayor and governor George Voinovich, who in 1998 moved on to the U.S. Senate. At this point, the greater problem seems to be getting credit for the turnaround in the markets of public opinion.

Politically, Ohio still shows some signs of its origins in the late 1700s. Early settlers included Yankees coming west from New England and southerners coming north from what had been the westernmost reaches of colonial Virginia. To this day, the cultural roots and speaking styles of southern Ohio are closer to those of Kentucky than to the shores of Lake Erie. In the first half of the 1800s, these two halves struck a rough balance, but after the Civil War the metal-bending progress was concentrated in the north. Apart from Cincinnati on the Ohio River and Columbus, the midstate capital where the state university was built, the southern counties were obliged to supply farm goods, coal, and other raw materials.

In the generations that followed there were boatloads of immigrants followed by trains and buses filled with African Americans coming north seeking work in Ohio's industries. The descendants of these workers are the base of urban and suburban Ohio today, especially in the north. Cleveland has long been known for its ethnic politicians, including former mayors Voinovich and Dennis Kucinich, a representative and presidential candidate in 2003. But today Ohio is less a magnet to immigrants. One big reason for this: the lack of appeal to Hispanics. The state's population is less than 2 percent Hispanic, ranking forty-first among the states. That compares to African Americans' 12 percent share of the state population, which ranks about average for the nation. Blacks have a larger share of the population in four congressional districts dominated by Cleveland (majority black), Cincinnati (about one-third black), Columbus (about one-quarter black), and Dayton (about one-fifth black).

The slow growth in Ohio has spelled problems primarily for Democrats because the remaining Ohio voter tends to live in a suburb, in a smaller city or town, or in the country. All these venues have been historically Republican in Ohio.

Complicating this trend for Democrats is the increase in Republican voting among social conservatives, including traditional Catholics in the blue-collar precincts of the big metro areas and white evangelical Protestants in the rural counties of southern Ohio. Both these constituencies have historical Democratic patterns, but both were disaffected in large measure by the social liberalism of President Bill Clinton. Clinton himself actually carried the state twice with a plurality, but his years in office brought problems for Democrats here as elsewhere.

As recently as 1994, Ohio Democrats had both Senate seats and ten of 19 House seats. A decade later they were shut out in the Senate, down to seven seats in the House, held no statewide offices, and were in the minority in both chambers of the state legislature. Equally discouraging were the numbers on party identification. Although Ohio does not register voters by party, a Gallup Poll in 2003 found 49 percent of those interviewed considered themselves Republicans or leaned toward the GOP. In 1993 that total had been below 40 percent. Democratic identification had dropped correspondingly from just under 50 percent to barely over 40 percent.

In presidential terms, Ohio has long vied with Virginia and New York as the prime nursery for presidential timber (although it must be said that all three states have been shut out since the 1940s). Ohio had a strong Republican Party almost as soon as the GOP began. In the national expansion years between the Civil War and the Depression of the 1930s, Ohio provided six Republican presidents (yet a seventh, Ulysses S. Grant, was born in Ohio but grew up in Illinois). Over the same period, three Ohio Republicans became chief justice of the United States. No state has lent more leaders to either party, although the GOP nominated Ohioans in part because Ohio was one of the few big states that either party could win. The last in Ohio's White House parade was Warren G. Harding, who died in office in 1923. Since then, the state has gone with the electoral college winner every time with two exceptions: choosing Republicans Thomas Dewey in 1944 (but not in 1948) and Richard Nixon in 1960.

Statewide voting for governor and senator has been equally subject to partisan tides. Counting back to the Civil War finds the GOP electing more governors and more senators by a ratio of about three-to-two for each office. But counting the years served by governors and senators of each party since World War II, the ratio is closer to even. Among governors the most memorable may have been James A. Rhodes, a Republican who served from 1963 to 1971, gave way to a Democrat for a term, then returned to serve again from 1975 to 1983. Recognizing Rhodes's 16 years in office, the state recently named its new office building on the Capitol Square for him, and the towering black monolith is known as the "Colossus of Rhodes."

Remarkable among recent senators are Democrats John Glenn, the astronaut who served four terms beginning in 1974, and Howard Metzenbaum, the Cleveland parking mogul who served from 1976 through 1994. The Senate still feels the impact of Republican Robert A. Taft, the revered Senate majority leader in the early 1950s who had lived in the White House during the term of his father, William Howard Taft.

But on the other side of the Capitol, in the House, the state has been feeling the debilitating effects of its slowing population growth. In its early decades Ohio grew fast and was the fourth largest state by 1830. Its presence in Congress peaked at 24 seats exactly 100 years later, when it was still the fourth largest state, and then again in 1960 (when it was tied for fourth with Illinois for the fourth largest House delegation). Since then, the state has lost one or two seats in each decennial reapportionment, reducing the 24 seats to 18.

In 2001 Ohio faced losing one seat when it dropped to 18 total (although the state was grateful to be losing just one this time). Republicans were in complete control of the state legislature and had their governor in Bob Taft (son and grandson of senators, great-grandson of the president). It was obvious that the lost seat would be charged to the Democrats (already the minority with just eight seats), but it also seemed possible that the overall squeeze might cost the Democrats a second seat as well.

In the end, two events eased the redistricting task. First, Rep. Tony Hall, a 12-term Democrat from Dayton, retired from the House to become director of the Bush administration's food programs. Hall's old 3rd District was redrawn to incorporate half of Warren County and all of Clinton and Highland Counties to the southwest. It was then won by Republican Mike Turner, a former two-term mayor of Dayton.

The other development that eased the redistricting process was the trial and conviction of Democratic representative James A. Traficant Jr. on charges of bribery, racketeering, and conspiracy. A former sheriff from Youngstown who had survived nine terms while holding various federal investigations at bay, Traficant refused to resign and was expelled from the House by a near unanimous vote. His heavily Democratic district in the Mahoning Valley was pieced out among neighboring districts, including the Akron-based 14th District of eight-term veteran Tom Sawyer. In the subsequent Democratic primary, Sawyer lost to Timothy J. Ryan, a 29-year-old former House aide making his first bid for office.

In November, the eleven Republican incumbents all won reelection in adjusted versions of their previous districts. The same was true of the six incumbent Democrats still on the ballot (including Stephanie Tubbs Jones of Cleveland, the only black member of the delegation). Ryan also won in November in the new 17th District, keeping the Democrats at seven seats and holding their losses to one.

Table 1 Population

District	Population	Population under 18	Voting-age population	Median age	Male*	Female*
1	630,730	166,300	464,430	34.6	47.8	52.2
2	630,730	165,428	465,302	36.1	48.5	51.5
3	630,730	157,653	473,077	36.5	48.4	51.6
4	630,730	163,443	467,287	36.5	49.8	50.2
5	630,730	166,180	464,550	35.9	49.0	51.0
6	630,730	144,811	485,919	38.5	48.7	51.3
7	630,730	160,214	470,516	35.8	49.7	50.3
8	630,730	165,575	465,155	35.1	48.9	51.1
9	630,730	161,941	468,789	36.2	48.3	51.7
10	630,730	147,814	482,916	37.8	48.0	52.0
11	630,730	165,569	465,161	36.0	46.2	53.8
12	630,730	171,797	458,933	34.1	48.1	51.9
13	630,730	162,797	467,933	37.3	48.4	51.6
14	630,730	163,836	466,894	38.4	48.8	51.2
15	630,730	147,774	482,956	32.4	49.5	50.5
16	630,730	162,352	468,378	37.4	48.5	51.5

District	Population	Population under 18	Voting-age population	Median age	Male*	Female*
17	630,730	150,706	480,024	37.0	48.4	51.6
18	630,730	164,149	466,581	36.7	49.0	51.0
State	11,353,140	2,888,339	8,464,801	36.2	48.6	51.4

*As percentage of total population.

Table 2   Voting-Age Persons by Race/Hispanic or Latino Origin

District	White*	Black or African American*	American Indian or Alaska Native*	Asian*	Other or multirace*	Hispanic or Latino*
1	71.7	24.7	0.2	1.4	1.0	1.0
2	92.2	4.6	0.2	1.3	0.7	0.9
3	81.3	15.6	0.2	1.1	0.9	1.0
4	92.5	5.0	0.2	0.6	0.7	1.0
5	94.8	1.0	0.2	0.4	0.5	3.1
6	95.5	2.4	0.2	0.5	0.6	0.7
7	89.4	7.3	0.3	1.0	1.0	1.0
8	92.7	4.0	0.2	1.2	0.7	1.1
9	82.5	12.1	0.2	1.1	1.1	3.1
10	89.4	3.5	0.2	1.7	1.2	4.0
11	43.2	51.6	0.2	1.8	1.3	2.0
12	74.7	19.9	0.2	2.2	1.4	1.5
13	83.9	11.0	0.2	1.1	0.9	2.9
14	94.8	2.3	0.1	1.1	0.5	1.1
15	86.2	6.8	0.2	3.4	1.3	2.1
16	93.5	4.2	0.2	0.6	0.7	0.7
17	86.5	10.3	0.2	0.7	0.8	1.4
18	96.3	1.9	0.2	0.3	0.7	0.5
State	85.7	10.4	0.2	1.2	1.0	1.6

*As percentage of voting-age population.

Table 3   Voting-Age Population by Age Groups

District	18 to 24*	25 to 44*	45 to 64*	Over 64*
1	14.2	39.8	28.3	17.7
2	10.6	42.0	30.8	16.6
3	12.3	39.0	30.6	18.1
4	12.2	38.5	31.1	18.3
5	13.8	37.7	30.7	17.8
6	13.3	35.1	31.6	20.0
7	13.3	39.4	31.2	16.0
8	14.0	39.7	30.3	16.0
9	12.7	38.3	30.6	18.3
10	10.0	40.0	28.9	21.1
11	11.8	38.6	28.6	20.9
12	12.6	43.7	30.3	13.4
13	10.3	39.6	31.8	18.2
14	9.3	38.7	33.9	18.0
15	17.0	44.5	25.5	13.0
16	11.5	37.8	31.9	18.8
17	13.6	36.9	30.1	19.4
18	12.1	37.9	31.4	18.6
State	12.5	39.3	30.4	17.8

*As percentage of voting-age population.

Table 4   Income and Occupation

District	Median family income	Families in poverty*	White collar†	Blue collar†	Service†	Farm†
1	$49,197	10.5	60.5	23.1	16.3	0.1
2	$56,695	6.3	63.7	23.2	12.8	0.3
3	$51,589	7.4	59.7	26.0	14.1	0.2
4	$47,106	7.1	47.1	37.5	14.9	0.6
5	$49,425	5.2	46.0	39.8	13.5	0.7
6	$40,511	10.2	51.7	31.3	16.4	0.6
7	$50,975	6.4	57.1	28.1	14.4	0.4
8	$51,726	6.0	56.0	29.9	13.6	0.4
9	$50,131	8.9	54.9	29.2	15.6	0.3
10	$51,808	6.7	62.5	23.3	14.0	0.1
11	$40,406	16.0	61.4	21.3	17.3	0.1
12	$58,305	7.8	68.4	18.0	13.4	0.2
13	$53,761	7.2	59.2	26.3	14.2	0.2
14	$60,292	4.0	62.0	25.1	12.5	0.4
15	$55,273	6.7	66.3	19.8	13.7	0.1
16	$50,000	6.1	54.7	30.5	14.2	0.6
17	$45,128	9.2	51.6	31.8	16.4	0.2
18	$40,760	9.7	45.8	37.5	15.8	0.8
State	$50,037	7.8	57.3	27.8	14.6	0.3

*As percentage of all families.   †As percentage of employed workers 16 years and over.

Table 5   Education: School Years Completed

District	Less than grade 9*	Grades 9–12 no diploma*	High school diploma no college*	Some college*	College bachelor's degree or higher*
1	5.0	15.0	31.4	26.4	22.3
2	5.3	11.4	30.2	24.1	29.0
3	4.4	11.8	31.9	29.1	22.7
4	4.5	13.1	45.0	24.2	13.1
5	4.2	11.5	45.0	24.7	14.6
6	5.4	13.4	43.5	23.5	14.2
7	3.9	12.6	38.2	26.7	18.7
8	4.6	12.9	37.7	26.0	18.7
9	4.0	12.7	34.7	28.8	19.8
10	4.4	12.9	32.5	26.9	23.3
11	5.1	16.7	28.8	26.0	23.4
12	2.9	9.6	28.0	27.4	32.1
13	3.6	11.8	34.3	28.0	22.3
14	3.5	9.3	32.8	27.3	27.1
15	3.6	10.9	27.6	25.7	32.1
16	4.6	11.6	40.8	23.8	19.2
17	4.0	13.8	41.7	24.6	15.8
18	7.5	15.0	45.3	20.9	11.3
State	4.5	12.6	36.1	25.8	21.1

*As percentage of persons age 25 and over.

Table 6   Housing and Residential Patterns

District	Median home value	Owner occupied*	Renter occupied*	Urban†	Rural†
1	$98,900	57.6	42.4	94.8	5.2
2	$117,600	71.5	28.5	73.0	27.0
3	$101,600	67.4	32.6	84.7	15.3
4	$87,700	73.8	26.2	58.6	41.4
5	$90,500	76.5	23.5	48.9	51.1
6	$74,800	75.1	24.9	50.0	50.0
7	$101,600	71.1	28.9	71.3	28.7
8	$103,900	71.2	28.8	78.1	21.9
9	$96,000	68.3	31.7	86.0	14.0
10	$113,400	68.0	32.0	99.4	0.6
11	$89,800	54.3	45.7	100.0	0.0

District	Median home value	Owner occupied*	Renter occupied*	Urban†	Rural†
12	$129,900	62.5	37.5	88.1	11.9
13	$116,400	72.7	27.3	92.7	7.3
14	$139,100	79.6	20.4	74.1	25.9
15	$117,000	59.1	40.9	91.3	8.8
16	$108,100	73.6	26.4	73.6	26.4
17	$84,500	70.0	30.0	84.3	15.7
18	$81,700	74.3	25.7	43.3	56.7
State	$100,500	69.1	30.9	77.3	22.7

*As percentage of occupied housing units.　　†As percentage of total population.

Ohio 1st District

Western Cincinnati and suburbs

Nestled in Ohio's southwest corner, the 1st contains about three-fourths of Cincinnati's residents. The city's 43 percent black population is critical to Democrats, as Cincinnati's traditional German Catholic conservatives, a growing suburban base, and GOP-friendly 2002 redistricting have made the Hamilton County-based 1st politically competitive.

The 1st's southern border is the Ohio River, which serves as a major thoroughfare for barges laden with cargo, helping Cincinnati earn its reputation as a regional center of commerce.

The city's diverse economy prevented it from suffering the degree of hardship that hit other industrial cities in the 1980s, although the region has not been immune to defense cutbacks. Aircraft engine manufacturing and machine tool-making account for a large portion of blue-collar jobs. The city also houses the headquarters of major U.S. companies (including Procter & Gamble) and is a magnet for research and development firms.

The district takes in Cincinnati's heavily black neighborhoods, including the West End (site of the Laurel Homes housing project, which is being redeveloped). The 1st also takes in the Over-the-Rhine neighborhood near downtown, where in April 2001 a white police officer shot an unarmed black man, leading to several days of riots.

Redistricting in 2002 drew the 1st to resemble closely its 1980s configuration, when the district also included most of Cincinnati and points north and west. Added to the 1st were GOP-friendly suburbs such as Reading and high-income Evendale and Springdale (which had been in the 2nd District). The redrawn 1st also includes a southwestern piece of Butler County, located north of Hamilton.

Major Industry

Consumer products development and manufacturing, service.

Notable

Talk show host Jerry Springer is a former council member and mayor of Cincinnati; the Red Stockings—now the Cincinnati Reds—were the nation's first professional baseball team; the National Underground Railroad Freedom Center was set to open in Cincinnati in 2004.

Election Returns

	Republican		Democratic		Other	
President 2000	136,372	51.3%	120,927	45.5%	8,463	3.2%
House 2002	110,760	64.8%	60,168	35.2%		

District Profile

Population　630,730

Total area (square miles)　420.0
　Land area (square miles)　416.2

Population per square mile　1,515.4

Counties (2000 population)
　Butler (pt.)　21,767
　Hamilton (pt.)　608,963

Cities and other areas over 10,000 (2000 population)
　Bridgetown North CDP　12,569
　Cincinnati (pt.)　257,122
　Finneytown CDP　13,492
　Forest Park　19,463
　Northbrook CDP　11,076
　North College Hill　10,082
　Norwood (pt.)　21,675
　Reading　11,292
　Springdale　10,563
　White Oak CDP　13,277

Race and Hispanic or Latino origin*
　White　68.6%
　Black or African American　27.4%
　American Indian or Alaska Native　0.2%
　Asian　1.3%
　Native Hawaiian or other Pacific Islander　0.0%
　Some other race　0.2%
　Hispanic or Latino origin　1.1%
　Two or more races　1.2%

*As percentage of total population.

Ancestry*

English　5.4%	Irish　9.8%
French　1.7%	Italian　3.0%
German　23.6%	USA/American　5.4%

*As estimated percentage of total population.

Universities and colleges, 2000–2001 enrollment
　Cincinnati Bible College and Seminary, Cincinnati　931
　Cincinnati State Technical and Community College, Cincinnati　6,675
　College of Mount St. Joseph, Cincinnati　2,221
　God's Bible School and College, Cincinnati　238
　Good Samaritan Hospital School of Nursing, Cincinnati　230
　Hebrew Union College-Jewish Institute of Religion, Cincinnati　403
　ITT Technical Institute, Norwood　498
　Southern Ohio College, Cincinnati　766
　Union Institute, Cincinnati　1,812
　University of Cincinnati, Cincinnati　27,327
　Xavier University, Cincinnati　6,523

Newspapers and circulation

	District circulation	Total circulation
Cincinnati Enquirer	71,658	189,326
Cincinnati Post	13,439	52,163
Hamilton Journal-News	6,793	22,691
USA Today*	7,711	1,674,376

*See Sources and Explanations in the front of the volume.

Television stations and affiliations

Cincinnati	100%	WCET	PBS
Cincinnati	100%	WCPO	ABC
Cincinnati	100%	WCVN	PBS
Cincinnati	100%	WKOI	Independent
Cincinnati	100%	WKON	PBS
Cincinnati	100%	WKRC	CBS
Cincinnati	100%	WLWT	NBC
Cincinnati	100%	WPTO	PBS
Cincinnati	100%	WSTR	WB
Cincinnati	100%	WXIX	FOX

Cable systems and subscribers

Adelphia   24,051
Time Warner   85,292

Businesses and other major employers

University of Cincinnati; Cincinnati   13,500
Good Samaritan Hospital of Cincinnati; Cincinnati   5,000
Children's Hospital; Cincinnati   3,650
U.S. Postal Service; Cincinnati   2,500
Cognis Corp.; Cincinnati; industrial inorganic chemicals   2,250
Convergys Corp.; Cincinnati; telemarketing   2,000
Tire Centers; Cincinnati; tire retreading/repair   2,000
Trihealth Sleep and Alertness Center; Cincinnati   2,000
Gannett Satellite Information Network Inc.; Cincinnati; newspaper   1,700
Cintas Corp.; Cincinnati; industrial uniforms   1,500
Deaconess Long Term Care of Missouri Inc.; Cincinnati; nursing home   1,500
General Electric Co.; Cincinnati   1,500
Health Alliance of Greater Cincinnati; Cincinnati; health services management   1,500
Procter & Gamble Co.; Cincinnati; product testing lab   1,500
Bethesda Hospital Inc.; Cincinnati   1,390
City of Cincinnati; Cincinnati; police dept.   1,316
Hamilton County; Cincinnati; social and human resources   1,300
Provident Bank; Cincinnati; state commercial banks   1,250
Campbell Hausfeld/Scott Fetzer Co.; Harrison; domestic water or sump pumps   1,200
Mercy Franciscan Mt. Airy Hospital; Cincinnati   1,154
Avon Products Inc.; Cincinnati; cosmetics   1,000
Formica Corp.; Cincinnati; table/counter tops   1,000
Kroger Co; Cincinnati; supermarkets   1,000
Deaconess Hospital of Cincinnati Ohio; Cincinnati   950
Hamilton County; Cincinnati; sheriff's office   950
Sara Lee Corp.; Cincinnati; meatpacking plants   900
Procter & Gamble Co.; Cincinnati; noncommercial research   850

Drake Center; Cincinnati; nursing care facilities   800
Hamilton County; Cincinnati; police dept.   740
Professional Maintenance of Cincinnati Inc.; Cincinnati; janitorial service   700
U.S. Veterans Hospital; Cincinnati   700
Union Central Life Insurance Co.; Cincinnati; mutual association life insurance   700
Viox Services Inc.; Cincinnati; facilities support services   700
Xavier University; Cincinnati   700
Bayer Corp.; Addyston; plastics   660
Federated Department Stores Inc.; Cincinnati   650
Allied Security Inc.; Cincinnati; security guard service   600
Aventis Pharmaceuticals Inc.; Cincinnati   600
Cincinnati Board of Education; Cincinnati   600
Cincinnati Inc.; Harrison; machine tool design   600
City of Cincinnati; Cincinnati; public service commission   600
City of Cincinnati; Cincinnati; public health agency   600
City of Cincinnati; Cincinnati; water, solid waste management   600
Givaudan Fragrances Inc.; Cincinnati; perfume materials   600
Siemens Energy and Automation Inc.; Cincinnati; electric motors   600
Hamilton County Educational Service Center; Cincinnati   589
Southwest Ohio Regional Transit Authority; Cincinnati   523
La Rosa's Inc.; Cincinnati; pizza franchise   515
American Building Maintenance Co. of Illinois; Cincinnati   500
Andrew Jergens Co.; Cincinnati; cosmetics   500
Cincom International Operations Inc.; Cincinnati; software development   500
Hamilton County; Cincinnati; government   500
Hillman Group Inc.; Cincinnati; hardware   500
Hyatt Corp.; Cincinnati; hotels   500
Kendle International Inc.; Cincinnati; biological research   500
Petermann; Cincinnati; local passenger transportation   500
Provident Consumer Financial Services Inc.; Cincinnati; mortgage bankers   500
U.S. Environmental Protection Agency; Cincinnati   500
XLC Services of Cincinnati Ohio Inc.; Cincinnati; employment agencies   500

Ohio 2nd District

Eastern Cincinnati and suburbs; Portsmouth

The 2nd stretches from some of Ohio's wealthiest communities in eastern Cincinnati and Hamilton County in southwest Ohio, to some economically struggling areas in rural southern Ohio. It is perhaps the most solidly Republican district in the state and one with a distinct split between its suburban and rural elements. While Cincinnati's wealthy Republican establishment—including the Taft family—has had significant political influence over the years, the district's rural counties have considerably less political pull.

The area economy revolves around light manufacturing and the retail and service industries, and the district's economic health has been boosted by construction around Cincinnati's downtown. Procter & Gamble, Ford Motor Co., and Chiquita Brands International are among the major employers.

The 2nd includes less than one-fourth of Cincinnati's residents, including those in the well-heeled neighborhoods of Hyde Park and Mount Lookout. Almost 40 percent of the population lives in Cincinnati or in Hamilton County, including the well-to-do communities of Indian Hills, Madeira, Mariemont, and Blue Ash.

To the east, fast-growing Clermont County has become more Republican as it has edged closer to Cincinnati's metropolitan orbit. Once-undeveloped farmland is bursting with development. To the north, Warren County is filling up with Dayton-area commuters.

Economically, rural Adams County has suffered, with one of the state's highest unemployment rates. Pike County and most of Scioto County (including its most populous city, Portsmouth), which were added in 2002 redistricting, also are struggling. Pike County includes a uranium enrichment facility that long provided good incomes but ceased operations in 2001.

Major Industry

Manufacturing, service, retail.

Notable

An Underground Railroad landmark in Ripley (Brown County): the Rev. John Rankin House, where Harriet Beecher Stowe is believed to have obtained ideas for *Uncle Tom's Cabin*; President Ulysses S. Grant was born in Point Pleasant (Clermont County).

Election Returns

	Republican		Democratic		Other	
President 2000	175,382	62.7%	96,027	34.3%	8,187	2.9%
House 2002	139,218	74.1%	48,785	25.9%	13	

District Profile

Population   630,730

Total area (square miles)   2,630.4
  Land area (square miles)   2,611.5

Population per square mile   241.5

Counties (2000 population)

Adams 27,330	Pike 27,695
Brown 42,285	Scioto (pt.) 44,937
Clermont 177,977	Warren (pt.) 74,166
Hamilton (pt.) 236,340	

Cities and other areas over 10,000 (2000 population)

Blue Ash 12,513	Loveland 11,677
Cincinnati (pt.) 74,163	Montgomery 10,163
Forestville CDP 10,978	Portsmouth 20,909
Landen CDP 12,766	Sharonville (pt.) 11,578
Lebanon 16,962	

Race and Hispanic or Latino origin*

White   91.7%
Black or African American   4.7%
American Indian or Alaska Native   0.2%
Asian   1.3%
Native Hawaiian or other Pacific Islander   0.0%
Some other race   0.1%
Hispanic or Latino origin   1.0%
Two or more races   0.9%

*As percentage of total population.

Ancestry*

Dutch 1.3%		Italian 2.9%	
English 8.3%		Polish 1.1%	
French 2.0%		Scotch-Irish 1.2%	
German 21.3%		Scottish 1.5%	
Irish 11.1%		USA/American 8.6%	

*As estimated percentage of total population.

Universities and colleges, 2000–2001 enrollment

Antonelli College, Cincinnati   350
Art Academy of Cincinnati, Cincinnati   246
Athenaeum of Ohio, Cincinnati   225
Chatfield College, St. Martin   251
Great Oaks Joint Vocational School-Scarlet Oaks, Cincinnati   503
Shawnee State University, Portsmouth   3,280
University of Cincinnati-Clermont College, Batavia   2,185
University of Cincinnati-Raymond Walters College, Blue Ash   3,668

Newspapers and circulation

	District circulation	Total circulation
Chillicothe Gazette	1,982	16,233
Cincinnati Enquirer	64,175	189,326
Cincinnati Post	9,227	52,163
Columbus Dispatch	1,117	245,310
Portsmouth Daily Times	7,347	14,915
*USA Today**	5,902	1,674,376

*See Sources and Explanations in the front of the volume.

Television stations and affiliations

Cincinnati	70%	WCET	PBS
Cincinnati	70%	WCPO	ABC
Cincinnati	70%	WCVN	PBS
Cincinnati	70%	WKOI	Independent
Cincinnati	70%	WKON	PBS
Cincinnati	70%	WKRC	CBS
Cincinnati	70%	WLWT	NBC
Cincinnati	70%	WPTO	PBS
Cincinnati	70%	WSTR	WB
Cincinnati	70%	WXIX	FOX
Columbus	17%	WBNS	CBS
Columbus	17%	WCMH	NBC
Columbus	17%	WOSU	PBS
Columbus	17%	WOUC	PBS
Columbus	17%	WSFJ	PAX
Columbus	17%	WSYX	ABC
Columbus	17%	WTTE	FOX
Columbus	17%	WWHO	UPN, WB
Charleston-Huntington, WV	13%	WCHS	ABC

Charleston-Huntington, WV	13%	WHCP	WB, UPN
Charleston-Huntington, WV	13%	WKAS	PBS
Charleston-Huntington, WV	13%	WKPI	PBS
Charleston-Huntington, WV	13%	WOUB	PBS
Charleston-Huntington, WV	13%	WOWK	CBS
Charleston-Huntington, WV	13%	WPBO	PBS
Charleston-Huntington, WV	13%	WPBY	PBS
Charleston-Huntington, WV	13%	WSAZ	NBC
Charleston-Huntington, WV	13%	WTSF	Independent
Charleston-Huntington, WV	13%	WVAH	FOX

Cable systems and subscribers
Adelphia   31,263
Time Warner   45,455

Military installations, September 2001
Kings Mills Memorial U.S. Army Reserve Center, Kings Mills   350

Businesses and other major employers
Procter & Gamble Co.; Cincinnati; toiletries   14,500
Ethicon Inc.; Cincinnati; medical supplies   4,000
Delta Airlines Inc.; Cincinnati   3,800
Federated Department Stores Inc.; Mason; personal credit institutions   3,000
Ford Motor Co.; Cincinnati   2,958
Jewish Hospital of Cincinnati Inc.; Cincinnati   2,480
Procter & Gamble Co.; Mason; commercial physical research   2,400
Belcan Corp.; Cincinnati; engineering help service   2,000
Southern Ohio Medical Center; Portsmouth   2,000
Fifth Third Bank; Cincinnati; state trust company   1,800
Mill's Pride Partnership; Waverly; kitchen cabinets   1,800
Cinergy Corp.; Cincinnati; electric power distribution   1,700
Community Insurance Co. Inc.; Mason; medical service plans   1,700
Fluor Fernald Inc.; Cincinnati; environmental cleanup   1,700
Ford Motor Co.; Batavia   1,600
Bethesda Hospital Inc.; Cincinnati   1,500
U.S. Enrichment Corp.; Piketon; public utilities consultant   1,470
Super Food Services Inc.; Cincinnati; food supplier   1,350
UNOVA Inc.; Cincinnati; metal cutting machine tools   1,300
ZF Batavia; Batavia; automotive power transmissions   1,300
Great American Insurance Co.; Cincinnati; fire, marine, casualty insurance   1,250
Convergys Corp.; Cincinnati; telemarketing   1,200
Hamilton County; Cincinnati; social and manpower programs   1,200
Senco Products Inc.; Cincinnati; power-driven handtools   1,200
U.S. Postal Service; Cincinnati   1,200
Firstar Bank NA; Cincinnati; commercial bank   1,150
Ohio Valley Bistros Inc.; Cincinnati; restaurant management   1,100

Chiquita Brands International Inc.; Cincinnati; bananas   1,000
Corning Precision Lens Inc.; Cincinnati; optical elements/assemblies   1,000
Griffey Uniforms Inc.; Cincinnati; work clothing   1,000
Ingersoll-Rand Co.; Cincinnati; warehousing   1,000
Luxottica Group; Cincinnati; glassware   1,000
Milacron Inc.; Batavia; plastics working machinery   1,000
Western and Southern Life Insurance Co.; Cincinnati   982
Coca-Cola Enterprises Inc.; Cincinnati; vending machines   950
Fidelity Brokerage Services; Cincinnati; mutual fund sales   950
Cincinnati Bell Telephone Co.; Cincinnati; telephone communication   900
PNC Bank National Assn.; Cincinnati; commercial bank   900
GE Capital Services; Mason; personal credit institutions   880
AT & T Corp.; Cincinnati; long-distance telephone   800
Midland-Guardian Co.; Amelia; life insurance   800
American Airlines Inc.; Cincinnati   750
American Modern Home Insurance Co.; Amelia; fire, marine, casualty insurance   750
Mercy Hospital Anderson; Cincinnati   728
Mercy Hospital Clermont; Batavia   720
Dillard's Inc.; Cincinnati; department stores   700
Pickard Enterprises; Cincinnati; fast-food restaurant   700
Siemens Business Services Inc.; Mason; computer systems resellers   700
Unigraphics Solutions Inc.; Milford; magnetic and optical recording media   700
P. J. L. Enterprises Inc.; Portsmouth; restaurant   681
U.S. Internal Revenue Service; Cincinnati   650
Arena Management Holdings; Cincinnati; sports clubs   600
ChoiceCare Health Plans Inc.; Cincinnati; group hospitalization   600
D. H. Packaging Co.; Cincinnati; gift-wrapping services   600
International Union UAW of America; Cincinnati; labor organization   600
Lenscrafters Inc.; Cincinnati; optical goods stores   600
LSI Industries Inc.; Cincinnati; lighting equipment   600
Time Warner Entertainment Co.; Cincinnati; cable TV   600
U.S. National Institutes of Health; Cincinnati   600
Dayton Power and Light Co.; Aberdeen; electric power generation   561
Adams County/Ohio Valley School District; West Union   560
Brisben Companies Inc.; Cincinnati; residential land development   500
Federated Department Stores Inc.; Cincinnati; warehousing   500
Miami Management/Downtown Inc.; Cincinnati; fast-food restaurants/stands   500
Milacron Inc.; Cincinnati; lubricating oil   500

SEI Brakes Inc.; Lebanon; brake systems/parts   500
Siemens Energy and Automation Inc.; Lebanon;
   electrical equipment and supplies   500
Sinergy Corp.; Cincinnati; electric, other services   500
Warren County; Lebanon; county government   500

Ohio 3rd District

Southwest — most of Dayton, Kettering

Once one of the state's most successful manufacturing centers, Dayton has suffered economic setbacks. A torrent of company departures has displaced its manufacturing base, and efforts to diversify have not yielded results. Montgomery County, which surrounds Dayton, lost population in the 1990s. Still, the area's defense industry, revolving around Wright-Patterson Air Force Base, in the adjacent 7th district, has had some success in attracting aerospace and technology research companies.

The 3rd leans Republican. Redistricting in 2002 excised parts of northeastern Montgomery County and added GOP territory in Warren County, a fast-growing area outside of Cincinnati, and mostly rural Clinton and Highland Counties to the southeast. These three counties give the 3rd its slight Republican tilt.

The district takes in most of Dayton and Montgomery County (both are shared with the 8th), and Dayton's southern suburbs include GOP-inclined, white-collar areas such as Kettering and Centerville. The urban vote—driven by Dayton's black population and large blue-collar workforce—makes Montgomery slightly Democratic overall. But the areas added in the remap more than balance this Democratic edge.

Major Industry
Auto manufacturing, defense, service.

Notable
The Dayton Peace Agreement to end fighting in the former Yugoslavia was signed in 1995 at Wright-Patterson; Dayton was home to the Wright brothers, who tested several airplanes nearby; Montgomery County claims to be birthplace of the refrigerator, the ice cream cone, and the stepladder.

Election Returns

	Republican		Democratic		Other	
President 2000	130,446	52.3%	112,102	44.9%	6,874	2.8%
House 2002	111,630	58.8%	78,307	41.2%		

District Profile

Population   630,730

Total area (square miles)   1,610.2
   Land area (square miles)   1,595.4

Population per square mile   395.3

Counties (2000 population)
Clinton 40,543		Montgomery (pt.) 465,095
Highland 40,875		Warren (pt.) 84,217

Cities and other areas over 10,000 (2000 population)
Centerville   23,024
Clayton   13,347
Dayton (pt.)   137,180
Englewood   12,235
Franklin   11,396
Kettering (pt.)   57,502
Mason (pt.)   14,393
Miamisburg   19,489
Shiloh CDP   11,272
Springboro   12,380
Trotwood   27,420
Vandalia (pt.)   14,603
West Carrollton City   13,818
Wilmington   11,921

Race and Hispanic or Latino origin*
White   79.5%
Black or African American   16.9%
American Indian or Alaska Native   0.2%
Asian   1.1%
Native Hawaiian or other Pacific Islander   0.0%
Some other race   0.1%
Hispanic or Latino origin   1.1%
Two or more races   1.2%

As percentage of total population.

Ancestry*
Dutch 1.4%	Italian 2.2%
English 7.4%	Polish 1.2%
French 1.9%	Scotch-Irish 1.1%
German 17.9%	Scottish 1.4%
Irish 9.1%	USA/American 8.5%

As estimated percentage of total population.

Universities and colleges, 2000–2001 enrollment
ITT Technical Institute, Dayton   480
Kettering College of Medical Arts, Kettering   498
Miami-Jacobs College, Dayton   326
Ohio Institute of Photography and Technology, Dayton   376
Rets Tech Center, Centerville   413
Sinclair Community College, Dayton   19,026
Southern State Community College, Hillsboro   1,847
Southwestern College of Business, Dayton   230
University of Dayton, Dayton   10,318
Wilmington College, Wilmington   1,930

Newspapers and circulation

	District circulation	Total circulation
Cincinnati Enquirer	6,133	189,326
Dayton Daily News	81,815	135,680
Middletown Journal	5,265	22,091
*USA Today**	8,126	1,674,376

See Sources and Explanations in the front of the volume.

Television stations and affiliations
Cincinnati	74%	WCET	PBS
Cincinnati	74%	WCPO	ABC
Cincinnati	74%	WCVN	PBS
Cincinnati	74%	WKOI	Independent

Cincinnati	74%	WKON	PBS
Cincinnati	74%	WKRC	CBS
Cincinnati	74%	WLWT	NBC
Cincinnati	74%	WPTO	PBS
Cincinnati	74%	WSTR	WB
Cincinnati	74%	WXIX	FOX
Dayton	26%	WBDT	WB, PAX
Dayton	26%	WDTN	ABC
Dayton	26%	WHIO	CBS
Dayton	26%	WKEF	NBC
Dayton	26%	WPTD	PBS
Dayton	26%	WRGT	FOX

Cable systems and subscribers

Adelphia   5,601
Time Warner   150,801

Businesses and other major employers

Delphi Corp.; Dayton; motor vehicle parts/accessories 5,000

General Motors Corp.; Dayton; motor trucks assembly 4,500

Reed Elsevier Inc.; Miamisburg; computer service bureau 4,300

Miami Valley Hospital; Dayton   3,792

NCR Corp.; Dayton; data processing 3,200

Emery Air Freight Corp.; Vandalia; air cargo carrier 3,000

Good Samaritan Hospital and Health Center; Dayton 2,165

Kettering Medical Center; Dayton   2,100

Meijer Inc.; Dayton; department stores   2,100

U.S. Veterans Hospital; Dayton   2,100

University of Dayton; Dayton   2,090

Relizon Industrial Inc.; Dayton; stationery and office supplies   2,000

Southern Bag Corp.; Lebanon   2,000

U.S. Postal Service; Dayton   2,000

Elder-Beerman Stores Corp.; Dayton; department stores 1,500

Lau Industries Inc.; Dayton; industrial fans   1,500

Victoria's Secret Stores Inc.; Dayton; women's specialty stores   1,300

Cintas Corp.; Mason; industrial uniforms   1,200

National City Mortgage Co.; Miamisburg; mortgage bankers   1,200

Dayton Osteopathic Hospital; Dayton   1,134

Lancaster Colony Corp.; Leesburg; food dips   1,100

BankOne Corp.; Springboro; commercial bank   1,012

Montgomery County; Dayton; county government 1,000

Sogeti USA; Dayton; online services technology   1,000

Dayton Progress Corp.; Dayton; forming/stamping punches   976

Montgomery County Community College District; Dayton   894

EG&G Optoelectronics; Miamisburg; energy research 880

DMAX; Dayton; diesel, dual-fuel engines   850

Greenwood Motor Lines Inc.; Wilmington; trucking 800

Monarch Marking Systems Inc.; Miamisburg; printing trades machinery repair   800

OneSource Facility Services Inc.; Dayton; building maintenance   800

Baker Concrete Construction Inc.; Monroe; concrete work   700

U.S. Dept. of Energy; Miamisburg   700

Mead Corp.; Dayton; stationery products   680

Dayton Power and Light Co.; Dayton; electric, other services   650

L. M. Berry and Co.; Dayton; advertising   650

Clinton Memorial Hospital; Wilmington   630

Blackhawk Automotive Plastics Inc.; Mason   600

City of Dayton; Dayton; city government   600

Green Tokai Co.; Brookville; motor vehicle body/frame 600

Meijer Inc.; Franklin; department stores   600

Ohio Dept. of Transportation; Lebanon   600

Standard Register Co.; Dayton; business forms   600

Textron Automotive Co.; Wilmington; plastics molding 600

Scitex Digital Printing Inc.; Dayton; printing trades machinery   595

City of Dayton; Dayton; police dept.   592

BWXT of Ohio Inc.; Miamisburg; management services 580

Micro Warehouse of Ohio Inc.; Wilmington; mail-order software   565

Lutheran Social Services of Miami Valley; Dayton; nursing care facilities   550

U.S. Defense Dept.; Dayton; payroll accounting service 537

American Showa Inc.; Blanchester; automotive steering systems   530

Home Care Network Inc.; Dayton; home health care 521

ABX Air Inc.; Wilmington; package delivery   500

American Tool Companies Inc.; Wilmington; screwdrivers, pliers, chisels   500

Dayton Newspapers Inc.; Dayton   500

DT Industries Inc.; Dayton; jobbing and machine repair shop   500

Electronic Data Systems Corp.; Dayton; data processing 500

Findlay Industries Inc.; Dayton; truck bodies and parts 500

Johnson Controls; Dayton; motor vehicle body/frame 500

Maria-Joseph Living Care Center; Dayton   500

Pinkerton's Inc.; Dayton; detective agency   500

Reynolds and Reynolds Co.; Dayton; business forms 500

Ohio 4th District

West central — Mansfield, Lima, Findlay

The 4th is a solid block of Ohio Corn Belt counties. The land supports soybeans, corn, livestock, and Republicans. Not one of the 11 counties in the 4th has supported a Democratic presidential candidate since 1964, and seven of them gave Republican George W. Bush at least 60 percent of the vote in 2000. Two of the three most populous, Allen and

Hancock Counties, last voted Democratic in the Roosevelt-Landon contest of 1936.

Democrats have oases of support, but they are few and far between. Democrats can normally count on votes in Mansfield, the district's largest city, which has a 20 percent black population. While those votes occasionally help a Democrat get elected to local office, they are rarely enough to swing the district in national elections.

Along with corn and soybeans, manufacturing is important to the 4th. While declines in the automobile industry in the 1980s and defense cutbacks in the 1990s caused economic hardships throughout parts of the district, the 4th's small industrial companies and large auto manufacturing plants—including a Ford engine plant in Lima, a General Motors plant in Mansfield, and Honda facilities in East Liberty (Logan County), Anna (Shelby County), and Marysville (Union County)—continue to spur the economy. Findlay, headquarters of Cooper Tire & Rubber Co. and the joint venture Marathon Ashland Petroleum, is the 4th's most prosperous city.

Redistricting in 2002 did not make significant changes to the 4th. The district picked up some territory in the southwest, adding the rest of Auglaize and Logan Counties and all of Champaign and Shelby Counties.

Major Industry

Agriculture, auto manufacturing, oil.

Notable

Lima was one of the original refinery centers for John D. Rockefeller's Standard Oil; Richland Carrousel Park in downtown Mansfield boasts one of the world's largest carousels; astronaut Neil Armstrong's hometown of Wapakoneta has a museum in his honor.

Election Returns

	Republican		Democratic		Other	
President 2000	158,862	62.1%	88,760	34.7%	8,244	3.2%
House 2002	120,001	67.5%	57,726	32.5%		

District Profile

Population   630,730

Total area (square miles)   4,642.0
  Land area (square miles)   4,619.9

Population per square mile   136.5

Counties (2000 population)

Allen	108,473	Marion 66,217
Auglaize	46,611	Morrow 31,628
Champaign	38,890	Richland 128,852
Hancock	71,295	Shelby 47,910
Hardin	31,945	Wyandot (pt.) 12,904
Logan	46,005	

Cities and other areas over 10,000 (2000 population)

Bellefontaine	13,069	Marion 35,318
Findlay	38,967	Sidney 20,211
Lima	40,081	Urbana 11,613
Mansfield	49,346	

Race and Hispanic or Latino origin*

White   91.7%
Black or African American   5.2%
American Indian or Alaska Native   0.2%
Asian   0.6%
Native Hawaiian or other Pacific Islander   0.0%
Some other race   0.1%
Hispanic or Latino origin   1.2%
Two or more races   1.0%

*As percentage of total population.

Ancestry*

Dutch	1.8%	Irish	8.1%
English	6.8%	Italian	2.0%
French	1.9%	Scottish	1.2%
German	23.4%	USA/American	9.7%

*As estimated percentage of total population.

Universities and colleges, 2000–2001 enrollment

Bluffton College, Bluffton   1,059
Lima Technical College, Lima   2,521
Marion Technical College, Marion   1,679
North Central Technical College, Mansfield   2,813
Northwestern College, Lima   2,046
Ohio Northern University, Ada   3,227
Ohio State University, Lima   1,238
Ohio State University, Mansfield   1,583
Ohio State University, Marion   1,276
Owens Community College, Findlay   1,689
University of Findlay, Findlay   4,510
Urbana University, Urbana   1,372

Newspapers and circulation

	District circulation	Total circulation
Bellefontaine Examiner	9,187	9,290
Columbus Dispatch	5,344	245,310
Dayton Daily News	3,355	135,680
Findlay Courier	18,735	22,636
Lima News	27,005	34,759
Mansfield News-Journal	27,122	33,575
Marion Star	12,783	14,269
Piqua Daily Call	1,083	6,679
Sidney Daily News	12,426	13,038
Springfield News-Sun	3,434	31,035
Toledo Blade	2,573	138,304
Urbana Daily Citizen	5,909	6,193
*USA Today**	6,042	1,674,376

*See Sources and Explanations in the front of the volume.

Television stations and affiliations

Columbus	28%	WBNS	CBS
Columbus	28%	WCMH	NBC
Columbus	28%	WOSU	PBS
Columbus	28%	WOUC	PBS
Columbus	28%	WSFJ	PAX
Columbus	28%	WSYX	ABC
Columbus	28%	WTTE	FOX
Columbus	28%	WWHO	UPN, WB
Dayton	28%	WBDT	WB, PAX
Dayton	28%	WDTN	ABC
Dayton	28%	WHIO	CBS
Dayton	28%	WKEF	NBC

Dayton	28%	WPTD	PBS
Dayton	28%	WRGT	FOX
Lima	17%	WLIO	NBC
Lima	17%	WTLW	Independent
Toledo	16%	WBGU	PBS
Toledo	16%	WGTE	PBS
Toledo	16%	WINM	Independent
Toledo	16%	WLMB	PAX
Toledo	16%	WNWO	NBC
Toledo	16%	WTOL	CBS
Toledo	16%	WTVG	ABC
Toledo	16%	WUPW	FOX
Cleveland-Akron (Canton)	11%	WBNX	WB
Cleveland-Akron (Canton)	11%	WDLI	Independent
Cleveland-Akron (Canton)	11%	WEAO	PBS
Cleveland-Akron (Canton)	11%	WEWS	ABC
Cleveland-Akron (Canton)	11%	WGGN	Independent
Cleveland-Akron (Canton)	11%	WJW	FOX
Cleveland-Akron (Canton)	11%	WKYC	NBC
Cleveland-Akron (Canton)	11%	WMFD	Independent
Cleveland-Akron (Canton)	11%	WOAC	Independent
Cleveland-Akron (Canton)	11%	WOIO	CBS
Cleveland-Akron (Canton)	11%	WQHS	Univision
Cleveland-Akron (Canton)	11%	WUAB	UPN
Cleveland-Akron (Canton)	11%	WVIZ	PBS
Cleveland-Akron (Canton)	11%	WVPX	PAX

Cable systems and subscribers
Adelphia   21,660
Charter   5,726
New Knoxville Cable   3,618
Time Warner   94,152

Military installations, September 2001
Beckley Municipal Airport Air National Guard Station, Springfield   1,044
Mansfield Lahm Airport Air National Guard Station, Mansfield   974

Businesses and other major employers
Honda of America Manufacturing Inc.; Marysville; automobiles, motorcycles   6,500
General Motors Corp.; Mansfield; automotive body parts   2,600
St. Rita's Medical Center; Lima   2,600
Crown Equipment Corp.; New Bremen; lift trucks   2,500
Whirlpool Corp.; Marion; laundry dryers   2,500
United Telephone Company of Indiana; Mansfield; local telephone communications   2,499
Honda of America Manufacturing Inc.; Anna; automotive parts/accessories   2,400
Copeland Corp.; Sidney; refrigeration/air conditioning   2,000
Whirlpool Corp.; Findlay; electric ranges   2,000
Ford Motor Co.; Lima; automotive engines/parts   1,949
Mansfield Hospital; Mansfield   1,900
Cooper Tire & Rubber Co.; Findlay; automobile tires   1,800
Honda of America Manufacturing Inc.; East Liberty; motor vehicles and car bodies   1,800
Bennett Enterprises Inc.; Lima; restaurants   1,500
Lima Memorial Hospital; Lima   1,455
Marion General Hospital Inc.; Marion   1,250

Consolidated Biscuit Co.; McComb; cookies   1,200
Blanchard Valley Regional Health Center; Findlay   1,196
Marathon Ashland Petroleum; Findlay; petroleum refining   1,015
Gorman-Rupp Co.; Mansfield; pumping equipment   1,000
Kohl's Department Stores Inc.; Findlay; warehousing   1,000
Siemens Energy and Automation Inc.; Bellefontaine; nonelectric transformers   1,000
United Steelworkers of America Union; Findlay; labor union   1,000
Midwest Express Inc.; East Liberty; materials handling machinery   950
AK Steel Corp.; Mansfield; blast furnaces and steel mills   900
Honeywell Inc.; Urbana; process control instruments   900
Therm-O-Disc Inc.; Mansfield; thermostats   900
Goodyear Tire and Rubber Co.; St. Marys; rubber products   850
American Trim; Sidney; automotive moldings or trim   800
Grimes Aerospace Co.; Urbana; aircraft parts, equipment   800
KTH Parts Industries Inc.; St. Paris; automotive parts/accessories   780
Ohio Dept. of Rehabilitation and Correction; Mansfield   769
DTR Industries Inc.; Bluffton; rubber products   750
PACE; Kenton; labor organization   750
Honda of America Manufacturing Inc.; Russells Point; automotive parts   723
Nash-Finch Co.; Bellefontaine; food supplier   715
ArvinMeritor Inc.; Kenton; motor vehicle axles   700
Newman Technology Inc.; Mansfield; automotive parts/accessories   700
Reliance Electric Industrial Co.; Kenton; electric motor, generator parts   700
Bluffton College; Bluffton   650
Sky Chefs Inc.; Delphos; food supplier   650
Blackhawk Automotive Plastics Inc.; Upper Sandusky   619
AFG Industries Inc.; Bellefontaine; safety glass   615
American Trim; Lima; metal stampings   600
BPI Communications Inc.; Marion; subscription fulfillment   600
Copperweld Tubing Products Co; Shelby; steel pipe and tubes   600
Findlay City School District; Findlay   600
Joint Township District Memorial Hospital; St. Marys   600
LTV Corp.; Shelby; pipe and tubing, steel   600
Shelby County Memorial Hospital Assn.; Sidney   600
Budd Co.; Carey; plastics   585
Ohio Northern University; Ada   570
Findlex Corp.; Findlay; automotive brakes/parts   565
CR/Pl Management Co. Inc.; Mansfield; plumbing fixtures, vitreous china   550
Roundy's Inc.; Lima; grocery store   550
Bridgestone APM Co.; Findlay; automotive rubber goods   533

Spicer Driveshaft Manufacturing Inc.; Lima; automotive drive shafts   512

Gates McDonald and Co.; Bellville; restaurants   500

Intersil Communications Inc.; Findlay; semiconductors   500

Stoneridge Inc.; Mansfield; ignition apparatus and distributors   500

Wal-Mart Stores Inc.; Findlay; department stores   500

Wyandot Inc.; Marion; snacks   500

Ohio 5th District

Northwest — Bowling Green, Tiffin, Fremont

A mixture of flat farmland, limestone plains, and small towns, the 5th runs from Ohio's northwest corner to the north-central portion of the state.

At the district's center is the university town of Bowling Green, located in Wood County, the largest and most populous jurisdiction in the 5th. The Maumee River divides Wood from Toledo-dominated Lucas County (most of which is in the 9th), and more people are finding northern Wood an attractive place to live. Perrysburg increased its population 35 percent in the 1990s. Still, most of Wood's land area is devoted to farming. The county is a top producer of wheat, tomatoes, soybeans, and corn.

The remaining constituents are almost evenly divided between counties west and east of Wood. Many of the counties are devoted almost exclusively to agriculture and food packaging. This area is the heart of Ohio's wheat-growing country: the state's five top producers are in northwestern Ohio (Wood, Fulton, Seneca, Henry, and Paulding). Migrant workers who live in farm camps during the harvesting months help boost the district's Hispanic population to 3.8 percent, double the state's average of about 2 percent. Manufacturing is important here as well, with General Motors, Whirlpool, and Heinz among the 5th's major manufacturers.

Redistricting in 2002 made some adjustments to the lines in the district's east. The 5th no longer borders Lake Erie; the district boundaries were moved south to give the 5th all of Crawford County and parts of Wyandot and Ashland Counties. Sandusky is now in the 9th.

The 5th is strong GOP territory. Fifteen of the 16 counties that lie wholly or partly within the 5th voted for Republican George W. Bush in the 2000 presidential election—the lone exception was Lucas County, a small southwestern chunk of which is in the 5th. Putnam County, located southwest of Wood, gave Bush his best showing in Ohio, 74 percent.

Major Industry

Agriculture, manufacturing.

Notable

President Rutherford B. Hayes lived in Fremont (Sandusky County), and the Hayes Presidential Center is located there.

Election Returns

	Republican		Democratic		Other	
President 2000	158,037	59.1%	99,818	37.4%	9,383	3.5%
House 2002	126,286	67.1%	51,872	27.6%	10,096	5.4%

District Profile

Population   630,730

Total area (square miles)   6,158.1
  Land area (square miles)   6,128.3

Population per square mile   102.9

Counties (2000 population)

Ashland (pt.) 11,883	Paulding 20,293
Crawford 46,966	Putnam 34,726
Defiance 39,500	Sandusky 61,792
Fulton 42,084	Seneca 58,683
Henry 29,210	Van Wert 29,659
Huron 59,487	Williams 39,188
Lucas (pt.) 16,475	Wood 121,065
Mercer (pt.) 9,715	Wyandot (pt.) 10,004

Cities and other areas over 10,000 (2000 population)

Bowling Green 29,636	Galion 11,341
Bucyrus 13,224	Norwalk 16,238
Defiance 16,465	Perrysburg 16,945
Fostoria (pt.) 10,877	Tiffin 18,135
Fremont 17,375	Van Wert 10,690

Race and Hispanic or Latino origin*

White   93.7%
Black or African American   1.1%
American Indian or Alaska Native   0.2%
Asian   0.4%
Native Hawaiian or other Pacific Islander   0.0%
Some other race   0.1%
Hispanic or Latino origin   3.8%
Two or more races   0.7%

*As percentage of total population.

Ancestry*

Dutch 1.7%	Italian 2.0%
English 6.4%	Polish 2.2%
French 2.5%	Scottish 1.1%
German 29.9%	USA/American 7.3%
Irish 7.5%	

*As estimated percentage of total population.

Universities and colleges, 2000–2001 enrollment

Bowling Green State University, Bowling Green   18,096
Defiance College, Defiance   991
Heidelberg College, Tiffin   1,452
Northwest State Community College, Archbold   2,720
Owens Community College, Toledo   15,845
Terra State Community College, Fremont   2,454
Tiffin University, Tiffin   1,543

Newspapers and circulation

	District circulation	Total circulation
Ashland Times Gazette	4,084	11,934
Bowling Green Sentinel-Tribune	11,641	11,724
Bryan Times	10,560	10,832
Bucyrus Telegraph-Forum	6,560	6,870
Cleveland Plain Dealer	1,147	362,446
Defiance Crescent-News	17,237	17,237
Findlay Courier	3,177	22,636

Fort Wayne Journal Gazette	2,878	58,705	
Fort Wayne Journal Gazette/ *News-Sentinel*	3,214	103,643	
Fremont News-Messenger	13,238	13,598	
Lima News	7,321	34,759	
Lorain Morning Journal	1,813	33,328	
Mansfield News-Journal	4,219	33,575	
Norwalk Reflector	7,492	8,706	
Sandusky Register	4,012	22,761	
Tiffin Advertiser Tribune	10,184	10,475	
Toledo Blade	33,175	138,304	
USA Today*	6,938	1,674,376	

*See Sources and Explanations in the front of the volume.

Television stations and affiliations

Toledo	65%	WBGU	PBS
Toledo	65%	WGTE	PBS
Toledo	65%	WINM	Independent
Toledo	65%	WLMB	PAX
Toledo	65%	WNWO	NBC
Toledo	65%	WTOL	CBS
Toledo	65%	WTVG	ABC
Toledo	65%	WUPW	FOX
Fort Wayne, IN	14%	WANE	CBS
Fort Wayne, IN	14%	WFFT	FOX
Fort Wayne, IN	14%	WFWA	PBS
Fort Wayne, IN	14%	WKJG	NBC
Fort Wayne, IN	14%	WPTA	ABC
Cleveland-Akron (Canton)	11%	WBNX	WB
Cleveland-Akron (Canton)	11%	WDLI	Independent
Cleveland-Akron (Canton)	11%	WEAO	PBS
Cleveland-Akron (Canton)	11%	WEWS	ABC
Cleveland-Akron (Canton)	11%	WGGN	Independent
Cleveland-Akron (Canton)	11%	WJW	FOX
Cleveland-Akron (Canton)	11%	WKYC	NBC
Cleveland-Akron (Canton)	11%	WMFD	Independent
Cleveland-Akron (Canton)	11%	WOAC	Independent
Cleveland-Akron (Canton)	11%	WOIO	CBS
Cleveland-Akron (Canton)	11%	WQHS	Univision
Cleveland-Akron (Canton)	11%	WUAB	UPN
Cleveland-Akron (Canton)	11%	WVIZ	PBS
Cleveland-Akron (Canton)	11%	WVPX	PAX
Columbus	6%	WBNS	CBS
Columbus	6%	WCMH	NBC
Columbus	6%	WOSU	PBS
Columbus	6%	WOUC	PBS
Columbus	6%	WSFJ	PAX
Columbus	6%	WSYX	ABC
Columbus	6%	WTTE	FOX
Columbus	6%	WWHO	UPN, WB
Dayton	4%	WBDT	WB, PAX
Dayton	4%	WDTN	ABC
Dayton	4%	WHIO	CBS
Dayton	4%	WKEF	NBC
Dayton	4%	WPTD	PBS
Dayton	4%	WRGT	FOX

Cable systems and subscribers

Adelphia   43,014
AmeriCable International   726
Buckeye Cablevision   12,095
Comcast   670
Mediacom   1,218

Orwell Cable Television Co.   2,607
Quality One Cable   744
Time Warner   64,272

Businesses and other major employers

General Motors Corp.; Defiance; gray iron castings   4,000

Whirlpool Corp.; Clyde; laundry dryers   3,800

Sauder Woodworking Co.; Archbold; home furniture   3,200

Bowling Green State University; Bowling Green   2,450

LG Philips Displays USA Inc.; Ottawa; TV tubes   1,770

DaimlerChrysler Corp.; Perrysburg; automotive transmissions   1,600

R. R. Donnelley and Sons Co.; Willard; directories publishing, printing   1,600

Eaton Corp.; Van Wert; rubber hose   1,000

Gem Industrial Inc.; Walbridge; mechanical contractor   1,000

Owens Community College; Perrysburg   1,000

Prestolite Wire Corp.; Clyde; engine electrical equipment   1,000

Timken Co.; Bucyrus; roller bearings and parts   975

Honeywell International Inc.; Fostoria; engine spark plugs   900

Norwalk Furniture Corp.; Norwalk   900

BAX Global Inc.; Swanton; air cargo carrier   800

Federal-Mogul Corp.; Van Wert; oil seals, rubber   800

MTD Products Inc.; Willard; lawn/garden equipment   800

NFO Worldwide Inc.; Northwood; market research/analysis   800

Tekni-Plex Inc.; Bucyrus; hose clamps and couplings   800

Bennett Enterprises Inc.; Perrysburg; franchised motel   768

Teleflex Inc.; Van Wert; automotive air conditioner parts   750

American Standard Inc.; Tiffin; plumbing fixtures, vitreous china   700

PPG Industries Inc.; Crestline; flat glass   700

Pepperidge Farm Inc.; Willard; breads and cakes   680

Norwalk Area Health Services; Norwalk; ambulance service   650

Kmart Corp.; Defiance; department stores   640

H. J. Heinz Co.; Fremont; catsup   620

Aeroquip-Inoac Co.; Fremont; plastics   600

Cedar Fair; Sandusky; theme park   600

Great Lakes Window Inc.; Walbridge; windows, plastics   600

Lear Corp.; Wauseon; automotive parts/accessories   600

Norplas Industries Inc.; Northwood; automotive stampings   600

Air-Ride Inc.; Swanton; trucking   550

Ingersoll-Rand Co.; Bryan; power-driven handtools   550

PECO II Inc.; Galion; telephone apparatus   517

Armstrong Air Conditioning Inc.; Bellevue; air conditioning equipment   500

Cooper-Standard Automotive Inc.; Bowling Green; automobile hose   500

Fisher-Titus Medical Center; Norwalk   500

Guardian Industries Corp.; Upper Sandusky; glass
  500
Plastech Exterior Systems Inc.; Bryan; plastics   500
Tenneco Automotive Operating Co.; Norwalk;
  automotive bearings   500
Williams County Community Hospitals; Bryan   500
Wood County Hospital Assn.; Bowling Green   500

Ohio 6th District

South and east — Boardman, Athens, Steubenville

The 6th parallels the Ohio River for more than 300 miles, bordering three states and enveloping the hardscrabble areas from southern Ohio's Appalachia to the Mahoning Valley near Youngstown.

Many of the district's counties, especially those along the Ohio River in old coal mining territory, suffer high unemployment and have difficulty retaining younger people. Meigs County had Ohio's lowest median household income in 1999; Athens, north of Meigs, Scioto (shared with the 2nd), and Lawrence, which form the southwest border of the 6th, were not far behind.

Athens County (shared with the 18th) is home to Ohio University and leans Democratic. The Green Party's Ralph Nader received a greater vote share in Athens than in any other Ohio county in the 2000 presidential election. East of Athens lies Washington County, which takes in Marietta and is one of the few solidly Republican areas in the district.

North of Washington, the district tilts Democratic. Monroe and Belmont Counties have supported Democrats for president since 1976. Jefferson County, which includes Steubenville, also votes dependably Democratic. Jefferson has lost population in the past four censuses and has the highest proportion of elderly residents of any Ohio county.

About one-third of residents live in the northern extreme of the district, in Mahoning and Columbiana Counties. The Mahoning portions take in Boardman and Poland, just south of Youngstown.

The 6th has a strong Democratic orientation, though it leans conservative on social issues, particularly on gun control. George W. Bush won seven of the 12 counties that lie wholly or partly within the 6th District in 2000. Redistricting following the 2000 census moved the district's boundaries east and north, strengthening the Democratic edge.

Major Industry
Service, manufacturing.

Notable
Marietta was the first European settlement in the Northwest Territories; entertainer Dean Martin was born in Steubenville.

Election Returns

	Republican		Democratic		Other	
President 2000	129,689	48.6%	125,292	46.9%	11,969	4.5%
House 2002	77,643	40.5%	113,972	59.5%		

District Profile

Population   630,730

Total area (square miles)   5,235.7
  Land area (square miles)   5,197.5

Population per square mile   121.4

Counties (2000 population)

Athens (pt.) 43,567	Mahoning (pt.) 102,809
Belmont (pt.) 55,178	Meigs 23,072
Columbiana 112,075	Monroe 15,180
Gallia 31,069	Noble 14,058
Jefferson 73,894	Scioto (pt.) 34,258
Lawrence 62,319	Washington 63,251

Cities and other areas over 10,000 (2000 population)

Athens 21,342	Marietta 14,515
Boardman CDP 37,215	Salem 12,197
East Liverpool 13,089	Steubenville 19,015
Ironton 11,211	

Race and Hispanic or Latino origin*
White   95.2%
Black or African American   2.4%
American Indian or Alaska Native   0.2%
Asian   0.5%
Native Hawaiian or other Pacific Islander   0.0%
Some other race   0.1%
Hispanic or Latino origin   0.8%
Two or more races   0.8%

*As percentage of total population.

Ancestry*

Dutch 1.5%	Polish 2.6%
English 7.7%	Scotch-Irish 1.6%
French 1.3%	Scottish 1.4%
German 15.2%	Slovak 1.6%
Irish 9.9%	USA/American 8.4%
Italian 5.8%	Welsh 1.1%

*As estimated percentage of total population.

Universities and colleges, 2000–2001 enrollment
Franciscan University, Steubenville   2,154
Jefferson Community College, Steubenville   1,482
Kent State University, East Liverpool   584
Kent State University, Salem   990
Marietta College, Marietta   1,238
O. C. Collins Career Center, Chesapeake   502
Ohio University, Athens   19,920
Ohio University, Ironton   2,250
University of Rio Grande, Rio Grande   2,107
Washington State Community College, Marietta
  1,911

Newspapers and circulation

	District circulation	Total circulation
Alliance Review	5,318	12,715
Athens Messenger	6,223	11,152
Cambridge Daily Jeffersonian	1,866	12,205
Canton Repository	1,172	64,499
Columbus Dispatch	3,214	245,310

East Liverpool Review	7,566	9,763
Gallipolis Daily Tribune	4,949	4,949
Huntington Herald Dispatch	7,304	35,241
Lisbon Morning Journal	12,758	13,310
Marietta Times	10,333	11,645
Martins Ferry Times Leader	13,608	18,408
Parkersburg News	4,016	20,956
Parkersburg News/Sentinel	4,746	27,185
Pittsburgh Post-Gazette	1,158	240,791
Pomeroy Daily Sentinel	4,360	4,360
Portsmouth Daily Times	6,400	14,915
Salem News	7,804	7,900
Steubenville Herald-Star	12,737	15,442
*USA Today**	7,044	1,674,376
Wheeling Intelligencer	6,678	20,126
Wheeling News-Register	9,305	52,757
Youngstown Vindicator	26,709	70,119

See Sources and Explanations in the front of the volume.

Television stations and affiliations

Charleston-Huntington, WV	38%	WCHS	ABC
Charleston-Huntington, WV	38%	WHCP	WB, UPN
Charleston-Huntington, WV	38%	WKAS	PBS
Charleston-Huntington, WV	38%	WKPI	PBS
Charleston-Huntington, WV	38%	WOUB	PBS
Charleston-Huntington, WV	38%	WOWK	CBS
Charleston-Huntington, WV	38%	WPBO	PBS
Charleston-Huntington, WV	38%	WPBY	PBS
Charleston-Huntington, WV	38%	WSAZ	NBC
Charleston-Huntington, WV	38%	WTSF	Independent
Charleston-Huntington, WV	38%	WVAH	FOX
Wheeling-Steubenville	33%	WTRF	CBS
Youngstown	17%	WFMJ	NBC
Youngstown	17%	WNEO	PBS
Youngstown	17%	WYTV	ABC
Parkersburg, WV	12%	WTAP	NBC

Cable systems and subscribers

Adelphia   20,343
Armstrong   26,604
CableVision Communications   5,472
Charter   18,408
Classic   979
Comcast   42,564
Community TV Systems   748
Jefferson Co. Cable   3,068
Nelsonville TV Cable   1,281
Powhatan Point Cable   13,555
Richards TV Cable   803
Thompson Cablevision   5,507
Time Warner   12,707

Businesses and other major employers

Ohio University; Athens; elementary and secondary schools   5,000
Ormet Corp.; Hannibal; aluminum products   2,500
Ohio University; Athens   1,812
Wheeling-Pittsburgh Steel Corp.; Mingo Junction; hot-rolled steel sheet or strip   1,000
Marietta Memorial Hospital Inc.; Marietta   900
Holzer Hospital Foundation Inc.; Gallipolis   898
Southern Ohio Coal Co.; Albany; anthracite mining   822

Trinity Medical Center West; Steubenville   800
Salem Community Hospital; Salem   790
Ohio Edison Co.; Stratton; electric power generation   785
Ohio Dept. of Rehabilitation and Correction; Lucasville   734
City Hospital Assn.; East Liverpool   700
Holzer Clinic; Gallipolis; medical services organization   700
Blackhawk Automotive Plastics Inc.; Salem; plastics molding   680
Fresh Mark Inc.; Salem; meatpacking plants   650
Wheeling-Pittsburgh Steel Corp.; Yorkville; cold finishing of steel shapes   650
Jefferson County; Steubenville; county government   600
Ohio Mental Health Dept.; Gallipolis   600
Eramet Marietta Inc.; Marietta; ferroalloys   550
Wal-Mart Stores Inc.; East Liverpool; department stores   540
Titanium Metals Corp.; Toronto; speed changers, drives, gears   527
Copeland Oaks; Sebring; convalescent home   500
Wheeling-Pittsburgh Steel Corp.; Steubenville; blast furnaces and steel mills   500

Ohio 7th District

Central — Springfield, Lancaster, part of Columbus

The 7th District begins in Clark County, located west of Columbus and just east of Dayton, then curls south and east past Columbus all the way to rural Perry County, near Zanesville. It exhibits a strong GOP lean, though the excision of several conservative rural counties in redistricting following the 2000 census marginally lessened the 7th's right-of-center voting tendencies.

The district's two most populous counties—Greene and Clark—form the western portion of the district. Wright-Patterson Air Force Base, most of which is in Greene, is the largest single-site employer in Ohio. Greene also has several colleges and universities.

Clark and its county seat, Springfield, suffered economically in the early 1980s but have seen a dramatic turnaround. New companies, including trucking and auto manufacturing plants, now call the area home. Major employers include International Truck and Engine Corp., Nortel, and Du Pont. Clark voted Democratic for president in 2000, one of just three Ohio counties west of Franklin County (Columbus) to do so.

Residential growth around Columbus has especially affected Clark and Fairfield Counties, which serve as bedroom communities and are filling up with white-collar commuters. Fairfield is solidly Republican, as are Fayette and Pickaway Counties to its west. Fayette, the least populous county wholly within the 7th, is a major horse-breeding area. Perry, the easternmost county in the 7th, has above-average unemployment.

The 7th was redrawn in 2002 to include about 86,000 people in southeast Franklin County, including a small portion of Columbus.

Major Industry

Auto manufacturing, military, technology research, agriculture.

Notable

Gen. William Tecumseh Sherman was born in Lancaster; the modern combine, invented in Springfield, helped revolutionize harvesting and the agriculture industry.

Election Returns

	Republican		Democratic		Other	
President 2000	137,548	55.5%	102,846	41.5%	7,644	3.1%
House 2002	113,252	67.6%	45,568	27.2%	8,812	5.3%

District Profile

Population   630,730

Total area (square miles)   2,865.6
Land area (square miles)   2,848.1

Population per square mile   221.5

Counties (2000 population)

Clark 144,742	Greene 147,886
Fairfield 122,759	Perry 34,078
Fayette 28,433	Pickaway 52,727
Franklin (pt.) 86,106	Ross (pt.) 13,999

Cities and other areas over 10,000 (2000 population)

Beavercreek 37,984	Springfield 65,358
Circleville 13,485	Washington 13,524
Columbus (pt.) 51,097	Whitehall 19,201
Fairborn 32,052	Xenia 24,164
Lancaster 35,335	

Race and Hispanic or Latino origin*

White   88.7%
Black or African American   7.5%
American Indian or Alaska Native   0.3%
Asian   1.0%
Native Hawaiian or other Pacific Islander   0.0%
Some other race   0.1%
Hispanic or Latino origin   1.1%
Two or more races   1.3%

*As percentage of total population.

Ancestry*

Dutch 1.8%	Italian 2.3%
English 7.4%	Polish 1.2%
French 1.6%	Scotch-Irish 1.2%
German 17.6%	Scottish 1.4%
Irish 9.3%	USA/American 10.1%

*As estimated percentage of total population.

Universities and colleges, 2000–2001 enrollment

Air Force Institute of Technology, Wright-Patterson Air Force Base   561
Antioch College, Yellow Springs   652
Cedarville University, Cedarville   2,855
Central State University, Wilberforce   1,103
Clark State Community College, Springfield   2,808
Ohio University, Lancaster   1,585
Payne Theological Seminary, Wilberforce   238
McGregor School of Antioch University, Yellow Springs   644
Wilberforce University, Wilberforce   925
Wittenberg University, Springfield   2,273
Wright State University, Dayton   13,964

Newspapers and circulation

	District circulation	Total circulation
Chillicothe Gazette	2,764	16,233
Circleville Herald	6,318	6,907
Columbus Dispatch	32,067	245,310
Dayton Daily News	22,362	135,680
Lancaster Eagle-Gazette	14,750	15,253
Springfield News-Sun	27,056	31,035
*USA Today**	7,435	1,674,376
Xenia Daily Gazette	6,104	6,189
Zanesville Times Recorder	2,309	21,051

*See Sources and Explanations in the front of the volume.

Television stations and affiliations

Columbus	71%	WBNS	CBS
Columbus	71%	WCMH	NBC
Columbus	71%	WOSU	PBS
Columbus	71%	WOUC	PBS
Columbus	71%	WSFJ	PAX
Columbus	71%	WSYX	ABC
Columbus	71%	WTTE	FOX
Columbus	71%	WWHO	UPN, WB
Dayton	29%	WBDT	WB, PAX
Dayton	29%	WDTN	ABC
Dayton	29%	WHIO	CBS
Dayton	29%	WKEF	NBC
Dayton	29%	WPTD	PBS
Dayton	29%	WRGT	FOX

Cable systems and subscribers

Adelphia   23,260
CableVision Communications   3,686
Insight   12,203
Time Warner   121,280

Military installations, September 2001

Wright-Patterson Air Force Base, Fairborn   17,718
Navy Air Reserve Center, Columbus   281

Businesses and other major employers

U.S. Defense Dept.; Columbus   6,000
International Truck and Engine Corp.; Springfield; truck/tractor truck assembly   4,000
Nortel Networks Inc.; Cedarville; telecommunication repair   3,000
Wright State University; Dayton   1,960
Army and Air Force Exchange Service; Dayton; Army-Navy goods stores, recreation   1,670
Fairfield Medical Center; Lancaster   1,587
JC Penney Corp.; Columbus; warehousing   1,500
Ohio National Guard; Columbus   1,500
Community Hospital of Springfield and Clark County; Springfield   1,300
U.S. Veterans Hospital; Chillicothe   1,300
Mercy Health System Western Ohio; Springfield; drug and proprietary stores   1,200
Springfield Board of Education; Springfield   1,200

Thomson Multimedia Inc.; Circleville; audio/video equipment 1,100

Anchor Hocking Corp.; Lancaster; glass containers 1,000

E. I. Du Pont De Nemours and Co.; Circleville; polyesters 1,000

Alliance Data Systems Corp.; Columbus; data processing 800

Meijer Inc.; Fairborn; department stores 800

Speedway SuperAmerica; Enon; gas stations 800

Adcare Health Systems Inc.; Springfield; health services consultant 650

Rittal Corp.; Springfield; electronic enclosures 635

Antioch College; Yellow Springs 600

Clark State Community College; Springfield; vocational schools 600

General Electric Co.; Circleville; commercial lighting 600

Greene Memorial Hospital Inc.; Xenia 600

Meijer Inc.; Springfield; department stores 600

Yusa Corp.; Washington Court House; motor mounting rings 600

SuperValu Inc.; Xenia; food supplier 565

Diamond Power International Inc.; Lancaster; space vehicle guidance systems 557

Oasis Corp.; Columbus; drinking fountains 550

Ohio Dept. of Rehabilitation and Correction; Orient 544

Sugar Creek Packing Co.; Washington Court House; bacon 529

Clark State Community College; Springfield 510

Cedarville University Inc.; Cedarville 500

Meijer Inc.; Columbus; department stores 500

Relizon Co.; Dayton; design services 500

RMA Intermediate Holdings Inc.; Columbus; collection agency 500

Science Applications International Corp.; Frankfort; management consulting 500

Ohio 8th District

Southwest — Hamilton, most of Middletown

Running along the state's western border, the 8th is fertile GOP ground that is anchored by Butler County, home to the district's two largest cities, Hamilton and Middletown.

Butler has long voted solidly Republican, but the expansion of its suburbs has escalated the rightward trend. The county is known for electing some of Ohio's more conservative state and congressional legislators. George W. Bush took 63 percent of Butler's vote in the 2000 presidential election. One exception to the GOP dominance is Oxford, which includes Miami University and voted narrowly for Al Gore in 2000.

Butler and Miami Counties have propelled the district's rapid growth. Union Township, in Butler County, is one of the state's fastest growing suburbs, and many residents there commute to Cincinnati or Dayton. While bad weather and low pork prices hurt the 8th's dominant agriculture industry in the late 1990s, the district's strong manufacturing base, along with new construction and commercial de-

velopment, helped prevent economic hardship. Honeywell, American Express, and AK Steel Corp. are among the largest employers.

About half the 8th's residents live outside Butler County in a string of fertile Corn Belt counties. Corn and soybeans are the major cash crops here, and poultry and livestock also are moneymakers. Mercer (shared with the 5th) and Darke are Ohio's two top-producing soybean and corn counties, and they also yield plenty of Republican votes, backing Bush with 68 percent and 64 percent respectively. Miami County, the district's second most populous, also is reliable GOP turf.

Redistricting in 2002 gave the 8th a bigger chunk of Montgomery County, including parts of northeast Dayton near Wright-Patterson Air Force Base. The new map ceded a small part of southwestern Butler County to the 1st District and moved the 8th's northeast border farther south.

Major Industry
Agriculture, manufacturing, higher education.

Notable
Hamilton once was known as the safe capital of the world for the burglar-resistant safes made there; Darke County hosts an Annie Oakley festival each year in honor of their home-grown sharpshooter.

Election Returns

	Republican		Democratic		Other	
President 2000	155,132	61.0%	91,744	36.1%	7,371	2.9%
House 2002	119,947	70.8%	49,444	29.2%		

District Profile

Population 630,730

Total area (square miles) 2,031.3
  Land area (square miles) 2,013.9

Population per square mile 313.2

Counties (2000 population)

Butler (pt.) 311,040	Miami 98,868
Darke 53,309	Montgomery (pt.) 93,967
Mercer (pt.) 31,209	Preble 42,337

Cities and other areas over 10,000 (2000 population)

Celina 10,303	Middletown (pt.) 49,574
Dayton (pt.) 28,999	Oxford 21,943
Fairfield (pt.) 42,097	Piqua 20,738
Greenville 13,294	Riverside (pt.) 17,868
Hamilton (pt.) 60,675	Troy 21,999
Huber Heights 38,212	

Race and Hispanic or Latino origin*
White 91.8%
Black or African American 4.4%
American Indian or Alaska Native 0.2%
Asian 1.2%
Native Hawaiian or other Pacific Islander 0.0%
Some other race 0.1%
Hispanic or Latino origin 1.3%
Two or more races 1.1%

As percentage of total population.

Ancestry*

Dutch	1.5%	Italian	2.4%
English	7.3%	Polish	1.2%
French	2.3%	Scotch-Irish	1.1%
German	22.0%	Scottish	1.3%
Irish	8.9%	USA/American	9.8%

*As estimated percentage of total population.

Universities and colleges, 2000–2001 enrollment

Edison State Community College, Piqua   2,877
Miami University, Hamilton   2,318
Miami University, Middletown   2,073
Miami University, Oxford   16,757
Wright State University-Lake, Celina   639

Newspapers and circulation

	District circulation	Total circulation
Cincinnati Enquirer	20,120	189,326
Dayton Daily News	27,689	135,680
Greenville Daily Advocate	6,926	7,029
Hamilton Journal-News	15,831	22,691
Middletown Journal	16,665	22,091
Piqua Daily Call	5,756	6,679
Richmond Palladium-Item	2,189	18,474
Troy Daily News	10,116	10,326
*USA Today**	3,681	1,674,376

*See Sources and Explanations in the front of the volume.

Television stations and affiliations

Dayton	84%	WBDT	WB, PAX
Dayton	84%	WDTN	ABC
Dayton	84%	WHIO	CBS
Dayton	84%	WKEF	NBC
Dayton	84%	WPTD	PBS
Dayton	84%	WRGT	FOX
Cincinnati	16%	WCET	PBS
Cincinnati	16%	WCPO	ABC
Cincinnati	16%	WCVN	PBS
Cincinnati	16%	WKOI	Independent
Cincinnati	16%	WKON	PBS
Cincinnati	16%	WKRC	CBS
Cincinnati	16%	WLWT	NBC
Cincinnati	16%	WPTO	PBS
Cincinnati	16%	WSTR	WB
Cincinnati	16%	WXIX	FOX

Cable systems and subscribers

Adelphia   2,738
Time Warner   113,471

Businesses and other major employers

West American Insurance Co.; Fairfield; workers' compensation insurance   3,280
AK Steel Corp.; Middletown; blast furnaces and steel mills   3,000
Miami University Inc.; Oxford   2,900
Cincinnati Insurance Co.; Fairfield; fire, marine, casualty insurance   2,600
Behr America Inc.; Dayton; roofing, siding, insulation   2,000
American Express Financial Advisors Inc.; Piqua; financial consultant   2,000
Reliance Resource Inc.; West Chester; employee leasing service   1,950
Middletown Regional Hospital; Middletown   1,609
International Paper Co.; Hamilton; paper mills   1,510
Delphi Corp.; Dayton; metal forming brakes   1,500
Dayton Children's Medical Center; Dayton   1,450
Ohio Casualty Corp.; Hamilton; fire, marine, casualty insurance   1,430
Lakota Local School District; Middletown   1,400
PaySource Inc.; Dayton; employee leasing service   1,400
Hobart Corp.; Troy; commercial dishwashers   1,300
Honeywell International Inc.; Greenville; automotive air, fuel, oil filters   1,300
Ohio Casualty Insurance Co.; Fairfield; automobile insurance   1,200
Fort Hamilton Hospital; Hamilton   1,196
Upper Valley Medical Center Inc.; Troy   1,120
Systemax Manufacturing Inc.; Fletcher; computer peripherals, software   1,000
Watkins Motor Lines Inc.; West Chester; trucking   1,000
Cornerstone Consolidated Services Group; West Chester; mail-order catalog   910
General Electric Co.; Cincinnati; aircraft electrical equipment repair   900
Hobart Brothers Co.; Troy; welding apparatus   900
Meijer Inc.; Dayton; department stores   879
Illinois Tool Works Inc.; Troy; molded plastics   800
Meijer Inc.; Hamilton; department stores   800
Meijer Inc.; Tipp City; warehousing   785
Goodrich Corp.; Troy; aircraft   750
Neaton Auto Products Manufacturing Inc.; Eaton; automotive parts/accessories   705
Spalding Sports Worlwide Inc.; Piqua; juvenile furniture   700
Buschman Co.; Cincinnati; conveyors and equipment   686
ABF Freight System Inc.; Dayton; contract haulers   600
Butler County of Ohio; Hamilton; county government   600
F&P America Manufacturing Inc.; Troy; automotive parts/accessories   600
Greenville Technology Inc.; Greenville; automotive parts/accessories   600
Miller Brewing Co.; Trenton; malt beverages   600
Roadway Express Inc.; Cincinnati; trucking terminals   600
Spectra Precision Inc.; Dayton; laser systems and equipment   600
Square D Co.; Oxford; electrical bus bars   600
Teamsters Local Union; Middletown; trade union   600
Pierre Foods Inc.; Cincinnati; biscuits   580
Alexson Services Inc.; Fairfield; health services   550
Contech Construction Products Inc.; Middletown; fabricated plate work   500
Corning Inc.; Greenville; pressed and blown glass   500
Illinois Tool Works Inc.; Troy; welding rods   500
Meijer Inc.; Fairfield; department stores   500
Meijer Inc.; West Chester; department stores   500
Merck-Medco Managed Care; Fairfield; mail-order pharmaceuticals   500
Midmark Corp.; Versailles; operating tables   500
Xerox Corp.; Cincinnati; photocopiers   500

Ohio 9th District

North — Toledo, Sandusky

The 9th surrounds Toledo, stretching from Lucas County on the Michigan border to southwestern Lorain County. About half of the district's residents live in Toledo, which sits at the mouth of the Maumee River, the largest river flowing into the Great Lakes. Toledo's large concentrations of ethnic blue-collar workers—Germans, Irish, Poles, and Hungarians—make it a lonely Democratic outpost in rural, Republican northwestern Ohio.

Republicans are concentrated in the more affluent suburbs on Toledo's west side, such as upscale Ottawa Hills. But Toledo's Democratic voters overwhelm Republicans elsewhere in the district.

Toledo's economy has long depended on the auto industry, which closed several area factories in the 1980s. But the industry is back, albeit in smaller form, with a DaimlerChrysler Jeep assembly plant and a General Motors parts facility. Growth in the city's petroleum and manufacturing industries, including glass and machinery, also has spurred some economic recovery.

To the east of Lucas is Ottawa County, which includes Port Clinton and some islands near Canada's Pelee Island, and Erie County, which includes Sandusky and has a blue-collar feel and a slight Democratic lean. The district's easternmost county is Lorain, parts of which were drawn into the 9th along with Erie County and Sandusky in redistricting following the 2000 census. There is a liberal area around Oberlin College, where residents took a strong antislavery stance in the nineteenth century and continue to crusade for social reforms.

Major Industry
Auto manufacturing, agriculture, health care.

Notable
Toledo's historic "Old West End" is known for its Victorian homes and claims to have been the nation's largest residential neighborhood at the turn of the century; Oberlin College, founded in 1833, was the first coeducational institution of higher learning in the United States.

Election Returns

	Republican		Democratic		Other	
President 2000	100,704	41.4%	134,907	55.4%	7,894	3.2%
House 2002	46,481	26.0%	132,236	74.0%		

District Profile

Population   630,730

Total area (square miles)   1,244.1
   Land area (square miles)   1,101.5

Population per square mile   572.6

Counties (2000 population)
Erie   79,551
Lorain (pt.)   71,615
Lucas (pt.)   438,579
Ottawa   40,985

Cities and other areas over 10,000 (2000 population)
Amherst   11,797
Maumee   15,237
Oregon (pt.)   19,355
Sandusky (pt.)   27,844
Sylvania   18,670
Toledo   313,619
Vermilion   10,927

Race and Hispanic or Latino origin*
White   79.6%
Black or African American   13.6%
American Indian or Alaska Native   0.2%
Asian   1.0%
Native Hawaiian or other Pacific Islander   0.0%
Some other race   0.1%
Hispanic or Latino origin   4.0%
Two or more races   1.5%

As percentage of total population.

Ancestry*
Dutch   1.2%
English   6.2%
French   3.2%
German   21.3%
Hungarian   1.9%
Irish   8.9%
Italian   3.2%
Polish   6.4%
Scottish   1.1%
USA/American   3.6%

As estimated percentage of total population.

Universities and colleges, 2000–2001 enrollment
Bowling Green State University-Firelands, Huron   1,471
Davis College, Toledo   434
Lourdes College, Sylvania   1,312
Medical College of Ohio, Toledo   974
Mercy College of Northwest Ohio, Toledo   208
Oberlin College, Oberlin   2,928
University of Toledo, Toledo   19,491

Newspapers and circulation

	District circulation	Total circulation
Cleveland Plain Dealer	6,865	362,446
Elyria Chronicle-Telegram	11,873	25,793
Lorain Morning Journal	12,490	33,328
Norwalk Reflector	1,083	8,706
Port Clinton News Herald	5,614	5,683
Sandusky Register	18,767	22,761
Toledo Blade	91,382	138,304
*USA Today**	7,494	1,674,376

See Sources and Explanations in the front of the volume.

Television stations and affiliations

Toledo	54%	WBGU	PBS
Toledo	54%	WGTE	PBS
Toledo	54%	WINM	Independent
Toledo	54%	WLMB	PAX
Toledo	54%	WNWO	NBC
Toledo	54%	WTOL	CBS
Toledo	54%	WTVG	ABC
Toledo	54%	WUPW	FOX
Cleveland-Akron (Canton)	46%	WBNX	WB
Cleveland-Akron (Canton)	46%	WDLI	Independent
Cleveland-Akron (Canton)	46%	WEAO	PBS
Cleveland-Akron (Canton)	46%	WEWS	ABC
Cleveland-Akron (Canton)	46%	WGGN	Independent
Cleveland-Akron (Canton)	46%	WJW	FOX

Cleveland-Akron (Canton)	46%	WKYC	NBC
Cleveland-Akron (Canton)	46%	WMFD	Independent
Cleveland-Akron (Canton)	46%	WOAC	Independent
Cleveland-Akron (Canton)	46%	WOIO	CBS
Cleveland-Akron (Canton)	46%	WQHS	Univision
Cleveland-Akron (Canton)	46%	WUAB	UPN
Cleveland-Akron (Canton)	46%	WVIZ	PBS
Cleveland-Akron (Canton)	46%	WVPX	PAX

Cable systems and subscribers
Adelphia   11,367
Buckeye Cablevision   113,293
Cable Co-Op   1,558
Comcast   4,659
Erie County Cablevision   15,445
South Shore Cable   1,131
Time Warner   1,309

Military installations, September 2001
Toledo Express Airport Air National Guard Station, Swanton   1,032
Toledo Area U.S. Army Reserve, Toledo   321
Camp Perry Air National Guard Station, Port Clinton 205
Camp Perry Training Site, Port Clinton   119
Cooney U.S. Army Reserve Center, Sandusky   108

Businesses and other major employers
Kellermeyer Building Services; Maumee; building maintenance   6,600
Toledo Hospital; Toledo   6,000
Mercy Health Partners; Toledo; hospital management 5,500
DaimlerChrysler Corp.; Toledo; motor vehicles and car bodies   5,000
General Motors Corp.; Toledo; electric power transmission   5,000
Franciscan Care Center Hospital; Sylvania   4,800
ProMedica Health System Inc.; Toledo; investment holding company   4,500
Medical College of Ohio; Toledo   3,200
St. Vincent Mercy Medical Center; Toledo   2,900
University of Toledo; Toledo   2,700
Owens-Brockway Glass Container Inc.; Toledo   2,500
TSL Ltd.; Toledo; truck driver services   2,495
Delphi Corp.; Sandusky; ball and roller bearings   2,000
Exel Logistics Inc.; Toledo; local trucking   2,000
Owens Corning; Toledo; fiberglass insulation   1,800
St. Charles Mercy Hospital; Oregon   1,681
United Parcel Service Inc.; Maumee; package delivery 1,600
St. Luke's Hospital; Maumee   1,540
U.S. Postal Service; Toledo   1,500
Camp Fire USA Firelands Council; Sandusky; individual and family services   1,000
Nordson Corp.; Amherst; compressor spraying equipment   1,000
AP Automotive Holdings; Toledo; automotive exhaust systems   925
Oberlin College; Oberlin   906
Job 1 USA Inc.; Toledo; security guard service   900
Flower Hospital; Sylvania   889
Riverside Mercy Hospital; Toledo   857
Ford Motor Co.; Maumee; automotive stampings   817

Allied Healthcare Products Inc.; Toledo; medical instruments   800
Magnum Management Corp.; Sandusky; toll-bridge operation   800
Toledo Edison Co.; Oak Harbor; electric power generation   800
Washington Local Schools; Toledo   800
Lucas County; Toledo; school for mentally retarded 750
Brush Wellman Inc.; Elmore; beryllium metal   700
FirstEnergy Corp.; Oak Harbor; electric services   700
Lear Corp.; Huron; molded plastics   700
Faurecia Exhaust Systems Inc.; Toledo; automotive exhaust systems   650
Firelands Regional Health System Hospital; Sandusky 603
Lucas County; Toledo; county government   600
Manor Care Inc.; Toledo; convalescent home   600
Xanterra Parks and Resorts; Oregon; restaurants   600
Seaway Food Town Inc.; Maumee; supermarkets   591
Lucas County; Toledo; public welfare administration 589
Toledo Clinic Inc.; Toledo   550
Sunoco Inc.; Oregon; petroleum refining   530
Phycor Inc.; Toledo; physicians' office   521
Pilkington North America Inc.; Toledo; plate/sheet glass 520
BP America Inc.; Toledo; gas stations   510
Toledo Building Services Co.; Toledo; commercial cleaning services   510
Concept Rehab Inc.; Toledo; outpatient rehabilitation center   500
Medical Mutual of Ohio Inc.; Toledo; medical service plans   500
Meijer Inc.; Oregon; department stores   500
Meijer Inc.; Toledo; department stores   500
Meijer Inc.; Sandusky; department stores   500
Product Design and Engineering Inc.; Toledo; engineering services   500
Reese Brothers Inc.; Norwalk; telemarketing services 500
Toledo Edison Co.; Toledo; electric power generation 500

Ohio 10th District

Cleveland — West Side and suburbs

The 10th includes the western portion of Cleveland and follows the migration of its ethnic residents into the western and southern suburbs. *(See map p. 725.)*

The district, composed mainly of Reagan Democrats, has successfully navigated the transition from an industrial to a service economy.

The line between the 10th and 11th Districts generally divides Cleveland's white and black neighborhoods. The 10th contains the state's largest concentration of ethnic voters, mostly Poles, Czechs, Italians, Irish, and Germans. Although industry still provides the backbone of the city's economy, the 10th has attracted smaller, high-tech companies and undergone a downtown restoration, helping the district maintain its steady employment base.

CLEVELAND AND COLUMBUS AREAS

Cleveland Area

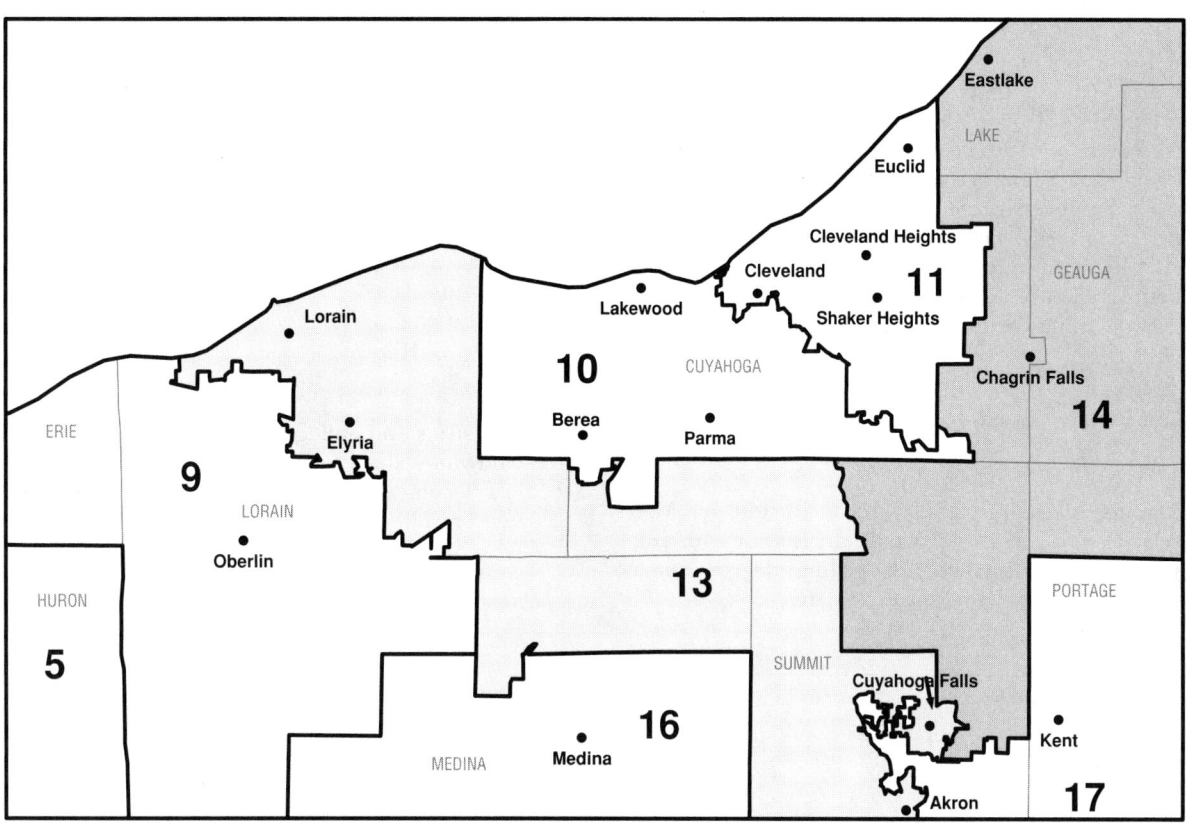

Columbus Area

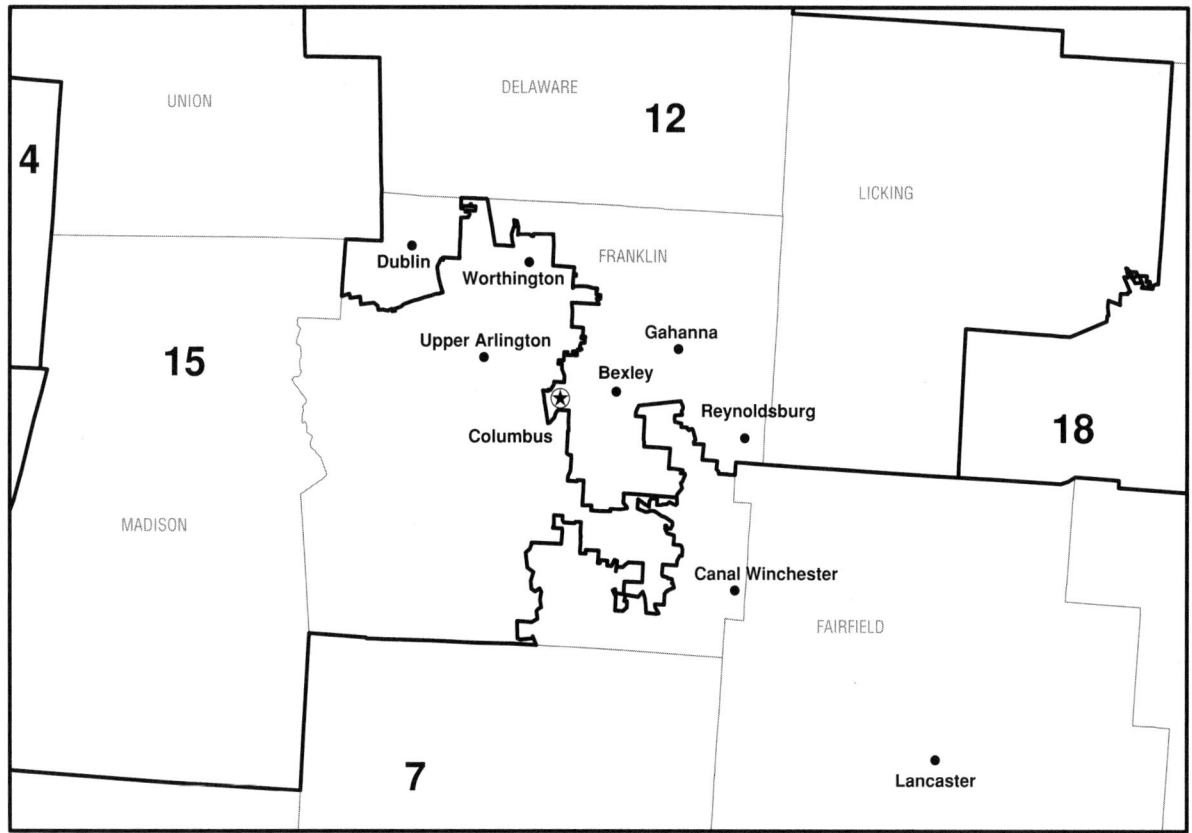

The immediate suburbs have a strong union presence and a Democratic lean. The communities of Brooklyn and Lakewood, which abut western Cleveland, are middle-income and lean Democratic. Farther west the incomes rise, as does the level of Republicanism: Bay Village and Westlake residents have above-average incomes and voted solidly for George W. Bush in the 2000 presidential election.

Redistricting following the 2000 census altered the 10th to take in some of central Cuyahoga County—including Brook Park, Middleburg Heights, and Parma Heights—that had been in the old 19th District. Brook Park is a blue-collar autoworkers' community that is decidedly Democratic. Ford Motor Co. has several large plants in the district.

The strong Democratic tendencies of Cleveland, coupled with the Republican leanings of some of the city's western and southern suburbs, combine to give the 10th a slight but not overwhelming Democratic lean.

Major Industry
Manufacturing, banking, technology, auto parts.

Notable
A publisher dropped an "a" from city founder Moses Cleaveland's name so that it would fit neatly on his page, giving the city's name its current spelling; the city is home to NASA's John H. Glenn Research Center.

Election Returns

	Republican		Democratic		Other	
President 2000	96,623	41.9%	122,219	53.1%	11,540	5.0%
House 2002	41,778	23.8%	129,997	74.1%	3,761	2.1%

District Profile

Population   630,730

Total area (square miles)   195.7
   Land area (square miles)   195.4

Population per square mile   3,227.9

Counties (2000 population)
   Cuyahoga (pt.)   630,730

Cities and other areas over 10,000 (2000 population)
   Bay Village (pt.)   16,087
   Berea   18,970
   Brooklyn   11,586
   Brook Park   21,218
   Cleveland (pt.)   190,224
   Fairview Park   17,572
   Garfield Heights (pt.)   26,577
   Lakewood (pt.)   56,646
   Middleburg Heights   15,542
   North Olmsted   34,113
   Parma   85,655
   Parma Heights   21,659
   Rocky River (pt.)   20,735
   Seven Hills   12,080
   Strongsville (pt.)   14,143
   Westlake   31,719

Race and Hispanic or Latino origin*
White   87.2%
Black or African American   4.2%
American Indian or Alaska Native   0.2%
Asian   1.7%
Native Hawaiian or other Pacific Islander   0.0%
Some other race   0.1%
Hispanic or Latino origin   5.0%
Two or more races   1.5%

*As percentage of total population.

Ancestry*
Arab-Misc. 1.2%	Italian 7.7%
English 5.3%	Polish 8.7%
French 1.4%	Scottish 1.1%
German 16.6%	Slovak 4.0%
Hungarian 3.1%	Ukrainian 1.3%
Irish 12.8%	USA/American 2.5%

*As estimated percentage of total population.

Universities and colleges, 2000–2001 enrollment
Baldwin-Wallace College, Berea   4,831
ITT Technical Institute, Strongsville   397
Sawyer College of Business-West, Cleveland   479
West Side Institute of Technology, Cleveland   262

Newspapers and circulation

	District circulation	Total circulation
Bedford Sun Banner	1,628	4,215
Berea News Sun	14,354	14,667
Brooklyn Sun Journal	6,860	7,099
Cleveland Plain Dealer	124,244	362,446
Garfield/Maple Heights Sun	4,014	7,629
Lakewood Sun Post	8,368	8,452
Parma Sun Post	22,135	22,397
Strongsville Sun Star	2,887	10,988
Sun Newspaper Group	86,290	167,715
*USA Today**	6,981	1,674,376
Valley View Sun Courier	1,769	6,575
Valley View Sun Herald	13,743	13,849
West Side Sun News	12,992	13,902

*See Sources and Explanations in the front of the volume.

Television stations and affiliations
Cleveland-Akron (Canton)	100%	WBNX	WB
Cleveland-Akron (Canton)	100%	WDLI	Independent
Cleveland-Akron (Canton)	100%	WEAO	PBS
Cleveland-Akron (Canton)	100%	WEWS	ABC
Cleveland-Akron (Canton)	100%	WGGN	Independent
Cleveland-Akron (Canton)	100%	WJW	FOX
Cleveland-Akron (Canton)	100%	WKYC	NBC
Cleveland-Akron (Canton)	100%	WMFD	Independent
Cleveland-Akron (Canton)	100%	WOAC	Independent
Cleveland-Akron (Canton)	100%	WOIO	CBS
Cleveland-Akron (Canton)	100%	WQHS	Univision
Cleveland-Akron (Canton)	100%	WUAB	UPN
Cleveland-Akron (Canton)	100%	WVIZ	PBS
Cleveland-Akron (Canton)	100%	WVPX	PAX

Cable systems and subscribers
Adelphia   42,231
Comcast   4,686
Cox   58,078

Businesses and other major employers

Ford Motor Co.; Cleveland; automotive engines and parts   6,000

LTV Steel Co.; Cleveland; steel sheets/strips   5,000

Ford Motor Co.; Cleveland; automotive parts/accessories   3,600

National Aeronautics and Space Admin.; Cleveland; space research/development   3,359

American Greetings Corp.; Cleveland; greeting cards   3,000

Cleveland Clinic Health System-Western Region; Cleveland   2,800

Alcoa Inc.; Cleveland; aluminum forgings   2,500

Southwest General Health Center Inc.; Cleveland   2,400

Ford Motor Co.; Cleveland; automotive stampings   2,200

Gibson Greetings Inc.; Cleveland; greeting cards   1,800

Parma Community General Hospital Assn.; Cleveland   1,667

JG Shopping Center Management; Cleveland; real estate managers   1,300

Baldwin Wallace College; Berea   1,103

Lakewood Hospital Assn.; Cleveland   1,100

Burns International Security Services Corp.; Cleveland; detective, armored car services   1,000

United Parcel Service Inc.; Cleveland; parcel delivery   1,000

Marymount Hospital Inc.; Cleveland   982

City of Cleveland; Cleveland; fire dept.   975

Arrow International Inc.; Cleveland; commercial printing   900

First Choice Medical Staffing of Ohio Inc.; Cleveland; personal service agents   850

Deaconess Hospital; Cleveland   818

Ford Motor Co.; Bedford; automotive stampings   817

Cuyahoga County; Cleveland; public special education school   800

Axia Inc.; Cleveland; insulated or armored steel wire   700

Sears Roebuck and Co. Inc.; Cleveland; department stores   700

PPG Industries Ohio Inc.; Cleveland; paints and allied products   602

Tersher Corp.; Cleveland; household goods transport   600

UHHS/CSAHS-Cuyahoga Inc. Hospital; Cleveland   600

Central Reserve Life Insurance Co.; Cleveland; life insurance   590

Industrial Security Service Inc.; Cleveland; security guard service   523

Bonne Bell Inc.; Cleveland; cosmetics   508

Birmingham Steel Corp.; Cleveland; blast furnaces and steel mills   500

Bridgestone/Firestone North American Tire; Cleveland; sales promotion   500

General Motors Corp.; Cleveland; automotive transmissions   500

Keybank National Assn.; Cleveland; commercial bank   500

Kirkwood Industries Inc.; Cleveland; motors and generators   500

May Department Stores Co.; Cleveland   500

Scott Fetzer Co.; Westlake; nonelectric transformers   500

Ohio 11th District

Cleveland — East Side and suburbs

The 11th consists of the poor, inner-city areas of Cleveland's East Side and fans out to the east to include upper-middle-class suburbs. The district's black-majority and liberal suburbanites combine to make it overwhelmingly Democratic. *(See map p. 725.)*

The 11th includes 60 percent of Cleveland's residents. Although suburban growth has lured many businesses and residents outside the city, there has been a smattering of commercial and residential development in the downtown area. Redistricting following the 2000 census moved the district line west to take in the Rock and Roll Hall of Fame and the sports stadiums for baseball's Indians, football's Browns, and basketball's Cavaliers.

Much of the district's black majority lives in inner-city neighborhoods, mostly below the poverty line. There are some middle-class neighborhoods toward Lake Erie, inhabited mostly by Italians and Eastern Europeans.

The upper-middle-class suburbs of Cleveland Heights, Shaker Heights, and University Heights to the east are home to large communities of Jews and young professionals, forming some of Ohio's most liberal and racially integrated areas. Redistricting pushed the 11th farther east to take in communities such as Mayfield Heights, Richmond Heights, Lyndhurst, and Pepper Pike, which has one of the highest incomes in the state. Case Western Reserve University is located in University Circle, Cleveland's cultural center.

From the circle area, commuters drive along historic Euclid Avenue to their jobs downtown. While the avenue now bears the marks of poverty, it was known as "Millionaire's Row" at the beginning of the 20th century. Few of the old mansions remain. The one belonging to John D. Rockefeller, founder of Standard Oil, was razed after his death in 1937.

Major Industry

Health care, manufacturing, utilities.

Notable

Shaker Historical Museum; the nation's first indoor shopping mall (1890).

Election Returns

	Republican		Democratic		Other	
President 2000	38,382	17.7%	172,146	79.2%	6,706	3.1%
House 2002	36,146	23.7%	116,590	76.3%		

District Profile

Population   630,730

Total area (square miles)   135.0
  Land area (square miles)   134.5

Population per square mile   4,689.4

Counties (2000 population)
  Cuyahoga (pt.)   630,730

Cities and other areas over 10,000 (2000 population)
Beachwood   12,186
Bedford   14,214
Bedford Heights   11,375
Cleveland (pt.)   288,179
Cleveland Heights   49,958
East Cleveland   27,217
Euclid (pt.)   52,717
Lyndhurst   15,279
Maple Heights   26,156
Mayfield Heights   19,386
Richmond Heights   10,944
Shaker Heights   29,405
South Euclid   23,537
University Heights   14,146
Warrensville Heights   15,109

Race and Hispanic or Latino origin*
White   38.8%
Black or African American   55.5%
American Indian or Alaska Native   0.1%
Asian   1.6%
Native Hawaiian or other Pacific Islander   0.0%
Some other race   0.2%
Hispanic or Latino origin   2.3%
Two or more races   1.4%

*As percentage of total population.

Ancestry*
English   2.9%   Polish   3.3%
German   6.5%   Russian   1.7%
Hungarian   1.8%   Subsaharan   1.2%
Irish   5.2%   USA/American   2.0%
Italian   4.9%

*As estimated percentage of total population.

Universities and colleges, 2000–2001 enrollment
Bryant and Stratton College, Cleveland   214
Case Western Reserve University, Cleveland   9,304
Cleveland Institute of Art, Cleveland   553
Cleveland Institute of Electronics, Cleveland   5,534
Cleveland Institute of Music, Cleveland   379
Cleveland State University, Cleveland   15,294
Cuyahoga Community College District, Cleveland   19,518
David N. Myers College, Cleveland   1,227
Education America-Remington College, Cleveland   324
John Carroll University, Cleveland   4,384
Notre Dame College of Ohio, South Euclid   215
Ohio College of Podiatric Medicine, Cleveland   359
Ohio Technical College, Cleveland   518
Sawyer College of Business, Cleveland Heights   221
Ursuline College, Pepper Pike   1,252
Yavne College For Women,* Cleveland

*Enrollment under 100. See Sources and Explanations in the front of the volume.

Newspapers and circulation

	District circulation	Total circulation
Bedford Sun Banner	2,523	4,215
Cleveland Plain Dealer	107,751	362,446
Euclid Sun Journal	9,070	9,743
Garfield/Maple Heights Sun	3,588	7,629
Lake County News Herald	2,776	47,060
Sun Newspaper Group	45,435	167,715
*USA Today**	4,386	1,674,376
Valley View Sun Messenger	10,193	12,559
Valley View Sun Press	17,564	17,805
Valley View Sun Scoop Journal	3,846	3,947

*See Sources and Explanations in the front of the volume.

Television stations and affiliations
Cleveland-Akron (Canton)   100%   WBNX   WB
Cleveland-Akron (Canton)   100%   WDLI   Independent
Cleveland-Akron (Canton)   100%   WEAO   PBS
Cleveland-Akron (Canton)   100%   WEWS   ABC
Cleveland-Akron (Canton)   100%   WGGN   Independent
Cleveland-Akron (Canton)   100%   WJW   FOX
Cleveland-Akron (Canton)   100%   WKYC   NBC
Cleveland-Akron (Canton)   100%   WMFD   Independent
Cleveland-Akron (Canton)   100%   WOAC   Independent
Cleveland-Akron (Canton)   100%   WOIO   CBS
Cleveland-Akron (Canton)   100%   WQHS   Univision
Cleveland-Akron (Canton)   100%   WUAB   UPN
Cleveland-Akron (Canton)   100%   WVIZ   PBS
Cleveland-Akron (Canton)   100%   WVPX   PAX

Cable systems and subscribers
Adelphia   186,222
East Cleveland Cable TV   5,539

Businesses and other major employers
Cleveland Clinic Foundation; Cleveland   13,000
Keybank National Assn.; Cleveland; commercial bank   8,000
Ohio Bell Telephone Co.; Cleveland; local/long-distance telephone   7,971
City of Cleveland; Cleveland; public finance and monetary policy   7,500
University Hospitals of Cleveland; Cleveland   4,600
City of Cleveland; Cleveland; public safety bureau   4,290
Case Western Reserve University; Cleveland   4,000
Metrohealth Medical Center; Cleveland   4,000
Tops Markets Inc.; Cleveland; supermarkets   3,500
Lincoln Electric Co.; Cleveland; welding generators   3,200
U.S. Coast Guard; Cleveland   2,557
Cleveland State University; Cleveland   2,400
Tenable Protective Service Inc.; Cleveland; security guard service   2,240
Sherwin-Williams Co.; Cleveland; paint, glass, wallpaper stores   2,000
City of Cleveland; Cleveland; police dept.   1,838
OfficeMax Inc.; Cleveland; office supplies   1,548
Plain Dealer Publishing Co. Inc.; Cleveland; newspaper   1,520
Medical Mutual of Ohio Inc.; Cleveland; medical service plans   1,500
Transportation Unlimited Inc.; Cleveland; truck driver services   1,450
McDonald Investments Inc.; Cleveland; financial management for business   1,400
U.S. Veterans Hospital; Cleveland   1,350

National City Bank; Cleveland; commercial bank
1,300

Cuyahoga County; Cleveland; sheriff's office   1,200

Cuyahoga County; Cleveland; employment agencies
1,200

General Electric Co.; Cleveland; commercial lighting
1,200

East Ohio Gas Co.; Cleveland; gas transmission,
distribution   1,051

City of Cleveland; Cleveland; fire dept.   1,000

Cuyahoga County; Cleveland; individual and family
services   1,000

Millenium Group Corp.; Cleveland; tourist agency
1,000

American Building Maintenance Co. of Illinois;
Cleveland; building maintenance   900

Ohio Savings Bank; Cleveland; federal savings and loan
874

Cuyahoga County; Cleveland; building maintenance
800

Forest City Enterprises Inc.; Cleveland; lumber,
plywood, and millwork   800

Kmart Corp.; Cleveland; department stores   800

Lutheran Medical Center; Cleveland   800

Volume Services America Inc.; Cleveland; food vending
machines   800

Menorah Park Center for Aging Bet Moshav Zekenim
Hadati; Cleveland; nursing care facilities   780

Federal Reserve Bank of Cleveland; Cleveland   760

Jones Day Reavis and Pogue; Cleveland; law office   750

LTV Corp.; Cleveland; steel sheets/strips   750

Penton Media Inc.; Cleveland; periodicals   750

Ohio Mental Health Dept.; Cleveland   738

Aramark Services Inc.; Cleveland; management services
700

Eaton Corp.; Cleveland; automotive electrical equipment
700

Washington Group International Inc.; Cleveland;
industrial buildings, warehouses   700

UHHS/CSAHS-Cuyahoga Inc. Hospital; Cleveland
675

Cleveland Clinic Health System-Western Region;
Cleveland   650

John Carroll University; Cleveland   650

Renaissance Hotel Group; Cleveland   650

Sysco Food Services; Cleveland; canned goods   650

Cuyahoga County; Cleveland; courts   630

Sears Roebuck and Co. Inc.; Cleveland; department
stores   612

Cap Gemini Ernst and Young; Cleveland; computer
consulting   600

Goodrich Corp.; Cleveland; aircraft landing gear   600

MBNA Marketing Systems Inc.; Cleveland; data
processing   600

Parker Hannifin Corp.; Cleveland; warehousing   600

TRW Inc.; Cleveland; automotive parts/accessories   600

Chase Manhattan Mortgage Corp.; Cleveland; mortgage
bankers   599

MetroHealth System Inc.; Cleveland; nursing care
facilities   550

Sunrise Home Health Care Inc.; Cleveland   513

Maxim Healthcare Services Inc.; Cleveland; medical help
service   508

AWS Inc.; Cleveland; vocational rehabilitation agency
500

Euclid; Cleveland; personnel agency   500

Greater Cleveland Regional Transit Authority; Cleveland
500

Progressive Casualty Insurance Co.; Cleveland;
management services   500

Sportservice Corp.; Cleveland; concessionaire   500

Ohio 12th District

Central — Eastern Columbus and suburbs

The 12th includes the eastern half of Columbus and the suburban counties to the north and east of the city. *(See map p. 725.)*

Columbus has become primarily white-collar, and its thriving service economy has led to significant growth in both the city and its adjacent areas. The district has a slight Republican lean, with the strong GOP influence in the Columbus suburbs overcoming the Democratic tilt of the city.

For Democrats to be successful in the 12th, they must command the urban portion of the district, which is heavily black and poorer than the surrounding areas. The 12th includes the bulk of Columbus's black population, which is concentrated east of High Street, near Bexley. These precincts gave large majorities to African American Democrat Michael B. Coleman in his successful 1999 Columbus mayoral race. Farther east along Broad Street and into the suburbs, black Democratic support diminishes and Republican support goes up. Blacks make up 21.7 percent of the overall district's residents.

Within Franklin County but outside Columbus, the 12th includes the comfortable suburbs of Dublin, an upscale, solidly Republican area in northwest Franklin that is known to many as the headquarters of Wendy's, whose founder, Dave Thomas, died in 2002. In eastern Franklin, the 12th also takes in Westerville, Gahanna, and Reynoldsburg, which also vote dependably Republican.

Delaware County, north of Franklin, has experienced enormous growth and startlingly low unemployment in recent years. Delaware County tops state levels of household income and educational attainment (41 percent have a bachelor's degree). It also experienced the fastest growth by far of any Ohio county in the 1990s, increasing its population by 64 percent. Republicans dominate local offices here. Western Licking County, where the remainder of constituents live, also is experiencing growth.

Major Industry

Financial services, manufacturing, service.

Notable

The Ohio State Fair is held every August at the Ohio Expo Center.

Election Returns

	Republican		Democratic		Other	
President 2000	129,840	51.5%	115,083	45.6%	7,340	2.9%
House 2002	116,982	64.4%	64,707	35.6%		

District Profile

Population   630,730

Total area (square miles)   1,030.7
   Land area (square miles)   1,016.0

Population per square mile   620.8

Counties (2000 population)
   Delaware   109,989
   Franklin (pt.)   433,264
   Licking (pt.)   87,477

Cities and other areas over 10,000 (2000 population)
   Bexley   13,203
   Columbus (pt.)   275,882
   Delaware   25,243
   Dublin (pt.)   31,370
   Gahanna   32,636
   Newark (pt.)   25,161
   Pataskala   10,249
   Reynoldsburg (pt.)   32,069
   Westerville   35,318

Race and Hispanic or Latino origin*
   White   72.1%
   Black or African American   21.7%
   American Indian or Alaska Native   0.2%
   Asian   2.1%
   Native Hawaiian or other Pacific Islander   0.0%
   Some other race   0.2%
   Hispanic or Latino origin   1.7%
   Two or more races   1.9%

As percentage of total population.

Ancestry*

Dutch 1.3%		Polish 1.8%	
English 7.5%		Scotch-Irish 1.2%	
French 1.7%		Scottish 1.7%	
German 16.8%		Subsaharan 1.4%	
Irish 9.3%		USA/American 5.6%	
Italian 3.8%		Welsh 1.3%	

As estimated percentage of total population.

Universities and colleges, 2000–2001 enrollment
   Capital University, Columbus   3,899
   Central Ohio Technical College, Newark   1,832
   Denison University, Granville   2,108
   Devry University, Columbus   3,570
   Methodist Theological School-Ohio, Delaware   264
   Ohio Dominican College, Columbus   2,085
   Ohio State University, Newark   2,025
   Ohio Wesleyan University, Delaware   1,880
   Otterbein College, Westerville   2,887
   Trinity Lutheran Seminary, Columbus   248

Newspapers and circulation

	District circulation	Total circulation
Columbus Dispatch	92,055	245,310
*USA Today**	12,788	1,674,376

See Sources and Explanations in the front of the volume.

Television stations and affiliations

Columbus	100%	WBNS	CBS
Columbus	100%	WCMH	NBC
Columbus	100%	WOSU	PBS
Columbus	100%	WOUC	PBS
Columbus	100%	WSFJ	PAX
Columbus	100%	WSYX	ABC
Columbus	100%	WTTE	FOX
Columbus	100%	WWHO	UPN, WB

Cable systems and subscribers
   Adelphia   4,147
   Insight   13,415
   Time Warner   42,287

Businesses and other major employers
   Limited Brands Inc.; Columbus; women's apparel   10,000
   U.S. Bancorp; Columbus; commercial bank   5,500
   U.S. Defense Dept.; Columbus   2,900
   Children's Hospital; Columbus   2,879
   BancOne Services Corp.; Columbus; financial services   2,855
   Lucent Technologies Inc.; Columbus; commercial physical research   2,172
   Victoria's Secret Direct; Columbus; lingerie   1,950
   Ohio Expositions Commission; Columbus   1,500
   Guardsmark Inc.; Columbus; security guard service   1,400
   Liebert Corp.; Columbus; air conditioning equipment   1,382
   State Farm Mutual Automobile Insurance Co.; Newark; insurance agents and brokers   1,200
   Mount Carmel East Hospital; Columbus   1,100
   American Fidelity Assurance Co.; Columbus; insurance agents and brokers   1,000
   Ashland Inc.; Dublin; chemicals and allied products   1,000
   Checkfree Services Corp.; Dublin; computer processing services   1,000
   Concord Financial Group Inc.; Columbus; security brokers, dealers   1,000
   Express; Columbus; women's apparel   1,000
   Qwest Corp.; Dublin; warehousing   1,000
   Structure Inc.; Columbus; clothing stores   1,000
   Victoria's Secret Stores Inc.; Reynoldsburg; lingerie   1,000
   Licking Memorial Hospital; Newark   990
   Celestica Corp.; Columbus; semiconductors and related devices   962
   OCLC Online Computer Library Center Inc.; Dublin; online database services   928
   Abbott Laboratories; Columbus; medical labs   900
   Anheuser-Busch Inc.; Columbus; malt beverages   900
   Value City Department Stores Inc.; Columbus; department stores   900
   Interim Healthcare of Columbus Inc.; Columbus; home health care   890
   Alliance Data Systems Corp.; Westerville; credit card service   850
   Ohio Dept. of Public Safety; Columbus   850
   Interbake Foods Inc.; Columbus; ice cream machinery   841

Ohio Dept. of Health; Columbus   800

St. Ann's Hospital of Columbus Inc.; Westerville   800

Lane Bryant Inc.; Reynoldsburg; women's apparel   780

Cardinal Health Inc.; Dublin; drugs, proprietaries, sundries   700

Limited Stores Inc.; Columbus; clothing stores   700

Micro Electronics Inc.; Westerville; computer and software stores   700

Ohio Dept. of Natural Resources; Columbus   700

Nationwide Mutual Insurance Co.; Columbus; fire, marine, casualty insurance   677

Pacer Global Logistics Inc.; Dublin; shipping agents   650

Ohio Wesleyan University; Delaware   630

Laboratory Corp. of America; Dublin; testing labs   608

Olentangy Local School District; Lewis Center   602

Aetna Inc.; New Albany; insurance agents and brokers   600

Airnet Systems Inc.; Columbus; air cargo carrier   600

Compuware Corp.; Columbus; software development   600

Crane Plastics Co.; Columbus   600

Dacco Detroit of Ohio Inc.; Columbus; airports   600

Meijer Inc.; Columbus; department stores   600

Payco-General American Credits Inc.; Dublin; collection agency   600

Trim Systems; Dublin; automotive parts   600

Wal-Mart Stores Inc.; Reynoldsburg; department stores   600

Wendy's International Inc.; Dublin; fast-food restaurant chain   600

McGraw-Hill Companies Inc.; Westerville; book publishing   579

Wal-Mart Stores Inc.; Columbus; department stores   550

Sanese Services Inc.; Delaware; lunchrooms and cafeterias   540

Anomatic Corp.; Newark; metal plating   500

Capital University; Columbus   500

Cendant Corp.; Westerville; buyers' club   500

Computer Sciences Corp.; Dublin; accounting services   500

Exel Inc.; Westerville; warehousing   500

McGraw-Hill Companies Inc.; Blacklick; book publishing   500

Meijer Inc.; Lewis Center; department stores   500

Nationwide Mutual Insurance Co.; Dublin; insurance agents and brokers   500

Ohio Attorney General; Columbus   500

Risk Management Alternatives Inc.; Columbus; insurance agents and brokers   500

Stanley Works Inc.; Columbus; hand and edge tools   500

Verizon Wireless Inc.; Dublin; cellular telephones   500

Ohio 13th District

Northeast — parts of Akron and suburbs, Cleveland suburbs

The lightning bolt-shaped 13th runs from the shores of Lake Erie west of Cleveland, southeast through the city's mostly middle-class suburbs to Akron. *(See map p. 725.)*

Redistricting following the 2000 census increased the district's Democratic heft by adding western Summit County, including part of Akron. Summit is the most populous county in the 13th, making up 44 percent of the population. The district includes more than 70 percent of Akron's residents, including much of its black population.

Akron had a long history as a blue-collar factory town and was known as the world's rubber capital. Although the tire companies have moved many of their factories, many of their corporate headquarters and research facilities remain, keeping the city alive through tough years.

The city also has been renovating its downtown and recreational areas along the Ohio & Erie Canal. Blue-collar descendants combine with blacks, ethnic whites, and the University of Akron's academic community to help the city retain its Democratic character from its blue-collar past.

Bordering Lake Erie at the district's other end is Lorain County, which includes one-third of the 13th's residents and has an industrial, blue-collar heritage. The 13th's portions of Lorain include staunchly Democratic Lorain and Sheffield Lake and Democratic-leaning Elyria. Farther northeast, the Avon and Avon Lake communities are upper middle-class and dependably Republican. Lorain and Avon Lake are home to some of the district's automotive plants.

In the district's middle are some Republican-leaning communities in southern Cuyahoga County and northern Medina County. But Summit and Lorain's dominance gives the 13th a Democratic tilt.

Major Industry

Auto and auto parts manufacturing, steel, polymer research.

Notable

The National Inventors Hall of Fame is in Akron; the All-American Soap Box Derby race has been held in Akron since 1935.

Election Returns

	Republican		Democratic		Other	
President 2000	110,812	43.7%	133,458	52.6%	9,559	3.8%
House 2002	55,357	31.0%	123,025	69.0%		

District Profile

Population   630,730

Total area (square miles)   537.2
  Land area (square miles)   530.5

Population per square mile   1,188.9

Counties (2000 population)
| Cuyahoga (pt.)   87,712 | Medina (pt.)   50,667 |
| Lorain (pt.)   213,049 | Summit (pt.)   279,302 |

Cities and other areas over 10,000 (2000 population)
Akron (pt.)   129,298
Avon   11,446
Avon Lake   18,145
Barberton   27,899
Brecksville   13,382
Broadview Heights   15,967
Brunswick   33,388

Cuyahoga Falls (pt.)   39,051
Elyria   55,953
Lorain (pt.)   68,652
North Ridgeville   22,338
North Royalton   28,648
Norton (pt.)   11,512
Strongsville (pt.)   29,715

Race and Hispanic or Latino origin*
White   81.5%
Black or African American   12.1%
American Indian or Alaska Native   0.2%
Asian   1.2%
Native Hawaiian or other Pacific Islander   0.0%
Some other race   0.1%
Hispanic or Latino origin   3.5%
Two or more races   1.3%

*As percentage of total population.

Ancestry*

Dutch	1.1%	Italian	6.1%
English	6.7%	Polish	5.4%
French	1.5%	Scotch-Irish	1.1%
German	17.2%	Scottish	1.4%
Hungarian	2.9%	Slovak	2.5%
Irish	10.1%	USA/American	3.8%

*As estimated percentage of total population.

Universities and colleges, 2000–2001 enrollment
Lorain County Community College, Elyria   7,106
Ohio College of Massotherapy, Akron   356
University of Akron, Akron   21,363

Newspapers and circulation

	District circulation	Total circulation
Akron Beacon Journal	55,916	141,144
Brunswick Sun Times	4,938	5,051
Cleveland Plain Dealer	39,287	362,446
Elyria Chronicle-Telegram	12,647	25,793
Lorain Morning Journal	18,761	33,328
Medina County Gazette	3,090	14,313
Strongsville Sun Star	8,110	10,988
Sun Newspaper Group	19,216	167,715
*USA Today**	3,685	1,674,376
Valley View Sun Courier	4,428	6,575

*See Sources and Explanations in the front of the volume.

Television stations and affiliations
Cleveland-Akron (Canton)	100%	WBNX	WB
Cleveland-Akron (Canton)	100%	WDLI	Independent
Cleveland-Akron (Canton)	100%	WEAO	PBS
Cleveland-Akron (Canton)	100%	WEWS	ABC
Cleveland-Akron (Canton)	100%	WGGN	Independent
Cleveland-Akron (Canton)	100%	WJW	FOX
Cleveland-Akron (Canton)	100%	WKYC	NBC
Cleveland-Akron (Canton)	100%	WMFD	Independent
Cleveland-Akron (Canton)	100%	WOAC	Independent
Cleveland-Akron (Canton)	100%	WOIO	CBS
Cleveland-Akron (Canton)	100%	WQHS	Univision
Cleveland-Akron (Canton)	100%	WUAB	UPN
Cleveland-Akron (Canton)	100%	WVIZ	PBS
Cleveland-Akron (Canton)	100%	WVPX	PAX

Cable systems and subscribers
Adelphia   58,517
Comcast   29,410
Cox   3,702
Time Warner   84,163

Businesses and other major employers
Cleveland Clinic; Strongsville   5,000
University of Akron; Akron   4,427
Noveon Inc.; Cleveland; chemical preparations   2,800
Akron General Medical Center Inc.; Akron   2,700
FirstMerit Bank NA; Akron; commercial bank   2,573
FirstEnergy Corp.; Akron; electric services   2,118
Bendix Commercial Vehicle Systems; Elyria; automotive supplies   1,900
Ford Motor Co.; Lorain; automobiles   1,745
Ford Motor Co.; Avon Lake; van bodies   1,729
EMH Regional Medical Center; Elyria   1,712
Akron Medical Center Children's Hospital; Akron   1,700
Alcoa Inc.; Barberton; automotive stampings   1,600
PPG Industries Ohio Inc.; Brunswick; coated fabrics   1,427
Barberton Citizens Hospital; Barberton   1,200
Cleveland Electric Illuminating Co.; Akron; electric power generation   1,100
Goodrich Corp.; Cleveland; pigments   1,100
Ohio Edison Co.; Akron; electric power generation   1,100
Sterling Jewelers Inc.; Akron   1,100
Lorain County Community College District; Elyria   1,019
PolyOne Corp.; Avon Lake; compound purchased resins   1,000
Babcock and Wilcox Co.; Barberton; boiler and furnace contractors   900
Community Health Partners; Lorain; health systems agency   900
Cuyahoga Falls General Hospital; Cuyahoga Falls   800
Ridge Tool Co.; Elyria; metal-cutting machine tools   800
Consolidated Freightways Corp. of Delaware; Richfield; trucking terminals   700
U.S. Postal Service; Akron   635
Beacon Journal Publishing Co.; Akron; newspaper   625
U.S. Veterans Hospital; Brecksville   600
U.S. Steel Corp.; Lorain; blast furnaces and steel mills   550
Roadway Express Inc.; Akron; contract haulers   525
City of Akron; Akron; police dept.   520
Mature Services Inc.; Akron; senior citizens' center   516
B&C Research Inc.; Barberton; jobbing and repair machine shop   500
City of Akron; Akron; water, solid waste management   500
City of Cuyahoga Falls; Cuyahoga Falls; housing programs   500
Invacare Corp.; Elyria; wheelchairs   500
Marconi Communications Holdings Inc.; Lorain; business management   500
MTD Products Inc.; Valley City; lawn/garden equipment   500

Murray Ridge Production Center Inc.; Elyria; vocational rehabilitation agency   500

Ohio Dept. of Rehabilitation and Correction; Grafton   500

Summit County; Akron; county government   500

Summit County; Akron; individual and family services   500

West Lamrite Inc.; Strongsville; art supplies   500

Ohio 14th District

Northeast — Cleveland and Akron suburbs

The Republican 14th begins south and east of Cleveland and then snakes along the Lake Erie shoreline to include all of Lake and Ashtabula Counties in Ohio's northeast corner. *(See map p. 725.)*

The depressed far northeastern communities remain reliant on the ailing steel, chemical, and automobile manufacturing industries but have seen some new life from migrants from Cleveland. Plants along Lake Erie have been hurt by foreign competition in steel and chemicals.

Lake County is the district's most populous area (more than one-third of residents live here), despite being Ohio's smallest county in land area. Mentor, the district's largest city and a traditionally industrial swing area, has seen an influx of Republicans with its recent growth. The GOP generally performs better in areas south of Mentor, such as the upper-income Kirtland. Democrats do well in Painesville, where more than half of Lake's blacks and Hispanics live, and in western Lake, including Wickliffe and Willowick.

Ashtabula County, a mostly agricultural region that borders Pennsylvania, is the state's largest county in land area and is known for its covered bridges.

South of Lake are Geauga County, a Republican-leaning, affluent, well-educated area, and northern Portage County. The 14th also includes northeastern Summit County, taking in Stow and Twinsburg.

The 14th is descended from the 1990s-era 19th District that included many of Cuyahoga County's eastern Cleveland suburbs. But redistricting following the 2000 census left the 14th with only a small portion of eastern Cuyahoga, including the upscale communities of Bentleyville and Moreland Hills.

Major Industry

Auto manufacturing, health care, chemicals.

Notable

Holden Arboretum, the nation's largest, is in Kirtland; Twinsburg hosts a gathering of twins each August that it calls the largest in the world; a President James A. Garfield Historic Site is in Mentor.

Election Returns

	Republican		Democratic		Other	
President 2000	147,148	52.0%	124,582	44.0%	11,360	4.0%
House 2002	134,413	72.2%	51,846	27.8%		

District Profile

Population   630,730

Total area (square miles)   1,819.7
Land area (square miles)   1,796.7

Population per square mile   351.0

Counties (2000 population)

Ashtabula	102,728	Portage (pt.)	28,048
Cuyahoga (pt.)	44,806	Summit (pt.)	124,912
Geauga	90,895	Trumbull (pt.)	11,830
Lake	227,511		

Cities and other areas over 10,000 (2000 population)

Ashtabula	20,962	Painesville	17,503
Aurora	13,556	Solon	21,802
Conneaut	12,485	Stow	32,139
Cuyahoga Falls (pt.)	10,323	Twinsburg	17,006
Eastlake (pt.)	20,255	Wickliffe	13,484
Hudson	22,439	Willoughby	22,621
Mentor	50,278	Willowick	14,361

Race and Hispanic or Latino origin*
White   94.0%
Black or African American   2.5%
American Indian or Alaska Native   0.1%
Asian   1.1%
Native Hawaiian or other Pacific Islander   0.0%
Some other race   0.1%
Hispanic or Latino origin   1.3%
Two or more races   0.8%

As percentage of total population.

Ancestry*

Dutch	1.1%	Italian	9.0%
English	8.7%	Polish	5.1%
French	1.6%	Scotch-Irish	1.3%
German	16.9%	Scottish	1.6%
Hungarian	3.2%	Slovak	2.1%
Irish	11.2%	USA/American	3.7%

As estimated percentage of total population.

Universities and colleges, 2000–2001 enrollment
Hiram College, Hiram   1,199
Kent State University, Ashtabula   1,236
Kent State University-Geauga, Burton   620
Lake Erie College, Painesville   815
Lakeland Community College, Kirtland   7,722

Newspapers and circulation

	District circulation	Total circulation
Akron Beacon Journal	15,187	141,144
Ashtabula Star-Beacon	20,149	20,279
Chagrin Herald Sun	1,229	1,494
Cleveland Plain Dealer	61,163	362,446
Lake County News Herald	44,192	47,060
Nordonia Hills Sun	1,358	1,371
Ravenna Record-Courier	2,334	18,595
Solon Herald Sun	2,521	2,896
Sun Newspaper Group	9,137	167,715

Twinsburg Sun	1,029	1,046
*USA Today**	4,822	1,674,376
Valley View Sun Messenger	2,220	12,559
Warren Tribune Chronicle	2,014	34,341

See Sources and Explanations in the front of the volume.

Television stations and affiliations

Cleveland-Akron (Canton)	94%	WBNX	WB
Cleveland-Akron (Canton)	94%	WDLI	Independent
Cleveland-Akron (Canton)	94%	WEAO	PBS
Cleveland-Akron (Canton)	94%	WEWS	ABC
Cleveland-Akron (Canton)	94%	WGGN	Independent
Cleveland-Akron (Canton)	94%	WJW	FOX
Cleveland-Akron (Canton)	94%	WKYC	NBC
Cleveland-Akron (Canton)	94%	WMFD	Independent
Cleveland-Akron (Canton)	94%	WOAC	Independent
Cleveland-Akron (Canton)	94%	WOIO	CBS
Cleveland-Akron (Canton)	94%	WQHS	Univision
Cleveland-Akron (Canton)	94%	WUAB	UPN
Cleveland-Akron (Canton)	94%	WVIZ	PBS
Cleveland-Akron (Canton)	94%	WVPX	PAX
Youngstown	6%	WFMJ	NBC
Youngstown	6%	WNEO	PBS
Youngstown	6%	WYTV	ABC

Cable systems and subscribers

Adelphia   117,500

Classic   4,812

Comcast   45,676

Orwell Cable Television Co.   1,100

Time Warner   11,101

Businesses and other major employers

Progressive Corp.; Cleveland; automobile insurance
7,251

House of Fabrics Inc.; Hudson; fabric stores   3,000

Kraftmaid Cabinetry Inc.; Middlefield; kitchen cabinets
3,000

Case Western Reserve University; Chagrin Falls   2,000

Philips Medical Systems Cleveland Inc.; Cleveland; x-ray
apparatus and tubes   1,580

Renaissance International Inc.; Cleveland; hotel,
franchised   1,500

Lubrizol Corp.; Wickliffe; oil treating compounds
1,300

Jo-Ann Stores Inc.; Hudson; arts and crafts supplies
1,200

Lake Hospital System Inc.; Painesville   1,200

Ashtabula County; Jefferson; county government
1,191

Lake County; Painesville; county government   1,000

Lake County Community College District; Willoughby
1,000

Lake Hospital System Inc.; Willoughby   1,000

Nestle USA-Prepared Foods Div. Inc.; Cleveland; frozen
dinners   1,000

DFG Holding Inc.; Willoughby; check-cashing agencies
940

FirstEnergy Corp.; Perry; electric power generation
900

Ashtabula County Medical Center; Ashtabula   800

Cole Vision Corp.; Twinsburg; eyeglasses   700

Eaton Corp.; Willoughby; data processing   700

Lake County; Mentor; job training and related services
700

Integrated Warranty Services; Cleveland; appraisers
650

L'Oreal USA Inc.; Cleveland; hair preparations   650

Molded Fiber Glass Companies Inc.; Ashtabula; molding
primary plastics   650

PCC Airfoils Inc.; Wickliffe; aircraft engines and parts
650

ALLTEL Ohio Inc.; Twinsburg; telephone
communication   600

Morgan Adhesives Co.; Stow   600

Kennametal Inc.; Solon; tools and machine tool
accessories   560

Allstate Insurance Co.; Hudson; insurance agents   550

Geauga Community Hospital Assn. Inc.; Chardon   550

Advanced Lighting Technologies Inc.; Cleveland; electric
lamps   500

Avery Dennison Corp.; Painesville; adhesive papers,
labels, or tapes   500

BankOne Corp.; Painesville; commercial bank   500

Fedex Supply Chain Services Inc.; Hudson;
transportation consultant   500

Pepsi-Cola Metropolitan Bottling Co.; Twinsburg; soft
drinks   500

Randstad North America; Hudson; automobiles   500

Reliance Electric Industrial Co.; Twinsburg; printed
circuit boards   500

Steris Corp.; Mentor; surgical and corrective belts   500

Sunbeam Corp.; Cleveland; electric housewares   500

Venture Lighting International Inc.; Solon; electric
lamps   500

Ohio 15th District

Western Columbus and suburbs

The 15th is centered on Columbus, the state's centrally
located capital. The district includes most of the city, taking
in all of Columbus that lies west of High Street, a major
north-south thoroughfare. *(See map p. 725.)*

The 15th takes in some city attractions, including the
State Capitol building (at High and Broad streets), City Hall,
Ohio State University, and the Columbus Museum of Art. It
also includes the stadium of professional soccer's Crew and
the arena of hockey's Blue Jackets.

Columbus is not known to draw large numbers of tourists
except on Saturdays in autumn, when Ohio State plays football at home. But the region is generally regarded as a good
place to raise a family. Covering much of Franklin County's
expanding service sector, which includes several large high-
tech research centers, the district has a steady employment
base. American Electric Power also is based in the 15th.

Columbus has continued to grow since surpassing Cleveland in the early 1980s to become Ohio's most populous
city. The 15th traditionally has been the more Republican of the two districts that divide the capital—the neighboring 12th includes most of the heavily black East Side.
Ohio State's academic community and neighborhoods in the
nearby West Side of Columbus support Democrats, but they
are more than offset by rock-ribbed Republican suburbs west
of the Olentangy and Scioto Rivers. GOP candidates are

strong in comfortable suburbs such as Upper Arlington and Worthington.

Almost 90 percent of district residents live in Franklin County. The rest reside in Madison County, a major corn-producing area to the west, and in Union County, located northwest of Columbus, which last voted Democratic for president in 1932. Although a major Honda auto plant is in the 4th District portion of Marysville, it employs many 12th District residents.

Major Industry

Retail trade, health care, research, higher education.

Notable

A full-scale replica of Christopher Columbus's ship, the *Santa Maria*, is in Columbus; the historic German Village reflects the architecture and character of a nineteenth-century German neighborhood.

Election Returns

	Republican		Democratic		Other	
President 2000	117,175	52.2%	98,204	43.8%	8,931	4.0%
House 2002	108,193	66.6%	54,286	33.4%		

District Profile

Population   630,730

Total area (square miles)   1,181.8
Land area (square miles)   1,178.3

Population per square mile   535.3

Counties (2000 population)
Franklin (pt.)   549,608   Union   40,909
Madison   40,213

Cities and other areas over 10,000 (2000 population)
Columbus (pt.)   384,491
Grove City   27,075
Hilliard (pt.)   23,853
Marysville   15,942
Upper Arlington   33,686
Worthington (pt.)   14,125

Race and Hispanic or Latino origin*
White   85.2%
Black or African American   7.2%
American Indian or Alaska Native   0.2%
Asian   3.3%
Native Hawaiian or other Pacific Islander   0.0%
Some other race   0.2%
Hispanic or Latino origin   2.3%
Two or more races   1.7%

As percentage of total population.

Ancestry*
Dutch	1.4%	Polish	1.7%
English	8.0%	Scotch-Irish	1.3%
French	1.8%	Scottish	1.6%
German	18.5%	USA/American	7.2%
Irish	10.4%	Welsh	1.4%
Italian	4.2%		

As estimated percentage of total population.

Universities and colleges, 2000–2001 enrollment
Columbus College of Art and Design, Columbus   1,416
Columbus State Community College, Columbus 18,094
Franklin University, Columbus   5,083
Mount Carmel College of Nursing, Columbus   295
Ohio State University, Columbus   47,952

Newspapers and circulation

	District circulation	Total circulation
Columbus Dispatch	95,367	245,310
*USA Today**	17,083	1,674,376

See Sources and Explanations in the front of the volume.

Television stations and affiliations
Columbus	100%	WBNS	CBS
Columbus	100%	WCMH	NBC
Columbus	100%	WOSU	PBS
Columbus	100%	WOUC	PBS
Columbus	100%	WSFJ	PAX
Columbus	100%	WSYX	ABC
Columbus	100%	WTTE	FOX
Columbus	100%	WWHO	UPN, WB

Cable systems and subscribers
Adelphia   792
Time Warner   182,443

Military installations, September 2001
Rickenbacker Air National Guard Base, Lockbourne 1,356
83rd Division Memorial U.S. Army Reserve Center/AMSA, Columbus   1,041
Rickenbacker Military Training Area, Columbus   873
Defense Construction Supply Center, Columbus   426
Fort Hayes Memorial U.S. Army Reserve Center, Columbus   326
Rickenbacker Storage Facility, Columbus   291

Businesses and other major employers
Ohio State University; Columbus   19,000
Ohio Dept. of Rehabilitation and Correction; Columbus 15,000
ABB Automation Inc.; Columbus; controllers for process variables   7,000
Columbus City School District; Columbus   7,000
Nationwide Mutual Insurance Co.; Columbus; fire, marine, casualty insurance   6,953
Grant/Riverside Methodist Hospitals Corp.; Columbus 6,000
C. S. Ross Co.; Columbus; variety stores   4,000
Ohio State University Hospital; Columbus   4,000
Ohio Bureau Workers Compensation; Columbus   3,600
Battelle Memorial Institute Inc.; Columbus; commercial physical research   3,000
Discover Financial Services Inc.; Columbus; credit card service   3,000
Abbott Laboratories; Columbus; pharmaceuticals 2,500
Buckeye Temporaries Inc.; Columbus; temporary help 2,500
City of Columbus; Columbus; police dept.   2,000
Hyponex Corp.; Marysville; peat mining   2,000

American Electric Power Service Corp.; Columbus; electric power generation 1,800

Doctors OhioHealth Corp. Hospital; Columbus 1,700

Ohio Dept. of Transportation; Columbus 1,700

Invensys Climate Controls; Plain City; air conditioning controls 1,600

Mount Carmel Hospital West; Columbus 1,600

Meijer Inc.; Columbus; department stores 1,400

American Chemical Society; Columbus; chemical consultant 1,334

Ohio Dept. of Public Safety; Columbus 1,300

B-F Processing Corp.; Columbus; fluid milk 1,200

Distribution Fulfillment Services Inc.; Groveport; warehousing 1,200

St. Jude Children's Research Hospital; Columbus 1,200

Wal-Mart Stores Inc.; Grove City; warehousing 1,200

CallTech Communications; Columbus; telephone/video communications 1,165

Delphi Corp.; Columbus; automotive parts 1,100

Columbus State Community College; Columbus 1,000

Employer Advantage Group Inc.; Columbus; employee leasing service 1,000

James Cancer Hospital; Columbus 1,000

MI Homes; Columbus; manufactured homes broker 1,000

Safelite Glass Corp.; Columbus; automotive glass 1,000

SBC Ameritech; Columbus; telecommunication repair 1,000

Ohio Dept. of Admin. Services; Columbus 900

National Electric Coil Inc.; Columbus; electronic coils and transformers 850

Alliance Data Systems Corp.; Columbus; credit card service 800

Banana Republic Inc.; Groveport; clothing stores 800

Camel Back Pizza Inc.; Columbus 800

Grange Mutual Casualty Co.; Columbus; automobile insurance 800

Ohio Dept. of Health; Columbus 800

Roxane Laboratories Inc.; Columbus; pharmaceuticals 800

Ohio Mental Health Dept.; Columbus 761

Huntington National Bank; Columbus; commercial trust company 760

Big Lots Inc.; Columbus; housewares 751

Buckeye Steel Castings Co.; Columbus; steel foundries 750

Franklin County; Columbus; sheriff's office 750

General Electric Co.; Columbus; abrasive products 750

Lakeside Building Maintenance Inc.; Columbus; building maintenance 750

Ohio Dept. of Jobs and Family Services; Columbus 750

Ohio National Guard; Columbus 750

Franklin County; Grove City; children's aid society 740

Goodwill Industries of Central Ohio Inc.; Columbus; job training services 710

Columbus Assn. for Performing Arts; Columbus; theater building operation 705

Kroger Co.; Columbus; bakery products 700

Merck-Medco Rx Services of Ohio; Columbus; mail-order pharmaceuticals 700

Micro Electronics Inc.; Hilliard; computers 700

Rich's Department Stores Inc.; Columbus; department stores 700

Yellow Transportation; Columbus; trucking terminals 695

Scotts Co.; Marysville; fertilizers 650

Stanley Electric U.S. Co.; London; automotive lighting 630

Columbus Fair Auto Auction Inc.; Columbus; automobile auction 620

Aetna Inc.; Columbus; insurance agents and brokers 600

Central Ohio Transit Authority; Columbus 600

DecisionOne Corp.; Grove City; computer maintenance/repair 600

Education Unlimited of Ohio Inc.; Columbus; elementary and secondary schools 600

Gates McDonald and Co.; Hilliard; insurance claim processing 600

Time Warner Entertainment Co.; Columbus; cable TV 600

U.S. Environmental Protection Agency; Columbus 600

Vorys, Sater, Seymour and Pease; Columbus; law office 575

AT&T Corp.; Worthington; long-distance telephone 550

Ricart Ford Inc.; Groveport; car dealers 550

Showa Aluminum Corp. of America; Mount Sterling; automotive parts/accessories 550

Columbia Gas of Ohio Inc.; Columbus; natural gas distribution 541

Motorists Mutual Insurance Co.; Columbus; fire, marine, casualty insurance 528

Fiesta Salons Inc.; Columbus; beauty shops 520

Arctic Express Inc.; Hilliard; trucking 500

Consolidated Rail Corp.; Columbus; freight hauling 500

Corna/Kokosing Construction Co.; Columbus; building construction 500

Dispatch Printing Co.; Columbus; newspaper 500

Farmers Group Inc.; Columbus; management services 500

Fedex Ground Inc.; Grove City; trucking 500

Hyatt Corp.; Columbus; hotels 500

Ohio Dept. of Development; Columbus 500

Ohio Dept. of Education; Columbus 500

Ohio Dept. of Taxation; Columbus 500

Rail Products International Inc.; Columbus; fuse devices 500

Roadway Express Inc.; Columbus; contract haulers 500

Sears Logistics Services Inc.; Columbus; warehousing 500

State Auto Property and Casualty Insurance Co.; Columbus; fire, marine, casualty insurance 500

Worthington Foods Inc.; Worthington; frozen specialties 500

Ohio 16th District

Northeast — Canton

A region of traditional midwestern values and work ethic, the 16th takes in Canton's Stark County and territory to the west.

Although the boundaries have changed over the years, the Canton-based 16th was represented by William McKinley from 1877 to 1884 and 1885 to 1891. McKinley launched his governorship from the area and ran much of his 1896 presidential campaign from a front porch in Canton.

Canton has a rich manufacturing and steel-producing history, and high-skill manufacturing remains at the core of the region's steadily prosperous economy. But it is a working-class city, with a median income more than $10,000 below the state average. That, coupled with a more than 20 percent black population, makes Canton solidly Democratic. The city backed Al Gore with 61 percent of the vote in 2000.

But Canton has been less important to the 16th's political outlook as its population has declined since the 1950s. The city now accounts for just one-fifth of Stark's population. Massillon and Alliance, the county's next-most-populous cities, grew only marginally in population in the 1990s and lean Democratic. Northern Stark County is upper-middle-class and GOP-leaning. Stark overall voted narrowly for George W. Bush.

West of Stark, the district becomes more rural and solidly Republican. Wayne County, just west of Stark, produced more oats than any other Ohio county in 2000. The 16th also takes in most of Ashland County, which is even more solidly conservative than Wayne.

Redistricting following the 2000 census added two-thirds of Medina County, a dependably Republican area that is northwest of Canton and west of Akron. The area solidified the 16th's GOP orientation.

Major Industry
Steel, bearings manufacturing, health care.

Notable
The Professional Football Hall of Fame is in Canton; President William McKinley's burial site is in a Canton park; Massillon was the hometown of Jacob Coxey, whose "army" of unemployed men marched to Washington, D.C., after the Panic of 1893.

Election Returns

	Republican		Democratic		Other	
President 2000	141,311	53.4%	112,270	42.4%	10,908	4.1%
House 2002	129,734	68.9%	58,644	31.1%		

District Profile

Population   630,730

Total area (square miles)   1,741.0
Land area (square miles)   1,732.0

Population per square mile   364.2

Counties (2000 population)
Ashland (pt.)	40,640	Stark	378,098
Medina (pt.)	100,428	Wayne	111,564

Cities and other areas over 10,000 (2000 population)
Alliance (pt.)	23,195	Medina	25,139
Ashland	21,249	North Canton	16,369
Canton	80,806	Wadsworth	18,437
Massillon	31,325	Wooster	24,811

Race and Hispanic or Latino origin*
White   92.4%
Black or African American   4.8%
American Indian or Alaska Native   0.2%
Asian   0.6%
Native Hawaiian or other Pacific Islander   0.0%
Some other race   0.1%
Hispanic or Latino origin   0.9%
Two or more races   1.1%

*As percentage of total population.

Ancestry*
Dutch	1.5%	Italian	5.6%
English	7.3%	Polish	2.3%
French	2.4%	Scotch-Irish	1.2%
German	21.9%	Scottish	1.5%
Hungarian	1.3%	Swiss	1.7%
Irish	9.5%	USA/American	5.5%

*As estimated percentage of total population.

Universities and colleges, 2000–2001 enrollment
Ashland University, Ashland   6,055
College of Wooster, Wooster   1,837
ETI Technical College, North Canton   330
Kent State University-Stark, North Canton   2,982
Malone College, Canton   2,162
Mount Union College, Alliance   2,334
Ohio State University Agricultural Technical Institute, Wooster   969
Stark State College of Technology, Canton   4,507
University of Akron-Wayne College, Orrville   1,515
Walsh University, North Canton   1,545

Newspapers and circulation

	District circulation	Total circulation
Akron Beacon Journal	26,617	141,144
Alliance Review	6,797	12,715
Ashland Times Gazette	7,001	11,934
Canton Repository	57,086	64,499
Cleveland Plain Dealer	7,040	362,446
Mansfield News-Journal	1,465	33,575
Massillon Independent	14,043	14,231
Medina County Gazette	11,130	14,313
Sun Newspaper Group	2,888	167,715
*USA Today**	3,942	1,674,376
Wooster Daily Record	18,829	22,805

*See Sources and Explanations in the front of the volume.

Television stations and affiliations
Cleveland-Akron (Canton)	100%	WBNX	WB
Cleveland-Akron (Canton)	100%	WDLI	Independent
Cleveland-Akron (Canton)	100%	WEAO	PBS

Cleveland-Akron (Canton)	100%	WEWS	ABC
Cleveland-Akron (Canton)	100%	WGGN	Independent
Cleveland-Akron (Canton)	100%	WJW	FOX
Cleveland-Akron (Canton)	100%	WKYC	NBC
Cleveland-Akron (Canton)	100%	WMFD	Independent
Cleveland-Akron (Canton)	100%	WOAC	Independent
Cleveland-Akron (Canton)	100%	WOIO	CBS
Cleveland-Akron (Canton)	100%	WQHS	Univision
Cleveland-Akron (Canton)	100%	WUAB	UPN
Cleveland-Akron (Canton)	100%	WVIZ	PBS
Cleveland-Akron (Canton)	100%	WVPX	PAX

Cable systems and subscribers

Adelphia   4,225
Armstrong   27,261
Clear Picture Inc.   17,025
Doylestown Cable TV   710
Massillon Cable TV   15,390
Time Warner   76,316

Businesses and other major employers

Timken Co.; Canton; roller bearings and parts   4,500
Aultman Hospital; Canton   2,900
Hoover Co.; Canton; electric sweepers   2,600
Republic Technologies International; Canton; steel bars   1,680
Westfield Insurance Co.; Westfield Center; property and casualty insurance   1,600
Alliance Hospital; Alliance   1,200
Amsted Industries Inc.; Alliance; iron and steel forgings   1,200
PCC Airfoils Inc.; Minerva; nonferrous foundries   1,200
Gerstenslager Co.; Wooster; automotive parts   900
Suarez Corp. Industries; Canton; mail-order catalog   900
Massillon Community Hospital; Massillon   875
Medina General Hospital Inc.; Medina   843
ArvinMeritor Inc.; Canton; automotive parts   800
Stark County; Canton; sewerage systems   790
J. M. Smucker Co.; Orrville; canned fruits/jams   750
U.S. Postal Service; Canton   750
Bosch Rexroth Corp.; Wooster; power transfer pumps   700
Heinz Frozen Food Co. Inc.; Massillon   700
North Canton Board of Education; Canton   700
Mansfield Plumbing Products; Perrysville   698
Fresh Mark Inc.; Canton; beef products   650
General Electric Capital Corp.; Canton; accounting services   650
Graco Children's Products Inc.; Canton; furniture   650
Wooster Hospital; Wooster   650
Ashland University; Ashland   600
College of Wooster; Wooster   600
Luk Inc.; Wooster; automotive parts   600
Nationwide Corp.; Canton; insurance agents   600
Stark County; Canton; mental health agency   600
Abbott Laboratories; Ashland; medical equipment   590
Fleming Companies Inc.; Massillon; cold storage   570
Alfred Nickles Bakery Inc.; Navarre   550
Ohio State University; Wooster   550
Timken Co.; Canton; ball and roller bearings   550
Wooster Brush Co.; Wooster; paintbrushes   525

Belden Brick Co.; Canton; management consulting   500
Diversified Employee Solutions Inc.; Medina; employee leasing service   500
Kmart Corp.; Medina; department stores   500
Ohio Agricultural Research; Wooster   500
PTC Alliance Corp.; Alliance; stainless tubing   500
Republic Storage Systems Co.; Canton; nonrefrigerated lockers   500
Stark County; Canton; social and human resources   500
Wal-Mart Stores Inc.; Wooster; department stores   500

Ohio 17th District

Northeast — Youngstown, Warren, part of Akron

Bordering Pennsylvania in the northeast part of the state, the 17th is a Democratic bastion that takes in part of the Mahoning Valley, including Youngstown. Once a leading steel-producing area, the valley now symbolizes industrial decline; the remaining steel mills are predominantly silent and abandoned.

Despite some economic diversification, young people searching for opportunities often look elsewhere, and the population of most cities has declined. Youngstown's population hovered around 170,000 from the 1930s to the 1960s; the 2000 census found just 82,000 people.

Officials hope the manufacturing industry is starting to turn around. Several auto plants are in the area, and the regional airport, which houses a large Air Force Reserve base, is undergoing expansion that is expected to turn it into an air cargo hub.

Trumbull County (shared with the 14th) is home to a plurality of residents. This area is staunchly Democratic: Warren, Trumbull's most populous city, backed Al Gore with 69 percent of the vote in 2000, and Niles and Girard backed Gore by more than two-to-one.

Redistricting in 2002 added parts of Summit and Portage Counties, which are west of Youngstown and are less solidly Democratic. The Portage portion includes Kent and Ravenna. The Summit portion includes the eastern half of Akron, a city that once produced 90 percent of the nation's tires.

Major Industry

Automobile assembly, manufacturing.

Notable

Mill Creek Park in Youngstown covers 2,530 acres; Kent State University was the site of four deaths during a 1970 antiwar protest.

Election Returns

	Republican		Democratic		Other	
President 2000	88,184	35.3%	150,748	60.4%	10,767	4.3%
House 2002	62,188	33.7%	94,441	51.1%	28,045	15.2%

District Profile

Population   630,730

Total area (square miles)   1,033.2
   Land area (square miles)   1,005.5

Population per square mile   627.3

Counties (2000 population)

Mahoning (pt.)	154,746	Summit (pt.)	138,685
Portage (pt.)	124,013	Trumbull (pt.)	213,286

Cities and other areas over 10,000 (2000 population)

Akron (pt.)	87,776	Ravenna	11,771
Austintown CDP	31,627	Streetsboro	12,311
Girard	10,902	Struthers	11,756
Green (pt.)	14,049	Tallmadge	16,390
Kent	27,906	Warren	46,832
Niles	20,932	Youngstown	82,026

Race and Hispanic or Latino origin*

White 84.5%
Black or African American 11.6%
American Indian or Alaska Native 0.2%
Asian 0.7%
Native Hawaiian or other Pacific Islander 0.0%
Some other race 0.1%
Hispanic or Latino origin 1.6%
Two or more races 1.2%

*As percentage of total population.

Ancestry*

Dutch	1.3%	Polish	3.1%
English	6.8%	Scotch-Irish	1.1%
French	1.4%	Scottish	1.3%
German	15.5%	Slovak	3.2%
Hungarian	2.0%	USA/American	4.6%
Irish	10.3%	Welsh	1.4%
Italian	9.2%		

*As estimated percentage of total population.

Universities and colleges, 2000–2001 enrollment

ETI Technical College, Niles 306
ITT Technical Institute, Youngstown 368
Kent State University, Kent 21,924
Kent State University-Trumbull, Warren 2,323
Northeastern Ohio Universities College of Medicine, Rootstown 421
Southern Ohio College-Northeast, Akron 373
Trumbull Business College, Warren 345
Youngstown State University, Youngstown 11,787

Newspapers and circulation

	District circulation	Total circulation
Akron Beacon Journal	39,949	141,144
Canton Repository	2,048	64,499
Cleveland Plain Dealer	7,616	362,446
Ravenna Record-Courier	16,045	18,595
Sharon Herald	1,328	20,696
*USA Today**	4,192	1,674,376
Warren Tribune Chronicle	31,818	34,341
Youngstown Vindicator	40,700	70,119

*See Sources and Explanations in the front of the volume.

Television stations and affiliations

Youngstown	53%	WFMJ	NBC
Youngstown	53%	WNEO	PBS
Youngstown	53%	WYTV	ABC
Cleveland-Akron (Canton)	47%	WBNX	WB
Cleveland-Akron (Canton)	47%	WDLI	Independent
Cleveland-Akron (Canton)	47%	WEAO	PBS
Cleveland-Akron (Canton)	47%	WEWS	ABC
Cleveland-Akron (Canton)	47%	WGGN	Independent
Cleveland-Akron (Canton)	47%	WJW	FOX
Cleveland-Akron (Canton)	47%	WKYC	NBC
Cleveland-Akron (Canton)	47%	WMFD	Independent
Cleveland-Akron (Canton)	47%	WOAC	Independent
Cleveland-Akron (Canton)	47%	WOIO	CBS
Cleveland-Akron (Canton)	47%	WQHS	Univision
Cleveland-Akron (Canton)	47%	WUAB	UPN
Cleveland-Akron (Canton)	47%	WVIZ	PBS
Cleveland-Akron (Canton)	47%	WVPX	PAX

Cable systems and subscribers

Adelphia 7,878
Armstrong 13,149
Classic 1,225
Time Warner 119,561

Military installations, September 2001

Youngstown-Warren Regional Airport Air Reserve Station, Vienna 1,635

Businesses and other major employers

Goodyear Tire and Rubber Co.; Akron; tires 7,077
General Motors Corp.; Warren; automobiles 7,000
Kent State University; Kent 4,500
Forum Health Trumbull Memorial Hospital; Warren 4,300
Trumbull Memorial Hospital; Warren 3,000
Akron City Hospital; Akron 2,621
St. Elizabeth Health Center; Youngstown 2,480
Youngstown State University Inc.; Youngstown 1,621
WCI Steel Inc.; Warren; steel sheets/strips 1,398
CSC; Warren; iron bars 1,250
Delphi Corp.; Warren; engineering services 1,200
HM Health Services Hospital; Warren 1,090
Roadway Express Inc.; Akron; off-highway trucks 1,000
Robinson Memorial Hospital; Ravenna 959
Trumbull County; Warren; county government 950
Diebold Inc.; Canton; automatic teller machines 900
Aircraft Braking Systems Corp.; Akron 769
Akwen; Uniontown; fast-food restaurant chain 700
Ohio Dept. of Transportation; Ravenna 610
General Electric Co.; Ravenna; electric lamps 600
General Electric Co.; Warren; sealed beam lamps 600
Lockheed Martin Integrated Systems Inc.; Akron; data processing 600
Summit County; Tallmadge; public health programs 600
Kmart Corp.; Warren; warehousing 556
Ravenna Aluminum Inc.; Ravenna; automotive parts 530
Fedex Custom Critical Inc.; Akron; trucking 508
Center 5; Akron; mental health clinic 500
Delphi Corp.; Warren; automotive parts 500
RTI International Metals Inc.; Niles; titanium 500
Step2 Co.; Streetsboro; plastics 500
Thomas Steel Strip Corp.; Warren; steel finishing 500

Ohio 18th District

East — Zanesville, Chillicothe

Ohio's most geographically vast district, the 18th envelops 12 whole counties and parts of four others in southern and eastern Ohio. It starts in the rolling hills just south of Canton and runs southwest to the rugged areas in Appalachia. The district, which roughly parallels but does not touch the Ohio River, depends on the steel and coal industries and includes a large Catholic population of Eastern European and Greek immigrants. It has a conservative lean, and contains the highest percentage of white residents (96 percent) and the smallest percentage of college graduates (11 percent) in the state.

The northern part of the 18th includes Tuscarawas County, the district's most populous. West of Tuscarawas (derived from an Indian word meaning "open mouth") are several solidly Republican counties. Newark (shared with the 12th), in Licking County, survived the closure of an Air Force base in the 1990s and has become a growing manufacturing and research center.

Carroll, Harrison, and Guernsey Counties on the district's eastern border are ancestrally Democratic areas that tend to be populist on economics but strongly conservative on cultural issues. Harrison in 2000 voted Republican for president for the first time since 1984. The district scoops up a northern sliver of Belmont County southeast of Harrison. In redistricting following the 2000 census, GOP mapmakers intentionally drew the 18th's boundaries to include the Republican incumbent's hometown of St. Clairsville and to place the bulk of Democratic-leaning Belmont in the 6th.

The 18th narrows south of Muskingum County (Zanesville) to reach Morgan County and northwestern Athens County (though not the portion that includes Ohio University). Moving westward, the 18th remains rural as it crosses forests to take in most of Ross County, including Chillicothe.

Major Industry
Steel, manufacturing, agriculture, coal.

Notable
Astronaut and former senator John Glenn was born in New Concord; a memorial to baseball pitcher Cy Young is in Newcomerstown; there was an Underground Railroad stop in Leesville; a basket-shaped building serves as headquarters for the Longaberger basket company in Newark.

Election Returns

	Republican		Democratic		Other	
President 2000	132,709	55.1%	98,328	40.8%	9,810	4.1%
House 2002	125,546	100.0%				

District Profile

Population   630,730

Total area (square miles)   6,876.4
  Land area (square miles)   6,826.4

Population per square mile   92.4

Counties (2000 population)

Athens (pt.)	18,656	Jackson	32,641
Belmont (pt.)	15,048	Knox	54,500
Carroll	28,836	Licking (pt.)	58,014
Coshocton	36,655	Morgan	14,897
Guernsey	40,792	Muskingum	84,585
Harrison	15,856	Ross (pt.)	59,346
Hocking	28,241	Tuscarawas	90,914
Holmes	38,943	Vinton	12,806

Cities and other areas over 10,000 (2000 population)

Cambridge	11,520	Mount Vernon	14,375
Chillicothe	21,796	Newark (pt.)	21,118
Coshocton	11,682	New Philadelphia	17,056
Dover	12,210	Zanesville	25,586

Race and Hispanic or Latino origin*
White   95.9%
Black or African American   1.9%
American Indian or Alaska Native   0.2%
Asian   0.3%
Native Hawaiian or other Pacific Islander   0.0%
Some other race   0.1%
Hispanic or Latino origin   0.6%
Two or more races   1.0%

As percentage of total population.

Ancestry*

Dutch	1.8%	Polish	1.2%
English	7.2%	Scotch-Irish	1.2%
French	1.4%	Scottish	1.2%
German	16.7%	Swiss	1.1%
Irish	8.7%	USA/American	10.2%
Italian	2.4%	Welsh	1.1%

As estimated percentage of total population.

Universities and colleges, 2000–2001 enrollment
Belmont Technical College, St. Clairsville   1,524
Hocking Technical College, Nelsonville   5,051
Kent State University-Tuscarawas, New Philadelphia   1,708
Kenyon College, Gambier   1,599
Mount Vernon Nazarene College, Mount Vernon   1,961
Muskingum Area Technical College, Zanesville   1,898
Muskingum College, New Concord   1,830
Ohio University, Chillicothe   1,726
Ohio University, Zanesville   1,516
Ohio University-Eastern, St. Clairsville   1,118

Newspapers and circulation

	District circulation	Total circulation
Akron Beacon Journal	1,376	141,144
Athens Messenger	4,805	11,152
Cambridge Daily Jeffersonian	10,325	12,205
Canton Repository	3,234	64,499
Chillicothe Gazette	11,105	16,233
Columbus Dispatch	14,502	245,310
Coshocton Tribune	7,112	7,124
Logan Daily News	4,137	4,241
Martins Ferry Times Leader	4,385	18,408
Mount Vernon News	8,571	9,324
New Philadelphia Times Reporter	22,771	23,450

USA Today*	4,207	1,674,376
Wheeling Intelligencer	1,424	20,126
Wheeling News-Register	1,901	36,471
Wooster Daily Record	3,776	22,805
Zanesville Times Recorder	18,776	21,051

See Sources and Explanations in the front of the volume.

Television stations and affiliations

Columbus	49%	WBNS	CBS
Columbus	49%	WCMH	NBC
Columbus	49%	WOSU	PBS
Columbus	49%	WOUC	PBS
Columbus	49%	WSFJ	PAX
Columbus	49%	WSYX	ABC
Columbus	49%	WTTE	FOX
Columbus	49%	WWHO	UPN, WB
Cleveland-Akron (Canton)	20%	WBNX	WB
Cleveland-Akron (Canton)	20%	WDLI	Independent
Cleveland-Akron (Canton)	20%	WEAO	PBS
Cleveland-Akron (Canton)	20%	WEWS	ABC
Cleveland-Akron (Canton)	20%	WGGN	Independent
Cleveland-Akron (Canton)	20%	WJW	FOX
Cleveland-Akron (Canton)	20%	WKYC	NBC
Cleveland-Akron (Canton)	20%	WMFD	Independent
Cleveland-Akron (Canton)	20%	WOAC	Independent
Cleveland-Akron (Canton)	20%	WOIO	CBS
Cleveland-Akron (Canton)	20%	WQHS	Univision
Cleveland-Akron (Canton)	20%	WUAB	UPN
Cleveland-Akron (Canton)	20%	WVIZ	PBS
Cleveland-Akron (Canton)	20%	WVPX	PAX
Charleston-Huntington, WV	14%	WCHS	ABC
Charleston-Huntington, WV	14%	WHCP	WB, UPN
Charleston-Huntington, WV	14%	WKAS	PBS
Charleston-Huntington, WV	14%	WKPI	PBS
Charleston-Huntington, WV	14%	WOUB	PBS
Charleston-Huntington, WV	14%	WOWK	CBS
Charleston-Huntington, WV	14%	WPBO	PBS
Charleston-Huntington, WV	14%	WPBY	PBS
Charleston-Huntington, WV	14%	WSAZ	NBC
Charleston-Huntington, WV	14%	WTSF	Independent
Charleston-Huntington, WV	14%	WVAH	FOX
Zanesville	10%	WHIZ	NBC
Wheeling-Steubenville	7%	WTRF	CBS

Cable systems and subscribers

Adelphia   102,766
CableVision Communications   2,671
Comcast   1,494
Nelsonville TV Cable   6,393
Time Warner   38,023

Businesses and other major employers

Longaberger Co.; Zanesville; fruit and vegetable baskets 7,000

Kent State University; Cambridge 5,466
Longaberger Co.; Frazeysburg; fruit and vegetable baskets 3,600
Genesis Bethesda Hospital; Zanesville 2,500
Ohio Workers Compensation Risk Field; Zanesville; insurance agents and brokers 2,400
Mead Corp.; Chillicothe; paper mills 2,200
Luiginos Inc.; Jackson; frozen dinners 1,100
Paccar Inc.; Chillicothe; truck and tractor truck assembly 1,000
Salt Fork Resort Club Inc.; Kimbolton; resort hotel 1,000
Zandex HealthCare; Zanesville; advisory services, insurance 950
Kitchen Collection Inc.; Zanesville; kitchenware 850
Merillat Corp.; Loudonville; kitchen cabinets 702
America Team Corp.; Dover; employee leasing service 700
Boeing Co.; Newark; search and navigation equipment 700
Guernsey Health Enterprises Inc.; Cambridge; ambulance service 700
Gradall Co.; New Philadelphia; excavation work 690
Owens-Brockway Glass Container Inc.; Zanesville 680
Pretty Products Inc.; Coshocton; mats/matting 679
Southeastern Ohio Regional Medical Center; Cambridge 653
Wayne-Dalton Corp.; Mount Hope; garage doors 650
ArvinMeritor Inc.; Newark; motor vehicle axles 600
MPW Industrial Services Inc.; Hebron; building cleaning 600
Ohio Dept. of Rehabilitation and Correction; Chillicothe 600
AK Steel Corp.; Coshocton; blast furnaces and steel mills 580
Muskingum County; Zanesville; police dept. 540
Ohio Dept. of Rehabilitation and Correction; St. Clairsville 535
Rocky Shoes and Boots Inc.; Nelsonville 530
Mount Vernon Nazarene College Inc.; Mount Vernon 528
Detroit Diesel Remanufacturing-East; Cambridge; diesel engine rebuilding 500
Holophane Corp.; Newark; lighting fixtures 500
Jeld-Wen Inc.; Mount Vernon; millwork 500
Kraft Foods Inc.; Coshocton; prepared meats 500
LDM Technologies Inc.; Byesville; plastics 500
Longaberger Co.; Newark; reed, rattan, wicker products 500
Tomkins Industries Inc.; Malta; window frames 500

OKLAHOMA

Districts established May 31, 2002, for elections first held in 2002.

5 members

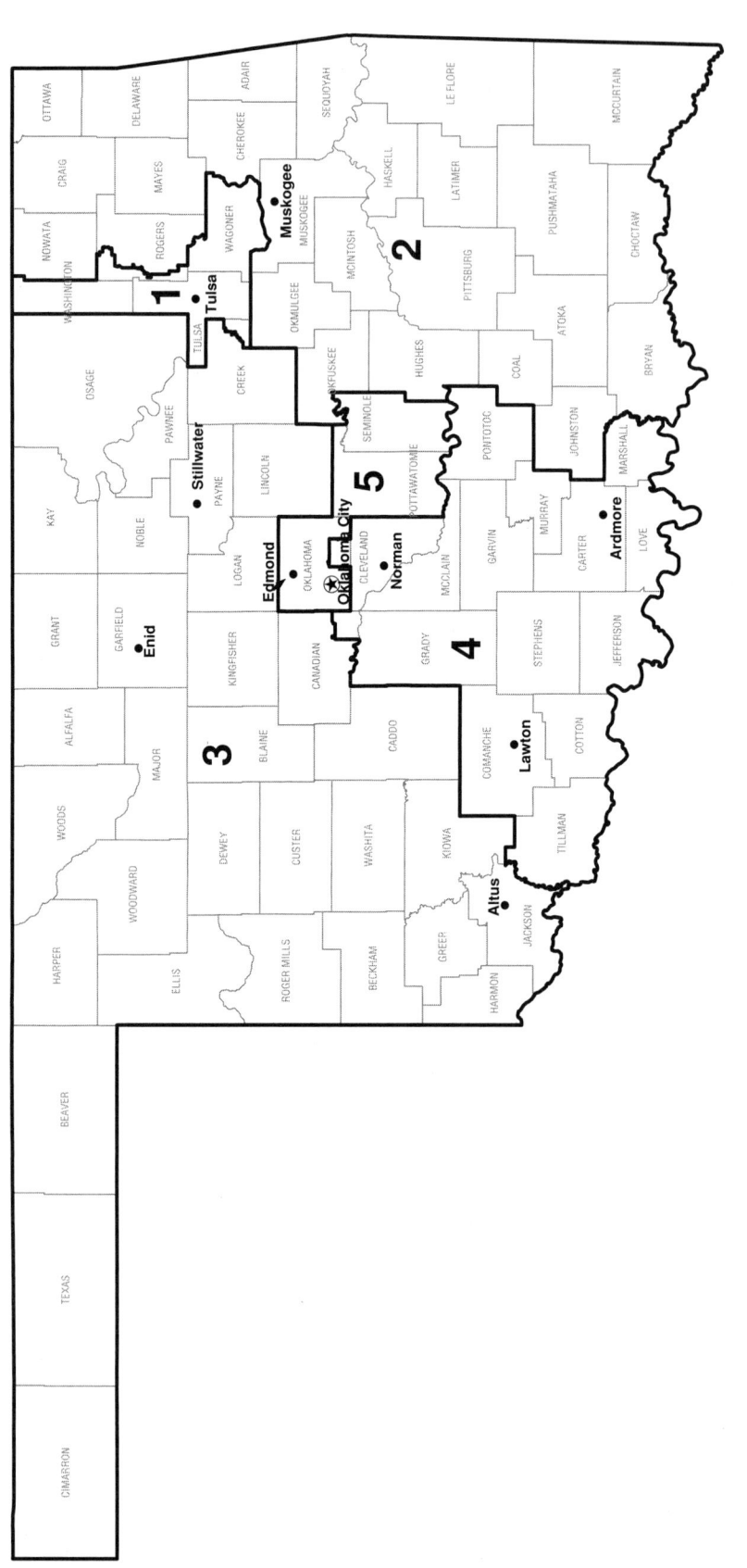

Oklahoma

Oklahoma constitutes a kind of land bridge connecting the Midwest to the South and the Southwest. The state's longest border is with Texas on the south, carved by the legendary Red River. But the northern line is all shared with Kansas, and the state also touches New Mexico and Colorado on the west and Arkansas and Missouri on the east. Aside from two low mountain chains that partly cross the eastern state line, Oklahoma shares topography with the midwestern states stacked neatly above it on the map, and its market basket is full of the same grains and beans and beef. For most of the twentieth century, Oklahoma expressed its passion for college football largely by playing (and usually beating) the big midwestern states to the north (Colorado, Kansas, Nebraska, Iowa, and Missouri).

But Oklahoma does not fit comfortably in the midwestern mode. There has been too much oil here, and the spirit of other cultural influences from the 1800s is too strong. Although there is just one Native American reservation, Oklahoma has a higher percentage of Native Americans than any other state by far (and the highest raw number behind California, a state nearly ten times as populous). Besides its own native tribes, Oklahoma has long harbored the Cherokee and other tribes (known as the Five Civilized Nations) driven over the "Trail of Tears" from the Deep South by General Andrew Jackson in the 1830s. Their descendants remain in the state's northeast, where as much as 40 percent of the population claims some Native American ancestry. The first white men of influence in Oklahoma came from the South, as did most of the homesteaders who took part in the great land rush in 1906 (including those who started early and were called "Sooners").

Even before statehood was conferred, Oklahoma was discovering oil and the sudden changes it brings. Growth in the first decades was rapid and haphazard. In 1930 the state had 2.5 million people, nine seats in the House, and all the bring-it-on attitude of the wildcatter. But the next decade brought the devastation of the Dust Bowl, a drought compounded by gales that gathered up the plow-broken prairie and carried it away. Thousands of busted farm families took to the highway, most famously to California, a harrowing trek recounted in John Steinbeck's *The Grapes of Wrath*. Surviving "Okies" are a demographic mainstay of that state's agricultural valleys to this day.

Oklahoma was able to come back from the devastation visited on its farm economy because it still had oil. That meant new hope during World War II, briefly, and again with the big leap in oil prices in the 1970s. But each time, the boom went bust. After World War II the energy business stagnated, and the boom that followed the Arab oil disruptions of the 1970s was only slightly longer in duration. The traditional gauge of the oil and gas industry's health is the count of drilling rigs at work on new wells. At the height of the most recent peak, the rig count approached 1,000. But in 1984 it fell below 200, and after 2000 it remained there. The amount of oil produced in Oklahoma in 1999 was less than it had been since 1919.

The state's difficulty getting beyond the cycles of farming and drilling has consigned it to the lower ranks of prosperity, despite the huge fortunes that were made by a few. In the 1990s the state had a small surge of high-tech investment, which also went sour as the computer-based bubble burst on Wall Street. Having played host to such high-flyers as WorldCom and Lucent, Oklahoma learned that not all economic illusions were based in natural resources. So while Oklahomans tend to keep working (the unemployment rate of 3.5 percent in 2002 was among the lowest in the country), they work at lower-level jobs (just one in five residents had a college degree in 2001, ranking the state forty-first in that category) and make less money. Oklahomans are more likely to be working in agriculture than the average American. Annual pay here was forty-third among the states in the 2000 census, and per capita income was only 84 percent of the national figure (down from 94 percent in 1980, when the rigs were all in the field). The percentage of state residents living in statistically defined poverty was over 15 percent in 2000, among the five worst states.

Growth managed to revive somewhat in the 1990s. Oklahoma City has broken into the top 30 cities (Tulsa was forty-third in 2000), with its metro area now larger than a million. The Census Bureau expects the state to grow another 20 percent by 2025, going from 20 percent minority to 27 percent over that period. Still, the lack of a first-tier metro area (or a likely candidate for one) will likely keep the state at five seats, just where it started.

As a southern-oriented and populist state, Oklahoma grew up voting Democratic. But as it grew older it grew more Republican. From 1908 to 1948 it went with the GOP presidential nominee only twice: for Warren Harding in 1920 and for Herbert Hoover in 1928. But after 1950 the voters turned around. In the dozen presidential elections since, Oklahoma has voted for every Republican except Barry Goldwater. The state voted for Dwight Eisenhower or Richard Nixon five times, for Ronald Reagan twice, for Gerald Ford in 1976, for George Bush in 1992, and even for Robert Dole in 1996. The capstone was the crushing win for George W. Bush in 2000. He carried 68 of the 77 counties and 60 percent of the vote (despite the fact that Green candidate Ralph Nader did not qualify for the ballot in the state).

Oklahoma did not elect a Republican governor until 1962 (Henry Bellmon) but then elected its second in 1966. Bellmon also came back to win another term in 1986, and Frank Keating served two terms from 1995 through 2002. Bellmon also broke the Democratic lock on the Senate seat, winning terms in the Republican year of 1968 and the Democratic year of 1974. Bellmon turned that job over in 1980 to a young admirer, Don Nickles, who surprised the state by winning the nomination. Nickles remained in the Senate as Budget Committee chair nearly a quarter century later. During this same era the Democrats came up with an exceptional champion of their own in David L. Boren, a Rhodes scholar who won the governorship in 1974, moved on to the Senate in 1978, and racked up some of the biggest election margins in state history. Boren resigned in 1994 to become president of the University of Oklahoma and was replaced by former Tulsa mayor and representative Jim Inhofe, a Republican.

As recently as 1994, Democrats still held four of the state's six seats. But the administration of Bill Clinton was not popular in Oklahoma, and as soon as the first House seat came open, in a special election held in May 1994, it went Republican. Over the course of the next two regular elections, the delegation became entirely Republican. In 1994 Oklahoma sent to the House two freshmen who had been college football heroes, J. C. Watts and Steve Largent. Watts, a stand-out quarterback at the University of Oklahoma, moved up quickly in Republican leadership and had a shot at being the first black Speaker. But in 2002 he became disillusioned with his House career and retired. Largent, a wide receiver at the University of Tulsa who later set the pro record for pass receptions, also went home in 2002, to run for governor. Most observers expected him to win, but his campaign lacked excitement, and he was upset by 39-year-old Democrat Brad Henry.

The state lost a seat in reapportionment after 2000, the dropping of a shoe that state demographers had been expecting for half a century. Healthy growth of nearly 10 percent in the 1990s was not enough to forestall the inevitable. The Democrats who still run the legislature in Oklahoma City drew a map that might have given them two or three seats but for the veto power of the governor, Frank Keating. So the final map was drawn by a state court, which combined most of the two easternmost districts into one and changed the other four districts hardly at all.

The new eastern district, numbered the 2nd, was won in 2002 by Brad Carson, the young Democrat who had integrated the delegation in 2000 by winning the old 2nd in the state's northeast corner. He should find the new district easier, as its new ground is the old "Little Dixie" district in the southeast part of the state that once produced Democratic Speaker Carl Albert, the pride of the town of Bug Tussle on the Texas line.

The new 1st District drawn by the court has added territory at its edges but remains, in essence, Tulsa and its immediate environs. The 5th comes close to aggregating all of metro Oklahoma City with Seminole and Pottawatomie Counties. The Fourth is a rough triangle formed by Norman (Oklahoma University) near Oklahoma City and reaching southwest to Lawton (home of Fort Sill) and southeast to Ardmore. The new 3rd is a renumbered reincarnation of the old 6th, beginning with the state's western extreme with the three counties of the Panhandle, then spilling out across nearly half the state. The new 3rd touches the Kansas and Texas lines and comes east past Stillwater (home of Oklahoma State) to the outskirts of metro Tulsa at one point, while stopping just outside of metro Oklahoma City at another.

Table 1 Population

District	Population	Population under 18	Voting-age population	Median age	Male*	Female*
1	690,131	182,345	507,786	35.0	48.6	51.4
2	690,130	179,577	510,553	37.2	49.2	50.8
3	690,131	175,998	514,133	36.3	49.8	50.2
4	690,131	177,869	512,262	34.6	49.7	50.3
5	690,131	176,571	513,560	34.4	48.5	51.5
State	3,450,654	892,360	2,558,294	35.5	49.1	50.9

*As percentage of total population.

Table 2 Voting-Age Persons by Race/Hispanic or Latino Origin

District	White*	Black or African American*	American Indian or Alaska Native*	Asian*	Other or multirace*	Hispanic or Latino*
1	77.1	8.2	5.2	1.4	3.6	4.6
2	74.2	3.9	14.5	0.3	5.2	1.9
3	83.4	3.8	5.1	0.9	2.5	4.2
4	80.4	6.0	4.8	1.9	2.9	4.0
5	71.8	12.2	4.0	2.8	2.7	6.7
State	77.4	6.8	6.7	1.5	3.3	4.3

*As percentage of voting-age population.

Table 3 Voting-Age Population by Age Groups

District	18 to 24*	25 to 44*	45 to 64*	Over 64*
1	13.0	40.5	30.2	16.4
2	12.2	35.4	31.9	20.5
3	14.6	36.2	30.2	19.1
4	15.4	38.8	29.5	16.3
5	14.6	39.7	28.9	16.8
State	14.0	38.1	30.1	17.8

*As percentage of voting-age population.

Table 4 Income and Occupation

District	Median family income	Families in poverty*	White collar†	Blue collar†	Service†	Farm†
1	$47,365	8.5	62.9	23.2	13.8	0.2
2	$33,907	14.6	48.3	33.2	16.7	1.8
3	$39,355	10.9	54.1	28.2	16.1	1.6
4	$42,429	9.7	57.2	26.4	15.7	0.7
5	$41,585	12.2	60.6	23.6	15.5	0.3
State	$40,709	11.2	56.9	26.7	15.5	0.9

*As percentage of all families.   †As percentage of employed workers 16 years and over.

Table 5 Education: School Years Completed

District	Less than grade 9*	Grades 9–12 no diploma*	High school diploma no college*	Some college*	College bachelor's degree or higher*
1	4.3	10.9	27.9	31.2	25.6
2	9.0	17.2	35.1	25.5	13.2

District	Less than grade 9*	Grades 9–12 no diploma*	High school diploma no college*	Some college*	College bachelor's degree or higher*
3	6.3	13.2	35.2	27.3	18.1
4	5.0	12.5	32.2	30.2	20.2
5	6.0	12.5	27.0	30.1	24.5
State	6.1	13.3	31.5	28.8	20.3

*As percentage of persons age 25 and over.

Table 6 Housing and Residential Patterns

District	Median home value	Owner occupied*	Renter occupied*	Urban†	Rural†
1	$83,200	64.8	35.2	89.6	10.4
2	$55,600	74.3	25.7	35.6	64.4
3	$59,000	72.5	27.5	50.7	49.3
4	$70,700	69.7	30.3	63.3	36.7
5	$71,800	61.2	38.8	87.5	12.5
State	$67,700	68.4	31.6	65.3	34.7

*As percentage of occupied housing units.   †As percentage of total population.

Oklahoma 1st District

Tulsa; Wagoner and Washington Counties

Wooden homes on small plots of land in the city's outskirts contrast with the skyscrapers of downtown Tulsa, the heart of the 1st and one of the most solidly Republican enclaves in Oklahoma. More insular and tied to old money than Oklahoma City and the rest of the state, Tulsans like to distinguish themselves from the "dust-on-their-boots" stereotype of the rest of Oklahoma.

Once the "oil capital of the world," Tulsa thrived on drilling for "black gold" until the market dried up in the 1980s. It is now a city seeking an economic identity to fit with its historic self-image. In the late 1980s, an effort to attract a diverse range of businesses through tax breaks and other incentives started to pay off. Tulsa has become a manufacturing hub of flight simulators. While aviation and aerospace manufacturing have remained productive, the telecommunications and financial services industries have helped prolong growth.

With the economy on the mend, real estate prices are beginning to rise as Tulsa expands to the east and south. Young professionals are moving into the more established sections of the city's center. South Tulsa is sprinkled with executive homes, and new subdivisions are springing up in the bedroom communities of Broken Arrow, Owasso, and Jenks. Redistricting after the 2000 census added Bartlesville in Washington County to the north and fast-growing suburbs in Wagoner County to the east.

Democrats split the votes in the 1st's local elections, but Republicans dominate at the federal level. The region has voted for a Democratic presidential candidate only twice since 1920. Socially conservative issues play well here, the home of Oral Roberts University.

Major Industry

Aerospace, defense manufacturing, oil, agriculture.

Notable

One of the deadliest race riots in American history took place in the Tulsa neighborhood of Greenwood in June 1921—nearly 300 people died; Oral Roberts University is known for its 200-foot prayer tower and "Praying Hands" sculpture.

Election Returns

	Republican		Democratic		Other	
President 2000	165,759	61.7%	99,283	37.0%	3,566	1.3%
House 2002	119,566	55.6%	90,649	42.2%	4,740	2.2%

District Profile

Population   690,131

Total area (square miles)   1,790.3
   Land area (square miles)   1,736.8

Population per square mile   397.4

Counties (2000 population)
   Creek (pt.)   5,670   Wagoner   57,491
   Rogers (pt.)   14,675   Washington   48,996
   Tulsa   563,299

Cities and other areas over 10,000 (2000 population)
   Bartlesville (pt.)   34,746
   Bixby   13,336
   Broken Arrow   74,859
   Owasso (pt.)   18,502
   Sand Springs (pt.)   17,172
   Tulsa (pt.)   387,419

Race and Hispanic or Latino origin*
   White   73.8%
   Black or African American   9.4%
   American Indian or Alaska Native   5.8%
   Asian   1.4%
   Native Hawaiian or other Pacific Islander   0.0%
   Some other race   0.1%
   Hispanic or Latino origin   5.3%
   Two or more races   4.2%

*As percentage of total population.

Ancestry*
   Dutch   1.7%   Italian   1.4%
   English   7.9%   Scotch-Irish   1.6%
   French   2.0%   Scottish   1.5%
   German   11.1%   USA/American   7.7%
   Irish   8.7%

*As estimated percentage of total population.

Universities and colleges, 2000–2001 enrollment
   Bartlesville Wesleyan College, Bartlesville   828
   College of Osteopathic Medicine of Oklahoma State University, Tulsa   352
   National Education Center-Spartan School of Aeronautics, Tulsa   1,653
   Oral Roberts University, Tulsa   3,607
   Phillips University, Enid   584
   Tulsa Community College, Tulsa   16,270
   Tulsa Welding School, Tulsa   327
   University of Tulsa, Tulsa   4,158

Newspapers and circulation

	District circulation	Total circulation
Bartlesville Examiner-Enterprise	8,006	11,251
Daily Oklahoman	3,513	208,321
Muskogee Phoenix-Times Democrat	1,538	18,787
USA Today*	4,639	1,674,376

*See Sources and Explanations in the front of the volume.

Television stations and affiliations

Tulsa	100%	KDOR	Independent
Tulsa	100%	KJRH	NBC
Tulsa	100%	KOED	PBS
Tulsa	100%	KOET	PBS
Tulsa	100%	KOKI	FOX
Tulsa	100%	KOTV	CBS
Tulsa	100%	KRSC	PBS
Tulsa	100%	KTFO	UPN
Tulsa	100%	KTPX	PAX
Tulsa	100%	KTUL	ABC
Tulsa	100%	KWBT	WB
Tulsa	100%	KWHB	Independent

Cable systems and subscribers

Cable ONE   13,674
Community Cablevision   3,529
Cox   152,056

Military installations, September 2001

Tulsa Army Aviation Support Facility No. 2 (Army Guard), Tulsa   280

Businesses and other major employers

American Airlines Inc.; Tulsa   11,625
Phillips Petroleum Co.; Bartlesville; petroleum refining   6,700
Hillcrest Healthcare System Hospital; Tulsa   6,150
Sabre Inc.; Collinsville; information retrieval services   6,100
Hillcrest Medical Center Inc.; Tulsa   6,000
Williams International Ventures Co.; Tulsa; coal pipeline operation   4,000
St. John Medical Center Inc.; Tulsa   3,675
St. Francis Hospital Inc.; Tulsa   3,095
Nordam Group Inc.; Tulsa; aircraft parts and service   2,850
ONEOK Services Co.; Tulsa; natural gas transmission   2,377
Vartec Telecom Inc.; Tulsa; information retrieval services   1,700
Amoco Fabrics and Fibers Co.; Tulsa; polyethylene resins   1,500
Boeing Co.; Tulsa; missile guidance systems   1,500
Hilti of America Inc.; Tulsa; nuts, rivets, and washers   1,500
WorldCom Inc.; Tulsa; telephone communication   1,500
Siegfried Inc.; Tulsa; holding company   1,463
TV Guide Inc.; Tulsa; cable TV equipment   1,400
BP Corp. North America Inc.; Tulsa; petroleum refining   1,300
City of Tulsa; Tulsa; water, solid waste management   1,300
Superstar/Netlink Group; Tulsa; cable TV   1,225

Arrow Trucking Co.; Tulsa; machinery transport   1,200
HCA Inc. Hospital; Tulsa   1,200
Jane Phillips Medical Center Inc.; Bartlesville   1,200
PricewaterhouseCoopers; Tulsa; certified public accountant   1,200
Avis Rent a Car Systems Inc.; Tulsa   1,000
Metris Companies Inc.; Tulsa; personal credit institutions   1,000
Oral Roberts University; Tulsa   1,000
University of Tulsa; Tulsa   1,000
West Telemarketing Corp.; Tulsa   1,000
Dollar Thrifty Automotive Group Inc.; Tulsa; automobile rental   984
Group Health Service of Oklahoma Inc.; Tulsa; health insurance   950
Citgo Petroleum Corp.; Tulsa; petroleum refining   940
U.S. Postal Service; Tulsa   900
Metropolitan Life Insurance Co.; Tulsa; insurance agents and brokers   850
Helmerich and Payne Inc.; Tulsa; drilling oil and gas wells   840
First Data Resources Inc.; Tulsa; credit card service   825
Bama Pie; Tulsa; frozen pies   800
First Data Corp.; Tulsa; data processing   800
Tulsa County; Tulsa; county government   800
Visteon Corp.; Tulsa; structural glass   800
City of Tulsa; Tulsa; police dept.   750
Oklahoma Congress PTA; Jenks; parent-teachers' association   723
AAON Inc.; Tulsa; air conditioning equipment   719
Burns International Security Services Corp.; Tulsa; protective services, guard   700
Pennwell Corp.; Tulsa; advertising, trade shows   700
Tulsa Fire Dept.; Tulsa   700
American Transportation of Oklahoma; Tulsa; truck and bus bodies   656
Oklahoma Fixture Co.; Tulsa; display cabinets   650
Owasso Public Schools District; Owasso   648
World Publishing Co.; Tulsa; newspaper   628
John Zink Co.; Tulsa; petroleum refinery equipment   625
BP America Inc.; Tulsa; petroleum products   600
DoAll Tulsa Co.; Tulsa; industrial machinery/equipment   600
Gatesway Foundation; Broken Arrow; sheltered workshop   600
Heritage Holding Inc.; Tulsa; propane gas   600
Interstate Brands West Corp.; Tulsa; bakeries   600
Sunoco Inc.; Tulsa; petroleum refining   600
Wal-Mart Stores Inc.; Broken Arrow; department stores   600
Braden Manufacturing; Tulsa; structural metal   575
Broken Arrow Independent School District 3; Broken Arrow   564
FlightSafety International Inc.; Broken Arrow; flight simulators   533
Burlington Northern and Santa Fe Railway Co.; Broken Arrow; switching and terminal services   500
CellXion; Wagoner; prefabricated portable buildings   500
City of Tulsa; Tulsa; city government   500
Independent School District of Tulsa County; Tulsa   500

NCO Financial Systems Inc.; Tulsa; collection agency
500

Oklahoma Dept. of Human Services; Tulsa 500

Public Service Company of Oklahoma; Tulsa; electric
power generation 500

Samson Operating LP; Tulsa; crude petroleum
production 500

TCIM Services; Tulsa; radio stations 500

Thrifty Rent-a-Car System Inc.; Tulsa 500

Zebco Federal Credit Union; Tulsa 500

Oklahoma 2nd District

East — Muskogee, "Little Dixie"

The 2nd has a definite Democratic lean—all nine Oklahoma counties that George W. Bush lost in the 2000 presidential election are here—but partisanship does not disguise a cultural split between the district's north and south regions. Running from Kansas to Texas and hugging Oklahoma's eastern border, the 2nd takes in outlying areas of Tulsa to the north and the "Little Dixie" region in the south. Southeastern Oklahoma relies on farming and is "Yellow Dog" Democratic territory, while Democrats in the northeastern part of the state are more liberal, at least by Oklahoma's conservative standards.

In "Little Dixie," a 1998 drought was as severe as any in the Dust Bowl era of the 1930s, but conservation techniques prevented similar sandstorms. The economy did suffer, however, as farmers were forced to use feed for grazing animals by midsummer, several months earlier than normal. In addition to beef and poultry, farmers cultivate peanuts and wheat, and in rocky southeastern McCurtain County, the timber industry thrives. Marginal oil and natural gas wells compose the energy businesses that survived the 1980s industry depression.

Up north, in the foothills of the Ozark Mountains, the thickly forested section of the 2nd provides northeast Oklahoma with its nickname, the Green Country. It is a poor rural area with Democratic sympathies. The lakes and waterways, the state's most extensive, attract tourists and the elderly, helping to boost the economy. Delaware County, which contains most of Grand Lake O' the Cherokees, was the state's fastest-growing county in the 1990s (32 percent). The 2nd also has one of the largest Native American population percentages in the nation (16.8 percent), and includes Tahlequah, the capital of the Cherokee Nation.

Major Industry

Timber, ranching, oil, and gas.

Notable

The Native American "Trail of Tears" of 1838–1839 ended in Tahlequah—nearly 20 percent of the Cherokee Nation died en route.

Election Returns

	Republican		Democratic		Other	
President 2000	123,952	52.0%	110,791	46.5%	3,438	1.4%
House 2002	51,234	25.9%	146,748	74.1%		

District Profile

Population 690,130

Total area (square miles) 21,224.9
Land area (square miles) 20,563.1

Population per square mile 33.6

Counties (2000 population)

Adair	21,038	Mayes	38,369
Atoka	13,879	McCurtain	34,402
Bryan	36,534	McIntosh	19,456
Cherokee	42,521	Muskogee	69,451
Choctaw	15,342	Nowata	10,569
Coal	6,031	Okfuskee	11,814
Craig	14,950	Okmulgee	39,685
Delaware	37,077	Ottawa	33,194
Haskell	11,792	Pittsburg	43,953
Hughes	14,154	Pushmataha	11,667
Johnston	10,513	Rogers (pt.)	55,966
Latimer	10,692	Sequoyah	38,972
Le Flore	48,109		

Cities and other areas over 10,000 (2000 population)

Claremore (pt.)	15,873	Muskogee	38,310
Durant	13,549	Okmulgee	13,022
McAlester	17,783	Tahlequah	14,458
Miami	13,704		

Race and Hispanic or Latino origin*
White 70.2%
Black or African American 4.0%
American Indian or Alaska Native 16.8%
Asian 0.3%
Native Hawaiian or other Pacific Islander 0.0%
Some other race 0.0%
Hispanic or Latino origin 2.4%
Two or more races 6.2%

*As percentage of total population.

Ancestry*

Dutch	1.6%	German	7.2%
English	5.0%	Irish	7.8%
French	1.5%	USA/American	10.2%

*As estimated percentage of total population.

Universities and colleges, 2000–2001 enrollment
Bacone College, Muskogee 830
Carl Albert State College, Poteau 1,847
Connors State College, Warner 1,979
Eastern Oklahoma State College, Wilburton 1,946
Kiamichi Technology Center, Idabel 211
Murray State College, Tishomingo 1,768
Northeastern Oklahoma A&M College, Miami 1,947
Northeastern State University, Tahlequah 8,082
Oklahoma State University, Okmulgee 2,419
Rogers University-Claremore, Claremore 2,640
Southeastern Oklahoma State University, Durant 3,746

Newspapers and circulation

	District circulation	Total circulation
Daily Oklahoman	15,193	208,321
*Fort Smith Times Record**	6,226	41,298

Joplin Globe		1,926	30,638
McAlester News-Capital & Democrat		10,933	10,982
Muskogee Phoenix-Times Democrat		17,139	18,787

*See Sources and Explanations in the front of the volume.

Television stations and affiliations

Tulsa	46%	KDOR	Independent
Tulsa	46%	KJRH	NBC
Tulsa	46%	KOED	PBS
Tulsa	46%	KOET	PBS
Tulsa	46%	KOKI	FOX
Tulsa	46%	KOTV	CBS
Tulsa	46%	KRSC	PBS
Tulsa	46%	KTFO	UPN
Tulsa	46%	KTPX	PAX
Tulsa	46%	KTUL	ABC
Tulsa	46%	KWBT	WB
Tulsa	46%	KWHB	Independent
Sherman-Ada	25%	KTEN	NBC
Sherman-Ada	25%	KXII	CBS
Fort Smith-Fayetteville-Springdale-Rogers	11%	KAFT	PBS
Fort Smith-Fayetteville-Springdale-Rogers	11%	KFAA	NBC
Fort Smith-Fayetteville-Springdale-Rogers	11%	KFSM	CBS
Fort Smith-Fayetteville-Springdale-Rogers	11%	KHBS	ABC
Fort Smith-Fayetteville-Springdale-Rogers	11%	KHOG	ABC
Fort Smith-Fayetteville-Springdale-Rogers	11%	KPOM	NBC
Fort Smith-Fayetteville-Springdale-Rogers	11%	KSBN	Independent
Shreveport, LA	9%	KLTS	PBS
Shreveport, LA	9%	KMSS	FOX
Shreveport, LA	9%	KPXJ	PAX
Shreveport, LA	9%	KSHV	WB, UPN
Shreveport, LA	9%	KSLA	CBS
Shreveport, LA	9%	KTAL	NBC
Shreveport, LA	9%	KTBS	ABC
Oklahoma City	7%	KAUT	UPN
Oklahoma City	7%	KETA	PBS
Oklahoma City	7%	KFOR	NBC
Oklahoma City	7%	KOCB	WB
Oklahoma City	7%	KOCO	ABC
Oklahoma City	7%	KOKH	FOX
Oklahoma City	7%	KOPX	PAX
Oklahoma City	7%	KSBI	Independent
Oklahoma City	7%	KTBO	Independent
Oklahoma City	7%	KWET	PBS
Oklahoma City	7%	KWTV	CBS
Joplin-Pittsburg	2%	KOAM	CBS
Joplin-Pittsburg	2%	KODE	ABC
Joplin-Pittsburg	2%	KOZJ	PBS
Joplin-Pittsburg	2%	KSNF	NBC

Cable systems and subscribers

Adelphia 2,318
Broken Bow Cable TV 1,257
Cable ONE 10,422
Charter 18,017
Classic 17,250
Communicomm 9,862
Cox 42,226
Mediacom 686
Omni III Cable TV 953
WEHCO Video 4,182

Military installations, September 2001

McAlester Army Ammunition Plant, McAlester 1,697

Businesses and other major employers

Choctaw Nation of Oklahoma; Durant; Native American reservation 1,633
Georgia-Pacific Corp.; Muskogee; tissue paper 1,200
Northrop Grumman Technical Services Inc.; Valliant; aircraft servicing 1,200
Staff One Inc.; Durant; employee leasing service 1,100

Muskogee Medical Center Authority; Muskogee 1,000
Northeastern State University; Tahlequah 980
OK Foods Inc.; Heavener; processed poultry 900
Weyerhaeuser Co.; Valliant; sawmills and planing mills 900
Cherokee Nation; Tahlequah; harness assemblies, electronic use 800
Harsco Corp.; Catoosa; coolers, condensers 800
Sundowner Trailers Inc.; Coleman; horse trailers 715
OK Foods Inc.; Muldrow; processed poultry 700
Reasor's Inc.; Tahlequah; grocery store 700
U.S. Veterans Hospital; Muskogee 700
Greenleaf Nursery Co.; Park Hill; nursery stock 650
McAlester Regional Health Center Authority; McAlester 625
Labinal Inc.; Pryor; aircraft parts 600
Weyerhaeuser Co.; Wright City; building materials 600
Tyson Foods Inc.; Stilwell; processed poultry 575
Oklahoma Dept. of Corrections; McAlester 520
ASEC Manufacturing Sales; Catoosa; automotive exhaust systems 500
Baptist Regional Health Center; Miami 500
Fenton Financial Group; McAlester; placement agencies 500
Indian Health Service; Tahlequah 500
Therma-Tru Corp.; Roland; metal doors 500

Oklahoma 3rd District

Panhandle, west and north-central Oklahoma

With nothing to stop it on the flat plains, the wind blows with constant force in the 3rd, an area devastated by the Dust Bowl of the 1930s. Few areas felt the boom or the bust of the 1980s oil market more than the 3rd, as those who had made fortunes on oil had their rigs and property auctioned and their Mercedes and Lincolns repossessed. Western Oklahoma had never fully recovered from the Dust Bowl, and the oil bust was another reason to leave the area.

The 3rd contains most of the old 6th District that existed before redistricting after the 2000 census, covering huge swaths of Oklahoma's land in the western and north-central parts of the state, including much of its border with Kansas. In the western areas, more than half of the district's counties lost population in the first half of the 1990s because of the oil market downturn. Locals are striving to diversify beyond agriculture and oil.

Midwestern plains become more evident in the eastern portions of the 3rd, north of Oklahoma City—an area characterized by Bible Belt conservatism.

The three panhandle counties—Cimarron, Texas, and Beaver—are perhaps the most heavily Republican-voting in the state: George W. Bush topped 80 percent in each of these counties in the 2000 presidential election, and 2002 GOP gubernatorial nominee Steve Largent surpassed 65 percent in each county. The southern part of the district is home to conservative Democrats whose families relocated from Texas.

Major Industry

Agriculture, oil.

Notable

In November 1868 Gen. George A. Custer led an Army contingent in the Battle of Washita, also referred to as the Black Kettle Massacre, in which 103 Native American men, women, and children died.

Election Returns

	Republican		Democratic		Other	
President 2000	163,302	65.1%	84,691	33.8%	2,805	1.1%
House 2002	148,206	75.6%			47,884	24.4%

District Profile

Population   690,131

Total area (square miles)   34,384.1
   Land area (square miles)   34,088.5

Population per square mile   20.2

Counties (2000 population)

Alfalfa 6,105	Jackson 28,439
Beaver 5,857	Kay 48,080
Beckham 19,799	Kingfisher 13,926
Blaine 11,976	Kiowa 10,227
Caddo 30,150	Lincoln 32,080
Canadian (pt.) 63,079	Logan 33,924
Cimarron 3,148	Major 7,545
Creek (pt.) 61,697	Noble 11,411
Custer 26,142	Osage 44,437
Dewey 4,743	Pawnee 16,612
Ellis 4,075	Payne 68,190
Garfield 57,813	Roger Mills 3,436
Grant 5,144	Texas 20,107
Greer 6,061	Washita 11,508
Harmon 3,283	Woods 9,089
Harper 3,562	Woodward 18,486

Cities and other areas over 10,000 (2000 population)

Altus   21,447
Elk City   10,510
El Reno   16,212
Enid   47,045
Guymon   10,472
Oklahoma City (pt.)   14,849
Ponca City   25,919
Sapulpa (pt.)   19,044
Stillwater   39,065
Woodward   11,853
Yukon   21,043

Race and Hispanic or Latino origin*

White   81.0%
Black or African American   3.8%
American Indian or Alaska Native   6.0%
Asian   0.8%
Native Hawaiian or other Pacific Islander   0.1%
Some other race   0.1%
Hispanic or Latino origin   5.2%
Two or more races   3.0%

*As percentage of total population.

Ancestry*

Dutch 1.9%	Irish 8.2%
English 6.8%	Scotch-Irish 1.4%
French 1.8%	Scottish 1.1%
German 12.4%	USA/American 10.0%

*As estimated percentage of total population.

Universities and colleges, 2000–2001 enrollment

Caddo-Kiowa Area Vocational Technical School, Fort Cobb   311
Langston University, Langston   2,826
Meridian Technology Center, Stillwater   662
Northern Oklahoma College, Tonkawa   2,690
Northwestern Oklahoma State University, Alva   1,984
Oklahoma Panhandle State University, Goodwell   1,183
Oklahoma State University, Stillwater   18,676
O. T. Autry Area Vocational Technical Center, Enid   208
Redlands Community College, El Reno   2,163
Southwestern Oklahoma State University, Weatherford   4,860
Western Oklahoma State College, Altus   2,296

Newspapers and circulation

	District circulation	Total circulation
Bartlesville Examiner-Enterprise	2,761	11,251
Daily Oklahoman	45,990	208,321
Enid News and Eagle	19,102	19,253
Lawton Constitution	1,878	23,410
Ponca City News	9,679	9,679
Stillwater News Press	8,896	8,896

*See Sources and Explanations in the front of the volume.

Television stations and affiliations

Oklahoma City	70%	KAUT	UPN
Oklahoma City	70%	KETA	PBS
Oklahoma City	70%	KFOR	NBC
Oklahoma City	70%	KOCB	WB
Oklahoma City	70%	KOCO	ABC
Oklahoma City	70%	KOKH	FOX
Oklahoma City	70%	KOPX	PAX
Oklahoma City	70%	KSBI	Independent
Oklahoma City	70%	KTBO	Independent
Oklahoma City	70%	KWET	PBS
Oklahoma City	70%	KWTV	CBS
Amarillo, TX	17%	KACV	PBS
Amarillo, TX	17%	KAMR	NBC
Amarillo, TX	17%	KCIT	FOX
Amarillo, TX	17%	KFDA	CBS
Amarillo, TX	17%	KVIH	ABC
Amarillo, TX	17%	KVII	ABC
Tulsa	11%	KDOR	Independent
Tulsa	11%	KJRH	NBC
Tulsa	11%	KOED	PBS
Tulsa	11%	KOET	PBS
Tulsa	11%	KOKI	FOX
Tulsa	11%	KOTV	CBS
Tulsa	11%	KRSC	PBS
Tulsa	11%	KTFO	UPN

Tulsa	11%	KTPX	PAX
Tulsa	11%	KTUL	ABC
Tulsa	11%	KWBT	WB
Tulsa	11%	KWHB	Independent
Wichita Falls-Lawton	2%	KAUZ	CBS
Wichita Falls-Lawton	2%	KFDX	NBC
Wichita Falls-Lawton	2%	KJTL	FOX
Wichita Falls-Lawton	2%	KSWO	ABC

Cable systems and subscribers
Cable ONE 33,556
Carnegie Cable 842
Charter 4,744
Cim Tel 5,525
Classic 30,795
Community Cablevision 2,661
Cox 62,583
Eagle Media 923
Galaxy 4,937
Hinton CATV 735

Military installations, September 2001
Altus Air Force Base, Altus 2,939
Vance Air Force Base, Enid 963

Businesses and other major employers
Oklahoma State University; Stillwater 3,709
Conoco Inc.; Ponca City; petroleum refining 2,000
Seaboard Farms Inc.; Guymon; livestock farm 2,000
Charles Machine Works Inc.; Perry; backhoes 1,311
Phillips Petroleum Co.; Bartlesville; petroleum bulk stations/terminals 1,300
Kwikset Corp.; Bristow; locks or lock sets 1,200
Northrop Grumman Technical Services Inc.; Enid; aircraft servicing 1,200
Brunswick Corp.; Stillwater; outboard motors 1,000
Advance Food Co.; Enid; cooked meats 900
Integris Rural Healthcare of Oklahoma Inc.; Enid 900
Southwestern Oklahoma State University; Weatherford 900
Hilti Inc.; Tulsa; power-driven handtools 800
Universal Health Services Inc.; Enid; hospital 650
Jackson County Memorial Hospital Trust Authority; Altus 624
International Trading Co.; Ponca City; prepared meats 600
Pioneer Business Solutions; Kingfisher; retail stores 600
Bar-S Foods Co.; Clinton; prepared meats 550
Oklahoma Dept. of Human Services; Enid 550
QIS Inc.; Goodwell; pipeline inspections 550
Sykes Enterprises Inc.; Ponca City; computer consulting services 550
John Christner Trucking Inc.; Sapulpa; trucking 540
Stillwater Medical Center Authority; Stillwater 523
Haines Construction Co. Inc.; Woodward; oil/gas pipeline construction 500
Indiana Glass Co.; Sapulpa; pressed and blown glass 500
St. Gobain-Container Inc.; Sapulpa; food containers, glass 500

Oklahoma 4th District
South central — Norman, Lawton, part of Oklahoma City

Home to the state's largest university and two military bases, the 4th contains part of Oklahoma City, its southern suburbs and the western edges of "Little Dixie," a part of the state named for its southern influence.

The 4th's once-booming oil economy suffered from the low prices of the 1990s, and a concurrent drought helped decimate the southwest. Still, agriculture remains an essential economic cog. Soybeans, cotton, wheat, and peanuts fill many of the district's family farms. Overall, the district's population increased by the close of the 1990s, as the military maintained its ubiquitous presence. The cancellation of the Crusader artillery system was a blow to Fort Sill and the town of Lawton, however, and many worry that Lawton's economy will collapse completely if Fort Sill does not survive the next round of base closures.

The district has epitomized the Oklahoman trend toward voting Republican in national elections. Although once confined in the 4th to presidential elections, this GOP swing now extends to congressional candidates and trickles down to some state legislators. But Democrats remain competitive, especially in the rural, southern parts of the district and around the University of Oklahoma in Norman. Republicans have strength in other parts of Norman. George W. Bush received 60.7 percent of the 4th District vote in the 2000 presidential election.

Major Industry
Military, higher education, oil, agriculture.

Notable
Apache warrior Geronimo was imprisoned at the Fort Sill Military Reservation.

Election Returns

	Republican		Democratic		Other	
President 2000	144,568	60.7%	91,078	38.2%	2,497	1.0%
House 2002	106,452	53.8%	91,322	46.2%		

District Profile

Population 690,131

Total area (square miles) 10,409.3
   Land area (square miles) 10,211.8

Population per square mile 67.6

Counties (2000 population)

Canadian (pt.)	24,618	Love	8,831
Carter	45,621	Marshall	13,184
Cleveland	208,016	McClain	27,740
Comanche	114,996	Murray	12,623
Cotton	6,614	Oklahoma (pt.)	60,732
Garvin	27,210	Pontotoc	35,143
Grady	45,516	Stephens	43,182
Jefferson	6,818	Tillman	9,287

Cities and other areas over 10,000 (2000 population)

Ada   15,691
Ardmore   23,711
Chickasha   15,850
Duncan   22,505
Lawton   92,757
Midwest City (pt.)   45,044
Moore   41,138
Mustang   13,156
Norman   95,694
Oklahoma City (pt.)   70,896

Race and Hispanic or Latino origin*

White   77.6%
Black or African American   6.6%
American Indian or Alaska Native   5.5%
Asian   1.7%
Native Hawaiian or other Pacific Islander   0.1%
Some other race   0.1%
Hispanic or Latino origin   4.8%
Two or more races   3.6%

*As percentage of total population.

Ancestry*

Dutch 1.5%	Italian 1.3%
English 6.8%	Scotch-Irish 1.3%
French 1.8%	Scottish 1.2%
German 9.9%	USA/American 10.0%
Irish 8.6%	

*As estimated percentage of total population.

Universities and colleges, 2000–2001 enrollment

Cameron University, Lawton   4,629
East Central University, Ada   4,067
Great Plains Area Vocational Technical School, Lawton   234
Mid America Bible College, Oklahoma City   357
Moore-Norman Area Vocational Technical School, Norman   209
Rose State College, Midwest City   7,471
University of Oklahoma, Norman   24,205
University of Science and Arts of Oklahoma, Chickasha   1,409

Newspapers and circulation

	District circulation	Total circulation
Daily Oklahoman	54,846	208,321
Dallas Morning News	2,014	495,624
Lawton Constitution	21,495	23,410
Norman Transcript	15,523	15,548
*USA Today**	1,955	1,674,376

*See Sources and Explanations in the front of the volume.

Television stations and affiliations

Wichita Falls-Lawton, TX	41%	KAUZ	CBS
Wichita Falls-Lawton, TX	41%	KFDX	NBC
Wichita Falls-Lawton, TX	41%	KJTL	FOX
Wichita Falls-Lawton, TX	41%	KSWO	ABC
Oklahoma City	35%	KAUT	UPN
Oklahoma City	35%	KETA	PBS
Oklahoma City	35%	KFOR	NBC
Oklahoma City	35%	KOCB	WB
Oklahoma City	35%	KOCO	ABC
Oklahoma City	35%	KOKH	FOX
Oklahoma City	35%	KOPX	PAX
Oklahoma City	35%	KSBI	Independent
Oklahoma City	35%	KTBO	Independent
Oklahoma City	35%	KWET	PBS
Oklahoma City	35%	KWTV	CBS
Sherman-Ada, TX	24%	KTEN	NBC
Sherman-Ada, TX	24%	KXII	CBS

Cable systems and subscribers

Cable ONE   32,016
Classic   13,415
Cox   37,462
Eagle Media   660
Galaxy   747
Lawton Cablevision   22,930
Southwestern CATV   894

Military installations, September 2001

Tinker Air Force Base, Midwest City   22,223
Fort Sill (Army), Lawton   16,175
Will Rogers World Airport Air National Guard Station, Oklahoma City   1,267
Midwest City (Twaddle), Oklahoma City   402
Lexington Army Aviation Support Facility No. 1 (Army Guard), Lexington   257

Businesses and other major employers

Wellness Center of Southern Oklahoma; Ardmore   6,000
General Motors Corp.; Oklahoma City; automobile bodies   5,800
Goodyear Tire and Rubber Co.; Lawton; pneumatic tires   4,000
University of Oklahoma; Norman   2,400
Sonic Corp.; Oklahoma City; restaurants   2,000
Michelin North America Inc.; Ardmore; automobile tires   1,945
CMI Corp.; Oklahoma City; road construction machinery   1,700
Comanche County Hospital Authority; Lawton   1,600
Norman Regional Hospital Authority; Norman   1,411
York International Corp.; Norman; oil/gas field machinery   1,400
Midwest City HMA Inc. Hospital; Oklahoma City   1,200
Chickasaw Foundation Upward Bound; Ada; educational research   1,000
Independent School District; Norman   1,000
Rose State College; Oklahoma City   1,000
Hudiburg Auto Group; Oklahoma City; automobiles   900
Oklahoma Dept. of Human Services; Pauls Valley   900
ArvinMeritor Inc.; Chickasha; automotive parts   700
Mercy Memorial Health Center; Ardmore   700
Valley View Hospital Authority; Ada   700
Veritas Software Technology Corp.; Oklahoma City; disk drives   700
Wal-Mart Stores Inc.; Moore; department stores   650
Cameron University; Lawton   625
Wal-Mart Stores Inc.; Lawton; department stores   600
Pre-Paid Legal Casualty Inc.; Ada; insurance agents and brokers   586

City of Lawton; Lawton; city government   573
Duncan Regional Hospital Inc.; Duncan   550
Oklahoma Dept. of Mental Health and Substance Abuse
  Services; Norman   550
Wal-Mart Stores Inc.; Ardmore; department stores   532
Dolgencorp Inc.; Ardmore; variety stores   511
Southwestern Medical Center; Lawton   507
Ardmore Independent School District; Ardmore   500
Halliburton Energy Services Inc.; Duncan; product
  testing lab   500
Solo Cup Co.; Ada; cups   500

Oklahoma 5th District

*Most of Oklahoma City; Pottawatomie and Seminole
Counties*

The 5th contains all of downtown Oklahoma City, which underwent many changes in the 1980s and 1990s. The early-1980s boom swelled the population, but the economic torpor that gripped the area at decade's end forced corporations to scale back, and the population declined in some areas.

By the early 1990s, Oklahoma City's economy diversified by necessity. While oil and gas still compose a large chunk of the economy along with some agriculture, energy corporations have had to expand their businesses to plastics and other industries. Telecommunications companies took hold in the district, though the recent economic downturn has caused some corporate layoffs. Lucent Technologies was once Oklahoma City's largest employer, but the ailing company sold its plant to an electronics company in 2001.

Oklahoma City is indelibly linked to the 1995 bombing at the Alfred P. Murrah Federal Building that killed 168 people. A memorial and the Institute for the Prevention of Terrorism commemorate the site.

The 5th contains the towns of Shawnee and Seminole, both home to large Native American populations. Though Tinker Air Force Base is in the 4th, many who work there live in the 5th. The district is also home to several colleges and universities in Oklahoma City.

Republicans have dominated federal elections in the 5th. The addition of Shawnee, Seminole County, and the largely black northeastern portion of Oklahoma City in redistricting following the 2000 census made the district more Democratic, but not enough to threaten the GOP hold. George W. Bush took 61.8 percent of the vote here in the 2000 presidential election.

Major Industry

Oil, computer hardware, state government, education.

Notable

Seminole County is the historic Seminole Nation territory, accepted by the tribes in exchange for their departure from the Florida Territory; the shopping cart and parking meter were invented in Oklahoma City.

Election Returns

	Republican		Democratic		Other	
President 2000	135,761	61.8%	82,584	37.6%	1,338	0.6%
House 2002	121,374	62.2%	63,208	32.4%	10,469	5.4%

District Profile

Population   690,131

Total area (square miles)   2,089.3
  Land area (square miles)   2,066.7

Population per square mile   333.9

Counties (2000 population)
  Oklahoma (pt.)   599,716
  Pottawatomie   65,521
  Seminole   24,894

Cities and other areas over 10,000 (2000 population)
  Bethany   20,307   Oklahoma City (pt.)   420,387
  Del City   22,128   Shawnee   28,692
  Edmond   68,315   The Village   10,157

Race and Hispanic or Latino origin*
  White   67.7%
  Black or African American   13.6%
  American Indian or Alaska Native   4.4%
  Asian   2.5%
  Native Hawaiian or other Pacific Islander   0.1%
  Some other race   0.1%
  Hispanic or Latino origin   8.3%
  Two or more races   3.3%

As percentage of total population.

Ancestry*

Dutch 1.4%	Italian 1.2%
English 7.2%	Scotch-Irish 1.5%
French 1.9%	Scottish 1.4%
German 9.7%	USA/American 7.6%
Irish 7.7%	

As estimated percentage of total population.

Universities and colleges, 2000–2001 enrollment
  American Bible College and Seminary, Bethany   278
  Francis Tuttle Area Vocational Technical Center,
    Oklahoma City   821
  Hillsdale Free Will Baptist College, Moore   262
  Oklahoma Baptist University, Shawnee   2,017
  Oklahoma Christian University of Science and Arts,
    Oklahoma City   1,752
  Oklahoma City Community College, Oklahoma City
    9,358
  Oklahoma City University, Oklahoma City   3,878
  Oklahoma State University, Oklahoma City   3,995
  Seminole State College, Seminole   2,033
  Southern Nazarene University, Bethany   2,064
  St. Gregory's University, Shawnee   633
  University of Central Oklahoma, Edmond   14,099
  University of Oklahoma Health Sciences Center,
    Oklahoma City   2,759
  University of Phoenix, Oklahoma City   1,154

Newspapers and circulation

	District circulation	Total circulation
Daily Oklahoman	84,700	208,321
Dallas Morning News	2,751	495,624
Oklahoma City Journal Record	2,379	2,865

Shawnee News-Star	8,786	9,834
*USA Today**	5,657	1,674,376

See Sources and Explanations in the front of the volume.

Television stations and affiliations
Oklahoma City	100%	KAUT	UPN
Oklahoma City	100%	KETA	PBS
Oklahoma City	100%	KFOR	NBC
Oklahoma City	100%	KOCB	WB
Oklahoma City	100%	KOCO	ABC
Oklahoma City	100%	KOKH	FOX
Oklahoma City	100%	KOPX	PAX
Oklahoma City	100%	KSBI	Independent
Oklahoma City	100%	KTBO	Independent
Oklahoma City	100%	KWET	PBS
Oklahoma City	100%	KWTV	CBS

Cable systems and subscribers
Charter   11,748
Cox   158,350

Military installations, September 2001
Tulsa International Airport, Tulsa   1,168
Oklahoma Regional Training Institute, Oklahoma City
111

Businesses and other major employers
Oklahoma Dept. of Human Services; Oklahoma City
8,000
Old Navy Inc.; Oklahoma City; clothing stores   5,000
U.S. Federal Aviation Admin.; Oklahoma City   5,000
Lucent Technologies Inc.; Oklahoma City; computer
peripheral equipment   4,200
Electronic Data Systems Corp.; Oklahoma City; billing,
bookkeeping service   3,500
Oklahoma Dept. of Human Services; Oklahoma City
3,200
Integris Southwest Medical Center; Oklahoma City
3,000
St. Anthony Hospital; Choctaw   3,000
University of Oklahoma; Oklahoma City   3,000
HCA Inc.; Oklahoma City; hospital   2,900
Everett Hospital; Oklahoma City   2,800
Integris Baptist Medical Center Inc.; Oklahoma City
2,694
Oklahoma Health Dept.; Oklahoma City   2,300
St. Anthony Hospital; Oklahoma City   2,000
U.S. Postal Service; Oklahoma City   2,000
Oklahoma City; Oklahoma City; police dept.   1,700
Mercy Health Center; Oklahoma City   1,630
Oklahoma County; Oklahoma City; county government
1,550
Veritas Software Technology Corp.; Oklahoma City;
computer storage devices   1,500
Unit Parts Co.; Oklahoma City; automotive alternators
1,480
U.S. Veterans Hospital; Oklahoma City   1,400
VF Jeanswear; Seminole; work clothing   1,350
American Fidelity Assurance Co.; Oklahoma City;
accident insurance carriers   1,250
Oklahoma Finance Office; Oklahoma City   1,200
Oklahoma Publishing Co.; Oklahoma City; newspaper
1,200

Kerr-McGee Corp.; Oklahoma City; pigments   1,200
University of Central Oklahoma; Edmond   1,200
Deaconess Hospital; Oklahoma City   1,180
Hobby Lobby Stores Inc.; Oklahoma City; arts and crafts
supplies   1,100
Fleming Companies Inc.; Oklahoma City; food supplier
1,035
America Online Inc.; Oklahoma City; Internet services
1,000
Fleming Wholesale Inc.; Oklahoma City; food supplier
1,000
Hertz Technologies Inc.; Oklahoma City; management
services   1,000
Oklahoma City; Oklahoma City; fire dept.   1,000
Southwest Airlines Co.; Oklahoma City   950
Macklanburg-Duncan Company of California Inc.;
Oklahoma City; adhesives and sealants   900
Oklahoma City Community College; Oklahoma City
887
Cameron Enterprises LP; Oklahoma City; trusts   850
Devon Energy Production Co.; Oklahoma City; crude
petroleum production   800
Oklahoma Dept. of Transportation; Oklahoma City
700
OGE Energy Corp.; Oklahoma City; electric power
generation   600
Oklahoma City; Oklahoma City; water, solid waste
management   600
Oklahoma Gas and Electric Co.; Oklahoma City; electric
power generation   600
Oklahoma Gas and Electric Co.; Oklahoma City; electric
services   600
St. Michael Hospital Inc.; Oklahoma City   600
Wolverine Tube Inc.; Shawnee; copper tubing   600
Oklahoma City Water Utilities Trust; Oklahoma City;
waste management agency   593
MidFirst Bank; Oklahoma City; savings and loan   578
A. M. Gilardi and Sons Inc.; Oklahoma City; refrigerated
pizza   550
Chesapeake Energy Corp.; Oklahoma City; crude
petroleum production   550
Oklahoma Employment Security Commission;
Oklahoma City   505
Carlisle Foodservice Products Inc.; Oklahoma City;
plastic containers   500
IFriendly Co. Inc.; Oklahoma City; Internet services
500
Integris Baptist Medical Center Inc.; Spencer; family
counseling   500
Mobil Chemical Co.; Shawnee; polypropylene film and
sheet   500
Oklahoma City University; Oklahoma City   500
Oklahoma Dept. of Public Safety; Oklahoma City   500
Oklahoma Gas and Electric Co.; Oklahoma City; gas and
other services   500
Oklahoma Tourism and Recreation Department;
Oklahoma City   500
Oxbow Enterprises; Oklahoma City; fast-food restaurant
chain   500
Pinkerton's Inc.; Oklahoma City; security guard service
500
Wal-Mart Stores Inc.; Oklahoma City; department stores
500

OREGON

Districts established October 19, 2001, for elections first held in 2002.

5 members

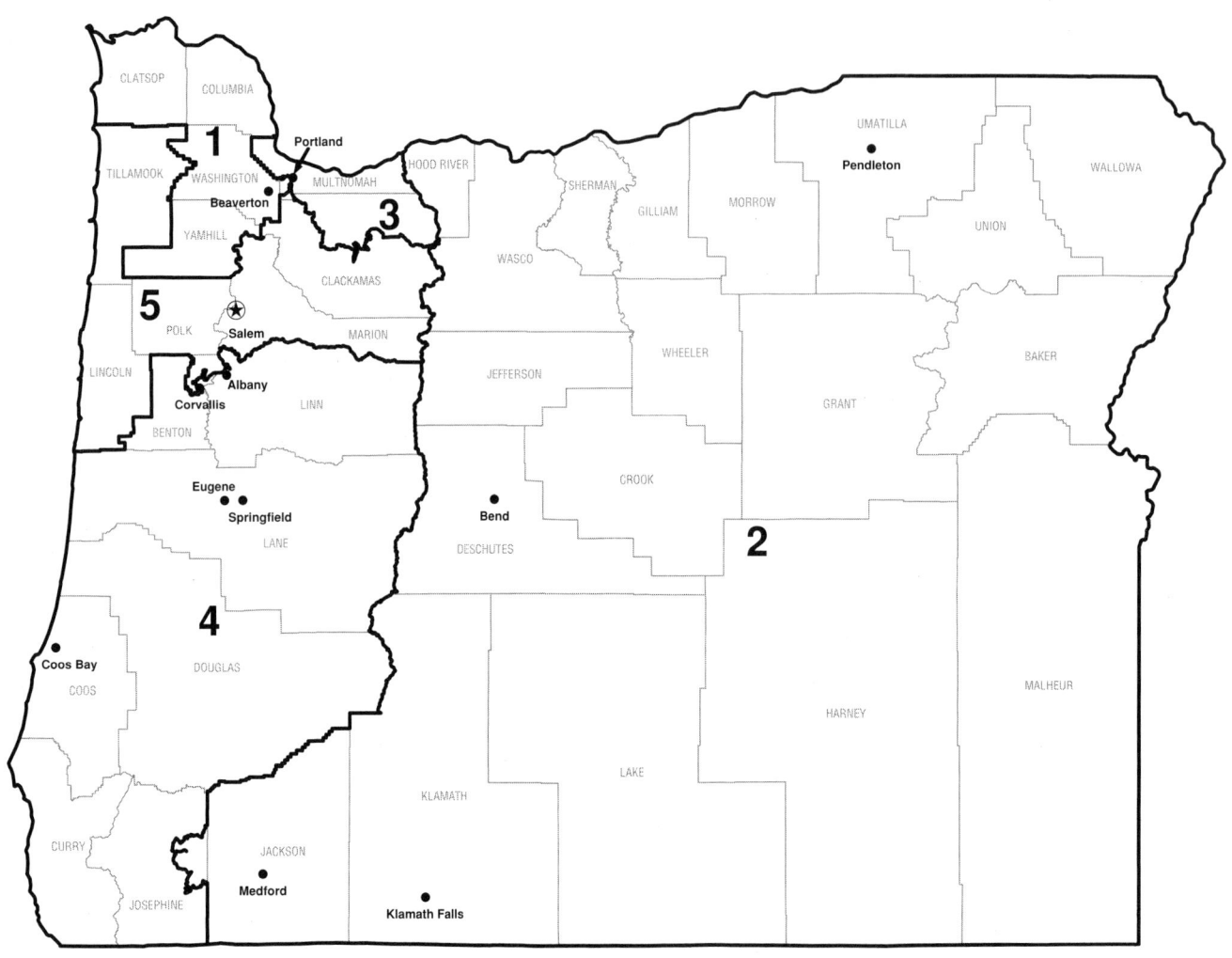

Oregon

Where the High Plains reach the Pacific Ocean, the demographics and sociology of the West meet those of the West Coast. The result is the geographically gorgeous and politically intriguing state of Oregon. The eastern part of the state is like its neighbors, Idaho and Nevada, a high and dry plateau where farmers grow wheat and potatoes and ranchers graze cattle and sheep. But further west the mountains of the Coastal Range march through, running parallel to the seashore and peaking at Mount Hood at 11,200 feet. On the slopes of this range, rainforest conditions have created some of the most magnificent stands of evergreen timber in the world. In the state's far northwest corner the great Columbia River meets the Pacific, creating such a wealth of natural harborage that the big town they built almost had to be called Portland.

For those who appreciate these eye-filling landscapes, deep green even under typically low and gray clouds, Oregon is a near paradise. White explorers, English and Spanish sailors in the sixteenth century, then Lewis and Clark on their riverboats in 1805, came looking for the fabled Northwest Passage. They returned instead with stories that eventually lured easterners and Europeans to settle here. The Oregon Trail was operational by the 1830s, and it took six months to cross from Independence, Missouri, by covered wagon. The early arrivals were mainly farmers. The coming of railroads allowed the transport of timber and ore, and Oregon went to work in its forests and mines. This early development enabled Oregon to enter the Union in the 1850s, before the Civil War and decades ahead of other western states.

These extraction industries brought wealth to Oregon and made Portland a boom town in the late 1800s and early 1900s. The city ranked sixty-first in population nationally in 1890 but had leaped to 28 by 1910. Something of an aristocracy developed in the upstart city, producing mansions and museums and a sense that manifest destiny had found its westernmost flower here. Portland was still in the top 25 cities when World War II began, while the postwar demand for lumber kept the economy booming through the 1940s.

Through the next generation, however, growth slowed. Oregon's raw materials found many competitors in the globalizing marketplace, and its neighbors to the north and south (Washington and California) became bigger manufacturing centers. Oregon came to be viewed as a comparatively rural, woodsy world with more appeal for a vacation than a plant location. Portland slipped back in the ranks of cities, competing with Toledo and Fort Worth. When the Portland Trail Blazers won the National Basketball Association title

in 1977 it seemed quaint that a city of this size would have a professional team at all, let alone a champion.

But in the last quarter of the twentieth century, Oregon and Portland made a comeback based in the high-tech and computer-based revolution. Portland, as with other West Coast cities, was ground zero for the industry and its research and production ends (there is an area west of Portland known as "Silicon Forest"). In 2000 Portland was at 453,000 and growing, but its suburbs, spilling over into six Oregon counties and across the river into Washington state, were almost four times as populous. Altogether, metro Portland was 2.2 million, and another decade of 20 percent growth will catapult it over metro St. Louis in the national rankings.

With the phases of growth have come eras of political change. The earliest statewide politicians were Democrats, and the Democrats won the presidential election of 1868 here. But there followed a GOP dominant era reflecting the state's demographic roots in New England and the Upper Midwest. Later, as lumber, mine, and factory workers multiplied in the late 1800s, the two-party competition got livelier. The state also had its share of radicals such as John Reed, a writer and speechmaker who made his way to Moscow in 1917 (where he would write *Seven Days that Shook the World* and be buried in the walls of the Kremlin). Still, no Democrat carried the state for president between 1868 and 1912, and apart from the landslides of Franklin D. Roosevelt and Lyndon B. Johnson, no Democrat carried it thereafter until 1988.

Similarly, the Republican candidates for governor and senator prevailed roughly two-thirds of the time (with streaks of even greater domination) until the mid-1990s. Much of the real competition took place within the GOP, where conservatives vied with moderate and even liberal factions at nomination time. Beginning in 1966, Republicans Mark Hatfield and Bob Packwood won ten straight Senate elections between them, in part because they voted with the Democrats on social and foreign issues. Republicans also won the governorship 10 times out of 12 in the 40 years after World War II, with governors who usually respected the state's preference for fiscal restraint and libertarian acceptance of individual liberty.

The GOP lock on the governor's office was broken in 1986, signaling a broader shift to come. Two years later, the nation took notice when Oregon was one of just ten states carried by Democrat Michael Dukakis in 1988. Thereafter the state was carried twice by Bill Clinton and again, barely, by Al Gore in 2000 (despite a 5 percent vote for the Green nominee Ralph Nader). The election of Gov. Ted Kulongoski in 2002 marked the fifth straight win for the Democrats in that office, from which they have dueled the Republican legislature.

The Senate seats have been split since the Hatfield-Packwood team left the field. Democrat Ron Wyden of Portland and Republican Gordon Smith of Pendleton represent the left and right lobes of Oregon's civic brain, respectively, yet they get along and do not campaign against one another, respectfully. One reason the state has such different senators is that Smith ran twice in 1996, first for the Packwood seat as a conservative and then for the Hatfield seat as a moderate. The second time, for example, he moderated his views on abortion limits and rejected the endorsement of the Oregon Citizens' Alliance, a group of social conservatives that has tended to highlight internal disagreements among Republicans and thus to aid the election of Democrats.

But the most notable change in Oregon's partisan mood may be the shift in the House delegation, which is one of the very few nationwide that has been moving in a Democratic direction. The 1990s ended with Democrats firmly in charge, four seats to one. That ratio was all but set in stone in 2001 by a state court, which rejected the redistricting approach of the Republicans in the state legislature.

The legislators had passed a plan aimed at packing more of the Portland metro Democratic vote into the area's most Democratic district, leaving at least one other district more vulnerable to takeover. The chosen ground was West Portland, in the Portland-based but largely suburban 1st District. This was justifiable, given that the 1st had grown 30 percent and the neighboring 3rd District (Portland proper), had grown only half as much. But a judge chose the Democrats' plan instead, preserving the status quo politically while redistributing residents to balance the new districts at 683,000 residents.

Somewhat surprising in the 2000 census was the growth of the state's 2nd District, which consists of the eastern two-thirds of the state's land mass. The 2nd grew by nearly a quarter, faster than any other district but the 1st, confounding the trend toward shrinking population in rural, inland venues. This part of the state has many longtime westerners, among them many Mormons (a characteristic shared with the neighboring sections of Idaho, Nevada, and northeastern California). It is home to the state's Republican Smith (a Mormon) and to its lone Republican House member.

There was little trouble dividing the 4th and 5th Districts, both represented by liberal Democrats although both gave pluralities to George W. Bush in 2000. The 5th is the southern portion of the Portland-Salem metro area, including Polk, Marion, and Clackamas Counties and centering on the city of Salem. The 4th is the Willamette Valley, named for its chief river, and includes the Eugene-Springfield metro area. Eugene is the capital and home of the University of Oregon. The 4th also includes the city of Corvallis, home of Oregon State. The years after 2000 have seen both schools return to the national top ten in football after decades in eclipse (an important achievement in a state that has no National Football League team nor Major League Baseball team).

Experimentation is as basic to twenty-first-century Oregon as machine politics have been to the big cities of the East. The state was an early exponent of presidential preference primaries (holding an important one in 1948, before the world took much notice of primaries) and ballot initiatives, which have grown so numerous that voters now vote by mail to facilitate reading the voluminous voter's guide.

The state has also been in the forefront of health care reform, assisted suicide, and environmental protection via statewide initiative.

Table 1 Population

District	Population	Population under 18	Voting-age population	Median age	Male*	Female*
1	684,280	172,958	511,322	34.2	50.1	49.9
2	684,280	174,678	509,602	38.3	49.7	50.3
3	684,279	163,916	520,363	34.9	49.3	50.7
4	684,280	159,708	524,572	38.6	49.3	50.7
5	684,280	175,266	509,014	36.2	49.6	50.4
State	3,421,399	846,526	2,574,873	36.3	49.6	50.4

*As percentage of total population.

Table 2 Voting-Age Persons by Race/Hispanic or Latino Origin

District	White*	Black or African American*	American Indian or Alaska Native*	Asian*	Other or multirace*	Hispanic or Latino*
1	83.1	1.1	0.7	5.3	1.8	8.0
2	88.7	0.4	1.7	0.9	1.5	6.7
3	80.2	4.6	0.8	5.5	2.5	6.3
4	91.2	0.5	1.1	1.7	2.1	3.4
5	86.2	0.6	1.0	2.2	1.8	8.3
State	85.9	1.4	1.1	3.2	1.9	6.5

*As percentage of voting-age population.

Table 3 Voting-Age Population by Age Groups

District	18 to 24*	25 to 44*	45 to 64*	Over 64*
1	12.9	44.0	29.7	13.5
2	11.2	35.2	33.3	20.3
3	12.9	43.1	29.6	14.4
4	13.1	34.3	33.0	19.7
5	13.7	37.2	32.0	17.1
State	12.7	38.7	31.5	17.0

*As percentage of voting-age population.

Table 4 Income and Occupation

District	Median family income	Families in poverty*	White collar†	Blue collar†	Service†	Farm†
1	$58,789	5.4	65.3	20.6	12.9	1.2
2	$41,606	9.4	54.0	26.3	17.0	2.7
3	$50,039	8.1	59.4	24.6	15.5	0.5
4	$42,976	9.4	55.2	26.3	16.5	2.0
5	$52,162	7.2	60.6	22.1	14.9	2.5
State	$48,680	7.9	59.1	23.9	15.3	1.7

*As percentage of all families.   †As percentage of employed workers 16 years and over.

Table 5 Education: School Years Completed

District	Less than grade 9*	Grades 9–12 no diploma*	High school diploma no college*	Some college*	College bachelor's degree or higher*
1	4.3	7.3	21.9	33.1	33.3
2	5.4	11.8	30.7	33.0	19.0
3	5.4	10.1	25.5	34.1	24.8

District	Less than grade 9*	Grades 9–12 no diploma*	High school diploma no college*	Some college*	College bachelor's degree or higher*
4	4.0	11.1	28.5	35.0	21.4
5	5.7	9.2	24.5	33.6	27.0
State	5.0	9.9	26.3	33.8	25.1

*As percentage of persons age 25 and over.

Table 6   Housing and Residential Patterns

District	Median home value	Owner occupied*	Renter occupied*	Urban†	Rural†
1	$176,200	59.7	40.3	86.7	13.3
2	$114,600	68.2	31.8	64.2	35.8
3	$154,200	61.3	38.7	93.1	6.9
4	$125,700	65.6	34.4	69.2	30.8
5	$157,800	66.6	33.4	80.4	19.6
State	$145,800	64.3	35.7	78.7	21.3

*As percentage of occupied housing units.   †As percentage of total population.

Oregon 1st District

Western Portland and suburbs; Beaverton

Nestled onto the west bank of the Willamette River, Portland's Silicon Forest hums with new companies assembling computer chips. Californians and other migrants have come to Portland in droves, looking for an urban economy with a leisurely lifestyle.

Many of the most affluent urbanites have settled in the city; others are filling up fast-growing suburbs in Washington and Yamhill Counties. Aided by a western light rail that stretches to Hillsboro, towns that were once bedroom communities have turned into satellite cities with their own streams of commuters. The populations of Hillsboro, Beaverton, and suburbs farther west exploded in the 1990s.

Outside the Portland metro area, the 1st is struggling to keep its traditional industries intact. A highly public battle between loggers and environmentalists over the fate of the spotted owl has dampened forestry. Salmon stocks are dwindling because of excessive harvests and hydroelectric dams. State officials are working to help workers in both fields move to emerging industries in the area.

Electronics, vineyards, and nurseries now lead the 1st's economy. Tourism and the remnants of the timber industry round out the job market. With a number of big businesses in the district, international trade is a hot issue.

Redistricting following the 2000 census removed the 1st's share of Clackamas County and reduced its share of Multnomah County (Portland). Washington County, which accounts for 65 percent of the population, epitomizes the 1st's competitiveness: Al Gore won the county by less than 3 percentage points in the 2000 presidential election. Democrats do well in Multnomah and in the far northwestern counties of Clatsop and Columbia, while the GOP has the edge in Yamhill.

Major Industry

Electronics, computer manufacturing, wine production, nurseries.

Notable

Nike is headquartered in Beaverton; the Lewis and Clark expedition set up a winter camp in 1805–1806 in what is now the Fort Clatsop National Memorial, near Astoria.

Election Returns

	Republican		Democratic		Other	
President 2000	131,808	46.6%	150,768	53.4%		
House 2002	80,917	34.0%	149,215	62.7%	7,904	3.3%

District Profile

Population   684,280

Total area (square miles)   3,236.2
     Land area (square miles)   2,941.3

Population per square mile   232.6

Counties (2000 population)
Clatsop 35,630	Washington 445,342
Columbia 43,560	Yamhill 84,992
Multnomah (pt.) 74,756	

Cities and other areas over 10,000 (2000 population)
Aloha CDP 41,741	Newberg 18,064
Beaverton 76,129	Portland (pt.) 74,097
Cedar Mill CDP 12,597	Sherwood 11,791
Forest Grove 17,708	St. Helens 10,019
Hillsboro 70,186	Tigard 41,223
McMinnville 26,499	Tualatin (pt.) 20,127

Race and Hispanic or Latino origin*
White 81.1%
Black or African American 1.1%
American Indian or Alaska Native 0.7%
Asian 5.0%
Native Hawaiian or other Pacific Islander 0.2%
Some other race 0.1%
Hispanic or Latino origin 9.4%
Two or more races 2.3%

*As percentage of total population.

Ancestry*
Dutch 1.9%	Norwegian 3.4%
English 9.5%	Polish 1.4%
French 2.6%	Scotch-Irish 1.5%
German 15.0%	Scottish 2.4%
Irish 8.4%	Swedish 2.4%
Italian 2.3%	USA/American 4.1%

*As estimated percentage of total population.

Universities and colleges, 2000–2001 enrollment
Art Institute International at Portland, Portland   666
Clatsop Community College, Astoria   1,743
George Fox University, Newberg   2,635
Heald College, Portland   344
Linfield College, McMinnville   1,534
Oregon Graduate Institute of Science and Tech, Beaverton   580
Oregon Health Sciences University, Portland   1,905
Pacific Northwest College of Art, Portland   325
Pacific University, Forest Grove   1,979
Pioneer Pacific College, Wilsonville   352

Portland Community College, Portland   24,209
Portland State University, Portland   18,889
University of Phoenix-Oregon, Tigard   1,081
Western Business College, Portland   450

Newspapers and circulation

	District circulation	Total circulation
Daily Astorian	7,213	8,236
Longview Daily News	1,736	22,786
Portland Oregonian	108,809	351,568
Salem Statesman Journal	2,232	57,279
*USA Today**	2,715	1,674,376

See Sources and Explanations in the front of the volume.

Television stations and affiliations

Portland	100%	KATU	ABC
Portland	100%	KGW	NBC
Portland	100%	KNMT	Independent
Portland	100%	KOIN	CBS
Portland	100%	KOPB	PBS
Portland	100%	KPDX	UPN
Portland	100%	KPTV	FOX
Portland	100%	KPXG	PAX
Portland	100%	KTVR	PBS
Portland	100%	KWBP	WB

Cable systems and subscribers
Charter   14,824
Comcast   192,995
USA Media Group   1,951
Uvision LLC   1,402

Military installations, September 2001
Camp Rilea Military Training Area, Warrenton   325

Businesses and other major employers
U.S. Postal Service; Portland   8,700
Intel Corp.; Hillsboro; wire products   8,000
Oregon Health and Science University; Portland   5,500
Portland State University; Portland   3,022
Providence Health System-Oregon Hospital; Portland   3,000
Tektronix Inc.; Beaverton; electronic/electric measuring test equipment   2,550
Ameriquest Mortgage Co.; Portland; mortgage bankers   2,500
Nike Inc.; Beaverton; athletic shoes   2,500
U.S. Veterans Hospital; Portland   2,500
Con-Way Western Express Inc.; Portland; trucking   2,000
Regence BlueCross BlueShield of Oregon; Portland; health insurance   1,815
Consolidated Freightways Corp. of Delaware; Portland; trucking terminals   1,800
Intel Corp.; Beaverton; semiconductors   1,700
Northwest Staffing Resources Inc.; Portland; temporary help service   1,523
All PEO Inc.; Tigard; employment agencies   1,500
Good Samaritan Hospital and Medical Center; Portland   1,478
McMenamins Inc.; Portland; restaurants   1,400
Mid-Valley Resources Inc.; Portland; business services   1,400

Wallace Theatre Corp.; Portland; movie theaters   1,400
CNF Inc.; Portland; trucking   1,200
Columbia Forest Products Corp.; Portland; wood panels   1,200
Fort James Operating Co.; Clatskanie; paper products   1,200
May Department Stores Co.; Portland   1,200
Standard Insurance Co.; Portland; life insurance   1,200
Georgia-Pacific Corp.; Clatskanie; pulp mills   1,122
Merix Corp.; Forest Grove; printed circuit boards   1,059
Tuality Community Hospital Inc.; Hillsboro   1,052
Washington County; Hillsboro; county government   1,050
International Business Machines Corp.; Beaverton; minicomputers   1,000
Maxim Integrated Products Inc.; Beaverton; integrated circuits, semiconductors   1,000
Qwest Corp.; Portland; local telephone communications   1,000
Stream International Inc.; Beaverton; software development   1,000
Tyco International Inc.; Wilsonville; current-carrying wiring services   1,000
Northwest Natural Gas Co.; Portland; natural gas distribution   975
A-Dec Inc.; Newberg; dental equipment   950
Intel Corp.; Beaverton; microprocessors   816
First Consumers National Bank; Beaverton; commercial bank   807
ESCO Corp.; Portland; mining machinery   800
U.S. Army Corps of Engineers; Portland   725
Liberty Insurance Services Inc.; Tualatin; loss prevention services, insurance   715
Health Services Group Inc.; Portland; investment holding company   700
Oregonian Publishing Co.; Portland; newspaper   700
Hillsboro School District; Hillsboro   621
EC Co.; Portland; electrical contractor   620
Nordstrom Inc.; Tigard; clothing stores   613
Automatic Data Processing Inc.; Portland   600
Boise Cascade Corp.; St. Helens; pulp mills   600
Ch2m Hill Industrial Design and Construction Inc.; Portland; engineering services   600
Mattel Inc.; Beaverton; mail-order catalog   600
Starplex Corp.; Portland; security guard service   575
Monrovia Nursery Co.; Dayton; nursery stock   567
Dole Food Co.; Portland; food supplier   555
U.S. Internal Revenue Service; Portland   550
Integrated Device Technology; Hillsboro; metal oxide silicon devices   531
Cascade Steel Rolling Mills Inc.; McMinnville; blast furnaces and steel mills   525
Sysco Food Services; Wilsonville; food supplier   510
City of Portland; Portland; water, solid waste management   502
City of Portland; Portland; city government   500
Columbia Sportswear Co.; Portland   500
Denkor Dental Management Corp.; Beaverton; dental insurance   500
Legacy Health System; Portland; hospital management   500

Leupold and Stevens Inc.; Beaverton; telescopic sights 500

Oregon Dental Service Inc.; Portland; dental insurance 500

Portland General Electric Co.; Portland; electric power distribution 500

PSC Inc.; Portland; magnetic ink recognition devices 500

Shriners Hospitals for Children; Portland 500

Stoel Rives; Portland; law office 500

Triquint Semiconductor Inc.; Beaverton; warehousing 500

Willamette Industries; Portland; foreign trade and international banks 500

Oregon 2nd District

East and Southwest — Medford, Bend

The 2nd covers the eastern two-thirds of Oregon, bordering Washington, Idaho, Nevada, and California. Most of the land is owned by the federal government, causing considerable strife with the district's residents, who depend on fishing, farming, and logging to make a living.

The 2nd lost timber jobs when the spotted owl was deemed an endangered species and its Oregon forest habitat was protected from clear-cutting. Those jobs have been difficult to replace in a district with few urban areas. Farmers produce fruit, wheat, and hay in the plateaus and river valleys, but cattle farmers have seen their access to public grazing lands limited. At the same time, the Columbia River's fishing industry has faced restrictions on salmon under the Endangered Species Act. Fishers, farmers, and environmentalists have staged high-profile battles over how federal regulators should allocate the Klamath River's water. Shortages led to the loss of crops and thousands of salmon.

During the 1980s, economic difficulties drove enough people from the district that it declined in population, but numbers rebounded in the 1990s as retired couples moved to the area.

With more than 60,000 people, Medford (Jackson County) is the largest city in the 2nd. It is surrounded by pear, cherry, and apple orchards in the Rogue River Valley. Less than 20 miles southeast of Medford is Ashland, which has played host to the Oregon Shakespeare Festival since 1935.

Hostility toward the federal government makes the 2nd Oregon's most reliably Republican district. Both George W. Bush in 2000 and gubernatorial nominee Kevin Mannix in 2002 won 19 of the 20 counties wholly or partly within the 2nd (Hood River County was the exception). Democrats are scattered through parts of Ashland and Bend, but they are too few to swing the district.

Major Industry

Agriculture, forestry, tourism.

Notable

Crater Lake National Park, designated in 1902, is in Klamath County; the Warm Springs Native American Reservation is in the northwest part of the district.

Election Returns

	Republican		Democratic		Other	
President 2000	182,924	63.3%	105,971	36.7%		
House 2002	181,295	71.9%	64,991	25.8%	5,998	2.3%

District Profile

Population   684,280

Total area (square miles)   70,227.2
  Land area (square miles)   69,491.4

Population per square mile   9.8

Counties (2000 population)

Baker	16,741	Klamath	63,775
Crook	19,182	Lake	7,422
Deschutes	115,367	Malheur	31,615
Gilliam	1,915	Morrow	10,995
Grant	7,935	Sherman	1,934
Harney	7,609	Umatilla	70,548
Hood River	20,411	Union	24,530
Jackson	181,269	Wallowa	7,226
Jefferson	19,009	Wasco	23,791
Josephine (pt.)	51,459	Wheeler	1,547

Cities and other areas over 10,000 (2000 population)
  Altamont CDP   19,603
  Ashland   19,522
  Bend   52,029
  Central Point   12,493
  City of The Dalles   12,156
  Grants Pass   23,003
  Hermiston   13,154
  Klamath Falls   19,462
  La Grande   12,327
  Medford   63,154
  Ontario   10,985
  Pendleton   16,354
  Redmond   13,481

Race and Hispanic or Latino origin*
  White   86.1%
  Black or African American   0.4%
  American Indian or Alaska Native   1.9%
  Asian   0.8%
  Native Hawaiian or other Pacific Islander   0.1%
  Some other race   0.1%
  Hispanic or Latino origin   8.8%
  Two or more races   1.8%

*As percentage of total population.

Ancestry*

Dutch	2.0%	Norwegian	2.5%
English	9.9%	Scotch-Irish	1.8%
French	2.7%	Scottish	2.3%
German	13.6%	Swedish	1.9%
Irish	8.7%	USA/American	5.7%
Italian	2.3%		

*As estimated percentage of total population.

Universities and colleges, 2000–2001 enrollment
  Blue Mountain Community College, Pendleton   1,934
  Central Oregon Community College, Bend   4,079

Columbia Gorge Community College, The Dalles   840
Eastern Oregon University, La Grande   2,778
Klamath Community College, Klamath Falls   448
Oregon Institute of Technology, Klamath Falls   2,815
Rogue Community College, Grants Pass   4,071
Southern Oregon University, Ashland   5,493
Treasure Valley Community College, Ontario   1,785

Newspapers and circulation

	District circulation	Total circulation
Ashland Daily Tidings	5,004	5,022
Bend Bulletin	26,296	26,296
Grants Pass Daily Courier	5,726	16,380
Klamath Falls Herald and News	15,115	16,752
La Grande Observer	6,463	6,463
Pendleton East Oregonian	11,396	11,396
Portland Oregonian	15,684	351,568
*USA Today**	1,543	1,674,376
Walla Walla Union-Bulletin	2,153	14,111

See Sources and Explanations in the front of the volume.

Television stations and affiliations

Portland	41%	KATU	ABC
Portland	41%	KGW	NBC
Portland	41%	KNMT	Independent
Portland	41%	KOIN	CBS
Portland	41%	KOPB	PBS
Portland	41%	KPDX	UPN
Portland	41%	KPTV	FOX
Portland	41%	KPXG	PAX
Portland	41%	KTVR	PBS
Portland	41%	KWBP	WB
Medford-Klamath Falls	25%	KDKF	ABC
Medford-Klamath Falls	25%	KDRV	ABC
Medford-Klamath Falls	25%	KFTS	PBS
Medford-Klamath Falls	25%	KMVU	FOX
Medford-Klamath Falls	25%	KOBI	NBC
Medford-Klamath Falls	25%	KOTI	NBC
Medford-Klamath Falls	25%	KSYS	PBS
Medford-Klamath Falls	25%	KTVL	CBS
Boise, ID	21%	KAID	PBS
Boise, ID	21%	KBCI	CBS
Boise, ID	21%	KIVI	ABC
Boise, ID	21%	KNIN	UPN
Boise, ID	21%	KTRV	FOX
Boise, ID	21%	KTVB	NBC
Yakima-Pasco-Richland-Kennewick	5%	KAPP	ABC
Yakima-Pasco-Richland-Kennewick	5%	KEPR	CBS, UPN
Yakima-Pasco-Richland-Kennewick	5%	KIMA	CBS, UPN
Yakima-Pasco-Richland-Kennewick	5%	KNDO	NBC
Yakima-Pasco-Richland-Kennewick	5%	KNDU	NBC
Yakima-Pasco-Richland-Kennewick	5%	KTNW	PBS
Yakima-Pasco-Richland-Kennewick	5%	KVEW	ABC
Yakima-Pasco-Richland-Kennewick	5%	KYVE	PBS
Bend	4%	KOAB	PBS
Bend	4%	KTVZ	NBC
Spokane, WA	4%	KAYU	FOX
Spokane, WA	4%	KCDT	PBS
Spokane, WA	4%	KHQ	NBC
Spokane, WA	4%	KLEW	CBS, UPN
Spokane, WA	4%	KREM	CBS
Spokane, WA	4%	KSKN	WB
Spokane, WA	4%	KSPS	PBS
Spokane, WA	4%	KUID	PBS
Spokane, WA	4%	KWSU	PBS
Spokane, WA	4%	KXLY	ABC

Cable systems and subscribers

Bend Cable Communications   17,727
Blue Mountain Cable   1,842
Cable ONE   3,544
Chambers Communications   2,898
Charter   93,911
Crestview Cable   9,225
Elgin TV Association   712
Heppner TV Inc.   665
J&N Cable   2,008
Mallard   10,749
USA Media Group   3,493

Military installations, September 2001

Umatilla Chemical Depot, Hermiston   790
Klamath Falls Airport-Kingsley Field, Klamath Falls   727

Businesses and other major employers

Rogue Valley Medical Center Inc.; Medford   1,778
St. Charles Medical Center and Hospital; Bend   1,722
Pet Protector Game Away; Elgin; safety equipment and supplies   1,300
Bright Wood Corp.; Madras; door frames   1,200
Cascade Health Services Inc. Hospital; Bend   1,152
Bear Creek Operations Inc.; Medford; confectionery products   1,100
Jeld-Wen Inc.; Klamath Falls; millwork   1,000
West Merle Medical Center; Klamath Falls   930
Bend Millwork Systems Inc.; Bend; window and door frames   900
Jeld-Wen Inc.; Bend; window and door frames   900
Les Schwab Tire Centers of Washington Inc.; Prineville; automotive tires   880
Providence Health System-Oregon Hospital; Medford   860
JR Simplot Co.; Hermiston; frozen specialties   750
Goldendale Aluminum Co.; The Dalles; aluminum   700
Oregon Dept. of Military; Tygh Valley   700
Southern Oregon University; Ashland   694
Jackson County School District; Eagle Point   660
Medford School District; Medford   656
Confederated Tribes of Warm Springs Reservation of Oregon; Warm Springs; timber tracts   650
Fleetwood Travel Trailers of Oregon Inc.; Pendleton; travel trailer chassis   607
Amalgamated Sugar Co.; Nyssa; beet sugar   600
Destination Hotels and Resorts Inc.; Bend; resort hotel   600
Forest Service; Bend; land conservation agencies   600
Three Rivers Community Hospital and Health Center; Grants Pass   600
Central Oregon Community College; Bend   560
Collins Products; Klamath Falls; veneer and plywood   542
Central Oregon Redi-Mix; Redmond; concrete   541
Northwest Aluminum Co.; The Dalles; aluminum ingots   512
iSKY Inc.; Bend; customer care services   500
Lamb-Weston Inc.; Hermiston; frozen/cold pack vegetables   500

Mid-Columbia Health Services Co. Inc.; The Dalles;
administrative management   500
Oregon Dept. of Corrections; Pendleton   500
Oregon National Guard; Klamath Falls   500

Oregon 3rd District

North and east Portland; eastern suburbs

Split by the Willamette River, the city of Portland has two personalities. The eastern portion, covered by the 3rd, still depends on the blue-collar economy that made the city a thriving international port for lumber and fruit. The Port of Portland and Portland International Airport make the city a leading center of trade and distribution. Computer chips and cappuccino drive the city's western side (in the 1st and 5th Districts).

Compared to the rest of Portland, the 3rd is a multicultural haven. There is a large African American population in precincts just east of the Willamette River, near Interstate 5 and Martin Luther King Jr. Blvd., where Democrats regularly win more than 80 percent of the vote in competitive statewide elections. A sizable Hispanic population resides in northeastern Portland and in Gresham and Wood Village east of the city. Asians are numerous in east-central Portland, near 82nd Avenue and Interstate 205.

The 3rd's second-largest city, Gresham, was once a thriving farm community. It is now the easternmost stop on Portland's light rail system and is growing rapidly. Beyond the Portland metropolitan area, the district quickly turns rural. Mount Hood National Forest covers the far eastern part of the district.

Portland's liberal leanings make the 3rd Oregon's most staunchly Democratic district. Democrat Theodore R. Kulongoski won 65 percent of the 3rd's share of Multnomah County in the 2002 gubernatorial election, which he won narrowly. Democrat Bill Bradbury took 56 percent even as he lost decisively statewide to Republican senator Gordon H. Smith in 2002. Redistricting following the 2000 census gave the 3rd a larger share of Clackamas County, which is more rural and politically competitive. But any Republican strength there is not large enough to weaken Portland's strong Democratic slant.

Major Industry
Wholesale trade and distribution, health care, education.

Notable
Forest Park is one of the largest urban parks in the nation; Mount Hood, Oregon's highest peak, reaches 11,239 feet.

Election Returns

	Republican		Democratic		Other	
President 2000	93,213	34.5%	176,831	65.5%		
House 2002	62,821	26.7%	156,851	66.8%	15,305	6.5%

District Profile

Population   684,279

Total area (square miles)   1,054.0
Land area (square miles)   1,020.7

Population per square mile   670.4

Counties (2000 population)
Clackamas (pt.)   124,972
Multnomah (pt.)   559,307

Cities and other areas over 10,000 (2000 population)
Gresham 90,205	Portland (pt.) 432,388
Milwaukie 20,490	Troutdale 13,777

Race and Hispanic or Latino origin*
White   77.2%
Black or African American   5.2%
American Indian or Alaska Native   0.9%
Asian   5.4%
Native Hawaiian or other Pacific Islander   0.3%
Some other race   0.2%
Hispanic or Latino origin   7.6%
Two or more races   3.3%

*As percentage of total population.

Ancestry*
Dutch 1.6%		Polish 1.2%	
English 8.4%		Russian 1.2%	
French 2.6%		Scotch-Irish 1.5%	
German 14.5%		Scottish 2.1%	
Irish 8.7%		Swedish 2.5%	
Italian 2.7%		USA/American 3.3%	
Norwegian 3.4%			

*As estimated percentage of total population.

Universities and colleges, 2000–2001 enrollment
Cascade College, Portland   321
Concordia University, Portland   1,040
ITT Technical Institute, Portland   471
Mt. Hood Community College, Gresham   8,556
Multnomah Bible College and Biblical Seminary, Portland   837
Reed College, Portland   1,385
University of Portland, Portland   2,926
Warner Pacific College, Portland   638
Western Seminary, Portland   732
Western States Chiropractic College, Portland   364

Newspapers and circulation

	District circulation	Total circulation
Portland Oregonian	122,615	351,568
USA Today*	6,298	1,674,376

*See Sources and Explanations in the front of the volume.

Television stations and affiliations
Portland	100%	KATU	ABC
Portland	100%	KGW	NBC
Portland	100%	KNMT	Independent
Portland	100%	KOIN	CBS
Portland	100%	KOPB	PBS
Portland	100%	KPDX	UPN
Portland	100%	KPTV	FOX
Portland	100%	KPXG	PAX
Portland	100%	KTVR	PBS
Portland	100%	KWBP	WB

Cable systems and subscribers
Cascade Cable   540
Charter   2,450
Comcast   61,930

Military installations, September 2001
Portland International Airport, Portland   2,414
Navy Marine Corps Reserve Center, Portland   362

Businesses and other major employers
Oregon Tri-County Metropolitan Transportation
   District; Portland   3,500
Providence Health System-Oregon Hospital; Portland
   2,541
PCC Structurals Inc.; Portland; aircraft parts, equipment
   2,075
NW Auto Consulting Inc.; Gresham; personal service
   agents   1,999
Legacy-Emanual Hospital and Health Center; Portland
   1,953
Consolidated Freightways Corp. of Delaware; Portland;
   trucking terminals   1,800
Roman Catholic Archbishop of Archdiocese of Portland
   in Oregon; Portland; religious organization   1,700
Portland Adventist Medical Center; Portland   1,450
Wacker Siltronic Corp.; Portland; silicon wafers   1,385
Fred Meyer Inc.; Portland; supermarkets   1,313
U.S. Bancorp; Portland; commercial bank   1,200
Mt. Hood Community College; Gresham   1,100
Gunderson Inc.; Portland; railroad equipment   1,050
Bonneville Power Admin.; Portland; electric power
   transmission   1,000
Kaiser Foundation Hospitals; Clackamas   1,000
Vanguard Marketing Services Inc.; Portland;
   management consulting   1,000
Freightliner; Portland; highway truck tractor assembly
   950
Oregon National Guard; Portland   906
Blount Inc.; Portland; sawing equipment   900
Unified Western Grocers Inc.; Portland; food supplier
   900
OECO; Milwaukie; magnetic cores   865
Hilton Hotels Corp.; Portland   800
North Pacific Group Inc.; Portland; lumber, plywood,
   and millwork   800
Multnomah County; Portland; police dept.   750
St. Johns Corp.; Portland; semitrailers   715
Adidas America Inc.; Portland; footwear   700
Horizon Air Industries Inc.; Portland; hangar   700
Multnomah County; Portland; county government   700
Oregon Electric Construction Inc.; Portland; electrical
   contractor   700
Oregon Steel Mills Inc.; Portland; blast furnaces and
   steel mills   700
Portland Habilitation Center Inc.; Portland; vocational
   rehabilitation   700
Roundup Co.; Clackamas; warehousing   656
Kraft Foods Inc.; Portland; cookies   650
Nationwide Mutual Insurance Co.; Portland; life
   insurance   650
Multnomah Education Service District; Portland   601
Albertson's Inc.; Portland; warehousing   600
Fujitsu Microelectronics Inc.; Gresham; semiconductors
   and related devices   500
Idaho Power Co.; Portland; electric services   500
Market Transport; Portland; contract haulers   500
May Department Stores Co.; Portland   500
Oregon Dept. of Human Services; Portland   500

Oregon Dept. of Human Services Health Services;
   Portland   500
U.S. Bakery; Portland; bakery goods   500
USF Reddaway Inc.; Clackamas; freight carrier   500

Oregon 4th District
Southwest — Eugene, part of Corvallis

Loggers, fishermen, and environmentalists combine to give the 4th a potentially combustible political mix. In the early 1990s, the district was a prime battleground in the fight between lumber mills and environmentalists over the fate of the spotted owl. But after the courts and the administration of President Bill Clinton turned against the lumber industry, the furor quieted down and most of the unionized mills closed shop.

Fishing, another of the district's economic mainstays, also has dwindled. Most commercial fishermen—in towns such as Charleston, Bandon, and Port Orford—are looking for a way out, having been harmed by frequent run closings, short seasons, and low prices. While this rural region's unemployment has been decreasing steadily, it is still higher than average, which may explain why the 4th experienced the slowest population growth of any Oregon district in the 1990s. The district increasingly has looked to tourists and expanding retirement communities to aid its economy.

Eugene and Springfield, the district's most populous cities, have fared better. Research at the University of Oregon in Eugene, still a hotbed of environmentalism, has lured high-tech companies. Computer manufacturers, software developers, retailers, and the service industry now drive the area's economy.

Eugene and Springfield make Lane County reliably Democratic. Linn and Douglas Counties vote solidly Republican, and Coos and Curry Counties, which once had a strong union tradition, now lean Republican as a result of upper-middle-class retirees flocking from outside the state. (Twenty-six percent of Curry's residents are 65 or older, the highest percentage in the state.) Redistricting following the 2000 census made minimal changes to the 4th, adding more of Benton County in the north and more of Josephine County in the south.

Major Industry
Forestry, agriculture, fishing, technology, tourism.

Notable
Much of the movie *Stand by Me* was filmed in Lane County.

Election Returns

	Republican		Democratic		Other	
President 2000	156,362	52.4%	142,123	47.6%		
House 2002	90,523	34.4%	168,150	63.8%	4,808	1.8%

District Profile

Population   684,280

Total area (square miles)   18,034.2
   Land area (square miles)   17,180.7

Population per square mile   39.8

Counties (2000 population)

Benton (pt.)	49,670	Josephine (pt.)	24,267
Coos	62,779	Lane	322,959
Curry	21,137	Linn	103,069
Douglas	100,399		

Cities and other areas over 10,000 (2000 population)

Albany (pt.)	36,950	Lebanon	12,950
Coos Bay	15,374	Roseburg	20,017
Corvallis (pt.)	32,076	Springfield	52,864
Eugene	137,893		

Race and Hispanic or Latino origin*

White 89.7%
Black or African American 0.5%
American Indian or Alaska Native 1.2%
Asian 1.5%
Native Hawaiian or other Pacific Islander 0.1%
Some other race 0.1%
Hispanic or Latino origin 4.2%
Two or more races 2.5%

As percentage of total population.

Ancestry*

Dutch	2.1%	Norwegian	3.0%
English	10.1%	Polish	1.1%
French	2.8%	Scotch-Irish	1.9%
German	14.7%	Scottish	2.4%
Irish	8.8%	Swedish	2.1%
Italian	2.1%	USA/American	5.3%

As estimated percentage of total population.

Universities and colleges, 2000–2001 enrollment

Lane Community College, Eugene 9,957
Linn-Benton Community College, Albany 4,443
Northwest Christian College, Eugene 490
Southwestern Oregon Community College, Coos Bay 3,326
Umpqua Community College, Roseburg 1,386
University of Oregon, Eugene 17,801

Newspapers and circulation

	District circulation	Total circulation
Albany Democrat-Herald	16,243	18,403
Corvallis Gazette-Times	7,084	12,298
Curry County Reporter	2,169	2,201
Eugene Register-Guard	72,464	73,237
Grants Pass Daily Courier	10,661	16,380
News Review of Douglas County	18,719	18,719
Portland Oregonian	12,670	351,568
Salem Statesman Journal	2,288	57,279
*USA Today**	1,940	1,674,376
World	13,930	13,972

See Sources and Explanations in the front of the volume.

Television stations and affiliations

Eugene	68%	KCBY	CBS
Eugene	68%	KEPB	PBS
Eugene	68%	KEZI	ABC
Eugene	68%	KLSR	FOX
Eugene	68%	KMTR	NBC
Eugene	68%	KMTX	NBC
Eugene	68%	KMTZ	NBC
Eugene	68%	KOAC	PBS
Eugene	68%	KPIC	CBS
Eugene	68%	KTVC	UPN
Eugene	68%	KVAL	CBS
Medford-Klamath Falls	19%	KDKF	ABC
Medford-Klamath Falls	19%	KDRV	ABC
Medford-Klamath Falls	19%	KFTS	PBS
Medford-Klamath Falls	19%	KMVU	FOX
Medford-Klamath Falls	19%	KOBI	NBC
Medford-Klamath Falls	19%	KOTI	NBC
Medford-Klamath Falls	19%	KSYS	PBS
Medford-Klamath Falls	19%	KTVL	CBS
Portland	13%	KATU	ABC
Portland	13%	KGW	NBC
Portland	13%	KNMT	Independent
Portland	13%	KOIN	CBS
Portland	13%	KOPB	PBS
Portland	13%	KPDX	UPN
Portland	13%	KPTV	FOX
Portland	13%	KPXG	PAX
Portland	13%	KTVR	PBS
Portland	13%	KWBP	WB

Cable systems and subscribers

Charter 56,269
Comcast 80,525
Green Acres TV Cable 4,242
Uvision LLC 696

Businesses and other major employers

University of Oregon; Eugene 6,600
Hewlett-Packard Co.; Corvallis; calculators 5,000
Peacehealth Sacred Heart Medical Center; Eugene 3,500
DeYoung and White; Philomath; accounting services 1,998
Roseburg Forest Products Co.; Dillard; plywood, softwood 1,829
Lane Community College; Eugene 1,800
McKenzie-Willamette Hospital; Springfield 1,400
Weyerhaeuser Co.; Springfield; paperboard mills 1,200
Mercy Medical Center; Roseburg 1,141
Lane County; Eugene; county government 1,050
Monaco Coach Corp.; Coburg; motor homes 1,000
Linn-Benton Community College; Albany 900
Good Samaritan Hospital; Corvallis 896
Bay Area Health District Inc. Hospital; Coos Bay 867
Country Coach Inc.; Junction City; motor homes 800
Roseburg Forest Products Co.; Riddle; plywood, softwood 800
Weyerhaeuser Co.; Cottage Grove; building materials 800
Cow Creek Band of Indians; Canyonville; gambling 750
Peacehealth Downtown Clinic; Eugene 750
Casey Industrial Inc.; Albany; industrial buildings construction 747
Mid Valley Hospital; Lebanon 740
HMT Technology Corp.; Eugene; computer disk drives 700
U.S. Postal Service; Eugene 650
Linn County; Albany; police dept. 630

U.S. Veterans Hospital; Roseburg   613
Physician Partners Inc.; Corvallis; medical clinic   600
TDY Industries Inc.; Albany; primary nonferrous metals   572
Albany General Hospital; Albany   550
Umpqua Community College; Roseburg   550
Union Pacific Corp.; Eugene; railroad terminals   550
Georgia-Pacific Corp.; Halsey; pulp mills   537
Oregon Freeze Dry Inc.; Albany; dried fruits   528
National Frozen Foods Corp.; Albany; frozen/cold pack vegetables   508
Allegheny Technologies Inc.; Albany; iron and steel forgings   500
Linn County; Albany; county government   500
Oregon Driver and Motor Vehicle Services; Cottage Grove   500

Oregon 5th District

Willamette Valley — Salem, part of Portland

Oregon City, the western terminus of the 2,000-mile Oregon Trail, in 1844 became the first incorporated city west of the Mississippi River. For settlers who made the five- to six-month journey from Independence, Missouri, the area marked the end of an arduous trek to Oregon's fertile Willamette Valley. The 5th takes in the northern part of that valley and the state capital of Salem, then spills over the Coast Range to cover two Pacific counties, Tillamook and Lincoln. It also includes a small part of Portland (shared with the 1st and 3rd Districts).

Clackamas, Marion, and Polk Counties are at the heart of the Willamette Valley, Oregon's most fertile farmland. The valley is the center of the state's profitable trade in greenhouse crops, seeds, and berries. Hops from Marion and Clackamas Counties go into some of the nation's finest beers. Polk County grows cherries and wine grapes; wineries dot Polk and Marion Counties.

Once exclusively dependent on agriculture and timber, the district's economy has diversified and now supports environmental research, high-tech manufacturing, and tourism. Portland's residential suburbs have begun expanding south into Clackamas County.

The 5th is highly competitive. Nearly 75 percent of district residents live in either Marion (Salem) or Clackamas Counties, which have many independent voters. Marion, the district's most populous jurisdiction, tends to vote narrowly Republican in competitive statewide races: Gubernatorial candidate Kevin Mannix in 2002 and George W. Bush in 2000 took 52 percent and 50.8 percent of the county vote in their respective races. Mannix also narrowly carried the 5th's share of Clackamas. Strong Democratic areas include Corvallis (split with the 4th District), which is home to Oregon State University, and southwestern Multnomah County, an area added in redistricting following the 2000 census that hosts some affluent Portland-area liberals around Lewis & Clark College.

Major Industry

Agriculture, lumber, paper, food processing, state government.

Notable

The Oregon Coast Aquarium is in Newport; Salem's Willamette University, established in 1842, was the first university in the West.

Election Returns

	Republican		Democratic		Other
President 2000	149,276	50.8%	144,657	49.2%	
House 2002	113,441	45.1%	137,713	54.8%	383

District Profile

Population   684,280

Total area (square miles)   5,828.7
   Land area (square miles)   5,362.4

Population per square mile   127.6

Counties (2000 population)
   Benton (pt.)   28,483
   Clackamas (pt.)   213,419
   Lincoln   44,479
   Marion   284,834
   Multnomah (pt.)   26,423
   Polk   62,380
   Tillamook   24,262

Cities and other areas over 10,000 (2000 population)
   Canby   12,790
   Corvallis (pt.)   17,246
   Dallas   12,459
   Four Corners CDP   13,922
   Gladstone   11,438
   Hayesville CDP   18,222
   Keizer   32,203
   Lake Oswego (pt.)   35,263
   Oak Grove CDP (pt.)   12,808
   Oatfield CDP (pt.)   12,355
   Oregon City (pt.)   25,744
   Portland (pt.)   22,636
   Salem   136,924
   West Linn   22,261
   Wilsonville (pt.)   13,987
   Woodburn   20,100

Race and Hispanic or Latino origin*
   White   83.6%
   Black or African American   0.6%
   American Indian or Alaska Native   1.1%
   Asian   1.9%
   Native Hawaiian or other Pacific Islander   0.2%
   Some other race   0.1%
   Hispanic or Latino origin   10.3%
   Two or more races   2.2%

*As percentage of total population.

Ancestry*
Dutch	1.9%	Norwegian	3.3%
English	9.7%	Polish	1.1%
French	2.7%	Scotch-Irish	1.6%
German	16.0%	Scottish	2.3%
Irish	8.1%	Swedish	2.3%
Italian	2.3%	USA/American	4.5%

*As estimated percentage of total population.

Universities and colleges, 2000–2001 enrollment
Chemeketa Community College, Salem   9,650
Clackamas Community College, Oregon City   6,369
Lewis & Clark College, Portland   3,018
Marylhurst University, Marylhurst   984
National College of Naturopathic Medicine, Portland
   578
Oregon Coast Community College, Newport   515
Oregon State University, Corvallis   16,758
Tillamook Bay Community College, Tillamook   277
Western Baptist College, Salem   696
Western Oregon University, Monmouth   4,729
Willamette University, Salem   2,415

Newspapers and circulation

	District circulation	Total circulation
Albany Democrat-Herald	2,055	18,403
Corvallis Gazette-Times	5,204	12,298
Portland Oregonian	63,450	351,568
Salem Statesman Journal	52,519	57,279
USA Today*	2,381	1,674,376

*See Sources and Explanations in the front of the volume.

Television stations and affiliations
Portland	98%	KATU	ABC
Portland	98%	KGW	NBC
Portland	98%	KNMT	Independent
Portland	98%	KOIN	CBS
Portland	98%	KOPB	PBS
Portland	98%	KPDX	UPN
Portland	98%	KPTV	FOX
Portland	98%	KPXG	PAX
Portland	98%	KTVR	PBS
Portland	98%	KWBP	WB
Eugene	2%	KCBY	CBS
Eugene	2%	KEPB	PBS
Eugene	2%	KEZI	ABC
Eugene	2%	KLSR	FOX
Eugene	2%	KMTR	NBC
Eugene	2%	KMTX	NBC
Eugene	2%	KMTZ	NBC
Eugene	2%	KOAC	PBS
Eugene	2%	KPIC	CBS
Eugene	2%	KTVC	UPN
Eugene	2%	KVAL	CBS

Cable systems and subscribers
Charter   45,365
Comcast   80,745

Direct Link   6,858
Millennium Digital Media   2,924
Telesystems West   792
Uvision LLC   3,939
Willamette Broadband   852

Military installations, September 2001
McNary Field Army Aviation Support, Salem   251

Businesses and other major employers
Oregon State University; Corvallis   6,998
Portland Community College Inc.; Portland   2,639
Clackamas Community College; Oregon City   1,550
Norpac Salads Inc.; Stayton; frozen fruits, fruit juices,
   vegetables   1,500
Salem Hospital; Salem   1,500
Spirit Mountain Gaming Inc.; Willamina; gambling
   1,450
Xerox Corp.; Wilsonville; commercial printing   1,300
Chemeketa Community College District; Salem   1,289
SUMCO; Salem; silicon wafers   1,260
Oregon Dept. of Human Services; Salem   1,200
Mentor Graphics Corp.; Wilsonville; computer-aided
   system services   1,000
Mentor Graphics Corp.; Keizer; computer systems
   1,000
City of Salem; Salem; city government   992
WinCo Foods Inc.; Woodburn; refrigerated transport
   965
Oregon State Police; Tillamook; police dept.   952
State Farm Mutual Automobile Insurance Co.; Salem;
   insurance agents and brokers   900
Tyco Printed Circuit Group Inc.; Dallas; circuit boards
   860
Oregon Consumer and Business Services Dept.; Salem
   850
Depuy Orthopaedics Inc.; Gladstone; orthopedic
   appliances   800
Oregon Dept. of Revenue; Salem   800
Oregon Driver and Motor Vehicle Services; Salem   700
Willamette Falls Hospital Inc.; Oregon City   700
Lewis & Clark College Inc.; Portland   690
Hollywood Entertainment Corp.; Wilsonville; video
   rental   687
Western Oregon University; Monmouth   637
GlaxoSmithKline; West Linn; pharmaceuticals   600
Marion County; Salem; county commissioner   600
Willamette University; Salem   600
Oregon Dept. of Employment; Salem   500
U.S. Postal Service; Salem   500

PENNSYLVANIA

Districts established April 18, 2002, for elections first held in 2002.

19 members

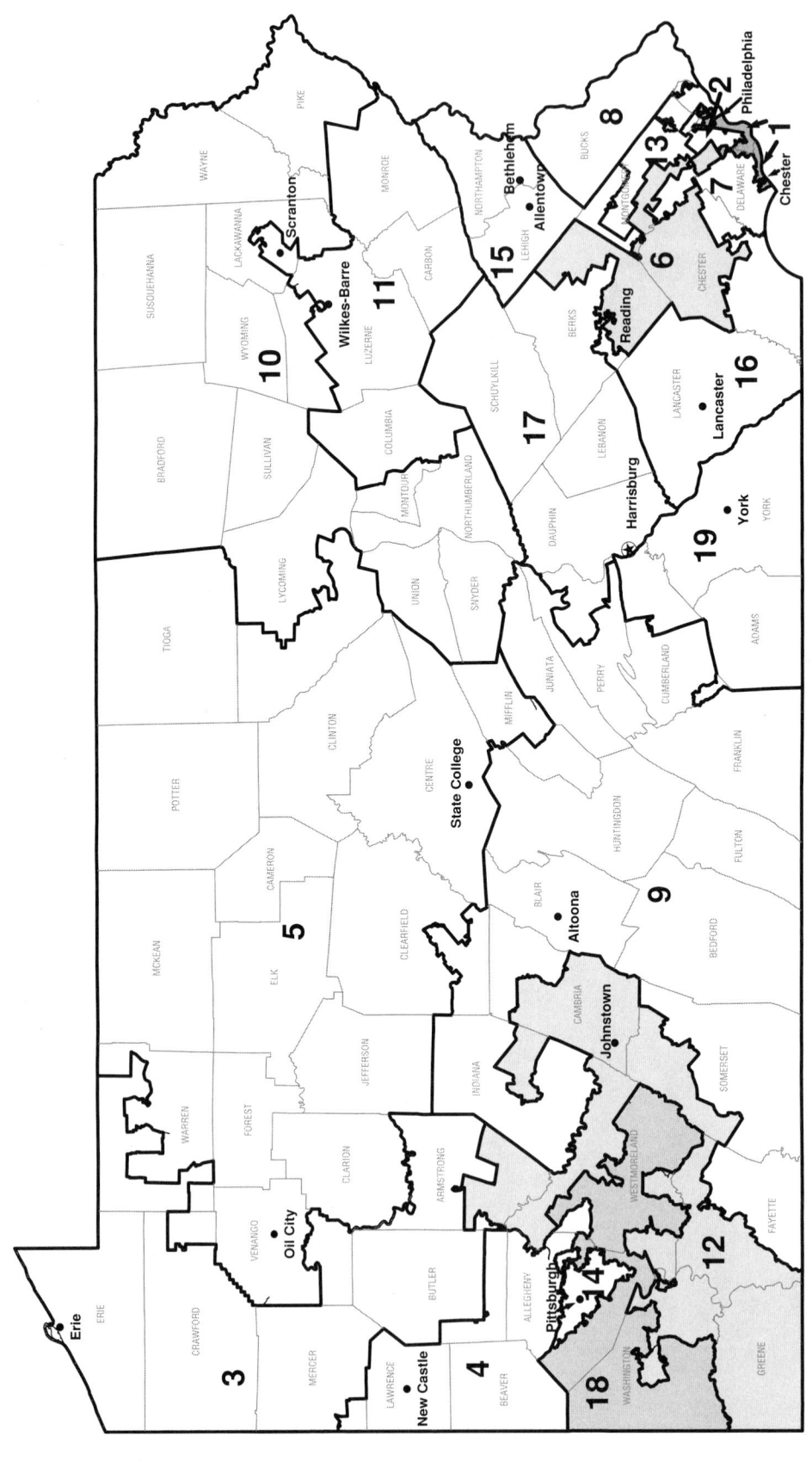

Pennsylvania

No state has been more important to American history than Pennsylvania. William Penn's arrival and establishment west of the Delaware signaled the willingness of the English crown to permit religious freedom in the colonies (or at least in its remote and forested portions). Penn was a Quaker, and the city he started on the Delaware's banks was called Philadelphia, literally the city of brotherly love. Never mind that the English had ousted the Dutch, who had ousted the Swedes who were here first. The founding of Penn's colony (literally "Penn's woods") was a beacon of hope to a Europe exhausted by religious civil wars.

In the middle and late 1700s, when colonials of all faiths had grown weary of their status in the Empire, they came to Philadelphia to conspire. This was the site of the First Continental Congress in 1774 and the Second in 1776, which declared independence. Eleven years later, the Constitution was drafted here, lending the sobriquet "Birthplace of the Nation" to the city. Penn may have been the colony's founder, but the enduring spirit may be Benjamin Franklin, the pragmatic Renaissance man who began publishing his *Pennsylvania Gazette* in Philadelphia in 1729, stuck around to help lead the Continental Congress, negotiated essential support from France, and even influenced the Constitutional Convention before dying in 1790.

Pennsylvanians put the first steamboat on the Delaware in 1787, and Robert Fulton launched his more famous version in Pittsburgh 24 years later. The state was an early leader, competing with New York, in canals and rail transport. Pennsylvania coal was the prime source of energy for America's industrial revolution. Edwin Drake drilled the first oil well that made money near Titusville in 1859.

In the Civil War, Pennsylvania furnished more Union troops than any state except New York and was the site of the war's most important battle, near Gettysburg, in July 1863. It was, of course, in Pittsburgh that Scottish immigrant Andrew Carnegie revolutionized steelmaking and amassed one of the great fortunes in history (which he proceeded to give away). Other innovative entrepreneurs made similar advances in glassmaking and other manufactures: In 1905 the world's largest chocolate factory was built in Hershey.

Unfortunately, reciting the glories of Pennsylvania's past tends to emphasize the degree to which they remain in the past. After 1900, the notion that Pennsylvania and New York stood alone atop the power pyramid of states became difficult to sustain. First it was Ohio and Illinois nipping at Pennsylvania's heels. But with World War II and its aftermath, the country moved in new directions. People went west and south to live. Industry went west and south looking for cheaper labor. Business followed, following the dictates of the market. New rivals from the Sun Belt arose and passed Pennsylvania in population: California in the 1940s, Texas in the 1970s, Florida in the 1980s, and Illinois, finally, in the late 1990s.

When America looked back from the year 2000, Pennsylvania appeared as if it had not kept pace. At one time, it had been a people magnet—attracting immigrants in great waves (especially Germans, often referred to as "Pennsylvania Dutch"). But in the twentieth century the magnet weakened. From 8 percent of the national total in 1900, the state fell to 4 percent in 2000. The great city of Philadelphia, once more than 2 million, had lost a quarter of its population and slid to number five on the national city list. Pittsburgh, which peaked at number eight, had lost more than half its population and fallen to number 52. Harrisburg, Allentown, Scranton, Erie, Lancaster, York, and a dozen other Pennsylvania cities that were once in the top 100 had all long since vanished from that list.

It is possible to overstate these losses, especially in relative rankings that may not always measure comparable entities. Philadelphia has lost much of its loft, to be sure, but its total metro population is larger than ever (more than 6 million, although much of that is in New Jersey and Delaware). The city's skyline has never been so replete with both classic and modern skyscrapers. The attachment of old money, cachet, and prestige to Philadelphia has helped to effectuate a recovery. To walk around the historic sections of the city today, approximating the route where Franklin took his storied first tour about the wharves, is to marvel at the determination of a great city to survive and prosper again. Similarly, Pittsburgh has become a model of redemption from economic doldrums and air pollution.

Pennsylvania has recently been led by a succession of ambitious, outspoken, and telegenic governors, including Democrat Bob Casey in the 1980s, Republican Tom Ridge in the 1990s, and Democrat Ed Rendell (elected in 2002). These men all dedicated themselves to bringing the benefits of high-tech industry to the state to replace the old metalbending arts and sciences of the past two centuries. Their work is in some measure displayed by the renewal of Harrisburg, the state's capital, which has revitalized its downtown, modernized its ornate capitol, and begun to expand its business base as well.

The population may also have stabilized for the time being (there was 3.4 percent growth in the 1990s), giving the state a solid base from which to expand again. But slow growth will remain a serious challenge, especially given the accelerating growth of the South and West. Pennsylvania was the fourth oldest state by median age in 2000, and it ranked second in residents above age 65 and forty-fourth in birth rates. That is why it grew only 3.4 percent in the 1990s (the third poorest growth in the country), and why it is expected to grow less than 6 percent over the first quarter of the new century, according to the Census Bureau. Only three states' growth percentages are lower. Part of the reason is the state's domination by whites with relatively low birth rates. Although the state is close to the national average for African Americans, it ranks thirty-third in Hispanics (about 3 percent in 2000 versus 12.5 percent nationally).

Whatever may come next for Pennsylvania, in the short term the consequences of negative growth must be dealt with, including a brutal round of reapportionment and redistricting. The 2000 census cost the state another two House seats, reducing the total from 21 to 19 (one more such downgrade and the state will be at less than half its 1910 peak of 36 seats). But if reapportionment hurt the state, redistricting was agony for the Democrats. With the state losing a pair of seats from a House delegation previously split as evenly as possible (11 Republicans, 10 Democrats), a bipartisan commission might have proposed taking one safe seat from each party. But that would not happen in any state relying instead on the partisan officeholders in the legislature and governor's office. In 2001 in Pennsylvania, the GOP had both. The result was an artful and highly effective new map that cost the Democrats dearly.

Geographically, Pennsylvania is a near-rectangle superimposed on a series of mountain ridges and valleys that cross the state diagonally. At its northwestern extreme, the state extends an appendage to touch Lake Erie, where the industrial city of Erie sits roughly midway up the lakeshore between Cleveland, Ohio, and Buffalo, New York. Southeast of Erie are the elevations of the Allegheny Plateau, followed in succession by the Allegheny Mountains, the Allegheny Front, then the main spine of the Appalachian Mountains, the Great Valley of the Susquehanna River, and the Piedmont plateau just above the Delaware.

The population is unevenly distributed across this topography, with most of the residents in the southeastern (Philadelphia), southwestern (Pittsburgh), and northeastern (Scranton, Wilkes-Barre) corners. Most state residents live in either the Philadelphia or Pittsburgh metro areas, which rank sixth and twentieth as market statistical areas nationally and spill into 12 of the state's 19 congressional districts.

The new congressional district map adopted in 2001 forced three pairs of Democratic incumbents to face off in the 2002 primaries and yet another Democrat to run against a senior Republican incumbent. The map also created one brand new district in the Philadelphia area and one heavily redrawn district on the south side of the Pittsburgh metro area—each with a clearly Republican tilt. Thus the Democrats would be forced to absorb not only both of the lost seats but more besides. The Republicans could count on picking up at least one newly drawn seat and had good prospects for gains elsewhere as well—all despite the overall downsizing of the delegation.

The plan mostly worked. Two long-term Democratic incumbents (one in the northeastern Philadelphia suburbs and one in the Pittsburgh metro area) retired rather than face Democratic colleagues. The dean of the Democratic delegation, John Murtha, defeated a fellow incumbent Democrat in the party primary in the southwest district (12th)

that includes Johnstown. This meant that three incumbent Democrats were gone before the general election. The GOP also got its desired result in both its newly drawn districts. The new 6th District, incorporating parts of three suburban counties outside Philadelphia, favored the Republican candidate who won. Outside Pittsburgh, the radically redrawn 18th, which in its old lines had given Al Gore 57 percent in the 2000 presidential election, went easily to another Republican newcomer.

But in the south-central 17th District (Harrisburg), where Republican incumbent George Gekas was pitted against Democratic incumbent Tim Holden, the Democrat proved the better campaigner. The 17th was redrawn to include Schuykill County and much of Berks, both of which went for George W. Bush in 2000. But Holden held his own. So the GOP wound up with two freshmen and retained 10 of 11 incumbents, while bidding goodbye to three veteran Democrats who probably would have won easily under the old lines. The new delegation in 2003 was 12 Republicans, seven Democrats.

In national elections, Pennsylvania has been viewed of late as a competitive state. Bill Clinton carried it twice and Al Gore even managed a 51 percent majority in 2000. But the state's larger historic context has been one of loyalty to the GOP. Before the Republican Party came to power in 1860, Pennsylvania had been as good a bellwether state as the nation had. Of course, the biggest states tend to go with the winner in part because their votes determine the winner. In 1832, for example, Pennsylvania and New York together accounted for a quarter of the electoral college; so winning both plus one more state guaranteed victory. From the 1790s to the Civil War, Pennsylvania voted for the winner every time the electoral college produced one.

But beginning in the 1880s, as the state's huge share of electoral votes diminished, so did its political weathervane power: the state went against Grover Cleveland both times he won, against Woodrow Wilson both times he won, and against Franklin D. Roosevelt in 1932, Harry S. Truman in 1948, Richard Nixon in 1968, and George W. Bush in 2000.

A glaring aspect of Pennsylvania's political history is its lack of representation in the White House. Neighboring New York saw its governors march to the nominating stage more often than not for a century after the Civil War. Ohio, Pennsylvania's less populous neighbor to the west, has produced six Republican presidents. But not one Pennsylvania native has been elected president since James Buchanan in 1856, and none has been elected vice president since George Dallas in 1844. Nor has either party nominated a Pennsylvanian for either office in the twentieth century. Because both parties often presumed Pennsylvania to lean Republican, it was thought unworthy of wooing—even with the running mate's slot. But there was also a paucity of Pennsylvanians who saw fit to drive their careers in this direction (an impression Pennsylvanians might like to correct in future presidential elections).

Despite its big cities, Pennsylvania's voting demographic is steeped in small-town, small-city Republicanism, topped off with heavy concentrations of Republican votes in the big cities' suburbs. This was evident in a long skein of Republican governors between the Civil War and World War II, interrupted by one Democratic term in the 1890s and another in the 1930s. In the postwar period, however, the state developed a reliable new rhythm, alternating the governorship between the parties once every eight years—like clockwork. The most recent demonstration: the election of Rendell in 2000 after Ridge had won two four-year terms. Before Ridge, Casey served eight years, before him Republican Richard Thornburgh had done the same—preceded by Democrat Milton Shapp, and so on.

In the same time frame, however, both of the state's U.S. Senate seats have been almost exclusively the property of the GOP. Democrat Joe Clark won two terms beginning in 1956, Harris Wofford won a special election to fill out an unexpired term in 1991 (losing his bid for a full term in 1994). Apart from those highly isolated incidents, the Republicans won the other 17 Senate elections between 1946 and 2000. Much of this Republican success has been because of the party's nomination of candidates who worked well with organized labor and pulled votes across party lines. But the latest Republican senator, Rick Santorum, is an outspoken exponent of the new Republican conservatism that came to Washington in the 1980s and 1990s, emphasizing social issues such as abortion and school prayer.

Table 1 Population

District	Population	Population under 18	Voting-age population	Median age	Male*	Female*
1	646,331	183,744	462,587	32.3	46.7	53.3
2	646,361	155,985	490,376	33.9	45.5	54.5
3	646,364	156,824	489,540	37.7	48.8	51.2
4	646,476	154,364	492,112	40.4	47.9	52.1
5	646,371	143,875	502,496	37.1	49.5	50.5
6	646,483	158,773	487,710	37.4	48.7	51.3
7	646,530	154,552	491,978	38.0	48.2	51.8
8	646,340	164,773	481,567	37.8	49.0	51.0
9	645,612	152,036	493,576	38.6	49.3	50.7
10	646,537	151,902	494,635	39.4	49.3	50.7
11	646,209	143,559	502,650	39.5	48.2	51.8
12	646,079	137,681	508,398	40.7	48.0	52.0
13	646,167	151,860	494,307	38.9	47.9	52.1
14	646,196	135,229	510,967	38.1	47.0	53.0
15	646,495	154,972	491,523	38.2	48.5	51.5
16	646,156	173,961	472,195	35.4	48.9	51.1
17	646,465	150,361	496,104	38.9	48.9	51.1
18	646,817	144,326	502,491	41.0	48.0	52.0
19	647,065	153,444	493,621	37.8	49.0	51.0
State	12,281,054	2,922,221	9,358,833	38.0	48.3	51.7

*As percentage of total population.

Table 2 Voting-Age Persons by Race/Hispanic or Latino Origin

District	White*	Black or African American*	American Indian or Alaska Native*	Asian*	Other or multirace*	Hispanic or Latino*
1	38.3	42.2	0.2	4.8	1.8	12.7
2	34.1	56.5	0.2	4.6	1.7	2.8
3	94.9	3.0	0.1	0.5	0.5	1.0
4	95.1	3.0	0.1	0.9	0.4	0.5
5	96.0	1.4	0.1	1.1	0.5	0.8
6	88.0	6.2	0.1	2.0	0.8	2.9
7	89.3	5.1	0.1	3.5	0.8	1.2
8	91.6	3.2	0.1	2.3	0.7	2.1
9	96.7	1.6	0.1	0.3	0.4	0.8
10	95.9	1.8	0.1	0.5	0.4	1.2
11	94.5	2.2	0.1	0.7	0.6	2.0
12	95.6	3.0	0.1	0.3	0.4	0.5
13	87.0	5.5	0.1	3.9	0.9	2.6
14	76.6	19.3	0.1	1.8	1.1	1.0
15	88.9	2.4	0.1	1.6	0.8	6.2
16	86.6	3.8	0.1	1.3	0.7	7.5
17	89.1	6.5	0.1	1.1	0.6	2.6
18	95.9	1.9	0.1	1.2	0.4	0.5
19	93.5	2.6	0.1	1.0	0.5	2.1
State	85.9	8.9	0.1	1.7	0.8	2.6

*As percentage of voting-age population.

Table 3 Voting-Age Population by Age Groups

District	18 to 24*	25 to 44*	45 to 64*	Over 64*
1	15.1	41.1	27.1	16.7
2	16.4	38.4	27.0	18.3
3	13.0	36.1	30.5	20.4
4	8.5	36.5	32.3	22.6
5	16.1	34.8	29.2	19.8
6	10.7	40.1	30.8	18.4
7	10.7	39.2	30.0	20.2
8	9.4	41.0	32.6	16.9
9	11.0	36.6	31.6	20.8
10	10.5	35.9	32.0	21.7
11	11.8	35.1	30.1	23.1
12	11.5	33.8	30.5	24.2
13	9.5	38.2	29.8	22.5
14	14.1	35.7	27.4	22.8
15	11.0	38.2	30.4	20.4
16	13.5	38.9	29.5	18.1
17	9.8	38.1	31.2	20.9
18	8.2	36.5	32.6	22.7
19	11.5	38.8	31.2	18.5
State	11.7	37.5	30.3	20.5

*As percentage of voting-age population.

Table 4 Income and Occupation

District	Median family income	Families in poverty*	White collar†	Blue collar†	Service†	Farm†
1	$32,273	22.8	56.8	21.4	21.6	0.2
2	$37,817	18.5	65.8	14.6	19.5	0.1
3	$43,381	8.1	52.3	30.7	16.3	0.7
4	$52,704	5.6	63.7	22.4	13.7	0.2
5	$41,141	8.3	51.2	32.4	15.5	1.0
6	$66,544	3.7	67.8	20.3	11.6	0.3
7	$68,639	3.6	72.6	16.1	11.2	0.1
8	$68,201	3.2	68.0	20.9	10.9	0.2
9	$41,051	8.0	48.7	34.4	15.6	1.3
10	$43,199	7.2	52.6	31.1	15.4	1.0
11	$43,860	7.8	54.0	29.8	15.9	0.2
12	$39,033	9.9	51.3	30.5	17.7	0.5
13	$61,115	5.1	68.3	19.2	12.5	0.1
14	$39,871	12.7	61.7	18.6	19.6	0.1
15	$54,604	5.9	59.5	26.4	13.9	0.2
16	$53,899	6.5	54.7	29.6	14.3	1.5
17	$48,864	6.1	55.1	30.1	14.1	0.7
18	$54,981	4.4	66.3	20.0	13.5	0.1
19	$53,039	4.4	57.1	29.3	13.1	0.6
State	$49,184	7.8	59.5	25.2	14.8	0.5

*As percentage of all families.   †As percentage of employed workers 16 years and over.

Table 5   Education: School Years Completed

District	Less than grade 9*	Grades 9–12 no diploma*	High school diploma no college*	Some college*	College bachelor's degree or higher*
1	9.8	23.4	33.9	19.0	13.8
2	5.8	19.9	29.2	20.8	24.2
3	4.8	11.5	44.3	21.4	18.0
4	3.8	9.0	36.4	23.6	27.2
5	5.4	12.4	46.2	18.9	17.0
6	4.1	10.1	30.8	21.1	33.9
7	3.0	7.9	30.0	22.9	36.1
8	2.8	8.9	32.6	25.0	30.6
9	7.4	13.7	48.4	17.7	12.9
10	5.5	12.9	43.2	21.3	17.1
11	5.6	13.9	42.5	22.0	15.9
12	6.9	13.0	46.6	19.9	13.6
13	4.3	12.4	32.3	22.3	28.7
14	4.5	13.2	36.8	24.2	21.3
15	6.2	12.6	36.0	22.9	22.3
16	9.0	13.3	36.4	18.3	23.0
17	6.2	13.8	43.0	19.7	17.3
18	3.6	7.9	34.8	24.3	29.3
19	5.9	11.8	39.8	21.3	21.3
State	5.5	12.6	38.1	21.4	22.4

*As percentage of persons age 25 and over.

Table 6   Housing and Residential Patterns

District	Median home value	Owner occupied*	Renter occupied*	Urban†	Rural†
1	$52,100	60.3	39.7	100.0	0.0
2	$60,200	53.4	46.6	100.0	0.0
3	$79,900	73.5	26.5	58.5	41.5
4	$97,600	78.6	21.4	78.2	21.8
5	$71,900	72.9	27.1	46.3	53.7
6	$140,700	74.2	25.8	84.8	15.2
7	$146,100	74.2	25.8	98.6	1.4
8	$157,000	77.5	22.5	90.9	9.1
9	$79,800	76.6	23.4	39.9	60.1
10	$90,400	75.7	24.3	44.6	55.4
11	$88,300	70.3	29.7	72.6	27.4
12	$66,100	73.4	26.6	62.5	37.5
13	$119,300	72.3	27.7	98.7	1.3
14	$61,500	58.0	42.0	99.8	0.2
15	$118,400	71.6	28.4	87.4	12.6
16	$122,800	69.5	30.5	76.0	24.0
17	$93,200	72.6	27.4	69.6	30.4
18	$99,200	77.2	22.8	84.2	15.8
19	$111,200	74.9	25.1	71.3	28.7
State	$94,800	71.3	28.7	77.0	23.0

*As percentage of occupied housing units.   †As percentage of total population.

Pennsylvania 1st District

South and central Philadelphia; Chester

Home of the Philly cheesesteak, the 1st is known for its patriotic attractions, including the Liberty Bell and Independence Hall, the birthplace of the Constitution. Its Italian population supports a famous market where vendors sell produce, meat, and cheese. Many Catholic churches still hold services in Italian. *(See map p. 773.)*

The W-shaped 1st, where almost 90 percent of residents live in Philadelphia, is the state's most racially and ethnically diverse district. Already home to Philadelphia's Chinatown, an influx of Vietnamese and Chinese residents and businesses has boosted the Asian presence. Nearly three-fourths of Philadelphia's Hispanic population resides in the 1st, with the highest concentration in the northern part of the district. But African Americans represent the largest population block, at 45 percent.

Veterans Stadium and First Union Center, home to the city's major sports teams, are in the 1st. Lincoln Financial Field, built to replace crumbling Veterans Stadium, was scheduled to house football's Eagles beginning with the 2003 season, and baseball's Phillies also are getting a new park.

Once home to factory workers and a large ethnic blue-collar workforce, factory closings have left swaths of the 1st with a bleak economic landscape. While Philadelphia overall won notice for substantial economic recovery in the 1990s and is seeing a surge of construction jobs, major sections have yet to recover from a long period of industrial decay. The 1st has the lowest median income in the state.

The nearby closed Philadelphia Naval Shipyard is home to the booming Kvaerner Philadelphia and Metro Machine shipyards. The region is working to become an important shipbuilding, refurbishing, and decommissioning center.

Its strong union presence and substantial minority population make the 1st a slam-dunk for Democratic candidates.

Major Industry
Government, service, health care.

Notable
Eastern State Penitentiary, the most expensive upon its opening in 1829, held gangster Al Capone; comedian Bill Cosby graduated from Temple University in 1977; the Liberty Bell has "Pennsylvania" spelled as "Pensylvania"; Sylvester Stallone's *Rocky* movies were filmed in south Philadelphia.

Election Returns

	Republican		Democratic		Other	
President 2000	31,722	14.7%	181,274	84.0%	2,679	1.2%
House 2002	17,444	12.5%	121,076	86.4%	1,570	1.1%

District Profile

Population   646,331

Total area (square miles)   67.6
   Land area (square miles)   58.8

Population per square mile   10,992.0

Counties (2000 population)
   Delaware (pt.)   75,227
   Philadelphia (pt.)   571,104

Cities and other areas over 10,000 (2000 population)
   Chester   36,854   Philadelphia (pt.)   571,104
   Darby borough   10,299   Yeadon borough   11,762

Race and Hispanic or Latino origin*

White   33.1%
Black or African American   44.9%
American Indian or Alaska Native   0.2%
Asian   4.8%
Native Hawaiian or other Pacific Islander   0.0%
Some other race   0.2%
Hispanic or Latino origin   15.0%
Two or more races   1.8%

*As percentage of total population.

Ancestry*

English	1.8%	Polish	2.7%
German	5.1%	Subsaharan	1.6%
Irish	8.9%	USA/American	1.5%
Italian	7.8%	West Indian	1.3%

*As estimated percentage of total population.

Universities and colleges, 2000–2001 enrollment

Center for Innovative Training and Education, Philadelphia   216
Community College of Philadelphia, Philadelphia   15,953
La Salle University, Philadelphia   5,567
Thomas Jefferson University, Philadelphia   2,256
Widener University, Chester   5,192

Newspapers and circulation

	District circulation	Total circulation
Delaware County Times	7,068	48,236
Philadelphia Daily News	35,362	151,682
Philadelphia Inquirer	30,933	371,901
*Philadelphia Tribune**	8,417	27,991
*USA Today**	3,945	1,674,376

*See Sources and Explanations in the front of the volume.

Television stations and affiliations

Philadelphia	100%	KYW	CBS
Philadelphia	100%	WBPH	Independent
Philadelphia	100%	WCAU	NBC
Philadelphia	100%	WFMZ	Independent
Philadelphia	100%	WHYY	PBS
Philadelphia	100%	WLVT	PBS
Philadelphia	100%	WMGM	NBC
Philadelphia	100%	WNJS	PBS
Philadelphia	100%	WNJT	PBS
Philadelphia	100%	WPHL	WB
Philadelphia	100%	WPPX	PAX
Philadelphia	100%	WPSG	UPN
Philadelphia	100%	WPVI	ABC
Philadelphia	100%	WTVE	Independent
Philadelphia	100%	WTXF	FOX
Philadelphia	100%	WWAC	Independent
Philadelphia	100%	WYBE	PBS

Cable systems and subscribers

Comcast   21,978

Military installations, September 2001

Naval Surface Warfare Center, Philadelphia   1,695

Businesses and other major employers

Boeing Co.; Eddystone; helicopters   15,000
Albert Einstein Medical Center; Philadelphia   6,000
Thomas Jefferson University Hospitals Systems; Philadelphia   4,000
Sheet Metal Workers International Assn. Local No. 19; Philadelphia; labor union   3,500
Temple University; Philadelphia   3,017
Aramark Services Inc.; Philadelphia; contract food services   2,500
City of Philadelphia; Philadelphia; water control agency   2,500
Southeastern Pennsylvania Transportation Authority; Philadelphia   2,000
City of Philadelphia; Philadelphia; gas production, distribution   1,900
United Parcel Service Inc.; Philadelphia; package delivery   1,700
U.S. Internal Revenue Service; Philadelphia   1,500
U.S. Social Security Admin.; Philadelphia   1,500
Community College of Philadelphia; Philadelphia   1,496
Philadelphia Housing Authority; Philadelphia   1,400
St. Christopher's Hospital for Children; Philadelphia   1,400
Presbyterian Medical Center of University of Pennsylvania Health System; Philadelphia   1,350
Pennsylvania Hospital of University of Pennsylvania Health System; Philadelphia   1,308
Aramark Uniform Services; Philadelphia; uniforms   1,300
Hunt International Trade Corp.; Philadelphia; paper handling machines   1,300
Pennsylvania General Insurance Co. Inc.; Philadelphia; fire, marine, casualty insurance   1,224
Keystone Mercy Health Plan; Philadelphia; medical service plans   1,200
Rohm and Haas Co.; Philadelphia; polyethylene resins   1,100
Frankford Hospital; Philadelphia   1,000
General Electric Co.; Philadelphia; data communication services   1,000
Kimberly-Clark Corp.; Chester; paper mills   1,000
National Railroad Passenger Corp.; Philadelphia; interurban railways   1,000
Sisters of Mercy of Merion Pennsylvania Hospital; Darby   1,000
Spectrum Arena LP; Philadelphia; auditorium and theater operations   1,000
La Salle University; Philadelphia   895
Philadelphia North Health System Hospital; Philadelphia   712
Philadelphia Kvaerner Shipyard Inc.; Philadelphia; freight transportation   704
Widener University; Chester   700
Crozer-Keystone Health System; Chester; home health care   675
American Red Cross; Philadelphia; emergency social services   660
12th Street Hotel Associates; Philadelphia; hotels and motels   600

American Medical Response Mid-Atlantic Inc.;
Philadelphia; ambulance service   600
City of Philadelphia; Philadelphia; convalescent home;
nursing care   600
Hewlett-Packard Co.; Philadelphia; computer
maintenance services   600
May Department Stores Co.; Philadelphia   600
Philadelphia Coca-Cola Bottling Co.; Philadelphia; soft
drinks   600
SIMLAR Corp.; Philadelphia; light fixtures   600
U.S. Mint; Philadelphia   560
Sysco Food Services; Philadelphia; food supplier   550
Automotive Remanufacturers Inc.; Philadelphia;
automotive parts   500
City of Philadelphia; Philadelphia; police dept.   500
Hertz Corp.; Philadelphia; car leasing   500
Levy United News Inc.; Philadelphia; newspaper   500

Pennsylvania 2nd District

West Philadelphia; Chestnut Hill; Cheltenham

From the vantage point of the William Penn statue atop
City Hall, one can see the 2nd stretching west and north over
some of Philadelphia's long-established neighborhoods. The
district encompasses Center City skyscrapers, then moves
west across the Schuylkill River past the University of Pennsylvania. West Philadelphia, once Irish, Greek, and Jewish,
is now nearly all black and features pockets of middle-class
and poor communities. Overall, African Americans represent
more than three-fifths of the 2nd's residents. *(See map p. 773.)*

Except for the Montgomery County township of Cheltenham, the 2nd is wholly within Philadelphia. The district takes in the affluent city neighborhoods of Rittenhouse
Square, one of five squares Penn included in his original design of the city, and Chestnut Hill, in the city's northwest
corner. It also includes Fairmount Park, which houses the
city's art museum, zoo, and "Boathouse Row." The park,
which flanks the Schuylkill River, runs north along diverse,
middle-class neighborhoods, some of which have seen some
recent gentrification, and ends in Chestnut Hill. Some of the
homes in Center City Philadelphia are among the oldest in
the United States.

Economic struggles continue to grip many areas of the
district; some of the city's lowest family incomes are found
in neighborhoods just north of downtown. The University of
Pennsylvania has invested in West Philadelphia, creating incentives for school staff members to live in the neighborhood.
This includes financial help for home buyers and the creation
of a University of Pennsylvania-assisted public school.

The 2nd's blue-collar workforce and large minority population give it an overwhelming Democratic majority. In
the 2002 gubernatorial election, Democrat Ed Rendell took
more than 85 percent of the vote in 26 of the 27 city wards
that are wholly within the district.

Major Industry
Education, health care, tourism.

Notable
The Philadelphia Zoo is home to the nation's only giant
river otters; the 30th Street Station is in West Philadelphia.

Election Returns

	Republican		Democratic		Other	
President 2000	29,458	11.6%	221,517	87.0%	3,529	1.4%
House 2002	20,988	12.2%	150,623	87.8%		

District Profile

Population   646,361

Total area (square miles)   60.0
Land area (square miles)   58.8

Population per square mile   10,992.5

Counties (2000 population)
Montgomery (pt.)   36,875
Philadelphia (pt.)   609,486

Cities and other areas over 10,000 (2000 population)
Philadelphia (pt.)   609,486

Race and Hispanic or Latino origin*
White   29.8%
Black or African American   60.8%
American Indian or Alaska Native   0.2%
Asian   4.3%
Native Hawaiian or other Pacific Islander   0.0%
Some other race   0.2%
Hispanic or Latino origin   3.0%
Two or more races   1.7%

As percentage of total population.

Ancestry*
English 2.3%	Russian 1.6%
German 4.7%	Subsaharan 1.8%
Irish 6.8%	USA/American 1.3%
Italian 5.4%	West Indian 1.3%
Polish 2.0%	

As estimated percentage of total population.

Universities and colleges, 2000–2001 enrollment
Allegheny University of the Health Sciences,
Philadelphia   2,500
Arcadia University, Glenside   2,736
Art Institute of Philadelphia, Philadelphia   2,516
Chestnut Hill College, Philadelphia   1,561
Computer Learning Center, Philadelphia   656
Drexel University, Philadelphia   13,128
Gratz College, Elkins Park   561
Lutheran Theological Seminary at Philadelphia,
Philadelphia   258
Metropolitan Career Center, Philadelphia   255
Moore College of Art and Design, Philadelphia   573
Peirce College, Philadelphia   2,236
Penn Council for Relationships, Philadelphia   238
Pennsylvania Academy of the Fine Arts, Philadelphia
256
Pennsylvania College of Optometry, Elkins Park   706
Philadelphia College of Osteopathic Medicine,
Philadelphia   1,386
Philadelphia University, Philadelphia   3,316
Philadelphia Wireless Technical Institute, Philadelphia
379
Restaurant School, Philadelphia   504

PHILADELPHIA AND PITTSBURGH AREAS

Philadelphia Area

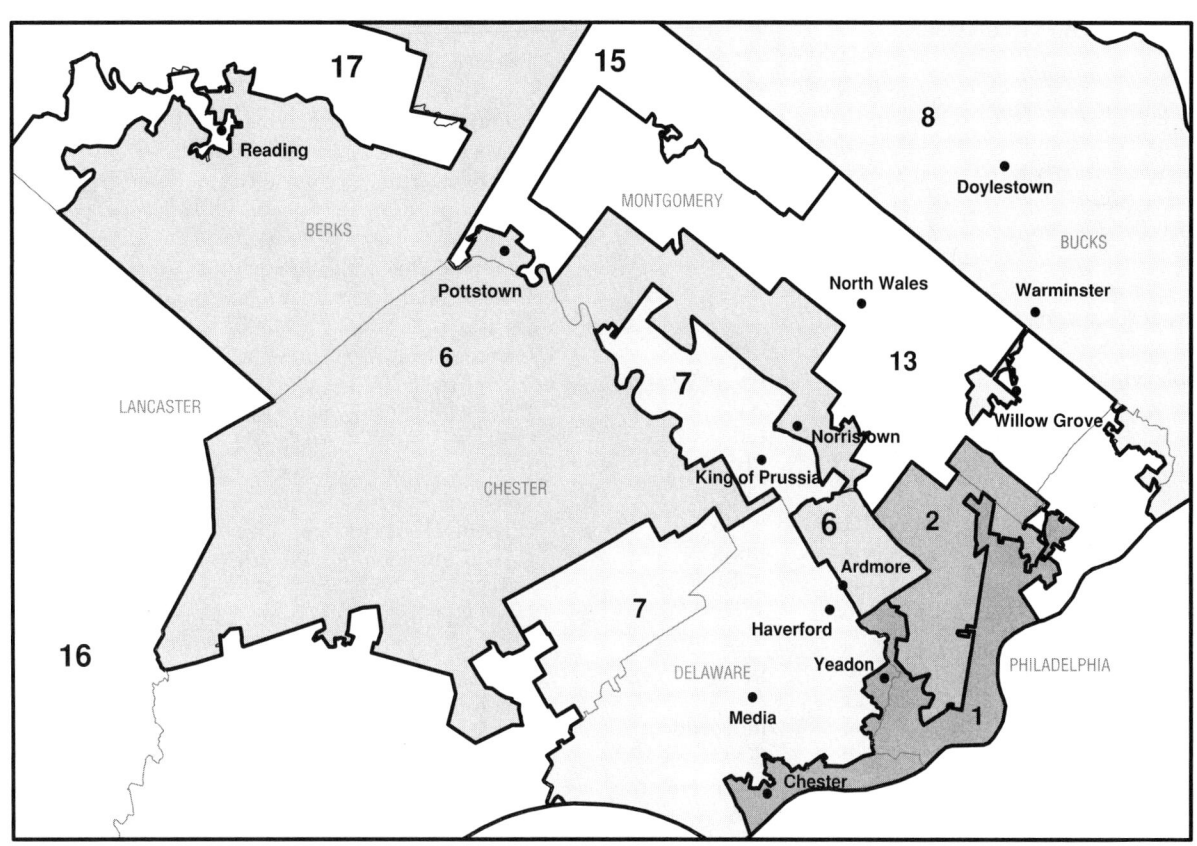

Pittsburgh Area

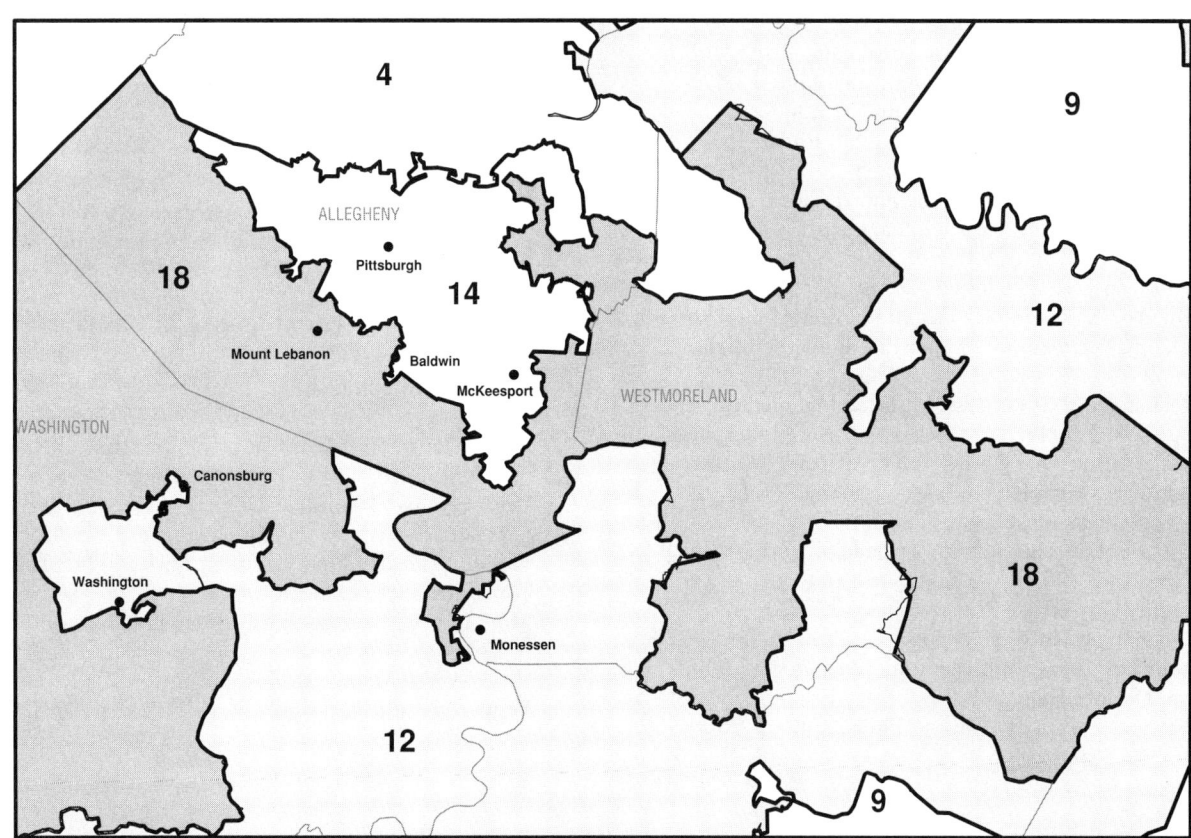

Temple University, Philadelphia   28,355
University of Pennsylvania, Philadelphia   21,853
University of the Arts, Philadelphia   2,037
University of the Sciences, Philadelphia   1,927
Westminster Theological Seminary, Glenside   224

Newspapers and circulation

	District circulation	Total circulation
Delaware County Times	1,032	48,236
Philadelphia Daily News	46,268	151,682
Philadelphia Inquirer	44,396	371,901
*Philadelphia Tribune**	9,041	27,991
*USA Today**	4,016	1,674,376

See Sources and Explanations in the front of the volume.

Television stations and affiliations

Philadelphia	100%	KYW	CBS
Philadelphia	100%	WBPH	Independent
Philadelphia	100%	WCAU	NBC
Philadelphia	100%	WFMZ	Independent
Philadelphia	100%	WHYY	PBS
Philadelphia	100%	WLVT	PBS
Philadelphia	100%	WMGM	NBC
Philadelphia	100%	WNJS	PBS
Philadelphia	100%	WNJT	PBS
Philadelphia	100%	WPHL	WB
Philadelphia	100%	WPPX	PAX
Philadelphia	100%	WPSG	UPN
Philadelphia	100%	WPVI	ABC
Philadelphia	100%	WTVE	Independent
Philadelphia	100%	WTXF	FOX
Philadelphia	100%	WWAC	Independent
Philadelphia	100%	WYBE	PBS

Cable systems and subscribers
Comcast   313,971

Businesses and other major employers
University of Pennsylvania; Philadelphia   13,572
U.S. Postal Service; Philadelphia   13,000
University of Pennsylvania Hospital; Philadelphia   12,001
City of Philadelphia; Philadelphia; police dept.   6,100
GlaxoSmithKline; Philadelphia; pharmaceuticals   5,000
Sunoco Inc.; Philadelphia; gas stations   5,000
Philadelphia Children's Hospital; Philadelphia   3,880
Atlantic Petroleum Corp.; Philadelphia; petroleum refining   3,000
Independence Blue Cross; Philadelphia; medical service plans   3,000
Drexel University; Philadelphia   2,760
Shop Rite; Philadelphia; grocery store   2,699
U.S. Veterans Hospital; Philadelphia   2,500
PNC Bank National Assn.; Philadelphia; commercial bank   2,400
Temple University; Philadelphia   2,296
Hahnemann University Hospital; Philadelphia   2,200
Budd Co.; Philadelphia; automotive parts   2,000
U.S. Defense Dept.; Philadelphia   1,800
U.S. Social Security Admin.; Philadelphia   1,800

Consolidated Rail Corp.; Philadelphia; freight hauling   1,700
Philadelphia Newspapers Inc.; Philadelphia   1,700
Cigna Corp.; Philadelphia; property damage insurance   1,600
Peco Energy Co.; Philadelphia; electric power generation   1,500
PricewaterhouseCoopers; Philadelphia; accounting services   1,500
Salomon Smith Barney Holdings Inc.; Philadelphia; stock option dealers   1,500
Pep Boys; Philadelphia; auto and home supplies   1,363
Fountains at Logans Square; Philadelphia; personal care home   1,300
Graduate Hospital; Philadelphia   1,300
United Pacific Insurance Co.; Philadelphia; property and casualty insurance   1,200
Genesis Health Ventures Inc.; Philadelphia; nursing care facilities   1,146
Philadelphia College of Osteopathic Medicine; Philadelphia   1,131
Bankers Standard Insurance Co.; Philadelphia; fire, marine, casualty insurance   1,000
Chestnut Hill Hospital; Philadelphia; hospital   1,000
City of Philadelphia; Philadelphia; city government   1,000
Day and Zimmermann International Inc.; Philadelphia; building construction consultant   1,000
International Business Machines Corp.; Philadelphia; computer peripherals, software   1,000
St. Joseph's University; Philadelphia   1,000
Stephen A. Cozen; Philadelphia; law office   1,000
Verizon Pennsylvania Inc.; Philadelphia; telephone communication   1,000
Accenture Inc.; Philadelphia; management information systems consultant   987
City of Philadelphia; Philadelphia; public library   912
Caribe Sun Oil Co.; Philadelphia; fuel oil dealers   900
Tasty Baking Co.; Philadelphia; breads and cakes   900
St. Agnes Medical Center; Philadelphia   840
Dechert LLP; Philadelphia; law office   814
National Railroad Passenger Corp.; Philadelphia; commuter rail operation   800
U.S. Veterans Hospital; Philadelphia   800
ATOFINA Chemicals Inc.; Philadelphia; chlorine   750
Comcast Cablevision of Mercer County Inc.; Philadelphia; cable TV   750
Ernst and Young; Philadelphia; certified public accountant   750
Reed Smith; Philadelphia; law office   722
FMC Corp.; Philadelphia; agricultural chemicals   700
Inglis House; Philadelphia; home for physically handicapped   700
Pennsylvania Hospital of University of Pennsylvania Health System; Philadelphia   700
Keystone Health Plan East Inc.; Philadelphia; health maintenance organization   696
Morgan Lewis and Bockius; Philadelphia; law office   680
Roxborough Memorial Hospital Inc.; Philadelphia   604
Pepper Hamilton; Philadelphia; law office   601

Greater Atlantic Health Service Inc.; Philadelphia; health maintenance organization   600

Institute for Scientific Information Inc.; Philadelphia; periodicals   600

Philadelphia University; Philadelphia   600

Ballard Spahr Andrews and Ingersoll; Philadelphia; law office   571

CSFS Philadelphia; Philadelphia; hotel, franchised   560

Delaware Management Holdings Inc.; Philadelphia; open-ended management investment   560

Episcopal Long Term Care; Philadelphia; nursing/personal care facility management   540

Friends Hospital; Philadelphia   520

Archdiocese of Philadelphia; Philadelphia; religious organization   500

City of Philadelphia; Philadelphia; recreational program   500

Deloitte and Touche; Philadelphia; certified public accountant   500

Fiserv Securities Inc.; Philadelphia; security brokers   500

J. J. White Inc.; Philadelphia; theater circuit management   500

KPMG; Philadelphia; accounting services   500

Seven Seventeen HB Corp.; Philadelphia; hotels   500

Pennsylvania 3rd District

Northwest — Erie

Located in the northwest corner of the state, the 3rd takes in all of Erie County and portions of six others. This historically blue-collar center includes Erie, the state's fourth-most-populous city. A port on Lake Erie, the city has been an industrial center for more than a century.

Although hard hit by economic restructuring in the 1980s, the 3rd remained an industrial area. The number of jobs in the services sector in Erie has nearly doubled since 1980. Fewer steel mills line Mercer County (a small portion of which is in the 4th District); those remaining now operate with a smaller employment base.

Despite those changes, Mercer boasts the largest concentration of pipe and tube production firms in the nation. In Crawford County, scores of tooling and machine shops dominate the landscape. Industrial expansion in Erie also is on the rise with a million-square-foot facility housing a distribution center and manufacturing plant.

Erie County's median household income is slightly below the state median, with the city of Erie well below and townships west and east of the city above the state median. The county, like the district overall, is largely white. Pockets of black residents in northern and central Erie help give the county a Democratic lean. Mercer County, home to one in six district residents, also has a Democratic lean, though George W. Bush nearly won the county in the 2000 presidential election after Bob Dole was trounced there in 1996.

Democratic tendencies in Erie and Mercer are offset by the Republican leanings in Butler and Crawford Counties. Overall, the district (numbered the 21st prior to redistricting following the 2000 census) voted narrowly for George W. Bush in 2000.

Major Industry

Manufacturing, law enforcement, service.

Notable

The reconstructed *US Brig Niagara,* a fighting ship from the War of 1812, is docked in Erie; Erie's Presque Isle State Park includes a Coast Guard station and Perry Monument, which is dedicated to those killed in the Battle of Lake Erie (1813).

Election Returns

	Republican		Democratic		Other	
President 2000	127,598	51.0%	116,118	46.5%	6,233	2.5%
House 2002	116,763	77.7%			33,566	22.3%

District Profile

Population   646,364

Total area (square miles)   4,761.8
Land area (square miles)   3,954.1

Population per square mile   163.5

Counties (2000 population)

Armstrong (pt.) 30,630	Mercer (pt.) 107,015
Butler (pt.) 113,160	Venango (pt.) 6,495
Crawford (pt.) 79,990	Warren (pt.) 28,231
Erie 280,843	

Cities and other areas over 10,000 (2000 population)

Butler 15,121	Meadville 13,685
Erie 103,717	Sharon 16,328
Hermitage (pt.) 14,643	Warren 10,259

Race and Hispanic or Latino origin*

White   93.7%
Black or African American   3.5%
American Indian or Alaska Native   0.1%
Asian   0.5%
Native Hawaiian or other Pacific Islander   0.0%
Some other race   0.1%
Hispanic or Latino origin   1.3%
Two or more races   0.8%

As percentage of total population.

Ancestry*

Dutch 1.6%	Polish 5.9%
English 6.8%	Scotch-Irish 2.3%
French 1.6%	Scottish 1.3%
German 20.8%	Slovak 1.3%
Irish 10.5%	Swedish 1.5%
Italian 7.1%	USA/American 4.0%

As estimated percentage of total population.

Universities and colleges, 2000–2001 enrollment

Allegheny College, Meadville   1,904
Butler County Community College, Butler   2,913
Edinboro University of Pennsylvania, Edinboro   7,278
Erie Business Center, Erie   459
Gannon University, Erie   3,377
Grove City College, Grove City   2,329
Lake Erie College of Osteopathic Medicine, Erie   620
Mercyhurst College, Erie   3,186

Northwest Pennsylvania Technical Institute, Erie
9,840
Pennsylvania State University-Erie Behrend College,
Erie   3,791
Pennsylvania State University-Penn State Shenango,
Sharon   1,032
Slippery Rock University of Pennsylvania, Slippery Rock
6,952
Thiel College, Greenville   994
Tri-State Business Institute, Erie   318

Newspapers and circulation

	District circulation	Total circulation
Butler Eagle	24,297	28,592
Erie Times-News	59,155	60,072
Greensburg Tribune Review	1,463	86,808
Kittanning Leader Times	6,150	10,014
Meadville Tribune	14,339	15,356
New Kensington Valley News Dispatch	1,269	31,270
Pittsburgh Post-Gazette	5,524	240,791
Sharon Herald	15,971	20,696
USA Today*	6,855	1,674,376
Warren Times Observer	4,164	11,042

*See Sources and Explanations in the front of the volume.

Television stations and affiliations

Erie	61%	WFXP	FOX
Erie	61%	WICU	NBC
Erie	61%	WJET	ABC
Erie	61%	WQLN	PBS
Erie	61%	WSEE	CBS
Pittsburgh	26%	KDKA	CBS
Pittsburgh	26%	WCWB	WB
Pittsburgh	26%	WGPT	PBS
Pittsburgh	26%	WNPA	UPN
Pittsburgh	26%	WNPB	PBS
Pittsburgh	26%	WPCB	Independent
Pittsburgh	26%	WPGH	FOX
Pittsburgh	26%	WPXI	NBC
Pittsburgh	26%	WQED	PBS
Pittsburgh	26%	WQEX	PBS
Pittsburgh	26%	WTAE	ABC
Pittsburgh	26%	WTOV	NBC
Pittsburgh	26%	WWCP	FOX
Youngstown, OH	13%	WFMJ	NBC
Youngstown, OH	13%	WNEO	PBS
Youngstown, OH	13%	WYTV	ABC

Cable systems and subscribers

Adelphia   42,997
Armstrong   28,660
CableVision Communications   3,518
Charter   6,499
Coaxial Cable TV   4,110
Comcast   545
Milestone Communications   2,790
Time Warner   42,537
Youngsville TV Corp.   932

Businesses and other major employers

AK Steel Corp.; Butler; stainless steel; steel bars   6,500
General Electric Co.; Erie; railroad-related equipment
5,500

United Refining Company of Pennsylvania; Warren; gas
stations   2,371
Hamot Medical Center; Erie   2,000
St. Vincent Health Center Inc.; Erie   1,644
Erie Insurance Exchange; Erie; fire, marine, casualty
interinsurance   1,600
Flying Aces Club; Erie; building scale models   1,500
Butler Memorial Hospital; Butler   1,300
Sharon Regional Hospital; Sharon   1,100
Erie County; Erie; county government   1,020
Verizon North Inc.; Erie; local/long-distance telephone
1,000
PPG Industries Inc.; Meadville; flat glass   900
Werner Co.; Greenville; metal ladders   900
Slippery Rock University; Slippery Rock   877
Armstrong County Memorial Hospital; Kittanning
868
Blair Corp.; Warren; mail-order catalog   800
University of Pittsburgh Medical Center Horizon;
Greenville   800
Edinboro University of Pennsylvania; Edinboro   780
Blair Corp.; Irvine; mail-order catalog   700
Gertrude Barber Center Inc.; Erie; school for physically
handicapped   700
John Maneely Co.; Sharon; steel pipe and tubes   700
Meadville Medical Center; Meadville   661
U.S. Veterans Hospital; Butler   650
John Maneely Co.; Wheatland; conduit   600
Plastek Industries Inc.; Erie; plastics molding   600
Spang and Co.; Butler; magnetic cores   600
Western Reserve Fish and Game Protective Office;
Mercer; hunting club   600
Concordia Lutheran Ministries; Cabot; extended health
care facility   560
Osram Sylvania Inc.; Warren; electric lamps   560
National Forge Co.; Irvine; iron and steel forgings   550
Penn United Technology Inc.; Cabot; carbides   550
AK Steel Corp.; Sharon; steel and iron tubes   520
Warren General Hospital; Warren   503
Creditron Financial Corp.; Erie; marketing consulting
services   500
General Electric Co.; Grove City; automotive
engines/parts   500
Kaiser Aluminum and Chemical Corp.; Erie; aluminum
die-castings   500
Lord Corp.; Erie; reclaimed rubber, specialty rubber
compounds   500
Pennsylvania Dept. of Corrections; Albion   500
Youngstown YMCA; North Springfield; sporting and
recreational camps   500

Pennsylvania 4th District

West — Pittsburgh suburbs, exurbs

The 4th starts at the western Pennsylvania border in Beaver and Lawrence Counties and wraps around the northern and eastern sides of Pittsburgh. Once a top producer of iron and steel, this traditionally blue-collar district is struggling to bounce back from hard economic times.

The area's major highways and proximity to Pittsburgh make the 4th attractive to commuters and expanding companies. Although abandoned steel mills still line the rivers, other sectors are beginning to prosper, bringing some much-needed diversity to the economy. Along with the health care industry, which is a major employer, the 4th has a growing number of computer firms. The district also is dabbling in the biotech industry as surrounding universities expand research grants in the field. The district has yet to regain the population of its booming steel days, but some areas, including parts of Butler County, are experiencing rapid residential growth.

Although union tradition has generally kept the district Democratic from the township level to the presidency, socially conservative Republicans can break the Democratic grip. That happened in 2000, when George W. Bush captured the 4th and a Republican easily won the open House seat. Much of the district's GOP base can be found in small farming communities, wealthy Pittsburgh suburbs such as Franklin Park, Fox Chapel, and Marshall Township, and the southern tier of Butler County. Redistricting following the 2000 census made the 4th slightly more Republican by moving the boundary farther into Alleghany County, where the GOP's strength has increased in recent years.

Major Industry
Health care, steel, manufacturing.

Notable
Oliver B. Shallenberger invented the electric meter, which indicated the amount of electrical energy dispensed or applied, in Rochester; there were several stops on the Underground Railroad in Lawrence County.

Election Returns

	Republican		Democratic		Other	
President 2000	152,313	52.0%	134,688	45.9%	6,167	2.1%
House 2002	130,534	64.6%	71,674	35.4%	10	

District Profile

Population   646,476

Total area (square miles)   1,339.6
   Land area (square miles)   1,323.6

Population per square mile   488.4

Counties (2000 population)
   Allegheny (pt.)   273,956
   Beaver   181,412
   Butler (pt.)   60,923
   Lawrence   94,643
   Mercer (pt.)   13,278
   Westmoreland (pt.)   22,264

Cities and other areas over 10,000 (2000 population)
   Aliquippa   11,734
   Fernway CDP   12,188
   Franklin Park borough   11,364
   Hampton Township CDP   17,526
   Harrison Township CDP   10,934
   McCandless Township CDP   29,022
   Municipality of Murrysville borough   18,872
   New Castle   26,309
   Plum borough   26,940

Ross Township CDP   32,551
Shaler Township CDP   29,757

Race and Hispanic or Latino origin*
White   94.3%
Black or African American   3.4%
American Indian or Alaska Native   0.1%
Asian   0.9%
Native Hawaiian or other Pacific Islander   0.0%
Some other race   0.1%
Hispanic or Latino origin   0.6%
Two or more races   0.7%

*As percentage of total population.

Ancestry*
English 6.4%		Polish 5.9%	
French 1.3%		Scotch-Irish 2.3%	
German 20.7%		Scottish 1.4%	
Irish 12.4%		Slovak 2.4%	
Italian 11.7%		USA/American 2.7%	

*As estimated percentage of total population.

Universities and colleges, 2000–2001 enrollment
Community College of Beaver County, Monaca   2,188
Geneva College, Beaver Falls   2,297
La Roche College, Pittsburgh   1,875
New Castle School of Trades, Pulaski   443
Pennsylvania State University-Penn State Beaver,
   Monaca   776
Trinity Episcopal School for Ministry, Ambridge   309
Westminster College, New Wilmington   1,659

Newspapers and circulation

	District circulation	Total circulation
Beaver County Times	40,226	42,448
Butler Eagle	3,901	28,592
Greensburg Tribune Review	12,421	86,808
New Castle News	17,616	18,463
New Kensington Valley News Dispatch	13,057	31,270
Pittsburgh Post-Gazette	56,459	240,791
Sharon Herald	3,235	20,696
*USA Today**	9,031	1,674,376
Youngstown Vindicator	1,301	70,119

*See Sources and Explanations in the front of the volume.

Television stations and affiliations
Pittsburgh	97%	KDKA	CBS
Pittsburgh	97%	WCWB	WB
Pittsburgh	97%	WGPT	PBS
Pittsburgh	97%	WNPA	UPN
Pittsburgh	97%	WNPB	PBS
Pittsburgh	97%	WPCB	Independent
Pittsburgh	97%	WPGH	FOX
Pittsburgh	97%	WPXI	NBC
Pittsburgh	97%	WQED	PBS
Pittsburgh	97%	WQEX	PBS
Pittsburgh	97%	WTAE	ABC
Pittsburgh	97%	WTOV	NBC
Pittsburgh	97%	WWCP	FOX
Youngstown, OH	3%	WFMJ	NBC
Youngstown, OH	3%	WNEO	PBS
Youngstown, OH	3%	WYTV	ABC

Cable systems and subscribers
Adelphia 57,302
Armstrong 11,074
Comcast 57,393
Ward Communications 710

Businesses and other major employers
U.S. Airways Inc.; Ambridge 3,400
Valley Medical Facilities Inc.; Sewickley 3,000
Heritage Valley Health System Hospital; Beaver 2,500
Jefferson Regional Medical Center; Pittsburgh 2,000
American Eagle Outfitters Inc.; Warrendale; apparel 1,500
Associated Cleaning Consultants and Services Inc.; Pittsburgh; janitorial service 1,500
University of Pittsburgh Medical Center Passavant; Pittsburgh 1,351
Alle-Kiski Medical Center Inc.; Natrona Heights 1,350
Logan's Roadhouse Inc.; Zelienople; restaurants 1,200
PJAX Inc.; Gibsonia; trucking 1,200
Jameson Health System Inc.; New Castle; management services 1,111
Delabarta Inc.; Pittsburgh; newspaper 975
Three Rivers Aluminum Co.; Cranberry Township; storm doors or windows 900
U.S. Postal Service; Warrendale 875
Eaton Corp.; Beaver; switchgear and switchboard apparatus 850
Lutheran Affiliated Services; Cranberry Township; hospital management 800
HealthSouth Corp.; Pittsburgh; rehabilitation center 795
Medrad Inc.; Indianola; medical instruments 733
Beaver County Community College; Monaca 705
Beaver County; Beaver; nursing home 700
Genco Co.; Pittsburgh; warehousing 700
Giant Eagle Inc.; Pittsburgh; supermarkets 700
Mercy Behavioral Health Center; Pittsburgh 700
Michael Baker Corp.; Beaver; civil engineering 620
Mine Safety Appliances Co.; Murrysville; safety equipment 620
St. Francis Hospital of New Castle; New Castle 620
Manheim's Pennsylvania Auction Services Inc.; Cranberry Township; automobile auction 595
Koppel Steel Corp.; Koppel; bar, rod, and wire products 575
Anchor Hocking Corp.; Monaca; tableware 550
Oberg Industries Inc.; Freeport; metal stampings 530
J&L Specialty Steel Inc.; Midland; stainless steel 516
Veka Inc.; Fombell; plastics 513
Allegheny County Port Authority; Gibsonia 500
Allegheny Ludlum Corp.; Brackenridge; blast furnaces and steel mills 500
American Architectural Products Corp.; Wexford; millwork 500
Duferco Farrell Corp.; Farrell; nonferrous rolling and drawing 500
Glidden Co.; Wexford; paint 500
Michael Baker Corp.; Pittsburgh; civil engineering 500
Mine Safety Appliances Co.; Monaca; safety equipment 500
Mine Safety Appliances Co.; Cranberry Township; safety equipment 500
Respironics Inc.; Murrysville; medical supplies 500

Pennsylvania 5th District
North central — State College

The giant, sprawling 5th encompasses part or all of 16 counties and the state's largest university, Pennsylvania State. The district's upper counties border New York state, and its westernmost point is only about 30 miles from the Ohio border. In land framed by the Appalachian Mountains sit struggling towns and pockets of poverty.

State College (Centre County), the district's largest city and home of Penn State, has hopped on the high-tech bandwagon, bringing in manufacturing firms that specialize in electronics and computer products. Its technology-driven development mimics the tide that brought the Silicon Valley to prominence, though on a much smaller scale. The district also boasts a contingent of more than 200 meteorologists.

While State College's workforce is technologically advanced, the 5th's other counties remain tied to timber production, manufacturing, and oil refining. The district's population is overwhelmingly white. At 96 percent, it has the second-highest percentage in the state.

Much of the 5th—particularly the northern counties—votes Republican, and George W. Bush won all of its counties in 2000. Some exceptions exist: Penn State keeps Centre County competitive for Democrats. Neighboring Clinton County and, farther west, Elk County lean toward Democrats in local elections (but toward Republicans in statewide and federal elections). Jefferson, Tioga, McKean, Clarion, and Potter Counties are staunchly Republican. Mike Fisher, the Republican gubernatorial nominee in 2002, took 71 percent in Potter and 69 percent in Tioga, his second- and fifth-best counties in the state.

Major Industry
Manufacturing, higher education, timber.

Notable
The town of Punxsutawney (Jefferson County) holds a yearly celebration for groundhog "Punxsutawney Phil," who becomes a national media star on Groundhog Day; situated amidst about 160,000 acres of the Tioga State Forest lies the Grand Canyon of Pennsylvania; Drake's Well, the first successful oil well in the nation, is on an artificial island in Oil Creek near Titusville.

Election Returns

	Republican		Democratic		Other	
President 2000	137,837	59.1%	89,180	38.2%	6,197	2.7%
House 2002	124,942	87.4%			18,269	12.6%

District Profile

Population 646,371

Total area (square miles) 11,058.3
  Land area (square miles) 10,992.3

Population per square mile 58.8

Counties (2000 population)

Cameron	5,974	Jefferson	45,932
Centre	135,758	Lycoming (pt.)	47,104
Clarion	41,765	McKean	45,936
Clearfield (pt.)	74,743	Mifflin (pt.)	34,656
Clinton	37,914	Potter	18,080
Crawford (pt.)	10,376	Tioga	41,373
Elk	35,112	Venango (pt.)	51,070
Forest	4,946	Warren (pt.)	15,632

Cities and other areas over 10,000 (2000 population)

Oil City   11,504
State College borough   38,420
St. Marys   14,502

Race and Hispanic or Latino origin*

White   96.1%
Black or African American   1.3%
American Indian or Alaska Native   0.1%
Asian   1.1%
Native Hawaiian or other Pacific Islander   0.0%
Some other race   0.1%
Hispanic or Latino origin   0.8%
Two or more races   0.6%

*As percentage of total population.

Ancestry*

Dutch	2.7%	Polish	3.1%
English	6.7%	Scotch-Irish	1.6%
French	1.6%	Scottish	1.3%
German	21.2%	Swedish	2.1%
Irish	9.1%	USA/American	6.1%
Italian	5.6%		

*As estimated percentage of total population.

Universities and colleges, 2000–2001 enrollment

Clarion University of Pennsylvania, Clarion   6,192
DuBois Business College, DuBois   445
Lock Haven University of Pennsylvania, Lock Haven   3,948
Mansfield University of Pennsylvania, Mansfield   3,113
Pennsylvania State University, DuBois   1,012
Pennsylvania State University, University Park   40,571
South Hills School of Business and Technology, State College   527
Triangle Tech, DuBois   301
University of Pittsburgh, Bradford   1,204
University of Pittsburgh, Titusville   509

Newspapers and circulation

	District circulation	Total circulation
DuBois Courier Express	10,142	10,236
Elmira Star Gazette	3,350	28,670
Lewistown Sentinel	7,669	12,724
Lock Haven Express	9,002	9,138
Pittsburgh Post-Gazette	1,669	240,791
State College Centre Daily Times	23,430	24,534
*USA Today**	6,899	1,674,376
Warren Times Observer	6,870	11,042
Williamsport Sun-Gazette	15,847	28,062

*See Sources and Explanations in the front of the volume.

Television stations and affiliations

Johnstown-Altoona	36%	WATM	ABC
Johnstown-Altoona	36%	WJAC	NBC
Johnstown-Altoona	36%	WKBS	Independent
Johnstown-Altoona	36%	WPSX	PBS
Johnstown-Altoona	36%	WTAJ	CBS
Buffalo	19%	WGRZ	NBC
Buffalo	19%	WIVB	CBS
Buffalo	19%	WKBW	ABC
Buffalo	19%	WNED	PBS
Buffalo	19%	WNYB	Independent
Buffalo	19%	WNYO	WB
Buffalo	19%	WUTV	FOX
Pittsburgh	14%	KDKA	CBS
Pittsburgh	14%	WCWB	WB
Pittsburgh	14%	WGPT	PBS
Pittsburgh	14%	WNPA	UPN
Pittsburgh	14%	WNPB	PBS
Pittsburgh	14%	WPCB	Independent
Pittsburgh	14%	WPGH	FOX
Pittsburgh	14%	WPXI	NBC
Pittsburgh	14%	WQED	PBS
Pittsburgh	14%	WQEX	PBS
Pittsburgh	14%	WTAE	ABC
Pittsburgh	14%	WTOV	NBC
Pittsburgh	14%	WWCP	FOX
Wilkes-Barre-Scranton	14%	WBRE	NBC
Wilkes-Barre-Scranton	14%	WILF	FOX
Wilkes-Barre-Scranton	14%	WNEP	ABC
Wilkes-Barre-Scranton	14%	WOLF	FOX
Wilkes-Barre-Scranton	14%	WQPX	PAX
Wilkes-Barre-Scranton	14%	WSWB	WB, UPN
Wilkes-Barre-Scranton	14%	WVIA	PBS
Wilkes-Barre-Scranton	14%	WYOU	CBS
Elmira	10%	WENY	ABC
Elmira	10%	WETM	NBC
Elmira	10%	WYDC	FOX
Erie	5%	WFXP	FOX
Erie	5%	WICU	NBC
Erie	5%	WJET	ABC
Erie	5%	WQLN	PBS
Erie	5%	WSEE	CBS
Harrisburg-Lancaster-Lebanon-York	2%	WGAL	NBC
Harrisburg-Lancaster-Lebanon-York	2%	WGCB	Independent
Harrisburg-Lancaster-Lebanon-York	2%	WHP	CBS
Harrisburg-Lancaster-Lebanon-York	2%	WHTM	ABC
Harrisburg-Lancaster-Lebanon-York	2%	WITF	PBS
Harrisburg-Lancaster-Lebanon-York	2%	WLYH	UPN
Harrisburg-Lancaster-Lebanon-York	2%	WPMT	FOX

Cable systems and subscribers

Adelphia   90,475
Blue Ridge   11,727
CableVision Communications   8,135
Charter   21,932
Comcast   794
Ducom Inc.   875
Harrison Valley TV   4,578
Johnsonburg Community TV   1,632
Milestone Communications   1,682
Morris TV Association   940
Mountainview TV Cable   905
Sheffield West Side TV Association   710
Suscom   14,794
Time Warner   10,891
Westfield CATV   1,250

Businesses and other major employers

Pennsylvania State University; State College   12,000

American Customer Care Inc.; Montoursville; help supply services   2,000

Northwest Health System; Franklin; nursing/personal care facility management   1,230

DuBois Regional Medical Center Inc.; DuBois   1,206

Corning Inc.; State College; glass TV tube blanks   1,200

Pennsylvania Dept. of Public Welfare; Polk   1,200

Premier Restaurant Management Co.; Clarion; restaurants   1,200

State Farm Mutual Automobile Insurance Co.; Aston; fire, marine, casualty insurance   1,000

Wal-Mart Stores Inc.; Woodland; warehousing   1,000

Ward Manufacturing Inc.; Blossburg; cast iron pipe, fittings   984

GKN Sinter Metals; Emporium; metal powder   900

Springs Window Fashions Division Inc.; Montgomery; vertical blinds   900

Centre Community Hospital; State College   882

Lewistown Hospital; Lewistown   825

Elk Regional Health Center; St. Marys   800

Joy Technologies Inc.; Franklin; mining machinery   800

Pennsylvania Dept. of Corrections; Bellefonte   800

Freedom Forge Corp.; Burnham; iron/steel forgings   750

Clearfield Area Hospital; Clearfield   728

Woolrich Inc.; Woolrich; men's/boys' coats   719

Osram Sylvania Inc.; St. Marys; incandescent lamps   710

Clarion University of Pennsylvania; Clarion   700

Pennsylvania Dept. of Public Welfare; North Warren   688

International Paper Co.; Lock Haven; paper mills   667

Cerro Metal Products Co.; Bellefonte; wire, copper and copper alloy   650

Keystone Powdered Metal Co.; St. Marys; metal powder   600

Metaldyne Sintered Components Inc.; St. Marys; metal powder   600

Willamette Industries Inc.; Johnsonburg; paper mills   600

Bradford Hospital Inc.; Bradford   580

Charles Navasky and Co.; Philipsburg; men's/boys' suits   550

Olympus Communications; Coudersport; cable TV   539

Mine Safety Appliances Co.; Cranberry; compressed and liquefied gases   500

Overhead Door Corp.; Lewistown; metal doors   500

Pennsylvania Dept. of Corrections; Houtzdale   500

Pennsylvania 6th District

Southeast — Philadelphia suburbs, part of Reading

The 6th takes in urban, suburban, and rural communities stretching from a slice of Montgomery County in the Philadelphia area through northern Chester County and southern and eastern portions of Berks County, including part of Reading and all of Kutztown. Most of the district's land is spread through sparsely populated towns. *(See map p. 773.)*

Once known for its rails and industrial prowess, the economy of Berks County has branched out in recent years to include service and retail jobs. With its share of historical sites and untouched land, the 6th enjoys a modest tourism industry. Reading is home to a minor league baseball team and, in the neighboring 16th District, a performing arts center, and minor league hockey team.

Growth and water-use issues dominate much of the political discussion in the region, which is mostly situated in the area triangulated by Philadelphia, Reading, and Lancaster.

Remnants of an earlier time are evident, as the 6th is home to numerous covered bridges, old mill towns, and Pennsylvania Dutch communities, as well as the Hopewell Furnace National Historic Site, a preserved iron plantation in Elverson that dates back to the eighteenth century.

The GOP-controlled legislature vastly altered the district during redistricting following the 2000 census, redrawing it to give a Republican candidate a small but significant edge. But the new 6th, now much closer to Philadelphia, certainly makes the nation's dwindling list of "swing" districts. Al Gore and George W. Bush ran neck-and-neck here in the 2000 presidential election, with Gore edging Bush by half a percentage point among the district's voters.

Major Industry

Manufacturing, tourism, retail.

Notable

Daniel Boone was born in Exeter Township.

Election Returns

	Republican		Democratic		Other	
President 2000	129,318	48.7%	130,472	49.2%	5,589	2.1%
House 2002	103,648	51.4%	98,128	48.6%	15	

District Profile

Population   646,483

Total area (square miles)   844.8
  Land area (square miles)   839.3

Population per square mile   770.3

Counties (2000 population)
  Berks (pt.)   213,355
  Chester (pt.)   242,361
  Montgomery (pt.)   190,767

Cities and other areas over 10,000 (2000 population)
  Coatesville   10,838
  East Norriton CDP   13,211
  Norristown borough   31,282
  Phoenixville borough   14,788
  Pottstown borough   21,859
  Reading (pt.)   36,706

Race and Hispanic or Latino origin*
  White   86.6%
  Black or African American   6.7%
  American Indian or Alaska Native   0.1%
  Asian   2.0%

Native Hawaiian or other Pacific Islander   0.0%
Some other race   0.1%
Hispanic or Latino origin   3.5%
Two or more races   1.0%

*As percentage of total population.

Ancestry*

Dutch 1.9%	Polish 4.7%
English 6.9%	Russian 1.5%
French 1.5%	Scotch-Irish 1.1%
German 19.0%	Scottish 1.3%
Irish 12.5%	USA/American 3.5%
Italian 9.8%	Welsh 1.1%

*As estimated percentage of total population.

Universities and colleges, 2000–2001 enrollment

Albright College, Reading   1,728
Alvernia College, Reading   1,574
Berks Technical Institute, Wyomissing   693
Bryn Mawr College, Bryn Mawr   1,784
Cabrini College, Radnor   2,039
Eastern Baptist Theological Seminary, Wynnewood 464
Harcum College, Bryn Mawr   545
Haverford College, Haverford   1,135
Immaculata College, Immaculata   2,922
Kutztown University of Pennsylvania, Kutztown 8,033
Pennsylvania State University-Great Valley, Malvern 1,613
Reading Area Community College, Reading   2,885
Rosemont College, Rosemont   1,179
St. Charles Borromeo Seminary-Overbrook, Wynnewood 482
St. Joseph's University, Philadelphia   6,961
Ursinus College, Collegeville   1,271
Valley Forge Christian College, Phoenixville   618

Newspapers and circulation

	District circulation	Total circulation
Allentown Morning Call	2,644	126,651
Ardmore Main Line Times	5,260	9,713
Lansdale Reporter	1,963	18,554
Norristown Times Herald	8,025	17,226
Philadelphia Daily News	7,567	151,682
Philadelphia Inquirer	41,423	371,901
Phoenixville Phoenix	2,845	3,543
Pottstown Mercury	14,531	24,659
Reading Eagle	40,568	82,493
*USA Today**	4,236	1,674,376
West Chester Daily Local News	15,287	29,214

*See Sources and Explanations in the front of the volume.

Television stations and affiliations

Philadelphia	100%	KYW	CBS
Philadelphia	100%	WBPH	Independent
Philadelphia	100%	WCAU	NBC
Philadelphia	100%	WFMZ	Independent
Philadelphia	100%	WHYY	PBS
Philadelphia	100%	WLVT	PBS
Philadelphia	100%	WMGM	NBC
Philadelphia	100%	WNJS	PBS
Philadelphia	100%	WNJT	PBS
Philadelphia	100%	WPHL	WB
Philadelphia	100%	WPPX	PAX
Philadelphia	100%	WPSG	UPN
Philadelphia	100%	WPVI	ABC
Philadelphia	100%	WTVE	Independent
Philadelphia	100%	WTXF	FOX
Philadelphia	100%	WWAC	Independent
Philadelphia	100%	WYBE	PBS

Cable systems and subscribers

Comcast   65,717
Service Electric Cablevision   3,945

Military installations, September 2001

Worcester U.S. Army Reserve Center, Norristown   291

Businesses and other major employers

Merck and Co. Inc.; Merion Station; pharmaceuticals 10,000
Vanguard Group Inc.; Malvern; mutual fund sales 8,250
Diakon Lutheran Social Ministries; Topton; individual and family services   4,000
Carpenter Technology Corp.; Reading; stainless steel 3,000
Bethlehem Lukens Plate Inc.; Coatesville; steel plate, pipe, and tubes   2,700
Ford Electronics and Refrigeration Corp.; Lansdale; electronic computers   2,700
Bethlehem Steel Corp.; Coatesville; blast furnaces and steel mills   2,500
Shared Medical Systems Corp.; Malvern; computer peripherals, software   2,000
David's Bridal Inc.; Collegeville; bridal shops   2,000
Triton PCS Operating Co.; Berwyn; radiotelephone communication   1,900
Main Line Hospitals; Wynnewood   1,531
Allstate Insurance Co.; Wayne; insurance agents and brokers   1,500
Unisys Corp.; Malvern; computers   1,500
Visteon Corp.; Lansdale; automotive parts   1,500
U.S. Veterans Hospital; Coatesville   1,400
XLConnect Systems Inc.; Exton; computer consulting 1,400
Montgomery Hospital; Norristown   1,300
St. Joseph's Hospital; Reading   1,300
St. Joseph Regional Health Network; Reading   1,300
Main Line Hospitals; Bryn Mawr   1,287
Brandywine Hospital; Coatesville   1,245
Parsons Power Group Inc.; Reading; engineering services 1,200
Pottstown Memorial Medical Center; Pottstown   1,050
Montgomery County; Norristown; county government 1,025
Centocor Inc.; Malvern; pharmaceuticals   1,000
Systems and Computer Technology Corp.; Malvern; software development   1,000
U.S. Postal Service; Southeastern   1,000
OneSource Facility Services Inc.; Bala Cynwyd; building maintenance   900
Weston Solutions Inc.; West Chester; business consulting   850

Boscov's Department Store; Reading   850

Chester County; Malvern; transportation regulation
   800

IMS Health Inc.; Plymouth Meeting; market analysis or
   research   800

Phoenixville Hospital of University of Pennsylvania
   Health System (Inc.); Phoenixville   789

Bryn Mawr College; Bryn Mawr   763

SCT Software and Resources Management Corp.;
   Malvern; software development/applications   750

Rubbermaid Inc.; Elverson; juvenile furniture   725

Wyeth Laboratories Inc.; Malvern; pharmaceuticals
   715

Suburban General Hospital; Norristown   707

Peoples Benefit Life Insurance Co.; Malvern   704

Micro Motion Inc.; Phoenixville; industrial magnetic
   flow meters   700

Pennsylvania Electric Co.; Reading; electric power
   transmission   628

Penske Truck Leasing Co.; Reading   620

U.S. Postal Service; Reading   620

De Lage Landen Financial Services Inc.; Wayne;
   machinery and equipment finance leasing   600

Provident Mutual Life and Financial Services Inc.;
   Berwyn; life insurance   600

Morgan Trailer Manufacturing Co.; Morgantown; truck
   bodies   600

Reading Station Partners; Reading; shopping center
   property operation   600

Cambridge-Lee Industries Inc.; Reading; steel   572

Sanofi-Synthelab Inc.; Malvern; chemical laboratory
   567

Golden American Life Insurance Co.; West Chester   550

Alcon Laboratories Inc.; Reading; ophthalmic
   instruments   550

Cambridge-Lee Industries Inc.; Reading; copper tubing
   540

Spicer Driveshaft Manufacturing Inc.; Pottstown;
   universal joints, motor vehicle   525

Maxwell Cab Co. Inc.; Ardmore; taxicabs   500

Karr-Barth Associates; Bala Cynwyd; investment advice
   500

Vanguard Group Inc.; Wayne; warehousing   500

Impact Merchandising Services Inc.; Exton;
   merchandising consultant   500

Aegon USA Inc.; Malvern; investment firm   500

DecisionOne Corp.; Malvern; computer maintenance and
   repair   500

Veterans Life Insurance Co. Inc.; Malvern   500

Sharp Corp.; Conshohocken; container packaging and
   boxboard   500

Research Pharmaceutical Search Inc.; Plymouth
   Meeting; executive placement   500

Shellville Services Inc.; Skippack; janitorial service   500

Cabot Corp.; Boyertown; primary nonferrous metals
   500

Pennsylvania 7th District

Suburban Philadelphia — most of Delaware County

Anchored in the suburbs south and west of Philadelphia, the politically competitive 7th takes in vast tracts of middle-class suburbia, including most of Delaware County, the district's population center, as well as southwestern Montgomery and eastern Chester Counties. *(See map p. 773.)*

The 7th attracted significant economic growth in the 1990s. Its defense industry, driven by Lockheed Martin and Boeing (located across district lines in the 1st), is a large employer, as are the pharmaceutical and technology sectors. New developments, many of which are springing up in the less-populated areas of Chester County, are attracting Philadelphia residents.

Upper Merion Township in Montgomery County has been expanding rapidly since the 1990s opening of the Blue Route (Interstate 476), which links Interstate 95 along the Delaware River with the Schuylkill Expressway near King of Prussia. Farther south, older suburbs such as Norwood, Ridley Park, Media, and Upper Darby are mostly white and working class. So is Marcus Hook, an old refinery town along the Delaware River. The 7th has the state's highest percentage of residents with Irish (31 percent) or Italian (20 percent) ancestry.

As recently as 1988, Delaware County voted Republican for president by 21 percentage points. But Delaware now votes Democratic in presidential elections. The county's hefty GOP registration advantage is shrinking, and Al Gore won Delaware in 2000 with 54 percent, the highest total for a Democratic presidential candidate since 1964. The county's strongest Democratic areas, including the mostly black city of Chester, are in the 1st District. The GOP still does well in the expanding, upper-income areas of Delaware County, including Radnor Township in the north and fast-growing Concord and Bethel townships in the southwest.

Major Industry

Pharmaceuticals, defense.

Notable

The Thomas Massey House, one of the state's oldest English Quaker homes, is in Marple Township; the King of Prussia Mall is the largest East Coast shopping center.

Election Returns

	Republican		Democratic		Other	
President 2000	140,862	47.2%	150,805	50.5%	6,945	2.3%
House 2002	146,296	66.1%	75,055	33.9%		

District Profile

Population   646,530

Total area (square miles)   293.4
   Land area (square miles)   289.9

Population per square mile   2,230.2

Counties (2000 population)
Chester (pt.)   73,689
Delaware (pt.)   475,637
Montgomery (pt.)   97,204

Cities and other areas over 10,000 (2000 population)
Broomall CDP   11,046
Drexel Hill CDP   29,364
King of Prussia CDP   18,511
Lansdowne borough   11,044
Nether Providence Township CDP   13,456
Radnor Township CDP   30,878
Springfield CDP   23,677
Upper Providence Township CDP   10,509
West Norriton CDP   14,901
Woodlyn CDP   10,036

Race and Hispanic or Latino origin*
White   88.4%
Black or African American   5.4%
American Indian or Alaska Native   0.1%
Asian   3.7%
Native Hawaiian or other Pacific Islander   0.0%
Some other race   0.1%
Hispanic or Latino origin   1.3%
Two or more races   0.9%

*As percentage of total population.

Ancestry*
English 8.2%	Polish 4.1%
French 1.5%	Russian 1.1%
German 13.3%	Scotch-Irish 1.4%
Irish 21.8%	Scottish 1.3%
Italian 14.3%	USA/American 2.2%

*As estimated percentage of total population.

Universities and colleges, 2000–2001 enrollment
American College, Bryn Mawr   547
Cheyney University of Pennsylvania, Cheyney   1,496
CHI Institute, Broomall   548
Delaware County Community College, Media   8,943
Eastern College, St. Davids   2,939
Neumann College, Aston   1,804
Pennsylvania Institute of Technology, Media   369
Pennsylvania State University-Delaware, Media   1,679
PJA School, Upper Darby   278
Swarthmore College, Swarthmore   1,428
Valley Forge Military College, Wayne   214
Villanova University, Villanova   10,017

Newspapers and circulation
	District circulation	Total circulation
Ardmore Main Line Times	4,442	9,713
Delaware County Times	38,691	48,236
Norristown Times Herald	5,962	17,226
Philadelphia Daily News	11,865	151,682
Philadelphia Inquirer	61,781	371,901
Pottstown Mercury	1,614	24,659
*USA Today**	2,993	1,674,376
West Chester Daily Local News	5,200	29,214

*See Sources and Explanations in the front of the volume.

Television stations and affiliations
Philadelphia	100%	KYW	CBS
Philadelphia	100%	WBPH	Independent
Philadelphia	100%	WCAU	NBC
Philadelphia	100%	WFMZ	Independent
Philadelphia	100%	WHYY	PBS
Philadelphia	100%	WLVT	PBS
Philadelphia	100%	WMGM	NBC
Philadelphia	100%	WNJS	PBS
Philadelphia	100%	WNJT	PBS
Philadelphia	100%	WPHL	WB
Philadelphia	100%	WPPX	PAX
Philadelphia	100%	WPSG	UPN
Philadelphia	100%	WPVI	ABC
Philadelphia	100%	WTVE	Independent
Philadelphia	100%	WTXF	FOX
Philadelphia	100%	WWAC	Independent
Philadelphia	100%	WYBE	PBS

Cable systems and subscribers
Comcast   116,739

Military installations, September 2001
Edgemont U.S. Army Reserve Center, Philadelphia   597

Businesses and other major employers
Universal Health Services Inc. Hospital; King of Prussia   25,000
AmeriGas Propane Inc.; King of Prussia; bottled propane   5,000
Mercy Health System of Southeastern Pennsylvania; Conshohocken; hospital management   5,000
General Electric Co.; King of Prussia; TV broadcasting   4,000
Crozer-Chester Medical Center; Chester   2,785
Delaware County; Media; county government   2,600
Aventis Pharmaceuticals Inc.; Collegeville   2,500
QVC Inc.; West Chester; TV home shopping   2,475
Guardian Assets Inc.; West Chester; semiconductors and related devices   2,000
Villanova University; Villanova   2,000
Wyeth Laboratories Inc.; Wayne; pharmaceuticals   1,936
Elwyn Inc.; Media; private special education school   1,500
HGO Inc.; King of Prussia; janitorial service   1,500
SmithKline Beecham Research Co.; Collegeville; biological research   1,400
Delaware County Memorial Hospital; Drexel Hill   1,365
SAP America Inc.; Newtown Square; software development   1,300
Delaware County; Glen Riddle Lima; geriatric residential care   1,200
Riddle Memorial Hospital; Media   1,200

Fair Acres Geriatric Center; Media   1,095

Crozer-Keystone Health System; Ridley Park; hospital
1,000

American Manufacturing Co.; King of Prussia; rope
950

Chester County Hospital; West Chester   925

Lockheed Martin Corp.; Brookhaven; satellite
communications equipment   800

Quest Diagnostics Clinical Laboratories Inc.; Norristown
800

TV Guide Magazine; Wayne; publishing and printing
800

Wyeth Laboratories Inc.; Paoli; pharmaceuticals   771

American Commercial Security Services Inc.; Media;
protective services, guard   750

Communications Test Design Inc.; West Chester;
telecommunication equipment repair   750

Arthur Jackson Co.; Upper Darby; janitorial service
750

First Consulting Group Inc.; Villanova; management
consulting   700

Reed Elsevier Inc.; King of Prussia; periodicals   700

Swarthmore College; Swarthmore   700

Montgomery County; Royersford; rehabilitation center
625

Hyatt Capital Management; West Chester; investment
advisory service   622

A. Duie Pyle Inc.; West Chester; local trucking   619

Upper Darby School District Inc.; Drexel Hill   613

BP Exploration and Oil Inc.; Marcus Hook; petroleum
products   600

GSI Commerce Inc.; King of Prussia; online services
600

Interboro School District; Prospect Park   600

NovaCare Inc.; King of Prussia; speech therapist   600

Pennsylvania Dept. of Public Welfare; Haverford   600

Cephalon Inc.; West Chester; pharmaceuticals   597

Macy's East Inc.; Springfield; department stores   560

Bryn Mawr Rehabilitation Hospital; Malvern   550

May Department Stores Co.; Springfield   550

Main Line Hospitals; Paoli   535

Aramark Services Inc.; Philadelphia; management
services   500

Bloomingdale's Inc.; King of Prussia; department stores
500

Eastern University; Wayne   500

ExxonMobil Oil Corp.; Glen Mills; drilling oil and gas
wells   500

GlaxoSmithKline; Audubon; administrative services
consultant   500

GlaxoSmithKline; King of Prussia; commercial physical
research   500

Lockheed Martin Corp.; King of Prussia; data processing
500

Mars Electronics International Inc.; West Chester;
mechanisms for coin-operated machines   500

Miller Anderson and Sherrerd; West Conshohocken;
open-ended management investment   500

Neiman Marcus Group Inc.; King of Prussia; clothing
stores   500

Nordstrom Inc.; King of Prussia; clothing stores   500

Quest Diagnostics Clinical Laboratories Inc.;
Collegeville   500

TV Guide Magazine Group Inc.; Radnor; TV schedules
500

Pennsylvania 8th District

Northern Philadelphia suburbs — Bucks County

Nestled mostly north of Philadelphia on the eastern edge of the state, the 8th includes all of Bucks County, a small portion of Montgomery County, and a sliver of northeastern Philadelphia. Established in 1682 by William Penn as one of the three original counties in Pennsylvania, Bucks features stately mansions such as Pennsbury Manor, Penn's home. The scenery and charm continue to attract wealthy new residents.

Bucks County grew about 10 percent in the 1990s, on par with its suburban neighbor, Montgomery County. The area's healthy, white-collar economy claims to support more than 20,000 small businesses. But the decade was not without economic problems. Blue-collar workers faced cutbacks in the steel industry, once a significant employer in Bucks County. A new deep-water port has helped, making the 8th something of a distribution and warehouse center. The district also is home to several hospitals. Voters in the 8th tend to be fiscally conservative but support environmentalism and hold moderate stances on some social issues.

Upper Bucks leans Republican—Bedminster Township in north-central Bucks was a rare Philadelphia suburb that did not vote for the former Philadelphia mayor, Democrat Edward G. Rendell, in the 2002 gubernatorial election. The GOP also does well in wealthy Upper and Lower Makefield townships. Democrats fare well in southeastern Bucks, near the Philadelphia line, and in the area just across the Delaware River from Trenton, New Jersey.

Though Republicans dominate elections for the state legislature in the 8th, Democrats can compete in statewide and federal elections here. Rendell won 63 percent of the Bucks County vote in 2002, and the district gave Al Gore a 5 percentage point cushion in the 2000 presidential election.

Major Industry

Health care, wholesale and retail trade, tourism.

Notable

George Washington's Delaware River crossing is reenacted in Washington Crossing each Christmas Day; Nobel Prize-winning author Pearl S. Buck lived in Bucks County.

Election Returns

	Republican		Democratic		Other	
President 2000	130,500	45.9%	144,878	50.9%	9,050	3.2%
House 2002	127,475	62.6%	76,178	37.4%	34	

District Profile

Population   646,340

Total area (square miles)   633.9
  Land area (square miles)   619.2

Population per square mile   1,043.8

Counties (2000 population)
Bucks   597,635
Montgomery (pt.)   17,156
Philadelphia (pt.)   31,549

Cities and other areas over 10,000 (2000 population)
Levittown CDP   53,966
Morrisville borough   10,023
Philadelphia (pt.)   31,549

Race and Hispanic or Latino origin*
White   90.8%
Black or African American   3.4%
American Indian or Alaska Native   0.1%
Asian   2.4%
Native Hawaiian or other Pacific Islander   0.0%
Some other race   0.1%
Hispanic or Latino origin   2.3%
Two or more races   0.9%

*As percentage of total population.

Ancestry*
English	7.6%	Russian	2.0%
French	1.4%	Scotch-Irish	1.1%
German	18.5%	Scottish	1.3%
Irish	18.1%	Ukrainian	1.1%
Italian	10.6%	USA/American	2.9%
Polish	5.5%		

*As estimated percentage of total population.

Universities and colleges, 2000–2001 enrollment
Bucks County Community College, Newtown   8,469
CHI Institute, Southampton   594
Delaware Valley College, Doylestown   1,833
Pennco Tech, Bristol   394
Philadelphia College of Bible, Langhorne   1,306
Ultrasound Diagnostic School, Trevose   244

Newspapers and circulation

	District circulation	Total circulation
Allentown Morning Call	5,654	126,651
Bucks County Courier Times	67,253	67,438
Doylestown Intelligencer	33,008	44,991
Greater Philadelphia Newspapers	101,325	152,790
Lansdale Reporter	1,605	18,554
Philadelphia Daily News	8,219	151,682
Philadelphia Inquirer	34,686	371,901
*Philadelphia Tribune**	1,184	27,991
Trenton Times	2,210	76,719
Trenton Trentonian	3,813	48,680
*USA Today**	3,310	1,674,376

*See Sources and Explanations in the front of the volume.

Television stations and affiliations
Philadelphia	100%	KYW	CBS
Philadelphia	100%	WBPH	Independent
Philadelphia	100%	WCAU	NBC
Philadelphia	100%	WFMZ	Independent
Philadelphia	100%	WHYY	PBS
Philadelphia	100%	WLVT	PBS
Philadelphia	100%	WMGM	NBC
Philadelphia	100%	WNJS	PBS
Philadelphia	100%	WNJT	PBS
Philadelphia	100%	WPHL	WB
Philadelphia	100%	WPPX	PAX
Philadelphia	100%	WPSG	UPN
Philadelphia	100%	WPVI	ABC
Philadelphia	100%	WTVE	Independent
Philadelphia	100%	WTXF	FOX
Philadelphia	100%	WWAC	Independent
Philadelphia	100%	WYBE	PBS

Cable systems and subscribers
Comcast   69,947
Service Electric Cablevision   2,994

Military installations, September 2001
Willow Grove Air Rescue Service (Air Force), Hatboro   2,349

Businesses and other major employers
Waste Management of Pennsylvania Inc.; Morrisville; street refuse systems   4,000
Woods Services Ltd.; Langhorne; residential treatment facility   3,000
Bucks County; Doylestown; county government   2,500
Union Fidelity Life Insurance Co.; Fort Washington   2,500
Prudential Insurance Company of America; Dresher; life insurance   2,000
Rohm and Haas Co.; Bristol; commercial research lab   1,500
Grand View Hospital; Sellersville   1,489
Frankford Hospital; Philadelphia   1,400
St. Mary Medical Center; Langhorne   1,382
Combined Insurance Company of America; Langhorne; insurance agents and brokers   1,200
Kmart Corp.; Fairless Hills; warehousing   1,200
U.S. Postal Service; Philadelphia   1,200
Edgcomb Metals Co.; Bensalem; metals service centers and offices   1,100
Kraft Foods Inc.; Philadelphia; biscuits   1,000
Doylestown Hospital; Doylestown   985
Lockheed Martin Corp.; Newtown; guided missiles and space vehicles   900
Advance Logistics Inc.; Morrisville; management consulting   800
Charming Shoppes Inc.; Bensalem; women's apparel   800
Keystone Turf Club Inc.; Bensalem; investment holding company   800
Silver Creek Athletic Assn.; Springtown; athletic organizations   800
Temple Lower Bucks Hospital; Bristol   770
Penn Engineering and Manufacturing Corp.; Danboro; metal fasteners   710
Atlantic Security International Investigations Inc.; Bensalem; security guard service   693
Courier Times Inc.; Levittown; newspaper   655
Simon and Schuster Inc.; Bristol; warehousing   650
Bucks County; Doylestown; education dept.   600
Hercules Inc.; Feasterville Trevose; water treating compounds   600
Prescolite Inc.; Bristol; light fixtures   600

ABB Inc.; Warminster; process control instruments 550

Wyndham International Inc.; Philadelphia; hotels and motels 550

L-3 Communications Corp.; Philadelphia; nonelectric transformers 508

Advertising Specialties Institute Inc.; Langhorne; book publishing 500

Pepsi-Cola Metropolitan Bottling Co.; Philadelphia; soft drinks 500

Pennsylvania 9th District

South central — Altoona

Situated in the south-central part of Pennsylvania, the 9th contains no booming metropolis—Altoona, the largest city, is tucked into the Allegheny Mountains and maintains a small-town feel. Most of the 9th's towns have populations under 5,000, making this one of the most rural districts in the nation. The district borders western Maryland and West Virginia to the south and expanded slightly in every other direction as a result of redistricting in 2002.

After decades of decline brought about by the waning of the railroad and mining industries, the area has begun to rebound, and once again residents can thank transportation-related industry for the growth. Bedford County saw its job creation rate shoot up as improvements began on the aging Pennsylvania Turnpike, which opened as the nation's first superhighway in 1940. And the city of Breezewood continues to draw in travelers with its garish display of signs adorning hotels and fast-food restaurants at the turnpike interchange.

Still, the bulk of the district's land is rural and dependent on agriculture. The 9th has a religious population, one of the most conservative in the state. Voters oppose most gun control and "big government" policies. Its small-business owners and farmers tend also to be fiscally conservative.

Voters went solidly for Republican presidential candidates in 1992, 1996, and 2000. The 9th includes George W. Bush's top two counties in the state in the 2000 election, Fulton (71 percent) and Bedford (70 percent), as well as part of Perry County (70 percent), which was Bush's fourth best. The GOP controls most local offices.

Major Industry
Agriculture, manufacturing, services.

Notable
A memorial to Flight 93 is in Shanksville, where the hijacked airplane crashed in a field September 11, 2001; President James Buchanan, a native of Mercersburg, vacationed at the Bedford Springs Hotel; architect Frank Lloyd Wright's Fallingwater house is in Fayette County.

Election Returns

	Republican		Democratic		Other	
President 2000	149,393	64.0%	80,008	34.3%	4,079	1.7%
House 2002	124,184	71.1%	50,558	28.9%	107	

District Profile

Population   645,612

Total area (square miles)   7,284.2
  Land area (square miles)   7,245.0

Population per square mile   89.1

Counties (2000 population)

Bedford 49,984	Fulton 14,261
Blair 129,144	Huntingdon 45,586
Cambria (pt.) 23,253	Indiana (pt.) 66,886
Clearfield (pt.) 8,639	Juniata 22,821
Cumberland (pt.) 39,652	Mifflin (pt.) 11,830
Fayette (pt.) 32,316	Perry (pt.) 21,834
Franklin 129,313	Somerset (pt.) 50,093

Cities and other areas over 10,000 (2000 population)
Altoona   49,523
Chambersburg borough   17,862

Race and Hispanic or Latino origin*
White   96.4%
Black or African American   1.6%
American Indian or Alaska Native   0.1%
Asian   0.4%
Native Hawaiian or other Pacific Islander   0.0%
Some other race   0.0%
Hispanic or Latino origin   0.9%
Two or more races   0.5%

As percentage of total population.

Ancestry*

Dutch 2.2%	Italian 4.2%
English 5.3%	Polish 2.4%
French 1.3%	Scotch-Irish 1.5%
German 24.4%	Scottish 1.1%
Irish 9.0%	USA/American 7.6%

As estimated percentage of total population.

Universities and colleges, 2000–2001 enrollment
Education America-Vale Technical Institute, Blairsville   231
Juniata College, Huntingdon   1,291
Pennsylvania State University, Altoona   3,765
Pennsylvania State University, Mont Alto   1,307
St. Francis University, Loretto   2,129
Wilson College, Chambersburg   764

Newspapers and circulation

	District circulation	Total circulation
Altoona Mirror	29,587	31,717
Carlisle Sentinel	8,623	15,388
Chambersburg Public Opinion	17,763	19,128
Connellsville Courier	2,134	10,225
Cumberland Times-News	1,128	30,232
Greensburg Tribune Review	2,181	86,808
Hagerstown Morning Herald	4,948	21,015
Hagerstown Morning Herald/ Daily Mail	5,160	35,668

Harrisburg Patriot News	8,652	101,633	
Indiana Gazette	10,214	15,563	
Johnstown Tribune-Democrat	6,814	42,734	
Lewistown Sentinel	4,643	12,724	
Pittsburgh Post-Gazette	1,744	240,791	
Somerset Daily American	7,993	13,431	
Uniontown Herald Standard	8,462	28,285	
*USA Today**	6,329	1,674,376	

*See Sources and Explanations in the front of the volume.

Television stations and affiliations

Johnstown-Altoona	50%	WATM	ABC
Johnstown-Altoona	50%	WJAC	NBC
Johnstown-Altoona	50%	WKBS	Independent
Johnstown-Altoona	50%	WPSX	PBS
Johnstown-Altoona	50%	WTAJ	CBS
Harrisburg-Lancaster-Lebanon-York	18%	WGAL	NBC
Harrisburg-Lancaster-Lebanon-York	18%	WGCB	Independent
Harrisburg-Lancaster-Lebanon-York	18%	WHP	CBS
Harrisburg-Lancaster-Lebanon-York	18%	WHTM	ABC
Harrisburg-Lancaster-Lebanon-York	18%	WITF	PBS
Harrisburg-Lancaster-Lebanon-York	18%	WLYH	UPN
Harrisburg-Lancaster-Lebanon-York	18%	WPMT	FOX
Washington, DC (Hagerstown)	17%	WBDC	WB
Washington, DC (Hagerstown)	17%	WDCA	UPN
Washington, DC (Hagerstown)	17%	WETA	PBS
Washington, DC (Hagerstown)	17%	WFPT	PBS
Washington, DC (Hagerstown)	17%	WHAG	NBC
Washington, DC (Hagerstown)	17%	WHSV	ABC
Washington, DC (Hagerstown)	17%	WHUT	PBS
Washington, DC (Hagerstown)	17%	WJAL	ABC
Washington, DC (Hagerstown)	17%	WJLA	ABC
Washington, DC (Hagerstown)	17%	WNVC	Independent
Washington, DC (Hagerstown)	17%	WNVT	PBS
Washington, DC (Hagerstown)	17%	WPXW	PAX
Washington, DC (Hagerstown)	17%	WRC	NBC
Washington, DC (Hagerstown)	17%	WTTG	FOX
Washington, DC (Hagerstown)	17%	WUSA	CBS
Washington, DC (Hagerstown)	17%	WVPY	PBS
Washington, DC (Hagerstown)	17%	WWPB	PBS
Washington, DC (Hagerstown)	17%	WWPX	PAX
Pittsburgh	15%	KDKA	CBS
Pittsburgh	15%	WCWB	WB
Pittsburgh	15%	WGPT	PBS
Pittsburgh	15%	WNPA	UPN
Pittsburgh	15%	WNPB	PBS
Pittsburgh	15%	WPCB	Independent
Pittsburgh	15%	WPGH	FOX
Pittsburgh	15%	WPXI	NBC
Pittsburgh	15%	WQED	PBS
Pittsburgh	15%	WQEX	PBS
Pittsburgh	15%	WTAE	ABC
Pittsburgh	15%	WTOV	NBC
Pittsburgh	15%	WWCP	FOX

Cable systems and subscribers

Adelphia   56,844
Armstrong   7,605
CableVision Communications   538
Charter   34,637
Comcast   29,353
Cooney Cable   5,175
Laurel Highland TV Co.   1,216
Nittany Media   802

Military installations, September 2001

Letterkenny Army Depot, Chambersburg   2,166
Carlisle Barracks (Army), Carlisle   1,179

Businesses and other major employers

Grove Worldwide; Greencastle; cranes   3,000
Leiss Tool and Die; Somerset; jobbing and repair machine shop   2,850
JLG Industries Inc.; McConnellsburg; conveyors and conveying equipment   2,300
Altoona Hospital; Altoona   1,600
Indiana University of Pennsylvania; Indiana   1,465
Chambersburg Hospital; Chambersburg   1,150
Empire Kosher Poultry Inc.; Mifflintown; poultry processing   1,006
Consolidated Rail Corp.; Altoona; freight hauling   1,000
York International Corp.; Waynesboro; refrigeration equipment   1,000
New Holland North America Inc.; Belleville; farm machinery   800
Norfolk Southern Corp.; Altoona; railroad freight hauling   800
Bon Secours Holy Family Regional Health System Inc.; Altoona   740
JLG Industries Inc.; Bedford; hoists, cranes, and monorails   733
Franklin County; Chambersburg; county government   700
Ingersoll-Rand Co.; Shippensburg; road construction/maintenance machinery   700
Smith Trucking Inc.; Roaring Spring; contract haulers   650
Pennsylvania Dept. of Corrections; Huntingdon   642
Advanced Glassfiber Yarns; Huntingdon; glass fibers, textile   600
Corning Inc.; Greencastle; warehousing   600
H. H. Brown Shoe Co.; Martinsburg; men's footwear   600
Hollidaysburg Veterans Home; Duncansville   600
Seton Co.; Saxton; leather tanning and finishing   600
St. Francis University; Loretto   600
Taylor Corp.; Waynesboro; invitations printing   600
Yokogawa Industrial Automation of America Inc.; Blairsville; process control instruments   600
Anchor Glass Container Corp.; Connellsville   591
Somerset Hospital Center for Health; Somerset   553
Nemacolin Woodlands Inc.; Farmington; resort hotel   550
North American Communications Inc.; Duncansville; envelopes   550
PPG Industries Inc.; Tipton; tempered glass   550
Consolidated Rail Corp.; Hollidaysburg; railroad car repair   520
Bear Air; Duncansville; air transportation   514
Appleton Papers Inc.; Roaring Spring; business forms   500
Cannondale Corp.; Bedford; tents   500
Chaparral Steel Co.; Petersburg; blast furnaces and steel mills   500
Pennsylvania Dept. of Corrections; Somerset   500
Pennsylvania State University; Altoona   500
Synertech Health System Solutions Inc.; Carlisle; administrative management   500
U.S. Foodservice Inc.; Altoona; grocery store   500
U.S. Veterans Hospital; Altoona   500

Wal-Mart Stores Inc.; Bedford; department stores   500
Wal-Mart Stores Inc.; Chambersburg; department stores 500
World Kitchen Inc.; Greencastle; pressed and blown glass   500

Pennsylvania 10th District

Northeast — Central Susquehanna Valley

Situated in the upper northeast corner of Pennsylvania, the 10th is home to a portion of the Pocono Mountains region, a popular honeymoon retreat known for its skiing, fishing, and golfing.

Redistricting in 2002 significantly expanded the 10th, which ceded Scranton to the neighboring 11th but stretched farther into east-central Pennsylvania to pick up four Central Susquehanna Valley counties—Montour, Northumberland, Union, and Snyder. While Scranton was once the 10th's major hub, the four new counties account for about 30 percent of the population. The district retained Williamsport, now its largest city, and Sunbury.

This region includes some of the state's best areas for lumber and agriculture. The latter is particularly prominent in Bradford County, which is among the state and national leaders in dairy production, and in Northumberland and Snyder Counties, known for their poultry. Tourism remains strong, especially during the summer months, when visitors come for the scenery and sporting in the eastern part of the district and for the Little League World Series held annually in Williamsport, in the western reaches. Pike County, which increased its population 66 percent in the 1990s, is rapidly filling up with early-rising commuters to New Jersey and New York City who prefer Pike's small-town setting, affordable land, and access to interstate highways.

The 10th has large swaths of rural, socially conservative heartland. With Scranton and its strong union ties no longer in the district, the district is more rural and Republican. Democrats still have a presence in areas such as Carbondale and Archbald in Lackawanna County and in parts of Northumberland County. But most voters are heavily inclined to support the GOP for federal and state offices. George W. Bush won the 10th by 16 percentage points in 2000.

Major Industry

Agriculture, manufacturing, tourism.

Notable

Little League baseball was founded in Williamsport in 1939.

Election Returns

	Republican		Democratic		Other	
President 2000	140,387	56.4%	100,754	40.5%	7,887	3.2%
House 2002	152,017	92.6%			12,142	7.4%

District Profile

Population   646,537

Total area (square miles)   6,689.3
   Land area (square miles)   6,584.3

Population per square mile   98.2

Counties (2000 population)

Bradford 62,761	Snyder 37,546
Lackawanna (pt.) 84,976	Sullivan 6,556
Luzerne (pt.) 63,000	Susquehanna 42,238
Lycoming (pt.) 72,940	Union 41,624
Montour 18,236	Wayne 47,722
Northumberland 94,556	Wyoming 28,080
Pike 46,302	

Cities and other areas over 10,000 (2000 population)
Back Mountain CDP (pt.)   22,237
Kingston borough   13,855
Sunbury   10,610
Williamsport   30,706

Race and Hispanic or Latino origin*
White   95.5%
Black or African American   1.9%
American Indian or Alaska Native   0.1%
Asian   0.5%
Native Hawaiian or other Pacific Islander   0.0%
Some other race   0.1%
Hispanic or Latino origin   1.4%
Two or more races   0.6%

As percentage of total population.

Ancestry*

Dutch 2.7%	Polish 7.2%
English 7.1%	Russian 1.2%
French 1.4%	Slovak 1.3%
German 18.5%	USA/American 5.0%
Irish 11.0%	Welsh 2.4%
Italian 7.4%	

As estimated percentage of total population.

Universities and colleges, 2000–2001 enrollment
Baptist Bible College and Seminary, Clarks Summit   920
Bucknell University, Lewisburg   3,592
College Misericordia, Dallas   1,798
Keystone College, La Plume   1,220
Lycoming College, Williamsport   1,396
Pennsylvania College of Technology, Williamsport   5,320
Pennsylvania State University-Wilkes-Barre, Lehman   877
Susquehanna University, Selinsgrove   1,824

Newspapers and circulation

	District circulation	Total circulation
Binghamton Press & Sun-Bulletin	2,432	58,790
Elmira Star Gazette	1,962	28,670
Middleton Times Herald Record	1,843	82,615
*New York Daily News**	1,172	723,155
New York Post	1,865	511,412
Scranton Times	41,509	97,130
Scranton Tribune	14,863	32,843
Shamokin News-Item	10,440	11,037
Stroudsburg Pocono Record	1,739	20,722
Sunbury Daily Item	22,750	23,219
*USA Today**	5,111	1,674,376
Wilkes-Barre Citizens' Voice	6,395	32,752

| *Wilkes-Barre Times Leader* | 12,491 | 44,338 |
| *Williamsport Sun-Gazette* | 11,947 | 28,062 |

See Sources and Explanations in the front of the volume.

Television stations and affiliations

Wilkes-Barre-Scranton	92%	WBRE	NBC
Wilkes-Barre-Scranton	92%	WILF	FOX
Wilkes-Barre-Scranton	92%	WNEP	ABC
Wilkes-Barre-Scranton	92%	WOLF	FOX
Wilkes-Barre-Scranton	92%	WQPX	PAX
Wilkes-Barre-Scranton	92%	WSWB	WB, UPN
Wilkes-Barre-Scranton	92%	WVIA	PBS
Wilkes-Barre-Scranton	92%	WYOU	CBS
New York	8%	WABC	ABC
New York	8%	WCBS	CBS
New York	8%	WEDW	PBS
New York	8%	WFME	Independent
New York	8%	WLIW	PBS
New York	8%	WLNY	Independent
New York	8%	WMBC	Independent
New York	8%	WNBC	NBC
New York	8%	WNET	PBS
New York	8%	WNJB	PBS
New York	8%	WNJN	PBS
New York	8%	WNJU	Telemundo
New York	8%	WNYE	PBS
New York	8%	WNYW	FOX
New York	8%	WPIX	WB
New York	8%	WPXN	PAX
New York	8%	WRNN	Independent
New York	8%	WTBY	Independent
New York	8%	WWOR	UPN
New York	8%	WXTV	Univision

Cable systems and subscribers

Adams CATV   41,361
Adelphia   33,025
Beaver Valley Cable Co.   1,567
Blue Ridge   45,033
Cablevision   830
CATV Services Inc.   11,481
Charter   2,283
Eagles Mere/Laporte Cablevision   590
Retel TV Cable Co.   4,158
Service Electric Cablevision   28,437
Service Electric Co.   6,619
Suscom   19,068
Time Warner   7,029

Businesses and other major employers

Geisinger Medical Center; Danville   5,100
Procter and Gamble Paper Products Co.; Mehoopany; towels, napkins, tissue paper   3,150
Wood-Mode Inc.; Kreamer; kitchen cabinets   1,775
ConAgra Grocery Products Co.; Milton; meatpacking plants   1,700
Pennsylvania College of Technology; Williamsport   1,510
Bucknell University; Lewisburg   1,500
E. I. Du Pont De Nemours and Co.; Towanda; electrical connectors and terminals   1,300
Robert Packer Hospital Inc.; Sayre   1,270

Osram Sylvania Inc.; Towanda; chemical preparations   1,200
PPL Electric Utilities Corp.; Wilkes-Barre; electric power generation   1,200
ConAgra Foods Inc.; Milton; meatpacking plants   1,100
Taylor Packing Co; Wyalusing; beef products   1,000
Williamsport Hospital and Medical Center; Williamsport   1,000
Geisinger Wyoming Valley Medical Center; Wilkes-Barre   825
Metropolitan Life Insurance Co.; Clarks Summit   825
Brodart Co.; Williamsport; books   800
Divine Providence Hospital of Sisters of Christian Charity; Williamsport   800
Shop-Vac Corp.; Williamsport; industrial vacuum cleaners   800
Evangelical Community Hospital; Lewisburg   750
Pennsylvania Dept. of Corrections; Waymart   700
Wayne Memorial Health Systems Inc.; Honesdale; health services consultant   700
Wundies Enterprises Inc.; Williamsport; undergarments   700
Offset Paperback Manufacturer Inc.; Dallas; book publishing   675
Leroy Township Supervisor; Canton; city government   620
Weis Markets Inc.; Sunbury; supermarkets   600
U.S. Bureau of Prisons; Lewisburg   579
Ingersoll-Rand Co.; Athens; keys   550
Pennsylvania House Inc.; Lewisburg; home furniture   540
Masonite Corp.; Towanda; hardboard   538
Merck and Co. Inc.; Riverside; medicinal chemicals   525
Lockheed Martin Corp.; Archbald; industrial, special purpose electron tubes   500
Pennsylvania Dept. of Public Welfare; Danville   500
Pennsylvania Dept. of Public Welfare; Clarks Summit   500
Sanmina-SCI Corp.; Lewisburg; commutators, electronic   500
Woodloch Pines Inc.; Hawley; resort hotel   500
Yorktowne Inc.; Mifflinburg; kitchen cabinets   500

Pennsylvania 11th District

Northeast — Scranton, Wilkes-Barre

Since the turn of the century, the health of the 11th District has been inextricably linked to the production, manufacturing, and sale of coal. Demand for the district's anthracite coal peaked in the 1910s and 1920s. Since then, a few cities in this district have disappeared with the long decline of the coal industry and the rise of oil and natural gas. Centralia, site of a burning underground mine, turned into a ghost town after a federally ordered evacuation.

Other towns, such as Jim Thorpe and Wilkes-Barre, have been more prosperous. Jim Thorpe, given that name in 1954 for the decathlon Olympic gold medalist who is buried in town, was a haven for millionaires and has maintained its historic charm as a preservation project of the Interior

Department. Economic development needs along with an elderly population help drive the push for federal dollars.

The 11th has a decided but not monolithic Democratic lean, the result of a large Irish population and a strong union tradition. Had the reconfigured 11th existed in the 2000 election, Al Gore would have won it by 10 percentage points. Redistricting in 2002 moved Scranton (Lackawanna County) from the neighboring 10th into the 11th, making it even more Democratic. Democrats also do well in Luzerne County, with strong showings in Wilkes-Barre and in smaller cities to the north and east, but not at a level commensurate with their wide registration advantage in the county.

The decline of coal and an investment in technology-driven businesses have helped the GOP, which does well in Columbia County and has a slight edge in voter registration and electoral performance in Monroe County, a fast-growing area in the Poconos where many newcomers commute via Interstate 80 to their jobs in New Jersey and New York.

Major Industry

Manufacturing, retail trade, tourism.

Notable

Berwick prides itself on its high school football team, a perennial power in Pennsylvania that has produced several professional players.

Election Returns

	Republican		Democratic		Other	
President 2000	101,629	43.1%	127,140	53.9%	6,983	3.0%
House 2002	71,543	42.4%	93,758	55.6%	3,314	2.0%

District Profile

Population 646,209

Total area (square miles) 2,248.6
   Land area (square miles) 2,217.9

Population per square mile 291.4

Counties (2000 population)
Carbon 58,802
Columbia 64,151
Lackawanna (pt.) 128,319
Luzerne (pt.) 256,250
Monroe 138,687

Cities and other areas over 10,000 (2000 population)
Berwick borough 10,774
Bloomsburg town 12,375
Dunmore borough 14,018
Hazleton 23,329
Mountain Top CDP 15,269
Nanticoke 10,955
Scranton 76,415
Wilkes-Barre 43,123

Race and Hispanic or Latino origin*
White 93.3%
Black or African American 2.5%
American Indian or Alaska Native 0.1%
Asian 0.7%
Native Hawaiian or other Pacific Islander 0.0%
Some other race 0.1%
Hispanic or Latino origin 2.5%
Two or more races 0.7%

As percentage of total population.

Ancestry*

Dutch	2.5%	Polish	11.4%
English	4.5%	Russian	1.7%
German	14.5%	Slovak	3.1%
Irish	13.2%	Ukrainian	1.1%
Italian	11.9%	USA/American	2.8%
Lithuanian	1.5%	Welsh	2.8%

As estimated percentage of total population.

Universities and colleges, 2000–2001 enrollment
Bloomsburg University, Bloomsburg 7,548
East Stroudsburg University, East Stroudsburg 5,811
King's College, Wilkes-Barre 2,233
Lackawanna Junior College, Scranton 877
Luzerne County Community College, Nanticoke 5,920
Marywood University, Scranton 2,859
Northampton County Area Community College-Monroe, Tannersville 799
Pennsylvania State University, Hazleton 1,377
Pennsylvania State University-Worthington Scranton, Dunmore 1,716
University of Scranton, Scranton 4,615
Wilkes University, Wilkes-Barre 3,570

Newspapers and circulation

	District circulation	Total circulation
Allentown Morning Call	7,264	126,651
Hazelton Standard-Speaker	17,329	21,380
Lehighton Times News	9,103	13,871
*New York Daily News**	1,286	723,155
New York Post	4,180	511,412
Philadelphia Inquirer	1,244	371,901
Scranton Times	57,169	95,708
Scranton Tribune	17,809	32,843
Stroudsburg Pocono Record	18,437	20,722
*USA Today**	3,394	1,674,376
Wilkes-Barre Citizens' Voice	26,139	32,752
Wilkes-Barre Times Leader	31,729	44,338

See Sources and Explanations in the front of the volume.

Television stations and affiliations

Wilkes-Barre-Scranton	100%	WBRE	NBC
Wilkes-Barre-Scranton	100%	WILF	FOX
Wilkes-Barre-Scranton	100%	WNEP	ABC
Wilkes-Barre-Scranton	100%	WOLF	FOX
Wilkes-Barre-Scranton	100%	WQPX	PAX
Wilkes-Barre-Scranton	100%	WSWB	WB, UPN
Wilkes-Barre-Scranton	100%	WVIA	PBS
Wilkes-Barre-Scranton	100%	WYOU	CBS

Cable systems and subscribers
Adelphia 87,715
Blue Ridge 29,352
Gans 11,337
Service Electric Cablevision 15,318
Service Electric Co. 19,470

Military installations, September 2001

Tobyhanna Army Depot, Scranton   3,505
Scranton Army Ammunition Plant, Scranton   383

Businesses and other major employers

Mercy Hospital of Scranton Inc.; Scranton   2,554
Allied Services Institute of Rehabilitation Medicine; Scranton   2,500
Wilkes-Barre General Hospital; Wilkes-Barre   1,550
U.S. Veterans Hospital; Wilkes-Barre   1,500
United Parcel Service Inc.; Stroudsburg; parcel delivery   1,500
United Parcel Service Inc.; Taylor; parcel delivery   1,500
Hospital Service Assn. of Northeastern Pennsylvania; Wilkes-Barre; group hospitalization   1,475
Aventis Pasteur; Swiftwater; biological products   1,200
FleetBoston Financial; Scranton; commercial bank   1,200
Pocono Medical Center; East Stroudsburg   1,200
Transcontinental Refrigerated Lines Inc.; Pittston; refrigerated transport   1,200
Coca-Cola Inc.; Pittston; soft drinks   1,198
U.S. Social Security Admin.; Wilkes-Barre   1,000
University of Scranton; Scranton   982
Roadway Express Inc.; Tannersville; trucking terminals   950
Camelback Ski Corp.; Tannersville; ski instruction   900
Luzerne County Community College; Nanticoke   900
Bloomsburg University of Pennsylvania Inc.; Bloomsburg   800
Excel Corp.; Hazleton; meatpacking plants   800
Hartford Fire Insurance Co.; Lehighton; fire, marine, casualty insurance   800
Prudential Trust Co.; Scranton; investment advice   800
Wise Foods Inc.; Berwick; snacks   800
Moses Taylor Hospital Inc.; Scranton   787
Star-Kist Foods Inc.; Bloomsburg; dog food   770
H. J. Heinz Co.; Bloomsburg; canned specialties   750
PPL Susquehanna; Berwick; electric power generation   735
Fairchild Semiconductor Corp.; Mountain Top; solid state electronic devices   700
Lackawanna County; Scranton; county government   700
Marywood University; Scranton   700
Pocono Palace Inc.; Scotrun; resort hotel   700
Ski Shawnee Inc.; Shawnee On Delaware; ski lodge   700
Thomson Corp.; Scranton; greeting cards   700
Magee Rieter Automotive Systems; Bloomsburg   694
East Stroudsburg University of Pennsylvania; East Stroudsburg   693
Mercy Hospital of Wilkes-Barre Pennsylvania; Wilkes-Barre   649
Kovatch Mobile Equipment Corp.; Nesquehoning; motor vehicle chassis   625
Pocono Mountain School District; Swiftwater   609
Allied Health Care Services Inc.; Wilkes-Barre; individual and family services   600
Carter Footwear Inc.; Wilkes-Barre; shoes   600
City of Scranton; Scranton; city government   600
Gnaden Huetten Memorial Hospital; Lehighton   600
May Department Stores Co.; Wilkes-Barre   600

Northeastern Pennsylvania Health Corp.; Hazleton; hospital   600
Warner Advanced Media Operation; Olyphant; compact laser discs   600
Berwick Hospital Center Inc.; Berwick   596
Pennsylvania Dept. of Public Welfare; White Haven   585
Bemis Co.; Hazleton; packaging paper   565
Laird Technologies Inc.; Delaware Water Gap; stamping metal   550
Wal-Mart Stores Inc.; Dickson City; department stores   550
Kraft Foods Inc.; Wilkes-Barre; management services   520
Frank Martz Coach Co.; East Stroudsburg; bus transportation   517
Harcourt Learning Direct Inc.; Scranton; correspondence school   511
Pennsylvania National Guard; Kingston   510
U.S. Postal Service; Scranton   510
Bloomsburg Hospital; Bloomsburg   500
First Union Arena at Casey Plaza; Wilkes-Barre; convention services   500
JC Penney Corp.; Mountain Top; telemarketing   500
Hazleton-St. Joseph Medical Center; Hazleton   500
King's College; Wilkes-Barre   500
Luzerne County; Wilkes-Barre; county government   500
Prudential Asset Management Co. Inc.; Moosic; life insurance   500
Sears Roebuck and Co. Inc.; Wilkes-Barre; department stores   500
Super Market Service Corp.; Scranton; grocery store   500
U.S. Postal Service; Wilkes-Barre   500

Pennsylvania 12th District

Southwest — Johnstown

Described as "an upside-down Chinese dragon," the strangely contorted 12th hopscotches in southwestern Pennsylvania across nine counties, eight of which are shared with other districts. A once-booming center of coal, steel, and iron production, this area is diversifying to escape economic distress and industrial loss.

The 12th has been the unfortunate victim of floods that devastated Johnstown (Cambria County), the district's largest city, three times in history. The Great Flood of 1889, the most severe, destroyed the town and killed 2,200 people. Again in 1936 and 1977, floods took lives and caused significant damage. The area just celebrated its 25th anniversary of being flood-free, featuring an advertising campaign saying, "The flood's over, come on back!" The 1980s recession also had a devastating effect on the economy. The coal and steel industries declined and the unemployment rate skyrocketed to more than 27 percent.

More recently, the district has bounced back, in part by attracting some high-tech industry and a number of defense and research firms. Capitalizing on past hardships, the Johnstown Flood Museum also draws tourists to the area, and the city's large health care base has remained stable. The unemployment rate in Johnstown has been in the single digits since early 1994, though it generally exceeds the national rate.

This district has been a Democratic stronghold since the New Deal, and Republican mapmakers in 2002 redistricting packed Democrats into the 12th to give the GOP an edge in adjacent districts. As with other towns in the state with an industrial past and an aging population, Johnstown wants federal help, but many voters are more socially conservative than the national Democratic Party. While George W. Bush lost both Cambria and Washington Counties in 2000, he received the highest vote share of any GOP presidential candidate there since Richard Nixon in 1972.

Major Industry
Manufacturing, service, health care.

Notable
The National Drug Intelligence Center in Johnstown tracks illegal drugs.

Election Returns

	Republican		Democratic		Other	
President 2000	105,451	43.8%	131,960	54.8%	3,595	1.5%
House 2002	44,818	26.5%	124,201	73.5%	9	

District Profile

Population   646,079

Total area (square miles)   2,783.0
   Land area (square miles)   2,753.5

Population per square mile   234.6

Counties (2000 population)
   Allegheny (pt.)   5,831
   Armstrong (pt.)   41,762
   Cambria (pt.)   129,345
   Fayette (pt.)   116,328
   Greene   40,672
   Indiana (pt.)   22,719
   Somerset (pt.)   29,930
   Washington (pt.)   103,027
   Westmoreland (pt.)   156,465

Cities and other areas over 10,000 (2000 population)
   Indiana borough (pt.)   11,325
   Johnstown   23,906
   Lower Burrell   12,608
   New Kensington   14,701
   Uniontown   12,422
   Washington   15,268

Race and Hispanic or Latino origin*
   White   94.9%
   Black or African American   3.3%
   American Indian or Alaska Native   0.1%
   Asian   0.3%
   Native Hawaiian or other Pacific Islander   0.0%
   Some other race   0.1%
   Hispanic or Latino origin   0.6%
   Two or more races   0.7%

   *As percentage of total population.

Ancestry*

Dutch	1.8%	Italian	9.2%
English	6.3%	Polish	6.6%
French	1.1%	Scotch-Irish	1.8%
German	17.2%	Scottish	1.2%
Hungarian	1.5%	Slovak	4.5%
Irish	9.9%	USA/American	3.7%

*As estimated percentage of total population.

Universities and colleges, 2000–2001 enrollment
   California University of Pennsylvania, California   5,899
   Cambria County Area Community College, Johnston   1,050
   Indiana University of Pennsylvania, Indiana   13,410
   Laurel Business Institute, Uniontown   249
   Mount Aloysius College, Cresson   1,297
   Pennsylvania State University, New Kensington   888
   Pennsylvania State University-Fayette, Uniontown   1,127
   St. Vincent College, Latrobe   1,206
   University of Pittsburgh, Johnstown   3,031
   Washington and Jefferson College, Washington   1,241
   Waynesburg College, Waynesburg   1,616

Newspapers and circulation

	District circulation	Total circulation
Altoona Mirror	1,253	31,717
Connellsville Courier	6,743	10,225
Greensburg Tribune Review	18,850	86,808
Indiana Gazette	4,957	15,563
Johnstown Tribune-Democrat	35,361	42,734
Kittanning Leader Times	3,577	10,014
Monessen Valley Independent	13,065	15,270
New Kensington Valley News Dispatch	16,080	31,270
Pittsburgh Post-Gazette	11,544	240,791
Somerset Daily American	5,459	13,431
Uniontown Herald Standard	19,682	28,285
*USA Today**	3,084	1,674,376
Washington Observer Reporter	16,126	36,673

*See Sources and Explanations in the front of the volume.

Television stations and affiliations

Pittsburgh	73%	KDKA	CBS
Pittsburgh	73%	WCWB	WB
Pittsburgh	73%	WGPT	PBS
Pittsburgh	73%	WNPA	UPN
Pittsburgh	73%	WNPB	PBS
Pittsburgh	73%	WPCB	Independent
Pittsburgh	73%	WPGH	FOX
Pittsburgh	73%	WPXI	NBC
Pittsburgh	73%	WQED	PBS
Pittsburgh	73%	WQEX	PBS
Pittsburgh	73%	WTAE	ABC
Pittsburgh	73%	WTOV	NBC
Pittsburgh	73%	WWCP	FOX
Johnstown-Altoona	27%	WATM	ABC
Johnstown-Altoona	27%	WJAC	NBC
Johnstown-Altoona	27%	WKBS	Independent
Johnstown-Altoona	27%	WPSX	PBS
Johnstown-Altoona	27%	WTAJ	CBS

Cable systems and subscribers
Adelphia   43,901
Armstrong   18,751
Bentleyville Telephone Co.   1,377
Charter   53,811
Comcast   64,731
Laurel Highland TV Co.   1,733

Businesses and other major employers
Bestform Group Inc.; Johnstown; lingerie   2,000
Conemaugh Valley Memorial Hospital; Johnstown   1,786
Latrobe Area Hospital Inc.; Latrobe   1,470
Washington Hospital; Washington   1,435
University of Pittsburgh Medical Center Lee Regional; Johnstown   1,300
National Envelope Corp.; Scottdale; printing   1,200
Monongahela Valley Hospital Inc.; Monongahela   1,000
SuperValu Inc.; Belle Vernon; food supplier   1,000
Uniontown Hospital Inc.; Uniontown   900
Indiana Hospital; Indiana   900
TeleTech Holdings Inc.; Uniontown; personal service agents   900
Pennsylvania Dept. of Public Welfare; Ebensburg   875
Johnstown America Corp.; Johnstown; freight cars and equipment   800
Citizens General Hospital; New Kensington   800
Seven Springs Farm Inc.; Champion; ski lodge   800
Timken Latrobe Steel; Latrobe; tool and die steel   800
Alcoa Inc.; New Kensington; aluminum   750
Corning Inc.; Charleroi; ceramic fiber   750
California University of Pennsylvania; California   747
Pennsylvania Dept. of Corrections; Waynesburg   714
Pennsylvania Dept. of Public Welfare; Torrance   660
Allegheny Ludlum Corp.; Leechburg; steel sheets/strips   625
Aramark Services Inc.; Indiana; contract food services   600
Concurrent Technologies Corp.; Johnstown; consulting engineer   600
Conemaugh Valley Memorial Hospital; Davidsville   600
Frick Hospital; Mount Pleasant   586
RAG Cumberland Resources Corp.; Waynesburg; coal mining   529
Washington County; Washington; county government   522
Invensys Metering Systems Inc.; Uniontown; water meters   500
Westmoreland Health System Inc.; Mount Pleasant; medical labs   500

Pennsylvania 13th District

East — northeast Philadelphia, part of Montgomery County suburbs

Nearly evenly divided between Montgomery County and northeast Philadelphia, the 13th combines white-collar suburbia with a portion of the city known for blue-collar grit. While registration is nearly evenly split between the parties, it belies the advantage Democrats have enjoyed in recent statewide and federal races. *(See map p. 773.)*

Prescription drugs and health care have become prevalent issues in the district thanks to a large senior citizen population in northeast Philadelphia. Education is drawing more attention, as Philadelphia public schools are in worse shape than Montgomery County schools. In the first test of the redrawn district's leanings, public housing has been a subject of debate—many residents are concerned about how federal housing assistance is being administered.

Numerous shopping centers, strip malls, and small businesses are housed in northeast Philadelphia, where a riverfront redevelopment project has sparked hopes of stimulating the 13th's dragging economy. This area votes Democratic, but not monolithically so.

Though the GOP still runs well at the local level in Montgomery County, Democrats have made major inroads here in state and federal races. In a dozen years Montgomery went from voting Republican for president by 22 percentage points to backing Al Gore by 10 points in 2000. Close-in Abington and Upper Dublin (shared with the 8th) now vote Democratic for president, while Republicans run well in northwestern Montgomery, in areas such as Upper and Lower Salford, Upper and Lower Frederick, and New Hanover.

Major Industry
Health and business services, chemicals.

Notable
Pennypack Park is known as the green heart of northeast Philadelphia.

Election Returns

	Republican		Democratic		Other	
President 2000	117,773	42.1%	155,903	55.7%	5,972	2.1%
House 2002	100,295	47.3%	107,945	50.9%	3,627	1.7%

District Profile

Population   646,167

Total area (square miles)   250.9
   Land area (square miles)   248.1

Population per square mile   2,604.5

Counties (2000 population)
   Montgomery (pt.)   340,756
   Philadelphia (pt.)   305,411

Cities and other areas over 10,000 (2000 population)
   Horsham CDP   14,779
   Lansdale borough   16,071
   Montgomeryville CDP   12,031
   Philadelphia (pt.)   305,411
   Willow Grove CDP (pt.)   12,464

Race and Hispanic or Latino origin*
   White   85.6%
   Black or African American   5.9%
   American Indian or Alaska Native   0.1%
   Asian   4.1%
   Native Hawaiian or other Pacific Islander   0.0%
   Some other race   0.1%

Hispanic or Latino origin   3.1%
Two or more races   1.0%

As percentage of total population.

Ancestry*

English	5.9%	Russian	2.6%
French	1.1%	Scotch-Irish	1.1%
German	15.5%	Scottish	1.1%
Irish	19.5%	Ukrainian	1.5%
Italian	10.4%	USA/American	2.7%
Polish	5.8%		

As estimated percentage of total population.

Universities and colleges, 2000–2001 enrollment

Biblical Theological Seminary, Hatfield   278
DPT Business School, Philadelphia   1,126
Gwynedd Mercy College, Gwynedd Valley   1,913
Holy Family College, Philadelphia   2,530
Lansdale School of Business, North Wales   449
Lincoln Technical Institute, Philadelphia   283
Manor Junior College, Jenkintown   684
Montgomery County Community College, Blue Bell 8,922
Pennsylvania State University, Abington   3,049

Newspapers and circulation

	District circulation	Total circulation
Doylestown Intelligencer	10,611	44,991
Greater Philadelphia Newspapers	10,564	152,790
Lansdale Reporter	12,399	18,554
Norristown Times Herald	3,051	17,226
Philadelphia Daily News	19,311	151,682
Philadelphia Inquirer	65,298	371,901
*Philadelphia Tribune**	6,902	27,991
Pottstown Mercury	2,109	24,659
*USA Today**	5,307	1,674,376

See Sources and Explanations in the front of the volume.

Television stations and affiliations

Philadelphia	100%	KYW	CBS
Philadelphia	100%	WBPH	Independent
Philadelphia	100%	WCAU	NBC
Philadelphia	100%	WFMZ	Independent
Philadelphia	100%	WHYY	PBS
Philadelphia	100%	WLVT	PBS
Philadelphia	100%	WMGM	NBC
Philadelphia	100%	WNJS	PBS
Philadelphia	100%	WNJT	PBS
Philadelphia	100%	WPHL	WB
Philadelphia	100%	WPPX	PAX
Philadelphia	100%	WPSG	UPN
Philadelphia	100%	WPVI	ABC
Philadelphia	100%	WTVE	Independent
Philadelphia	100%	WTXF	FOX
Philadelphia	100%	WWAC	Independent
Philadelphia	100%	WYBE	PBS

Cable systems and subscribers

Comcast   43,321

Military installations, September 2001

Willow Grove Naval Air Station, Willow Grove   2,284

Businesses and other major employers

Merck and Co. Inc.; Hatfield; pharmaceuticals   14,000
Crown Beverage Packaging Inc.; Philadelphia; metal cans   12,000
Merck and Co. Inc.; West Point; pharmaceuticals   10,000
Albert Einstein Healthcare Network Hospital; Glenside   5,251
Abington Memorial Hospital Inc.; Abington   3,900
Unisys Corp.; Blue Bell; systems integration services   3,400
Complete Care Services; Horsham; nursing care facilities   3,000
MSSC Co.; Glenside; radar systems   2,800
City of Philadelphia; Philadelphia; fire dept.   2,500
City of Philadelphia; Philadelphia; correctional institutions   2,012
GlaxoSmithKline; Conshohocken; medical labs   2,000
Fox Chase Cancer Center; Philadelphia   1,800
Holy Redeemer Hospital and Medical Center Inc.; Jenkintown   1,600
Frankford Hospital; Philadelphia   1,500
Clemens Family Corp.; Hatfield; pork products   1,450
Packaging Coordinators Inc.; Philadelphia; packaging and labeling services   1,400
Jeanes Hospital; Philadelphia   1,340
Philadelphia Newspapers Inc.; Conshohocken   1,300
Nazareth Hospital; Philadelphia   1,250
Defense Logistics Agency; Philadelphia   1,200
Prudential Financial; Fort Washington; life insurance   1,200
Harleysville Mutual Insurance Co. Inc.; Harleysville; life insurance   1,100
Rohm and Haas Co.; Spring House; commercial physical research   1,100
Fleet National Bank; Horsham; commercial bank   1,000
GMAC Mortgage Corp.; Horsham; mortgage bankers   1,000
Madlyn and Leonard Abramson Center for Jewish Life; North Wales; extended care facility   1,000
NCO Group Inc.; Horsham; adjustment and collection services   1,000
SPS Technologies Inc.; Jenkintown; metal screws   1,000
Johnson and Johnson; Spring House; commercial medical research   900
McNeil Consumer Healthcare Co.; Fort Washington; pharmaceuticals   900
Manufacturers Alliance Insurance Co.; Blue Bell; workers' compensation insurance   896
Medical Management Systems Inc.; Horsham; personal service agents   850
Siemens Moore Process Automation Inc.; Spring House; process control instruments   810
Aetna Inc.; Blue Bell; medical service plans   800
Central Montgomery Medical Center; Lansdale   730
BISYS Group Inc.; Ambler; data processing   700
Tenet Healthcare Corp. Hospital; Elkins Park   700
New Seasons Assisted Living Communities Inc.; Blue Bell; community development   684
Northeastern Hospital of Philadelphia; Philadelphia   650
Webcraft; Chalfont; printing paper   650

R&B Inc.; Colmar; automotive parts   641

VerticalNet Inc.; Horsham; computer graphics service
629

BISYS Group Inc.; Fort Washington; pension and
retirement plan consultants   600

Fox Chase Cancer Center; Jenkintown   600

Weight Watchers of Philadelphia Inc.; Fort Washington;
diet center   600

Tuscan/Lehigh Dairies; Lansdale; fluid milk   584

BAE Systems Aerospace Electronics Inc.; Lansdale;
defense systems   530

Dietz and Watson Inc.; Philadelphia; beef products
500

Henkels and McCoy Inc.; Blue Bell; electric power line
construction   500

Jet Plastica Industries Inc.; Hatfield; plastics molding
500

Macy's East Inc.; North Wales; department stores   500

Merck and Co. Inc.; Blue Bell; commercial medical
research   500

Penn Mutual Life Insurance Co.; Horsham   500

Reimbursement Technologies Inc.; Conshohocken;
bookkeeping service   500

Greene Tweed and Co. Inc.; Kulpsville; gaskets and
sealing devices   500

Pennsylvania 14th District

Pittsburgh and some close-in suburbs

The 14th, which includes all of Pittsburgh and some of
its close-in suburbs, has undergone an economic transformation while maintaining its Democratic tradition and ethnic
character. *(See map p. 773.)*

Medical centers and universities, parks, skyscrapers, and
high-tech industry have replaced the smoke stacks from the
steel industry once nestled between the Allegheny, Monongahela, and Ohio Rivers. A thriving, corporate downtown has
grown up in the "Golden Triangle," where the Allegheny and
Monongahela Rivers meet. Major League Baseball's Pittsburgh Pirates played their first game in their new stadium,
PNC Park, in April 2001, and the National Football League's
Pittsburgh Steelers also play in a new stadium, Heinz Field,
which opened in 2001.

Towns such as Monroeville and Penn Hills, only parts
of which are in the district, have seen commercial development and some technology jobs move in, while others
have languished. Many of Pittsburgh's neighborhoods, such
as Bloomfield and Lawrenceville, retain their ethnic roots—
mainly German, Italian, Irish, and Polish. Squirrel Hill long
has been the center of the city's Jewish population.

Even with the diversification of the 14th's economy, the
district retains strong Democratic roots. Union strength
translates into lopsided Democratic margins, and Democrats
far outnumber Republicans, whose outposts in the region
are found mostly in the neighboring 4th and 18th Districts.
Pittsburgh is staunchly Democratic, and the party's candidates also rack up big margins in Wilkinsburg, a heavily
black area that abuts Pittsburgh to the east, and McKeesport,
West Mifflin, and Duquesne, south of the city. Al Gore took
73 percent of the Pittsburgh vote and 69.6 percent of the

district vote in 2000. Democrat Edward G. Rendell took 67
percent in Pittsburgh in the 2002 gubernatorial election.

Major Industry

Banking, government, health care.

Notable

Artist Andy Warhol was born in Pittsburgh; in the 1980s
a bad economy forced Clairton, setting for the movie *The Deer
Hunter,* to furlough its police and turn off streetlights.

Election Returns

	Republican		Democratic		Other	
President 2000	74,085	28.1%	183,640	69.6%	6,007	2.3%
House 2002			123,323	100.0%	89	

District Profile

Population   646,196

Total area (square miles)   168.5
  Land area (square miles)   160.4

Population per square mile   4,028.7

Counties (2000 population)
  Allegheny (pt.)   646,196

Cities and other areas over 10,000 (2000 population)
  Baldwin borough (pt.)   13,416
  McKeesport   24,040
  Munhall borough   12,264
  North Versailles CDP (pt.)   10,468
  Penn Hills CDP (pt.)   35,864
  Pittsburgh   334,563
  West Mifflin borough   22,464
  Wilkinsburg borough   19,196

Race and Hispanic or Latino origin*
  White   72.9%
  Black or African American   22.5%
  American Indian or Alaska Native   0.2%
  Asian   1.7%
  Native Hawaiian or other Pacific Islander   0.0%
  Some other race   0.3%
  Hispanic or Latino origin   1.1%
  Two or more races   1.4%

As percentage of total population.

Ancestry*

English 4.1%	Polish 6.2%
German 15.5%	Russian 1.2%
Hungarian 1.4%	Scotch-Irish 1.1%
Irish 12.1%	Slovak 3.1%
Italian 9.8%	USA/American 2.0%

As estimated percentage of total population.

Universities and colleges, 2000–2001 enrollment
  Art Institute, Pittsburgh   2,497
  Bradford School, Pittsburgh   479
  Carlow College, Pittsburgh   1,925
  Carnegie Mellon University, Pittsburgh   8,514
  Chatham College, Pittsburgh   1,002

Community College of Allegheny County, Pittsburgh
15,556
Computer Tech, Pittsburgh   1,296
Duffs Business Institute, Pittsburgh   581
Duquesne University, Pittsburgh   9,667
ICM School of Business and Medical Careers, Pittsburgh
675
Median School of Allied Health Careers, Pittsburgh
272
Pennsylvania Institute of Culinary Arts, Pittsburgh
1,599
Pennsylvania State University, McKeesport   901
Pittsburgh Institute of Aeronautics, West Mifflin   441
Pittsburgh Technical Institute, Pittsburgh   1,861
Pittsburgh Theological Seminary, Pittsburgh   333
Point Park College, Pittsburgh   2,816
Sawyer School, Pittsburgh   675
Triangle Tech, Pittsburgh   234
University of Pittsburgh, Pittsburgh   26,329
Western School of Health and Business Careers,
Pittsburgh   474

Newspapers and circulation

	District circulation	Total circulation
Greensburg Tribune Review	10,110	86,808
McKeesport Daily News	13,296	20,756
Pittsburgh Post-Gazette	87,788	240,791
*USA Today**	3,946	1,674,376

See Sources and Explanations in the front of the volume.

Television stations and affiliations

Pittsburgh	100%	KDKA	CBS
Pittsburgh	100%	WCWB	WB
Pittsburgh	100%	WGPT	PBS
Pittsburgh	100%	WNPA	UPN
Pittsburgh	100%	WNPB	PBS
Pittsburgh	100%	WPCB	Independent
Pittsburgh	100%	WPGH	FOX
Pittsburgh	100%	WPXI	NBC
Pittsburgh	100%	WQED	PBS
Pittsburgh	100%	WQEX	PBS
Pittsburgh	100%	WTAE	ABC
Pittsburgh	100%	WTOV	NBC
Pittsburgh	100%	WWCP	FOX

Cable systems and subscribers
Adelphia   32,366
Comcast   178,419

Military installations, September 2001
Pittsburgh International Airport Air National Guard
Station, Coraopolis   1,453
Pittsburgh International Airport Air Force Reserve,
Coraopolis   1,359
Naval and Marine Corps Reserve Center, Pittsburgh
316

Businesses and other major employers
Highmark Inc.; Pittsburgh; medical service plans
11,000
Mellon Bank; Pittsburgh; commercial trust company
10,200

University of Pittsburgh; Pittsburgh   8,793
PNC Mortgage Bank National Assn.; Pittsburgh;
mortgage bankers   8,000
Salvation Army; Pittsburgh; individual and family
services   7,998
Allegheny County; Pittsburgh; county government
7,013
Allegheny General Hospital; Pittsburgh; extended care
facility   5,000
University of Pittsburgh; Pittsburgh   5,000
Philadelphia Health and Education Corp. Hospital;
Pittsburgh   4,000
Western Pennsylvania Hospital; Pittsburgh   2,800
Bechtel Bettis Inc.; West Mifflin; commercial physical
research   2,771
St. Francis Medical Center; Pittsburgh   2,591
Bombardier Transportation Systems; West Mifflin;
switching and terminal services   2,500
Mercy Hospital of Pittsburgh; Pittsburgh   2,450
Art Institute International; Pittsburgh   2,400
City of Pittsburgh; Pittsburgh; city government   2,304
Bechtel Bettis Inc.; Pittsburgh; economic research
2,100
Anthony F. Jeselnik; Pittsburgh; law office   2,000
Federated Investors Management Co.; Pittsburgh;
open-ended management investment   2,000
University of Pittsburgh Medical Center Shadyside;
Pittsburgh   1,987
Duquesne University of Holy Ghost; Pittsburgh   1,899
U.S. Veterans Hospital; Pittsburgh   1,840
Magee-Women's Hospital; Pittsburgh   1,800
Pittsburgh Children's Hospital; Pittsburgh   1,800
U.S. Steel Corp.; West Mifflin; steel slabs   1,800
U.S. Steel Corp.; Clairton; blast furnaces and steel mills
1,700
U.S. Steel Corp.; Pittsburgh; blast furnaces and steel
mills   1,700
Diversified Services Inc.; Pittsburgh; individual and
family services   1,600
H. J. Heinz Co.; Pittsburgh food products   1,500
Marathon Oil Corp.; Dravosburg; blast furnaces and steel
mills   1,500
May Department Stores Co.; Pittsburgh   1,500
PPG Industries Inc.; Pittsburgh; building glass   1,500
University of Pittsburgh Medical Center Presbyterian;
Pittsburgh   1,500
University of Pittsburgh Medical Center; McKeesport
1,400
Alcoa Inc.; Pittsburgh; aluminum sheets/strips   1,300
Marathon Oil Corp.; Houston; crude petroleum
production   1,300
PG Publishing Co.; Pittsburgh; newspaper   1,300
Avon Inc.; Pittsburgh; licensing and permits for retail
trade   1,000
Marathon Oil Corp.; Braddock; steel foundries   1,000
Verizon Communications Inc.; Pittsburgh; telephone
communication   1,000
Verizon Pennsylvania Inc.; Pittsburgh; personal service
agents   1,000
West Penn Allegheny Health Systems Inc.; Pittsburgh;
management services   1,000
Duquesne Light Co.; Pittsburgh; electric power
generation   900

Central Property Services Inc.; Pittsburgh; industrial, commercial cleaning services   850

Kvaerner U.S. Inc.; Pittsburgh; engineering services   850

DaimlerChrysler Rail Systems Inc.; Pittsburgh; railroad equipment   800

General Nutrition Corp.; Pittsburgh; vitamin/food stores   800

PNC Bank National Assn.; Pittsburgh; commercial trust company   800

Dollar Bank; Pittsburgh; federal savings banks   796

Pennsylvania Dept. of Corrections; Pittsburgh   725

General Motors Corp.; West Mifflin; motor vehicles and car bodies   700

McKeesport Area School District; McKeesport   700

Carnegie Institute; Pittsburgh; museum   688

FreeMarkets Inc.; Pittsburgh; software development   660

Giant Eagle Inc.; Pittsburgh; grocery store   650

Com-Net Critical Communications Inc.; Pittsburgh; communications specialization   625

Hilton Hotels Corp.; Pittsburgh; hotels   603

Cauley Detective Agency Inc.; Pittsburgh; security guard service   600

ComPro Inc.; Pittsburgh; community action agency   600

International Business Machines Corp.; Pittsburgh; data processing   600

Kirkpatrick and Lockhart; Pittsburgh; legal services   600

TCI of Pennsylvania Inc.; Pittsburgh; cable TV   600

University of Pittsburgh Medical Center Braddock; Braddock; hospital   600

Westinghouse Process Control Inc.; Pittsburgh; electric motor, generator parts   600

Management Science Associates Inc.; Pittsburgh; management consulting   580

Suburban General Hospital; Pittsburgh   570

Allegheny County Port Authority; Pittsburgh; intercity bus line   550

Kraft Foods Inc.; Pittsburgh; crackers   550

United Healthcare Insurance Co.; Pittsburgh; medical service plans   550

Allegheny County; Pittsburgh; correctional institutions   500

Allegheny County Port Authority; Pittsburgh   500

Aramark Services Inc.; Pittsburgh; restaurants   500

Aramark Services Inc.; Pittsburgh; merchandising machine operators   500

Buchanan Ingersoll Professional Corp.; Pittsburgh; accounting services   500

Carnegie Mellon University; Pittsburgh   500

Chicago Bridge and Iron Co.; Pittsburgh; fabricated plate work   500

DaimlerChrysler Rail Systems Inc.; West Mifflin; cargo loading, unloading   500

Fiserv Solutions Inc.; Pittsburgh; electrical work   500

LifeCare Hospitals of Pittsburgh Inc.; Pittsburgh   500

Mellon Arena Pittsburgh; Pittsburgh; auditorium operation   500

PRN Health Services Inc.; East Pittsburgh; nurses' registry   500

Sargent Electric Co.; Pittsburgh; electrical contractor   500

Star MultiCare Services Inc.; Pittsburgh; medical help service   500

U.S. Dept. of Veterans Affairs; Pittsburgh   500

U.S. Postal Service; East Pittsburgh   500

Pennsylvania 15th District

East — Allentown, Bethlehem

Centered in the Lehigh Valley about 60 miles north of Philadelphia and abutting the Delaware River, the 15th takes in the cities of Allentown, Bethlehem, and Easton—longtime strongholds of heavy industry.

The region once suffered from Rust Belt blues that singer Billy Joel enshrined in his 1982 song "Allentown." But the area began to reinvent its economy in the 1990s after unsuccessful attempts to revive the economic might of Bethlehem Steel and Mack Trucks. Bethlehem Steel filed for bankruptcy in 2001 and its company board in 2003 approved a takeover offer by International Steel Group.

Technology office parks and highway freight centers now cover a landscape where factories and small farms once were mainstays. Major employers include Agere Systems, Air Products and Chemicals, and the Lehigh Valley Hospital complex.

Many of the district's towns date to colonial times, some with well-established Pennsylvania Dutch heritages. But the 250-year-old German influence has been diluted by a century of immigration and recent migration from New Jersey and New York. Allentown—the only city among the state's top four not to lose residents in the 1990s—passed Erie during the decade to become Pennsylvania's third-largest city.

Blue-collar, ethnic workers provide a dwindling yet still-powerful base for Democrats. But the increasing white-collar constituency and a socially conservative streak among blue-collar Democrats have helped Republicans win 15th District House contests.

George W. Bush and Al Gore made multiple trips to the 15th during the 2000 presidential campaign, prompting then-governor Tom Ridge to declare, "If Pennsylvania is a battleground state, the Lehigh Valley is the bull's eye." Gore ultimately captured the district by 1 percentage point.

Major Industry

Manufacturing, technology, health care.

Notable

The Liberty Bell was hidden from the British in an Allentown church; Easton is home to the Crayola crayon factory; Just Born, based in Bethlehem, makes more than 600 million Peeps (brightly colored marshmallow candies) around Easter.

Election Returns

	Republican		Democratic		Other	
President 2000	116,817	47.7%	119,393	48.7%	8,865	3.6%
House 2002	98,493	57.4%	73,212	42.6%	8	

District Profile

Population 646,495

Total area (square miles) 817.4
  Land area (square miles) 810.8

Population per square mile 797.4

Counties (2000 population)
  Lehigh 312,090
  Montgomery (pt.) 67,339
  Northampton 267,066

Cities and other areas over 10,000 (2000 population)
  Allentown 106,632
  Bethlehem 71,329
  Easton 26,263
  Emmaus borough 11,313
  Fullerton CDP 14,268

Race and Hispanic or Latino origin*
  White 86.4%
  Black or African American 2.8%
  American Indian or Alaska Native 0.1%
  Asian 1.7%
  Native Hawaiian or other Pacific Islander 0.0%
  Some other race 0.1%
  Hispanic or Latino origin 7.9%
  Two or more races 1.0%

*As percentage of total population.

Ancestry*

Austrian 1.2%	Italian 8.1%
Dutch 2.5%	Polish 3.8%
English 4.8%	Slovak 2.2%
French 1.3%	Ukrainian 1.3%
German 21.9%	USA/American 3.4%
Hungarian 2.2%	Welsh 1.5%
Irish 9.0%	

*As estimated percentage of total population.

Universities and colleges, 2000–2001 enrollment
  Allentown Business School, Allentown 1,561
  Cedar Crest College, Allentown 1,519
  DeSales University, Center Valley 2,549
  Lafayette College, Easton 2,279
  Lehigh Carbon Community College, Schnecksville 3,768
  Lehigh University, Bethlehem 6,476
  Lincoln Technical Institute, Allentown 631
  Moravian College and Theological Seminary, Bethlehem 1,912
  Muhlenberg College, Allentown 2,543
  Northampton County Area Community College, Bethlehem 4,797
  Pennsylvania State University-Lehigh Valley, Fogelsville 693

Newspapers and circulation

	District circulation	Total circulation
Allentown Morning Call	108,388	126,651
Easton Express-Times	29,908	48,585
Lansdale Reporter	2,349	18,554
Philadelphia Daily News	1,178	151,682
Philadelphia Inquirer	2,247	371,901
Pottstown Mercury	5,869	24,659
*USA Today**	4,564	1,674,376

*See Sources and Explanations in the front of the volume.

Television stations and affiliations

Philadelphia	100%	KYW	CBS
Philadelphia	100%	WBPH	Independent
Philadelphia	100%	WCAU	NBC
Philadelphia	100%	WFMZ	Independent
Philadelphia	100%	WHYY	PBS
Philadelphia	100%	WLVT	PBS
Philadelphia	100%	WMGM	NBC
Philadelphia	100%	WNJS	PBS
Philadelphia	100%	WNJT	PBS
Philadelphia	100%	WPHL	WB
Philadelphia	100%	WPPX	PAX
Philadelphia	100%	WPSG	UPN
Philadelphia	100%	WPVI	ABC
Philadelphia	100%	WTVE	Independent
Philadelphia	100%	WTXF	FOX
Philadelphia	100%	WWAC	Independent
Philadelphia	100%	WYBE	PBS

Cable systems and subscribers
  Blue Ridge 2,399
  Comcast 11,150
  Service Electric Cablevision 121,099

Businesses and other major employers
  Air Products; Allentown; industrial gases 4,500
  Lehigh Valley Hospital Inc.; Allentown 3,300
  Lucent Technologies Inc.; Allentown; integrated microcircuits 3,000
  Air Products and Chemicals Inc.; Allentown; liquid petroleum transport 2,600
  St. Luke's Hospital of Bethlehem; Bethlehem 2,270
  PLP Corp.; Allentown; electric power generation 1,650
  Easton Hospital; Easton 1,412
  Guardian Life Insurance Company of America; Bethlehem; pension, health, welfare funds 1,400
  Victaulic Co. of America Inc.; Easton; couplings 1,400
  Lehigh University; Bethlehem 1,360
  Knoll Inc.; East Greenville; office panel systems and partitions 1,350
  FLS U.S. Holdings Inc.; Bethlehem; cement-making machinery 1,243
  Moyer Packing Co.; Souderton; beef products 1,200
  Prudential Insurance Company of America; Fogelsville; insurance agents and brokers 1,200
  Lehigh County; Allentown; county government 1,026
  KidsPeace National Centers for Kids in Crisis Inc.; Orefield; child guidance agency 1,000
  Sacred Heart Hospital of Allentown; Allentown 1,000
  City of Allentown; Allentown; city government 964
  Rodale Inc.; Emmaus; book publishing 950
  Good Shepherd Home-Long Term Care Facility Inc.; Allentown; rehabilitation center 900
  Mack Trucks Inc.; Allentown; motor trucks assembly 862
  Dun and Bradstreet Inc.; Bethlehem; credit reporting bureau 850

Northampton County; Nazareth; convalescent home
850

Mack Trucks Inc.; Macungie; highway truck tractor
assembly   840

Day-Timers Inc.; East Texas; calendar and card printing
800

Morning Call Inc.; Allentown; newspaper   800

Lehigh County; Allentown; social and human resources
780

Carbon-Lehigh Intermediate School District;
Schnecksville   750

Kraft Foods Inc.; Allentown; cheese products   750

Northampton County Area Community College;
Bethlehem   750

Pilgrim's Pride Corp.; Franconia; poultry processing
750

Binney and Smith Inc.; Easton; pencils and art goods
747

Good Shepherd Home Inc.; Allentown; rehabilitation
center   720

Bethlehem Steel Corp.; Bethlehem; blast furnaces and
steel mills   700

Pilgrim's Pride Corp.; Souderton; poultry processing
700

Lafayette College; Easton   675

Fleet National Bank; Bethlehem; state trust company
657

Bosch Rexroth Corp.; Bethlehem; tanks and tank
components   650

PPL Electric Utilities Corp.; Allentown; electric services
650

Sure Fit Inc.; Allentown; slip covers and pads   650

U.S. Postal Service; Lehigh Valley   650

Walgreen Eastern Co.; Bethlehem; trucking terminals
640

C. F. Martin and Co. Inc.; Nazareth; musical instruments
624

B. Braun Medical Inc.; Bethlehem; medical instruments
600

B. Braun Medical Inc.; Allentown; medical instruments
600

City of Bethlehem; Bethlehem; city government   600

Day-Timers Inc.; Allentown; mail-order catalog   600

Gruner and Jahr Printing and Publishing Co.; East
Greenville; commercial printing   600

Lehigh Carbon Community College; Schnecksville   590

Northampton County; Easton; county government   587

St. Luke's Hospital of Bethlehem; Allentown   580

Laurel Pipe Line Co.; Allentown; refined petroleum
pipelines   543

Agere Systems Inc.; Breinigsville; electronic research
540

National Assn. of Letter Carriers; Allentown; labor union
539

D&M Properties; Bethlehem; subdividers and developers
530

Colonial Intermediate School District; Easton   525

Muhlenberg College; Allentown   522

Cadmus Communications Corp.; Easton; offset printing
507

ProQuest Co.; Allentown; mailing, letter handling,
addressing machines   500

Pennsylvania 16th District

Southeast — Lancaster, part of Reading

Located in southeast Pennsylvania and bordering
Delaware and Maryland to the south, the 16th includes all of
Lancaster County, the southern half of Chester County, and
a slice of Berks County, including part of Reading. Containing much of the so-called "Pennsylvania Dutch Country," the
16th is a Republican bastion.

The strong work ethic of the local workforce and the district's proximity to major roadways attract companies to the
area, which is central to the mid-Atlantic's major markets.
Economic expansion has attracted new residents, and some
of the area's farmland has been built over with tract housing.
Rolling and pastoral Chester County was the seventh-fastest-
growing county in the state in the 1990s.

Although the 16th welcomes the development, farm
preservation remains a major concern, especially in Lancaster,
an area ranked among the top nationally in agricultural product sales. Tourism also enhances the 16th's robust economy.
Some 4.5 million visitors annually flock to Dutch Country to
gaze at Amish horse-drawn carriages, browse at quilt shops,
and dine in family-style restaurants.

Since the dawn of the Civil War, the areas in the 16th
have favored the GOP at all levels. Lancaster County, which
accounts for more than 70 percent of the district population,
sets the district's conservative political tone with its Amish
heritage: George W. Bush won 66 percent of the county vote
in the 2000 presidential election. Chester County is more
socially moderate, but Bush won nearly every jurisdiction in
the 16th's share of the county and topped 60 percent in several townships in western Chester. The only real Democratic
strength is in Reading, which is shared with the 6th District
and is heavily Democratic as a result of its large Hispanic
and black population.

Major Industry

Agriculture, tourism, manufacturing.

Notable

Frank Woolworth's original five-and-ten-cent store
opened in Lancaster in 1879; one of the architects of the
U.S. Capitol designed the Chester County Courthouse.

Election Returns

	Republican		Democratic		Other	
President 2000	144,862	62.1%	82,729	35.5%	5,713	2.4%
House 2002	119,046	88.5%			15,551	11.5%

District Profile

Population   646,156

Total area (square miles)   1,329.9
   Land area (square miles)   1,293.7

Population per square mile   499.5

Counties (2000 population)
   Berks (pt.)   58,047
   Chester (pt.)   117,451
   Lancaster   470,658

Cities and other areas over 10,000 (2000 population)
Columbia borough   10,311
Elizabethtown borough   11,887
Ephrata borough   13,213
Lancaster   56,348
Reading (pt.)   44,501
West Chester borough   17,861

Race and Hispanic or Latino origin*
White   84.3%
Black or African American   4.0%
American Indian or Alaska Native   0.1%
Asian   1.4%
Native Hawaiian or other Pacific Islander   0.0%
Some other race   0.1%
Hispanic or Latino origin   9.2%
Two or more races   0.9%

*As percentage of total population.

Ancestry*
Dutch 1.2%	Polish 2.2%
English 6.1%	Scotch-Irish 1.4%
French 1.4%	Scottish 1.3%
German 25.2%	Swiss 1.9%
Irish 8.8%	USA/American 6.1%
Italian 4.7%	

*As estimated percentage of total population.

Universities and colleges, 2000–2001 enrollment
Elizabethtown College, Elizabethtown   1,825
Franklin and Marshall College, Lancaster   1,892
Harrisburg Area Community College, Lancaster   1,603
Lancaster Bible College, Lancaster   749
Lincoln University, Lincoln University   1,842
Millersville University, Millersville   7,378
Pace Institute, Reading   210
Pennsylvania State University, Reading   2,197
Thaddeus Stevens State School of Technology, Lancaster 543
West Chester University, West Chester   12,272

Newspapers and circulation
	District circulation	Total circulation
Lancaster Intelligencer Journal	43,157	44,929
Lancaster New Era	43,894	44,684
Philadelphia Inquirer	6,013	371,901
Reading Eagle	14,373	82,493
USA Today *	4,418	1,674,376
West Chester Daily Local News	8,678	29,214
Wilmington News Journal	2,950	121,217

*See Sources and Explanations in the front of the volume.

Television stations and affiliations
Harrisburg-Lancaster-Lebanon-York	74%	WGAL	NBC
Harrisburg-Lancaster-Lebanon-York	74%	WGCB	Independent
Harrisburg-Lancaster-Lebanon-York	74%	WHP	CBS
Harrisburg-Lancaster-Lebanon-York	74%	WHTM	ABC
Harrisburg-Lancaster-Lebanon-York	74%	WITF	PBS
Harrisburg-Lancaster-Lebanon-York	74%	WLYH	UPN
Harrisburg-Lancaster-Lebanon-York	74%	WPMT	FOX
Philadelphia	26%	KYW	CBS
Philadelphia	26%	WBPH	Independent
Philadelphia	26%	WCAU	NBC
Philadelphia	26%	WFMZ	Independent
Philadelphia	26%	WHYY	PBS
Philadelphia	26%	WLVT	PBS
Philadelphia	26%	WMGM	NBC
Philadelphia	26%	WNJS	PBS
Philadelphia	26%	WNJT	PBS
Philadelphia	26%	WPHL	WB
Philadelphia	26%	WPPX	PAX
Philadelphia	26%	WPSG	UPN
Philadelphia	26%	WPVI	ABC
Philadelphia	26%	WTVE	Independent
Philadelphia	26%	WTXF	FOX
Philadelphia	26%	WWAC	Independent
Philadelphia	26%	WYBE	PBS

Cable systems and subscribers
Armstrong   1,917
Blue Ridge   32,695
Comcast   112,861

Businesses and other major employers
SCT Software and Resources Management Corp.; West Chester; software development   6,000
Armstrong World Industries Inc.; Lancaster; floor coverings   3,800
Reading Medical Center; Reading   3,600
Lancaster General Hospital Inc.; Lancaster   2,821
Chester County; West Chester; county government 2,442
Genesis Elder Care Rehabilitation Services Inc.; Kennett Square   2,100
New Holland North America Inc.; New Holland; farm machinery   1,729
R. R. Donnelley and Sons Co.; Lancaster; offset printing 1,500
Rosenbluth International Inc.; Lancaster; travel agency 1,250
Amergen Energy Co.; Kennett Square; electric power generation   1,200
Ephrata Community Hospital; Ephrata   1,200
Tyson Foods Inc.; New Holland; frozen specialties 1,200
West Chester University; West Chester   1,150
Lancaster Regional Medical Center; Lancaster   1,100
Masonic Homes; Elizabethtown; convalescent home 1,099
Millersville University of Pennsylvania; Millersville 1,036
Yellow Transportation; East Petersburg; trucking terminals   1,022
Anvil International Inc.; Columbia; valves and pipe fittings   1,000
Berks County; Reading; county government   1,000
Pepperidge Farm Inc.; Denver; bread baking   1,000
Reading Area Community College; Reading   991
Alumax Inc.; Lancaster; aluminum   900
Community Hospital of Lancaster Foundation Inc.; Lancaster   887
Pfizer Corp.; Lititz; pharmaceuticals   875
Baldwin Hardware Corp.; Reading; builders' hardware 816
Conestoga Wood Specialties Corp.; East Earl; wood doors 775
Hershey Foods Corp.; Lancaster; licorice candy   767
Allstate Insurance Co.; Reading; insurance agents and brokers   700

Dart Container Corp. of Pennsylvania; Leola; plastic cups
700

Lancaster County; Lancaster; county government   700

Lancaster Laboratories Inc.; Lancaster; commercial
research lab   670

ING Life Insurance and Annuity Co.; Reading   650

Arrow International Inc.; Reading; catheters   600

Bollman Industries Inc.; Adamstown; scouring fibers
600

CBRL Group Inc.; Lancaster; restaurant   600

City of Reading; Reading; city government   600

Interstate Brands Corp.; Lancaster; breads and cakes
600

Willow Valley Associates Inc.; Lancaster; resort hotel
600

Armstrong World Industries Inc.; Marietta; light
fixtures   550

City of Lancaster; Lancaster; education programs   540

Brethren Village Inc.; Lancaster; nursing care facilities
530

Franklin and Marshall College; Lancaster   525

Burnham Corp.; Lancaster; heating system boilers   510

Kellogg Co.; Lancaster; breakfast cereals   508

Fulton Financial Corp.; Lancaster; bank holding
companies   500

Herr Foods Inc.; Nottingham; snacks   500

Lancaster County; Lancaster; nursing care facilities   500

M&M/Mars Inc.; Elizabethtown; chocolate bars   500

QVC Inc.; Lancaster; mail-order catalog   500

Pennsylvania 17th District

East central — Harrisburg, Lebanon, Pottsville

Anchored in the eastern part of south-central Pennsylvania, the 17th is home to Harrisburg, the state capital, which sits 100 miles west of Philadelphia and 200 miles east of Pittsburgh. Here, in GOP-minded central Pennsylvania, state government and manufacturing remain key sources of employment. The district contains all of Dauphin, Lebanon, and Schuylkill Counties along with parts of Berks and Perry Counties.

Harrisburg's skyline is dominated by the state capitol building, with a dome inspired by St. Peter's Basilica in Rome. With many state government employees and an African American majority, the city typically votes Democratic, though the rest of Dauphin County favors Republicans. Those wanting a real taste of Dauphin County skip Harrisburg and go to Hershey, also known as "Chocolatetown, U.S.A." The chocolate factory stands at Hershey's center, emitting the most pleasant of industrial odors.

Computer and electrical components manufacturing drive the economy in Dauphin and Lebanon Counties. The proliferation of service, health care, and state government jobs has helped mitigate the impact of other losses. Officials look to balance the needs of agricultural producers with those of industrial workers, making trade a potent issue in the 17th.

The district has a distinct Republican lean, but Rep. Holden demonstrated in 2002 that moderate Democrats can play here. The GOP runs strongly in Lebanon County and in the areas of Dauphin outside Harrisburg. Democrats do well in Schuylkill County, long a coal mining powerhouse, with

comfortable margins in Pottsville, Mahanoy, and Shenandoah. Holden also easily won the 17th's share of Berks.

Major Industry
Government, services, manufacturing, agriculture.

Notable
Streetlights in the town of Hershey are shaped like Hershey Kisses; Pottsville is home to Yuengling, America's oldest active brewery.

Election Returns

	Republican		Democratic		Other	
President 2000	139,932	55.9%	103,603	41.4%	6,994	2.8%
House 2002	97,802	48.6%	103,483	51.4%	6	

District Profile

Population   646,465

Total area (square miles)   2,333.7
Land area (square miles)   2,290.7

Population per square mile   282.2

Counties (2000 population)
Berks (pt.)   102,236   Perry (pt.)   21,768
Dauphin   251,798   Schuylkill   150,336
Lebanon   120,327

Cities and other areas over 10,000 (2000 population)
Colonial Park CDP   13,259   Lebanon   24,461
Harrisburg   48,950   Pottsville   15,549
Hershey CDP   12,771

Race and Hispanic or Latino origin*
White   87.3%
Black or African American   7.3%
American Indian or Alaska Native   0.1%
Asian   1.1%
Native Hawaiian or other Pacific Islander   0.0%
Some other race   0.1%
Hispanic or Latino origin   3.2%
Two or more races   0.9%

As percentage of total population.

Ancestry*
Dutch   2.8%   Lithuanian   1.3%
English   4.1%   Polish   3.8%
French   1.1%   Slovak   1.1%
German   26.0%   USA/American   5.0%
Irish   8.7%   Welsh   1.4%
Italian   5.2%

As estimated percentage of total population.

Universities and colleges, 2000–2001 enrollment
Academy of Medical Arts and Business, Harrisburg
213
Harrisburg Area Community College, Harrisburg
7,572
Harrisburg Area Community College, Lebanon   785
Lebanon Valley College, Annville   2,099
McCann School of Business, Mahanoy City   206
Pennsylvania State University, Schuylkill Haven   1,124

Pennsylvania State University-Harrisburg, Middletown
3,258
Pennsylvania State University-Hershey Medical Center,
Hershey   644
Thompson Institute, Harrisburg   431
Widener University-Harrisburg, Harrisburg   422

Newspapers and circulation

	District circulation	Total circulation
Allentown Morning Call	1,817	126,651
Harrisburg Patriot News	55,231	101,633
Hazelton Standard-Speaker	4,101	21,380
Lancaster Intelligencer Journal	1,260	44,929
Lebanon Daily News	20,508	20,694
Lehighton Times News	3,423	13,871
Philadelphia Inquirer	1,701	371,901
Pottsville Republican & Evening Herald	28,564	29,044
Reading Eagle	25,742	82,493
*USA Today**	6,413	1,674,376

See Sources and Explanations in the front of the volume.

Television stations and affiliations

Harrisburg-Lancaster-Lebanon-York	46%	WGAL	NBC
Harrisburg-Lancaster-Lebanon-York	46%	WGCB	Independent
Harrisburg-Lancaster-Lebanon-York	46%	WHP	CBS
Harrisburg-Lancaster-Lebanon-York	46%	WHTM	ABC
Harrisburg-Lancaster-Lebanon-York	46%	WITF	PBS
Harrisburg-Lancaster-Lebanon-York	46%	WLYH	UPN
Harrisburg-Lancaster-Lebanon-York	46%	WPMT	FOX
Wilkes-Barre-Scranton	34%	WBRE	NBC
Wilkes-Barre-Scranton	34%	WILF	FOX
Wilkes-Barre-Scranton	34%	WNEP	ABC
Wilkes-Barre-Scranton	34%	WOLF	FOX
Wilkes-Barre-Scranton	34%	WQPX	PAX
Wilkes-Barre-Scranton	34%	WSWB	WB, UPN
Wilkes-Barre-Scranton	34%	WVIA	PBS
Wilkes-Barre-Scranton	34%	WYOU	CBS
Philadelphia	20%	KYW	CBS
Philadelphia	20%	WBPH	Independent
Philadelphia	20%	WCAU	NBC
Philadelphia	20%	WFMZ	Independent
Philadelphia	20%	WHYY	PBS
Philadelphia	20%	WLVT	PBS
Philadelphia	20%	WMGM	NBC
Philadelphia	20%	WNJS	PBS
Philadelphia	20%	WNJT	PBS
Philadelphia	20%	WPHL	WB
Philadelphia	20%	WPPX	PAX
Philadelphia	20%	WPSG	UPN
Philadelphia	20%	WPVI	ABC
Philadelphia	20%	WTVE	Independent
Philadelphia	20%	WTXF	FOX
Philadelphia	20%	WWAC	Independent
Philadelphia	20%	WYBE	PBS

Cable systems and subscribers
Adelphia   4,678
Blue Ridge   3,947
Comcast   98,806
JB Cable   4,883
Service Electric Co.   13,241
Shen Heights Cable   3,284
Wire Tele View   1,787

Military installations, September 2001
Harrisburg International Airport Air National Guard,
Middletown   1,112
Fort Indiantown Gap Air National Guard Station,
Lickdale   557

Businesses and other major employers
Hershey Foods Corp.; Hershey; chocolate and cocoa
products   8,000
Pennsylvania State University Hospital; Hershey   5,100
Pinnacle Health Hospitals; Harrisburg   4,837
East Penn Manufacturing Co. Inc.; Lyon Station; storage
batteries   3,800
Pennsylvania Dept. of Transportation; Harrisburg
3,000
Pennsylvania Environmental Protection Dept.;
Harrisburg   3,000
Pennsylvania Dept. of Revenue; Harrisburg   2,400
Higher Education Assistance Agency; Harrisburg
2,150
Capital Blue Cross; Harrisburg; health insurance   2,000
Pinnacle Health Hospitals; Harrisburg   2,000
Pennsylvania Dept. of Public Welfare; Harrisburg
1,925
Ranger Hose Co.; Girardville; fire dept.   1,900
Pennsylvania Legislative Office; Harrisburg   1,800
Carlos R. Leffler Inc.; Richland; fuel oil dealers   1,668
Dauphin County; Harrisburg; county government
1,640
Hershey Entertainment and Resorts Co.; Hershey;
amusement parks   1,500
House of Representatives Pennsylvania; Harrisburg;
legislative bodies   1,500
U.S. Postal Service; Harrisburg   1,500
Pennsylvania Steel Technologies Inc.; Steelton; steel or
iron rails   1,400
Pennsylvania Dept. of Labor and Industry; Harrisburg
1,317
Pennsylvania Dept. of Health; Harrisburg   1,300
Country Meadows Associates; Hershey; nursing care
facilities   1,225
U.S. Veterans Hospital; Lebanon   1,222
Alcoa Extrusions Inc.; Cressona; aluminum products
1,200
Amergen Energy Co.; Middletown; electric power
generation   1,200
Harrisburg Area Community College Inc.; Harrisburg
1,200
Ames Department Stores Inc.; Leesport; warehousing
1,037
Pennsylvania Bureau of Planning; Harrisburg   1,000
Good Samaritan Hospital; Lebanon   950
Kutztown University of Pennsylvania; Kutztown   831
AM Care Health Services; Dauberville; nurses, medical
assistants   800
Berks County; Leesport; nursing care facilities   800
Good Samaritan Regional Medical Center; Pottsville
800
Hershey Foods Corp.; Palmyra; candy   800

Associated Wholesalers Inc.; Robesonia; food supplier
780

Tyco Electronics Corp.; Harrisburg; administrative management   756

Tyco International Inc.; Middletown; administrative management   756

Nationwide Mutual Insurance Co.; Harrisburg; fire, marine, casualty insurance   750

Pennsylvania Dept. of General Services; Harrisburg 750

Synertech Health System Solutions Inc.; Harrisburg; administrative management   750

United Concordia Companies Inc.; Harrisburg; dental insurance   750

Pottsville Hospital and Warne Clinic; Pottsville   720

Jetson Direct Mail Services Inc.; Hamburg; addressing service   700

Watkins Motor Lines Inc.; Middletown; trucking   700

Farmers Pride Inc.; Fredericksburg; poultry processing 675

Pennsylvania Dept. of Public Welfare; Harrisburg   626

Milton Hershey School; Hershey   625

J. E. Morgan Knitting Mills Inc.; Tamaqua; underwear 600

Pennsylvania National Mutual Casualty Insurance; Harrisburg; insurance agents and brokers   600

Pennsylvania State Police; Harrisburg   600

Pennsylvania Dept. of Public Welfare; Hamburg   590

Pinnacle Health Hospital at Community General; Harrisburg   580

Lowe's Home Centers Inc.; Pottsville; home improvement centers   575

Guilford Mills Inc.; Pine Grove; lace goods, fabrics   550

Pennsylvania Dept. of Education; Harrisburg   519

Cabot Corp.; Boyertown; primary nonferrous metals 500

Campbell Soup Co.; Fleetwood   500

City of Harrisburg; Harrisburg; city government   500

Dauphin County; Harrisburg; convalescent home   500

Goulds Pumps Inc.; Ashland; pumping equipment 500

Highmark; Harrisburg; health insurance   500

Jersey Central Power and Light Co.; Reading; electric power generation   500

Lebanon County; Lebanon; residential care   500

Nursefinders Inc.; Harrisburg; home health care   500

Pennsylvania Dept. of Corrections; Frackville   500

Pennsylvania Liquor Control Board; Harrisburg   500

Pennsylvania State Treasury; Harrisburg   500

Philhaven; Mount Gretna; outpatient clinics   500

Tyco Electronics Corp.; Jonestown; electronic connectors 500

Weaber Inc.; Lebanon; hardwood dimension and flooring mills   500

Pennsylvania 18th District

West — Pittsburgh suburbs, part of Westmoreland County

The 18th is a socially conservative, ancestrally Democratic area that takes in parts of Allegheny, Washington, and Westmoreland Counties in the orbit of Pittsburgh. The area's access to major waterways made the first half of the twentieth century prosperous for parts of the 18th, which was once a prodigious producer of steel. Now, many areas are struggling to make an economic comeback. *(See map p. 773.)*

The presence of universities and hospitals in the district has led some new technology companies to relocate to the area. However, an economic downturn early in the twenty-first century and the troubles of several high-tech companies have left the region grasping for a way to deal with unemployment. High property taxes are a volatile issue here.

About 55 percent of the 18th's residents live in Allegheny County, which is dominated by Pittsburgh. The Democratic-leaning city is in the 14th District, and most of Allegheny's wealthy Republican suburbs are in the 4th. The 18th's share includes well-off areas in southwestern Allegheny such as Upper St. Clair and Bethel Park, which went solidly for Republican Mike Fisher in the 2002 governor's race, as well as middle- and working-class Democratic enclaves such as Carnegie and Dormont, which are just southwest of Pittsburgh. The 18th also includes most of Westmoreland County, a former Democratic bastion that has moved to the right. George W. Bush won the county by 6 percentage points in the 2000 presidential election.

Major Industry
Health care, technology, manufacturing, air cargo, steel.

Notable
Singer Perry Como was born in Canonsburg (shared with the 12th).

Election Returns

	Republican		Democratic		Other	
President 2000	154,252	51.6%	139,346	46.6%	5,240	1.8%
House 2002	119,885	60.1%	79,451	39.9%	13	

District Profile

Population   646,817

Total area (square miles)   1,433.1
  Land area (square miles)   1,427.0

Population per square mile   453.3

Counties (2000 population)
  Allegheny (pt.)   355,683
  Washington (pt.)   99,870
  Westmoreland (pt.)   191,264

Cities and other areas over 10,000 (2000 population)
  Bethel Park borough   33,556
  Brentwood borough   10,466
  Carnot-Moon CDP   10,637
  Greensburg   15,889
  Jeannette   10,654
  Mount Lebanon CDP   33,017
  Municipality of Monroeville borough (pt.)   24,294
  Penn Hills CDP (pt.)   10,945
  Robinson Township CDP (pt.)   10,510
  Scott Township CDP   17,288
  South Park Township CDP   14,340
  Upper St. Clair CDP   20,053
  Whitehall borough   14,444

Race and Hispanic or Latino origin*

White 95.4%
Black or African American 2.0%
American Indian or Alaska Native 0.1%
Asian 1.3%
Native Hawaiian or other Pacific Islander 0.0%
Some other race 0.1%
Hispanic or Latino origin 0.6%
Two or more races 0.6%

*As percentage of total population.

Ancestry*

English	6.8%	Polish	6.4%
French	1.5%	Scotch-Irish	2.3%
German	19.4%	Scottish	1.5%
Hungarian	1.3%	Slovak	3.0%
Irish	12.3%	USA/American	2.6%
Italian	11.8%		

*As estimated percentage of total population.

Universities and colleges, 2000–2001 enrollment

ITT Technical Institute, Monroeville 438
ITT Technical Institute, Pittsburgh 336
Robert Morris College, Moon Township 4,620
Seton Hill College, Greensburg 1,356
University of Pittsburgh, Greensburg 1,587
Westmoreland County Community College, Youngwood 5,272
Wilma Boyd Career Schools, Moon Township 624

Newspapers and circulation

	District circulation	Total circulation
Beaver County Times	1,869	42,448
Connellsville Courier	1,260	10,225
Greensburg Tribune Review	41,181	86,808
McKeesport Daily News	6,897	20,756
Monessen Valley Independent	2,013	15,270
Pittsburgh Post-Gazette	72,576	240,791
*USA Today**	8,773	1,674,376
Washington Observer Reporter	20,388	36,673

*See Sources and Explanations in the front of the volume.

Television stations and affiliations

Pittsburgh	100%	KDKA	CBS
Pittsburgh	100%	WCWB	WB
Pittsburgh	100%	WGPT	PBS
Pittsburgh	100%	WNPA	UPN
Pittsburgh	100%	WNPB	PBS
Pittsburgh	100%	WPCB	Independent
Pittsburgh	100%	WPGH	FOX
Pittsburgh	100%	WPXI	NBC
Pittsburgh	100%	WQED	PBS
Pittsburgh	100%	WQEX	PBS
Pittsburgh	100%	WTAE	ABC
Pittsburgh	100%	WTOV	NBC
Pittsburgh	100%	WWCP	FOX

Cable systems and subscribers

Adelphia 36,008
Anchor Communications Co. 3,835
Blue Devil 910
Comcast 130,872

Laurel Highland TV Co. 6,358
Pitcain Municipal Electric/TV 1,600

Military installations, September 2001

Charles E. Kelly Support Facility (Army), Pittsburgh 314

Businesses and other major employers

FedEx Ground Inc.; Coraopolis; contract haulers 5,000
Westinghouse Electric Co.; Monroeville; electrical or electronic engineering 4,500
Michael Baker Corp.; Coraopolis; architectural engineering 3,700
Westinghouse Government Service Co.; Aiken; bridge construction 2,500
PNC Bank National Assn.; Bethel Park; commercial bank 2,000
United Steel Enterprises Inc.; Library; steel wire and related products 2,000
Bayer Corp.; Pittsburgh; polypropylene resins 1,900
Jefferson Health Services; Pittsburgh; hospital 1,850
Pennsylvania Dept. of Public Welfare; Bridgeville 1,700
Westmoreland Regional Hospital; Greensburg 1,600
St. Clair Health Corp.; Pittsburgh; hospital management 1,500
United Parcel Service Inc.; New Stanton; parcel delivery 1,500
West Penn Allegheny Health Systems Inc.; Monroeville 1,500
Westmoreland County Community College Inc.; Youngwood 1,280
Consol Pennsylvania Coal Co.; Pittsburgh; coal mining 1,200
Emplifi Inc.; Pittsburgh; computer integrated systems design 1,200
Marathon Oil Corp.; Irwin; real estate agents and managers 1,200
Monongahela Power Co.; Greensburg; electric services 1,200
SuperValu Inc.; New Stanton; food supplier 1,200
Elliott Turbomachinery Co.; Jeannette; steam turbines 1,198
Westmoreland County; Greensburg; county government 1,140
CBS Corp.; Monroeville; TV broadcasting 1,000
Dick Corp.; Clairton; highway and street paving contractor 1,000
Pinkerton's Inc.; Pittsburgh; detective agency 1,000
Cutler-Hammer Inc.; Pittsburgh; electronic research 975
Kennametal Exports Inc.; Latrobe; machine tools and machinery 900
SpectaGuard Acquisition; Pittsburgh; detective services 850
Duluth Missabe and Iron Range Railway Co.; Monroeville; freight hauling 750
Burns International Security Services Corp.; Pittsburgh; security guard service 700
Jeannette District Memorial Hospital Inc.; Jeannette 700
Wexford Health Sources Inc.; Pittsburgh; management services 664

Westmoreland County; Greensburg; convalescent home 650

Premium Retail Services Inc.; Pittsburgh; merchandising consultant   640

Consolidated Rail Corp.; Pittsburgh; freight hauling 600

EMCON; Monroeville; sanitary engineers   600

Island Creek Coal Inc.; Pittsburgh; coal mining   565

Black Box Corp. of Pennsylvania; Lawrence; computer peripheral equipment   553

Bechtel Plant Machinery Inc.; Pittsburgh; industrial plant construction   550

Development Dimensions International Inc.; Bridgeville; training and development consultant   550

MEC Pennsylvania Racing; Meadow Lands; horse racing 550

Buckeye Pipeline Holdings; Coraopolis; petroleum/chemical bulk stations/terminals   539

North American Telecom Services; Canonsburg; telephone equipment and systems   530

Quality Services Inc.; Pittsburgh; industrial, commercial cleaning services   525

Keystone Coal Mining Corp.; Pittsburgh   521

CBS Corp.; Madison; test development and evaluation service   520

American Bridge Holding Co.; Coraopolis; structural steel erection   500

American Video Glass Co.; Mount Pleasant; flat glass 500

Cutler-Hammer Inc.; Coraopolis; electrical equipment 500

Fisher Scientific Co.; Pittsburgh; lab equipment   500

iGATE Corp.; Pittsburgh; software development   500

Mine Safety Appliances Co.; Tarrs; safety equipment 500

National City Bank; Pittsburgh; state commercial banks 500

Pennsylvania Dept. of Corrections; Cresson   500

Pennsylvania Dept. of Public Welfare; Canonsburg   500

St. Moritz Security Services Inc.; Pittsburgh; security guard service   500

U.S. Airways; Pittsburgh   500

Wal-Mart Stores Inc.; Pittsburgh; department stores 500

Wal-Mart Stores Inc.; Washington; department stores 500

Pennsylvania 19th District

South central — York, Gettysburg

Situated west of the Susquehanna River, mostly east of the South Mountains and mostly south of Harrisburg, the 19th's historic landscape has a reliably Republican constituency and flourishing agricultural and manufacturing industries.

Located along several major highways, the district is a prime location for manufacturing and distribution centers, including depots and logistical support facilities for the Department of Defense. York County, where 60 percent of residents live, serves as the 19th's industrial hub. Residential growth, a more recent trend, also can be attributed to the district's location—Marylanders have moved here for the lower

taxes and affordable real estate. But many residents, or their forefathers, traveled much farther than from a neighboring state—the 19th has the highest percentage of residents with German ancestry in the state.

Tourism also plays a major role. Nearly 2 million visitors a year come to see the site of the 1863 Battle of Gettysburg in Adams County, a largely agricultural area. Many come for the annual reenactment of one of the Civil War's most significant battles.

George W. Bush won 61.4 percent of the 19th's vote in the 2000 presidential election. Cumberland County, which is shared with the 9th, is strongly Republican, with Bush winning all but two precincts in the county. York and Adams also have strong GOP leans, with Democrats only finding strength in the city of York, where blacks and Hispanics together are more than 40 percent of the population, and Gettysburg, which has a large college-age population.

Major Industry

Agriculture, manufacturing, distribution.

Notable

Birthplace of the Articles of Confederation; York served as the U.S. Capitol from 1777–1778 while the British occupied Philadelphia; Harley Davidson's largest manufacturing facility is in York; President Abraham Lincoln gave his famed Gettysburg Address in Adams County.

Election Returns

	Republican		Democratic		Other	
President 2000	153,892	61.4%	90,125	35.9%	6,766	2.7%
House 2002	143,097	91.1%			14,048	8.9%

District Profile

Population   647,065

Total area (square miles)   1,656.5
   Land area (square miles)   1,648.4

Population per square mile   392.5

Counties (2000 population)
   Adams   91,292
   Cumberland (pt.)   174,022
   York   381,751

Cities and other areas over 10,000 (2000 population)
   Carlisle borough   17,970
   Hanover borough   14,535
   Shiloh CDP   10,192
   Weigelstown CDP   10,117
   York   40,862

Race and Hispanic or Latino origin*
   White   92.2%
   Black or African American   2.9%
   American Indian or Alaska Native   0.1%
   Asian   1.1%
   Native Hawaiian or other Pacific Islander   0.0%
   Some other race   0.1%
   Hispanic or Latino origin   2.7%
   Two or more races   0.9%

*As percentage of total population.

Ancestry*

Dutch	1.6%	Italian	4.0%
English	6.2%	Polish	2.2%
French	1.5%	Scotch-Irish	1.6%
German	28.1%	Scottish	1.3%
Irish	9.0%	USA/American	6.7%

As estimated percentage of total population.

Universities and colleges, 2000–2001 enrollment

Bradley Academy for the Visual Arts, York   465
Central Pennsylvania Business School, Summerdale   579
Dickinson College, Carlisle   2,115
Dickinson School of Law, Carlisle   544
Gettysburg College, Gettysburg   2,234
ITT Technical Institute, Mechanicsburg   277
Messiah College, Grantham   2,797
Pennsylvania State University, York   2,006
Shippensburg University, Shippensburg   7,011
York College Pennsylvania, York   5,254
York Technical Institute, York   1,097
Yorktowne Business Institute, York   300

Newspapers and circulation

	District circulation	Total circulation
Baltimore Sun	1,637	268,280
Carlisle Sentinel	6,360	15,388
Chambersburg Public Opinion	1,419	19,128
Gettysburg Times	9,374	9,519
Hanover Evening Sun	19,518	20,470
Harrisburg Patriot News	29,097	101,633
*USA Today**	4,110	1,674,376
York Daily Record	42,968	43,172
York Daily Record/York Dispatch/News	83,041	83,310
York Dispatch/News	40,073	40,158

See Sources and Explanations in the front of the volume.

Television stations and affiliations

Harrisburg-Lancaster-Lebanon-York	100%	WGAL	NBC
Harrisburg-Lancaster-Lebanon-York	100%	WGCB	Independent
Harrisburg-Lancaster-Lebanon-York	100%	WHP	CBS
Harrisburg-Lancaster-Lebanon-York	100%	WHTM	ABC
Harrisburg-Lancaster-Lebanon-York	100%	WITF	PBS
Harrisburg-Lancaster-Lebanon-York	100%	WLYH	UPN
Harrisburg-Lancaster-Lebanon-York	100%	WPMT	FOX

Cable systems and subscribers

Adelphia   19,563
Blue Ridge   2,237
Clearview Partners   4,244
Comcast   24,290
Suscom   57,637

Military installations, September 2001

Defense Distribution Depot, New Cumberland   1,213
Naval Support Activity, Mechanicsburg   196

Businesses and other major employers

U.S. Navy; Mechanicsburg   5,200
York Hospital; York   4,500
Harley-Davidson Inc.; York; motorcycles   2,300
Framatome Connectors International Inc.; Etters; electronic connectors   2,200
U.S. Defense Dept.; New Cumberland   2,200
York International Corp.; York; refrigeration and heating equipment   2,000
Trans Healthcare Inc.; Camp Hill; group health association   1,600
Holy Spirit Hospital of Sisters of Christian Charity; Camp Hill   1,459
Roadway Express Inc.; Carlisle; trucking terminals   1,400
Fleming Gannett Inc.; Camp Hill; engineering services   1,300
Capital Blue Cross; Lemoyne; health insurance   1,200
PH Glatfelter Co.; Spring Grove; printing paper   1,200
Executive Office of Pennsylvania; Mechanicsburg; education programs   1,100
Utz Quality Foods Inc.; Hanover; snacks   1,100
Lincoln Intermediate School District; New Oxford   1,096
Fry Communications Inc.; Mechanicsburg; commercial printing, newspaper publishing   1,050
Hanover Direct Inc.; Hanover; mail-order books   1,000
Hanover Direct Inc.; Littlestown; mail-order catalog   1,000
Pennsylvania Dept. of Corrections; Camp Hill   1,000
Venator Group Retail Inc.; Camp Hill; shoe stores   1,000
Hanover Hospital Inc.; Hanover   950
Exel Holdings; Mechanicsburg; warehousing   900
Venator Group Retail Inc.; Carlisle; men's footwear   890
Carlisle Regional Medical Center; Carlisle   852
Peco Energy Co.; Delta; electric services   851
Gettysburg College; Gettysburg   850
R. H. Sheppard Co. Inc.; Hanover; automotive gears   850
Merck Medco Rx Services of Pennsylvania Inc.; Mechanicsburg; mail order   812
ABF Freight System Inc.; Carlisle; trucking terminals   800
Rite Aid Corp.; Camp Hill; drug stores   800
Ross Stores Inc.; Carlisle; textile warehousing   800
United Defense Industries Inc.; York; tanks and tank components   800
Pennsylvania Shippensburg University; Shippensburg   780
Snyder's of Hanover Inc.; Hanover; pretzels   760
FedEx Ground Inc.; Lewisberry; delivery service   700
Hersha Hospitality Management; New Cumberland; hotel or motel management   700
Shaffer Trucking Inc.; New Kingstown; trucking   700
Brethren Home Community; New Oxford; nursing care facilities   669
Hanover Foods Corp.; Hanover; canned foods   655
HealthSouth Sub-Acute Center of Mechanicsburg Inc.; Mechanicsburg   650
York College of Pennsylvania Inc.; York   645
Carlisle Tire and Wheel Co.; Carlisle; pneumatic tires   630
Messiah College; Grantham   626
Gettysburg Hospital Inc.; Gettysburg   617
Dickinson College; Carlisle   615
Memorial Hospital; York   608

Consolidated Freightways Corp. of Delaware; York; trucking terminals   600
Cumberland Valley School District; Mechanicsburg   600
Dentsply International Inc.; York; dental equipment   600
Overnite Transportation Co.; Mechanicsburg; trucking   600
PPG Industries Inc.; Carlisle; flat glass   600
USF Glen Moore Inc.; Carlisle; heavy hauling   600
Washington Group International Inc.; Mechanicsburg; bridge construction   600
Woodloch Pines Resort; Hawley; resort hotel   600
Maple Press Co.; York; book printing and binding   595
Appleton Papers Inc.; Camp Hill; paper coating/finishing machinery   550
Cumberland County Nursing Home; Carlisle   550
DONSCO Inc.; Wrightsville; iron castings   550
Giant Food Stores; Carlisle; supermarkets   550
Tenet Healthcare Corp. Hospital; Mechanicsburg   550
Olin Corp.; Red Lion; ordnance and accessories   539
Quaker Oats Co.; Shiremanstown; breakfast cereals   525

Susquehanna Pfaltzgraff Co.; Thomasville; tableware   525
White Tail Mountain Operating Corp.; York; hotels and motels   525
Keystone Health Plan Central; Camp Hill; health maintenance organization   521
Bon-Ton Stores Inc.; York; department stores   500
ESAB Group Inc.; Hanover; welding apparatus   500
Graham Packaging Holdings Co.; York; plastic containers   500
Hoffman Mills Inc.; Shippensburg; fabrics   500
International Business Machines Corp.; Mechanicsburg; computer peripherals, software   500
MasterBrand Cabinets Inc.; Littlestown   500
Quebecor Printing Fairfield Inc.; Fairfield; book printing and binding   500
Rite Aid of Pennsylvania Inc.; Etters; accounting services   500
Schaad Detective Agency Inc.; York   500
D. F. Stauffer Biscuit Co.; York; cookies   500
Strine Printing Co.; York; offset printing   500

RHODE ISLAND

Districts established February 20, 2002, for elections first held in 2002.

2 members

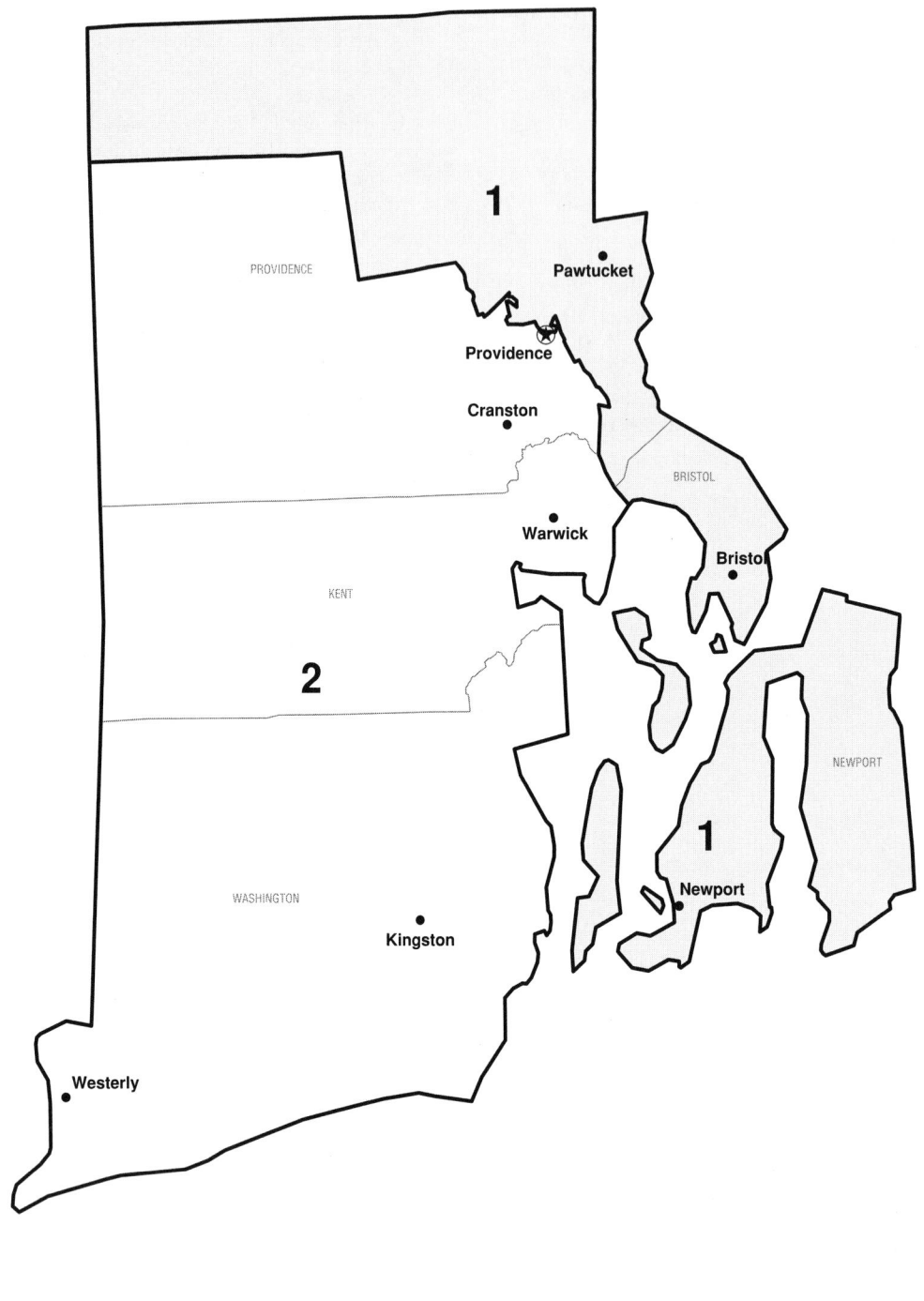

Rhode Island

Originally and legally known as Rhode Island and Providence Plantations, this is a state rife with ironies. For starters, the part that is actually Rhode Island has only a vestigial population today compared with what was founded as Providence Plantations. In recent decades, that majority has been concentrated more and more in the city and suburbs of Providence (the term plantation having long since fallen out of favor).

Although it has just a million residents overall, Rhode Island is among the more crowded states because it is, famously, the smallest in area (1,045 square miles). Despite its diminutive size, or perhaps because of it, Rhode Island has been feisty from its earliest relations with its neighbors. It was the first colony to declare itself free from England—locals were burning British revenue ships here years before Lexington and Concord—and the only state not to send delegates to the Constitutional Convention in 1787. It was also the last state to ratify the product of that convention. Constantly mindful of its larger neighbors, Rhode Island has been a fierce defender of the rights of the individual and the individual state.

Rhode Island has long been known for the great wealth of its most elite residents (those who summer in Newport, still following the custom of the moguls in the Gilded Age) but also for its high proportion of union families, blue-collar workers, and Democratic voters. Obviously, the fortunes represented at Newport of a summer's festival season were mostly made elsewhere. But the voters who are around in November are more likely drawing paychecks from factories and machine shops in Woonsocket and Cranston.

Through most of the twentieth century the state's politics pitted its New England Republican legacy against its rising Democratic tide, composed largely of Catholic blue-collar wage earners. While the state voted Republican in five of the first six elections of the 1900s, it went for Al Smith, the first Catholic nominee, in 1928. Since then, it has voted consistently Democratic for president except in the big GOP landslides for Dwight Eisenhower, Richard Nixon (1972 only), and Ronald Reagan (1984 only). Al Gore got 61 percent of the vote in this, his best state, despite a 6 percent showing for Green nominee Ralph Nader.

In the governorship contests, the two parties were more evenly represented over the course of the century. Republicans dominated early, with Democrats taking over in the harrowing early days of the Depression. Democrats would elect eight of ten governors from the early 1940s to the mid-1980s before Republicans made another comeback. Most recently, Myrth York won the Democratic nomination for governor three times from 1994 through 2002 but lost each time in November.

There was little suspense in the other major contests in 2002. Jack Reed, the senior senator who is a West Point graduate and Vietnam vet with a Harvard law degree, won a second term without breaking a sweat, as did both the state's Democratic House members, including Patrick J. Kennedy, son of the Massachusetts senator, nephew of the former president.

Like other small states, Rhode Island has maximized its power in Washington by clinging to its congressional incumbents, who often serve 20 years and more. Its elected senators have included such multiterm Democrats as Peter Gerry, Theodore Green (who was elected at 69 and served until he was 93), John Pastore, and Claiborne Pell, a blueblood who spoke fluently the languages of the state's ethnic minorities. When the state does elect a Republican it tends to be a moderate-to-liberal one who does well with union families. Such was John Chafee, an affable aristocrat who served as governor and won four terms in the U.S. Senate. When he died in office in 1999, his son, Lincoln, was his appointed and then elected successor. Although a Republican, Chafee the younger proved one of the more reliable votes in the Senate for the Democrats. The two Chafees are literally the only Republicans elected to the Senate from the state since 1930.

The task of redrawing the district line between the two House incumbents was largely a matter of moving the dividing line inside Providence, which is split between the two. Kennedy represents the northern side of Providence, city and county, with the seaside counties of Bristol and Newport to the southeast. James Langevin has the southern side of Providence and the western part of the state: Kent and Washington Counties and Block Island in Narragansett Bay.

Rhode Island's near-static population may soon mean the loss of its two-century status as a multiple-seat state. Although Providence saw respectable 8 percent growth in the 1990s, the state as a whole grew little more than half that much. Warwick, Cranston, Pawtucket, and East Providence barely changed their numbers at all. The state's two congressional districts are now about 100,000 below the national average population for districts (in states with more than one). All seven of the states with smaller populations are already down to one district. Like the one-district states, Rhode Island has very small minority populations and relatively low birth rates. Only 4 percent of the state is African American and 5 percent Hispanic.

Table 1 Population

District	Population	Population under 18	Voting-age population	Median age	Male*	Female*
1	524,157	119,220	404,937	36.8	47.7	52.3
2	524,162	128,602	395,560	36.7	48.4	51.6
State	1,048,319	247,822	800,497	36.7	48.0	52.0

*As percentage of total population.

Table 2 Voting-Age Persons by Race/Hispanic or Latino Origin

District	White*	Black or African American*	American Indian or Alaska Native*	Asian*	Other or multirace*	Hispanic or Latino*
1	85.3	3.5	0.2	1.9	3.1	5.9
2	84.2	3.6	0.5	2.3	1.5	8.0
State	84.7	3.5	0.3	2.1	2.3	7.0

*As percentage of voting-age population.

Table 3 Voting-Age Population by Age Groups

District	18 to 24*	25 to 44*	45 to 64*	Over 64*
1	14.0	38.1	28.0	19.9
2	12.6	39.6	29.7	18.1
State	13.3	38.8	28.8	19.0

*As percentage of voting-age population.

Table 4 Income and Occupation

District	Median family income	Families in poverty*	White collar†	Blue collar†	Service†	Farm†
1	$51,918	8.9	61.3	23.2	15.2	0.2
2	$53,764	8.8	60.8	22.6	16.1	0.5
State	$52,781	8.9	61.1	22.9	15.7	0.3

*As percentage of all families.   †As percentage of employed workers 16 years and over.

Table 5 Education: School Years Completed

District	Less than grade 9*	Grades 9–12 no diploma*	High school diploma no college*	Some college*	College bachelor's degree or higher*
1	9.1	14.6	26.8	23.5	26.0
2	7.1	13.2	28.8	25.7	25.2
State	8.1	13.9	27.8	24.6	25.6

*As percentage of persons age 25 and over.

Table 6 Housing and Residential Patterns

District	Median home value	Owner occupied*	Renter occupied*	Urban†	Rural†
1	$133,700	55.7	44.3	95.5	4.5
2	$127,300	64.6	35.4	86.3	13.7
State	$130,500	60.0	40.0	90.9	9.1

*As percentage of occupied housing units.   †As percentage of total population.

Rhode Island 1st District

East — Pawtucket, part of Providence, Newport

The Democratic 1st occupies the top of Rhode Island, along the Massachusetts border, then moves south to take in Pawtucket and the northeastern part of Providence, the capital, before running along Narragansett Bay to pick up Newport and the island communities in the southeast.

The 1st's industry is mostly centered in northern Rhode Island's Blackstone Valley. Woonsocket, a manufacturing city, is home to the headquarters of CVS, the largest drugstore in the nation.

The district's portion of Providence takes in several colleges, such as Brown University and Providence College, and includes the state capitol. Students and government workers push the 1st's political lean to the left.

The coastal economy south of Providence relies largely on maritime defense. Companies such as Raytheon, which makes components for Navy submarines in Portsmouth, as well as a large naval base and training center in Newport fuel the industry. Large numbers of visitors to Newport, as well as to Providence, make tourism an important economic component.

Democrats dominate the district, getting support from ethnic minorities as well as the area's large Catholic majority. Some small, wealthy coastal towns support the GOP, but larger towns lean Democratic. In statewide elections, however, the district has supported Republicans for governor, such as Donald L. Carcieri in 2002, and for U.S. senator, such as Lincoln Chafee in 2000.

Major Industry

Defense, higher education, manufacturing, tourism, government.

Notable

One of the nation's oldest taverns, the White Horse Tavern, opened in Newport before 1673; Touro Synagogue in Newport, designed by colonial architect Peter Harrison and dedicated in 1762, is the oldest U.S. synagogue.

Election Returns

	Republican		Democratic		Other	
President 2000	61,396	30.8%	125,174	62.8%	12,705	6.4%
House 2002	59,316	37.3%	95,233	59.9%	4,314	2.7%

District Profile

Population 524,157

Total area (square miles) 564.7
  Land area (square miles) 324.6

Population per square mile 1,614.8

Counties (2000 population)
Bristol   50,648
Newport   85,433
Providence (pt.)   388,076

Cities and other areas over 10,000 (2000 population)
Barrington CDP   16,819
Bristol CDP   22,469
Central Falls   18,928
East Providence   48,688
Newport   26,475
Newport East CDP   11,463
North Providence CDP   32,411
Pawtucket   72,958
Providence (pt.)   72,102
Valley Falls CDP   11,599
Woonsocket   43,224

Race and Hispanic or Latino origin*
White   82.6%
Black or African American   4.1%
American Indian or Alaska Native   0.3%
Asian   1.9%
Native Hawaiian or other Pacific Islander   0.0%
Some other race   1.3%
Hispanic or Latino origin   7.5%
Two or more races   2.3%

*As percentage of total population.

Ancestry*
English 8.0%	Polish 3.4%
Fr. Canadian 6.2%	Portuguese 9.3%
French 8.8%	Scottish 1.4%
German 3.9%	Subsaharan 2.4%
Irish 12.9%	USA/American 2.4%
Italian 11.4%	

*As estimated percentage of total population.

Universities and colleges, 2000–2001 enrollment
Brown University, Providence   7,723
Bryant College, Smithfield   3,373
Providence College, Providence   5,336
Roger Williams University, Bristol   3,750
Roger Williams University School of Law, Bristol   365
Salve Regina University, Newport   2,251
St. Joseph Hospital School of Nurse Anesthesia, North Providence   224
Zion Bible Institute, Barrington   401

Newspapers and circulation
	District circulation	Total circulation
Boston Globe	1,227	465,248
Boston Herald	1,728	257,071
Fall River Herald News	1,839	22,943
Newport Daily News	12,428	12,446
Pawtucket Times	12,611	13,533
Providence Journal	65,943	161,108
*USA Today**	3,711	1,674,376
Woonsocket Call	12,448	15,580

*See Sources and Explanations in the front of the volume.

Television stations and affiliations
Providence-New Bedford	100%	WJAR	NBC
Providence-New Bedford	100%	WLNE	ABC
Providence-New Bedford	100%	WLWC	UPN, WB
Providence-New Bedford	100%	WNAC	FOX
Providence-New Bedford	100%	WPRI	CBS
Providence-New Bedford	100%	WPXQ	PAX
Providence-New Bedford	100%	WSBE	PBS

Cable systems and subscribers
Cox   98,513
Full Channel TV   11,125

Military installations, September 2001
Newport Naval Station, Newport   778
Naval and Marine Corps Reserve Center, Newport   395

Businesses and other major employers
Brown University; Providence   2,758
Raytheon Co.; Portsmouth; defense systems   2,100
Hasbro Inc.; Pawtucket; board games   2,000
City of Pawtucket; Pawtucket; city government   1,710
DB Marketing Inc.; Pawtucket; gas stations   1,600
Memorial Hospital; Pawtucket   1,564
CVS Pharmacy Inc.; Woonsocket; drug stores   1,500
Roger Williams Medical Center; Providence   1,470
Lifespan Corp. Miriam Hospital; Providence   1,413
City of Woonsocket; Woonsocket; city government   1,385
St. Joseph Hospital; Providence   1,000
U.S. Postal Service; Providence   1,000
U.S. Veterans Hospital; Providence   1,000
Chinet Co.; Rumford; packaging and boxboard   900
East Providence; Riverside; city government   850
Lifespan Corp. Newport Hospital; Newport   817
Landmark Medical Center; Woonsocket   815
American Postal Workers Union; North Providence; labor organization   800
Providence College; Providence   800
Town of North Providence; North Providence; city government   760
AT Cross Co.; Lincoln; computer peripheral equipment   750
Citizens Financial Group Inc.; Riverside; bank holding companies   742
Butler Hospital; Providence   700
Lifespan Corp. Bradley Hospital; Riverside   677
Elmwood Sensors Inc.; Pawtucket; thermostats   650
Teknor Apex Co.; Pawtucket; compound resins   650
Burrillville Racing Assn. Inc.; Lincoln; dog racing   600
City of Bristol; Bristol; city government   600
International Packaging Corp.; Pawtucket; packing, shipping boxes   600
Fleet National Bank; Smithfield; financial services   550
Osram Sylvania Inc.; Central Falls; industrial glassware   535
Rhode Island Dept. of Environmental Management; Providence   530
ACS Industries Inc.; Woonsocket; scouring sponges   500

Burns International Security Services Corp.; East
Providence; security guard service   500
Paramount Cards Inc.; Pawtucket; greeting cards   500
Victoria & Co.; Rumford; costume jewelry   500

Rhode Island 2nd District

West — part of Providence, Warwick, Cranston

Bordering Connecticut on one side and the Narragansett Bay on the other, the 2nd occupies the western two-thirds of Rhode Island, covering the upstate rolling hills and most of the metropolitan area around Providence. Washington County, the southernmost part of the district, has beaches and lakes that attract tourists and residents alike. Twelve miles off the southern coast lies Block Island, a scenic vacation spot with more than 365 ponds.

The 2nd's economy is shifting from manufacturing to service. The change has caused a population shift, with people leaving Providence (shared with the 1st District) for Washington County, attracted by the growing businesses centered in the county's idyllic landscape. As white residents have departed the Providence area, more blacks and Hispanics have moved in, increasing the city's already Democratic tendency. The 2nd's portion of Providence includes a few schools, including Johnson & Wales University and Rhode Island College.

General Dynamics' Electric Boat has a submarine facility near Quonset Point in Washington County, and some county residents commute to the company's Groton, Connecticut, plant as well. Most of the district experienced modest growth during the 1990s, though the median age of the population is getting younger.

The 2nd is home to many working- and middle-class towns, with a substantial union presence that votes Democratic. No Republican presidential candidate has carried the district since Ronald Reagan in 1984. Despite the Democratic dominance, the district's large Catholic population has made abortion a key issue. Redistricting following the 2000 census shifted a few Providence neighborhoods into the 1st District, but the change did not affect the 2nd's political makeup.

Major Industry

Defense, banking, higher education, government, tourism.

Notable

The first armed conflict of the American Revolution took place near Warwick in 1772, when patriots in eight longboats captured and burned two British revenue ships.

Election Returns

	Republican		Democratic		Other	
President 2000	69,076	33.2%	124,314	59.8%	14,366	6.9%
House 2002	37,740	22.3%	129,312	76.3%	2,323	1.4%

District Profile

Population   524,162

Total area (square miles)   980.3
  Land area (square miles)   720.2

Population per square mile   727.8

Counties (2000 population)
  Kent   167,090
  Providence (pt.)   233,526
  Washington   123,546

Cities and other areas over 10,000 (2000 population)
  Cranston   79,269
  Providence (pt.)   101,516
  Warwick   85,808
  Westerly CDP   17,682
  West Warwick CDP   29,581

Race and Hispanic or Latino origin*
  White   81.2%
  Black or African American   3.9%
  American Indian or Alaska Native   0.5%
  Asian   2.6%
  Native Hawaiian or other Pacific Islander   0.0%
  Some other race   0.3%
  Hispanic or Latino origin   9.8%
  Two or more races   1.6%

As percentage of total population.

Ancestry*
English 9.8%	Polish 2.8%
Fr. Canadian 3.3%	Portuguese 3.8%
French 7.4%	Scottish 1.5%
German 4.1%	Swedish 1.7%
Irish 14.4%	USA/American 2.1%
Italian 16.7%	

As estimated percentage of total population.

Universities and colleges, 2000–2001 enrollment
  Community College of Rhode Island, Warwick   15,583
  Johnson & Wales University, Providence   9,172
  New England Institute of Technology, Warwick   2,712
  Rhode Island College, Providence   8,513
  Rhode Island School of Design, Providence   2,086
  University of Rhode Island, Kingston   14,362

Newspapers and circulation

	District circulation	Total circulation
Boston Globe	1,259	465,248
Boston Herald	1,177	257,071
Kent County Daily Times	4,656	4,661
Providence Journal	82,233	161,108
*USA Today**	4,946	1,674,376
Westerly Sun	7,893	10,398

See Sources and Explanations in the front of the volume.

Television stations and affiliations
  Providence-New Bedford   100%   WJAR   NBC
  Providence-New Bedford   100%   WLNE   ABC
  Providence-New Bedford   100%   WLWC   UPN, WB
  Providence-New Bedford   100%   WNAC   FOX
  Providence-New Bedford   100%   WPRI   CBS
  Providence-New Bedford   100%   WPXQ   PAX
  Providence-New Bedford   100%   WSBE   PBS

Cable systems and subscribers
  Cox   144,677

Military installations, September 2001

Quonset State Airport Air National Guard Station, North Kingston   945

Camp Fogarty Training Site, East Greenwich   590

Coventry Air National Guard Station, Coventry   268

Businesses and other major employers

Care New England Health System Inc.; Providence; investment holding company   5,500

Rhode Island Hospital; Providence   4,000

Providence School Dept.; Providence   2,500

University of Rhode Island; Kingston   2,000

Kent County Memorial Hospital; Warwick   1,840

Women and Infants Hospital of Rhode Island; Providence   1,800

American Power Conversion Corp.; West Kingston; AC/DC power conversion units   1,400

GTECH Corp.; Warwick; lottery operation   1,400

Metropolitan Group Properties and Casualty; Warwick; property damage insurance   1,350

GTECH Corp.; West Greenwich; lottery operation   1,200

Rhode Island Dept. of Mental Health Retardation and Hospitals; Cranston   1,200

Stanley-Bostitch Inc.; East Greenwich; stapling machines   1,100

Fleet Capital Corp.; Providence; real estate leasing and rentals   1,000

ON Semiconductor Corp.; Exeter; semiconductors and related devices   968

Blue Cross and Blue Shield of Rhode Island; Providence; medical service plans   950

Rhode Island School of Design Inc.; Providence   948

Providence Journal Co.; Providence; newspaper   870

Rhode Island College; Providence   841

Fleet Services Corp.; Providence; data processing   801

Leviton Manufacturing Co.; Warwick; electric sockets   800

K&M Associates; Providence; jewelry   746

AFCO Inc.; Johnston; corrugated display items   700

Brown and Sharpe International Capital Corp.; North Kingstown; machine tool accessories   700

Johnson and Wales University Inc.; Providence   700

Pritchard Industries Inc.; Cranston; commercial cleaning services   700

Toray Plastics America Inc.; North Kingstown; polypropylene film and sheet   675

City of Providence; Providence; police dept.   650

Swarovski North America; Cranston; costume jewelry   650

Amtrol Inc.; West Warwick; lined metal plate tanks   600

Harvard Pilgrim Health Care Inc.; Providence; health insurance   600

Metropolitan Tower Corp.; West Warwick; fire, marine, casualty insurance   600

South County Hospital Inc.; Wakefield   600

Cranston International Sales Corp.; Cranston; chemicals and allied products   550

Southern Union Co.; Providence; natural gas distribution   517

Citizens Bank of Rhode Island; Cranston; state commercial banks   500

Citizens Bank of Rhode Island; Providence; state commercial banks   500

City of Westerly; Westerly; city government   500

Davol Inc.; Cranston; medical supplies   500

Kenney Manufacturing Co.; Warwick; window shades   500

Rhode Island Dept. of Children, Youth, and Families; Providence   500

Rhode Island Public Transit Authority; Providence   500

Shaw's Supermarkets Inc.; Warwick   500

West Warwick School District; West Warwick   500

SOUTH CAROLINA

Districts established March 20, 2002, for elections first held in 2002.

6 members

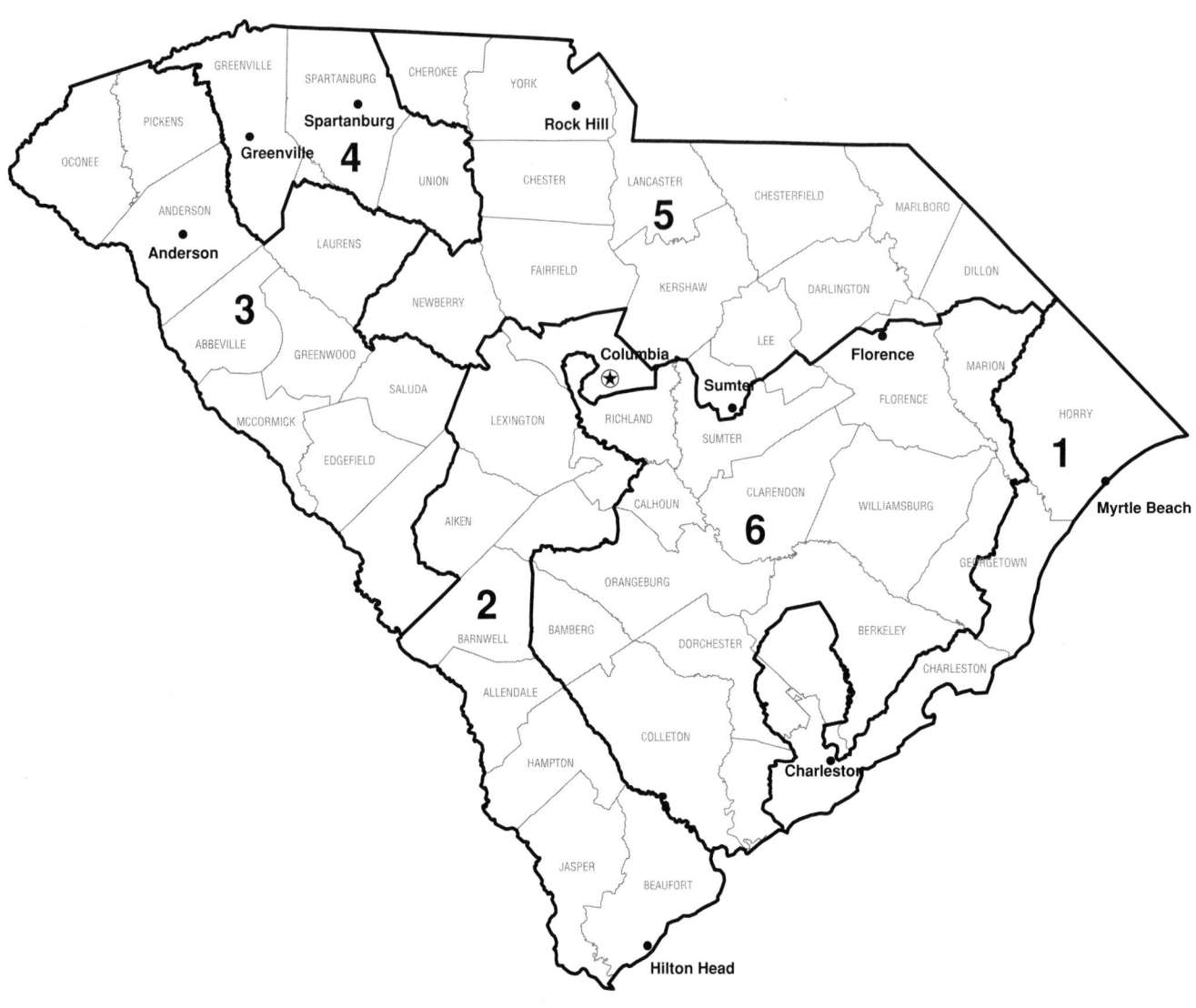

South Carolina

While it has never been among the larger southern states, South Carolina has always been pivotal in defense of the southern cause. As far back as the Revolutionary War, the residents of South Carolina put up a fight against British occupying forces, first as guerillas and then in conventional battle at Kings Mountain (1780). In the years when slavery preoccupied Congress, South Carolina's senator John C. Calhoun was the foremost exponent of state's rights (including the right to nullify acts of the national government). In 1860 South Carolina was the first state to secede, and in 1861 it commenced the bloody conflict between the states by firing on Fort Sumter in Charleston Bay.

More recently, South Carolina has been a leader in the transformation of the South from a one-party system based on the Democratic Party to a two-party system dominated by Republicans. The key figure in that transformation was Strom Thurmond, who was born in Edgefield in 1902 and began running for public office in the 1920s. He was an airborne Army officer on D-Day in 1944, returned to South Carolina and was elected governor in 1946 as a Democrat. In 1948 he bolted the Democratic convention in protest of the civil rights plank in the platform and accepted the presidential nomination of the States' Rights Party. In the splintered election of 1948 he won his home state with 70 percent of the vote and carried three others by wide margins. After finishing his governor's term he ran for the Senate as a Democrat in 1956 and won.

In 1964, protesting the Civil Rights Act, Thurmond became a Republican and endorsed Barry Goldwater for president. South Carolina was one of the five states in Dixie that Goldwater carried (and one of six overall). Thereafter, Thurmond had to wait 16 years to return to majority status in the Senate but when his patience was rewarded in 1980 he was elevated to Senate president pro tempore, a largely honorific post he would hold most of the time until he retired in 2003, having broken the Senate records for age and length of service. In his later years, Thurmond kept his political focus on "law and order" rather than race and found a certain rapprochement with blacks in his state.

It took time for other South Carolinians to follow Thurmond into the GOP. His successor, elected in 2002, was just the second Republican to occupy a Senate seat from the state. The first Republican governor since Reconstruction was James Edwards, elected in 1974, but there have been three since. It took until the 1980s for Republicans to reach parity in the House and until the mid-1990s for them to dominate the delegation, but they seemed entrenched there in the years after 2000. They also controlled both chambers of the legislature.

The 1980s also marked the emergence of the Palmetto State as a kingmaker in the Republican primaries. It was here, on a March Saturday in 1980, that Ronald Reagan knocked out his conservative rival, John Connally of Texas. Having established himself as the southern champion, Reagan swept Florida, Georgia, and Alabama three days later and breezed to the nomination. In 1988, South Carolina performed a similar service for George Bush, whose campaign was run by South Carolinian Lee Atwater. In 1996, South Carolina was where Bob Dole put a lock on his GOP nomination. In 2000 George W. Bush turned his fortunes around in South Carolina after a bad loss in New Hampshire. More than any other state, South Carolina has become the place where Republican nominees are anointed.

One reason Dole won over Pat Buchanan and his antiglobalization themes in 1996 was that South Carolina has grown more internationally oriented. Long dependent on raw materials and textiles, South Carolina has begun to build cars for European automakers and move itself higher on the chain of added value. While resentments remain, more and more of the state's younger residents want to view themselves as winners in the new world economy.

This is not to say the long-depressed rural areas of the state have banished poverty. About 10 percent of the population is below the poverty line, a figure very near the national average. The gross state product is still forty-first in the nation, per capita personal income is fortieth, and average hourly earnings are dead last in the 50 states. But unemployment is among the lowest, and the overall direction of the economy is clearly upward. The statewide population rose by 15 percent in the 1990s, with the principal reason the bloom in the western upland counties of Anderson, Greenville, and Spartanburg on the Piedmont Plateau. Taken together, these and adjacent counties are now a market statistical area of more than 960,000—growing faster than the state as a whole and verging on being among the 50 largest metro areas.

The largest individual city is still the state capital of Columbia (116,000), at the center of the state. Second is historic Charleston (89,000), still a jewel of a seaport, somewhat akin to Savannah and New Orleans in its architectural charm, replete with wrought iron porches and cobblestone streets. But its economic vitality has been severely challenged by the closing of its Navy base in the mid-1990s. Centuries old, the Charleston Bay base had been second only to Norfolk on the East Coast. But the Navy's decision to consolidate at

Norfolk could not be swayed, even by Thurmond's influence on the Senate Armed Services Committee.

South Carolina was long a mainstay of the Democratic column in presidential elections. It voted for the Democrat every time from the end of Reconstruction until 1948, even in 1928 when much of the South deserted the party for nominating New York's Catholic governor Al Smith. In 1948 South Carolina voted for Thurmond, then returned to voting for Democrats until 1964, the year Thurmond led the switch to Goldwater's GOP. Since then, the state has gone for every Republican nominee except Gerald R. Ford in 1976 (the year Jimmy Carter from nearby Georgia successfully ran as a southern Democrat).

South Carolina is now recognized as a GOP stronghold, perhaps its best in the South east of the Mississippi. In 2000 it gave nearly 57 percent of its vote to George W. Bush (and nearly 70 percent of its white vote), better than any southern state except Texas and Oklahoma. In 2002 it defeated its one-term Democratic governor, elected a new Republican senator (Graham), and reelected its 4–2 Republican House delegation. The Democratic Party was further set back in August 2003, when its highest-profile leader, six-term incumbent Sen. Ernest F. Hollings, announced plans to retire when his term ended in 2005.

The redistricting of 2001 in the GOP-controlled legislature was controversial largely as it pertained to state legislative districts. It was vetoed by the Democratic governor of that year and an override effort failed. So a three-judge federal panel stepped in and approved a congressional map with very few changes. On a practical plane, there was not much the Republicans could do to dislodge Democrat John Spratt in the north-central Sand Hills and tidewater counties of the 5th District (which shares lines with each of the other five districts). Even less likely to be molested was the central 6th District of Democrat Jim Clyburn, the delegation's one African American, who had the cities of Florence and Sumter and black neighborhoods of Columbia and Charleston. In November 2002 the state elected four Republicans and two Democrats for the fifth straight time, although all four of the Republican members had changed since the GOP first took over the majority in the mid-1990s.

South Carolina is 30 percent black, meaning it might well sustain two black districts. But drawing the second one would require far greater contortions than the artfully drawn 1st, and the Supreme Court has looked askance at such exertions. Clyburn's district is more than 60 percent African American, and no other district in the state is less than two-thirds white.

Table 1 Population

District	Population	Population under 18	Voting-age population	Median age	Male*	Female*
1	668,668	160,985	507,683	35.5	48.9	51.1
2	668,668	169,038	499,630	34.9	49.3	50.7
3	668,669	162,596	506,073	36.4	48.7	51.3
4	668,669	164,999	503,670	35.8	48.6	51.4
5	668,668	176,022	492,646	35.5	48.3	51.7
6	668,670	176,001	492,669	34.5	47.6	52.4
State	4,012,012	1,009,641	3,002,371	35.4	48.6	51.4

*As percentage of total population.

Table 2 Voting-Age Persons by Race/Hispanic or Latino Origin

District	White*	Black or African American*	American Indian or Alaska Native*	Asian*	Other or multirace*	Hispanic or Latino*
1	76.6	18.5	0.4	1.4	0.9	2.4
2	70.7	23.9	0.3	1.3	0.8	3.2
3	77.9	19.0	0.2	0.6	0.5	1.7
4	76.7	18.1	0.2	1.3	0.6	3.1
5	66.8	29.9	0.5	0.5	0.5	1.7
6	43.6	53.5	0.3	0.6	0.6	1.4
State	68.8	27.0	0.3	0.9	0.6	2.2

*As percentage of voting-age population.

Table 3 Voting-Age Population by Age Groups

District	18 to 24*	25 to 44*	45 to 64*	Over 64*
1	13.8	40.2	30.5	15.6
2	13.5	41.5	30.0	15.1
3	13.7	37.5	31.2	17.8
4	12.5	40.6	30.8	16.2
5	12.4	39.9	31.5	16.2
6	15.8	37.3	30.6	16.3
State	13.6	39.5	30.8	16.2

*As percentage of voting-age population.

Table 4 Income and Occupation

District	Median family income	Families in poverty*	White collar†	Blue collar†	Service†	Farm†
1	$48,001	8.2	59.7	23.0	16.9	0.5
2	$51,175	8.1	63.1	22.6	13.9	0.5
3	$43,177	9.6	48.7	36.8	13.9	0.5
4	$47,252	8.6	56.0	30.8	12.9	0.3
5	$41,549	11.9	48.5	37.5	13.3	0.8
6	$34,961	18.4	48.1	33.0	17.9	1.0
State	$44,227	10.7	54.2	30.4	14.7	0.6

*As percentage of all families.   †As percentage of employed workers 16 years and over.

Table 5 Education: School Years Completed

District	Less than grade 9*	Grades 9–12 no diploma*	High school diploma no college*	Some college*	College bachelor's degree or higher*
1	5.0	11.2	27.7	30.7	25.4
2	5.3	11.2	26.5	28.6	28.5
3	10.1	16.7	32.5	23.7	17.1
4	8.3	15.2	28.2	25.9	22.3
5	10.5	18.4	32.7	23.5	14.8
6	10.9	19.5	32.4	23.1	14.1
State	8.3	15.4	30.0	25.9	20.4

*As percentage of persons age 25 and over.

Table 6 Housing and Residential Patterns

District	Median home value	Owner occupied*	Renter occupied*	Urban†	Rural†
1	$102,800	69.4	30.6	78.4	21.6
2	$96,400	73.4	26.6	66.0	34.0
3	$77,400	75.5	24.5	50.3	49.7
4	$92,000	70.1	29.9	73.5	26.5
5	$71,400	74.6	25.4	46.7	53.3
6	$62,800	70.2	29.8	48.0	52.0
State	$83,100	72.2	27.8	60.5	39.5

*As percentage of occupied housing units.   †As percentage of total population.

South Carolina 1st District

East — part of Charleston, Myrtle Beach

Taking in the northeast half of the state's coastline, the 1st is marked by two of South Carolina's landmark tourism cities, Charleston and Myrtle Beach. Horry County, which envelops Myrtle Beach, still has plenty of farmland but is one of the state's fastest-growing areas. The 1st is the least rural of South Carolina's six congressional districts.

Hurricane Hugo wrought devastation all along the state's coastline in 1989, and defense downsizing further hurt Charleston in the early 1990s. But these events also heralded a wave of redevelopment, as the city shifted its economy to manufacturing, shipping, health care, and technology. Charleston (80 percent of whose residents live in the 1st) is an icon of the New South but retains its traditional culture. Surrounded by reminders of antebellum history, it is nicknamed the "Holy City" because of the church steeples marking its skyline.

Moving north, tourism and agriculture dominate the 1st. Myrtle Beach's tourist-resort economy welcomes 13 million visitors a year. Horry County voted similarly to South Carolina in the 2002 elections, backing Republicans for governor and the U.S. Senate by solid but not overwhelming margins.

The district's demographics—mostly white, suburban, and comfortably middle class—make it reliable Republican territory. One exception is the strong environmental and antidevelopment sentiment shared by many coastal residents in response to rapid population growth, rising pollution, and beach erosion.

Major Industry

Tourism, shipping, health care.

Notable

Charleston Harbor is home to Fort Sumter, where the Civil War began in April 1861; Fort Moultrie on Sullivan's Island nearby marks the first decisive victory in the War for Independence; 18-year-old Edgar Allan Poe arrived in Charleston in 1827 to enlist at Fort Moultrie.

Election Returns

	Republican		Democratic		Other	
President 2000	139,758	60.4%	91,510	39.6%		
House 2002	127,562	89.6%			14,863	10.4%

District Profile

Population 668,668

Total area (square miles) 3,418.6
   Land area (square miles) 2,644.5

Population per square mile 252.9

Counties (2000 population)
   Berkeley (pt.) 111,464   Georgetown (pt.) 37,667
   Charleston (pt.) 245,954   Horry 196,629
   Dorchester (pt.) 76,954

Cities and other areas over 10,000 (2000 population)
   Charleston (pt.) 77,434
   Conway 11,788
   Goose Creek 29,208
   Hanahan 12,937
   Ladson CDP 13,264
   Mount Pleasant town 47,609
   Myrtle Beach 22,759
   North Charleston (pt.) 45,530
   North Myrtle Beach 10,974
   Red Hill CDP 10,509
   Socastee CDP 14,295
   Summerville town 27,752

Race and Hispanic or Latino origin*
   White 73.7%
   Black or African American 20.9%
   American Indian or Alaska Native 0.4%
   Asian 1.2%
   Native Hawaiian or other Pacific Islander 0.1%
   Some other race 0.1%
   Hispanic or Latino origin 2.5%
   Two or more races 1.1%

*As percentage of total population.

Ancestry*
   English 8.9%   Polish 1.4%
   French 2.4%   Scotch-Irish 2.3%
   German 9.6%   Scottish 2.1%
   Irish 8.5%   USA/American 9.3%
   Italian 3.1%

*As estimated percentage of total population.

Universities and colleges, 2000–2001 enrollment
   Charleston Southern University, Charleston 2,603
   Coastal Carolina University, Conway 4,653
   College of Charleston, Charleston 11,129
   Horry-Georgetown Technical College, Conway 3,693
   Johnson & Wales University, Charleston 1,396
   Medical University of South Carolina, Charleston 2,346
   Trident Technical College, Charleston 10,246

Newspapers and circulation

	District circulation	Total circulation
Charleston Post and Courier	76,474	104,054
Columbia State	2,050	118,929
Myrtle Beach Sun News	44,011	48,171
*USA Today**	7,123	1,674,376

*See Sources and Explanations in the front of the volume.

Television stations and affiliations

Charleston	63%	WCBD	NBC
Charleston	63%	WCIV	ABC
Charleston	63%	WCSC	CBS
Charleston	63%	WITV	PBS
Charleston	63%	WJWJ	PBS
Charleston	63%	WMMP	UPN
Charleston	63%	WTAT	FOX
Florence-Myrtle Beach	37%	WBTW	CBS
Florence-Myrtle Beach	37%	WFPX	PAX
Florence-Myrtle Beach	37%	WFXB	FOX
Florence-Myrtle Beach	37%	WHMC	PBS
Florence-Myrtle Beach	37%	WJPM	PBS
Florence-Myrtle Beach	37%	WPDE	ABC
Florence-Myrtle Beach	37%	WUNU	PBS
Florence-Myrtle Beach	37%	WWMB	UPN

Cable systems and subscribers

Berkley Cable   15,337
Comcast   58,914
Horry Telephone Cable   27,877
Time Warner   73,879
U.S. Cable   5,626

Military installations, September 2001

Charleston Air Force Base, Charleston   6,064
Charleston Naval Weapons Station, Goose Creek   700

Businesses and other major employers

PeopLease Corp.; Mount Pleasant; employment agencies   5,400
CareAlliance Marketing; Charleston; marketing consulting   4,000
Charleston Memorial Hospital; Charleston   3,500
AVX Corp.; Myrtle Beach; electronic capacitors   2,075
Trident Medical Center; Charleston   1,992
Employee Resource Management Inc.; Charleston; employee leasing service   1,960
Granite Professional Technical Services Inc.; Summerville; industrial help service   1,571
Cummins Inc.; Charleston; combustion engines   1,250
Bayer Corp.; Goose Creek; chemicals and allied products   1,100
Conway Hospital Inc.; Conway   1,075
AGFA Corp.; Goose Creek; photographic equipment, supplies   1,065
Wal-Mart Stores Inc.; Myrtle Beach; department stores   1,030
College of Charleston; Charleston   1,028
U.S. Dept. of Veterans Affairs; Charleston   1,000
Horry County; Conway; county government   910
Coastal Carolina University; Conway   900
International Paper Co.; Georgetown; paper mills   860
Talbots Inc.; Charleston; mail-order catalog   825
Myrtle Beach Hospital Inc.; Myrtle Beach   811
Williams Technologies Inc.; Summerville; automotive transmissions   810
Bon-Secours St. Francis Xavier Hospital; Charleston   800
Behr Heat Transfer Systems Inc.; Charleston; automotive radiators   700
Campground at James Island; Charleston; trailer parks and campsites   700
Sands Investments Inc.; Myrtle Beach; subdividers and developers   700
Praxair Inc.; Georgetown; nitrogen   670
Loris Community Hospital District; Loris   650
LINQ Industrial Fabrics Inc.; Summerville; nonwoven fabrics   630
Georgetown Steel Corp.; Georgetown; iron and steel rods   625
Alumax of South Carolina Inc.; Goose Creek; primary aluminum   620
Georgetown Memorial Hospital; Georgetown   613
Destination Hotels and Resorts Inc.; Isle of Palms; hotels and motels   600
Horry Telephone Cooperative Inc.; Conway; telephone communication   600
Six Continental Hotels; Charleston; hotel, franchised   600
Charleston Center; Charleston; hotels and motels   575
South Carolina State Ports Authority; Charleston   531
Blue Cross and Blue Shield of South Carolina; Myrtle Beach; medical service plans   500
East Cooper Community Hospital Inc.; Mount Pleasant   500
H&C Racing Inc.; Myrtle Beach; restaurants   500
Legends Group Inc.; Myrtle Beach; real estate managers   500
Ness Motley Loadholt Richardson and Poole; Mount Pleasant; law office   500

South Carolina 2nd District

Central and south — part of Columbia and suburbs, Hilton Head Island

---

The oddly shaped 2nd winds from the state capital of Columbia down through the middle of the state to a sandy stretch along the coast. The two ends of the district encapsulate some of the state's wealthiest communities: the suburbs of Columbia, in Richland and Lexington Counties, and Beaufort and Hilton Head Island on the southern tip.

Columbia's suburbs have grown steadily. While state and local government are still the city's largest employers, its private sector is becoming more of a force. At the southern end of the 2nd, retirees and tourists are drawn to Hilton Head Island. Surrounding Beaufort was the fastest-growing county in population in South Carolina in the 1990s.

Military issues are important here. Just up the shore from the swank resorts, recruits sweat at the Parris Island Marine Corps camp. Fort Jackson in Richland County at the district's northern end and another Marine installation also contribute to the military presence.

The areas between Columbia and Hilton Head are dotted with smaller towns and rural areas that are considerably poorer. Many families in the black-majority counties of Allendale, Hampton, and Jasper live below the poverty line, relying on tenant farming and sharecropping.

Heavy Democratic support in the poor areas is offset by wealthy white-collar professionals in the north and south, who push the district firmly into the GOP column. Lexington County, the 2nd's most-populous, voted two-to-one for Republican gubernatorial and senatorial candidates in 2002.

Major Industry

Tourism, government, military, agriculture.

Notable

The first federally authorized black unit to fight for the Union, the First South Carolina Volunteers, camped in Beaufort; Hilton Head Island is the site of the largest naval engagement of the Civil War.

Election Returns

	Republican		Democratic		Other	
President 2000	145,953	59.8%	97,985	40.2%		
House 2002	144,149	84.1%			27,210	15.9%

District Profile

Population   668,668

Total area (square miles)   5,237.3
   Land area (square miles)   4,767.3

Population per square mile   140.3

Counties (2000 population)

Aiken (pt.) 26,953	Hampton 21,386
Allendale 11,211	Jasper 20,678
Barnwell 23,478	Lexington 216,014
Beaufort 120,937	Orangeburg (pt.) 22,389
Calhoun (pt.) 6,895	Richland (pt.) 198,727

Cities and other areas over 10,000 (2000 population)

Beaufort   12,950
Cayce   12,150
Columbia (pt.)   59,771
Forest Acres (pt.)   10,558
Hilton Head Island town   33,862
Irmo town   11,039
Seven Oaks CDP   15,755
St. Andrews CDP   21,814
West Columbia   13,064

Race and Hispanic or Latino origin*

White   68.0%
Black or African American   26.2%
American Indian or Alaska Native   0.3%
Asian   1.1%
Native Hawaiian or other Pacific Islander   0.0%
Some other race   0.1%
Hispanic or Latino origin   3.3%
Two or more races   0.9%

*As percentage of total population.

Ancestry*

English 7.9%	Italian 2.1%
French 1.8%	Scotch-Irish 2.5%
German 10.0%	Scottish 1.8%
Irish 7.3%	USA/American 9.9%

*As estimated percentage of total population.

Universities and colleges, 2000–2001 enrollment

Midlands Technical College, Columbia   9,702
Technical College of the Lowcountry, Beaufort   1,776
University of South Carolina, Beaufort   1,175
University of South Carolina at Salkehatchie, Allendale   785

Newspapers and circulation

	District circulation	Total circulation
Aiken Standard	4,799	14,002
Augusta Chronicle	2,585	68,807
Beaufort Gazette	11,530	11,747
Columbia State	71,300	118,929
Hilton Head Island Packet	17,040	17,098
Orangeburg Times & Democrat	4,327	17,597
Savannah Morning News	3,758	58,145
*USA Today**	8,000	1,674,376

*See Sources and Explanations in the front of the volume.

Television stations and affiliations

Savannah, GA	42%	WGSA	UPN
Savannah, GA	42%	WJCL	ABC
Savannah, GA	42%	WSAV	NBC
Savannah, GA	42%	WTGS	FOX
Savannah, GA	42%	WTOC	CBS
Savannah, GA	42%	WVAN	PBS
Columbia	30%	WACH	FOX
Columbia	30%	WIS	NBC
Columbia	30%	WLTX	CBS
Columbia	30%	WOLO	ABC
Columbia	30%	WQHB	UPN, WB
Columbia	30%	WRJA	PBS
Columbia	30%	WRLK	PBS
Augusta, GA	28%	WAGT	NBC
Augusta, GA	28%	WCES	PBS
Augusta, GA	28%	WEBA	PBS
Augusta, GA	28%	WFXG	FOX
Augusta, GA	28%	WJBF	ABC
Augusta, GA	28%	WRDW	CBS

Cable systems and subscribers

Adelphia   20,000
Charter   11,947
Comcast   1,575
G-Force   3,085
Hargray CATV   2,093
Pine Tree Cablevision   1,626
Time Warner   42,887

Military installations, September 2001

Fort Jackson (Army), Columbia   9,290
Beaufort Marine Corps Air Station, Beaufort   5,368
Marine Corps Recruitment Depot Activity, Parris Island   4,200
Beaufort Naval Hospital, Beaufort   259

Businesses and other major employers

Blue Cross and Blue Shield of South Carolina; Columbia; medical service plans   3,000
Signum LLC; Columbia; temporary help service   2,500
Lexington Medical Center; West Columbia   1,800
South Carolina Public Service Authority; Bluffton; electric services   1,700
South Carolina University; Columbia   1,653
Washington Group International Inc.; Aiken; energy development, conservation   1,500
Owens Corning; Aiken; mineral wool   1,200
Concurrent Technologies Corp.; Hilton Head Island; engineering services   1,141

Dixie-Narco Inc.; Williston; vending machines   1,100
Advanced Glassfiber Yarns; Aiken; fiberglass fabrics   1,000
APAC Customer Services Inc.; Columbia; telemarketing   1,000
Shaw Industries Inc.; Fairfax; carpet finishing   1,000
Colonial Life and Accident Insurance Co.; Columbia   940
Amick Farms Inc.; Batesburg; poultry and poultry products   900
Beaufort County; Beaufort; county government   850
Bose Corp.; Blythewood; audio/video equipment   800
U.S. Postal Service; West Columbia   800
Beaufort County Memorial Hospital; Beaufort   780
Eastman Chemical Co.; West Columbia; industrial chemicals   710
International Paper Co.; Hampton; packing materials, plastics sheet   632
FiberBuys.com; Columbia; Internet services   600
Midlands Technical College Inc.; West Columbia   546
Collette Travel Service Inc.; Barnwell; tour operators   525
Hyatt Corp.; Hilton Head Island; hotels   500
Midlands Technical College Inc.; Columbia   500
PYA/Monarch Inc.; Lexington; food brokers   500
Wal-Mart Stores Inc.; Columbia; department stores   500

South Carolina 3rd District

West — Anderson, Aiken

Encompassing the northwest corner of the state, the 3rd is one of South Carolina's most rural districts. Many voters here are converts to the Republican Party, having shifted over from "Yellow Dog" Democrat status. Former representative (and now senator) Lindsey Graham was the first Republican to win this seat since Reconstruction in 1994.

The brimming economy has further boosted opportunities for the GOP. The base of engineers surrounding the Savannah River nuclear complex near Aiken, the district's largest employer, has helped attract Fortune 500 firms to the area, as well as several U.S. divisions of international companies. An example is Fujifilm in Greenwood, which employs 1,500 South Carolinians and has invested more than $1.3 billion in the state. Fujifilm's new medical products plant is the first built outside of Japan.

To the northwest, Anderson has built a more industrial economy, moving away from its rural roots. Many area textile mills have successfully shifted to high-tech fiber manufacturing. Clemson University provides the economic and social nexus for Pickens County at the 3rd's northern tip.

The district votes solidly Republican in federal and statewide races. The 3rd's most populous voting jurisdictions—Anderson, Aiken, and Pickens Counties—are heavily Republican. Pickens County gave 71 percent of its vote to George W. Bush in 2000. The counties in the 3rd's midsection are more rural, less prosperous, and less Republican-leaning. This area includes McCormick County, where the majority of the population is black.

Major Industry

Manufacturing, textiles, cotton.

Notable

The 70,000-acre Lake Thurmond, previously known as Clarks Hill Lake, was renamed after Republican senator Strom Thurmond; Aiken is known as the polo center of the South.

Election Returns

	Republican		Democratic		Other	
President 2000	142,414	64.7%	77,694	35.3%		
House 2002	119,644	67.1%	55,743	31.3%	2,808	1.6%

District Profile

Population   668,669

Total area (square miles)   5,567.5
Land area (square miles)   5,392.3

Population per square mile   124.0

Counties (2000 population)
Abbeville 26,167	Laurens (pt.) 64,186
Aiken (pt.) 115,599	McCormick 9,958
Anderson 165,740	Oconee 66,215
Edgefield 24,595	Pickens 110,757
Greenwood 66,271	Saluda 19,181

Cities and other areas over 10,000 (2000 population)
Aiken (pt.) 22,810	Easley 17,754
Anderson 25,514	Greenwood 22,071
Clemson 11,939	North Augusta 17,574

Race and Hispanic or Latino origin*
White   76.0%
Black or African American   20.5%
American Indian or Alaska Native   0.2%
Asian   0.6%
Native Hawaiian or other Pacific Islander   0.0%
Some other race   0.1%
Hispanic or Latino origin   1.9%
Two or more races   0.7%

As percentage of total population.

Ancestry*
English 7.3%	Italian 1.3%
French 1.4%	Scotch-Irish 2.8%
German 7.0%	Scottish 1.5%
Irish 8.0%	USA/American 15.0%

As estimated percentage of total population.

Universities and colleges, 2000–2001 enrollment
Aiken Technical College, Aiken   2,268
Anderson College, Anderson   1,398
Clemson University, Clemson   17,465
Erskine College and Seminary, Due West   858
Forrest Junior College, Anderson   229
Lander University, Greenwood   2,935
Piedmont Technical College, Greenwood   4,104
Presbyterian College, Clinton   1,148

Southern Wesleyan University, Central   1,803
Tri-County Technical College, Pendleton   3,612
University of South Carolina, Aiken   3,278

Newspapers and circulation

	District circulation	Total circulation
Aiken Standard	9,282	14,002
Anderson Independent-Mail	30,086	38,854
Atlanta Journal-Constitution	1,670	857,088
Augusta Chronicle	13,792	68,807
Columbia State	3,428	118,929
Greenville News	31,095	95,391
Greenwood Index Journal	14,460	14,498
*USA Today**	2,251	1,674,376

See Sources and Explanations in the front of the volume.

Television stations and affiliations

Greenville-Spartanburg-Asheville-Anderson	65%	WASV	UPN
Greenville-Spartanburg-Asheville-Anderson	65%	WBSC	WB
Greenville-Spartanburg-Asheville-Anderson	65%	WGGS	Independent
Greenville-Spartanburg-Asheville-Anderson	65%	WHNS	FOX
Greenville-Spartanburg-Asheville-Anderson	65%	WLOS	ABC
Greenville-Spartanburg-Asheville-Anderson	65%	WNEG	CBS
Greenville-Spartanburg-Asheville-Anderson	65%	WNEH	PBS
Greenville-Spartanburg-Asheville-Anderson	65%	WNTV	PBS
Greenville-Spartanburg-Asheville-Anderson	65%	WRET	PBS
Greenville-Spartanburg-Asheville-Anderson	65%	WSPA	CBS
Greenville-Spartanburg-Asheville-Anderson	65%	WUNF	PBS
Greenville-Spartanburg-Asheville-Anderson	65%	WYFF	NBC
Augusta, GA	27%	WAGT	NBC
Augusta, GA	27%	WCES	PBS
Augusta, GA	27%	WEBA	PBS
Augusta, GA	27%	WFXG	FOX
Augusta, GA	27%	WJBF	ABC
Augusta, GA	27%	WRDW	CBS
Columbia	8%	WACH	FOX
Columbia	8%	WIS	NBC
Columbia	8%	WLTX	CBS
Columbia	8%	WOLO	ABC
Columbia	8%	WQHB	UPN, WB
Columbia	8%	WRJA	PBS
Columbia	8%	WRLK	PBS

Cable systems and subscribers

Charter   57,686
Comcast   6,684
G-Force   19,185
Northland   49,913

Businesses and other major employers

Clemson University; Clemson   16,000
CBS Corp.; North Augusta; electrical work   15,000
Centex Corp.; Piedmont; operative builders   13,526
U.S. Dept. of Energy; Aiken   13,500
Springs Industries Inc.; Honea Path; fabric mills   4,429
Pickens Roofing Inc.; Anderson; roofing contractor   3,845
Anderson Area Medical Center Inc.; Anderson   2,420
Westinghouse Savannah River Co.; Aiken; hazardous waste clean up   2,300
WestPoint Stevens Inc.; Clemson; fabric mills   2,200
Duke Energy Corp.; Seneca; electric services   2,000
Electrolux Home Products Inc.; Anderson; refrigerators   2,000
Self Memorial Hospital Regional Health Services Inc.; Greenwood   2,000
CMI Industries Inc.; Clinton; throwing and winding mills   1,900

Michelin North America Inc.; Sandy Springs; tires and inner tubes   1,700
Fujifilm; Greenwood; photographic equipment, supplies   1,500
BASF Corp.; Anderson; pharmaceuticals   1,300
Wal-Mart Stores Inc.; Laurens; warehousing   1,300
Solutia Inc.; Greenwood; organic fibers   1,200
Torrington Co.; Clinton; ball bearings and parts   1,104
Kimberly-Clark Corp.; Beech Island; tissue paper   1,050
OWT Industries Inc.; Pickens; power tools   1,000
South Carolina Mental Health Dept.; Clinton   930
Aiken Regional Medical Centers; Aiken   925
Oconee Memorial Hospital Inc.; Seneca   850
Schlumberger ElectriCities Inc.; West Union; electrical meters   850
Bridgestone/Firestone North American Tire; Graniteville; tires and inner tubes   800
Faurecia Interior Systems; Fountain Inn; automotive supplies, parts   800
Square D Co.; Seneca; switchgear apparatus   800
Beacon Blankets Inc.; Westminster; blankets   700
Torrington Co.; Honea Path; ball bearings and parts   660
Milliken & Co.; Williamston; fabric mills   650
Tyco Healthcare Group; Seneca; elastic braces   617
Greenwood Mills Inc.; Greenwood; fabric mills   600
Greenwood Packing Plant Inc.; Greenwood; meatpacking plants   600
Loris Community Hospital; Laurens   600
National Textiles; Hodges; yarn mills   600
Wal-Mart Stores Inc.; Aiken; department stores   560
Rug Barn Inc.; Abbeville; fabric mills   550
Tri-County Technical College; Pendleton   550
Aramark Services Inc.; Clemson; contract food services   500
Beaulieu Group; Aiken; yarn mills   500
Dispoz-O Products Inc.; Fountain Inn; molded plastics   500
Flexible Technologies Inc.; Abbeville; plastic ducting   500
Milliken & Co.; Abbeville; fabric mills   500
Milliken & Co.; Greenwood; fabric mills   500
Milliken & Co.; Honea Path; fabric mills   500
Mount Vernon Mills Inc.; La France; fabrics   500
Nutritia Manufacturing USA Inc.; Anderson; vitamin preparations   500
Pfizer Corp.; Greenwood; gelatin capsules   500

South Carolina 4th District

Northwest — Greenville, Spartanburg

The 4th is South Carolina's most compact district and is centered on Greenville County, the state's most-populous. Greenville and Spartanburg Counties together account for 95 percent of the district population. The 4th also takes in Union County, a heavily forested but lightly populated area, and a tiny part of Laurens County.

Successful manufacturing and warehousing ventures have transformed the area from its textile past. The cities of Greenville and Spartanburg are national leaders in per capita investment by foreign corporations. Michelin's North American headquarters are in Greenville, and BMW is a major presence in Spartanburg.

Although no longer the textile capital of the world, the 4th retains a strong textile presence. Industry giant Milliken & Co. is headquartered in Spartanburg. Trade issues are important in the district, though textile companies have less political influence since the industry has declined. Agriculture also plays a role in the Spartanburg area; its sprawling orchards yield one of the biggest peach crops in the South.

Air pollution, however, is a developing problem for the Greenville-Spartanburg area. A 2003 environmental study found that the region had suffered a 175 percent increase in smog levels from the early 1990s to 2002, the greatest increase nationwide.

Spreading wealth has helped keep this district solidly Republican. But the local GOP has two distinct camps: mainstream, business-oriented conservatives and social conservatives focused around Greenville-based Bob Jones University. In recent years, an influx of professionals has diluted the influence of social conservatives.

With its rank-and-file textile workers and farm laborers, Spartanburg is less heavily Republican than Greenville. Nonetheless, both counties voted for GOP candidates in key 2002 races by landslide margins. Mark Sanford took 62 percent in Greenville and 59 percent in Spartanburg in the gubernatorial election, and Lindsey Graham took 64 percent and 60 percent in those counties in the Senate election.

Major Industry
Engineering, manufacturing, textiles, agriculture.

Notable
Vietnam War general William C. Westmoreland was born in Spartanburg County; baseball player "Shoeless" Joe Jackson grew up in Greenville.

Election Returns

	Republican		Democratic		Other	
President 2000	151,975	66.0%	78,449	34.0%		
House 2002	122,422	69.0%	52,635	29.7%	2,360	1.3%

District Profile

Population   668,669

Total area (square miles)   2,165.4
Land area (square miles)   2,150.5

Population per square mile   310.9

Counties (2000 population)

Greenville	379,616	Spartanburg	253,791
Laurens (pt.)	5,381	Union	29,881

Cities and other areas over 10,000 (2000 population)
Berea CDP   14,158
Gantt CDP   13,962
Greenville   56,002
Greer   16,843
Mauldin   15,224
Parker CDP   10,760
Simpsonville   14,352
Spartanburg   39,673
Taylors CDP   20,125
Wade Hampton CDP   20,458

Race and Hispanic or Latino origin*
White   74.6%
Black or African American   19.7%
American Indian or Alaska Native   0.2%
Asian   1.3%
Native Hawaiian or other Pacific Islander   0.0%
Some other race   0.1%
Hispanic or Latino origin   3.2%
Two or more races   0.8%

*As percentage of total population.

Ancestry*

English	8.0%	Italian	1.8%
French	1.6%	Scotch-Irish	2.8%
German	7.1%	Scottish	1.7%
Irish	7.5%	USA/American	13.7%

*As estimated percentage of total population.

Universities and colleges, 2000–2001 enrollment
Bob Jones University, Greenville   3,706
Converse College, Spartanburg   1,412
Furman University, Greenville   3,272
Greenville Technical College, Greenville   10,786
North Greenville College, Tigerville   1,279
Sherman College of Straight Chiropractic, Spartanburg   352
Spartanburg Methodist College, Spartanburg   583
Spartanburg Technical College, Spartanburg   3,030
University of South Carolina, Spartanburg   3,709
University of South Carolina, Union   363
Woford College, Spartanburg   1,087

Newspapers and circulation

	District circulation	Total circulation
Greenville News	62,911	95,391
Spartanburg Herald-Journal	45,252	52,383
*USA Today**	4,413	1,674,376

*See Sources and Explanations in the front of the volume.

Television stations and affiliations

Greenville-Spartanburg-Asheville-Anderson	100%	WASV	UPN
Greenville-Spartanburg-Asheville-Anderson	100%	WBSC	WB
Greenville-Spartanburg-Asheville-Anderson	100%	WGGS	Independent
Greenville-Spartanburg-Asheville-Anderson	100%	WHNS	FOX
Greenville-Spartanburg-Asheville-Anderson	100%	WLOS	ABC
Greenville-Spartanburg-Asheville-Anderson	100%	WNEG	CBS
Greenville-Spartanburg-Asheville-Anderson	100%	WNEH	PBS
Greenville-Spartanburg-Asheville-Anderson	100%	WNTV	PBS
Greenville-Spartanburg-Asheville-Anderson	100%	WRET	PBS
Greenville-Spartanburg-Asheville-Anderson	100%	WSPA	CBS
Greenville-Spartanburg-Asheville-Anderson	100%	WUNF	PBS
Greenville-Spartanburg-Asheville-Anderson	100%	WYFF	NBC

Cable systems and subscribers
Charter   140,049

Businesses and other major employers
BMW Manufacturing Corp.; Greer; automobiles   4,500
Greenville Hospital System Inc.; Greenville   4,000
Spartanburg Regional Medical Center; Spartanburg   3,340
Advantica Restaurant Group Inc.; Spartanburg; vending machines   3,000

General Electric Co.; Greenville; gas turbines   2,800

Fluor Enterprises Inc.; Greenville; building site preparation   2,500

Arteva Specialties S.A.R.L. Ltd.; Spartanburg; polyesters and organic fibers   1,800

KEMET Electronics Corp.; Simpsonville; electronic capacitors   1,529

City of Greenville; Greenville; city government   1,500

MCI WorldCom Network Services Inc.; Greenville; communications specialization   1,500

St. Francis Hospital Inc.; Greenville   1,382

Bob Jones University Inc.; Greenville   1,380

Michelin Corp.; Greenville; automobile tires   1,300

Mary Black Center for Rehabilitative Medicine; Spartanburg   1,238

Lockheed Martin Aircraft and Logistic Center; Greenville; aircraft   1,200

Springs Industries Inc.; Lyman; fabric mills   1,180

Greenville Technical College; Greenville   1,140

BI-LO Foods; Greenville; supermarkets   1,000

Davis Electrical Constructors Inc.; Greenville; electrical contractor   1,000

Milliken & Co.; Spartanburg; fabric mills   1,000

Michelin Americas Research and Development Corp.; Greenville; commercial physical research   900

Inman Mills; Enoree; fabrics   883

KEMET Electronics Corp.; Fountain Inn; electronic capacitors   856

Kohler Co.; Spartanburg; plumbing fixtures, vitreous china   840

Carrier Corp.; Spartanburg; refrigeration equipment   830

Ideal Solutions Inc.; Greenville; executive placement   800

Jacobs Engineering Group Inc.; Greenville; engineering services   775

Conso International Corp.; Union; fabric mills   725

HomeGold Inc.; Greenville; urban mortgage   700

Spartanburg County; Spartanburg; county government   700

Furman University; Greenville   695

House of Raeford Farms Inc.; Greenville; processed turkey   650

R. R. Donnelley and Sons Co.; Spartanburg; commercial printing   650

Multimedia Publishing of South Carolina Inc.; Greenville; newspaper   630

Spartanburg Automotive Steel Inc.; Spartanburg; automotive stampings   618

BMG Music; Duncan; records and tapes   600

Reliance Electric Industrial Co.; Greenville; electric motor, generator parts   600

TeleTech Holdings Inc.; Greenville; mailing and messenger services   600

Tietex International; Spartanburg; fabrics   600

One Price Clothing Stores Inc.; Duncan   550

Delta Mills Inc.; Piedmont; fabric mills   533

Greenville County; Greenville; purchasing service   527

Ahold U.S.A. Inc.; Greenville; data processing   500

American Fibers and Yarns Co.; Spartanburg; organic fibers   500

Drive Automotive Industries of America Inc.; Piedmont; automotive stampings   500

International Paper Co.; Spartanburg; paper bags   500

Reeves Brothers Inc.; Spartanburg; cotton finishing plants   500

Torrington Co.; Union; roller bearings and parts   500

Winn-Dixie Charlotte Inc.; Taylors; supermarkets   500

South Carolina 5th District

North central — Rock Hill

The 5th spans all or part of 14 mostly rural counties in the north-central part of the state, stretching from near Charlotte, North Carolina, to the Columbia suburbs, with considerable territory spreading east and west. Redistricting following the 2000 census added even more rural sections to the area. The combination of tobacco farmers, white-collar Charlotte commuters, and textile workers makes this a conservative district, though it still clings to its traditional Southern Democrat roots.

In the midsection and west, rural counties such as Newberry, Chester, Lancaster, and Kershaw produce cotton for the textile mills that historically have dominated the region's economy. The two largest cities, Rock Hill and Sumter (shared with the 6th), add immigrants from the North. Rock Hill, once dependent on the textile industry, now serves as a home for white-collar commuters and Winthrop University.

Many residents of Fairfield County—an area that already had a double-digit unemployment rate—have lost their jobs because of businesses downsizing or moving overseas.

The city of Sumter, once the center of a large agricultural area, is shifting toward industry. Seven miles west of Sumter, Shaw Air Force Base makes up one-third of the area's economy. In the east, Darlington, Dillon, and Marlboro Counties depend heavily on tobacco farming.

Politically, the 5th tends to vote narrowly Republican in federal races, but conservative Democrats who appeal to the district's numerous poor and rural residents can win here. Democrats also are helped by the district's 32 percent black population, the largest of any South Carolina district except the black-majority 6th.

Major Industry
Cotton, textiles, tobacco.

Notable
The Lee County Cotton Festival, held every October, celebrates the agricultural history of "King Cotton"; televangelist Jim Bakker's PTL ministries were located in Fort Mill.

Election Returns

	Republican		Democratic		Other	
President 2000	119,052	56.0%	93,637	44.0%		
House 2002			121,912	85.9%	20,060	14.1%

District Profile

Population   668,668

Total area (square miles)   7,141.0
   Land area (square miles)   7,034.9

Population per square mile   95.1

Counties (2000 population)

Cherokee	52,537	Kershaw	52,647
Chester	34,068	Lancaster	61,351
Chesterfield	42,768	Lee (pt.)	17,534
Darlington	67,394	Marlboro	28,818
Dillon	30,722	Newberry	36,108
Fairfield	23,454	Sumter (pt.)	44,144
Florence (pt.)	12,509	York	164,614

Cities and other areas over 10,000 (2000 population)

Gaffney	12,968	Rock Hill	49,765
Newberry town	10,580	Sumter (pt.)	20,518

Race and Hispanic or Latino origin*

White 64.1%
Black or African American 32.2%
American Indian or Alaska Native 0.6%
Asian 0.5%
Native Hawaiian or other Pacific Islander 0.0%
Some other race 0.1%
Hispanic or Latino origin 1.8%
Two or more races 0.7%

*As percentage of total population.

Ancestry*

English	5.6%	Italian	1.2%
French	1.1%	Scotch-Irish	3.2%
German	5.5%	Scottish	1.3%
Irish	5.6%	USA/American	14.8%

*As estimated percentage of total population.

Universities and colleges, 2000–2001 enrollment

Central Carolina Technical College, Sumter 2,546
Chesterfield-Marlboro Technical College, Cheraw 982
Coker College, Hartsville 1,002
Florence Darlington Technical College, Florence 3,814
Limestone College, Gaffney 1,967
Newberry College, Newberry 724
University of South Carolina, Lancaster 837
University of South Carolina, Sumter 1,173
Winthrop University, Rock Hill 6,061
York Technical College, Rock Hill 3,597

Newspapers and circulation

	District circulation	Total circulation
Charlotte Observer	16,903	237,693
Columbia State	17,420	118,929
Florence Morning News	14,179	32,871
Rock Hill Herald	30,931	31,081
Spartanburg Herald-Journal	5,793	52,383
Sumter Item	6,094	21,598
*USA Today**	2,005	1,674,376

*See Sources and Explanations in the front of the volume.

Television stations and affiliations

Charlotte	37%	WAXN	Independent
Charlotte	37%	WBTV	CBS
Charlotte	37%	WCCB	FOX
Charlotte	37%	WCNC	NBC
Charlotte	37%	WHKY	Independent
Charlotte	37%	WJZY	UPN
Charlotte	37%	WNSC	PBS
Charlotte	37%	WSOC	ABC
Charlotte	37%	WTVI	PBS
Charlotte	37%	WUNE	PBS
Charlotte	37%	WUNG	PBS
Columbia	36%	WACH	FOX
Columbia	36%	WIS	NBC
Columbia	36%	WLTX	CBS
Columbia	36%	WOLO	ABC
Columbia	36%	WQHB	UPN, WB
Columbia	36%	WRJA	PBS
Columbia	36%	WRLK	PBS
Florence-Myrtle Beach	21%	WBTW	CBS
Florence-Myrtle Beach	21%	WFPX	PAX
Florence-Myrtle Beach	21%	WFXB	FOX
Florence-Myrtle Beach	21%	WHMC	PBS
Florence-Myrtle Beach	21%	WJPM	PBS
Florence-Myrtle Beach	21%	WPDE	ABC
Florence-Myrtle Beach	21%	WUNU	PBS
Florence-Myrtle Beach	21%	WWMB	UPN
Greenville-Spartanburg-Asheville-Anderson	6%	WASV	UPN
Greenville-Spartanburg-Asheville-Anderson	6%	WBSC	WB
Greenville-Spartanburg-Asheville-Anderson	6%	WGGS	Independent
Greenville-Spartanburg-Asheville-Anderson	6%	WHNS	FOX
Greenville-Spartanburg-Asheville-Anderson	6%	WLOS	ABC
Greenville-Spartanburg-Asheville-Anderson	6%	WNEG	CBS
Greenville-Spartanburg-Asheville-Anderson	6%	WNEH	PBS
Greenville-Spartanburg-Asheville-Anderson	6%	WNTV	PBS
Greenville-Spartanburg-Asheville-Anderson	6%	WRET	PBS
Greenville-Spartanburg-Asheville-Anderson	6%	WSPA	CBS
Greenville-Spartanburg-Asheville-Anderson	6%	WUNF	PBS
Greenville-Spartanburg-Asheville-Anderson	6%	WYFF	NBC

Cable systems and subscribers

Adelphia 18,163
Catawba Services 38,052
Charter 17,599
Comcast 4,592
Galaxy 1,482
Northland 4,944
Palmetto Cable TV 5,155
Pine Tree Cablevision 2,271
Time Warner 2,217

Businesses and other major employers

ESAB Group Inc.; Florence; welding apparatus 2,200
Sonoco Products Co.; Hartsville; fiber cans, drums, similar products 2,100
E. I. Du Pont De Nemours and Co.; Camden; textured yarns 2,000
Duke Energy Corp.; York; electric services 1,200
Piedmont Medical Center; Rock Hill 1,200
Kraft Foods Inc.; Newberry; processed turkey 1,100
Sumter County School District; Sumter 1,100
Gillette Co.; Lancaster; alkaline batteries 1,047
Galey and Lord Industries Inc.; Society Hill; cotton finishing plants 1,000
Perdue Farms Inc.; Dillon; poultry processing 1,000
Timken Co.; Gaffney; roller bearings and parts 1,000
A. O. Smith Corp.; McBee; household water heaters 936
Springs Industries Inc.; Chester; piques, cotton 833
South Carolina University; Sumter 820
Becton Dickinson and Co.; Sumter; medical instruments 800
Cone Mills Corp.; Carlisle; cotton finishing plants 800
Mack Trucks Inc.; Winnsboro; motor vehicles and car bodies 800
Carolina Power and Light Co.; Hartsville; electric power generation 700
Leiner Health Products Inc.; Fort Mill; vitamin, nutrient, hematinic preparations 700
Maytag Corp.; Florence; electric ranges 700
Milliken & Co.; Blacksburg; woven goods 700

Wal-Mart Stores Inc.; Pageland; warehousing   700

Sanders Bros. Inc.; Gaffney; machine moving and rigging   670

Freightliner Custom Chassis Corp.; Gaffney; highway truck tractor assembly   660

Lancaster Hospital Corp.; Lancaster   660

United Dominion Industries Ltd.; Bennettsville; blowers, fans, air purification   650

Wellman Inc.; Darlington; organic fibers   650

South Carolina Electric and Gas Co.; Jenkinsville; electric, other services   618

Aladdin Manufacturing Corp.; Bennettsville; throwing and winding mills   600

Black and Decker Corp.; Fort Mill; TV and radios   600

Polygram Holding Inc.; Grover; phonograph record cutting styli   600

Standard Corp.; Lugoff; automobile storage   600

Ostrow Co.; Rock Hill; business management   560

Springs Industries Inc.; Lancaster; linen fabrics   560

Champion Products Inc.; Gaffney; athletic clothing   550

Dillon Yarn Corp.; Dillon   550

INA USA Corp.; Cheraw; roller bearings and parts   550

Overnite Transportation Co.; Gaffney; trucking   550

Fort James Corp.; Darlington; paper mills   535

Pedro Land Inc.; Hamer; amusement parks   530

Springs Industries Inc.; Fort Lawn; comforters and quilts   526

E. I. Du Pont De Nemours and Co.; Florence; polyethylene film   520

York Technical College; Rock Hill   512

Kershaw County Medical Center; Camden   510

Allegiance Healthcare Corp.; Fort Mill; drugs, proprietaries, sundries   500

La-Z-Boy Inc.; Florence; home furniture   500

Nestle USA-Prepared Foods Division Inc.; Gaffney; frozen specialties   500

Second Chance International; Greenville; apparel accessories   500

South Carolina Dept. of Corrections; Bishopville   500

South Carolina Mental Health Dept.; Florence   500

Stowe-Pharr Mills Inc.; Clover; carpet yarn   500

Tyco Electronics Corp.; Rock Hill; computer and software stores   500

South Carolina 6th District

Central and east — parts of Columbia, Florence, and Charleston

A black-majority district designed to take in African American areas in Columbia, Charleston, and elsewhere in the state, the 6th includes all or part of 15 counties in the eastern half of the state, starting near the North Carolina border and reaching the southeastern coast. With five of South Carolina's six poorest counties, the 6th has the state's lowest median household income.

In the rural portions of the district, many families depend on tobacco and tobacco-related agribusiness for their incomes. In the 1980s, Bamberg, Marion, and Williamsburg Counties lost population as residents left farms and jobs in the textile industry disappeared. For those who remain, agri-

culture continues to be the economic mainstay. Many others who live in the district find work in Charleston (shared with the 1st) and Columbia (shared with the 2nd).

Other sectors of the district's economy have fared better. Plastics, pharmaceuticals, textiles, and paperboard manufacturing sustain many in the city of Florence (shared with the 5th), which is more middle-class than most of the rest of the 6th. In the coastal parts of the district, maritime industries and tourism provide the economic base. Government services, higher education, and manufacturing create jobs in the 6th's midsection.

The 6th gives solid and consistent support to Democrats at all levels. The district's black-majority areas—including the 6th's shares of Columbia and North Charleston, which are more than two-thirds African American—make this seat a Democratic lock.

Major Industry

Agriculture, government, textiles, tourism.

Notable

All of the state's four historically black colleges and universities are in the district; Clarendon County can claim five South Carolina governors—and all were related.

Election Returns

	Republican		Democratic		Other	
President 2000	87,252	40.9%	126,287	59.1%		
House 2002	55,760	32.0%	116,586	67.0%	1,720	1.0%

District Profile

Population   668,670

Total area (square miles)   8,490.0
Land area (square miles)   8,119.7

Population per square mile   82.4

Counties (2000 population)

Bamberg 16,658	Georgetown (pt.) 18,130
Berkeley (pt.) 31,187	Lee (pt.) 2,585
Calhoun (pt.) 8,290	Marion 35,466
Charleston (pt.) 64,015	Orangeburg (pt.) 69,193
Clarendon 32,502	Richland (pt.) 121,950
Colleton 38,264	Sumter (pt.) 60,502
Dorchester (pt.) 19,459	Williamsburg 37,217
Florence (pt.) 113,252	

Cities and other areas over 10,000 (2000 population)
Charleston (pt.)   19,216
Columbia (pt.)   56,507
Florence (pt.)   26,623
North Charleston (pt.)   34,111
Orangeburg (pt.)   10,260
Sumter (pt.)   19,125

Race and Hispanic or Latino origin*
White   40.3%
Black or African American   56.7%
American Indian or Alaska Native   0.3%
Asian   0.5%
Native Hawaiian or other Pacific Islander   0.0%
Some other race   0.1%

Hispanic or Latino origin   1.5%
Two or more races   0.7%

*As percentage of total population.

Ancestry*

English 4.1%	Scotch-Irish 1.5%
German 3.7%	Subsaharan 1.1%
Irish 3.5%	USA/American 9.0%

*As estimated percentage of total population.

Universities and colleges, 2000–2001 enrollment

Allen University, Columbia   371
Benedict College, Columbia   2,966
Citadel Military College, Charleston   3,872
Claflin College, Orangeburg   1,130
Columbia College, Columbia   1,399
Columbia International University, Columbia   1,054
Denmark Technical College, Denmark   1,240
Francis Marion University, Florence   3,567
Morris College, Sumter   940
Nielsen Electronics Institute, North Charleston   409
Orangeburg Calhoun Technical College, Orangeburg
   1,861
South Carolina State University, Orangeburg   4,525
University of South Carolina, Columbia   23,728
Voorhees College, Denmark   677
Williamsburg Technical College, Kingstree   661

Newspapers and circulation

	District circulation	Total circulation
Charleston Post and Courier	19,183	104,054
Columbia State	24,025	118,929
Florence Morning News	18,668	32,871
Myrtle Beach Sun News	1,572	48,171
Orangeburg Times & Democrat	13,295	17,597
Sumter Item	15,448	21,598
*USA Today**	5,537	1,674,376

*See Sources and Explanations in the front of the volume.

Television stations and affiliations

Charleston	48%	WCBD	NBC
Charleston	48%	WCIV	ABC
Charleston	48%	WCSC	CBS
Charleston	48%	WITV	PBS
Charleston	48%	WJWJ	PBS
Charleston	48%	WMMP	UPN
Charleston	48%	WTAT	FOX
Columbia	32%	WACH	FOX
Columbia	32%	WIS	NBC
Columbia	32%	WLTX	CBS
Columbia	32%	WOLO	ABC
Columbia	32%	WQHB	UPN, WB
Columbia	32%	WRJA	PBS
Columbia	32%	WRLK	PBS
Florence-Myrtle Beach	15%	WBTW	CBS
Florence-Myrtle Beach	15%	WFPX	PAX
Florence-Myrtle Beach	15%	WFXB	FOX
Florence-Myrtle Beach	15%	WHMC	PBS
Florence-Myrtle Beach	15%	WJPM	PBS
Florence-Myrtle Beach	15%	WPDE	ABC
Florence-Myrtle Beach	15%	WUNU	PBS
Florence-Myrtle Beach	15%	WWMB	UPN
Augusta, GA	5%	WAGT	NBC
Augusta, GA	5%	WCES	PBS
Augusta, GA	5%	WEBA	PBS
Augusta, GA	5%	WFXG	FOX
Augusta, GA	5%	WJBF	ABC
Augusta, GA	5%	WRDW	CBS

Cable systems and subscribers

Adelphia   4,810
Berkley Cable   13,005
Comcast   15,428
Galaxy   633
G-Force   1,708
Mallard   1,898
Pine Tree Cablevision   1,101
Time Warner   105,158
U.S. Cable   1,980

Military installations, September 2001

McEntire Air Force Guard Station, Eastover   1,228
McEntire Army Aviation Support Facility, Eastover
   884
Charleston Branch Clinic Naval Hospital, Charleston
   620
Columbia (Bluff Road) (Army Guard), Columbia   615

Businesses and other major employers

Safety-Kleen Services Inc.; Columbia; building
   maintenance   9,618
South Carolina Mental Health Dept.; Columbia   6,000
Medical University of South Carolina; Charleston
   4,000
Gold Kist Inc.; Sumter; poultry hatcheries   2,500
McLeod Regional Medical Center of Pee Dee Inc.;
   Florence   2,345
Polymer Group Inc.; North Charleston; fabrics   2,023
Electrolux Home Products Inc.; Orangeburg; electrical
   appliances   2,000
Florence General Hospital; Florence   1,600
Blue Cross and Blue Shield of South Carolina; Columbia;
   medical service plans   1,500
Tuomey Health Care Systems Hospital; Sumter   1,279
South Carolina State University; Orangeburg   1,259
Employment and Training Program; Columbia; job
   training and related services   1,250
Orangeburg/Calhoun Counties Regional Medical Center;
   Orangeburg   1,200
Sisters of Charity Providence Hospitals; Columbia
   1,200
Wellman Inc.; Johnsonville; wool tops   1,200
Santee Print Works; Sumter; cotton finishing   1,100
South Carolina Electric and Gas Co.; Columbia   1,100
Richland County; Columbia   1,043
Bayer Corp.; Charleston; polypropylene resins   1,000
Bosh Braking Systems Inc.; Sumter   1,000
CBS Corp.; Columbia; TV broadcasting   1,000
Robert Bosch Corp.; Sumter; motor vehicle brake
   systems/parts   1,000
Scooter Store; North Charleston; medical equipment and
   supplies   1,000
South Carolina Dept. of Health and Environmental
   Control; Columbia   1,000
South Carolina Transportation Dept.; Columbia   1,000

Midwest Express Inc.; Timmonsville; materials handling machinery   950

South Carolina Natural Resource Dept.; Columbia   900

Blue Cross and Blue Shield of South Carolina; Florence; medical service plans   877

ESAB Group Inc.; Florence; welding and cutting apparatus   850

International Paper Co.; Eastover; paper mills   850

City of North Charleston; North Charleston; city government   825

ArvinMeritor Inc.; Marion; automotive parts/accessories   820

Nucor Corp.; Huger; blast furnaces and steel mills   800

South Carolina Dept. of Revenue; Columbia; commercial regulation   800

South Carolina Dept. of Social Services; Columbia   800

South Carolina University; Columbia   800

Alternative Staffing Inc.; North Charleston; temporary help services   785

Cullum Constructors Inc.; North Charleston; industrial buildings, warehouses   750

Sara Lee Corp.; Marion; undergarments   730

Super Transport; Walterboro; trucking   712

Anvil Knitwear Inc.; Mullins; undergarments   700

Federal-Mogul Corp.; Summerton; gaskets and sealing devices   700

South Carolina Dept. of Transportation; Florence   700

Washington Mutual Inc.; Columbia; mortgage bankers   700

Nan Ya Plastics Corp. America; Lake City; organic fibers   686

Tupperware U.S. Inc.; Hemingway; plastic containers   675

Sears Roebuck and Co. Inc.; Columbia; department stores   650

Blackbaud Inc.; Charleston; software   620

South Carolina Employment Security Commission; Columbia   600

U.S. Postal Service; Charleston   600

Evening Post Publishing Co.; Charleston; newspaper   585

Citadel Military College; Charleston   572

Square D Co.; Columbia; power switchboards and parts   556

Stone Container Corp.; Florence; kraft linerboard   554

Marion County Hospital District; Mullins   550

Rockford Manufacturing; Walterboro; prefabricated buildings   525

Cutler-Hammer Inc.; Sumter; switchgear and switchgear accessories   500

Florence County; Florence; county government   500

Korn Industries Inc.; Sumter; wood household dressers   500

South Carolina Dept. of Health and Human Services; Florence   500

South Carolina Electric and Gas Co.; Charleston; utilities   500

State-Record Co.; Columbia; newspaper   500

Trinity Healthcare Staffing Group Inc.; Florence; employment agencies   500

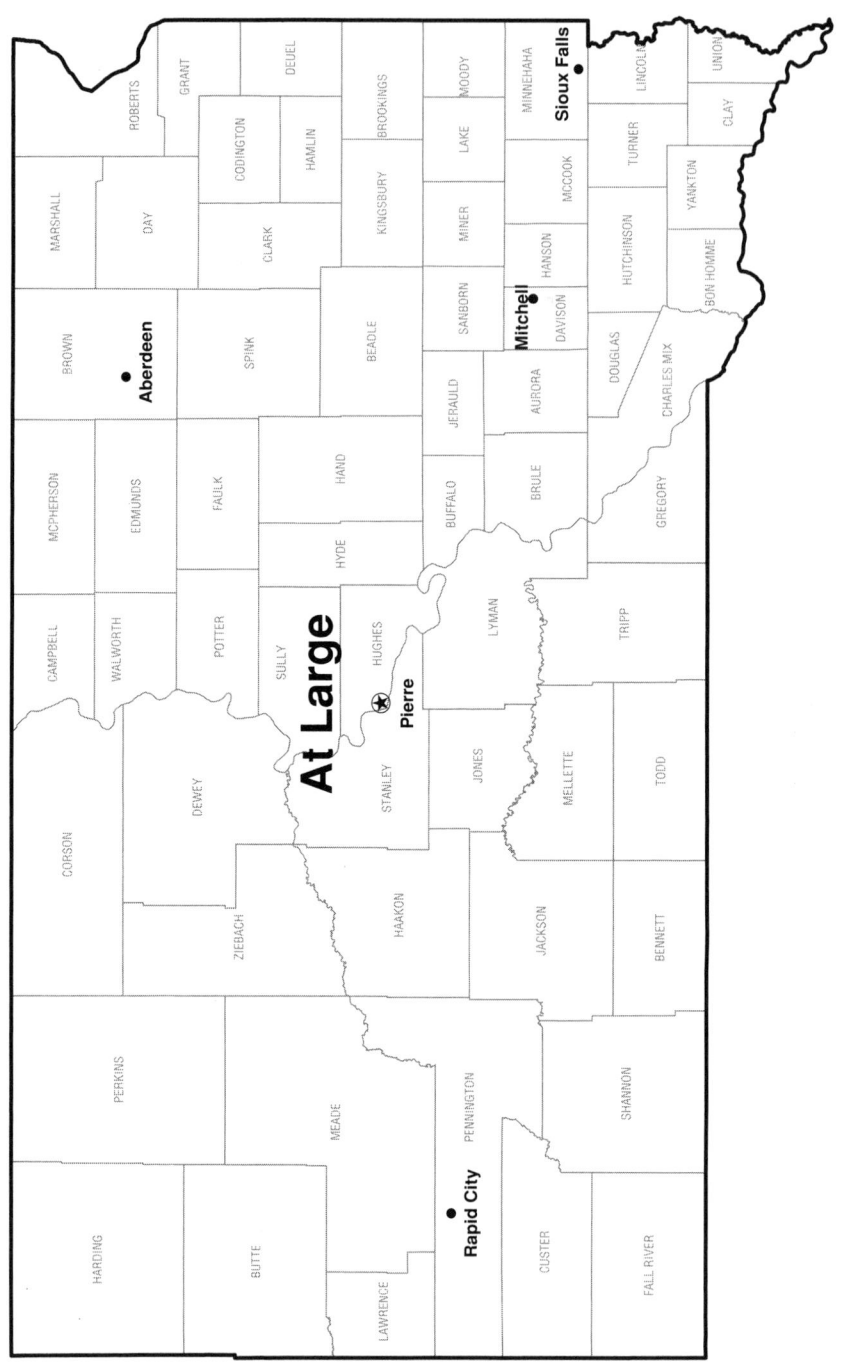

South Dakota

In the southwestern corner of South Dakota, something sudden and extraordinary happens. The Black Hills, a range of exotic and unsettling mountains, rise up and tower over the gradual plain that is the state. The highest point is Mount Harney, some 7,242 feet above sea level, one of the very few elevations of this magnitude between the Appalachians in the east (which can only top 6,000) and the twice-higher behemoths of the Rockies and the Sierras in the west. Few Americans think of South Dakota as mountainous, but in this rocky corner of a sparsely populated state, dramatic scenery abounds.

The high places for which South Dakota is best known are north of both Harney and the Badlands National Park, near Rapid City, where granite bluffs have been carved into memorials by sculptors. Mount Rushmore depicts the Presidents George Washington, Thomas Jefferson, Abraham Lincoln, and Theodore Roosevelt. Taking shape not too far away is the vastly larger carving of Chief Crazy Horse, a Native American leader. To the southeast are the Badlands, a region both forbidding and intriguing for generations of explorers and tourists. Rapid City continues to grow as a result.

This part of the state has often been its most alluring. In 1874, General George Armstrong Custer discovered gold in these hills, with predictable results including raucous boomtowns and outraged Sioux, who had been promised the land in the Laramie Treaty. This led to the massacre of Custer and his Seventh Cavalry at the Little Big Horn, Montana, in 1876. Violent struggles between the settlers and the Sioux continued until federal troops killed approximately 300 men, women, and children at Wounded Knee, in the Black Hills, in 1890. Much of the state became a reservation thereafter, and trouble has flared again as recently as the 1970s and 1980s near Wounded Knee. The boomtowns of the old gold rush days have since made a comeback, most particularly Deadwood, the town made famous by the death of the legendary Wild Bill Hickock. Nowadays Deadwood is a modern gambling center with a frontier flavor, and one more reason tourism spending is up.

South Dakota remains a state with one of the highest percentages of Native Americans, at just more than 8 percent of the population, in the nation. The traditionally poor Native American communities found a bright spot in casinos in the 1990s; all nine of the state's reservations grew in population over the decade. But poverty is still a major problem. Shannon County, home of the Pine Ridge Reservation, is one of the poorest counties in the nation.

The Missouri River, which splits the state, sometimes is considered a political divide as well. On the more Democratic east side of the river are familiar-looking farms laid out in conventional, reasonably well-watered sections. Here Dakotans have grown grains and beans and raised cattle and sheep for more than 150 years, since building their first homes of sod. In the western part of the state, ranching Republicans outnumber eastern urban and agricultural Democrats by about 46,000 registered voters. Native Americans, found predominantly in the west, traditionally support Democrats.

Nestled in a crook of the Missouri River, is the state capital of Pierre, roughly at the center of the state. The capital marks one of the points of progress on the journey of Lewis and Clark in 1804–1806. Low crop prices wounded eastern South Dakota's agriculture-based economy in the 1990s, adding to a steady migration into cities, where finance, computers, and health care gradually have overtaken meatpacking as the primary industries. Citibank, Gateway, and others moved into the state during the 1990s to take advantage of low taxes and wages.

Like its namesake neighbor to the north, with which it entered the union in 1889, South Dakota peaked at three congressional districts in the sanguine census of 1910 and lost the third seat almost immediately. The second seat lasted until 1980, after which the state's two incumbent representatives had to run against each other to survive. The winner was a soft-spoken second-term Democrat, Tom Daschle, who soon ran for the Senate and won and soon became part of the leadership. In 1994, after the Democrats had lost their majority in the Senate, Daschle was elected as their leader.

Daschle and his Democratic colleague Tim Johnson, re-elected by a hair's breadth in 2002, have now won five of the nine Senate terms won by Democrats in this state since World War II. Three of the other four were won by George S. McGovern, who held one seat from 1962 to 1980 and was the Democratic nominee for president in 1972 (losing 49 states, including South Dakota). McGovern could scarcely have expected much better. This is as Republican a state in presidential contests as can be found in the nation. Since statehood it has voted for only three Democrats for the White House: William Jennings Bryan in 1896, Franklin D. Roosevelt (two times out of four), and Lyndon B. Johnson in 1964. The state also has an independent streak, giving Ross Perot 22 percent in 1992 and 10 percent in 1996.

But as a populist Democrat, Daschle is not entirely out of the state's political tradition. The first ten governors elected after statehood included nine Republicans and one populist.

The next ten included eight Republicans and two Democrats. The last seven have been six Republican, one Democrat. Among the recent governors, by far the most important has been Republican William J. Janklow, who served two terms in the 1970s and 1980s, left politics for a time, then returned to win two more in the 1990s. Term-limited in the governor's office, he won the state's sole House seat in 2002. Janklow's political future, however, became clouded in 2003 when he sped through a stop sign on a country road and hit and killed a motorcyclist.

As governor, Janklow was credited with bringing Citibank to the state, where the nation's largest bank now operates an enormous processing center for its credit card holders that employs more people than any other private business in the state. It has helped to make Sioux Falls the state's great generator of population growth. Situated in the southeastern corner, near the three-way meeting point with Iowa and Minnesota, Sioux Falls grew by nearly one fourth (to more than 123,000) in the 1990s, providing nearly half the state's overall growth.

Major Industry

Agriculture, finance, tourism.

Notable

More than 200 Sioux were massacred in one day at Wounded Knee in 1890.

Table 1   Population

District	Population	Population under 18	Voting-age population	Median age	Male*	Female*
At Large	754,844	202,649	552,195	35.6	49.6	50.4

*As percentage of total population.

Table 2   Voting-Age Persons by Race/Hispanic or Latino Origin

District	White*	Black or African American*	American Indian or Alaska Native*	Asian*	Other or multirace*	Hispanic or Latino*
At Large	90.8	0.5	6.1	0.6	0.8	1.2

*As percentage of voting-age population.

Table 3   Voting-Age Population by Age Groups

District	18 to 24*	25 to 44*	45 to 64*	Over 64*
At Large	14.1	37.4	29.0	19.6

*As percentage of voting-age population.

Table 4   Income and Occupation

District	Median family income	Families in poverty*	White collar†	Blue collar†	Service†	Farm†
At Large	$43,237	9.3	59.1	23.3	15.6	1.9

*As percentage of all families.   †As percentage of employed workers 16 years and over.

Table 5   Education: School Years Completed

District	Less than grade 9*	Grades 9–12 no diploma*	High school diploma no college*	Some college*	College bachelor's degree or higher*
At Large	7.5	8.0	32.9	30.2	21.5

*As percentage of persons age 25 and over.

Table 6   Housing and Residential Patterns

District	Median home value	Owner occupied*	Renter occupied*	Urban†	Rural†
At Large	$74,300	68.2	31.8	51.9	48.1

*As percentage of occupied housing units.   †As percentage of total population.

Election Returns

	Republican		Democratic		Other	
President 2000	190,700	60.3%	118,804	37.6%	6,765	2.1%
House 2002	180,023	53.4%	153,656	45.6%	3,128	0.9%

District Profile

Population   754,844

Total area (square miles)   77,116.4
    Land area (square miles)   75,884.6

Population per square mile   9.9

Counties (2000 population)

Aurora	3,058	Faulk	2,640
Beadle	17,023	Grant	7,847
Bennett	3,574	Gregory	4,792
Bon Homme	7,260	Haakon	2,196
Brookings	28,220	Hamlin	5,540
Brown	35,460	Hand	3,741
Brule	5,364	Hanson	3,139
Buffalo	2,032	Harding	1,353
Butte	9,094	Hughes	16,481
Campbell	1,782	Hutchinson	8,075
Charles Mix	9,350	Hyde	1,671
Clark	4,143	Jackson	2,930
Clay	13,537	Jerauld	2,295
Codington	25,897	Jones	1,193
Corson	4,181	Kingsbury	5,815
Custer	7,275	Lake	11,276
Davison	18,741	Lawrence	21,802
Day	6,267	Lincoln	24,131
Deuel	4,498	Lyman	3,895
Dewey	5,972	Marshall	4,576
Douglas	3,458	McCook	5,832
Edmunds	4,367	McPherson	2,904
Fall River	7,453	Meade	24,253

Mellette	2,083	Spink	7,454
Miner	2,884	Stanley	2,772
Minnehaha	148,281	Sully	1,556
Moody	6,595	Todd	9,050
Pennington	88,565	Tripp	6,430
Perkins	3,363	Turner	8,849
Potter	2,693	Union	12,584
Roberts	10,016	Walworth	5,974
Sanborn	2,675	Yankton	21,652
Shannon	12,466	Ziebach	2,519

Cities and other areas over 10,000 (2000 population)

Aberdeen	24,658	Rapid City	59,607
Brookings	18,504	Sioux Falls	123,975
Huron	11,893	Watertown	20,237
Mitchell	14,558	Yankton	13,528
Pierre	13,876		

Race and Hispanic or Latino origin*

White 88.0%
Black or African American 0.6%
American Indian or Alaska Native 8.1%
Asian 0.6%
Native Hawaiian or other Pacific Islander 0.0%
Some other race 0.0%
Hispanic or Latino origin 1.4%
Two or more races 1.2%

*As percentage of total population.

Ancestry*

Danish	1.9%	Irish	7.4%
Dutch	3.4%	Norwegian	10.9%
English	5.0%	Polish	1.1%
French	2.1%	Swedish	2.8%
German	29.1%	USA/American	2.8%

*As estimated percentage of total population.

Universities and colleges, 2000–2001 enrollment

Augustana College, Sioux Falls 1,783
Black Hills State University, Spearfish 4,171
Colorado Technical University, Sioux Falls 840
Dakota State University, Madison 1,806
Dakota Wesleyan University, Mitchell 676
Huron University, Huron 598
Kilian Community College, Sioux Falls 212
Lake Area Technical Institute, Watertown 571
Mitchell Technical Institute, Mitchell 905
Mount Marty College, Yankton 1,125
National American University, Rapid City 1,005
National American University, Sioux Falls 261
Northern State University, Aberdeen 3,283
Oglala Lakota College, Kyle 1,174
Presentation College, Aberdeen 468
Sinte Gleska University, Rosebud 900
Sisseton-Wahpeton Community College, Agency Village 250
South Dakota School of Mines and Technology, Rapid City 2,307
South Dakota State University, Brookings 8,695
Southeast Technical Institute, Sioux Falls 2,283
University of Sioux Falls, Sioux Falls 1,272
University of South Dakota, Vermillion 7,487
Western Dakota Technical Institute, Rapid City 966

Newspapers and circulation

	District circulation	Total circulation
Aberdeen American News	14,911	15,705
Brookings Register	4,700	4,700
Huron Plainsman	6,653	6,653
Rapid City Journal	27,241	28,126
Sioux City Journal	1,949	46,030
Sioux Falls Argus Leader	47,657	51,753
USA Today*	2,442	1,674,376
Watertown Public Opinion	12,015	12,633

*See Sources and Explanations in the front of the volume.

Television stations and affiliations

Sioux Falls (Mitchell)	60%	KABY	ABC
Sioux Falls (Mitchell)	60%	KCSD	PBS
Sioux Falls (Mitchell)	60%	KDLO	CBS
Sioux Falls (Mitchell)	60%	KDLV	NBC
Sioux Falls (Mitchell)	60%	KDSD	PBS
Sioux Falls (Mitchell)	60%	KELO	CBS
Sioux Falls (Mitchell)	60%	KESD	PBS
Sioux Falls (Mitchell)	60%	KPLO	CBS
Sioux Falls (Mitchell)	60%	KPRY	ABC
Sioux Falls (Mitchell)	60%	KQSD	PBS
Sioux Falls (Mitchell)	60%	KRNE	PBS
Sioux Falls (Mitchell)	60%	KSFY	ABC
Sioux Falls (Mitchell)	60%	KSMN	PBS
Sioux Falls (Mitchell)	60%	KTSD	PBS
Sioux Falls (Mitchell)	60%	KTTM	FOX
Sioux Falls (Mitchell)	60%	KTTW	FOX
Rapid City	35%	KBHE	PBS
Rapid City	35%	KCLO	CBS
Rapid City	35%	KEVN	FOX
Rapid City	35%	KHSD	ABC
Rapid City	35%	KIVV	FOX
Rapid City	35%	KOTA	ABC
Rapid City	35%	KPSD	PBS
Rapid City	35%	KSGW	ABC
Rapid City	35%	KTNE	PBS
Rapid City	35%	KZSD	PBS
Minot-Bismarck-Dickinson	4%	KBME	PBS
Minot-Bismarck-Dickinson	4%	KBMY	ABC
Minot-Bismarck-Dickinson	4%	KDSE	PBS
Minot-Bismarck-Dickinson	4%	KFYR	NBC
Minot-Bismarck-Dickinson	4%	KMOT	NBC
Minot-Bismarck-Dickinson	4%	KQCD	NBC
Minot-Bismarck-Dickinson	4%	KSRE	PBS
Minot-Bismarck-Dickinson	4%	KUMV	NBC
Minot-Bismarck-Dickinson	4%	KWSE	PBS
Minot-Bismarck-Dickinson	4%	KXMA	CBS
Minot-Bismarck-Dickinson	4%	KXMB	CBS
Minot-Bismarck-Dickinson	4%	KXMC	CBS
Minot-Bismarck-Dickinson	4%	KXMD	CBS
Sioux City	1%	KCAU	ABC
Sioux City	1%	KMEG	CBS, UPN
Sioux City	1%	KSIN	PBS
Sioux City	1%	KTIV	NBC
Sioux City	1%	KUSD	PBS
Sioux City	1%	KXNE	PBS

Cable systems and subscribers

Beresford Cablevision 710
Cable ONE 902

Dakota Telecom   2,869
Golden West Cablevision   2,440
James Valley Telecommunications   756
Mediacom   27,768
Midcontinent Cable   96,301
Midstate Communications   1,260
Pine Ridge Cable TV   915
Platte Community Cable TV   526
Rosebud Community Cable TV   852
Rural Television Network   697
Savage Communications   521
Splitrock Telecom Co-op   1,826
Sully Buttes Co-op   1,706
Valley Cablevision   1,057
Valley Telco   578
Village Cable   2,587

Military installations, September 2001
Ellsworth Air Force Base, Box Elder   3,665
Joe Foss Field Air National Guard Station, Sioux Falls   982
Camp Rapid Military Training Area, Rapid City   419
Rapid City Armory, Rapid City   128

Businesses and other major employers
IBP Inc.; North Sioux City; boxed beef   6,000
Citibank NA; Sioux Falls; commercial bank   3,200
Sioux Valley Hospitals and Health Systems; Sioux Falls   2,900
Rapid City Regional Hospital Inc.; Rapid City   2,565
Avera McKennan and University Health Center; Sioux Falls   2,100
Sasker Repair; Chancellor; farm machinery repair   1,989
State Farm Mutual Automobile Insurance Co.; North Sioux City; insurance agents   1,973
Northwestern Growth Corp.; Sioux Falls; heating/air conditioning contractor   1,937
South Dakota State University; Brookings   1,600
Gateway Inc.; Sioux Falls; computers   1,400
Gehl Power Products Inc.; Yankton; forklift trucks   956
Associates First Capital Corp.; Sioux Falls; consumer finance companies   900
Household Credit Services Inc.; Sioux Falls; personal credit institutions   800

University of South Dakota; Vermillion   800
Wells Fargo Education Financial Services; Sioux Falls; financial services   800
Northern State University; Aberdeen   795
Larson Manufacturing Co.; Brookings; metal doors, sash, and trim   750
Sacred Heart Hospital; Yankton   750
U.S. Dept. of Veterans Affairs; Sioux Falls   750
Associates Commerce Solutions; Sioux Falls; data processing   700
Avera St. Luke's Hospital; Aberdeen   700
Bankfirst Corp. Inc.; Sioux Falls; bank holding companies   700
Daktronics Inc.; Brookings; signs and advertising specialties   700
Hutchinson Technology Inc.; Sioux Falls; computer peripheral equipment   700
U.S. Veterans Hospital; Fort Meade   700
Orion Food Systems Inc.; Sioux Falls; franchise   670
3M Co.; Brookings; pharmaceuticals   650
U.S. Geological Survey Agency; Sioux Falls   630
South Dakota Dept. of Human Services; Redfield   609
Conseco Finance Corp. Inc.; Rapid City; personal credit institutions   600
Avera Queen of Peace Hospital; Mitchell   545
Beef Products Inc.; North Sioux City; meatpacking plants   533
LodgeNet Entertainment Corp.; Sioux Falls; subscription TV services   525
3M Co.; Aberdeen; respiratory protection equipment   500
Hy-Vee Inc.; Sioux Falls; grocery store   500
Interbake Foods Inc.; North Sioux City; cookies   500
Northwestern Public Service; Huron; electric power line construction   500
Oglala Sioux Tribe of Pine Ridge Reservation; Pine Ridge; public health programs   500
Raytheon Technical Services Co.; Sioux Falls; software design   500
U.S. Dept. of Veterans Affairs; Hot Springs   500
Yankton Sioux Tribe; Lake Andes; gambling   500

Tennessee

The Volunteer State was so named for the willingness of its men to enter the fray against any and all foes: Native American, British, Mexican, or Yankee. Andrew Jackson of Tennessee came to national attention fighting Native Americans before, during, and after the War of 1812, which he capped by winning the Battle of New Orleans. Davey Crockett and Sam Houston, a former representative and governor of Tennessee, were the headliner heroes when Texas won its independence from Mexico in 1836.

As the Civil War began, however, Tennessee's hybrid nature came to the fore. The settlers in rugged East Tennessee, dominated by the massive Blue and Appalachian Ridges, were small-plot farmers and woodsmen. They had neither the land nor the inclination to support slave-labor agriculture such as that of the state's central and western river basins. So secession was more controversial here: Tennessee was the last of the 11 Confederate states to leave the Union and the first to return. Nonetheless, the state gave generously to the fight, and more Civil War battles were fought here than in any state except Virginia (including Shiloh with 23,000 casualties). Tennessee also provided three presidents between 1828 and 1868: Jackson, James K. Polk (who squeaked past Henry Clay in 1844 despite losing Tennessee), and Andrew Johnson, who became president after the assassination of Abraham Lincoln in 1865.

Tennessee has benefited from being economically more diverse than most of the South. It had assets from coal mining in the east, timber in the mountains and upland ridges, and good farmland in the central and western basins. In the 1930s, much of its watershed was transformed by the coming of the Tennessee Valley Authority (TVA), taming rivers and producing cheap power. World War II brought the Manhattan Project that developed the atomic bomb and the huge federal research labs at Oak Ridge. In the last two decades of the 1900s the state began attracting industrial gems such as auto assembly plants (Saturn and Nissan), partly on its availability of cheap land and power, partly on its lower wages and weaker unions. Even today the state ranks low in hourly earnings and personal income, and high in percentage of its people in poverty. In 2001, when the national poverty rate was 11.6 percent, Tennessee was 13.2 percent and eleventh nationally.

The fast growth has been concentrated in the cities—Nashville, Memphis, Knoxville—which together averaged better than 15 percent growth in the decade, leading the state as a whole to nearly 17 percent growth. The biggest hit has been Nashville, which has gotten bigger and more glamorous, just like the country music industry for which it has long been the capital (and for which it recently opened a $37 million museum). The Nashville-Davidson metro area grew a remarkable 25 percent to top 1.23 million in the 2000 census, propelling it past metropolitan Memphis.

Memphis, on the Mississippi, has traditionally been the state's largest and most important commercial city, although the economy over which it presides is largely in Arkansas and Mississippi. Memphis is still the single largest entity in the state at about 600,000 people, and its metro area was up about 10 percent to 1.1 million in the 1990s. This city has been an enormous part of southern black history, not least for the blues and jazz heritage of Beale Street and the recording studios that brought the world rhythm and blues and Elvis Presley (whose mansion remains a major tourist attraction). Memphis was the big city to many rural people in the blackest parts of the South. The congressional district centered in Memphis was 59 percent black after 2000 and home to about 40 percent of the state's 950,000 African Americans. Nashville has slightly more Hispanics and Asians, two groups that together still account for less than 3 percent of the state's population. The best sign of growth and health for Tennessee in recent years may be that both Nashville and Memphis added professional sports franchises: football and hockey in Nashville, basketball in Memphis.

Politically, Tennessee was an early example of two-party politics in the South. All three Tennessee presidents were Jeffersonians, and in the generations after the Civil War the state mostly followed the Southern Democratic tradition. After Reconstruction, a shorter ordeal here than elsewhere, the Democrats dominated in Nashville, holding the governorship for a century from 1871 until 1971 with time out for just three widely-spaced Republicans to serve a total of four two-year terms. The state also elected only Democrats to the Senate from 1874 to 1966, although one Republican served briefly as an appointee. The change came with Howard Baker Jr., a representative who won with nearly 57 percent of the vote over the Democratic governor of the time.

Baker was reelected twice and retired as Senate majority leader in 1984. In 1970 Albert Gore Sr. lost his Senate seat to another Republican, Bill Brock, giving the state two Republican senators and a Republican governor for the first time in its history. Since the early 1970s, the state has been one of the most competitive in the country for both parties. Between 1974 and 2002 the governorship was won four times by each party, while Republicans won six Senate elections to the Democrats' five.

Tennessee was primed to shed its Democratic fealty sooner than other southern states in part because the old pro-Union

Districts established January 17, 2002, for elections first held in 2002.

9 members

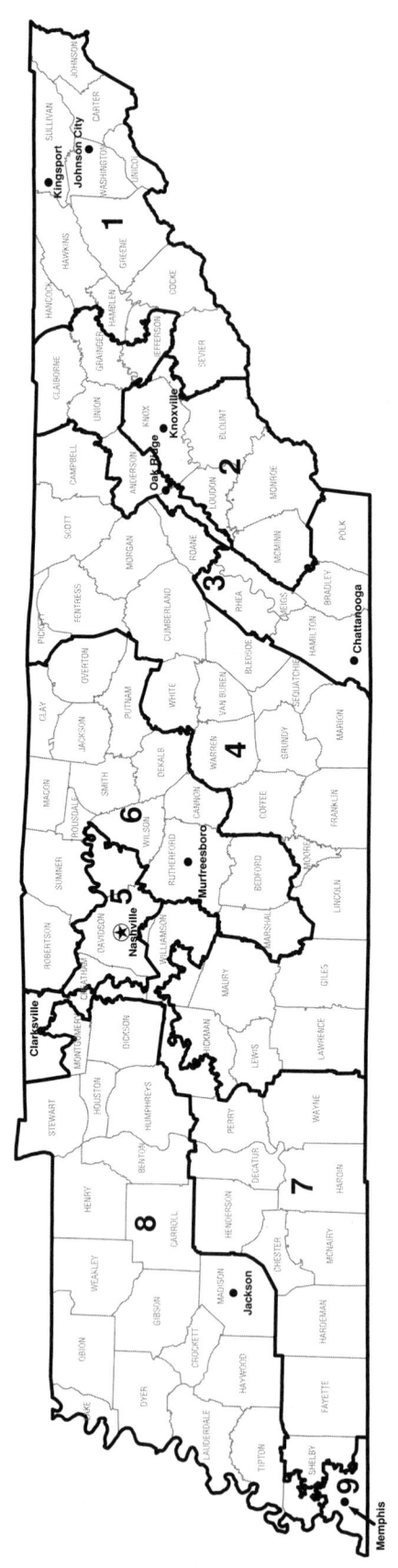

counties of East Tennessee kept the GOP alive in the state, especially in Knoxville. So, in the later phase of the twentieth century, as air conditioning and mobile service industries brought new residents from all directions, Republicans had an infrastructure in place to take advantage. There had even been enough of a GOP base here to swing the state in good Republican presidential years. This happened first in 1920, when Tennessee was the only state from the old Confederacy to vote for Warren G. Harding, an Ohio Republican, over John Cox, an Ohio Democrat. Tennessee repeated this apostasy in 1928, voting for Herbert Hoover.

In 1948 Tennessee stuck with Democrat Harry S. Truman, making it five Democratic presidential votes in a row. But it also gave 13 percent of its vote that year to States' Rights Democrat Strom Thurmond of South Carolina, who was carrying much of the Deep South. In 1952 Tennessee's shift to the Republicans began in earnest. The state went for Eisenhower in 1952 and 1956, and for Richard Nixon in 1960, 1968, and 1972. As with other southern states, Tennessee liked Jimmy Carter in 1976 but deserted him in 1980, beginning another string of three cycles with the GOP. Bill Clinton managed to carry Tennessee twice for the Democrats in the 1990s, thanks in part to his running mate, Al Gore, who was a former Tennessee senator and son of the former Tennessee senator. In 2000 Gore ran his own campaign for president from Nashville, but he spent little time in the state and saw it slip away—with enough electoral votes to have made him president—by four percentage points.

In terms of seats in the U.S. House, Tennessee has had two recent struggles: one between the parties and the other for more seats. In the latter effort, Tennessee has been striving to regain a stature it once held. As just the third state added to the fledgling nation after the original thirteen, Tennessee was voting when America chose its second president in 1796. Tennessee also grew quickly in the early 1800s, arguably the period of its greatest national influence. But through most of a century after the Civil War, the state seemed to be slowly losing in national standing as its cities and towns grew only gradually compared with the nation at large.

In fact, Tennessee has had one of the most stable House delegation sizes in U.S. history. Several factors affect this: the House itself grew throughout the nineteenth century before reaching its current 435 seats in 1910. So while Tennessee's population shrank as a percentage of the national total, and its relative share of the House did likewise, its number of seats remained at ten (give or take a seat). In the twentieth century, with the House size finally frozen at 435, Tennessee has seen some ebb and flow, with eight seats the low point after the 1970 census. With renewed growth, however, the state was back to nine in 1980. Another decade of growth like the 1990s would almost surely bring back the tenth seat in 2010. (The Census Bureau projects Tennessee will grow more slowly in the early decades of the new century.)

With just nine districts to redraw, the conflict in post-2000 redistricting was primarily partisan. Democrats held both chambers of the legislature and had the power to override a veto by the Republican governor with a simple majority. So they drew the map to facilitate a return to the majority in the House delegation in November of 2002—and it worked. The basic idea was to add Democrats to the 4th District, the state's poorest and least educated, which connected upland counties on the Kentucky line with sim-

ilar ones on the Alabama line via the Eastern Ridge east of Nashville. It had been represented by a Republican who was running for governor. So the Democrats redrew it, removing several percentage points of the margin George W. Bush received in 2000 while adding Morgan and Roane Counties west of Oak Ridge. The new district elected a Democrat, which flipped the delegation back to a Democratic majority for the first time since the big Republican takeover year in 1994.

The Democrats had also sought to strengthen 20-year veteran Bart Gordon in his 6th District east of Nashville and to keep the Nashville-based 5th solid. They managed to help Gordon improve his winning margin in 2002 to 66 percent, and they filled the vacated 5th by bringing back an old hand, Jim Cooper, who had previously served six terms in the 4th District before losing a Senate bid in 1994.

Table 1   Population

District	Population	Population under 18	Voting-age population	Median age	Male*	Female*
1	632,143	139,338	492,805	38.7	48.8	51.2
2	632,144	143,471	488,673	36.9	48.4	51.6
3	632,143	147,743	484,400	37.4	48.3	51.7
4	632,143	152,710	479,433	37.9	49.0	51.0
5	632,143	144,468	487,675	34.2	48.6	51.4
6	632,143	161,171	470,972	34.7	49.4	50.6
7	632,139	171,974	460,165	35.6	49.6	50.4
8	632,142	163,960	468,182	35.7	48.5	51.5
9	632,143	173,686	458,457	32.1	47.5	52.5
State	5,689,283	1,398,521	4,290,762	35.9	48.7	51.3

As percentage of total population.

Table 2   Voting-Age Persons by Race/Hispanic or Latino Origin

District	White*	Black or African American*	American Indian or Alaska Native*	Asian*	Other or multirace*	Hispanic or Latino*
1	95.5	2.0	0.2	0.4	0.6	1.3
2	91.1	5.7	0.3	1.0	0.8	1.1
3	86.6	10.0	0.3	0.8	0.8	1.4
4	93.2	4.2	0.3	0.3	0.6	1.4
5	71.1	21.3	0.3	2.1	1.3	3.9
6	89.9	6.0	0.3	0.9	0.6	2.4
7	84.7	10.8	0.2	1.6	0.8	2.0
8	77.3	19.9	0.3	0.5	0.6	1.4
9	39.5	55.0	0.2	1.6	0.8	2.9
State	81.2	14.8	0.2	1.0	0.7	2.0

As percentage of voting-age population.

Table 3   Voting-Age Population by Age Groups

District	18 to 24*	25 to 44*	45 to 64*	Over 64*
1	10.9	37.4	33.0	18.7
2	13.3	38.5	31.1	17.1
3	12.4	37.7	32.1	17.8
4	11.2	37.3	32.5	19.1
5	14.6	43.8	27.6	14.0
6	14.0	41.4	30.0	14.6
7	11.1	42.8	32.7	13.5
8	13.0	38.8	30.4	17.9
9	14.8	43.1	27.4	14.7
State	12.8	40.1	30.8	16.4

As percentage of voting-age population.

Table 4 Income and Occupation

District	Median family income	Families in poverty*	White collar†	Blue collar†	Service†	Farm†
1	$37,898	11.3	50.0	34.4	15.0	0.6
2	$45,810	8.5	59.6	25.9	14.1	0.4
3	$42,518	10.4	54.3	31.7	13.6	0.4
4	$37,490	11.9	45.1	40.4	13.1	1.3
5	$49,617	9.3	64.2	21.9	13.7	0.1
6	$46,699	7.9	52.9	33.9	12.3	0.8
7	$57,275	6.2	64.0	24.0	11.6	0.5
8	$39,932	11.9	47.7	37.0	14.6	0.8
9	$40,066	16.1	60.4	24.0	15.5	0.1
State	$43,517	10.3	55.6	30.2	13.7	0.6

*As percentage of all families. †As percentage of employed workers 16 years and over.

Table 5 Education: School Years Completed

District	Less than grade 9*	Grades 9–12 no diploma*	High school diploma no college*	Some college*	College bachelor's degree or higher*
1	13.0	15.2	34.1	22.7	15.0
2	8.0	12.8	30.4	25.4	23.3
3	10.2	14.6	30.2	26.1	18.9
4	14.1	16.9	36.9	20.7	11.3
5	5.9	13.2	26.5	26.5	27.9
6	10.7	14.6	35.0	23.4	16.3
7	6.2	10.1	26.6	27.9	29.2
8	10.7	17.5	37.1	22.2	12.5
9	7.2	15.4	27.0	28.2	22.1
State	9.6	14.5	31.6	24.8	19.6

*As percentage of persons age 25 and over.

Table 6 Housing and Residential Patterns

District	Median home value	Owner occupied*	Renter occupied*	Urban†	Rural†
1	$80,000	74.2	25.8	55.4	44.6
2	$92,500	70.9	29.1	71.4	28.6
3	$85,500	70.5	29.5	64.2	35.8
4	$74,300	76.7	23.3	32.1	67.9
5	$113,700	58.1	41.9	88.7	11.3
6	$98,500	73.3	26.7	53.2	46.8
7	$126,300	79.3	20.7	61.0	39.0
8	$71,700	70.3	29.7	47.0	53.0
9	$76,900	56.9	43.1	99.6	0.4
State	$88,300	69.9	30.1	63.6	36.4

*As percentage of occupied housing units. †As percentage of total population.

Tennessee 1st District

Northeast — Tri-Cities, Morristown

Rolling hills and mountains cover the 1st, which borders Virginia and North Carolina. Thanks to Tennessee Valley Authority power, what were once isolated highland towns and tobacco patches are now scattered small cities with moderate economic growth.

Kingsport, Johnson City, and Bristol, known collectively as the Tri-Cities, center their industry on plastics, chemicals, and drug manufacturing. East Tennessee State University, a major employer in Johnson City, is a regional medical hub for much of the lower Appalachian region. The Tri-Cities have grown to become the area's economic anchor, while rural areas have lost clout.

Campers, hikers, and other visitors seeking the serenity of Great Smoky Mountains National Park must pass through an area jam-packed with large hotels, outlet shopping malls, and neon amusement parks. Pigeon Forge and Gatlinburg bring in millions of dollars each year through a booming tourist industry.

In the district's northwest, Hancock and Hawkins Counties are severely impoverished. Farmers here raise tobacco, poultry, and livestock. There also is zinc and limestone mining, though the coal mining industry's long-ago shutdown has left the area poor.

Like the rest of East Tennessee, the 1st has an overwhelming GOP lean, having sent a Republican to the House for more than a century (since the 1880 election). The rural areas almost always elect Republican state representatives, and the urban areas only sporadically send a Democrat to Nashville. However, mayoral and other local elections are usually nonpartisan.

Major Industry

Manufacturing, tourism.

Notable

Dollywood, in Pigeon Forge, is country music star Dolly Parton's theme park; Jonesborough is the state's oldest settlement and is home to the National Storytelling Festival; the Star Cars Museum in Gatlinburg has famous cars from movies; Bristol Motor Speedway, which seats 160,000, has become a major attraction, paralleling the rise of NASCAR.

Election Returns

	Republican		Democratic		Other	
President 2000	132,304	60.9%	81,335	37.5%	3,441	1.6%
House 2002	127,300	98.8%			1,586	0.2%

District Profile

Population 632,143

Total area (square miles) 4,174.1
  Land area (square miles) 4,093.2

Population per square mile 154.4

Counties (2000 population)

Carter	56,742	Jefferson (pt.)	11,095
Cocke	33,565	Johnson	17,499
Greene	62,909	Sevier (pt.)	53,943
Hamblen	58,128	Sullivan	153,048
Hancock	6,786	Unicoi	17,667
Hawkins	53,563	Washington	107,198

Cities and other areas over 10,000 (2000 population)

Bloomingdale CDP	10,350	Johnson City	55,469
Bristol	24,821	Kingsport	44,905
Elizabethton	13,372	Morristown	24,965
Greeneville town	15,198	Sevierville (pt.)	10,636

Race and Hispanic or Latino origin*
White 95.0%
Black or African American 2.1%

American Indian or Alaska Native   0.2%
Asian   0.4%
Native Hawaiian or other Pacific Islander   0.0%
Some other race   0.1%
Hispanic or Latino origin   1.5%
Two or more races   0.7%

As percentage of total population.

Ancestry*

Dutch 1.5%	Italian 1.1%
English 8.1%	Scotch-Irish 2.5%
French 1.2%	Scottish 1.5%
German 7.6%	USA/American 18.9%
Irish 7.8%	

As estimated percentage of total population.

Universities and colleges, 2000–2001 enrollment

East Tennessee State University, Johnson City   11,063
King College, Bristol   600
Milligan College, Milligan College   906
Northeast State Technical Community College, Blountville   4,125
Tusculum College, Greeneville   1,682
Walters State Community College, Morristown   6,163

Newspapers and circulation

	District circulation	Total circulation
Bristol Herald Courier	11,275	41,509
Greeneville Sun	14,732	14,747
Johnson City Press	29,816	30,007
Kingsport Times-News	31,421	42,469
Knoxville News-Sentinel	11,437	116,635
Morristown Citizen Tribune	14,677	18,538
*USA Today**	3,235	1,674,376

See Sources and Explanations in the front of the volume.

Television stations and affiliations

Bristol-Johnson City-Kingsport	65%	WCYB	NBC
Bristol-Johnson City-Kingsport	65%	WEMT	FOX
Bristol-Johnson City-Kingsport	65%	WJHL	CBS
Bristol-Johnson City-Kingsport	65%	WKPT	ABC
Bristol-Johnson City-Kingsport	65%	WLFG	Independent
Bristol-Johnson City-Kingsport	65%	WMSY	PBS
Bristol-Johnson City-Kingsport	65%	WSBN	PBS
Bristol-Johnson City-Kingsport	65%	WSJK	PBS
Knoxville	35%	WATE	ABC
Knoxville	35%	WBIR	NBC
Knoxville	35%	WBXX	WB
Knoxville	35%	WKOP	PBS
Knoxville	35%	WPXK	PAX
Knoxville	35%	WTNZ	FOX
Knoxville	35%	WVLT	CBS

Cable systems and subscribers

Adelphia   13,845
Charter   129,202
Comcast   15,076
STC Holdings Inc.   6,515

Military installations, September 2001

Holston Army Ammunition Plant, Kingsport   327

Businesses and other major employers

Johnson City Medical Center Inc.; Johnson City   2,300
Wellmont Health System Inc.; Kingsport; hospital   2,200
Citicorp Credit Services Inc.; Gray; savings institutions   1,800
East Tennessee State University; Johnson City   1,800
Berkline; Morristown; home furniture   1,730
Mahle Inc.; Morristown; pistons and piston rings   1,550
U.S. Veterans Hospital; Mountain Home   1,400
Five Rivers Electronic Innovations; Greeneville; TV receiving sets   1,200
Tennessee Dept. of Mental Health and Mental Retardation; Greeneville   1,124
Fingerhut Corp.; Piney Flats; warehouse club stores   1,100
Quebecor World Kingsport Inc.; Kingsport; book printing   1,100
Washington County Dept. of Education; Jonesborough   1,100
Landair Transport Inc.; Greeneville; trucking   1,025
American Water Heater Co.; Johnson City; household water heaters   1,000
Eastman Chemical Co.; Kingsport; plastics materials and resins   1,000
Shelby Williams Industries Inc.; Morristown; hotel furniture   1,000
A&L Industrial Construction and Maintenance Inc.; Kingsport; industrial buildings, warehouses   950
Exide Technologies; Bristol; batteries   800
TRW Inc.; Rogersville; automotive gears   800
City of Kingsport; Kingsport; city government   779
AFG Industries Inc.; Church Hill; float glass   750
Lear Corp.; Morristown; automobile seats   700
Nuclear Fuel Services Inc.; Erwin; nuclear fuel and cores   692
Monarch Pharmaceuticals Inc.; Bristol; mail-order pharmaceuticals   667
Quebecor Printing Kingsport Inc.; Church Hill; book publishing   652
NBTY Inc.; Morristown; health food stores   650
Morristown-Hamblen Healthcare System Hospital; Morristown   600
Plus Mark Inc.; Afton; wrapping paper   600
TPI Corp.; Gray; industrial electric heating units, devices   600
Indian Path Hospital Inc.; Kingsport   585
Monitor Systems Inc.; Blountville; restaurants   550
Wal-Mart Stores Inc.; Morristown; department stores   550
Prestolite Wire Corp.; Bristol; automotive parts   546
Toyoda Automotive Inc.; Morristown; automotive power steering equipment   545
Dan River Inc.; Sevierville; fabric mills   541
Deere and Co.; Greeneville; lawn and garden equipment   525
Disabled American Veterans; Johnson City; civic and social associations   525
J. W. Allen and Co. Inc.; Morristown; bakery goods   507
City of Greeneville; Greeneville; city government   500

ConAgra Grocery Products Co.; Newport; tomato
products   500
MECO Corp.; Greeneville; metal stampings   500
Philips Electronics North America Corp.; Greeneville;
electronic parts   500
Rockwell Automation Inc.; Rogersville; ball bearings
and parts   500

Tennessee 2nd District

East — Knoxville

Nestled in the valley of the Great Smoky Mountains at the mouth of the Tennessee River, the 2nd envelopes Knoxville and stretches south and west to include several conservative, rural counties.

State and federal jobs in the district are abundant for residents despite their well-voiced distaste for big government. The Tennessee Valley Authority is headquartered in Knoxville, and the Pellissippi Parkway enables commuters to quickly travel west of Knoxville to the Oak Ridge National Laboratory, in the 3rd District.

Knoxville residents will tell you their pride and joy is University of Tennessee athletics. Restaurants, hotels, and other businesses thrive on the fans who flock to the university's gargantuan football stadium and basketball arenas each year.

Nonetheless, Knoxville has struggled to revitalize its downtown since playing host to the World's Fair in 1982, after which businesses and hotels began to depart. The Women's Basketball Hall of Fame that opened in 1999 has helped, as have medical facilities that take up the slack from shuttered hospitals outside the city. The rural areas have attracted tourists, while Knoxville itself opened a new convention center in 2002. A major problem affecting the area, however, is air pollution. A 2003 report listed Knoxville in the top ten of U.S. cities with the worst air pollution.

Like all of East Tennessee, the mountainous 2nd has a long history of voting Republican. The GOP is entrenched in the district, which has not sent a Democrat to Congress since before the Civil War. In fact, rarely does the Republican incumbent sweat an election. Republicans who are somewhat more moderate mingle freely with a new strain of conservative activist here.

Major Industry
Higher education, medical services, tourism.

Notable
On home football game days, the University of Tennessee's Neyland Stadium becomes the state's fifth-largest city, with more than 104,000 in attendance; a statue in Haley Heritage Square honors *Roots* author Alex Haley, who made his home in Knoxville.

Election Returns

	Republican		Democratic		Other	
President 2000	144,412	59.2%	95,100	39.0%	4,246	1.7%
House 2002	146,887	79.0%	37,035	19.9%	2,059	1.1%

District Profile

Population   632,144

Total area (square miles)   2,491.8
Land area (square miles)   2,426.8

Population per square mile   260.5

Counties (2000 population)

Blount	105,823	McMinn	49,015
Knox	382,032	Monroe	38,961
Loudon	39,086	Sevier (pt.)	17,227

Cities and other areas over 10,000 (2000 population)

Athens	13,220	Knoxville	173,890
Farragut town	17,720	Maryville	23,120

Race and Hispanic or Latino origin*
White   90.1%
Black or African American   6.2%
American Indian or Alaska Native   0.3%
Asian   1.0%
Native Hawaiian or other Pacific Islander   0.0%
Some other race   0.1%
Hispanic or Latino origin   1.3%
Two or more races   1.0%

As percentage of total population.

Ancestry*

Dutch	1.6%	Italian	1.4%
English	8.9%	Scotch-Irish	3.2%
French	1.5%	Scottish	2.0%
German	8.9%	USA/American	14.0%
Irish	8.6%		

As estimated percentage of total population.

Universities and colleges, 2000–2001 enrollment
Hiwassee College, Madisonville   379
ITT Technical Institute, Knoxville   446
Johnson Bible College, Knoxville   626
Knoxville Business College, Knoxville   296
Maryville College, Maryville   982
Pellissippi State Technical Community College, Knoxville   7,859
Tennessee Wesleyan College, Athens   795
University of Tennessee, Knoxville   25,890

Newspapers and circulation

	District circulation	Total circulation
Athens Daily Post-Athenian	9,477	10,859
Chattanooga Times Free Press	1,458	72,730
Knoxville News-Sentinel	80,326	116,635
Maryville Daily Times	20,764	20,854
*USA Today**	5,131	1,674,376

See Sources and Explanations in the front of the volume.

Television stations and affiliations

Knoxville	83%	WATE	ABC
Knoxville	83%	WBIR	NBC
Knoxville	83%	WBXX	WB
Knoxville	83%	WKOP	PBS
Knoxville	83%	WPXK	PAX

Knoxville	83%	WTNZ	FOX
Knoxville	83%	WVLT	CBS
Chattanooga	17%	WCLP	PBS
Chattanooga	17%	WDEF	CBS
Chattanooga	17%	WDSI	FOX
Chattanooga	17%	WELF	Independent
Chattanooga	17%	WFLI	WB
Chattanooga	17%	WRCB	NBC
Chattanooga	17%	WTCI	PBS
Chattanooga	17%	WTVC	ABC

Cable systems and subscribers
Adelphia   2,133
Charter   41,831
Comcast   113,458

Military installations, September 2001
McGhee Tyson Airport Air Force Guard Station, Alcoa
1,184

Businesses and other major employers
University of Tennessee; Knoxville   4,000
Alcoa Inc.; Alcoa; aluminum smelting and refining
3,500
East Tennessee Baptist Hospital; Knoxville   2,500
DENSO Manufacturing Tennessee Inc.; Maryville;
automotive alternators   2,350
GJC Construction Co. Inc.; Knoxville; special trade
contractors   1,992
St. Mary's Health System Inc.; Knoxville; hospital
management   1,750
United Parcel Service Inc.; Knoxville   1,600
Fort Sanders Regional Medical Center; Knoxville
1,500
Tennessee Valley Authority; Knoxville; electric power
generation   1,250
Blount County; Maryville; public schools   1,144
Blount Memorial Hospital; Maryville   1,140
Fort Sanders-Parkwest Medical Center; Knoxville
1,100
Johnson Controls Inc.; Athens; automobile seats   1,100
Peebles Inc.; Knoxville; department stores   1,100
Honeywell International Inc.; Knoxville; automobile and
aircraft seat belts   1,000
Levi Strauss and Co.; Powell; sportswear   1,000
Collins and Aikman Corp.; Athens; automotive
moldings or trim   900
East Tennessee Childrens Hospital Assn. Inc.; Knoxville
900
Pellissippi State Technical Community College;
Knoxville   858
Knox County; Knoxville; county government   800
TRW Koyo Steering Systems Co.; Vonore; automotive
parts   780
United Brotherhood of Carpenters and Joiners of
America; Knoxville; trade union   750
National Seating Co.; Vonore; public conveyance seats
740
Norfolk Southern Railway Co.; Knoxville; railroad ticket
offices   700
Philips Electronics North America Corp.; Knoxville;
radio/TV communications equipment   675
Levi Strauss and Co.; Knoxville; computer integrated
systems design   650

Goody's Family Clothing Inc.; Knoxville; clothing stores
641
Aramark Corp.; Knoxville; direct selling   600
Plasti-Line Inc.; Powell; electric signs   600
Tennesse Dept. of Mental Health and Developmental
Disabilities; Knoxville   600
Knoxville News-Sentinel Co.; Knoxville; newspaper
580
City of Maryville; Maryville; elementary and secondary
schools   565
Employers Security Corp.; Knoxville; security guard
service   550
Wal-Mart Stores Inc.; Alcoa; supermarkets   550
Matsushita Electronic Components Corp.; Knoxville;
audio electronic systems   540
Mayfield Dairy Farms Inc.; Athens; milk processing
525
Loudon County; Loudon; county government   515
Bike Athletic Co.; Knoxville; athletic clothing   500
City of Knoxville; Knoxville; police dept.   500
E. W. Scripps Co.; Knoxville; TV film production   500
Hillcrest Medical Nursing Institute Inc.; Knoxville
500
Mastercraft Boat Co. Inc.; Vonore; jet skis   500
Tennessee National Guard; Alcoa   500
Tennessee National Guard; Louisville   500
Thomas and Betts Corp.; Athens; electric switch boxes
500
Travelers Property Casualty Corp.; Knoxville; fire,
marine, casualty insurance   500

Tennessee 3rd District

East — Chattanooga, Oak Ridge

The skinny 3rd stretches from Georgia to Kentucky and
Virginia but is dominated by Hamilton County, home to
the district's largest city, Chattanooga. It was altered in
redistricting to give it a more East Tennessee—and hence
Republican—flavor.

Once mostly industrial, Chattanooga is attempting to attract high-tech jobs with a "Technology Corridor" similar to
Research Triangle Park in North Carolina. The plan encour-
ages collaboration among high-tech companies in Knoxville
(in the neighboring 2nd District), Chattanooga, and Oak
Ridge, and an extensive highway system makes such commuting practical. A new highway linking the Knoxville airport to Oak Ridge—home of nuclear laboratories established
during World War II—has boosted growth.

Oak Ridge, once full of scientists and heavily dependent
on federal dollars, has diversified as wealth has moved west of
Knoxville. Chattanooga has injected life into its downtown
through projects such as the Tennessee Aquarium, the world's
largest freshwater aquarium, and new downtown apartments,
nightlife, and museums. Since the aquarium opened in 1992,
the city has attracted hundreds of millions of dollars in downtown investments.

The 3rd historically gives its representatives long tenures
in Washington. Republican dominance in the 1960s and
early 1970s gave way to Watergate-era disillusionment that
led to a ten-term run for Democrats. But Republicans won
the House seat in 1994 and continue to win reelection by

large margins. Middle Tennessee counties were cut out of the district in remapping following the 2000 census to ensure a Republican hold. George W. Bush captured 57 percent of the district's vote in the 2000 presidential election.

Major Industry
Nuclear and high-tech research, technology.

Notable
Popularized by the Glenn Miller song, the Chattanooga Choo-Choo has been restored as a historic landmark; the Scopes "monkey trial" in Dayton in 1925 upheld a ruling making it illegal to teach evolution.

Election Returns

	Republican		Democratic		Other	
President 2000	132,792	57.0%	96,441	41.4%	3,843	1.6%
House 2002	112,254	64.5%	58,824	33.8%	2,843	1.7%

District Profile

Population   632,143

Total area (square miles)   3,596.8
Land area (square miles)   3,410.7

Population per square mile   185.3

Counties (2000 population)

Anderson 71,330	Meigs 11,086
Bradley 87,965	Polk 16,050
Claiborne 29,862	Rhea 28,400
Grainger 20,659	Roane (pt.) 7,888
Hamilton 307,896	Union 17,808
Jefferson (pt.) 33,199	

Cities and other areas over 10,000 (2000 population)
Chattanooga (pt.)   155,554
Cleveland   37,192
East Brainerd CDP   14,132
East Ridge   20,640
Middle Valley CDP   11,854
Oak Ridge (pt.)   27,387
Red Bank   12,418
Soddy-Daisy   11,530

Race and Hispanic or Latino origin*
White   85.2%
Black or African American   11.1%
American Indian or Alaska Native   0.3%
Asian   0.9%
Native Hawaiian or other Pacific Islander   0.0%
Some other race   0.1%
Hispanic or Latino origin   1.6%
Two or more races   1.0%

*As percentage of total population.

Ancestry*

Dutch 1.3%	Italian 1.1%
English 7.9%	Scotch-Irish 2.1%
French 1.3%	Scottish 1.6%
German 7.0%	USA/American 16.4%
Irish 8.0%	

*As estimated percentage of total population.

Universities and colleges, 2000–2001 enrollment
Bryan College, Dayton   613
Carson-Newman College, Jefferson City   2,230
Chattanooga State Technical Community College, Chattanooga   7,873
Church of Theological Seminary, Cleveland   292
Cleveland State Community College, Cleveland   3,056
Lee University, Cleveland   3,361
Lincoln Memorial University, Harrogate   1,753
Southern Adventist University, Collegedale   2,041
Tennessee Temple University, Chattanooga   770
University of Tennessee, Chattanooga   8,319

Newspapers and circulation

	District circulation	Total circulation
Athens Daily Post-Athenian	1,262	10,859
Atlanta Journal-Constitution	1,460	857,088
Chattanooga Times Free Press	50,670	72,730
Cleveland Daily Banner	13,748	13,830
Knoxville News-Sentinel	15,808	116,635
Morristown Citizen Tribune	3,323	18,538
*USA Today**	3,538	1,674,376

*See Sources and Explanations in the front of the volume.

Television stations and affiliations
Chattanooga	53%	WCLP	PBS
Chattanooga	53%	WDEF	CBS
Chattanooga	53%	WDSI	FOX
Chattanooga	53%	WELF	Independent
Chattanooga	53%	WFLI	WB
Chattanooga	53%	WRCB	NBC
Chattanooga	53%	WTCI	PBS
Chattanooga	53%	WTVC	ABC
Knoxville	47%	WATE	ABC
Knoxville	47%	WBIR	NBC
Knoxville	47%	WBXX	WB
Knoxville	47%	WKOP	PBS
Knoxville	47%	WPXK	PAX
Knoxville	47%	WTNZ	FOX
Knoxville	47%	WVLT	CBS

Cable systems and subscribers
Charter   32,053
Comcast   82,774
Communicomm   11,343
Spring City Cable TV   614
Tele-Media   799

Military installations, September 2001
Volunteer Army Ammunition Plant, Chattanooga   392

Businesses and other major employers
US Xpress Inc.; Chattanooga; trucking   8,100
BWXT Y-12; Oak Ridge; missile warheads   4,420
Lockheed Martin Energy Research Corp.; Oak Ridge; noncommercial research organization   4,000
UT-Battelle; Oak Ridge; energy research   4,000
Catholic Health Initiative Hospital; Chattanooga   3,800
McKee Foods Corp.; Collegedale; bakery products   3,795
BlueCross and BlueShield of Tennessee Inc.; Chattanooga; medical service plans   3,347

Tennessee Valley Authority; Spring City; electric services
3,000

Anderson County; Clinton; county government   2,300

Erlanger Medical Center; Chattanooga   2,300

La-Z-Boy Inc.; Dayton; home furniture   2,016

Cigna Healthcare; Chattanooga; medical service plans
1,900

Maytag Corp.; Cleveland; indoor cooking equipment
1,888

Advantage Personnel Consultants Inc.; Chattanooga;
personnel management consultant   1,500

Dupont Sabanci International Inc.; Chattanooga; yarn
1,500

England/Corsair Inc.; New Tazewell; home furniture
1,500

Provident Life and Accident Insurance Co.; Chattanooga;
accident insurance carriers   1,500

Methodist Medical Center of Oak Ridge Inc.; Oak Ridge
1,442

Hamilton County; Chattanooga; county government
1,300

Baptist International Missions Inc.; Harrison; religious
organization   1,100

Bradley County Memorial Hospital Inc.; Cleveland
1,000

Covenant Transport Inc.; Chattanooga; trucking   1,000

Tennessee Valley Authority; Chattanooga; electric
services   1,000

Bechtel Jacobs Co.; Oak Ridge; environmental
remediation   980

Stellar Management Group Inc.; Chattanooga; garbage
disposals   947

Boeing Co.; Oak Ridge; aircraft   900

Kroger Co.; Cleveland; variety store merchandise   900

North American Royalties Inc.; Chattanooga; iron
foundry   836

ConAgra Poultry Co.; Chattanooga; poultry processing
800

Gillette Co.; Cleveland; dry cell batteries   800

University of Tennessee; Chattanooga   800

Parkridge Hospital Inc.; Chattanooga   785

Kindred Healthcare Inc. Hospital; Chattanooga   750

Security Consultants Group Inc.; Oak Ridge; security
systems services   750

U.S. Pipe and Foundry Co.; Chattanooga; iron foundry
722

Astec Inc.; Chattanooga; construction machinery   720

Musa Holdings Inc.; Chattanooga; personal credit
institutions   700

U.S. Dept. of Energy; Oak Ridge energy development,
conservation   700

Olin Corp.; Charleston; alkalies and chlorine   680

Hamilton County; Chattanooga; land redevelopment
agency   679

Mars Inc.; Cleveland; confectionery goods   678

Venator Group Retail Inc.; Cleveland; shoe stores   610

Alstom Power Inc.; Chattanooga; engineering services
600

Brach's Confections Inc.; Chattanooga; confectionery
goods   600

Eagle Bend Manufacturing Inc.; Clinton; automotive
parts   600

Komatsu America Corp.; Chattanooga; construction
machinery   600

Olan Mills Inc.; Chattanooga; photographer   600

T. C. Thompson Children's Hospital; Chattanooga   600

Tennessee National Guard; Chattanooga   600

Volunteer Behavioral Health System; Chattanooga;
mental health clinic   600

Mueller Co.; Chattanooga; fire hydrant valves   585

Catholic Health Initiative Hospital; Hixson   580

Dixie Group Inc.; Lupton City; cotton yarn   580

North American Royalties Inc.; Chattanooga; ductile
iron castings   579

Orange Grove Center Inc.; Chattanooga; vocational
training agency   575

Wal-Mart Stores Inc.; Cleveland; department stores
530

City of Chattanooga; Chattanooga; police dept.   504

Kayser-Roth Corp.; Dayton; hosiery   503

Carson-Newman College; Jefferson City   500

City of Chattanooga; Chattanooga; city government
500

City of Chattanooga; Chattanooga; utility regulation
500

DeRoyal Industries Inc.; Tazewell; medical diagnostic
apparatus   500

Olan Mills Inc.; Chattanooga; photographic studios
500

Philips Electronics North America Corp.; Jefferson City;
factory cabinets   500

Tennessee 4th District

Middle Tennessee — northeast and south

Predominantly rural and poor, the 4th touches Alabama, Georgia, and Kentucky and grabs suburbs southwest of Nashville as well as those west of Oak Ridge and Chattanooga. The conservative-leaning district is a melting pot of Tennessee's three regions, as plains turn east into rolling hills that merge with the Cumberland Plateau and eventually the Appalachian Mountains.

The sparsely populated district includes tobacco farms, many of them small, a Saturn plant that employs 7,800 in Spring Hill, and light manufacturing in the south.

The north is equally bereft of economic development. Campbell County in the district's northeast corner has high unemployment and sometimes halts school bus service for lack of funds. Campbell favored Al Gore in the 2000 presidential election, despite sending Republicans to the state legislature. Economic struggles in isolated rural areas such as Morgan and Grundy Counties leave water and electricity service unreliable.

Opposition to gun control and abortion, along with a strong religious sentiment, typifies the socially conservative constituency. With the exception of Republican Williamson County (shared with the 7th), the district's conservatives often are Democrats. But Gore lost the district narrowly in 2000.

Major Industry

Agriculture, auto parts, manufacturing.

Notable

Jack Daniel's sour mash whiskey distillery in Lynchburg is located in a dry county (Moore); President James K. Polk's home is in Columbia; Mule Day in Columbia attracts 250,000 every April.

Election Returns

	Republican		Democratic		Other	
President 2000	111,639	49.7%	109,559	48.8%	3,507	1.6%
House 2002	85,680	46.5%	95,989	52.1%	2,631	1.4%

District Profile

Population   632,143

Total area (square miles)   10,155.2
  Land area (square miles)   10,038.2

Population per square mile   63.0

Counties (2000 population)

Bledsoe 12,367	Marion 27,776
Campbell 39,854	Maury 69,498
Coffee 48,014	Moore 5,740
Cumberland 46,802	Morgan 19,757
Fentress 16,625	Pickett 4,945
Franklin 39,270	Roane (pt.) 44,022
Giles 29,447	Scott 21,127
Grundy 14,332	Sequatchie 11,370
Hickman (pt.) 13,045	Van Buren 5,508
Lawrence 39,926	Warren 38,276
Lewis 11,367	White 23,102
Lincoln 31,340	Williamson (pt.) 18,633

Cities and other areas over 10,000 (2000 population)

Columbia 33,055	McMinnville 12,749
Lawrenceburg 10,796	Tullahoma 17,994

Race and Hispanic or Latino origin*

White   92.6%
Black or African American   4.4%
American Indian or Alaska Native   0.3%
Asian   0.3%
Native Hawaiian or other Pacific Islander   0.0%
Some other race   0.0%
Hispanic or Latino origin   1.6%
Two or more races   0.8%

*As percentage of total population.

Ancestry*

Dutch 1.1%	Irish 8.1%
English 7.2%	Scotch-Irish 1.8%
French 1.2%	Scottish 1.3%
German 6.4%	USA/American 20.0%

*As estimated percentage of total population.

Universities and colleges, 2000–2001 enrollment

Columbia State Community College, Columbia   4,261
Martin Methodist College, Pulaski   582
Motlow State Community College, Tullahoma   3,331
Roane State Community College, Harriman   5,099
Tennessee Technology Center, Harriman   230
Tennessee Technology Center, Pulaski   285
University of the South, Sewanee   1,494

Newspapers and circulation

	District circulation	Total circulation
Chattanooga Times Free Press	6,043	72,730
Columbia Daily Herald	11,435	12,243
Knoxville News-Sentinel	9,101	116,635
Nashville Tennessean	21,726	182,088
*USA Today**	3,014	1,674,376

*See Sources and Explanations in the front of the volume.

Television stations and affiliations

Nashville	49%	WCTE	PBS
Nashville	49%	WHTN	Independent
Nashville	49%	WJFB	Independent
Nashville	49%	WKRN	ABC
Nashville	49%	WNAB	WB
Nashville	49%	WNPX	PAX
Nashville	49%	WPGD	Independent
Nashville	49%	WSMV	NBC
Nashville	49%	WTVF	CBS
Nashville	49%	WUXP	UPN
Nashville	49%	WZTV	FOX
Knoxville	30%	WATE	ABC
Knoxville	30%	WBIR	NBC
Knoxville	30%	WBXX	WB
Knoxville	30%	WKOP	PBS
Knoxville	30%	WPXK	PAX
Knoxville	30%	WTNZ	FOX
Knoxville	30%	WVLT	CBS
Chattanooga	15%	WCLP	PBS
Chattanooga	15%	WDEF	CBS
Chattanooga	15%	WDSI	FOX
Chattanooga	15%	WELF	Independent
Chattanooga	15%	WFLI	WB
Chattanooga	15%	WRCB	NBC
Chattanooga	15%	WTCI	PBS
Chattanooga	15%	WTVC	ABC
Huntsville-Decatur (Florence)	6%	WAAY	ABC
Huntsville-Decatur (Florence)	6%	WAFF	NBC
Huntsville-Decatur (Florence)	6%	WFIQ	PBS
Huntsville-Decatur (Florence)	6%	WHDF	UPN
Huntsville-Decatur (Florence)	6%	WHIQ	PBS
Huntsville-Decatur (Florence)	6%	WHNT	CBS
Huntsville-Decatur (Florence)	6%	WYLE	Independent
Huntsville-Decatur (Florence)	6%	WZDX	FOX

Cable systems and subscribers

Bledsoe Telephone Co-op   2,014
Charter   68,515
Comcast   37,114
Mediacom   2,675
Petersburg Cable   1,536

Military installations, September 2001

Arnold Air Station (Air Force), Manchester   268

Businesses and other major employers

Saturn Corp.; Spring Hill; motor vehicles and car bodies   8,268
Carrier Corp.; Morrison; air conditioning equipment   1,600
Tennessee Assn. of Middle Schools; Whitwell   1,500
Maury Regional Hospital; Columbia   1,407

Aerospace Center Support; Tullahoma; facilities support services 1,200

Goodman Manufacturing Co.; Fayetteville; air conditioning equipment 1,100

Thyssen Elevator Co.; Kingston; elevators and equipment 1,000

Yorozu Automotive Tennessee Inc.; Morrison; automotive moldings or trim 1,000

A. O. Smith Corp.; McMinnville; electric motors 998

Cumberland Medical Center Inc.; Crossville 850

United Steelworkers of America International Union; Morrison; labor organization 800

Dura Operating Corp.; Lawrenceburg; windows, plastics 760

Roane County; Kingston; elementary and secondary schools 750

Bridgestone/Firestone North American Tire; Morrison; tires and inner tubes 745

White County; Sparta; county government 700

Sunbeam Products Inc.; McMinnville; cooking equipment 670

Lawrence County; Lawrenceburg; elementary and secondary schools 669

Hartco Flooring Co.; Oneida; hardwood flooring 667

Tecumseh Products Co.; Dunlap; internal combustion engines 650

TEPRO Inc.; Winchester; automotive rubber goods 648

Batesville Casket Co.; Manchester; burial caskets 600

M-Tek Inc.; Manchester; molded plastics 600

Plus Mark Inc.; Franklin; ribbons and bows 600

Torrington Co.; Pulaski; industrial supplies 600

Hickman County; Centerville; county government 599

National Medical Hospitals of Tullahoma Inc.; Tullahoma 500

Tennessee 5th District

Nashville

Home to state capital Nashville, the 5th is Tennessee's second-smallest district geographically, but it looms large in economic, political, and cultural value.

"Music City U.S.A." is known for the Grand Ole Opry and homes of country music stars. While country music is unquestionably Nashville's most famous industry, state government is its top employer. Vanderbilt University and 16 other schools make the district a hub for higher education in the state. As a national health care center, the district hosts several insurance companies and research facilities, including the Vanderbilt University Medical Center.

A population boom in Middle Tennessee has kept businesses in downtown Nashville while settlers flock to the Davidson County suburbs. Two large sports stadiums—home to football's Titans and hockey's Predators—opened downtown in the late-1990s. The 5th takes in 96 percent of the county's residents.

Bargain retail stores and other attractions have drawn tourists and locals to suburban Nashville. The Belle Meade suburb long has been one of the state's wealthiest areas, and the hilly district includes parts of more-rural Wilson and Cheatham Counties.

The area's economic boom attracted young, Republican-leaning upper-class couples to neighborhoods such as Bellevue and the Hermitage. But the city core, home to many government employees, academics, and labor unions, is so strongly Democratic that control of the seat is not in doubt. No Republican won Nashville's congressional seat in the twentieth century.

Major Industry

Government, music, higher education, religious publishing, auto manufacturing.

Notable

"The Hermitage" was the home of President Andrew Jackson; Nashville is home to a life-size reproduction of the Parthenon and to the Country Music Hall of Fame.

Election Returns

	Republican		Democratic		Other	
President 2000	95,309	41.5%	130,111	56.7%	4,015	1.8%
House 2002	56,825	33.3%	108,903	63.7%	5,158	3.0%

District Profile

Population 632,143

Total area (square miles) 932.0
Land area (square miles) 893.8

Population per square mile 707.3

Counties (2000 population)
Cheatham (pt.) 24,389
Davidson (pt.) 542,831
Wilson (pt.) 64,923

Cities and other areas over 10,000 (2000 population)
Lebanon (pt.) 12,718
Mount Juliet 12,366
Nashville-Davidson (pt.) 524,339

Race and Hispanic or Latino origin*
White 68.2%
Black or African American 23.4%
American Indian or Alaska Native 0.3%
Asian 2.0%
Native Hawaiian or other Pacific Islander 0.1%
Some other race 0.2%
Hispanic or Latino origin 4.2%
Two or more races 1.6%

*As percentage of total population.

Ancestry*

English	7.6%	Italian	1.5%
French	1.6%	Scotch-Irish	2.4%
German	7.5%	Scottish	1.7%
Irish	7.6%	USA/American	10.8%

*As estimated percentage of total population.

Universities and colleges, 2000–2001 enrollment
Aquinas College, Nashville 477
Belmont University, Nashville 2,976
Cumberland University, Lebanon 1,492
David Lipscomb University, Nashville 2,528

Fisk University, Nashville   973
Free Will Baptist Bible College, Nashville   319
Fugazzi College, Nashville   450
ITT Technical Institute, Nashville   498
Meharry Medical College, Nashville   905
Nashville Auto Diesel College, Nashville   1,298
Nashville School of Law*, Nashville
Nashville State Technical Institute, Nashville   7,315
Tennessee State University, Nashville   8,640
Trevecca Nazarene University, Nashville   1,709
Vanderbilt University, Nashville   10,092
Watkins Institute College of Art and Design, Nashville
338

*Enrollment under 100. See Sources and Explanations in the front of the volume.

Newspapers and circulation

	District circulation	Total circulation
Nashville Tennessean	82,960	182,088
*USA Today**	10,376	1,674,376

*See Sources and Explanations in the front of the volume.

Television stations and affiliations

Nashville	100%	WCTE	PBS
Nashville	100%	WHTN	Independent
Nashville	100%	WJFB	Independent
Nashville	100%	WKRN	ABC
Nashville	100%	WNAB	WB
Nashville	100%	WNPX	PAX
Nashville	100%	WPGD	Independent
Nashville	100%	WSMV	NBC
Nashville	100%	WTVF	CBS
Nashville	100%	WUXP	UPN
Nashville	100%	WZTV	FOX

Cable systems and subscribers
Charter   14,115
Comcast   136,349

Military installations, September 2001
Nashville International Airport Air Force Guard Station, Nashville   1,184
Lyell Armed Forces Reserve Center, Nashville   875

Businesses and other major employers
Nortel Networks Inc.; Nashville; telephone switching equipment   20,000
General Parts Inc.; Lebanon; automotive supplies 13,118
Vanderbilt University; Nashville   9,000
Kinny Systems of Atlantic City Inc.; Nashville; parking lots   4,500
Vanderbilt University Hospital; Nashville   4,200
Bradley Coatings Inc.; Nashville; commercial painting 4,030
HCA Inc. Hospital; Nashville   4,000
Willis Group; Nashville; insurance information, consulting services   3,900
Gaylord Entertainment Co.; Nashville; hotels and motels 3,622
Ardent Health Services; Nashville; psychiatric hospitals 3,000
St. Thomas Hospital; Nashville   3,000

Baptist Hospital Inc.; Nashville   2,900
United Parcel Service Inc.; Nashville; parcel delivery 2,500
Insource Electronics Inc.; Nashville; circuit board repair 2,001
CompuCom Systems Inc.; Nashville; computer systems resellers   2,000
State Industries Inc.; Ashland City; household water heaters   1,811
Columbia Healthcare of Central Virginia Inc. Hospital; Nashville   1,800
Sprint Corp.; Nashville; cellular telephones   1,600
Lifeway Christian Resources of Southern Baptist Convention; Nashville; religious books   1,454
American General Life and Accident Insurance Co.; Nashville   1,300
City of Nashville; Nashville; police dept.   1,200
PACCAR Inc.; Madison; motor vehicles and car bodies 1,200
U.S. Dept. of Veterans Affairs; Nashville   1,200
Meharry Medical College; Nashville   1,100
Summit Medical Center; Hermitage   1,100
Tennessee State University; Nashville   1,100
Alcoa Fujikura Inc.; Nashville; wire, copper and copper alloy   1,060
CNA Insurance Corp.; Nashville; fire, marine, casualty insurance   1,000
Jones Bros. Inc.; Mount Juliet; bridge construction 1,000
Tennesse Dept. of Environment and Conservation; Nashville   1,000
Tennessee Dept. of Human Services; Nashville   1,000
City of Nashville; Nashville; water supply   970
Quickway Distribution Services Co.; Nashville; refrigerated products transport   950
Skyline Medical Center; Nashville   950
Cracker Barrel Old Country Store Inc.; Lebanon; restaurant chain   900
Tennessee Christian Medical Center; Madison   900
Whirlpool Corp.; La Vergne; refrigeration and heating equipment   900
Wilson County Board of Education; Lebanon   821
Continental Assurance Co.; Old Hickory; fire, marine, casualty insurance   800
U.S. Army Corps of Engineers; Nashville   800
First Union Corp. of Tennessee; Nashville; commercial trust company   785
National Federation of Independent Business; Nashville; business associations   720
Dana Corp.; Antioch; automotive engines and parts 700
Dollar General Corp.; Goodlettsville; variety stores   700
E. I. Du Pont De Nemours and Co.; Old Hickory; leather processing   700
Mica Energy Systems; Nashville; testing labs   700
Nashville/Davidson County Electric Power Board; Nashville; electric power distribution   700
United Methodist Publishing House; Nashville; book publishing and printing   700
Sysco Food Services; Nashville; frozen foods   694
Metro Nashville City Hospital; Nashville   692
Southern Hills Medical Center Inc.; Nashville   650

Steiner-Liff Textile Products Inc.; Nashville; textile mill waste and remnant processing   650

TRW Inc.; Lebanon; automotive steering mechanisms   650

Wright RTS Industries; Nashville; assembly machines   650

Yellow Freight System Inc.; Nashville; contract haulers   631

Cigna Health Corp.; Nashville; medical assistance program administration   630

National Medical Hospital of Wilson County Inc.; Lebanon   625

Belmont University; Nashville   600

DB Services Tennessee Inc.; Nashville; management consulting   600

Horace Small Manufacturing Co.; Nashville; men's/boys' uniforms   600

JC Penney Corp.; Nashville; catalog sales   600

Manheim Auctions Inc.; Nashville; automobile auction   600

Rock City Mechanical Inc.; Nashville; mechanical contractor   600

U.S. Postal Service; Antioch   600

City of Nashville; Nashville; convalescent home   562

Thomas Nelson Inc.; Nashville; book publishing   560

Meridian Comp of New York; Nashville; medical offices   559

Aladdin Industries; Nashville; plastic materials and resins   550

Tennessee Dept. of Corrections; Nashville   550

City of Nashville; Nashville; utility regulation   542

City of Nashville; Nashville; city government   500

City of Nashville; Nashville; recreation services   500

Dell Computer Corp.; Nashville; electronic computers   500

Deloitte and Touche; Hermitage; accounting services   500

Galaxy Logistics Inc.; Nashville; warehousing   500

Nashville Machine; Nashville; mechanical engineering   500

Reemay Inc.; Old Hickory; yarn   500

Renaissance Hotel Group; Nashville; hotels   500

Roadway Express Inc.; Antioch; trucking   500

Shoney's Inc.; Nashville; real estate brokers and agents   500

Tennessee Dept. of Commerce and Insurance; Nashville   500

Tennessee Dept. of Transportation; Nashville   500

Tennessee National Guard; Nashville   500

Wackenhut Corp.; Nashville; security guard service   500

Tennessee 6th District

Middle Tennessee — Murfreesboro

Nearby Nashville's population boom has spilled over into much of the 6th District, which wraps around Nashville to the north and east before swinging south.

The hilly countryside includes two university communities: Murfreesboro, which is home to Middle Tennessee State University and has grown rapidly, and Cookeville, where

Tennessee Tech University is located. Rutherford County, which includes Murfreesboro, grew by more than 50 percent in the 1990s, and Wilson County east of Nashville grew by almost one-third during the decade. The district has remained fairly loyal to the Democratic Party since the days of Andrew Jackson, who built his political career in the area. Redistricting following the 2000 census allowed the 6th to shed growing conservative areas in Williamson County and increased the chance the seat will stay in Democratic hands. A rural, tobacco-farming base added in northern Robertson County remains staunchly Democratic, as does Bedford County, which was added to the district's southern end.

In the Nashville area's orbit, the economy was strong in the 1990s. A well-developed highway system makes commuting from Nashville, in the 5th District, to Murfreesboro easy. Some residents have government jobs, but employment relies more on automobile parts manufacturers spurred by a Nissan plant in Smyrna and a Saturn plant in the 4th District. Tobacco farming and book distribution also are big businesses.

The 6th supports a Democratic but socially conservative constituency that favors prayer in schools. Though Al Gore represented this area in Congress, the 2000 presidential election was essentially a dead heat. Reconfigured voting results from the new district show Gore losing to George W. Bush by just over 200 votes.

Major Industry

Auto and textile manufacturing, book and video distribution.

Notable

Cordell Hull practiced law in Celina before beginning his political career, during which he became President Franklin D. Roosevelt's secretary of state from 1933 until 1944; Shelbyville in Bedford County is the heart of Tennessee Walking Horse country; Carthage is the hometown of former vice president and presidential candidate Al Gore.

Election Returns

	Republican		Democratic		Other	
President 2000	112,096	49.2%	111,872	49.1%	3,729	1.6%
House 2002	57,401	32.3%	117,034	65.9%	3,112	1.7%

District Profile

Population   632,143

Total area (square miles)   5,575.7
   Land area (square miles)   5,480.1

Population per square mile   115.4

Counties (2000 population)

Bedford	37,586	Putnam	62,315
Cannon	12,826	Robertson	54,433
Clay	7,976	Rutherford	182,023
DeKalb	17,423	Smith	17,712
Jackson	10,984	Sumner	130,449
Macon	20,386	Trousdale	7,259
Marshall	26,767	Wilson (pt.)	23,886
Overton	20,118		

Cities and other areas over 10,000 (2000 population)

Cookeville	23,923	Murfreesboro	68,816
Gallatin	23,230	Shelbyville	16,105
Hendersonville	40,620	Smyrna town	25,569
La Vergne	18,687	Springfield	14,329
Lewisburg	10,413		

Race and Hispanic or Latino origin*

White 89.0%
Black or African American 6.3%
American Indian or Alaska Native 0.3%
Asian 0.9%
Native Hawaiian or other Pacific Islander 0.0%
Some other race 0.1%
Hispanic or Latino origin 2.6%
Two or more races 0.8%

*As percentage of total population.

Ancestry*

English	8.1%	Italian	1.4%
French	1.5%	Scotch-Irish	2.1%
German	7.0%	Scottish	1.5%
Irish	8.1%	USA/American	19.0%

*As estimated percentage of total population.

Universities and colleges, 2000–2001 enrollment

Middle Tennessee State University, Murfreesboro 19,121
Tennessee Technological University, Cookeville 8,410
Tennessee Technology Center, Shelbyville 323
Volunteer State Community College, Gallatin 6,567

Newspapers and circulation

	District circulation	Total circulation
Cookeville Herald Citizen	10,577	10,893
Murfreesboro Daily News Journal	15,249	15,249
Nashville Tennessean	42,994	182,088
*USA Today**	2,958	1,674,376

*See Sources and Explanations in the front of the volume.

Television stations and affiliations

Nashville	100%	WCTE	PBS
Nashville	100%	WHTN	Independent
Nashville	100%	WJFB	Independent
Nashville	100%	WKRN	ABC
Nashville	100%	WNAB	WB
Nashville	100%	WNPX	PAX
Nashville	100%	WPGD	Independent
Nashville	100%	WSMV	NBC
Nashville	100%	WTVF	CBS
Nashville	100%	WUXP	UPN
Nashville	100%	WZTV	FOX

Cable systems and subscribers

Celina Cable 1,146
Charter 26,822
Comcast 64,095
Tele-Media 1,053

Military installations, September 2001

Symrna Airport (Army Guard), Smyrna 860

Businesses and other major employers

Nissan Motor Manufacturing Corp. USA; Smyrna; automobiles 6,300
Middle Tennessee State University; Murfreesboro 2,482
Sumner County; Gallatin; county government 2,375
Ingram Book Group Inc.; La Vergne; video and audio equipment 2,050
Perdue Farms Inc.; Monterey; poultry processing 1,694
Rutherford County; Murfreesboro 1,390
Tyson Foods Inc.; Shelbyville; poultry processing 1,200
Middle Tennessee Medical Center Inc.; Murfreesboro 1,050
Cookeville Regional Medical Center; Cookeville 1,000
Cumberland Swan Holdings Inc.; Smyrna; toiletries 1,000
Fleetguard Inc.; Cookeville; automotive parts 1,000
Calsonic North America Inc.; Shelbyville; automotive air conditioning 1,000
Sanford-Shelbyville; Shelbyville; pencils, art goods 1,000
Tennessee National Guard; Smyrna 1,000
Tennessee Technological University; Cookeville 1,000
Imperial Group; Portland; fabricated plate work 837
Cosmolab Inc.; Lewisburg; cosmetics 800
Federal-Mogul Corp.; Smithville; automotive parts 800
R. R. Donnelley and Sons Co.; Gallatin; offset printing 800
Electrolux Home Products Inc.; Springfield; electric ranges 750
Sanford-Lewisburg; Lewisburg; pens and pencils 750
Perrigo of Tennessee; Smyrna; toiletries 736
City of Murfreesboro; Murfreesboro; city government 719
Furnishings International Inc.; Livingston; home furniture 700
Kantus Corp.; Lewisburg; automotive radiators 640
Sumner Regional Health Systems Inc. Hospital; Gallatin 609
Rexam Beverage Can Co.; Shelbyville; unsupported plastic tubes 600
Unipres USA Inc.; Portland; automotive body parts 600
CPI of Tennessee Inc.; Lebanon; employee leasing service 560
Wal-Mart Stores Inc.; Cookeville; department stores 560
Eaton Corp.; Shelbyville; electric power transmission 550
TRW Inc.; Cookeville; automotive steering mechanisms 550
Warnaco Inc.; Murfreesboro; undergarments 550
Tutco Inc.; Cookeville; electric appliances 526
Square D Co.; Smyrna; electrical bus bars 519
MI Home Products Inc.; Smyrna; metal doors, sash, and trim 500
Pechiney Plastic Packaging Inc.; Shelbyville; plastic foam products 500
Stratus Javelin Boats; Murfreesboro; fiberglass boats 500
Walker Die Casting Inc.; Lewisburg; aluminum die-castings 500

Tennessee 7th District

Eastern Memphis suburbs; most of Clarksville and Franklin

Bordering Kentucky to the north and Mississippi and Alabama to the south, the 7th is anchored by two wealthy, conservative suburban communities: Memphis' Shelby County in the southwest and the Nashville area's Williamson County in the east. It also includes most of the moderately sized city of Clarksville.

White flight from Memphis (in the 9th) has driven growth in suburban Shelby County, where many children attend parochial schools. The migration has transformed traditionally Democratic West Tennessee into a Republican-leaning area dominated by small churches. The new strain of GOP activism is strongly antitax and socially conservative.

Heading east and north, agriculture makes for rural counties, where corn, tobacco, hogs, and cattle dominate. The rural areas between Memphis and Nashville also are a solid base for Republicans.

"Yellow Dog" Democrats still outweigh Republican voters in Clarksville and surrounding rural sectors. A few miles from the Kentucky border, Clarksville has benefited from diverse manufacturing and the expansion of Fort Campbell, one-third of which is in Kentucky.

The GOP has held the congressional seat since 1973, with support from socially conservative suburban, rural, and military contingents.

Major Industry
Tobacco, cattle, military.

Notable
Shiloh National Military Park memorializes those who died in one of the bloodiest battles of the Civil War.

Election Returns

	Republican		Democratic		Other	
President 2000	146,213	58.8%	99,423	40.0%	3,098	1.2%
House 2002	138,314	70.7%	51,790	26.5%	5,454	2.8%

District Profile

Population   632,139

Total area (square miles)   6,349.1
  Land area (square miles)   6,291.7

Population per square mile   100.5

Counties (2000 population)

Cheatham (pt.) 11,523	Hickman (pt.) 9,250
Chester 15,540	McNairy 24,653
Davidson (pt.) 27,060	Montgomery (pt.) 102,740
Decatur 11,731	Perry 7,631
Fayette 28,806	Shelby (pt.) 189,153
Hardeman 28,105	Wayne 16,842
Hardin 25,578	Williamson (pt.) 108,005
Henderson 25,522	

Cities and other areas over 10,000 (2000 population)
Bartlett (pt.)   40,409
Brentwood   23,445
Clarksville (pt.)   83,680
Collierville town (pt.)   27,779
Franklin (pt.)   33,627
Germantown (pt.)   34,200
Memphis (pt.)   25,359
Nashville-Davidson (pt.)   21,185

Race and Hispanic or Latino origin*
White   83.5%
Black or African American   11.4%
American Indian or Alaska Native   0.2%
Asian   1.5%
Native Hawaiian or other Pacific Islander   0.1%
Some other race   0.1%
Hispanic or Latino origin   2.2%
Two or more races   1.1%

As percentage of total population.

Ancestry*

Dutch 1.1%	Italian 2.2%
English 9.1%	Polish 1.1%
French 1.9%	Scotch-Irish 2.4%
German 8.8%	Scottish 2.0%
Irish 9.1%	USA/American 12.3%

As estimated percentage of total population.

Universities and colleges, 2000–2001 enrollment
Draughons Junior College, Clarksville   254
Freed-Hardeman University, Henderson   1,886
Tennessee Technology Center, Crump   272

Newspapers and circulation

	District circulation	Total circulation
Clarksville Leaf Chronicle	14,150	21,341
Jackson Sun	7,481	35,921
Memphis Commercial Appeal	32,500	157,808
Nashville Tennessean	27,689	182,088
*USA Today**	5,474	1,674,376

See Sources and Explanations in the front of the volume.

Television stations and affiliations

Nashville	37%	WCTE	PBS
Nashville	37%	WHTN	Independent
Nashville	37%	WJFB	Independent
Nashville	37%	WKRN	ABC
Nashville	37%	WNAB	WB
Nashville	37%	WNPX	PAX
Nashville	37%	WPGD	Independent
Nashville	37%	WSMV	NBC
Nashville	37%	WTVF	CBS
Nashville	37%	WUXP	UPN
Nashville	37%	WZTV	FOX
Memphis	35%	KVTJ	Independent
Memphis	35%	WBUY	Independent
Memphis	35%	WHBQ	FOX
Memphis	35%	WKNO	PBS
Memphis	35%	WMAE	PBS
Memphis	35%	WMAV	PBS
Memphis	35%	WMC	NBC
Memphis	35%	WPTY	ABC, WB
Memphis	35%	WPXX	PAX

Memphis	35%	WREG	CBS
Jackson, MS	28%	WBBJ	ABC
Jackson, MS	28%	WLJT	PBS

Cable systems and subscribers
Charter 18,624
Comcast 19,163
STC Holdings Inc. 582
Time Warner 18,928

Businesses and other major employers
Diversicare Leasing Corp.; Franklin; nursing/personal care facility management 4,000

Raygar International; Brentwood; investment holding company 3,189

AHOM Holdings Inc.; Brentwood; home health care 1,891

Trane Co.; Clarksville; air conditioning equipment 1,780

Primus Automotive Financial Services Inc.; Franklin; automobile loans 1,700

Aabakus Inc.; Brentwood; employee leasing service 1,200

International Staff Management Inc.; Memphis; management consulting 1,100

Service Merchandise Co.; Brentwood; catalog showroom stores 1,050

Agricultural Marketing Service; Memphis; agricultural marketing regulation 1,000

Aqua Glass Corp.; Adamsville; bath, shower, laundry tubs 1,000

Comdata Network Inc.; Brentwood; data entry service 1,000

Gateway Health System Hospital; Clarksville 1,000

Tom James of New Orleans Inc.; Franklin; clothing stores 1,000

Quebecor World Inc.; Clarksville; commercial printing 1,000

Williamson Medical Center; Franklin 980

Tennessee Dept. of Mental Health and Mental Retardation; Arlington 843

ThyssenKrupp Elevator Corp.; Middleton; elevator installation and conversion 825

Coca-Cola Bottling Co.; Brentwood; soft drinks 800

Army and Air Force Exchange Service; Fort Campbell; Army-Navy goods stores 750

Magnum International Freight; Nashville; heavy hauling 710

J&A Mechanical Inc.; Cordova; plumbing contractors 650

Johnson Controls Inc.; Lexington; automotive parts 630

AIM Healthcare Services Inc.; Franklin; financial management for business 600

Johnson Controls Inc.; Linden; automotive parts 600

Precision Printing and Packaging Inc.; Clarksville; labels and seals 575

Packaging Corp. of America; Counce; corrugated boxes 550

Manufacturers Industrial Group; Lexington; automobile seat frames 515

DynCorp; Fort Campbell; pilot service 510

Brother Industries Inc.; Memphis; typewriters and parts 500

Central Church Inc.; Collierville; religious organization 500

Fayette County; Somerville; elementary and secondary schools 500

Jostens Inc.; Clarksville; book publishing and printing 500

Ryder Integrated Logistics Inc.; Franklin; truck rental 500

Wal-Mart Stores Inc.; Memphis; department stores 500

Wright Medical Technology Inc.; Arlington; medical supplies 500

Tennessee 8th District

West — Jackson, parts of Memphis and Clarksville

The mighty Mississippi to the west and the Tennessee and Cumberland rivers to the east frame the rolling hills and flat farmland that make up the 8th. Except for Memphis' northern suburbs and Jackson, the district is predominantly rural, Democratic, and working-class. Democrats, often conservative ones, have held this district seat since Reconstruction. Redistricting following the 2000 census sliced away some growing Republican parts of Shelby County north of Memphis, adding to the Democratic lean. Al Gore carried the 8th in the 2000 presidential contest with 50.8 percent of the vote.

The district is poor, but a few manufacturing plants prevent the economy from slipping further. A Procter and Gamble Pringles potato chip plant employs more than 1,100 people in Jackson, and tire, auto, and textile manufacturers are scattered throughout less-populated sectors. Mechanization has decreased factory employment but increased production on small farms. Chicken-processing plants give the area some value-added agriculture, while the boll weevil is a longtime scourge to cotton farmers.

State and federal government also provide much-needed jobs via two large state prisons and a downsized, but still significant, naval air station in Millington. Redistricting moved the 8th's eastern border into Clarksville and closer to Nashville.

The northern section of the Tennessee River feeds into Kentucky Lake in the northeast. Tennessee Valley Authority dams and power plants are here, and these waterways also draw many avid hunters and fishermen to the district. Thousands of birdwatchers flock to Reelfoot Lake in the northwest each winter to view the migration of hundreds of bald eagles.

Major Industry
Manufacturing, agriculture, government.

Notable
Civil War battles were fought at Fort Donelson, Fort Henry, and Fort Pillow; a 60-foot-tall replica of the Eiffel Tower is in Paris, which also is home to the World's Biggest Fish Fry.

Election Returns

	Republican		Democratic		Other	
President 2000	102,998	47.9%	109,221	50.8%	2,633	1.2%
House 2002	45,853	27.3%	117,811	70.1%	4,306	2.6%

District Profile

Population 632,142

Total area (square miles) 8,528.4
 Land area (square miles) 8,261.7

Population per square mile 76.5

Counties (2000 population)

Benton 16,537	Lake 7,954
Carroll 29,475	Lauderdale 27,101
Crockett 14,532	Madison 91,837
Dickson 43,156	Montgomery (pt.) 32,028
Dyer 37,279	Obion 32,450
Gibson 48,152	Shelby (pt.) 76,176
Haywood 19,797	Stewart 12,370
Henry 31,115	Tipton 51,271
Houston 8,088	Weakley 34,895
Humphreys 17,929	

Cities and other areas over 10,000 (2000 population)

Brownsville 10,748	Martin 10,515
Clarksville (pt.) 19,775	Memphis (pt.) 53,080
Dickson 12,244	Millington (pt.) 10,433
Dyersburg 17,452	Union City 10,876
Jackson 59,643	

Race and Hispanic or Latino origin*
 White 74.4%
 Black or African American 22.3%
 American Indian or Alaska Native 0.3%
 Asian 0.4%
 Native Hawaiian or other Pacific Islander 0.0%
 Some other race 0.1%
 Hispanic or Latino origin 1.6%
 Two or more races 0.8%

*As percentage of total population.

Ancestry*

English 6.3%	Italian 1.1%
French 1.1%	Scotch-Irish 1.7%
German 5.3%	USA/American 15.8%
Irish 7.6%	

*As estimated percentage of total population.

Universities and colleges, 2000–2001 enrollment
 Austin Peay State University, Clarksville 7,121
 Bethel College, McKenzie 843
 Dyersburg State Community College, Dyersburg 2,278
 Jackson State Community College, Jackson 3,726
 Lambuth University, Jackson 979
 Lane College, Jackson 702
 Tennessee Technology Center, Covington 215
 Tennessee Technology Center, Jackson 515
 Union University, Jackson 2,373
 University of Tennessee, Martin 5,870

Newspapers and circulation

	District circulation	Total circulation
Clarksville Leaf Chronicle	6,493	21,341
Jackson Sun	28,319	35,921
Memphis Commercial Appeal	15,230	157,808
Nashville Tennessean	5,816	182,088
*USA Today**	3,724	1,674,376

*See Sources and Explanations in the front of the volume.

Television stations and affiliations

Memphis	36%	KVTJ	Independent
Memphis	36%	WBUY	Independent
Memphis	36%	WHBQ	FOX
Memphis	36%	WKNO	PBS
Memphis	36%	WMAE	PBS
Memphis	36%	WMAV	PBS
Memphis	36%	WMC	NBC
Memphis	36%	WPTY	ABC, WB
Memphis	36%	WPXX	PAX
Memphis	36%	WREG	CBS
Nashville	35%	WCTE	PBS
Nashville	35%	WHTN	Independent
Nashville	35%	WJFB	Independent
Nashville	35%	WKRN	ABC
Nashville	35%	WNAB	WB
Nashville	35%	WNPX	PAX
Nashville	35%	WPGD	Independent
Nashville	35%	WSMV	NBC
Nashville	35%	WTVF	CBS
Nashville	35%	WUXP	UPN
Nashville	35%	WZTV	FOX
Paducah-Cape Girardeau-Harrisburg-Mt. Vernon	15%	KBSI	FOX
Paducah-Cape Girardeau-Harrisburg-Mt. Vernon	15%	KFVS	CBS
Paducah-Cape Girardeau-Harrisburg-Mt. Vernon	15%	KPOB	ABC
Paducah-Cape Girardeau-Harrisburg-Mt. Vernon	15%	WDKA	WB
Paducah-Cape Girardeau-Harrisburg-Mt. Vernon	15%	WKMU	PBS
Paducah-Cape Girardeau-Harrisburg-Mt. Vernon	15%	WKPD	PBS
Paducah-Cape Girardeau-Harrisburg-Mt. Vernon	15%	WPSD	NBC
Paducah-Cape Girardeau-Harrisburg-Mt. Vernon	15%	WSIL	ABC
Paducah-Cape Girardeau-Harrisburg-Mt. Vernon	15%	WSIU	PBS
Paducah-Cape Girardeau-Harrisburg-Mt. Vernon	15%	WTCT	Independent
Jackson, MS	14%	WBBJ	ABC
Jackson, MS	14%	WLJT	PBS

Cable systems and subscribers
 Cable ONE 9,593
 CableVision Communications 1,835
 Charter 98,003
 Comcast 7,227
 Dresden Cable Inc. 800
 Infostructure Cable 4,332
 Mediacom 624
 Millington CATV Inc. 6,937
 Peoples CATV Inc. 3,095
 Trenton TV Cable Co. 2,134

Military installations, September 2001
 Naval Support Activity, Millington 1,622
 NSA Memphis U.S. Army Reserve Center, Memphis 898
 Milan Army Ammunition Plant, Milan 813
 Millington Medical Clinic, Millington 324

Businesses and other major employers
 University of Tennessee; Martin 3,200
 West Tennessee Healthcare Inc. Hospital; Jackson 2,627
 Jackson-Madison County General Hospital; Jackson 2,600
 Murray Inc.; Jackson; lawn and garden equipment 2,050

Siegel-Robert Inc.; Ripley; plastics   1,900
Madison County; Jackson; county government   1,720
Dana Corp.; Paris; mechanical rubber goods   1,500
Quebecor World Dickson Inc.; Dickson; publication
   printing, lithographic   1,300
Procter and Gamble Co.; Jackson; snacks   1,100
Porter Cable/Delta Corp.; Jackson; power-driven
   handtools   1,000
Quebecor World Inc.; Dyersburg; offset printing   1,000
American Ordnance; Milan; ammunition plant   910
Dyersburg Fabric LP; Dyersburg; synthetic fabrics   900
Tennessee Dept. of Transportation; Jackson   900
Tyson Foods Inc.; Union City; chicken hatchery   900
E. I. Du Pont De Nemours and Co.; New Johnsonville;
   industrial organic chemicals   850
Sara Lee Corp.; Newbern; meats and meat products   850
Copeland Electric Corp.; Humboldt; electric motors
   800
Quebecor World Inc.; Covington; periodicals   800
E. I. Du Pont De Nemours and Co.; Memphis; industrial
   inorganic chemicals   775
Marvin Windows of Tennessee Inc.; Ripley; wood doors
   700
Austin Peay State University; Clarksville   685
DeVilbiss Air Power Co.; Jackson; air and gas
   compressors   678
Weakley County; Dresden; county government   666
Haywood Co.; Brownsville; custom compound resins
   650
MTD Products Inc.; Martin; lawnmowers   650
Tennsco Corp.; Dickson; office furniture   650
Wilson Sporting Goods Co.; Humboldt; baseball
   equipment   625
ASSA ABLOY Door Group; Milan; metal doors   600
Durango Apparel Manufacturing Inc.; South Fulton;
   men's, boys' clothing   600
Maytag Corp.; Jackson; dishwashers   600
Armstrong Wood Products Inc.; Jackson; flooring   550
Intier Automotive Seating of America Inc.; Milan;
   public building and related furniture   550
Lennox Hearth Products Inc.; Union City; silverware
   540
Dal-Tile Corp.; Jackson; wall and floor tile   522
Aurora Foods Inc.; Jackson; frozen bakery products   500
Fru-Con Construction Corp.; Jackson; residential
   construction   500
Henry County Medical Center; Paris   500
Kellwood Co.; Rutherford; women's apparel   500
Kohler Co.; Union City; products of purchased glass
   500
McDonald's Restaurants; Paris   500
Procter and Gamble Pharmaceuticals Inc.; Memphis
   500

Tennessee 9th District

Memphis

The 9th includes most of Tennessee's largest city, Memphis, which sits atop the bluffs of the Mississippi River. Memphis continues to struggle with racial tension that has hindered its growth since the 1960s, though it grew during the 1990s. The district is almost 60 percent black and gave 63 percent of its vote to Democratic presidential candidate Al Gore in 2000. Much of the white population has moved north and east to the Shelby County suburbs. However, revitalization efforts have paved the way for inner-city economic development and integrated downtown residences such as Harbourtown and South Bluffs.

Memphis is a key distribution center. Federal Express is based at the Memphis International Airport, making it the world's busiest cargo airport and attracting international companies to the area. The economy also depends on St. Jude Children's Research Hospital, one of the nation's top pediatric care centers.

It remains to be seen whether Memphis has fully recovered from the industrial decline that began in the 1970s, but tourism has remained an economic mainstay, with people flocking to honor two American icons—Elvis Presley and Martin Luther King Jr. The hotel where King was assassinated is now a museum.

The area first sent an African American to Congress in 1974, initiating the reign of Democratic black political power in Memphis. In 1998 more than 40 percent of white voters, who traditionally support Republicans, cast their vote for Rep. Harold E. Ford Jr., a black Democrat. Republicans have not fielded a challenger since 1998.

Major Industry

Distribution, health care, government.

Notable

Graceland was the home of Elvis Presley; W. C. Handy developed the blues musical style on Beale Street; Memphis takes its name from the Egyptian city with ports on the banks of another meandering waterway, the Nile; the Peabody hotel in downtown Memphis has ducks that ride the elevator from the rooftop to the ground floor twice each day.

Election Returns

	Republican		Democratic		Other	
President 2000	83,531	35.7%	147,898	63.2%	2,758	1.2%
House 2002			120,904	83.8%	23,356	16.2%

District Profile

Population   632,143

Total area (square miles)   339.8
   Land area (square miles)   320.5

Population per square mile   1,972.4

Counties (2000 population)
   Shelby (pt.)   632,143

Cities and other areas over 10,000 (2000 population)
   Memphis (pt.)   571,661

Race and Hispanic or Latino origin*
   White   34.9%
   Black or African American   59.5%
   American Indian or Alaska Native   0.2%
   Asian   1.5%
   Native Hawaiian or other Pacific Islander   0.0%
   Some other race   0.1%

Hispanic or Latino origin   3.0%
Two or more races   0.9%

*As percentage of total population.

Ancestry*

English	4.9%	Italian	1.6%
French	1.1%	Scotch-Irish	1.6%
German	4.0%	Subsaharan	1.5%
Irish	4.7%	USA/American	4.5%

*As estimated percentage of total population.

Universities and colleges, 2000–2001 enrollment
Baptist Memorial College of Health Sciences, Memphis   432
Christian Brothers University, Memphis   2,167
Concorde Career Institute, Memphis   755
Crichton College, Memphis   963
ITT Technical Institute, Memphis   237
Le Moyne-Owen College, Memphis   1,018
Memphis College of Art, Memphis   289
Memphis Theological Seminary, Memphis   269
Rhodes College, Memphis   1,553
Shelby State Community College, Memphis   12,194
Southeast College of Technology, Memphis   534
Southern College of Optometry, Memphis   481
Southwest Tennessee Community College, Memphis   12,194
University of Memphis, Memphis   19,986
University of Tennessee, Memphis   2,069

Newspapers and circulation

	District circulation	Total circulation
Memphis Commercial Appeal	76,882	157,808
*USA Today**	3,679	1,674,376

*See Sources and Explanations in the front of the volume.

Television stations and affiliations

Memphis	100%	KVTJ	Independent
Memphis	100%	WBUY	Independent
Memphis	100%	WHBQ	FOX
Memphis	100%	WKNO	PBS
Memphis	100%	WMAE	PBS
Memphis	100%	WMAV	PBS
Memphis	100%	WMC	NBC
Memphis	100%	WPTY	ABC, WB
Memphis	100%	WPXX	PAX
Memphis	100%	WREG	CBS

Cable systems and subscribers
Time Warner   167,571

Military installations, September 2001
Memphis International Airport Air Force Guard Station, Oakville   1,111

Businesses and other major employers
Federal Express Corp.; Memphis; package delivery   31,680
Central Memphis Hospital; Memphis   5,575
U.S. Internal Revenue Service; Memphis   5,000
Baptist Memorial Hospital; Memphis   4,000
Defense Logistics Agency; Memphis; national security   2,500

Northwest Airlines Inc.; Memphis   2,335
University of Memphis; Memphis   2,300
Birthplace Hospital; Memphis   2,200
Morgan Keegan Co.; Memphis; management consulting   2,000
U.S. Veterans Hospital; Memphis   2,000
St. Jude Children's Research Hospital; Memphis   1,850
LeBonheur Children's Medical Center; Memphis   1,830
St. Francis Hospital; Memphis   1,700
AutoZone Inc.; Memphis; automotive parts   1,608
Carrier Corp.; Collierville; air conditioning equipment   1,600
Shelby County; Memphis; sheriff's office   1,500
Tennessee Dept. of Military; Memphis; national guard   1,500
American Residential Services Inc.; Memphis; plumbing contractors   1,300
Promus Operating Co.; Memphis; hotels and motels   1,300
Nike Inc.; Memphis; athletic shoes   1,200
MCI WorldCom Network Services Inc.; Bartlett; long-distance telephone   1,100
City of Memphis; Memphis; city government   1,000
First Tennessee Bank National Assn.; Memphis; commercial bank   1,000
Memphis Publishing Co.; Memphis; newspaper   1,000
Rehabcare Group; Memphis; outpatient clinics   1,000
Roadway Express Inc.; Memphis; trucking terminals   1,000
Shelby County; Memphis; correctional institutions   1,000
United Parcel Service Inc.; Memphis; parcel delivery   1,000
Imperial Guard and Detective Services Inc.; Memphis; detective agency   900
Interstate Brands Corp.; Memphis; breads and cakes   850
Conwood Co.; Memphis; snuff   800
Kroger Co.; Memphis; refrigerated storage   800
Mid-South Health Care Services Inc.; Memphis; employment agencies   800
Shelby County; Memphis; public health programs   800
EFS National Bank; Memphis; commercial bank   750
Fred's Inc.; Memphis; variety stores   750
Kellogg Co.; Memphis; breakfast cereals   750
Pinnacle Airlines Corp.; Memphis; airport terminal   750
Shelby County; Memphis; county government   750
American Building Maintenance Co. of Georgia; Memphis; janitorial service   700
Corporate Security Inc.; Memphis; security guard service   700
Hotel Peabody; Memphis; hotels   700
Thomas and Betts Corp.; Memphis; electrical connectors and terminals   675
Mueller Streamline Co.; Memphis; copper products   659
Ozark Motor Lines Inc.; Memphis; trucking   650
Priority Fulfillment Services Inc.; Memphis; management services   650
Sanitors Southwest of Memphis Inc.; Memphis; janitorial service   626

Texas

At the beginning of the millennium in the United States, the time has come for Texas. Long the dominant presence in its region and a major factor in the nation's politics and popular culture, the Lone Star State has taken its importance to a new level. Texas is more populous, prosperous, and powerful than ever, competing with New York and California for primacy in defining the nation's identity and direction.

Until Alaska became a state in 1959, Texas was number one in geographic size and renowned for taking pride in the fact. But many of those 261,797 square miles were subject to drought and baking heat. Thus this grand expanse of space still seemed relatively unpopulated (fewer than 37 people per square mile in 1959), and the state's image remained remote, rural, and dominated by Hollywood notions of the cowboy. A variety of forces were at work, however, both nationally and locally, transforming the metropolitan areas of the South and the Southwest. Texas, the meeting point of these two dynamic regions, was the main focus of those forces.

One of these was a torrent of newcomers. Texas had known rapid in-migration before, of course, starting with its first full decade after statehood, when the population nearly tripled. Thereafter the ranks of Texans grew steadily, reaching 3 million by 1900. At that juncture the state was heavily dependent on farming, ranching, and mining—and many of its people lived at a subsistence level. The technologies that would lift its fortunes in the century to come had yet to emerge. Yet Texas was already the sixth most populous state in that census taken more than a century ago. Growth continued at an average of about 850,000 over the next four decades. Still, at the time of World War II, Texas remained only sixth in population, trailing the same five states it had in 1900. But the war spurred a great shift to the Sun Belt and the suburbs. Air conditioning made life more pleasant, even as labor-management struggles sent industries in search of states with lower wages, fewer regulations, and weaker unions.

So Texas took off. Waves of growth raised the population by an average of more than 2 million per decade (1940 to 1990)—and then by a stunning 3.8 million in the 1990s. The number of Texans has more than doubled since Alaska became a state, and the state's rank in population density has risen from the bottom dozen to the middle ranks as some of those wide open spaces have begun to fill up. Moreover, Texas clearly is not finished growing. It had the second lowest median age in the country in 2000, meaning it could count on fewer deaths and more babies than the country at large. But it will have trouble sustaining the torrid pace of recent decades. The Census Bureau projects it will grow more slowly in the first quarter of the new century but still increase by roughly 30 percent (6.4 million people) by the year 2025. Economically, Texas looks strong enough to support this growth. But it may need to work harder at distributing its wealth. The 2000 census found about 15 percent of the population was poor, the eighth highest percentage in the country.

The state's solution to poverty and joblessness has always been to encourage more business activity, and often to involve the federal government in making that happen. The 1960s made Texas the heart of the space program, the 1970s and 1980s brought the semiconductor revolution, the personal computer boom, and the surge in demand for telecommunications equipment. Texas also became a hub for the growing air transportation industry. All these blossoming industries contributed not only direct employment but a wide range of employee wages and tremendous multiplier benefits for the larger economy.

Still, the great base beneath the state's economy has remained its energy industry, one of the great engines of growth in the twentieth century, dating back to the first, transforming discovery of oil in East Texas in 1901. Never was that transforming power stronger than in the 1970s, after the Arab oil embargo spiked the price of a barrel of oil up by fivefold almost overnight and spawned nearly 20 years of expansion. Through most of that time, the assumption in Texas was that oil would keep going up and taking the price of everything else in the same direction—including real estate in Houston, Dallas, and the rest of the state.

When this boom, too, came to bust, and the number of drilling rigs active in the field dropped by 80 percent, Texas went through a long and wrenching retrenchment. The collateral damage was everywhere: the state's savings and loan industry, overextended in the belief that oil prices would climb indefinitely, came to grief in the late 1980s. The resulting collapse reverberated throughout the country, cost the federal taxpayer hundreds of billions of dollars, and ended the savings and loan business as it had been known for generations. Much more recently, the state received a blow when one of its most prominent and politically connected companies, Enron, proved to have been falsifying transactions to sweeten its profit. An early user of the Internet as a marketing device, Enron had grown up suddenly as a seller and transporter of natural gas. By the late 1990s it was selling and speculating in various energy futures on a worldwide scale. When the collapse came, leaving tens of thousands of employees without jobs and jeopardizing their pensions, it

TEXAS

Districts established November 14, 2001, for elections first held in 2002.

32 members

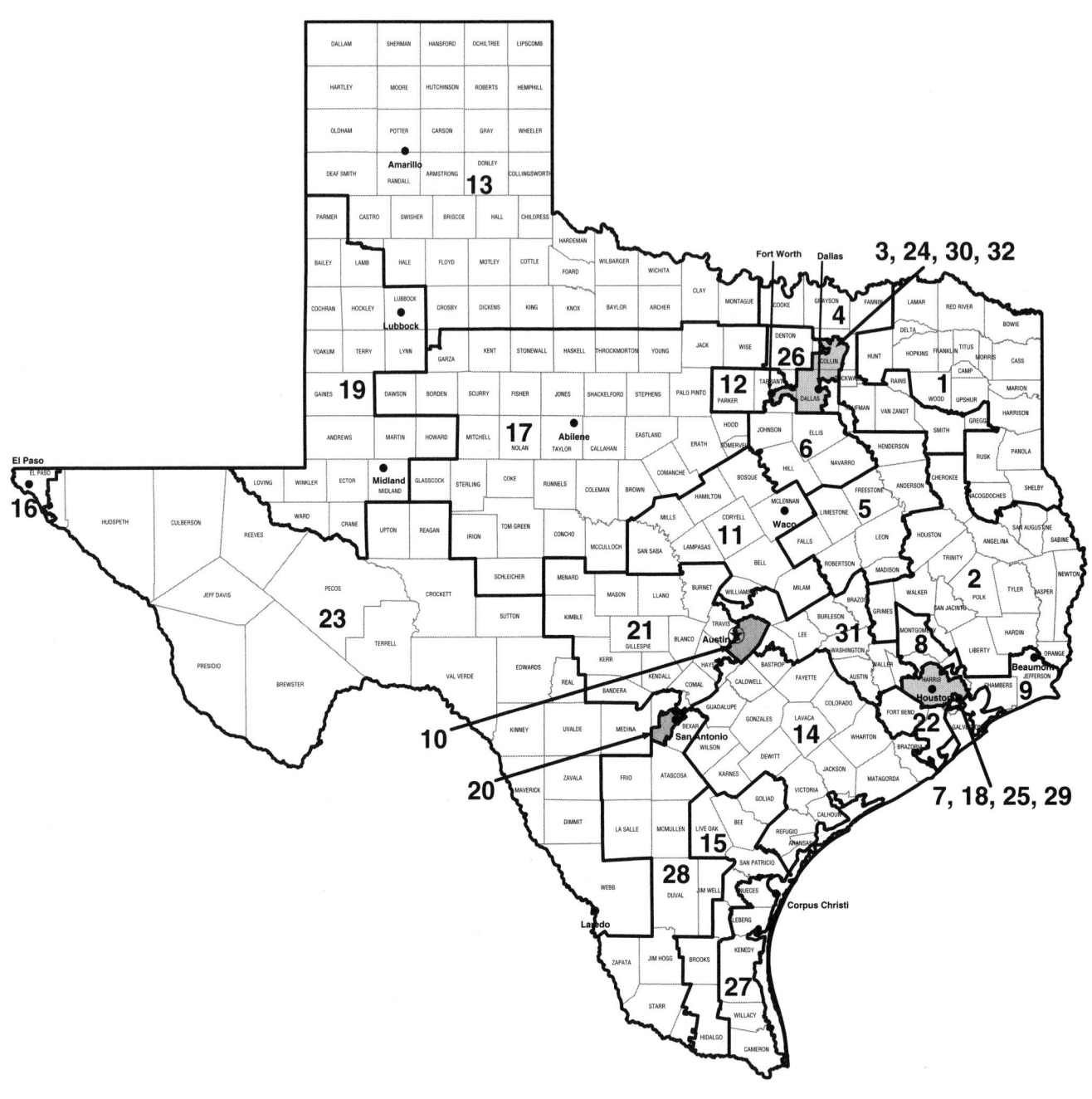

seemed for a time that a popular uprising would target the company.

Yet, even in the down times of the later 1980s and early 1990s, Texas still looked like a good move for millions. The state still came out of the 1980s with a net gain of 2.75 million. In 1994 Texas roared past New York to become the second most populous state in the land, after California. Subsequent growth in the years before 2000 was not only the greatest in state history numerically, it was also the most diverse. The jobs that drew new residents were found in many industries, but still centered largely on the energy metros of Houston and Dallas, both of which are now among the nation's top ten population centers. Each grew about 20 percent in the 1990s: Dallas-Fort Worth to about 5 million, Houston-Galveston to about 4.5 million. Taken together, the two are now more populous than greater Chicago.

But if oil and high-tech industry have made Texans out of millions of Americans, the state's momentum has been sustained in large part by its continuing appeal to non-Americans. This is one of the main destinations for immigrants crossing the Rio Grande from Mexico and countries further south. Texas has long been a state with enough Spanish-speaking residents to be almost bilingual, but in the past generation the entire country has begun using the phrase Tex-Mex, and not just to refer to a local variant on Mexican food. The state had 6.7 million Hispanic residents in 2000, second only to California. In percentage terms, the two states are tied at 32 percent Hispanic. Only New Mexico, which is more than 42 percent Hispanic, has a larger percentage of Hispanic residents.

The large Hispanic influx has helped fuel the growth of the state's other three large metropolitan areas. Metro San Antonio, long the capital of Spanish-speaking Texas, grew by 20 percent in the 1990s and entered the list of 30 most populous market statistical areas with 1.6 million people. Not far behind is Austin, considered by many the most livable and culturally rewarding place to settle in Texas. The Austin-San Marcos metro area has kept pace with its bigger neighbors in growth and now has 1.25 million people. One new congressional district drawn after the 2000 census actually combined some southeastern Austin suburbs with some of the northwestern suburbs of Houston, suggesting a future metro area of truly grand proportions.

At the far western tip of the state, the city of El Paso has reached 680,000 in population while sharing its daily life across the Bridge of the Americas with its sister city, Ciudad Juarez, Mexico.

People drawn to Texas for its high-tech industries often tend to be Republicans, based on their business interests and consonant with their education and income levels. The new Hispanic voters tend to favor Democrats, although not by the margins seen recently in California. The bigger problem for Democrats counting on these new voters is that the citizenship process can take years, and many new residents do not even attempt it. Still, the allocation of the Hispanic population is one of the key elements in the state's long-running fight to redraw its congressional districts. In the 1990s the legislature's map was thrown out by a federal court, which redrew 14 districts that had substantial Hispanic population. But that was only a warm-up for what was coming after 2000.

In one sense at least, the remapping after 2000 should have been easy. Reapportionment after the census had given Texas two new seats, bringing its total to 32 (exactly twice as many as the state was awarded after the census taken 100 years earlier). But the political power situation in Austin was complicated. The governor, Rick Perry, was a Republican who acceded to office when his predecessor, George W. Bush, went to the White House. The state House in Austin had a slight Democratic edge, the state Senate was narrowly Republican. Republicans in the legislature devised a plan that would have assigned more black and Hispanic residents to metro-area districts already held by Democrats, leaving adjacent districts more likely to favor Republicans. It was the same strategy used successfully elsewhere in the South in the 1990s to concentrate black voters in a few districts while leaving more of the surrounding districts relatively white and heavily Republican.

But the plan bogged down in the divided legislature and Rick Perry, then the acting governor and seeking election, refused to call a special session. The state courts also failed to produce a plan after the Texas supreme court spiked one attempt. Finally, a panel of three federal judges drew a map of their own. It protected the incumbents and fashioned two new districts, one in the suburbs of Dallas and one between Houston and Austin. Both were won by Republicans in November 2002, cutting the Democrats' edge in the U.S. House delegation to 17 to 15, the closest it had been since Reconstruction.

The remap for 2002 left the 15th and 16th Districts both over 75 percent Hispanic, the most Hispanic districts in the nation (and among the most poverty stricken). Two others were drawn more than 70 percent Hispanic and three more over 60 percent. The delegation before the remap had six Hispanic members (five of them Democrats): one fifth of the delegation. There were also two African American Democrats (the state is about 12 percent black, just below the national average), one each from the cores of Houston and Dallas. The new map drawn by the federal panel in 2001 left all eight of these incumbents in place (plus one Anglo Democrat representing a 62 percent Hispanic district). But the panel did not create any new majority-minority districts, so the black and Hispanic populations, together totaling more than two-fifths of the state, had just one-fourth of the House seats.

But on the same day the court-map was producing the new 17 to 15 congressional delegation, the voters were electing Perry and installing clear Republican majorities in both chambers of the state legislature. So early in 2003, the Republicans in Austin, against historical precedent, reopened the redistricting issue, largely at the urging of the Washington delegation's leading Republican, Tom DeLay. A 20-year veteran from suburban Houston who had risen to the number two power position in the House, DeLay had long been incensed that Texas still sent a Democratic majority delegation to Congress while voting so Republican in other elections.

The DeLay-influenced plan in 2003 was another effort at redividing the residents of Austin, Dallas, Houston, and Beaumont-Galveston so as to thin out the minority vote for four Anglo Democrats. Also targeted were five Anglo Democrats outside the big metro areas, incumbents who have hung on in ancestral Democratic territory around Abilene and Waco and in East and Northeast Texas. The seats of some of these senior Democrats such as Ralph Hall and Charles Stenholm have long been expected to fall to the GOP when the incumbents retire. That is because fewer and fewer rural Texans are willing to call themselves Democrats, even in congressional voting. The conversion of what were once called "Yellow Dog" Democrats (who would supposedly vote for a yellow dog over a Republican) has been as important a factor as any in making Texas a Republican state.

Even without those retirements, however, DeLay's remap was designed to reduce the number of Democrats in the House to a dozen or fewer. Rather than allow that to happen, the Democrats in Austin hit on a desperate plan. More than 50 House Democrats in May 2003 left the state to Oklahoma, denying legislative leaders a quorum to do business. When the deadline for the session passed, the legislators returned. Not to be obstructed by the end of the regular session, Perry then called two special sessions during the summer. Each time, however, it was the Democratic members of the state Senate who bolted—this time to New Mexico—to prevent a quorum.

In September, however, after one of the Democrats broke ranks and returned home, the remaining holdouts returned to Texas. Perry called a third special session, and the legislature passed a GOP remap that Perry signed in October. Democrats and a Mexican American group immediately launched legal challenges that were likely to keep the new map in the courts well into 2004.

In statewide voting, Texas was a typical southern state for nearly a century after Reconstruction. But in recent decades it has fully shifted its loyalties. There was no Republican senator popularly elected until 1961, when John Tower won a special election in a large field with no official party designations. But Tower held the seat until 1984 and turned it over to Republican Phil Gramm, who held it three terms and turned it over to Republican John Cornyn. The state's second Senate seat was first won in another special election, this one in 1993, by Republican Kay Bailey Hutchison, who won reelection by huge margins in 1994 and 2000.

In presidential voting, Texas was Democratic from statehood to 1928, when it preferred the GOP's Herbert Hoover to the Catholic governor of New York, Al Smith. Thereafter it returned to the Democratic column until the 1950s, when it went twice for Dwight Eisenhower, the war hero who was born in Texas. In the 1960s the state was loyal to Lyndon B. Johnson and his party, in 1972 it helped reelect Richard Nixon, and in 1976 it was part of the big southern shift for Democrat Jimmy Carter. But in 1980, Ronald Reagan raised the curtain on a new era. Beginning in that year, there has been a Texan named George Bush on the national ticket five times in six presidential cycles. The GOP has won the state's electoral votes by big margins in all cycles, including nearly 60 percent for George W. Bush in 2000.

Strange as it may seem, the second president Bush was actually the first Texan to win the presidency without first being vice president. Many have tried, including Gov. John Connally (1980) and senators such as Gramm (2000) and Democrat Lloyd Bentsen (1976). All these began their bids well-funded and highly touted, but none made it past the early primaries. Another Texan, Ross Perot, ran twice in the 1990s, receiving 19 percent as an independent in 1992 and 8 percent as the nominee of the Reform Party in 1996.

Table 1 Population

District	Population	Population under 18	Voting-age population	Median age	Male*	Female*
1	651,619	166,383	485,236	36.8	49.0	51.0
2	651,619	167,100	484,519	36.0	50.9	49.1
3	651,620	189,269	462,351	32.7	49.8	50.2
4	651,620	174,176	477,444	36.2	48.9	51.1
5	651,620	175,570	476,050	34.0	50.2	49.8
6	651,620	190,967	460,653	33.5	49.3	50.7
7	651,620	171,379	480,241	32.4	49.3	50.7
8	651,619	191,191	460,428	34.2	49.4	50.6
9	651,619	172,328	479,291	35.0	49.8	50.2
10	651,619	149,921	501,698	29.3	51.5	48.5
11	651,620	177,880	473,740	31.2	49.7	50.3
12	651,619	177,413	474,206	33.6	49.6	50.4
13	651,619	177,005	474,614	34.7	50.0	50.0
14	651,620	178,096	473,524	34.6	49.8	50.2
15	651,619	213,859	437,760	29.0	49.4	50.6
16	651,619	206,020	445,599	30.2	48.2	51.8
17	651,619	166,958	484,661	36.3	49.8	50.2
18	651,620	177,470	474,150	31.8	50.0	50.0
19	651,619	185,114	466,505	32.4	49.1	50.9
20	651,619	187,434	464,185	30.0	49.1	50.9
21	651,619	162,523	489,096	38.5	48.8	51.2
22	651,619	196,397	455,222	34.2	50.5	49.5
23	651,619	210,021	441,598	30.7	49.0	51.0
24	651,619	194,986	456,633	29.5	50.2	49.8
25	651,619	187,064	464,555	30.4	49.1	50.9
26	651,619	181,942	469,677	32.1	49.7	50.3
27	651,619	203,278	448,341	30.8	48.5	51.5
28	651,620	211,657	439,963	30.4	48.8	51.2
29	651,620	216,554	435,066	27.4	50.8	49.2
30	651,620	191,638	459,982	30.0	49.4	50.6
31	651,620	183,148	468,472	30.5	49.9	50.1
32	651,619	152,018	499,601	32.0	51.0	49.0
State	20,851,820	5,886,759	14,965,061	32.3	49.6	50.4

As percentage of total population.

Table 2 Voting-Age Persons by Race/Hispanic or Latino Origin

District	White*	Black or African American*	American Indian or Alaska Native*	Asian*	Other or multirace*	Hispanic or Latino*
1	77.1	15.2	0.5	0.4	0.7	6.0
2	77.3	13.4	0.4	0.4	0.7	7.7
3	71.9	6.1	0.4	7.5	1.2	12.9
4	79.3	11.0	0.6	0.6	0.9	7.7
5	66.8	14.6	0.4	1.7	1.1	15.3
6	74.7	9.4	0.4	2.7	1.1	11.7
7	53.1	10.2	0.2	11.3	1.9	23.3
8	79.1	4.8	0.3	3.1	1.0	11.6
9	63.2	19.9	0.3	2.7	1.0	12.9
10	54.5	9.9	0.3	4.8	1.6	29.0
11	68.0	14.3	0.5	1.9	1.3	14.1
12	74.5	4.4	0.5	2.4	1.2	17.1
13	73.9	5.5	0.6	1.1	0.9	17.9
14	62.2	7.5	0.3	0.8	0.8	28.4
15	22.9	1.6	0.1	0.7	0.3	74.3
16	20.1	2.9	0.3	1.2	0.7	74.8
17	77.8	3.8	0.4	0.6	0.8	16.6

District	White*	Black or African American*	American Indian or Alaska Native*	Asian*	Other or multirace*	Hispanic or Latino*
18	25.3	41.4	0.2	3.1	0.9	29.1
19	63.1	5.3	0.4	0.9	0.7	29.6
20	27.4	5.4	0.3	1.6	1.1	64.3
21	79.5	1.9	0.3	2.0	1.0	15.2
22	62.4	9.9	0.3	8.3	1.2	18.0
23	33.4	1.5	0.3	1.1	0.7	63.0
24	40.7	20.8	0.4	3.3	1.2	33.6
25	41.2	21.2	0.2	5.3	1.3	30.7
26	79.3	4.8	0.5	4.2	1.2	10.0
27	28.7	2.2	0.2	0.8	0.6	67.5
28	24.8	7.7	0.2	0.9	0.7	65.7
29	24.2	14.2	0.2	2.4	0.8	58.2
30	28.9	39.6	0.3	2.4	1.0	27.7
31	72.1	8.6	0.3	3.3	1.0	14.9
32	59.2	8.6	0.3	6.3	1.4	24.1
State	56.3	10.9	0.3	2.9	1.0	28.6

*As percentage of voting-age population.

Table 3 Voting-Age Population by Age Groups

District	18 to 24*	25 to 44*	45 to 64*	Over 64*
1	13.3	35.8	30.8	20.1
2	13.3	38.0	30.5	18.1
3	11.1	51.8	29.1	8.1
4	12.3	38.1	30.9	18.7
5	12.6	43.7	27.9	15.7
6	12.3	44.6	30.3	12.8
7	12.9	48.9	27.9	10.3
8	11.3	44.9	33.4	10.4
9	12.9	41.9	30.0	15.2
10	21.9	48.1	21.4	8.6
11	18.3	40.5	25.7	15.6
12	13.4	44.2	28.4	14.0
13	14.3	38.1	28.8	18.9
14	14.6	38.1	29.5	17.8
15	16.8	41.5	26.1	15.6
16	15.5	42.8	27.1	14.6
17	14.2	36.0	29.5	20.4
18	15.3	44.3	27.3	13.2
19	16.7	38.8	28.1	16.5
20	17.6	43.7	24.7	14.1
21	9.3	39.2	33.3	18.2
22	11.0	46.9	32.4	9.7
23	14.5	42.6	29.3	13.6
24	17.0	46.9	25.4	10.8
25	15.5	47.3	26.1	11.1
26	13.9	50.7	28.2	7.2
27	15.4	40.3	28.0	16.3
28	14.7	41.7	28.0	15.6
29	18.7	47.6	24.5	9.2
30	16.3	46.5	25.9	11.4
31	19.4	44.3	26.2	10.1
32	14.5	49.5	25.2	10.9
State	14.7	43.3	28.1	13.9

*As percentage of voting-age population.

Table 4 Income and Occupation

District	Median family income	Families in poverty*	White collar†	Blue collar†	Service†	Farm†
1	$38,838	12.8	51.0	31.9	15.5	1.6
2	$39,266	12.3	48.2	33.3	16.8	1.7
3	$74,314	3.9	75.9	14.8	9.1	0.1
4	$46,086	9.5	56.4	28.6	14.3	0.8
5	$45,097	9.7	58.1	26.5	14.9	0.6
6	$55,584	6.3	62.2	25.4	12.0	0.3
7	$57,494	8.3	71.8	15.5	12.6	0.1
8	$68,134	4.9	70.0	18.6	11.3	0.1
9	$49,761	10.9	60.3	24.0	15.2	0.4
10	$50,548	9.5	66.2	19.6	14.0	0.2
11	$42,179	10.1	57.1	25.6	16.5	0.7
12	$51,916	7.1	61.2	25.5	13.2	0.2
13	$40,252	11.2	53.3	26.7	17.7	2.3
14	$42,501	11.3	52.1	30.3	16.0	1.6
15	$30,024	25.8	53.5	25.5	18.6	2.5
16	$33,810	20.2	58.1	24.7	16.9	0.3
17	$39,126	11.3	53.9	26.8	17.6	1.6
18	$34,707	20.1	55.2	27.3	17.3	0.1
19	$39,184	13.5	57.8	24.4	16.4	1.4
20	$35,455	17.0	56.7	24.3	18.8	0.2
21	$62,437	4.9	72.6	15.7	11.2	0.5
22	$69,714	5.0	69.3	19.7	10.7	0.3
23	$40,043	17.9	61.0	21.8	15.7	1.4
24	$41,000	14.1	55.0	30.4	14.4	0.2
25	$42,310	13.7	60.0	24.2	15.7	0.2
26	$73,453	3.6	73.5	15.8	10.5	0.1
27	$33,168	22.1	55.1	25.0	18.9	1.0
28	$31,417	22.8	48.6	30.3	19.5	1.6
29	$34,415	18.8	43.1	40.4	16.3	0.2
30	$38,499	15.9	54.4	29.3	16.0	0.2
31	$60,407	6.8	67.7	19.9	12.0	0.5
32	$60,426	8.3	71.3	16.4	12.3	0.1
State	$45,861	12.0	60.6	24.1	14.6	0.7

*As percentage of all families.   †As percentage of employed workers 16 years and over.

Table 5 Education: School Years Completed

District	Less than grade 9*	Grades 9–12 no diploma*	High school diploma no college*	Some college*	College bachelor's degree or higher*
1	8.6	16.6	33.3	26.7	14.8
2	9.7	17.8	36.1	25.0	11.4
3	5.0	6.3	17.3	29.8	41.6
4	7.3	14.0	29.0	30.9	18.7
5	8.6	15.9	28.9	28.4	18.2
6	5.8	11.6	27.1	32.5	23.0
7	7.4	8.5	16.6	27.7	39.8
8	4.4	8.5	22.7	31.5	32.9
9	6.9	12.2	28.6	31.4	20.9
10	9.1	9.4	19.3	27.1	35.1
11	7.7	11.9	28.7	32.7	19.0
12	7.9	12.6	26.0	30.9	22.7
13	9.7	14.5	29.4	28.9	17.4
14	12.6	14.5	31.3	26.6	15.0

District	Less than grade 9*	Grades 9–12 no diploma*	High school diploma no college*	Some college*	College bachelor's degree or higher*
15	26.8	15.1	23.0	21.0	14.1
16	21.0	12.6	22.5	26.9	17.0
17	9.6	15.0	31.6	27.0	16.8
18	15.4	19.0	25.0	22.4	18.2
19	12.7	14.2	26.3	28.1	18.7
20	15.4	14.4	26.0	28.6	15.6
21	4.1	6.3	20.7	30.0	38.9
22	5.9	8.6	21.7	30.6	33.2
23	20.4	12.4	20.1	24.0	23.2
24	15.7	16.3	24.4	25.3	18.2
25	12.5	13.2	21.2	25.0	28.0
26	3.5	5.8	19.0	32.9	38.9
27	21.4	14.5	22.5	25.8	15.8
28	22.1	16.8	27.8	23.5	9.8
29	26.0	21.7	24.7	19.5	8.1
30	15.2	17.9	25.7	24.9	16.3
31	6.6	8.9	23.7	29.1	31.6
32	9.7	8.3	14.0	24.9	43.2
State	11.5	12.9	24.8	27.6	23.2

As percentage of persons age 25 and over.

Table 6 Housing and Residential Patterns

District	Median home value	Owner occupied*	Renter occupied*	Urban†	Rural†
1	$58,300	73.9	26.1	40.1	59.9
2	$54,700	77.7	22.3	38.1	61.9
3	$132,300	68.9	31.1	96.0	4.0
4	$75,600	72.2	27.8	54.2	45.8
5	$76,000	65.7	34.3	76.7	23.3
6	$87,300	74.3	25.7	75.6	24.4
7	$104,500	49.5	50.5	99.9	0.1
8	$110,400	74.4	25.6	83.8	16.2
9	$74,800	65.7	34.3	89.6	10.4
10	$107,400	45.7	54.3	95.6	4.4
11	$73,700	61.4	38.6	72.6	27.4
12	$83,600	65.3	34.7	88.7	11.3
13	$57,000	68.4	31.6	73.2	26.8
14	$65,900	71.0	29.0	55.1	44.9
15	$49,600	70.8	29.2	87.3	12.7
16	$67,900	62.8	37.2	98.3	1.7
17	$55,800	70.7	29.3	61.0	39.0
18	$62,800	51.1	48.9	99.9	0.1
19	$53,400	66.7	33.3	81.3	18.7
20	$58,700	52.7	47.3	97.7	2.3
21	$126,400	73.3	26.7	69.4	30.6
22	$105,300	79.2	20.8	87.5	12.5
23	$74,600	72.2	27.8	80.4	19.6
24	$68,000	52.9	47.1	99.5	0.5
25	$78,700	46.5	53.5	99.5	0.5
26	$135,400	64.5	35.5	91.7	8.3
27	$56,800	64.2	35.8	90.1	9.9
28	$47,500	71.9	28.1	82.1	17.9
29	$54,600	53.0	47.0	99.5	0.5
30	$70,000	49.6	50.4	99.1	0.9
31	$105,500	69.1	30.9	77.0	23.0
32	$158,000	42.9	57.1	99.8	0.2
State	$77,800	63.8	36.2	82.5	17.5

As percentage of occupied housing units.   †As percentage of total population.*

Texas 1st District

Northeast — Texarkana, Nacogdoches, Paris

The 1st wraps around Texas's northeast corner along the Oklahoma and Arkansas borders to take in Texarkana, then stretches south along the Louisiana border to take in most of Nacogdoches County. Mostly removed from the Dallas-Fort Worth suburbs, the 1st has a rural southern feel that is harder to find in other Texas districts.

The economic dominance of natural resources—timber, oil, and natural gas—has diminished since the oil bust of the 1980s and the rise of the manufacturing sector, which now drives the economy. The 1st still faces some economic challenges from foreign timber companies and cattle ranchers who can sell their products at lower prices. A small but significant defense industry is centered around Greenville. Slow population growth and miles of forests and agricultural land are hallmarks of the district but do less to improve its economy than the highways that connect the district to the outside world.

Residents of the 1st tend to be conservative, even among Democrats, and the region associates itself with the Bible Belt that stretches through much of the South. A bastion of political populism, the district has one of the largest percentages of elderly residents in the state.

Counties in the district's west and south—such as Hunt, Wood, Nacogdoches, and Rusk—vote reliably Republican. But conservative Democrats can win in the 1st, especially in the east. In 2002 Republican governor Rick Perry lost just Cass, Morris, and Marion Counties, and GOP Senate nominee John Cornyn lost only Morris and Marion. Morris, home to a big Lone Star Steel plant, was the only county in the 1st—and the only Texas county in a 170-mile radius—not to back George W. Bush in 2000.

Major Industry

Timber, light manufacturing, agriculture, oil.

Notable

"Uncle Jesse's Memorial Big Bass Classic," is an annual event in Paris; Texarkana is split between Texas and Arkansas—it has two mayors, two police forces, and two school systems—and is the birthplace of Ross Perot.

Election Returns

	Republican		Democratic		Other
President 2000	142,544	64.1%	79,801	35.9%	
House 2002	66,654	43.6%	86,384	56.4%	

District Profile

Population 651,619

Total area (square miles) 12,899.6
  Land area (square miles) 12,542.8

Population per square mile 52.0

Counties (2000 population)

Bowie	89,306	Morris	13,048
Camp	11,549	Nacogdoches (pt.)	54,262
Cass	30,438	Panola	22,756
Delta	5,327	Red River	14,314
Franklin	9,458	Rusk	47,372
Harrison	62,110	Shelby	25,224
Hopkins	31,960	Titus	28,118
Hunt (pt.)	74,894	Upshur	35,291
Lamar	48,499	Wood	36,752
Marion	10,941		

Cities and other areas over 10,000 (2000 population)

Greenville	23,960	Nacogdoches	29,914
Henderson	11,273	Paris	25,898
Marshall	23,935	Sulphur Springs	14,551
Mount Pleasant	13,935	Texarkana	34,782

Race and Hispanic or Latino origin*

White 74.7%
Black or African American 16.2%
American Indian or Alaska Native 0.5%
Asian 0.3%
Native Hawaiian or other Pacific Islander 0.0%
Some other race 0.1%
Hispanic or Latino origin 7.4%
Two or more races 0.9%

As percentage of total population.

Ancestry*

Dutch	1.2%	Irish	7.8%
English	6.7%	Scotch-Irish	1.5%
French	1.6%	USA/American	13.0%
German	5.9%		

As estimated percentage of total population.

Universities and colleges, 2000–2001 enrollment

East Texas Baptist University, Marshall 1,402
Jarvis Christian College, Hawkins 537
Northeast Texas Community College, Mount Pleasant 1,832
Panola College, Carthage 1,424
Paris Junior College, Paris 2,942
Stephen F. Austin State University, Nacogdoches 11,484
Texarkana College, Texarkana 3,735
Texas A&M University, Commerce 7,508
Texas A&M University, Texarkana 1,198
Texas State Technical College, Marshall 489
Wiley College, Marshall 552

Newspapers and circulation

	District circulation	Total circulation
Dallas Morning News	19,193	495,624
Greenville Herald-Banner	6,836	7,315
Longview News-Journal	14,915	29,041
Marshall News Messenger	6,734	6,734
Shreveport Times	1,270	66,644
Texarkana Gazette	18,981	30,429
Tyler Telegraph-Courier Times	5,030	43,387

See Sources and Explanations in the front of the volume.

Television stations and affiliations

Shreveport, LA	43%	KLTS	PBS
Shreveport, LA	43%	KMSS	FOX
Shreveport, LA	43%	KPXJ	PAX
Shreveport, LA	43%	KSHV	WB, UPN
Shreveport, LA	43%	KSLA	CBS
Shreveport, LA	43%	KTAL	NBC
Shreveport, LA	43%	KTBS	ABC
Dallas-Fort Worth	30%	KDAF	WB
Dallas-Fort Worth	30%	KDFI	Independent
Dallas-Fort Worth	30%	KDFW	FOX
Dallas-Fort Worth	30%	KDTN	PBS
Dallas-Fort Worth	30%	KDTX	Independent
Dallas-Fort Worth	30%	KERA	PBS
Dallas-Fort Worth	30%	KFWD	Independent
Dallas-Fort Worth	30%	KMPX	Independent
Dallas-Fort Worth	30%	KPXD	PAX
Dallas-Fort Worth	30%	KSTR	Telefutura
Dallas-Fort Worth	30%	KTAQ	Independent
Dallas-Fort Worth	30%	KTVT	CBS
Dallas-Fort Worth	30%	KTXA	UPN
Dallas-Fort Worth	30%	KUVN	Univision
Dallas-Fort Worth	30%	KXAS	NBC
Dallas-Fort Worth	30%	KXTX	Telemundo
Dallas-Fort Worth	30%	WFAA	ABC
Tyler-Longview (Lufkin-Nacogdoches)	27%	KETK	NBC
Tyler-Longview (Lufkin-Nacogdoches)	27%	KFXK	FOX
Tyler-Longview (Lufkin-Nacogdoches)	27%	KLSB	NBC
Tyler-Longview (Lufkin-Nacogdoches)	27%	KLTV	ABC
Tyler-Longview (Lufkin-Nacogdoches)	27%	KTRE	ABC

Cable systems and subscribers

Cable ONE 13,881
Charter 9,118
Classic 18,905
Comcast 7,685
Cox 47,638
Gilmer Cable TV 945
Time Warner 4,820

Military installations, September 2001

Red River Army Depot, Texarkana 2,497
Lone Star Army Ammunition Plant, Texarkana 420

Businesses and other major employers

L-3 Communications Corp.; Greenville; aircraft control systems 4,598
Stephen F. Austin State University; Nacogdoches 2,900
Dallas Morning News; Greenville; newspaper 2,500
CHRISTUS St. Michael Hospital; Texarkana 1,500
Good Shepherd Hospital Inc.; Longview 1,457
Tyson Foods Inc.; Center; processed poultry 1,300
Wadley Regional Medical Center; Texarkana 1,250
Campbell Soup Co.; Paris; canned goods 1,000
Clay Energy Development Co. Inc.; Paris; oil/gas exploration 1,000
Texas A&M University; Commerce 872
Lone Star Steel Co.; Lone Star; steel sheets/strips 860
Texas Criminal Justice Dept.; New Boston 806
LeTourneau Inc.; Longview; mining trucks (dollies) 800
CHRISTUS St. Joseph's Hospital; Paris 790
U.S. Defense Dept.; Texarkana 750
Tyson Foods Inc.; Carthage; processed poultry 730
Sara Lee Bakery Group Inc.; Paris; bread baking 700
Titus County Hospital District; Mount Pleasant 693

Nacogdoches County Hospital District; Nacogdoches 650

TXU Mining Co.; Tatum; coal mining 645

Hunt Memorial Hospital District; Greenville 640

TXU Mining Co.; Beckville; natural gas distribution 600

Wal-Mart Stores Inc.; Mount Pleasant; department stores 600

Nacogdoches Medical Center Hospital; Nacogdoches 597

Harrison County Hospital Assn.; Marshall 593

Pilgrim's Pride Corp.; Mount Pleasant; poultry processing 588

Republic Industries Inc.; Marshall; kitchen cabinets 570

Texas Health System Inc. Hospital; Paris 550

Kimberly-Clark Corp.; Paris; disposable diapers 530

Turner International Piping Systems Inc.; Paris; concrete lined pipe 525

Sulphur Springs Independent School District; Sulphur Springs 507

Dana Corp.; Longview; automotive frames 500

GSC Enterprises Inc.; Sulphur Springs; food supplier 500

Neiman Marcus Group Inc.; Longview; warehousing 500

Tenet Health System Hospitals Inc.; Nacogdoches 500

Texas 2nd District

East — Huntsville, Lufkin, Orange

A sprawling mass of east Texas territory, the 2nd borders Louisiana to the east and reaches west to near Bryan. Its southern border skirts the oil city of Beaumont in the 9th and suburbs northeast of Houston. A mostly rural district, the 2nd's most populous cities are Huntsville, just off Interstate 45 in the southwestern part of the district, and Lufkin, located in the north and surrounded by vast timber forests.

The 2nd's economy has been split between the eastern and southern portions, which rely on the chemical and shipping industries based in Orange and nearby Beaumont and Port Arthur, and the northern and western sections, where timber still reigns. Government jobs and contracts became increasingly important to the region as its industrial and manufacturing economies slipped somewhat during the late 1980s and early 1990s. Slow population growth and a high percentage of blue-collar workers have made it difficult to attract higher-paying service jobs. The Texas State Penitentiary at Huntsville, home of the state's death row, is one economic factor in the district.

The southern end of the district is in the orbit of Houston. Liberty and San Jacinto Counties experienced robust population growth in the 1990s, and many Liberty residents make a long commute to work in Houston.

A court-drawn redistricting plan following the 2000 census kept the 2nd's shape mostly intact. The plan tweaked the boundaries of the 2nd's share of Nacogdoches and Montgomery Counties and moved Shelby County, located on the Louisiana border, to the 1st. The 2nd tends to vote like Texas overall—mostly conservative and Republican, but not overwhelmingly enough to shut out Democrats. In 2002 the

16 counties wholly in the district together voted for Senate and gubernatorial candidates in the same proportion as the state at large (56 percent to 43 percent for John Cornyn and 58 percent to 40 percent for Rick Perry).

Major Industry

Timber, petrochemicals, shipping.

Notable

Cut and Shoot, a town in Montgomery County, is said to be named after a confrontation in 1912; Huntsville's favorite son is Sam Houston, the first president of the Republic of Texas.

Election Returns

	Republican		Democratic		Other	
President 2000	133,641	63.0%	78,493	37.0%		
House 2002	53,656	38.2%	85,492	60.8%	1,353	1.0%

District Profile

Population 651,619

Total area (square miles) 14,213.7
Land area (square miles) 13,710.1

Population per square mile 47.5

Counties (2000 population)

Angelina	80,130	Newton	15,072
Cherokee	46,659	Orange	84,966
Grimes	23,552	Polk	41,133
Hardin	48,073	Sabine	10,469
Houston	23,185	San Augustine	8,946
Jasper	35,604	San Jacinto	22,246
Liberty	70,154	Trinity	13,779
Montgomery (pt.)	40,081	Tyler	20,871
Nacogdoches (pt.)	4,941	Walker	61,758

Cities and other areas over 10,000 (2000 population)

Huntsville	35,078	Orange	18,643
Jacksonville	13,868	Vidor	11,440
Lufkin	32,709		

Race and Hispanic or Latino origin*

White 75.6%
Black or African American 13.8%
American Indian or Alaska Native 0.4%
Asian 0.4%
Native Hawaiian or other Pacific Islander 0.0%
Some other race 0.0%
Hispanic or Latino origin 8.8%
Two or more races 0.9%

*As percentage of total population.

Ancestry*

English	5.8%	Italian	1.1%
French	3.4%	Scotch-Irish	1.4%
German	6.5%	USA/American	12.5%
Irish	7.5%		

*As estimated percentage of total population.

Universities and colleges, 2000–2001 enrollment

Angelina College, Lufkin 4,412
Jacksonville College, Jacksonville 275

Lamar University, Orange   1,939
Lon Morris College, Jacksonville   364
Sam Houston State University, Huntsville   12,358

Newspapers and circulation

	District circulation	Total circulation
*Beaumont Enterprise**	21,910	54,940
Dallas Morning News	2,033	495,624
Houston Chronicle	13,756	548,437
Orange Leader	7,003	7,636
Plano Star Courier	2,236	10,862
Tyler Telegraph-Courier Times	3,632	43,387

See Sources and Explanations in the front of the volume.

Television stations and affiliations

Tyler-Longview (Lufkin-Nacogdoches)	37%	KETK	NBC
Tyler-Longview (Lufkin-Nacogdoches)	37%	KFXK	FOX
Tyler-Longview (Lufkin-Nacogdoches)	37%	KLSB	NBC
Tyler-Longview (Lufkin-Nacogdoches)	37%	KLTV	ABC
Tyler-Longview (Lufkin-Nacogdoches)	37%	KTRE	ABC
Houston	34%	KAVU	ABC
Houston	34%	KBTX	CBS
Houston	34%	KETH	Independent
Houston	34%	KHOU	CBS
Houston	34%	KHWB	WB
Houston	34%	KLTJ	Independent
Houston	34%	KNWS	Independent
Houston	34%	KPRC	NBC
Houston	34%	KPXB	PAX
Houston	34%	KRIV	FOX
Houston	34%	KTBU	Independent
Houston	34%	KTMD	Telemundo
Houston	34%	KTRK	ABC
Houston	34%	KTXH	UPN
Houston	34%	KUHT	PBS
Houston	34%	KXLN	Univision
Houston	34%	KZJL	Independent Spanish
Beaumont-Port Arthur	29%	KBMT	ABC
Beaumont-Port Arthur	29%	KBTV	NBC
Beaumont-Port Arthur	29%	KFDM	CBS, UPN
Beaumont-Port Arthur	29%	KITU	Independent

Cable systems and subscribers

Cequel III   2,794
Classic   14,819
Communicomm   2,338
Cox   30,192
National Cable   688
Northland   5,476
Timber Lake Cablevision   569
Time Warner   27,475
Tri City Cable   7,401

Military installations, September 2001

Conroe Army Support Facility (Army Reserve), Conroe   364

Businesses and other major employers

Texas Criminal Justice Dept.; Huntsville   3,500
University of Texas Medical Clinic; Woodville   1,494
Lufkin Industries Inc.; Lufkin; truck semitrailers   1,200
Texas Mental Health and Mental Retardation Dept.; Lufkin   1,100
Temple-Inland Inc.; Diboll; forestry services   1,000
Texas Dept. of Public Safety; Coldspring   1,000
Texas Mental Health and Mental Retardation Dept.; Rusk   949
Texas Criminal Justice Dept.; Livingston   833

Donohue Industries Inc.; Lufkin; newsprint paper   800
Grant Prideco Inc.; Navasota; pipe sections   800
Specialty Retailers Inc.; Jacksonville; clothing stores   800
Memorial Health Systems Hospital; Lufkin   770
Texas Criminal Justice Dept.; Lovelady   708
International Paper Co.; Camden; hardwood panels   700
Louisiana-Pacific Corp.; New Waverly; plywood, softwood   700
Texas Foundries; Lufkin; iron foundries   650
Sam Houston State University; Huntsville   629
West Orange Cove School District; Orange   600
Baxter Healthcare Corp.; Jacksonville; medical instruments   550
Woodland Heights General Hospital Inc.; Lufkin   540
DXP Enterprises Inc.; Jasper; industrial machinery/equipment   511
Chevron Phillips Chemical Co.; Orange; polyethylene resins   500
Huntsville Memorial Hospital; Huntsville   500

Texas 3rd District

Northeast Dallas suburbs — Plano

The 3rd has moved steadily northward since 1990. It used to be a Dallas-based district, home to some of the city's wealthiest areas, but redistricting in 1996 and 2001 moved the district to the city's northern suburbs, including most of Collin County. Collin—the state's fastest-growing county in the 1990s—includes most of the suburban cities of Plano, Frisco, and McKinney. The district still takes in part of northeast Dallas County, including most of the suburbs of Richardson and Garland. Collin has two-thirds and Dallas one-third of the district population. *(See map p. 862.)*

Despite demographic changes, the district remains economically well-off, white, and Republican. Many corporate headquarters have moved into the Plano area, and wealthy executives have built expensive homes in sections such as Deerfield. The concentration of electronic and telecommunications firms along Interstate 75 has earned that area the name "Telecom Corridor." Texas Instruments and Electronic Data Systems are a major presence along the corridor. Just off the Lyndon B. Johnson Freeway along Interstate 75, Richardson has benefited greatly from high-tech firms and is growing at a rapid rate. Frisco also is undergoing a population and development boom. The district has middle-class areas such as Garland, which grew at a steady pace in the 1980s and 1990s. About two-thirds of Garland is in the 3rd. Although downtown Dallas is in the 30th, its white-collar companies rely heavily on the 3rd for their workforce.

The district is solidly Republican—Collin County is filled with young, upwardly mobile professionals and is even more Republican than suburbs that are closer to Dallas. In the 2002 Senate race, Republican John Cornyn won 70 percent of the 3rd's share of Collin, capturing all but two precincts in the county, and 68 percent overall. Republican governor Rick Perry took 72 percent of the vote in the 3rd.

Major Industry

Telecommunications, transportation, banking.

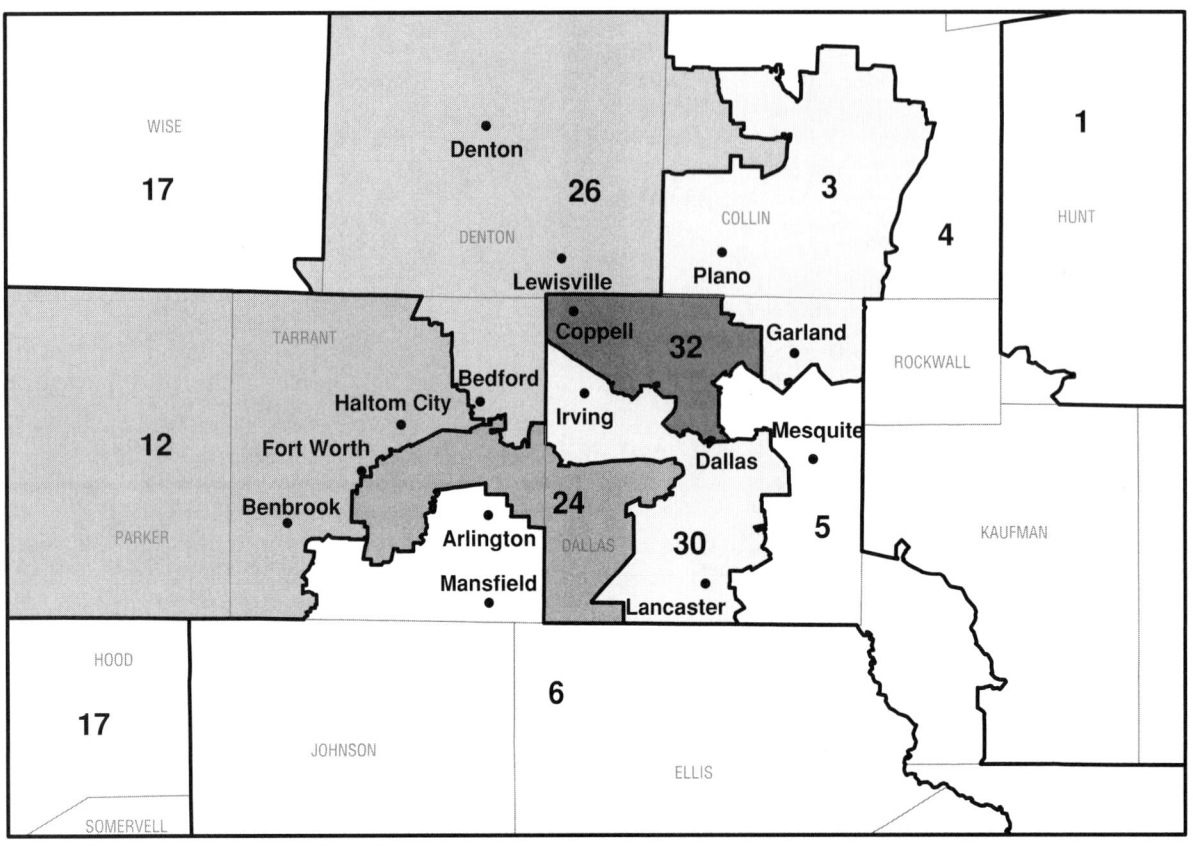

Notable

Southfork Ranch, the fictional home of the Ewing family in the long-running television program *Dallas,* is located in Parker.

Election Returns

	Republican		Democratic		Other	
President 2000	154,525	72.2%	59,357	27.8%		
House 2002	113,974	73.9%	37,503	24.3%	2,656	1.7%

District Profile

Population   651,620

Total area (square miles)   489.0
   Land area (square miles)   462.4

Population per square mile   1,409.2

Counties (2000 population)
   Collin (pt.)   432,045
   Dallas (pt.)   219,575

Cities and other areas over 10,000 (2000 population)
   Allen   43,554
   Dallas (pt.)   45,162
   Frisco (pt.)   25,618
   Garland (pt.)   146,118
   McKinney (pt.)   27,346
   Plano (pt.)   219,890
   Richardson (pt.)   47,347
   Rowlett (pt.)   37,462
   Wylie (pt.)   14,805

Race and Hispanic or Latino origin*
   White   69.6%
   Black or African American   6.6%
   American Indian or Alaska Native   0.4%
   Asian   7.4%
   Native Hawaiian or other Pacific Islander   0.0%
   Some other race   0.1%
   Hispanic or Latino origin   14.4%
   Two or more races   1.5%

As percentage of total population.

Ancestry*
   English   8.3%
   French   2.3%
   German   11.3%
   Irish   8.3%
   Italian   2.6%
   Polish   1.5%
   Scotch-Irish   1.6%
   Scottish   1.8%
   USA/American   6.9%

As estimated percentage of total population.

Universities and colleges, 2000–2001 enrollment
   Amber University, Garland   1,548
   Collin County Community College-Central Park, McKinney   12,996
   Collin County Community College-Preston Ridge*, Frisco
   Collin County Community College-Spring Creek*, Plano
   Education America-Dallas, Garland   483
   ITT Technical Institute, Garland   391
   University of Texas-Dallas, Richardson   10,945

Enrollment under 100. See Sources and Explanations in the front of the volume.

Newspapers and circulation

	District circulation	Total circulation
Dallas Morning News	77,920	495,624
*USA Today**	3,066	1,674,376

See Sources and Explanations in the front of the volume.

Television stations and affiliations
Dallas-Fort Worth	100%	KDAF	WB
Dallas-Fort Worth	100%	KDFI	Independent
Dallas-Fort Worth	100%	KDFW	FOX
Dallas-Fort Worth	100%	KDTN	PBS
Dallas-Fort Worth	100%	KDTX	Independent
Dallas-Fort Worth	100%	KERA	PBS
Dallas-Fort Worth	100%	KFWD	Independent
Dallas-Fort Worth	100%	KMPX	Independent
Dallas-Fort Worth	100%	KPXD	PAX
Dallas-Fort Worth	100%	KSTR	Telefutura
Dallas-Fort Worth	100%	KTAQ	Independent
Dallas-Fort Worth	100%	KTVT	CBS
Dallas-Fort Worth	100%	KTXA	UPN
Dallas-Fort Worth	100%	KUVN	Univision
Dallas-Fort Worth	100%	KXAS	NBC
Dallas-Fort Worth	100%	KXTX	Telemundo
Dallas-Fort Worth	100%	WFAA	ABC

Cable systems and subscribers
   Classic   1,838
   Comcast   95,548

Businesses and other major employers
   Electronic Data Systems Corp.; Plano; systems integration   15,000
   Nortel Networks Inc.; Richardson; warehousing   7,000
   Alcatel USA Inc.; Plano; telephones   4,500
   JC Penney Corp.; Plano; department stores   3,500
   Perot Systems Corp.; Plano; computer facilities management   2,811
   Fujitsu Network Communications Inc.; Richardson; fiber optics   2,500
   Fossil Inc.; Richardson; watches, clocks, watchcases   2,000
   Frito-Lay Inc.; Plano; snacks   2,000
   Texas Instruments Inc.; McKinney; electrical equipment   2,000
   Steak and Ale of Georgia Inc.; Plano; restaurant   1,728
   SBC Communications Inc.; Richardson; telephone, telecommunication   1,690
   Ericsson Inc.; Richardson; electronic parts, equipment   1,600
   JC Penney Life Insurance Co.; Richardson   1,520
   Ericsson Inc.; Plano; radio broadcast equipment   1,500
   SVA Networks Inc.; Plano; security systems services   1,500
   University of Texas at Dallas; Richardson   1,420
   Medical Center of Plano; Plano   1,400
   State Farm Insurance Co.; Dallas; insurance agents   1,368
   Grubb and Ellis Co.; Richardson; real estate agents   1,300

Blockbuster Inc.; McKinney; video rental   1,200

Cingular Wireless; Richardson; cellular telephones
1,200

Hewlett-Packard Co.; Richardson; computer consulting
services   1,200

JC Penney Life Insurance Co.; Plano   1,200

Presbyterian Hospital of Dallas; Plano   1,100

Aegon Direct Marketing Services Inc.; Plano; financial
services   1,000

Callin County Community College; McKinney   1,000

Capital One Auto Finance; Plano; automobile loans
1,000

Cingular Wireless; Dallas; mobile telephones and
equipment   1,000

Janssen Pharmaceutica; Plano; pharmaceuticals   1,000

Fabtech Industries Corp.; Garland; structural metal
975

Litton Systems Inc.; Garland; search and detection
systems   950

Baylor Medical Center; Garland   875

City of Plano; Plano; city government   850

Dallas Morning News; Plano; newspaper   800

Rockwell Collins Inc.; Richardson; aircraft   800

Transwestern Publishing Co.; Frisco; telephone
directories   780

HCA Inc. Hospital; Plano   751

MCI WorldCom Network Services Inc.; Richardson;
long-distance telephone   750

North Central Medical Center; McKinney   750

Sanden International (USA) Inc.; Wylie; automotive air
conditioning   735

BeneCorp Business Services Inc.; Allen; employee leasing
service   719

Beverly Enterprises Inc.; McKinney; local trucking   700

Kaneb Services; Richardson; petroleum pipelines   623

Global Commercial Services Inc.; Plano; building
maintenance   620

Intervoice Services Inc.; Dallas; business consulting
600

Richardson Hospital Authority; Richardson   600

Samsung Telecommunications; Richardson; telephone
equipment   600

Software Spectrum Inc.; Garland; computer software
600

Telvista Co.; Dallas; telephone/video communications
600

United Parcel Service Inc.; Allen; courier services   600

Verizon Communications Inc.; Garland; telephone
installation   600

Wal-Mart Stores Inc.; Garland; department stores   600

Southwestern Bell; Plano; electronic equipment   599

Accucom Technical Services Inc.; Richardson; telephone
equipment installation   570

Collin County Community College; Frisco   550

Atlantic Richfield Co.; Plano; petroleum, natural gas
525

Collin County; McKinney; county government   503

AdvancePCS; Richardson; health services consultant
500

Alliance Data Systems Corp.; Dallas; credit card service
500

Compass Bank Credit Card Services Inc.; Richardson;
commercial banking   500

Datron Inc.; Garland; aircraft assemblies, parts   500

Dr Pepper/Cadbury; Plano; beverage bases   500

General Electric Co.; Richardson; finance companies
500

iNet Technologies Inc.; Richardson; telephone apparatus
500

Kraft Foods Inc.; Garland; jams   500

Nachi America Inc.; Garland; industrial
machinery/equipment   500

National Spirit Group; Garland; sports clubs   500

TGH Companies; Plano; janitorial service   500

United American Insurance Co.; McKinney; accident
insurance   500

Texas 4th District

Northeast — Tyler, Sherman, most of Longview

The 4th covers a wide swath of the Red River Valley area
north and east of Dallas, which was once the bailiwick of
former Democratic House Speaker Sam Rayburn but now is
fertile territory for the GOP. The district extends from the
Oklahoma border down to skirt suburban Dallas, and then
moves east to take in the oil cities of Tyler and Longview.

East Texas, and the 4th District in particular, has an
older, more rural, and more blue-collar population than
most other areas of the state, and many residents espouse
economic conservatism and gun rights. The 4th is mostly
white but is one of the few Texas districts where blacks outnumber Hispanics. In Smith and Gregg Counties, the two
most-populous in the district, nearly one in five residents is
black.

Voters in the 4th elect conservatives of both parties to
local and national offices, but the GOP has made dramatic
inroads since the 1980s. In 2000 George W. Bush garnered
70 percent of the two-party vote in the district, his ninth-
highest percentage in Texas, and Republicans John Cornyn
and Rick Perry also topped two-thirds of the district vote in
their 2002 races for senator and governor, respectively. The
district's GOP advantage runs from slight in Fannin County,
on the Oklahoma border, to overwhelming in burgeoning
Rockwall County, which in the 1990s had the third-fastest
population growth rate of Texas's 254 counties.

Many Rockwall residents commute to jobs in Dallas,
while those in other counties farm the land for peanuts and
other crops that became popular after the cotton industry's
decline. The oil bust in the mid-1980s hurt the economy near
Tyler and Longview, but other areas have rebounded with the
help of several electronics manufacturing plants located in or
near the district. Both the agricultural and manufacturing
sectors have since posted large gains, offsetting the oil decline.

Major Industry

Health care, electronics manufacturing, agriculture, oil.

Notable

Tyler bills itself as the "Rose Capital of the World" and
hosts a weeklong festival each October; former House Speaker
Rayburn hailed from Bonham (Fannin County), which is now
home to the Sam Rayburn Library and Museum.

Election Returns

	Republican		Democratic		Other	
President 2000	157,678	70.2%	66,995	29.8%		
House 2002	67,939	40.4%	97,304	57.8%	3,042	1.8%

District Profile

Population 651,620

Total area (square miles) 6,335.1
  Land area (square miles) 6,141.0

Population per square mile 106.1

Counties (2000 population)

Collin (pt.)	25,074	Kaufman (pt.)	60,200
Cooke	36,363	Rains	9,139
Fannin	31,242	Rockwall	43,080
Grayson	110,595	Smith	174,706
Gregg	111,379	Van Zandt	48,140
Hunt (pt.)	1,702		

Cities and other areas over 10,000 (2000 population)

Denison	22,773	Sherman	35,082
Gainesville	15,538	Terrell	13,606
Longview (pt.)	71,746	Tyler	83,650
Rockwall	17,976		

Race and Hispanic or Latino origin*

White 76.6%
Black or African American 11.7%
American Indian or Alaska Native 0.6%
Asian 0.6%
Native Hawaiian or other Pacific Islander 0.0%
Some other race 0.1%
Hispanic or Latino origin 9.4%
Two or more races 1.1%

As percentage of total population.

Ancestry*

Dutch	1.2%	Irish	7.9%
English	7.1%	Scotch-Irish	1.6%
French	1.8%	Scottish	1.3%
German	7.9%	USA/American	12.4%

As estimated percentage of total population.

Universities and colleges, 2000–2001 enrollment

Austin College, Sherman 1,234
Grayson County College, Denison 3,318
Kilgore College, Kilgore 4,000
Letourneau University, Longview 2,981
North Central Texas College, Gainesville 4,844
Southwestern Christian College, Terrell 211
Tyler Junior College, Tyler 8,319
University of Texas, Tyler 3,594

Newspapers and circulation

	District circulation	Total circulation
Dallas Morning News	29,367	495,624
Herald Democrat	23,059	24,146
Longview News-Journal	14,131	29,041
Tyler Telegraph-Courier Times	30,185	43,387
*USA Today**	1,925	1,674,376

See Sources and Explanations in the front of the volume.

Television stations and affiliations

Dallas-Fort Worth	65%	KDAF	WB
Dallas-Fort Worth	65%	KDFI	Independent
Dallas-Fort Worth	65%	KDFW	FOX
Dallas-Fort Worth	65%	KDTN	PBS
Dallas-Fort Worth	65%	KDTX	Independent
Dallas-Fort Worth	65%	KERA	PBS
Dallas-Fort Worth	65%	KFWD	Independent
Dallas-Fort Worth	65%	KMPX	Independent
Dallas-Fort Worth	65%	KPXD	PAX
Dallas-Fort Worth	65%	KSTR	Telefutura
Dallas-Fort Worth	65%	KTAQ	Independent
Dallas-Fort Worth	65%	KTVT	CBS
Dallas-Fort Worth	65%	KTXA	UPN
Dallas-Fort Worth	65%	KUVN	Univision
Dallas-Fort Worth	65%	KXAS	NBC
Dallas-Fort Worth	65%	KXTX	Telemundo
Dallas-Fort Worth	65%	WFAA	ABC
Tyler-Longview (Lufkin-Nacogdoches)	19%	KETK	NBC
Tyler-Longview (Lufkin-Nacogdoches)	19%	KFXK	FOX
Tyler-Longview (Lufkin-Nacogdoches)	19%	KLSB	NBC
Tyler-Longview (Lufkin-Nacogdoches)	19%	KLTV	ABC
Tyler-Longview (Lufkin-Nacogdoches)	19%	KTRE	ABC
Sherman-Ada	16%	KTEN	NBC
Sherman-Ada	16%	KXII	CBS

Cable systems and subscribers

Cable ONE 28,217
Charter 8,395
Classic 8,574
Comcast 929
Cox 42,449
East Texas Cable 1,287
Kilgore Cable TV 4,035
Longview Cable TV 24,793
Nortex Communications 1,179
Northland 6,867

Businesses and other major employers

East Texas Medical Center; Tyler 2,355
Mother Frances Hospital; Tyler 2,141
American Standard Inc.; Tyler; refrigeration, heating equipment 2,000
University of Texas Health Center; Tyler 1,500
Goodyear Tire and Rubber Co.; Tyler; pneumatic tires 1,415
MEMC Southwest Inc.; Sherman; silicon wafers 1,400
Brookshire Grocery Co.; Tyler; supermarkets 1,250
Carrier Corp.; Tyler; air conditioning equipment 1,200
Texas Mental Health and Mental Retardation Dept.; Terrell 1,200
Texoma Medical Center Inc.; Denison 1,200
United Technologies Corp.; Tyler; air conditioning equipment 1,100
Weber Aircraft; Gainesville; aircraft parts, equipment 1,075
Ransom Industries; Tyler; iron foundry 1,000
Advanced Temporaries Inc.; Tyler; temporary help service 983
Dolgencorp of Texas Inc.; Gainesville; variety stores 980
Butler Manufacturing Co.; Terrell; metal doors, sash, trim 900
Grayson County Junior College; Denison 900
Staff One Inc.; Denison; travel agency 886
Sitel Corp.; Longview; telemarketing 800
Universal Cable Holdings Inc.; Tyler; cable TV 750

Wilson N. Jones Memorial Hospital; Sherman   725

Johnson and Johnson Medical Inc.; Sherman; surgical supplies   700

Tyler Junior College; Tyler   700

Madix Inc.; Terrell nonwood partitions, fixtures   700

Helping Hands Homecare Inc.; Tyler; home health care   600

Longview Regional Hospital Inc.; Longview   600

Fleetwood Travel Trailers of Texas Inc.; Longview; travel trailer chassis   571

Mansfield Plumbing Products; Kilgore   518

Gregg County; Longview; county government   500

Maurice's Inc.; Sherman; clothing stores   500

Steel Corp.; Longview; tank freight cars, equipment   500

Woodman of World Life Insurance Society; Longview; life insurance   500

Texas 5th District

East central — part of Dallas, east and south suburbs

The 5th begins in Dallas and its suburbs, then winds more than 150 miles south through all or part of ten other counties, reaching almost to Bryan and College Station (both of which are in the 31st). Dallas County is home to 63 percent of the 5th's residents. *(See map p. 862.)*

The district's part of Dallas differs from the glitz and wealth that characterizes the portion in the 32nd. The 5th takes in eastern and northeastern Dallas, which has more of a working-class flavor and is home to many small businesses. Mesquite, a suburb east of the city, also is a major voting base.

Many of the city's suburbs have growing populations and provide easy access to a bustling metropolis while supplying the benefits of small-town life. Prisons are a large employer in rural parts of the district. Cattle, natural gas, and coal continue to be big industries as well. Many of the smaller towns previously relied on steel or lumber and were hit hard when those markets declined. Brownfields revitalization efforts are now taking place in the district.

The 5th generally favors Republicans. GOP areas abound in northeastern Dallas, in neighborhoods on both sides of the L. B. J. Freeway, and in Anderson and Henderson Counties well southeast of the city. Some heavily minority precincts in the district's northwestern periphery vote solidly Democratic, and Mesquite often is politically competitive. Down south, Falls and Robertson Counties have large black populations and vote Democratic, which helps keep the party's candidates competitive in some tight statewide races.

Major Industry
Technology, prisons, service.

Notable
The Dallas Arboretum and Botanical Garden; Resistol Arena is home to the Mesquite Championship Rodeo.

Election Returns

	Republican		Democratic		Other	
President 2000	118,703	62.1%	72,507	37.9%		
House 2002	81,439	58.2%	56,330	40.3%	2,139	1.5%

District Profile

Population   651,620

Total area (square miles)   7,455.4
　Land area (square miles)   7,296.8

Population per square mile   89.3

Counties (2000 population)

Anderson 55,109	Leon 15,335
Dallas (pt.) 407,727	Limestone 22,051
Falls 18,576	Madison 12,940
Freestone 17,867	McLennan (pt.) 1,625
Henderson 73,277	Robertson 16,000
Kaufman (pt.) 11,113	

Cities and other areas over 10,000 (2000 population)

Athens 11,297	Mesquite (pt.) 123,948
Balch Springs 19,375	Palestine 17,598
Dallas (pt.) 188,480	Seagoville (pt.) 10,816
Garland (pt.) 54,729	

Race and Hispanic or Latino origin*
White   63.0%
Black or African American   15.8%
American Indian or Alaska Native   0.4%
Asian   1.8%
Native Hawaiian or other Pacific Islander   0.0%
Some other race   0.1%
Hispanic or Latino origin   17.7%
Two or more races   1.2%

As percentage of total population.

Ancestry*

English 6.6%	Italian 1.2%
French 1.7%	Scotch-Irish 1.5%
German 7.5%	Scottish 1.1%
Irish 7.1%	USA/American 9.2%

As estimated percentage of total population.

Universities and colleges, 2000–2001 enrollment
Eastfield College, Mesquite   7,873
Trinity Valley Community College, Athens   4,780

Newspapers and circulation

	District circulation	Total circulation
Bryan-College Station Eagle	2,539	24,358
Dallas Morning News	49,789	495,624
Palestine Herald-Press	7,504	7,950
Tyler Telegraph-Courier Times	4,540	43,387
*USA Today**	6,359	1,674,376
Waco Tribune-Herald	2,998	40,354

See Sources and Explanations in the front of the volume.

Television stations and affiliations

Waco-Temple-Bryan	55%	KAMU	PBS
Waco-Temple-Bryan	55%	KCEN	NBC
Waco-Temple-Bryan	55%	KNCT	PBS
Waco-Temple-Bryan	55%	KWKT	FOX,WB
Waco-Temple-Bryan	55%	KWTX	CBS
Waco-Temple-Bryan	55%	KXXV	ABC
Waco-Temple-Bryan	55%	KYLE	FOX,WB

Dallas-Fort Worth	45%	KDAF	WB
Dallas-Fort Worth	45%	KDFI	Independent
Dallas-Fort Worth	45%	KDFW	FOX
Dallas-Fort Worth	45%	KDTN	PBS
Dallas-Fort Worth	45%	KDTX	Independent
Dallas-Fort Worth	45%	KERA	PBS
Dallas-Fort Worth	45%	KFWD	Independent
Dallas-Fort Worth	45%	KMPX	Independent
Dallas-Fort Worth	45%	KPXD	PAX
Dallas-Fort Worth	45%	KSTR	Telefutura
Dallas-Fort Worth	45%	KTAQ	Independent
Dallas-Fort Worth	45%	KTVT	CBS
Dallas-Fort Worth	45%	KTXA	UPN
Dallas-Fort Worth	45%	KUVN	Univision
Dallas-Fort Worth	45%	KXAS	NBC
Dallas-Fort Worth	45%	KXTX	Telemundo
Dallas-Fort Worth	45%	WFAA	ABC

Cable systems and subscribers

Charter   1,899
Classic   4,806
Comcast   22,550
Cox   6,313
Galaxy   1,161
Northland   14,567

Businesses and other major employers

Crossmark Inc.; Dallas; sales promotion   10,000

Tyco Electronics Corp.; Mesquite; telephone apparatus   3,000

United Parcel Service Inc.; Mesquite; package delivery   2,500

Fahler and Riels DDS; Jewett; dental offices   2,000

United Parcel Service Inc.; Garland; package delivery   2,000

George Braswell Heating and Air; Chilton; contractors   1,961

Hawkins Associates Inc.; Dallas; help supply services   1,606

Mexia State School; Mexia   1,500

Wal-Mart Stores Inc.; Palestine; department stores   1,200

Texas Criminal Justice Dept.; Tennessee Colony   1,017

McKesson Corp.; Garland; warehousing   1,000

Texas Dept. of Transportation; Mesquite   1,000

TA Operating Corp.; Mesquite; truck stops   979

Ericsson Hewlett-Packard; Dallas; business software   900

Texas Criminal Justice Dept.; Midway   730

Dallas Morning News; Dallas; newspaper   650

Zachry Construction Corp.; Fairfield; housing construction   650

Southwestern Bell Telephone Co.; Dallas; data telephone communications   649

HCR Manorcare Mesquite; Mesquite; hospital   597

Monterey Mushrooms Inc.; Madisonville; mushroom production   550

Tenet Health System-Dallas Inc.; Dallas; hospital   550

Ashland Inc.; Mesquite; petroleum refining   510

Atlantic Southeast Airlines Inc.; Dallas; helicopter carrier   500

Maxxim Medical Inc.; Athens; surgical supplies   500

U.S. Bureau of Customs and Border Protection; Dallas   500

Texas 6th District

Suburban Dallas — parts of Fort Worth and Arlington; southern suburbs

Once a snaking district that included Republican areas in and outside Fort Worth, the 6th, as redrawn in 2001 redistricting, became a cohesive block of counties just south of the Dallas-Fort Worth metroplex. The district takes in southern Tarrant County, including about one-eighth of Fort Worth and most of the suburb of Arlington. While the old district was urban-suburban, the new district is mostly suburban-rural.

More than half of the district population comes out of Tarrant, while most of the rest lives in Johnson and Ellis Counties. Rapidly growing Johnson has become a bedroom community for Fort Worth and is home to many of the city's southern suburbs. Ellis County, which includes Waxahachie and Ennis, used to be dependent on cotton farming, but the cement industry has taken hold there. The other two counties in the district—Hill and Navarro—are rural and less-populated, and are sustained by oil, ranching, and farming.

Fort Worth's economy has diversified and expanded in recent years, while population growth in Arlington has leveled out after a tremendous boom from the 1950s through the 1990s. There are some black and Hispanic areas in the district, and the Vietnamese and Samoan populations have increased. But the 6th is generally white, financially secure, and suburban.

It is also heavily Republican. Most of the Tarrant precincts are aligned with the GOP, though there is some Democratic strength in southern Fort Worth and eastern Arlington. But the overwhelming GOP advantage in Ellis and Johnson, which went for John Cornyn and Rick Perry by better than two-to-one ratios in 2002, makes the 6th a safe haven for Republican candidates.

Major Industry

Transportation, home building, technology, agriculture.

Notable

A superconducting supercollider—or "atom smasher"—was to be located in Waxahachie, but Congress cut all funding for the project in 1993 after $2 billion had already been spent.

Election Returns

	Republican		Democratic		Other	
President 2000	146,931	66.9%	72,754	33.1%		
House 2002	115,396	70.3%	45,404	27.7%	3,237	2.0%

District Profile

Population   651,620

Total area (square miles)   3,961.1
  Land area (square miles)   3,836.5

Population per square mile   169.8

Counties (2000 population)

Ellis 111,360
Hill 32,321
Johnson 126,811
Navarro 45,124
Tarrant (pt.) 336,004

Cities and other areas over 10,000 (2000 population)

Arlington (pt.) 191,470
Burleson 20,976
Cleburne 26,005
Corsicana 24,485
Ennis 16,045
Fort Worth (pt.) 64,649
Grand Prairie (pt.) 10,466
Mansfield 28,031
Waxahachie 21,426

Race and Hispanic or Latino origin*

White 71.8%
Black or African American 10.2%
American Indian or Alaska Native 0.4%
Asian 2.6%
Native Hawaiian or other Pacific Islander 0.1%
Some other race 0.1%
Hispanic or Latino origin 13.5%
Two or more races 1.3%

As percentage of total population.

Ancestry*

Dutch 1.1%
English 7.5%
French 2.0%
German 9.3%
Irish 7.8%
Italian 1.6%
Scotch-Irish 1.6%
Scottish 1.5%
USA/American 9.4%

As estimated percentage of total population.

Universities and colleges, 2000–2001 enrollment

Hill College, Hillsboro 2,512
International Aviation and Travel Academy, Arlington 525
Navarro College, Corsicana 4,048
Southwestern Adventist University, Keene 1,187
Southwestern Assemblies of God University, Waxahachie 1,782

Newspapers and circulation

	District circulation	Total circulation
Dallas Morning News	20,382	495,624
Fort Worth Star-Telegram	55,094	224,885
*USA Today**	1,325	1,674,376
Waco Tribune-Herald	1,746	40,354

See Sources and Explanations in the front of the volume.

Television stations and affiliations

Dallas-Fort Worth	100%	KDAF	WB
Dallas-Fort Worth	100%	KDFI	Independent
Dallas-Fort Worth	100%	KDFW	FOX
Dallas-Fort Worth	100%	KDTN	PBS
Dallas-Fort Worth	100%	KDTX	Independent
Dallas-Fort Worth	100%	KERA	PBS
Dallas-Fort Worth	100%	KFWD	Independent
Dallas-Fort Worth	100%	KMPX	Independent
Dallas-Fort Worth	100%	KPXD	PAX
Dallas-Fort Worth	100%	KSTR	Telefutura
Dallas-Fort Worth	100%	KTAQ	Independent
Dallas-Fort Worth	100%	KTVT	CBS
Dallas-Fort Worth	100%	KTXA	UPN
Dallas-Fort Worth	100%	KUVN	Univision
Dallas-Fort Worth	100%	KXAS	NBC
Dallas-Fort Worth	100%	KXTX	Telemundo
Dallas-Fort Worth	100%	WFAA	ABC

Cable systems and subscribers

Charter 27,133
Comcast 1,238
National Cable 977
Northland 6,962

Businesses and other major employers

AT&T Corp.; Red Oak; telephone communication 1,500
Huguley Memorial Hospital Burleson; Burleson 1,500
Texas Industries Inc.; Midlothian; blast furnaces, steel mills 1,200
National Semiconductor Corp.; Arlington; computer chips 1,100
Asplundh Tree Expert Co.; Mansfield; tree trimming 1,000
JP Morgan Chase Bank; Arlington; commercial bank 1,000
Chaparral Steel Co.; Midlothian; blast furnaces, steel mills 950
Star-Telegram Operating; Fort Worth; newspaper 870
Doskocil Manufacturing Co.; Arlington; molded plastics 866
Medical Center of Arlington; Arlington 800
Russell Stover Candies Inc.; Corsicana; candy, nut stores 800
Johnson and Johnson Medical Inc.; Sherman; medical supplies 700
Oakwood Homes Corp.; Hillsboro; mobile homes 600
Silverleaf Resorts Inc.; Arlington; condominium manager 600
TIC-The Industrial Co.; Midlothian; industrial buildings construction 600
Wal-Mart Stores Inc.; Arlington; department stores 600
Harris Methodist Hospital; Fort Worth 585
Disability Services of Southwest Inc.; Fort Worth; outpatient clinics 567
Toys R Us Inc.; Midlothian; hobby, toy shops 550
Alamo Rent-a-Car; Grand Prairie 500
Arlington Independent School District; Arlington 500
Carrier Commercial Refrigeration Inc.; Waxahachie; refrigeration equipment 500
Everman Independent School District; Fort Worth 500
Martin Sprocket and Gear Inc.; Arlington; transmission gears 500

Texas 7th District

Western Houston; northwestern suburbs

Based in western Houston and split in two by Interstate 10, the 7th is removed from downtown Houston's oil and gas companies but nonetheless has several important corporate residents and the Galleria, a huge shopping and office complex that provides jobs and a major retail presence. Like other areas around Houston, the district rebounded slowly after the oil industry's troubles in the 1980s. But an increasing

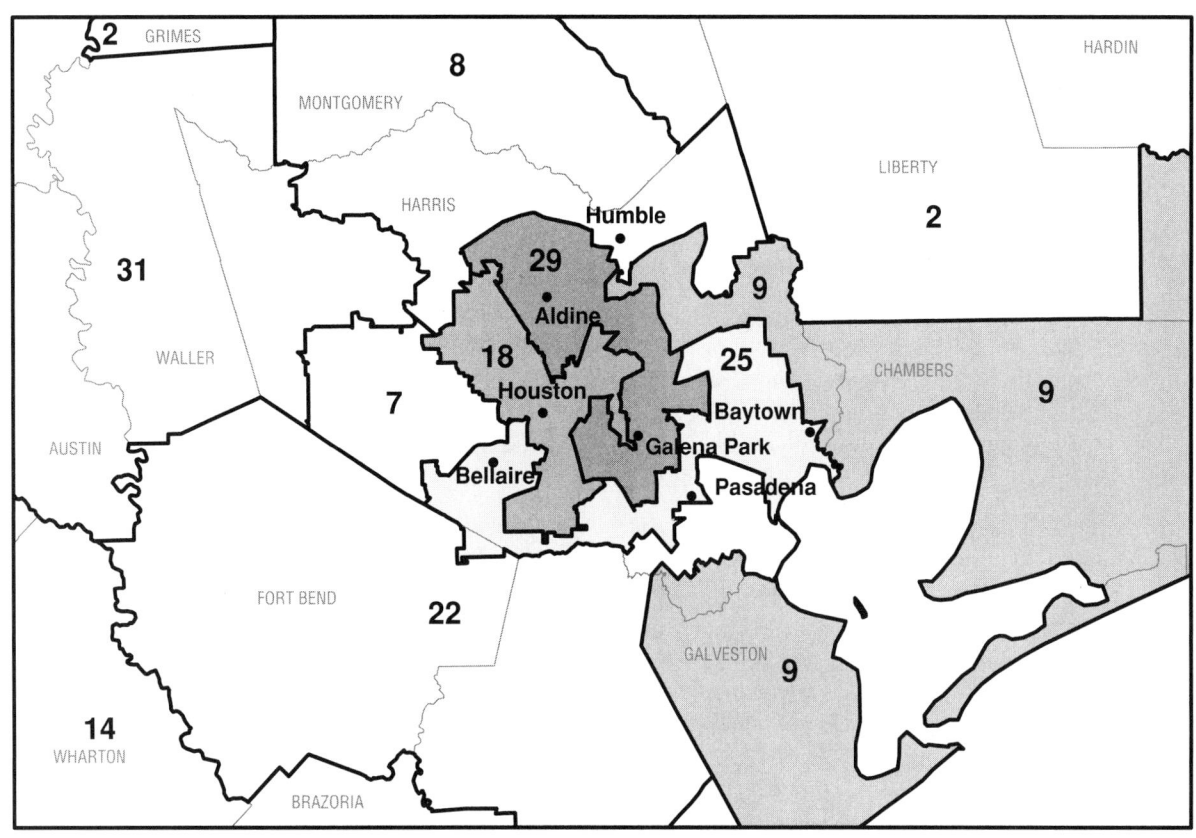

emphasis on high-tech firms and corporate headquarters enabled the 7th to enjoy sustained economic growth during the 1990s. *(See map p. 869.)*

The 7th is more racially diverse than it was prior to redistricting in 2001. The new map pushed the 7th farther east, inside the Interstate 610 beltway encircling Houston, to make room for the newly drawn 31st. At its easternmost point, the redrawn 7th nearly touches Compaq Center, the arena where the NBA's Rockets play.

Nearly seven in ten district residents live in Houston. The 7th's share of the city is mostly middle class and heavily minority: whites (46 percent) are outnumbered by Hispanics (26 percent), blacks (12 percent), and Asians (12 percent) taken together. Northwest Houston includes a large Hispanic population, particularly between Interstate 10 and the Northwest Freeway, and there are sizable black and Asian populations in southwest Houston. Alief, picked up in redistricting, has a large Vietnamese population.

Much of the district is characterized by white-collar executives, good schools, and religious conservatism. The 7th's median income is brought up by wealthy villages like Piney Point, Bunker Hill, and Hunters Creek, which are near Interstate 10 and surrounded on all sides by Houston.

Redistricting only marginally lessened the 7th's strong Republican lean. In 2002 statewide races, Republicans John Cornyn and Gov. Rick Perry each took more than two-thirds of the vote in the district.

Major Industry
Technology, retail, health care.

Notable
George Bush, who later served as vice president and president, represented the 7th from 1967 to 1971; the Galleria, dubbed "a city within a city," is the fifth-largest mall in the nation.

Election Returns

	Republican		Democratic		Other	
President 2000	130,053	67.9%	61,498	32.1%		
House 2002	96,795	89.2%			11,732	10.8%

District Profile

Population 651,620

Total area (square miles) 193.9
Land area (square miles) 193.8

Population per square mile 3,362.3

Counties (2000 population)
Harris (pt.) 651,620

Cities and other areas over 10,000 (2000 population)
Houston (pt.) 449,641
Mission Bend CDP (pt.) 11,673

Race and Hispanic or Latino origin*
White 49.6%
Black or African American 11.3%
American Indian or Alaska Native 0.2%
Asian 10.9%
Native Hawaiian or other Pacific Islander 0.0%
Some other race 0.2%
Hispanic or Latino origin 25.9%
Two or more races 2.0%

As percentage of total population.

Ancestry*

Arab-Misc.	1.1%	Polish	1.3%
English	7.1%	Scotch-Irish	1.5%
French	2.4%	Scottish	1.6%
German	8.4%	Subsaharan	1.4%
Irish	5.9%	USA/American	4.2%
Italian	2.3%		

As estimated percentage of total population.

Universities and colleges, 2000–2001 enrollment
Art Institute of Houston, Houston 551
College of Biblical Studies, Houston 983
ITT Technical Institute, Houston 540
MTI College of Business and Technology, Houston 409

Newspapers and circulation

	District circulation	Total circulation
Houston Chronicle	79,427	548,437
*USA Today**	1,908	1,674,376

See Sources and Explanations in the front of the volume.

Television stations and affiliations

Houston	100%	KAVU	ABC
Houston	100%	KBTX	CBS
Houston	100%	KETH	Independent
Houston	100%	KHOU	CBS
Houston	100%	KHWB	WB
Houston	100%	KLTJ	Independent
Houston	100%	KNWS	Independent
Houston	100%	KPRC	NBC
Houston	100%	KPXB	PAX
Houston	100%	KRIV	FOX
Houston	100%	KTBU	Independent
Houston	100%	KTMD	Telemundo
Houston	100%	KTRK	ABC
Houston	100%	KTXH	UPN
Houston	100%	KUHT	PBS
Houston	100%	KXLN	Univision
Houston	100%	KZJL	Independent Spanish

Cable systems and subscribers
Time Warner 2,997

Military installations, September 2001
New Addicks National Guard, Houston 563

Businesses and other major employers
Canamere Inc.; Houston; mutual fund sales 15,000
SK Construction; Houston; home remodeling 11,993
Arethusa Off-Shore Co.; Houston; oil/gas exploration 4,300
Duke Energy Corp.; Houston; natural gas transmission 3,000
CHRISTUS Houston Health Support Center; Houston 2,800
Conoco Inc.; Houston; petroleum refining 2,500

Cumberland Maritime Corp.; Houston; drilling oil and gas wells   2,500

Diamond Offshore General Co.; Houston; drilling oil and gas wells   2,500

NetVersant Solutions Inc.; Houston; fiber-optic cable installation   2,500

ABB Lummus Global Inc.; Houston; engineering services   2,000

Mustang Engineers and Constructors; Houston; consulting engineer   1,900

ABB Lummus Global Inc.; Houston; fabricated plate work   1,600

Cliffs Drilling Co.; Houston; oil, gas well drilling   1,572

Pool Company Inc.; Houston; oil, gas well servicing   1,527

Reading and Bates Exploration Co. Inc.; Houston; oil, gas well drilling   1,500

Shell Deepwater Production Holding Inc.; Houston; service station supplies   1,500

Shell Oil Co.; Houston; gas refinery   1,500

Texas Dept. of Protective and Regulatory Services; Houston   1,500

BMC Software Inc.; Houston; utility computer software   1,464

City of Houston; Houston; police dept.   1,400

Global Santa Fe Drilling Co.; Houston; drilling oil and gas wells   1,324

Vastar Resources Inc.; Houston; natural gas production   1,250

May Department Stores Co.; Houston; department stores   1,230

Igloo Holdings Inc.; Houston; ice chests or coolers   1,205

Shell Oil Co.; Houston; gasoline service stations   1,200

WesternGeco; Houston; oil/gas exploration   1,200

Columbia Spring Branch Medical Center; Houston   1,100

Jacobs Engineering Group Inc.; Houston; engineering services   1,100

Willbros West Africa Inc.; Houston; oil/gas pipeline construction   1,100

Global Offshore International; Houston; water, sewer, utility lines   1,056

Fisk Corp.; Houston; electrical contractor   1,000

Kellogg Brown and Root Inc.; Houston; oil refinery construction   1,000

Marathon Oil Corp.; Houston; oil well machinery   1,000

Occidental Permian; Houston; crude oil   1,000

Prime Staff; Houston; health care staffing   1,000

Pritchard Industries Southwest Inc.; Houston; janitorial service   1,000

Republic Waste Services of Texas; Houston; refuse systems   1,000

Verizon Communications Inc.; Houston; telephone communication   1,000

Stone and Webster Engineering Corp.; Houston; engineering services   940

Toshiba International Corp.; Houston; motors and generators   920

Rowan Drill Inc.; Houston; directional oil, gas well drilling   915

Galleria; Houston; building operation   900

IKON Office Solutions Inc.; Houston; copying equipment   900

Mitsubishi Caterpillar Forklift; Houston; forklift trucks   850

Superior Protection Inc.; Houston; personal service agents   820

International Business Machines Corp.; Houston; office equipment   800

Sodexho Inc.; Houston; restaurants   800

Sysco Food Services; Houston; information bureau   800

Urban Shopping Centers Inc.; Houston; hotels and motels   800

BP America Inc.; Houston; petroleum products   750

Baker/MO Services Inc.; Houston; construction, repair   744

ExxonMobil Oil Corp.; Houston; industrial chemicals   700

Foster Wheeler USA Corp.; Houston; chemical engineering   700

Landmark Finance Co.; Houston; oil/gas field services   700

NextiraOne; Houston; telephone equipment   700

Redstone Hotels Inc.; Houston; hotels   700

Starwood Hotels; Houston; hotels   700

Augusta Foods Holdings; Houston   650

Transcontinental Gas Pipe Line Corp.; Houston; gas transmission   650

Wal-Mart Stores Inc.; Houston; department stores   650

Grey Wolf Inc.; Houston; oil, gas well drilling   650

NYLCare Health Plan of Gulf Coast Inc.; Houston; health maintenance organization   625

Aetna Inc.; Houston; medical service plans   620

TeleCheck Services Inc.; Houston; check validation service   620

Cameron Cooper Corp.; Houston; valves and pipe fittings   600

HBE Corp.; Houston; hotels   600

HCA West Houston Medical Center; Houston   600

Litton Loan Servicing; Houston; mortgage bankers   600

Tenet Healthcare Hospital; Houston   600

Stewart Information Services Corp.; Houston; title insurance   591

Pace Entertainment Corp.; Houston; theatrical production   574

Southwestern Bell Telephone Co.; Houston; telephone communications   564

Professional Janitorial Service of Houston Inc.; Houston; janitorial service   550

CSO Aker Maritime Inc.; Houston; engineering services   539

Hines Interests LP; Houston; commercial land development   525

Second Baptist Church Inc.; Houston; religious organization   520

Apache Corp.; Houston; crude petroleum production   507

Air Liquide America Corp.; Houston; industrial gases   500

AON Service Corp.; Houston; insurance brokers   500

AquaSource Inc.; Houston; combination utilities   500

BFI Medical Waste Systems of Iowa Inc.; Houston; medical waste disposal   500

BHP Minerals International Inc.; Houston; oil/gas
    exploration services   500
Coca-Cola Co.; Houston; frozen foods   500
Daniel Measurement Control Inc.; Houston; industrial
    gas meters   500
Greystar Corp.; Houston; gas field services   500
Harris County; Houston; child aid society   500
Neiman Marcus Group Inc.; Houston; department stores
    500
Netstaff Inc.; Houston; employee leasing service   500
PrimeCo Personal Communications; Houston; cellular
    telephones   500
Schlumberger Technology Corp.; Houston; meters:
    electric, panelboard   500
Talbert Hotel Corp.; Houston; hotel, motel management
    500
Van Kampen Asset Management Inc.; Houston; mutual
    funds   500

Texas 8th District

Part of Houston; northern Houston suburbs

Made up of northern Harris County and Houston's rapidly growing northern suburbs in Montgomery County, the 8th is a Republican bastion. In the past three major statewide elections—the 2002 gubernatorial and senatorial races and the 2000 presidential race—the 8th gave the GOP candidate more than 75 percent of the vote, each time topping every other district in the state in its support for the GOP. *(See map p. 869.)*

Redistricting following the 2000 census chopped the districts' land mass substantially, as a result of strong population growth in the 1990s. Portions removed included rural areas northeast of Houston and Texas A&M University. The district is now much more homogeneous, home to planned communities that house executives from the Houston Advanced Research Center and the region's many medical facilities.

About 60 percent of the district's residents live in Harris County, with the remainder in Montgomery. The Harris County portion of the district contains some of the Houston region's wealthiest areas, including Jersey Village, located just off the Northwest Freeway, and parts of northeastern Houston near Lake Houston.

The 8th's share of Montgomery includes The Woodlands, a large planned community in the county that gets its name from its proximity to Sam Houston National Forest. The Woodlands consists of several villages, each with its residential neighborhoods and local shops. The area has aggressively courted business, and several petroleum and biotechnology companies make their home here.

The timber industry and some cattle ranches populate the northern part of Montgomery County, though these areas are quickly becoming Houston suburbs. Montgomery County added 112,000 people and grew by 61 percent in the 1990s, a rate that was exceeded by just five of Texas's other 253 counties.

Major Industry
    Health care, education, retail.

Notable
    Texas's Lone Star flag was designed in Montgomery County in 1839.

Election Returns

	Republican		Democratic		Other	
President 2000	187,243	77.7%	53,843	22.3%		
House 2002	140,575	93.1%			10,351	6.9%

District Profile

Population   651,619

Total area (square miles)   1,192.5
    Land area (square miles)   1,146.0

Population per square mile   568.6

Counties (2000 population)
    Harris (pt.)   397,932
    Montgomery (pt.)   253,687

Cities and other areas over 10,000 (2000 population)
    Atascocita CDP (pt.)   18,234
    Conroe (pt.)   36,811
    Houston (pt.)   60,058
    Humble (pt.)   12,253
    Spring CDP   36,385
    The Woodlands CDP   55,649

Race and Hispanic or Latino origin*
    White   77.2%
    Black or African American   5.2%
    American Indian or Alaska Native   0.3%
    Asian   3.0%
    Native Hawaiian or other Pacific Islander   0.1%
    Some other race   0.1%
    Hispanic or Latino origin   13.0%
    Two or more races   1.2%

As percentage of total population.

Ancestry*

Dutch 1.1%	Italian 3.0%
English 8.6%	Polish 1.9%
French 3.3%	Scotch-Irish 1.8%
German 12.8%	Scottish 1.8%
Irish 9.0%	USA/American 7.2%

As estimated percentage of total population.

Newspapers and circulation

	District circulation	Total circulation
Houston Chronicle	76,857	548,437
Plano Star Courier	8,637	10,862
*USA Today**	4,323	1,674,376

See Sources and Explanations in the front of the volume.

Television stations and affiliations

Houston	100%	KAVU	ABC
Houston	100%	KBTX	CBS
Houston	100%	KETH	Independent
Houston	100%	KHOU	CBS

Houston	100%	KHWB	WB
Houston	100%	KLTJ	Independent
Houston	100%	KNWS	Independent
Houston	100%	KPRC	NBC
Houston	100%	KPXB	PAX
Houston	100%	KRIV	FOX
Houston	100%	KTBU	Independent
Houston	100%	KTMD	Telemundo
Houston	100%	KTRK	ABC
Houston	100%	KTXH	UPN
Houston	100%	KUHT	PBS
Houston	100%	KXLN	Univision
Houston	100%	KZJL	Independent Spanish

Cable systems and subscribers

Cequel III   18,432
Charter   5,138
Classic   4,505
Cox   10,415
Northland   1,240
Time Warner   6,800

Businesses and other major employers

Concord Insurance Services; Houston; insurance agents   16,000

Compaq Computer Corp.; Houston; personal computers   7,800

Global Knowledge; Humble; computer peripherals, software   1,600

Houston Northwest Medical Center Inc.; Houston   1,600

CB&I Constructors Inc.; Spring; structural steel erection   1,300

Russell-Stanley Corp.; Conroe; plastic pallets   1,300

Dillard's Inc.; Spring; department stores   1,200

Hewitt Associates; The Woodlands; management consulting   1,200

Reliant Energy Inc.; Houston; electricity, energy   1,200

Tomball Hospital Authority; Tomball   1,100

Conroe Hospital Corp.; Conroe   1,000

Woodlands Operating Co.; The Woodlands; subdividers, developers   1,000

Northeast Hospital Authority; Humble   850

RMH Teleservices Inc.; Humble; telemarketing   761

Chicago Bridge and Iron Co.; Houston; structural steel erection   700

North Harris Montgomery Community College District; Conroe   700

North Harris Montgomery Community College District; Kingwood   700

North Harris Montgomery Community College District; Tomball   700

Wal-Mart Stores Inc.; Conroe; department stores   700

New Caney Independent School District; New Caney   650

HCA Health Services of Texas Inc. Hospital; Kingwood   570

Stewart Builders; Houston; concrete work   560

Memorial Hermann Hospital System; The Woodlands   520

Champion Window Inc.; Houston; metal storm doors, windows   500

Cypress-Fairbanks Independent School District; Houston   500

National Sales Services Inc.; Houston; retail trade consultant   500

Wal-Mart Stores Inc.; Houston; department stores   500

Texas 9th District

Southeast — Beaumont, Galveston

From the suburbs east of Houston to the Gulf of Mexico, the 9th is oil country. Its largest cities, Beaumont, Galveston, and Port Arthur, are heavily involved in the production and distribution of petroleum products. When the bottom fell out of the industry in the 1980s, unemployment skyrocketed. Many of the district's towns lost population, though they slowly regained people throughout the 1990s. *(See map p. 869.)*

The 9th's large number of factory jobs makes it one of the few Texas districts where unions wield significant political power. But while the unions underpin the area's economically liberal outlook, residents also tend to be socially conservative. Republicans have attracted votes from Galveston and the "Golden Triangle"—the area bounded by Beaumont, Port Arthur, and Orange (in the 2nd District)—by appealing to voters' opposition to gun control. The district is politically competitive: the GOP has a slight edge in Galveston County and dominates the 9th's share of the Houston suburbs, while Democrats run well in Jefferson County, where there are large black populations in Beaumont and Port Arthur.

The sometimes marshy land between Houston and the coast does not yield many crops. Instead, it contains the National Aeronautics and Space Administration's Lyndon B. Johnson Space Center, refineries, and shipbuilding facilities. The 9th also relies on coastal industries, including ship repair and commercial fishing.

Although the 1980s oil bust hurt the 9th's economy, the rapid growth of the petrochemical industry in the 1990s helped the district. Shipbuilders rely on the government, as does the Space Center, located 20 miles southeast of Houston. A growing service sector near Galveston has helped diversify the economy. Galveston, with its nearby beaches, also has emerged as a tourist destination.

Major Industry

Petrochemicals, shipbuilding, health care.

Notable

Johnson Space Center serves as the lead NASA center for the International Space Station; Galveston is known for the devastating flood of 1900.

Election Returns

	Republican		Democratic		Other	
President 2000	124,758	55.3%	100,778	44.7%		
House 2002	59,635	40.3%	86,710	58.6%	1,613	1.1%

District Profile

Population   651,619

Total area (square miles)   3,022.5
  Land area (square miles)   2,059.2

Population per square mile   316.4

Counties (2000 population)

Chambers	26,031	Harris (pt.)	123,379
Galveston	250,158	Jefferson	252,051

Cities and other areas over 10,000 (2000 population)

Atascocita CDP (pt.)   17,523
Baytown (pt.)   23,379
Beaumont   113,866
Dickinson   17,093
Friendswood   29,037
Galveston   57,247
Groves   15,733
Houston (pt.)   27,358
La Marque   13,682
League City   45,444
Nederland   17,422
Port Arthur (pt.)   57,755
Port Neches   13,601
Texas City   41,521

Race and Hispanic or Latino origin*

White   60.1%
Black or African American   21.1%
American Indian or Alaska Native   0.3%
Asian   2.7%
Native Hawaiian or other Pacific Islander   0.0%
Some other race   0.1%
Hispanic or Latino origin   14.4%
Two or more races   1.1%

As percentage of total population.

Ancestry*

English	6.1%	Italian	2.6%
French	4.4%	Scotch-Irish	1.4%
German	8.4%	Scottish	1.1%
Irish	6.9%	USA/American	6.2%

As estimated percentage of total population.

Universities and colleges, 2000–2001 enrollment

College of the Mainland, Texas City   3,358
Galveston College, Galveston   2,255
ITT Technical Institute, Houston   389
Lamar University, Beaumont   11,550
Lamar University, Port Arthur   482
MTI College of Business and Technology, Houston   346
Texas A&M University-Galveston, Galveston   1,363
University of Houston-Clear Lake, Houston   7,580
University of Texas Medical Branch, Galveston   1,927

Newspapers and circulation

	District circulation	Total circulation
Beaumont Enterprise	32,777	54,940
Houston Chronicle	36,491	548,437
Port Arthur News	15,410	16,155
*USA Today**	3,460	1,674,376

See Sources and Explanations in the front of the volume.

Television stations and affiliations

Houston	63%	KAVU	ABC
Houston	63%	KBTX	CBS
Houston	63%	KETH	Independent
Houston	63%	KHOU	CBS
Houston	63%	KHWB	WB
Houston	63%	KLTJ	Independent
Houston	63%	KNWS	Independent
Houston	63%	KPRC	NBC
Houston	63%	KPXB	PAX
Houston	63%	KRIV	FOX
Houston	63%	KTBU	Independent
Houston	63%	KTMD	Telemundo
Houston	63%	KTRK	ABC
Houston	63%	KTXH	UPN
Houston	63%	KUHT	PBS
Houston	63%	KXLN	Univision
Houston	63%	KZJL	Independent Spanish
Beaumont-Port Arthur	37%	KBMT	ABC
Beaumont-Port Arthur	37%	KBTV	NBC
Beaumont-Port Arthur	37%	KFDM	CBS, UPN
Beaumont-Port Arthur	37%	KITU	Independent

Cable systems and subscribers

Classic   18,887
Timber Lake Cablevision   607
Time Warner   113,017

Businesses and other major employers

National Aeronautics and Space Admin.; Houston; space research, technology   17,000
University of Texas Medical Branch; Galveston   8,000
St. Elizabeth Hospital; Beaumont   3,000
Lockheed Martin Services Inc.; Houston; engineering services   2,800
BP Corp. North America Inc.; Texas City; petroleum refining   2,300
Memorial Hermann Hospital System; Houston   2,300
ExxonMobil Oil Corp.; Beaumont; petroleum refining   1,700
E. I. Du Pont De Nemours and Co.; Beaumont; synthetic rubber   1,500
University of Texas System; Galveston   1,494
U.S. Bureau of Prisons; Beaumont   1,300
American National Insurance Co.; Galveston; life insurance   1,200
CHRISTUS St. Mary Hospital; Port Arthur   1,100
Honeywell Technology Solutions Inc.; Houston; engineering services   1,100
International Business Machines Corp.; Houston; computer programming   1,100
Motiva Enterprises; Port Arthur; petroleum refining   1,100
Vinson and Elkins; Houston; law office   1,040
Texas Criminal Justice Dept.; Beaumont   903
HCS Holdings Inc.; Beaumont; medical equipment rental   900
Ameripol Synpol Corp.; Port Neches; synthetic rubber   850

Premcor Refining Group Inc.; Port Arthur; petroleum products   850

Baptist Hospital Inc.; Beaumont   800

Entergy Gulf States Inc.; Beaumont; electric power generation   800

Unisys Corp.; League City; consulting engineer   800

Gulf Greyhound Partners; La Marque; dog race track operation   763

Sanserve Building Service; Beaumont; janitorial service   750

Texas City Independent School District; Texas City   730

Clear Lake Regional Medical Center Inc.; Webster   700

Mainland Medical Center; La Marque   700

Danforth Hospital Inc.; Texas City   698

Chevron Phillips Chemical Co.; Baytown; polyethylene resins   650

Computer Sciences Corp.; Houston; computer software   650

Goodyear Tire and Rubber Co.; Beaumont; synthetic rubber   640

Beaumont Hospital Inc.; Beaumont   620

Brock Specialty Services; Beaumont; industrial chemicals   600

Helena Laboratories Corp.; Beaumont; optical instruments   600

International Maintenance Corp.; Nederland; industrial buildings renovation   600

Jefferson County; Beaumont; government   600

Newpark Shipbuilding; Galveston; shipbuilding, repairing   600

Tenet Healthcare Corp. Hospital; Port Arthur   600

Lamar University; Beaumont   576

Petrocon Engineering Inc.; Beaumont; engineering services   550

BP Amoco Chemical Co.; Texas City; petroleum refining   545

Amed Medical Inc.; Texas City; home health care   500

BP Corp. North America Inc.; Houston; warehouses   500

Burns International Security Services Corp.; Houston; security guard service   500

CHRISTUS St. John Hospital; Houston   500

Clear Creek Independent School District; Houston   500

Johnson Engineering Corp.; Webster; commercial physical research   500

Spindletop Mental Health Services; Beaumont; mental health clinic   500

Sterling Chemicals Holdings Inc.; Texas City; cyclic crudes   500

University of Houston System; Houston   500

Wal-Mart Stores Inc.; Galveston; department stores   500

Texas 10th District

Central — Austin

The once expansive rural district that Lyndon B. Johnson represented in the House in the 1940s has been shrinking in size and growing in population ever since he left. Today, the 10th is limited to Austin and eastern Travis County, where the population explosion has brought new inhabitants, many drawn to the area's burgeoning computer industry. The district takes in 80 percent of Travis County's residents (shared with the 21st), and about 85 percent of Austin's population.

Austin is a liberal Democratic island in the vast conservative Republican sea of the Lone Star State. A kind of Seattle for the South, Austin has been attracting music lovers and computer programmers in search of a hip, youthful place in a warm climate. State government workers and the University of Texas at Austin add to the city's liberal political bent, as does the 10th's sizable minority population (Hispanics and blacks, taken together, nearly equal whites).

The troubled oil industry of the mid-1980s did not permanently wound the 10th's economy, which was buoyed by its university and state government employers. In the 1990s, the area became a hub for high-tech startup firms, and its technology sector grew rapidly before hitting a small slump. Dell Computer is based in the town of Round Rock, shared with the 31st District. In 1999, the city opened a new municipal airport on the site of the former Bergstrom Air Force Base—Austin-Bergstrom International Airport. In 2000 *Money* magazine called Austin one of the nation's ten best places to live.

The fast-growing 10th was made more Democratic through redistricting following the 2000 census, which excised GOP precincts in western Travis. In 2002 Democrats Ron Kirk and Tony Sanchez won 64 percent and 57 percent of the district's vote in their races for senator and governor.

Major Industry
Software, technology, service, state government.

Notable
Austin's country music scene gets national exposure on the weekly public television show *Austin City Limits*; South by Southwest, a huge pop and rock music festival in Austin, is held each spring; Austin is home to North America's largest urban colony of Mexican free-tailed bats.

Election Returns

	Republican		Democratic		Other	
President 2000	89,738	46.9%	101,534	53.1%		
House 2002			114,428	84.4%	21,196	15.6%

District Profile

Population   651,619

Total area (square miles)   554.5
Land area (square miles)   549.9

Population per square mile   1,185.0

Counties (2000 population)
Travis (pt.)   651,619

Cities and other areas over 10,000 (2000 population)
Austin (pt.)   554,906
Pflugerville (pt.)   16,335
Wells Branch CDP   11,271

Race and Hispanic or Latino origin*
White   49.7%
Black or African American   10.9%
American Indian or Alaska Native   0.3%

Asian   4.3%
Native Hawaiian or other Pacific Islander   0.0%
Some other race   0.2%
Hispanic or Latino origin   33.0%
Two or more races   1.6%

As percentage of total population.

Ancestry*
English 6.5%	Polish 1.1%
French 2.1%	Scotch-Irish 1.8%
German 10.1%	Scottish 1.7%
Irish 6.6%	USA/American 3.4%
Italian 1.9%	

As estimated percentage of total population.

Universities and colleges, 2000–2001 enrollment
Austin Business College, Austin   461
Austin Community College, Austin   25,735
Austin Presbyterian Theological Seminary, Austin   291
Concordia University, Austin   795
Huston-Tillotson College, Austin   602
ITT Technical Institute, Austin   594
St. Edwards University, Austin   3,824
University of Texas, Austin   49,996

Newspapers and circulation
	District circulation	Total circulation
Austin American Statesman	84,989	186,020
Dallas Morning News	3,469	495,624
*USA Today**	2,990	1,674,376

See Sources and Explanations in the front of the volume.

Television stations and affiliations
Austin	100%	KAKW	Univision
Austin	100%	KEYE	CBS
Austin	100%	KLRU	PBS
Austin	100%	KNVA	WB
Austin	100%	KTBC	FOX
Austin	100%	KVUE	ABC
Austin	100%	KXAM	NBC
Austin	100%	KXAN	NBC

Cable systems and subscribers
Cox   5,414
Time Warner   155,151

Military installations, September 2001
Camp Mabry (Army Guard), Austin   2,081
Armed Forces Reserve Center, Austin   347

Businesses and other major employers
Fastenal Co.; Austin; manufacturing consultant   5,100
Seton Hospital; Austin   5,000
Austin Community College; Austin   3,669
Texas Dept. of Health; Austin   3,000
University of Texas Club; Austin   3,000
Texas Comptroller; Austin   2,760
Dell Computer Corp.; Round Rock   2,750
University of Texas System; Austin   2,500
Texas Natural Resource Conservation Commission; Austin   2,318
Solectron Texas; Austin; computers   2,300
Whole Foods Market Southwest Inc.; Austin; grocery store   2,199
Texas Attorney General; Austin   2,000
Texas Executive Office; Austin   2,000
Texas Legislative Office; Austin   1,997
Texas Dept. of Public Safety; Austin   1,973
Texas Workforce Commission; Austin   1,800
Nextel Communications Inc.; Austin; radiotelephone communication   1,700
Applied Materials Inc.; Austin; semiconductor manufacturing machinery   1,600
Texas Dept. of Transportation; Austin   1,500
Golfsmith International; Austin; fitness and sporting goods   1,300
U.S. Internal Revenue Service; Austin   1,300
Multek Multilayer Technology Inc.; Austin; printed circuit boards   1,200
Commemorative Brands Inc.; Austin; precious metal finger rings   1,100
Advanced Micro Devices Inc.; Austin; semiconductors   1,000
City of Austin; Austin; fire dept.   1,000
Cox Texas Publications Inc.; Austin; newspaper   1,000
Texas Child Support Division; Austin   1,000
Texas Dept. of Human Services; Austin   1,000
Travis County; Austin; county government   1,000
Travis County; Austin; sheriff's office   1,000
First Market Research Corp.; Austin; market analysis or research   985
Texas Mental Health and Mental Retardation Dept.; Austin   962
Samsung Austin Semiconductor; Austin; microprocessors   950
North Austin Medical Center; Austin   940
Cirrus Logic Inc.; Austin; computer microcircuits   910
City of Austin; Austin; recreation   900
Fisher-Rosemount Systems Inc.; Austin; relays, industrial controls   900
Michael Angelo's Gourmet Foods Inc.; Austin; frozen dinners   900
Texas Dept. of Parks and Wildlife; Austin   861
Texas Education Agency; Austin   844
Sell-Thru Services Inc.; Austin; food supplier   800
Texas Dept. of Insurance; Austin   800
Texas General Service Commission; Austin   800
Texas Workers' Compensation Commission; Austin   800
National Instruments Corp.; Austin; software   762
Autonation Inc.; Austin; car dealers   750
Compaq Computer Corp.; Austin; research services   700
Farmers Insurance Group of Companies; Austin; accident, health insurance   700
Foodservice Management System; Austin; restaurant management   700
Texas Mutual Insurance Co.; Austin   677
South Austin Medical Center Inc.; Austin   625
GSD&M; Austin; advertising   600
Lower Colorado River Authority; Austin   600
Outback Steakhouse of Florida Inc.; Austin; restaurants   600
Siemens Information and Communication Networks Inc.; Austin; electronic computers   600

Sulzer Orthopedics Inc.; Austin; heart-lung machine
600

Texas Commission for Blind; Austin   583

H. E. Butt Grocery Co.; Austin; grocery store   550

PPD Development Inc.; Austin; commercial physical
research   550

Xetel Corp.; Austin; printed circuit boards   535

Southwestern Bell Telephone Co.; Austin; telephone
communications   507

3M Co.; Austin; electronic test equipment   500

Arthritis Foundation; Austin; fund-raising organization
500

City of Austin; Austin; public health programs   500

Dresser Inc.; Austin; gas pumps   500

Dynamic Systems Inc.; Austin; mechanical contractor
500

Electronic Arts; Austin; home entertainment software
500

Janus Investment Fund; Austin; mutual fund sales   500

National Heritage Insurance Co.; Austin; medical
insurance claim processing   500

Railroad Commission of Texas; Austin   500

Texas Dept. of Agriculture; Austin; agricultural
marketing regulation   500

Travis County; Austin; probation office   500

TXU US Holdings Co.; Austin; electrical work   500

U.S. Security Associates Inc.; Austin; security guard
service   500

URS Group Inc.; Austin; engineering services   500

Texas 11th District

Central — Waco

The 11th is home to President George W. Bush's ranch, located in Crawford. The ranch has given the area a new level of recognition and has contributed to small boosts in the economy whenever Bush—and his many media followers—traveled here from the White House.

Bush's attachment to the area and the district's Republican lean make it a GOP target in most every cycle. But the Democratic incumbent has won the seat seven times, as the district is populated with conservative "Yellow Dog" Democrats and ticket splitters. Voters here embrace longevity in their House members—in 66 years, the district has had just three representatives.

Redistricting following the 2000 census made the 11th slightly more Republican-leaning. The addition of parts of Williamson County, which contains fast-growing suburbs of Austin, probably will quicken the district's GOP trend. Bush received 67.5 percent of the two-party vote here in 2000, and Republican governor Rick Perry took 66 percent in 2002.

About 70 percent of the district population comes out of Bell and McLennan Counties. Waco, in McLennan County, is the district's most populous city and is the largest marketing center between Austin and Dallas. Fort Hood, the 11th's massive military base in Bell and Coryell Counties, is an economic mainstay that has yet to be substantially affected by defense cutbacks. It has drawn many retired veterans who come to the 11th for its mild climate and the veterans' medical centers.

Major Industry
Military, agriculture, light manufacturing.

Notable
Ranger Museum in Waco includes Billy the Kid's rifle and guns; in 1993, a complex outside Waco known as Ranch Apocalypse was the scene of a deadly standoff between federal agents and members of the Branch Davidian religious group.

Election Returns

	Republican		Democratic		Other	
President 2000	129,701	67.5%	62,465	32.5%		
House 2002	68,236	47.1%	74,678	51.6%	1,943	1.3%

District Profile

Population   651,620

Total area (square miles)   9,074.2
Land area (square miles)   8,993.3

Population per square mile   72.5

Counties (2000 population)

Bell 237,974	McLennan (pt.) 211,892
Bosque 17,204	Milam 24,238
Coryell 74,978	Mills 5,151
Hamilton 8,229	San Saba 6,186
Lampasas 17,762	Williamson (pt.) 48,006

Cities and other areas over 10,000 (2000 population)

Belton 14,623	Harker Heights 17,308
Copperas Cove 29,592	Hewitt 11,085
Fort Hood CDP 33,711	Killeen 86,911
Gatesville 15,591	Temple 54,514
Georgetown (pt.) 24,005	Waco 113,726

Race and Hispanic or Latino origin*
White   64.2%
Black or African American   15.4%
American Indian or Alaska Native   0.4%
Asian   1.5%
Native Hawaiian or other Pacific Islander   0.2%
Some other race   0.1%
Hispanic or Latino origin   16.4%
Two or more races   1.7%

As percentage of total population.

Ancestry*

English 6.3%	Italian 1.4%
French 1.8%	Scotch-Irish 1.6%
German 11.4%	Scottish 1.4%
Irish 7.1%	USA/American 7.1%

As estimated percentage of total population.

Universities and colleges, 2000–2001 enrollment
Baylor University, Waco   13,719
Central Texas College, Killeen   14,636
McLennan Community College, Waco   5,731
Southwestern University, Georgetown   1,309
Temple College, Temple   3,404
Texas State Technical College, Waco   3,814
University of Central Texas, Killeen   1,117
University of Mary Hardin Baylor, Belton   2,590

Newspapers and circulation

	District circulation	Total circulation
Austin American Statesman	11,759	186,020
Dallas Morning News	5,825	495,624
Killeen Daily Herald	18,378	18,443
Temple Daily Telegram	21,205	21,701
*USA Today**	1,759	1,674,376
Waco Tribune-Herald	35,776	40,354

See Sources and Explanations in the front of the volume.

Television stations and affiliations

Waco-Temple-Bryan	75%	KAMU	PBS
Waco-Temple-Bryan	75%	KCEN	NBC
Waco-Temple-Bryan	75%	KNCT	PBS
Waco-Temple-Bryan	75%	KWKT	FOX,WB
Waco-Temple-Bryan	75%	KWTX	CBS
Waco-Temple-Bryan	75%	KXXV	ABC
Waco-Temple-Bryan	75%	KYLE	FOX,WB
Dallas-Fort Worth	20%	KDAF	WB
Dallas-Fort Worth	20%	KDFI	Independent
Dallas-Fort Worth	20%	KDFW	FOX
Dallas-Fort Worth	20%	KDTN	PBS
Dallas-Fort Worth	20%	KDTX	Independent
Dallas-Fort Worth	20%	KERA	PBS
Dallas-Fort Worth	20%	KFWD	Independent
Dallas-Fort Worth	20%	KMPX	Independent
Dallas-Fort Worth	20%	KPXD	PAX
Dallas-Fort Worth	20%	KSTR	Telefutura
Dallas-Fort Worth	20%	KTAQ	Independent
Dallas-Fort Worth	20%	KTVT	CBS
Dallas-Fort Worth	20%	KTXA	UPN
Dallas-Fort Worth	20%	KUVN	Univision
Dallas-Fort Worth	20%	KXAS	NBC
Dallas-Fort Worth	20%	KXTX	Telemundo
Dallas-Fort Worth	20%	WFAA	ABC
Austin	5%	KAKW	Univision
Austin	5%	KEYE	CBS
Austin	5%	KLRU	PBS
Austin	5%	KNVA	WB
Austin	5%	KTBC	FOX
Austin	5%	KVUE	ABC
Austin	5%	KXAM	NBC
Austin	5%	KXAN	NBC

Cable systems and subscribers

Centrovision 1,265
Charter 1,883
Classic 6,726
Cox 9,334
Galaxy 2,730
Northland 1,590
Time Warner 117,748

Military installations, September 2001

Fort Hood (Army), Killeen 50,229
Temple National Guard, Temple 372

Businesses and other major employers

Scott and White Memorial Hospital; Temple 5,600
Killeen Independent School District; Killeen 5,000
Crompton Technology Group; Waco; computer consulting services 4,000
Hillcrest Baptist Medical Center; Waco 2,018
L-3 Communications Corp.; Waco; search/navigation equipment 2,000
U.S. Veterans Hospital; Temple 2,000
Raytheon E-Systems Inc.; Waco; guidance systems 1,700
Texas Criminal Justice Dept.; Gatesville 1,672
Alcoa Inc.; Rockdale; aluminum smelting, refining 1,500
U.S. Veterans Hospital; Waco 1,425
Wilsonart International Inc.; Temple; plastic materials, resins 1,400
Cargill Inc.; Waco; turkeys, turkey eggs 1,300
Wal-Mart Stores Inc.; Waco; department stores 1,300
Central Texas College; Killeen 1,200
Providence Health Services of Waco; Waco; hospital 1,187
Baylor University; Waco 1,170
Mars Inc.; Waco; confectionery products 1,000
McLane Co.; Temple; department stores 878
Mobil Chemical Co.; Temple; plastic products 800
Willis Shaw Express Inc.; Waco; refrigerated transport 800
Metroplex Adventist Hospital; Killeen 750
United Steelworkers of America International Union; Rockdale; labor organization 750
Williamson County; Georgetown; county government 700
Sallie Mae Servicing Corp.; Killeen; student loans 683
Austin Diagnostic Clinic Assn.; Georgetown 650
McLennan County Junior College District; Waco 592
Texas State Technical College; Waco 586
McLennan County; Waco; correctional facilities 509
West Telemarketing Corp.; Killeen; telemarketing 505
Allergan Inc.; Waco; pharmaceuticals 500
MPS Group Inc.; Killeen; help supply services 500
Sikorsky Aircraft Corp.; Fort Hood; aircraft engines, parts 500
Southern Farm Bureau Casualty Insurance Co.; Waco; property, casualty insurance 500
Texas Dept. of Veterans Affairs; Waco 500
Wal-Mart Stores Inc.; Temple; department stores 500

Texas 12th District

Part of Fort Worth and suburbs; Parker County

The Republican-leaning 12th includes much of Tarrant County, including a large segment of Fort Worth, and all of rural Parker County. The mostly white, middle-class district contains downtown Fort Worth but also takes in a mix of suburban and rural areas. *(See map p. 862.)*

The 12th's solid economy is built around transportation. Three major airports, an Air Force base, three railroad lines, and several interstate highways are in or adjacent to the district, supporting myriad businesses. The Union Pacific and now-combined Burlington Northern Santa Fe railroads both are active in the district, but the air industry has far surpassed rail. Large government defense contracts—including those from Lockheed Martin, which has a facility in the district—have helped create jobs and fuel economic growth.

Parker County includes Weatherford, which is becoming more Republican as it undergoes a transition from a rural town into part of Fort Worth's suburbs. Though Parker County covers more than half the district's land mass, it only contains 14 percent of the district's voters.

Redistricting following the 2000 census changed the 12th from a politically competitive district to one dominated by Republicans. Mapmakers gave the neighboring 24th Democratic areas south of downtown Fort Worth. The 12th still includes some Democratic areas downtown, but the parts of Tarrant outside the city are overwhelmingly Republican, as is Parker County. Had the redrawn 12th existed in the 2000 presidential election, George W. Bush would have won two-thirds of the vote.

Major Industry

Defense technology, transportation, medicine.

Notable

The National Cowgirl Museum in Fort Worth showcases women rodeo riders and contributors to Western heritage; Cowtown Coliseum, in the historic Stockyards district of Fort Worth, was the site of the world's first indoor rodeo and the world's first live radio broadcast of a rodeo.

Election Returns

	Republican		Democratic		Other	
President 2000	141,032	66.6%	70,751	33.4%		
House 2002	121,208	91.9%			10,723	8.1%

District Profile

Population   651,619

Total area (square miles)   1,362.6
Land area (square miles)   1,331.5

Population per square mile   489.4

Counties (2000 population)
Parker   88,495
Tarrant (pt.)   563,124

Cities and other areas over 10,000 (2000 population)
Benbrook   20,208
Fort Worth (pt.)   270,210
Haltom City (pt.)   39,002
Hurst (pt.)   31,336
Keller (pt.)   23,689
North Richland Hills (pt.)   55,634
Saginaw   12,374
Watauga   21,908
Weatherford   19,000
White Settlement   14,831

Race and Hispanic or Latino origin*
White   71.4%
Black or African American   4.5%
American Indian or Alaska Native   0.5%
Asian   2.3%
Native Hawaiian or other Pacific Islander   0.1%
Some other race   0.1%
Hispanic or Latino origin   19.9%
Two or more races   1.3%

*As percentage of total population.

Ancestry*

Dutch	1.2%	Italian	1.6%
English	7.8%	Scotch-Irish	1.7%
French	2.0%	Scottish	1.5%
German	9.4%	USA/American	9.0%
Irish	8.1%		

*As estimated percentage of total population.

Universities and colleges, 2000–2001 enrollment
Southwestern Baptist Theological Seminary, Fort Worth   3,149
Tarrant County Junior College, Fort Worth   26,868
Texas Christian University, Fort Worth   7,775
University of North Texas-Health Science Center, Fort Worth   729
Weatherford College, Weatherford   2,788

Newspapers and circulation

	District circulation	Total circulation
Dallas Morning News	9,492	495,624
Fort Worth Star-Telegram	85,332	224,885
*USA Today**	2,705	1,674,376

*See Sources and Explanations in the front of the volume.

Television stations and affiliations

Dallas-Fort Worth	100%	KDAF	WB
Dallas-Fort Worth	100%	KDFI	Independent
Dallas-Fort Worth	100%	KDFW	FOX
Dallas-Fort Worth	100%	KDTN	PBS
Dallas-Fort Worth	100%	KDTX	Independent
Dallas-Fort Worth	100%	KERA	PBS
Dallas-Fort Worth	100%	KFWD	Independent
Dallas-Fort Worth	100%	KMPX	Independent
Dallas-Fort Worth	100%	KPXD	PAX
Dallas-Fort Worth	100%	KSTR	Telefutura
Dallas-Fort Worth	100%	KTAQ	Independent
Dallas-Fort Worth	100%	KTVT	CBS
Dallas-Fort Worth	100%	KTXA	UPN
Dallas-Fort Worth	100%	KUVN	Univision
Dallas-Fort Worth	100%	KXAS	NBC
Dallas-Fort Worth	100%	KXTX	Telemundo
Dallas-Fort Worth	100%	WFAA	ABC

Cable systems and subscribers
Charter   30,647
Classic   691
Comcast   13,921
Mallard   1,067
Southtel   1,955

Military installations, September 2001
Saginaw National Guard, Saginaw   125
Fort Wolters National Guard, Mineral Wells   104

Businesses and other major employers
Lockheed Martin Corp.; Fort Worth; aircraft   10,000
Fort Worth Independent School District; Fort Worth   7,000
Bell Helicopter Textron Inc.; Hurst; helicopters   6,500
American Airlines Inc.; Fort Worth   4,200
U.S. Postal Service; Fort Worth   4,000
University of Texas; Fort Worth   4,000

Nokia; Fort Worth; cellular telephone   2,620

Texas Pacific Group Inc.; Fort Worth; venture capital
2,419

RadioShack Corp.; Fort Worth; electronic stores   2,300

Baylor All Saints Medical Centers; Fort Worth   2,200

Sprint Spectrum; Fort Worth; telephone communication
2,000

Kimberly-Clark Corp.; Fort Worth; medical supplies
1,870

United Parcel Service Inc.; Fort Worth; package delivery
1,850

Burlington Northern and Santa Fe Railway Co.; Fort
Worth; freight hauling   1,800

Computer Sciences Corp.; Fort Worth; computer systems
design   1,600

U.S. Army Corps of Engineers; Fort Worth   1,591

Harris Methodist Hospital; Fort Worth   1,537

University of North Texas Health Center; Fort Worth
1,400

Motorola Inc.; Fort Worth; communications equipment
1,200

Cook Children's Medical Center; Fort Worth   1,169

Texas Christian University Inc.; Fort Worth   1,100

Columbia Plaza Medical Center; Fort Worth   1,000

DynCorp International; Fort Worth; administrative
management   1,000

U.S. Federal Aviation Admin.; Fort Worth   1,000

City of Fort Worth; Fort Worth; city government   950

Smith Temporaries Inc.; Fort Worth; employment
agency   947

APAC Customer Services Inc.; Fort Worth;
telemarketing   800

City of Fort Worth; Fort Worth; fire dept.   800

UICI Insurance; Fort Worth; insurance agents   800

Southwestern Baptist Theological Seminary; Fort Worth
785

First State Bank of Texas; Denton; state commercial
banks   779

Pier 1 Imports Inc.; Fort Worth; home furnishings   750

Texas Dept. of Transportation; Fort Worth   750

Fort Worth Osteopathic Hospital Inc.; Fort Worth   700

Star-Telegram Operating; Fort Worth; newspaper   700

U.S. Treasury Dept.; Fort Worth   650

Carter and Burgess Inc.; Fort Worth; engineering
services   622

Southwestern Bell Telephone Co.; Fort Worth; telephone
communication   617

Bimar Foods Corp.; Fort Worth; bakery products   600

Tarrant County Junior College District; Fort Worth
589

Haggar Clothing Co.; Fort Worth; trousers, slacks   570

Aftermarket Technology Corp.; Fort Worth; automotive
supplies   550

Wal-Mart Stores Inc.; Fort Worth; department stores
525

AmeriCredit Financial Service Inc.; Fort Worth;
automobile loans   500

AT&T Wireless Services Inc.; Fort Worth;
radiotelephone communication   500

Coca-Cola Co.; Fort Worth; soft drinks   500

Dillard's Inc.; Fort Worth; department stores   500

Texas-New Mexico Power Co.; Fort Worth; electric
power generation   500

Texas 13th District

Panhandle — Amarillo; Wichita Falls

The conservative 13th takes in almost all of the Texas Panhandle, including the city of Amarillo, then extends east along the southern Oklahoma border to include the South Plains and much of the Red River Valley. It contains Wichita Falls and reaches as far east as Montague County, about 60 miles northwest of Fort Worth and Dallas. A monstrous and mainly rural district, the 13th takes in all or part of 43 counties, 39 of which have a population of under 25,000.

Oil and cotton dominate the district's economy, and both industries suffered during the 1980s and early 1990s as oil prices dropped and droughts starved the land. Thanks to other industries, the main cities weathered the difficulties. In Amarillo, Pantex is the nation's only nuclear weapons assembly and disassembly plant. The city also has a hand in producing the military's V-22 Osprey, which takes off like a helicopter but flies like a plane. After several crashes during testing, the aircraft's future is uncertain.

In Wichita Falls, factories are numerous, but the jewel of the economy is Sheppard Air Force Base, which so far has escaped downsizing. Many of the district's rural counties depend on the Ogallala Aquifer to grow wheat, sorghum, sugar beets, corn, and hay.

The 13th is one of the most Republican districts in Texas. The GOP does especially well in many of the rural small towns that dot the district, particularly around Amarillo. Ochiltree County, a Panhandle county on the Oklahoma border, gave 91 percent to George W. Bush in the 2000 presidential election. Closer to blue-collar Wichita Falls, voters have traditionally favored Democrats at the local level, but even this area votes solidly Republican in state and national elections. In 2002, the 13th gave Republican governor Rick Perry 71 percent of the vote.

Major Industry

Agriculture, oil, defense.

Notable

A stretch of Route 66, made famous by songs and television, cuts through the 13th.

Election Returns

	Republican		Democratic		Other
President 2000	156,330	74.6%	53,146	25.4%	
House 2002	119,401	79.3%	31,218	20.7%	

District Profile

Population   651,619

Total area (square miles)   39,620.5
   Land area (square miles)   39,461.8

Population per square mile   16.5

Counties (2000 population)

Archer	8,854	Hardeman	4,724
Armstrong	2,148	Hartley	5,537
Baylor	4,093	Hemphill	3,351
Briscoe	1,790	Hutchinson	23,857
Carson	6,516	King	356
Castro	8,285	Knox	4,253
Childress	7,688	Lamb (pt.)	528
Clay	11,006	Lipscomb	3,057
Collingsworth	3,206	Montague	19,117
Cottle	1,904	Moore	20,121
Crosby	7,072	Motley	1,426
Dallam	6,222	Ochiltree	9,006
Deaf Smith	18,561	Oldham	2,185
Dickens	2,762	Potter	113,546
Donley	3,828	Randall	104,312
Floyd	7,771	Roberts	887
Foard	1,622	Sherman	3,186
Garza (pt.)	343	Swisher	8,378
Gray	22,744	Wheeler	5,284
Hale	36,602	Wichita	131,664
Hall	3,782	Wilbarger	14,676
Hansford	5,369		

Cities and other areas over 10,000 (2000 population)

Amarillo	173,627	Hereford	14,597
Borger	14,302	Pampa	17,887
Burkburnett	10,927	Plainview	22,336
Canyon	12,875	Vernon	11,660
Dumas	13,747	Wichita Falls	104,197

Race and Hispanic or Latino origin*

White 70.0%
Black or African American 5.6%
American Indian or Alaska Native 0.6%
Asian 1.1%
Native Hawaiian or other Pacific Islander 0.0%
Some other race 0.1%
Hispanic or Latino origin 21.6%
Two or more races 1.1%

*As percentage of total population.

Ancestry*

Dutch	1.3%	Irish	7.3%
English	6.8%	Scotch-Irish	1.6%
French	1.5%	Scottish	1.2%
German	9.0%	USA/American	10.2%

*As estimated percentage of total population.

Universities and colleges, 2000–2001 enrollment

Amarillo College, Amarillo 8,422
Clarendon College, Clarendon 999
Frank Phillips College, Borger 1,155
Midwestern State University, Wichita Falls 5,809
Vernon Regional Junior College, Vernon 2,095
Wayland Baptist University, Plainview 5,093
West Texas A&M University, Canyon 6,775

Newspapers and circulation

	District circulation	Total circulation
Amarillo Globe-News	49,801	51,596
Dallas Morning News	4,061	495,624
Lubbock Avalanche Journal	5,020	54,669
*USA Today**	1,008	1,674,376
Wichita Falls Times-Record News	31,362	34,182

*See Sources and Explanations in the front of the volume.

Television stations and affiliations

Amarillo	65%	KACV	PBS
Amarillo	65%	KAMR	NBC
Amarillo	65%	KCIT	FOX
Amarillo	65%	KFDA	CBS
Amarillo	65%	KVIH	ABC
Amarillo	65%	KVII	ABC
Wichita Falls-Lawton	20%	KAUZ	CBS
Wichita Falls-Lawton	20%	KFDX	NBC
Wichita Falls-Lawton	20%	KJTL	FOX
Wichita Falls-Lawton	20%	KSWO	ABC
Lubbock	13%	KAMC	ABC
Lubbock	13%	KCBD	NBC
Lubbock	13%	KJTV	FOX
Lubbock	13%	KLBK	CBS
Lubbock	13%	KPTB	Independent
Lubbock	13%	KTXT	PBS
Abilene-Sweetwater	2%	KPCB	Independent
Abilene-Sweetwater	2%	KRBC	NBC
Abilene-Sweetwater	2%	KTAB	CBS
Abilene-Sweetwater	2%	KTXS	ABC

Cable systems and subscribers

Cable ONE 19,322
Charter 726
Classic 34,078
Communicomm 4,156
Cox 58,931
Hereford Cablevision 4,043
High Plains Cablevision 958
Time Warner 27,079

Military installations, September 2001

Sheppard Air Force Base, Wichita Falls 4,803

Businesses and other major employers

Baptist St. Anthony's Hospital Corp.; Amarillo 3,400
Mason and Hanger Corp.; Amarillo; ammunition 3,000
ConAgra Wet Blue; Cactus; leather tanning, finishing 2,400
BWXT Pantex LLC; Amarillo; ammunition 2,300
Burlington Northern and Santa Fe Railway Co.; Amarillo; freight hauling 2,000
City of Amarillo; Amarillo; city government 2,000
Wichita Falls General Hospital; Wichita Falls 2,000
Northwest Texas Hospital; Amarillo 1,720
Excel Corp.; Plainview; meats, meat products 1,700
Pavilion Counseling Center Hospital; Amarillo 1,500
Texas Mental Health and Mental Retardation Dept.; Wichita Falls 1,283
Southwestern Public Service Co.; Amarillo; electric power generation 1,200
XCEL Energy Inc.; Amarillo; electric services 1,200
Texas Mental Health and Mental Retardation Dept.; Vernon 1,161
Texas Criminal Justice Dept.; Amarillo 1,105
Certainteed Corp.; Wichita Falls; fiberglass building materials 1,100

Wal-Mart Stores Inc.; Amarillo; department stores
1,100

Howmet Corp.; Wichita Falls; aerospace castings   1,050

St. Gobain Vetrotex America Inc.; Wichita Falls; glass,
fiberglass fabrics   1,000

Texas Tech University Health Sciences Center; Amarillo
1,000

Phillips Petroleum Co.; Borger; aromatic chemical
products   950

Affiliated Foods Inc.; Amarillo; food supplier   917

Amarillo Junior College District Inc.; Amarillo   910

Chevron Phillips Chemical Co.; Borger; commercial
research lab   890

Bankers National Life Insurance Co.; Amarillo   771

Plainview Independent School District; Plainview   750

West Texas A&M University; Canyon   700

U.S. Veterans Hospital; Amarillo   650

Owens Corning; Amarillo; fiberglass insulation   600

ASARCO Inc.; Amarillo; copper smelting, refining
576

Wal-Mart Stores Inc.; Wichita Falls; variety stores   550

Work Services Corp.; Wichita Falls; sheltered workshop
526

Clinics of North Texas; Wichita Falls; medical offices
500

Delphi Corp.; Wichita Falls; chemical analyzers   500

Infinium Software Inc.; Amarillo; computer
programming   500

Stanley Works Inc.; Wichita Falls; power-driven
handtools   500

Texas 14th District

Southeast — Victoria, San Marcos

Spanning a roughly 15,000-square-mile area framed on the outside by San Antonio, Austin, Houston, and Corpus Christi, the 14th takes in a stretch of coastal land from near Galveston to Rockport. Inland, it stretches to eastern San Antonio and southern Austin suburbs. Redistricting after the 2000 census moved the district slightly westward, away from Houston and toward San Antonio.

Despite some suburban areas, the district is overwhelmingly coastal and agricultural. Only two cities in the district, Victoria and San Marcos, have more than 25,000 people, and nearly 80 percent of residents are native-born Texans.

Chemical companies, such as Dow, have facilities near the Gulf Coast, where they rode the 1980s oil glut to success by making antifreeze and other products. Victoria is a leading oil and chemical center. Mingled with the chemical producers on the coast are fishermen who haul in boatloads of shrimp.

Farmers in the 14th's interior grow rice, grain, and sorghum, while the northwest reaches of the district benefit from Austin's health care and government sectors. The district also holds attraction for nature lovers, who can visit Goose Island State Park, the Aransas National Wildlife Refuge, and several bird sanctuaries.

Dominated by farms and petrochemical plants, the 14th leans Republican but has Democratic roots and a sizable minority population. Roughly one-third of residents are of Hispanic origin. The 14th tends to elect Republicans, but not by the overwhelming margins the more solidly Republican sub-urban Houston districts rack up. Locally, Republicans tend to do very well in the southern portions of the 14th, while the areas around Austin have taken on some of that city's more liberal leanings.

Major Industry

Petrochemicals, agriculture, shrimping.

Notable

Stephen F. Austin, Texas's founder, was from Jones Creek, near the city of Freeport; West Columbia was chosen by the founders of the Republic of Texas to be the fledgling nation's first capital.

Election Returns

	Republican		Democratic		Other
President 2000	136,460	65.6%	71,434	34.4%	
House 2002	102,905	68.1%	48,224	31.9%	

District Profile

Population   651,620

Total area (square miles)   16,067.2
Land area (square miles)   14,458.2

Population per square mile   45.1

Counties (2000 population)

Aransas 22,497	Hays (pt.) 57,278
Bastrop (pt.) 32,382	Jackson 14,391
Brazoria (pt.) 64,248	Karnes 15,446
Caldwell 32,194	Lavaca 19,210
Calhoun 20,647	Matagorda 37,957
Colorado 20,390	Refugio 7,828
DeWitt 20,013	Victoria 84,088
Fayette 21,804	Wharton 41,188
Gonzales 18,628	Wilson 32,408
Guadalupe 89,023	

Cities and other areas over 10,000 (2000 population)

Bay City 18,667	Port Lavaca 12,035
Clute (pt.) 10,422	San Marcos (pt.) 34,733
El Campo 10,945	Schertz (pt.) 17,333
Freeport (pt.) 12,517	Seguin 22,011
Lockhart 11,615	Victoria 60,603

Race and Hispanic or Latino origin*

White   58.2%
Black or African American   7.7%
American Indian or Alaska Native   0.3%
Asian   0.8%
Native Hawaiian or other Pacific Islander   0.0%
Some other race   0.1%
Hispanic or Latino origin   32.0%
Two or more races   0.9%

As percentage of total population.

Ancestry*

English 5.3%	Italian 1.1%
French 1.8%	Polish 1.6%
German 14.1%	Scotch-Irish 1.4%
Irish 6.2%	USA/American 5.0%

As estimated percentage of total population.

Universities and colleges, 2000–2001 enrollment

Brazosport College, Lake Jackson   3,855
Southwest Texas State University, San Marcos   22,423
Texas Lutheran University, Seguin   1,460
University of Houston, Victoria   1,698
Victoria College, Victoria   4,022
Wharton County Junior College, Wharton   4,571

Newspapers and circulation

	District circulation	Total circulation
Austin American Statesman	9,490	186,020
Clute Facts	7,260	16,682
Houston Chronicle	8,256	548,437
New Braunfels Herald-Zeitung	3,090	7,573
San Antonio Express-News	12,485	216,752
Victoria Advocate	37,389	38,822

Television stations and affiliations

Houston	40%	KAVU	ABC
Houston	40%	KBTX	CBS
Houston	40%	KETH	Independent
Houston	40%	KHOU	CBS
Houston	40%	KHWB	WB
Houston	40%	KLTJ	Independent
Houston	40%	KNWS	Independent
Houston	40%	KPRC	NBC
Houston	40%	KPXB	PAX
Houston	40%	KRIV	FOX
Houston	40%	KTBU	Independent
Houston	40%	KTMD	Telemundo
Houston	40%	KTRK	ABC
Houston	40%	KTXH	UPN
Houston	40%	KUHT	PBS
Houston	40%	KXLN	Univision
Houston	40%	KZJL	Independent Spanish
San Antonio	32%	KABB	FOX
San Antonio	32%	KENS	CBS
San Antonio	32%	KHCE	Independent
San Antonio	32%	KLRN	PBS
San Antonio	32%	KRRT	WB
San Antonio	32%	KSAT	ABC
San Antonio	32%	KTRG	Independent Spanish
San Antonio	32%	KVAW	Independent Spanish
San Antonio	32%	KVDA	Telemundo
San Antonio	32%	KWEX	Univision
Austin	14%	KAKW	Univision
Austin	14%	KEYE	CBS
Austin	14%	KLRU	PBS
Austin	14%	KNVA	WB
Austin	14%	KTBC	FOX
Austin	14%	KVUE	ABC
Austin	14%	KXAM	NBC
Austin	14%	KXAN	NBC
Corpus Christi	8%	KEDT	PBS
Corpus Christi	8%	KIII	ABC
Corpus Christi	8%	KORO	Univision
Corpus Christi	8%	KRIS	NBC
Corpus Christi	8%	KZTV	CBS
Victoria	6%	KVCT	FOX

Cable systems and subscribers

Cable ONE   4,618
Charter   10,162
Classic   10,704
CMA   4,793
Cox   19,664
Mid Coast Cable   6,661
National Cable   1,170
Northland   6,208
Time Warner   43,844

Businesses and other major employers

Southwest Texas State University; San Marcos   2,049
Donna School District; Donna   2,000
Reliant Energy Inc.; Wadsworth; electric services   1,898
Inteplast Group; Lolita; plastic film and sheets   1,800
U.S. Contractors; Clute; plant, refinery construction   1,800
Kaspar Wire Works Inc.; Shiner; merchandise display/storage racks   1,750
Motorola Inc.; Seguin; radio/TV communications equipment   1,500
South Texas Project Electric Generating Station; Wadsworth; electric services   1,250
America Buckhead Corp.; Wharton; hotels and motels   1,200
E. I. Du Pont De Nemours and Co.; Victoria; inorganic chemicals   1,200
Phillips Petroleum Co.; Old Ocean; petroleum refining   1,200
Citizens Medical Center; Victoria   1,195
Alcoa Inc.; Point Comfort; primary aluminum   1,000
Edward D. Jones and Co.; Edna; security brokers   999
Structural Metals Inc.; Seguin; blast furnaces, steel mills   810
TIC-Industrial Co.; San Marcos; industrial buildings, warehouses   800
Tyson Foods Inc.; Seguin; poultry   800
Texas Criminal Justice Dept.; Kenedy   790
GS Group Inc.; Clute; mechanical contractor   700
Plains Cotton Cooperative Assn.; New Braunfels; cotton merchants   700
Victoria Hospital Corp.; Victoria   700
Guadalupe Valley Hospital; Seguin   690
Benchmark Electronics Inc.; Angleton; printed circuit boards   550
Management and Training Corp.; San Marcos; job training   550
Alstom Power Inc.; San Marcos; engineering services   533
Central Texas Medical Center; San Marcos   500
H. E. Butt Grocery Co.; San Marcos; warehousing   500
Tandy Brands Accessories Inc.; Yoakum; men's/boy's clothing   500
Texas Cable Partners; Lockhart; cable TV   500
Thermon Industries Inc.; San Marcos; wiring services   500

Texas 15th District

South — most of Hidalgo County, McAllen

Situated in southern Texas, the convoluted boundaries of the 15th take in the agricultural and cattle areas north of Corpus Christi and then dip down to the Texas-Mexico border. The 15th has a 78.3 percent Hispanic population, making it the most heavily Hispanic district in the nation. The large minority influence contributes to the district's overall Democratic lean.

The 15th also is one of the poorest districts in the nation. Community leaders struggle to bring jobs to the region and to provide job training. Hidalgo County, an agricultural area, is the most populous and fastest-growing in the district. Along the U.S.-Mexico border *maquiladoras*—assembly or manufacturing plants that use low-cost labor and import many parts from the United States—are the mainstay. The economy is on the rise since the passage of the North American Free Trade Agreement, and trade with Mexican border cities, such as Reynosa, also adds jobs.

Transportation is an issue—the region is said to be the largest populated area that does not have easy access to an interstate highway. Plans are in the works to build a new interstate called I-69 that would connect South Texas to Indianapolis.

The 15th's congressional seat has never been held by a Republican. While Republicans became more competitive in the 1990s, Democrats continue to dominate. George W. Bush took just 45.5 percent of the two-party vote in the 2000 presidential election, even as he swept the state with 59 percent. Democrats Ron Kirk and Tony Sanchez took more than 60 percent of the two-party vote in their 2002 races for senator and governor.

Major Industry
Small business, trade, manufacturing.

Notable
In 1836 Colonel James Walker Fannin of the Texas independence movement was executed with members of his troop in what was known as the "Goliad Massacre."

Election Returns

	Republican		Democratic		Other
President 2000	63,495	45.5%	76,161	54.5%	
House 2002			66,311	100.0%	

District Profile

Population 651,619

Total area (square miles) 6,435.0
  Land area (square miles) 6,355.8

Population per square mile 102.5

Counties (2000 population)

Bee	32,359	Kleberg (pt.)	28,163
Brooks	7,976	Live Oak	12,309
Goliad	6,928	Nueces (pt.)	21,135
Hidalgo (pt.)	475,611	San Patricio	67,138

Cities and other areas over 10,000 (2000 population)

Alamo	14,760	Mercedes	13,649
Beeville	13,129	Mission (pt.)	32,037
Donna	14,768	Pharr	46,660
Edinburg	48,465	Portland (pt.)	14,827
Kingsville (pt.)	25,494	San Juan	26,229
McAllen (pt.)	106,406	Weslaco	26,935

Race and Hispanic or Latino origin*
White 19.2%
Black or African American 1.3%
American Indian or Alaska Native 0.1%
Asian 0.6%
Native Hawaiian or other Pacific Islander 0.0%
Some other race 0.0%
Hispanic or Latino origin 78.3%
Two or more races 0.4%

As percentage of total population.

Ancestry*

English	2.5%	Irish	2.5%
German	4.3%	USA/American	2.7%

As estimated percentage of total population.

Universities and colleges, 2000–2001 enrollment
Coastal Bend College, Beeville 3,259
South Texas Community College, McAllen 11,319
Texas A&M University, Kingsville 5,948
University of Texas-Pan American, Edinburg 12,759

Newspapers and circulation

	District circulation	Total circulation
Harlingen Valley Morning Star	3,161	24,654
McAllen Monitor	32,279	42,010
San Antonio Express-News	2,390	216,752
Victoria Advocate	1,404	38,822

Television stations and affiliations

Corpus Christi	68%	KEDT	PBS
Corpus Christi	68%	KIII	ABC
Corpus Christi	68%	KORO	Univision
Corpus Christi	68%	KRIS	NBC
Corpus Christi	68%	KZTV	CBS
Harlingen-Weslaco-Brownsville-McAllen	19%	KGBT	CBS
Harlingen-Weslaco-Brownsville-McAllen	19%	KLUJ	Independent
Harlingen-Weslaco-Brownsville-McAllen	19%	KMBH	PBS
Harlingen-Weslaco-Brownsville-McAllen	19%	KNVO	Univision
Harlingen-Weslaco-Brownsville-McAllen	19%	KRGV	ABC
Harlingen-Weslaco-Brownsville-McAllen	19%	KTLM	Telemundo
Harlingen-Weslaco-Brownsville-McAllen	19%	KVEO	NBC
San Antonio	13%	KABB	FOX
San Antonio	13%	KENS	CBS
San Antonio	13%	KHCE	Independent
San Antonio	13%	KLRN	PBS
San Antonio	13%	KRRT	WB
San Antonio	13%	KSAT	ABC
San Antonio	13%	KTRG	Independent Spanish
San Antonio	13%	KVAW	Independent Spanish
San Antonio	13%	KVDA	Telemundo
San Antonio	13%	KWEX	Univision

Cable systems and subscribers
Cable ONE 4,827
Charter 4,154
CMA 5,291
Time Warner 50,804

Military installations, September 2001
Ingleside Naval Station, Ingleside 3,300
Kingsville Naval Air Station, Kingsville 680

Businesses and other major employers

Celanese Americas Corp.; Bishop; chemicals, metallic salts   4,000

SETC De Mexico SA De CV; Pharr; masonry materials, supplies   2,500

McAllen Medical Center Inc.; Edinburg   2,248

University of Texas-Pan American; Edinburg   1,680

U.S. Bureau of Customs and Border Protection; McAllen   1,400

Texas Criminal Justice Dept.; Beeville   1,081

Southwest Marine Inc.; Ingleside; shipbuilding, repairing   1,000

Ticketmaster Corp.; Pharr; sports ticket sales   1,000

Knapp Medical Center; Weslaco   950

BPU Reynolds; Gregory; alumina fused refractories   826

Invacare Corp.; Hidalgo; medical supplies   800

Levi Strauss and Co.; McAllen; men's/boys' jeans   800

Gulf Marine Fabricators; Aransas Pass; fabricated structural metal   750

Calzado Deportivo De Reynosa SA De CV; Hidalgo; athletic shoes   700

Edinburg Regional Medical Center; Edinburg   513

National Service Direct Inc.; McAllen; telephone communication   500

Nurses That Care Sitter Services Inc.; McAllen   500

Rio Grande Regional Hospital; McAllen   500

Texas Dept. of Protective and Regulatory Services; Edinburg   500

West Telemarketing Corp.; McAllen; telemarketing   500

Williamson-Dickie Manufacturing Co.; Weslaco; work pants   500

Texas 16th District

West — El Paso and suburbs

Looking more toward Mexico than Texas, the solidly Democratic 16th includes most of El Paso and some suburbs. Joined to Mexico by the Bridge of the Americas, the 16th has a 77.7 percent Hispanic population, more than any other district in the nation except for south Texas's 15th.

Redistricting following the 2000 census pushed the district north, removing some of the 16th's border with Mexico and taking out a few small towns. Remapping also gave the 16th all of Fort Bliss, removing it entirely from the 23rd. The base, a major employer, gives the area a military flavor.

Mexico has had a long and deep effect on the 16th's economy. El Paso's growth was credited to trade with Mexico long before free-trade zones and global markets flourished. Companies on the U.S. side of the border provide supplies and services to manufacturing plants in Mexico, and residents from El Paso's sister city, Ciudad Juarez, regularly cross the border to spend money in El Paso's stores. In recent years, leaders have been concerned with the effects of the North American Free Trade Agreement, which they blame for displacing American workers. The trade agreement has been partially responsible for an explosion of *maquiladoras,* twin plants in which Mexican workers do the bulk of the manufacturing labor and Americans complete the products with final details.

Democrats held the 16th's congressional seat for all but two years in the twentieth century, often unchallenged by Republicans since the 1960s. In 2002 Democratic Senate nominee Ron Kirk won 71 percent of the two-party vote in the 16th, his third-best district in the state.

Major Industry

Manufacturing, apparel, defense.

Notable

The Border Patrol Museum displays aircraft and vehicles used by the patrol as well as surveillance equipment and confiscated items; Fort Bliss, the largest air defense artillery training center in the world, occupies an area larger than Rhode Island.

Election Returns

	Republican		Democratic		Other
President 2000	56,276	40.7%	81,860	59.3%	
House 2002			72,383	100.0%	

District Profile

Population   651,619

Total area (square miles)   582.3
Land area (square miles)   580.8

Population per square mile   1,121.9

Counties (2000 population)
El Paso (pt.)   651,619

Cities and other areas over 10,000 (2000 population)
El Paso   563,662
San Elizario CDP (pt.)   11,011
Socorro   27,152

Race and Hispanic or Latino origin*
White   17.4%
Black or African American   2.9%
American Indian or Alaska Native   0.3%
Asian   0.9%
Native Hawaiian or other Pacific Islander   0.1%
Some other race   0.1%
Hispanic or Latino origin   77.7%
Two or more races   0.7%

As percentage of total population.

Ancestry*

English 2.4%	Irish 2.6%
German 3.9%	USA/American 2.4%

As estimated percentage of total population.

Universities and colleges, 2000–2001 enrollment
Computer Career Center, El Paso   204
El Paso Community College, El Paso   18,001
University of Texas, El Paso   15,224
Western Technical Institute, El Paso   700

Newspapers and circulation

	District circulation	Total circulation
El Paso Times	64,685	74,595
*USA Today**	1,449	1,674,376

See Sources and Explanations in the front of the volume.

Television stations and affiliations

El Paso	100%	KCOS	PBS
El Paso	100%	KDBC	CBS
El Paso	100%	KFOX	FOX
El Paso	100%	KINT	Univision
El Paso	100%	KRWG	PBS
El Paso	100%	KSCE	Independent
El Paso	100%	KTSM	NBC
El Paso	100%	KVIA	ABC

Cable systems and subscribers

Time Warner   113,247

Military installations, September 2001

Fort Bliss (Army), El Paso   15,860

Businesses and other major employers

Tenet Health System Hospitals Inc.; El Paso   4,000

University of Texas at El Paso; El Paso   3,700

Philips Electronics Corp.; El Paso; computer components 2,500

William Beaumont Army Medical Center; El Paso 2,500

General Electric Co.; El Paso; motors, generators, condensers   2,400

El Paso County Community College District; El Paso 2,054

City of El Paso; El Paso; police dept.   1,900

Electronic Data Management; El Paso; data processing 1,800

City of El Paso; El Paso; recreational program   1,700

Del Sol Medical Center; El Paso   1,500

ELAMEX Logistics Inc.; El Paso; engine electrical equipment   1,500

TECMA Group; El Paso; brokers' services   1,500

VF Jeanswear; El Paso; jeans, slacks   1,500

R. E. Thomason General Hospital; El Paso   1,400

Las Palmas Medical Center; El Paso   1,300

U.S. Bureau of Customs and Border Protection; El Paso 1,200

Union Pacific Railroad Co.; El Paso; freight hauling 1,200

West Corp.; El Paso; telemarketing   1,200

U.S. Postal Service; El Paso   1,123

R. M. Personnel Inc.; El Paso; employment agencies 1,100

T&T Staff Management Inc.; El Paso; employment agencies   1,100

Carrier Corp.; El Paso; air conditioning equipment 1,000

Ysleta del Sur Pueblo; El Paso; bingo hall   1,000

El Paso County; El Paso; sheriff's office   1,000

Greater Texas Finishing Corp.; El Paso; electronic circuits   1,000

WorldCom Inc.; El Paso; telephone communication 1,000

El Paso Electric Co.; El Paso; electric power generation 920

Levi Strauss and Co.; El Paso; men's/boys' sportswear 902

3M Co.; El Paso; pressure-sensitive tape   900

Datamark Inc.; El Paso; data entry   900

Philips Electronics North America Corp.; El Paso; audio/video equipment   900

UPS Freight Services Inc.; El Paso; package delivery 900

Tony Lama Co.; El Paso; men's boots   870

Onsite International Inc.; El Paso; sportswear   860

Osram Sylvania Inc.; El Paso; vehicle headlights   800

Philips Electronics North America Corp.; El Paso; electronic capacitors   800

Federal-Mogul Corp.; El Paso; automotive lighting 750

Stoneridge Inc.; El Paso; electronic connectors   750

Big 8 Foods; El Paso; specialty foods   700

Brylane Inc.; El Paso; mail-order apparel   700

Conexant Systems Inc.; El Paso; semiconductors   700

Greater Texas Finishing Corp.; El Paso; cleaning and dyeing   700

Texas Education Agency; El Paso   653

Allegiance Corp.; El Paso; medical supplies   650

National Center for Employment of Disabled; El Paso; employment agencies   650

City of El Paso; El Paso; transportation   630

El Paso County Community College District; El Paso 613

City of El Paso; El Paso; city government   600

First Choice Subscribers of Texas Inc.; El Paso; employee leasing service   600

GC Services LP; El Paso; telecommunications consultant 600

General Assembly Corp.; El Paso; harness assemblies 600

Lear Corp.; El Paso; automotive parts   600

Pinkerton's Inc.; El Paso; security guard service   600

Sun Apparel Inc.; El Paso; dress slacks   600

Toro Co.; El Paso; plastics injection molding   600

Visiting Nurse Assn. Inc.; El Paso   600

Catholic Diocese of El Paso Inc.; El Paso; religious organization   575

Leviton Manufacturing Co.; El Paso; wiring services 575

Waste Connections Inc.; El Paso; rubbish collection 554

Philips Electronics North America Corp.; El Paso; warehousing   550

SC Group Inc.; El Paso; real estate consultant   542

JC Viramontes Inc.; El Paso; cotton finishing plants 530

Wal-Mart Stores Inc.; El Paso; department stores   525

Eaton Corp.; El Paso; relays, industrial controls   500

Gail Darling Inc.; El Paso; temporary help service   500

Kessler Industries Inc.; El Paso; novelty furniture   500

Phelps Dodge Refining Corp.; El Paso; copper ore   500

Stone Container Corp.; El Paso; corrugated boxes   500

VF Jeanswear; Fabens   500

Texas 17th District

Central — Abilene, San Angelo

Starting west of Fort Worth, the conservative 17th takes in the central Texas plains and heads through Abilene until reaching the outer edges of Lubbock in western Texas. The culture of the Old West lingers in this part of the Lone Star State with ranches, cotton, and cowboys. The district contains all or part of 36 counties.

When the 1980s oil glut hit home in Texas, refineries covered the 17th's prairie. Today, there is only a fraction of the rigs that once blanketed the area, and some of those oil-producing towns have disappeared. Abilene, the district's largest city, has made an effort to revitalize its downtown. Three church-sponsored colleges nurture a powerful evangelical community.

Cattle and cotton are still big in the 17th, but low cattle prices and droughts have jeopardized both. Adding a measure of stability to the economy are Air Force bases near Abilene and San Angelo. The prison industry also has done well, with several state and contract facilities around the district.

The 17th became even more Republican after redistricting following the 2000 census, picking up the city of San Angelo and some of its wealthier suburbs. While the 17th is socially conservative, economic hardships have sent it in search of government assistance in agriculture. At the local level, voters tend to favor Republicans, but conservative Democrats do well in some areas north and west of Abilene. The 17th includes George W. Bush's top-performing county in the nation in 2000—Glasscock, a lightly populated area east of Midland where he received 92 percent of the vote. Republicans John Cornyn and Rick Perry topped two-thirds of the district vote in the 2002 Senate and gubernatorial races.

Major Industry

Cattle, cotton, defense, oil.

Notable

Abilene is named after the famous cattle shipping center in Abilene, Kansas; the first Hilton hotel was built in Cisco.

Election Returns

	Republican		Democratic		Other	
President 2000	161,877	72.2%	62,241	27.8%		
House 2002	77,622	47.4%	84,136	51.4%	2,046	1.2%

District Profile

Population   651,619

Total area (square miles)   33,836.0
Land area (square miles)   33,564.2

Population per square mile   19.4

Counties (2000 population)

Borden	729	Concho	3,966
Brown	37,674	Dawson	14,985
Callahan	12,905	Eastland	18,297
Coke	3,864	Erath	33,001
Coleman	9,235	Fisher	4,344
Comanche	14,026	Garza (pt.)	4,529

Glasscock	1,406	Schleicher	2,935
Haskell	6,093	Scurry	16,361
Hood	41,100	Shackelford	3,302
Irion	1,771	Somervell	6,809
Jack	8,763	Stephens	9,674
Jones	20,785	Sterling	1,393
Kent	859	Stonewall	1,693
McCulloch	8,205	Taylor	126,555
Mitchell	9,698	Throckmorton	1,850
Nolan	15,802	Tom Green	104,010
Palo Pinto	27,026	Wise (pt.)	48,536
Runnels	11,495	Young	17,943

Cities and other areas over 10,000 (2000 population)

Abilene	115,930	Snyder	10,783
Brownwood	18,813	Stephenville	14,921
Mineral Wells (pt.)	14,770	Sweetwater	11,415
San Angelo	88,439		

Race and Hispanic or Latino origin*

White   74.7%
Black or African American   3.8%
American Indian or Alaska Native   0.4%
Asian   0.5%
Native Hawaiian or other Pacific Islander   0.0%
Some other race   0.1%
Hispanic or Latino origin   19.6%
Two or more races   1.0%

As percentage of total population.

Ancestry*

Dutch	1.2%	Irish	7.6%
English	7.0%	Scotch-Irish	1.7%
French	1.5%	Scottish	1.3%
German	8.6%	USA/American	11.4%

As estimated percentage of total population.

Universities and colleges, 2000–2001 enrollment

Abilene Christian University, Abilene   4,739
Angelo State University, San Angelo   6,308
Cisco Junior College, Cisco   2,642
Hardin-Simmons University, Abilene   2,304
Howard Payne University, Brownwood   1,480
McMurry University, Abilene   1,344
Ranger College, Ranger   847
Tarleton State University, Stephenville   7,545
Texas State Technical College-Sweetwater, Sweetwater   948
Western Texas College, Snyder   1,233

Newspapers and circulation

	District circulation	Total circulation
Abilene Reporter-News	33,657	34,435
Dallas Morning News	6,874	495,624
Fort Worth Star-Telegram	15,267	224,885
Lubbock Avalanche Journal	2,022	54,669
San Angelo Standard-Times	23,414	27,823
Wichita Falls Times-Record News	1,956	34,182

Television stations and affiliations

Abilene-Sweetwater	42%	KPCB	Independent
Abilene-Sweetwater	42%	KRBC	NBC
Abilene-Sweetwater	42%	KTAB	CBS

Abilene-Sweetwater	42%	KTXS	ABC
San Angelo	23%	KACB	NBC
San Angelo	23%	KIDY	FOX, UPN
San Angelo	23%	KLST	CBS
Dallas-Fort Worth	16%	KDAF	WB
Dallas-Fort Worth	16%	KDFI	Independent
Dallas-Fort Worth	16%	KDFW	FOX
Dallas-Fort Worth	16%	KDTN	PBS
Dallas-Fort Worth	16%	KDTX	Independent
Dallas-Fort Worth	16%	KERA	PBS
Dallas-Fort Worth	16%	KFWD	Independent
Dallas-Fort Worth	16%	KMPX	Independent
Dallas-Fort Worth	16%	KPXD	PAX
Dallas-Fort Worth	16%	KSTR	Telefutura
Dallas-Fort Worth	16%	KTAQ	Independent
Dallas-Fort Worth	16%	KTVT	CBS
Dallas-Fort Worth	16%	KTXA	UPN
Dallas-Fort Worth	16%	KUVN	Univision
Dallas-Fort Worth	16%	KXAS	NBC
Dallas-Fort Worth	16%	KXTX	Telemundo
Dallas-Fort Worth	16%	WFAA	ABC
Lubbock	10%	KAMC	ABC
Lubbock	10%	KCBD	NBC
Lubbock	10%	KJTV	FOX
Lubbock	10%	KLBK	CBS
Lubbock	10%	KPTB	Independent
Lubbock	10%	KTXT	PBS
Wichita Falls-Lawton	6%	KAUZ	CBS
Wichita Falls-Lawton	6%	KFDX	NBC
Wichita Falls-Lawton	6%	KJTL	FOX
Wichita Falls-Lawton	6%	KSWO	ABC
Odessa-Midland	3%	KMID	ABC
Odessa-Midland	3%	KMLM	Independent
Odessa-Midland	3%	KOCV	PBS
Odessa-Midland	3%	KOSA	CBS
Odessa-Midland	3%	KPEJ	FOX, UPN
Odessa-Midland	3%	KWAB	NBC
Odessa-Midland	3%	KWES	NBC

Cable systems and subscribers
Big Country Cablevision   1,486
Brownwood TV Cable   9,496
Charter   11,880
Classic   18,224
Comcast   3,565
Communicomm   4,599
Cox   84,880
National Cable   1,419
Northland   10,182
Southtel   648
Time Warner   2,845
West Texas Cablevision   1,559

Military installations, September 2001
Dyess Air Force Base, Abilene   5,350
Goodfellow Air Force Base, San Angelo   1,898

Businesses and other major employers
Santa Fe Crossing Senior; San Angelo; amusement/recreation   5,000
Allied Staffing Inc.; Abilene; employment agencies   2,799

GTE Southwest Inc.; San Angelo; telephone communication   2,200
Hendrick Medical Center; Abilene   2,200
TXU US Holdings Co.; Glen Rose; electric services   2,000
Ethicon Inc.; San Angelo; surgical appliances   1,900
Church of Jesus Christ of Latter-Day Saints Corp.; San Angelo; religious organization   1,500
Kohler Co.; Brownwood; plumbing fixtures   1,500
Patterson Drilling Co.; San Angelo; oil, gas well drilling   1,400
Shannon Medical Center Inc.; San Angelo   1,100
Verizon Communications Inc.; San Angelo; telecommunications consultant   1,000
Western Wireless Corp.; San Angelo; telephone equipment   1,000
Housley Communications Inc.; San Angelo; telephone installation   945
Texas A&M University; Stephenville   906
Texas Criminal Justice Dept.; Abilene   900
Texas Mental Health and Mental Retardation Dept.; Carlsbad   800
Abilene Regional Medical Center; Abilene   770
3M Co.; Brownwood; traffic signals   750
MAL Enterprises Inc.; Abilene; grocery store   750
Tarleton State University; Stephenville   700
Abilene Christian University Inc.; Abilene   640
St. Gobain Abrasives Inc.; Stephenville; sandpaper   600
Brownwood Regional Hospital Inc.; Brownwood   596
Accenture Inc.; Cisco; management consulting   575
National Energy Production Corp.; Granbury; power plant construction   550
San Angelo Community Medical Center; San Angelo   550
Wilks Masonry Corp.; Cisco; masonry/stonework   546
San Angelo State University; San Angelo   531
Wal-Mart Stores Inc.; Abilene; department stores   530
Eagle Mountain International Church Inc.; Newark; religious organization   500
Richeson Management Inc.; Graham; motels   500
Superior Telecom Inc.; Brownwood; communication wire   500

Texas 18th District

Downtown Houston

Downtown Houston's older black neighborhoods and more-progressive residents make up the 18th, which includes one of the city's poorest areas. Though economically struggling, the district has seen revitalization as the downtown experiences a resurgence in construction, with new baseball and basketball stadiums inside its boundaries. *(See map p. 869.)*

The 18th is diverse: 42 percent of residents are African American and 33 percent are Hispanic, and a large portion of the city's gay and lesbian residents live in the district. Some of the district's most heavily black areas are just south of downtown, and heavily Hispanic neighborhoods can be found just north of downtown, between Interstate 45 and the Eastex Freeway. Texas Southern University and the University of Houston add to the area's liberal tendencies.

Though the district is overwhelmingly inner-city urban, it does include some areas around downtown, as well as the Heights, a trendier neighborhood populated with some young professionals.

Downtown office buildings are filled with oil and gas employees and other white-collar businesses and service workers, but most commute from outside the district. Downtown also houses some corporate giants and was home to the once-powerful Enron Corp. This area includes the city's Theater District, where the Hobby Center for the Performing Arts opened in 2002, and part of the Museum District (shared with the 25th).

The large black and Hispanic populations make the 18th perhaps the most strongly Democratic district in Texas. In 2002, it gave Democratic Senate nominee Ron Kirk 77 percent of the two-party vote, more than any other district. In the 2000 presidential contest, George W. Bush had his worst showing in Texas (26 percent) in the 18th.

Major Industry

Energy, government, business services, entertainment.

Notable

The district was once represented by the late representative Barbara Jordan, D-Texas in the 1970s; Minute Maid Park, home of the Houston Astros baseball team, was originally named Enron Field but was renamed in 2002 after the collapse of the energy giant.

Election Returns

	Republican		Democratic		Other	
President 2000	47,335	25.5%	138,059	74.5%		
House 2002	27,980	21.7%	99,161	76.9%	1,785	1.4%

District Profile

Population 651,620

Total area (square miles) 186.1
 Land area (square miles) 186.0

Population per square mile 3,503.3

Counties (2000 population)
 Harris (pt.) 651,620

Cities and other areas over 10,000 (2000 population)
 Houston (pt.) 577,190

Race and Hispanic or Latino origin*
 White 21.2%
 Black or African American 42.2%
 American Indian or Alaska Native 0.2%
 Asian 2.8%
 Native Hawaiian or other Pacific Islander 0.0%
 Some other race 0.1%
 Hispanic or Latino origin 32.6%
 Two or more races 0.9%

As percentage of total population.

Ancestry*

English	2.9%	Irish	2.7%
French	1.2%	Italian	1.1%
German	4.0%	USA/American	2.5%

As estimated percentage of total population.

Universities and colleges, 2000–2001 enrollment
 Houston Community College System, Houston 40,929
 South Texas College of Law, Houston 1,231
 Texas Southern University, Houston 6,886
 University of Houston-Downtown, Houston 8,951
 University of Houston-University Park, Houston 32,123
 University of St. Thomas, Houston 4,073

Newspapers and circulation

	District circulation	Total circulation
Houston Chronicle	85,142	548,437
*USA Today**	1,832	1,674,376

See Sources and Explanations in the front of the volume.

Television stations and affiliations

Houston	100%	KAVU	ABC
Houston	100%	KBTX	CBS
Houston	100%	KETH	Independent
Houston	100%	KHOU	CBS
Houston	100%	KHWB	WB
Houston	100%	KLTJ	Independent
Houston	100%	KNWS	Independent
Houston	100%	KPRC	NBC
Houston	100%	KPXB	PAX
Houston	100%	KRIV	FOX
Houston	100%	KTBU	Independent
Houston	100%	KTMD	Telemundo
Houston	100%	KTRK	ABC
Houston	100%	KTXH	UPN
Houston	100%	KUHT	PBS
Houston	100%	KXLN	Univision
Houston	100%	KZJL	Independent Spanish

Cable systems and subscribers
 Time Warner 286,837

Businesses and other major employers
 ExxonMobil Oil Corp.; Houston; petroleum refining 5,000
 Kellogg Brown and Root Inc.; Houston; industrial plant construction 5,000
 Hearst Corp.; Houston; newspaper 4,300
 Harris County; Houston; county government 4,227
 Continental Airlines Inc.; Houston 4,000
 Equistar Chemicals; Houston; chemicals, polymers, polyolefins 3,656
 U.S. Veterans Hospital; Houston 3,500
 Reliant Energy Inc.; Houston; electric power transmission 3,000
 Kenny Industrial Service; Houston; industrial painting 2,500
 Halliburton Co.; Houston; bridge, tunnel, highway construction 2,400
 Shell Oil Co.; Houston; crude petroleum production 2,400
 St. Joseph Hospital; Houston 2,271
 Associated Building Services Co.; Houston; janitorial service 2,000
 Chevron Phillips Chemical Co.; Houston; plastic materials, resins 2,000
 Cornerstone Gas Gathering Co. Inc.; Houston; petroleum refining 2,000

Texas Dept. of Transportation; Houston   2,000
Vinson and Elkins; Houston; law office   2,000
HCA Inc.; Houston; hospital   1,910
Harris County Hospital District; Houston   1,900
Goodman Manufacturing Co.; Houston; air conditioning equipment   1,725
Accenture Inc.; Houston; management consulting   1,500
American General Life Insurance Co.; Houston; life insurance   1,500
El Paso Tennessee Pipeline Co.; Houston; natural gas transmission   1,500
Fulbright and Jaworski; Houston; law office   1,500
Grocers Supply Co. Inc.; Houston; food supplier   1,500
University of Houston System; Houston   1,423
Xserv Inc.; Houston; scaffolding   1,297
Baker Botts LLP; Houston; law office   1,200
Enron Operations Services Corp.; Houston; natural gas transmission   1,200
Memorial Hermann Hospital System; Houston   1,200
Pennzoil-Quaker State Co.; Houston; lubricants   1,200
Virginia International Co.; Houston; oil/gas exploration services   1,195
Tenet Healthcare Corp. Hospital; Houston   1,100
Anheuser-Busch Inc.; Houston; malt beverages   1,000
Cingular Wireless; Houston; cellular telephones   1,000
City of Houston; Houston; courts   1,000
Coral Energy Co.; Houston; natural gas transmission   1,000
Equiva Services; Houston; management services   1,000
Houston McLane Co.; Houston; baseball club   1,000
Riviana Foods Inc.; Houston; milled rice   1,000
Royal Window Coverings; Houston; vertical blinds   1,000
Texas Southern University; Houston   1,000
Waste Management Holdings Inc.; Houston; dump operations   1,000
Houston Community College System; Houston   980
Baker Hughes Inc.; Houston; oil field machinery   970
Cunningham Lindsey US Inc.; Houston; insurance adjusters   930
International Trading Co.; Houston; pork products   907
Bank of America Corp.; Houston; commercial bank   900
ExxonMobil Oil Corp.; Houston; petroleum, natural gas   900
Harris County Metropolitan Transit Authority; Houston   900
Williams Brothers Construction Co.; Houston; highway construction   900
Fisk Electric Co.; Houston; electrical contractor   880
Trees Inc.; Houston; tree trimming   860
MacGregor Medical Assn.; Houston   801
City of Houston; Houston; water, solid waste management   800
Dynegy Inc.; Houston; natural gas distribution   800
SCI International Ltd.; Houston; funeral services   800
Universal Computer Systems Holding Inc.; Houston; computer peripherals   800
Health Care Temporaries Inc.; Houston; home health care   763

Dril-Quip Inc.; Houston; oil/gas drilling tools   759
Sysco Food Services; Houston; canned goods   750
Harris County Metropolitan Transit Authority; Houston   734
ABB Vetco Gray Inc.; Houston; oil field machinery   700
El Paso Natural Gas Co.; Houston; natural gas transmission   700
Kraft Foods Inc.; Houston; snacks   700
Specialty Piping Components Inc.; Houston; pipe fittings   700
UBS/Warburg; Houston; security traders   700
Enterprise Products Co.; Houston; natural gas liquids   657
City of Houston; Houston; public library   652
Cameron Cooper Corp.; Houston; oil/gas field machinery   600
Central Parking Corp.; Houston; parking lots   600
Corporate Express Inc.; Houston; office supplies   600
Marek Brothers Systems Inc.; Houston; drywall   600
Tennessee Gas Pipeline Co.; Houston; natural gas pipelines   600
U.S. Internal Revenue Service; Houston   600
SBC Communications Inc.; Houston; telephone communication   590
Select Specialty Hospital; Houston   566
Mrs Baird's Bakeries Business Trust; Houston; bakery products   560
Bracewell and Patterson; Houston; law office   550
Burns International Security Services Corp.; Houston; security guard service   543
Shell Pipe Line Corp.; Houston; crude petroleum pipelines   540
Wal-Mart Stores Inc.; Houston; department stores   530
Amerada Hess Corp.; Houston; natural gas production   500
Bridgeline Gas Distribution; Houston; natural gas distribution   500
City of Houston; Houston; city government   500
CMS Energy Corp.; Houston; oil/gas exploration   500
Deloitte and Touche; Houston; accounting services   500
Equiva Trading Co.; Houston; petroleum products   500
Harris County Mental Health and Mental Retardation Authority; Houston   500
KPMG; Houston; certified public accountant   500
McLemore Building Maintenance Inc.; Houston; janitorial service   500
Mustang Tractor and Equipment Co.; Houston; construction, mining machinery   500
Rushlake Hotels Inc.; Houston; hotel, franchised   500
U.S. Federal Bureau of Investigation; Houston   500
University of Texas Health Science Center; Houston   500
Varco International Inc.; Houston; measuring, controlling devices   500
W. S. Bellows Construction Corp.; Houston; building construction   500
Wackenhut Corp.; Houston; security guard service   500
Woman's Hospital of Texas Inc.; Houston   500

Texas 19th District

West — Lubbock, Midland

The conservative 19th starts in the panhandle and extends south through cattle and cotton country until reaching oil field operations near Midland and Odessa. With ranches, cattle, and remnants of the cowboy lifestyle, the 19th offers a taste of the Wild West and feels little like the Old South, which never reached this far west.

While the northern part of the district, which includes Lubbock, is more agricultural, the southern part of the 19th—called the Permian Basin, home to Midland and Odessa—is oil country. The differences set the district up for competing interests, but redistricting following the 2000 census pushed the 19th farther south, giving energy producers more clout.

The district's largest city, Lubbock thrives on the acres upon acres of cotton surrounding it. The city calls itself the world's largest cottonseed-processing center and is home to Texas Tech University. Because the 19th's economy is so dependent on agriculture and oil, it was nearly devastated during the worldwide oil glut of the 1980s and bad weather in the 1990s. Famine and drought have been detrimental to cattle and cotton, and continued low prices have dampened the oil industry. Reese Air Force Base was another major employer, but it was shut down under the 1995 military restructuring.

Conservative Democrats used to dominate the 19th: as recently as 1978, George W. Bush lost a race for this House seat to Democrat Kent Hance. More recently, Republicans have done well at all levels and routinely receive between 60 percent and 70 percent of the vote. The 19th gave Bush 75.5 percent of the vote in the 2000 presidential contest, his second-highest percentage among the state's congressional districts.

Major Industry

Cattle, agriculture, oil, and gas.

Notable

Singer Buddy Holly was born and raised in Lubbock; Odessa boasts the world's largest barbecue pit.

Election Returns

	Republican		Democratic		Other	
President 2000	149,350	75.5%	48,400	24.5%		
House 2002	117,092	91.6%			10,684	8.4%

District Profile

Population   651,619

Total area (square miles)   17,527.9
  Land area (square miles)   17,508.4

Population per square mile   37.2

Counties (2000 population)

Andrews 13,004	Lubbock 242,628
Bailey 6,594	Lynn 6,550
Cochran 3,730	Martin 4,746
Crane 3,996	Midland 116,009
Ector 121,123	Parmer 10,016
Gaines 14,467	Terry 12,761
Hockley 22,716	Ward 10,909
Howard 33,627	Winkler 7,173
Lamb (pt.) 14,181	Yoakum 7,322
Loving 67	

Cities and other areas over 10,000 (2000 population)

Big Spring 25,233	Midland 94,996
Levelland 12,866	Odessa 90,943
Lubbock 199,564	West Odessa CDP 17,799

Race and Hispanic or Latino origin*

White   58.2%
Black or African American   5.6%
American Indian or Alaska Native   0.4%
Asian   0.8%
Native Hawaiian or other Pacific Islander   0.0%
Some other race   0.0%
Hispanic or Latino origin   34.1%
Two or more races   0.8%

As percentage of total population.

Ancestry*

English 6.5%	Scotch-Irish 1.5%
French 1.3%	Scottish 1.2%
German 7.4%	USA/American 8.4%
Irish 6.1%	

As estimated percentage of total population.

Universities and colleges, 2000–2001 enrollment

Howard County Junior College District, Big Spring   2,260
International Business College, Lubbock   661
Lubbock Christian University, Lubbock   1,617
Midland College, Midland   4,842
Odessa College, Odessa   4,568
South Plains College, Levelland   6,731
Texas Tech University, Lubbock   24,558
Texas Tech University Health Sciences Center, Lubbock   1,719
University of Texas of the Permian Basin, Odessa   2,224

Newspapers and circulation

	District circulation	Total circulation
Big Spring Herald	4,559	4,559
Dallas Morning News	6,131	495,624
Lubbock Avalanche Journal	46,191	54,669
Midland Reporter-Telegram	19,412	19,468
Odessa American	23,664	25,714
*USA Today**	1,671	1,674,376

See Sources and Explanations in the front of the volume.

Television stations and affiliations

Lubbock	48%	KAMC	ABC
Lubbock	48%	KCBD	NBC
Lubbock	48%	KJTV	FOX
Lubbock	48%	KLBK	CBS
Lubbock	48%	KPTB	Independent
Lubbock	48%	KTXT	PBS
Odessa-Midland	47%	KMID	ABC
Odessa-Midland	47%	KMLM	Independent
Odessa-Midland	47%	KOCV	PBS
Odessa-Midland	47%	KOSA	CBS
Odessa-Midland	47%	KPEJ	FOX, UPN
Odessa-Midland	47%	KWAB	NBC
Odessa-Midland	47%	KWES	NBC
Amarillo	5%	KACV	PBS
Amarillo	5%	KAMR	NBC
Amarillo	5%	KCIT	FOX
Amarillo	5%	KFDA	CBS
Amarillo	5%	KVIH	ABC
Amarillo	5%	KVII	ABC

Cable systems and subscribers

Cable ONE   22,731
Charter   12,416
Classic   14,873
Cox   85,847
National Cable   576
U.S. Cable   4,193

Businesses and other major employers

Covenant Health System Inc.; Lubbock; rehabilitation center   6,000
Texas Tech Unversity System; Lubbock   4,000
Texas Tech University Health Sciences Center; Lubbock   3,723
Excel Corp.; Friona; meatpacking plants   3,000
City of Lubbock; Lubbock; zoning board   2,000
Methodist Hospital; Lubbock   1,998
Lubbock County Hospital District; Lubbock   1,900
Ector County Hospital District; Odessa   1,600
Memorial Hospital and Medical Center; Midland   1,500
University of Texas System; Lubbock   1,494
City of Lubbock; Lubbock; city government   1,329
Texas Mental Health and Mental Retardation Dept.; Lubbock   950
Texas Criminal Justice Dept.; Lubbock   847
Texas Mental Health and Mental Retardation Dept.; Big Spring   840
Basic Energy Services Inc.; Midland; oil field services   800
International Union of Operating Engineers Local 351; Big Spring; trade union   800
Acme Energy Services Inc.; Midland; oil field haulage   700
Huntsman Polymers Corp.; Odessa; polyethylene resins   700
OSC Long Distance Inc.; Lubbock; telephone communication   700
First West Texas Bancshares; Midland; bank holding   650
Odessa Junior College District; Odessa   600
West Corp.; Lubbock; telemarketing   600

Midland College; Midland   595
Caprock Home Health Services Inc.; Lubbock; visiting nurse service   550
Atlantic Richfield Co.; Midland; petroleum production   500
Halliburton Energy Services Inc.; Midland; oil field services   500
Huntsman Polymers Corp.; Odessa; plastics materials   500
Plains Cotton Cooperative Assn.; Littlefield; denims   500
UTI Drilling; Midland; oil, gas well drilling   500

Texas 20th District

Downtown San Antonio

A city rich in history, San Antonio witnessed the death of Davy Crockett and the famed fall of the Alamo. Since those rugged days in the early 1800s, San Antonio has grown into one of the nation's largest cities (9th, according to the 2000 census). The strongly Democratic 20th takes in most of the city, including the heavily Hispanic west side, downtown San Antonio, and some surrounding communities.

A huge military presence in San Antonio makes up the biggest chunk of the economy, but mid-1990s downsizing caused the city some economic pains. Kelly Air Force Base, one of the city's largest employers, has closed. Leaders have redeveloped it as a business park, bringing some jobs back to the area. Two other bases are still significant employers.

Although tourism does not make up for the defense industry's losses, it continues to be a reliable moneymaker. The Alamo, site of the 1836 battle with Mexico, is in the heart of downtown. The city's scenic Paseo del Rio, or Riverwalk, also is a popular draw with its shops, restaurants, and hotels winding along the San Antonio River. The most urban of San Antonio's four districts, the 20th has felt pressure on its roads, courts, and schools as trade has increased because of the North American Free Trade Agreement. The city also is working to become a base for cybersecurity efforts.

Democrats dominate most of this Hispanic-majority district. Ron Kirk, the 2002 Democratic Senate nominee, carried the 20th with 60 percent of the vote. The only significant Republican presence in the district is in the largely white, higher-income areas northwest and northeast of San Antonio.

Major Industry

Military, tourism, trade.

Notable

Sculptor Gutzon Borglum designed Mount Rushmore presidential carvings in a studio in San Antonio; St. Anthony Hotel in San Antonio is said to have been the first fully air conditioned hotel in the world, in 1941.

Election Returns

	Republican		Democratic		Other
President 2000	64,659	42.9%	86,133	57.1%	
House 2002			68,685	100.0%	

District Profile

Population   651,619

Total area (square miles)   304.1
   Land area (square miles)   303.2

Population per square mile   2,149.1

Counties (2000 population)
   Bexar (pt.)   651,619

Cities and other areas over 10,000 (2000 population)
   San Antonio (pt.)   600,760

Race and Hispanic or Latino origin*
   White   23.7%
   Black or African American   5.3%
   American Indian or Alaska Native   0.2%
   Asian   1.3%
   Native Hawaiian or other Pacific Islander   0.1%
   Some other race   0.1%
   Hispanic or Latino origin   68.2%
   Two or more races   1.1%

*As percentage of total population.

Ancestry*

English	3.0%	Irish	3.6%
French	1.2%	Italian	1.3%
German	6.1%	USA/American	2.4%

*As estimated percentage of total population.

Universities and colleges, 2000–2001 enrollment
   Hallmark Institute of Technology, San Antonio   425
   Northwest Vista College, San Antonio   3,893
   Our Lady of the Lake University, San Antonio   3,474
   San Antonio College, San Antonio   19,253
   St. Mary's University, San Antonio   4,137
   Trinity University, San Antonio   2,571
   University of Texas Health Science, San Antonio   2,543

Newspapers and circulation

	District circulation	Total circulation
San Antonio Express-News	65,901	216,752
*USA Today**	1,581	1,674,376

*See Sources and Explanations in the front of the volume.

Television stations and affiliations

San Antonio	100%	KABB	FOX
San Antonio	100%	KENS	CBS
San Antonio	100%	KHCE	Independent
San Antonio	100%	KLRN	PBS
San Antonio	100%	KRRT	WB
San Antonio	100%	KSAT	ABC
San Antonio	100%	KTRG	Independent Spanish
San Antonio	100%	KVAW	Independent Spanish
San Antonio	100%	KVDA	Telemundo
San Antonio	100%	KWEX	Univision

Cable systems and subscribers
   Time Warner   186,932

Military installations, September 2001
   Fort Sam Houston (Army), San Antonio   13,178
   Lackland Air Force Base, San Antonio   167

Businesses and other major employers

City of San Antonio; San Antonio; city government 12,000

Baptist Health System Hospital; San Antonio   5,989

Cingular Wireless; San Antonio; radiotelephone communication   5,000

Trans Western Commercial Services; San Antonio; real estate leasing   5,000

University of Texas Health Science Center; San Antonio 4,257

Santa Rosa Children's Hospital; San Antonio   3,000

U.S. Postal Service; San Antonio   3,000

H. E. Butt Grocery Co.; San Antonio; grocery store 2,800

U.S. Veterans Hospital; San Antonio   2,700

Southwest Research Institute Inc.; San Antonio; commercial physical research   2,424

Baptist Health System; San Antonio; hospital, medical school   2,300

Bexar County Hospital District; San Antonio   2,252

AT&T Corp.; San Antonio; long-distance telephone 2,100

Pacific Telesis Group; San Antonio; telephone communication   2,000

City of San Antonio; San Antonio; water, solid waste management   1,893

Methodist Healthcare System; San Antonio; hospital 1,744

VIA Metropolitan Transit; San Antonio; bus line operations   1,685

Dee Howard Aircraft Maintenance; San Antonio; aircraft maintenance   1,600

Bexar County; San Antonio; sheriff's office   1,500

City Public Service; San Antonio; electric power transmission   1,500

Frost National Bank; San Antonio; commercial bank 1,500

Hawkins Associates Inc.; San Antonio; temporary help 1,500

Procter and Gamble Co.; San Antonio; detergents 1,500

QVC Inc.; San Antonio; TV home shopping   1,468

Alamo Community College District; San Antonio 1,400

Goodwill Industries of San Antonio; San Antonio; job training   1,300

OnPoint; San Antonio; travel agency   1,300

Valero Refining Co.; San Antonio; petroleum refining 1,263

Bank of America Corp.; San Antonio; commercial bank 1,183

Bexar County; San Antonio; county government   1,173

USAA Federal Savings Bank; San Antonio; federal savings banks   1,124

Texas Dept. of Human Services; San Antonio   1,083

Calling Solutions Inc.; San Antonio; telemarketing 1,062

Staff Professionals Inc.; San Antonio; employee leasing 1,000

SBC Telecom Inc.; San Antonio; telephone communications   900

USAA Life Insurance Co.; San Antonio; life reinsurance carriers   850

Boeing Co.; San Antonio; airplanes   800

Hearst Corp.; San Antonio; newspaper   800

Sanitors Southwest of San Antonio Inc.; San Antonio;
  janitorial service   800

Selrico Services Inc.; San Antonio; caterers   800

Fairchild Dornier Corp.; San Antonio; airplanes   780

Norwood Promotional Products Inc.; San Antonio;
  plastic foam products   750

St. Mary's University of San Antonio; San Antonio   750

Pabst Brewing Co.; San Antonio; beer   700

Radio Cap Co.; San Antonio; advertising   700

Sony Corp.; San Antonio; semiconductor circuit
  networks   700

Southwestern Bell Telephone Co.; San Antonio;
  telephone communications   669

Philips Semiconductor VLSI Inc.; San Antonio;
  semiconductors   650

Standard Aero Inc.; San Antonio; engine repair   642

Army and Air Force Exchange Service; San Antonio;
  Army-Navy goods stores   625

Lockheed Martin; San Antonio; aircraft   600

U.S. Defense Dept.; San Antonio   600

Burns International Security Services Corp.; San
  Antonio; security guard   550

Hyatt Corp.; San Antonio; hotel, franchised   550

University of Incarnate Word; San Antonio   550

Accord Medical Management Inc.; San Antonio; hospital
  500

Air Force Insurance Fund; San Antonio; Army-Navy
  goods stores   500

Associated Payroll Control Inc.; San Antonio; payroll
  support   500

DPT Laboratories; San Antonio; personal service agents
  500

KCI New Technologies Inc.; San Antonio; medical
  equipment rental   500

MCMI Food Co.; San Antonio; investment holding
  company   500

OneSource Facility Services Inc.; San Antonio; janitorial
  service   500

Union Pacific Railroad Co.; San Antonio; freight hauling
  500

Texas 21st District

Central — parts of San Antonio, Austin, and suburbs

The 21st is a staunchly Republican, mostly suburban and rural district that connects the cities of San Antonio and Austin via Interstate 35, with the so-called Hill Country and some rural ranching communities in between and to the west.

About 30 percent of the 21st's population comes from San Antonio's Bexar County (pronounced BEAR), with the district taking in the mostly comfortable north and northeast parts of the city and its suburbs, and cupping the airport (located in the 20th). Another 25 percent of the population comes from Austin's Travis County, mostly in suburbs populated with workers in the high-tech industry. Comal County, the only other jurisdiction with at least 50,000 people, is located northeast of San Antonio and takes in almost all of New Braunfels, which was founded by German immigrants

in the 1840s. Nearly one in five district residents claims some German ancestry, more than any other Texas district.

Military installations contribute to the 12th's economy, and the city of Kerrville has an active veterans hospital. Hill Country is home to many retirees who once lived in Austin or San Antonio. Llano County, in the northern part of the district, has the highest percentage of elderly residents in the state (31 percent). Kerr and Gillespie Counties, southwest of Llano, also have large over-65 populations.

The 21st produces a consistent GOP vote at all levels. In 2002, Republican governor Rick Perry won 73 percent of the district vote, his third-highest total among Texas's 32 districts.

Major Industry

Agriculture, technology, government.

Notable

The Admiral Nimitz Museum and Historical Center in Fredericksburg has a major collection of Allied and Japanese aircraft, guns, and other artifacts from World War II; former president Lyndon B. Johnson was born in Blanco County.

Election Returns

	Republican		Democratic		Other	
President 2000	206,157	72.8%	77,056	27.2%		
House 2002	161,836	72.9%	56,206	25.3%	4,051	1.8

District Profile

Population   651,619

Total area (square miles)   11,088.1
  Land area (square miles)   10,978.6

Population per square mile   59.4

Counties (2000 population)

Bandera	17,645	Kendall	23,743
Bexar (pt.)	196,596	Kerr	43,653
Blanco	8,418	Kimble	4,468
Burnet	34,147	Llano	17,044
Comal	78,021	Mason	3,738
Gillespie	20,814	Menard	2,360
Hays (pt.)	40,311	Travis (pt.)	160,661

Cities and other areas over 10,000 (2000 population)
  Austin (pt.)   89,846
  Canyon Lake CDP   16,870
  Kerrville   20,425
  New Braunfels (pt.)   35,328
  San Antonio (pt.)   162,956

Race and Hispanic or Latino origin*
  White   77.2%
  Black or African American   2.1%
  American Indian or Alaska Native   0.3%
  Asian   2.0%
  Native Hawaiian or other Pacific Islander   0.1%
  Some other race   0.1%
  Hispanic or Latino origin   17.2%
  Two or more races   1.1%

As percentage of total population.

Ancestry*

Dutch	1.1%	Italian	2.1%
English	10.1%	Polish	1.6%
French	2.7%	Scotch-Irish	2.6%
German	16.2%	Scottish	2.0%
Irish	8.7%	USA/American	5.4%

As estimated percentage of total population.

Universities and colleges, 2000–2001 enrollment

Schreiner College, Kerrville   780
University of the Incarnate Word, San Antonio   3,702

Newspapers and circulation

	District circulation	Total circulation
Austin American Statesman	47,285	186,020
Dallas Morning News	1,518	495,624
New Braunfels Herald-Zeitung	4,476	7,573
San Angelo Standard-Times	1,134	27,823
San Antonio Express-News	51,818	216,752
*USA Today**	3,533	1,674,376

See Sources and Explanations in the front of the volume.

Television stations and affiliations

Austin	51%	KAKW	Univision
Austin	51%	KEYE	CBS
Austin	51%	KLRU	PBS
Austin	51%	KNVA	WB
Austin	51%	KTBC	FOX
Austin	51%	KVUE	ABC
Austin	51%	KXAM	NBC
Austin	51%	KXAN	NBC
San Antonio	30%	KABB	FOX
San Antonio	30%	KENS	CBS
San Antonio	30%	KHCE	Independent
San Antonio	30%	KLRN	PBS
San Antonio	30%	KRRT	WB
San Antonio	30%	KSAT	ABC
San Antonio	30%	KTRG	Independent Spanish
San Antonio	30%	KVAW	Independent Spanish
San Antonio	30%	KVDA	Telemundo
San Antonio	30%	KWEX	Univision
San Angelo	19%	KACB	NBC
San Angelo	19%	KIDY	FOX, UPN
San Angelo	19%	KLST	CBS

Cable systems and subscribers

Classic   5,445
Guadalupe Valley Communications   5,580
Northland   6,255
Time Warner   39,046

Military installations, September 2001

Lackland Training Annex, San Antonio   18,441
Bee Cave (Army Guard), Austin   140

Businesses and other major employers

Methodist Healthcare System Hospital; San Antonio   5,400
Motorola Inc.; Austin; semiconductors   2,500
Tivoli Systems Inc.; Austin; computer software   2,000
Broadwing Communication Services Inc.; Austin; data communication   1,783
Lance Inc.; San Antonio; snacks   1,470

San Antonio State Hospital; San Antonio   1,300
Guaranty Bank; Austin; federal savings institutions   1,200
Miller Curtain Co.; San Antonio; draperies   1,100
Computer Sciences Corp.; Austin; computer programming   1,000
Texas Mental Health and Mental Retardation Dept.; Kerrville   880
Barton Creek Resort and Clubs Inc.; Austin; membership hotel   800
TNL Flight Services Inc.; Austin; air transportation   750
McKenna Memorial Hospital; New Braunfels   741
Hilti Inc.; San Antonio; metal fasteners   725
First USA Bank; Austin; commercial bank   700
Guaranty Residential Lending Inc.; Austin; mortgage bankers   700
WorldCom Inc.; San Antonio; telephone communication   700
LCRA Transmission Services; Johnson City; electric distribution transformers   680
Alamo Cement Co.; San Antonio; cement   672
Sid Peterson Memorial Hospital; Kerrville   670
Trinity University; San Antonio   618
BMC Software Inc.; Austin; utility computer software   600
Heart Employee Leasing Inc.; Austin; employee leasing   600
Southwest Airlines; Bulverde   600
U.S. Veterans Hospital; Kerrville   600
Plains Cotton Cooperative Assn.; New Braunfels; apparel, fabrics   581
Southwestern Bell Telephone Co.; Austin; telephone communication   526
Professional Contract Services Inc.; Austin; building maintenance   500

Texas 22nd District

Southeast Houston and southern suburbs; most of Fort Bend and Brazoria Counties

The solidly Republican 22nd includes nearly all of Brazoria and Fort Bend Counties south of Houston, plus a small slice of the city itself. Most residents live in fast-growing Houston suburbs outside Harris County or in more-rural settings. The district contains booming communities such as Sugar Land, as well as upscale homes surrounding the Lyndon B. Johnson Space Center, where many NASA scientists and astronauts live. Numerous residents work at the space center, located in the neighboring 9th District. *(See map p. 869.)*

About half of the population resides in Fort Bend County, which includes Rep. Tom DeLay's hometown of Sugar Land. Since the 1960s, the area has changed from a sugar-growing center into suburbia. Sugar refiner Imperial Holly still maintains its presence in Sugar Land, but the city has welcomed new planned developments and a range of corporations. It is not uncommon to find six-figure earners living in Sugar Land.

Brazoria County, where more than one-fourth of the population lives, has retained much of its agrarian feel. Many residents grow rice and sorghum and raise cattle. The 22nd's portions of Brazoria are not as upscale as Fort Bend but nonetheless have a median income more than $10,000 above the national mark.

Moving east, the 22nd takes up parts of southeastern Harris County, including a chunk of Houston. This part of Harris tends toward the upscale: Some of the wealthiest areas in the county are in southeast Houston, near Ellington Field, a former Air Force base that now houses the space center's aircraft operations.

Major Industry

Aerospace, agriculture, retail.

Notable

The annual "Texian Market Days" in Fort Bend County include reenactments of 1830s pioneer life, when the area was settled by some of the "Old 300" families led by Stephen F. Austin; George Observatory in Brazos Bend State Park includes a memorial to the seven astronauts who died aboard the space shuttle *Challenger* in 1986.

Election Returns

	Republican		Democratic		Other	
President 2000	156,219	68.2%	72,806	31.8%		
House 2002	100,499	63.2%	55,716	35.0%	2,869	1.8%

District Profile

Population   651,619

Total area (square miles)   1,706.4
  Land area (square miles)   1,670.1

Population per square mile   390.2

Counties (2000 population)
Brazoria (pt.)   177,519
Fort Bend (pt.)   321,994
Harris (pt.)   152,106

Cities and other areas over 10,000 (2000 population)
Alvin (pt.)   21,413
Angleton (pt.)   17,178
Deer Park (pt.)   28,493
Houston (pt.)   46,678
Lake Jackson (pt.)   26,384
La Porte (pt.)   24,275
Mission Bend CDP (pt.)   19,158
Missouri City (pt.)   47,419
New Territory CDP   13,861
Pasadena (pt.)   17,238
Pearland (pt.)   37,630
Pecan Grove CDP   13,551
Richmond   11,081
Rosenberg   24,043
Stafford (pt.)   15,371
Sugar Land   63,328

Race and Hispanic or Latino origin*
White   60.1%
Black or African American   10.1%
American Indian or Alaska Native   0.3%
Asian   8.3%
Native Hawaiian or other Pacific Islander   0.0%
Some other race   0.1%
Hispanic or Latino origin   19.7%
Two or more races   1.4%

As percentage of total population.

Ancestry*
English	6.9%	Polish	1.4%
French	2.9%	Scotch-Irish	1.4%
German	10.5%	Scottish	1.3%
Irish	6.8%	USA/American	5.8%
Italian	2.2%		

As estimated percentage of total population.

Universities and colleges, 2000–2001 enrollment
Alvin Community College, Alvin   3,665
San Jacinto College, Houston   6,086
San Jacinto College, Pasadena   10,507

Newspapers and circulation
	District circulation	Total circulation
Clute Facts	9,280	16,682
Houston Chronicle	73,433	548,437
*USA Today**	1,672	1,674,376

See Sources and Explanations in the front of the volume.

Television stations and affiliations
Houston	100%	KAVU	ABC
Houston	100%	KBTX	CBS
Houston	100%	KETH	Independent
Houston	100%	KHOU	CBS
Houston	100%	KHWB	WB
Houston	100%	KLTJ	Independent
Houston	100%	KNWS	Independent
Houston	100%	KPRC	NBC
Houston	100%	KPXB	PAX
Houston	100%	KRIV	FOX
Houston	100%	KTBU	Independent
Houston	100%	KTMD	Telemundo
Houston	100%	KTRK	ABC
Houston	100%	KTXH	UPN
Houston	100%	KUHT	PBS
Houston	100%	KXLN	Univision
Houston	100%	KZJL	Independent Spanish

Cable systems and subscribers
Charter   828
Classic   1,110
CMA   4,331
Time Warner   228,470

Military installations, September 2001
Ellington Field (Air National Guard), Genoa   1,022

Businesses and other major employers
Schlumberger Technology Corp.; Sugar Land; oil, gas exploration   7,000
Schlumberger Ltd.; Missouri City; construction, repair services   4,000
Fluor Corp.; Sugar Land; petroleum engineering   2,500
Shell Oil Co.; Deer Park; chemicals   2,500

Fort Bend County; Richmond; county government
2,400

BMC Software Inc.; Pearland; software   2,000

Texas Instruments Inc.; Stafford; semiconductors   1,800

United Parcel Service Inc.; Stafford; parcel delivery
1,200

E. I. Du Pont De Nemours and Co.; La Porte; x-ray film,
supplies   1,100

Suntron Corp.; Sugar Land; harness assemblies,
electronic use   1,100

Union Oil Company of California; Sugar Land; oil, gas
well drilling   1,000

BASF Corp.; Freeport; industrial chemicals   850

BP Amoco Chemical Co.; Alvin; oil/gas drilling
equipment   850

Computer Camp; Sugar Land; educational software   822

Industrial Specialists Inc.; Clute; building insulation
800

Noble Drilling Inc.; Sugar Land; drilling oil and gas
wells   800

Imperial Sugar Co.; Sugar Land; granulated cane sugar
715

American Leader Technology; Freeport; telephone
equipment   700

Solutia Inc.; Alvin; chemicals   680

Memorial Hermann Hospital System; Houston   650

Input/Output Inc.; Alvin; testing equipment   630

Texas Criminal Justice Dept.; Rosharon   626

Lubrizol Corp.; Deer Park; chemical preparations   611

Celanese Americas Corp.; Pasadena; industrial chemicals
600

Encompass Services Corp.; Freeport; plumbing, heating,
air-conditioning   600

Wal-Mart Stores Inc.; Alvin; department stores   600

Reliant Energy Inc.; Thompsons; electric services   582

Texas Criminal Justice Dept.; Richmond   571

Brazoport Community Hospital; Lake Jackson   565

Alpha Tech International Inc.; Stafford; pressure
measurement instruments   550

Babcock and Wilcox Co.; Richmond; boiler and furnace
contractors   550

Boeing Co.; Houston; aviation, aeronautical engineering
530

Clear Lake Regional Medical Center Inc.; Alvin   500

General Pipe Service Inc.; Pearland; oil field services
500

Hines Horticulture Inc.; Fulshear; flowers and florists
supplies   500

Igloo Products Corp.; Katy; ice chests or coolers   500

Schlumberger Technology Corp.; Rosharon; process
control instruments   500

WorldCom Inc.; Sugar Land; local/long-distance
telephone   500

Texas 23rd District

Southwest — Laredo, San Antonio suburbs

The 23rd District is larger than most states east of the Mississippi River—residents like to say the area encompasses two time zones and three climates. Taking up 800 miles of the U.S. border with Mexico along the Rio Grande River,

the politically moderate 23rd skims El Paso in the west and heads over to San Antonio in the east. The largest district in a state that boasts of doing everything bigger and better, the 23rd includes all or part of 24 counties. The district's population is 67 percent Hispanic.

The 23rd includes some of the nation's poorest counties along its southern border. Seasonal employment, the influx of legal and illegal immigrants, and an abundance of cheaper Mexican labor contribute to high unemployment. Manufacturing operations along the border known as *maquiladoras* are an integral part of the economy. An increase in trade and manufacturing in the 1990s has benefited the area.

Border communities often seem to have more in common with their Mexican neighbors than with the rest of Texas. Laredo celebrates Mexican Independence Day, and three bridges connect it to its Mexican sister city, Nuevo Laredo.

The 23rd is politically competitive, with Republicans holding a huge advantage in the San Antonio region and Democrats holding an edge in Laredo's Webb County and in some heavily Hispanic counties farther south and in the west. George W. Bush handily won the 23rd in the 2000 presidential election. But the district swung Democratic in 2002, largely because of a strong turnout in Laredo, the hometown of Democratic gubernatorial nominee Tony Sanchez. He won the 23rd with 54 percent of the two-party vote, a bit higher than Democratic Senate nominee Ron Kirk's 53 percent showing.

Major Industry

Agriculture, trade, tourism, defense.

Notable

Texas's largest county, Brewster, is roughly 6,200 square miles, about the size of Connecticut and Rhode Island combined.

Election Returns

	Republican		Democratic		Other	
President 2000	105,789	58.6%	74,727	41.4%		
House 2002	77,573	51.5%	71,067	47.2%	1,912	1.3%

District Profile

Population   651,619

Total area (square miles)   55,536.4
   Land area (square miles)   55,414.9

Population per square mile   11.8

Counties (2000 population)

Bexar (pt.)	172,051	Pecos	16,809
Brewster	8,866	Presidio	7,304
Crockett	4,099	Reagan	3,326
Culberson	2,975	Real	3,047
Dimmit	10,248	Reeves	13,137
Edwards	2,162	Sutton	4,077
El Paso (pt.)	28,003	Terrell	1,081
Hudspeth	3,344	Upton	3,404
Jeff Davis	2,207	Uvalde	25,926
Kinney	3,379	Val Verde	44,856
Maverick	47,297	Webb	193,117
Medina	39,304	Zavala	11,600

Cities and other areas over 10,000 (2000 population)

Del Rio	33,867	San Antonio (pt.)	133,432
Eagle Pass	22,413	Uvalde	14,929
Laredo	176,576		

Race and Hispanic or Latino origin*

White   29.8%
Black or African American   1.4%
American Indian or Alaska Native   0.3%
Asian   1.0%
Native Hawaiian or other Pacific Islander   0.0%
Some other race   0.1%
Hispanic or Latino origin   66.8%
Two or more races   0.7%

*As percentage of total population.

Ancestry*

English	4.2%	Irish	3.9%
French	1.2%	Italian	1.2%
German	6.8%	USA/American	3.5%

*As estimated percentage of total population.

Universities and colleges, 2000–2001 enrollment

ITT Technical Institute, San Antonio   695
Laredo Community College, Laredo   7,322
Southwest Texas Junior College, Uvalde   3,715
Sul Ross State University, Alpine   2,838
Texas A&M International University, Laredo   3,038
University of Texas, San Antonio   18,830

Newspapers and circulation

	District circulation	Total circulation
El Paso Times	2,428	74,595
Laredo Morning Times	19,572	20,540
Odessa American	1,859	25,714
San Angelo Standard-Times	2,499	27,823
San Antonio Express-News	40,612	216,752
*USA Today**	3,108	1,674,376

*See Sources and Explanations in the front of the volume.

Television stations and affiliations

Odessa-Midland	44%	KMID	ABC
Odessa-Midland	44%	KMLM	Independent
Odessa-Midland	44%	KOCV	PBS
Odessa-Midland	44%	KOSA	CBS
Odessa-Midland	44%	KPEJ	FOX, UPN
Odessa-Midland	44%	KWAB	NBC
Odessa-Midland	44%	KWES	NBC
San Antonio	26%	KABB	FOX
San Antonio	26%	KENS	CBS
San Antonio	26%	KHCE	Independent
San Antonio	26%	KLRN	PBS
San Antonio	26%	KRRT	WB
San Antonio	26%	KSAT	ABC
San Antonio	26%	KTRG	Independent Spanish
San Antonio	26%	KVAW	Independent Spanish
San Antonio	26%	KVDA	Telemundo
San Antonio	26%	KWEX	Univision
El Paso	16%	KCOS	PBS
El Paso	16%	KDBC	CBS
El Paso	16%	KFOX	FOX
El Paso	16%	KINT	Univision
El Paso	16%	KRWG	PBS
El Paso	16%	KSCE	Independent
El Paso	16%	KTSM	NBC
El Paso	16%	KVIA	ABC
San Angelo	8%	KACB	NBC
San Angelo	8%	KIDY	FOX, UPN
San Angelo	8%	KLST	CBS
Laredo	6%	KGNS	NBC
Laredo	6%	KLDO	Univision
Laredo	6%	KVTV	CBS

Cable systems and subscribers

Charter   4,498
Circle Bar Cable TV   1,408
Classic   7,331
Marfa TV Cable   860
Presidio TV Cable   615
Time Warner   52,087
U.S. Cable   7,929

Military installations, September 2001

Laughlin Air Force Base, Del Rio   1,957

Businesses and other major employers

Bank of America Corp.; San Antonio; commercial bank   57,000
United Services Automobile Assn.; San Antonio; property damage insurance   17,069
West Telemarketing Corp.; San Antonio; telemarketing   2,844
University of Texas at San Antonio; San Antonio   2,800
Six Flags San Antonio; San Antonio; theme park   1,775
City of Laredo; Laredo; city government   1,759
Mercy Hospital of Laredo; Laredo   1,300
Robertshaw Holdings Corp.; Laredo; warehousing   1,300
Clarke American Checks Inc.; San Antonio; checkbooks   1,050
Electrolux Home Products Inc.; El Paso; vacuum cleaners   1,000
Northside Independent School District; Helotes   1,000
Phoenix Assembly; Laredo; printed circuit boards   1,000
Sunbeam Products Inc.; Del Rio; purchasing service   1,000
WorldCom Inc.; San Antonio; telephone communication   1,000
International Data; Del Rio; coupon redemption service   967
Sony Electronics Inc.; Laredo; audio/video equipment   800
TK Holdings Inc.; Del Rio; warehousing   800
Ultramar Inc.; San Antonio; petroleum refining   800
South Texas Primary Care Inc.; Laredo; home health care   775
San Antonio Shoe Inc.; Del Rio; shoe stores   625
Travel-Ease Inc.; San Antonio; employee leasing   600
U.S. Bureau of Customs and Border Protection; Laredo; immigration services   558
Village Farms; Fort Davis; construction, civil engineering   538
Agrilink Foods Inc.; Uvalde; canned fruits   500

Army and Air Force Exchange Service; El Paso;
  Army-Navy goods stores   500
Del Monte Corp.; Crystal City; canned fruits   500
HCA Inc. Hospital; Laredo   500
Laredo Community College; Laredo   500
Pecos Barstow Toyah Independent School District; Pecos;
  500

Texas 24th District

Parts of Dallas, Fort Worth, and Arlington

The 24th is a swath of working-class neighborhoods that takes in mostly black areas in Fort Worth, Hispanic areas in Dallas, and white areas in between. Hispanics make up a plurality of district residents (38 percent), followed by whites (35 percent), and blacks (22 percent). *(See map p. 862.)*

Nearly 90 percent of district residents live in Arlington, Dallas, Fort Worth, or Grand Prairie, all of which the 24th shares with other districts. In Arlington and Grand Prairie, which lie along the Interstate 30 corridor between Fort Worth and Dallas, many residents are unionized workers who work at the General Motors plant in the district or at nearby defense contractors Bell Helicopter, Northrop Grumman, and Lockheed Martin. Blue-collar workers in the 24th have borne the brunt of military cutbacks and defense contractor layoffs. The city was dealt a setback in 1998 when Dallas Naval Air Station was shut down.

Arlington's entertainment venues—including the Ballpark at Arlington, home of the Texas Rangers—are large employers in the district, and the University of Texas at Arlington to the southwest benefits the local economy as well. The Fort Worth part of the 24th takes in the city's hospital district, which includes five different medical facilities.

The large urban minority vote propels Democratic candidates to victory in the 24th, even when Republicans win handily statewide. Fort Worth's Tarrant County has a stronger Democratic lean than Dallas County because of the heavily black precincts in southeastern Fort Worth. There is some GOP strength in northeastern Arlington and just southwest of Dallas. But overall, the 24th is solid Democratic territory: In the 2002 Senate race, Democrat Ron Kirk carried the 24th by nearly 20 percentage points, taking 63 percent in Tarrant and 54 percent in Dallas.

Major Industry
Defense, transportation, entertainment.

Notable
Six Flags over Texas amusement park is home to the Texas Giant, often referred to as the No. 1 wooden roller coaster in the world; the Ballpark at Arlington is home to a baseball museum and a children's learning center.

Election Returns

	Republican		Democratic		Other	
President 2000	70,665	45.7%	83,806	54.3%		
House 2002	38,332	34.0%	73,002	64.7%	1,560	1.4%

District Profile

Population   651,619

Total area (square miles)   261.4
  Land area (square miles)   248.5

Population per square mile   2,622.2

Counties (2000 population)
  Dallas (pt.)   288,358
  Tarrant (pt.)   363,261

Cities and other areas over 10,000 (2000 population)
  Arlington (pt.)   140,407
  Cedar Hill (pt.)   19,665
  Dallas (pt.)   139,111
  Duncanville (pt.)   30,665
  Forest Hill (pt.)   12,906
  Fort Worth (pt.)   192,305
  Grand Prairie (pt.)   111,637

Race and Hispanic or Latino origin*
  White   35.3%
  Black or African American   21.7%
  American Indian or Alaska Native   0.4%
  Asian   3.1%
  Native Hawaiian or other Pacific Islander   0.1%
  Some other race   0.1%
  Hispanic or Latino origin   38.0%
  Two or more races   1.3%

As percentage of total population.

Ancestry*
English 4.5%	Irish 4.4%
French 1.1%	USA/American 4.8%
German 5.3%	

As estimated percentage of total population.

Universities and colleges, 2000–2001 enrollment
  Dallas Baptist University, Dallas   4,032
  Education America, Fort Worth   516
  ITT Technical Institute, Arlington   401
  Mountain View College, Dallas   5,491
  Northwood University, Cedar Hill   1,014
  Texas Wesleyan University, Fort Worth   3,133
  University of Texas, Arlington   20,424

Newspapers and circulation

	District circulation	Total circulation
Dallas Morning News	30,158	495,624
Fort Worth Star-Telegram	36,163	224,885
*USA Today**	4,181	1,674,376

See Sources and Explanations in the front of the volume.

Television stations and affiliations
Dallas-Fort Worth	100%	KDAF	WB
Dallas-Fort Worth	100%	KDFI	Independent
Dallas-Fort Worth	100%	KDFW	FOX
Dallas-Fort Worth	100%	KDTN	PBS

Dallas–Fort Worth	100%	KDTX	Independent
Dallas–Fort Worth	100%	KERA	PBS
Dallas–Fort Worth	100%	KFWD	Independent
Dallas–Fort Worth	100%	KMPX	Independent
Dallas–Fort Worth	100%	KPXD	PAX
Dallas–Fort Worth	100%	KSTR	Telefutura
Dallas–Fort Worth	100%	KTAQ	Independent
Dallas–Fort Worth	100%	KTVT	CBS
Dallas–Fort Worth	100%	KTXA	UPN
Dallas–Fort Worth	100%	KUVN	Univision
Dallas–Fort Worth	100%	KXAS	NBC
Dallas–Fort Worth	100%	KXTX	Telemundo
Dallas–Fort Worth	100%	WFAA	ABC

Cable systems and subscribers
Charter 61,520
Comcast 95,473

Military installations, September 2001
Grand Prairie Reserve Complex, Grand Prairie 216

Businesses and other major employers
Lockheed Martin Corp.; Grand Prairie; missiles, space vehicles 4,000

Vought Aircraft Industries Inc.; Dallas; industrial/commercial equipment inspection service 3,600

Mrs Baird's Bakeries Business Trust; Fort Worth; breads and cakes 3,500

Falcon Pharmaceuticals; Fort Worth 3,000

University of Texas at Arlington; Arlington 3,000

L-3 Communications Corp.; Arlington; radio/TV communications equipment 2,400

Tarrant County Hospital District; Fort Worth 2,100

General Motors Corp.; Arlington; motor vehicles, car bodies 2,000

Vought Aircraft Industries Inc.; Dallas; aircraft 2,000

Methodist Hospitals of Dallas Inc.; Dallas 1,825

Texwood Industries; Duncanville; kitchen cabinets 1,750

Arlington Memorial Hospital Foundation Inc.; Arlington 1,700

Tarrant County Junior College District; Fort Worth 1,487

Huguley Behavioral Health Hospital; Fort Worth 1,008

Bell Helicopter Textron Inc.; Grand Prairie; helicopters 1,000

Poly-America; Grand Prairie; polyethylene film 1,000

Raytheon Training; Arlington; electronic training devices 850

FedEx Ground Inc.; Fort Worth; trucking 800

Sweetheart Cup Co.; Dallas; cups 800

Albertson's Inc.; Fort Worth; warehousing 790

Siemens Dematic Postal Automation; Arlington; letter handling, addressing machines 735

Potter Concrete Co.; Fort Worth; concrete work 710

Nissan Motor Acceptance Corp.; Arlington; finance companies 700

Summer Institute of Linguistics Inc.; Dallas; noncommercial research 700

Halliburton Energy Services Inc.; Fort Worth; oil field machinery 650

Miller Brewing Co.; Fort Worth; beer 636

Dallas Baptist University; Dallas 620

ATCO Rubber Products Inc.; Fort Worth; plastic pipes 600

J. B. Hunt Transport Inc.; Dallas; trucking 600

Wal-Mart Stores Inc.; Grand Prairie; department stores 600

Aramark Sports and Entertainment Services Inc.; Arlington; concessionaire 550

Fairfield Properties; Grand Prairie; real estate managers 550

Bell Helicopter Textron Inc.; Hurst; helicopter parts 505

BG Distribution Partners; Grand Prairie; warehousing 500

City of Grand Prairie; Grand Prairie; police 500

GRUMA Corp.; Dallas; tortilla chips 500

Tandycrafts Inc.; Fort Worth; picture and mirror frames 500

Williamson-Dickie Manufacturing Co.; Fort Worth; work clothing 500

Texas 25th District

Southern Houston and suburbs

The 25th encompasses many of Houston's working-class suburbs as well as some of its wealthy estates. It is a semicircle carved through south and southeast Harris County and a small part of Fort Bend County, stretching from the petrochemical suburbs of Baytown and Pasadena to the multimillion-dollar estates of Bellaire. It contains a mix of blue-collar union supporters, suburban blacks, Reagan Democrats, and a sizable portion of Houston's Jewish population. *(See map p. 869.)*

Redistricting after the 2000 census modified its boundaries, but the 25th still leans Democratic. The redraw reinforced its left-leaning tendencies by removing some more conservative western precincts.

The 25th has been known as a swing district, and often its residents are the quintessential Texas ticket-splitters—they tend to be fiscally conservative but socially progressive, supporting issues such as abortion and gay rights. The 25th's eastern edges have refineries, honky-tonk bars, and union Democrats who voted for Ronald Reagan in 1980 and for Al Gore in 2000. Stances on issues, not party affiliation, often decide close elections.

Once mostly agricultural, the district's land was converted long ago to industrial purposes, including refining and plastics production. The 25th also includes most of the Texas Medical Center and the Port of Houston, which are important to Houston's economy. Many residents commute to NASA's nearby Lyndon B. Johnson Space Center (located in the 9th). The district also claims Rice University, the Houston Zoo, the Astrodome, and Reliant Stadium, home to the Texans football team.

Major Industry
Energy, shipping, health care, research.

Notable

Gilley's, a country and western bar featured in the 1980 movie *Urban Cowboy,* was in Pasadena; the club closed and later burned.

Election Returns

	Republican		Democratic		Other	
President 2000	81,359	48.4%	86,764	51.6%		
House 2002	50,041	43.1%	63,590	54.8%	2,495	2.1%

District Profile

Population 651,619

Total area (square miles) 279.9
  Land area (square miles) 259.0

Population per square mile 2,515.9

Counties (2000 population)
  Fort Bend (pt.) 32,458
  Harris (pt.) 619,161

Cities and other areas over 10,000 (2000 population)
  Baytown (pt.) 43,051
  Bellaire 15,642
  Houston (pt.) 453,368
  Pasadena (pt.) 77,786
  West University Place 14,211

Race and Hispanic or Latino origin*
  White 36.6%
  Black or African American 22.7%
  American Indian or Alaska Native 0.2%
  Asian 4.8%
  Native Hawaiian or other Pacific Islander 0.0%
  Some other race 0.1%
  Hispanic or Latino origin 34.3%
  Two or more races 1.3%

As percentage of total population.

Ancestry*

English	4.9%	Italian	1.3%
French	1.9%	Scotch-Irish	1.2%
German	5.8%	Subsaharan	1.8%
Irish	4.3%	USA/American	4.5%

As estimated percentage of total population.

Universities and colleges, 2000–2001 enrollment
  Baylor College of Medicine, Houston 1,192
  Houston Baptist University, Houston 2,673
  Lee College, Baytown 5,932
  Rice University, Houston 4,205
  Texas Chiropractic College, Pasadena 388
  University of Texas Health Science Center, Houston 3,143

Newspapers and circulation

	District circulation	Total circulation
Houston Chronicle	71,677	548,437
*USA Today**	2,681	1,674,376

See Sources and Explanations in the front of the volume.

Television stations and affiliations

Houston	100%	KAVU	ABC
Houston	100%	KBTX	CBS
Houston	100%	KETH	Independent
Houston	100%	KHOU	CBS
Houston	100%	KHWB	WB
Houston	100%	KLTJ	Independent
Houston	100%	KNWS	Independent
Houston	100%	KPRC	NBC
Houston	100%	KPXB	PAX
Houston	100%	KRIV	FOX
Houston	100%	KTBU	Independent
Houston	100%	KTMD	Telemundo
Houston	100%	KTRK	ABC
Houston	100%	KTXH	UPN
Houston	100%	KUHT	PBS
Houston	100%	KXLN	Univision
Houston	100%	KZJL	Independent Spanish

Cable systems and subscribers
  Time Warner 27,152

Businesses and other major employers
  University of Texas Hospital; Houston 11,000
  Baylor College of Medicine Inc.; Houston 8,075
  Houston Independent School District; Houston 6,000
  Baker Hughes Oilfield Operations Inc.; Houston; oil, gas well drilling 5,000
  St. Luke's Episcopal Hospital; Houston 4,500
  Methodist Hospital; Houston 3,780
  Texas Children's Hospital; Houston 2,600
  Harris County Hospital District; Houston 2,200
  Contemporary Services Corp.; Houston; protective services 2,000
  Parsons Energy and Chemicals Group Inc.; Houston; ship, boat, machine designing 2,000
  University of Texas; Houston 2,000
  KS Management Services; Houston; shoe stores 1,700
  Rice University Inc.; Houston 1,689
  Memorial Hermann Hospital System; Houston 1,650
  AT&T Corp.; Houston; telephone communication 1,500
  Tenet Healthcare Corp. Hospital; Houston 1,500
  Transocean Offshore Deepwater Drilling Inc.; Houston; oil, gas well drilling 1,500
  Stage Stores Inc.; Houston; clothing stores 1,341
  ExxonMobil Oil Corp.; Houston; petroleum refining 1,250
  Pasadena Bayshore Hospital Inc.; Pasadena 1,200
  San Jacinto Methodist Hospital; Baytown 1,097
  AIM Management Group Inc.; Houston; management investment 1,060
  Austin Maintenance and Construction Inc.; Houston; building construction 1,000
  Exxon Coal USA Inc.; Baytown; energy resources 1,000
  ExxonMobil Upstream Research Co.; Houston; commercial physical research 1,000
  Rohm and Haas Texas Inc.; Deer Park; industrial chemicals 1,000
  Variable Annuity Life Insurance Co.; Houston 998
  Southwestern Bell Telephone Co.; Bellaire; local telephone 911

Styles and Styles Inc.; Houston; investment holding company   900

Lyondell Chemical Worldwide Inc.; Channelview; industrial chemicals   850

Reliant Energy Inc.; Houston; electric services   850

Coastal Holding Corp.; Houston; petroleum refining   848

Bayer Corp.; Baytown; industrial chemicals   830

Harris County Mental Health and Mental Retardation Authority; Houston   759

Industrial Security Services Corp.; Houston; security guard service   750

Phillips Petroleum Co.; Bellaire; oil/gas exploration   750

ExxonMobil Oil Corp.; Baytown; petroleum refining   700

First Homecare-Houston Inc.; Houston; home health care   700

Donohue Industries Inc.; Houston; paper mills   650

Alcon Laboratories Inc.; Houston; ophthalmic goods   600

Entergy-Koch; Houston; gas transmission   600

GE Packaged Power Inc.; Houston; power generators   600

Protherm Services Group; Pasadena; painting and paper hanging   600

Rosenbluth International Inc.; Houston; travel agency   600

Schlumberger International Inc.; Houston; oil field services   600

Shell Oil Co.; Houston; industry consultants   600

Union Tank Car Co.; Houston; train cars, equipment   600

Stolt-Nielsen Transportation Group Inc.; Houston; security brokers   599

V&M Star; Houston; steel pipe and tubes   561

Auchan USA Inc.; Houston; supermarkets   550

Wal-Mart Stores Inc.; Baytown; department stores   534

Columbia Bellaire Medical Center; Houston   530

American General Life Co.; Houston; computer programming   500

Bellaire General Hospital; Bellaire   500

City of Houston; Houston; environmental health program   500

Diagnostic Center Hospital Corp.; Houston   500

Dreco Inc.; Houston; oil field machinery   500

Kelsey-Seybold Clinic; Houston   500

Mobley Industrial Painters Inc.; La Porte; residential painting   500

O'Reilly Automotive Inc.; Houston; automotive parts   500

Randall's Food and Drugs Inc.; Baytown; grocery store   500

River Oaks Diagnostic Network; Houston; nuclear MRI device   500

Social Security Admin.; Houston   500

Stone and Webster Engineering Corp.; Houston; professional engineer   500

Texaco Inc.; Bellaire; purchasing service   500

Texas Iron Works Inc.; Houston; oil field equipment   500

Veritas DGC Inc.; Houston; seismograph surveys   500

Waukesha-Pearce Industries Inc.; Houston; oil field equipment   500

Texas 26th District

Dallas suburbs — Denton County

Tremendous growth in the suburbs north of Dallas pushed the 26th farther from the city in redistricting following the 2000 census. The district now is centered in Denton County, but takes in small parts of Tarrant, Collin, and Wise Counties. Denton County is home to two-thirds of the district's residents. *(See map p. 862.)*

As the Dallas-Fort Worth area grew in the 1990s, residents moved north into rural Denton and Collin Counties. Denton's population started expanding in the 1970s and continues to grow as upper-middle-class families build large homes. The district takes in northeastern Tarrant County, including the wealthy Fort Worth suburbs of Colleyville and Southlake, as well as the wealthier parts of Hurst, Euless, and Bedford (all shared with the 12th). In Collin County, once-rural towns such as Frisco and McKinney (both shared with the 3rd) have caught the overgrowth from the Plano area. However, the north and much of the west edge of the district remain rural and depend on cotton, eggs, cattle, and corn.

Transportation is a major economic force here. Part of Dallas-Fort Worth International Airport lies in the 26th, and the airport—one of the three largest in the nation—employs many residents. American Airlines' headquarters is at the airport. A major shipping artery, Interstate 35, which runs from the Mexican border, crosses the district. Alliance Airport, the first airport in the nation to be built specifically to serve the needs of business, also is in the district.

Overall, the 26th is predominantly white, upper-class, and suburban. Residents voted more than two-to-one for George W. Bush in the 2000 presidential election. The area tends to be socially and fiscally conservative, but local issues—such as highway congestion—remain the top priority for many.

Major Industry

Transportation, telecommunications.

Notable

Texas Motor Speedway, the nation's second-largest sports facility, is in Denton County.

Election Returns

	Republican		Democratic		Other	
President 2000	166,762	73.3%	60,771	26.7%		
House 2002	123,195	74.8%	37,485	22.8%	3,998	2.4%

District Profile

Population   651,619

Total area (square miles)   1,147.6
   Land area (square miles)   1,074.5

Population per square mile   606.4

Counties (2000 population)

Collin (pt.)	34,556	Tarrant (pt.)	183,830
Denton	432,976	Wise (pt.)	257

Cities and other areas over 10,000 (2000 population)

Bedford (pt.)   41,719
Carrollton (pt.)   59,754
Colleyville   19,636
The Colony   26,531
Corinth   11,325
Dallas (pt.)   22,273
Denton   80,537
Euless (pt.)   42,033
Flower Mound town   50,702
Grapevine (pt.)   42,059
Highland Village   12,173
Lewisville (pt.)   77,735
McKinney (pt.)   27,016
Southlake (pt.)   21,444

Race and Hispanic or Latino origin*

White   77.8%
Black or African American   5.0%
American Indian or Alaska Native   0.5%
Asian   4.0%
Native Hawaiian or other Pacific Islander   0.2%
Some other race   0.1%
Hispanic or Latino origin   11.0%
Two or more races   1.4%

As percentage of total population.

Ancestry*

Dutch	1.3%	Italian	2.6%
English	9.1%	Polish	1.5%
French	2.4%	Scotch-Irish	1.8%
German	12.9%	Scottish	2.0%
Irish	9.3%	USA/American	7.2%

As estimated percentage of total population.

Universities and colleges, 2000–2001 enrollment

Texas Woman's University, Denton   8,404
University of North Texas, Denton   27,054

Newspapers and circulation

	District circulation	Total circulation
Dallas Morning News	51,747	495,624
Fort Worth Star-Telegram	23,417	224,885
*USA Today**	1,947	1,674,376

See Sources and Explanations in the front of the volume.

Television stations and affiliations

Dallas-Fort Worth	100%	KDAF	WB
Dallas-Fort Worth	100%	KDFI	Independent
Dallas-Fort Worth	100%	KDFW	FOX
Dallas-Fort Worth	100%	KDTN	PBS
Dallas-Fort Worth	100%	KDTX	Independent
Dallas-Fort Worth	100%	KERA	PBS
Dallas-Fort Worth	100%	KFWD	Independent
Dallas-Fort Worth	100%	KMPX	Independent
Dallas-Fort Worth	100%	KPXD	PAX
Dallas-Fort Worth	100%	KSTR	Telefutura
Dallas-Fort Worth	100%	KTAQ	Independent
Dallas-Fort Worth	100%	KTVT	CBS
Dallas-Fort Worth	100%	KTXA	UPN
Dallas-Fort Worth	100%	KUVN	Univision
Dallas-Fort Worth	100%	KXAS	NBC
Dallas-Fort Worth	100%	KXTX	Telemundo
Dallas-Fort Worth	100%	WFAA	ABC

Cable systems and subscribers

Charter   19,763
Classic   2,377
Comcast   52,052

Businesses and other major employers

American Airlines Inc.; Fort Worth   12,500
Odyssey Resource Management Inc.; Euless; employee leasing   12,000
GameStop Corp.; Grapevine; mail-order computer software   8,000
Delta Airlines Inc.; Dallas   6,000
Con-Way Southern Express Inc.; Fort Worth; freight carrier   5,000
University of North Texas; Denton   4,000
Sabre Inc.; Fort Worth; airline schedules   3,000
American Eagle Airlines Inc.; Fort Worth   2,500
Hillcrest Medical Center Inc.; Lewisville   2,126
Sabre Inc.; Southlake; airline schedules   2,100
Certainteed Corp.; McKinney; mineral wool insulation   2,000
TXU Corp.; Carrollton; engineering services   2,000
Fleming Companies Inc.; Lewisville; food supplier   1,800
Star-Telegram Operating; Bedford; newspaper   1,800
Boeing Corinth Co.; Lake Dallas; electronic circuits   1,737
Dallas-Fort Worth International Airport Board; Dallas   1,700
Verizon Information Services Inc.; Dallas; telephone directories   1,500
Wal-Mart Stores Inc.; Sanger; warehousing   1,500
Travelocity.com; Fort Worth; Internet connections   1,200
Intel Corp.; Fort Worth; semiconductors   1,100
PACCAR Inc.; Denton; motor vehicles, car bodies   1,100
McKesson Corp.; Roanoke; warehousing   1,000
Texas Woman's University; Denton   1,000
Harris Methodist HEB Hospital; Bedford   924
Wherehouse Entertainment Inc.; Lewisville; tape stores   911
Denton Regional Medical Center Inc.; Denton   900
Texas Cable Partners; Flower Mound; cable TV   900
Unisource Worldwide Inc.; Carrollton; paper products   900
BankOne Corp.; Bedford; commercial bank   859
DaimlerChrysler Services; Roanoke; automotive dealer financing   850
Lewisville Independent School District; Lewisville   750
Electronic Data Systems Corp.; Fort Worth; computer software   702
Capital One Services Inc.; Fort Worth; credit card service   700

Marconi Communications Holdings Inc.; Bedford;
  telephone apparatus   700
Stonegate Senior Care; Flower Mound; skilled nursing
  care   700
Genuity Inc.; Lewisville; online service providers   686
Dallas Airmotive Inc.; Grapevine; aircraft, heavy
  equipment repair   670
City of Denton; Denton; city government   662
City of Lewisville; Lewisville; city government   641
AdvancePCS; Fort Worth; management consulting
  600
Merck-Medco Rx Services of Texas Inc.; Fort Worth;
  personal service agents   600
Denton Hospital Inc.; Denton   550
Wal-Mart Stores Inc.; Lewisville; department stores
  550
Tenet Health System Hospitals Inc.; Carrollton   540
Denton County Electric Cooperative Inc.; Lake Dallas;
  electric power distribution   517
Aftermarket Technology Corp.; Fort Worth; automotive
  supplies   500
American Eagle Holding Corp.; Dallas; air passenger
  carrier   500
Associates Corp. of North America; Bedford; consumer
  finance companies   500
Lennox Industries Inc.; Carrollton; heating and air
  conditioning   500
U.S. Federal Aviation Admin.; Fort Worth   500
WorldPoint Logistics Inc.; Grapevine; delivery service
  500

Texas 27th District

Gulf Coast — Corpus Christi, Brownsville

Anchored by Corpus Christi in the north, the 27th runs south to the Rio Grande River, with the Gulf of Mexico on its eastern coast. Ranches are the mainstay between the two largest cities, Corpus Christi, and Brownsville, which together contain more than half of the 27th's population. But much of the district is coastal, and the district's two deep-water ports are major economic generators.

Corpus Christi has a solid economy fueled by its reliable tourism industry and a military presence that grew in the 1990s. Oil and gas used to be among the biggest industries in the city in the 1980s, but now petrochemical refining, which is also found up and down the coast, is more common. Farther south, the port city of Brownsville struggles with an influx of illegal immigrants and high poverty, but new manufacturing plants and *maquiladoras*—assembly or manufacturing plants that use low-cost labor and import many parts from the United States—have brightened the area and lowered unemployment rates. Visitors coming from Mexico boost Brownsville's retail industry, and "ecotourism" also adds to the economy by drawing bird and turtle watchers to the area's wetlands. Willacy County is competing to be the location of a new spaceport that would launch satellites and planes into space.

Created after the 1980 census, the 27th has been represented by the same Democrat since its creation. The district's 72 percent Hispanic population gives it a decided Demo-

cratic lean, though some affluent areas in Harlingen and Corpus Christi lean Republican. In 2002 statewide races, Democrats Tony Sanchez and Ron Kirk carried the 27th by percentage point margins in the double digits.

Major Industry
Manufacturing, trade, tourism.

Notable
Padre Island is a popular college spring break location; Port Isabel served as a supply depot during the U.S.-Mexican War in the 1840s.

Election Returns

	Republican		Democratic		Other	
President 2000	75,600	48.7%	79,716	51.3%		
House 2002	41,004	36.5%	68,559	61.1%	2,646	2.4%

District Profile

Population   651,619

Total area (square miles)   5,530.5
  Land area (square miles)   3,937.9

Population per square mile   165.5

Counties (2000 population)
Cameron	335,227	Nueces (pt.)	292,510
Kenedy	414	Willacy	20,082
Kleberg (pt.)	3,386		

Cities and other areas over 10,000 (2000 population)
Brownsville   139,722
Corpus Christi (pt.)   270,677
Harlingen   57,564
Robstown (pt.)   12,599
San Benito   23,444

Race and Hispanic or Latino origin*
White   24.6%
Black or African American   2.1%
American Indian or Alaska Native   0.2%
Asian   0.8%
Native Hawaiian or other Pacific Islander   0.0%
Some other race   0.1%
Hispanic or Latino origin   71.6%
Two or more races   0.6%

As percentage of total population.

Ancestry*
English	3.4%	Irish	3.4%
French	1.1%	USA/American	3.2%
German	4.9%		

As estimated percentage of total population.

Universities and colleges, 2000–2001 enrollment
Del Mar College, Corpus Christi   9,936
Texas A&M University, Corpus Christi   6,823
Texas Southmost College, Brownsville   7,776
Texas State Technical College, Harlingen   3,265
University of Texas, Brownsville   9,072

Newspapers and circulation

	District circulation	Total circulation
Brownsville Herald	15,210	15,210
Harlingen Valley Morning Star	21,456	24,654
San Antonio Express-News	1,868	216,752
*USA Today**	1,668	1,674,376

See Sources and Explanations in the front of the volume.

Television stations and affiliations

Corpus Christi	63%	KEDT	PBS
Corpus Christi	63%	KIII	ABC
Corpus Christi	63%	KORO	Univision
Corpus Christi	63%	KRIS	NBC
Corpus Christi	63%	KZTV	CBS
Harlingen-Weslaco-Brownsville-McAllen	37%	KGBT	CBS
Harlingen-Weslaco-Brownsville-McAllen	37%	KLUJ	Independent
Harlingen-Weslaco-Brownsville-McAllen	37%	KMBH	PBS
Harlingen-Weslaco-Brownsville-McAllen	37%	KNVO	Univision
Harlingen-Weslaco-Brownsville-McAllen	37%	KRGV	ABC
Harlingen-Weslaco-Brownsville-McAllen	37%	KTLM	Telemundo
Harlingen-Weslaco-Brownsville-McAllen	37%	KVEO	NBC

Cable systems and subscribers

Charter   809
Time Warner   89,662

Military installations, September 2001

Corpus Christi Naval Air Station, Corpus Christi   2,313
Corpus Christi Naval Hospital, Corpus Christi   207

Businesses and other major employers

Delphi Corp.; Brownsville; automotive parts   3,000
CHRISTUS Spohn Hospital Shoreline; Corpus Christi   2,200
Valley Baptist Medical Center Inc.; Harlingen   2,088
Susser Co.; Corpus Christi; real estate brokers   2,000
HCA Inc. Hospital; Corpus Christi   1,600
Union Underwear Co.; Harlingen; shirts, t-shirts   1,600
AMFELS Inc.; Brownsville; oil refinery construction   1,528
University of Texas at Brownsville; Brownsville   1,494
Driscoll Children's Hospital; Corpus Christi   1,358
Citgo Petroleum Corp.; Corpus Christi; petroleum refining   1,325
CHRISTUS Health System Hospital; Corpus Christi   1,304
Berry Contracting; Corpus Christi; oil refinery construction   1,000
Tyco Electronics Corp.; Brownsville; electronic parts, equipment   1,000
General Instrument Corp.; Brownsville; television sets   980
Birch Telecom Inc.; Corpus Christi; online service providers   900
Koch Industries Inc.; Corpus Christi; oil refining machinery   900
UETA Inc.; Brownsville; liquor   883
Texas Mental Health and Mental Retardation Dept.; Corpus Christi   850
Central Power and Light Co.; Corpus Christi; electric power generation   845
Flint Hills Resources; Corpus Christi; petroleum refining   840
APC Home Health Service Inc.; Harlingen; nurses   805

Invensys Building Systems Inc.; Brownsville; environmental controls   800
Cameron County; Brownsville; county government   785
First Data Resources Inc.; Corpus Christi; telephone services   750
Texas A&M University; Corpus Christi   700
Vicki Roy Home Health Care Inc.; Harlingen   700
Albertson's Inc.; Corpus Christi; supermarkets   680
Brownsville-Valley Regional Medical Center Inc.; Brownsville   672
Sam Kane Beef Processors Inc.; Corpus Christi; meatpacking plants   670
Levi Strauss and Co.; Brownsville; jeans   650
MC Fabrication Industries Inc.; Harlingen; machine shop work   650
Corpus Christi Medical Center; Corpus Christi   600
H&S Constructors Inc.; Corpus Christi; mechanical contractor   600
Trico Products Corp.; Brownsville; automotive parts   600
City of Corpus Christi; Corpus Christi; city government   550
William Carter Co.; Harlingen; undergarments   550
Dillard's Inc.; Harlingen; department stores   525
Levi Strauss and Co.; San Benito; sportswear   500
Omni Southwest Operating Co.; Corpus Christi; hotels   500

Texas 28th District

South San Antonio; Alice; Zapata

The 28th starts in southern San Antonio and heads south through brush country to the Mexico border. The district's population center is in the low- and middle-class communities of San Antonio, while the southern part of the district is mostly sparsely populated agricultural land.

Many residents in this Hispanic-majority district face economic struggles. Median household income in the 28th is under $30,000, and less than 10 percent of residents 25 and over have a bachelor's degree. In Starr County, the nation's most heavily Hispanic county (97.5 percent), nearly half of all families live below the poverty line.

San Antonio's five military bases sustain the economy in the northern part of the 28th. The area was dealt a blow by the 2001 closure of Kelly Air Force Base, the largest base in the 20th and a major employer for the 28th's Hispanic residents.

But while other industries help keep San Antonio afloat, there is not as much in the way of enterprise in the south, where the unemployment rate remains high. The North American Free Trade Agreement has stimulated the economy somewhat, and towns such as Mission, in Hidalgo County, have lower unemployment rates than they did several years ago. Hidalgo is one of the fastest-growing areas in the state, and the economy is getting better as the number of small businesses has risen. A small technology industry is growing. Citrus growing also is a mainstay here.

Democrats do well in the 28th at every level, though a large Catholic influence gives the district a socially conservative bent. Al Gore received 59.2 percent of the 28th's vote in the 2000 presidential election.

Major Industry
Defense, agriculture, tourism.

Notable
San Antonio Missions National Historical Park; Caro Brown, the first woman to win a Pulitzer Prize for journalism, worked at the *Alice Daily News* during the 1940s and 1950s.

Election Returns

	Republican		Democratic		Other	
President 2000	62,275	40.8%	90,202	59.2%		
House 2002	26,973	26.9%	71,393	71.1%	2,054	2.0%

District Profile

Population 651,620

Total area (square miles) 11,929.6
  Land area (square miles) 11,804.8

Population per square mile 55.2

Counties (2000 population)
Atascosa 38,628	Jim Wells 39,326
Bexar (pt.) 372,665	La Salle 5,866
Duval 13,120	McMullen 851
Frio 16,252	Starr 53,597
Hidalgo (pt.) 93,852	Zapata 12,182
Jim Hogg 5,281	

Cities and other areas over 10,000 (2000 population)
Alice 19,010	Mission (pt.) 13,371
Converse 11,508	Rio Grande City 11,923
La Homa CDP 10,433	San Antonio (pt.) 247,498

Race and Hispanic or Latino origin*
White 21.2%
Black or African American 7.5%
American Indian or Alaska Native 0.2%
Asian 0.7%
Native Hawaiian or other Pacific Islander 0.0%
Some other race 0.1%
Hispanic or Latino origin 69.6%
Two or more races 0.7%

*As percentage of total population.

Ancestry*
English 2.4%	Polish 1.1%
German 5.4%	USA/American 2.7%
Irish 2.8%	

*As estimated percentage of total population.

Universities and colleges, 2000–2001 enrollment
Palo Alto College, San Antonio 5,951
St. Philips College, San Antonio 7,921

Newspapers and circulation

	District circulation	Total circulation
McAllen Monitor	9,633	42,010
San Antonio Express-News	40,335	216,752
*USA Today**	2,600	1,674,376

*See Sources and Explanations in the front of the volume.

Television stations and affiliations

San Antonio	46%	KABB	FOX
San Antonio	46%	KENS	CBS
San Antonio	46%	KHCE	Independent
San Antonio	46%	KLRN	PBS
San Antonio	46%	KRRT	WB
San Antonio	46%	KSAT	ABC
San Antonio	46%	KTRG	Independent Spanish
San Antonio	46%	KVAW	Independent Spanish
San Antonio	46%	KVDA	Telemundo
San Antonio	46%	KWEX	Univision
Corpus Christi	32%	KEDT	PBS
Corpus Christi	32%	KIII	ABC
Corpus Christi	32%	KORO	Univision
Corpus Christi	32%	KRIS	NBC
Corpus Christi	32%	KZTV	CBS
Harlingen-Weslaco-Brownsville-McAllen	13%	KGBT	CBS
Harlingen-Weslaco-Brownsville-McAllen	13%	KLUJ	Independent
Harlingen-Weslaco-Brownsville-McAllen	13%	KMBH	PBS
Harlingen-Weslaco-Brownsville-McAllen	13%	KNVO	Univision
Harlingen-Weslaco-Brownsville-McAllen	13%	KRGV	ABC
Harlingen-Weslaco-Brownsville-McAllen	13%	KTLM	Telemundo
Harlingen-Weslaco-Brownsville-McAllen	13%	KVEO	NBC
Laredo	9%	KGNS	NBC
Laredo	9%	KLDO	Univision
Laredo	9%	KVTV	CBS

Cable systems and subscribers
Charter 1,900
Time Warner 87,748

Military installations, September 2001
Randolph Air Force Base, Universal City 8,812
Brooks Air Force Base, San Antonio 2,574

Businesses and other major employers
La Joya Independent School District; Mission 2,300
Austin Coca-Cola Bottling Co.; San Antonio; soft drinks 2,000
Cold Drink Service; San Antonio; vending machines 2,000
B. J. Tidwell Industries Inc.; San Antonio; kitchen cabinets 1,850
Lancer Partnership; San Antonio; market analysis 1,200
Texas Mental Health and Mental Retardation Dept.; San Antonio 900
Texas Dept. of Protective and Regulatory Services; San Antonio 800
San Antonio Shoe Inc.; San Antonio; footwear 800
Mission Hospital Inc.; Mission 710
Baptist Health System Hospital; San Antonio 707
La Joya Independent School District; La Joya 676
Zachry Construction Corp.; San Antonio; industrial buildings 600
Alamo Community College District; San Antonio 600
San Antonio Independent School District; San Antonio 550

Cox Enterprises Inc.; San Antonio; automobile auction
500

United Parcel Service Inc.; San Antonio; parcel delivery
500

Nabors Drilling USA Inc.; Alice; oil, gas well drilling
500

Rio Grande City Independent School District; Rio
Grande City   500

Texas 29th District

Part of Houston and eastern suburbs

Located on the eastern side of Houston's downtown, the 29th is a blue-collar, working-class, Hispanic-majority district near refineries and factories that employ many union members. *(See map p. 869.)*

The district resembles a backward "C" and arcs from northern to southeastern Houston (slightly more than half of district residents live in the city). In the north the 29th takes in George Bush Intercontinental Airport, a source of employment for many district residents, and part of the comfortable suburb of Humble. It also includes part of the Houston Ship Channel, a major shipping route that has seen increased business since the North American Free Trade Agreement. The district also takes in most of middle-class Channelview, east of Houston. In the bottom half, the 29th includes working-class areas near Interstate 10 such as Jacinto City, Galena Park, south Houston, and part of Pasadena.

The 29th was originally drawn in 1992 as a Hispanic-majority district, and Hispanics now make up 62 percent of the district population. The heaviest concentrations of Hispanics are in South Houston, Jacinto City, Houston, and Pasadena. Nearly 60 percent of district residents speak a language other than English at home.

The 29th has the largest blue-collar workforce (40.4 percent) and lowest median age (27.4 years). It was severely affected in 2001 by one of Houston's worst floods, Tropical Storm Allison.

The district is solidly Democratic, even with the traditionally poor voter turnout in the Hispanic community. In the 2002 senatorial and gubernatorial races, the 29th backed Democrats Ron Kirk and Tony Sanchez by a better than two-to-one ratio. Republicans can win only a few precincts up north, near the airport.

Major Industry

Chemicals, energy, construction, aviation.

Notable

The district houses much of the city's $15 billion petrochemical complex, which rivals Rotterdam in the Netherlands as the world's largest.

Election Returns

	Republican		Democratic		Other	
President 2000	42,770	39.4%	65,863	60.6%		
House 2002			55,760	95.2%	2,833	4.8%

District Profile

Population   651,620

Total area (square miles)   239.8
   Land area (square miles)   238.5

Population per square mile   2,732.2

Counties (2000 population)
   Harris (pt.)   651,620

Cities and other areas over 10,000 (2000 population)
   Aldine CDP   13,979
   Channelview CDP (pt.)   20,451
   Cloverleaf CDP   23,508
   Galena Park (pt.)   10,592
   Houston (pt.)   339,295
   Jacinto City (pt.)   10,302
   Pasadena (pt.)   46,643
   South Houston   15,833

Race and Hispanic or Latino origin*
   White   20.0%
   Black or African American   14.7%
   American Indian or Alaska Native   0.2%
   Asian   2.1%
   Native Hawaiian or other Pacific Islander   0.0%
   Some other race   0.1%
   Hispanic or Latino origin   62.2%
   Two or more races   0.8%

As percentage of total population.

Ancestry*

English	2.0%	Irish	2.7%
German	2.9%	USA/American	3.7%

As estimated percentage of total population.

Universities and colleges, 2000–2001 enrollment
   ITT Technical Institute, Houston   459
   North Harris Montgomery Community College,
      Houston   24,554
   San Jacinto College, Houston   4,947
   Universal Technical Institute, Houston   1,625

Newspapers and circulation

	District circulation	Total circulation
Houston Chronicle	43,216	548,437
*USA Today**	2,360	1,674,376

See Sources and Explanations in the front of the volume.

Television stations and affiliations

Houston	100%	KAVU	ABC
Houston	100%	KBTX	CBS
Houston	100%	KETH	Independent
Houston	100%	KHOU	CBS
Houston	100%	KHWB	WB
Houston	100%	KLTJ	Independent
Houston	100%	KNWS	Independent
Houston	100%	KPRC	NBC

Houston	100%	KPXB	PAX
Houston	100%	KRIV	FOX
Houston	100%	KTBU	Independent
Houston	100%	KTMD	Telemundo
Houston	100%	KTRK	ABC
Houston	100%	KTXH	UPN
Houston	100%	KUHT	PBS
Houston	100%	KXLN	Univision
Houston	100%	KZJL	Independent Spanish

Cable systems and subscribers
Time Warner   132,516

Businesses and other major employers
Arteva Specialties S.A.R.L. Ltd.; Houston; polyethylene resins   5,000

Labor Ready Central; Houston; temporary help service   5,000

EGL Eagle Global Logistics; Houston; freight forwarding   4,000

Anadarko Petroleum Corp.; Houston; oil/gas exploration   3,000

Reliant Energy Inc.; Houston; nonelectric transformers   3,000

S&B Engineers and Constructors Inc.; Houston; engineering services   2,000

Smith International South America Inc.; Houston; oil, gas drilling bits   2,000

Schlumberger Technology Corp.; Houston; oil, gas well servicing   1,800

Nabors Drilling International Ltd.; Houston; oil, gas well drilling   1,639

Baker Hughes Oilfield Operations Inc.; Houston; oil, gas drilling tools   1,500

May Department Stores Co.; Houston; warehousing   1,500

U.S. Postal Service; North Houston   1,500

NHM Community College District; Houston   1,400

Kellogg Brown and Root Inc.; Houston; marine construction   1,300

Halliburton Co.; Houston; oil/gas field machinery   1,250

City of Houston; Houston; airport   1,243

Aldine Independent School District; Houston   1,100

DHL Airways Inc.; Houston; courier service   1,100

RME Holding Co.; Houston; crude petroleum production   1,079

PD Holdings (USA) Inc.; Houston; investment holding company   1,031

Continental Airlines Inc.; Houston   1,000

Convergys Corp.; Houston; telemarketing   1,000

ExxonMobil Development Co.; Houston; oil, gas well drilling   1,000

Houston Community College System; Houston   1,000

Texas Dept. of Protective and Regulatory Services; Houston   1,000

United Parcel Service Inc.; Houston; package delivery   1,000

Spring Independent School District; Houston   988

Kindred Healthcare Inc.; Pasadena; specialty hospitals   950

FMC Technologies Inc.; Houston; oil field machinery   900

IKON Office Solutions Inc.; Houston; photocopying   880

Chevron Phillips Chemical Co.; Pasadena; agricultural chemicals   800

Pedus Service Inc.; Houston; janitorial service   800

U.S. Federal Aviation Admin.; Houston   800

City of Pasadena; Pasadena; city government   771

Harris County Metropolitan Transit Authority; Humble   733

Albemarle Corp.; Pasadena; plastics materials   700

American Bureau of Shipping Inc.; Houston; transportation inspection   700

Anadarko Petroleum Corp.; The Woodlands; petroleum production   700

Castle Dental Centers of Texas Inc.; Houston   700

Equistar Chemicals; Channelview; olefins   700

North Harris Montgomery Community College District; Houston   700

U.S. Federal Emergency Management Agency; Houston   700

Kraft Foods Inc.; Houston; roasted coffee   650

International Total Services Inc.; Houston; airports   600

Phillips Petroleum Co.; Houston; tax title dealers   600

Memorial Hermann Hospital System; Pasadena   550

Smith International Inc.; Houston; oil/gas field machinery   550

Harris County Dept. of Education; Houston   507

Initial Security Inc.; Houston; security guard service   500

Lucia Inc.; Houston; masonry/stonework   500

Valero Refining-Texas; Houston; petroleum refining   500

Texas 30th District

Downtown Dallas; part of Irving

Confined to Dallas County, the 30th stretches from the Dallas-Fort Worth International Airport southeast through Irving and into downtown Dallas. It then dips south to take in some suburbs, such as Lancaster, where many African American families have relocated after leaving the city. *(See map p. 862.)*

When the district was drawn after the 1990 census, blacks made up 50 percent of the 30th's constituency. Now they account for just 41 percent, but the district is still largely minority, as 31 percent of residents are Hispanic. There has been a rise in Asian populations because of corporate expansions. As the population grows, road congestion and air pollution have become concerns. Leaders hope a recent expansion of the city's light rail system into the suburbs will alleviate some of the problems.

Once a quiet suburb, Irving boomed in the 1980s and 1990s. The massive ExxonMobil Corp. made its corporate home in Irving in late 1999 (in the neighboring 32nd), and the city has been growing fast enough that officials decided in 1999 to overturn Irving's more than 20-year refusal of public housing money, which had been based on concerns over what federal strings would accompany the funds. Many residents make their living in the aviation industry. The district includes Love Field Airport and shares the Dallas-Fort Worth

International Airport, one of the nation's busiest, with the 26th and 32nd.

The 30th is overwhelmingly Democratic. In the 2002 election, it gave 74 percent of its vote to Democratic Senate nominee Ron Kirk, a former Dallas mayor, and 71 percent to Democratic gubernatorial nominee Tony Sanchez. Democrats run strongly in the heavily black precincts just south of Illinois Avenue, and in largely Hispanic precincts near Love Field, giving the party a big edge in a district where the only significant Republican vote is in Irving.

Major Industry

Banking, technology, transportation.

Notable

Dealey Plaza and the Texas School Book Depository, where President John F. Kennedy was assassinated in 1963; the Texas State Fair attracts 3 million people and features Big Tex—a 52-foot-tall talking cowboy; Texas Stadium in Irving is home to the NFL's Dallas Cowboys.

Election Returns

	Republican		Democratic		Other	
President 2000	48,916	30.9%	109,507	69.1%		
House 2002	28,981	24.2%	88,980	74.3%	1,856	1.5%

District Profile

Population   651,620

Total area (square miles)   290.3
   Land area (square miles)   288.7

Population per square mile   2,257.1

Counties (2000 population)
   Dallas (pt.)   651,620

Cities and other areas over 10,000 (2000 population)
   Cedar Hill (pt.)   12,379   Irving (pt.)   165,467
   Dallas (pt.)   386,837   Lancaster (pt.)   25,854
   DeSoto   37,646

Race and Hispanic or Latino origin*
   White   24.7%
   Black or African American   40.5%
   American Indian or Alaska Native   0.3%
   Asian   2.2%
   Native Hawaiian or other Pacific Islander   0.0%
   Some other race   0.1%
   Hispanic or Latino origin   31.1%
   Two or more races   1.0%

*As percentage of total population.

Ancestry*
   English   3.0%   Subsaharan   1.4%
   German   3.7%   USA/American   3.6%
   Irish   3.1%

*As estimated percentage of total population.

Universities and colleges, 2000–2001 enrollment
   Cedar Valley College, Lancaster   3,280
   Court Reporting Institute-Wheeler Institute of Texas, Dallas   501

El Centro College, Dallas   4,333
North Lake College, Irving   8,615
Paul Quinn College, Dallas   674
Texas A&M University-Baylor College of Dentistry, Dallas   1,014
Ultrasound Diagnostic School, Irving   264
University of Dallas, Irving   3,738

Newspapers and circulation

	District circulation	Total circulation
Dallas Morning News	69,379	495,624
Fort Worth Star-Telegram	1,396	224,885
*USA Today**	7,542	1,674,376

*See Sources and Explanations in the front of the volume.

Television stations and affiliations

Dallas-Fort Worth	100%	KDAF	WB
Dallas-Fort Worth	100%	KDFI	Independent
Dallas-Fort Worth	100%	KDFW	FOX
Dallas-Fort Worth	100%	KDTN	PBS
Dallas-Fort Worth	100%	KDTX	Independent
Dallas-Fort Worth	100%	KERA	PBS
Dallas-Fort Worth	100%	KFWD	Independent
Dallas-Fort Worth	100%	KMPX	Independent
Dallas-Fort Worth	100%	KPXD	PAX
Dallas-Fort Worth	100%	KSTR	Telefutura
Dallas-Fort Worth	100%	KTAQ	Independent
Dallas-Fort Worth	100%	KTVT	CBS
Dallas-Fort Worth	100%	KTXA	UPN
Dallas-Fort Worth	100%	KUVN	Univision
Dallas-Fort Worth	100%	KXAS	NBC
Dallas-Fort Worth	100%	KXTX	Telemundo
Dallas-Fort Worth	100%	WFAA	ABC

Cable systems and subscribers
   Charter   602
   Comcast   169,129

Businesses and other major employers
   Flowserve US Corp.; Irving; pumping equipment   9,030
   Bank of America Corp.; Dallas; commercial bank   8,000
   New Path Media; Dallas; radio broadcasting stations   8,000
   American Staff Resources Corp.; Dallas; administrative management   7,000
   Dallas County Hospital District; Dallas   5,700
   Dallas County Community College District; Dallas   5,000
   Global Industrial Technologies Services Co.; Dallas; financial services   5,000
   U.S. Veterans Hospital; Dallas   5,000
   Baylor University Medical Center; Dallas   4,425
   Associates First Capital Corp.; Irving; consumer finance companies   4,000
   Southwest Airlines Co.; Dallas   3,064
   Fieldcrest Cannon Inc.; Dallas; cotton towels   3,000
   Verizon Communications Inc.; Irving; telephone communication   3,000
   DDFS Inc.; Irving; courier services   2,950
   Centex Homes Partnership; Dallas; commercial land development   2,542

Fidelity Brokerage Services; Irving; investment advisors 2,500

First American Corp.; Dallas; real estate title insurance 2,500

U.S. Postal Service; Dallas   2,500

U.S. Internal Revenue Service; Dallas   2,460

Dallas Morning News; Dallas; newspaper   2,400

Army and Air Force Exchange Service; Dallas; Army-Navy goods stores   2,386

Vartec Telecom Inc.; Dallas; long-distance telephone 2,255

City of Dallas; Dallas; city government   2,000

City of Dallas; Dallas; waste management   2,000

EQR/Lincoln LP; Dallas; residential land development 2,000

ExxonMobil Oil Corp.; Dallas; petroleum products 2,000

Interstate FiberNet; Dallas; telephone communication 2,000

Dallas Children's Medical Center; Dallas   1,924

City of Dallas; Dallas; water supply   1,700

Center Operating Co.; Dallas; sports stadium operator 1,625

Anatole Hotel Investors LP; Dallas; hotels   1,600

City of Dallas; Dallas; fire dept.   1,600

ABM Industries Inc.; Dallas; janitorial service   1,500

AT&T Corp.; Dallas; telephone communication   1,500

Baylor Medical Center at Irving; Irving   1,500

City of Dallas; Dallas; automotive repair shops   1,500

Contel Federal Systems Inc.; Irving; telephone apparatus 1,500

Pilgrim's Pride Corp.; Dallas; poultry processing 1,500

TXU US Holdings Co.; Dallas; electric power generation 1,402

Frito-Lay Inc.; Dallas; snacks   1,400

Novation; Irving; management consulting   1,400

St. Paul Medical Center; Dallas   1,388

Delta Airlines Inc.; Irving   1,300

Abbott Laboratories; Irving; medical instruments 1,200

Benemax; Irving; employee leasing   1,200

JPI Lifestyle Apartment Communities; Irving; apartment building operators   1,200

Vertis Inc.; Irving; commercial photography   1,200

Yellow Transportation; Dallas; freight transportation 1,200

Hunt Overseas Oil Co.; Dallas; petroleum production 1,139

Teccor Electronics Inc.; Irving; semiconductors   1,129

SWS Securities Inc.; Dallas; security brokers, dealers 1,100

Ernst and Young; Dallas; certified public accountant 1,050

Atlantic Southeast Airlines Inc.; Dallas   1,000

Central Freight Lines Inc.; Irving; trucking   1,000

Dal-Tile Corp.; Dallas; ceramic tile   1,000

Dr. Pepper/Seven Up Bottling Group Inc.; Irving; soft drinks   1,000

Dual Holding Co.; Dallas; oil, gas well drilling   1,000

Gulfstream Aerospace Corp.; Dallas; aircraft   1,000

Haggar Corp.; Dallas; trousers and slacks   1,000

NEC America Inc.; Irving; warehousing   1,000

Site Concrete Inc.; Grand Prairie; excavation work 1,000

U.S. Environmental Protection Agency; Dallas   1,000

Zale Corp.; Irving; jewelry   1,000

Federal Reserve Bank of Dallas; Dallas; banking regulation   946

Aetna Inc.; Dallas; insurance agents   900

Federal Deposit Insurance Corp.; Dallas   900

KPMG; Dallas; certified public accountant   900

Trinity Industries International Inc.; Dallas; railway motor cars   900

Brae Staffing; Irving; secretarial service   850

Builders FirstSource Inc.; Dallas; lumber   850

Capital Entertainment Video; Dallas; video rental   850

Dallas Airmotive Inc.; Dallas; aircraft, heavy equipment repair   800

Deloitte and Touche; Dallas; accounting services   800

Four Season Hotels; Irving; hotels   800

Frito-Lay Inc.; Irving; snacks   800

Hyatt Corp.; Dallas; hotels   800

Mary Kay Inc.; Dallas; cosmetics   800

Silverleaf Resorts Inc.; Dallas; condominium manager 800

TIG American Specialty Insurance Co.; Irving; workers' compensation insurance   800

Transamerica Real Estate Tax Service; Dallas; real estate appraiser   800

Visiting Nurse Assn. of Texas; Dallas; home health care 760

Blockbuster Inc.; Dallas; video rental   750

Military Sales and Service Co.; Dallas; computer software 750

Taylor Publishing Co.; Dallas; book publishing   725

Austin Coca-Cola Bottling Co.; Dallas; soft drinks   700

Culinaire of Florida Inc.; Dallas; food services consultants   700

Dallas County; Dallas; district attorney's office   700

David McDade Used Cars; Irving   700

DFW Airport Hotel Associates; Dallas; hotels and motels   700

Lone Star Race Park; Grand Prairie; race track operation 700

Paymentech Management Resources Inc.; Dallas; credit card services   700

VHA Inc.; Irving; health services consultant   700

Burns International Security Services Corp.; Dallas; security guard   687

Las Colinas-USAA LP; Irving; hotels   675

American Airlines Inc.; Dallas; freight handling   650

GTE Corp.; Irving; telephone communication   650

International Airmotive Holding Co. Inc.; Grapevine; aircraft engines, parts   650

Archon Residential Management; Irving; real estate managers   637

First USA Financial Inc.; Dallas; credit card services 605

NCH Corp.; Irving; specialty cleaning   605

Allen Telecom Inc.; Dallas; radio/TV communications 600

BancTec Inc.; Irving; computer systems design   600

Dallas Area Rapid Transit; Dallas   600

GE Aircraft Engines Holdings Inc.; Dallas; aircraft servicing   600

Greyhound Lines Inc.; Dallas; transit   600
GTE Corp.; Dallas; telephone equipment   600
Microsoft Corp.; Irving; computer processing   600
Mastec North America Inc.; Dallas; underground
    utilities contractor   600
Pinkerton's Inc.; Dallas; security guard service   600
Raytheon Co.; Dallas; radar systems   600
S Group Inc.; Dallas; bond dealers and brokers   600
Southwest Airlines Co.; Grand Prairie   600
Trammell Crow Co.; Dallas; real estate agents   600
Dr. Pepper-Seven Up Bottling Group Inc.; Dallas; soft
    drinks   550
Precept Transportation Services; Dallas; administrative
    management   550
Potter Concrete; Dallas; concrete work   540
Boy Scouts of America; Irving; boys' organization   520
Jenkens and Gilchrist; Dallas; law office   517
City of Dallas; Dallas; public library   515
Ennis Business Forms Inc.; DeSoto; special dies, tools
    502
Atlantic Southeast Airlines Inc.; Irving   500
Baylor Health Care System; Dallas; information retrieval
    500
CHRISTUS Health Hospital; Irving   500
City of Irving; Irving; correctional facilities   500
Dalfort Aerospace; Dallas; aircraft, heavy equipment
    repair   500
Dallas Airmotive Inc.; Grapevine; engine repair,
    replacement   500
Dallas County; Dallas; county government   500
Dallas Independent School District; Dallas   500
Delta Airlines Inc.; Dallas; travel agency   500
Electronic Data Systems Corp.; Dallas; computer systems
    500
Fairmont Hotel Management; Dallas; hotels and motels
    500
Federal Express Corp.; Dallas; letter, package delivery
    500
Gables Residential Trust; Irving; real estate brokers
    500
Genuity Inc.; Irving; computer systems   500
Hanson Building Materials America Inc.; Grand Prairie;
    construction machinery   500
Hazel Staffing Inc.; Irving; temporary help   500
Jones, Day, Reavis, & Pogue; Dallas; law office   500
Maintenance of Dallas Inc.; Dallas; building
    maintenance   500
Mechanical Interiors Inc.; Dallas; mechanical contractor
    500
MedSynergies Inc.; Irving; management services   500
Mobil Exploration; Dallas; petroleum production   500
Oracle Corp.; Irving; software   500
Rosewood Property Co.; Dallas; hotels   500
Sky Chefs Inc.; Dallas; caterers   500
Southwestern Bell Telephone Co.; Dallas; data processing
    500
Spherion Corp.; Dallas; help supply   500
Sterling Commerce Inc.; Irving; business software   500
Thompson & Knight; Dallas; law office   500

Texas 31st District

*East central — Houston and Austin suburbs, College
Station, Bryan*

The 31st is made up of suburbs and rural areas in a large
swath of central Texas extending from Austin to Houston
and up to College Station.

In the west, the district takes in part of Williamson
County, its largest population base. A bedroom enclave north
of Austin, the county is home to many who left the city for
a more suburban lifestyle. The district's Harris County portion, in its eastern end, features similar Houston suburbs.
Ranches and rural areas dominate in between. To the north,
the 31st takes in all of Brazos County, including Bryan and
College Station, home of Texas A&M University. These areas
all strongly favor Republicans.

The district's portions of Williamson and Harris Counties are two of the fastest-growing areas of the state. Texas
A&M—including the George Bush Presidential Library—
also is a major employer. Unlike the more liberal University
of Texas at Austin, Texas A&M has a conservative agricultural and military tradition that complements local values
such as free-market economics and pro-defense sentiments.
As a result, the 31st has given Republicans some of their
largest margins in the state at every level.

Two of the district's rural counties, Lee and Burleson, lean
Democratic but are sparsely populated.

Major Industry
Technology, agriculture, education.

Notable
Blue Bell Creameries, maker of Texas's most famous ice
cream, is in Brenham; former baseball pitcher Nolan Ryan
owns the Round Rock Express, a minor-league team of the
Houston Astros.

Election Returns

	Republican		Democratic		Other	
President 2000	160,802	71.6%	63,903	28.4%		
House 2002	111,556	69.1%	44,183	27.4%	5,745	3.6%

District Profile

Population   651,620

Total area (square miles)   5,089.9
  Land area (square miles)   5,033.9

Population per square mile   129.4

Counties (2000 population)
Austin 23,590	Lee 15,657
Bastrop (pt.) 25,351	Waller 32,663
Brazos 152,415	Washington 30,373
Burleson 16,470	Williamson (pt.) 201,961
Harris (pt.) 153,140	

Cities and other areas over 10,000 (2000 population)
Austin (pt.)   11,810
Brenham   13,507
Brushy Creek CDP   15,371
Bryan   65,660
Cedar Park (pt.)   25,508
College Station   67,890
Jollyville CDP (pt.)   14,801
Katy (pt.)   10,886
Round Rock (pt.)   60,060
Taylor   13,575

Race and Hispanic or Latino origin*
White   69.4%
Black or African American   9.0%
American Indian or Alaska Native   0.3%
Asian   3.1%
Native Hawaiian or other Pacific Islander   0.0%
Some other race   0.1%
Hispanic or Latino origin   16.9%
Two or more races   1.2%

As percentage of total population.

Ancestry*
English   7.5%   Polish   1.8%
French   2.4%   Scotch-Irish   1.8%
German   14.7%   Scottish   1.6%
Irish   7.6%   USA/American   5.2%
Italian   2.3%

As estimated percentage of total population.

Universities and colleges, 2000–2001 enrollment
Blinn College, Brenham   11,588
Prairie View A&M University, Prairie View   6,609
Texas A&M University, College Station   44,026

Newspapers and circulation

	District circulation	Total circulation
Austin American Statesman	31,453	186,020
Bryan-College Station Eagle	20,820	24,358
Dallas Morning News	1,602	495,624
Houston Chronicle	24,165	548,437
USA Today*	3,630	1,674,376

See Sources and Explanations in the front of the volume.

Television stations and affiliations
Houston	40%	KAVU
Houston	40%	KBTX
Houston	40%	KETH
Houston	40%	KHOU
Houston	40%	KHWB
Houston	40%	KLTJ
Houston	40%	KNWS
Houston	40%	KPRC
Houston	40%	KPXB
Houston	40%	KRIV
Houston	40%	KTBU
Houston	40%	KTMD
Houston	40%	KTRK
Houston	40%	KTXH
Houston	40%	KUHT
Houston	40%	KXLN
Houston	40%	KZJL
Austin	35%	KAKW
Austin	35%	KEYE
Austin	35%	KLRU
Austin	35%	KNVA
Austin	35%	KTBC
Austin	35%	KVUE
Austin	35%	KXAM
Austin	35%	KXAN
Waco-Temple-Bryan	25%	KAMU
Waco-Temple-Bryan	25%	KCEN
Waco-Temple-Bryan	25%	KNCT
Waco-Temple-Bryan	25%	KWKT
Waco-Temple-Bryan	25%	KWTX
Waco-Temple-Bryan	25%	KXXV
Waco-Temple-Bryan	25%	KYLE

Cable systems and subscribers
Classic   1,856
CMA   3,226
Cox   62,724
Northland   5,270
Time Warner   18,230

Businesses and other major employers
Assn. of Engineering Geologists; College Station; noncommercial research   30,000
Texas A&M University; College Station   15,000
St. Joseph Hospital; Bryan   1,600
Sanderson Farms Inc.; Bryan; chickens   1,600
Alenco Window Holding; Bryan; window, door frames   1,500
Texas A&M University; Prairie View   1,494
Sears Roebuck and Co. Inc.; Round Rock; department stores   1,200
Texas Mental Health and Mental Retardation Dept.; Brenham   1,000
Rental Systems Inc.; College Station; computer rental   900
Wyman-Gordon Forgings Inc.; Houston; iron, steel forgings   872
Fairbanks Cypress Medical Center Inc.; Houston   850
Texas Transportation Institute; College Station   800
Blue Bell Creameries LP; Brenham; ice cream   750
URS Corp.; Austin; engineering services   700
Maxwell Dodge; Austin; automobiles   600
Texas Mental Health and Mental Retardation Dept.; Bryan   530
Wal-Mart Stores Inc.; Bryan; department stores   514
NCI Building Systems Inc.; Houston; nonresidential construction   500
Stewart and Stevenson Services Inc.; Sealy; oil well, field pumps   500
Classic Fleet and Commercial Sales; Round Rock; automobiles   500
Tellabs Operations Inc.; Round Rock; telephone apparatus   500

Texas 32nd District

Northwest Dallas County

Though it does not include downtown Dallas, the 32nd is home to much of the Dallas business community. Many who work downtown live here, and several Fortune 500 companies are located off the Lyndon B. Johnson Freeway, which encircles the city. *(See map p. 862.)*

The 32nd is located in the northwest corner of Dallas County, which contains a northern chunk of the city of Dallas and some of the city's north and west suburbs. The district begins on the edge of downtown, a growing haven for younger workers living in luxury apartments along McKinney Avenue. Nearby is Oak Lawn, home to much of the city's gay community. The district then moves north to take in the exclusive "Park Cities," made up of the cities of Highland Park and University Park. The Park Cities area, which is almost entirely white, has its own school system and local government. The 32nd continues north to the county line, through less exclusive but equally wealthy neighborhoods. Some middle-class neighborhoods exist in the northern part of the district along the L. B. J. Freeway.

The city's "telecom corridor" is in the north part of Dallas, where Texas Instruments is the standard bearer. ExxonMobil is in the 32nd, based in Irving (shared with the 30th), along with other oil companies.

Transportation issues are important to residents, as several highways run through the district, which also takes in a small portion of Dallas-Fort Worth International Airport. Many employees of Dallas-Fort Worth International Airport and Dallas Love Field airport—which borders the district—live here.

The 32nd is solidly Republican. George W. Bush took 65 percent of the district's two-party vote in 2000, and Republicans running statewide routinely garner more than 60 percent here. The GOP is particularly strong in precincts around University Park and Southern Methodist University, while Democrats do well in the far southern reaches of the district near downtown Dallas.

Major Industry

Telecommunications, oil, retail.

Notable

Ross Perot lives in the 32nd; the Dallas Theater Center is located here.

Election Returns

	Republican		Democratic		Other	
President 2000	129,527	64.9%	70,029	35.1%		
House 2002	100,226	67.8%	44,886	30.3%	2,790	1.9%

District Profile

Population   651,619

Total area (square miles)   166.0
  Land area (square miles)   164.6

Population per square mile   3,958.8

Counties (2000 population)

Dallas (pt.)   651,619

Cities and other areas over 10,000 (2000 population)

Addison town 14,166	Garland (pt.) 14,921
Carrollton (pt.) 49,822	Irving (pt.) 26,148
Coppell (pt.) 35,734	Richardson (pt.) 44,455
Dallas (pt.) 406,696	University Park 23,324
Farmers Branch 27,508	

Race and Hispanic or Latino origin*

White   55.2%
Black or African American   9.1%
American Indian or Alaska Native   0.3%
Asian   6.3%
Native Hawaiian or other Pacific Islander   0.0%
Some other race   0.1%
Hispanic or Latino origin   27.4%
Two or more races   1.5%

As percentage of total population.

Ancestry*

English 8.2%	Polish 1.3%
French 2.1%	Scotch-Irish 1.8%
German 8.7%	Scottish 1.9%
Irish 6.7%	Subsaharan 1.2%
Italian 1.9%	USA/American 4.7%

As estimated percentage of total population.

Universities and colleges, 2000–2001 enrollment

Art Institute of Dallas, Dallas   1,463
ATI Career Training Center, Dallas   664
Brookhaven College, Farmers Branch   8,556
Dallas Christian College, Dallas   255
Dallas Theological Seminary, Dallas   1,561
Devry University, Irving   3,462
Executive Secretarial School of Texas, Dallas   542
ITT Technical Institute, Richardson   495
Parker College of Chiropractic, Dallas   809
Richland College, Dallas   12,537
Southern Methodist University, Dallas   10,064
University of Texas Southwest Medical Center, Dallas   1,505

Newspapers and circulation

	District circulation	Total circulation
Dallas Morning News	90,819	495,624
*USA Today**	4,314	1,674,376

See Sources and Explanations in the front of the volume.

Television stations and affiliations

Dallas-Fort Worth	100%	KDAF	WB
Dallas-Fort Worth	100%	KDFI	Independent
Dallas-Fort Worth	100%	KDFW	FOX
Dallas-Fort Worth	100%	KDTN	PBS
Dallas-Fort Worth	100%	KDTX	Independent
Dallas-Fort Worth	100%	KERA	PBS
Dallas-Fort Worth	100%	KFWD	Independent
Dallas-Fort Worth	100%	KMPX	Independent
Dallas-Fort Worth	100%	KPXD	PAX

Dallas-Fort Worth	100%	KSTR	Telefutura
Dallas-Fort Worth	100%	KTAQ	Independent
Dallas-Fort Worth	100%	KTVT	CBS
Dallas-Fort Worth	100%	KTXA	UPN
Dallas-Fort Worth	100%	KUVN	Univision
Dallas-Fort Worth	100%	KXAS	NBC
Dallas-Fort Worth	100%	KXTX	Telemundo
Dallas-Fort Worth	100%	WFAA	ABC

Cable systems and subscribers
Comcast   62,183

Businesses and other major employers
Texas Instruments Inc.; Dallas; microprocessors   9,900

Texas Health Resources Inc.; Arlington; hospital management   9,384

International Brotherhood of Electrical Workers; Dallas; labor union   7,700

Presbyterian Hospital of Dallas; Dallas   6,727

Computer Media and Services Corp.; Carrollton; software   6,000

Raytheon Co.; McKinney; radar systems   5,800

University of Texas Southwestern Medical Center; Dallas   4,800

McLane Foodservice Distribution Inc.; Carrollton; packaged frozen goods   3,111

Palm Harbor Homes; Addison; modular homes   3,000

Health Care Professionals Inc.; Richardson; health insurance   2,500

Medical City Dallas Hospital Inc.; Dallas   2,300

Trader Publishing Co.; Carrollton; shopping news publishing   2,100

Tenet Health Care Hospitals Inc.; Dallas; medical centers   2,015

Affiliated Computer Services Inc.; Dallas; data processing   2,000

Associates First Capital Corp.; Irving; fire, marine, casualty insurance   2,000

Community Health Corp.; Dallas; medical plans   2,000

Neiman Marcus Group Inc.; Irving; clothing stores   2,000

United Parcel Service Inc.; Dallas; parcel delivery   2,000

Accubanc Mortgage Corp.; Dallas; mortgage bankers   1,844

Mary Kay Inc.; Addison; perfumes, cosmetics   1,800

Mobil Corp.; Irving; petroleum refining   1,645

STMicroelectronics Inc.; Carrollton; semiconductors   1,601

Southern Methodist University Inc.; Dallas   1,600

Tuesday Morning Corp.; Addison; gift shop   1,597

Capital Senior Living Inc.; Dallas; rest home with health care   1,558

Chili's of Minnesota Inc.; Dallas; restaurants   1,500

International Business Machines Corp.; Dallas; computers   1,500

Laboratory Corp. of America; Dallas; testing labs   1,500

Southern Methodist University; Dallas   1,500

Dallas Semiconductor Corp.; Dallas; integrated microcircuits   1,450

MBNA Hallmark Information Services Inc.; Addison; data processing   1,400

General Instrument Corp.; Carrollton; security systems   1,200

Sprint Corp.; Dallas; telephone communication   1,180

Allstate Insurance Co.; Irving; insurance agents   1,000

AT&T Corp.; Dallas; long-distance telephone   1,000

Fidelity Brokerage Services; Dallas; investment advice   1,000

Raytheon Co.; Dallas; radar systems   1,000

Staff Extension Inc.; Dallas; help supply services   1,000

Texstore Properties Corp.; Dallas; real property lessors   1,000

Aegis Communications Group Inc.; Irving; telemarketing   983

Pinnacle Restaurant Group; Dallas; restaurants   965

Dickey's Barbecue Inc.; Dallas; restaurant   952

Zale Lipshy University Hospital Inc.; Dallas   950

First Horizon Home Loans Corp.; Irving; mortgage bankers   900

Pizza Hut of Charles County Inc.; Dallas; pizzeria chain   900

Quick Learning; Dallas; public speaking school   900

TD Industries; Dallas; mechanical contractor   900

Bombardier Aerospace Corp.; Dallas; aircraft and parts   878

WebLink Wireless Inc.; Dallas; radiotelephone communication   878

American Realty Investors Inc.; Dallas; real estate investment trusts   870

Maersk Inc.; Dallas; shipping agents   850

Alliance Data Systems Corp.; Dallas; credit card service   800

Brink's Home Security Inc.; Irving; security systems   800

CompUSA Inc.; Dallas; computer stores   800

Oxidental Chemical Corp.; Dallas; alkalies and chlorine   800

Silverleaf Resorts Inc.; Carrollton; resort hotel   800

Sky Chefs Inc.; Dallas; caterers   800

Third Stevenson Properties Corp.; Dallas; subdividers, developers   800

Nokia Telecommunications Inc.; Irving; radiotelephone communication   790

Merck-Medco Rx Services of Texas Inc.; Irving; mail-order pharmaceuticals   750

Nissan Motor Acceptance Corp.; Irving; auto purchase financing   750

Thomson Professional and Regulatory Inc.; Carrollton; software development   750

Medical Edge Health Care Group Inc.; Dallas; management services   725

7-Eleven Inc.; Dallas; convenience stores   718

Austin Commercial; Dallas; office building contractors   700

General Aluminum Corp.; Carrollton; window, door frames   700

GTE Corp.; Irving; telephone communication   700

Sears Roebuck and Co. Inc.; Dallas; group day care center   700

UBM Inc.; Dallas; building maintenance   700

Hensley Industries Inc.; Dallas; alloy steel castings   690

Security National Insurance Co.; Dallas; fire, marine, casualty insurance   690

GEICO; Dallas; life insurance   686

Kingtex Inc.; Dallas; fast-food restaurant   660

Essilor Laboratory of America Inc.; Dallas; eyeglasses, lenses, frames   650

Manhattan Construction Co.; Dallas; institutional building construction   650

Mills Electrical Contractors Inc.; Dallas; electrical contractor   650

Temerlin McClain Inc.; Irving; advertising   650

Mrs Baird's Bakeries Business Trust; Dallas; retail bakeries   640

Sysco Food Services; Dallas; food supplier   632

GlobalSantaFe Corp.; Houston; oil, gas well drilling   630

Austin Bridge and Road Inc.; Dallas; highway paving   600

Block Management; Dallas; tax preparation   600

Cap Gemini America Inc.; Irving; computer consulting   600

CitiFinancial Credit Co.; Irving; consumer finance companies   600

Danvid Window Co.; Carrollton; metal doors, sash, trim   600

Deloitte and Touche; Dallas; accounting services   600

Hilton Reservations Worldwide; Carrollton; hotel, motel reservations   600

IKON Office Solutions Inc.; Dallas; office equipment   600

McKesson Corp.; Carrollton; warehousing   600

Minyard Food Stores Inc.; Coppell; grocery store   600

Omega Optical General Inc.; Dallas; investment holding company   600

Quebecor World Dallas; Dallas; commercial printing   600

SierraCities.com Inc.; Dallas; financial services   600

Texas Scottish Rite Hospital for Crippled Children; Dallas   600

TXU US Holdings Co.; Dallas; electric services   600

Encompass Electrical Technologies Inc.; Dallas; electrical contractor   580

Western Extrusions Corp.; Carrollton; aluminum products   572

Cameron and Barkley Co.; Dallas; industrial supplies   567

Dynamic Details Inc.; Dallas; printed circuit boards   561

i2 Technologies Inc.; Dallas; business computer software   550

Staubach Co.; Addison; real estate consultant   550

Sanmina Cable Systems Inc.; Carrollton; current-carrying wiring services   540

Neiman Marcus Group Inc.; Dallas; department stores   530

Stanley Works Inc.; Dallas; hand and edge tools   520

Computer Sciences Corp.; Dallas; consumer credit reporting bureau   508

American Heart Assn. Inc.; Dallas; health systems agency   500

Associated Building Services-Dallas Inc.; Dallas; janitorial service   500

Auto One Funding Corp.; Dallas; automobile loans   500

Brandt Mechanical Services Inc.; Dallas; plumbing, heating, air-conditioning   500

Cingular Wireless; Dallas; cellular telephones   500

ClubCorp Financial Management Co.; Dallas; auditing services   500

Columbia Medical Center of Las Colinas; Irving   500

CompuCom Systems Inc.; Dallas; computer software   500

Dallas County Community College District; Dallas   500

DFW Airport Hotel Associates; Dallas; hotels   500

Excel Communications Inc.; Dallas; long-distance telephone   500

ExxonMobil; Dallas; commercial nonphysical research   500

General Electric Capital Corp.; Addison; credit card service   500

JC Penney Corp.; Dallas; credit card service   500

Kinko's Inc.; Dallas; photocopying   500

Nordstrom Inc.; Dallas; clothing stores   500

Texas Instruments Inc.; Dallas; electrical equipment   500

Viacom Inc.; Dallas; video rental   500

UTAH

Districts established October 11, 2001, for elections first held in 2002.

3 members

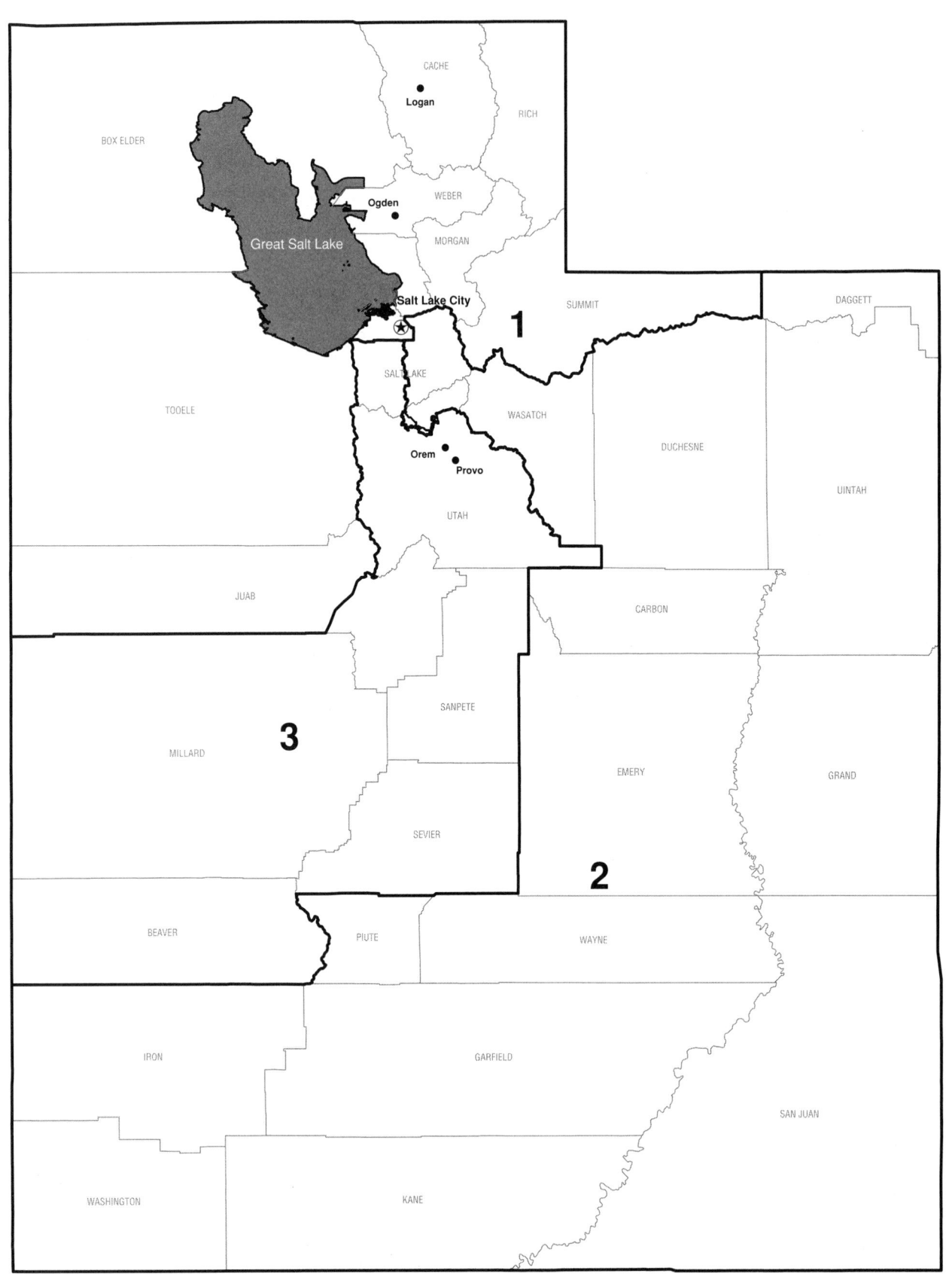

Utah

The state of Utah is unique in the contemporary American polity because it is the only state whose history is dominated by a church. The Church of Jesus Christ of Latter-Day Saints, commonly called the Mormon church, was the founding institution in what had been a nearly deserted territory at the heart of the Interior West. The Mormons arrived here in the late 1840s, having been driven out of Missouri and Illinois. Their arduous journey across the plains and Rocky Mountains to settle this unclaimed land is the stuff of legend and the inspiration for the Mormon community's achievements ever since.

Relations were difficult for a time between the federal government and the Mormons, who had their own governance structure and considered it a higher authority. In the 1850s, as thousands of Mormons made the trek west, federal troops were also dispatched to Utah to deal with its apparent sense of autonomy. This led to a compromise between the civil and church hierarchies and that of the church, a compromise that has been evolving ever since. One issue that blocked statehood for Utah for many years was polygamy, or more precisely polygyny, the taking of multiple wives. While this practice had contributed mightily to the populating of the desert, the Mormons were compelled to renounce it in 1890 before they entered the Union in 1896. Today the Mormon church is one of the largest in the country, with 11,500 congregations and 5.2 million members in the U.S. alone (the church also claims nearly 6 million overseas). Two-thirds of the American Mormons live outside of Utah, with large and politically active concentrations in Idaho, Oregon, California, Nevada, and Arizona.

More than 150 years after the first Mormons arrived, Utah remains a sparsely populated state. At 27 people per square mile, it is forty-first in population density. The mountains that march through the northern half of the state and the unyielding desert in the state's southern corners have limited the agriculture and thus the population prospects here. For many generations the one source of growth was the fecundity of the Mormon stock. But in the postwar era, the appeal of the high plains has brought increasing economic and demographic diversity to Salt Lake City and its suburbs. The state's voting-age population was just over 8 percent Hispanic in the 2000 census and a little under 1 percent African American. Both figures are below the national average, but the minority population in Salt Lake has begun to have a political impact.

The biggest population jump yet came in the 1990s, as Utah prepared to host the 2002 Winter Olympics and welcomed a wave of high-tech industry lured largely by the high education level and the remarkable skiing and other recreation opportunities. In that one decade the state grew nearly 30 percent—the fourth fastest state growth rate in the country—and passed the 2.2 million mark. Most observers expected that to mean a fourth congressional district (the first addition since 1980). The state would have gotten that fourth seat in the reapportionment after 2000 had it been able to count the tens of thousands of Utahans absent on Mormon missions at census time. But the federal courts turned back the state's appeal, and it will be 2010 before the fourth seat arrives. Further growth seems assured beyond that, as Utahans' median age is the youngest in the country.

Mormons, and Utah residents in general, tend to regard themselves as independent entrepreneurs in economic matters and supporters of traditional values in social and cultural matters. Moreover, the federal government owns 34 million acres of Utah, largely in national forests. Only three states have more federal land, which as a rule tends to engender anti-Washington feelings among a state's residents. Thus it is no surprise that contemporary Utah has become one of the top Republican bastions of the nation. In a Gallup Poll done early in 2003, more than 63 percent of Utahans identified themselves as Republican or leaning to Republican. That was a 14 point increase over 1993, and it was the highest percentage of GOP identification in any state (nine points higher than Mississippi at number two).

Oddly enough, however, Utah began its presidential voting history by opting for William Jennings Bryan in 1896. Bryan's promise of free silver was music in the ears of western landowners, and the Democratic Party had supported Utah's entrance into the Union. But the fledgling state soon turned its loyalty to the era's dominant national party, the Republicans, who carried the state in each presidential election from 1900 to 1932 save one, the 1916 reelection of Woodrow Wilson (an election Wilson barely won on support from usually Republican states in the West). Franklin D. Roosevelt was popular enough to win here four times himself and leave enough to carry Harry S. Truman over the top here in 1948. But thereafter the Republican hegemony returned. Utah has been in the GOP's column in every presidential election since, excepting only the 1964 landslide by Lyndon B. Johnson. Moreover, the era of President Bill Clinton made Utah more Republican than ever. In 1992 Clinton got less than one-fourth of the vote here—finishing in third place behind independent Ross Perot—and in 2000 Al Gore did scarcely better.

The pattern in statewide offices has been similar. Utah's strain of populism, evident a century ago and in the 1930s, helped elect Democrat William H. King four times starting in 1916 and Democrat Elbert Thomas in 1932 (defeating Reed Smoot, Republican senator who helped push through punitive tariffs in the wake of the stock market crash of 1929). After World War II, however, the populist power waned. The only Democrat elected to the Senate since has been Frank Moss, who won in a three-way special election in 1958 and was reelected twice before losing to Orrin Hatch in 1976. Hatch has since represented the mix of economic and social conservatism the state has come to symbolize, working to block President Clinton's appointees to federal judgeships and then to boost those of President George W. Bush.

Democrats could claim to have held their own a little better in races for governor. Since statehood, Democrats have elected four of the first eight governors and two of the last four. But the last two Republicans, Norman Bangerter and Mike Leavitt, combined for five straight wins from 1984 through 2000, making it hard to remember when the Democrats were competitive.

Similarly, Democrats in Utah held both the state's House seats as recently as 1976. Since 1980, Republicans have held at least one of the seats and usually two or three (the state gained its third in time for the 1982 election). From 1986 to 1992, two Democrats managed to win based on a shared base in Salt Lake City and environs, but thereafter the GOP had the upper hand. The latest Democrat to make a dent was Jim Matheson, elected in the Salt Lake 2nd District in 2000. Matheson's father was Scott Matheson, a highly popular two-term Democratic governor in the 1970s and 1980s. Redistricting is usually not a major issue in states with just three districts, but in 2001 the Republican legislature in Salt Lake decided to make it one. The mapmakers radically redrew Matheson's 2nd District, which had consisted of Salt Lake City and its immediate suburbs since the 1980 census.

The new 2nd includes Salt Lake City proper but then goes straight east to the Colorado line, drops south to Arizona and doubles back to the west, picking up new population centers in Utah's southwest corner (not far from the Grand Canyon and Las Vegas). All in all, the new 2nd makes up about half the state's land mass. Matheson had already been bucking a substantial Republican lean in his old district (56 percent for Bush in 2000), but his new district was tougher yet (63 percent for Bush). Matheson barely survived in November 2002 against a lightly regarded challenger. The other two districts divide the western and northern suburbs of Salt Lake City, with the northwestern 1st District getting Ogden and Provo, the west-central 3rd District taking in Provo. These venues are heavily Republican (both over two-thirds for Bush in 2000), and both easily reelected their incumbents in 2002.

Table 1 Population

District	Population	Population under 18	Voting-age population	Median age	Male*	Female*
1	744,389	240,699	503,690	27.6	50.3	49.7
2	744,390	221,034	523,356	30.1	50.0	50.0
3	744,390	256,965	487,425	24.5	50.0	50.0
State	2,233,169	718,698	1,514,471	27.1	50.1	49.9

*As percentage of total population.

Table 2 Voting-Age Persons by Race/Hispanic or Latino Origin

District	White*	Black or African American*	American Indian or Alaska Native*	Asian*	Other or multirace*	Hispanic or Latino*
1	84.8	1.1	0.7	2.4	1.1	10.0
2	89.1	0.5	1.9	2.0	1.1	5.4
3	85.8	0.4	0.6	2.8	1.1	9.2
State	86.6	0.7	1.1	2.4	1.1	8.1

*As percentage of voting-age population.

Table 3 Voting-Age Population by Age Groups

District	18 to 24*	25 to 44*	45 to 64*	Over 64*
1	19.9	42.3	25.2	12.6
2	17.9	39.4	27.3	15.4
3	25.4	42.6	22.7	9.4
State	21.0	41.4	25.1	12.6

*As percentage of voting-age population.

Table 4 Income and Occupation

District	Median family income	Families in poverty*	White collar†	Blue collar†	Service†	Farm†
1	$50,927	6.6	58.7	26.2	14.4	0.6
2	$51,981	6.6	65.6	20.1	13.9	0.4
3	$50,245	6.2	59.7	26.2	13.6	0.5
State	$51,022	6.5	61.4	24.1	14.0	0.5

*As percentage of all families.   †As percentage of employed workers 16 years and over.

Table 5 Education: School Years Completed

District	Less than grade 9*	Grades 9–12 no diploma*	High school diploma no college*	Some college*	College bachelor's degree or higher*
1	4.1	9.2	25.6	36.4	24.7
2	2.3	8.3	22.6	35.9	30.9
3	3.3	9.9	25.7	39.1	22.1
State	3.2	9.1	24.6	37.0	26.1

*As percentage of persons age 25 and over.

Table 6 Housing and Residential Patterns

District	Median home value	Owner occupied*	Renter occupied*	Urban†	Rural†
1	$135,100	70.7	29.3	88.7	11.3
2	$158,300	70.6	29.4	84.9	15.1
3	$138,200	73.5	26.5	91.2	8.8
State	$142,600	71.5	28.5	88.3	11.7

*As percentage of occupied housing units.   †As percentage of total population.

Utah 1st District

North — part of Salt Lake City, Ogden

In the 1840s, Mormon pioneers journeyed into the mountainous terrain of northern Utah. Today, the 1st retains that

Mormon influence. Redistricting following the 2000 census added more than half of Salt Lake City, bringing in most of downtown and Temple Square, which includes the Tabernacle and the headquarters of the Church of Jesus Christ of Latter-Day Saints.

Ogden, the 1st's second-largest city, was once a lively railroad town but today looks more toward defense. Hill Air Force Base is one of the state's largest employers. The 1st also contains much of Utah's ski country, including Park City, a wealthy resort town.

Despite the district's overall GOP tilt, many of the added areas in Salt Lake City lean Democratic. George W. Bush received 72 percent of the 2000 vote in the old 1st, but dropped to 67 percent under the new lines. The new 1st combines some of Utah's poorest urban areas with some of its most wealthy, including the heavily populated Davis County, a solidly Republican suburb. Most of the rural areas favor Republicans, though Democrats pick up some votes in Park City and in Weber County—once a center of railroad-related work.

In rural parts of the district, agriculture is king. The aerospace industry also employs many residents. The 2002 Winter Olympics provided an influx of tourism dollars.

Major Industry

Manufacturing, defense, technology.

Notable

Great Salt Lake is the world's second-largest saltwater lake; Park City is home to the U.S. Ski and Snowboard Team.

Election Returns

	Republican		Democratic		Other	
President 2000	167,716	67.6%	66,792	26.9%	13,415	5.4%
House 2002	109,265	60.9%	66,104	36.8%	4,043	2.2%

District Profile

Population   744,389

Total area (square miles)   22,699.7
    Land area (square miles)   20,768.4

Population per square mile   35.8

Counties (2000 population)

Box Elder 42,745	Rich 1,961
Cache 91,391	Salt Lake (pt.) 94,103
Davis 238,994	Summit 29,736
Juab (pt.) 1,062	Tooele 40,735
Morgan 7,129	Weber 196,533

Cities and other areas over 10,000 (2000 population)

Bountiful 41,301	Logan 42,670
Brigham City 17,411	North Ogden 15,026
Centerville 14,585	Ogden 77,226
Clearfield 25,974	Roy 32,885
Clinton 12,585	Salt Lake City (pt.) 94,049
Farmington 12,081	South Ogden 14,377
Kaysville 20,351	Tooele 22,502
Layton 58,474	

Race and Hispanic or Latino origin*

White   83.3%
Black or African American   1.1%
American Indian or Alaska Native   0.7%
Asian   1.6%
Native Hawaiian or other Pacific Islander   0.6%
Some other race   0.1%
Hispanic or Latino origin   11.1%
Two or more races   1.4%

*As percentage of total population.

Ancestry*

Danish 4.6%		Norwegian 2.0%
Dutch 1.9%		Scottish 3.3%
English 20.9%		Swedish 2.9%
French 1.6%		Swiss 1.1%
German 8.3%		USA/American 5.0%
Irish 4.2%		Welsh 1.5%
Italian 1.9%		

*As estimated percentage of total population.

Universities and colleges, 2000–2001 enrollment

Davis Applied Technology Center, Kaysville   324
Latter Day Saints Business College, Salt Lake City   824
Stevens-Henager College of Business, Ogden   298
Utah State University, Logan   21,490
Weber State University, Ogden   16,050
Western Governors University, Salt Lake City   205

Newspapers and circulation

	District circulation	Total circulation
Logan Herald Journal	13,456	14,458
Ogden Standard-Examiner	62,257	62,373
Salt Lake City Deseret News	18,508	66,857
Salt Lake Tribune	34,265	134,140
Salt Lake Tribune/Deseret News	52,776	201,353
*USA Today**	4,399	1,674,376

*See Sources and Explanations in the front of the volume.

Television stations and affiliations

Salt Lake City	100%	KBYU	PBS
Salt Lake City	100%	KCSG	PAX
Salt Lake City	100%	KENV	NBC
Salt Lake City	100%	KGWR	CBS
Salt Lake City	100%	KJZZ	Independent
Salt Lake City	100%	KSL	NBC
Salt Lake City	100%	KSTU	FOX
Salt Lake City	100%	KTVX	ABC
Salt Lake City	100%	KUED	PBS
Salt Lake City	100%	KULC	PBS
Salt Lake City	100%	KUTV	CBS
Salt Lake City	100%	KUWB	WB

Cable systems and subscribers

All West Cable TV   754
Comcast   63,908

Military installations, September 2001
  - Hill Air Force Base, Clearfield   16,441
  - Deseret Chemical Depot, Tooele   1,453
  - Salt Lake City International Airport Air National Guard, Salt Lake City   1,449
  - Dugway Proving Ground (Army), Salt Lake City   1,133
  - Tooele Army Depot, Tooele   738
  - Defense District Depot, Ogden   242

Businesses and other major employers
  - Steiner Corp.; Salt Lake City; uniform supply   5,043
  - U.S. Internal Revenue Service; Ogden   5,000
  - Utah State University; Logan   5,000
  - MarketStar Corp.; Ogden; marketing consulting   4,000
  - Church of Jesus Christ of Latter-Day Saints Corp.; Clearfield; religious organization   3,800
  - Icon Health and Fitness Inc.; Logan; exercise equipment   3,600
  - Snake River Sugar Co.; Ogden; growers' associations   2,923
  - Salt Lake City School District; Salt Lake City   2,848
  - Weber State University; Ogden   2,557
  - McKay-Dee Hospital; Ogden   2,300
  - International Alliance Theatrical Stage Employee; Salt Lake City; labor organization   2,000
  - Iomega Corp.; Ogden; computer hardware   2,000
  - Char's Kountry Quilts; Clearfield; comforters and quilts   1,998
  - O. C. Tanner Manufacturing; Salt Lake City; jewelry   1,800
  - Church of Jesus Christ of Latter-Day Saints Corp.; Salt Lake City; religious organization   1,783
  - Alliant Techsystems Inc.; Brigham City; fuel propellants   1,500
  - Convergys Corp.; Ogden; telemarketing   1,500
  - L-3 Communications Corp.; Salt Lake City; electronic equipment   1,500
  - Central Refrigerated Services Inc.; Salt Lake City refrigerated transport   1,444
  - Alliant Techsystems Inc.; Clearfield; fuel propellants   1,428
  - Church of Jesus Christ of Latter-Day Saints Corp.; Layton; religious organization   1,400
  - Railworks Track Systems Inc.; Salt Lake City; railway construction   1,400
  - Wasatch Constructors; Salt Lake City; road construction   1,383
  - Supplemental Health Care Services Ltd.; Park City   1,300
  - Associated Foods; Salt Lake City; milk supplier   1,200
  - Boeing Co.; Clearfield; aircraft assemblies, parts   1,200
  - Autoliv Inc.; Ogden; automotive and apparel trimmings   1,100
  - La-Z-Boy Inc.; Tremonton; furniture   1,060
  - Associates Commerce Solutions; Layton; savings institutions   1,000
  - Southwest Airlines Co.; Salt Lake City   1,000
  - HCA Ogden Medical Center Inc.; Ogden   950
  - Alliant Techsystems Inc.; Layton; missile warheads   900
  - Citicorp Credit Services Inc.; Layton; credit card services   900
  - Management and Training Corp.; Syracuse; job training services   900
  - Litton Systems Inc.; Salt Lake City; search, navigation equipment   875
  - Smith's Food and Drug Centers Inc.; Layton; drug stores   850
  - FMR Corp.; Salt Lake City; insurance brokers   839
  - Compeq International Corp.; Salt Lake City; printed circuit boards   800
  - Iomega Corp.; Roy; computer storage   800
  - Utah Tax Commission; Salt Lake City   765
  - Wells Fargo Bank; Salt Lake City; commercial bank   763
  - Logan Regional Hospital; Logan   720
  - Baker Hughes Inc.; Salt Lake City; document embossing   700
  - Manufacturers Services Ltd.; Salt Lake City; computer peripherals   700
  - Parker Hannifin Corp.; Ogden; aircraft control systems   700
  - Sinclair Oil Corp.; Salt Lake City   700
  - U.S. Postal Service; Salt Lake City   700
  - University of Utah; Ogden   700
  - Caterpillar Inc.; Salt Lake City; construction machinery   650
  - Moore North America Inc.; Logan; business forms   650
  - Salt Lake County; Salt Lake City; sheriff's office   650
  - Sinclair Oil Corp.; Salt Lake City; petroleum refining   650
  - Huish Detergents Inc.; Salt Lake City   614
  - Autoliv ASP Inc.; Ogden; motor vehicle parts/accessories   600
  - Associates Capital Bank Inc.; Salt Lake City; credit institutions   600
  - Bonneville International Corp.; Salt Lake City; radio broadcasting   600
  - EG&G Defense Materials Inc.; Tooele; engineering services   600
  - Kimberly-Clark Corp.; Ogden; disposable diapers   600
  - Questar Corp.; Salt Lake City; natural gas distribution   600
  - United Parcel Service Inc.; Salt Lake City; courier services   600
  - Utah Dept. of Natural Resources; Salt Lake City   600
  - Varsity Contractors Inc.; Salt Lake City; janitorial service   600
  - America First Credit Union; Ogden; state credit unions   575
  - Nordstrom Inc.; Salt Lake City; clothing stores   574
  - FMC Corp.; Ogden; elevators and equipment   550
  - Hospital Corp. of Utah Inc.; Bountiful   550
  - Davis Hospital and Medical Center Inc.; Layton   540
  - Magnesium Corp. of America; Salt Lake City; magnesium smelting, refining   530
  - Autoliv ASP Inc.; Ogden; textile bags   525
  - Miller Arena Corp.; Salt Lake City; convention services   520
  - American Skiing Co; Park City; resort hotel   500
  - Boeing Co.; Salt Lake City; airplanes   500
  - Kennecott Minerals Co.; Salt Lake City; metal mining services   500
  - Kennecott Utah Copper Corp.; Magna; copper foundries   500
  - Management and Training Corp.; Clearfield; job training services   500

McLoud USA; Salt Lake City; telephone communication
500

Solaray Inc.; Ogden; vitamins   500

Toole Regional Medical Center; Tooele   500

Utah Dept. of Work Force Services; Salt Lake City   500

Varian Medical Systems Inc.; Salt Lake City; TV tubes
500

Wells Fargo Bank; Salt Lake City; commercial bank
500

White Cloud Consulting Inc.; Kaysville; management
consulting   500

Utah 2nd District

South and east — part of Salt Lake City, rural Utah

The 2nd was a compact Salt Lake County district for 20 years before redistricting following the 2000 census dramatically altered it to be much more rural. The 2nd now forms a reverse "L" shape, moving south from Salt Lake City to take in the eastern half of the state and moving westward to take in the state's southwest corner, a ranching center and growing retirement hub.

While some of the 2nd's rural eastern communities saw sharp population declines during the 1980s, these areas have begun to rebound. Grand County, once devastated by the collapse of the uranium mining industry, has seen new life since telecommuter and artist communities have sprung up in the town of Moab. However, the area has not yet fully recovered—it is still losing some of its population and unemployment is high.

Democratic areas of Salt Lake City used to make the 2nd a swing district, but the part of Salt Lake County that remains in the redrawn district—and totals about 60 percent of the 2nd's voters—is now more Republican. In the old 2nd, George W. Bush took 56 percent of the vote in the 2000 presidential election, subpar in a state that gave him a total of 67 percent. But under the new 2nd District lines, Bush received 66.9 percent. The eastern portion of Salt Lake County provides some Democratic votes, as does Carbon County, a mining center in the middle of the state. Washington and Iron Counties, in the southwest, are the district's most Republican.

Land-use issues are important in the district, which includes all five of the state's national parks—Arches, Bryce Canyon, Canyonlands, Capitol Reef, and Zion. Much of the district is federal land. President Bill Clinton's designation of the 1.7 million-acre Grand Staircase-Escalante as a national monument in 1996 angered many in the state.

Major Industry

Financial services, manufacturing, tourism, ranching.

Notable

Zion National Park near Springdale was designated in 1919.

Election Returns

	Republican		Democratic		Other	
President 2000	183,387	66.9%	84,266	30.7%	6,573	2.4%
House 2002	109,123	48.7%	110,764	49.4%	4,211	1.9%

District Profile

Population   744,390

Total area (square miles)   46,034.4
  Land area (square miles)   45,624.2

Population per square mile   16.3

Counties (2000 population)

Carbon 20,422	Piute 1,435
Daggett 921	Salt Lake (pt.) 437,894
Duchesne 14,371	San Juan 14,413
Emery 10,860	Uintah 25,224
Garfield 4,735	Utah (pt.) 57,727
Grand 8,485	Wasatch 15,215
Iron 33,779	Washington 90,354
Kane 6,046	Wayne 2,509

Cities and other areas over 10,000 (2000 population)

American Fork   21,941
Canyon Rim CDP   10,428
Cedar City   20,527
Cottonwood Heights CDP   27,569
Cottonwood West CDP   18,727
Draper   25,220
East Millcreek CDP   21,385
Holladay   14,561
Lehi (pt.)   19,026
Midvale   27,029
Millcreek CDP   30,377
Murray   34,024
Salt Lake City (pt.)   87,694
Sandy   88,418
South Salt Lake   22,038
St. George   49,663

Race and Hispanic or Latino origin*

White   88.0%
Black or African American   0.6%
American Indian or Alaska Native   2.2%
Asian   1.5%
Native Hawaiian or other Pacific Islander   0.3%
Some other race   0.1%
Hispanic or Latino origin   5.9%
Two or more races   1.4%

As percentage of total population.

Ancestry*

Danish 4.5%	Norwegian 2.2%
Dutch 1.7%	Scottish 3.4%
English 21.8%	Swedish 3.4%
French 1.8%	Swiss 1.2%
German 9.0%	USA/American 4.8%
Irish 5.0%	Welsh 1.6%
Italian 2.1%	

As estimated percentage of total population.

Universities and colleges, 2000–2001 enrollment

College of Eastern Utah, Price   2,704
Dixie College, St. George   6,350
Mountain West College, Salt Lake City   405
Southern Utah University, Cedar City   5,963

University of Phoenix, Salt Lake City   2,021
University of Utah, Salt Lake City   24,948
Westminster College, Salt Lake City   2,403

Newspapers and circulation

	District circulation	Total circulation
Provo Daily Herald	2,860	30,797
Salt Lake City Deseret News	26,267	66,857
Salt Lake Tribune	64,433	134,140
Salt Lake Tribune/Deseret News	90,706	201,353
St. George Spectrum	19,965	21,196
*USA Today**	4,075	1,674,376

See Sources and Explanations in the front of the volume.

Television stations and affiliations

Salt Lake City	100%	KBYU	PBS
Salt Lake City	100%	KCSG	PAX
Salt Lake City	100%	KENV	NBC
Salt Lake City	100%	KGWR	CBS
Salt Lake City	100%	KJZZ	Independent
Salt Lake City	100%	KSL	NBC
Salt Lake City	100%	KSTU	FOX
Salt Lake City	100%	KTVX	ABC
Salt Lake City	100%	KUED	PBS
Salt Lake City	100%	KULC	PBS
Salt Lake City	100%	KUTV	CBS
Salt Lake City	100%	KUWB	WB

Cable systems and subscribers

Bresnan   5,015
Charter   7,386
Comcast   48,794
Mallard   3,223
Precis Communications   11,013

Military installations, September 2001

Stephen A. Douglas Armed Forces Reserve Center, Salt Lake City   1,663

Businesses and other major employers

Huntsman ICI Holdings; Salt Lake City; plastics, resins   5,600
PacifiCorp; Ferron; electric power distribution   5,000
Utah National Guard; Draper   5,000
University of Utah Hospital; Salt Lake City   3,200
Haulaway Storage Container; Salt Lake City; bins and containers   3,000
Primary Children's Medical Center; Salt Lake City   2,150
Novus Services Inc.; Sandy; business services   1,800
Southern Utah University; Cedar City   1,660
Cottonwood Medical Center; Salt Lake City   1,600
Affiliated Computer Services Inc.; Sandy; computer consulting   1,500
U.S. Veterans Hospital; Salt Lake City   1,500
HB Boys; Salt Lake City; fast-food chain   1,311
Albertson's Inc.; Salt Lake City; supermarkets   1,200
Becton Dickinson and Co.; Sandy; medical instruments   1,200
HCA St. Mark's Hospital; Salt Lake City   1,200
Delta Airlines Inc.; Salt Lake City   1,100
Utah Transit Authority; Salt Lake City   1,075
Dixie Regional Medical Center; St. George   1,000

Salt Lake County; Salt Lake City; detention center   1,000
Utah Dept. of Human Services; American Fork   1,000
Utah State Prison; Draper   1,000
AT&T; Sandy; cable TV   930
Corporate Consultants Inc.; American Fork; management services   840
Evans and Sutherland Computer Corp.; Salt Lake City; electronic computers   781
Boyne USA Inc.; Salt Lake City; resort hotel   700
CompHealth Inc.; Sandy; employment agencies   700
Energy West Mining Co.; Huntington; coal mining services   700
Regence Blue Cross Blue Shield of Utah; Salt Lake City; health maintenance organization   700
3M Co.; Salt Lake City; computer software   600
College of Eastern Utah; Price   600
Feature Films for Families Inc.; Salt Lake City; video tapes   600
Salt Lake Regional Medical Center Inc.; Salt Lake City   600
Convergys Corp.; Cedar City; telemarketing   550
Layton Construction Co. Inc.; Sandy; building construction   500
Northwest Pipeline Corp.; Salt Lake City; gas transmission   500
Salt Lake City Corp.; Salt Lake City; airport   500
Skywest Airlines Inc.; St. George   500
University of Utah; Salt Lake City   500
Utah Dept. of Corrections; Draper   500
Workforce Solutions Inc.; Salt Lake City; help supply services   500

Utah 3rd District

Central — part of Salt Lake County, Provo

Utah's conservative 3rd is located in the central part of the state, taking in some Salt Lake City suburbs and heading south on Interstate 15 to Provo and Orem, the district's economic centers. It also stretches west to pick up rural Millard and Beaver Counties on the state's western border. A heavily Mormon-influenced district, the 3rd has one of the highest concentrations of married couples and has the lowest median age (24.5) of any district in the nation.

The Provo-Orem area has a flourishing computer industry. Newly minted graduates from the 3rd's colleges have helped make the area attractive to some of the industry's big-name companies. Brigham Young University, located in Provo, is one of the largest employers in the state. Outside Utah County, cattle ranching, mining, and tourism sustain small-town life.

The 3rd included the state's eastern half for 20 years, but redistricting after the 2000 census made the district smaller. The boundary change did not affect the 3rd's GOP lean—George W. Bush received 74.6 percent of the vote in 2000.

Salt Lake County's residents make up slightly less than half of the 3rd's population. These western suburbs grew rapidly in the 1990s. Many are lower income, socially conservative areas that tend to vote Republican. Most of the state's Asian population is located in this part of the district. The 3rd also takes in some of the city's southern suburbs, which recently have attracted younger married couples.

Ranchers in Millard County and hog farmers in Beaver County also tend to vote Republican. Small Democratic pockets exist in the mining community of Magna, the Salt Lake City suburb of West Valley City, and the railroad town of Milford.

Major Industry

Technology, mining, education, ranching.

Notable

Philo T. Farnsworth, credited with inventing TV, lived in Provo; Brigham Young University was founded on an acre of land on October 16, 1875.

Election Returns

	Republican		Democratic		Other	
President 2000	163,983	74.6%	51,878	23.6%	4,002	1.8%
House 2002	103,598	67.4%	44,533	29.0%	5,512	3.6%

District Profile

Population 744,390

Total area (square miles) 16,164.6
  Land area (square miles) 15,750.9

Population per square mile 47.3

Counties (2000 population)

Beaver 6,005	Sanpete 22,763
Juab (pt.) 7,176	Sevier 18,842
Millard 12,405	Utah (pt.) 310,809
Salt Lake (pt.) 366,390	

Cities and other areas over 10,000 (2000 population)

Kearns CDP 33,659	Riverton 25,011
Magna CDP 22,770	South Jordan 29,437
Oquirrh CDP 10,390	Spanish Fork 20,246
Orem 84,324	Springville 20,424
Payson 12,716	Taylorsville 57,439
Pleasant Grove 23,468	West Jordan 68,336
Provo 105,166	West Valley City 108,896

Race and Hispanic or Latino origin*

White 84.5%
Black or African American 0.5%
American Indian or Alaska Native 0.7%
Asian 1.7%
Native Hawaiian or other Pacific Islander 1.1%
Some other race 0.1%
Hispanic or Latino origin 10.0%
Two or more races 1.4%

*As percentage of total population.

Ancestry*

Danish 5.2%	Italian 1.7%
Dutch 1.6%	Norwegian 1.8%
English 21.5%	Scottish 3.1%
French 1.6%	Swedish 3.1%
German 8.2%	USA/American 5.2%
Irish 3.9%	Welsh 1.7%

*As estimated percentage of total population.

Universities and colleges, 2000–2001 enrollment

Brigham Young University, Provo 32,554
ITT Technical Institute, Murray 503
Provo College, Provo 464
Salt Lake Community College, Salt Lake City 21,596
Sevier Valley Applied Technology Center, Richfield 304
Snow College, Ephraim 2,999
Stevens-Henager College of Business, Provo 242
Utah Valley State College, Orem 20,946

Newspapers and circulation

	District circulation	Total circulation
Provo Daily Herald	27,940	30,797
Salt Lake City Deseret News	22,241	66,857
Salt Lake Tribune	34,909	134,140
Salt Lake Tribune/Deseret News	57,154	201,353
*USA Today**	3,454	1,674,376

*See Sources and Explanations in the front of the volume.

Television stations and affiliations

Salt Lake City	100%	KBYU	PBS
Salt Lake City	100%	KCSG	PAX
Salt Lake City	100%	KENV	NBC
Salt Lake City	100%	KGWR	CBS
Salt Lake City	100%	KJZZ	Independent
Salt Lake City	100%	KSL	NBC
Salt Lake City	100%	KSTU	FOX
Salt Lake City	100%	KTVX	ABC
Salt Lake City	100%	KUED	PBS
Salt Lake City	100%	KULC	PBS
Salt Lake City	100%	KUTV	CBS
Salt Lake City	100%	KUWB	WB

Cable systems and subscribers

Comcast 96,184
Mallard 1,428
Precis Communications 5,249

Military installations, September 2001

E. J. Garn Aviation Complex, West Jordan 659

Businesses and other major employers

Brigham Young University; Provo 11,000
Team Mucho Inc.; South Jordan; payroll accounting 3,200
Granite School District; Salt Lake City 3,000
U.S. Postal Service; Riverton 3,000
Salt Lake City School District; Salt Lake City 2,500
Kennecott Utah Copper Corp.; Magna; copper ore 2,400
Utah Valley State College Inc.; Orem 2,200
Convergys Corp.; Salt Lake City; telemarketing 2,000
Nu Skin Enterprises Inc.; Provo; cosmetics, drugs 1,900
Utah Dept. of Transportation; Salt Lake City 1,800
Franklin Covey Co.; Salt Lake City; publishing 1,616
Salt Lake Community College; Salt Lake City 1,580
Geneva Steel Holdings Corp.; Orem; steel mills 1,535
Abbott Laboratories; Salt Lake City; medical instruments 1,425

Alliant Techsystems Inc.; West Jordan; guided missiles, rockets   1,200

Media Modus International Inc.; Lindon; software   1,200

Micron Technology Inc.; Lehi; semiconductors   1,200

Novell Inc.; Provo; software   1,108

Alpine School District; Orem   1,080

ATK Aerospace Co. Inc.; Magna; small arms ammunition   1,000

Utah Bowmens Assn.; Salt Lake City; sports clubs   1,000

Utah Dept. of Health; Provo   810

Alliant Techsystems Inc.; Riverton; guided missile rocket motors   800

Salt Lake County; Riverton; police dept.   800

Jacobsen/Power; Salt Lake City; building construction   680

Merit Medical Systems Inc.; South Jordan; medical appliances   680

CR England Inc.; Salt Lake City; refrigerated transport   650

Ingenix Inc.; Salt Lake City; management consulting   650

Ultradent Products Inc.; South Jordan; dental equipment   650

Saturn Solutions Corp.; Orem; software   646

City of Provo; Provo; city government   600

Fairchild Semiconductor Corp.; West Jordan; calculators   600

Moroni Feed Co.; Moroni; poultry processing   600

Sysco Food Services; West Jordan; food supplier   598

Moog Inc.; Salt Lake City; navigational systems and instruments   579

Nature's Sunshine Products Inc.; Provo; botanicals   578

Sento Corp.; American Fork; software   537

Consolidated Freightways Corp. of Delaware; Salt Lake City; contract haulers   510

Nestle USA; Springville; frozen specialties   500

Pioneer Valley Hospital; Salt Lake City   500

Vermont

Resting on the shores of Lake Champlain and rolling through the rustic Green Mountains, Vermont began its postcolony life not as a state but as an independent republic (just as Texas, California, and Hawaii would do later). The colonists set up shop on their own after Ethan Allen and the Green Mountain Boys beat back the British forces sent to occupy the frontier forts in the state's highlands in 1777 (and secured their cannon for George Washington). Vermont did not join the United States until 1791, after all 13 original states had already ratified the Constitution. The time apart may have helped the early Vermonters develop their sense of doing things their way, a spirit that continues to inform the state's politics.

The state has been through another revolution of sorts in recent years. As a typical New England state—small farms and small manufacturing—Vermont had long been conservative in the classic meaning. When the Republican Party was formed in the 1850s, Vermont embraced it immediately: the first Republican governor took the oath in 1854; the first Republican vote for president occurred in 1856. The state then stuck with that party preference for both offices (and virtually all others) for more than a century. But in the 1960s, Vermont began to grow more populous; and the newcomers soon brought about a political conversion. In a mirror image of the change overtaking the southern states during the same 40 years, Vermont went from being the single most reliably Republican state in the Union to being one of the most dependable for the Democrats.

What happened was not mysterious. As people began to leave the postwar cities in search of cleaner air and a simpler life, the sparsely populated hills and woods of Vermont (the name means green mountain) were a natural magnet. Many of these new folk had been influenced by the counterculture of the 1960s and 1970s. Not all were ex-hippies, by any means, but Vermont was a place to "get back to the land and try to get my soul free" (to borrow lyrics from Joni Mitchell's "Woodstock"). By the 1970s, Democrat Pat Leahy could get elected to the Senate and still tell people his favorite band was the Grateful Dead. In the 1980s, a New York native named Bernie Sanders could call himself a socialist and still get elected mayor of the state's largest town. In the 1990s Sanders became a fixture in the state's U.S. House seat as an independent caucusing with the Democrats. As of 2003, another New York native named Howard Dean, who had been Vermont's governor for the previous decade, was running as an antiwar candidate for the Democratic presidential nomination.

Like Sanders and Dean, many of the new Vermonters came from the Boston and New York metro areas and other examples of urban sprawl further south and west. Some had come to New England first to attend one of its myriad liberal arts colleges. These include many successful entrepreneurs, such as the makers of Ben & Jerry's ice cream and a number of high-tech innovators and catalog retailers. They were looking for lifestyle and a sense of community government, and not for the antitax and antigovernment attitude of neighboring New Hampshire. A common interest of many newcomers and visitors is the sense of pristine environment and gentle recreation (hiking, cross-country skiing). In recent years state officials have been trying to convince tourists, so prevalent on the ski slopes in winter, to visit the state year round, though none of Vermont's attractions are advertised on roadside billboards—state law prohibits them.

Vermont may also have seemed more welcoming because it needed people. The state's population had first reached the 300,000 plateau in the census of 1850 (good at that time for three seats in the U.S. House), but it had yet to reach 400,000 in the census taken 110 years later. Therefore the net gain of about 220,000 in the next 40 years seemed huge by local standards, even if it was only about average by national standards. Vermont is still forty-ninth in population—only Wyoming has fewer people—but it is hard to find anyone here who minds.

Economically, Vermont began as a farming state. That soon came to mean growing hay to feed dairy cows and grass to feed sheep. It is hard to do much more with a short growing season and rocky soil. (There was a reason the first Vermonters built their fences of stone, which some say is still the state's best crop.) Vermont retains its dairy industry, and that drives the legislative agendas of its delegation in Congress. When lifelong Republican James Jeffords, the junior senator first elected in 1988, became an independent and voted with the Democrats in 2001, it was in part because the George W. Bush administration had refused to accommodate his demands regarding dairy prices. Leahy, despite strong interests in judicial and foreign issues, remained chair or ranking Democratic member of the Senate Agriculture Committee until his fifth term in the Senate.

In state and federal elections, the strong progressive contingency based in Burlington and surrounding Chittenden County usually outvotes the numerous Yankee libertarian conservatives, based mostly in East Montpelier and some of the Burlington suburbs. Rural areas of the state, especially the northeast corner, also hold a few Republican votes.

GRAND ISLE

FRANKLIN

ORLEANS

ESSEX

● St. Albans City

LAMOILLE

CALEDONIA

Burlington ●

CHITTENDEN

South Burlington ●

St. Johnsbury ●

WASHINGTON

☆ Montpelier

● Barre City

ADDISON

ORANGE

At Large

Middlebury ●

Rutland City ●

WINDSOR

RUTLAND

BENNINGTON

WINDHAM

Bennington ●

Brattleboro ●

Democrats dominate the central swath of land along Interstates 89 and 91, as well as the southeast corner. Many small urban centers, such as Montpelier and Rutland, once reliably Republican, now have more Democrats.

The less conservative newcomers to the state who have been changing Vermont have provoked a backlash. Conflicts over gun laws are common, as hunters with rifles remain a big part of the cultural landscape (statistically, residents in Vermont are more likely to be hunters with firearms than those in Texas or Tennessee). When in 2000 the general assembly (as the state legislature is called) gave its approval for gay couples to have "civil unions" in lieu of marriages, many of the more traditional Vermonters rebelled, formed ad hoc political organizations such as Take Back Vermont and recalled a number of legislators. Although efforts to defeat Democrats at the statewide slate failed in 2002, the newly elected legislature had a narrow Republican majority in its lower chamber. Many of the state's Democrats have acknowledged that they moved farther and faster than the state was ready to accept.

But the direction of the state's politics is clear. Vermont once had voted Republican in the face of all four of Franklin D. Roosevelt's landslides. (After his 1936 win, FDR crowed: "As Maine goes, so goes Vermont.") Vermont joined in rejecting Barry Goldwater in 1964 but returned to the GOP fold in 1968 and stayed another two decades. It was, quite simply, the bedrock of the GOP base for more than 130 years. The first glimmer of change came in 1988, when George Bush won with just 51 percent over Michael Dukakis of Massachusetts. In the 1990s Democrat Bill Clinton carried the state twice, the second time with an outright majority. Al Gore managed to do the same in 2000.

Similarly, Democrats have now won six gubernatorial elections in a row in Vermont and nine of the last ten. Leahy's five wins are the only ones Democrats have had for that office since the popular election of senators began in 1914. It is doubly remarkable to see Democrats win in this fashion in a state that has virtually no minority vote to speak of. Vermont ranked forty-eighth in 2000 in its percentage of blacks and Hispanics.

Major Industry
Manufacturing, tourism, dairy farming.

Notable
In Bristol, the Lord's Prayer Rock stands beside a road—Dr. Joseph Greene had the prayer carved in the rock in 1891, hoping wagon drivers would stop cursing their horses during the muddy season; Ben & Jerry's ice cream was started in Burlington in an old gas station.

Table 1 Population

District	Population	Population under 18	Voting-age population	Median age	Male*	Female*
At Large	608,827	147,523	461,304	37.7	49.0	51.0

*As percentage of total population.

Table 2 Voting-Age Persons by Race/Hispanic or Latino Origin

District	White*	Black or African American*	American Indian or Alaska Native*	Asian*	Other or multirace*	Hispanic or Latino*
At Large	96.6	0.4	0.4	0.8	1.0	0.8

*As percentage of voting-age population.

Table 3 Voting-Age Population by Age Groups

District	18 to 24*	25 to 44*	45 to 64*	Over 64*
At Large	12.3	38.3	32.7	16.8

*As percentage of voting-age population.

Table 4 Income and Occupation

District	Median family income	Families in poverty*	White collar†	Blue collar†	Service†	Farm†
At Large	$48,625	6.3	60.8	23.3	14.6	1.3

*As percentage of all families.   †As percentage of employed workers 16 years and over.

Table 5 Education: School Years Completed

District	Less than grade 9*	Grades 9–12 no diploma*	High school diploma no college*	Some college*	College bachelor's degree or higher*
At Large	5.1	8.4	32.4	24.6	29.4

*As percentage of persons age 25 and over.

Table 6 Housing and Residential Patterns

District	Median home value	Owner occupied*	Renter occupied*	Urban†	Rural†
At Large	$111,200	70.6	29.4	38.2	61.8

*As percentage of occupied housing units.   †As percentage of total population.

Election Returns

	Republican		Democratic		Other	
President 2000	119,775	40.7%	149,022	50.6%	25,511	8.7%
House 2002*	72,813	32.3%			152,663	67.7%

*Independent Bernard Sanders received 144,880 votes (64.3%).

District Profile

Population   608,827

Total area (square miles)   9,614.2
    Land area (square miles)   9,249.5

Population per square mile   65.8

Counties (2000 population)

Addison	35,974	Lamoille	23,233
Bennington	36,994	Orange	28,226
Caledonia	29,702	Orleans	26,277
Chittenden	146,571	Rutland	63,400
Essex	6,459	Washington	58,039
Franklin	45,417	Windham	44,216
Grand Isle	6,901	Windsor	57,418

Cities and other areas over 10,000 (2000 population)

Burlington   38,889
Rutland   17,292
South Burlington   15,814

Race and Hispanic or Latino origin*

White   96.2%
Black or African American   0.5%
American Indian or Alaska Native   0.4%
Asian   0.8%
Native Hawaiian or other Pacific Islander   0.0%
Some other race   0.1%
Hispanic or Latino origin   0.9%
Two or more races   1.1%

*As percentage of total population.

Ancestry*

English	13.1%	Polish	2.4%
Fr. Canadian	6.3%	Scotch-Irish	1.5%
French	10.3%	Scottish	3.2%
German	6.5%	Swedish	1.2%
Irish	11.7%	USA/American	5.9%
Italian	4.5%		

*As estimated percentage of total population.

Universities and colleges, 2000–2001 enrollment

Bennington College, Bennington   632
Burlington College, Burlington   206
Castleton State College, Castleton   1,605
Champlain College, Burlington   2,530
College of St. Joseph, Rutland   529
Community College of Vermont, Waterbury   4,412
Goddard College, Plainfield   589
Green Mountain College, Poultney   631
Johnson State College, Johnson   1,527
Landmark College, Putney   265
Lyndon State College, Lyndonville   1,214
Marlboro College, Marlboro   416
Middlebury College, Middlebury   2,298
Norwich University, Northfield   2,652
School for International Training, Brattleboro   490
Southern Vermont College, Bennington   455
St. Michael's College, Colchester   2,687
Trinity College, Burlington   961
University of Vermont and State Agricultural College, Burlington   10,118
Vermont Law School, South Royalton   573
Vermont Technical College, Randolph Center   1,145

Newspapers and circulation

	District circulation	Total circulation
Barre Times Argus	10,305	10,464
Bennington Banner	6,283	7,356
Boston Globe	2,082	465,248
Brattleboro Reformer	9,006	10,178
Burlington Free Press	49,380	49,824
Claremont Eagle Times	1,809	7,049
Lebanon Valley News	7,899	17,284
Rutland Herald	20,539	21,417
St. Johnsbury Caledonian-Record	7,578	10,315
*USA Today**	4,389	1,674,376

*See Sources and Explanations in the front of the volume.

Television stations and affiliations

Burlington-Plattsburgh	85%	WCAX	CBS
Burlington-Plattsburgh	85%	WCFE	PBS
Burlington-Plattsburgh	85%	WETK	PBS
Burlington-Plattsburgh	85%	WLED	PBS
Burlington-Plattsburgh	85%	WNNE	NBC
Burlington-Plattsburgh	85%	WPTZ	NBC
Burlington-Plattsburgh	85%	WVER	PBS
Burlington-Plattsburgh	85%	WVNY	ABC
Burlington-Plattsburgh	85%	WVTB	PBS
Boston (Manchester)	8%	WBPX	PAX
Boston (Manchester)	8%	WBZ	CBS
Boston (Manchester)	8%	WCVB	ABC
Boston (Manchester)	8%	WDPX	PAX
Boston (Manchester)	8%	WEKW	PBS
Boston (Manchester)	8%	WFXT	FOX
Boston (Manchester)	8%	WGBH	PBS
Boston (Manchester)	8%	WGBX	PBS
Boston (Manchester)	8%	WHDH	NBC
Boston (Manchester)	8%	WLVI	WB
Boston (Manchester)	8%	WMFP	Independent
Boston (Manchester)	8%	WMUR	ABC
Boston (Manchester)	8%	WNDS	Independent
Boston (Manchester)	8%	WPXB	Independent
Boston (Manchester)	8%	WPXG	PAX
Boston (Manchester)	8%	WSBK	UPN
Boston (Manchester)	8%	WUNI	Univision
Boston (Manchester)	8%	WWDP	Independent
Boston (Manchester)	8%	WYDN	Independent
Albany-Schenectady-Troy, NY	7%	WCDC	ABC
Albany-Schenectady-Troy, NY	7%	WEWB	WB
Albany-Schenectady-Troy, NY	7%	WMHT	PBS
Albany-Schenectady-Troy, NY	7%	WRGB	CBS
Albany-Schenectady-Troy, NY	7%	WTEN	ABC
Albany-Schenectady-Troy, NY	7%	WXXA	FOX
Albany-Schenectady-Troy, NY	7%	WYPX	PAX

Cable systems and subscribers

Adelphia   102,482
Area TeleCable   1,796
Charter   15,888
North Country Cablevision Inc.   939
North Valley Cable   1,086
Southern Vermont Cable Co.   826
Trans Video Inc.   1,620
Waitsfield Cable   2,403

Military installations, September 2001

Burlington International Airport Air National Guard, South Burlington   997
Camp Johnson (Army Guard), Colchester   419

Businesses and other major employers

International Business Machines Corp.; Essex Junction; integrated microcircuits   7,500
University of Vermont Health Center; Burlington   5,000

University of Vermont and State Agricultural College; Burlington 3,250

All Cycle Transfer Inc.; Williston; refuse collection 3,189

University of Vermont Medical Center; Burlington 3,100

Computer Sciences Corp.; Burlington; computer consulting services 2,000

General Electric Co.; Rutland; aircraft engines, parts 1,600

General Electric Co.; North Clarendon; aircraft engines, parts 1,500

Vermont Agency of Transportation; Montpelier 1,200

C&S Wholesale Grocers Inc.; Brattleboro; food supplier 1,000

Rutland Hospital Inc.; Rutland 1,000

Middlebury College; Middlebury 970

Casella Waste Systems Inc.; Rutland; rubbish collection 908

Stratton Corp.; South Londonderry; ski lodge 900

U.S. Bureau of Customs and Border Protection; St. Albans 900

National Life Insurance Co.; Montpelier 850

Visiting Nurse Assn. Inc.; Colchester; visiting nurse service 800

Goodrich Corp.; Vergennes; aircraft parts, equipment 800

Chittenden Trust Co.; Brattleboro; commercial bank 769

Southwestern Vermont Medical Center Inc.; Bennington 750

Essex Community Educational Center; Essex Junction 700

Central Vermont Hospital Inc.; Montpelier 683

Ethan Allen Inc.; Beecher Falls; furniture 680

Vermont Agency of Natural Resources; Waterbury 570

Ethan Allen Inc.; Orleans; furniture 550

U.S. Postal Service; White River Junction 500

Brattleboro Retreat Hospital; Brattleboro 500

South Burlington School District; South Burlington 500

Summit Ventures; Warren; investment holding company 500

VIRGINIA

Districts established July 19, 2001, for elections first held in 2002.

11 members

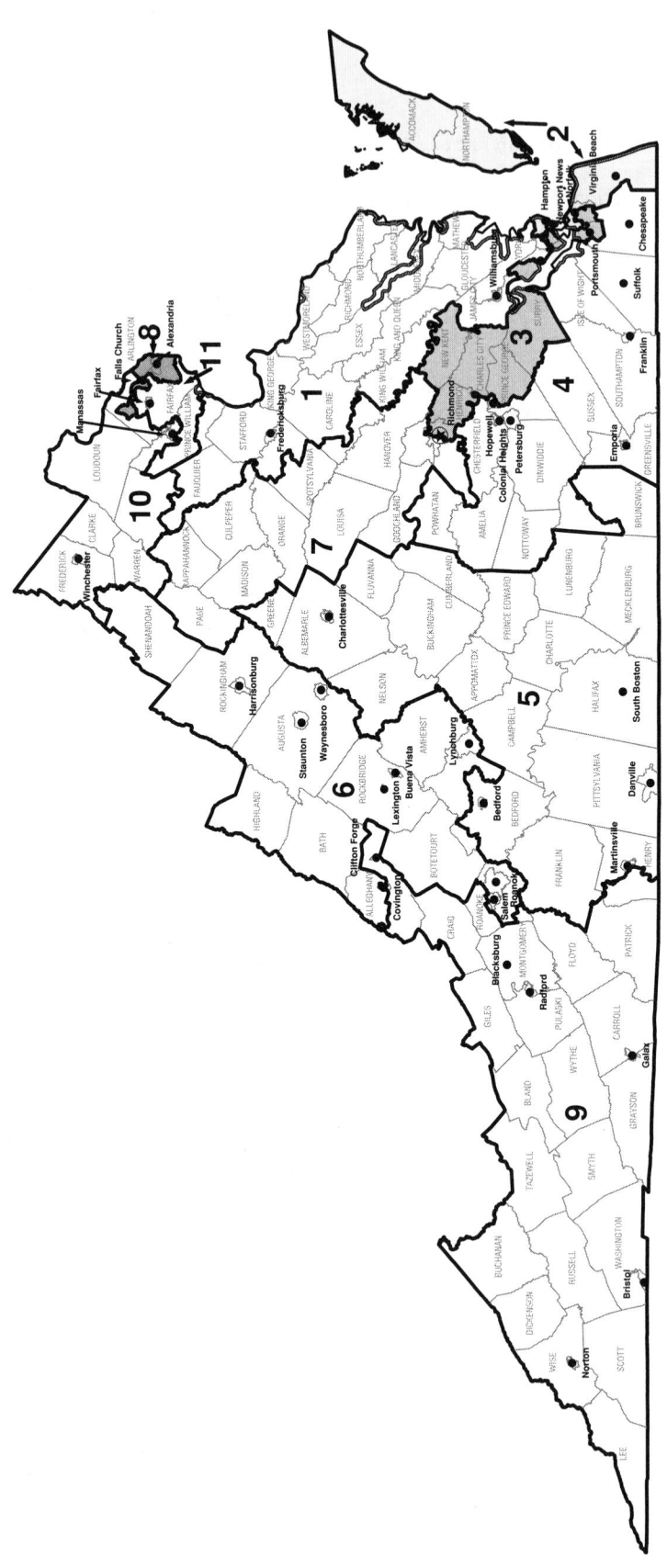

Virginia

It is not hard to understand why Virginians show an almost European penchant for preserving the past. The Commonwealth of Virginia (as it is still called) was the first, largest, richest, most populous, and most powerful of the colonies that became the United States of America. Virginia still uses the sobriquet "The Old Dominion," recalling its loyalty to the king in the English civil wars of the 1640s. It captures the tone of the early Virginians, who fancied themselves cavaliers, creatures of the English aristocracy, whether they were highborn or not. They were also ambitious about their real estate: as late as 1783, Virginia claimed not only its present territory but everything that is now West Virginia and Kentucky plus portions of what is now Ohio, Indiana, Michigan, Illinois, Wisconsin, and Minnesota. Virginia was where much of America's story began: the barter with Native Americans, the tobacco trade, the representative House of Burgesses and, in the same year of 1619, the first purchase of slaves.

The American Revolutionary War ended at Yorktown in 1781, with a Virginia general the victor. That general would be the new nation's first president and the first of eight native Virginians to hold the office (more than any other state). Although it did not have a city to compete with Boston, Philadelphia, New York, or Baltimore, Virginia was well settled to the fall line and even beyond. It easily led the 1790 census with 692,000 residents to Pennsylvania's second place 434,000. In the first Congress, Virginia's ten-member delegation was the only one in double digits.

But this dominance continued for little more than a generation. After Washington, three of the next four presidents also were Virginians. But challenges were arising. In the census of 1820, Virginia's 938,000 residents entitled the state to 22 seats in the House. But Pennsylvania had more than a million people, New York more than 1.3 million, and these northern upstarts got 26 seats and 34 seats respectively. Without a major city, Virginia was far less a magnet for new immigrants, and it was starting to lose ground.

As the nineteenth century wore on and the conflict over slavery intensified, leading citizens of the commonwealth such as Robert E. Lee sensed its destiny in the balance and feared war. But when the war came, hastened by other states, Richmond became the Confederacy's capital and Lee its reluctant general. The war was fought in Virginia more than any other state, Richmond was burned to the ground, and Lee surrendered at Appomattox, Virginia, in 1865. The economy and infrastructure were devastated even before the emancipation of the slaves took legal effect. During and after the war, anti-Southern elements in the federal government wanted to inflict special indignities on the state they saw as having led the rebellion. The family estate of Lee and his wife Mary Custis was expropriated for use as a burial ground for war dead, and became the Arlington National Cemetery. (The Lee-Custis home still stands amidst the graves.)

In 1860 Virginia still had 11 seats in a U.S. House of 243 seats. Over the next half century, as the House grew to 435 seats, Virginia's delegation would actually shrink—hitting a low point of nine. As with the rest of the South, Virginia was starved for postwar capital and consigned to a kind of agricultural peonage. It still had its farms, mines, and forests—and shipbuilding and textiles would become increasingly important—but Virginia did not develop much of the heavy manufacturing that characterized the industrial age. Richmond, its biggest city at the time, spent much of the postwar period rebuilding from ruins. When the Rockefellers made a project of restoring Colonial Williamsburg in the 1920s, it appeared to some that the state's best hopes lay in tourism. Many of Virginia's sons and daughters, black and white, went to seek economic and social opportunity elsewhere. While in these doldrums, Virginia elected Dixie Democrats, established Jim Crow laws to restrict the former slaves and their progeny, and reelected its few representatives to Congress so they would gain power through seniority.

But change did come to Virginia in the mid-1900s, driven by World War II and the explosion of growth in and around Washington, D.C. The war built up the area around Norfolk and Hampton Roads as the Navy gradually made this its main base of operations on the Atlantic (eclipsing both Philadelphia to the north and Charleston Bay to the south). World War II, in particular, also wrought immense changes in the nation's capital city and the neighboring counties of Virginia. Toward the close of the century, these counties would also host an explosion of economic activity linked to telecommunications, personal computers, software, and Internet communication (including the headquarters of AOL, which would merge with Time Warner to form the largest media company in the world). Although "NoVa" did not have the kind of universities and research institutes that spawned Silicon Valley and its counterparts, it did have the Pentagon. That meant a base of applied science professionals and facilities left over from the cold war and the big military buildup of President Ronald Reagan's administration in the 1980s.

The key to all this was the city of Washington. Although located across the Potomac in what would otherwise be Maryland, the capital always had close ties to Virginians (George Washington helped site the Capitol) and, after 150 years, finally became the population center Virginia had long lacked. Washington had been a small town at the time of Civil War but doubled in population to nearly 280,000 by the year 1900. By 1950, it had peaked at 800,000.

With such swelling demand for housing the city burst at its seams, spilling population into Maryland but also over new, modern bridges into the Old Dominion. Fairfax County, which half-encircles the older suburbs of Arlington and Alexandria, had nearly a million residents by 2000. But the growth continued outward, to Prince William County (nearly 300,000 in 2000), Loudon (190,000), and Fauquier and Stafford Counties as well. In the 1860s, Lee had called his forces the Army of Northern Virginia and dreamed of occupying Washington. A century later, an army of Northern Virginia commuters was battling its way into Washington every day.

This dynamic changed life in Richmond as well. Nearly 30 percent of the state vote is now cast within what is considered the Washington area. At times, its elected representatives join forces with those from the second largest metro area in the state, which consists of the Tidewater cities of Newport News, Norfolk, Hampton Roads, and Virginia Beach (a fast-growing retirement center and vacation draw that surpassed Richmond as the most populous municipality in 1990). Counting in the resort communities just over the line in North Carolina, this metro area had 1.57 million people in 2000. Even the long-depressed Richmond-Petersburg metro area turned out to have passed the million people mark by 2000, having grown 15 percent in the 1990s.

Overall, Virginia doubled in population between 1950 and 2000, exceeding the national growth rate for the first time since the early 1800s. As this era reinvigorated the state, it also brought social upheaval, particularly on the issue of race. While other states tried to deal with the integration imperative of the Supreme Court's 1953 decision in *Brown vs. Board of Education,* much of Virginia's white hierarchy preferred the policy of "massive resistance," even to the point of closing public schools. As the administrations of presidents John F. Kennedy and Lyndon B. Johnson pressed the Civil Rights Act of 1964 and the Voting Rights Act of 1965, Virginia's Democrats were still led by Sen. Harry F. Byrd, their most powerful figure since he became governor in the mid-1920s. A scion one of the state's first big land-owning families, Byrd had been in the Senate since 1933. Byrd's son would succeed him in 1966 and serve 16 years as an independent rather than follow the national Democrats or join the party of Lincoln.

Soon enough, though, the state's preference for conservatives in statewide office led to a more general party switch. The state elected its first Republican governors since Reconstruction in the late 1960s and early 1970s and its first Republican senator (John Warner) in 1978. The 1980s brought the first majority-Republican delegation to the U.S. House and a second Republican to the Senate (Paul Trible).

The GOP takeover was slowed in the 1980s by the career of Chuck Robb, who won the governorship in 1981 and helped two Democratic successors win it too. Robb later served two terms in the Senate. But after 2000, Robb was gone and both Senate seats were Republican, as were eight of the 11 U.S. House seats, both chambers of the General Assembly, and all three of the top state offices.

Virginia had prefigured all this Republican success in its presidential voting. It first happened in 1928: the presence of New York's Catholic governor Al Smith atop the Democratic ticket was too much for the Old Dominion, which voted to elect Herbert Hoover. It was a shock at the time: Virginia was still the ancestral home of Jeffersonian Democrats and the capital of the Confederacy. But after a series of votes for Franklin D. Roosevelt and Harry S. Truman, the state moved more-or-less permanently into the Republican column and stayed there for the next 50 years (setting aside the typical exception for Lyndon Johnson's 1964 landslide).

George W. Bush won a majority here, although his 52 percent was not as impressive as earlier Republican winners. Al Gore won 60 percent or more in Alexandria and Arlington and in the largely black cities of Norfolk, Richmond, and Petersburg. Bush won the big prize of Fairfax County, but by less than two percentage points. He survived by running up better margins in populous Virginia Beach, suburban Richmond County, the newer Washington suburbs of Loudon and Prince William Counties, and the rural counties of Southside Virginia, south of Richmond.

Race has remained an issue in Virginia politics, even after the 1989 triumph of Doug Wilder, the first African American to be elected governor of any state. Robert Scott was elected to Congress in 1992, the first African American to serve from Virginia since his own great-grandfather, George Washington Murray, did so in the 1890s. But Scott in the 3rd District is still the lone African American in the 11-member delegation for a state that is one-fifth black. The old 4th District had been 39 percent black, allowing a Democratic African American state senator to run a close, but unsuccessful, race there against Republican Randy Forbes in 2000. But the 2001 remap was the first since Reconstruction to be done by a fully Republican General Assembly with a Republican governor. Their goal was to preserve the party's recent gains (eight seats of 11 are now in GOP hands), even at the cost of shoring up a Democrat here and there. So the new map reduced the black share of the 4th District to 34 percent. The Justice Department, which is required to sign off on remapping here (and in 15 other states adjudged to have histories of racial discrimination) registered no objections.

Virginia has also begun to have a notable Hispanic presence, which in 2000 amounted to 5 percent of the population, mostly concentrated in the immediate Washington suburbs, where about a fifth of the people now speak Spanish. But the concerns of minority voters were not the central focus of redistricting in 2001. The main business was incumbent protection, which was pursued on a bipartisan basis. Republicans and Democrats were redistricted in the Washington suburbs, both making Republican Tom Davis and Democrat Jim Moran safer. The same was done in the state's southeastern corner, where the 2nd District had been considered marginal but should now be safe indefinitely for Republican Ed Schrock. In the 2002 election the state once again elected eight Republicans and three Democrats to the U.S. House.

Table 1 Population

District	Population	Population under 18	Voting-age population	Median age	Male*	Female*
1	643,514	170,161	473,353	35.7	49.0	51.0
2	643,510	164,979	478,531	32.5	50.8	49.2
3	643,476	166,199	477,277	33.2	47.7	52.3
4	643,477	171,539	471,938	35.8	49.2	50.8
5	643,497	145,077	498,420	38.3	48.5	51.5
6	643,504	143,892	499,612	37.8	48.1	51.9
7	643,499	161,143	482,356	37.1	48.2	51.8
8	643,503	126,594	516,909	34.7	49.4	50.6
9	643,514	133,538	509,976	38.0	49.2	50.8
10	643,512	181,657	461,855	34.6	49.7	50.3
11	643,509	173,483	470,026	35.7	49.6	50.4
State	7,078,515	1,738,262	5,340,253	35.7	49.0	51.0

*As percentage of total population.

Table 2 Voting-Age Persons by Race/Hispanic or Latino Origin

District	White*	Black or African American*	American Indian or Alaska Native*	Asian*	Other or multirace*	Hispanic or Latino*
1	76.6	17.5	0.4	1.8	1.2	2.6
2	70.0	19.8	0.4	4.3	1.6	3.9
3	41.5	52.7	0.5	1.6	1.3	2.4
4	63.6	32.1	0.3	1.3	0.9	1.8
5	74.1	22.6	0.2	1.0	0.7	1.4
6	86.2	10.1	0.2	0.9	0.8	1.7
7	79.4	15.4	0.3	2.3	0.9	1.8
8	60.4	12.4	0.2	9.5	2.7	14.7
9	93.6	3.8	0.1	0.8	0.6	1.0
10	78.3	6.5	0.2	6.7	1.5	6.7
11	68.6	9.5	0.2	11.2	2.1	8.4
State	72.2	18.3	0.3	3.7	1.3	4.2

*As percentage of voting-age population.

Table 3 Voting-Age Population by Age Groups

District	18 to 24*	25 to 44*	45 to 64*	Over 64*
1	12.4	41.5	30.7	15.3
2	16.6	44.6	26.2	12.7
3	16.0	41.0	27.3	15.6
4	11.4	42.8	31.2	14.6
5	12.5	36.6	31.9	19.1
6	14.2	35.7	30.8	19.3
7	10.1	41.6	32.2	16.1
8	11.1	49.9	28.0	11.0
9	15.1	35.1	31.5	18.4
10	9.9	48.3	31.5	10.3
11	10.4	44.5	34.7	10.3
State	12.7	41.9	30.5	14.8

*As percentage of voting-age population.

Table 4 Income and Occupation

District	Median family income	Families in poverty*	White collar†	Blue collar†	Service†	Farm†
1	$57,518	4.8	62.8	22.1	14.4	0.6
2	$50,060	6.6	63.0	21.1	15.3	0.6
3	$38,319	15.3	55.4	25.8	18.5	0.2
4	$51,721	7.6	57.8	27.6	14.1	0.5
5	$42,900	9.2	53.3	31.7	14.0	0.9
6	$46,177	7.3	55.9	28.5	14.7	0.9
7	$60,384	4.4	68.4	19.4	11.8	0.4
8	$75,302	5.2	77.0	10.7	12.2	0.1
9	$36,972	11.2	49.1	35.3	14.6	0.9
10	$81,119	2.8	72.5	15.9	11.3	0.3
11	$88,612	2.5	76.5	11.7	11.7	0.1
State	$54,169	7.0	63.7	22.1	13.7	0.5

*As percentage of all families.   †As percentage of employed workers 16 years and over.

Table 5 Education: School Years Completed

District	Less than grade 9*	Grades 9–12 no diploma*	High school diploma no college*	Some college*	College bachelor's degree or higher*
1	5.1	10.3	28.2	29.6	26.8
2	3.6	9.0	27.4	34.6	25.5
3	7.5	17.4	29.7	28.3	17.2
4	7.6	13.9	30.1	28.7	19.6
5	11.3	16.3	30.8	22.6	19.0
6	8.9	13.5	32.1	24.8	20.8
7	5.2	9.9	25.5	26.3	33.2
8	6.3	6.6	13.8	19.6	53.8
9	15.5	15.7	32.0	22.7	14.0
10	4.7	7.1	20.2	24.8	43.1
11	3.5	4.8	17.0	25.8	48.9
State	7.2	11.3	26.0	26.0	29.5

*As percentage of persons age 25 and over.

Table 6 Housing and Residential Patterns

District	Median home value	Owner occupied*	Renter occupied*	Urban†	Rural†
1	$127,500	72.7	27.3	64.0	36.0
2	$111,200	63.4	36.6	91.7	8.3
3	$83,300	52.2	47.8	92.2	7.8
4	$102,200	73.5	26.5	70.9	29.1
5	$87,500	72.4	27.6	36.0	64.0
6	$98,400	69.2	30.8	64.7	35.3
7	$128,600	72.8	27.2	70.0	30.0
8	$198,800	50.1	49.9	100.0	0.0
9	$67,500	74.2	25.8	34.1	65.9
10	$187,100	75.3	24.7	83.3	16.7
11	$205,500	76.7	23.3	95.9	4.1
State	$118,800	68.1	31.9	73.0	27.0

*As percentage of occupied housing units.   †As percentage of total population.

Virginia 1st District

East — parts of Newport News and Hampton, Fredericksburg

The Republican-friendly 1st lies along Virginia's coast, stretching from outer Northern Virginia suburbs and exurbs of Washington, D.C., all the way south to the shipbuilding cities of Hampton and Newport News. (*See map p. 936.*)

Industry in the 1st revolves around its military installations and NASA sites, which have attracted a growing technology private sector. Colleges and universities also contribute to the district's economic base, as do shipbuilding and tourism. The most popular tourist destinations—Williamsburg, Jamestown, and Yorktown—recall Virginia's colonial past. Inland, agriculture and chickens help drive the economy.

Virginia's population expansion is not confined to the Washington suburbs. Spotsylvania County (one-fifth of which is in the neighboring 7th) has experienced rapid growth as a result of its proximity to both Richmond and Washington and its location on the Interstate 95 corridor. Spotsylvania's 58 percent growth in the 1990s was the third-fastest clip in the state. Stafford County, located just north of Fredericksburg, grew by nearly 50 percent in the 1990s, and is now the most populous county in the 1st.

Redistricting following the 2000 census shifted the 1st slightly north toward Washington. The new map removed parts of Newport News and Hampton and added parts of Prince William and Fauquier Counties. The changes kept the 1st's solidly GOP orientation intact: George W. Bush took 58.4 percent in the 2000 presidential election, third-best in the state.

Major Industry
Defense, technology, agriculture, tourism.

Notable
Jamestown was the first English settlement in North America; George Washington and Robert E. Lee were born in Westmoreland County.

Election Returns

	Republican		Democratic		Other	
President 2000	146,914	58.4%	98,731	39.2%	6,060	2.4%
House 2002	113,168	95.9%			4,829	0.1%

District Profile

Population   643,514

Total area (square miles)   4,611.6
  Land area (square miles)   3,772.7

Population per square mile   170.6

Counties (2000 population)
  Caroline (pt.)   12,019
  Essex   9,989
  Fauquier (pt.)   28,577
  Fredericksburg city   19,279
  Gloucester   34,780
  Hampton city (pt.)   31,755
  James City   48,102
  King and Queen   6,630
  King George   16,803
  King William   13,146
  Lancaster   11,567
  Mathews   9,207
  Middlesex   9,932
  Newport News city (pt.)   71,800
  Northumberland   12,259
  Poquoson city   11,566

Prince William (pt.)   38,265
Richmond   8,809
Spotsylvania (pt.)   71,570
Stafford   92,446
Westmoreland   16,718
Williamsburg city   11,998
York   56,297

Cities and other areas over 10,000 (2000 population)
Fredericksburg   19,279   Poquoson   11,566
Hampton (pt.)   31,755   Williamsburg   11,998
Newport News (pt.)   71,800

Race and Hispanic or Latino origin*
White   74.7%
Black or African American   18.4%
American Indian or Alaska Native   0.4%
Asian   1.7%
Native Hawaiian or other Pacific Islander   0.1%
Some other race   0.2%
Hispanic or Latino origin   3.0%
Two or more races   1.6%

*As percentage of total population.

Ancestry*

Dutch 1.1%		Italian 3.3%	
English 10.7%		Polish 1.7%	
French 1.9%		Scotch-Irish 1.9%	
German 10.4%		Scottish 1.9%	
Irish 8.8%		USA/American 8.6%	

*As estimated percentage of total population.

Universities and colleges, 2000–2001 enrollment
Christopher Newport University, Newport News   5,314
College of William and Mary, Williamsburg   7,530
Mary Washington College, Fredericksburg   4,282
Rappahannock Community College, Glenns   1,774
Strayer University, Fredericksburg   797
Thomas Nelson Community College, Hampton   7,379

Newspapers and circulation

	District circulation	Total circulation
Fauquier Democrat	7,777	16,459
Fredericksburg Free Lance-Star	38,290	46,135
Gloucester-Mathews Gazette-Journal	9,975	10,336
Newport News Daily Press	52,161	92,132
Norfolk Virginian-Pilot	1,138	192,929
Potomac News	3,144	15,331
Potomac News/Manassas Journal Messenger	3,168	20,274
Richmond Times-Dispatch	10,410	193,688
Times Community Newspapers	7,722	34,552
*USA Today**	3,653	1,674,376
Washington Post	15,366	779,632
Washington Times	2,033	101,367

*See Sources and Explanations in the front of the volume.

Television stations and affiliations

Richmond-Petersburg	49%	WCVE	PBS
Richmond-Petersburg	49%	WCVW	PBS
Richmond-Petersburg	49%	WRIC	ABC
Richmond-Petersburg	49%	WRLH	FOX

Richmond-Petersburg	49%	WTVR	CBS
Richmond-Petersburg	49%	WUPV	UPN
Richmond-Petersburg	49%	WWBT	NBC
Washington, DC (Hagerstown)	28%	WBDC	WB
Washington, DC (Hagerstown)	28%	WDCA	UPN
Washington, DC (Hagerstown)	28%	WETA	PBS
Washington, DC (Hagerstown)	28%	WFPT	PBS
Washington, DC (Hagerstown)	28%	WHAG	NBC
Washington, DC (Hagerstown)	28%	WHSV	ABC
Washington, DC (Hagerstown)	28%	WHUT	PBS
Washington, DC (Hagerstown)	28%	WJAL	ABC
Washington, DC (Hagerstown)	28%	WJLA	ABC
Washington, DC (Hagerstown)	28%	WNVC	Independent
Washington, DC (Hagerstown)	28%	WNVT	PBS
Washington, DC (Hagerstown)	28%	WPXW	PAX
Washington, DC (Hagerstown)	28%	WRC	NBC
Washington, DC (Hagerstown)	28%	WTTG	FOX
Washington, DC (Hagerstown)	28%	WUSA	CBS
Washington, DC (Hagerstown)	28%	WVPY	PBS
Washington, DC (Hagerstown)	28%	WWPB	PBS
Washington, DC (Hagerstown)	28%	WWPX	PAX
Norfolk-Portsmouth-Newport News	23%	WAVY	NBC
Norfolk-Portsmouth-Newport News	23%	WGNT	UPN
Norfolk-Portsmouth-Newport News	23%	WHRO	PBS
Norfolk-Portsmouth-Newport News	23%	WPXV	PAX
Norfolk-Portsmouth-Newport News	23%	WTKR	CBS
Norfolk-Portsmouth-Newport News	23%	WTVZ	WB
Norfolk-Portsmouth-Newport News	23%	WVBT	FOX
Norfolk-Portsmouth-Newport News	23%	WVEC	ABC

Cable systems and subscribers
Adelphia   7,610
Charter   5,264
Comcast   3,573
Cox   63,712
Gans   3,098

Military installations, September 2001
Langley Air Force Base, Hampton   10,727
Quantico Marine Corps Base, Quantico   9,877
Naval Surface Weapons Center, Dahlgren   4,059
Weapons Support Facility, Yorktown   1,572
Fort AP Hill (Army), Bowling Green   737

Businesses and other major employers
Busch Entertainment Corp.; Williamsburg; theme park   3,140
U.S. Defense Dept.; Dumfries   3,000
Riverside Hospital Inc.; Newport News   2,995
Colonial Williamsburg Foundation; Williamsburg; historical site   2,400
College of William and Mary; Williamsburg   2,067
Canon Virginia Inc.; Newport News; photo equipment   2,000
GEICO Inc.; Fredericksburg; automobile insurance   2,000
Virginia Mental Health Services; Williamsburg   1,400
Mary Washington Hospital Inc.; Fredericksburg   1,395
SRA International Inc.; Stafford; computer graphics   1,300
Anheuser-Busch Inc.; Williamsburg; malt beverages   1,200
U.S. Marine Corps.; Quantico personnel support   1,100
Siemens Automotive Corp.; Newport News; automotive parts   1,035
Gloucester County; Gloucester; county government   1,000

National Geographic Society; Triangle; periodicals   1,000
Riverside Healthcare Assn. Inc.; Newport News; nursing care   1,000
Riverside Wellness Associates Hospital; Newport News   949
Williamsburg Community Hospital Inc.; Williamsburg   916
APAC Customer Services Inc.; Newport News; telemarketing   900
Gloucester County School Board; Hayes   900
St. Laurent Paper Products Corp.; West Point; container board   900
Mary Immaculate Hospital Inc.; Newport News   825
Nextel Communications Inc.; Hampton; wireless phones   813
United Parcel Service Inc.; Newport News; delivery service   800
McLane/Mid Atlantic Inc.; Fredericksburg; department stores   785
Christopher Newport University; Newport News   760
Busch Properties Inc.; Williamsburg; public golf courses   700
Virginia Dept. of Transportation; Fredericksburg   700
Polly Lowe Group Inc.; Newport News; employment agencies   675
GTSI Corp.; Remington; computer peripherals   608
CVS Inc.; Fredericksburg; warehousing   600
Energy Services Group International Inc.; Williamsburg; help supply services   600
GE Capital Montgomery Ward; Hampton; short-term business credit   575
Capital One Services Inc.; Fredericksburg; credit card service   500
Southeastern Universities Research Assn. Inc.; Newport News; noncommercial research   500
Virginia Community College System; Hampton   500
Wal-Mart Stores Inc.; Newport News; department stores   500

Virginia 2nd District

Southeast — Virginia Beach, parts of Norfolk and Hampton

The 2nd is dominated by Virginia Beach, a center for white-collar, suburban military families and retirees. It also extends north to include parts of Norfolk and Hampton and crosses the Chesapeake Bay inlet to reach Virginia's portion of the Eastern Shore. *(See map p. 936.)*

Virginia Beach's tourism-driven population boom of the 1980s is over, but the area has held its ground in the face of military base closings. The Norfolk Naval Base continues to dominate the economy, which also is bolstered by shipbuilding and shipping companies. About two-thirds of the district's population lives in Virginia Beach.

The 2nd includes half of the city of Norfolk (shared with the 3rd), a largely blue-collar and Democratic-leaning area that was surpassed by Virginia Beach in the early 1980s as Virginia's most populous city. Norfolk has lost population at about the same rate Virginia Beach has gained residents.

The district is home to Pat Robertson's religious broadcast network. But the 2nd's conservatism derives more from

NORTHERN VIRGINIA AND HAMPTON ROADS-VIRGINIA BEACH AREAS

Northern Virginia Area

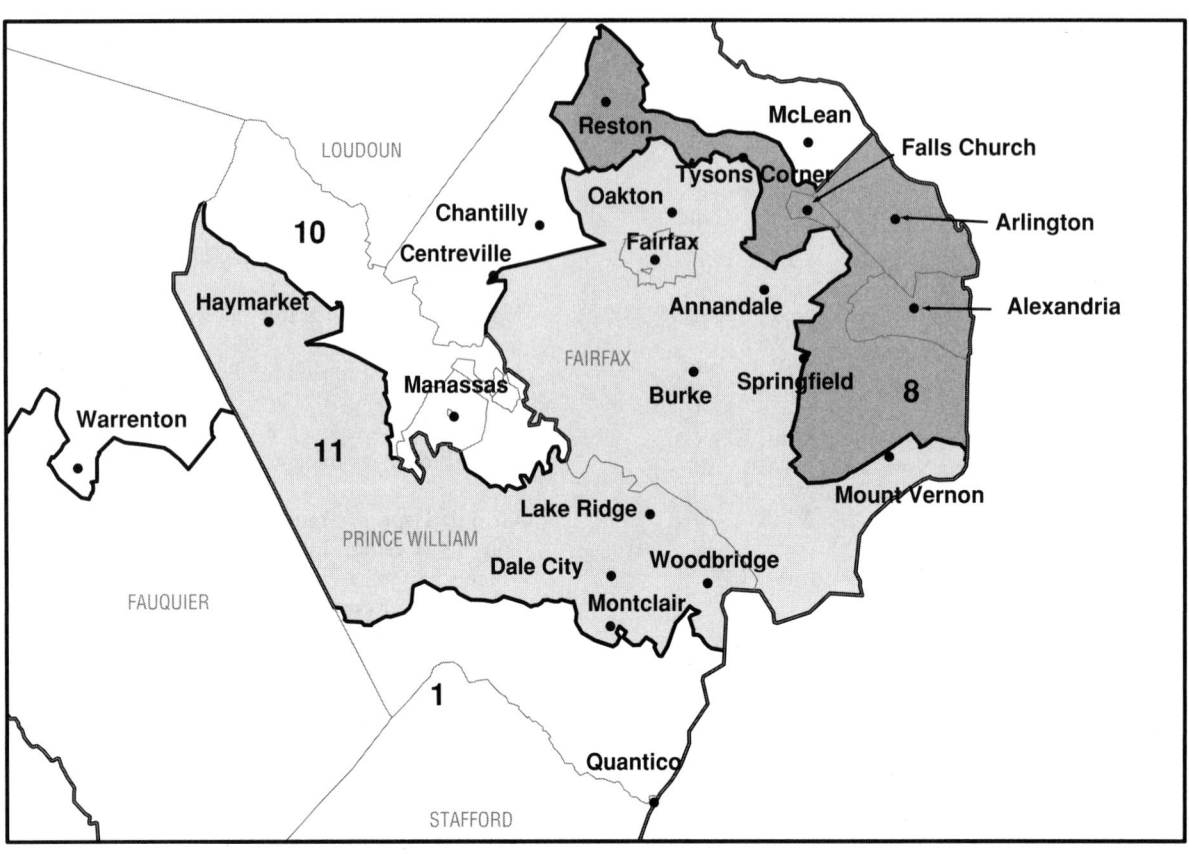

Hampton Roads-Virginia Beach Area

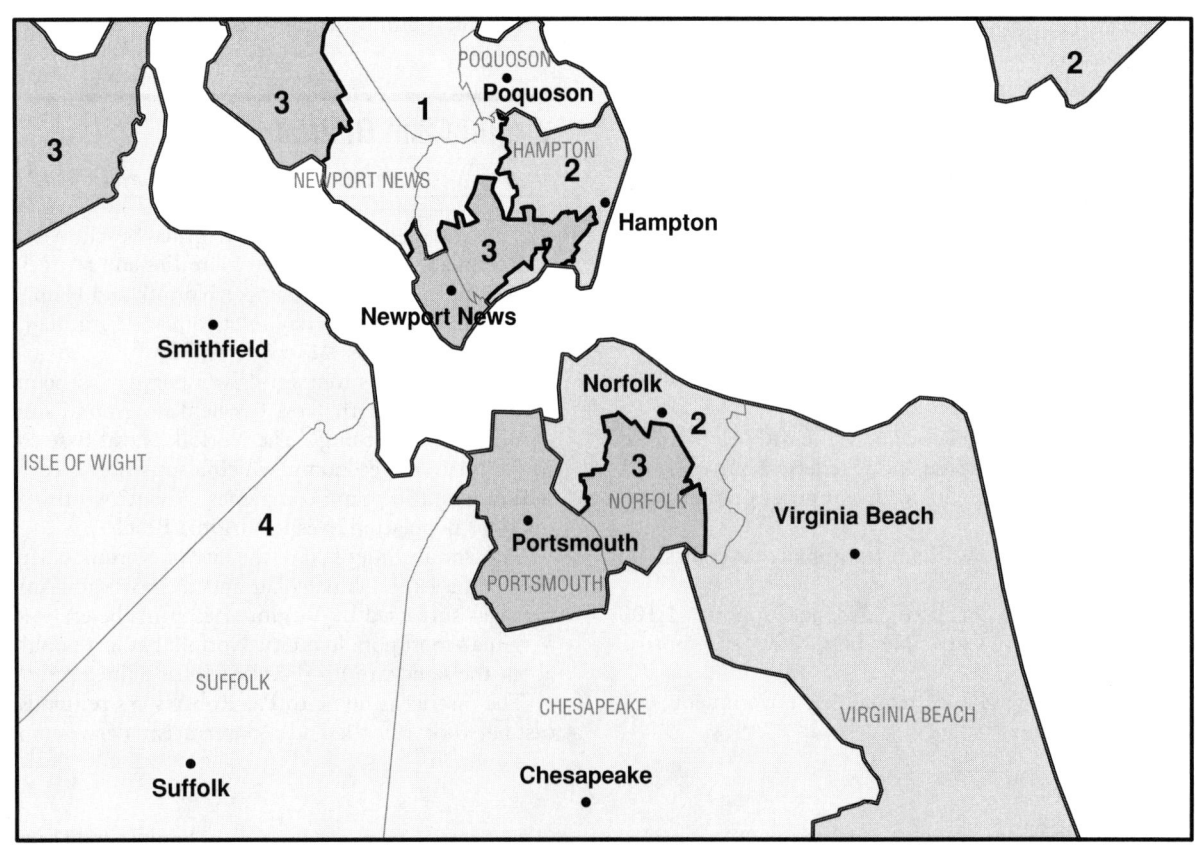

military and economic issues than social questions. Voters here typically side with the GOP: Republicans hold all state legislative seats in Virginia Beach and have made major inroads in Norfolk.

Redistricting following the 2000 census, which added the Eastern Shore and part of Hampton, made the 2nd slightly more Republican-leaning.

Major Industry

Military, tourism, shipbuilding.

Notable

Cape Henry Lighthouse in Virginia Beach was the first government-built lighthouse in the United States, finished about 1791.

Election Returns

	Republican		Democratic		Other	
President 2000	115,512	54.8%	90,256	42.8%	4,940	2.3%
House 2002	103,807	83.1%			21,039	16.9%

District Profile

Population   643,510

Total area (square miles)   2,776.3
  Land area (square miles)   961.0

Population per square mile   669.6

Counties (2000 population)
  Accomack   38,305
  Hampton city (pt.)   54,753
  Norfolk city (pt.)   112,102
  Northampton   13,093
  Virginia Beach city   425,257

Cities and other areas over 10,000 (2000 population)
  Hampton (pt.)   54,753
  Norfolk (pt.)   112,102
  Virginia Beach   425,257

Race and Hispanic or Latino origin*
  White   67.4%
  Black or African American   21.4%
  American Indian or Alaska Native   0.4%
  Asian   4.0%
  Native Hawaiian or other Pacific Islander   0.1%
  Some other race   0.2%
  Hispanic or Latino origin   4.4%
  Two or more races   2.2%

*As percentage of total population.

Ancestry*
English 9.0%	Polish 1.8%
French 2.2%	Scotch-Irish 1.6%
German 10.1%	Scottish 1.9%
Irish 9.1%	USA/American 6.3%
Italian 4.1%	

*As estimated percentage of total population.

Universities and colleges, 2000–2001 enrollment
  Eastern Shore Community College, Melfa   773
  ECPI College of Technology, Virginia Beach   2,895
  ITT Technical Institute, Norfolk   326
  Johnson & Wales University, Norfolk   619
  Old Dominion University, Norfolk   18,969
  Rav School of Professional Studies, Virginia Beach   200
  Regent University, Virginia Beach   2,449
  Tidewater Tech, Virginia Beach   251
  Virginia Wesleyan College, Norfolk   1,421

Newspapers and circulation

	District circulation	Total circulation
Newport News Daily Press	8,671	92,132
Norfolk Virginian-Pilot	95,154	192,929
*USA Today**	4,294	1,674,376

*See Sources and Explanations in the front of the volume.

Television stations and affiliations
Norfolk-Portsmouth-Newport News	100%	WAVY	NBC
Norfolk-Portsmouth-Newport News	100%	WGNT	UPN
Norfolk-Portsmouth-Newport News	100%	WHRO	PBS
Norfolk-Portsmouth-Newport News	100%	WPXV	PAX
Norfolk-Portsmouth-Newport News	100%	WTKR	CBS
Norfolk-Portsmouth-Newport News	100%	WTVZ	WB
Norfolk-Portsmouth-Newport News	100%	WVBT	FOX
Norfolk-Portsmouth-Newport News	100%	WVEC	ABC

Cable systems and subscribers
  Charter   97,035
  Cox   134,614

Military installations, September 2001
  Naval Base Norfolk, Norfolk   47,665
  Oceana Naval Air Station, Virginia Beach   13,141
  Little Creek Naval Amphibious Base, Norfolk   10,850
  Fort Monroe (Army), Hampton   2,910
  Norfolk Fleet and Industrial Supply Center, Norfolk   2,910
  Public Works Center Norfolk (Navy), Norfolk   2,794
  Fort Story (Army), Norfolk   1,936
  Naval Facilities Engineering Command, Norfolk   1,050
  Surface Combat Systems Center, Wallops Island   141

Businesses and other major employers
  City of Virginia Beach; Virginia Beach; city government   3,500
  Old Dominion University; Norfolk   3,268
  Perdue Farms Inc.; Accomac; poultry   1,800
  AMSEC LLC; Virginia Beach; ship cleaning   1,725
  Newport News Shipbuilding Co.; Norfolk; shipbuilding   1,700
  Sentara Virginia Beach General Hospital; Virginia Beach   1,700
  Management Consulting Inc.; Virginia Beach; shipping packing   1,500
  Virginia International Terminals Inc.; Norfolk; marine terminals   1,450
  United Services Automobile Assn.; Norfolk; life insurance   1,342
  Bernard C. Harris Publishing Co.; Norfolk; directories publishing   1,200
  National Aeronautics and Space Admin.; Chincoteague   1,000
  Navy Exchange Service Command; Norfolk; Army-Navy goods stores   1,000

Sentara Leigh Memorial Hospital; Norfolk   991
S3 Ltd.; Virginia Beach; help supply services   900
Lillian Vernon Fulfillment Services Inc.; Virginia Beach;
  telemarketing   900
Navy Exchange Service Command; Virginia Beach;
  Army-Navy stores   850
Stihl Inc.; Virginia Beach; chain saws   850
Special Markets Inc.; Virginia Beach; bakery products
  800
Tyson Foods Inc.; Temperanceville; poultry   800
Swissport CFE Inc.; Virginia Beach; air freight handling
  750
Sentara Bayside Hospital; Virginia Beach   650
Christian Broadcasting Network Inc.; Virginia Beach;
  religious organization   600
Southeastern Tidewater Opportunity Project Inc.;
  Norfolk; community development   600
Verizon Communications Inc.; Virginia Beach; telephone
  communication   600
Wal-Mart Stores Inc.; Virginia Beach; department stores
  580
Shore Memorial Hospital; Nassawadox   567
City of Norfolk; Norfolk; city government   500
City of Virginia Beach; Virginia Beach; public schools
  500
Computer Sciences Corp.; Hampton; computer systems
  500
Household Recovery Services Corp.; Virginia Beach;
  business consulting   500
Pinkerton's Inc.; Norfolk; security guard   500

Virginia 3rd District

*Southeast — parts of Richmond, Norfolk,
Newport News, Portsmouth*

The black-majority 3rd begins in historic Richmond and
reaches southeast into military and shipbuilding territory,
including parts of Newport News, Hampton, and Norfolk.
Redistricting following the 2000 census added the city of
Portsmouth, which had been in the 4th District. The 3rd
is the strongest Democratic district in the state. *(See map
p. 936.)*

Originally drawn as a 64 percent black district, the 3rd
has been the focal point of Virginia redistricting since 1991.
It saw its black population reduced under a court-ordered
remap in 1998, then slightly increased under 2001 redistricting. Richmond, Portsmouth, and Norfolk, which have
substantial black populations, all gave Al Gore more than
60 percent of their vote in the 2000 presidential election.
One heavily black precinct in Richmond backed Gore over
George W. Bush by 639 to 5.

The 3rd long has benefited from one of the nation's largest
ports at Hampton Roads and from growing financial firms
in Richmond. State government also drives the economy of
Richmond and its vicinity, as does manufacturing. Richmond
boasts one of the largest cigarette plants in the nation (Philip
Morris).

The Hampton Roads area has a heavy concentration of
naval installations as well as shipbuilding and ship repair
companies. Among these is the nation's largest privately
owned shipyard—Newport News Shipbuilding—which
builds Navy aircraft carriers and submarines.

Major Industry

Defense, shipbuilding and repair, shipping, tobacco.

Notable

The Edgar Allen Poe Museum is in Richmond, where the
author lived and worked.

Election Returns

	Republican		Democratic		Other	
President 2000	65,724	32.3%	134,020	65.9%	3,603	1.8%
House 2002			87,521	96.1%	3,552	3.9%

District Profile

Population   643,476

Total area (square miles)   1,305.9
  Land area (square miles)   1,117.9

Population per square mile   575.6

Counties (2000 population)
  Charles City   6,926
  Hampton city (pt.)   59,929
  Henrico (pt.)   65,420
  New Kent   13,462
  Newport News city (pt.)   108,350
  Norfolk city (pt.)   122,301
  Portsmouth city   100,565
  Prince George (pt.)   15,174
  Richmond city (pt.)   144,520
  Surry   6,829

Cities and other areas over 10,000 (2000 population)
  East Highland Park CDP (pt.)   10,842
  Hampton (pt.)   59,929
  Highland Springs CDP   15,137
  Newport News (pt.)   108,350
  Norfolk (pt.)   122,301
  Portsmouth   100,565
  Richmond (pt.)   144,520

Race and Hispanic or Latino origin*
  White   37.7%
  Black or African American   56.0%
  American Indian or Alaska Native   0.5%
  Asian   1.4%
  Native Hawaiian or other Pacific Islander   0.1%
  Some other race   0.2%
  Hispanic or Latino origin   2.6%
  Two or more races   1.6%

As percentage of total population.

Ancestry*

English	5.6%	Scotch-Irish	1.1%
French	1.1%	Scottish	1.1%
German	5.3%	Subsaharan	1.1%
Irish	4.7%	USA/American	5.3%
Italian	1.8%		

As estimated percentage of total population.

Universities and colleges, 2000–2001 enrollment
Eastern Virginia Medical School, Norfolk   699
Hampton University, Hampton   5,743
Norfolk State University, Norfolk   6,668
Tidewater Community College, Norfolk   20,184
Virginia Commonwealth University, Richmond 24,066
Virginia Union University, Richmond   1,538

Newspapers and circulation
	District circulation	Total circulation
Newport News Daily Press	28,202	92,132
Norfolk Virginian-Pilot	34,788	192,929
Petersburg Progress-Index	1,704	15,424
Richmond Times-Dispatch	35,030	193,688
*USA Today**	4,665	1,674,376
Washington Post	1,662	779,632

See Sources and Explanations in the front of the volume.

Television stations and affiliations
Richmond-Petersburg	60%	WCVE	PBS
Richmond-Petersburg	60%	WCVW	PBS
Richmond-Petersburg	60%	WRIC	ABC
Richmond-Petersburg	60%	WRLH	FOX
Richmond-Petersburg	60%	WTVR	CBS
Richmond-Petersburg	60%	WUPV	UPN
Richmond-Petersburg	60%	WWBT	NBC
Norfolk-Portsmouth-Newport News	40%	WAVY	NBC
Norfolk-Portsmouth-Newport News	40%	WGNT	UPN
Norfolk-Portsmouth-Newport News	40%	WHRO	PBS
Norfolk-Portsmouth-Newport News	40%	WPXV	PAX
Norfolk-Portsmouth-Newport News	40%	WTKR	CBS
Norfolk-Portsmouth-Newport News	40%	WTVZ	WB
Norfolk-Portsmouth-Newport News	40%	WVBT	FOX
Norfolk-Portsmouth-Newport News	40%	WVEC	ABC

Cable systems and subscribers
Adelphia   1,161
Comcast   44,104
Cox   162,397
Tele-Media   3,688

Military installations, September 2001
Norfolk Naval Station, Norfolk   13,324
Fort Eustis (Army), Newport News   9,865
Norfolk Naval Shipyard, Portsmouth   8,619
Portsmouth Naval Medical Center, Portsmouth   4,632
Richmond Defense General Supply Center, Richmond 3,308
Richmond International Airport Air National Guard, Sandston   1,031
Byrd Field (Army Guard), Sandston   328
Sandston Armory (Army Guard), Sandston   278

Businesses and other major employers
Philip Morris Inc.; Richmond; cigarettes, research 27,000
First Union; Richmond; commercial bank   20,000
Dominion Resources Inc.; Richmond; natural gas production   7,800
Virginia Commonwealth University; Richmond   7,000
City of Newport News; Newport News; city government 5,600

National Aeronautics and Space Admin.; Hampton 5,000
U.S. Postal Service; Richmond   4,000
City of Richmond; Richmond; city government   3,840
Bank of America Corp.; Norfolk; short-term business credit   3,000
Medical College of Virginia Hospital; Richmond   3,000
Sentara Norfolk General Hospital; Norfolk   3,000
Wyeth-Ayerst International Inc.; Richmond; pharmaceuticals   2,500
U.S. Veterans Hospital; Richmond   2,285
Ford Motor Co.; Norfolk; truck and tractor truck assembly   2,230
Virginia Dept. of Social Services; Richmond   1,600
Virginia Dept. of Transportation; Richmond   1,590
Children's Hospital of Kings Daughters Inc.; Norfolk 1,500
City of Norfolk; Norfolk; city government   1,500
U.S. Coast Guard; Portsmouth   1,500
Bon Secours-DePaul Medical Center Inc.; Norfolk 1,400
Landmark Communications Inc.; Norfolk; newspaper 1,400
U.S. Postal Service; Norfolk   1,400
Virginia Electric and Power Co.; Richmond; electric power generation   1,400
Federal Reserve Bank of Richmond; Richmond   1,300
Maryview Hospital; Portsmouth   1,300
Whitehall Robins Inc.; Richmond; pharmaceuticals 1,205
American Chemical Society; Sandston; scientific association   1,200
Norfolk State University; Norfolk   1,200
U.S. Veterans Hospital; Hampton   1,200
City of Richmond; Richmond; police dept.   1,000
Hampton Training School for Nurses; Hampton   1,000
Hampton University; Hampton   1,000
Howmet Corp.; Hampton; commercial castings   1,000
Hunting and Williams; Richmond; legal services 1,000
Medical College of Hampton Roads; Norfolk   1,000
Troutman Sanders LLP; Richmond; law office   1,000
U.S. Marine Repair Inc.; Norfolk; shipbuilding, repairing   1,000
Virginia Motor Vehicles Dept.; Richmond   1,000
Virginia Electric and Power Co.; Surry; electric power generation   922
Army and Air Force Exchange Service; Newport News; Army-Navy goods stores   800
Excel Services Inc.; Richmond; janitorial service   800
Hunton & Williams; Richmond; legal services   800
Infineon Technologies Richmond; Sandston semiconductors, related devices   800
Media General Operations Inc.; Richmond; newspaper 800
Overnite Transportation Co.; Richmond; trucking   800
United House of Prayer for All People; Newport News; religious organization   800
Pines Residential Treatment Center Inc.; Portsmouth 775
General Foam Plastics Corp.; Norfolk; artificial Christmas trees   750

Reynolds Metals Co.; Richmond; aluminum products 750

Prince George's County; Prince George; county government 710

Virginia Dept. of Taxation; Richmond 700

Westvaco Corp.; Richmond; paperboard boxes 700

McGuire Woods; Richmond; law office 685

Virginia Dept. of Health; Richmond 650

E. I. Du Pont De Nemours and Co.; Hopewell; plastics materials and resins 610

City of Hampton; Hampton; city government 609

Encompass Constructors Inc.; Richmond; machinery installation 600

U.S. Internal Revenue Service; Richmond 600

Virginia Employment Commission; Richmond 600

Virginia State Corp. Commission; Richmond 600

Daily Press Inc.; Newport News; newspaper publishing 575

Virginia Dept. of Corrections; Richmond 550

Westminster-Canterbury Corp.; Richmond; residential care 550

Virginia Farm Bureau Mutual Insurance Co.; Richmond; insurance 540

Wal-Mart Stores Inc.; Hampton; department stores 537

Virginia Community College System; Portsmouth 523

Naptheon Inc.; Newport News; systems integration services 510

City of Hampton; Hampton; utility regulation 500

Fluor Enterprises Inc.; Surry; housing construction 500

Interbake Foods Inc.; Richmond; retail bakeries 500

Interstate Brands Corp.; Richmond; breads and cakes 500

U.S. Army Corps of Engineers; Norfolk 500

U.S. Merchants Financial Group Inc.; Richmond; personal service agents 500

Virginia Department Agriculture Community Office; Richmond 500

Virginia Electric and Power Co.; Norfolk; electricity services 500

Williams Mullen Clark and Dobbins; Richmond; law office 500

Virginia 4th District

Southeast — Chesapeake

Located in southeast and south-central Virginia, the 4th includes burgeoning Chesapeake and rural tobacco-growing areas to the west.

Redistricting following the 2000 census transformed the 4th from highly competitive territory to a Republican-leaning district that comfortably backed George W. Bush for president in 2000. Mapmakers removed the heavily black, strongly Democratic city of Portsmouth and reduced the district's black population from 39 percent to 33 percent.

Chesapeake, the 4th's most populous city, grew by nearly one-third in the 1990s. Chesapeake votes dependably Republican, as do the portions of Chesterfield County south of Richmond that are in the northern part of the district.

Democrats fare better in areas with sizable black voting blocks. Petersburg, which is four-fifths African American,

gave Al Gore his best vote percentage (79 percent) in the state in 2000. Across the Appomattox River from Petersburg is Colonial Heights, which is largely white and gave 71 percent of the vote to Bush.

Although the 4th's military installations lost civilian employees in the 1990s wave of downsizing, the overall effect on the district was negligible, as Chesapeake compensated by attracting new manufacturing businesses. Outside of the 4th's population centers, tobacco, and peanut farming play a central role in the economy.

Major Industry

Military, agriculture, health care, manufacturing.

Notable

Suffolk is considered the peanut capital of the world—the town has a small museum dedicated to Planters' Mr. Peanut and hosts an annual "peanut fest."

Election Returns

	Republican		Democratic		Other	
President 2000	131,834	54.2%	107,553	44.2%	3,690	1.5%
House 2002	108,733	97.9%			2,308	2.1%

District Profile

Population 643,477

Total area (square miles) 4,575.4
 Land area (square miles) 4,488.7

Population per square mile 143.4

Counties (2000 population)
 Amelia 11,400
 Brunswick (pt.) 3,318
 Chesapeake city 199,184
 Chesterfield (pt.) 127,114
 Colonial Heights city 16,897
 Dinwiddie 24,533
 Emporia city 5,665
 Franklin city 8,346
 Greensville 11,560
 Hopewell city 22,354
 Isle of Wight 29,728
 Nottoway 15,725
 Petersburg city 33,740
 Powhatan 22,377
 Prince George (pt.) 17,873
 Southampton 17,482
 Suffolk city 63,677
 Sussex 12,504

Cities and other areas over 10,000 (2000 population)
 Chesapeake 199,184
 Chester CDP 17,890
 Colonial Heights 16,897
 Hopewell 22,354
 Petersburg 33,740
 Suffolk 63,677

Race and Hispanic or Latino origin*
 White 62.0%
 Black or African American 33.1%
 American Indian or Alaska Native 0.3%

Asian   1.3%
Native Hawaiian or other Pacific Islander   0.0%
Some other race   0.1%
Hispanic or Latino origin   2.0%
Two or more races   1.1%

As percentage of total population.

Ancestry*

English	8.6%	Polish	1.2%
French	1.5%	Scotch-Irish	1.5%
German	7.2%	Scottish	1.4%
Irish	6.3%	USA/American	10.0%
Italian	2.3%		

As estimated percentage of total population.

Universities and colleges, 2000–2001 enrollment

John Tyler Community College, Chester   5,238
Paul D. Camp Community College, Franklin   1,540
Richard Bland College-College of William & Mary,
   Petersburg   1,267
Southside Virginia Community College, Alberta   3,755
Virginia State University, Petersburg   4,353

Newspapers and circulation

	District circulation	Total circulation
Newport News Daily Press	4,201	92,132
Norfolk Virginian-Pilot	48,005	192,929
Petersburg Progress-Index	13,659	15,424
Richmond Times-Dispatch	34,099	193,688
*USA Today**	2,129	1,674,376

See Sources and Explanations in the front of the volume.

Television stations and affiliations

Richmond-Petersburg	62%	WCVE	PBS
Richmond-Petersburg	62%	WCVW	PBS
Richmond-Petersburg	62%	WRIC	ABC
Richmond-Petersburg	62%	WRLH	FOX
Richmond-Petersburg	62%	WTVR	CBS
Richmond-Petersburg	62%	WUPV	UPN
Richmond-Petersburg	62%	WWBT	NBC
Norfolk-Portsmouth-Newport News	38%	WAVY	NBC
Norfolk-Portsmouth-Newport News	38%	WGNT	UPN
Norfolk-Portsmouth-Newport News	38%	WHRO	PBS
Norfolk-Portsmouth-Newport News	38%	WPXV	PAX
Norfolk-Portsmouth-Newport News	38%	WTKR	CBS
Norfolk-Portsmouth-Newport News	38%	WTVZ	WB
Norfolk-Portsmouth-Newport News	38%	WVBT	FOX
Norfolk-Portsmouth-Newport News	38%	WVEC	ABC

Cable systems and subscribers

Adelphia   8,676
Charter   30,914
Comcast   61,005
Nesbe Cable TV   2,064
Tele-Media   8,273

Military installations, September 2001

Fort Lee (Army), Petersburg   7,221
Fort Pickett Army National Guard, Blackstone   1,293

Businesses and other major employers

Smithfield Packing Co.; Smithfield; hams   4,636
E. I. Du Pont De Nemours and Co.; Richmond; fabric
   finishing   3,300
Rosenbluth International Inc.; Richmond; travel agency
   3,000
U.S. Defense Dept.; Richmond   3,000
Raytheon Co.; Chesapeake; navigational systems   2,500
Gwaltney of Smithfield Inc.; Smithfield; meatpacking
   2,100
Chesapeake General Hospital; Chesapeake   1,900
Virginia Mental Health Services; Petersburg   1,700
City of Chesapeake; Chesapeake; city government
   1,512
Virginia Dept. of Transportation; Suffolk   1,500
Petersburg Hospital Authority; Petersburg   1,350
QVC Inc.; Chesapeake; TV shopping network   1,300
Louise Obici Memorial Hospital; Suffolk   1,120
Virginia State University; Petersburg   1,100
Honeywell International Inc.; Hopewell; organic fibers
   1,000
United Parcel Service Inc.; Richmond; parcel delivery
   995
Virginia Dept. of Corrections; Jarratt   985
Virginia Dept. of Corrections; Waverly   900
Kraft Foods Inc.; Suffolk; nuts   800
QVC Inc.; Suffolk; warehousing   727
Heartland Express Inc.; Chester; trucking   708
Boar's Head Provision Co. Inc.; Jarratt; meat products
   700
Pinkerton's Inc.; Richmond; security guard   687
John Randolph Medical Center; Hopewell   665
Church and Dwight Co. Inc.; Colonial Heights;
   perfumes, cosmetics   613
City of Suffolk; Suffolk; city government   600
Philip Morris Inc.; Chester; tobacco   600
Hill Phoenix Inc.; Colonial Heights; refrigeration
   equipment   550
Rehrig International Inc.; Richmond; fabricated wire
   550
Honeywell International Inc.; Chesterfield; cellulosic
   fibers   545
Wal-Mart Stores Inc.; Colonial Heights; department
   stores   525
Canon Information Technology Services Inc.;
   Chesapeake; computer maintenance   500
Carroll's Foods of Virginia Inc.; Waverly; hogs   500
Food Lion; Disputanta; supermarkets   500

Virginia 5th District

South central — Charlottesville, Danville

Rich in Civil War landmarks, the 5th extends from just north of Charlottesville, in the central part of the state, to the south-central tier bordering North Carolina, an area known as "Southside."

The mostly rural 5th is relatively poor, and the district relies heavily on agriculture and textiles. Known as the heart of tobacco country, the 5th still supports a vast tobacco industry, but in recent years manufacturing has taken a more prominent role. Danville, the district's largest city, is a tobacco and textile center on the North Carolina border. To the west is Martinsville, a textile and furniture town.

The seasonal nature of the economy led to above-average unemployment during some of the 1990s in the district's southwest corner. But the 5th's economy also saw some strong performances during the decade. Bedford County, between Roanoke and Lynchburg (both of which are in the 6th), and Fluvanna County, in the orbit of Charlottesville, have grown by attracting commuters as well as many small businesses. Fluvanna County grew by 61 percent in the 1990s, and Greene County, located north of Charlottesville, grew by 48 percent.

Redistricting following the 2000 census made minor changes to the reliably conservative district, which typically gives GOP candidates vote percentages hovering in the mid-50s. One notable exception to the district's conservative posture is the city of Charlottesville, which is home to the University of Virginia and almost always backs Democrats. But the conservative rural areas also can support Democratic candidates, provided they express right-of-center views on issues such as gun owners' rights. Democrat Mark Warner employed such a strategy with success in the 5th District during his successful 2001 gubernatorial bid.

Major Industry
Agriculture, manufacturing, textiles, service.

Notable
Appomattox Court House is where Gen. Robert E. Lee surrendered to Gen. Ulysses S. Grant, ending the Civil War; Thomas Jefferson's estate, Monticello, and James Monroe's estate, Ash Lawn-Highland, are just south of Charlottesville.

Election Returns

	Republican		Democratic		Other	
President 2000	137,223	55.1%	102,814	41.3%	8,907	3.6%
House 2002	95,360	63.5%	54,805	36.5%	68	

District Profile

Population   643,497

Total area (square miles)   9,053.5
  Land area (square miles)   8,922.0

Population per square mile   72.1

Counties (2000 population)
Albemarle 79,236	Fluvanna 20,047
Appomattox 13,705	Franklin 47,286
Bedford (pt.) 35,637	Greene 15,244
Bedford city 6,299	Halifax 37,355
Brunswick (pt.) 15,101	Henry (pt.) 35,085
Buckingham 15,623	Lunenburg 13,146
Campbell 51,078	Martinsville city 15,416
Charlotte 12,472	Mecklenburg 32,380
Charlottesville city 45,049	Nelson 14,445
Cumberland 9,017	Pittsylvania 61,745
Danville city 48,411	Prince Edward 19,720

Cities and other areas over 10,000 (2000 population)
Charlottesville 45,049	Martinsville 15,416
Danville 48,411	Timberlake CDP 10,683

Race and Hispanic or Latino origin*
White   72.4%
Black or African American   23.9%
American Indian or Alaska Native   0.2%
Asian   1.0%
Native Hawaiian or other Pacific Islander   0.0%
Some other race   0.1%
Hispanic or Latino origin   1.6%
Two or more races   0.8%

*As percentage of total population.

Ancestry*
English 9.0%	Italian 1.7%
French 1.3%	Scotch-Irish 1.8%
German 6.6%	Scottish 1.6%
Irish 5.9%	USA/American 14.7%

*As estimated percentage of total population.

Universities and colleges, 2000–2001 enrollment
Averett College, Danville   2,296
Danville Community College, Danville   3,554
Hampden-Sydney College, Hampden-Sydney   976
Longwood College, Farmville   3,961
Patrick Henry Community College, Martinsville   2,936
Piedmont Virginia Community College, Charlottesville   4,277
St. Pauls College, Lawrenceville   518
University of Virginia, Charlottesville   22,411

Newspapers and circulation

	District circulation	Total circulation
Charlottesville Progress	26,213	30,084
Danville Register & Bee	20,389	21,896
Lynchburg News & Advance	17,782	37,361
Martinsville Bulletin	10,858	17,549
Nelson County Times	2,186	3,138
Richmond Times-Dispatch	12,380	193,688
Roanoke Times	15,016	99,140
*USA Today**	4,569	1,674,376
Washington Post	4,392	779,632

*See Sources and Explanations in the front of the volume.

Television stations and affiliations
Roanoke-Lynchburg	56%	WBRA	PBS
Roanoke-Lynchburg	56%	WDBJ	CBS
Roanoke-Lynchburg	56%	WFXR	FOX
Roanoke-Lynchburg	56%	WJPR	FOX
Roanoke-Lynchburg	56%	WPXR	PAX
Roanoke-Lynchburg	56%	WSET	ABC
Roanoke-Lynchburg	56%	WSLS	NBC
Roanoke-Lynchburg	56%	WVVA	NBC
Richmond-Petersburg	23%	WCVE	PBS
Richmond-Petersburg	23%	WCVW	PBS
Richmond-Petersburg	23%	WRIC	ABC
Richmond-Petersburg	23%	WRLH	FOX
Richmond-Petersburg	23%	WTVR	CBS
Richmond-Petersburg	23%	WUPV	UPN
Richmond-Petersburg	23%	WWBT	NBC
Charlottesville	13%	WHTJ	PBS
Charlottesville	13%	WVIR	NBC
Raleigh-Durham (Fayetteville)	8%	WGPX	PAX
Raleigh-Durham (Fayetteville)	8%	WKFT	Independent
Raleigh-Durham (Fayetteville)	8%	WLFL	WB
Raleigh-Durham (Fayetteville)	8%	WNCN	NBC
Raleigh-Durham (Fayetteville)	8%	WRAL	CBS
Raleigh-Durham (Fayetteville)	8%	WRAY	Independent
Raleigh-Durham (Fayetteville)	8%	WRAZ	FOX

Raleigh-Durham (Fayetteville)	8%	WRDC	UPN
Raleigh-Durham (Fayetteville)	8%	WRPX	PAX
Raleigh-Durham (Fayetteville)	8%	WTVD	ABC
Raleigh-Durham (Fayetteville)	8%	WUNC	PBS
Raleigh-Durham (Fayetteville)	8%	WUNP	PBS

Cable systems and subscribers
Adelphia   83,977
Appomattox Cable TV   1,308
Charter   86,028
Chatmoss Cablevision   1,581

Businesses and other major employers
University of Virginia; Charlottesville   4,700
University of Virginia Medical Center; Charlottesville 4,248
Bedford County School Board; Bedford   3,000
State Farm Insurance Co.; Charlottesville; automobile insurance   2,600
BWX Technologies Inc.; Lynchburg; management engineering   2,024
Albemarle County Public Schools; Charlottesville 2,000
Bassett Furniture Industries Inc.; Collinsville   2,000
McDermott International Inc.; Lynchburg; industrial chemicals   2,000
Campbell County; Rustburg; county government 1,798
GE Fanuc Automation North America Inc.; Charlottesville; numerical controls   1,500
VF Imagewear Inc.; Martinsville; jogging suits   1,500
Burlington Industries Inc.; Hurt; fabric mills   1,400
Danville Regional Medical Center; Danville   1,300
Stanley Furniture Co.; Stanleytown   1,300
American Furniture Corp.; Martinsville   1,200
Martha Jefferson Hospital; Charlottesville   1,100
Burlington Industries Inc.; Clarksville; dyeing/finishing wool   1,050
Babcock and Wilcox Co.; Lynchburg; nuclear fuels 1,000
Campbell County; Rustburg; public schools   1,000
M. W. Manufacturers Inc.; Rocky Mount; window frames   1,000
RBX Industries Inc.; Bedford; rubber products   900
Hooker Furniture Corp.; Martinsville   850
Abbott Laboratories; Altavista; baby formulas   800
Burlington Industries Inc.; Halifax; worsted fabrics 800
INTERMET Corp.; Lynchburg; iron foundry   800
Memorial Hospital of Martinsville and Henry County; Martinsville   790
Community Memorial Health Center; South Hill   750
Russell Stover Candies Inc.; Clarksville   703
City of Martinsville; Martinsville; city government   700
Litton Marine Systems Inc.; Charlottesville; marine propulsion equipment   700
Reed Elsevier Inc.; Charlottesville; book publishing 700
Times Fiber Communications Inc.; Chatham; wiredrawing and insulating   629
BGF Industries Inc.; Altavista; fiberglass fabrics   600
Lane Furniture Industries Inc.; Rocky Mount   600
VF Playwear Inc.; Danville; children's outerwear   600

Halifax Regional Hospital Inc.; South Boston   590
American Postal Workers Union; Charlottesville; labor union   550
Klockner Pentaplast of America Inc.; Gordonsville; plastic film, sheets   550
O'Sullivan Industries-Virginia Inc.; South Boston; home furniture   550
American Management Technologies Inc.; Rocky Mount; financial services   522
Albemarle County Charlottesville; county government 500
Comdial Business Communications Corp.; Charlottesville; telephone apparatus   500
Debbie's Staffing Services Inc.; Danville; temporary help service   500

Virginia 6th District
Northwest — Roanoke, Lynchburg

Running along the Shenandoah Valley, the conservative 6th is a collage of mountainous terrain, small towns, medium-size cities, and natural beauty. Beginning in Roanoke, the district's most populous city, one can drive 160 miles northeast along Interstate 81 to Interstate 66, without leaving the 6th District.

The 6th has one of the largest populations of senior citizens in the state, a mostly white-collar workforce, and a generous dose of Republicans. George W. Bush and Sen. George Allen both won 60 percent of the vote in the 2000 presidential and senatorial elections. Augusta and Rockingham Counties gave Bush more than 70 percent of their votes.

The brand of Republicanism in the rural valley traditionally has been a moderate one. The 1992 election of Republicans ended the Democrats' decade-long domination of the 6th seat, but Democrats still won in local elections in the 1990s. Roanoke has a strong Democratic base with union ties. But Republicans have done well in Roanoke's suburbs, in Lynchburg, and in most rural areas.

Roanoke has a variety of industries, including furniture and electrical products manufacturing. Both Roanoke and Lynchburg saw their populations shrink slightly in the 1990s, but the manufacturing economy was generally solid. Several colleges are in the district as well.

Outside the Roanoke and Lynchburg metropolitan areas, the 6th depends mainly on dairy farming, livestock, and poultry. In the north, Rockingham County leads the state in livestock and hay production. Tourists traveling to the district's national parks and caverns also help boost the economy. There are some chemical plants and pulpwood and paper mills in the area north of Roanoke.

Major Industry
Agriculture, livestock, manufacturing.

Notable
Lynchburg is the home of evangelist Jerry Falwell's Liberty University and Thomas Road Baptist Church; President Woodrow Wilson was born in Staunton (pronounced "Stanton").

Election Returns

	Republican		Democratic		Other	
President 2000	147,961	59.8%	92,407	37.4%	6,984	2.8%
House 2002	105,530	97.1%			3,202	2.9%

District Profile

Population 643,504

Total area (square miles) 5,663.5
  Land area (square miles) 5,646.9

Population per square mile 114.0

Counties (2000 population)

Alleghany (pt.) 5,154	Lexington city 6,867
Amherst 31,894	Lynchburg city 65,269
Augusta 65,615	Roanoke (pt.) 71,157
Bath 5,048	Roanoke city 94,911
Bedford (pt.) 24,734	Rockbridge 20,808
Botetourt 30,496	Rockingham 67,725
Buena Vista city 6,349	Salem city 24,747
Covington city (pt.) 1,278	Shenandoah 35,075
Harrisonburg city 40,468	Staunton city 23,853
Highland 2,536	Waynesboro city 19,520

Cities and other areas over 10,000 (2000 population)

Cave Spring CDP 24,941	Roanoke 94,911
Harrisonburg 40,468	Salem 24,747
Hollins CDP (pt.) 11,274	Staunton 23,853
Lynchburg 65,269	Waynesboro 19,520
Madison Heights CDP 11,584	

Race and Hispanic or Latino origin*

White 84.8%
Black or African American 10.9%
American Indian or Alaska Native 0.2%
Asian 0.9%
Native Hawaiian or other Pacific Islander 0.0%
Some other race 0.1%
Hispanic or Latino origin 2.0%
Two or more races 1.0%

As percentage of total population.

Ancestry*

English 8.9%	Italian 1.9%
French 1.4%	Scotch-Irish 2.6%
German 11.9%	Scottish 1.7%
Irish 7.1%	USA/American 13.4%

As estimated percentage of total population.

Universities and colleges, 2000–2001 enrollment

Blue Ridge Community College, Weyers Cave 2,873
Bridgewater College, Bridgewater 1,223
Central Virginia Community College, Lynchburg 3,919
Community Hospital of Roanoke Valley College of Health Sciences, Roanoke 508
Dominion College, Roanoke 221
Eastern Mennonite University, Harrisonburg 1,398
ECPI Technical College, Roanoke 379
Hollins University, Roanoke 1,043
James Madison University, Harrisonburg 15,326
Liberty University, Lynchburg 6,192
Lynchburg College, Lynchburg 1,982
Mary Baldwin College, Staunton 1,451
National Business College, Salem 2,455
Randolph-Macon Woman's College, Lynchburg 741
Roanoke College, Salem 1,677
Southern Virginia College, Buena Vista 412
Sweet Briar College, Sweet Briar 749
Virginia Military Institute, Lexington 1,300
Virginia Western Community College, Roanoke 7,307
Washington and Lee University, Lexington 2,067

Newspapers and circulation

	District circulation	Total circulation
Amherst New Era-Progress	3,574	3,931
Covington Virginian Review	2,892	7,492
Elkton Valley Banner	2,615	4,014
Harrisonburg Daily News Record	27,003	31,367
Lexington News-Gazette	7,547	7,547
Lynchburg News & Advance	19,420	37,361
Northern Virginia Daily	6,802	14,675
Richmond Times-Dispatch	2,728	193,688
Roanoke Times	47,910	99,140
*Shenandoah Valley-Herald**	4,662	4,662
*Staunton Daily News Leader**	18,367	18,367
*USA Today**	4,271	1,674,376
Washington Post	3,357	779,632
Waynesboro News-Virginian	7,260	7,774

See Sources and Explanations in the front of the volume.

Television stations and affiliations

Roanoke-Lynchburg	58%	WBRA	PBS
Roanoke-Lynchburg	58%	WDBJ	CBS
Roanoke-Lynchburg	58%	WFXR	FOX
Roanoke-Lynchburg	58%	WJPR	FOX
Roanoke-Lynchburg	58%	WPXR	PAX
Roanoke-Lynchburg	58%	WSET	ABC
Roanoke-Lynchburg	58%	WSLS	NBC
Roanoke-Lynchburg	58%	WVVA	NBC
Harrisonburg	33%	WVPT	PBS
Washington, DC (Hagerstown)	9%	WBDC	WB
Washington, DC (Hagerstown)	9%	WDCA	UPN
Washington, DC (Hagerstown)	9%	WETA	PBS
Washington, DC (Hagerstown)	9%	WFPT	PBS
Washington, DC (Hagerstown)	9%	WHAG	NBC
Washington, DC (Hagerstown)	9%	WHSV	ABC
Washington, DC (Hagerstown)	9%	WHUT	PBS
Washington, DC (Hagerstown)	9%	WJAL	ABC
Washington, DC (Hagerstown)	9%	WJLA	ABC
Washington, DC (Hagerstown)	9%	WNVC	Independent
Washington, DC (Hagerstown)	9%	WNVT	PBS
Washington, DC (Hagerstown)	9%	WPXW	PAX
Washington, DC (Hagerstown)	9%	WRC	NBC
Washington, DC (Hagerstown)	9%	WTTG	FOX
Washington, DC (Hagerstown)	9%	WUSA	CBS
Washington, DC (Hagerstown)	9%	WVPY	PBS
Washington, DC (Hagerstown)	9%	WWPB	PBS
Washington, DC (Hagerstown)	9%	WWPX	PAX

Cable systems and subscribers

Adelphia 82,010
Charter 569
Cooney Cable TV 1,190
Cox 64,441
Rapid Communications 5,537
Shenandoah Cable TV 5,945

Businesses and other major employers

Carilion Roanoke Memorial Hospital; Roanoke   5,000
General Electric Co.; Greenville; turbines, generators   2,900
Centra Health Inc.; Lynchburg; hospital   2,453
Carilion Transplant Clinic; Roanoke   2,340
First Union Corp. of Virginia; Roanoke; commercial bank   2,200
Carilion Roanoke Community Hospital; Roanoke   2,000
Westvaco Corp.; Covington; paperboard mills   1,900
James Madison University; Harrisonburg   1,700
Rocco Poultry Operations Inc.; Timberville; turkey   1,600
E. I. Du Pont De Nemours and Co.; Waynesboro; throwing, winding mills   1,500
McDermott International Inc.; Lynchburg; turbines, generators   1,500
U.S. Veterans Hospital; Salem   1,500
Liberty University Inc.; Lynchburg   1,398
Rockingham Memorial Hospital Inc.; Harrisonburg   1,390
Burlington Industries Inc.; Glasgow; carpets, rugs   1,350
Augusta Hospital Corp.; Fishersville; hospital   1,342
Lewis Gale Medical Center; Salem   1,300
Manpower Inc.; Lynchburg; temporary help   1,200
Rocco Poultry Operations Inc.; Edinburg; poultry   1,200
City of Lynchburg; Lynchburg; city government   1,080
Precision Fabrics Group Inc.; Vinton; weaving mill   1,000
R. R. Donnelley and Sons Co.; Harrisonburg; book printing   1,000
Lear Corp.; Strasburg; automobile seats   918
ITT Industries Inc.; Roanoke; defense systems   900
Norfolk Southern Railway Co.; Roanoke; freight hauling   900
Tenneco Automotive Operating Co.; Harrisonburg; automotive exhaust systems   900
Trigon Insurance Co.; Roanoke; life insurance   878
R. R. Donnelley and Sons Co.; Lynchburg; printing   860
First Colony Life Insurance Co.; Lynchburg; life insurance   851
Perry Judd's Inc.; Strasburg; offset printing   850
RPS Teleservice Center Inc.; Roanoke; telephone services   850
U.S. Postal Service; Roanoke   850
Virginia Mental Health Services; Staunton   850
Perdue Farms Inc.; Bridgewater; processed poultry   800
Roanoke County; Roanoke; board of supervisors   800
Merck and Co. Inc.; Elkton; industrial chemicals   766
Pilgrim's Pride Corp.; Hinton; poultry processing   750
Yokohama Tire Corp.; Salem; tread rubber   750
Lynchburg Foundry Co.; Lynchburg; iron foundry   700
Washington and Lee University; Lexington   700
Homestead; Hot Springs; resort hotel   650
American Postal Workers Union; Roanoke; labor union   600
Atlantic Mutual Insurance Co.; Roanoke; insurance   600
Conopco Inc.; Roanoke; plastics processing   600

Home Shopping Network Inc.; Salem; TV shopping   600
Orvis Co.; Roanoke; mail order   600
Virginia Fuels Inc.; Lynchburg   600
AAF-McQuay Inc.; Verona; air conditioning equipment   550
Allstate Insurance Co.; Roanoke; insurance agents   550
WT Industries Inc.; Waynesboro; polypropylene fabrics   540
City of Salem; Salem; city government   534
Advance Auto Parts Inc.; Roanoke   527
American Safety Razor Co.; Verona; razors, blades   500
Amsted Industries Inc.; Lynchburg; brass, bronze pipe   500
Asplundh Tree Expert Co.; Roanoke; tree services   500
Framatome ANP; Lynchburg; process control instruments   500
Hanover Direct Inc.; Roanoke; mail-order catalog   500
Kroger Co.; Salem; meat products   500
Roanoke Electric Steel Corp.; Roanoke; iron bars   500
United Parcel Service Inc.; Roanoke; parcel delivery   500
Virginia Dept. of Corrections; Craigsville   500
Virginia Dept. of Transportation; Lynchburg   500
Vishay Vitramon Inc.; Roanoke; capacitors, condensers   500
Wal-Mart Stores Inc.; Staunton; department stores   500

Virginia 7th District

Central — part of Richmond and suburbs

The solidly Republican 7th contains parts of Richmond and its affluent old-money suburbs, and then reaches northwest into farmlands.

Many of the 7th's residents work in Richmond, which grew steadily in the 1990s on the strength of banking and manufacturing. The longtime center of state government and commerce, Richmond also was one of the South's early manufacturing centers, concentrating on tobacco processing. Nearby Philip Morris continues to employ thousands of workers who live in the district.

The largest population block is in Henrico County (shared with the 3rd), which cups Richmond and has a backward C-shape. Henrico generally leans Republican, though it backed Democrat Mark Warner in the 2001 gubernatorial election. Chesterfield County, half of which is in the 4th, borders Richmond to the south and west and also has a strong GOP lean. Richmonders who live in the 7th are generally strong Republican voters who live in the city's western end.

The northern stretch of the 7th is home to traditional farming communities that gradually are being taken over by people who take long commutes to jobs in metropolitan Washington, D.C.

The 7th is a Republican bastion that gave George W. Bush 61 percent of its 2000 presidential vote—his statewide high—and gave 60 percent to Sen. George Allen in the 2000 Senate race. Redistricting following the 2000 census made the 7th slightly less Republican by adding some Democratic precincts in Richmond and Henrico County. But the district is still reliably Republican territory.

Major Industry

Agriculture, government, manufacturing.

Notable

Luray Caverns is in Page County; the late tennis star Arthur Ashe was born in Richmond in 1943; during a 1960 presidential campaign stop in Culpeper, Lyndon B. Johnson famously asked, "What has Richard Nixon ever done for Culpeper?"

Election Returns

	Republican		Democratic		Other	
President 2000	172,425	60.7%	105,504	37.1%	6,261	2.2%
House 2002	113,658	69.5%	49,854	30.5%	153	

District Profile

Population   643,499

Total area (square miles)   3,556.1
    Land area (square miles)   3,514.2

Population per square mile   183.1

Counties (2000 population)
    Caroline (pt.)   10,102
    Chesterfield (pt.)   132,789
    Culpeper   34,262
    Goochland   16,863
    Hanover   86,320
    Henrico (pt.)   196,880
    Louisa   25,627
    Madison   12,520
    Orange   25,881
    Page   23,177
    Rappahannock   6,983
    Richmond city (pt.)   53,270
    Spotsylvania (pt.)   18,825

Cities and other areas over 10,000 (2000 population)
    Bon Air CDP   16,213
    Glen Allen CDP   12,562
    Lakeside CDP   11,157
    Laurel CDP   14,875
    Mechanicsville CDP   30,464
    Richmond (pt.)   53,270
    Tuckahoe CDP   43,242

Race and Hispanic or Latino origin*
    White   78.2%
    Black or African American   16.1%
    American Indian or Alaska Native   0.3%
    Asian   2.3%
    Native Hawaiian or other Pacific Islander   0.0%
    Some other race   0.1%
    Hispanic or Latino origin   2.0%
    Two or more races   1.1%

*As percentage of total population.

Ancestry*

English	12.0%	Polish	1.3%
French	1.9%	Scotch-Irish	2.3%
German	10.2%	Scottish	2.2%
Irish	8.4%	USA/American	10.6%
Italian	3.1%		

*As estimated percentage of total population.

Universities and colleges, 2000–2001 enrollment
    Baptist Theological Seminary, Richmond   226
    Bryant and Stratton College, Richmond   238
    ECPI Technical College, Richmond   1,423
    Germanna Community College, Locust Grove   3,856
    J. Sargeant Reynolds Community College, Richmond   10,091
    Randolph-Macon College, Ashland   1,171
    Rav School of Professional Studies, Richmond   346
    Strayer University-Henrico, Glen Allen   499
    Union Theological Seminary and Presbyterian School, Richmond   327
    University of Richmond, Richmond   4,325

Newspapers and circulation

	District circulation	Total circulation
Charlottesville Progress	3,378	30,084
Elkton Valley Banner	1,305	4,014
Fredericksburg Free Lance-Star	7,702	46,135
Harrisonburg Daily News Record	3,087	31,367
Page News and Courier	6,107	6,107
Rappahannock News	1,999	2,463
Richmond Times-Dispatch	96,093	193,688
Times Community Newspapers	3,209	34,552
*USA Today**	3,458	1,674,376
Washington Post	3,956	779,632

*See Sources and Explanations in the front of the volume.

Television stations and affiliations

Richmond-Petersburg	57%	WCVE	PBS
Richmond-Petersburg	57%	WCVW	PBS
Richmond-Petersburg	57%	WRIC	ABC
Richmond-Petersburg	57%	WRLH	FOX
Richmond-Petersburg	57%	WTVR	CBS
Richmond-Petersburg	57%	WUPV	UPN
Richmond-Petersburg	57%	WWBT	NBC
Washington, DC (Hagerstown)	34%	WBDC	WB
Washington, DC (Hagerstown)	34%	WDCA	UPN
Washington, DC (Hagerstown)	34%	WETA	PBS
Washington, DC (Hagerstown)	34%	WFPT	PBS
Washington, DC (Hagerstown)	34%	WHAG	NBC
Washington, DC (Hagerstown)	34%	WHSV	ABC
Washington, DC (Hagerstown)	34%	WHUT	PBS
Washington, DC (Hagerstown)	34%	WJAL	ABC
Washington, DC (Hagerstown)	34%	WJLA	ABC
Washington, DC (Hagerstown)	34%	WNVC	Independent
Washington, DC (Hagerstown)	34%	WNVT	PBS
Washington, DC (Hagerstown)	34%	WPXW	PAX
Washington, DC (Hagerstown)	34%	WRC	NBC

Washington, DC (Hagerstown)	34%	WTTG	FOX
Washington, DC (Hagerstown)	34%	WUSA	CBS
Washington, DC (Hagerstown)	34%	WVPY	PBS
Washington, DC (Hagerstown)	34%	WWPB	PBS
Washington, DC (Hagerstown)	34%	WWPX	PAX
Charlottesville	9%	WHTJ	PBS
Charlottesville	9%	WVIR	NBC

Cable systems and subscribers
Adelphia 33,993
Comcast 15,447

Businesses and other major employers
SuperValu Inc.; Glen Allen; grocery store 15,141
International Mission Board; Richmond; religious organization 4,586
Henrico County; Richmond; county government 2,665
Columbia Chippenham Medical Center and Johnston-Willis Hospitals Inc.; Richmond 2,216
Bon Secours Memorial Regional Medical Center; Richmond 1,700
St. Mary's Hospital of Richmond Inc.; Richmond 1,650
Henrico Doctors Hospital; Richmond 1,300
Reynolds Metals Co.; Richmond; aluminum cans 1,300
VF Jeanswear; Luray; overalls, coveralls 1,107
Bank of America Corp.; Richmond; data processing 1,100
Trigon Insurance Co.; Richmond; group hospitalization 1,100
Tyson Foods Inc.; Glen Allen; poultry 1,060
University of Richmond; Richmond 1,055
Circuit City Stores Inc.; Richmond; electronic stores 1,000
Dominion Resources Services Inc.; Glen Allen; electric power generation 1,000
First Union Securities Inc.; Glen Allen; stock brokers, dealers 1,000
SuperValu Inc.; Mechanicsville; food supplier 1,000
Virginia Electric and Power Co.; Glen Allen; electric power generation 1,000
Virginia Electric and Power Co.; Mineral; electric services 917
American Critical Care Services Inc.; Richmond 900
William Byrd Press Inc.; Richmond; commercial printing 830
Henrico Doctors' Hospital-Parham; Richmond 787
Performance Food Group Co.; Richmond; food brokers 750
Bon Secours Memorial Regional Medical Center; Mechanicsville 700
GE Life Annuity Assurance Co.; Richmond; life insurance 700
Southern States Cooperative Inc.; Richmond; prepared feeds 700
SkateNation Inc.; Glen Allen; recreation club 697
Hanover County; Hanover; county government 634
Louisa County; Mineral; public schools 617
Heilig-Meyers Co.; Richmond; furniture stores 609
Cadmus Communications Corp.; Richmond; trade journals 600
Colonial Mechanical Corp.; Richmond; mechanical contractor 600

First Health Services Corp.; Glen Allen 600
Patient First Corp.; Glen Allen; management services 600
Henrico County; Richmond; recreational program 550
Virginia Dept. of Corrections; State Farm 550
Kellogg Brown and Root Inc.; Richmond; street paving 521
Asplundh Tree Expert Co; Glen Allen; tree services 500
Culpeper Memorial Hospital Inc.; Culpeper 500
JC Penney Corp.; Midlothian; catalog sales 500
Media General Operations Inc.; Mechanicsville; newspaper 500
National Nurses Service; Richmond; nursing facility management 500
Virginia Dept. of Corrections; Richmond 500
Wal-Mart Stores Inc.; Mechanicsville; department stores 500

Virginia 8th District

Washington suburbs — Arlington, Alexandria, part of Fairfax County

Taking in the close-in Washington, D.C., suburbs in Northern Virginia, the Democratic 8th is one of the wealthiest districts in the state, though poorer pockets exist along the Route 1 corridor. The area is racially diverse, especially in Arlington County, where nearly one in five residents is Hispanic, and in Alexandria, where nearly one in four is black. *(See map p. 936.)*

A smattering of landmarks gives the district a colonial flavor, but the area is far from old-fashioned. The 8th bustles with technology businesses and defense contractors, drawn to the district's substantial military presence, including the Pentagon. While government and defense-related employment is important to the economy, technology took off as the hot industry of the 1990s.

The 8th votes heavily Democratic. Alexandria and Arlington give Democrats some of their highest vote percentages in the state and contrast sharply with Virginia's overall Republican lean. In the 2001 gubernatorial election, Democrat Mark Warner won 68 percent of the vote in Arlington and Alexandria, compared with 52 percent statewide.

Half of the 8th's residents live in Fairfax County, where redistricting altered boundaries following the 2000 census. Mapmakers made the 8th's portion of Fairfax more Democratic, and it now stretches west from the county's border with Alexandria past Falls Church and the Tysons Corner area to Reston, instead of south to the Prince William County line.

Major Industry
Government, technology, defense, service.

Notable
The U.S. Capitol could fit into any one of the Pentagon's five wedge-shaped sections; despite the Pentagon's 17.5 miles of corridors, it takes only seven minutes to walk between any two points.

Election Returns

	Republican		Democratic		Other	
President 2000	101,788	38.2%	152,940	57.4%	11,692	4.4%
House 2002	64,121	37.3%	102,759	59.8%	4,919	2.7%

District Profile

Population 643,503

Total area (square miles) 124.8
  Land area (square miles) 123.1

Population per square mile 5,227.5

Counties (2000 population)
Alexandria city 128,283   Fairfax (pt.) 315,390
Arlington 189,453   Falls Church city 10,377

Cities and other areas over 10,000 (2000 population)
Alexandria 128,283
Arlington CDP 189,453
Bailey's Crossroads CDP (pt.) 21,259
Falls Church 10,377
Franconia CDP 31,907
Groveton CDP 21,296
Hybla Valley CDP 16,721
Idylwood CDP 16,005
Jefferson CDP (pt.) 23,366
Lincolnia CDP 15,788
Mount Vernon CDP (pt.) 18,007
Reston CDP (pt.) 56,275
Rose Hill CDP 15,058
Springfield CDP (pt.) 14,106
Tysons Corner CDP (pt.) 14,075

Race and Hispanic or Latino origin*
White 57.1%
Black or African American 13.4%
American Indian or Alaska Native 0.2%
Asian 9.5%
Native Hawaiian or other Pacific Islander 0.1%
Some other race 0.3%
Hispanic or Latino origin 16.4%
Two or more races 3.0%

As percentage of total population.

Ancestry*
Arab-Misc. 1.6%   Polish 2.0%
English 8.4%   Russian 1.2%
French 1.8%   Scotch-Irish 1.6%
German 9.6%   Scottish 2.1%
Irish 9.0%   Subsaharan 2.8%
Italian 3.7%   USA/American 3.0%

As estimated percentage of total population.

Universities and colleges, 2000–2001 enrollment
American School of Professional Psychology-Virginia, Arlington 318
Computer Learning Center, Alexandria 1,486
Keller Graduate School of Management, McLean 246
Marymount University, Arlington 3,422
Strayer University, Alexandria 1,244
Strayer University, Arlington 1,575
University of Northern Virginia, Falls Church 327

Newspapers and circulation

	District circulation	Total circulation
*USA Today**	10,637	1,674,376
Washington Post	119,727	779,632
Washington Times	13,412	101,367

See Sources and Explanations in the front of the volume.

Television stations and affiliations
Washington, DC (Hagerstown) 100% WBDC WB
Washington, DC (Hagerstown) 100% WDCA UPN
Washington, DC (Hagerstown) 100% WETA PBS
Washington, DC (Hagerstown) 100% WFPT PBS
Washington, DC (Hagerstown) 100% WHAG NBC
Washington, DC (Hagerstown) 100% WHSV ABC
Washington, DC (Hagerstown) 100% WHUT PBS
Washington, DC (Hagerstown) 100% WJAL ABC
Washington, DC (Hagerstown) 100% WJLA ABC
Washington, DC (Hagerstown) 100% WNVC Independent
Washington, DC (Hagerstown) 100% WNVT PBS
Washington, DC (Hagerstown) 100% WPXW PAX
Washington, DC (Hagerstown) 100% WRC NBC
Washington, DC (Hagerstown) 100% WTTG FOX
Washington, DC (Hagerstown) 100% WUSA CBS
Washington, DC (Hagerstown) 100% WVPY PBS
Washington, DC (Hagerstown) 100% WWPB PBS
Washington, DC (Hagerstown) 100% WWPX PAX

Cable systems and subscribers
Comcast 52,224

Military installations, September 2001
Fort Belvoir (Army), Alexandria 16,181
Marine Corps Headquarters, Arlington 6,178
Fort Myer (Army), Arlington 3,132
Army Guard Readiness Center, Arlington 429

Businesses and other major employers
U.S. Defense Dept./Pentagon; Arlington 26,000
ITT Defense; McLean; electronic circuits 14,000
Gap Inc.; Arlington; clothing stores 13,080
U.S. Defense Information Systems Agency; Arlington 8,500
DynCorp Systems and Solutions; Reston; information services, consumer 6,350
MCI WorldCom Communications Inc.; Arlington; communications 5,700
U.S. Defense Dept.; Fort Belvoir 5,183
U.S. Patent and Trademark Office; Arlington 5,100
Old Navy Inc.; Springfield; clothing stores 5,000
ExxonMobil Oil Corp.; Fairfax; petroleum products 4,000
U.S. Defense Logistics Agency; Alexandria 3,200
Nextel del Peru SA; Reston; cell phones 3,000
Nextel Communications Inc.; Reston; cell phones 3,000
U.S. Drug Enforcement Admin.; Arlington 3,000
First Virginia Banks Inc.; Falls Church; state commercial bank 2,700
Equant Inc.; Reston; data communication 2,474
Federal Home Loan Mortgage Corp.; McLean 2,200
Washington Gas Light Co.; Springfield; natural gas distribution 2,100
Unification Church International; Falls Church; book publishing 2,006

Science Applications International Corp.; McLean; commercial research   2,000

U.S. Geological Survey; Reston   2,000

Raytheon Co.; Falls Church; radar systems, equipment   1,975

City of Alexandria; Alexandria; city government   1,968

Verizon Services Corp.; Arlington; telephones   1,800

Virginia Hospital Center-Arlington Health Systems; Arlington   1,800

Accenture Inc.; Reston; business management consultant   1,790

Alexandria Inova Hospital; Alexandria   1,750

America Talk; Reston; local/long-distance telephone   1,700

Sallie Mae Inc.; Reston; student loan marketing association   1,700

CACI Inc. Federal; Arlington; computer systems   1,665

Booz Allen and Hamilton Inc.; McLean; management consulting   1,600

Inova Alexandria Hospital; Alexandria   1,500

Ringling Brothers Barnum and Bailey; Vienna; circus company   1,500

Mills LP; Arlington; retail property operation   1,400

EarthLink Inc.; Reston; Internet services   1,300

KPMG Consulting; McLean; management consulting   1,200

Verizon Communications Inc.; Reston; local telephones   1,200

Washington Team Inc.; Alexandria; pizzeria chain   1,200

Computer Sciences Corp.; Falls Church; data processing   1,150

BAE Systems Enterprise Systems Inc.; McLean; quality assurance consultant   1,100

MVM Inc.; McLean; detective, armored car services   1,100

Nordstrom Inc.; McLean; clothing stores   1,100

Reston Hospital; Reston   1,100

Fairfax County; Springfield; nutrition services   1,000

Geneva Management Inc.; Arlington; business management   1,000

Nextel Communications Inc.; McLean; cell phones   1,000

Vision Technologies Systems Inc.; Alexandria; personal services   1,000

MicroStrategy Inc.; McLean; computer software   985

Gannett Co. Inc.; McLean; newspapers   900

GTS Carrier Services Inc.; Arlington; telephones   883

Argenbright Security Inc.; Arlington; security guard service   800

Fourth Crystal Park Associate; Arlington; building operators   800

Gannett Satellite Information Network Inc.; Springfield; commercial printing   800

Institute for Defense Analyses; Alexandria; noncommercial research   800

Lockheed Martin Corp.; Reston; data processing   800

Oracle Corp.; Reston; educational software   800

U.S. Marshals Service; Arlington   800

Matcom International Corp.; Alexandria; computer systems   750

U.S. Airways Inc.; Arlington   750

PricewaterhouseCoopers; Arlington; certified public accountant   701

Arlington County; Arlington; county government   700

Marriott International Inc.; Arlington; hotels   700

Mitretek Systems Inc.; Falls Church; noncommercial research   700

U.S. Postal Service; Arlington   700

Unisys Corp.; McLean; computer systems   700

Boat America Corp.; Alexandria; marine supplies   650

MCI WorldCom International Inc.; McLean; telephone communication   650

Raytheon Technical Services Co.; Reston; electrical equipment repair   650

Rowe Companies; McLean; home furniture   649

CNA Corp.; Alexandria; research services   629

Combined Communications Corp.; McLean; investment holding company   600

Deloitte and Touche; McLean; accounting services   600

Federal Home Loan Mortgage Corp.; Vienna   600

Gannett Satellite Information Network Inc.; McLean; newspaper   600

Northrop Grumman Information Technology Inc.; McLean; management consulting   600

Pentagon Federal Credit Union; Alexandria; federal credit unions   600

Teleglobe USA Inc.; Reston; long-distance telephone   600

Washington Metropolitan Area Transit Authority; Alexandria   600

West 1 Real Estate Inc.; Alexandria; real estate agents   592

Arya Corp.; Falls Church; general merchandise   580

Bloomingdale's Inc.; McLean; department stores   550

Science Applications International Corp.; Falls Church; computer systems   550

Virginia Community College System; Alexandria   530

Hyatt Corp.; Arlington; hotel, franchised   525

National Wildlife Federation Inc.; Reston; environmental protection   524

Federal Deposit Insurance Corp.; Arlington   516

Public Broadcasting Service; Alexandria; TV broadcasting   510

Computer Sciences Corp.; Springfield; data processing   500

CRS Facility Services LLP; Alexandria; cleaning services   500

DynCorp Aviation Services Inc.; Reston; airports   500

Falls Church Public Schools; Falls Church   500

Kwajalein Services Inc.; Reston; computer systems   500

May Department Stores Co.; McLean   500

Nature Conservancy; Arlington; environmental protection   500

PricewaterhouseCoopers; McLean; accounting services   500

SRA International Inc.; Arlington; systems analysis   500

Sun Microsystems Inc.; McLean; computer maintenance   500

VSE Corp.; Alexandria; engineering services   500

Virginia 9th District

Southwest — Blacksburg, Bristol

Covered with forests, mountainous terrain, and a slew of small factory and coal towns, the Democratic-leaning 9th is rich in beauty but also is Virginia's poorest district. Located in the southwestern part of the state, the 9th has struggled with high poverty rates and a weak economic base. The median income here is less than $30,000.

Coal mining provides jobs in counties at the western tip of the 9th, which also is the most economically depressed part of the district. Elsewhere, manufacturing is the major industry.

Diversifying the economy and ensuring clean drinking water for the thousands of residents who lack it are priorities in the 9th. Leaders have targeted the Internet as a way to get community exposure and to offer residents new learning opportunities. Although the district's overall population was stagnant in the 1990s, Craig County grew with Salem and Roanoke commuters. Blacksburg remains the largest city and is home to the state's largest university—Virginia Tech. Surrounding Montgomery County is economically atypical of the 9th.

The district is known as the "Fighting 9th," a name that reflects the area's fiercely competitive politics and its ornery isolation from the political establishment in Richmond. In the post–World War II era, when Democrats routinely dominated Virginia politics, the 9th was one of the only areas in which Republicans were consistently strong. Now that the statewide trend has flipped, the 9th has been in Democratic hands since 1983.

Bill Clinton carried the 9th in the 1992 and 1996 presidential elections, but social issues such as gun control compelled many voters to back George W. Bush in 2000. Wise County, which borders Kentucky, narrowly backed Bush after supporting Democratic presidential candidates in 1988, 1992, and 1996. Bush narrowly lost Russell County, which abuts Wise, but he received a higher percentage there than Ronald Reagan did in 1984.

Major Industry

Manufacturing, coal mining, agriculture.

Notable

Brass markers placed through the city of Bristol mark the Virginia-Tennessee state line.

Election Returns

	Republican		Democratic		Other	
President 2000	129,110	54.6%	100,298	42.4%	7,011	3.0%
House 2002	52,076	34.2%	100,075	65.8%	32	

District Profile

Population   643,514

Total area (square miles)   8,838.0
 Land area (square miles)   8,803.3

Population per square mile   73.1

Counties (2000 population)

Alleghany (pt.) 7,772	Lee 23,589
Bland 6,871	Montgomery 83,629
Bristol city 17,367	Norton city 3,904
Buchanan 26,978	Patrick 19,407
Carroll 29,245	Pulaski 35,127
Clifton Forge city 4,289	Radford city 15,859
Covington city (pt.) 5,025	Roanoke (pt.) 14,621
Craig 5,091	Russell 30,308
Dickenson 16,395	Scott 23,403
Floyd 13,874	Smyth 33,081
Galax city 6,837	Tazewell 44,598
Giles 16,657	Washington 51,103
Grayson 17,917	Wise 40,123
Henry (pt.) 22,845	Wythe 27,599

Cities and other areas over 10,000 (2000 population)

Blacksburg town   39,573
Bristol   17,367
Christiansburg town   16,947
Radford   15,859

Race and Hispanic or Latino origin*

White   93.3%
Black or African American   3.8%
American Indian or Alaska Native   0.1%
Asian   0.8%
Native Hawaiian or other Pacific Islander   0.0%
Some other race   0.1%
Hispanic or Latino origin   1.1%
Two or more races   0.7%

*As percentage of total population.

Ancestry*

Dutch 1.1%	Italian 1.3%
English 7.7%	Scotch-Irish 2.2%
German 7.7%	Scottish 1.4%
Irish 6.8%	USA/American 20.0%

*As estimated percentage of total population.

Universities and colleges, 2000–2001 enrollment

Bluefield College, Bluefield   820
Dabney S. Lancaster Community College, Clifton Forge   1,453
Emory and Henry College, Emory   977
Ferrum College, Ferrum   914
Mountain Empire Community College, Big Stone Gap   2,741
New River Community College, Dublin   3,692
Radford University, Radford   8,837
Southwest Virginia Community College, Richlands   3,819
University of Virginia-Clinch Valley College, Wise   1,447
Virginia Highlands Community College, Abingdon   2,254
Virginia Intermont College, Bristol   537
Virginia Polytechnic Institute and State University, Blacksburg   27,869
Wytheville Community College, Wytheville   2,339

Newspapers and circulation

	District circulation	Total circulation
Bluefield Daily Telegraph	6,212	20,938
Bristol Herald Courier	30,239	41,509
Coalfield Progress	6,034	6,100
Covington Virginian Review	4,452	7,492
Kingsport Times-News	11,059	42,469
Martinsville Bulletin	6,626	17,549
Roanoke Times	36,312	99,140
*USA Today**	2,454	1,674,376

*See Sources and Explanations in the front of the volume.

Television stations and affiliations

Roanoke-Lynchburg	46%	WBRA	PBS
Roanoke-Lynchburg	46%	WDBJ	CBS
Roanoke-Lynchburg	46%	WFXR	FOX
Roanoke-Lynchburg	46%	WJPR	FOX
Roanoke-Lynchburg	46%	WPXR	PAX
Roanoke-Lynchburg	46%	WSET	ABC
Roanoke-Lynchburg	46%	WSLS	NBC
Roanoke-Lynchburg	46%	WVVA	NBC
Bristol-Johnson City-Kingsport	42%	WCYB	NBC
Bristol-Johnson City-Kingsport	42%	WEMT	FOX
Bristol-Johnson City-Kingsport	42%	WJHL	CBS
Bristol-Johnson City-Kingsport	42%	WKPT	ABC
Bristol-Johnson City-Kingsport	42%	WLFG	Independent
Bristol-Johnson City-Kingsport	42%	WMSY	PBS
Bristol-Johnson City-Kingsport	42%	WSBN	PBS
Bristol-Johnson City-Kingsport	42%	WSJK	PBS
Bluefield-Beckley-Oak Hill	6%	WOAY	ABC
Bluefield-Beckley-Oak Hill	6%	WSWP	PBS
Greensboro-High Point-Winston-Salem	6%	WDRL	UPN
Greensboro-High Point-Winston-Salem	6%	WFMY	CBS
Greensboro-High Point-Winston-Salem	6%	WGHP	FOX
Greensboro-High Point-Winston-Salem	6%	WLXI	Independent
Greensboro-High Point-Winston-Salem	6%	WUNL	PBS
Greensboro-High Point-Winston-Salem	6%	WUPN	UPN
Greensboro-High Point-Winston-Salem	6%	WXII	NBC
Greensboro-High Point-Winston-Salem	6%	WXLV	ABC

Cable systems and subscribers

Adelphia   65,579
Charter   30,621
Clearview TV Cable   2,193
Comcast   20,289
Phoenix Cable   2,632
Rapid Communications   3,476
Rural Retreat Cable TV Inc.   690
Scott County Telephone & Cable   7,444
Time Warner   1,349

Military installations, September 2001

Radford Army Ammunition Plant, Radford   2,250

Businesses and other major employers

Virginia Polytechnic Institute and State University; Blacksburg   4,800
Celanese Americas Corp.; Narrows; acetate, triacetate fibers   3,000
Bassett Furniture Industries Inc.; Bassett   2,700
Pittston Coal Management Co.; Lebanon   1,500
Volvo Trucks North America Inc.; Dublin; truck assembly   1,450
E. I. Du Pont De Nemours and Co.; Martinsville; organic fibers   1,200
Virginia Dept. of Transportation; Bristol   1,200
Pillowtex Corp.; Fieldale; cotton towels   1,000

VF Imagewear Inc.; Bassett; knit outerwear mills   1,000
Cimarron Coach of Virginia Inc.; Falls Mills; local passenger transportation   900
Consolidation Coal Co.; Oakwood; coal mining   800
Advanced Technical Products Inc.; Marion; plastics materials and resins   750
Marley Mouldings; Marion; molding primary plastics   750
Aerus LLC; Bristol; vacuum cleaners   700
Bucannan School District; Grundy   700
CP Films Inc.; Fieldale; consulting engineer   700
Utility Trailer Manufacturing Co.; Atkins; truck trailers   700
Federal-Mogul Corp.; Blacksburg; automotive parts   625
Clinch Valley Medical Center; Richlands   600
Ethan Allen Inc.; Dublin; furniture   600
National Textiles; Galax; underwear fabrics   600
Renfro Corp.; Pulaski; hosiery   600
Rowe Furniture Inc.; Elliston   600
Sprint Corp.; Wytheville; telephone communication   590
Vaughan-Bassett Furniture Co.; Galax; bed frames   556
American Furniture Corp.; Chilhowie   550
Consolidated Glass and Mirror Corp.; Galax; glass products   550
Twin County Regional Hospital; Galax   550
Johnston Memorial Hospital Inc.; Abingdon   510
Technical Products Group Inc.; Marion; prefabricated plastic buildings   509
CMI Industries Inc.; Stuart; elastic narrow fabrics   500
Hubbell Lighting Inc.; Christiansburg; lighting equipment   500
Magnolia Manufacturing Co.; Hillsville; yarn   500
Montgomery Regional Hospital Inc.; Blacksburg   500
Virginia Mental Health Services; Marion   500

Virginia 10th District

North — part of Fairfax County, Loudoun County

Located in the northern part of Virginia, the Republican-friendly 10th bridges a dizzying range of economies and lifestyles, with mountains and farmland at one end and congested Washington, D.C., suburbs at the other. A hotbed of economic activity in the 1990s, the 10th is a mostly white-collar area that includes some of the state's wealthiest counties—Loudoun and parts of Fauquier and Fairfax. *(See map p. 936.)*

Most of the district's population resides in suburban Northern Virginia, and many residents commute to jobs in Washington or the inner suburbs just outside the nation's capital.

Nearly all of the 10th's counties grew substantially in the 1990s. Technology-magnet Loudoun County, which includes Leesburg and Washington Dulles International Airport, is home to more than one-fourth of district residents and nearly doubled in population during the decade. The area is grappling with its expansion, and slow-growth advocates have fared well in recent local elections. About one-third of residents live in Fairfax County (shared with the 8th and 11th), which includes Chantilly.

Beyond suburbia, agriculture and manufacturing fuel the economy. Clarke and Frederick Counties produce about half of Virginia's apples and peaches. Winchester (Frederick County), the center of the state's apple-growing industry, is the home base of the Byrd family, which dominated Democratic politics in Virginia for decades. But the district has long since abandoned its Democratic roots.

Robust population growth required mapmakers to shrink the 10th's borders in redistricting following the 2000 census. As redrawn, the district includes a bit more of Fairfax County but decidedly less of Prince William County, which is located south and west of Fairfax. Several northern Shenandoah Valley counties were stripped from the 10th and given to the 6th or 7th Districts.

Major Industry
Federal government, technology, manufacturing, agriculture.

Notable
The CIA headquarters are in Langley; Manassas National Battlefield Park is the site of two Civil War battles.

Election Returns

	Republican		Democratic		Other	
President 2000	148,211	55.8%	109,063	41.1%	8,106	3.1%
House 2002	115,917	71.7%	45,464	28.1%	234	0.2%

District Profile

Population 643,512

Total area (square miles) 1,864.2
Land area (square miles) 1,856.2

Population per square mile 346.7

Counties (2000 population)
Clarke 12,652
Fairfax (pt.) 222,296
Fauquier (pt.) 26,562
Frederick 59,209
Loudoun 169,599
Manassas city 35,135
Manassas Park city 10,290
Prince William (pt.) 52,600
Warren 31,584
Winchester city 23,585

Cities and other areas over 10,000 (2000 population)
Bull Run CDP 11,337
Centreville CDP (pt.) 33,053
Chantilly CDP 41,041
Front Royal town 13,589
Herndon town 21,655
Leesburg town 28,311
Manassas 35,135
Manassas Park 10,290
McLean CDP (pt.) 37,427
Winchester 23,585

Race and Hispanic or Latino origin*
White 77.2%
Black or African American 6.7%
American Indian or Alaska Native 0.2%
Asian 6.6%
Native Hawaiian or other Pacific Islander 0.0%
Some other race 0.2%
Hispanic or Latino origin 7.1%
Two or more races 1.9%

*As percentage of total population.

Ancestry*
English 9.5%	Polish 2.2%
French 1.9%	Scotch-Irish 1.7%
German 12.9%	Scottish 2.0%
Irish 10.5%	USA/American 6.6%
Italian 4.4%	

*As estimated percentage of total population.

Universities and colleges, 2000–2001 enrollment
American Military University, Manassas Park 934
Christendom College, Front Royal 356
Lord Fairfax Community College, Middletown 3,945
Shenandoah University, Winchester 2,428
Strayer University, Ashburn 1,033
Strayer University, Manassas 1,000

Newspapers and circulation

	District circulation	Total circulation
Clarke Times-Courier	1,829	1,829
Fauquier Democrat	4,533	16,459
Loudoun Times-Mirror	15,892	18,798
Manassas Journal Messenger	3,606	4,943
Northern Virginia Daily	6,985	14,675
Potomac News	1,753	15,331
Potomac News/Manassas Journal Messenger	5,359	20,274
Times Community Newspapers	22,161	34,552
USA Today*	4,170	1,674,376
Warren Sentinel	4,289	4,289
Washington Post	75,141	779,632
Washington Times	7,279	101,367
Winchester Star	19,477	20,841

*See Sources and Explanations in the front of the volume.

Television stations and affiliations
Washington, DC (Hagerstown)	100%	WBDC	WB
Washington, DC (Hagerstown)	100%	WDCA	UPN
Washington, DC (Hagerstown)	100%	WETA	PBS
Washington, DC (Hagerstown)	100%	WFPT	PBS
Washington, DC (Hagerstown)	100%	WHAG	NBC
Washington, DC (Hagerstown)	100%	WHSV	ABC
Washington, DC (Hagerstown)	100%	WHUT	PBS
Washington, DC (Hagerstown)	100%	WJAL	ABC
Washington, DC (Hagerstown)	100%	WJLA	ABC
Washington, DC (Hagerstown)	100%	WNVC	Independent
Washington, DC (Hagerstown)	100%	WNVT	PBS
Washington, DC (Hagerstown)	100%	WPXW	PAX
Washington, DC (Hagerstown)	100%	WRC	NBC
Washington, DC (Hagerstown)	100%	WTTG	FOX
Washington, DC (Hagerstown)	100%	WUSA	CBS

Washington, DC (Hagerstown)	100%	WVPY	PBS
Washington, DC (Hagerstown)	100%	WWPB	PBS
Washington, DC (Hagerstown)	100%	WWPX	PAX

Cable systems and subscribers

Adelphia 56,988
Comcast 13,437
Cox 2,709

Businesses and other major employers

Northrop Grumman Commercial Information Services Inc.; Herndon; aircraft 40,000

Electronic Data Systems Corp.; Herndon; data processing 10,000

America Online Inc.; Dulles; online service providers 3,000

Checks and Balances Inc.; Manassas; payroll accounting 3,000

Winchester Medical Center Inc.; Winchester 2,700

Vinnell-Brown and Root; Fairfax; building maintenance 2,200

UUNET Technologies Inc.; Ashburn; Internet host 2,000

Verizon Communications Inc.; Chantilly; data communication 1,500

United Air Lines Inc.; Chantilly 1,300

Network Solutions Inc.; Sterling; local area network systems 1,200

NVR Inc.; McLean; mortgage bankers 1,200

VeriSign Inc.; Sterling; computer programming 1,200

Frederick County; Winchester; county government 1,158

International Business Machines Corp.; Manassas 1,150

Micron Technology Inc.; Manassas; computer peripheral equipment 1,000

New Custom Service Companies Inc.; Sterling; insurance agents, brokers 1,000

Rubbermaid Commercial Products; Winchester; plastic containers 1,000

DynCorp Information Systems; Chantilly; engineering services 900

Internet Global; Herndon; online service providers 900

Lear Corp.; Winchester; automotive parts 900

Orbital Sciences Corp.; Sterling; space vehicles 900

U.S. Postal Service; Dulles 900

United Air Lines Inc.; Sterling 900

United Air Lines Inc.; Ashburn 875

American Management Systems Inc.; Fairfax; computer consulting services 851

Continental Building Maintenance Co.; Chantilly; janitor service 800

Federal-Mogul Corp.; Winchester; automotive parts 800

Medical Laboratories Corp.; Chantilly; pathology lab 800

Seavin; Fairfax; base maintenance 800

Siemens VDO Automotive Corp.; Winchester; instrument relays 800

Systems Research and Applications Corp.; Fairfax; systems engineering consultant 800

TRW Inc.; Chantilly; administrative management 800

Oberthur Card Systems and Services Inc.; Chantilly; security systems services 790

Loudoun Hospital Center; Leesburg 770

Anteon Corp.; Chantilly; engineering services 750

Berryville Graphics Inc.; Berryville; book printing 750

Fauquier Hospital Inc.; Warrenton 700

Laboratory Corp. of America; Herndon; testing labs 700

Polyone Engineered Films Group; Winchester; vinyl film and sheet 680

TRW Inc.; Fairfax; administrative management 635

Kohl's Department Stores Inc.; Winchester; warehousing 600

Lockheed Martin Corp.; Manassas; computer software design 600

PSINet Inc.; Ashburn; computer systems 600

Prince William Hospital Corp.; Manassas 600

Cavalier Telephone; Herndon; business consulting 500

Computer Associates International Inc.; Herndon; prepackaged software 500

First Union National Bank; McLean; commercial bank 500

General Electric Co.; Winchester; electric lamps 500

Getronics Government Solutions; Herndon; systems integration services 500

HealthScribe Inc.; Sterling; data processing 500

Mantech Advanced Systems International Inc.; Chantilly; engineering services 500

National Fruit Product Co.; Winchester 500

ORBCOMM Global; Dulles; data communication services 500

Prince William County; Manassas; county police 500

Sitel Support Services Inc.; Herndon; telemarketing 500

Sordoni/Skanska Construction Co.; Fairfax; industrial buildings 500

Teligent Inc.; Herndon; radiotelephone communication 500

U.S. Federal Aviation Admin.; Leesburg 500

United Parcel Service Inc.; Chantilly; parcel delivery 500

Xerox Corp.; Leesburg 500

Virginia 11th District

Washington suburbs — parts of Fairfax and Prince William Counties

Anchored in the suburbs of Washington, D.C., the 11th is home to well-educated, middle- and upper-class suburbanites. It also is racially diverse, with more Asians—11 percent of residents—than any other Virginia district. Only the inner-suburb 8th has more Hispanic residents. *(See map p. 936.)*

The district is tailor-made for a moderate Republican, especially one who hews to the center on social issues. The 11th leans to the right on fiscal matters, but traffic congestion is a large problem here, and some residents support tax increases to pay for improvements. Democrat Mark Warner carried the 11th in the 2001 gubernatorial race in part because of his strong support of increased transportation spending for the region.

Fairfax County, including Vienna and Burke, accounts for two-thirds of residents. The rest live in Prince William

County, which grew by 30 percent in the 1990s to become Virginia's third-most-populous jurisdiction (after Fairfax County and Virginia Beach), or in Fairfax city.

Many residents work in downtown Washington, either for the federal government or for companies whose business is linked to the government. Despite the public sector influence, technology is the district's fastest-growing industry, and dozens of companies have put down roots in office park developments in Fairfax County. A growing number of workers telecommute, and the 11th has the highest median income (more than $80,000) of any district in the nation.

The 11th was a quintessential swing district in the 1990s. But a GOP-controlled redistricting plan following the 2000 census turned the district into Republican-leaning territory, mainly by revising the 11th's portions of Fairfax County. Democratic-leaning areas such as Reston and Bailey's Crossroads were removed, and Republican areas were added.

Major Industry
Federal government, technology, service.

Notable
Fairfax Court House is where George and Martha Washington's wills were recorded and still are kept.

Election Returns

	Republican		Democratic		Other	
President 2000	140,961	51.7%	123,702	45.4%	8,087	3.0%
House 2002	135,379	82.9%			27,919	17.1%

District Profile

Population   643,509

Total area (square miles)   404.4
   Land area (square miles)   387.7

Population per square mile   1,659.8

Counties (2000 population)
   Fairfax (pt.)   432,063
   Fairfax city   21,498
   Prince William (pt.)   189,948

Cities and other areas over 10,000 (2000 population)
   Annandale CDP (pt.)   51,350
   Burke CDP   57,737
   Centreville CDP (pt.)   15,608
   Dale City CDP   55,971
   Fairfax   21,498
   Lake Ridge CDP   30,404
   Lorton CDP   17,786
   Merrifield CDP   11,170
   Montclair CDP (pt.)   13,528
   Mount Vernon CDP (pt.)   10,575
   Newington CDP (pt.)   16,946
   Oakton CDP   29,348
   Springfield CDP (pt.)   16,311
   Vienna town   14,453
   West Springfield CDP   28,378
   Woodbridge CDP (pt.)   29,506

Race and Hispanic or Latino origin*
White   66.8%
Black or African American   10.1%
American Indian or Alaska Native   0.2%
Asian   10.9%
Native Hawaiian or other Pacific Islander   0.1%
Some other race   0.2%
Hispanic or Latino origin   9.1%
Two or more races   2.6%

*As percentage of total population.

Ancestry*

English 9.4%	Polish 2.3%
French 2.0%	Scotch-Irish 1.7%
German 11.5%	Scottish 2.0%
Irish 10.0%	Subsaharan 1.1%
Italian 4.4%	USA/American 4.4%

*As estimated percentage of total population.

Universities and colleges, 2000–2001 enrollment
George Mason University, Fairfax   23,408
Northern Virginia Community College, Annandale   37,073
Strayer University, Woodbridge   1,170

Newspapers and circulation

	District circulation	Total circulation
Manassas Journal Messenger	1,110	4,943
Potomac News	10,468	15,331
Potomac News/Manassas Journal Messenger	11,583	20,274
*USA Today**	16,182	1,674,376
Washington Post	94,790	779,632
Washington Times	11,124	101,367

*See Sources and Explanations in the front of the volume.

Television stations and affiliations
Washington, DC (Hagerstown)	100%	WBDC	WB
Washington, DC (Hagerstown)	100%	WDCA	UPN
Washington, DC (Hagerstown)	100%	WETA	PBS
Washington, DC (Hagerstown)	100%	WFPT	PBS
Washington, DC (Hagerstown)	100%	WHAG	NBC
Washington, DC (Hagerstown)	100%	WHSV	ABC
Washington, DC (Hagerstown)	100%	WHUT	PBS
Washington, DC (Hagerstown)	100%	WJAL	ABC
Washington, DC (Hagerstown)	100%	WJLA	ABC
Washington, DC (Hagerstown)	100%	WNVC	Independent
Washington, DC (Hagerstown)	100%	WNVT	PBS
Washington, DC (Hagerstown)	100%	WPXW	PAX
Washington, DC (Hagerstown)	100%	WRC	NBC
Washington, DC (Hagerstown)	100%	WTTG	FOX
Washington, DC (Hagerstown)	100%	WUSA	CBS
Washington, DC (Hagerstown)	100%	WVPY	PBS
Washington, DC (Hagerstown)	100%	WWPB	PBS
Washington, DC (Hagerstown)	100%	WWPX	PAX

Cable systems and subscribers
Comcast   48,055
Cox   156,847

Businesses and other major employers

ArmorGroup North America Inc.; Vienna; armored car services 4,437

George Mason University; Fairfax 4,300

American Red Cross; Falls Church; individual and family services 3,000

Fairfax County; Fairfax; county government 3,000

Navy Federal Credit Union; Vienna 2,800

Prince William County School Board; Manassas 2,265

AT&T Corp.; Oakton; long-distance telephone 2,000

Pro Tech Plumbing and Heating; Springfield; heating, air conditioning 1,995

Virginia Community College System; Annandale 1,944

Progressive Nursing Staffers Inc.; Springfield; temporary help 1,800

Cable and Wireless USA Inc.; Vienna; long-distance telephone 1,300

Church of Jesus Christ of Latter-Day Saints Corp.; Mount Vernon; religious organization 1,200

Fairfax County; Fairfax; public schools 1,200

U.S. Bureau of Customs and Border Protection; Springfield 1,200

AT&T Corp.; Vienna; telephone equipment 1,000

Verizon Services Corp.; Oakton; telephones 1,000

Potomac Hospital Corp. of Prince William; Woodbridge 922

Kaiser Engineers Group Inc.; Fairfax; dams, waterways, docks 910

ICF Consulting Group Holdings; Fairfax; management consulting 900

Cavalier Maintenance Services Inc.; Fairfax; building maintenance 850

Potomac District Council of Assemblies of God; Fairfax; religious organization 813

BTG Inc.; Fairfax; computer software 800

Dewberry and Davis; Fairfax; consulting engineer 800

District of Columbia Dept. of Corrections; Lorton 800

Lockheed Martin Corp.; Fairfax; aircraft 800

Atlantic Research Corp.; Gainesville; missile, rocket engines 700

Paxton Van Lines Inc.; Springfield; local trucking, storage 700

Computer Sciences Corp.; Falls Church; computer-aided design systems 675

GRC International Inc.; Vienna; systems analysis or design 650

Anteon International Corp.; Fairfax; computer maintenance 646

Tech Enterprises Inc.; Fairfax; typesetting 600

Rodgers Co.; Gainesville; building site preparation 550

Fairfax County; Fairfax; sheriff's office 500

Life With Cancer Family Center; Merrifield 500

Lockheed Martin Corp.; Springfield; missiles and space vehicles 500

MCI WorldCom Network Services Inc.; Fairfax; long-distance telephone 500

Teligent Inc.; Fairfax; radiotelephone communication 500

US Food Service; Manassas; food services 500

WASHINGTON

Districts established January 1, 2002, for elections first held in 2002.

9 members

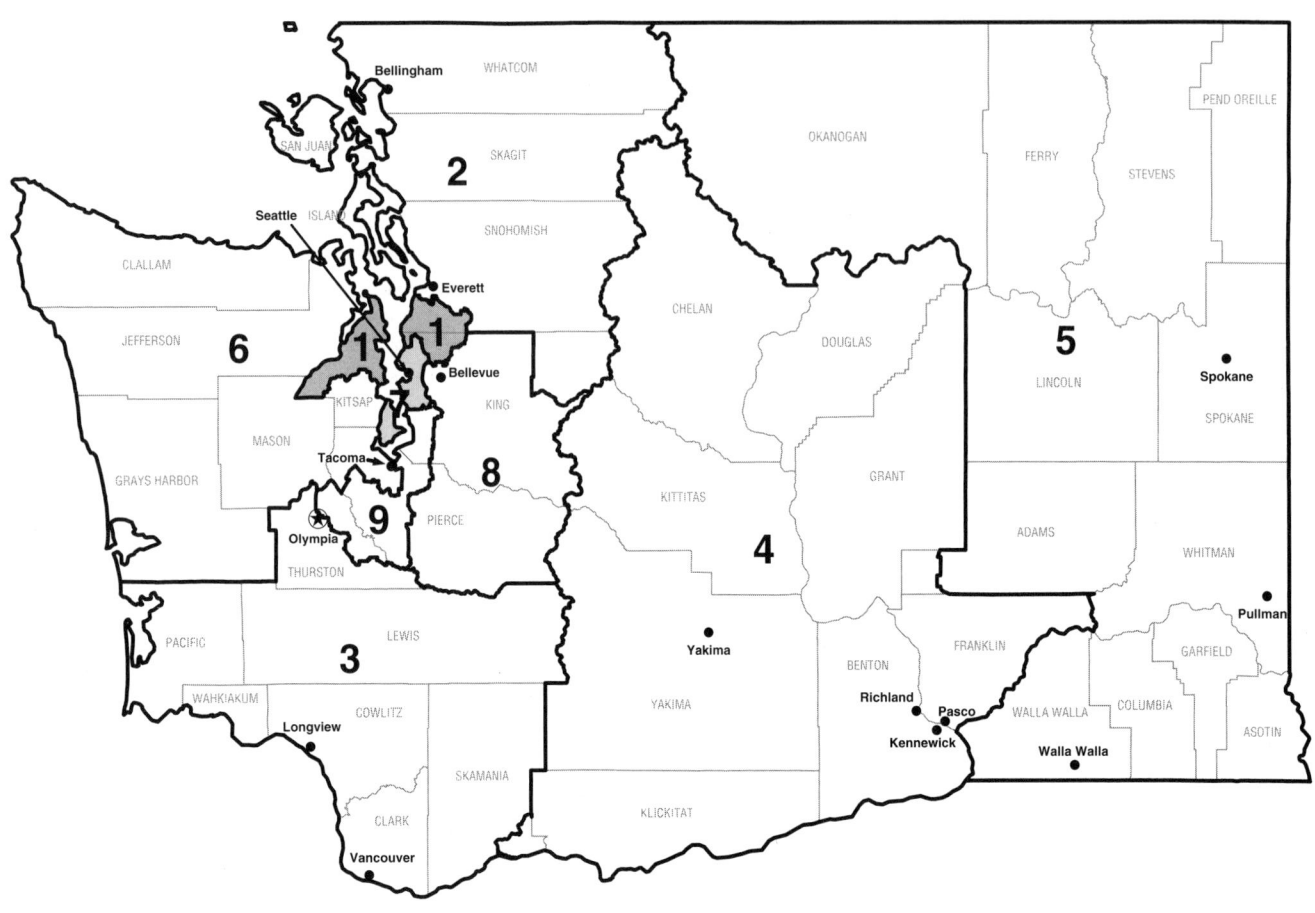

Washington

As with much of the West, Washington state was built largely on agriculture and the extraction industries: mining and timber. These economic bases were subject to classic boom and bust cycles, sometimes quite severe. For a century, the state's economic and political leaders tried to escape the tyranny of these cycles. They made Puget Sound a great seaport, one of the first fully converted to containerized cargo. Shipping, shipbuilding, and the servicing of Navy vessels thrived from Bremerton around the southern end of the Sound at Tacoma and on up the eastern side through Seattle and north to Everett and beyond. They also made the metro area a manufacturing center through Boeing, the world's biggest aircraft maker and America's biggest exporting company—a source of quality jobs and community pride for generations.

But state leaders really thought they had finessed the cycles when Washington became the world capital of something called software. Bill Gates, a native son, developed an operating system for computers just as computer manufacturers were making them small enough and cheap enough for the home. Gates and his firm, Microsoft, became the wellspring not only of a new industry but of a new economy. Gates became the world's richest man. His top lieutenants became billionaires in their own right, buying sports franchises and building stadiums for them to play in. Thousands of software spin-offs and related vendors sprang up in the Seattle area (as well as worldwide), especially after the Internet emerged in the 1990s. In the ensuing welter of dot-com businesses, the quintessential winner was a Web site called Amazon.com, which sold books, and later much else also. The company, too, was based in Seattle.

In this "new economy," Washington had it all: high-paying jobs, limitless future, capital formation in soaring stock prices, community reinvestment, and minimal pollution. Moreover, it seemed immune to the old cycle of boom and bust. Some observers said the popular perception of a bust-proof new economy was the best sign that a bust was coming. When the bust came in spring 2000, the stock markets that had previously pounced on any new dot-com were no longer content to wait for promised profit. Computer sales slumped. The new economy was suddenly just the shiny part of the old one, and the laws of gravity had not been repealed.

The story was familiar. The other industries that had been built up to smooth out the cycle had not been immune to it either. The ports of Seattle and Tacoma, among the world's busiest in recent decades, have seen their business fall off with downturns in Asian business and global trade. The Navy has shifted its reliance to its main Pacific base in San Diego. The weakening of the airline industry after the September 2001 terrorist attacks has again brought cutbacks at Boeing—an echo of the years after Vietnam and the cold war. (At one point in the 1970s, signs around town asked, "Will the last person leaving Seattle please turn out the lights?")

The trends after 2000 coincided with a period of pronounced weakness in the traditional industries (mining, timber, and agriculture), which are suffering from soft demand, world competition, and price depression. So Washington state, after a decade as an international success story, actually had the lowest rate of employment and the highest rate of unemployment in the country at the time of the 2000 census.

It should be said, however, that Puget Sound and the state as a whole continue to grow in population—if not quite as fast as once expected. Where jobs can be found, the wages are good (second highest in the nation), contributing to the state's high standing in average annual pay (eighth) and per capita income (eleventh). Also, something about the up-and-down economy seems to inform and express what is life in the West, especially on the Pacific Coast itself. Those who come here to live are often risk takers (the state was first in the nation in new company startups in 2000), and those who stick it out through the bad patches are often rewarded over time. Surely that is true of those who have wagered on real estate in the Puget Sound area over time. This metro area has bounded forward to vie with Atlanta, Miami, and Phoenix to see which will enter the top ten metro areas list in the years after 2000. Housing costs have gotten so high here in recent years that home ownership rates have plunged (only eight states have higher percentages of renters).

It was against this variegated backdrop that the state held pivotal elections in the year 2000. Washington had been trending Democratic for more than a decade, largely on issues of social and economic freedom (the state GOP had taken some strikingly conservative positions on these issues in the 1980s and 1990s). But in 2000 the social agenda was joined to economic insecurity, with potent results. The state went for Al Gore, who carried six of its nine congressional districts and held Ralph Nader to 4 percent in a state the Green Party had targeted. This fourth consecutive victory for the Democrats was the first such string in the state since the era of Franklin D. Roosevelt and Harry S. Truman, and it reversed a skein of four GOP victories from 1972 through 1984.

Washington state in 2000 also elected a second Democratic woman senator in Maria Cantwell, who joined Patty Murray (first elected 1992), reelected its Democratic governor, Gary Locke, the first Asian American governor on the mainland, and awarded six of its nine congressional seats to Democrats. The results of this watershed election were generally confirmed in 2002, when the state reelected the same nine House members and kept the legislature divided almost perfectly balanced between the parties.

Cantwell, who won by one-tenth of 1 percent, was making a comeback in a career that illustrates the switchbacks in the state's recent congressional voting. She had first been elected to Congress from the suburban 1st District in 1992, winning a traditionally Republican seat in a year when Democrats captured eight of the nine. Two years later, in a backlash election nationally and locally, Democrats shed six of its seats in the state and Cantwell's was one of them. Through the rest of the decade the Democrats slowly recovered, reclaiming one of the lost seats in 1996, two in 1998, one more in 2000. In the meantime, Cantwell had worked for a startup computer software firm and cashed in some of her stock to finance a challenge to incumbent Republican Slade Gorton in 2000.

Gorton's career had been a measure of change in the state and in the Senate. He made history by defeating the legendary six-term Democrat Warren G. Magnuson in 1980, becoming the first Republican to win a Senate election in the state since the early 1940s. Defeated for reelection in 1986, Gorton was back in 1988, winning the seat that had once belonged to the influential Democrat Henry "Scoop" Jackson, who died in 1983.

The Murray-Cantwell combination is the first Democratic brace of senators since Jackson worked in tandem with Magnuson through more than three decades of political and legislative success. They remembered the state's early history of confrontational left-labor politics, of Scandinavian immigrants and others who had fought the "timber bosses." Between them, Maggie and Scoop, as they were popularly known, won a dozen Senate elections from 1944 through 1982. But far from being firebrands, they were committee-and-cloakroom operators of the first order. Chairing such committees as Appropriations, Commerce, Interior, and Energy, they did everything they could for labor and cheap hydropower electricity (essential to aluminum making and therefore to Boeing), continuing the tradition of the Columbia River dams such as the Grand Coulee, built in the Roosevelt years.

But in the 1980s, Ronald Reagan and a Republican Senate set a different course. Gorton and Evans, moderates by standards of the day, did what they could for the state's industries while addressing high taxes and regulations, raising the priority of "sagebrush rebellion" issues popular among the state's more rural voters, who live in the farm and range lands east of the Cascade Mountains. This is typically the agenda for the three districts in the state that are not dominated by the Puget Sound metro area. The first is the southwestern 3rd, which begins at the state capital of Olympia (south of Tacoma) and extends south to the city of Vancouver on the Oregon line while also running west all the way to the Pacific. This is the home of the timber industry in the state and remains depressed by weakened demand and environmental conflicts that wind up in court.

Further inland is the mountainous central 4th, with Yakima at its center and a strong Republican bent throughout (62 percent for George W. Bush in 2000, by far his best

showing in the state). The 4th is loyally Republican, as befits a largely rural and agricultural district. The district has by far the largest Hispanic presence in the state (more than one-fourth its population), but so few of the Hispanic residents vote that they have relatively little political impact. The state's easternmost third is the 5th District, where the population center of Spokane has continued to grow (10 percent in the 1990s), in part because it is the largest city on the road due east from Seattle until one reaches Minneapolis. Spokane is a classic western wheat-stacking, meatpacking town that has grown to nearly 200,000 people (passing Tacoma as the state's second largest city).

Although Washington's population rose 21 percent in the 1990s, the state did not receive a new congressional seat in 2000 (as it had in the reapportionments of 1980 and 1990). All nine incumbents were seeking reelection, and there were few issues of race to consider. (The state's African American population is 3 percent, far below the national average of 12 percent; while Hispanics, at 7 percent, are at little more than half their national proportion. Asians are 5 percent of the state, substantially higher than their 4 percent share nationwide.) So it was not surprising that the state's four-member redistricting commission, which had drawn the lines after 1980 and 1990, failed to reach a compromise. Commission Republicans wanted to redress imbalance between the raw vote statewide and seats won in recent House elections (Democrats had been getting a little more than half the vote and holding six of the nine seats). The GOP has also been especially vexed to see the southwestern 3rd District (which voted for George W. Bush) elect a Democrat, along with the northwestern 2nd District (which nearly went for Bush).

So they tried to remove parts of Olympia, the state capital near Tacoma, from the 3rd District, which has been Democratic since 1998 and extends south to the Oregon line and west to the Pacific. They also tried to move the Democratic city of Everett from the 2nd to the 1st District, making life easier for the Democratic incumbent in the 1st but harder for his colleague in the 2nd District further north. They also tried to move some of the 9th District's Democrats in Tacoma, where they sustain an incumbent in a marginal district, westward into the safer Democratic venue of the 6th. But when the commission was deadlocked, the decision went to the state supreme court, which did what many judicial authorities did in the redistricting cycle after 2000. It tinkered at the margins to balance the population between the districts and preserved the partisan status quo.

Table 1 Population

District	Population	Population under 18	Voting-age population	Median age	Male*	Female*
1	654,904	167,003	487,901	36.0	49.7	50.3
2	654,903	173,132	481,771	35.2	49.9	50.1
3	654,898	177,768	477,130	35.8	49.6	50.4
4	654,901	199,289	455,612	32.5	50.2	49.8
5	654,904	166,779	488,125	35.6	49.4	50.6
6	654,902	163,840	491,062	37.0	49.3	50.7
7	654,902	111,426	543,476	35.5	49.9	50.1
8	654,905	181,998	472,907	35.8	50.0	50.0
9	654,902	172,608	482,294	34.1	50.1	49.9
State	5,894,121	1,513,843	4,380,278	35.3	49.8	50.2

*As percentage of total population.

Table 2　Voting-Age Persons by Race/Hispanic or Latino Origin

District	White*	Black or African American*	American Indian or Alaska Native*	Asian*	Other or multirace*	Hispanic or Latino*
1	83.3	1.7	0.8	8.3	2.2	3.8
2	87.7	1.0	1.6	3.0	1.9	4.7
3	89.6	1.1	1.0	2.8	1.9	3.7
4	73.4	0.8	1.8	1.4	1.5	21.1
5	89.4	1.2	2.0	2.0	1.8	3.6
6	80.9	5.0	2.0	5.0	2.9	4.1
7	70.4	7.3	0.9	13.2	3.2	5.0
8	83.6	1.8	0.8	8.3	2.1	3.5
9	76.4	5.7	1.1	8.1	3.0	5.7
State	81.5	2.9	1.3	5.9	2.3	6.0

*As percentage of voting-age population.

Table 3　Voting-Age Population by Age Groups

District	18 to 24*	25 to 44*	45 to 64*	Over 64*
1	11.0	43.9	32.3	12.8
2	13.5	40.3	30.5	15.7
3	11.7	40.0	32.6	15.7
4	14.2	39.5	30.2	16.1
5	15.2	36.9	30.5	17.3
6	12.5	37.6	31.3	18.6
7	13.7	45.3	26.8	14.3
8	9.8	45.5	32.7	12.2
9	13.2	43.8	29.5	13.5
State	12.8	41.5	30.7	15.1

*As percentage of voting-age population.

Table 4　Income and Occupation

District	Median family income	Families in poverty*	White collar†	Blue collar†	Service†	Farm†
1	$67,249	3.8	69.4	18.0	12.3	0.3
2	$52,617	6.6	55.1	27.6	15.7	1.6
3	$51,005	7.7	57.0	26.8	14.9	1.4
4	$43,603	12.0	52.8	23.7	15.8	7.7
5	$44,161	9.6	60.0	21.1	17.2	1.7
6	$46,156	9.5	54.8	25.3	18.5	1.4
7	$60,614	7.0	70.9	14.7	14.1	0.3
8	$71,459	3.5	68.6	19.7	11.4	0.3
9	$53,190	6.7	59.4	24.7	15.5	0.4
State	$53,760	7.3	61.4	22.1	14.9	1.6

*As percentage of all families.　　†As percentage of employed workers 16 years and over.

Table 5　Education: School Years Completed

District	Less than grade 9*	Grades 9–12 no diploma*	High school diploma no college*	Some college*	College bachelor's degree or higher*
1	1.8	5.4	20.1	36.2	36.4
2	3.5	9.2	27.4	37.4	22.4
3	3.5	10.1	28.1	36.9	21.4
4	12.6	12.2	26.7	29.7	18.7
5	3.9	9.0	27.5	35.8	23.8
6	3.9	10.4	29.4	36.2	20.1
7	4.6	6.9	16.8	27.6	44.1
8	2.2	5.7	21.7	33.1	37.4
9	3.5	9.1	27.8	37.4	22.3
State	4.3	8.6	24.9	34.4	27.7

*As percentage of persons age 25 and over.

Table 6　Housing and Residential Patterns

District	Median home value	Owner occupied*	Renter occupied*	Urban†	Rural†
1	$217,800	67.9	32.1	95.4	4.6
2	$165,300	67.2	32.8	69.4	30.6
3	$142,400	68.0	32.0	70.9	29.1
4	$111,800	66.0	34.0	70.5	29.5
5	$107,700	66.0	34.0	71.9	28.1
6	$127,700	63.5	36.5	78.8	21.2
7	$237,400	50.6	49.4	98.5	1.5
8	$221,700	75.6	24.4	87.6	12.4
9	$152,300	59.5	40.5	95.0	5.0
State	$158,800	64.6	35.4	82.0	18.0

*As percentage of occupied housing units.　　†As percentage of total population.

Washington 1st District

Puget Sound (west and east) — north Seattle suburbs

The technology boom, though dulled in recent years, continues to drive growth in the suburban 1st. Microsoft's main Redmond campus, which is just over the district line in the 8th, is the best known of many technology and biotechnology companies in the region. Suburban areas around Lake Washington and Puget Sound have continued to expand, with many of the "Microsoft millionaires" moving into the crescent north of Seattle. *(See map p. 960.)*

Military bases spur the economy on the west side of Puget Sound, but the high-tech companies—especially along Interstate 405—and home buyers in Seattle's first ring of suburbs are what have attracted newcomers. More than 80 percent of the district's population is on the east side of Puget Sound, in King and Snohomish Counties. Redistricting in 2002 gave the 1st a greater share of Snohomish, including a small part of Everett and most of Monroe, and a smaller share of King. The 1st was given a smaller share of Seattle.

Democrats have the edge in the district, with its well-educated, socially liberal professionals. The Snohomish portion is probably the most politically competitive of the three counties; the King and Kitsap portions are slightly more Democratic.

Major Industry
Software, military, aviation.

Notable
Bainbridge Island is a 35-minute ferry ride from downtown Seattle; the city of Lynnwood hosts an annual Trolley Days Festival; Mill Creek is a master-planned community, complete with a new high school, middle school, and 18-hole golf course; Poulsbo is home to the annual Scandinavian celebration Viking Fest.

Election Returns

	Republican		Democratic		Other	
President 2000	123,879	42.4%	154,583	52.9%	13,803	4.7%
House 2002	84,696	41.3%	114,087	55.6%	6,251	3.0%

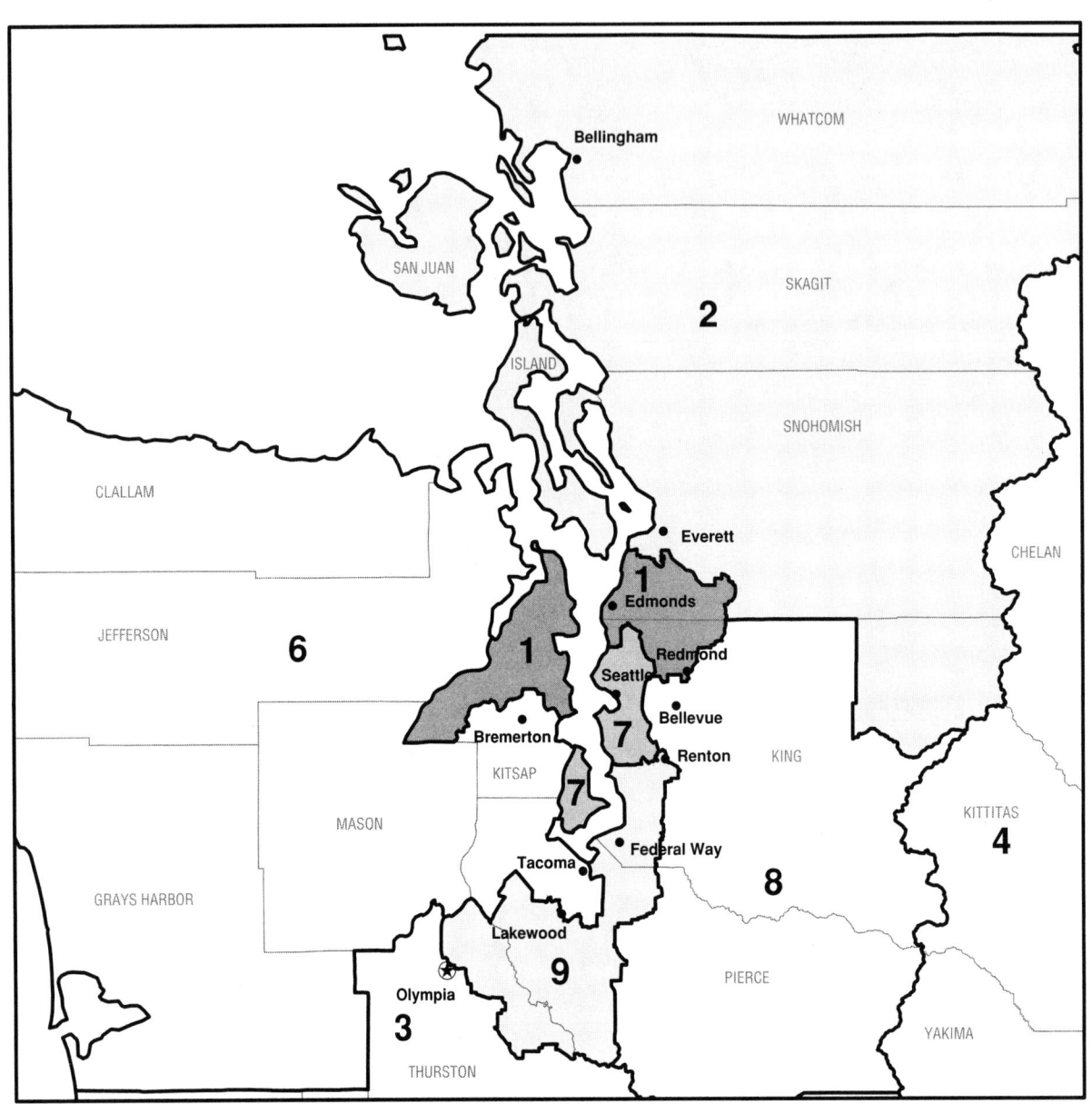

Population 654,904

Total area (square miles) 616.4
  Land area (square miles) 439.2

Population per square mile 1,491.1

Counties (2000 population)
  King (pt.)   238,531
  Kitsap (pt.)   109,184
  Snohomish (pt.)   307,189

Cities and other areas over 10,000 (2000 population)
  Alderwood Manor CDP   15,329
  Bainbridge Island   20,308
  Bothell   30,150
  Cottage Lake CDP   24,330
  Edmonds   39,515
  Inglewood-Finn Hill CDP   22,661
  Kenmore   18,678
  Kingsgate CDP   12,222
  Kirkland (pt.)   44,406
  Lynnwood   33,847
  Martha Lake CDP   12,633
  Mill Creek   11,525
  Mountlake Terrace   20,362
  Mukilteo (pt.)   13,174
  North Creek CDP   25,742
  Paine Field-Lake Stickney CDP (pt.)   23,334
  Picnic Point-North Lynnwood CDP   22,953
  Redmond (pt.)   34,759
  Seattle (pt.)   10,540
  Seattle Hill-Silver Firs CDP   35,311
  Shoreline (pt.)   35,694
  Silverdale CDP   15,816

Race and Hispanic or Latino origin*
  White   81.6%
  Black or African American   1.8%
  American Indian or Alaska Native   0.8%
  Asian   7.9%
  Native Hawaiian or other Pacific Islander   0.3%
  Some other race   0.2%
  Hispanic or Latino origin   4.3%
  Two or more races   3.1%

*As percentage of total population.

Ancestry*

Dutch	1.6%	Norwegian	5.6%
English	10.0%	Polish	1.4%
French	2.7%	Scotch-Irish	1.6%
German	13.6%	Scottish	2.6%
Irish	8.7%	Swedish	3.2%
Italian	2.6%	USA/American	3.2%

*As estimated percentage of total population.

Universities and colleges, 2000–2001 enrollment
  Bastyr University, Kenmore   1,075
  Edmonds Community College, Lynnwood   8,094
  ITT Technical Institute, Bothell   252
  Lake Washington Technical College, Kirkland   3,917
  Northwest College of the Assemblies of God, Kirkland   1,039
  Shoreline Community College, Seattle   6,600
  University of Washington, Bothell   1,422

Newspapers and circulation

	District circulation	Total circulation
Bremerton Sun	1,124	31,988
Eastside Business Journal	7,722	26,435
Everett Herald	6,708	50,880
Seattle Post-Intelligencer	47,222	222,671
Seattle Times/Post-Intelligencer (Sunday)	141,193	753,860
*USA Today**	1,274	1,674,376

*See Sources and Explanations in the front of the volume.

Television stations and affiliations

Seattle-Tacoma	100%
Seattle-Tacoma	100%
Seattle-Tacoma	100%
Seattle-Tacoma	100%
Seattle-Tacoma	100%
Seattle-Tacoma	100%
Seattle-Tacoma	100%
Seattle-Tacoma	100%
Seattle-Tacoma	100%
Seattle-Tacoma	100%
Seattle-Tacoma	100%
Seattle-Tacoma	100%
Seattle-Tacoma	100%
Seattle-Tacoma	100%
Seattle-Tacoma	100%
Seattle-Tacoma	100%

Cable systems and subscribers
  Charter   7,573
  Comcast   100,348
  Northland   6,573

Military installations, September 2001
  Bangor Naval Submarine Base, Bangor   4,273
  Naval Undersea Warfare Engineering Station, Keyport   1,575
  Joe R. Hooper U.S. Army Reserve Center, Bothell   194

Businesses and other major employers
  United Parcel Service Inc.; Kirkland; parcel delivery   5,000
  Warehouse Demo Service Inc.; Kirkland; demonstration service   4,000
  King County Public Hospital District; Kirkland   2,600
  Advanced Technology Laboratories Inc.; Bothell; medical equipment   2,500
  Premera Blue Cross Blue Shield; Mountlake Terrace; medical service plans   2,100
  AT&T Wireless Services Inc.; Redmond; cellular telephones   2,000
  Boeing Co.; Lynnwood; aircraft parts, equipment   2,000
  Emerald City Pizza; Lynnwood; restaurants   1,800
  Philips Medical Systems North America Inc.; Bothell; x-ray machines and tubes   1,525
  Shoreline School District; Seattle   1,400
  Public Hospital District Snohomish County; Edmonds   1,280
  Edmonds Community College; Lynnwood   1,182

Everett Clinic; Mukilteo   1,000
Washington Dept. of Corrections; Monroe   1,000
Crista Ministries; Seattle; individual, family services
  900
Spacelabs Medical Inc.; Redmond; patient monitoring
  apparatus   900
Nintendo of America Inc.; Redmond; video games   855
Washington Superintendent of Public Instruction;
  Seattle   850
General Dynamics Ordnance and Tactical Systems Inc.;
  Redmond; ammunition   809
Allstate Insurance Co.; Bothell; insurance   800
ELDEC Corp.; Lynnwood; search and navigation   800
Johnson Controls World Services Inc.; Silverdale;
  management services   800
Matsushita Avionics Systems Corp.; Bothell;
  transportation equipment   800
Washington Dept. of Transportation; Seattle   800
Safeco Life Insurance Co.; Redmond   750
Holmes-Hally Industries; Kirkland; masonry/stonework
  749
Medtronic Physio-Control Corp.; Redmond;
  electromedical apparatus   600
Mackie Designs Inc.; Woodinville; audio/video
  equipment   585
Bastyr University; Kenmore   535
National Energy Production Corp.; Bothell; power plant
  construction   530
Coca-Cola Co.; Bothell; soft drinks   500
Oracle Corp.; Woodinville; software and accessories
  500
Precor Inc.; Woodinville; exercise equipment   500
Siemens Business Services Inc.; Redmond; computer
  maintenance   500

Washington 2nd District

Puget Sound — Bellingham, most of Everett

West of the Cascade Mountains, in the northwest corner of the state, the 2nd covers an area that is mostly rural in its topography and moderate in its politics. Most of the district's population lives along Interstate 5, a technology corridor that runs up the state's coast, while the rural areas just west of the mountains provide residents with open expanses of land, much of it national forest. Between lies a fertile agricultural plain. *(See map p. 960.)*

Aspects of the district's economy that were dependent on natural resources—logging, farming, and paper production—have continued to decline. But the technology explosion in the 1980s and 1990s helped grow the economy and population. Thousands of Boeing employees work at the company's plant in Everett, but to the east, the district has struggled to find well-paying jobs for those formerly employed in farming and logging. The area seeks to diversify, though technology companies have made inroads as far north as Bellingham.

Traffic congestion into the Seattle area has become such a problem that it is often faster to drive from northern parts of the district into Everett than from Everett south to Seattle. These northwestern areas are home to many retirees who leave Seattle; San Juan County, a collection of islands southwest of

Bellingham, has the highest median age in the state (47 years). At the northern border, beefed-up security has slowed trade to Canada.

The 2nd is highly competitive. The western urban centers of Everett in the south and Bellingham in the north are liberal, while the eastern rural sections lean conservative. Al Gore narrowly won the 2nd in 2000.

Major Industry
Aviation, computer software, shipping.

Notable
Skagit County, home to the world's largest tulip fields, hosts a tulip festival every April; the San Juan Islands are known for their funky, liberal residents, including musician Steve Miller.

Election Returns

	Republican		Democratic		Other	
President 2000	129,027	46.2%	133,216	47.7%	16,765	6.0%
House 2002	92,528	45.8%	101,219	50.1%	8,403	4.2%

District Profile

Population   654,903

Total area (square miles)   7,976.4
  Land area (square miles)   6,564.3

Population per square mile   99.8

Counties (2000 population)
Island 71,558	Skagit 102,979
King (pt.) 640	Snohomish (pt.) 298,835
San Juan 14,077	Whatcom 166,814

Cities and other areas over 10,000 (2000 population)
Anacortes   14,557
Arlington   11,713
Bellingham   67,171
Camano CDP   13,347
Everett (pt.)   87,329
Marysville   25,315
Mount Vernon   26,232
North Marysville CDP   21,161
Oak Harbor   19,795
West Lake Stevens CDP   18,071

Race and Hispanic or Latino origin*
White   85.6%
Black or African American   1.1%
American Indian or Alaska Native   1.9%
Asian   2.8%
Native Hawaiian or other Pacific Islander   0.2%
Some other race   0.2%
Hispanic or Latino origin   5.8%
Two or more races   2.4%

As percentage of total population.

Ancestry*
Dutch 3.3%	German 13.7%
English 9.2%	Irish 8.4%
French 2.7%	Italian 2.2%

Norwegian	6.1%	Scottish	2.6%
Polish	1.1%	Swedish	3.2%
Scotch-Irish	1.8%	USA/American	4.0%

*As estimated percentage of total population.

Universities and colleges, 2000–2001 enrollment

Bellingham Technical College, Bellingham 3,682
Everett Community College, Everett 6,102
Henry Cogswell College, Everett 249
Northwest Indian College, Bellingham 524
Skagit Valley College, Mount Vernon 5,488
Western Washington University, Bellingham 12,307
Whatcom Community College, Bellingham 3,832

Newspapers and circulation

	District circulation	Total circulation
*Bellingham Herald**	24,245	24,245
*Mount Vernon Skagit Valley Herald**	19,294	19,332
*USA Today**	5,934	1,674,376
*Wenatchee World**	13,148	24,906

*See Sources and Explanations in the front of the volume.

Television stations and affiliations

Seattle-Tacoma	100%	KBCB	Independent
Seattle-Tacoma	100%	KBTC	PBS
Seattle-Tacoma	100%	KCKA	PBS
Seattle-Tacoma	100%	KCPQ	FOX
Seattle-Tacoma	100%	KCTS	PBS
Seattle-Tacoma	100%	KHCV	Independent
Seattle-Tacoma	100%	KING	NBC
Seattle-Tacoma	100%	KIRO	CBS
Seattle-Tacoma	100%	KOMO	ABC
Seattle-Tacoma	100%	KONG	Independent
Seattle-Tacoma	100%	KSTW	UPN
Seattle-Tacoma	100%	KTBW	Independent
Seattle-Tacoma	100%	KTWB	WB
Seattle-Tacoma	100%	KVOS	Independent
Seattle-Tacoma	100%	KWPX	PAX

Cable systems and subscribers

Adelphia 1,090
Comcast 147,392
Delta Cablevision 900
Millennium Digital Media 1,764
Northland 1,024

Military installations, September 2001

Whidbey Island Naval Air Station, Oak Harbor 8,819

Businesses and other major employers

Intermec International Inc.; Everett; computer peripheral equipment 3,000
Fluke Electronics Corp.; Everett; electronic test equipment 1,500
Verizon Northwest Inc.; Everett; telephone communication 1,500
Snohomish County; Everett; county government 1,440
Kimberly-Clark Corp.; Everett; pulp wood 1,275
Intalco Aluminum Corp.; Ferndale; primary aluminum 1,180
St. Joseph Hospital; Bellingham 1,100
Public Hospital District Skagit County; Mount Vernon 1,072

Billingham School District; Bellingham 1,000
Washington Dept. of Labor and Industries; Everett 1,000
Mukilteo School District; Everett 876
Austin Co.; Everett; industrial buildings construction 800
Tulalip Casino Inc.; Marysville 800
Skagit County; Mount Vernon; county commissioner 780
Whatcom County; Bellingham; county government 507
Draper Valley Farms Inc.; Mount Vernon; poultry processing 500
Marriott International Inc.; Bellingham; contract food services 500
Skagit Valley Casino; Bow; casino hotel 500

Washington 3rd District

Southwest — Vancouver, most of Olympia

The 3rd is an eclectic, politically competitive district in southwest Washington that scoops up liberals in the state capital of Olympia and suburbanites in Vancouver, which is just across the Columbia River from Portland, Oregon. Joining the two cities and bifurcating the district is Interstate 5, west and east of which lies considerable rural territory.

The district's population center is Clark County (Vancouver), where 54 percent of the 3rd's residents live. Clark's population grew 45 percent in the 1990s, as Portland residents flocked across the river to buy cheaper land. Trees and farmland are being cleared to make way for suburban developments, and voters have demanded infrastructure improvements to relieve traffic congestion and school overcrowding.

The 3rd still has vast stretches of woodlands, including the scenic Coastal Range and much of the Cascade Mountains, with Mount Rainier just outside the district's borders in the 8th. Though the timber trade has declined in the Cascade Mountains in the east, the western part of the district still sustains hearty logging. Many former timber workers have transferred to the technology sector.

Clark, like the district at large, is politically competitive. The Democratic vote in Vancouver is offset by Republican strength outside the city, in areas such as Battle Ground, Yacolt, and La Center. George W. Bush and Sen. Slade Gorton narrowly won Clark in 2000, even as they lost statewide.

Thurston County, which includes Olympia, is more favorable to Democrats. A redistricting commission in 2002 gave about one-sixth of the capital city to the 9th District. Of the other counties in the 3rd, Lewis is strongly Republican and Cowlitz and Pacific vote Democratic, though Bush substantially narrowed the big vote margins Bill Clinton enjoyed.

Major Industry

Timber, mining, computer hardware.

Notable

Mount St. Helens erupted May 18, 1980, killing 57 people and destroying enough lumber for 300,000 two-bedroom homes; Lewis and Clark used the Columbia River, the 3rd's southern boundary, to reach the Pacific Ocean in 1805.

Election Returns

	Republican		Democratic		Other	
President 2000	131,958	48.0%	127,292	46.3%	15,732	5.7%
House 2002	74,065	38.3%	119,264	61.7%		

District Profile

Population   654,898

Total area (square miles)   7,960.5
   Land area (square miles)   7,515.3

Population per square mile   87.1

Counties (2000 population)

Clark 345,238	Skamania (pt.) 7,015
Cowlitz 92,948	Thurston (pt.) 116,289
Lewis 68,600	Wahkiakum 3,824
Pacific 20,984	

Cities and other areas over 10,000 (2000 population)

Camas   12,534
Centralia   14,742
Five Corners CDP   12,207
Kelso   11,895
Longview   34,660
Olympia (pt.)   35,230
Orchards CDP   17,852
Salmon Creek CDP   16,767
Tumwater   12,698
Vancouver   143,560

Race and Hispanic or Latino origin*

White   87.7%
Black or African American   1.2%
American Indian or Alaska Native   1.0%
Asian   2.6%
Native Hawaiian or other Pacific Islander   0.3%
Some other race   0.1%
Hispanic or Latino origin   4.6%
Two or more races   2.5%

*As percentage of total population.

Ancestry*

Dutch 1.7%	Norwegian 4.1%
English 8.9%	Polish 1.3%
Finnish 1.2%	Scotch-Irish 1.6%
French 2.7%	Scottish 2.1%
German 14.3%	Swedish 2.6%
Irish 8.3%	USA/American 5.0%
Italian 2.1%	

*As estimated percentage of total population.

Universities and colleges, 2000–2001 enrollment

Business Computer Training Institute, Vancouver   210
Centralia College, Centralia   3,063
Clark College, Vancouver   8,241
Evergreen State College, Olympia   4,125
Lower Columbia College, Longview   3,248
South Puget Sound Community College, Olympia   4,442
Western Business College, Vancouver   215

Newspapers and circulation

	District circulation	Total circulation
*Aberdeen Daily World**	1,392	15,402
*Centralia Chronicle**	13,251	13,710
*Olympia Olympian**	26,343	38,197
*USA Today**	2,224	1,674,376

*See Sources and Explanations in the front of the volume.

Television stations and affiliations

Seattle-Tacoma	54%	KBCB	Independent
Seattle-Tacoma	54%	KBTC	PBS
Seattle-Tacoma	54%	KCKA	PBS
Seattle-Tacoma	54%	KCPQ	FOX
Seattle-Tacoma	54%	KCTS	PBS
Seattle-Tacoma	54%	KHCV	Independent
Seattle-Tacoma	54%	KING	NBC
Seattle-Tacoma	54%	KIRO	CBS
Seattle-Tacoma	54%	KOMO	ABC
Seattle-Tacoma	54%	KONG	Independent
Seattle-Tacoma	54%	KSTW	UPN
Seattle-Tacoma	54%	KTBW	Independent
Seattle-Tacoma	54%	KTWB	WB
Seattle-Tacoma	54%	KVOS	Independent
Seattle-Tacoma	54%	KWPX	PAX
Portland, OR	46%	KATU	ABC
Portland, OR	46%	KGW	NBC
Portland, OR	46%	KNMT	Independent
Portland, OR	46%	KOIN	CBS
Portland, OR	46%	KOPB	PBS
Portland, OR	46%	KPDX	UPN
Portland, OR	46%	KPTV	FOX
Portland, OR	46%	KPXG	PAX
Portland, OR	46%	KTVR	PBS
Portland, OR	46%	KWBP	WB

Cable systems and subscribers

Adelphia   17,031
Charter   3,042
Comcast   107,433
Computel Cablevision   2,015
Mikes TV   749
Millennium Digital Media   2,749
RGA Cable   4,688

Military installations, September 2001

Vancouver Barracks (Army Reserve), Vancouver   907

Businesses and other major employers

Southwest Washington Medical Center; Vancouver   3,000
Washington Dept. of Employment Security; Olympia   2,500
Longview Fibre Co.; Longview; corrugated boxes   2,100
Pet Break; Vancouver; pets, pet supplies   1,991
Portland Adventist Medical Center; Vancouver   1,800
Shin-Etsu Handotai America Inc.; Vancouver; wafers (semiconductor devices)   1,690
Washington Dept. of Labor and Industries; Tumwater   1,675
St. John Medical Center; Longview   1,600

Liquor Control Board Washington State; Olympia
1,500
U.S. Dept. of Energy; Vancouver   1,400
Washington Dept. of Licensing; Olympia   1,200
Washington Dept. of Natural Resources; Olympia
1,200
Washington Fish and Wildlife Dept.; Olympia   1,100
Georgia-Pacific Resins Inc.; Skamokawa; paper mills
1,100
Sea Mar Dental Clinic; Olympia   1,000
Washington Dept. of Social and Health Services;
Olympia   1,000
Weyerhaeuser Co.; Longview; railroad freight hauling
1,000
WaferTech; Camas; semiconductor circuit networks
920
Hewlett-Packard Co.; Vancouver; printers, computers
850
TransAlta Centralia Mining; Centralia; mining services
800
Fosters Poultry Farms; Kelso; poultry, poultry products
800
Providence Centralia Hospital; Centralia   731
Washington Dept. of Social and Health Services;
Olympia   700
Washington Dept. of Transportation; Olympia   700
Washington General Admin. Dept.; Olympia   700
Goldendale Aluminum Corp.; Vancouver; primary
aluminum   700
Bonneville Power Admin.; Vancouver; electric services
700
Clark College; Vancouver   700
Vanalco Inc.; Vancouver; primary aluminum   680
Frito-Lay Inc.; Vancouver; snacks   600
GST Telecom Inc.; Vancouver; telephone communication
600
American Medical Response Inc.; Vancouver; ambulance
service   600
Columbia Lower College; Longview   580
Evergreen State College; Olympia   550
Lucky Eagle Casino; Rochester   550
Clark County; Vancouver; county government   550
Matsushita Kotobuki Electronic Industries of America
Inc.; Vancouver; video recorders   526
Cowlitz County; Kelso; county government   525
North Pacific Paper Corp.; Longview; newsprint paper
524
U.S. Veterans Hospital; Vancouver   520
Vancouver Clinic Inc.; Vancouver   500

Washington 4th District

Central — Yakima and Tri-Cities

Lying just east of the Cascade Mountains, the 4th covers a
huge swath of central Washington that includes the Yakima
Valley, known as the fruit bowl of the Northwest, and the
Tri-Cities area, which is home to the Hanford Nuclear Reservation.

Yakima County is the district's largest, both in land area
and population. To the east and south is Benton County,
which takes in the district's other population center, the Tri-

Cities of Pasco, Kennewick, and Richland on the Columbia
River.

Heavily irrigated agriculture drives the district, which
contains an older irrigation area in the Yakima Valley, full of
apple orchards and the world's largest producer of hops. It
also includes the Columbia Basin project, fed by the Grand
Coulee Dam, which has bred hundreds of wineries and potato,
corn, and fruit farms.

Many of these agricultural areas have attracted large Hispanic populations. Mattawa and Royal City (Grant County)
and Mabton, Granger, and Toppenish (Yakima) are more than
75 percent Hispanic.

The Hanford reservation and the Pacific Northwest National Laboratory, the district's largest employer, take up a
570-square-mile tract on the Columbia. Hanford's jobs drove
the region during the cold war, but in 1988 the plutonium
plant was shut down. Hanford is now the nation's most con-
taminated nuclear site, with 54 million gallons of deadly
material stored in aging underground tanks.

The 4th is the state's most conservative district. George W.
Bush won every county in the district in the 2000 presidential
election, most by overwhelming margins.

Major Industry

Scientific research, timber, fruit orchards.

Notable

The oldest skeleton ever found in North America was discovered along the banks of the Columbia River in Richland
in 1996. Dubbed the "Kennewick Man," he is believed to be
more than 9,300 years old.

Election Returns

	Republican		Democratic		Other	
President 2000	141,891	61.9%	78,768	34.4%	8,629	3.8%
House 2002	108,257	66.9%	53,572	33.1%		

District Profile

Population   654,901

Total area (square miles)   19,429.7
Land area (square miles)   19,051.4

Population per square mile   34.4

Counties (2000 population)

Adams (pt.)	11,201	Grant	74,698
Benton	142,475	Kittitas	33,362
Chelan	66,616	Klickitat	19,161
Douglas	32,603	Skamania (pt.)	2,857
Franklin	49,347	Yakima	222,581

Cities and other areas over 10,000 (2000 population)
East Wenatchee Bench CDP   13,658
Ellensburg   15,414
Kennewick   54,693
Moses Lake   14,953
Pasco   32,066
Richland   38,708
Sunnyside   13,905
Wenatchee   27,856
West Valley CDP   10,433
Yakima   71,845

Race and Hispanic or Latino origin*
White   67.8%
Black or African American   0.8%
American Indian or Alaska Native   1.9%
Asian   1.2%
Native Hawaiian or other Pacific Islander   0.1%
Some other race   0.1%
Hispanic or Latino origin   26.4%
Two or more races   1.7%

As percentage of total population.

Ancestry*
Dutch 1.8%		Norwegian 3.0%	
English 7.8%		Scotch-Irish 1.4%	
French 2.5%		Scottish 1.6%	
German 13.1%		Swedish 1.9%	
Irish 6.9%		USA/American 4.9%	
Italian 1.5%			

As estimated percentage of total population.

Universities and colleges, 2000–2001 enrollment
Big Bend Community College, Moses Lake   1,854
Central Washington University, Ellensburg   8,050
Columbia Basin College, Pasco   5,714
Heritage College, Toppenish   1,185
Perry Technical Institute, Yakima   446
Wenatchee Valley College, Wenatchee   2,777
Yakima Valley Community College, Yakima   3,916

Newspapers and circulation
	District circulation	Total circulation
Pasco Tri-City Herald	37,677	41,010
*USA Today**	1,844	1,674,376
Wenatchee World	8,268	24,906
Yakima Herald-Republic	39,034	39,034

See Sources and Explanations in the front of the volume.

Television stations and affiliations
Yakima-Pasco-Richland-Kennewick	50%	KAPP	ABC
Yakima-Pasco-Richland-Kennewick	50%	KEPR	CBS, UPN
Yakima-Pasco-Richland-Kennewick	50%	KIMA	CBS, UPN
Yakima-Pasco-Richland-Kennewick	50%	KNDO	NBC
Yakima-Pasco-Richland-Kennewick	50%	KNDU	NBC
Yakima-Pasco-Richland-Kennewick	50%	KTNW	PBS
Yakima-Pasco-Richland-Kennewick	50%	KVEW	ABC
Yakima-Pasco-Richland-Kennewick	50%	KYVE	PBS
Seattle-Tacoma	25%	KBCB	Independent
Seattle-Tacoma	25%	KBTC	PBS
Seattle-Tacoma	25%	KCKA	PBS
Seattle-Tacoma	25%	KCPQ	FOX
Seattle-Tacoma	25%	KCTS	PBS
Seattle-Tacoma	25%	KHCV	Independent
Seattle-Tacoma	25%	KING	NBC
Seattle-Tacoma	25%	KIRO	CBS
Seattle-Tacoma	25%	KOMO	ABC
Seattle-Tacoma	25%	KONG	Independent
Seattle-Tacoma	25%	KSTW	UPN
Seattle-Tacoma	25%	KTBW	Independent
Seattle-Tacoma	25%	KTWB	WB
Seattle-Tacoma	25%	KVOS	Independent
Seattle-Tacoma	25%	KWPX	PAX
Spokane	15%	KAYU	FOX
Spokane	15%	KCDT	PBS
Spokane	15%	KHQ	NBC
Spokane	15%	KLEW	CBS, UPN
Spokane	15%	KREM	CBS
Spokane	15%	KSKN	WB
Spokane	15%	KSPS	PBS
Spokane	15%	KUID	PBS
Spokane	15%	KWSU	PBS
Spokane	15%	KXLY	ABC
Portland, OR	10%	KATU	ABC
Portland, OR	10%	KGW	NBC
Portland, OR	10%	KNMT	Independent
Portland, OR	10%	KOIN	CBS
Portland, OR	10%	KOPB	PBS
Portland, OR	10%	KPDX	UPN
Portland, OR	10%	KPTV	FOX
Portland, OR	10%	KPXG	PAX
Portland, OR	10%	KTVR	PBS
Portland, OR	10%	KWBP	WB

Cable systems and subscribers
Charter   87,597
Comcast   92,087
Community Antenna Systems   556
Millennium Digital Media   11,446
Northland   8,390
R&R Cable   817
USA Media Group   14,835

Military installations, September 2001
Yakima Training Center (Army), Yakima   582

Businesses and other major employers
Gateway Inc.; Kennewick; computer and software stores   12,300
Fluor Hanford; Richland; environmental remediation   4,500
Battelle Memorial Institute Inc.; Richland; commercial physical research   4,000
Ski Lifts Inc.; Snoqualmie Pass; ski lodge   1,600
Ch2m Hill Hanford Group Inc.; Richland; engineering services   1,325
Yakima Valley Memorial Hospital; Yakima   1,099
Energy Northwest; Richland; electric power generation   1,098
Bechtel National Inc.; Richland; engineering services   1,000
Providence Medical Center; Yakima   1,000
Tree Top Inc.; Selah; fruit juices   900
Columbia Basin Community College; Pasco   883
Kadlec Medical Center; Richland   781
Central Washington Hospital; Wenatchee   740
Central Washington University Inc.; Ellensburg   712
Framatome Inc.; Richland; gas generators   700
Yakima County; Yakima; county government   700
Washington Beef Inc.; Toppenish; beef products   620
City of Yakima; Yakima; city government   605
Alcoa Inc.; Malaga; primary aluminum   600
Lamb-Weston Inc.; Richland; frozen vegetables   600
McCain Foods Inc.; Othello; frozen potato products   600
Wenatchee Valley Medical Center; Wenatchee   575
Dole Fresh Fruit Co.; East Wenatchee   555
Goldendale Aluminum Co.; Goldendale; primary aluminum   500
Lamb-Weston Inc.; Pasco; frozen specialties   500
Lockheed Martin Corp.; Richland; commercial physical research   500
Pacific Aerospace and Electronics Inc.; Wenatchee; electronic hermetic seals   500

Washington 5th District

East — Spokane

The fertile soil of eastern Washington makes the 5th's protein-rich wheat some of the most desired in the world. Politically conservative, the state's largest district has suffered the decline of some of its traditional industries and enjoyed the emergence of others.

Spokane is a trade hub for the inland Northwest. Largely dependent on manufacturing, the area has suffered intermittent layoffs. Increases in electronics manufacturing and the health care industry offered opportunities for workers to retrain. Slightly less than two-thirds of district residents live in Spokane or surrounding Spokane County.

Okanogan County, in the northwest corner of the district, has been particularly hard-hit as the logging and mining industries have slowed and a looming water shortage keeps farmers on edge. But the district remains a top apple producer. Unlike the neighboring Yakima and Columbia irrigation systems, the 5th's agriculture, based in the southern part of the district, is centered mostly on staple crops such as wheat, which receive federal subsidies.

The 5th's politics more closely resemble neighboring Idaho's than western Washington's. Rural communities and the natural resource-dependent economy make for residents who eschew federal interference and support private property rights. Spokane can be politically competitive: George W. Bush won the county by 9 percentage points in 2000 after Bill Clinton narrowly won it in 1996. But the rural areas are heavily Republican. Bush took 74 percent in Garfield County and 72 percent in Columbia County in 2000, his highest percentages in the state.

Major Industry

Agriculture, electronics manufacturing, health care.

Notable

Spokane hosts Bloomsday, the largest timed foot race in North America; Sonora Smart Dodd of Spokane thought up the idea for Father's Day while listening to a Mother's Day sermon in 1909; the Grand Coulee Dam created the 130-mile-long Lake Roosevelt on the Columbia River.

Election Returns

	Republican		Democratic		Other	
President 2000	150,013	55.6%	106,610	39.5%	13,262	4.9%
House 2002	126,757	62.7%	65,146	32.2%	10,379	5.1%

District Profile

Population 654,904

Total area (square miles) 23,165.8
  Land area (square miles) 22,863.9

Population per square mile 28.6

Counties (2000 population)

Adams (pt.)	5,227	Ferry	7,260
Asotin	20,551	Garfield	2,397
Columbia	4,064	Lincoln	10,184
Okanogan	39,564	Stevens	40,066
Pend Oreille	11,732	Walla Walla	55,180
Spokane	417,939	Whitman	40,740

Cities and other areas over 10,000 (2000 population)

Dishman CDP	10,031	Spokane	195,629
Opportunity CDP	25,065	Walla Walla	29,686
Pullman	24,675		

Race and Hispanic or Latino origin*

White 87.7%
Black or African American 1.3%
American Indian or Alaska Native 2.3%
Asian 1.7%
Native Hawaiian or other Pacific Islander 0.1%
Some other race 0.2%
Hispanic or Latino origin 4.5%
Two or more races 2.3%

As percentage of total population.

Ancestry*

Dutch	1.6%	Norwegian	4.3%
English	8.8%	Scotch-Irish	1.7%
French	2.9%	Scottish	2.1%
German	16.5%	Swedish	2.5%
Irish	9.0%	USA/American	4.6%
Italian	2.5%		

As estimated percentage of total population.

Universities and colleges, 2000–2001 enrollment

Eastern Washington University, Cheney 8,597
Gonzaga University, Spokane 4,548
ITT Technical Institute, Spokane 390
Spokane Community College, Spokane 7,767
Spokane Falls Community College, Spokane 9,872
Walla Walla College, College Place 1,795
Walla Walla Community College, Walla Walla 4,568
Washington State University, Pullman 20,492
Whitman College, Walla Walla 1,424
Whitworth College, Spokane 2,026

Newspapers and circulation

	District circulation	Total circulation
Pasco Tri-City Herald	2,438	41,010
*USA Today**	2,056	1,674,376
Wenatchee World	3,490	24,906

See Sources and Explanations in the front of the volume.

Television stations and affiliations

Spokane	94%	KAYU	FOX
Spokane	94%	KCDT	PBS
Spokane	94%	KHQ	NBC
Spokane	94%	KLEW	CBS, UPN
Spokane	94%	KREM	CBS
Spokane	94%	KSKN	WB
Spokane	94%	KSPS	PBS
Spokane	94%	KUID	PBS
Spokane	94%	KWSU	PBS
Spokane	94%	KXLY	ABC
Yakima-Pasco-Richland-Kennewick	6%	KAPP	ABC
Yakima-Pasco-Richland-Kennewick	6%	KEPR	CBS, UPN
Yakima-Pasco-Richland-Kennewick	6%	KIMA	CBS, UPN
Yakima-Pasco-Richland-Kennewick	6%	KNDO	NBC

Yakima-Pasco-Richland-Kennewick	6%	KNDU	NBC
Yakima-Pasco-Richland-Kennewick	6%	KTNW	PBS
Yakima-Pasco-Richland-Kennewick	6%	KVEW	ABC
Yakima-Pasco-Richland-Kennewick	6%	KYVE	PBS

Cable systems and subscribers

Adelphia   7,410
Cable Montana   620
Charter   27,444
Cheney TV Cable   2,639
Comcast   89,955
Concept Cable   657
Hood Canal   2,402
Millennium Digital Media   883
Touchet Valley TV   1,174
USA Media Group   1,338

Military installations, September 2001

Fairchild Air Force Base, Airway Heights   4,691
Geiger Field (Army Guard), Spokane   550
Naval Marine Corps Reserve Center, Spokane   530
Spokane International Airport Air Force Guard Station, Spokane   135
Four Lakes Air Force Guard Station, Cheney   129

Businesses and other major employers

Washington State University; Pullman   8,696
Sacred Heart Medical Center; Spokane   3,700
West Telemarketing Corp.; Spokane   2,700
IBP Inc.; Wallula; meatpacking plants   2,500
Empire Health Centers Group; Spokane   2,020
Kaiser Aluminum and Chemical Corp.; Spokane; aluminum products   1,700
Spokane County; Spokane; county government   1,440
Broetje Orchards; Prescott; apples   1,200
City of Spokane; Spokane; city government   1,183
Kaiser Aluminum and Chemical Corp.; Mead; primary aluminum   1,100
Eastern Washington University Inc.; Cheney   1,057
Hewlett-Packard Co.; Liberty Lake; electronic test equipment   1,000
Holy Family Hospital; Spokane   1,000
Honeywell Electronic Materials Inc.; Spokane; electronic circuits   1,000
Washington Dept. of Corrections; Walla Walla   1,000
Westcoast Hospitality Corp.; Spokane; hotels   1,000
Avista Corp.; Spokane; electric power generation   900
Genesis Services Portland Inc.; Spokane; investment holding company   900
Telect Inc.; Liberty Lake; telephones and apparatus   850
JC Penney Corp.; Spokane; department stores   800
United Steelworkers of America International Union; Spokane; labor union   750
Guardian Life Insurance Company of America; Spokane; insurance agents, brokers   700
System TWT Transportation; Cheney; trucking   700
U.S. Postal Service; Spokane   700
URM Stores Inc.; Spokane; food supplier   700
Walla Walla Community College Inc.; Walla Walla   695
Alera Lighting; Spokane; light fixtures   650
Gonzaga University; Spokane   650
Washington Dept. of Social and Health Services; Medical Lake   650

Central Valley School District; Greenacres   644
Boeing Co.; Spokane; aircraft engines and parts   600
Eastern State Hospital Advisory Board; Medical Lake   600
Sysco Food Services; Kent; meat and fish markets   600
Boise Cascade Corp.; Wallula; pulp mills   500
ICT Group Inc.; Spokane; telephone services   500
Metropolitan Mortgage and Securities Co.; Spokane; life insurance   500
OLSY North America Inc.; Liberty Lake; computer systems integration   500
Premera Blue Cross Blue Shield; Spokane; medical service plans   500
Software Spectrum Inc.; Liberty Lake; computer software   500
U.S. Veterans Hospital; Spokane   500

Washington 6th District

West — Bremerton, Tacoma, Olympic Peninsula

The green, lush habitation of the 6th is part of what gives Washington its nickname, the Evergreen State. Olympic National Park and Olympic National Forest constitute more than half of the district's land, about 2 million protected acres. Along the coast, the mountains drop to the Pacific Ocean.

Logging and fishing remain major industries in the west, but fights over protection for the spotted owl and other endangered species have forced some companies to cut back their work forces.

Communities are trying to diversify their economies and mostly have had success in attracting high-tech companies. Trade has increased in the port towns of Grays Harbor County. Bremerton, with the Puget Sound Naval Shipyard and Naval Station Bremerton, depends heavily on the military. The 6th also has a substantial Coast Guard presence. The district's representative must balance environmental concerns with labor and defense spending needs.

The 6th includes most of Tacoma and its suburbs. The industrial city's blue-collar, heavily unionized electorate generally gives Democrats the edge in Pierce County, where half of the district population lives. Bremerton, in Kitsap County (19 percent of the 6th's population), leans Democratic, as do Grays Harbor and Jefferson Counties. Al Gore won by 51.6 percent to 42.8 percent in the 6th, which was marginally redrawn in 2002 by the state's redistricting commission.

Major Industry

Lumber, fishing, shipping, health care.

Notable

The *USS Missouri,* the battleship on which the Japanese signed their surrender ending World War II, was based in Bremerton from the end of the war until 1998, when it was moved to Hawaii.

Election Returns

	Republican		Democratic		Other	
President 2000	115,736	42.8%	139,643	51.6%	15,098	5.6%
House 2002	61,584	31.3%	126,116	64.2%	8,744	4.5%

District Profile

Population   654,902

Total area (square miles)   8,592.1
   Land area (square miles)   6,781.4

Population per square mile   96.6

Counties (2000 population)

Clallam 64,525	Kitsap (pt.) 122,785
Grays Harbor 67,194	Mason 49,405
Jefferson 25,953	Pierce (pt.) 325,040

Cities and other areas over 10,000 (2000 population)

Aberdeen 16,461	Port Angeles 18,397
Bremerton 37,259	Tacoma (pt.) 176,853
Lakewood (pt.) 26,878	University Place 29,933
Parkland CDP (pt.) 15,206	

Race and Hispanic or Latino origin*

White   77.7%
Black or African American   5.5%
American Indian or Alaska Native   2.2%
Asian   4.4%
Native Hawaiian or other Pacific Islander   0.7%
Some other race   0.2%
Hispanic or Latino origin   5.1%
Two or more races   4.1%

As percentage of total population.

Ancestry*

Dutch 1.5%	Norwegian 4.6%
English 8.5%	Polish 1.3%
French 2.8%	Scotch-Irish 1.7%
German 13.2%	Scottish 2.2%
Irish 8.5%	Swedish 2.7%
Italian 2.4%	USA/American 4.2%

As estimated percentage of total population.

Universities and colleges, 2000–2001 enrollment

Bates Technical College, Tacoma   6,230
Business Computer Training Institute, Tacoma   318
Clover Park Technical College, Lakewood   7,921
Grays Harbor College, Aberdeen   1,950
Olympic College, Bremerton   5,613
Pacific Lutheran University, Tacoma   3,515
Peninsula College, Port Angeles   3,808
Tacoma Community College, Tacoma   5,302
University of Puget Sound, Tacoma   2,865
University of Washington, Tacoma   1,689
Washington Baptist College of Biblical Education, Tacoma   797

Newspapers and circulation

	District circulation	Total circulation
*Aberdeen Daily World**	14,010	15,402
*Olympia Olympian**	4,212	38,197
*Peninsula Daily News**	15,631	15,631
*USA Today**	1,457	1,674,376

See Sources and Explanations in the front of the volume.

Television stations and affiliations

Seattle-Tacoma	100%	KBCB	Independent
Seattle-Tacoma	100%	KBTC	PBS
Seattle-Tacoma	100%	KCKA	PBS
Seattle-Tacoma	100%	KCPQ	FOX
Seattle-Tacoma	100%	KCTS	PBS
Seattle-Tacoma	100%	KHCV	Independent
Seattle-Tacoma	100%	KING	NBC
Seattle-Tacoma	100%	KIRO	CBS
Seattle-Tacoma	100%	KOMO	ABC
Seattle-Tacoma	100%	KONG	Independent
Seattle-Tacoma	100%	KSTW	UPN
Seattle-Tacoma	100%	KTBW	Independent
Seattle-Tacoma	100%	KTWB	WB
Seattle-Tacoma	100%	KVOS	Independent
Seattle-Tacoma	100%	KWPX	PAX

Cable systems and subscribers

Charter   11,699
Coast Communications   2,656
Comcast   102,811
Millennium Digital Media   6,017
Northland   14,455

Military installations, September 2001

Puget Sound Naval Shipyard, Bremerton   14,372
McChord Air Force Base, Tacoma   6,883
Bremerton Naval Hospital, Bremerton   2,467
Puget Sound Bremerton Fleet and Industrial Supply Center, Bremerton   657

Businesses and other major employers

Tacoma General Hospital; Tacoma   5,000
City of Tacoma; Tacoma; electric services   3,000
Weyerhaeuser Co.; Tacoma; lumber products   3,000
St. Joseph Medical Center; Tacoma   1,642
Washington Judiciary Courts; Tacoma   1,586
Associated Health Services; Tacoma   1,200
Tacoma Community College; Tacoma   1,100
Harrison Memorial Hospital Inc.; Bremerton   995
Washington State Community College; Bremerton   809
University of Puget Sound; Tacoma   800
Simpson Timber Co.; Shelton; wood building materials   800
Pierce Transit; Tacoma; bus transportation   700
Clallam County Public Hospital District; Port Angeles   665
Concurrent Technologies Corp.; Bremerton; engineering services   600
Washington Dept. of Corrections; Shelton   550
St. Clare Hospital; Tacoma   549
Armstrong Uniserve Inc.; Tacoma; geriatric social service   517
Mutual Materials; Port Orchard; concrete building products   500
Davita Inc.; Tacoma; kidney dialysis centers   500
City of Tacoma; Tacoma; city government   500
Rainier Shows Inc.; Tacoma; carnival operation   500
Pierce County; Tacoma; county government   500

Washington 7th District

Seattle and suburbs

Framed by mountains, lakes, and Puget Sound, the 7th provides a serene atmosphere for Seattle. Although more rain falls here than in almost any other part of the nation, it is considered one of the most desirable places to live. Despite economic downturns that have killed off parts of Seattle's technology boom, the area remains wealthy, diverse, liberal, and cosmopolitan. *(See map p. 960.)*

The district is still home to high-tech startups and industry leaders, including retailer Amazon.com and software manufacturer Adobe. Microsoft's headquarters is in the neighboring 8th. The aviation and biotechnology industries also are big employers.

Economic downturns doomed many technology startups, and Boeing's decision in 2001 to move its corporate headquarters out of the state, along with subsequent layoffs, also hurt. The cost of housing remains high, forcing most low-income residents out of the city. But top-end restaurants and nightlife abound, catering to young singles and empty nesters. In Seattle, one is almost as likely to live alone as with a family.

The 2000 census measured Seattle's population at just more than its 1960 peak. Asians, at 13 percent of the city's population, are roughly equal to Seattle's combined black and Hispanic populations. The percentage of Seattle residents who describe themselves as members of two races is nearly twice the national average. But the city's population growth has not kept pace with the suburbs, especially in the north.

The Port of Seattle is one of the nation's major gateways to Asian markets and makes the 7th's economy dependent on trade.

The 7th's urban setting and large populations of minorities and singles make it a liberal bastion. Democratic candidates regularly dominate the district, and in 2000 the Green Party's Ralph Nader outpolled George W. Bush in some Seattle precincts.

Major Industry
Aviation, computer software, health care.

Notable
In 1971, the first Starbucks Coffee opened at Pike's Place Market.

Election Returns

	Republican		Democratic		Other	
President 2000	66,066	20.7%	228,988	71.8%	23,952	7.5%
House 2002	46,256	21.9%	156,300	74.1%	8,447	4.0%

District Profile

Population 654,902

Total area (square miles) 246.4
  Land area (square miles) 141.3

Population per square mile 4,634.8

Counties (2000 population)
  King (pt.) 654,902

Cities and other areas over 10,000 (2000 population)
  Bryn Mawr-Skyway CDP (pt.) 13,970
  Burien (pt.) 14,377
  Riverton-Boulevard Park CDP 11,188
  Seattle (pt.) 552,834
  Shoreline (pt.) 17,331
  Vashon CDP 10,123
  White Center CDP 20,975

Race and Hispanic or Latino origin*
  White 66.9%
  Black or African American 8.3%
  American Indian or Alaska Native 0.9%
  Asian 13.2%
  Native Hawaiian or other Pacific Islander 0.6%
  Some other race 0.3%
  Hispanic or Latino origin 5.8%
  Two or more races 3.9%

As percentage of total population.

Ancestry*

Dutch 1.4%	Polish 1.6%
English 8.2%	Russian 1.2%
French 2.5%	Scotch-Irish 1.6%
German 11.1%	Scottish 2.5%
Irish 8.5%	Subsaharan 1.3%
Italian 2.8%	Swedish 2.5%
Norwegian 4.2%	USA/American 2.0%

As estimated percentage of total population.

Universities and colleges, 2000–2001 enrollment
  Antioch University, Seattle 877
  Art Institute of Seattle, Seattle 2,561
  Cornish College of the Arts, Seattle 634
  Golden Gate University-Seattle, Seattle 238
  ITT Technical Institute, Seattle 521
  Northwest Institute of Acupuncture & Oriental
    Medicine, Seattle 233
  Pima Medical Institute, Seattle 297
  Seattle Community College-Central, Seattle 6,567
  Seattle Community College-North, Seattle 5,847
  Seattle Community College-South, Seattle 5,738
  Seattle Pacific University, Seattle 3,491
  Seattle University, Seattle 5,852
  University of Washington, Seattle 36,139

Newspapers and circulation

	District circulation	Total circulation
Seattle Post-Intelligencer	73,099	222,671
Seattle Times/Post-Intelligencer (Sunday)	242,266	753,860
Tacoma News Tribune	1,125	128,497
*USA Today**	1,608	1,674,376

See Sources and Explanations in the front of the volume.

Television stations and affiliations

Seattle-Tacoma	100%	KBCB	Independent
Seattle-Tacoma	100%	KBTC	PBS
Seattle-Tacoma	100%	KCKA	PBS
Seattle-Tacoma	100%	KCPQ	FOX
Seattle-Tacoma	100%	KCTS	PBS
Seattle-Tacoma	100%	KHCV	Independent

Seattle-Tacoma	100%	KING	NBC
Seattle-Tacoma	100%	KIRO	CBS
Seattle-Tacoma	100%	KOMO	ABC
Seattle-Tacoma	100%	KONG	Independent
Seattle-Tacoma	100%	KSTW	UPN
Seattle-Tacoma	100%	KTBW	Independent
Seattle-Tacoma	100%	KTWB	WB
Seattle-Tacoma	100%	KVOS	Independent
Seattle-Tacoma	100%	KWPX	PAX

Cable systems and subscribers
Comcast   149,839

Military installations, September 2001
Pier 71 (Army Guard), Seattle   720
Fort Lawton Army Complex, Seattle   623

Businesses and other major employers
Providence Health System Inc.; Seattle; health systems agency   33,000
Washington University; Seattle   25,000
Boeing Co.; Seattle; airplanes   12,100
Washington University Medical Center; Seattle   5,000
Swedish Medical Center; Seattle   4,400
RUI One Corp.; Seattle; restaurant   3,500
Clinic Harborview Medical Center; Seattle   3,000
Virginia Mason Medical Center; Seattle   2,800
Childrens Hospital and Regional Medical Center; Seattle   2,400
Providence Family Medicine WIC-Capital Hill; Seattle   2,393
Fred Hutchinson Cancer Research Center; Seattle   2,140
Amazon.com Inc.; Seattle; book, record sales   2,000
Providence Medical Center; Seattle   2,000
Regence Blue Shield; Seattle; medical service plans   1,800
U.S. Veterans Hospital; Seattle   1,600
Nordstrom Inc.; Seattle; clothing stores   1,500
Seattle Times Co.; Seattle; newspaper   1,500
Safeco Corp.; Seattle; property damage insurance   1,400
King County; Seattle; county government   1,350
Ackerley Media Group Inc.; Seattle; TV broadcast stations   1,336
Holland America Line Inc.; Seattle; excursion boat operators   1,300
Washington Dept. of Transportation; Seattle   1,300
Northwest Hospital; Seattle   1,217
Airborne Express Inc.; Seattle; air courier   1,200
White Pass and Yukon Motor Coaches Inc.; Seattle; bus charter   1,200
Shaun Watchie Perry Law Offices; Seattle   1,199
Group Health Permanente Inc.; Seattle; medical help service   1,100
American Seafoods Co.; Seattle; management services   1,040
Associated Grocers Inc.; Seattle; food supplier   1,000
Interstate Brands West Corp.; Seattle; bakery products   1,000
Pepsi-Cola Metropolitan Bottling Co.; Seattle; soft drinks   1,000
U.S. Army Corps of Engineers; Seattle   1,000
U.S. Dept. of Commerce; Seattle   1,000

RealNetworks Inc.; Seattle; software development   905
City of Seattle; Seattle; recreational program   900
City of Seattle; Seattle; public health programs   900
King County; Seattle; sheriff's office   900
Todd Pacific Shipyards Corp.; Seattle; shipbuilding, repairing   900
Pemco Mutual Insurance Co.; Seattle   850
Cray Inc.; Seattle; electronic computers   830
Group Health Co-Operative of Puget Sound Inc.; Seattle; health maintenance organization   800
Starbucks Corp.; Seattle; coffee shops   763
American Medical Response Inc.; Seattle; ambulance service   750
Assn. of University Physicians; Seattle; medical associations   750
Boeing Employees Credit Union; Tukwila; state credit unions   750
Sea-Mar Community Health Center; Seattle   714
Pacific Medical Center; Seattle   701
Baugh Construction Co. Inc.; Seattle; building construction   700
Immunex Corp.; Seattle; pharmaceuticals   700
MacDonald-Miller Co. Inc.; Seattle; heating/air conditioning   700
Washington State Community College District; Seattle   700
Korry Electronics Co.; Seattle; switchgear apparatus   675
Perkins Coie; Seattle; law office   660
Seattle Housing Authority; Seattle   659
Seattle City Light; Seattle; city government   650
U.S. Bakery; Seattle; bakery products   650
Dynacare Northwest Inc.; Seattle; medical labs   640
Aramark Services Inc.; Seattle; concessionaire   600
ITT Sheraton Corp.; Seattle; hotels   600
St. Gobain-Container Inc.; Seattle; glass containers   600
Starwood Hotels and Resorts Worldwide Inc.; Seattle; resort hotel   600
United Air Lines Inc.; Seattle   600
Urban Four Seasons Hotel Venture LP; Seattle; hotels and motels   600
URS Greiner Woodward-Clyde Inc.; Seattle; architectural services   600
Preston Gates and Ellis; Seattle; law office   588
Deloitte and Touche; Seattle; certified public accountant   560
Adobe Systems Inc.; Seattle; software development   550
Seattle University; Seattle   525
Accenture Inc.; Seattle; business consulting   524
Washington Mutual Bank; Seattle; federal savings institutions   513
AT&T Wireless Services Inc.; Seattle; cellular telephones   500
Avanade Inc.; Seattle; online services   500
Four Season Olympic Hotel; Seattle; hotels and motels   500
IDX Systems Corp.; Seattle; software design   500
McKinstry Co.; Seattle; plumbing contractors   500
Poly Clinic; Seattle; medical offices   500
Recreational Equipment Inc.; Seattle; sporting and athletic goods   500
Seattle Cancer Care Alliance; Seattle   500

Sellen Construction Co. Inc.; Seattle; building
construction   500
Westin Hotel Seattle; Seattle; hotel, franchised   500
Windermere Real Estate Co. Inc.; Seattle; real estate
agent   500

Washington 8th District

Eastside Seattle suburbs; Bellevue; eastern Pierce County

Home to some of suburban Seattle's most prosperous areas, the 8th takes in King County's Eastside suburbs east of Lake Washington, where million-dollar homes dot the lakeshore in wealthy hamlets like Hunts Point, Clyde Hill, Yarrow Point, and Medina, where Microsoft founder Bill Gates lives. Commuters continue to fill out the exurban land as they are priced out of more-central neighborhoods. The expansion has caused huge traffic problems and ignited debates on smart growth and preservation. *(See map p. 960.)*

The Eastside suburbs were once farmland but have become fertile ground for the Northwest's technology companies. While attracting residents who work for companies such as Microsoft (whose main campus lies just within the district's boundaries), the 8th also is home to higher-paid, blue-collar workers. Russian and Native American communities also are growing as they take on the area's high-tech jobs. Boeing remains a dominant employer, but its influence on the district waned after the 2001 decision to move its headquarters out of state. Subsequent rounds of layoffs caused some workers to leave the district.

In addition to its near-in Seattle suburbs, the 8th continues east to the border of King County and heads south to take in a mostly rural part of Pierce County, which includes Mount Rainier National Park.

The 8th's once strongly Republican politics are changing as the first-ring suburbs begin to resemble the urban core. Generally fiscally conservative and socially moderate, the 8th is politically competitive, backing Al Gore narrowly in 2000. Southeast Asian and Middle Eastern immigrants are diversifying the area and will influence future elections.

Major Industry
Logging, aviation manufacturing, software.

Notable
A pontoon bridge made of reinforced concrete was finished July 2, 1940, connecting Mercer Island and Seattle.

Election Returns

	Republican		Democratic		Other	
President 2000	136,575	47.3%	140,387	48.6%	11,838	4.1%
House 2002	121,633	59.8%	75,931	37.3%	5,771	2.8%

District Profile

Population   654,905

Total area (square miles)   2,621.3
   Land area (square miles)   2,579.2

Population per square mile   253.9

Counties (2000 population)
King (pt.)   524,733
Pierce (pt.)   130,172

Cities and other areas over 10,000 (2000 population)
Auburn (pt.)   17,043
Bellevue   109,569
Cascade-Fairwood CDP (pt.)   17,337
Covington   13,783
East Hill-Meridian CDP (pt.)   23,866
East Renton Highlands CDP   13,264
Enumclaw   11,116
Issaquah   11,212
Kent (pt.)   35,620
Lea Hill CDP   10,871
Maple Valley   14,209
Mercer Island   22,036
Prairie Ridge CDP   11,688
Redmond (pt.)   10,497
Renton (pt.)   29,264
Sammamish   34,104
South Hill CDP   31,623
Union Hill-Novelty Hill CDP (pt.)   11,260

Race and Hispanic or Latino origin*
White   82.1%
Black or African American   2.0%
American Indian or Alaska Native   0.8%
Asian   7.8%
Native Hawaiian or other Pacific Islander   0.3%
Some other race   0.2%
Hispanic or Latino origin   4.0%
Two or more races   2.8%

As percentage of total population.

Ancestry*

Dutch 1.5%	Norwegian 4.7%
English 9.4%	Polish 1.5%
French 2.7%	Scotch-Irish 1.4%
German 14.0%	Scottish 2.3%
Irish 8.3%	Swedish 2.9%
Italian 2.8%	USA/American 3.7%

As estimated percentage of total population.

Universities and colleges, 2000–2001 enrollment
Bellevue Community College, Bellevue   11,234
City University, Bellevue   8,339
Green River Community College, Auburn   6,566
Renton Technical College, Renton   5,065
University of Phoenix, Bellevue   1,114

Newspapers and circulation

	District circulation	Total circulation
Eastside Business Journal	16,889	26,435
Seattle Post-Intelligencer	45,629	222,671
Seattle Times/Post-Intelligencer (Sunday)	136,314	753,860
South County Journal	13,144	22,173
Tacoma News Tribune	2,174	128,497
*USA Today**	10,592	1,674,376

See Sources and Explanations in the front of the volume.

Television stations and affiliations

Seattle-Tacoma	100%	KBCB	Independent
Seattle-Tacoma	100%	KBTC	PBS
Seattle-Tacoma	100%	KCKA	PBS
Seattle-Tacoma	100%	KCPQ	FOX
Seattle-Tacoma	100%	KCTS	PBS
Seattle-Tacoma	100%	KHCV	Independent
Seattle-Tacoma	100%	KING	NBC
Seattle-Tacoma	100%	KIRO	CBS
Seattle-Tacoma	100%	KOMO	ABC
Seattle-Tacoma	100%	KONG	Independent
Seattle-Tacoma	100%	KSTW	UPN
Seattle-Tacoma	100%	KTBW	Independent
Seattle-Tacoma	100%	KTWB	WB
Seattle-Tacoma	100%	KVOS	Independent
Seattle-Tacoma	100%	KWPX	PAX

Cable systems and subscribers

Comcast   191,694

Millennium Digital Media   921

Military installations, September 2001

Everett Naval Station, Everett   5,829

Businesses and other major employers

VoiceStream Wireless Corp.; Bellevue; radiotelephone communication   10,387

Microsoft Corp.; Redmond; computer software   4,700

TCI West Inc.; Bellevue; cable TV   4,250

Group Health Eastside Hospital; Redmond   2,250

Costco Wholesale Corp.; Issaquah; warehouse club stores   2,100

Puget Sound Energy; Bellevue; electric power generation   2,009

Overlake Hospital Medical Center; Bellevue   1,850

Boeing Co.; Puyallup; airplane equipment   1,500

Washington Dept. of Social and Health Services; Buckley   1,100

Eddie Bauer Inc.; Redmond; clothing stores   1,000

Western Wireless Corp.; Bellevue; cellular telephones   1,000

Nordstrom Inc.; Bellevue; clothing stores   998

California 9 Cellular Corp.; Issaquah; cellular telephones   900

Green River Community College Inc.; Auburn   875

Renton Technical College; Renton   800

City of Bellevue; Bellevue; city government   770

Honeywell International Inc.; Redmond; plastic materials and resins   754

King County; Issaquah; public library   750

Safeway Inc.; Bellevue; warehousing   700

Attachmate Corp.; Bellevue; systems integration services   600

Compass Group USA Inc.; Issaquah; restaurants   600

KPMG; Bellevue; accounting services   600

Solucient; Bellevue; computer systems design   600

Winterthur US Holdings Inc.; Bellevue; insurance agents and brokers   600

Bellevue Community College; Bellevue   590

Farmers New World Life Insurance Co.; Mercer Island   520

Interflight Services Inc.; Bellevue; transportation consultant   505

Boeing Co.; Bellevue; aircraft   500

Boeing Co.; Maple Valley; aircraft   500

IKON Office Solutions Inc.; Bellevue; office equipment   500

Microsoft Corp.; Issaquah; computer software   500

PACCAR Inc.; Bellevue; truck parts and accessories   500

TTM Technologies Inc.; Redmond; printed circuit boards   500

Unigard Service Corp. of California; Bellevue; personal credit institutions   500

Washington 9th District

South Seattle suburbs; small part of Tacoma

The 9th is a politically competitive, mostly suburban district south of Seattle that runs along Interstate 5, picking up small parts of Tacoma and the capital of Olympia en route to rural areas that afford great views of the 14,410-foot Mount Rainier (in the 8th), the state's highest point. *(See map p. 960.)*

The district's northern area, just south of the Seattle line, takes in predominantly middle-class King County suburbs, including most of Burien, SeaTac, and Tukwila (shared with the 7th) and Renton (shared with the 8th). SeaTac (a partial concatenation of the names of the area's major cities) includes the region's major airport. Boeing has a commercial airplane production facility in Renton. Farther south are slightly more prosperous areas like Kent (shared with the 8th) and Des Moines. Federal Way, in southwest King, includes the headquarters of paper giant Weyerhaeuser.

King County accounts for about half of the 9th's population. The rest live in Pierce County, south of King, or in Thurston County, including northeastern Olympia. In Pierce, the 9th takes in the deep-water Port of Tacoma, which has diversified an economy once dominated by Boeing. The corridor along Interstate 5 has become a magnet for technology companies that provide high-paying jobs for well-educated residents.

Redistricting in 2002 made small changes to the 9th, which during the 1990s was a quintessential swing district that elected a Democratic representative in 1992, a Republican in 1994, and a Democrat in 1996. Democrats fare better in the King and Thurston portions of the district than in Pierce.

Major Industry

Aviation manufacturing, computer software, hardware.

Notable

Before becoming commander of the American forces in the Persian Gulf, Gen. Norman Schwarzkopf was commander of Fort Lewis; Puyallup Valley claims to be the nation's No. 1 producer of rhubarb.

Election Returns

	Republican		Democratic		Other	
President 2000	104,549	42.9%	128,076	52.6%	10,874	4.5%
House 2002	63,146	38.6%	95,805	58.5%	4,759	2.9%

District Profile

Population   654,902

Total area (square miles)   690.6
 Land area (square miles)   607.7

Population per square mile   1,077.7

Counties (2000 population)
King (pt.)   318,228
Pierce (pt.)   245,608
Thurston (pt.)   91,066

Cities and other areas over 10,000 (2000 population)
Auburn (pt.)   23,271
Burien (pt.)   17,504
Cascade-Fairwood CDP (pt.)   17,243
Des Moines   29,267
Elk Plain CDP   15,697
Federal Way   83,259
Fort Lewis CDP   19,089
Kent (pt.)   43,904
Lacey (pt.)   28,829
Lakeland North CDP   15,085
Lakeland South CDP   11,436
Lakewood (pt.)   31,333
Puyallup (pt.)   33,011
Renton (pt.)   20,788
SeaTac (pt.)   22,847
Spanaway CDP   21,588
Tacoma (pt.)   16,703
Tukwila (pt.)   11,211

Race and Hispanic or Latino origin*
White   73.3%
Black or African American   6.3%
American Indian or Alaska Native   1.1%
Asian   7.1%
Native Hawaiian or other Pacific Islander   0.9%
Some other race   0.3%
Hispanic or Latino origin   6.7%
Two or more races   4.2%

*As percentage of total population.

Ancestry*
Dutch 1.4%	Norwegian 4.2%
English 7.7%	Polish 1.4%
French 2.5%	Scotch-Irish 1.4%
German 13.2%	Scottish 1.9%
Irish 7.9%	Swedish 2.2%
Italian 2.4%	USA/American 3.6%

*As estimated percentage of total population.

Universities and colleges, 2000–2001 enrollment
Highline Community College, Des Moines   6,327
Pierce College, Lakewood   9,238
Resource Center for the Handicapped, Renton   270
St. Martins College, Lacey   1,408

Newspapers and circulation

	District circulation	Total circulation
*Olympia Olympian**	7,641	38,197
Seattle Post-Intelligencer	20,229	222,671
Seattle Times/Post-Intelligencer (Sunday)	68,574	753,860
South County Journal	8,074	22,173
Tacoma News Tribune	7,118	128,497
*USA Today**	1,422	1,674,376

*See Sources and Explanations in the front of the volume.

Television stations and affiliations
Seattle-Tacoma	100%	KBCB	Independent
Seattle-Tacoma	100%	KBTC	PBS
Seattle-Tacoma	100%	KCKA	PBS
Seattle-Tacoma	100%	KCPQ	FOX
Seattle-Tacoma	100%	KCTS	PBS
Seattle-Tacoma	100%	KHCV	Independent
Seattle-Tacoma	100%	KING	NBC
Seattle-Tacoma	100%	KIRO	CBS
Seattle-Tacoma	100%	KOMO	ABC
Seattle-Tacoma	100%	KONG	Independent
Seattle-Tacoma	100%	KSTW	UPN
Seattle-Tacoma	100%	KTBW	Independent
Seattle-Tacoma	100%	KTWB	WB
Seattle-Tacoma	100%	KVOS	Independent
Seattle-Tacoma	100%	KWPX	PAX

Cable systems and subscribers
Comcast   118,905

Military installations, September 2001
Fort Lewis (Army), Tacoma   28,274
Camp Murray Military Training Area, Tacoma   1,169
Kent Armory (Army Guard), Kent   702
Camp Murray Air National Guard Station, Tacoma   418

Businesses and other major employers
Weyerhaeuser Co.; Federal Way; lumber, plywood   4,000
Alaska Airlines Inc.; Seattle   2,500
PACCAR Inc.; Renton; truck and tractor assembly   2,500
Providence St. Peter Hospital; Olympia   2,300
Washington Dept. of Social and Health Services; Tacoma   2,200
U.S. Veterans Hospital; Tacoma   2,000
King County Public Hospital District; Renton   1,628
Good Samaritan Hospital; Puyallup   1,500
Intel Corp.; DuPont; computers   1,500
Puyallup School District; Puyallup   1,433
Boeing Co.; Renton; job training   1,000
Delta Airlines Inc.; Seattle   1,000
Great Pacific News Co.; Tacoma; publishing   1,000
Manpower Inc.; Kent; manpower pools   1,000

Washington Dept. of Ecology; Olympia   1,000
Weyerhaeuser Co.; Federal Way; lumber   1,000
Pacific Lutheran University Inc.; Tacoma   959
SuperValu Inc.; Tacoma; food supplier   850
State Farm Mutual Automobile Insurance Co.; DuPont; life insurance   800
Highline Community College Inc.; Des Moines   772
Highline Community Hospital Inc.; Seattle   770
Gordon Trucking Inc.; Pacific   700
King County; Kent; correctional institutions   700
United Air Lines Inc.; Seattle; helicopter carrier   700
Recreational Equipment Inc.; Kent; warehousing   680
Stewart Information Services Corp.; Kent; title insurance   670
Cubic Applications Inc.; Lacey; computer systems design   669
Milgard Manufacturing Inc.; Tacoma; windows, plastics   650
Army and Air Force Exchange Service; Fort Lewis   600

Family Medical Center; Auburn   600
United Air Lines Inc.; Kent   600
City of Kent; Kent; city government   581
Pierce College; Lakewood   580
Hilton Hotels Corp.; Seattle; resort hotel   575
Auburn General Hospital Inc.; Auburn   551
City of Renton; Renton; city government   530
Hasbro Inc.; Renton; board games   500
Interstate Brands West Corp.; Kent; bakery products   500
JC Penney Corp.; Seattle; department stores   500
Mikron Industries Inc.; Kent; plastics hardware   500
Simpson Tacoma Kraft Co.; Tacoma; paperboard mills   500
Sysco Food Services; Kent; food supplier   500
U.S. Postal Service; Federal Way   500
Wizards of Coast Inc.; Renton; board games   500
Yelm Community Schools; Yelm   500

WEST VIRGINIA

Districts established October 4, 2001, for elections first held in 2002.

3 members

West Virginia

This state will always represent a painful memory for Al Gore. Had he carried it and its precious five electoral votes in November 2000, there would have been no need for a five-week delay in determining who had won the presidency. Gore suffered other disappointments that day, but no state was so far from its moorings in voting for Republican winner George W. Bush. This was the first time West Virginia had favored a nonincumbent Republican for the White House since 1928, when it rejected the Democrats' first Catholic nominee.

But it can also be said that Gore represented a painful memory for West Virginia. His presence atop the Democratic ticket was, for many traditional voters here, an indication of how much the old Democratic Party had changed. There had been a time when Democrats were always for jobs, even jobs digging coal. But the Clinton-Gore administration opposed the "mountain top" mining that decapitated hills and filled streams with rock and silt—the kind of mining that still creates jobs here. Gore also favored gun control and got poor marks from the National Rifle Association, a group well represented in the woods and towns of West Virginia.

Gore may have been so closely and personally tied to anticoal and antigun policies that he could not have carried West Virginia in 2000. But losing here also highlighted how Democrats in general have reduced their reliance on blue-collar working people, particularly those who are neither ideologically liberal nor culturally attuned to the new Democrat themes. Such voters, known in the 1980s as "Reagan Democrats," have been associated with ethnic working-class neighborhoods in the big cities; but they abound as well in Anglo-Saxon rural America, especially in West Virginia.

Historically, West Virginia was a breakaway subset of Virginia during the Civil War. The counties beyond the Blue Ridge where plantation farming was unknown had little use for slaves or for the institution of slavery. Like the voters in other highland areas—in states all the way down the Appalachian spine to Alabama—the voters here developed a Republican habit and stuck with it. The governors in the early 1900s tended to be Republicans. But as the unions caught on and held on, the state developed a two-party politics that became more Democratic with each downturn in the economy or in the fortunes of coal. Since 1933, only two Republicans have won the office, and only one (Arch Moore) was able to win consecutive terms. The other, Cecil Underwood, was elected in the Eisenhower landslide of 1956 when he was just 34: the youngest governor in the country. Much later, in 1996, he returned and was elected again at the age of 74, becoming the nation's oldest governor.

Senate races have been a simpler matter. With the exception of Chapman Revercomb, who won a special election in 1956 and served just two years, the state has had all Democrats in the Senate since the New Deal. Some of these had characteristics of the party's Dixiecrat strain. The state's current senior senator, the remarkable Robert C. Byrd, first came to Congress in 1953 and to the Senate six years later. He was an old-fashioned southern politician. He played the fiddle to draw a crowd to hear him speak and helped to filibuster against civil rights bills.

Byrd has traveled a great distance since then, becoming a champion for many social and economic causes and a leading voice against the war in Iraq in 2003 (making him a hero to a generation not born when he first came to the Senate). But his supreme cause has always been West Virginia. Byrd served as his party's Senate leader in the 1970s and 1980s and more recently has been the top Democrat on Appropriations, where he has worked hard at moving as much of the federal government as possible to West Virginia.

After 1984, Byrd's Democratic colleague in the Senate was a Democrat bearing the extraordinary name of John D. Rockefeller IV (he prefers "Jay"). He likes to say he had a lot of reasons to be a Republican, pausing to stress the words "a lot of reasons." He came to the state as a VISTA volunteer and politician, rose to governor and senator, flirted with a presidential bid in 1992, and decided to stick to the Senate. He has not sought a place in leadership, preferring the low-light labors of tax, trade, health policy, and oversight of the intelligence agencies.

The redistricting plan for West Virginia was a wholly Democratic project that did the party little apparent good. The Democratic legislature drew, and Gov. Bob Wise, another Democrat, signed a new map that did nothing to weaken the state's one Republican House member, Shelley Moore Capito, a freshman from the state capital of Charleston. Capito's maiden name (her father was former governor Moore) was an important asset, but she proved a strong candidate in 2000, winning the 2nd District seat that had belonged to Wise. Capito won again in 2002 in a slightly refashioned 2nd that rambled from the easternmost point of the state (Martinsburg) through its eastern panhandle, a corridor at times just one county wide, before spilling out into the center of the state. The 2nd includes Charleston and reaches the western state line between Parkersburg and Huntington (without including either town).

While not exactly Republican heaven, the district is 94 percent white (the whole state is just 3 percent black, with 1 percent each for Asians and Hispanics) and gave Bush the nod by a spread of 10 percentage points over Gore (the statewide divide was just four). Capito won reelection with 60 percent of the vote, a substantial improvement over the 48.5 percent she managed in 2000. Meanwhile, her two Democratic colleagues in the House, Nick J. Rahall and Alan B. Mollohan, each won reelection easily as well. Mollohan might have had more trouble in his northern 1st District had he been given some of Capito's Republican voters from her part of the eastern panhandle. But instead the new map required the 2nd to give up Gilmer County to the 1st and Nicholas County to the 3rd District (Rahall) to balance the numbers and make all three incumbents safer. Although they knew they were making Capito secure, Mollohan and Rahall endorsed the plan.

Table 1 Population

District	Population	Population under 18	Voting-age population	Median age	Male*	Female*
1	602,545	131,442	471,103	38.7	48.5	51.5
2	602,243	139,063	463,180	38.7	48.8	51.2
3	603,556	131,888	471,668	39.3	48.5	51.5
State	1,808,344	402,393	1,405,951	38.9	48.6	51.4

*As percentage of total population.

Table 2 Voting-Age Persons by Race/Hispanic or Latino Origin

District	White*	Black or African American*	American Indian or Alaska Native*	Asian*	Other or multirace*	Hispanic or Latino*
1	96.2	1.7	0.2	0.7	0.6	0.6
2	94.6	3.3	0.2	0.5	0.7	0.6
3	94.3	4.0	0.2	0.4	0.6	0.5
State	95.0	3.0	0.2	0.5	0.6	0.6

*As percentage of voting-age population.

Table 3 Voting-Age Population by Age Groups

District	18 to 24*	25 to 44*	45 to 64*	Over 64*
1	13.6	34.7	31.6	20.2
2	11.0	37.2	32.9	18.9
3	12.3	35.1	32.7	20.0
State	12.3	35.7	32.4	19.7

*As percentage of voting-age population.

Table 4 Income and Occupation

District	Median family income	Families in poverty*	White collar†	Blue collar†	Service†	Farm†
1	$37,913	12.3	54.0	28.5	16.9	0.6
2	$40,003	11.6	55.1	28.9	15.3	0.8
3	$31,928	17.7	52.6	28.8	17.7	0.9
State	$36,484	13.9	54.0	28.7	16.6	0.7

*As percentage of all families.   †As percentage of employed workers 16 years and over.

Table 5 Education: School Years Completed

District	Less than grade 9*	Grades 9–12 no diploma*	High school diploma no college*	Some college*	College bachelor's degree or higher*
1	7.7	12.9	40.9	22.3	16.3
2	9.2	14.0	39.6	21.1	16.2
3	13.2	17.5	37.8	19.5	12.0
State	10.0	14.8	39.4	21.0	14.8

*As percentage of persons age 25 and over.

Table 6 Housing and Residential Patterns

District	Median home value	Owner occupied*	Renter occupied*	Urban†	Rural†
1	$66,500	74.0	26.0	53.7	46.3
2	$76,200	75.5	24.5	46.2	53.8
3	$56,100	76.0	24.0	38.4	61.6
State	$66,000	75.2	24.8	46.1	53.9

*As percentage of occupied housing units.   †As percentage of total population.

West Virginia 1st District

North — Parkersburg, Wheeling, Morgantown

Located in the northernmost part of the state, the Democratic-leaning 1st has a large rural component but is the most urban of West Virginia's three districts. It contains six of the state's ten largest cities and West Virginia University, the state's largest school. Wheeling, an industrial town and commercial center in the north, and Parkersburg, a regional trade center in the west, are two of the main urban areas.

The district was hit hard by economic depression in the 1980s, losing population as factories shut down and coal mines mechanized. Unemployment remained high in the early 1990s—topping 10 percent in some counties—and 12 of the district's 20 counties lost population during the decade. Coal and steel are still the district's biggest employers, but a budding technology sector has brightened economic prospects. The Federal Bureau of Investigation and the U.S. Department of Energy have facilities in the district, and Morgantown, home to West Virginia University, is attracting high-tech firms. Located amid the coal fields of Monongalia County (one of the state's leading coal-producing counties), Morgantown also is home to Software Valley, an organization that promotes technology and research activity.

The 1st long has elected Democrats to Congress and has more registered Democrats than Republicans, but Parkersburg and Wheeling have some Republican-leaning state House districts. The 1st gave George W. Bush 54 percent of the vote in the 2000 presidential election, helping him win by a 6-point statewide margin over Democratic nominee Al Gore. The loss of West Virginia, a traditional Democratic state, was seen by many analysts as the central event that cost Gore the election.

Major Industry

Coal, steel, technology, chemicals.

Notable

Prabhupada's Palace of Gold was built in Moundsville by the International Society for Krishna Consciousness; the Capitol Music Hall in Wheeling hosts Jamboree USA, a country music program that has aired on radio station WWVA since 1933; 1984 Olympic gold medalist Mary Lou Retton is from Marion County.

Election Returns

	Republican		Democratic		Other	
President 2000	122,827	54.0%	97,432	42.8%	7,399	3.3%
House 2002			110,941	99.7%	320	0.3%

District Profile

Population 602,545

Total area (square miles) 6,343.6
   Land area (square miles) 6,286.2

Population per square mile 95.9

Counties (2000 population)

Barbour	15,557	Monongalia	81,866
Brooke	25,447	Ohio	47,427
Doddridge	7,403	Pleasants	7,514
Gilmer	7,160	Preston	29,334
Grant	11,299	Ritchie	10,343
Hancock	32,667	Taylor	16,089
Harrison	68,652	Tucker	7,321
Marion	56,598	Tyler	9,592
Marshall	35,519	Wetzel	17,693
Mineral	27,078	Wood	87,986

Cities and other areas over 10,000 (2000 population)

Clarksburg	16,743	Vienna	10,861
Fairmont	19,097	Weirton	20,411
Morgantown	26,809	Wheeling	31,419
Parkersburg	33,099		

Race and Hispanic or Latino origin*

White 95.8%
Black or African American 1.7%
American Indian or Alaska Native 0.2%
Asian 0.7%
Native Hawaiian or other Pacific Islander 0.0%
Some other race 0.1%
Hispanic or Latino origin 0.7%
Two or more races 0.8%

*As percentage of total population.

Ancestry*

Dutch	2.0%	Italian	5.0%
English	7.9%	Polish	2.2%
French	1.2%	Scotch-Irish	1.8%
German	14.1%	Scottish	1.3%
Irish	10.0%	USA/American	10.7%

*As estimated percentage of total population.

Universities and colleges, 2000–2001 enrollment

Alderson Broaddus College, Philippi 751
Bethany College, Bethany 750
Fairmont State College, Fairmont 6,496
Glenville State College, Glenville 2,126
Ohio Valley College, Parkersburg 419
Potomac State College of West Virginia University, Keyser 1,109
Salem International University, Salem 601
West Liberty State College, West Liberty 2,606
West Virginia Northern Community College, Wheeling 2,486
West Virginia University, Morgantown 21,987
West Virginia University, Parkersburg 3,278
Wheeling Jesuit University, Wheeling 1,515

Newspapers and circulation

	District circulation	Total circulation
Clarksburg Exponent & Telegram	14,658	16,286
Cumberland Times-News	5,094	30,232
East Liverpool Review	1,861	9,763
Elkins Inter Mountain	2,273	10,244
Fairmont Times West Virginian	11,749	11,925
Morgantown Dominion Post	18,853	19,410
Parkersburg News	14,634	20,956
Parkersburg News/Sentinel	19,828	27,185
Parkersburg Sentinel	5,194	6,010
Pittsburgh Post-Gazette	1,435	240,791
Steubenville Herald-Star	2,029	15,442
*USA Today**	4,863	1,674,376
Weirton Daily Times	5,958	6,121
Wheeling Intelligencer	11,813	20,126
Wheeling News Register	38,163	52,757

*See Sources and Explanations in the front of the volume.

Television stations and affiliations

Clarksburg-Weston	44%	WBOY	NBC
Clarksburg-Weston	44%	WDTV	CBS
Clarksburg-Weston	44%	WVFX	FOX
Wheeling-Steubenville	19%	WTRF	CBS
Pittsburgh	16%	KDKA	CBS
Pittsburgh	16%	WCWB	WB
Pittsburgh	16%	WGPT	PBS
Pittsburgh	16%	WNPA	UPN
Pittsburgh	16%	WNPB	PBS
Pittsburgh	16%	WPCB	Independent
Pittsburgh	16%	WPGH	FOX
Pittsburgh	16%	WPXI	NBC
Pittsburgh	16%	WQED	PBS
Pittsburgh	16%	WQEX	PBS
Pittsburgh	16%	WTAE	ABC
Pittsburgh	16%	WTOV	NBC
Pittsburgh	16%	WWCP	FOX
Washington, DC (Hagerstown)	13%	WBDC	WB
Washington, DC (Hagerstown)	13%	WDCA	UPN
Washington, DC (Hagerstown)	13%	WETA	PBS
Washington, DC (Hagerstown)	13%	WFPT	PBS
Washington, DC (Hagerstown)	13%	WHAG	NBC
Washington, DC (Hagerstown)	13%	WHSV	ABC
Washington, DC (Hagerstown)	13%	WHUT	PBS
Washington, DC (Hagerstown)	13%	WJAL	ABC
Washington, DC (Hagerstown)	13%	WJLA	ABC
Washington, DC (Hagerstown)	13%	WNVC	Independent
Washington, DC (Hagerstown)	13%	WNVT	PBS

Washington, DC (Hagerstown)	13%	WPXW	PAX
Washington, DC (Hagerstown)	13%	WRC	NBC
Washington, DC (Hagerstown)	13%	WTTG	FOX
Washington, DC (Hagerstown)	13%	WUSA	CBS
Washington, DC (Hagerstown)	13%	WVPY	PBS
Washington, DC (Hagerstown)	13%	WWPB	PBS
Washington, DC (Hagerstown)	13%	WWPX	PAX
Parkersburg	8%	WTAP	NBC

Cable systems and subscribers
Adelphia   26,025
Blue Devil Cable   980
CableVision Communications   8,963
Charter   75,754
CMA Cablevision   6,495
Comcast   43,769
CT&R Cable   888
Manningtin TV   1,208
Philippi Comm   1,578
Time Warner   28,892

Military installations, September 2001
Camp Dawson-Kingwood Military Training Area, Kingwood   433

Businesses and other major employers
West Virginia University; Morgantown   5,000
Weirton Steel Corp.; Weirton; steel sheets, strips   4,200
E. I. Du Pont De Nemours and Co.; Washington; plastics processing   2,500
Federal Bureau of Investigation; Clarksburg   2,400
Virginia West University Hospitals Inc.; Morgantown   2,250
Ohio Valley General Hospital; Wheeling   1,825
Oglebay Resort; Wheeling; resort hotel   1,700
United Hospital Center Inc.; Clarksburg   1,700
New Castle Refractories; Newell; ceramic kilns and furnaces   1,479
West Virginia Public Debt Bureau; Parkersburg   1,415
Wheeling Hospital Inc.; Wheeling   1,228
Homer Laughlin China Co.; Newell; kitchenware   1,145
TeleTech Customer Care Management Inc.; Morgantown; telemarketing   1,100
Monongalia County General Hospital Co.; Morgantown   1,098
Bayer Corp.; New Martinsville; inorganic chemicals   1,035
Camden-Clark Memorial Hospital Corp.; Parkersburg   1,000
Simonton Building Products Inc.; Pennsboro; window frames and sash   1,000
Weirton Medical Center Inc.; Weirton   999
Mylan Pharmaceuticals Inc.; Morgantown; proprietary drug products   974
St. Joseph Hospital; Parkersburg   900
Wheeling Park Commission; Wheeling   900
General Electric Co.; Parkersburg; plastics materials, resins   850
Ames True Temper Inc.; Parkersburg; garden, farm tools   800
PNC Bancorp Inc.; Wellsburg; commercial bank   800
Fairmont General Hospital Inc.; Fairmont   752
WesBanco Inc.; Wheeling; commercial bank   734

Coldwater Creek Inc.; Mineral Wells; warehousing   700
Aegis Communications Group Inc.; Fairmont; telemarketing   659
Alliant Missile Products Co.; Keyser; missiles, space vehicles   654
Crompton Corp.; Friendly; surface active agents   634
Fenton Art Glass Co.; Williamstown; decorative glass   600
Wal-Mart Stores Inc.; Clarksburg; department stores   600
U.S. Dept. of Veterans Affairs; Clarksburg   580
Wal-Mart Stores Inc.; Vienna; department stores   560
Advantage Foods; Petersburg; poultry processing   520
Perdue Farms Inc.; Petersburg; poultry processing   520
Centers for Disease Control and Prevention; Morgantown   500
Consolidation Coal Co.; Mannington; coal mining   500
U.S. Dept. of Energy; Morgantown   500

West Virginia 2nd District

Center — Charleston, Eastern Panhandle

The economically diverse 2nd stretches across the mountainous state from the Ohio border to the Eastern Panhandle at Harpers Ferry. The 2nd is home to poor coal mining areas and isolated towns, as well as the more prosperous capital city of Charleston and commuters in the Eastern Panhandle.

Charleston, the district's dominant city, is a center for chemical plants, state employees, and retail shopping. But chemical plants cut back in the late 1990s and a tough economy hit manufacturing companies hard. Much of the recent job growth has come from a boom in telemarketing companies moving to the state and from the expansion of retail around Charleston. The mainly Democratic mountain regions north and east of Kanawha County remain heavily dependent on coal. Putnam County, west of Kanawha County, is the site of a Toyota plant in Buffalo.

Economic depression in the 1980s drove residents from the 2nd. But in the 1990s, eastern counties within commuting distance of Washington, D.C., grew rapidly. That growth forced the 2nd to shed two counties—Nicholas and Gilmer—in redistricting following the 2000 census.

The 2nd was loyal to Democrats in congressional elections for 18 years before electing a Republican in 2000. Pockets of Republicans dot the district, particularly in the Panhandle, where GOP voters register in strong numbers and where they can be reached through Washington's media market. The National Republican Campaign Committee's late ads in that market helped the GOP take the seat in 2000.

Major Industry
Chemicals, lumber, manufacturing.

Notable
Abolitionist John Brown was hanged after attempting to incite a slave revolt in Harpers Ferry in 1859; as of 2002, there were no stoplights in Calhoun County; the U.S. Geological Survey's Leetown Science Center, located near Kearneysville, is the oldest federal fishery research facility.

Election Returns

	Republican		Democratic		Other	
President 2000	118,839	54.0%	96,524	43.8%	4,787	2.2%
House 2002	98,276	60.0%	65,400	40.0%		

District Profile

Population   602,243

Total area (square miles)   8,511.5
Land area (square miles)   8,459.3

Population per square mile   71.2

Counties (2000 population)

Berkeley 75,905	Lewis 16,919
Braxton 14,702	Mason 25,957
Calhoun 7,582	Morgan 14,943
Clay 10,330	Pendleton 8,196
Hampshire 20,203	Putnam 51,589
Hardy 12,669	Randolph 28,262
Jackson 28,000	Roane 15,446
Jefferson 42,190	Upshur 23,404
Kanawha 200,073	Wirt 5,873

Cities and other areas over 10,000 (2000 population)

Charleston 53,421	South Charleston 13,390
Cross Lanes CDP 10,353	St. Albans 11,567
Martinsburg 14,972	Teays Valley CDP 12,704

Race and Hispanic or Latino origin*

White   93.9%
Black or African American   3.6%
American Indian or Alaska Native   0.2%
Asian   0.5%
Native Hawaiian or other Pacific Islander   0.0%
Some other race   0.1%
Hispanic or Latino origin   0.8%
Two or more races   0.9%

*As percentage of total population.

Ancestry*

Dutch 1.5%	Italian 2.3%
English 8.0%	Scotch-Irish 1.5%
French 1.2%	Scottish 1.3%
German 11.7%	USA/American 14.7%
Irish 8.1%	

*As estimated percentage of total population.

Universities and colleges, 2000–2001 enrollment

Ben Franklin Career Center, Dunbar   362
Carver Career Center, Charleston   212
Davis and Elkins College, Elkins   668
National Institute of Technology, Cross Lanes   491
Shepherd College, Shepherdstown   4,703
University of Charleston, Charleston   1,096
West Virginia Career College, Charleston   204
West Virginia State College, Institute   4,824
West Virginia Wesleyan College, Buckhannon   1,622

Newspapers and circulation

	District circulation	Total circulation
Charleston Daily Mail	32,022	36,591
Charleston Gazette	36,510	50,216
Charleston Gazette/Daily Mail	68,536	87,087
Clarksburg Exponent & Telegram	1,439	16,286
Cumberland Times-News	2,007	30,232
Elkins Inter Mountain	7,469	10,244
Hagerstown Morning Herald	3,069	21,015
Hagerstown Morning Herald/ Daily Mail	3,187	35,668
Huntington Herald Dispatch	1,331	35,241
Martinsburg Journal	18,357	18,924
Parkersburg News	2,160	20,956
Parkersburg News/Sentinel	2,423	27,185
Point Pleasant Register	4,842	4,842
*USA Today**	3,204	1,674,376
Washington Post	1,982	779,632
Winchester Star	1,078	20,841

*See Sources and Explanations in the front of the volume.

Television stations and affiliations

Charleston-Huntington	47%	WCHS	ABC
Charleston-Huntington	47%	WHCP	WB, UPN
Charleston-Huntington	47%	WKAS	PBS
Charleston-Huntington	47%	WKPI	PBS
Charleston-Huntington	47%	WOUB	PBS
Charleston-Huntington	47%	WOWK	CBS
Charleston-Huntington	47%	WPBO	PBS
Charleston-Huntington	47%	WPBY	PBS
Charleston-Huntington	47%	WSAZ	NBC
Charleston-Huntington	47%	WTSF	Independent
Charleston-Huntington	47%	WVAH	FOX
Washington, DC (Hagerstown)	24%	WBDC	WB
Washington, DC (Hagerstown)	24%	WDCA	UPN
Washington, DC (Hagerstown)	24%	WETA	PBS
Washington, DC (Hagerstown)	24%	WFPT	PBS
Washington, DC (Hagerstown)	24%	WHAG	NBC
Washington, DC (Hagerstown)	24%	WHSV	ABC
Washington, DC (Hagerstown)	24%	WHUT	PBS
Washington, DC (Hagerstown)	24%	WJAL	ABC
Washington, DC (Hagerstown)	24%	WJLA	ABC
Washington, DC (Hagerstown)	24%	WNVC	Independent
Washington, DC (Hagerstown)	24%	WNVT	PBS
Washington, DC (Hagerstown)	24%	WPXW	PAX
Washington, DC (Hagerstown)	24%	WRC	NBC
Washington, DC (Hagerstown)	24%	WTTG	FOX
Washington, DC (Hagerstown)	24%	WUSA	CBS
Washington, DC (Hagerstown)	24%	WVPY	PBS
Washington, DC (Hagerstown)	24%	WWPB	PBS
Washington, DC (Hagerstown)	24%	WWPX	PAX
Clarksburg-Weston	21%	WBOY	NBC
Clarksburg-Weston	21%	WDTV	CBS
Clarksburg-Weston	21%	WVFX	FOX
Harrisonburg, VA	8%	WVPT	PBS

Cable systems and subscribers

Adelphia   29,978
Basco Electronics   1,006
CableVision Communications   13,020

Charter   76,473
CMA Cablevision   1,987
Comcast   1,369
Econoco Inc.   698
Quick Cable   1,720
Thompson Cablevision   2,663
Valley Cable   740
Valley Head TV Cable   1,012

Military installations, September 2001

Shepherd Field Regional Airport Air Force Guard Station, Martinsburg   1,182

Yeager Airport Air Force Guard Station, Charleston   938

Naval Security Group, Sugar Grove   220

Businesses and other major employers

Charleston Area Medical Center Inc.; Charleston   2,500

West Virginia Dept. of Public Safety; Charleston   1,577

Pechiney Rolled Products; Ravenswood; aluminum sheets, strips   1,500

Aventis CropScience USA; Institute; insecticides   1,350

U.S. Veterans Hospital; Martinsburg   1,200

West Virginia Dept. of Health and Human Resources; Charleston   1,170

E. I. Du Pont De Nemours and Co.; Belle; inorganic chemicals   1,066

Quad Graphics Inc.; Martinsburg; commercial printing   1,000

Royal Vendors Inc.; Kearneysville; vending machines   1,000

United Parcel Service Inc.; South Charleston; parcel delivery   1,000

Verizon Communications Inc.; Nitro; telephones   1,000

West Virginia Dept. of Transportation; Charleston   1,000

West Virginia Judiciary Courts; Charleston   1,000

Thomas Memorial Hospital Assn.; Charleston   975

General Motors Corp.; Martinsburg; automotive supplies   900

West Virginia Division of Natural Resources; Charleston   868

Mayflower Vehicle Systems Inc.; South Charleston; automotive stampings   850

Acordia of West Virginia Inc.; Charleston; insurance agents   820

United Steel Workers Local; South Charleston; labor union   803

City Hospital Inc.; Martinsburg   800

Penn National Gaming Inc.; Charles Town; race track operation   800

Sheperd College; Shepherdstown   800

U.S. Internal Revenue Service; Martinsburg   800

U.S. Postal Service; Charleston   800

American Woodmark Corp.; Moorefield; kitchen cabinets   700

Columbia Energy Group Inc.; Charleston; natural gas transmission   700

Hester Industries Inc.; Moorefield; poultry processing   675

Century Aluminum Co.; Ravenswood; aluminum ingots   650

Columbia St. Francis Hospital; Charleston   645

AT&T Corp.; Charleston; telephone services   600

Davis Memorial Hospital; Elkins   575

Mayflower Inc.; Hurricane; truck cabs   550

Toyota Motor Manufacturing West Virginia Inc.; Buffalo; engines, transmissions   550

West Virginia Bureau of Employment Programs; Charleston   550

Pleasant Valley Hospital Inc.; Point Pleasant   530

C&J Clark America Inc.; Franklin; footwear   525

Lyondell Chemical Worldwide Inc.; South Charleston; plastics materials   500

Rite Aid of West Virginia Inc.; Poca; warehousing   500

Verizon West Virginia Inc.; Charleston; telephones   500

Wal-Mart Stores Inc.; Dunbar; department stores   500

West Virginia Dept. of Taxation and Revenue; Charleston   500

West Virginia 3rd District

South — Huntington, Beckley

The 3rd is a largely rural region taking in the state's southern counties. Known as the coal district, it is home to six of the state's ten leading coal-producing counties, including the top two, Boone and Mingo.

In the 1980s technological advances in coal mining sharply reduced the need for manpower, and the 3rd has struggled to create new jobs. The decline, which also took a toll on the 3rd's population, added misery to a region that always has had pockets of Appalachian poverty. The situation improved in the 1990s and some counties grew slightly, though other counties continued to see residents leave as unemployment rates remained high. In 1999 the district had the third-lowest median income of any congressional district in the nation, at slightly more than $25,600.

The 3rd contributes to the state's tourism industry with its ski resorts, whitewater rafting, and the Greenbrier, a luxury resort hotel in White Sulphur Springs that plays host to congressional party retreats. Huntington, the district's largest city, is cushioned by its location on the Ohio River and a diversified economy that includes tobacco growers as well as oil and steel companies.

While Huntington's white-collar sector and tobacco growers help make Cabell County the most Republican part of the 3rd, overall Democrats have held a lock on the district and continue to register in large numbers. Eight of Al Gore's ten best West Virginia counties in the 2000 presidential race were in the 3rd, topped by McDowell with 66 percent. Still, George W. Bush made major inroads in the 3rd, losing the district by just over 3 percentage points after Bill Clinton won handily in 1992 and 1996.

Major Industry

Coal, wood products, tourism.

Notable

There is a now-closed nuclear bomb shelter for Congress under the Greenbrier; Sunshine Farm & Gardens, in Renick, houses one of the nation's most extensive plant collections; Mingo County, site of the West Virginia Mine Wars of the 1920s, is also the site of part of the feuding between the Hatfields and McCoys.

Election Returns

	Republican		Democratic		Other	
President 2000	94,809	47.3%	101,541	50.7%	3,942	2.0%
House 2002	37,229	29.8%	87,783	70.2%		

District Profile

Population   603,556

Total area (square miles)   9,374.5
  Land area (square miles)   9,332.2

Population per square mile   64.7

Counties (2000 population)

Boone	25,535	Monroe	14,583
Cabell	96,784	Nicholas	26,562
Fayette	47,579	Pocahontas	9,131
Greenbrier	34,453	Raleigh	79,220
Lincoln	22,108	Summers	12,999
Logan	37,710	Wayne	42,903
McDowell	27,329	Webster	9,719
Mercer	62,980	Wyoming	25,708
Mingo	28,253		

Cities and other areas over 10,000 (2000 population)

Beckley   17,254
Bluefield   11,451
Huntington   51,475

Race and Hispanic or Latino origin*

White   93.9%
Black or African American   4.1%
American Indian or Alaska Native   0.2%
Asian   0.4%
Native Hawaiian or other Pacific Islander   0.0%
Some other race   0.0%
Hispanic or Latino origin   0.6%
Two or more races   0.8%

*As percentage of total population.

Ancestry*

Dutch	1.4%	Italian	1.7%
English	7.1%	Scotch-Irish	1.5%
German	7.0%	Scottish	1.1%
Irish	7.7%	USA/American	19.7%

*As estimated percentage of total population.

Universities and colleges, 2000–2001 enrollment

Appalachian Bible College, Bradley   302
Bluefield State College, Bluefield   2,648
College of West Virginia, Beckley   2,076
Concord College, Athens   3,048
Huntington Junior College, Huntington   463
Marshall University, Huntington   15,640
Southern West Virginia Community and Technical College, Mount Gay   2,574
West Virginia School of Osteopathic Medicine, Lewisburg   285
West Virginia University Institute of Technology, Montgomery   2,326

Newspapers and circulation

	District circulation	Total circulation
Beckley Register/Herald	28,682	29,436
Bluefield Daily Telegraph	14,806	20,938
Charleston Daily Mail	4,463	36,591
Charleston Gazette	11,883	50,216
Charleston Gazette/Daily Mail	16,348	87,087
Huntington Herald Dispatch	24,020	35,241
*USA Today**	1,635	1,674,376

*See Sources and Explanations in the front of the volume.

Television stations and affiliations

Bluefield-Beckley-Oak Hill	59%	WOAY	ABC
Bluefield-Beckley-Oak Hill	59%	WSWP	PBS
Charleston-Huntington	35%	WCHS	ABC
Charleston-Huntington	35%	WHCP	WB, UPN
Charleston-Huntington	35%	WKAS	PBS
Charleston-Huntington	35%	WKPI	PBS
Charleston-Huntington	35%	WOUB	PBS
Charleston-Huntington	35%	WOWK	CBS
Charleston-Huntington	35%	WPBO	PBS
Charleston-Huntington	35%	WPBY	PBS
Charleston-Huntington	35%	WSAZ	NBC
Charleston-Huntington	35%	WTSF	Independent
Charleston-Huntington	35%	WVAH	FOX
Clarksburg-Weston	6%	WBOY	NBC
Clarksburg-Weston	6%	WDTV	CBS
Clarksburg-Weston	6%	WVFX	FOX

Cable systems and subscribers

Adelphia   24,156
Armstrong   3,820
Bradley's Inc.   1,982
Charter   114,777
Comcast   11,489
Cooney Cable   3,229
Milestone Communications   1,527
Nesbe Cable   4,040
Ronceverte TV Corp.   3,262
Ron's Cable TV   2,169
Tele-Media   6,357
Thompson Cablevision   7,548

Businesses and other major employers

St. Mary's Hospital of Huntington Inc.; Huntington   2,000
Marshall University; Huntington   1,750
CSX Corp.; White Sulphur Spring; railroad freight hauling   1,683
Huntington Cabell Hospital; Huntington   1,600
Inco Alloys International Inc.; Huntington; nickel and nickel alloy   1,153
Fayette County District; Ansted   1,150
Bluefield Regional Medical Center Inc.; Bluefield   1,040
Raleigh General Hospital; Beckley   930
Applied Card Systems Inc.; Huntington; credit card service   908

Princeton Community Hospital; Princeton   900
Logan General Hospital; Logan   803
Mercer County Board of Education; Princeton   747
Boone County School District; Madison   700
U.S. Steel Mining Co.; Pineville; coal mining   700
CSX Transportation Inc.; Huntington; railroad freight hauling   650
Cooper Community Development; Daniels; residential land development   600

Elk Run Coal Co.; Whitesville; coal mining   600
SWVA Inc.; Huntington; steel billets   570
Greenbrier County Board of Education; Lewisburg   538
Echostar Communications Corp.; Bluefield; satellite broadcast services   500
TeleSpectrum Worldwide Inc.; Huntington; telemarketing   500
U.S. Dept. of Veterans Affairs; Huntington   500
Wal-Mart Stores Inc.; Logan; department stores   500

Wisconsin

In the twentieth century, Wisconsin projected two distinctly different characters on the national political stage. The first was based on Robert M. LaFollette, a progressive Republican known at home as "Fighting Bob," the scourge of the railroads and other corporate monopolies. First elected governor in 1900, LaFollette later served three terms in the Senate and ran for president in 1924, receiving more votes than any third-party candidate for the White House between Teddy Roosevelt (1912) and Ross Perot (1992). He and his sons, who followed him into the governorship and the Senate, would give the state nearly half a century of their style of leadership.

The other touchstone figure for the state's politics came along as the LaFollette era waned after World War II. His name was Joseph R. McCarthy, and he was from neither the state's strait-laced old Yankee stock nor its array of Nordic immigrants but rather from a family of Irish Catholic Democrats. A vigorous campaigner, McCarthy wrested the GOP nomination from incumbent senator Robert LaFollette Jr. in 1946 and went to Washington. His crusade to uncover communists in government careened out of control in the 1950s, bringing many careers to grief—including his own. But within the state his politics presaged a shift from the progressive style to the populist among the state's Republicans. In an even broader sense, his politics looked ahead to the alliance of socially conservative Catholics with rural and suburban white Protestants that would drive the rightward movement in national politics later in the century.

In the meantime, a resurgent state Democratic Party in the 1950s picked up LaFollette's old philosophy of reliance on government as a wise and just arbiter in society. Allied with the considerable forces of organized labor in the state, these Democrats began to win statewide offices for the first time since the 1800s—in fact winning most of them for 30 years after McCarthy's death in 1957. His seat in the Senate has been in Democratic hands since he died, and the other Senate seat was Democratic from 1962 through 1980, and again after 1992. In addition, from 1958 through 1986, five of the seven governors would be Democrats.

But in 1986 the state elected a new Republican governor who changed the political climate. His name was Tommy Thompson, and like McCarthy he was a Catholic country lawyer who appealed to people as a populist of the right—a critic of the cerebral and didactic liberals and their welfare state. But he also believed in the assertive use of government to press his case. Although a narrow winner in 1986 (a Democratic year in which he nonetheless ousted a Democratic incumbent), Thompson went after his issues as if he had

been elected by a Reaganesque landslide. He lowered taxes, reduced regulation, championed school choice in Milwaukee, and pushed for radical welfare reform. While he did not always prevail, Thompson drove visible change and saw the state's economic fortunes improve dramatically during his tenure. He was reelected three times, shattering all records for longevity. In 2001 he became the secretary of Health and Human Services in the George W. Bush administration.

One of the main reasons Thompson was well regarded was that he came to office in an era when most observers thought the state's best economic times were behind it. Founded on timber and mining (the state's mascot, the badger, was adopted for its burrowing prowess), Wisconsin became known for its dairy products (it still leads the nation in cheese), meatpacking, beer brewing, and heavy manufacturing. Milwaukee and the smaller cities around the state had countless machine shops and factories of all sizes, assembling cars and farm equipment, construction machinery, and all kinds of small motors. But the energy crises of the 1970s, combined with a strong dollar and foreign wage competition, made Wisconsin look downright inhospitable to manufacturing. Plants closed and payrolls shrank. Milwaukee saw its population drop and its pride wounded by jokes about the "Rust Belt" and the "Frost Belt." There were those who looked at the miner and the plowman on the state seal and thought the state was reverting to its nineteenth-century economy (throwing in perhaps a fisherman to salute tourism and recreation).

All that changed when reinvestment dollars returned to the state in the late 1980s and in the 1990s. New applications were found for the state's traditional work ethic and high education quotient, and industries modernized enough to restore competitiveness. Employment went back up, and the state became attractive to newcomers again. In the 1990s, its population began growing again after three relatively static decades. Thompson got much of the credit for the improving numbers, but he was not a completely partisan governor. He often was at his best working with the Democrats in the legislature—or with Democratic mayor John Norquist of Milwaukee—rather than against them.

In Thompson's 14-year reign, the Republicans usually controlled at least one chamber of the legislature if not both and at times had a majority in the U.S. House delegation as well (peaking at six seats of the nine in 1995–1996). But the GOP could not translate this success in the presidential elections of the era, losing four in a row from 1988 through 2000. The margin in the last of these, however, was slim. It was a measure of Al Gore's tenuous grasp on the Democratic

WISCONSIN   Districts established March 27, 2002, for elections first held in 2002.

8 members

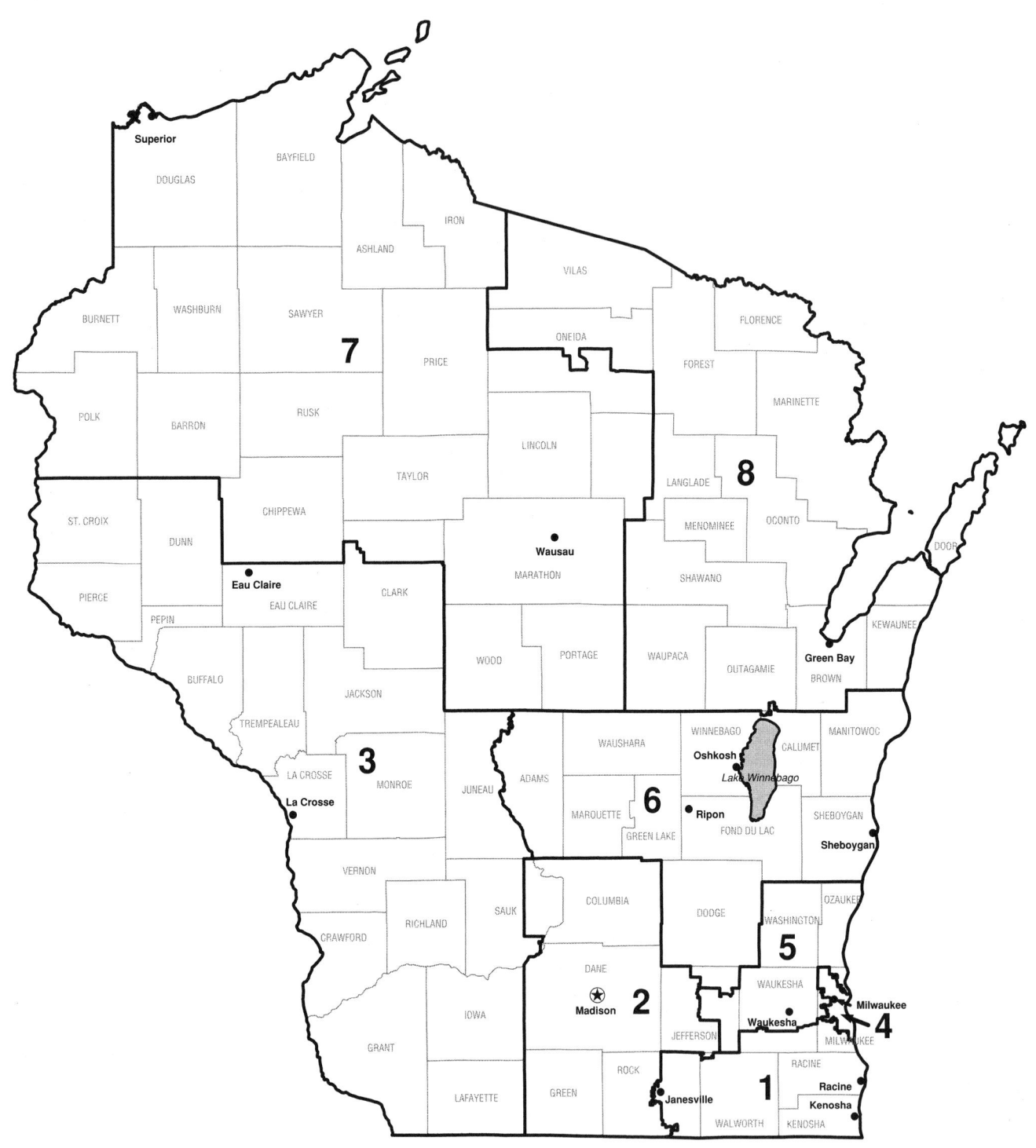

coalition built up in the 1990s that he quite nearly lost a state that had been among the meager ten won by Michael Dukakis in 1988. Before that, Wisconsin had been a swing state and a bellwether, voting with the winner for 60 years with just one exception (John F. Kennedy lost the state in 1960).

To win four presidential races is remarkable for Democrats in a state where they have remarkably little base among minority voters. As minorities approached 30 percent of the national population in 2000, Wisconsin's Hispanic, Asian, and African Americans were just 12 percent of their state's total. Census projections put the national minority share at more than 37 percent in 2025, but Wisconsin's at less than 17 percent. Most of the growth is expected to come among Hispanics, who have in recent years dispersed well beyond their original base on Milwaukee's South Side. Most of the state's African Americans live on the North Side of Milwaukee in contiguous neighborhoods. They account for more than a third of the city's population and well over half its public school children.

The 2001 redistricting had one central and distasteful mission. The state had grown nearly 10 percent in population in the 1990s but that was not sufficient growth to protect the ninth district in reapportionment. The state had barely kept its ninth seat in 1990 and so could afford to lag the national growth by even a few percentage points in yet another decade. That meant dropping from nine congressional seats to eight (the state had peaked at 11 in 1900 and still enjoyed ten from 1930 until 1970). The difficult task facing the split-control legislature (and the Republican interim governor who had succeeded Thompson) was eased when veteran Democratic representative Tom Barrett decided to run for governor (he lost narrowly in the primary to eventual winner Jim Doyle). Barrett had represented the most Democratic district in the state, the old 5th, dominated by the North and Northwest Sides of Milwaukee and its most immediate suburbs in Milwaukee County. The 5th was also a target because it had lost population, while the other eight mostly gained.

So the new map's main change was to subsume the Milwaukee portions of the old 5th with the city portions of the old 4th District (traditionally the South Side, a collection of Polish, Slavic, Italian, and German enclaves). The new district, numbered the 4th, will soon be the state's first majority-minority district, as it is already 33 percent black, 11 percent Hispanic, and 3 percent Asian. It still includes all or part of the blue-collar suburbs of South Milwaukee and West Allis. In 2000, the precincts now included in the new 4th gave Al Gore two votes of every three.

Meanwhile, the suburban portions of the old 5th were conjoined with suburbs and exurbs from the old 9th District, which had long been the state's most affluent and Republican district. The new amalgam has assumed the number of the old 5th District while preserving the demographics and politics of the old 9th. The 9th includes Ozaukee, Washington, and Waukesha Counties—the fastest growing counties in recent decades of Wisconsin history. The voting booths in this new district gave 62 percent of their votes to George W. Bush in 2000 and can be counted on to reelect the state's senior Republican, F. James Sensenbrenner Jr., chair of the House Judiciary Committee.

The state's other five districts did not need much tinkering. Just south of the Milwaukee metro area, the 1st District on the Illinois line consists of a triangle of factory towns—Racine, Kenosha, and Janesville—the southernmost suburbs of Milwaukee and the last of the dairy farms that once dominated the region. To the west, the 2nd District constricted a little more around Madison, the state's capital and second largest city, pushing its outlying counties into adjacent districts such as the southwestern 3rd District. The 3rd expanded but remained oriented to the Mississippi River on the west and to the towns of La Crosse and Eau Claire. The 3rd has historically been the one district in the country with the highest ratio of cows to people.

The northwestern 7th, home of senior Democrat David Obey, picked up Barron County and parts of three others to make the population level (about 670,000 residents). And the northeastern 8th District expanded slightly, picking up Waupaca County, but remained centered on Green Bay. Moving clockwise, the map moved the 6th District eastward. The 6th remains the Fox River Valley and Lake Fond du Lac district, but it has lost its two westernmost counties in exchange for Dodge County on the south and the city of Sheboygan on the east (on the shore of Lake Michigan).

Table 1 Population

District	Population	Population under 18	Voting-age population	Median age	Male*	Female*
1	670,458	174,938	495,520	36.5	49.5	50.5
2	670,457	157,310	513,147	34.3	49.4	50.6
3	670,462	169,696	500,766	35.5	49.7	50.3
4	670,458	187,695	482,763	31.3	47.9	52.1
5	670,458	169,821	500,637	38.4	48.8	51.2
6	670,440	166,097	504,343	37.2	50.1	49.9
7	670,462	169,906	500,556	38.0	49.7	50.3
8	670,480	173,293	497,187	36.6	49.8	50.2
State	5,363,675	1,368,756	3,994,919	36.0	49.4	50.6

*As percentage of total population.

Table 2 Voting-Age Persons by Race/Hispanic or Latino Origin

District	White*	Black or African American*	American Indian or Alaska Native*	Asian*	Other or multirace*	Hispanic or Latino*
1	89.5	4.1	0.3	0.9	0.6	4.6
2	90.6	3.0	0.3	2.3	0.9	2.9
3	97.0	0.4	0.5	0.8	0.4	0.8
4	58.5	27.8	0.7	2.3	1.3	9.4
5	94.9	1.2	0.2	1.4	0.4	1.8
6	95.1	1.2	0.4	1.0	0.5	1.9
7	96.4	0.2	1.3	0.9	0.5	0.6
8	93.9	0.5	2.2	1.0	0.5	1.8
State	89.6	4.7	0.7	1.3	0.6	2.9

*As percentage of voting-age population.

Table 3 Voting-Age Population by Age Groups

District	18 to 24*	25 to 44*	45 to 64*	Over 64*
1	11.1	41.3	30.9	16.7
2	16.8	40.6	28.3	14.3
3	16.0	36.8	29.2	18.0
4	16.4	42.2	25.5	15.9
5	9.1	39.8	32.8	18.3
6	11.9	39.1	29.9	19.1
7	11.5	36.9	31.3	20.3
8	11.5	40.0	30.3	18.2
State	13.0	39.6	29.8	17.6

*As percentage of voting-age population.

Table 4　Income and Occupation

District	Median family income	Families in poverty*	White collar†	Blue collar†	Service†	Farm†
1	$59,264	4.3	57.4	29.4	12.9	0.3
2	$58,332	4.2	63.6	22.3	13.5	0.6
3	$48,147	5.6	53.3	29.2	15.6	1.9
4	$39,567	15.9	54.0	27.8	18.1	0.2
5	$68,756	2.2	68.2	21.3	10.3	0.2
6	$52,213	3.8	49.1	35.4	14.2	1.2
7	$46,865	5.7	51.5	31.8	14.9	1.8
8	$51,548	4.6	53.9	31.3	13.6	1.2
State	$52,911	5.6	56.6	28.4	14.0	0.9

*As percentage of all families.　　†As percentage of employed workers 16 years and over.

Table 5　Education: School Years Completed

District	Less than grade 9*	Grades 9–12 no diploma*	High school diploma no college*	Some college*	College bachelor's degree or higher*
1	4.2	10.4	33.2	30.7	21.5
2	3.9	7.0	28.3	28.7	32.1
3	6.3	8.2	37.3	28.7	19.5
4	7.4	16.8	31.1	26.8	17.8
5	2.9	6.1	27.0	28.9	35.0
6	5.8	10.1	40.7	26.2	17.1
7	6.7	9.5	39.7	27.5	16.6
8	5.8	8.9	39.1	27.1	19.1
State	5.4	9.6	34.6	28.1	22.4

*As percentage of persons age 25 and over.

Table 6　Housing and Residential Patterns

District	Median home value	Owner occupied*	Renter occupied*	Urban†	Rural†
1	$125,200	70.8	29.2	84.4	15.6
2	$134,400	62.3	37.7	75.6	24.4
3	$92,400	72.1	27.9	43.1	56.9
4	$83,700	46.6	53.4	100.0	0.0
5	$159,400	73.4	26.6	84.9	15.1
6	$98,900	73.3	26.7	60.7	39.3
7	$86,200	76.1	23.9	42.0	58.0
8	$102,500	73.3	26.7	56.0	44.0
State	$109,900	68.4	31.6	68.3	31.7

*As percentage of occupied housing units.　　†As percentage of total population.

Wisconsin 1st District

Southeast — Kenosha, Racine

From the wealthy Milwaukee suburbs on the coast of Lake Michigan to the center of Rock County, the 1st blends rural communities with some of the state's largest industrial areas. The district's two largest cities are sandwiched between Milwaukee and Chicago along the lake: Racine, originally settled by Danish immigrants, and Kenosha, with a large Italian community.

A major manufacturing producer of heavy equipment and other goods, the economy fares best when a weak dollar attracts international buyers. A high foreign exchange rate in the 1990s—compounded by the shutdown of several manufacturing plants—weakened the economy and depressed real estate prices. This attracted commuters, forming large bedroom communities for Milwaukee and Chicago—both less than an hour's drive away. The influx helped the counties along the Illinois border grow almost twice as fast as the state average in the 1990s. On the other side of the district, Janesville has struggled in recent years as demand has softened for trucks from its General Motors plant.

Resorts catering to wealthy vacationers from nearby cities ring Lake Geneva and Lake Delavan (Walworth County), while Kenosha lures gamblers with Dairyland Greyhound Park, a dog-racing track.

Wisconsin lost one seat in the 2000 reapportionment, and redistricting revised the 1st's boundaries to exclude blue-collar, heavily Democratic Beloit (Rock County) and to add more of GOP-leaning Waukesha County and part of Milwaukee County. The district is about evenly split between the two parties: Of the six counties wholly or partly in the 1st, two are strongly Democratic (Kenosha and Rock), two are strongly Republican (Walworth and Waukesha), and two are highly competitive (Racine and Milwaukee). In the 2002 gubernatorial race, Democrat James E. Doyle and Republican Scott McCallum fought to a near-tie in the 1st, with Doyle prevailing by just one-tenth of a percentage point.

Major Industry
Automotive manufacturing, heavy machine manufacturing, farming.

Notable
Racine's Salmon-A-Rama fishing match; Orson Welles was born in Kenosha.

Election Returns

	Republican		Democratic		Other	
President 2000	163,040	53.1%	144,138	46.9%		
House 2002	140,176	67.2%	63,895	30.6%	4,542	2.1%

District Profile

Population　670,458

Total area (square miles)　1,723.5
　Land area (square miles)　1,679.9

Population per square mile　399.1

Counties (2000 population)
Kenosha	149,577	Rock (pt.)	79,353
Milwaukee (pt.)	115,596	Walworth (pt.)	81,187
Racine	188,831	Waukesha (pt.)	55,914

Cities and other areas over 10,000 (2000 population)
Franklin　29,494
Greendale village　14,405
Greenfield　35,476
Janesville (pt.)　59,474
Kenosha (pt.)　90,352
Muskego　21,397
Oak Creek　28,456
Pleasant Prairie village　16,136
Racine (pt.)　81,855

Race and Hispanic or Latino origin*

White   87.4%
Black or African American   4.6%
American Indian or Alaska Native   0.3%
Asian   1.0%
Native Hawaiian or other Pacific Islander   0.0%
Some other race   0.1%
Hispanic or Latino origin   5.7%
Two or more races   1.0%

*As percentage of total population.

Ancestry*

Danish   1.9%   Italian   4.2%
Dutch   1.4%   Norwegian   4.2%
English   5.1%   Polish   8.5%
French   2.6%   Swedish   1.9%
German   27.0%   USA/American   2.4%
Irish   8.3%

*As estimated percentage of total population.

Universities and colleges, 2000–2001 enrollment

Carthage College, Kenosha   2,222
Gateway Technical College, Kenosha   5,741
ITT Technical Institute, Greenfield   419
Midwest Center for the Study of Oriental Medicine,
    Racine   224
University of Wisconsin-Parkside, Kenosha   4,884

Newspapers and circulation

	District circulation	Total circulation
Franklin Hub	4,546	4,560
Greendale Village Life	2,707	2,756
Greenfield Observer	2,150	3,471
Janesville Gazette	10,992	24,784
Kenosha News	25,417	25,882
Milwaukee Journal Sentinel	42,262	271,551
Muskego Sun	3,401	3,464
New Berlin Citizen	1,230	4,096
Oak Creek Pictorial	4,153	4,224
Racine Journal Times	28,454	28,544
*USA Today**	3,587	1,674,376
Waukesha Freeman	1,933	15,798

*See Sources and Explanations in the front of the volume.

Television stations and affiliations

Milwaukee	89%	WCGV	UPN
Milwaukee	89%	WDJT	CBS
Milwaukee	89%	WISN	ABC
Milwaukee	89%	WITI	FOX
Milwaukee	89%	WJJA	Independent
Milwaukee	89%	WMVS	PBS
Milwaukee	89%	WMVT	PBS
Milwaukee	89%	WPXE	PAX
Milwaukee	89%	WTMJ	NBC
Milwaukee	89%	WVCY	Independent
Milwaukee	89%	WVTV	WB
Milwaukee	89%	WWRS	Independent
Madison	11%	KFXB	FOX
Madison	11%	WHA	PBS
Madison	11%	WISC	CBS
Madison	11%	WKOW	ABC
Madison	11%	WMSN	FOX
Madison	11%	WMTV	NBC

Cable systems and subscribers

Charter   30,279
Time Warner   107,536

Businesses and other major employers

General Motors Corp.; Janesville; truck, tractor assembly   6,000
General Motors Corp.; Janesville; automobiles   5,500
Banc One Wisconsin; Burlington; state commercial banks   3,308
IDSC Holding Inc.; Pleasant Prairie; mechanics' tools   3,000
All Saints-St. Mary's Medical Center Inc.; Racine   2,661
Case Corp.; Racine; farm machinery   2,000
DaimlerChrysler Corp.; Kenosha; diesel, dual-fuel engines   1,800
Mercy Health System Corp.; Janesville; hospital management   1,764
Delphi Corp.; Oak Creek; hardware   1,500
S. C. Johnson and Son Inc.; Sturtevant; floor waxes   1,500
United Parcel Service Inc.; Oak Creek; parcel delivery   1,500
S. C. Johnson and Son Inc.; Racine; floor waxes   1,400
City of Kenosha; Kenosha; city government   1,000
Demolay International; Kenosha; charitable organization   1,000
Intermet Corp.; Sturtevant; aluminum die-castings   1,000
Morris Material Handling Inc.; Oak Creek; hoists, cranes, monorails   1,000
Snap-On Inc.; Pleasant Prairie; tools   1,000
City of Racine; Racine; city government   940
Kenosha Hospital; Kenosha   900
STA-Rite Industries Inc.; Delavan; pumping equipment   900
Lear Corp.; Janesville; furniture   870
SSI Technologies Inc.; Janesville; electric control equipment   860
St. Luke's Memorial Hospital; Racine   850
Kindred Healthcare Inc.; Milwaukee; nursing care   800
Sanmina-SCI Corp.; Pleasant Prairie; circuit boards   800
St. Catherine's Hospital Inc.; Kenosha   800
SuperValu Inc.; Kenosha; food supplier   800
Lab Safety Supply; Janesville; safety equipment   758
Modine Manufacturing Co.; Racine; radiators, condensers   750
Wisconsin Dept. of Health and Family Services; Union Grove   700
Krones Inc.; Hales Corners; industrial labeling machines   657
Snap-On Inc.; East Troy; tools   651
PPG Industries Inc.; Oak Creek; paints   650
Twin Disc Inc.; Racine; transmission equipment   650
Cherry Corp.; Pleasant Prairie; electric switches   600
E-Funds Corp.; Milwaukee; data processing   600

Newell Rubbermaid Inc.; Janesville; pens, desk sets
   600
U.S. Postal Service; Oak Creek   600
Wal-Mart Stores Inc.; Racine; supermarkets   600
Warren Industries Inc.; Racine; packaging, labeling
   600
Wisconsin Dept. of Veterans; King   560
Case Corp.; Racine; construction tractors   550
Lake Lawn Lodge Inc.; Delavan; resort hotel   550
Textron Inc.; Racine; lawn, garden equipment   540
Franklin Public School District; Franklin   525
Charter Manufacturing Co.; Saukville; steel mills   500
Lemans Corp.; Janesville; automotive supplies   500
Tennessee Gas Pipeline Co.; Racine; natural gas
   transmission   500

Wisconsin 2nd District

South — Madison

Once described by former Republican governor Lee Dreyfus as "23 square miles surrounded by reality," Madison long has been Wisconsin's liberal centerpiece. But in the suburbs around Wisconsin's university- and government-dominated capital, growing numbers of socially liberal, fiscally conservative young professionals keep Democrats on their toes.

Many magazines have named Madison as one of the nation's most livable cities, citing the bitter winters as the only negative. The state university system's main campus is a major influence on the city. The stable economy is fueled by an educated, white-collar population, while university-associated industries such as biotechnology have been boosted by school resources and expertise. Other large employers include state government, insurance companies, and some light-manufacturing firms.

Outside of Madison, the 2nd resembles most of the rest of the state. Dane County's dairy and beef farms have declined, but it is still the second-largest farming region in the state. Tourists are attracted to the district by "Little Switzerland" in Green County, while the Wisconsin Dells—ancient natural limestone formations along the Wisconsin River—attract visitors to the north. Remapping following the 2000 census gave the 2nd Beloit, a struggling blue-collar manufacturing town near the Illinois border.

Only the Milwaukee-based 4th District exceeds the 2nd in its Democratic proclivities. In 2002 Republican governor Scott McCallum took just 19 percent of the vote in Madison, where he finished behind the Democratic, Green, and Libertarian candidates in some precincts. McCallum captured 24 percent overall in Dane County, his worst showing in the state. The addition of Beloit adds to the 2nd's Democratic heft.

Major Industry
Higher education, farming, insurance.

Notable
The Ringling brothers were from Baraboo, where the Circus World Museum is located; painter Georgia O'Keeffe was raised in Sun Prairie.

Election Returns

	Republican		Democratic		Other
President 2000	125,442	38.3%	201,738	61.7%	
House 2002	83,694	33.9%	163,313	66.1%	403

District Profile

Population   670,457

Total area (square miles)   3,601.6
   Land area (square miles)   3,511.4

Population per square mile   190.9

Counties (2000 population)
Columbia 52,468	Rock (pt.) 72,954
Dane 426,526	Sauk (pt.) 28,486
Green 33,647	Walworth (pt.) 12,572
Jefferson (pt.) 43,804	

Cities and other areas over 10,000 (2000 population)
Baraboo 10,711	Middleton 15,770
Beloit 35,775	Monroe 10,843
Fitchburg 20,501	Stoughton 12,354
Fort Atkinson 11,621	Sun Prairie 20,369
Madison 208,054	Whitewater 13,437

Race and Hispanic or Latino origin*
White   89.0%
Black or African American   3.6%
American Indian or Alaska Native   0.3%
Asian   2.4%
Native Hawaiian or other Pacific Islander   0.0%
Some other Race   0.1%
Hispanic or Latino origin   3.4%
Two or more races   1.3%

*As percentage of total population.

Ancestry*
Dutch 1.5%	Norwegian 9.1%
English 6.6%	Polish 3.2%
French 2.2%	Scottish 1.1%
German 28.4%	Swedish 1.7%
Irish 9.4%	Swiss 2.2%
Italian 2.0%	USA/American 2.4%

*As estimated percentage of total population.

Universities and colleges, 2000–2001 enrollment
Beloit College, Beloit   1,262
Blackhawk Technical College, Janesville   2,472
Edgewood College, Madison   2,062
Herzing College of Technology, Madison   527
Madison Area Technical College, Madison   14,474
Madison Media Institute, Madison   233
University of Wisconsin, Madison   51,925
University of Wisconsin, Whitewater   10,671

Newspapers and circulation

	District circulation	Total circulation
Baraboo News Republic	2,788	3,710
Janesville Gazette	12,656	24,784
Madison Capital Times	18,859	19,000

Madison Wisconsin State Journal	67,953	86,293
Milwaukee Journal Sentinel	5,346	271,551
Portage Daily Register	3,829	4,280
*USA Today**	4,881	1,674,376

*See Sources and Explanations in the front of the volume.

Television stations and affiliations

Madison	91%	KFXB	FOX
Madison	91%	WHA	PBS
Madison	91%	WISC	CBS
Madison	91%	WKOW	ABC
Madison	91%	WMSN	FOX
Madison	91%	WMTV	NBC
Milwaukee	9%	WCGV	UPN
Milwaukee	9%	WDJT	CBS
Milwaukee	9%	WISN	ABC
Milwaukee	9%	WITI	FOX
Milwaukee	9%	WJJA	Independent
Milwaukee	9%	WMVS	PBS
Milwaukee	9%	WMVT	PBS
Milwaukee	9%	WPXE	PAX
Milwaukee	9%	WTMJ	NBC
Milwaukee	9%	WVCY	Independent
Milwaukee	9%	WVTV	WB
Milwaukee	9%	WWRS	Independent

Cable systems and subscribers
Centurytel Televideo   1,745
Charter   133,575
Mediacom   1,332

Military installations, September 2001
Truax Field (Air National Guard), Madison   1,021

Businesses and other major employers
University of Wisconsin Hospital and Clinics; Madison
6,000
Wisconsin Dept. of Health and Social Services; Madison
6,000
Wisconsin Dept. of Transportation; Madison   4,000
Kraft Foods Inc.; Madison; luncheon meat   3,500
American Family Mutual Insurance Co. Inc.; Madison
3,000
City of Madison; Madison; city government   2,776
CUNA Mutual Insurance Society; Madison; accident,
health insurance   2,700
University of Wisconsin System; Madison   2,100
Meriter Hospital Inc.; Madison   1,933
Ho-Chunk Nation; Baraboo; bingo hall   1,500
Wisconsin Dept. of Health and Family Services; Madison
1,500
St. Mary's Hospital; Madison   1,400
University of Wisconsin Medical Foundation; Madison
1,300
Covance Laboratories Inc.; Madison; biological research
1,250
Trek Bicycle Corp.; Waterloo; bicycles, parts   1,250
U.S. Veterans Hospital; Madison   1,200
Springs Window Fashions; Middleton; window blinds
1,199
Wisconsin Dept. of Natural Resources; Madison   1,179
Central Wisconsin Developmentally Disabled; Madison
1,000

Madison Area Technical College District; Madison
1,000
TDS Telecommunications Corp.; Madison; telephone
service   1,000
Verizon North Inc.; Sun Prairie; telephone service
1,000
Wisconsin Dept. of Admin.; Madison   1,000
Wisconsin Workforce Development Dept.; Madison
1,000
Metso Paper USA Inc.; Beloit; paper manufacturing
machines   900
Beloit Memorial Hospital Inc.; Beloit   898
Monroe Clinic Inc.; Monroe   887
Pizza Hut of Southern Wisconsin Inc.; Madison;
restaurant management   876
Great Lakes Companies Inc.; Madison; subdividers,
developers   850
Central State Telephone Co.; Madison; local telephone
communications   800
Lands' End Inc.; Cross Plains; mail-order catalog   800
University of Wisconsin; Menomonie   800
Wisconsin Dept. of Revenue; Madison   800
Wisconsin Physicians Service Insurance Corp.; Madison;
hospital service plans   800
Anchor Bancorp Wisconsin Inc.; Madison; state savings
bank   750
Sitel Support Services Inc.; Madison; telemarketing
750
Alliant Energy Corp.; Madison; electric power
generation   700
Perry Judd's Inc.; Waterloo; commercial printing   700
Goodrich Corp.; Beloit; diesel, dual-fuel engines   683
Madison Gas and Electric Co.; Madison; utilities   671
Wisconsin Early Autism Project; Madison   657
Datex-Ohmeda Inc.; Madison; electrotherapeutic
apparatus   650
Kenexa Corp.; Madison; employment agencies   650
Pleasant Co.; Middleton; toys, games   650
Business First Inc.; Madison; newspaper   640
Madison Newspapers Inc.; Madison   634
Dane County; Madison; legislative bodies   620
Epic Systems Corp.; Madison; prepackaged software
600
Flambeau Corp.; Baraboo; molding primary plastics
600
General Casualty Co.; Sun Prairie; property damage
insurance   600
Madison-Kipp Corp.; Madison; aluminum die-castings
600
Philips Electronics North America Corp.; Monroe; light
fixtures ballasts   600
Sub-Zero Freezer Co.; Madison; refrigerators, freezers
600
Swiss Colony Inc.; Monroe; mail-order cheese   600
Sysco Food Services; Baraboo; food supplier   600
Fort Atkinson Memorial Hospital; Fort Atkinson   597
Marshall Erdman and Associates; Madison; hospital
construction   590
Wisconsin Power and Light Co.; Madison; electric, other
services   575
Perry Judd's Holdings Inc.; Baraboo; commercial
printing   560

WebCrafters Inc.; Madison; textbooks   540

Barry-Wehmiller Companies Inc.; Madison; paper
   industries machinery   500

Electronic Theatre Controls Inc.; Middleton; stage
   lighting equipment   500

Promega Corp.; Madison; biological products   500

Stoughton Trailers Inc.; Evansville; truck trailers   500

Stoughton Trailers Inc.; Stoughton; semitrailers for truck
   tractors   500

Wisconsin State Times Library; Madison   500

Wisconsin 3rd District

West — Eau Claire, La Crosse

In the 1930s, President Franklin D. Roosevelt declared Eau Claire the heart of the nation's milk industry, establishing a system that pays dairy producers more for their milk the farther they are from the 3rd's biggest city. Today, the district still has more cows than people, but the Roosevelt system has become outdated and contributed to the shutdown of family farms, forcing the 3rd to look elsewhere to boost its economy.

Despite the flat prairie land and nutrient-rich soil, the rural southwestern part of the district has been hardest hit by the lagging dairy industry. In the north, Eau Claire and La Crosse have seen declines in their manufacturing industries as well. But the five branches of Wisconsin's state university system in the 3rd have placed an emphasis on computer and technology education, and both cities have experienced recent growth in their technology sectors. Meanwhile, bedroom communities in St. Croix County—inhabited by commuters to Minneapolis-St. Paul, just across the Minnesota state line—grew rapidly during the 1990s.

Recreational tourism also contributes to the 3rd's economy. The 200 miles of Mississippi River that the district takes in along the western border with Minnesota and Iowa provide bird-watchers an opportunity to spot bald eagles perched on bluffs. Lakes in the north attract sports enthusiasts and retirees.

The 3rd has a slight Democratic lean and voted narrowly for Democrat James E. Doyle in the 2002 gubernatorial election. But most of the 19 counties wholly or partly in the district are politically competitive; in the 2000 presidential contest, all but four gave the winner a margin of victory of less than 10 percentage points.

Major Industry

Dairy farming, heavy manufacturing, tourism.

Notable

Laura Ingalls Wilder, author of the *Little House on the Prairie* books, was born in Pepin; Taliesin, Frank Lloyd Wright's estate, is in Spring Green.

Election Returns

	Republican		Democratic		Other	
President 2000	144,948	48.2%	155,832	51.8%		
House 2002	69,955	33.5%	131,038	62.8%	7,588	3.7%

District Profile

Population   670,462

Total area (square miles)   13,849.1
   Land area (square miles)   13,565.4

Population per square mile   49.4

Counties (2000 population)

Buffalo 13,804	Lafayette 16,137
Clark (pt.) 19,565	Monroe 40,899
Crawford 17,243	Pepin 7,213
Dunn 39,858	Pierce 36,804
Eau Claire 93,142	Richland 17,924
Grant 49,597	Sauk (pt.) 26,739
Iowa 22,780	St. Croix 63,155
Jackson 19,100	Trempealeau 27,010
Juneau 24,316	Vernon 28,056
La Crosse 107,120	

Cities and other areas over 10,000 (2000 population)

Eau Claire (pt.) 59,794	Onalaska 14,839
La Crosse 51,818	River Falls 12,560
Menomonie 14,937	

Race and Hispanic or Latino origin*

White   96.1%
Black or African American   0.5%
American Indian or Alaska Native   0.5%
Asian   1.2%
Native Hawaiian or other Pacific Islander   0.0%
Some other race   0.0%
Hispanic or Latino origin   0.9%
Two or more races   0.7%

As percentage of total population.

Ancestry*

Dutch 1.3%	Italian 1.2%
English 5.4%	Norwegian 14.1%
French 2.4%	Polish 3.5%
German 29.7%	Swedish 2.3%
Irish 8.5%	USA/American 2.7%

As estimated percentage of total population.

Universities and colleges, 2000–2001 enrollment

Chippewa Valley Technical College, Eau Claire   4,503
Southwest Wisconsin Technical College, Fennimore   1,264
University of Wisconsin, Eau Claire   10,647
University of Wisconsin, La Crosse   9,409
University of Wisconsin, Platteville   5,559
University of Wisconsin, River Falls   5,899
University of Wisconsin, Menomonie   7,877
Viterbo College, La Crosse   2,941
Western Wisconsin Technical College, La Crosse   4,928

Newspapers and circulation

	District circulation	Total circulation
Dubuque Telegraph Herald	4,541	28,283
Eau Claire Leader-Telegram	20,929	27,574
Juneau County Star Times	2,403	2,491

La Crosse Tribune	28,129	31,589	
Madison Wisconsin State Journal	13,533	86,293	
Marshfield News-Herald	2,402	13,469	
Milwaukee Journal Sentinel	3,118	271,551	
Minneapolis Star Tribune	1,343	341,251	
Reedsburg Times Press	1,123	1,181	
St. Paul Pioneer Press	13,027	200,578	
*USA Today**	2,560	1,674,376	
Winona Daily News	2,058	11,538	

See Sources and Explanations in the front of the volume.

Television stations and affiliations

La Crosse-Eau Claire	57%	WEAU	NBC
La Crosse-Eau Claire	57%	WEUX	FOX
La Crosse-Eau Claire	57%	WEUX	FOX
La Crosse-Eau Claire	57%	WHLA	PBS
La Crosse-Eau Claire	57%	WHWC	PBS
La Crosse-Eau Claire	57%	WKBT	CBS
La Crosse-Eau Claire	57%	WLAX	FOX
La Crosse-Eau Claire	57%	WQOW	ABC
La Crosse-Eau Claire	57%	WXOW	ABC
Madison	33%	KFXB	FOX
Madison	33%	WHA	PBS
Madison	33%	WISC	CBS
Madison	33%	WKOW	ABC
Madison	33%	WMSN	FOX
Madison	33%	WMTV	NBC
Minneapolis-St. Paul	10%	KARE	NBC
Minneapolis-St. Paul	10%	KAWB	PBS
Minneapolis-St. Paul	10%	KAWE	PBS
Minneapolis-St. Paul	10%	KCCO	CBS
Minneapolis-St. Paul	10%	KCCW	CBS
Minneapolis-St. Paul	10%	KMSP	FOX
Minneapolis-St. Paul	10%	KMWB	WB
Minneapolis-St. Paul	10%	KPXM	PAX
Minneapolis-St. Paul	10%	KRWF	ABC
Minneapolis-St. Paul	10%	KSAX	ABC
Minneapolis-St. Paul	10%	KSTP	ABC
Minneapolis-St. Paul	10%	KTCA	PBS
Minneapolis-St. Paul	10%	KTCI	PBS
Minneapolis-St. Paul	10%	KWCM	PBS
Minneapolis-St. Paul	10%	WFTC	UPN

Cable systems and subscribers
Baldwin Telecom   1,944
Centurytel Televideo   2,695
Charter   74,303
Comcast   5,939
Community Antenna   1,503
Durand Cable TV   2,328
Frontier Cable of Wisconsin   1,882
KRM Cablevision   920
Mediacom   15,706
U.S. Cable   1,419
Western Wisconsin Community Co-op   6,345

Military installations, September 2001
Fort McCoy (Army), Sparta   3,268
Volk Field (Air National Guard), Camp Douglas   253

Businesses and other major employers
Gundersen Lutheran Medical Center Inc.; La Crosse; hospital   4,000
Lands' End Inc.; Dodgeville; mail-order catalog   3,420

Franciscan Skemp Medical Center Inc.; La Crosse   3,300
Trane Co.; La Crosse; refrigeration, heating   3,100
Horace Mann Educators Corp.; Platteville; fire, marine, casualty insurance   2,700
Ashley Furniture Industries Inc.; Arcadia   2,480
Menard Inc.; Eau Claire; lumber, building materials   2,400
City of La Crosse; La Crosse; city government   1,500
Hutchinson Technology Inc.; Eau Claire; computer storage devices   1,500
La Crosse County; La Crosse; county government   1,300
University of Wisconsin System; Eau Claire   1,300
Luther Hospital-Mayo Health System; Eau Claire   1,230
University of Wisconsin System; Menomonie   1,200
Wal-Mart Stores Inc.; Menomonie; warehousing   1,200
Marten Transport; Mondovi; refrigerated transport   1,100
Chippewa Valley Technical College District; Eau Claire   1,050
Sacred Heart Hospital; Eau Claire   1,000
Midelfort Clinic-Mayo Health System; Eau Claire   986
Village Bake Shop Inc.; La Crosse; grocery store   800
U.S. Veterans Hospital; Tomah   750
UnitedHealth Group; Eau Claire; insurance claim processing   750
Millis Transfer Inc.; Black River Falls; contract haulers   700
Philips Electronics North America Corp.; Boscobel; switchgear apparatus   700
University of Wisconsin System; Platteville   700
Wisconsin Public Safety Dept.; River Falls   700
University of Wisconsin System; River Falls   697
McMillan Electric Co.; Woodville; electric motors   650
3M Co.; Prairie Du Chien; abrasive products   600
Black Bear Casino and Hotel; Eau Claire   600
Equitable Life Assurance Society of U.S.; Eau Claire; insurance agents and brokers   600
Fleming Companies Inc.; La Crosse; food supplier   600
Ho-Chunk Nation; Black River Falls; Native American reservation   600
Kwik Trip Inc.; La Crosse; gas stations   600
LaCrosse Footwear Inc.; La Crosse; rubber and plastic footwear   600
Toro Co.; Tomah; lawn and garden equipment   600
Carlisle Walker Group; New Lisbon; lined metal plate tanks   600
Western Wisconsin Technical College; La Crosse   600
APAC Customer Services Inc.; La Crosse; telemarketing   560
Rockwell Automation Inc.; Richland Center; electric control equipment   560
Grede Foundries Inc.; Reedsburg; gray iron castings   510
APAC Customer Services Inc.; Onalaska; telemarketing   500
Derosa Development Inc.; Eau Claire; fast-food restaurant chain   500
Northern Automotive Systems; West Salem; plastics processing   500
Northern Engraving Corp.; Sparta; metal stampings   500
Rayovac Corp.; Fennimore; alkaline batteries   500

Wisconsin 4th District

Milwaukee

As Father James Groppi led civil rights protesters across Milwaukee's 16th Street Bridge over the Menomonee Valley in the 1960s, observers called it the "longest bridge in the world"—quipping that it stretched all the way from Poland to Africa. After redistricting following the 2000 census put all of Milwaukee into a single district for the first time, the 4th must confront the stark racial, cultural, and economic differences that divide its northern and southern parts.

Polish immigrants flocked to the southern side of the valley in the early twentieth century as Milwaukee grew into one of the nation's larger cities. Then a large black population migrated to the area following World War II, but regulations forced them to the northern side of the valley. As population has declined since the 1960s, the pronounced social and economic differences between the two communities have remained.

Milwaukee today is minority-majority, with blacks (37 percent) and Hispanics (12 percent) together outnumbering whites. Milwaukee was once tagged as "hypersegregated," but city officials say it is becoming more integrated. Still, it is not uncommon to find almost completely black areas in north-central Milwaukee and almost exclusively white areas in the southern part of the city.

As the growing Hispanic population displaces wealthier white-collar workers migrating to suburbs west of Milwaukee, the city's manufacturing industries—especially some of the breweries and tanneries that defined the economy—continue to decline, leaving the city struggling to find a new identity. Milwaukee's large minority population and strong union presence make the 4th staunchly Democratic.

Major Industry
Machinery manufacturing, service.

Notable
The world's largest four-sided clock is on the Allen-Bradley building; Milwaukee's Holler House is the nation's oldest sanctioned bowling alley; Schlitz, "the beer that made Milwaukee famous," closed its Milwaukee brewery in 1981.

Election Returns

	Republican		Democratic		Other	
President 2000	84,823	31.6%	183,810	68.4%		
House 2002			122,031	86.3%	19,336	13.7%

District Profile

Population 670,458

Total area (square miles) 112.5
   Land area (square miles) 111.9

Population per square mile 5,991.6

Counties (2000 population)
   Milwaukee (pt.) 670,458

Cities and other areas over 10,000 (2000 population)
Cudahy	18,429	South Milwaukee	21,256
Milwaukee (pt.)	596,974	West Allis (pt.)	20,936

Race and Hispanic or Latino origin*
White 50.4%
Black or African American 33.0%
American Indian or Alaska Native 0.7%
Asian 2.7%
Native Hawaiian or other Pacific Islander 0.0%
Some other race 0.2%
Hispanic or Latino origin 11.2%
Two or more races 1.8%

As percentage of total population.

Ancestry*
English	2.2%	Italian	2.6%
French	1.7%	Norwegian	1.8%
German	18.3%	Polish	8.9%
Irish	5.4%	USA/American	1.6%

As estimated percentage of total population.

Universities and colleges, 2000–2001 enrollment
Alverno College, Milwaukee 1,932
Keller Graduate School of Management, Milwaukee 332
Marquette University, Milwaukee 10,892
Milwaukee Area Technical College, Milwaukee 14,296
Milwaukee Institute of Art Design, Milwaukee 646
Milwaukee School of Engineering, Milwaukee 2,620
Mount Mary College, Milwaukee 1,246
University of Wisconsin, Milwaukee 23,578
Wisconsin Lutheran College, Milwaukee 634

Newspapers and circulation

	District circulation	Total circulation
Cudahy Reminder Enterprise	4,143	4,293
Greenfield Observer	1,300	3,471
Milwaukee Journal Sentinel	76,549	271,551
Shorewood Herald	2,807	9,642
South Milwaukee Voice Graphic	3,230	3,380
Wauwatosa News Times	1,316	6,269
West Allis Star	2,139	4,799

See Sources and Explanations in the front of the volume.

Television stations and affiliations
Milwaukee	100%	WCGV	UPN
Milwaukee	100%	WDJT	CBS
Milwaukee	100%	WISN	ABC
Milwaukee	100%	WITI	FOX
Milwaukee	100%	WJJA	Independent
Milwaukee	100%	WMVS	PBS
Milwaukee	100%	WMVT	PBS
Milwaukee	100%	WPXE	PAX
Milwaukee	100%	WTMJ	NBC
Milwaukee	100%	WVCY	Independent
Milwaukee	100%	WVTV	WB
Milwaukee	100%	WWRS	Independent

Cable systems and subscribers
Time Warner 120,284

Military installations, September 2001

W. Silver Spring Complex (Army Reserve), Milwaukee
1,733

General Mitchell International Airport Air Force
Reserve, Milwaukee   1,549

General Mitchell International Airport Air Force Guard
Station, Milwaukee   873

Businesses and other major employers

Miller Brewing Co.; Milwaukee; beer and ale   8,000

Northwestern Financial Group; Milwaukee; land
developers   5,000

U.S. Postal Service; Milwaukee   4,000

St. Luke's Medical Center; Milwaukee   3,148

Tower Automotive Inc.; Milwaukee; automotive
parts/accessories   2,840

Wisconsin Children's Hospital; Milwaukee   2,600

Baymont Inns Hospitality Corp.; Milwaukee; franchised
motel   2,567

U.S. Dept. of Veterans Affairs; Milwaukee   2,052

Wisconsin Energy Corp.; Milwaukee; electric power
generation   2,000

Fortis Insurance Co.; Milwaukee; life insurance   1,847

City of Milwaukee; Milwaukee; city government   1,800

Columbia-St. Mary's Hospital of Milwaukee; Milwaukee
1,800

Marquette University; Milwaukee   1,600

St. Joseph Hospital; Milwaukee   1,587

V&J National Enterprises; Milwaukee; fast-food
restaurant chain   1,538

Aqua-Chem Inc.; Milwaukee; engineering services
1,500

Potawatomi Bingo; Milwaukee; bingo hall   1,500

Journal Sentinel Inc.; Milwaukee; newspaper publishing
1,500

Milwaukee County; Milwaukee; aircraft regulating
agencies   1,500

St. Francis Hospital Inc.; Milwaukee   1,500

Milwaukee Area Technical College Foundation Inc.;
Milwaukee   1,450

Columbia Hospital Inc.; Milwaukee   1,412

Northern Health Facilities Inc.; Milwaukee; nursing care
1,394

John Alden Life Insurance Co.; Milwaukee   1,368

Milwaukee County; Milwaukee; social service center
1,350

Mortgage Guaranty Insurance Corp.; Milwaukee   1,100

Patrick Cudahy Inc.; Cudahy; sausages   1,100

Milwaukee County; Milwaukee; county government
1,045

Blue Cross and Blue Shield; Milwaukee; medical plans
1,000

Harnischfeger Corp.; Milwaukee; power shovels   1,000

Rockwell Automation Inc.; Milwaukee; shipping agents
1,000

St. Michael Hospital; Milwaukee   1,000

University of Wisconsin System; Milwaukee   1,000

Falk Corp.; Milwaukee; automobile parts   950

Sinai Samaritan Medical Center Inc.; Milwaukee   950

Ladish Co. Inc.; Cudahy iron and steel forgings   941

Emmber Foods Inc.; Milwaukee; beef products   900

GE Medical Systems Information Technologies;
Milwaukee; patient monitoring apparatus   900

Milwaukee County; Milwaukee; transportation
department   850

Marcus Theatres Corp.; Milwaukee; movie theaters   834

Instant Help Inc.; Milwaukee; temporary help service
825

Bucyrus International Inc.; South Milwaukee; powered
draglines   813

E Z Paintr Corp.; Milwaukee; paint rollers   800

Foley and Lardner; Milwaukee; law office   800

Harley-Davidson Inc.; Milwaukee; motorcycles   760

Schneider Automation Inc.; Milwaukee; process control
instruments   750

Alverno College; Milwaukee   722

Burns International Security Services Corp.; Milwaukee;
security guard   722

Eaton Corp.; Milwaukee; industrial electric controls
700

Milwaukee School of Engineering Inc.; Milwaukee   700

Saks Inc.; Milwaukee; department stores   700

St. Luke's Medical Center; Cudahy   700

ADT Security Services Inc.; Milwaukee; alarm systems
682

Aurora Health Care Inc.; Milwaukee; hospital
management   675

MGIC Investment Corp.; Milwaukee; mortgage
guarantee insurance   648

Aldrich Chemical Co.; Milwaukee; industrial organic
chemicals   630

Compuware Corp.; Milwaukee; software   600

Master Lock Co.; Milwaukee; padlocks   600

Bradley Center Corp.; Milwaukee; auditorium operation
560

Johnson Controls Inc.; Milwaukee; air-conditioning
pressure controllers   550

Quarles and Brady; Milwaukee; law office   531

West Allis City; Milwaukee; city government   520

Baird Capital Partners Management Co.; Milwaukee;
venture capital companies   500

Brady Corp.; Milwaukee; name plates   500

City of Milwaukee; Milwaukee; city government   500

Cooper Power Systems Inc.; South Milwaukee; electronic
generation equipment   500

Professionally Speaking Inc.; Milwaukee; fund-raising
organizations   500

Rodney Dow; Milwaukee; law office   500

SBC Communications Inc.; Milwaukee; telephone
communication   500

U.S. Internal Revenue Service; Milwaukee   500

Wisconsin 5th District

Southeast — Milwaukee suburbs

Residents of Waukesha and Ozaukee Counties joke that more people commute from Milwaukee to the suburbs that make up the 5th District than the other way around. Indeed, the affluent counties to the west and north of the city have continued to experience rapid growth as Milwaukee middle managers leave downtown and newly transferred white-collar workers settle in the city's outskirts.

As the suburbs expand, they are becoming increasingly self-sufficient, providing employment in all sectors. Most of the manufacturing jobs outside of the city are located in Waukesha County, west of Milwaukee. Quad Graphics, a major printing company, is headquartered in Pewaukee, while engine manufacturer Briggs and Stratton is located in Wauwatosa. Most residents in Ozaukee County, to the north of the city, hold service and legal-related jobs. Waukesha County's population grew by 18 percent in the 1990s; Washington County, to Waukesha's north, grew by 23 percent, the fourth-fastest in the state.

While the northern and western outskirts of the 5th are still mostly rural and populated with dairy farms and cattle ranches, urban sprawl has started to encroach upon them as well. Most residents of the 5th still proudly celebrate their diverse European heritages—German, Belgian, Dutch, and Eastern European folk festivals attract tourists almost every weekend of the summer. Vacationers also travel here for the recreational fishing and boating opportunities along Lake Michigan.

The present-day 5th is descended from the 9th District that existed in the 1990s; the renumbering was required after redistricting following the 2000 census dismantled a Milwaukee-based district (the old 5th). The strong GOP lean in Ozaukee, Washington, and Waukesha makes the new 5th the state's most heavily Republican district: it gave 63.8 percent to George W. Bush in the 2000 presidential election. Democrats are competitive only in Milwaukee County.

Major Industry
Service, manufacturing, retail.

Notable
Harley-Davidson has a product development center in Wauwatosa.

Election Returns

	Republican		Democratic		Other	
President 2000	233,005	63.8%	132,310	36.2%		
House 2002	191,224	86.1%			30,788	13.9%

District Profile

Population   670,458

Total area (square miles)   1,300.8
   Land area (square miles)   1,273.2

Population per square mile   526.6

Counties (2000 population)

Jefferson (pt.)	11,685	Washington	117,493
Milwaukee (pt.)	154,110	Waukesha (pt.)	304,853
Ozaukee	82,317		

Cities and other areas over 10,000 (2000 population)
Brookfield   38,649
Brown Deer village   12,170
Cedarburg   10,908
Germantown village   18,260
Glendale   13,367
Grafton village   10,312
Hartford (pt.)   10,895
Menomonee Falls village   32,647
Mequon   21,823
New Berlin (pt.)   31,636
Oconomowoc   12,382
Pewaukee   11,783
Port Washington (pt.)   10,467
Shorewood village   13,763
Waukesha   64,825
Wauwatosa   47,271
West Allis (pt.)   40,318
West Bend   28,152
Whitefish Bay village   14,163

Race and Hispanic or Latino origin*
White   94.0%
Black or African American   1.3%
American Indian or Alaska Native   0.2%
Asian   1.5%
Native Hawaiian or other Pacific Islander   0.0%
Some other race   0.1%
Hispanic or Latino origin   2.2%
Two or more races   0.7%

*As percentage of total population.

Ancestry*

Dutch	1.4%	Italian	3.7%
English	5.0%	Norwegian	3.3%
French	2.5%	Polish	7.7%
German	34.6%	Swedish	1.5%
Irish	8.8%	USA/American	2.4%

*As estimated percentage of total population.

Universities and colleges, 2000–2001 enrollment
Cardinal Stritch University, Milwaukee   6,041
Carroll College, Waukesha   2,902
Concordia University, Mequon   4,603
Medical College of Wisconsin, Milwaukee   1,181
Ottawa University, Brookfield   205
Waukesha County Technical College, Pewaukee   7,943

Newspapers and circulation

	District circulation	Total circulation
Brookfield News	5,821	5,830
Elm Grove Elm Leaves	1,451	1,453
German Town Banner Press	2,225	2,225
Menomonee Falls News	3,883	3,881
Mequon-Thiensville Courant	1,401	1,401
Milwaukee Journal Sentinel	105,738	271,551
New Berlin Citizen	2,883	4,096
Ozaukee County News Graphic	7,692	7,718
Shorewood Herald	6,809	9,642
*USA Today**	8,774	1,674,376
Waukesha Freeman	13,595	15,798
Wauwatosa News Times	4,869	6,269
West Allis Star	2,438	4,799
West Bend Daily News	9,639	9,966

*See Sources and Explanations in the front of the volume.

Television stations and affiliations

Milwaukee	100%	WCGV	UPN
Milwaukee	100%	WDJT	CBS
Milwaukee	100%	WISN	ABC
Milwaukee	100%	WITI	FOX
Milwaukee	100%	WJJA	Independent
Milwaukee	100%	WMVS	PBS

Milwaukee	100%	WMVT	PBS
Milwaukee	100%	WPXE	PAX
Milwaukee	100%	WTMJ	NBC
Milwaukee	100%	WVCY	Independent
Milwaukee	100%	WVTV	WB
Milwaukee	100%	WWRS	Independent

Cable systems and subscribers

Charter 21,027
Time Warner 102,031

Businesses and other major employers

Pick 'n Save Warehouse Foods Inc.; Pewaukee; grocery store 5,446

Wisconsin Hospitality Group; Milwaukee; health services consultant 5,000

Western Power Products Inc.; Waukesha; insulation materials 4,269

Metavante Corp.; Milwaukee; data processing 2,700

Medical College of Wisconsin Inc.; Milwaukee 2,359

Briggs and Stratton Corp.; Milwaukee; internal combustion engines 2,152

Waukesha Memorial Hospital Inc.; Waukesha 2,046

ProHealth Care Inc.; Waukesha; data processing 2,045

Mark Travel Corp.; Milwaukee; tour operators 2,000

JC Penney Corp.; Milwaukee; warehousing 1,700

Germantown-45 Inc.; Milwaukee; fast-food restaurant chain 1,600

Milwaukee Mental Health Clinic; Milwaukee 1,600

Waukesha County; Waukesha; county government 1,550

Kohl's Department Stores Inc.; Menomonee Falls 1,500

Allis West Memorial Hospital Inc.; Milwaukee 1,400

Quad Graphics Inc.; Hartford; commercial printing 1,200

Menomonee Falls Community Memorial Hospital; Menomonee Falls 1,050

Brady Worldwide Inc.; Milwaukee; industrial labeling machines 1,000

Cooper Power Systems Inc.; Waukesha; electric power transformers 1,000

Rockwell Automation Inc.; Mequon; PBX equipment 1,000

Serigraph Inc.; West Bend; screen printing 1,000

United Parcel Service Inc.; Elm Grove; parcel delivery 1,000

Wisconsin Evangelical Lutheran Synod; Milwaukee 912

Johnson Controls Inc.; Milwaukee; thermostats 900

Manpower Inc.; Milwaukee; temporary help service 900

West Bend Co.; West Bend; cooking appliances 850

Dresser Inc.; Waukesha; internal combustion engines 800

Elmbrook Memorial Hospital Inc.; Brookfield 800

Menasha Material Handling Corp.; Oconomowoc; synthetic resin finished products 800

Quad Graphics Inc.; Milwaukee; commercial printing 800

Target Corp.; Oconomowoc; warehousing 800

St. Mary's Hospital Ozaukee Inc.; Thiensville 763

Benevolent Corp. Cedar Campuses; West Bend; religious instruction 750

Broan-NuTone; Hartford; exhaust and ventilating fans 750

Milwaukee Electric Tool Corp.; Brookfield; power-driven handtools 750

Strattec Security Corp.; Milwaukee; automotive parts/accessories 750

Leggett and Platt Inc.; Grafton; bed frames 716

Clean Power Inc.; Milwaukee; janitorial service 710

Arandell Corp.; Menomonee Falls; commercial printing 700

Leeson Electric Corp.; Grafton; electric motors 700

Pinkerton's Inc.; Milwaukee; security guard service 700

Quad/Graphics Inc.; Sussex; commercial printing 700

St. Joseph's Community Hospital; West Bend 688

CBT; New Berlin; restaurants 650

United Lutheran Program for Aging Inc.; Milwaukee; nursing care facilities 630

Strong Capital Management Inc.; Menomonee Falls; investment research 611

Oconomowoc Memorial Hospital; Oconomowoc 604

Allen-Edmonds Shoe Corp.; Port Washington; nonathletic shoes 600

Citation Custom Products; Menomonee Falls; repair machine shop 600

General Electric Co.; Waukesha; x-ray apparatus and tubes 600

Harley-Davidson Inc.; Milwaukee; motorcycles 600

Husco International Inc.; Waukesha; control valves, fluid power 600

Milwaukee Sportservice Inc.; Milwaukee; concessionaire 600

Thomson Financial Inc.; Brookfield; computer software 600

Waukesha Electric Systems Inc.; Waukesha; electric power transformers 585

Western States Envelope Co.; Butler 560

Kilian Management Services Inc.; West Bend; fast-food restaurant chain 550

MetalTek International Inc.; Waukesha; iron foundry 550

West Bend Mutual Insurance Co.; West Bend; fire, marine, casualty insurance 544

SC Advanced Healthcare; Milwaukee; medical clinic 525

Gehl Co.; West Bend; farm machinery 510

Charter Manufacturing Co.; Saukville; nonferrous rolling and drawing 502

Wacker Corp.; Menomonee Falls; backfillers, self-propelled 502

Ameritech Services Inc.; Waukesha; purchasing service 500

Badger Meter Inc.; Milwaukee; process control instruments 500

Cooper Power Systems Inc.; Waukesha; nonelectric transformers 500

Eaton Corp.; Oconomowoc; electric control equipment 500

Fiserv Solutions Inc.; Brookfield; data processing 500

Generac Power Systems Inc.; Waukesha; electric generators 500

International Truck and Engine Corp.; Waukesha; iron foundries 500

Milwaukee Mutual Insurance Co.; Brookfield; fire, marine, casualty insurance   500

Regal Ware Inc.; Kewaskum; engineering services   500

Tecumseh Products Co.; Grafton; refrigeration and heating   500

Wisconsin 6th District

East central — Oshkosh, Sheboygan, Fond du Lac

In 1854 a group of dissatisfied Whigs, Free Soilers, and Democrats met in a Ripon schoolhouse in central Fond du Lac County and created the Republican Party. Today, the rural areas west of Ripon still carry on the GOP tradition of their forefathers, but the blue-collar communities along Lake Michigan's shores, characterized by manufacturing and processing plants, vote Democratic.

On Lake Michigan, Manitowoc County has a long-standing reputation as a shipbuilding center. Sheboygan County is famed for its meat processing—it considers itself the bratwurst capital of the world—and also for its manufacturing, including the plumbing company Kohler. Around Lake Winnebago, Oshkosh produces heavy trucks while Neenah and Menasha are major paper-product manufacturers.

The west is farming territory, though family dairy farms have struggled. Some have been assimilated by large corporate farms and others have turned to crops such as beans, peas, and corn. Marquette County, located in the southwest, is the least-populous county in the 6th but the fastest-growing in the state (28.5 percent in the 1990s). It is popular among retirees from the Milwaukee and Chicago areas.

Many of the 6th's residents are descendants of German immigrants who settled the area in the 1850s, and the district claims more people of German ancestry (54 percent) than any other in the nation. Although these socially conservative Lutherans combine with a Catholic community to dominate much of the district, some of the state's traditional progressivism remains. The Hmong population—immigrants from East Asia—nearly doubled in the 1990s.

The 6th leans Republican, but not overwhelmingly so. In 2000, George W. Bush won every county here except for Adams, located in the far west. Republican Scott McCallum won the 6th in the 2002 gubernatorial election, narrowly winning Sheboygan and Winnebago.

Major Industry
Paper, dairy, tourism.

Notable
The Wisconsin Maritime Museum is in Manitowoc.

Election Returns

	Republican		Democratic		Other	
President 2000	170,134	55.8%	134,926	44.2%		
House 2002	169,834	99.2%			1,327	0.8%

District Profile

Population   670,440

Total area (square miles)   5,816.4
    Land area (square miles)   5,641.1

Population per square mile   118.8

Counties (2000 population)

Adams 18,643	Manitowoc 82,887
Calumet (pt.) 29,619	Marquette 15,832
Dodge 85,897	Outagamie (pt.) 10,066
Fond du Lac 97,296	Sheboygan 112,646
Green Lake 19,105	Waushara 23,154
Jefferson (pt.) 18,532	Winnebago 156,763

Cities and other areas over 10,000 (2000 population)

Beaver Dam 15,169	Oshkosh (pt.) 62,916
Fond du Lac (pt.) 42,203	Sheboygan 50,792
Manitowoc 34,053	Two Rivers 12,639
Menasha (pt.) 16,331	Watertown 21,598
Neenah 24,507	Waupun 10,718

Race and Hispanic or Latino origin*
White   94.1%
Black or African American   1.0%
American Indian or Alaska Native   0.4%
Asian   1.5%
Native Hawaiian or other Pacific Islander   0.0%
Some other race   0.0%
Hispanic or Latino origin   2.3%
Two or more races   0.7%

*As percentage of total population.

Ancestry*

Dutch 3.7%	Italian 1.4%
English 4.0%	Norwegian 3.2%
French 2.9%	Polish 5.4%
German 38.8%	Swedish 1.3%
Irish 6.8%	USA/American 3.0%

*As estimated percentage of total population.

Universities and colleges, 2000–2001 enrollment
Lakeland College, Sheboygan   3,565
Lakeshore Technical College, Cleveland   2,742
Maranatha Baptist Bible College, Watertown   503
Marian College of Fond du Lac, Fond du Lac   2,557
Moraine Park Technical College, Fond du Lac   6,921
Ripon College, Ripon   862
Silver Lake College, Manitowoc   938
University of Wisconsin, Oshkosh   10,744

Newspapers and circulation

	District circulation	Total circulation
Appleton Post-Crescent	20,096	52,578
Beaver Dam Daily Citizen	9,202	10,034
Fond du Lac Reporter	17,758	17,758
Green Bay Press Gazette	1,072	55,568
Madison Wisconsin State Journal	2,733	86,293
Manitowoc Herald Times Reporter	15,909	16,165
Milwaukee Journal Sentinel	19,165	271,551
Oshkosh Northwestern	22,453	22,453
Sheboygan Press	23,495	23,649
*USA Today**	3,356	1,674,376
Wisconsin Rapids Daily Tribune	1,237	12,585

*See Sources and Explanations in the front of the volume.

Television stations and affiliations

Green Bay-Appleton	55%	WACY	UPN
Green Bay-Appleton	55%	WBAY	ABC
Green Bay-Appleton	55%	WFRV	CBS
Green Bay-Appleton	55%	WGBA	NBC
Green Bay-Appleton	55%	WIWB	WB, PAX
Green Bay-Appleton	55%	WJFW	NBC
Green Bay-Appleton	55%	WLUK	FOX
Green Bay-Appleton	55%	WPNE	PBS
Milwaukee	30%	WCGV	UPN
Milwaukee	30%	WDJT	CBS
Milwaukee	30%	WISN	ABC
Milwaukee	30%	WITI	FOX
Milwaukee	30%	WJJA	Independent
Milwaukee	30%	WMVS	PBS
Milwaukee	30%	WMVT	PBS
Milwaukee	30%	WPXE	PAX
Milwaukee	30%	WTMJ	NBC
Milwaukee	30%	WVCY	Independent
Milwaukee	30%	WVTV	WB
Milwaukee	30%	WWRS	Independent
Wausau-Rhinelander	9%	WAOW	NBC
Wausau-Rhinelander	9%	WHRM	PBS
Wausau-Rhinelander	9%	WLEF	PBS
Wausau-Rhinelander	9%	WSAW	CBS
Wausau-Rhinelander	9%	WYOW	ABC
Madison	6%	KFXB	FOX
Madison	6%	WHA	PBS
Madison	6%	WISC	CBS
Madison	6%	WKOW	ABC
Madison	6%	WMSN	FOX
Madison	6%	WMTV	NBC

Cable systems and subscribers

Centurytel Televideo   1,042
Charter   73,149
Comcast   10,817
Dodge County Cable   734
Time Warner   45,155

Businesses and other major employers

Kohler Co.; Kohler; plumbing fixtures   7,500
Mercury Marine International; Fond du Lac; outboard motors   3,800
Kimberly-Clark Corp.; Neenah; paper mills   2,000
Quad Graphics Inc.; Lomira; commercial printing   2,000
Sweetheart Cup Co.; Oshkosh; paper plates   1,739
Bemis Manufacturing Co.; Sheboygan Falls; molded plastics products   1,600
Deere and Co.; Horicon; lawn, garden equipment   1,600
Electronic Assembly Corp.; Neenah; circuit boards   1,500
J. L. French Automotive Castings Inc.; Sheboygan; aluminum die-castings   1,325
Oshkosh Truck Corp.; Oshkosh; motor vehicles, car bodies   1,300
Mercy Medical Center; Oshkosh   1,250
Theda Clark Memorial Hospital; Neenah   1,200
Fisher Hamilton; Two Rivers; lab furniture   1,200
St. Agnes Hospital of Fond du Lac; Fond du Lac   1,200

Banner Packaging Inc.; Oshkosh; polyethylene film   1,075
Brillion Iron Works Inc.; Brillion; gray iron castings   1,000
Curwood Inc.; Oshkosh; packaging paper   1,000
Stora Enso Corp.; Kimberly; coated paper   1,000
Tecumseh Products Co.; New Holstein; internal combustion engines   1,000
Patricia Lapine; Oshkosh; demonstration service   980
Travelers Protective Assn.; Cleveland   921
United Steel Workers of America-Local; Manitowoc; labor union   900
J. J. Keller and Associates Inc.; Neenah; guide publishing   890
Holy Family Memorial Hospital; Manitowoc   870
Alliance Laundry Systems; Ripon; commercial laundry equipment   850
Banta Corp.; Menasha; book printing/binding   800
Lear Corp.; Sheboygan; automobile seats   800
Beaver Dam Community Hospitals Inc.; Beaver Dam   790
Ariens Co.; Brillion; tractors   730
Montclair Hotel Investors Inc.; Oshkosh; resort hotel   700
SCA Tissue North America; Neenah; paper napkin stock   700
Wisconsin Dept. of Health and Family Services; Winnebago   700
Manitowoc Cranes Inc.; Manitowoc; construction machinery   650
Lakeshore Technical College Foundation Inc.; Cleveland   625
Aurora Sheboygan Memorial Medical Center; Sheboygan   600
Mayville Engineering Co. Inc.; Mayville; stamping metal   600
Wisconsin Dept. of Corrections; Waupun   600
Wisconsin Dept. of Corrections; Oshkosh   600
Dodge County; Juneau; convalescent home   580
Sargento Foods Inc.; Plymouth; cheese   570
N&M Transfer Co. Inc.; Neenah; local trucking   550
Bremner Inc.; Ripon; cookies   500
Encompass Services Corp.; Appleton; plumbing contractors   500
Federal-Mogul Corp.; Manitowoc; pistons/piston rings   500
Habitat for Humanity International Inc.; Wautoma; individual, family services   500
Kalahari Development; Wisconsin Dells; hotels   500
Lear Corp.; Sheboygan; automotive parts/accessories   500
Metalcraft of Mayville Inc.; Mayville; mowing equipment   500
Milwaukee Transport Services Inc.; Fond du Lac; bus terminals   500
Raytheon Co.; Ripon; TVs and radios   500
Rockline Industries Inc.; Sheboygan; paper towels   500
Venator Group Specialty Inc.; Oshkosh; mail-order catalog   500
Vollrath Co.; Sheboygan; silverware and plateware   500

Wisconsin 7th District

Northwest — Wausau, Superior, Stevens Point

Wisconsin's most rural district, the 7th stretches north and west from the state's central counties to the Apostle Islands along the southern coast of Lake Superior. Small towns and family farms checker the district, carrying a populist flavor and still retaining some threads of midcentury LaFollette progressivism.

Farming sustains the district's economy, although cold weather in the north shaves a full month off the growing season. The dairy industry has declined since the 1980s, but small, 60-cow farms still populate the northern half of the 7th. The more nutrient-rich soil in the Central Sands country in the state's midsection produces seed potatoes, cranberries, beans, and ginseng. Some small metalworking and paper factories—the industries that attracted immigrants to the 7th in the nineteenth century—still produce their goods. The insurance industry has waned in recent years.

The tranquil lifestyle in small towns and along hundreds of lakes in the north attracts a particularly large number of senior citizens to the 7th. Young people migrate south to cities, such as Milwaukee and Madison, to find jobs or to take advantage of the University of Wisconsin's main branch, while Hmong immigrants from Asia's eastern coast have settled in the region in large numbers. One fast-growing area is Polk County, on the St. Croix River northeast of the Minneapolis-St. Paul metro area.

Blue-collar regions around Stevens Point and Wausau and along Lake Superior in the north consistently vote Democratic, but the rest of the area is more politically competitive. Descendants of Scandinavian immigrants in north-central Wisconsin and an emerging Christian Right contingent keep the region competitive. Redistricting following the 2000 census did not significantly alter the 7th's political leanings.

Major Industry

Agriculture, paper, manufacturing.

Notable

The American Birkebeiner, from Cable to Hayward, is North America's largest cross-country ski marathon; Poniatowski is the center of the northern half of the western hemisphere; Colby cheese is named after a district town.

Election Returns

	Republican		Democratic		Other
President 2000	150,068	49.7%	152,177	50.3%	
House 2002	81,518	35.8%	146,364	64.2%	73

District Profile

Population   670,462

Total area (square miles)   19,390.8
   Land area (square miles)   18,786.5

Population per square mile   35.7

Counties (2000 population)

Ashland	16,866	Marathon	125,834
Barron	44,963	Oneida (pt.)	20,111
Bayfield	15,013	Polk	41,319
Burnett	15,674	Portage	67,182
Chippewa	55,195	Price	15,822
Clark (pt.)	13,992	Rusk	15,347
Douglas	43,287	Sawyer	16,196
Iron	6,861	Taylor	19,680
Langlade (pt.)	15,888	Washburn	16,036
Lincoln	29,641	Wood	75,555

Cities and other areas over 10,000 (2000 population)

Chippewa Falls	12,925	Superior (pt.)	27,368
Marshfield	18,800	Wausau	38,426
Merrill	10,146	Weston village	12,079
Plover village	10,520	Wisconsin Rapids	18,435
Stevens Point	24,551		

Race and Hispanic or Latino origin*

White   95.1%
Black or African American   0.3%
American Indian or Alaska Native   1.5%
Asian   1.5%
Native Hawaiian or other Pacific Islander   0.0%
Some other race   0.0%
Hispanic or Latino origin   0.9%
Two or more races   0.8%

*As percentage of total population.

Ancestry*

Danish	1.1%	Irish	6.5%
Dutch	1.4%	Italian	1.5%
English	4.1%	Norwegian	7.6%
Finnish	1.3%	Polish	8.6%
Fr. Canadian	1.2%	Swedish	4.0%
French	3.1%	USA/American	2.5%
German	30.4%		

*As estimated percentage of total population.

Universities and colleges, 2000–2001 enrollment

Lac Courte Oreilles Ojibwa Community College, Hayward   489
Mid-State Technical College, Wisconsin Rapids   2,584
Mount Senario College, Ladysmith   829
Nicolet Area Technical College, Rhinelander   1,415
Northcentral Technical College, Wausau   3,821
Northland College, Ashland   773
University of Wisconsin, Stevens Point   8,757
University of Wisconsin, Superior   2,881
Wisconsin Indianhead Technical College, Shell Lake   3,350

Newspapers and circulation

	District circulation	Total circulation
Chippewa Herald	6,191	6,506
Duluth News-Tribune	5,451	45,647
Eau Claire Leader-Telegram	6,340	27,574

Marshfield News-Herald	11,031	13,469	
Milwaukee Journal Sentinel	8,584	271,551	
Stevens Point Journal	13,011	13,456	
St. Paul Pioneer Press	9,864	200,578	
*USA Today**	2,200	1,674,376	
Wausau Daily Herald	21,554	22,051	
Wisconsin Daily Tribune	10,948	12,585	

*See Sources and Explanations in the front of the volume.

Television stations and affiliations

Duluth-Superior	37%	KBJR	NBC, UPN
Duluth-Superior	37%	KDLH	CBS
Duluth-Superior	37%	KQDS	FOX
Duluth-Superior	37%	WDIO	ABC
Duluth-Superior	37%	WDSE	PBS
Duluth-Superior	37%	WIRT	ABC
Wausau-Rhinelander	35%	WAOW	NBC
Wausau-Rhinelander	35%	WHRM	PBS
Wausau-Rhinelander	35%	WLEF	PBS
Wausau-Rhinelander	35%	WSAW	CBS
Wausau-Rhinelander	35%	WYOW	ABC
Minneapolis-St. Paul	17%	KARE	NBC
Minneapolis-St. Paul	17%	KAWB	PBS
Minneapolis-St. Paul	17%	KAWE	PBS
Minneapolis-St. Paul	17%	KCCO	CBS
Minneapolis-St. Paul	17%	KCCW	CBS
Minneapolis-St. Paul	17%	KMSP	FOX
Minneapolis-St. Paul	17%	KMWB	WB
Minneapolis-St. Paul	17%	KPXM	PAX
Minneapolis-St. Paul	17%	KRWF	ABC
Minneapolis-St. Paul	17%	KSAX	ABC
Minneapolis-St. Paul	17%	KSTP	ABC
Minneapolis-St. Paul	17%	KTCA	PBS
Minneapolis-St. Paul	17%	KTCI	PBS
Minneapolis-St. Paul	17%	KWCM	PBS
Minneapolis-St. Paul	17%	WFTC	UPN
La Crosse-Eau Claire	11%	WEAU	NBC
La Crosse-Eau Claire	11%	WEUX	FOX
La Crosse-Eau Claire	11%	WEUX	FOX
La Crosse-Eau Claire	11%	WHLA	PBS
La Crosse-Eau Claire	11%	WHWC	PBS
La Crosse-Eau Claire	11%	WKBT	CBS
La Crosse-Eau Claire	11%	WLAX	FOX
La Crosse-Eau Claire	11%	WQOW	ABC
La Crosse-Eau Claire	11%	WXOW	ABC

Cable systems and subscribers
Charter   88,421
CTC Telecom CATV   2,450
HLM Cable   998
KRM Cablevision   1,125
Northwest Community Communications   1,772
Price County Telephone   808
Time Warner   572
Vision Communications   2,672

Businesses and other major employers
Stora Enso North America Corp.; Wisconsin Rapids; paper mills   6,000
Employers Insurance of Wausau; Wausau; workers' compensation insurance   3,500
Wausau Service Corp.; Wausau; fire, marine, casualty insurance   3,000

Marshfield Clinic; Marshfield   2,245
St. Joseph's Hospital of Marshfield Inc.; Marshfield   2,200
Community Health Care Wausau Hospital; Wausau   2,060
Foot Locker.com Inc.; Wausau; athletic wear   2,000
Turkey Store Co.; Barron; turkey processing   1,800
Wausau Hospital Inc.; Wausau   1,711
Kolbe and Kolbe Millwork Co.; Wausau; window frames   1,450
Roehl Transport Inc.; Marshfield; trucking   1,422
Sentry Insurance; Stevens Point; fire, marine, casualty insurance   1,388
Greenheck Fan Corp.; Schofield; sheet metal specialties   1,300
Weather Shield Manufacturing Inc.; Medford; wood window frames   1,300
Silicon Graphics Inc.; Holcombe; mainframe computers   1,200
Security Health Plan of Wisconsin Inc.; Marshfield; health maintenance organization   1,006
Honeywell Electronic Materials Inc.; Chippewa Falls; semiconductors   1,000
Silicon Graphics Inc.; Chippewa Falls; computer peripherals, software   1,000
St. Croix Tribal Council; Turtle Lake; casino hotel   950
Lac Courte Oreilles Tribal Governing Board; Hayward; Native American reservation   922
Heyde Hospitality Inc.; Chippewa Falls; restaurants   903
Domtar Industries Inc.; Port Edwards; paper mills   850
Eastbay Inc.; Wausau; catalog sales   850
McCain Foods Inc.; Plover; potato products   850
Wisconsin Dept. of Health and Family Services; Chippewa Falls   850
Marathon Electric Manufacturing Corp.; Wausau; electric motors   838
Polaris Industries Inc.; Osceola; fabricated plate work   800
Domtar Industries Inc.; Nekoosa; paper mills   750
Marathon Cheese Corp.; Marathon; packaging, labeling services   750
Marshfield DoorSystems Inc.; Marshfield; wood doors   750
Weyerhaeuser Co.; Marshfield; wood doors   750
Nekoosa Papers Inc.; Nekoosa; wrapping paper   700
SNE Enterprises Inc.; Mosinee; millwork   700
FKI Industries Inc.; Rice Lake; metal doors   670
Rhinelander Paper Co.; Rhinelander; specialty papers   625
Hurd Millwork Co.; Medford; window frames   609
Apogee Wausau Group Inc.; Wausau; metal doors, sash, trim   600
Northland College; Ashland   600
St. Joseph's Hospital; Chippewa Falls   600
Wick Building Systems Inc.; Marshfield; mobile homes   600
Mason Shoe Manufacturing Co.; Chippewa Falls; men's shoes   550
Petersen Healthcare of Wisconsin Inc.; Rhinelander; nursing care facilities   550
Sacred Heart-St. Mary's Hospital Inc.; Tomahawk   550
North Central Health Care Facilities; Wausau   530

Land O'Lakes Inc.; Spencer; cheese products   528
Sacred Heart-St. Mary's Hospital Inc.; Rhinelander   526
C. G. Bretting Manufacturing Co.; Ashland; paper
   industries machinery   520
Superior School District; Superior   504
Jeld-Wen Inc.; Hawkins; windows, parts, and trim   500
McCain Foods Inc.; Rice Lake; food preparations   500
Packaging Corp. of America; Tomahawk; corrugating
   medium   500
Seneca Foods Corp.; Cumberland; packaged vegetables
   500
Weyerhaeuser Co.; Rothschild; paper mills   500

Wisconsin 8th District

Northeast — Green Bay, Appleton

Each autumn Sunday, all eyes in Wisconsin turn to the 8th's center to watch football's Green Bay Packers. Regardless of the team's fortunes, the Packers represent the emotional heart of the state—and they draw international attention and pull in millions of dollars. But the district's blue-collar feel stems from the paper industry that stretches southwest from Green Bay along the Fox River Valley, an area with more paper mills than anywhere else in the world.

Much of the economy is stable and dependent on natural resources. The sparsely populated north contains the state's largest tracts of forests, supplying the local paper industry. More-fertile land in the southern part of the district supports grain and dairy farming, with some high-skill manufacturing in Green Bay and Appleton. The district is also home to six federally recognized Native American tribes—each of which boasts a reservation-based casino.

The area is famed for its natural beauty and draws large numbers of tourists from Milwaukee and Chicago during the more temperate seasons. Forests and lakes in Vilas County, near the Michigan border, lure outdoorsmen and nature lovers, while Door County, the peninsula jutting into Lake Michigan, attracts wealthier vacationers with upscale second homes, scenic apple orchards, and a bustling art community.

The 8th leans slightly Republican. Though blue-collar throughout, the district is largely Catholic, anti-big government, and socially conservative. It has been home to some far-right icons such as Joseph R. McCarthy and the John Birch Society in Appleton. Brown County, which includes Green Bay, tends to be politically competitive. Waupaca and Shawano Counties, in the district's southwest corner, vote Republican. The GOP runs well in the less-populated northern counties of Vilas and Florence, while Democrats dominate in Menominee County, which is conterminous with an Indian reservation.

Major Industry
Paper products, casinos, farming.

Notable
About 56,000 people are on the waiting list for Packers season tickets.

Election Returns

	Republican		Democratic		Other	
President 2000	165,819	54.6%	138,056	45.4%		
House 2002	152,745	72.6%	50,284	23.9%	4,718	3.5%

District Profile

Population   670,480

Total area (square miles)   10,117.8
Land area (square miles)   9,740.4

Population per square mile   68.8

Counties (2000 population)

Brown 226,778	Menominee 4,562
Calumet (pt.) 11,012	Oconto 35,634
Door 27,961	Oneida (pt.) 16,665
Florence 5,088	Outagamie (pt.) 150,905
Forest 10,024	Shawano 40,664
Kewaunee 20,187	Vilas 21,033
Langlade (pt.) 4,852	Waupaca 51,731
Marinette 43,384	

Cities and other areas over 10,000 (2000 population)
Allouez village   15,443
Appleton (pt.)   69,270
Ashwaubenon village   17,634
Bellevue Town CDP   11,828
De Pere   20,559
Green Bay (pt.)   102,313
Howard village (pt.)   13,546
Kaukauna   12,983
Little Chute village   10,476
Marinette   11,749

Race and Hispanic or Latino origin*
White   92.2%
Black or African American   0.6%
American Indian or Alaska Native   2.6%
Asian   1.4%
Native Hawaiian or other Pacific Islander   0.0%
Some other race   0.0%
Hispanic or Latino origin   2.2%
Two or more races   0.9%

As percentage of total population.

Ancestry*

Belgian 4.2%	Irish 6.9%
Dutch 4.3%	Italian 1.5%
English 3.6%	Norwegian 3.5%
Fr. Canadian 1.7%	Polish 6.5%
French 4.0%	Swedish 2.0%
German 30.8%	USA/American 2.7%

As estimated percentage of total population.

Universities and colleges, 2000–2001 enrollment
College of the Menominee Nation, Keshena   371
Fox Valley Technical College, Appleton   6,806

Lawrence University, Appleton 1,228
Northeast Wisconsin Technical College, Green Bay
7,500
St. Norbert College, De Pere 2,133
University of Wisconsin, Green Bay 5,657

Newspapers and circulation

	District circulation	Total circulation
Appleton Post-Crescent	32,313	52,578
Green Bay Press Gazette	54,109	55,568
Iron Mountain Daily News	1,441	9,616
Milwaukee Journal Sentinel	8,533	271,551
Shawano Leader	5,377	5,377
*USA Today**	2,769	1,674,376

See Sources and Explanations in the front of the volume.

Television stations and affiliations

Green Bay-Appleton	72%	WACY	UPN
Green Bay-Appleton	72%	WBAY	ABC
Green Bay-Appleton	72%	WFRV	CBS
Green Bay-Appleton	72%	WGBA	NBC
Green Bay-Appleton	72%	WIWB	WB, PAX
Green Bay-Appleton	72%	WJFW	NBC
Green Bay-Appleton	72%	WLUK	FOX
Green Bay-Appleton	72%	WPNE	PBS
Wausau-Rhinelander	24%	WAOW	NBC
Wausau-Rhinelander	24%	WHRM	PBS
Wausau-Rhinelander	24%	WLEF	PBS
Wausau-Rhinelander	24%	WSAW	CBS
Wausau-Rhinelander	24%	WYOW	ABC
Marquette	4%	WBKP	ABC
Marquette	4%	WJMN	CBS
Marquette	4%	WLUC	NBC
Marquette	4%	WNMU	PBS

Cable systems and subscribers

Centurytel Televideo 832
Charter 25,341
Howard Cable 789
Mediacom 577
Net Cable 761
Niagara CMTV Co-op 740
Oconto Falls Cable 800
Time Warner 78,635

Military installations, September 2001

Denis J. Murphy U.S. Army Reserve Center, Green Bay
328

Businesses and other major employers

ShopKo Properties Inc.; Green Bay; department stores
4,294
ThedaCare Inc.; Appleton; hospital management 4,000
Oneida Tribe of Indians of Wisconsin; Green Bay; casino
hotel 3,000
Waupaca Foundry Inc.; Waupaca; gray iron castings
3,000
Wisconsin Water Ski Federation; Appleton; tour
operators 3,000
Schneider National Inc.; Green Bay; trucking 2,600
Green Bay Public Schools; Green Bay 2,546
Air Wisconsin Airlines Corp.; Appleton 2,115

Aid Assn. for Lutherans; Appleton; fraternal life
insurance 2,100
Northeast Wisconsin Technical College District; Green
Bay 2,056
American Medical Security Inc.; Green Bay; medical
service plans 2,000
Cellcom Green Bay Marathon; Green Bay; planning
consultant 2,000
Humana Insurance Co.; Green Bay; life insurance
1,784
Procter and Gamble Paper Products Co.; Green Bay;
sanitary paper products 1,650
Packerland Packing Co.; Green Bay; boxed beef 1,550
Bellin Health Systems Inc.; Green Bay; hospital 1,500
Appleton Papers Inc.; Appleton; paper mills 1,400
Miller Electric Manufacturing Co.; Appleton; welding
apparatus 1,400
St. Elizabeth Hospital Inc.; Appleton 1,368
APAC Customer Services Inc.; Green Bay; telemarketing
1,300
Wisconsin Public Service Corp.; Green Bay; electric
services 1,300
Green Bay City; Green Bay; city government 1,286
Appleton Medical Center; Appleton 1,230
Green Bay Dressed Beef Inc.; Green Bay; meatpacking
plants 1,200
International Paper Co.; Kaukauna; kraft paper 1,200
Krueger International Inc.; Green Bay; office chairs
1,200
Anchor Food Products Inc.; Appleton; frozen specialties
1,000
Guides4me Inc.; Appleton; marketing consulting
1,000
Oneida Tribe of Indians of Wisconsin; Oneida 1,000
KCS International Inc.; Oconto; fiberglass boats 950
Paper Converting Machine Co.; Green Bay; paper
industries machinery 900
Karl Schmidt Unisia Inc.; Marinette; pistons and piston
rings 874
Marinette Marine Corp.; Marinette;
shipbuilding/repairing 840
Carver Boat Corp.; Pulaski; fiberglass boats 800
Georgia-Pacific Corp.; Green Bay; paper mills 800
Lac du Flambeau Band of Lake Superior Chippewa
Indians; Lac du Flambeau; casino hotel 800
Schreiber Foods Inc.; Green Bay; cheese 760
Boldt Co.; Appleton; warehouses 750
MEGTEC Systems Inc.; De Pere; industrial driers 707
Aurora BayCare Medical Center; Green Bay 700
Moore North America Inc.; De Pere; advertising 700
SMTC Inc.; Appleton; electronic products 700
Outagamie County; Appleton; county government 650
University of Wisconsin System; Green Bay 650
Appleton Coated; Combined Locks; paper mills 640
Ansul Inc.; Marinette; firefighting equipment 600
City of Appleton; Appleton; city government 600
Curwood Inc.; New London; wrapping paper 600
Genex Cooperative Inc.; Shawano; livestock services
600
Howard Young Medical Center Inc.; Woodruff 600
Stora Enso North America Corp.; Niagara; coated paper
600

Waupaca Foundry Inc.; Marinette; gray iron castings
600
Fox Valley Technical College; Appleton   575
Krause Publications Inc.; Iola; periodicals   573
St. Mary's Hospital and Medical Center; Green Bay
571
Fox Midwest Transport Inc.; Green Bay; contract haulers
550
Menominee Tribal Gaming Corp.; Keshena; gambling
550
Voith Paper Inc.; Appleton; paper industries machinery
550

Bay Area Medical Center; Marinette   510
Brown County; Green Bay; county government   500
Brown County; Green Bay; airport   500
Door County Memorial Hospital; Sturgeon Bay   500
Emerson Electric Co.; Keshena; electrical work   500
IDS Property Casualty Insurance Co.; Green Bay;
automobile insurance   500
Reynolds Consumer Products Inc.; Appleton; plastic,
laminated packaging   500
Stockbridge-Munsee Community Inc.; Bowler;
gambling   500

Wyoming

Wyoming, the least populated state, basks in its wide open spaces, which define its libertarian politics and natural resource-based economy. Yellowstone National Park is one of the most visited parks in the nation, and tourism is an essential part of Wyoming's economy. The jagged peaks of the Grand Tetons rise more than 5,000 feet from the Jackson Hole Valley floor to their 13,000-foot apex, less than ten miles from the nation's steepest ski slopes at Jackson Hole Mountain.

The state's name was borrowed from Delaware Native Americans in the East, for whom it meant "across the Great Plain." These Native Americans, of course, were thinking of a plain in what is now Pennsylvania (where there is a Wyoming County). The plain across which the state of Wyoming would be born was farther away and far greater. It was the awe-inspiring expanse that pioneers had to traverse on the historic trails that led west through the Rockies and on to Utah and California and Oregon. Today, as the ninth-largest state in area and absolute smallest in population, Wyoming still defines the open West and the surviving spirit of the frontier. There are places in the mountain passes here where one can see and touch today the ruts cut in the rock by the wagon wheels of pioneers in the 1800s.

Wyoming has two nicknames that aptly summarize its competing histories. For some, this is the Equality State because it was here that American women first voted, served on juries, and ran for public office. All three rights were granted by the territorial legislature in 1869 and were exercised widely in the 1870s. The first woman elected governor of any state was Wyoming's Nellie Tayloe Ross, who won that office in 1924. The most recent example is Barbara Cubin, the state's lone member of Congress as of 2003.

The other nickname is the Cowboy State, evoking the history of cattle drives chronicled in countless stories from the later 1800s through the twentieth century. Richard B. Cheney, the Wyoming boy who had risen to be vice president of the United States, said in 2003 that to be a cowboy meant to be plain-spoken and direct in negotiation, saying and doing just what one meant to say and do.

Wyoming has been a sparsely populated state since its inception and has always seemed in search of an economic ticket to ride. Agriculture here has been primarily a matter of feeding livestock for slaughter. Mining and timber and oil and—more recently, tourism in the northwestern corner—have been the economic mainstays. Here as elsewhere, oil and gas have brought both prosperity and disappointment in cycles that began practically with the state's first well (drilled in 1883, seven years before statehood). Nearly a century later,

on the heels of the 1973 Arab oil embargo, the mad search for secure sources of oil brought tens of thousands of new residents to Wyoming. What had been literally the slowest growing state in the nation in the preceding decade was suddenly growing faster than all but two other states.

But then came the oil bust of the early 1980s: prices fell, exploration and development stopped. Efforts at developing alternative sources, such as mining oil shale to be rendered into petroleum, faltered and then died. At the end of that decade, Wyoming had not only failed to grow, it had actually lost about 16,000 people.

The 1990s were a better time as several Wyoming industries flourished once again. In recent decades, the Grand Tetons have lured millionaires of many kinds to the northwestern area around Jackson Hole, where the original rustic appeal was broadened by luxurious resorts and villas. Some elements of the state's energy and agriculture sectors also began to come back. The state is the nation's top source of low-sulfur coal. After several years of budget shortfalls, the state experienced surpluses because of rising prices of oil and natural gas, and the increase in coal mining. The population grew 9 percent in the 1990s, bringing the state once again to the threshold of half a million residents. It seems unlikely Wyoming will ever have a second congressional seat, and it may not even escape the negative distinction of being the nation's single least populous state.

In terms of human diversity, Wyoming is nearly homogeneous. The state has few blacks (less than 1 percent) or Asians (less than 1 percent), and the Hispanic presence (6 percent) is less than half the national average. The lack of even one city or big town (Cheyenne is number one at 53,000 and the top four together are about 150,000) has been a brake on the state's growth from its early days to the present.

Residents savor their land and resources and abhor government intrusion of any kind, especially in dictating how land may be used. In most regions, residents are happy with the state's relative seclusion and tranquil lifestyle and are not particularly warm to population growth anyway. The state's lawmakers are loath to raise taxes and dare not entertain a dreaded income tax. Wyoming has no corporate or personal income taxes and has a statewide 4 percent sales tax.

Cheney symbolized the ethos of Wyoming. A five-term Wyoming representative who served as secretary of defense from 1989 to 1993, Cheney took the oath as George W. Bush's vice president in 2001. He bespeaks the state's Republican tradition, which dates back to the transcontinental railroad in the intensely Republican era after the Civil War. Voter registration in 2003 was 62 percent Republican, one

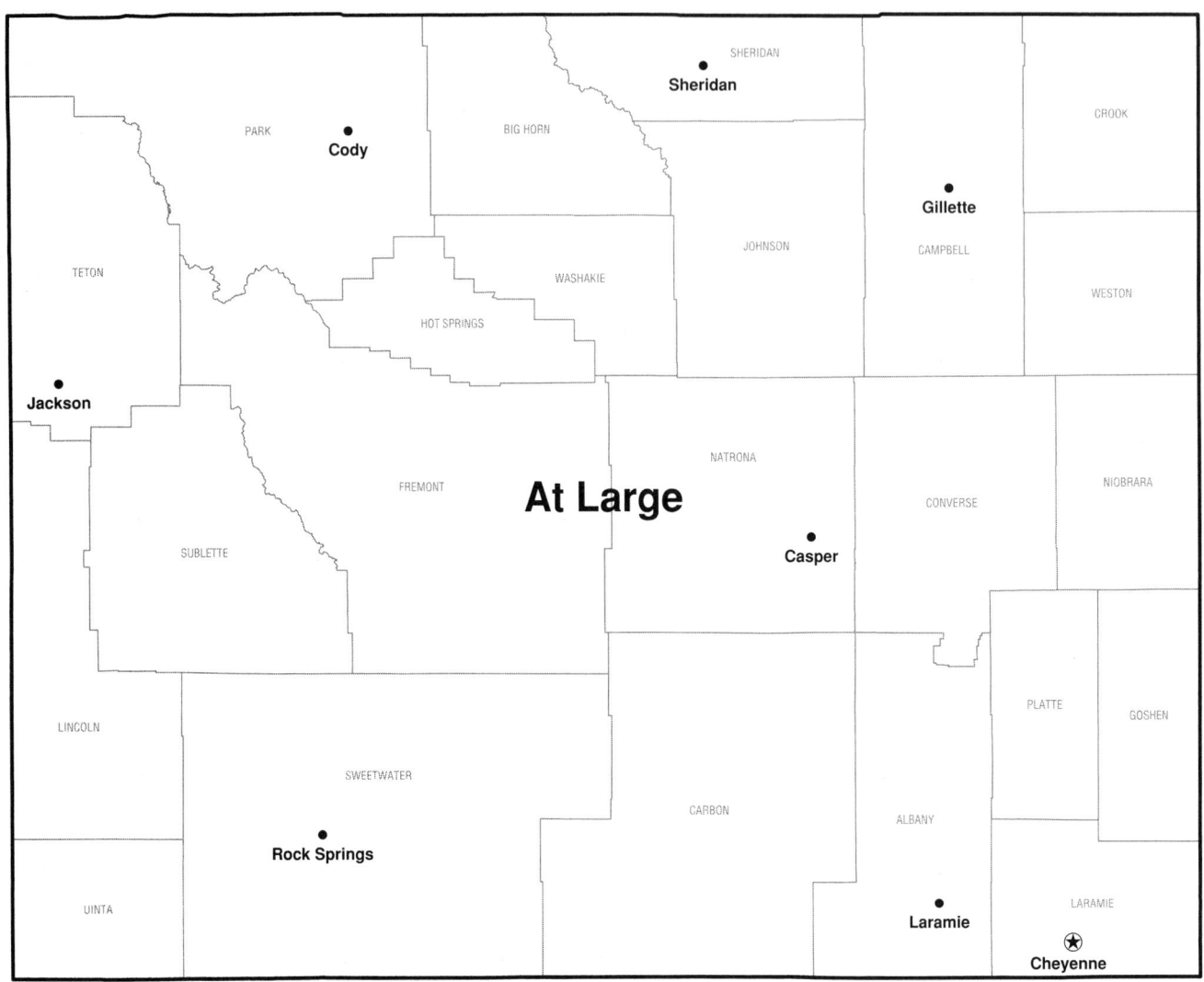

SHERIDAN
Sheridan

PARK
Cody

CROOK

BIG HORN

TETON

JOHNSON

GILLETTE
Gillette

CAMPBELL

WASHAKIE

WESTON

HOT SPRINGS

Jackson

FREMONT

At Large

NATRONA

CONVERSE

NIOBRARA

SUBLETTE

Casper

LINCOLN

SWEETWATER

PLATTE

GOSHEN

CARBON

ALBANY

Rock Springs

UINTA

Laramie

LARAMIE

Cheyenne

of the highest percentages for either party in the nation. Wyoming has gone Republican for president in every cycle beginning with 1952 (setting apart only the Lyndon Johnson landslide of 1964). In 2000 George W. Bush won here with more than two-thirds of the vote. The same Republican tilt has been evident in the state's legislatures (where Democrats are outnumbered two to one or even three to one) and in its congressional delegations.

Democrats were last truly competitive for the Senate here in the 1950s, when the mines were still employing big numbers of union workers and the southern counties cast a more lopsided Democratic vote. Gale McGee won three Senate terms as a Democrat, running well-timed campaigns in Democratic years: 1958, 1964, and 1970. But as of 2003, no Democrat had won a Senate seat since. Republicans had racked up 11 straight victories for that office, three each for Malcolm Wallop and Alan K. Simpson. The state's lone House seat, a statewide office, has been in Republican hands continuously since 1978.

Wyoming has had some Democratic tradition, too. Some of the first workers brought to the state came to build the transcontinental railroad in the 1860s (the line ran straight through the five southern Wyoming counties on the Colorado state line). Some of the railroad workers stayed to work mining gold and other more reliable ores. (More recently, the most consistently rewarding mine product has been low-sulfur coal.) In time, the ranks of these miners were unionized and became the backbone of the state's Democratic Party—giving it some success in races for the House and for governor. Democrats elected their first governor here in 1892 and have had at least one in each decade of the twentieth century (most for two-year terms). Ex-Marine Ed Herschler held the job for a dozen years at the height of the right-populist "Sagebrush Rebellion" in the 1970s and 1980s, handing it off to another Democrat in 1987. The most recent Democratic governor, Dave Freudenthal, was elected in 2002 by two percentage points.

Major Industry

Mining, tourism, agriculture.

Notable

Wyoming was the first state with a national park (Yellowstone was begun in 1872) or a national monument (Devil's Tower); Jackson was the first U.S. town ever to elect an all-female slate—mayor, council, and marshal—in 1920; Wyoming has more cars per capita than any other state, 1.17.

Table 1　Population

District	Population	Population under 18	Voting-age population	Median age	Male*	Female*
At Large	493,782	128,873	364,909	36.2	50.3	49.7

*As percentage of total population.

Table 2　Voting-Age Persons by Race/Hispanic or Latino Origin

District	White*	Black or African American*	American Indian or Alaska Native*	Asian*	Other or multirace*	Hispanic or Latino*
At Large	90.3	0.7	1.8	0.7	1.1	5.5

*As percentage of voting-age population.

Table 3　Voting-Age Population by Age Groups

District	18 to 24*	25 to 44*	45 to 64*	Over 64*
At Large	13.7	38.0	32.5	15.8

*As percentage of voting-age population.

Table 4　Income and Occupation

District	Median family income	Families in poverty*	White collar†	Blue collar†	Service†	Farm†
At Large	$45,685	8.0	54.2	27.5	16.7	1.5

*As percentage of all families.　　†As percentage of employed workers 16 years and over.

Table 5　Education: School Years Completed

District	Less than grade 9*	Grades 9–12 no diploma*	High school diploma no college*	Some college*	College bachelor's degree or higher*
At Large	3.4	8.8	31.0	35.0	21.9

*As percentage of persons age 25 and over.

Table 6　Housing and Residential Patterns

District	Median home value	Owner occupied*	Renter occupied*	Urban†	Rural†
At Large	$91,500	70.0	30.0	65.2	34.8

*As percentage of occupied housing units.　　†As percentage of total population.

Election Returns

	Republican		Democratic		Other	
President 2000	147,947	69.2%	60,481	28.3%	5,298	2.5%
House 2002	110,229	60.5%	65,961	36.2%	5,962	3.3%

District Profile

Population　493,782

Total area (square miles)　97,813.5
　Land area (square miles)　97,100.4

Population per square mile　5.1

Counties (2000 population)

Albany	32,014	Natrona	66,533
Big Horn	11,461	Niobrara	2,407
Campbell	33,698	Park	25,786
Carbon	15,639	Platte	8,807
Converse	12,052	Sheridan	26,560
Crook	5,887	Sublette	5,920
Fremont	35,804	Sweetwater	37,613
Goshen	12,538	Teton	18,251
Hot Springs	4,882	Uinta	19,742
Johnson	7,075	Washakie	8,289
Laramie	81,607	Weston	6,644
Lincoln	14,573		

Cities and other areas over 10,000 (2000 population)

Casper	49,644	Green River	11,808
Cheyenne	53,011	Laramie	27,204
Evanston	11,507	Rock Springs	18,708
Gillette	19,646	Sheridan	15,804

Race and Hispanic or Latino origin*

White 88.9%
Black or African American 0.7%
American Indian or Alaska Native 2.1%
Asian 0.5%
Native Hawaiian or other Pacific Islander 0.1%
Some other race 0.1%
Hispanic or Latino origin 6.4%
Two or more races 1.2%

*As percentage of total population.

Ancestry*

Danish	1.4%	Norwegian	3.0%
Dutch	1.8%	Polish	1.4%
English	11.3%	Scotch-Irish	1.8%
French	2.5%	Scottish	2.3%
German	18.4%	Swedish	2.5%
Irish	9.4%	USA/American	4.6%
Italian	2.2%		

*As estimated percentage of total population.

Universities and colleges, 2000–2001 enrollment

Casper College, Casper 3,972
Central Wyoming College, Riverton 1,644
Eastern Wyoming College, Torrington 1,420
Laramie County Community College, Cheyenne 3,394
Northwest Community College, Powell 1,289
Sheridan College, Sheridan 2,674
University of Wyoming, Laramie 11,743
Western Wyoming Community College, Rock Springs 2,579
Wyoming Technical Institute, Laramie 1,289

Newspapers and circulation

	District circulation	Total circulation
Billings Gazette	5,403	46,010
Casper Star-Tribune	30,565	31,019
Cheyenne Wyoming Tribune-Eagle	16,116	16,311
Laramie Daily Boomerang	5,241	5,342
Rock Springs Daily Rocket-Miner	6,982	6,982
Scottsbluff Star-Herald	1,331	15,180
Sheridan Press	5,638	5,709
*USA Today**	2,401	1,674,376

*See Sources and Explanations in the front of the volume.

Television stations and affiliations

Denver	27%	KBDI	PBS
Denver	27%	KCEC	Univision
Denver	27%	KCNC	CBS
Denver	27%	KDUH	ABC
Denver	27%	KDVR	FOX
Denver	27%	KFCT	FOX
Denver	27%	KFNR	ABC
Denver	27%	KMGH	ABC
Denver	27%	KPXC	PAX
Denver	27%	KREG	CBS
Denver	27%	KRMA	CBS
Denver	27%	KRMT	Independent
Denver	27%	KTVD	UPN
Denver	27%	KUSA	NBC
Denver	27%	KWGN	WB
Denver	27%	KWHD	Independent
Casper-Riverton	24%	KCWC	PBS
Casper-Riverton	24%	KFNB	ABC
Casper-Riverton	24%	KFNE	ABC
Casper-Riverton	24%	KGWC	CBS
Casper-Riverton	24%	KGWL	CBS
Casper-Riverton	24%	KTWO	NBC
Salt Lake City	22%	KBYU	PBS
Salt Lake City	22%	KCSG	PAX
Salt Lake City	22%	KENV	NBC
Salt Lake City	22%	KGWR	CBS
Salt Lake City	22%	KJZZ	Independent
Salt Lake City	22%	KSL	NBC
Salt Lake City	22%	KSTU	FOX
Salt Lake City	22%	KTVX	ABC
Salt Lake City	22%	KUED	PBS
Salt Lake City	22%	KULC	PBS
Salt Lake City	22%	KUTV	CBS
Salt Lake City	22%	KUWB	WB
Billings, MT	10%	KHMT	FOX
Billings, MT	10%	KSVI	ABC
Billings, MT	10%	KTVQ	CBS
Billings, MT	10%	KULR	NBC
Billings, MT	10%	KYUS	NBC
Rapid City, SD	8%	KBHE	PBS
Rapid City, SD	8%	KCLO	CBS
Rapid City, SD	8%	KEVN	FOX
Rapid City, SD	8%	KHSD	ABC
Rapid City, SD	8%	KIVV	FOX
Rapid City, SD	8%	KOTA	ABC
Rapid City, SD	8%	KPSD	PBS
Rapid City, SD	8%	KSGW	ABC
Rapid City, SD	8%	KTNE	PBS
Rapid City, SD	8%	KZSD	PBS
Cheyenne-Scottsbluff	5%	KGWN	CBS
Cheyenne-Scottsbluff	5%	KKTU	NBC
Cheyenne-Scottsbluff	5%	KLWY	FOX
Cheyenne-Scottsbluff	5%	KSTF	CBS
Idaho Falls-Pocatello, ID	4%	KIDK	CBS, UPN
Idaho Falls-Pocatello, ID	4%	KIFI	ABC
Idaho Falls-Pocatello, ID	4%	KISU	PBS
Idaho Falls-Pocatello, ID	4%	KJWY	NBC
Idaho Falls-Pocatello, ID	4%	KPVI	NBC

Cable systems and subscribers

Adelphia 3,097
Bresnan 89,033
CommuniComm 8,630
Lovell Cable 820
Mallard 4,418
Sweetwater Cable TV 12,812
Tounge River Cable TV 995
Union Cable TV 778

Military installations, September 2001

Francis E. Warren Air Force Base, Cheyenne 3,900

Cheyenne Municipal Airport Air National Guard, Cheyenne 1,105

Camp Guernsey Military Training Area, Guernsey 123

Businesses and other major employers

Stalkup's RV Superstore Inc.; Casper; recreational vehicle dealers 2,328

Wyoming Medical Center Inc.; Casper 1,018

Union Pacific Railroad Co.; Cheyenne; freight hauling 1,000

University of Wyoming; Laramie 1,000

FMC Wyoming Corp.; Green River; soda ash, sodium carbonate 900

Memorial Hospital of Laramie County; Cheyenne 830

AMFAC Recreational Services Inc.; Yellowstone National; hotels 800

Peabody Coal Co.; Gillette; administrative management 670

Wyoming Dept. of Transportation; Cheyenne 650

City of Casper; Casper; city government 650

General Chemical Corp.; Green River; potash, soda, and borate minerals 650

Powder River Coal Co.; Wright; surface mining, bituminous 604

Western States Equipment Co.; Jackson; automotive repair shops 600

Wyoming State Training School; Lander 585

Key Energy Services Inc.; Casper; servicing oil and gas wells 540

Qwest Corp.; Cheyenne; telephone communication 500

Wal-Mart Stores Inc.; Casper; department stores 500

Kennecott Energy Co.; Newcastle; coal mining services 500

OCI Chemical Corp.; Green River; soda ash mining 500

Appendix

National Census Tables

National Table 1   Population

State	Population	Population under 18	Voting-age population	Median age	Male*	Female*
Alabama	4,447,100	1,123,422	3,323,678	35.8	48.3	51.7
Alaska	626,932	190,717	436,215	32.4	51.7	48.3
Arizona	5,130,632	1,366,947	3,763,685	34.2	49.9	50.1
Arkansas	2,673,400	680,369	1,993,031	36.0	48.8	51.2
California	33,871,648	9,249,829	24,621,819	33.3	49.8	50.2
Colorado	4,301,261	1,100,795	3,200,466	34.3	50.4	49.6
Connecticut	3,405,565	841,688	2,563,877	37.4	48.4	51.6
Delaware	783,600	194,587	589,013	36.0	48.6	51.4
District of Columbia	572,059	114,992	457,067	34.6	47.1	52.9
Florida	15,982,378	3,646,340	12,336,038	38.7	48.8	51.2
Georgia	8,186,453	2,169,234	6,017,219	33.4	49.2	50.8
Hawaii	1,211,537	295,767	915,770	36.2	50.2	49.8
Idaho	1,293,953	369,030	924,923	33.2	50.1	49.9
Illinois	12,419,293	3,245,451	9,173,842	34.7	49.0	51.0
Indiana	6,080,485	1,574,396	4,506,089	35.2	49.0	51.0
Iowa	2,926,324	733,638	2,192,686	36.6	49.1	50.9
Kansas	2,688,418	712,993	1,975,425	35.2	49.4	50.6
Kentucky	4,041,769	994,818	3,046,951	35.9	48.9	51.1
Louisiana	4,468,976	1,219,799	3,249,177	34.0	48.4	51.6
Maine	1,274,923	301,238	973,685	38.6	48.7	51.3
Maryland	5,296,486	1,356,172	3,940,314	36.0	48.3	51.7
Massachusetts	6,349,097	1,500,064	4,849,033	36.5	48.2	51.8
Michigan	9,938,444	2,595,767	7,342,677	35.5	49.0	51.0
Minnesota	4,919,479	1,286,894	3,632,585	35.4	49.5	50.5
Mississippi	2,844,658	775,187	2,069,471	33.8	48.3	51.7
Missouri	5,595,211	1,427,692	4,167,519	36.1	48.6	51.4
Montana	902,195	230,062	672,133	37.5	49.8	50.2
Nebraska	1,711,263	450,242	1,261,021	35.3	49.3	50.7
Nevada	1,998,257	511,799	1,486,458	35.0	50.9	49.1
New Hampshire	1,235,786	309,562	926,224	37.1	49.2	50.8
New Jersey	8,414,350	2,087,558	6,326,792	36.7	48.5	51.5
New Mexico	1,819,046	508,574	1,310,472	34.6	49.2	50.8
New York	18,976,457	4,690,107	14,286,350	35.9	48.2	51.8
North Carolina	8,049,313	1,964,047	6,085,266	35.3	49.0	51.0
North Dakota	642,200	160,849	481,351	36.2	49.9	50.1
Ohio	11,353,140	2,888,339	8,464,801	36.2	48.6	51.4
Oklahoma	3,450,654	892,360	2,558,294	35.5	49.1	50.9
Oregon	3,421,399	846,526	2,574,873	36.3	49.6	50.4
Pennsylvania	12,281,054	2,922,221	9,358,833	38.0	48.3	51.7
Rhode Island	1,048,319	247,822	800,497	36.7	48.0	52.0
South Carolina	4,012,012	1,009,641	3,002,371	35.4	48.6	51.4
South Dakota	754,844	202,649	552,195	35.6	49.6	50.4
Tennessee	5,689,283	1,398,521	4,290,762	35.9	48.7	51.3
Texas	20,851,820	5,886,759	14,965,061	32.3	49.6	50.4
Utah	2,233,169	718,698	1,514,471	27.1	50.1	49.9
Vermont	608,827	147,523	461,304	37.7	49.0	51.0
Virginia	7,078,515	1,738,262	5,340,253	35.7	49.0	51.0
Washington	5,894,121	1,513,843	4,380,278	35.3	49.8	50.2
West Virginia	1,808,344	402,393	1,405,951	38.9	48.6	51.4
Wisconsin	5,363,675	1,368,756	3,994,919	36.0	49.4	50.6
Wyoming	493,782	128,873	364,909	36.2	50.3	49.7
United States	281,421,906	72,293,812	209,128,094	35.3	49.1	50.9

*As percentage of total population.

National Table 2   Voting-Age Persons by Race/Hispanic or Latino Origin

State	White*	Black or African American*	American Indian or Alaska Native*	Asian*	Other or multirace*	Hispanic or Latino*
Alabama	72.7	23.8	0.5	0.7	0.7	1.5
Alaska	71.4	3.2	13.7	4.6	3.5	3.6
Arizona	69.0	2.7	3.8	1.9	1.2	21.3
Arkansas	81.0	13.9	0.6	0.8	0.9	2.8
California	51.1	6.2	0.5	11.6	2.4	28.1
Colorado	77.3	3.5	0.7	2.3	1.4	14.9
Connecticut	80.1	7.9	0.2	2.4	1.4	8.0
Delaware	75.2	17.4	0.3	2.1	1.0	4.0
District of Columbia	31.8	55.7	0.2	2.9	1.9	7.3
Florida	68.4	12.3	0.3	1.6	1.3	16.1
Georgia	65.2	26.4	0.2	2.1	1.0	5.0
Hawaii	25.4	1.7	0.2	52.6	14.3	5.7
Idaho	89.9	0.4	1.1	1.1	1.2	6.4
Illinois	70.9	13.7	0.1	3.5	1.1	10.7
Indiana	87.3	7.6	0.2	1.0	0.7	3.1
Iowa	93.9	1.8	0.2	1.2	0.5	2.3
Kansas	85.3	5.2	0.8	1.7	1.2	5.8
Kentucky	90.2	6.7	0.2	0.7	0.7	1.3
Louisiana	65.5	29.5	0.5	1.2	0.8	2.4
Maine	97.1	0.4	0.5	0.7	0.7	0.6
Maryland	64.2	26.2	0.3	4.1	1.3	4.0
Massachusetts	83.9	4.6	0.2	3.7	2.0	5.6
Michigan	80.7	13.0	0.5	1.7	1.3	2.7
Minnesota	90.3	2.9	0.9	2.4	1.0	2.4
Mississippi	64.2	33.0	0.4	0.6	0.5	1.3
Missouri	85.4	10.1	0.4	1.1	1.1	1.8
Montana	91.5	0.3	4.9	0.5	1.3	1.6
Nebraska	89.3	3.5	0.7	1.3	0.7	4.5
Nevada	69.1	6.1	1.0	5.1	2.0	16.7
New Hampshire	95.7	0.6	0.2	1.3	0.8	1.4
New Jersey	68.2	12.2	0.1	5.6	1.5	12.3
New Mexico	49.5	1.7	7.8	1.2	1.4	38.7
New York	64.4	13.8	0.2	5.6	2.0	13.8
North Carolina	72.6	19.9	1.1	1.3	0.8	4.3
North Dakota	93.5	0.5	3.8	0.6	0.7	1.0
Ohio	85.7	10.4	0.2	1.2	1.0	1.6
Oklahoma	77.4	6.8	6.7	1.5	3.3	4.3
Oregon	85.9	1.4	1.1	3.2	1.9	6.5
Pennsylvania	85.9	8.9	0.1	1.7	0.8	2.6
Rhode Island	84.7	3.5	0.3	2.1	2.3	7.0
South Carolina	68.8	27.0	0.3	0.9	0.6	2.2
South Dakota	90.8	0.5	6.1	0.6	0.8	1.2
Tennessee	81.2	14.8	0.2	1.0	0.7	2.0
Texas	56.3	10.9	0.3	2.9	1.0	28.6
Utah	86.6	0.7	1.1	2.4	1.1	8.1
Vermont	96.6	0.4	0.4	0.8	1.0	0.8
Virginia	72.2	18.3	0.3	3.7	1.3	4.2
Washington	81.5	2.9	1.3	5.9	2.3	6.0
West Virginia	95.0	3.0	0.2	0.5	0.6	0.6
Wisconsin	89.6	4.7	0.7	1.3	0.6	2.9
Wyoming	90.3	0.7	1.8	0.7	1.1	5.5
United States	72.0	11.2	0.7	3.8	1.4	11.0

*As percentage of voting-age population.

National Table 3 Voting-Age Population by Age Groups

State	18 to 24*	25 to 44*	45 to 64*	Over 64*
Alabama	13.2	38.8	30.6	17.4
Alaska	13.1	46.7	32.0	8.2
Arizona	13.7	40.2	28.4	17.7
Arkansas	13.1	37.7	30.4	18.8
California	13.7	43.5	28.2	14.6
Colorado	13.4	43.8	29.8	13.0
Connecticut	10.6	40.3	30.8	18.3
Delaware	12.8	40.1	29.8	17.3
District of Columbia	15.9	41.5	27.4	15.3
Florida	10.8	37.0	29.4	22.8
Georgia	13.9	44.1	28.9	13.1
Hawaii	12.6	39.6	30.4	17.5
Idaho	15.0	39.2	30.0	15.8
Illinois	13.2	41.4	29.1	16.4
Indiana	13.6	39.8	29.9	16.7
Iowa	13.6	36.9	29.7	19.9
Kansas	14.0	38.9	29.1	18.0
Kentucky	13.2	39.7	30.5	16.6
Louisiana	14.6	39.8	29.7	15.9
Maine	10.7	38.1	32.4	18.8
Maryland	11.4	42.3	31.1	15.2
Massachusetts	12.0	41.0	29.3	17.7
Michigan	12.7	40.3	30.4	16.6
Minnesota	13.0	41.2	29.5	16.4
Mississippi	15.0	39.0	29.4	16.6
Missouri	12.9	39.0	30.0	18.1
Montana	12.8	36.5	32.8	18.0
Nebraska	13.8	38.6	29.1	18.4
Nevada	12.1	42.3	30.9	14.7
New Hampshire	11.2	41.2	31.7	16.0
New Jersey	10.7	41.5	30.2	17.6
New Mexico	13.6	39.4	30.9	16.2
New York	12.4	40.8	29.7	17.1
North Carolina	13.3	41.1	29.7	15.9
North Dakota	15.2	36.3	28.9	19.6
Ohio	12.5	39.3	30.4	17.8
Oklahoma	14.0	38.1	30.1	17.8
Oregon	12.7	38.7	31.5	17.0
Pennsylvania	11.7	37.5	30.3	20.5
Rhode Island	13.3	38.8	28.8	19.0
South Carolina	13.6	39.5	30.8	16.2
South Dakota	14.1	37.4	29.0	19.6
Tennessee	12.8	40.1	30.8	16.4
Texas	14.7	43.3	28.1	13.9
Utah	21.0	41.4	25.1	12.6
Vermont	12.3	38.3	32.7	16.8
Virginia	12.7	41.9	30.5	14.8
Washington	12.8	41.5	30.7	15.1
West Virginia	12.3	35.7	32.4	19.7
Wisconsin	13.0	39.6	29.8	17.6
Wyoming	13.7	38.0	32.5	15.8
United States	13.0	40.7	29.6	16.7

*As percentage of voting-age population.

National Table 4 Income and Occupation

State	Median family income	Families in poverty*	White collar†	Blue collar†	Service†	Farm†
Alabama	$41,657	12.5	55.4	30.3	13.5	0.8
Alaska	$59,036	6.7	60.5	22.4	15.6	1.5
Arizona	$46,723	9.9	61.2	21.9	16.2	0.6
Arkansas	$38,663	12.0	52.8	31.6	14.1	1.5
California	$53,025	10.6	62.7	21.2	14.8	1.3
Colorado	$55,883	6.2	64.5	21.0	13.9	0.6
Connecticut	$65,521	5.6	65.6	19.9	14.3	0.2
Delaware	$55,257	6.5	62.9	22.0	14.6	0.5
District of Columbia	$46,283	16.7	73.9	10.0	16.1	0.1
Florida	$45,625	9.0	61.1	21.1	16.9	0.9
Georgia	$49,280	9.9	59.5	26.5	13.4	0.6
Hawaii	$56,961	7.6	60.3	17.5	20.9	1.3
Idaho	$43,490	8.3	56.7	25.0	15.6	2.7
Illinois	$55,545	7.8	61.8	24.0	13.9	0.3
Indiana	$50,261	6.7	54.0	31.4	14.2	0.4
Iowa	$48,005	6.0	57.2	27.0	14.8	1.1
Kansas	$49,624	6.7	59.7	24.9	14.4	1.0
Kentucky	$40,939	12.7	54.1	30.7	14.3	0.9
Louisiana	$39,774	15.8	56.6	25.8	16.7	0.8
Maine	$45,179	7.8	57.4	25.6	15.3	1.7
Maryland	$61,876	6.1	67.7	18.1	13.9	0.3
Massachusetts	$61,664	6.7	67.0	18.7	14.1	0.2
Michigan	$53,457	7.4	57.1	27.6	14.8	0.5
Minnesota	$56,874	5.1	62.3	23.3	13.7	0.7
Mississippi	$37,406	16.0	52.3	31.6	14.9	1.2
Missouri	$46,044	8.6	58.3	26.0	15.0	0.6
Montana	$40,487	10.5	58.6	22.0	17.2	2.2
Nebraska	$48,032	6.7	59.4	24.4	14.6	1.6
Nevada	$50,849	7.5	53.3	21.8	24.6	0.3
New Hampshire	$57,575	4.3	62.4	24.1	13.0	0.4
New Jersey	$65,370	6.3	66.5	19.7	13.6	0.2
New Mexico	$39,425	14.5	59.9	22.2	17.0	1.0
New York	$51,691	11.5	63.8	19.3	16.6	0.3
North Carolina	$46,335	9.0	56.0	29.7	13.5	0.8
North Dakota	$43,654	8.3	59.4	22.2	16.7	1.7
Ohio	$50,037	7.8	57.3	27.8	14.6	0.3
Oklahoma	$40,709	11.2	56.9	26.7	15.5	0.9
Oregon	$48,680	7.9	59.1	23.9	15.3	1.7
Pennsylvania	$49,184	7.8	59.5	25.2	14.8	0.5
Rhode Island	$52,781	8.9	61.1	22.9	15.7	0.3
South Carolina	$44,227	10.7	54.2	30.4	14.7	0.6
South Dakota	$43,237	9.3	59.1	23.3	15.6	1.9
Tennessee	$43,517	10.3	55.6	30.2	13.7	0.6
Texas	$45,861	12.0	60.6	24.1	14.6	0.7
Utah	$51,022	6.5	61.4	24.1	14.0	0.5
Vermont	$48,625	6.3	60.8	23.3	14.6	1.3
Virginia	$54,169	7.0	63.7	22.1	13.7	0.5
Washington	$53,760	7.3	61.4	22.1	14.9	1.6
West Virginia	$36,484	13.9	54.0	28.7	16.6	0.7
Wisconsin	$52,911	5.6	56.6	28.4	14.0	0.9
Wyoming	$45,685	8.0	54.2	27.5	16.7	1.5
United States	$50,046	9.2	60.3	24.1	14.9	0.7

*As percentage of all families.   †As percentage of employed workers 16 years and over.

National Table 5 Education: School Years Completed

State	Less than grade 9*	Grades 9–12 no diploma*	High school diploma no college*	Some college*	College bachelor's degree or higher*
Alabama	8.3	16.4	30.4	25.9	19.0
Alaska	4.1	7.5	27.9	35.7	24.7
Arizona	7.8	11.2	24.3	33.1	23.5
Arkansas	9.4	15.3	34.1	24.5	16.7
California	11.5	11.7	20.1	30.0	26.6
Colorado	4.8	8.2	23.2	31.0	32.7
Connecticut	5.8	10.2	28.5	24.1	31.4
Delaware	5.0	12.4	31.4	26.1	25.0
District of Columbia	7.8	14.4	20.6	18.2	39.1
Florida	6.7	13.4	28.7	28.8	22.3
Georgia	7.6	13.8	28.7	25.6	24.3
Hawaii	7.2	8.2	28.5	29.9	26.2
Idaho	5.2	10.1	28.5	34.6	21.7
Illinois	7.5	11.1	27.7	27.6	26.1
Indiana	5.3	12.6	37.2	25.5	19.4
Iowa	5.6	8.3	36.1	28.8	21.2
Kansas	5.2	8.8	29.8	30.4	25.8
Kentucky	11.7	14.2	33.6	23.4	17.1
Louisiana	9.3	15.9	32.4	23.7	18.7
Maine	5.4	9.2	36.2	26.3	22.9
Maryland	5.1	11.1	26.7	25.7	31.4
Massachusetts	5.8	9.4	27.3	24.3	33.2
Michigan	4.7	11.9	31.3	30.3	21.8
Minnesota	5.0	7.0	28.8	31.7	27.4
Mississippi	9.6	17.5	29.4	26.6	16.9
Missouri	6.5	12.1	32.7	27.0	21.6
Montana	4.3	8.6	31.3	31.5	24.4
Nebraska	5.4	8.0	31.3	31.6	23.7
Nevada	6.4	12.9	29.3	33.2	18.2
New Hampshire	3.9	8.7	30.1	28.7	28.7
New Jersey	6.6	11.3	29.4	22.9	29.8
New Mexico	9.3	11.9	26.6	28.8	23.5
New York	8.0	12.9	27.8	23.9	27.4
North Carolina	7.8	14.0	28.4	27.2	22.5
North Dakota	8.7	7.4	27.9	34.0	22.0
Ohio	4.5	12.6	36.1	25.8	21.1
Oklahoma	6.1	13.3	31.5	28.8	20.3
Oregon	5.0	9.9	26.3	33.8	25.1
Pennsylvania	5.5	12.6	38.1	21.4	22.4
Rhode Island	8.1	13.9	27.8	24.6	25.6
South Carolina	8.3	15.4	30.0	25.9	20.4
South Dakota	7.5	8.0	32.9	30.2	21.5
Tennessee	9.6	14.5	31.6	24.8	19.6
Texas	11.5	12.9	24.8	27.6	23.2
Utah	3.2	9.1	24.6	37.0	26.1
Vermont	5.1	8.4	32.4	24.6	29.4
Virginia	7.2	11.3	26.0	26.0	29.5
Washington	4.3	8.6	24.9	34.4	27.7
West Virginia	10.0	14.8	39.4	21.0	14.8
Wisconsin	5.4	9.6	34.6	28.1	22.4
Wyoming	3.4	8.8	31.0	35.0	21.9
United States	7.5	12.1	28.6	27.4	24.4

*As percentage of persons age 25 and over.

National Table 6 Housing and Residential Patterns

State	Median home value	Owner occupied*	Renter occupied*	Urban†	Rural†
Alabama	$76,700	72.5	27.5	55.4	44.6
Alaska	$137,400	62.5	37.5	65.7	34.3
Arizona	$109,400	68.0	32.0	88.2	11.8
Arkansas	$67,400	69.4	30.6	52.4	47.6
California	$198,900	56.9	43.1	94.5	5.5
Colorado	$160,100	67.3	32.7	84.5	15.5
Connecticut	$160,600	66.8	33.2	87.7	12.3
Delaware	$122,000	72.3	27.7	80.0	20.0
District of Columbia	$153,500	40.8	59.2	100.0	0.0
Florida	$93,200	70.1	29.9	89.3	10.7
Georgia	$100,600	67.5	32.5	71.7	28.3
Hawaii	$249,300	56.5	43.5	91.6	8.4
Idaho	$102,100	72.4	27.6	66.4	33.6
Illinois	$127,800	67.3	32.7	87.8	12.2
Indiana	$92,500	71.4	28.6	70.8	29.2
Iowa	$82,100	72.3	27.7	61.1	38.9
Kansas	$81,000	69.2	30.8	71.4	28.6
Kentucky	$79,600	70.8	29.2	55.7	44.3
Louisiana	$77,500	67.9	32.1	72.7	27.3
Maine	$94,300	71.6	28.4	40.2	59.8
Maryland	$143,300	67.7	32.3	86.1	13.9
Massachusetts	$182,800	61.7	38.3	91.4	8.6
Michigan	$110,300	73.8	26.2	74.7	25.3
Minnesota	$118,100	74.6	25.4	70.9	29.1
Mississippi	$64,700	72.3	27.7	48.8	51.2
Missouri	$86,900	70.3	29.7	69.4	30.6
Montana	$95,800	69.1	30.9	54.0	46.0
Nebraska	$86,900	67.4	32.6	69.7	30.3
Nevada	$132,500	60.9	39.1	91.6	8.4
New Hampshire	$127,500	69.7	30.3	59.2	40.8
New Jersey	$167,900	65.6	34.4	94.3	5.7
New Mexico	$94,600	70.0	30.0	75.0	25.0
New York	$147,600	53.0	47.0	87.5	12.5
North Carolina	$95,800	69.4	30.6	60.2	39.8
North Dakota	$68,300	66.6	33.4	55.8	44.2
Ohio	$100,500	69.1	30.9	77.3	22.7
Oklahoma	$67,700	68.4	31.6	65.3	34.7
Oregon	$145,800	64.3	35.7	78.7	21.3
Pennsylvania	$94,800	71.3	28.7	77.0	23.0
Rhode Island	$130,500	60.0	40.0	90.9	9.1
South Carolina	$83,100	72.2	27.8	60.5	39.5
South Dakota	$74,300	68.2	31.8	51.9	48.1
Tennessee	$88,300	69.9	30.1	63.6	36.4
Texas	$77,800	63.8	36.2	82.5	17.5
Utah	$142,600	71.5	28.5	88.3	11.7
Vermont	$111,200	70.6	29.4	38.2	61.8
Virginia	$118,800	68.1	31.9	73.0	27.0
Washington	$158,800	64.6	35.4	82.0	18.0
West Virginia	$66,000	75.2	24.8	46.1	53.9
Wisconsin	$109,900	68.4	31.6	68.3	31.7
Wyoming	$91,500	70.0	30.0	65.2	34.8
United States	$111,800	66.2	33.8	79.0	21.0

*As percentage of occupied housing units.   †As percentage of total population.

Measuring Congressional Districts in the 2000s

The seven categories of information in the following table provide a snapshot of the racial, economic, and educational makeup of congressional districts throughout the United States. Important demographic divisions that often affect voting behavior are in the first three groups under Race and Hispanic or Latino origin. The family income and poverty levels in the next group give an indication of the economic level—and needs—of a district. The high school or college achievements shown in the third group are a guide to the overall educational level. All of these sets of data have correlations to voting behavior.

The table lists all districts alphabetically by state and then in numerical order within each state. Each data group includes a column to the right that ranks a district compared to other districts. Many districts have the same percentage or dollar amount and are assigned the same rank. As a result there are fewer ranks in total than the number of districts in the House. The bottom rank for each group is shown at the end of the table on page 1025.

The race and origin columns are expressed as a percentage of the voting-age population, not the entire population. This measure was used to give a more accurate picture of the potential voting strength of each group. The data on family poverty are expressed as a percentage of all families. The educational levels are expressed as a percentage of persons age 25 years or over.

A portion of each data set was extracted and sorted separately to show the highest and lowest rankings for approximately 50 to 100 ranking levels. Those rankings are shown in the table that begins on page 1026.

The District of Columbia, although not a congressional district with House voting privileges, is included in the table for comparison purposes.

State	CD	Non-Hispanic white[1]	National rank	Non-Hispanic black[1]	National rank	Hispanic[1]	National rank	Median family income, 1999	National rank	Families in poverty[2]	National rank	High school diploma, no college[3]	National rank	College bachelor's degree or higher[3]	National rank
Alabama	1	70.7%	170	25.4%	50	1.2%	185	$41,406	333	13.7%	53	32.1%	70	18.5%	174
Alabama	2	69.6%	177	27.1%	47	1.4%	183	$40,062	356	13.6%	54	30.1%	89	18.0%	179
Alabama	3	67.4%	186	29.9%	42	1.1%	186	$38,959	375	13.8%	52	30.8%	82	16.7%	191
Alabama	4	91.4%	44	4.7%	156	2.5%	172	$37,916	385	11.4%	71	33.1%	60	11.3%	228
Alabama	5	79.4%	122	15.8%	82	1.7%	180	$46,350	258	9.7%	86	28.6%	104	23.5%	132
Alabama	6	89.5%	58	7.2%	134	1.5%	182	$56,307	126	5.9%	124	27.0%	120	29.6%	81
Alabama	7	39.5%	257	57.8%	7	1.2%	185	$33,398	418	20.4%	14	31.1%	79	15.1%	203
Alaska	AL	71.4%	168	3.2%	171	3.6%	161	$59,036	105	6.7%	116	27.9%	111	24.7%	121
Arizona	1	64.3%	200	1.3%	190	14.8%	82	$38,113	384	15.0%	45	27.2%	118	17.5%	183
Arizona	2	82.1%	106	1.9%	184	11.4%	101	$49,150	218	5.9%	124	29.1%	99	19.3%	166
Arizona	3	81.4%	109	2.1%	182	11.9%	98	$57,053	119	5.7%	126	22.3%	158	30.3%	76
Arizona	4	35.6%	266	7.3%	133	51.8%	20	$31,933	424	21.1%	12	24.7%	141	10.2%	230
Arizona	5	79.7%	119	2.5%	178	11.3%	102	$63,729	73	4.8%	135	17.9%	186	39.6%	29
Arizona	6	80.1%	117	1.8%	185	14.4%	85	$53,537	147	5.4%	129	25.1%	138	23.6%	131
Arizona	7	45.3%	247	2.7%	176	44.5%	26	$34,287	408	17.2%	30	26.7%	122	13.3%	217
Arizona	8	77.6%	132	2.8%	175	15.3%	78	$49,568	209	7.3%	110	21.9%	160	30.6%	74
Arkansas	1	82.9%	101	14.2%	93	1.4%	183	$34,949	403	14.4%	49	35.9%	41	12.3%	223
Arkansas	2	78.3%	127	17.3%	77	2.1%	176	$44,403	284	9.5%	88	31.0%	80	23.2%	135
Arkansas	3	89.1%	62	1.8%	185	5.2%	146	$40,169	353	9.9%	85	33.1%	60	17.9%	180
Arkansas	4	73.8%	154	22.3%	59	2.3%	174	$35,915	397	14.2%	50	36.4%	38	13.3%	217
California	1	74.6%	147	1.4%	189	15.0%	80	$47,667	234	9.7%	86	23.2%	152	25.0%	118
California	2	80.0%	118	1.1%	192	11.4%	101	$40,408	347	12.0%	66	25.9%	130	17.4%	184
California	3	77.0%	137	4.2%	161	9.1%	116	$59,574	99	5.8%	125	23.4%	150	27.0%	102
California	4	85.7%	83	1.2%	191	7.6%	126	$57,310	115	6.1%	122	23.6%	148	25.2%	117
California	5	49.3%	239	13.0%	95	18.0%	67	$41,011	339	15.3%	43	23.2%	152	21.4%	148
California	6	78.9%	125	2.0%	183	12.4%	96	$69,561	43	4.4%	139	17.2%	190	37.9%	36
California	7	47.3%	242	15.9%	81	18.7%	66	$59,656	97	7.5%	108	23.8%	146	22.4%	141
California	8	46.6%	243	7.8%	129	14.1%	87	$59,037	104	8.8%	95	13.8%	204	44.0%	15
California	9	39.3%	258	24.5%	54	16.2%	74	$53,315	150	12.3%	63	16.9%	192	37.4%	37

1015

State	CD	Race and Hispanic or Latino origin						Income and Poverty				Education Levels			
		Non-Hispanic white[1]	National rank	Non-Hispanic black[1]	National rank	Hispanic[1]	National rank	Median family income, 1999	National rank	Families in poverty[2]	National rank	High school diploma, no college[3]	National rank	College bachelor's degree or higher[3]	National rank
California	10	68.7%	181	5.1%	152	12.9%	91	$74,079	28	4.3%	140	19.7%	177	36.2%	42
California	11	67.5%	185	3.3%	170	17.2%	69	$70,734	38	6.2%	121	21.4%	163	29.1%	86
California	12	50.9%	234	2.5%	178	14.0%	88	$80,658	18	3.2%	150	17.5%	188	40.7%	25
California	13	42.1%	252	5.9%	145	18.7%	66	$69,228	45	5.0%	133	21.3%	164	31.8%	67
California	14	62.3%	207	3.0%	173	15.2%	79	$91,249	2	3.8%	145	12.2%	207	52.2%	5
California	15	50.1%	235	2.3%	180	15.2%	79	$82,246	12	4.4%	139	16.2%	198	41.6%	23
California	16	35.5%	267	3.4%	169	33.8%	36	$71,400	34	6.7%	116	19.1%	180	26.9%	103
California	17	51.8%	233	2.8%	175	37.0%	33	$53,318	149	9.0%	93	18.5%	184	24.9%	119
California	18	44.8%	248	5.5%	148	37.5%	32	$37,281	391	18.1%	25	25.1%	138	9.7%	233
California	19	64.8%	198	3.2%	171	24.1%	53	$46,636	255	11.0%	75	23.8%	146	20.3%	157
California	20	26.0%	286	7.9%	128	58.7%	15	$27,800	430	27.4%	4	23.2%	152	6.3%	239
California	21	52.3%	232	2.0%	183	38.1%	31	$39,710	363	15.8%	39	23.0%	154	15.0%	204
California	22	70.5%	171	5.3%	150	18.0%	67	$48,470	225	10.8%	77	25.7%	132	18.3%	176
California	23	54.8%	224	2.0%	183	35.5%	34	$51,509	178	9.4%	89	18.8%	183	26.2%	107
California	24	71.7%	167	1.7%	186	19.6%	63	$68,648	49	5.0%	133	20.0%	175	30.0%	77
California	25	61.4%	210	7.2%	134	24.0%	54	$53,522	148	9.9%	85	25.1%	138	18.8%	171
California	26	56.2%	221	4.3%	160	21.5%	60	$66,539	59	6.2%	121	18.9%	182	32.4%	62
California	27	49.7%	237	4.3%	160	31.8%	39	$52,228	161	10.1%	84	20.6%	170	25.8%	111
California	28	37.2%	262	4.2%	161	49.2%	21	$41,622	328	16.0%	37	16.6%	195	23.7%	130
California	29	42.0%	253	5.6%	147	23.2%	57	$49,831	203	11.6%	70	17.5%	188	33.4%	56
California	30	77.2%	135	2.6%	177	7.7%	125	$85,703	8	4.8%	135	13.0%	206	53.5%	4
California	31	12.1%	308	4.5%	158	65.5%	9	$26,927	431	27.5%	3	16.5%	196	13.7%	214
California	32	17.7%	302	2.5%	178	57.4%	17	$42,785	310	14.6%	47	21.3%	164	13.6%	215
California	33	23.2%	293	29.6%	43	30.2%	42	$35,695	398	19.9%	18	18.1%	185	26.9%	103
California	34	13.9%	306	5.0%	153	72.9%	3	$32,003	423	22.1%	11	19.1%	180	8.7%	236
California	35	13.0%	307	35.0%	35	42.7%	27	$34,063	411	23.2%	8	21.2%	165	13.3%	217
California	36	53.0%	230	3.8%	165	25.8%	48	$60,049	94	9.7%	86	16.9%	192	36.9%	39
California	37	21.4%	296	24.7%	53	38.2%	30	$35,681	399	22.1%	11	20.6%	170	15.2%	202
California	38	16.5%	304	3.6%	167	66.3%	7	$44,772	280	13.3%	57	22.6%	156	12.5%	222
California	39	25.1%	288	6.0%	144	56.3%	18	$47,373	237	12.5%	61	22.1%	159	14.7%	206
California	40	53.4%	228	2.1%	182	25.6%	49	$59,625	98	7.1%	112	20.9%	167	26.4%	105
California	41	68.4%	183	4.7%	156	19.6%	63	$44,625	281	11.8%	68	26.2%	127	18.1%	178
California	42	56.6%	219	3.0%	173	21.6%	59	$77,088	22	4.2%	141	18.5%	184	34.8%	48
California	43	28.2%	283	11.9%	101	53.7%	19	$39,688	364	17.4%	29	25.5%	134	8.8%	235
California	44	55.8%	223	5.4%	149	30.6%	41	$57,132	117	8.7%	96	22.1%	159	21.1%	151
California	45	56.8%	218	5.7%	146	32.2%	38	$45,707	269	11.3%	72	24.4%	143	17.4%	184
California	46	66.1%	191	1.5%	188	14.4%	85	$71,863	32	5.0%	133	16.7%	194	36.4%	41
California	47	21.2%	297	1.6%	187	59.5%	14	$40,870	342	15.4%	42	19.2%	179	10.0%	231
California	48	70.4%	172	1.3%	190	12.7%	93	$82,172	13	3.7%	146	13.3%	205	46.5%	12
California	49	63.1%	204	4.7%	156	25.1%	51	$51,111	182	8.7%	96	23.4%	150	20.7%	154
California	50	69.4%	178	1.7%	186	15.9%	77	$67,489	54	5.0%	133	15.7%	200	40.0%	27

State	CD	Race and Hispanic or Latino origin						Income and Poverty						Education Levels			
		Non-Hispanic white[1]	National rank	Non-Hispanic black[1]	National rank	Hispanic[1]	National rank	Median family income, 1999	National rank	Families in poverty[2]	National rank	High school diploma, no college[3]	National rank	College bachelor's degree or higher[3]	National rank
California	51	25.1%	288	9.5%	117	49.0%	22	$42,118	323	13.8%	52	23.1%	153	15.2%	202
California	52	76.0%	143	3.3%	170	11.7%	99	$60,116	93	5.7%	126	22.3%	158	28.6%	91
California	53	57.3%	217	6.6%	139	24.0%	54	$41,189	336	15.4%	42	17.7%	187	32.2%	64
Colorado	1	60.3%	212	9.1%	120	25.3%	50	$48,541	223	10.1%	84	20.4%	172	34.3%	50
Colorado	2	81.4%	109	0.9%	194	12.8%	92	$64,006	72	4.0%	143	21.2%	165	39.3%	31
Colorado	3	77.3%	134	0.7%	196	19.0%	65	$42,668	311	9.2%	91	28.6%	104	23.8%	129
Colorado	4	82.2%	105	0.8%	195	14.3%	86	$51,590	175	6.7%	116	25.2%	137	28.7%	90
Colorado	5	79.6%	120	5.5%	148	9.8%	110	$52,482	159	5.9%	124	24.4%	143	29.8%	79
Colorado	6	89.0%	63	1.8%	185	5.1%	147	$80,910	16	1.9%	158	16.5%	196	46.8%	11
Colorado	7	72.7%	160	5.2%	151	16.9%	71	$53,624	146	6.4%	119	26.3%	126	26.0%	109
Connecticut	1	75.3%	144	11.4%	104	9.3%	114	$61,187	82	7.3%	110	29.4%	96	28.2%	93
Connecticut	2	89.7%	56	3.3%	170	3.7%	160	$64,772	64	3.7%	146	30.8%	82	28.8%	89
Connecticut	3	79.1%	124	10.1%	113	6.6%	135	$61,106	85	6.4%	119	31.3%	78	28.0%	94
Connecticut	4	73.3%	157	10.0%	114	11.7%	99	$80,284	19	5.4%	129	22.1%	159	42.2%	22
Connecticut	5	82.8%	102	4.8%	155	8.7%	118	$65,204	61	5.5%	128	28.7%	103	29.9%	78
Delaware	AL	75.2%	145	17.4%	76	4.0%	157	$55,257	132	6.5%	118	31.4%	77	25.0%	118
District of Columbia	AL	31.8%	276	55.7%	12	7.3%	128	$46,283	259	16.7%	33	20.6%	170	39.1%	32
Florida	1	80.1%	117	12.5%	97	2.8%	169	$42,656	312	10.3%	82	29.4%	96	20.2%	158
Florida	2	73.2%	158	20.8%	64	3.1%	166	$43,496	298	11.1%	74	28.8%	102	24.1%	126
Florida	3	43.2%	251	45.1%	26	7.5%	127	$34,216	410	17.4%	29	31.4%	77	12.9%	220
Florida	4	79.6%	120	12.4%	98	3.9%	158	$51,472	179	6.6%	117	28.7%	103	24.4%	124
Florida	5	89.3%	60	4.0%	163	4.8%	150	$40,204	352	7.6%	107	36.6%	37	14.3%	208
Florida	6	80.9%	112	10.5%	110	4.8%	150	$44,815	278	8.3%	100	31.3%	78	21.4%	148
Florida	7	83.4%	98	7.9%	128	6.2%	138	$48,369	226	7.0%	113	28.7%	103	24.5%	123
Florida	8	72.8%	159	6.3%	141	16.0%	76	$48,078	229	6.9%	114	27.6%	114	25.9%	110
Florida	9	87.2%	74	3.0%	173	6.9%	132	$49,756	205	6.0%	123	29.0%	100	24.6%	122
Florida	10	89.7%	56	2.9%	174	3.8%	159	$47,118	244	5.8%	125	30.2%	88	22.6%	140
Florida	11	53.0%	230	23.9%	56	19.0%	65	$39,492	367	13.4%	56	27.5%	115	21.2%	150
Florida	12	76.1%	142	11.3%	105	10.1%	107	$43,389	299	9.0%	93	32.5%	66	16.6%	192
Florida	13	88.5%	67	3.6%	167	6.3%	137	$47,780	233	6.1%	122	31.3%	78	23.7%	130
Florida	14	86.8%	76	4.0%	163	7.5%	127	$49,608	208	5.9%	124	30.6%	84	24.4%	124
Florida	15	80.6%	114	6.3%	141	9.9%	109	$45,860	266	7.1%	112	29.8%	92	22.3%	142
Florida	16	84.6%	91	4.9%	154	8.5%	120	$45,950	265	6.7%	116	31.6%	75	20.0%	160
Florida	17	21.5%	295	51.3%	19	22.0%	58	$33,677	416	20.0%	17	28.6%	104	13.5%	216
Florida	18	29.6%	279	4.7%	156	63.9%	11	$38,509	379	14.5%	48	20.1%	174	25.6%	113
Florida	19	80.8%	113	4.9%	154	11.1%	103	$51,689	172	5.2%	131	30.3%	87	25.7%	112
Florida	20	69.1%	180	7.0%	136	19.8%	62	$54,631	136	6.8%	115	26.3%	126	29.6%	81
Florida	21	19.1%	300	6.1%	143	72.2%	4	$44,799	279	10.6%	79	21.5%	162	22.9%	138
Florida	22	84.2%	94	3.2%	171	9.7%	111	$64,685	66	4.6%	137	23.9%	145	34.1%	51
Florida	23	35.0%	269	46.2%	24	13.2%	90	$35,126	401	18.3%	24	29.8%	92	12.8%	221
Florida	24	81.8%	107	5.7%	146	8.9%	117	$50,858	187	5.5%	128	27.6%	114	25.5%	114

State	CD	Non-Hispanic white[1]	National rank	Non-Hispanic black[1]	National rank	Hispanic[1]	National rank	Median family income, 1999	National rank	Families in poverty[2]	National rank	High school diploma, no college[3]	National rank	College bachelor's degree or higher[3]	National rank
Florida	25	23.3%	292	9.2%	119	64.3%	10	$46,820	252	11.0%	75	24.1%	144	20.3%	157
Georgia	1	73.6%	155	20.6%	65	3.7%	160	$42,042	324	11.7%	69	32.7%	64	17.9%	180
Georgia	2	54.2%	227	40.9%	30	3.2%	165	$34,793	404	18.3%	24	33.0%	61	13.9%	212
Georgia	3	59.2%	213	37.2%	34	2.3%	174	$38,410	381	15.9%	38	36.6%	37	12.8%	221
Georgia	4	36.5%	263	48.8%	22	8.5%	120	$54,221	138	7.6%	107	20.4%	172	35.9%	44
Georgia	5	39.2%	259	51.0%	21	5.9%	140	$43,324	301	16.5%	34	21.0%	166	37.3%	38
Georgia	6	83.9%	95	6.5%	140	4.4%	153	$86,640	4	2.4%	155	15.8%	199	50.7%	6
Georgia	7	83.4%	98	6.5%	140	5.1%	147	$68,828	47	3.2%	150	25.3%	136	31.9%	66
Georgia	8	83.9%	95	11.8%	102	2.0%	177	$59,258	103	4.6%	137	31.5%	76	23.4%	133
Georgia	9	82.8%	102	12.8%	96	2.3%	174	$46,212	261	8.6%	97	33.2%	59	18.5%	174
Georgia	10	87.0%	75	3.2%	171	8.2%	123	$47,474	236	7.5%	108	31.8%	73	15.9%	198
Georgia	11	65.0%	196	25.8%	49	6.7%	134	$42,834	308	10.7%	78	32.0%	71	16.9%	189
Georgia	12	56.1%	222	38.4%	32	2.7%	170	$38,566	378	15.9%	38	30.8%	82	19.3%	166
Georgia	13	46.1%	245	37.3%	33	9.8%	110	$47,840	231	8.8%	95	29.5%	95	19.4%	165
Hawaii	1	19.3%	299	1.9%	184	4.4%	153	$60,609	88	6.6%	117	26.6%	123	28.9%	88
Hawaii	2	31.9%	275	1.5%	188	7.2%	129	$53,852	142	8.7%	96	30.6%	84	23.1%	136
Idaho	1	90.8%	49	0.2%	201	5.5%	143	$44,109	291	7.9%	104	30.0%	90	20.3%	157
Idaho	2	89.0%	63	0.5%	198	7.2%	129	$42,800	309	8.7%	96	26.8%	121	23.1%	136
Illinois	1	29.8%	278	63.2%	1	4.2%	155	$44,422	283	15.9%	38	28.0%	110	18.7%	172
Illinois	2	29.4%	280	59.4%	3	9.3%	114	$47,809	232	12.3%	63	27.7%	113	18.1%	178
Illinois	3	72.4%	163	5.1%	152	18.0%	67	$57,104	118	6.4%	119	30.5%	85	20.5%	155
Illinois	4	23.6%	291	3.6%	167	69.0%	5	$37,143	393	17.8%	27	21.9%	160	13.6%	215
Illinois	5	70.0%	174	2.1%	182	19.2%	64	$56,881	122	6.2%	121	23.5%	149	33.9%	52
Illinois	6	77.4%	133	2.4%	179	11.0%	104	$71,991	31	3.0%	152	23.8%	146	34.6%	49
Illinois	7	32.8%	272	55.9%	11	5.4%	144	$43,748	293	20.5%	13	20.5%	171	32.1%	65
Illinois	8	81.0%	111	2.8%	175	9.4%	113	$71,398	35	3.2%	150	25.7%	132	32.1%	65
Illinois	9	65.7%	193	9.7%	116	9.9%	109	$60,033	95	7.7%	106	20.4%	172	39.6%	29
Illinois	10	77.3%	134	4.9%	154	10.9%	105	$85,990	6	3.1%	151	17.3%	189	47.5%	10
Illinois	11	85.9%	81	6.9%	137	5.6%	142	$56,971	120	5.7%	126	34.8%	47	18.5%	174
Illinois	12	82.1%	106	14.4%	91	1.6%	181	$43,580	297	11.4%	71	32.0%	71	16.8%	190
Illinois	13	82.8%	102	4.7%	156	4.9%	149	$82,413	11	1.9%	158	20.7%	169	42.4%	20
Illinois	14	77.0%	137	4.2%	161	16.1%	75	$64,330	71	4.6%	137	27.0%	120	26.3%	106
Illinois	15	89.3%	60	5.2%	151	2.0%	177	$48,961	219	6.6%	117	33.5%	57	23.2%	135
Illinois	16	87.9%	70	4.6%	157	5.4%	144	$57,434	114	5.2%	131	32.9%	62	21.1%	151
Illinois	17	89.3%	60	6.2%	142	3.0%	167	$43,200	303	9.0%	93	37.8%	28	14.7%	206
Illinois	18	91.4%	44	5.6%	147	1.3%	184	$51,009	183	6.2%	121	34.3%	51	20.7%	154
Illinois	19	94.3%	21	3.6%	167	0.9%	188	$47,058	247	6.6%	117	34.3%	51	17.1%	187
Indiana	1	72.5%	162	17.0%	79	8.7%	118	$52,076	165	8.1%	102	38.3%	25	17.1%	187
Indiana	2	86.6%	78	7.2%	134	4.2%	155	$48,153	227	6.9%	114	38.1%	27	17.2%	186
Indiana	3	89.2%	61	5.0%	153	3.9%	158	$51,664	173	5.5%	128	36.4%	38	18.4%	175
Indiana	4	94.0%	24	1.3%	190	2.3%	174	$54,668	135	4.9%	134	38.4%	24	22.1%	143
Indiana	5	93.9%	25	2.5%	178	1.4%	183	$62,335	78	3.5%	148	31.9%	72	30.6%	74

State	CD	Race and Hispanic or Latino origin						Income and Poverty						Education Levels			
		Non-Hispanic white[1]	National rank	Non-Hispanic black[1]	National rank	Hispanic[1]	National rank	Median family income, 1999	National rank	Families in poverty[2]	National rank	High school diploma, no college[3]	National rank	College bachelor's degree or higher[3]	National rank
Indiana	6	94.1%	23	3.5%	168	1.1%	186	$46,778	253	6.7%	116	42.0%	11	14.7%	206
Indiana	7	66.5%	188	26.7%	48	4.1%	156	$43,721	294	10.6%	79	31.4%	77	21.2%	150
Indiana	8	94.2%	22	3.5%	168	0.8%	189	$45,199	273	7.7%	106	39.3%	19	15.9%	198
Indiana	9	94.5%	19	2.2%	181	1.4%	183	$47,129	243	6.7%	116	38.9%	21	17.3%	185
Iowa	1	93.7%	27	3.1%	172	1.6%	181	$47,321	241	6.9%	114	37.5%	31	20.0%	160
Iowa	2	93.6%	28	1.8%	185	2.2%	175	$50,101	199	6.0%	123	33.2%	59	25.0%	118
Iowa	3	91.7%	41	2.8%	175	2.6%	171	$52,260	160	5.4%	129	34.2%	52	24.6%	122
Iowa	4	95.5%	12	0.7%	196	2.0%	177	$46,867	250	5.5%	128	36.1%	39	20.4%	156
Iowa	5	95.0%	14	0.5%	198	2.9%	168	$44,322	285	6.3%	120	39.3%	19	16.1%	196
Kansas	1	87.3%	73	2.0%	183	8.6%	119	$42,292	317	7.8%	105	32.9%	62	18.0%	179
Kansas	2	88.7%	66	4.7%	156	3.2%	165	$47,095	246	7.1%	112	34.2%	52	23.2%	135
Kansas	3	81.5%	108	8.0%	127	6.0%	139	$62,695	76	4.9%	134	21.7%	161	39.1%	32
Kansas	4	83.5%	97	6.2%	142	5.4%	144	$49,650	206	7.0%	113	30.5%	85	23.0%	137
Kentucky	1	90.9%	48	6.6%	139	1.3%	184	$37,022	394	12.7%	60	37.2%	33	11.8%	226
Kentucky	2	91.5%	43	5.3%	150	1.5%	182	$42,124	322	10.3%	82	37.6%	30	13.9%	212
Kentucky	3	78.5%	126	17.2%	78	1.7%	180	$49,426	212	9.5%	88	28.8%	102	25.3%	116
Kentucky	4	95.5%	12	2.2%	181	1.0%	187	$47,648	235	9.1%	92	35.3%	43	17.5%	183
Kentucky	5	97.2%	1	1.2%	191	0.6%	191	$26,627	432	24.0%	7	32.8%	63	9.6%	234
Kentucky	6	88.0%	69	7.8%	129	2.0%	177	$46,939	249	9.6%	87	29.9%	91	24.6%	122
Louisiana	1	81.3%	110	11.4%	104	4.6%	152	$50,317	194	9.1%	92	28.0%	110	27.4%	98
Louisiana	2	32.7%	273	59.3%	4	3.9%	158	$32,306	420	22.8%	9	27.1%	119	19.4%	165
Louisiana	3	72.7%	160	22.2%	60	2.0%	177	$39,990	359	15.6%	40	38.2%	26	10.8%	229
Louisiana	4	65.1%	195	30.5%	40	1.9%	178	$37,414	390	16.0%	37	34.7%	48	16.7%	191
Louisiana	5	66.3%	190	30.8%	37	1.3%	184	$34,260	409	18.7%	21	34.1%	53	15.5%	201
Louisiana	6	65.3%	194	30.7%	38	1.6%	181	$46,699	254	12.5%	61	31.3%	78	24.1%	126
Louisiana	7	74.5%	148	22.6%	58	1.3%	184	$38,189	383	16.2%	35	33.6%	56	16.6%	192
Maine	1	97.0%	2	0.5%	198	0.7%	190	$50,419	193	6.2%	121	32.8%	63	27.5%	97
Maine	2	97.2%	1	0.3%	200	0.5%	192	$40,113	354	9.5%	88	39.8%	16	17.7%	182
Maryland	1	85.6%	84	10.8%	108	1.4%	183	$60,620	86	5.2%	131	30.7%	83	27.3%	99
Maryland	2	69.8%	176	24.3%	55	1.9%	178	$51,916	168	7.5%	108	32.0%	71	20.3%	157
Maryland	3	77.7%	131	14.9%	88	2.7%	170	$63,408	75	5.2%	131	23.6%	148	36.5%	40
Maryland	4	29.6%	279	55.3%	13	7.1%	130	$65,107	62	5.5%	128	24.8%	140	32.7%	61
Maryland	5	62.5%	205	28.5%	45	3.1%	166	$70,571	39	3.4%	149	28.8%	102	28.7%	90
Maryland	6	92.1%	40	4.9%	154	1.3%	184	$59,362	101	4.6%	137	34.2%	52	23.7%	130
Maryland	7	36.2%	264	57.0%	8	1.6%	181	$48,649	221	13.6%	54	25.4%	135	27.5%	97
Maryland	8	58.2%	215	15.7%	83	12.6%	94	$81,922	14	4.2%	141	14.6%	201	53.7%	3
Massachusetts	1	90.8%	49	1.5%	188	4.8%	150	$52,561	158	7.3%	110	32.2%	69	25.4%	115
Massachusetts	2	85.4%	85	4.9%	154	7.2%	129	$54,851	134	8.2%	101	32.1%	70	23.1%	136
Massachusetts	3	88.1%	68	2.3%	180	4.9%	149	$61,768	81	6.6%	117	26.7%	122	30.8%	73
Massachusetts	4	88.8%	65	1.9%	184	2.7%	170	$65,100	63	6.2%	121	23.8%	146	36.9%	39
Massachusetts	5	82.3%	104	1.7%	186	9.9%	109	$67,846	53	6.7%	116	26.5%	124	33.6%	54

State	CD	Race and Hispanic or Latino origin						Income and Poverty				Education Levels			
		Non-Hispanic white[1]	National rank	Non-Hispanic black[1]	National rank	Hispanic[1]	National rank	Median family income, 1999	National rank	Families in poverty[2]	National rank	High school diploma, no college[3]	National rank	College bachelor's degree or higher[3]	National rank
Massachusetts	6	91.4%	44	1.7%	186	3.6%	161	$70,858	37	4.3%	140	27.4%	116	35.1%	45
Massachusetts	7	85.2%	87	3.0%	173	4.2%	155	$69,501	44	4.6%	137	26.1%	128	39.5%	30
Massachusetts	8	54.6%	225	18.7%	72	13.4%	89	$42,246	318	15.6%	40	21.5%	162	39.8%	28
Massachusetts	9	81.8%	107	7.1%	135	3.9%	158	$67,060	57	5.4%	129	28.2%	108	33.8%	53
Massachusetts	10	92.8%	35	1.5%	188	1.1%	186	$63,464	74	4.1%	142	28.0%	110	33.5%	55
Michigan	1	94.5%	19	1.2%	191	0.7%	190	$41,241	335	7.8%	105	38.6%	23	15.6%	200
Michigan	2	89.4%	59	4.1%	162	4.1%	156	$50,227	196	6.3%	120	35.1%	45	18.3%	176
Michigan	3	84.5%	92	7.2%	134	5.3%	145	$54,123	139	6.2%	121	29.9%	91	23.9%	128
Michigan	4	93.6%	28	2.1%	182	2.0%	177	$46,500	257	6.6%	117	35.9%	41	18.6%	173
Michigan	5	78.3%	127	16.4%	80	2.9%	168	$47,051	248	10.6%	79	34.8%	47	15.1%	203
Michigan	6	86.7%	77	7.7%	130	2.9%	168	$49,402	214	7.5%	108	32.3%	68	21.1%	151
Michigan	7	89.8%	55	5.4%	149	2.6%	171	$53,227	151	5.4%	129	33.8%	55	19.1%	168
Michigan	8	89.1%	62	4.5%	158	2.9%	168	$64,336	70	4.9%	134	26.8%	121	29.0%	87
Michigan	9	83.3%	99	7.3%	133	2.6%	171	$80,897	17	3.5%	148	20.0%	175	43.5%	17
Michigan	10	94.4%	20	1.4%	189	1.7%	180	$61,930	80	4.3%	140	34.6%	49	16.9%	189
Michigan	11	90.4%	52	3.6%	167	1.7%	180	$70,224	40	3.0%	152	28.0%	110	28.5%	92
Michigan	12	83.3%	99	11.2%	106	1.2%	185	$56,748	123	5.4%	129	31.4%	77	19.5%	164
Michigan	13	32.5%	274	57.9%	6	6.6%	135	$37,220	392	19.8%	19	29.3%	97	14.1%	210
Michigan	14	35.1%	268	58.9%	5	1.7%	180	$41,967	326	15.9%	38	31.1%	79	14.2%	209
Michigan	15	80.9%	112	10.6%	109	2.5%	172	$59,541	100	6.3%	120	28.7%	103	27.5%	97
Minnesota	1	94.5%	19	0.8%	195	2.4%	173	$50,143	197	5.3%	130	32.7%	64	21.6%	146
Minnesota	2	93.1%	32	1.4%	189	2.2%	175	$68,944	46	2.5%	154	26.8%	121	31.2%	70
Minnesota	3	90.5%	51	3.2%	171	1.5%	182	$75,042	25	2.3%	156	21.3%	164	40.1%	26
Minnesota	4	82.8%	102	5.4%	149	4.3%	154	$58,913	106	6.6%	117	26.1%	128	33.0%	59
Minnesota	5	76.9%	138	10.2%	112	5.2%	146	$53,149	154	8.2%	101	23.3%	151	34.9%	47
Minnesota	6	95.6%	11	0.9%	194	1.0%	187	$64,348	69	2.8%	153	31.1%	79	24.5%	123
Minnesota	7	94.7%	17	0.3%	200	1.9%	178	$44,925	277	6.8%	115	34.5%	50	16.4%	193
Minnesota	8	95.7%	10	0.5%	198	0.6%	191	$46,275	260	6.9%	114	35.1%	45	17.7%	182
Mississippi	1	74.0%	152	23.7%	57	1.3%	184	$39,449	368	12.9%	58	31.7%	74	13.9%	212
Mississippi	2	38.8%	260	58.9%	5	1.2%	185	$32,114	422	22.7%	10	26.2%	127	16.8%	190
Mississippi	3	66.8%	187	30.2%	41	1.1%	186	$38,626	377	15.4%	42	28.6%	104	20.2%	158
Mississippi	4	76.0%	143	20.0%	66	1.7%	180	$39,063	373	13.4%	56	30.8%	82	16.7%	191
Missouri	1	50.0%	236	45.8%	25	1.2%	185	$44,444	282	12.4%	62	28.5%	105	22.4%	141
Missouri	2	93.9%	25	2.1%	182	1.2%	185	$70,863	36	2.5%	154	23.5%	149	38.3%	35
Missouri	3	87.7%	71	7.6%	131	1.6%	181	$50,835	188	7.4%	109	29.8%	92	23.2%	135
Missouri	4	93.0%	33	3.2%	171	1.6%	181	$40,995	341	8.9%	94	38.7%	22	15.6%	200
Missouri	5	69.9%	175	21.8%	61	4.9%	149	$47,363	239	9.4%	89	30.1%	89	22.9%	138
Missouri	6	93.1%	32	2.8%	175	2.0%	177	$49,428	211	6.2%	121	36.4%	38	21.2%	150
Missouri	7	93.8%	26	1.2%	191	2.1%	176	$39,859	362	9.0%	93	34.6%	49	18.8%	171
Missouri	8	93.6%	28	3.6%	167	0.8%	189	$33,951	412	13.7%	53	37.3%	32	11.9%	225
Missouri	9	93.2%	31	3.8%	165	0.9%	188	$45,159	274	7.7%	106	35.7%	42	19.9%	161

State	CD	Race and Hispanic or Latino origin						Income and Poverty				Education Levels			
		Non-Hispanic white[1]	National rank	Non-Hispanic black[1]	National rank	Hispanic[1]	National rank	Median family income, 1999	National rank	Families in poverty[2]	National rank	High school diploma, no college[3]	National rank	College bachelor's degree or higher[3]	National rank
Montana	AL	91.5%	43	0.3%	200	1.6%	181	$40,487	346	10.5%	80	31.3%	78	24.4%	124
Nebraska	1	92.1%	40	1.3%	190	3.4%	163	$49,295	215	5.9%	124	32.0%	71	23.9%	128
Nebraska	2	82.2%	105	9.0%	121	5.4%	144	$55,674	128	6.0%	123	25.9%	130	30.5%	75
Nebraska	3	93.5%	29	0.2%	201	4.8%	150	$41,316	334	8.1%	102	35.7%	42	17.1%	187
Nevada	1	56.4%	220	11.0%	107	24.3%	52	$45,242	272	10.3%	82	30.2%	88	14.6%	207
Nevada	2	78.0%	128	2.3%	180	12.7%	93	$50,813	189	7.1%	112	28.4%	106	19.3%	166
Nevada	3	72.6%	161	5.1%	152	13.2%	90	$55,902	127	5.4%	129	29.4%	96	20.4%	156
New Hampshire	1	95.7%	10	0.7%	196	1.3%	184	$58,351	109	4.4%	139	29.3%	97	28.5%	92
New Hampshire	2	95.6%	11	0.6%	197	1.4%	183	$56,966	121	4.2%	141	30.8%	82	28.9%	88
New Jersey	1	74.1%	151	15.2%	87	6.9%	132	$56,329	125	7.6%	107	34.8%	47	20.7%	154
New Jersey	2	74.4%	149	12.8%	96	8.9%	117	$52,213	162	7.6%	107	36.0%	40	17.9%	180
New Jersey	3	84.9%	88	7.9%	128	3.4%	163	$64,418	68	3.5%	148	32.7%	64	27.2%	100
New Jersey	4	82.8%	102	7.0%	136	6.9%	132	$64,505	67	4.5%	138	32.4%	67	25.4%	115
New Jersey	5	87.3%	73	1.4%	189	4.1%	156	$83,194	9	2.3%	156	27.3%	117	38.6%	34
New Jersey	6	64.4%	199	14.8%	89	10.7%	106	$65,888	60	6.2%	121	29.5%	95	29.7%	80
New Jersey	7	80.2%	116	4.3%	160	6.5%	136	$86,430	5	2.2%	157	25.8%	131	41.5%	24
New Jersey	8	57.4%	216	11.7%	103	23.5%	55	$61,172	83	8.1%	102	28.8%	102	28.0%	94
New Jersey	9	63.9%	201	6.3%	141	17.2%	69	$62,187	79	5.6%	127	29.4%	96	29.5%	82
New Jersey	10	24.2%	290	54.3%	15	14.5%	84	$45,403	271	14.9%	46	31.4%	77	18.3%	176
New Jersey	11	83.6%	96	2.7%	176	6.5%	136	$91,571	1	2.2%	157	23.4%	150	45.2%	13
New Jersey	12	74.1%	151	10.8%	108	5.0%	148	$82,529	10	3.4%	149	23.8%	146	42.3%	21
New Jersey	13	35.7%	265	10.5%	110	44.9%	23	$40,326	350	15.6%	40	27.1%	119	20.5%	155
New Mexico	1	52.8%	231	2.3%	180	38.8%	29	$45,837	267	10.4%	81	25.2%	137	29.5%	82
New Mexico	2	49.5%	238	1.6%	187	42.5%	28	$33,637	417	17.9%	26	28.2%	108	16.9%	189
New Mexico	3	45.9%	246	1.1%	192	34.6%	35	$39,673	365	15.2%	44	26.4%	125	23.7%	130
New York	1	85.7%	83	3.7%	166	6.8%	133	$69,971	41	4.0%	143	31.5%	76	27.2%	100
New York	2	73.9%	153	8.9%	122	12.7%	93	$77,224	21	3.9%	144	29.2%	98	30.6%	74
New York	3	87.9%	70	2.0%	183	6.3%	137	$78,874	20	2.8%	153	30.4%	86	31.3%	69
New York	4	64.9%	197	16.4%	80	12.7%	93	$75,653	23	4.4%	139	27.9%	111	31.0%	71
New York	5	46.3%	244	5.1%	152	22.0%	58	$58,694	108	9.4%	89	23.9%	145	33.6%	54
New York	6	14.5%	305	51.1%	20	16.2%	74	$49,563	210	12.1%	65	29.6%	94	18.0%	179
New York	7	30.8%	277	15.8%	82	37.0%	33	$42,003	325	14.9%	46	29.0%	100	19.8%	162
New York	8	70.5%	171	5.0%	153	10.7%	106	$50,615	190	15.5%	41	17.7%	187	47.8%	9
New York	9	66.4%	189	3.7%	166	12.3%	97	$53,950	140	9.9%	85	27.6%	114	31.0%	71
New York	10	16.8%	303	60.0%	2	16.5%	73	$33,698	415	25.8%	5	27.8%	112	17.5%	183
New York	11	23.6%	291	56.8%	9	11.6%	100	$36,637	396	21.1%	12	25.6%	133	25.0%	118
New York	12	26.9%	285	8.1%	126	44.7%	25	$30,215	427	25.5%	6	23.2%	152	17.1%	187
New York	13	73.8%	154	5.4%	149	9.6%	112	$59,749	96	9.6%	87	31.9%	72	24.0%	127
New York	14	68.6%	182	4.2%	161	12.5%	95	$72,594	30	9.4%	89	13.9%	203	56.9%	1
New York	15	19.0%	301	30.5%	40	44.8%	24	$29,416	429	27.6%	2	19.8%	176	25.0%	118
New York	16	3.6%	309	30.6%	39	61.5%	13	$20,924	433	39.9%	1	23.2%	152	7.8%	238

State	CD	Non-Hispanic white[1]	National rank	Non-Hispanic black[1]	National rank	Hispanic[1]	National rank	Median family income, 1999	National rank	Families in poverty[2]	National rank	High school diploma, no college[3]	National rank	College bachelor's degree or higher[3]	National rank
New York	17	44.1%	249	29.3%	44	18.7%	66	$53,201	152	13.4%	56	25.0%	139	28.5%	92
New York	18	69.2%	179	9.1%	120	15.0%	80	$85,771	7	5.5%	128	20.8%	168	43.8%	16
New York	19	84.3%	93	5.1%	152	7.2%	129	$74,699	26	4.2%	141	27.2%	118	32.3%	63
New York	20	93.8%	26	2.5%	178	2.0%	177	$52,099	164	5.5%	128	32.3%	68	24.7%	121
New York	21	87.6%	72	6.5%	140	2.6%	171	$51,647	174	7.8%	105	30.6%	84	27.0%	102
New York	22	82.1%	106	6.9%	137	6.7%	134	$48,489	224	9.3%	90	30.9%	81	23.9%	128
New York	23	92.9%	34	2.9%	174	2.1%	176	$41,845	327	9.5%	88	37.5%	31	16.0%	197
New York	24	92.9%	34	3.2%	171	2.0%	177	$44,280	286	8.8%	95	33.8%	55	19.3%	166
New York	25	88.8%	65	6.0%	144	1.8%	179	$53,779	143	7.2%	111	29.7%	93	27.8%	96
New York	26	92.6%	37	3.2%	171	1.7%	180	$55,616	129	4.7%	136	31.5%	76	25.5%	114
New York	27	90.6%	50	3.7%	166	3.6%	161	$46,520	256	8.8%	95	33.1%	60	19.9%	161
New York	28	67.4%	186	24.9%	52	4.4%	153	$40,361	349	15.3%	43	30.6%	84	21.2%	150
New York	29	93.3%	30	2.6%	177	1.2%	185	$50,475	192	6.8%	115	32.0%	71	26.1%	108
North Carolina	1	47.9%	241	47.6%	23	2.8%	169	$34,523	406	17.1%	31	33.0%	61	12.0%	224
North Carolina	2	61.9%	209	28.5%	45	7.0%	131	$42,230	319	10.9%	76	31.1%	79	15.9%	198
North Carolina	3	78.3%	127	15.5%	85	3.9%	158	$44,273	287	8.8%	95	30.4%	86	20.1%	159
North Carolina	4	70.3%	173	19.6%	69	4.8%	150	$67,201	56	5.7%	126	16.3%	197	48.0%	8
North Carolina	5	89.3%	60	6.2%	142	3.1%	166	$47,339	240	6.5%	118	30.5%	85	20.1%	159
North Carolina	6	86.8%	76	8.1%	126	3.3%	164	$51,119	181	5.8%	125	29.4%	96	22.7%	139
North Carolina	7	66.3%	190	21.2%	63	3.5%	162	$40,612	344	12.7%	60	30.5%	85	17.8%	181
North Carolina	8	65.1%	195	24.5%	54	6.0%	139	$44,245	288	9.7%	86	29.7%	93	18.2%	177
North Carolina	9	84.3%	93	9.4%	118	3.3%	164	$64,759	65	4.3%	140	21.4%	163	35.9%	44
North Carolina	10	86.6%	78	8.4%	124	3.2%	165	$44,138	290	7.8%	105	31.9%	72	14.1%	210
North Carolina	11	91.0%	47	4.2%	161	2.2%	175	$41,579	331	8.4%	99	30.4%	86	20.5%	155
North Carolina	12	48.1%	240	41.9%	28	6.7%	134	$42,127	321	12.4%	62	29.2%	98	19.2%	167
North Carolina	13	66.0%	192	25.1%	51	5.6%	142	$49,168	217	8.1%	102	25.9%	130	27.3%	99
North Dakota	AL	93.5%	29	0.5%	198	1.0%	187	$43,654	295	8.3%	100	27.9%	111	22.0%	144
Ohio	1	71.7%	167	24.7%	53	1.0%	187	$49,197	216	10.5%	80	31.4%	77	22.3%	142
Ohio	2	92.2%	39	4.6%	157	0.9%	188	$56,695	124	6.3%	120	30.2%	88	29.0%	87
Ohio	3	81.3%	110	15.6%	84	1.0%	187	$51,589	176	7.4%	109	31.9%	72	22.7%	139
Ohio	4	92.5%	38	5.0%	153	1.0%	187	$47,106	245	7.1%	112	45.0%	5	13.1%	219
Ohio	5	94.8%	16	1.0%	193	3.1%	166	$49,425	213	5.2%	131	45.0%	5	14.6%	207
Ohio	6	95.5%	12	2.4%	179	0.7%	190	$40,511	345	10.2%	83	43.5%	7	14.2%	209
Ohio	7	89.4%	59	7.3%	133	1.0%	187	$50,975	185	6.4%	119	38.2%	26	18.7%	172
Ohio	8	92.7%	36	4.0%	163	1.1%	186	$51,726	170	6.0%	123	37.7%	29	18.7%	172
Ohio	9	82.5%	103	12.1%	100	3.1%	166	$50,131	198	8.9%	94	34.7%	48	19.8%	162
Ohio	10	89.4%	59	3.5%	168	4.0%	157	$51,808	169	6.7%	116	32.5%	66	23.3%	134
Ohio	11	43.2%	251	51.6%	18	2.0%	177	$40,406	348	16.0%	37	28.8%	102	23.4%	133
Ohio	12	74.7%	146	19.9%	67	1.5%	182	$58,305	111	7.8%	105	28.0%	110	32.1%	65
Ohio	13	83.9%	95	11.0%	107	2.9%	168	$53,761	145	7.2%	111	34.3%	51	22.3%	142
Ohio	14	94.8%	16	2.3%	180	1.1%	186	$60,292	92	4.0%	143	32.8%	63	27.1%	101

State	CD	Non-Hispanic white[1]	National rank	Non-Hispanic black[1]	National rank	Hispanic[1]	National rank	Median family income, 1999	National rank	Families in poverty[2]	National rank	High school diploma, no college[3]	National rank	College bachelor's degree or higher[3]	National rank
Ohio	15	86.2%	80	6.8%	138	2.1%	176	$55,273	131	6.7%	116	27.6%	114	32.1%	65
Ohio	16	93.5%	29	4.2%	161	0.7%	190	$50,000	202	6.1%	122	40.8%	14	19.2%	167
Ohio	17	86.5%	79	10.3%	111	1.4%	183	$45,128	275	9.2%	91	41.7%	12	15.8%	199
Ohio	18	96.3%	6	1.9%	184	0.5%	192	$40,760	343	9.7%	86	45.3%	4	11.3%	228
Oklahoma	1	77.1%	136	8.2%	125	4.6%	152	$47,365	238	8.5%	98	27.9%	111	25.6%	113
Oklahoma	2	74.2%	150	3.9%	164	1.9%	178	$33,907	413	14.6%	47	35.1%	45	13.2%	218
Oklahoma	3	83.4%	98	3.8%	165	4.2%	155	$39,355	369	10.9%	76	35.2%	44	18.1%	178
Oklahoma	4	80.4%	115	6.0%	144	4.0%	157	$42,429	315	9.7%	86	32.2%	69	20.2%	158
Oklahoma	5	71.8%	166	12.2%	99	6.7%	134	$41,585	330	12.2%	64	27.0%	120	24.5%	123
Oregon	1	83.1%	100	1.1%	192	8.0%	124	$58,789	107	5.4%	129	21.9%	160	33.3%	57
Oregon	2	88.7%	66	0.4%	199	6.7%	134	$41,606	329	9.4%	89	30.7%	83	19.0%	169
Oregon	3	80.2%	116	4.6%	157	6.3%	137	$50,039	201	8.1%	102	25.5%	134	24.8%	120
Oregon	4	91.2%	45	0.5%	198	3.4%	163	$42,976	306	9.4%	89	28.5%	105	21.4%	148
Oregon	5	86.2%	80	0.6%	197	8.3%	122	$52,162	163	7.2%	111	24.5%	142	27.0%	102
Pennsylvania	1	38.3%	261	42.2%	27	12.7%	93	$32,273	421	22.8%	9	33.9%	54	13.8%	213
Pennsylvania	2	34.1%	270	56.5%	10	2.8%	169	$37,817	388	18.5%	22	29.2%	98	24.2%	125
Pennsylvania	3	94.9%	15	3.0%	173	1.0%	187	$43,381	300	8.1%	102	44.3%	6	18.0%	179
Pennsylvania	4	95.1%	13	3.0%	173	0.5%	192	$52,704	156	5.6%	127	36.4%	38	27.2%	100
Pennsylvania	5	96.0%	8	1.4%	189	0.8%	189	$41,141	337	8.3%	100	46.2%	3	17.0%	188
Pennsylvania	6	88.0%	69	6.2%	142	2.9%	168	$66,544	58	3.7%	146	30.8%	82	33.9%	52
Pennsylvania	7	89.3%	60	5.1%	152	1.2%	185	$68,639	50	3.6%	147	30.0%	90	36.1%	43
Pennsylvania	8	91.6%	42	3.2%	171	2.1%	176	$68,201	51	3.2%	150	32.6%	65	30.6%	74
Pennsylvania	9	96.7%	3	1.6%	187	0.8%	189	$41,051	338	8.0%	103	48.4%	1	12.9%	220
Pennsylvania	10	95.9%	9	1.8%	185	1.2%	185	$43,199	304	7.2%	111	43.2%	8	17.1%	187
Pennsylvania	11	94.5%	19	2.2%	181	2.0%	177	$43,860	292	7.8%	105	42.5%	10	15.9%	198
Pennsylvania	12	95.6%	11	3.0%	173	0.5%	192	$39,033	374	9.9%	85	46.6%	2	13.6%	215
Pennsylvania	13	87.0%	75	5.5%	148	2.6%	171	$61,115	84	5.1%	132	32.3%	68	28.7%	90
Pennsylvania	14	76.6%	140	19.3%	70	1.0%	187	$39,871	361	12.7%	60	36.8%	36	21.3%	149
Pennsylvania	15	88.9%	64	2.4%	179	6.2%	138	$54,604	137	5.9%	124	36.0%	40	22.3%	142
Pennsylvania	16	86.6%	78	3.8%	165	7.5%	127	$53,899	141	6.5%	118	36.4%	38	23.0%	137
Pennsylvania	17	89.1%	62	6.5%	140	2.6%	171	$48,864	220	6.1%	122	43.0%	9	17.3%	185
Pennsylvania	18	95.9%	9	1.9%	184	0.5%	192	$54,981	133	4.4%	139	34.8%	47	29.3%	84
Pennsylvania	19	93.5%	29	2.6%	177	2.1%	176	$53,039	155	4.4%	139	39.8%	16	21.3%	149
Rhode Island	1	85.3%	86	3.5%	168	5.9%	140	$51,918	167	8.9%	94	26.8%	121	26.0%	109
Rhode Island	2	84.2%	94	3.6%	167	8.0%	124	$53,764	144	8.8%	95	28.8%	102	25.2%	117
South Carolina	1	76.6%	140	18.5%	73	2.4%	173	$48,001	230	8.2%	101	27.7%	113	25.4%	115
South Carolina	2	70.7%	170	23.9%	56	3.2%	165	$51,175	180	8.1%	102	26.5%	124	28.5%	92
South Carolina	3	77.9%	129	19.0%	71	1.7%	180	$43,177	305	9.6%	87	32.5%	66	17.1%	187
South Carolina	4	76.7%	139	18.1%	74	3.1%	166	$47,252	242	8.6%	97	28.2%	108	22.3%	142
South Carolina	5	66.8%	187	29.9%	42	1.7%	180	$41,549	332	11.9%	67	32.7%	64	14.8%	205
South Carolina	6	43.6%	250	53.5%	16	1.4%	183	$34,961	402	18.4%	23	32.4%	67	14.1%	210

State	CD	Race and Hispanic or Latino origin						Income and Poverty				Education Levels			
		Non-Hispanic white[1]	National rank	Non-Hispanic black[1]	National rank	Hispanic[1]	National rank	Median family income, 1999	National rank	Families in poverty[2]	National rank	High school diploma, no college[3]	National rank	College bachelor's degree or higher[3]	National rank
South Dakota	AL	90.8%	49	0.5%	198	1.2%	185	$43,237	302	9.3%	90	32.9%	62	21.5%	147
Tennessee	1	95.5%	12	2.0%	183	1.3%	184	$37,898	387	11.3%	72	34.1%	53	15.0%	204
Tennessee	2	91.1%	46	5.7%	146	1.1%	186	$45,810	268	8.5%	98	30.4%	86	23.3%	134
Tennessee	3	86.6%	78	10.0%	114	1.4%	183	$42,518	313	10.4%	81	30.2%	88	18.9%	170
Tennessee	4	93.2%	31	4.2%	161	1.4%	183	$37,490	389	11.9%	67	36.9%	35	11.3%	228
Tennessee	5	71.1%	169	21.3%	62	3.9%	158	$49,617	207	9.3%	90	26.5%	124	27.9%	95
Tennessee	6	89.9%	54	6.0%	144	2.4%	173	$46,699	254	7.9%	104	35.0%	46	16.3%	194
Tennessee	7	84.7%	90	10.8%	108	2.0%	177	$57,275	116	6.2%	121	26.6%	123	29.2%	85
Tennessee	8	77.3%	134	19.9%	67	1.4%	183	$39,932	360	11.9%	67	37.1%	34	12.5%	222
Tennessee	9	39.5%	257	55.0%	14	2.9%	168	$40,066	355	16.1%	36	27.0%	120	22.1%	143
Texas	1	77.1%	136	15.2%	87	6.0%	139	$38,838	376	12.8%	59	33.3%	58	14.8%	205
Texas	2	77.3%	134	13.4%	94	7.7%	125	$39,266	370	12.3%	63	36.1%	39	11.4%	227
Texas	3	71.9%	165	6.1%	143	12.9%	91	$74,314	27	3.9%	144	17.3%	189	41.6%	23
Texas	4	79.3%	123	11.0%	107	7.7%	125	$46,086	264	9.5%	88	29.0%	100	18.7%	172
Texas	5	66.8%	187	14.6%	90	15.3%	78	$45,097	276	9.7%	86	28.9%	101	18.2%	177
Texas	6	74.7%	146	9.4%	118	11.7%	99	$55,584	130	6.3%	120	27.1%	119	23.0%	137
Texas	7	53.1%	229	10.2%	112	23.3%	56	$57,494	113	8.3%	100	16.6%	195	39.8%	28
Texas	8	79.1%	124	4.8%	155	11.6%	100	$68,134	52	4.9%	134	22.7%	155	32.9%	60
Texas	9	63.2%	203	19.9%	67	12.9%	91	$49,761	204	10.9%	76	28.6%	104	20.9%	152
Texas	10	54.5%	226	9.9%	115	29.0%	45	$50,548	191	9.5%	88	19.3%	178	35.1%	45
Texas	11	68.0%	184	14.3%	92	14.1%	87	$42,179	320	10.1%	84	28.7%	103	19.0%	169
Texas	12	74.5%	148	4.4%	159	17.1%	70	$51,916	168	7.1%	112	26.0%	129	22.7%	139
Texas	13	73.9%	153	5.5%	148	17.9%	68	$40,252	351	11.2%	73	29.4%	96	17.4%	184
Texas	14	62.2%	208	7.5%	132	28.4%	46	$42,501	314	11.3%	72	31.3%	78	15.0%	204
Texas	15	22.9%	294	1.6%	187	74.3%	2	$30,024	428	25.8%	5	23.0%	154	14.1%	210
Texas	16	20.1%	298	2.9%	174	74.8%	1	$33,810	414	20.2%	15	22.5%	157	17.0%	188
Texas	17	77.8%	130	3.8%	165	16.6%	72	$39,126	372	11.3%	72	31.6%	75	16.8%	190
Texas	18	25.3%	287	41.4%	29	29.1%	44	$34,707	405	20.1%	16	25.0%	139	18.2%	177
Texas	19	63.1%	204	5.3%	150	29.6%	43	$39,184	371	13.5%	55	26.3%	126	18.7%	172
Texas	20	27.4%	284	5.4%	149	64.3%	10	$35,455	400	17.0%	32	26.0%	129	15.6%	200
Texas	21	79.5%	121	1.9%	184	15.2%	79	$62,437	77	4.9%	134	20.7%	169	38.9%	33
Texas	22	62.4%	206	9.9%	115	18.0%	67	$69,714	42	5.0%	133	21.7%	161	33.2%	58
Texas	23	33.4%	271	1.5%	188	63.0%	12	$40,043	357	17.9%	26	20.1%	174	23.2%	135
Texas	24	40.7%	256	20.8%	64	33.6%	37	$41,000	340	14.1%	51	24.4%	143	18.2%	177
Texas	25	41.2%	255	21.2%	63	30.7%	40	$42,310	316	13.7%	53	21.2%	165	28.0%	94
Texas	26	79.3%	123	4.8%	155	10.0%	108	$73,453	29	3.6%	147	19.0%	181	38.9%	33
Texas	27	28.7%	282	2.2%	181	67.5%	6	$33,168	419	22.1%	11	22.5%	157	15.8%	199
Texas	28	24.8%	289	7.7%	130	65.7%	8	$31,417	426	22.8%	9	27.8%	112	9.8%	232
Texas	29	24.2%	290	14.2%	93	58.2%	16	$34,415	407	18.8%	20	24.7%	141	8.1%	237
Texas	30	28.9%	281	39.6%	31	27.7%	47	$38,499	380	15.9%	38	25.7%	132	16.3%	194
Texas	31	72.1%	164	8.6%	123	14.9%	81	$60,407	90	6.8%	115	23.7%	147	31.6%	68

State	CD	Race and Hispanic or Latino origin						Income and Poverty				Education Levels			
		Non-Hispanic white[1]	National rank	Non-Hispanic black[1]	National rank	Hispanic[1]	National rank	Median family income, 1999	National rank	Families in poverty[2]	National rank	High school diploma, no college[3]	National rank	College bachelor's degree or higher[3]	National rank
Texas	32	59.2%	213	8.6%	123	24.1%	53	$60,426	89	8.3%	100	14.0%	202	43.2%	18
Utah	1	84.8%	89	1.1%	192	10.0%	108	$50,927	186	6.6%	117	25.6%	133	24.7%	121
Utah	2	89.1%	62	0.5%	198	5.4%	144	$51,981	166	6.6%	117	22.6%	156	30.9%	72
Utah	3	85.8%	82	0.4%	199	9.2%	115	$50,245	195	6.2%	121	25.7%	132	22.1%	143
Vermont	AL	96.6%	4	0.4%	199	0.8%	189	$48,625	222	6.3%	120	32.4%	67	29.4%	83
Virginia	1	76.6%	140	17.5%	75	2.6%	171	$57,518	112	4.8%	135	28.2%	108	26.8%	104
Virginia	2	70.0%	174	19.8%	68	3.9%	158	$50,060	200	6.6%	117	27.4%	116	25.5%	114
Virginia	3	41.5%	254	52.7%	17	2.4%	173	$38,319	382	15.3%	43	29.7%	93	17.2%	186
Virginia	4	63.6%	202	32.1%	36	1.8%	179	$51,721	171	7.6%	107	30.1%	89	19.6%	163
Virginia	5	74.1%	151	22.6%	58	1.4%	183	$42,900	307	9.2%	91	30.8%	82	19.0%	169
Virginia	6	86.2%	80	10.1%	113	1.7%	180	$46,177	262	7.3%	110	32.1%	70	20.8%	153
Virginia	7	79.4%	122	15.4%	86	1.8%	179	$60,384	91	4.4%	139	25.5%	134	33.2%	58
Virginia	8	60.4%	211	12.4%	98	14.7%	83	$75,302	24	5.2%	131	13.8%	204	53.8%	2
Virginia	9	93.6%	28	3.8%	165	1.0%	187	$36,972	395	11.2%	73	32.0%	71	14.0%	211
Virginia	10	78.3%	127	6.5%	140	6.7%	134	$81,119	15	2.8%	153	20.2%	173	43.1%	19
Virginia	11	68.6%	182	9.5%	117	8.4%	121	$88,612	3	2.5%	154	17.0%	191	48.9%	7
Washington	1	83.3%	99	1.7%	186	3.8%	159	$67,249	55	3.8%	145	20.1%	174	36.4%	41
Washington	2	87.7%	71	1.0%	193	4.7%	151	$52,617	157	6.6%	117	27.4%	116	22.4%	141
Washington	3	89.6%	57	1.1%	192	3.7%	160	$51,005	184	7.7%	106	28.1%	109	21.4%	148
Washington	4	73.4%	156	0.8%	195	21.1%	61	$43,603	296	12.0%	66	26.7%	122	18.7%	172
Washington	5	89.4%	59	1.2%	191	3.6%	161	$44,161	289	9.6%	87	27.5%	115	23.8%	129
Washington	6	80.9%	112	5.0%	153	4.1%	156	$46,156	263	9.5%	88	29.4%	96	20.1%	159
Washington	7	70.4%	172	7.3%	133	5.0%	148	$60,614	87	7.0%	113	16.8%	193	44.1%	14
Washington	8	83.6%	96	1.8%	185	3.5%	162	$71,459	33	3.5%	148	21.7%	161	37.4%	37
Washington	9	76.4%	141	5.7%	146	5.7%	141	$53,190	153	6.7%	116	27.8%	112	22.3%	142
West Virginia	1	96.2%	7	1.7%	186	0.6%	191	$37,913	386	12.3%	63	40.9%	13	16.3%	194
West Virginia	2	94.6%	18	3.3%	170	0.6%	191	$40,003	358	11.6%	70	39.6%	18	16.2%	195
West Virginia	3	94.3%	21	4.0%	163	0.5%	192	$31,928	425	17.7%	28	37.8%	28	12.0%	224
Wisconsin	1	89.5%	58	4.1%	162	4.6%	152	$59,264	102	4.3%	140	33.2%	59	21.5%	147
Wisconsin	2	90.6%	50	3.0%	173	2.9%	168	$58,332	110	4.2%	141	28.3%	107	32.1%	65
Wisconsin	3	97.0%	2	0.4%	199	0.8%	189	$48,147	228	5.6%	127	37.3%	32	19.5%	164
Wisconsin	4	58.5%	214	27.8%	46	9.4%	113	$39,567	366	15.9%	38	31.1%	79	17.8%	181
Wisconsin	5	94.9%	15	1.2%	191	1.8%	179	$68,756	48	2.2%	157	27.0%	120	35.0%	46
Wisconsin	6	95.1%	13	1.2%	191	1.9%	178	$52,213	162	3.8%	145	40.7%	15	17.1%	187
Wisconsin	7	96.4%	5	0.2%	201	0.6%	191	$46,865	251	5.7%	126	39.7%	17	16.6%	192
Wisconsin	8	93.9%	25	0.5%	198	1.8%	179	$51,548	177	4.6%	137	39.1%	20	19.1%	168
Wyoming	AL	90.3%	53	0.7%	196	5.5%	143	$45,685	270	8.0%	103	31.0%	80	21.9%	145
Bottom rank			309		201		192		433		158		207		239

[1] As percentage of the voting-age population.
[2] As percentage of all families.
[3] As percentage of persons age 25 years or over.

High and Low Congressional District Rankings

The following tables present a selection of rankings for demographic and economic data that are often used to analyze and characterize a congressional district. The groups of data are presented by their rank compared to other districts in the United States. Districts with the same percentage or dollar amount are given the same ranking. The tables are based on information from the 2000 census or from 1999 for median family income. The tables include the District of Columbia.

Black Districts

Listed below are the districts with the largest percentage of voting-age blacks. Several districts have the same percentage.

State	District	Black*	Rank
Illinois	1	63.2%	1
New York	10	60.0%	2
Illinois	2	59.4%	3
Louisiana	2	59.3%	4
Michigan	14	58.9%	5
Mississippi	2	58.9%	5
Michigan	13	57.9%	6
Alabama	7	57.8%	7
Maryland	7	57.0%	8
New York	11	56.8%	9
Pennsylvania	2	56.5%	10
Illinois	7	55.9%	11
District of Columbia	AL	55.7%	12
Maryland	4	55.3%	13
Tennessee	9	55.0%	14
New Jersey	10	54.3%	15
South Carolina	6	53.5%	16
Virginia	3	52.7%	17
Ohio	11	51.6%	18
Florida	17	51.3%	19
New York	6	51.1%	20
Georgia	5	51.0%	21
Georgia	4	48.8%	22
North Carolina	1	47.6%	23
Florida	23	46.2%	24
Missouri	1	45.8%	25
Florida	3	45.1%	26
Pennsylvania	1	42.2%	27
North Carolina	12	41.9%	28
Texas	18	41.4%	29
Georgia	2	40.9%	30
Texas	30	39.6%	31
Georgia	12	38.4%	32
Georgia	13	37.3%	33
Georgia	3	37.2%	34
California	35	35.0%	35
Virginia	4	32.1%	36
Louisiana	5	30.8%	37
Louisiana	6	30.7%	38
New York	16	30.6%	39
Louisiana	4	30.5%	40
New York	15	30.5%	40

State	District	Black*	Rank
Mississippi	3	30.2%	41
Alabama	3	29.9%	42
South Carolina	5	29.9%	42
California	33	29.6%	43
New York	17	29.3%	44
Maryland	5	28.5%	45
North Carolina	2	28.5%	45
Wisconsin	4	27.8%	46
Alabama	2	27.1%	47
Indiana	7	26.7%	48
Georgia	11	25.8%	49
Alabama	1	25.4%	50
North Carolina	13	25.1%	51
New York	28	24.9%	52
California	37	24.7%	53
Ohio	1	24.7%	53
California	9	24.5%	54
North Carolina	8	24.5%	54
Maryland	2	24.3%	55
Florida	11	23.9%	56
South Carolina	2	23.9%	56
Mississippi	1	23.7%	57
Louisiana	7	22.6%	58
Virginia	5	22.6%	58
Arkansas	4	22.3%	59
Louisiana	3	22.2%	60
Missouri	5	21.8%	61
Tennessee	5	21.3%	62
North Carolina	7	21.2%	63
Texas	25	21.2%	63
Florida	2	20.8%	64
Texas	24	20.8%	64
Georgia	1	20.6%	65
Mississippi	4	20.0%	66
Ohio	12	19.9%	67
Tennessee	8	19.9%	67
Texas	9	19.9%	67
Virginia	2	19.8%	68
North Carolina	4	19.6%	69
Pennsylvania	14	19.3%	70
South Carolina	3	19.0%	71
Massachusetts	8	18.7%	72
South Carolina	1	18.5%	73
South Carolina	4	18.1%	74
Virginia	1	17.5%	75
Delaware	AL	17.4%	76
Arkansas	2	17.3%	77
Kentucky	3	17.2%	78
Indiana	1	17.0%	79
Michigan	5	16.4%	80
New York	4	16.4%	80
California	7	15.9%	81
Alabama	5	15.8%	82
New York	7	15.8%	82
Maryland	8	15.7%	83
Ohio	3	15.6%	84
North Carolina	3	15.5%	85

State	District	Black*	Rank
Virginia	7	15.4%	86
New Jersey	1	15.2%	87
Texas	1	15.2%	87
Maryland	3	14.9%	88
New Jersey	6	14.8%	89
Texas	5	14.6%	90
Illinois	12	14.4%	91
Texas	11	14.3%	92
Arkansas	1	14.2%	93
Texas	29	14.2%	93
Texas	2	13.4%	94
California	5	13.0%	95
Georgia	9	12.8%	96
New Jersey	2	12.8%	96
Florida	1	12.5%	97
Florida	4	12.4%	98
Virginia	8	12.4%	98
Oklahoma	5	12.2%	99
Ohio	9	12.1%	100

As percentage of voting-age population.

Hispanic Districts

Listed below are the districts with the largest percentage of voting-age Hispanics. Several districts have the same percentage.

State	District	Hispanic*	Rank
Texas	16	74.8%	1
Texas	15	74.3%	2
California	34	72.9%	3
Florida	21	72.2%	4
Illinois	4	69.0%	5
Texas	27	67.5%	6
California	38	66.3%	7
Texas	28	65.7%	8
California	31	65.5%	9
Florida	25	64.3%	10
Texas	20	64.3%	10
Florida	18	63.9%	11
Texas	23	63.0%	12
New York	16	61.5%	13
California	47	59.5%	14
California	20	58.7%	15
Texas	29	58.2%	16
California	32	57.4%	17
California	39	56.3%	18
California	43	53.7%	19
Arizona	4	51.8%	20
California	28	49.2%	21
California	51	49.0%	22
New Jersey	13	44.9%	23
New York	15	44.8%	24
New York	12	44.7%	25
Arizona	7	44.5%	26
California	35	42.7%	27
New Mexico	2	42.5%	28
New Mexico	1	38.8%	29

State	District	Hispanic*	Rank
California	37	38.2%	30
California	21	38.1%	31
California	18	37.5%	32
California	17	37.0%	33
New York	7	37.0%	33
California	23	35.5%	34
New Mexico	3	34.6%	35
California	16	33.8%	36
Texas	24	33.6%	37
California	45	32.2%	38
California	27	31.8%	39
Texas	25	30.7%	40
California	44	30.6%	41
California	33	30.2%	42
Texas	19	29.6%	43
Texas	18	29.1%	44
Texas	10	29.0%	45
Texas	14	28.4%	46
Texas	30	27.7%	47
California	36	25.8%	48
California	40	25.6%	49
Colorado	1	25.3%	50
California	49	25.1%	51
Nevada	1	24.3%	52
California	19	24.1%	53
Texas	32	24.1%	53
California	25	24.0%	54
California	53	24.0%	54
New Jersey	8	23.5%	55
Texas	7	23.3%	56
California	29	23.2%	57
Florida	17	22.0%	58
New York	5	22.0%	58
California	42	21.6%	59
California	26	21.5%	60
Washington	4	21.1%	61
Florida	20	19.8%	62
California	24	19.6%	63
California	41	19.6%	63
Illinois	5	19.2%	64
Colorado	3	19.0%	65
Florida	11	19.0%	65
California	7	18.7%	66
California	13	18.7%	66
New York	17	18.7%	66
California	5	18.0%	67
California	22	18.0%	67
Illinois	3	18.0%	67
Texas	22	18.0%	67
Texas	13	17.9%	68
California	11	17.2%	69
New Jersey	9	17.2%	69
Texas	12	17.1%	70
Connecticut	1	16.9%	71
Texas	17	16.6%	72
New York	10	16.5%	73
California	9	16.2%	74
New York	6	16.2%	74
Illinois	14	16.1%	75
Florida	8	16.0%	76
California	50	15.9%	77
Arizona	8	15.3%	78

State	District	Hispanic*	Rank
Texas	5	15.3%	78
California	14	15.2%	79
California	15	15.2%	79
Texas	21	15.2%	79
California	1	15.0%	80
New York	18	15.0%	80
Texas	31	14.9%	81
Arizona	1	14.8%	82
Virginia	8	14.7%	83
New Jersey	10	14.5%	84
Arizona	6	14.4%	85
California	46	14.4%	85
Colorado	4	14.3%	86
California	8	14.1%	87
Texas	11	14.1%	87
California	12	14.0%	88
Massachusetts	8	13.4%	89
Florida	23	13.2%	90
Nevada	3	13.2%	90
California	10	12.9%	91
Texas	3	12.9%	91
Texas	9	12.9%	91
Colorado	2	12.8%	92
California	48	12.7%	93
Nevada	2	12.7%	93
New York	2	12.7%	93
New York	4	12.7%	93
Pennsylvania	1	12.7%	93
Maryland	8	12.6%	94
New York	14	12.5%	95
California	6	12.4%	96
New York	9	12.3%	97
Arizona	3	11.9%	98
California	52	11.7%	99
Connecticut	5	11.7%	99
Texas	6	11.7%	99
New York	11	11.6%	100

*As percentage of voting-age population.

Median Family Income

Listed below are the districts with the highest median family income and the lowest median family income.

Highest Median Family Income Districts

State	District	Median family income, 1999	Rank
New Jersey	11	$91,571	1
California	14	$91,249	2
Virginia	11	$88,612	3
Georgia	6	$86,640	4
New Jersey	7	$86,430	5
Illinois	10	$85,990	6
New York	18	$85,771	7
California	30	$85,703	8
New Jersey	5	$83,194	9
New Jersey	12	$82,529	10
Illinois	13	$82,413	11
California	15	$82,246	12
California	48	$82,172	13
Maryland	8	$81,922	14
Virginia	10	$81,119	15

State	District	Median family income, 1999	Rank
Colorado	6	$80,910	16
Michigan	9	$80,897	17
California	12	$80,658	18
Connecticut	5	$80,284	19
New York	3	$78,874	20
New York	2	$77,224	21
California	42	$77,088	22
New York	4	$75,653	23
Virginia	8	$75,302	24
Minnesota	3	$75,042	25
New York	19	$74,699	26
Texas	3	$74,314	27
California	10	$74,079	28
Texas	26	$73,453	29
New York	14	$72,594	30
Illinois	6	$71,991	31
California	46	$71,863	32
Washington	8	$71,459	33
California	16	$71,400	34
Illinois	8	$71,398	35
Missouri	2	$70,863	36
Massachusetts	6	$70,858	37
California	11	$70,734	38
Maryland	5	$70,571	39
Michigan	11	$70,224	40
New York	1	$69,971	41
Texas	22	$69,714	42
California	6	$69,561	43
Massachusetts	7	$69,501	44
California	13	$69,228	45
Minnesota	2	$68,944	46
Georgia	7	$68,828	47
Wisconsin	5	$68,756	48
California	24	$68,648	49
Pennsylvania	7	$68,639	50

Lowest Median Family Income Districts

State	District	Median family income, 1999	Rank
New York	16	$20,924	1
Kentucky	5	$26,627	2
California	31	$26,927	3
California	20	$27,800	4
New York	15	$29,416	5
Texas	15	$30,024	6
New York	12	$30,215	7
Texas	28	$31,417	8
West Virginia	3	$31,928	9
Arizona	4	$31,933	10
California	34	$32,003	11
Mississippi	2	$32,114	12
Pennsylvania	1	$32,273	13
Louisiana	2	$32,306	14
Texas	27	$33,168	15
Alabama	7	$33,398	16
New Mexico	2	$33,637	17
Florida	17	$33,677	18
New York	10	$33,698	19
Texas	16	$33,810	20
Oklahoma	2	$33,907	21
Missouri	8	$33,951	22
California	35	$34,063	23
Florida	3	$34,216	24

Lowest Median Family Income Districts

State	District	Median family income, 1999	Rank
Louisiana	5	$34,260	25
Arizona	7	$34,287	26
Texas	29	$34,415	27
North Carolina	1	$34,523	28
Texas	18	$34,707	29
Georgia	2	$34,793	30
Arkansas	1	$34,949	31
South Carolina	6	$34,961	32
Florida	23	$35,126	33
Texas	20	$35,455	34
California	37	$35,681	35
California	33	$35,695	36
Arkansas	4	$35,915	37
New York	11	$36,637	38
Virginia	9	$36,972	39
Kentucky	1	$37,022	40
Illinois	4	$37,143	41
Michigan	13	$37,220	42
California	18	$37,281	43
Louisiana	4	$37,414	44
Tennessee	4	$37,490	45
Pennsylvania	2	$37,817	46
Tennessee	1	$37,898	47
West Virginia	1	$37,913	48
Alabama	4	$37,916	49
Arizona	1	$38,113	50

Families in Poverty

Listed below are the districts with the highest level of families in poverty, under federal poverty standards, as a percentage of all families. Several districts have the same percentage.

State	District	Families in poverty	Rank
New York	16	39.9%	1
New York	15	27.6%	2
California	31	27.5%	3
California	20	27.4%	4
New York	10	25.8%	5
Texas	15	25.8%	5
New York	12	25.5%	6
Kentucky	5	24.0%	7
California	35	23.2%	8
Louisiana	2	22.8%	9
Pennsylvania	1	22.8%	9
Texas	28	22.8%	9
Mississippi	2	22.7%	10
California	34	22.1%	11
California	37	22.1%	11
Texas	27	22.1%	11
Arizona	4	21.1%	12
New York	11	21.1%	12
Illinois	7	20.5%	13
Alabama	7	20.4%	14
Texas	16	20.2%	15
Texas	18	20.1%	16
Florida	17	20.0%	17
California	33	19.9%	18
Michigan	13	19.8%	19
Texas	29	18.8%	20
Louisiana	5	18.7%	21

State	District	Families in poverty	Rank
Pennsylvania	2	18.5%	22
South Carolina	6	18.4%	23
Florida	23	18.3%	24
Georgia	2	18.3%	24
California	18	18.1%	25
New Mexico	2	17.9%	26
Texas	23	17.9%	26
Illinois	4	17.8%	27
West Virginia	3	17.7%	28
California	43	17.4%	29
Florida	3	17.4%	29
Arizona	7	17.2%	30
North Carolina	1	17.1%	31
Texas	20	17.0%	32
District of Columbia	AL	16.7%	33
Georgia	5	16.5%	34
Louisiana	7	16.2%	35
Tennessee	9	16.1%	36
California	28	16.0%	37
Louisiana	4	16.0%	37
Ohio	11	16.0%	37
Georgia	3	15.9%	38
Georgia	12	15.9%	38

High School Education

Listed below are the districts with the lowest percentage of persons 25 years or older with a high school diploma only. Several districts have the same percentage.

State	District	High school diploma only	Rank
California	14	12.2%	1
California	30	13.0%	2
California	48	13.3%	3
California	8	13.8%	4
Virginia	8	13.8%	4
New York	14	13.9%	5
Texas	32	14.0%	6
Maryland	8	14.6%	7
California	50	15.7%	8
Georgia	6	15.8%	9
California	15	16.2%	10
North Carolina	4	16.3%	11
California	31	16.5%	12
Colorado	6	16.5%	12
California	28	16.6%	13
Texas	7	16.6%	13
California	46	16.7%	14
Washington	7	16.8%	15
California	9	16.9%	16
California	36	16.9%	16
Virginia	11	17.0%	17
California	6	17.2%	18
Illinois	10	17.3%	19
Texas	3	17.3%	19
California	12	17.5%	20
California	29	17.5%	20
California	53	17.7%	21
New York	8	17.7%	21
Arizona	5	17.9%	22
California	33	18.1%	23

State	District	High school diploma only	Rank
California	17	18.5%	24
California	42	18.5%	24
California	23	18.8%	25
California	26	18.9%	26
Texas	26	19.0%	27
California	16	19.1%	28
California	34	19.1%	28
California	47	19.2%	29
Texas	10	19.3%	30
California	10	19.7%	31
New York	15	19.8%	32
California	24	20.0%	33
Michigan	9	20.0%	33
Florida	18	20.1%	34
Texas	23	20.1%	34
Washington	1	20.1%	34
Virginia	10	20.2%	35
Colorado	1	20.4%	36
Georgia	4	20.4%	36
Illinois	9	20.4%	36

College Education

Listed below are the districts with the highest percentage of persons 25 years or older with a bachelor's or higher college degree. Several districts have the same percentage.

State	District	College degree or higher	Rank
New York	14	56.9%	1
Virginia	8	53.8%	2
Maryland	8	53.7%	3
California	30	53.5%	4
California	14	52.2%	5
Georgia	6	50.7%	6
Virginia	11	48.9%	7
North Carolina	4	48.0%	8
New York	8	47.8%	9
Illinois	10	47.5%	10
Colorado	6	46.8%	11
California	48	46.5%	12
New Jersey	11	45.2%	13
Washington	7	44.1%	14
California	8	44.0%	15
New York	18	43.8%	16
Michigan	9	43.5%	17
Texas	32	43.2%	18
Virginia	10	43.1%	19
Illinois	13	42.4%	20
New Jersey	12	42.3%	21
Connecticut	5	42.2%	22
California	15	41.6%	23
Texas	3	41.6%	23
New Jersey	7	41.5%	24
California	12	40.7%	25
Minnesota	3	40.1%	26
California	50	40.0%	27
Massachusetts	8	39.8%	28
Texas	7	39.8%	28
Arizona	5	39.6%	29
Illinois	9	39.6%	29
Massachusetts	7	39.5%	30
Colorado	2	39.3%	31

State	District	College degree or higher	Rank	State	District	College degree or higher	Rank	State	District	College degree or higher	Rank
District of Columbia	AL	39.1%	32	Missouri	2	38.3%	35	Massachusetts	4	36.9%	39
Kansas	3	39.1%	32	California	6	37.9%	36	Maryland	3	36.5%	40
Texas	21	38.9%	33	California	9	37.4%	37	California	46	36.4%	41
Texas	26	38.9%	33	Washington	8	37.4%	37	Washington	1	36.4%	41
New Jersey	5	38.6%	34	Georgia	5	37.3%	38	California	10	36.2%	42
				California	36	36.9%	39				

Redistricting Court Cases in the United States

Litigation over the shape and composition of House districts became commonplace in the latter decades of the twentieth century. Redistricting is fundamentally a political process in which a party in power in a state will attempt to draw district lines after each decennial census to enhance the chances of one of its members winning a House seat or—increasingly frequently—to protect an incumbent of either party, particularly one who has been in Congress for a lengthy period and accumulated influential seniority. (Redistricting may also be done to consider local or community interests, such as keeping a city or town together in the same district.)

Court cases, however, have proliferated as aggrieved individuals or groups believe they have been unfairly, and often illegally, discriminated against by the map drawers. This trend strengthened as state legislators, and an expanding army of political consultants; used computers to draw ever more exact lines to place voters inside or outside a district where they most likely would benefit the party that is drawing the maps. Also, voting rights laws from the 1960s onward have made clear that minorities cannot be discriminated against in drawing district lines. These laws have given rise to some of the most important Supreme Court decisions, particularly a number occurring in North Carolina in the 1990s.

Below is a list of more than 200 court cases that dealt broadly with reapportionment and redistricting. Most are federal cases, but a few important state legislative cases are also included. The cases are organized by state (sections for the District of Columbia and the federal government are also included). Each case is accompanied by its official citation to facilitate additional research.

The earliest case came in 1904 followed by a handful of decisions until the 1960s. Beginning in that decade the court challenges accelerated markedly, particularly after 1970.

Alabama

Barnett v. Alabama, 171 F. Supp. 2d 1292 (2001)
Kelley v. Bennett, 96 F. Supp. 2d 1301 (2000)
McKee v. James, 1998 U.S. Dist. LEXIS 21568 (1998)
Montiel v. Davis, 215 F. Supp. 2d 1279 (2002)
Moore v. Moore, 246 F. Supp. 578 (1965)
Wesch v. Hunt, 785 F. Supp. 1491 (1992)

Arizona

Arizonans for Fair Representation v. Symington, 828 F. Supp. 684 (1992)
Goddard v. Bobbitt, 536 F. Supp. 538 (1982)
Klahr v. Goddard, 250 F. Supp. 537 (1966)
Klahr v. Williams, 339 F. Supp. 922 (1972)
Navajo Nation v. Arizona Independent Redistricting Commission,
    230 F. Supp. 2d 998 (2002)

Arkansas

Doulin v. White, 528 F. Supp. 1323 (1982)
Doulin v. White, 535 F. Supp. 450 (1982)
Doulin v. White, 549 F. Supp. 152 (1982)
Park v. Faubus, 238 F. Supp. 62 (1965)
Turner v. Arkansas, 784 F. Supp. 553 (1991)
Turner v. State, 784 F. Supp. 585 (1991)

California

Badham v. March Fong Eu, 568 F. Supp. 156 (1983)
Badham v. March Fong Eu, 694 F. Supp. 664 (1988)
Badham v. United States District Court for Northern District of California,
    721 F.2d 1170 (1983)
Cano v. Davis, 211 F. Supp. 2d 1208 (2002)
DeWitt v. Foley, 1992 U.S. Dist. LEXIS 14571 (1992)
DeWitt v. Wilson, 856 F. Supp. 1409 (1994)
Members of the California Democratic Congressional Delegation v. Eu,
    790 F. Supp. 925 (1992)

Colorado

Carstens v. Lamm, 543 F. Supp. 68 (1982)

Connecticut

Donnelly v. Meskill, 345 F. Supp. 962 (1972)

District of Columbia

Adams v. Clinton, 26 F. Supp. 2d 156 (1998)
Adams v. Clinton, 90 F. Supp. 2d 27 (2000)
Busbee v. Smith, 549 F. Supp. 494 (1982)
Giles v. Ashcroft, 193 F. Supp. 2d 258 (2002)
Virginia v. Reno, 117 F. Supp. 2d 46 (2000)

Federal Government

Federation for American Immigration Reform v. Klutznick, 486 F. Supp. 564 (1980)
United States House of Representatives v. United States Department of Commerce,
    11 F. Supp. 2d 76 (1998)

Florida

Brown v. Florida, 208 F. Supp. 2d 1344 (2002)
DeGrandy v. Wetherell, 794 F. Supp. 1076 (1992)
DeGrandy v. Wetherell, 815 F. Supp. 1550 (1992)
Gong v. Bryant, 230 F. Supp. 917 (1964)
Gong v. Kirk, 278 F. Supp. 133 (1967)
Gong v. Kirk, 375 F.2d 728 (1967)
Johnson v. DeGrandy, 512 U.S. 997 (1994)
Johnson v. Mortham, 915 F. Supp. 1529 (1995)
Johnson v. Mortham, 926 F. Supp. 1460 (1996)
Johnson v. Smith, 1994 U.S. Dist. LEXIS 20765 (1994)
Martinez v. Bush, 234 F. Supp. 1275 (2002)
Wendler v. Stone, 350 F. Supp. 838 (1972)

Georgia

Abrams v. Johnson, 521 U.S. 74 (1997)
Georgia v. Ashcroft, 195 F. Supp. 2d 25 (2002)
Georgia v. Ashcroft, 539 U.S. __ (2003)
Georgia v. United States, 411 U.S. 526 (1973)
Gray v. Sanders, 372 U.S. 368 (1961)
Johnson v. Miller, 864 F. Supp. 1354 (1994)
Johnson v. Miller, 922 F. Supp. 1556 (1995)
Johnson v. Miller, 929 F. Supp. 1529 (1996)
Miller v. Johnson, 515 U.S. 900 (1995)
Wesberry v. Sanders, 376 U.S. 1 (1964)
Wesberry v. Vandiver, 206 F. Supp. 276 (1962)

Hawaii

Travis v. King, 552 F. Supp. 554 (1982)

Illinois

Colegrove v. Green, 64 F. Supp. 632 (1946)
Colegrove v. Green, 328 U.S. 549 (1946)
Grivetti v. Illinois State Electoral Board, 335 F. Supp. 779 (1971)
Hastert v. Illinois State Board of Election Commissioners, 28 F.3d 1430 (1993)
Hastert v. Illinois State Board of Election Commissioners,
    1994 U.S. App. LEXIS 13101 (1994)
Hastert v. State Board of Elections, 777 F. Supp. 634 (1991)
Hastert v. State Board of Elections, 794 F. Supp. 254 (1992)
King v. State Board of Elections, 979 F. Supp. 582 (1996)
Otto v. Kasper, 1981 U.S. Dist. LEXIS 18449 (1981)
PAC for Middle America v. State Board of Elections,
    1995 U.S. Dist. LEXIS 14011 (1995)
PAC for Middle America v. State Board of Elections,
    1995 U.S. Dist. LEXIS 14021 (1995)
Ryan v. State Board of Elections, 661 F.2d 1130 (1981)
Skolnick v. State Electoral Board, 336 F. Supp. 839 (1971)

Indiana

Davis v. Bandemer, 478 U.S. 109 (1986)
Grills v. Branigin, 255 F. Supp. 155 (1966)

Kansas

Anthony v. Burrow, 129 F. 783 (1904)
Graham v. Thornburgh, 207 F. Supp. 2d 1280 (2002)
Meeks v. Anderson, 229 F. Supp. 271 (1964)
Meeks v. Avery, 251 F. Supp. 245 (1966)
O'Sullivan v. Brier, 540 F. Supp. 1200 (1982)
State ex rel. Stephan v. Graves, 796 F. Supp. 468 (1992)

Kentucky

Clarke v. Carter, 218 F. Supp. 448 (1963)
Hume v. Mahan, 1 F. Supp. 142 (1932)
Richardson v. McChesney, 218 U.S. 487 (1910)

Louisiana

Couhig v. Brown, 538 F. Supp. 1086 (1982)
Hays v. Louisiana, 839 F. Supp. 1188 (1993)
Hays v. Louisiana, 862 F. Supp. 119 (1994)
Hays v. Louisiana, 936 F. Supp. 360 (1996)
Major v. Treen, 574 F. Supp. 325 (1983)
United States v. Hays, 515 U.S. 737 (1995)

Maryland

Anne Arundel Republican Central Commission v. State Advisory Board of Election Laws, 781 F. Supp. 394 (1991)
Duckworth v. State Board of Elections, 213 F. Supp. 2d 543 (2002)
Marylanders for Fair Representation v. Schaefer, 144 F. R. D. 292 (1992)
Shapiro v. Maryland, 336 F. Supp. 1205 (1972)

Massachusetts

Black Political Task Force v. Connolly, 679 F. Supp. 109 (1988)
Dinis v. Volpe, 264 F. Supp. 425 (1967)
Franklin v. Massachusetts, 505 U.S. 788 (1992)
Massachusetts v. Mashbacher, 785 F. Supp. 230 (1992)

Michigan

Calkins v. Hare, 228 F. Supp. 824 (1964)
City of Detroit v. Secretary of Commerce, 4 F.3d 1367 (1993)
Detroit v. Franklin, 800 F. Supp. 539 (1992)
Dunnell v. Austin, 344 F. Supp. 210 (1972)
Good v. Austin, 800 F. Supp. 557 (1992)
O'Lear v. Miller, 222 F. Supp. 2d 850 (2002)
Young v. Klutznick, 497 F. Supp. 1318 (1980)
Young v. Klutznick, 652 F.2d 617 (1981)

Minnesota

Emison v. Growe, 782 F. Supp. 427 (1992)
Growe v. Emison, 507 U.S. 25 (1993)
LaComb v. Growe, 541 F. Supp. 145 (1982)
Smiley v. Holm, 285 U.S. 355 (1932)

Mississippi

Branch v. Smith, 538 U.S. __, 123 S. Ct. 1429 (2003)
Brown v. Wood, 1 F. Supp. 134 (1932)
Connor v. Johnson, 256 F. Supp. 962 (1966)
Jordan v. Winter, 604 F. Supp. 807 (1984)
Mississippi v. Smith, 541 F. Supp. 1329 (1982)
Smith v. Clark, 189 F. Supp. 2d 548 (2002)
Wood v. Broom, 287 U.S. 1 (1932)

Missouri

Carroll v. Becker, 285 U.S. 380 (1932)
Kirkpatrick v. Preisler, 394 U.S. 526 (1969)
Preisler v. Secretary of Missouri, 238 F. Supp. 187 (1965)
Preisler v. Secretary of State, 279 F. Supp. 952 (1967)
Shayer v. Kirkpatrick, 541 F. Supp. 922 (1982)

Montana

Montana v. United States Department of Commerce, 775 F. Supp. 1358 (1991)
Roberts v. Babcock, 246 F. Supp. 396 (1965)
United States Department of Commerce v. Montana, 503 U.S. 442 (1992)

Nebraska

Exon v. Tiemann, 279 F. Supp. 603 (1967)

New Jersey

Daggett v. Kimmelman, 535 F. Supp. 978 (1982)
Daggett v. Kimmelman, 580 F. Supp. 1259 (1984)
Daggett v. Kimmelman, 617 F. Supp. 1269 (1985)
David v. Cahill, 342 F. Supp. 463 (1972)
Karcher v. Daggett, 455 U.S. 1303 (1982)
Karcher v. Daggett, 535 F. Supp. 978 (1982)
Karcher v. Daggett, 462 U.S. 725 (1983)
Karcher v. Daggett, 466 U.S. 910 (1984)

New Mexico

Adams v. Richardson, 871 F. Supp. 43 (1994)
Norton v. Campbell, 359 F.2d 608 (1966)

New York

Carey v. Klutznick, 508 F. Supp. 404 (1980)
City of New York v. United States Department of Commerce, 34 F.3d 111 (1972)
City of New York v. United States Department of Commerce, 822 F. Supp. 906 (1993)

Cooper v. Power, 260 F. Supp. 207 (1966)
Diaz v. Silver, 932 F. Supp. 462 (1996)
Diaz v. Silver, 978 F. Supp. 96 (1997)
Flateau v. Anderson, 537 F. Supp. 257 (1982)
Honeywood v. Rockefeller, 214 F. Supp. 897 (1963)
Koenig v. Flynn, 285 U.S. 375 (1932)
Puerto Rican Legal Defense and Education Fund, Inc. v. Gantt, 796 F. Supp. 681 (1992)
Rodriguez v. Pataki, 2002 U.S. Dist. LEXIS 9272 (2002)
Sharrow v. Fish, 501 F. Supp. 202 (1980)
Sharrow v. Peyser, 443 F. Supp. 321 (1977)
United Jewish Organizations v. Carey, 430 U.S. 144 (1977)
Wells v. Rockefeller, 273 F. Supp. 984 (1967)
Wells v. Rockefeller, 281 F. Supp. 821 (1968)
Wells v. Rockefeller, 394 U.S. 542 (1969)
Wells v. Rockefeller, 311 F. Supp. 48 (1970)
Wells v. Rockefeller, 398 U.S. 901 (1970)
Wisconsin v. New York, 517 U.S. 1 (1996)
W. M. C. A., Inc. v. Simon, 202 F. Supp. 741 (1962)
Wright v. Rockefeller, 211 F. Supp. 460 (1962)
Wright v. Rockefeller, 376 U.S. 52 (1964)

North Carolina

Cromartie v. Hunt, 1998 U.S. Dist. LEXIS 7767 (1998)
Cromartie v. Hunt, 133 F. Supp. 2d 407 (2000)
Drum v. Seawell, 271 F. Supp. 193 (1967)
Easley v. Cromartie, 532 U.S. 234 (2001)
Hunt v. Cromartie, 526 U.S. 541 (1999)
Shaw v. Barr, 808 F. Supp. 461 (1992)
Shaw v. Hunt, 517 U.S. 899 (1996)
Shaw v. Hunt, 861 F. Supp. 408 (1994)
Shaw v. Reno, 509 U.S. 630 (1993)
Thornburg v. Gingles, 478 U.S. 30 (1986)

Ohio

Flanagan v. Gillmor, 561 F. Supp. 36 (1982)
Ohio ex rel. Davis v. Hildebrant, 241 U.S. 565 (1916)
Quilter v. Voinovich, 912 F. Supp. 1006 (1995)
Quilter v. Voinovich, 1995 U.S. Dist. LEXIS 19740 (1995)
Quilter v. Voinovich, 981 F. Supp. 1032 (1997)

Pennsylvania

Bethel Park v. Stars, 319 F. Supp. 971 (1970)
In re Pennsylvania Cong. Dist. Reapportionment Cases, 535 F. Supp. 191 (1982)
In re Pennsylvania Cong. Dist. Reapportionment Cases, 567 F. Supp. 1507 (1982)
Ridge v. Verity, 715 F. Supp. 1308 (1989)
Valentini v. Mitchel, 790 F. Supp. 534 (1992)
Vieth v. Pennsylvania, 188 F. Supp. 2d 532 (2002)
Vieth v. Pennsylvania, 195 F. Supp. 2d 672 (2002)
Vieth v. Pennsylvania, 241 F. Supp. 2d 532 (2002)

South Carolina

Burton ex rel. Republican Party v. Sheheen, 793 F. Supp. 1329 (1992)
Colleton County Council v. McConnell, 201 F. Supp. 2d 618 (2002)
Smith v. Beasley, 946 F. Supp. 1174 (1996)

Tennessee

Baker v. Carr, 369 U.S. 186 (1962)
Baker v. Clement, 247 F. Supp. 886 (1965)
Baker v. Ellington, 273 F. Supp. 174 (1967)
Crone v. Darnell, 176 F. Supp. 2d 814 (2001)
Dixon v. Hassler, 412 F. Supp. 1036 (1976)

Texas

Balderas v. Texas, 2001 U.S. Dist. LEXIS 25003 (2001)
Balderas v. Texas, 2001 U.S. Dist. LEXIS 25006 (2001)
Bush v. Martin, 224 F. Supp. 499 (1963)
Bush v. Martin, 251 F. Supp. 484 (1966)
Bush v. Vera, 517 U.S. 952 (1996)
Martin v. Bush, 376 U.S. 222 (1964)
Mayfield v. Texas, 206 F. Supp. 820 (2001)
Seamon v. Upham, 536 F. Supp. 931 (1982)
Seamon v. Upham, 536 F. Supp. 1030 (1982)
Upham v. Seamon, 456 U.S. 37 (1982)
Vera v. Bush, 933 F. Supp. 1341 (1996)
Vera v. Richards, 861 F. Supp. 1304 (1994)
White v. Weiser, 412 U.S. 783 (1973)

Utah

Utah v. Evans, 143 F. Supp. 2d 1290 (2001)
Utah v. Evans, 536 U.S. 452 (2002)

Virginia

Department of Commerce v. United States House of Representatives,
  525 U.S. 316 (1999)
Glavin v. Clinton, 19 F. Supp. 2d 543 (1998)
Moon v. Meadows, 952 F. Supp. 1141 (1997)

Washington

Thigpen v. Meyers, 211 F. Supp. 826 (1962)

West Virginia

Stone v. Hechler, 782 F. Supp. 1116 (1992)
West Virginia Civil Liberties Union v. Rockefeller, 336 F. Supp. 395 (1972)

Wisconsin

Arrington v. Elections Board, 173 F. Supp. 2d 856 (2001)
Wisconsin v. Zimmerman, 209 F. Supp. 183 (1962)

District of Columbia

Washington, DC is one of the most famous cities in the world, yet it is not what most people think it is. Overseas, many imagine it as they would a European capital—the seat of government and the mainspring of commerce and culture. Within the United States, many envision Washington as the National Mall, a collection of monuments, museums, and marble palaces that represent the idea of the nation and recall its past. But the real Washington is neither the cultural capital on the European model nor the narrow strip of tourist attractions in the popular American conception.

Washington is the quintessential government town, ground zero for federal command and control. Late in the twentieth century, a high-tech economy sprang up in its suburbs, becoming increasingly important to the local economy. But that has not altered the city's focus on making the laws, rules, and policies for the nation. As for culture, Washington has far more offerings in performing arts and restaurants than it did a generation ago, and many media organizations have headquarters here—but no one will mistake it for New York City.

At the same time, Washington is far more than what the average tourist sees. A modern city enfolds the Mall on three sides, a city of tree-lined boulevards and choking traffic, grand old embassies, and deteriorating neighborhoods. The city has some sophistication and international flavor; but it is also riven by dramatic disparity in income and lifestyle. If it were a state, the District of Columbia would be tops in the country in average annual pay. The high end of the earnings scale lifts the mean to $56,024 (2001 Census Bureau estimate), which is half again higher than the national average. Factoring in family size knocks the District down a bit, so that it ranked second behind Connecticut in personal income per capita ($38,374) in 2001 (30 percent above the national average). The 2000 census showed median family income at $46,283. All of these different measures of income indicate that DC residents have substantial earning power.

Washington also has a high percentage of adults with college degrees, reflecting the presence of a professional caste, living predominantly in the city's northwest quadrant. But most of the city's territory is dominated by middle-class and working-class neighborhoods of African Americans and, increasingly, new arrivals speaking Spanish. The poorer areas, particularly those across the Anacostia River, suffer the full panoply of urban ills and a deep bruise from historic segregation. Despite the high pay for some at the top, the DC unemployment rate is above the national average. The percentage of families in poverty—16.7 percent according to

the 2000 census—would rank it thirty-third in the list of districts with the most poverty. For the United States as a whole, the rate for families in poverty was 9.2 percent.

The Census Bureau now considers Washington's metro area (greater than 4 million) to have grown together with Baltimore's, making the combined market statistical area more than 7 million—the largest in the country after New York, Los Angeles, and Chicago. This meta-metro has major league pro franchises in every sport and two in several. The residents of this area live and recreate over a four-state area, winding their way into West Virginia's hills and surging across the Chesapeake Bay Bridge into the Delaware-Maryland-Virginia peninsula.

Yet it all begins with Washington, a compact area of 68 square miles where barely more than 572,000 people lived at the 2000 census count but where several times that many come to work or visit each day. Washington is unique among U.S. cities because it exists by fiat. Politics created it of necessity, because the southern states did not wish to be under the rule of Philadelphia or New York (or any other northern city). George Washington himself persuaded the original landowners of this swampy real estate to sell to the government. The city grew up along the streets between the Capitol (under construction for most of a century) and the White House, and it was more haphazard than grand for several generations.

The city's history was further distorted by its ambivalent relationship with slavery. Emancipation formally came to Washington far earlier than it did to the rest of the South (and Washington, well below the Mason-Dixon line, has always been part of the South). But the second-class citizenship to which former slaves were often consigned was largely institutionalized here. The residents of this city, alone among Americans, can neither vote for a member of Congress nor run their own community without the oversight of Congress.

There is a historical reason for this and a partisan one. The framers of the Constitution feared the growth of a central authority in an all-powerful capital such as London or Paris. So they dictated that residents of the capital should not be enfranchised. This was not originally targeted at African Americans. But Washington evolved into a black-majority city after World War II—for a time more than two-thirds of its residents were African American, more than any U.S. city save Detroit. Here, as elsewhere, the black vote has tilted heavily to the Democratic Party. So statehood would mean giving the District another vote in the House and two senators—all presumably Democratic.

Washington residents have been allowed to vote for president since the early 1960s. "Home rule," enacted in the wake of the civil rights movement, allowed Washington a mayor and a city council after a century of being run directly by subcommittees of Congress. But the city has only a nonvoting delegate in the House. City residents have adopted the colonial rebels' rallying cry of "No taxation without representation" in their pursuit of statehood, even printing it on their license plates.

Washington's first mayor in the 1970s, Walter Washington, was a transitional figure who did not rock the boat too hard. Thereafter, the voters elected Marion Barry, a former radical and political organizer from Mississippi who had come to the city to go to school. Barry was often called "mayor for life" before he was arrested using crack cocaine in 1990. Barry lost his office and did real time, but once out of jail he won a seat on the City Council and soon won another term as mayor in 1994. This prompted a partial repeal of home rule by Congress, which appointed a control board to manage the city's affairs.

When Barry retired again in 1998, the voters turned to an Ivy-educated accountant named Tony Williams, who had helped straighten out some of the city's more pressing fiscal problems. In 1998 the bow-tied Williams won the first of two four-year terms as mayor in his own right. He made visible progress in spurring economic growth—particularly in downtown Washington—but struggled against corruption and mismanagement in various city agencies.

From a peak just above 800,000 residents in the 1950 census, Washington had fallen by nearly 30 percent by 2000—a more precipitous drop than any state suffered in that half century (although not nearly the worst suffered by any city). Much of the decline was because of the enduring fallout from the riots of 1968 (sparked by the assassination of Dr. Martin Luther King Jr. in Memphis), a searing event that ravaged blocks of commercial districts that had been the vibrant heart of the city's black community.

At first, the city lost people to classic white flight. The white working class found their old neighborhoods less hospitable and the exclusive neighborhoods west of Rock Creek Park too expensive, so they moved to Maryland and Virginia. But since the 1968 riots, the exodus has also included many of the city's more mobile blacks in northeast and northwest Washington, who made the move across Eastern Avenue into Prince Georges County (Maryland) in search of better schools and housing. By the 1990s, "P-G County" had become the largest suburban county in America with a black majority. In the city, some of the homes and neighborhoods these people left behind were taken over by Hispanics, who were arriving in big numbers for the first time in the 1980s and 1990s.

By 2001 Census estimates, the city was just 60 percent black, with whites above 30 percent and Hispanics rising to 8 percent (an official figure many thought too low). Although Asian Americans were somewhat more common in the suburbs, the city was about 3 percent Asian as well. The new arrivals helped the city arrest its decline at the beginning of the new century. After losing badly in the early to mid-1990s, the city slowed the hemorrhage in the late 1990s and stabilized its population after 2000.

Major Industry

Government, professional services.

Notable

Since residents began casting votes for president in 1964, the Republican candidate's share has ranged from a high of 22 percent in 1972 to 9 percent in 2000.

Table 1 Population

District	Population	Population under 18	Voting-age population	Median age	Male*	Female*
D.C.	572,059	114,992	457,067	34.6	47.1	52.9

*As percentage of total population.

Table 2 Voting-Age Persons by Race/Hispanic or Latino Origin

District	White*	Black or African American*	American Indian or Alaska Native*	Asian*	Other or multirace*	Hispanic or Latino*
D.C.	31.8	55.7	0.2	2.9	1.9	7.3

*As percentage of voting-age population.

Table 3 Voting-Age Population by Age Groups

District	18 to 24*	25 to 44*	45 to 64*	Over 64*
D.C.	15.9	41.5	27.4	15.3

*As percentage of voting-age population.

Table 4 Income and Occupation

District	Median family income	Families in poverty*	White collar†	Blue collar†	Service†	Farm†
D.C.	$46,283	16.7	73.9	10.0	16.1	0.1

*As percentage of all families.   †As percentage of employed workers 16 years and over.

Table 5 Education: School Years Completed

District	Less than grade 9*	Grades 9–12 no diploma*	High school diploma no college*	Some college*	College bachelor's degree or higher*
D.C.	7.8	14.4	20.6	18.2	39.1

*As percentage of persons age 25 and over.

Table 6 Housing and Residential Patterns

District	Median home value	Owner occupied*	Renter occupied*	Urban†	Rural†
D.C.	$153,500	40.8	59.2	100.0	0.0

*As percentage of occupied housing units.   †As percentage of total population.

Election Returns

	Republican		Democratic		Other	
President 2000	18,073	9.0%	171,923	85.4%	11,898	5.6%
House 2002*			119,268	93.9%	7,733	6.1%

*Non-voting delegate.

Population 572,059

Total area (square miles) 68.3
Land area (square miles) 61.4

Population per square mile 9,316.9

Counties (2000 population)
District of Columbia 572,059

Cities and other areas over 10,000 (2000 population)
Washington, DC 572,059

Race and Hispanic or Latino origin*
White 27.8%
Black or African American 59.4%
American Indian or Alaska Native 0.2%
Asian 2.6%
Native Hawaiian or other Pacific Islander 0.0%
Some other race 0.3%
Hispanic or Latino origin 7.9%
Two or more races 1.7%

*As percentage of total population.

Ancestry*
English 3.9%
French 1.1%
German 4.2%
Irish 4.3%
Italian 1.9%
Polish 1.2%
Russian 1.3%
Subsaharan 2.5%
USA/American 1.5%
West Indian 1.2%

*As estimated percentage of total population.

Universities and colleges, 2000–2001 enrollment
American University, Washington, DC 10,776
Catholic University, Washington, DC 5,493
Corcoran School of Art, Washington, DC 332
Gallaudet University, Washington, DC 1,689
George Washington University, Washington, DC
20,527
Georgetown University, Washington, DC 12,427
Howard University, Washington, DC 10,010
Joint Military Intelligence College, Washington, DC
421
Mount Vernon College, Washington, DC 597
National Defense University, Fort McNair 716
Potomac College, Washington, DC 404
Southeastern University, Washington, DC 1,058
Strayer University, Washington, DC 1,425
Strayer University-Takoma Park, Washington, DC
1,062
Trinity College, Washington, DC 1,295
University of the District of Columbia, Washington, DC
5,358
Washington Theological Union, Washington, DC 221
Wesley Theological Seminary, Washington, DC 384

Newspapers and circulation

	District circulation	Total circulation
Baltimore Sun	1,572	268,280
New York Post	1,213	511,412
*USA Today**	21,150	1,674,376
Washington Post	137,245	779,632
Washington Times	22,563	101,367

Television stations and affiliations
Washington, DC (Hagerstown) 100% WBDC WB
Washington, DC (Hagerstown) 100% WDCA UPN
Washington, DC (Hagerstown) 100% WETA PBS
Washington, DC (Hagerstown) 100% WFPT PBS
Washington, DC (Hagerstown) 100% WHAG NBC
Washington, DC (Hagerstown) 100% WHSV ABC
Washington, DC (Hagerstown) 100% WHUT PBS
Washington, DC (Hagerstown) 100% WJAL ABC
Washington, DC (Hagerstown) 100% WJLA ABC
Washington, DC (Hagerstown) 100% WNVC Independent
Washington, DC (Hagerstown) 100% WNVT PBS
Washington, DC (Hagerstown) 100% WPXW PAX
Washington, DC (Hagerstown) 100% WRC NBC
Washington, DC (Hagerstown) 100% WTTG FOX
Washington, DC (Hagerstown) 100% WUSA CBS
Washington, DC (Hagerstown) 100% WVPY PBS
Washington, DC (Hagerstown) 100% WWPB PBS
Washington, DC (Hagerstown) 100% WWPX PAX

Cable systems and subscribers
Comcast 88,756

Military installations, September 2001
Naval Headquarters, Washington, DC 20,328
Walter Reed Army Medical Center, Silver Spring 5,771
Naval Research Laboratory, Washington, DC 2,821
Bolling Air Force Base, Washington, DC 2,385
Fort Leslie J. McNair (Army), Washington, DC 1,394

Businesses and other major employers
U.S. Dept. of Commerce; Washington, DC 19,000
U.S. Treasury; Washington, DC 15,000
U.S. House of Representatives; Washington, DC
10,000
U.S. Dept. of Agriculture; Washington, DC 9,718
Federal Bureau of Investigation; Washington, DC
7,250
U.S. Environmental Protection Agency; Washington,
DC 6,500
U.S. Dept. of Labor; Washington, DC 6,400
Howard University; Washington, DC 6,100
International Bank for Reconstruction and Development;
Washington, DC; foreign trade and banks 6,000
White House Office; Washington, DC 6,000
I2 Technologies; Washington, DC; computer software
5,500
U.S. Dept. of Transportation; Washington, DC 5,500
Pepco Inc.; Washington, DC; public utilities 5,000
Washington Hospital Center; Washington, DC 5,000
George Washington University; Washington, DC
5,000
U.S. Internal Revenue Service; Washington, DC 5,000

Washington Metropolitan Area Transit Authority; Washington, DC 4,691

U.S. Secret Service; Washington, DC 4,610

Federal Deposit Insurance Corp.; Washington, DC 4,000

Medstar-Georgetown Medical Center Inc.; Washington, DC 3,700

U.S. Dept. of Defense; Washington, DC 3,700

U.S. Dept. of State; Washington, DC 3,700

U.S. Dept. of Veterans Affairs; Washington, DC 3,501

U.S. Postal Service; Washington, DC 3,500

U.S. Dept. of Education; Washington, DC 3,461

Akin Gump Strauss Hauer and Feld; Washington, DC; law office 3,000

Catholic University of America Inc.; Washington, DC 3,000

U.S. Dept. of Health and Human Services; Washington, DC 3,000

U.S. Dept. of Housing and Urban Development; Washington, DC 3,000

U.S. Federal Aviation Admin.; Washington, DC 3,000

National Assn. of State Depts. of Agriculture; Washington, DC; trade associations 2,952

U.S. Government Printing Office; Washington, DC 2,900

U.S. Dept. of Energy; Washington, DC 2,800

Children's Hospital Corp.; Washington, DC 2,757

Howard University Hospital; Washington, DC 2,716

U.S. Bureau of Engraving and Printing; Washington, DC 2,700

U.S. National Park Service; Washington, DC 2,620

International Monetary Fund; Washington, DC; international development agency 2,600

Architect of the Capitol; Washington, DC 2,512

District of Columbia; Washington, DC; city government 2,500

Federal National Mortgage Assn. (Fannie Mae); Washington, DC 2,500

GEICO Corp.; Washington, DC; fire, marine, casualty insurance 2,500

General Accounting Office; Washington, DC 2,400

George Washington University Hospital; Washington, DC 2,200

Providence Hospital; Washington, DC 2,100

U.S. Forest Service; Washington, DC 2,078

Global Trade Corp.; Washington, DC; oil/gas lease brokers 2,000

WorldCom Inc.; Washington, DC; local/long-distance telephone 2,000

U.S. Office of Personnel Management; Washington, DC 2,000

U.S. Agency for International Development; Washington, DC; economic development 2,000

Securities and Exchange Commission; Washington, DC 1,877

Federal Reserve Board; Washington, DC 1,700

MCI World Com Inc.; Washington, DC; telephone communication 1,650

Inter-American Development Bank; Washington, DC; foreign trade and banks 1,604

U.S. Veterans Hospital; Washington, DC 1,600

American University; Washington, DC 1,550

Washington Sports and Entertainment; Washington, DC; sports/recreation clubs 1,500

Washington Post Co.; Washington, DC; newspaper 1,500

KPMG; Washington, DC; certified public accountant 1,500

Embassy of U.S. of America; Washington, DC; embassies 1,500

U.S. Dept. of Justice; Washington, DC 1,500

U.S. Coast Guard; Washington, DC 1,500

Pan American Health Organization Inc.; Washington, DC; health and welfare council 1,475

District of Columbia; Washington, DC; water supply 1,474

U.S. Bureau of Customs and Border Protection; Washington, DC 1,463

U.S. Bureau of Prisons; Washington, DC 1,400

Federal Communications Commission; Washington, DC 1,400

Verizon Washington, DC Inc.; Washington, DC; telephone communication 1,367

Atlantic Coast Airlines Inc.; Washington, DC 1,362

National Geographic Society Inc.; Washington, DC; magazine publishing 1,326

Pitney Bowes Inc.; Washington, DC; photocopying services 1,300

Lucy Webb Hayes Training School; Washington, DC 1,300

National Archives and Records Admin.; Washington, DC 1,213

National Railroad Passenger Corp.; Washington, DC; train services 1,200

Greater Southeast Community Hospital Corp.; Washington, DC 1,200

Bureau of National Affairs Inc.; Washington, DC; law periodicals 1,200

Group Hospitalization and Medical Services Inc.; Washington, DC; group hospitalization 1,200

U.S. General Services Admin.; Washington, DC 1,200

Gallaudet University; Washington, DC 1,152

John F. Kennedy Center for Performing Arts; Washington, DC 1,144

Potomac Electric Power Co.; Washington, DC; electric power generation 1,100

International Finance Corp.; Washington, DC; foreign trade and banks 1,100

Marriott Wardman Park Hotel; Washington, DC 1,000

AARP; Washington, DC; elder citizen organization 1,000

U.S. Financial Management Service; Washington, DC 1,000

U.S. Veterans Admin.; Washington, DC 1,000

National Gallery of Art; Washington, DC 1,000

Mirant Mid-Atlantic; Washington, DC; power generators 980

U.S. Peace Corps; Washington, DC 979

Washington Terminal Co.; Washington, DC 950

National Aeronautics and Space Admin.; Washington, DC 945

University of District of Columbia; Washington, DC 914

Electronic Data Systems Corp.; Washington, DC; insurance agents   900

News World Communications Inc.; Washington, DC; newspaper   900

Covington and Burling; Washington, DC; law office   900

U.S. Army Corps of Engineers; Washington, DC   900

Federal Emergency Management Agency; Washington, DC   900

Administrative Office of U.S. Courts; Washington, DC   900

Hilton Hotels Corp.; Washington, DC   830

Hogan and Hartson; Washington, DC; law office   800

Howrey Simon Arnold & White; Washington, DC; law office   800

Marriott International Inc.; Washington, DC; hotels   800

Financial Management Service; Washington, DC; treasurer's office   800

Intelsat Global Service Corp.; Washington, DC; data communication services   800

U.S. Comptroller of Currency; Washington, DC   800

U.S. Bureau of Alcohol Tobacco and Firearms; Washington, DC   800

U.S. Small Business Admin.; Washington, DC   800

Federal Trade Commission; Washington, DC   775

Corporate Executive Board Co.; Washington, DC; research services   768

Pension Benefit Guaranty Corp.; Washington, DC; economic programs   758

Tenet Healthcare Corp.; Washington, DC; psychiatric hospitals   750

Palm Management Corp.; Washington, DC; restaurant management   750

U.S. Equal Employment Opportunity Commission; Washington, DC   728

CPF Corp.; Washington, DC; janitorial service   715

Unlimited Security Inc.; Washington, DC; security guard service   700

District of Columbia; Washington, DC; family services   700

Arnold and Porter; Washington, DC; law office   700

VMT Long Term Care Management Inc.; Washington, DC; health services consultant   700

Bureau of Diplomatic Security; Washington, DC   700

World Wildlife Fund Inc.; Washington, DC; environmental protection   650

U.S. Bureau of Labor Statistics; Washington, DC   650

Conservation International Foundation; Washington, DC; environmental protection   627

Protestant Episcopal Cathedral Foundation; Washington, DC; religious organization   624

SPACEHAB Inc.; Washington, DC; commercial physical research   619

National Public Radio; Washington, DC   615

American Airlines; Washington, DC   600

Jones Day Reavis and Pogue; Washington, DC; law office   600

MRCO Inc.; Washington, DC; mortgage bankers   600

Renaissance Hotel Group; Washington, DC   600

District of Columbia; Washington, DC; public schools   600

District of Columbia; Washington, DC; corrections department   600

Crowell and Moring LLP; Washington, DC; law office   600

Watson Wyatt and Co. Holdings; Washington, DC; benefits planning   600

Horton and Barber Professional Services; Washington, DC; janitorial service   600

Ernst and Young; Washington, DC; certified public accountant   600

Dickstein Shapiro Morin and Oshinsky; Washington, DC; law office   600

U.S. Senate; Washington, DC   600

Employment Standards Admin.; Washington, DC   594

Organization of American States; Washington, DC; economic development   590

Shaw Pittman; Washington, DC; law office   585

National Labor Relations Board; Washington, DC   580

Wilmer Cutler and Pickering; Washington, DC; law office   575

Academy for Educational Development; Washington, DC; educational research   560

National Education Assn. of U.S.; Washington, DC; labor union   555

Omni Hotels Management Corp.; Washington, DC   550

Davis Memorial Goodwill Industries Inc.; Washington, DC; surplus and salvage stores   534

Thayer Capital Partners; Washington, DC; security brokers, dealers   530

International Brotherhood of Teamsters; Washington, DC; labor organization   520

Hyatt Corp.; Washington, DC; hotels   500

Union Labor Life Insurance Co.; Washington, DC   500

Zenith Administrators Inc.; Washington, DC; pension funds   500

National Children's Center Inc.; Washington, DC; services for disabled   500

Parsons Infrastructure and Technology Group Inc.; Washington, DC; engineering services   500

PricewaterhouseCoopers; Washington, DC; accounting services   500

AT&T Corp.; Washington, DC; telecommunications consultant   500

Allied Riser Operations Corp.; Washington, DC; telephone communication   500

Swidler Berlin Shereff Friedman; Washington, DC; law office   500

Embassy of United Kingdom; Washington, DC; foreign embassy   500

Fort Myer Construction Corp.; Washington, DC; road construction   500

ABC Inc.; Washington, DC; news organization   500

Arent Fox Kintner Plotkin and Kahn; Washington, DC; law office   500

American Chemical Society; Washington, DC; scientific association   500

B'nai B'rith Housing Inc.; Washington, DC; counseling services   500

Steptoe & Johnson LLP; Washington, DC; law office   500

Smithsonian Institution; Washington, DC   500

Indexes

Business Index

This index covers most private employers listed in this book. Excluded are federal, state, and local government agencies, including school districts, municipal transportation agencies, and military installations; legal and medical professional groups; hospitals, health maintenance organizations, and health insurers; universities; and newspapers. Universities and military installations are indexed separately. Legal identifications, such as Corp., Inc., or Co., generally have been omitted from the business names in the index but will be found at the listings. An asterisk (*) indicates that the organization appears more than once in the congressional district, usually because of multiple plants or offices at different locations. Employer names have been edited so that national business firms appears together. For example, Hyatt Hotels are always indexed under the word "Hyatt," even though the actual hotel name may begin with another word. For additional information, consult Sources and Explanations in the front of the volume.

Business	State-District	Page
A		
A Z 3	CA-34	134
A&E Products Group	MI-2	466
A&L Industrial Construction	TN-1	837
A&R Security Services	IL-1	299
A. C. Nielsen	IL-8	312
A. C. Nielsen	IL-14	324
A. Duda and Sons	FL-16	236
A. Duie Pyle	PA-7	784
A. E. Staley Manufacturing	IL-17	330
A. G. Edwards and Sons	MO-1	526
A. M. Best	NJ-7	590
A. M. E. Services	LA-3	402
A. M. Gilardi and Sons	OK-5	753
A. O. Smith	KY-1	384
A. O. Smith	SC-5	824
A. O. Smith	TN-4	843
A-1 Temporary Services	AL-6	34
AAA Cooper Transportation	AL-2	27
AAA Cooper Transportation	GA-13	280
AAA South Central New England	MA-1	440
Aabakus	TN-7	848
AAF-McQuay	NY-24	660
AAF-McQuay	VA-6	945
AAI	MD-2	424
Aalfs Manufacturing	AR-4	68
Aames Financial	CA-34	134
AAON	OK-1	746
AAR International	IL-6	307
Aargus Security Systems	IL-3	301
AARP	DC-AL	1036
AARP	IA-3	363
Aavid Thermalloy	NH-1	570
AB Cellular Holding	CA-39	143
AB Chance	MO-9	541
AB Dick	IL-9	314
Abacus	MD-3	425
ABB	GA-12	278
ABB	MI-9	479
ABB	MO-4	532
ABB	NJ-12	600
ABB	OH-15	735
ABB	PA-8	786
ABB	TX-7	871*

Business	State-District	Page
ABB	TX-18	890
Abbott Laboratories	CA-11	94
Abbott Laboratories	IL-10	316
Abbott Laboratories	MA-6	450
Abbott Laboratories	NC-8	688
Abbott Laboratories	OH-12	730
Abbott Laboratories	OH-15	735
Abbott Laboratories	OH-16	738
Abbott Laboratories	TX-30	910
Abbott Laboratories	UT-3	923
Abbott Laboratories	VA-5	943
Abbott Resorts	FL-2	212
ABC Family Worldwide	CA-30	127
ABC News	DC-AL	1037
Aberdeen Sportswear	NJ-4	583
ABF Freight System	FL-3	214
ABF Freight System	IL-2	300
ABF Freight System	OH-8	722
ABF Freight System	PA-19	806
Abitibi Consolidated Sales	AZ-1	46
ABM Janitorial Services	CA-34	133
ABM Janitorial Services	CA-36	138
ABM Janitorial Services	MN-5	503
ABM Janitorial Services	TX-30	910
ABM Security Services	CA-8	89
ABM Security Services	CA-33	132
ABN Amro	IL-4	303
ABN Amro	IL-7	309*
ABN Amro	NY-14	640
ABR Benefits Services	FL-11	228
ABT Associates	MA-8	455
ABX Air	OH-3	713
AC	NC-12	695
Accent Maintenance	NY-18	648
Accenture	AL-6	34
Accenture	CA-36	137
Accenture	CO-1	172
Accenture	FL-10	226
Accenture	GA-5	265
Accenture	IL-7	309
Accenture	MA-4	446
Accenture	MA-7	452
Accenture	MI-13	486
Accenture	MN-3	499
Accenture	MN-5	504
Accenture	NC-12	695
Accenture	NJ-11	597
Accenture	PA-2	774
Accenture	TX-17	888
Accenture	TX-18	890
Accenture	VA-8	949
Accenture	WA-7	971
Accessory	NY-14	640
Accessory Plating	CA-27	122
ACCO Brands	NY-14	641
Account	MN-4	501
Accubanc Mortgage	TX-32	914
Accucom Technical Services	TX-3	864
Accuride	KY-1	384
Ace	DE-AL	204
Ace	GA-8	271
Ace Hardware	IL-13	322
Ace-Tex	MI-13	486
ACH Financing	FL-6	218
Ackerley Media Group	WA-7	971
Acme Bus	NY-2	618
Acme Energy Services	TX-19	892
Acme Steel	IL-2	300
Acordia of West Virginia	WV-2	982
Acordis	AL-1	25
Acordis	AL-5	32
Acorn Engineering	CA-38	141
ACS Government Services	MD-8	434
ACS Industries	RI-1	811

Business	State-District	Page
ACS State and Local Solutions	NJ-9	593
Act Manufacturing	MA-3	444
Act Manufacturing	MS-1	515
Acterna	CO-6	181
Acterna	MD-4	427*
Acterna	NC-4	681
Acuity Specialty Products	GA-5	266
Acushnet	MA-4	446*
Acuson	CA-14	99*
Acxiom	AR-2	64
Acxiom	IL-6	306
Adamar of New Jersey	NJ-2	579
Adaptec	CA-15	102
ADC Telecommunications	CT-3	195
ADC Telecommunications	GA-6	268
ADC Telecommunications	MN-3	499
Addington Mining	KY-4	390
Addison Wesley	IL-10	316
Addison Wesley	NJ-5	585
A-Dec	OR-1	758
Adecco Staffing	NY-2	618
Adesa	NJ-7	590
Adidas America	OR-3	762
Adminastar Federal	IN-5	347
Adobe Systems	CA-16	104
Adobe Systems	WA-7	971
AdobeAir	AZ-4	51
ADP Claims Solutions Group	CA-11	94
ADP Marshall	NC-4	681
ADP Total Source	FL-23	248
ADP Total Source	MI-9	479
ADT Security Services	IL-13	322
ADT Security Services	MI-5	471
ADT Security Services	MI-8	476
ADT Security Services	NE-2	554
ADT Security Services	WI-4	995
Adtran	AL-5	32
Advance Auto Parts	VA-6	945
Advance Building Maintenance	CA-30	127
Advance Dial	IL-6	306
Advance Food	OK-3	750
Advance Logistics	PA-8	785
Advance Magazine Publishers	NY-8	629
Advance Polybag	LA-1	399
Advanced Cardiovascular Systems	CA-15	102
Advanced Data	CA-24	116
Advanced Data-Comm	IA-1	360
Advanced Distributor Products	MS-1	515
Advanced Energy Industries	CO-4	178
Advanced Fibre Communications	CA-6	84
Advanced Glassfiber Yarns	PA-9	787
Advanced Glassfiber Yarns	SC-2	820
Advanced Lighting Technologies	OH-14	734
Advanced Medical Optics	CA-48	157
Advanced Micro Devices	CA-14	99
Advanced Micro Devices	TX-10	876
Advanced Technical Products	VA-9	951
Advanced Technology Lab	WA-1	961
Advanced Temporaries	TX-4	865
Advanta USA	IA-4	365
Advantage Foods	WV-1	980
Advantage Logistics Southwest	AZ-4	51
Advantage Logistics-Michigan	MI-11	482
Advantage Personnel	TN-3	841
Advantage-Crown	CA-48	157
Advantek	MN-3	499
Advantica Restaurant Group	SC-4	822
Advent Software	CA-8	89
Advertising Specialties Institute	PA-8	786
Aearo	MA-2	442
Aegis Communications	AZ-8	57
Aegis Communications	FL-16	236
Aegis Communications	GA-4	264

Business	State-District	Page	Business	State-District	Page	Business	State-District	Page
Coca-Cola	MO-2	529	Command Security	NY-6	626	Computer Sciences	VA-8	949*
Coca-Cola	OH-2	711	Command Security	NY-14	642	Computer Sciences	VA-11	955
Coca-Cola	PA-1	771	Commemorative Brands	TX-10	876	Computer Sciences	VT-AL	929
Coca-Cola	PA-11	791	Commerce Bank	MO-5	534	Computer Systems Technology	AL-5	32
Coca-Cola	TN-7	848	Commerce Group	MA-2	442	Compuware	MI-9	479
Coca-Cola	TX-7	872	Commercial Building			Compuware	MN-3	500
Coca-Cola	TX-12	880	Maintenance	NY-2	619	Compuware	OH-12	731
Coca-Cola	TX-28	906	Commercial Communications	FL-16	236	Compuware	WI-4	995
Coca-Cola	TX-30	910	Commercial Credit Plan	MD-7	432	Comverse Network Systems	MA-5	448
Coca-Cola	WA-1	962	Commercial Federal Bank	NE-2	554	Comverse Network Systems	MA-6	450
Cochrane Furniture	NC-10	691	Commodities	IL-10	316	ConAgra	AL-2	27
CoEnergy MidContinent	MI-13	486	Commonwealth Aluminum	KY-2	386	ConAgra	AL-5	32
Cognis	OH-1	709	Commonwealth Edison	IL-3	301	ConAgra	AR-1	62
Coherent	CA-4	81	Commonwealth Edison	IL-7	308	ConAgra	AR-3	65*
Coherent	CA-15	102	Commonwealth Edison	IL-11	318	ConAgra	AR-4	68
Cold Drink Service	TX-28	906	Commonwealth Edison	IL-17	330	ConAgra	CA-17	106
Cold Spring Granite	MN-6	506*	Commonwealth Maintenance			ConAgra	CA-19	108
Cold Spring Harbor Laboratory	NY-3	621	Systems	MA-7	452	ConAgra	CA-20	110
Coldwater Creek	ID-1	290*	Commonwealth Service Sales	MI-14	487	ConAgra	CA-40	145
Coldwater Creek	WV-1	980	CommScope	NC-10	691*	ConAgra	CA-48	157
Coldwell Banker	CA-42	148	Communications and Power			ConAgra	CO-4	178
Cole Vision	OH-14	734	Industries	CA-14	100	ConAgra	DE-AL	203
Coleman	KS-4	379	Communications Data Services	IA-3	363	ConAgra	FL-11	228
Coleman and Associates	MD-7	433	Communications Data Services	IA-5	368	ConAgra	GA-7	270
Colgate-Palmolive	KS-3	377	Communications Test Design	PA-7	784	ConAgra	GA-9	273
Colgate-Palmolive	NJ-6	587	Com-Net Critical			ConAgra	GA-10	274*
Colgate-Palmolive	NY-14	640	Communications	PA-14	797	ConAgra	GA-12	278
Collette Travel Service	SC-2	820	Compaq Computer	CA-13	97	ConAgra	IA-5	367
Collins and Aikman	MI-7	475	Compaq Computer	CA-14	100	ConAgra	IL-6	307
Collins and Aikman	NC-1	675	Compaq Computer	CA-15	102	ConAgra	KS-1	373
Collins and Aikman	NC-8	688	Compaq Computer	GA-6	268	ConAgra	KY-1	384
Collins and Aikman	NC-11	693	Compaq Computer	MA-5	448*	ConAgra	LA-4	404
Collins and Aikman	NC-13	697	Compaq Computer	NE-2	554	ConAgra	LA-5	406
Collins and Aikman	NH-1	570	Compaq Computer	NH-2	571	ConAgra	MN-3	499
Collins and Aikman	TN-2	839	Compaq Computer	TX-8	873	ConAgra	MO-4	532
Collins Building Services	NY-14	641	Compaq Computer	TX-10	876	ConAgra	MO-5	535
Collins Products	OR-2	760	Compaq Federal	MD-5	429	ConAgra	MO-6	536
Collins Signs	AL-2	27	Compass Bank Credit			ConAgra	MO-7	538
Colonial Bank	AL-2	27	Card Services	TX-3	864	ConAgra	MO-9	542
Colonial Gardens	CO-1	173	Compass Facility Management	IA-4	365	ConAgra	NC-7	686
Colonial Life and Accident			Compass Group	CA-30	127	ConAgra	NE-1	552
Insurance	SC-2	820	Compass Group	IL-6	306	ConAgra	NE-2	553
Colonial Mechanical	VA-7	947	Compass Group	LA-6	408	ConAgra	NE-3	556
Colonial Williamsburg			Compass Group	MO-1	527	ConAgra	PA-10	789*
Foundation	VA-1	935	Compass Group	NC-12	695	ConAgra	TN-1	838
Colorado Belle	NV-3	565	Compass Group	NY-1	617	ConAgra	TN-3	841
Colorado Interstate Production	CO-5	180	Compass Group	NY-3	621	ConAgra	TX-13	881
Colorado Leasing Systems	CO-2	175	Compass Group	WA-8	973	Concessions International	GA-5	266
Colorado Rockies Baseball Club	CO-1	172	Compeq International	UT-1	920	Concord Financial Group	OH-12	730
Colt's Manufacturing	CT-1	191	ComPro	PA-14	797	Concord Insurance Services	TX-8	873
Columbia Energy Group	WV-2	982	CompuCom Systems	TN-5	844	Concord Telephone	NC-8	688
Columbia Falls Aluminum	MT-AL	547	CompuCom Systems	TX-32	915	Concrete Forming	GA-5	266
Columbia Forest Products	OR-1	758	Compus Logistics	CO-1	172	Concurrent Technologies	PA-12	793
Columbia Gas	OH-15	736	CompUSA	TX-32	914	Concurrent Technologies	SC-2	819
Columbia House	CO-3	177	Computer Aid	DE-AL	204	Concurrent Technologies	WA-6	969
Columbia House	IN-8	353	Computer Associates	NY-2	618*	Cone Mills	NC-10	691
Columbia Pictures Industries	CA-29	125	Computer Associates	VA-10	953	Cone Mills	NC-12	695
Columbia Properties Ozark	MO-4	532	Computer Camp	TX-22	897	Cone Mills	NC-13	697
Columbia Sportswear	OR-1	758	Computer Curriculum	CA-14	100	Cone Mills	SC-5	824
Columbus Fair Auto Auction	OH-15	736	Computer Curriculum	NY-23	658	Conestoga Wood Specialties	PA-16	800
Columbus Internet Foundry	GA-11	276	Computer Media and Services	TX-32	914	Conexant Systems	CA-48	157
Comark	IL-6	306	Computer Network Technology	IL-19	334	Conexant Systems	TX-16	886
Combat Support Associates	CA-40	144	Computer Network Technology	MN-3	500	Confish	MS-2	517
Combined Communications	VA-8	949	Computer Programs and			Congoleum	LA-1	399
Combined Insurance	IL-7	309	Systems	AL-1	25	ConMed	NY-24	660
Combined Insurance	PA-8	785	Computer Sciences	AL-5	32	Connecticut General	CT-1	191
Combined Life Insurance	NY-21	654	Computer Sciences	CA-37	139	Connecticut Light and Power	CT-1	192
Combined Management	ME-2	416	Computer Sciences	CA-40	144	Connecticut Light and Power	CT-2	193
Comdata Network	TN-7	848	Computer Sciences	CA-52	164	Connoisseur Communications	CT-4	197
Comdial	FL-13	230	Computer Sciences	CT-2	193	Conoco	LA-7	409
Comdial Business			Computer Sciences	MD-2	423	Conoco	OK-3	750
Communications	VA-5	943	Computer Sciences	NJ-3	581	Conoco	TX-7	870
Comdisco	IL-9	314	Computer Sciences	OH-12	731	Conopco	CT-2	193
Comerica Bank	MI-9	479	Computer Sciences	TX-9	875	Conopco	CT-4	197
Comerica Bank	MI-11	482	Computer Sciences	TX-12	880	Conopco	IN-1	339
Comforce	NY-2	618	Computer Sciences	TX-21	895	Conopco	MD-2	424
Comfort Inn of Lee's Summit	MO-5	533	Computer Sciences	TX-32	915	Conopco	MO-1	527
Command Security	CA-35	136	Computer Sciences	VA-2	938	Conopco	MO-4	532

Business	State-District	Page
Dreamworks	CA-29	125
Dreco	TX-25	902
Dresser	CT-3	195
Dresser	MD-1	421
Dresser	TX-10	877
Dresser	WI-5	997
Dresser-Rand	NY-29	668*
Drexel Heritage Furnishings	NC-11	693
Dreyfus	NY-14	641
Dreyfus Service	NY-4	623
Dril-Quip	TX-18	890
Drive Automotive Industries of America	SC-4	823
Drivers Management	NE-1	551
Drummond	AL-6	34
Dry Storage	IL-7	310
DSM Pharmaceuticals	NC-1	675
DST Systems	CA-4	81
DST Systems	MO-5	534*
DT Industries	OH-3	713
DTE Energy	MI-13	485
DTR Industries	OH-4	715
Du Pont Pharmaceutical	NJ-2	579
Dual Holding	TX-30	910
Duck Head Apparel	GA-9	273
Duckrey Enterprises II	NJ-3	581
Duferco Farrell	PA-4	778
Dukane	IL-14	324
Duke Capital	NC-12	695
Duke Energy	NC-9	689
Duke Energy	NC-12	695
Duke Energy	SC-3	821
Duke Energy	SC-5	824
Duke Energy	TX-7	870
Duluth Missabe and Iron Range Railway	MN-8	510*
Duluth Missabe and Iron Range Railway	PA-18	804
Dun and Bradstreet	PA-15	798
Duncan Aviation	MI-6	473
Duncan Aviation	MI-7	475
Duncan Aviation	NE-1	552
Dundee Citrus Growers Assn.	FL-12	230
Dundee Mills	GA-13	279
Dunkin' Donuts	MA-9	458
Dunn Industries	MO-5	534
Dupont Dow Elastomers	LA-5	406
Dupont Sabanci	TN-3	841
Duquesne Light	PA-14	796
Dura Automotive Systems	MO-9	542*
Dura Operating	FL-4	215
Dura Operating	TN-4	843
Durand Glass Manufacturing	NJ-2	579
Durango Apparel Manufacturing	TN-8	850
Durango-Georgia Paper	GA-1	257
Duron	MD-5	429
Durst Organization	NY-14	642
Dutch Housing	IN-3	343
DXP Enterprises	TX-2	861
Dyersburg Fabric	TN-8	850
Dynagear	IL-13	322
Dynamic Cooking Systems	CA-46	154
Dynamic Details	CA-15	102
Dynamic Details	CA-40	145
Dynamic Details	TX-32	915
Dynamic Gunver Technologies	CT-1	191
Dynamic Systems	TX-10	877
DynCorp	CA-25	118
DynCorp	CO-1	173
DynCorp	MD-5	429
DynCorp	TN-7	848
DynCorp	TX-12	880
DynCorp	VA-8	948*
DynCorp	VA-10	953
Dynegy	TX-18	890
Dyneon	AL-5	32

Business	State-District	Page
Dynetics	AL-5	32
DynMcDermott Petroleum Operations	LA-1	399

E

Business	State-District	Page
E & J Gallo Winery	CA-18	107
E Entertainment Television	CA-30	127
E Trade Group	CA-14	100
E Trade Group	GA-6	268
E Z Paintr	WI-4	995
E. C. Aviation Services	MI-2	466
E. I. Du Pont De Nemours	DE-AL	203*
E. I. Du Pont De Nemours	LA-3	403
E. I. Du Pont De Nemours	MI-9	479
E. I. Du Pont De Nemours	MI-12	484
E. I. Du Pont De Nemours	MS-4	521
E. I. Du Pont De Nemours	NC-1	675
E. I. Du Pont De Nemours	NC-7	686
E. I. Du Pont De Nemours	NJ-6	587
E. I. Du Pont De Nemours	NY-27	665
E. I. Du Pont De Nemours	NY-28	667*
E. I. Du Pont De Nemours	OH-7	721
E. I. Du Pont De Nemours	PA-10	789
E. I. Du Pont De Nemours	SC-5	824*
E. I. Du Pont De Nemours	TN-5	844
E. I. Du Pont De Nemours	TN-8	850*
E. I. Du Pont De Nemours	TX-9	874
E. I. Du Pont De Nemours	TX-14	883
E. I. Du Pont De Nemours	TX-22	897
E. I. Du Pont De Nemours	VA-3	940
E. I. Du Pont De Nemours	VA-4	941
E. I. Du Pont De Nemours	VA-6	945
E. I. Du Pont De Nemours	VA-9	951
E. I. Du Pont De Nemours	WV-1	980
E. I. Du Pont De Nemours	WV-2	982
E. W. Scripps	TN-2	839
E.piphany	CA-12	96
Eagan McAllister Associates	MD-5	429
Eagle Alliance	MD-3	425
Eagle Bend Manufacturing	TN-3	841
Eagle Comtronics	NY-25	662
Eagle Industries	KY-2	386
Eagle Ottawa Rochester Hills	MI-9	479
Eagle Ridge Lease	IL-16	328
Eagle Window and Door	IA-1	360
Eagle-Picher Technologies	MO-7	538
Earl L. Henderson Trucking	IL-19	334
Earlybird Delivery Systems	NY-14	642
Earnhardt's Gilbert Dodge	AZ-6	54
EarthLink	CA-4	81
EarthLink	CA-29	124
EarthLink	GA-5	266
EarthLink	VA-8	949
Eassist Global Solutions	CA-50	161
East Jordan Iron Works	MI-1	465
East Ohio Gas	OH-11	729
East Penn Manufacturing	PA-17	802
Eastbay	KS-1	373
Eastbay	WI-7	1001
Eastern Band of Cherokee Indians	NC-11	693
Eastern Bank	MA-6	450
Eastern Omni Constructors	NC-12	696
Eastman Chemical	AR-1	62
Eastman Chemical	IL-14	324
Eastman Chemical	SC-2	820
Eastman Chemical	TN-1	837
Eastman Kodak	IL-9	314
Eastman Kodak	MN-4	501
Eastman Kodak	NY-28	666
Easton Sports	CA-27	122
Eaton	AR-2	64
Eaton	FL-13	230
Eaton	IA-5	367
Eaton	IL-18	332
Eaton	KS-1	373
Eaton	MI-6	473

Business	State-District	Page
Eaton	MI-7	474*
Eaton	MI-9	479
Eaton	MI-15	489
Eaton	MN-3	499*
Eaton	MS-2	517
Eaton	NC-10	691
Eaton	NE-3	556
Eaton	OH-5	717
Eaton	OH-11	729
Eaton	OH-14	734
Eaton	PA-4	778
Eaton	TN-6	846
Eaton	TX-16	886
Eaton	WI-4	995
Eaton	WI-5	997
EBSCO Industries	AL-6	34
EC	OR-1	758
Echo	IL-8	312
EchoStar Communications	CO-6	181
EchoStar Communications	WV-3	984
Eckerd	FL-10	226
Eckerd	GA-5	266
Eckerd	GA-8	272
Ecolab	LA-6	407
Ecolab	MN-2	496
Ecolab	MN-4	501
Ecolab	ND-AL	702
E-Commerce Support Centers	NC-3	678
Economy Fire and Casualty	IL-16	328
Ed Fund	CA-3	79
ED&F Man	IL-7	310
Eddie Bauer	WA-8	973
Edelman Public Relations	IL-7	310
Edgewater Hotel	NV-3	565
Edison	CA-30	126
Edison Capital Housing Management	CA-48	157
Edison Chouest Offshore	LA-3	402
Edison Housing South Carolina	CA-48	158
Edix	CA-53	165
EDS Personal Communications	MA-7	452
Edsal Manufacturing	IL-4	303
Educational Testing Service	NJ-12	599
Edward D. Jones & Co.	MO-2	529
Edward D. Jones & Co.	TX-14	883
Edwin Knowles China	IL-9	314
EFCO	MO-7	538
EFS National Bank	TN-9	851
E-Funds	AZ-5	53
E-Funds	MN-4	501
E-Funds	WI-1	989
EG&G	OH-3	713
EG&G	UT-1	920
EGL Eagle Global Logistics	TX-29	908
El Conquistador Hotel Associates	AZ-8	57
El Dorado Resorts	NV-2	563
El Paso Electric	TX-16	886
El Paso Natural Gas	TX-18	890*
ELAMEX Logistics	TX-16	886
Elastic of America	AL-6	34
ELDEC	WA-1	962
Elder-Beerman Stores	OH-3	713*
Eldorado Stone	CA-50	161
Electric Boat	CT-2	193
Electric Machinery Enterprises	FL-11	228
Electric Power Research Institute	CA-14	100
Electrolux Home Products	AL-4	30
Electrolux Home Products	AR-4	68*
Electrolux Home Products	MI-4	470
Electrolux Home Products	MN-6	506
Electrolux Home Products	NC-3	678
Electrolux Home Products	NJ-6	587
Electrolux Home Products	SC-3	821
Electrolux Home Products	SC-6	826*
Electrolux Home Products	TN-6	846

Business	State-District	Page	Business	State-District	Page	Business	State-District	Page
Gold Kist	SC-6	826	Graybar Electric	MO-3	530	GTS Carrier Services	VA-8	949
Gold River Operating	NV-3	565	Grayhill	IL-3	302	GTSI	FL-13	230
Gold Toe Brands	NC-6	684	GRC International	VA-11	955	GTSI	VA-1	935
Golden American Life Insurance	PA-6	782	Great American Insurance	OH-2	711	Guarantee Electrical		
Golden Eagle Insurance	CA-53	165	Great Atlantic and Pacific Tea	NJ-5	584	Construction	MO-3	530
Golden Road Motor Inn	NV-2	563	Great Atlantic and Pacific Tea	NY-20	652	Guaranty Bank	TX-21	895*
Golden Rod Broilers	AL-4	31	Great Dane	GA-12	278	Guard Management	CA-52	164
Golden Rule Farms	MO-6	536	Great Dane	IN-8	353	Guardian Assets	PA-7	783
Golden Rule Insurance	IN-7	351	Great Dane	MS-2	517	Guardian Automotive Products	MI-9	479
Golden West Financial	CA-9	91	Great Hawaiian	HI-1	285	Guardian Industries	MI-15	489
Goldendale Aluminum	OR-2	760	Great Hawaiian	IL-7	309	Guardian Industries	OH-5	718
Goldendale Aluminum	WA-3	965	Great Lakes Companies	WI-2	991	Guardian Life Insurance	NY-8	629
Goldendale Aluminum	WA-4	966	Great Lakes Window	OH-5	717	Guardian Life Insurance	PA-15	798
Goldman Sachs	NY-8	629	Great Northern Paper	ME-2	416	Guardian Life Insurance	WA-5	968
Gold'n Plump Poultry	MN-6	506	Greate Bay Hotel and Casino	NJ-2	579	Guardian Protective Services	MI-3	468
Golf Host Resorts	FL-9	224	Greater Nevada Auto Auction	NV-3	565	Guardsmark	IL-6	306
Golfsmith	TX-10	876	Greater Omaha Packing	NE-2	554	Guardsmark	MO-5	534
Golub	NY-21	654	Greater Texas Finishing	TX-16	886	Guardsmark	NC-13	698
Goodman Manufacturing	TN-4	843	Great-West Life	CO-6	181	Guardsmark	OH-12	730
Goodman Manufacturing	TX-18	890	Great-West Life	NJ-6	588	Guess	CA-34	134
Goodmark Foods	NC-2	677	Grede Foundries	MI-1	465	Guidant	CA-14	100
Goodrich	AZ-5	53	Grede Foundries	WI-3	993	Guidant	CA-15	102
Goodrich	CT-5	199	Greektown Casino	MI-13	486	Guidant	CA-49	159
Goodrich	OH-8	722	Green Bay Dressed Beef	WI-8	1003	Guideone Life Insuance	IA-3	364
Goodrich	OH-11	729	Green Bus Lines	NY-6	626	Guides4me	WI-8	1003
Goodrich	OH-13	732	Green Capital Investors	GA-5	265	Guilford Mills	NC-7	686
Goodrich	VT-AL	929	Green Island Associates	NY-20	652	Guilford Mills	NC-13	697*
Goodrich	WI-2	991	Green Isle Partners	FL-17	238	Guilford Mills	NY-21	654
Goody Products	GA-11	276	Green Leaf Acquisitions	IN-1	339	Guilford Mills	PA-17	803
Goodyear Tire and Rubber	AL-4	30	Green Tokai	OH-3	713	Gulf Capital Services	GA-4	263
Goodyear Tire and Rubber	AL-5	32	Green Tree Financial	MN-4	502	Gulf Coast Travel World	FL-14	232
Goodyear Tire and Rubber	GA-11	276	Greene Tweed	PA-13	795	Gulf Greyhound Partners	TX-9	875
Goodyear Tire and Rubber	IL-14	324	Greenheck Fan	WI-7	1001	Gulf Marine Fabricators	TX-15	885
Goodyear Tire and Rubber	IL-16	328	Greenleaf Nursery	OK-2	748	Gulf Power	GA-7	270
Goodyear Tire and Rubber	KS-2	375	Greenville Technology	OH-8	722	Gulf States Paper	AL-7	36
Goodyear Tire and Rubber	NE-1	551	Greenwich Capital Markets	CT-4	197	Gulf Stream Coach	IN-3	343
Goodyear Tire and Rubber	OH-4	715	Greenwood Mills	GA-11	276	Gulfport Building	MS-4	521
Goodyear Tire and Rubber	OH-17	739*	Greenwood Mills	SC-3	821	Gulfside Casinos	MS-4	521
Goodyear Tire and Rubber	OK-4	751	Greenwood Motor Lines	OH-3	713	Gulfstream Aerospace	GA-12	278
Goodyear Tire and Rubber	TX-4	865	Greenwood Packing Plant	SC-3	821	Gulfstream Aerospace	TX-30	910
Goodyear Tire and Rubber	TX-9	875	Gregory Poole Equipment	NC-13	697	Gulfstream International		
Goody's Family Clothing	TN-2	839	Gress Foods	GA-10	274	Airlines	FL-20	243
Gordon Food Service	MI-3	468	Grey Global Group	NY-14	640	Gunderson	OR-3	762
Gordon Gaming	NV-1	561	Grey Wolf	TX-7	871	Gunlocke	NY-29	668
Gordon Trucking	WA-9	975	Greyhound Lines	NE-2	554	Guthrie North America	MA-6	450
Gorilla	AZ-6	54	Greyhound Lines	TX-30	911	Guy's Foods	MO-6	536
Gorman-Rupp	OH-4	715	Greystar	TX-7	872	Gwaltney of Smithfield	VA-4	941
Gothic Landscaping	CA-25	118	Griffey Uniforms	OH-2	711	GWI	CA-30	127
Goulds Pumps	NY-24	660	Grimes Aerospace	OH-4	715			
Goulds Pumps	PA-17	803	Grinnell Mutual Reinsurance	IA-3	364	**H**		
GPX	NV-1	561	Grocers Supply	TX-18	890			
Grace Brothers	IL-9	314	Grolier	CT-5	199	H&C Racing	SC-1	818
Graco	MN-5	504	Grosvenor Properties	FL-8	222	H&R Block	MI-13	486
Graco Children's Products	OH-16	738	Grote Industries	IN-9	355	H&S Constructors	TX-27	905
Gradall	OH-18	741	Ground Round of Minn.	MA-9	457	H. C. Beck	GA-5	267
Grafton	KS-3	377	Grove Park Inn Resort Spa	NC-11	693	H. E. Butt Grocery	TX-10	877
Graham Packaging	PA-19	807	Grove Worldwide	PA-9	787	H. E. Butt Grocery	TX-14	883
Grain Processing	IA-2	362	Grubb and Ellis	TX-3	863	H. E. Butt Grocery	TX-20	893
Grand Casinos	LA-4	404	GRUMA	CA-34	134	H. H. Brown Shoe	PA-9	787
Grand Casinos	MS-2	517	GRUMA	TX-24	900	H. J. Heinz	CA-11	94
Grand Casinos	MS-4	520	Gruner and Jahr	IL-8	312	H. J. Heinz	OH-5	717
Grand Island Liederkranz	NE-3	556	Gruner and Jahr	NY-14	642*	H. J. Heinz	OH-16	738
Grand Lux Cafe	NV-1	561	Gruner and Jahr	PA-15	799	H. J. Heinz	PA-11	791
Grand Traverse Band	MI-4	470	Gruntal Financial	NY-14	642	H. J. Heinz	PA-14	796
Grand Trunk Western Railroad	MI-7	475	GS Group	TX-14	883	H. N. Bull Information Systems	MA-5	448
Grand Victoria Casino	IL-14	323	GSC Enterprises	TX-1	860	Hach	CO-4	178
Grand Victoria Casino	IN-9	355	GSD&M	TX-10	876	Hachette Filipacchi Magazines	NY-8	630
Grandview Hotel	KY-4	390	GSF Safeway	IN-7	351	Hadco	AZ-4	51
Grange Mutual Casualty	OH-15	736	GSI Commerce	PA-7	784	Hadco	CA-15	101
Granite Broadcasting	NY-14	641	GSI Group	IL-19	334	Hadco	NY-22	656
Granite Professional Technical	SC-1	818	GST Telecom	WA-3	965	Haden MacLellan	MI-9	479
Granite Rock	CA-15	102	GTE	CT-4	197	Haemonetics	MA-9	457
Granite Rock	CA-17	106	GTE	FL-11	228	Hagadone Hospitality	ID-1	290
Granite State Credit Union	NH-2	572	GTE	MO-2	529	Hager & Sons Hinge	AL-3	29
Grant Prideco	TX-2	861	GTE	TX-17	888	Haggar	TX-12	880
Grant Thornton	IL-7	311	GTE	TX-30	910*	Haggar	TX-30	910
Graphic Arts Mutual Insurance	NY-24	659	GTE	TX-32	914	Haines Construction	OK-3	750
Graphic Controls	NY-27	665	GTECH	RI-2	813*	Halekulani Hotel	HI-1	285

Business	State-District	Page	Business	State-District	Page	Business	State-District	Page
Hilton Hotels	NV-2	563	Honeywell	NJ-9	593	Hubbard Broadcasting	MN-4	502
Hilton Hotels	OR-3	762	Honeywell	NJ-11	596	Hubbard Construction	FL-8	222
Hilton Hotels	PA-14	797	Honeywell	NM-1	607	Hubbell	CT-4	197
Hilton Hotels	TX-32	915	Honeywell	NM-2	609*	Hubbell Lighting	VA-9	951
Hilton Hotels	WA-9	975	Honeywell	OH-4	715	Hudiburg Auto Group	OK-4	751
Hines Horticulture	TX-22	897	Honeywell	OH-5	717	Hudson General	NY-7	627
Hines Interests	TX-7	871	Honeywell	OH-8	722	Hudson Group	NJ-13	602
Hines Nurseries	CA-48	158	Honeywell	TN-2	839	Hudson United Bancorp	NJ-5	585
Hitachi Automotive Products	KY-6	393	Honeywell	TX-9	874	Huen New York	NY-25	662
Hitchiner Manufacturing	NH-2	571*	Honeywell	VA-4	941*	Huffy	MO-8	540
Hitech Metal Fabrication	CA-47	155	Honeywell	WA-5	968	Hughes Electronics	CA-36	137
HMT Technology	CA-13	97	Honeywell	WA-8	973	Hughes Electronics	MD-8	435
HMT Technology	OR-4	763	Honeywell	WI-7	1001	Hughes Network Systems	MD-8	434
HNB Auto Exchange	AL-7	36	Hooker Furniture	VA-5	943	Hughes Supply	FL-8	222
HND/Hawaiian Dredging	HI-1	285	Hoosier Park	IN-6	349	Huhtamaki	NY-23	658
HNS Management	CT-1	191	Hoover	OH-16	738	Huhtamkaki	ME-1	415
Hobart	OH-8	722	Hoover Universal	GA-7	270	Huish Detergents	KY-2	386
Hobart Brothers	OH-8	722	Hoover Universal	MI-11	482	Huish Detergents	UT-1	920
Hobbico	IL-15	326	Horace Mann Educators	IL-18	331	Human Capital	MI-12	484
Hobby Lobby Stores	OK-5	753	Horace Mann Educators	WI-3	993	Human Genome Sciences	MD-8	434
Ho-Chunk Nation	WI-2	991	Horace Small Manufacturing	TN-5	845	Humana Insurance	WI-8	1003
Hoffman Enclosures	MN-6	506	Horizon Air Industries	OR-3	762	Humana Source	MD-3	425
Hoffman Mills	PA-19	807	Horizon Pharmacies	MO-6	536	Hunt International Trade	PA-1	771
Hoffmann-La Roche	NJ-8	591	Hormel Foods	MN-1	494	Hunt Overseas Oil	TX-30	910
Hofmann Laces	NY-24	660	Horry Telephone Cooperative	SC-1	818	Hunter Fan	CT-2	193
Holiday	MN-3	499	Horsemen's Quarter Horse Racing	CA-40	145	Hunter Douglas	CO-2	174
Holiday Pacific Partners	GA-4	263	Horseshoe Club Operating	NV-1	561	Hunter Douglas	MD-6	431
Holiday Statistics	NY-14	641	Horseshoe Entertainement	LA-4	404	Hunter Douglas Fashions	CA-31	128
Holland America Line	WA-7	971	Horseshoe Gaming Holding	MS-2	517	Hunter Industries	CA-50	161
Holley Performance Products	KY-2	386	Horton and Barber	DC-AL	1037	Huntington National Bank	OH-15	736
Hollinger International Publishing	IL-7	309	Horton Homes	GA-9	273	Huntsman	UT-2	922
Hollywood Casino	IL-14	323	Hospitality Enterprises	LA-2	401	Huntsman Polymers	TX-19	892*
Hollywood Casino	MS-2	517	Host International	AZ-4	51	Hurd Millwork	WI-7	1001
Hollywood Entertainment	OR-5	765	Host International	FL-11	228	Hurley of America	MA-7	452
Holmes Group	MO-4	532	Host International	FL-21	245	Huron Concrete	MI-1	465
Holmes-Hally Industries	WA-1	962	Host International	IL-6	306	Husco	WI-5	997
Holophane	OH-18	741	Host International	MA-8	455	Hussmann	CA-42	147
Holt Cargo Systems	NJ-1	578	Host International	MD-2	424	Hussmann	MO-1	526
Holtzbrinck Publishers	NY-14	642	Host International	MD-3	426	Hutchinson Technology	MN-7	507
Home Lumber	CO-6	181	Hotel Nikko	NY-14	641	Hutchinson Technology	SD-AL	832
Home Shopping Network	NY-14	640	Hotel Peabody	TN-9	851	Hutchinson Technology	WI-3	993
Home Shopping Network	VA-6	945	Houghton Mifflin	MA-8	454	Hyatt	AZ-4	51
Home Supply	KY-3	388	House of Fabrics	OH-14	734	Hyatt	AZ-5	53
HomeGold	SC-4	823	House of Raeford Farms	NC-7	686	Hyatt	CA-8	88*
Homeq Servicing	CA-5	82	House of Raeford Farms	NC-8	688	Hyatt	CA-45	152
Homer Laughlin China	WV-1	980	House of Raeford Farms	SC-4	823	Hyatt	CA-46	154
Homeside Lending	FL-4	215	House2home	CA-48	158	Hyatt	CA-53	166
Homestead	VA-6	945	Household Financial Group	CA-38	141	Hyatt	DC-AL	1037
Hometown Communications	MI-11	482	Household Financial Group	CA-50	161	Hyatt	FL-3	213
Hon Industries	GA-11	276	Household Financial Group	FL-12	230	Hyatt	FL-8	221*
Honda Manufacturing	AL-3	29	Household Financial Group	IL-6	306	Hyatt	FL-11	228
Honda Manufacturing	OH-4	715*	Household Financial Group	IL-10	316	Hyatt	HI-1	284
Honeywell	AZ-2	48*	Household Financial Group	NV-1	561	Hyatt	HI-2	286
Honeywell	AZ-3	49*	Household Financial Group	SD-AL	832	Hyatt	IL-7	309
Honeywell	AZ-4	50	Household Recovery Services	VA-2	938	Hyatt	IL-9	314
Honeywell	AZ-5	52	Housley Communications	TX-17	888	Hyatt	LA-2	401
Honeywell	AZ-8	57	Houston McLane	TX-18	890	Hyatt	MI-15	489
Honeywell	CA-15	102*	Howard Delivery Service	MI-11	482	Hyatt	MN-5	504
Honeywell	CA-36	137*	Howard Industries	MS-4	520*	Hyatt	MO-5	534
Honeywell	CO-5	180	Howard Miller Clock	MI-2	466	Hyatt	NE-2	554
Honeywell	CT-3	195	Howmedica Osteonics	NJ-5	584	Hyatt	NV-2	563*
Honeywell	FL-4	215	Howmedica Osteonics	NJ-9	593	Hyatt	NY-14	640
Honeywell	FL-10	226*	Howmet	IN-2	341	Hyatt	OH-1	709
Honeywell	FL-11	228	Howmet	NJ-11	597	Hyatt	OH-15	736
Honeywell	IL-9	314	Howmet	TX-13	882	Hyatt	PA-7	784
Honeywell	IL-16	327	Howmet	VA-3	939	Hyatt	SC-2	820
Honeywell	IN-2	341*	HPM-Stadco	CA-31	128	Hyatt	TX-20	894
Honeywell	KS-3	376*	HR Network	FL-22	247	Hyatt	TX-30	910
Honeywell	LA-3	402	HR Serve Enterprises	CA-46	154	Hyatt	VA-8	949
Honeywell	MD-3	426	HR Solutions	NJ-2	579	Hyco Holdings	GA-6	268
Honeywell	MD-5	429	HR Textron	CA-25	118	Hydro-Aire	CA-27	122
Honeywell	MN-3	499*	HSBC	NY-8	629*	Hydro-Electric Associates	NY-14	642
Honeywell	MN-5	504*	HSBC	NY-25	662	Hydrolic Research	CA-25	118
Honeywell	MO-5	534*	HSBC	NY-27	664*	Hygrade Food Products	MI-12	484
Honeywell	NC-1	675	HSBC Arena	NY-27	665	Hypercom	AZ-3	49*
Honeywell	NC-4	681	HSN	FL-10	226	Hyperion Solutions	CT-4	197
Honeywell	NC-11	693	HTH	HI-1	285	Hypermetallics	CA-51	162
						Hyponex	OH-15	735

Business	State-District	Page
Oracle	CO-6	184
Oracle	FL-15	234
Oracle	GA-6	268*
Oracle	MA-7	452
Oracle	MD-8	435
Oracle	TX-30	911
Oracle	VA-8	949
Oracle	WA-1	962
Orange and Rockland Utilities	NY-24	660
ORBCOMM Global	VA-10	953
Orbital Sciences	AZ-6	54
Orbital Sciences	MD-4	427
Orbital Sciences	VA-10	953
Oregon Electric Construction	OR-3	762
Oregon Freeze Dry	OR-4	764
Oregon Steel Mills	OR-3	762
O'Reilly Automotive	MO-7	538
O'Reilly Automotive	TX-25	902
Organon	NJ-8	591
Orgill	TN-9	852
Oriental Trading	NE-2	553
Orient-Express Hotels	LA-2	401
Orilio and Associates	CA-50	161
Orion Bus Industries Parts	NY-24	660
Orion Food Systems	SD-AL	832
Orion Refining	LA-1	399
OrionAuto	CO-6	184
Orman Grubb	CA-40	145
Ormco	CA-26	120
Ormet	OH-6	719
Orval Kent Food	IL-10	317
Orvis	VA-6	945
Osborne Construction	GA-2	259
OSC Long Distance	TX-19	892
Oshkosh Truck	WI-6	999
Osmose	NY-28	666
Osram Sylvania	KY-6	393
Osram Sylvania	MA-6	450
Osram Sylvania	NH-1	570
Osram Sylvania	NH-2	571
Osram Sylvania	PA-3	776
Osram Sylvania	PA-5	780
Osram Sylvania	PA-10	789
Osram Sylvania	RI-1	811
Osram Sylvania	TX-16	886
Ostrow	SC-5	825
O'Sullivan Industries	MO-4	532
O'Sullivan Industries	VA-5	943
Otaka	HI-1	285
Otis Elevator	CT-5	199
Outback Steakhouse	TX-10	876
Outlet Square of Atlanta	MD-7	433
Outokumpu American Brass	NY-27	665
Outrigger Hotels	HI-1	284
Overhead Door	PA-5	780
Overnite Transportation	PA-19	807
Overnite Transportation	SC-5	825
Overnite Transportation	VA-3	939
Owens Corning	GA-13	280
Owens Corning	KS-3	377
Owens Corning	NC-13	697
Owens Corning	OH-9	724
Owens Corning	SC-2	819
Owens Corning	TX-13	882
Owens-Brockway Glass Container	CA-9	91
Owens-Brockway Glass Container	CA-11	94
Owens-Brockway Glass Container	CA-34	134
Owens-Brockway Glass Container	CA-38	141
Owens-Brockway Glass Container	GA-5	266
Owens-Brockway Glass Container	IL-19	334

Business	State-District	Page
Owens-Brockway Glass Container	IN-6	349
Owens-Brockway Glass Container	OH-9	724
Owens-Brockway Glass Container	OH-18	741
Owens-Brockway Plastics Products	CA-39	143
OWT Industries	SC-3	821
Oxbow Enterprises	OK-5	753
Oxford Applied Research	NJ-10	594
Oxidental Chemical	TX-32	914
Oxnard Harvest	CA-24	116
Ozark Motor Lines	TN-9	851

P

Business	State-District	Page
P&T Products	CA-6	84
PA Acquisition	CA-15	102
Pabst Brewing	TX-20	894
PACCAR	OH-18	741
PACCAR	TN-5	844
PACCAR	TX-26	903
PACCAR	WA-8	973
PACCAR	WA-9	974
Pace Entertainment	TX-7	871
Pace Industries	AR-3	66
Pacer	NV-2	563
Pacer Global Logistics	OH-12	731
Pacesetter	CA-27	122
Pacific Aerospace and Electronics	WA-4	966
Pacific Beach	HI-1	285
Pacific Bell	CA-3	79
Pacific Bell	CA-8	88*
Pacific Bell	CA-10	92*
Pacific Bell	CA-11	94*
Pacific Bell	CA-13	98
Pacific Bell	CA-16	104*
Pacific Bell	CA-20	110
Pacific Bell	CA-21	111
Pacific Bell	CA-24	116
Pacific Bell	CA-29	125
Pacific Bell	CA-30	127
Pacific Bell	CA-31	129*
Pacific Bell	CA-32	130*
Pacific Bell	CA-34	134*
Pacific Bell	CA-40	145
Pacific Bell	CA-47	155*
Pacific Bell	CA-48	157
Pacific Bell	CA-50	161
Pacific Bell	CA-52	164
Pacific Bell	CA-53	166
Pacific Building Care	CA-48	157
Pacific Gas and Electric	CA-8	88
Pacific Gas and Electric	CA-9	90
Pacific Gas and Electric	CA-10	92
Pacific Gas and Electric	CA-12	96
Pacific Gas and Electric	CA-13	97
Pacific Gas and Electric	CA-23	114
Pacific Life Insurance	CA-48	157
Pacific Telesis Group	TX-20	893
Pacific Tomato Growers	FL-11	228
PacifiCorp	UT-2	922
Packaging Coordinators	PA-13	794
Packaging Dynamics	IL-4	303
Packaging of America	TN-7	848
Packaging of America	WI-7	1002
Packer Hughes Interconnect	CA-51	162
Packerland Packing	WI-8	1003
PacPizza	CA-11	94
Pactiv	GA-13	280
Pactiv	IL-10	316*
Pactiv	IL-18	332
Paddock Restaurant	FL-23	248
Padilla Construction	CA-40	145
Palace	NY-14	641
Palace Hotel	CA-8	89
Palace Station Hotel	NV-1	561

Business	State-District	Page
Pall	NY-5	624
Pall	NY-24	660
Pall Aeropower	FL-5	217
Palm	CA-15	102
Palm Coast Data	FL-7	220
Palm Harbor Homes	AL-4	31
Palm Harbor Homes	TX-32	914
Palm Management	DC-AL	1037
Palo Verde Nuclear Generating	AZ-7	56
PAM Transport	AR-3	66
Pamida	NE-2	554
Pampered Chef	IL-6	306
Pampered Chef	IL-18	332
Pampered Chef	LA-1	399
Pan American Airways	NH-1	570
Pan American Life Insurance	LA-2	401
Pan Global Partners	HI-2	286
Panametrics	MA-7	452
Panduit	IL-1	298
Panduit	IL-11	318
Panolam Industries	ME-2	416
Panthers BRHC	FL-22	246
Paoli	IN-9	355
Paper Converting Machine	WI-8	1003
Paper-Pak Products	NC-1	675
Papetti's Hygrade Egg Products	NJ-13	602
Par-a-Dice Gaming	IL-18	332
Paradise Point Resort	CA-53	166
Paragon Produce	FL-25	251
Paragon Water Services	FL-10	226
Parametric Technology	MA-9	456
Paramount Cards	RI-1	812
Paramount Communications	NY-14	639
Paramount Farms	CA-20	110
Paramount Pictures	CA-33	131
Parco Foods	IL-1	299
Paribas	NY-14	642
Paris Hotel Casino	NV-1	560
Park Electrochemical	AZ-5	53
Park Hyatt Beaver Creek	GA-5	266
Park Hyatt Beaver Creek	IL-7	308
Park Hyatt Beaver Creek	NY-14	640
Park Place Entertainment	LA-2	401
Park Place Entertainment	NV-1	560*
Park Place Entertainment	NV-3	565
Parkdale America	NC-9	689
Parker Drilling	LA-3	403
Parker Hannifin	CA-42	148
Parker Hannifin	CA-48	157
Parker Hannifin	IN-3	343*
Parker Hannifin	MA-7	452
Parker Hannifin	ME-1	415
Parker Hannifin	MI-6	473*
Parker Hannifin	NY-2	618
Parker Hannifin	NY-25	662
Parker Hannifin	OH-11	729
Parker Hannifin	UT-1	920
Parking Service	IL-7	310
Parks Mechanical Construction	CA-36	138
Parochial Bus System	NY-17	647
Parsec	CA-34	134
Parsons	CA-29	125*
Parsons Brinckerhoff	NY-8	631
Parsons Communications	NC-9	690
Parsons Energy and Chemicals	MA-9	458
Parsons Energy and Chemicals	TX-25	901
Parsons Infrastructure and Technology Group	CA-29	125
Parsons Infrastructure and Technology Group	DC-AL	1037
Parsons Power Group	PA-6	781
Pasco Beverage	FL-11	228
Pasco Beverage	FL-12	230
Paslode	IL-10	316
Pass and Seymour	NC-8	688
Patricia Lapine	WI-6	999
Patrick Cudahy	WI-4	995
Patrick Ruff	MI-5	471

Business	State-District	Page	Business	State-District	Page	Business	State-District	Page
Veritas Software Technology	CA-13	97	VF Imagewear	VA-5	943	Vivendi Universal	NY-14	642
Veritas Software Technology	CA-14	99*	VF Imagewear	VA-9	951	Vivendi Universal	NY-15	644
Veritas Software Technology	CA-15	101	VF Jeanswear	AL-4	30*	VNU Business Media	IL-7	310
Veritas Software Technology	CA-16	104	VF Jeanswear	AL-5	32	VNU Business Media	NY-8	630
Veritas Software Technology	CO-4	178	VF Jeanswear	MO-4	532	VoiceStream Wireless	IL-9	314
Veritas Software Technology	MN-3	499	VF Jeanswear	NC-1	675	VoiceStream Wireless	NM-1	607
Veritas Software Technology	OK-4	751	VF Jeanswear	NC-12	696	VoiceStream Wireless	WA-8	973
Veritas Software Technology	OK-5	753	VF Jeanswear	NC-13	697	Voith Paper	WI-8	1004
Verizon	CA-10	93	VF Jeanswear	OK-5	753	Volex Interconnect Systems	CA-14	100
Verizon	CA-23	114	VF Jeanswear	TX-16	886*	Volkert and Associates	NC-6	685
Verizon	CA-24	116	VF Jeanswear	VA-7	947	Vollrath	WI-6	999
Verizon	CA-25	118	VF Playwear	VA-5	943	Volume Services America	CA-8	89
Verizon	CA-32	'130	VGP	NY-8	630	Volume Services America	MN-5	504
Verizon	CA-40	145	Viacom	NY-14	640	Volume Services America	MO-5	534
Verizon	CA-46	154	Viacom	TX-32	915	Volume Services America	NY-16	645
Verizon	CA-48	157	Viasat	CA-50	161	Volume Services America	OH-11	729
Verizon	CT-4	197	Vickers	NE-2	553	Voluntary Enterprises	IN-5	347
Verizon	DC-AL	1036	Vicor	MA-5	448	Volvo Trucks	NC-12	695
Verizon	FL-5	217	Victaulic of America	PA-15	798	Volvo Trucks	VA-9	951
Verizon	FL-8	222	Victor Forstmann	GA-3	261	Von Duprin	IN-7	351
Verizon	FL-9	224	Victoria & Company	RI-1	812	Von Hoffmann	MO-3	530
Verizon	FL-10	226	Victoria Partners	NV-1	561	Von Hoffmann	MO-4	532
Verizon	FL-11	228*	Victoria's Secret Stores	NM-1	607	Vons	CA-26	119
Verizon	IL-15	325	Victoria's Secret Stores	OH-3	713	Vons	CA-38	141
Verizon	IN-3	342*	Victoria's Secret Stores	OH-12	730*	Vopak	GA-6	268
Verizon	IN-5	347	Victory Packaging	GA-13	279	Vought Aircraft Industries	GA-3	261
Verizon	KY-6	393	Video Monitoring Services	NY-8	631	Vought Aircraft Industries	TX-24	900*
Verizon	MA-3	444	Videojet Technologies	IL-6	306	VPA	CA-6	84
Verizon	MA-4	446	Viejas Casino	CA-52	163	VSE	VA-8	949
Verizon	MA-5	448	Viele Manufacturing	NY-16	645	VSS Enterprises	NV-1	561
Verizon	MA-6	450	Viking Freight	CA-38	141	VT Administrative	MA-9	457
Verizon	MA-7	452	Viking Pump	IA-1	360	VTech Innovation	NJ-11	596
Verizon	MA-9	456	Viking Pump	MI-7	474	Vulcan Construction Materials	AL-6	34
Verizon	MD-1	421	Viking Yacht	NJ-2	579	Vulcan Life Insurance	IN-5	347
Verizon	MD-3	425	Village Bake Shop	WI-3	993	Vulcan Materials	KS-4	379
Verizon	MD-4	427	Village Farms	TX-23	898	Vystar Credit Union	FL-6	218
Verizon	MD-7	432	Villager Franchise Systems	NJ-11	597			
Verizon	ME-1	415	Villages of Lake-Sumter	FL-5	216	**W**		
Verizon	MO-2	529	Villages of Lake-Sumter	FL-6	218			
Verizon	NC-4	681	Vinnell-Brown and Root	VA-10	953	W&R Insurance Agency	KS-3	377
Verizon	NH-1	570	Vinoy Investments	FL-10	226	W&A Schafer Enterprises	AZ-6	54
Verizon	NJ-11	597*	Viox Services	OH-1	709	W. B. Johnson Properties	MA-9	458
Verizon	NJ-12	600	Viracon	GA-12	278	W. F. Cinema	CA-28	123
Verizon	NJ-13	601	Viracon	MN-1	494	W. G. Yates and Sons	MS-3	519
Verizon	NY-4	623	Virco Manufacturing	AR-2	63	W. L. Sparkay O'Caine	GA-3	261
Verizon	NY-5	624	Virco Manufacturing	CA-36	138	W. S. Badcock	FL-12	230
Verizon	NY-6	626*	Virgin River Hotel and Casino	NV-2	563	W. S. Bellows Construction	TX-18	890
Verizon	NY-10	634	Virginia Electric and Power	NC-1	675	W. W. Gay Mechanical	FL-3	213
Verizon	NY-14	640*	Virginia Electric and Power	VA-3	939*	W. W. Grainger	IL-10	316
Verizon	NY-17	647*	Virginia Electric and Power	VA-7	947*	Wabash National	IN-4	345
Verizon	NY-18	649	Virginia Farm Bureau Mutual	VA-3	940	Wabash Technologies	IN-5	347
Verizon	NY-25	662	Virginia Fuels	VA-6	945	Wabtec	ID-2	292
Verizon	NY-27	665	Virginia International	TX-18	890	Wachovia Bank	NC-12	694*
Verizon	OH-12	731	Virginia International Terminals	VA-2	937	Wachovia Bank	GA-5	266
Verizon	PA-2	774	Virginia Surety	IL-7	309	Wackenhut	CA-33	132
Verizon	PA-3	776	VISA	AZ-5	53	Wackenhut	CA-40	144
Verizon	PA-14	796*	VISA	CA-12	96*	Wackenhut	FL-22	247
Verizon	TX-3	864	Vishay Siliconics	CA-15	102	Wackenhut	IL-6	306
Verizon	TX-7	871	Vishay Vitramon	VA-6	945	Wackenhut	MD-4	427
Verizon	TX-17	888	Vishay-Dale Electronics	NE-1	552	Wackenhut	MD-7	433
Verizon	TX-26	903	Vision Technologies Systems	VA-8	949	Wackenhut	MD-8	434
Verizon	TX-30	909	Vision-X	CA-33	132	Wackenhut	NC-4	681
Verizon	VA-2	938	Vista Bakery	IA-2	362	Wackenhut	NJ-12	600
Verizon	VA-8	949*	Vista International	IL-7	310	Wackenhut	TN-5	845
Verizon	VA-10	953	Vistakon Vision Products	FL-4	215	Wackenhut	TN-9	852
Verizon	VA-11	955	Visteon	IN-4	345	Wackenhut	TX-18	890
Verizon	WA-2	963	Visteon	IN-6	349	Wacker	WI-5	997
Verizon	WI-2	991	Visteon	MI-10	481	Wacker Chemical Holding	MI-7	475
Verizon	WV-2	982*	Visteon	MI-11	482	Wacker Siltronic	OR-3	762
Vermeer Manufacturing	IA-3	363	Visteon	MI-14	487*	Waddell and Reed	KS-3	377
Vernon	IA-3	364	Visteon	MI-15	489*	WaferTech	WA-3	965
Vertical Systems	MN-3	499	Visteon	OK-1	746	Wagner Equipment	CO-7	185
VerticalNet	PA-13	795	Visteon	PA-6	781	Wagner Industries	MO-6	536
Vertis	TX-30	910	Visual Services	MI-9	479	Wahl Clipper	IL-17	330
Vertis Direct Marketing	NJ-12	600	Vita Quest	NJ-11	597	Wakefern Food	NJ-12	600
Vetcor Professional Practices	MA-10	459	Vital Processing Services	AZ-5	53	Wakefern Food	NY-19	650
Veterans Life Insurance	PA-6	782	Vitamin World	NJ-8	591	Walbro Engine Management	AZ-8	57
VF Imagewear	FL-11	228	Vivendi Universal	CA-35	136	Waldorf Astoria Hotel	NY-14	640

Cable System Index

This index lists cable television companies that appear in this book.

Franchise	State-District	Page	Franchise	State-District	Page
Cable ONE	ND-AL	702	CableVision Communications	IN-8	352
Cable ONE	NE-1	551	CableVision Communications	MD-6	430
Cable ONE	NE-3	556	CableVision Communications	MO-8	539
Cable ONE	NM-2	608	CableVision Communications	OH-6	719
Cable ONE	NM-3	610	CableVision Communications	OH-7	720
Cable ONE	OK-1	746	CableVision Communications	OH-18	741
Cable ONE	OK-2	748	CableVision Communications	PA-3	776
Cable ONE	OK-3	750	CableVision Communications	PA-5	779
Cable ONE	OK-4	751	CableVision Communications	PA-9	787
Cable ONE	OR-2	760	CableVision Communications	TN-8	849
Cable ONE	SD-AL	831	CableVision Communications	WV-1	980
Cable ONE	TN-8	849	CableVision Communications	WV-2	981
Cable ONE	TX-1	859	Callais Cablevision	LA-3	402
Cable ONE	TX-4	865	Cam-Tel Co.	AR-4	67
Cable ONE	TX-13	881	Capital Cable	IN-8	352
Cable ONE	TX-14	883	Carnegie Cable	OK-3	750
Cable ONE	TX-15	884	Carolina Cable	NC-7	686
Cable ONE	TX-19	892	Carolina Cable Partners	NC-6	684
Cable Services Inc.	ND-AL	702	Carolina Country Cable	NC-11	693
Cable South Inc.	AL-1	25	Carson Communications	KS-1	373
Cable South Inc.	LA-3	402	Carson Communications	KS-2	375
Cable South Inc.	LA-6	407	Cascade Cable	OR-3	761
Cable South Inc.	LA-7	409	Casco Cable Television Inc.	ME-1	414
Cable South Inc.	MS-1	515	Caspian Community TV	MI-1	465
Cable South Inc.	MS-3	518	Cass Cable TV	IL-18	331
Cable TV	NC-11	693	Cass Cable TV	IL-19	333
Cable TV Inc.	MS-3	518	Cass County Cable	MO-9	541
Cable TV of Belzoni	MS-2	516	Castle Cable TV	NY-23	658
Cable TV of Stanton	NE-1	551	Catalina Cable TV	CA-46	153
Cable TV Services	HI-1	284	Catawba Services	SC-5	824
Cable USA	CA-49	159	CATV Services Inc.	PA-10	789
Cable USA	CA-51	162	Cedar Vision	NE-3	556
Cable USA	CA-52	163	Celina Cable	TN-6	846
Cable USA	CO-4	178	Center Municipal Cable	CO-3	176
Cable Vu TV	GA-1	257	Central Valley Cable	CA-1	76
Cablevision	AZ-1	46	Central Valley Cable	CA-2	77
Cablevision	AZ-2	47	Central Valley Cable	CA-6	84
Cablevision	AZ-7	55	Central Valley Cable	CA-20	110
Cablevision	CT-3	195	Centrovision	TX-11	878
Cablevision	CT-4	196	Centurytel Televideo	WI-2	991
Cablevision	CT-5	199	Centurytel Televideo	WI-3	993
Cablevision	MS-2	517	Centurytel Televideo	WI-6	999
Cablevision	NJ-3	581	Centurytel Televideo	WI-8	1003
Cablevision	NJ-4	583	Cequel III	TX-2	861
Cablevision	NJ-5	584	Cequel III	TX-8	873
Cablevision	NJ-6	587	Chambers Communications	OR-2	760
Cablevision	NJ-7	589	Chaparral Cable Co.	NM-2	608
Cablevision	NJ-8	591	Charter	AL-1	25
Cablevision	NJ-9	592	Charter	AL-2	26
Cablevision	NJ-10	594	Charter	AL-3	28
Cablevision	NJ-11	596	Charter	AL-4	30
Cablevision	NJ-12	599	Charter	AL-5	32
Cablevision	NJ-13	601	Charter	AL-6	34
Cablevision	NY-1	616	Charter	AL-7	35
Cablevision	NY-2	618	Charter	AR-1	62
Cablevision	NY-3	621	Charter	AR-2	63
Cablevision	NY-4	622	Charter	AR-4	67
Cablevision	NY-5	624	Charter	CA-1	76
Cablevision	NY-7	627	Charter	CA-2	77
Cablevision	NY-8	628	Charter	CA-4	81
Cablevision	NY-9	632	Charter	CA-10	92
Cablevision	NY-10	633	Charter	CA-11	94
Cablevision	NY-11	635	Charter	CA-15	101
Cablevision	NY-12	636	Charter	CA-17	105
Cablevision	NY-13	637	Charter	CA-18	107
Cablevision	NY-16	645	Charter	CA-19	108
Cablevision	NY-17	646	Charter	CA-21	111
Cablevision	NY-18	648	Charter	CA-22	112
Cablevision	NY-19	650	Charter	CA-23	114
Cablevision	NY-20	652	Charter	CA-25	118
Cablevision	NY-22	656	Charter	CA-26	119
Cablevision	PA-10	789	Charter	CA-29	124
CableVision Communications	AR-1	62	Charter	CA-32	130
CableVision Communications	IL-15	325	Charter	CA-34	133
CableVision Communications	IL-17	329	Charter	CA-37	139
CableVision Communications	IL-18	331	Charter	CA-38	141
CableVision Communications	IL-19	333	Charter	CA-39	142
CableVision Communications	IN-6	348	Charter	CA-41	146

Franchise	State-District	Page	Franchise	State-District	Page
Charter	WA-3	964	Clearview CATV Inc.	MD-1	421
Charter	WA-4	966	Clearview Partners	PA-19	806
Charter	WA-5	968	Clearview TV Cable	VA-9	951
Charter	WA-6	969	Clearwater Cablevision	KS-4	378
Charter	WI-1	989	Clinton Cable TV	AR-2	63
Charter	WI-2	991	Clinton Cable TV	IN-8	352
Charter	WI-3	993	CLR Video	KS-2	375
Charter	WI-5	997	CMA	TX-14	883
Charter	WI-6	999	CMA	TX-15	884
Charter	WI-7	1001	CMA	TX-22	896
Charter	WI-8	1003	CMA	TX-31	912
Charter	WV-1	980	CMA Cablevision	WV-1	980
Charter	WV-2	982	CMA Cablevision	WV-2	982
Charter	WV-3	983	Coast Communications	WA-6	969
Chatmoss Cablevision	VA-5	943	Coaxial Cable TV	PA-3	776
Chautauqua Cable Inc.	NY-27	664	Collins Communications	MS-3	519
Cheney TV Cable	WA-5	968	Columbus Municipal Cable TV	KS-2	375
Cherokee Cablevision	NC-11	693	Comcast	AL-1	25
Chula Vista Cable	CA-51	162	Comcast	AL-2	26
Cim Tel	OK-3	750	Comcast	AL-3	28
Circle Bar Cable TV	TX-23	898	Comcast	AL-4	30
Citizens Cable	CA-41	146	Comcast	AL-5	32
Citizens Cable TV	GA-2	258	Comcast	AL-7	35
Citizens Utility	AZ-1	46	Comcast	AR-2	63
Citizens Utility	NM-3	610	Comcast	AZ-7	55
City Cable	AR-1	62	Comcast	AZ-8	57
City Cablevision	AL-2	26	Comcast	CA-1	76
City of Morganton	NC-10	691	Comcast	CA-2	77
City of Newberry	FL-6	218	Comcast	CA-3	79
City of Unionville Cable	MO-6	536	Comcast	CA-4	81
City TV Cable	NM-2	608	Comcast	CA-5	82
Clairborne Cablevision	LA-4	404	Comcast	CA-6	84
Clark Cablevision	NV-2	563	Comcast	CA-7	86
Clark Cablevision	NV-3	564	Comcast	CA-8	88
Classic	AR-1	62	Comcast	CA-9	90
Classic	AR-2	63	Comcast	CA-10	92
Classic	AR-3	65	Comcast	CA-11	94
Classic	AR-4	67	Comcast	CA-12	95
Classic	CO-4	178	Comcast	CA-13	97
Classic	KS-1	373	Comcast	CA-14	99
Classic	KS-2	375	Comcast	CA-15	101
Classic	KS-3	376	Comcast	CA-16	103
Classic	KS-4	378	Comcast	CA-17	105
Classic	LA-3	402	Comcast	CA-18	107
Classic	LA-4	404	Comcast	CA-19	108
Classic	LA-5	406	Comcast	CA-20	110
Classic	LA-7	409	Comcast	CA-21	111
Classic	MO-4	532	Comcast	CA-23	114
Classic	MO-6	536	Comcast	CA-24	116
Classic	MO-7	538	Comcast	CA-28	123
Classic	MO-8	539	Comcast	CA-31	128
Classic	NE-3	556	Comcast	CA-33	131
Classic	NM-2	608	Comcast	CA-34	133
Classic	OH-6	719	Comcast	CA-35	135
Classic	OH-14	734	Comcast	CA-36	137
Classic	OH-17	739	Comcast	CA-37	139
Classic	OK-2	748	Comcast	CA-38	141
Classic	OK-3	750	Comcast	CA-39	142
Classic	OK-4	751	Comcast	CA-40	144
Classic	TX-1	859	Comcast	CA-44	150
Classic	TX-2	861	Comcast	CA-45	152
Classic	TX-3	863	Comcast	CA-46	153
Classic	TX-4	865	Comcast	CA-48	157
Classic	TX-5	867	Comcast	CA-49	159
Classic	TX-8	873	Comcast	CO-1	172
Classic	TX-9	874	Comcast	CO-2	174
Classic	TX-11	878	Comcast	CO-3	176
Classic	TX-12	879	Comcast	CO-4	178
Classic	TX-13	881	Comcast	CO-6	181
Classic	TX-14	883	Comcast	CO-7	185
Classic	TX-17	888	Comcast	CT-1	190
Classic	TX-19	892	Comcast	CT-2	193
Classic	TX-21	895	Comcast	CT-3	195
Classic	TX-22	896	Comcast	CT-4	196
Classic	TX-23	898	Comcast	CT-5	199
Classic	TX-26	903	Comcast	DC-AL	1035
Classic	TX-31	912	Comcast	DE-AL	203
Clear Picture Inc.	OH-16	738	Comcast	FL-1	210

Franchise	State-District	Page
Cox	TX-2	861
Cox	TX-4	865
Cox	TX-5	867
Cox	TX-8	873
Cox	TX-10	876
Cox	TX-11	878
Cox	TX-13	881
Cox	TX-14	883
Cox	TX-17	888
Cox	TX-19	892
Cox	TX-31	912
Cox	VA-1	935
Cox	VA-2	937
Cox	VA-3	939
Cox	VA-6	944
Cox	VA-10	953
Cox	VA-11	954
Crestview Cable	OR-2	760
Crosslake Cablevision	MN-8	509
Crystal Cable TV	MI-4	470
CT&R Cable	WV-1	980
CTC Telecom CATV	WI-7	1001
Cunningham Cable	KS-1	373

D

Franchise	State-District	Page
Dakota Telecom	SD-AL	832
Data Video Systems	MN-7	507
Delta Cablevision	LA-5	406
Delta Cablevision	WA-2	963
Demopolis CATV	AL-7	35
Dickey Rural Cable	ND-AL	702
Direct Link	OR-5	765
Diverse Communications	IL-17	329
Dixie Cable Television	GA-1	257
Dixon Telephone	IA-1	359
Dodge County Cable	WI-6	999
Doylestown Cable TV	OH-16	738
Dresden Cable Inc.	TN-8	849
Ducom Inc.	PA-5	779
Durand Cable TV	WI-3	993

E

Franchise	State-District	Page
Eagle Communications	KS-1	373
Eagle Media	OK-3	750
Eagle Media	OK-4	751
Eagle West	AZ-1	46
Eagle West	AZ-3	49
Eagle West	NV-2	563
Eagles Mere/Laporte Cablevision	PA-10	789
East Arkansas Video	AR-1	62
East Cleveland Cable TV	OH-11	728
East Texas Cable	TX-4	865
Eastern Cable Corp.	KY-5	391
Eastern Connecticut Cable TV	CT-2	193
Easton Utilities	MD-1	421
Econoco Inc.	WV-2	982
Elgin TV Assn.	OR-2	760
Epic Touch	KS-1	373
Erie County Cablevision	OH-9	724
Eyecom Inc.	AK-AL	40

F

Franchise	State-District	Page
Fibervision	MT-AL	546
Fidelity Cablevision	MO-8	539
Five Star Cable	KS-1	373
Flint Cable TV	GA-3	260
Florida Cable	FL-3	213
Forsyth Municipal	GA-3	260
Frankfort Community Cable Service	KY-6	393
Frontier Cable of Wisconsin	WI-3	993
Frontier Communications	IN-4	345
FSN Cable	FL-5	216
Full Channel TV	RI-1	811

G

Franchise	State-District	Page
Galaxy	AL-1	25
Galaxy	AL-4	30
Galaxy	AL-7	35
Galaxy	CO-2	174
Galaxy	CO-3	176
Galaxy	CO-4	178
Galaxy	FL-5	216
Galaxy	FL-6	218
Galaxy	GA-9	273
Galaxy	IA-2	361
Galaxy	IA-5	367
Galaxy	IL-11	318
Galaxy	IL-12	320
Galaxy	IL-15	325
Galaxy	IL-17	329
Galaxy	IL-19	333
Galaxy	IN-1	339
Galaxy	IN-2	340
Galaxy	IN-3	342
Galaxy	IN-4	345
Galaxy	IN-5	346
Galaxy	IN-6	348
Galaxy	IN-8	352
Galaxy	IN-9	354
Galaxy	KS-1	373
Galaxy	KS-2	375
Galaxy	KS-4	378
Galaxy	KY-1	384
Galaxy	LA-1	399
Galaxy	MO-4	532
Galaxy	MO-5	533
Galaxy	MO-6	536
Galaxy	MO-9	541
Galaxy	MS-1	515
Galaxy	MS-2	517
Galaxy	MS-3	519
Galaxy	MS-4	520
Galaxy	NE-1	551
Galaxy	NE-2	553
Galaxy	NE-3	556
Galaxy	OK-3	750
Galaxy	OK-4	751
Galaxy	SC-5	824
Galaxy	SC-6	826
Galaxy	TX-5	867
Galaxy	TX-11	878
Gans	MD-1	421
Gans	MD-5	428
Gans	PA-11	790
Gans	VA-1	935
Garden Valley Telephone	MN-7	507
GBT Communications	KS-1	373
GCI Cable Inc.	AK-AL	40
G-Force	SC-2	819
G-Force	SC-3	821
G-Force	SC-6	826
Gilmer Cable TV	TX-1	859
Glenwood Telecommunications	NE-3	556
Golden West Cablevision	SD-AL	832
Great Plains Cable TV	NE-1	551
Great Plains Cable TV	NE-3	556
Green Acres TV Cable	OR-4	763
Green County Cable	IL-17	329
Green County Cable	IL-18	331
Green County Cable	IL-19	333
Green Hills Communications	MO-6	536
Guadalupe Valley Communications	TX-21	895
Gulfshores Communications	FL-2	211

H

Franchise	State-District	Page
H&B Cable Services	KS-1	373
Haefele TV Inc.	NY-22	656
Haefele TV Inc.	NY-24	659
Haefele TV Inc.	NY-29	668

Franchise	State-District	Page
Mediacom	CA-1	76
Mediacom	CA-22	112
Mediacom	CA-25	118
Mediacom	CA-49	159
Mediacom	DE-AL	203
Mediacom	FL-1	210
Mediacom	FL-2	211
Mediacom	GA-1	257
Mediacom	GA-2	258
Mediacom	GA-3	260
Mediacom	GA-8	271
Mediacom	GA-13	279
Mediacom	IA-1	359
Mediacom	IA-2	361
Mediacom	IA-3	363
Mediacom	IA-4	365
Mediacom	IA-5	367
Mediacom	IL-8	312
Mediacom	IL-11	318
Mediacom	IL-12	320
Mediacom	IL-14	323
Mediacom	IL-15	325
Mediacom	IL-16	327
Mediacom	IL-17	329
Mediacom	IL-18	331
Mediacom	IL-19	333
Mediacom	IN-1	339
Mediacom	IN-2	341
Mediacom	IN-3	342
Mediacom	IN-5	346
Mediacom	IN-6	348
Mediacom	KS-2	375
Mediacom	KS-4	378
Mediacom	KY-1	384
Mediacom	KY-2	386
Mediacom	MD-1	421
Mediacom	MI-6	473
Mediacom	MN-1	494
Mediacom	MN-2	496
Mediacom	MN-3	498
Mediacom	MN-6	505
Mediacom	MN-7	507
Mediacom	MN-8	509
Mediacom	MO-4	532
Mediacom	MO-6	536
Mediacom	MO-7	538
Mediacom	MO-8	540
Mediacom	MO-9	541
Mediacom	MS-1	515
Mediacom	MS-3	519
Mediacom	MS-4	520
Mediacom	NC-1	675
Mediacom	NC-3	678
Mediacom	NC-5	682
Mediacom	NC-11	693
Mediacom	OH-5	717
Mediacom	OK-2	748
Mediacom	SD-AL	832
Mediacom	TN-4	842
Mediacom	TN-8	849
Mediacom	WI-2	991
Mediacom	WI-3	993
Mediacom	WI-8	1003
Mediapolis Cablevision	IA-2	361
Metrocast	ME-1	414
Metrocast	NH-1	569
Metrocast	NH-2	571
Meyerhoff Cable	CA-19	108
Mid Coast Cable	TX-14	883
Mid-America Cablevision	IL-19	333
Midcontinent Cable	MN-7	507
Midcontinent Cable	ND-AL	702
Midcontinent Cable	NE-3	556
Midcontinent Cable	SD-AL	832
Mid-Hudson Cablevision	NY-20	652
Mid-Hudson Cablevision	NY-21	653
Mid-Rivers Cable TV	MT-AL	546
Mid-South Cablevision	MS-2	517

Franchise	State-District	Page
Midstate Communications	SD-AL	832
Mid-State Community TV	NE-3	556
MidTel Cable TV	NY-21	653
Mike's TV	WA-3	964
Milestone Communications	PA-3	776
Milestone Communications	PA-5	779
Milestone Communications	WV-3	983
Milford Cable TV	IA-5	367
Millennium Digital Media	ID-2	292
Millennium Digital Media	MI-3	468
Millennium Digital Media	MI-7	474
Millennium Digital Media	MI-8	476
Millennium Digital Media	OR-5	765
Millennium Digital Media	WA-2	963
Millennium Digital Media	WA-3	964
Millennium Digital Media	WA-4	966
Millennium Digital Media	WA-5	968
Millennium Digital Media	WA-6	969
Millennium Digital Media	WA-8	973
Millington CATV Inc.	TN-8	849
Modern Communications	IA-5	367
Montezuma Telephone	IA-3	363
Moosehead Enterprises	ME-2	416
Morris TV Assn.	PA-5	779
Mountain Cablevision	CA-22	112
Mountainview TV Cable	PA-5	779
MTC Cable	NY-20	652

N

Franchise	State-District	Page
National Cable	KS-2	375
National Cable	TX-2	861
National Cable	TX-6	868
National Cable	TX-14	883
National Cable	TX-17	888
National Cable	TX-19	892
Negaunee Cable TV	MI-1	465
Nelsonville TV Cable	OH-6	719
Nelsonville TV Cable	OH-18	741
Nesbe Cable	WV-3	983
Nesbe Cable TV	VA-4	941
Net Cable	WI-8	1003
New Century Communications	IA-5	367
New Hope Telephone Co-op	AL-5	32
New Knoxville Cable	OH-4	715
Nex-Tech	KS-1	373
Niagara CMTV Co-op	WI-8	1003
Nittany Media	PA-9	787
Nortex Communications	TX-4	865
North American Communications Corp.	MN-1	494
North American Communications Corp.	MN-2	496
North Country Cablevision Inc.	VT-AL	928
North Valley Cable	VT-AL	928
Northeast Iowa Telephone	IA-1	359
Northeast Louisiana Cablevision	LA-4	404
Northland	AL-4	30
Northland	AL-7	35
Northland	CA-2	77
Northland	CA-19	108
Northland	GA-3	260
Northland	GA-9	273
Northland	GA-12	277
Northland	ID-1	290
Northland	MS-2	517
Northland	MS-3	519
Northland	NC-10	691
Northland	NC-11	693
Northland	SC-3	821
Northland	SC-5	824
Northland	TX-2	861
Northland	TX-4	865
Northland	TX-5	867
Northland	TX-6	868
Northland	TX-8	873
Northland	TX-11	878
Northland	TX-14	883
Northland	TX-17	888
Northland	TX-21	895

Franchise	State-District	Page
Northland	TX-31	912
Northland	WA-1	961
Northland	WA-2	963
Northland	WA-4	966
Northland	WA-6	969
Northwest Communications	IA-4	365
Northwest Communications	MO-6	536
Northwest Community Communications	WI-7	1001
Northwest Iowa Telephone	IA-5	367
Northwoods Cable TV	MI-1	465
Norway CATV	MI-1	465
NPG Cable	CA-25	118
NPG Cable	CA-45	152
NU-View TV	NY-24	659

O

Franchise	State-District	Page
Oak Hill Cablevision	IN-5	346
Oconto Falls Cable	WI-8	1003
Ogden Telephone	IA-4	365
Omni III Cable TV	OK-2	748
Opp Cablevision	AL-2	26
Optel Cable	IL-13	321
Orwell Cable Television Co.	OH-5	717
Orwell Cable Television Co.	OH-14	734
Otel Co.	AL-4	30

P

Franchise	State-District	Page
Palmetto Cable TV	SC-5	824
Parish Communications	MI-6	473
Patriot Media	NJ-6	587
Patriot Media	NJ-7	589
Patriot Media	NJ-11	596
Patriot Media	NJ-12	599
Peoples CATV Inc.	TN-8	849
Petersburg Cable	TN-4	842
Phenix City CATV	AL-3	28
Philippi Comm.	WV-1	980
Phoenix Cable	VA-9	951
Pine Bluff Cable TV	AR-4	67
Pine Island Telephone	MN-2	496
Pine Ridge Cable TV	SD-AL	832
Pine Tree Cablevision	ME-2	416
Pine Tree Cablevision	NH-2	571
Pine Tree Cablevision	SC-2	819
Pine Tree Cablevision	SC-5	824
Pine Tree Cablevision	SC-6	826
Pinpoint Communications	NE-3	556
Pioneer Communications	KS-1	373
Pitcain Municipal Electric/TV	PA-18	804
Plantation Cablevision	GA-9	273
Plaquemines Cablevision	LA-3	402
Platte Community Cable TV	SD-AL	832
Pleasant Vision	LA-4	404
Polar Cablevision	ND-AL	702
Ponderosa Cable Systems	CA-11	94
Ponderosa Cablevision	CA-19	108
Powhatan Point Cable	OH-6	719
Prairiewave	MN-1	494
Precis Communications	NV-2	563
Precis Communications	UT-2	922
Precis Communications	UT-3	923
Premier Center	IA-5	367
Premier Communications	IA-5	367
Prescott Video	AR-4	67
Presidio TV Cable	TX-23	898
Price County Telephone	WI-7	1001

Q

Franchise	State-District	Page
Quality One Cable	OH-5	717
Quick Cable	WV-2	982
Quincy Community TV	CA-4	81

R

Franchise	State-District	Page
R&R Cable	WA-4	966
Rainbow Cable	NV-2	563
Rancho Murietta Assn.	CA-3	79
Range TV Cable	MN-8	509
Rapid Communications	VA-6	944
Rapid Communications	VA-9	951
RCN of Southeast New York	NY-19	650
Reservation Telephone Co-op	ND-AL	702
Resort TV Cable	AR-4	67
Retel TV Cable Co.	PA-10	789
RGA Cable	WA-3	964
Richards TV Cable	OH-6	719
Ripley Video Cable	MS-1	515
Riviera Utility Cable TV	AL-1	25
Rock Port Cablevision	MO-6	536
Rocky Mountain Cable	CO-2	174
Rocky Mountain Cable	CO-3	176
Ronceverte TV Corp.	WV-3	983
Ron's Cable TV	WV-3	983
Ropir Cablevision	CO-2	174
Rosebud Community Cable TV	SD-AL	832
Runestone Communications	MN-7	507
Rural Retreat Cable TV Inc.	VA-9	951
Rural Television Network	SD-AL	832

S

Franchise	State-District	Page
Salem Community Cablevision	AR-1	62
San Bruno Cable TV	CA-12	95
San Carlos Cablevision	AZ-1	46
Savage Communications	MN-8	509
Savage Communications	SD-AL	832
Scott County Telephone & Cable	VA-9	951
Selectavision of Cazadonia	NY-23	658
Semo Communications	MO-8	540
Seneca Cable TV	IL-11	318
Service Electric Cablevision	PA-6	781
Service Electric Cablevision	PA-8	785
Service Electric Cablevision	PA-10	789
Service Electric Cablevision	PA-11	790
Service Electric Cablevision	PA-15	798
Service Electric Co.	NJ-5	584
Service Electric Co.	NJ-7	589
Service Electric Co.	NJ-11	596
Service Electric Co.	NJ-12	599
Service Electric Co.	PA-10	789
Service Electric Co.	PA-11	790
Service Electric Co.	PA-17	802
Shaw Communications	FL-7	219
Shaw Communications	FL-22	246
Shaw Communications	FL-23	248
Sheffield West Side TV Assn.	PA-5	779
Shellsburg Cablevision	IA-1	359
Shellsburg Cablevision	IA-2	361
Shen Heights Cable	PA-17	802
Shenandoah Cable TV	VA-6	944
Shrewsbury Community Television	MA-3	443
Siskiyou Cablevision	CA-2	77
Sjoberg's Cable TV	MN-7	507
Sky Cablevision	AL-7	35
Sky Scan Cable	NE-3	556
Souris River Telephone Co-op	ND-AL	702
South Shore Cable	OH-9	724
Southeast Cable TV	GA-2	258
Southern Cable	NC-7	686
Southern Kansas Telephone	KS-4	378
Southern Vermont Cable Co.	VT-AL	928
Southtel	TX-12	879
Southtel	TX-17	888
Southtel Communications	MS-1	515
Southwest Cablevision	LA-5	406
Southwestern CATV	OK-4	751
Spillway Communications	LA-5	406
Splitrock Telecom Co-op	SD-AL	832
Spring City Cable TV	TN-3	840

Franchise	State-District	Page	Franchise	State-District	Page
Springville Cable	IA-2	361	Time Warner	CA-29	124
St. Joseph Cablevision	MO-6	536	Time Warner	CA-35	135
St. Joseph Cablevision	MO-9	541	Time Warner	CA-36	137
Stambaugh Cable	MI-1	465	Time Warner	CA-40	144
Star Video	NY-20	652	Time Warner	CA-41	146
Starvision	NC-2	676	Time Warner	CA-45	152
Starvision	NC-7	686	Time Warner	CA-46	153
Starwest Cable	IA-2	361	Time Warner	CA-47	155
STC Holdings Inc.	TN-1	837	Time Warner	CA-49	159
STC Holdings Inc.	TN-7	848	Time Warner	CA-50	160
Stephen Cable TV	MN-7	507	Time Warner	CA-52	163
Sully Buttes Co-op	SD-AL	832	Time Warner	CA-53	165
Sumner Cable TV	KS-4	378	Time Warner	FL-1	210
Sun Country Cable	CA-19	108	Time Warner	FL-2	211
Sunflower Cablevision	KS-2	375	Time Warner	FL-3	213
Sunflower Cablevision	KS-3	376	Time Warner	FL-4	215
SunTel Communications	AL-6	34	Time Warner	FL-6	218
SunTel Communications	CA-4	81	Time Warner	FL-7	219
SunTel Communications	GA-3	260	Time Warner	FL-14	232
SunTel Communications	GA-11	276	Time Warner	FL-16	236
Suscom	IL-12	320	Time Warner	FL-25	251
Suscom	IL-19	333	Time Warner	GA-2	258
Suscom	IN-5	346	Time Warner	HI-1	284
Suscom	IN-6	348	Time Warner	HI-2	286
Suscom	IN-9	354	Time Warner	IN-6	348
Suscom	ME-1	414	Time Warner	IN-8	352
Suscom	ME-2	416	Time Warner	KS-1	373
Suscom	MS-2	517	Time Warner	KS-2	375
Suscom	MS-3	519	Time Warner	KS-3	376
Suscom	PA-5	779	Time Warner	LA-3	402
Suscom	PA-10	789	Time Warner	LA-4	404
Suscom	PA-19	806	Time Warner	LA-5	406
Sweetwater Cable TV	WY-AL	1008	Time Warner	MA-1	440
Sylvan Valley CATV	NC-11	693	Time Warner	ME-1	414
			Time Warner	ME-2	416
			Time Warner	MI-1	465
T			Time Warner	MN-1	494
			Time Warner	MN-2	496
			Time Warner	MN-3	498
Tallulah Cable TV	LA-5	406	Time Warner	MN-5	503
Tekstar	MN-7	507	Time Warner	MO-4	532
Tekstar Cablevision	MN-8	509	Time Warner	MO-5	533
Tele-Media	CT-3	195	Time Warner	MO-6	536
Tele-Media	CT-4	196	Time Warner	MO-8	540
Tele-Media	CT-5	199	Time Warner	MS-1	515
Tele-Media	KY-1	384	Time Warner	MS-2	517
Tele-Media	KY-5	391	Time Warner	MS-3	519
Tele-Media	MD-6	430	Time Warner	NC-1	675
Tele-Media	NC-11	693	Time Warner	NC-2	676
Tele-Media	TN-3	840	Time Warner	NC-3	678
Tele-Media	TN-6	846	Time Warner	NC-4	680
Tele-Media	VA-3	939	Time Warner	NC-5	682
Tele-Media	VA-4	941	Time Warner	NC-6	684
Tele-Media	WV-3	983	Time Warner	NC-7	686
Telepartners	IA-4	365	Time Warner	NC-8	688
Telepartners	IA-5	367	Time Warner	NC-9	689
Telepartners	NE-1	551	Time Warner	NC-10	691
Telesystems West	OR-5	765	Time Warner	NC-12	694
Telnet	IA-1	359	Time Warner	NC-13	697
Telnet Communications	IA-4	365	Time Warner	NE-1	551
Telnet South	IA-3	363	Time Warner	NE-3	556
Telnet South	IA-5	367	Time Warner	NH-2	571
Terril Cable System	MN-1	494	Time Warner	NJ-9	592
Thompson Cablevision	KY-4	390	Time Warner	NM-2	608
Thompson Cablevision	OH-6	719	Time Warner	NY-5	624
Thompson Cablevision	WV-2	982	Time Warner	NY-6	625
Thompson Cablevision	WV-3	983	Time Warner	NY-7	627
Timber Lake Cablevision	TX-2	861	Time Warner	NY-8	628
Timber Lake Cablevision	TX-9	874	Time Warner	NY-9	632
Time Warner	AL-1	25	Time Warner	NY-10	633
Time Warner	AL-2	26	Time Warner	NY-11	635
Time Warner	AL-6	34	Time Warner	NY-12	636
Time Warner	AL-7	35	Time Warner	NY-13	637
Time Warner	AR-1	62	Time Warner	NY-14	639
Time Warner	CA-20	110	Time Warner	NY-15	644
Time Warner	CA-25	118	Time Warner	NY-17	646
Time Warner	CA-26	119	Time Warner	NY-19	650
Time Warner	CA-27	122	Time Warner	NY-20	652
Time Warner	CA-28	123			

City Index

Cities and other areas with populations greater than 10,000 or parts of such locations are indexed here by district and page number. Census Bureau designations of localities such as "town" or "village" or "Census Designated Place" (CDP) have been retained. In Alaska, the designation is "Census Area" or "Borough." See Sources and Explanation for information on these designations and terms. "(Pt.)" indicates that the city or other area is split between districts. Thus a locality may have two or more entries. A locality with only one "(pt.)" entry indicates that the remaining part has a population of less than 10,000 and is not listed in this book.

City	State-District	Page
Burbank (pt.)	CA-27	120
Burbank (pt.)	CA-29	124
Burien (pt.)	WA-7	970
Burien (pt.)	WA-9	974
Burkburnett	TX-13	881
Burke CDP	VA-11	954
Burleson	TX-6	868
Burlingame	CA-12	95
Burlington	IA-2	361
Burlington	VT-AL	928
Burlington (pt.)	NC-6	683
Burlington (pt.)	NC-13	696
Burlington CDP	KY-4	389
Burlington CDP	MA-6	449
Burnsville	MN-2	495
Burton	MI-5	471
Butler	PA-3	775
Butte-Silver Bow	MT-AL	545

C

City	State-District	Page
Cabot	AR-1	61
Cadillac	MI-2	465
Cahokia village	IL-12	319
Calabasas	CA-30	126
Caldwell	ID-1	290
Calexico	CA-51	161
Calhoun	GA-10	274
Callaway	FL-2	211
Calumet City	IL-2	299
Camano CDP	WA-2	962
Camarillo	CA-24	115
Camas	WA-3	964
Cambridge	MA-8	453
Cambridge	OH-18	740
Cambridge (pt.)	MD-1	420
Camden	AR-4	67
Camden	NJ-1	577
Cameron Park CDP	CA-4	80
Camp Springs CDP (pt.)	MD-4	426
Campbell	CA-15	101
Campbellsville	KY-2	385
Canandaigua	NY-29	667
Canby	OR-5	764
Candler-McAfee CDP	GA-4	261
Canon City	CO-5	179
Canton	IL-17	328
Canton	OH-16	737
Canton (pt.)	MS-2	516
Canton CDP	MI-11	481
Canyon	TX-13	881
Canyon Lake CDP	TX-21	894
Canyon Rim CDP	UT-2	921
Cape Coral	FL-14	232
Cape Girardeau	MO-8	539
Capitola	CA-17	105
Carbondale	IL-12	319
Carlisle borough	PA-19	805
Carlsbad	CA-50	160
Carlsbad	NM-2	607
Carmel	IN-5	346
Carmichael CDP	CA-3	78
Carney CDP (pt.)	MD-2	423
Carnot-Moon CDP	PA-18	803
Carol City CDP (pt.)	FL-17	236
Carol City CDP (pt.)	FL-21	244
Carol Stream village	IL-6	305
Carpentersville village	IL-14	323
Carpinteria	CA-23	113
Carrboro town	NC-4	680
Carroll	IA-5	366
Carrollton (pt.)	GA-11	275
Carrollton (pt.)	TX-26	903
Carrollton (pt.)	TX-32	913
Carson	CA-37	138
Carson City	NV-2	562
Carteret borough	NJ-13	601
Cartersville (pt.)	GA-11	275

City	State-District	Page
Carthage	MO-7	537
Cary town (pt.)	NC-4	680
Cary town (pt.)	NC-13	696
Cary village	IL-16	327
Casa de Oro-Mount Helix CDP	CA-52	163
Casa Grande	AZ-1	45
Casas Adobes CDP	AZ-8	57
Cascade-Fairwood CDP (pt.)	WA-8	972
Cascade-Fairwood CDP (pt.)	WA-9	974
Casper	WY-AL	1008
Casselberry (pt.)	FL-7	219
Casselberry (pt.)	FL-24	249
Castle Rock town	CO-6	180
Castlewood CDP	CO-6	180
Castro Valley CDP (pt.)	CA-9	90
Catalina Foothills CDP	AZ-8	57
Cathedral City	CA-45	151
Catonsville CDP	MD-7	432
Cave Spring CDP	VA-6	944
Cayce	SC-2	819
Cedar City	UT-2	921
Cedar Falls	IA-1	359
Cedar Grove CDP	NJ-8	590
Cedar Hill (pt.)	TX-24	899
Cedar Hill (pt.)	TX-30	909
Cedar Mill CDP	OR-1	757
Cedar Park (pt.)	TX-31	912
Cedar Rapids	IA-2	361
Cedarburg	WI-5	996
Celina	OH-8	721
Center Point CDP (pt.)	AL-7	35
Centereach CDP	NY-1	616
Centerville	OH-3	712
Centerville	UT-1	919
Central Falls	RI-1	811
Central Islip CDP	NY-2	617
Central Manchester CDP	CT-1	190
Central Point	OR-2	759
Centralia	IL-19	333
Centralia	WA-3	964
Centreville CDP (pt.)	VA-10	952
Centreville CDP (pt.)	VA-11	954
Ceres	CA-18	106
Cerritos	CA-39	142
Chalmette CDP	LA-3	402
Chambersburg borough	PA-9	786
Champaign	IL-15	324
Champlin	MN-3	498
Chandler (pt.)	AZ-5	52
Chandler (pt.)	AZ-6	54
Chanhassen	MN-2	495
Channelview CDP (pt.)	TX-29	907
Chantilly CDP	VA-10	952
Chapel Hill town	NC-4	680
Charleston	IL-15	324
Charleston	WV-2	981
Charleston (pt.)	SC-1	817
Charleston (pt.)	SC-6	825
Charlotte (pt.)	NC-8	687
Charlotte (pt.)	NC-9	689
Charlotte (pt.)	NC-12	694
Charlottesville	VA-5	942
Chaska	MN-2	495
Chattanooga (pt.)	TN-3	840
Cheektowaga CDP	NY-27	664
Chelsea	MA-8	453
Cherry Hill Mall CDP	NJ-3	580
Cherryland CDP (pt.)	CA-9	90
Chesapeake	VA-4	940
Chesapeake Ranch Estates-Drum Point CDP (pt.)	MD-5	428
Chester	PA-1	770
Chester CDP	VA-4	940
Chesterfield	MO-2	528
Chesterton town (pt.)	IN-1	338
Cheyenne	WY-AL	1008
Chicago (pt.)	IL-1	298
Chicago (pt.)	IL-2	299

City	State-District	Page
Chicago (pt.)	IL-3	301
Chicago (pt.)	IL-4	302
Chicago (pt.)	IL-5	303
Chicago (pt.)	IL-7	307
Chicago (pt.)	IL-9	313
Chicago Heights	IL-2	299
Chicago Ridge village	IL-3	301
Chickasha	OK-4	751
Chico	CA-2	77
Chicopee	MA-2	441
Chillicothe	OH-18	740
Chillum CDP (pt.)	MD-4	426
Chillum CDP (pt.)	MD-8	433
Chino	CA-42	147
Chino Hills	CA-42	147
Chippewa Falls	WI-7	1000
Chowchilla	CA-19	108
Christiansburg town	VA-9	950
Chula Vista	CA-51	161
Cicero town (pt.)	IL-3	301
Cicero town (pt.)	IL-4	302
Cimarron Hills CDP	CO-5	179
Cincinnati (pt.)	OH-1	708
Cincinnati (pt.)	OH-2	710
Circleville	OH-7	720
Citrus Heights	CA-3	78
Citrus Park CDP (pt.)	FL-11	227
City of The Dalles	OR-2	759
Claremont	CA-26	118
Claremont	NH-2	570
Claremore (pt.)	OK-2	747
Clark CDP	NJ-7	588
Clarksburg	WV-1	979
Clarksdale	MS-2	516
Clarksville (pt.)	TN-7	847
Clarksville (pt.)	TN-8	849
Clarksville town	IN-9	354
Clawson	MI-9	478
Clayton	CA-7	86
Clayton	OH-3	712
Clayton (pt.)	MO-3	530
Clearfield	UT-1	919
Clearlake	CA-1	75
Clearwater (pt.)	FL-9	224
Clearwater (pt.)	FL-10	225
Cleburne	TX-6	868
Clemmons village	NC-5	682
Clemson	SC-3	820
Cleveland	MS-2	516
Cleveland	TN-3	840
Cleveland (pt.)	OH-10	726
Cleveland (pt.)	OH-11	728
Cleveland (pt.)	OH-11	728
Cleveland Heights	OH-11	728
Cliffside Park borough	NJ-9	592
Clifton	NJ-8	590
Clifton CDP	CO-3	175
Clinton	IA-1	359
Clinton	MS-2	516
Clinton	UT-1	919
Clinton CDP	MD-5	428
Clinton CDP	MI-14	483
Clive (pt.)	IA-3	362
Cloquet	MN-8	508
Cloverleaf CDP	TX-29	907
Clovis	CA-21	111
Clovis	NM-3	609
Clute (pt.)	TX-14	882
Coachella	CA-45	151
Coalinga	CA-20	109
Coatesville	PA-6	780
Cockeysville CDP (pt.)	MD-2	423
Cocoa (pt.)	FL-15	233
Cocoa Beach	FL-15	233
Coconut Creek (pt.)	FL-19	241
Coconut Creek (pt.)	FL-22	246
Coeur d'Alene	ID-1	290
Coffeyville	KS-4	378
Cohoes	NY-21	653

1114 **City Index**

City	State-District	Page	City	State-District	Page	City	State-District	Page
Marshall	MO-4	531	Mercerville-Hamilton Square			Mission Viejo	CA-42	147
Marshall	TX-1	859	CDP	NJ-4	582	Missoula	MT-AL	545
Marshalltown	IA-4	365	Meriden	CT-5	198	Missouri City (pt.)	TX-22	896
Marshfield	WI-7	1000	Meridian	ID-1	290	Mitchell	SD-AL	831
Martha Lake CDP	WA-1	961	Meridian	MS-3	518	Moberly	MO-9	541
Martin	TN-8	849	Merriam	KS-3	376	Mobile	AL-1	24
Martinez	CA-7	86	Merrick CDP (pt.)	NY-3	619	Modesto (pt.)	CA-18	106
Martinez CDP	GA-9	272	Merrifield CDP	VA-11	954	Modesto (pt.)	CA-19	108
Martinsburg	WV-2	981	Merrill	WI-7	1000	Mohave Valley CDP	AZ-2	47
Martinsville	IN-4	344	Merrillville town	IN-1	338	Mokena village	IL-11	317
Martinsville	VA-5	942	Merritt Island CDP (pt.)	FL-15	233	Moline	IL-17	328
Maryland Heights (pt.)	MO-1	526	Merrydale CDP	LA-6	407	Monroe	LA-5	405
Maryland Heights (pt.)	MO-2	528	Mesa (pt.)	AZ-5	52	Monroe	MI-15	488
Marysville	CA-2	77	Mesa (pt.)	AZ-6	54	Monroe	WI-2	990
Marysville	OH-15	735	Mesquite (pt.)	TX-5	866	Monroe (pt.)	NC-8	687
Marysville	WA-2	962	Metairie CDP (pt.)	LA-1	398	Monrovia	CA-26	119
Maryville	MO-6	535	Methuen	MA-5	447	Monsey CDP	NY-17	646
Maryville	TN-2	838	Metuchen borough	NJ-6	585	Montclair	CA-26	119
Mason (pt.)	OH-3	712	Mexico	MO-9	541	Montclair CDP (pt.)	NJ-8	590
Mason City	IA-4	365	Miami	OK-2	747	Montclair CDP (pt.)	NJ-10	594
Masonboro CDP	NC-7	685	Miami (pt.)	FL-17	238	Montclair CDP (pt.)	VA-11	954
Massapequa CDP	NY-3	619	Miami (pt.)	FL-18	239	Montebello	CA-38	140
Massapequa Park village	NY-3	619	Miami (pt.)	FL-20	242	Monterey	CA-17	105
Massena village	NY-23	657	Miami Beach (pt.)	FL-18	239	Monterey Park (pt.)	CA-29	124
Massillon	OH-16	737	Miami Beach (pt.)	FL-20	242	Monterey Park (pt.)	CA-32	129
Mastic Beach CDP	NY-1	616	Miami Lakes CDP (pt.)	FL-21	244	Montgomery	OH-2	710
Mastic CDP	NY-1	616	Miami Springs (pt.)	FL-21	244	Montgomery (pt.)	AL-2	26
Matteson village (pt.)	IL-2	299	Miamisburg	OH-3	712	Montgomery (pt.)	AL-3	28
Matthews town	NC-9	689	Michigan City	IN-2	340	Montgomery Village CDP (pt.)	MD-4	426
Mattoon	IL-15	324	Middle River CDP (pt.)	MD-2	423	Montgomery Village CDP (pt.)	MD-8	433
Mauldin	SC-4	822	Middle Valley CDP	TN-3	840	Montgomeryville CDP	PA-13	793
Maumee	OH-9	723	Middleburg CDP	FL-6	217	Montrose	CO-3	175
Maumelle	AR-2	63	Middleburg Heights	OH-10	726	Moore	OK-4	751
Mayfield	KY-1	383	Middlesborough	KY-5	391	Moorestown-Lenola CDP	NJ-3	580
Mayfield Heights	OH-11	728	Middlesex borough	NJ-6	585	Mooresville town (pt.)	NC-10	690
Maynard CDP	MA-5	447	Middleton	WI-2	990	Moorhead	MN-7	507
Maywood	CA-34	132	Middletown	NY-22	655	Moorpark	CA-24	115
Maywood village (pt.)	IL-7	307	Middletown (pt.)	CT-3	194	Moraga town	CA-10	91
McAlester	OK-2	747	Middletown (pt.)	OH-8	721	Moreno Valley	CA-45	151
McAllen (pt.)	TX-15	884	Midland	TX-19	891	Morgan City	LA-3	402
McCandless Township CDP	PA-4	777	Midland (pt.)	MI-4	469	Morgan Hill	CA-11	93
McComb	MS-3	518	Midlothian village	IL-1	298	Morganton	NC-10	690
McHenry	IL-8	311	Midvale	UT-2	921	Morgantown	WV-1	979
McKeesport	PA-14	795	Midwest City (pt.)	OK-4	751	Morris	IL-11	317
McKinleyville CDP	CA-1	75	Milford	CT-3	194	Morristown	TN-1	836
McKinney (pt.)	TX-3	863	Milford CDP	MA-2	441	Morristown town	NJ-11	595
McKinney (pt.)	TX-26	903	Milford Mill CDP (pt.)	MD-7	432	Morrisville borough	PA-8	785
McLean CDP (pt.)	VA-10	952	Mililani Town CDP	HI-1	283	Morro Bay	CA-23	113
McMinnville	OR-1	757	Mill Creek	WA-1	961	Morton Grove village	IL-9	313
McMinnville	TN-4	842	Mill Valley	CA-6	83	Morton village	IL-18	331
McPherson	KS-1	372	Millbrae	CA-12	95	Moscow	ID-1	290
Meadow Woods CDP	FL-8	221	Millbrook	AL-2	26	Moses Lake	WA-4	965
Meadville	PA-3	775	Millburn CDP (pt.)	NJ-10	594	Moss Bluff CDP	LA-7	408
Mechanicsville CDP	VA-7	946	Millcreek CDP	UT-2	921	Moss Point	MS-4	520
Medford	MA-7	451	Milledgeville	GA-3	260	Moultrie (pt.)	GA-1	256
Medford	OR-2	759	Miller Place CDP	NY-1	616	Mounds View	MN-4	500
Medford CDP	NY-1	616	Millington (pt.)	TN-8	849	Mount Clemens	MI-12	483
Medina	OH-16	737	Millville	NJ-2	578	Mount Juliet	TN-5	843
Mehlville CDP (pt.)	MO-3	530	Milpitas	CA-15	101	Mount Lebanon CDP	PA-18	803
Melbourne	FL-15	233	Milton CDP	MA-9	456	Mount Pleasant	MI-4	469
Melrose	MA-7	451	Milwaukee (pt.)	WI-4	994	Mount Pleasant	TX-1	859
Melrose Park village (pt.)	IL-5	303	Milwaukie	OR-3	761	Mount Pleasant town	SC-1	817
Melville CDP	NY-2	617	Minden	LA-4	403	Mount Prospect village (pt.)	IL-6	305
Melvindale	MI-14	487	Mineola village	NY-4	622	Mount Prospect village (pt.)	IL-10	315
Memphis (pt.)	TN-7	847	Mineral Wells (pt.)	TX-17	887	Mount Vernon	IL-19	333
Memphis (pt.)	TN-8	849	Minneapolis	MN-5	503	Mount Vernon	NY-17	646
Memphis (pt.)	TN-9	850	Minnetonka	MN-3	498	Mount Vernon	OH-18	740
Menasha (pt.)	WI-6	998	Minot	ND-AL	702	Mount Vernon	WA-2	962
Mendota Heights	MN-4	500	Mint Hill town	NC-9	689	Mount Vernon CDP (pt.)	VA-8	948
Menlo Park	CA-14	98	Mira Loma CDP	CA-44	150	Mount Vernon CDP (pt.)	VA-11	954
Menomonee Falls village	WI-5	996	Miramar (pt.)	FL-17	238	Mountain Brook	AL-6	33
Menomonie	WI-3	992	Miramar (pt.)	FL-21	244	Mountain Home	AR-1	61
Mentor	OH-14	733	Miramar (pt.)	FL-23	247	Mountain Home	ID-2	291
Mequon	WI-5	996	Mishawaka	IN-2	340	Mountain Top CDP	PA-11	790
Meraux CDP	LA-3	402	Mission (pt.)	TX-15	884	Mountain View	CA-14	98
Merced	CA-18	106	Mission (pt.)	TX-28	906	Mountlake Terrace	WA-1	961
Mercedes	TX-15	884	Mission Bend CDP (pt.)	TX-7	870	Mukilteo (pt.)	WA-1	961
Mercer Island	WA-8	972	Mission Bend CDP (pt.)	TX-22	896	Muncie	IN-6	348

City	State-District	Page	City	State-District	Page	City	State-District	Page
Oceanside CDP (pt.)	NY-4	622	Oxon Hill-Glassmanor CDP	MD-4	426	Pecan Grove CDP	TX-22	896
Ocoee (pt.)	FL-8	221	Ozark	AL-2	26	Pedley CDP	CA-44	150
Oconomowoc	WI-5	996				Peekskill	NY-19	649
Odenton CDP (pt.)	MD-3	424	**P**			Pekin	IL-18	331
Odessa	TX-19	891				Pelham	AL-6	33
O'Fallon	IL-12	319	Pacific Grove	CA-17	105	Pembroke Pines (pt.)	FL-17	238
O'Fallon (pt.)	MO-2	528	Pacifica	CA-12	95	Pembroke Pines (pt.)	FL-20	242
Ogden	UT-1	919	Paducah	KY-1	383	Pembroke Pines (pt.)	FL-21	244
Ogdensburg	NY-23	657	Pahrump CDP	NV-2	562	Pembroke Pines (pt.)	FL-23	247
Oil City	PA-5	779	Paine Field-Lake Stickney			Pendleton	OR-2	759
Oildale CDP	CA-22	112	CDP (pt.)	WA-1	961	Penn Hills CDP (pt.)	PA-14	795
Ojus CDP	FL-17	238	Painesville	OH-14	733	Penn Hills CDP (pt.)	PA-18	803
Okemos CDP	MI-8	475	Palatine village (pt.)	IL-8	311	Pennsauken CDP	NJ-1	577
Oklahoma City (pt.)	OK-3	749	Palatine village (pt.)	IL-10	315	Pennsville CDP	NJ-2	578
Oklahoma City (pt.)	OK-4	751	Palestine	TX-5	866	Pensacola	FL-1	209
Oklahoma City (pt.)	OK-5	752	Palisades Park borough	NJ-9	592	Peoria	AZ-2	47
Okmulgee	OK-2	747	Palm Bay	FL-15	233	Peoria	IL-18	331
Okolona CDP (pt.)	KY-3	387	Palm Beach Gardens (pt.)	FL-22	246	Perris	CA-49	158
Olathe	KS-3	376	Palm Beach town	FL-22	246	Perry Hall CDP (pt.)	MD-1	420
Old Bridge CDP (pt.)	NJ-12	598	Palm City CDP	FL-16	235	Perry Hall CDP (pt.)	MD-2	423
Oldsmar	FL-9	224	Palm Coast	FL-7	219	Perrysburg	OH-5	716
Olean	NY-29	667	Palm Desert	CA-45	151	Perth Amboy	NJ-13	601
Olive Branch	MS-1	514	Palm Harbor CDP (pt.)	FL-9	224	Peru	IN-5	346
Olivehurst CDP	CA-2	77	Palm Harbor CDP (pt.)	FL-10	225	Petaluma	CA-6	83
Olney CDP	MD-4	426	Palm River-Clair Mel CDP	FL-11	227	Petersburg	VA-4	940
Olympia (pt.)	WA-3	964	Palm Springs	CA-45	151	Pewaukee	WI-5	996
Olympia Heights CDP (pt.)	FL-21	244	Palm Valley CDP	FL-7	219	Pflugerville (pt.)	TX-10	875
Omaha	NE-2	552	Palmdale	CA-25	117	Pharr	TX-15	884
Onalaska	WI-3	992	Palo Alto	CA-14	98	Phenix City	AL-3	28
Oneida	NY-23	657	Palos Hills	IL-3	301	Philadelphia (pt.)	PA-1	770
Oneonta	NY-24	659	Palos Verdes Estates	CA-46	153	Philadelphia (pt.)	PA-2	772
Ontario	CA-43	148	Pampa	TX-13	881	Philadelphia (pt.)	PA-8	785
Ontario	OR-2	759	Panama City	FL-2	211	Philadelphia (pt.)	PA-13	793
Opa-locka (pt.)	FL-17	238	Panthersville CDP	GA-4	261	Phillipsburg town	NJ-5	583
Opelika	AL-3	28	Papillion	NE-2	552	Phoenix (pt.)	AZ-2	47
Opelousas	LA-7	408	Paradise CDP (pt.)	NV-1	560	Phoenix (pt.)	AZ-3	48
Opportunity CDP	WA-5	967	Paradise CDP (pt.)	NV-3	564	Phoenix (pt.)	AZ-4	50
Oquirrh CDP	UT-3	923	Paradise town	CA-2	77	Phoenix (pt.)	AZ-5	52
Orange	CA-40	143	Paradise Valley town	AZ-3	48	Phoenix (pt.)	AZ-7	55
Orange	TX-2	860	Paragould	AR-1	61	Phoenixville borough	PA-6	780
Orange CDP	CT-3	194	Paramount	CA-39	142	Picayune	MS-4	520
Orange CDP	NJ-10	594	Paramus borough	NJ-5	583	Picnic Point-North Lynnwood		
Orangeburg (pt.)	SC-6	825	Paris	TX-1	859	CDP	WA-1	961
Orangevale CDP	CA-4	80	Park Forest village	IL-2	299	Pico Rivera	CA-38	140
Orchards CDP	WA-3	964	Park Ridge	IL-9	313	Piedmont	CA-9	90
Orcutt CDP	CA-24	115	Parker CDP	SC-4	822	Pierre	SD-AL	831
Oregon (pt.)	OH-9	723	Parker town	CO-6	181	Pike Creek CDP	DE-AL	202
Oregon City (pt.)	OR-5	764	Parkersburg	WV-1	979	Pikesville CDP (pt.)	MD-3	424
Orem	UT-3	923	Parkland (pt.)	FL-22	246	Pine Bluff	AR-4	67
Orinda	CA-10	91	Parkland CDP (pt.)	WA-6	969	Pine Hill borough	NJ-1	577
Orland Park village (pt.)	IL-1	298	Parkville CDP (pt.)	MD-2	423	Pine Hills CDP	FL-3	212
Orland Park village (pt.)	IL-13	321	Parkville CDP (pt.)	MD-3	424	Pinecrest village (pt.)	FL-18	239
Orlando (pt.)	FL-3	212	Parkway-South Sacramento CDP	CA-5	81	Pinellas Park	FL-10	225
Orlando (pt.)	FL-8	221	Parlier	CA-20	109	Pineville	LA-5	405
Ormond Beach	FL-7	219	Parma	OH-10	726	Pinewood CDP	FL-17	238
Oro Valley town	AZ-8	57	Parma Heights	OH-10	726	Piney Green CDP	NC-3	677
Oroville	CA-4	80	Parole CDP (pt.)	MD-3	424	Pinole	CA-7	86
Oshkosh (pt.)	WI-6	998	Parsons	KS-2	374	Piqua	OH-8	721
Oskaloosa	IA-3	363	Pasadena	CA-29	124	Pittsburg	CA-7	86
Ossining village	NY-18	647	Pasadena (pt.)	TX-22	896	Pittsburg	KS-2	374
Oswego	NY-23	657	Pasadena (pt.)	TX-25	901	Pittsburgh	PA-14	795
Oswego village	IL-14	323	Pasadena (pt.)	TX-29	907	Pittsfield	MA-1	439
Ottawa	IL-11	317	Pascagoula	MS-4	520	Placentia (pt.)	CA-40	143
Ottawa	KS-2	374	Pasco	WA-4	965	Plainfield	NJ-6	585
Ottumwa	IA-2	361	Passaic	NJ-8	590	Plainfield town	IN-4	344
Overland	MO-1	526	Pataskala	OH-12	730	Plainfield village (pt.)	IL-13	321
Overland Park	KS-3	376	Patchogue village	NY-1	616	Plainview	TX-13	881
Overlea CDP (pt.)	MD-3	424	Paterson	NJ-8	590	Plainview CDP (pt.)	NY-2	617
Oviedo	FL-24	249	Patterson	CA-18	106	Plano (pt.)	TX-3	863
Owasso (pt.)	OK-1	745	Pawtucket	RI-1	811	Plant City (pt.)	FL-9	224
Owatonna	MN-1	493	Payson	UT-3	923	Plantation (pt.)	FL-20	242
Owensboro	KY-2	385	Payson town	AZ-1	45	Plattsburgh	NY-23	657
Owings Mills CDP (pt.)	MD-3	424	Peabody	MA-6	449	Pleasant Grove	UT-3	923
Owosso	MI-4	469	Peachtree City	GA-8	271	Pleasant Hill	CA-10	91
Oxford	AL-3	28	Pearl	MS-3	518	Pleasant Prairie village	WI-1	988
Oxford	MS-1	514	Pearl City CDP	HI-1	283	Pleasanton (pt.)	CA-11	93
Oxford	OH-8	721	Pearl River CDP	NY-17	646	Pleasantville	NJ-2	578
Oxnard	CA-23	113	Pearland (pt.)	TX-22	896	Pleasure Ridge Park CDP	KY-3	387

City	State-District	Page
Tooele	UT-1	919
Topeka	KS-2	374
Torrance	CA-36	136
Torrington (pt.)	CT-1	190
Torrington (pt.)	CT-5	198
Town and Country (pt.)	MO-2	528
Town 'n' Country CDP	FL-11	227
Towson CDP (pt.)	MD-2	423
Towson CDP (pt.)	MD-3	425
Tracy	CA-11	93
Traverse City (pt.)	MI-4	469
Trenton (pt.)	MI-14	487
Trenton (pt.)	NJ-4	582
Trenton (pt.)	NJ-12	598
Trotwood	OH-3	712
Troutdale	OR-3	761
Troy	AL-2	26
Troy	MI-9	478
Troy	NY-21	653
Troy	OH-8	721
Truckee town	CA-4	80
Trumbull CDP	CT-4	196
Trussville (pt.)	AL-6	33
Tualatin (pt.)	OR-1	757
Tuckahoe CDP	VA-7	946
Tucker CDP	GA-4	261
Tucson (pt.)	AZ-7	55
Tucson (pt.)	AZ-8	57
Tukwila (pt.)	WA-9	974
Tulare	CA-21	111
Tullahoma	TN-4	842
Tulsa (pt.)	OK-1	745
Tumwater	WA-3	964
Tupelo	MS-1	514
Turlock	CA-19	108
Tuscaloosa (pt.)	AL-7	35
Tuskegee	AL-3	28
Tustin	CA-48	156
Tustin Foothills CDP	CA-48	156
Twentynine Palms	CA-41	145
Twin Falls	ID-2	291
Twinsburg	OH-14	733
Two Rivers	WI-6	998
Tyler	TX-4	865
Tysons Corner CDP (pt.)	VA-8	948

U

City	State-District	Page
Ukiah	CA-1	75
Union CDP (pt.)	NJ-7	588
Union CDP (pt.)	NJ-10	594
Union City	CA-13	97
Union City	GA-13	279
Union City	NJ-13	601
Union City	TN-8	849
Union Hill-Novelty Hill CDP (pt.)	WA-8	972
Uniondale CDP	NY-4	622
Uniontown	PA-12	792
University CDP	FL-11	227
University City (pt.)	MO-1	526
University City (pt.)	MO-3	530
University Heights	OH-11	728
University Park	TX-32	913
University Park CDP	FL-21	244
University Place	WA-6	969
Upland	CA-26	119
Upper Arlington	OH-15	735
Upper Grand Lagoon CDP	FL-2	211
Upper Providence Township CDP	PA-7	783
Upper St. Clair CDP	PA-18	803
Urbana	IL-15	324
Urbana	OH-4	714
Urbandale (pt.)	IA-3	363
Utica	NY-24	659
Uvalde	TX-23	898

V

City	State-District	Page
Vacaville	CA-7	86
Vadnais Heights	MN-4	500
Valdosta (pt.)	GA-1	256
Valdosta (pt.)	GA-2	258
Valinda CDP (pt.)	CA-38	140
Valle Vista CDP	CA-41	145
Vallejo	CA-7	86
Valley Falls CDP	RI-1	811
Valley Station CDP	KY-3	387
Valley Stream village	NY-4	622
Valparaiso (pt.)	IN-1	338
Van Buren	AR-3	65
Van Wert	OH-5	716
Vancouver	WA-3	964
Vandalia (pt.)	OH-3	712
Vashon CDP	WA-7	970
Venice	FL-13	230
Ventnor City	NJ-2	578
Vermilion	OH-9	723
Vernon	TX-13	881
Vernon Hills village (pt.)	IL-10	315
Vero Beach	FL-15	233
Vero Beach South CDP	FL-15	233
Verona CDP	NJ-8	590
Vestavia Hills	AL-6	33
Vicksburg	MS-2	516
Victoria	TX-14	882
Victorville	CA-25	117
Vidalia	GA-3	260
Vidor	TX-2	860
Vienna	WV-1	979
Vienna town	VA-11	954
View Park-Windsor Hills CDP	CA-33	131
Villa Park village	IL-6	305
Villas CDP	FL-14	232
Vincennes	IN-8	352
Vincent CDP	CA-32	129
Vineland	NJ-2	578
Vineyard CDP	CA-3	78
Virginia Beach	VA-2	937
Visalia	CA-21	111
Vista	CA-49	158

W

City	State-District	Page
Wabash	IN-5	346
Waco	TX-11	877
Wade Hampton CDP	SC-4	822
Wadsworth	OH-16	737
Wahiawa CDP	HI-2	285
Waianae CDP	HI-2	285
Wailuku CDP	HI-2	285
Waimalu CDP	HI-1	283
Waipahu CDP	HI-1	283
Waipio CDP	HI-1	283
Wake Forest town	NC-13	696
Wakefield CDP	MA-6	449
Waldorf CDP	MD-5	428
Walker	MI-3	467
Walker Mill CDP	MD-4	426
Walla Walla	WA-5	967
Wallingford Center CDP	CT-3	194
Wallington borough	NJ-9	592
Walnut	CA-26	119
Walnut Creek	CA-10	91
Walnut Park CDP	CA-34	132
Waltham	MA-7	451
Wanaque borough	NJ-5	584
Wantagh CDP	NY-3	619
Warner Robins (pt.)	GA-3	260
Warren	MI-12	483
Warren	OH-17	739
Warren	PA-3	775
Warrensburg	MO-4	531
Warrensville Heights	OH-11	728

City	State-District	Page
Warrington CDP	FL-1	209
Warsaw	IN-3	342
Warwick	RI-2	812
Wasco	CA-20	109
Washington	DC-AL	1035
Washington	IL-18	331
Washington	IN-8	352
Washington	MO-9	541
Washington	OH-7	720
Washington	PA-12	792
Watauga	TX-12	879
Waterbury (pt.)	CT-3	194
Waterbury (pt.)	CT-5	198
Waterford CDP (pt.)	MI-9	478
Waterloo	IA-1	359
Watertown	MA-7	451
Watertown	NY-23	657
Watertown	SD-AL	831
Watertown	WI-6	998
Waterville	ME-1	414
Watervliet	NY-21	653
Watsonville	CA-17	105
Waukegan (pt.)	IL-10	315
Waukesha	WI-5	996
Waupun	WI-6	998
Wausau	WI-7	1000
Wauwatosa	WI-5	996
Waverly CDP	MI-7	474
Waxahachie	TX-6	868
Waycross	GA-1	256
Wayne	MI-11	481
Wayne CDP	NJ-8	590
Waynesboro	VA-6	944
Weatherford	TX-12	879
Webster CDP	MA-2	441
Webster Groves	MO-3	530
Weigelstown CDP	PA-19	805
Weirton	WV-1	979
Wekiwa Springs CDP	FL-7	219
Welby CDP (pt.)	CO-2	174
Wellesley CDP	MA-4	444
Wellington village (pt.)	FL-16	235
Wells Branch CDP	TX-10	875
Wenatchee	WA-4	965
Weslaco	TX-15	884
West Allis (pt.)	WI-4	994
West Allis (pt.)	WI-5	996
West and East Lealman CDP	FL-10	225
West Babylon CDP (pt.)	NY-2	617
West Babylon CDP (pt.)	NY-3	619
West Bend	WI-5	996
West Bloomfield Township CDP	MI-9	478
West Caldwell CDP	NJ-11	595
West Carrollton City	OH-3	712
West Carson CDP (pt.)	CA-36	136
West Chester borough	PA-16	800
West Chicago (pt.)	IL-14	323
West Columbia	SC-2	819
West Covina	CA-32	129
West Des Moines (pt.)	IA-3	363
West Fargo	ND-AL	702
West Freehold CDP	NJ-4	582
West Hartford CDP	CT-1	190
West Haven	CT-3	194
West Hempstead CDP	NY-4	622
West Hollywood	CA-30	126
West Islip CDP (pt.)	NY-3	619
West Jordan	UT-3	923
West Lafayette	IN-4	344
West Lake Stevens CDP	WA-2	962
West Linn	OR-5	764
West Little River CDP (pt.)	FL-17	238
West Memphis	AR-1	61
West Mifflin borough	PA-14	795
West Milford CDP	NJ-5	584
West Monroe	LA-5	405
West New York town	NJ-13	601
West Norriton CDP	PA-7	783

County Index

All counties are indexed here by district and page number. "(Pt.)" indicates counties that are split between districts. Thus a county may have two or more entries. For Alaska, which has no counties, the major political divisions of boroughs and census areas are listed. For Louisiana, parishes (the political equivalents of counties) are listed. A few states, including Maryland, Missouri, Nevada, and Virginia, have cities that are independent of counties. These "independent cities" are considered county equivalents and are listed with the word "city" following the city name.

County	State-District	Page
Beaver	UT-3	923
Beaverhead	MT-AL	545
Becker	MN-7	506
Beckham	OK-3	749
Bedford	PA-9	786
Bedford	TN-6	845
Bedford (pt.)	VA-5	942
Bedford (pt.)	VA-6	944
Bedford city	VA-5	942
Bee	TX-15	884
Belknap (pt.)	NH-1	568
Belknap (pt.)	NH-2	570
Bell	KY-5	391
Bell	TX-11	877
Belmont (pt.)	OH-6	718
Belmont (pt.)	OH-18	740
Beltrami (pt.)	MN-7	506
Beltrami (pt.)	MN-8	508
Ben Hill	GA-1	256
Benewah	ID-1	290
Bennett	SD-AL	830
Bennington	VT-AL	928
Benson	ND-AL	701
Bent	CO-4	177
Benton	AR-3	65
Benton	IA-3	362
Benton	IN-1	338
Benton	MN-6	505
Benton	MO-4	531
Benton	MS-1	514
Benton	TN-8	849
Benton	WA-4	965
Benton (pt.)	OR-4	763
Benton (pt.)	OR-5	764
Benzie (pt.)	MI-2	465
Bergen (pt.)	NJ-5	583
Bergen (pt.)	NJ-9	592
Berkeley	WV-2	981
Berkeley (pt.)	SC-1	817
Berkeley (pt.)	SC-6	825
Berks (pt.)	PA-6	780
Berks (pt.)	PA-16	799
Berks (pt.)	PA-17	801
Berkshire	MA-1	439
Bernalillo (pt.)	NM-1	606
Bernalillo (pt.)	NM-2	607
Bernalillo (pt.)	NM-3	609
Berrien	GA-1	256
Berrien (pt.)	MI-6	472
Bertie	NC-1	674
Bethel Census Area	AK-AL	39
Bexar (pt.)	TX-20	893
Bexar (pt.)	TX-21	894
Bexar (pt.)	TX-23	897
Bexar (pt.)	TX-28	906
Bibb	AL-6	33
Bibb (pt.)	GA-3	259
Bibb (pt.)	GA-8	271
Bienville Parish	LA-4	403
Big Horn	MT-AL	545
Big Horn	WY-AL	1007
Big Stone	MN-7	506
Billings	ND-AL	701
Bingham	ID-2	291
Black Hawk	IA-1	359
Blackford	IN-6	348
Bladen	NC-7	685
Blaine	ID-2	291
Blaine	MT-AL	545
Blaine	NE-3	554
Blaine	OK-3	749
Blair	PA-9	786
Blanco	TX-21	894
Bland	VA-9	950
Bleckley	GA-3	259
Bledsoe	TN-4	842
Blount	AL-4	30
Blount	TN-2	838
Blue Earth	MN-1	493
Boise	ID-1	290
Bolivar	MS-2	516
Bollinger	MO-8	539
Bon Homme	SD-AL	830
Bond	IL-19	332
Bonner	ID-1	290
Bonneville	ID-2	291
Boone	AR-3	65
Boone	IA-4	365
Boone	IL-16	327
Boone	IN-4	344
Boone	KY-4	389
Boone	MO-9	540
Boone	NE-3	554
Boone	WV-3	983
Borden	TX-17	887
Bosque	TX-11	877
Bossier Parish	LA-4	403
Botetourt	VA-6	944
Bottineau	ND-AL	701
Boulder (pt.)	CO-2	174
Boulder (pt.)	CO-4	177
Boundary	ID-1	290
Bourbon	KS-2	374
Bourbon	KY-6	392
Bowie	TX-1	859
Bowman	ND-AL	701
Box Butte	NE-3	554
Box Elder	UT-1	919
Boyd	KY-4	389
Boyd	NE-3	554
Boyle	KY-6	392
Bracken	KY-4	389
Bradford	FL-6	217
Bradford	PA-10	788
Bradley	AR-4	67
Bradley	TN-3	840
Branch	MI-7	474
Brantley	GA-1	256
Braxton	WV-2	981
Brazoria (pt.)	TX-14	882
Brazoria (pt.)	TX-22	896
Brazos	TX-31	911
Breathitt	KY-5	391
Breckinridge	KY-2	385
Bremer	IA-1	359
Brevard (pt.)	FL-15	233
Brevard (pt.)	FL-24	249
Brewster	TX-23	897
Briscoe	TX-13	881
Bristol	RI-1	811
Bristol (pt.)	MA-3	443
Bristol (pt.)	MA-4	444
Bristol (pt.)	MA-9	455
Bristol Bay Borough	AK-AL	39
Bristol city	VA-9	950
Broadwater	MT-AL	545
Bronx (pt.)	NY-7	626
Bronx (pt.)	NY-15	643
Bronx (pt.)	NY-16	644
Bronx (pt.)	NY-17	646
Brooke	WV-1	979
Brookings	SD-AL	830
Brooks	GA-2	258
Brooks	TX-15	884
Broome (pt.)	NY-22	655
Broome (pt.)	NY-24	659
Broward (pt.)	FL-17	236
Broward (pt.)	FL-19	241
Broward (pt.)	FL-20	242
Broward (pt.)	FL-21	244
Broward (pt.)	FL-22	246
Broward (pt.)	FL-23	247
Brown	IL-18	330
Brown	IN-9	354
Brown	KS-2	374
Brown	MN-1	493
Brown	NE-3	554
Brown	OH-2	710
Brown	SD-AL	830
Brown	TX-17	887
Brown (pt.)	WI-8	1002
Brule	SD-AL	830
Brunswick	NC-7	685
Brunswick (pt.)	VA-4	940
Brunswick (pt.)	VA-5	942
Bryan	OK-2	747
Bryan (pt.)	GA-1	256
Bryan (pt.)	GA-12	277
Buchanan	IA-1	359
Buchanan	MO-6	535
Buchanan	VA-9	950
Buckingham	VA-5	942
Bucks	PA-8	785
Buena Vista	IA-5	366
Buena Vista city	VA-6	944
Buffalo	NE-3	554
Buffalo	SD-AL	830
Buffalo	WI-3	992
Bullitt	KY-2	385
Bulloch	GA-12	277
Bullock	AL-2	26
Buncombe	NC-11	692
Bureau (pt.)	IL-11	317
Bureau (pt.)	IL-14	323
Bureau (pt.)	IL-18	330
Burke	GA-12	277
Burke	NC-10	690
Burke	ND-AL	701
Burleigh	ND-AL	701
Burleson	TX-31	911
Burlington (pt.)	NJ-1	577
Burlington (pt.)	NJ-2	578
Burlington (pt.)	NJ-3	580
Burlington (pt.)	NJ-4	582
Burnet	TX-21	894
Burnett	WI-7	1000
Burt	NE-1	551
Butler	AL-2	26
Butler	IA-1	359
Butler	KS-4	378
Butler	KY-1	383
Butler	MO-8	539
Butler	NE-1	551
Butler (pt.)	OH-1	708
Butler (pt.)	OH-8	721
Butler (pt.)	PA-3	775
Butler (pt.)	PA-4	777
Butte	ID-2	291
Butte	SD-AL	830
Butte (pt.)	CA-2	77
Butte (pt.)	CA-4	80
Butts (pt.)	GA-8	271
Butts (pt.)	GA-13	279

C

County	State-District	Page
Cabarrus (pt.)	NC-8	687
Cabarrus (pt.)	NC-12	694
Cabell	WV-3	983
Cache	UT-1	919
Caddo	OK-3	749
Caddo Parish	LA-4	403
Calaveras	CA-3	78
Calcasieu Parish	LA-7	408
Caldwell	KY-1	383
Caldwell	MO-6	535
Caldwell	NC-10	690
Caldwell	TX-14	882
Caldwell Parish	LA-5	405
Caledonia	VT-AL	928
Calhoun	AL-3	28
Calhoun	AR-4	67
Calhoun	FL-2	211
Calhoun	GA-2	258

County	State-District	Page	County	State-District	Page	County	State-District	Page
Pierce	ND-AL	701	Portsmouth city	VA-3	938	Ralls	MO-9	540
Pierce	NE-3	555	Posey	IN-8	352	Ramsey	ND-AL	701
Pierce	WI-3	992	Pottawatomie	KS-2	374	Ramsey (pt.)	MN-4	500
Pierce (pt.)	WA-6	969	Pottawatomie	OK-5	752	Ramsey (pt.)	MN-5	502
Pierce (pt.)	WA-8	972	Pottawattamie	IA-5	366	Randall	TX-13	881
Pierce (pt.)	WA-9	974	Potter	PA-5	779	Randolph	AL-3	28
Pike	AL-2	26	Potter	SD-AL	831	Randolph	AR-1	61
Pike	AR-4	67	Potter	TX-13	881	Randolph	GA-2	258
Pike	GA-8	271	Powder River	MT-AL	545	Randolph	IL-12	319
Pike	IN-8	352	Powell	KY-6	392	Randolph	IN-6	348
Pike	KY-5	391	Powell	MT-AL	545	Randolph	MO-9	540
Pike	MO-9	540	Power	ID-2	291	Randolph	NC-6	683
Pike	MS-3	518	Poweshiek	IA-3	362	Randolph	WV-2	981
Pike	OH-2	710	Powhatan	VA-4	940	Rankin	MS-3	518
Pike	PA-10	788	Prairie	AR-1	61	Ransom	ND-AL	701
Pike (pt.)	IL-17	328	Prairie	MT-AL	545	Rapides Parish	LA-5	405
Pike (pt.)	IL-18	331	Pratt	KS-1	372	Rappahannock	VA-7	946
Pima (pt.)	AZ-7	55	Preble	OH-8	721	Ravalli	MT-AL	545
Pima (pt.)	AZ-8	57	Prentiss	MS-1	514	Rawlins	KS-1	372
Pinal (pt.)	AZ-1	45	Presidio	TX-23	897	Ray	MO-4	531
Pinal (pt.)	AZ-6	54	Presque Isle (pt.)	MI-1	464	Reagan	TX-23	897
Pinal (pt.)	AZ-7	55	Preston	WV-1	979	Real	TX-23	897
Pinal (pt.)	AZ-8	57	Price	WI-7	1000	Red Lake	MN-7	506
Pine	MN-8	508	Prince Edward	VA-5	942	Red River	TX-1	859
Pinellas (pt.)	FL-9	224	Prince George (pt.)	VA-3	938	Red River Parish	LA-4	403
Pinellas (pt.)	FL-10	225	Prince George (pt.)	VA-4	940	Red Willow	NE-3	555
Pinellas (pt.)	FL-11	227	Prince George's (pt.)	MD-4	426	Redwood	MN-7	506
Pipestone	MN-1	493	Prince George's (pt.)	MD-5	428	Reeves	TX-23	897
Piscataquis	ME-2	415	Prince George's (pt.)	MD-8	433	Refugio	TX-14	882
Pitkin	CO-3	175	Prince of Wales-Outer			Reno	KS-1	372
Pitt (pt.)	NC-1	674	Ketchikan Census Area	AK-AL	39	Rensselaer (pt.)	NY-20	651
Pitt (pt.)	NC-3	677	Prince William (pt.)	VA-1	934	Rensselaer (pt.)	NY-21	653
Pittsburg	OK-2	747	Prince William (pt.)	VA-10	952	Renville	MN-7	506
Pittsylvania	VA-5	942	Prince William (pt.)	VA-11	954	Renville	ND-AL	701
Piute	UT-2	921	Providence (pt.)	RI-1	811	Republic	KS-1	372
Placer	CA-4	80	Providence (pt.)	RI-2	812	Reynolds	MO-8	539
Plaquemines Parish	LA-3	402	Prowers	CO-4	177	Rhea	TN-3	840
Platte	MO-6	535	Pueblo	CO-3	175	Rice	KS-1	372
Platte	NE-3	555	Pulaski	AR-2	63	Rice	MN-2	495
Platte	WY-AL	1007	Pulaski	IL-12	319	Rich	UT-1	919
Pleasants	WV-1	979	Pulaski	IN-2	340	Richardson	NE-1	551
Plumas	CA-4	80	Pulaski	KY-5	391	Richland	IL-19	332
Plymouth	IA-5	366	Pulaski	MO-4	531	Richland	MT-AL	545
Plymouth (pt.)	MA-4	444	Pulaski	VA-9	950	Richland	ND-AL	701
Plymouth (pt.)	MA-9	455	Pulaski (pt.)	GA-1	256	Richland	OH-4	714
Plymouth (pt.)	MA-10	458	Pulaski (pt.)	GA-3	260	Richland	WI-3	992
Pocahontas	IA-4	365	Pushmataha	OK-2	747	Richland (pt.)	SC-2	819
Pocahontas	WV-3	983	Putnam	GA-9	272	Richland (pt.)	SC-6	825
Poinsett	AR-1	61	Putnam	IL-18	331	Richland Parish	LA-5	405
Pointe Coupee Parish (pt.)	LA-5	405	Putnam	IN-8	352	Richmond	NC-8	687
Pointe Coupee Parish (pt.)	LA-6	407	Putnam	MO-6	535	Richmond	NY-13	637
Polk	AR-4	67	Putnam	NY-19	649	Richmond	VA-1	934
Polk	GA-11	275	Putnam	OH-5	716	Richmond (pt.)	GA-9	272
Polk	IA-3	362	Putnam	TN-6	845	Richmond (pt.)	GA-12	277
Polk	MN-7	506	Putnam	WV-2	981	Richmond city (pt.)	VA-3	938
Polk	NC-11	692	Putnam (pt.)	FL-3	212	Richmond city (pt.)	VA-7	946
Polk	NE-3	555	Putnam (pt.)	FL-7	219	Riley	KS-2	374
Polk	OR-5	764				Ringgold	IA-5	366
Polk	TN-3	840	**Q**			Rio Arriba	NM-3	609
Polk	TX-2	860				Rio Blanco	CO-3	175
Polk	WI-7	1000	Quay	NM-3	609	Rio Grande	CO-3	175
Polk (pt.)	FL-5	216	Queen Anne's (pt.)	MD-1	420	Ripley	IN-9	354
Polk (pt.)	FL-12	229	Queens (pt.)	NY-5	624	Ripley	MO-8	539
Polk (pt.)	FL-15	233	Queens (pt.)	NY-6	625	Ritchie	WV-1	979
Polk (pt.)	MO-4	531	Queens (pt.)	NY-7	626	Riverside (pt.)	CA-41	145
Polk (pt.)	MO-7	537	Queens (pt.)	NY-9	632	Riverside (pt.)	CA-44	150
Pondera	MT-AL	545	Queens (pt.)	NY-12	636	Riverside (pt.)	CA-45	151
Pontotoc	MS-1	514	Queens (pt.)	NY-14	638	Riverside (pt.)	CA-49	158
Pontotoc	OK-4	750	Quitman	GA-2	258	Roane	WV-2	981
Pope	AR-3	65	Quitman	MS-2	516	Roane (pt.)	TN-3	840
Pope	IL-19	332				Roane (pt.)	TN-4	842
Pope	MN-7	506	**R**			Roanoke (pt.)	VA-6	944
Poquoson city	VA-1	934				Roanoke (pt.)	VA-9	950
Portage	WI-7	1000	Rabun	GA-9	272	Roanoke city	VA-6	944
Portage (pt.)	OH-14	733	Racine (pt.)	WI-1	988	Roberts	SD-AL	831
Portage (pt.)	OH-17	739	Radford city	VA-9	950	Roberts	TX-13	881
Porter (pt.)	IN-1	338	Rains	TX-4	865	Robertson	KY-4	389
Porter (pt.)	IN-2	340	Raleigh	WV-3	983	Robertson	TN-6	845

Military Installation Index

All major U.S. military installations (as of September 2001) are indexed by district and page number.

Installation	State-District	Page
U		
U.S. Adelphi Laboratory Center, Adelphi	MD-5	428
U.S. Naval Academy, Annapolis	MD-1	421
Umatilla Chemical Depot, Hermiston	OR-2	760
United States Air Force Academy, Colorado Springs	CO-5	179
V		
Vance Air Force Base, Enid	OK-3	750
Vancouver Barracks (Army Reserve), Vancouver	WA-3	964
Vandenberg Air Force Base, Lompoc	CA-22	112
Vietnam Veterans Memorial U.S. Army Reserve Center, Homewood	IL-2	300
Volk Field (Air National Guard), Camp Douglas	WI-3	993
Volunteer Army Ammunition Plant, Chattanooga	TN-3	840
W		
W. Silver Spring Complex (Army Reserve), Milwaukee	WI-4	995
W. K. Kellogg Airport (Air National Guard), Battle Creek	MI-6	473
Walter Reed Army Medical Center, Washington	DC-AL	1035
Watervliet Arsenal, Watervliet	NY-21	653
Weapons Support Facility, Earle	NJ-4	583

Installation	State-District	Page
Weapons Support Facility, Yorktown	VA-1	935
West Point Military Reservation, New York	NY-19	650
Westover Air Reserve Base, Chicopee	MA-2	441
Westover Armed Forces Reserve Center, Chicopee	MA-2	441
Wheeler Army Airfield, Wahiawa	HI-1	284
Whidbey Island Naval Air Station, Oak Harbor	WA-2	963
White Sands Missile Range, Las Cruces	NM-2	608
Whiteman Air Force Base, Knob Noster	MO-4	532
Whiting Field Naval Air Station, Milton	FL-1	210
Will Rogers World Airport Air National Guard Station, Oklahoma City	OK-4	751
Willow Grove Air Rescue Service (Air Force), Hatboro	PA-8	785
Willow Grove Naval Air Station, Willow Grove	PA-13	794
Winter Harbor Naval Security Group Activity, Winter Harbor	ME-2	416
Worcester U.S. Army Reserve Center, Norristown	PA-6	781
Wright-Patterson Air Force Base, Fairborn	OH-7	720
Y		
Yakima Training Center (Army), Yakima	WA-4	966
Yeager Airport Air Force Guard Station, Charleston	WV-2	982
Youngstown-Warren Regional Airport Air Reserve Station, Vienna	OH-17	739
Yuma Marine Corps Air Station, Yuma	AZ-7	55
Yuma Proving Ground (Army), Yuma	AZ-7	55

University and College Index

Universities and colleges are indexed here by the first word in their name. For example, the University of Wisconsin will be found under the U's; John Marshall Law School will be found under the J's.

School	State-District	Page

A

School	State-District	Page
Abilene Christian University, Abilene	TX-17	887
Abraham Baldwin Agricultural College, Tifton	GA-2	258
Academy Education Center, Minneapolis	MN-3	498
Academy of Art College, San Francisco	CA-8	87
Academy of Medical Arts and Business, Harrisburg	PA-17	801
Academy of Medical Careers, Las Vegas	NV-1	560
Adams State College, Alamosa	CO-3	176
Adelphi University, Garden City	NY-4	622
Adirondack Community College, Queensbury	NY-20	651
Adler School of Professional Psychology, Chicago	IL-7	307
Adrian College, Adrian	MI-7	474
Advertising Arts College, San Diego	CA-50	160
Agnes Scott College, Atlanta	GA-4	263
Aiken Technical College, Aiken	SC-3	820
Aims Community College, Greeley	CO-4	177
Air Force Institute of Technology, Wright-Patterson AFB	OH-7	720
Al Collins Graphic Design School, Tempe	AZ-5	52
Alabama A&M University, Normal	AL-5	31
Alabama Southern Community College, Monroeville	AL-1	24
Alabama State University, Montgomery	AL-3	28
Alamance Community College, Graham	NC-13	696
Alaska Pacific University, Anchorage	AK-AL	40
Albany College of Pharmacy, Albany	NY-21	653
Albany Law School, Albany	NY-21	653
Albany Medical College, Albany	NY-21	653
Albany State University, Albany	GA-2	258
Albany Technical Institute, Albany	GA-2	258
Albertson College of Idaho, Caldwell	ID-1	290
Albertus Magnus College, New Haven	CT-3	194
Albion College, Albion	MI-7	474
Albright College, Reading	PA-6	781
Albuquerque Technical Vocational Institute, Albuquerque	NM-1	606
Alcorn State University, Alcorn State	MS-2	516
Alderson-Broaddus College, Philippi	WV-1	979
Alexandria Technical College, Alexandria	MN-7	507
Alfred University, Alfred	NY-29	668
Alice Lloyd College, Pippa Passes	KY-5	391
Allan Hancock College, Santa Maria	CA-23	114
Allegany College of Maryland, Cumberland	MD-6	430
Allegheny College, Meadville	PA-3	775
Allegheny University of the Health Sciences, Philadelphia	PA-2	772
Allen College, Waterloo	IA-1	359
Allen County Community College, Iola	KS-2	374
Allen University, Columbia	SC-6	826
Allentown Business School, Allentown	PA-15	798
Alma College, Alma	MI-4	469
Alpena Community College, Alpena	MI-1	464
Altamaha Technical Institute, Jesup	GA-1	256
Alvernia College, Reading	PA-6	781
Alverno College, Milwaukee	WI-4	994
Alvin Community College, Alvin	TX-22	896
Amarillo College, Amarillo	TX-13	881
Amber University, Garland	TX-3	863
American Academy of Art, Chicago	IL-7	307
American Academy of Dramatic Arts-West, Pasadena	CA-29	124
American Bible College and Seminary, Bethany	OK-5	752
American Business Academy, Hackensack	NJ-9	592
American College, Bryn Mawr	PA-7	783
American College of Law, Anaheim	CA-47	155
American College of Traditional Chinese Medicine, San Francisco	CA-8	87
American Film Institute, Los Angeles	CA-33	131
American Graduate School of International Management, Glendale	AZ-2	47
American Institute of Business, Des Moines	IA-3	363
American Institute of Commerce, Cedar Falls	IA-1	359

School	State-District	Page
American Institute of Commerce, Davenport	IA-1	359
American Institute of Health Technology, Boise	ID-2	291
American Intercontinental University, Atlanta	GA-5	264
American Intercontinental University, Los Angeles	CA-30	126
American International College, Springfield	MA-2	441
American Military University, Manassas Park	VA-10	952
American Musical and Dramatic Academy, New York	NY-8	628
American River College, Sacramento	CA-3	79
American School of Professional Psychology, Arlington	VA-8	948
American School of Professional Psychology, Honolulu	HI-1	284
American University, Washington	DC-AL	1035
Amherst College, Amherst	MA-1	439
Ancilla College, Donaldson	IN-2	340
Anderson College, Anderson	SC-3	820
Anderson University, Anderson	IN-6	348
Andon College, Modesto	CA-18	107
Andover College, Portland	ME-1	414
Andover Newton Theological School, Newton Centre	MA-4	446
Andrew College, Cuthbert	GA-2	258
Andrew Jackson University, Birmingham	AL-6	33
Andrews University, Berrien Springs	MI-6	472
Angelina College, Lufkin	TX-2	860
Angelo State University, San Angelo	TX-17	887
Anna Maria College, Paxton	MA-3	443
Anne Arundel Community College, Arnold	MD-1	420
Anoka-Hennepin Technical College, Anoka	MN-6	505
Anoka-Ramsey Community College, Coon Rapids	MN-3	498
Antelope Valley College, Lancaster	CA-22	112
Antioch College, Yellow Springs	OH-7	720
Antioch New England Graduate School, Keene	NH-2	571
Antioch University, Los Angeles	CA-36	137
Antioch University, Santa Barbara	CA-23	114
Antioch University, Seattle	WA-7	970
Antonelli College, Cincinnati	OH-2	710
Antonelli College, Jackson	MS-2	516
Apollo College, Phoenix	AZ-3	48
Appalachian Bible College, Bradley	WV-3	983
Appalachian State University, Boone	NC-5	682
Aquinas College, Grand Rapids	MI-3	467
Aquinas College, Nashville	TN-5	843
Aquinas Institute of Theology, St. Louis	MO-1	526
Arapahoe Community College, Littleton	CO-6	181
Arcadia University, Glenside	PA-2	772
Argosy University, Chicago	IL-7	307
Arizona Institute of Business and Technology, Mesa	AZ-6	54
Arizona Institute of Business and Technology, Phoenix	AZ-4	50
Arizona State University, Tempe	AZ-5	52
Arizona State University-East, Mesa	AZ-6	54
Arizona State University-West, Phoenix	AZ-3	48
Arizona Western College, Yuma	AZ-7	55
Arkansas Baptist College, Little Rock	AR-2	63
Arkansas State University, Mountain Home	AR-1	61
Arkansas State University-Beebe Branch, Beebe	AR-2	63
Arkansas Tech University, Russellville	AR-3	65
Armstrong Atlantic State University, Savannah	GA-1	256
Art Academy of Cincinnati, Cincinnati	OH-2	710
Art Center, Albuquerque	NM-1	606
Art Center, Tucson	AZ-8	57
Art Center College of Design, Pasadena	CA-29	124
Art Institute , Pittsburgh	PA-14	795
Art Institute International at Portland, Portland	OR-1	757
Art Institute of Atlanta, Atlanta	GA-5	264
Art Institute of Boston, Boston	MA-8	453
Art Institute of Dallas, Dallas	TX-32	913
Art Institute of Fort Lauderdale, Fort Lauderdale	FL-22	246
Art Institute of Houston, Houston	TX-7	870
Art Institute of Los Angeles, Santa Monica	CA-30	126
Art Institute of Philadelphia, Philadelphia	PA-2	772
Art Institute of Phoenix, Phoenix	AZ-3	48
Art Institute of Seattle, Seattle	WA-7	970
Art Institute of Southern California, Laguna Beach	CA-48	156
Art Institutes International at Minnesota, Minneapolis	MN-5	503
Art Institutes International at San Francisco, San Francisco	CA-8	87

School	State-District	Page
Concordia University, Seward	NE-1	551
Concordia University, St. Paul	MN-4	501
Connecticut College, New London	CT-2	192
Connors State College, Warner	OK-2	747
Contra Costa College, San Pablo	CA-7	86
Converse College, Spartanburg	SC-4	822
Cooking and Hospitality Institute of Chicago, Chicago	IL-7	307
Cooper Career Institute, West Palm Beach	FL-23	248
Cooper Union for the Advancement of Science and Art, New York	NY-8	628
Coosa Valley Technical Institute, Rome	GA-11	275
Cope Institute, New York	NY-8	628
Copiah-Lincoln Community College, Natchez	MS-3	518
Copiah-Lincoln Community College, Wesson	MS-2	516
Coppin State College, Baltimore	MD-7	432
Corcoran School of Art, Washington	DC-AL	1035
Cornell College, Mt. Vernon	IA-2	361
Cornell University, Ithaca	NY-22	655
Cornell University Medical College, New York	NY-14	639
Cornerstone College, Grand Rapids	MI-3	467
Corning Community College, Corning	NY-29	668
Cornish College of the Arts, Seattle	WA-7	970
Cossatot Technical College, De Queen	AR-4	67
Cosumnes River College, Sacramento	CA-5	82
Cottey College, Nevada	MO-4	531
County College of Morris, Randolph	NJ-11	596
Court Reporting Institute-Wheeler Institute of Texas, Dallas	TX-30	909
Covenant College, Lookout Mountain	GA-10	274
Covenant Theological Seminary, St. Louis	MO-1	526
Cowley County Community College, Arkansas City	KS-4	378
Crafton Hills College, Yucaipa	CA-41	146
Craven Community College, New Bern	NC-3	678
Creighton University, Omaha	NE-2	553
Crichton College, Memphis	TN-9	851
Crowder College, Neosho	MO-7	537
Crown College, St. Bonifacius	MN-3	498
Crownpoint Institute of Technology, Crownpoint	NM-3	609
Cuesta College, San Luis Obispo	CA-23	114
Culinary Institute of America, Hyde Park	NY-20	651
Culver-Stockton College, Canton	MO-9	541
Cumberland College, Williamsburg	KY-5	391
Cumberland County College, Vineland	NJ-2	579
Cumberland University, Lebanon	TN-5	843
Curry College, Milton	MA-9	456
Cuyahoga Community College District, Cleveland	OH-11	728
Cuyamaca College, El Cajon	CA-52	163
Cypress College, Cypress	CA-40	144

D

School	State-District	Page
D. G. Erwin Technical Center, Tampa	FL-11	227
Dabney S. Lancaster Community College, Clifton Forge	VA-9	950
Daemen College, Amherst	NY-26	663
Dakota County Technical College, Rosemount	MN-2	495
Dakota State University, Madison	SD-AL	831
Dakota Wesleyan University, Mitchell	SD-AL	831
Dallas Baptist University, Dallas	TX-24	899
Dallas Christian College, Dallas	TX-32	913
Dallas Theological Seminary, Dallas	TX-32	913
Dalton College, Dalton	GA-10	274
Dana College, Blair	NE-1	551
Daniel Webster College, Nashua	NH-2	571
Danville Area Community College, Danville	IL-15	325
Danville Community College, Danville	VA-5	942
Dartmouth College, Hanover	NH-2	571
Darton College, Albany	GA-2	258
Data Institute, East Hartford	CT-1	190
Davenport College, Grand Rapids	MI-3	467
Davenport College, Kalamazoo	MI-6	472
Davenport College, Lansing	MI-8	476
Davenport College, Merrillville	IN-1	338
Davenport College of Business, Holland	MI-2	466
Davenport College-South Bend-Mishawaka, Granger	IN-2	340
David Lipscomb University, Nashville	TN-5	843
David N. Myers College, Cleveland	OH-11	728
Davidson College, Davidson	NC-12	694
Davidson County Community College, Lexington	NC-6	684

School	State-District	Page
Davis and Elkins College, Elkins	WV-2	981
Davis Applied Technology Center, Kaysville	UT-1	919
Davis College, Toledo	OH-9	723
Dawson Community College, Glendive	MT-AL	546
Daytona Beach Community College, Daytona Beach	FL-7	219
De Anza College, Cupertino	CA-15	101
Deaconess College of Nursing, St. Louis	MO-3	530
Dean College, Franklin	MA-3	443
Deep Springs College, Dyer	NV-2	562
Defiance College, Defiance	OH-5	716
DeKalb Technical Institute, Clarkston	GA-4	263
Del Mar College, Corpus Christi	TX-27	904
Delaware County Community College, Media	PA-7	783
Delaware State University, Dover	DE-AL	203
Delaware Technical & Community College-Owens, Georgetown	DE-AL	203
Delaware Technical & Community College-Stanton-Wilmington, Newark	DE-AL	203
Delaware Technical & Community College-Terry, Dover	DE-AL	203
Delaware Valley College, Doylestown	PA-8	785
Delgado Community College, New Orleans	LA-1	398
Delta College, University Center	MI-5	471
Delta College of Arts and Technology, Baton Rouge	LA-6	407
Delta School of Business and Technology, Lake Charles	LA-7	409
Delta State University, Cleveland	MS-2	516
Delta Technical Institute, Marked Tree	AR-1	61
Delta-Ouachita Regional Technical Institute, West Monroe	LA-5	405
Denison University, Granville	OH-12	730
Denmark Technical College, Denmark	SC-6	826
Denver Academy of Court Reporting, Denver	CO-7	185
Denver Automotive and Diesel College, Denver	CO-1	171
Denver Seminary, Englewood	CO-1	171
Denver Technical College, Denver	CO-1	171
Denver Technical College at Colorado Springs, Colorado Springs	CO-5	179
DePaul University, Chicago	IL-7	307
DePauw University, Greencastle	IN-8	352
Des Moines Community College, Ankeny	IA-3	363
DeSales University, Center Valley	PA-15	798
Design Institute of San Diego, San Diego	CA-50	160
Detroit College of Business, Dearborn	MI-14	487
Detroit College of Business, Flint	MI-5	471
Detroit College of Business, Warren	MI-12	483
Detroit College of Law at Michigan State University, East Lansing	MI-8	476
Devry University, Addison	IL-6	305
Devry University, Chicago	IL-5	304
Devry University, Columbus	OH-12	730
Devry University, Decatur	GA-4	263
Devry University, Fremont	CA-13	97
Devry University, Irving	TX-32	913
Devry University, Kansas City	MO-5	533
Devry University, Long Beach	CA-37	139
Devry University, Long Island City	NY-14	639
Devry University, North Brunswick	NJ-6	587
Devry University, Phoenix	AZ-3	48
Devry University, Pomona	CA-38	140
Diablo Valley College, Pleasant Hill	CA-10	92
Dickinson College, Carlisle	PA-19	806
Dickinson School of Law, Carlisle	PA-19	806
Dickinson State University, Dickinson	ND-AL	702
Dillard University, New Orleans	LA-2	400
Diné College, Tsaile	AZ-1	45
Dixie College, St. George	UT-2	921
Doane College, Crete	NE-3	555
Dodge City Community College, Dodge City	KS-1	372
Dominican College of Blauvelt, Orangeburg	NY-17	646
Dominican College of San Rafael, San Rafael	CA-6	83
Dominican University, River Forest	IL-7	307
Dominion College, Roanoke	VA-6	944
Don Bosco Technical Institute, Rosemead	CA-32	129
Dongguk Royal University, Los Angeles	CA-33	131
Donnelly College, Kansas City	KS-3	376
Dordt College, Sioux Center	IA-5	367
Douglas MacArthur State Technical College, Opp	AL-2	26
Dowling College, Oakdale	NY-2	618
DPT Business School, Philadelphia	PA-13	794
Dr. William Scholl College of Podiatric Medicine, Chicago	IL-7	307

University and College Index 1159

School	State-District	Page	School	State-District	Page
Messiah College, Grantham	PA-19	806	Mississippi University for Women, Columbus	MS-1	514
Methodist College, Fayetteville	NC-7	685	Mississippi Valley State University, Itta Bena	MS-2	516
Methodist Theological School-Ohio, Delaware	OH-12	730	Missouri Baptist College, St. Louis	MO-1	526
Metropolitan Career Center, Philadelphia	PA-2	772	Missouri College, St. Louis	MO-2	528
Metropolitan College of Court Reporting, Albuquerque	NM-1	606	Missouri Southern State College, Joplin	MO-7	537
Metropolitan Community College, East St. Louis	IL-12	320	Missouri Technical School, St. Louis	MO-1	526
Metropolitan Community College Area, Omaha	NE-2	553	Missouri Valley College, Marshall	MO-4	531
Metropolitan State College of Denver, Denver	CO-1	171	Missouri Western State College, St. Joseph	MO-6	535
Metropolitan State University, St. Paul	MN-4	501	Mitchell College, New London	CT-2	192
Metropolitan Technical Institute, Fairfield	NJ-11	596	Mitchell Community College, Statesville	NC-5	682
MGH Institute of Health Professions, Boston	MA-9	456	Mitchell Technical Institute, Mitchell	SD-AL	831
Miami Lakes Technical Education Center, Miami	FL-21	244	Moberly Area Community College, Moberly	MO-9	541
Miami University, Hamilton	OH-8	722	Modern Technology College, North Hollywood	CA-28	123
Miami University, Middletown	OH-8	722	Modesto Junior College, Modesto	CA-18	107
Miami University, Oxford	OH-8	722	Mohave Community College, Kingman	AZ-2	47
Miami-Dade Community College, Miami	FL-18	239	Mohawk Valley Community College, Utica	NY-24	659
Miami-Jacobs College, Dayton	OH-3	712	Molloy College, Rockville Center	NY-4	622
Michigan Institute of Aeronautics, Belleville	MI-11	482	Monmouth College, Monmouth	IL-17	329
Michigan State University, East Lansing	MI-8	476	Monmouth University, West Long Branch	NJ-6	587
Michigan Technological University, Houghton	MI-1	464	Monroe College, Bronx	NY-16	645
Mid America Bible College, Oklahoma City	OK-4	751	Monroe College, New Rochelle	NY-18	648
Mid Plains Community College, North Platte	NE-3	555	Monroe Community College, Rochester	NY-28	666
Midamerica Nazarene University, Olathe	KS-3	376	Monroe Community College, Rochester	NY-29	668
Mid-Continent College, Mayfield	KY-1	383	Monroe County Community College, Monroe	MI-15	488
Middle Georgia College, Cochran	GA-3	260	Montana State University, Billings	MT-AL	546
Middle Georgia Technical Institute, Warner Robins	GA-1	256	Montana State University, Bozeman	MT-AL	546
Middle Tennessee State University, Murfreesboro	TN-6	846	Montana State University-College of Technology, Billings	MT-AL	546
Middlebury College, Middlebury	VT-AL	928	Montana State University-Northern, Havre	MT-AL	546
Middlesex Community College, Bedford	MA-6	449	Montana Tech of the University of Montana, Butte	MT-AL	546
Middlesex Community Technical College, Middletown	CT-3	194	Montana Tech-College of Technology, Butte	MT-AL	546
Middlesex County College, Edison	NJ-6	587	Montcalm Community College, Sidney	MI-4	469
Mid-Florida Tech, Orlando	FL-3	213	Montclair State University, Upper Montclair	NJ-8	590
Midland College, Midland	TX-19	891	Monterey Institute of International Studies, Monterey	CA-17	105
Midland Lutheran College, Fremont	NE-1	551	Monterey Peninsula College, Monterey	CA-17	105
Midlands Technical College, Columbia	SC-2	819	Montgomery College, Germantown	MD-8	434
Mid-Michigan Community College, Harrison	MI-4	469	Montgomery College, Rockville	MD-8	434
Midstate College, Peoria	IL-18	331	Montgomery College, Takoma Park	MD-8	434
Mid-State Technical College, Wisconsin Rapids	WI-7	1000	Montgomery Community College, Troy	NC-8	687
Midway College, Midway	KY-6	393	Montgomery County Community College, Blue Bell	PA-13	794
Midwest Center for the Study of Oriental Medicine, Racine	WI-1	989	Montreat College, Montreat	NC-11	692
Midwestern Baptist Theological Seminary, Kansas City	MO-5	533	Montserrat College of Art, Beverly	MA-6	449
Midwestern State University, Wichita Falls	TX-13	881	Moody Bible Institute, Chicago	IL-7	308
Midwestern University, Downers Grove	IL-6	305	Moore College of Art and Design, Philadelphia	PA-2	772
Midwestern University, Glendale	AZ-2	47	Moore-Norman Area Vocational Technical School, Norman	OK-4	751
Mildred Elley School, Latham	NY-21	653	Moorhead State University, Moorhead	MN-7	507
Miles College, Fairfield	AL-7	35	Moorpark College, Moorpark	CA-24	115
Miller-Motte Business College, Wilmington	NC-7	685	Moraine Park Technical College, Fond du Lac	WI-6	998
Millersville University, Millersville	PA-16	800	Moraine Valley Community College, Palos Hills	IL-3	301
Milligan College, Milligan College	TN-1	837	Moravian College and Theological Seminary, Bethlehem	PA-15	798
Millikin University, Decatur	IL-17	329	Morehead State University, Morehead	KY-5	391
Mills College, Oakland	CA-9	90	Morehouse College, Atlanta	GA-5	265
Millsaps College, Jackson	MS-3	518	Morehouse School of Medicine, Atlanta	GA-5	265
Milwaukee Area Technical College, Milwaukee	WI-4	994	Morgan Community College, Fort Morgan	CO-4	177
Milwaukee Institute of Art Design, Milwaukee	WI-4	994	Morgan State University, Baltimore	MD-7	432
Milwaukee School of Engineering, Milwaukee	WI-4	994	Morningside College, Sioux City	IA-5	367
Mineral Area College, Park Hills	MO-8	539	Morris Brown College, Atlanta	GA-5	265
Minneapolis Business College, Roseville	MN-4	501	Morris College, Sumter	SC-6	826
Minneapolis College of Art and Design, Minneapolis	MN-5	503	Morton College, Cicero	IL-3	301
Minneapolis Community and Technical College, Minneapolis	MN-5	503	Motlow State Community College, Tullahoma	TN-4	842
Minnesota School of Business, Brooklyn Center	MN-3	498	Mott Community College, Flint	MI-5	471
Minnesota School of Business, Richfield	MN-5	503	Moultrie Area Technical Institute, Moultrie	GA-1	256
Minnesota School of Professional Psychology, Minneapolis	MN-3	498	Mount Aloysius College, Cresson	PA-12	792
Minnesota State College, Red Wing	MN-2	496	Mount Carmel College of Nursing, Columbus	OH-15	735
Minnesota State Unversity, Mankato	MN-1	493	Mount Holyoke College, South Hadley	MA-2	441
Minnesota West Community and Technical College, Granite Falls	MN-7	507	Mount Ida College, Newton Centre	MA-4	446
			Mount Marty College, Yankton	SD-AL	831
Minnesota West Community and Technical College, Worthington	MN-1	493	Mount Mary College, Milwaukee	WI-4	994
			Mount Mercy College, Cedar Rapids	IA-2	361
Minot State University, Bottineau	ND-AL	702	Mount Olive College, Mt. Olive	NC-3	678
Minot State University, Minot	ND-AL	702	Mount Senario College, Ladysmith	WI-7	1000
Mira Costa College, Oceanside	CA-49	159	Mount Sinai School of Medicine, New York	NY-14	639
Mirrer Yeshiva Cent Institute, Brooklyn	NY-11	635	Mount St. Clare College, Clinton	IA-1	359
Mission College, Santa Clara	CA-15	101	Mount St. Mary College, Newburgh	NY-22	655
Mississippi College, Clinton	MS-2	516	Mount St. Mary's College, Los Angeles	CA-30	126
Mississippi County Community College, Blytheville	AR-1	61	Mount St. Mary's College, Emmitsburg	MD-6	430
Mississippi Delta Community College, Moorhead	MS-2	516	Mount Union College, Alliance	OH-16	737
Mississippi Gulf Coast Community College, Perkinston	MS-4	520	Mount Vernon College, Washington	DC-AL	1035
Mississippi State University, Mississippi State	MS-3	518	Mount Vernon Nazarene College, Mt. Vernon	OH-18	740

School	State-District	Page	School	State-District	Page
Salem State College, Salem	MA-6	449	Seton Hall University, South Orange	NJ-10	594
Salina Area Vocational Technical School, Salina	KS-1	372	Seton Hill College, Greensburg	PA-18	804
Salisbury State University, Salisbury	MD-1	420	Sevier Valley Applied Technology Center, Richfield	UT-3	923
Salish Kootenai College, Pablo	MT-AL	546	Seward County Community College, Liberal	KS-1	372
Salt Lake Community College, Salt Lake City	UT-3	923	Shasta College, Redding	CA-2	77
Salve Regina University, Newport	RI-1	811	Shaw University, Raleigh	NC-13	696
Sam Houston State University, Huntsville	TX-2	861	Shawnee Community College, Ullin	IL-12	320
Samford University, Birmingham	AL-6	33	Shawnee State University, Portsmouth	OH-2	710
Sampson Community College, Clinton	NC-2	676	Shelby State Community College, Memphis	TN-9	851
Samra University of Oriental Medicine, Los Angeles	CA-33	131	Shelton State Community College, Tuscaloosa	AL-7	35
San Antonio College, San Antonio	TX-20	893	Shenandoah University, Winchester	VA-10	952
San Bernardino Valley College, San Bernardino	CA-43	148	Shepherd College, Shepherdstown	WV-2	981
San Diego City College, San Diego	CA-53	165	Sheridan College, Sheridan	WY-AL	1008
San Diego Mesa College, San Diego	CA-53	165	Sheridan Vocational Center, Hollywood	FL-20	243
San Diego Miramar College, San Diego	CA-52	163	Sherman College of Straight Chiropractic, Spartanburg	SC-4	822
San Diego State University, San Diego	CA-53	165	Shippensburg University, Shippensburg	PA-19	806
San Francisco Art Institute, San Francisco	CA-8	87	Shoreline Community College, Seattle	WA-1	961
San Francisco Conservatory of Music, San Francisco	CA-12	95	Shorter College, Rome	GA-11	275
San Francisco Law School, San Francisco	CA-8	87	Siena College, Loudonville	NY-21	653
San Francisco State University, San Francisco	CA-12	95	Siena Heights College, Adrian	MI-7	474
San Francisco Theological Seminary, San Anselmo	CA-6	83	Sierra Academy of Aeronautics Technical Institute, Oakland	CA-9	90
San Jacinto College, Houston	TX-22	896	Sierra College, Rocklin	CA-4	80
San Jacinto College, Houston	TX-29	907	Sierra Nevada College, Incline Village	NV-2	562
San Jacinto College, Pasadena	TX-22	896	Silicon Valley College, Fremont	CA-13	97
San Joaquin College of Law, Clovis	CA-21	111	Silver Lake College, Manitowoc	WI-6	998
San Joaquin Delta College, Stockton	CA-11	93	Simmons College, Boston	MA-8	453
San Joaquin Valley College, Bakersfield	CA-22	112	Simons Rock College of Bard, Great Barrington	MA-1	439
San Joaquin Valley College, Fresno	CA-19	108	Simpson College, Indianola	IA-4	365
San Joaquin Valley College, Visalia	CA-21	111	Simpson College, Redding	CA-2	77
San Jose Christian College, San Jose	CA-16	103	Sinclair Community College, Dayton	OH-3	712
San Jose City College, San Jose	CA-15	101	Sinte Gleska University, Rosebud	SD-AL	831
San Jose State University, San Jose	CA-16	103	Sisseton-Wahpeton Community College, Agency Village	SD-AL	831
San Juan Basin Area Vocational School, Cortez	CO-3	176	Skagit Valley College, Mt. Vernon	WA-2	963
San Juan College, Farmington	NM-3	609	Skidmore College, Saratoga Springs	NY-20	651
Sandersville Regional Technical Institute, Sandersville	GA-3	260	Skills and Business Education Center, Sacramento	CA-5	82
Sandhills Community College, Pinehurst	NC-6	684	Skyline College, San Bruno	CA-12	95
Sanford-Brown College, Des Peres	MO-2	528	Slippery Rock University of Pennsylvania, Slippery Rock	PA-3	776
Sanford-Brown College, Hazelwood	MO-1	526	Smith College, Northampton	MA-2	441
Santa Ana College, Santa Ana	CA-47	155	Snead State Community College, Boaz	AL-4	30
Santa Barbara Business College, Fremont	CA-13	97	Snow College, Ephraim	UT-3	923
Santa Barbara City College, Santa Barbara	CA-23	114	Sojourner-Douglas College, Baltimore	MD-7	432
Santa Clara University, Santa Clara	CA-15	101	Somerset Community College, Somerset	KY-5	391
Santa Fe Community College, Gainesville	FL-6	217	Somerset County Technical Institute, Bridgewater	NJ-11	596
Santa Fe Community College, Santa Fe	NM-3	609	Somerset Technical College, Somerset	KY-5	391
Santa Monica College, Santa Monica	CA-30	126	Sonoma State University, Rohnert Park	CA-6	83
Santa Rosa Junior College, Santa Rosa	CA-6	83	South Arkansas Community College, El Dorado	AR-4	67
Santiago Canyon College, Orange	CA-40	144	South Baylo University, Anaheim	CA-47	155
Sarah Lawrence College, Bronxville	NY-18	648	South Carolina State University, Orangeburg	SC-6	826
Sarasota County Technical Institute, Sarasota	FL-13	231	South Central Technical College, North Mankato	MN-1	493
Sauk Valley Community College, Dixon	IL-14	323	South College, Montgomery	AL-2	26
Savannah College of Art and Design, Savannah	GA-12	277	South College, Savannah	GA-12	277
Savannah State University, Savannah	GA-12	277	South College, West Palm Beach	FL-23	248
Savannah Technical Institute, Savannah	GA-12	277	South Dakota School of Mines and Technology, Rapid City	SD-AL	831
Sawyer College of Business, Cleveland Heights	OH-11	728	South Dakota State University, Brookings	SD-AL	831
Sawyer College of Business-West, Cleveland	OH-10	726	South Florida Community College, Avon Park	FL-16	235
Sawyer School, Pittsburgh	PA-14	796	South Georgia College, Douglas	GA-1	256
Saybrook Institute, San Francisco	CA-8	87	South Georgia Technical Institute, Americus	GA-2	258
Schenectady County Community College, Schenectady	NY-21	653	South Hills School of Business and Technology, State College	PA-5	779
Schiller International University, Dunedin	FL-10	225	South Louisiana Community College, New Iberia	LA-3	402
School for International Training, Brattleboro	VT-AL	928	South Mountain Community College, Phoenix	AZ-4	50
School of Art Institute of Chicago, Chicago	IL-7	308	South Piedmont Community College, Polkton	NC-8	687
School of the Museum of Fine Arts, Boston	MA-8	453	South Plains College, Levelland	TX-19	891
School of Visual Arts, New York	NY-14	639	South Puget Sound Community College, Olympia	WA-3	964
Schoolcraft College, Livonia	MI-11	482	South Suburban College, South Holland	IL-2	300
Schreiner College, Kerrville	TX-21	895	South Texas College of Law, Houston	TX-18	889
Scottsdale Community College, Scottsdale	AZ-5	52	South Texas Community College, McAllen	TX-15	884
Scottsdale Culinary Institute, Scottsdale	AZ-5	52	Southeast Arkansas College, Pine Bluff	AR-4	67
Scripps College, Claremont	CA-26	119	Southeast College of Technology, Memphis	TN-9	851
Scripps Research Institute, La Jolla	CA-53	165	Southeast College of Technology, Mobile	AL-1	24
Seattle Community College-Central, Seattle	WA-7	970	Southeast Community College, Cumberland	KY-5	391
Seattle Community College-North, Seattle	WA-7	970	Southeast Community College Area, Lincoln	NE-1	551
Seattle Community College-South, Seattle	WA-7	970	Southeast Missouri State University, Cape Girardeau	MO-8	539
Seattle Pacific University, Seattle	WA-7	970	Southeast Technical Institute, Sioux Falls	SD-AL	831
Seattle University, Seattle	WA-7	970	Southeastern Baptist Theological Seminary, Wake Forest	NC-13	696
Selma University, Selma	AL-7	35	Southeastern College, Lakeland	FL-12	229
Seminole Community College, Sanford	FL-7	219	Southeastern Community College, West Burlington	IA-2	361
Seminole State College, Seminole	OK-5	752	Southeastern Community College, Whiteville	NC-7	685
Sequoia Institute, Fremont	CA-13	97	Southeastern Illinois College, Harrisburg	IL-19	333

School	State-District	Page
Wayne State University, Detroit	MI-13	485
Waynesburg College, Waynesburg	PA-12	792
Weatherford College, Weatherford	TX-12	879
Webber College, Babson Park	FL-12	229
Weber State University, Ogden	UT-1	919
Webster College, Ocala	FL-6	217
Webster University, St. Louis	MO-3	530
Wellesley College, Wellesley	MA-4	446
Wells College, Aurora	NY-24	659
Wenatchee Valley College, Wenatchee	WA-4	966
Wentworth Institute of Technology, Boston	MA-8	453
Wentworth Military Academy, Lexington	MO-4	531
Wesley College, Dover	DE-AL	203
Wesley Theological Seminary, Washington	DC-AL	384
Wesleyan College, Macon	GA-8	271
Wesleyan University, Middletown	CT-3	194
West Chester University, West Chester	PA-16	800
West Georgia Technical Institute, Lagrange	GA-11	275
West Hills Community College, Coalinga	CA-20	109
West Kentucky Technical College, Paducah	KY-1	383
West Liberty State College, West Liberty	WV-1	979
West Los Angeles College, Culver City	CA-33	131
West Shore Community College, Scottville	MI-2	466
West Side Institute of Technology, Cleveland	OH-10	726
West Texas A&M University, Canyon	TX-13	881
West Valley College, Saratoga	CA-14	99
West Virginia Career College, Charleston	WV-2	981
West Virginia Northern Community College, Wheeling	WV-1	979
West Virginia School of Osteopathic Medicine, Lewisburg	WV-3	983
West Virginia State College, Institute	WV-2	981
West Virginia University, Morgantown	WV-1	979
West Virginia University, Parkersburg	WV-1	979
West Virginia University Institute of Technology, Montgomery	WV-3	983
West Virginia Wesleyan College, Buckhannon	WV-2	981
Westark College, Fort Smith	AR-3	65
Westchester Business Institute, White Plains	NY-18	648
Western Baptist College, Salem	OR-5	765
Western Business College, Portland	OR-1	758
Western Business College, Vancouver	WA-3	964
Western Career College, Sacramento	CA-5	82
Western Career College, San Leandro	CA-13	97
Western Carolina University, Cullowhee	NC-11	692
Western Connecticut State University, Danbury	CT-5	198
Western Dakota Technical Institute, Rapid City	SD-AL	831
Western Governors University, Salt Lake City	UT-1	919
Western Illinois University, Macomb	IL-17	329
Western International University, Phoenix	AZ-3	48
Western Iowa Tech Community College, Sioux City	IA-5	367
Western Kentucky University, Bowling Green	KY-2	385
Western Maryland College, Westminster	MD-6	430
Western Michigan University, Kalamazoo	MI-6	472
Western Montana College-University of Montana, Dillon	MT-AL	546
Western Nebraska Community College, Scottsbluff	NE-3	555
Western Nevada Community College, Carson City	NV-2	562
Western New England College, Springfield	MA-2	441
Western New Mexico University, Silver City	NM-2	608
Western Oklahoma State College, Altus	OK-3	749
Western Oregon University, Monmouth	OR-5	765
Western Piedmont Community College, Morganton	NC-10	690
Western School of Health and Business Careers, Pittsburgh	PA-14	796
Western Seminary, Portland	OR-3	761
Western State College Colorado, Gunnison	CO-3	176
Western State University College of Law, Fullerton	CA-40	144
Western States Chiropractic College, Portland	OR-3	761
Western Technical Institute, El Paso	TX-16	885
Western Texas College, Snyder	TX-17	887
Western University of Health Sciences, Pomona	CA-38	140
Western Washington University, Bellingham	WA-2	963
Western Wisconsin Technical College, La Crosse	WI-3	992
Western Wyoming Community College, Rock Springs	WY-AL	1008
Westfield State College, Westfield	MA-1	439
Westminster College, Fulton	MO-9	541
Westminster College, New Wilmington	PA-4	777
Westminster College, Salt Lake City	UT-2	922
Westminster Theological Seminary, Glenside	PA-2	774

School	State-District	Page
Westmont College, Santa Barbara	CA-23	114
Westmoreland County Community College, Youngwood	PA-18	804
Westwood College of Technology, Denver	CO-1	171
Westwood College of Technology, Denver	CO-2	174
Wharton County Junior College, Wharton	TX-14	883
Whatcom Community College, Bellingham	WA-2	963
Wheaton College, Norton	MA-4	446
Wheaton College, Wheaton	IL-6	305
Wheeling Jesuit University, Wheeling	WV-1	979
Wheelock College, Boston	MA-8	453
White Earth Tribal and Community College, Mahnomen	MN-7	507
Whitman College, Walla Walla	WA-5	967
Whittier College, Whittier	CA-42	147
Whitworth College, Spokane	WA-5	967
Wichita Area Technical College, Wichita	KS-4	378
Wichita State University, Wichita	KS-4	378
Widener University, Chester	PA-1	771
Widener University, Harrisburg	PA-17	802
Widener University-Delaware, Wilmington	DE-AL	203
Wilberforce University, Wilberforce	OH-7	720
Wiley College, Marshall	TX-1	859
Wilkes Community College, Wilkesboro	NC-5	682
Wilkes University, Wilkes Barre	PA-11	790
Willamette University, Salem	OR-5	765
William Carey College, Hattiesburg	MS-4	520
William Howard Taft University, Santa Ana	CA-47	155
William Jewell College, Liberty	MO-6	536
William Mitchell College of Law, St. Paul	MN-4	501
William Paterson University of New Jersey, Wayne	NJ-8	590
William Penn College, Oskaloosa	IA-3	363
William Rainey Harper College, Palatine	IL-10	315
William T. McFatter Vocational Technical Center, Davie	FL-20	243
William Tyndale College, Farmington Hills	MI-9	478
William Woods University, Fulton	MO-9	541
Williams Baptist College, Walnut Ridge	AR-1	61
Williams College, Williamstown	MA-1	439
Williamsburg Technical College, Kingstree	SC-6	826
Wilma Boyd Career Schools, Moon Township	PA-18	804
Wilmington College, New Castle	DE-AL	203
Wilmington College, Wilmington	OH-3	712
Wilson College, Chambersburg	PA-9	786
Wilson Technical Community College, Wilson	NC-1	674
Windward Community College, Kaneohe	HI-2	285
Wingate University, Wingate	NC-8	687
Winona State University, Winona	MN-1	494
Winston Salem State University, Winston-Salem	NC-12	694
Winter Park Tech, Winter Park	FL-3	213
Winthrop University, Rock Hill	SC-5	824
Wisconsin Indianhead Technical College, Shell Lake	WI-7	1000
Wisconsin Lutheran College, Milwaukee	WI-4	994
Withlacoochee Technical Institute, Inverness	FL-5	216
Wittenberg University, Springfield	OH-7	720
Woford College, Spartanburg	SC-4	822
Wood Tobé Coburn School, New York	NY-14	639
Woodbury University, Burbank	CA-27	120
Worcester Polytechnic Institute, Worcester	MA-3	443
Worcester State College, Worcester	MA-3	443
Worcester Technical Institute, Worcester	MA-3	443
Word of Life Bible Institute, Pottersville	NY-20	651
Wor-Wic Community College, Salisbury	MD-1	420
Wright Institute, Berkeley	CA-9	90
Wright State University, Dayton	OH-7	720
Wright State University-Lake, Celina	OH-8	722
Wyoming Technical Institute, Laramie	WY-AL	1008
Wytheville Community College, Wytheville	VA-9	950

X

School	State-District	Page
Xavier University, Cincinnati	OH-1	708
Xavier University of Louisiana, New Orleans	LA-2	400

Y

School	State-District	Page
Yakima Valley Community College, Yakima	WA-4	966
Yale University, New Haven	CT-3	194
Yavapai College, Prescott	AZ-1	46

WITHDRAWAL